The Wisden Book of Test Cricket 1876-77 to 1977-78

THE
WISDEN
BOOK OF
TEST
CRICKET
1876-77 to 1977-78

Compiled and edited by
BILL FRINDALL

MACDONALD AND JANE'S, LONDON

# THE
# WISDEN
## BOOK OF
# TEST CRICKET
### 1876-77 to 1977-78

## Compiled and edited by
# BILL FRINDALL

MACDONALD AND JANE'S · LONDON

© W.H. Frindall 1979

First published in 1979 by Macdonald and Jane's Publishers Ltd,
Paulton House, 8 Shepherdess Walk, London N1 7LW

ISBN 0354 08535 2

Typeset by Computer Graphics, 18/19 Clerkenwell Green, London EC1

Printed and bound in Great Britain by
The Garden City Press Ltd, Letchworth and London

## FOREWORD BY JOHN ARLOTT

No man can work shoulder to shoulder with another through the Test matches of a dozen years in England without coming to know much about him. Bill Frindall, following such distinguished BBC scorers as the late Arthur Wrigley and Roy Webber, had a high standard to meet. After some initial self-doubt, he met it completely.

His merits as a scorer for broadcasting are, first, accuracy; once or twice, perhaps, he has made a mistake – and been duly ribbed for it – but I cannot recall one of them, which means that none was important. Then, his enthusiasm prompts him to provide more information than his job actually demands. Interested himself, he passes on the items that interest him – but has learnt not to be hurt when the commentator prefers to follow a line of his own. The essential aspect here is that any commentator who needs it always has a constant flow of material to his hand. Thirdly, ask Bill for a specific piece of information and he will produce it, either from his own meticulous record of the match in progress, or from the positive library of books he transports to matches in a series of dispatch cases.

He has made that kind of precise information available in this book. Most of us are convinced that the cricket reference book without error does not exist. If there are errors in this one, it is not for want of checking. There has been a need for this book ever since the Webber volumes fell out of date. Arthur Wrigley's subsequent record, because it grouped the countries, was more difficult to follow than the Webber-Frindall chronological method – and did not so easily reveal the story of development. Everyone who works in cricket, indeed everyone who follows the game with any degree of interest, will want to be able to turn to this collection of Test facts. They are not available anywhere else, except through a bulky collection of annuals to bridge the gap – far wider than most would appreciate – from the previous collections. Such is the proliferation of Test cricket in recent years that, between the end of Webber's Volume Two (1953) and the end of this book there were 453 Test matches (55 per cent of all ever played); and, even since Wrigley's last entry, 259 (or 31 per cent). It is, too, the first of such books to indicate the type – right hand or left, and so on – of batsmen and bowlers.

If this can be kept up-to-date by regular supplements, it must become as essential a part of the cricket reference shelf as the *Wisden Cricketers' Almanack* whose name it bears.

*John Arlott*

England, 1978

# FOREWORD BY RAY ROBINSON

English minds created cricket and contributions from its most fruitful transplant have mostly been to heighten Test cricket as a spectacle. This is just as it should be in a sunnier land where wickets roll out harder and more spin or cut is needed to persuade the ball to change course.

Three Australians, Trumper, Macartney and Bradman, were the first to begin a Test match with 100 before lunch. Jack Gregory ripped off the fastest Test ton. Australians made the four quickest double-centuries and were the first to approach 500 runs in a day.

In research for *On Top Down Under* I found that an Australian captain urged MCC to allow six runs for boundary-clearing strokes until then worth five. He was Joe Darling, first man to hit 20 fours in a Test 100. Spofforth brought off the first hat-trick and Grimmett was first to collect 200 Test wickets. Davidson alone has a record of 10 wickets and 100 runs in one Test.

Products of spacious grounds, Australians have usually out-fielded opponents, especially in throwing. Another fielder has yet to equal Gregory's 15 slip-catches in a rubber or Greg Chappell's seven catches in a Test. Simpson and Ian Chappell brought off 100 catches each in fewer Tests than other countries' star slip-fielders.

Strategically, Australia was first to confront Test batsmen with fast bowlers from each end (1921) and first to pack eight men into the umbrella field (1953). Captains Blackham and Grace agreed to six-ball overs in Australia in 1891, ahead of laws changing from five. The first time a toss-winner sent opponents in was in Melbourne. Sydney has been the only scene of a team winning after having followed-on.

Australian crowds have formed the world's largest cricket throng, 90,800, the biggest match attendance, 350,000, and drew closest to a million at a rubber.

In case these scattered samples of statistics might be thought to have a vainglorious ring, I should mention that the tallest Test total was taken off Australian bowling. It led to the most crushing of Australia's 23 defeats by an innings.

*Ray Robinson*

Australia, 1978

# CONTENTS

# CONTENTS – *continued*

# INTRODUCTION

The phrase 'Test match' was coined during the first English tour to Australia in 1861-62 to describe games between H.H. Stephenson's team and each of the colonies. Those matches were against odds, i.e. with the opposition batting and fielding more than eleven men, and it was not until the fourth expedition to Australia, by James Lillywhite's professionals in 1877-78, that an English team played on level terms overseas. The first such contest, against a combined eleven from Melbourne and Sydney, has become accepted as the first official Test match.

This first volume of the new Wisden Cricket Library contains the full scores of the 824 Test matches played before June 1978. Although purists may object to the inclusion of matches in which England was represented by privately arranged teams in Australia and South Africa prior to the first official MCC tours to those countries in 1903-04 and 1905-06 respectively, the status of those matches has now been sanctified by time and no purpose would be served by omitting them. Similarly, the coincidental England rubbers in New Zealand and the West Indies in the early months of 1930 have also been accepted and should not now have their status challenged. The one major decision facing compilers of Test match records since 1970 has been whether to include the England v Rest of the World matches which were substituted for the cancelled rubber against South Africa. Space allows only for me to state that I have excluded these unofficial Tests because the International Cricket Conference, who have control of the title 'Test match', ruled that they should not be included in Test match records. Spare a thought for Alan Jones of Glamorgan who won a full England cap for appearing in the first match of that 'rubber' but whose name does not appear elsewhere in this book because he was never selected for an official Test match.

With two exceptions, the matches are arranged chronologically by rubber; to ensure that each player's Test career is shown in unbroken chronological order, the nine matches constituting the 1912 Triangular Tournament and England's eight matches in Pakistan and India in 1961-62 are set strictly in the order in which they were played. Each match has a reference number to show its position in the general order and its place in that particular series; e.g. 638/200 is the 638th match listed and was the 200th in the series between England and Australia. Only the prefix of each match number is used in the Index of Test Cricketers which follows the Records section.

Ideally each score should be an exact reproduction of the match details recorded in the original scorebook. Where that document has been unobtainable, research has turned to contemporary press reports and I am particularly indebted to the British Museum Newspaper Library. Thanks to the characteristically thorough and precise research of Geoffrey Saulez, the current Sussex and England scorer, who has checked virtually every relevant scorebook in all the Test-playing countries, a host of errors have been corrected and several new features introduced. For the first time in a volume covering all Test matches substitute catchers are identified, all but one set of umpires are named, and changes of batting order for the second innings are shown (by bracketed figures). Innovations include noting days when no play was possible and listing those players making their Test debut in that particular match.

I have also endeavoured to denote left-handers by annotating symbols in the career records section. This I must confess was something of an afterthought and I do not claim to have found every left-hander – particularly amongst the early South Africans. Only where I have been certain that the player was left-handed have I marked his batting or bowling columns. Additional entries, indeed corrections of any kind, are warmly invited. The publishers plan to bring out a new edition of this title every five years.

Besides recording my immense gratitude to Geoffrey Saulez for much sound advice, capacious information and stoic proof-checking, I want to add my thanks to Kirsty Ennever of Macdonald and Jane's for her incredible patience, encouragement, good humour, conscientiousness and expertise; to Malcolm McInnes of Computer Graphics for computerising the entire manuscript and for many calm and dextrous changes of schedule; to John Arlott and Ray Robinson for good counsel and for honouring this volume with their forewords; to Jacky Frindall for her literary assistance; to Roy Wilkinson, Michael Fordham, Denys Heesom, Bob Spence and Mike Ringham for valuable help and information; to Maureen White for wielding the typewriter; and, above all, to Alan Smith for his enthusiasm and courage in publishing this long-overdue volume.

*Bill Frindall*

Fortis Green, London
August 1978

---

## BALLS TO AN OVER
### *(Test Matches only)*

| In England | Balls | In Australia | Balls | In South Africa | Balls |
|---|---|---|---|---|---|
| 1880-88 | 4 | 1876-77 to 1887-88 | 4 | As in England to 1937-38 | |
| 1890-99 | 5 | 1891-92 to 1920-21 | 6 | 1938-39 to 1969-70 | 8 |
| 1902-38 | 6 | 1924-25 | 8 | | |
| 1939 | 8 | 1928-29 to 1932-33 | 6 | **In West Indies** | |
| 1946-78 | 6 | 1936-37 to 1977-78 | 8 | All Tests | 6 |

| In New Zealand | Balls | In India | Balls | In Pakistan | Balls |
|---|---|---|---|---|---|
| As in England to 1967-68 | | All Tests | 6 | 1952-53 to 1972-73 | 6 |
| 1968-69 to 1977-78 | 8 | | | 1973-74 to 1977-78 | 8 |

## KEY TO TEST MATCH GROUNDS
### *(Where more than one ground has been used at a centre)*

| | | | |
|---|---|---|---|
| Bombay[1] | Gymkhana | Johannesburg[1] | Old Wanderers |
| Bombay[2] | Brabourne Stadium | Johannesburg[2] | Ellis Park |
| Bombay[3] | Wankhede Stadium | Johannesburg[3] | New Wanderers |
| Brisbane[1] | Exhibition Ground | Lahore[1] | Bagh-i-Jinnah |
| Brisbane[2] | Woolloongabba | Lahore[2] | Lahore (Gaddafi) Stadium |
| Durban[1] | Lord's | Madras[1] | Chepauk |
| Durban[2] | Kingsmead | Madras[2] | Corporation (Nehru) Stadium |

## KEY TO SYMBOLS

Throughout this volume the symbol * is used to denote a 'not out' innings or an unbroken partnership. In the Match Scores, * denotes the Captain and † shows the Wicket-Keeper.

All other symbols are explained within the section in which they appear.

# Test Match Scores 1876-77 to 1977-78

# AUSTRALIA v ENGLAND 1876–77 (1st Test)

Played at Melbourne Cricket Ground on 15, 16, 17, 19 March.
Toss: Australia.   Result: AUSTRALIA won by 45 runs.
Debuts: All.

The first match played on level terms between English and Australian teams was only subsequently given the label of 'Australia v England' and recognised as the first Test match. In fact it was between a combined Melbourne and Sydney XI and James Lillywhite's professional touring team. The Australians lacked three of their best bowlers in Allan, Evans and Spofforth, while the leading English batsmen were absent amateurs and the tourists' only wicket-keeper, Pooley, had been 'confiscated' by the authorities in New Zealand – whence the team had returned somewhat sea-sick the previous day.

Note that the match continued into the fourth day (most recent publications list only three), that Horan was dismissed by Hill (not Ulyett, as most scores show), that Selby and not Jupp kept wicket for England, and that overs were of four balls.

## AUSTRALIA

| | | | | |
|---|---|---:|---|---:|
| C. Bannerman | retired hurt | 165 | b Ulyett | 4 |
| N. Thompson | b Hill | 1 | c Emmett b Shaw | 7 |
| T.P. Horan | c Hill b Shaw | 12 | c Selby b Hill | 20 |
| D.W. Gregory* | run out | 1 | (9) b Shaw | 3 |
| B.B. Cooper | b Southerton | 15 | b Shaw | 3 |
| W.E. Midwinter | c Ulyett b Southerton | 5 | c Southerton b Ulyett | 17 |
| E.J. Gregory | c Greenwood b Lillywhite | 0 | c Emmett b Ulyett | 11 |
| J.M. Blackham† | b Southerton | 17 | lbw b Shaw | 6 |
| T.W. Garrett | not out | 18 | (4) c Emmett b Shaw | 0 |
| T. Kendall | c Southerton b Shaw | 3 | not out | 17 |
| J.H. Hodges | b Shaw | 0 | b Lillywhite | 8 |
| Extras | (B 4, LB 2, W 2) | 8 | (B 5, LB 3) | 8 |
| **Total** | | **245** | | **104** |

## ENGLAND

| | | | | |
|---|---|---:|---|---:|
| H. Jupp | lbw b Garrett | 63 | (3) lbw b Midwinter | 4 |
| J. Selby† | c Cooper b Hodges | 7 | (5) c Horan b Hodges | 38 |
| H.R.J. Charlwood | c Blackham b Midwinter | 36 | (4) b Kendall | 13 |
| G. Ulyett | lbw b Thompson | 10 | (6) b Kendall | 24 |
| A. Greenwood | c E.J. Gregory b Midwinter | 1 | (2) c Midwinter b Kendall | 5 |
| T. Armitage | c Blackham b Midwinter | 9 | (8) c Blackham b Kendall | 3 |
| A. Shaw | b Midwinter | 10 | st Blackham b Kendall | 2 |
| T. Emmett | b Midwinter | 8 | (9) b Kendall | 9 |
| A. Hill | not out | 35 | (1) c Thompson b Kendall | 0 |
| James Lillywhite* | c and b Kendall | 10 | b Hodges | 4 |
| J. Southerton | c Cooper b Garrett | 6 | not out | 1 |
| Extras | (LB 1) | 1 | (B 4, LB 1) | 5 |
| **Total** | | **196** | | **108** |

| ENGLAND | O | M | R | W | O | M | R | W | | | | | |
|---|---|---|---|---|---|---|---|---|---|---|---|---|---|
| Shaw | 55·3 | 34 | 51 | 3 | 34 | 16 | 38 | 5 | | | | | |
| Hill | 23 | 10 | 42 | 1 | 14 | 6 | 18 | 1 | | | | | |
| Ulyett | 25 | 12 | 36 | 0 | 19 | 7 | 39 | 3 | | | | | |
| Southerton | 37 | 17 | 61 | 3 | | | | | | | | | |
| Armitage | 3 | 0 | 15 | 0 | | | | | | | | | |
| Lillywhite | 14 | 5 | 19 | 1 | 1 | 0 | 1 | 1 | | | | | |
| Emmett | 12 | 7 | 13 | 0 | | | | | | | | | |

| FALL OF WICKETS | | | | |
|---|---|---|---|---|
| | A | E | A | E |
| Wkt | 1st | 1st | 2nd | 2nd |
| 1st | 2 | 23 | 7 | 0 |
| 2nd | 40 | 79 | 27 | 7 |
| 3rd | 41 | 98 | 31 | 20 |
| 4th | 118 | 109 | 31 | 22 |
| 5th | 142 | 121 | 35 | 62 |
| 6th | 143 | 135 | 58 | 68 |
| 7th | 197 | 145 | 71 | 92 |
| 8th | 243 | 145 | 75 | 93 |
| 9th | 245 | 168 | 75 | 100 |
| 10th | – | 196 | 104 | 108 |

| AUSTRALIA | O | M | R | W | O | M | R | W |
|---|---|---|---|---|---|---|---|---|
| Hodges | 9 | 0 | 27 | 1 | 7 | 5 | 7 | 2 |
| Garrett | 18·1 | 10 | 22 | 2 | 2 | 0 | 9 | 0 |
| Kendall | 38 | 16 | 54 | 1 | 33·1 | 12 | 55 | 7 |
| Midwinter | 54 | 23 | 78 | 5 | 19 | 7 | 23 | 1 |
| Thompson | 17 | 10 | 14 | 1 | | | | |
| D.W. Gregory | | | | | 5 | 1 | 9 | 0 |

Umpires: C.A. Reid and R.B. Terry.

In his seventh first-class match (tenth innings), Charles Bannerman, born in Kent 25 years earlier, faced the first ball in Test cricket from the round-arm, 'length' bowler, Alfred Shaw, scored the first run (second ball) and the first hundred by an Australian against any English team. He reached the only first-class century of his career in 160 minutes (playing hours the first day were 1.05 to 5.00 p.m. with lunch 2.00 to 2.40 p.m.) and, when a rising ball from Ulyett split the second finger of his right hand, he retired hurt with 165 of Australia's total of 240 for 7 after batting chancelessly for 4¾ hours and hitting 18 fours. His score remains the highest by an Australian on debut against England; it was the Test record until W.L. Murdoch scored 211 in 1884 (*Test No. 16*) and the record score in Australia until S.E. Gregory made 201 for Australia in 1894-95 (*Test No. 42*). He scored 67·3 per cent of his side's total (69·6 per cent of the runs scored from the bat) – this remains the highest individual proportion of any Test innings.

One hundred years later this result and its margin were exactly emulated on the same ground in the Centenary Test (*Test No. 803*).

## THE FIRST TEST CRICKETERS

| AUSTRALIA | Born | Died |
|---|---|---|
| BANNERMAN, Charles | Woolwich, England | Surry Hills, Sydney |
| | 3 July 1851 | 20 August 1930 |
| BLACKHAM, John McCarthy | Fitzroy, Melbourne | Melbourne |
| | 11 May 1854 | 28 December 1932 |
| COOPER, Bransby Beauchamp | India | Geelong, Victoria |
| | 15 March 1844 | 7 August 1914 |
| GARRETT, Thomas William | Wollongong, N.S.W. | Warrawee, Sydney |
| | 26 July 1858 | 6 August 1943 |
| GREGORY, David William | Wollongong, N.S.W. | Turramurra, Sydney |
| | 15 April 1845 | 4 August 1919 |
| GREGORY, Edward James | Waverley, Sydney | S.C.G., Sydney |
| | 29 May 1839 | 22 April 1922 |
| HODGES, John Henry | Collingwood, Victoria | Collingwood, Victoria |
| | 31 July 1856 | 17 January 1933 |
| HORAN, Thomas Patrick | Middleton, Eire | Malvern, Melbourne |
| | 3 March 1854 | 16 April 1916 |
| KENDALL, Thomas | Bedford, England | Hobart |
| | 24 August 1851 | 17 August 1924 |
| MIDWINTER, William Evans | St Briavels, Glos, England | Melbourne |
| | 19 June 1851 | 3 December 1890 |
| THOMPSON, Nathaniel | Birmingham, England | Burwood, Sydney |
| | 21 April 1838 | 2 September 1896 |

| ENGLAND | | |
|---|---|---|
| ARMITAGE, Thomas | Sheffield, Yorkshire | Pullman, U.S.A. |
| | 25 April 1848 | 21 September 1922 |
| CHARLWOOD, Henry Rupert James | Horsham, Sussex | Scarborough, Yorkshire |
| | 19 December 1846 | 6 June 1888 |
| EMMETT, Thomas | Halifax, Yorkshire | Leicester |
| | 3 September 1841 | 29 June 1904 |
| GREENWOOD, Andrew | Lepton, Yorkshire | Huddersfield, Yorkshire |
| | 20 August 1847 | 12 February 1889 |
| HILL, Allen | Kirkheaton, Yorkshire | Leyland, Lancs |
| | 14 November 1845 | 29 August 1910 |
| JUPP, Henry | Dorking, Surrey | Bermondsey, London |
| | 19 November 1841 | 8 April 1889 |
| LILLYWHITE, James | West Hampnett, Sussex | Chichester, Sussex |
| | 23 February 1842 | 25 October 1929 |
| SELBY, John | Nottingham | Nottingham |
| | 1 July 1849 | 11 March 1894 |
| SHAW, Alfred | Burton Joyce, Notts | Gedling, Notts |
| | 29 August 1842 | 16 January 1907 |
| SOUTHERTON, James | Petworth, Sussex | Mitcham, Surrey |
| | 16 November 1827 | 16 June 1880 |
| ULYETT, George | Sheffield, Yorkshire | Sheffield, Yorkshire |
| | 21 October 1851 | 18 June 1898 |

# AUSTRALIA v ENGLAND 1876–77 (2nd Test)

Played at Melbourne Cricket Ground on 31 March, 2, 3, 4 April.
Toss: Australia.　Result: ENGLAND won by four wickets.
Debuts: Australia – T.J.D. Kelly, W.L. Murdoch, F.R. Spofforth.

This return match was played for the benefit of the English professionals, and attracted a total attendance of about 15,000. H. Jupp took over as England's wicket-keeper after lunch on the first day. In Australia's second innings Kelly made eight successive scoring strokes for four, and Bannerman scored 30 in thirteen minutes.

## AUSTRALIA

| | | | | | |
|---|---|---|---|---|---|
| N. Thompson | lbw b Hill | 18 | | b Lillywhite | 41 |
| C. Bannerman | b Hill | 10 | (3) | c Jupp b Ulyett | 30 |
| J.M. Blackham† | c Lillywhite b Hill | 5 | (10) | lbw b Southerton | 26 |
| T.W. Garrett | b Hill | 12 | (7) | c Jupp b Lillywhite | 18 |
| T.J.D. Kelly | b Ulyett | 19 | (4) | b Southerton | 35 |
| W.E. Midwinter | c Emmett b Lillywhite | 31 | | c Greenwood b Lillywhite | 12 |
| F.R. Spofforth | b Ulyett | 0 | (8) | b Hill | 17 |
| W.L. Murdoch | run out | 3 | (5) | c Shaw b Southerton | 8 |
| T. Kendall | b Lillywhite | 7 | | b Southerton | 12 |
| D.W. Gregory* | not out | 1 | (2) | c Ulyett b Lillywhite | 43 |
| '.H. Hodges | run out | 2 | | not out | 0 |
| Extras | (B 8, LB 5, W 1) | 14 | | (B 10, LB 7) | 17 |
| **Total** | | **122** | | | **259** |

## ENGLAND

| | | | | | |
|---|---|---|---|---|---|
| H. Jupp | b Kendall | 0 | | b Kendall | 1 |
| A. Shaw | st Blackham b Spofforth | 1 | (8) | not out | 0 |
| A. Greenwood | b Hodges | 49 | | c Murdoch b Hodges | 22 |
| H.R.J. Charlwood | c Kelly b Kendall | 14 | | b Kendall | 0 |
| J. Selby† | b Kendall | 7 | (2) | b Spofforth | 2 |
| G. Ulyett | b Spofforth | 52 | (5) | c Spofforth b Hodges | 63 |
| T. Emmett | c Kendall b Spofforth | 48 | (6) | b Midwinter | 8 |
| A. Hill | run out | 49 | (7) | not out | 17 |
| T. Armitage | c Thompson b Midwinter | 21 | | | |
| James Lillywhite* | not out | 2 | | | |
| J. Southerton | c Thompson b Kendall | 0 | | | |
| Extras | (B 5, LB 12, NB 1) | 18 | | (B 8, LB 1) | 9 |
| **Total** | | **261** | | (6 wickets) | **122** |

| ENGLAND | O | M | R | W | O | M | R | W | | FALL OF WICKETS | | | |
|---|---|---|---|---|---|---|---|---|---|---|---|---|---|
| Shaw | 42 | 27 | 30 | 0 | 32 | 19 | 27 | 0 | | A | E | A | E |
| Lillywhite | 29 | 17 | 36 | 2 | 41 | 15 | 70 | 4 | *Wkt* | *1st* | *1st* | *2nd* | *2nd* |
| Hill | 27 | 12 | 27 | 4 | 21 | 9 | 43 | 1 | 1st | 29 | 0 | 88 | 2 |
| Ulyett | 14·1 | 6 | 15 | 2 | 19 | 9 | 33 | 1 | 2nd | 29 | 4 | 112 | 8 |
| Emmett | | | | | 13 | 6 | 23 | 0 | 3rd | 50 | 55 | 135 | 9 |
| Southerton | | | | | 28·3 | 13 | 46 | 4 | 4th | 60 | 72 | 164 | 54 |
| | | | | | | | | | 5th | 96 | 88 | 169 | 76 |
| AUSTRALIA | | | | | | | | | 6th | 104 | 162 | 196 | 112 |
| Kendall | 52·2 | 21 | 82 | 4 | 17 | 7 | 24 | 2 | 7th | 108 | 196 | 203 | |
| Spofforth | 29 | 6 | 67 | 3 | 15 | 3 | 44 | 1 | 8th | 114 | 255 | 221 | |
| Midwinter | 21 | 8 | 30 | 1 | 13·1 | 6 | 25 | 1 | 9th | 119 | 259 | 259 | |
| Hodges | 12 | 2 | 37 | 1 | 6 | 2 | 13 | 2 | 10th | 122 | 261 | 259 | |
| Garrett | 5 | 2 | 10 | 0 | 1 | 0 | 7 | 0 | | | | | |
| Thompson | 11 | 6 | 17 | 0 | | | | | | | | | |

Umpires: B. Terry and S. Cosstick.

# AUSTRALIA v ENGLAND 1878–79 (Only Test)

Played at Melbourne Cricket Ground on 2, 3, 4 January.
Toss: England.   Result: AUSTRALIA won by ten wickets.
Debuts: Australia – F.E. Allan, A.C. Bannerman, H.F. Boyle; England – C.A. Absolom, The Fourth
  Lord Harris, L. Hone, A.N. Hornby, A.P. Lucas, F.A. Mackinnon (The Mackinnon of
  Mackinnon, 35th Chief of the Clan Mackinnon), V.P.F.A. Royle, S.S. Schultz, A.J. Webbe.

Originally billed as 'Gentlemen of England (with Ulyett and Emmett) v The Australian XI', this match has
become accepted as the third Test match between the two countries. F.R. Spofforth achieved the first Test match
hat-trick when he dismissed Royle, Mackinnon and Emmett in the first innings.

## ENGLAND

| | | | | | |
|---|---|---|---|---|---|
| G. Ulyett | b Spofforth | 0 | b Spofforth | | 14 |
| A.P. Lucas | b Allan | 6 | c Boyle b Allan | | 13 |
| A.J. Webbe | b Allan | 4 | lbw b Allan | | 0 |
| A.N. Hornby | b Spofforth | 2 | b Spofforth | | 4 |
| Lord Harris* | b Garrett | 33 | c Horan b Spofforth | | 36 |
| V.P.F.A. Royle | b Spofforth | 3 | c Spofforth b Boyle | | 18 |
| F.A. Mackinnon | b Spofforth | 0 | b Spofforth | | 5 |
| T. Emmett | c Horan b Spofforth | 0 | (9) not out | | 24 |
| C.A. Absolom | c A.C. Bannerman b Boyle | 52 | (8) c and b Spofforth | | 6 |
| L. Hone† | c Blackham b Spofforth | 7 | b Spofforth | | 6 |
| S.S. Schultz | not out | 0 | c and b Spofforth | | 20 |
| Extras | (B 4, LB 2) | 6 | (B 10, LB 4) | | 14 |
| **Total** | | **113** | | | **160** |

## AUSTRALIA

| | | | | |
|---|---|---|---|---|
| C. Bannerman | b Emmett | 15 | not out | 15 |
| W.L. Murdoch | c Webbe b Ulyett | 4 | not out | 4 |
| T.P. Horan | c Hone b Emmett | 10 | | |
| A.C. Bannerman | b Schultz | 73 | | |
| F.R. Spofforth | c Royle b Emmett | 39 | | |
| T.W. Garrett | c Hone b Emmett | 26 | | |
| F.E. Allan | b Hornby | 5 | | |
| H.F. Boyle | c Royle b Emmett | 28 | | |
| J.M. Blackham† | b Emmett | 6 | | |
| T.J.D. Kelly | c Webbe b Emmett | 10 | | |
| D.W. Gregory* | not out | 12 | | |
| Extras | (B19, LB 2, W 7) | 28 | | |
| **Total** | | **256** | (0 wickets) | **19** |

| AUSTRALIA | O | M | R | W | O | M | R | W |
|---|---|---|---|---|---|---|---|---|
| Spofforth | 25 | 9 | 48 | 6 | 35 | 16 | 62 | 7 |
| Allan | 17 | 4 | 30 | 2 | 28 | 11 | 50 | 2 |
| Garrett | 5 | 0 | 18 | 1 | 10 | 6 | 18 | 0 |
| Boyle | 7 | 1 | 11 | 1 | 10 | 4 | 16 | 1 |
| ENGLAND | | | | | | | | |
| Emmett | 59 | 31 | 68 | 7 | | | | |
| Ulyett | 62 | 24 | 93 | 1 | 1 | 0 | 9 | 0 |
| Lucas | 18 | 6 | 31 | 0 | | | | |
| Schultz | 6·3 | 3 | 16 | 1 | 2 | 0 | 10 | 0 |
| Hornby | 7 | 7 | 0 | 1 | | | | |
| Royle | 4 | 1 | 6 | 0 | | | | |
| Lord Harris | 3 | 0 | 14 | 0 | | | | |

### FALL OF WICKETS

| Wkt | E 1st | A 1st | E 2nd | A 2nd |
|---|---|---|---|---|
| 1st | 0 | 16 | 26 | – |
| 2nd | 7 | 30 | 28 | – |
| 3rd | 10 | 37 | 28 | – |
| 4th | 14 | 101 | 34 | – |
| 5th | 26 | 131 | 78 | – |
| 6th | 26 | 158 | 103 | – |
| 7th | 26 | 215 | 103 | – |
| 8th | 89 | 224 | 118 | – |
| 9th | 113 | 234 | 128 | – |
| 10th | 113 | 256 | 160 | – |

Umpires: G. Coulthard and P. Coady.

# ENGLAND v AUSTRALIA 1880 (Only Test)

Played at Kennington Oval, London, on 6, 7, 8 September.
Toss: England.   Result: ENGLAND won by five wickets.
Debuts: England – W. Barnes, E.M. Grace, G.F. Grace, W.G. Grace, Hon. A. Lyttelton, F. Morley,
   F. Penn, A.G. Steel; Australia – G. Alexander, G.J. Bonnor, T.U. Groube, P.S. McDonnell,
   W.H. Moule, G.E. Palmer, J. Slight.

William Gilbert Grace, who scored England's first Test century, and his two brothers, Edward Mills and George
Frederick, provided the first instance of three brothers playing in the same Test. 'W.G.' and Lucas shared the first
hundred partnership in Test cricket – 120 for the second wicket.

## ENGLAND

| | | | | |
|---|---|---|---|---|
| E.M. Grace | c Alexander b Bannerman | 36 | (6) b Boyle | 0 |
| W.G. Grace | b Palmer | 152 | (7) not out | 9 |
| A.P. Lucas | b Bannerman | 55 | c Blackham b Palmer | 2 |
| W. Barnes | b Alexander | 28 | (5) c Moule b Boyle | 5 |
| Lord Harris* | c Bonnor b Alexander | 52 | | |
| F. Penn | b Bannerman | 23 | (4) not out | 27 |
| A.G. Steel | c Boyle b Moule | 42 | | |
| Hon. A. Lyttelton† | not out | 11 | (1) b Palmer | 13 |
| G.F. Grace | c Bannerman b Moule | 0 | (2) b Palmer | 0 |
| A. Shaw | b Moule | 0 | | |
| F. Morley | run out | 2 | | |
| Extras | (B 8, LB 11) | 19 | (NB 1) | 1 |
| **Total** | | **420** | (5 wickets) | **57** |

## AUSTRALIA

| | | | | |
|---|---|---|---|---|
| A.C. Bannerman | b Morley | 32 | c Lucas b Shaw | 8 |
| W.L. Murdoch* | c Barnes b Steel | 0 | (3) not out | 153 |
| T.U. Groube | b Steel | 11 | (4) c Shaw b Morley | 0 |
| P.S. McDonnell | c Barnes b Morley | 27 | (5) lbw b W.G. Grace | 43 |
| J. Slight | c G.F. Grace b Morley | 11 | (6) c Harris b W.G. Grace | 0 |
| J.M. Blackham† | c and b Morley | 0 | (7) c E.M. Grace b Morley | 19 |
| G.J. Bonnor | c G.F. Grace b Shaw | 2 | (8) b Steel | 16 |
| H.F. Boyle | not out | 36 | (2) run out | 3 |
| G.E. Palmer | b Morley | 6 | c and b Steel | 4 |
| G. Alexander | c W.G. Grace b Steel | 6 | c Shaw b Morley | 33 |
| W.H. Moule | c Morley b W.G. Grace | 6 | b Barnes | 34 |
| Extras | (B 9, LB 3) | 12 | (B 7, LB 7) | 14 |
| **Total** | | **149** | | **327** |

| AUSTRALIA | O | M | R | W | O | M | R | W |
|---|---|---|---|---|---|---|---|---|
| Boyle | 44 | 17 | 71 | 0 | 17 | 7 | 21 | 2 |
| Palmer | 70 | 27 | 116 | 1 | 16·3 | 5 | 35 | 3 |
| Alexander | 32 | 10 | 69 | 2 | | | | |
| Bannerman | 50 | 12 | 111 | 3 | | | | |
| McDonnell | 2 | 0 | 11 | 0 | | | | |
| Moule | 12·3 | 4 | 23 | 3 | | | | |
| **ENGLAND** | | | | | | | | |
| Morley | 32 | 9 | 56 | 5 | 61 | 30 | 90 | 3 |
| Steel | 29 | 9 | 58 | 3 | 31 | 6 | 73 | 2 |
| Shaw | 13 | 5 | 21 | 1 | 33 | 18 | 42 | 1 |
| W.G. Grace | 1·1 | 0 | 2 | 1 | 28 | 10 | 66 | 2 |
| Barnes | | | | | 8·3 | 3 | 17 | 1 |
| Lucas | | | | | 12 | 7 | 23 | 0 |
| Penn | | | | | 3 | 1 | 2 | 0 |

### FALL OF WICKETS

| | E | A | A | E |
|---|---|---|---|---|
| Wkt | 1st | 1st | 2nd | 2nd |
| 1st | 91 | 28 | 8 | 2 |
| 2nd | 211 | 39 | 13 | 10 |
| 3rd | 269 | 59 | 14 | 22 |
| 4th | 281 | 84 | 97 | 31 |
| 5th | 322 | 84 | 101 | 31 |
| 6th | 404 | 89 | 143 | – |
| 7th | 410 | 97 | 181 | – |
| 8th | 410 | 113 | 187 | – |
| 9th | 413 | 126 | 239 | – |
| 10th | 420 | 149 | 327 | – |

Umpires: H.H. Stephenson and R. Thoms.

# AUSTRALIA v ENGLAND 1881–82 (1st Test)

Played at Melbourne Cricket Ground on 31 December, 2, 3, 4 January.
Toss: England.   Result: MATCH DRAWN.
Debuts: Australia – W.H. Cooper, E. Evans, G. Giffen, H.H. Massie; England – R.G. Barlow, W. Bates, E. Peate, R. Pilling, A. Shrewsbury, W.H. Scotton. *W.E. Midwinter made his debut for England having played for Australia in the first two Test matches.*

Horan and Giffen recorded Australia's first century-partnership: 107 for the fifth wicket. Ulyett scored 80 not out in two hours before lunch on the first day. His second-wicket partnership of 137 with Selby was a new Test record for any wicket.

## ENGLAND

| | | | | | |
|---|---|--:|---|---|--:|
| R.G. Barlow | c Bannerman b Palmer | 0 | st Blackham b Palmer | | 33 |
| G. Ulyett | c McDonnell b Cooper | 87 | st Blackham b Cooper | | 23 |
| J. Selby | run out | 55 | c Boyle b Cooper | | 70 |
| W. Bates | c Giffen b Boyle | 58 | c Bannerman b Cooper | | 47 |
| A. Shrewsbury | c Blackham b Evans | 11 | b Cooper | | 16 |
| W.E. Midwinter | b Evans | 36 | c Massie b Cooper | | 4 |
| T. Emmett | b Evans | 5 | b Cooper | | 6 |
| W.H. Scotton | run out | 21 | not out | | 50 |
| A. Shaw* | c Boyle b Cooper | 5 | c Cooper b Boyle | | 40 |
| R. Pilling† | c Giffen b Cooper | 5 | b Palmer | | 3 |
| E. Peate | not out | 4 | run out | | 2 |
| Extras | (LB 6, NB 1) | 7 | (B 7, LB 2, NB 5) | | 14 |
| **Total** | | **294** | | | **308** |

## AUSTRALIA

| | | | | | |
|---|---|--:|---|---|--:|
| H.H. Massie | st Pilling b Midwinter | 2 | | | |
| A.C. Bannerman | b Ulyett | 38 | b Ulyett | | 8 |
| W.L. Murdoch* | b Ulyett | 39 | (4) not out | | 22 |
| P.S. McDonnell | b Midwinter | 19 | (5) not out | | 33 |
| T.P. Horan | run out | 124 | (3) c Emmett b Bates | | 26 |
| G. Giffen | b Emmett | 30 | | | |
| J.M. Blackham† | b Emmett | 2 | (1) b Bates | | 25 |
| G.E. Palmer | c Pilling b Bates | 34 | | | |
| E. Evans | b Bates | 3 | | | |
| H.F. Boyle | not out | 4 | | | |
| W.H. Cooper | st Pilling b Peate | 7 | | | |
| Extras | (B 4, LB 11, W 3) | 18 | (B 9, LB 3, W 1) | | 13 |
| **Total** | | **320** | (3 wickets) | | **127** |

| AUSTRALIA | O | M | R | W | O | M | R | W |
|---|--:|--:|--:|--:|--:|--:|--:|--:|
| Palmer | 36 | 9 | 73 | 1 | 77 | 19 | 77 | 2 |
| Boyle | 18 | 9 | 18 | 1 | 15 | 6 | 19 | 1 |
| Bannerman | 10 | 3 | 23 | 0 | | | | |
| Evans | 71 | 35 | 81 | 3 | 75·2 | 45 | 63 | 0 |
| Cooper | 32·2 | 8 | 80 | 3 | 66 | 19 | 120 | 6 |
| Giffen | 3 | 0 | 12 | 0 | | | | |
| McDonnell | | | | | 4 | 1 | 15 | 0 |
| ENGLAND | | | | | | | | |
| Peate | 59 | 24 | 64 | 1 | 11 | 5 | 22 | 0 |
| Midwinter | 39 | 21 | 50 | 2 | | | | |
| Bates | 41 | 20 | 43 | 2 | 13 | 3 | 43 | 2 |
| Emmett | 35 | 12 | 61 | 2 | 16 | 11 | 19 | 0 |
| Ulyett | 20 | 5 | 41 | 2 | 15 | 3 | 30 | 1 |
| Barlow | 23 | 13 | 22 | 0 | | | | |
| Shaw | 20 | 11 | 21 | 0 | | | | |

### FALL OF WICKETS

| | E | A | E | A |
|---|--:|--:|--:|--:|
| *Wkt* | *1st* | *1st* | *2nd* | *2nd* |
| 1st | 5 | 9 | 37 | 35 |
| 2nd | 142 | 82 | 96 | 70 |
| 3rd | 151 | 97 | 179 | 72 |
| 4th | 187 | 113 | 183 | – |
| 5th | 227 | 220 | 188 | – |
| 6th | 232 | 226 | 197 | – |
| 7th | 277 | 305 | 217 | – |
| 8th | 284 | 309 | 300 | – |
| 9th | 289 | 309 | 305 | – |
| 10th | 294 | 320 | 308 | – |

Umpires: J. Swift and James Lillywhite, jr.

# AUSTRALIA v ENGLAND 1881–82 (2nd Test)

Played at Sydney Cricket Ground on 17, 18, 20, 21 February.
Toss: England.   Result: AUSTRALIA won by five wickets.
Debuts: Australia – G. Coulthard, S.P. Jones.

Ulyett and Barlow scored 122 for England's first wicket in the second innings – the first hundred opening partnership in Test cricket. Blackham kept wicket for part of England's second innings. Palmer and Evans bowled unchanged throughout England's first innings which lasted over three hours.

## ENGLAND

| | | | | | |
|---|---|---|---|---|---|
| G. Ulyett | c Murdoch b Evans | 25 | lbw b Palmer | | 67 |
| R.G. Barlow | b Palmer | 31 | c Boyle b Garrett | | 62 |
| J. Selby | c and b Evans | 6 | c Blackham b Palmer | | 2 |
| W. Bates | st Murdoch b Palmer | 4 | b Palmer | | 5 |
| A. Shrewsbury | b Palmer | 7 | c McDonnell b Garrett | | 22 |
| W.E. Midwinter | c Blackham b Palmer | 4 | b Palmer | | 8 |
| W.H. Scotton | b Palmer | 30 | lbw b Garrett | | 12 |
| T. Emmett | b Evans | 10 | c McDonnell b Garrett | | 9 |
| A. Shaw* | c Massie b Palmer | 11 | b Evans | | 30 |
| R. Pilling† | b Palmer | 3 | b Jones | | 9 |
| E. Peate | not out | 1 | not out | | 1 |
| Extras | (LB 1) | 1 | (B 3, LB 2) | | 5 |
| **Total** | | **133** | | | **232** |

## AUSTRALIA

| | | | | | |
|---|---|---|---|---|---|
| H.H. Massie | c Shrewsbury b Bates | 49 | b Ulyett | | 22 |
| J.M. Blackham | c Shaw b Midwinter | 40 | c and b Bates | | 4 |
| E. Evans | run out | 11 | | | |
| W.L. Murdoch*† | c Emmett b Bates | 10 | (3) Barlow b Midwinter | | 49 |
| T.P. Horan | run out | 4 | (4) b Ulyett | | 21 |
| P.S. McDonnell | b Bates | 14 | (5) b Shaw | | 25 |
| S.P. Jones | c Emmett b Ulyett | 37 | (6) not out | | 13 |
| T.W. Garrett | c Shrewsbury b Peate | 4 | (7) not out | | 31 |
| G.E. Palmer | b Bates | 16 | | | |
| H.F. Boyle | c Shrewsbury b Ulyett | 0 | | | |
| G. Coulthard | not out | 6 | | | |
| Extras | (B 1, LB 2, W 2, NB 1) | 6 | (B 3, LB 1) | | 4 |
| **Total** | | **197** | (5 wickets) | | **169** |

| AUSTRALIA | O | M | R | W | O | M | R | W | | FALL OF WICKETS | | | |
|---|---|---|---|---|---|---|---|---|---|---|---|---|---|
| Palmer | 58 | 36 | 68 | 7 | 66 | 29 | 97 | 4 | | E | A | E | A |
| Evans | 57 | 32 | 64 | 3 | 40·1 | 19 | 49 | 1 | *Wkt* | *1st* | *1st* | *2nd* | *2nd* |
| Garrett | | | | | 36 | 12 | 62 | 4 | 1st | 39 | 78 | 122 | 10 |
| Jones | | | | | 11 | 4 | 19 | 1 | 2nd | 47 | 102 | 124 | 28 |
| | | | | | | | | | 3rd | 64 | 103 | 130 | 67 |
| ENGLAND | | | | | | | | | 4th | 73 | 111 | 156 | 113 |
| Peate | 52 | 28 | 53 | 1 | 20 | 12 | 22 | 0 | 5th | 77 | 132 | 165 | 127 |
| Midwinter | 34 | 16 | 43 | 1 | 18 | 8 | 23 | 1 | 6th | 90 | 133 | 175 | – |
| Emmett | 6 | 2 | 24 | 0 | 6 | 3 | 17 | 0 | 7th | 115 | 140 | 183 | – |
| Ulyett | 22·2 | 16 | 11 | 2 | 15 | 4 | 48 | 2 | 8th | 123 | 167 | 204 | – |
| Bates | 72 | 43 | 52 | 4 | 24 | 11 | 37 | 1 | 9th | 132 | 168 | 230 | – |
| Barlow | 8 | 4 | 8 | 0 | 4 | 1 | 6 | 0 | 10th | 133 | 197 | 232 | – |
| Shaw | | | | | 21 | 15 | 12 | 1 | | | | | |

Umpires: J. Swift and James Lillywhite, jr.

# AUSTRALIA v ENGLAND 1881–82 (3rd Test)

Played at Sydney Cricket Ground on 3, 4, 6, 7 March.
Toss: England.   Result: AUSTRALIA won by six wickets.
Debuts: Nil.

The partnership of 199 between A.C. Bannerman and McDonnell remained the highest for any wicket in Test matches until W.L. Murdoch and H.J.H. Scott added 207 in 1884 (*Test No. 16*). It remains the fourth-wicket record by either side in Australia v England Tests in Australia.

## ENGLAND

| | | | | | |
|---|---|---|---|---|---|
| G. Ulyett | b Palmer | 0 | b Garrett | | 23 |
| R.G. Barlow | c Blackham b Garrett | 4 | c and b Garrett | | 8 |
| J. Selby | c Massie b Palmer | 13 | b Palmer | | 1 |
| W. Bates | c and b Palmer | 1 | c Bannerman b Garrett | | 2 |
| A. Shrewsbury | c and b Boyle | 82 | c Boyle b Garrett | | 47 |
| W.E. Midwinter | b Palmer | 12 | b Palmer | | 10 |
| W.H. Scotton | c Jones b Garrett | 18 | b Palmer | | 1 |
| T. Emmett | b Garrett | 4 | b Garrett | | 2 |
| A. Shaw* | b Boyle | 3 | b Garrett | | 6 |
| R. Pilling† | b Palmer | 12 | b Palmer | | 23 |
| E. Peate | not out | 11 | not out | | 8 |
| Extras | (B 22, LB 6) | 28 | (B 2, NB 1) | | 3 |
| **Total** | | **188** | | | **134** |

## AUSTRALIA

| | | | | | |
|---|---|---|---|---|---|
| A.C. Bannerman | b Midwinter | 70 | c Pilling b Peate | | 14 |
| H.H. Massie | b Bates | 0 | c Midwinter b Peate | | 9 |
| W.L. Murdoch* | c Ulyett b Bates | 6 | c Midwinter b Bates | | 4 |
| T.P. Horan | c and b Bates | 1 | not out | | 16 |
| P.S. McDonnell | c Midwinter b Peate | 147 | c Emmett b Peate | | 4 |
| G. Giffen | c Pilling b Peate | 2 | | | |
| J.M. Blackham† | b Peate | 4 | | | |
| T.W. Garrett | b Peate | 0 | | | |
| G.E. Palmer | b Midwinter | 6 | | | |
| S.P. Jones | not out | 7 | (6) not out | | 10 |
| H.F. Boyle | c Pilling b Peate | 3 | | | |
| Extras | (B 6, LB 8) | 14 | (B 2, LB 5, W 1, NB 1) | | 9 |
| **Total** | | **260** | (4 wickets) | | **66** |

| AUSTRALIA | O | M | R | W | O | M | R | W |
|---|---|---|---|---|---|---|---|---|
| Palmer | 45·2 | 23 | 46 | 5 | 40 | 19 | 44 | 4 |
| Garrett | 60 | 25 | 85 | 3 | 36·1 | 10 | 78 | 6 |
| Boyle | 27 | 18 | 18 | 2 | 4 | 1 | 9 | 0 |
| Jones | 8 | 5 | 11 | 0 | | | | |
| ENGLAND | | | | | | | | |
| Peate | 45 | 24 | 43 | 5 | 25 | 18 | 14 | 3 |
| Bates | 38 | 17 | 67 | 3 | 24·3 | 13 | 43 | 1 |
| Ulyett | 3 | 1 | 10 | 0 | | | | |
| Midwinter | 62 | 25 | 75 | 2 | | | | |
| Shaw | 8 | 4 | 14 | 0 | | | | |
| Emmett | 16 | 6 | 37 | 0 | | | | |

FALL OF WICKETS

| Wkt | E 1st | A 1st | E 2nd | A 2nd |
|---|---|---|---|---|
| 1st | 2 | 0 | 28 | 14 |
| 2nd | 8 | 10 | 29 | 21 |
| 3rd | 17 | 16 | 32 | 39 |
| 4th | 35 | 215 | 42 | 49 |
| 5th | 56 | 228 | 60 | – |
| 6th | 148 | 235 | 70 | – |
| 7th | 154 | 244 | 73 | – |
| 8th | 159 | 245 | 79 | – |
| 9th | 164 | 252 | 113 | – |
| 10th | 188 | 260 | 134 | – |

Umpires: J. Swift and James Lillywhite, jr.

# AUSTRALIA v ENGLAND 1881–82 (4th Test)

Played at Melbourne Cricket Ground on 10, 11, 13, 14 (*no play*) March.
Toss: England.   Result: MATCH DRAWN.
Debuts: Nil.

This was the last drawn Test in Australia until 1946-47. G. Ulyett's 149 was the first Test hundred for England in Australia and it was the highest score for England on the first day of a Test in Australia until R.W. Barber scored 185 in 1965-66 (*Test No. 599*).

## ENGLAND

| | | | | | |
|---|---|---|---|---|---|
| G. Ulyett | c Blackham b Garrett | 149 | c Palmer b Boyle | | 64 |
| R.G. Barlow | c Blackham b Garrett | 16 | run out | | 56 |
| J. Selby | b Spofforth | 7 | not out | | 48 |
| W. Bates | st Blackham b Garrett | 23 | not out | | 52 |
| A. Shrewsbury | lbw b Palmer | 1 | | | |
| W.E. Midwinter | c Palmer b Boyle | 21 | | | |
| W.H. Scotton | st Blackham b Giffen | 26 | | | |
| T. Emmett | b Giffen | 27 | | | |
| A. Shaw* | c Murdoch b Garrett | 3 | | | |
| R. Pilling† | not out | 6 | | | |
| E. Peate | c and b Garrett | 13 | | | |
| Extras | (B 10, LB 7) | 17 | (B 12, LB 2) | | 14 |
| **Total** | | **309** | (2 wickets) | | **234** |

## AUSTRALIA

| | | |
|---|---|---|
| W.L. Murdoch* | b Midwinter | 85 |
| A.C. Bannerman | c and b Midwinter | 37 |
| T.P. Horan | c and b Midwinter | 20 |
| P.S. McDonnell | c Barlow b Ulyett | 52 |
| H.H. Massie | c Emmett b Shaw | 19 |
| G. Giffen | c Scotton b Peate | 14 |
| J.M. Blackham† | c Pilling b Midwinter | 6 |
| T.W. Garrett | c Ulyett b Bates | 10 |
| G.E. Palmer | c Ulyett b Bates | 32 |
| H.F. Boyle | c Shrewsbury b Bates | 6 |
| F.R. Spofforth | not out | 3 |
| Extras | (B 2, LB 7, W 6, NB 1) | 16 |
| **Total** | | **300** |

| AUSTRALIA | O | M | R | W | O | M | R | W | | FALL OF WICKETS | | | |
|---|---|---|---|---|---|---|---|---|---|---|---|---|---|
| | | | | | | | | | | | E | A | E |
| Garrett | 54·2 | 23 | 80 | 5 | 27 | 6 | 62 | 0 | *Wkt* | *1st* | *1st* | *2nd* | |
| Spofforth | 51 | 14 | 92 | 1 | 15 | 3 | 36 | 0 | 1st | 32 | 110 | 98 | |
| Boyle | 18 | 4 | 33 | 1 | 25 | 9 | 38 | 1 | 2nd | 49 | 149 | 152 | |
| Palmer | 23 | 5 | 70 | 1 | 20 | 5 | 47 | 0 | 3rd | 98 | 153 | – | |
| Giffen | 13 | 6 | 17 | 2 | 8·3 | 1 | 25 | 0 | 4th | 109 | 189 | – | |
| Bannerman | | | | | 2 | 0 | 12 | 0 | 5th | 177 | 228 | – | |
| | | | | | | | | | 6th | 239 | 237 | – | |
| ENGLAND | | | | | | | | | 7th | 281 | 247 | – | |
| Bates | 28·1 | 14 | 49 | 3 | | | | | 8th | 284 | 280 | – | |
| Peate | 20 | 6 | 38 | 1 | | | | | 9th | 288 | 297 | – | |
| Emmett | 19 | 14 | 22 | 0 | | | | | 10th | 309 | 300 | – | |
| Ulyett | 24 | 8 | 40 | 1 | | | | | | | | | |
| Barlow | 15 | 6 | 25 | 0 | | | | | | | | | |
| Shaw | 16 | 6 | 29 | 1 | | | | | | | | | |
| Midwinter | 41 | 9 | 81 | 4 | | | | | | | | | |

Umpires: James Lillywhite, jr and C. Coulthard.

# ENGLAND v AUSTRALIA 1882 (Only Test)

Played at Kennington Oval, London, on 28, 29 August.
Toss: Australia.   Result: AUSTRALIA won by 7 runs.
Debuts: England – J.M. Read, C.T. Studd.

The Ashes came into being as a result of this first Australian victory over a full-strength England side in England. The *Sporting Times* carried a mock obituary notice stating that the body of English cricket would be cremated and the Ashes taken to Australia.

## AUSTRALIA

| | | | | |
|---|---|---|---|---|
| A.C. Bannerman | c Grace b Peate | 9 | c Studd b Barnes | 13 |
| H.H. Massie | b Ulyett | 1 | b Steel | 55 |
| W.L. Murdoch* | b Peate | 13 | (4) run out | 29 |
| G.J. Bonnor | b Barlow | 1 | (3) b Ulyett | 2 |
| T.P. Horan | b Barlow | 3 | c Grace b Peate | 2 |
| G. Giffen | b Peate | 2 | c Grace b Peate | 0 |
| J.M. Blackham† | c Grace b Barlow | 17 | c Lyttelton b Peate | 7 |
| T.W. Garrett | c Read b Peate | 10 | (10) not out | 2 |
| H.F. Boyle | b Barlow | 2 | (11) b Steel | 0 |
| S.P. Jones | c Barnes b Barlow | 0 | (8) run out | 6 |
| F.R. Spofforth | not out | 4 | (9) b Peate | 0 |
| Extras | (B 1) | 1 | (B 6) | 6 |
| **Total** | | **63** | | **122** |

## ENGLAND

| | | | | |
|---|---|---|---|---|
| R.G. Barlow | c Bannerman b Spofforth | 11 | (3) b Spofforth | 0 |
| W.G. Grace | b Spofforth | 4 | c Bannerman b Boyle | 32 |
| G. Ulyett | st Blackham b Spofforth | 26 | (4) c Blackham b Spofforth | 11 |
| A.P. Lucas | c Blackham b Boyle | 9 | (5) b Spofforth | 5 |
| Hon. A. Lyttelton† | c Blackham b Spofforth | 2 | (6) b Spofforth | 12 |
| C.T. Studd | b Spofforth | 0 | (10) not out | 0 |
| J.M. Read | not out | 19 | (8) b Spofforth | 0 |
| W. Barnes | b Boyle | 5 | (9) c Murdoch b Boyle | 2 |
| A.G. Steel | b Garrett | 14 | (7) c and b Spofforth | 0 |
| A.N. Hornby* | b Spofforth | 2 | (1) b Spofforth | 9 |
| E. Peate | c Boyle b Spofforth | 0 | b Boyle | 2 |
| Extras | (B 6, LB 2, NB 1) | 9 | (B 3, NB 1) | 4 |
| **Total** | | **101** | | **77** |

| ENGLAND | O | M | R | W | O | M | R | W | | FALL OF WICKETS | | | |
|---|---|---|---|---|---|---|---|---|---|---|---|---|---|
| | | | | | | | | | | A | E | A | E |
| Peate | 38 | 24 | 31 | 4 | 21 | 9 | 40 | 4 | *Wkt* | *1st* | *1st* | *2nd* | *2nd* |
| Ulyett | 9 | 5 | 11 | 1 | 6 | 2 | 10 | 1 | 1st | 6 | 13 | 66 | 15 |
| Barlow | 31 | 22 | 19 | 5 | 13 | 5 | 27 | 0 | 2nd | 21 | 18 | 70 | 15 |
| Steel | 2 | 1 | 1 | 0 | 7 | 0 | 15 | 2 | 3rd | 22 | 57 | 70 | 51 |
| Barnes | | | | | 12 | 5 | 15 | 1 | 4th | 26 | 59 | 79 | 53 |
| Studd | | | | | 4 | 1 | 9 | 0 | 5th | 30 | 60 | 79 | 66 |
| | | | | | | | | | 6th | 30 | 63 | 99 | 70 |
| AUSTRALIA | | | | | | | | | 7th | 48 | 70 | 114 | 70 |
| Spofforth | 36·3 | 18 | 46 | 7 | 28 | 15 | 44 | 7 | 8th | 53 | 96 | 117 | 75 |
| Garrett | 16 | 7 | 22 | 1 | 7 | 2 | 10 | 0 | 9th | 59 | 101 | 122 | 75 |
| Boyle | 19 | 7 | 24 | 2 | 20 | 11 | 19 | 3 | 10th | 63 | 101 | 122 | 77 |

Umpires: R. Thoms and L. Greenwood.

## AUSTRALIA v ENGLAND 1882–83 (1st Test)

Played at Melbourne Cricket Ground on 30 December, 1, 2 January.
Toss: Australia.   Result: AUSTRALIA won by nine wickets.
Debuts: England – Hon. Ivo Bligh, C.F.H. Leslie, W.W. Read, G.B. Studd, E.F.S. Tylecote,
G.F. Vernon. *The Hon. I.F.W. Bligh later became the eighth Earl of Darnley.*

### AUSTRALIA

| | | | | | |
|---|---|---|---|---|---|
| A.C. Bannerman | st Tylecote b Leslie | 30 | not out | | 25 |
| H.H. Massie | c and b C.T. Studd | 4 | c and b Barnes | | 0 |
| W.L. Murdoch* | b Leslie | 48 | not out | | 33 |
| T.P. Horan | c Barlow b Leslie | 0 | | | |
| P.S. McDonnell | b Bates | 43 | | | |
| G. Giffen | st Tylecote b Steel | 36 | | | |
| G.J. Bonnor | c Barlow b Barnes | 85 | | | |
| J.M. Blackham† | c Tylecote b C.T. Studd | 25 | | | |
| F.R. Spofforth | c Steel b Barnes | 9 | | | |
| T.W. Garrett | c C.T. Studd b Steel | 0 | | | |
| G.E. Palmer | not out | 0 | | | |
| Extras | (B 4, LB 2, W 2, NB 3) | 11 | | | |
| **Total** | | **291** | (1 wicket) | | **58** |

### ENGLAND

| | | | | | |
|---|---|---|---|---|---|
| R.G. Barlow | st Blackham b Palmer | 10 | b Spofforth | | 28 |
| Hon. Ivo Bligh* | b Palmer | 0 | (5) b Spofforth | | 3 |
| C.F.H. Leslie | c Garrett b Palmer | 4 | (7) b Giffen | | 4 |
| C.T. Studd | b Spofforth | 0 | (3) b Palmer | | 21 |
| A.G. Steel | b Palmer | 27 | (4) lbw b Giffen | | 29 |
| W.W. Read | b Palmer | 19 | b Giffen | | 29 |
| W.Bates | c Bannerman b Garrett | 28 | (8) c Massie b Palmer | | 11 |
| E.F.S. Tylecote† | b Palmer | 33 | (2) b Spofforth | | 38 |
| G.B. Studd | run out | 7 | c Palmer b Giffen | | 0 |
| W. Barnes | b Palmer | 26 | not out | | 2 |
| G.F. Vernon | not out | 11 | lbw b Palmer | | 3 |
| Extras | (B 8, LB 1, NB 3) | 12 | (LB 1) | | 1 |
| **Total** | | **177** | | | **169** |

| ENGLAND | O | M | R | W | O | M | R | W | | FALL OF WICKETS | | | |
|---|---|---|---|---|---|---|---|---|---|---|---|---|---|
| C.T. Studd | 46 | 30 | 35 | 2 | 14 | 11 | 7 | 0 | | A | E | E | A |
| Barnes | 30 | 11 | 51 | 2 | 13 | 8 | 6 | 1 | *Wkt* | *1st* | *1st* | *2nd* | *2nd* |
| Steel | 33 | 16 | 68 | 2 | 9 | 4 | 17 | 0 | 1st | 5 | 2 | 64 | 0 |
| Barlow | 20 | 6 | 37 | 0 | 4 | 2 | 6 | 0 | 2nd | 81 | 7 | 75 | – |
| Bates | 21 | 7 | 31 | 1 | 13·1 | 7 | 22 | 0 | 3rd | 81 | 8 | 105 | – |
| Read | 8 | 2 | 27 | 0 | | | | | 4th | 96 | 36 | 108 | – |
| Leslie | 11 | 1 | 31 | 3 | | | | | 5th | 162 | 45 | 132 | – |
| AUSTRALIA | | | | | | | | | 6th | 190 | 96 | 150 | – |
| Spofforth | 28 | 11 | 56 | 1 | 41 | 15 | 65 | 3 | 7th | 251 | 96 | 164 | – |
| Palmer | 52·2 | 25 | 65 | 7 | 36·1 | 11 | 61 | 3 | 8th | 289 | 117 | 164 | – |
| Garrett | 27 | 6 | 44 | 1 | 2 | 1 | 4 | 0 | 9th | 289 | 156 | 164 | – |
| Giffen | | | | | 20 | 7 | 38 | 4 | 10th | 291 | 177 | 169 | – |

Umpires: J. Swift and E.H. Elliott.

# AUSTRALIA v ENGLAND 1882–83 (2nd Test)

Played at Melbourne Cricket Ground on 19, 20, 22 January.
Toss: England.    Result: ENGLAND won by an innings and 27 runs.
Debuts: Nil.

W. Bates achieved the first Test hat-trick by an England bowler when he dismissed McDonnell, Giffen and Bonnor in the first innings. He went on to become the first player to score a fifty and take ten or more wickets in the same Test match. This was the first victory by an innings margin in Test cricket.

### ENGLAND

| | | |
|---|---|---|
| R.G. Barlow | b Palmer | 14 |
| C.T. Studd | b Palmer | 14 |
| C.F.H. Leslie | run out | 54 |
| A.G. Steel | c McDonnell b Giffen | 39 |
| W.W. Read | c and b Palmer | 75 |
| W. Barnes | b Giffen | 32 |
| E.F.S. Tylecote† | b Giffen | 0 |
| Hon. Ivo Bligh* | b Giffen | 0 |
| W. Bates | c Horan b Palmer | 55 |
| G.B. Studd | b Palmer | 1 |
| F. Morley | not out | 0 |
| Extras | (B 3, LB 3, NB 4) | 10 |
| **Total** | | **294** |

### AUSTRALIA

| | | | | | |
|---|---|---|---|---|---|
| H.H. Massie | b Barlow | 43 | (7) c C.T. Studd b Barlow | | 10 |
| A.C. Bannerman | b Bates | 14 | c Bligh b Bates | | 14 |
| W.L. Murdoch* | not out | 19 | (1) b Bates | | 17 |
| T.P. Horan | c and b Barnes | 3 | (5) c Morley b Bates | | 15 |
| P.S. McDonnell | b Bates | 3 | (6) b Bates | | 13 |
| G. Giffen | c and b Bates | 0 | (8) c Bligh b Bates | | 19 |
| G.J. Bonnor | c Read b Bates | 0 | (4) c Morley b Barlow | | 34 |
| J.M. Blackham† | b Barnes | 5 | (3) b Barlow | | 6 |
| T.W. Garrett | b Bates | 10 | c Barnes b Bates | | 6 |
| G.E. Palmer | b Bates | 7 | c G.B. Studd b Bates | | 4 |
| F.R. Spofforth | b Bates | 0 | not out | | 14 |
| Extras | (B 6, LB 3, NB 1) | 10 | (B 1) | | 1 |
| **Total** | | **114** | | | **153** |

| AUSTRALIA | O | M | R | W | O | M | R | W |
|---|---|---|---|---|---|---|---|---|
| Spofforth | 34 | 11 | 57 | 0 | | | | |
| Palmer | 66·3 | 25 | 103 | 5 | | | | |
| Giffen | 49 | 13 | 89 | 4 | | | | |
| Garrett | 34 | 16 | 35 | 0 | | | | |
| ENGLAND | | | | | | | | |
| C.T. Studd | 4 | 1 | 22 | 0 | | | | |
| Morley | 23 | 16 | 13 | 0 | 2 | 0 | 7 | 0 |
| Barnes | 23 | 7 | 32 | 2 | 3 | 1 | 4 | 0 |
| Barlow | 22 | 18 | 9 | 1 | 31 | 6 | 67 | 3 |
| Bates | 26·2 | 14 | 28 | 7 | 33 | 14 | 74 | 7 |

### FALL OF WICKETS

| | E | A | A |
|---|---|---|---|
| Wkt | 1st | 1st | 2nd |
| 1st | 28 | 56 | 21 |
| 2nd | 35 | 72 | 28 |
| 3rd | 106 | 75 | 66 |
| 4th | 131 | 78 | 72 |
| 5th | 193 | 78 | 93 |
| 6th | 199 | 78 | 104 |
| 7th | 199 | 85 | 113 |
| 8th | 287 | 104 | 132 |
| 9th | 293 | 114 | 139 |
| 10th | 294 | 114 | 153 |

Umpires: J. Swift and E.H. Elliott.

# AUSTRALIA v ENGLAND 1882–83 (3rd Test)

Played at Sydney Cricket Ground on 26, 27, 29, 30 January.
Toss: England.   Result: ENGLAND won by 69 runs.
Debuts: Nil.

After this match, the last of the rubber originally scheduled, some Australian ladies burned a bail, sealed the ashes in an urn and presented it to the victorious captain of the English team. The urn, together with its embroidered velvet bag, is housed in the Memorial Gallery at Lord's.

## ENGLAND

| | | | | |
|---|---|---|---|---|
| R.G. Barlow | c Murdoch b Spofforth | 28 | (3) c Palmer b Horan | 24 |
| C.T. Studd | c Blackham b Garrett | 21 | b Spofforth | 25 |
| C.F.H. Leslie | b Spofforth | 0 | (1) b Spofforth | 8 |
| A.G. Steel | b Garrett | 17 | lbw b Spofforth | 6 |
| W.W. Read | c Massie b Bannerman | 66 | b Horan | 21 |
| W. Barnes | b Spofforth | 2 | lbw b Spofforth | 3 |
| E.F.S. Tylecote† | run out | 66 | c Bonnor b Spofforth | 0 |
| W. Bates | c McDonnell b Spofforth | 17 | c Murdoch b Horan | 4 |
| G.B. Studd | b Palmer | 3 | (10) c Garrett b Spofforth | 8 |
| Hon. Ivo Bligh* | b Palmer | 13 | (9) not out | 17 |
| F. Morley | not out | 2 | b Spofforth | 0 |
| Extras | (B 8, LB 3, NB 1) | 12 | (B 5, LB 2) | 7 |
| **Total** | | **247** | | **123** |

## AUSTRALIA

| | | | | |
|---|---|---|---|---|
| A.C. Bannerman | c Bates b Morley | 94 | c Bligh b Barlow | 5 |
| G. Giffen | st Tylecote b Bates | 41 | b Barlow | 7 |
| W.L. Murdoch* | lbw b Steel | 19 | c G.B. Studd b Morley | 0 |
| P.S. McDonnell | b Steel | 0 | (5) c Bligh b Morley | 0 |
| T.P. Horan | c Steel b Morley | 19 | (4) run out | 8 |
| H.H. Massie | c Bligh b Steel | 1 | c C.T. Studd b Barlow | 11 |
| G.J. Bonnor | c G.B. Studd b Morley | 0 | b Barlow | 8 |
| J.M. Blackham† | b Barlow | 27 | b Barlow | 26 |
| T.W. Garrett | c Barlow b Morley | 0 | (11) b Barlow | 0 |
| G.E. Palmer | c G.B. Studd b Barnes | 7 | not out | 2 |
| F.R. Spofforth | not out | 0 | (9) c Steel b Barlow | 7 |
| Extras | (B 6, LB 2, W 1, NB 1) | 10 | (B 6, LB 2, W 1) | 9 |
| **Total** | | **218** | | **83** |

| AUSTRALIA | O | M | R | W | O | M | R | W | | | | | |
|---|---|---|---|---|---|---|---|---|---|---|---|---|---|
| Giffen | 12 | 3 | 37 | 0 | | | | | | | | | |
| Palmer | 38 | 21 | 38 | 2 | 9 | 3 | 19 | 0 | | | | | |
| Spofforth | 51 | 19 | 73 | 4 | 41·1 | 23 | 44 | 7 | | | | | |
| Garrett | 27 | 8 | 54 | 2 | 13 | 3 | 31 | 0 | | | | | |
| Bannerman | 11 | 2 | 17 | 1 | | | | | | | | | |
| McDonnell | 4 | 0 | 16 | 0 | | | | | | | | | |
| Horan | | | | | 17 | 10 | 22 | 3 | | | | | |

**FALL OF WICKETS**

| Wkt | E 1st | A 1st | E 2nd | A 2nd |
|---|---|---|---|---|
| 1st | 41 | 76 | 13 | 11 |
| 2nd | 44 | 140 | 45 | 12 |
| 3rd | 67 | 140 | 55 | 18 |
| 4th | 69 | 176 | 87 | 18 |
| 5th | 75 | 177 | 92 | 30 |
| 6th | 191 | 178 | 94 | 33 |
| 7th | 223 | 196 | 97 | 56 |
| 8th | 224 | 196 | 98 | 72 |
| 9th | 244 | 218 | 115 | 80 |
| 10th | 247 | 218 | 123 | 83 |

| ENGLAND | O | M | R | W | O | M | R | W |
|---|---|---|---|---|---|---|---|---|
| Morley | 34 | 16 | 47 | 4 | 35 | 19 | 34 | 2 |
| Barlow | 47·1 | 31 | 52 | 1 | 34·2 | 20 | 40 | 7 |
| Bates | 45 | 20 | 55 | 1 | | | | |
| Barnes | 13 | 6 | 22 | 1 | | | | |
| C.T. Studd | 14 | 11 | 5 | 0 | | | | |
| Steel | 26 | 14 | 27 | 3 | | | | |

Umpires: J. Swift and E.H. Elliott.

# AUSTRALIA v ENGLAND 1882–83 (4th Test)

Played at Sydney Cricket Ground on 17, 19, 20, 21 February.
Toss: England.    Result: AUSTRALIA won by four wickets.
Debuts: Nil.

Having completed the three-match rubber against W.L. Murdoch's 1882 touring team, England played a fourth match against a combined side. For this match the captains decided to experiment by using a separate pitch for each of the four innings.

## ENGLAND

| | | | | | |
|---|---|---|---|---|---|
| R.G. Barlow | c Murdoch b Midwinter | 2 | c Bonnor b Midwinter | 20 |
| C.T. Studd | run out | 48 | c Murdoch b Midwinter | 31 |
| C.F.H. Leslie | c Bonnor b Boyle | 17 | b Horan | 19 |
| A.G. Steel | not out | 135 | b Spofforth | 21 |
| W.W. Read | c Bonnor b Boyle | 11 | b Spofforth | 7 |
| E.F.S. Tylecote† | b Boyle | 5 | b Palmer | 0 |
| W. Barnes | b Spofforth | 2 | (9) c and b Boyle | 20 |
| W.Bates | c Bonnor b Midwinter | 9 | (7) not out | 48 |
| Hon. Ivo Bligh* | b Palmer | 19 | (8) c Murdoch b Horan | 10 |
| G.B. Studd | run out | 3 | c Murdoch b Boyle | 9 |
| F. Morley | b Palmer | 0 | c Blackham b Palmer | 2 |
| Extras | (B 4, LB 7, NB 1) | 12 | (B 8, LB 1, NB 1) | 10 |
| **Total** | | **263** | | **197** |

## AUSTRALIA

| | | | | | |
|---|---|---|---|---|---|
| A.C. Bannerman | c Barlow b Morley | 10 | c Bligh b C.T. Studd | 63 |
| G.J. Bonnor | c Barlow b Steel | 87 | (3) c G.B. Studd b Steel | 3 |
| W.L. Murdoch* | b Barlow | 0 | (2) c Barlow b Bates | 17 |
| T.P. Horan | c G.B. Studd b Morley | 4 | c and b Bates | 0 |
| G. Giffen | c G.B. Studd b Leslie | 27 | st Tylecote b Steel | 32 |
| W.E. Midwinter | b Barlow | 10 | (8) not out | 8 |
| J.M. Blackham† | b Bates | 57 | (6) not out | 58 |
| G.E. Palmer | c Bligh b Steel | 0 | | |
| E. Evans | not out | 22 | (7) c Leslie b Steel | 0 |
| F.R. Spofforth | c Bates b Steel | 1 | | |
| H.F. Boyle | c G.B. Studd b Barlow | 29 | | |
| Extras | (B 10, LB 3, W 2) | 15 | (B 10, LB 4, W 4) | 18 |
| **Total** | | **262** | (6 wickets) | **199** |

| AUSTRALIA | O | M | R | W | O | M | R | W |
|---|---|---|---|---|---|---|---|---|
| Palmer | 24 | 9 | 52 | 2 | 43·3 | 19 | 59 | 2 |
| Midwinter | 47 | 24 | 50 | 2 | 23 | 13 | 21 | 2 |
| Spofforth | 21 | 8 | 56 | 1 | 28 | 6 | 57 | 2 |
| Boyle | 40 | 19 | 52 | 3 | 23 | 6 | 35 | 2 |
| Horan | 12 | 4 | 26 | 0 | 9 | 2 | 15 | 2 |
| Evans | 11 | 3 | 15 | 0 | | | | |
| ENGLAND | | | | | | | | |
| Barlow | 48 | 21 | 88 | 3 | 37·1 | 20 | 44 | 0 |
| Morley | 44 | 25 | 45 | 2 | 12 | 9 | 4 | 0 |
| Barnes | 10 | 2 | 33 | 0 | 16 | 5 | 22 | 0 |
| Bates | 15 | 6 | 24 | 1 | 39 | 19 | 52 | 2 |
| Leslie | 5 | 2 | 11 | 1 | 8 | 7 | 2 | 0 |
| Steel | 19 | 6 | 34 | 3 | 43 | 9 | 49 | 3 |
| C.T. Studd | 6 | 2 | 12 | 0 | 8 | 4 | 8 | 1 |

| | FALL OF WICKETS | | | |
|---|---|---|---|---|
| | E | A | E | A |
| Wkt | 1st | 1st | 2nd | 2nd |
| 1st | 13 | 31 | 54 | 44 |
| 2nd | 37 | 34 | 55 | 51 |
| 3rd | 110 | 39 | 77 | 51 |
| 4th | 150 | 113 | 99 | 107 |
| 5th | 156 | 128 | 100 | 162 |
| 6th | 159 | 160 | 112 | 164 |
| 7th | 199 | 164 | 137 | – |
| 8th | 236 | 220 | 178 | – |
| 9th | 263 | 221 | 192 | – |
| 10th | 263 | 262 | 197 | – |

Umpires: J. Swift and E.H. Elliott.

# ENGLAND v AUSTRALIA 1884 (1st Test)

Played at Old Trafford, Manchester, on 10 (*no play*), 11, 12 July.
Toss: England.   Result: MATCH DRAWN.
Debuts: England – T.C. O'Brien; Australia – H.J.H. Scott. *O'Brien later became Sir Timothy Carew O'Brien, Third Baronet.*

Old Trafford immediately established its unenviable reputation as the rain-centre of Britain when the first day of Test match cricket there was washed out. This was the first rubber of more than one match to be played in England.

## ENGLAND

| | | | | | |
|---|---|---|---|---|---|
| W.G. Grace | c Palmer b Boyle | 8 | | b Palmer | 31 |
| A.N. Hornby* | st Blackham b Boyle | 0 | (9) | st Blackham b Palmer | 4 |
| G. Ulyett | b Spofforth | 5 | | c Bannerman b Boyle | 1 |
| A. Shrewsbury | b Boyle | 43 | | b Palmer | 25 |
| A.G. Steel | c Midwinter b Spofforth | 15 | | c Blackham b Bonnor | 18 |
| A.P. Lucas | not out | 15 | (2) | b Giffen | 24 |
| W. Barnes | c and b Boyle | 0 | (6) | b Palmer | 8 |
| T.C. O'Brien | b Spofforth | 0 | | c Bannerman b Spofforth | 20 |
| R.G. Barlow | c Bonnor b Boyle | 6 | (7) | not out | 14 |
| R. Pilling† | c Scott b Boyle | 0 | | b Spofforth | 3 |
| E. Peate | b Spofforth | 2 | | not out | 8 |
| Extras | (LB 1) | 1 | | (B 18, LB 5, NB 1) | 24 |
| **Total** | | **95** | | (9 wickets) | **180** |

## AUSTRALIA

| | | |
|---|---|---|
| P.S. McDonnell | c Pilling b Steel | 36 |
| A.C. Bannerman | lbw b Ulyett | 6 |
| W.L. Murdoch* | c Grace b Peate | 28 |
| G. Giffen | c and b Barnes | 16 |
| W.E. Midwinter | c Grace b Ulyett | 37 |
| G.J. Bonnor | hit wkt b Peate | 6 |
| J.M. Blackham† | lbw b Steel | 8 |
| H.J.H. Scott | b Grace | 12 |
| G.E. Palmer | not out | 14 |
| F.R. Spofforth | c Shrewsbury b Peate | 13 |
| H.F. Boyle | b Ulyett | 4 |
| Extras | (LB 2) | 2 |
| **Total** | | **182** |

| AUSTRALIA | O | M | R | W | O | M | R | W |
|---|---|---|---|---|---|---|---|---|
| Spofforth | 32 | 10 | 42 | 4 | 41 | 17 | 5 | 2 |
| Boyle | 25 | 9 | 42 | 6 | 20 | 8 | 27 | 1 |
| Palmer | 6 | 2 | 10 | 0 | 36 | 17 | 47 | 4 |
| Giffen | | | | | 29 | 15 | 25 | 1 |
| Bonnor | | | | | 4 | 1 | 5 | 1 |

| ENGLAND | O | M | R | W |
|---|---|---|---|---|
| Peate | 49 | 25 | 62 | 3 |
| Ulyett | 30 | 17 | 41 | 3 |
| Barlow | 8 | 3 | 18 | 0 |
| Steel | 13 | 5 | 32 | 2 |
| Barnes | 19 | 10 | 25 | 1 |
| Grace | 11 | 10 | 2 | 1 |

FALL OF WICKETS

| | E | A | E |
|---|---|---|---|
| Wkt | 1st | 1st | 2nd |
| 1st | 6 | 10 | 41 |
| 2nd | 13 | 56 | 44 |
| 3rd | 13 | 86 | 70 |
| 4th | 45 | 90 | 106 |
| 5th | 83 | 97 | 108 |
| 6th | 83 | 118 | 114 |
| 7th | 84 | 141 | 139 |
| 8th | 93 | 157 | 145 |
| 9th | 93 | 172 | 154 |
| 10th | 95 | 182 | – |

Umpires: J. Rowbotham and C.K. Pullin.

# ENGLAND v AUSTRALIA 1884 (2nd Test)

Played at Lord's, London, on 21, 22, 23 July.
Toss: Australia.   Result: ENGLAND won by an innings and 5 runs.
Debuts: England – S. Christopherson.

The first Test to be played at Thomas Lord's third ground.

## AUSTRALIA

| | | | | | |
|---|---|---|---|---|---|
| P.S. McDonnell | b Peate | 0 | b Steel | | 20 |
| A.C. Bannerman | b Peate | 12 | c and b Ulyett | | 27 |
| W.L. Murdoch* | lbw b Peate | 10 | c Shrewsbury b Ulyett | | 17 |
| G. Giffen | b Peate | 63 | c Peate b Ulyett | | 5 |
| W.E. Midwinter | b Peate | 3 | (7) b Ulyett | | 6 |
| G.J. Bonnor | c Grace b Christopherson | 25 | (5) c and b Ulyett | | 4 |
| J.M. Blackham† | run out | 0 | (8) retired hurt | | 0 |
| H.J.H. Scott | c sub (W.L. Murdoch) b Steel | 75 | (6) not out | | 31 |
| G.E. Palmer | c Grace b Peate | 7 | b Ulyett | | 13 |
| F.R. Spofforth | c Barlow b Grace | 0 | c Shrewsbury b Barlow | | 11 |
| H.F. Boyle | not out | 26 | b Ulyett | | 10 |
| Extras | (B 5, LB 3) | 8 | (B 1) | | 1 |
| **Total** | | **229** | | | **145** |

## ENGLAND

| | | |
|---|---|---|
| W.G. Grace | c Bonnor b Palmer | 14 |
| A.P. Lucas | c Bonnor b Palmer | 28 |
| A. Shrewsbury | st Blackham b Giffen | 27 |
| G. Ulyett | b Palmer | 32 |
| A.G. Steel | b Palmer | 148 |
| Lord Harris* | b Spofforth | 4 |
| R.G. Barlow | c Palmer b Bonnor | 38 |
| W.W. Read | b Palmer | 12 |
| Hon. A. Lyttelton† | b Palmer | 31 |
| E. Peate | not out | 8 |
| S. Christopherson | c Bonnor b Spofforth | 17 |
| Extras | (B 15, LB 5) | 20 |
| **Total** | | **379** |

| ENGLAND | O | M | R | W | O | M | R | W | FALL OF WICKETS | | | |
|---|---|---|---|---|---|---|---|---|---|---|---|---|
| Peate | 40 | 14 | 85 | 6 | 16 | 4 | 34 | 0 | | A | E | A |
| Barlow | 20 | 6 | 44 | 0 | 21 | 8 | 31 | 1 | Wkt | 1st | 1st | 2nd |
| Ulyett | 11 | 3 | 21 | 0 | 39·1 | 23 | 36 | 7 | 1st | 0 | 37 | 33 |
| Christopherson | 26 | 10 | 52 | 1 | 8 | 3 | 17 | 0 | 2nd | 25 | 56 | 60 |
| Grace | 7 | 4 | 13 | 1 | | | | | 3rd | 32 | 90 | 65 |
| Steel | 1·2 | 0 | 6 | 1 | 10 | 2 | 26 | 1 | 4th | 46 | 120 | 73 |
| | | | | | | | | | 5th | 88 | 135 | 84 |
| AUSTRALIA | | | | | | | | | 6th | 93 | 233 | 90 |
| Spofforth | 55·1 | 19 | 112 | 2 | | | | | 7th | 132 | 272 | 118 |
| Palmer | 75 | 26 | 111 | 6 | | | | | 8th | 155 | 348 | 133 |
| Giffen | 22 | 4 | 68 | 1 | | | | | 9th | 160 | 351 | 145 |
| Boyle | 11 | 3 | 16 | 0 | | | | | 10th | 229 | 379 | – |
| Bonnor | 8 | 1 | 23 | 1 | | | | | | | | |
| Midwinter | 13 | 2 | 29 | 0 | | | | | | | | |

Umpires: F.H. Farrands and C.K. Pullin.

# ENGLAND v AUSTRALIA 1884 (3rd Test)

Played at Kennington Oval, London, on 11, 12, 13 August.
Toss: Australia.   Result: MATCH DRAWN.
Debuts: Nil.

W.L. Murdoch scored the first double-century in Test cricket. His stand with Scott of 207 was a Test record for any wicket. W.W. Read reached his hundred in 113 minutes with 36 scoring strokes; it remains the highest Test innings by a No. 10 batsman. For the only time in Test cricket all eleven players bowled during Australia's innings, Grace keeping wicket while Lyttelton took four wickets with lobs. Declarations were not permitted until 1889.

## AUSTRALIA

| | | |
|---|---|---|
| A.C. Bannerman | c Read b Peate | 4 |
| P.S. McDonnell | c Ulyett b Peate | 103 |
| W.L. Murdoch* | c Peate b Barnes | 211 |
| H.J.H. Scott | c Lyttelton b Barnes | 102 |
| G. Giffen | c Steel b Ulyett | 32 |
| G.J. Bonnor | c Read b Grace | 8 |
| W.E. Midwinter | c Grace b Lyttelton | 30 |
| J.M. Blackham† | lbw b Lyttelton | 31 |
| G.E. Palmer | not out | 8 |
| F.R. Spofforth | b Lyttelton | 4 |
| H.F. Boyle | c Harris b Lyttelton | 1 |
| Extras | (B 7, LB 10) | 17 |
| **Total** | | **551** |

## ENGLAND

| | | | | |
|---|---|---|---|---|
| W.G. Grace | run out | 19 | | |
| W.H. Scotton | c Scott b Giffen | 90 | | |
| W.Barnes | c Midwinter b Spofforth | 19 | | |
| A. Shrewsbury | c Blackham b Midwinter | 10 | (3) c Scott b Giffen | 37 |
| A.G. Steel | lbw b Palmer | 31 | | |
| G. Ulyett | c Bannerman b Palmer | 10 | | |
| R.G. Barlow | c Murdoch b Palmer | 0 | (1) not out | 21 |
| Lord Harris* | lbw b Palmer | 14 | (4) not out | 6 |
| Hon. A. Lyttelton† | b Spofforth | 8 | (2) b Boyle | 17 |
| W.W. Read | b Boyle | 117 | | |
| E. Peate | not out | 4 | | |
| Extras | (B 8, LB 7, W 6, NB 3) | 24 | (B 3, LB 1) | 4 |
| **Total** | | **346** | (2 wickets) | **85** |

| ENGLAND | O | M | R | W | O | M | R | W |
|---|---|---|---|---|---|---|---|---|
| Peate | 63 | 25 | 99 | 2 | | | | |
| Ulyett | 56 | 24 | 96 | 1 | | | | |
| Steel | 34 | 7 | 71 | 0 | | | | |
| Barnes | 52 | 25 | 81 | 2 | | | | |
| Barlow | 50 | 22 | 72 | 0 | | | | |
| Grace | 24 | 14 | 23 | 1 | | | | |
| Read | 7 | 0 | 36 | 0 | | | | |
| Scotton | 5 | 1 | 20 | 0 | | | | |
| Harris | 5 | 1 | 15 | 0 | | | | |
| Lyttelton | 12 | 5 | 19 | 4 | | | | |
| Shrewsbury | 3 | 2 | 2 | 0 | | | | |
| AUSTRALIA | | | | | | | | |
| Bonnor | 13 | 4 | 33 | 0 | | | | |
| Palmer | 54 | 19 | 90 | 4 | 2 | 1 | 2 | 0 |
| Spofforth | 58 | 31 | 81 | 2 | 6 | 2 | 14 | 0 |
| Boyle | 13 | 7 | 24 | 1 | 8 | 1 | 32 | 1 |
| Midwinter | 31 | 16 | 41 | 1 | 3 | 0 | 15 | 0 |
| Giffen | 26 | 13 | 36 | 1 | 7 | 1 | 18 | 1 |
| Scott | 3 | 0 | 17 | 0 | | | | |

### FALL OF WICKETS

| | A | E | E |
|---|---|---|---|
| Wkt | 1st | 1st | 2nd |
| 1st | 15 | 32 | 22 |
| 2nd | 158 | 60 | 73 |
| 3rd | 365 | 75 | – |
| 4th | 432 | 120 | – |
| 5th | 454 | 136 | – |
| 6th | 494 | 136 | – |
| 7th | 532 | 160 | – |
| 8th | 545 | 181 | – |
| 9th | 549 | 332 | – |
| 10th | 551 | 346 | – |

Umpires: F.H. Farrands and C.K. Pullin.

# AUSTRALIA v ENGLAND 1884–85 (1st Test)

Played at Adelaide Oval on 12, 13, 15, 16 December.
Toss: Australia.    Result: ENGLAND won by eight wickets.
Debuts: England – W. Attewell, J. Briggs, W. Flowers, J. Hunter, R. Peel.

McDonnell became the first batsman to score two hundreds in successive Test innings. This was the first Test to be played at Adelaide.

## AUSTRALIA

| | | | | |
|---|---|---|---|---|
| A.C. Bannerman | lbw b Peel | 2 | absent hurt | – |
| P.S. McDonnell | b Attewell | 124 | run out | 83 |
| W.L. Murdoch* | c Hunter b Peel | 5 | b Peel | 7 |
| H.J.H. Scott | b Peel | 19 | (5) lbw b Peel | 1 |
| J.M. Blackham† | c Attewell b Bates | 66 | (1) b Peel | 11 |
| G. Giffen | b Bates | 4 | (4) c Shrewsbury b Peel | 47 |
| G.J. Bonnor | c Read b Bates | 4 | c Peel b Barnes | 19 |
| G.E. Palmer | c Shrewsbury b Bates | 6 | b Barnes | 0 |
| H.F. Boyle | c Hunter b Bates | 1 | (10) not out | 0 |
| G. Alexander | run out | 3 | (9) st Hunter b Peel | 10 |
| W.H. Cooper | not out | 0 | (6) c Shrewsbury b Barnes | 6 |
| Extras | (B 7, W 2) | 9 | (B 7) | 7 |
| **Total** | | **243** | | **191** |

## ENGLAND

| | | | | |
|---|---|---|---|---|
| W.H. Scotton | st Blackham b Giffen | 82 | c Scott b Boyle | 2 |
| A. Shrewsbury* | b Boyle | 0 | (3) not out | 26 |
| G.Ulyett | c Alexander b Boyle | 68 | | |
| W. Barnes | b Palmer | 134 | (4) not out | 28 |
| W. Bates | c Giffen b Palmer | 18 | | |
| W. Flowers | lbw b Palmer | 15 | (2) c Scott b Palmer | 7 |
| J.M. Read | c and b Giffen | 14 | | |
| J. Briggs | c Blackham b Palmer | 1 | | |
| W. Attewell | not out | 12 | | |
| R. Peel | b Palmer | 4 | | |
| J. Hunter† | run out | 1 | | |
| Extras | (B 18, LB 1, NB 1) | 20 | (B 4) | 4 |
| **Total** | | **369** | (2 wickets) | **67** |

| ENGLAND | O | M | R | W | O | M | R | W | | FALL OF WICKETS | | | |
|---|---|---|---|---|---|---|---|---|---|---|---|---|---|
| Peel | 41 | 15 | 68 | 3 | 40·1 | 15 | 51 | 5 | | A | E | A | E |
| Attewell | 50 | 23 | 48 | 1 | 18 | 10 | 26 | 0 | *Wkt* | *1st* | *1st* | *2nd* | *2nd* |
| Ulyett | 10 | 3 | 23 | 0 | 2 | 1 | 3 | 0 | 1st | 33 | 11 | 28 | 8 |
| Flowers | 10 | 1 | 27 | 0 | 16 | 4 | 27 | 0 | 2nd | 47 | 107 | 56 | 14 |
| Barnes | 14 | 2 | 37 | 0 | 31 | 10 | 51 | 3 | 3rd | 95 | 282 | 125 | – |
| Bates | 24·1 | 10 | 31 | 5 | 9 | 3 | 26 | 0 | 4th | 190 | 306 | 139 | – |
| | | | | | | | | | 5th | 224 | 325 | 160 | – |
| AUSTRALIA | | | | | | | | | 6th | 227 | 344 | 171 | – |
| Boyle | 63 | 25 | 95 | 2 | 9 | 3 | 21 | 1 | 7th | 233 | 349 | 182 | – |
| Giffen | 56·2 | 26 | 80 | 2 | 6 | 0 | 19 | 0 | 8th | 239 | 349 | 191 | – |
| Cooper | 18 | 4 | 26 | 0 | | | | | 9th | 242 | 361 | 191 | – |
| Bonnor | 16 | 10 | 23 | 0 | | | | | 10th | 243 | 369 | – | – |
| Palmer | 73 | 37 | 81 | 5 | 16 | 5 | 23 | 1 | | | | | |
| McDonnell | 3 | 0 | 11 | 0 | | | | | | | | | |
| Scott | 4 | 1 | 9 | 0 | | | | | | | | | |
| Alexander | 10 | 3 | 24 | 0 | | | | | | | | | |

Umpires: I. Fisher and J. Travers.

## AUSTRALIA v ENGLAND 1884–85 (2nd Test)

Played at Melbourne Cricket Ground on 1, 2, 3, 5 January.
Toss: England.   Result: ENGLAND won by ten wickets.
Debuts: Australia – W. Bruce, A.H. Jarvis, A.P. Marr, S. Morris, H. Musgrove, R.J. Pope,
W.R. Robertson, J.W. Trumble, J. Worrall.

Australia's team showed eleven changes as a result of the 1884 touring team (who had contested the 1st Test) demanding fifty per cent of the gate money for this match. Thus was ended the unique run of J.M. Blackham who played in each of the first 17 Test matches. For the first time players from the same county (Shrewsbury, Scotton and Barnes of Nottinghamshire) occupied the first three places in England's batting order.

### ENGLAND

| | | | | |
|---|---|---|---|---|
| A. Shrewsbury* | c Worrall b Morris | 72 | not out | 0 |
| W.H. Scotton | b Bruce | 13 | not out | 7 |
| W. Barnes | b Morris | 58 | | |
| W. Bates | b Bruce | 35 | | |
| W. Flowers | c Worrall b Bruce | 5 | | |
| J.M. Read | b Jones | 3 | | |
| J. Briggs | c Horan b Jones | 121 | | |
| G. Ulyett | b Jones | 0 | | |
| W. Attewell | c Jones b Worrall | 30 | | |
| R. Peel | b Jones | 5 | | |
| J. Hunter† | not out | 39 | | |
| Extras | (B 7, LB 12, NB 1) | 20 | | |
| **Total** | | **401** | (0 wickets) | 7 |

### AUSTRALIA

| | | | | |
|---|---|---|---|---|
| S.P. Jones | lbw b Peel | 19 | b Ulyett | 9 |
| S. Morris | lbw b Attewell | 4 | (10) not out | 10 |
| T.P. Horan* | c Shrewsbury b Peel | 63 | c Hunter b Barnes | 16 |
| J.W. Trumble | c and b Barnes | 59 | c and b Barnes | 11 |
| A.H. Jarvis† | c Briggs b Flowers | 82 | lbw b Peel | 10 |
| R.J. Pope | c Flowers b Attewell | 0 | b Peel | 3 |
| A.P. Marr | b Barnes | 0 | c and b Barnes | 5 |
| H. Musgrove | c Read b Barnes | 4 | c Bates b Peel | 9 |
| J. Worrall | b Flowers | 34 | c and b Barnes | 6 |
| W. Bruce | not out | 3 | (2) c Hunter b Barnes | 45 |
| W.R. Robertson | c Barnes b Peel | 0 | b Barnes | 2 |
| Extras | (B 3, LB 4, W 2, NB 2) | 11 | | |
| **Total** | | **279** | | **126** |

| AUSTRALIA | O | M | R | W | O | M | R | W |
|---|---|---|---|---|---|---|---|---|
| Bruce | 55 | 22 | 88 | 3 | 0·1 | 0 | 4 | 0 |
| Worrall | 56 | 28 | 97 | 1 | | | | |
| Marr | 11 | 6 | 11 | 0 | 1 | 0 | 3 | 0 |
| Trumble | 23 | 9 | 41 | 0 | | | | |
| Robertson | 11 | 3 | 24 | 0 | | | | |
| Morris | 34 | 14 | 73 | 2 | | | | |
| Jones | 25·2 | 9 | 47 | 4 | | | | |
| Horan | 1 | 1 | 0 | 0 | | | | |
| ENGLAND | | | | | | | | |
| Flowers | 29 | 12 | 46 | 2 | 11 | 6 | 11 | 0 |
| Attewell | 61 | 35 | 54 | 2 | 5 | 2 | 7 | 0 |
| Barnes | 50 | 27 | 50 | 3 | 38·3 | 26 | 31 | 6 |
| Peel | 102·1 | 56 | 78 | 3 | 44 | 26 | 45 | 3 |
| Bates | 17 | 11 | 17 | 0 | | | | |
| Ulyett | 15 | 7 | 23 | 0 | 8 | 3 | 19 | 1 |
| Briggs | | | | | 8 | 3 | 13 | 0 |

### FALL OF WICKETS

| | E | A | A | E |
|---|---|---|---|---|
| Wkt | 1st | 1st | 2nd | 2nd |
| 1st | 28 | 4 | 29 | – |
| 2nd | 144 | 46 | 66 | – |
| 3rd | 161 | 124 | 80 | – |
| 4th | 191 | 190 | 83 | – |
| 5th | 194 | 193 | 86 | – |
| 6th | 204 | 193 | 95 | – |
| 7th | 204 | 203 | 99 | – |
| 8th | 254 | 276 | 108 | – |
| 9th | 303 | 278 | 116 | – |
| 10th | 401 | 279 | 126 | – |

Umpires: James Lillywhite, jr and E.H. Elliott.

# AUSTRALIA v ENGLAND 1884–85 (3rd Test)

Played at Sydney Cricket Ground on 20, 21, 23, 24 February.
Toss: Australia.   Result: AUSTRALIA won by 6 runs.
Debuts: Nil.

This match resulted in the smallest margin of victory in a Test until Australia beat England by three runs in 1902 (*Test No. 73*). F.R. Spofforth took England's first three first innings wickets in four balls.

## AUSTRALIA

| | | | | | |
|---|---|---|---|---|---|
| A.C. Bannerman | c Peel b Flowers | 13 | | c Shrewsbury b Ulyett | 16 |
| S.P. Jones | st Hunter b Flowers | 28 | (4) | b Attewell | 22 |
| T.P. Horan | c Hunter b Attewell | 7 | | b Bates | 36 |
| H.J.H. Scott | c Ulyett b Attewell | 5 | (5) | c Barnes b Attewell | 4 |
| G.J. Bonnor | c Barnes b Flowers | 18 | (2) | b Ulyett | 29 |
| J.W. Trumble | c Read b Attewell | 13 | | c Ulyett b Bates | 32 |
| H.H. Massie* | c Scotton b Flowers | 2 | | b Bates | 21 |
| A.H. Jarvis† | b Attewell | 0 | | c and b Peel | 2 |
| F.R. Spofforth | st Hunter b Flowers | 3 | (11) | c Attewell b Bates | 0 |
| T.W. Garrett | not out | 51 | | not out | 0 |
| E. Evans | c Hunter b Ulyett | 33 | (9) | b Bates | 1 |
| Extras | (B 3, LB 5) | 8 | | (B 1, LB 1) | 2 |
| **Total** | | **181** | | | **165** |

## ENGLAND

| | | | | | |
|---|---|---|---|---|---|
| W.H. Scotton | c Jarvis b Horan | 22 | | b Spofforth | 2 |
| A. Shrewsbury* | c and b Spofforth | 18 | | b Spofforth | 24 |
| G.Ulyett | b Spofforth | 2 | | run out | 4 |
| W. Barnes | st Jarvis b Spofforth | 0 | | c Jarvis b Trumble | 5 |
| W. Bates | c Evans b Horan | 12 | | c Jarvis b Spofforth | 31 |
| J. Briggs | c Scott b Horan | 3 | | b Spofforth | 1 |
| W. Flowers | c Jarvis b Spofforth | 24 | | c Evans b Spofforth | 56 |
| J.M. Read | c Evans b Horan | 4 | | b Spofforth | 56 |
| W. Attewell | b Horan | 14 | | run out | 0 |
| R. Peel | not out | 8 | | c Jarvis b Trumble | 3 |
| J. Hunter† | b Horan | 13 | | not out | 5 |
| Extras | (B 8, LB 3, NB 2) | 13 | | (B 7, LB 9, W 1, NB 3) | 20 |
| **Total** | | **133** | | | **207** |

| ENGLAND | O | M | R | W | O | M | R | W |
|---|---|---|---|---|---|---|---|---|
| Attewell | 71 | 47 | 53 | 4 | 58 | 36 | 54 | 2 |
| Ulyett | 12·2 | 8 | 17 | 1 | 39 | 25 | 42 | 2 |
| Flowers | 46 | 24 | 46 | 5 | 20 | 14 | 19 | 0 |
| Bates | 6 | 2 | 6 | 0 | 20 | 10 | 24 | 5 |
| Peel | 32 | 13 | 51 | 0 | 20 | 10 | 24 | 1 |
| **AUSTRALIA** | | | | | | | | |
| Spofforth | 48 | 23 | 54 | 4 | 48·1 | 22 | 90 | 6 |
| Garrett | 6 | 2 | 17 | 0 | 16 | 8 | 31 | 0 |
| Horan | 37·1 | 22 | 40 | 6 | 9 | 4 | 23 | 0 |
| Evans | 4 | 1 | 9 | 0 | 4 | 1 | 8 | 0 |
| Trumble | | | | | 26 | 13 | 26 | 2 |
| Jones | | | | | 3 | 0 | 9 | 0 |

FALL OF WICKETS

| Wkt | A 1st | E 1st | A 2nd | E 2nd |
|---|---|---|---|---|
| 1st | 45 | 31 | 36 | 14 |
| 2nd | 46 | 33 | 56 | 18 |
| 3rd | 56 | 33 | 91 | 29 |
| 4th | 73 | 46 | 95 | 59 |
| 5th | 77 | 56 | 119 | 61 |
| 6th | 83 | 70 | 151 | 92 |
| 7th | 83 | 82 | 161 | 194 |
| 8th | 94 | 111 | 165 | 194 |
| 9th | 101 | 111 | 165 | 199 |
| 10th | 181 | 133 | 165 | 207 |

Umpires: E. Payne and J. Bryant.

# AUSTRALIA v ENGLAND 1884–85 (4th Test)

Played at Sydney Cricket Ground on 14, 16, 17 March.
Toss: England.   Result: AUSTRALIA won by eight wickets.
Debuts: Nil.

Bonnor, 6 ft. 6 in. tall, scored his hundred in 100 minutes and it remained the fastest in Tests until J.T. Brown reached his in 95 minutes in 1894-95 (*Test No. 46*). Note that in the second innings Australia's total was 40 (not 38), the two additional runs being byes.

## ENGLAND

| | | | | | |
|---|---|---|---|---|---|
| G. Ulyett | b Giffen | 10 | c Garrett b Palmer | | 2 |
| A. Shrewsbury* | b Giffen | 40 | c Bonnor b Spofforth | | 16 |
| W.H. Scotton | c Blackham b Giffen | 4 | c Jones b Spofforth | | 0 |
| W. Barnes | b Giffen | 50 | c Bannerman b Spofforth | | 20 |
| W. Bates | c and b Jones | 64 | c Blackham b Palmer | | 1 |
| J.M. Read | b Giffen | 47 | c Bannerman b Spofforth | | 6 |
| W. Flowers | b Giffen | 14 | c Jones b Palmer | | 7 |
| J. Briggs | c Palmer b Spofforth | 3 | run out | | 5 |
| W. Attewell | b Giffen | 1 | not out | | 1 |
| R. Peel | not out | 17 | c and b Spofforth | | 0 |
| J. Hunter† | b Spofforth | 13 | b Palmer | | 4 |
| Extras | (B 5, NB 1) | 6 | (B 14, NB 1) | | 15 |
| **Total** | | **269** | | | **77** |

## AUSTRALIA

| | | | | | |
|---|---|---|---|---|---|
| G.E. Palmer | b Ulyett | 0 | | | |
| T.W. Garrett | b Barnes | 32 | | | |
| J.W. Trumble | b Peel | 5 | | | |
| P.S. McDonnell | c Attewell b Ulyett | 20 | (1) c Flowers b Peel | | 3 |
| A.C. Bannerman | c Shrewsbury b Flowers | 51 | (2) b Barnes | | 8 |
| G. Giffen | c Attewell b Barnes | 1 | | | |
| T.P. Horan | c Barnes b Ulyett | 9 | (3) not out | | 12 |
| G.J. Bonnor | c Bates b Barnes | 128 | | | |
| S.P. Jones | run out | 40 | (4) not out | | 15 |
| J.M. Blackham*† | not out | 11 | | | |
| F.R. Spofforth | c Read b Barnes | 1 | | | |
| Extras | (B 5, LB 1, W 2, NB 3) | 11 | (B 2) | | 2 |
| **Total** | | **309** | (2 wickets) | | **40** |

| AUSTRALIA | O | M | R | W | O | M | R | W |
|---|---|---|---|---|---|---|---|---|
| Giffen | 52 | 14 | 117 | 7 | | | | |
| Palmer | 16 | 5 | 35 | 0 | 19·1 | 7 | 32 | 4 |
| Spofforth | 29 | 10 | 61 | 2 | 20 | 8 | 30 | 5 |
| Garrett | 2 | 1 | 5 | 0 | | | | |
| Trumble | 12 | 5 | 16 | 0 | | | | |
| Horan | 5 | 2 | 12 | 0 | | | | |
| Jones | 10 | 5 | 17 | 1 | | | | |
| ENGLAND | | | | | | | | |
| Ulyett | 54 | 25 | 91 | 3 | | | | |
| Peel | 31 | 12 | 53 | 1 | 9 | 4 | 16 | 1 |
| Attewell | 18 | 13 | 22 | 0 | 3 | 1 | 4 | 0 |
| Bates | 17 | 5 | 44 | 0 | | | | |
| Barnes | 35·3 | 17 | 61 | 4 | 9 | 3 | 15 | 1 |
| Flowers | 14 | 5 | 27 | 1 | 3·3 | 2 | 3 | 0 |

| FALL OF WICKETS | | | | |
|---|---|---|---|---|
| | E | A | E | A |
| Wkt | 1st | 1st | 2nd | 2nd |
| 1st | 19 | 0 | 5 | 7 |
| 2nd | 52 | 16 | 16 | 16 |
| 3rd | 76 | 40 | 19 | – |
| 4th | 159 | 98 | 20 | – |
| 5th | 186 | 108 | 27 | – |
| 6th | 219 | 119 | 42 | – |
| 7th | 222 | 134 | 63 | – |
| 8th | 229 | 288 | 69 | – |
| 9th | 252 | 308 | 69 | – |
| 10th | 269 | 309 | 77 | – |

Umpires: E.H. Elliott and P.G. McShane.

# AUSTRALIA v ENGLAND 1884–85 (5th Test)

Played at Melbourne Cricket Ground on 21, 23, 24, 25 March.
Toss: Australia.    Result: ENGLAND won by an innings and 98 runs.
Debuts: Australia – P.G. McShane, F.H. Walters.

A. Shrewsbury became the first England captain to score a Test match hundred. T.W. Garrett deputised for umpire J. Hodges when the latter refused to stand after tea on the third day because of England's complaints about his decisions. J.C. Allen stood for J. Phillips on third and fourth days. McShane played in this Test after umpiring in the previous one. Bates retired ill with 54 not out when England were 214-4. England fielded an unchanged team throughout the five-match rubber.

## AUSTRALIA

| | | | | | |
|---|---|---|---|---|---|
| A.C. Bannerman | c Peel b Ulyett | 5 | | c sub (G.F. Vernon) b Ulyett | 2 |
| W. Bruce | c Briggs b Peel | 15 | (6) | c Bates b Attewell | 35 |
| G. Giffen | b Ulyett | 13 | | c Peel b Ulyett | 12 |
| T.P. Horan* | lbw b Ulyett | 0 | (5) | b Attewell | 20 |
| S.P. Jones | lbw b Peel | 0 | (4) | b Peel | 17 |
| F.H. Walters | b Ulyett | 7 | (8) | c Attewell b Flowers | 5 |
| A.H. Jarvis† | c Hunter b Peel | 15 | (9) | c Peel b Flowers | 1 |
| J.W. Trumble | not out | 34 | (7) | lbw b Attewell | 10 |
| P.G. McShane | c Hunter b Barnes | 9 | (11) | not out | 12 |
| T.W. Garrett | c Briggs b Barnes | 6 | (2) | b Ulyett | 5 |
| F.R. Spofforth | b Attewell | 50 | (10) | c sub (A.H. Jarvis) b Flowers | 1 |
| Extras | (B 5, LB 1, NB 3) | 9 | | (B 5) | 5 |
| **Total** | | **163** | | | **125** |

## ENGLAND

| | | |
|---|---|---|
| W.H. Scotton | b Bruce | 27 |
| W. Barnes | c Horan b Bruce | 74 |
| J.M. Read | b Giffen | 13 |
| G. Ulyett | b Spofforth | 1 |
| A. Shrewsbury* | not out | 105 |
| W. Bates | c Walters b Bruce | 61 |
| W. Flowers | b Spofforth | 16 |
| J. Briggs | c Walters b Trumble | 43 |
| W. Attewell | c Bannerman b Trumble | 0 |
| R. Peel | b Trumble | 0 |
| J. Hunter† | b Giffen | 18 |
| Extras | (B 10, LB 14, NB 4) | 28 |
| **Total** | | **386** |

| ENGLAND | O | M | R | W | O | M | R | W | | FALL OF WICKETS | | |
|---|---|---|---|---|---|---|---|---|---|---|---|---|
| Peel | 41 | 26 | 28 | 3 | 30 | 16 | 37 | 1 | | A | E | A |
| Ulyett | 23 | 7 | 52 | 4 | 15 | 7 | 25 | 3 | *Wkt* | *1st* | *1st* | *2nd* |
| Barnes | 28 | 12 | 47 | 2 | | | | | 1st | 21 | 60 | 4 |
| Flowers | 9 | 6 | 9 | 0 | 21 | 7 | 34 | 3 | 2nd | 21 | 96 | 17 |
| Attewell | 5 | 1 | 18 | 1 | 36·1 | 22 | 24 | 3 | 3rd | 21 | 97 | 26 |
| | | | | | | | | | 4th | 34 | 141 | 60 |
| AUSTRALIA | | | | | | | | | 5th | 34 | 256 | 60 |
| Giffen | 74·3 | 31 | 132 | 2 | | | | | 6th | 45 | 324 | 91 |
| Bruce | 51 | 13 | 99 | 3 | | | | | 7th | 67 | 324 | 100 |
| Spofforth | 49 | 21 | 71 | 2 | | | | | 8th | 87 | 335 | 106 |
| Trumble | 28 | 14 | 29 | 3 | | | | | 9th | 99 | 337 | 108 |
| Garrett | 8 | 6 | 12 | 0 | | | | | 10th | 163 | 386 | 125 |
| McShane | 3 | 2 | 3 | 0 | | | | | | | | |
| Jones | 5 | 2 | 7 | 0 | | | | | | | | |
| Horan | 3 | 0 | 5 | 0 | | | | | | | | |

Umpires: J. Hodges and J. Phillips.

WBOTMR—2 **

# ENGLAND v AUSTRALIA 1886 (1st Test)

Played at Old Trafford, Manchester, on 5, 6, 7 July.
Toss: Australia.   Result: ENGLAND won by four wickets.
Debuts: England – G.A. Lohmann.

## AUSTRALIA

| | | | | | |
|---|---|---|---|---|---|
| S.P. Jones | lbw b Grace | 87 | c Ulyett b Steel | | 12 |
| H.J.H. Scott* | c Barlow b Ulyett | 21 | b Barlow | | 47 |
| G. Giffen | b Steel | 3 | c Shrewsbury b Barlow | | 1 |
| A.H. Jarvis | c Scotton b Ulyett | 45 | c Lohmann b Barlow | | 2 |
| G.J. Bonnor | c Lohmann b Barlow | 4 | c Barlow b Peate | | 2 |
| J.W. Trumble | c Scotton b Steel | 24 | c Ulyett b Barlow | | 4 |
| W. Bruce | run out | 2 | (8) c Grace b Barlow | | 0 |
| T.W. Garrett | c Pilling b Lohmann | 5 | (9) c Grace b Ulyett | | 22 |
| J.M. Blackham† | not out | 7 | (7) lbw b Barlow | | 2 |
| G.E. Palmer | c Lohmann b Ulyett | 4 | c Pilling b Barlow | | 8 |
| F.R. Spofforth | c Barlow b Ulyett | 2 | not out | | 20 |
| Extras | (W1) | 1 | (B 3) | | 3 |
| **Total** | | **205** | | | **123** |

## ENGLAND

| | | | | | |
|---|---|---|---|---|---|
| W.H. Scotton | c Trumble b Garrett | 21 | b Palmer | | 20 |
| W.G. Grace | c Bonnor b Spofforth | 8 | c Palmer b Giffen | | 4 |
| A. Shrewsbury | b Spofforth | 31 | c and b Giffen | | 4 |
| W.W. Read | c Scott b Garrett | 51 | c Jones b Spofforth | | 9 |
| A.G. Steel* | c Jarvis b Palmer | 12 | (6) not out | | 19 |
| R.G. Barlow | not out | 38 | (5) c Palmer b Spofforth | | 30 |
| G. Ulyett | b Spofforth | 17 | c Scott b Garrett | | 8 |
| J. Briggs | c Garrett b Spofforth | 1 | not out | | 2 |
| G.A. Lohmann | b Giffen | 32 | | | |
| E. Peate | st Jarvis b Palmer | 6 | | | |
| R. Pilling† | c Bruce b Palmer | 2 | | | |
| Extras | (B 2, LB 2) | 4 | (B 10, LB 1) | | 11 |
| **Total** | | **223** | (6 wickets) | | **107** |

| ENGLAND | O | M | R | W | O | M | R | W |
|---|---|---|---|---|---|---|---|---|
| Peate | 19 | 7 | 30 | 0 | 46 | 35 | 45 | 1 |
| Lohmann | 23 | 9 | 41 | 1 | 5 | 3 | 14 | 0 |
| Steel | 27 | 5 | 47 | 2 | 8 | 3 | 9 | 1 |
| Ulyett | 36·1 | 20 | 46 | 4 | 6·3 | 3 | 7 | 1 |
| Barlow | 23 | 15 | 19 | 1 | 52 | 24 | 44 | 7 |
| Grace | 9 | 3 | 21 | 1 | 1 | 0 | 1 | 0 |
| AUSTRALIA | | | | | | | | |
| Spofforth | 53 | 22 | 82 | 4 | 29·2 | 13 | 40 | 2 |
| Giffen | 32 | 15 | 44 | 1 | 24 | 9 | 31 | 2 |
| Garrett | 45 | 23 | 43 | 2 | 17 | 9 | 14 | 1 |
| Palmer | 17·2 | 4 | 41 | 3 | 7 | 3 | 11 | 1 |
| Bruce | 9 | 6 | 9 | 0 | | | | |

### FALL OF WICKETS

| | A | E | A | E |
|---|---|---|---|---|
| Wkt | 1st | 1st | 2nd | 2nd |
| 1st | 58 | 9 | 37 | 7 |
| 2nd | 71 | 51 | 42 | 15 |
| 3rd | 134 | 80 | 44 | 24 |
| 4th | 141 | 109 | 53 | 62 |
| 5th | 181 | 131 | 68 | 90 |
| 6th | 187 | 156 | 70 | 105 |
| 7th | 188 | 160 | 70 | – |
| 8th | 192 | 206 | 73 | – |
| 9th | 201 | 219 | 103 | – |
| 10th | 205 | 223 | 123 | – |

Umpires: J. West and C.K. Pullin.

# ENGLAND v AUSTRALIA 1886 (2nd Test)

Played at Lord's, London, on 19, 20, 21 July.
Toss: England.    Result: ENGLAND won by an innings and 106 runs.
Debuts: Nil.

A. Shrewsbury's 164 was an England Test record for only one match – W.G. Grace regained it with 170 in the 3rd Test.

## ENGLAND

| | | |
|---|---|---:|
| W.G. Grace | c Jarvis b Palmer | 18 |
| W.H. Scotton | b Garrett | 19 |
| A. Shrewsbury | c Bonnor b Trumble | 164 |
| W.W. Read | c Spofforth b Giffen | 22 |
| A.G. Steel* | lbw b Spofforth | 5 |
| W. Barnes | c Palmer b Garrett | 58 |
| R.G. Barlow | c Palmer b Spofforth | 12 |
| G. Ulyett | b Spofforth | 19 |
| E.F.S. Tylecote† | b Spofforth | 0 |
| J. Briggs | c Jones b Trumble | 0 |
| G.A. Lohmann | not out | 7 |
| Extras | (B 24, LB 4, NB 1) | 29 |
| **Total** | | **353** |

## AUSTRALIA

| | | | | | |
|---|---|---:|---|---|---:|
| S.P. Jones | c Grace b Briggs | 25 | (4) b Briggs | | 17 |
| H.J.H. Scott* | lbw b Briggs | 30 | (5) b Briggs | | 2 |
| G. Giffen | b Steel | 3 | (6) b Barlow | | 1 |
| A.H. Jarvis† | b Briggs | 3 | (7) not out | | 13 |
| G.J. Bonnor | c Grace b Steel | 0 | (8) b Briggs | | 3 |
| J.W. Trumble | c Tylecote b Briggs | 0 | (3) c Tylecote b Barnes | | 20 |
| G.E. Palmer | c Shrewsbury b Barnes | 20 | (1) c Lohmann b Barlow | | 48 |
| J.M. Blackham | b Briggs | 23 | (9) b Briggs | | 5 |
| T.W. Garrett | not out | 7 | (2) b Briggs | | 4 |
| F.R. Spofforth | b Barnes | 5 | (11) c and b Briggs | | 0 |
| E. Evans | c Ulyett b Barnes | 0 | (10) run out | | 0 |
| Extras | (B 4, LB 1) | 5 | (B 13) | | 13 |
| **Total** | | **121** | | | **126** |

| AUSTRALIA | O | M | R | W | O | M | R | W | | FALL OF WICKETS | | |
|---|---:|---:|---:|---:|---:|---:|---:|---:|---|---|---|---|
| Garrett | 72 | 40 | 77 | 2 | | | | | | E | A | A |
| Evans | 36 | 20 | 37 | 0 | | | | | *Wkt* | *1st* | *1st* | *2nd* |
| Palmer | 38 | 15 | 45 | 1 | | | | | 1st | 27 | 45 | 6 |
| Spofforth | 56 | 26 | 73 | 4 | | | | | 2nd | 77 | 52 | 56 |
| Trumble | 14 | 4 | 27 | 2 | | | | | 3rd | 112 | 59 | 91 |
| Giffen | 40 | 18 | 63 | 1 | | | | | 4th | 119 | 60 | 95 |
| Jones | 3 | 1 | 2 | 0 | | | | | 5th | 280 | 62 | 98 |
| ENGLAND | | | | | | | | | 6th | 303 | 67 | 105 |
| Barnes | 14·3 | 7 | 25 | 3 | 10 | 5 | 18 | 1 | 7th | 333 | 99 | 120 |
| Lohmann | 7 | 3 | 21 | 0 | 14 | 9 | 11 | 0 | 8th | 333 | 109 | 126 |
| Briggs | 34 | 22 | 29 | 5 | 38·1 | 17 | 45 | 6 | 9th | 340 | 121 | 126 |
| Steel | 21 | 8 | 34 | 2 | 16 | 9 | 14 | 0 | 10th | 353 | 121 | 126 |
| Barlow | 6 | 3 | 7 | 0 | 25 | 20 | 12 | 2 | | | | |
| Ulyett | | | | | 8 | 3 | 13 | 0 | | | | |

Umpires: F.H. Farrands and C.K. Pullin.

# ENGLAND v AUSTRALIA 1886 (3rd Test)

Played at Kennington Oval, London, on 12, 13, 14 August.
Toss: England.   Result: ENGLAND won by an innings and 217 runs.
Debuts: Australia – J. McIlwraith.

W.G. Grace (170) recaptured the record England Test score which A. Shrewsbury had claimed in the previous match. The opening partnership of 170 between Grace and Scotton was the highest first-wicket stand by either country and a record for any England wicket. At one stage of his innings, Scotton did not add to his score for 67 minutes.

## ENGLAND

| | | |
|---|---|---|
| W.G. Grace | c Blackham b Spofforth | 170 |
| W.H. Scotton | b Garrett | 34 |
| A. Shrewsbury | c Jones b Trumble | 44 |
| W.W. Read | c Jones b Spofforth | 94 |
| W. Barnes | c Evans b Trumble | 3 |
| A.G. Steel* | st Blackham b Trumble | 9 |
| R.G. Barlow | c Trumble b Garrett | 3 |
| G. Ulyett | c McIlwraith b Garrett | 0 |
| J. Briggs | c Trumble b Spofforth | 53 |
| E.F.S. Tylecote† | not out | 10 |
| G.A. Lohmann | b Spofforth | 7 |
| Extras | (B 3, LB 2, NB 2) | 7 |
| **Total** | | **434** |

## AUSTRALIA

| | | | | | |
|---|---|---|---|---|---|
| S.P. Jones | c Grace b Lohmann | 2 | (3) c Read b Lohmann | | 2 |
| G.E. Palmer | c Barlow b Briggs | 15 | (6) st Tylecote b Steel | | 35 |
| G. Giffen | c Shrewsbury b Briggs | 5 | (4) c and b Lohmann | | 47 |
| H.J.H. Scott* | c Tylecote b Lohmann | 6 | (5) c Grace b Lohmann | | 4 |
| J.W. Trumble | c Read b Lohmann | 13 | (7) c Read b Briggs | | 18 |
| J. McIlwraith | b Lohmann | 2 | (1) c Tylecote b Briggs | | 7 |
| J.M. Blackham† | c and b Briggs | 0 | (8) c Grace b Briggs | | 5 |
| T.W. Garrett | c Grace b Lohmann | 2 | (10) c Shrewsbury b Lohmann | | 4 |
| W. Bruce | c Ulyett b Lohmann | 9 | b Lohmann | | 11 |
| E. Evans | not out | 9 | (2) run out | | 3 |
| F.R. Spofforth | b Lohmann | 1 | not out | | 5 |
| Extras | (B 4) | 4 | (B 7, LB 1) | | 8 |
| **Total** | | **68** | | | **149** |

| AUSTRALIA | O | M | R | W | O | M | R | W |
|---|---|---|---|---|---|---|---|---|
| Giffen | 62 | 32 | 96 | 0 | | | | |
| Garrett | 99 | 55 | 88 | 3 | | | | |
| Palmer | 47 | 21 | 80 | 0 | | | | |
| Bruce | 6 | 2 | 9 | 0 | | | | |
| Spofforth | 30·1 | 12 | 65 | 4 | | | | |
| Evans | 13 | 10 | 6 | 0 | | | | |
| Trumble | 47 | 14 | 83 | 3 | | | | |
| ENGLAND | | | | | | | | |
| Lohmann | 30·2 | 17 | 36 | 7 | 37 | 14 | 68 | 5 |
| Briggs | 30 | 17 | 28 | 3 | 32 | 19 | 30 | 3 |
| Barlow | | | | | 14 | 8 | 13 | 0 |
| Barnes | | | | | 7 | 4 | 10 | 0 |
| Steel | | | | | 7 | 1 | 20 | 1 |

### FALL OF WICKETS

| | E | A | A |
|---|---|---|---|
| Wkt | 1st | 1st | 2nd |
| 1st | 170 | 2 | 11 |
| 2nd | 216 | 11 | 14 |
| 3rd | 287 | 22 | 26 |
| 4th | 293 | 34 | 30 |
| 5th | 305 | 35 | 84 |
| 6th | 314 | 35 | 120 |
| 7th | 320 | 44 | 129 |
| 8th | 410 | 49 | 131 |
| 9th | 418 | 67 | 137 |
| 10th | 434 | 68 | 149 |

Umpires: F.H. Farrands and R. Carpenter.

# AUSTRALIA v ENGLAND 1886–87 (1st Test)

Played at Sydney Cricket Ground on 28, 29, 31 January.
Toss: Australia.   Result: ENGLAND won by 13 runs.
Debuts: Australia – J.J. Ferris, H. Moses, C.T.B. Turner; England – W. Gunn, M. Sherwin.

England were dismissed for what is still their lowest total in any Test match and by two bowlers who bowled unchanged through the innings on their first appearance at Test level. P.S. McDonnell was the first captain to invite the opposition to bat on winning the toss in a Test match.

### ENGLAND

| | | | | |
|---|---|--:|---|--:|
| W. Bates | c Midwinter b Ferris | 8 | b Ferris | 24 |
| A. Shrewsbury* | c McShane b Ferris | 2 | b Ferris | 29 |
| W. Barnes | c Spofforth b Turner | 0 | c Moses b Garrett | 32 |
| R.G. Barlow | b Turner | 2 | c Jones b Ferris | 4 |
| J.M. Read | c Spofforth b Ferris | 5 | b Ferris | 0 |
| W. Gunn | b Turner | 0 | b Turner | 4 |
| W.H. Scotton | c Jones b Turner | 1 | (9) c Spofforth b Garrett | 6 |
| J. Briggs | c Midwinter b Turner | 5 | b Spofforth | 33 |
| G.A. Lohmann | c Garrett b Ferris | 17 | (7) lbw b Ferris | 3 |
| W. Flowers | b Turner | 2 | c McDonnell b Turner | 14 |
| M. Sherwin† | not out | 0 | not out | 21 |
| Extras | (B2, LB 1) | 3 | (B 9, LB 5) | 14 |
| **Total** | | **45** | | **184** |

### AUSTRALIA

| | | | | |
|---|---|--:|---|--:|
| J.M. Blackham† | c Sherwin b Lohmann | 4 | b Barnes | 5 |
| P.S. McDonnell* | b Barnes | 14 | lbw b Barnes | 0 |
| H. Moses | b Barlow | 31 | c Shrewsbury b Barnes | 24 |
| S.P. Jones | c Shrewsbury b Bates | 31 | c Read b Barnes | 18 |
| C.T.B. Turner | b Barlow | 3 | c and b Barnes | 7 |
| A.C. Bannerman | not out | 15 | b Lohmann | 4 |
| P.G. McShane | lbw b Briggs | 5 | b Briggs | 0 |
| W.E. Midwinter | c Shrewsbury b Barlow | 0 | lbw b Barnes | 10 |
| T.W. Garrett | b Lohmann | 12 | c Gunn b Lohmann | 10 |
| F.R. Spofforth | b Lohmann | 2 | b Lohmann | 5 |
| J.J. Ferris | c Barlow b Barnes | 1 | not out | 0 |
| Extras | (B 1) | 1 | (B 12, LB 2) | 14 |
| **Total** | | **119** | | **97** |

| AUSTRALIA | O | M | R | W | O | M | R | W | | FALL OF WICKETS | | | |
|---|--:|--:|--:|--:|--:|--:|--:|--:|---|---|---|---|---|
| Turner | 18 | 11 | 15 | 6 | 44·2 | 22 | 53 | 2 | | **E** | **A** | **E** | **A** |
| Ferris | 17·3 | 7 | 27 | 4 | 61 | 30 | 76 | 5 | *Wkt* | *1st* | *1st* | *2nd* | *2nd* |
| Spofforth | | | | | 12 | 3 | 17 | 1 | 1st | 11 | 8 | 31 | 4 |
| Midwinter | | | | | 4 | 1 | 10 | 0 | 2nd | 11 | 18 | 80 | 5 |
| Garrett | | | | | 12 | 7 | 8 | 2 | 3rd | 13 | 64 | 92 | 29 |
| McShane | | | | | 3 | 0 | 6 | 0 | 4th | 13 | 67 | 92 | 38 |
| | | | | | | | | | 5th | 13 | 86 | 98 | 58 |
| ENGLAND | | | | | | | | | 6th | 17 | 95 | 99 | 61 |
| Barnes | 22·1 | 16 | 19 | 2 | 46 | 29 | 28 | 6 | 7th | 21 | 96 | 103 | 80 |
| Lohmann | 21 | 12 | 30 | 3 | 24 | 11 | 20 | 3 | 8th | 29 | 116 | 128 | 83 |
| Briggs | 14 | 5 | 25 | 1 | 7 | 5 | 7 | 1 | 9th | 41 | 118 | 153 | 95 |
| Barlow | 35 | 23 | 25 | 3 | 13 | 6 | 20 | 0 | 10th | 45 | 119 | 184 | 97 |
| Bates | 21 | 9 | 19 | 1 | 17 | 11 | 8 | 0 | | | | | |

Umpires: C. Bannerman and H. Rawlinson.

# AUSTRALIA v ENGLAND 1886-87 (2nd Test)

Played at Sydney Cricket Ground on 25, 26, 28 February, 1 March.
Toss: England.   Result: ENGLAND won by 71 runs.
Debuts: Australia – R.C. Allen, F.J. Burton, J.T. Cottam, W.F. Giffen, J.J. Lyons; England – R. Wood.

G.A. Lohmann became the first bowler to take eight wickets in an innings of a Test match. W. Gunn both played and umpired in this match.

## ENGLAND

| | | | | |
|---|---|---|---|---|
| A. Shrewsbury* | b Turner | 9 | b Turner | 6 |
| W. Bates | c Ferris b Turner | 8 | b Turner | 30 |
| J.M. Read | b Turner | 11 | (4) st Burton b Ferris | 2 |
| W. Gunn | b Turner | 9 | (5) c Cottam b Ferris | 10 |
| G.A. Lohmann | b Ferris | 2 | (6) b Ferris | 6 |
| W.H. Scotton | b Turner | 0 | (7) b Ferris | 2 |
| J. Briggs | b Ferris | 17 | (8) b Garrett | 16 |
| R.G. Barlow | c Allen b Ferris | 34 | (3) not out | 42 |
| W. Flowers | c Allen b Ferris | 37 | b Turner | 18 |
| R. Wood | lbw b Ferris | 6 | hit wkt b Midwinter | 0 |
| M. Sherwin† | not out | 4 | b Turner | 5 |
| Extras | (B 9, LB 3, NB 2) | 14 | (B 12, LB 5) | 17 |
| **Total** | | **151** | | **154** |

## AUSTRALIA

| | | | | |
|---|---|---|---|---|
| W.F. Giffen | b Lohmann | 2 | (6) b Briggs | 0 |
| J.J. Lyons | b Lohmann | 11 | (4) c Gunn b Bates | 0 |
| H. Moses | b Flowers | 28 | (2) st Sherwin b Bates | 33 |
| R.C. Allen | b Lohmann | 14 | (3) c sub (C.T.B. Turner) b Bates | 30 |
| P.S. McDonnell* | c Gunn b Lohmann | 10 | (1) c Gunn b Lohmann | 35 |
| W.E. Midwinter | b Lohmann | 1 | (7) c Sherwin b Lohmann | 4 |
| J.T. Cottam | hit wkt b Lohmann | 1 | (5) st Sherwin b Briggs | 3 |
| C.T.B. Turner | c and b Flowers | 9 | c Briggs b Bates | 9 |
| T.W. Garrett | b Lohmann | 1 | c Sherwin b Briggs | 20 |
| J.J. Ferris | b Lohmann | 1 | run out | 2 |
| F.J. Burton† | not out | 0 | not out | 2 |
| Extras | (B 5, LB 1) | 6 | (B 9, LB 3) | 12 |
| **Total** | | **84** | | **150** |

| AUSTRALIA | O | M | R | W | O | M | R | W |
|---|---|---|---|---|---|---|---|---|
| Ferris | 45 | 16 | 71 | 5 | 60 | 33 | 69 | 4 |
| Turner | 53 | 29 | 41 | 5 | 64·1 | 33 | 52 | 4 |
| Garrett | 6 | 2 | 12 | 0 | 10 | 6 | 7 | 1 |
| Midwinter | 3 | 1 | 2 | 0 | 6 | 3 | 9 | 1 |
| Lyons | 2 | 0 | 11 | 0 | | | | |
| ENGLAND | | | | | | | | |
| Lohmann | 25 | 12 | 35 | 8 | 40 | 16 | 52 | 2 |
| Briggs | 20 | 6 | 34 | 0 | 22 | 9 | 31 | 3 |
| Flowers | 8 | 3 | 9 | 2 | 13 | 5 | 17 | 0 |
| Bates | | | | | 26 | 13 | 26 | 4 |
| Barlow | | | | | 9 | 2 | 12 | 0 |

### FALL OF WICKETS

| | E | A | E | A |
|---|---|---|---|---|
| Wkt | 1st | 1st | 2nd | 2nd |
| 1st | 14 | 12 | 21 | 51 |
| 2nd | 19 | 15 | 42 | 86 |
| 3rd | 35 | 40 | 47 | 86 |
| 4th | 38 | 56 | 59 | 95 |
| 5th | 43 | 59 | 73 | 95 |
| 6th | 50 | 65 | 77 | 106 |
| 7th | 73 | 82 | 98 | 121 |
| 8th | 130 | 83 | 136 | 129 |
| 9th | 145 | 83 | 137 | 135 |
| 10th | 151 | 84 | 154 | 150 |

Umpires: C. Bannerman, J. Swift and W. Gunn.

# AUSTRALIA v ENGLAND 1887-88 (Only Test)

Played at Sydney Cricket Ground on 10, 11, 13, 14, 15, February.
Toss: Australia.   Result: ENGLAND won by 126 runs.
Debuts: England – W. Newham, A.E. Stoddart.

Two English touring teams in Australia during the 1887-88 season combined to play this match. Australia's total of 42 remains their lowest in any Test in Australia and was their lowest in all Tests until they were dismissed for 36 by England in 1902 (*Test No. 70*). Turner's match analysis of 12 for 87 remains the record for any Test at Sydney.

## ENGLAND

| | | | | | |
|---|---|---|---|---|---|
| A.E. Stoddart | c McShane b Turner | 16 | | c Blackham b Turner | 17 |
| A. Shrewsbury | c Turner b Ferris | 44 | (6) | b Ferris | 1 |
| G. Ulyett | c Burton b Turner | 5 | (2) | b Ferris | 5 |
| W.W. Read* | b Turner | 10 | (3) | b Turner | 8 |
| J.M. Read | c and b Turner | 0 | (4) | c Bannerman b Turner | 39 |
| R. Peel | hit wkt b Ferris | 3 | (5) | st Blackham b Turner | 9 |
| W. Newham | c Worrall b Ferris | 9 | (9) | lbw b Turner | 17 |
| G.A. Lohmann | c Jones b Ferris | 12 | (7) | c Blackham b Turner | 0 |
| J. Briggs | b Turner | 0 | (8) | c Worrall b McShane | 14 |
| W. Attewell | not out | 7 | | not out | 10 |
| R. Pilling† | run out | 3 | | b Turner | 5 |
| Extras | (B 4) | 4 | | (B 7, LB 5) | 12 |
| **Total** | | **113** | | | **137** |

## AUSTRALIA

| | | | | | |
|---|---|---|---|---|---|
| A.C. Bannerman | c Ulyett b Lohmann | 2 | | c Attewell b Lohmann | 2 |
| S.P. Jones | c Shrewsbury b Peel | 0 | (4) | c Shrewsbury b Lohmann | 15 |
| H. Moses | c W.W. Read b Lohmann | 3 | | c Briggs b Lohmann | 11 |
| F.J. Burton | c Stoddart b Lohmann | 1 | (5) | c Pilling b Peel | 1 |
| J. Worrall | st Pilling b Peel | 6 | (10) | b Lohmann | 1 |
| P.G. McShane | c Shrewsbury b Peel | 0 | (8) | b Peel | 0 |
| P.S. McDonnell* | b Lohmann | 3 | (2) | b Peel | 6 |
| J.M. Blackham† | c Shrewsbury b Peel | 2 | (9) | not out | 25 |
| T.W. Garrett | c Pilling b Lohmann | 10 | (7) | c Shrewsbury b Peel | 1 |
| C.T.B. Turner | not out | 8 | (6) | lbw b Attewell | 12 |
| J.J. Ferris | c W.W. Read b Peel | 0 | | c Shrewsbury b Peel | 5 |
| Extras | (B 6, W 1) | 7 | | (B 2, LB 1) | 3 |
| **Total** | | **42** | | | **82** |

| AUSTRALIA | O | M | R | W | O | M | R | W |
|---|---|---|---|---|---|---|---|---|
| Turner | 50 | 27 | 44 | 5 | 38 | 23 | 43 | 7 |
| Ferris | 47 | 25 | 60 | 4 | 16 | 4 | 43 | 2 |
| Garrett | 3 | 1 | 5 | 0 | | | | |
| McShane | | | | | 21 | 7 | 39 | 1 |
| ENGLAND | | | | | | | | |
| Lohmann | 19 | 13 | 17 | 5 | 32 | 18 | 35 | 4 |
| Peel | 18·3 | 9 | 18 | 5 | 33 | 14 | 40 | 5 |
| Attewell | | | | | 4·2 | 2 | 4 | 1 |

Umpires: C. Bannerman and J. Phillips.

### FALL OF WICKETS

| | E | A | E | A |
|---|---|---|---|---|
| Wkt | 1st | 1st | 2nd | 2nd |
| 1st | 27 | 2 | 9 | 8 |
| 2nd | 36 | 2 | 15 | 8 |
| 3rd | 54 | 10 | 27 | 20 |
| 4th | 54 | 16 | 54 | 21 |
| 5th | 57 | 18 | 82 | 44 |
| 6th | 88 | 21 | 82 | 47 |
| 7th | 102 | 23 | 84 | 53 |
| 8th | 103 | 26 | 111 | 60 |
| 9th | 103 | 37 | 131 | 61 |
| 10th | 113 | 42 | 137 | 82 |

# ENGLAND v AUSTRALIA 1888 (1st Test)

Played at Lord's, London, 16, 17 July.
Toss: Australia.   Result: AUSTRALIA won by 61 runs.
Debuts: England – R. Abel; Australia – J.D. Edwards, G.H.S. Trott, S.M.J. Woods.

A wet pitch resulted in the lowest aggregate for any completed Test between England and Australia – 291 – the match ending at 4.25 p.m. on the second day. There has been only one lower aggregate in a completed Test match: 234 (29 wickets), Australia v South Africa at Melbourne in 1931-32 (*Test No. 216*).

## AUSTRALIA

| | | | | |
|---|---|--:|---|--:|
| A.C. Bannerman | c Grace b Lohmann | 0 | b Peel | 0 |
| P.S. McDonnell* | c O'Brien b Peel | 22 | b Lohmann | 1 |
| G.H.S. Trott | c Lohmann b Peel | 0 | b Lohmann | 3 |
| G.J. Bonnor | b Lohmann | 6 | c Lohmann b Peel | 8 |
| J.M. Blackham† | b Briggs | 22 | run out | 1 |
| S.M.J. Woods | c Gunn b Briggs | 18 | c Grace b Peel | 3 |
| C.T.B. Turner | c Lohmann b Peel | 3 | c Grace b Briggs | 12 |
| J.D. Edwards | not out | 21 | c Sherwin b Lohmann | 0 |
| A.H. Jarvis | c Lohmann b Peel | 3 | (11) c Barnes b Peel | 4 |
| J. Worrall | c Abel b Briggs | 2 | b Lohmann | 4 |
| J.J. Ferris | c Sherwin b Steel | 14 | (9) not out | 20 |
| Extras | (B 5) | 5 | (B 3, LB 1) | 4 |
| **Total** | | **116** | | **60** |

## ENGLAND

| | | | | |
|---|---|--:|---|--:|
| W.G. Grace | c Woods b Ferris | 10 | c Bannerman b Ferris | 24 |
| R. Abel | b Ferris | 3 | c Bonnor b Ferris | 8 |
| W. Barnes | c Jarvis b Turner | 3 | (9) st Blackham b Ferris | 1 |
| G.A. Lohmann | lbw b Turner | 2 | (10) st Blackham b Ferris | 0 |
| W.W. Read | st Blackham b Turner | 4 | (4) b Turner | 3 |
| T.C. O'Brien | b Turner | 0 | (5) b Turner | 4 |
| R. Peel | run out | 8 | (3) b Turner | 4 |
| A.G. Steel* | st Blackham b Turner | 3 | (6) not out | 10 |
| W. Gunn | c Blackham b Ferris | 2 | (7) b Ferris | 8 |
| J. Briggs | b Woods | 17 | (8) b Turner | 0 |
| M. Sherwin† | not out | 0 | c Ferris b Turner | 0 |
| Extras | (LB 1) | 1 | | |
| **Total** | | **53** | | **62** |

| ENGLAND | O | M | R | W | O | M | R | W | | FALL OF WICKETS | | | |
|---|--:|--:|--:|--:|--:|--:|--:|--:|---|---|---|---|---|
| Lohmann | 20 | 9 | 28 | 2 | 14 | 4 | 33 | 4 | | A | E | A | E |
| Peel | 21 | 7 | 36 | 4 | 10·2 | 3 | 14 | 4 | *Wkt* | *1st* | *1st* | *2nd* | *2nd* |
| Briggs | 21 | 8 | 26 | 3 | 4 | 1 | 9 | 1 | 1st | 0 | 5 | 1 | 29 |
| Barnes | 6 | 0 | 17 | 0 | | | | | 2nd | 3 | 14 | 1 | 34 |
| Steel | 3·2 | 2 | 4 | 1 | 1 | 1 | 0 | 0 | 3rd | 28 | 18 | 13 | 38 |
| | | | | | | | | | 4th | 32 | 22 | 15 | 39 |
| AUSTRALIA | | | | | | | | | 5th | 65 | 22 | 18 | 44 |
| Turner | 25 | 9 | 27 | 5 | 24 | 8 | 36 | 5 | 6th | 76 | 22 | 18 | 55 |
| Ferris | 21 | 13 | 19 | 3 | 23 | 11 | 26 | 5 | 7th | 76 | 26 | 18 | 56 |
| Woods | 4 | 2 | 6 | 1 | | | | | 8th | 79 | 35 | 42 | 57 |
| | | | | | | | | | 9th | 82 | 49 | 49 | 57 |
| | | | | | | | | | 10th | 116 | 53 | 60 | 62 |

Umpires: F.H. Farrands and C.K. Pullin.

# ENGLAND v AUSTRALIA 1888 (2nd Test)

Played at Kennington Oval, London, on 13, 14 August.
Toss: Australia.   Result: ENGLAND won by an innings and 137 runs.
Debuts: England – J. Shuter, F.H. Sugg, H. Wood.

## AUSTRALIA

| | | | | |
|---|---|---|---|---|
| A.C. Bannerman | c Lohmann b Barnes | 13 | b Barnes | 5 |
| P.S. McDonnell* | c Lohmann b Peel | 0 | b Peel | 32 |
| G.H.S. Trott | b Briggs | 13 | st Wood b Peel | 4 |
| G.J. Bonnor | b Briggs | 0 | c Wood b Barnes | 5 |
| J.D. Edwards | b Lohmann | 26 | c Read b Barnes | 0 |
| A.H. Jarvis | b Briggs | 5 | (9) b Peel | 8 |
| S.M.J. Woods | run out | 0 | c Abel b Barnes | 7 |
| C.T.B. Turner | b Briggs | 0 | b Peel | 18 |
| J.M. Blackham† | b Briggs | 0 | (10) c Lohmann b Barnes | 4 |
| J. Worrall | c Grace b Barnes | 8 | (11) not out | 0 |
| J.J. Ferris | not out | 13 | (6) run out | 16 |
| Extras | (B 1, LB 1) | 2 | (LB 1) | 1 |
| **Total** | | **80** | | **100** |

## ENGLAND

| | | |
|---|---|---|
| W.G. Grace* | c Edwards b Turner | 1 |
| J. Shuter | b Turner | 28 |
| G. Ulyett | c Blackham b Turner | 0 |
| W.W. Read | b Turner | 18 |
| R. Abel | run out | 70 |
| W. Barnes | c Worrall b Turner | 62 |
| F.H. Sugg | b Turner | 31 |
| R. Peel | b Woods | 25 |
| J. Briggs | b Woods | 0 |
| G.A. Lohmann | not out | 62 |
| H. Wood† | c Bannerman b Ferris | 8 |
| Extras | (B 6, LB 4, W 2) | 12 |
| **Total** | | **317** |

| ENGLAND | O | M | R | W | O | M | R | W |
|---|---|---|---|---|---|---|---|---|
| Lohmann | 29·3 | 21 | 21 | 1 | 6 | 4 | 11 | 0 |
| Peel | 8 | 4 | 14 | 1 | 28·2 | 13 | 49 | 4 |
| Briggs | 37 | 24 | 25 | 5 | 6 | 3 | 7 | 0 |
| Barnes | 16 | 9 | 18 | 2 | 29 | 16 | 32 | 5 |
| AUSTRALIA | | | | | | | | |
| Turner | 60 | 24 | 112 | 6 | | | | |
| Ferris | 35·2 | 15 | 73 | 1 | | | | |
| Trott | 7 | 2 | 25 | 0 | | | | |
| Woods | 32 | 10 | 80 | 2 | | | | |
| Worrall | 4 | 1 | 15 | 0 | | | | |

## FALL OF WICKETS

| | A | E | A |
|---|---|---|---|
| Wkt | 1st | 1st | 2nd |
| 1st | 0 | 2 | 34 |
| 2nd | 22 | 6 | 38 |
| 3rd | 22 | 46 | 43 |
| 4th | 40 | 53 | 45 |
| 5th | 49 | 165 | 62 |
| 6th | 49 | 191 | 62 |
| 7th | 50 | 241 | 72 |
| 8th | 50 | 242 | 89 |
| 9th | 63 | 259 | 98 |
| 10th | 80 | 317 | 100 |

Umpires: F.H. Farrands and R. Carpenter.

# ENGLAND v AUSTRALIA 1888 (3rd Test)

Played at Old Trafford, Manchester, on 30, 31 August.
Toss: England.   Result: ENGLAND won by an innings and 21 runs.
Debuts: Nil.

This was the shortest Test match in which there was a result, England completing their victory before lunch – at 1.55 p.m. – on the second day.

## ENGLAND

| | | |
|---|---|---|
| W.G. Grace* | c Bonnor b Turner | 38 |
| R. Abel | b Turner | 0 |
| G. Ulyett | b Turner | 0 |
| W.W. Read | b Turner | 19 |
| W. Barnes | b Ferris | 24 |
| F.H. Sugg | b Woods | 24 |
| W. Gunn | lbw b Turner | 15 |
| R. Peel | lbw b Ferris | 11 |
| J. Briggs | not out | 22 |
| G.A. Lohmann | run out | 0 |
| R. Pilling† | c Bonnor b Woods | 17 |
| Extras | (B 2) | 2 |
| **Total** | | **172** |

## AUSTRALIA

| | | | | | |
|---|---|---|---|---|---|
| P.S. McDonnell* | c Grace b Peel | 15 | | b Lohmann | 0 |
| A.C. Bannerman | b Peel | 1 | | c Grace b Peel | 0 |
| G.H.S. Trott | st Pilling b Peel | 17 | | run out | 0 |
| G.J. Bonnor | run out | 5 | | c Grace b Peel | 0 |
| J.D. Edwards | b Peel | 0 | (9) | c Grace b Peel | 1 |
| C.T.B. Turner | b Peel | 0 | (8) | b Briggs | 26 |
| S.M.J. Woods | c Read b Briggs | 4 | | b Lohmann | 0 |
| J.M. Blackham† | c Read b Lohmann | 15 | (5) | b Lohmann | 5 |
| J.J. Lyons | c Lohmann b Peel | 22 | (6) | b Briggs | 32 |
| J. Worrall | b Peel | 0 | (11) | not out | 0 |
| J.J. Ferris | not out | 0 | (10) | c Abel b Peel | 3 |
| Extras | (B 2) | 2 | | (B 2, LB 1) | 3 |
| **Total** | | **81** | | | **70** |

| AUSTRALIA | O | M | R | W | O | M | R | W |
|---|---|---|---|---|---|---|---|---|
| Ferris | 40 | 20 | 49 | 2 | | | | |
| Turner | 59 | 21 | 86 | 5 | | | | |
| Woods | 18·1 | 6 | 35 | 2 | | | | |
| ENGLAND | | | | | | | | |
| Peel | 26·2 | 17 | 31 | 7 | 16 | 4 | 37 | 4 |
| Lohmann | 17 | 9 | 31 | 1 | 8 | 3 | 20 | 3 |
| Briggs | 9 | 4 | 1·7 | 1 | 7·1 | 2 | 10 | 2 |

Umpires: F.H. Farrands and C.K. Pullin.

| | FALL OF WICKETS | | |
|---|---|---|---|
| | E | A | A |
| Wkt | 1st | 1st | 2nd |
| 1st | 0 | 16 | 0 |
| 2nd | 6 | 32 | 0 |
| 3rd | 58 | 35 | 1 |
| 4th | 59 | 39 | 7 |
| 5th | 96 | 39 | 7 |
| 6th | 115 | 43 | 7 |
| 7th | 127 | 45 | 55 |
| 8th | 135 | 81 | 56 |
| 9th | 136 | 81 | 70 |
| 10th | 172 | 81 | 70 |

# SOUTH AFRICA v ENGLAND 1888-89 (1st Test)

Played at St George's Park, Port Elizabeth, on 12, 13 March.
Toss: South Africa.   Result: ENGLAND won by eight wickets.
Debuts: South Africa – All; England – M.P. Bowden, Hon. C.J. Coventry, A.J. Fothergill, B.A.F.
Grieve, F. Hearne, C.A. Smith. *Coventry and Grieve were making their debuts in first-class cricket;*
*both ended their first-class careers with the 2nd Test of this series. C.A. Smith (later Sir Aubrey*
*Smith) of Hollywood fame is the only player to captain England on his only appearance in Test*
*cricket.*

South Africa's introduction to Test cricket ended in a comprehensive defeat by Major Warton's touring team.
The match, played on matting, finished just before 3.30 p.m. on the second day. Milton kept wicket for South
Africa in the second innings and was in turn caught by Bowden who deputised for Wood after lunch on the second
day.

## SOUTH AFRICA

| | | | | |
|---|---|---|---|---|
| A.R. Innes | b Briggs | 0 | b Smith | 13 |
| A.B. Tancred | b Smith | 29 | c and b Briggs | 29 |
| P.Hutchinson | b Briggs | 0 | (5) b Smith | 11 |
| C.H. Vintcent | c Abel b Briggs | 3 | c and b Ulyett | 4 |
| A.H. Ochse | c Abel b Briggs | 4 | (3) lbw b Fothergill | 8 |
| W.H. Milton | c Abel b Fothergill | 1 | (7) c Bowden b Briggs | 19 |
| O.R. Dunell* | not out | 26 | (6) c and b Ulyett | 11 |
| R.B. Stewart | lbw b Smith | 4 | c Ulyett b Fothergill | 9 |
| F.W. Smith† | b Smith | 7 | b Fothergill | 12 |
| C.E. Finlason | b Smith | 0 | b Fothergill | 6 |
| G.A. Kempis | c Hearne b Smith | 0 | not out | 0 |
| Extras | (B 8, W 2) | 10 | (B 7) | 7 |
| **Total** | | **84** | | **129** |

## ENGLAND

| | | | | |
|---|---|---|---|---|
| R. Abel | c Milton b Innes | 46 | not out | 23 |
| G. Ulyett | b Kempis | 4 | b Vintcent | 22 |
| J.M. Read | c Dunell b Kempis | 1 | b Kempis | 3 |
| F. Hearne | c Stewart b Innes | 27 | | |
| H. Wood† | c Hutchinson b Innes | 3 | | |
| M.P. Bowden | run out | 0 | | |
| J. Briggs | c Smith b Innes | 0 | | |
| C.A. Smith* | c Stewart b Kempis | 3 | | |
| B.A.F. Grieve | not out | 14 | (4) not out | 12 |
| Hon. C.J. Coventry | c Smith b Innes | 12 | | |
| A.J. Fothergill | c Tancred b Milton | 32 | | |
| Extras | (B 5, W 1) | 6 | (B 7) | 7 |
| **Total** | | **148** | (2 wickets) | **67** |

| ENGLAND | O | M | R | W | O | M | R | W | | FALL OF WICKETS | | | |
|---|---|---|---|---|---|---|---|---|---|---|---|---|---|
| Briggs | 37 | 21 | 39 | 4 | 27 | 14 | 34 | 2 | | SA | E | SA | E |
| Fothergill | 24 | 15 | 15 | 1 | 18·1 | 11 | 19 | 4 | *Wkt* | *1st* | *1st* | *2nd* | *2nd* |
| Smith | 13·2 | 6 | 19 | 5 | 25 | 10 | 42 | 2 | 1st | 0 | 10 | 21 | 32 |
| Ulyett | 1 | 0 | 1 | 0 | 20 | 9 | 27 | 2 | 2nd | 0 | 14 | 42 | 35 |
| SOUTH AFRICA | | | | | | | | | 3rd | 10 | 65 | 51 | – |
| | | | | | | | | | 4th | 16 | 75 | 67 | – |
| Kempis | 31 | 14 | 53 | 3 | 11 | 3 | 23 | 1 | 5th | 17 | 75 | 67 | – |
| Finlason | 3 | 0 | 7 | 0 | | | | | 6th | 58 | 77 | 88 | – |
| Vintcent | 12 | 4 | 34 | 0 | 8·1 | 2 | 21 | 1 | 7th | 66 | 85 | 110 | – |
| Innes | 18 | 5 | 43 | 5 | 2 | 0 | 16 | 0 | 8th | 78 | 87 | 116 | – |
| Milton | 2·2 | 1 | 5 | 1 | | | | | 9th | 82 | 103 | 126 | – |
| | | | | | | | | | 10th | 84 | 148 | 129 | – |

Umpires: R.G. Warton, C.R. Deare and H.H. Webster.

# SOUTH AFRICA v ENGLAND 1888-89 (2nd Test)

Played at Newlands, Cape Town, on 25, 26 March.
Toss: England.   Result: ENGLAND won by an innings and 202 runs.
Debuts: South Africa – W.H. Ashley, W.H.M. Richards, N.H. Theunissen; England – J.E.P. McMaster.

Abel scored the first hundred in a Test match in and against South Africa and Tancred became the first batsman to carry his bat through a completed Test innings. Briggs set new Test records by taking 8 for 11 (all bowled) in the second innings and 15 for 28 in the match – still the record for a Cape Town Test. The latter still stands as the most wickets in one day of Test cricket. Ashley took 7 for 95 in his only Test.

## ENGLAND

| | | |
|---|---|---:|
| R. Abel | b Ashley | 120 |
| G. Ulyett | b Ashley | 22 |
| J. Briggs | b Vintcent | 6 |
| J.M. Read | c Hutchinson b Ashley | 12 |
| F. Hearne | b Vintcent | 20 |
| H. Wood† | c Innes b Vintcent | 59 |
| M.P. Bowden* | c Hutchinson b Ashley | 25 |
| B.A.F. Grieve | c Tancred b Ashley | 14 |
| J.E.P. McMaster | c Innes b Ashley | 0 |
| Hon. C.J. Coventry | not out | 1 |
| A.J. Fothergill | b Ashley | 1 |
| Extras | (B 12) | 12 |
| **Total** | | **292** |

## SOUTH AFRICA

| | | | | | |
|---|---|---:|---|---|---:|
| A.B. Tancred | not out | 26 | b Briggs | | 3 |
| A.R. Innes | lbw b Fothergill | 1 | run out | | 0 |
| A.E. Ochse | run out | 1 | b Briggs | | 3 |
| P. Hutchinson | b Briggs | 3 | b Briggs | | 0 |
| O.R. Dunell | b Briggs | 0 | b Fothergill | | 5 |
| W.H. Milton* | b Briggs | 7 | b Briggs | | 4 |
| W.H.M. Richards | c Abel b Fothergill | 0 | b Briggs | | 4 |
| C.H. Vintcent | b Briggs | 4 | b Briggs | | 9 |
| F.W. Smith† | b Briggs | 0 | b Briggs | | 11 |
| N.H. Theunissen | lbw b Briggs | 0 | not out | | 2 |
| W.H. Ashley | b Briggs | 1 | b Briggs | | 0 |
| Extras | (B 2, NB 2) | 4 | (B 2) | | 2 |
| **Total** | | **47** | | | **43** |

| SOUTH AFRICA | O | M | R | W | O | M | R | W |
|---|---|---|---|---|---|---|---|---|
| Theunissen | 20 | 5 | 51 | 0 | | | | |
| Innes | 12 | 3 | 30 | 0 | | | | |
| Ashley | 43·1 | 18 | 95 | 7 | | | | |
| Vintcent | 42 | 9 | 88 | 3 | | | | |
| Milton | 6 | 2 | 16 | 0 | | | | |
| **ENGLAND** | | | | | | | | |
| Fothergill | 24 | 12 | 26 | 2 | 14 | 4 | 30 | 1 |
| Ulyett | 4 | 4 | 0 | 0 | | | | |
| Briggs | 19·1 | 11 | 17 | 7 | 14·2 | 5 | 11 | 8 |

Umpires: R.G. Warton and J. Hickson.

FALL OF WICKETS

| | E | SA | SA |
|---|---|---|---|
| Wkt | 1st | 1st | 2nd |
| 1st | 54 | 2 | 1 |
| 2nd | 62 | 3 | 4 |
| 3rd | 79 | 11 | 6 |
| 4th | 110 | 19 | 12 |
| 5th | 215 | 31 | 16 |
| 6th | 257 | 32 | 20 |
| 7th | 287 | 41 | 20 |
| 8th | 287 | 41 | 37 |
| 9th | 288 | 41 | 43 |
| 10th | 292 | 47 | 43 |

# ENGLAND v AUSTRALIA 1890 (1st Test)

Played at Lord's, London, on 21, 22, 23 July.
Toss: Australia.    Result: ENGLAND won by seven wickets.
Debuts: England – G. MacGregor; Australia – J.E. Barrett, K.E. Burn, P.C. Charlton, S.E. Gregory, H. Trumble.

Barrett, playing his first Test match, became the first to carry his bat through a completed innings in a Test between Australia and England. Lyons took only 36 minutes to reach his fifty and set the record for Australia's fastest half-century against England (equalled by J. Ryder in 1928-29 in *Test No. 177*). For the first time no byes were conceded in a Test match.

## AUSTRALIA

| | | | | | |
|---|---|---|---|---|---|
| J.J. Lyons | b Barnes | 55 | (4) c Attewell b Peel | | 33 |
| C.T.B. Turner | b Attewell | 24 | lbw b Peel | | 2 |
| W.L. Murdoch* | c and b Attewell | 9 | (5) b Lohmann | | 19 |
| J.E. Barrett | c Grace b Ulyett | 9 | (1) not out | | 67 |
| G.H.S. Trott | run out | 12 | (3) b Peel | | 0 |
| S.E. Gregory | b Attewell | 0 | c Lohmann b Barnes | | 9 |
| P.C. Charlton | st MacGregor b Peel | 6 | lbw b Grace | | 2 |
| J.M. Blackham† | b Peel | 5 | c Barnes b Grace | | 10 |
| J.J. Ferris | b Attewell | 8 | lbw b Lohmann | | 8 |
| K.E. Burn | st MacGregor b Peel | 0 | (11) c MacGregor b Attewell | | 19 |
| H. Trumble | not out | 1 | (10) c Barnes b Lohmann | | 5 |
| Extras | (LB 3) | 3 | (LB 2) | | 2 |
| **Total** | | **132** | | | **176** |

## ENGLAND

| | | | | |
|---|---|---|---|---|
| W.G. Grace* | c and b Turner | 0 | not out | 75 |
| A. Shrewsbury | st Blackham b Ferris | 4 | lbw b Ferris | 13 |
| W. Gunn | run out | 14 | c and b Ferris | 34 |
| W.W. Read | c and b Ferris | 1 | b Trumble | 13 |
| J.M. Read | b Lyons | 34 | not out | 2 |
| G. Ulyett | b Lyons | 74 | | |
| R. Peel | c and b Trumble | 16 | | |
| W. Barnes | b Lyons | 9 | | |
| G.A. Lohmann | c and b Lyons | 19 | | |
| G. MacGregor† | b Lyons | 0 | | |
| W. Attewell | not out | 0 | | |
| Extras | (LB 2) | 2 | | |
| **Total** | | **173** | (3 wickets) | **137** |

| ENGLAND | O | M | R | W | O | M | R | W |
|---|---|---|---|---|---|---|---|---|
| Lohmann | 21 | 10 | 43 | 0 | 29 | 19 | 28 | 3 |
| Peel | 24 | 11 | 28 | 3 | 43 | 23 | 59 | 3 |
| Attewell | 32 | 15 | 42 | 4 | 42·2 | 22 | 54 | 1 |
| Barnes | 6 | 2 | 16 | 1 | 6 | 3 | 10 | 1 |
| Ulyett | 3 | 3 | 0 | 1 | 6 | 2 | 11 | 0 |
| Grace | | | | | 14 | 10 | 12 | 2 |
| AUSTRALIA | | | | | | | | |
| Turner | 35 | 17 | 53 | 1 | 22 | 12 | 31 | 0 |
| Ferris | 40 | 17 | 55 | 2 | 25 | 11 | 42 | 2 |
| Trott | 3 | 0 | 16 | 0 | | | | |
| Lyons | 20·1 | 7 | 30 | 5 | 20 | 6 | 43 | 0 |
| Trumble | 12 | 7 | 17 | 1 | 8 | 1 | 21 | 1 |

FALL OF WICKETS

| | A | E | A | E |
|---|---|---|---|---|
| Wkt | 1st | 1st | 2nd | 2nd |
| 1st | 66 | 0 | 6 | 27 |
| 2nd | 82 | 14 | 8 | 101 |
| 3rd | 93 | 20 | 48 | 135 |
| 4th | 109 | 20 | 84 | – |
| 5th | 111 | 92 | 106 | – |
| 6th | 113 | 133 | 109 | – |
| 7th | 120 | 147 | 119 | – |
| 8th | 131 | 162 | 136 | – |
| 9th | 131 | 166 | 142 | – |
| 10th | 132 | 173 | 176 | – |

Umpires: A. Hill and C.K. Pullin.

# ENGLAND v AUSTRALIA 1890 (2nd Test)

Played at Kennington Oval, London, on 11, 12 August.
Toss: Australia.   Result: ENGLAND won by two wickets.
Debuts: England – J. Cranston, F. Martin, J.W. Sharpe.

Martin, a left-arm, medium-fast bowler from Kent, became the first to take twelve wickets on debut. His record remained until 1972 when R.A.L. Massie took 16 for 137 in his first Test (*No. 699*). England won the match from an overthrow when Barrett missed an easy run-out.

## AUSTRALIA

| | | | | | |
|---|---|---|---|---|---|
| J.J. Lyons | c W.W. Read b Martin | 13 | (4) b Martin | | 21 |
| C.T.B. Turner | c Sharpe b Lohmann | 12 | (7) b Martin | | 0 |
| W.L. Murdoch* | b Martin | 2 | (5) b Lohmann | | 6 |
| J.E. Barrett | c Lohmann b Martin | 0 | (1) b Martin | | 4 |
| G.H.S. Trott | c MacGregor b Martin | 39 | (6) c Cranston b Martin | | 25 |
| K.E. Birn | c MacGregor b Lohmann | 7 | (2) b Martin | | 15 |
| J.M. Blackham† | b Martin | 1 | (8) b Lohmann | | 1 |
| J.J. Ferris | c Lohmann b Sharpe | 6 | b Lohmann | | 1 |
| P.C. Charlton | b Martin | 10 | b Sharpe | | 11 |
| S.E. Gregory | b Lohmann | 2 | (11) not out | | 4 |
| H. Trumble | not out | 0 | (10) b Martin | | 6 |
| Extras | | | (B 7, LB 1) | | 8 |
| **Total** | | **92** | | | **102** |

## ENGLAND

| | | | | | |
|---|---|---|---|---|---|
| W.G. Grace* | c Trumble b Ferris | 0 | c Trumble b Ferris | | 16 |
| A. Shrewsbury | c Trott b Turner | 4 | lbw b Ferris | | 9 |
| W. Gunn | b Ferris | 32 | st Blackham b Ferris | | 1 |
| W.W. Read | b Turner | 1 | b Turner | | 6 |
| J. Cranston | run out | 16 | (6) c Trumble b Turner | | 15 |
| J.M. Read | c Murdoch b Charlton | 19 | (5) c Barrett b Turner | | 35 |
| W. Barnes | c Murdoch b Charlton | 5 | (8) lbw b Ferris | | 5 |
| G.A. Lohmann | c Gregory b Ferris | 3 | (7) c Blackham b Ferris | | 2 |
| G. MacGregor† | c Turner b Ferris | 1 | not out | | 2 |
| J.W. Sharpe | not out | 5 | not out | | 2 |
| F. Martin | c Turner b Charlton | 1 | | | |
| Extras | (B 9, LB 3, NB 1) | 13 | (LB 1, NB 1) | | 2 |
| **Total** | | **100** | (8 wickets) | | **95** |

| ENGLAND | O | M | R | W | O | M | R | W | | FALL OF WICKETS | | | |
|---|---|---|---|---|---|---|---|---|---|---|---|---|---|
| Martin | 27 | 9 | 50 | 6 | 30·2 | 12 | 52 | 6 | | A | E | A | E |
| Lohmann | 32·2 | 19 | 34 | 3 | 21 | 8 | 32 | 3 | Wkt | 1st | 1st | 2nd | 2nd |
| Sharpe | 6 | 3 | 8 | 1 | 9 | 5 | 10 | 1 | 1st | 16 | 0 | 4 | 24 |
| | | | | | | | | | 2nd | 27 | 10 | 5 | 25 |
| AUSTRALIA | | | | | | | | | 3rd | 27 | 16 | 36 | 28 |
| Turner | 22 | 12 | 37 | 2 | 25 | 9 | 38 | 3 | 4th | 32 | 55 | 43 | 32 |
| Ferris | 25 | 14 | 25 | 4 | 23 | 8 | 49 | 5 | 5th | 39 | 79 | 49 | 83 |
| Trumble | 2 | 0 | 7 | 0 | | | | | 6th | 46 | 90 | 53 | 83 |
| Charlton | 6 | 0 | 18 | 3 | 3 | 1 | 6 | 0 | 7th | 70 | 91 | 54 | 86 |
| | | | | | | | | | 8th | 85 | 93 | 90 | 93 |
| Umpires: J. Street and C.K. Pullin. | | | | | | | | | 9th | 92 | 94 | 92 | – |
| | | | | | | | | | 10th | 92 | 100 | 102 | – |

**The Third Test at Old Trafford, scheduled for 25, 26, 27 August, was abandoned without a ball being bowled. The teams are shown on page 837.**

# AUSTRALIA v ENGLAND 1891-92 (1st Test)

Played at Melbourne Cricket Ground on 1, 2, 4, 5, 6 January.
Toss: Australia.    Result: AUSTRALIA won by 54 runs.
Debuts: Australia – S.T. Callaway, H. Donnan, R.W. McLeod; England – G. Bean.

Bannerman batted for 435 minutes for 86 runs in this match which was W.G. Grace's first Test in Australia.

### AUSTRALIA

| | | | | |
|---|---|---|---|---|
| A.C. Bannerman | c Read b Sharpe | 45 | c Grace b Sharpe | 41 |
| J.J. Lyons | c Grace b Peel | 19 | c Abel b Briggs | 51 |
| G. Giffen | lbw b Peel | 2 | b Attewell | 1 |
| W. Bruce | b Sharpe | 57 | c Lohmann b Sharpe | 40 |
| H. Donnan | b Sharpe | 9 | (9) c and b Lohmann | 2 |
| H. Moses | c Lohmann b Sharpe | 23 | run out | 15 |
| G.H.S. Trott | c MacGregor b Sharpe | 6 | lbw b Attewell | 23 |
| R.W. McLeod | b Sharpe | 14 | b Peel | 31 |
| S.T. Callaway | b Attewell | 21 | (10) not out | 13 |
| C.T.B. Turner | b Peel | 29 | (5) c Peel b Lohmann | 19 |
| J.M. Blackham*† | not out | 4 | c MacGregor b Peel | 0 |
| Extras | B 5, LB 6) | 11 | | |
| **Total** | | **240** | | **236** |

### ENGLAND

| | | | | |
|---|---|---|---|---|
| W.G. Grace* | b McLeod | 50 | c Bannerman b Turner | 25 |
| R. Abel | b McLeod | 32 | (5) c Blackham b Turner | 28 |
| A.E. Stoddart | c Giffen b McLeod | 0 | (2) b Callaway | 35 |
| G. Bean | c Bruce b Giffen | 50 | (3) c McLeod b Trott | 3 |
| J.M. Read | c and b Giffen | 38 | (4) b Trott | 11 |
| R.Peel | b McLeod | 19 | b Turner | 6 |
| G.A. Lohmann | lbw b Giffen | 3 | c Bannerman b Turner | 0 |
| J.Briggs | c Bruce b Turner | 41 | c Trott b McLeod | 4 |
| W.Attewell | c Bannerman b Turner | 8 | (10) c Donnan b Turner | 24 |
| J.W. Sharpe | c Blackham b McLeod | 2 | (11) not out | 5 |
| G. MacGregor† | not out | 9 | (9) c sub (S.E. Gregory) b Trott | 16 |
| Extras | (B 7, LB 2, NB 3) | 12 | (B 1) | 1 |
| **Total** | | **264** | | **158** |

| ENGLAND | O | M | R | W | O | M | R | W |
|---|---|---|---|---|---|---|---|---|
| Sharpe | 51 | 20 | 84 | 6 | 54 | 25 | 81 | 2 |
| Peel | 43 | 23 | 54 | 3 | 16·5 | 7 | 25 | 2 |
| Attewell | 21·1 | 11 | 28 | 1 | 61 | 32 | 51 | 2 |
| Lohmann | 28 | 14 | 40 | 0 | 39 | 15 | 53 | 2 |
| Briggs | 3 | 1 | 13 | 0 | 21 | 9 | 26 | 1 |
| Stoddart | 5 | 2 | 10 | 0 | | | | |
| AUSTRALIA | | | | | | | | |
| Trott | 10 | 2 | 25 | 0 | 19 | 2 | 52 | 3 |
| Giffen | 20 | 3 | 75 | 3 | 3 | 0 | 8 | 0 |
| Turner | 16 | 3 | 40 | 2 | 33·2 | 14 | 51 | 5 |
| McLeod | 28·4 | 12 | 55 | 5 | 23 | 8 | 39 | 1 |
| Callaway | 14 | 2 | 39 | 0 | 4 | 1 | 7 | 1 |
| Bruce | 3 | 0 | 18 | 0 | | | | |

### FALL OF WICKETS

| | A | E | A | E |
|---|---|---|---|---|
| Wkt | 1st | 1st | 2nd | 2nd |
| 1st | 32 | 84 | 66 | 60 |
| 2nd | 36 | 85 | 67 | 60 |
| 3rd | 123 | 85 | 120 | 71 |
| 4th | 136 | 171 | 152 | 75 |
| 5th | 136 | 179 | 152 | 93 |
| 6th | 148 | 187 | 182 | 93 |
| 7th | 164 | 232 | 197 | 98 |
| 8th | 191 | 249 | 210 | 125 |
| 9th | 232 | 256 | 236 | 139 |
| 10th | 240 | 264 | 236 | 158 |

Umpires: J. Phillips and T. Flynn.

# AUSTRALIA v ENGLAND 1891-92 (2nd Test)

Played at Sydney Cricket Ground on 29, 30 January, 1, 2, 3 February.
Toss: Australia.   Result: AUSTRALIA won by 72 runs.
Debuts: Nil.

Abel became the first England player to carry his bat through a completed Test innings. Briggs ended Australia's second innings with a hat-trick, dismissing W.F. Giffen, Callaway and Blackham. Bannerman scored only 67 runs in the complete third day's play.

## AUSTRALIA

| | | | | |
|---|---|---|---|---|
| A.C. Bannerman | c Abel b Lohmann | 12 | c Grace b Briggs | 91 |
| J.J. Lyons | c Grace b Lohmann | 41 | (3) c Grace b Lohmann | 134 |
| G. Giffen | c Abel b Lohmann | 6 | (4) lbw b Attewell | 49 |
| H. Moses | c Grace b Lohmann | 29 | absent hurt | – |
| C.T.B. Turner | c MacGregor b Lohmann | 15 | (7) not out | 14 |
| W. Bruce | c Bean b Attewell | 15 | (5) c Briggs b Sharpe | 72 |
| G.H.S. Trott | b Lohmann | 2 | (2) c Sharpe b Lohmann | 1 |
| R.W. McLeod | c Attewell b Lohmann | 13 | (6) c Read b Peel | 18 |
| W.F. Giffen | c and b Lohmann | 1 | (8) b Briggs | 3 |
| S.T. Callaway | run out | 1 | c Grace b Briggs | 0 |
| J.M. Blackham*† | not out | 3 | (9) lbw b Briggs | 0 |
| Extras | (B 6, W 1) | 7 | (B 6, LB 2, W 1) | 9 |
| **Total** | | **145** | | **391** |

## ENGLAND

| | | | | |
|---|---|---|---|---|
| R. Abel | not out | 132 | c W.F. Giffen b G.Giffen | 1 |
| W.G. Grace* | b Turner | 26 | c Blackham b Turner | 5 |
| G. Bean | b G. Giffen | 19 | c Lyons b Turner | 4 |
| A.E. Stoddart | c Blackham b McLeod | 27 | b Turner | 69 |
| J.M. Read | c Turner b G. Giffen | 3 | c and b G. Giffen | 22 |
| R. Peel | c G. Giffen b Turner | 20 | st Blackham b G. Giffen | 6 |
| G.A. Lohmann | b G. Giffen | 10 | c Bruce b G. Giffen | 15 |
| G. MacGregor† | lbw b McLeod | 3 | c and b G. Giffen | 12 |
| J. Briggs | lbw b Trott | 28 | c Trott b Turner | 12 |
| W. Attewell | b Trott | 0 | c and b G. Giffen | 0 |
| J.W. Sharpe | c Bannerman b G. Giffen | 26 | not out | 4 |
| Extras | (B 10, LB 2, W 1) | 13 | (B 5, LB 2) | 7 |
| **Total** | | **307** | | **157** |

| ENGLAND | O | M | R | W | O | M | R | W |
|---|---|---|---|---|---|---|---|---|
| Lohmann | 43·2 | 18 | 58 | 8 | 51 | 14 | 84 | 2 |
| Attewell | 31 | 20 | 25 | 1 | 46 | 24 | 43 | 1 |
| Briggs | 10 | 2 | 24 | 0 | 32·4 | 8 | 69 | 4 |
| Sharpe | 10 | 1 | 31 | 0 | 35 | 7 | 91 | 1 |
| Peel | | | | | 35 | 13 | 49 | 1 |
| Grace | | | | | 15·3 | 2 | 34 | 0 |
| Stoddart | | | | | 4 | 1 | 12 | 0 |
| AUSTRALIA | | | | | | | | |
| Turner | 37 | 11 | 90 | 2 | 23·2 | 7 | 46 | 4 |
| McLeod | 18 | 6 | 55 | 2 | | | | |
| G. Giffen | 28·2 | 5 | 88 | 4 | 28 | 10 | 72 | 6 |
| Trott | 14 | 3 | 42 | 2 | 5 | 0 | 11 | 0 |
| Callaway | 17 | 10 | 19 | 0 | 10 | 6 | 21 | 0 |

### FALL OF WICKETS

| | A | E | A | E |
|---|---|---|---|---|
| Wkt | 1st | 1st | 2nd | 2nd |
| 1st | 31 | 50 | 1 | 2 |
| 2nd | 57 | 79 | 175 | 6 |
| 3rd | 62 | 123 | 254 | 11 |
| 4th | 90 | 127 | 347 | 64 |
| 5th | 117 | 152 | 364 | 83 |
| 6th | 123 | 167 | 376 | 117 |
| 7th | 126 | 178 | 391 | 133 |
| 8th | 132 | 235 | 391 | 140 |
| 9th | 141 | 235 | 391 | 140 |
| 10th | 145 | 307 | – | 157 |

Umpires: J. Tooher and T. Flynn.

# AUSTRALIA v ENGLAND 1891-92 (3rd Test)

Played at Adelaide Oval on 24, 25, 26, 28 March.
Toss: England.   Result: ENGLAND won by an innings and 230 runs.
Debuts: England – H. Philipson.

England gained their biggest margin of victory in any Test so far. Throughout this rubber – and those of 1894-95 and 1897-98 – six-ball overs were bowled.

## ENGLAND

| | | |
|---|---|---|
| W.G. Grace* | b McLeod | 58 |
| R. Abel | st Blackham b Trott | 24 |
| A.E. Stoddart | lbw b G. Giffen | 134 |
| J.M. Read | c Gregory b Turner | 57 |
| G. Bean | c McLeod b Lyons | 16 |
| R. Peel | c G. Giffen b Turner | 83 |
| G.A. Lohmann | lbw b G. Giffen | 0 |
| J. Briggs | b Turner | 39 |
| H. Philipson† | c Blackham b McLeod | 1 |
| G. MacGregor | run out | 31 |
| W. Attewell | not out | 43 |
| Extras | (B 5, LB 7, W 1) | 13 |
| **Total** | | **499** |

## AUSTRALIA

| | | | | | |
|---|---|---|---|---|---|
| A.C. Bannerman | c Bean b Lohmann | 12 | b Briggs | | 1 |
| J.J. Lyons | c Peel b Briggs | 23 | c Stoddart b Briggs | | 19 |
| G. Giffen | run out | 5 | c Bean b Attewell | | 27 |
| W. Bruce | lbw b Lohmann | 5 | lbw b Attewell | | 37 |
| C.T.B. Turner | c Lohmann b Briggs | 10 | c Grace b Briggs | | 5 |
| S.E. Gregory | c Abel b Briggs | 3 | c Peel b Briggs | | 7 |
| R.W. McLeod | b Briggs | 20 | c Grace b Lohmann | | 30 |
| G.H.S. Trott | b Briggs | 0 | st Philipson b Briggs | | 16 |
| W.F. Giffen | b Lohmann | 3 | c Peel b Briggs | | 2 |
| H. Donnan | c Bean b Briggs | 7 | not out | | 11 |
| J.M. Blackham*† | not out | 7 | b Attewell | | 9 |
| Extras | (B 5) | 5 | (B 3, LB 2) | | 5 |
| **Total** | | **100** | | | **169** |

| AUSTRALIA | O | M | R | W | O | M | R | W |
|---|---|---|---|---|---|---|---|---|
| G. Giffen | 51·1 | 17 | 154 | 2 | | | | |
| McLeod | 41 | 11 | 78 | 2 | | | | |
| Trott | 12 | 0 | 80 | 1 | | | | |
| Turner | 46 | 17 | 111 | 3 | | | | |
| Donnan | 9 | 2 | 22 | 0 | | | | |
| Lyons | 5 | 0 | 22 | 1 | | | | |
| Bruce | 4 | 3 | 19 | 0 | | | | |
| **ENGLAND** | | | | | | | | |
| Briggs | 21·5 | 4 | 49 | 6 | 28 | 7 | 87 | 6 |
| Lohmann | 21 | 8 | 46 | 3 | 6 | 2 | 8 | 1 |
| Attewell | | | | | 34 | 10 | 69 | 3 |

## FALL OF WICKETS

| | E | A | A |
|---|---|---|---|
| Wkt | 1st | 1st | 2nd |
| 1st | 47 | 30 | 1 |
| 2nd | 121 | 38 | 42 |
| 3rd | 218 | 48 | 51 |
| 4th | 272 | 48 | 85 |
| 5th | 327 | 51 | 91 |
| 6th | 333 | 66 | 99 |
| 7th | 412 | 66 | 120 |
| 8th | 425 | 73 | 124 |
| 9th | 425 | 90 | 157 |
| 10th | 499 | 100 | 169 |

Umpires: W.O. Whitridge and G. Downes.

# SOUTH AFRICA v ENGLAND 1891-92 (Only Test)

Played at Newlands, Cape Town, on 19, 21, 22 March.
Toss: South Africa.   Result: ENGLAND won by an innings and 189 runs.
Debuts: South Africa – G. Cripps, J.F. du Toit, C.G. Fichardt, E.A. Halliwell, C. Mills, D.C. Parkin, T.W. Routledge, S.C. Wimble; England – V.A. Barton, W. Chatterton, A. Hearne, G.G. Hearne, J.T. Hearne, A.D. Pougher. *F. Hearne was making his debut for South Africa after playing twice for England. J.J. Ferris and W.L. Murdoch were making their debuts for England after appearing for Australia.*

The Hearnes provided the second instance of three brothers playing in the same match: Alec and George Gibbons for England, and Frank for South Africa. John Thomas was their cousin. Murdoch, the former Australian captain, kept wicket for England in the second innings.

## SOUTH AFRICA

| | | | | | |
|---|---|--:|---|---|--:|
| T.W. Routledge | b Ferris | 5 | c Pougher b Ferris | | 1 |
| F. Hearne | b Pougher | 24 | b Ferris | | 23 |
| C.G. Fichardt | c and b Pougher | 0 | run out | | 10 |
| C. Mills | b Ferris | 4 | b Ferris | | 21 |
| E.A. Halliwell† | c J.T. Hearne b Ferris | 8 | b Ferris | | 0 |
| C.S. Wimble | c Wood b Pougher | 0 | (10) st Murdoch b Martin | | 0 |
| G. Cripps | b J.T. Hearne | 18 | b Ferris | | 3 |
| W.H. Milton* | c Martin b Ferris | 21 | c A. Hearne b Ferris | | 16 |
| C.H. Vintcent | lbw b Ferris | 6 | (6) b Ferris | | 0 |
| D.C. Parkin | b Ferris | 6 | (9) c and b Martin | | 0 |
| J.F. du Toit | not out | 0 | not out | | 2 |
| Extras | (B 5) | 5 | (B 7) | | 7 |
| **Total** | | **97** | | | **83** |

## ENGLAND

| | | |
|---|---|--:|
| W. Chatterton | c Du Toit b Mills | 48 |
| A. Hearne | lbw b Parkin | 9 |
| W.L. Murdoch | c and b Parkin | 12 |
| G.G. Hearne | c Mills b Parkin | 0 |
| V.A. Barton | c Vintcent b Mills | 23 |
| W.W. Read* | b Du Toit | 40 |
| A.D. Pougher | b Hearne | 17 |
| H. Wood† | not out | 134 |
| J.J. Ferris | run out | 16 |
| J.T. Hearne | c Fichardt b Milton | 40 |
| F. Martin | c Mills b Hearne | 13 |
| Extras | (B 13, NB 4) | 17 |
| **Total** | | **369** |

| ENGLAND | O | M | R | W | O | M | R | W |
|---|--:|--:|--:|--:|--:|--:|--:|--:|
| Ferris | 29·2 | 11 | 54 | 6 | 25 | 16 | 37 | 7 |
| Pougher | 21 | 8 | 26 | 3 | | | | |
| J.T. Hearne | 8 | 2 | 12 | 1 | | | | |
| Martin | | | | | 24·3 | 9 | 39 | 2 |
| **SOUTH AFRICA** | | | | | | | | |
| Vintcent | 24 | 8 | 50 | 0 | | | | |
| Parkin | 26 | 4 | 82 | 3 | | | | |
| Mills | 28 | 7 | 83 | 2 | | | | |
| Hearne | 12·2 | 0 | 40 | 2 | | | | |
| Du Toit | 17 | 5 | 47 | 1 | | | | |
| Milton | 9 | 2 | 27 | 1 | | | | |
| Cripps | 3 | 0 | 23 | 0 | | | | |

### FALL OF WICKETS

| | SA | E | SA |
|---|--:|--:|--:|
| Wkt | 1st | 1st | 2nd |
| 1st | 7 | 19 | 1 |
| 2nd | 14 | 33 | 30 |
| 3rd | 29 | 33 | 40 |
| 4th | 33 | 86 | 45 |
| 5th | 39 | 110 | 45 |
| 6th | 47 | 144 | 59 |
| 7th | 78 | 215 | 70 |
| 8th | 89 | 280 | 79 |
| 9th | 93 | 351 | 81 |
| 10th | 97 | 369 | 83 |

Umpires: J. Leaney and C.N. Thomas.

# ENGLAND v AUSTRALIA 1893 (1st Test)

Played at Lord's, London, on 17, 18, 19 July.
Toss: England.   Result: MATCH DRAWN.
Debuts: England – F.S. Jackson, W.H. Lockwood, A. Mold, E. Wainwright; Australia – H. Graham.
*Jackson was to become Colonel the Honourable Sir Francis Stanley Jackson, P.C., G.C.I.E.*

Shrewsbury became the first to score three Test hundreds for England and the first batsman from either country to score 1,000 runs in England v Australia Tests. Graham became the second Australian after C. Bannerman (*Test No. 1*) to score a hundred in his first Test. Stoddart was the first captain to declare a Test innings closed. Rain prevented play after lunch on the third day.

## ENGLAND

| | | | | | |
|---|---|---|---|---|---|
| A. Shrewsbury | c Blackham b Turner | 106 | b Giffen | | 81 |
| A.E. Stoddart* | b Turner | 24 | b Turner | | 13 |
| W. Gunn | c Lyons b Turner | 2 | c Graham b Giffen | | 77 |
| F.S. Jackson | c Blackham b Turner | 91 | c Bruce b Giffen | | 5 |
| J.M. Read | b Bruce | 6 | c McLeod b Bruce | | 1 |
| R. Peel | c Bruce b Trumble | 12 | (9) not out | | 0 |
| W. Flowers | b McLeod | 35 | (6) b Turner | | 4 |
| E. Wainwright | c Giffen b Turner | 1 | b Giffen | | 26 |
| W.H. Lockwood | b Bruce | 22 | (7) b Giffen | | 0 |
| G. MacGregor† | not out | 5 | | | |
| A. Mold | b Turner | 0 | | | |
| Extras | (B 19, LB 9, NB 2) | 30 | (B 16, LB 9, W 1, NB 1) | | 27 |
| **Total** | | **334** | (8 wickets declared) | | **234** |

## AUSTRALIA

| | | |
|---|---|---|
| J.J. Lyons | b Lockwood | 7 |
| A.C. Bannerman | c Shrewsbury b Lockwood | 17 |
| G. Giffen | b Lockwood | 0 |
| G.H.S. Trott | c MacGregor b Lockwood | 33 |
| R.W. McLeod | b Lockwood | 5 |
| S.E. Gregory | c MacGregor b Lockwood | 57 |
| H. Graham | c MacGregor b Mold | 107 |
| W. Bruce | c Peel b Mold | 23 |
| C.T.B. Turner | b Flowers | 0 |
| H. Trumble | not out | 2 |
| J.M. Blackham*† | lbw b Mold | 2 |
| Extras | (B 15, LB 1) | 16 |
| **Total** | | **269** |

| AUSTRALIA | O | M | R | W | O | M | R | W | | FALL OF WICKETS | | |
|---|---|---|---|---|---|---|---|---|---|---|---|---|
| Turner | 36 | 16 | 67 | 6 | 32 | 15 | 64 | 2 | | E | A | E |
| Bruce | 22 | 4 | 58 | 2 | 20 | 10 | 34 | 1 | *Wkt* | *1st* | *1st* | *2nd* |
| Trumble | 19 | 7 | 42 | 1 | 11 | 2 | 33 | 0 | 1st | 29 | 7 | 27 |
| Trott | 9 | 2 | 38 | 0 | 2 | 0 | 5 | 0 | 2nd | 31 | 7 | 179 |
| McLeod | 21 | 6 | 51 | 1 | 25 | 11 | 28 | 0 | 3rd | 168 | 50 | 195 |
| Giffen | 18 | 3 | 48 | 0 | 26·4 | 6 | 43 | 5 | 4th | 189 | 60 | 198 |
| | | | | | | | | | 5th | 213 | 75 | 198 |
| ENGLAND | | | | | | | | | 6th | 293 | 217 | 198 |
| Peel | 22 | 12 | 36 | 0 | | | | | 7th | 298 | 264 | 234 |
| Lockwood | 45 | 11 | 101 | 6 | | | | | 8th | 313 | 265 | 234 |
| Mold | 20·1 | 7 | 44 | 3 | | | | | 9th | 333 | 265 | – |
| Jackson | 5 | 1 | 10 | 0 | | | | | 10th | 334 | 269 | – |
| Wainwright | 11 | 3 | 41 | 0 | | | | | | | | |
| Flowers | 11 | 3 | 21 | 1 | | | | | | | | |

Umpires: J. Phillips and W. Hearn.

# ENGLAND v AUSTRALIA 1893 (2nd Test)

Played at Kennington Oval, London, on 14, 15, 16 August.
Toss: England.    Result: ENGLAND won by an innings and 43 runs.
Debuts: England – Albert Ward.

Jackson's hundred, which took 135 minutes, was the first in a Test in England to be completed with a hit over the boundary (then worth only four runs). Bannerman became the first Australian to score 1,000 runs in Tests. This match was awarded as a benefit to J.M. Read and produced takings of £1,200.

## ENGLAND

| | | |
|---|---|---|
| W.G. Grace* | c Giffen b Trumble | 68 |
| A.E. Stoddart | b Turner | 83 |
| A. Shrewsbury | c Graham b Giffen | 66 |
| W. Gunn | b Giffen | 16 |
| A. Ward | c and b Giffen | 55 |
| W.W. Read | b Giffen | 52 |
| F.S. Jackson | run out | 103 |
| J. Briggs | b Giffen | 0 |
| W.H. Lockwood | c and b Giffen | 10 |
| G. MacGregor† | lbw b Giffen | 5 |
| A. Mold | not out | 0 |
| Extras | (B 19, LB 4, W 2) | 25 |
| **Total** | | **483** |

## AUSTRALIA

| | | | | | |
|---|---|---|---|---|---|
| A.C. Bannerman | c MacGregor b Lockwood | 10 | | c Read b Lockwood | 55 |
| J.J. Lyons | b Briggs | 19 | (7) | c Grace b Lockwood | 31 |
| G.H.S. Trott | b Lockwood | 0 | (4) | c Read b Lockwood | 92 |
| S.E. Gregory | lbw b Briggs | 9 | (5) | c Shrewsbury b Briggs | 6 |
| H. Graham | c MacGregor b Lockwood | 0 | (6) | b Briggs | 42 |
| G. Giffen | c MacGregor b Lockwood | 4 | (3) | b Lockwood | 53 |
| W. Bruce | not out | 10 | (2) | c Jackson b Mold | 22 |
| H. Trumble | b Briggs | 5 | | b Briggs | 8 |
| R.W. McLeod | c Lockwood b Briggs | 2 | | c Jackson b Briggs | 5 |
| C.T.B. Turner | b Briggs | 7 | | b Briggs | 0 |
| J.M. Blackham*† | run out | 17 | | not out | 2 |
| Extras | (B 5, LB 3) | 8 | | (B 18, LB 15) | 33 |
| **Total** | | **91** | | | **349** |

| AUSTRALIA | O | M | R | W | O | M | R | W |
|---|---|---|---|---|---|---|---|---|
| Turner | 47 | 18 | 94 | 1 | | | | |
| Trumble | 47 | 16 | 101 | 1 | | | | |
| McLeod | 23 | 6 | 57 | 0 | | | | |
| Giffen | 54 | 17 | 128 | 7 | | | | |
| Trott | 6 | 1 | 33 | 0 | | | | |
| Bruce | 3 | 0 | 19 | 0 | | | | |
| Lyons | 7 | 1 | 26 | 0 | | | | |
| ENGLAND | | | | | | | | |
| Lockwood | 19 | 9 | 37 | 4 | 29 | 7 | 96 | 4 |
| Mold | 4 | 0 | 12 | 0 | 23 | 8 | 73 | 1 |
| Briggs | 14·3 | 5 | 34 | 5 | 35 | 6 | 114 | 5 |
| Jackson | | | | | 11 | 3 | 33 | 0 |

### FALL OF WICKETS

| Wkt | 1st | 1st | 2nd |
|---|---|---|---|
| | E | A | A |
| 1st | 151 | 30 | 54 |
| 2nd | 151 | 31 | 126 |
| 3rd | 200 | 32 | 165 |
| 4th | 303 | 32 | 189 |
| 5th | 311 | 40 | 295 |
| 6th | 442 | 48 | 311 |
| 7th | 442 | 57 | 340 |
| 8th | 456 | 59 | 342 |
| 9th | 478 | 69 | 342 |
| 10th | 483 | 91 | 349 |

Umpires: H. Draper and C.K. Pullin.

# ENGLAND v AUSTRALIA 1893 (3rd Test)

Played at Old Trafford, Manchester, on 24, 25, 26 August.
Toss: Australia.   Result: MATCH DRAWN.
Debuts: England – W. Brockwell, T. Richardson.

Gunn's hundred took 250 minutes and was the first in a Test at Old Trafford.

## AUSTRALIA

| | | | | |
|---|---|--:|---|--:|
| A.C. Bannerman | c MacGregor b Briggs | 19 | b Richardson | 60 |
| J.J. Lyons | c MacGregor b Briggs | 27 | b Mold | 33 |
| G. Giffen | b Richardson | 17 | c Brockwell b Richardson | 17 |
| G.H.S. Trott | c Grace b Richardson | 9 | b Mold | 12 |
| W. Bruce | c Read b Richardson | 68 | (6) c Shrewsbury b Richardson | 36 |
| H. Graham | lbw b Mold | 18 | (7) st MacGregor b Briggs | 3 |
| S.E. Gregory | b Briggs | 0 | (8) lbw b Richardson | 3 |
| H. Trumble | b Richardson | 35 | (9) run out | 8 |
| R.W. McLeod | b Briggs | 2 | (5) c Read b Richardson | 6 |
| C.T.B. Turner | b Richardson | 0 | c Mold b Briggs | 27 |
| J.M. Blackham*† | not out | 0 | not out | 23 |
| Extras | (B 5, LB 4) | 9 | (B 4, LB 4) | 8 |
| **Total** | | **204** | | **236** |

## ENGLAND

| | | | | |
|---|---|--:|---|--:|
| A.E. Stoddart | run out | 0 | c Gregory b Trumble | 42 |
| W.G. Grace* | b Bruce | 40 | c Trott b McLeod | 45 |
| A. Shrewsbury | c Bruce b Giffen | 12 | not out | 19 |
| W. Gunn | not out | 102 | b Trumble | 11 |
| A. Ward | c Blackham b Turner | 13 | b Trumble | 0 |
| W.W. Read | b Giffen | 12 | not out | 0 |
| W. Brockwell | c Gregory b Giffen | 11 | | |
| J. Briggs | b Giffen | 2 | | |
| G. MacGregor† | st Blackham b Turner | 12 | | |
| T. Richardson | b Bruce | 16 | | |
| A. Mold | b Trumble | 0 | | |
| Extras | (B 17, LB 6) | 23 | (B 1) | 1 |
| **Total** | | **243** | (4 wickets) | **118** |

| ENGLAND | O | M | R | W | O | M | R | W |
|---|--:|--:|--:|--:|--:|--:|--:|--:|
| Mold | 28 | 11 | 48 | 1 | 23 | 6 | 57 | 2 |
| Richardson | 23·4 | 5 | 49 | 5 | 44 | 15 | 107 | 5 |
| Briggs | 42 | 18 | 81 | 4 | 28·3 | 11 | 64 | 2 |
| Brockwell | 3 | 0 | 17 | 0 | | | | |
| **AUSTRALIA** | | | | | | | | |
| Giffen | 67 | 30 | 113 | 4 | 6 | 3 | 10 | 0 |
| Turner | 53 | 22 | 72 | 2 | 7 | 1 | 18 | 0 |
| Bruce | 17 | 5 | 26 | 2 | 9 | 4 | 19 | 0 |
| Trumble | 3·2 | 1 | 9 | 1 | 25 | 4 | 49 | 3 |
| McLeod | | | | | 16 | 7 | 21 | 1 |

## FALL OF WICKETS

| | A | E | A | E |
|---|--:|--:|--:|--:|
| Wkt | 1st | 1st | 2nd | 2nd |
| 1st | 32 | 4 | 56 | 78 |
| 2nd | 59 | 43 | 79 | 100 |
| 3rd | 69 | 73 | 92 | 117 |
| 4th | 73 | 93 | 99 | 117 |
| 5th | 129 | 112 | 153 | – |
| 6th | 130 | 136 | 170 | – |
| 7th | 194 | 165 | 173 | – |
| 8th | 198 | 196 | 182 | – |
| 9th | 201 | 238 | 200 | – |
| 10th | 204 | 243 | 236 | – |

Umpires: J. Phillips and C. Clements.

# AUSTRALIA v ENGLAND 1894–95 (1st Test)

Played at Sydney Cricket Ground on 14, 15, 17, 18, 19, 20 December.
Toss: Australia.   Result: ENGLAND won by 10 runs.
Debuts: Australia – J. Darling, F.A. Iredale, E. Jones, C.E. McLeod, J.C. Reedman; England –
   J.T. Brown, F.G.J. Ford, L.H.Gay, A.C. MacLaren.

This first Test of the first five-match rubber ever played was the first to go into the sixth day. It resulted in the only
instance in Test cricket of a team winning after following on. S.E. Gregory scored the first Test double-century in
Australia. G. Giffen is the only player to score 200 runs and take eight wickets in the same Test between these two
countries. Blackham was unable to keep wicket after splitting a finger in the first innings.

## AUSTRALIA

| | | | | |
|---|---|---|---|---|
| J.J. Lyons | b Richardson | 1 | b Richardson | 25 |
| G.H.S. Trott | b Richardson | 12 | c Gay b Peel | 8 |
| G Giffen | c Ford b Brockwell | 161 | lbw b Briggs | 41 |
| J. Darling | b Richardson | 0 | c Brockwell b Peel | 53 |
| F.A. Iredale | c Stoddart b Ford | 81 | (6) c and b Briggs | 5 |
| S.E. Gregory | c Peel b Stoddart | 201 | (5) c Gay b Peel | 16 |
| J.C. Reedman | c Ford b Peel | 17 | st Gay b Peel | 4 |
| C.E. McLeod | b Richardson | 15 | not out | 2 |
| C.T.B. Turner | c Gay b Peel | 1 | c Briggs b Peel | 2 |
| J.M. Blackham*† | b Richardson | 74 | (11) c and b Peel | 2 |
| E. Jones | not out | 11 | (10) c MacLaren b Briggs | 1 |
| Extras | (B 8, LB 3, W 1) | 12 | (B 2, LB 1, NB 4) | 7 |
| **Total** | | **586** | | **166** |

## ENGLAND

| | | | | |
|---|---|---|---|---|
| A.C. MacLaren | c Reedman b Turner | 4 | b Giffen | 20 |
| A. Ward | c Iredale b Turner | 75 | b Giffen | 117 |
| A.E. Stoddart* | c Jones b Giffen | 12 | c Giffen b Turner | 36 |
| J.T. Brown | run out | 22 | c Jones b Giffen | 53 |
| W. Brockwell | c Blackham b Jones | 49 | b Jones | 37 |
| R. Peel | c Gregory b Giffen | 4 | b Giffen | 17 |
| F.G.J. Ford | st Blackham b Giffen | 30 | c and b McLeod | 48 |
| J. Briggs | b Giffen | 57 | b McLeod | 42 |
| W.H. Lockwood | c Giffen b Trott | 18 | b Trott | 29 |
| L.H. Gay† | c Gregory b Reedman | 33 | b Trott | 4 |
| T. Richardson | not out | 0 | not out | 12 |
| Extras | (B 17, LB 3, W 1) | 21 | (B 14, LB 8) | 22 |
| **Total** | | **325** | | **437** |

| ENGLAND | O | M | R | W | O | M | R | W | | FALL OF WICKETS | | | |
|---|---|---|---|---|---|---|---|---|---|---|---|---|---|
| Richardson | 55·3 | 13 | 181 | 5 | 11 | 3 | 27 | 1 | | A | E | E | A |
| Peel | 53 | 14 | 140 | 2 | 30 | 9 | 67 | 6 | Wkt | 1st | 1st | 2nd | 2nd |
| Briggs | 25 | 4 | 96 | 0 | 11 | 2 | 25 | 3 | 1st | 10 | 14 | 44 | 26 |
| Brockwell | 22 | 7 | 78 | 1 | | | | | 2nd | 21 | 43 | 115 | 45 |
| Lockwood | 3 | 2 | 1 | 0 | 16 | 3 | 40 | 0 | 3rd | 21 | 78 | 217 | 130 |
| Ford | 11 | 2 | 47 | 1 | | | | | 4th | 192 | 149 | 245 | 135 |
| Stoddart | 3 | 0 | 31 | 1 | | | | | 5th | 331 | 155 | 290 | 147 |
| | | | | | | | | | 6th | 379 | 211 | 296 | 158 |
| AUSTRALIA | | | | | | | | | 7th | 400 | 211 | 385 | 159 |
| Turner | 44 | 16 | 89 | 2 | 35 | 14 | 78 | 1 | 8th | 409 | 252 | 398 | 161 |
| Jones | 18 | 6 | 44 | 1 | 19 | 0 | 57 | 1 | 9th | 563 | 325 | 420 | 162 |
| Giffen | 43 | 17 | 75 | 4 | 75 | 25 | 164 | 4 | 10th | 586 | 325 | 437 | 166 |
| McLeod | 14 | 2 | 25 | 0 | 30 | 6 | 67 | 2 | | | | | |
| Trott | 15 | 4 | 59 | 1 | 12·4 | 3 | 22 | 2 | | | | | |
| Reedman | 3·3 | 1 | 12 | 1 | 6 | 1 | 12 | 0 | | | | | |
| Lyons | 2 | 2 | 0 | 0 | 2 | 0 | 12 | 0 | | | | | |
| Iredale | | | | | 2 | 1 | 3 | 0 | | | | | |

Umpires: J. Phillips and C. Bannerman.

# AUSTRALIA v ENGLAND 1894–95 (2nd Test)

Played at Melbourne Cricket Ground on 29, 31 December, 1, 2, 3 January.
Toss: Australia.    Result: ENGLAND won by 94 runs.
Debuts: Australia – A. Coningham.

Giffen was the first captain to give his opponents first innings on winning the toss. Stoddart's 173 was the highest score for England in Tests, beating W.G. Grace's 170 in 1886 (*Test No. 24*). It remained the England record until K.S. Ranjitsinhji scored 175 in 1897-98 (*Test No. 53*) and the highest by an England captain in Australia until 1974-75 when M.H. Denness scored 188 (*Test No. 755*). Coningham took MacLaren's wicket with his first ball. In England's second innings all eleven batsmen reached double figures for the first time in a Test match innings.

## ENGLAND

| | | | | | |
|---|---|---|---|---|---|
| A.C. MacLaren | c Trott b Coningham | 0 | b Turner | | 15 |
| A. Ward | c Darling b Trumble | 30 | b Turner | | 41 |
| A.E. Stoddart* | b Turner | 10 | b Giffen | | 173 |
| J.T. Brown | c Trumble b Turner | 0 | c Jarvis b Bruce | | 37 |
| W. Brockwell | c Iredale b Coningham | 0 | b Turner | | 21 |
| R. Peel | c Trumble b Turner | 6 | st Jarvis b Giffen | | 53 |
| F.G.J. Ford | c Giffen b Trumble | 9 | c Trott b Giffen | | 24 |
| W.H. Lockwood | not out | 3 | (9) not out | | 33 |
| J. Briggs | c Bruce b Turner | 5 | (8) lbw b Giffen | | 31 |
| H. Philipson† | c Darling b Turner | 1 | b Giffen | | 30 |
| T. Richardson | c Iredale b Trumble | 0 | c Gregory b Giffen | | 11 |
| Extras | (LB 9, NB 2) | 11 | (B 1, LB 2, NB 3) | | 6 |
| **Total** | | **75** | | | **475** |

## AUSTRALIA

| | | | | | |
|---|---|---|---|---|---|
| J.J. Lyons | b Richardson | 2 | (7) b Peel | | 14 |
| W. Bruce | c Ford b Peel | 4 | c Stoddart b Peel | | 54 |
| G. Giffen* | c Philipson b Briggs | 32 | c Brown b Brockwell | | 43 |
| S.E. Gregory | c Ward b Richardson | 2 | b Richardson | | 12 |
| J. Darling | b Lockwood | 32 | b Brockwell | | 5 |
| F.A. Iredale | b Richardson | 10 | b Peel | | 68 |
| G.H.S. Trott | run out | 16 | (1) c and b Brockwell | | 95 |
| A. Coningham | c Philipson b Richardson | 10 | (9) b Peel | | 3 |
| H. Trumble | b Richardson | 1 | (10) run out | | 2 |
| A.H. Jarvis† | c Brown b Briggs | 11 | (8) b Richardson | | 4 |
| C.T.B. Turner | not out | 1 | not out | | 26 |
| Extras | (W 2) | 2 | (B 5, LB 1, NB 1) | | 7 |
| **Total** | | **123** | | | **333** |

| AUSTRALIA | O | M | R | W | O | M | R | W | | FALL OF WICKETS | | | |
|---|---|---|---|---|---|---|---|---|---|---|---|---|---|
| | | | | | | | | | | E | A | E | A |
| Coningham | 11 | 5 | 17 | 2 | 20 | 4 | 59 | 0 | *Wkt* | *1st* | *1st* | *2nd* | *2nd* |
| Turner | 20 | 9 | 32 | 5 | 55 | 21 | 99 | 3 | 1st | 0 | 4 | 24 | 98 |
| Trumble | 9·1 | 4 | 15 | 3 | 26 | 6 | 72 | 0 | 2nd | 19 | 12 | 101 | 191 |
| Giffen | | | | | 78·2 | 21 | 155 | 6 | 3rd | 23 | 14 | 191 | 206 |
| Lyons | | | | | 2 | 1 | 3 | 0 | 4th | 26 | 53 | 222 | 214 |
| Trott | | | | | 17 | 0 | 60 | 0 | 5th | 44 | 80 | 320 | 216 |
| Bruce | | | | | 4 | 0 | 21 | 1 | 6th | 58 | 96 | 362 | 241 |
| ENGLAND | | | | | | | | | 7th | 60 | 108 | 385 | 254 |
| Richardson | 23 | 6 | 57 | 5 | 40 | 10 | 100 | 2 | 8th | 70 | 110 | 402 | 263 |
| Peel | 14 | 4 | 21 | 1 | 40·1 | 9 | 77 | 4 | 9th | 71 | 116 | 455 | 268 |
| Lockwood | 5 | 0 | 17 | 1 | 25 | 5 | 60 | 0 | 10th | 75 | 123 | 475 | 333 |
| Briggs | 13·5 | 2 | 26 | 2 | 12 | 0 | 49 | 0 | | | | | |
| Ford | | | | | 6 | 2 | 7 | 0 | | | | | |
| Brockwell | | | | | 14 | 3 | 33 | 3 | | | | | |

Umpires: J. Phillips and T. Flynn.

# AUSTRALIA v ENGLAND 1894–95 (3rd Test)

Played at Adelaide Oval on 11, 12, 14, 15 January.
Toss: Australia.   Result: AUSTRALIA won by 382 runs.
Debuts: Australia – J. Harry, A.E. Trott.

This match, played in tremendous heat, was notable for the all-round performance of A.E. Trott who scored 110 runs without being dismissed and bowled unchanged throughout the second innings to take 8 for 43. Only two other bowlers have taken eight wickets in an innings of their maiden Test: A.L. Valentine for West Indies in 1950 (*Test No. 323*) and R.A.L. Massie (twice) for Australia in 1972 (*Test No. 699*).

## AUSTRALIA

| | | | | | |
|---|---|---|---|---|---|
| W. Bruce | b Richardson | 11 | c Brockwell b Briggs | | 80 |
| G.H.S. Trott | run out | 48 | b Peel | | 0 |
| G. Giffen* | c Lockwood b Brockwell | 58 | c Ford b Peel | | 24 |
| F.A. Iredale | b Richardson | 7 | c and b Peel | | 140 |
| J. Darling | c Philipson b Briggs | 10 | c Philipson b Lockwood | | 3 |
| S.E. Gregory | c Brown b Richardson | 6 | b Richardson | | 20 |
| J. Harry | b Richardson | 2 | b Richardson | | 6 |
| J. Worrall | run out | 0 | c Peel b Briggs | | 11 |
| A.H. Jarvis† | c and b Lockwood | 13 | c Brown b Peel | | 29 |
| A.E. Trott | not out | 38 | not out | | 72 |
| S.T. Callaway | b Richardson | 41 | b Richardson | | 11 |
| Extras | (B 2, W 1, NB 1) | 4 | (B 7, LB 7, NB 1) | | 15 |
| **Total** | | **238** | | | **411** |

## ENGLAND

| | | | | | |
|---|---|---|---|---|---|
| J. Briggs | b Callaway | 12 | (9) b A.E. Trott | | 0 |
| A.C. MacLaren | b Callaway | 25 | c Iredale b A.E. Trott | | 35 |
| W. Brockwell | c Harry b Callaway | 12 | (6) c and b A.E. Trott | | 24 |
| A. Ward | c Bruce b Giffen | 5 | (1) b A.E. Trott | | 13 |
| A.E. Stoddart* | b Giffen | 1 | (3) not out | | 34 |
| J.T. Brown | not out | 39 | (5) b A.E. Trott | | 2 |
| R. Peel | b Callaway | 0 | (7) c and b A.E. Trott | | 0 |
| F.G.J. Ford | c Worrall b Giffen | 21 | c G.H.S. Trott b A.E. Trott | | 14 |
| W.H. Lockwood | c Worrall b Giffen | 0 | (10) c Iredale b A.E. Trott | | 1 |
| H. Philipson† | c Gregory b Giffen | 7 | (4) b Giffen | | 1 |
| T. Richardson | c Worrall b Callaway | 0 | c A.E. Trott b Giffen | | 12 |
| Extras | (B 2) | 2 | (B 5, LB 2) | | 7 |
| **Total** | | **124** | | | **143** |

| ENGLAND | O | M | R | W | O | M | R | W | | FALL OF WICKETS | | | |
|---|---|---|---|---|---|---|---|---|---|---|---|---|---|
| Richardson | 21 | 4 | 75 | 5 | 31·2 | 8 | 89 | 3 | | A | E | A | E |
| Peel | 16 | 1 | 43 | 0 | 34 | 6 | 96 | 4 | *Wkt* | *1st* | *1st* | *2nd* | *2nd* |
| Brockwell | 20 | 13 | 30 | 1 | 10 | 1 | 50 | 0 | 1st | 31 | 14 | 0 | 52 |
| Ford | 8 | 2 | 19 | 0 | 6 | 0 | 33 | 0 | 2nd | 69 | 30 | 44 | 52 |
| Briggs | 8 | 2 | 34 | 1 | 19 | 3 | 57 | 2 | 3rd | 84 | 49 | 142 | 53 |
| Lockwood | 8 | 2 | 33 | 1 | 15 | 2 | 71 | 1 | 4th | 103 | 50 | 145 | 64 |
| | | | | | | | | | 5th | 120 | 56 | 197 | 102 |
| AUSTRALIA | | | | | | | | | 6th | 124 | 64 | 215 | 102 |
| A.E. Trott | 3 | 1 | 9 | 0 | 27 | 10 | 43 | 8 | 7th | 137 | 111 | 238 | 128 |
| Giffen | 28 | 11 | 76 | 5 | 22·1 | 12 | 74 | 2 | 8th | 157 | 111 | 283 | 128 |
| Callaway | 26·3 | 13 | 37 | 5 | 7 | 1 | 19 | 0 | 9th | 157 | 124 | 347 | 130 |
| | | | | | | | | | 10th | 238 | 124 | 411 | 143 |

Umpires: J. Phillips and G. Searcy.

# AUSTRALIA v ENGLAND 1894–95 (4th Test)

Played at Sydney Cricket Ground on 1, 2 (*no play*), 4 February.
Toss: England.    Result: AUSTRALIA won by an innings and 147 runs.
Debuts: Nil.

England were dismissed twice on the third day. There has been only one similar occurrence – in 1952 when India scored 58 and 82 on the third day at Old Trafford (*Test No. 353*). J. Briggs became the first bowler to take 100 Test wickets when he had Jarvis stumped in the first innings. On the third day C.T.B. Turner became the first Australian bowler to reach that aggregate when he took his third wicket; it was his last Test. Lancashire players occupied the first three places in England's batting order in the first innings.

## AUSTRALIA

| | | |
|---|---|---:|
| G.H.S. Trott | c Brown b Peel | 1 |
| W. Bruce | c Brockwell b Peel | 15 |
| G Giffen* | b Peel | 8 |
| H. Moses | b Richardson | 1 |
| H. Graham | st Philipson b Briggs | 105 |
| S.E. Gregory | st Philipson b Briggs | 5 |
| F.A. Iredale | c and b Briggs | 0 |
| J. Darling | b Richardson | 31 |
| A.E. Trott | not out | 85 |
| A.H. Jarvis† | c Philipson b Briggs | 5 |
| C.T.B. Turner | c Richardson b Lockwood | 22 |
| Extras | (B 3, LB 1, W 1, NB 1) | 6 |
| **Total** | | **284** |

## ENGLAND

| | | | | |
|---|---|---:|---|---:|
| A.C. MacLaren | st Jarvis b G.H.S. Trott | 1 | (4) c Bruce b Giffen | 0 |
| A. Ward | c and b Turner | 7 | c Darling b Giffen | 6 |
| J. Briggs | b G.H.S. Trott | 11 | (8) c Bruce b Giffen | 6 |
| A.E. Stoddart* | st Jarvis b G.H.S. Trott | 7 | (3) c Iredale b Turner | 0 |
| J.T. Brown | not out | 20 | (1) b Giffen | 0 |
| W. Brockwell | c Darling b Turner | 1 | (5) c Bruce b Turner | 17 |
| F.G.J. Ford | c G.H.S. Trott b Giffen | 0 | c Darling b Giffen | 11 |
| R. Peel | st Jarvis b Turner | 0 | (6) st Jarvis b Turner | 0 |
| H. Philipson† | c Graham b Giffen | 4 | c and b Turner | 9 |
| T. Richardson | c and b Giffen | 2 | not out | 10 |
| W.H. Lockwood | absent hurt | – | absent hurt | – |
| Extras | (B 7, LB 3, NB 2) | 12 | (B 5, LB 7, NB 1) | 13 |
| **Total** | | **65** | | **72** |

| ENGLAND | O | M | R | W | O | M | R | W |
|---|---|---|---|---|---|---|---|---|
| Peel | 24 | 5 | 74 | 3 | | | | |
| Richardson | 22 | 5 | 78 | 2 | | | | |
| Briggs | 22 | 4 | 65 | 4 | | | | |
| Brockwell | 5 | 1 | 25 | 0 | | | | |
| Ford | 2 | 0 | 14 | 0 | | | | |
| Lockwood | 8·2 | 3 | 22 | 1 | | | | |
| AUSTRALIA | | | | | | | | |
| G.H.S. Trott | 14 | 5 | 21 | 3 | | | | |
| Turner | 19 | 10 | 18 | 3 | 14·1 | 6 | 33 | 4 |
| Giffen | 5·5 | 1 | 14 | 3 | 15 | 7 | 26 | 5 |

| FALL OF WICKETS | | | |
|---|---|---|---|
| | A | E | E |
| Wkt | 1st | 1st | 2nd |
| 1st | 2 | 2 | 0 |
| 2nd | 20 | 20 | 5 |
| 3rd | 26 | 24 | 5 |
| 4th | 26 | 31 | 12 |
| 5th | 51 | 40 | 14 |
| 6th | 51 | 43 | 29 |
| 7th | 119 | 56 | 47 |
| 8th | 231 | 63 | 52 |
| 9th | 239 | 65 | 72 |
| 10th | 284 | – | – |

Umpires: J. Phillips and C. Bannerman.

# AUSTRALIA v ENGLAND 1894–95 (5th Test)

Played at Melbourne Cricket Ground on 1, 2, 4, 5, 6 March.
Toss: Australia.    Result: ENGLAND won by six wickets.
Debuts: Australia – T.R. McKibbin.

J.T. Brown (140) scored his first fifty in only 28 minutes – the fastest half-century in all Test cricket to date. His hundred took 95 minutes and was the fastest Test century. Brown's third-wicket partnership of 210 with Ward set a new Test record for any wicket. G. Giffen achieved the best all-round performance for a Test rubber by scoring 475 runs and taking 34 wickets.

## AUSTRALIA

| | | | | |
|---|---|--:|---|--:|
| G.H.S. Trott | b Briggs | 42 | b Peel | 42 |
| W. Bruce | c MacLaren b Peel | 22 | c and b Peel | 11 |
| G. Giffen* | b Peel | 57 | b Richardson | 51 |
| F.A. Iredale | b Richardson | 8 | b Richardson | 18 |
| S.E. Gregory | c Philipson b Richardson | 70 | b Richardson | 30 |
| J. Darling | c Ford b Peel | 74 | b Peel | 50 |
| J.J. Lyons | c Philipson b Lockwood | 55 | b Briggs | 15 |
| H. Graham | b Richardson | 6 | lbw b Richardson | 10 |
| A.E. Trott | c Lockwood b Peel | 10 | b Richardson | 0 |
| A.H. Jarvis† | not out | 34 | not out | 14 |
| T.R. McKibbin | c Peel b Briggs | 23 | c Philipson b Richardson | 13 |
| Extras | (B 3, LB 10) | 13 | (B 5, LB 6, NB 2) | 13 |
| **Total** | | **414** | | **267** |

## ENGLAND

| | | | | |
|---|---|--:|---|--:|
| A. Ward | b McKibbin | 32 | b G.H.S. Trott | 93 |
| W. Brockwell | st Jarvis b G.H.S. Trott | 5 | c and b Giffen | 5 |
| A.E. Stoddart* | st Jarvis b G.H.S. Trott | 68 | lbw b G.H.S. Trott | 11 |
| J.T. Brown | b A.E. Trott | 30 | c Giffen b McKibbin | 140 |
| A.C. MacLaren | hit wkt b G.H.S. Trott | 120 | not out | 20 |
| R. Peel | c Gregory b Giffen | 73 | not out | 15 |
| W.H. Lockwood | c G.H.S. Trott b Giffen | 5 | | |
| F.G.J. Ford | c A.E. Trott b Giffen | 11 | | |
| J. Briggs | c G.H.S. Trott b Giffen | 0 | | |
| H. Philipson† | not out | 10 | | |
| T. Richardson | lbw b G.H.S. Trott | 11 | | |
| Extras | (B 8, LB 8, W 4) | 20 | (B 6, LB 5, W 2, NB 1) | 14 |
| **Total** | | **385** | (4 wickets) | **298** |

| ENGLAND | O | M | R | W | O | M | R | W | FALL OF WICKETS | | | | |
|---|--:|--:|--:|--:|--:|--:|--:|--:|---|--:|--:|--:|--:|
| Richardson | 42 | 7 | 138 | 3 | 45·2 | 7 | 104 | 6 | | A | E | A | E |
| Peel | 48 | 13 | 114 | 4 | 46 | 16 | 89 | 3 | Wkt | 1st | 1st | 2nd | 2nd |
| Lockwood | 27 | 7 | 72 | 1 | 16 | 7 | 24 | 0 | 1st | 40 | 6 | 32 | 5 |
| Briggs | 23·4 | 5 | 46 | 2 | 16 | 3 | 37 | 1 | 2nd | 101 | 110 | 75 | 28 |
| Brockwell | 6 | 1 | 22 | 0 | | | | | 3rd | 126 | 112 | 125 | 238 |
| Ford | 2 | 0 | 9 | 0 | | | | | 4th | 142 | 166 | 148 | 278 |
| | | | | | | | | | 5th | 284 | 328 | 179 | — |
| AUSTRALIA | | | | | | | | | 6th | 286 | 342 | 200 | — |
| Giffen | 45 | 13 | 130 | 4 | 31 | 4 | 106 | 1 | 7th | 304 | 364 | 219 | — |
| G.H.S. Trott | 24 | 5 | 71 | 4 | 20 | 1 | 63 | 2 | 8th | 335 | 364 | 219 | — |
| A.E. Trott | 30 | 4 | 84 | 1 | 19 | 2 | 56 | 0 | 9th | 367 | 366 | 248 | — |
| McKibbin | 29 | 6 | 73 | 1 | 14 | 2 | 47 | 1 | 10th | 414 | 385 | 267 | — |
| Bruce | 5 | 1 | 7 | 0 | 3 | 1 | 10 | 0 | | | | | |
| Lyons | | | | | 1 | 0 | 2 | 0 | | | | | |

Umpires: J. Phillips and T. Flynn.

# SOUTH AFRICA v ENGLAND 1895–96 (1st Test)

Played at St George's Park, Port Elizabeth, on 13, 14 February.
Toss: South Africa.    Result: ENGLAND won by 288 runs.
Debuts: South Africa – F.J. Cook, R.A. Gleeson, C.F.W. Hime, J. Middleton, R.M. Poore, J.H. Sinclair, J.T. Willoughby; England – H.R. Bromley-Davenport, H.R. Butt, C.B. Fry, The Seventh Lord Hawke, T.W. Hayward, A.J.L. Hill, A.M. Miller, C.W. Wright. *S.M.J. Woods was making his debut for England after playing for Australia.*

South Africa were dismissed in only 94 balls for 30 – the lowest total in Test cricket until 1954-55 when New Zealand were dismissed for 26 (*Test No. 402*). Lohmann's analysis of 8 for 7 set a new Test record and he ended the match – on the second day – with a hat-trick. His match figures of 15 for 45 remain the best in any Test at Port Elizabeth.

## ENGLAND

| | | | | | |
|---|---|---|---|---|---|
| Sir T.C. O'Brien* | c Gleeson b Willoughby | 17 | (3) b Sinclair | | 16 |
| G.A. Lohmann | c Routledge b Willoughby | 0 | (6) b Willoughby | | 0 |
| T.W. Hayward | c Sinclair b Middleton | 30 | (4) c Halliwell b Willoughby | | 6 |
| C.B. Fry | b Middleton | 43 | (5) c Halliwell b Middleton | | 15 |
| A.J.L. Hill | run out | 25 | (7) b Middleton | | 37 |
| S.M.J. Woods | b Hime | 7 | (8) c Poore b Sinclair | | 53 |
| H.R. Bromley-Davenport | c Fichardt b Middleton | 26 | (9) c Poore b Middleton | | 7 |
| Lord Hawke | b Middleton | 0 | (10) c Gleeson b Poore | | 30 |
| C.W. Wright | b Sinclair | 19 | (1) b Sinclair | | 33 |
| A.M. Miller | not out | 4 | (11) not out | | 20 |
| H.R. Butt† | c Halliwell b Middleton | 1 | (2) b Middleton | | 0 |
| Extras | (B 13) | 13 | (B 9) | | 9 |
| **Total** | | **185** | | | **226** |

## SOUTH AFRICA

| | | | | | |
|---|---|---|---|---|---|
| T.W. Routledge | b Bromley-Davenport | 22 | b Lohmann | | 2 |
| F. Hearne | c O'Brien b Bromley-Davenport | 23 | b Lohmann | | 5 |
| R.M. Poore | b Lohmann | 11 | c O'Brien b Lohmann | | 10 |
| J.H. Sinclair | b Lohmann | 4 | b Lohmann | | 0 |
| C.F.W. Hime | b Lohmann | 0 | (6) b Hayward | | 8 |
| E.A. Halliwell*† | b Lohmann | 13 | (7) c Hayward b Lohmann | | 3 |
| C.G. Fichardt | b Lohmann | 4 | (5) lbw b Bromley-Davenport | | 1 |
| R.A. Gleeson | c Lohmann b Hayward | 3 | not out | | 1 |
| F.J. Cook | b Lohmann | 7 | b Lohmann | | 0 |
| J. Middleton | not out | 4 | b Lohmann | | 0 |
| J.T. Willoughby | b Lohmann | 0 | c Hayward b Lohmann | | 0 |
| Extras | (B 2) | 2 | | | – |
| **Total** | | **93** | | | **30** |

| SOUTH AFRICA | O | M | R | W | O | M | R | W | | FALL OF WICKETS | | | |
|---|---|---|---|---|---|---|---|---|---|---|---|---|---|
| Sinclair | 16 | 5 | 34 | 1 | 20 | 2 | 68 | 3 | | E | SA | E | SA |
| Willoughby | 22 | 6 | 54 | 2 | 19 | 4 | 68 | 2 | Wkt | 1st | 1st | 2nd | 2nd |
| Middleton | 25·4 | 6 | 64 | 5 | 36 | 12 | 66 | 4 | 1st | 0 | 29 | 0 | 4 |
| Hime | 7 | 3 | 20 | 1 | 4 | 1 | 11 | 0 | 2nd | 25 | 58 | 39 | 11 |
| Poore | | | | | 1·4 | 0 | 4 | 1 | 3rd | 68 | 58 | 52 | 11 |
| | | | | | | | | | 4th | 120 | 62 | 68 | 18 |
| ENGLAND | | | | | | | | | 5th | 125 | 62 | 68 | 18 |
| Lohmann | 15·4 | 6 | 38 | 7 | 9·4 | 5 | 7 | 8 | 6th | 131 | 77 | 72 | 28 |
| Bromley-Davenport | 12 | 2 | 46 | 2 | 7 | 1 | 23 | 1 | 7th | 140 | 80 | 161 | 29 |
| Hayward | 3 | 1 | 7 | 1 | 2 | 2 | 0 | 1 | 8th | 145 | 80 | 169 | 30 |
| | | | | | | | | | 9th | 184 | 92 | 184 | 30 |
| Umpires: Not known. | | | | | | | | | 10th | 185 | 93 | 226 | 30 |

# SOUTH AFRICA v ENGLAND 1895–96 (2nd Test)

Played at Old Wanderers, Johannesburg, on 2, 3, 4 March.
Toss: England.   Result: ENGLAND won by an innings and 197 runs.
Debuts: South Africa – W.H.B. Frank, C.L. Johnson, C.B. Llewellyn, G.A. Rowe, G.H. Shepstone;
England – C. Heseltine.

Lohmann improved on his record analysis of the previous match by becoming the first bowler to take nine wickets in a Test match. Only J.C. Laker with 10 for 53 against Australia in 1956 (*Test No. 428*) has returned better figures at Test level. Lohmann took his hundredth Test wicket during the second innings of this his 16th Test. Wright kept wicket after Butt had injured his hand during South Africa's first innings.

### ENGLAND

| | | |
|---|---|---:|
| Sir T.C. O'Brien | b Rowe | 0 |
| G.A. Lohmann | c Hearne b Sinclair | 2 |
| T.W. Hayward | c Routledge b Rowe | 122 |
| C.B. Fry | c and b Rowe | 64 |
| A.J.L. Hill | b Sinclair | 65 |
| S.M.J. Woods | c Rowe b Sinclair | 32 |
| Lord Hawke* | lbw b Sinclair | 4 |
| C.W. Wright | b Frank | 71 |
| H.R. Bromley-Davenport | c Johnson b Rowe | 84 |
| C. Heseltine | lbw b Rowe | 0 |
| H.R. Butt† | not out | 8 |
| Extras | (B 22, LB 4, W 1, NB 3) | 30 |
| **Total** | | **482** |

### SOUTH AFRICA

| | | | | | |
|---|---|---:|---|---|---:|
| T.W. Routledge | b Woods | 14 | c sub (H.F. Mosenthal) b Heseltine | | 0 |
| J.H. Sinclair | c and b Lohmann | 40 | c sub (H.F. Mosenthal) b Woods | | 29 |
| R.M. Poore | b Lohmann | 20 | b Heseltine | | 10 |
| F. Hearne | c Butt b Lohmann | 0 | c Heseltine b Lohmann | | 16 |
| E.A. Halliwell*† | c O'Brien b Lohmann | 13 | c Hawke b Heseltine | | 41 |
| C.L. Johnson | b Lohmann | 3 | run out | | 7 |
| G.H. Shepstone | b Lohmann | 21 | c Fry b Lohmann | | 9 |
| F.W. Smith | b Lohmann | 4 | not out | | 11 |
| W.H.B. Frank | c and b Lohmann | 5 | c Hill b Lohmann | | 2 |
| C.B. Llewellyn | c Heseltine b Lohmann | 24 | c Lohmann b Heseltine | | 4 |
| G.A. Rowe | not out | 0 | b Heseltine | | 0 |
| Extras | (W 2, NB 5) | 7 | (LB 3, NB 2) | | 5 |
| **Total** | | **151** | | | **134** |

| SOUTH AFRICA | O | M | R | W | O | M | R | W |
|---|---:|---:|---:|---:|---:|---:|---:|---:|
| Rowe | 49 | 9 | 115 | 5 | | | | |
| Sinclair | 35 | 6 | 118 | 4 | | | | |
| Frank | 11·3 | 3 | 52 | 1 | | | | |
| Llewellyn | 14 | 3 | 71 | 0 | | | | |
| Johnson | 28 | 12 | 57 | 0 | | | | |
| Shepstone | 20 | 8 | 39 | 0 | | | | |
| ENGLAND | | | | | | | | |
| Heseltine | 9 | 0 | 29 | 0 | 16·2 | 3 | 38 | 5 |
| Woods | 20 | 2 | 74 | 1 | 6 | 1 | 27 | 1 |
| Lohmann | 14·2 | 6 | 28 | 9 | 17 | 4 | 43 | 3 |
| Bromley-Davenport | 3 | 0 | 13 | 0 | | | | |
| Hayward | | | | | 4 | 1 | 21 | 0 |

FALL OF WICKETS

| | E | SA | SA |
|---|---:|---:|---:|
| *Wkt* | *1st* | *1st* | *2nd* |
| 1st | 0 | 19 | 0 |
| 2nd | 8 | 70 | 23 |
| 3rd | 127 | 70 | 48 |
| 4th | 249 | 77 | 63 |
| 5th | 291 | 85 | 83 |
| 6th | 304 | 101 | 116 |
| 7th | 307 | 105 | 118 |
| 8th | 461 | 111 | 124 |
| 9th | 461 | 142 | 134 |
| 10th | 482 | 151 | 134 |

Umpires: A.M. Miller and (probably) G. Allsop.

# SOUTH AFRICA v ENGLAND 1895–96 (3rd Test)

Played at Newlands, Cape Town, on 21, 23 March.
Toss: England.   Result. ENGLAND won by an innings and 33 runs.
Debuts: South Africa – G.K. Glover, A.R. Richards, A.W. Seccull; England – E.J. Tyler.

Lohmann took his total of wickets for the three-match rubber to 35 at 5.8 runs apiece.

## SOUTH AFRICA

| | | | | | |
|---|---|--:|---|---|--:|
| T.W. Routledge | b Lohmann | 24 | (5) b Woods | | 4 |
| F. Hearne | c and b Lohmann | 0 | c Hayward b Tyler | | 30 |
| R.M. Poore | c Woods b Lohmann | 17 | b Woods | | 8 |
| J.H. Sinclair | c Woods b Tyler | 2 | (6) c Hawke b Bromley-Davenport | | 28 |
| A.R. Richards* | c Woods b Lohmann | 6 | (1) b Woods | | 0 |
| E.A. Halliwell† | c Heseltine b Tyler | 23 | (7) b Hill | | 11 |
| A.W. Seccull | c and b Lohmann | 6 | (8) not out | | 17 |
| G.K. Glover | not out | 18 | (4) c Woods b Lohmann | | 3 |
| J. Middleton | c Hayward b Tyler | 2 | c Hawke b Hill | | 6 |
| J.T. Willoughby | b Lohmann | 5 | st Butt b Hill | | 3 |
| G.A. Rowe | b Lohmann | 5 | b Hill | | 3 |
| Extras | (B 5, W 1, NB 1) | 7 | (B 2, NB 2) | | 4 |
| **Total** | | **115** | | | **117** |

## ENGLAND

| | | |
|---|---|--:|
| C.W. Wright | c Seccull b Willoughby | 2 |
| A.J.L. Hill | c Poore b Middleton | 124 |
| T.W. Hayward | b Seccull | 31 |
| H.R. Bromley-Davenport | b Seccull | 7 |
| S.M.J. Woods | b Rowe | 30 |
| Sir T.C. O'Brien | c sub (J.H. Anderson) b Glover | 2 |
| G.A. Lohmann | b Willoughby | 8 |
| C. Heseltine | c Hearne b Rowe | 18 |
| Lord Hawke* | not out | 12 |
| E.J. Tyler | b Middleton | 0 |
| H.R. Butt† | c Sinclair b Middleton | 13 |
| Extras | (B 12, LB 4, NB 2) | 18 |
| **Total** | | **265** |

| ENGLAND | O | M | R | W | O | M | R | W | | FALL OF WICKETS | | |
|---|--:|--:|--:|--:|--:|--:|--:|--:|---|:--:|:--:|:--:|
| | | | | | | | | | | SA | E | SA |
| Lohmann | 24 | 9 | 42 | 7 | 23 | 8 | 45 | 1 | Wkt | 1st | 1st | 2nd |
| Tyler | 18 | 3 | 49 | 3 | 11 | 3 | 16 | 1 | 1st | 6 | 2 | 1 |
| Heseltine | 6 | 0 | 17 | 0 | | | | | 2nd | 43 | 79 | 13 |
| Woods | | | | | 13 | 5 | 28 | 3 | 3rd | 48 | 95 | 28 |
| Bromley-Davenport | | | | | 9 | 3 | 16 | 1 | 4th | 48 | 159 | 35 |
| Hill | | | | | 8 | 4 | 8 | 4 | 5th | 74 | 168 | 75 |
| | | | | | | | | | 6th | 80 | 190 | 80 |
| SOUTH AFRICA | | | | | | | | | 7th | 90 | 226 | 97 |
| Willoughby | 14 | 2 | 37 | 2 | | | | | 8th | 98 | 244 | 105 |
| Rowe | 32 | 9 | 72 | 2 | | | | | 9th | 104 | 244 | 111 |
| Seccull | 12 | 2 | 37 | 2 | | | | | 10th | 115 | 265 | 117 |
| Sinclair | 7 | 1 | 23 | 0 | | | | | | | | |
| Middleton | 23·4 | 6 | 50 | 3 | | | | | | | | |
| Glover | 13 | 4 | 28 | 1 | | | | | | | | |

Umpires: A.M. Miller and (probably) G. Beves.

# ENGLAND v AUSTRALIA 1896 (1st Test)

Played at Lord's, London, on 22, 23, 24 June.
Toss: Australia.   Result: ENGLAND won by six wickets.
Debuts: England – A.F.A. Lilley; Australia – C.J. Eady, C. Hill, J.J. Kelly.

The fourth-wicket partnership of 221 between Trott and Gregory was a new record for any wicket in Test matches.

## AUSTRALIA

| | | | | | |
|---|---|---|---|---|---|
| H. Donnan | run out | | 1 | (11) b Hearne | 8 |
| J. Darling | b Richardson | | 22 | b Richardson | 0 |
| G. Giffen | c Lilley b Lohmann | | 0 | b Richardson | 32 |
| G.H.S. Trott* | b Richardson | | 0 | c Hayward b Richardson | 143 |
| S.E. Gregory | b Richardson | | 14 | c Lohmann b Hearne | 103 |
| H. Graham | b Richardson | | 0 | b Richardson | 10 |
| C. Hill | b Lohmann | | 1 | b Hearne | 5 |
| C.J. Eady | not out | | 10 | (1) c Lilley b Richardson | 2 |
| H. Trumble | b Richardson | | 0 | (8) c Lilley b Hearne | 4 |
| J.J. Kelly† | c Lilley b Lohmann | | 0 | (9) not out | 24 |
| E. Jones | b Richardson | | 4 | (10) c Jackson b Hearne | 4 |
| Extras | (B 1) | | 1 | (B 7, LB 4, W 1) | 12 |
| **Total** | | | **53** | | **347** |

## ENGLAND

| | | | | | |
|---|---|---|---|---|---|
| W.G. Grace* | c Trumble b Giffen | | 66 | c Hill b Trumble | 7 |
| A.E. Stoddart | b Eady | | 17 | (5) not out | 30 |
| R. Abel | b Eady | | 94 | (2) c sub (F.A. Iredale) b Jones | 4 |
| J.T. Brown | b Jones | | 9 | c Kelly b Eady | 36 |
| W. Gunn | c Kelly b Trumble | | 25 | (6) not out | 13 |
| F.S. Jackson | c Darling b Giffen | | 44 | (3) b Jones | 13 |
| T.W. Hayward | not out | | 12 | | |
| A.F.A. Lilley† | b Eady | | 0 | | |
| G.A. Lohmann | c sub (F.A. Iredale) b Giffen | | 1 | | |
| J.T. Hearne | c Giffen b Trott | | 11 | | |
| T. Richardson | c Hill b Trot. | | 6 | | |
| Extras | (B 5, LB 2) | | 7 | (B 3, LB 4, W 1) | 8 |
| **Total** | | | **292** | (4 wickets) | **111** |

| ENGLAND | O | M | R | W | O | M | R | W |
|---|---|---|---|---|---|---|---|---|
| Richardson | 11·3 | 3 | 39 | 6 | 47 | 15 | 134 | 5 |
| Lohmann | 11 | 6 | 13 | 3 | 22 | 6 | 39 | 0 |
| Hayward | | | | | 11 | 3 | 44 | 0 |
| Hearne | | | | | 36 | 14 | 76 | 5 |
| Jackson | | | | | 11 | 5 | 28 | 0 |
| Grace | | | | | 6 | 1 | 14 | 0 |
| AUSTRALIA | | | | | | | | |
| Jones | 26 | 6 | 64 | 1 | 23 | 10 | 42 | 2 |
| Giffen | 26 | 5 | 95 | 3 | 1 | 0 | 9 | 0 |
| Eady | 29 | 12 | 58 | 3 | 3 | 0 | 11 | 1 |
| Trott | 7·4 | 2 | 13 | 2 | 0·1 | 0 | 4 | 0 |
| Trumble | 19 | 3 | 55 | 1 | 20 | 10 | 37 | 1 |

### FALL OF WICKETS

| | A | E | A | E |
|---|---|---|---|---|
| Wkt | 1st | 1st | 2nd | 2nd |
| 1st | 3 | 38 | 0 | 16 |
| 2nd | 3 | 143 | 3 | 20 |
| 3rd | 4 | 152 | 62 | 42 |
| 4th | 26 | 197 | 283 | 82 |
| 5th | 26 | 256 | 289 | – |
| 6th | 31 | 266 | 300 | – |
| 7th | 41 | 266 | 304 | – |
| 8th | 45 | 267 | 308 | – |
| 9th | 46 | 286 | 318 | – |
| 10th | 53 | 292 | 347 | – |

Umpires: W.A.J. West and J. Phillips.

# ENGLAND v AUSTRALIA 1896 (2nd Test)

Played at Old Trafford, Manchester, on 16, 17, 18 July.
Toss: Australia.    Result: AUSTRALIA won by three wickets.
Debuts: England – K.S. Ranjitsinhji (*Kumar Shri Ranjitsinhji, later His Highness The Jam Saheb of Nawanagar*).

'Ranji', the first Indian to play Test cricket, became the second batsman after W.G. Grace (*Test No. 4*) to score a hundred on debut for England. He was the first player to score a hundred before lunch in a Test match; on the third morning he took his overnight score of 41* to 154*, adding 113 runs in 130 minutes and setting a record that remains unbeaten for the most runs in a pre-lunch session in Tests between these two countries. Brown kept wicket when Lilley's leg-breaks were required to break a stand.

## AUSTRALIA

| | | | | | |
|---|---|---:|---|---|---:|
| F.A. Iredale | b Briggs | 108 | b Richardson | | 11 |
| J. Darling | c Lilley b Richardson | 27 | c Lilley b Richardson | | 16 |
| G. Giffen | c and b Richardson | 80 | c Ranjitsinhji b Richardson | | 6 |
| G.H.S. Trott* | c Brown b Lilley | 53 | c Lilley b Richardson | | 2 |
| S.E. Gregory | c Stoddart b Briggs | 25 | c Ranjitsinhji b Briggs | | 33 |
| H. Donnan | b Richardson | 12 | c Jackson b Richardson | | 15 |
| C. Hill | c Jackson b Richardson | 9 | c Lilley b Richardson | | 14 |
| H. Trumble | b Richardson | 24 | not out | | 17 |
| J.J. Kelly† | c Lilley b Richardson | 27 | not out | | 8 |
| T.R. McKibbin | not out | 28 | | | |
| E. Jones | b Richardson | 4 | | | |
| Extras | (B 6, LB 8, W 1) | 15 | (LB 3) | | 3 |
| **Total** | | **412** | (7 wickets) | | **125** |

## ENGLAND

| | | | | | |
|---|---|---:|---|---|---:|
| W.G. Grace* | st Kelly b Trott | 2 | c Trott b Jones | | 11 |
| A.E. Stoddart | st Kelly b Trott | 15 | b McKibbin | | 41 |
| K.S. Ranjitsinhji | c Trott b McKibbin | 62 | not out | | 154 |
| R. Abel | c Trumble b McKibbin | 26 | c McKibbin b Giffen | | 13 |
| F.S. Jackson | run out | 18 | c McKibbin b Giffen | | 1 |
| J.T. Brown | c Kelly b Trumble | 22 | c Iredale b Jones | | 19 |
| A.C. MacLaren | c Trumble b McKibbin | 0 | c Jones b Trumble | | 15 |
| A.F.A. Lilley† | not out | 65 | c Trott b Giffen | | 19 |
| J. Briggs | b Trumble | 0 | st Kelly b McKibbin | | 16 |
| J.T. Hearne | c Trumble b Giffen | 18 | c Kelly b McKibbin | | 9 |
| T. Richardson | run out | 2 | c Jones b Trumble | | 1 |
| Extras | (B 1) | 1 | (B 2, LB 3, W 1) | | 6 |
| **Total** | | **231** | | | **305** |

| ENGLAND | O | M | R | W | O | M | R | W | | FALL OF WICKETS | | | |
|---|---:|---:|---:|---:|---:|---:|---:|---:|---|---|---|---|---|
| Richardson | 68 | 23 | 168 | 7 | 42·3 | 16 | 76 | 6 | | A | E | E | A |
| Briggs | 40 | 18 | 99 | 2 | 18 | 8 | 24 | 1 | Wkt | 1st | 1st | 2nd | 2nd |
| Jackson | 16 | 6 | 34 | 0 | | | | | 1st | 41 | 2 | 33 | 20 |
| Hearne | 28 | 11 | 53 | 0 | 24 | 13 | 22 | 0 | 2nd | 172 | 23 | 76 | 26 |
| Grace | 7 | 3 | 11 | 0 | | | | | 3rd | 242 | 104 | 97 | 28 |
| Stoddart | 6 | 2 | 9 | 0 | | | | | 4th | 294 | 111 | 109 | 45 |
| Lilley | 5 | 1 | 23 | 1 | | | | | 5th | 294 | 140 | 132 | 79 |
| | | | | | | | | | 6th | 314 | 140 | 179 | 95 |
| AUSTRALIA | | | | | | | | | 7th | 325 | 154 | 232 | 100 |
| Jones | 5 | 2 | 11 | 0 | 17 | 0 | 78 | 2 | 8th | 362 | 166 | 268 | – |
| Trott | 10 | 0 | 46 | 2 | 7 | 1 | 17 | 0 | 9th | 403 | 219 | 304 | – |
| Giffen | 19 | 3 | 48 | 1 | 16 | 1 | 65 | 3 | 10th | 412 | 231 | 305 | – |
| Trumble | 37 | 14 | 80 | 2 | 29·1 | 12 | 78 | 2 | | | | | |
| McKibbin | 19 | 8 | 45 | 3 | 21 | 4 | 61 | 3 | | | | | |

Umpires: J. Phillips and A. Chester.

# ENGLAND v AUSTRALIA 1896 (3rd Test)

Played at Kennington Oval, London, on 10, 11, 12 August.
Toss: England.   Result: ENGLAND won by 66 runs.
Debuts: England – E.G. Wynyard.

Rain prevented play until 4.55 p.m. on the first day, caused 24 wickets to fall on the second, and led to Australia being dismissed for their lowest total in England until 1902 (36 in *Test No. 70*). R. Peel ended his Test career with the splendid analysis of 6 for 23; the fourth of those wickets was his hundredth in Test matches.

## ENGLAND

| | | | | |
|---|---|---|---|---|
| W.G. Grace* | c Trott b Giffen | 24 | b Trumble | 9 |
| F.S. Jackson | c McKibbin b Trumble | 45 | b Trumble | 2 |
| K.S. Ranjitsinhji | b Giffen | 8 | st Kelly b McKibbin | 11 |
| R. Abel | c and b Trumble | 26 | c Giffen b Trumble | 21 |
| A.C. MacLaren | b Trumble | 20 | b Jones | 6 |
| T.W. Hayward | b Trumble | 0 | c Trott b Trumble | 13 |
| E.G. Wynyard | c Darling b McKibbin | 10 | c Kelly b McKibbin | 3 |
| R. Peel | b Trumble | 0 | b Trumble | 0 |
| A.F.A. Lilley† | c Iredale b Trumble | 2 | c McKibbin b Trumble | 6 |
| J.T. Hearne | b McKibbin | 8 | b McKibbin | 1 |
| T. Richardson | not out | 1 | not out | 10 |
| Extras | (LB 1) | 1 | (LB 2) | 2 |
| **Total** | | **145** | | **84** |

## AUSTRALIA

| | | | | |
|---|---|---|---|---|
| J. Darling | c MacLaren b Hearne | 47 | b Hearne | 0 |
| F.A. Iredale | run out | 30 | c Jackson b Hearne | 3 |
| G. Giffen | b Hearne | 0 | (4) b Hearne | 1 |
| G.H.S. Trott* | b Peel | 5 | (3) c sub (W. Brockwell) b Peel | 3 |
| S.E. Gregory | b Hearne | 1 | c Richardson b Peel | 6 |
| C. Hill | run out | 1 | b Peel | 0 |
| H. Donnan | b ghearne | 10 | c Hayward b Peel | 0 |
| J.J. Kelly† | not out | 10 | lbw b Peel | 3 |
| H. Trumble | b Hearne | 3 | not out | 7 |
| E. Jones | c MacLaren b Peel | 3 | b Peel | 3 |
| T.R. McKibbin | b Hearne | 0 | c Abel b Hearne | 16 |
| Extras | (B 8, LB 1) | 9 | (B 2) | 2 |
| **Total** | | **119** | | **44** |

| AUSTRALIA | O | M | R | W | O | M | R | W |
|---|---|---|---|---|---|---|---|---|
| Giffen | 32 | 12 | 64 | 2 | 1 | 0 | 4 | 0 |
| Trumble | 40 | 10 | 59 | 6 | 25 | 9 | 30 | 6 |
| McKibbin | 9·3 | 0 | 21 | 2 | 20 | 8 | 35 | 3 |
| Jones | | | | | 3 | 0 | 13 | 1 |
| ENGLAND | | | | | | | | |
| Peel | 20 | 9 | 30 | 2 | 12 | 5 | 23 | 6 |
| Hearne | 26·1 | 10 | 41 | 6 | 13 | 8 | 19 | 4 |
| Richardson | 5 | 0 | 22 | 0 | 1 | 1 | 0 | 0 |
| Hayward | 2 | 0 | 17 | 0 | | | | |

FALL OF WICKETS

| Wkt | E 1st | A 1st | E 2nd | A 2nd |
|---|---|---|---|---|
| 1st | 54 | 75 | 11 | 0 |
| 2nd | 78 | 77 | 12 | 3 |
| 3rd | 78 | 82 | 24 | 7 |
| 4th | 114 | 83 | 50 | 7 |
| 5th | 114 | 84 | 56 | 11 |
| 6th | 131 | 85 | 67 | 11 |
| 7th | 132 | 112 | 67 | 14 |
| 8th | 135 | 116 | 67 | 19 |
| 9th | 138 | 119 | 68 | 25 |
| 10th | 145 | 119 | 84 | 44 |

Umpires: J. Phillips and W. Hearn.

# AUSTRALIA v ENGLAND 1897–98 (1st Test)

Played at Sydney Cricket Ground on 13, 14, 15, 16, 17 December.
Toss: England.   Result: ENGLAND won by nine wickets.
Debuts: England – N.F. Druce, G.H. Hirst, J.R. Mason, W. Storer.

Ranjitsinhji, although ill, emulated H. Graham by scoring a hundred in his first Test in Australia having also done so in England. His 175 set a new England record which stood until R.E. Foster scored 287 in 1903-04 (*Test No. 78*). J. Darling had the distinction of being the first left-hander to score a hundred in a Test match.

## ENGLAND

| | | | | |
|---|---|---:|---|---:|
| J.R. Mason | b Jones | 6 | b McKibbin | 32 |
| A.C. MacLaren* | c Kelly b McLeod | 109 | not out | 50 |
| T.W. Hayward | c Trott b Trumble | 72 | | |
| W. Storer† | c and b Trott | 43 | | |
| N.F. Druce | c Gregory b McLeod | 20 | | |
| G.H. Hirst | b Jones | 62 | | |
| K.S. Ranjitsinhji | c Gregory b McKibbin | 175 | (3) not out | 8 |
| E. Wainwright | b Jones | 10 | | |
| J.T. Hearne | c and b McLeod | 17 | | |
| J. Briggs | run out | 1 | | |
| T. Richardson | not out | 24 | | |
| Extras | (LB 11, W 1) | 12 | (B 5, NB 1) | 6 |
| **Total** | | **551** | (1 wicket) | **96** |

## AUSTRALIA

| | | | | |
|---|---|---:|---|---:|
| J. Darling | c Druce b Richardson | 7 | c Druce b Briggs | 101 |
| J.J. Lyons | b Richardson | 3 | (7) c Hayward b Hearne | 25 |
| F.A. Iredale | c Druce b Hearne | 25 | (2) b Briggs | 18 |
| C. Hill | b Hearne | 19 | b Hearne | 96 |
| S.E. Gregory | c Mason b Hearne | 46 | run out | 31 |
| G.H.S. Trott* | b Briggs | 10 | (8) b Richardson | 27 |
| J.J. Kelly† | b Richardson | 1 | (9) not out | 46 |
| H. Trumble | c Storer b Mason | 70 | (6) c Druce b Hearne | 2 |
| C.E. McLeod | not out | 50 | (3) run out | 26 |
| T.R. McKibbin | b Hearne | 0 | (11) b Hearne | 6 |
| E. Jones | c Richardson b Hearne | 0 | (10) lbw b Richardson | 3 |
| Extras | (B 1, LB 1, NB 4) | 6 | (B 12, LB 1, W 4, NB 10) | 27 |
| **Total** | | **237** | | **408** |

| AUSTRALIA | O | M | R | W | O | M | R | W |
|---|---|---|---|---|---|---|---|---|
| McKibbin | 34 | 5 | 113 | 1 | 5 | 1 | 22 | 1 |
| Jones | 50 | 8 | 130 | 3 | 9 | 1 | 28 | 0 |
| McLeod | 28 | 12 | 80 | 3 | | | | |
| Trumble | 40 | 7 | 138 | 1 | 14 | 4 | 40 | 0 |
| Trott | 23 | 2 | 78 | 1 | | | | |
| **ENGLAND** | | | | | | | | |
| Richardson | 27 | 8 | 71 | 3 | 41 | 9 | 121 | 2 |
| Hirst | 28 | 7 | 57 | 0 | 13 | 3 | 49 | 0 |
| Hearne | 20·1 | 7 | 42 | 5 | 38 | 8 | 99 | 4 |
| Briggs | 20 | 7 | 42 | 1 | 22 | 3 | 86 | 2 |
| Hayward | 3 | 1 | 11 | 0 | 5 | 1 | 16 | 0 |
| Mason | 2 | 1 | 8 | 1 | 2 | 0 | 10 | 0 |

### FALL OF WICKETS

| | E | A | A | E |
|---|---|---|---|---|
| Wkt | 1st | 1st | 2nd | 2nd |
| 1st | 26 | 8 | 37 | 80 |
| 2nd | 162 | 24 | 135 | – |
| 3rd | 224 | 56 | 191 | – |
| 4th | 256 | 57 | 269 | – |
| 5th | 258 | 86 | 271 | – |
| 6th | 382 | 87 | 318 | – |
| 7th | 422 | 138 | 321 | – |
| 8th | 471 | 228 | 382 | – |
| 9th | 477 | 237 | 390 | – |
| 10th | 551 | 237 | 408 | – |

Umpires: C. Bannerman and J. Phillips.

# AUSTRALIA v ENGLAND 1897–98 (2nd Test)

Played at Melbourne Cricket Ground on 1, 3, 4, 5 January.
Toss: Australia.   Result: AUSTRALIA won by an innings and 55 runs.
Debuts: Australia – M.A. Noble.

Jones was the first bowler to be no-balled for throwing in a Test match – umpire Phillips called him once.

## AUSTRALIA

| | | |
|---|---|---|
| J. Darling | c Hirst b Briggs | 36 |
| C.E. McLeod | b Storer | 112 |
| C. Hill | c Storer b Hayward | 58 |
| S.E. Gregory | b Briggs | 71 |
| F.A. Iredale | c Ranjitsinhji b Hirst | 89 |
| G.H.S. Trott* | c Wainwright b Briggs | 79 |
| M.A. Noble | b Richardson | 17 |
| H. Trumble | c Hirst b Mason | 14 |
| J.J. Kelly† | c Richardson b Hearne | 19 |
| E. Jones | run out | 7 |
| T.R. McKibbin | not out | 2 |
| Extras | (B 14, W 1, NB 1) | 16 |
| **Total** | | **520** |

## ENGLAND

| | | | | | |
|---|---|---|---|---|---|
| A.C. MacLaren* | c Trumble b McKibbin | 35 | | c Trott b Trumble | 38 |
| J.R. Mason | b McKibbin | 3 | | b Trumble | 3 |
| E. Wainwright | c Jones b Noble | 21 | (8) | b Noble | 11 |
| K.S. Ranjitsinhji | b Trumble | 71 | (3) | b Noble | 27 |
| T.W. Hayward | c Jones b Trott | 23 | (4) | c Trumble b Noble | 33 |
| W. Storer† | c Kelly b Trumble | 51 | (5) | c Trumble b Noble | 1 |
| G.H. Hirst | b Jones | 0 | (6) | lbw b Trumble | 3 |
| N.F. Druce | lbw b Trumble | 44 | (7) | c McLeod b Noble | 15 |
| J.T. Hearne | b Jones | 1 | (10) | c Jones b Noble | 0 |
| J. Briggs | not out | 46 | (9) | c Trott b Trumble | 12 |
| T. Richardson | b Trumble | 3 | | not out | 2 |
| Extras | (B 10, LB 3, NB 4) | 17 | | (B 3, LB 1, W 1) | 5 |
| **Total** | | **315** | | | **150** |

| ENGLAND | O | M | R | W | O | M | R | W |
|---|---|---|---|---|---|---|---|---|
| Richardson | 48 | 12 | 114 | 1 | | | | |
| Hirst | 25 | 1 | 89 | 1 | | | | |
| Briggs | 40 | 10 | 96 | 3 | | | | |
| Hearne | 36 | 6 | 94 | 1 | | | | |
| Mason | 11 | 1 | 33 | 1 | | | | |
| Hayward | 9 | 4 | 23 | 1 | | | | |
| Storer | 16 | 4 | 55 | 1 | | | | |
| AUSTRALIA | | | | | | | | |
| McKibbin | 28 | 7 | 66 | 2 | 4 | 0 | 13 | 0 |
| Trumble | 26·5 | 5 | 54 | 4 | 30·4 | 12 | 53 | 4 |
| Jones | 22 | 5 | 54 | 2 | | | | |
| Trott | 17 | 3 | 49 | 1 | 7 | 0 | 17 | 0 |
| Noble | 12 | 3 | 31 | 1 | 17 | 1 | 49 | 6 |
| McLeod | 14 | 2 | 44 | 0 | 7 | 2 | 13 | 0 |

FALL OF WICKETS

| | A | E | E |
|---|---|---|---|
| Wkt | 1st | 1st | 2nd |
| 1st | 43 | 10 | 10 |
| 2nd | 167 | 60 | 65 |
| 3rd | 244 | 74 | 71 |
| 4th | 310 | 133 | 75 |
| 5th | 434 | 203 | 80 |
| 6th | 453 | 208 | 115 |
| 7th | 478 | 223 | 123 |
| 8th | 509 | 224 | 141 |
| 9th | 515 | 311 | 148 |
| 10th | 520 | 315 | 150 |

Umpires: C Bannerman and J. Phillips.

# AUSTRALIA v ENGLAND 1897–98 (3rd Test)

Played at Adelaide Oval on 14, 15, 17, 18, 19 January.
Toss: Australia.   Result: AUSTRALIA won by an innings and 13 runs.
Debuts: Australia – W.P. Howell.

J. Darling became the first batsman to score two hundreds in the same rubber (A.C. MacLaren equalled this feat later in the match), the first to hit 20 fours in a Test innings (he hit 26), and the first to reach his century with a six which in those days involved hitting the ball right out of the ground as opposed to over the boundary. This was the first six ever hit in Test cricket without the aid of overthrows.

## AUSTRALIA

| | | |
|---|---|---:|
| C.E. McLeod | b Briggs | 31 |
| J. Darling | c Storer b Richardson | 178 |
| C. Hill | c Storer b Richardson | 81 |
| S.E. Gregory | c Storer b Hirst | 52 |
| F.A. Iredale | b Richardson | 84 |
| G.H.S. Trott* | b Hearne | 3 |
| M.A. Noble | b Richardson | 39 |
| H. Trumble | not out | 37 |
| J.J. Kelly† | b Stoddart | 22 |
| E. Jones | run out | 8 |
| W.P. Howell | b Hearne | 16 |
| Extras | (B 16, LB 5, NB 1) | 22 |
| **Total** | | **573** |

## ENGLAND

| | | | | | |
|---|---|---:|---|---|---:|
| A.C. MacLaren | b Howell | 14 | c Kelly b Noble | | 124 |
| J.R. Mason | b Jones | 11 | c Jones b Noble | | 0 |
| K.S. Ranjitsinhji | c Noble b Trumble | 6 | c Trumble b McLeod | | 77 |
| W. Storer† | b Howell | 4 | (5) c Hill b McLeod | | 6 |
| T.W. Hayward | b Jones | 70 | (4) c and b McLeod | | 1 |
| N.F Druce | c Darling b Noble | 24 | b Noble | | 27 |
| G.H. Hirst | c Trumble b Noble | 85 | lbw b McLeod | | 6 |
| A.E. Stoddart* | c Jones b Howell | 15 | c Jones b McLeod | | 24 |
| J. Briggs | c Kelly b Noble | 14 | not out | | 0 |
| J.T. Hearne | b Howell | 0 | c and b Noble | | 4 |
| T. Richardson | not out | 25 | c Jones b Noble | | 0 |
| Extras | (B 2, LB 6, W 2) | 10 | (B 2, LB 6, W 3, NB 2) | | 13 |
| **Total** | | **278** | | | **282** |

| ENGLAND | O | M | R | W | O | M | R | W |
|---|---:|---:|---:|---:|---:|---:|---:|---:|
| Richardson | 56 | 11 | 164 | 4 | | | | |
| Briggs | 63 | 26 | 128 | 1 | | | | |
| Hearne | 44·1 | 15 | 94 | 2 | | | | |
| Hirst | 22 | 6 | 62 | 1 | | | | |
| Hayward | 8. | 1 | 36 | 0 | | | | |
| Mason | 11 | 2 | 41 | 0 | | | | |
| Storer | 3 | 0 | 16 | 0 | | | | |
| Stoddart | 4 | 1 | 10 | 1 | | | | |
| **AUSTRALIA** | | | | | | | | |
| Howell | 54 | 23 | 70 | 4 | 40 | 18 | 60 | 0 |
| Jones | 27 | 3 | 67 | 2 | 1 | 0 | 5 | 0 |
| Trumble | 17 | 3 | 39 | 1 | 16 | 5 | 37 | 0 |
| Noble | 24·5 | 5 | 78 | 3 | 33 | 7 | 84 | 5 |
| Trott | 4 | 0 | 14 | 0 | 6 | 0 | 18 | 0 |
| McLeod | | | | | 48 | 24 | 65 | 5 |

| FALL OF WICKETS | | | |
|---|---:|---:|---:|
| | A | E | E |
| Wkt | 1st | 1st | 2nd |
| 1st | 97 | 24 | 10 |
| 2nd | 245 | 30 | 152 |
| 3rd | 310 | 34 | 154 |
| 4th | 374 | 42 | 160 |
| 5th | 389 | 106 | 212 |
| 6th | 474 | 172 | 235 |
| 7th | 493 | 206 | 262 |
| 8th | 537 | 223 | 278 |
| 9th | 552 | 224 | 282 |
| 10th | 573 | 278 | 282 |

Umpires: C. Bannerman and J. Phillips.

# AUSTRALIA v ENGLAND 1897–98 (4th Test)

Played at Melbourne Cricket Ground on 29, 31 January, 1, 2 February.
Toss: Australia.   Result: AUSTRALIA won by eight wickets.
Debuts: Nil.

Hill's 188 remains the highest score by a batsman under 21 in Tests between England and Australia; he was 20 years 317 days old. His 182 not out was the highest score on the first day of a Test in Australia and his partnership of 165 with Trumble is still the best for Australia's seventh wicket against England.

## AUSTRALIA

| | | | | |
|---|---|---|---|---|
| C.E. McLeod | b Hearne | 1 | not out | 64 |
| J. Darling | c Hearne b Richardson | 12 | c Druce b Hayward | 29 |
| C. Hill | c Stoddart b Hearne | 188 | lbw b Hayward | 0 |
| S.E. Gregory | b Richardson | 0 | not out | 21 |
| F.A. Iredale | c Storer b Hearne | 0 | | |
| M.A. Noble | c and b Hearne | 4 | | |
| G.H.S. Trott* | c Storer b Hearne | 7 | | |
| H. Trumble | c Mason b Storer | 46 | | |
| J.J. Kelly† | c Storer b Briggs | 32 | | |
| E. Jones | c Hayward b Hearne | 20 | | |
| W.P. Howell | not out | 9 | | |
| Extras | (B 3, W 1) | 4 | (NB 1) | 1 |
| **Total** | | **323** | (2 wickets) | **115** |

## ENGLAND

| | | | | |
|---|---|---|---|---|
| A.C. MacLaren | b Howell | 8 | (3) c Iredale b Trumble | 45 |
| E. Wainwright | c Howell b Trott | 6 | c McLeod b Jones | 2 |
| K.S. Ranjitsinhji | c Iredale b Trumble | 24 | (4) b Noble | 55 |
| T.W.Hayward | c Gregory b Noble | 22 | (5) c and b Trumble | 25 |
| N.F. Druce | lbw b Jones | 24 | (9) c Howell b Trott | 16 |
| W. Storer† | c and b Trumble | 2 | (7) c Darling b McLeod | 26 |
| J.R. Mason | b Jones | 30 | (8) b Howell | 26 |
| A.E. Stoddart* | c Darling b Jones | 17 | (6) b Jones | 25 |
| J. Briggs | not out | 21 | (1) c Darling b Howell | 23 |
| J.T. Hearne | c Trott b Jones | 0 | not out | 4 |
| T. Richardson | b Trott | 20 | c Trumble b McLeod | 2 |
| Extras | | – | (B 1, LB 11, W 1, NB 1) | 14 |
| **Total** | | **174** | | **263** |

| ENGLAND | O | M | R | W | O | M | R | W |
|---|---|---|---|---|---|---|---|---|
| Richardson | 26 | 2 | 102 | 2 | | | | |
| Hearne | 35·4 | 13 | 98 | 6 | 7 | 3 | 19 | 0 |
| Hayward | 10 | 4 | 24 | 0 | 10 | 4 | 24 | 2 |
| Briggs | 17 | 4 | 38 | 1 | 6 | 1 | 31 | 0 |
| Stoddart | 6 | 1 | 22 | 0 | | | | |
| Storer | 4 | 0 | 24 | 1 | | | | |
| Wainwright | 3 | 1 | 11 | 0 | 9 | 2 | 21 | 0 |
| Mason | | | | | 4 | 1 | 10 | 0 |
| Ranjitsinhji | | | | | 3·4 | 1 | 9 | 0 |
| AUSTRALIA | | | | | | | | |
| Howell | 16 | 7 | 34 | 1 | 30 | 12 | 58 | 2 |
| Trott | 11·1 | 1 | 33 | 2 | 12 | 2 | 39 | 1 |
| Noble | 7 | 1 | 21 | 1 | 16 | 6 | 31 | 1 |
| Trumble | 15 | 4 | 30 | 2 | 23 | 6 | 40 | 2 |
| Jones | 12 | 2 | 56 | 4 | 25 | 7 | 70 | 2 |
| McLeod | | | | | 8·2 | 4 | 11 | 2 |

## FALL OF WICKETS

| | A | E | E | A |
|---|---|---|---|---|
| Wkt | 1st | 1st | 2nd | 2nd |
| 1st | 1 | 14 | 7 | 50 |
| 2nd | 25 | 16 | 63 | 50 |
| 3rd | 25 | 60 | 94 | – |
| 4th | 26 | 60 | 147 | – |
| 5th | 32 | 67 | 157 | – |
| 6th | 58 | 103 | 192 | – |
| 7th | 223 | 121 | 211 | – |
| 8th | 283 | 148 | 259 | – |
| 9th | 303 | 148 | 259 | – |
| 10th | 323 | 174 | 263 | – |

Umpires: C. Bannerman and J. Phillips.

# AUSTRALIA v ENGLAND 1897–98 (5th Test)

Played at Sydney Cricket Ground on 26, 28 February, 1, 2 March.
Toss: England.   Result: AUSTRALIA won by six wickets.
Debuts: Nil.

Darling's hundred took only 91 minutes and remains the fastest for Australia against England. Only G.L. Jessop (75 minutes in *Test No. 74*) has scored a faster hundred in Tests between England and Australia. Darling was the first batsman to score three hundreds in the same Test rubber and the first to aggregate 500 runs in one.

## ENGLAND

| | | | | | |
|---|---|---|---|---|---|
| A.C. MacLaren* | b Trott | 65 | c Darling b Jones | | 0 |
| E. Wainwright | c Hill  b Trumble | 49 | b Noble | | 6 |
| K.S. Ranjitsinhji | c Gregory b Trott | 2 | lbw b Jones | | 12 |
| T.W. Hayward | b Jones | 47 | c Worrall b Trumble | | 43 |
| W. Storer† | b Jones | 44 | c Gregory b Trumble | | 31 |
| N.F. Druce | lbw b Noble | 64 | c Howell b Trumble | | 18 |
| G.H. Hirst | b Jones | 44 | c Trott b Jones | | 7 |
| J.R. Mason | c Howell b Jones | 7 | b Trumble | | 11 |
| J. Briggs | b Jones | 0 | b Howell | | 29 |
| J.T. Hearne | not out | 2 | not out | | 3 |
| T. Richardson | b Jones | 1 | b Howell | | 6 |
| Extras | (B 2, LB 5, W 2, NB 1) | 10 | (LB 12) | | 12 |
| **Total** | | **335** | | | **178** |

## AUSTRALIA

| | | | | | |
|---|---|---|---|---|---|
| C.E. McLeod | b Richardson | 64 | b Hearne | | 4 |
| J. Darling | c Mason b Briggs | 14 | c Wainwright b Richardson | | 160 |
| C. Hill | b Richardson | 8 | b Richardson | | 2 |
| J. Worrall | c Ranjitsinhji b Richardson | 26 | c Hirst b Hayward | | 62 |
| S.E. Gregory | c Storer b Richardson | 21 | not out | | 22 |
| M.A. Noble | c Storer b Richardson | 31 | not out | | 15 |
| G.H.S. Trott* | c Ranjitsinhji b Hearne | 18 | | | |
| H. Trumble | b Richardson | 12 | | | |
| J.J. Kelly† | not out | 27 | | | |
| W.P. Howell | c MacLaren b Richardson | 10 | | | |
| E. Jones | c Storer b Richardson | 1 | | | |
| Extras | (B 5, W 1, NB 1) | 7 | (B 6, W 1, NB 4) | | 11 |
| **Total** | | **239** | (4 wickets) | | **276** |

| AUSTRALIA | O | M | R | W | O | M | R | W | FALL OF WICKETS | | | | |
|---|---|---|---|---|---|---|---|---|---|---|---|---|---|
| | | | | | | | | | | E | A | E | A |
| Noble | 26 | 6 | 57 | 1 | 15 | 4 | 34 | 1 | *Wkt* | *1st* | *1st* | *2nd* | *2nd* |
| Howell | 17 | 6 | 40 | 0 | 6·1 | 0 | 22 | 2 | 1st | 111 | 36 | 0 | 23 |
| Trumble | 26 | 4 | 67 | 4 | 24 | 7 | 37 | 4 | 2nd | 117 | 45 | 16 | 40 |
| Jones | 26·2 | 3 | 82 | 6 | 26 | 3 | 61 | 3 | 3rd | 119 | 99 | 30 | 233 |
| Trott | 23 | 6 | 56 | 2 | 7 | 1 | 12 | 0 | 4th | 197 | 132 | 99 | 252 |
| McLeod | 11 | 4 | 23 | 0 | | | | | 5th | 230 | 137 | 104 | – |
| | | | | | | | | | 6th | 308 | 188 | 121 | – |
| ENGLAND | | | | | | | | | 7th | 318 | 188 | 137 | – |
| Richardson | 36·1 | 7 | 94 | 8 | 21·4 | 1 | 110 | 2 | 8th | 324 | 221 | 148 | – |
| Briggs | 17 | 4 | 39 | 1 | 5 | 1 | 25 | 0 | 9th | 334 | 232 | 172 | – |
| Hearne | 21 | 9 | 40 | 1 | 15 | 5 | 52 | 1 | 10th | 335 | 239 | 178 | – |
| Storer | 5 | 1 | 13 | 0 | | | | | | | | | |
| Mason | 13 | 7 | 20 | 0 | 11 | 1 | 27 | 0 | | | | | |
| Hayward | 4 | 0 | 12 | 0 | 3 | 0 | 18 | 1 | | | | | |
| Hirst | 4 | 1 | 14 | 0 | 7 | 0 | 33 | 0 | | | | | |

Umpires: C. Bannerman and J. Phillips.

# SOUTH AFRICA v ENGLAND 1898–99 (1st Test)

Played at Old Wanderers, Johannesburg, on 14, 15, 16 February.
Toss: England.   Result: ENGLAND won by 32 runs.
Debuts: South Africa – M. Bisset, R.R. Dower, H.H. Francis, R. Graham, W.R.T. Solomon, V.M. Tancred; England – J.H. Board, W.R. Cuttell, S. Haigh, F.W. Milligan, F. Mitchell, J.T. Tyldesley, P.F. Warner, C.E.M. Wilson. *A.E. Trott was making his debut for England after appearing in three Tests for Australia. A knighthood was conferred on Warner (Sir Pelham) in the 1937 Coronation Honours List for his services to cricket.*

Warner was the first to score a hundred in his first Test, that match being against South Africa, and the first to carry his bat through a completed innings on debut for England (J.E. Barrett did so for Australia in *Test No. 33*).

## ENGLAND

| | | | | | |
|---|---|---:|---|---|---:|
| F. Mitchell | b Graham | 28 | lbw b Llewellyn | | 1 |
| P.F. Warner | c and b Llewellyn | 21 | not out | | 132 |
| J.T. Tyldesley | run out | 17 | c Shepstone b Middleton | | 17 |
| C.E.M. Wilson | b Middleton | 8 | b Middleton | | 18 |
| W.R. Cuttell | c Llewellyn b Graham | 19 | c Dower b Middleton | | 21 |
| A.E. Trott | run out | 0 | c Solomon b Rowe | | 6 |
| F.W. Milligan | c Graham b Middleton | 11 | (8) st Bisset b Llewellyn | | 8 |
| Lord Hawke* | c Bisset b Llewellyn | 0 | (9) b Llewellyn | | 5 |
| J.H. Board† | c Dower b Rowe | 29 | (10) c and b Middleton | | 17 |
| H.R. Bromley-Davenport | c Graham b Rowe | 4 | (11) b Middleton | | 0 |
| S. Haigh | not out | 2 | (7) c Shepstone b Rowe | | 1 |
| Extras | (B 4, LB 1, W 1) | 6 | (B 9, NB 2) | | 11 |
| **Total** | | **145** | | | **237** |

## SOUTH AFRICA

| | | | | | |
|---|---|---:|---|---|---:|
| J.H. Sinclair | run out | 86 | c Cuttell b Haigh | | 4 |
| V.M. Tancred | b Haigh | 18 | c Board b Haigh | | 7 |
| H.H. Francis | lbw b Trott | 7 | b Cuttell | | 29 |
| R.R. Dower | b Trott | 0 | c Cuttell b Trott | | 9 |
| M. Bisset*† | b Haigh | 35 | not out | | 21 |
| W.R.T. Solomon | c Tyldesley b Haigh | 2 | (8) b Cuttell | | 0 |
| G.H. Shepstone | b Cuttell | 8 | lbw b Cuttell | | 0 |
| C.B. Llewellyn | st Board b Trott | 38 | (6) b Trott | | 0 |
| R. Graham | c Board b Cuttell | 4 | (10) c Tyldesley b Trott | | 0 |
| J. Middleton | c Mitchell b Trott | 22 | (9) c Bromley-Davenport b Trott | | 14 |
| G.A. Rowe | not out | 13 | b Trott | | 0 |
| Extras | (B 5, LB 11, NB 2) | 18 | (B 4, LB 5, NB 4) | | 13 |
| **Total** | | **251** | | | **99** |

| SOUTH AFRICA | O | M | R | W | O | M | R | W |
|---|---|---|---|---|---|---|---|---|
| Middleton | 23 | 9 | 48 | 2 | 26 | 8 | 51 | 5 |
| Rowe | 18·2 | 6 | 34 | 2 | 28 | 12 | 40 | 2 |
| Graham | 16 | 7 | 22 | 2 | 11 | 2 | 38 | 0 |
| Llewellyn | 20 | 6 | 35 | 2 | 36 | 11 | 89 | 3 |
| Shepstone | | | | | 3 | 1 | 8 | 0 |
| ENGLAND | | | | | | | | |
| Trott | 30·1 | 13 | 61 | 4 | 33·1 | 14 | 49 | 5 |
| Haigh | 30 | 5 | 101 | 3 | 12 | 5 | 20 | 2 |
| Cuttell | 17 | 5 | 42 | 2 | 32 | 24 | 17 | 3 |
| Milligan | 7 | 0 | 29 | 0 | | | | |

| FALL OF WICKETS | | | | |
|---|---|---|---|---|
| | E | SA | E | SA |
| *Wkt* | *1st* | *1st* | *2nd* | *2nd* |
| 1st | 51 | 46 | 1 | 13 |
| 2nd | 53 | 55 | 41 | 21 |
| 3rd | 77 | 59 | 104 | 58 |
| 4th | 77 | 114 | 139 | 62 |
| 5th | 81 | 118 | 149 | 65 |
| 6th | 96 | 143 | 153 | 66 |
| 7th | 96 | 169 | 171 | 78 |
| 8th | 138 | 183 | 189 | 97 |
| 9th | 138 | 224 | 233 | 99 |
| 10th | 145 | 251 | 237 | 99 |

Umpires: A.A. White and A. Soames.

# SOUTH AFRICA v ENGLAND 1898–99 (2nd Test)

Played at Newlands, Cape Town, on 1, 3, 4 April.
Toss: England.   Result: ENGLAND won by 210 runs.
Debuts: South Africa – F. Kuys, A.W. Powell, C.F.H. Prince, W.A. Shalders;
  England – A.G. Archer.

Sinclair, having scored South Africa's first Test fifty in the previous match, hit his country's first Test hundred. He also became the first player to score a century and take six wickets in the first innings of the same Test and the only one to do so for South Africa. This was South Africa's eighth consecutive defeat – a record equalled by England in the 1920-21 and 1921 series against Australia.

## ENGLAND

| | | | | | |
|---|---|--:|---|---|--:|
| F. Mitchell | c Rowe b Middleton | 18 | lbw b Rowe | | 41 |
| P.F. Warner | c Halliwell b Sinclair | 31 | b Rowe | | 23 |
| J.T. Tyldesley | b Sinclair | 13 | c Shalders b Kuys | | 112 |
| C.E.M. Wilson | not out | 10 | b Powell | | 6 |
| W.R. Cuttell | b Sinclair | 7 | b Kuys | | 18 |
| A.E. Trott | c Powell b Sinclair | 1 | b Rowe | | 16 |
| S. Haigh | c Halliwell b Middleton | 0 | c Francis b Sinclair | | 25 |
| F.W. Milligan | b Sinclair | 1 | b Sinclair | | 38 |
| J.H. Board† | b Sinclair | 0 | b Graham | | 6 |
| A.G. Archer | c Powell b Middleton | 7 | not out | | 24 |
| Lord Hawke* | b Middleton | 1 | c and b Sinclair | | 3 |
| Extras | (LB 3) | 3 | (B 6, LB 10, W 1, NB 1) | | 18 |
| **Total** | | **92** | | | **330** |

## SOUTH AFRICA

| | | | | | |
|---|---|--:|---|---|--:|
| W.A. Shalders | b Haigh | 9 | lbw b Haigh | | 8 |
| H.H. Francis | b Trott | 1 | (5) c Haigh b Trott | | 2 |
| M Bisset* | b Haigh | 15 | b Trott | | 1 |
| J.H. Sinclair | c Tyldesley b Trott | 106 | c Milligan b Haigh | | 4 |
| A.W. Powell | c Haigh b Trott | 5 | (2) b Haigh | | 11 |
| E.A. Halliwell† | st Board b Haigh | 0 | (7) b Haigh | | 1 |
| F. Kuys | b Cuttell | 26 | (6) b Trott | | 0 |
| C.F.H. Prince | run out | 5 | b Haigh | | 1 |
| R. Graham | b Trott | 0 | b Trott | | 2 |
| J. Middleton | run out | 3 | not out | | 0 |
| G.A. Rowe | not out | 1 | c Mitchell b Haigh | | 0 |
| Extras | (B 4, W 1, NB 1) | 6 | (B 5) | | 5 |
| **Total** | | **177** | | | **35** |

| SOUTH AFRICA | O | M | R | W | O | M | R | W | | FALL OF WICKETS | | | |
|---|--:|--:|--:|--:|--:|--:|--:|--:|---|---|---|---|---|
| Graham | 5 | 0 | 26 | 0 | 16 | 4 | 41 | 1 | | E | SA | E | SA |
| Rowe | 12 | 4 | 19 | 0 | 41 | 8 | 93 | 3 | *Wkt* | *1st* | *1st* | *2nd* | *2nd* |
| Middleton | 19 | 9 | 18 | 4 | 28 | 7 | 74 | 0 | 1st | 36 | 1 | 63 | 18 |
| Sinclair | 12 | 4 | 26 | 6 | 31·2 | 8 | 63 | 3 | 2nd | 61 | 27 | 68 | 21 |
| Powell | | | | | 4 | 1 | 10 | 1 | 3rd | 62 | 34 | 96 | 21 |
| Kuys | | | | | 12 | 4 | 31 | 2 | 4th | 70 | 60 | 146 | 27 |
| | | | | | | | | | 5th | 72 | 61 | 178 | 27 |
| ENGLAND | | | | | | | | | 6th | 74 | 110 | 234 | 28 |
| Trott | 20·2 | 5 | 69 | 4 | 11 | 5 | 19 | 4 | 7th | 81 | 115 | 281 | 28 |
| Haigh | 27· | 4 | 88 | 3 | 11·4 | 6 | 11 | 6 | 8th | 81 | 127 | 288 | 31 |
| Cuttell | 8 | 3 | 14 | 1 | | | | | 9th | 90 | 173 | 322 | 35 |
| Milligan | 2 | 2 | 0 | 0 | | | | | 10th | 92 | 177 | 330 | 35 |

Umpires: A.A. White and F. Hearne.

# ENGLAND v AUSTRALIA 1899 (1st Test)

Played at Trent Bridge, Nottingham, on 1, 2, 3 June.
Toss: Australia.    Result: MATCH DRAWN.
Debuts: England – W. Rhodes; Australia – F. Laver, V.T. Trumper.

The first five-match rubber in England began with the first Test ever staged at Nottingham. W.G. Grace, playing his last Test was 50 years and 320 days old when the match ended; only Wilfred Rhodes played Test cricket at a greater age, and by coincidence, he was making his debut in Grace's last match.

## AUSTRALIA

| | | | | | |
|---|---|---|---|---|---|
| J. Darling* | b Hearne | 47 | b Rhodes | | 14 |
| F.A. Iredale | c Hayward b Hearne | 6 | (4) run out | | 20 |
| M.A. Noble | b Rhodes | 41 | (2) lbw b Rhodes | | 45 |
| S.E. Gregory | b Hirst | 48 | b Noble | | |
| C. Hill | run out | 52 | (3) c Grace b Jackson | | 80 |
| V.T. Trumper | b Hearne | 0 | (5) b Jackson | | 11 |
| J.J. Kelly† | c Hirst b Hearne | 26 | (9) not out | | 11 |
| F. Laver | b Rhodes | 3 | (7) b Jackson | | 3 |
| W.P. Howell | c Hayward b Rhodes | 0 | (10) not out | | 4 |
| H. Trumble | not out | 16 | (8) c Ranjitsinhji b Rhodes | | 38 |
| E. Jones | c Fry b Rhodes | 4 | (6) c Ranjitsinhji b Hearne | | 3 |
| Extras | (B 8, LB 1) | 9 | (LB 1) | | 1 |
| **Total** | | **252** | (8 wickets declared) | | **230** |

## ENGLAND

| | | | | | |
|---|---|---|---|---|---|
| W.G. Grace* | c Kelly b Noble | 28 | b Howell | | 1 |
| C.B. Fry | b Jones | 50 | c Jones b Trumble | | 9 |
| F.S. Jackson | c Darling b Noble | 8 | b Howell | | 0 |
| W. Gunn | b Jones | 14 | b Jones | | 3 |
| K.S. Ranjitsinhji | b Jones | 42 | not out | | 93 |
| T.W. Hayward | run out | 0 | b Trumble | | 28 |
| J.T. Tyldesley | c Laver b Howell | 22 | c Kelly b Trumble | | 10 |
| W. Storer† | b Jones | 4 | lbw b Jones | | 3 |
| G.H. Hirst | b Howell | 6 | | | |
| W. Rhodes | c Kelly b Jones | 6 | | | |
| J.T. Hearne | not out | 4 | | | |
| Extras | (LB 3, NB 6) | 9 | (B 5, W 1, NB 2) | | 8 |
| **Total** | | **193** | (7 wickets) | | **155** |

| ENGLAND | O | M | R | W | O | M | R | W | | FALL OF WICKETS | | | |
|---|---|---|---|---|---|---|---|---|---|---|---|---|---|
| Rhodes | 35·2 | 13 | 58 | 4 | 20 | 3 | 60 | 3 | | | A | E | A | E |
| Hearne | 59 | 28 | 71 | 4 | 29 | 10 | 70 | 1 | Wkt | 1st | 1st | 2nd | 2nd |
| Grace | 20 | 8 | 31 | 0 | 2 | 0 | 6 | 0 | 1st | 14 | 75 | 18 | 1 |
| Hirst | 24 | 9 | 42 | 1 | 11 | 4 | 20 | 0 | 2nd | 85 | 91 | 111 | 1 |
| Jackson | 11 | 3 | 27 | 0 | 26 | 8 | 57 | 3 | 3rd | 109 | 93 | 151 | 10 |
| Hayward | 3 | 0 | 14 | 0 | 6 | 2 | 16 | 0 | 4th | 166 | 116 | 170 | 19 |
| | | | | | | | | | 5th | 167 | 117 | 173 | 82 |
| AUSTRALIA | | | | | | | | | 6th | 229 | 172 | 177 | 140 |
| Jones | 33 | 6 | 88 | 5 | 22 | 9 | 31 | 2 | 7th | 229 | 176 | 180 | 155 |
| Howell | 28·4 | 12 | 43 | 2 | 37 | 18 | 54 | 2 | 8th | 229 | 178 | 226 | – |
| Trumble | 13 | 7 | 17 | 0 | 29 | 16 | 39 | 3 | 9th | 248 | 185 | – | – |
| Noble | 16 | 4 | 36 | 2 | 11 | 5 | 23 | 0 | 10th | 252 | 193 | – | – |

Umpires: R.G. Barlow and V.A. Titchmarsh.

# ENGLAND v AUSTRALIA 1899 (2nd Test)

Played at Lord's, London, on 15, 16, 17 June.
Toss: England.   Result: AUSTRALIA won by ten wickets.
Debuts: England – G.L. Jessop, W. Mead, C.L. Townsend.

Trumper, aged 21, scored a chanceless 135 not out in his second Test match.

## ENGLAND

| | | | | |
|---|---|---|---|---|
| C.B. Fry | c Trumble b Jones | 13 | b Jones | 4 |
| A.C. MacLaren* | b Jones | 4 | (6) not out | 88 |
| K.S. Ranjitsinhji | c and b Jones | 8 | c Noble b Howell | 0 |
| C.L. Townsend | st Kelly b Howell | 5 | b Jones | 8 |
| F.S. Jackson | b Jones | 73 | c and b Trumble | 37 |
| T.W. Hayward | b Noble | 1 | (2) c Trumble b Laver | 77 |
| J.T. Tyldesley | c Darling b Jones | 14 | c Gregory b Laver | 4 |
| G.L. Jessop | c Trumper b Trumble | 51 | c Trumble b Laver | 4 |
| A.F.A. Lilley† | not out | 19 | b Jones | 12 |
| W. Mead | b Jones | 7 | (11) lbw b Noble | 0 |
| W. Rhodes | b Jones | 2 | (10) c and b Noble | 2 |
| Extras | (B 2, LB 6, W 1) | 9 | (B 2, LB 2) | 4 |
| **Total** | | **206** | | **240** |

## AUSTRALIA

| | | | | |
|---|---|---|---|---|
| J. Worrall | c Hayward b Rhodes | 18 | not out | 11 |
| J. Darling* | c Ranjitsinhji b Rhodes | 9 | not out | 17 |
| C. Hill | c Fry b Townsend | 135 | | |
| S.E. Gregory | c Lilley b Jessop | 15 | | |
| M.A. Noble | c Lilley b Rhodes | 54 | | |
| V.T. Trumper | not out | 135 | | |
| J.J. Kelly† | c Lilley b Mead | 9 | | |
| H. Trumble | c Lilley b Jessop | 24 | | |
| F. Laver | b Townsend | 0 | | |
| E. Jones | c Mead b Townsend | 17 | | |
| W.P. Howell | b Jessop | 0 | | |
| Extras | (LB 4, NB 1) | 5 | | |
| **Total** | | **421** | (0 wickets) | **28** |

| AUSTRALIA | O | M | R | W | O | M | R | W | | FALL OF WICKETS | | | |
|---|---|---|---|---|---|---|---|---|---|---|---|---|---|
| | | | | | | | | | | E | A | E | A |
| Jones | 36·1 | 11 | 88 | 7 | 36 | 15 | 76 | 3 | Wkt | 1st | 1st | 2nd | 2nd |
| Howell | 14 | 4 | 43 | 1 | 31 | 12 | 67 | 1 | 1st | 4 | 27 | 5 | – |
| Noble | 15 | 7 | 39 | 1 | 19·4 | 8 | 37 | 2 | 2nd | 4 | 28 | 6 | – |
| Trumble | 15 | 9 | 27 | 1 | 15 | 6 | 20 | 1 | 3rd | 20 | 59 | 23 | – |
| Laver | | | | | 16 | 4 | 36 | 3 | 4th | 44 | 189 | 94 | – |
| | | | | | | | | | 5th | 45 | 271 | 160 | – |
| ENGLAND | | | | | | | | | 6th | 66 | 306 | 166 | – |
| Jessop | 37·1 | 10 | 105 | 3 | 6 | 0 | 19 | 0 | 7th | 161 | 386 | 170 | – |
| Mead | 53 | 24 | 91 | 1 | | | | | 8th | 184 | 387 | 212 | – |
| Rhodes | 39 | 10 | 108 | 3 | 5 | 1 | 9 | 0 | 9th | 194 | 421 | 240 | – |
| Jackson | 18 | 6 | 31 | 0 | | | | | 10th | 206 | 421 | 240 | – |
| Townsend | 15 | 1 | 50 | 3 | | | | | | | | | |
| Ranjitsinhji | 2 | 0 | 6 | 0 | | | | | | | | | |
| Hayward | 6 | 0 | 25 | 0 | | | | | | | | | |

Umpires: W.A.J. West and T. Mycroft.

# ENGLAND v AUSTRALIA 1899 (3rd Test)

Played at Headingley, Yorkshire, 29, 30 June, 1 (*no play*) July.
Toss: Australia.   Result: MATCH DRAWN.
Debuts: England – W.G. Quaife, H.I. Young.

Briggs suffered a violent fit on the first night of this first Test in Yorkshire, was detained in Cheadle Asylum and played no further cricket until the next season. J.T. Hearne did the hat-trick in the second innings when he dismissed Hill, Gregory and Noble for 'ducks'.

## AUSTRALIA

| | | | | | |
|---|---|---|---|---|---|
| J. Worrall | run out | 76 | c sub (J.T. Tyldesley) b Young | 16 |
| J.J. Kelly† | c Fry b Briggs | 0 | (7) c Lilley b Hayward | 33 |
| M.A. Noble | run out | 0 | (5) c Ranjitsinhji b Hearne | 0 |
| S.E. Gregory | c Lilley b Hearne | 0 | (4) c MacLaren b Hearne | 0 |
| C. Hill | c Lilley b Young | 34 | (3) b Hearne | 0 |
| J. Darling* | c Young b Briggs | 9 | (2) c Fry b Young | 16 |
| V.T. Trumper | b Young | 12 | (6) c Ranjitsinhji b Jackson | 32 |
| H. Trumble | not out | 20 | run out | 56 |
| F. Laver | st Lilley b Briggs | 7 | c Lilley b Hearne | 45 |
| E. Jones | b Young | 5 | c Brown b Hayward | 2 |
| W.P. Howell | c Ranjitsinhji b Young | 7 | not out | 2 |
| Extras | (B 2) | 2 | (B 17, LB 3, W 1, NB 1) | 22 |
| **Total** | | **172** | | **224** |

## ENGLAND

| | | | | | |
|---|---|---|---|---|---|
| J.T. Brown | c Trumble b Noble | 27 | not out | 14 |
| A.C. MacLaren* | c and b Trumble | 9 | | |
| K.S. Ranjitsinhji | c Worrall b Noble | 11 | | |
| W.G. Quaife | b Jones | 20 | (2) not out | 1 |
| F.S. Jackson | b Trumble | 9 | | |
| C.B. Fry | b Noble | 38 | | |
| T.W. Hayward | not out | 40 | | |
| A.F.A. Lilley† | c Hill b Trumble | 55 | | |
| J.T. Hearne | b Trumble | 3 | | |
| H.I. Young | c Kelly b Trumble | 0 | | |
| J. Briggs | absent ill | – | | |
| Extras | (B 3, LB 5) | 8 | (LB 4) | 4 |
| **Total** | | **220** | (0 wickets) | **19** |

| ENGLAND | O | M | R | W | O | M | R | W |
|---|---|---|---|---|---|---|---|---|
| Hearne | 23 | 5 | 69 | 1 | 31·3 | 12 | 50 | 4 |
| Briggs | 30 | 11 | 53 | 3 | | | | |
| Young | 19·1 | 11 | 30 | 4 | 26 | 5 | 72 | 2 |
| Jackson | 5 | 1 | 18 | 0 | 11 | 6 | 13 | 1 |
| Brown | | | | | 7 | 0 | 22 | 0 |
| Hayward | | | | | 10 | 1 | 45 | 2 |
| AUSTRALIA | | | | | | | | |
| Trumble | 39·3 | 16 | 60 | 5 | | | | |
| Noble | 42 | 17 | 82 | 3 | 3 | 1 | 8 | 0 |
| Howell | 13 | 3 | 29 | 0 | | | | |
| Jones | 21 | 9 | 34 | 1 | 4 | 2 | 7 | 0 |
| Laver | 3 | 1 | 7 | 0 | | | | |

### FALL OF WICKETS

| Wkt | A 1st | E 1st | A 2nd | E 2nd |
|---|---|---|---|---|
| 1st | 8 | 27 | 34 | – |
| 2nd | 17 | 38 | 34 | – |
| 3rd | 24 | 53 | 34 | – |
| 4th | 95 | 69 | 34 | – |
| 5th | 114 | 119 | 39 | – |
| 6th | 131 | 119 | 97 | – |
| 7th | 132 | 212 | 140 | – |
| 8th | 151 | 220 | 213 | – |
| 9th | 164 | 220 | 215 | – |
| 10th | 172 | – | 224 | – |

Umpires: W. Hearn and M. Sherwin.

# ENGLAND v AUSTRALIA 1899 (4th Test)

Played at Old Trafford, Manchester, on 17, 18, 19 July.
Toss: England.   Result: MATCH DRAWN.
Debuts: England – W.M. Bradley.

This match provoked a change in the follow-on law, which was then applied automatically in cases of first innings arrears of 120 runs and which often inadvertently penalised the ascendant team.

## ENGLAND

| | | | | | |
|---|---|---|---|---|---|
| W.G. Quaife | c Darling b Noble | 8 | c Iredale b Jones | | 15 |
| C.B. Fry | b Jones | 9 | c Iredale b Trumble | | 4 |
| K.S. Ranjitsinhji | c Worrall b Jones | 21 | not out | | 49 |
| A.C. MacLaren* | b Noble | 8 | c Iredale b Trumble | | 6 |
| F.S. Jackson | c Trumble b Jones | 44 | not out | | 14 |
| T.W. Hayward | c Jones b Howell | 130 | | | |
| W. Brockwell | c Worrall b Noble | 20 | | | |
| A.F.A. Lilley† | lbw b Laver | 58 | | | |
| H.I. Young | b Howell | 43 | | | |
| J.T. Hearne | c Iredale b Trumble | 1 | | | |
| W.M. Bradley | not out | 23 | | | |
| Extras | (B 3, LB 3, W 1) | 7 | (B4, NB 2) | | 6 |
| **Total** | | **372** | (3 wickets) | | **94** |

## AUSTRALIA

| | | | | | |
|---|---|---|---|---|---|
| J.J. Kelly† | b Young | 9 | (8) c Lilley b Ranjitsinhji | | 26 |
| F. Laver | c Lilley b Bradley | 0 | (9) not out | | 14 |
| W.P. Howell | b Bradley | 0 | | | |
| J. Worrall | b Bradley | 14 | (1) c Brockwell b Young | | 53 |
| M.A. Noble | not out | 60 | (2) c and b Hearne | | 89 |
| S.E. Gregory | lbw b Young | 5 | (5) c Ranjitsinhji b Hearne | | 1 |
| V.T. Trumper | b Young | 14 | (4) b Hearne | | 63 |
| J. Darling* | b Young | 4 | (6) c sub (W. Rhodes) b Young | | 39 |
| H. Trumble | c MacLaren b Bradley | 44 | (3) c Ranjitsinhji b Bradley | | 7 |
| F.A. Iredale | c Lilley b Bradley | 31 | (7) not out | | 36 |
| E. Jones | b Jackson | 0 | | | |
| Extras | (B 14, W 1) | 15 | (B 14, LB 2, W 1, NB 1) | | 18 |
| **Total** | | **196** | (7 wickets declared) | | **346** |

| AUSTRALIA | O | M | R | W | O | M | R | W |
|---|---|---|---|---|---|---|---|---|
| Jones | 42 | 9 | 136 | 3 | 8 | 0 | 33 | 1 |
| Noble | 28 | 19 | 85 | 3 | | | | |
| Trumble | 29 | 10 | 72 | 1 | 13 | 3 | 33 | 2 |
| Howell | 19·1 | 7 | 45 | 2 | 6 | 2 | 22 | 0 |
| Laver | 13 | 2 | 27 | 1 | | | | |
| **ENGLAND** | | | | | | | | |
| Young | 29 | 10 | 79 | 4 | 37 | 12 | 81 | 2 |
| Bradley | 33 | 13 | 67 | 5 | 46 | 16 | 82 | 1 |
| Brockwell | 6 | 2 | 18 | 0 | 15 | 3 | 36 | 0 |
| Hearne | 10 | 6 | 7 | 0 | 47 | 26 | 54 | 3 |
| Jackson | 3·3 | 1 | 9 | 1 | 18 | 8 | 36 | 0 |
| Ranjitsinhji | 1 | 0 | 1 | 0 | 12 | 5 | 23 | 1 |
| Hayward | | | | | 3 | 1 | 10 | 0 |
| Quaife | | | | | 3 | 1 | 6 | 0 |

### FALL OF WICKETS

| | E | A | A | E |
|---|---|---|---|---|
| Wkt | 1st | 1st | 2nd | 2nd |
| 1st | 14 | 1 | 93 | 12 |
| 2nd | 18 | 6 | 117 | 39 |
| 3rd | 47 | 14 | 205 | 54 |
| 4th | 47 | 26 | 213 | – |
| 5th | 107 | 35 | 255 | – |
| 6th | 154 | 53 | 278 | – |
| 7th | 267 | 57 | 319 | – |
| 8th | 324 | 139 | – | – |
| 9th | 337 | 195 | – | – |
| 10th | 372 | 196 | – | – |

Umpires: James Lillywhite, jr and A. Hide.

# ENGLAND v AUSTRALIA 1899 (5th Test)

Played at Kennington Oval, London, on 14, 15, 16 August.
Toss: England.   Result: MATCH DRAWN.
Debuts: England – A.O. Jones.

Hayward and Jackson, both opening a Test innings for the first time, shared a partnership of 185, then England's highest for any wicket in England and the best opening stand by either country in these matches. Hayward's hundred was his second in successive innings. England scored 435 for 4 on the first day and went on to record the highest total in a Test in England until 1930 (*Test No. 195*).

## ENGLAND

| | | | | |
|---|---|---|---|---|
| F.S. Jackson | b Jones | 118 | | |
| T.W. Hayward | c Iredale b McLeod | 137 | | |
| K.S. Ranjitsinhji | c Howell b Jones | 54 | | |
| C.B. Fry | c Worrall b Jones | 60 | | |
| A.C. MacLaren* | c Trumper b Trumble | 49 | | |
| C.L. Townsend | b Jones | 38 | | |
| W.M. Bradley | run out | 0 | | |
| W.H. Lockwood | b Trumble | 24 | | |
| A.O. Jones | b Noble | 31 | | |
| A.F.A. Lilley† | c Iredale b Noble | 37 | | |
| W. Rhodes | not out | 8 | | |
| Extras | (B 9, LB 6, W 4, NB 1) | 20 | | |
| **Total** | | **576** | | |

## AUSTRALIA

| | | | | | |
|---|---|---|---|---|---|
| J. Worrall | c Hayward b Lockwood | 55 | c Lilley b Hayward | 75 |
| H. Trumble | c and b Jones | 24 | (7) not out | 3 |
| V.T. Trumper | c Lilley b Jones | 6 | (4) c and b Rhodes | 7 |
| M.A. Noble | b Lockwood | 9 | (3) not out | 69 |
| J. Darling* | c Fry b Lockwood | 71 | (6) run out | 6 |
| S.E. Gregory | c Jones b Lockwood | 117 | (5) b Rhodes | 2 |
| F.A. Iredale | b Lockwood | 9 | | |
| J.J. Kelly† | lbw b Jones | 4 | | |
| C.E. McLeod | not out | 31 | (2) b Rhodes | 77 |
| E. Jones | b Lockwood | 0 | | |
| W.P. Howell | b Lockwood | 4 | | |
| Extras | (B 5, LB 10, W 1, NB 6) | 22 | (B 7, W 4, NB 4) | 15 |
| **Total** | | **352** | (5 wickets) | **254** |

| AUSTRALIA | O | M | R | W | O | M | R | W |
|---|---|---|---|---|---|---|---|---|
| Jones | 53 | 12 | 164 | 4 | | | | |
| Noble | 35·4 | 12 | 96 | 2 | | | | |
| Trumble | 39 | 11 | 107 | 2 | | | | |
| McLeod | 48 | 15 | 131 | 1 | | | | |
| Howell | 15 | 3 | 43 | 0 | | | | |
| Worrall | 3 | 0 | 15 | 0 | | | | |
| ENGLAND | | | | | | | | |
| Bradley | 29 | 12 | 52 | 0 | 17 | 8 | 32 | 0 |
| Rhodes | 25 | 2 | 79 | 0 | 22 | 8 | 27 | 3 |
| Lockwood | 40·3 | 17 | 71 | 7 | 15 | 7 | 33 | 0 |
| Jones | 30 | 12 | 73 | 3 | 12 | 2 | 43 | 0 |
| Townsend | 5 | 0 | 16 | 0 | 8 | 4 | 9 | 0 |
| Jackson | 14 | 7 | 39 | 0 | 13 | 2 | 54 | 0 |
| Hayward | | | | | 11 | 3 | 38 | 1 |
| Fry | | | | | 2 | 1 | 3 | 0 |

### FALL OF WICKETS

| | E | A | A |
|---|---|---|---|
| Wkt | 1st | 1st | 2nd |
| 1st | 185 | 38 | 116 |
| 2nd | 316 | 44 | 208 |
| 3rd | 318 | 85 | 224 |
| 4th | 428 | 120 | 228 |
| 5th | 436 | 220 | 243 |
| 6th | 436 | 242 | – |
| 7th | 479 | 257 | – |
| 8th | 511 | 340 | – |
| 9th | 551 | 340 | – |
| 10th | 576 | 352 | – |

Umpires: A.A. White and W. Richards.

# AUSTRALIA v ENGLAND 1901–02 (1st Test)

Played at Sydney Cricket Ground on 13, 14, 16 December.
Toss: England.   Result: ENGLAND won by an innings and 124 runs.
Debuts: England – S.F. Barnes, C. Blythe, L.C. Braund, J. Gunn.

MacLaren became the first batsman to score four centuries in Test cricket. Not until 1958–59 did another England captain score a Test hundred in Australia (P.B.H. May in *Test No. 465*).

### ENGLAND

| | | |
|---|---|---:|
| A.C. MacLaren* | lbw b McLeod | 116 |
| T.W. Hayward | c Hill b Trumble | 69 |
| J.T. Tyldesley | c McLeod b Laver | 1 |
| W.G. Quaife | b Howell | 21 |
| G.L. Jessop | b McLeod | 24 |
| A.O. Jones | c Kelly b Noble | 9 |
| A.F.A. Lilley† | c Laver b McLeod | 84 |
| L.C. Braund | c Jones b McLeod | 58 |
| J.Gunn | c and b Jones | 21 |
| S.F. Barnes | not out | 26 |
| C. Blythe | c Trumble b Laver | 20 |
| Extras | (B 6, LB 7, W 1, NB 1) | 15 |
| **Total** | | **464** |

### AUSTRALIA

| | | | | | |
|---|---|---:|---|---|---:|
| S.E. Gregory | c Braund b Blythe | 48 | (5) c MacLaren b Braund | | 43 |
| V.T. Trumper | c and b Barnes | 2 | c Lilley b Blythe | | 34 |
| C. Hill | b Barnes | 46 | b Braund | | 0 |
| M.A. Noble | st Lilley b Braund | 2 | c Lilley b Blythe | | 14 |
| W.P. Howell | c Braund b Blythe | 9 | (10) not out | | 31 |
| C.E. McLeod | b Barnes | 0 | b Blythe | | 0 |
| J.J. Kelly† | b Blythe | 0 | c Barnes b Blythe | | 12 |
| J. Darling* | c Quaife b Barnes | 39 | (1) c Jessop b Braund | | 3 |
| F. Laver | c Quaife b Braund | 6 | st Lilley b Braund | | 0 |
| H. Trumble | not out | 5 | (8) c Lilley b Barnes | | 26 |
| E. Jones | c Jessop b Barnes | 5 | c Jones b Braund | | 2 |
| Extras | (B 1, LB 3, NB 2) | 6 | (B 5, LB 2) | | 7 |
| **Total** | | **168** | | | **172** |

| AUSTRALIA | O | M | R | W | O | M | R | W |
|---|---:|---:|---:|---:|---:|---:|---:|---:|
| Jones | 36 | 8 | 98 | 1 | | | | |
| Noble | 33 | 17 | 91 | 1 | | | | |
| McLeod | 44 | 17 | 84 | 4 | | | | |
| Howell | 21 | 8 | 52 | 1 | | | | |
| Trumble | 34 | 12 | 85 | 1 | | | | |
| Laver | 17 | 6 | 39 | 2 | | | | |
| Trumper | 1 | 1 | 0 | 0 | | | | |
| ENGLAND | | | | | | | | |
| Barnes | 35·1 | 9 | 65 | 5 | 16 | 2 | 74 | 1 |
| Braund | 15 | 4 | 40 | 2 | 28·4 | 8 | 61 | 5 |
| Gunn | 5 | 0 | 27 | 0 | | | | |
| Blythe | 16 | 8 | 26 | 3 | 13 | 5 | 30 | 4 |
| Jessop | 1 | 0 | 4 | 0 | | | | |

### FALL OF WICKETS

| Wkt | E 1st | A 1st | A 2nd |
|---|---:|---:|---:|
| 1st | 154 | 3 | 12 |
| 2nd | 163 | 89 | 12 |
| 3rd | 193 | 97 | 52 |
| 4th | 220 | 112 | 59 |
| 5th | 236 | 112 | 59 |
| 6th | 272 | 112 | 89 |
| 7th | 396 | 112 | 129 |
| 8th | 405 | 142 | 136 |
| 9th | 425 | 163 | 147 |
| 10th | 464 | 168 | 172 |

Umpires: R. Callaway and R.W. Crockett.

# AUSTRALIA v ENGLAND 1901–02 (2nd Test)

Played at Melbourne Cricket Ground on 1, 2, 3, 4 January.
Toss: England. Result: AUSTRALIA won by 229 runs.
Debuts: Australia – W.W. Armstrong, R.A. Duff.

R.A. Duff, top-scorer in both innings, became the third Australian to score a hundred on his Test debut. He remains the only Australian to score a century against England batting at No. 10. He and Armstrong had been held back until the pitch eased and they responded with the first hundred partnership for the tenth wicket in Tests. H. Trumble completed Australia's victory by taking a hat-trick to dismiss Jones, Gunn and Barnes.

## AUSTRALIA

| | | | | |
|---|---|---|---|---|
| V.T. Trumper | c Tyldesley b Barnes | 0 | (8) c Lilley b Barnes | 16 |
| J. Darling* | c Lilley b Blythe | 19 | c Tyldesley b Barnes | 23 |
| C. Hill | b Barnes | 15 | (7) c Jones b Barnes | 99 |
| H. Trumble | c Braund b Blythe | 16 | (1) c Braund b Barnes | 16 |
| M.A. Noble | c Lilley b Blythe | 0 | (9) lbw b Blythe | 16 |
| S.E. Gregory | st Lilley b Blythe | 0 | c Jones b Barnes | 17 |
| R.A. Duff | c Braund b Barnes | 32 | (10) b Braund | 104 |
| J.J. Kelly† | c Quaife b Barnes | 5 | (4) run out | 3 |
| W.W. Armstrong | not out | 4 | (11) not out | 45 |
| W.P. Howell | b Barnes | 1 | (3) c Hayward b Barnes | 0 |
| E. Jones | c MacLaren b Barnes | 14 | (5) c MacLaren b Barnes | 5 |
| Extras | (B 6) | 6 | (B 7, LB 1, NB 1) | 9 |
| **Total** | | **112** | | **353** |

## ENGLAND

| | | | | |
|---|---|---|---|---|
| A.C. MacLaren* | c Jones b Trumble | 13 | c Trumble b Noble | 1 |
| T.W. Hayward | c Darling b Trumble | 0 | st Kelly b Trumble | 12 |
| J.T. Tyldesley | c Gregory b Trumble | 2 | c Trumble b Noble | 66 |
| W.G. Quaife | b Noble | 0 | b Noble | 25 |
| G.L. Jessop | st Kelly b Noble | 27 | c Gregory b Noble | 32 |
| J.Gunn | st Kelly b Noble | 0 | (9) c Jones b Trumble | 2 |
| A.F.A. Lilley† | c Trumper b Noble | 6 | (6) c Darling b Noble | 0 |
| A.O. Jones | c Kelly b Noble | 0 | c Darling b Trumble | 6 |
| L.C. Braund | not out | 2 | (7) c Darling b Noble | 25 |
| S.F. Barnes | c and b Noble | 1 | c and b Trumble | 0 |
| C. Blythe | c Trumper b Noble | 4 | not out | 0 |
| Extras | (B 6) | 6 | (B 1, LB 1, NB 4) | 6 |
| **Total** | | **61** | | **175** |

| ENGLAND | O | M | R | W | O | M | R | W |
|---|---|---|---|---|---|---|---|---|
| Barnes | 16·1 | 5 | 42 | 6 | 64 | 17 | 121 | 7 |
| Blythe | 16 | 2 | 64 | 4 | 31 | 7 | 85 | 1 |
| Braund | | | | | 53·2 | 17 | 114 | 1 |
| Jessop | | | | | 1 | 0 | 9 | 0 |
| Gunn | | | | | 6 | 1 | 13 | 0 |
| Jones | | | | | 1 | 0 | 2 | 0 |

| AUSTRALIA | O | M | R | W | O | M | R | W |
|---|---|---|---|---|---|---|---|---|
| Trumble | 8 | 1 | 38 | 3 | 22·5 | 10 | 49 | 4 |
| Noble | 7·4 | 2 | 17 | 7 | 26 | 5 | 60 | 6 |
| Jones | | | | | 12 | 2 | 33 | 0 |
| Howell | | | | | 15 | 6 | 23 | 0 |
| Armstrong | | | | | 2 | 1 | 3 | 0 |
| Trumper | | | | | 2 | 1 | 1 | 0 |

## FALL OF WICKETS

| | A | E | A | E |
|---|---|---|---|---|
| Wkt | 1st | 1st | 2nd | 2nd |
| 1st | 0 | 5 | 32 | 2 |
| 2nd | 32 | 16 | 42 | 29 |
| 3rd | 34 | 16 | 42 | 80 |
| 4th | 34 | 24 | 42 | 123 |
| 5th | 38 | 36 | 48 | 123 |
| 6th | 81 | 51 | 98 | 156 |
| 7th | 85 | 51 | 128 | 173 |
| 8th | 90 | 56 | 167 | 175 |
| 9th | 94 | 57 | 233 | 175 |
| 10th | 112 | 61 | 353 | 175 |

Umpires: R. Callaway and R.W. Crockett.

# AUSTRALIA v ENGLAND 1901–02 (3rd Test)

Played at Adelaide Oval on 17, 18, 20, 21, 22, 23 January.
Toss: England.   Result: AUSTRALIA won by four wickets.
Debuts: Nil.

C. Hill became the only batsman to be dismissed for three successive nineties in Test matches: 99, 98 and 97.

## ENGLAND

| | | | | | |
|---|---|---|---|---|---|
| A.C. MacLaren* | run out | 67 | | b Trumble | 44 |
| T.W. Hayward | run out | 90 | | b Trumble | 47 |
| J.T. Tyldesley | c and b Trumble | 0 | | run out | 25 |
| G.L. Jessop | c Trumper b Trumble | 1 | (5) | b Trumble | 16 |
| A.F.A. Lilley† | lbw b Trumble | 10 | (7) | b McLeod | 21 |
| W.G. Quaife | c Kelly b Howell | 68 | (4) | lbw b Trumble | 44 |
| L.C. Braund | not out | 103 | (6) | b Howell | 17 |
| A.O. Jones | run out | 5 | | c and b Trumble | 11 |
| J. Gunn | b Noble | 24 | | lbw b Trumble | 5 |
| S.F. Barnes | c Hill b Noble | 5 | | absent hurt | – |
| C. Blythe | c Hill b Noble | 2 | (10) | not out | 10 |
| Extras | (B 9, W 1, NB 3) | 13 | | (B 7) | 7 |
| **Total** | | **388** | | | **247** |

## AUSTRALIA

| | | | | | |
|---|---|---|---|---|---|
| J. Darling* | c MacLaren b Blythe | 1 | (5) | c Hayward b Jessop | 69 |
| V.T. Trumper | run out | 65 | | b Gunn | 25 |
| C. Hill | c Tyldesley b Braund | 98 | | b Jessop | 97 |
| R.A. Duff | lbw b Braund | 43 | (1) | hit wkt b Gunn | 4 |
| S.E. Gregory | c Blythe b Braund | 55 | (4) | c Braund b Gunn | 23 |
| W.W. Armstrong | c and b Gunn | 9 | (8) | not out | 9 |
| H. Trumble | b Gunn | 13 | (6) | not out | 62 |
| W.P. Howell | c Braund b Gunn | 3 | | | |
| M.A. Noble | b Gunn | 14 | (7) | run out | 13 |
| J.J. Kelly† | not out | 5 | | | |
| C.E. McLeod | b Gunn | 7 | | | |
| Extras | (B 2, LB 6) | 8 | | (B 9, LB 3, NB 1) | 13 |
| **Total** | | **321** | | (6 wickets) | **315** |

| AUSTRALIA | O | M | R | W | O | M | R | W |
|---|---|---|---|---|---|---|---|---|
| Trumble | 65 | 23 | 124 | 3 | 44 | 18 | 74 | 6 |
| Noble | 26 | 10 | 58 | 3 | 21 | 7 | 72 | 0 |
| Howell | 36 | 10 | 82 | 1 | 27 | 9 | 54 | 1 |
| Armstrong | 18 | 5 | 45 | 0 | 5 | 0 | 9 | 0 |
| Trumper | 6 | 3 | 17 | 0 | | | | |
| McLeod | 19 | 5 | 49 | 0 | 14 | 3 | 31 | 1 |
| ENGLAND | | | | | | | | |
| Braund | 46 | 9 | 143 | 3 | 14 | 5 | 79 | 0 |
| Blythe | 11 | 3 | 54 | 1 | 23 | 16 | 66 | 0 |
| Barnes | 7 | 0 | 21 | 0 | | | | |
| Gunn | 42 | 14 | 76 | 5 | 22 | 14 | 88 | 3 |
| Jessop | 7 | 0 | 19 | 0 | 13 | 9 | 41 | 2 |
| Hayward | | | | | 4 | 0 | 28 | 0 |

FALL OF WICKETS

| | E | A | E | A |
|---|---|---|---|---|
| Wkt | 1st | 1st | 2nd | 2nd |
| 1st | 149 | 2 | 80 | 5 |
| 2nd | 160 | 138 | 113 | 50 |
| 3rd | 164 | 197 | 126 | 98 |
| 4th | 171 | 229 | 144 | 194 |
| 5th | 186 | 260 | 165 | 255 |
| 6th | 294 | 288 | 204 | 287 |
| 7th | 302 | 289 | 218 | – |
| 8th | 371 | 302 | 224 | – |
| 9th | 384 | 309 | 247 | – |
| 10th | 388 | 321 | – | – |

Umpires: R.W. Crockett and P. Argall.

# AUSTRALIA v ENGLAND 1901–02 (4th Test)

Played at Sydney Cricket Ground on 14, 15, 17, 18 February.
Toss: England.   Result: AUSTRALIA won by seven wickets.
Debuts: Australia – A.J.Y. Hopkins, J.V. Saunders; England – C.P. McGahey.

Howell scored 35 in 14 minutes, being out to his 15th ball; he hit 23 off his first eight balls. Saunders took nine wickets in his first Test but was not selected for the next match.

## ENGLAND

| | | | | |
|---|---|---|---|---|
| A.C. MacLaren* | c Duff b Saunders | 92 | c Kelly b Noble | 5 |
| T.W. Hayward | b Saunders | 41 | b Noble | 12 |
| J.T. Tyldesley | c Kelly b Noble | 79 | c Trumble b Saunders | 10 |
| W.G. Quaife | c Kelly b Saunders | 4 | lbw b Noble | 15 |
| G.L. Jessop | c Noble b Saunders | 0 | b Saunders | 15 |
| L.C. Braund | lbw b Trumble | 17 | b Saunders | 0 |
| C.P. McGahey | b Trumble | 18 | c Kelly b Saunders | 13 |
| A.F.A. Lilley† | c Kelly b Noble | 40 | c Trumble b Noble | 0 |
| A.O. Jones | c Kelly b Trumble | 15 | c Kelly b Noble | 6 |
| J. Gunn | not out | 0 | not out | 13 |
| C. Blythe | b Noble | 4 | c Kelly b Saunders | 8 |
| Extras | (B 5, NB 2) | 7 | (LB 2) | 2 |
| **Total** | | **317** | | **99** |

## AUSTRALIA

| | | | | |
|---|---|---|---|---|
| H. Trumble* | c MacLaren b Jessop | 6 | | |
| V.T. Trumper | c Braund b Jessop | 7 | lbw b Blythe | 25 |
| C. Hill | c Jones b Jessop | 21 | c Lilley b Gunn | 30 |
| S.E. Gregory | c Braund b Jessop | 5 | (5) not out | 12 |
| M.A. Noble | lbw b Braund | 56 | (1) not out | 51 |
| R.A. Duff | c Lilley b Blythe | 39 | | |
| W.W. Armstrong | b Braund | 55 | | |
| A.J.Y. Hopkins | c Lilley b Braund | 43 | | |
| J.J. Kelly† | not out | 24 | | |
| W.P. Howell | c MacLaren b Gunn | 35 | (4) c sub (H.G. Garnett) b Gunn | 0 |
| J.V. Saunders | b Braund | 0 | | |
| Extras | (B 7, NB 1) | 8 | (LB 1, NB 2) | 3 |
| **Total** | | **299** | (3 wickets) | **121** |

| AUSTRALIA | O | M | R | W | O | M | R | W | | FALL OF WICKETS | | | |
|---|---|---|---|---|---|---|---|---|---|---|---|---|---|
| Noble | 33·2 | 12 | 78 | 3 | 24 | 7 | 54 | 5 | | | E | A | E | A |
| Saunders | 43 | 11 | 119 | 4 | 24·1 | 8 | 43 | 5 | *Wkt* | *1st* | *1st* | *2nd* | *2nd* |
| Howell | 22 | 10 | 40 | 0 | | | | | 1st | 73 | 7 | 5 | 50 |
| Trumble | 38 | 18 | 65 | 3 | | | | | 2nd | 179 | 18 | 24 | 105 |
| Armstrong | 2 | 1 | 8 | 0 | | | | | 3rd | 188 | 30 | 36 | 105 |
| | | | | | | | | | 4th | 188 | 48 | 57 | – |
| ENGLAND | | | | | | | | | 5th | 225 | 119 | 57 | – |
| Braund | 60 | 25 | 118 | 4 | 15 | 2 | 55 | 0 | 6th | 245 | 160 | 57 | – |
| Gunn | 16 | 5 | 48 | 1 | 8·3 | 1 | 17 | 2 | 7th | 267 | 205 | 60 | – |
| Jessop | 26 | 5 | 68 | 4 | 7 | 0 | 23 | 0 | 8th | 312 | 252 | 78 | – |
| Blythe | 37 | 17 | 57 | 1 | 6 | 0 | 23 | 1 | 9th | 312 | 288 | 88 | – |
| | | | | | | | | | 10th | 317 | 299 | 99 | – |

Umpires: C. Bannerman and R. Callaway.

# AUSTRALIA v ENGLAND 1901–02 (5th Test)

Played at Melbourne Cricket Ground on 28 February, 1, 3, 4 March.
Toss: Australia.   Result: AUSTRALIA won by 32 runs.
Debuts: Australia – J.P.F. Travers.

C. Hill became the first player to score 500 runs in a series without making a century; C.C. Hunte (550 for West Indies v Australia in 1964–65) is the only other batsman to do so.

## AUSTRALIA

| | | | | | |
|---|---|---|---|---|---|
| V.T. Trumper | b Blythe | 27 | c McGahey b Braund | | 18 |
| R.A. Duff | b Braund | 10 | c and b Braund | | 28 |
| C. Hill | c Jones b Gunn | 28 | c Lilley b Hayward | | 87 |
| S.E. Gregory | c Jones b Gunn | 25 | b Gunn | | 41 |
| M.A. Noble | lbw b Hayward | 7 | c MacLaren b Gunn | | 16 |
| H. Trumble* | c Quaife b Hayward | 3 | (7) b Blythe | | 22 |
| W.W. Armstrong | not out | 17 | (6) lbw b Braund | | 20 |
| A.J.Y. Hopkins | c Lilley b Hayward | 4 | c MacLaren b Blythe | | 0 |
| J.J. Kelly† | c Gunn b Hayward | 0 | not out | | 11 |
| C.J. Eady | b Gunn | 5 | c Gunn b Braund | | 3 |
| J.P.F. Travers | c Braund b Gunn | 9 | c and b Braund | | 1 |
| Extras | (B 7, W 1, NB 1) | 9 | (B 3, LB 1, NB 4) | | 8 |
| **Total** | | **144** | | | **255** |

## ENGLAND

| | | | | | |
|---|---|---|---|---|---|
| A.C. MacLaren* | c and b Trumble | 25 | run out | | 49 |
| G.L. Jessop | c Hopkins b Trumble | 35 | (4) c Trumper b Trumble | | 16 |
| W.G. Quaife | c Trumble b Noble | 3 | lbw b Noble | | 4 |
| J.T. Tyldesley | c Kelly b Eady | 13 | (5) c Eady b Trumble | | 36 |
| T.W. Hayward | c Trumper b Travers | 19 | (2) c Travers b Trumble | | 15 |
| L.C. Braund | c Hopkins b Trumble | 32 | c Hill b Noble | | 2 |
| A.F.A. Lilley† | c Eady b Trumble | 41 | c Duff b Noble | | 9 |
| C.P. McGahey | b Trumble | 0 | c Hill b Noble | | 7 |
| A.O. Jones | c Kelly b Eady | 10 | c and b Noble | | 28 |
| J.Gunn | lbw b Eady | 8 | c Hill b Noble | | 4 |
| C. Blythe | not out | 0 | not out | | 5 |
| Extras | (B 1, LB 2) | 3 | (LB 2, NB 1) | | 3 |
| **Total** | | **189** | | | **178** |

| ENGLAND | O | M | R | W | O | M | R | W | FALL OF WICKETS | | | | |
|---|---|---|---|---|---|---|---|---|---|---|---|---|---|
| Jessop | 1 | 0 | 13 | 0 | | | | | | A | E | A | E |
| Braund | 10 | 2 | 33 | 1 | 26·1 | 4 | 95 | 5 | Wkt | 1st | 1st | 2nd | 2nd |
| Blythe | 9 | 2 | 29 | 1 | 13 | 3 | 36 | 2 | 1st | 16 | 50 | 30 | 40 |
| Hayward | 16 | 9 | 22 | 4 | 22 | 4 | 63 | 1 | 2nd | 54 | 62 | 52 | 64 |
| Gunn | 17 | 6 | 38 | 4 | 28 | 11 | 53 | 2 | 3rd | 81 | 64 | 131 | 87 |
| | | | | | | | | | 4th | 98 | 91 | 149 | 87 |
| AUSTRALIA | | | | | | | | | 5th | 104 | 96 | 208 | 93 |
| Noble | 26 | 4 | 80 | 1 | 33 | 4 | 98 | 6 | 6th | 108 | 164 | 224 | 104 |
| Trumble | 25 | 4 | 62 | 5 | 30·3 | 7 | 64 | 3 | 7th | 112 | 168 | 249 | 120 |
| Travers | 8 | 2 | 14 | 1 | | | | | 8th | 112 | 173 | 249 | 157 |
| Eady | 8·3 | 2 | 30 | 3 | 2 | 0 | 13 | 0 | 9th | 124 | 186 | 255 | 161 |
| | | | | | | | | | 10th | 144 | 189 | 255 | 178 |

Umpires: C. Bannerman and R.W. Crockett.

# ENGLAND v AUSTRALIA 1902 (1st Test)

Played at Edgbaston, Birmingham, on 29, 30, 31 May.
Toss: England.   Result: MATCH DRAWN.
Debuts: Nil.

MacLaren's team in this, Birmingham's first Test match, is usually considered to be the strongest batting side ever to represent England – all eleven scored centuries in first-class cricket. Australia were dismissed in 85 minutes for their lowest score in Tests. Rain delayed the start on the third day until 5.15 p.m. and restricted play to 75 minutes.

### ENGLAND

| | | |
|---|---|---|
| A.C. MacLaren* | run out | 9 |
| C.B. Fry | c Kelly b Jones | 0 |
| K.S. Ranjitsinhji | b Armstrong | 13 |
| Hon. F.S. Jackson | b Jones | 53 |
| J.T. Tyldesley | lbw b Howell | 138 |
| A.F.A. Lilley† | c Jones b Noble | 2 |
| G.H. Hirst | c Armstrong b Trumper | 48 |
| G.L. Jessop | c Hopkins b Trumper | 6 |
| L.C. Braund | b Jones | 14 |
| W.H. Lockwood | not out | 52 |
| W. Rhodes | not out | 38 |
| Extras | (LB 3) | 3 |
| **Total** | (9 wickets declared) | **376** |

### AUSTRALIA

| | | | | |
|---|---|---|---|---|
| V.T. Trumper | b Hirst | 18 | c Braund b Rhodes | 14 |
| R.A. Duff | c Jessop b Rhodes | 2 | c Fry b Braund | 15 |
| C. Hill | c Braund b Hirst | 1 | not out | 10 |
| S.E. Gregory | lbw b Hirst | 0 | not out | 1 |
| J. Darling* | c Jessop b Rhodes | 3 | | |
| M.A. Noble | st Lilley b Rhodes | 3 | | |
| W.W. Armstrong | c Lilley b Rhodes | 0 | | |
| A.J.Y. Hopkins | c Lilley b Rhodes | 5 | | |
| J.J. Kelly† | not out | 1 | | |
| E. Jones | c Jackson b Rhodes | 0 | | |
| W.P. Howell | c Fry b Rhodes | 0 | | |
| Extras | (B 3) | 3 | (LB 4, W 1, NB 1) | 6 |
| **Total** | | **36** | (2 wickets) | **46** |

| AUSTRALIA | O | M | R | W | O | M | R | W |
|---|---|---|---|---|---|---|---|---|
| Jones | 28 | 9 | 76 | 3 | | | | |
| Noble | 44 | 15 | 112 | 1 | | | | |
| Trumper | 13 | 5 | 35 | 2 | | | | |
| Armstrong | 25 | 6 | 64 | 1 | | | | |
| Howell | 26 | 8 | 58 | 1 | | | | |
| Hopkins | 6 | 2 | 28 | 0 | | | | |
| ENGLAND | | | | | | | | |
| Hirst | 11 | 4 | 15 | 3 | 9 | 6 | 10 | 0 |
| Rhodes | 11 | 3 | 17 | 7 | 10 | 5 | 9 | 1 |
| Braund | 1 | 0 | 1 | 0 | 5 | 0 | 14 | 1 |
| Jackson | | | | | 4 | 2 | 7 | 0 |

### FALL OF WICKETS

| Wkt | E 1st | A 1st | A 2nd |
|---|---|---|---|
| 1st | 5 | 9 | 16 |
| 2nd | 13 | 10 | 41 |
| 3rd | 35 | 14 | – |
| 4th | 112 | 17 | – |
| 5th | 121 | 25 | – |
| 6th | 212 | 25 | – |
| 7th | 230 | 31 | – |
| 8th | 264 | 35 | – |
| 9th | 295 | 35 | – |
| 10th | – | 36 | – |

Umpires: J. Phillips and W. Hearn.

# ENGLAND v AUSTRALIA 1902 (2nd Test)

Played at Lord's, London, on 12, 13 (*no play*), 14 (*no play*) June.
Toss: England.   Result: MATCH DRAWN.
Debuts: Nil.

Rain delayed the start until 2.45 p.m., restricted play to 105 minutes on the first day, completely washed out the second, and caused the match to be abandoned before the scheduled start of the third and final day.

## ENGLAND

| | | |
|---|---|---|
| A.C. MacLaren* | not out | 47 |
| C.B. Fry | c Hill b Hopkins | 0 |
| K.S. Ranjitsinhji | b Hopkins | 0 |
| Hon. F.S. Jackson | not out | 55 |
| J.T. Tyldesley | ) | |
| A.F.A. Lilley† | ) | |
| G.H. Hirst | ) | |
| G.L. Jessop | ) did not bat | |
| L.C. Braund | ) | |
| W.H. Lockwood | ) | |
| W. Rhodes | ) | |
| Extras | | 0 |
| **Total** | (2 wickets) | **102** |

## AUSTRALIA

V.T. Trumper
R.A. Duff
A.J.Y. Hopkins
C. Hill
S.E. Gregory
J. Darling*
M.A. Noble
W.W. Armstrong
J.J. Kelly†
E. Jones
J.V. Saunders

| AUSTRALIA | O | M | R | W |
|---|---|---|---|---|
| Jones | 11 | 4 | 31 | 0 |
| Hopkins | 9 | 3 | 18 | 2 |
| Saunders | 3 | 0 | 15 | 0 |
| Trumper | 8 | 1 | 33 | 0 |
| Armstrong | 5 | 0 | 5 | 0 |
| Noble | 2 | 2 | 0 | 0 |

Umpires: V.A. Titchmarsh and C.E. Richardson.

## FALL OF WICKETS

| | E |
|---|---|
| Wkt | 1st |
| 1st | 0 |
| 2nd | 0 |

# ENGLAND v AUSTRALIA 1902 (3rd Test)

Played at Bramall Lane, Sheffield, on 3, 4, 5 July.
Toss: Australia.   Result: AUSTRALIA won by 143 runs.
Debuts: Nil.

C. Hill had the distinction of scoring the only hundred in Sheffield's only Test. Now solely the home of Sheffield United Football Club, Bramall Lane staged its last first-class cricket match in 1973. Trumper made 50 in 40 minutes, taking only 50 minutes to score 62.

## AUSTRALIA

| | | | | | |
|---|---|---|---|---|---|
| V.T. Trumper | b Braund | 1 | c Lilley b Jackson | | 62 |
| R.A. Duff | c Lilley b Barnes | 25 | c Hirst b Rhodes | | 1 |
| C. Hill | c Rhodes b Barnes | 18 | c MacLaren b Jackson | | 119 |
| J. Darling* | c Braund b Barnes | 0 | c Braund b Barnes | | 0 |
| S.E. Gregory | c Abel b Barnes | 11 | run out | | 29 |
| M.A. Noble | c Braund b Rhodes | 47 | b Jackson | | 8 |
| A.J.Y. Hopkins | c Braund b Barnes | 27 | not out | | 40 |
| W.W. Armstrong | c and b Braund | 25 | b Rhodes | | 26 |
| J.J. Kelly† | b Barnes | 0 | c Hirst b Rhodes | | 0 |
| H. Trumble | c and b Jackson | 32 | b Rhodes | | 1 |
| J.V. Saunders | not out | 0 | b Rhodes | | 0 |
| Extras | (B 3, LB 5) | 8 | (LB 3) | | 3 |
| **Total** | | **194** | | | **289** |

## ENGLAND

| | | | | | |
|---|---|---|---|---|---|
| A.C. MacLaren* | b Noble | 31 | (4) c Trumper b Noble | | 63 |
| R. Abel | b Noble | 38 | c Hill b Noble | | 8 |
| J.T. Tyldesley | c Armstrong b Noble | 22 | b Trumble | | 14 |
| Hon. F.S. Jackson | c Gregory b Saunders | 3 | (6) b Noble | | 14 |
| C.B. Fry | st Kelly b Saunders | 1 | lbw b Trumble | | 4 |
| A.F.A. Lilley† | b Noble | 8 | (7) b Noble | | 9 |
| L.C. Braund | st Kelly b Saunders | 0 | (8) c Armstrong b Noble | | 9 |
| G.H. Hirst | c Trumble b Saunders | 8 | (9) b Noble | | 0 |
| G.L. Jessop | c Saunders b Noble | 12 | (1) lbw b Trumble | | 55 |
| W. Rhodes | not out | 7 | not out | | 7 |
| S.F. Barnes | c Darling b Saunders | 7 | b Trumble | | 5 |
| Extras | (B 4, LB 3, NB 1) | 8 | (B 4, LB 1, W 1, NB 1) | | 7 |
| **Total** | | **145** | | | **195** |

| ENGLAND | O | M | R | W | O | M | R | W | | FALL OF WICKETS | | | |
|---|---|---|---|---|---|---|---|---|---|---|---|---|---|
| Hirst | 15 | 1 | 59 | 0 | 10 | 1 | 40 | 0 | | A | E | A | E |
| Braund | 13 | 4 | 34 | 2 | 12 | 0 | 58 | 0 | Wkt | 1st | 1st | 2nd | 2nd |
| Barnes | 20 | 9 | 49 | 6 | 12 | 4 | 50 | 1 | 1st | 3 | 61 | 20 | 14 |
| Jackson | 5·1 | 1 | 11 | 1 | 17 | 2 | 60 | 3 | 2nd | 39 | 86 | 80 | 75 |
| Rhodes | 13 | 3 | 33 | 1 | 17·1 | 3 | 63 | 5 | 3rd | 39 | 101 | 80 | 84 |
| Jessop | | | | | 4 | 0 | 15 | 0 | 4th | 52 | 101 | 187 | 98 |
| | | | | | | | | | 5th | 73 | 102 | 214 | 162 |
| AUSTRALIA | | | | | | | | | 6th | 127 | 106 | 225 | 165 |
| Trumble | 18 | 10 | 21 | 0 | 21·5 | 3 | 49 | 4 | 7th | 137 | 110 | 277 | 174 |
| Saunders | 15·3 | 4 | 50 | 5 | 12 | 0 | 68 | 0 | 8th | 137 | 130 | 287 | 174 |
| Trumper | 4 | 1 | 8 | 0 | 6 | 0 | 19 | 0 | 9th | 194 | 131 | 287 | 186 |
| Noble | 19 | 6 | 51 | 5 | 21 | 4 | 52 | 6 | 10th | 194 | 145 | 289 | 195 |
| Armstrong | 5 | 2 | 7 | 0 | | | | | | | | | |

Umpires: J. Phillips and W. Richards.

# ENGLAND v AUSTRALIA 1902 (4th Test)

Played at Old Trafford, Manchester, on 24, 25, 26 July.
Toss: Australia.   Result: AUSTRALIA won by 3 runs.
Debuts: England – L.C.H. Palairet, F.W. Tate.

V.T. Trumper reached his century in 108 minutes before lunch on the first day – a feat since equalled on only three occasions: C.G. Macartney in 1926 (*Test No. 165*), D.G. Bradman in 1930 (*196*), and Majid Khan in 1976–77 (*784*). At lunch Trumper was 103 not out and Australia's score was 173–1. This result remains the closest by a runs margin in Test cricket.

## AUSTRALIA

| | | | | | |
|---|---|---|---|---|---|
| V.T. Trumper | c Lilley b Rhodes | 104 | c Braund b Lockwood | | 4 |
| R.A. Duff | c Lilley b Lockwood | 54 | b Lockwood | | 3 |
| C. Hill | c Rhodes b Lockwood | 65 | b Lockwood | | 0 |
| M.A. Noble | c and b Rhodes | 2 | (6) c Lilley b Lockwood | | 4 |
| S.E. Gregory | c Lilley b Rhodes | 3 | lbw b Tate | | 24 |
| J. Darling* | c MacLaren b Rhodes | 51 | (4) c Palairet b Rhodes | | 37 |
| A.J.Y. Hopkins | c Palairet b Lockwood | 0 | c Tate b Lockwood | | 2 |
| W.W. Armstrong | b Lockwood | 5 | b Rhodes | | 3 |
| J.J. Kelly† | not out | 4 | not out | | 2 |
| H. Trumble | c Tate b Lockwood | 0 | lbw b Tate | | 4 |
| J.V. Saunders | b Lockwood | 3 | c Tyldesley b Rhodes | | 0 |
| Extras | (B 5, LB 2, W 1) | 8 | (B 1, LB 1, NB .) | | 3 |
| **Total** | | **299** | | | **86** |

## ENGLAND

| | | | | | |
|---|---|---|---|---|---|
| L.C.H. Palairet | c Noble b Saunders | 6 | b Saunders | | 17 |
| R. Abel | c Armstrong b Saunders | 6 | (5) b Trumble | | 21 |
| J.T. Tyldesley | c Hopkins b Saunders | 22 | c Armstrong b Saunders | | 16 |
| A.C. MacLaren* | b Trumble | 1 | (2) c Duff b Trumble | | 35 |
| K.S. Ranjitsinhji | lbw b Trumble | 2 | (4) lbw b Trumble | | 4 |
| Hon. F.S. Jackson | c Duff b Trumble | 128 | c Gregory b Saunders | | 7 |
| L.C. Braund | b Noble | 65 | st Kelly b Trumble | | 3 |
| A.F.A. Lilley† | b Noble | 7 | c Hill b Trumble | | 4 |
| W.H. Lockwood | run out | 7 | b Trumble | | 0 |
| W. Rhodes | c and b Trumble | 5 | not out | | 4 |
| F.W. Tate | not out | 5 | b Saunders | | 4 |
| Extras | (B 6, LB 2) | 8 | (B 5) | | 5 |
| **Total** | | **262** | | | **120** |

| ENGLAND | O | M | R | W | O | M | R | W |
|---|---|---|---|---|---|---|---|---|
| Rhodes | 25 | 3 | 104 | 4 | 14·4 | 5 | 26 | 3 |
| Jackson | 11 | 0 | 58 | 0 | | | | |
| Tate | 11 | 1 | 44 | 0 | 5 | 3 | 7 | 2 |
| Braund | 9 | 0 | 37 | 0 | 11 | 3 | 22 | 0 |
| Lockwood | 20·1 | 5 | 48 | 6 | 17 | 5 | 28 | 5 |
| **AUSTRALIA** | | | | | | | | |
| Trumble | 43 | 16 | 75 | 4 | 25 | 9 | 53 | 6 |
| Saunders | 34 | 5 | 104 | 3 | 19·4 | 4 | 52 | 4 |
| Noble | 24 | 8 | 47 | 2 | 5 | 3 | 10 | 0 |
| Trumper | 6 | 4 | 6 | 0 | | | | |
| Armstrong | 5 | 2 | 19 | 0 | | | | |
| Hopkins | 2 | 0 | 3 | 0 | | | | |

### FALL OF WICKETS

| | A | E | A | E |
|---|---|---|---|---|
| Wkt | 1st | 1st | 2nd | 2nd |
| 1st | 135 | 12 | 7 | 44 |
| 2nd | 175 | 13 | 9 | 68 |
| 3rd | 179 | 14 | 10 | 72 |
| 4th | 183 | 30 | 64 | 92 |
| 5th | 256 | 44 | 74 | 97 |
| 6th | 256 | 185 | 76 | 107 |
| 7th | 288 | 203 | 77 | 109 |
| 8th | 292 | 214 | 79 | 109 |
| 9th | 292 | 235 | 85 | 116 |
| 10th | 299 | 262 | 86 | 120 |

Umpires: J. Moss and T. Mycroft.

# ENGLAND v AUSTRALIA 1902 (5th Test)

Played at Kennington Oval, London, on 11, 12, 13 August.
Toss: Australia.    Result: ENGLAND won by one wicket.
Debuts: Nil.

G.L. Jessop hit fifty in 43 minutes and went on to record the fastest century in Test cricket in 85 minutes. There has been only one faster Test hundred since – J.M. Gregory reaching his in just 70 minutes in 1921–22 (*Test No. 146*). Trumble became the first Australian to score a fifty and take ten wickets in the same Test. This was the first of five one-wicket victories in Test cricket and the only one in England.

## AUSTRALIA

| | | | | |
|---|---|---|---|---|
| V.T. Trumper | b Hirst | 42 | run out | 2 |
| R.A. Duff | c Lilley b Hirst | 23 | b Lockwood | 6 |
| C. Hill | b Hirst | 11 | c MacLaren b Hirst | 34 |
| J. Darling* | c Lilley b Hirst | 3 | c MacLaren b Lockwood | 15 |
| M.A. Noble | c and b Jackson | 52 | b Braund | 13 |
| S.E. Gregory | b Hirst | 23 | b Braund | 9 |
| W.W. Armstrong | b Jackson | 17 | b Lockwood | 21 |
| A.J.Y. Hopkins | c MacLaren b Lockwood | 40 | c Lilley b Lockwood | 3 |
| H. Trumble | not out | 64 | (10) not out | 7 |
| J.J. Kelly† | c Rhodes b Braund | 39 | (11) lbw b Lockwood | 0 |
| J.V. Saunders | lbw b Braund | 0 | (9) c Tyldesley b Rhodes | 2 |
| Extras | (B 5, LB 3, NB 2) | 10 | (B 7, LB 2) | 9 |
| **Total** | | **324** | | **121** |

## ENGLAND

| | | | | |
|---|---|---|---|---|
| A.C. MacLaren* | c Armstrong b Trumble | 10 | b Saunders | 2 |
| L.C.H. Palairet | b Trumble | 20 | b Saunders | 6 |
| J.T. Tyldesley | b Trumble | 33 | b Saunders | 0 |
| T.W. Hayward | b Trumble | 0 | c Kelly b Saunders | 7 |
| Hon. F.S. Jackson | c Armstrong b Saunders | 2 | c and b Trumble | 49 |
| L.C. Braund | c Hill b Trumble | 22 | c Kelly b Trumble | 2 |
| G.L. Jessop | b Trumble | 13 | c Noble b Armstrong | 104 |
| G.H. Hirst | c and b Trumble | 43 | not out | 58 |
| W.H. Lockwood | c Noble b Saunders | 25 | lbw b Trumble | 2 |
| A.F.A. Lilley† | c Trumper b Trumble | 0 | c Darling b Trumble | 16 |
| W. Rhodes | not out | 0 | not out | 6 |
| Extras | (B 13, LB 2) | 15 | (B 5, LB 6) | 11 |
| **Total** | | **183** | (9 wickets) | **263** |

| ENGLAND | O | M | R | W | O | M | R | W | FALL OF WICKETS | | | | |
|---|---|---|---|---|---|---|---|---|---|---|---|---|---|
| Lockwood | 24 | 2 | 85 | 1 | 20 | 6 | 45 | 5 | | A | E | A | E |
| Rhodes | 28 | 9 | 46 | 0 | 22 | 7 | 38 | 1 | *Wkt* | *1st* | *1st* | *2nd* | *2nd* |
| Hirst | 29 | 5 | 77 | 5 | 5 | 1 | 7 | 1 | 1st | 47 | 31 | 6 | 5 |
| Braund | 16·5 | 5 | 29 | 2 | 9 | 1 | 15 | 2 | 2nd | 63 | 36 | 9 | 5 |
| Jackson | 20 | 4 | 66 | 2 | 4 | 3 | 7 | 0 | 3rd | 69 | 67 | 31 | 10 |
| Jessop | 6 | 2 | 11 | 0 | | | | | 4th | 82 | 67 | 71 | 31 |
| | | | | | | | | | 5th | 126 | 67 | 75 | 48 |
| AUSTRALIA | | | | | | | | | 6th | 174 | 83 | 91 | 157 |
| Trumble | 31 | 13 | 65 | 8 | 33·5 | 4 | 108 | 4 | 7th | 175 | 137 | 99 | 187 |
| Saunders | 23 | 7 | 79 | 2 | 24 | 3 | 105 | 4 | 8th | 256 | 179 | 114 | 214 |
| Noble | 7 | 3 | 24 | 0 | 5 | 0 | 11 | 0 | 9th | 324 | 183 | 115 | 248 |
| Armstrong | | | | | 4 | 0 | 28 | 1 | 10th | 324 | 183 | 121 | – |

Umpires: C.E. Richardson and A.A. White.

# SOUTH AFRICA v AUSTRALIA 1902–03 (1st Test)

Played at Old Wanderers, Johannesburg, on 11, 13, 14 October.
Toss: South Africa.   Result: MATCH DRAWN.
Debuts: South Africa – C.M.H. Hathorn, A.W. Nourse, C.J.E. Smith, H.M. Taberer, L.J. Tancred,
   P.G. Thornton. *Arthur William Nourse was known as 'Dave' and he is usually incorrectly shown as
   'A.D. Nourse, sr' to differentiate him from his son, Arthur Dudley.*

The 1902 Australians sailed home via the Cape and this match was played almost immediately after their arrival –
on matting at an altitude of nearly 6,000 feet. Taberer emulated C.A. Smith of England (*Test No. 31*) by
captaining his country in his only Test.

## SOUTH AFRICA

| | | | | | |
|---|---|---|---|---|---|
| W.A. Shalders | c and b Jones | 19 | c Kelly b Jones | | 0 |
| L.J. Tancred | c Duff b Trumper | 97 | b Armstrong | | 24 |
| C.B. Llewellyn | b Trumper | 90 | (6) not out | | 4 |
| J.H. Sinclair | c and b Hopkins | 44 | b Armstrong | | 19 |
| C.M.H. Hathorn | c Gregory b Jones | 45 | (3) c Armstrong b Noble | | 31 |
| C.J.E. Smith | b Hopkins | 13 | (5) not out | | 16 |
| H.M. Taberer* | b Hopkins | 2 | | | |
| A.W. Nourse | c Hopkins b Noble | 72 | | | |
| E.A. Halliwell† | c Darling b Jones | 57 | | | |
| P.G. Thornton | not out | 1 | | | |
| G.A. Rowe | c Jones b Noble | 4 | | | |
| Extras | (B 5, LB 4, NB 1) | 10 | (B 4, LB 3) | | 7 |
| **Total** | | **454** | (4 wickets) | | **101** |

## AUSTRALIA

| | | | | | |
|---|---|---|---|---|---|
| V.T. Trumper | c Rowe b Llewellyn | 63 | b Taberer | | 37 |
| W.W. Armstrong | b Sinclair | 11 | (4) c Halliwell b Thornton | | 59 |
| C. Hill | c Nourse b Sinclair | 76 | c and b Sinclair | | 142 |
| R.A. Duff | not out | 82 | (2) c Halliwell b Rowe | | 15 |
| M.A. Noble | b Sinclair | 1 | (6) not out | | 53 |
| J. Darling* | st Halliwell b Sinclair | 0 | (5) b Llewellyn | | 14 |
| S.E. Gregory | lbw b Llewellyn | 0 | b Llewellyn | | 4 |
| A.J.Y. Hopkins | c Tancred b Llewellyn | 1 | lbw b Llewellyn | | 30 |
| H. Trumble | c Thornton b Llewellyn | 13 | not out | | 0 |
| J.J. Kelly† | c Halliwell b Llewellyn | 25 | | | |
| E. Jones | c Sinclair b Llewellyn | 0 | | | |
| Extras | (B 22, LB 2) | 24 | (B 13, LB 5) | | 18 |
| **Total** | | **296** | (7 wickets declared) | | **372** |

| AUSTRALIA | O | M | R | W | O | M | R | W |
|---|---|---|---|---|---|---|---|---|
| Jones | 21 | 5 | 78 | 3 | 7 | 3 | 22 | 1 |
| Armstrong | 13 | 3 | 88 | 0 | 7 | 2 | 24 | 2 |
| Trumble | 23 | 1 | 103 | 0 | 11 | 3 | 24 | 0 |
| Trumper | 12 | 0 | 62 | 2 | | | | |
| Hopkins | 12 | 1 | 59 | 3 | 2 | 0 | 17 | 0 |
| Noble | 14 | 2 | 54 | 2 | 5 | 1 | 7 | 1 |
| SOUTH AFRICA | | | | | | | | |
| Rowe | 5 | 1 | 28 | 0 | 11 | 1 | 55 | 1 |
| Taberer | 4 | 1 | 23 | 0 | 6 | 1 | 25 | 1 |
| Llewellyn | 22 | 3 | 92 | 6 | 26 | 3 | 124 | 3 |
| Sinclair | 20 | 1 | 129 | 4 | 23 | 2 | 115 | 1 |
| Nourse | | | | | 8 | 2 | 15 | 0 |
| Thornton | | | | | 4 | 0 | 20 | 1 |

| | FALL OF WICKETS | | | |
|---|---|---|---|---|
| | SA | A | A | SA |
| Wkt | 1st | 1st | 2nd | 2nd |
| 1st | 31 | 60 | 42 | 5 |
| 2nd | 204 | 106 | 67 | 44 |
| 3rd | 223 | 195 | 231 | 74 |
| 4th | 296 | 196 | 277 | 90 |
| 5th | 304 | 196 | 281 | – |
| 6th | 306 | 199 | 297 | – |
| 7th | 325 | 217 | 354 | – |
| 8th | 449 | 242 | – | – |
| 9th | 449 | 296 | – | – |
| 10th | 454 | 296 | – | – |

Umpires: F. Hearne and A. Soames.

# SOUTH AFRICA v AUSTRALIA 1902–03 (2nd Test)

Played at Old Wanderers, Johannesburg, on 18, 20, 21 October.
Toss: Australia.   Result: AUSTRALIA won by 159 runs.
Debuts: South Africa – J.H. Anderson, J.J. Kotze.

W.W. Armstrong became the second Australian after J.E. Barrett (*Test No. 33*) to carry his bat through a completed innings and the only one to do so against South Africa. Anderson emulated H.M. Taberer (*Test No. 75*) by captaining South Africa in his only Test.

## AUSTRALIA

| | | | | |
|---|---|---|---|---|
| V.T. Trumper | b Kotze | 18 | (3) c Shalders b Sinclair | 13 |
| R.A. Duff | b Middleton | 43 | (4) b Sinclair | 44 |
| C. Hill | st Halliwell b Kotze | 6 | (8) c Kotze b Llewellyn | 12 |
| W.W. Armstrong | run out | 49 | (1) not out | 159 |
| M.A. Noble | c Kotze b Llewellyn | 5 | lbw b Llewellyn | 24 |
| J. Darling* | c Anderson b Llewellyn | 6 | b Llewellyn | 4 |
| S.E. Gregory | b Kotze | 1 | (2) c Llewellyn b Kotze | 13 |
| A.J.Y. Hopkins | c Nourse b Llewellyn | 20 | (9) c Llewellyn b Nourse | 8 |
| J.J. Kelly† | c Halliwell b Llewellyn | 16 | (10) c Hathorn b Llewellyn | 9 |
| W.P. Howell | c Nourse b Llewellyn | 0 | (11) b Llewellyn | 9 |
| J.V. Saunders | not out | 0 | (7) b Sinclair | 1 |
| Extras | (B 10, W 1) | 11 | (B 8, LB 5) | 13 |
| **Total** | | **175** | | **309** |

## SOUTH AFRICA

| | | | | |
|---|---|---|---|---|
| L.J. Tancred | lbw b Noble | 19 | c Kelly b Howell | 29 |
| W.A. Shalders | b Howell | 42 | (3) b Saunders | 3 |
| C.M.H. Hathorn | c Armstrong b Noble | 12 | (2) b Saunders | 1 |
| J.H. Sinclair | b Howell | 101 | b Howell | 18 |
| C.J.E. Smith | c Kelly b Trumper | 12 | (6) b Howell | 4 |
| C.B. Llewellyn | c and b Trumper | 10 | (5) b Saunders | 0 |
| A.W. Nourse | c and b Trumper | 5 | (8) not out | 18 |
| E.A. Halliwell† | c Kelly b Noble | 4 | (9) b Saunders | 0 |
| J.H. Anderson* | c Howell b Saunders | 32 | (7) c Darling b Saunders | 11 |
| J.J. Kotze | b Saunders | 0 | (11) st Kelly b Saunders | 0 |
| J. Middleton | not out | 0 | (10) b Saunders | 0 |
| Extras | (B 3) | 3 | (LB 1) | 1 |
| **Total** | | **240** | | **85** |

| SOUTH AFRICA | O | M | R | W | O | M | R | W | | FALL OF WICKETS | | | |
|---|---|---|---|---|---|---|---|---|---|---|---|---|---|
| Kotze | 20 | 2 | 64 | 3 | 17 | 2 | 71 | 1 | | A | SA | A | SA |
| Middleton | 13 | 3 | 27 | 1 | 4 | 0 | 15 | 0 | *Wkt* | *1st* | *1st* | *2nd* | *2nd* |
| Llewellyn | 18·1 | 3 | 43 | 5 | 31·4 | 9 | 73 | 5 | 1st | 29 | 58 | 40 | 4 |
| Sinclair | 4 | 0 | 30 | 0 | 26 | 0 | 118 | 3 | 2nd | 35 | 66 | 87 | 26 |
| Nourse | | | | | 3 | 0 | 19 | 1 | 3rd | 125 | 91 | 143 | 46 |
| | | | | | | | | | 4th | 125 | 136 | 180 | 51 |
| AUSTRALIA | | | | | | | | | 5th | 138 | 154 | 188 | 51 |
| Trumper | 12 | 1 | 60 | 3 | 3 | 0 | 27 | 0 | 6th | 138 | 170 | 201 | 66 |
| Saunders | 9 | 1 | 32 | 2 | 11 | 2 | 34 | 7 | 7th | 140 | 179 | 238 | 66 |
| Howell | 13 | 1 | 52 | 2 | 8 | 3 | 23 | 3 | 8th | 172 | 231 | 263 | 77 |
| Noble | 15 | 2 | 75 | 3 | | | | | 9th | 172 | 240 | 290 | 77 |
| Armstrong | 2 | 0 | 16 | 0 | | | | | 10th | 175 | 240 | 309 | 85 |
| Hopkins | 2 | 1 | 2 | 0 | | | | | | | | | |

Umpires: F. Hearne and F.E. Smith.

# SOUTH AFRICA v AUSTRALIA 1902–03 (3rd Test)

Played at Newlands, Cape Town, on 8, 10, 11 November.
Toss: Australia.    Result: AUSTRALIA won by ten wickets.
Debuts: South Africa – P.S.T. Jones (P.S. Twentyman-Jones).

J.H. Sinclair scored his century in only 80 minutes – still the fastest for South Africa and the fourth-fastest in all Tests; it included six sixes. He scored South Africa's first three hundreds; not until South Africa's 14th match (*Test No. 90*) did another batsman score a century. Howell took three wickets in four balls.

### AUSTRALIA

| | | | | |
|---|---|---|---|---|
| R.A. Duff | c Tancred b Kotze | 34 | not out | 20 |
| V.T. Trumper | b Llewellyn | 70 | not out | 38 |
| C. Hill | not out | 91 | | |
| W.W. Armstrong | b Llewellyn | 3 | | |
| M.A. Noble | c Smith b Sinclair | 9 | | |
| A.J.Y. Hopkins | b Llewellyn | 16 | | |
| S.E. Gregory | c Smith b Llewellyn | 11 | | |
| J. Darling* | b Llewellyn | 1 | | |
| J.J. Kelly† | b Kotze | 1 | | |
| W.P. Howell | b Llewellyn | 2 | | |
| J.V. Saunders | run out | 4 | | |
| Extras | (B 6, LB 4) | 10 | (NB 1) | 1 |
| **Total** | | **252** | (0 wickets) | **59** |

### SOUTH AFRICA

| | | | | |
|---|---|---|---|---|
| L.J. Tancred | b Howell | 0 | c and b Howell | 2 |
| W.A. Shalders | c Darling b Saunders | 11 | c Darling b Hopkins | 40 |
| C.J.E. Smith | b Saunders | 16 | c and b Trumper | 45 |
| J.H. Sinclair | b Howell | 0 | st Kelly b Saunders | 104 |
| P.S.T. Jones | b Howell | 0 | b Hopkins | 0 |
| C.B. Llewellyn | b Howell | 1 | st Kelly b Howell | 8 |
| C.M.H. Hathorn | run out | 19 | st Kelly b Saunders | 18 |
| A.W. Nourse | b Saunders | 15 | b Howell | 5 |
| E.A. Halliwell*† | run out | 13 | b Howell | 1 |
| J.J. Kotze | b Saunders | 2 | b Howell | 0 |
| J. Middleton | not out | 1 | not out | 0 |
| Extras | (B 4, LB 3) | 7 | (LB 1, NB 1) | 2 |
| **Total** | | **85** | | **225** |

| SOUTH AFRICA | O | M | R | W | O | M | R | W |
|---|---|---|---|---|---|---|---|---|
| Llewellyn | 30·5 | 4 | 97 | 6 | 4 | 1 | 19 | 0 |
| Kotze | 17 | 1 | 49 | 2 | 2·5 | 1 | 16 | 0 |
| Sinclair | 12 | 0 | 55 | 1 | 2 | 0 | 22 | 0 |
| Middleton | 8 | 1 | 28 | 0 | 1 | 0 | 1 | 0 |
| Nourse | 3 | 0 | 13 | 0 | | | | |
| AUSTRALIA | | | | | | | | |
| Howell | 17 | 6 | 18 | 4 | 26 | 6 | 81 | 5 |
| Saunders | 12·2 | 2 | 37 | 4 | 17·1 | 3 | 73 | 2 |
| Noble | 4 | 0 | 23 | 0 | 6 | 3 | 6 | 0 |
| Trumper | | | | | 6 | 1 | 26 | 1 |
| Hopkins | | | | | 8 | 0 | 37 | 2 |

| | FALL OF WICKETS | | | |
|---|---|---|---|---|
| | A | SA | SA | A |
| Wkt | 1st | 1st | 2nd | 2nd |
| 1st | 100 | 12 | 2 | – |
| 2nd | 121 | 12 | 81 | – |
| 3rd | 129 | 12 | 115 | – |
| 4th | 142 | 12 | 115 | – |
| 5th | 179 | 14 | 134 | – |
| 6th | 223 | 36 | 216 | – |
| 7th | 226 | 60 | 221 | – |
| 8th | 227 | 79 | 225 | – |
| 9th | 230 | 83 | 225 | – |
| 10th | 252 | 85 | 225 | – |

Umpires: F. Hearne and W.H. Creese.

# AUSTRALIA v ENGLAND 1903–04 (1st Test)

Played at Sydney Cricket Ground on 11, 12, 14, 15, 16, 17 December.
Toss: Australia.   Result: ENGLAND won by five wickets.
Debuts: England – E.G. Arnold, B.J.T. Bosanquet, R.E. Foster, A.E. Relf.

This was the first touring team to be selected and managed by the M.C.C.   R.E. Foster's 287 was the highest score in Test cricket until A. Sandham scored 325 in 1929-30 (*Test No. 193*) and remains the highest by any player in his first Test, and the highest for England in Australia. He was the first batsman to share in three century partnerships in the same Test innings and his tenth-wicket stand of 130 with W. Rhodes remains the record for either country in this series. Arnold took Trumper's wicket with his first ball.

## AUSTRALIA

| | | | | |
|---|---|--:|---|--:|
| R.A. Duff | c Lilley b Arnold | 3 | (3) c Relf b Rhodes | 84 |
| V.T. Trumper | c Foster b Arnold | 1 | (5) not out | 185 |
| C. Hill | c Lilley b Hirst | 5 | (4) run out | 51 |
| M.A. Noble* | c Foster b Arnold | 133 | (6) st Lilley b Bosanquet | 22 |
| W.W. Armstrong | b Bosanquet | 48 | (7) c Bosanquet b Rhodes | 27 |
| A.J.Y. Hopkins | b Hirst | 39 | (8) c Arnold b Rhodes | 20 |
| W.P. Howell | c Relf b Arnold | 5 | (10) c Lilley b Arnold | 4 |
| S.E. Gregory | b Bosanquet | 23 | (1) c Lilley b Rhodes | 43 |
| F. Laver | lbw b Rhodes | 4 | c Relf b Rhodes | 6 |
| J.J. Kelly† | c Braund b Rhodes | 10 | (2) b Arnold | 13 |
| J.V. Saunders | not out | 11 | run out | 2 |
| Extras | (NB 3) | 3 | (B 10, LB 15, W 2, NB 1) | 28 |
| **Total** | | **285** | | **485** |

## ENGLAND

| | | | | |
|---|---|--:|---|--:|
| T.W. Hayward | b Howell | 15 | st Kelly b Saunders | 91 |
| P.F. Warner* | c Kelly b Laver | 0 | b Howell | 8 |
| J.T. Tyldesley | b Noble | 53 | c Noble b Saunders | 9 |
| E.G. Arnold | c Laver b Armstrong | 27 | | |
| R.E. Foster | c Noble b Saunders | 287 | (4) st Kelly b Armstrong | 19 |
| L.C. Braund | b Howell | 102 | (5) c Noble b Howell | 0 |
| G.H. Hirst | b Howell | 0 | (6) not out | 60 |
| B.J.T. Bosanquet | c Howell b Noble | 2 | (7) not out | 1 |
| A.F.A. Lilley† | c Hill b Noble | 4 | | |
| A.E. Relf | c Armstrong b Saunders | 31 | | |
| W. Rhodes | not out | 40 | | |
| Extras | (B 6, LB 7, W 1, NB 2) | 16 | (B 3, LB 1, W 2) | 6 |
| **Total** | | **577** | (5 wickets) | **194** |

| ENGLAND | O | M | R | W | O | M | R | W | | FALL OF WICKETS | | | |
|---|--:|--:|--:|--:|--:|--:|--:|--:|---|---|---|---|---|
| Hirst | 24 | 8 | 47 | 2 | 29 | 1 | 79 | 0 | | A | E | A | E |
| Arnold | 32 | 7 | 76 | 4 | 28 | 2 | 93 | 2 | *Wkt* | *1st* | *1st* | *2nd* | *2nd* |
| Braund | 26 | 9 | 39 | 0 | 12 | 2 | 56 | 0 | 1st | 2 | 0 | 36 | 21 |
| Bosanquet | 13 | 0 | 52 | 2 | 23 | 1 | 100 | 1 | 2nd | 9 | 49 | 108 | 39 |
| Rhodes | 17·2 | 3 | 41 | 2 | 40·2 | 10 | 94 | 5 | 3rd | 12 | 73 | 191 | 81 |
| Relf | 6 | 1 | 27 | 0 | 13 | 5 | 35 | 0 | 4th | 118 | 117 | 254 | 82 |
| | | | | | | | | | 5th | 200 | 309 | 334 | 181 |
| AUSTRALIA | | | | | | | | | 6th | 207 | 311 | 393 | – |
| Saunders | 36·2 | 8 | 125 | 2 | 18·5 | 3 | 51 | 2 | 7th | 259 | 318 | 441 | – |
| Laver | 37 | 12 | 119 | 1 | 16 | 4 | 37 | 0 | 8th | 263 | 332 | 468 | – |
| Howell | 31 | 7 | 111 | 3 | 31 | 18 | 35 | 2 | 9th | 271 | 447 | 473 | – |
| Noble | 34 | 8 | 99 | 3 | 12 | 2 | 37 | 0 | 10th | 285 | 577 | 485 | – |
| Armstrong | 23 | 3 | 47 | 1 | 18 | 6 | 28 | 1 | | | | | |
| Hopkins | 11 | 1 | 40 | 0 | | | | | | | | | |
| Trumper | 7 | 2 | 12 | 0 | | | | | | | | | |
| Gregory | 2 | 0 | 8 | 0 | | | | | | | | | |

Umpires: R.W. Crockett and A.C. Jones.

# AUSTRALIA v ENGLAND 1903–04 (2nd Test)

Played at Melbourne Cricket Ground on 1, 2, 4, 5 January.
Toss: England.   Result: ENGLAND won by 185 runs.
Debuts: England – A. Fielder, A.E. Knight.

W. Rhodes set an England record against Australia by taking 15 wickets in the match – despite having eight catches dropped! His record stood until 1934 when H. Verity slightly improved the figures with 15-104 (*Test No. 234*). Rhodes' match analysis of 15 for 124 remains the best in any Melbourne Test.

## ENGLAND

| | | | | | |
|---|---|--:|---|---|--:|
| P.F. Warner* | c Duff b Trumble | 68 | c Trumper b Saunders | | 3 |
| T.W. Hayward | c Gregory b Hopkins | 58 | c Trumper b Trumble | | 0 |
| J.T. Tyldesley | c Trumble b Howell | 97 | c Trumble b Howell | | 62 |
| R.E. Foster | retired ill | 49 | absent ill | | – |
| L.C. Braund | c Howell b Trumble | 20 | (4) b Saunders | | 3 |
| A.E. Knight | b Howell | 2 | (7) lbw b Trumble | | 0 |
| G.H. Hirst | c Noble b Howell | 7 | (5) c Gregory b Howell | | 4 |
| W. Rhodes | lbw b Trumble | 2 | (6) lbw b Trumble | | 9 |
| A.F.A. Lilley† | c Howell b Trumble | 4 | (8) st Kelly b Trumble | | 0 |
| A.E. Relf | not out | 3 | (9) not out | | 10 |
| A. Fielder | b Howell | 1 | (10) c Hill b Trumble | | 4 |
| Extras | (LB 3, W 1) | 4 | (B 7, LB 1) | | 8 |
| **Total** | | **315** | | | **103** |

## AUSTRALIA

| | | | | | |
|---|---|--:|---|---|--:|
| V.T. Trumper | c Tyldesley b Rhodes | 74 | c Relf b Rhodes | | 35 |
| R.A. Duff | st Lilley b Rhodes | 10 | c Braund b Rhodes | | 8 |
| C. Hill | c Rhodes b Hirst | 5 | c Relf b Rhodes | | 20 |
| M.A. Noble* | c sub (H. Strudwick) b Rhodes | 0 | not out | | 31 |
| S.E. Gregory | c Hirst b Rhodes | 1 | c Rhodes b Hirst | | 0 |
| A.J.Y. Hopkins | c sub (H. Strudwick) b Relf | 18 | c and b Rhodes | | 7 |
| H. Trumble | c sub (H. Strudwick) b Rhodes | 2 | c Braund b Rhodes | | 0 |
| W.W. Armstrong | c Braund b Rhodes | 1 | c Hayward b Rhodes | | 0 |
| J.J. Kelly† | run out | 8 | c Lilley b Rhodes | | 7 |
| W.P. Howell | c Fielder b Rhodes | 0 | c Hirst b Rhodes | | 3 |
| J.V. Saunders | not out | 2 | c Fielder b Hirst | | 0 |
| Extras | (LB 1) | 1 | | | |
| **Total** | | **122** | | | **111** |

| AUSTRALIA | O | M | R | W | O | M | R | W |
|---|--:|--:|--:|--:|--:|--:|--:|--:|
| Trumble | 50 | 10 | 107 | 4 | 10·5 | 2 | 34 | 5 |
| Noble | 6 | 3 | 4 | 0 | | | | |
| Saunders | 16 | 3 | 60 | 0 | 8 | 0 | 33 | 2 |
| Howell | 34·5 | 14 | 43 | 4 | 8 | 3 | 25 | 2 |
| Armstrong | 25 | 6 | 43 | 0 | | | | |
| Hopkins | 20 | 2 | 50 | 1 | 2 | 1 | 3 | 0 |
| Trumper | 1 | 0 | 4 | 0 | | | | |
| **ENGLAND** | | | | | | | | |
| Rhodes | 15·2 | 3 | 56 | 7 | 15 | 0 | 68 | 8 |
| Hirst | 8 | 1 | 33 | 1 | 14·4 | 4 | 38 | 2 |
| Relf | 2 | 0 | 12 | 1 | 1 | 0 | 5 | 0 |
| Braund | 5 | 0 | 20 | 0 | | | | |

### FALL OF WICKETS

| Wkt | E 1st | A 1st | E 2nd | A 2nd |
|---|--:|--:|--:|--:|
| 1st | 122 | 14 | 5 | 14 |
| 2nd | 132 | 23 | 7 | 59 |
| 3rd | 277 | 23 | 27 | 73 |
| 4th | 279 | 33 | 40 | 77 |
| 5th | 297 | 67 | 74 | 86 |
| 6th | 306 | 73 | 74 | 90 |
| 7th | 306 | 97 | 74 | 90 |
| 8th | 314 | 105 | 90 | 102 |
| 9th | 315 | 116 | 103 | 105 |
| 10th | – | 122 | – | 111 |

Umpires: R.W. Crockett and P. Argall.

# AUSTRALIA v ENGLAND 1903–04 (3rd Test)

Played at Adelaide Oval on 15, 16, 18, 19, 20 January.
Toss: Australia.   Result: AUSTRALIA won by 216 runs.
Debuts: Nil.

V.T. Trumper was the first to score four Test hundreds against England. It was the fourth successive Test innings in which he had made top score. S.E. Gregory equalled Trumper's record in the second innings with his own fourth hundred which took 115 minutes.

## AUSTRALIA

| | | | | | |
|---|---|---|---|---|---|
| V.T. Trumper | b Hirst | 113 | lbw b Rhodes | | 59 |
| R.A. Duff | b Hirst | 79 | c Braund b Hirst | | 14 |
| C. Hill | c Lilley b Arnold | 88 | b Fielder | | 16 |
| M.A. Noble* | st Lilley b Arnold | 59 | c Bosanquet b Braund | | 65 |
| S.E. Gregory | c Tyldesley b Arnold | 8 | c Rhodes b Braund | | 112 |
| A.J.Y. Hopkins | b Bosanquet | 0 | (7) run out | | 7 |
| W.W. Armstrong | lbw b Rhodes | 10 | (6) c Hirst b Bosanquet | | 39 |
| H. Trumble | b Bosanquet | 4 | c and b Bosanquet | | 9 |
| C.E. McLeod | run out | 8 | b Bosanquet | | 2 |
| J.J. Kelly† | lbw b Bosanquet | 1 | st Lilley b Bosanquet | | 13 |
| W.P. Howell | not out | 3 | not out | | 1 |
| Extras | (B 7, LB 5, W 3) | 15 | (B 8, LB 2, W 3, NB 1) | | 14 |
| **Total** | | **388** | | | **351** |

## ENGLAND

| | | | | | |
|---|---|---|---|---|---|
| P.F. Warner* | c McLeod b Trumble | 48 | c and b Trumble | | 79 |
| T.W. Hayward | b Howell | 20 | lbw b Hopkins | | 67 |
| J.T. Tyldesley | c Kelly b Hopkins | 0 | (4) c Noble b Hopkins | | 10 |
| R.E. Foster | c Howell b Noble | 21 | (5) b McLeod | | 16 |
| L.C. Braund | c Duff b Hopkins | 13 | (6) b Howell | | 25 |
| G.H. Hirst | c Trumper b Trumble | 58 | (7) b Trumble | | 44 |
| B.J.T. Bosanquet | c Duff b Hopkins | 10 | (9) c Trumper b Hopkins | | 10 |
| W. Rhodes | c Armstrong b McLeod | 9 | (10) run out | | 8 |
| E.G. Arnold | not out | 23 | (3) b Hopkins | | 1 |
| A.F.A. Lilley† | run out | 28 | (8) c and b Howell | | 0 |
| A. Fielder | b Trumble | 6 | not out | | 14 |
| Extras | (B 4, LB 1, W 4) | 9 | (LB 2, W 2) | | 4 |
| **Total** | | **245** | | | **278** |

| ENGLAND | O | M | R | W | O | M | R | W | | FALL OF WICKETS | | | |
|---|---|---|---|---|---|---|---|---|---|---|---|---|---|
| Fielder | 7 | 0 | 33 | 0 | 25 | 11 | 51 | 1 | | A | E | A | E |
| Arnold | 27 | 4 | 93 | 3 | 19 | 3 | 74 | 0 | Wkt | 1st | 1st | 2nd | 2nd |
| Rhodes | 14 | 3 | 45 | 1 | 21 | 4 | 46 | 1 | 1st | 129 | 47 | 48 | 148 |
| Bosanquet | 30·1 | 4 | 95 | 3 | 15·5 | 0 | 73 | 4 | 2nd | 272 | 48 | 81 | 150 |
| Braund | 13 | 1 | 49 | 0 | 21 | 6 | 57 | 2 | 3rd | 296 | 88 | 101 | 160 |
| Hirst | 15 | 1 | 58 | 2 | 13 | 1 | 36 | 1 | 4th | 308 | 99 | 263 | 160 |
| | | | | | | | | | 5th | 310 | 116 | 289 | 195 |
| AUSTRALIA | | | | | | | | | 6th | 343 | 146 | 320 | 231 |
| McLeod | 24 | 6 | 56 | 1 | 25 | 4 | 46 | 1 | 7th | 360 | 173 | 324 | 231 |
| Trumble | 28 | 9 | 49 | 3 | 33 | 8 | 73 | 2 | 8th | 384 | 199 | 326 | 256 |
| Howell | 13 | 4 | 28 | 1 | 20 | 5 | 52 | 2 | 9th | 384 | 234 | 350 | 256 |
| Hopkins | 24 | 5 | 68 | 3 | 28·1 | 9 | 81 | 4 | 10th | 388 | 245 | 351 | 278 |
| Armstrong | 10 | 3 | 25 | 0 | 7 | 2 | 15 | 0 | | | | | |
| Noble | 3 | 0 | 10 | 1 | | | | | | | | | |
| Trumper | | | | | 4 | 0 | 7 | 0 | | | | | |

Umpires: R.W. Crockett and P. Argall.

# AUSTRALIA v ENGLAND 1903–04 (4th Test)

Played at Sydney Cricket Ground on 26, 27, 29 (*no play*) February, 1, 2, 3 March.
Toss: England.   Result: ENGLAND won by 157 runs.
Debuts: Australia – A. Cotter, P.A. McAlister.

Frequent interruptions by rain – there was no play at all on the third day and the fourth day's start was delayed until 4 p.m. – extended this comparatively low-scoring game into the sixth morning.

## ENGLAND

| | | | | |
|---|---|---:|---|---:|
| P.F. Warner* | b Noble | 0 | (9) not out | 31 |
| T.W. Hayward | c McAlister b Trumble | 18 | lbw b Trumble | 52 |
| J.T. Tyldesley | c Gregory b Noble | 16 | (4) b Cotter | 5 |
| R.E. Foster | c McAlister b Noble | 19 | (1) c Noble b Hopkins | 27 |
| A.E. Knight | not out | 70 | c McAlister b Cotter | 9 |
| L.C. Braund | c Trumble b Noble | 39 | c McLeod b Hopkins | 19 |
| G.H. Hirst | b Noble | 25 | c Kelly b McLeod | 18 |
| B.J.T. Bosanquet | b Hopkins | 12 | c Hill b McLeod | 7 |
| E.G. Arnold | lbw b Noble | 0 | (3) c Kelly b Noble | 0 |
| A.F.A. Lilley† | c Hopkins b Trumble | 24 | b McLeod | 6 |
| W. Rhodes | st Kelly b Noble | 10 | c McAlister b Cotter | 29 |
| Extras | (B 6, LB 7, W 2, NB 1) | 16 | (B 1, LB 6) | 7 |
| **Total** | | **249** | | **210** |

## AUSTRALIA

| | | | | |
|---|---|---:|---|---:|
| V.T. Trumper | b Braund | 7 | (4) lbw b Arnold | 12 |
| R.A. Duff | b Arnold | 47 | b Arnold | 19 |
| C. Hill | c Braund b Arnold | 33 | st Lilley b Bosanquet | 26 |
| P.A. McAlister | c Arnold b Rhodes | 2 | (1) b Hirst | 1 |
| A.J.Y. Hopkins | b Braund | 9 | (7) st Lilley b Bosanquet | 0 |
| C.E. McLeod | b Rhodes | 18 | (8) c Lilley b Bosanquet | 6 |
| J.J. Kelly† | c Foster b Arnold | 5 | (10) c Foster b Bosanquet | 10 |
| M.A. Noble* | not out | 6 | (5) not out | 53 |
| S.E. Gregory | c Foster b Rhodes | 2 | (6) lbw b Bosanquet | 0 |
| H. Trumble | c Lilley b Rhodes | 0 | (9) st Lilley b Bosanquet | 0 |
| A. Cotter | c Tyldesley b Arnold | 0 | b Hirst | 34 |
| Extras | (B 1, W 1) | 2 | (B 10) | 10 |
| **Total** | | **131** | | **171** |

| AUSTRALIA | O | M | R | W | O | M | R | W | FALL OF WICKETS | | | | |
|---|---|---|---|---|---|---|---|---|---|---|---|---|---|
| | | | | | | | | | | E | A | E | A |
| Cotter | 14 | 1 | 44 | 0 | 17·3 | 3 | 41 | 3 | Wkt | 1st | 1st | 2nd | 2nd |
| Noble | 41·1 | 10 | 100 | 7 | 19 | 8 | 40 | 1 | 1st | 4 | 28 | 49 | 7 |
| Trumble | 43 | 20 | 58 | 2 | 28 | 10 | 49 | 1 | 2nd | 34 | 61 | 50 | 35 |
| Hopkins | 8 | 3 | 22 | 1 | 14 | 5 | 31 | 2 | 3rd | 42 | 72 | 57 | 59 |
| McLeod | 8 | 5 | 9 | 0 | 20 | 5 | 42 | 3 | 4th | 66 | 97 | 73 | 76 |
| ENGLAND | | | | | | | | | 5th | 155 | 101 | 106 | 76 |
| Hirst | 13 | 1 | 36 | 0 | 12·5 | 2 | 32 | 2 | 6th | 185 | 116 | 120 | 76 |
| Braund | 11 | 2 | 27 | 2 | 16 | 3 | 24 | 0 | 7th | 207 | 124 | 138 | 86 |
| Rhodes | 11 | 3 | 33 | 4 | 11 | 7 | 12 | 0 | 8th | 208 | 126 | 141 | 90 |
| Arnold | 15·3 | 5 | 28 | 4 | 12 | 3 | 42 | 2 | 9th | 237 | 130 | 155 | 114 |
| Bosanquet | 2 | 1 | 5 | 0 | 15 | 1 | 51 | 6 | 10th | 249 | 131 | 210 | 171 |

Umpires: R.W. Crockett and P. Argall.

# AUSTRALIA v ENGLAND 1903–04 (5th Test)

Played at Melbourne Cricket Ground on 5, 7, 8 March.
Toss: Australia.   Result: AUSTRALIA won by 218 runs.
Debuts: Australia – D.R.A. Gehrs.

Rain during the first night of the match delayed the next day's start until 4 p.m. and greatly affected the wicket – the 20-year-old fast bowler, Cotter, being particularly dangerous. Trumble took his second Test hat-trick in his final match, dismissing Bosanquet, Warner and Lilley.

## AUSTRALIA

| | | | | | |
|---|---|---|---|---|---|
| R.A. Duff | b Braund | 9 | (7) c Warner b Rhodes | | 31 |
| V.T. Trumper | c and b Braund | 88 | (5) b Hirst | | 0 |
| C. Hill | c Braund b Rhodes | 16 | (6) c Warner b Hirst | | 16 |
| M.A. Noble* | c Foster b Arnold | 29 | (8) st Lilley b Rhodes | | 19 |
| P.A. McAlister | st Lilley b Braund | 36 | (1) c Foster b Arnold | | 9 |
| D.R.A. Gehrs | c and b Braund | 3 | (10) c and b Hirst | | 5 |
| A.J.Y. Hopkins | c Knight b Braund | 32 | (9) not out | | 25 |
| C.E. McLeod | c Rhodes b Braund | 8 | (2) c Bosanquet b Braund | | 0 |
| H. Trumble | c Foster b Braund | 6 | (11) c Arnold b Hirst | | 0 |
| J.J. Kelly† | not out | 6 | (3) c and b Arnold | | 24 |
| A. Cotter | b Braund | 6 | (4) b Hirst | | 0 |
| Extras | (B 4, LB 4) | 8 | (B 1, LB 3) | | 4 |
| **Total** | | **247** | | | **133** |

## ENGLAND

| | | | | | |
|---|---|---|---|---|---|
| T.W. Hayward | b Noble | 0 | absent ill | | – |
| W. Rhodes | c Gehrs b Cotter | 3 | (8) not out | | 16 |
| E.G. Arnold | c Kelly b Noble | 0 | (10) c Duff b Trumble | | 19 |
| P.F. Warner* | c McAlister b Cotter | 1 | (5) c and b Trumble | | 11 |
| J.T. Tyldesley | c Gehrs b Noble | 10 | (3) c Hopkins b Cotter | | 15 |
| R.E. Foster | b Cotter | 18 | (2) c Trumper b Trumble | | 30 |
| G.H. Hirst | c Trumper b Cotter | 0 | (6) c McAlister b Trumble | | 1 |
| L.C. Braund | c Hopkins b Noble | 5 | (1) c McAlister b Cotter | | 0 |
| A.E. Knight | b Cotter | 0 | (4) c Kelly b Trumble | | 0 |
| B.J.T. Bosanquet | c Noble b Cotter | 16 | (7) c Gehrs b Trumble | | 4 |
| A.F.A. Lilley† | not out | 6 | (9) lbw b Trumble | | 0 |
| Extras | (B 1, NB 1) | 2 | (B 1, LB 4) | | 5 |
| **Total** | | **61** | | | **101** |

| ENGLAND | O | M | R | W | O | M | R | W |
|---|---|---|---|---|---|---|---|---|
| Hirst | 19 | 6 | 44 | 0 | 16·5 | 4 | 48 | 5 |
| Braund | 28·5 | 6 | 81 | 8 | 4 | 1 | 6 | 1 |
| Rhodes | 12 | 1 | 41 | 1 | 15 | 2 | 52 | 2 |
| Arnold | 18 | 4 | 46 | 1 | 8 | 3 | 23 | 2 |
| Bosanquet | 4 | 0 | 27 | 0 | | | | |
| AUSTRALIA | | | | | | | | |
| Noble | 15 | 8 | 19 | 4 | 6 | 2 | 19 | 0 |
| Cotter | 15·2 | 2 | 40 | 6 | 5 | 0 | 25 | 2 |
| McLeod | 1 | 1 | 0 | 0 | 5 | 0 | 24 | 0 |
| Trumble | | | | | 6·5 | 0 | 28 | 7 |

### FALL OF WICKETS

| | A | E | A | E |
|---|---|---|---|---|
| Wkt | 1st | 1st | 2nd | 2nd |
| 1st | 13 | 0 | 9 | 0 |
| 2nd | 67 | 0 | 9 | 24 |
| 3rd | 142 | 4 | 13 | 38 |
| 4th | 144 | 5 | 13 | 47 |
| 5th | 159 | 23 | 43 | 54 |
| 6th | 218 | 26 | 49 | 61 |
| 7th | 221 | 36 | 92 | 61 |
| 8th | 231 | 36 | 115 | 61 |
| 9th | 235 | 48 | 133 | 101 |
| 10th | 247 | 61 | 133 | – |

Umpires: R.W. Crockett and P. Argall.

# ENGLAND v AUSTRALIA 1905 (1st Test)

Played at Trent Bridge, Nottingham, on 29, 30, 31 May.
Toss: England.    Result: ENGLAND won by 213 runs.
Debuts: Nil.

A.C. MacLaren's hundred was the first in Tests at Nottingham and the fifth of his Test career – a record. Trumper retired hurt at 23 for 1. Hill and Noble added 106 for the second wicket. Jackson dismissed Noble, Hill and Darling in one over: WO1WOW.

## ENGLAND

| | | | | |
|---|---|--:|---|--:|
| T.W. Hayward | b Cotter | 5 | c Darling b Armstrong | 47 |
| A.O. Jones | b Laver | 4 | (4) b Duff | 30 |
| J.T. Tyldesley | c Duff b Laver | 56 | c and b Duff | 61 |
| A.C. MacLaren | c Kelly b Laver | 2 | (2) c Duff b Laver | 140 |
| Hon. F.S. Jackson* | b Cotter | 0 | not out | 82 |
| B.J.T. Bosanquet | b Laver | 27 | b Cotter | 6 |
| J. Gunn | b Cotter | 8 | | |
| G.L. Jessop | b Laver | 0 | | |
| A.F.A. Lilley† | c and b Laver | 37 | | |
| W. Rhodes | c Noble b Laver | 29 | (7) not out | 39 |
| E.G. Arnold | not out | 2 | | |
| Extras | (B 21, LB 5) | 26 | (B 11, LB 9, W 1) | 21 |
| **Total** | | **196** | (5 wickets declared) | **426** |

## AUSTRALIA

| | | | | |
|---|---|--:|---|--:|
| R.A. Duff | c Hayward b Gunn | 1 | c and b Bosanquet | 25 |
| V.T. Trumper | retired hurt | 13 | absent hurt | – |
| C. Hill | b Jackson | 54 | (5) c and b Bosanquet | 8 |
| M.A. Noble | c Lilley b Jackson | 50 | (3) st Lilley b Bosanquet | 7 |
| W.W. Armstrong | st Lilley b Rhodes | 27 | (4) c Jackson b Bosanquet | 6 |
| J. Darling* | c Bosanquet b Jackson | 0 | (2) b Bosanquet | 40 |
| A. Cotter | c and b Jessop | 45 | b Rhodes | 18 |
| S.E. Gregory | c Jones b Jackson | 2 | (6) c Arnold b Bosanquet | 51 |
| C.E. McLeod | b Arnold | 4 | lbw b Bosanquet | 13 |
| F. Laver | c Jones b Jackson | 5 | (8) st Lilley b Bosanquet | 5 |
| J.J. Kelly† | not out | 1 | (10) not out | 6 |
| Extras | (B 16, LB 2, W 1) | 19 | (B 4, LB 3, L 2) | 9 |
| **Total** | | **221** | | **188** |

| AUSTRALIA | O | M | R | W | O | M | R | W |
|---|--|--|--|--|--|--|--|--|
| Cotter | 23 | 2 | 64 | 3 | 17 | 1 | 59 | 1 |
| Laver | 31·3 | 14 | 64 | 7 | 34 | 7 | 121 | 1 |
| McLeod | 8 | 2 | 19 | 0 | 28 | 9 | 84 | 0 |
| Armstrong | 6 | 3 | 4 | 0 | 52 | 24 | 67 | 1 |
| Noble | 3 | 0 | 19 | 0 | 7 | 1 | 31 | 0 |
| Duff | | | | | 15 | 2 | 43 | 2 |
| ENGLAND | | | | | | | | |
| Arnold | 11 | 2 | 39 | 1 | 4 | 2 | 7 | 0 |
| Gunn | 6 | 2 | 27 | 1 | | | | |
| Jessop | 7 | 2 | 18 | 1 | 1 | 0 | 1 | 0 |
| Bosanquet | 7 | 0 | 29 | 0 | 32·4 | 2 | 107 | 8 |
| Rhodes | 18 | 6 | 37 | 1 | 30 | 8 | 58 | 1 |
| Jackson | 14·5 | 2 | 52 | 5 | 5 | 3 | 6 | 0 |

### FALL OF WICKETS

| Wkt | E 1st | A 1st | E 2nd | A 2nd |
|---|--|--|--|--|
| 1st | 6 | 1 | 145 | 62 |
| 2nd | 24 | 129 | 222 | 75 |
| 3rd | 40 | 130 | 276 | 82 |
| 4th | 49 | 130 | 301 | 93 |
| 5th | 98 | 200 | 313 | 100 |
| 6th | 119 | 204 | – | 139 |
| 7th | 119 | 209 | – | 144 |
| 8th | 139 | 216 | – | 175 |
| 9th | 187 | 221 | – | 188 |
| 10th | 196 | – | – | – |

Umpires: J. Carlin and J. Phillips.

# ENGLAND v AUSTRALIA 1905 (2nd Test)

Played at Lord's, London, on 15, 16, 17 (*no play*) June.
Toss: England.    Result: MATCH DRAWN.
Debuts: Nil.

Rain, which had accounted for the last two days of the 1902 Lord's Test, took its tally at Headquarters to three days out of the last five in Test matches.

## ENGLAND

| | | | | | |
|---|---|--:|---|---|--:|
| A.C. MacLaren | b Hopkins | 56 | b Armstrong | | 79 |
| T.W. Hayward | lbw b Duff | 16 | c Laver b McLeod | | 8 |
| J.T. Tyldesley | c Laver b Armstrong | 43 | b Noble | | 12 |
| C.B. Fry | c Kelly b Hopkins | 73 | not out | | 36 |
| Hon. F.S. Jackson* | c Armstrong b Laver | 29 | b Armstrong | | 0 |
| A.O. Jones | b Laver | 1 | c Trumper b Armstrong | | 5 |
| B.J.T. Bosanquet | c and b Armstrong | 6 | not out | | 4 |
| W. Rhodes | b Hopkins | 15 | | | |
| A.F.A. Lilley† | lbw b McLeod | 0 | | | |
| S.Haigh | b Laver | 14 | | | |
| E.G. Arnold | not out | 7 | | | |
| Extras | (B 20, LB 2) | 22 | (B 2, LB 4, NB 1) | | 7 |
| **Total** | | **282** | (5 wickets) | | **151** |

## AUSTRALIA

| | | |
|---|---|--:|
| V.T. Trumper | b Jackson | 31 |
| R.A. Duff | c Lilley b Rhodes | 27 |
| C. Hill | c Bosanquet b Jackson | 7 |
| M.A. Noble | c Fry b Jackson | 7 |
| W.W. Armstrong | lbw b Jackson | 33 |
| J. Darling* | c Haigh b Arnold | 41 |
| S.E. Gregory | c Jones b Rhodes | 5 |
| A.J.Y. Hopkins | b Haigh | 16 |
| C.E. McLeod | b Haigh | 0 |
| F. Laver | not out | 4 |
| J.J. Kelly† | lbw b Rhodes | 2 |
| Extras | (B 3, LB 5) | 8 |
| **Total** | | **181** |

| AUSTRALIA | O | M | R | W | O | M | R | W | | FALL OF WICKETS | | | |
|---|--:|--:|--:|--:|--:|--:|--:|--:|---|---|--:|--:|--:|
| McLeod | 20 | 7 | 40 | 1 | 15 | 5 | 33 | 1 | | | E | A | E |
| Laver | 34 | 8 | 64 | 3 | 10 | 4 | 39 | 0 | *Wkt* | *1st* | *1st* | *2nd* | |
| Armstrong | 30 | 11 | 41 | 2 | 10 | 2 | 30 | 3 | 1st | 59 | 57 | 18 | |
| Noble | 34 | 13 | 61 | 0 | 13 | 2 | 31 | 1 | 2nd | 97 | 73 | 63 | |
| Duff | 7 | 4 | 14 | 1 | | | | | 3rd | 149 | 73 | 136 | |
| Hopkins | 15 | 4 | 40 | 3 | 2 | 0 | 11 | 0 | 4th | 208 | 95 | 136 | |
| | | | | | | | | | 5th | 210 | 131 | 146 | |
| ENGLAND | | | | | | | | | 6th | 227 | 138 | – | |
| Haigh | 12 | 3 | 40 | 2 | | | | | 7th | 257 | 171 | – | |
| Rhodes | 16·1 | 1 | 70 | 3 | | | | | 8th | 258 | 175 | – | |
| Jackson | 15 | 0 | 50 | 4 | | | | | 9th | 258 | 175 | – | |
| Arnold | 7 | 3 | 13 | 1 | | | | | 10th | 282 | 181 | – | |

Umpires: J. Phillips and W. Richards.

# ENGLAND v AUSTRALIA 1905 (3rd Test)

Played at Headingley, Leeds, on 3, 4, 5 July.
Toss: England.   Result: MATCH DRAWN.
Debuts: England – D. Denton, A.R. Warren.

Jackson's hundred was the first in a Test at Leeds. Warren took five wickets in the first innings of his only Test match.

## ENGLAND

| | | | | | |
|---|---|---|---|---|---|
| T.W. Hayward | b McLeod | 26 | c Hopkins b Armstrong | | 60 |
| C.B. Fry | c Noble b McLeod | 32 | c Kelly b Armstrong | | 30 |
| J.T. Tyldesley | b Laver | 0 | st Kelly b Armstrong | | 100 |
| D. Denton | c Duff b McLeod | 0 | c Hill b Armstrong | | 12 |
| Hon.F.S. Jackson* | not out | 144 | c Duff b Armstrong | | 17 |
| G.H. Hirst | c Trumper b Laver | 35 | not out | | 40 |
| B.J.T. Bosanquet | b Duff | 20 | not out | | 22 |
| A.F.A. Lilley† | b Noble | 11 | | | |
| S. Haigh | c Noble b Armstrong | 11 | | | |
| A.R. Warren | run out | 7 | | | |
| C. Blythe | b Armstrong | 0 | | | |
| Extras | (B 10, LB 1, W 2, NB 2) | 15 | (B 1, LB 6, W 6, NB 1) | | 14 |
| **Total** | | **301** | (5 wickets declared) | | **295** |

## AUSTRALIA

| | | | | | |
|---|---|---|---|---|---|
| V.T. Trumper | b Warren | 8 | c Hirst b Warren | | 0 |
| R.A. Duff | c Lilley b Blythe | 48 | b Hirst | | 17 |
| C Hill | c and b Hirst | 7 | c Warren b Haigh | | 33 |
| M.A. Noble | c Hayward b Warren | 2 | st Lilley b Bosanquet | | 62 |
| W.W. Armstrong | c Hayward b Warren | 66 | lbw b Blythe | | 32 |
| J. Darling* | c Bosanquet b Warren | 5 | b Blythe | | 2 |
| A.J.Y. Hopkins | c Lilley b Jackson | 36 | b Blythe | | 17 |
| S.E. Gregory | run out | 4 | not out | | 32 |
| C.E. McLeod | b Haigh | 8 | not out | | 10 |
| J.J. Kelly† | not out | 1 | | | |
| F. Laver | b Warren | 3 | | | |
| Extras | (B 4, LB 1, W 2) | 7 | (B 11, W 6, NB 2) | | 19 |
| **Total** | | **195** | (7 wickets) | | **224** |

| AUSTRALIA | O | M | R | W | O | M | R | W | | FALL OF WICKETS | | | |
|---|---|---|---|---|---|---|---|---|---|---|---|---|---|
| Armstrong | 26·3 | 6 | 44 | 2 | 51 | 14 | 122 | 5 | | | E | A | E | A |
| Noble | 23 | 6 | 59 | 1 | 20 | 3 | 68 | 0 | Wkt | 1st | 1st | 2nd | 2nd |
| Laver | 29 | 10 | 61 | 2 | 10 | 4 | 29 | 0 | 1st | 51 | 26 | 80 | 0 |
| McLeod | 37 | 13 | 88 | 3 | 23 | 6 | 62 | 0 | 2nd | 54 | 33 | 126 | 36 |
| Hopkins | 9 | 4 | 2i | 0 | | | | | 3rd | 57 | 36 | 170 | 64 |
| Duff | 4 | 1 | 13 | 1 | | | | | 4th | 64 | 96 | 202 | 117 |
| | | | | | | | | | 5th | 133 | 105 | 258 | 121 |
| ENGLAND | | | | | | | | | 6th | 201 | 161 | – | 152 |
| Hirst | 7 | 1 | 37 | 1 | 10 | 2 | 26 | 1 | 7th | 232 | 166 | – | 199 |
| Warren | 19·2 | 5 | 57 | 5 | 20 | 4 | 56 | 1 | 8th | 282 | 191 | – | – |
| Blythe | 8 | 0 | 36 | 1 | 24 | 11 | 41 | 3 | 9th | 301 | 191 | – | – |
| Jackson | 4 | 0 | 10 | 1 | 8 | 2 | 10 | 0 | 10th | 301 | 195 | – | – |
| Haigh | 11 | 5 | 19 | 1 | 14 | 4 | 36 | 1 | | | | | |
| Bosanquet | 4 | 0 | 29 | 0 | 15 | 1 | 36 | 1 | | | | | |

Umpires: J. Phillips and V.A. Titchmarsh.

# ENGLAND v AUSTRALIA 1905 (4th Test)

Played at Old Trafford, Manchester, 24, 25, 26 July.
Toss: England.   Result: ENGLAND won by an innings and 80 runs.
Debuts: England – W. Brearley, R.H. Spooner.

Jackson hit his second hundred in successive Tests and became the first to score five Test hundreds in England.
He is the only England batsman to score five hundreds against Australia in England.

## ENGLAND

| | | | |
|---|---|---:|---|
| A.C. MacLaren | c Hill b McLeod | 14 | |
| T.W. Hayward | c Gehrs b McLeod | 82 | |
| J.T. Tyldesley | b Laver | 24 | |
| C.B. Fry | b Armstrong | 17 | |
| Hon. F.S. Jackson* | c Cotter b McLeod | 113 | |
| R.H. Spooner | c and b McLeod | 52 | |
| G.H. Hirst | c Laver b McLeod | 25 | |
| E.G. Arnold | run out | 25 | |
| W. Rhodes | not out | 27 | |
| A.F.A. Lilley† | lbw b Noble | 28 | |
| W. Brearley | c Darling b Noble | 0 | |
| Extras | (B 17, LB 20, W 1, NB 1) | 39 | |
| **Total** | | **446** | |

## AUSTRALIA

| | | | | | |
|---|---|---:|---|---|---:|
| M.A. Noble | b Brearley | 7 | (4) c Rhodes b Brearley | | 10 |
| V.T. Trumper | c Rhodes b Brearley | 11 | lbw b Rhodes | | 30 |
| C. Hill | c Fry b Arnold | 0 | c sub (A.O. Jones) b Arnold | | 27 |
| W.W. Armstrong | b Rhodes | 29 | (5) b Brearley | | 9 |
| R.A. Duff | c MacLaren b Brearley | 11 | (1) c Spooner b Brearley | | 60 |
| J. Darling* | c Tyldesley b Jackson | 73 | c Rhodes b Brearley | | 0 |
| D.R.A. Gehrs | b Arnold | 0 | (8) c and b Rhodes | | 11 |
| C.E. McLeod | b Brearley | 6 | (9) c Arnold b Rhodes | | 6 |
| A. Cotter | c Fry b Jackson | 11 | (10) run out | | 0 |
| F. Laver | b Rhodes | 24 | (11) not out | | 6 |
| J.J. Kelly† | not out | 16 | (7) c Rhodes b Arnold | | 5 |
| Extras | (B 9) | 9 | (B 4, NB 1) | | 5 |
| **Total** | | **197** | | | **169** |

| AUSTRALIA | O | M | R | W | O | M | R | W | | FALL OF WICKETS | | |
|---|---:|---:|---:|---:|---:|---:|---:|---:|---|---|---|---|
| Cotter | 26 | 4 | 83 | 0 | | | | | | E | A | A |
| McLeod | 47 | 8 | 125 | 5 | | | | | Wkt | 1st | 1st | 2nd |
| Armstrong | 48 | 14 | 93 | 1 | | | | | 1st | 24 | 20 | 55 |
| Laver | 21 | 5 | 73 | 1 | | | | | 2nd | 77 | 21 | 121 |
| Noble | 15·5 | 3 | 33 | 2 | | | | | 3rd | 136 | 27 | 122 |
| | | | | | | | | | 4th | 176 | 41 | 133 |
| ENGLAND | | | | | | | | | 5th | 301 | 88 | 133 |
| Hirst | 2 | 0 | 12 | 0 | 7 | 2 | 19 | 0 | 6th | 347 | 93 | 146 |
| Brearley | 17 | 3 | 72 | 4 | 14 | 3 | 54 | 4 | 7th | 382 | 146 | 146 |
| Arnold | 14 | 2 | 53 | 2 | 15 | 5 | 35 | 2 | 8th | 387 | 146 | 158 |
| Rhodes | 5·5 | 1 | 25 | 2 | 11·3 | 3 | 36 | 3 | 9th | 446 | 166 | 158 |
| Jackson | 7 | 0 | 26 | 2 | 5 | 0 | 20 | 0 | 10th | 446 | 197 | 169 |

Umpires: J. Carlin and J.E. West.

# ENGLAND v AUSTRALIA 1905 (5th Test)

Played at Kennington Oval, London, on 14, 15, 16 August.
Toss: England.    Result: MATCH DRAWN.
Debuts: Nil.

Jackson became the first captain to win every toss in a five-match rubber. Duff was the first of four batsman (W.H. Ponsford, M. Leyland and R. Subba Row being the others) to score centuries on both their first and their last appearances in Tests between England and Australia. A.O. Jones was the first substitute to keep wicket in a Test and the first such to make a dismissal (Armstrong). Spooner kept wicket in the second innings and caught Trumper.

## ENGLAND

| | | | | | |
|---|---|---|---|---|---|
| A.C. MacLaren | c Laver b Cotter | 6 | (3) c Kelly b Armstrong | | 6 |
| T.W. Hayward | hit wkt b Hopkins | 59 | lbw b Armstrong | | 2 |
| J.T. Tyldesley | b Cotter | 16 | (4) not out | | 112 |
| C.B. Fry | b Cotter | 144 | (5) c Armstrong b Noble | | 16 |
| Hon. F.S. Jackson* | c Armstrong b Laver | 76 | (6) b Cotter | | 31 |
| R.H. Spooner | b Cotter | 0 | (7) c sub (D.R.A. Gehrs) b Noble | | 79 |
| G.H. Hirst | c Noble b Laver | 5 | | | |
| E.G. Arnold | c Trumper b Cotter | 40 | (1) b Cotter | | 0 |
| W. Rhodes | b Cotter | 36 | | | |
| A.F.A. Lilley† | b Cotter | 17 | | | |
| W. Brearley | not out | 11 | | | |
| Extras | (B 11, LB 1, W 1, NB 7) | 20 | (B 4, LB 5, W 1, NB 5) | | 15 |
| **Total** | | **430** | (6 wickets declared) | | **261** |

## AUSTRALIA

| | | | | | |
|---|---|---|---|---|---|
| V.T. Trumper | b Brearley | 4 | c Spooner b Brearley | | 28 |
| R.A. Duff | c and b Hirst | 146 | b Arnold | | 34 |
| C. Hill | c Rhodes b Brearley | 18 | b Hirst | | 3 |
| M.A. Noble | c MacLaren b Jackson | 25 | not out | | 32 |
| W.W. Armstrong | c sub (A.O. Jones) b Hirst | 18 | not out | | 12 |
| J. Darling* | b Hirst | 57 | (2) run out | | 10 |
| A.J.Y. Hopkins | b Brearley | 1 | | | |
| C.E. McLeod | b Brearley | 0 | | | |
| J.J. Kelly† | run out | 42 | | | |
| A. Cotter | c Fry b Brearley | 6 | | | |
| F. Laver | not out | 15 | | | |
| Extras | (B 17, LB 9, W 1, NB 4) | 31 | (B 4, LB 1) | | 5 |
| **Total** | | **363** | (4 wickets) | | **124** |

| AUSTRALIA | O | M | R | W | O | M | R | W |
|---|---|---|---|---|---|---|---|---|
| Cotter | 40 | 4 | 148 | 7 | 21 | 2 | 73 | 2 |
| Noble | 18 | 6 | 51 | 0 | 14·3 | 3 | 56 | 2 |
| Armstrong | 27 | 7 | 76 | 0 | 30 | 13 | 61 | 2 |
| McLeod | 13 | 2 | 47 | 0 | 11 | 2 | 27 | 0 |
| Laver | 17 | 3 | 41 | 2 | 3 | 0 | 18 | 0 |
| Hopkins | 11 | 2 | 32 | 1 | 1 | 0 | 11 | 0 |
| Duff | 4 | 1 | 15 | 0 | | | | |
| ENGLAND | | | | | | | | |
| Hirst | 23 | 6 | 86 | 3 | 9 | 2 | 32 | 1 |
| Brearley | 31·1 | 8 | 110 | 5 | 11 | 2 | 41 | 1 |
| Arnold | 9 | 0 | 50 | 0 | 9 | 2 | 17 | 1 |
| Rhodes | 21 | 2 | 59 | 0 | 8 | 0 | 29 | 0 |
| Jackson | 9 | 1 | 27 | 1 | | | | |

| | FALL OF WICKETS | | | |
|---|---|---|---|---|
| | E | A | E | A |
| Wkt | 1st | 1st | 2nd | 2nd |
| 1st | 12 | 5 | 0 | 27 |
| 2nd | 32 | 44 | 8 | 49 |
| 3rd | 132 | 159 | 13 | 58 |
| 4th | 283 | 214 | 48 | 92 |
| 5th | 291 | 237 | 103 | – |
| 6th | 306 | 247 | 261 | – |
| 7th | 322 | 265 | – | – |
| 8th | 394 | 293 | – | – |
| 9th | 418 | 304 | – | – |
| 10th | 430 | 363 | – | – |

Umpires: J. Phillips and W.A.J. West.

# SOUTH AFRICA v ENGLAND 1905–06 (1st Test)

Played at Old Wanderers, Johannesburg, on 2, 3, 4 January.
Toss: England.    Result: SOUTH AFRICA won by one wicket.
Debuts: South Africa – G.A. Faulkner, R.O. Schwarz, P.W. Sherwell, S.J. Snooke, A.E.E. Vogler,
  G.C. White; England – J.N. Crawford, F.L. Fane, E.G. Hayes, W.S. Lees.

South Africa's first Test victory came in their twelfth match. They defeated the first official M.C.C. team by a margin which has occurred only five times in Tests. Nourse, who shared the decisive last-wicket stand with Sherwell, made the highest score for South Africa on debut against England.

## ENGLAND

| | | | | | |
|---|---|---:|---|---|---:|
| P.F. Warner* | c Snooke b Schwarz | 6 | b Vogler | | 51 |
| F.L. Fane | c Schwarz b Faulkner | 1 | b Snooke | | 3 |
| D. Denton | c Faulkner b Schwarz | 0 | b Faulkner | | 34 |
| E.G. Wynyard | st Sherwell b Schwarz | 29 | b Vogler | | 0 |
| E.G. Hayes | c and b Vogler | 20 | c Schwarz b Snooke | | 3 |
| J.N. Crawford | c Nourse b Sinclair | 44 | b Nourse | | 43 |
| A.E. Relf | b White | 8 | c Sherwell b Faulkner | | 17 |
| S. Haigh | b Faulkner | 23 | lbw b Nourse | | 0 |
| J.H. Board† | not out | 9 | lbw b Faulkner | | 7 |
| W.S. Lees | st Sherwell b White | 11 | not out | | 1 |
| C. Blythe | b Sinclair | 17 | b Faulkner | | 0 |
| Extras | (B 6, LB 9, NB 1) | 16 | (B 23, LB 8) | | 31 |
| **Total** | | **184** | | | **190** |

## SOUTH AFRICA

| | | | | | |
|---|---|---:|---|---|---:|
| L.J. Tancred | c Board b Lees | 3 | c Warner b Blythe | | 10 |
| W.A. Shalders | c Haigh b Blythe | 4 | run out | | 38 |
| C.M.H. Hathorn | b Lees | 5 | c Crawford b Lees | | 4 |
| G.C. White | c Blythe b Lees | 8 | b Relf | | 81 |
| S.J. Snooke | c Board b Blythe | 19 | lbw b Lees | | 9 |
| J.H. Sinclair | c and b Lees | 0 | c Fane b Lees | | 5 |
| G.A. Faulkner | b Blythe | 4 | run out | | 6 |
| A.W. Nourse | not out | 18 | not out | | 93 |
| A.E.E. Vogler | b Crawford | 14 | b Hayes | | 2 |
| R.O. Schwarz | c Relf b Crawford | 5 | c and b Relf | | 2 |
| P.W. Sherwell*† | lbw b Lees | 1 | not out | | 22 |
| Extras | (B 9, LB 1) | 10 | (B 6, LB 2, NB 7) | | 15 |
| **Total** | | **91** | (9 wickets) | | **287** |

| SOUTH AFRICA | O | M | R | W | O | M | R | W |
|---|---|---|---|---|---|---|---|---|
| Schwarz | 21 | 5 | 72 | 3 | 8 | 1 | 24 | 0 |
| Faulkner | 22 | 7 | 35 | 2 | 12·5 | 5 | 26 | 4 |
| Sinclair | 11 | 1 | 36 | 2 | 5 | 1 | 25 | 0 |
| Vogler | 3 | 0 | 10 | 1 | 11 | 3 | 24 | 2 |
| White | 5 | 1 | 13 | 2 | 4 | 0 | 15 | 0 |
| Nourse | 1 | 0 | 2 | 0 | 6 | 4 | 7 | 2 |
| Snooke | | | | | 12 | 4 | 38 | 2 |
| ENGLAND | | | | | | | | |
| Lees | 23·1 | 10 | 34 | 5 | 33 | 10 | 74 | 3 |
| Blythe | 16 | 5 | 33 | 3 | 28 | 12 | 50 | 1 |
| Crawford | 7 | 1 | 14 | 2 | 17 | 4 | 49 | 0 |
| Haigh | | | | | 1 | 0 | 9 | 0 |
| Relf | | | | | 21·5 | 7 | 47 | 2 |
| Wynyard | | | | | 3 | 0 | 15 | 0 |
| Hayes | | | | | 9 | 1 | 28 | 1 |

## FALL OF WICKETS

| | E | SA | E | SA |
|---|---|---|---|---|
| Wkt | 1st | 1st | 2nd | 2nd |
| 1st | 6 | 5 | 3 | 11 |
| 2nd | 6 | 11 | 55 | 22 |
| 3rd | 15 | 13 | 56 | 68 |
| 4th | 53 | 35 | 73 | 81 |
| 5th | 76 | 39 | 113 | 89 |
| 6th | 97 | 43 | 166 | 105 |
| 7th | 145 | 44 | 174 | 226 |
| 8th | 147 | 62 | 185 | 230 |
| 9th | 159 | 82 | 190 | 239 |
| 10th | 184 | 91 | 190 | – |

Umpires: J. Phillips and F.E. Smith.

# SOUTH AFRICA v ENGLAND 1905–06 (2nd Test)

Played at Old Wanderers, Johannesburg, on 6, 7, 8 March.
Toss: England.    Result: SOUTH AFRICA won by nine wickets.
Debuts: England – L.J. Moon.

## ENGLAND

| | | | | | |
|---|---|---|---|---|---|
| P.F. Warner* | c White b Snooke | 2 | b Snooke | | 0 |
| J.N. Crawford | c Faulkner b Schwarz | 23 | c Sherwell b Snooke | | 6 |
| D. Denton | c and b Sinclair | 1 | c Sherwell b Snooke | | 4 |
| F.L. Fane | c and b Faulkner | 8 | b Sinclair | | 65 |
| L.J. Moon | lbw b Sinclair | 30 | c Sherwell b Sinclair | | 0 |
| E.G. Wynyard | b Vogler | 0 | c and b Vogler | | 30 |
| A.E. Relf | c White b Faulkner | 24 | c White b Schwarz | | 37 |
| S. Haigh | c Hathorn b Faulkner | 3 | (10) not out | | 0 |
| J.H. Board† | b Sinclair | 0 | b Schwarz | | 2 |
| W.S. Lees | not out | 25 | (8) b Schwarz | | 4 |
| C. Blythe | b Schwarz | 12 | b Schwarz | | 0 |
| Extras | (B 10, LB 5, NB 5) | 20 | (B 12) | | 12 |
| **Total** | | **148** | | | **160** |

## SOUTH AFRICA

| | | | | |
|---|---|---|---|---|
| L.J. Tancred | b Crawford | 28 | not out | 18 |
| W.A. Shalders | b Crawford | 37 | c Board b Lees | 0 |
| G.C. White | b Relf | 21 | not out | 9 |
| A.W. Nourse | c Denton b Haigh | 21 | | |
| C.M.H. Hathorn | run out | 17 | | |
| G.A. Faulkner | c Denton b Lees | 17 | | |
| J.H. Sinclair | st Board b Blythe | 66 | | |
| S.J. Snooke | b Haigh | 24 | | |
| R.O. Schwarz | b Haigh | 2 | | |
| P.W. Sherwell*† | not out | 20 | | |
| A.E.E. Vogler | b Haigh | 6 | | |
| Extras | (B 9, LB 8, NB 1) | 18 | (B 2, LB 4, NB 1) | 7 |
| **Total** | | **277** | (1 wicket) | **34** |

| SOUTH AFRICA | O | M | R | W | O | M | R | W |
|---|---|---|---|---|---|---|---|---|
| Snooke | 7 | 2 | 15 | 1 | 15 | 3 | 40 | 3 |
| Sinclair | 25 | 11 | 35 | 3 | 22 | 6 | 36 | 2 |
| Faulkner | 17 | 6 | 38 | 3 | 7 | 0 | 19 | 0 |
| Schwarz | 5·2 | 0 | 16 | 2 | 14·5 | 3 | 30 | 4 |
| Vogler | 9 | 3 | 18 | 1 | 6 | 2 | 7 | 1 |
| Nourse | 3 | 1 | 6 | 0 | 6 | 1 | 16 | 0 |
| ENGLAND | | | | | | | | |
| Lees | 26 | 13 | 47 | 1 | 4 | 0 | 16 | 1 |
| Blythe | 25 | 6 | 66 | 1 | 4·5 | 3 | 7 | 0 |
| Haigh | 19·2 | 4 | 64 | 4 | | | | |
| Relf | 18 | 4 | 36 | 1 | | | | |
| Crawford | 11 | 1 | 44 | 2 | 2 | 1 | 4 | 0 |
| Wynyard | 1 | 0 | 2 | 0 | | | | |

| FALL OF WICKETS | | | | |
|---|---|---|---|---|
| | E | SA | E | SA |
| Wkt | 1st | 1st | 2nd | 2nd |
| 1st | 2 | 70 | 0 | 0 |
| 2nd | 13 | 71 | 10 | – |
| 3rd | 28 | 100 | 19 | – |
| 4th | 62 | 131 | 25 | – |
| 5th | 66 | 133 | 97 | – |
| 6th | 102 | 175 | 138 | – |
| 7th | 109 | 232 | 151 | – |
| 8th | 109 | 242 | 157 | – |
| 9th | 111 | 252 | 160 | – |
| 10th | 148 | 277 | 160 | – |

Umpires: J. Phillips and F.E. Smith.

# SOUTH AFRICA v ENGLAND 1905–06 (3rd Test)

Played at Old Wanderers, Johannesburg, on 10, 12, 13, 14 March.
Toss: South Africa.    Result: SOUTH AFRICA won by 243 runs.
Debuts: England – J.C. Hartley.

S.J. Snooke was the first South African bowler to take eight wickets in a Test innings – no other did so until 1956-57. All eleven batsmen reached double figures in South Africa's first innings.

## SOUTH AFRICA

| | | | | | |
|---|---|---|---|---|---|
| L.J. Tancred | c Hartley b Blythe | 13 | | c Fane b Lees | 73 |
| W.A. Shalders | c Denton b Lees | 13 | | c Hartley b Blythe | 11 |
| G.C. White | c Relf b Lees | 46 | | c Crawford b Lees | 147 |
| A.W. Nourse | c Moon b Relf | 61 | | c Denton b Haigh | 55 |
| C.M.H. Hathorn | c Haigh b Hartley | 102 | | | |
| J.H. Sinclair | b Blythe | 28 | (5) | c Denton b Lees | 48 |
| G.A. Faulkner | c and b Lees | 19 | | not out | 0 |
| S.J. Snooke | b Lees | 29 | | | |
| P.W. Sherwell*† | b Lees | 11 | | | |
| R.O. Schwarz | c Haigh b Lees | 10 | | | |
| A.E.E. Vogler | not out | 28 | (6) | not out | 4 |
| Extras | (B 10, LB 9, NB 6) | 25 | | (B 9, LB 2) | 11 |
| **Total** | | **385** | | (5 wickets declared) | **349** |

## ENGLAND

| | | | | | |
|---|---|---|---|---|---|
| P.F. Warner* | b Schwarz | 19 | | b Schwarz | 2 |
| J.N. Crawford | b Schwarz | 4 | (7) | c White b Sinclair | 34 |
| D. Denton | b Schwarz | 4 | (6) | c Sherwell b Snooke | 61 |
| F.L. Fane | c Vogler b Snooke | 143 | (5) | c Sherwell b Snooke | 7 |
| L.J. Moon† | b Schwarz | 36 | (8) | b Snooke | 15 |
| E.G. Hayes | c Snooke b Sinclair | 35 | (9) | not out | 11 |
| A.E. Relf | c Schwarz b Snooke | 33 | (3) | c Schwarz b Snooke | 18 |
| J.C. Hartley | b Shalders | 0 | (2) | c Vogler b Snooke | 9 |
| S. Haigh | c Sherwell b Snooke | 0 | (4) | c Sherwell b Snooke | 16 |
| W.S. Lees | c Sherwell b Snooke | 6 | | c Vogler b Snooke | 3 |
| C. Blythe | not out | 3 | | c Shalders b Snooke | 7 |
| Extras | (B 3, LB 3, W 2, NB 4) | 12 | | (B 8, LB 3, NB 2) | 13 |
| **Total** | | **295** | | | **196** |

| ENGLAND | O | M | R | W | O | M | R | W |
|---|---|---|---|---|---|---|---|---|
| Lees | 31·3 | 7 | 78 | 6 | 26 | 6 | 85 | 3 |
| Blythe | 26 | 8 | 72 | 2 | 31 | 6 | 96 | 1 |
| Haigh | 15 | 2 | 50 | 0 | 24 | 5 | 72 | 1 |
| Relf | 14 | 1 | 47 | 1 | 9 | 0 | 37 | 0 |
| Crawford | 13 | 1 | 51 | 0 | 4 | 0 | 17 | 0 |
| Hartley | 19 | 1 | 62 | 1 | 7 | 1 | 31 | 0 |
| SOUTH AFRICA | | | | | | | | |
| Snooke | 21·2 | 1 | 57 | 4 | 31·4 | 8 | 70 | 8 |
| Schwarz | 20 | 2 | 67 | 4 | 15 | 4 | 31 | 1 |
| Vogler | 19 | 8 | 33 | 0 | 7 | 5 | 9 | 0 |
| Faulkner | 15 | 3 | 46 | 0 | 8 | 0 | 21 | 0 |
| Nourse | 4 | 2 | 11 | 0 | | | | |
| Sinclair | 12 | 0 | 61 | 1 | 17 | 3 | 52 | 1 |
| White | 2 | 0 | 2 | 0 | | | | |
| Shalders | 8 | 3 | 6 | 1 | | | | |

### FALL OF WICKETS

| | SA | E | SA | E |
|---|---|---|---|---|
| Wkt | 1st | 1st | 2nd | 2nd |
| 1st | 27 | 7 | 24 | 3 |
| 2nd | 29 | 16 | 134 | 14 |
| 3rd | 126 | 51 | 254 | 34 |
| 4th | 157 | 135 | 341 | 48 |
| 5th | 209 | 223 | 345 | 75 |
| 6th | 253 | 280 | – | 139 |
| 7th | 325 | 284 | – | 171 |
| 8th | 339 | 285 | – | 171 |
| 9th | 349 | 288 | – | 182 |
| 10th | 385 | 295 | – | 196 |

Umpires: J. Phillips and F.E. Smith.

# SOUTH AFRICA v ENGLAND 1905–06 (4th Test)

Played at Newlands, Cape Town, on 24, 26, 27 March.
Toss: South Africa.    Result: ENGLAND won by four wickets.
Debuts: Nil.

## SOUTH AFRICA

| | | | | | |
|---|---|---|---|---|---|
| L.J. Tancred | lbw b Blythe | 11 | c Haigh b Blythe | | 10 |
| W.A. Shalders | lbw b Blythe | 16 | c Blythe b Crawford | | 0 |
| G.C. White | c Board b Lees | 41 | b Lees | | 73 |
| A.W. Nourse | c Hayes b Blythe | 2 | c Crawford b Blythe | | 3 |
| C.M.H. Hathorn | b Blythe | 3 | b Lees | | 10 |
| J.H. Sinclair | c Board b Blythe | 0 | b Lees | | 1 |
| G.A. Faulkner | b Blythe | 34 | b Blythe | | 4 |
| S.J. Snooke | b Crawford | 44 | b Blythe | | 5 |
| R.O. Schwarz | c Moon b Relf | 33 | c Haigh b Lees | | 8 |
| A.E.E. Vogler | b Haigh | 9 | (11) not out | | 12 |
| P.W. Sherwell*† | not out | 0 | (10) b Blythe | | 9 |
| Extras | (B 20, LB 3, W 2) | 25 | (LB 3) | | 3 |
| **Total** | | **218** | | | **138** |

## ENGLAND

| | | | | | |
|---|---|---|---|---|---|
| J.H. Board† | b Snooke | 0 | (8) not out | | 14 |
| A.E. Relf | lbw b Faulkner | 28 | (6) b Vogler | | 18 |
| C. Blythe | b Faulkner | 27 | | | |
| F.L. Fane | b Sinclair | 9 | (4) not out | | 66 |
| D. Denton | c Vogler b Snooke | 34 | (3) b Snooke | | 20 |
| P.F. Warner* | c Snooke b Faulkner | 1 | (1) b Sinclair | | 4 |
| J.N. Crawford | not out | 36 | (2) b Sinclair | | 4 |
| L.J. Moon | b Sinclair | 33 | (5) lbw b Faulkner | | 28 |
| E.G. Hayes | lbw b Sinclair | 0 | (7) b Sinclair | | 0 |
| S. Haigh | c Nourse b Sinclair | 0 | | | |
| W.S. Lees | c Hathorn b Faulkner | 5 | | | |
| Extras | (B 14, LB 6, W 1, NB 4) | 25 | (B 3, LB 2, NB 1) | | 6 |
| **Total** | | **198** | (6 wickets) | | **160** |

| ENGLAND | O | M | R | W | O | M | R | W | | FALL OF WICKETS | | | |
|---|---|---|---|---|---|---|---|---|---|---|---|---|---|
| Lees | 27 | 12 | 42 | 1 | 14 | 5 | 27 | 4 | | | SA | E | SA | E |
| Blythe | 32 | 13 | 68 | 6 | 28·5 | 10 | 50 | 5 | Wkt | 1st | 1st | 2nd | 2nd |
| Crawford | 13·3 | 3 | 28 | 1 | 15 | 5 | 46 | 1 | 1st | 28 | 0 | 0 | 5 |
| Haigh | 19 | 8 | 38 | 1 | 2 | 0 | 12 | 0 | 2nd | 34 | 59 | 28 | 20 |
| Relf | 6 | 2 | 17 | 1 | | | | | 3rd | 40 | 70 | 40 | 34 |
| | | | | | | | | | 4th | 44 | 98 | 94 | 100 |
| SOUTH AFRICA | | | | | | | | | 5th | 44 | 101 | 97 | 131 |
| Snooke | 18 | 5 | 41 | 2 | 19 | 6 | 41 | 1 | 6th | 116 | 137 | 102 | 134 |
| Schwarz | 12 | 2 | 34 | 0 | 2 | 0 | 6 | 0 | 7th | 136 | 193 | 106 | – |
| Sinclair | 27 | 10 | 41 | 4 | 26·1 | 5 | 67 | 3 | 8th | 199 | 193 | 115 | – |
| Faulkner | 25·5 | 11 | 49 | 4 | 5 | 0 | 21 | 1 | 9th | 218 | 193 | 121 | – |
| Vogler | 5 | 3 | 7 | 0 | 6 | 1 | 13 | 1 | 10th | 218 | 198 | 138 | – |
| Nourse | 2 | 1 | 1 | 0 | 1 | 0 | 6 | 0 | | | | | |

Umpires: J. Phillips and F. Hearne.

# SOUTH AFRICA v ENGLAND 1905–06 (5th Test)

Played at Newlands, Cape Town, on 30, 31 March, 2 April.
Toss: England.   Result: SOUTH AFRICA won by an innings and 16 runs.
Debuts: Nil.

South Africa's selectors had named the side for all five matches at the start of the series. On only one other occasion (England in Australia in 1884–85) has a team remained unchanged throughout a five-match rubber. Vogler's 62 not out remained the highest score by a number eleven batsman until 1972-73 when R.O. Collinge scored 68 not out (*Test No. 713*).

## ENGLAND

| | | | | | |
|---|---|---|---|---|---|
| J.N. Crawford | b Sinclair | 74 | | b Snooke | 13 |
| P.F. Warner* | b Schwarz | 0 | (7) | c Snooke b Schwarz | 4 |
| D. Denton | b Snooke | 4 | | b Vogler | 10 |
| F.L. Fane | b Vogler | 30 | | b Nourse | 10 |
| L.J. Moon | lbw b Vogler | 7 | (2) | lbw b Sinclair | 33 |
| A.E. Relf | c Faulkner b Sinclair | 25 | (5) | b Nourse | 21 |
| J.H. Board† | c Nourse b Snooke | 20 | (6) | b Nourse | 4 |
| J.C. Hartley | run out | 6 | (9) | c Vogler b Schwarz | 0 |
| W.S. Lees | not out | 9 | (8) | b Nourse | 2 |
| S. Haigh | c Tancred b Sinclair | 1 | | c Nourse b Schwarz | 2 |
| C. Blythe | b Sinclair | 1 | | not out | 11 |
| Extras | (B 6, NB 4) | 10 | | (B 14, LB 2, W 2, NB 2) | 20 |
| **Total** | | **187** | | | **130** |

## SOUTH AFRICA

| | | |
|---|---|---|
| L.J. Tancred | c Moon b Crawford | 26 |
| W.A. Shalders | c and b Crawford | 21 |
| G.C. White | c Crawford b Lees | 11 |
| A.W. Nourse | c Relf b Crawford | 36 |
| C.M.H. Hathorn | c Board b Blythe | 1 |
| J.H. Sinclair | b Blythe | 12 |
| G.A. Faulkner | c Moon b Relf | 45 |
| S.J. Snooke | lbw b Relf | 60 |
| R.O. Schwarz | c Crawford b Relf | 15 |
| P.W. Sherwell*† | c Blythe b Lees | 30 |
| A.E.E. Vogler | not out | 62 |
| Extras | (B 12, LB 1, NB 1) | 14 |
| **Total** | | **333** |

| SOUTH AFRICA | O | M | R | W | O | M | R | W |
|---|---|---|---|---|---|---|---|---|
| Snooke | 12 | 4 | 41 | 2 | 9 | 3 | 26 | 1 |
| Schwarz | 7 | 2 | 14 | 1 | 8·2 | 2 | 16 | 3 |
| Sinclair | 21·2 | 8 | 45 | 4 | 11 | 4 | 20 | 1 |
| Vogler | 19 | 6 | 63 | 2 | 8 | 3 | 17 | 1 |
| Faulkner | 4 | 1 | 11 | 0 | 3 | 1 | 6 | 0 |
| Nourse | 2 | 1 | 3 | 0 | 10 | 3 | 25 | 4 |
| ENGLAND | | | | | | | | |
| Lees | 24·4 | 6 | 64 | 2 | | | | |
| Blythe | 35 | 11 | 106 | 2 | | | | |
| Crawford | 18 | 3 | 69 | 3 | | | | |
| Haigh | 6 | 1 | 18 | 0 | | | | |
| Hartley | 6 | 0 | 22 | 0 | | | | |
| Relf | 21 | 6 | 40 | 3 | | | | |

### FALL OF WICKETS

| Wkt | E 1st | SA 1st | E 2nd |
|---|---|---|---|
| 1st | 0 | 45 | 33 |
| 2nd | 5 | 52 | 62 |
| 3rd | 91 | 65 | 64 |
| 4th | 108 | 66 | 90 |
| 5th | 137 | 87 | 94 |
| 6th | 160 | 140 | 103 |
| 7th | 176 | 182 | 105 |
| 8th | 176 | 226 | 106 |
| 9th | 181 | 239 | 109 |
| 10th | 187 | 333 | 130 |

Umpires: J. Phillips and F. Hearne.

# ENGLAND v SOUTH AFRICA 1907 (1st Test)

Played at Lord's, London, on 1, 2, 3 (*no play*) July.
Toss: England.    Result: MATCH DRAWN.
Debuts: Nil.

On their first Test appearance in England, South Africa lost their last six first-innings wickets in the course of 24 balls. Jessop and Braund scored 145 for the sixth wicket in 75 minutes.

## ENGLAND

| | | |
|---|---|---|
| C.B Fry | b Vogler | 33 |
| T.W. Hayward | st Sherwell b Vogler | 21 |
| J.T. Tyldesley | b Vogler | 52 |
| R.E. Foster* | st Sherwell b Vogler | 8 |
| L.C. Braund | c Kotze b Faulkner | 104 |
| G.H. Hirst | b Vogler | 7 |
| G.L. Jessop | c Faulkner b Vogler | 93 |
| J.N. Crawford | c Sherwell b Schwarz | 22 |
| E.G. Arnold | b Schwarz | 4 |
| A.F.A. Lilley† | c Nourse b Vogler | 48 |
| C. Blythe | not out | 4 |
| Extras | (B 24, LB 6, W 2) | 32 |
| **Total** | | **428** |

## SOUTH AFRICA

| | | | | | |
|---|---|---|---|---|---|
| W.A. Shalders | c Lilley b Arnold | 2 | b Hirst | | 0 |
| P.W. Sherwell*† | run out | 6 | b Blythe | | 115 |
| C.M.H. Hathorn | c Foster b Hirst | 6 | c Fry b Blythe | | 30 |
| A.W. Nourse | b Blythe | 62 | not out | | 11 |
| G.A. Faulkner | c Jessop b Braund | 44 | not out | | 12 |
| S.J. Snooke | lbw b Blythe | 5 | | | |
| G.C. White | b Arnold | 0 | | | |
| J.H. Sinclair | b Arnold | 0 | | | |
| R.O. Schwarz | not out | 0 | | | |
| A.E.E. Vogler | c Lilley b Arnold | 3 | | | |
| J.J. Kotze | b Arnold | 0 | | | |
| Extras | (B 9, LB 2, W 1) | 12 | (B 15, LB 2) | | 17 |
| **Total** | | **140** | (3 wickets) | | **185** |

| SOUTH AFRICA | O | M | R | W | O | M | R | W | | FALL OF WICKETS | | |
|---|---|---|---|---|---|---|---|---|---|---|---|---|
| Kotze | 12 | 2 | 43 | 0 | | | | | | E | SA | SA |
| Schwarz | 34 | 7 | 90 | 2 | | | | | Wkt | 1st | 1st | 2nd |
| Vogler | 47·2 | 12 | 128 | 7 | | | | | 1st | 54 | 8 | 1 |
| White | 15 | 2 | 52 | 0 | | | | | 2nd | 55 | 8 | 140 |
| Nourse | 1 | 0 | 2 | 0 | | | | | 3rd | 79 | 18 | 153 |
| Faulkner | 12 | 1 | 59 | 1 | | | | | 4th | 140 | 116 | – |
| Sinclair | 6 | 1 | 22 | 0 | | | | | 5th | 158 | 134 | – |
| ENGLAND | | | | | | | | | 6th | 303 | 135 | – |
| | | | | | | | | | 7th | 335 | 135 | – |
| Hirst | 18 | 7 | 35 | 1 | 16 | 8 | 26 | 1 | 8th | 347 | 137 | – |
| Arnold | 22 | 7 | 37 | 5 | 13 | 2 | 41 | 0 | 9th | 401 | 140 | – |
| Jessop | 2 | 0 | 8 | 0 | | | | | 10th | 428 | 140 | – |
| Crawford | 8 | 1 | 20 | 0 | 4 | 0 | 19 | 0 | | | | |
| Blythe | 8 | 3 | 18 | 2 | 21 | 5 | 56 | 2 | | | | |
| Braund | 7 | 4 | 10 | 1 | 4 | 0 | 26 | 0 | | | | |

Umpires: A. Millward and A.A. White.

# ENGLAND v SOUTH AFRICA 1907 (2nd Test)

Played at Headingley, Leeds, on 29, 30, 31 July.
Toss: England.   Result: ENGLAND won by 53 runs.
Debuts: England – N.A. Knox.

Blythe is the only bowler to take 15 South African wickets in a Test in England. His match analysis of 15 for 99 remains the record for a Test at Leeds.

## ENGLAND

| | | | | |
|---|---|---|---|---|
| T.W. Hayward | st Sherwell b Faulkner | 24 | st Sherwell b Vogler | 15 |
| C.B. Fry | b Vogler | 2 | lbw b White | 54 |
| J.T. Tyldesley | b Faulkner | 12 | c Snooke b Schwarz | 30 |
| R.E. Foster* | b Sinclair | 0 | lbw b Faulkner | 22 |
| L.C. Braund | lbw b Faulkner | 1 | c Schwarz b White | 0 |
| G.H. Hirst | c Hathorn b Sinclair | 17 | b White | 2 |
| G.L. Jessop | c Sherwell b Faulkner | 0 | c Hathorn b Faulkner | 10 |
| E.G. Arnold | b Faulkner | 0 | c Schwarz b Faulkner | 12 |
| A.F.A. Lilley† | c Schwarz b Faulkner | 3 | lbw b White | 0 |
| C. Blythe | not out | 5 | not out | 4 |
| N.A. Knox | c Faulkner b Sinclair | 8 | run out | 5 |
| Extras | (B 1, LB 2, NB 1) | 4 | (B 7, LB 1) | 8 |
| **Total** | | **76** | | **162** |

## SOUTH AFRICA

| | | | | | |
|---|---|---|---|---|---|
| L.J. Tancred | st Lilley b Blythe | 0 | | run out | 0 |
| P.W. Sherwell*† | lbw b Blythe | 26 | | c Foster b Blythe | 1 |
| C.M.H. Hathorn | c Lilley b Hirst | 0 | | b Arnold | 7 |
| A.W. Nourse | c Arnold b Blythe | 18 | | lbw b Blythe | 2 |
| G.C. White | c Hirst b Blythe | 3 | | c Arnold b Blythe | 7 |
| J.H. Sinclair | st Lilley b Blythe | 2 | (7) | c Braund b Blythe | 15 |
| G.A. Faulkner | c Braund b Blythe | 6 | (6) | c Foster b Blythe | 11 |
| S.J. Snooke | c Lilley b Knox | 13 | | c Hirst b Blythe | 14 |
| W.A. Shalders | c Fry b Blythe | 21 | | lbw b Hirst | 5 |
| A.E.E. Vogler | c Hayward b Blythe | 11 | | c Tyldesley b Blythe | 9 |
| R.O. Schwarz | not out | 5 | | not out | 0 |
| Extras | (B 3, LB 1, NB 1) | 5 | | (B 3, NB 1) | 4 |
| **Total** | | **110** | | | **75** |

| SOUTH AFRICA | O | M | R | W | O | M | R | W |
|---|---|---|---|---|---|---|---|---|
| Vogler | 8 | 3 | 14 | 1 | 4 | 0 | 18 | 1 |
| Schwarz | 7 | 0 | 18 | 0 | 5·4 | 0 | 18 | 1 |
| Faulkner | 11 | 4 | 17 | 6 | 20 | 3 | 58 | 3 |
| Sinclair | 10·3 | 2 | 23 | 3 | 4 | 0 | 13 | 0 |
| White | | | | | 16 | 3 | 47 | 4 |
| ENGLAND | | | | | | | | |
| Hirst | 9 | 3 | 22 | 1 | 9 | 2 | 21 | 1 |
| Blythe | 15·5 | 1 | 59 | 8 | 22·4 | 9 | 40 | 7 |
| Arnold | 4 | 1 | 11 | 0 | 13 | 7 | 10 | 1 |
| Knox | 3 | 0 | 13 | 1 | | | | |

| FALL OF WICKETS | | | | |
|---|---|---|---|---|
| | E | SA | E | SA |
| Wkt | 1st | 1st | 2nd | 2nd |
| 1st | 9 | 6 | 37 | 0 |
| 2nd | 41 | 9 | 100 | 3 |
| 3rd | 42 | 34 | 106 | 10 |
| 4th | 42 | 47 | 107 | 16 |
| 5th | 53 | 49 | 115 | 18 |
| 6th | 53 | 56 | 126 | 38 |
| 7th | 57 | 59 | 151 | 56 |
| 8th | 63 | 73 | 152 | 66 |
| 9th | 63 | 102 | 154 | 75 |
| 10th | 76 | 110 | 162 | 75 |

Umpires: J. Moss and J. Carlin.

# ENGLAND v SOUTH AFRICA 1907 (3rd Test)

Played at Kennington Oval, London, on 19, 20, 21 August.
Toss: England.    Result: MATCH DRAWN.
Debuts: South Africa – S.D. Snooke.

## ENGLAND

| | | | | |
|---|---|---:|---|---:|
| C.B. Fry | c and b Faulkner | 129 | b Vogler | 3 |
| T.W. Hayward | lbw b Vogler | 0 | c Sherwell b Nourse | 3 |
| J.T. Tyldesley | b Faulkner | 8 | c White b Nourse | 11 |
| R.E. Foster* | lbw b Vogler | 51 | c and b S.J. Snooke | 35 |
| L.C. Braund | b Schwarz | 18 | c Schwarz b Vogler | 34 |
| G.H. Hirst | c S.J. Snooke b Schwarz | 4 | (7) hit wkt b Schwarz | 16 |
| G.L. Jessop | c S.D. Snooke b Sinclair | 2 | (6) st Sherwell b Schwarz | 11 |
| J.N. Crawford | c S.D. Snooke b Schwarz | 2 | c Nourse b Vogler | 2 |
| A.F.A. Lilley† | b Nourse | 42 | not out | 9 |
| C. Blythe | b Nourse | 10 | b Schwarz | 0 |
| N.A. Knox | not out | 8 | b Vogler | 3 |
| Extras | (B 6, LB 12, W 1, NB 2) | 21 | (B 3, LB 6, NB 2) | 11 |
| **Total** | | **295** | | **138** |

## SOUTH AFRICA

| | | | | |
|---|---|---:|---|---:|
| P.W. Sherwell*† | b Blythe | 6 | | |
| G.A. Faulkner | c and b Hirst | 2 | b Hirst | 42 |
| S.J. Snooke | c Jessop b Hirst | 63 | c Foster b Blythe | 36 |
| A.W. Nourse | c Lilley b Knox | 34 | (7) not out | 0 |
| J.H. Sinclair | c Crawford b Knox | 22 | (1) b Hirst | 28 |
| W.A. Shalders | c Jessop b Blythe | 31 | not out | 24 |
| A.E.E. Vogler | b Blythe | 5 | (5) b Blythe | 19 |
| R.O. Schwarz | c Blythe b Hirst | 2 | | |
| G.C. White | st Lilley b Blythe | 4 | (4) b Hirst | 1 |
| C.M.H. Hathorn | not out | 3 | | |
| S.D. Snooke | c Foster b Blythe | 0 | | |
| Extras | (B 3, LB 1, NB 2) | 6 | (B 5, LB 3, NB 1) | 9 |
| **Total** | | **178** | (5 wickets) | **159** |

| SOUTH AFRICA | O | M | R | W | O | M | R | W |
|---|---|---|---|---|---|---|---|---|
| Vogler | 31 | 7 | 86 | 2 | 14·3 | 2 | 49 | 4 |
| Faulkner | 27 | 2 | 78 | 2 | 3 | 1 | 6 | 0 |
| Schwarz | 27 | 8 | 45 | 3 | 14 | 7 | 21 | 3 |
| White | 9 | 2 | 28 | 0 | | | | |
| Sinclair | 14 | 4 | 27 | 1 | | | | |
| Nourse | 4 | 1 | 10 | 2 | 18 | 6 | 43 | 2 |
| S.J. Snooke | | | | | 5 | 3 | 8 | 1 |
| **ENGLAND** | | | | | | | | |
| Blythe | 20·3 | 5 | 61 | 5 | 12·3 | 3 | 36 | 2 |
| Hirst | 22 | 7 | 39 | 3 | 13 | 1 | 42 | 3 |
| Crawford | 11 | 2 | 33 | 0 | 6 | 3 | 14 | 0 |
| Knox | 10 | 2 | 39 | 2 | 8 | 0 | 53 | 0 |
| Braund | | | | | 1 | 0 | 5 | 0 |

### FALL OF WICKETS

| Wkt | E 1st | SA 1st | E 2nd | SA 2nd |
|---|---|---|---|---|
| 1st | 0 | 8 | 6 | 61 |
| 2nd | 19 | 8 | 6 | 72 |
| 3rd | 105 | 69 | 20 | 76 |
| 4th | 154 | 105 | 89 | 110 |
| 5th | 170 | 149 | 100 | 159 |
| 6th | 177 | 160 | 108 | – |
| 7th | 181 | 163 | 118 | – |
| 8th | 271 | 174 | 131 | – |
| 9th | 274 | 175 | 131 | – |
| 10th | 295 | 178 | 138 | – |

Umpires: W. Richards and W.A.J. West.

# AUSTRALIA v ENGLAND 1907–08 (1st Test)

Played at Sydney Cricket Ground on 13, 14, 16, 17, 18, 19 December.
Toss: England.   Result: AUSTRALIA won by two wickets.
Debuts: Australia – H. Carter, G.R. Hazlitt, C.G. Macartney, V.S. Ransford; England – G. Gunn,
J. Hardstaff, sr, K.L. Hutchings, R.A. Young.

G.Gunn, in Australia for health reasons and not a member of the M.C.C. touring team, was a last minute selection
and made top score in both innings, becoming the fifth batsman to score a century for England on debut.

## ENGLAND

| | | | | | |
|---|---|---|---|---|---|
| F.L. Fane* | c Trumper b Cotter | 2 | | c Noble b Saunders | 33 |
| R.A. Young† | c Carter b Cotter | 13 | (7) | b Noble | 3 |
| G. Gunn | c Hazlitt b Cotter | 119 | | c Noble b Cotter | 74 |
| K.L. Hutchings | c and b Armstrong | 42 | | c Armstrong b Saunders | 17 |
| L.C. Braund | b Cotter | 30 | (6) | not out | 32 |
| J. Hardstaff, sr | b Armstrong | 12 | (5) | b Noble | 63 |
| W. Rhodes | run out | 1 | (2) | c McAlister b Macartney | 29 |
| J.N. Crawford | b Armstrong | 31 | | c Hazlitt b Cotter | 5 |
| S.F. Barnes | b Cotter | 1 | | b Saunders | 11 |
| C. Blythe | b Cotter | 5 | | c Noble b Saunders | 15 |
| A. Fielder | not out | 1 | | lbw b Armstrong | 6 |
| Extras | (B 7, LB 6, W 1, NB 2) | 16 | | (B 2, W 3, NB 7) | 12 |
| **Total** | | **273** | | | **300** |

## AUSTRALIA

| | | | | | |
|---|---|---|---|---|---|
| V.T. Trumper | b Fielder | 43 | | b Barnes | 3 |
| P.A. McAlister | c Hutchings b Barnes | 3 | (7) | b Crawford | 41 |
| C. Hill | c Gunn b Fielder | 87 | | b Fielder | 1 |
| M.A. Noble* | c Braund b Fielder | 37 | | b Barnes | 27 |
| W.W. Armstrong | c Braund b Fielder | 7 | | b Crawford | 44 |
| V.S. Ransford | c Braund b Rhodes | 24 | | c and b Blythe | 13 |
| C.G. Macartney | c Young b Fielder | 35 | (2) | c Crawford b Fielder | 9 |
| H. Carter† | b Braund | 25 | | c Young b Fielder | 61 |
| G.R. Hazlitt | not out | 18 | (10) | not out | 34 |
| A. Cotter | b Braund | 2 | (9) | not out | 33 |
| J.V. Saunders | c Braund b Fielder | 9 | | | |
| Extras | (B 4, LB 2, W 2, NB 2) | 10 | | (B 6, NB 3) | 9 |
| **Total** | | **300** | | (8 wickets) | **275** |

| AUSTRALIA | O | M | R | W | O | M | R | W | | FALL OF WICKETS | | | |
|---|---|---|---|---|---|---|---|---|---|---|---|---|---|
| Cotter | 21·5 | 0 | 101 | 6 | 26 | 1 | 101 | 2 | | E | A | E | A |
| Saunders | 11 | 0 | 42 | 0 | 23 | 6 | 68 | 4 | Wkt | 1st | 1st | 2nd | 2nd |
| Hazlitt | 9 | 2 | 32 | 0 | 4 | 2 | 24 | 0 | 1st | 11 | 4 | 56 | 7 |
| Armstrong | 26 | 10 | 63 | 3 | 27 | 14 | 33 | 1 | 2nd | 18 | 72 | 82 | 12 |
| Macartney | 3 | 0 | 5 | 0 | 14 | 2 | 39 | 1 | 3rd | 91 | 164 | 105 | 27 |
| Noble | 6 | 1 | 14 | 0 | 15 | 5 | 23 | 2 | 4th | 208 | 171 | 218 | 75 |
| | | | | | | | | | 5th | 221 | 184 | 223 | 95 |
| ENGLAND | | | | | | | | | 6th | 223 | 222 | 227 | 124 |
| Fielder | 30·2 | 4 | 82 | 6 | 27·3 | 4 | 88 | 3 | 7th | 246 | 253 | 241 | 185 |
| Barnes | 22 | 3 | 74 | 1 | 30 | 7 | 63 | 2 | 8th | 253 | 279 | 262 | 219 |
| Blythe | 12 | 1 | 33 | 0 | 19 | 5 | 55 | 1 | 9th | 271 | 281 | 293 | – |
| Braund | 17 | 2 | 74 | 2 | 7 | 2 | 14 | 0 | 10th | 273 | 300 | 300 | – |
| Crawford | 5 | 1 | 14 | 0 | 8 | 2 | 33 | 2 | | | | | |
| Rhodes | 5 | 2 | 13 | 1 | 7 | 3 | 13 | 0 | | | | | |

Umpires: R.W. Crockett and W. Hannah.

# AUSTRALIA v ENGLAND 1907–08 (2nd Test)

Played at Melbourne Cricket Ground on 1, 2, 3, 4, 6, 7 January.
Toss: Australia.    Result: ENGLAND won by one wicket.
Debuts: England – J.B. Hobbs, J. Humphries.

Had cover-point (Hazlitt) thrown accurately as the winning run was being scampered, this match would have provided Test cricket with its first tie.

## AUSTRALIA

| | | | | | |
|---|---|---|---|---|---|
| V.T. Trumper | c Humphries b Crawford | 49 | | lbw b Crawford | 63 |
| C.G. Macartney | b Crawford | 37 | (6) | c Humphries b Barnes | 54 |
| C. Hill | b Fielder | 16 | | b Fielder | 3 |
| M.A. Noble* | c Braund b Rhodes | 61 | (2) | b Crawford | 64 |
| W.W. Armstrong | c Hutchings b Crawford | 31 | | b Barnes | 77 |
| P.A. McAlister | run out | 10 | (4) | run out | 15 |
| V.S. Ransford | run out | 27 | | c Hutchings b Barnes | 18 |
| A. Cotter | b Crawford | 17 | (9) | lbw b Crawford | 27 |
| H. Carter† | not out | 15 | (8) | c Fane b Barnes | 53 |
| G.R. Hazlitt | b Crawford | 1 | | b Barnes | 3 |
| J.V. Saunders | b Fielder | 0 | | not out | 0 |
| Extras | (LB 1, W 1) | 2 | | (B 12, LB 8) | 20 |
| **Total** | | **266** | | | **397** |

## ENGLAND

| | | | | |
|---|---|---|---|---|
| F.L. Fane* | b Armstrong | 13 | b Armstrong | 50 |
| J.B. Hobbs | b Cotter | 83 | b Noble | 28 |
| G. Gunn | lbw b Cotter | 15 | lbw b Noble | 0 |
| K.L. Hutchings | b Cotter | 126 | c Cotter b Macartney | 39 |
| L.C. Braund | b Cotter | 49 | b Armstrong | 30 |
| J. Hardstaff, sr | b Saunders | 12 | c Ransford b Cotter | 19 |
| W. Rhodes | b Saunders | 32 | run out | 15 |
| J.N. Crawford | c Ransford b Saunders | 16 | c Armstrong b Saunders | 10 |
| S.F. Barnes | c Hill b Armstrong | 14 | not out | 38 |
| J. Humphries† | b Cotter | 6 | lbw b Armstrong | 16 |
| A. Fielder | not out | 6 | not out | 18 |
| Extras | (B 3, LB 3, W 1, NB 3) | 10 | (B 9, LB 7, W 1, NB 2) | 19 |
| **Total** | | **382** | (9 wickets) | **282** |

| ENGLAND | O | M | R | W | O | M | R | W | | FALL OF WICKETS | | | |
|---|---|---|---|---|---|---|---|---|---|---|---|---|---|
| Fielder | 27·5 | 4 | 77 | 2 | 27 | 6 | 74 | 1 | | A | E | A | E |
| Barnes | 17 | 7 | 30 | 0 | 27·4 | 4 | 72 | 5 | *Wkt* | *1st* | *1st* | *2nd* | *2nd* |
| Rhodes | 11 | 0 | 37 | 1 | 16 | 6 | 38 | 0 | 1st | 84 | 27 | 126 | 54 |
| Braund | 16 | 5 | 41 | 0 | 18 | 2 | 68 | 0 | 2nd | 93 | 61 | 131 | 54 |
| Crawford | 29 | 1 | 79 | 5 | 33 | 6 | 125 | 3 | 3rd | 111 | 160 | 135 | 121 |
| | | | | | | | | | 4th | 168 | 268 | 162 | 131 |
| AUSTRALIA | | | | | | | | | 5th | 197 | 287 | 268 | 162 |
| Cotter | 33 | 4 | 142 | 5 | 28 | 3 | 82 | 1 | 6th | 214 | 325 | 303 | 196 |
| Saunders | 34 | 7 | 100 | 3 | 30 | 9 | 58 | 1 | 7th | 240 | 353 | 312 | 198 |
| Noble | 9 | 3 | 26 | 0 | 22 | 7 | 41 | 2 | 8th | 261 | 360 | 361 | 209 |
| Armstrong | 34·2 | 15 | 36 | 2 | 30·4 | 10 | 53 | 3 | 9th | 265 | 369 | 392 | 243 |
| Hazlitt | 13 | 1 | 34 | 0 | 2 | 1 | 8 | 0 | 10th | 266 | 382 | 397 | – |
| Macartney | 12 | 2 | 34 | 0 | 9 | 3 | 21 | 1 | | | | | |

Umpires: R.W. Crockett and P. Argall.

# AUSTRALIA v ENGLAND 1907–08 (3rd Test)

Played at Adelaide Oval on 10, 11, 13, 14, 15, 16 January.
Toss: Australia.   Result: AUSTRALIA won by 245 runs.
Debuts: Australia – R.J. Hartigan, J.D.A. O'Connor.

R.J. Hartigan became the fourth Australian to score a century on debut. His partnership of 243 with Hill set a new Test record for any wicket and remains Australia's highest eighth-wicket stand in all Test matches. Hobbs resumed his innings after retiring on the last day because of a strain.

## AUSTRALIA

| | | | | | |
|---|---|---|---|---|---|
| V.T. Trumper | b Fielder | 4 | | b Barnes | 0 |
| M.A. Noble* | c Hutchings b Barnes | 15 | | c Gunn b Fielder | 65 |
| C.G. Macartney | lbw b Braund | 75 | | b Barnes | 9 |
| P.A. McAlister | c Hutchings b Crawford | 28 | | c Hutchings b Crawford | 17 |
| W.W. Armstrong | c Humphries b Fielder | 17 | | c Hutchings b Braund | 34 |
| V.S. Ransford | b Barnes | 44 | (7) | c Rhodes b Braund | 25 |
| C. Hill | c Humphries b Barnes | 5 | (9) | c Gunn b Crawford | 160 |
| R.J. Hartigan | b Fielder | 48 | | c sub (R.A. Young) b Barnes | 116 |
| H. Carter† | lbw b Hutchings | 24 | (10) | not out | 31 |
| J.D.A. O'Connor | not out | 10 | (6) | b Crawford | 20 |
| J.V. Saunders | b Fielder | 1 | | run out | 0 |
| Extras | (B 3, LB 5, W 3, NB 3) | 14 | | (B 20, LB 7, W 2) | 29 |
| **Total** | | **285** | | | **506** |

## ENGLAND

| | | | | |
|---|---|---|---|---|
| J.B. Hobbs | c Carter b Saunders | 26 | not out | 23 |
| F.L. Fane* | run out | 48 | b Saunders | 0 |
| G. Gunn | b O'Connor | 65 | c Trumper b O'Connor | 11 |
| K.L. Hutchings | c and b Macartney | 23 | b O'Connor | 0 |
| L.C. Braund | b Macartney | 0 | c Hartigan b O'Connor | 47 |
| J. Hardstaff, sr | b O'Connor | 61 | c Macartney b Saunders | 72 |
| W. Rhodes | c Carter b O'Connor | 38 | c Armstrong b O'Connor | 9 |
| J.N. Crawford | b Armstrong | 62 | c and b Saunders | 7 |
| S.F. Barnes | c and b Armstrong | 12 | c McAlister b Saunders | 8 |
| J. Humphries† | run out | 7 | b O'Connor | 1 |
| A. Fielder | not out | 0 | c Ransford b Saunders | 1 |
| Extras | (B 12, LB 2, W 2, NB 5) | 21 | (B 3, NB 1) | 4 |
| **Total** | | **363** | | **183** |

| ENGLAND | O | M | R | W | O | M | R | W |
|---|---|---|---|---|---|---|---|---|
| Barnes | 27 | 8 | 60 | 3 | 42 | 9 | 83 | 3 |
| Fielder | 27·5 | 5 | 80 | 4 | 23 | 3 | 81 | 1 |
| Rhodes | 15 | 5 | 35 | 0 | 27 | 9 | 81 | 0 |
| Crawford | 14 | 0 | 65 | 1 | 45·5 | 4 | 113 | 3 |
| Braund | 9 | 1 | 26 | 1 | 23 | 3 | 85 | 2 |
| Hutchings | 2 | 1 | 5 | 1 | 7 | 0 | 34 | 0 |
| AUSTRALIA | | | | | | | | |
| Saunders | 36 | 6 | 83 | 1 | 21·4 | 4 | 65 | 5 |
| Macartney | 18 | 3 | 49 | 2 | 4 | 1 | 17 | 0 |
| O'Connor | 40 | 8 | 110 | 3 | 21 | 6 | 40 | 5 |
| Noble | 18 | 4 | 38 | 0 | 7 | 1 | 14 | 0 |
| Armstrong | 18 | 4 | 55 | 2 | 10 | 1 | 43 | 0 |
| Hartigan | 2 | 0 | 7 | 0 | | | | |

## FALL OF WICKETS

| | A | E | A | E |
|---|---|---|---|---|
| Wkt | 1st | 1st | 2nd | 2nd |
| 1st | 11 | 58 | 7 | 8 |
| 2nd | 35 | 98 | 35 | 9 |
| 3rd | 114 | 138 | 71 | 15 |
| 4th | 140 | 138 | 127 | 128 |
| 5th | 160 | 194 | 135 | 138 |
| 6th | 191 | 277 | 179 | 146 |
| 7th | 215 | 282 | 180 | 162 |
| 8th | 273 | 320 | 423 | 177 |
| 9th | 275 | 363 | 501 | 182 |
| 10th | 285 | 363 | 506 | 183 |

Umpires: R.W. Crockett and T. Laing.

# AUSTRALIA v ENGLAND 1907–08 (4th Test)

Played at Melbourne Cricket Ground on 7, 8, 10, 11 February.
Toss: Australia.   Result: AUSTRALIA won by 308 runs.
Debuts: Nil.

## AUSTRALIA

| | | | | | |
|---|---|---|---|---|---|
| M.A. Noble* | b Crawford | 48 | b Crawford | | 10 |
| V.T. Trumper | c Crawford b Fielder | 0 | b Crawford | | 0 |
| C. Hill | b Barnes | 7 | run out | | 25 |
| P.A. McAlister | c Jones b Fielder | 37 | c Humphries b Fielder | | 4 |
| S.E. Gregory | c Fielder b Crawford | 10 | lbw b Fielder | | 29 |
| W.W. Armstrong | b Crawford | 32 | not out | | 133 |
| V.S. Ransford | c Braund b Fielder | 51 | c Humphries b Rhodes | | 54 |
| C.G. Macartney | c Hardstaff b Fielder | 12 | c Gunn b Crawford | | 29 |
| H. Carter† | c and b Crawford | 2 | c Braund b Fielder | | 66 |
| J.D.A. O'Connor | c Fielder b Crawford | 2 | c Humphries b Barnes | | 18 |
| J.V. Saunders | not out | 1 | c Jones b Fielder | | 2 |
| Extras | (B 1, LB 10, NB 1) | 12 | (B 7, LB 2, NB 6) | | 15 |
| **Total** | | **214** | | | **385** |

## ENGLAND

| | | | | | |
|---|---|---|---|---|---|
| J.B. Hobbs | b Noble | 57 | c and b Saunders | | 0 |
| G. Gunn | c and b Saunders | 13 | b Saunders | | 43 |
| J. Hardstaff, sr | c Carter b O'Connor | 8 | c Carter b Saunders | | 39 |
| K.L. Hutchings | b Saunders | 8 | b Noble | | 3 |
| L.C. Braund | run out | 4 | b Macartney | | 10 |
| W. Rhodes | c McAlister b Saunders | 0 | c Carter b O'Connor | | 2 |
| J.N. Crawford | b Saunders | 1 | c Carter b O'Connor | | 0 |
| A.O. Jones* | b Noble | 3 | c Saunders b O'Connor | | 31 |
| S.F. Barnes | c O'Connor b Noble | 3 | not out | | 22 |
| J. Humphries† | not out | 3 | c Carter b Saunders | | 11 |
| A. Fielder | st Carter b Saunders | 1 | b Armstrong | | 20 |
| Extras | (B 1, LB 2, NB 1) | 4 | (LB 4, NB 1) | | 5 |
| **Total** | | **105** | | | **186** |

| ENGLAND | O | M | R | W | O | M | R | W |
|---|---|---|---|---|---|---|---|---|
| Fielder | 22 | 3 | 54 | 4 | 31 | 2 | 91 | 4 |
| Barnes | 23 | 11 | 37 | 1 | 35 | 13 | 69 | 1 |
| Braund | 12 | 3 | 42 | 0 | 7 | 0 | 48 | 0 |
| Crawford | 23·5 | 3 | 48 | 5 | 25 | 5 | 72 | 3 |
| Rhodes | 5 | 0 | 21 | 0 | 24 | 5 | 66 | 1 |
| Hutchings | | | | | 2 | 0 | 24 | 0 |
| AUSTRALIA | | | | | | | | |
| O'Connor | 6 | 1 | 40 | 1 | 21 | 3 | 58 | 3 |
| Armstrong | 1 | 0 | 4 | 0 | 3·1 | 0 | 18 | 1 |
| Macartney | 6 | 1 | 18 | 0 | 6 | 1 | 15 | 1 |
| Saunders | 15·2 | 8 | 28 | 5 | 26 | 2 | 76 | 4 |
| Noble | 6 | 0 | 11 | 3 | 12 | 6 | 14 | 1 |

### FALL OF WICKETS

| | A | E | A | E |
|---|---|---|---|---|
| Wkt | 1st | 1st | 2nd | 2nd |
| 1st | 1 | 58 | 4 | 0 |
| 2nd | 14 | 69 | 21 | 61 |
| 3rd | 84 | 88 | 28 | 64 |
| 4th | 100 | 90 | 65 | 79 |
| 5th | 105 | 90 | 77 | 85 |
| 6th | 196 | 92 | 162 | 85 |
| 7th | 196 | 96 | 217 | 128 |
| 8th | 198 | 100 | 329 | 132 |
| 9th | 212 | 103 | 374 | 146 |
| 10th | 214 | 105 | 385 | 186 |

Umpires: R.W. Crockett and P. Argall.

# AUSTRALIA v ENGLAND 1907–08 (5th Test)

Played at Sydney Cricket Ground on 21, 22, 24, 25, 26, 27 February.
Toss: England.    Result: AUSTRALIA won by 49 runs.
Debuts: Nil.

## AUSTRALIA

| | | | | | |
|---|---|---:|---|---|---:|
| M.A. Noble* | b Barnes | 35 | | lbw b Rhodes | 34 |
| C.G. Macartney | c Crawford b Barnes | 1 | (5) | c Jones b Crawford | 12 |
| J.D.A. O'Connor | c Young b Crawford | 9 | (2) | b Barnes | 6 |
| S.E. Gregory | c and b Barnes | 44 | | b Crawford | 56 |
| C. Hill | c Hutchings b Barnes | 12 | (6) | c Young b Crawford | 44 |
| W.W. Armstrong | c and b Crawford | 3 | (7) | c Gunn b Crawford | 32 |
| V.T. Trumper | c Braund b Barnes | 10 | (3) | c Gunn b Rhodes | 166 |
| V.S. Ransford | c Gunn b Barnes | 11 | | not out | 21 |
| R.J. Hartigan | c and b Crawford | 1 | | b Crawford | 5 |
| H. Carter† | not out | 1 | | c Hobbs b Rhodes | 22 |
| J.V. Saunders | c Young b Barnes | 0 | | c Young b Rhodes | 0 |
| Extras | (B 9, LB 1) | 10 | | (B 21, LB 3) | 24 |
| **Total** | | **137** | | | **422** |

## ENGLAND

| | | | | | |
|---|---|---:|---|---|---:|
| J.B. Hobbs | b Saunders | 72 | | c Gregory b Saunders | 13 |
| F.L. Fane | b Noble | 0 | | b Noble | 46 |
| G. Gunn | not out | 122 | | b Macartney | 0 |
| K.L. Hutchings | run out | 13 | | b Macartney | 2 |
| J. Hardstaff, sr | c O'Connor b Saunders | 17 | | b Saunders | 8 |
| J.N. Crawford | c Hill b Saunders | 6 | (10) | not out | 24 |
| L.C. Braund | st Carter b Macartney | 31 | (6) | c Noble b Saunders | 0 |
| W. Rhodes | c Noble b Armstrong | 10 | (7) | b Noble | 69 |
| R.A. Young† | st Carter b Macartney | 0 | (8) | c O'Connor b Saunders | 11 |
| A.O. Jones* | b Macartney | 0 | (9) | b Armstrong | 34 |
| S.F. Barnes | run out | 1 | | b Saunders | 11 |
| Extras | (B 6, LB 3) | 9 | | (B 5, LB 6) | 11 |
| **Total** | | **281** | | | **229** |

| ENGLAND | O | M | R | W | O | M | R | W |
|---|---|---|---|---|---|---|---|---|
| Barnes | 22·4 | 6 | 60 | 7 | 27 | 6 | 78 | 1 |
| Rhodes | 10 | 5 | 15 | 0 | 37·4 | 7 | 102 | 4 |
| Crawford | 18 | 4 | 52 | 3 | 36 | 10 | 141 | 5 |
| Braund | | | | | 20 | 3 | 64 | 0 |
| Hobbs | | | | | 7 | 3 | 13 | 0 |
| AUSTRALIA | | | | | | | | |
| Noble | 28 | 9 | 62 | 1 | 24 | 6 | 56 | 2 |
| Saunders | 35 | 5 | 114 | 3 | 35·1 | 5 | 82 | 5 |
| O'Connor | 6 | 0 | 23 | 0 | 13 | 3 | 29 | 0 |
| Macartney | 15·1 | 3 | 44 | 3 | 15 | 4 | 24 | 2 |
| Armstrong | 12 | 2 | 29 | 1 | 18 | 7 | 27 | 1 |

| | FALL OF WICKETS | | | |
|---|---|---|---|---|
| | A | E | A | E |
| Wkt | 1st | 1st | 2nd | 2nd |
| 1st | 10 | 1 | 25 | 21 |
| 2nd | 46 | 135 | 52 | 26 |
| 3rd | 46 | 168 | 166 | 30 |
| 4th | 64 | 189 | 192 | 51 |
| 5th | 73 | 197 | 300 | 57 |
| 6th | 94 | 245 | 342 | 87 |
| 7th | 124 | 264 | 373 | 123 |
| 8th | 129 | 271 | 387 | 176 |
| 9th | 137 | 271 | 422 | 198 |
| 10th | 137 | 281 | 422 | 229 |

Umpires: A.C. Jones and W. Hannah.

# ENGLAND v AUSTRALIA 1909 (1st Test)

Played at Edgbaston, Birmingham, on 27, 28, 29 May.
Toss: Australia.    Result: ENGLAND won by ten wickets.
Debuts: England – G.J. Thompson; Australia – W. Bardsley, W.J. Whitty.

England's selectors called upon 25 players during the series and invited fifteen to Birmingham. W. Brearley, H.A. Gilbert, T.W. Hayward and A.E. Relf were eventually omitted.

## AUSTRALIA

| | | | | | |
|---|---|---|---|---|---|
| A. Cotter | c Hirst b Blythe | 2 | (9) c Tyldesley b Hirst | | 15 |
| W. Bardsley | c MacLaren b Hirst | 2 | (6) c Thompson b Blythe | | 6 |
| W.W. Armstrong | b Hirst | 24 | (7) c Jessop b Blythe | | 0 |
| V.T. Trumper | c Hirst b Blythe | 10 | (5) c Rhodes b Hirst | | 1 |
| M.A. Noble* | c Jessop b Blythe | 15 | (1) c Jones b Hirst | | 11 |
| S.E. Gregory | c Rhodes b Blythe | 0 | (3) c Thompson b Blythe | | 43 |
| V.S. Ransford | b Hirst | 1 | (4) b Blythe | | 43 |
| C.G. Macartney | c MacLaren b Blythe | 10 | (2) lbw b Blythe | | 1 |
| H. Carter† | lbw b Hirst | 0 | (8) c Hobbs b Hirst | | 1 |
| J.D.A. O'Connor | lbw b Blythe | 8 | c Lilley b Hirst | | 13 |
| W.J. Whitty | not out | 0 | not out | | 9 |
| Extras | (LB 1, NB 1) | 2 | (B 7, LB 1) | | 8 |
| **Total** | | **74** | | | **151** |

## ENGLAND

| | | | | | |
|---|---|---|---|---|---|
| A.C. MacLaren* | b Macartney | 5 | | | |
| J.B. Hobbs | lbw b Macartney | 0 | (1) not out | | 62 |
| J.T. Tyldesley | b O'Connor | 24 | | | |
| C.B. Fry | b Macartney | 0 | (2) not out | | 35 |
| A.O. Jones | c Carter b Armstrong | 28 | | | |
| G.H. Hirst | lbw b Armstrong | 15 | | | |
| G.L. Jessop | b Armstrong | 22 | | | |
| W. Rhodes | not out | 15 | | | |
| A.F.A. Lilley† | c Ransford b Armstrong | 0 | | | |
| G.J. Thompson | run out | 6 | | | |
| C. Blythe | c Macartney b Armstrong | 1 | | | |
| Extras | (B 4, LB 1) | 5 | (B 5, LB 3) | | 8 |
| **Total** | | **121** | (0 wickets) | | **105** |

| ENGLAND | O | M | R | W | O | M | R | W |
|---|---|---|---|---|---|---|---|---|
| Hirst | 23 | 8 | 28 | 4 | 23·5 | 4 | 58 | 5 |
| Blythe | 23 | 6 | 44 | 6 | 24 | 3 | 58 | 5 |
| Thompson | | | | | 4 | 0 | 19 | 0 |
| Rhodes | | | | | 1 | 0 | 8 | 0 |

| AUSTRALIA | O | M | R | W | O | M | R | W |
|---|---|---|---|---|---|---|---|---|
| Whitty | 17 | 5 | 43 | 0 | 5 | 1 | 18 | 0 |
| Macartney | 17 | 6 | 21 | 3 | 11 | 2 | 35 | 0 |
| Noble | 1 | 0 | 2 | 0 | | | | |
| O'Connor | 5 | 2 | 23 | 1 | 3·2 | 1 | 17 | 0 |
| Armstrong | 15·3 | 7 | 27 | 5 | 13 | 5 | 27 | 0 |

Umpires: J. Carlin and F. Parris.

### FALL OF WICKETS

| | A | E | A | E |
|---|---|---|---|---|
| Wkt | 1st | 1st | 2nd | 2nd |
| 1st | 5 | 0 | 4 | – |
| 2nd | 7 | 13 | 16 | – |
| 3rd | 30 | 13 | 97 | – |
| 4th | 46 | 61 | 99 | – |
| 5th | 47 | 61 | 103 | – |
| 6th | 52 | 90 | 103 | – |
| 7th | 58 | 103 | 106 | – |
| 8th | 59 | 107 | 123 | – |
| 9th | 71 | 116 | 125 | – |
| 10th | 74 | 121 | 151 | – |

# ENGLAND v AUSTRALIA 1909 (2nd Test)

Played at Lord's, London, on 14, 15, 16 June.
Toss: Australia.   Result: AUSTRALIA won by nine wickets.
Debuts: England – J.H. King.

## ENGLAND

| | | | | | |
|---|---|---|---|---|---|
| T.W. Hayward | st Carter b Laver | 16 | run out | | 6 |
| J.B. Hobbs | c Carter b Laver | 19 | c and b Armstrong | | 9 |
| J.T. Tyldesley | lbw b Laver | 46 | st Carter b Armstrong | | 3 |
| G. Gunn | lbw b Cotter | 1 | b Armstrong | | 0 |
| J.H. King | c Macartney b Cotter | 60 | b Armstrong | | 4 |
| A.C. MacLaren* | c Armstrong b Noble | 7 | (8) b Noble | | 24 |
| G.H. Hirst | b Cotter | 31 | b Armstrong | | 1 |
| A.O. Jones | b Cotter | 8 | (6) lbw b Laver | | 26 |
| A.E. Relf | c Armstrong b Noble | 17 | (10) b Armstrong | | 3 |
| A.F.A. Lilley† | c Bardsley b Noble | 47 | (9) not out | | 25 |
| S. Haigh | not out | 1 | run out | | 5 |
| Extras | (B 8, LB 3, W 3, NB 2) | 16 | (B 2, LB 3, NB 10) | | 15 |
| **Total** | | **269** | | | **121** |

## AUSTRALIA

| | | | | | |
|---|---|---|---|---|---|
| P.A. McAlister | lbw b King | 22 | not out | | 19 |
| F. Laver | b Hirst | 14 | | | |
| W. Bardsley | b Relf | 46 | (2) c Lilley b Relf | | 0 |
| W.W. Armstrong | c Lilley b Relf | 12 | | | |
| V.S. Ransford | not out | 143 | | | |
| V.T. Trumper | c MacLaren b Relf | 28 | | | |
| M.A. Noble* | c Lilley b Relf | 32 | | | |
| S.E. Gregory | c Lilley b Relf | 14 | (3) not out | | 18 |
| A.Cotter | run out | 0 | | | |
| C.G. Macartney | b Hirst | 5 | | | |
| H. Carter† | b Hirst | 7 | | | |
| Extras | (B 16, LB 8, W 1, NB 2) | 27 | (B 4) | | 4 |
| **Total** | | **350** | (1 wicket) | | **41** |

| AUSTRALIA | O | M | R | W | O | M | R | W | FALL OF WICKETS | | | | |
|---|---|---|---|---|---|---|---|---|---|---|---|---|---|
| Laver | 32 | 9 | 75 | 3 | 13 | 4 | 24 | 1 | | E | A | E | A |
| Macartney | 8 | 3 | 10 | 0 | | | | | Wkt | 1st | 1st | 2nd | 2nd |
| Cotter | 23 | 1 | 80 | 4 | 18 | 3 | 35 | 0 | 1st | 23 | 18 | 16 | 4 |
| Noble | 24·2 | 9 | 42 | 3 | 5 | 1 | 12 | 1 | 2nd | 41 | 84 | 22 | — |
| Armstrong | 20 | 6 | 46 | 0 | 24·5 | 11 | 35 | 6 | 3rd | 44 | 90 | 22 | — |
| | | | | | | | | | 4th | 123 | 119 | 23 | — |
| ENGLAND | | | | | | | | | 5th | 149 | 198 | 34 | — |
| Hirst | 26·5 | 2 | 83 | 3 | 8 | 1 | 28 | 0 | 6th | 175 | 269 | 41 | — |
| King | 27 | 5 | 99 | 1 | | | | | 7th | 199 | 317 | 82 | — |
| Relf | 45 | 14 | 85 | 5 | 7·4 | 4 | 9 | 1 | 8th | 205 | 317 | 90 | — |
| Haigh | 19 | 5 | 41 | 0 | | | | | 9th | 258 | 342 | 101 | — |
| Jones | 2 | 0 | 15 | 0 | | | | | 10th | 269 | 350 | 121 | — |

Umpires: J. Moss and C.E. Dench.

# ENGLAND v AUSTRALIA 1909 (3rd Test)

Played at Headingley, Leeds, on 1, 2, 3 July.
Toss: Australia.   Result: AUSTRALIA won by 126 runs.
Debuts: England – J. Sharp.

### AUSTRALIA

| | | | | |
|---|---|---|---|---|
| P.A. McAlister | lbw b Hirst | 3 | c Sharp b Barnes | 5 |
| S.E. Gregory | b Barnes | 46 | b Hirst | 0 |
| V.S. Ransford | run out | 45 | lbw b Barnes | 24 |
| M.A. Noble* | b Hirst | 3 | (5) c Rhodes b Barnes | 31 |
| W. Bardsley | hit wkt b Rhodes | 30 | (7) c Lilley b Barnes | 2 |
| W.W. Armstrong | c Lilley b Brearley | 21 | (4) b Rhodes | 45 |
| V.T. Trumper | not out | 27 | (6) b Barnes | 2 |
| C.G. Macartney | c Fry b Rhodes | 4 | b Brearley | 18 |
| A. Cotter | b Rhodes | 2 | c MacLaren b Rhodes | 19 |
| H. Carter† | lbw b Rhodes | 1 | c Lilley b Barnes | 30 |
| F. Laver | c Lilley b Brearley | 0 | not out | 13 |
| Extras | (LB 4, W 1, NB 1) | 6 | (B 15, LB 2, NB 1) | 18 |
| **Total** | | **188** | | **207** |

### ENGLAND

| | | | | |
|---|---|---|---|---|
| C.B. Fry | lbw b Cotter | 1 | b Cotter | 7 |
| J.B. Hobbs | b Macartney | 12 | b Cotter | 30 |
| J.T. Tyldesley | c Armstrong b Macartney | 55 | c and b Macartney | 7 |
| J. Sharp | st Carter b Macartney | 61 | b Cotter | 11 |
| A.C. MacLaren* | b Macartney | 17 | c Cotter b Macartney | 1 |
| W. Rhodes | c Carter b Laver | 12 | c Armstrong b Macartney | 16 |
| G.H. Hirst | b Macartney | 4 | (8) b Cotter | 0 |
| A.F.A. Lilley† | not out | 4 | (7) lbw b Cotter | 2 |
| S.F. Barnes | b Macartney | 1 | b Macartney | 1 |
| W. Brearley | b Macartney | 6 | not out | 4 |
| G.L. Jessop | absent hurt | – | absent hurt | – |
| Extras | (B 1, LB 4, NB 4) | 9 | (B 1, LB 1, W 1, NB 5) | 8 |
| **Total** | | **182** | | **87** |

| ENGLAND | O | M | R | W | O | M | R | W | | FALL OF WICKETS | | | |
|---|---|---|---|---|---|---|---|---|---|---|---|---|---|
| | | | | | | | | | | A | E | A | E |
| Hirst | 26 | 6 | 65 | 2 | 17 | 3 | 39 | 1 | *Wkt* | *1st* | *1st* | *2nd* | *2nd* |
| Barnes | 25 | 12 | 37 | 1 | 35 | 16 | 63 | 6 | 1st | 6 | 8 | 0 | 17 |
| Brearley | 14·1 | 1 | 42 | 2 | 24·1 | 6 | 36 | 1 | 2nd | 86 | 31 | 14 | 26 |
| Rhodes | 8 | 2 | 38 | 4 | 19 | 3 | 44 | 2 | 3rd | 100 | 137 | 52 | 60 |
| Sharp | | | | | 1 | 0 | 7 | 0 | 4th | 104 | 146 | 118 | 61 |
| | | | | | | | | | 5th | 140 | 157 | 122 | 61 |
| AUSTRALIA | | | | | | | | | 6th | 154 | 169 | 126 | 82 |
| Cotter | 17 | 1 | 45 | 1 | 16 | 2 | 38 | 5 | 7th | 167 | 171 | 127 | 82 |
| Macartney | 25·3 | 6 | 58 | 7 | 16·5 | 5 | 27 | 4 | 8th | 169 | 174 | 150 | 82 |
| Armstrong | 16 | 5 | 33 | 0 | 3 | 1 | 8 | 0 | 9th | 171 | 182 | 183 | 87 |
| Laver | 13 | 4 | 15 | 1 | 2 | 0 | 6 | 0 | 10th | 188 | – | 207 | – |
| Noble | 13 | 5 | 22 | 0 | | | | | | | | | |

Umpires: W.A.J. West and W. Richards.

# ENGLAND v AUSTRALIA 1909 (4th Test)

Played at Old Trafford, Manchester, on 26, 27, 28 July.
Toss: Australia.    Result: MATCH DRAWN.
Debuts: Nil.

## AUSTRALIA

| | | | | |
|---|---|---|---|---|
| S.E. Gregory | b Blythe | 21 | b Hirst | 5 |
| W. Bardsley | b Barnes | 9 | c MacLaren b Blythe | 35 |
| V.S. Ransford | lbw b Barnes | 4 | (7) not out | 54 |
| M.A. Noble* | b Blythe | 17 | b Blythe | 13 |
| V.T. Trumper | c Hutchings b Barnes | 2 | (6) c Tyldesley b Rhodes | 48 |
| W.W. Armstrong | not out | 32 | (5) lbw b Rhodes | 30 |
| A.J.Y. Hopkins | b Blythe | 3 | (8) c Barnes b Rhodes | 9 |
| C.G. Macartney | b Barnes | 5 | (3) b Rhodes | 51 |
| A. Cotter | c Tyldesley b Blythe | 17 | c MacLaren b Rhodes | 4 |
| H. Carter† | lbw b Barnes | 13 | lbw b Barnes | 12 |
| F. Laver | b Blythe | 11 | | |
| Extras | (B 6, LB 7) | 13 | (B 9, LB 8, NB 1) | 18 |
| **Total** | | **147** | (9 wickets declared) | **279** |

## ENGLAND

| | | | | |
|---|---|---|---|---|
| P.F. Warner | b Macartney | 9 | b Hopkins | 25 |
| R.H. Spooner | c and b Cotter | 25 | b Laver | 58 |
| J.T. Tyldesley | c Armstrong b Laver | 15 | b Hopkins | 11 |
| J. Sharp | c Armstrong b Laver | 3 | not out | 8 |
| W. Rhodes | c Carter b Laver | 5 | not out | 0 |
| K.L. Hutchings | b Laver | 9 | | |
| A.C. MacLaren* | lbw b Laver | 16 | | |
| A.F.A. Lilley† | not out | 26 | | |
| G.H. Hirst | c Hopkins b Laver | 1 | | |
| S.F. Barnes | b Laver | 0 | | |
| C. Blythe | b Laver | 1 | | |
| Extras | (B 2, LB 3, NB 4) | 9 | (B 2, LB 4) | 6 |
| **Total** | | **119** | (3 wickets) | **108** |

| ENGLAND | O | M | R | W | O | M | R | W |
|---|---|---|---|---|---|---|---|---|
| Hirst | 7 | 0 | 15 | 0 | 12 | 3 | 32 | 1 |
| Barnes | 27 | 9 | 56 | 5 | 22·3 | 5 | 66 | 1 |
| Blythe | 20·3 | 5 | 63 | 5 | 24 | 5 | 77 | 2 |
| Sharp | | | | | 1 | 0 | 3 | 0 |
| Rhodes | | | | | 25 | 0 | 83 | 5 |
| AUSTRALIA | | | | | | | | |
| Noble | 8 | 2 | 11 | 0 | | | | |
| Macartney | 18 | 6 | 31 | 1 | 7 | 2 | 16 | 0 |
| Laver | 18·2 | 7 | 31 | 8 | 21 | 12 | 25 | 1 |
| Cotter | 8 | 1 | 37 | 1 | 5 | 0 | 14 | 0 |
| Armstrong | | | | | 10 | 6 | 16 | 0 |
| Hopkins | | | | | 12 | 4 | 31 | 2 |

## FALL OF WICKETS

| | A | E | A | E |
|---|---|---|---|---|
| Wkt | 1st | 1st | 2nd | 2nd |
| 1st | 13 | 24 | 16 | 78 |
| 2nd | 21 | 39 | 77 | 90 |
| 3rd | 45 | 44 | 106 | 102 |
| 4th | 48 | 50 | 126 | — |
| 5th | 58 | 63 | 148 | — |
| 6th | 66 | 72 | 237 | — |
| 7th | 86 | 99 | 256 | — |
| 8th | 110 | 103 | 262 | — |
| 9th | 128 | 103 | 279 | — |
| 10th | 147 | 119 | — | — |

Umpires: W.A.J. West and W. Richards.

# ENGLAND v AUSTRALIA 1909 (5th Test)

Played at Kennington Oval, London, on 9, 10, 11 August.
Toss: Australia.   Result: MATCH DRAWN.
Debuts: England – D.W. Carr, F.E. Woolley.

M.A. Noble emulated Jackson's feat of 1905 by winning all five tosses in the series. D.W. Carr, aged 37 and a googly bowler in his first season of county cricket, took 3 for 19 in the first seven overs of his only Test but was then grossly overbowled. W. Bardsley became the first batsman to score a hundred in each innings of a Test match.

## AUSTRALIA

| | | | | | |
|---|---|---|---|---|---|
| S.E. Gregory | b Carr | 1 | run out | | 74 |
| W. Bardsley | b Sharp | 136 | lbw b Barnes | | 130 |
| M.A. Noble* | lbw b Carr | 2 | c MacLaren b Barnes | | 55 |
| W.W. Armstrong | lbw b Carr | 15 | c Woolley b Carr | | 10 |
| V.S. Ransford | b Barnes | 3 | not out | | 36 |
| V.T. Trumper | c Rhodes b Barnes | 73 | st Lilley b Carr | | 20 |
| C.G. Macartney | c Rhodes b Sharp | 50 | not out | | 4 |
| A.J.Y. Hopkins | c Rhodes b Sharp | 21 | | | |
| A. Cotter | b Carr | 7 | | | |
| H. Carter† | lbw b Carr | 4 | | | |
| F. Laver | not out | 8 | | | |
| Extras | (B 1, LB 3, NB 1) | 5 | (B 4, LB 3, W 1, NB 2) | | 10 |
| **Total** | | **325** | (5 wickets declared) | | **339** |

## ENGLAND

| | | | | | |
|---|---|---|---|---|---|
| R.H. Spooner | b Cotter | 13 | c and b Macartney | | 3 |
| A.C. MacLaren* | lbw b Cotter | 15 | | | |
| W. Rhodes | c Carter b Cotter | 66 | (2) st Carter b Armstrong | | 54 |
| C.B. Fry | run out | 62 | not out | | 35 |
| J. Sharp | c Gregory b Hopkins | 105 | not out | | 0 |
| F.E. Woolley | b Cotter | 8 | | | |
| E.G. Hayes | lbw b Armstrong | 4 | (3) c sub (R.J. Hartigan) b Armstrong | | 9 |
| K.L. Hutchings | c Macartney b Cotter | 59 | | | |
| A.F.A. Lilley† | not out | 2 | | | |
| S.F. Barnes | c Carter b Hopkins | 0 | | | |
| D.W. Carr | b Cotter | 0 | | | |
| Extras | (B 8, LB 4, NB 6) | 18 | (LB 2, NB 1) | | 3 |
| **Total** | | **352** | (3 wickets) | | **104** |

| ENGLAND | O | M | R | W | O | M | R | W |
|---|---|---|---|---|---|---|---|---|
| Carr | 34 | 2 | 146 | 5 | 35 | 1 | 136 | 2 |
| Barnes | 19 | 3 | 57 | 2 | 27 | 7 | 61 | 2 |
| Sharp | 16·3 | 3 | 67 | 3 | 12 | 0 | 34 | 0 |
| Woolley | 4 | 1 | 6 | 0 | 6 | 0 | 31 | 0 |
| Hayes | 4 | 0 | 10 | 0 | 2 | 0 | 14 | 0 |
| Rhodes | 12 | 3 | 34 | 0 | 14 | 1 | 35 | 0 |
| Hutchings | | | | | 4 | 0 | 18 | 0 |
| AUSTRALIA | | | | | | | | |
| Cotter | 27·4 | 1 | 95 | 6 | 8 | 1 | 21 | 0 |
| Armstrong | 31 | 7 | 93 | 1 | 7 | 4 | 8 | 2 |
| Laver | 8 | 1 | 13 | 0 | | | | |
| Macartney | 16 | 2 | 49 | 0 | 8 | 2 | 11 | 1 |
| Hopkins | 15 | 2 | 51 | 2 | 8 | 0 | 40 | 0 |
| Noble | 8 | 1 | 29 | 0 | | | | |
| Gregory | 1 | 0 | 4 | 0 | 2 | 0 | 21 | 0 |

FALL OF WICKETS

| Wkt | A 1st | E 1st | A 2nd | E 2nd |
|---|---|---|---|---|
| 1st | 9 | 15 | 180 | 14 |
| 2nd | 27 | 36 | 267 | 27 |
| 3rd | 55 | 140 | 268 | 88 |
| 4th | 58 | 187 | 294 | – |
| 5th | 176 | 201 | 335 | – |
| 6th | 259 | 206 | – | – |
| 7th | 289 | 348 | – | – |
| 8th | 300 | 348 | – | – |
| 9th | 304 | 351 | – | – |
| 10th | 325 | 352 | – | – |

Umpires: J. Moss and W. Richards.

# SOUTH AFRICA v ENGLAND 1909–10 (1st Test)

Played at Old Wanderers, Johannesburg, on 1, 3, 4, 5 January.
Toss: South Africa.   Result: SOUTH AFRICA won by 19 runs.
Debuts: South Africa – T. Campbell, J.M.M. Commaille, L.A. Stricker, J.W. Zulch;
  England – M.C. Bird, C.P. Buckenham, H.D.G. Leveson-Gower, G.H.T. Simpson-Hayward,
  H. Strudwick.

Faulkner became the only player ever to score 200 runs and take eight wickets in the same Test match.
Simpson-Hayward, a lob bowler, took 6 for 43 in his first Test innings.

## SOUTH AFRICA

| | | | | | |
|---|---|--:|---|---|--:|
| J.W. Zulch | b Simpson-Hayward | 19 | | lbw b Buckenham | 27 |
| L.A. Stricker | b Buckenham | 12 | | b Simpson-Hayward | 17 |
| G.A. Faulkner | lbw b Simpson-Hayward | 78 | (6) | b Bird | 123 |
| A.W. Nourse | c Leveson-Gower b Rhodes | 53 | | c Strudwick b Buckenham | 34 |
| S.J. Snooke* | c Strudwick b Buckenham | 12 | (7) | c Rhodes b Buckenham | 47 |
| G.C. White | c Woolley b Buckenham | 0 | (3) | c Woolley b Buckenham | 39 |
| J.H. Sinclair | b Simpson-Hayward | 3 | (8) | b Simpson-Hayward | 0 |
| J.M.M. Commaille | st Strudwick b Simpson-Hayward | 8 | (9) | b Bird | 19 |
| R.O. Schwarz | b Simpson-Hayward | 0 | (11) | not out | 6 |
| A.E.E. Vogler | c Denton b Simpson-Hayward | 10 | | c Rhodes b Bird | 14 |
| T. Campbell† | not out | 8 | (5) | b Thompson | 8 |
| Extras | (B 1, LB 2, NB 2) | 5 | | (B 2, W 1, NB 8) | 11 |
| **Total** | | **208** | | | **345** |

## ENGLAND

| | | | | | |
|---|---|--:|---|---|--:|
| J.B. Hobbs | c Campbell b Vogler | 89 | | b Vogler | 35 |
| W. Rhodes | b Vogler | 66 | | c Nourse b Vogler | 2 |
| D. Denton | c Vogler b Faulkner | 28 | | c and b Vogler | 26 |
| F.L. Fane | c Vogler b Faulkner | 23 | | lbw b Vogler | 0 |
| F.E. Woolley | c Schwarz b Vogler | 14 | | b Vogler | 25 |
| G.J. Thompson | lbw b Vogler | 16 | | b Faulkner | 63 |
| M.C. Bird | c Vogler b Faulkner | 4 | | c Snooke b Faulkner | 5 |
| C.P. Buckenham | b Faulkner | 0 | | b Vogler | 1 |
| H.D.G. Leveson-Gower* | c Campbell b Faulkner | 17 | | b Faulkner | 31 |
| G.H.T. Simpson-Hayward | not out | 29 | | c White b Vogler | 14 |
| H. Strudwick† | b Vogler | 7 | | not out | 1 |
| Extras | (B 9, LB 8) | 17 | | (B 14, LB 2, W 1, NB 4) | 21 |
| **Total** | | **310** | | | **224** |

| ENGLAND | O | M | R | W | O | M | R | W | | FALL OF WICKETS | | | |
|---|--:|--:|--:|--:|--:|--:|--:|--:|---|--:|--:|--:|--:|
| Buckenham | 19 | 1 | 77 | 3 | 39 | 5 | 110 | 4 | | SA | E | SA | E |
| Hobbs | 6 | 1 | 20 | 0 | 6 | 2 | 16 | 0 | *Wkt* | *1st* | *1st* | *2nd* | *2nd* |
| Simpson-Hayward | 16 | 3 | 43 | 6 | 24 | 3 | 59 | 2 | 1st | 25 | 159 | 30 | 36 |
| Thompson | 11 | 3 | 25 | 0 | 28 | 6 | 100 | 1 | 2nd | 33 | 190 | 88 | 47 |
| Rhodes | 9 | 1 | 34 | 1 | 9 | 3 | 25 | 0 | 3rd | 133 | 206 | 95 | 47 |
| Woolley | 1 | 0 | 4 | 0 | 4 | 1 | 13 | 0 | 4th | 155 | 237 | 129 | 91 |
| Bird | 1 | 1 | 0 | 0 | 4 | 1 | 11 | 3 | 5th | 155 | 241 | 143 | 94 |
| | | | | | | | | | 6th | 164 | 245 | 242 | 102 |
| SOUTH AFRICA | | | | | | | | | 7th | 187 | 247 | 247 | 108 |
| Vogler | 30·1 | 4 | 87 | 5 | 22 | 2 | 94 | 7 | 8th | 187 | 265 | 321 | 178 |
| Snooke | 6 | 1 | 28 | 0 | 3 | 0 | 10 | 0 | 9th | 195 | 275 | 332 | 210 |
| Nourse | 9 | 3 | 13 | 0 | 5 | 0 | 20 | 0 | 10th | 208 | 310 | 345 | 224 |
| Faulkner | 33 | 4 | 120 | 5 | 17·2 | 7 | 40 | 3 | | | | | |
| White | 3 | 0 | 15 | 0 | 4 | 0 | 33 | 0 | | | | | |
| Sinclair | 4 | 0 | 10 | 0 | | | | | | | | | |
| Schwarz | 2 | 0 | 8 | 0 | 1 | 0 | 4 | 0 | | | | | |
| Stricker | 3 | 0 | 12 | 0 | 1 | 0 | 2 | 0 | | | | | |

Umpires: A.J. Atfield and F.W. Grey.

# SOUTH AFRICA v ENGLAND 1909–10 (2nd Test)

Played at Lord's, Durban, on 21, 22, 24, 25, 26 January.
Toss: South Africa.   Result: SOUTH AFRICA won by 95 runs.
Debuts: Nil.

N.C. Tufnell, who made his only Test appearance in the final match of this rubber, was the first substitute to make a stumping in a Test match; he kept wicket after Strudwick had been hit in the face.

## SOUTH AFRICA

| Batsman | Dismissal 1st | Runs | Dismissal 2nd | Runs |
|---|---|---|---|---|
| L.A. Stricker | b Buckenham | 31 | c Strudwick b Thompson | 5 |
| J.W. Zulch | b Thompson | 13 | c Rhodes b Buckenham | 3 |
| G.C. White | c Hobbs b Thompson | 7 | (5) b Simpson-Hayward | 118 |
| A.W. Nourse | c Strudwick b Buckenham | 0 | c Rhodes b Bird | 69 |
| G.A. Faulkner | c Woolley b Thompson | 47 | (3) c Fane b Backenham | 9 |
| T. Campbell† | b Simpson-Hayward | 48 | (9) b Simpson-Hayward | 1 |
| S.J. Snooke* | b Woolley | 19 | st sub (N.C. Tufnell) b Thompson | 53 |
| J.H. Sinclair | b Simpson-Hayward | 12 | b Woolley | 22 |
| J.M.M. Commaille | c Thompson b Simpson-Hayward | 3 | (6) b Buckenham | 30 |
| R.O. Schwarz | b Simpson-Hayward | 0 | (11) not out | 9 |
| A.E.E. Vogler | not out | 7 | (10) c Woolley b Simpson-Hayward | 11 |
| Extras | (B 7, LB 5) | 12 | (B 12, LB 1, NB 4) | 17 |
| **Total** | | **199** | | **347** |

## ENGLAND

| Batsman | Dismissal 1st | Runs | Dismissal 2nd | Runs |
|---|---|---|---|---|
| J.B. Hobbs | b Sinclair | 53 | c Vogler b Faulkner | 70 |
| W. Rhodes | c Schwarz b Vogler | 44 | c White b Sinclair | 17 |
| D. Denton | run out | 0 | c Vogler b Faulkner | 6 |
| F.L. Fane | c and b Vogler | 6 | c Schwarz b Vogler | 6 |
| F.E. Woolley | c Zulch b Vogler | 22 | c Vogler b Faulkner | 4 |
| G.J. Thompson | c and b Vogler | 38 | not out | 46 |
| M.C. Bird | c Stricker b Nourse | 1 | c Nourse b Faulkner | 42 |
| C.P. Buckenham | b Faulkner | 16 | c Faulkner b Vogler | 3 |
| H.D.G. Leveson-Gower* | not out | 6 | b Nourse | 23 |
| G.H.T. Simpson-Hayward | c Campbell b Vogler | 0 | lbw b Faulkner | 16 |
| H. Strudwick† | hit wkt b Faulkner | 1 | c Vogler b Faulkner | 7 |
| Extras | (B 4, LB 6, NB 2) | 12 | (B 9, LB 1, NB 2) | 12 |
| **Total** | | **199** | | **252** |

| ENGLAND | O | M | R | W | O | M | R | W |
|---|---|---|---|---|---|---|---|---|
| Buckenham | 27 | 4 | 51 | 2 | 31 | 4 | 94 | 3 |
| Hobbs | 5 | 2 | 5 | 0 | 2 | 0 | 5 | 0 |
| Simpson-Hayward | 23·5 | 3 | 42 | 4 | 23 | 4 | 66 | 3 |
| Thompson | 28 | 13 | 52 | 3 | 38·2 | 13 | 78 | 2 |
| Woolley | 15 | 5 | 23 | 1 | 10 | 3 | 34 | 1 |
| Rhodes | 5 | 1 | 11 | 0 | 19 | 6 | 43 | 0 |
| Bird | 3 | 2 | 3 | 0 | 7 | 3 | 10 | 1 |
| SOUTH AFRICA | | | | | | | | |
| Snooke | 6 | 1 | 11 | 0 | 1 | 0 | 9 | 0 |
| Vogler | 30 | 6 | 83 | 5 | 29 | 6 | 93 | 2 |
| Faulkner | 17·1 | 4 | 51 | 2 | 33·4 | 8 | 87 | 6 |
| Sinclair | 16 | 4 | 32 | 1 | 5 | 0 | 18 | 1 |
| White | 4 | 1 | 9 | 0 | 6 | 3 | 10 | 0 |
| Stricker | 1 | 0 | 1 | 0 | | | | |
| Nourse | 1 | 1 | 0 | 1 | 6 | 2 | 11 | 1 |
| Schwarz | | | | | 2 | 0 | 12 | 0 |

## FALL OF WICKETS

| | SA | E | SA | E |
|---|---|---|---|---|
| Wkt | 1st | 1st | 2nd | 2nd |
| 1st | 20 | 94 | 6 | 48 |
| 2nd | 36 | 95 | 16 | 59 |
| 3rd | 37 | 108 | 23 | 84 |
| 4th | 76 | 117 | 166 | 106 |
| 5th | 116 | 138 | 245 | 111 |
| 6th | 150 | 148 | 269 | 174 |
| 7th | 187 | 188 | 302 | 180 |
| 8th | 190 | 198 | 305 | 220 |
| 9th | 192 | 198 | 317 | 244 |
| 10th | 199 | 199 | 347 | 252 |

Umpires: F.E. Smith and F.W. Grey.

## SOUTH AFRICA v ENGLAND 1909–10 (3rd Test)

Played at Old Wanderers, Johannesburg, on 26, 28 February, 1, 2, 3 March.
Toss: South Africa.   Result: ENGLAND won by three wickets.
Debuts: South Africa – C.E. Floquet, S.J. Pegler.

Denton scored his 104 in 100 minutes.

### SOUTH AFRICA

| | | | | | |
|---|---|--:|---|---|--:|
| L.A. Stricker | c Woolley b Buckenham | 1 | | b Thompson | 12 |
| J.W. Zulch | c Woolley b Thompson | 3 | | run out | 34 |
| G.C. White | c Buckenham b Simpson-Hayward | 72 | (7) | c Woolley b Simpson-Hayward | 2 |
| A.W. Nourse | b Thompson | 12 | (6) | c Thompson b Simpson-Hayward | 5 |
| G.A. Faulkner | c Rhodes b Buckenham | 76 | | c Thompson b Simpson-Hayward | 44 |
| J.M.M. Commaille | c Strudwick b Buckenham | 39 | (3) | b Simpson-Hayward | 2 |
| S.J. Snooke* | c Rhodes b Buckenham | 13 | (8) | b Thompson | 52 |
| A.E.E. Vogler | c Woolley b Rhodes | 65 | (9) | b Thompson | 22 |
| C.E. Floquet | b Buckenham | 1 | (11) | not out | 11 |
| S.J. Pegler | not out | 11 | | run out | 28 |
| T. Campbell† | c Strudwick b Woolley | 0 | (4) | b Simpson-Hayward | 19 |
| Extras | (B 9, LB 1, W 1, NB 1) | 12 | | (B 1, LB 3, NB 2) | 6 |
| **Total** | | **305** | | | **237** |

### ENGLAND

| | | | | | |
|---|---|--:|---|---|--:|
| W. Rhodes | c Faulkner b Vogler | 14 | (4) | c Snooke b Faulkner | 1 |
| F.L. Fane | c Campbell b Pegler | 39 | (6) | b Faulkner | 17 |
| D. Denton | b Vogler | 104 | | c White b Vogler | 24 |
| G.J. Thompson | c Vogler b Faulkner | 21 | (1) | lbw b Vogler | 10 |
| M.C. Bird | b Faulkner | 20 | (8) | run out | 45 |
| H.D.G. Leveson-Gower* | lbw b Vogler | 6 | (9) | not out | 12 |
| J.B. Hobbs | b Faulkner | 11 | (5) | not out | 93 |
| F.E. Woolley | not out | 58 | (7) | c Nourse b Vogler | 0 |
| G.H.T. Simpson-Hayward | c Zulch b Vogler | 5 | | | |
| C.P. Buckenham | c Pegler b Faulkner | 1 | | | |
| H. Strudwick† | c Snooke b Pegler | 18 | (2) | b Vogler | 5 |
| Extras | (B 17, LB 7, NB 1) | 25 | | (B 10, LB 3, NB 1) | 14 |
| **Total** | | **322** | | (7 wickets) | **221** |

| ENGLAND | O | M | R | W | O | M | R | W |
|---|--:|--:|--:|--:|--:|--:|--:|--:|
| Buckenham | 31 | 2 | 115 | 5 | 23 | 4 | 73 | 0 |
| Thompson | 17 | 6 | 74 | 2 | 23 | 9 | 54 | 3 |
| Simpson-Hayward | 14 | 1 | 46 | 1 | 22 | 2 | 69 | 5 |
| Woolley | 21 | 4 | 54 | 1 | 18 | 6 | 29 | 0 |
| Rhodes | 1 | 0 | 4 | 1 | 4 | 1 | 6 | 0 |
| Bird | | | | | 1 | 1 | 0 | 0 |
| SOUTH AFRICA | | | | | | | | |
| Vogler | 28 | 4 | 98 | 4 | 25 | 2 | 109 | 4 |
| Faulkner | 30 | 4 | 89 | 4 | 23·4 | 5 | 75 | 2 |
| Pegler | 9·4 | 0 | 40 | 2 | 4 | 1 | 15 | 0 |
| White | 4 | 0 | 28 | 0 | | | | |
| Floquet | 8 | 2 | 24 | 0 | | | | |
| Nourse | 3 | 1 | 18 | 0 | | | | |
| Snooke | | | | | 6 | 3 | 8 | 0 |

### FALL OF WICKETS

| | SA | E | SA | E |
|---|--:|--:|--:|--:|
| Wkt | 1st | 1st | 2nd | 2nd |
| 1st | 4 | 32 | 24 | 16 |
| 2nd | 4 | 96 | 57 | 37 |
| 3rd | 30 | 187 | 61 | 42 |
| 4th | 144 | 193 | 104 | 42 |
| 5th | 198 | 201 | 119 | 92 |
| 6th | 212 | 233 | 120 | 93 |
| 7th | 239 | 234 | 123 | 188 |
| 8th | 245 | 251 | 178 | — |
| 9th | 304 | 253 | 214 | — |
| 10th | 305 | 322 | 237 | — |

Umpires: A.J. Atfield and F.W. Grey.

# SOUTH AFRICA v ENGLAND 1909–10 (4th Test)

Played at Newlands, Cape Town, on 7, 8, 9 March.
Toss: England.   Result: SOUTH AFRICA won by four wickets.
Debuts: Nil.

## ENGLAND

| | | | | | |
|---|---|---|---|---|---|
| J.B. Hobbs | c Faulkner b Vogler | 1 | c Campbell b Snooke | | 0 |
| W. Rhodes | c Faulkner b Snooke | 0 | b Snooke | | 5 |
| D. Denton | c Commaille b Snooke | 0 | c Faulkner b Vogler | | 10 |
| F.L. Fane* | c Campbell b Sinclair | 14 | c Snooke b Faulkner | | 37 |
| F.E. Woolley | c Zulch b Sinclair | 69 | b Vogler | | 64 |
| G.J. Thompson | run out | 16 | c Snooke b Faulkner | | 6 |
| M.C. Bird | c Campbell b White | 57 | c Schwarz b Vogler | | 11 |
| G.H.T. Simpson-Hayward | b Faulkner | 13 | c Faulkner b Vogler | | 9 |
| C.P. Buckenham | b Vogler | 5 | (10) c Faulkner b Vogler | | 17 |
| H. Strudwick† | c and b White | 7 | (9) c Nourse b Faulkner | | 3 |
| C. Blythe | not out | 1 | not out | | 4 |
| Extras | (B 13, LB 5, NB 2) | 20 | (B 4, LB 8) | | 12 |
| **Total** | | **203** | | | **178** |

## SOUTH AFRICA

| | | | | | |
|---|---|---|---|---|---|
| J.W. Zulch | b Simpson-Hayward | 30 | c Strudwick b Thompson | | 13 |
| J.M.M. Commaille | c and b Buckenham | 42 | b Buckenham | | 3 |
| G.C. White | b Bird | 15 | c Woolley b Thompson | | 31 |
| A.W. Nourse | b Thompson | 27 | c Rhodes b Blythe | | 24 |
| G.A. Faulkner | c Fane b Buckenham | 10 | not out | | 49 |
| S.J. Snooke* | b Woolley | 9 | lbw b Blythe | | 7 |
| J.H. Sinclair | b Thompson | 10 | b Thompson | | 19 |
| L.A. Stricker | lbw b Thompson | 0 | | | |
| R.O. Schwarz | c Rhodes b Thompson | 27 | (8) not out | | 9 |
| A.E.E. Vogler | b Buckenham | 23 | | | |
| T. Campbell† | not out | 3 | | | |
| Extras | (B 10, NB 1,) | 11 | (B 15, LB 3, NB 2) | | 20 |
| **Total** | | **207** | (6 wickets) | | **175** |

| SOUTH AFRICA | O | M | R | W | O | M | R | W |
|---|---|---|---|---|---|---|---|---|
| Snooke | 8 | 1 | 35 | 2 | 8 | 0 | 23 | 2 |
| Vogler | 11 | 3 | 28 | 2 | 21·3 | 3 | 72 | 5 |
| Faulkner | 15 | 1 | 61 | 1 | 14 | 6 | 40 | 3 |
| Sinclair | 15 | 3 | 41 | 2 | 4 | 1 | 16 | 0 |
| Nourse | 3 | 0 | 13 | 0 | | | | |
| White | 1 | 0 | 5 | 2 | 4 | 1 | 15 | 0 |
| ENGLAND | | | | | | | | |
| Buckenham | 20 | 3 | 61 | 3 | 7 | 2 | 12 | 1 |
| Blythe | 15 | 7 | 26 | 0 | 20 | 7 | 38 | 2 |
| Simpson-Hayward | 9 | 1 | 33 | 1 | 5 | 0 | 12 | 0 |
| Thompson | 16 | 3 | 50 | 4 | 20·3 | 2 | 62 | 3 |
| Bird | 1 | 0 | 3 | 1 | 1 | 0 | 5 | 0 |
| Woolley | 6 | 2 | 23 | 1 | 3 | 0 | 24 | 0 |
| Rhodes | | | | | 3 | 2 | 2 | 0 |

### FALL OF WICKETS

| | E | SA | E | SA |
|---|---|---|---|---|
| Wkt | 1st | 1st | 2nd | 2nd |
| 1st | 1 | 47 | 10 | 18 |
| 2nd | 1 | 93 | 15 | 18 |
| 3rd | 2 | 101 | 17 | 76 |
| 4th | 43 | 113 | 117 | 76 |
| 5th | 112 | 131 | 125 | 91 |
| 6th | 118 | 143 | 140 | 162 |
| 7th | 146 | 143 | 142 | – |
| 8th | 161 | 160 | 146 | – |
| 9th | 198 | 195 | 167 | – |
| 10th | 203 | 207 | 178 | – |

Umpires: A.J. Atfield and S.L. Harris.

## SOUTH AFRICA v ENGLAND 1909–10 (5th Test)

Played at Newlands, Cape Town, on 11, 12, 14 March.
Toss: England.   Result: ENGLAND won by nine wickets.
Debuts: South Africa – N.O. Norton, S.V. Samuelson; England – N.C. Tufnell.

Zulch became the second South African to carry his bat through a completed innings against England; both instances took place at Newlands (also *Test No. 32*).

### ENGLAND

| | | | | |
|---|---|---|---|---|
| J.B. Hobbs | hit wkt b Norton | 187 | | |
| W. Rhodes | b Nourse | 77 | not out | 0 |
| D. Denton | c Samuelson b Nourse | 26 | not out | 16 |
| F.L. Fane* | b Norton | 6 | | |
| F.E. Woolley | b Norton | 0 | | |
| G.J. Thompson | c Sinclair b Faulkner | 51 | | |
| M.C. Bird | b Norton | 0 | (1) c Bisset b Vogler | 0 |
| G.H.T. Simpson-Hayward | c Snooke b Faulkner | 19 | | |
| N.C. Tufnell† | c and b Vogler | 14 | | |
| H. Strudwick | c Zulch b Faulkner | 2 | | |
| C. Blythe | not out | 2 | | |
| Extras | (B 30, LB 3) | 33 | | |
| **Total** | | **417** | (1 wicket) | **16** |

### SOUTH AFRICA

| | | | | |
|---|---|---|---|---|
| J.W. Zulch | not out | 43 | b Woolley | 14 |
| J.M.M. Commaille | b Blythe | 4 | lbw b Thompson | 5 |
| S.J. Snooke* | b Blythe | 0 | b Woolley | 47 |
| A.W. Nourse | lbw b Thompson | 8 | c Simpson-Hayward b Woolley | 0 |
| G.A. Faulkner | c Rhodes b Blythe | 10 | c Woolley b Thompson | 99 |
| J.H. Sinclair | c Denton b Thompson | 1 | st Tufnell b Blythe | 37 |
| M. Bisset† | c Rhodes b Blythe | 4 | not out | 27 |
| A.E.E. Vogler | b Blythe | 0 | b Thompson | 2 |
| R.O. Schwarz | c Denton b Blythe | 13 | c Bird b Hobbs | 44 |
| N.O. Norton | b Blythe | 2 | c Fane b Blythe | 7 |
| S.V. Samuelson | b Simpson-Hayward | 15 | b Blythe | 7 |
| Extras | (LB 2, NB 1) | 3 | (B 25, LB 5, NB 8) | 38 |
| **Total** | | **103** | | **327** |

| SOUTH AFRICA | O | M | R | W | O | M | R | W |
|---|---|---|---|---|---|---|---|---|
| Snooke | 5 | 0 | 17 | 0 | 2 | 2 | 0 | 0 |
| Vogler | 26 | 2 | 103 | 1 | 2·1 | 1 | 16 | 1 |
| Faulkner | 25·2 | 6 | 72 | 3 | | | | |
| Samuelson | 18 | 2 | 64 | 0 | | | | |
| Norton | 15 | 4 | 47 | 4 | | | | |
| Sinclair | 8 | 1 | 36 | 0 | | | | |
| Nourse | 8 | 1 | 35 | 2 | | | | |
| Schwarz | 3 | 0 | 10 | 0 | | | | |

| ENGLAND | O | M | R | W | O | M | R | W |
|---|---|---|---|---|---|---|---|---|
| Hobbs | 4 | 0 | 11 | 0 | 8 | 3 | 19 | 1 |
| Blythe | 18 | 5 | 46 | 7 | 30 | 13 | 58 | 3 |
| Thompson | 12 | 6 | 28 | 2 | 30 | 5 | 96 | 3 |
| Simpson-Hayward | 4·5 | 0 | 15 | 1 | 8 | 1 | 35 | 0 |
| Woolley | | | | | 13 | 3 | 47 | 3 |
| Bird | | | | | 3 | 0 | 12 | 0 |
| Rhodes | | | | | 7 | 0 | 22 | 0 |

### FALL OF WICKETS

| | E | SA | SA | E |
|---|---|---|---|---|
| Wkt | 1st | 1st | 2nd | 2nd |
| 1st | 221 | 4 | 25 | 0 |
| 2nd | 265 | 4 | 29 | – |
| 3rd | 286 | 23 | 31 | – |
| 4th | 286 | 30 | 151 | – |
| 5th | 327 | 41 | 199 | – |
| 6th | 327 | 48 | 226 | – |
| 7th | 381 | 48 | 229 | – |
| 8th | 406 | 83 | 296 | – |
| 9th | 413 | 86 | 307 | – |
| 10th | 417 | 103 | 327 | – |

Umpires: A.J. Atfield and S.L. Harris.

# AUSTRALIA v SOUTH AFRICA 1910–11 (1st Test)

Played at Sydney Cricket Ground on 9, 10, 12 (*no play*), 13, 14 December.
Toss: Australia.   Result: AUSTRALIA won by an innings and 114 runs.
Debuts: Australia – C. Kelleway; South Africa – C.O.C. Pearse.

Australia scored 494 for 6 on the first day of this first match between these countries in Australia. This is still the highest total for the first day of any Test match and there has been only one instance of more runs being scored in one day's play – England scoring 503 for 2 v South Africa on the second day at Lord's in 1924 (*Test No. 154*).

## AUSTRALIA

| | | |
|---|---|---|
| V.T. Trumper | run out | 27 |
| W. Bardsley | b Pearse | 132 |
| C. Hill* | b Pearse | 191 |
| D.R.A. Gehrs | b Pearse | 67 |
| W.W. Armstrong | b Schwarz | 48 |
| V.S. Ransford | b Schwarz | 11 |
| C.G. Macartney | b Schwarz | 1 |
| C. Kelleway | not out | 14 |
| H. Carter† | st Sherwell b Schwarz | 5 |
| A. Cotter | st Sherwell b Schwarz | 0 |
| W.J. Whitty | c Snooke b Sinclair | 15 |
| Extras | (B 12, LB 4, NB 1) | 17 |
| **Total** | | **528** |

## SOUTH AFRICA

| | | | | | |
|---|---|---|---|---|---|
| L.A. Stricker | b Cotter | 2 | (7) lbw b Whitty | 4 |
| J.W. Zulch | b Cotter | 4 | (4) run out | 1 |
| C.O.C. Pearse | c Trumper b Cotter | 16 | (10) run out | 31 |
| A.W. Nourse | c Kelleway b Cotter | 5 | (6) not out | 64 |
| G.A. Faulkner | c Kelleway b Whitty | 62 | c Bardsley b Whitty | 43 |
| C.B. Llewellyn | b Cotter | 0 | (8) c Macartney b Whitty | 19 |
| S.J. Snooke | b Whitty | 3 | (3) b Cotter | 4 |
| J.H. Sinclair | b Cotter | 1 | (2) b Cotter | 6 |
| R.O. Schwarz | c Trumper b Whitty | 61 | c Carter b Whitty | 0 |
| P.W. Sherwell*† | not out | 8 | (1) c Whitty b Kelleway | 60 |
| A.E.E. Vogler | b Whitty | 0 | b Kelleway | 0 |
| Extras | (LB 7, NB 5) | 12 | (LB 1, NB 7) | 8 |
| **Total** | | **174** | | **240** |

| SOUTH AFRICA | O | M | R | W | O | M | R | W |
|---|---|---|---|---|---|---|---|---|
| Llewellyn | 14 | 0 | 54 | 0 | | | | |
| Sinclair | 19·4 | 0 | 80 | 1 | | | | |
| Schwarz | 25 | 6 | 102 | 5 | | | | |
| Nourse | 12 | 0 | 61 | 0 | | | | |
| Vogler | 15 | 0 | 87 | 0 | | | | |
| Faulkner | 12 | 0 | 71 | 0 | | | | |
| Pearse | 12 | 0 | 56 | 3 | | | | |
| AUSTRALIA | | | | | | | | |
| Cotter | 20 | 2 | 69 | 6 | 17 | 2 | 73 | 2 |
| Whitty | 24 | 11 | 33 | 4 | 21 | 4 | 75 | 4 |
| Armstrong | 8 | 3 | 16 | 0 | 9 | 1 | 35 | 0 |
| Kelleway | 9 | 1 | 33 | 0 | 15·1 | 4 | 37 | 2 |
| Macartney | 7 | 4 | 11 | 0 | 5 | 1 | 12 | 0 |

| FALL OF WICKETS | | | |
|---|---|---|---|
| | A | SA | SA |
| Wkt | 1st | 1st | 2nd |
| 1st | 52 | 5 | 24 |
| 2nd | 276 | 10 | 28 |
| 3rd | 420 | 29 | 44 |
| 4th | 427 | 38 | 98 |
| 5th | 445 | 38 | 124 |
| 6th | 453 | 44 | 144 |
| 7th | 499 | 49 | 183 |
| 8th | 511 | 149 | 185 |
| 9th | 511 | 174 | 237 |
| 10th | 528 | 174 | 240 |

Umpires: R.W. Crockett and W. Curran.

# AUSTRALIA v SOUTH AFRICA 1910–11 (2nd Test)

Played at Melbourne Cricket Ground on 31 December, 2, 3, 4 January.
Toss: Australia.   Result: AUSTRALIA won by 89 runs.
Debuts: Nil.

Faulkner scored South Africa's first double-century.

## AUSTRALIA

| | | | | |
|---|---|---|---|---|
| V.T. Trumper | b Pegler | 34 | b Faulkner | 159 |
| W. Bardsley | c Snooke b Sinclair | 85 | st Sherwell b Schwarz | 14 |
| C. Hill* | b Llewellyn | 39 | b Schwarz | 0 |
| D.R.A. Gehrs | b Llewellyn | 4 | st Sherwell b Schwarz | 22 |
| C.G. Macartney | run out | 7 | c Snooke b Llewellyn | 5 |
| V.S. Ransford | run out | 58 | c Sinclair b Schwarz | 23 |
| W.W. Armstrong | c Sherwell b Faulkner | 75 | (8) b Llewellyn | 29 |
| C. Kelleway | c Faulkner b Stricker | 18 | (7) b Pegler | 48 |
| H. Carter† | not out | 15 | c Sherwell b Llewellyn | 0 |
| A. Cotter | c Stricker b Schwarz | 3 | c sub (J.M.M. Commaille) b Llewellyn | 1 |
| W.J. Whitty | c Nourse b Faulkner | 6 | not out | |
| Extras | (LB 3, NB 1) | 4 | (LB 6, NB 1) | 32? |
| **Total** | | **348** | | |

## SOUTH AFRICA

| | | | | |
|---|---|---|---|---|
| P.W. Sherwell*† | c Carter b Cotter | 24 | b Whitty | 1? |
| J.W. Zulch | b Cotter | 42 | (8) not out | |
| G.A. Faulkner | c Armstrong b Whitty | 204 | c Kelleway b Whitty | |
| A.W. Nourse | b Kelleway | 33 | lbw b Cotter | |
| L.A. Stricker | b Armstrong | 26 | (2) lbw b Cotter | |
| C.B. Llewellyn | b Armstrong | 5 | b Cotter | 1? |
| S.J. Snooke | b Whitty | 77 | c Armstrong b Whitty | |
| J.H. Sinclair | not out | 58 | (5) lbw b Whitty | |
| R.O. Schwarz | b Whitty | 0 | c Kelleway b Cotter | |
| C.O.C. Pearse | b Armstrong | 6 | c Kelleway b Whitty | |
| S.J. Pegler | lbw b Armstrong | 8 | lbw b Whitty | |
| Extras | (B 2, LB 10, W 2, NB 9) | 23 | (B 6, LB 3, NB 3) | 1? |
| **Total** | | **506** | | 8? |

| SOUTH AFRICA | O | M | R | W | O | M | R | W |
|---|---|---|---|---|---|---|---|---|
| Nourse | 8 | 3 | 24 | 0 | 5 | 1 | 18 | 0 |
| Snooke | 5 | 1 | 19 | 0 | 8 | 1 | 24 | 0 |
| Pegler | 10 | 0 | 43 | 1 | 6·3 | 1 | 24 | 1 |
| Schwarz | 13 | 0 | 66 | 1 | 22 | 2 | 76 | 4 |
| Llewellyn | 10 | 0 | 69 | 2 | 16 | 0 | 81 | 4 |
| Sinclair | 13 | 1 | 53 | 1 | 8 | 0 | 32 | 0 |
| Stricker | 10 | 0 | 36 | 1 | 2 | 1 | 10 | 0 |
| Faulkner | 10·4 | 0 | 34 | 2 | 12 | 1 | 55 | 1 |
| **AUSTRALIA** | | | | | | | | |
| Cotter | 43 | 5 | 158 | 2 | 15 | 3 | 47 | 4 |
| Whitty | 29 | 6 | 81 | 3 | 16 | 7 | 17 | 6 |
| Kelleway | 17 | 3 | 67 | 1 | | | | |
| Armstrong | 48 | 9 | 134 | 4 | 1 | 0 | 4 | 0 |
| Macartney | 16 | 5 | 43 | 0 | | | | |

### FALL OF WICKETS

| | A | SA | A | SA |
|---|---|---|---|---|
| Wkt | 1st | 1st | 2nd | 2n? |
| 1st | 59 | 34 | 35 | |
| 2nd | 160 | 141 | 35 | 2? |
| 3rd | 164 | 251 | 89 | 3? |
| 4th | 164 | 298 | 94 | 3? |
| 5th | 183 | 312 | 176 | 4? |
| 6th | 262 | 402 | 237 | 6? |
| 7th | 309 | 469 | 279 | 6? |
| 8th | 337 | 469 | 279 | 7? |
| 9th | 340 | 482 | 305 | 8? |
| 10th | 348 | 506 | 327 | 8? |

Umpires: R.W. Crockett and W. Hannah.

# AUSTRALIA v SOUTH AFRICA 1910–11 (3rd Test)

Played at Adelaide Oval on 7, 9, 10, 11, 12, 13 January.
Toss: South Africa.   Result: SOUTH AFRICA won by 38 runs.
Debuts: Nil.

South Africa gained their first win against Australia in a match which produced the highest aggregate to date in Test cricket: 1,646 runs for 40 wickets. It remains the record for any Test between Australia and South Africa. Trumper's 214 not out was a new Test record for Australia.

## SOUTH AFRICA

| | | | | | |
|---|---|---|---|---|---|
| P.W. Sherwell*† | lbw b Armstrong | 11 | | lbw b Whitty | 1 |
| J.W. Zulch | c Macartney b Whitty | 105 | | c Carter b Whitty | 14 |
| G.A. Faulkner | c Hill b Armstrong | 56 | | c Armstrong b Whitty | 115 |
| A.W. Nourse | b Cotter | 10 | | c Armstrong b Kelleway | 39 |
| C.M.H. Hathorn | b Whitty | 9 | (10) | b Whitty | 2 |
| C.B. Llewellyn | run out | 43 | | b Whitty | 80 |
| S.J. Snooke | c Kelleway b Cotter | 103 | (8) | run out | 25 |
| J.H. Sinclair | c Armstrong b Kelleway | 20 | (9) | c Hill b Whitty | 29 |
| L.A. Stricker | c Kelleway b Armstrong | 48 | (5) | b Macartney | 6 |
| R.O. Schwarz | b Armstrong | 15 | (11) | not out | 11 |
| S.J. Pegler | not out | 24 | (7) | c Cotter b Kelleway | 26 |
| Extras | (B 6, LB 10, W 4, NB 18) | 38 | | (B 4, LB 2, W 1, NB 5) | 12 |
| **Total** | | **482** | | | **360** |

## AUSTRALIA

| | | | | | |
|---|---|---|---|---|---|
| C.G. Macartney | b Llewellyn | 2 | (9) | lbw b Schwarz | 0 |
| C. Kelleway | c Sherwell b Llewellyn | 47 | (4) | c Sherwell b Sinclair | 65 |
| V.S. Ransford | b Llewellyn | 50 | (5) | c Llewellyn b Schwarz | 0 |
| W. Bardsley | lbw b Nourse | 54 | (2) | c and b Faulkner | 58 |
| V.T. Trumper | not out | 214 | (1) | b Llewellyn | 28 |
| D.R.A. Gehrs | c Schwarz b Faulkner | 20 | (8) | c Sherwell b Schwarz | 22 |
| C. Hill* | c Snooke b Schwarz | 16 | (3) | c Schwarz b Sinclair | 55 |
| W.W. Armstrong | b Sinclair | 30 | (7) | b Schwarz | 48 |
| H. Carter† | lbw b Schwarz | 17 | (6) | c Llewellyn b Faulkner | 11 |
| A. Cotter | c Snooke b Llewellyn | 8 | | not out | 36 |
| W.J. Whitty | c Sherwell b Sinclair | 1 | | c Schwarz b Pegler | 11 |
| Extras | (B 4, LB 2) | 6 | | (LB 5) | 5 |
| **Total** | | **465** | | | **339** |

| AUSTRALIA | O | M | R | W | O | M | R | W |
|---|---|---|---|---|---|---|---|---|
| Cotter | 38 | 4 | 100 | 2 | 23 | 3 | 64 | 0 |
| Whitty | 34 | 7 | 114 | 2 | 39·2 | 5 | 104 | 6 |
| Armstrong | 42·4 | 9 | 103 | 4 | 33 | 9 | 90 | 0 |
| Kelleway | 24 | 6 | 72 | 1 | 23 | 4 | 64 | 2 |
| Macartney | 27 | 9 | 51 | 0 | 12 | 3 | 26 | 1 |
| Gehrs | 1 | 0 | 4 | 0 | | | | |
| **SOUTH AFRICA** | | | | | | | | |
| Llewellyn | 31 | 4 | 107 | 4 | 12 | 0 | 48 | 1 |
| Schwarz | 19 | 2 | 68 | 2 | 15 | 3 | 48 | 4 |
| Sinclair | 25·5 | 3 | 86 | 2 | 21 | 2 | 72 | 2 |
| Pegler | 20 | 2 | 92 | 0 | 10·4 | 0 | 58 | 1 |
| Faulkner | 11 | 0 | 59 | 1 | 15 | 3 | 56 | 2 |
| Nourse | 12 | 2 | 43 | 1 | 5 | 0 | 31 | 0 |
| Stricker | 1 | 0 | 4 | 0 | | | | |
| Snooke | | | | | 5 | 0 | 21 | 0 |

### FALL OF WICKETS

| | SA | A | SA | A |
|---|---|---|---|---|
| Wkt | 1st | 1st | 2nd | 2nd |
| 1st | 31 | 7 | 10 | 63 |
| 2nd | 166 | 94 | 29 | 122 |
| 3rd | 189 | 111 | 106 | 170 |
| 4th | 191 | 229 | 119 | 171 |
| 5th | 205 | 276 | 228 | 187 |
| 6th | 303 | 319 | 273 | 263 |
| 7th | 338 | 384 | 317 | 285 |
| 8th | 400 | 430 | 319 | 285 |
| 9th | 429 | 458 | 327 | 292 |
| 10th | 482 | 465 | 360 | 339 |

Umpires: R.W. Crockett and G.A. Watson.

# AUSTRALIA v SOUTH AFRICA 1910–11 (4th Test)

Played at Melbourne Cricket Ground on 17, 18, 20, 21 February.
Toss: South Africa.   Result: AUSTRALIA won by 530 runs.
Debuts: Australia – H.V. Hordern.

Australia gained the first Test win by a margin exceeding 500 runs.

## AUSTRALIA

| | | | | | |
|---|---|---|---|---|---|
| V.T. Trumper | b Faulkner | 7 | (6) c Sherwell b Vogler | 87 |
| W. Bardsley | c Schwarz b Pegler | 82 | (3) run out | 15 |
| C. Hill* | b Llewellyn | 11 | (5) st Sherwell b Pegler | 100 |
| W.W. Armstrong | run out | 48 | (4) c Sherwell b Vogler | 132 |
| D.R.A. Gehrs | st Sherwell b Vogler | 9 | (2) c Snooke b Faulkner | 58 |
| C. Kelleway | run out | 59 | (1) run out | 18 |
| V.S. Ransford | lbw b Schwarz | 75 | b Faulkner | 95 |
| A. Cotter | b Pegler | 10 | c sub (C.O.C. Pearse) b Vogler | 0 |
| H.V. Hordern | c Vogler b Pegler | 7 | c sub (C.O.C. Pearse) b Schwarz | 24 |
| H. Carter† | run out | 5 | c Snooke b Faulkner | 2 |
| W.J. Whitty | not out | 0 | not out | 39 |
| Extras | (B 7, LB 7, W 1) | 15 | (B 4, LB 3, NB 1) | 8 |
| **Total** | | **328** | | **578** |

## SOUTH AFRICA

| | | | | | |
|---|---|---|---|---|---|
| J.W. Zulch | run out | 2 | c Trumper b Cotter | 15 |
| L.A. Stricker | b Hordern | 4 | c Carter b Cotter | 0 |
| G.A. Faulkner | c Gehrs b Hordern | 20 | b Whitty | 80 |
| A.W. Nourse | not out | 92 | c and b Hordern | 28 |
| S.J. Snooke | b Whitty | 1 | b Hordern | 7 |
| J.H. Sinclair | b Hordern | 0 | lbw b Hordern | 19 |
| R.O. Schwarz | b Whitty | 18 | c Carter b Whitty | 1 |
| P.W. Sherwell*† | c sub (T.J. Matthews) b Whitty | 41 | c Kelleway b Hordern | 0 |
| C.B. Llewellyn | b Whitty | 7 | absent hurt | – |
| S.J. Pegler | c Hill b Cotter | 15 | (9) c Gehrs b Hordern | 8 |
| A.E.E. Vogler | b Cotter | 0 | (10) not out | 2 |
| Extras | (B 4, LB 1) | 5 | (B 7, LB 1, W 2, NB 1) | 11 |
| **Total** | | **205** | | **171** |

| SOUTH AFRICA | O | M | R | W | O | M | R | W |
|---|---|---|---|---|---|---|---|---|
| Llewellyn | 15 | 1 | 65 | 1 | | | | |
| Faulkner | 18 | 2 | 82 | 1 | 28·2 | 5 | 101 | 3 |
| Schwarz | 15 | 2 | 34 | 1 | 38 | 4 | 168 | 1 |
| Vogler | 8 | 2 | 30 | 1 | 15 | 3 | 59 | 3 |
| Sinclair | 14 | 2 | 40 | 0 | 13 | 1 | 71 | 0 |
| Pegler | 17·4 | 3 | 40 | 3 | 17 | 1 | 88 | 1 |
| Stricker | 5 | 1 | 18 | 0 | 3 | 0 | 14 | 0 |
| Nourse | 2 | 0 | 4 | 0 | 7 | 0 | 31 | 0 |
| Zulch | | | | | 3 | 0 | 26 | 0 |
| Snooke | | | | | 2 | 0 | 12 | 0 |
| AUSTRALIA | | | | | | | | |
| Cotter | 6·5 | 0 | 16 | 2 | 6 | 1 | 22 | 2 |
| Whitty | 22 | 5 | 78 | 4 | 9 | 2 | 32 | 2 |
| Hordern | 15 | 1 | 39 | 3 | 14·2 | 2 | 66 | 5 |
| Armstrong | 8 | 2 | 25 | 0 | 3 | 0 | 15 | 0 |
| Kelleway | 11 | 1 | 42 | 0 | 8 | 0 | 25 | 0 |

### FALL OF WICKETS

| Wkt | A 1st | SA 1st | A 2nd | SA 2nd |
|---|---|---|---|---|
| 1st | 9 | 7 | 48 | 2 |
| 2nd | 24 | 23 | 88 | 25 |
| 3rd | 126 | 36 | 106 | 88 |
| 4th | 146 | 37 | 260 | 108 |
| 5th | 182 | 38 | 403 | 151 |
| 6th | 289 | 65 | 418 | 158 |
| 7th | 310 | 156 | 420 | 161 |
| 8th | 317 | 171 | 491 | 165 |
| 9th | 328 | 205 | 496 | 171 |
| 10th | 328 | 205 | 578 | – |

Umpires: R.W. Crockett and D. Elder.

# AUSTRALIA v SOUTH AFRICA 1910–11 (5th Test)

Played at Sydney Cricket Ground on 3, 4, 6, 7 March.
Toss: South Africa.   Result: AUSTRALIA won by seven wickets.
Debuts: Nil.

## AUSTRALIA

| | | | | |
|---|---|---|---|---|
| C. Kelleway | c Snooke b Llewellyn | 2 | (5) not out | 24 |
| C.G. Macartney | lbw b Schwarz | 137 | c Nourse b Schwarz | 56 |
| H.V. Hordern | lbw b Sinclair | 50 | | |
| W. Bardsley | c and b Sinclair | 94 | (1) b Nourse | 39 |
| W.J. Whitty | c Nourse b Llewellyn | 13 | | |
| V.T. Trumper | b Schwarz | 31 | (3) not out | 74 |
| C. Hill* | st Sherwell b Schwarz | 13 | | |
| W.W. Armstrong | c Pearse b Schwarz | 0 | | |
| V.S. Ransford | st Sherwell b Schwarz | 6 | (4) b Nourse | 0 |
| A. Cotter | st Sherwell b Schwarz | 8 | | |
| H. Carter† | not out | 1 | | |
| Extras | (B 7, LB 2) | 9 | (B 1, LB 3, W 1) | 5 |
| **Total** | | **364** | (3 wickets) | **198** |

## SOUTH AFRICA

| | | | | |
|---|---|---|---|---|
| C.O.C. Pearse | b Whitty | 0 | (11) lbw b Hordern | 2 |
| J.W. Zulch | st Carter b Hordern | 15 | b Ransford | 150 |
| G.A. Faulkner | b Armstrong | 52 | (4) b Cotter | 92 |
| A.W. Nourse | b Armstrong | 3 | (5) c Cotter b Whitty | 28 |
| L.A. Stricker | c Macartney b Hordern | 19 | (6) b Cotter | 42 |
| J.H. Sinclair | c Ransford b Hordern | 1 | (8) c and b Whitty | 12 |
| S.J. Snooke | b Hordern | 18 | c Carter b Whitty | 12 |
| C.B. Llewellyn | c Carter b Kelleway | 24 | (9) b Whitty | 3 |
| R.O. Schwarz | run out | 13 | (10) not out | 6 |
| P.W. Sherwell*† | c Bardsley b Whitty | 5 | (1) b Armstrong | 14 |
| S.J. Pegler | not out | 0 | (3) c Cotter b Hordern | 26 |
| Extras | (B 1, LB 9) | 10 | (B 3, LB 4, W 2, NB 5) | 14 |
| **Total** | | **160** | | **401** |

| SOUTH AFRICA | O | M | R | W | O | M | R | W |
|---|---|---|---|---|---|---|---|---|
| Llewellyn | 25 | 0 | 92 | 2 | 8 | 1 | 43 | 0 |
| Faulkner | 12 | 2 | 38 | 0 | 5 | 0 | 18 | 0 |
| Sinclair | 27 | 6 | 83 | 2 | 6 | 1 | 22 | 0 |
| Pegler | 6 | 1 | 31 | 0 | 4 | 0 | 22 | 0 |
| Schwarz | 11·4 | 0 | 47 | 6 | 9 | 0 | 42 | 1 |
| Nourse | 5 | 1 | 26 | 0 | 8·1 | 0 | 32 | 2 |
| Pearse | 9 | 0 | 36 | 0 | 3 | 0 | 14 | 0 |
| Zulch | 1 | 0 | 2 | 0 | | | | |

| AUSTRALIA | O | M | R | W | O | M | R | W |
|---|---|---|---|---|---|---|---|---|
| Cotter | 8 | 2 | 24 | 0 | 18 | 1 | 60 | 2 |
| Whitty | 11·1 | 3 | 32 | 2 | 27 | 5 | 66 | 4 |
| Hordern | 21 | 3 | 73 | 4 | 30·1 | 1 | 117 | 2 |
| Kelleway | 4 | 1 | 4 | 1 | 7 | 1 | 46 | 0 |
| Armstrong | 6 | 1 | 17 | 2 | 26 | 4 | 68 | 1 |
| Macartney | | | | | 10 | 0 | 21 | 0 |
| Ransford | | | | | 4 | 2 | 9 | 1 |

### FALL OF WICKETS

| Wkt | A 1st | SA 1st | SA 2nd | A 2nd |
|---|---|---|---|---|
| 1st | 2 | 4 | 19 | 74 |
| 2nd | 126 | 47 | 64 | 134 |
| 3rd | 271 | 70 | 207 | 134 |
| 4th | 296 | 81 | 278 | – |
| 5th | 317 | 87 | 357 | – |
| 6th | 346 | 115 | 368 | – |
| 7th | 346 | 128 | 385 | – |
| 8th | 351 | 144 | 392 | – |
| 9th | 361 | 160 | 398 | – |
| 10th | 364 | 160 | 401 | – |

Umpires: R.W. Crockett and D. Elder.

# AUSTRALIA v ENGLAND 1911–12 (1st Test)

Played at Sydney Cricket Ground on 15, 16, 18, 19, 20, 21 December.
Toss: Australia.   Result: AUSTRALIA won by 146 runs.
Debuts: Australia – R.B. Minnett; England – J.W.H.T. Douglas, F.R. Foster, J.W. Hearne, S.P. Kinneir, C.P. Mead.

Trumper's century was his eighth in Tests and his sixth against England – both being records at the time. The googly bowler, Hordern, took twelve wickets in his first Test against England (he had played twice against South Africa in the previous season).

## AUSTRALIA

| | | | | | |
|---|---|---|---|---|---|
| W. Bardsley | c Strudwick b Douglas | 30 | | b Foster | 12 |
| C. Kelleway | c and b Woolley | 20 | | b Douglas | 70 |
| C. Hill* | run out | 46 | | b Foster | 65 |
| W.W. Armstrong | st Strudwick b Hearne | 60 | | b Foster | 28 |
| V.T. Trumper | c Hobbs b Woolley | 113 | | c and b Douglas | 14 |
| V.S. Ransford | c Hearne b Barnes | 26 | | c Rhodes b Barnes | 34 |
| R.B. Minnett | c Foster b Barnes | 90 | (8) | b Douglas | 17 |
| H.V. Hordern | not out | 17 | (7) | b Foster | 18 |
| A. Cotter | c and b Barnes | 6 | | lbw b Douglas | 2 |
| H. Carter† | b Foster | 13 | | c Gunn b Foster | 15 |
| W.J. Whitty | b Foster | 0 | | not out | 9 |
| Extras | (B 9, LB 15, NB 2) | 26 | | (B 16, LB 7, NB 1) | 24 |
| **Total** | | **447** | | | **308** |

## ENGLAND

| | | | | | |
|---|---|---|---|---|---|
| J.B. Hobbs | c Hill b Whitty | 63 | | c Carter b Cotter | 22 |
| S.P. Kinneir | b Kelleway | 22 | | c Trumper b Hordern | 30 |
| G. Gunn | b Cotter | 4 | | c Whitty b Hordern | 62 |
| W. Rhodes | c Hill b Hordern | 41 | (5) | c Trumper b Hordern | 0 |
| C.P. Mead | c and b Hordern | 0 | (4) | run out | 25 |
| J.W. Hearne | c Trumper b Kelleway | 76 | (7) | b Hordern | 43 |
| F.R. Foster | b Hordern | 56 | (6) | c Ransford b Hordern | 21 |
| F.E. Woolley | b Hordern | 39 | | c Armstrong b Cotter | 7 |
| J.W.H.T. Douglas* | c Trumper b Hordern | 0 | | b Hordern | 32 |
| S.F. Barnes | b Kelleway | 9 | | b Hordern | 14 |
| H. Strudwick† | not out | 0 | | not out | 12 |
| Extras | (B 3, LB 3, W 1, NB 1) | 8 | | (B 14, LB 8, NB 1) | 23 |
| **Total** | | **318** | | | **291** |

| ENGLAND | O | M | R | W | O | M | R | W |
|---|---|---|---|---|---|---|---|---|
| Foster | 29 | 6 | 105 | 2 | 31·3 | 5 | 92 | 5 |
| Douglas | 24 | 5 | 62 | 1 | 21 | 3 | 50 | 4 |
| Barnes | 35 | 5 | 107 | 3 | 30 | 8 | 72 | 1 |
| Hearne | 10 | 1 | 44 | 1 | 13 | 2 | 51 | 0 |
| Woolley | 21 | 2 | 77 | 2 | 6 | 1 | 15 | 0 |
| Rhodes | 8 | 0 | 26 | 0 | 3 | 1 | 4 | 0 |
| AUSTRALIA | | | | | | | | |
| Cotter | 19 | 0 | 88 | 1 | 27 | 3 | 71 | 2 |
| Whitty | 28 | 13 | 60 | 1 | 20 | 8 | 41 | 0 |
| Kelleway | 16·5 | 3 | 46 | 3 | 19 | 6 | 27 | 0 |
| Hordern | 27 | 4 | 85 | 5 | 42·2 | 11 | 90 | 7 |
| Armstrong | 9 | 3 | 28 | 0 | 15 | 3 | 39 | 0 |
| Minnett | 2 | 1 | 3 | 0 | | | | |

### FALL OF WICKETS

| | A | E | A | E |
|---|---|---|---|---|
| Wkt | 1st | 1st | 2nd | 2nd |
| 1st | 44 | 45 | 29 | 29 |
| 2nd | 77 | 53 | 150 | 6? |
| 3rd | 121 | 115 | 169 | 14? |
| 4th | 198 | 129 | 191 | 14? |
| 5th | 278 | 142 | 218 | 14? |
| 6th | 387 | 231 | 246 | 16? |
| 7th | 420 | 293 | 268 | 17? |
| 8th | 426 | 293 | 274 | 26? |
| 9th | 447 | 310 | 283 | 27? |
| 10th | 447 | 318 | 308 | 29? |

Umpires: R.W. Crockett and W. Curran.

# AUSTRALIA v ENGLAND 1911–12 (2nd Test)

Played at Melbourne Cricket Ground on 30 December, 1, 2, 3 January.
Toss: Australia.   Result: ENGLAND won by eight wickets.
Debuts: England – J.W. Hitch, E.J. Smith.

Barnes gave the match a sensational start by dismissing Kelleway (with his first ball), Bardsley, Hill, and Armstrong for just one run in five overs. Hearne's hundred was scored in his second Test and at the age of 20 years 324 days. Only D.C.S. Compton, who was 20 years 19 days old when he scored 102 at Nottingham in 1938 (*Test No. 263*), has scored a century for England against Australia at an earlier age.

## AUSTRALIA

| | | | | | |
|---|---|---:|---|---|---:|
| C. Kelleway | lbw b Barnes | 2 | c Gunn b Foster | | 13 |
| W. Bardsley | b Barnes | 0 | run out | | 16 |
| C. Hill* | b Barnes | 4 | c Gunn b Barnes | | 0 |
| W.W. Armstrong | c Smith b Barnes | 4 | b Foster | | 90 |
| V.T. Trumper | b Foster | 13 | b Barnes | | 2 |
| V.S. Ransford | c Smith b Hitch | 43 | c Smith b Foster | | 32 |
| R.B. Minnett | c Hobbs b Barnes | 2 | (8) b Foster | | 34 |
| H.V. Hordern | not out | 49 | (7) c Mead b Foster | | 31 |
| A. Cotter | run out | 14 | c Hobbs b Foster | | 41 |
| H. Carter† | c Smith b Douglas | 29 | b Barnes | | 16 |
| W.J. Whitty | b Woolley | 14 | not out | | 0 |
| Extras | (B 5, LB 4, NB 1) | 10 | (B 14, LB 7, W 1, NB 2) | | 24 |
| **Total** | | **184** | | | **299** |

## ENGLAND

| | | | | | |
|---|---|---:|---|---|---:|
| W. Rhodes | c Trumper b Cotter | 61 | c Carter b Cotter | | 28 |
| J.B. Hobbs | c Carter b Cotter | 6 | not out | | 126 |
| J.W. Hearne | c Carter b Cotter | 114 | (4) not out | | 12 |
| G. Gunn | lbw b Armstrong | 10 | (3) c Carter b Whitty | | 43 |
| C.P. Mead | c Armstrong b Whitty | 11 | | | |
| F.R. Foster | c Hill b Cotter | 9 | | | |
| J.W.H.T. Douglas* | b Hordern | 9 | | | |
| F.E. Woolley | c Ransford b Hordern | 23 | | | |
| E.J. Smith† | b Hordern | 5 | | | |
| S.F. Barnes | lbw b Hordern | 1 | | | |
| J.W. Hitch | not out | 0 | | | |
| Extras | (B 2, LB 10, NB 4) | 16 | (B 5, LB 5) | | 10 |
| **Total** | | **265** | (2 wickets) | | **219** |

| ENGLAND | O | M | R | W | O | M | R | W | | FALL OF WICKETS | | | |
|---|---:|---:|---:|---:|---:|---:|---:|---:|---|---|---|---|---|
| Foster | 16 | 2 | 52 | 1 | 38 | 9 | 91 | 6 | | A | E | A | E |
| Barnes | 23 | 9 | 44 | 5 | 32·1 | 7 | 96 | 3 | *Wkt* | *1st* | *1st* | *2nd* | *2nd* |
| Hitch | 7 | 0 | 57 | 1 | 5 | 0 | 21 | 0 | 1st | 0 | 10 | 28 | 57 |
| Douglas | 15 | 4 | 33 | 1 | 10 | 0 | 38 | 0 | 2nd | 5 | 137 | 34 | 169 |
| Hearne | 1 | 0 | 8 | 0 | 1 | 0 | 5 | 0 | 3rd | 8 | 174 | 34 | – |
| Woolley | 0·1 | 0 | 0 | 1 | 3 | 0 | 21 | 0 | 4th | 11 | 213 | 38 | – |
| Rhodes | | | | | 3 | 1 | 3 | 0 | 5th | 33 | 224 | 135 | – |
| | | | | | | | | | 6th | 38 | 227 | 168 | – |
| AUSTRALIA | | | | | | | | | 7th | 80 | 258 | 232 | – |
| Cotter | 22 | 2 | 73 | 4 | 14 | 5 | 45 | 1 | 8th | 97 | 260 | 235 | – |
| Whitty | 19 | 2 | 47 | 1 | 18 | 3 | 37 | 1 | 9th | 140 | 262 | 298 | – |
| Hordern | 23·1 | 1 | 66 | 4 | 17 | 0 | 66 | 0 | 10th | 184 | 265 | 299 | – |
| Kelleway | 15 | 7 | 27 | 0 | 7 | 0 | 15 | 0 | | | | | |
| Armstrong | 15 | 6 | 20 | 1 | 8 | 1 | 22 | 0 | | | | | |
| Minnett | 5 | 0 | 16 | 0 | 2 | 0 | 13 | 0 | | | | | |
| Ransford | | | | | 1·1 | 0 | 11 | 0 | | | | | |

Umpires: R.W. Crockett and D. Elder.

# AUSTRALIA v ENGLAND 1911–12 (3rd Test)

Played at Adelaide Oval on 12, 13, 15, 16, 17 January.
Toss: Australia.   Result: ENGLAND won by seven wickets.
Debuts: Australia – T.J. Matthews.

J.B. Hobbs scored his second hundred in successive Test innings. It was the highest of his twelve centuries against Australia and it remains England's highest score at Adelaide. Ransford retired at 17 for 2 when 6 not out and resumed at 113 for 8.

## AUSTRALIA

| | | | | | |
|---|---|---|---|---|---|
| W. Bardsley | c Smith b Barnes | 5 | | b Foster | 63 |
| C. Kelleway | b Foster | 1 | | b Douglas | 37 |
| H.V. Hordern | c Rhodes b Foster | 25 | (7) | c and b Barnes | 5 |
| V.S. Ransford | not out | 8 | (8) | b Hitch | 38 |
| W.W. Armstrong | b Foster | 33 | | b Douglas | 25 |
| V.T. Trumper | b Hitch | 26 | (11) | not out | 1 |
| C. Hill* | st Smith b Foster | 0 | (4) | c Hitch b Barnes | 98 |
| R.B. Minnett | b Foster | 0 | (6) | c Hobbs b Barnes | 38 |
| T.J. Matthews | c Mead b Barnes | 5 | | b Barnes | 53 |
| A. Cotter | b Barnes | 11 | | b Barnes | 15 |
| H. Carter† | c Gunn b Douglas | 8 | (3) | c Smith b Woolley | 72 |
| Extras | (B 3, LB 6, NB 2) | 11 | | (B 26, LB 3, NB 2) | 31 |
| **Total** | | **133** | | | **476** |

## ENGLAND

| | | | | | |
|---|---|---|---|---|---|
| J.B. Hobbs | c Hordern b Minnett | 187 | | lbw b Hordern | 3 |
| W. Rhodes | lbw b Cotter | 59 | | not out | 57 |
| G. Gunn | c Hill b Cotter | 29 | | c Cotter b Kelleway | 45 |
| J.W. Hearne | c Hill b Kelleway | 12 | | c Kelleway b Matthews | 2 |
| C.P. Mead | c and b Hordern | 46 | | not out | 2 |
| F.R. Foster | b Armstrong | 71 | | | |
| J.W.H.T. Douglas* | b Minnett | 35 | | | |
| F.E. Woolley | b Cotter | 20 | | | |
| E.J. Smith† | c sub (J. Vine) b Cotter | 22 | | | |
| S.F. Barnes | not out | 2 | | | |
| J.W. Hitch | c sub (C.G. Macartney) b Hordern | 0 | | | |
| Extras | (B 7, LB 8, NB 3) | 18 | | (B 1, LB 1, NB 1) | 3 |
| **Total** | | **501** | | (3 wickets) | **112** |

| ENGLAND | O | M | R | W | O | M | R | W |
|---|---|---|---|---|---|---|---|---|
| Foster | 26 | 9 | 36 | 5 | 49 | 15 | 103 | 1 |
| Barnes | 23 | 4 | 71 | 3 | 46·4 | 7 | 105 | 5 |
| Douglas | 7 | 2 | 7 | 1 | 29 | 10 | 71 | 2 |
| Hearne | 2 | 0 | 6 | 0 | 10 | 0 | 61 | 0 |
| Hitch | 2 | 1 | 2 | 1 | 11 | 0 | 69 | 1 |
| Woolley | | | | | 7 | 1 | 30 | 1 |
| Rhodes | | | | | 1 | 0 | 6 | 0 |

| AUSTRALIA | O | M | R | W | O | M | R | W |
|---|---|---|---|---|---|---|---|---|
| Cotter | 43 | 11 | 125 | 4 | 5 | 0 | 21 | 0 |
| Hordern | 47·1 | 5 | 143 | 2 | 11 | 3 | 32 | 1 |
| Kelleway | 23 | 3 | 46 | 1 | 7 | 3 | 8 | 1 |
| Matthews | 33 | 8 | 72 | 0 | 9·2 | 3 | 24 | 1 |
| Minnett | 17 | 3 | 54 | 2 | 4 | 1 | 12 | 0 |
| Armstrong | 14 | 0 | 43 | 1 | 6 | 1 | 12 | 0 |

FALL OF WICKETS

| | A | E | A | E |
|---|---|---|---|---|
| Wkt | 1st | 1st | 2nd | 2nd |
| 1st | 6 | 147 | 86 | 5 |
| 2nd | 6 | 206 | 122 | 102 |
| 3rd | 65 | 260 | 279 | 105 |
| 4th | 84 | 323 | 303 | – |
| 5th | 88 | 350 | 342 | – |
| 6th | 88 | 435 | 360 | – |
| 7th | 97 | 455 | 363 | – |
| 8th | 113 | 492 | 447 | – |
| 9th | 123 | 501 | 475 | – |
| 10th | 133 | 501 | 476 | – |

Umpires: R.W. Crockett and G.A. Watson.

# AUSTRALIA v ENGLAND 1911–12 (4th Test)

Played at Melbourne Cricket Ground on 9, 10, 12, 13 February.
Toss: England.   Result: ENGLAND won by an innings and 225 runs.
Debuts: England – J. Vine.

England's total of 589 and the first wicket partnership of 323 between Hobbs and Rhodes set new Test records.
That partnership took 268 minutes and remains the highest opening stand by either country in Tests between
England and Australia, and England's highest stand for any wicket in Australia. There has been only one higher
opening partnership for England, L. Hutton and C. Washbrook scoring 359 against South Africa in 1948-49
(*Test No. 310*).

## AUSTRALIA

| | | | | | |
|---|---|---|---|---|---|
| C. Kelleway | c Hearne b Woolley | 29 | | c Smith b Barnes | 5 |
| H.V. Hordern | b Barnes | 19 | (11) | c Foster b Douglas | 5 |
| W. Bardsley | b Foster | 0 | | b Foster | 3 |
| V.T. Trumper | b Foster | 17 | | b Barnes | 28 |
| C. Hill* | c Hearne b Barnes | 22 | | b Douglas | 11 |
| W.W. Armstrong | b Barnes | 7 | | b Douglas | 11 |
| R.B. Minnett | c Rhodes b Foster | 56 | | b Douglas | 7 |
| V.S. Ransford | c Rhodes b Foster | 4 | | not out | 29 |
| T.J. Matthews | c Gunn b Barnes | 3 | (10) | b Foster | 10 |
| A. Cotter | b Barnes | 15 | (9) | c Mead b Foster | 8 |
| H. Carter† | not out | 6 | (2) | c Hearne b Douglas | 38 |
| Extras | (B 1, LB 5, NB 7) | 13 | | (B 9, LB 2, NB 7) | 18 |
| **Total** | | **191** | | | **173** |

## ENGLAND

| | | |
|---|---|---|
| J.B. Hobbs | c Carter b Hordern | 178 |
| W. Rhodes | c Carter b Minnett | 179 |
| G. Gunn | c Hill b Armstrong | 75 |
| J.W. Hearne | c Armstrong b Minnett | 0 |
| F.R. Foster | c Hordern b Armstrong | 50 |
| J.W.H.T. Douglas* | c Bardsley b Armstrong | 0 |
| F.E. Woolley | c Kelleway b Minnett | 56 |
| C.P. Mead | b Hordern | 21 |
| J. Vine | not out | 4 |
| E.J. Smith† | c Matthews b Kelleway | 7 |
| S.F. Barnes | c Hill b Hordern | 0 |
| Extras | (B 2, LB 4, W 4, NB 9) | 19 |
| **Total** | | **589** |

| ENGLAND | O | M | R | W | O | M | R | W | | FALL OF WICKETS | | |
|---|---|---|---|---|---|---|---|---|---|---|---|---|
| Foster | 22 | 2 | 77 | 4 | 19 | 3 | 38 | 3 | | A | E | A |
| Barnes | 29·1 | 4 | 74 | 5 | 20 | 6 | 47 | 2 | *Wkt* | *1st* | *1st* | *2nd* |
| Woolley | 11 | 3 | 22 | 1 | 2 | 0 | 7 | 0 | 1st | 53 | 323 | 12 |
| Rhodes | 2 | 1 | 1 | 0 | | | | | 2nd | 53 | 425 | 20 |
| Hearne | 1 | 0 | 4 | 0 | 3 | 0 | 17 | 0 | 3rd | 69 | 425 | 76 |
| Douglas | | | | | 17·5 | 6 | 46 | 5 | 4th | 74 | 486 | 86 |
| | | | | | | | | | 5th | 83 | 486 | 101 |
| AUSTRALIA | | | | | | | | | 6th | 124 | 513 | 112 |
| Cotter | 37 | 5 | 125 | 0 | | | | | 7th | 152 | 565 | 117 |
| Kelleway | 26 | 2 | 80 | 1 | | | | | 8th | 165 | 579 | 127 |
| Armstrong | 36 | 12 | 93 | 3 | | | | | 9th | 170 | 589 | 156 |
| Matthews | 22 | 1 | 68 | 0 | | | | | 10th | 191 | 589 | 173 |
| Hordern | 47·5 | 5 | 137 | 3 | | | | | | | | |
| Minnett | 20 | 5 | 59 | 3 | | | | | | | | |
| Ransford | 2 | 1 | 8 | 0 | | | | | | | | |

Umpires: R.W. Crockett and W. Young.

## AUSTRALIA v ENGLAND 1911–12 (5th Test)

Played at Sydney Cricket Ground on 23, 24, 26 (*no play*), 27, 28, 29 (*no play*) February, 1 March.
Toss: England.   Result: ENGLAND won by 70 runs.
Debuts: Australia – J.W. McLaren.

F.E. Woolley's hundred was the first by an England left-hander against Australia. His partnership of 143 with
J. Vine remains the England seventh-wicket record against Australia.

### ENGLAND

| | | | | | |
|---|---|---|---|---|---|
| J.B. Hobbs | c Ransford b Hordern | 32 | c Hazlitt b Hordern | | 45 |
| W. Rhodes | b Macartney | 8 | lbw b Armstrong | | 30 |
| G. Gunn | st Carter b Hordern | 52 | b Hordern | | 61 |
| J.W. Hearne | c Macartney b Armstrong | 4 | b Hordern | | 18 |
| F.R. Foster | st Carter b Hazlitt | 15 | b McLaren | | 4 |
| J.W.H.T. Douglas* | c Ransford b Hordern | 18 | b Armstrong | | 8 |
| F.E. Woolley | not out | 133 | c Armstrong b Hazlitt | | 11 |
| J. Vine | b Hordern | 36 | not out | | 6 |
| E.J. Smith† | b Hordern | 0 | b Hordern | | 13 |
| S.F. Barnes | c Hordern b Hazlitt | 5 | b Hordern | | 4 |
| J.W. Hitch | c Hill b Hazlitt | 4 | c Ransford b Armstrong | | 4 |
| Extras | (B 10, LB 4, W 1, NB 2) | 17 | (B 8, NB 2) | | 10 |
| **Total** | | **324** | | | **214** |

### AUSTRALIA

| | | | | | |
|---|---|---|---|---|---|
| V.T. Trumper | c Woolley b Barnes | 5 | c Woolley b Barnes | | 50 |
| S.E. Gregory | c Gunn b Douglas | 32 | c Smith b Barnes | | 40 |
| C. Hill* | c Smith b Hitch | 20 | b Foster | | 8 |
| W.W. Armstrong | lbw b Barnes | 33 | b Barnes | | 33 |
| R.B. Minnett | c Douglas b Hitch | 0 | c Woolley b Barnes | | 61 |
| V.S. Ransford | c Hitch b Foster | 29 | b Woolley | | 9 |
| H. Carter† | c sub (C.P. Mead) b Barnes | 11 | c Woolley b Foster | | 23 |
| C.G. Macartney | c and b Woolley | 26 | c Woolley b Foster | | 27 |
| H.V. Hordern | b Woolley | 0 | run out | | 4 |
| G.R. Hazlitt | run out | 1 | c Rhodes b Foster | | 4 |
| J.W. McLaren | not out | 0 | not out | | 0 |
| Extras | (B 14, LB 2, W 2, NB 1) | 19 | (B 22, LB 8, W 1, NB 2) | | 33 |
| **Total** | | **176** | | | **292** |

| AUSTRALIA | O | M | R | W | O | M | R | W | | FALL OF WICKETS | | | |
|---|---|---|---|---|---|---|---|---|---|---|---|---|---|
| McLaren | 16 | 2 | 47 | 0 | 8 | 1 | 23 | 1 | | E | A | E | A |
| Macartney | 12 | 3 | 26 | 1 | 7 | 0 | 28 | 0 | *Wkt* | *1st* | *1st* | *2nd* | *2nd* |
| Hordern | 37 | 8 | 95 | 5 | 25 | 5 | 66 | 5 | 1st | 15 | 17 | 76 | 88 |
| Hazlitt | 31 | 6 | 75 | 3 | 12 | 2 | 52 | 1 | 2nd | 69 | 59 | 76 | 101 |
| Armstrong | 25 | 8 | 42 | 1 | 17·3 | 7 | 35 | 3 | 3rd | 83 | 81 | 105 | 117 |
| Minnett | 8 | 1 | 22 | 0 | 1 | 1 | 0 | 0 | 4th | 114 | 82 | 110 | 209 |
| | | | | | | | | | 5th | 125 | 133 | 146 | 220 |
| ENGLAND | | | | | | | | | 6th | 162 | 133 | 178 | 231 |
| Foster | 16 | 0 | 55 | 1 | 30·1 | 7 | 43 | 4 | 7th | 305 | 171 | 186 | 278 |
| Barnes | 19 | 2 | 56 | 3 | 39 | 12 | 106 | 4 | 8th | 305 | 175 | 201 | 287 |
| Hitch | 9 | 0 | 31 | 2 | 6 | 1 | 23 | 0 | 9th | 312 | 176 | 209 | 287 |
| Douglas | 7 | 0 | 14 | 1 | 9 | 0 | 34 | 0 | 10th | 324 | 176 | 214 | 292 |
| Woolley | 2 | 1 | 1 | 2 | 16 | 5 | 36 | 1 | | | | | |
| Rhodes | | | | | 2 | 0 | 17 | 0 | | | | | |

Umpires: R.W. Crockett and A.C. Jones.

# AUSTRALIA v SOUTH AFRICA 1912 (1st Test)
## Triangular Tournament – 1st Match

Played at Old Trafford, Manchester, on 27, 28 May.
Toss: Australia.   Result: AUSTRALIA won by an innings and 88 runs.
Debuts: Australia – W. Carkeek, S.H. Emery, C.B. Jennings; South Africa – R. Beaumont,
G.P.D. Hartigan, H.W. Taylor, T.A. Ward. *F. Mitchell was playing in his first Test match for South Africa having made his debut for England in* Test No. 58.

T.J. Matthews created a unique Test record by taking a hat-trick in each innings – both instances being on the second day. Ward bagged a 'king pair', being the third victim of both hat-tricks. This was the first of nine Test matches between England, Australia and South Africa which constituted the Triangular Tournament of 1912.

### AUSTRALIA

| | | |
|---|---|---|
| C.B. Jennings | c Schwarz b Pegler | 32 |
| C. Kelleway | c Ward b Pegler | 114 |
| C.G. Macartney | b Pegler | 21 |
| W. Bardsley | c and b White | 121 |
| S.E. Gregory* | st Ward b Pegler | 37 |
| R.B. Minnett | c and b Schwarz | 12 |
| T.J. Matthews | not out | 49 |
| S.H. Emery | b Schwarz | 1 |
| G.R. Hazlitt | lbw b Schwarz | 0 |
| W. Carkeek† | b Pegler | 4 |
| W.J. Whitty | st Ward b Pegler | 33 |
| Extras | (B 14, LB 9, W 1) | 24 |
| **Total** | | **448** |

### SOUTH AFRICA

| | | | | | |
|---|---|---|---|---|---|
| G.P.D. Hartigan | c Carkeek b Emery | 25 | | b Kelleway | 4 |
| H.W. Taylor | c Carkeek b Whitty | 0 | (5) | b Matthews | 21 |
| A.W. Nourse | b Whitty | 17 | | c Bardsley b Whitty | 18 |
| S.J. Snooke | b Whitty | 7 | | b Whitty | 9 |
| G.A. Faulkner | not out | 122 | (2) | b Kelleway | 0 |
| G.C. White | lbw b Whitty | 22 | | c Carkeek b Kelleway | 9 |
| F. Mitchell* | b Whitty | 11 | | b Kelleway | 0 |
| R.O. Schwarz | b Hazlitt | 19 | | c and b Matthews | 0 |
| R. Beaumont | b Matthews | 31 | (10) | b Kelleway | 17 |
| S.J. Pegler | lbw b Matthews | 0 | (11) | not out | 8 |
| T.A. Ward† | lbw b Matthews | 0 | (9) | c and b Matthews | 0 |
| Extras | (B 2, LB 5, W 1, NB 3) | 11 | | (B 5, LB 1, NB 3) | 9 |
| **Total** | | **265** | | | **95** |

| SOUTH AFRICA | O | M | R | W | O | M | R | W |
|---|---|---|---|---|---|---|---|---|
| Faulkner | 16 | 2 | 55 | 0 | | | | |
| Nourse | 14 | 1 | 62 | 0 | | | | |
| Pegler | 45·3 | 9 | 105 | 6 | | | | |
| Schwarz | 32 | 0 | 142 | 3 | | | | |
| Hartigan | 9 | 0 | 31 | 0 | | | | |
| White | 6 | 1 | 29 | 1 | | | | |
| **AUSTRALIA** | | | | | | | | |
| Hazlitt | 16 | 4 | 46 | 1 | | | | |
| Whitty | 34 | 12 | 55 | 5 | 6 | 3 | 15 | 2 |
| Emery | 37 | 10 | 94 | 1 | | | | |
| Kelleway | 11 | 3 | 27 | 0 | 14·2 | 4 | 33 | 5 |
| Matthews | 12 | 3 | 16 | 3 | 8 | 1 | 38 | 3 |
| Minnett | 6 | 2 | 16 | 0 | | | | |

FALL OF WICKETS

| Wkt | A 1st | SA 1st | SA 2nd |
|---|---|---|---|
| 1st | 62 | 4 | 1 |
| 2nd | 92 | 30 | 22 |
| 3rd | 294 | 42 | 22 |
| 4th | 314 | 54 | 43 |
| 5th | 328 | 143 | 70 |
| 6th | 375 | 167 | 70 |
| 7th | 376 | 200 | 70 |
| 8th | 376 | 265 | 70 |
| 9th | 385 | 265 | 78 |
| 10th | 448 | 265 | 95 |

Umpires: G. Webb and A.A. White.

# ENGLAND v SOUTH AFRICA 1912 (1st Test)
## Triangular Tournament – 2nd Match

Played at Lord's, London, on 10, 11, 12 June.
Toss: South Africa.   Result: ENGLAND won by an innings and 62 runs.
Debuts: South Africa – C.P. Carter.

Following their two-day defeat by Australia, South Africa were bowled out by England in 90 minutes for the lowest total of the Tournament.

## SOUTH AFRICA

| Batsman | Dismissal 1 | Score | Dismissal 2 | Score |
|---|---|---|---|---|
| G.P.D. Hartigan | c Foster b Barnes | 0 | b Foster | |
| H.W. Taylor | lbw b Barnes | 1 | b Barnes | |
| A.W. Nourse | b Foster | 13 | run out | 1 |
| C.B. Llewellyn | b Foster | 9 | c Smith b Foster | 7 |
| G.A. Faulkner | b Foster | 7 | b Barnes | 1 |
| S.J. Snooke | b Barnes | 2 | b Foster | 1 |
| F. Mitchell* | c and b Barnes | 1 | b Barnes | |
| R.O. Schwarz | c Foster b Barnes | 4 | b Barnes | 28 |
| S.J. Pegler | b Foster | 4 | b Barnes | 10 |
| C.P. Carter | b Foster | 0 | not out | 27 |
| T. Campbell† | not out | 0 | c Jessop b Barnes | |
| Extras | (B 12, LB 3, NB 2) | 17 | (B 17, LB 1, NB 1) | 19 |
| **Total** | | **58** | | **217** |

## ENGLAND

|  |  |  |
|---|---|---|
| J.B. Hobbs | b Nourse | 4 |
| W. Rhodes | b Nourse | 36 |
| R.H. Spooner | c Llewellyn b Nourse | 119 |
| C.B. Fry* | b Pegler | 29 |
| P.F. Warner | st Campbell b Pegler | 39 |
| F.E. Woolley | b Pegler | 73 |
| G.L. Jessop | b Pegler | 3 |
| F.R. Foster | lbw b Pegler | 11 |
| E.J. Smith† | b Pegler | 2 |
| S.F. Barnes | not out | 0 |
| W. Brearley | b Pegler | 0 |
| Extras | (B 11, LB 9, W 1) | 21 |
| **Total** | | **337** |

| ENGLAND | O | M | R | W | O | M | R | W |
|---|---|---|---|---|---|---|---|---|
| Foster | 13·1 | 7 | 16 | 5 | 27 | 10 | 54 | 3 |
| Barnes | 13 | 3 | 25 | 5 | 34 | 9 | 85 | 6 |
| Brearley | | | | | 6 | 2 | 4 | 0 |
| Woolley | | | | | 4 | 0 | 19 | 0 |
| Hobbs | | | | | 11 | 2 | 36 | 0 |

| SOUTH AFRICA | O | M | R | W |
|---|---|---|---|---|
| Nourse | 16 | 5 | 46 | 3 |
| Pegler | 31 | 8 | 65 | 7 |
| Faulkner | 29 | 6 | 72 | 0 |
| Carter | 4 | 0 | 15 | 0 |
| Llewellyn | 9 | 0 | 60 | 0 |
| Schwarz | 20 | 3 | 44 | 0 |
| Hartigan | 10 | 2 | 14 | 0 |

### FALL OF WICKETS

| Wkt | SA 1st | E 1st | SA 2nd |
|---|---|---|---|
| 1st | 2 | 4 | 5 |
| 2nd | 3 | 128 | 17 |
| 3rd | 28 | 183 | 36 |
| 4th | 35 | 207 | 104 |
| 5th | 36 | 320 | 132 |
| 6th | 42 | 323 | 135 |
| 7th | 45 | 324 | 147 |
| 8th | 54 | 330 | 176 |
| 9th | 55 | 337 | 197 |
| 10th | 58 | 337 | 217 |

Umpires: W.A.J. West and W. Richards.

# ENGLAND v AUSTRALIA 1912 (1st Test)
## Triangular Tournament – 3rd Match

Played at Lord's, London, on 24, 25, 26 June.
Toss: England.    Result: MATCH DRAWN.
Debuts: England – H. Dean; Australia – D.B.M. Smith.

The weather at Lord's consolidated its unenviable Test record by restricting play in this match to 3½ hours on the first day and to twenty minutes on the second.

### ENGLAND

| | | |
|---|---|---:|
| J.B. Hobbs | b Emery | 107 |
| W. Rhodes | c Carkeek b Kelleway | 59 |
| R.H. Spooner | c Bardsley b Kelleway | 1 |
| C.B. Fry* | run out | 42 |
| P.F. Warner | b Emery | 4 |
| F.E. Woolley | c Kelleway b Hazlitt | 20 |
| F.R. Foster | c Macartney b Whitty | 20 |
| J.W. Hearne | not out | 21 |
| E.J. Smith† | not out | 14 |
| S.F. Barnes | ) did not bat | |
| H. Dean | ) | |
| Extras | (B 16, LB 4, NB 2) | 22 |
| **Total** | **(7 wickets declared)** | **310** |

### AUSTRALIA

| | | |
|---|---|---:|
| C.B. Jennings | c Smith b Foster | 21 |
| C. Kelleway | b Rhodes | 61 |
| C.G. Macartney | c Smith b Foster | 99 |
| W. Bardsley | lbw b Rhodes | 21 |
| S.E. Gregory* | c Foster b Dean | 10 |
| D.B.M. Smith | not out | 24 |
| T.J. Matthews | b Dean | 0 |
| G.R. Hazlitt | b Rhodes | 19 |
| S.H. Emery | ) | |
| W.J. Whitty | ) did not bat | |
| W. Carkeek† | ) | |
| Extras | (B 17, LB 5, W 1, NB 4) | 27 |
| **Total** | **(7 wickets)** | **282** |

| AUSTRALIA | O | M | R | W | | FALL OF WICKETS | | |
|---|---|---|---|---|---|---|---|---|
| | | | | | | | E | A |
| Whitty | 12 | 2 | 69 | 1 | | Wkt | 1st | 1st |
| Hazlitt | 25 | 6 | 68 | 1 | | 1st | 112 | 27 |
| Matthews | 13 | 4 | 26 | 0 | | 2nd | 123 | 173 |
| Kelleway | 21 | 5 | 66 | 2 | | 3rd | 197 | 226 |
| Emery | 12 | 1 | 46 | 2 | | 4th | 211 | 233 |
| Macartney | 7 | 1 | 13 | 0 | | 5th | 246 | 243 |
| | | | | | | 6th | 255 | 243 |
| ENGLAND | | | | | | 7th | 285 | 282 |
| Foster | 36 | 18 | 42 | 2 | | 8th | – | – |
| Barnes | 31 | 10 | 74 | 0 | | 9th | – | – |
| Dean | 29 | 10 | 49 | 2 | | 10th | – | – |
| Hearne | 12 | 1 | 31 | 0 | | | | |
| Rhodes | 19·2 | 5 | 59 | 3 | | | | |

Umpires: J. Moss and A.E. Street.

# ENGLAND v SOUTH AFRICA 1912 (2nd Test)
## Triangular Tournament – 4th Match

Played at Headingley, Leeds, on 8, 9, 10 July.
Toss: England.   Result: ENGLAND won by 174 runs.
Debuts: Nil.

### ENGLAND

| | | | | | |
|---|---|--:|---|---|--:|
| J.B. Hobbs | c Ward b Nourse | 27 | c Nourse b Faulkner | | 55 |
| W. Rhodes | c and b Pegler | 7 | b Pegler | | 10 |
| R.H. Spooner | c Stricker b Nourse | 21 | b Faulkner | | 82 |
| C.B. Fry* | lbw b Pegler | 10 | c Nourse b Pegler | | 7 |
| J.W. Hearne | b Pegler | 45 | b Nourse | | 35 |
| F.E. Woolley | b Nourse | 57 | c Nourse b Pegler | | 4 |
| G.L. Jessop | b Faulkner | 16 | b Nourse | | 1 |
| F.R. Foster | c Pegler b Nourse | 30 | b Nourse | | 0 |
| E.J. Smith† | run out | 13 | c Ward b Faulkner | | 11 |
| S.F. Barnes | b Faulkner | 0 | not out | | 15 |
| H. Dean | not out | 2 | b Faulkner | | 8 |
| Extras | (B 12, LB 2) | 14 | (B 5, LB 5) | | 10 |
| **Total** | | **242** | | | **238** |

### SOUTH AFRICA

| | | | | | |
|---|---|--:|---|---|--:|
| L.J. Tancred* | c Spooner b Barnes | 15 | st Smith b Barnes | | 39 |
| H.W. Taylor | c Hobbs b Dean | 31 | c Smith b Foster | | 2 |
| A.W. Nourse | b Barnes | 5 | (6) c Foster b Dean | | 15 |
| C.B. Llewellyn | c Smith b Barnes | 0 | b Barnes | | 4 |
| G.A. Faulkner | c and b Barnes | 5 | b Barnes | | 0 |
| L.A. Stricker | b Dean | 10 | (7) run out | | 0 |
| G.C. White | c Barnes b Woolley | 6 | (3) c and b Foster | | 17 |
| S.J. Snooke | b Barnes | 23 | b Dean | | 8 |
| S.J. Pegler | not out | 35 | b Hearne | | 32 |
| C.P. Carter | c Dean b Barnes | 5 | b Barnes | | 31 |
| T.A. Ward† | b Dean | 0 | not out | | 0 |
| Extras | (B 4, LB 3, NB 5) | 12 | (B 5, LB 3, NB 3) | | 11 |
| **Total** | | **147** | | | **159** |

| SOUTH AFRICA | O | M | R | W | O | M | R | W |
|---|--:|--:|--:|--:|--:|--:|--:|--:|
| Nourse | 26·1 | 8 | 52 | 4 | 30 | 11 | 52 | 3 |
| Pegler | 35 | 6 | 112 | 3 | 31 | 0 | 110 | 3 |
| Faulkner | 13 | 2 | 50 | 2 | 24·2 | 2 | 50 | 4 |
| Carter | 4 | 0 | 14 | 0 | 5 | 1 | 16 | 0 |
| **ENGLAND** | | | | | | | | |
| Foster | 16 | 7 | 29 | 0 | 23 | 4 | 51 | 2 |
| Barnes | 22 | 7 | 52 | 6 | 21·2 | 5 | 63 | 4 |
| Dean | 12·3 | 1 | 41 | 3 | 8 | 3 | 15 | 2 |
| Woolley | 6 | 2 | 13 | 1 | | | | |
| Rhodes | | | | | 4 | 1 | 14 | 0 |
| Hearne | | | | | 2 | 0 | 5 | 1 |

| FALL OF WICKETS | | | | |
|---|--:|--:|--:|--:|
| | E | SA | E | SA |
| Wkt | 1st | 1st | 2nd | 2nd |
| 1st | 20 | 18 | 46 | 18 |
| 2nd | 44 | 25 | 78 | 38 |
| 3rd | 67 | 25 | 95 | 44 |
| 4th | 68 | 43 | 165 | 49 |
| 5th | 179 | 69 | 180 | 67 |
| 6th | 181 | 76 | 181 | 69 |
| 7th | 198 | 80 | 181 | 85 |
| 8th | 226 | 130 | 207 | 110 |
| 9th | 227 | 146 | 224 | 159 |
| 10th | 242 | 147 | 238 | 159 |

Umpires: W. Richards and A.A. White.

# AUSTRALIA v SOUTH AFRICA 1912 (2nd Test)
## Triangular Tournament – 5th Match

Played at Lord's, London, on 15, 16, 17 July.
Toss: South Africa.   Result: AUSTRALIA won by ten wickets.
Debuts: Australia – E.R. Mayne.

### SOUTH AFRICA

| | | | | | |
|---|---|---:|---|---|---:|
| G.A. Faulkner | b Whitty | 56 | (6) c and b Matthews | | 6 |
| L.J. Tancred | lbw b Matthews | 31 | c Bardsley b Hazlitt | | 19 |
| G.C. White | c Carkeek b Minnett | 0 | b Matthews | | 18 |
| C.B. Llewellyn | c Jennings b Minnett | 8 | b Macartney | | 59 |
| A.W. Nourse | b Hazlitt | 11 | lbw b Kelleway | | 10 |
| H.W. Taylor | c Kelleway b Hazlitt | 93 | (7) not out | | 10 |
| L.A. Stricker | lbw b Kelleway | 48 | (1) b Hazlitt | | 13 |
| F. Mitchell* | b Whitty | 12 | b Matthews | | 3 |
| R.O. Schwarz | b Whitty | 0 | c Macartney b Matthews | | 1 |
| S.J. Pegler | c Bardsley b Whitty | 25 | c Kelleway b Macartney | | 14 |
| T.A. Ward† | not out | 1 | b Macartney | | 7 |
| Extras | (B 12, LB 14, W 1, NB 2) | 29 | (B 9, LB 4) | | 13 |
| **Total** | | **263** | | | **173** |

### AUSTRALIA

| | | | | | |
|---|---|---:|---|---|---:|
| C.B. Jennings | b Nourse | 0 | not out | | 22 |
| C. Kelleway | lbw b Faulkner | 102 | | | |
| C.G. Macartney | b Nourse | 9 | | | |
| W. Bardsley | lbw b Llewellyn | 164 | | | |
| S.E. Gregory* | b Llewellyn | 5 | | | |
| E.R. Mayne | st Ward b Pegler | 23 | (2) not out | | 25 |
| R.B. Minnett | b Pegler | 39 | | | |
| T.J. Matthews | c Faulkner b Pegler | 9 | | | |
| G.R. Hazlitt | b Nourse | 0 | | | |
| W. Carkeek† | not out | 6 | | | |
| W.J. Whitty | lbw b Pegler | 3 | | | |
| Extras | (B 24, LB 3, W 2, NB 1) | 30 | (B 1) | | 1 |
| **Total** | | **390** | (0 wickets) | | **48** |

| AUSTRALIA | O | M | R | W | O | M | R | W | | FALL OF WICKETS | | | |
|---|---|---|---|---|---|---|---|---|---|---|---|---|---|
| | | | | | | | | | | | SA | A | SA | A |
| Minnett | 15 | 6 | 49 | 2 | | | | | | | | | |
| Whitty | 31 | 9 | 68 | 4 | 9 | 0 | 41 | 0 | | *Wkt* | *1st* | *1st* | *2nd* | *2nd* |
| Hazlitt | 19 | 9 | 47 | 2 | 13 | 1 | 39 | 2 | | 1st | 24 | 0 | 28 | – |
| Matthews | 13 | 5 | 32 | 1 | 13 | 2 | 29 | 4 | | 2nd | 25 | 14 | 54 | – |
| Kelleway | 11 | 3 | 38 | 1 | 8 | 1 | 22 | 1 | | 3rd | 35 | 256 | 62 | – |
| Macartney | | | | | 14·1 | 5 | 29 | 3 | | 4th | 56 | 277 | 102 | – |
| | | | | | | | | | | 5th | 74 | 316 | 134 | – |
| SOUTH AFRICA | | | | | | | | | | 6th | 171 | 353 | 136 | – |
| Nourse | 36 | 12 | 60 | 3 | 6·1 | 2 | 22 | 0 | | 7th | 203 | 375 | 142 | – |
| Pegler | 29·5 | 7 | 79 | 4 | 4 | 1 | 15 | 0 | | 8th | 213 | 379 | 146 | – |
| Schwarz | 11 | 1 | 44 | 0 | | | | | | 9th | 250 | 381 | 163 | – |
| Faulkner | 28 | 3 | 86 | 1 | 2 | 0 | 10 | 0 | | 10th | 263 | 390 | 173 | – |
| Llewellyn | 19 | 2 | 71 | 2 | | | | | | | | | |
| Taylor | 2 | 0 | 12 | 0 | | | | | | | | | |
| Stricker | 3 | 1 | 8 | 0 | | | | | | | | | |

Umpires: J. Moss and A.E. Street.

# ENGLAND v AUSTRALIA 1912 (2nd Test)
## Triangular Tournament – 6th Match

Played at Old Trafford, Manchester, on 29, 30, 31 (*no play*) July.
Toss: England.    Result: MATCH DRAWN.
Debuts: Nil.

Rain restricted play to 3¾ hours on the first day and to 75 minutes on the second, before completely washing out the third.

### ENGLAND

| | | |
|---|---|---:|
| J.D. Hobbs | b Whitty | 19 |
| W. Rhodes | b Whitty | 92 |
| R.H. Spooner | b Whitty | 1 |
| C.B. Fry* | c sub (J.W. McLaren) b Matthews | 19 |
| J.W. Hearne | b Hazlitt | 9 |
| F.E. Woolley | c Kelleway b Whitty | 13 |
| F.R. Foster | c and b Matthews | 13 |
| E.J. Smith | c Emery b Hazlitt | 4 |
| S. Haigh | c Kelleway b Hazlitt | 9 |
| S.F. Barnes | not out | 1 |
| J.W. Hitch | b Hazlitt | 4 |
| Extras | (B 9, LB 9, NB 1) | 19 |
| **Total** | | **203** |

### AUSTRALIA

| | | |
|---|---|---:|
| C.B. Jennings | not out | 9 |
| C. Kelleway | not out | 3 |
| W. Bardsley | ) | |
| S.E. Gregory* | ) | |
| C.G. Macartney | ) | |
| E.R. Mayne | ) | |
| T.J. Matthews | ) did not bat | |
| S.H. Emery | ) | |
| W.J. Whitty | ) | |
| G.R. Hazlitt | ) | |
| W. Carkeek† | ) | |
| Extras | (B 2) | 2 |
| **Total** | (0 wickets) | **14** |

| AUSTRALIA | O | M | R | W |
|---|---|---|---|---|
| Hazlitt | 40·5 | 12 | 77 | 4 |
| Whitty | 27 | 15 | 43 | 4 |
| Kelleway | 6 | 1 | 19 | 0 |
| Matthews | 12 | 4 | 23 | 2 |
| Emery | 7 | 1 | 22 | 0 |
| ENGLAND | | | | |
| Foster | 1 | 0 | 3 | 0 |
| Haigh | 6 | 4 | 3 | 0 |
| Wooley | 6 | 3 | 6 | 0 |

Umpires: G. Webb and W.A.J. West.

### FALL OF WICKETS

| Wkt | E 1st | A 1st |
|---|---|---|
| 1st | 37 | – |
| 2nd | 39 | – |
| 3rd | 83 | – |
| 4th | 140 | – |
| 5th | 155 | – |
| 6th | 181 | – |
| 7th | 185 | – |
| 8th | 189 | – |
| 9th | 199 | – |
| 10th | 203 | – |

# AUSTRALIA v SOUTH AFRICA 1912 (3rd Test)
## Triangular Tournament – 7th Match

Played at Trent Bridge, Nottingham, on 5, 6, 7 (*no play*) August.
Toss: South Africa.    Result: MATCH DRAWN.
Debuts: Nil.

### SOUTH AFRICA

| | | |
|---|---|---|
| L.J. Tancred* | c Kelleway b Matthews | 30 |
| H.W. Taylor | b Whitty | 2 |
| A.W. Nourse | b Whitty | 64 |
| G.A. Faulkner | c Kelleway b Emery | 15 |
| C.B. Llewellyn | b Emery | 12 |
| L.A. Stricker | lbw b Macartney | 37 |
| S.J. Snooke | b Kelleway | 20 |
| G.C. White | not out | 59 |
| R. Beaumont | b Hazlitt | 2 |
| S.J. Pegler | b Hazlitt | 26 |
| T.A. Ward† | c Emery b Matthews | 24 |
| Extra | (B 30, LB 7, NB 1) | 38 |
| **Total** | | **329** |

### AUSTRALIA

| | | |
|---|---|---|
| C.B. Jennings | run out | 9 |
| C. Kelleway | c Faulkner b Pegler | 37 |
| C.G. Macartney | c Faulkner b Llewellyn | 34 |
| W. Bardsley | run out | 56 |
| S.E. Gregory* | b Pegler | 18 |
| R.B. Minnett | c Nourse b Faulkner | 31 |
| T.J. Matthews | b Pegler | 21 |
| S.H. Emery | b Faulkner | 5 |
| G.R. Hazlitt | not out | 2 |
| W.J. Whitty | b Pegler | 0 |
| W. Carkeek† | st Ward b Faulkner | 1 |
| Extras | (B 2, LB 3) | 5 |
| **Total** | | **219** |

| AUSTRALIA | O | M | R | W |
|---|---|---|---|---|
| Whitty | 30 | 10 | 64 | 2 |
| Minnett | 8 | 3 | 12 | 0 |
| Hazlitt | 28 | 10 | 48 | 2 |
| Matthews | 20·5 | 7 | 27 | 2 |
| Emery | 21 | 1 | 87 | 2 |
| Kelleway | 8 | 2 | 18 | 1 |
| Macartney | 13 | 2 | 35 | 1 |
| SOUTH AFRICA | | | | |
| Pegler | 36 | 6 | 80 | 4 |
| Faulkner | 20·1 | 2 | 43 | 3 |
| Taylor | 12 | 5 | 19 | 0 |
| Llewellyn | 22 | 3 | 60 | 1 |
| Nourse | 4 | 1 | 12 | 0 |

### FALL OF WICKETS

| | SA | A |
|---|---|---|
| Wkt | 1st | 1st |
| 1st | 2 | 19 |
| 2nd | 79 | 61 |
| 3rd | 116 | 101 |
| 4th | 140 | 127 |
| 5th | 154 | 171 |
| 6th | 196 | 199 |
| 7th | 225 | 212 |
| 8th | 232 | 216 |
| 9th | 282 | 216 |
| 10th | 329 | 219 |

Umpires: W.A.J. West and G. Webb.

# ENGLAND v SOUTH AFRICA 1912 (3rd Test)
## Triangular Tournament – 8th Match

Played at Kennington Oval, London, on 12, 13 August.
Toss: South Africa.   Result: ENGLAND won by ten wickets.
Debuts: Nil.

As at Manchester in 1888 *(Test No. 30)*, when Australia were their victims, England completed their victory before lunch on the second day. Barnes, who bowled unchanged through both South African innings, recorded the best analysis (8 for 29) for any Oval Test.

## SOUTH AFRICA

| | | | | | |
|---|---|---|---|---|---|
| L.J. Tancred* | b Barnes | 0 | | st Smith b Woolley | 0 |
| H.W. Taylor | c Foster b Woolley | 23 | | lbw b Barnes | 6 |
| A.W. Nourse | lbw b Woolley | 8 | | c and b Foster | 42 |
| G.A. Faulkner | c Hayes b Barnes | 9 | (5) | b Barnes | 10 |
| L.A. Stricker | b Barnes | 5 | (4) | c Spooner b Barnes | 0 |
| C.B. Llewellyn | c Rhodes b Woolley | 0 | | c Hitch b Barnes | 0 |
| G.C. White | b Barnes | 4 | | c Smith b Barnes | 1 |
| S.J. Snooke | c Foster b Woolley | 23 | | c Hearne b Barnes | 7 |
| R. Beaumont | c Hearne b Barnes | 3 | | b Barnes | 6 |
| S.J. Pegler | c Hitch b Woolley | 3 | | b Barnes | 0 |
| T.A. Ward† | not out | 6 | | not out | 0 |
| Extras | (B 8, LB 3) | 11 | | (B 18, LB 3) | 21 |
| **Total** | | **95** | | | **93** |

## ENGLAND

| | | | | | |
|---|---|---|---|---|---|
| J.B. Hobbs | c and b Faulkner | 68 | | not out | 9 |
| W. Rhodes | b Faulkner | 0 | | | |
| R.H. Spooner | c Nourse b Llewellyn | 26 | | | |
| C.B. Fry* | c Snooke b Faulkner | 9 | | | |
| E.G. Hayes | b Faulkner | 4 | | | |
| F.E. Woolley | b Pegler | 13 | | | |
| J.W. Hearne | lbw b Faulkner | 20 | (2) | not out | 5 |
| F.R. Foster | st Ward b Faulkner | 8 | | | |
| E.J. Smith† | b Faulkner | 9 | | | |
| S.F. Barnes | c Taylor b Pegler | 8 | | | |
| J.W. Hitch | not out | 0 | | | |
| Extras | (B 10, LB 1) | 11 | | | |
| **Total** | | **176** | | (0 wickets) | **14** |

| ENGLAND | O | M | R | W | O | M | R | W |
|---|---|---|---|---|---|---|---|---|
| Foster | 6 | 2 | 15 | 0 | 7 | 2 | 19 | 1 |
| Barnes | 21 | 10 | 28 | 5 | 16·4 | 4 | 29 | 8 |
| Woolley | 15·3 | 1 | 41 | 5 | 9 | 2 | 24 | 1 |
| SOUTH AFRICA | | | | | | | | |
| Pegler | 19 | 3 | 53 | 2 | | | | |
| Faulkner | 27·1 | 4 | 84 | 7 | 2 | 0 | 4 | 0 |
| Llewellyn | 10 | 1 | 28 | 1 | | | | |
| Nourse | | | | | 2·3 | 0 | 10 | 0 |

Umpires: A.A. White and W. Richards.

### FALL OF WICKETS

| | SA | E | SA | E |
|---|---|---|---|---|
| Wkt | 1st | 1st | 2nd | 2nd |
| 1st | 2 | 4 | 0 | – |
| 2nd | 31 | 65 | 10 | – |
| 3rd | 38 | 85 | 10 | – |
| 4th | 47 | 89 | 54 | – |
| 5th | 50 | 111 | 54 | – |
| 6th | 53 | 127 | 58 | – |
| 7th | 76 | 135 | 70 | – |
| 8th | 86 | 163 | 89 | – |
| 9th | 86 | 176 | 93 | – |
| 10th | 95 | 176 | 93 | – |

# ENGLAND v AUSTRALIA 1912 (3rd Test)
## Triangular Tournament – 9th Match

Played at Kennington Oval, London, on 19, 20, 21, 22 August.
Toss: England.   Result: ENGLAND won by 244 runs.
Debuts: Nil.

This was the first 'Timeless' Test to be staged in England – a result was essential to decide the winners of the Tournament. Woolley became the third player after W. Bates and H. Trumble to score a fifty and take ten wickets in an England-Australia Test.

| TOURNAMENT | RESULTS | *Played* | *Won* | *Lost* | *Drawn* |
|---|---|---|---|---|---|
| | ENGLAND | 6 | 4 | 0 | 2 |
| | Australia | 6 | 2 | 1 | 3 |
| | South Africa | 6 | 0 | 5 | 1 |

### ENGLAND

| | | | | | |
|---|---|---|---|---|---|
| J.B. Hobbs | c Carkeek b Macartney | 66 | c Matthews b Whitty | 32 |
| W. Rhodes | b Minnett | 49 | b Whitty | 4 |
| R.H. Spooner | c Hazlitt b Macartney | 1 | c Jennings b Whitty | 0 |
| C.B. Fry* | c Kelleway b Whitty | 5 | c Jennings b Hazlitt | 79 |
| F.E. Woolley | lbw b Minnett | 62 | b Hazlitt | 4 |
| J.W. Hearne | c Jennings b Whitty | 1 | c Matthews b Hazlitt | 14 |
| J.W.H.T. Douglas | lbw b Whitty | 18 | lbw b Hazlitt | 24 |
| F.R. Foster | b Minnett | 19 | not out | 3 |
| E.J. Smith† | b Whitty | 4 | b Hazlitt | 0 |
| S.F. Barnes | c Jennings b Minnett | 7 | c Whitty b Hazlitt | 0 |
| H. Dean | not out | 0 | b Hazlitt | 0 |
| Extras | (B 2, LB 10, NB 1) | 13 | (B 14, NB 1) | 15 |
| **Total** | | **245** | | **175** |

### AUSTRALIA

| | | | | | |
|---|---|---|---|---|---|
| S.E. Gregory* | c Rhodes b Barnes | 1 | (5) c Douglas b Dean | 1 |
| C. Kelleway | lbw b Woolley | 43 | c Douglas b Dean | 0 |
| C.G. Macartney | b Barnes | 4 | b Dean | 30 |
| W. Bardsley | b Barnes | 30 | run out | 0 |
| C.B. Jennings | c and b Woolley | 0 | (1) c Fry b Woolley | 14 |
| R.B. Minnett | c Rhodes b Woolley | 0 | lbw b Woolley | 4 |
| D.B.M. Smith | c Smith b Woolley | 6 | c Douglas b Dean | 0 |
| T.J. Matthews | c Fry b Barnes | 2 | c and b Woolley | 1 |
| W.J. Whitty | c Foster b Barnes | 0 | b Woolley | 3 |
| G.R. Hazlitt | not out | 2 | c Dean b Woolley | 5 |
| W. Carkeek† | c Barnes b Woolley | 5 | not out | 0 |
| Extras | (B 12, LB 6) | 18 | (B 1, LB 5, W 1) | 7 |
| **Total** | | **111** | | **65** |

| AUSTRALIA | O | M | R | W | O | M | R | W |
|---|---|---|---|---|---|---|---|---|
| Whitty | 38 | 12 | 69 | 4 | 33 | 13 | 71 | 3 |
| Matthews | 14 | 5 | 43 | 0 | 10 | 3 | 21 | 0 |
| Hazlitt | 26 | 10 | 48 | 0 | 21·4 | 8 | 25 | 7 |
| Macartney | 19 | 6 | 22 | 2 | 22 | 5 | 43 | 0 |
| Minnett | 10·1 | 3 | 34 | 4 | | | | |
| Kelleway | 7 | 2 | 16 | 0 | | | | |
| **ENGLAND** | | | | | | | | |
| Barnes | 27 | 15 | 30 | 5 | 4 | 1 | 18 | 0 |
| Dean | 16 | 7 | 29 | 0 | 9 | 2 | 19 | 4 |
| Foster | 2 | 0 | 5 | 0 | | | | |
| Woolley | 9·4 | 3 | 29 | 5 | 7·4 | 1 | 20 | 5 |
| Rhodes | | | | | 2 | 1 | 1 | 0 |

### FALL OF WICKETS

| Wkt | E 1st | A 1st | E 2nd | A 2nd |
|---|---|---|---|---|
| 1st | 107 | 9 | 7 | 0 |
| 2nd | 109 | 19 | 7 | 46 |
| 3rd | 127 | 90 | 51 | 46 |
| 4th | 131 | 90 | 56 | 47 |
| 5th | 144 | 92 | 91 | 51 |
| 6th | 180 | 96 | 170 | 51 |
| 7th | 216 | 104 | 171 | 51 |
| 8th | 233 | 104 | 171 | 54 |
| 9th | 239 | 104 | 175 | 65 |
| 10th | 245 | 111 | 175 | 65 |

Umpires: J. Moss and A.E. Street.

# SOUTH AFRICA v ENGLAND 1913-14 (1st Test)

Played at Lord's, Durban, 13, 15, 16, 17 December.
Toss: South Africa.   Result: ENGLAND won by an innings and 157 runs.
Debuts: South Africa – H.V. Baumgartner, J.M. Blanckenberg, A.H.C. Cooper, J.L. Cox, P.A.M.
Hands, P.T. Lewis, G.L. Tapscott; England – M.W. Booth, Hon. L.H. Tennyson (*later The Third Baron Tennyson*).

This match provided the first instance of both captains scoring hundreds, Taylor doing so on his first appearance in that role.

## SOUTH AFRICA

| | | | | | |
|---|---|---|---|---|---|
| H.W. Taylor* | c Strudwick b Douglas | 109 | | lbw b Barnes | 8 |
| G.P.D. Hartigan | c Strudwick b Barnes | 0 | (3) | c Hobbs b Woolley | 13 |
| P.A.M. Hands | c Barnes b Booth | 3 | (2) | lbw b Relf | 14 |
| A.W. Nourse | b Douglas | 19 | | hit wkt b Barnes | 46 |
| P.T. Lewis | c Woolley b Barnes | 0 | | c Woolley b Barnes | 0 |
| A.H.C. Cooper | b Barnes | 6 | | c Strudwick b Barnes | 0 |
| G.L. Tapscott | b Barnes | 4 | | c Relf b Woolley | 1 |
| T.A. Ward† | c Woolley b Booth | 9 | | c Rhodes b Barnes | 12 |
| H.V. Baumgartner | lbw b Woolley | 16 | | b Relf | 3 |
| J.M. Blanckenberg | not out | 6 | | not out | 0 |
| J.L. Cox | b Barnes | 1 | | c and b Relf | 0 |
| Extras | (B 6, LB 1, NB 2) | 9 | | (B 6, LB 6, W 2) | 14 |
| **Total** | | **182** | | | **111** |

## ENGLAND

| | | |
|---|---|---|
| J.B. Hobbs | b Baumgartner | 82 |
| W. Rhodes | c Tapscott b Cox | 18 |
| A.E. Relf | c Baumgartner b Cox | 1 |
| Hon. L.H. Tennyson | lbw b Nourse | 52 |
| C.P. Mead | c and b Blanckenberg | 41 |
| J.W.H.T. Douglas* | b Baumgartner | 119 |
| F.E. Woolley | c Cooper b Hartigan | 31 |
| M.C. Bird | c Ward b Nourse | 61 |
| M.W. Booth | run out | 14 |
| S.F. Barnes | run out | 0 |
| H. Strudwick† | not out | 2 |
| Extras | (B 25, LB 2, W 2) | 29 |
| **Total** | | **450** |

| ENGLAND | O | M | R | W | O | M | R | W |
|---|---|---|---|---|---|---|---|---|
| Barnes | 19·4 | 1 | 57 | 5 | 25 | 11 | 48 | 5 |
| Booth | 10 | 0 | 38 | 2 | | | | |
| Woolley | 7 | 0 | 24 | 1 | 9 | 3 | 16 | 2 |
| Relf | 5 | 2 | 9 | 0 | 16·2 | 3 | 31 | 3 |
| Douglas | 8 | 2 | 19 | 2 | 2 | 1 | 2 | 0 |
| Rhodes | 7 | 0 | 26 | 0 | | | | |

| SOUTH AFRICA | O | M | R | W |
|---|---|---|---|---|
| Cox | 43 | 9 | 123 | 2 |
| Nourse | 29 | 7 | 74 | 2 |
| Hartigan | 18 | 5 | 72 | 1 |
| Baumgartner | 27·4 | 3 | 99 | 2 |
| Blanckenberg | 21 | 5 | 46 | 1 |
| Taylor | 6 | 3 | 7 | 0 |

### FALL OF WICKETS

| | SA | E | SA |
|---|---|---|---|
| Wkt | 1st | 1st | 2nd |
| 1st | 5 | 24 | 21 |
| 2nd | 22 | 40 | 31 |
| 3rd | 62 | 136 | 57 |
| 4th | 65 | 173 | 71 |
| 5th | 73 | 236 | 77 |
| 6th | 77 | 301 | 78 |
| 7th | 113 | 416 | 104 |
| 8th | 144 | 448 | 111 |
| 9th | 181 | 448 | 111 |
| 10th | 182 | 450 | 111 |

Umpires: A.J. Atfield and F.W. Grey.

# SOUTH AFRICA v ENGLAND 1913-14 (2nd Test)

Played at Old Wanderers, Johannesburg, on 26, 27, 29, 30 December.
Toss: South Africa.    Result: ENGLAND won by an innings and 12 runs.
Debuts: South Africa – C.J. Newberry.

By taking seventeen wickets, S.F. Barnes established a Test record which stood until 1956 when J.C. Laker took 19 for 90 against Australia at Manchester (*Test No. 428*). The only previous instance of nine wickets in an innings, by G.A. Lohmann in 1895-96, also took place at Johannesburg (*Test No. 48*).

## SOUTH AFRICA

| | | | | | |
|---|---|---|---|---|---|
| J.W. Zulch | c Woolley b Barnes | 14 | | c Relf b Barnes | 34 |
| H.W. Taylor* | b Barnes | 29 | | c Rhodes b Barnes | 40 |
| P.A.M. Hands | c Rhodes b Barnes | 0 | (6) | c Rhodes b Barnes | 40 |
| R. Beaumont | c Strudwick b Barnes | 0 | (3) | c Strudwick b Relf | 5 |
| A.W. Nourse | b Barnes | 17 | (4) | c Strudwick b Barnes | 56 |
| L.J. Tancred | st Strudwick b Barnes | 13 | (7) | b Barnes | 20 |
| G.P.D. Hartigan | c Smith b Rhodes | 51 | (5) | lbw b Barnes | 2 |
| T.A. Ward† | b Woolley | 19 | | b Barnes | 0 |
| C.J. Newberry | st Strudwick b Barnes | 1 | | st Strudwick b Barnes | 5 |
| J.M. Blanckenberg | not out | 0 | | not out | 12 |
| J.L. Cox | c Strudwick b Barnes | 0 | | b Barnes | 0 |
| Extras | (B 10, LB 4, NB 2) | 16 | | (B 9, LB 6, NB 2) | 17 |
| **Total** | | **160** | | | **231** |

## ENGLAND

| | | |
|---|---|---|
| W. Rhodes | c and b Blanckenberg | 152 |
| A.E. Relf | b Blanckenberg | 63 |
| J.B. Hobbs | lbw b Newberry | 23 |
| C.P. Mead | c Beaumont b Blanckenberg | 102 |
| Hon. L.H. Tennyson | lbw b Cox | 13 |
| J.W.H.T. Douglas* | c Taylor b Blanckenberg | 3 |
| F.E. Woolley | b Newberry | 0 |
| M.C. Bird | c Ward b Newberry | 1 |
| E.J. Smith | lbw b Cox | 9 |
| H. Strudwick† | c Cox b Blanckenberg | 14 |
| S.F. Barnes | not out | 0 |
| Extras | (B 18, LB 4, W 1) | 23 |
| **Total** | | **403** |

| ENGLAND | O | M | R | W | O | M | R | W | | FALL OF WICKETS | | |
|---|---|---|---|---|---|---|---|---|---|---|---|---|
| | | | | | | | | | | SA | E | SA |
| Douglas | 2 | 0 | 11 | 0 | 6 | 0 | 27 | 0 | *Wkt* | *1st* | *1st* | *2nd* |
| Barnes | 26·5 | 9 | 56 | 8 | 38·4 | 7 | 103 | 9 | 1st | 22 | 141 | 70 |
| Relf | 14 | 1 | 34 | 0 | 9 | 3 | 19 | 1 | 2nd | 22 | 181 | 77 |
| Woolley | 3 | 1 | 5 | 1 | 21 | 5 | 45 | 0 | 3rd | 24 | 333 | 93 |
| Rhodes | 13 | 5 | 23 | 1 | 9 | 2 | 20 | 0 | 4th | 56 | 354 | 106 |
| Bird | 4 | 1 | 15 | 0 | | | | | 5th | 63 | 373 | 177 |
| | | | | | | | | | 6th | 78 | 374 | 194 |
| SOUTH AFRICA | | | | | | | | | 7th | 155 | 376 | 201 |
| Cox | 30 | 8 | 74 | 2 | | | | | 8th | 159 | 376 | 212 |
| Nourse | 21 | 2 | 62 | 0 | | | | | 9th | 160 | 395 | 223 |
| Blanckenberg | 38 | 13 | 83 | 5 | | | | | 10th | 160 | 403 | 231 |
| Newberry | 26 | 2 | 93 | 3 | | | | | | | | |
| Hartigan | 5 | 0 | 24 | 0 | | | | | | | | |
| Hands | 6 | 0 | 17 | 0 | | | | | | | | |
| Taylor | 8 | 0 | 27 | 0 | | | | | | | | |
| Beaumont | 1 | 1 | 0 | 0 | | | | | | | | |

Umpires: A.J. Atfield and F.W. Grey.

# SOUTH AFRICA v ENGLAND 1913-14 (3rd Test)

Played at Old Wanderers, Johannesburg, on 1, 2, 3, 5 January.
Toss: England.   Result: ENGLAND won by 91 runs.
Debuts: South Africa – C.D. Dixon, L.R. Tuckett.

## ENGLAND

| | | | | |
|---|---|---|---|---|
| J.B. Hobbs | c Ward b Dixon | 92 | c Nourse b Dixon | 41 |
| W. Rhodes | lbw b Taylor | 35 | c Ward b Taylor | 0 |
| J.W. Hearne | c and b Dixon | 27 | (4) lbw b Newberry | 0 |
| C.P. Mead | b Blanckenberg | 0 | (3) c Tuckett b Newberry | 86 |
| Hon. L.H. Tennyson | b Nourse | 21 | (6) c Beaumont b Nourse | 6 |
| J.W.H.T. Douglas* | c Ward b Blanckenberg | 30 | (5) b Newberry | 77 |
| F.E. Woolley | lbw b Taylor | 7 | st Ward b Newberry | 37 |
| A.E. Relf | lbw b Nourse | 0 | b Blanckenberg | 25 |
| M.C. Bird | st Ward b Taylor | 1 | not out | 20 |
| S.F. Barnes | b Blanckenberg | 5 | b Blanckenberg | 0 |
| H. Strudwick† | not out | 9 | c Tuckett b Blanckenberg | 0 |
| Extras | (B 4, LB 7) | 11 | (B 10, LB 5, W1) | 16 |
| **Total** | | **238** | | **308** |

## SOUTH AFRICA

| | | | | |
|---|---|---|---|---|
| H.W. Taylor* | c Woolley b Relf | 14 | c Tennyson b Relf | 70 |
| J.W. Zulch | c and b Hearne | 38 | c and b Relf | 82 |
| T.A. Ward† | b Hearne | 15 | (6) c Strudwick b Douglas | 40 |
| R. Beaumont | c Rhodes b Hearne | 6 | (5) b Barnes | 0 |
| A.W. Nourse | b Hearne | 1 | (4) c Strudwick b Barnes | 6 |
| P.A.M. Hands | hit wkt b Hearne | 26 | (3) c Tennyson b Barnes | 7 |
| G.P.D. Hartigan | b Barnes | 18 | c Douglas b Barnes | 0 |
| C.J. Newberry | c Hearne b Rhodes | 15 | b Barnes | 13 |
| C.D. Dixon | c Rhodes b Barnes | 0 | (10) b Hearne | 0 |
| L.R. Tuckett | b Barnes | 0 | (11) not out | 0 |
| J.M. Blanckenberg | not out | 4 | (9) b Douglas | 59 |
| Extras | (B 4, LB 9, NB 1) | 14 | (B 17, LB 8, NB 2) | 27 |
| **Total** | | **151** | | **304** |

| SOUTH AFRICA | O | M | R | W | O | M | R | W | | FALL OF WICKETS | | | |
|---|---|---|---|---|---|---|---|---|---|---|---|---|---|
| Nourse | 9 | 1 | 22 | 2 | 13 | 4 | 36 | 1 | | E | SA | E | SA |
| Dixon | 19 | 2 | 62 | 2 | 21 | 4 | 56 | 1 | *Wkt* | *1st* | *1st* | *2nd* | *2nd* |
| Blanckenberg | 22·1 | 4 | 54 | 3 | 21·3 | 7 | 66 | 3 | 1st | 100 | 24 | 4 | 153 |
| Tuckett | 10 | 1 | 45 | 0 | 10 | 3 | 24 | 0 | 2nd | 158 | 67 | 83 | 162 |
| Newberry | 10 | 1 | 29 | 0 | 22 | 2 | 72 | 4 | 3rd | 159 | 81 | 84 | 167 |
| Taylor | 10 | 5 | 15 | 3 | 6 | 1 | 38 | 1 | 4th | 163 | 82 | 177 | 170 |
| | | | | | | | | | 5th | 201 | 91 | 198 | 173 |
| ENGLAND | | | | | | | | | 6th | 208 | 112 | 250 | 173 |
| Barnes | 16 | 3 | 26 | 3 | 38 | 8 | 102 | 5 | 7th | 209 | 143 | 262 | 217 |
| Hearne | 16 | 4 | 49 | 5 | 14 | 2 | 58 | 1 | 8th | 210 | 143 | 304 | 295 |
| Relf | 14 | 7 | 24 | 1 | 29 | 12 | 40 | 2 | 9th | 219 | 147 | 304 | 300 |
| Douglas | 7 | 2 | 16 | 0 | 13·4 | 2 | 34 | 2 | 10th | 238 | 151 | 308 | 304 |
| Woolley | 5 | 1 | 13 | 0 | 7 | 0 | 24 | 0 | | | | | |
| Rhodes | 3·5 | 1 | 9 | 1 | 6 | 1 | 17 | 0 | | | | | |
| Bird | | | | | 2 | 1 | 2 | 0 | | | | | |

Umpires: A.J. Atfield and F.W. Grey.

# SOUTH AFRICA v ENGLAND 1913-14 (4th Test)

Played at Lord's, Durban, on 14, 16, 17, 18 February.
Toss: South Africa.   Result: MATCH DRAWN.
Debuts: South Africa – H.W. Chapman, F.L. le Roux, D. Taylor.

This was S.F. Barnes' last Test appearance. His fourteen wickets brought his total in the rubber to 49. In seven Tests against South Africa (this rubber and the Triangular Tournament), Barnes took 83 wickets, average 9·85, with six instances of ten or more wickets in a match, and twelve of five or more in an innings. His match analysis of 14 for 144 remains the record for a Test at Durban.

## SOUTH AFRICA

| | | | | | |
|---|---|---|---|---|---|
| H.W. Taylor* | c Strudwick b Barnes | 16 | lbw b Barnes | | 93 |
| T.A. Ward† | b Barnes | 5 | b Barnes | | 1 |
| D. Taylor | c Rhodes b Barnes | 36 | c Strudwick b Barnes | | 36 |
| A.W. Nourse | b Barnes | 9 | c Tennyson b Rhodes | | 45 |
| F.L. le Roux | b Barnes | 1 | c and b Barnes | | 0 |
| P.A.M. Hands | st Strudwick b Rhodes | 51 | c Rhodes b Barnes | | 8 |
| C.J. Newberry | b Rhodes | 0 | c Bird b Barnes | | 16 |
| H.W. Chapman | b Barnes | 17 | (9) not out | | 16 |
| J.M. Blanckenberg | c Douglas b Rhodes | 4 | (10) c Tennyson b Barnes | | 13 |
| C.P. Carter | not out | 19 | (8) b Douglas | | 45 |
| J.L. Cox | c Strudwick b Barnes | 4 | not out | | 12 |
| Extras | (B 6, LB 2) | 8 | ( B12, LB 5, NB 3) | | 20 |
| **Total** | | **170** | (9 wickets declared) | | **305** |

## ENGLAND

| | | | | | |
|---|---|---|---|---|---|
| J.B. Hobbs | c Nourse b Blanckenberg | 64 | b Blanckenberg | | 97 |
| W. Rhodes | lbw b Carter | 22 | lbw b Carter | | 35 |
| J.W. Hearne | c Newberry b Carter | 2 | not out | | 8 |
| C.P. Mead | c Newberry b Blanckenberg | 31 | c Blanckenberg b Newberry | | 1 |
| Hon. L.H. Tennyson | c and b Newberry | 1 | (6) b Blanckenberg | | 0 |
| J.W.H.T. Douglas* | c and b Carter | 0 | (5) lbw b Blanckenberg | | 7 |
| F.E. Woolley | c Hands b Newberry | 9 | not out | | 0 |
| M.C. Bird | b Carter | 8 | | | |
| A.E. Relf | b Carter | 11 | | | |
| S.F. Barnes | not out | 4 | | | |
| H. Strudwick† | b Carter | 0 | | | |
| Extras | (B 7, LB 3, NB 1) | 11 | (B 2, LB 4) | | 6 |
| **Total** | | **163** | (5 wickets) | | **154** |

| ENGLAND | O | M | R | W | O | M | R | W |
|---|---|---|---|---|---|---|---|---|
| Barnes | 29·5 | 7 | 56 | 7 | 32 | 10 | 88 | 7 |
| Woolley | 10 | 3 | 27 | 0 | 13 | 2 | 26 | 0 |
| Relf | 8 | 3 | 15 | 0 | | | | |
| Rhodes | 14 | 5 | 33 | 3 | 26 | 6 | 53 | 1 |
| Douglas | 7 | 0 | 31 | 0 | 14 | 1 | 51 | 1 |
| Hearne | | | | | 11 | 0 | 46 | 0 |
| Bird | | | | | 6 | 1 | 21 | 0 |
| SOUTH AFRICA | | | | | | | | |
| Le Roux | 6 | 1 | 19 | 0 | 3 | 2 | 5 | 0 |
| Cox | 10 | 1 | 30 | 0 | 13 | 6 | 18 | 0 |
| Carter | 28 | 8 | 50 | 6 | 29 | 12 | 27 | 1 |
| Blanckenberg | 20 | 4 | 35 | 2 | 15 | 4 | 43 | 3 |
| Newberry | 11 | 4 | 18 | 2 | 10 | 4 | 22 | 1 |
| Nourse | | | | | 6 | 0 | 13 | 0 |
| Chapman | | | | | 4 | 0 | 20 | 0 |

### FALL OF WICKETS

| | SA | E | SA | E |
|---|---|---|---|---|
| Wkt | 1st | 1st | 2nd | 2nd |
| 1st | 20 | 92 | 15 | 133 |
| 2nd | 25 | 92 | 84 | 141 |
| 3rd | 35 | 104 | 181 | 142 |
| 4th | 45 | 109 | 183 | 152 |
| 5th | 84 | 116 | 195 | 154 |
| 6th | 84 | 127 | 203 | – |
| 7th | 135 | 146 | 244 | – |
| 8th | 145 | 146 | 269 | – |
| 9th | 164 | 163 | 283 | – |
| 10th | 170 | 163 | – | – |

Umpires: A.J. Atfield and F.W. Grey.

## SOUTH AFRICA v ENGLAND 1913-14 (5th Test)

Played at St George's Park, Port Elizabeth, on 27, 28 February, 2, 3 March.
Toss: South Africa.   Result: ENGLAND won by ten wickets.
Debuts: South Africa – R.H.M. Hands, E.B. Lundie.

### SOUTH AFRICA

| | | | | | |
|---|---|---|---|---|---|
| H.W. Taylor* | c Strudwick b Woolley | 42 | | c Rhodes b Bird | 87 |
| J.W. Zulch | c Strudwick b Booth | 11 | | c Rhodes b Booth | 60 |
| D. Taylor | b Relf | 12 | | b Bird | 1 |
| A.W. Nourse | b Hearne | 26 | | c Relf b Bird | 0 |
| P.A.M. Hands | c Bird b Douglas | 83 | | c Woolley b Booth | 49 |
| R.H.M. Hands | st Strudwick b Woolley | 0 | | st Strudwick b Douglas | 7 |
| C.J. Newberry | b Woolley | 11 | (8) | c Hearne b Relf | 1 |
| T.A. Ward† | c Bird b Douglas | 3 | (7) | c Woolley b Booth | 1 |
| C.P. Carter | c Bird b Douglas | 0 | | b Booth | 5 |
| J.M. Blanckenberg | b Douglas | 0 | | not out | 6 |
| E.B. Lundie | not out | 0 | | c Strudwick b Relf | 1 |
| Extras | (B 2, LB 2, NB 1) | 5 | | (B 6, LB 3, NB 1) | 10 |
| **Total** | | **193** | | | **228** |

### ENGLAND

| | | | | |
|---|---|---|---|---|
| J.B. Hobbs | c Nourse b Lundie | 33 | not out | 11 |
| W. Rhodes | b Carter | 27 | not out | 0 |
| H. Strudwick† | b Carter | 3 | | |
| J.W. Hearne | c H.W. Taylor b Blanckenberg | 32 | | |
| C.P. Mead | c and b Blanckenberg | 117 | | |
| F.E. Woolley | lbw b Newberry | 54 | | |
| J.W.H.T. Douglas* | c Blanckenberg b Lundie | 30 | | |
| Hon. L.H. Tennyson | lbw b Lundie | 23 | | |
| M.C. Bird | run out | 4 | | |
| M.W. Booth | b Lundie | 32 | | |
| A.E. Relf | not out | 23 | | |
| Extras | (B20, LB 6, NB 7) | 33 | | |
| **Total** | | **411** | (0 wickets) | **11** |

| ENGLAND | O | M | R | W | O | M | R | W | | FALL OF WICKETS | | | |
|---|---|---|---|---|---|---|---|---|---|---|---|---|---|
| | | | | | | | | | | SA | E | SA | E |
| Relf | 11 | 5 | 26 | 1 | 23·1 | 11 | 29 | 2 | *Wkt* | *1st* | *1st* | *2nd* | *2nd* |
| Booth | 18 | 3 | 43 | 1 | 24 | 5 | 49 | 4 | 1st | 19 | 48 | 129 | – |
| Woolley | 22 | 4 | 71 | 3 | 5 | 2 | 23 | 0 | 2nd | 36 | 52 | 133 | – |
| Hearne | 9 | 2 | 34 | 1 | 12 | 4 | 30 | 0 | 3rd | 95 | 90 | 133 | – |
| Douglas | 5·4 | 2 | 14 | 4 | 9 | 1 | 34 | 1 | 4th | 116 | 134 | 173 | – |
| Bird | | | | | 11 | 1 | 38 | 3 | 5th | 116 | 238 | 204 | – |
| Tennyson | | | | | 1 | 0 | 1 | 0 | 6th | 167 | 317 | 213 | – |
| Rhodes | | | | | 10 | 4 | 14 | 0 | 7th | 176 | 329 | 215 | – |
| | | | | | | | | | 8th | 176 | 353 | 215 | – |
| SOUTH AFRICA | | | | | | | | | 9th | 180 | 361 | 223 | – |
| Lundie | 46·3 | 9 | 101 | 4 | 1·1 | 0 | 6 | 0 | 10th | 193 | 411 | 228 | – |
| Nourse | 9 | 1 | 31 | 0 | | | | | | | | | |
| Carter | 41 | 9 | 111 | 2 | | | | | | | | | |
| Blanckenberg | 34 | 7 | 101 | 2 | | | | | | | | | |
| Newberry | 14 | 2 | 34 | 1 | | | | | | | | | |
| H.W. Taylor | | | | | 1 | 0 | 5 | 0 | | | | | |

Umpires: F.W. Grey and Douglas Smith.

# AUSTRALIA v ENGLAND 1920-21 (1st Test)

Played at Sydney Cricket Ground on 17, 18, 20, 21, 22 December.
Toss: Australia.   Result: AUSTRALIA won by 377 runs.
Debuts: Australia – H.L. Collins, J.M. Gregory, A.A. Mailey, W.A.S. Oldfield, C.E. Pellew,
J. Ryder, J.M. Taylor; England – E.H. Hendren, C.H. Parkin, C.A.G. Russell, A. Waddington.
*Note that Ryder has no second initial. Russell has usually appeared as 'A.C. Russell'.*

H.L. Collins was the fifth Australian to score a hundred against England in his first Test match. At the age of 31,
he was the oldest to do so. Australia's total of 581 was a record for the second innings of any Test match.

## AUSTRALIA

| | | | | | |
|---|---|---|---|---|---|
| C.G. Macartney | b Waddington | 19 | (3) b Douglas | | 69 |
| H.L. Collins | run out | 70 | c Waddington b Douglas | | 104 |
| W. Bardsley | c Strudwick b Hearne | 22 | (1) b Hearne | | 57 |
| C. Kelleway | run out | 33 | (6) c Russell b Woolley | | 78 |
| W.W. Armstrong* | st Strudwick b Woolley | 12 | (7) b Parkin | | 158 |
| J.M. Gregory | c Strudwick b Woolley | 8 | (9) run out | | 0 |
| J.M. Taylor | lbw b Hearne | 34 | (4) c Woolley b Parkin | | 51 |
| C.E. Pellew | c Hendren b Hearne | 36 | (5) lbw b Woolley | | 16 |
| J. Ryder | run out | 5 | (8) run out | | 6 |
| W.A.S. Oldfield† | c Hobbs b Parkin | 7 | c Strudwick b Parkin | | 16 |
| A.A. Mailey | not out | 10 | not out | | 0 |
| Extras | (B 4, LB 6, NB 1) | 11 | (B 17, LB 7, NB 2) | | 26 |
| **Total** | | **267** | | | **581** |

## ENGLAND

| | | | | | |
|---|---|---|---|---|---|
| J.B. Hobbs | b Gregory | 49 | lbw b Armstrong | | 59 |
| C.A.G. Russell | b Kelleway | 0 | c Oldfield b Gregory | | 5 |
| J.W. Hearne | c Gregory b Mailey | 14 | b Gregory | | 57 |
| E.H. Hendren | c Gregory b Ryder | 28 | b Kelleway | | 56 |
| F.E. Woolley | c Mailey b Ryder | 52 | st Oldfield b Mailey | | 16 |
| J.W.H.T. Douglas* | st Oldfield b Mailey | 21 | c Armstrong b Mailey | | 7 |
| W. Rhodes | c Gregory b Mailey | 3 | c Ryder b Mailey | | 45 |
| J.W. Hitch | c Kelleway b Gregory | 3 | c Taylor b Gregory | | 19 |
| A. Waddington | run out | 7 | b Kelleway | | 3 |
| C.H. Parkin | not out | 4 | b Kelleway | | 4 |
| H. Strudwick† | lbw b Gregory | 2 | not out | | 1 |
| Extras | (B 3, LB 4) | 7 | (B 6, LB 3) | | 9 |
| **Total** | | **190** | | | **281** |

| ENGLAND | O | M | R | W | O | M | R | W |
|---|---|---|---|---|---|---|---|---|
| Hitch | 10 | 0 | 37 | 0 | 8 | 0 | 40 | 0 |
| Waddington | 18 | 3 | 35 | 1 | 23 | 4 | 53 | 0 |
| Parkin | 26·5 | 5 | 58 | 1 | 35·3 | 5 | 102 | 3 |
| Hearne | 34 | 8 | 77 | 3 | 42 | 7 | 124 | 1 |
| Douglas | 3 | 0 | 14 | 0 | 26 | 3 | 79 | 2 |
| Woolley | 23 | 7 | 35 | 2 | 36 | 10 | 90 | 2 |
| Rhodes | | | | | 22 | 2 | 67 | 0 |
| AUSTRALIA | | | | | | | | |
| Kelleway | 6 | 2 | 10 | 1 | 15·5 | 3 | 45 | 3 |
| Gregory | 23·1 | 3 | 56 | 3 | 33 | 6 | 70 | 3 |
| Mailey | 23 | 4 | 95 | 3 | 24 | 2 | 105 | 3 |
| Ryder | 6 | 1 | 20 | 2 | 17 | 6 | 24 | 0 |
| Armstrong | 1 | 0 | 2 | 0 | 10 | 0 | 21 | 1 |
| Macartney | | | | | 3 | 0 | 7 | 0 |

## FALL OF WICKETS

| | A | E | A | E |
|---|---|---|---|---|
| Wkt | 1st | 1st | 2nd | 2nd |
| 1st | 40 | 0 | 123 | 5 |
| 2nd | 80 | 50 | 234 | 105 |
| 3rd | 140 | 70 | 241 | 149 |
| 4th | 162 | 144 | 282 | 170 |
| 5th | 173 | 145 | 332 | 178 |
| 6th | 176 | 158 | 519 | 231 |
| 7th | 244 | 165 | 536 | 264 |
| 8th | 249 | 180 | 540 | 271 |
| 9th | 250 | 188 | 578 | 279 |
| 10th | 267 | 190 | 581 | 281 |

Umpires: A.C. Jones and R.W. Crockett.

## AUSTRALIA v ENGLAND 1920-21 (2nd Test)

Played at Melbourne Cricket Ground on 31 December, 1, 3, 4 January.
Toss: Australia.   Result: AUSTRALIA won by an innings and 91 runs.
Debuts: Australia – R.L. Park; England – H. Howell, W.H.R. Makepeace *(usually given as 'H. Makepeace')*.

Pellew and Gregory each scored their maiden Test centuries in their second match. Gregory equalled G. Giffen's record *(Test No. 42)* by scoring a hundred and taking eight wickets in the same Test. Hobbs scored his third century in successive innings at Melbourne.

### AUSTRALIA

| | | |
|---|---|---|
| H.L. Collins | c Hearne b Howell | 64 |
| W. Bardsley | c Strudwick b Woolley | 51 |
| R.L. Park | b Howell | 0 |
| J.M. Taylor | c Woolley b Parkin | 68 |
| W.W. Armstrong* | lbw b Douglas | 39 |
| C. Kelleway | c Strudwick b Howell | 9 |
| C.E. Pellew | b Parkin | 116 |
| J. Ryder | c Woolley b Douglas | 13 |
| J.M. Gregory | c Russell b Woolley | 100 |
| W.A.S. Oldfield† | c and b Rhodes | 24 |
| A.A. Mailey | not out | 8 |
| Extras | (B 1, LB 3, W 1, NB 2) | 7 |
| **Total** | | **499** |

### ENGLAND

| | | | | | |
|---|---|---|---|---|---|
| J.B. Hobbs | c Ryder b Gregory | 122 | b Kelleway | | 20 |
| W. Rhodes | b Gregory | 7 | c Collins b Armstrong | | 28 |
| W.H.R. Makepeace | lbw b Armstrong | 4 | c Gregory b Armstrong | | 4 |
| E.H. Hendren | c Taylor b Gregory | 67 | c and b Collins | | 1 |
| C.A.G. Russell | c Collins b Gregory | 0 | c Armstrong b Collins | | 5 |
| F.E. Woolley | b Gregory | 5 | b Ryder | | 50 |
| J.W.H.T. Douglas* | lbw b Gregory | 15 | b Gregory | | 9 |
| C.H. Parkin | c Mailey b Gregory | 4 | c Taylor b Armstrong | | 9 |
| H. Strudwick† | not out | 21 | c Oldfield b Armstrong | | 24 |
| H. Howell | st Oldfield b Armstrong | 5 | not out | | 0 |
| J.W. Hearne | absent ill | – | absent ill | | – |
| Extras | (NB 1) | 1 | (B 3, LB 3, NB 1) | | 7 |
| **Total** | | **251** | | | **157** |

| ENGLAND | O | M | R | W | O | M | R | W |
|---|---|---|---|---|---|---|---|---|
| Howell | 37 | 5 | 142 | 3 | | | | |
| Douglas | 24 | 1 | 83 | 2 | | | | |
| Parkin | 27 | 0 | 116 | 2 | | | | |
| Hearne | 14 | 0 | 38 | 0 | | | | |
| Woolley | 27 | 8 | 87 | 2 | | | | |
| Rhodes | 8·3 | 1 | 26 | 1 | | | | |
| AUSTRALIA | | | | | | | | |
| Gregory | 20 | 1 | 69 | 7 | 12 | 0 | 32 | 1 |
| Kelleway | 19 | 1 | 54 | 0 | 12 | 1 | 25 | 1 |
| Armstrong | 24·3 | 8 | 50 | 2 | 15·2 | 5 | 26 | 4 |
| Ryder | 14 | 2 | 31 | 0 | 10 | 2 | 17 | 1 |
| Park | 1 | 0 | 9 | 0 | | | | |
| Collins | 9 | 0 | 37 | 0 | 17 | 5 | 47 | 2 |
| Pellew | | | | | 1 | 0 | 3 | 0 |

FALL OF WICKETS

| | A | E | E |
|---|---|---|---|
| Wkt | 1st | 1st | 2nd |
| 1st | 116 | 20 | 36 |
| 2nd | 116 | 32 | 53 |
| 3rd | 118 | 174 | 54 |
| 4th | 194 | 185 | 58 |
| 5th | 220 | 201 | 70 |
| 6th | 251 | 208 | 104 |
| 7th | 282 | 213 | 141 |
| 8th | 455 | 232 | 151 |
| 9th | 469 | 251 | 157 |
| 10th | 499 | – | – |

Umpires: R.W. Crockett and D. Elder.

# AUSTRALIA v ENGLAND 1920-21 (3rd Test)

Played at Adelaide Oval on 14, 15, 17, 18, 19, 20 January.
Toss: Australia.   Result: AUSTRALIA won by 119 runs.
Debuts: Australia – E.A. McDonald; England – P.G.H. Fender.

This match produced six centuries – a record which stood until 1938 when seven were scored at Nottingham (*Test No. 263*). Australia's total of 582 beat by one run the record set in the 1st Test of this rubber and remains the second innings record for Tests between England and Australia – as does the match aggregate of 1,753 runs.

## AUSTRALIA

| | | | | | |
|---|---|---|---|---|---|
| H.L. Collins | c Rhodes b Parkin | 162 | | c Hendren b Parkin | 24 |
| W. Bardsley | st Strudwick b Douglas | 14 | | b Howell | 16 |
| C. Kelleway | c Fender b Parkin | 4 | | b Howell | 147 |
| J.M. Taylor | run out | 5 | (6) | c Strudwick b Fender | 38 |
| W.W. Armstrong* | c Strudwick b Douglas | 11 | | b Howell | 121 |
| C.E. Pellew | run out | 35 | (7) | c Strudwick b Parkin | 104 |
| J.M. Gregory | c Strudwick b Fender | 10 | (8) | not out | 78 |
| J. Ryder | c Douglas b Parkin | 44 | (4) | c Woolley b Howell | 3 |
| W.A.S. Oldfield† | lbw b Parkin | 50 | | b Rhodes | 10 |
| E.A. McDonald | b Parkin | 2 | | b Rhodes | 4 |
| A.A. Mailey | not out | 3 | | b Rhodes | 13 |
| Extras | (B 6, LB 8) | 14 | | (B 5, LB 10, W 4, NB 5) | 24 |
| **Total** | | **354** | | | **582** |

## ENGLAND

| | | | | |
|---|---|---|---|---|
| J.B. Hobbs | c and b Mailey | 18 | b Gregory | 123 |
| W. Rhodes | run out | 16 | lbw b McDonald | 4 |
| W.H.R. Makepeace | c Gregory b Armstrong | 60 | c and b McDonald | 30 |
| E.H. Hendren | b Gregory | 36 | b Mailey | 51 |
| F.E. Woolley | c Kelleway b Gregory | 79 | b Gregory | 0 |
| C.A.G. Russell | not out | 135 | b Mailey | 59 |
| J.W.H.T. Douglas* | lbw b Mailey | 60 | c Armstrong b Gregory | 32 |
| P.G.H. Fender | b McDonald | 2 | c Ryder b Mailey | 42 |
| C.H. Parkin | st Oldfield b Mailey | 12 | st Oldfield b Mailey | 17 |
| H. Strudwick† | c Pellew b Mailey | 9 | c Armstrong b Mailey | 1 |
| H. Howell | c Gregory b Mailey | 2 | not out | 4 |
| Extras | (B 8, LB 5, NB 5) | 18 | (LB 3, NB 4) | 7 |
| **Total** | | **447** | | **370** |

| ENGLAND | O | M | R | W | O | M | R | W | | FALL OF WICKETS | | | |
|---|---|---|---|---|---|---|---|---|---|---|---|---|---|
| Howell | 26 | 1 | 89 | 0 | 34 | 6 | 115 | 4 | | A | E | A | E |
| Douglas | 24 | 6 | 69 | 2 | 19 | 2 | 61 | 0 | *Wkt* | *1st* | *1st* | *2nd* | *2nd* |
| Parkin | 20 | 2 | 60 | 5 | 40 | 8 | 109 | 2 | 1st | 32 | 25 | 34 | 20 |
| Woolley | 21 | 6 | 47 | 0 | 38 | 4 | 91 | 0 | 2nd | 45 | 49 | 63 | 125 |
| Fender | 12 | 0 | 52 | 1 | 22 | 0 | 105 | 1 | 3rd | 55 | 111 | 71 | 183 |
| Rhodes | 5 | 1 | 23 | 0 | 25·5 | 8 | 61 | 3 | 4th | 96 | 161 | 265 | 185 |
| Hobbs | | | | | 7 | 2 | 16 | 0 | 5th | 176 | 250 | 328 | 243 |
| | | | | | | | | | 6th | 209 | 374 | 454 | 292 |
| AUSTRALIA | | | | | | | | | 7th | 285 | 391 | 477 | 308 |
| McDonald | 24 | 1 | 78 | 1 | 24 | 0 | 95 | 2 | 8th | 347 | 416 | 511 | 321 |
| Gregory | 36 | 5 | 108 | 2 | 20 | 2 | 50 | 3 | 9th | 349 | 437 | 570 | 341 |
| Kelleway | 11 | 4 | 25 | 0 | 8 | 2 | 16 | 0 | 10th | 354 | 447 | 582 | 370 |
| Mailey | 32·1 | 3 | 160 | 5 | 29·2 | 3 | 142 | 5 | | | | | |
| Armstrong | 23 | 10 | 29 | 1 | 16 | 1 | 41 | 0 | | | | | |
| Ryder | 6 | 0 | 29 | 0 | 9 | 2 | 19 | 0 | | | | | |

Umpires: R.W. Crockett and D. Elder.

# AUSTRALIA v ENGLAND 1920-21 (4th Test)

Played at Melbourne Cricket Ground on 11, 12, 14, 15, 16 February.
Toss: England. Result: AUSTRALIA won by eight wickets.
Debuts: England – A. Dolphin.

Mailey's analysis of 9 for 121 remains Australia's record in all Test matches and the record in any Test at Melbourne. No other Australian bowler has taken nine wickets in a Test innings. At 38 years 173 days, Makepeace was the oldest player to score a maiden Test hundred.

## ENGLAND

| | | | | | |
|---|---|---|---|---|---|
| J.B. Hobbs | c Carter b McDonald | 27 | | lbw b Mailey | 13 |
| W. Rhodes | c Carter b Gregory | 11 | | c Gregory b Mailey | 73 |
| W.H.R. Makepeace | c Collins b Mailey | 117 | | lbw b Mailey | 54 |
| E.H. Hendren | c Carter b Mailey | 30 | | b Kelleway | 32 |
| F.E. Woolley | lbw b Kelleway | 29 | | st Carter b Mailey | 0 |
| J.W.H.T. Douglas* | c and b Mailey | 50 | | st Carter b Mailey | 60 |
| A. Waddington | b Mailey | 0 | (8) | st Carter b Mailey | 6 |
| P.G.H. Fender | c Gregory b Kelleway | 3 | (7) | c Collins b Mailey | 59 |
| A. Dolphin† | b Kelleway | 1 | | c Gregory b Mailey | 0 |
| C.H. Parkin | run out | 10 | | c Bardsley b Mailey | 4 |
| H. Howell | not out | 0 | | not out | 0 |
| Extras | (B 1, LB 5) | 6 | | (B 5, LB 5, W 1, NB 3) | 14 |
| **Total** | | **284** | | | **315** |

## AUSTRALIA

| | | | | | |
|---|---|---|---|---|---|
| H.L. Collins | c Rhodes b Woolley | 59 | | c Rhodes b Parkin | 32 |
| W. Bardsley | b Fender | 56 | | run out | 38 |
| J. Ryder | lbw b Woolley | 7 | | not out | 52 |
| J.M. Taylor | hit wkt b Fender | 2 | | | |
| J.M. Gregory | c Dolphin b Parkin | 77 | (4) | not out | 76 |
| C.E. Pellew | b Fender | 12 | | | |
| W.W. Armstrong* | not out | 123 | | | |
| C. Kelleway | b Fender | 27 | | | |
| H. Carter† | b Fender | 0 | | | |
| A.A. Mailey | run out | 13 | | | |
| E.A. McDonald | b Woolley | 0 | | | |
| Extras | (B 1, LB 6, W 1, NB 5) | 13 | | (B 5, LB 5, W 2, NB 1) | 13 |
| **Total** | | **389** | | (2 wickets) | **211** |

| AUSTRALIA | O | M | R | W | O | M | R | W |
|---|---|---|---|---|---|---|---|---|
| McDonald | 19 | 2 | 46 | 1 | 23 | 2 | 77 | 0 |
| Gregory | 18 | 1 | 61 | 1 | 14 | 4 | 31 | 0 |
| Mailey | 29·2 | 1 | 115 | 4 | 47 | 8 | 121 | 9 |
| Ryder | 10 | 5 | 10 | 0 | 10 | 3 | 25 | 0 |
| Armstrong | 5 | 1 | 9 | 0 | | | | |
| Kelleway | 18 | 2 | 37 | 3 | 23 | 8 | 47 | 1 |
| ENGLAND | | | | | | | | |
| Howell | 17 | 2 | 86 | 0 | 10 | 1 | 36 | 0 |
| Douglas | 4 | 0 | 17 | 0 | 5 | 1 | 13 | 0 |
| Waddington | 5 | 0 | 31 | 0 | | | | |
| Parkin | 22 | 5 | 64 | 1 | 12 | 2 | 46 | 1 |
| Fender | 32 | 3 | 122 | 5 | 13·2 | 2 | 39 | 0 |
| Woolley | 32·1 | 14 | 56 | 3 | 14 | 4 | 39 | 0 |
| Rhodes | | | | | 10 | 2 | 25 | 0 |

FALL OF WICKETS

| | E | A | E | A |
|---|---|---|---|---|
| Wkt | 1st | 1st | 2nd | 2nd |
| 1st | 18 | 117 | 32 | 71 |
| 2nd | 61 | 123 | 145 | 81 |
| 3rd | 104 | 128 | 152 | – |
| 4th | 164 | 133 | 152 | – |
| 5th | 270 | 153 | 201 | – |
| 6th | 270 | 298 | 305 | – |
| 7th | 273 | 335 | 307 | – |
| 8th | 274 | 335 | 307 | – |
| 9th | 275 | 376 | 315 | – |
| 10th | 284 | 389 | 315 | – |

Umpires: R.W. Crockett and D. Elder.

# AUSTRALIA v ENGLAND 1920-21 (5th Test)

Played at Sydney Cricket Ground on 25, 26, 28 February, 1 March.
Toss: England.   Result: AUSTRALIA won by nine wickets.
Debuts: England – E.R. Wilson.

This victory gave Australia an unprecedented and unequalled five wins in one rubber between these two countries. Mailey's total of 36 wickets remains Australia's record in any rubber against England. Gregory is the only non-wicket-keeper to make 15 catches in a Test rubber.

## ENGLAND

| | | | | | |
|---|---|--:|---|---|--:|
| J.B. Hobbs | lbw b Gregory | 40 | (5) c Taylor b Mailey | | 34 |
| W. Rhodes | c Carter b Kelleway | 26 | run out | | 25 |
| W.H.R. Makepeace | c Gregory b Mailey | 3 | c Gregory b Kelleway | | 7 |
| E.H. Hendren | c Carter b Gregory | 5 | (6) st Carter b Mailey | | 13 |
| F.E. Woolley | b McDonald | 53 | (1) c and b Kelleway | | 1 |
| C.A.G. Russell | c Gregory b Mailey | 19 | (8) c Gregory b Armstrong | | 35 |
| J.W.H.T. Douglas* | not out | 32 | c and b Mailey | | 68 |
| P.G.H. Fender | c Gregory b Kelleway | 2 | (9) c Kelleway b McDonald | | 40 |
| E.R. Wilson | c Carter b Kelleway | 5 | (4) st Carter b Mailey | | 5 |
| C.H. Parkin | c Taylor b Kelleway | 9 | c Gregory b Mailey | | 36 |
| H. Strudwick† | b Gregory | 2 | not out | | 5 |
| Extras | (B 3, LB 2, W 1, NB 2) | 8 | (B 3, LB 5, NB 3) | | 11 |
| **Total** | | **204** | | | **280** |

## AUSTRALIA

| | | | | | |
|---|---|--:|---|---|--:|
| H.L. Collins | c Fender b Parkin | 5 | c Strudwick b Wilson | | 37 |
| W. Bardsley | c Fender b Douglas | 7 | not out | | 50 |
| C.G. Macartney | c Hobbs b Fender | 170 | not out | | 2 |
| J.M. Taylor | c Hendren b Douglas | 32 | | | |
| J.M. Gregory | c Strudwick b Fender | 93 | | | |
| W.W. Armstrong* | c Woolley b Fender | 0 | | | |
| J. Ryder | b Fender | 2 | | | |
| C. Kelleway | c Strudwick b Wilson | 32 | | | |
| H. Carter† | c Woolley b Fender | 17 | | | |
| A.A. Mailey | b Wilson | 5 | | | |
| E.A. McDonald | not out | 3 | | | |
| Extras | (B 18, LB 6, NB 2) | 26 | (B 3, NB 1) | | 4 |
| **Total** | | **392** | (1 wicket) | | **93** |

| AUSTRALIA | O | M | R | W | O | M | R | W | | FALL OF WICKETS | | | |
|---|--:|--:|--:|--:|--:|--:|--:|--:|---|---|---|---|---|
| Gregory | 16·1 | 4 | 42 | 3 | 16 | 3 | 37 | 0 | | E | A | E | A |
| McDonald | 11 | 2 | 38 | 1 | 25 | 3 | 58 | 1 | Wkt | 1st | 1st | 2nd | 2nd |
| Kelleway | 20 | 6 | 27 | 4 | 14 | 3 | 29 | 2 | 1st | 54 | 16 | 1 | 91 |
| Mailey | 23 | 1 | 89 | 2 | 36·2 | 5 | 119 | 5 | 2nd | 70 | 22 | 14 | – |
| Ryder | | | | | 2 | 2 | 0 | 0 | 3rd | 74 | 89 | 29 | – |
| Armstrong | | | | | 8 | 2 | 26 | 1 | 4th | 76 | 287 | 75 | – |
| ENGLAND | | | | | | | | | 5th | 125 | 287 | 82 | – |
| Douglas | 16 | 0 | 84 | 2 | | | | | 6th | 161 | 313 | 91 | – |
| Parkin | 19 | 1 | 83 | 1 | 9 | 1 | 32 | 0 | 7th | 164 | 356 | 160 | – |
| Woolley | 15 | 1 | 58 | 0 | 11 | 3 | 27 | 0 | 8th | 172 | 384 | 224 | – |
| Wilson | 14·3 | 4 | 28 | 2 | 6 | 1 | 8 | 1 | 9th | 201 | 384 | 251 | – |
| Fender | 20 | 1 | 90 | 5 | 1 | 0 | 2 | 0 | 10th | 204 | 392 | 280 | – |
| Rhodes | 7 | 0 | 23 | 0 | 7·2 | 1 | 20 | 0 | | | | | |

Umpires: R.W. Crockett and D. Elder.

# ENGLAND v AUSTRALIA 1921 (1st Test)

Played at Trent Bridge, Nottingham, on 28, 30 May.
Toss: England.   Result: AUSTRALIA won by ten wickets.
Debuts: England – P. Holmes, V.W.C. Jupp, D.J. Knight, T.L. Richmond, E. Tyldesley; Australia –
T.J.E. Andrews, H.S.T.L. Hendry.

The hundredth match in this series ended on the second afternoon.

## ENGLAND

| | | | | | |
|---|---|---|---|---|---|
| D.J. Knight | c Carter b Gregory | 8 | run out | | 38 |
| P. Holmes | b McDonald | 30 | c Taylor b McDonald | | 8 |
| E. Tyldesley | b Gregory | 0 | b Gregory | | 7 |
| E.H. Hendren | b Gregory | 0 | b McDonald | | 7 |
| J.W.H.T. Douglas* | c Gregory b Armstrong | 11 | c Hendry b McDonald | | 13 |
| F.E. Woolley | c Hendry b McDonald | 20 | c Carter b Hendry | | 34 |
| V.W.C. Jupp | c Armstrong b McDonald | 8 | c Pellew b Gregory | | 15 |
| W. Rhodes | c Carter b Gregory | 19 | c Carter b McDonald | | 10 |
| H. Strudwick† | c Collins b Gregory | 0 | b Hendry | | 0 |
| H. Howell | not out | 0 | not out | | 4 |
| T.L. Richmond | c and b Gregory | 4 | b McDonald | | 2 |
| Extras | (B 6, LB 6) | 12 | (B 4, LB 3, NB 2) | | 9 |
| **Total** | | **112** | | | **147** |

## AUSTRALIA

| | | | | | |
|---|---|---|---|---|---|
| W. Bardsley | lbw b Woolley | 66 | not out | | 8 |
| H.L. Collins | lbw b Richmond | 17 | | | |
| C.G. Macartney | lbw b Douglas | 20 | (2) not out | | 22 |
| J.M. Taylor | c Jupp b Douglas | 4 | | | |
| W.W. Armstrong* | b Jupp | 11 | | | |
| J.M. Gregory | lbw b Richmond | 14 | | | |
| C.E. Pellew | c and b Rhodes | 25 | | | |
| H. Carter† | b Woolley | 33 | | | |
| T.J.E. Andrews | c and b Rhodes | 6 | | | |
| H.S.T.L. Hendry | not out | 12 | | | |
| E.A. McDonald | c Knight b Woolley | 10 | | | |
| Extras | (B 8, LB 5, NB 1) | 14 | | | |
| **Total** | | **232** | (0 wickets) | | **30** |

| AUSTRALIA | O | M | R | W | O | M | R | W | FALL OF WICKETS | | | | |
|---|---|---|---|---|---|---|---|---|---|---|---|---|---|
| Gregory | 19 | 5 | 58 | 6 | 22 | 8 | 45 | 2 | | E | A | E | A |
| McDonald | 15 | 5 | 42 | 3 | 22·4 | 10 | 32 | 5 | Wkt | 1st | 1st | 2nd | 2nd |
| Armstrong | 3 | 3 | 0 | 1 | 27 | 10 | 33 | 0 | 1st | 18 | 49 | 23 | – |
| Macartney | | | | | 5 | 2 | 10 | 0 | 2nd | 18 | 86 | 41 | – |
| Hendry | | | | | 9 | 1 | 18 | 2 | 3rd | 18 | 98 | 60 | – |
| | | | | | | | | | 4th | 43 | 126 | 63 | – |
| | | | | | | | | | 5th | 77 | 138 | 76 | – |
| ENGLAND | | | | | | | | | 6th | 78 | 152 | 110 | – |
| Howell | 9 | 3 | 22 | 0 | | | | | 7th | 101 | 183 | 138 | – |
| Douglas | 13 | 2 | 34 | 2 | | | | | 8th | 107 | 202 | 138 | – |
| Richmond | 16 | 3 | 69 | 2 | 3 | 0 | 17 | 0 | 9th | 108 | 212 | 140 | – |
| Woolley | 22 | 8 | 46 | 3 | | | | | 10th | 112 | 232 | 147 | – |
| Jupp | 5 | 0 | 14 | 1 | 3·1 | 0 | 13 | 0 | | | | | |
| Rhodes | 13 | 3 | 33 | 2 | | | | | | | | | |

Umpires: J. Moss and H.R. Butt.

# ENGLAND v AUSTRALIA 1921 (2nd Test)

Played at Lord's, London, on 11, 13, 14 June.
Toss: England.   Result: AUSTRALIA won by eight wickets.
Debuts: England – A.E. Dipper, F.J. Durston, A.J. Evans, N.E. Haig.

## ENGLAND

| | | | | | |
|---|---|---|---|---|---|
| D.J. Knight | c Gregory b Armstrong | 7 | c Carter b Gregory | 1 |
| A.E. Dipper | b McDonald | 11 | b McDonald | 40 |
| F.E. Woolley | st Carter b Mailey | 95 | c Hendry b Mailey | 93 |
| E.H. Hendren | b McDonald | 0 | c Gregory b Mailey | 10 |
| J.W.H.T. Douglas* | b McDonald | 34 | b Gregory | 14 |
| A.J. Evans | b McDonald | 4 | lbw b McDonald | 14 |
| Hon. L.H. Tennyson | st Carter b Mailey | 5 | not out | 74 |
| N.E. Haig | c Carter b Gregory | 3 | b McDonald | 0 |
| C.H. Parkin | b Mailey | 0 | c Pellew b McDonald | 11 |
| H. Strudwick† | c McDonald b Mailey | 8 | b Gregory | 12 |
| F.J. Durston | not out | 6 | b Gregory | 2 |
| Extras | (B 1, LB 11, W 1, NB 1) | 14 | (B 4, LB 3, NB 5) | 12 |
| **Total** | | **187** | | **283** |

## AUSTRALIA

| | | | | | |
|---|---|---|---|---|---|
| W. Bardsley | c Woolley b Douglas | 88 | not out | 63 |
| T.J.E. Andrews | c Strudwick b Durston | 9 | lbw b Parkin | 49 |
| C.G. Macartney | c Strudwick b Durston | 31 | b Durston | 8 |
| C.E. Pellew | b Haig | 43 | not out | 5 |
| J.M. Taylor | lbw b Douglas | 36 | | |
| W.W. Armstrong* | b Durston | 0 | | |
| J.M. Gregory | c and b Parkin | 52 | | |
| H.S.T.L. Hendry | b Haig | 5 | | |
| H. Carter† | b Durston | 46 | | |
| A.A. Mailey | c and b Parkin | 5 | | |
| E.A. McDonald | not out | 17 | | |
| Extras | (B 2, LB 5, NB 3) | 10 | (B 3, LB 2, NB 1) | 6 |
| **Total** | | **342** | (2 wickets) | **131** |

| AUSTRALIA | O | M | R | W | O | M | R | W |
|---|---|---|---|---|---|---|---|---|
| Gregory | 16 | 1 | 51 | 1 | 26·2 | 4 | 76 | 4 |
| McDonald | 20 | 2 | 58 | 4 | 23 | 3 | 89 | 4 |
| Armstrong | 18 | 12 | 9 | 1 | 12 | 6 | 19 | 0 |
| Mailey | 14·2 | 1 | 55 | 4 | 25 | 4 | 72 | 2 |
| Hendry | | | | | 4 | 0 | 15 | 0 |
| ENGLAND | | | | | | | | |
| Durston | 24·1 | 2 | 102 | 4 | 9·3 | 0 | 34 | 1 |
| Douglas | 9 | 1 | 53 | 2 | 6 | 0 | 23 | 0 |
| Parkin | 20 | 5 | 72 | 2 | 9 | 0 | 31 | 1 |
| Haig | 20 | 4 | 61 | 2 | 3 | 0 | 27 | 0 |
| Woolley | 11 | 2 | 44 | 0 | 3 | 0 | 10 | 0 |

### FALL OF WICKETS

| Wkt | E 1st | A 1st | E 2nd | A 2nd |
|---|---|---|---|---|
| 1st | 20 | 19 | 3 | 103 |
| 2nd | 24 | 73 | 97 | 114 |
| 3rd | 25 | 145 | 124 | – |
| 4th | 108 | 191 | 165 | – |
| 5th | 120 | 192 | 165 | – |
| 6th | 145 | 230 | 198 | – |
| 7th | 156 | 263 | 202 | – |
| 8th | 157 | 277 | 235 | – |
| 9th | 170 | 289 | 263 | – |
| 10th | 187 | 342 | 283 | – |

Umpires: J. Moss and W. Phillips.

# ENGLAND v AUSTRALIA 1921 (3rd Test)

Played at Headingley, Leeds, on 2, 4, 5 July.
Toss: Australia.   Result: AUSTRALIA won by 219 runs.
Debuts: England – G. Brown, A. Ducat, H.T.W. Hardinge, J.C. White.

Hobbs, having missed the first two Tests because of injury, was taken ill with appendicitis on the first afternoon of the match. Macartney's hundred was his fourth in successive first-class innings, Australia's only century of the rubber, and the first for Australia at Leeds. This was Australia's eighth successive win which still stands as the record number of consecutive victories by any Test-playing country. England thus equalled South Africa's record of eight consecutive defeats (1888-89 to 1898-99).

## AUSTRALIA

| | | | | | |
|---|---|---|---|---|---|
| W. Bardsley | c Woolley b Douglas | 6 | b Jupp | | 25 |
| T.J.E. Andrews | c Woolley b Douglas | 19 | b Jupp | | 92 |
| C.G. Macartney | lbw b Parkin | 115 | c and b Woolley | | 30 |
| C.E. Pellew | c Hearne b Woolley | 52 | (5) c Ducat b White | | 16 |
| J.M. Taylor | c Douglas b Jupp | 50 | (6) c Tennyson b White | | 4 |
| J.M. Gregory | b Parkin | 1 | (8) c Jupp b White | | 3 |
| W.W. Armstrong* | c Brown b Douglas | 77 | not out | | 28 |
| H.S.T.L. Hendry | b Parkin | 0 | (9) not out | | 11 |
| H. Carter† | b Jupp | 34 | (4) lbw b Parkin | | 47 |
| E.A. McDonald | not out | 21 | | | |
| A.A. Mailey | c and b Parkin | 6 | | | |
| Extras | (B 16, LB 7, NB 3) | 26 | (B 10, LB 4, NB 3) | | 17 |
| **Total** | | **407** | (7 wickets declared) | | **273** |

## ENGLAND

| | | | | | |
|---|---|---|---|---|---|
| F.E. Woolley | b Gregory | 0 | (4) b Mailey | | 37 |
| H.T.W. Hardinge | lbw b Armstrong | 25 | c Gregory b McDonald | | 5 |
| J.W. Hearne | b McDonald | 7 | c Taylor b McDonald | | 27 |
| A. Ducat | c Gregory b McDonald | 3 | (6) st Carter b Mailey | | 2 |
| J.W.H.T. Douglas | b Armstrong | 75 | b Gregory | | 8 |
| V.W.C. Jupp | c Carter b Gregory | 14 | (7) c Carter b Armstrong | | 28 |
| G. Brown† | c Armstrong b Mailey | 57 | (1) lbw b Gregory | | 46 |
| J.C. White | b McDonald | 1 | (9) not out | | 6 |
| Hon. L.H. Tennyson* | c Gregory b McDonald | 63 | (8) b Armstrong | | 36 |
| C.H. Parkin | not out | 5 | b Mailey | | 4 |
| J.B. Hobbs | absent ill | – | absent ill | | |
| Extras | (LB 3, NB 6) | 9 | (B 3) | | 3 |
| **Total** | | **259** | | | **202** |

| ENGLAND | O | M | R | W | O | M | R | W | | | FALL OF WICKETS | | | |
|---|---|---|---|---|---|---|---|---|---|---|---|---|---|---|
| Douglas | 20 | 3 | 80 | 3 | 11 | 0 | 38 | 0 | | | A | E | A | E |
| White | 25 | 4 | 70 | 0 | 11 | 3 | 37 | 3 | Wkt | 1st | 1st | 2nd | 2nd |
| Parkin | 20·1 | 0 | 106 | 4 | 20 | 0 | 91 | 1 | 1st | 22 | 0 | 71 | 15 |
| Hearne | 5 | 0 | 21 | 0 | | | | | 2nd | 45 | 13 | 139 | 57 |
| Jupp | 18 | 2 | 70 | 2 | 13 | 2 | 45 | 2 | 3rd | 146 | 30 | 193 | 98 |
| Woolley | 5 | 0 | 34 | 1 | 18 | 4 | 45 | 1 | 4th | 255 | 47 | 223 | 124 |
| | | | | | | | | | 5th | 256 | 67 | 227 | 126 |
| AUSTRALIA | | | | | | | | | 6th | 271 | 164 | 227 | 128 |
| Gregory | 21 | 6 | 47 | 2 | 14 | 1 | 55 | 2 | 7th | 271 | 165 | 230 | 190 |
| McDonald | 26·1 | 0 | 105 | 4 | 15 | 2 | 67 | 2 | 8th | 333 | 253 | – | 197 |
| Armstrong | 19 | 4 | 44 | 2 | 3 | 0 | 6 | 2 | 9th | 388 | 259 | – | 202 |
| Mailey | 17 | 4 | 38 | 1 | 20·2 | 3 | 71 | 3 | 10th | 407 | – | – | – |
| Hendry | 10 | 4 | 16 | 0 | | | | | | | | | |

Umpires: H.R. Butt and A. Millward.

# ENGLAND v AUSTRALIA 1921 (4th Test)

Played at Old Trafford, Manchester, on 23 (*no play*), 25, 26 July.
Toss: England.   Result: MATCH DRAWN.
Debuts: England – C. Hallows, C.W.L. Parker.

When Tennyson attempted to close England's innings at 5.50 p.m. on the second day, the first having been washed out, Armstrong pointed out that, under two-day rules, no declaration was permissible unless 100 minutes batting was available to the fielding side on that day. The players left the field, 25 minutes were lost, and, when the England innings eventually resumed, Armstrong bowled his second consecutive over – one either side of the hiatus.

## ENGLAND

| | | | | |
|---|---|---|---|---|
| C.A.G. Russell | b Gregory | 101 | | |
| G. Brown† | c Gregory b Armstrong | 31 | | |
| F.E. Woolley | c Pellew b Armstrong | 41 | | |
| C.P. Mead | c Andrews b Hendry | 47 | | |
| E. Tyldesley | not out | 78 | | |
| P.G.H. Fender | not out | 44 | | |
| C. Hallows | | | (1) not out | 16 |
| C.H. Parkin | | | (2) c Collins b Andrews | 23 |
| C.W.L. Parker | | | (3) not out | 3 |
| Hon. L.H. Tennyson* | ) did not bat | | | |
| J.W.H.T. Douglas | ) | | | |
| Extras | (B 12, LB 5, NB 3) | 20 | (LB 2) | 2 |
| **Total** | (4 wickets declared) | **362** | (1 wicket) | **44** |

## AUSTRALIA

| | | |
|---|---|---|
| W. Bardsley | b Parkin | 3 |
| H.L. Collins | lbw b Parkin | 40 |
| C.G. Macartney | b Parker | 13 |
| T.J.E. Andrews | c Tennyson b Fender | 6 |
| J.M. Taylor | b Fender | 4 |
| C.E. Pellew | c Tyldesley b Parker | 17 |
| W.W. Armstrong* | b Douglas | 17 |
| J.M. Gregory | b Parkin | 29 |
| H. Carter† | b Parkin | 0 |
| H.S.T.L. Hendry | c Russell b Parkin | 4 |
| E.A. McDonald | not out | 8 |
| Extras | (B 22, LB 5, NB 7) | 34 |
| **Total** | | **175** |

| AUSTRALIA | O | M | R | W | O | M | R | W |
|---|---|---|---|---|---|---|---|---|
| Gregory | 23 | 5 | 79 | 1 | | | | |
| McDonald | 31 | 1 | 112 | 0 | | | | |
| Macartney | 8 | 2 | 20 | 0 | | | | |
| Hendry | 25 | 5 | 74 | 1 | 4 | 1 | 12 | 0 |
| Armstrong | 33 | 13 | 57 | 2 | | | | |
| Andrews | | | | | 5 | 0 | 23 | 1 |
| Pellew | | | | | 3 | 0 | 6 | 0 |
| Taylor | | | | | 1 | 0 | 1 | 0 |

| ENGLAND | O | M | R | W |
|---|---|---|---|---|
| Parkin | 29·4 | 12 | 38 | 5 |
| Woolley | 39 | 22 | 38 | 0 |
| Parker | 28 | 16 | 32 | 2 |
| Fender | 15 | 6 | 30 | 2 |
| Douglas | 5 | 2 | 3 | 1 |

### FALL OF WICKETS

| | E | A | E |
|---|---|---|---|
| Wkt | 1st | 1st | 2nd |
| 1st | 65 | 9 | 36 |
| 2nd | 145 | 33 | – |
| 3rd | 217 | 44 | – |
| 4th | 260 | 48 | – |
| 5th | – | 78 | – |
| 6th | – | 125 | – |
| 7th | – | 161 | – |
| 8th | – | 161 | – |
| 9th | – | 166 | – |
| 10th | – | 175 | – |

Umpires: J. Moss and A.E. Street.

# ENGLAND v AUSTRALIA 1921 (5th Test)

Played at Kennington Oval, London, on 13, 15, 16 August.
Toss: England.   Result: MATCH DRAWN.
Debuts: England – A. Sandham.

England's selectors employed 30 players during this five-match rubber – two more than have played in any rubber before or since. Mead's 182 not out was a new record for England against Australia at home and stood until 1938. Although 471 runs were scored on the third day, the match quickly declined from being a serious contest to a farce. Hitch reached his fifty in 35 minutes – the second-fastest in this series of Tests.

## ENGLAND

| | | | | | |
|---|---|---|---|---|---|
| C.A.G. Russell | c Oldfield b McDonald | 13 | not out | | 102 |
| G. Brown† | b Mailey | 32 | c Mailey b Taylor | | 84 |
| E. Tyldesley | c Macartney b Gregory | 39 | | | |
| F.E. Woolley | run out | 23 | | | |
| C.P. Mead | not out | 182 | | | |
| A. Sandham | b McDonald | 21 | | | |
| Hon. L.H. Tennyson* | b McDonald | 51 | | | |
| P.G.H. Fender | c Armstrong b McDonald | 0 | (3) c Armstrong b Mailey | | 6 |
| J.W. Hitch | b McDonald | 18 | (4) not out | | 51 |
| J.W.H.T. Douglas | not out | 21 | | | |
| C.H. Parkin | did not bat | | | | |
| Extras | (LB 3) | 3 | (B 1) | | 1 |
| **Total** | (8 wickets declared) | **403** | (2 wickets) | | **244** |

## AUSTRALIA

| | | |
|---|---|---|
| H.L. Collins | hit wkt b Hitch | 14 |
| W. Bardsley | b Hitch | 22 |
| C.G. Macartney | b Douglas | 61 |
| T.J.E. Andrews | lbw b Parkin | 94 |
| J.M. Taylor | c Woolley b Douglas | 75 |
| C.E. Pellew | c Woolley b Parkin | 1 |
| W.W. Armstrong* | c Brown b Douglas | 19 |
| J.M. Gregory | st Brown b Parkin | 27 |
| W.A.S. Oldfield† | not out | 28 |
| E.A. McDonald | st Brown b Woolley | 36 |
| A.A. Mailey | b Woolley | 0 |
| Extras | (B 6, LB 3, W 2, NB 1) | 12 |
| **Total** | | **389** |

| AUSTRALIA | O | M | R | W | O | M | R | W |
|---|---|---|---|---|---|---|---|---|
| Gregory | 38 | 5 | 128 | 1 | 3 | 0 | 13 | 0 |
| McDonald | 47 | 9 | 143 | 5 | 6 | 0 | 20 | 0 |
| Mailey | 30 | 4 | 85 | 1 | 18 | 2 | 77 | 1 |
| Armstrong | 12 | 2 | 44 | 0 | | | | |
| Pellew | | | | | 9 | 3 | 25 | 0 |
| Andrews | | | | | 8 | 0 | 44 | 0 |
| Taylor | | | | | 7 | 1 | 25 | 1 |
| Collins | | | | | 7 | 0 | 39 | 0 |
| ENGLAND | | | | | | | | |
| Hitch | 19 | 3 | 65 | 2 | | | | |
| Douglas | 30 | 2 | 117 | 3 | | | | |
| Fender | 19 | 3 | 82 | 0 | | | | |
| Parkin | 23 | 4 | 82 | 3 | | | | |
| Woolley | 11 | 2 | 31 | 2 | | | | |

### FALL OF WICKETS

| | E | A | E |
|---|---|---|---|
| Wkt | 1st | 1st | 2nd |
| 1st | 27 | 33 | 158 |
| 2nd | 54 | 54 | 173 |
| 3rd | 84 | 162 | – |
| 4th | 121 | 233 | – |
| 5th | 191 | 239 | – |
| 6th | 312 | 288 | – |
| 7th | 312 | 311 | – |
| 8th | 339 | 338 | – |
| 9th | – | 389 | – |
| 10th | – | 389 | – |

Umpires: J. Moss and W. Phillips.

# SOUTH AFRICA v AUSTRALIA 1921-22 (1st Test)

Played at Lord's, Durban, on 5, 7, 8, 9 November.
Toss: Australia.   Result: MATCH DRAWN.
Debuts: South Africa – C.N. Frank, W.V.S. Ling, W.F.E. Marx, E.P. Nupen.

The 1921 Australians played three Tests in South Africa on their way home. Armstrong handed over the captaincy to Collins.

## AUSTRALIA

| | | | | | |
|---|---|---|---|---|---|
| H.L. Collins* | b Carter | 31 | c Chapman b Nupen | | 47 |
| J.M. Gregory | b Blanckenberg | 51 | (4) b Blanckenberg | | 6 |
| C.G. Macartney | c Nourse b Nupen | 59 | c Ward b Marx | | 116 |
| W. Bardsley | b Blanckenberg | 5 | (2) lbw b Carter | | 23 |
| T.J.E. Andrews | b Blanckenberg | 3 | (6) not out | | 35 |
| J. Ryder | not out | 78 | (5) b Blanckenberg | | 58 |
| J.M. Taylor | b Carter | 18 | b Carter | | 11 |
| H.S.T.L. Hendry | c Nourse b Chapman | 23 | b Carter | | 13 |
| H. Carter† | c Nourse b Blanckenberg | 9 | not out | | 1 |
| E.A. McDonald | b Carter | 2 | | | |
| A.A. Mailey | b Blanckenberg | 2 | | | |
| Extras | (B 16, LB 2) | 18 | (B 12, LB 1, NB 1) | | 14 |
| **Total** | | **299** | (7 wickets declared) | | **324** |

## SOUTH AFRICA

| | | | | | |
|---|---|---|---|---|---|
| H.W. Taylor* | c Hendry b Gregory | 1 | (4) c and b McDonald | | 29 |
| J.W. Zulch | c Gregory b Macartney | 80 | (5) c Taylor b McDonald | | 17 |
| C.N. Frank | c Gregory b McDonald | 1 | (1) c Gregory b Mailey | | 38 |
| A.W. Nourse | c Hendry b Gregory | 32 | (6) not out | | 31 |
| W.V.S. Ling | b Gregory | 33 | (7) c Gregory b McDonald | | 28 |
| W.F.E. Marx | c Macartney b Gregory | 0 | (3) c Carter b Mailey | | 28 |
| H.W. Chapman | c Gregory b Hendry | 4 | (8) b Gregory | | 2 |
| E.P. Nupen | c and b Hendry | 6 | (9) not out | | 0 |
| T.A. Ward† | not out | 22 | (2) b Gregory | | 0 |
| J.M. Blanckenberg | c Ryder b Gregory | 28 | | | |
| C.P. Carter | c Mailey b Gregory | 14 | | | |
| Extras | (B 4, LB 3, NB 4) | 11 | (LB 8, NB 3) | | 11 |
| **Total** | | **232** | (7 wickets) | | **184** |

| SOUTH AFRICA | O | M | R | W | O | M | R | W |
|---|---|---|---|---|---|---|---|---|
| Marx | 3 | 0 | 6 | 0 | 6 | 0 | 20 | 1 |
| Nourse | 11 | 1 | 36 | 0 | 8 | 1 | 32 | 0 |
| Nupen | 15 | 2 | 42 | 1 | 16 | 3 | 59 | 1 |
| Chapman | 11 | 0 | 51 | 1 | 6 | 1 | 33 | 0 |
| Blanckenberg | 24·4 | 6 | 78 | 5 | 30 | 3 | 100 | 2 |
| Carter | 20 | 1 | 68 | 3 | 21 | 3 | 66 | 3 |
| AUSTRALIA | | | | | | | | |
| Gregory | 25·1 | 4 | 77 | 6 | 19 | 7 | 28 | 2 |
| McDonald | 20 | 5 | 55 | 1 | 34 | 17 | 64 | 3 |
| Mailey | 17 | 2 | 55 | 0 | 31 | 10 | 54 | 2 |
| Macartney | 11 | 6 | 13 | 1 | | | | |
| Hendry | 7 | 0 | 21 | 2 | 4 | 0 | 20 | 0 |
| Ryder | | | | | 8 | 3 | 7 | 0 |

### FALL OF WICKETS

| Wkt | A 1st | SA 1st | A 2nd | SA 2nd |
|---|---|---|---|---|
| 1st | 85 | 2 | 44 | 1 |
| 2nd | 95 | 9 | 118 | 43 |
| 3rd | 116 | 62 | 144 | 82 |
| 4th | 128 | 136 | 250 | 112 |
| 5th | 175 | 136 | 270 | 131 |
| 6th | 214 | 154 | 283 | 179 |
| 7th | 276 | 154 | 314 | 182 |
| 8th | 291 | 163 | – | – |
| 9th | 296 | 214 | – | – |
| 10th | 299 | 232 | – | – |

Umpires: A.G. Laver and F.W. Grey.

# SOUTH AFRICA v AUSTRALIA 1921-22 (2nd Test)

Played at Old Wanderers, Johannesburg, on 12, 14, 15, 16 November.
Toss: Australia.   Result: MATCH DRAWN.
Debuts: South Africa – N.V. Lindsay.

Collins scored Australia's only double-century in a Test in South Africa. Gregory took only 70 minutes to reach his hundred; it is still the fastest century in Test cricket. C.N. Frank took 518 minutes to score 152; his partnership of 206 with Nourse remains South Africa's highest for the fourth wicket against Australia.

### AUSTRALIA

| | | | | |
|---|---|---|---|---|
| H.L. Collins* | c Lindsay b Carter | 203 | not out | 5 |
| W. Bardsley | b Marx | 8 | not out | 2 |
| J. Ryder | b Blanckenberg | 56 | | |
| J.M. Gregory | st Ward b Carter | 119 | | |
| T.J.E. Andrews | st Ward b Carter | 3 | | |
| J.M. Taylor | c Nupen b Marx | 11 | | |
| E.R. Mayne | b Carter | 1 | | |
| H.S.T.L. Hendry | b Carter | 15 | | |
| W.A.S. Oldfield† | b Marx | 2 | | |
| E.A. McDonald | not out | 9 | | |
| A.A. Mailey | st Ward b Carter | 4 | | |
| Extras | (B 3, LB 15, NB 1) | 19 | | |
| **Total** | | **450** | (0 wickets) | **7** |

### SOUTH AFRICA

| | | | | | |
|---|---|---|---|---|---|
| J.W. Zulch | hit wkt b McDonald | 4 | | b Gregory | 2 |
| C.N. Frank | run out | 1 | | c Collins b Mailey | 152 |
| N.V. Lindsay | hit wkt b Gregory | 6 | | b Gregory | 29 |
| H.W. Taylor* | c Mailey b Gregory | 47 | | c Hendry b Gregory | 80 |
| A.W. Nourse | c sub (C.E. Pellew) b McDonald | 64 | | c Gregory b Ryder | 111 |
| W.V.S. Ling | c Hendry b Gregory | 0 | | st Oldfield b Ryder | 19 |
| W.F.E. Marx | c Collins b Mailey | 36 | (8) | c Bardsley b Mailey | 34 |
| T.A. Ward† | c Taylor b Collins | 7 | (9) | not out | 9 |
| J.M. Blanckenberg | b Gregory | 45 | (7) | c Andrews b Mailey | 4 |
| E.P. Nupen | b Mailey | 22 | | not out | 13 |
| C.P. Carter | not out | 0 | | | |
| Extras | (B 4, LB 4, NB 3) | 11 | | (B10, LB 5, NB 4) | 19 |
| **Total** | | **243** | | (8 wickets declared) | **472** |

| SOUTH AFRICA | O | M | R | W | O | M | R | W |
|---|---|---|---|---|---|---|---|---|
| Marx | 21 | 0 | 85 | 3 | 1 | 0 | 4 | 0 |
| Nupen | 16 | 0 | 86 | 0 | 0·4 | 0 | 3 | 0 |
| Carter | 29·5 | 4 | 91 | 6 | | | | |
| Blanckenberg | 21 | 2 | 105 | 1 | | | | |
| Nourse | 7 | 1 | 44 | 0 | | | | |
| Ling | 3 | 0 | 20 | 0 | | | | |
| AUSTRALIA | | | | | | | | |
| Gregory | 19·3 | 1 | 71 | 4 | 28 | 7 | 68 | 3 |
| McDonald | 19 | 7 | 43 | 2 | 44 | 14 | 121 | 0 |
| Mailey | 22 | 4 | 72 | 2 | 43 | 8 | 113 | 3 |
| Hendry | 12 | 2 | 37 | 0 | 23 | 6 | 58 | 0 |
| Collins | 6 | 2 | 9 | 1 | 15 | 12 | 7 | 0 |
| Taylor | | | | | 11 | 4 | 19 | 0 |
| Mayne | | | | | 1 | 0 | 1 | 0 |
| Ryder | | | | | 30 | 9 | 66 | 2 |

### FALL OF WICKETS

| | A | SA | SA | A |
|---|---|---|---|---|
| Wkt | 1st | 1st | 2nd | 2nd |
| 1st | 15 | 6 | 6 | – |
| 2nd | 128 | 6 | 44 | – |
| 3rd | 337 | 16 | 149 | – |
| 4th | 347 | 95 | 355 | – |
| 5th | 382 | 109 | 387 | – |
| 6th | 383 | 135 | 393 | – |
| 7th | 407 | 164 | 446 | – |
| 8th | 422 | 189 | 450 | – |
| 9th | 446 | 243 | – | – |
| 10th | 450 | 243 | – | – |

Umpires: A.G. Laver and S.L. Harris.

# SOUTH AFRICA v AUSTRALIA 1921-22 (3rd Test)

Played at Newlands, Cape Town, on 26, 28, 29 November.
Toss: South Africa.   Result: AUSTRALIA won by ten wickets.
Debuts: South Africa – N. Reid.

### SOUTH AFRICA

| | | | | |
|---|---|---|---|---|
| C.N. Frank | b Ryder | 21 | b Macartney | 23 |
| J.W. Zulch | c Ryder b Macartney | 50 | (3) c and b Macartney | 40 |
| P.A.M. Hands | c Gregory b Ryder | 0 | (6) c Andrews b Macartney | 19 |
| H.W. Taylor* | c Andrews b McDonald | 26 | run out | 17 |
| A.W. Nourse | c Mayne b Mailey | 11 | st Carter b Mailey | 31 |
| W.V.S. Ling | b McDonald | 0 | (7) b Macartney | 35 |
| W.F.E. Marx | st Carter b Mailey | 11 | (8) run out | 16 |
| J.M. Blanckenberg | st Carter b Mailey | 25 | (9) c Carter b Mailey | 20 |
| T.A. Ward† | b McDonald | 2 | (2) b McDonald | 4 |
| C.P. Carter | not out | 19 | not out | 1 |
| N. Reid | c Mayne b Mailey | 11 | b Macartney | 6 |
| Extras | (LB 2, NB 2) | 4 | (B 1, LB 2, NB 1) | 4 |
| **Total** | | **180** | | **216** |

### AUSTRALIA

| | | |
|---|---|---|
| H.L. Collins* | b Blanckenberg | 54 |
| W. Bardsley | lbw b Blanckenberg | 30 |
| C.G. Macartney | c Nourse b Blanckenberg | 44 |
| J. Ryder | c Taylor b Carter | 142 |
| J.M. Gregory | c Hands b Blanckenberg | 29 |
| E.R. Mayne | lbw b Reid | 15 |
| J.E. Andrews | c Hands b Carter | 10 |
| C.E. Pellew | c Nourse b Reid | 6 |
| H. Carter† | not out | 31 | (2) not out | 0 |
| E.A. McDonald | c Ward b Carter | 4 |
| A.A. Mailey | c Taylor b Nourse | 14 | (1) not out | 1 |
| Extras | (B 9, LB 5, NB 3) | 17 |
| **Total** | | **396** | (0 wickets) | **1** |

| AUSTRALIA | O | M | R | W | O | M | R | W |
|---|---|---|---|---|---|---|---|---|
| Gregory | 15 | 9 | 11 | 0 | 9 | 1 | 29 | 0 |
| McDonald | 19 | 3 | 53 | 3 | 13 | 2 | 35 | 1 |
| Macartney | 24 | 10 | 47 | 1 | 24·3 | 10 | 44 | 5 |
| Ryder | 16 | 7 | 25 | 2 | 7 | 0 | 15 | 0 |
| Mailey | 14 | 1 | 40 | 4 | 26 | 0 | 89 | 2 |
| Collins | | | | | 1 | 1 | 0 | 0 |
| SOUTH AFRICA | | | | | | | | |
| Marx | 7 | 1 | 29 | 0 |
| Nourse | 30 | 5 | 89 | 1 |
| Blanckenberg | 31 | 5 | 82 | 4 |
| Carter | 26 | 5 | 104 | 3 |
| Reid | 21 | 3 | 63 | 2 |
| Taylor | 5 | 2 | 12 | 0 |
| Hands | | | | | 0·1 | 0 | 1 | 0 |

| FALL OF WICKETS | | | | |
|---|---|---|---|---|
| | SA | A | SA | A |
| Wkt | 1st | 1st | 2nd | 2nd |
| 1st | 50 | 71 | 10 | – |
| 2nd | 54 | 108 | 58 | – |
| 3rd | 82 | 153 | 84 | – |
| 4th | 106 | 201 | 92 | – |
| 5th | 107 | 242 | 122 | – |
| 6th | 110 | 281 | 162 | – |
| 7th | 143 | 320 | 182 | – |
| 8th | 146 | 358 | 203 | – |
| 9th | 151 | 361 | 209 | – |
| 10th | 180 | 396 | 216 | – |

Umpires: A.G. Laver and H.V. Adams.

# SOUTH AFRICA v ENGLAND 1922-23 (1st Test)

Played at Old Wanderers, Johannesburg, on 23, 26, 27, 28 December.
Toss: South Africa.   Result: SOUTH AFRICA won by 168 runs.
Debuts: South Africa – W.H. Brann, I.D. Buys, R.H. Catterall, C.M. Francois, G.A.L. Hearne;
   England – A.W. Carr, A.E.R. Gilligan, A.S. Kennedy, F.T. Mann, G.T.S. Stevens.

South Africa scored their highest total to date against England. Taylor's innings of 176 remains the highest for his country in a home Test against England.

## SOUTH AFRICA

| | | | | | |
|---|---|---|---|---|---|
| R.H. Catterall | c and b Kennedy | 39 | c Woolley b Gilligan | | 17 |
| G.A.L. Hearne | b Jupp | 28 | c Kennedy b Gilligan | | 27 |
| H.W. Taylor* | c Brown b Fender | 21 | c Gilligan b Kennedy | | 176 |
| A.W. Nourse | c Brown b Kennedy | 14 | c Fender b Jupp | | 20 |
| W.V.S. Ling | b Kennedy | 0 | b Kennedy | | 38 |
| W.H. Brann | lbw b Kennedy | 1 | c Fender b Gilligan | | 50 |
| C.M. Francois | c Fender b Jupp | 19 | (8) c Mann b Jupp | | 9 |
| J.M. Blanckenberg | lbw b Jupp | 1 | (9) b Kennedy | | 30 |
| E.P. Nupen | c Kennedy b Jupp | 0 | (10) st Brown b Kennedy | | 23 |
| T.A. Ward† | not out | 13 | (7) b Jupp | | 10 |
| I.D. Buys | run out | 0 | not out | | 4 |
| Extras | (B 5, LB 2, NB 5) | 12 | (B 14, LB 1, W 1) | | 16 |
| **Total** | | **148** | | | **420** |

## ENGLAND

| | | | | | |
|---|---|---|---|---|---|
| A. Sandham | b Blanckenberg | 26 | lbw b Blanckenberg | | 25 |
| F.T. Mann* | c Francois b Nupen | 4 | (6) not out | | 28 |
| F.E. Woolley | lbw b Francois | 26 | (4) c Nupen b Francois | | 15 |
| A.W. Carr | b Francois | 27 | (3) c Taylor b Nupen | | 27 |
| C.P. Mead | b Blanckenberg | 1 | (2) b Nupen | | 49 |
| P.G.H. Fender | c Brann b Blanckenberg | 0 | (7) run out | | 9 |
| V.W.C. Jupp | c and b Blanckenberg | 1 | (9) st Ward b Blanckenberg | | 33 |
| G.T.S. Stevens | b Francois | 11 | (10) c Nourse b Nupen | | 2 |
| G. Brown† | b Blanckenberg | 22 | (8) b Blanckenberg | | 1 |
| A.S. Kennedy | not out | 41 | (5) c Blanckenberg b Nupen | | 0 |
| A.E.R. Gilligan | b Blanckenberg | 18 | b Nupen | | 7 |
| Extras | (B 3, LB 1, W 1) | 5 | (B 14, LB 6, NB 2) | | 22 |
| **Total** | | **182** | | | **218** |

| ENGLAND | O | M | R | W | O | M | R | W |
|---|---|---|---|---|---|---|---|---|
| Gilligan | 7 | 1 | 23 | 0 | 20 | 3 | 69 | 3 |
| Kennedy | 20·4 | 5 | 37 | 4 | 41·3 | 9 | 132 | 4 |
| Jupp | 21 | 6 | 59 | 4 | 31 | 7 | 87 | 3 |
| Fender | 7 | 1 | 17 | 1 | 12 | 0 | 64 | 0 |
| Woolley | | | | | 16 | 4 | 33 | 0 |
| Stevens | | | | | 4 | 0 | 19 | 0 |
| SOUTH AFRICA | | | | | | | | |
| Buys | 7 | 1 | 20 | 0 | 17 | 3 | 32 | 0 |
| Nupen | 17 | 3 | 58 | 1 | 30 | 11 | 53 | 5 |
| Blanckenberg | 22·5 | 5 | 76 | 6 | 24 | 3 | 59 | 3 |
| Francois | 10 | 1 | 23 | 3 | 29 | 9 | 52 | 1 |

### FALL OF WICKETS

| | SA | E | SA | E |
|---|---|---|---|---|
| Wkt | 1st | 1st | 2nd | 2nd |
| 1st | 55 | 15 | 33 | 56 |
| 2nd | 92 | 45 | 52 | 99 |
| 3rd | 97 | 79 | 91 | 114 |
| 4th | 97 | 84 | 202 | 114 |
| 5th | 111 | 84 | 300 | 124 |
| 6th | 120 | 85 | 326 | 147 |
| 7th | 121 | 93 | 352 | 161 |
| 8th | 121 | 100 | 380 | 207 |
| 9th | 145 | 152 | 393 | 210 |
| 10th | 148 | 182 | 420 | 218 |

Umpires: A.G. Laver and F.W. Grey.

# SOUTH AFRICA v ENGLAND 1922-23 (2nd Test)

Played at Newlands, Cape Town, on 1, 2, 3, 4 January.
Toss: South Africa.   Result: ENGLAND won by one wicket.
Debuts: South Africa – A.E. Hall; England – G.G. Macaulay.

Macaulay took the wicket of Hearne with his first ball in Test cricket and also made the winning hit in one of only five Test matches to be won by the margin of one wicket. Hall, the other debutant in this match, took eleven wickets and came within the narrowest possible margin of winning the game for South Africa. Hearne kept wicket for part of the match.

## SOUTH AFRICA

| | | | | |
|---|---|---|---|---|
| R.H. Catterall | c Brown b Fender | 10 | b Macaulay | 76 |
| G.A.L. Hearne | c Fender b Macaulay | 0 | b Kennedy | 0 |
| H.W. Taylor* | b Fender | 9 | c Jupp b Macaulay | 68 |
| A.W. Nourse | lbw b Fender | 16 | b Fender | 19 |
| W.V.S. Ling | c Mann b Fender | 13 | c Fender b Macaulay | 2 |
| W.H. Brann | b Kennedy | 0 | lbw b Macaulay | 4 |
| J.M. Blanckenberg | c Carr b Jupp | 9 | (8) b Kennedy | 5 |
| C.M. Francois | run out | 28 | (7) c and b Macaulay | 19 |
| T.A. Ward† | b Jupp | 4 | not out | 15 |
| E.P. Nupen | c and b Macaulay | 2 | b Kennedy | 6 |
| A.E. Hall | not out | 0 | b Kennedy | 5 |
| Extras | (B 14, LB 6, NB 2) | 22 | (B 15, LB 6, NB 2) | 23 |
| **Total** | | **113** | | **242** |

## ENGLAND

| | | | | |
|---|---|---|---|---|
| C.A.G. Russell | c Catterall b Hall | 39 | lbw b Blanckenberg | 8 |
| A. Sandham | c Francois b Blanckenberg | 19 | lbw b Hall | 17 |
| F.E. Woolley | c Francois b Hall | 0 | b Hall | 5 |
| C.P. Mead | c Francois b Blanckenberg | 21 | lbw b Hall | 31 |
| A.W. Carr | c Ward b Hall | 42 | c Brann b Hall | 6 |
| F.T. Mann* | lbw b Blanckenberg | 4 | (7) c Blanckenberg b Hall | 45 |
| P.G.H. Fender | c Hearne b Hall | 3 | (6) c Nourse b Hall | 2 |
| V.W.C. Jupp | c Hearne b Nupen | 12 | st Ward b Hall | 38 |
| A.S. Kennedy | c Hearne b Blanckenberg | 2 | not out | 11 |
| G. Brown† | not out | 10 | run out | 0 |
| G.G. Macaulay | b Blanckenberg | 19 | not out | 1 |
| Extras | (B 5, LB 4, W 1, NB 2) | 12 | (B 4, LB 5) | 9 |
| **Total** | | **183** | (9 wickets) | **173** |

| ENGLAND | O | M | R | W | O | M | R | W | FALL OF WICKETS | | | | |
|---|---|---|---|---|---|---|---|---|---|---|---|---|---|
| | | | | | | | | | | SA | E | SA | E |
| Kennedy | 18 | 10 | 24 | 1 | 35·2 | 13 | 58 | 4 | *Wkt* | *1st* | *1st* | *2nd* | *2nd* |
| Macaulay | 13 | 5 | 19 | 2 | 37 | 11 | 64 | 5 | 1st | 0 | 59 | 2 | 20 |
| Fender | 14 | 4 | 29 | 4 | 20 | 3 | 52 | 1 | 2nd | 22 | 59 | 157 | 29 |
| Woolley | 2 | 1 | 1 | 0 | 11 | 3 | 22 | 0 | 3rd | 31 | 60 | 158 | 49 |
| Jupp | 9 | 3 | 18 | 2 | 11 | 3 | 23 | 0 | 4th | 60 | 128. | 162 | 56 |
| SOUTH AFRICA | | | | | | | | | 5th | 67 | 134 | 170 | 59 |
| Nupen | 15 | 2 | 48 | 1 | 24 | 8 | 41 | 0 | 6th | 67 | 137 | 200 | 86 |
| Hall | 25 | 8 | 49 | 4 | 37·3 | 12 | 63 | 7 | 7th | 96 | 147 | 212 | 154 |
| Blanckenberg | 24·1 | 5 | 61 | 5 | 24 | 7 | 56 | 1 | 8th | 108 | 149 | 212 | 167 |
| Francois | 4 | 1 | 13 | 0 | 3 | 0 | 4 | 0 | 9th | 111 | 155 | 224 | 168 |
| | | | | | | | | | 10th | 113 | 183 | 242 | – |

Umpires: A.G. Laver and G.J. Thompson.

# SOUTH AFRICA v ENGLAND 1922-23 (3rd Test)

Played at Kingsmead, Durban, on 18, 19, 20 (*no play*), 22 January.
Toss: England.   Result: MATCH DRAWN.
Debuts: England – G.B. Street.

This was the first Test to be played on the Kingsmead Ground in Durban. Mead scored the first Test hundred on the new ground but his innings of 181 took 454 minutes. Ling was summoned home to Kimberley when his mother became seriously ill; it proved to be his last Test.

## ENGLAND

| | | | | | |
|---|---|---|---|---|---|
| C.A.G. Russell | c Ward b Nupen | 34 | | | |
| A. Sandham | c Nourse b Snooke | 0 | | | |
| F.E. Woolley | c Nourse b Hall | 0 | | | |
| C.P. Mead | c Nourse b Blanckenberg | 181 | | | |
| A.W. Carr | c Snooke b Nupen | 7 | (3) not out | | 2 |
| P.G.H. Fender | c Ling b Hall | 60 | | | |
| F.T. Mann* | c Snooke b Hall | 84 | | | |
| V.W.C. Jupp | st Ward b Blanckenberg | 16 | | | |
| A.S. Kennedy | c Catterall b Blanckenberg | 8 | | | |
| G.B. Street† | c Nourse b Hall | 4 | (1) not out | | 7 |
| G.G. Macaulay | not out | 3 | (2) c Blanckenberg b Hall | | 2 |
| Extras | (B 16, LB 6, NB 9) | 31 | | | |
| **Total** | | **428** | (1 wicket) | | **11** |

## SOUTH AFRICA

| | | |
|---|---|---|
| R.H. Catterall | c Woolley b Kennedy | 52 |
| H.W. Taylor* | c Woolley b Macaulay | 91 |
| S.J. Snooke | lbw b Kennedy | 8 |
| A.W. Nourse | c Woolley b Kennedy | 52 |
| W.H. Brann | c Kennedy b Fender | 16 |
| C.M. Francois | c Jupp b Kennedy | 72 |
| T.A. Ward† | b Jupp | 26 |
| J.M. Blanckenberg | b Kennedy | 8 |
| E.P. Nupen | st Street b Jupp | 6 |
| A.E. Hall | not out | 1 |
| W.V.S. Ling | absent | – |
| Extras | (B 15, LB 8, NB 13) | 36 |
| **Total** | | **368** |

| SOUTH AFRICA | O | M | R | W | O | M | R | W |
|---|---|---|---|---|---|---|---|---|
| Snooke | 9 | 1 | 20 | 1 | 2 | 0 | 9 | 0 |
| Hall | 53·5 | 23 | 105 | 4 | 2 | 1 | 2 | 1 |
| Blanckenberg | 48 | 12 | 122 | 3 | | | | |
| Francois | 30 | 13 | 55 | 0 | | | | |
| Nupen | 41 | 9 | 86 | 2 | | | | |
| Nourse | 4 | 0 | 9 | 0 | | | | |
| **ENGLAND** | | | | | | | | |
| Kennedy | 39 | 14 | 88 | 5 | | | | |
| Macaulay | 29 | 8 | 55 | 1 | | | | |
| Fender | 29 | 7 | 72 | 1 | | | | |
| Jupp | 22·4 | 6 | 70 | 2 | | | | |
| Woolley | 15 | 3 | 47 | 0 | | | | |

### FALL OF WICKETS

| | E | SA | E |
|---|---|---|---|
| Wkt | 1st | 1st | 2nd |
| 1st | 1 | 110 | 8 |
| 2nd | 2 | 120 | – |
| 3rd | 63 | 220 | – |
| 4th | 71 | 228 | – |
| 5th | 225 | 263 | – |
| 6th | 381 | 338 | – |
| 7th | 397 | 360 | – |
| 8th | 418 | 362 | – |
| 9th | 421 | 368 | – |
| 10th | 428 | – | – |

Umpires: W. Wainwright and G.J. Thompson.

# SOUTH AFRICA v ENGLAND 1922-23 (4th Test)

Played at Old Wanderers, Johannesburg, on 9, 10, 12, 13 February.
Toss: England.   Result: MATCH DRAWN.
Debuts: South Africa – D.J. Meintjes, L.E. Tapscott.

## ENGLAND

| | | | | | |
|---|---|---|---|---|---|
| C.A.G. Russell | b Hall | 8 | c Hall b Nupen | 96 |
| A. Sandham | c Ward b Meintjes | 6 | lbw b Hall | 58 |
| F.E. Woolley | c Nourse b Hall | 15 | not out | 115 |
| A.W. Carr | lbw b Blanckenberg | 63 | c Ward b Meintjes | 6 |
| C.P. Mead | b Nupen | 38 | c and b Meintjes | 0 |
| P.G.H. Fender | c Hall b Blanckenberg | 44 | b Meintjes | 9 |
| F.T. Mann* | c Catterall b Hall | 34 | c Meintjes b Blanckenberg | 59 |
| V.W.C. Jupp | c Nourse b Hall | 7 | not out | 10 |
| A.S. Kennedy | c Nourse b Hall | 16 | | |
| G. Brown† | b Hall | 0 | | |
| G.G. Macaulay | not out | 1 | | |
| Extras | (B 4, LB 7, NB 1) | 12 | (B 12, LB 8, NB 3) | 23 |
| **Total** | | **244** | (6 wickets declared) | **376** |

## SOUTH AFRICA

| | | | | | |
|---|---|---|---|---|---|
| D.J. Meintjes | c Russell b Kennedy | 3 | | |
| T.A. Ward† | b Jupp | 64 | (3) c Macaulay b Kennedy | 8 |
| R.H. Catterall | b Fender | 31 | (1) c Brown b Macaulay | 8 |
| H.W. Taylor* | c Russell b Fender | 11 | (2) c Russell b Kennedy | 101 |
| A.W. Nourse | c Woolley b Jupp | 51 | (4) c Fender b Kennedy | 63 |
| S.J. Snooke | lbw b Jupp | 2 | (5) not out | 39 |
| C.M. Francois | c Brown b Kennedy | 41 | (6) not out | 3 |
| L.E. Tapscott | not out | 50 | | |
| J.M. Blanckenberg | c Russell b Kennedy | 7 | | |
| E.P. Nupen | c Mann b Macaulay | 12 | | |
| A.E. Hall | c Kennedy b Macaulay | 0 | | |
| Extras | (B 11, LB 6, NB 6) | 23 | (B 16, LB 3, NB 6) | 25 |
| **Total** | | **295** | (4 wickets) | **247** |

| SOUTH AFRICA | O | M | R | W | O | M | R | W |
|---|---|---|---|---|---|---|---|---|
| Meintjes | 8 | 1 | 31 | 1 | 11 | 3 | 38 | 3 |
| Snooke | 3 | 0 | 10 | 0 | 6 | 3 | 11 | 0 |
| Hall | 36·4 | 11 | 82 | 6 | 44 | 8 | 114 | 1 |
| Blanckenberg | 30 | 10 | 46 | 2 | 29 | 6 | 78 | 1 |
| Nupen | 16 | 4 | 50 | 1 | 28 | 4 | 88 | 1 |
| Francois | 10 | 6 | 13 | 0 | 9 | 3 | 17 | 0 |
| Nourse | | | | | 5 | 3 | 7 | 0 |
| Taylor | | | | | 2 | 2 | 0 | 0 |
| ENGLAND | | | | | | | | |
| Kennedy | 24 | 5 | 68 | 3 | 27·5 | 7 | 70 | 3 |
| Macaulay | 27 | 5 | 80 | 2 | 17 | 6 | 27 | 1 |
| Woolley | 6 | 3 | 10 | 0 | 6 | 2 | 26 | 0 |
| Fender | 20 | 4 | 78 | 2 | 17 | 2 | 60 | 0 |
| Jupp | 15 | 5 | 36 | 3 | 12 | 3 | 39 | 0 |

### FALL OF WICKETS

| | E | SA | E | SA |
|---|---|---|---|---|
| Wkt | 1st | 1st | 2nd | 2nd |
| 1st | 9 | 16 | 153 | 19 |
| 2nd | 19 | 78 | 189 | 32 |
| 3rd | 35 | 116 | 203 | 166 |
| 4th | 108 | 139 | 209 | 238 |
| 5th | 177 | 157 | 221 | – |
| 6th | 192 | 212 | 345 | – |
| 7th | 207 | 220 | – | – |
| 8th | 237 | 230 | – | – |
| 9th | 243 | 293 | – | – |
| 10th | 244 | 295 | – | – |

Umpires: A.G. Laver and S.L. Harris.

# SOUTH AFRICA v ENGLAND 1922-23 (5th Test)

Played at Kingsmead, Durban, on 16, 17, 19, 20, 21, 22 February.
Toss: England.· Result: ENGLAND won by 109 runs.
Debuts: South Africa – D.P. Conyngham.

Russell, in what proved to be his final Test match, emulated W. Bardsley of Australia (*Test No. 105*) by scoring a hundred in each innings of a Test. Russell's last three scores in Test cricket were 96, 140 and 111. His stand of 92 with Gilligan remains England's best for the tenth wicket against South Africa.

## ENGLAND

| | | | | | |
|---|---|---:|---|---|---:|
| C.A.G. Russell | c Catterall b Blanckenberg | 140 | (6) c Francois b Blanckenberg | | 111 |
| A. Sandham | c Ward b Snooke | 1 | (4) b Francois | | 40 |
| F.E. Woolley | c and b Meintjes | 2 | c Nourse b Snooke | | 8 |
| C.P. Mead | lbw b Francois | 66 | (5) c Conyngham b Meintjes | | 5 |
| A.W. Carr | lbw b Conyngham | 14 | (7) b Blanckenberg | | 5 |
| P.G.H. Fender | b Hall | 1 | (8) b Blanckenberg | | 0 |
| F.T. Mann* | b Nourse | 8 | (9) lbw b Conyngham | | 15 |
| A.S. Kennedy | c Nourse b Snooke | 14 | (2) c Taylor b Hall | | 1 |
| G.G. Macaulay | lbw b Snooke | 0 | (10) b Hall | | 1 |
| G. Brown† | not out | 15 | (1) lbw b Snooke | | 1 |
| A.E.R. Gilligan | c Taylor b Hall | 4 | not out | | 39 |
| Extras | (B 12, LB 3, NB 1) | 16 | (B 13, LB 1, NB 1) | | 15 |
| **Total** | | **281** | | | **241** |

## SOUTH AFRICA

| | | | | | |
|---|---|---:|---|---|---:|
| R.H. Catterall | b Macaulay | 17 | c Macaulay b Gilligan | | 22 |
| H.W. Taylor* | c Russell b Gilligan | 3 | (4) c Fender b Kennedy | | 102 |
| T.A. Ward† | c Macaulay b Gilligan | 1 | b Macaulay | | 10 |
| A.W. Nourse | c Mann b Fender | 44 | (5) c Brown b Kennedy | | 25 |
| S.J. Snooke | c Woolley b Kennedy | 4 | (7) lbw b Kennedy | | 1 |
| C.M. Francois | c Fender b Gilligan | 43 | b Gilligan | | 18 |
| L.E. Tapscott | c Brown b Macaulay | 2 | (8) b Macaulay | | 6 |
| D.J. Meintjes | run out | 19 | (2) lbw b Kennedy | | 21 |
| J.M. Blanckenberg | c Mead b Kennedy | 21 | b Gilligan | | 9 |
| D.P. Conyngham | not out | 3 | not out | | 3 |
| A.E. Hall | c Fender b Macaulay | 0 | c Woolley b Kennedy | | 0 |
| Extras | (B 14, LB 2, NB 6) | 22 | (B 11, LB 3, NB 3) | | 17 |
| **Total** | | **179** | | | **234** |

| SOUTH AFRICA | O | M | R | W | O | M | R | W |
|---|---|---|---|---|---|---|---|---|
| Meintjes | 13 | 1 | 33 | 1 | 9 | 2 | 13 | 1 |
| Snooke | 12 | 3 | 17 | 3 | 23 | 6 | 41 | 2 |
| Conyngham | 31 | 10 | 63 | 1 | 30 | 12 | 40 | 1 |
| Blanckenberg | 24 | 5 | 65 | 1 | 25·4 | 7 | 50 | 3 |
| Hall | 24·5 | 9 | 31 | 2 | 27 | 10 | 55 | 2 |
| Francois | 11 | 1 | 33 | 1 | 8 | 2 | 15 | 1 |
| Nourse | 11 | 4 | 23 | 1 | 6 | 2 | 10 | 0 |
| Tapscott | | | | | 2 | 1 | 2 | 0 |
| **ENGLAND** | | | | | | | | |
| Gilligan | 23 | 7 | 35 | 3 | 36 | 10 | 78 | 3 |
| Kennedy | 25 | 9 | 46 | 2 | 49·1 | 19 | 76 | 5 |
| Macaulay | 20 | 5 | 42 | 3 | 18 | 6 | 39 | 2 |
| Fender | 11 | 3 | 25 | 1 | 11 | 3 | 21 | 0 |
| Woolley | 6 | 3 | 9 | 0 | 3 | 2 | 3 | 0 |

| FALL OF WICKETS | | | | |
|---|---|---|---|---|
| | E | SA | E | SA |
| Wkt | 1st | 1st | 2nd | 2nd |
| 1st | 14 | 7 | 2 | 42 |
| 2nd | 17 | 13 | 10 | 48 |
| 3rd | 156 | 41 | 14 | 64 |
| 4th | 191 | 58 | 26 | 122 |
| 5th | 194 | 97 | 102 | 149 |
| 6th | 224 | 107 | 111 | 150 |
| 7th | 253 | 135 | 111 | 175 |
| 8th | 253 | 169 | 148 | 204 |
| 9th | 268 | 178 | 149 | 232 |
| 10th | 281 | 179 | 241 | 234 |

Umpires: A.G. Laver and J. Reid.

# ENGLAND v SOUTH AFRICA 1924 (1st Test)

Played at Edgbaston, Birmingham, on 14, 16, 17 June.
Toss: South Africa.   Result: ENGLAND won by an innings and 18 runs.
Debuts: England – A.P.F. Chapman, R. Kilner, H. Sutcliffe, M.W. Tate, G.E.C. Wood; South
Africa – H.G. Deane, G.M. Parker, M.J. Susskind.

Parker, a Bradford League cricketer who was not a member of the touring team, was called up to strengthen the bowling and responded with six wickets. South Africa equalled their own record for the lowest Test score set in 1895-96 (*Test No. 47*). It stood until England dismissed New Zealand for 26 in 1954-55 (*Test No. 402*). The innings was over in 75 balls and took 75 minutes. Tate dismissed Susskind with his first ball in Test cricket.

## ENGLAND

| | | |
|---|---|---|
| J.B. Hobbs | lbw b Blanckenberg | 76 |
| H. Sutcliffe | b Parker | 64 |
| F.E. Woolley | c Ward b Parker | 64 |
| E.H. Hendren | c Nourse b Parker | 74 |
| A.P.F. Chapman | b Parker | 8 |
| P.G.H. Fender | c Taylor b Blanckenberg | 36 |
| R. Kilner | c and b Pegler | 59 |
| M.W. Tate | c Taylor b Parker | 19 |
| A.E.R. Gilligan* | b Pegler | 13 |
| G.E.C. Wood† | b Parker | 1 |
| C.H. Parkin | not out | 8 |
| Extras | (B 4, LB 11, NB 1) | 16 |
| **Total** | | **438** |

## SOUTH AFRICA

| | | | | | |
|---|---|---|---|---|---|
| H.W. Taylor* | b Tate | 7 | | c and b Tate | 34 |
| R.H. Catterall | b Gilligan | 0 | (5) | c Hobbs b Tate | 120 |
| M.J. Susskind | c Kilner b Tate | 3 | | b Gilligan | 51 |
| A.W. Nourse | lbw b Gilligan | 1 | | c Wood b Gilligan | 34 |
| J.M.M. Commaille | not out | 1 | (2) | c Hendren b Tate | 29 |
| J.M. Blanckenberg | b Tate | 4 | | c Chapman b Gilligan | 56 |
| H.G. Deane | b Gilligan | 2 | | run out | 5 |
| E.P. Nupen | b Gilligan | 0 | | lbw b Tate | 5 |
| S.J. Pegler | b Tate | 0 | (10) | c Hobbs b Gilligan | 6 |
| T.A. Ward† | b Gilligan | 1 | (9) | b Gilligan | 19 |
| G.M. Parker | lbw b Gilligan | 0 | | not out | 2 |
| Extras | (B 1, LB 7, NB 3) | 11 | | (B 4, LB 18, W 1, NB 6) | 29 |
| **Total** | | **30** | | | **390** |

| SOUTH AFRICA | O | M | R | W | O | M | R | W |
|---|---|---|---|---|---|---|---|---|
| Parker | 37 | 2 | 152 | 6 | | | | |
| Pegler | 36 | 8 | 106 | 2 | | | | |
| Blanckenberg | 32 | 5 | 95 | 2 | | | | |
| Nupen | 18 | 2 | 66 | 0 | | | | |
| Nourse | 1 | 0 | 3 | 0 | | | | |
| **ENGLAND** | | | | | | | | |
| Gilligan | 6·3 | 4 | 7 | 6 | 28 | 6 | 83 | 5 |
| Tate | 6 | 1 | 12 | 4 | 50·4 | 19 | 103 | 4 |
| Parkin | | | | | 16 | 5 | 38 | 0 |
| Kilner | | | | | 22 | 10 | 40 | 0 |
| Fender | | | | | 17 | 5 | 56 | 0 |
| Woolley | | | | | 10 | 2 | 41 | 0 |

### FALL OF WICKETS

| Wkt | E 1st | SA 1st | SA 2nd |
|---|---|---|---|
| 1st | 136 | 1 | 54 |
| 2nd | 164 | 4 | 101 |
| 3rd | 247 | 6 | 152 |
| 4th | 255 | 14 | 161 |
| 5th | 315 | 20 | 275 |
| 6th | 356 | 23 | 284 |
| 7th | 386 | 23 | 295 |
| 8th | 407 | 24 | 350 |
| 9th | 410 | 30 | 372 |
| 10th | 438 | 30 | 390 |

Umpires: H.R. Butt and W. Reeves.

# ENGLAND v SOUTH AFRICA 1924 (2nd Test)

Played at Lord's, London, on 28, 30 June, 1 July.
Toss: South Africa.   Result: ENGLAND won by an innings and 18 runs.
Debuts: England – R.K. Tyldesley.

Catterall made his second successive top-score of 120 and his country suffered their second successive defeat by the identical margin of an innings and 18 runs. England gained their victory for the loss of only two wickets; no other country has equalled this record. On the second day England became the only Test team to score 500 runs in a day (503-2).

## SOUTH AFRICA

| | | | | |
|---|---|---|---|---|
| H.W. Taylor* | c Wood b Gilligan | 4 | (5) b Gilligan | 8 |
| J.M.M. Commaille | b Gilligan | 0 | lbw b Tyldesley | 37 |
| M.J. Susskind | c Tate b Hearne | 64 | lbw b Tyldesley | 53 |
| A.W. Nourse | c Woolley b Tate | 4 | lbw b Gilligan | 11 |
| R.H. Catterall | b Gilligan | 120 | (6) c Gilligan b Tyldesley | 45 |
| J.M. Blanckenberg | b Tate | 12 | (7) c Hobbs b Fender | 15 |
| H.G. Deane | b Tylesley | 33 | (1) c Sutcliffe b Hearne | 24 |
| G.A. Faulkner | b Fender | 25 | run out | 12 |
| T.A. Ward† | b Tyldesley | 1 | (10) not out | 3 |
| S.J. Pegler | c Fender b Tyldesley | 0 | (9) b Tate | 8 |
| G.M. Parker | not out | 1 | b Tate | 0 |
| Extras | (B 3, LB 2, NB 4) | 9 | (B 13, LB 8, NB 3) | 24 |
| **Total** | | **273** | | **240** |

## ENGLAND

| | | |
|---|---|---|
| J.B. Hobbs | c Taylor b Parker | 211 |
| H. Sutcliffe | b Parker | 122 |
| F.E. Woolley | not out | 134 |
| E.H. Hendren | not out | 50 |
| J.W. Hearne | ) | |
| A.P.F. Chapman | ) | |
| P.G.H. Fender | ) | |
| A.E.R. Gilligan* | ) did not bat | |
| G.E.C. Wood† | ) | |
| M.W. Tate | ) | |
| R.K. Tyldesley | ) | |
| Extras | (B 11, LB 1, NB 2) | 14 |
| **Total** | (2 wickets declared) | **531** |

| ENGLAND | O | M | R | W | O | M | R | W |
|---|---|---|---|---|---|---|---|---|
| Gilligan | 31 | 7 | 70 | 3 | 24 | 6 | 54 | 2 |
| Tate | 34 | 12 | 62 | 2 | 26·4 | 8 | 43 | 2 |
| Tyldesley | 24 | 10 | 52 | 3 | 36 | 18 | 50 | 3 |
| Hearne | 18 | 3 | 35 | 1 | 19 | 4 | 35 | 1 |
| Fender | 9 | 1 | 45 | 1 | 14 | 5 | 25 | 1 |
| Woolley | | | | | 4 | 1 | 9 | 0 |
| SOUTH AFRICA | | | | | | | | |
| Parker | 24 | 0 | 121 | 2 | | | | |
| Blanckenberg | 28 | 3 | 113 | 0 | | | | |
| Pegler | 31 | 4 | 120 | 0 | | | | |
| Nourse | 15 | 1 | 57 | 0 | | | | |
| Faulkner | 17 | 0 | 87 | 0 | | | | |
| Catterall | 3 | 0 | 19 | 0 | | | | |

FALL OF WICKETS

| Wkt | SA 1st | E 1st | SA 2nd |
|---|---|---|---|
| 1st | 4 | 268 | 50 |
| 2nd | 5 | 410 | 78 |
| 3rd | 17 | – | 103 |
| 4th | 129 | – | 117 |
| 5th | 182 | – | 171 |
| 6th | 212 | – | 204 |
| 7th | 265 | – | 224 |
| 8th | 271 | – | 231 |
| 9th | 272 | – | 240 |
| 10th | 273 | – | 240 |

Umpires: F. Chester and H. Young.

# ENGLAND v SOUTH AFRICA 1924 (3rd Test)

Played at Headingley, Leeds, on 12, 14, 15 July.
Toss: England.   Result: ENGLAND won by nine wickets.
Debuts: Nil.

## ENGLAND

| | | | | |
|---|---|---|---|---|
| J.B. Hobbs | c Pegler b Nourse | 31 | b Blanckenberg | 7 |
| H. Sutcliffe | c Nupen b Blanckenberg | 83 | not out | 29 |
| J.W. Hearne | lbw b Pegler | 20 | not out | 23 |
| F.E. Woolley | b Pegler | 0 | | |
| E.H. Hendren | c Deane b Nupen | 132 | | |
| E. Tyldesley | run out | 15 | | |
| M.W. Tate | c Taylor b Carter | 29 | | |
| A.E.R. Gilligan* | c Catterall b Pegler | 28 | | |
| R.K. Tyldesley | c Carter b Pegler | 29 | | |
| G.E.C. Wood† | run out | 6 | | |
| G.G. Macaulay | not out | 0 | | |
| Extras | (B 13, LB 8, W 1, NB 1) | 23 | (LB 1) | 1 |
| **Total** | | **396** | (1 wicket) | **60** |

## SOUTH AFRICA

| | | | | |
|---|---|---|---|---|
| J.M.M. Commaille | run out | 4 | st Wood b R.K. Tyldesley | 31 |
| H.G. Deane | c and b Tate | 2 | (7) not out | 47 |
| T.A. Ward† | b Tate | 17 | (2) lbw b Hearne | 25 |
| M.J. Susskind | b Gilligan | 4 | lbw b R.K. Tyldesley | 23 |
| A.W. Nourse | run out | 3 | (3) c Wood b R.K. Tyldesley | 30 |
| H.W. Taylor* | not out | 59 | (5) run out | 56 |
| R.H. Catterall | c Wood b Tate | 29 | (6) b Tate | 56 |
| E.P. Nupen | c Wood b Tate | 0 | (9) b Macaulay | 11 |
| S.J. Pegler | lbw b Tate | 0 | (10) run out | 14 |
| J.M. Blanckenberg | b Tate | 0 | (8) b Tate | 6 |
| C.P. Carter | c Hendren b Macaulay | 11 | b Tate | 0 |
| Extras | (LB 1, NB 2) | 3 | (B 14, LB 7, NB 3) | 24 |
| **Total** | | **132** | | **323** |

| SOUTH AFRICA | O | M | R | W | O | M | R | W |
|---|---|---|---|---|---|---|---|---|
| Nupen | 30 | 8 | 85 | 1 | 1 | 0 | 6 | 0 |
| Pegler | 35 | 6 | 116 | 4 | 11·2 | 3 | 30 | 0 |
| Nourse | 24 | 7 | 67 | 1 | | | | |
| Blanckenberg | 12 | 0 | 58 | 1 | 10 | 2 | 23 | 1 |
| Carter | 15 | 2 | 47 | 1 | | | | |
| ENGLAND | | | | | | | | |
| Gilligan | 10 | 3 | 27 | 1 | 18 | 7 | 37 | 0 |
| Tate | 17 | 4 | 42 | 6 | 30 | 6 | 64 | 3 |
| Macaulay | 11·3 | 2 | 23 | 1 | 27 | 8 | 60 | 1 |
| R.K. Tyldesley | 13 | 4 | 37 | 0 | 24 | 8 | 63 | 3 |
| Hearne | | | | | 19 | 3 | 54 | 1 |
| Woolley | | | | | 9 | 2 | 21 | 0 |

### FALL OF WICKETS

| Wkt | E 1st | SA 1st | SA 2nd | E 2nd |
|---|---|---|---|---|
| 1st | 72 | 6 | 35 | 17 |
| 2nd | 130 | 10 | 81 | – |
| 3rd | 130 | 16 | 82 | – |
| 4th | 201 | 30 | 135 | – |
| 5th | 248 | 34 | 234 | – |
| 6th | 305 | 88 | 238 | – |
| 7th | 350 | 88 | 244 | – |
| 8th | 365 | 90 | 276 | – |
| 9th | 386 | 90 | 318 | – |
| 10th | 396 | 132 | 323 | – |

Umpires: W. Reeves and A.E. Street.

# ENGLAND v SOUTH AFRICA 1924 (4th Test)

Played at Old Trafford, Manchester, on 26, 28 (*no play*), 29 (*no play*) July.
Toss: South Africa.   Result: MATCH DRAWN.
Debuts: England – G. Duckworth, G. Geary, J.C.W. MacBryan.

Manchester's weather restricted play to a total of 165 minutes.

## SOUTH AFRICA

| | | |
|---|---|---|
| J.M.M. Commaille | lbw b Tate | 8 |
| T.A. Ward† | b Tate | 50 |
| M.J. Susskind | lbw b Tyldesley | 5 |
| A.W. Nourse | b Tate | 18 |
| H.W. Taylor* | not out | 18 |
| R. Catterall | not out | 6 |
| H.G. Deane | ) | |
| P.A.M. Hands | ) | |
| J.M. Blanckenberg | ) did not bat | |
| S.J. Pegler | ) | |
| C.P. Carter | ) | |
| Extras | (B 8, LB 3) | 11 |
| **Total** | (4 wickets) | **116** |

## ENGLAND

H. Sutcliffe
A. Sandham
J.C.W. MacBryan
F.E. Woolley
E.H. Hendren
J.W.H.T. Douglas*
R. Kilner
M.W. Tate
G. Geary
R.K. Tyldesley
G. Duckworth†

| ENGLAND | O | M | R | W |
|---|---|---|---|---|
| Tate | 24 | 8 | 34 | 3 |
| Douglas | 8 | 2 | 20 | 0 |
| Geary | 11 | 5 | 21 | 0 |
| Tyldesley | 11·5 | 4 | 11 | 1 |
| Kilner | 12 | 6 | 19 | 0 |

Umpires: H.R. Butt and A.E. Street.

| | FALL OF WICKETS | |
|---|---|---|
| | | SA |
| Wkt | | 1st |
| 1st | | 8 |
| 2nd | | 40 |
| 3rd | | 71 |
| 4th | | 98 |
| 5th | | – |
| 6th | | – |
| 7th | | – |
| 8th | | – |
| 9th | | – |
| 10th | | – |

# ENGLAND v SOUTH AFRICA 1924 (5th Test)

Played at Kennington Oval, London, on 16, 18, 19 August.
Toss: South Africa.   Result: MATCH DRAWN.
Debuts: Nil.

Rain prevented a finish, the equivalent of a complete day's play being lost.

## SOUTH AFRICA

| | | |
|---|---|---|
| J.M.M. Commaille | b Tate | 3 |
| G.A.L. Hearne | run out | 4 |
| M.J. Susskind | c Woolley b Hearne | 65 |
| A.W. Nourse | c Sutcliffe b Woolley | 37 |
| H.W. Taylor* | c and b Tyldesley | 11 |
| R.H. Catterall | c sub (R. Kilner) b Tate | 95 |
| H.G. Deane | c Strudwick b Hearne | 30 |
| J.M. Blanckenberg | not out | 46 |
| T.A. Ward† | lbw b Tate | 5 |
| S.J. Pegler | b Tyldesley | 25 |
| C.P. Carter | c Sandham b Hearne | 4 |
| Extras | (B 4, LB 9, W 1, NB 3) | 17 |
| **Total** | | **342** |

## ENGLAND

| | | |
|---|---|---|
| J.B. Hobbs | c Ward b Pegler | 30 |
| H. Sutcliffe | c Ward b Nourse | 5 |
| J.W. Hearne | c Susskind b Pegler | 35 |
| F.E. Woolley | b Carter | 51 |
| A. Sandham | c Ward b Nourse | 46 |
| E.H. Hendren | c Nourse b Carter | 142 |
| M.W. Tate | b Carter | 50 |
| A.E.R. Gilligan* | c Nourse b Pegler | 36 |
| R.K. Tyldesley | not out | 1 |
| H. Strudwick† | not out | 2 |
| H. Howell | did not bat | |
| Extras | (B 8, LB 13, NB 2) | 23 |
| **Total** | (8 wickets) | **421** |

| ENGLAND | O | M | R | W |
|---|---|---|---|---|
| Gilligan | 16 | 5 | 44 | 0 |
| Tate | 29 | 10 | 64 | 3 |
| Howell | 20 | 5 | 69 | 0 |
| Tyldesley | 22 | 6 | 36 | 2 |
| Hearne | 23 | 3 | 90 | 3 |
| Woolley | 14 | 4 | 22 | 1 |
| SOUTH AFRICA | | | | |
| Nourse | 24 | 3 | 63 | 2 |
| Blanckenberg | 36 | 2 | 122 | 0 |
| Carter | 23 | 2 | 85 | 3 |
| Pegler | 48 | 14 | 128 | 3 |

| | FALL OF WICKETS | |
|---|---|---|
| | SA | E |
| *Wkt* | *1st* | *1st* |
| 1st | 7 | 5 |
| 2nd | 7 | 72 |
| 3rd | 86 | 79 |
| 4th | 108 | 137 |
| 5th | 181 | 238 |
| 6th | 259 | 328 |
| 7th | 259 | 402 |
| 8th | 268 | 418 |
| 9th | 337 | – |
| 10th | 342 | – |

Umpires: H.R. Butt and F. Chester.

# AUSTRALIA v ENGLAND 1924-25 (1st Test)

Played at Sydney Cricket Ground on 19, 20, 22, 23, 24, 26, 27 December.
Toss: Australia.    Result: AUSTRALIA won by 193 runs.
Debuts: Australia – W.H. Ponsford, A.J. Richardson, V.Y. Richardson; England – A.P. Freeman.

This rubber, in which the 8-ball over was introduced to Test cricket, saw the start of the famous association between Hobbs (aged 42) and Sutcliffe (30) against Australia. It began with opening partnerships of 157 and 110 in this match. At the other end of the scale, the stand of 127 between Taylor and Mailey remains the best for Australia's last-wicket against England. Hearne injured his hand and was unable to complete his over in the first innings.

## AUSTRALIA

| | | | | |
|---|---|---|---|---|
| H.L. Collins* | c Hendren b Tate | 114 | (4) c Chapman b Tate | 60 |
| W. Bardsley | c Woolley b Freeman | 21 | b Tate | 22 |
| W.H. Ponsford | b Gilligan | 110 | (5) c Woolley b Freeman | 27 |
| A.J. Richardson | b Hearne | 22 | (1) c and b Freeman | 98 |
| J.M. Taylor | c Strudwick b Tate | 43 | (8) b Tate | 108 |
| V.Y. Richardson | b Freeman | 42 | c Hendren b Tate | 18 |
| C. Kelleway | c Woolley b Tate | 17 | (3) b Gilligan | 23 |
| H.S.T.L. Hendry | c Strudwick b Tate | 3 | (7) c Strudwick b Tate | 22 |
| J.M. Gregory | c Strudwick b Tate | 0 | c Woolley b Freeman | 2 |
| W.A.S. Oldfield† | not out | 39 | c Strudwick b Gilligan | 18 |
| A.A. Mailey | b Tate | 21 | not out | 46 |
| Extras | (B 10, LB 8) | 18 | (B 2, LB 5, W 1) | 8 |
| **Total** | | **450** | | **452** |

## ENGLAND

| | | | | |
|---|---|---|---|---|
| J.B. Hobbs | c Kelleway b Gregory | 115 | c Hendry b Mailey | 57 |
| H. Sutcliffe | c V.Y. Richardson b Mailey | 59 | c Gregory b Mailey | 115 |
| J.W. Hearne | c sub (T.J.E. Andrews) b Mailey | 7 | b Gregory | 0 |
| F.E. Woolley | b Gregory | 0 | (6) c Mailey b Gregory | 123 |
| E.H. Hendren | not out | 74 | c Gregory b Hendry | 9 |
| A. Sandham | b Mailey | 7 | (7) c Oldfield b Mailey | 2 |
| A.P.F. Chapman | run out | 13 | (4) c Oldfield b Hendry | 44 |
| M.W. Tate | c sub (T.J.E. Andrews) b Mailey | 7 | c Ponsford b Kelleway | 0 |
| A.E.R. Gilligan* | b Gregory | 1 | b Kelleway | 1 |
| A.P. Freeman | b Gregory | 0 | not out | 50 |
| H. Strudwick† | lbw b Gregory | 6 | c Oldfield b Hendry | 2 |
| Extras | (B 1, LB 5, NB 3) | 9 | (B 4, LB 3, NB 1) | 8 |
| **Total** | | **298** | | **411** |

| ENGLAND | O | M | R | W | O | M | R | W | | | | | |
|---|---|---|---|---|---|---|---|---|---|---|---|---|---|
| Tate | 55·1 | 11 | 130 | 6 | 33·7 | 8 | 98 | 5 | | | | | |
| Gilligan | 23 | 0 | 92 | 1 | 27 | 6 | 114 | 2 | | | | | |
| Freeman | 49 | 11 | 124 | 2 | 37 | 4 | 134 | 3 | | | | | |
| Hearne | 12·1 | 3 | 28 | 1 | 25 | 2 | 88 | 0 | | | | | |
| Woolley | 9 | 0 | 35 | 0 | | | | | | | | | |
| Hobbs | 2 | 0 | 13 | 0 | | | | | | | | | |
| Chapman | 2 | 0 | 10 | 0 | 3 | 1 | 10 | 0 | | | | | |

| FALL OF WICKETS | | | | |
|---|---|---|---|---|
| | A | E | A | E |
| Wkt | 1st | 1st | 2nd | 2nd |
| 1st | 46 | 157 | 40 | 110 |
| 2nd | 236 | 171 | 115 | 127 |
| 3rd | 275 | 172 | 168 | 195 |
| 4th | 286 | 202 | 210 | 212 |
| 5th | 364 | 235 | 241 | 263 |
| 6th | 374 | 254 | 260 | 269 |
| 7th | 387 | 272 | 281 | 270 |
| 8th | 387 | 274 | 286 | 276 |
| 9th | 388 | 274 | 325 | 404 |
| 10th | 450 | 298 | 452 | 411 |

| AUSTRALIA | O | M | R | W | O | M | R | W |
|---|---|---|---|---|---|---|---|---|
| Gregory | 28·7 | 2 | 111 | 5 | 28 | 2 | 115 | 2 |
| Kelleway | 14 | 3 | 44 | 0 | 21 | 5 | 60 | 2 |
| Mailey | 31 | 2 | 129 | 4 | 32 | 0 | 179 | 3 |
| Hendry | 5 | 1 | 5 | 0 | 10·7 | 2 | 36 | 3 |
| A.J. Richardson | 1 | 1 | 0 | 0 | 5 | 0 | 13 | 0 |

Umpires: A.C. Jones and A.P. Williams.

# AUSTRALIA v ENGLAND 1924-25 (2nd Test)

Played at Melbourne Cricket Ground on 1, 2, 3, 5, 6, 7, 8 January.
Toss: Australia.    Result: AUSTRALIA won by 81 runs.
Debuts: Australia – A.E.V. Hartkopf.

Sutcliffe was the first batsman to score a hundred in each innings of a Test against Australia and became the first to score three successive hundreds in Test cricket; his first four innings against Australia were 59, 115, 176 and 127, and his first three partnerships with Hobbs against Australia produced stands of 157, 110 and 283. Ponsford was the first to score hundreds in each of his first two Tests. Australia's total of 600 set a record in Tests.

## AUSTRALIA

| | | | | | |
|---|---|---:|---|---|---:|
| H.L. Collins* | c Strudwick b Tate | 9 | b Hearne | | 30 |
| W. Bardsley | c Strudwick b Gilligan | 19 | lbw b Tate | | 2 |
| A.J. Richardson | run out | 14 | b Tate | | 9 |
| W.H. Ponsford | b Tate | 128 | b Tate | | 4 |
| J.M. Taylor | run out | 72 | b Tate | | 90 |
| V.Y. Richardson | run out | 138 | c Strudwick b Hearne | | 8 |
| C. Kelleway | c Strudwick b Gilligan | 32 | c and b Hearne | | 17 |
| A.E.V. Hartkopf | c Chapman b Gilligan | 80 | lbw b Tate | | 0 |
| J.M. Gregory | c Gilligan b Tate | 44 | not out | | 36 |
| W.A.S. Oldfield† | not out | 39 | lbw b Hearne | | 39 |
| A.A. Mailey | lbw b Douglas | 1 | b Tate | | 3 |
| Extras | (B 18, LB 5, NB 1) | 24 | (B 11, LB 1) | | 12 |
| **Total** | | **600** | | | **250** |

## ENGLAND

| | | | | | |
|---|---|---:|---|---|---:|
| J.B. Hobbs | b Mailey | 154 | lbw b Mailey | | 22 |
| H. Sutcliffe | b Kelleway | 176 | c Gregory b Mailey | | 127 |
| F.E. Woolley | b Gregory | 0 | (5) lbw b A.J. Richardson | | 50 |
| J.W. Hearne | b Mailey | 9 | lbw b Gregory | | 23 |
| E.H. Hendren | c Oldfield b Kelleway | 32 | (6) b Gregory | | 18 |
| A.P.F. Chapman | c Oldfield b Gregory | 28 | (9) not out | | 4 |
| J.W.H.T. Douglas | c Collins b A.J. Richardson | 8 | (8) b Mailey | | 14 |
| R.K. Tyldesley | c Collins b Gregory | 5 | (7) c Ponsford b Mailey | | 0 |
| M.W. Tate | b A.J. Richardson | 34 | (11) b Gregory | | 0 |
| A.E.R. Gilligan* | not out | 17 | c and b Mailey | | 0 |
| H. Strudwick† | b Hartkopf | 4 | (3) lbw b Gregory | | 22 |
| Extras | (B 4, LB 4, NB 4) | 12 | (B 6, LB 2, NB 2) | | 10 |
| **Total** | | **479** | | | **290** |

| ENGLAND | O | M | R | W | O | M | R | W |
|---|---:|---:|---:|---:|---:|---:|---:|---:|
| Tate | 45 | 10 | 142 | 3 | 33·3 | 8 | 99 | 6 |
| Douglas | 19·5 | 0 | 95 | 1 | 4 | 0 | 9 | 0 |
| Tyldesley | 35 | 3 | 130 | 0 | 2 | 0 | 6 | 0 |
| Gilligan | 26 | 1 | 114 | 3 | 11 | 2 | 40 | 0 |
| Hearne | 13 | 1 | 69 | 0 | 29 | 5 | 84 | 4 |
| Woolley | 11 | 3 | 26 | 0 | | | | |
| AUSTRALIA | | | | | | | | |
| Gregory | 34 | 4 | 124 | 3 | 27·3 | 6 | 87 | 4 |
| Kelleway | 30 | 10 | 62 | 2 | 18 | 4 | 42 | 0 |
| Mailey | 34 | 5 | 141 | 2 | 24 | 2 | 92 | 5 |
| Hartkopf | 26 | 1 | 120 | 1 | 4 | 1 | 14 | 0 |
| A.J. Richardson | 14 | 6 | 20 | 2 | 22 | 7 | 35 | 1 |
| Collins | | | | | 11 | 3 | 10 | 0 |

FALL OF WICKETS

| | A | E | A | E |
|---|---:|---:|---:|---:|
| _Wkt_ | _1st_ | _1st_ | _2nd_ | _2nd_ |
| 1st | 22 | 283 | 3 | 36 |
| 2nd | 47 | 284 | 13 | 75 |
| 3rd | 47 | 305 | 27 | 121 |
| 4th | 208 | 373 | 106 | 211 |
| 5th | 301 | 404 | 126 | 254 |
| 6th | 424 | 412 | 166 | 255 |
| 7th | 439 | 418 | 168 | 280 |
| 8th | 499 | 453 | 168 | 289 |
| 9th | 599 | 458 | 239 | 289 |
| 10th | 600 | 479 | 250 | 290 |

Umpires: R.W. Crockett and C. Garing.

# AUSTRALIA v ENGLAND 1924-25 (3rd Test)

Played at Adelaide Oval on 16, 17, 19, 20, 21, 22, 23 January.
Toss: Australia.   Result: AUSTRALIA won by 11 runs.
Debuts: England – W.W. Whysall.

Ryder (201) equalled S.E. Gregory's record score against England in Australia. It remained until D.G. Bradman scored 270 in 1936-37 (*Test No. 257* ). Gilligan (strained thigh) retired after bowling seven balls of his eighth over.

## AUSTRALIA

| | | | | | |
|---|---|---|---|---|---|
| H.L. Collins* | b Tate | 3 | b Freeman | | 26 |
| A.J. Richardson | b Kilner | 69 | c Kilner b Woolley | | 14 |
| J.M. Gregory | b Freeman | 6 | (9) c Hendren b Woolley | | 2 |
| J.M. Taylor | lbw b Tate | 0 | b Freeman | | 34 |
| W.H. Ponsford | c Strudwick b Gilligan | 31 | c Hendren b Kilner | | 43 |
| V.Y. Richardson | c Whysall b Kilner | 4 | (7) c Tate b Woolley | | 0 |
| J. Ryder | not out | 201 | (3) c and b Woolley | | 88 |
| T.J.E. Andrews | b Kilner | 72 | (6) c Whysall b Kilner | | 1 |
| C. Kelleway | c Strudwick b Woolley | 16 | (8) not out | | 22 |
| W.A.S. Oldfield† | lbw b Kilner | 47 | b Kilner | | 4 |
| A.A. Mailey | st Strudwick b Hendren | 27 | c Sutcliffe b Kilner | | 5 |
| Extras | (LB 9, NB 4) | 13 | (B 4, LB 4, NB 3) | | 11 |
| **Total** | | **489** | | | **250** |

## ENGLAND

| | | | | | |
|---|---|---|---|---|---|
| W.W. Whysall | b Gregory | 9 | (5) c and b Gregory | | 75 |
| M.W. Tate | c Andrews b Mailey | 27 | (8) b Mailey | | 21 |
| H. Strudwick† | c Gregory b Kelleway | 1 | (11) not out | | 2 |
| A.P.F. Chapman | b Gregory | 26 | (6) c Ryder b Kelleway | | 58 |
| J.B. Hobbs | c Gregory b Mailey | 119 | (1) c Collins b A. J. Richardson | | 27 |
| H. Sutcliffe | c Oldfield b Ryder | 33 | (2) c Ponsford b Mailey | | 59 |
| F.E. Woolley | c Andrews b Mailey | 16 | (3) b Kelleway | | 21 |
| E.H. Hendren | c Taylor b Gregory | 92 | (4) lbw b Kelleway | | 4 |
| R. Kilner | lbw b A.J. Richardson | 6 | (7) c V.Y. Richardson b A.J. Richardson | | 24 |
| A.E.R. Gilligan* | c Collins b A.J. Richardson | 9 | (9) c V.Y. Richardson b Gregory | | 31 |
| A.P. Freeman | not out | 6 | (10) c Oldfield b Mailey | | 24 |
| Extras | (B 8, LB 10, NB 3) | 21 | (B 5, LB 5, W 1, NB 6) | | 17 |
| **Total** | | **365** | | | **363** |

| ENGLAND | O | M | R | W | O | M | R | W |
|---|---|---|---|---|---|---|---|---|
| Tate | 18 | 4 | 43 | 2 | 10 | 4 | 17 | 0 |
| Gilligan | 7·7 | 1 | 17 | 1 | | | | |
| Freeman | 18 | 0 | 107 | 1 | 17 | 1 | 94 | 2 |
| Woolley | 43 | 5 | 135 | 1 | 19 | 1 | 77 | 4 |
| Kilner | 56 | 7 | 127 | 4 | 22·1 | 7 | 51 | 4 |
| Hobbs | 3 | 0 | 11 | 0 | | | | |
| Hendren | 5·1 | 0 | 27 | 1 | | | | |
| Whysall | 2 | 0 | 9 | 0 | | | | |
| AUSTRALIA | | | | | | | | |
| Gregory | 26·2 | 0 | 111 | 3 | 23 | 6 | 71 | 2 |
| Kelleway | 15 | 6 | 24 | 1 | 22 | 4 | 57 | 3 |
| Mailey | 44 | 5 | 133 | 3 | 30·2 | 4 | 126 | 3 |
| A.J. Richardson | 21 | 7 | 42 | 2 | 25 | 5 | 62 | 2 |
| Ryder | 6 | 2 | 15 | 1 | 2 | 0 | 11 | 0 |
| Collins | 5 | 1 | 19 | 0 | 9 | 4 | 19 | 0 |

### FALL OF WICKETS

| Wkt | A 1st | E 1st | A 2nd | E 2nd |
|---|---|---|---|---|
| 1st | 10 | 15 | 36 | 63 |
| 2nd | 19 | 18 | 63 | 92 |
| 3rd | 22 | 67 | 126 | 96 |
| 4th | 114 | 69 | 215 | 155 |
| 5th | 118 | 159 | 216 | 244 |
| 6th | 119 | 180 | 217 | 254 |
| 7th | 253 | 297 | 217 | 279 |
| 8th | 308 | 316 | 220 | 312 |
| 9th | 416 | 326 | 242 | 357 |
| 10th | 489 | 365 | 250 | 363 |

Umpires: R.W. Crockett and D. Elder.

# AUSTRALIA v ENGLAND 1924-25 (4th Test)

Played at Melbourne Cricket Ground on 13, 14, 16, 17, 18 February.
Toss: England.    Result: ENGLAND won by an innings and 29 runs.
Debuts: Nil.

Sutcliffe was the first to score four hundreds in one rubber of Test matches. This was his third century in consecutive Test innings at Melbourne. England's long-awaited victory ended Australia's run of 16 Tests without defeat against both England and South Africa since August 1912 (*Test No. 129*).

### ENGLAND

| | | |
|---|---|---:|
| J.B. Hobbs | st Oldfield b Ryder | 66 |
| H. Sutcliffe | lbw b Mailey | 143 |
| J.W. Hearne | c Bardsley b Richardson | 44 |
| F.E. Woolley | st Oldfield b Mailey | 40 |
| E.H. Hendren | b Ryder | 65 |
| A.P.F. Chapman | st Oldfield b Mailey | 12 |
| W.W. Whysall | st Oldfield b Kelleway | 76 |
| R. Kilner | lbw b Kelleway | 74 |
| A.E.R. Gilligan* | c Oldfield b Kelleway | 0 |
| M.W. Tate | c Taylor b Mailey | 8 |
| H. Strudwick† | not out | 7 |
| Extras | (B 6, LB 2, W 3, NB 2) | 13 |
| **Total** | | **548** |

### AUSTRALIA

| | | | | |
|---|---|---:|---|---:|
| H.L. Collins* | c Kilner b Tate | 22 | c Whysall b Kilner | 1 |
| A.J. Richardson | b Hearne | 19 | (9) lbw b Hearne | 3 |
| J. Ryder | b Tate | 0 | (5) lbw b Woolley | 38 |
| W. Bardsley | run out | 24 | (2) b Tate | 0 |
| W.H. Ponsford | c Strudwick b Hearne | 21 | (8) b Tate | 19 |
| J.M. Taylor | c Hendren b Woolley | 86 | (4) c Woolley b Gilligan | 68 |
| T.J.E. Andrews | c Hearne b Kilner | 35 | (6) c Strudwick b Tate | 3 |
| C. Kelleway | lbw b Kilner | 1 | (7) c Strudwick b Tate | 42 |
| J.M. Gregory | c Woolley b Hearne | 38 | (3) c Sutcliffe b Kilner | 45 |
| W.A.S. Oldfield† | c Chapman b Kilner | 3 | b Tate | 8 |
| A.A. Mailey | not out | 4 | not out | 8 |
| Extras | (B 13, LB 2, NB 1) | 16 | (B 15) | 15 |
| **Total** | | **269** | | **250** |

| AUSTRALIA | O | M | R | W | O | M | R | W |
|---|---|---|---|---|---|---|---|---|
| Gregory | 22 | 1 | 102 | 0 | | | | |
| Kelleway | 29 | 5 | 70 | 3 | | | | |
| Mailey | 43·6 | 2 | 186 | 4 | | | | |
| Ryder | 25 | 3 | 83 | 2 | | | | |
| Richardson | 26 | 8 | 76 | 1 | | | | |
| Collins | 6 | 1 | 18 | 0 | | | | |
| ENGLAND | | | | | | | | |
| Tate | 16 | 2 | 70 | 2 | 25·5 | 6 | 75 | 5 |
| Gilligan | 6 | 1 | 24 | 0 | 7 | 0 | 26 | 1 |
| Hearne | 19·3 | 1 | 77 | 3 | 20 | 0 | 76 | 1 |
| Kilner | 13 | 1 | 29 | 3 | 16 | 3 | 41 | 2 |
| Woolley | 9 | 1 | 53 | 1 | 6 | 0 | 17 | 1 |

### FALL OF WICKETS

| Wkt | E 1st | A 1st | A 2nd |
|---|---|---|---|
| 1st | 126 | 38 | 5 |
| 2nd | 232 | 38 | 5 |
| 3rd | 284 | 64 | 64 |
| 4th | 307 | 74 | 133 |
| 5th | 346 | 109 | 190 |
| 6th | 394 | 170 | 195 |
| 7th | 527 | 172 | 225 |
| 8th | 527 | 244 | 234 |
| 9th | 529 | 257 | 238 |
| 10th | 548 | 269 | 250 |

Umpires: R.W. Crockett and D. Elder.

## AUSTRALIA v ENGLAND 1924–25 (5th Test)

Played at Sydney Cricket Ground on 27, 28 February, 2, 3, 4 March.
Toss: Australia.   Result: AUSTRALIA won by 307 runs.
Debuts: Australia – C.V. Grimmett, A.F. Kippax.

Grimmett took eleven wickets in his first Test match; Sutcliffe set a new record aggregate for any Test rubber (734 runs, average 81·55); and Tate's total of 38 wickets remains the record for any Test rubber in Australia.

### AUSTRALIA

| | | | | |
|---|---|---|---|---|
| H.L. Collins* | c Strudwick b Gilligan | 1 | (7) lbw b Tate | 28 |
| J. Ryder | b Kilner | 29 | b Gilligan | 7 |
| J.M. Gregory | run out | 29 | (1) lbw b Hearne | 22 |
| T.J.E. Andrews | c Whysall b Kilner | 26 | (3) c Woolley b Hearne | 80 |
| J.M. Taylor | c Whysall b Tate | 15 | (4) st Strudwick b Tate | 25 |
| W.H. Ponsford | c Woolley b Kilner | 80 | (5) run out | 5 |
| A.F. Kippax | b Kilner | 42 | (6) c Whysall b Woolley | 8 |
| C. Kelleway | lbw b Tate | 9 | c Whysall b Tate | 73 |
| W.A.S. Oldfield† | c Strudwick b Tate | 29 | not out | 65 |
| A.A. Mailey | b Tate | 14 | b Tate | 0 |
| C.V. Grimmett | not out | 12 | b Tate | 0 |
| Extras | (B 2, LB 5, NB 2) | 9 | (B 6, LB 4, W 1, NB 1) | 12 |
| **Total** | | **295** | | **325** |

### ENGLAND

| | | | | |
|---|---|---|---|---|
| J.B. Hobbs | c Oldfield b Gregory | 0 | st Oldfield b Grimmett | 13 |
| H. Sutcliffe | c Mailey b Kelleway | 22 | b Gregory | 0 |
| A. Sandham | run out | 4 | lbw b Grimmett | 15 |
| F.E. Woolley | b Grimmett | 47 | c Andrews b Kelleway | 28 |
| E. H. Hendren | c Ponsford b Gregory | 10 | c Oldfield b Grimmett | 10 |
| J. W. Hearne | lbw b Grimmett | 16 | lbw b Grimmett | 24 |
| W.W. Whysall | lbw b Grimmett | 8 | st Oldfield b Grimmett | 18 |
| R. Kilner | st Oldfield b Grimmett | 24 | c Ponsford b Collins | 1 |
| M.W. Tate | b Ryder | 25 | c Mailey b Kelleway | 33 |
| A.E.R. Gilligan* | st Oldfield b Grimmett | 5 | not out | 0 |
| H. Strudwick† | not out | 1 | c Mailey b Grimmett | 0 |
| Extras | (LB 4, NB 1) | 5 | (B 1, LB 3) | 4 |
| **Total** | | **167** | | **146** |

| ENGLAND | O | M | R | W | O | M | R | W | | FALL OF WICKETS | | | |
|---|---|---|---|---|---|---|---|---|---|---|---|---|---|
| Tate | 39·5 | 6 | 92 | 4 | 39·3 | 6 | 115 | 5 | | A | E | A | E |
| Gilligan | 13 | 1 | 46 | 1 | 15 | 2 | 46 | 1 | Wkt | 1st | 1st | 2nd | 2nd |
| Kilner | 38 | 4 | 97 | 4 | 34 | 13 | 54 | 0 | 1st | 3 | 0 | 7 | 3 |
| Hearne | 7 | 0 | 33 | 0 | 22 | 0 | 84 | 2 | 2nd | 55 | 15 | 43 | 31 |
| Woolley | 5 | 0 | 18 | 0 | 8 | 1 | 14 | 1 | 3rd | 64 | 28 | 110 | 32 |
| | | | | | | | | | 4th | 99 | 58 | 130 | 60 |
| AUSTRALIA | | | | | | | | | 5th | 103 | 96 | 152 | 84 |
| Gregory | 9 | 1 | 42 | 2 | 10 | 0 | 53 | 1 | 6th | 208 | 109 | 156 | 99 |
| Kelleway | 15 | 1 | 38 | 1 | 7 | 1 | 16 | 2 | 7th | 239 | 122 | 209 | 100 |
| Mailey | 5 | 0 | 13 | 0 | | | | | 8th | 239 | 157 | 325 | 146 |
| Ryder | 7 | 0 | 24 | 1 | | | | | 9th | 264 | 163 | 325 | 146 |
| Grimmett | 11·7 | 2 | 45 | 5 | 19·4 | 3 | 37 | 6 | 10th | 295 | 167 | 325 | 146 |
| Collins | | | | | 8 | 2 | 36 | 1 | | | | | |

Umpires: R.W. Crockett and D. Elder.

# ENGLAND v AUSTRALIA 1926 (1st Test)

Played at Trent Bridge, Nottingham, on 12, 14 (*no play*), 15 (*no play*) June.
Toss: England.    Result: MATCH DRAWN.
Debuts: England – C.F. Root; Australia – W.M. Woodfull.

Following a delayed start there was only fifty minutes of play on the first day before heavy rain ended the match.

## ENGLAND

| | | |
|---|---|---|
| J.B. Hobbs | not out | 19 |
| H. Sutcliffe | not out | 13 |
| F.E. Woolley | ) | |
| J.W. Hearne | ) | |
| E.H. Hendren | ) | |
| A.P.F. Chapman | ) | |
| R. Kilner | ) did not bat | |
| A.W. Carr* | ) | |
| M.W. Tate | ) | |
| C.F. Root | ) | |
| H. Strudwick† | ) | |
| Extras | | – |
| **Total** | (0 wickets) | **32** |

## AUSTRALIA

H.L. Collins*
W. Bardsley
C.G. Macartney
J.M. Taylor
T.J.E. Andrews
W.M. Woodfull
J. Ryder
J.M. Gregory
A.J. Richardson
W.A.S. Oldfield
A.A. Mailey

| AUSTRALIA | O | M | R | W |
|---|---|---|---|---|
| Gregory | 8 | 1 | 18 | 0 |
| Macartney | 8·2 | 2 | 14 | 0 |
| Richardson | 1 | 1 | 0 | 0 |

Umpires: R.D. Burrows and F. Chester.

# ENGLAND v AUSTRALIA 1926 (2nd Test)

Played at Lord's, London, on 26, 28, 29 June.
Toss: Australia.   Result: MATCH DRAWN.
Debuts: England – H. Larwood.

Bardsley carried his bat through Australia's first innings and, at the age of 42 years 201 days, remains the oldest to score a hundred for Australia against England.

## AUSTRALIA

| | | | | | |
|---|---|---|---|---|---|
| H.L. Collins* | b Root | 1 | | c Sutcliffe b Larwood | 24 |
| W. Bardsley | not out | 193 | | | |
| C.G. Macartney | c Sutcliffe b Larwood | 39 | | not out | 133 |
| W.M. Woodfull | c Strudwick b Root | 13 | (6) | c Root b Woolley | 0 |
| T.J.E. Andrews | c and b Kilner | 10 | (4) | b Root | 9 |
| J.M. Gregory | b Larwood | 7 | (2) | c Sutcliffe b Root | 0 |
| J.M. Taylor | c Carr b Tate | 9 | | | |
| A.J. Richardson | b Kilner | 35 | | | |
| J. Ryder | c Strudwick b Tate | 28 | (7) | not out | 0 |
| W.A.S. Oldfield† | c Sutcliffe b Kilner | 19 | (5) | c Sutcliffe b Tate | 11 |
| A.A. Mailey | lbw b Kilner | 1 | | | |
| Extras | (B 12, LB 16) | 28 | | (B 5, LB 12) | 17 |
| **Total** | | **383** | | (5 wickets) | **194** |

## ENGLAND

| | | |
|---|---|---|
| J.B. Hobbs | c Richardson b Macartney | 119 |
| H. Sutcliffe | b Richardson | 82 |
| F.E. Woolley | lbw b Ryder | 87 |
| E.H. Hendren | not out | 127 |
| A.P.F. Chapman | not out | 50 |
| A.W. Carr* | ) | |
| R. Kilner | ) | |
| M.W. Tate | ) | |
| H. Larwood | } did not bat | |
| C.F. Root | ) | |
| H. Strudwick† | ) | |
| Extras | (B 4, LB 4, W 1, NB 1) | 10 |
| **Total** | (3 wickets declared) | **475** |

| ENGLAND | O | M | R | W | O | M | R | W |
|---|---|---|---|---|---|---|---|---|
| Tate | 50 | 12 | 111 | 2 | 25 | 11 | 38 | 1 |
| Root | 36 | 11 | 70 | 2 | 19 | 9 | 40 | 2 |
| Kilner | 34·5 | 11 | 70 | 4 | 22 | 2 | 49 | 0 |
| Larwood | 32 | 2 | 99 | 2 | 15 | 3 | 37 | 1 |
| Woolley | 2 | 0 | 5 | 0 | 7 | 1 | 13 | 1 |

| AUSTRALIA | O | M | R | W |
|---|---|---|---|---|
| Gregory | 30 | 3 | 125 | 0 |
| Macartney | 33 | 8 | 90 | 1 |
| Mailey | 30 | 6 | 96 | 0 |
| Richardson | 48 | 18 | 73 | 1 |
| Ryder | 25 | 3 | 70 | 1 |
| Collins | 2 | 0 | 11 | 0 |

| FALL OF WICKETS | | | |
|---|---|---|---|
| | A | E | A |
| Wkt | 1st | 1st | 2nd |
| 1st | 11 | 182 | 2 |
| 2nd | 84 | 219 | 125 |
| 3rd | 127 | 359 | 163 |
| 4th | 158 | – | 187 |
| 5th | 187 | – | 194 |
| 6th | 208 | – | – |
| 7th | 282 | – | – |
| 8th | 338 | – | – |
| 9th | 379 | – | – |
| 10th | 383 | – | – |

Umpires: L.C. Braund and A.E. Street.

# ENGLAND v AUSTRALIA 1926 (3rd Test)

Played at Headingley, Leeds, on 10, 12, 13 July.
Toss: England.    Result: MATCH DRAWN.
Debuts: Nil.

Macartney, who had been dropped fourth ball, reached his hundred in 103 minutes and scored 112 not out in 116 minutes before lunch on the first day. He was the second of four batsmen to achieve this feat in Test matches and his was the highest pre-lunch score. In the second innings, Hobbs broke C. Hill's record aggregate of 2,660 in Tests between England and Australia.

## AUSTRALIA

| | | |
|---|---|---:|
| W. Bardsley* | c Sutcliffe b Tate | 0 |
| W.M. Woodfull | b Tate | 141 |
| C.G. Macartney | c Hendren b Macaulay | 151 |
| T.J.E. Andrews | lbw b Kilner | 4 |
| A.J. Richardson | run out | 100 |
| J.M. Taylor | c Strudwick b Geary | 4 |
| J.M. Gregory | c Geary b Kilner | 26 |
| J. Ryder | b Tate | 42 |
| W.A.S. Oldfield† | lbw b Tate | 14 |
| C.V. Grimmett | c Sutcliffe b Geary | 1 |
| A.A. Mailey | not out | 1 |
| Extras | (B 2, LB 4, NB 4) | 10 |
| **Total** | | **494** |

## ENGLAND

| | | | | | |
|---|---|---:|---|---|---:|
| J.B. Hobbs | c Andrews b Mailey | 49 | b Grimmett | | 88 |
| H. Sutcliffe | c and b Grimmett | 26 | b Richardson | | 94 |
| F.E. Woolley | run out | 27 | c Macartney b Grimmett | | 20 |
| E.H. Hendren | c Andrews b Mailey | 0 | not out | | 4 |
| A.W. Carr* | lbw b Macartney | 13 | | | |
| A.P.F. Chapman | b Macartney | 15 | (5) not out | | 42 |
| R. Kilner | c Ryder b Grimmett | 36 | | | |
| M.W. Tate | st Oldfield b Grimmett | 5 | | | |
| G. Geary | not out | 35 | | | |
| G.G. Macaulay | c and b Grimmett | 76 | | | |
| H. Strudwick† | c Gregory b Grimmett | 1 | | | |
| Extras | (B 4, LB 6, NB 1) | 11 | (B 5, LB 1) | | 6 |
| **Total** | | **294** | (3 wickets) | | **254** |

| ENGLAND | O | M | R | W | O | M | R | W |
|---|---|---|---|---|---|---|---|---|
| Tate | 51 | 13 | 99 | 4 | | | | |
| Macaulay | 32 | 8 | 123 | 1 | | | | |
| Kilner | 37 | 6 | 106 | 2 | | | | |
| Geary | 41 | 5 | 130 | 2 | | | | |
| Woolley | 4 | 0 | 26 | 0 | | | | |
| **AUSTRALIA** | | | | | | | | |
| Gregory | 17 | 5 | 37 | 0 | 6 | 2 | 12 | 0 |
| Macartney | 31 | 13 | 51 | 2 | 4 | 1 | 13 | 0 |
| Grimmett | 39 | 11 | 88 | 5 | 29 | 10 | 59 | 2 |
| Richardson | 20 | 5 | 44 | 0 | 16 | 7 | 22 | 1 |
| Mailey | 21 | 4 | 63 | 2 | 18 | 2 | 80 | 0 |
| Ryder | | | | | 9 | 2 | 26 | 0 |
| Andrews | | | | | 4 | 0 | 36 | 0 |

### FALL OF WICKETS

| | A | E | E |
|---|---|---|---|
| Wkt | 1st | 1st | 2nd |
| 1st | 0 | 59 | 156 |
| 2nd | 235 | 104 | 208 |
| 3rd | 249 | 108 | 210 |
| 4th | 378 | 110 | – |
| 5th | 385 | 131 | – |
| 6th | 423 | 140 | – |
| 7th | 452 | 175 | – |
| 8th | 485 | 182 | – |
| 9th | 492 | 290 | – |
| 10th | 494 | 294 | – |

Umpires: H.R. Butt and W. Reeves.

# ENGLAND v AUSTRALIA 1926 (4th Test)

Played at Old Trafford, Manchester, on 24, 26, 27 July.
Toss: Australia.   Result: MATCH DRAWN.
Debuts: Nil.

Manchester's weather permitted ten balls to be bowled on the first afternoon. Macartney scored his third hundred in successive Test innings and became the first to score three hundreds in a Test rubber in England. Woodfull's century was his second in consecutive innings. Hobbs took over the captaincy on the second and third days after Carr developed tonsillitis.

## AUSTRALIA

| | | |
|---|---|---:|
| L.M. Woodfull | c Hendren b Root | 117 |
| W. Bardsley* | c Tyldesley b Stevens | 15 |
| C.G. Macartney | b Root | 109 |
| T.J.E. Andrews | c sub (A.P.F. Chapman) b Stevens | 8 |
| W.H. Ponsford | c and b Kilner | 23 |
| A.J. Richardson | c Woolley b Stevens | 0 |
| J. Ryder | c Strudwick b Root | 3 |
| J.M. Gregory | c Kilner b Root | 34 |
| W.A.S. Oldfield† | not out | 12 |
| C.V. Grimmett | c Stevens b Tate | 6 |
| A.A. Mailey | b Tate | 1 |
| Extras | (B 2, LB 1, W 1, NB 3) | 7 |
| **Total** | | **335** |

## ENGLAND

| | | |
|---|---|---:|
| J.B. Hobbs | c Ryder b Grimmett | 74 |
| H. Sutcliffe | c Oldfield b Mailey | 20 |
| E. Tyldesley | c Oldfield b Macartney | 81 |
| F.E. Woolley | c Ryder b Mailey | 58 |
| E.H. Hendren | not out | 32 |
| G.T.S. Stevens | c Bardsley b Mailey | 24 |
| R. Kilner | not out | 9 |
| A.W. Carr* | ) | |
| M.W. Tate | ) did not bat | |
| C.F. Root | ) | |
| H. Strudwick† | ) | |
| Extras | (B 4, LB 3) | 7 |
| **Total** | (5 wickets) | **305** |

| ENGLAND | O | M | R | W |
|---|---|---|---|---|
| Tate | 36·2 | 7 | 88 | 2 |
| Root | 52 | 27 | 84 | 4 |
| Kilner | 28 | 12 | 51 | 1 |
| Stevens | 32 | 3 | 86 | 3 |
| Woolley | 2 | 0 | 19 | 0 |
| AUSTRALIA | | | | |
| Gregory | 11 | 4 | 17 | 0 |
| Grimmett | 38 | 9 | 85 | 1 |
| Mailey | 27 | 4 | 87 | 3 |
| Ryder | 15 | 3 | 46 | 0 |
| Richardson | 17 | 3 | 43 | 0 |
| Macartney | 8 | 5 | 7 | 1 |
| Andrews | 9 | 5 | 13 | 0 |

### FALL OF WICKETS

| | A | E |
|---|---|---|
| Wkt | 1st | 1st |
| 1st | 29 | 58 |
| 2nd | 221 | 135 |
| 3rd | 252 | 225 |
| 4th | 256 | 243 |
| 5th | 257 | 272 |
| 6th | 266 | – |
| 7th | 300 | – |
| 8th | 317 | – |
| 9th | 329 | – |
| 10th | 335 | – |

Umpires: H. Young and H. Chidgey.

# ENGLAND v AUSTRALIA 1926 (5th Test)

Played at Kennington Oval, London, on 14, 16, 17, 18 August.
Toss: England.   Result: ENGLAND won by 289 runs.
Debuts: Nil.

England appointed Chapman as captain, recalled Rhodes at the age of 48 and gained one of their finest victories. The highlight was the opening partnership of 172 between Hobbs and Sutcliffe on a rain-affected pitch; it was Hobbs's only Test hundred against Australia on his home ground. This match ended a remarkable unbroken run of 52 Test appearances by Woolley; he had played in every England Test since the 5th Test of 1909.

## ENGLAND

| | | | | |
|---|---|---|---|---|
| J.B. Hobbs | b Mailey | 37 | b Gregory | 100 |
| H. Sutcliffe | b Mailey | 76 | b Mailey | 161 |
| F.E. Woolley | b Mailey | 18 | lbw b Richardson | 27 |
| E.H. Hendren | b Gregory | 8 | c Oldfield b Grimmett | 15 |
| A.P.F. Chapman* | st Oldfield b Mailey | 49 | b Richardson | 19 |
| G.T.S. Stevens | c Andrews b Mailey | 17 | c Mailey b Grimmett | 22 |
| W. Rhodes | c Oldfield b Mailey | 28 | lbw b Grimmett | 14 |
| G. Greary | run out | 9 | c Oldfield b Gregory | 1 |
| M.W. Tate | b Grimmett | 23 | not out | 33 |
| H. Larwood | c Andrews b Grimmett | 0 | b Mailey | 5 |
| H. Strudwick† | not out | 4 | c Andrews b Mailey | 2 |
| Extras | (B 6, LB 5) | 11 | (B 19, LB 18) | 37 |
| **Total** | | **280** | | **436** |

## AUSTRALIA

| | | | | |
|---|---|---|---|---|
| W.M. Woodfull | b Rhodes | 35 | c Geary b Larwood | 0 |
| W. Bardsley | c Strudwick b Larwood | 2 | (4) c Woolley b Rhodes | 21 |
| C.G. Macartney | b Stevens | 25 | c Geary b Larwood | 16 |
| W.H. Ponsford | run out | 2 | (2) c Larwood b Rhodes | 12 |
| T.J.E. Andrews | b Larwood | 3 | (6) c Tate b Larwood | 15 |
| H.L. Collins* | c Stevens b Larwood | 61 | (5) c Woolley b Rhodes | 4 |
| A.J. Richardson | c Geary b Rhodes | 16 | (8) b Rhodes | 4 |
| J.M. Gregory | c Stevens b Tate | 73 | (7) c Sutcliffe b Tate | 9 |
| W.A.S. Oldfield† | not out | 33 | b Stevens | 23 |
| C.V. Grimmett | b Tate | 35 | not out | 8 |
| A.A. Mailey | c Strudwick b Tate | 0 | b Geary | 6 |
| Extras | (B 5, LB 12) | 17 | (LB 7) | 7 |
| **Total** | | **302** | | **125** |

| AUSTRALIA | O | M | R | W | O | M | R | W | | FALL OF WICKETS | | | |
|---|---|---|---|---|---|---|---|---|---|---|---|---|---|
| | | | | | | | | | | E | A | E | A |
| Gregory | 15 | 4 | 31 | 1 | 18 | 1 | 58 | 2 | *Wkt* | *1st* | *1st* | *2nd* | *2nd* |
| Grimmett | 33 | 12 | 74 | 2 | 55 | 17 | 108 | 3 | 1st | 53 | 9 | 172 | 1 |
| Mailey | 33·5 | 3 | 138 | 6 | 42·5 | 6 | 128 | 3 | 2nd | 91 | 44 | 220 | 31 |
| Macartney | 6 | 3 | 16 | 0 | 26 | 16 | 24 | 0 | 3rd | 108 | 5. | 277 | 31 |
| Richardson | 7 | 2 | 10 | 0 | 41 | 21 | 81 | 2 | 4th | 189 | 59 | 316 | 35 |
| | | | | | | | | | 5th | 213 | 90 | 373 | 63 |
| ENGLAND | | | | | | | | | 6th | 214 | 122 | 375 | 83 |
| Tate | 37·1 | 17 | 40 | 3 | 9 | 4 | 12 | 1 | 7th | 231 | 229 | 382 | 83 |
| Larwood | 34 | 11 | 82 | 3 | 14 | 3 | 34 | 3 | 8th | 266 | 231 | 425 | 87 |
| Geary | 27 | 8 | 43 | 0 | 6·3 | 2 | 15 | 1 | 9th | 266 | 298 | 430 | 114 |
| Stevens | 29 | 3 | 85 | 1 | 3 | 1 | 13 | 1 | 10th | 280 | 302 | 436 | 125 |
| Rhodes | 25 | 15 | 35 | 2 | 20 | 9 | 44 | 4 | | | | | |

Umpires: F. Chester and H. Young.

# SOUTH AFRICA v ENGLAND 1927–28 (1st Test)

Played at Old Wanderers, Johannesburg, on 24, 26, 27 December.
Toss: South Africa.   Result: ENGLAND won by ten wickets.
Debuts: South Africa – H.B. Cameron, S.K. Coen, J.P. Duminy, D.P.B. Morkel, H.L.E. Promnitz, C.L. Vincent; England – W.E. Astill, W.R. Hammond, G.B. Legge, I.A.R. Peebles, R.T. Stanyforth, R.E.S. Wyatt.

Four players dominated this match: Hammond took three wickets in 23 balls and finished with five wickets and a fifty in his maiden Test; Sutcliffe and Tyldesley scored 230 in a second-wicket partnership; while Geary claimed twelve wickets.

## SOUTH AFRICA

| | | | | | |
|---|---|---|---|---|---|
| H.W. Taylor | c and b Stevens | 31 | (3) | b Hammond | 3 |
| J.P. Duminy | b Geary | 0 | | b Hammond | 4 |
| J.M.M. Commaille | lbw b Stevens | 23 | (1) | c Stanyforth b Geary | 4 |
| R.H. Catterall | c and b Geary | 86 | | b Hammond | 1 |
| H.G. Deane* | b Geary | 7 | | b Geary | 5 |
| D.P.B. Morkel | lbw b Geary | 2 | (7) | lbw b Geary | 29 |
| S.K. Coen | b Geary | 7 | (10) | not out | 41 |
| H.B. Cameron† | lbw b Stevens | 20 | (6) | lbw b Geary | 5 |
| E.P. Nupen | b Geary | 6 | (8) | b Geary | 1 |
| C.L. Vincent | not out | 2 | (9) | lbw b Hammond | 53 |
| H.L.E. Promnitz | b Geary | 4 | | b Hammond | 5 |
| Extras | (LB 6, NB 2) | 8 | | (B 5, LB 13, NB 1) | 19 |
| **Total** | | **196** | | | **170** |

## ENGLAND

| | | | | | |
|---|---|---|---|---|---|
| P. Holmes | lbw b Morkel | 0 | | not out | 15 |
| H. Sutcliffe | c Vincent b Promnitz | 102 | | not out | 41 |
| E. Tyldesley | lbw b Duminy | 122 | | | |
| W.R. Hammond | c Promnitz b Vincent | 51 | | | |
| R.E.S. Wyatt | lbw b Promnitz | 0 | | | |
| G.T.S. Stevens | c Nupen b Promnitz | 0 | | | |
| G.B. Legge | c and b Nupen | 0 | | | |
| W.E. Astill | c Cameron b Promnitz | 7 | | | |
| R.T. Stanyforth*† | c Cameron b Promnitz | 1 | | | |
| G. Geary | lbw b Vincent | 3 | | | |
| I.A.R. Peebles | not out | 2 | | | |
| Extras | (B 11, LB 10, W 1, NB 3) | 25 | | (B 1) | 1 |
| **Total** | | **313** | | (0 wickets) | **57** |

| ENGLAND | O | M | R | W | O | M | R | W |
|---|---|---|---|---|---|---|---|---|
| Geary | 27·3 | 7 | 70 | 7 | 27 | 9 | 60 | 5 |
| Hammond | 8 | 2 | 21 | 0 | 21·2 | 9 | 36 | 5 |
| Stevens | 19 | 3 | 58 | 3 | 8 | 3 | 13 | 0 |
| Peebles | 12 | 5 | 22 | 0 | 7 | 1 | 25 | 0 |
| Wyatt | 4 | 1 | 6 | 0 | | | | |
| Astill | 8 | 4 | 11 | 0 | 6 | 0 | 17 | 0 |
| SOUTH AFRICA | | | | | | | | |
| Morkel | 14 | 3 | 38 | 1 | | | | |
| Nupen | 49 | 12 | 111 | 1 | 11 | 1 | 29 | 0 |
| Vincent | 31·3 | 5 | 57 | 2 | | | | |
| Promnitz | 37 | 14 | 58 | 5 | 6 | 1 | 14 | 0 |
| Coen | 2 | 0 | 7 | 0 | | | | |
| Duminy | 4 | 0 | 17 | 1 | 4 | 0 | 13 | 0 |

### FALL OF WICKETS

| | SA | E | SA | E |
|---|---|---|---|---|
| Wkt | 1st | 1st | 2nd | 2nd |
| 1st | 1 | 0 | 10 | – |
| 2nd | 53 | 230 | 10 | – |
| 3rd | 58 | 252 | 11 | – |
| 4th | 89 | 252 | 20 | – |
| 5th | 93 | 254 | 20 | – |
| 6th | 120 | 263 | 26 | – |
| 7th | 170 | 280 | 38 | – |
| 8th | 185 | 292 | 78 | – |
| 9th | 190 | 308 | 158 | – |
| 10th | 196 | 313 | 170 | – |

Umpires: A.G. Laver and G.B. Treadwell.

# SOUTH AFRICA v ENGLAND 1927–28 (2nd Test)

Played at Newlands, Cape Town, on 31 December, 2, 3, 4 January.
Toss: South Africa.   Result: ENGLAND won by 87 runs.
Debuts: South Africa – G.F. Bissett, A.W. Palm.

## ENGLAND

| | | | | | |
|---|---|---|---|---|---|
| P. Holmes | b Bissett | 9 | c Vincent b Nupen | 88 |
| H. Sutcliffe | c Nupen b Bissett | 29 | b Bissett | 99 |
| E. Tyldesley | b Bissett | 0 | lbw b Promnitz | 87 |
| W.R. Hammond | lbw b Morkel | 43 | c Palm b Promnitz | 14 |
| G.T.S. Stevens | c Cameron b Bissett | 0 | c Morkel b Bissett | 2 |
| R.E.S. Wyatt | lbw b Bissett | 2 | c Promnitz b Bissett | 91 |
| W.E. Astill | lbw b Vincent | 25 | c Cameron b Vincent | 9 |
| R.T. Stanyforth*† | b Vincent | 4 | b Vincent | 1 |
| G. Geary | lbw b Vincent | 0 | b Vincent | 1 |
| I.A.R. Peebles | not out | 3 | c Vincent b Promnitz | 6 |
| A.P. Freeman | st Cameron b Vincent | 7 | not out | 0 |
| Extras | (B 5, LB 1, NB 5) | 11 | (B 19, LB 5, NB 6) | 30 |
| **Total** | | **133** | | **428** |

## SOUTH AFRICA

| | | | | | |
|---|---|---|---|---|---|
| H.W. Taylor | hit wkt b Freeman | 68 | run out | 71 |
| J.M.M. Commaille | lbw b Freeman | 13 | c Astill b Hammond | 47 |
| H.B. Cameron† | c Geary b Stevens | 19 | b Hammond | 19 |
| R.H. Catterall | b Hammond | 9 | lbw b Astill | 10 |
| D.P.B. Morkel | b Freeman | 36 | c Holmes b Astill | 23 |
| A.W. Palm | c Stevens b Freeman | 2 | (7) c Hammond b Freeman | 13 |
| H.G. Deane* | c Stanyforth b Hammond | 41 | (6) c Hammond b Freeman | 4 |
| C.L. Vincent | b Astill | 13 | c Hammond b Freeman | 11 |
| E.P. Nupen | not out | 39 | b Astill | 1 |
| G.F. Bissett | b Hammond | 3 | not out | 11 |
| H.L.E. Promnitz | run out | 3 | b Peebles | 2 |
| Extras | (B 2, LB 2) | 4 | (B 6, LB 4, NB 2) | 12 |
| **Total** | | **250** | | **224** |

| SOUTH AFRICA | O | M | R | W | O | M | R | W |
|---|---|---|---|---|---|---|---|---|
| Bissett | 17 | 5 | 37 | 5 | 31·5 | 5 | 99 | 3 |
| Morkel | 9 | 3 | 20 | 1 | 21 | 4 | 60 | 0 |
| Vincent | 15·1 | 4 | 22 | 4 | 40 | 10 | 93 | 3 |
| Nupen | 3 | 0 | 10 | 0 | 36 | 8 | 90 | 1 |
| Promnitz | 15 | 5 | 33 | 0 | 30 | 10 | 56 | 3 |
| **ENGLAND** | | | | | | | | |
| Geary | 23 | 2 | 50 | 0 | | | | |
| Hammond | 17 | 4 | 53 | 3 | 30 | 13 | 50 | 2 |
| Freeman | 29 | 12 | 58 | 4 | 22 | 7 | 66 | 3 |
| Peebles | 14 | 3 | 27 | 0 | 12·1 | 4 | 26 | 1 |
| Stevens | 10 | 1 | 26 | 1 | 5 | 0 | 17 | 0 |
| Astill | 8 | 0 | 32 | 1 | 29 | 11 | 48 | 3 |
| Wyatt | | | | | 3 | 0 | 5 | 0 |

| FALL OF WICKETS | | | | |
|---|---|---|---|---|
| | E | SA | E | SA |
| *Wkt* | *1st* | *1st* | *2nd* | *2nd* |
| 1st | 14 | 32 | 140 | 115 |
| 2nd | 14 | 72 | 233 | 126 |
| 3rd | 50 | 99 | 278 | 147 |
| 4th | 59 | 128 | 282 | 161 |
| 5th | 66 | 140 | 326 | 166 |
| 6th | 97 | 153 | 348 | 190 |
| 7th | 106 | 197 | 350 | 197 |
| 8th | 106 | 211 | 360 | 206 |
| 9th | 123 | 221 | 415 | 210 |
| 10th | 133 | 250 | 428 | 224 |

Umpires: H.V. Adams and G.B. Treadwell.

# SOUTH AFRICA v ENGLAND 1927–28 (3rd Test)

Played at Kingsmead, Durban, on 21, 23, 24, 25 January.
Toss: South Africa.   Result: MATCH DRAWN.
Debuts: South Africa – A.L. Ochse, J.F.W. Nicolson, I.J. Siedle; England – S.J. Staples.

## SOUTH AFRICA

| | | | | | |
|---|---|--:|---|---|--:|
| H.W. Taylor | b Wyatt | 7 | c Astill b Peebles | | 60 |
| I.J. Siedle | lbw b Staples | 11 | st Stanyforth b Freeman | | 10 |
| H.B. Cameron† | b Peebles | 21 | c Stanyforth b Freeman | | 9 |
| J.F.W. Nicolson | c Astill b Staples | 39 | c Hammond b Astill | | 78 |
| R.H. Catterall | b Staples | 14 | b Staples | | 76 |
| D.P.B. Morkel | b Peebles | 14 | b Freeman | | 42 |
| H.G. Deane* | st Stanyforth b Wyatt | 77 | lbw b Astill | | 73 |
| C.L. Vincent | c Stevens b Peebles | 2 | (9) not out | | 8 |
| E.P. Nupen | lbw b Wyatt | 51 | (8) b Staples | | 69 |
| A.L. Ochse | b Freeman | 4 | not out | | 4 |
| G.F. Bissett | not out | 1 | | | |
| Extras | (B 1, LB 1, NB 3) | 5 | (B 22, LB 12, NB 1) | | 35 |
| **Total** | | **246** | (8 wickets declared) | | **464** |

## ENGLAND

| | | | | | |
|---|---|--:|---|---|--:|
| P. Holmes | c Catterall b Nupen | 70 | c Catterall b Vincent | | 56 |
| H. Sutcliffe | b Vincent | 25 | c Morkel b Nupen | | 8 |
| E. Tyldesley | c Siedle b Vincent | 78 | not out | | 62 |
| W.R. Hammond | b Vincent | 90 | not out | | 1 |
| R.E.S. Wyatt | lbw b Vincent | 0 | | | |
| G.T.S. Stevens | b Vincent | 69 | | | |
| W.E. Astill | c Ochse b Vincent | 40 | | | |
| R.T. Stanyforth*† | c Vincent b Nupen | 0 | | | |
| S.J. Staples | b Nupen | 11 | | | |
| I.A.R. Peebles | not out | 18 | | | |
| A.P. Freeman | b Nupen | 3 | | | |
| Extras | (B 15, LB 9, NB 2) | 26 | (B 5) | | 5 |
| **Total** | | **430** | (2 wickets) | | **132** |

| ENGLAND | O | M | R | W | O | M | R | W |
|---|--:|--:|--:|--:|--:|--:|--:|--:|
| Hammond | 16 | 3 | 54 | 0 | 16 | 2 | 37 | 0 |
| Wyatt | 13 | 10 | 4 | 3 | 15 | 6 | 31 | 0 |
| Freeman | 16·3 | 3 | 44 | 1 | 33 | 3 | 122 | 3 |
| Staples | 36 | 17 | 50 | 3 | 47 | 9 | 111 | 2 |
| Peebles | 16 | 3 | 69 | 3 | 11 | 2 | 29 | 1 |
| Stevens | 4 | 0 | 12 | 0 | 11 | 0 | 58 | 0 |
| Astill | 3 | 1 | 8 | 0 | 24 | 6 | 41 | 2 |
| SOUTH AFRICA | | | | | | | | |
| Bissett | 30 | 4 | 89 | 0 | 11 | 2 | 41 | 0 |
| Ochse | 11 | 1 | 45 | 0 | | | | |
| Vincent | 45 | 10 | 131 | 6 | 13 | 0 | 31 | 1 |
| Nupen | 44·3 | 9 | 94 | 4 | 10·2 | 2 | 29 | 1 |
| Morkel | 3 | 0 | 17 | 0 | 8 | 0 | 26 | 0 |
| Nicolson | 2 | 0 | 5 | 0 | | | | |
| Catterall | 2 | 0 | 15 | 0 | | | | |
| Taylor | 2 | 0 | 8 | 0 | | | | |

### FALL OF WICKETS

| | SA | E | SA | E |
|---|--:|--:|--:|--:|
| Wkt | 1st | 1st | 2nd | 2nd |
| 1st | 13 | 67 | 30 | 25 |
| 2nd | 22 | 131 | 50 | 127 |
| 3rd | 55 | 258 | 118 | – |
| 4th | 93 | 260 | 225 | – |
| 5th | 98 | 303 | 284 | – |
| 6th | 135 | 365 | 307 | – |
| 7th | 146 | 365 | 430 | – |
| 8th | 241 | 379 | 454 | – |
| 9th | 242 | 421 | – | – |
| 10th | 246 | 430 | – | – |

Umpires: A.G. Laver and C. Saunders.

# SOUTH AFRICA v ENGLAND 1927–28 (4th Test)

Played at Old Wanderers, Johannesburg, on 28, 30, 31 January, 1 February.
Toss: South Africa.   Result: SOUTH AFRICA won by four wickets.
Debuts: Nil.

Freeman took over as wicket-keeper when Stanyforth retired after being hit under the right eye in the second innings.

## ENGLAND

| | | | | | |
|---|---|---|---|---|---|
| P. Holmes | b Bissett | 1 | b Vincent | | 63 |
| H. Sutcliffe | lbw b Hall | 37 | c Vincent b Bissett | | 3 |
| E. Tyldesley | lbw b Bissett | 42 | c Morkel b Nupen | | 8 |
| W.R. Hammond | c Cameron b Hall | 28 | lbw b Vincent | | 25 |
| R.E.S. Wyatt | c Cameron b Hall | 58 | lbw b Bissett | | 39 |
| G.T.S. Stevens | c Vincent b Hall | 14 | c Deane b Bissett | | 20 |
| W.E. Astill | c Hall b Bissett | 3 | c Duminy b Bissett | | 17 |
| I.A.R. Peebles | c Deane b Hall | 26 | lbw b Hall | | 7 |
| S.J. Staples | b Bissett | 39 | b Hall | | 6 |
| R.T. Stanyforth*† | b Hall | 1 | not out | | 6 |
| A.P. Freeman | not out | 9 | lbw b Hall | | 4 |
| Extras | (LB 5, NB 2) | 7 | (B 16, LB 1) | | 17 |
| **Total** | | **265** | | | **215** |

## SOUTH AFRICA

| | | | | | |
|---|---|---|---|---|---|
| H.W. Taylor | b Hammond | 101 | c Stanyforth b Hammond | | 6 |
| J.P. Duminy | c Stevens b Hammond | 7 | (4) b Freeman | | 5 |
| D.P.B. Morkel | b Hammond | 0 | lbw b Staples | | 45 |
| J.F.W. Nicolson | b Staples | 13 | (2) c Hammond b Staples | | 28 |
| R.H. Catterall | c Stanyforth b Astill | 39 | lbw b Staples | | 23 |
| H.B. Cameron† | c and b Astill | 64 | c Wyatt b Astill | | 18 |
| H.G. Deane* | c and b Wyatt | 39 | not out | | 8 |
| E.P. Nupen | c Stanyforth b Staples | 0 | not out | | 4 |
| C.L. Vincent | not out | 26 | | | |
| G.F. Bissett | c Stevens b Freeman | 23 | | | |
| A.E. Hall | c Stanyforth b Staples | 5 | | | |
| Extras | (B 8, LB 3) | 11 | (B 16, LB 3) | | 19 |
| **Total** | | **328** | (6 wickets) | | **156** |

| SOUTH AFRICA | O | M | R | W | O | M | R | W |
|---|---|---|---|---|---|---|---|---|
| Bissett | 23 | 5 | 43 | 4 | 17 | 1 | 70 | 4 |
| Hall | 42·4 | 9 | 100 | 6 | 26 | 6 | 67 | 3 |
| Nupen | 38 | 8 | 52 | 0 | 19 | 4 | 39 | 1 |
| Vincent | 20 | 2 | 54 | 0 | 10 | 5 | 22 | 2 |
| Duminy | 2 | 0 | 9 | 0 | | | | |
| ENGLAND | | | | | | | | |
| Hammond | 22 | 4 | 62 | 3 | 9 | 3 | 20 | 1 |
| Wyatt | 11 | 0 | 44 | 1 | 2 | 0 | 6 | 0 |
| Staples | 32·3 | 7 | 81 | 3 | 21 | 1 | 67 | 3 |
| Peebles | 12 | 0 | 48 | 0 | | | | |
| Freeman | 3 | 0 | 18 | 1 | 13 | 2 | 34 | 1 |
| Astill | 11 | 0 | 55 | 2 | 3·2 | 1 | 10 | 1 |
| Stevens | 1 | 0 | 9 | 0 | 1 | 1 | 0 | 0 |

### FALL OF WICKETS

| | E | SA | E | SA |
|---|---|---|---|---|
| Wkt | 1st | 1st | 2nd | 2nd |
| 1st | 6 | 33 | 21 | 14 |
| 2nd | 83 | 33 | 83 | 85 |
| 3rd | 83 | 62 | 83 | 98 |
| 4th | 136 | 152 | 141 | 124 |
| 5th | 167 | 170 | 172 | 126 |
| 6th | 174 | 259 | 185 | 151 |
| 7th | 198 | 268 | 192 | – |
| 8th | 253 | 268 | 198 | – |
| 9th | 254 | 313 | 209 | – |
| 10th | 265 | 328 | 215 | – |

Umpires: G.A. Verheyen and J. Page.

## SOUTH AFRICA v ENGLAND 1927–28 (5th Test)

Played at Kingsmead, Durban on 4, 6, 7, 8 February.
Toss: South Africa.   Result: SOUTH AFRICA won by eight wickets.
Debuts: England – E.W. Dawson, H. Elliott.

Deane became the third captain to win all five tosses in a rubber; on two occasions out of three South Africa won after he had put England in to bat. Wyatt retired hurt and later resumed his second innings.

### ENGLAND

| | | | | |
|---|---|--:|---|--:|
| P. Holmes | c Cameron b Bissett | 0 | lbw b Bissett | 0 |
| H. Sutcliffe | c Cameron b Vincent | 51 | lbw b Nupen | 23 |
| E. Tyldesley | c Morkel b Vincent | 100 | c Deane b Bissett | 21 |
| W.R. Hammond | c Catterall b Nupen | 66 | c Vincent b Bissett | 3 |
| R.E.S. Wyatt | c Catterall b Bissett | 22 | not out | 20 |
| G.T.S. Stevens* | c Taylor b Vincent | 13 | c Deane b Bissett | 18 |
| E.W. Dawson | lbw b Nupen | 14 | c Vincent b Bissett | 9 |
| W.E. Astill | lbw b Nupen | 1 | c Coen b Bissett | 0 |
| S.J. Staples | b Nupen | 2 | b Bissett | 7 |
| H. Elliott† | c Catterall b Nupen | 1 | b Vincent | 3 |
| A.P. Freeman | not out | 0 | c Hall b Vincent | 1 |
| Extras | (B 4, LB 4, NB 4) | 12 | (B 10, LB 1, NB 2) | 13 |
| **Total** | | **282** | | **118** |

### SOUTH AFRICA

| | | | | |
|---|---|--:|---|--:|
| H.W. Taylor | lbw b Staples | 36 | c Wyatt b Staples | 29 |
| S.K. Coen | b Astill | 28 | not out | 25 |
| D.P.B. Morkel | c Hammond b Staples | 2 | | |
| J.F.W. Nicolson | b Astill | 21 | | |
| R.H. Catterall | c Holmes b Astill | 119 | (4) not out | 2 |
| H.B. Cameron† | c Holmes b Freeman | 53 | | |
| H.G. Deane* | b Staples | 23 | | |
| E.P. Nupen | not out | 19 | (3) c Freeman b Hammond | 10 |
| C.L. Vincent | not out | 19 | | |
| G.F. Bissett | ) did not bat | | | |
| A.E. Hall | ) | | | |
| Extras | (B 1, LB 9, NB 2) | 12 | (B 3) | 3 |
| **Total** | (7 wickets declared) | **332** | (2 wickets) | **69** |

| SOUTH AFRICA | O | M | R | W | O | M | R | W | | FALL OF WICKETS | | | |
|---|--:|--:|--:|--:|--:|--:|--:|--:|---|--:|--:|--:|--:|
| Bissett | 16 | 1 | 61 | 2 | 19 | 5 | 29 | 7 | | E | SA | E | SA |
| Hall | 18 | 0 | 48 | 0 | 10 | 3 | 18 | 0 | *Wkt* | *1st* | *1st* | *2nd* | *2nd* |
| Nupen | 33·5 | 9 | 83 | 5 | 9 | 2 | 14 | 1 | 1st | 2 | 57 | 0 | 51 |
| Vincent | 31 | 4 | 63 | 3 | 17 | 3 | 44 | 2 | 2nd | 132 | 60 | 40 | 66 |
| Morkel | 2 | 0 | 3 | 0 | | | | | 3rd | 177 | 87 | 43 | – |
| Nicolson | 2 | 0 | 12 | 0 | | | | | 4th | 240 | 95 | 70 | – |
| ENGLAND | | | | | | | | | 5th | 262 | 230 | 89 | – |
| Hammond | 12 | 2 | 41 | 0 | 10 | 2 | 25 | 1 | 6th | 264 | 278 | 90 | – |
| Staples | 44 | 13 | 96 | 3 | 11 | 3 | 30 | 1 | 7th | 265 | 296 | 90 | – |
| Wyatt | 3 | 0 | 16 | 0 | | | | | 8th | 269 | – | 103 | – |
| Freeman | 16 | 2 | 57 | 1 | | | | | 9th | 282 | – | 114 | – |
| Astill | 36 | 10 | 99 | 3 | 2 | 0 | 9 | 0 | 10th | 282 | – | 118 | – |
| Stevens | 2 | 0 | 11 | 0 | | | | | | | | | |
| Tyldesley | | | | | 0·3 | 0 | 2 | 0 | | | | | |

Umpires: A.G. Laver and G.B. Treadwell.

# ENGLAND v WEST INDIES 1928 (1st Test)

Played at Lord's, London, 23, 25, 26 June.
Toss: England.   Result: ENGLAND won by an innings and 58 runs.
Debuts: England – D.R. Jardine, H. Smith; West Indies – All.

Tyldesley's hundred took 160 minutes and was the first against West Indies – scored in their first official Test match.

## ENGLAND

| | | |
|---|---|---|
| H. Sutcliffe | c Constantine b Francis | 48 |
| C. Hallows | c Griffith b Constantine | 26 |
| E. Tyldesley | c Constantine b Francis | 122 |
| W.R. Hammond | b Constantine | 45 |
| D.R. Jardine | lbw b Griffith | 22 |
| A.P.F. Chapman* | c Constantine b Small | 50 |
| V.W.C. Jupp | b Small | 14 |
| M.W. Tate | c Browne b Griffith | 22 |
| H. Smith† | b Constantine | 7 |
| H. Larwood | not out | 17 |
| A.P. Freeman | b Constantine | 1 |
| Extras | (B 6, LB 19, NB 2) | 27 |
| **Total** | | **401** |

## WEST INDIES

| | | | | | |
|---|---|---|---|---|---|
| G. Challenor | c Smith b Larwood | 29 | b Tate | | 0 |
| F.R. Martin | lbw b Tate | 44 | b Hammond | | 12 |
| M.P. Fernandes | b Tate | 0 | c Hammond b Freeman | | 8 |
| R.K. Nunes*† | b Jupp | 37 | lbw b Jupp | | 10 |
| W.H. St Hill | c Jardine b Jupp | 4 | lbw b Freeman | | 9 |
| C.A. Roach | run out | 0 | c Chapman b Tate | | 16 |
| L.N. Constantine | c Larwood b Freeman | 13 | b Freeman | | 0 |
| J.A. Small | lbw b Jupp | 10 | c Hammond b Jupp | | 52 |
| C.R. Browne | b Jupp | 10 | b Freeman | | 44 |
| G.N. Francis | not out | 19 | c Jardine b Jupp | | 0 |
| H.C. Griffith | c Sutcliffe b Freeman | 2 | not out | | 0 |
| Extras | (B 13, LB 6) | 19 | (B 10, LB 5) | | 15 |
| **Total** | | **177** | | | **166** |

| WEST INDIES | O | M | R | W | O | M | R | W |
|---|---|---|---|---|---|---|---|---|
| Francis | 25 | 4 | 72 | 2 | | | | |
| Constantine | 26·4 | 9 | 82 | 4 | | | | |
| Griffith | 29 | 9 | 78 | 2 | | | | |
| Browne | 22 | 5 | 53 | 0 | | | | |
| Small | 15 | 1 | 67 | 2 | | | | |
| Martin | 8 | 2 | 22 | 0 | | | | |
| ENGLAND | | | | | | | | |
| Larwood | 15 | 4 | 27 | 1 | | | | |
| Tate | 27 | 8 | 54 | 2 | 22 | 10 | 28 | 2 |
| Freeman | 18·3 | 5 | 40 | 2 | 21·1 | 10 | 37 | 4 |
| Jupp | 23 | 9 | 37 | 4 | 15 | 4 | 66 | 3 |
| Hammond | | | | | 15 | 6 | 20 | 1 |

## FALL OF WICKETS

| Wkt | E 1st | WI 1st | WI 2nd |
|---|---|---|---|
| 1st | 51 | 86 | 0 |
| 2nd | 97 | 86 | 22 |
| 3rd | 174 | 88 | 35 |
| 4th | 231 | 95 | 43 |
| 5th | 327 | 96 | 44 |
| 6th | 339 | 112 | 44 |
| 7th | 360 | 123 | 100 |
| 8th | 380 | 151 | 147 |
| 9th | 389 | 156 | 147 |
| 10th | 401 | 177 | 166 |

Umpires: L.C. Braund and F. Chester.

# ENGLAND v WEST INDIES 1928 (2nd Test)

Played at Old Trafford, Manchester, on 21, 23, 24 July.
Toss: West Indies.   Result: ENGLAND won by an innings and 30 runs.
Debuts: West Indies – E.L.G. Hoad, O.C. Scott.

J.C. White captained England in West Indies' second innings after Chapman had strained a muscle batting.

## WEST INDIES

| | | | | | |
|---|---|---|---|---|---|
| G. Challenor | run out | 24 | c Elliott b Hammond | | 0 |
| C.A. Roach | lbw b Freeman | 50 | c Jardine b Tate | | 0 |
| F.R. Martin | run out | 21 | c Hammond b Freeman | | 32 |
| W.H. St Hill | c Jupp b Tate | 3 | c Hammond b White | | 38 |
| E.L.G. Hoad | lbw b Jupp | 13 | lbw b Freeman | | 4 |
| R.K. Nunes*† | b Freeman | 17 | (7) c sub (M.L. Taylor) b Freeman | | 11 |
| L.N. Constantine | lbw b Jupp | 4 | (8) c Sutcliffe b Freeman | | 18 |
| C.R. Browne | c White b Freeman | 23 | (9) c Elliott b White | | 7 |
| O.C. Scott | c Chapman b Freeman | 32 | (10) not out | | 3 |
| G.N. Francis | b Freeman | 1 | (6) c Tate b Freeman | | 0 |
| H.C. Griffith | not out | 1 | c Hammond b White | | 0 |
| Extras | (B 10, LB 7) | 17 | (B 1, LB1) | | 2 |
| **Total** | | **206** | | | **115** |

## ENGLAND

| | | |
|---|---|---|
| J.B. Hobbs | c St Hill b Browne | 53 |
| H. Sutcliffe | c Nunes b Griffith | 54 |
| E. Tyldesley | b Browne | 3 |
| W.R. Hammond | c Roach b Constantine | 63 |
| D.R. Jardine | run out | 83 |
| A.P.F. Chapman* | retired hurt | 3 |
| M.W. Tate | b Griffith | 28 |
| V.W.C. Jupp | c Constantine b Griffith | 12 |
| J.C. White | not out | 21 |
| H. Elliott† | lbw b Scott | 6 |
| A.P. Freeman | lbw b Scott | 0 |
| Extras | (B 15, LB 3, W 1, NB 6) | 25 |
| **Total** | | **351** |

| ENGLAND | O | M | R | W | O | M | R | W | | FALL OF WICKETS | | |
|---|---|---|---|---|---|---|---|---|---|---|---|---|
| | | | | | | | | | | WI | E | WI |
| Tate | 35 | 13 | 68 | 1 | 9 | 4 | 10 | 1 | *Wkt* | *1st* | *1st* | *2nd* |
| Hammond | 6 | 2 | 16 | 0 | 6 | 0 | 23 | 1 | 1st | 48 | 119 | 0 |
| Freeman | 33·4 | 18 | 54 | 5 | 18 | 5 | 39 | 5 | 2nd | 100 | 124 | 2 |
| Jupp | 18 | 5 | 39 | 2 | | | | | 3rd | 105 | 131 | 57 |
| White | 13 | 6 | 12 | 0 | 14·3 | 4 | 41 | 3 | 4th | 113 | 251 | 67 |
| | | | | | | | | | 5th | 129 | 285 | 71 |
| WEST INDIES | | | | | | | | | 6th | 133 | 311 | 79 |
| Francis | 23 | 4 | 68 | 0 | | | | | 7th | 158 | 326 | 93 |
| Constantine | 25 | 7 | 89 | 1 | | | | | 8th | 185 | 351 | 108 |
| Browne | 25 | 2 | 72 | 2 | | | | | 9th | 203 | 351 | 115 |
| Griffith | 25 | 7 | 69 | 3 | | | | | 10th | 206 | – | 115 |
| Scott | 9·2 | 0 | 28 | 2 | | | | | | | | |

Umpires: A. Morton and W.R. Parry.

# ENGLAND v WEST INDIES 1928 (3rd Test)

Played at Kennington Oval, London, 11, 13, 14 August.
Toss: West Indies.   Result: ENGLAND won by an innings and 71 runs.
Debuts: England – M. Leyland; West Indies – E.L. Bartlett, C.V. Wight.

### WEST INDIES

| | | | | |
|---|---|---|---|---|
| G. Challenor | c Hammond b Leyland | 46 | c Hammond b Freeman | 2 |
| C.A. Roach | b Larwood | 53 | b Larwood | 12 |
| F.R. Martin | c Chapman b Freeman | 25 | b Tate | 41 |
| R.K. Nunes*† | b Tate | 0 | c Hendren b Larwood | 12 |
| E.L. Bartlett | b Larwood | 13 | c Larwood b Freeman | 8 |
| O.C. Scott | c Duckworth b Tate | 35 | c Duckworth b Larwood | 4 |
| L.N. Constantine | c Chapman b Hammond | 37 | c Larwood b Tate | 17 |
| C.V. Wight | c Chapman b Tate | 23 | not out | 12 |
| J.A. Small | lbw b Freeman | 0 | c Freeman b Tate | 2 |
| H.C. Griffith | not out | 0 | c Hammond b Freeman | 5 |
| G.N. Francis | c Chapman b Tate | 4 | c Hammond b Freeman | 4 |
| Extras | (B 2) | 2 | (B 6, LB 4) | 10 |
| **Total** | | **238** | | **129** |

### ENGLAND

| | | |
|---|---|---|
| J.B. Hobbs | c Small b Francis | 159 |
| H. Sutcliffe | b Francis | 63 |
| E. Tyldesley | c Constantine b Griffith | 73 |
| W.R. Hammond | c Small b Griffith | 3 |
| M. Leyland | b Griffith | 0 |
| E.H. Hendren | c Roach b Griffith | 14 |
| A.P.F. Chapman* | c Constantine b Griffith | 5 |
| M.W. Tate | c Griffith b Francis | 54 |
| H. Larwood | c and b Francis | 32 |
| G. Duckworth† | not out | 7 |
| A.P. Freeman | c Francis b Griffith | 19 |
| Extras | (B 1, LB 2, NB 6) | 9 |
| **Total** | | **438** |

| ENGLAND | O | M | R | W | O | M | R | W |
|---|---|---|---|---|---|---|---|---|
| Larwood | 21 | 6 | 46 | 2 | 14 | 3 | 41 | 3 |
| Tate | 21 | 4 | 59 | 4 | 13 | 4 | 27 | 3 |
| Freeman | 27 | 8 | 85 | 2 | 21·4 | 4 | 47 | 4 |
| Hammond | 8 | 0 | 40 | 1 | 4 | 2 | 4 | 0 |
| Leyland | 3 | 0 | 6 | 1 | | | | |
| **WEST INDIES** | | | | | | | | |
| Francis | 27 | 4 | 112 | 4 | | | | |
| Constantine | 20 | 3 | 91 | 0 | | | | |
| Griffith | 25·5 | 4 | 103 | 6 | | | | |
| Scott | 14 | 1 | 75 | 0 | | | | |
| Small | 15 | 2 | 39 | 0 | | | | |
| Martin | 2 | 1 | 9 | 0 | | | | |

| FALL OF WICKETS | | | |
|---|---|---|---|
| | WI | E | WI |
| Wkt | 1st | 1st | 2nd |
| 1st | 91 | 155 | 12 |
| 2nd | 112 | 284 | 26 |
| 3rd | 113 | 305 | 46 |
| 4th | 132 | 305 | 59 |
| 5th | 160 | 310 | 70 |
| 6th | 177 | 322 | 102 |
| 7th | 231 | 333 | 102 |
| 8th | 234 | 394 | 110 |
| 9th | 234 | 413 | 123 |
| 10th | 238 | 438 | 129 |

Umpires: T.W. Oates and J. Hardstaff, sr.

# AUSTRALIA v ENGLAND 1928–29 (1st Test)

Played at Exhibition Ground, Brisbane, on 30 November, 1, 3, 4, 5 December.
Toss: England.   Result: ENGLAND won by 675 runs.
Debuts: Australia – D.G. Bradman, H. Ironmonger.

Brisbane's introduction to Test cricket brought the first declaration in a Test in Australia and the record margin of victory by runs alone. Woodfull carried his bat through Australia's completed second innings in which two men (Kelleway with food poisoning, Gregory through cartilage problems) were absent. Gregory was unable to play cricket again.

## ENGLAND

| | | | | |
|---|---|---|---|---|
| J.B. Hobbs | run out | 49 | lbw b Grimmett | 11 |
| H. Sutcliffe | c Ponsford b Gregory | 38 | c sub (R.K. Oxenham) | |
| | | | b Ironmonger | 32 |
| C.P. Mead | lbw b Grimmett | 8 | lbw b Grimmett | 73 |
| W.R. Hammond | c Woodfull b Gregory | 44 | c sub (F.C. Thompson) | |
| | | | b Ironmonger | 28 |
| D.R. Jardine | c Woodfull b Ironmonger | 35 | not out | 65 |
| E.H. Hendren | c Ponsford b Ironmonger | 169 | c Ponsford b Grimmett | 45 |
| A.P.F. Chapman* | c Kelleway b Gregory | 50 | c Oldfield b Grimmett | 27 |
| M.W. Tate | c Ryder b Grimmett | 26 | c Bradman b Grimmett | 20 |
| H. Larwood | lbw b Hendry | 70 | c Ponsford b Grimmett | 37 |
| J.C. White | lbw b Grimmett | 14 | | |
| G. Duckworth† | not out | 5 | | |
| Extras | (LB 10, NB 3) | 13 | (LB 3, NB 1) | 4 |
| **Total** | | **521** | (8 wickets declared) | **342** |

## AUSTRALIA

| | | | | |
|---|---|---|---|---|
| W.M. Woodfull | c Chapman b Larwood | 0 | not out | 30 |
| W.H. Ponsford | b Larwood | 2 | c Duckworth b Larwood | 0 |
| A.F. Kippax | c and b Tate | 16 | c and b Larwood | 15 |
| H.S.T.L. Hendry | lbw b Larwood | 30 | c Larwood b White | |
| C. Kelleway | b Larwood | 8 | absent ill | – |
| J. Ryder* | c Jardine b Larwood | 33 | (5) c Larwood b Tate | 1 |
| D.G. Bradman | lbw b Tate | 18 | (6) c Chapman b White | 1 |
| W.A.S. Oldfield† | lbw b Tate | 2 | (7) c Larwood b Tate | |
| C.V. Grimmett | not out | 7 | (8) c Chapman b White | 1 |
| H. Ironmonger | b Larwood | 4 | (9) c Chapman b White | 0 |
| J.M. Gregory | absent hurt | – | absent hurt | – |
| Extras | (B 1, LB 1) | 2 | (NB 1) | 1 |
| **Total** | | **122** | | **66** |

| AUSTRALIA | O | M | R | W | O | M | R | W | FALL OF WICKETS | | | | |
|---|---|---|---|---|---|---|---|---|---|---|---|---|---|
| | | | | | | | | | | E | A | E | A |
| Gregory | 41 | 3 | 142 | 3 | | | | | Wkt | 1st | 1st | 2nd | 2nd |
| Kelleway | 34 | 9 | 77 | 0 | | | | | 1st | 85 | 0 | 25 | 6 |
| Grimmett | 40 | 2 | 167 | 3 | 44·1 | 9 | 131 | 6 | 2nd | 95 | 7 | 69 | 33 |
| Ironmonger | 44·3 | 18 | 79 | 2 | 50 | 20 | 85 | 2 | 3rd | 108 | 24 | 117 | 46 |
| Ryder | 6 | 2 | 23 | 0 | 14 | 3 | 43 | 0 | 4th | 161 | 40 | 165 | 47 |
| Hendry | 10 | 1 | 20 | 1 | 27 | 6 | 79 | 0 | 5th | 217 | 71 | 228 | 49 |
| ENGLAND | | | | | | | | | 6th | 291 | 101 | 263 | 62 |
| Larwood | 14·4 | 4 | 32 | 6 | 7 | 0 | 30 | 2 | 7th | 319 | 105 | 285 | 66 |
| Tate | 21 | 6 | 50 | 3 | 11 | 3 | 26 | 2 | 8th | 443 | 116 | 342 | 66 |
| Hammond | 15 | 5 | 38 | 0 | 1 | 0 | 2 | 0 | 9th | 495 | 122 | – | – |
| White | | | | | 6·3 | 2 | 7 | 4 | 10th | 521 | – | – | – |

Umpires: D. Elder and G.A. Hele.

# AUSTRALIA v ENGLAND 1928–29 (2nd Test)

Played at Sydney Cricket Ground on 14, 15, 17, 18, 19, 20 December.
Toss: Australia.   Result: ENGLAND won by eight wickets.
Debuts: Australia – D.D.J. Blackie, O.E. Nothling.

England's total of 636 established a new Test record. All England's batsmen reached double figures for the second time in these matches (*also Test No. 43*). Hammond's 251 came in his second match against Australia, in 461 minutes, and included 30 fours. Ryder reached his fifty in 36 minutes to equal J.J. Lyon's record for the fastest Australia fifty against England set in *Test No. 33*. Following his unsuccessful debut at Brisbane, the selectors dropped Bradman for this match.

## AUSTRALIA

| | | | | | |
|---|---|---|---|---|---|
| W.M. Woodfull | lbw b Geary | 68 | | run out | 111 |
| V.Y. Richardson | b Larwood | 27 | | c Hendren b Tate | 0 |
| A.F. Kippax | b Geary | 9 | (4) | lbw b Tate | 10 |
| W.H. Ponsford | retired hurt | 5 | | absent hurt | – |
| H.S.T.L. Hendry | b Geary | 37 | (3) | lbw b Tate | 112 |
| J. Ryder* | lbw b Geary | 25 | (5) | c Chapman b Larwood | 79 |
| O.E. Nothling | b Larwood | 8 | (6) | run out | 44 |
| W.A.S. Oldfield† | not out | 41 | (7) | lbw b Tate | 0 |
| C.V. Grimmett | run out | 9 | (8) | c Chapman b Geary | 18 |
| D.D.J. Blackie | b Geary | 8 | (9) | not out | 11 |
| H. Ironmonger | c Duckworth b Larwood | 1 | (10) | b Geary | 0 |
| Extras | (B 4, LB 9, W 2) | 15 | | (B 5, LB 6, W 1) | 12 |
| **Total** | | **253** | | | **397** |

## ENGLAND

| | | | | | |
|---|---|---|---|---|---|
| J.B. Hobbs | c Oldfield b Grimmett | 40 | | | |
| H. Sutcliffe | c Hendry b Ironmonger | 11 | | | |
| W.R. Hammond | b Ironmonger | 251 | | | |
| D.R. Jardine | run out | 28 | | | |
| E.H. Hendren | c Richardson b Blackie | 74 | | | |
| A.P.F. Chapman* | c Ryder b Blackie | 20 | | | |
| H. Larwood | c Ryder b Grimmett | 43 | | | |
| G. Geary | lbw b Blackie | 66 | (1) | b Hendry | 8 |
| M.W. Tate | lbw b Blackie | 25 | (2) | c sub (D.G. Bradman) b Hendry | 4 |
| G. Duckworth† | not out | 39 | (3) | not out | 2 |
| J.C. White | st Oldfield b Hendry | 29 | (4) | not out | 2 |
| Extras | (B 2, LB 3, W 4, NB 1) | 10 | | | |
| **Total** | | **636** | | (2 wickets) | **16** |

| ENGLAND | O | M | R | W | O | M | R | W |
|---|---|---|---|---|---|---|---|---|
| Larwood | 26·2 | 4 | 77 | 3 | 35 | 5 | 105 | 1 |
| Tate | 21 | 9 | 29 | 0 | 46 | 14 | 99 | 4 |
| White | 38 | 10 | 79 | 0 | 30 | 5 | 83 | 0 |
| Geary | 18 | 5 | 35 | 5 | 31·4 | 11 | 55 | 2 |
| Hammond | 5 | 0 | 18 | 0 | 9 | 0 | 43 | 0 |
| AUSTRALIA | | | | | | | | |
| Nothling | 42 | 15 | 60 | 0 | 4 | 0 | 12 | 0 |
| Grimmett | 64 | 14 | 191 | 2 | | | | |
| Ironmonger | 68 | 21 | 142 | 2 | | | | |
| Blackie | 59 | 10 | 148 | 4 | | | | |
| Hendry | 23·1 | 4 | 52 | 1 | 3 | 2 | 4 | 2 |
| Ryder | 11 | 3 | 22 | 0 | | | | |
| Kippax | 5 | 3 | 11 | 0 | | | | |

### FALL OF WICKETS

| | A | E | A | E |
|---|---|---|---|---|
| Wkt | 1st | 1st | 2nd | 2nd |
| 1st | 51 | 37 | 0 | 8 |
| 2nd | 65 | 65 | 215 | 13 |
| 3rd | 152 | 148 | 234 | – |
| 4th | 153 | 293 | 246 | – |
| 5th | 171 | 341 | 347 | – |
| 6th | 192 | 432 | 348 | – |
| 7th | 222 | 496 | 370 | – |
| 8th | 251 | 523 | 397 | – |
| 9th | 253 | 592 | 397 | – |
| 10th | – | 636 | – | – |

Umpires: D. Elder and G.A. Hele.

## AUSTRALIA v ENGLAND 1928–29 (3rd Test)

Played at Melbourne Cricket Ground on 29, 31 December, 1, 2, 3, 4, 5 January.
Toss: Australia.   Result: ENGLAND won by three wickets.
Debuts: Australia – E.L. a'Beckett, R.K. Oxenham.

Hammond, whose innings of 200 lasted 398 minutes and included 17 fours, was the first to score double-centuries in consecutive Test innings. Bradman, playing in his second match, scored the first of his record 29 Test hundreds at the age of 20 years 129 days. Sutcliffe's fourth hundred in five successive Test innings at Melbourne was chanceless and began on one of the most spiteful rain-affected pitches experienced in these matches.

### AUSTRALIA

| | | | | |
|---|---|---|---|---|
| W.M. Woodfull | c Jardine b Tate | 7 | c Duckworth b Tate | 107 |
| V.Y. Richardson | c Duckworth b Larwood | 3 | b Larwood | 5 |
| H.S.T.L. Hendry | c Jardine b Larwood | 23 | st Duckworth b White | 12 |
| A.F. Kippax | c Jardine b Larwood | 100 | b Tate | 41 |
| J. Ryder* | c Hendren b Tate | 112 | b Geary | 5 |
| D.G. Bradman | b Hammond | 79 | c Duckworth b Geary | 112 |
| W.A.S. Oldfield† | b Geary | 3 | b White | 7 |
| E.L. a'Beckett | c Duckworth b White | 41 | b White | 6 |
| R.K. Oxenham | b Geary | 15 | b White | 39 |
| C.V. Grimmett | c Duckworth b Geary | 5 | not out | 4 |
| D.D.J. Blackie | not out | 2 | b White | 0 |
| Extras | (B 4, LB 3) | 7 | (B 6, LB 7) | 13 |
| **Total** | | **397** | | **351** |

### ENGLAND

| | | | | |
|---|---|---|---|---|
| J.B. Hobbs | c Oldfield b A'Beckett | 20 | lbw b Blackie | 49 |
| H. Sutcliffe | b Blackie | 58 | lbw b Grimmett | 135 |
| W.R. Hammond | c A'Beckett b Blackie | 200 | (4) run out | 32 |
| A.P.F. Chapman* | b Blackie | 24 | (6) c Woodfull b Ryder | 5 |
| E.H. Hendren | c A'Beckett b Hendry | 19 | b Oxenham | 45 |
| D.R. Jardine | c and b Blackie | 62 | (3) b Grimmett | 33 |
| H. Larwood | c and b Blackie | 0 | | |
| G. Geary | lbw b Grimmett | 1 | not out | 4 |
| M.W. Tate | c Kippax b Grimmett | 21 | (7) run out | 0 |
| G. Duckworth† | b Blackie | 3 | (9) not out | 0 |
| J.C. White | not out | 8 | | |
| Extras | (B 1) | 1 | (B 15, LB 14) | 29 |
| **Total** | | **417** | (7 wickets) | **332** |

| ENGLAND | O | M | R | W | O | M | R | W | | FALL OF WICKETS | | | |
|---|---|---|---|---|---|---|---|---|---|---|---|---|---|
| | | | | | | | | | | A | E | A | E |
| Larwood | 37 | 3 | 127 | 3 | 16 | 3 | 37 | 1 | *Wkt* | *1st* | *1st* | *2nd* | *2nd* |
| Tate | 46 | 17 | 87 | 2 | 47 | 15 | 70 | 2 | 1st | 5 | 28 | 7 | 105 |
| Geary | 31·5 | 4 | 83 | 3 | 30 | 4 | 94 | 2 | 2nd | 15 | 161 | 60 | 199 |
| Hammond | 8 | 4 | 19 | 1 | 16 | 6 | 30 | 0 | 3rd | 57 | 201 | 138 | 257 |
| White | 57 | 30 | 64 | 1 | 56·5 | 20 | 107 | 5 | 4th | 218 | 238 | 143 | 318 |
| Jardine | 1 | 0 | 10 | 0 | | | | | 5th | 282 | 364 | 201 | 326 |
| | | | | | | | | | 6th | 287 | 364 | 226 | 328 |
| AUSTRALIA | | | | | | | | | 7th | 373 | 381 | 252 | 328 |
| A'Beckett | 37 | 7 | 92 | 1 | 22 | 5 | 39 | 0 | 8th | 383 | 385 | 345 | – |
| Hendry | 20 | 8 | 35 | 1 | 23 | 5 | 33 | 0 | 9th | 394 | 391 | 351 | – |
| Grimmett | 55 | 14 | 114 | 2 | 42 | 12 | 96 | 2 | 10th | 397 | 417 | 351 | – |
| Oxenham | 35 | 11 | 67 | 0 | 28 | 10 | 44 | 1 | | | | | |
| Blackie | 44 | 13 | 94 | 6 | 39 | 11 | 75 | 1 | | | | | |
| Ryder | 4 | 0 | 14 | 0 | 5·5 | 1 | 16 | 1 | | | | | |

Umpires: D. Elder and G.A. Hele.

# AUSTRALIA v ENGLAND 1928–29 (4th Test)

Played at Adelaide Oval on 1, 2, 4, 5, 6, 7, 8 February.
Toss: England.   Result: ENGLAND won by 12 runs.
Debuts: Australia – A. Jackson (not A.A.).

At 19 years 152 days of age, Jackson, playing his first Test match, became the youngest player to score a century in Tests between England and Australia. Hammond was the fourth batsman to score a hundred in each innings of a Test and the second after H. Sutcliffe (1924-25) to score four centuries in a rubber. His aggregate of 779 runs in five innings remains the record for England v Australia and included four centuries, two of them double-hundreds.

## ENGLAND

| | | | | |
|---|---|---|---|---|
| J.B. Hobbs | c Ryder b Hendry | 74 | c Oldfield b Hendry | 1 |
| H. Sutcliffe | st Oldfield b Grimmett | 64 | c Oldfield b A'Beckett | 17 |
| W.R. Hammond | not out | 119 | c and b Ryder | 177 |
| D.R. Jardine | lbw b Grimmett | 1 | c Woodfull b Oxenham | 98 |
| E.H. Hendren | b Blackie | 13 | c Bradman b Blackie | 11 |
| A.P.F. Chapman* | c A'Beckett b Ryder | 39 | c Woodfull b Blackie | 0 |
| G. Duckworth† | c Ryder b Grimmett | 5 | (11) lbw b Oxenham | 1 |
| H. Larwood | b Hendry | 3 | (7) lbw b Oxenham | 5 |
| G. Geary | run out | 3 | (8) c and b Grimmett | 6 |
| M.W. Tate | b Grimmett | 2 | (9) lbw b Oxenham | 47 |
| J.C. White | c Ryder b Grimmett | 0 | (10) not out | 4 |
| Extras | (B 3, LB 7, W 1) | 11 | (B 6, LB 10) | 16 |
| **Total** | | **334** | | **383** |

## AUSTRALIA

| | | | | |
|---|---|---|---|---|
| W.M. Woodfull | c Duckworth b Tate | 1 | c Geary b White | 30 |
| A. Jackson | lbw b White | 164 | c Duckworth b Geary | 36 |
| H.S.T.L. Hendry | c Duckworth b Larwood | 2 | c Tate b White | 5 |
| A.F. Kippax | b White | 3 | c Hendren b White | 51 |
| J. Ryder* | lbw b White | 63 | c and b White | 87 |
| D.G. Bradman | c Larwood b Tate | 40 | run out | 58 |
| E.L. a'Beckett | hit wkt b White | 36 | c Hammond b White | 21 |
| R.K. Oxenham | c Chapman b White | 15 | c Chapman b White | 12 |
| W.A.S. Oldfield† | b Tate | 32 | not out | 15 |
| C.V. Grimmett | b Tate | 4 | c Tate b White | 9 |
| D.D.J. Blackie | not out | 3 | c Larwood b White | 0 |
| Extras | (LB 5, W 1) | 6 | (B 9, LB 3) | 12 |
| **Total** | | **369** | | **336** |

| AUSTRALIA | O | M | R | W | O | M | R | W |
|---|---|---|---|---|---|---|---|---|
| A'Beckett | 31 | 8 | 44 | 0 | 27 | 9 | 41 | 1 |
| Hendry | 31 | 14 | 49 | 2 | 28 | 11 | 56 | 1 |
| Grimmett | 52·1 | 12 | 102 | 5 | 52 | 15 | 117 | 1 |
| Oxenham | 35 | 14 | 51 | 0 | 47·4 | 21 | 67 | 4 |
| Blackie | 29 | 6 | 57 | 1 | 39 | 11 | 70 | 2 |
| Ryder | 5 | 1 | 20 | 1 | 5 | 1 | 13 | 1 |
| Kippax | | | | | 2 | 0 | 3 | 0 |
| ENGLAND | | | | | | | | |
| Larwood | 37 | 6 | 92 | 1 | 20 | 4 | 60 | 0 |
| Tate | 42 | 10 | 77 | 4 | 37 | 9 | 75 | 0 |
| White | 60 | 16 | 130 | 5 | 64·5 | 21 | 126 | 8 |
| Geary | 12 | 3 | 32 | 0 | 16 | 2 | 42 | 1 |
| Hammond | 9 | 1 | 32 | 0 | 14 | 3 | 21 | 0 |

FALL OF WICKETS

| | E | A | E | A |
|---|---|---|---|---|
| Wkt | 1st | 1st | 2nd | 2nd |
| 1st | 143 | 1 | 1 | 65 |
| 2nd | 143 | 6 | 21 | 71 |
| 3rd | 149 | 19 | 283 | 74 |
| 4th | 179 | 145 | 296 | 211 |
| 5th | 246 | 227 | 297 | 224 |
| 6th | 263 | 287 | 302 | 258 |
| 7th | 270 | 323 | 327 | 308 |
| 8th | 308 | 336 | 337 | 320 |
| 9th | 312 | 365 | 381 | 336 |
| 10th | 334 | 369 | 383 | 336 |

Umpires: D. Elder and G.A. Hele.

# AUSTRALIA v ENGLAND 1928–29 (5th Test)

Played at Melbourne Cricket Ground on 8, 9, 11, 12, 13, 14, 15, 16 March.
Toss: England.   Result: AUSTRALIA won by five wickets.
Debuts: Australia – A.G. Fairfax, P.M. Hornibrook, T.W. Wall.

This was the first Test to be played on eight days. At the age of 46 years 83 days, Hobbs became the oldes batsman to score a century in a Test between England and Australia. It was his twelfth hundred against Australia and this remains the record for England. Five of his centuries were scored in his aggregate of 1,178 runs a Melbourne.

## ENGLAND

| Batsman | Dismissal | Runs | 2nd innings | Runs |
|---|---|---|---|---|
| J.B. Hobbs | lbw b Ryder | 142 | c Fairfax b Grimmett | 6? |
| D.R. Jardine | c Oldfield b Wall | 19 | c Oldfield b Wall | |
| W.R. Hammond | c Fairfax b Wall | 38 | (4) c Ryder b Fairfax | 1? |
| E. Tyldesley | c Hornibrook b Ryder | 31 | (5) c Oldfield b Wall | 2? |
| G. Duckworth† | c Fairfax b Hornibrook | 12 | (11) lbw b Oxenham | |
| E.H. Hendren | c Hornibrook b Fairfax | 95 | b Grimmett | |
| M. Leyland | c Fairfax b Oxenham | 137 | not out | 5? |
| H. Larwood | b Wall | 4 | (3) b Wall | 1? |
| G. Geary | b Hornibrook | 4 | (9) b Wall | |
| M.W. Tate | c sub (E.L. a'Beckett) b Hornibrook | 15 | (8) c Fairfax b Hornibrook | 5 |
| J.C. White* | not out | 9 | (10) c Oxenham b Wall | |
| Extras | (B 4, LB 6, W 1, NB 2) | 13 | (B 19, LB 1) | 2? |
| **Total** | | **519** | | **25?** |

## AUSTRALIA

| Batsman | Dismissal | Runs | 2nd innings | Runs |
|---|---|---|---|---|
| W.M. Woodfull | c Geary b Larwood | 102 | (3) b Hammond | 3? |
| A. Jackson | run out | 30 | (4) b Geary | 4? |
| A.F. Kippax | c Duckworth b White | 38 | (5) run out | 2? |
| J. Ryder* | c Tate b Hammond | 30 | (6) not out | 5? |
| D.G. Bradman | c Tate b Geary | 123 | (7) not out | 3 |
| A.G. Fairfax | lbw b Geary | 65 | | |
| R.K. Oxenham | c Duckworth b Geary | 7 | | |
| W.A.S. Oldfield† | c and b Gary | 6 | (1) b Hammond | 4? |
| C.V. Grimmett | not out | 38 | | |
| T.W. Wall | c Duckworth b Geary | 9 | | |
| P.M. Hornibrook | lbw b White | 26 | (2) b Hammond | 1? |
| Extras | (B 6, LB 9, W 2) | 17 | (B 12, LB 6) | 1? |
| **Total** | | **491** | (5 wickets) | **28?** |

| AUSTRALIA | O | M | R | W | O | M | R | W |
|---|---|---|---|---|---|---|---|---|
| Wall | 49 | 8 | 123 | 3 | 26 | 5 | 66 | 5 |
| Hornibrook | 48 | 8 | 142 | 3 | 19 | 5 | 51 | 1 |
| Oxenham | 45·1 | 15 | 86 | 1 | 10·1 | 1 | 34 | 1 |
| Grimmett | 25 | 11 | 40 | 0 | 24 | 7 | 66 | 2 |
| Fairfax | 27 | 4 | 84 | 1 | 7 | 0 | 20 | 1 |
| Ryder | 18 | 5 | 29 | 2 | | | | |
| Kippax | 3 | 1 | 2 | 0 | | | | |
| ENGLAND | | | | | | | | |
| Larwood | 34 | 7 | 83 | 1 | 32·1 | 5 | 81 | 0 |
| Tate | 62 | 26 | 108 | 0 | 38 | 13 | 76 | 0 |
| Geary | 81 | 36 | 105 | 5 | 20 | 5 | 31 | 1 |
| White | 75·3 | 22 | 136 | 2 | 18 | 8 | 28 | 0 |
| Hammond | 16 | 3 | 31 | 1 | 26 | 8 | 53 | 3 |
| Leyland | 3 | 0 | 11 | 0 | | | | |

### FALL OF WICKETS

| Wkt | E 1st | A 1st | E 2nd | A 2nd |
|---|---|---|---|---|
| 1st | 64 | 54 | 1 | 5? |
| 2nd | 146 | 143 | 19 | 8? |
| 3rd | 235 | 203 | 75 | 129 |
| 4th | 240 | 203 | 119 | 158 |
| 5th | 261 | 386 | 123 | 204 |
| 6th | 401 | 399 | 131 | – |
| 7th | 409 | 409 | 212 | – |
| 8th | 428 | 420 | 217 | – |
| 9th | 470 | 432 | 231 | – |
| 10th | 519 | 491 | 257 | – |

Umpires: G.A. Hele and A.C. Jones.

# ENGLAND v SOUTH AFRICA 1929 (1st Test)

Played at Edgbaston, Birmingham, on 15, 17, 18 June.
Toss: England.   Result: MATCH DRAWN.
Debuts: England – K.S. Duleepsinhji, E.T. Killick; South Africa – J.A.J. Christy, B. Mitchell,
H.G. Owen-Smith, N.A. Quinn.

Mitchell shared in opening partnerships of 119 and 171 in his first Test but took 575 minutes to score his 149 runs
in the match.

## ENGLAND

| | | | | | |
|---|---|---|---|---|---|
| H. Sutcliffe | c Cameron b Ochse | 26 | b Morkel | | 114 |
| E.T. Killick | c Morkel b Ochse | 31 | b Quinn | | 23 |
| W.R. Hammond | b Quinn | 18 | not out | | 138 |
| K.S. Duleepsinhji | c Vincent b Morkel | 12 | (5) lbw b Ochse | | 1 |
| E.H. Hendren | b Morkel | 70 | (6) not out | | 8 |
| M. Leyland | c Taylor b Ochse | 3 | | | |
| P.G.H. Fender | c Cameron b Quinn | 6 | (4) c Vincent b Ochse | | 12 |
| M.W. Tate | c Mitchell b Morkel | 40 | | | |
| H. Larwood | lbw b Ochse | 6 | | | |
| J.C. White* | run out | 5 | | | |
| G. Duckworth† | not out | 11 | | | |
| Extras | (B 9, LB 3, W 4, NB 1) | 17 | (LB 10, W 2) | | 12 |
| **Total** | | **245** | (4 wickets declared) | | **308** |

## SOUTH AFRICA

| | | | | | |
|---|---|---|---|---|---|
| R.H. Catterall | lbw b Fender | 67 | c White b Fender | | 98 |
| B. Mitchell | b Tate | 88 | not out | | 61 |
| J.A.J. Christy | b Larwood | 1 | | | |
| H.W. Taylor | b Larwood | 2 | | | |
| D.P.B. Morkel | b Tate | 5 | | | |
| H.G. Deane* | c and b Fender | 29 | | | |
| H.B. Cameron† | b Larwood | 5 | | | |
| H.G. Owen-Smith | b Tate | 25 | | | |
| C.L. Vincent | not out | 14 | | | |
| N.A. Quinn | b Larwood | 1 | | | |
| A.L. Ochse | b Larwood | 2 | | | |
| Extras | (B 6, LB 2, W 1, NB 2) | 11 | (B 9, NB 3) | | 12 |
| **Total** | | **250** | (1 wicket) | | **171** |

| SOUTH AFRICA | O | M | R | W | O | M | R | W |
|---|---|---|---|---|---|---|---|---|
| Morkel | 20 | 4 | 40 | 3 | 22 | 6 | 54 | 1 |
| Quinn | 27 | 8 | 62 | 2 | 20 | 2 | 55 | 1 |
| Ochse | 25·1 | 2 | 79 | 4 | 28 | 2 | 88 | 2 |
| Vincent | 7 | 0 | 37 | 0 | 19 | 3 | 55 | 0 |
| Mitchell | 2 | 0 | 10 | 0 | | | | |
| Owen-Smith | | | | | 6 | 0 | 29 | 0 |
| Christy | | | | | 5 | 1 | 15 | 0 |
| ENGLAND | | | | | | | | |
| Larwood | 42·4 | 17 | 57 | 5 | 11 | 6 | 12 | 0 |
| Tate | 44 | 14 | 65 | 3 | 16 | 4 | 43 | 0 |
| Fender | 32 | 10 | 64 | 2 | 15·4 | 3 | 55 | 1 |
| Hammond | 22 | 12 | 25 | 0 | 3 | 0 | 19 | 0 |
| White | 32 | 19 | 28 | 0 | 13 | 5 | 23 | 0 |
| Duleepsinhji | | | | | 1 | 0 | 7 | 0 |

FALL OF WICKETS

| Wkt | E 1st | SA 1st | E 2nd | SA 2nd |
|---|---|---|---|---|
| 1st | 59 | 119 | 34 | 171 |
| 2nd | 66 | 120 | 255 | – |
| 3rd | 92 | 122 | 278 | – |
| 4th | 96 | 130 | 280 | – |
| 5th | 111 | 174 | – | – |
| 6th | 128 | 182 | – | – |
| 7th | 215 | 224 | – | – |
| 8th | 215 | 239 | – | – |
| 9th | 222 | 248 | – | – |
| 10th | 245 | 250 | – | – |

Umpires: T.W. Oates and J. Hardstaff, sr.

# ENGLAND v SOUTH AFRICA 1929 (2nd Test)

Played at Lord's, London, on 29 June, 1, 2 July.
Toss: England.   Result: MATCH DRAWN.
Debuts: England – J. O'Connor, R.W.V. Robins; South Africa – A.J. Bell, E.L. Dalton, Q. McMillan.

Bad light ended this match at 5.45 pm on the third day when an England victory appeared highly probable.

### ENGLAND

| | | | | | |
|---|---|---|---|---|---|
| H. Sutcliffe | c Mitchell b Bell | 100 | | c Catterall b Morkel | 10 |
| E.T. Killick | b Morkel | 3 | | c Morkel b Christy | 24 |
| W.R. Hammond | c Christy b Morkel | 8 | (5) | b Morkel | 5 |
| J. O'Connor | b Morkel | 0 | (6) | c Cameron b Ochse | 11 |
| E.H. Hendren | b Morkel | 43 | (4) | b Morkel | 11 |
| M. Leyland | b Bell | 73 | (3) | c Cameron b Ochse | 102 |
| M.W. Tate | c Cameron b Bell | 15 | | not out | 100 |
| R.W.V. Robins | c Mitchell b Bell | 4 | | c Mitchell b Ochse | 0 |
| H. Larwood | b Bell | 35 | | b Ochse | 9 |
| J.C. White* | b Bell | 8 | | not out | 18 |
| G. Duckworth† | not out | 8 | | | |
| Extras | (LB 4, W 1) | 5 | | (B 11, LB 6, W 2, NB 3) | 22 |
| **Total** | | **302** | | (8 wickets declared) | **312** |

### SOUTH AFRICA

| | | | | | |
|---|---|---|---|---|---|
| R.H. Catterall | b Larwood | 0 | | b Tate | 3 |
| B. Mitchell | st Duckworth b Hammond | 29 | | c Hendren b Robins | 22 |
| J.A.J. Christy | run out | 70 | | c Hendren b Robins | 41 |
| D.P.B. Morkel | lbw b Tate | 88 | | not out | .7 |
| H.G. Deane* | b Tate | 1 | (6) | st Duckworth b Robins | 2 |
| H.B. Cameron† | c Leyland b Robins | 32 | (7) | retired hurt | 0 |
| H.G. Owen-Smith | not out | 52 | (8) | not out | 1 |
| E.L. Dalton | b Tate | 6 | (5) | c Killick b Larwood | 1 |
| Q. McMillan | c Killick b White | 17 | | | |
| A.L. Ochse | c Duckworth b White | 1 | | | |
| A.J. Bell | b Robins | 13 | | | |
| Extras | (B 9, LB 4) | 13 | | (B 2, LB 1) | 3 |
| **Total** | | **322** | | (5 wickets) | **90** |

| SOUTH AFRICA | O | M | R | W | O | M | R | W | | | | | |
|---|---|---|---|---|---|---|---|---|---|---|---|---|---|
| Ochse | 24 | 5 | 51 | 0 | 20 | 0 | 99 | 4 | | FALL OF WICKETS | | | |
| Morkel | 31 | 6 | 93 | 4 | 24 | 6 | 63 | 3 | | E | SA | | SA |
| Bell | 30·4 | 7 | 99 | 6 | 18·2 | 2 | 60 | 0 | *Wkt* | *1st* | *1st* | *2nd* | *2nd* |
| Christy | 6 | 2 | 20 | 0 | 3 | 0 | 15 | 1 | 1st | 8 | 0 | 28 | 9 |
| McMillan | 7 | 0 | 31 | 0 | 13 | 0 | 34 | 0 | 2nd | 18 | 82 | 46 | 60 |
| Owen-Smith | 1 | 0 | 3 | 0 | | | | | 3rd | 18 | 125 | 83 | 77 |
| Mitchell | | | | | 4 | 0 | 19 | 0 | 4th | 111 | 126 | 93 | 82 |
| | | | | | | | | | 5th | 199 | 189 | 117 | 85 |
| ENGLAND | | | | | | | | | 6th | 243 | 237 | 246 | – |
| Larwood | 20 | 4 | 65 | 1 | 12 | 3 | 17 | 1 | 7th | 249 | 253 | 250 | – |
| Tate | 39 | 9 | 108 | 3 | 11 | 3 | 27 | 1 | 8th | 252 | 272 | 260 | – |
| Hammond | 8 | 3 | 19 | 1 | | | | | 9th | 287 | 279 | – | – |
| White | 35 | 12 | 61 | 2 | 9 | 3 | 11 | 0 | 10th | 302 | 322 | – | – |
| Robins | 24 | 5 | 47 | 2 | 19 | 4 | 32 | 3 | | | | | |
| Leyland | 5 | 2 | 9 | 0 | | | | | | | | | |

Umpires: W. Bestwick and F. Chester.

# ENGLAND v SOUTH AFRICA 1929 (3rd Test)

Played at Headingley, Leeds, on 13, 15, 16 July.
Toss: South Africa.   Result: ENGLAND won by five wickets.
Debuts: England – E.H. Bowley; South Africa – E.A. van der Merwe.

Woolley and Tate scored 76 in 45 minutes to take England to victory. The partnership of 103 in 65 minutes between Owen-Smith and Bell remains South Africa's record for the tenth wicket in all Tests.

## SOUTH AFRICA

| | | | | |
|---|---|---|---|---|
| R.H. Catterall | b Freeman | 74 | b Tate | 10 |
| I.J. Siedle | b Larwood | 0 | c White b Freeman | 14 |
| B. Mitchell | b Tate | 22 | lbw b White | 24 |
| D.P.B. Morkel | st Duckworth b Freeman | 17 | lbw b Freeman | 14 |
| J.P. Duminy | b Freeman | 2 | b Woolley | 12 |
| H.G. Deane* | c Duckworth b Tate | 20 | b White | 4 |
| H.G. Owen-Smith | c Hammond b Freeman | 6 | c Sutcliffe b Woolley | 129 |
| C.L. Vincent | b Freeman | 60 | b Woolley | 0 |
| N.A. Quinn | c Leyland b Freeman | 5 | st Duckworth b White | 28 |
| E.A. van der Merwe† | c Hammond b Freeman | 19 | c Duckworth b Freeman | 1 |
| A.J. Bell | not out | 2 | not out | 26 |
| Extras | (LB 9) | 9 | (B 6, LB 6, NB 1) | 13 |
| **Total** | | **236** | | **275** |

## ENGLAND

| | | | | |
|---|---|---|---|---|
| H. Sutcliffe | c Mitchell b Quinn | 37 | c Owen-Smith b Morkel | 4 |
| E.H. Bowley | c Bell b Quinn | 31 | c Mitchell b Vincent | 46 |
| W.R. Hammond | c Van der Merwe b Quinn | 65 | c and b Morkel | 0 |
| G. Duckworth† | b Bell | 21 | | |
| F.E. Woolley | b Vincent | 83 | (4) not out | 95 |
| E.H. Hendren | c Van der Merwe b Quinn | 0 | (5) c Owen-Smith b Vincent | 5 |
| M. Leyland | c Duminy b Quinn | 45 | (6) b Vincent | 0 |
| M.W. Tate | c Owen-Smith b Vincent | 3 | (7) not out | 24 |
| J.C. White* | not out | 20 | | |
| H. Larwood | c Deane b Mitchell | 0 | | |
| A.P. Freeman | b Quinn | 15 | | |
| Extras | (B 2, LB 4, NB 2) | 8 | (B 8, LB 4) | 12 |
| **Total** | | **328** | (5 wickets) | **186** |

| ENGLAND | O | M | R | W | O | M | R | W | FALL OF WICKETS | | | |
|---|---|---|---|---|---|---|---|---|---|---|---|---|
| | | | | | | | | | | SA | E | SA | E |
| Larwood | 17 | 4 | 35 | 1 | | | | | | | | |
| Tate | 26 | 8 | 40 | 2 | 26 | 5 | 50 | 1 | *Wkt* | *1st* | *1st* | *2nd* | *2nd* |
| Freeman | 32·3 | 6 | 115 | 7 | 35 | 7 | 92 | 3 | 1st | 1 | 42 | 15 | 13 |
| Hammond | 8 | 2 | 13 | 0 | 7 | 0 | 19 | 0 | 2nd | 75 | 94 | 25 | 13 |
| White | 17 | 6 | 24 | 0 | 23 | 7 | 40 | 3 | 3rd | 120 | 149 | 66 | 98 |
| Bowley | | | | | 4 | 1 | 7 | 0 | 4th | 124 | 170 | 66 | 110 |
| Woolley | | | | | 13·1 | 3 | 35 | 3 | 5th | 125 | 170 | 73 | 110 |
| Leyland | | | | | 3 | 0 | 19 | 0 | 6th | 143 | 276 | 116 | – |
| | | | | | | | | | 7th | 151 | 285 | 116 | – |
| SOUTH AFRICA | | | | | | | | | 8th | 170 | 295 | 167 | – |
| Morkel | 19 | 5 | 41 | 0 | 14 | 1 | 43 | 2 | 9th | 219 | 300 | 172 | – |
| Bell | 14 | 0 | 58 | 1 | 2 | 0 | 12 | 0 | 10th | 236 | 328 | 275 | – |
| Quinn | 29·5 | 5 | 92 | 6 | 17 | 2 | 46 | 0 | | | | | |
| Vincent | 30 | 5 | 76 | 2 | 19 | 0 | 67 | 3 | | | | | |
| Owen-Smith | 2 | 0 | 8 | 0 | | | | | | | | | |
| Mitchell | 13 | 1 | 45 | 1 | 0·4 | 0 | 6 | 0 | | | | | |

Umpires: L.C. Braund and W.R. Parry.

# ENGLAND v SOUTH AFRICA 1929 (4th Test)

Played at Old Trafford, Manchester, on 27, 29, 30 July.
Toss: England.   Result: ENGLAND won by an innings and 32 runs.
Debuts: England – F. Barratt.

## ENGLAND

| | | |
|---|---|---|
| H. Sutcliffe | b Morkel | 9 |
| E.H. Bowley | b Bell | 13 |
| R.E.S. Wyatt | c Cameron b Vincent | 113 |
| F.E. Woolley | c and b Vincent | 154 |
| E.H. Hendren | b Quinn | 12 |
| M. Leyland | c Cameron b Mitchell | 55 |
| A.W. Carr* | c Bell b Quinn | 10 |
| G. Geary | not out | 31 |
| F. Barratt | not out | 2 |
| A.P. Freeman | } did not bat | |
| G. Duckworth† | } | |
| Extras | (B 16, LB 10, NB 2) | 28 |
| **Total** | (7 wickets declared) | **427** |

## SOUTH AFRICA

| | | | | | |
|---|---|---|---|---|---|
| I.J. Siedle | lbw b Freeman | 6 | | b Barratt | 1 |
| R.H. Catterall | c Sutcliffe b Barratt | 3 | | b Geary | 1 |
| B. Mitchell | c Geary b Freeman | 1 | | b Geary | 2 |
| H.W. Taylor | b Freeman | 28 | | c Leyland b Freeman | 70 |
| H.G. Deane* | st Duckworth b Freeman | 0 | (9) | c Duckworth b Wyatt | 29 |
| H.B. Cameron† | c Bowley b Freeman | 13 | (7) | c Woolley b Freeman | 83 |
| D.P.B. Morkel | lbw b Geary | 63 | (6) | st Duckworth b Woolley | 36 |
| H.G. Owen-Smith | c Barratt b Freeman | 6 | | st Duckworth b Freeman | 7 |
| C.L. Vincent | c Geary b Freeman | 6 | (10) | c Duckworth b Freeman | 4 |
| N.A. Quinn | not out | 1 | (5) | b Freeman | 11 |
| A.J. Bell | c Duckworth b Geary | 0 | | not out | 0 |
| Extras | (LB 2, NB 1) | 3 | | (B 13, LB 3, NB 5) | 21 |
| **Total** | | **130** | | | **265** |

| SOUTH AFRICA | O | M | R | W | O | M | R | W |
|---|---|---|---|---|---|---|---|---|
| Morkel | 18 | 5 | 61 | 1 | | | | |
| Quinn | 31 | 3 | 95 | 2 | | | | |
| Bell | 32 | 3 | 113 | 1 | | | | |
| Vincent | 34 | 4 | 93 | 2 | | | | |
| Owen-Smith | 5 | 0 | 16 | 0 | | | | |
| Mitchell | 8 | 3 | 21 | 1 | | | | |
| **ENGLAND** | | | | | | | | |
| Barratt | 10 | 4 | 8 | 1 | 20 | 7 | 30 | 1 |
| Geary | 22·3 | 13 | 18 | 2 | 37 | 18 | 50 | 2 |
| Freeman | 32 | 12 | 71 | 7 | 39·4 | 13 | 100 | 5 |
| Woolley | 9 | 3 | 22 | 0 | 18 | 5 | 51 | 1 |
| Wyatt | 2 | 1 | 8 | 0 | 4 | 0 | 13 | 1 |

FALL OF WICKETS

| Wkt | E 1st | SA 1st | SA 2nd |
|---|---|---|---|
| 1st | 30 | 4 | 1 |
| 2nd | 36 | 7 | 3 |
| 3rd | 281 | 34 | 13 |
| 4th | 304 | 34 | 66 |
| 5th | 342 | 39 | 113 |
| 6th | 365 | 65 | 145 |
| 7th | 424 | 84 | 180 |
| 8th | – | 98 | 245 |
| 9th | – | 130 | 256 |
| 10th | – | 130 | 265 |

Umpires: J. Hardstaff, sr and W.R. Parry.

# ENGLAND v SOUTH AFRICA 1929 (5th Test)

Played at Kennington Oval, London, on 17, 19, 20 August.
Toss: South Africa.   Result: MATCH DRAWN.
Debuts: England – L.E.G. Ames, E.W. Clark.

Sutcliffe became the first batsman to twice score a hundred in each innings of a Test match (also *Test No. 159*).

## ENGLAND

| | | | | | |
|---|---|---|---|---|---|
| J.B. Hobbs | c Quinn b McMillan | 10 | c Mitchell b Vincent | | 52 |
| H. Sutcliffe | c Owen-Smith b Vincent | 104 | not out | | 109 |
| W.R. Hammond | st Cameron b Vincent | 17 | not out | | 101 |
| F.E. Woolley | hit wkt b Vincent | 46 | | | |
| R.E.S. Wyatt | c Deane b Vincent | 6 | | | |
| M. Leyland | b Vincent | 16 | | | |
| A.W. Carr* | c Morkel b McMillan | 15 | | | |
| L.E.G. Ames† | c Mitchell b McMillan | 0 | | | |
| G. Geary | not out | 12 | | | |
| A.P. Freeman | c Cameron b Quinn | 15 | | | |
| E.W. Clark | b Quinn | 7 | | | |
| Extras | (B 9, NB 1) | 10 | (B 1, LB 1) | | 2 |
| **Total** | | **258** | (1 wicket) | | **264** |

## SOUTH AFRICA

| | | |
|---|---|---|
| R.H. Catterall | c Carr b Clark | 0 |
| I.J. Siedle | b Geary | 14 |
| B. Mitchell | b Geary | 2 |
| H.W. Taylor | c Ames b Clark | 121 |
| H.G. Deane* | c Woolley b Wyatt | 93 |
| H.B. Cameron† | c Freeman b Geary | 62 |
| D.P.B. Morkel | c Ames b Clark | 81 |
| H.G. Owen-Smith | b Woolley | 26 |
| Q. McMillan | not out | 50 |
| C.L. Vincent | not out | 24 |
| N.A. Quinn | did not bat | |
| Extras | (B 4, LB 12, W 2, NB 1) | 19 |
| **Total** | (8 wickets declared) | **492** |

| SOUTH AFRICA | O | M | R | W | O | M | R | W |
|---|---|---|---|---|---|---|---|---|
| Morkel | 9 | 2 | 20 | 0 | 16 | 6 | 43 | 0 |
| Quinn | 15·3 | 4 | 30 | 2 | 24 | 3 | 61 | 0 |
| Vincent | 45 | 10 | 105 | 5 | 15 | 3 | 42 | 1 |
| McMillan | 28 | 7 | 78 | 3 | 10 | 1 | 39 | 0 |
| Owen-Smith | 4 | 0 | 15 | 0 | 8 | 0 | 42 | 0 |
| Mitchell | | | | | 4 | 0 | 17 | 0 |
| Catterall | | | | | 3 | 0 | 18 | 0 |

| ENGLAND | O | M | R | W |
|---|---|---|---|---|
| Clark | 36 | 8 | 79 | 3 |
| Geary | 49 | 15 | 121 | 3 |
| Freeman | 49 | 9 | 169 | 0 |
| Woolley | 13 | 4 | 25 | 1 |
| Leyland | 9 | 4 | 25 | 0 |
| Wyatt | 16 | 4 | 54 | 1 |

## FALL OF WICKETS

| | E | SA | E |
|---|---|---|---|
| Wkt | 1st | 1st | 2nd |
| 1st | 38 | 0 | 77 |
| 2nd | 69 | 9 | – |
| 3rd | 140 | 20 | – |
| 4th | 166 | 234 | – |
| 5th | 194 | 246 | – |
| 6th | 217 | 326 | – |
| 7th | 221 | 397 | – |
| 8th | 222 | 439 | – |
| 9th | 239 | – | – |
| 10th | 258 | – | – |

Umpires: W. Bestwick and T.W. Oates.

# NEW ZEALAND v ENGLAND 1929-30 (1st Test)

Played at Lancaster Park, Christchurch, on 10, 11 (*no play*), 13 January.
Toss: New Zealand. Result: ENGLAND won by eight wickets.
Debuts: New Zealand – All; England – M.J.C. Allom, W.L. Cornford, A.H.H. Gilligan, M.S. Nichols, M.J.L. Turnbull, T.S. Worthington.

New Zealand's first Test match began just a day before another England team began a four-match rubber in the West Indies – the first and only occasion when one country has simultaneously played official Test matches in two different countries. Allom, playing in his first Test match, took four wickets in five balls, including the hat-trick.

## NEW ZEALAND

| | | | | | |
|---|---|---|---|---|---|
| C.S. Dempster | b Allom | 11 | c Duleepsinhji b Allom | | 25 |
| H. Foley | c Duleepsinhji b Nichols | 2 | c Nichols b Allom | | 2 |
| A.W. Roberts | c Duleepsinhji b Nichols | 3 | (6) c and b Worthington | | 5 |
| M.L. Page | c and b Nichols | 1 | st Cornford b Barratt | | 21 |
| R.C. Blunt | not out | 45 | (3) c Legge b Woolley | | 7 |
| T.C. Lowry* | lbw b Allom | 0 | (5) b Nichols | | 40 |
| K.C. James† | c Cornford b Allom | 0 | lbw b Worthington | | 0 |
| F.T. Badcock | b Allom | 0 | (9) b Nichols | | 0 |
| G.R. Dickinson | b Nichols | 11 | (8) c Barratt b Woolley | | 8 |
| W.E. Merritt | b Allom | 19 | b Allom | | 2 |
| M. Henderson | b Worthington | 6 | not out | | 2 |
| Extras | (B 7, LB 4, NB 3) | 14 | (B 9, LB 6, NB 4) | | 19 |
| **Total** | | **112** | | | **131** |

## ENGLAND

| | | | | | |
|---|---|---|---|---|---|
| E.W. Dawson | c Lowry b Henderson | 7 | lbw b Blunt | | 10 |
| A.H.H. Gilligan* | c Henderson b Badcock | 10 | b Blunt | | 4 |
| K.S. Duleepsinhji | c Dickinson b Henderson | 49 | not out | | 33 |
| F.E. Woolley | c Merritt b Dickinson | 31 | not out | | 17 |
| G.B. Legge | b Blunt | 36 | | | |
| M.S. Nichols | c Dickinson b Page | 21 | | | |
| T.S. Worthington | b Blunt | 0 | | | |
| M.J.L. Turnbull | c Merritt b Badcock | 7 | | | |
| F. Barratt | st James b Merritt | 4 | | | |
| W.L. Cornford† | c Lowry b Blunt | 6 | | | |
| M.J.C. Allom | not out | 4 | | | |
| Extras | (B 3, LB 1, NB 2) | 6 | (W 1, NB 1) | | 2 |
| **Total** | | **181** | (2 wickets) | | **66** |

| ENGLAND | O | M | R | W | O | M | R | W |
|---|---|---|---|---|---|---|---|---|
| Nichols | 17 | 5 | 28 | 4 | 14·3 | 6 | 23 | 2 |
| Allom | 19 | 4 | 38 | 5 | 15 | 6 | 17 | 3 |
| Barratt | 4 | 1 | 8 | 0 | 9 | 2 | 16 | 1 |
| Worthington | 7·1 | 1 | 24 | 1 | 13 | 4 | 19 | 2 |
| Woolley | | | | | 9 | 2 | 37 | 2 |

| NEW ZEALAND | O | M | R | W | O | M | R | W |
|---|---|---|---|---|---|---|---|---|
| Badcock | 18 | 7 | 29 | 2 | | | | |
| Dickinson | 11 | 1 | 40 | 1 | 2 | 0 | 4 | 0 |
| Merritt | 13 | 1 | 48 | 1 | 2 | 0 | 7 | 0 |
| Henderson | 8 | 1 | 38 | 2 | 7 | 2 | 26 | 0 |
| Blunt | 11·1 | 4 | 17 | 3 | 7 | 1 | 17 | 2 |
| Page | 2 | 1 | 3 | 1 | | | | |
| Dempster | | | | | 0·5 | 0 | 10 | 0 |

## FALL OF WICKETS

| | NZ | E | NZ | E |
|---|---|---|---|---|
| Wkt | 1st | 1st | 2nd | 2nd |
| 1st | 5 | 20 | 8 | 14 |
| 2nd | 11 | 20 | 28 | 17 |
| 3rd | 15 | 81 | 65 | – |
| 4th | 21 | 113 | 79 | – |
| 5th | 21 | 148 | 86 | – |
| 6th | 21 | 148 | 86 | – |
| 7th | 21 | 163 | 111 | – |
| 8th | 64 | 168 | 111 | – |
| 9th | 103 | 172 | 125 | – |
| 10th | 112 | 181 | 131 | – |

Umpires: W. Butler and K.H. Cave.

# NEW ZEALAND v ENGLAND 1929-30 (2nd Test)

Played at Basin Reserve, Wellington, on 24, 25, 27 January.
Toss: New Zealand.   Result: MATCH DRAWN.
Debuts: New Zealand – E.G. McLeod, J.E. Mills, G.L. Weir.

Mills was the first New Zealander to score a hundred in his first Test. His opening partnership of 276 with Dempster is still New Zealand's highest stand for any wicket against England; there has been only one higher partnership by a New Zealand pair, G.M. Turner and T.W. Jarvis scoring 387 for the first wicket against West Indies in 1971-72 (*Test No.696*).

## NEW ZEALAND

| | | | | | |
|---|---|--:|---|---|--:|
| C.S. Dempster | st Cornford b Woolley | 136 | not out | | 80 |
| J.E. Mills | b Woolley | 117 | b Nichols | | 7 |
| T.C. Lowry* | c Duleepsinhji b Woolley | 6 | | | |
| M.L. Page | c Cornford b Allom | 67 | c Bowley b Woolley | | 32 |
| R.C. Blunt | c Duleepsinhji b Woolley | 36 | b Worthington | | 12 |
| E.G. McLeod | b Woolley | 16 | not out | | 2 |
| G.L. Weir | lbw b Woolley | 3 | (3) c Duleepsinhji b Woolley | | 21 |
| K.C. James† | c Cornford b Worthington | 7 | | | |
| G.R. Dickinson | c Worthington b Woolley | 5 | | | |
| W.E. Merritt | lbw b Worthington | 0 | | | |
| F.T. Badcock | not out | 4 | | | |
| Extras | (B 17, LB 18, NB 8) | 43 | (B 1, LB 2, NB 7) | | 10 |
| **Total** | | **440** | (4 wickets declared) | | **164** |

## ENGLAND

| | | | | | |
|---|---|--:|---|---|--:|
| E.H. Bowley | b Blunt | 9 | c Weir b Dickinson | | 2 |
| E.W. Dawson | b Badcock | 44 | c Lowry b Badcock | | 7 |
| K.S. Duleepsinhji | c Blunt b Badcock | 40 | not out | | 56 |
| F.E. Woolley | c Lowry b Dickinson | 6 | b Merritt | | 23 |
| G.B. Legge | c James b Dickinson | 39 | c Lowry b Weir | | 9 |
| M.S. Nichols | not out | 78 | not out | | 3 |
| T.S. Worthington | st James b Merritt | 32 | | | |
| A.H.H. Gilligan* | b Merritt | 32 | | | |
| F. Barratt | b Badcock | 5 | | | |
| W.L. Cornford† | c Page b Badcock | 10 | | | |
| M.J.C. Allom | c Lowry b Dickinson | 2 | | | |
| Extras | (B 11, LB 4, NB 8) | 23 | (B 4, LB 2, NB 1) | | 7 |
| **Total** | | **320** | (4 wickets) | | **107** |

| ENGLAND | O | M | R | W | O | M | R | W |
|---|--:|--:|--:|--:|--:|--:|--:|--:|
| Nichols | 20 | 5 | 66 | 0 | 9 | 1 | 22 | 1 |
| Allom | 28 | 4 | 73 | 1 | 6 | 1 | 21 | 0 |
| Barratt | 33 | 4 | 87 | 0 | | | | |
| Worthington | 22 | 3 | 63 | 2 | 10 | 0 | 44 | 1 |
| Bowley | 5 | 0 | 32 | 0 | 5 | 0 | 19 | 0 |
| Woolley | 28·3 | 5 | 76 | 7 | 23 | 9 | 48 | 2 |
| NEW ZEALAND | | | | | | | | |
| Dickinson | 19·5 | 3 | 66 | 3 | 8 | 0 | 24 | 1 |
| Badcock | 36 | 6 | 80 | 4 | 17 | 8 | 22 | 1 |
| Blunt | 14 | 3 | 44 | 1 | 3 | 0 | 12 | 0 |
| Page | 2 | 0 | 8 | 0 | | | | |
| Merritt | 34 | 3 | 94 | 2 | 9 | 1 | 41 | 1 |
| McLeod | 2 | 0 | 5 | 0 | | | | |
| Weir | | | | | 2 | 1 | 1 | 1 |

FALL OF WICKETS

| Wkt | NZ 1st | E 1st | NZ 2nd | E 2nd |
|---|--:|--:|--:|--:|
| 1st | 276 | 20 | 23 | 8 |
| 2nd | 288 | 81 | 91 | 12 |
| 3rd | 295 | 91 | 135 | 58 |
| 4th | 385 | 135 | 155 | 98 |
| 5th | 407 | 149 | – | – |
| 6th | 410 | 219 | – | – |
| 7th | 425 | 288 | – | – |
| 8th | 431 | 293 | – | – |
| 9th | 431 | 303 | – | – |
| 10th | 440 | 320 | – | – |

Umpires: K.H. Cave and L.T. Cobcroft.

## NEW ZEALAND v ENGLAND 1929-30 (3rd Test)

Played at Eden Park, Auckland, on 14 (*no play*), 15 (*no play*), 17 February.
Toss: New Zealand.   Result: MATCH DRAWN.
Debuts: New Zealand – C.F.W. Allcott, H.M. McGirr.

Rain prevented play on the first two days and the M.C.C's itinerary was changed to accommodate an extra Test match at Auckland the following week-end.

### ENGLAND

| | | |
|---|---|---|
| E.H. Bowley | st James b Merritt | 109 |
| E.W. Dawson | b Merritt | 23 |
| K.S. Duleepsinhji | c and b Allcott | 117 |
| F.E. Woolley | run out | 59 |
| G.B. Legge | not out | 19 |
| M.S. Nichols | not out | 1 |
| A.H.H. Gilligan* | ) | |
| M.J.C. Allom | ) | |
| F. Barratt | ) did not bat | |
| T.S. Worthington | ) | |
| W.L. Cornford† | ) | |
| Extras | (LB 2) | 2 |
| **Total** | (4 wickets declared) | **330** |

### NEW ZEALAND

| | | |
|---|---|---|
| C.S. Dempster | not out | 62 |
| J.E. Mills | lbw b Barratt | 3 |
| G.L. Weir | not out | 27 |
| T.C. Lowry* | ) | |
| R.C. Blunt | ) | |
| M.L. Page | ) | |
| K.C. James† | ) did not bat | |
| C.F.W. Allcott | ) | |
| H.M. McGirr | ) | |
| F.T. Badcock | ) | |
| W.E. Merritt | ) | |
| Extras | (LB 3, NB 1) | 4 |
| **Total** | (1 wicket) | **96** |

| NEW ZEALAND | O | M | R | W |
|---|---|---|---|---|
| McGirr | 12 | 2 | 46 | 0 |
| Badcock | 11 | 2 | 22 | 0 |
| Merritt | 28 | 1 | 119 | 2 |
| Blunt | 6 | 2 | 16 | 0 |
| Page | 5 | 1 | 16 | 0 |
| Weir | 4 | 0 | 20 | 0 |
| Allcott | 22 | 2 | 89 | 1 |

| ENGLAND | O | M | R | W |
|---|---|---|---|---|
| Nichols | 5 | 0 | 18 | 0 |
| Allom | 6 | 4 | 3 | 0 |
| Barratt | 12 | 3 | 26 | 1 |
| Worthington | 6 | 1 | 11 | 0 |
| Legge | 5 | 0 | 34 | 0 |

### FALL OF WICKETS

| Wkt | E 1st | NZ 1st |
|---|---|---|
| 1st | 82 | 27 |
| 2nd | 193 | – |
| 3rd | 286 | – |
| 4th | 320 | – |
| 5th | – | – |
| 6th | – | – |
| 7th | – | – |
| 8th | – | – |
| 9th | – | – |
| 10th | – | – |

Umpires: K.H. Cave and L.T. Cobcroft.

# NEW ZEALAND v ENGLAND 1929-30 (4th Test)

Played at Eden Park, Auckland, on 21, 22, 24 February.
Toss: England.   Result: MATCH DRAWN.
Debuts: New Zealand – A.M. Matheson.

### ENGLAND

| | | | | |
|---|---|---|---|---|
| E.H. Bowley | run out | 42 | | |
| E.W. Dawson | c Allcott b Blunt | 55 | b Matheson | 6 |
| K.S. Duleepsinhji | b Allcott | 63 | | |
| F.E. Woolley | b Allcott | 10 | | |
| G.B. Legge | c Matheson b Weir | 196 | (4) b Blunt | 0 |
| M.S. Nichols | b McGirr | 75 | (3) not out | 7 |
| T.S. Worthington | b Merritt | 0 | | |
| A.H.H. Gilligan* | b Merritt | 25 | | |
| F. Barratt | c Mills b Blunt | 17 | | |
| W.L. Cornford† | c Matheson b Page | 18 | (1) b Matheson | 2 |
| M.J.C. Allom | not out | 8 | | |
| Extras | (B 19, LB 11, NB 1) | 31 | (B 6, LB 1) | 7 |
| **Total** | | **540** | (3 wickets) | **22** |

### NEW ZEALAND

| | | |
|---|---|---|
| C.S. Dempster | c Cornford b Allom | 27 |
| J.E. Mills | c Duleepsinhji b Allom | 12 |
| G.L. Weir | b Barratt | 63 |
| M.L. Page | c Cornford b Woolley | 25 |
| R.C. Blunt | b Nichols | 0 |
| C.F.W. Allcott | run out | 33 |
| T.C. Lowry* | lbw b Allom | 80 |
| H.M. McGirr | st Cornford b Woolley | 51 |
| K.C. James† | lbw b Worthington | 14 |
| W.E. Merritt | not out | 18 |
| A.M. Matheson | b Allom | 7 |
| Extras | (B 31, LB 16, NB 10) | 57 |
| **Total** | | **387** |

| NEW ZEALAND | O | M | R | W | O | M | R | W | | FALL OF WICKETS | | |
|---|---|---|---|---|---|---|---|---|---|---|---|---|
| | | | | | | | | | | E | NZ | E |
| McGirr | 15 | 2 | 65 | 1 | 3 | 1 | 4 | 0 | Wkt | 1st | 1st | 2nd |
| Matheson | 30 | 6 | 89 | 0 | 5 | 2 | 7 | 2 | 1st | 60 | 20 | 12 |
| Merritt | 34 | 2 | 127 | 2 | | | | | 2nd | 150 | 71 | 21 |
| Allcott | 47 | 17 | 102 | 2 | | | | | 3rd | 170 | 127 | 22 |
| Weir | 10 | 1 | 29 | 1 | | | | | 4th | 190 | 131 | – |
| Blunt | 21 | 8 | 61 | 2 | 3·3 | 2 | 4 | 1 | 5th | 374 | 186 | – |
| Page | 14·4 | 4 | 36 | 1 | | | | | 6th | 375 | 193 | – |
| Lowry | | | | | 1 | 1 | 0 | 0 | 7th | 432 | 293 | – |
| | | | | | | | | | 8th | 475 | 349 | – |
| ENGLAND | | | | | | | | | 9th | 526 | 373 | – |
| Nichols | 19 | 4 | 45 | 1 | | | | | 10th | 540 | 387 | – |
| Barratt | 37 | 12 | 60 | 1 | | | | | | | | |
| Allom | 26·1 | 5 | 42 | 4 | | | | | | | | |
| Woolley | 41 | 10 | 100 | 2 | | | | | | | | |
| Bowley | 28 | 6 | 58 | 0 | | | | | | | | |
| Worthington | 15 | 5 | 25 | 1 | | | | | | | | |

Umpires: K.H. Cave and L.T. Cobcroft.

# WEST INDIES v ENGLAND 1929-30 (1st Test)

Played at Kensington Oval, Bridgetown, Barbados, on 11, 13, 14, 15, 16 January.
Toss: West Indies.   Result: MATCH DRAWN.
Debuts: West Indies – F.I. de Caires, G.A. Headley, E.A.C. Hunte, E.L. St. Hill, J.E.D. Sealy,
L.A. Walcott; England – Hon. F.S.G. Calthorpe, W. Voce.

At 17 years 121 days, Sealy became the youngest Test cricketer to date. He remains the youngest apart from four
Pakistan players whose birthdates have never been verified. Roach was the first West Indian to score a Test
century, and Headley, aged 20 years 230 days, remains the youngest to do so. Stevens' match analysis of 10 for
195 remains the best in any Bridgetown Test.

## WEST INDIES

| | | | | | |
|---|---|---|---|---|---|
| C.A. Roach | c Hendren b Astill | 122 | c Rhodes b Haig | | 77 |
| E.L.G. Hoad* | c Rhodes b Voce | 24 | c Astill b Calthorpe | | 0 |
| A.G. Headley | b O'Connor | 21 | c O'Connor b Rhodes | | 176 |
| F.I. de Caires | c Sandham b Voce | 80 | c and b Stevens | | 70 |
| J.E.D. Sealy | c Haig b Stevens | 58 | (6) b Rhodes | | 15 |
| L.N. Constantine | lbw b Stevens | 13 | (5) c sub (L.F. Townsend) b Stevens | | 6 |
| C.R. Browne | b Stevens | 0 | (8) c Hendren b Rhodes | | 0 |
| L.A. Walcott | run out | 24 | (7) not out | | 16 |
| E.L. St. Hill | c Calthorpe b Stevens | 0 | c Ames b Stevens | | 12 |
| H.C. Griffith | lbw b Stevens | 8 | c O'Connor b Stevens | | 0 |
| E.A.C. Hunte† | not out | 10 | lbw b Stevens | | 1 |
| Extras | (B 6, LB 3) | 9 | (B 4, LB 6, W 1) | | 11 |
| **Total** | | **369** | | | **384** |

## ENGLAND

| | | | | | |
|---|---|---|---|---|---|
| G. Gunn | lbw b St. Hill | 35 | b Walcott | | 29 |
| A. Sandham | lbw b Constantine | 152 | b Griffith | | 51 |
| G.T.S. Stevens | run out | 9 | c Constantine b Griffith | | 5 |
| E.H. Hendren | c Constantine b St. Hill | 80 | not out | | 36 |
| J. O'Connor | c Constantine b Griffith | 37 | | | |
| L.E.G. Ames† | b Constantine | 16 | (5) not out | | 44 |
| N.E. Haig | c Hunte b Browne | 47 | | | |
| W.E. Astill | c Constantine b Griffith | 1 | | | |
| Hon. F.S.G. Calthorpe* | b Constantine | 40 | | | |
| W. Rhodes | not out | 14 | | | |
| W. Voce | c Hoad b Browne | 10 | | | |
| Extras | (B 20, LB 3, NB 3) | 26 | (W 2) | | 2 |
| **Total** | | **467** | (3 wickets) | | **167** |

| ENGLAND | O | M | R | W | O | M | R | W | | FALL OF WICKETS | | | |
|---|---|---|---|---|---|---|---|---|---|---|---|---|---|
| Voce | 27 | 1 | 120 | 2 | 3 | 0 | 15 | 0 | | WI | E | WI | E |
| Haig | 10 | 4 | 27 | 0 | 20 | 4 | 40 | 1 | *Wkt* | *1st* | *1st* | *2nd* | *2nd* |
| Rhodes | 27·1 | 9 | 44 | 0 | 51 | 10 | 110 | 3 | 1st | 90 | 78 | 6 | 77 |
| Stevens | 27 | 5 | 105 | 5 | 26·4 | 1 | 90 | 5 | 2nd | 157 | 96 | 162 | 85 |
| O'Connor | 10 | 0 | 31 | 1 | | | | | 3rd | 179 | 264 | 304 | 98 |
| Astill | 9 | 1 | 19 | 1 | 30 | 10 | 72 | 0 | 4th | 303 | 307 | 320 | – |
| Calthorpe | 4 | 0 | 14 | 0 | 20 | 7 | 38 | 1 | 5th | 320 | 333 | 352 | – |
| Gunn | | | | | 2 | 0 | 8 | 0 | 6th | 320 | 349 | 360 | – |
| | | | | | | | | | 7th | 327 | 353 | 362 | – |
| WEST INDIES | | | | | | | | | 8th | 327 | 431 | 381 | – |
| Constantine | 39 | 9 | 121 | 3 | 12 | 3 | 47 | 0 | 9th | 343 | 448 | 381 | – |
| Griffith | 36 | 11 | 102 | 2 | 15 | 4 | 37 | 2 | 10th | 369 | 467 | 384 | – |
| St. Hill | 35 | 7 | 110 | 2 | 11 | 3 | 24 | 0 | | | | | |
| Browne | 37 | 8 | 83 | 2 | 13 | 6 | 19 | 0 | | | | | |
| Headley | 3 | 0 | 10 | 0 | 2 | 0 | 6 | 0 | | | | | |
| Walcott | 3 | 0 | 15 | 0 | 5 | 1 | 17 | 1 | | | | | |
| Roach | | | | | 5 | 1 | 6 | 0 | | | | | |
| De Caires | | | | | 2 | 0 | 9 | 0 | | | | | |

Umpires: J. Hardstaff, sr and W. Badley.

# WEST INDIES v ENGLAND 1929-30 (2nd Test)

Played at Queen's Park Oval, Port-of-Spain, Trinidad, on 1, 3, 4, 5, 6 February.
Toss: England.   Result: ENGLAND won by 167 runs.
Debuts: West Indies – E.E. Achong, N. Betancourt, M.G. Grell.

Hendren scored the first double-century in Tests between England and West Indies. Previous versions of this score have included 'R.L.' and not 'E.A.C.' Hunte in the West Indies side. This error was caused by a copy typist mishearing 'Errol' as 'R.L.' and resulted in E.A.C. Hunte being given two separate career records! Betancourt captained West Indies in his only Test match.

## ENGLAND

| | | | | | |
|---|---|---|---|---|---|
| G. Gunn | run out | 1 | | c Achong b Constantine | 23 |
| A. Sandham | b Griffith | 0 | | b Griffith | 5 |
| G.T.S. Stevens | c Small b Constantine | 8 | (6) | c De Caires b Griffith | 29 |
| E.H. Hendren | b Achong | 77 | | not out | 205 |
| J.O'Connor | c Headley b Achong | 30 | (3) | c Headley b Constantine | 21 |
| L.E.G. Ames† | c Achong b Constantine | 42 | (5) | c sub (J.E.D. Sealy) b Small | 105 |
| N.E. Haig | c Grell b Griffith | 5 | | c and b Constantine | 5 |
| W.E. Astill | c sub (J.E.D. Sealy) b Griffith | 19 | | c Griffith b Constantine | 14 |
| Hon.F.S.G. Calthorpe* | c Constantine b Griffith | 12 | | c sub (J.E.D. Sealy) b Griffith | 0 |
| W. Rhodes | lbw b Griffith | 2 | | not out | 6 |
| W. Voce | not out | 2 | | | |
| Extras | (B 7, LB 2, NB 1) | 10 | | (B 9, LB 2, W 1) | 12 |
| **Total** | | **208** | | (8 wickets declared) | **425** |

## WEST INDIES

| | | | | | |
|---|---|---|---|---|---|
| C.A. Roach | b Voce | 0 | (4) | c Sandham b Voce | 0 |
| E.A.C. Hunte† | c Hendren b Astill | 58 | | b Stevens | 30 |
| W.H. St. Hill | lbw b Astill | 33 | (1) | c Ames b Voce | 30 |
| G.A. Headley | hit wkt b Voce | 8 | (3) | c Ames b Haig | 39 |
| F.I. de Caires | c and b Voce | 0 | (6) | c Astill b Voce | 45 |
| M.G. Grell | c Ames b Haig | 21 | (7) | b Voce | 13 |
| J.A. Small | c Voce b Astill | 20 | (8) | c Calthorpe b Haig | 5 |
| L.N. Constantine | c Hendren b Voce | 52 | (5) | c Gunn b Voce | 16 |
| N. Betancourt* | lbw b Rhodes | 39 | | c sub (L.F. Townsend) b Voce | 13 |
| H.C. Griffith | not out | 3 | | st Ames b Voce | 3 |
| E.E. Achong | c sub (L.F. Townsend) b Astill | 1 | | not out | 4 |
| Extras | (B 4, LB 14, NB 1) | 19 | | (B 8, LB 4, NB 2) | 14 |
| **Total** | | **254** | | | **212** |

| WEST INDIES | O | M | R | W | O | M | R | W | FALL OF WICKETS | | | | |
|---|---|---|---|---|---|---|---|---|---|---|---|---|---|
| Griffith | 22 | 4 | 63 | 5 | 38 | 8 | 99 | 3 | | E | WI | E | WI |
| Constantine | 16·1 | 3 | 42 | 2 | 40 | 4 | 165 | 4 | *Wkt* | *1st* | *1st* | *2nd* | *2nd* |
| Small | 12 | 6 | 22 | 0 | 19 | 2 | 56 | 1 | 1st | 1 | 0 | 9 | 57 |
| Achong | 20 | 3 | 64 | 2 | 4 | 0 | 12 | 0 | 2nd | 3 | 89 | 49 | 79 |
| Grell | 2 | 0 | 7 | 0 | 3 | 1 | 10 | 0 | 3rd | 12 | 104 | 52 | 85 |
| Headley | | | | | 11 | 2 | 30 | 0 | 4th | 61 | 104 | 289 | 109 |
| St. Hill | | | | | 2 | 0 | 9 | 0 | 5th | 142 | 110 | 375 | 135 |
| Roach | | | | | 8 | 1 | 32 | 0 | 6th | 147 | 141 | 380 | 165 |
| | | | | | | | | | 7th | 180 | 160 | 408 | 183 |
| ENGLAND | | | | | | | | | 8th | 200 | 231 | 409 | 193 |
| Voce | 28 | 5 | 79 | 4 | 37·2 | 15 | 70 | 7 | 9th | 206 | 253 | – | 207 |
| Haig | 8 | 1 | 33 | 1 | 21 | 8 | 33 | 2 | 10th | 208 | 254 | – | 212 |
| Stevens | 7 | 1 | 25 | 0 | 8 | 2 | 21 | 1 | | | | | |
| Astill | 24·2 | 6 | 58 | 4 | 20 | 3 | 34 | 0 | | | | | |
| Rhodes | 20 | 5 | 40 | 1 | 22 | 12 | 31 | 0 | | | | | |
| O'Connor | | | | | 4 | 1 | 9 | 0 | | | | | |

Umpires: J. Hardstaff, sr and K.L. Grant.

# WEST INDIES v ENGLAND 1929-30 (3rd Test)

Played at Bourda, Georgetown, British Guiana, on 21, 22, 24, 25, 26 February.
Toss: West Indies.   Result: WEST INDIES won by 289 runs.
Debuts: West Indies – C.M. Jones; England – L.F. Townsend.

West Indies gained their first Test match victory after Roach had scored their first double-century and Headley had become the first West Indian to score a hundred in each innings of a Test. He was also the first batsman to score three Test hundreds before his 21st birthday; he added a fourth in the next Test.

## WEST INDIES

| | | | | |
|---|---|--:|---|--:|
| C.A. Roach | c Haig b Townsend | 209 | st Ames b Astill | 22 |
| E.A.C. Hunte† | c Townsend b Wyatt | 53 | hit wkt b Townsend | 14 |
| G.A. Headley | run out | 114 | c Townsend b Haig | 112 |
| M.P. Fernandes* | c Ames b Rhodes | 22 | c Calthorpe b Rhodes | 19 |
| J.E.D. Sealy | c and b Rhodes | 0 | c Hendren b Rhodes | 10 |
| C.V. Wight | b Townsend | 10 | (8) b Haig | 22 |
| L.N. Constantine | st Ames b Wyatt | 13 | (6) b Astill | 0 |
| C.R. Browne | b Voce | 22 | (9) not out | 70 |
| C.M. Jones | c Ames b Voce | 6 | (11) b Townsend | 2 |
| G.N. Francis | not out | 5 | lbw b Astill | 2 |
| E.L. St. Hill | st Ames b Haig | 3 | (7) b Astill | 3 |
| Extras | (B 3, LB 11) | 14 | (B 9, LB 5) | 14 |
| **Total** | | **471** | | **290** |

## ENGLAND

| | | | | |
|---|---|--:|---|--:|
| G. Gunn | hit wkt b Francis | 11 | c Hunte b Francis | 45 |
| A. Sandham | c Hunte b Browne | 9 | c and b Constantine | 0 |
| R.E.S. Wyatt | c Francis b Constantine | 0 | c Jones b Constantine | 28 |
| E.H. Hendren | b Constantine | 56 | lbw b St. Hill | 123 |
| L.E.G. Ames† | c Hunte b Francis | 31 | c Francis b Constantine | 3 |
| L.F. Townsend | c Hunte b Francis | 3 | b Constantine | 21 |
| N.E. Haig | b Constantine | 4 | b Browne | 0 |
| W.E. Astill | run out | 0 | hit wkt b Constantine | 5 |
| Hon. F.S.G. Calthorpe* | c Headley b Constantine | 15 | c Jones b Roach | 49 |
| W. Rhodes | b Francis | 0 | not out | 10 |
| W. Voce | not out | 1 | lbw b Francis | 2 |
| Extras | (B 11, LB 2, NB 2) | 15 | (B 30, LB 5, W 3, NB 3) | 41 |
| **Total** | | **145** | | **327** |

| ENGLAND | O | M | R | W | O | M | R | W |
|---|--:|--:|--:|--:|--:|--:|--:|--:|
| Voce | 26 | 4 | 81 | 2 | 16 | 4 | 44 | 0 |
| Haig | 23 | 7 | 61 | 1 | 10 | 1 | 44 | 2 |
| Townsend | 16 | 6 | 48 | 2 | 7·3 | 2 | 25 | 2 |
| Rhodes | 40 | 8 | 96 | 2 | 51 | 23 | 93 | 2 |
| Astill | 28 | 3 | 92 | 0 | 43 | 17 | 70 | 4 |
| Calthorpe | 6 | 0 | 23 | 0 | | | | |
| Wyatt | 9 | 0 | 56 | 2 | | | | |
| **WEST INDIES** | | | | | | | | |
| Francis | 21 | 5 | 40 | 4 | 26·5 | 11 | 69 | 2 |
| Constantine | 16·3 | 6 | 35 | 4 | 40 | 17 | 87 | 5 |
| Browne | 10 | 2 | 29 | 1 | 33 | 15 | 32 | 1 |
| St. Hill | 14 | 4 | 26 | 0 | 33 | 15 | 61 | 1 |
| Roach | | | | | 9 | 2 | 18 | 1 |
| Headley | | | | | 2 | 0 | 8 | 0 |
| Jones | | | | | 10 | 7 | 5 | 0 |
| Wight | | | | | 5 | 1 | 6 | 0 |

FALL OF WICKETS

| Wkt | WI 1st | E 1st | WI 2nd | E 2nd |
|---|--:|--:|--:|--:|
| 1st | 144 | 19 | 23 | 0 |
| 2nd | 336 | 20 | 76 | 82 |
| 3rd | 400 | 33 | 135 | 82 |
| 4th | 406 | 103 | 138 | 106 |
| 5th | 417 | 107 | 138 | 162 |
| 6th | 427 | 117 | 155 | 168 |
| 7th | 446 | 120 | 209 | 181 |
| 8th | 459 | 126 | 248 | 269 |
| 9th | 464 | 141 | 281 | 320 |
| 10th | 471 | 145 | 290 | 327 |

Umpires: J. Hardstaff, sr and R.D.R. Hill.

# WEST INDIES v ENGLAND 1929-30 (4th Test)

Played at Sabina Park, Kingston, Jamaica, on 3, 4, 5, 7, 8, 9, 10, 11 (*no play*), 12 (*no play*) April.
Toss: England.   Result: MATCH DRAWN.
Debuts: West Indies – I. Barrow, O.C. Da Costa, G. Gladstone, C.C. Passailaigue.

This Test set records, all subsequently beaten, for the longest Test match, highest total, highest individual score, and highest individual match aggregate in Test cricket. Headley was the youngest to score a double-century in Tests until Javed Miandad did so at the age of 19 years 141 days (*Test No. 784*). He remains the only batsman to score four Test hundreds before attaining the age of 21.

## ENGLAND

| | | | | | |
|---|---|---|---|---|---|
| G. Gunn | st Barrow b Martin | 85 | | run out | 47 |
| A. Sandham | b Griffith | 325 | (7) | lbw b Griffith | 50 |
| R.E.S. Wyatt | c Barrow b Da Costa | 58 | (2) | c Passailaigue b Da Costa | 10 |
| E.H. Hendren | c Passailaigue b Scott | 61 | | b Roach | 55 |
| L.E.G. Ames† | b Griffith | 149 | | c Nunes b Scott | 27 |
| J. O'Connor | c Da Costa b Scott | 51 | (3) | c Headley b Scott | 3 |
| Hon.F.S.G. Calthorpe* | c Griffith b Scott | 5 | (8) | st Barrow b Scott | 8 |
| N.E. Haig | c Da Costa b Gladstone | 28 | (6) | c Passailaigue b Scott | 34 |
| W.E. Astill | b Scott | 39 | | b Griffith | 10 |
| W. Rhodes | not out | 8 | | not out | 11 |
| W. Voce | c Da Costa b Scott | 20 | | not out | 6 |
| Extras | (B 6, LB 12, W 1, NB 1) | 20 | | (B 5, LB 6) | 11 |
| **Total** | | **849** | | (9 wickets declared) | **272** |

## WEST INDIES

| | | | | | |
|---|---|---|---|---|---|
| R.K. Nunes* | c Ames b Voce | 66 | | b Astill | 92 |
| C.A. Roach | lbw b Haig | 15 | | c Gunn b Rhodes | 22 |
| G.A. Headley | c Haig b Voce | 10 | | st Ames b Wyatt | 223 |
| F.R. Martin | lbw b Haig | 33 | (5) | c Sandham b Wyatt | 24 |
| F.I. de Caires | run out | 21 | (4) | b Haig | 16 |
| C.C. Passailaigue | b Haig | 44 | | not out | 2 |
| I. Barrow† | b Astill | 0 | | | |
| O.C. Da Costa | c Haig b Astill | 39 | | | |
| O.C. Scott | c and b Astill | 8 | | | |
| H.C. Griffith | c Hendren b Rhodes | 7 | | | |
| G. Gladstone | not out | 12 | | | |
| Extras | (B 19, LB 5, W 2, NB 5) | 31 | | (B 17, LB 11, NB 1) | 29 |
| **Total** | | **286** | | (5 wickets) | **408** |

| WEST INDIES | O | M | R | W | O | M | R | W |
|---|---|---|---|---|---|---|---|---|
| Griffith | 58 | 6 | 155 | 2 | 21·1 | 5 | 52 | 2 |
| Da Costa | 21 | 0 | 81 | 1 | 6 | 2 | 14 | 1 |
| Gladstone | 42 | 5 | 139 | 1 | 8 | 0 | 50 | 0 |
| Scott | 80·2 | 13 | 266 | 5 | 25 | 0 | 108 | 4 |
| Martin | 45 | 6 | 128 | 1 | 9 | 1 | 12 | 0 |
| Headley | 5 | 0 | 23 | 0 | | | | |
| Roach | 5 | 0 | 22 | 0 | 10 | 1 | 25 | 1 |
| Passailaigue | 2 | 0 | 15 | 0 | | | | |
| **ENGLAND** | | | | | | | | |
| Voce | 22 | 3 | 81 | 2 | 29 | 3 | 94 | 0 |
| Haig | 30 | 10 | 73 | 3 | 26 | 15 | 49 | 1 |
| Rhodes | 20·5 | 12 | 17 | 1 | 24 | 13 | 22 | 1 |
| Astill | 33 | 12 | 73 | 3 | 46 | 13 | 108 | 1 |
| Wyatt | 4 | 0 | 11 | 0 | 24·3 | 7 | 58 | 2 |
| O'Connor | 2 | 2 | 0 | 0 | 11 | 3 | 32 | 0 |
| Calthorpe | | | | | 4 | 1 | 16 | 0 |

FALL OF WICKETS

| Wkt | E 1st | WI 1st | E 2nd | WI 2nd |
|---|---|---|---|---|
| 1st | 173 | 53 | 22 | 44 |
| 2nd | 321 | 80 | 35 | 271 |
| 3rd | 418 | 141 | 116 | 320 |
| 4th | 667 | 156 | 121 | 397 |
| 5th | 720 | 181 | 176 | 408 |
| 6th | 748 | 181 | 180 | – |
| 7th | 755 | 254 | 198 | – |
| 8th | 813 | 265 | 233 | – |
| 9th | 821 | 270 | 256 | – |
| 10th | 849 | 286 | – | – |

Umpires: J. Hardstaff, sr and E. Knibbs.

# ENGLAND v AUSTRALIA 1930 (1st Test)

Played at Trent Bridge, Nottingham, on 13, 14, 16, 17 June.
Toss: England.   Result: ENGLAND won by 93 runs.
Debuts: Australia – S.J. McCabe.

In the second innings, Sutcliffe retired hurt at 134-1. S.H. Copley, a 23-year-old member of the Nottinghamshire ground staff, 'made a lot of ground, took the ball at full-length and, although rolling over, retained possession' (*Wisden*).

## ENGLAND

| | | | | |
|---|---|---|---|---|
| J.B. Hobbs | c Richardson b McCabe | 78 | st Oldfield b Grimmett | 74 |
| H. Sutcliffe | c Hornibrook b Fairfax | 29 | retired hurt | 58 |
| W.R. Hammond | lbw b Grimmett | 8 | lbw b Grimmett | 4 |
| F.E. Woolley | st Oldfield b Grimmett | 0 | b Wall | 5 |
| E.H. Hendren | b Grimmett | 5 | c Richardson b Wall | 72 |
| A.P.F. Chapman* | c Ponsford b Hornibrook | 52 | b Wall | 29 |
| H. Larwood | b Grimmett | 18 | (9) b Grimmett | 7 |
| R.W.V. Robins | not out | 50 | b McCabe | 4 |
| M.W. Tate | b Grimmett | 13 | (7) c Kippax b Grimmett | 24 |
| R.K. Tyldesley | c Fairfax b Wall | 1 | b Grimmett | 5 |
| G. Duckworth† | lbw b Fairfax | 4 | not out | 14 |
| Extras | (B 4, LB 7, NB 1) | 12 | (B 5, LB 1) | 6 |
| **Total** | | **270** | | **302** |

## AUSTRALIA

| | | | | |
|---|---|---|---|---|
| W.M. Woodfull* | c Chapman b Tate | 2 | c Chapman b Larwood | 4 |
| W.H. Ponsford | b Tate | 3 | b Tate | 39 |
| A.G. Fairfax | c Hobbs b Robins | 14 | (7) c Robins b Tate | 14 |
| D.G. Bradman | b Tate | 8 | (3) b Robins | 131 |
| A.F. Kippax | not out | 64 | (4) c Hammond b Robins | 23 |
| S.J. McCabe | c Hammond b Robins | 4 | (5) c sub (S.H. Copley) b Tate | 49 |
| V.Y. Richardson | b Tyldesley | 37 | (6) lbw b Tyldesley | 29 |
| W.A.S. Oldfield† | c Duckworth b Robins | 4 | c Hammond b Tyldesley | 11 |
| C.V. Grimmett | st Duckworth b Robins | 0 | c Hammond b Tyldesley | 0 |
| P.M. Hornibrook | lbw b Larwood | 0 | c Duckworth b Robins | 5 |
| T.W. Wall | b Tyldesley | 0 | not out | 8 |
| Extras | (B 4, LB 4) | 8 | (B 17, LB 5) | 22 |
| **Total** | | **144** | | **335** |

| AUSTRALIA | O | M | R | W | O | M | R | W |
|---|---|---|---|---|---|---|---|---|
| Wall | 17 | 4 | 47 | 1 | 26 | 4 | 67 | 3 |
| Fairfax | 21·4 | 5 | 51 | 2 | 15 | 4 | 58 | 0 |
| Grimmett | 32 | 6 | 107 | 5 | 30 | 4 | 94 | 5 |
| Hornibrook | 12 | 3 | 30 | 1 | 11 | 4 | 35 | 0 |
| McCabe | 7 | 3 | 23 | 1 | 14 | 3 | 42 | 1 |
| ENGLAND | | | | | | | | |
| Larwood | 15 | 8 | 12 | 1 | 5 | 1 | 9 | 1 |
| Tate | 19 | 8 | 20 | 3 | 50 | 20 | 69 | 3 |
| Tyldesley | 21 | 8 | 53 | 2 | 35 | 10 | 77 | 3 |
| Robins | 17 | 4 | 51 | 4 | 17·2 | 1 | 81 | 3 |
| Hammond | | | | | 29 | 5 | 74 | 0 |
| Woolley | | | | | 3 | 1 | 3 | 0 |

FALL OF WICKETS

| Wkt | E 1st | A 1st | E 2nd | A 2nd |
|---|---|---|---|---|
| 1st | 53 | 4 | 125 | 12 |
| 2nd | 63 | 6 | 137 | 93 |
| 3rd | 63 | 16 | 147 | 152 |
| 4th | 71 | 57 | 211 | 229 |
| 5th | 153 | 61 | 250 | 267 |
| 6th | 188 | 105 | 260 | 296 |
| 7th | 218 | 134 | 283 | 296 |
| 8th | 241 | 140 | 283 | 322 |
| 9th | 242 | 141 | 302 | 324 |
| 10th | 270 | 144 | – | 335 |

Umpires: J. Hardstaff, sr and W.R. Parry.

# ENGLAND v AUSTRALIA 1930 (2nd Test)

Played at Lord's, London, on 27, 28, 30 June, 1 July.
Toss: England.   Result: AUSTRALIA won by seven wickets.
Debuts: England – G.O.B. Allen.

Ponsford lost his wicket immediately after the teams had been presented to H.M. King George V. Australia's 729 remains the highest total in any cricket match at Lord's and their highest against England. Duleepsinhji emulated his uncle, K.S. Ranjitsinhji, by scoring a hundred in his first Test against Australia. Bradman batted for 339 minutes and hit 25 fours in what remains the highest innings in any Test at Lord's.

## ENGLAND

| | | | | | |
|---|---|--:|---|---|--:|
| J.B. Hobbs | c Oldfield b Fairfax | 1 | b Grimmett | | 19 |
| F.E. Woolley | c Wall b Fairfax | 41 | hit wkt b Grimmett | | 28 |
| W.R. Hammond | b Grimmett | 38 | c Fairfax b Grimmett | | 32 |
| K.S. Duleepsinhji | c Bradman b Grimmett | 173 | c Oldfield b Hornibrook | | 48 |
| E.H. Hendren | c McCabe b Fairfax | 48 | c Richardson b Grimmett | | 9 |
| A.P.F. Chapman* | c Oldfield b Wall | 11 | c Oldfield b Fairfax | | 121 |
| G.O.B. Allen | b Fairfax | 3 | lbw b Grimmett | | 57 |
| M.W. Tate | c McCabe b Wall | 54 | c Ponsford b Grimmett | | 10 |
| R.W.V. Robins | c Oldfield b Hornibrook | 5 | not out | | 11 |
| J.C. White | not out | 23 | run out | | 10 |
| G. Duckworth† | c Oldfield b Wall | 18 | lbw b Fairfax | | 0 |
| Extras | (B 2, LB 7, NB 1) | 10 | (B 16, LB 13, W 1) | | 30 |
| **Total** | | **425** | | | **375** |

## AUSTRALIA

| | | | | |
|---|---|--:|---|--:|
| W.M. Woodfull* | st Duckworth b Robins | 155 | not out | 26 |
| W.H. Ponsford | c Hammond b White | 81 | b Robins | 14 |
| D.G. Bradman | c Chapman b White | 254 | c Chapman b Tate | 1 |
| A.F. Kippax | b White | 83 | c Duckworth b Robins | 3 |
| S.J. McCabe | c Woolley b Hammond | 44 | not out | 25 |
| V.Y. Richardson | c Hobbs b Tate | 30 | | |
| W.A.S. Oldfield† | not out | 43 | | |
| A.G. Fairfax | not out | 20 | | |
| C.V. Grimmett | ) | | | |
| P.M. Hornibrook | ) did not bat | | | |
| T.W. Wall | ) | | | |
| Extras | (B 6, LB 8, W 5) | 19 | (B 1, LB 2) | 3 |
| **Total** | (6 wickets declared) | **729** | (3 wickets) | **72** |

| AUSTRALIA | O | M | R | W | O | M | R | W |
|---|--:|--:|--:|--:|--:|--:|--:|--:|
| Wall | 29·4 | 2 | 118 | 3 | 25 | 2 | 80 | 0 |
| Fairfax | 31 | 6 | 101 | 4 | 12·4 | 2 | 37 | 2 |
| Grimmett | 33 | 4 | 105 | 2 | 53 | 13 | 167 | 6 |
| Hornibrook | 26 | 6 | 62 | 1 | 22 | 6 | 49 | 1 |
| McCabe | 9 | 1 | 29 | 0 | 3 | 1 | 11 | 0 |
| Bradman | | | | | 1 | 0 | 1 | 0 |
| **ENGLAND** | | | | | | | | |
| Allen | 34 | 7 | 115 | 0 | | | | |
| Tate | 64 | 16 | 148 | 1 | 13 | 6 | 21 | 1 |
| White | 51 | 7 | 158 | 3 | 2 | 0 | 8 | 0 |
| Robins | 42 | 1 | 172 | 1 | 9 | 1 | 34 | 2 |
| Hammond | 35 | 8 | 82 | 1 | 4·2 | 1 | 6 | 0 |
| Woolley | 6 | 0 | 35 | 0 | | | | |

## FALL OF WICKETS

| | E | A | E | A |
|---|--:|--:|--:|--:|
| Wkt | 1st | 1st | 2nd | 2nd |
| 1st | 13 | 162 | 45 | 16 |
| 2nd | 53 | 393 | 58 | 17 |
| 3rd | 105 | 585 | 129 | 22 |
| 4th | 209 | 588 | 141 | – |
| 5th | 236 | 643 | 147 | – |
| 6th | 239 | 672 | 272 | – |
| 7th | 337 | – | 329 | – |
| 8th | 363 | – | 354 | – |
| 9th | 387 | – | 372 | – |
| 10th | 425 | – | 375 | – |

Umpires: F. Chester and T.W. Oates.

# ENGLAND v AUSTRALIA 1930 (3rd Test)

Played at Headingley, Leeds, on 11, 12, 14, 15 July.
Toss: Australia.   Result: MATCH DRAWN.
Debuts: Nil.

Bradman scored 309 runs on the first day (still a record for all Test cricket); he made 105 before lunch, 115 between lunch and tea, and 89 in the final session. His 334 was the highest Test innings to date. At 21 years 318 days he remains the youngest to score a triple-century in Test cricket. With his score 138, he reached 1,000 runs in only seven Test matches (13 innings). His double-century took 214 minutes and remains the fastest in Test cricket.

### AUSTRALIA

| | | |
|---|---|---|
| W.M. Woodfull* | b Hammond | 50 |
| A. Jackson | c Larwood b Tate | 1 |
| D.G. Bradman | c Duckworth b Tate | 334 |
| A.F. Kippax | c Chapman b Tate | 77 |
| S.J. McCabe | b Larwood | 30 |
| V.Y. Richardson | c Larwood b Tate | 1 |
| E.L. a'Beckett | c Chapman b Geary | 29 |
| W.A.S. Oldfield† | c Hobbs b Tate | 2 |
| C.V. Grimmett | c Duckworth b Tyldesley | 24 |
| T.W. Wall | b Tyldesley | 3 |
| P.M. Hornibrook | not out | 1 |
| Extras | (B 5, LB 8, W 1) | 14 |
| **Total** | | **566** |

### ENGLAND

| | | | | | |
|---|---|---|---|---|---|
| J.B. Hobbs | c A'Beckett b Grimmett | 29 | run out | | 13 |
| H. Sutcliffe | c Hornibrook b Grimmett | 32 | not out | | 28 |
| W.R. Hammond | c Oldfield b McCabe | 113 | c Oldfield b Grimmett | | 35 |
| K.S. Duleepsinhji | b Hornibrook | 35 | c Grimmett b Hornibrook | | 10 |
| M. Leyland | c Kippax b Wall | 44 | not out | | 1 |
| G. Geary | run out | 0 | | | |
| G. Duckworth† | c Oldfield b A'Beckett | 33 | | | |
| A.P.F. Chapman* | b Grimmett | 45 | | | |
| M.W. Tate | c Jackson b Grimmett | 22 | | | |
| H. Larwood | not out | 10 | | | |
| R.K. Tyldesley | c Hornibrook b Grimmett | 6 | | | |
| Extras | (B 9, LB 10, NB 3) | 22 | (LB 8) | | 8 |
| **Total** | | **391** | (3 wickets) | | **95** |

| ENGLAND | O | M | R | W | O | M | R | W |
|---|---|---|---|---|---|---|---|---|
| Larwood | 33 | 3 | 139 | 1 | | | | |
| Tate | 39 | 9 | 124 | 5 | | | | |
| Geary | 35 | 10 | 95 | 1 | | | | |
| Tyldesley | 33 | 5 | 104 | 2 | | | | |
| Hammond | 17 | 3 | 46 | 1 | | | | |
| Leyland | 11 | 0 | 44 | 0 | | | | |
| AUSTRALIA | | | | | | | | |
| Wall | 40 | 12 | 70 | 1 | 10 | 3 | 20 | 0 |
| A'Beckett | 28 | 8 | 47 | 1 | 11 | 4 | 19 | 0 |
| Grimmett | 56·2 | 16 | 135 | 5 | 17 | 3 | 33 | 1 |
| Hornibrook | 41 | 7 | 94 | 1 | 11·5 | 5 | 14 | 1 |
| McCabe | 10 | 4 | 23 | 1 | 2 | 1 | 1 | 0 |

### FALL OF WICKETS

| | A | E | E |
|---|---|---|---|
| Wkt | 1st | 1st | 2nd |
| 1st | 2 | 53 | 24 |
| 2nd | 194 | 64 | 72 |
| 3rd | 423 | 123 | 94 |
| 4th | 486 | 206 | – |
| 5th | 491 | 206 | – |
| 6th | 508 | 289 | – |
| 7th | 519 | 319 | – |
| 8th | 544 | 370 | – |
| 9th | 565 | 375 | – |
| 10th | 566 | 391 | – |

Umpires: W. Bestwick and T.W. Oates.

# ENGLAND v AUSTRALIA 1930 (4th Test)

Played at Old Trafford, Manchester, on 25, 26, 28, 29 (*no play*) July.
Toss: Australia.   Result: MATCH DRAWN.
Debuts: England – T.W.J. Goddard.

Hobbs and Sutcliffe shared their eleventh and last first-wicket hundred partnership against Australia. Only 45 minutes' play was possible on the third day and none at all on the fourth.

## AUSTRALIA

| | | |
|---|---|---:|
| W.M. Woodfull* | c Duckworth b Tate | 54 |
| W.H. Ponsford | b Hammond | 83 |
| D.G. Bradman | c Duleepsinhji b Peebles | 14 |
| A.F. Kippax | c Chapman b Nichols | 51 |
| S.J. McCabe | lbw b Peebles | 4 |
| V.Y. Richardson | b Hammond | 1 |
| A.G. Fairfax | lbw b Goddard | 49 |
| W.A.S. Oldfield† | b Nichols | 2 |
| C.V. Grimmett | c Sutcliffe b Peebles | 50 |
| P.M. Hornibrook | c Duleepsinhji b Goddard | 3 |
| T.W. Hall | not out | 1 |
| Extras | (B 23, LB 3, NB 7) | 33 |
| **Total** | | **345** |

## ENGLAND

| | | |
|---|---|---:|
| J.B. Hobbs | c Oldfield b Wall | 31 |
| H. Sutcliffe | c Bradman b Wall | 74 |
| W.R. Hammond | b Wall | 3 |
| K.S. Duleepsinhji | c Hornibrook b McCabe | 54 |
| M. Leyland | b McCabe | 35 |
| A.P.F. Chapman* | c Grimmett b Hornibrook | 1 |
| M.W. Tate | c Ponsford b McCabe | 15 |
| M.S. Nichols | not out | 7 |
| I.A.R. Peebles | c Richardson b McCabe | 6 |
| G. Duckworth† | not out | 0 |
| T.W.J. Goddard | did not bat | |
| Extras | (B 13, LB 12) | 25 |
| **Total** | (8 wickets) | **251** |

| ENGLAND | O | M | R | W |
|---|---|---|---|---|
| Nichols | 21 | 5 | 33 | 2 |
| Tate | 30 | 11 | 39 | 1 |
| Goddard | 32·1 | 14 | 49 | 2 |
| Peebles | 55 | 9 | 150 | 3 |
| Leyland | 8 | 2 | 17 | 0 |
| Hammond | 21 | 6 | 24 | 2 |
| **AUSTRALIA** | | | | |
| Wall | 33 | 9 | 70 | 3 |
| Fairfax | 13 | 5 | 15 | 0 |
| Grimmett | 19 | 2 | 59 | 0 |
| Hornibrook | 26 | 9 | 41 | 1 |
| McCabe | 17 | 3 | 41 | 4 |

FALL OF WICKETS

| | A | E |
|---|---|---|
| *Wkt* | *1st* | *1st* |
| 1st | 106 | 108 |
| 2nd | 138 | 115 |
| 3rd | 184 | 119 |
| 4th | 189 | 192 |
| 5th | 190 | 199 |
| 6th | 239 | 222 |
| 7th | 243 | 237 |
| 8th | 330 | 247 |
| 9th | 338 | – |
| 10th | 345 | – |

Umpires: F. Chester and J. Hardstaff, sr.

# ENGLAND v AUSTRALIA 1930 (5th Test)

Played at Kennington Oval, London, on 16, 18, 19, 20, 21 (*no play*), 22 August.
Toss: England.   Result: AUSTRALIA won by an innings and 39 runs.
Debuts: Nil.

Australia regained the Ashes on their captain's birthday. Bradman's aggregate of 974, average 139.14, for the rubber still stands as the record for any Test series.

## ENGLAND

| | | | | |
|---|---|---|---|---|
| J.B. Hobbs | c Kippax b Wall | 47 | b Fairfax | 9 |
| H. Sutcliffe | c Oldfield b Fairfax | 161 | c Fairfax b Hornibrook | 54 |
| W.W. Whysall | lbw b Wall | 13 | c Hornibrook b Grimmett | 10 |
| K.S. Duleepsinhji | c Fairfax b Grimmett | 50 | c Kippax b Hornibrook | 46 |
| W.R. Hammond | b McCabe | 13 | c Fairfax b Hornibrook | 60 |
| M. Leyland | b Grimmett | 3 | b Hornibrook | 20 |
| R.E.S. Wyatt* | c Oldfield b Fairfax | 64 | b Hornibrook | 7 |
| M.W. Tate | st Oldfield b Grimmett | 10 | run out | 0 |
| H. Larwood | lbw b Grimmett | 19 | c McCabe b Hornibrook | 9 |
| G. Duckworth† | b Fairfax | 3 | b Hornibrook | 15 |
| I.A.R. Peebles | not out | 3 | not out | 0 |
| Extras | LB 17, NB 2) | 19 | (B 16, LB 3, NB 2) | 21 |
| **Total** | | **405** | | **251** |

## AUSTRALIA

| | | |
|---|---|---|
| W.M. Woodfull* | c Duckworth b Peebles | 54 |
| W.H. Ponsford | b Peebles | 110 |
| D.G. Bradman | c Duckworth b Larwood | 232 |
| A.F. Kippax | c Wyatt b Peebles | 28 |
| A. Jackson | c Sutcliffe b Wyatt | 73 |
| S.J. McCabe | c Duckworth b Hammond | 54 |
| A.G. Fairfax | not out | 53 |
| W.A.S. Oldfield† | c Larwood b Peebles | 34 |
| C.V. Grimmett | lbw b Peebles | 6 |
| T.W. Wall | lbw b Peebles | 0 |
| P.M. Hornibrook | c Duckworth b Tate | 7 |
| Extras | (B 22, LB 18, NB 4) | 44 |
| **Total** | | **695** |

| AUSTRALIA | O | M | R | W | O | M | R | W |
|---|---|---|---|---|---|---|---|---|
| Wall | 37 | 6 | 96 | 2 | 12 | 2 | 25 | 0 |
| Fairfax | 31 | 9 | 52 | 3 | 10 | 3 | 21 | 1 |
| Grimmett | 66·2 | 18 | 135 | 4 | 43 | 12 | 90 | 1 |
| McCabe | 22 | 4 | 49 | 1 | 3 | 1 | 2 | 0 |
| Hornibrook | 15 | 1 | 54 | 0 | 31·2 | 9 | 92 | 7 |
| **ENGLAND** | | | | | | | | |
| Larwood | 48 | 6 | 132 | 1 | | | | |
| Tate | 65·1 | 12 | 153 | 1 | | | | |
| Peebles | 71 | 8 | 204 | 6 | | | | |
| Wyatt | 14 | 1 | 58 | 1 | | | | |
| Hammond | 42 | 12 | 70 | 1 | | | | |
| Leyland | 16 | 7 | 34 | 0 | | | | |

### FALL OF WICKETS

| Wkt | E 1st | A 1st | E 2nd |
|---|---|---|---|
| 1st | 68 | 159 | 17 |
| 2nd | 97 | 190 | 37 |
| 3rd | 162 | 263 | 118 |
| 4th | 190 | 506 | 135 |
| 5th | 197 | 570 | 189 |
| 6th | 367 | 594 | 207 |
| 7th | 379 | 670 | 208 |
| 8th | 379 | 684 | 220 |
| 9th | 391 | 684 | 248 |
| 10th | 405 | 695 | 251 |

Umpires: J. Hardstaff, sr and W.R. Parry.

# AUSTRALIA v WEST INDIES 1930-31 (1st Test)

Played at Adelaide Oval on 12, 13, 15, 16 December.
Toss: West Indies.   Result: AUSTRALIA won by ten wickets.
Debuts: Australia – A. Hurwood; West Indies – L.S. Birkett, G.C. Grant.

Playing in West Indies' first match against Australia, Grant was the first to score a not out fifty in each innings of any Test Match.

## WEST INDIES

| | | | | |
|---|---|---|---|---|
| C.A. Roach | st Oldfield b Hurwood | 56 | b Hurwood | 9 |
| L.S. Birkett | c and b Grimmett | 27 | st Oldfield b Grimmett | 64 |
| G.A. Headley | c Wall b Grimmett | 0 | st Oldfield b Grimmett | 11 |
| F.R. Martin | b Grimmett | 39 | run out | 3 |
| L.N. Constantine | c Wall b Grimmett | 1 | b Grimmett | 14 |
| G.C. Grant* | not out | 53 | not out | 71 |
| E.L. Bartlett | lbw b Grimmett | 84 | c Grimmett b Hurwood | 11 |
| I. Barrow† | c Bradman b Grimmett | 12 | lbw b Bradman | 27 |
| G.N. Francis | lbw b Hurwood | 5 | b Hurwood | 3 |
| O.C. Scott | c Fairfax b Grimmett | 3 | c Kippax b Hurwood | 8 |
| H.C. Griffith | b Hurwood | 1 | st Oldfield b Grimmett | 10 |
| Extras | (B 6, LB 8, NB 1) | 15 | (B 16, LB 2) | 18 |
| **Total** | | **296** | | **249** |

## AUSTRALIA

| | | | | |
|---|---|---|---|---|
| W.H. Ponsford | c Birkett b Francis | 24 | not out | 92 |
| A. Jackson | c Barrow b Francis | 31 | not out | 70 |
| D.G. Bradman | c Grant b Griffith | 4 | | |
| A.F. Kippax | c Barrow b Griffith | 146 | | |
| S.J. McCabe | c and b Constantine | 90 | | |
| W.M. Woodfull* | run out | 6 | | |
| A.G. Fairfax | not out | 41 | | |
| W.A.S. Oldfield† | c Francis b Scott | 15 | | |
| C.V. Grimmett | c Barrow b Scott | 0 | | |
| A. Hurwood | c Martin b Scott | 0 | | |
| T.W. Hall | lbw b Scott | 0 | | |
| Extras | (B 2, LB 10, NB 7) | 19 | (B 8, W 1, NB 1) | 10 |
| **Total** | | **376** | (0 wickets) | **172** |

| AUSTRALIA | O | M | R | W | O | M | R | W |
|---|---|---|---|---|---|---|---|---|
| Wall | 16 | 0 | 64 | 0 | 10 | 1 | 20 | 0 |
| Fairfax | 11 | 1 | 36 | 0 | 3 | 2 | 6 | 0 |
| Grimmett | 48 | 19 | 87 | 7 | 38 | 7 | 96 | 4 |
| Hurwood | 36·1 | 14 | 55 | 3 | 34 | 11 | 86 | 4 |
| McCabe | 12 | 3 | 32 | 0 | 8 | 2 | 15 | 0 |
| Bradman | 4 | 0 | 7 | 0 | 5 | 1 | 8 | 1 |
| **WEST INDIES** | | | | | | | | |
| Francis | 18 | 7 | 43 | 2 | 10 | 1 | 30 | 0 |
| Constantine | 22 | 0 | 89 | 1 | 9·3 | 3 | 27 | 0 |
| Griffith | 28 | 4 | 69 | 2 | 10 | 1 | 20 | 0 |
| Martin | 29 | 3 | 73 | 0 | 11 | 0 | 28 | 0 |
| Scott | 20·5 | 2 | 83 | 4 | 13 | 0 | 55 | 0 |
| Birkett | | | | | 2 | 0 | 2 | 0 |

| FALL OF WICKETS | | | | |
|---|---|---|---|---|
| | WI | A | WI | A |
| Wkt | 1st | 1st | 2nd | 2nd |
| 1st | 58 | 56 | 15 | – |
| 2nd | 58 | 59 | 47 | – |
| 3rd | 118 | 64 | 52 | – |
| 4th | 123 | 246 | 74 | – |
| 5th | 131 | 269 | 115 | – |
| 6th | 245 | 341 | 138 | – |
| 7th | 269 | 374 | 203 | – |
| 8th | 290 | 374 | 208 | – |
| 9th | 295 | 374 | 220 | – |
| 10th | 296 | 376 | 249 | – |

Umpires: G.A. Hele and A.G. Jenkins.

# AUSTRALIA v WEST INDIES 1930-31 (2nd Test)

Played at Sydney Cricket Ground on 1, 2 (*no play*), 3, 5 January.
Toss: Australia.    Result: AUSTRALIA won by an innings and 172 runs.
Debuts: Nil.

Bartlett crushed a finger against his boot in catching Kippax at mid-on and was unable to bat.

## AUSTRALIA

| | | |
|---|---|---:|
| W.H. Ponsford | b Scott | 183 |
| A. Jackson | c Francis b Griffith | 8 |
| D.G. Bradman | c Barrow b Francis | 25 |
| A.F. Kippax | c Bartlett b Griffith | 10 |
| S.J. McCabe | lbw b Scott | 31 |
| W.M. Woodfull* | c Barrow b Constantine | 58 |
| A.G. Fairfax | c Constantine b Francis | 15 |
| W.A.S. Oldfield† | run out | 0 |
| C.V. Grimmett | b Scott | 12 |
| A. Hurwood | c Martin b Scott | 5 |
| H. Ironmonger | not out | 3 |
| Extras | (B 6, LB 5, W 5, NB 3) | 19 |
| **Total** | | **369** |

## WEST INDIES

| | | | | |
|---|---|---:|---|---:|
| C.A. Roach | run out | 7 | c Kippax b McCabe | 25 |
| L.S. Birkett | c Hurwood b Fairfax | 3 | c McCabe b Hurwood | 8 |
| G.A. Headley | b Fairfax | 14 | c Jackson b Hurwood | 2 |
| F.R. Martin | lbw b Grimmett | 10 | c McCabe b Hurwood | 0 |
| G.C. Grant* | c Hurwood b Ironmonger | 6 | not out | 15 |
| L.N. Constantine | c Bradman b Grimmett | 12 | b Hurwood | 8 |
| I. Barrow† | c Jackson b Fairfax | 17 | c McCabe b Ironmonger | 10 |
| G.N. Francis | b Grimmett | 8 | c Oldfield b Ironmonger | 0 |
| O.C. Scott | not out | 15 | c Woodfull b Ironmonger | 17 |
| H.C. Griffith | c Kippax b Grimmett | 8 | lbw b Grimmett | 0 |
| E.L. Bartlett | absent hurt | – | absent hurt | – |
| Extras | (B 6, NB 1) | 7 | (B 1, LB 2, W 1, NB 1) | 5 |
| **Total** | | **107** | | **90** |

| WEST INDIES | O | M | R | W | O | M | R | W | FALL OF WICKETS | | | |
|---|---|---|---|---|---|---|---|---|---|---|---|---|
| Griffith | 28 | 4 | 57 | 2 | | | | | | A | WI | WI |
| Constantine | 18 | 2 | 56 | 1 | | | | | *Wkt* | *1st* | *1st* | *2nd* |
| Francis | 27 | 3 | 70 | 2 | | | | | 1st | 12 | 3 | 26 |
| Scott | 15·4 | 0 | 66 | 4 | | | | | 2nd | 52 | 26 | 32 |
| Martin | 18 | 1 | 60 | 0 | | | | | 3rd | 69 | 36 | 32 |
| Birkett | 10 | 1 | 41 | 0 | | | | | 4th | 140 | 36 | 42 |
| | | | | | | | | | 5th | 323 | 57 | 53 |
| AUSTRALIA | | | | | | | | | 6th | 341 | 63 | 67 |
| Fairfax | 13 | 4 | 19 | 3 | 5 | 1 | 21 | 0 | 7th | 344 | 80 | 67 |
| Hurwood | 5 | 1 | 7 | 0 | 11 | 2 | 22 | 4 | 8th | 361 | 88 | 90 |
| Grimmett | 19·1 | 3 | 54 | 4 | 3·3 | 11 | 9 | 1 | 9th | 364 | 107 | 90 |
| Ironmonger | 13 | 3 | 20 | 1 | 4 | 1 | 13 | 3 | 10th | 369 | – | – |
| McCabe | | | | | 7 | 0 | 20 | 1 | | | | |

Umpires: G. Borwick and W.G. French.

# AUSTRALIA v WEST INDIES 1930-31 (3rd Test)

Played at Exhibition Ground Brisbane, on 16, 17, 19, 20 January.
Toss: Australia.   Result: AUSTRALIA won by an innings and 217 runs.
Debuts: Nil.

Missed in the slips when four, Bradman batted for five hours and hit 24 fours in making the highest score to date by an Australian in a home Test. Headley scored West Indies' first hundred against Australia.

## AUSTRALIA

| | | |
|---|---|---:|
| W.H. Ponsford | c Birkett b Francis | 109 |
| A. Jackson | lbw b Francis | 0 |
| D.G. Bradman | c Grant b Constantine | 223 |
| A.F. Kippax | b Birkett | 84 |
| S.J. McCabe | c Constantine b Griffith | 8 |
| W.M. Woodfull* | c Barrow b Griffith | 17 |
| A.G. Fairfax | c Sealy b Scott | 9 |
| R.K. Oxenham | lbw b Griffith | 48 |
| W.A.S. Oldfield† | not out | 38 |
| C.V. Grimmett | c Constantine b Francis | 4 |
| H. Ironmonger | c Roach b Griffith | 2 |
| Extras | (B 2, LB 7, NB 7) | 16 |
| **Total** | | **558** |

## WEST INDIES

| | | | | | |
|---|---|---:|---|---|---:|
| C.A. Roach | lbw b Oxenham | 4 | b McCabe | | 1 |
| F.R. Martin | lbw b Grimmett | 21 | lbw b Oxenham | | 11 |
| G.A. Headley | not out | 102 | c Oldfield b Ironmonger | | 28 |
| J.E.D. Sealy | c McCabe b Ironmonger | 3 | (9) not out | | 16 |
| G.C. Grant* | c McCabe b Grimmett | 8 | (6) run out | | 10 |
| L.N. Constantine | c Fairfax b Ironmonger | 9 | (4) lbw b Oxenham | | 7 |
| L.S. Birkett | lbw b Oxenham | 8 | (5) b Grimmett | | 13 |
| I. Barrow† | st Oldfield b Grimmett | 19 | (7) st Oldfield b Grimmett | | 17 |
| O.C. Scott | b Oxenham | 0 | (8) lbw b Grimmett | | 15 |
| G.N. Francis | b Oxenham | 8 | c Oldfield b Grimmett | | 7 |
| H.G. Griffith | lbw b Grimmett | 8 | c Bradman b Grimmett | | 12 |
| Extras | (B 1, LB 2) | 3 | (B 5, LB 4, NB 2) | | 11 |
| **Total** | | **193** | | | **148** |

| WEST INDIES | O | M | R | W | O | M | R | W |
|---|---:|---:|---:|---:|---:|---:|---:|---:|
| Francis | 26 | 4 | 76 | 3 | | | | |
| Constantine | 26 | 2 | 74 | 1 | | | | |
| Griffith | 33 | 4 | 133 | 4 | | | | |
| Scott | 24 | 1 | 125 | 1 | | | | |
| Martin | 27 | 3 | 85 | 0 | | | | |
| Sealy | 3 | 0 | 32 | 0 | | | | |
| Birkett | 7 | 0 | 16 | 1 | | | | |
| Grant | 1 | 0 | 1 | 0 | | | | |
| AUSTRALIA | | | | | | | | |
| Fairfax | 7 | 2 | 13 | 0 | 6 | 2 | 6 | 0 |
| Oxenham | 30 | 15 | 39 | 4 | 18 | 5 | 37 | 2 |
| Ironmonger | 26 | 15 | 43 | 2 | 15 | 8 | 29 | 1 |
| Grimmett | 41·3 | 9 | 95 | 4 | 14·3 | 4 | 49 | 5 |
| McCabe | | | | | 7 | 1 | 16 | 1 |

## FALL OF WICKETS

| | A | WI | WI |
|---|---:|---:|---:|
| *Wkt* | *1st* | *1st* | *2nd* |
| 1st | 1 | 5 | 13 |
| 2nd | 230 | 36 | 29 |
| 3rd | 423 | 41 | 47 |
| 4th | 431 | 60 | 58 |
| 5th | 441 | 94 | 72 |
| 6th | 462 | 116 | 82 |
| 7th | 468 | 159 | 94 |
| 8th | 543 | 162 | 112 |
| 9th | 551 | 182 | 128 |
| 10th | 558 | 193 | 148 |

Umpires: J.P. Orr and A.E. Wyeth.

# AUSTRALIA v WEST INDIES 1930-31 (4th Test)

Played at Melbourne Cricket Ground on 13, 14 February.
Toss: West Indies.   Result: AUSTRALIA won by an innings and 122 runs.
Debuts: Nil.

## WEST INDIES

| | | | | | |
|---|---|--:|---|---|--:|
| C.A. Roach | c Kippax b Grimmett | 20 | | lbw b Fairfax | 7 |
| F.R. Martin | lbw b Ironmonger | 17 | (6) | c Oldfield b Fairfax | 10 |
| G.A. Headley | c Jackson b Ironmonger | 33 | | c Fairfax b Ironmonger | 11 |
| L.S. Birkett | c McCabe b Ironmonger | 0 | | c Jackson b Ironmonger | 13 |
| E.L. Bartlett | st Oldfield b Ironmonger | 9 | (7) | b Fairfax | 6 |
| G.C. Grant* | c Oldfield b Ironmonger | 0 | (5) | c McCabe b Ironmonger | 3 |
| L.N. Constantine | c Jackson b Grimmett | 7 | (2) | c Kippax b Fairfax | 10 |
| I. Barrow† | c Fairfax b Ironmonger | 0 | | c Oxenham b Ironmonger | 13 |
| O.C. Scott | run out | 11 | | not out | 20 |
| G.N. Francis | not out | 0 | (11) | c Jackson b Grimmett | 0 |
| H.C. Griffith | c Fairfax b Ironmonger | 0 | (10) | b Grimmett | 4 |
| Extras | (NB 2) | 2 | | (B 3, LB 6, NB 1) | 10 |
| **Total** | | **99** | | | **107** |

## AUSTRALIA

| | | |
|---|---|--:|
| W.M. Woodfull* | run out | 83 |
| W.H. Ponsford | st Barrow b Constantine | 24 |
| D.G. Bradman | c Roach b Martin | 152 |
| A. Jackson | c Birkett b Constantine | 15 |
| S.J. McCabe | run out | 2 |
| A.G. Fairfax | c Birkett b Martin | 16 |
| A.F. Kippax | b Martin | 24 |
| R.K. Oxenham | c Constantine b Griffith | 0 |
| W.A.S. Oldfield† | not out | 1 |
| H. Ironmonger | } did not bat | |
| C.V. Grimmett | | |
| Extras | (B 7, LB 3, NB 1) | 11 |
| **Total** | (8 wickets declared) | **328** |

| AUSTRALIA | O | M | R | W | O | M | R | W |
|---|--:|--:|--:|--:|--:|--:|--:|--:|
| Fairfax | 5 | 0 | 14 | 0 | 14 | 2 | 31 | 4 |
| Oxenham | 6 | 1 | 14 | 0 | | | | |
| Ironmonger | 20 | 7 | 23 | 7 | 17 | 4 | 56 | 4 |
| Grimmett | 19 | 7 | 46 | 2 | 4·4 | 0 | 10 | 2 |

| WEST INDIES | O | M | R | W |
|---|--:|--:|--:|--:|
| Francis | 13 | 0 | 51 | 0 |
| Griffith | 8 | 1 | 33 | 1 |
| Scott | 11 | 0 | 47 | 0 |
| Constantine | 25 | 4 | 83 | 2 |
| Martin | 30·2 | 3 | 91 | 3 |
| Birkett | 2 | 0 | 12 | 0 |

## FALL OF WICKETS

| | WI | A | WI |
|---|--:|--:|--:|
| *Wkt* | *1st* | *1st* | *2nd* |
| 1st | 32 | 50 | 8 |
| 2nd | 51 | 206 | 32 |
| 3rd | 53 | 265 | 36 |
| 4th | 81 | 275 | 49 |
| 5th | 81 | 286 | 60 |
| 6th | 88 | 325 | 60 |
| 7th | 88 | 326 | 67 |
| 8th | 88 | 328 | 92 |
| 9th | 99 | – | 97 |
| 10th | 99 | – | 107 |

Umpires: A.N. Barlow and J. Richards.

# AUSTRALIA v WEST INDIES 1930-31 (5th Test)

Played at Sydney Cricket Ground on 27, 28 February, 2, 3, 4 March.
Toss: West Indies.   Result: WEST INDIES won by 30 runs.
Debuts: Australia – K.E. Rigg.

After losing their first four Tests against Australia, West Indies gained a surprise victory when Grant timed his declarations to allow his bowlers maximum asssistance from a 'sticky' pitch.

## WEST INDIES

| | | | | | |
|---|---|--:|---|---|--:|
| F.R. Martin | not out | 123 | c McCabe b Grimmett | | 20 |
| C.A. Roach | lbw b Grimmett | 31 | c Oldfield b Ironmonger | | 34 |
| G.A. Headley | lbw b McCabe | 105 | b Oxenham | | 30 |
| G.C. Grant* | c McCabe b Ironmonger | 62 | not out | | 27 |
| J.E.D. Sealy | c Kippax b Grimmett | 4 | run out | | 7 |
| L.N. Constantine | c McCabe b Ironmonger | 0 | c Bradman b Ironmonger | | 4 |
| E.L. Bartlett | b Grimmett | 0 | not out | | 0 |
| I. Barrow† | not out | 7 | | | |
| O.C. Scott | ) | | | | |
| G.N. Francis | ) did not bat | | | | |
| H.C. Griffith | ) | | | | |
| Extras | (B 6, LB 5, W 1, NB 6) | 18 | (B 1, LB 1) | | 2 |
| **Total** | (6 wickets declared) | **350** | (5 wickets declared) | | **124** |

## AUSTRALIA

| | | | | | |
|---|---|--:|---|---|--:|
| W.M. Woodfull* | c Constantine b Martin | 22 | c Constantine b Griffith | | 18 |
| W.H. Ponsford | c Bartlett b Francis | 7 | c Constantine b Martin | | 28 |
| D.G. Bradman | c Francis b Martin | 43 | b Griffith | | 0 |
| A.F. Kippax | c Sealy b Constantine | 3 | (5) c Roach b Constantine | | 10 |
| K.E. Rigg | c Barrow b Francis | 14 | (6) c Barrow b Constantine | | 16 |
| S.J. McCabe | c Headley b Francis | 21 | (7) c Grant b Martin | | 44 |
| A.G. Fairfax | st Barrow b Scott | 54 | (8) not out | | 60 |
| R.K. Oxenham | c Barrow b Francis | 0 | (9) lbw b Scott | | 14 |
| W.A.S. Oldfield† | run out | 36 | (4) lbw b Griffith | | 0 |
| C.V. Grimmett | not out | 15 | c Constantine b Griffith | | 12 |
| H. Ironmonger | b Griffith | 1 | run out | | 4 |
| Extras | (B 1, LB 7) | 8 | (B 3, LB 7, W 2, NB 2) | | 14 |
| **Total** | | **224** | | | **220** |

| AUSTRALIA | O | M | R | W | O | M | R | W | FALL OF WICKETS | | | | |
|---|--:|--:|--:|--:|--:|--:|--:|--:|---|--:|--:|--:|--:|
| | | | | | | | | | | WI | A | WI | A |
| Fairfax | 21 | 2 | 60 | 0 | | | | | *Wkt* | *1st* | *1st* | *2nd* | *2nd* |
| Oxenham | 24 | 10 | 51 | 0 | 10 | 4 | 14 | 1 | 1st | 70 | 7 | 46 | 49 |
| Ironmonger | 42 | 16 | 95 | 2 | 16 | 7 | 44 | 2 | 2nd | 222 | 66 | 66 | 49 |
| Grimmett | 33 | 7 | 100 | 3 | 18 | 4 | 47 | 1 | 3rd | 332 | 69 | 103 | 53 |
| McCabe | 15 | 5 | 26 | 1 | 7 | 2 | 17 | 0 | 4th | 337 | 89 | 113 | 53 |
| | | | | | | | | | 5th | 338 | 89 | 124 | 65 |
| WEST INDIES | | | | | | | | | 6th | 341 | 130 | – | 76 |
| Francis | 19 | 6 | 48 | 4 | 16 | 2 | 32 | 0 | 7th | – | 134 | – | 155 |
| Griffith | 13·2 | 3 | 31 | 1 | 13·3 | 3 | 50 | 4 | 8th | – | 196 | – | 180 |
| Martin | 27 | 3 | 67 | 2 | 18 | 4 | 44 | 2 | 9th | – | 215 | – | 214 |
| Constantine | 10 | 2 | 28 | 1 | 17 | 2 | 50 | 2 | 10th | – | 224 | – | 220 |
| Scott | 10 | 1 | 42 | 1 | 11 | 0 | 30 | 1 | | | | | |

Umpires: H. Armstrong and W.G. French.

# SOUTH AFRICA v ENGLAND 1930-31 (1st Test)

Played at Old Wanderers, Johannesburg, on 24, 26, 27 December.
Toss: England.   Result: SOUTH AFRICA won by 28 runs.
Debuts: South Africa – X.C. Balaskas, S.H. Curnow, E.S. Newson, K.G. Viljoen.

### SOUTH AFRICA

| | | | | | |
|---|---|---|---|---|---|
| I.J. Siedle | b Voce | 13 | | lbw b Voce | 35 |
| S.H. Curnow | lbw b Tate | 13 | | run out | 8 |
| B. Mitchell | c Hammond b Voce | 6 | | c Duckworth b Hammond | 72 |
| R.H. Catterall | b Voce | 5 | | c Hendren b Hammond | 54 |
| K.G. Viljoen | c Duckworth b Peebles | 7 | (6) | b Hammond | 44 |
| X.C. Balaskas | lbw b Peebles | 7 | (5) | lbw b Tate | 3 |
| H.B. Cameron† | b Peebles | 0 | | c Duckworth b Voce | 51 |
| Q. McMillan | not out | 45 | | b Voce | 14 |
| E.P. Nupen* | b Peebles | 0 | | b Hammond | 1 |
| C.L. Vincent | c Hammond b Voce | 2 | | b Voce | 1 |
| E.S. Newson | b Tate | 10 | | not out | 0 |
| Extras | (B 12, LB 5, NB 1) | 18 | | (B 16, LB 7) | 23 |
| **Total** | | **126** | | | **306** |

### ENGLAND

| | | | | | |
|---|---|---|---|---|---|
| R.E.S. Wyatt | lbw b Nupen | 8 | | c McMillan b Catterall | 5 |
| M. Leyland | c Cameron b Nupen | 29 | | c and b Catterall | 15 |
| W.R. Hammond | lbw b Nupen | 49 | | st Cameron b Vincent | 63 |
| E.H. Hendren | c Cameron b McMillan | 8 | | c Mitchell b Nupen | 3 |
| M.J.L. Turnbull | st Cameron b Vincent | 28 | | b Nupen | 61 |
| A.P.F. Chapman* | c Newson b Vincent | 28 | | c Mitchell b Nupen | 11 |
| J.C. White | c Curnow b Nupen | 14 | | lbw b Nupen | 2 |
| M.W. Tate | c Mitchell b Vincent | 8 | | c Mitchell b Nupen | 28 |
| I.A.R. Peebles | b Nupen | 0 | (11) | not out | 13 |
| W. Voce | run out | 8 | (9) | c Nupen b Vincent | 0 |
| G. Duckworth† | not out | 0 | (10) | lbw b Nupen | 4 |
| Extras | (B 9, LB 3, W 1) | 13 | | (LB 6) | 6 |
| **Total** | | **193** | | | **211** |

| ENGLAND | O | M | R | W | O | M | R | W |
|---|---|---|---|---|---|---|---|---|
| Tate | 12·2 | 4 | 20 | 2 | 18 | 2 | 47 | 1 |
| Voce | 26 | 11 | 45 | 4 | 27·2 | 8 | 59 | 4 |
| Peebles | 14 | 2 | 43 | 4 | 7 | 0 | 41 | 0 |
| Hammond | | | | | 25 | 5 | 63 | 4 |
| White | | | | | 16 | 3 | 53 | 0 |
| Wyatt | | | | | 2 | 0 | 20 | 0 |
| SOUTH AFRICA | | | | | | | | |
| Newson | 8 | 2 | 11 | 0 | 14 | 2 | 30 | 0 |
| Viljoen | 4 | 1 | 10 | 0 | | | | |
| McMillan | 9 | 0 | 47 | 1 | 4 | 0 | 25 | 0 |
| Nupen | 26·1 | 1 | 63 | 5 | 25·3 | 3 | 87 | 6 |
| Vincent | 21 | 8 | 49 | 3 | 17 | 1 | 44 | 2 |
| Catterall | | | | | 5 | 0 | 12 | 2 |
| Balaskas | | | | | 2 | 0 | 7 | 0 |

FALL OF WICKETS

| Wkt | SA 1st | E 1st | SA 2nd | E 2nd |
|---|---|---|---|---|
| 1st | 19 | 33 | 34 | 13 |
| 2nd | 28 | 42 | 50 | 22 |
| 3rd | 37 | 51 | 172 | 30 |
| 4th | 42 | 103 | 174 | 131 |
| 5th | 51 | 149 | 182 | 152 |
| 6th | 53 | 176 | 263 | 154 |
| 7th | 78 | 179 | 291 | 164 |
| 8th | 78 | 185 | 305 | 169 |
| 9th | 81 | 193 | 306 | 195 |
| 10th | 126 | 193 | 306 | 211 |

Umpires: W.B. Ryan and G.B. Treadwell.

# SOUTH AFRICA v ENGLAND 1930-31 (2nd Test)

Played at Newlands, Cape Town, on 1, 2, 3, 5 January.
Toss: South Africa.     Result: MATCH DRAWN.
Debuts: Nil.

The partnership of 260 between Mitchell and Siedle remains the highest by South Africa for the first wicket in all Tests.

## SOUTH AFRICA

| | | |
|---|---|---|
| B. Mitchell | b Tate | 123 |
| I.J. Siedle | c Chapman b White | 141 |
| E.P. Nupen | b Tate | 12 |
| H.W. Taylor | c White b Leyland | 117 |
| R.H. Catterall | b Tate | 56 |
| H.B. Cameron† | c Peebles b White | 26 |
| X.C. Balaskas | c Turnbull b Leyland | 0 |
| H.G. Deane* | b Leyland | 7 |
| Q. McMillan | not out | 7 |
| C.L. Vincent | not out | 3 |
| A.J. Bell | did not bat | |
| Extras | (B 8, LB 12, NB 1) | 21 |
| **Total** | (8 wickets declared) | **513** |

## ENGLAND

| | | | | | |
|---|---|---|---|---|---|
| R.E.S. Wyatt | b McMillan | 40 | | b Bell | 29 |
| W.R. Hammond | c and b McMillan | 57 | | c Deane b Vincent | 65 |
| M. Leyland | b Bell | 52 | | c Mitchell b McMillan | 28 |
| E.H. Hendren | b Balaskas | 93 | | b Vincent | 86 |
| M.J.L. Turnbull | b Bell | 7 | | b McMillan | 14 |
| A.P.F. Chapman* | b Bell | 0 | (8) | b Catterall | 4 |
| J.C. White | lbw b Balaskas | 23 | (6) | lbw b Catterall | 8 |
| M.W. Tate | c Taylor b McMillan | 15 | (9) | lbw b Nupen | 3 |
| W. Voce | c and b Vincent | 30 | (10) | not out | 1 |
| I.A.R. Peebles | not out | 7 | (7) | b Catterall | 0 |
| G. Duckworth† | lbw b Vincent | 0 | | absent hurt | – |
| Extras | (B9, LB 16, NB 1) | 26 | | (B 9, LB 4, NB 1) | 14 |
| **Total** | | **350** | | | **252** |

| ENGLAND | O | M | R | W | O | M | R | W |
|---|---|---|---|---|---|---|---|---|
| Tate | 43 | 13 | 79 | 3 | | | | |
| Hammond | 10 | 2 | 27 | 0 | | | | |
| Voce | 33 | 11 | 95 | 0 | | | | |
| Peebles | 28 | 2 | 95 | 0 | | | | |
| White | 46 | 15 | 101 | 2 | | | | |
| Leyland | 30 | 6 | 91 | 3 | | | | |
| Wyatt | 2 | 0 | 4 | 0 | | | | |
| SOUTH AFRICA | | | | | | | | |
| Bell | 27 | 9 | 53 | 3 | 29 | 8 | 58 | 1 |
| Catterall | 5 | 3 | 2 | 0 | 12 | 2 | 15 | 3 |
| Nupen | 22 | 7 | 43 | 0 | 17 | 2 | 26 | 1 |
| Balaskas | 16 | 0 | 75 | 2 | 9 | 1 | 29 | 0 |
| Vincent | 17·4 | 4 | 40 | 2 | 17 | 6 | 26 | 2 |
| McMillan | 33 | 6 | 111 | 3 | 32 | 7 | 64 | 2 |
| Mitchell | | | | | 8 | 0 | 20 | 0 |

### FALL OF WICKETS

| Wkt | SA 1st | E 1st | E 2nd |
|---|---|---|---|
| 1st | 260 | 75 | 58 |
| 2nd | 280 | 120 | 105 |
| 3rd | 299 | 202 | 152 |
| 4th | 447 | 214 | 184 |
| 5th | 473 | 214 | 225 |
| 6th | 479 | 288 | 225 |
| 7th | 502 | 293 | 235 |
| 8th | 506 | 312 | 250 |
| 9th | – | 350 | 252 |
| 10th | – | 350 | – |

Umpires: W.T. Ryan and J.C. Collings.

# SOUTH AFRICA v ENGLAND 1930-31 (3rd Test)

Played at Kingsmead, Durban, on 16, 17 (*no play*), 19, 20 January.
Toss: South Africa.   Result: MATCH DRAWN.
Debuts: Nil.

## SOUTH AFRICA

| | | | | | |
|---|---|---|---|---|---|
| I.J. Siedle | b White | 38 | | lbw b Tate | 0 |
| B. Mitchell | c Duckworth b Tate | 5 | (3) | c Chapman b White | 13 |
| S.H. Curnow | c Duckworth b Voce | 2 | (2) | c Hammond b Voce | 9 |
| H.W. Taylor | c Duckworth b Voce | 3 | | not out | 64 |
| R.H. Catterall | b White | 11 | | b Hammond | 19 |
| H.B. Cameron† | c Voce b Tate | 41 | | b Hammond | 8 |
| H.G. Dane* | b Voce | 15 | | c Duckworth b Allom | 8 |
| Q. McMillan | c Wyatt b White | 20 | | c Chapman b White | 1 |
| C.L. Vincent | c Duckworth b Voce | 18 | | c sub (H.W. Lee) b White | 5 |
| N.A. Quinn | b Voce | 3 | | | |
| A.J. Bell | not out | 0 | (10) | not out | 0 |
| Extras | (B 5, LB 8, NB 8) | 21 | | (B 8, LB 8, NB 2) | 18 |
| **Total** | | **177** | | (8 wickets) | **145** |

## ENGLAND

| | | |
|---|---|---|
| R.E.S. Wyatt | c Siedle b Vincent | 54 |
| W.R. Hammond | not out | 136 |
| M. Leyland | not out | 31 |
| E.H. Hendren | ) | |
| M.J.L. Turnbull | ) | |
| A.P.F. Chapman* | ) | |
| J.C. White | ) did not bat | |
| M.J.C. Allom | ) | |
| M.W. Tate | ) | |
| W. Voce | ) | |
| G. Duckworth† | ) | |
| Extras | (LB 2) | 2 |
| **Total** | (1 wicket declared) | **223** |

| ENGLAND | O | M | R | W | O | M | R | W |
|---|---|---|---|---|---|---|---|---|
| Tate | 27 | 13 | 33 | 2 | 9 | 3 | 12 | 1 |
| Allom | 25 | 4 | 44 | 0 | 11 | 0 | 27 | 1 |
| Voce | 29·2 | 3 | 58 | 5 | 12 | 3 | 14 | 1 |
| White | 16 | 6 | 21 | 3 | 18 | 4 | 33 | 3 |
| Hammond | | | | | 11 | 6 | 9 | 2 |
| Leyland | | | | | 9 | 1 | 32 | 0 |

| SOUTH AFRICA | O | M | R | W |
|---|---|---|---|---|
| Bell | 22 | 3 | 45 | 0 |
| Catterall | 10 | 0 | 37 | 0 |
| Quinn | 19 | 4 | 42 | 0 |
| Vincent | 25 | 7 | 66 | 1 |
| McMillan | 6 | 0 | 31 | 0 |

### FALL OF WICKETS

| Wkt | SA 1st | E 1st | SA 2nd |
|---|---|---|---|
| 1st | 14 | 160 | 0 |
| 2nd | 23 | – | 27 |
| 3rd | 33 | – | 47 |
| 4th | 51 | – | 106 |
| 5th | 86 | – | 116 |
| 6th | 118 | – | 136 |
| 7th | 141 | – | 137 |
| 8th | 161 | – | 145 |
| 9th | 172 | – | – |
| 10th | 177 | – | – |

Umpires: A.C. King and J.C. Collings.

# SOUTH AFRICA v ENGLAND 1930-31 (4th Test)

Played at Old Wanderers, Johannesburg, on 13, 14, 16, 17 February.
Toss: England.   Result: MATCH DRAWN.
Debuts: England – W. Farrimond, H.W. Lee.

## ENGLAND

| | | | | |
|---|---|--:|---|--:|
| R.E.S. Wyatt | lbw b Nupen | 37 | lbw b Vincent | 7 |
| H.W. Lee | lbw b Nupen | 8 | c Mitchell b Catterall | 1 |
| W.R. Hammond | c McMillan b Hall | 75 | c Mitchell b Catterall | 15 |
| E.H. Hendren | c Cameron b Hall | 64 | c Vincent b Nupen | 45 |
| M. Leyland | lbw b Hall | 91 | c Mitchell b Nupen | 46 |
| M.J.L. Turnbull | st wcameron b McMillan | 25 | (9) not out | 0 |
| W. Farrimond† | c Mitchell b McMillan | 28 | | |
| I.A.R. Peebles | c Nupen b Vincent | 3 | (10) c and b Nupen | 2 |
| A.P.F. Chapman* | b Nupen | 5 | (7) c Taylor b Nupen | 3 |
| M.W. Tate | c Mitchell b Hall | 26 | (6) c McMillan b Nupen | 38 |
| W. Voce | not out | 41 | (8) c Siedle b Nupen | 5 |
| Extras | (B 21, LB 8) | 29 | (B 1, LB 6) | 7 |
| **Total** | | **442** | (9 wickets declared) | **169** |

## SOUTH AFRICA

| | | | | |
|---|---|--:|---|--:|
| S.H. Curnow | lbw b Hammond | 7 | lbw b Tate | 12 |
| I.J. Siedle | lbw b Peebles | 62 | c Hammond b Tate | 8 |
| B. Mitchell | lbw b Tate | 68 | c Hammond b Voce | 74 |
| H.W. Taylor | hit wkt b Peebles | 72 | b Voce | 13 |
| R.H. Catterall | c Hammond b Tate | 11 | lbw b Peebles | 21 |
| K.G. Viljoen | b Voce | 30 | (7) c Hammond b Voce | 31 |
| H.B. Cameron*† | b Peebles | 2 | (6) not out | 69 |
| Q. McMillan | c Hendren b Peebles | 12 | c Hendren b Voce | 24 |
| E.P. Nupen | not out | 11 | not out | 11 |
| C.L. Vincent | lbw b Peebles | 0 | | |
| A.E. Hall | b Peebles | 0 | | |
| Extras | (B 6, LB 14) | 20 | (B 6, LB 9, NB 2) | 17 |
| **Total** | | **295** | (7 wickets) | **280** |

| SOUTH AFRICA | O | M | R | W | O | M | R | W | FALL OF WICKETS | | | | |
|---|--:|--:|--:|--:|--:|--:|--:|--:|---|--:|--:|--:|--:|
| | | | | | | | | | | E | SA | E | SA |
| Hall | 37 | 5 | 105 | 4 | 9 | 2 | 47 | 0 | Wkt | 1st | 1st | 2nd | 2nd |
| Catterall | 7 | 1 | 16 | 0 | 10 | 1 | 28 | 2 | 1st | 41 | 16 | 3 | 14 |
| Nupen | 51 | 7 | 148 | 3 | 16·1 | 1 | 46 | 6 | 2nd | 64 | 112 | 23 | 63 |
| McMillan | 16·4 | 1 | 62 | 2 | 2 | 0 | 12 | 0 | 3rd | 183 | 167 | 23 | 102 |
| Vincent | 26 | 8 | 69 | 1 | 14 | 4 | 29 | 1 | 4th | 231 | 185 | 120 | 135 |
| Viljoen | 4 | 0 | 13 | 0 | | | | | 5th | 329 | 243 | 125 | 153 |
| | | | | | | | | | 6th | 337 | 249 | 135 | 209 |
| ENGLAND | | | | | | | | | 7th | 341 | 280 | 167 | 261 |
| Tate | 27 | 9 | 46 | 2 | 22 | 6 | 52 | 2 | 8th | 352 | 295 | 167 | – |
| Hammond | 28 | 6 | 50 | 1 | 11 | 2 | 27 | 0 | 9th | 385 | 295 | 169 | – |
| Voce | 42 | 11 | 106 | 1 | 32 | 7 | 87 | 4 | 10th | 442 | 295 | – | – |
| Peebles | 38·5 | 10 | 63 | 6 | 27 | 6 | 86 | 1 | | | | | |
| Wyatt | 2 | 0 | 10 | 0 | | | | | | | | | |
| Leyland | | | | | 4 | 0 | 11 | 0 | | | | | |

Umpires: A.C. King and J.C. Collings.

# SOUTH AFRICA v ENGLAND 1930-31 (5th Test)

Played at Kingsmead, Durban, on 21, 23, 24, 25 February.
Toss: England.   Result: MATCH DRAWN.
Debuts: South Africa – J.A.K. Cochran.

The start of this match was delayed by 70 minutes because the correct size of bails was unavailable and the umpires had to make two sets.

## SOUTH AFRICA

|  |  | |  |  |  |
|---|---|---|---|---|---|
| I.J. Siedle | c and b White | | 57 | c Chapman b White | 3( |
| B. Mitchell | b Hammond | | 73 | c Hammond b Voce | 2 |
| J.A.J. Christy | b Peebles | | 16 | st Farrimond b Peebles | 3 |
| H.W. Taylor | c and b Peebles | | 16 | lbw b Peebles | 1 |
| K.G. Viljoen | c Hammond b Tate | | 16 | c Chapman b Voce | 1 |
| H.B. Cameron*† | b Voce | | 4 | (7) not out | 4 |
| E.L. Dalton | c Farrimond b Hammond | | 31 | (6) st Farrimond b Peebles | 1 |
| Q. McMillan | not out | | 29 | c Chapman b Wyatt | 2 |
| C.L. Vincent | c Chapman b Peebles | | 6 | not out | |
| A.J. Bell | b Voce | | 0 | | |
| J.A.K. Cochran | b Peebles | | 4 | | |
| Extras | | | | (B 8, LB 3, NB 3) | 1 |
| **Total** | | | **252** | (7 wickets declared) | 21 |

## ENGLAND

|  |  |  |  |  |
|---|---|---|---|---|
| R.E.S. Wyatt | c Cameron b Bell | 24 | c Mitchell b Christy | |
| W.R. Hammond | c Mitchell b Vincent | 29 | c Vincent b Bell | 2 |
| M. Leyland | lbw b Bell | 8 | | |
| E.H. Hendren | c McMillan b Vincent | 30 | | |
| M.J.L. Turnbull | b McMillan | 6 | (4) c and b Siedle | |
| W. Farrimond† | c Taylor b Vincent | 35 | (3) c Cameron b Taylor | |
| A.P.F. Chapman* | c McMillan b Vincent | 24 | | |
| M.W. Tate | b Vincent | 50 | (5) not out | 2 |
| W. Voce | c Bell b McMillan | 0 | | |
| J.C. White | c and b Vincent | 10 | | |
| I.A.R. Peebles | not out | 2 | | |
| Extras | (B 5, LB 4, NB 3) | 12 | (B 2, LB 1) | |
| **Total** | | **230** | (4 wickets) | 7 |

| ENGLAND | O | M | R | W | O | M | R | W | | FALL OF WICKETS | | | |
|---|---|---|---|---|---|---|---|---|---|---|---|---|---|
| | | | | | | | | | | SA | E | SA | E |
| Tate | 22 | 6 | 35 | 1 | 9 | 2 | 17 | 0 | Wkt | 1st | 1st | 2nd | 2nd |
| Hammond | 19 | 6 | 36 | 2 | 5 | 0 | 28 | 0 | 1st | 127 | 56 | 43 | 7 |
| Voce | 27 | 10 | 51 | 2 | 22 | 1 | 46 | 2 | 2nd | 131 | 56 | 64 | 3 |
| Peebles | 27·4 | 3 | 67 | 4 | 25 | 4 | 71 | 3 | 3rd | 157 | 87 | 91 | 4 |
| White | 35 | 9 | 63 | 1 | 17 | 6 | 37 | 1 | 4th | 163 | 101 | 110 | 7 |
| Wyatt | | | | | 4 | 2 | 6 | 1 | 5th | 168 | 101 | 126 | – |
| | | | | | | | | | 6th | 203 | 126 | 143 | – |
| SOUTH AFRICA | | | | | | | | | 7th | 221 | 188 | 208 | – |
| Bell | 30 | 4 | 63 | 2 | 3 | 0 | 14 | 1 | 8th | 242 | 188 | – | – |
| Cochran | 23 | 5 | 47 | 0 | | | | | 9th | 243 | 223 | – | – |
| Vincent | 31·2 | 9 | 51 | 6 | | | | | 10th | 252 | 230 | – | – |
| McMillan | 17 | 3 | 57 | 2 | | | | | | | | | |
| Christy | | | | | 4 | 1 | 17 | 1 | | | | | |
| Taylor | | | | | 3 | 0 | 13 | 1 | | | | | |
| Siedle | | | | | 3·1 | 1 | 7 | 1 | | | | | |
| Mitchell | | | | | 1 | 0 | 18 | 0 | | | | | |

Umpires: A.C. King and J.C. Collings.

# ENGLAND v NEW ZEALAND 1931 (1st Test)

Played at Lord's, London, on 27, 29, 30 June.
Toss: New Zealand.   Result: MATCH DRAWN.
Debuts: England – J. Arnold, A.H. Bakewell; New Zealand – I.B. Cromb, J.L. Kerr.

Although this was the only Test originally scheduled, New Zealand's form resulted in an extra two matches being arranged. The partnership of 246 between Ames and Allen is still the eighth-wicket record for all Test cricket.

## NEW ZEALAND

| | | | | |
|---|---|---:|---|---:|
| C.S. Dempster | lbw b Peebles | 53 | b Hammond | 120 |
| J.E. Mills | b Peebles | 34 | b Allen | 0 |
| G.L. Weir | lbw b Peebles | 37 | b Allen | 40 |
| J.L. Kerr | st Ames b Robins | 2 | (6) lbw b Peebles | 0 |
| R.C. Blunt | c Hammond b Robins | 7 | b Robins | 96 |
| M.L. Page | b Allen | 23 | (4) c and b Peebles | 104 |
| T.C. Lowry* | c Hammond b Robins | 1 | (9) b Peebles | 34 |
| I.B. Cromb | c Ames b Peebles | 20 | (7) c Voce b Robins | 14 |
| C.F.W. Allcott | c Hammond b Peebles | 13 | (10) not out | 20 |
| W.E. Merritt | c Jardine b Hammond | 17 | (8) b Peebles | 5 |
| K.C. James† | not out | 1 | | |
| Extras | (B 2, LB 12, W 1, NB 1) | 16 | (B 23, LB 10, W 1, NB 2) | 36 |
| **Total** | | **224** | (9 wickets declared) | **469** |

## ENGLAND

| | | | | |
|---|---|---:|---|---:|
| J. Arnold | c Page b Cromb | 0 | c and b Blunt | 34 |
| A.H. Bakewell | lbw b Cromb | 9 | c Blunt b Cromb | 27 |
| W.R. Hammond | b Cromb | 7 | run out | 46 |
| K.S. Duleepsinhji | c Kerr b Merritt | 25 | c James b Allcott | 11 |
| D.R. Jardine* | c Blunt b Merritt | 38 | (7) not out | 0 |
| F.E. Woolley | lbw b Merritt | 80 | (5) b Cromb | 9 |
| L.E.G. Ames† | c James b Weir | 137 | (6) not out | 17 |
| R.A.R. Peebles | st James b Merritt | 0 | | |
| G.O.B. Allen | c Lowry b Weir | 122 | | |
| R.W.V. Robins | c Lowry b Weir | 12 | | |
| W. Voce | not out | 1 | | |
| Extras | (B 15, LB 8) | 23 | (LB 2) | 2 |
| **Total** | | **454** | (5 wickets) | **146** |

| ENGLAND | O | M | R | W | O | M | R | W | | FALL OF WICKETS | | | |
|---|---:|---:|---:|---:|---:|---:|---:|---:|---|---|---|---|---|
| Voce | 10 | 1 | 40 | 0 | 32 | 11 | 60 | 0 | | NZ | E | NZ | E |
| Allen | 15 | 2 | 45 | 1 | 25 | 8 | 47 | 2 | *Wkt* | *1st* | *1st* | *2nd* | *2nd* |
| Hammond | 10·1 | 5 | 8 | 1 | 21 | 2 | 50 | 1 | 1st | 58 | 5 | 1 | 62 |
| Peebles | 26 | 3 | 77 | 5 | 42·4 | 6 | 150 | 4 | 2nd | 130 | 14 | 100 | 62 |
| Robins | 13 | 3 | 38 | 3 | 37 | 5 | 126 | 2 | 3rd | 136 | 31 | 218 | 94 |
| | | | | | | | | | 4th | 140 | 62 | 360 | 105 |
| NEW ZEALAND | | | | | | | | | 5th | 153 | 129 | 360 | 144 |
| Cromb | 37 | 7 | 113 | 3 | 25 | 5 | 44 | 2 | 6th | 161 | 188 | 389 | – |
| Weir | 8 | 1 | 38 | 3 | 5 | 1 | 18 | 0 | 7th | 190 | 190 | 404 | – |
| Blunt | 46 | 9 | 124 | 0 | 14 | 5 | 54 | 1 | 8th | 191 | 436 | 406 | – |
| Allcott | 17 | 3 | 34 | 0 | 10 | 2 | 26 | 1 | 9th | 209 | 447 | 469 | – |
| Merritt | 23 | 2 | 104 | 4 | 1 | 0 | 2 | 0 | 10th | 224 | 454 | – | – |
| Page | 3 | 0 | 18 | 0 | | | | | | | | | |

Umpires: F. Chester and J. Hardstaff, sr.

# ENGLAND v NEW ZEALAND 1931 (2nd Test)

Played at Kennington Oval, London, on 29, 30, 31 July.
Toss: England.   Result: ENGLAND won by an innings and 26 runs.
Debuts: England – F.R. Brown, H. Verity; New Zealand – H.G. Vivian.

### ENGLAND

| | | |
|---|---|---|
| H. Sutcliffe | st James b Vivian | 117 |
| A.H. Bakewell | run out | 40 |
| K.S. Duleepsinhji | c Weir b Allcott | 109 |
| W.R. Hammond | not out | 100 |
| L.E.G. Ames† | c James b Vivian | 41 |
| D.R. Jardine* | not out | 7 |
| F.R. Brown | ) | |
| G.O.B. Allen | ) | |
| M.W. Tate | ) did not bat | |
| I.A.R. Peebles | ) | |
| H. Verity | ) | |
| Extras | (B 1, LB 1) | 2 |
| **Total** | (4 wickets declared) | **416** |

### NEW ZEALAND

| | | | | | |
|---|---|---|---|---|---|
| J.E. Mills | b Allen | 27 | | b Brown | 30 |
| G.L. Weir | b Allen | 13 | | b Peebles | 6 |
| R.C. Blunt | c Ames b Allen | 2 | (4) | b Peebles | 43 |
| M.L. Page | c Peebles b Tate | 12 | (3) | b Tate | 3 |
| H.G. Vivian | c Ames b Allen | 3 | | c Brown b Peebles | 51 |
| T.C. Lowry* | c Jardine b Brown | 62 | | c Duleepsinhji b Peebles | 0 |
| J.L. Kerr | c Ames b Allen | 34 | | b Tate | 28 |
| K.C. James† | lbw b Brown | 4 | | c Peebles b Verity | 10 |
| I.B. Cromb | c Hammond b Verity | 8 | | not out | 3 |
| W.E. Merritt | c Hammond b Verity | 8 | | lbw b Tate | 4 |
| C.F.W. Allcott | not out | 5 | | c Allen b Verity | 1 |
| Extras | (B 2, LB 9, NB 4) | 15 | | (B 6, LB 10, NB 2) | 18 |
| **Total** | | **193** | | | **197** |

| NEW ZEALAND | O | M | R | W | O | M | R | W |
|---|---|---|---|---|---|---|---|---|
| Cromb | 30 | 5 | 97 | 0 | | | | |
| Allcott | 44 | 7 | 108 | 1 | | | | |
| Vivian | 34·3 | 8 | 96 | 2 | | | | |
| Weir | 10 | 1 | 36 | 0 | | | | |
| Merritt | 12 | 0 | 75 | 0 | | | | |
| Blunt | 1 | 0 | 2 | 0 | | | | |
| **ENGLAND** | | | | | | | | |
| Tate | 18 | 9 | 15 | 1 | 21 | 6 | 22 | 3 |
| Brown | 29 | 12 | 52 | 2 | 16 | 6 | 38 | 1 |
| Verity | 22·1 | 8 | 52 | 2 | 12·3 | 4 | 33 | 2 |
| Peebles | 12 | 3 | 35 | 0 | 22 | 4 | 63 | 4 |
| Allen | 13 | 7 | 14 | 5 | 13 | 4 | 23 | 0 |
| Hammond | 1 | 0 | 10 | 0 | | | | |

| FALL OF WICKETS | E | NZ | NZ |
|---|---|---|---|
| Wkt | 1st | 1st | 2nd |
| 1st | 84 | 42 | 19 |
| 2nd | 262 | 44 | 38 |
| 3rd | 271 | 45 | 51 |
| 4th | 401 | 53 | 139 |
| 5th | – | 92 | 143 |
| 6th | – | 157 | 162 |
| 7th | – | 167 | 189 |
| 8th | – | 168 | 189 |
| 9th | – | 188 | 196 |
| 10th | – | 193 | 197 |

Umpires: F. Chester and J. Hardstaff, sr.

# ENGLAND v NEW ZEALAND 1931 (3rd Test)

Played at Old Trafford, Manchester, on 15 (*no play*), 17 (*no play*), 18 August.
Toss: New Zealand.   Result: MATCH DRAWN.
Debuts: England – E. Paynter.

Manchester's rainfall relented in time for a 3 p.m. start on the third day.

## ENGLAND

| | | |
|---|---|---:|
| H. Sutcliffe | not out | 109 |
| E. Paynter | c James b Cromb | 3 |
| K.S. Duleepsinhji | c Allcott b Vivian | 63 |
| W.R. Hammond | c Cromb b Vivian | 16 |
| D.R. Jardine* | not out | 28 |
| L.E.G. Ames† | ) | |
| G.O.B. Allen | ) | |
| F.R. Brown | ) did not bat | |
| H. Larwood | ) | |
| L.A.R. Peebles | ) | |
| H. Verity | ) | |
| Extras | (B 4, NB 1) | 5 |
| **Total** | (3 wickets) | **224** |

## NEW ZEALAND

T.C. Lowry*
C.S. Dempster
J.E. Mills
M.L. Page
G.L. Weir
K.C. James†
A.M. Matheson
J.B. Cromb
C.F.W. Allcott
H.G. Vivian
R.C. Blunt

| NEW ZEALAND | O | M | R | W |
|---|---|---|---|---|
| Matheson | 12 | 1 | 40 | 0 |
| Cromb | 16 | 6 | 33 | 1 |
| Allcott | 27 | 6 | 75 | 0 |
| Vivian | 14 | 1 | 54 | 2 |
| Blunt | 1 | 0 | 12 | 0 |
| Lowry | 1 | 0 | 5 | 0 |

### FALL OF WICKETS

| | E |
|---|---|
| Wkt | *1st* |
| 1st | 8 |
| 2nd | 134 |
| 3rd | 166 |

Umpires: F. Chester and J. Hardstaff, sr.

# AUSTRALIA v SOUTH AFRICA 1931-32 (1st Test)

Play at Woolloongabba, Brisbane, on 27, 28, 30 (*no play*) November, 1 (*no play*), 2, 3 December.
Toss: Australia.   Result: AUSTRALIA won by an innings and 163 runs.
Debuts: Australia – H.C. Nitschke.

Bradman, missed when 11 and 15, marked the introduction of Test cricket to the 'Gabba' by exceeding his own record score by an Australian in a home Test. It remains the highest innings in a Test at Brisbane. South Africa 126 for 3 at Saturday's close, had to wait until 4 p.m. on Wednesday before resuming their innings on a rain-soaked pitch.

### AUSTRALIA

| | | |
|---|---|---|
| W.M. Woodfull* | lbw b Vincent | 76 |
| W.H. Ponsford | c Mitchell b Bell | 19 |
| D.G. Bradman | lbw b Vincent | 226 |
| A.F. Kippax | c Cameron b Vincent | 1 |
| S.J. McCabe | c Vincent b Morkel | 27 |
| H.C. Nitschke | c Cameron b Bell | 6 |
| R.K. Oxenham | b Bell | 1 |
| W.A.S. Oldfield† | not out | 56 |
| C.V. Grimmett | b Bell | 14 |
| T.W. Wall | lbw b Quinn | 14 |
| H. Ironmonger | b Quinn | 2 |
| Extras | (B 5, LB 1, W 1, NB 1) | 8 |
| **Total** | | **450** |

### SOUTH AFRICA

| | | | | | |
|---|---|---|---|---|---|
| J.A.J. Christy | b Wall | 24 | c McCabe b Ironmonger | | 1 |
| S.H. Curnow | b Ironmonger | 11 | b Grimmett | | |
| B. Mitchell | run out | 58 | b Wall | | |
| H.B. Cameron*† | st Oldfield b Grimmett | 4 | b Ironmonger | | 2 |
| H.W. Taylor | b Wall | 41 | c Oxenham b Ironmonger | | 4 |
| E.L. Dalton | c and b Ironmonger | 11 | b Wall | | |
| Q. McMillan | c Oxenham b Ironmonger | 0 | (8) c Nitschke b Wall | | |
| D.P.B. Morkel | c McCabe b Ironmonger | 3 | (7) b Wall | | |
| C.L. Vincent | c Nitschke b Grimmett | 10 | c sub (K.E. Rigg) b Wall | | |
| N.A. Quinn | c sub (K.E. Rigg) b Ironmonger | 1 | c McCabe b Ironmonger | | |
| A.J. Bell | not out | 1 | not out | | |
| Extras | (B 2, LB 4) | 6 | (B 6, LB 5, NB 3) | | 14 |
| **Total** | | **170** | | | **117** |

| SOUTH AFRICA | O | M | R | W | O | M | R | W |
|---|---|---|---|---|---|---|---|---|
| Bell | 42 | 5 | 120 | 4 | | | | |
| Morkel | 13 | 1 | 57 | 1 | | | | |
| Quinn | 38·3 | 6 | 113 | 2 | | | | |
| Vincent | 34 | 0 | 100 | 3 | | | | |
| McMillan | 10 | 0 | 52 | 0 | | | | |
| **AUSTRALIA** | | | | | | | | |
| Wall | 28 | 14 | 39 | 2 | 15·1 | 7 | 14 | 5 |
| McCabe | 11 | 4 | 16 | 0 | | | | |
| Grimmett | 41·1 | 21 | 49 | 2 | 15 | 3 | 45 | 1 |
| Ironmonger | 47 | 29 | 42 | 5 | 30 | 16 | 44 | 4 |
| Oxenham | 11 | 5 | 18 | 0 | | | | |

### FALL OF WICKETS

| | A | SA | SA |
|---|---|---|---|
| Wkt | 1st | 1st | 2nd |
| 1st | 32 | 25 | 16 |
| 2nd | 195 | 44 | 29 |
| 3rd | 211 | 49 | 34 |
| 4th | 292 | 129 | 78 |
| 5th | 316 | 140 | 97 |
| 6th | 320 | 140 | 111 |
| 7th | 380 | 152 | 111 |
| 8th | 407 | 157 | 117 |
| 9th | 446 | 169 | 117 |
| 10th | 450 | 170 | 117 |

Umpires: G. Borwick and G.A. Hele.

# AUSTRALIA v SOUTH AFRICA 1931-32 (2nd Test)

Played at Sydney Cricket Ground on 18, 19, 21 December.
Toss: South Africa.   Result: AUSTRALIA won by an innings and 155 runs.
Debuts: Australia – P.K. Lee; South Africa – L.S. Brown.

## SOUTH AFRICA

| | | | | | |
|---|---|---|---|---|---|
| J.A.J. Christy | c Nitschke b Grimmett | 14 | c Woodfull b Ironmonger | 41 |
| B. Mitchell | b McCabe | 1 | c Oldfield b Wall | 24 |
| D.P.B. Morkel | st Oldfield b Grimmett | 20 | lbw b Grimmett | 17 |
| H.B. Cameron*† | b Wall | 11 | b Wall | 0 |
| H.W. Taylor | c Lee b Grimmett | 7 | c Grimmett b Ironmonger | 6 |
| K.G. Viljoen | b Ironmonger | 37 | b Grimmett | 0 |
| E.L. Dalton | b Grimmett | 21 | c Bradman b Ironmonger | 14 |
| C.L. Vincent | not out | 31 | c Ponsford b Grimmett | 35 |
| L.S. Brown | b McCabe | 2 | c Wall b Lee | 8 |
| N.A. Quinn | lbw b McCabe | 5 | st Oldfield b Grimmett | 1 |
| A.J. Bell | b McCabe | 0 | not out | 1 |
| Extras | (LB 3, W 1) | 4 | (B 5, LB 8, NB 1) | 14 |
| **Total** | | **153** | | **161** |

## AUSTRALIA

| | | |
|---|---|---|
| W.M. Woodfull* | c Mitchell b Vincent | 58 |
| W.H. Ponsford | b Quinn | 5 |
| K.E. Rigg | b Bell | 127 |
| D.G. Bradman | c Viljoen b Morkel | 112 |
| S.J. McCabe | c Christy b Vincent | 79 |
| H.C. Nitschke | b Bell | 47 |
| P.K. Lee | c Cameron b Brown | 0 |
| W.A.S. Oldfield† | c Cameron b Bell | 8 |
| C.V. Grimmett | not out | 9 |
| T.W. Wall | c Morkel b Bell | 6 |
| H. Ironmonger | c Cameron b Bell | 0 |
| Extras | (B 5, LB 12, W 1) | 18 |
| **Total** | | **469** |

| AUSTRALIA | O | M | R | W | O | M | R | W | | FALL OF WICKETS | | |
|---|---|---|---|---|---|---|---|---|---|---|---|---|
| Wall | 18 | 4 | 46 | 1 | 18 | 5 | 31 | 2 | | SA | A | SA |
| McCabe | 12 | 5 | 13 | 4 | 3 | 0 | 25 | 0 | *Wkt* | *1st* | *1st* | *2nd* |
| Grimmett | 24 | 12 | 28 | 4 | 20·3 | 7 | 44 | 4 | 1st | 6 | 6 | 70 |
| Ironmonger | 12 | 1 | 38 | 1 | 19 | 10 | 22 | 3 | 2nd | 31 | 143 | 89 |
| Lee | 7 | 1 | 24 | 0 | 13 | 4 | 25 | 1 | 3rd | 36 | 254 | 89 |
| | | | | | | | | | 4th | 54 | 347 | 100 |
| SOUTH AFRICA | | | | | | | | | 5th | 62 | 432 | 100 |
| Bell | 46·5 | 6 | 140 | 5 | | | | | 6th | 91 | 433 | 100 |
| Quinn | 42 | 10 | 95 | 1 | | | | | 7th | 136 | 444 | 122 |
| Brown | 29 | 3 | 100 | 1 | | | | | 8th | 143 | 457 | 144 |
| Vincent | 24 | 5 | 75 | 2 | | | | | 9th | 153 | 469 | 160 |
| Morkel | 12 | 2 | 33 | 1 | | | | | 10th | 153 | 469 | 161 |
| Mitchell | 1 | 0 | 8 | 0 | | | | | | | | |

Umpires: G. Borwick and G.A. Hele.

# AUSTRALIA v SOUTH AFRICA 1931-32 (3rd Test)

Played at Melbourne Cricket Ground on 31 December, 1, 2, 4, 5, 6 January.
Toss: Australia.   Result: AUSTRALIA won by 169 runs.
Debuts: Nil.

The partnership of 274 between Woodfull and Bradman was Australia's highest to date for the second wicket against all countries.

## AUSTRALIA

| | | | | | |
|---|---|---|---|---|---|
| W.M. Woodfull* | c Cameron b Bell | 7 | c Mitchell b McMillan | | 161 |
| W.H. Ponsford | b Bell | 7 | c Mitchell b Bell | | 34 |
| D.G. Bradman | c Cameron b Quinn | 2 | lbw b Vincent | | 167 |
| A.F. Kippax | c Bell b Quinn | 52 | c Curnow b McMillan | | 67 |
| S.J. McCabe | c Morkel b Bell | 22 | c Mitchell b McMillan | | 71 |
| K.E. Rigg | c Mitchell b Bell | 68 | c Mitchell b Vincent | | 1 |
| E.L. a'Beckett | c Mitchell b Quinn | 6 | b Vincent | | 4 |
| W.A.S. Oldfield† | c Vincent b Quinn | 0 | lbw b McMillan | | 0 |
| C.V. Grimmett | c Morkel b Bell | 9 | not out | | 16 |
| T.W. Wall | not out | 6 | b Vincent | | 12 |
| H. Ironmonger | run out | 12 | b Quinn | | 0 |
| Extras | (B 1, LB 4, W 1, NB 1) | 7 | (B 17, LB 3, NB 1) | | 21 |
| **Total** | | **198** | | | **554** |

## SOUTH AFRICA

| | | | | | |
|---|---|---|---|---|---|
| S.H. Curnow | b Grimmett | 47 | b Grimmett | | 9 |
| B. Mitchell | c McCabe b Wall | 17 | c and b Grimmett | | 46 |
| J.A.J. Christy | c McCabe b Ironmonger | 16 | c Oldfield b Ironmonger | | 63 |
| H.W. Taylor | lbw b Grimmett | 11 | b Grimmett | | 38 |
| D.P.B. Morkel | lbw b Ironmonger | 33 | b Ironmonger | | 4 |
| H.B. Cameron*† | st Oldfield b Ironmonger | 39 | lbw b Ironmonger | | 13 |
| K.G. Viljoen | c Wall b McCabe | 111 | b Ironmonger | | 2 |
| C.L. Vincent | c Oldfield b Wall | 16 | c Ponsford b Grimmett | | 34 |
| Q. McMillan | c Oldfield b Wall | 29 | c Wall b Grimmett | | 1 |
| N.A. Quinn | b McCabe | 11 | not out | | 0 |
| A.J. Bell | not out | 10 | b Grimmett | | 0 |
| Extras | (B 3, LB 13, NB 2) | 18 | (B 8, LB 6, NB 1) | | 15 |
| **Total** | | **358** | | | **225** |

| SOUTH AFRICA | O | M | R | W | O | M | R | W |
|---|---|---|---|---|---|---|---|---|
| Bell | 26·1 | 9 | 69 | 5 | 36 | 6 | 101 | 1 |
| Quinn | 31 | 13 | 42 | 4 | 36·4 | 6 | 113 | 1 |
| Morkel | 3 | 0 | 12 | 0 | 4 | 0 | 15 | 0 |
| Vincent | 12 | 1 | 32 | 0 | 55 | 16 | 154 | 4 |
| McMillan | 2 | 0 | 22 | 0 | 33 | 3 | 150 | 4 |
| Christy | 3 | 0 | 14 | 0 | | | | |
| AUSTRALIA | | | | | | | | |
| Wall | 37 | 5 | 98 | 3 | 13 | 3 | 35 | 0 |
| A'Beckett | 18 | 5 | 29 | 0 | 3 | 1 | 6 | 0 |
| Grimmett | 63 | 23 | 100 | 2 | 46 | 14 | 92 | 6 |
| Ironmonger | 49 | 26 | 72 | 3 | 42 | 18 | 54 | 4 |
| McCabe | 21·3 | 4 | 41 | 2 | 10 | 1 | 21 | 0 |
| Bradman | | | | | 1 | 0 | 2 | 0 |

### FALL OF WICKETS

| | A | SA | A | SA |
|---|---|---|---|---|
| Wkt | 1st | 1st | 2nd | 2nd |
| 1st | 11 | 39 | 54 | 18 |
| 2nd | 16 | 79 | 328 | 120 |
| 3rd | 25 | 89 | 408 | 133 |
| 4th | 74 | 108 | 519 | 138 |
| 5th | 135 | 163 | 521 | 178 |
| 6th | 143 | 183 | 521 | 186 |
| 7th | 143 | 225 | 524 | 188 |
| 8th | 173 | 329 | 530 | 208 |
| 9th | 179 | 336 | 550 | 225 |
| 10th | 198 | 358 | 554 | 225 |

Umpires: G. Borwick and G.A. Hele.

# AUSTRALIA v SOUTH AFRICA 1931-32 (4th Test)

Played at Adelaide Oval on 29, 30 January, 1, 2 February.
Toss: South Africa.   Result: AUSTRALIA won by ten wickets.
Debuts: Australia – W.A. Hunt, W.J. O'Reilly, H.M. Thurlow.

Bradman ran out his last partner when attempting the vital single off the last ball of an over. His innings remains the highest in any Test at Adelaide and was the highest for Australia in a home Test until R.M. Cowper scored 311 at Melbourne in 1965-66. Grimmett's match analysis of 14 for 199 is still the Test record for Adelaide.

## SOUTH AFRICA

| | | | | |
|---|---|---|---|---|
| S.H. Curnow | c Ponsford b Grimmett | 20 | b McCabe | 3 |
| B. Mitchell | c and b McCabe | 75 | c O'Reilly b Grimmett | 95 |
| J.A.J. Christy | b O'Reilly | 7 | b Grimmett | 51 |
| H.W. Taylor | c Rigg b Grimmett | 78 | b O'Reilly | 84 |
| H.B. Cameron*† | lbw b Grimmett | 52 | b O'Reilly | 4 |
| D.P.B. Morkel | c and b Grimmett | 0 | (8) b Grimmett | 15 |
| K.G. Viljoen | c and b Grimmett | 0 | b Grimmett | 1 |
| C.L. Vincent | not out | 48 | (6) b Grimmett | 5 |
| Q. McMillan | b Grimmett | 19 | c Hunt b Grimmett | 3 |
| N.A. Quinn | c Ponsford b Grimmett | 1 | b Grimmett | 1 |
| A.J. Bell | lbw b O'Reilly | 2 | not out | 0 |
| Extras | (LB 2, NB 4) | 6 | (B 4, LB 3, NB 5) | 12 |
| **Total** | | **308** | | **274** |

## AUSTRALIA

| | | | | |
|---|---|---|---|---|
| W.M. Woodfull* | c Morkel b Bell | 82 | not out | 37 |
| W.H. Ponsford | b Quinn | 5 | not out | 27 |
| D.G. Bradman | not out | 299 | | |
| A.F. Kippax | run out | 0 | | |
| S.J. McCabe | c Vincent b Bell | 2 | | |
| K.E. Rigg | c Taylor b Bell | 35 | | |
| W.A.S. Oldfield† | lbw b Vincent | 23 | | |
| C.V. Grimmett | b Bell | 21 | | |
| W.A. Hunt | c Vincent b Quinn | 0 | | |
| W.J. O'Reilly | b Bell | 23 | | |
| H.M. Thurlow | run out | 0 | | |
| Extras | (B 18, LB 3, W 1, NB 1) | 23 | (B 4, LB 5) | 9 |
| **Total** | | **513** | (0 wickets) | **73** |

| AUSTRALIA | O | M | R | W | O | M | R | W |
|---|---|---|---|---|---|---|---|---|
| Thurlow | 27 | 6 | 53 | 0 | 12 | 1 | 33 | 0 |
| McCabe | 17 | 6 | 34 | 1 | 14 | 1 | 51 | 1 |
| O'Reilly | 39·4 | 10 | 74 | 2 | 42 | 13 | 81 | 2 |
| Grimmett | 47 | 11 | 116 | 7 | 49·2 | 17 | 83 | 7 |
| Hunt | 10 | 1 | 25 | 0 | 6 | 1 | 14 | 0 |
| SOUTH AFRICA | | | | | | | | |
| Bell | 40 | 2 | 142 | 5 | | | | |
| Quinn | 37 | 5 | 114 | 2 | 3 | 0 | 5 | 0 |
| Vincent | 34 | 5 | 110 | 1 | 7 | 0 | 31 | 0 |
| McMillan | 9 | 0 | 53 | 0 | 7·2 | 0 | 23 | 0 |
| Morkel | 18 | 1 | 71 | 0 | 2 | 0 | 5 | 0 |

### FALL OF WICKETS

| | SA | A | SA | A |
|---|---|---|---|---|
| Wkt | 1st | 1st | 2nd | 2nd |
| 1st | 27 | 9 | 22 | – |
| 2nd | 45 | 185 | 103 | – |
| 3rd | 165 | 191 | 224 | – |
| 4th | 202 | 194 | 232 | – |
| 5th | 204 | 308 | 240 | – |
| 6th | 204 | 357 | 246 | – |
| 7th | 243 | 418 | 262 | – |
| 8th | 286 | 421 | 268 | – |
| 9th | 300 | 499 | 274 | – |
| 10th | 308 | 513 | 274 | – |

Umpires: G. Borwick and G.A. Hele.

# AUSTRALIA v SOUTH AFRICA 1931-32 (5th Test)

Played at Melbourne Cricket Ground on 12, 13 (*no play*), 15 February.
Toss: South Africa.   Result: AUSTRALIA won by an innings and 72 runs.
Debuts: Australia – J.H.W. Fingleton, L.J. Nash.

A vicious Melbourne 'sticky' produced the lowest aggregate (81) by any side losing all twenty wickets in a Test match. The match aggregate of 234 is still the lowest in all Test cricket.

## SOUTH AFRICA

| | | | | | |
|---|---|---:|---|---|---:|
| B. Mitchell | c Rigg b McCabe | 2 | (4) c Oldfield b Ironmonger | | 4 |
| S.H. Curnow | c Oldfield b Nash | 3 | c Fingleton b Ironmonger | | 16 |
| J.A.J. Christy | c Grimmett b Nash | 4 | (1) c and b Nash | | 0 |
| H.W. Taylor | c Kippax b Nash | 0 | (7) c Bradman b Ironmonger | | 2 |
| K.G. Viljoen | c sub (L.S. Darling) b Ironmonger | 1 | (8) c Oldfield b O'Reilly | | 0 |
| H.B. Cameron*† | c McCabe b Nash | 11 | (5) c McCabe b O'Reilly | | 0 |
| D.P.B. Morkel | c Nash b Ironmonger | 1 | (6) c Rigg b Ironmonger | | 0 |
| C.L. Vincent | c Nash b Ironmonger | 1 | (9) not out | | 8 |
| Q. McMillan | st Oldfield b Ironmonger | 0 | (10) c Oldfield b Ironmonger | | 0 |
| N.A. Quinn | not out | 5 | (11) c Fingleton b Ironmonger | | 5 |
| A.J. Bell | st Oldfield b Ironmonger | 0 | (3) c McCabe b O'Reilly | | 6 |
| Extras | (B 2, LB 3, NB 3) | 8 | (B 3, LB 1) | | 4 |
| **Total** | | **36** | | | **45** |

## AUSTRALIA

| | | |
|---|---|---:|
| W.M. Woodfull* | b Bell | 0 |
| J.H.W. Fingleton | c Vincent b Bell | 40 |
| K.E. Rigg | c Vincent b Quinn | 22 |
| A.F. Kippax | c Curnow b McMillan | 42 |
| S.J. McCabe | c Cameron b Bell | 0 |
| L.J. Nash | b Quinn | 13 |
| W.A.S. Oldfield† | c Curnow b McMillan | 11 |
| C.V. Grimmett | c Cameron b Quinn | 9 |
| W.J. O'Reilly | c Curnow b McMillan | 13 |
| H. Ironmonger | not out | 0 |
| D.G. Bradman | absent hurt | – |
| Extras | (LB 3) | 3 |
| **Total** | | **153** |

| AUSTRALIA | O | M | R | W | O | M | R | W |
|---|---:|---:|---:|---:|---:|---:|---:|---:|
| Nash | 12 | 6 | 18 | 4 | 7 | 4 | 4 | 1 |
| McCabe | 4 | 1 | 4 | 1 | | | | |
| Ironmonger | 7·2 | 5 | 6 | 5 | 15·3 | 7 | 18 | 6 |
| O'Reilly | | | | | 9 | 5 | 19 | 3 |

| SOUTH AFRICA | O | M | R | W |
|---|---:|---:|---:|---:|
| Bell | 16 | 0 | 52 | 3 |
| Quinn | 19·3 | 4 | 29 | 3 |
| Vincent | 11 | 2 | 40 | 0 |
| McMillan | 8 | 0 | 29 | 3 |

Umpires: G. Borwick and G.A. Hele.

## FALL OF WICKETS

| | SA | A | SA |
|---|---:|---:|---:|
| *Wkt* | *1st* | *1st* | *2nd* |
| 1st | 7 | 0 | 0 |
| 2nd | 16 | 51 | 12 |
| 3rd | 16 | 75 | 25 |
| 4th | 17 | 75 | 30 |
| 5th | 19 | 112 | 30 |
| 6th | 25 | 125 | 30 |
| 7th | 31 | 131 | 32 |
| 8th | 31 | 148 | 32 |
| 9th | 33 | 153 | 33 |
| 10th | 36 | – | 45 |

# NEW ZEALAND v SOUTH AFRICA 1931-32 (1st Test)

Played at Lancaster Park, Christchurch, on 27, 29 February, 1 March.
Toss: New Zealand.   Result: SOUTH AFRICA won by an innings and 12 runs.
Debuts: New Zealand – D.C. Cleverley, J. Newman.

This first match between South Africa and New Zealand was the last of H.W. Taylor's Test career. Of the pre-First-World-War players only F.E. Woolley (who played his last Test in 1934) remained in Test cricket longer. The partnership of 196 between Christy and Mitchell remains the highest for the first wicket by either side in this series.

## NEW ZEALAND

| | | | | | |
|---|---|--:|---|---|--:|
| C.S. Dempster | b McMillan | 8 | b Quinn | | 12 |
| J.L. Kerr | b Bell | 0 | c Vincent b Bell | | 3 |
| R.C. Blunt | run out | 23 | c Mitchell b Vincent | | 17 |
| G.L. Weir | c Mitchell b Vincent | 46 | not out | | 74 |
| A.W. Roberts | st Cameron b Mitchell | 54 | c and b McMillan | | 17 |
| M.L. Page* | c Taylor b McMillan | 22 | st Cameron b McMillan | | 0 |
| F.T. Badcock | c Dalton b Bell | 64 | st Cameron b McMillan | | 5 |
| K.C. James† | c Cameron b McMillan | 3 | (9) lbw b Quinn | | 0 |
| I.B. Cromb | c Morkel b McMillan | 25 | (8) c Vincent b McMillan | | 0 |
| D.C. Cleverley | not out | 10 | b Quinn | | 7 |
| J. Newman | c Balaskas b Mitchell | 19 | lbw b McMillan | | 4 |
| Extras | (B 4, LB 13, NB 2) | 19 | (B 1, LB 5, NB 1) | | 7 |
| **Total** | | **293** | | | **146** |

## SOUTH AFRICA

| | | |
|---|---|--:|
| J.A.J. Christy | run out | 103 |
| B. Mitchell | c James b Cromb | 113 |
| H.W. Taylor | b Badcock | 9 |
| H.B. Cameron*† | c James b Badcock | 47 |
| X.C. Balaskas | run out | 5 |
| E.L. Dalton | c Page b Newman | 82 |
| D.P.B. Morkel | b Newman | 51 |
| C.L. Vincent | c Page b Blunt | 3 |
| Q. McMillan | c Badcock b Blunt | 6 |
| N.A. Quinn | run out | 3 |
| A.J. Bell | not out | 2 |
| Extras | (B 14, LB 10, NB 3) | 27 |
| **Total** | | **451** |

| SOUTH AFRICA | O | M | R | W | O | M | R | W |
|---|--:|--:|--:|--:|--:|--:|--:|--:|
| Bell | 32 | 8 | 64 | 2 | 9 | 3 | 11 | 1 |
| Quinn | 29 | 7 | 46 | 0 | 15 | 6 | 17 | 3 |
| McMillan | 19 | 2 | 61 | 4 | 20·5 | 4 | 66 | 5 |
| Vincent | 25 | 7 | 57 | 1 | 14 | 3 | 33 | 1 |
| Mitchell | 7·4 | 0 | 31 | 2 | 1 | 0 | 6 | 0 |
| Balaskas | 4 | 0 | 15 | 0 | | | | |
| Morkel | | | | | 2 | 0 | 6 | 0 |
| NEW ZEALAND | | | | | | | | |
| Cleverley | 22 | 2 | 79 | 0 | | | | |
| Badcock | 38 | 8 | 88 | 2 | | | | |
| Newman | 28·5 | 4 | 76 | 2 | | | | |
| Blunt | 16 | 0 | 60 | 2 | | | | |
| Cromb | 26 | 4 | 94 | 1 | | | | |
| Page | 6 | 0 | 27 | 0 | | | | |

## FALL OF WICKETS

| | NZ | SA | NZ |
|---|--:|--:|--:|
| Wkt | 1st | 1st | 2nd |
| 1st | 1 | 196 | 16 |
| 2nd | 26 | 227 | 16 |
| 3rd | 38 | 249 | 41 |
| 4th | 128 | 262 | 70 |
| 5th | 149 | 299 | 70 |
| 6th | 189 | 378 | 76 |
| 7th | 198 | 397 | 94 |
| 8th | 251 | 423 | 103 |
| 9th | 265 | 432 | 117 |
| 10th | 293 | 451 | 146 |

Umpires: J.T. Forrester and W. Butler.

# NEW ZEALAND v SOUTH AFRICA 1931-32 (2nd Test)

Played at Basin Reserve, Wellington, on 4, 5, 7 March.
Toss: New Zealand.   Result: SOUTH AFRICA won by eight wickets.
Debuts: Nil.

Vivian, who hit his country's first hundred against South Africa and who was top-scorer in both innings, shared in a partnership of 100 with Badcock which remains the highest for the sixth wicket by either side in this series.

### NEW ZEALAND

| | | | | | |
|---|---|---|---|---|---|
| C.S. Dempster | c Vincent b McMillan | 64 | | c Cameron b Quinn | 20 |
| G.L. Weir | b McMillan | 8 | | b Quinn | 1 |
| R.C. Blunt | lbw b Quinn | 25 | | b Brown | 17 |
| H.G. Vivian | c Dalton b McMillan | 100 | | c Vincent b Balaskas | 73 |
| A.W. Roberts | lbw b Quinn | 1 | | b Quinn | 26 |
| M.L. Page* | c Mitchell b Brown | 7 | (7) | c and b Balaskas | 23 |
| F.T. Badcock | c and b McMillan | 53 | (6) | run out | 0 |
| G.R. Dickinson | st Cameron b McMillan | 2 | | b McMillan | 5 |
| C.F.W. Allcott | c Dalton b Mitchell | 26 | (10) | b Quinn | 15 |
| I.B. Cromb | not out | 51 | (9) | c Christy b McMillan | 2 |
| K.C. James† | b Mitchell | 11 | | not out | 0 |
| Extras | (B 12, LB 4) | 16 | | (B 4, LB 6, NB 1) | 11 |
| **Total** | | **364** | | | **193** |

### SOUTH AFRICA

| | | | | |
|---|---|---|---|---|
| J.A.J. Christy | c Dempster b Badcock | 62 | c Roberts b Badcock | 53 |
| B. Mitchell | b Cromb | 0 | c James b Dickinson | 53 |
| H.B. Cameron*† | c Blunt b Vivian | 44 | not out | 22 |
| K.G. Viljoen | b Page | 81 | not out | 16 |
| E.L. Dalton | c James b Dickinson | 42 | | |
| X.C. Balaskas | not out | 122 | | |
| Q. McMillan | c Dickinson b Allcott | 1 | | |
| C.L. Vincent | c and b Vivian | 33 | | |
| L.S. Brown | c Page b Vivian | 7 | | |
| N.A. Quinn | b Vivian | 8 | | |
| A.J. Bell | lbw b Dickinson | 2 | | |
| Extras | (B 3, LB 1, W 1, NB 3) | 8 | (LB 6) | 6 |
| **Total** | | **410** | (2 wickets) | **150** |

| SOUTH AFRICA | O | M | R | W | O | M | R | W |
|---|---|---|---|---|---|---|---|---|
| Bell | 16 | 1 | 47 | 0 | 10 | 0 | 30 | 0 |
| Quinn | 28 | 6 | 51 | 2 | 24 | 9 | 37 | 4 |
| Brown | 14 | 1 | 59 | 1 | 10 | 3 | 30 | 1 |
| McMillan | 29 | 2 | 125 | 5 | 21 | 2 | 71 | 2 |
| Vincent | 6 | 1 | 32 | 0 | | | | |
| Christy | 2 | 0 | 11 | 0 | | | | |
| Mitchell | 4·5 | 0 | 23 | 2 | | | | |
| Balaskas | | | | | 7 | 2 | 14 | 2 |
| NEW ZEALAND | | | | | | | | |
| Dickinson | 26·2 | 7 | 78 | 2 | 8 | 2 | 33 | 1 |
| Cromb | 23 | 9 | 48 | 1 | 3 | 0 | 13 | 0 |
| Badcock | 24 | 6 | 70 | 1 | 11 | 2 | 31 | 1 |
| Allcott | 27 | 4 | 80 | 1 | 7 | 0 | 27 | 0 |
| Blunt | 10 | 0 | 38 | 0 | 2·2 | 0 | 11 | 0 |
| Vivian | 20 | 7 | 58 | 4 | 7 | 0 | 15 | 0 |
| Page | 11 | 3 | 30 | 1 | 3 | 0 | 14 | 0 |

FALL OF WICKETS

| | NZ | SA | NZ | SA |
|---|---|---|---|---|
| Wkt | 1st | 1st | 2nd | 2nd |
| 1st | 42 | 2 | 14 | 104 |
| 2nd | 79 | 78 | 23 | 115 |
| 3rd | 135 | 133 | 66 | – |
| 4th | 139 | 220 | 122 | – |
| 5th | 158 | 256 | 122 | – |
| 6th | 258 | 257 | 157 | – |
| 7th | 269 | 362 | 171 | – |
| 8th | 270 | 386 | 186 | – |
| 9th | 339 | 394 | 192 | – |
| 10th | 364 | 410 | 193 | – |

Umpires: K.H. Cave and W.P. Page.

# ENGLAND v INDIA 1932 (Only Test)

Played at Lord's, London, on 25, 27, 28 June.
Toss: England.   Result: ENGLAND won by 158 runs.
Debuts: England – W.E. Bowes; India – All.

In the absence of their captain, the Maharajah of Porbander, and vice-captain, K.S. Ganshyamsinhji, India were led by C.K. Nayudu in their first official Test match. Nayudu badly damaged his hand attempting a catch in the first innings, and India were further weakened by leg injuries to Nazir Ali and Palia. Amar Singh scored India's first fifty and added 74 in 40 minutes with Lall Singh.

## ENGLAND

| | | | | |
|---|---|---|---|---|
| P. Holmes | b Nissar | 6 | b Jahangir Khan | 11 |
| H. Sutcliffe | b Nissar | 3 | c Nayudu b Amar Singh | 19 |
| F.E. Woolley | run out | 9 | c Colah b Jahangir Khan | 21 |
| W.R. Hammond | b Amar Singh | 35 | b Jahangir Khan | 12 |
| D.R. Jardine* | c Navle b Nayudu | 79 | not out | 85 |
| E. Paynter | lbw b Nayudu | 14 | b Jahangir Khan | 54 |
| L.E.G. Ames† | b Nissar | 65 | b Amar Singh | 6 |
| R.W.V. Robins | c Lall Singh b Nissar | 21 | c Jahangir Khan b Nissar | 30 |
| F.R. Brown | c Amar Singh b Nissar | 1 | c Colah b Naoomal | 29 |
| W. Voce | not out | 4 | not out | 0 |
| W.E. Bowes | c Nissar b Amar Singh | 7 | | |
| Extras | (B 3, LB 9, NB 3) | 15 | (B 2, LB 6) | 8 |
| **Total** | | **259** | (8 wickets declared) | **275** |

## INDIA

| | | | | |
|---|---|---|---|---|
| J.G. Navle† | b Bowes | 12 | lbw b Robins | 13 |
| Naoomal Jeoomal | lbw b Robins | 33 | b Brown | 25 |
| S. Wazir Ali | lbw b Brown | 31 | c Hammond b Voce | 39 |
| C.K. Nayudu* | c Robins b Voce | 40 | b Bowes | 10 |
| S.H.M. Colah | c Robins b Bowes | 22 | b Brown | 4 |
| S. Nazir Ali | b Bowes | 13 | c Jardine b Bowes | 6 |
| P.E. Palia | b Voce | 1 | (11) not out | 1 |
| Lall Singh | c Jardine b Bowes | 15 | (7) b Hammond | 29 |
| M. Jahangir Khan | b Robins | 1 | (8) b Voce | 0 |
| L. Amar Singh | c Robins b Voce | 5 | (9) c and b Hammond | 51 |
| Mahomed Nissar | not out | 1 | (10) b Hammond | 0 |
| Extras | (B 5, LB 7, W 1, NB 2) | 15 | (B 5, LB 2, NB 2) | 9 |
| **Total** | | **189** | | **187** |

| INDIA | O | M | R | W | O | M | R | W | | | FALL OF WICKETS | | |
|---|---|---|---|---|---|---|---|---|---|---|---|---|---|
| Nissar | 26 | 3 | 93 | 5 | 18 | 5 | 42 | 1 | | E | I | E | I |
| Amar Singh | 31·1 | 10 | 75 | 2 | 41 | 13 | 84 | 2 | Wkt | 1st | 1st | 2nd | 2nd |
| Jahangir Khan | 17 | 7 | 26 | 0 | 30 | 12 | 60 | 4 | 1st | 8 | 39 | 30 | 41 |
| Nayudu | 24 | 8 | 40 | 2 | 9 | 0 | 21 | 0 | 2nd | 11 | 63 | 34 | 41 |
| Palia | 4 | 3 | 2 | 0 | 3 | 0 | 11 | 0 | 3rd | 19 | 110 | 54 | 52 |
| Naoomal | 3 | 0 | 8 | 0 | 8 | 0 | 40 | 1 | 4th | 101 | 139 | 67 | 65 |
| Wazir Ali | | | | | 1 | 0 | 9 | 0 | 5th | 149 | 160 | 156 | 83 |
| | | | | | | | | | 6th | 166 | 165 | 169 | 108 |
| ENGLAND | | | | | | | | | 7th | 229 | 181 | 222 | 108 |
| Bowes | 30 | 13 | 49 | 4 | 14 | 5 | 30 | 2 | 8th | 231 | 182 | 271 | 182 |
| Voce | 17 | 6 | 23 | 3 | 12 | 3 | 28 | 2 | 9th | 252 | 188 | – | 182 |
| Brown | 25 | 7 | 48 | 1 | 14 | 1 | 54 | 2 | 10th | 259 | 189 | – | 187 |
| Robins | 17 | 4 | 39 | 2 | 14 | 5 | 57 | 1 | | | | | |
| Hammond | 4 | 0 | 15 | 0 | 5·3 | 3 | 9 | 3 | | | | | |

Umpires: F. Chester and J. Hardstaff, sr.

# AUSTRALIA v ENGLAND 1932-33 (1st Test)

Played at Sydney Cricket Ground on 2, 3, 5, 6, 7 December.
Toss: Australia.   Result: ENGLAND won by ten wickets.
Debuts: Australia – L.E. Nagel; England – Nawab Iftikhar Ali of Pataudi.

Illness prevented Bradman from playing in the opening match of what has become known as 'The Bodyline
Series'. McCabe's innings was the greatest (in both senses) against such bowling. He batted for 242 minutes, hi
25 fours and scored his last 51 runs out of a tenth-wicket stand of 55 in 33 minutes. Pataudi, the third India
Prince to play cricket for England, emulated 'Ranji' and 'Duleep' by scoring a hundred in his first Test agains
Australia.

### AUSTRALIA

| | | | | | |
|---|---|---|---|---|---|
| W.M. Woodfull* | c Ames b Voce | 7 | | b Larwood | |
| W.H. Ponsford | b Larwood | 32 | | b Voce | |
| J.H.W. Fingleton | c Allen b Larwood | 26 | | c Voce b Larwood | 4( |
| A.F. Kippax | lbw b Larwood | 8 | (6) | b Larwood | 1 |
| S.J. McCabe | not out | 187 | (4) | lbw b Hammond | 3 |
| V.Y. Richardson | c Hammond b Voce | 49 | (5) | c Voce b Hammond | ( |
| W.A.S. Oldfield† | c Ames b Larwood | 4 | | c Leyland b Larwood | |
| C.V. Grimmett | c Ames b Voce | 19 | | c Allen b Larwood | |
| L.E. Nagel | b Larwood | 0 | | not out | 2 |
| W.J. O'Reilly | b Voce | 4 | (11) | b Voce | |
| T.W. Wall | c Allen b Hammond | 4 | (10) | c Ames b Allen | 2( |
| Extras | (B 12, LB 4, NB 4) | 20 | | (B 12, LB 2, W 1, NB 2) | 1 |
| **Total** | | **360** | | | 16 |

### ENGLAND

| | | | |
|---|---|---|---|
| H. Sutcliffe | lbw b Wall | 194 | not out |
| R.E.S. Wyatt | lbw b Grimmett | 38 | not out |
| W.R. Hammond | c Grimmett b Nagel | 112 | |
| Nawab of Pataudi, sr | b Nagel | 102 | |
| M.Leyland | c Oldfield b Wall | 0 | |
| D.R. Jardine* | c Oldfield b McCabe | 27 | |
| H. Verity | lbw b Wall | 2 | |
| G.O.B. Allen | c and b O'Reilly | 19 | |
| L.E.G. Ames† | c McCabe b O'Reilly | 0 | |
| H.Larwood | lbw b O'Reilly | 0 | |
| W. Voce | not out | 0 | |
| Extras | (B 7, LB 17, NB 6) | 30 | |
| **Total** | | **524** | (0 wickets) |

| ENGLAND | O | M | R | W | O | M | R | W | | FALL OF WICKETS | | | |
|---|---|---|---|---|---|---|---|---|---|---|---|---|---|
| | | | | | | | | | | A | E | A | E |
| Larwood | 31 | 5 | 96 | 5 | 18 | 4 | 28 | 5 | Wkt | 1st | 1st | 2nd | 2nd |
| Voce | 29 | 4 | 110 | 4 | 17·3 | 5 | 54 | 2 | 1st | 22 | 112 | 2 | – |
| Allen | 15 | 1 | 65 | 0 | 9 | 5 | 13 | 1 | 2nd | 65 | 300 | 10 | – |
| Hammond | 14·2 | 0 | 34 | 1 | 15 | 6 | 37 | 2 | 3rd | 82 | 423 | 61 | – |
| Verity | 13 | 4 | 35 | 0 | 4 | 1 | 15 | 0 | 4th | 87 | 423 | 61 | – |
| | | | | | | | | | 5th | 216 | 470 | 100 | – |
| AUSTRALIA | | | | | | | | | 6th | 231 | 479 | 104 | – |
| Wall | 38 | 4 | 104 | 3 | | | | | 7th | 299 | 519 | 105 | – |
| Nagel | 43·4 | 9 | 110 | 2 | | | | | 8th | 300 | 522 | 113 | – |
| O'Reilly | 67 | 32 | 117 | 3 | | | | | 9th | 305 | 522 | 151 | – |
| Grimmett | 64 | 22 | 118 | 1 | | | | | 10th | 360 | 524 | 164 | – |
| McCabe | 15 | 2 | 42 | 1 | 0·1 | 0 | 1 | 0 | | | | | |
| Kippax | 2 | 1 | 3 | 0 | | | | | | | | | |

Umpires: G. Borwick and G.A. Hele.

# AUSTRALIA v ENGLAND 1932-33 (2nd Test)

Played at Melbourne Cricket Ground on 30, 31 December, 2, 3 January.
Toss: Australia.   Result: AUSTRALIA won by 111 runs.
Debuts: Australia – L.P.J. O'Brien.

Bradman, who played on trying to hook his first ball in the first innings, batted for 185 minutes and hit seven fours. Australia's total of 191 remains their lowest against England to contain a century.

## AUSTRALIA

| | | | | | |
|---|---|---|---|---|---|
| J.H.W. Fingleton | b Allen | 83 | c Ames b Allen | | 1 |
| W.M. Woodfull* | b Allen | 10 | c Allen b Larwood | | 26 |
| L.P.J. O'Brien | run out | 10 | b Larwood | | 11 |
| D.G. Bradman | b Bowes | 0 | not out | | 103 |
| S.J. McCabe | c Jardine b Voce | 32 | b Allen | | 0 |
| V.Y. Richardson | c Hammond b Voce | 34 | lbw b Hammond | | 32 |
| W.A.S. Oldfield† | not out | 27 | b Voce | | 6 |
| C.V. Grimmett | c Sutcliffe b Voce | 2 | b Voce | | 0 |
| T.W. Wall | run out | 1 | lbw b Hammond | | 3 |
| W.J. O'Reilly | b Larwood | 15 | c Ames b Hammond | | 0 |
| H. Ironmonger | b Larwood | 4 | run out | | 0 |
| Extras | (B 5, LB 1, W 2, NB 2) | 10 | (B 3, LB 1, W 4, NB 1) | | 9 |
| **Total** | | **228** | | | **191** |

## ENGLAND

| | | | | | |
|---|---|---|---|---|---|
| H. Sutcliffe | c Richardson b Wall | 52 | b O'Reilly | | 33 |
| R.E.S. Wyatt | lbw b O'Reilly | 13 | (7) lbw b O'Reilly | | 25 |
| W.R. Hammond | b Wall | 8 | (4) c O'Brien b O'Reilly | | 23 |
| Nawab of Pataudi, Sr | b O'Reilly | 15 | (3) c Fingleton b Ironmonger | | 5 |
| M. Leyland | b O'Reilly | 22 | (2) b Wall | | 19 |
| D.R. Jardine* | c Oldfield b Wall | 1 | (5) c McCabe b Ironmonger | | 0 |
| L.E.G. Ames† | b Wall | 4 | (6) c Fingleton b O'Reilly | | 2 |
| G.O.B. Allen | c Richardson b O'Reilly | 30 | st Oldfield b Ironmonger | | 23 |
| H. Larwood | b O'Reilly | 9 | c Wall b Ironmonger | | 4 |
| W. Voce | c McCabe b Grimmett | 6 | c O'Brien b O'Reilly | | 0 |
| W.E. Bowes | not out | 4 | not out | | 0 |
| Extras | (B 1, LB 2, NB 2) | 5 | (LB 4, NB 1) | | 5 |
| **Total** | | **169** | | | **139** |

| ENGLAND | O | M | R | W | O | M | R | W | FALL OF WICKETS | | | | |
|---|---|---|---|---|---|---|---|---|---|---|---|---|---|
| Larwood | 20·3 | 2 | 52 | 2 | 15 | 2 | 50 | 2 | | A | E | A | E |
| Voce | 20 | 3 | 54 | 3 | 15 | 2 | 47 | 2 | Wkt | 1st | 1st | 2nd | 2nd |
| Allen | 17 | 3 | 41 | 2 | 12 | 1 | 44 | 2 | 1st | 29 | 30 | 1 | 53 |
| Hammond | 10 | 3 | 21 | 0 | 10·5 | 2 | 21 | 3 | 2nd | 67 | 43 | 27 | 53 |
| Bowes | 19 | 2 | 50 | 1 | 4 | 0 | 20 | 0 | 3rd | 67 | 83 | 78 | 70 |
| | | | | | | | | | 4th | 131 | 98 | 81 | 70 |
| AUSTRALIA | | | | | | | | | 5th | 156 | 104 | 135 | 77 |
| Wall | 21 | 4 | 52 | 4 | 8 | 2 | 23 | 1 | 6th | 188 | 110 | 150 | 85 |
| O'Reilly | 34·3 | 17 | 63 | 5 | 24 | 5 | 66 | 5 | 7th | 194 | 122 | 156 | 135 |
| Grimmett | 16 | 4 | 21 | 1 | 4 | 0 | 19 | 0 | 8th | 200 | 138 | 184 | 137 |
| Ironmonger | 14 | 4 | 28 | 0 | 19·1 | 8 | 26 | 4 | 9th | 222 | 161 | 186 | 138 |
| | | | | | | | | | 10th | 228 | 169 | 191 | 139 |

Umpires: G. Borwick and G.A. Hele.

## AUSTRALIA v ENGLAND 1932-33 (3rd Test)

Played at Adelaide Oval on 13, 14, 16, 17, 18, 19 January.
Toss: England, Result: ENGLAND won by 338 runs.
Debuts: Nil.

This match brought the 'bodyline' controversy to its crest. Woodfull was twice hit by bouncers and Oldfield deflected a ball from Larwood into his face. When the governing bodies of the two countries exchanged terse cables it seemed that the tour might be abandoned. Woodfull carried his bat through a completed innings against England for the second time.

### ENGLAND

| | | | | | |
|---|---|---|---|---|---|
| H. Sutcliffe | c Wall b O'Reilly | 9 | c sub (L.P.J. O'Brien) b Wall | | 7 |
| D.R. Jardine* | b Wall | 3 | lbw b Ironmonger | | 56 |
| W.R. Hammond | c Oldfield b Wall | 2 | (5) b Bradman | | 85 |
| L.E.G. Ames† | b Ironmonger | 3 | (7) b O'Reilly | | 69 |
| M. Leyland | b O'Reilly | 83 | (6) c Wall b Ironmonger | | 42 |
| R.E.S. Wyatt | c Richardson b Grimmett | 78 | (3) c Wall b O'Reilly | | 49 |
| E. Paynter | c Fingleton b Wall | 77 | (10) not out | | 1 |
| G.O.B. Allen | lbw b Grimmett | 15 | (4) lbw b Grimmett | | 15 |
| H. Verity | c Richardson b Wall | 45 | (8) lbw b O'Reilly | | 40 |
| W. Voce | b Wall | 8 | (11) b O'Reilly | | 8 |
| H. Larwood | not out | 3 | (9) c Bradman b Ironmonger | | 8 |
| Extras | (B 1, LB 7, NB 7) | 15 | (B 17, LB 11, NB 4) | | 32 |
| **Total** | | **341** | | | **412** |

### AUSTRALIA

| | | | | | |
|---|---|---|---|---|---|
| J.H.W. Fingleton | c Ames b Allen | 0 | b Larwood | | 0 |
| W.M. Woodfull* | b Allen | 22 | not out | | 73 |
| D.G. Bradman | c Allen b Larwood | 8 | (4) c and b Verity | | 66 |
| S.J. McCabe | c Jardine b Larwood | 8 | (5) c Leyland b Allen | | 7 |
| W.H. Ponsford | b Voce | 85 | (3) c Jardine b Larwood | | 3 |
| V.Y. Richardson | b Allen | 28 | c Allen b Larwood | | 21 |
| W.A.S. Oldfield† | retired hurt | 41 | absent hurt | | – |
| C.V. Grimmett | c Voce b Allen | 10 | (7) b Allen | | 6 |
| T.W. Wall | b Hammond | 6 | (8) b Allen | | 0 |
| W.J. O'Reilly | b Larwood | 0 | (9) b Larwood | | 5 |
| H. Ironmonger | not out | 0 | (10) b Allen | | 0 |
| Extras | (B 2, LB 11, NB 1) | 14 | (B 4, LB 2, W 1, NB 5) | | 12 |
| **Total** | | **222** | | | **193** |

| AUSTRALIA | O | M | R | W | O | M | R | W | | FALL OF WICKETS | | | |
|---|---|---|---|---|---|---|---|---|---|---|---|---|---|
| Wall | 34·1 | 10 | 72 | 5 | 29 | 6 | 75 | 1 | | E | A | E | A |
| O'Reilly | 50 | 19 | 82 | 2 | 50·3 | 21 | 79 | 4 | Wkt | 1st | 1st | 2nd | 2nd |
| Ironmonger | 20 | 6 | 50 | 1 | 57 | 21 | 87 | 3 | 1st | 4 | 1 | 7 | 3 |
| Grimmett | 28 | 6 | 94 | 2 | 35 | 9 | 74 | 1 | 2nd | 16 | 18 | 91 | 12 |
| McCabe | 14 | 3 | 28 | 0 | 16 | 0 | 42 | 0 | 3rd | 16 | 34 | 123 | 100 |
| Bradman | | | | | 4 | 0 | 23 | 1 | 4th | 30 | 51 | 154 | 116 |
| | | | | | | | | | 5th | 186 | 131 | 245 | 171 |
| ENGLAND | | | | | | | | | 6th | 196 | 194 | 296 | 183 |
| Larwood | 25 | 6 | 55 | 3 | 19 | 3 | 71 | 4 | 7th | 228 | 212 | 394 | 183 |
| Allen | 23 | 4 | 71 | 4 | 17·2 | 5 | 50 | 4 | 8th | 324 | 222 | 395 | 192 |
| Hammond | 17·4 | 4 | 30 | 1 | 9 | 3 | 27 | 0 | 9th | 336 | 222 | 403 | 193 |
| Voce | 14 | 5 | 21 | 1 | 4 | 1 | 7 | 0 | 10th | 341 | – | 412 | – |
| Verity | 16 | 7 | 31 | 0 | 20 | 12 | 26 | 1 | | | | | |

Umpires: G. Borwick and G.A. Hele.

## AUSTRALIA v ENGLAND 1932-33 (4th Test)

Played at Woolloongabba, Brisbane, on 10, 11, 13, 14, 15, 16 February.
Toss: Australia.   Result: ENGLAND won by six wickets.
Debuts: Australia – E.H. Bromley, L.S. Darling, H.S.B. Love; England – T.B. Mitchell.

Suffering from tonsillitis, Paynter left a hospital bed to play an historic four-hour innings of 83. Later he struck the six which won the match and regained the Ashes on the day when Archie Jackson had died in Brisbane at the age of 23.

### AUSTRALIA

| | | | | |
|---|---|---|---|---|
| V.Y. Richardson | st Ames b Hammond | 83 | c Jardine b Verity | 32 |
| W.M. Woodfull* | b Mitchell | 67 | c Hammond b Mitchell | 19 |
| D.G. Bradman | b Larwood | 76 | c Mitchell b Larwood | 24 |
| S.J. McCabe | c Jardine b Allen | 20 | (5) b Verity | 22 |
| W.H. Ponsford | b Larwood | 19 | (4) c Larwood b Allen | 0 |
| L.S. Darling | c Ames b Allen | 17 | run out | 39 |
| E.H. Bromley | c Verity b Larwood | 26 | c Hammond b Allen | 7 |
| H.S.B. Love† | lbw b Mitchell | 5 | lbw b Larwood | 3 |
| T.W. Wall | not out | 6 | c Jardine b Allen | 2 |
| W.J. O'Reilly | c Hammond b Larwood | 6 | b Larwood | 4 |
| H. Ironmonger | st Ames b Hammond | 8 | not out | 0 |
| Extras | (B 5, LB 1, NB 1) | 7 | (B 13, LB 9, NB 1) | 23 |
| **Total** | | **340** | | **175** |

### ENGLAND

| | | | | |
|---|---|---|---|---|
| D.R. Jardine* | c Love b O'Reilly | 46 | lbw b Ironmonger | 24 |
| H. Sutcliffe | lbw b O'Reilly | 86 | c Darling b Wall | 2 |
| W.R. Hammond | b McCabe | 20 | (4) c Bromley b Ironmonger | 14 |
| R.E.S. Wyatt | c Love b Ironmonger | 12 | | |
| M. Leyland | c Bradman b O'Reilly | 12 | (3) c McCabe b O'Reilly | 86 |
| L.E.G. Ames† | c Darling b Ironmonger | 17 | (5) not out | 14 |
| G.O.B. Allen | c Love b Wall | 13 | | |
| E. Paynter | c Richardson b Ironmonger | 83 | (6) not out | 14 |
| H. Larwood | b McCabe | 23 | | |
| H. Verity | not out | 23 | | |
| T.B. Mitchell | lbw b O'Reilly | 0 | | |
| Extras | (B 6, LB 12, NB 3) | 21 | (B 2, LB 4, NB 2) | 8 |
| **Total** | | **356** | (4 wickets) | **162** |

| ENGLAND | O | M | R | W | O | M | R | W | | FALL OF WICKETS | | | |
|---|---|---|---|---|---|---|---|---|---|---|---|---|---|
| Larwood | 31 | 7 | 101 | 4 | 17·3 | 3 | 49 | 3 | | A | E | A | E |
| Allen | 24 | 4 | 83 | 2 | 17 | 3 | 44 | 3 | Wkt | 1st | 1st | 2nd | 2nd |
| Hammond | 23 | 5 | 61 | 2 | 10 | 4 | 18 | 0 | 1st | 133 | 114 | 46 | 5 |
| Mitchell | 16 | 5 | 49 | 2 | 5 | 0 | 11 | 1 | 2nd | 200 | 157 | 79 | 78 |
| Verity | 27 | 12 | 39 | 0 | 19 | 6 | 30 | 2 | 3rd | 233 | 165 | 81 | 118 |
| AUSTRALIA | | | | | | | | | 4th | 264 | 188 | 91 | 138 |
| | | | | | | | | | 5th | 267 | 198 | 136 | – |
| Wall | 33 | 6 | 66 | 1 | 7 | 1 | 17 | 1 | 6th | 292 | 216 | 163 | – |
| O'Reilly | 67·4 | 27 | 120 | 4 | 30 | 11 | 65 | 1 | 7th | 315 | 225 | 169 | – |
| Ironmonger | 43 | 19 | 69 | 3 | 35 | 13 | 47 | 2 | 8th | 317 | 264 | 169 | – |
| McCabe | 23 | 7 | 40 | 2 | 7·4 | 2 | 25 | 0 | 9th | 329 | 356 | 171 | – |
| Bromley | 10 | 4 | 19 | 0 | | | | | 10th | 340 | 356 | 175 | – |
| Bradman | 7 | 1 | 17 | 0 | | | | | | | | | |
| Darling | 2 | 0 | 4 | 0 | | | | | | | | | |

Umpires: G. Borwick and G.A. Hele.

# AUSTRALIA v ENGLAND 1932-33 (5th Test)

Played at Sydney Cricket Ground on 23, 24, 25, 27, 28 February.
Toss: Australia.   Result: ENGLAND won by eight wickets.
Debuts: Australia – H.H. Alexander.

Larwood's innings of 98 in 135 minutes was the highest by a 'night-watchman' in Tests until 1977-78 when A.L. Mann scored 105 for Australia against India (*Test No. 810*). Hammond won the match with a six.

## AUSTRALIA

| | | | | |
|---|---|---|---|---|
| V.Y. Richardson | c Jardine b Larwood | 0 | c Allen b Larwood | ( |
| W.M. Woodfull* | b Larwood | 14 | b Allen | 67 |
| D.G. Bradman | b Larwood | 48 | b Verity | 71 |
| L.P.J. O'Brien | c Larwood b Voce | 61 | c Verity b Voce | 5 |
| S.J. McCabe | c Hammond b Verity | 73 | c Jardine b Voce | 4 |
| L.S. Darling | b Verity | 85 | c Wyatt b Verity | |
| W.A.S. Oldfield† | run out | 52 | c Wyatt b Verity | |
| P.K. Lee | c Jardine b Verity | 42 | b Allen | 1 |
| W.J. O'Reilly | b Allen | 19 | b Verity | |
| H.H. Alexander | not out | 17 | lbw b Verity | ( |
| H. Ironmonger | b Larwood | 1 | not out | ( |
| Extras | (B 13, LB 9, W 1) | 23 | (B 4, NB 3) | |
| **Total** | | **435** | | **182** |

## ENGLAND

| | | | | |
|---|---|---|---|---|
| D.R. Jardine* | c Oldfield b O'Reilly | 18 | c Richardson b Ironmonger | 24 |
| H. Sutcliffe | c Richardson b O'Reilly | 56 | | |
| W.R. Hammond | lbw b Lee | 101 | (4) not out | 75 |
| H. Larwood | c Ironmonger b Lee | 98 | | |
| M. Leyland | run out | 42 | (3) b Ironmonger | 0 |
| R.E.S. Wyatt | c Ironmonger b O'Reilly | 51 | (2) not out | 61 |
| L.E.G. Ames† | run out | 4 | | |
| E. Paynter | b Lee | 9 | | |
| G.O.B. Allen | c Bradman b Lee | 48 | | |
| H. Verity | c Oldfield b Alexander | 4 | | |
| W. Voce | not out | 7 | | |
| Extras | (B 7, LB 7, NB 2) | 16 | (B 6, LB 1, NB 1) | 8 |
| **Total** | | **454** | (2 wickets) | **168** |

| ENGLAND | O | M | R | W | O | M | R | W |
|---|---|---|---|---|---|---|---|---|
| Larwood | 32·2 | 10 | 98 | 4 | 11 | 0 | 44 | 1 |
| Voce | 24 | 4 | 80 | 1 | 10 | 0 | 34 | 2 |
| Allen | 25 | 1 | 128 | 1 | 11·4 | 2 | 54 | 2 |
| Hammond | 8 | 0 | 32 | 0 | 3 | 0 | 10 | 0 |
| Verity | 17 | 3 | 62 | 3 | 19 | 9 | 33 | 5 |
| Wyatt | 2 | 0 | 12 | 0 | | | | |
| **AUSTRALIA** | | | | | | | | |
| Alexander | 35 | 1 | 129 | 1 | 11 | 2 | 25 | 0 |
| McCabe | 12 | 1 | 27 | 0 | 5 | 2 | 10 | 0 |
| O'Reilly | 45 | 7 | 100 | 3 | 15 | 5 | 32 | 0 |
| Ironmonger | 31 | 13 | 64 | 0 | 26 | 12 | 34 | 2 |
| Lee | 40·2 | 11 | 111 | 4 | 12·2 | 3 | 52 | 2 |
| Darling | 7 | 5 | 3 | 0 | 2 | 0 | 7 | 0 |
| Bradman | 1 | 0 | 4 | 0 | | | | |

| | FALL OF WICKETS | | | |
|---|---|---|---|---|
| | A | E | A | E |
| *Wkt* | *1st* | *1st* | *2nd* | *2nd* |
| 1st | 0 | 31 | 0 | 43 |
| 2nd | 59 | 153 | 115 | 43 |
| 3rd | 64 | 245 | 135 | – |
| 4th | 163 | 310 | 139 | – |
| 5th | 244 | 330 | 148 | – |
| 6th | 328 | 349 | 161 | – |
| 7th | 385 | 374 | 177 | – |
| 8th | 414 | 418 | 178 | – |
| 9th | 430 | 434 | 178 | – |
| 10th | 435 | 454 | 182 | – |

Umpires: G. Borwick and G.A. Hele.

# NEW ZEALAND v ENGLAND 1932-33 (1st Test)

Played at Lancaster Park, Christchurch, on 24, 25, 27 March.
Toss: England.    Result: MATCH DRAWN.
Debuts: New Zealand – D.L. Freeman, H.D. Smith, P.E. Whitelaw.

Smith took Paynter's wicket with his first ball in his only Test match. Hammond and Ames added 242 runs in 145 minutes in the record fifth-wicket partnership for this series, England's score being 418 for 5 at the first day's close. A violent dust storm, poor light and, eventually, rain ended the match prematurely.

## ENGLAND

| | | | |
|---|---|---|---|
| H. Sutcliffe | c James b Badcock | 0 | |
| E. Paynter | b Smith | 0 | |
| W.R. Hammond | b Badcock | 227 | |
| R.E.S. Wyatt | run out | 20 | |
| D.R. Jardine* | c James b Badcock | 45 | |
| L.E.G. Ames† | b Vivian | 103 | |
| F.R. Brown | c Kerr b Page | 74 | |
| W. Voce | c Dempster b Page | 66 | |
| M.W. Tate | not out | 10 | |
| G.O.B. Allen | ) did not bat | | |
| H. Verity | ) | | |
| Extras | (B 8, LB 7) | 15 | |
| **Total** | **(8 wickets declared)** | **560** | |

## NEW ZEALAND

| | | | | | |
|---|---|---|---|---|---|
| C.S. Dempster | c Wyatt b Allen | 8 | not out | 14 | |
| P.E. Whitelaw | c Brown b Verity | 30 | not out | 17 | |
| G.L. Weir | c Hammond b Voce | 66 | | | |
| J.L. Kerr | c Hammond b Brown | 59 | | | |
| M.L. Page* | c Voce b Allen | 22 | | | |
| K.C. James† | lbw b Tate | 2 | | | |
| H.D. Smith | b Tate | 4 | | | |
| J. Newman | b Voce | 5 | | | |
| D.L. Freeman | b Voce | 1 | | | |
| F.T. Badcock | not out | 10 | | | |
| H.G. Vivian | absent hurt | – | | | |
| Extras | (B 3, LB 10, NB 3) | 16 | (LB 1 NB 3) | 4 | |
| **Total** | | **223** | **(0 wickets)** | **35** | |

| NEW ZEALAND | O | M | R | W | O | M | R | W | | FALL OF WICKETS | | |
|---|---|---|---|---|---|---|---|---|---|---|---|---|
| Badcock | 54 | 11 | 142 | 3 | | | | | | E | NZ | NZ |
| Smith | 20 | 0 | 113 | 1 | | | | | Wkt | 1st | 1st | 2nd |
| Newman | 25 | 5 | 91 | 0 | | | | | 1st | 0 | 25 | – |
| Freeman | 20 | 2 | 78 | 0 | | | | | 2nd | 4 | 59 | – |
| Vivian | 19 | 1 | 72 | 1 | | | | | 3rd | 46 | 153 | – |
| Page | 2·3 | 0 | 21 | 2 | | | | | 4th | 133 | 186 | – |
| Weir | 7 | 0 | 28 | 0 | | | | | 5th | 375 | 194 | – |
| | | | | | | | | | 6th | 424 | 205 | – |
| ENGLAND | | | | | | | | | 7th | 532 | 211 | – |
| Tate | 37 | 16 | 42 | 2 | 3 | 1 | 5 | 0 | 8th | 560 | 212 | – |
| Voce | 17·1 | 3 | 27 | 3 | 4 | 0 | 13 | 0 | 9th | – | 223 | – |
| Allen | 20 | 5 | 46 | 2 | 4·1 | 1 | 5 | 0 | 10th | – | – | – |
| Brown | 19 | 10 | 34 | 1 | | | | | | | | |
| Verity | 23 | 7 | 58 | 1 | 3 | 1 | 6 | 0 | | | | |
| Hammond | | | | | 2 | 0 | 2 | 0 | | | | |

Umpires: T. Burgess and R. Torrance.

# NEW ZEALAND v ENGLAND 1932-33 (2nd Test)

Played at Eden Park, Auckland, on 31 March, 1, 3 April.
Toss: New Zealand.    Result: MATCH DRAWN.
Debuts: New Zealand – J.A. Dunning.

Hammond's innings set a new record for the highest score in Test matches and was made out of 492 in only 318 minutes. He hit ten sixes, three of them off successive balls from Newman, and 34 fours. His 300 took 287 minutes and remains the fastest Test triple century. His third hundred took only 47 minutes. Rain caused the match to be abandoned after New Zealand had doubled their overnight total on the final morning.

## NEW ZEALAND

| | | | | |
|---|---|---|---|---|
| P.E. Whitelaw | b Bowes | 12 | not out | 5 |
| J.E. Mills | b Bowes | 0 | not out | 11 |
| G.L. Weir | b Bowes | 0 | | |
| C.S. Dempster | not out | 83 | | |
| J.L. Kerr | lbw b Voce | 10 | | |
| M.L. Page* | st Duckworth b Mitchell | 20 | | |
| F.T. Badcock | b Bowes | 1 | | |
| K.C. James† | b Bowes | 0 | | |
| J.A. Dunning | b Bowes | 12 | | |
| J. Newman | b Voce | 5 | | |
| D.L. Freeman | run out | 1 | | |
| Extras | (B 9, LB 4, NB 1) | 14 | | |
| **Total** | | **158** | (0 wickets) | **16** |

## ENGLAND

| | | |
|---|---|---|
| H. Sutcliffe | c Weir b Freeman | 24 |
| R.E.S. Wyatt* | b Dunning | 60 |
| W.R. Hammond | not out | 336 |
| E. Paynter | b Dunning | 36 |
| L.E.G. Ames | b Badcock | 26 |
| G.O.B. Allen | b Badcock | 12 |
| F.R. Brown | c Page b Weir | 13 |
| W. Voce | b Weir | 16 |
| G. Duckworth† | not out | 6 |
| W.E. Bowes ) | did not bat | |
| T.B. Mitchell ) | | |
| Extras | (B 7, LB 6, W 1, NB 5) | 19 |
| **Total** | (7 wickets declared) | **548** |

| ENGLAND | O | M | R | W | O | M | R | W |
|---|---|---|---|---|---|---|---|---|
| Allen | 5 | 2 | 11 | 0 | 3 | 1 | 4 | 0 |
| Bowes | 19 | 5 | 34 | 6 | 2 | 0 | 4 | 0 |
| Mitchell | 18 | 1 | 49 | 1 | | | | |
| Voce | 9·5 | 3 | 20 | 2 | 1·3 | 0 | 2 | 0 |
| Brown | 2 | 0 | 19 | 0 | | | | |
| Hammond | 3 | 0 | 11 | 0 | 2 | 0 | 6 | 0 |

| NEW ZEALAND | O | M | R | W |
|---|---|---|---|---|
| Badcock | 59 | 16 | 126 | 2 |
| Dunning | 43 | 5 | 156 | 2 |
| Freeman | 20 | 1 | 91 | 1 |
| Newman | 17 | 2 | 87 | 0 |
| Page | 6 | 2 | 30 | 0 |
| Weir | 11 | 2 | 39 | 2 |

### FALL OF WICKETS

| Wkt | NZ 1st | E 1st | NZ 2nd |
|---|---|---|---|
| 1st | 0 | 56 | – |
| 2nd | 0 | 139 | – |
| 3rd | 31 | 288 | – |
| 4th | 62 | 347 | – |
| 5th | 98 | 407 | – |
| 6th | 101 | 456 | – |
| 7th | 103 | 500 | – |
| 8th | 123 | – | – |
| 9th | 149 | – | – |
| 10th | 158 | – | – |

Umpires: K.H. Cave and J.T. Forrester.

# ENGLAND v WEST INDIES 1933 (1st Test)

Played at Lord's, London, on 24, 26, 27 June.
Toss: England.   Result: ENGLAND won by an innings and 27 runs.
Debuts: England – C.F. Walters; West Indies – E.A. Martindale, C.A. Merry.

The Nelson Club refused to release Constantine for this match. Francis, currently professional to Radcliffe in the Bolton League was brought in to strengthen the bowling. Rain allowed only 45 minutes' play in two instalments on the first day. Roach was out to the first ball of the second innings.

## ENGLAND

| | | |
|---|---|---|
| C.F. Walters | c Barrow b Martindale | 51 |
| H. Sutcliffe | c Grant b Martindale | 21 |
| W.R. Hammond | c Headley b Griffith | 29 |
| M. Leyland | c Barrow b Griffith | 1 |
| D.R. Jardine* | c Da Costa b Achong | 21 |
| M.J.L. Turnbull | c Barrow b Achong | 28 |
| L.E.G. Ames† | not out | 83 |
| G.O.B. Allen | run out | 16 |
| R.W.V. Robins | b Martindale | 8 |
| H. Verity | c Achong b Griffith | 21 |
| G.G. Macaulay | lbw b Martindale | 9 |
| Extras | (B 3, LB 5) | 8 |
| **Total** | | **296** |

## WEST INDIES

| | | | | | |
|---|---|---|---|---|---|
| C.A. Roach | b Allen | 0 | c Sutcliffe b Macaulay | | 0 |
| I. Barrow† | c and b Verity | 7 | lbw b Robins | | 12 |
| G.A. Headley | lbw b Allen | 13 | b Allen | | 50 |
| E.L.G. Hoad | lbw b Robins | 6 | c and b Verity | | 36 |
| G.C. Grant* | hit wkt b Robins | 26 | lbw b Macaulay | | 28 |
| O.C. Da Costa | b Robins | 6 | lbw b Verity | | 1 |
| C.A. Merry | lbw b Macaulay | 9 | b Macaulay | | 1 |
| E.E. Achong | b Robins | 15 | c Hammond b Verity | | 10 |
| G.N. Francis | b Robins | 4 | (10) not out | | 11 |
| E.A. Martindale | b Robins | 4 | (9) b Macaulay | | 4 |
| H.C. Griffith | not out | 1 | b Verity | | 18 |
| Extras | (B 3, LB 1, NB 2) | 6 | (B 1) | | 1 |
| **Total** | | **97** | | | **172** |

| WEST INDIES | O | M | R | W | O | M | R | W | FALL OF WICKETS | | | |
|---|---|---|---|---|---|---|---|---|---|---|---|---|
| | | | | | | | | | | E | WI | WI |
| Martindale | 24 | 3 | 85 | 4 | | | | | Wkt | 1st | 1st | 2nd |
| Francis | 18 | 3 | 52 | 0 | | | | | 1st | 49 | 1 | 0 |
| Griffith | 20 | 7 | 48 | 3 | | | | | 2nd | 103 | 17 | 56 |
| Achong | 35 | 9 | 88 | 2 | | | | | 3rd | 105 | 27 | 64 |
| Da Costa | 4 | 0 | 15 | 0 | | | | | 4th | 106 | 31 | 116 |
| ENGLAND | | | | | | | | | 5th | 154 | 40 | 119 |
| Macaulay | 18 | 7 | 25 | 1 | 20 | 6 | 57 | 4 | 6th | 155 | 51 | 120 |
| Allen | 13 | 6 | 13 | 2 | 11 | 2 | 33 | 1 | 7th | 194 | 87 | 133 |
| Verity | 16 | 8 | 21 | 1 | 18·1 | 4 | 45 | 4 | 8th | 217 | 92 | 138 |
| Robins | 11·5 | 1 | 32 | 6 | 12 | 2 | 36 | 1 | 9th | 265 | 96 | 146 |
| | | | | | | | | | 10th | 296 | 97 | 172 |

Umpires: F. Chester and A. Dolphin.

# ENGLAND v WEST INDIES 1933 (2nd Test)

Played at Old Trafford, Manchester, on 22, 24, 25 July.
Toss: West Indies.   Result: MATCH DRAWN.
Debuts: England – James Langridge (*elder brother of John George Langridge, also of Sussex*); West Indies – V.A. Valentine, C.A. Wiles.

Martindale and Constantine gave England's batsmen an exhibition of the 'bodyline' bowling which their bowlers had indulged in in Australia earlier that year. Hammond retired with a cut chin but Jardine gave the perfect rejoinder.

## WEST INDIES

| | | | | | |
|---|---|---|---|---|---|
| C.A. Roach | b Clark | 13 | lbw b Langridge | | 64 |
| I. Barrow† | b Wyatt | 105 | c Langridge b Clark | | 0 |
| G.A. Headley | not out | 169 | c and b Langridge | | 24 |
| E.L.G. Hoad | b Clark | 1 | c Hammond b Langridge | | 14 |
| G.C. Grant* | c Ames b Robins | 16 | c Hammond b Langridge | | 14 |
| L.N. Constantine | c Robins b Clark | 31 | (7) b Langridge | | 64 |
| C.A. Wiles | c Hammond b Verity | 0 | (6) st Ames b Langridge | | 2 |
| O.C. Da Costa | b Clark | 20 | c Sutcliffe b Clark | | 0 |
| E.E. Achong | b Verity | 6 | c Ames b Langridge | | 10 |
| V.A. Valentine | b Robins | 6 | not out | | 19 |
| E.A. Martindale | b Robins | 2 | c Verity b Robins | | 1 |
| Extras | (LB 6) | 6 | (B 8, LB 4, NB 1) | | 13 |
| **Total** | | **375** | | | **225** |

## ENGLAND

| | | |
|---|---|---|
| C.F. Walters | lbw b Martindale | 46 |
| H. Sutcliffe | run out | 20 |
| W.R. Hammond | c Martindale b Constantine | 34 |
| R.E.S. Wyatt | c Constantine b Martindale | 18 |
| D.R. Jardine* | c Constantine b Martindale | 127 |
| L.E.G. Ames† | c Headley b Martindale | 47 |
| James Langridge | c Grant b Achong | 9 |
| R.W.V. Robins | st Barrow b Achong | 55 |
| H. Verity | not out | 0 |
| E.W. Clark | b Martindale | 0 |
| G.G. Macaulay | absent hurt | – |
| Extras | (B 7, LB 6, W 1, NB 4) | 18 |
| **Total** | | **374** |

| ENGLAND | O | M | R | W | O | M | R | W |
|---|---|---|---|---|---|---|---|---|
| Clark | 40 | 8 | 99 | 4 | 15 | 1 | 64 | 2 |
| Macaulay | 14 | 2 | 48 | 0 | | | | |
| Robins | 28·4 | 2 | 111 | 3 | 11·1 | 0 | 41 | 1 |
| Verity | 32 | 14 | 47 | 2 | 13 | 2 | 40 | 0 |
| Hammond | 5 | 0 | 27 | 0 | | | | |
| Langridge | 9 | 1 | 23 | 0 | 17 | 4 | 56 | 7 |
| Wyatt | 7 | 1 | 14 | 1 | 4 | 1 | 11 | 0 |
| WEST INDIES | | | | | | | | |
| Martindale | 23·4 | 4 | 73 | 5 | | | | |
| Constantine | 25 | 5 | 55 | 1 | | | | |
| Valentine | 28 | 8 | 49 | 0 | | | | |
| Achong | 37 | 9 | 90 | 2 | | | | |
| Headley | 15 | 1 | 65 | 0 | | | | |
| Grant | 2 | 0 | 12 | 0 | | | | |
| Da Costa | 10 | 6 | 12 | 0 | | | | |

### FALL OF WICKETS

| | WI | E | WI |
|---|---|---|---|
| Wkt | 1st | 1st | 2nd |
| 1st | 26 | 63 | 5 |
| 2nd | 226 | 83 | 86 |
| 3rd | 227 | 118 | 95 |
| 4th | 266 | 134 | 112 |
| 5th | 302 | 217 | 118 |
| 6th | 306 | 234 | 131 |
| 7th | 341 | 374 | 132 |
| 8th | 354 | 374 | 191 |
| 9th | 363 | 374 | 214 |
| 10th | 375 | – | 225 |

Umpires: J. Hardstaff, sr and E.J. Smith.

# ENGLAND v WEST INDIES 1933 (3rd Test)

Played at Kennington Oval, London, on 12, 14, 15 August.
Toss: England.   Result: ENGLAND won by an innings and 17 runs.
Debuts: England – C.J. Barnett, C.S. Marriott; West Indies – B.J. Sealy.

Marriott took eleven wickets in his only Test match.

## ENGLAND

| | | |
|---|---|---:|
| C.F. Walters | c Merry b Martindale | 2 |
| A.H. Bakewell | c Headley b Sealy | 107 |
| W.R. Hammond | c Barrow b Valentine | 11 |
| R.E.S. Wyatt* | c Achong b Martindale | 15 |
| M.J.L. Turnbull | b Martindale | 4 |
| James Langridge | c Barrow b Da Costa | 22 |
| L.E.G. Ames† | c Headley b Martindale | 37 |
| C.J. Barnett | run out | 52 |
| M.S. Nichols | b Achong | 49 |
| E.W. Clark | not out | 8 |
| C.S. Marriott | b Martindale | 0 |
| Extras | (LB 5) | 5 |
| **Total** | | **312** |

## WEST INDIES

| | | | | | |
|---|---|---:|---|---|---:|
| C.A. Roach | c Bakewell b Clark | 8 | | lbw b Marriott | 56 |
| I. Barrow† | c Ames b Clark | 3 | | c Ames b Clark | 16 |
| G.A. Headley | st Ames b Marriott | 9 | (5) | c Ames b Clark | 12 |
| O.C. Da Costa | c Bakewell b Clark | 8 | (3) | b Marriott | 35 |
| B.J. Sealy | c Ames b Nichols | 29 | (4) | b Marriott | 12 |
| C.A. Merry | b Marriott | 13 | (7) | c Barnett b Nichols | 11 |
| G.C. Grant* | b Marriott | 4 | (6) | c Ames b Nichols | 14 |
| E.E. Achong | run out | 4 | | c Ames b Marriott | 22 |
| V.A. Valentine | c Langridge b Marriott | 10 | | c Barnett b Marriott | 0 |
| E.A. Martindale | not out | 1 | | not out | 9 |
| H.C. Griffith | st Ames b Marriott | 0 | | c and b Marriott | 0 |
| Extras | (B 1, LB 10) | 11 | | (LB 7, NB 1) | 8 |
| **Total** | | **100** | | | **195** |

| WEST INDIES | O | M | R | W | O | M | R | W | | FALL OF WICKETS | | |
|---|---|---|---|---|---|---|---|---|---|---|---|---|
| Martindale | 24·5 | 2 | 93 | 5 | | | | | | E | WI | WI |
| Griffith | 20 | 4 | 44 | 0 | | | | | Wkt | 1st | 1st | 2nd |
| Valentine | 20 | 6 | 55 | 1 | | | | | 1st | 2 | 7 | 77 |
| Da Costa | 12 | 2 | 30 | 1 | | | | | 2nd | 27 | 26 | 79 |
| Achong | 23 | 3 | 59 | 1 | | | | | 3rd | 64 | 38 | 113 |
| Headley | 4 | 0 | 16 | 0 | | | | | 4th | 68 | 44 | 138 |
| Sealy | 5 | 1 | 10 | 1 | | | | | 5th | 147 | 68 | 138 |
| | | | | | | | | | 6th | 194 | 74 | 151 |
| ENGLAND | | | | | | | | | 7th | 208 | 88 | 160 |
| Clark | 8 | 3 | 16 | 3 | 21 | 10 | 54 | 2 | 8th | 303 | 95 | 183 |
| Nichols | 10 | 1 | 36 | 1 | 14 | 3 | 51 | 2 | 9th | 305 | 100 | 195 |
| Marriott | 11·5 | 2 | 37 | 5 | 29·2 | 6 | 59 | 6 | 10th | 312 | 100 | 195 |
| Langridge | | | | | 7 | 1 | 23 | 0 | | | | |

Umpires: F. Chester and J. Hardstaff, sr.

# INDIA v ENGLAND 1933-34 (1st Test)

Played at Gymkhana Ground, Bombay, on 15, 16, 17, 18 December.
Toss: India.   Result: ENGLAND won by nine wickets.
Debuts: India – L. Amarnath, L.P. Jai, R.J. Jamshedji, V.M. Merchant, L. Ramji;
England – A. Mitchell, B.H. Valentine.

India's first official home Test was played on the first of three Test match grounds in Bombay. It was the first Test match to include Sunday play. Valentine and Amarnath scored their respective countries' first centuries of this series, both achieving the feat on debut.

## INDIA

| | | | | | |
|---|---|---|---|---|---|
| S. Wazir Ali | lbw b Nichols | 36 | c Nichols b Clark | | 5 |
| J.G. Navle† | c Nichols b Verity | 13 | c Elliott b Clark | | 4 |
| L. Amarnath | lbw b Langridge | 38 | c Nichols b Clark | | 118 |
| C.K. Nayudu* | lbw b Clark | 28 | c Valentine b Nichols | | 67 |
| L.P. Jai | c Mitchell b Langridge | 19 | c Jardine b Nichols | | 0 |
| V.M. Merchant | lbw b Nichols | 23 | c Elliott b Langridge | | 30 |
| S.H.M. Colah | c Elliott b Nichols | 31 | (8) c Elliott b Nichols | | 12 |
| L. Amar Singh | st Elliott b Langridge | 0 | (7) lbw b Verity | | 1 |
| Mahomed Nissar | c Mitchell b Verity | 13 | lbw b Nichols | | 1 |
| L. Ramji | b Verity | 1 | (11) lbw b Nichols | | 0 |
| R.J. Jamshedji | not out | 4 | (10) not out | | 1 |
| Extras | (B 2, LB 5, NB 6) | 13 | (B 4, LB 6, W 1, NB 8) | | 19 |
| **Total** | | **219** | | | **258** |

## ENGLAND

| | | | | | |
|---|---|---|---|---|---|
| A. Mitchell | b Nissar | 5 | lbw b Amar Singh | | 9 |
| C.F. Walters | c Merchant b Amar Singh | 78 | not out | | 14 |
| C.J. Barnett | c and b Jamshedji | 33 | not out | | 17 |
| James Langridge | lbw b Nissar | 31 | | | |
| D.R. Jardine* | b Nissar | 60 | | | |
| B.H. Valentine | c Merchant b Jamshedji | 136 | | | |
| L.F. Townsend | c and b Jamshedji | 15 | | | |
| M.S. Nichols | run out | 2 | | | |
| H. Verity | c Ramji b Nissar | 24 | | | |
| H. Elliott† | not out | 37 | | | |
| E.W. Clark | b Nissar | 1 | | | |
| Extras | (B 7, LB 9) | 16 | | | |
| **Total** | | **438** | (1 wicket) | | **40** |

| ENGLAND | O | M | R | W | O | M | R | W | | FALL OF WICKETS | | | |
|---|---|---|---|---|---|---|---|---|---|---|---|---|---|
| Nichols | 23·2 | 8 | 53 | 3 | 23·5 | 7 | 55 | 5 | | I | E | I | E |
| Clark | 13 | 3 | 41 | 1 | 19 | 5 | 69 | 3 | Wkt | 1st | 1st | 2nd | 2nd |
| Barnett | 2 | 1 | 1 | 0 | | | | | 1st | 44 | 12 | 9 | 15 |
| Verity | 27 | 11 | 44 | 3 | 20 | 9 | 50 | 1 | 2nd | 71 | 67 | 21 | – |
| Langridge | 17 | 4 | 42 | 3 | 16 | 7 | 32 | 1 | 3rd | 117 | 143 | 207 | – |
| Townsend | 9 | 2 | 25 | 0 | 12 | 5 | 33 | 0 | 4th | 135 | 164 | 208 | – |
| | | | | | | | | | 5th | 148 | 309 | 208 | – |
| INDIA | | | | | | | | | 6th | 175 | 362 | 214 | – |
| Nissar | 33·5 | 3 | 90 | 5 | 4 | 1 | 25 | 0 | 7th | 186 | 371 | 248 | – |
| Ramji | 23 | 5 | 64 | 0 | | | | | 8th | 209 | 373 | 249 | – |
| Amar Singh | 36 | 5 | 119 | 1 | 3·2 | 1 | 15 | 1 | 9th | 212 | 431 | 258 | – |
| Jamshedji | 35 | 4 | 137 | 3 | | | | | 10th | 219 | 438 | 258 | – |
| Nayudu | 7 | 2 | 10 | 0 | | | | | | | | | |
| Amarnath | 2 | 1 | 2 | 0 | | | | | | | | | |

Umpires: F.A. Tarrant and J.W. Hitch.

# INDIA v ENGLAND 1933-34 (2nd Test)

Played at Eden Gardens, Calcutta, on 5, 6, 7, 8 January.
Toss: England.   Result: MATCH DRAWN.
Debuts: India – Dilawar Hussain, M.J. Gopalan, Mushtaq Ali, C.S. Nayudu;
England – W.H.V. Levett.

Dilawar Hussain retired hurt, struck on the back of the head by a ball from Nichols, after scoring 11 in the first innings.

## ENGLAND

| | | | | |
|---|---|---|---|---|
| C.F. Walters | c Gopalan b Amar Singh | 29 | not out | 2 |
| A. Mitchell | c Gopalan b C.K. Nayudu | 47 | | |
| C.J. Barnett | lbw b Amar Singh | 8 | (2) c Gopalan b Nissar | 0 |
| James Langridge | c Nissar b Gopalan | 70 | | |
| D.R. Jardine* | c C.S. Nayudu b Mushtaq Ali | 61 | | |
| B.H. Valentine | lbw b C.K. Nayudu | 40 | (3) st Hussain b Naoomal | 3 |
| W.H.V. Levett† | b C.K. Nayudu | 5 | (4) not out | 2 |
| M.S. Nichols | lbw b Nissar | 13 | | |
| L.F. Townsend | c Hussain b Amar Singh | 40 | | |
| H. Verity | not out | 55 | | |
| E.W. Clark | c Merchant b Amar Singh | 10 | | |
| Extras | (B 13, LB 10, NB 2) | 25 | | |
| **Total** | | **403** | (2 wickets) | **7** |

## INDIA

| | | | | |
|---|---|---|---|---|
| Naoomal Jeoomal | c Jardine b Nichols | 2 | c Levett b Townsend | 43 |
| Dilawar Hussain† | c Jardine b Clark | 59 | (7) b Clark | 57 |
| S. Wazir Ali | c Nichols b Verity | 39 | c Nichols b Verity | 0 |
| C.K. Nayudu* | b Clark | 5 | lbw b Verity | 38 |
| L. Amarnath | c Jardine b Clark | 0 | c Levett b Clark | 9 |
| V.M. Merchant | b Verity | 54 | c Jardine b Verity | 17 |
| Mushtaq Ali | lbw b Nichols | 9 | (2) c Barnett b Nichols | 18 |
| C.S. Nayudu | c Verity b Nichols | 36 | lbw b Verity | 15 |
| L. Amar Singh | c Nichols b Verity | 10 | c Jardine b Townsend | 18 |
| M.J. Gopalan | not out | 11 | c Levett b Clark | 7 |
| Mahomed Nissar | c Walters b Verity | 2 | not out | 0 |
| Extras | (B 5, LB 5, NB 10) | 20 | (B 10, LB 4, NB 1) | 15 |
| **Total** | | **247** | | **237** |

| INDIA | O | M | R | W | O | M | R | W | | FALL OF WICKETS | | | |
|---|---|---|---|---|---|---|---|---|---|---|---|---|---|
| Nissar | 34 | 6 | 112 | 1 | 2 | 1 | 2 | 1 | | E | I | I | E |
| Amar Singh | 54·5 | 13 | 106 | 4 | 2 | 1 | 1 | 0 | Wkt | 1st | 1st | 2nd | 2nd |
| Gopalan | 19 | 7 | 39 | 1 | | | | | 1st | 45 | 12 | 57 | 0 |
| Mushtaq Ali | 19 | 5 | 45 | 1 | | | | | 2nd | 55 | 23 | 58 | 5 |
| Amarnath | 2 | 0 | 10 | 0 | | | | | 3rd | 135 | 27 | 76 | – |
| C.S. Nayudu | 8 | 1 | 26 | 0 | | | | | 4th | 185 | 90 | 88 | – |
| C.K. Nayudu | 23 | 7 | 40 | 3 | | | | | 5th | 256 | 131 | 129 | – |
| Naoomal | | | | | 1 | 0 | 4 | 1 | 6th | 281 | 158 | 149 | – |
| | | | | | | | | | 7th | 281 | 211 | 201 | – |
| ENGLAND | | | | | | | | | 8th | 301 | 223 | 214 | – |
| Clark | 26 | 8 | 39 | 3 | 19·3 | 4 | 50 | 3 | 9th | 371 | 236 | 230 | – |
| Nichols | 28 | 6 | 78 | 3 | 20 | 6 | 48 | 1 | 10th | 403 | 247 | 237 | – |
| Verity | 28·4 | 13 | 64 | 4 | 31 | 12 | 76 | 4 | | | | | |
| Langridge | 17 | 7 | 27 | 0 | 10 | 4 | 19 | 0 | | | | | |
| Townsend | 8 | 4 | 19 | 0 | 8 | 3 | 22 | 2 | | | | | |
| Barnett | | | | | 2 | 0 | 7 | 0 | | | | | |

Umpires: F.A. Tarrant and J.W. Hitch.

# INDIA v ENGLAND 1933-34 (3rd Test)

Played at Chepauk, Madras, on 10, 11, 12, 13 February.
Toss: England.   Result: ENGLAND won by 202 runs.
Debuts: India – The Yuvaraj of Patiala (*later Lt-Col Yadavendra Singh, Maharaja of Patiala*).

Naoomal Jeoomal played no further part in the match after retiring with a gashed head when he edged a ball from Clark.

## ENGLAND

| | | | | |
|---|---|--:|---|--:|
| A.H. Bakewell | c C.S. Nayudu b Amarnath | 85 | c Patiala b Amar Singh | 4 |
| C.F. Walters | lbw b Amar Singh | 59 | c sub (M.J. Gopalan) b Amarnath | 102 |
| A. Mitchell | lbw b Amarnath | 25 | (8) c and b Amarnath | 28 |
| James Langridge | lbw b Amar Singh | 1 | (6) c Hussain b Nazir Ali | 46 |
| D.R. Jardine* | c Wazir Ali b Amar Singh | 65 | (7) not out | 35 |
| C.J. Barnett | c Patiala b Amar Singh | 4 | (3) c Mushtaq Ali b Nazir Ali | 26 |
| M.S. Nichols | b Amar Singh | 1 | (5) c Hussain b Nazir Ali | 8 |
| L.F. Townsend | b Amar Singh | 10 | (4) c C.K. Nayudu b Nazir Ali | 8 |
| H. Verity | lbw b Mushtaq Ali | 42 | | |
| H. Elliott† | c Mushtaq Ali b Amar Singh | 14 | | |
| E.W. Clark | not out | 4 | | |
| Extras | (B 22, LB 2, NB 1) | 25 | (B 1, LB 3) | 4 |
| **Total** | | **335** | (7 wickets declared) | **261** |

## INDIA

| | | | | |
|---|---|--:|---|--:|
| Dilawar Hussain† | c Barnett b Verity | 13 | b Langridge | 36 |
| Naoomal Jeoomal | retired hurt | 5 | absent hurt | – |
| S. Wazir Ali | b Nichols | 2 | c Mitchell b Verity | 21 |
| C.K. Nayudu* | b Verity | 20 | (5) st Elliott b Langridge | 2 |
| L. Amarnath | c Elliott b Langridge | 12 | (8) not out | 26 |
| V.M. Merchant | b Verity | 26 | c and b Verity | 28 |
| Yuvaraj of Patiala | b Verity | 24 | c Elliott b Langridge | 60 |
| S. Nazir Ali | c Mitchell b Verity | 3 | (9) c Nicholls b Langridge | 8 |
| C.S. Nayudu | c Nichols b Verity | 11 | (10) st Elliott b Verity | 0 |
| Mushtaq Ali | not out | 7 | (2) c Mitchell b Verity | 8 |
| L. Amar Singh | c Barnett b Verity | 16 | (4) c Barnett b Langridge | 48 |
| Extras | (B 1, LB 3, NB 2) | 6 | (B 10, LB 1, NB 1) | 12 |
| **Total** | | **145** | | **249** |

| INDIA | O | M | R | W | O | M | R | W | | FALL OF WICKETS | | | |
|---|--:|--:|--:|--:|--:|--:|--:|--:|---|---|---|---|---|
| Amar Singh | 44·4 | 13 | 86 | 7 | 23 | 6 | 55 | 1 | | E | I | E | I |
| C.K. Nayudu | 11 | 1 | 32 | 0 | 9 | 0 | 38 | 0 | *Wkt* | *1st* | *1st* | *2nd* | *2nd* |
| Amarnath | 31 | 14 | 69 | 2 | 11·5 | 3 | 32 | 2 | 1st | 111 | 15 | 10 | 16 |
| Mushtaq Ali | 25 | 3 | 64 | 1 | 4 | 0 | 16 | 0 | 2nd | 167 | 39 | 76 | 45 |
| C.S. Nayudu | 13 | 1 | 43 | 0 | 2 | 0 | 17 | 0 | 3rd | 170 | 42 | 90 | 119 |
| Naoomal | 6 | 0 | 16 | 0 | | | | | 4th | 174 | 66 | 102 | 120 |
| Wazir Ali | 1 | 1 | 0 | 0 | 3 | 0 | 16 | 0 | 5th | 178 | 99 | 184 | 125 |
| Nazir Ali | | | | | 23 | 1 | 83 | 4 | 6th | 182 | 107 | 209 | 209 |
| | | | | | | | | | 7th | 208 | 122 | 261 | 237 |
| ENGLAND | | | | | | | | | 8th | 305 | 127 | – | 248 |
| Clark | 15 | 4 | 37 | 0 | 8 | 2 | 27 | 0 | 9th | 317 | 145 | – | 249 |
| Nichols | 12 | 3 | 30 | 1 | 6 | 1 | 23 | 0 | 10th | 335 | – | – | – |
| Verity | 23·5 | 10 | 49 | 7 | 27·2 | 6 | 104 | 4 | | | | | |
| Langridge | 6 | 1 | 9 | 1 | 24 | 5 | 63 | 5 | | | | | |
| Townsend | 3 | 0 | 14 | 0 | 3 | 0 | 19 | 0 | | | | | |
| Barnett | | | | | 1 | 0 | 1 | 0 | | | | | |

Umpires: J.B. Higgins and J.W. Hitch.

# ENGLAND v AUSTRALIA 1934 (1st Test)

Played at Trent Bridge, Nottingham, on 8, 9, 11, 12 June.
Toss: Australia.   Result: AUSTRALIA won by 238 runs.
Debuts: England – K. Farnes; Australia – W.A. Brown, A.G. Chipperfield.

This was Australia's only victory against England between 1928 and 1938 gained without Bradman contributing a century, and it was completed with only ten minutes to spare. Walters captained England in his first Test against Australia. Chipperfield was the first batsman to miss a hundred on Test debut by just one run; not out 99 at lunch, he was dismissed by the third ball afterwards.

## AUSTRALIA

| | | | | |
|---|---|---|---|---|
| W.M. Woodfull* | c Verity b Farnes | 26 | b Farnes | 2 |
| W.H. Ponsford | c Ames b Farnes | 53 | b Hammond | 5 |
| W.A. Brown | lbw b Geary | 22 | c Ames b Verity | 73 |
| D.G. Bradman | c Hammond b Geary | 29 | c Ames b Farnes | 25 |
| S.J. McCabe | c Leyland b Farnes | 65 | c Hammond b Farnes | 88 |
| L.S. Darling | b Verity | 4 | c Hammond b Farnes | 14 |
| A.G. Chipperfield | c Ames b Farnes | 99 | c Hammond b Farnes | 4 |
| W.A.S. Oldfield† | c Hammond b Mitchell | 20 | not out | 10 |
| C.V. Grimmett | b Geary | 39 | (10) not out | 3 |
| W.J. O'Reilly | b Farnes | 7 | (9) c Verity b Geary | 18 |
| T.W. Wall | not out | 0 | | |
| Extras | (B 4, LB 5, NB 1) | 10 | (B 22, LB 9) | 31 |
| **Total** | | **374** | (8 wickets declared) | **273** |

## ENGLAND

| | | | | |
|---|---|---|---|---|
| C.F. Walters* | lbw b Grimmett | 17 | b O'Reilly | 46 |
| H. Sutcliffe | c Chipperfield b Grimmett | 62 | c Chipperfield b O'Reilly | 24 |
| W.R. Hammond | c McCabe b O'Reilly | 25 | st Oldfield b Grimmett | 16 |
| Nawab of Pataudi, sr | c McCabe b Wall | 12 | c Ponsford b Grimmett | 10 |
| M. Leyland | c and b Grimmett | 6 | (6) c Oldfield b O'Reilly | 18 |
| E.H. Hendren | b O'Reilly | 79 | (5) c Chipperfield b O'Reilly | 3 |
| L.E.G. Ames† | c Wall b O'Reilly | 7 | b O'Reilly | 12 |
| G. Geary | st Oldfield b Grimmett | 53 | c Chipperfield b Grimmett | 0 |
| H. Verity | b O'Reilly | 0 | not out | 0 |
| K. Farnes | b Grimmett | 1 | c Oldfield b O'Reilly | 0 |
| T.B. Mitchell | not out | 1 | lbw b O'Reilly | 4 |
| Extras | (B 5) | 5 | (B 4, LB 3, NB 1) | 8 |
| **Total** | | **268** | | **141** |

| ENGLAND | O | M | R | W | O | M | R | W | FALL OF WICKETS | | | | |
|---|---|---|---|---|---|---|---|---|---|---|---|---|---|
| Farnes | 40·2 | 10 | 102 | 5 | 25 | 3 | 77 | 5 | | A | E | A | E |
| Geary | 43 | 8 | 101 | 3 | 23 | 5 | 46 | 1 | Wkt | 1st | 1st | 2nd | 2nd |
| Hammond | 13 | 4 | 29 | 0 | 12 | 5 | 25 | 1 | 1st | 77 | 45 | 2 | 51 |
| Verity | 34 | 9 | 65 | 1 | 17 | 8 | 48 | 1 | 2nd | 88 | 102 | 32 | 83 |
| Mitchell | 21 | 4 | 62 | 1 | 13 | 2 | 46 | 0 | 3rd | 125 | 106 | 69 | 91 |
| Leyland | 1 | 0 | 5 | 0 | | | | | 4th | 146 | 114 | 181 | 103 |
| | | | | | | | | | 5th | 153 | 145 | 219 | 110 |
| AUSTRALIA | | | | | | | | | 6th | 234 | 165 | 231 | 134 |
| Wall | 33 | 7 | 82 | 1 | 13 | 2 | 27 | 0 | 7th | 281 | 266 | 244 | 135 |
| McCabe | 7 | 2 | 7 | 0 | 2 | 0 | 7 | 0 | 8th | 355 | 266 | 267 | 137 |
| Grimmett | 58·3 | 24 | 81 | 5 | 47 | 28 | 39 | 3 | 9th | 374 | 266 | – | 137 |
| O'Reilly | 37 | 16 | 75 | 4 | 41·4 | 24 | 54 | 7 | 10th | 374 | 268 | – | 141 |
| Chipperfield | 3 | 0 | 18 | 0 | 4 | 1 | 6 | 0 | | | | | |

Umpires: F. Chester and A. Dolphin.

# ENGLAND v AUSTRALIA 1934 (2nd Test)

Played at Lord's, London, on 22, 23, 25 June.
Toss: England. Result: ENGLAND won by an innings and 38 runs.
Debuts: Nil.

Verity took 14 wickets for 80 runs on the third day – six of them in the last hour – to give England their first win against Australia at Lord's since 1896. His performance still stands as the record for most Test wickets in a day in Tests between England and Australia and led to the B.B.C. allowing commentator Howard Marshall a scorer/assistant (Arthur Wrigley) at the next Test. Ames scored the first hundred by a wicket-keeper in this series.

## ENGLAND

| | | |
|---|---|---|
| C.F. Walters | c Bromley b O'Reilly | 82 |
| H. Sutcliffe | lbw b Chipperfield | 20 |
| W.R. Hammond | c and b Chipperfield | 2 |
| E.H. Hendren | c McCabe b Wall | 13 |
| R.E.S. Wyatt* | c Oldfield b Chipperfield | 33 |
| M. Leyland | b Wall | 109 |
| L.E.G. Ames† | c Oldfield b McCabe | 120 |
| G. Geary | c Chipperfield b Wall | 9 |
| H. Verity | st Oldfield b Grimmett | 29 |
| K. Farnes | b Wall | 1 |
| W.E. Bowes | not out | 10 |
| Extras | (LB 12) | 12 |
| **Total** | | **440** |

## AUSTRALIA

| | | | | | |
|---|---|---|---|---|---|
| W.M. Woodfull* | b Bowes | 22 | | c Hammond b Verity | 43 |
| W.A. Brown | c Ames b Bowes | 105 | | c Walters b Bowes | 2 |
| D.G. Bradman | c and b Verity | 36 | (4) | c Ames b Verity | 13 |
| S.J. McCabe | c Hammond b Verity | 34 | (3) | c Hendren b Verity | 19 |
| L.S. Darling | c Sutcliffe b Verity | 0 | | b Hammond | 10 |
| A.G. Chipperfield | not out | 37 | | c Geary b Verity | 14 |
| E.H. Bromley | c Geary b Verity | 4 | | c and b Verity | 1 |
| W.A.S. Oldfield† | c Sutcliffe b Verity | 23 | | lbw b Verity | 0 |
| C.V. Grimmett | b Bowes | 9 | | c Hammond b Verity | 0 |
| W.J. O'Reilly | b Verity | 4 | | not out | 8 |
| T.W. Wall | lbw b Verity | 0 | | c Hendren b Verity | 1 |
| Extras | (B 1, LB 9) | 10 | | (B 6, NB 1) | 7 |
| **Total** | | **284** | | | **118** |

| AUSTRALIA | O | M | R | W | O | M | R | W |
|---|---|---|---|---|---|---|---|---|
| Wall | 49 | 7 | 108 | 4 | | | | |
| McCabe | 18 | 3 | 38 | 1 | | | | |
| Grimmett | 53·3 | 13 | 102 | 1 | | | | |
| O'Reilly | 38 | 15 | 70 | 1 | | | | |
| Chipperfield | 34 | 10 | 91 | 3 | | | | |
| Darling | 6 | 2 | 19 | 0 | | | | |
| ENGLAND | | | | | | | | |
| Farnes | 12 | 3 | 43 | 0 | 4 | 2 | 6 | 0 |
| Bowes | 31 | 5 | 98 | 3 | 14 | 4 | 24 | 1 |
| Geary | 22 | 4 | 56 | 0 | | | | |
| Verity | 36 | 15 | 61 | 7 | 22·3 | 8 | 43 | 8 |
| Hammond | 4 | 1 | 6 | 0 | 13 | 0 | 38 | 1 |
| Leyland | 4 | 1 | 10 | 0 | | | | |

FALL OF WICKETS

| | E | A | A |
|---|---|---|---|
| Wkt | 1st | 1st | 2nd |
| 1st | 70 | 68 | 10 |
| 2nd | 78 | 141 | 43 |
| 3rd | 99 | 203 | 57 |
| 4th | 130 | 204 | 94 |
| 5th | 182 | 205 | 94 |
| 6th | 311 | 218 | 95 |
| 7th | 359 | 258 | 95 |
| 8th | 409 | 273 | 95 |
| 9th | 410 | 284 | 112 |
| 10th | 440 | 284 | 118 |

Umpires: F. Chester and J. Hardstaff, sr.

# ENGLAND v AUSTRALIA 1934 (3rd Test)

Played at Old Trafford, Manchester, on 6, 7, 9, 10 July.
Toss: England.   Result: MATCH DRAWN.
Debuts: England – J.L. Hopwood.

Allen's first over in the second innings lasted thirteen balls; he was called for three wides and four no-balls. Possibly he was overcome by the phenomenal Manchester weather. 'From first to last the sun blazed down, the heat being at times almost unbearable.' (*Wisden*)

## ENGLAND

| | | | | |
|---|---|---|---|---|
| C.F. Walters | c Darling b O'Reilly | 52 | not out | 50 |
| H. Sutcliffe | c Chipperfield b O'Reilly | 63 | not out | 69 |
| R.E.S. Wyatt* | b O'Reilly | 0 | | |
| W.R. Hammond | b O'Reilly | 4 | | |
| E.H. Hendren | c and b O'Reilly | 132 | | |
| M. Leyland | c sub (B.A. Barnett) b O'Reilly | 153 | | |
| L.E.G. Ames† | c Ponsford b Grimmett | 72 | | |
| J.L. Hopwood | b O'Reilly | 2 | | |
| G.O.B. Allen | b McCabe | 61 | | |
| H. Verity | not out | 60 | | |
| E.W. Clark | not out | 2 | | |
| Extras | (B 6, LB 18, W 2) | 26 | (B 2, LB 1, W 1) | 4 |
| **Total** | (9 wickets declared) | **627** | (0 wickets declared) | **123** |

## AUSTRALIA

| | | | | |
|---|---|---|---|---|
| W.A. Brown | c Walters b Clark | 72 | c Hammond b Allen | 0 |
| W.H. Ponsford | c Hendren b Hammond | 12 | not out | 30 |
| S.J. McCabe | c Verity b Hammond | 137 | not out | 33 |
| W.M. Woodfull* | run out | 73 | | |
| L.S. Darling | b Verity | 37 | | |
| D.G. Bradman | c Ames b Hammond | 30 | | |
| W.A.S. Oldfield† | c Wyatt b Verity | 13 | | |
| A.G. Chipperfield | c Walters b Verity | 26 | | |
| C.V. Grimmett | b Verity | 0 | | |
| W.J. O'Reilly | not out | 30 | | |
| T.W. Wall | run out | 18 | | |
| Extras | (B 20, LB 13, W 4, NB 6) | 43 | (B 1, LB 2) | 3 |
| **Total** | | **491** | (1 wicket) | **66** |

| AUSTRALIA | O | M | R | W | O | M | R | W |
|---|---|---|---|---|---|---|---|---|
| Wall | 36 | 3 | 131 | 0 | 9 | 0 | 31 | 0 |
| McCabe | 32 | 3 | 98 | 1 | 13 | 4 | 35 | 0 |
| Grimmett | 57 | 20 | 122 | 1 | 17 | 5 | 28 | 0 |
| O'Reilly | 59 | 9 | 189 | 7 | 13 | 4 | 25 | 0 |
| Chipperfield | 7 | 0 | 29 | 0 | | | | |
| Darling | 10 | 0 | 32 | 0 | | | | |
| ENGLAND | | | | | | | | |
| Clark | 40 | 9 | 100 | 1 | 4 | 1 | 16 | 0 |
| Allen | 31 | 3 | 113 | 0 | 6 | 0 | 23 | 1 |
| Hammond | 28·3 | 6 | 111 | 3 | 2 | 1 | 2 | 0 |
| Verity | 53 | 24 | 78 | 4 | 5 | 4 | 2 | 0 |
| Hopwood | 38 | 20 | 46 | 0 | 9 | 5 | 16 | 0 |
| Hendren | | | | | 1 | 0 | 4 | 0 |

### FALL OF WICKETS

| Wkt | E 1st | A 1st | E 2nd | A 2nd |
|---|---|---|---|---|
| 1st | 68 | 34 | – | 1 |
| 2nd | 68 | 230 | – | – |
| 3rd | 72 | 242 | – | – |
| 4th | 149 | 320 | – | – |
| 5th | 340 | 378 | – | – |
| 6th | 482 | 409 | – | – |
| 7th | 492 | 411 | – | – |
| 8th | 510 | 419 | – | – |
| 9th | 605 | 454 | – | – |
| 10th | – | 491 | – | – |

Umpires: J. Hardstaff, sr and F. Walden.

# ENGLAND v AUSTRALIA 1934 (4th Test)

Played at Headingley, Leeds, on 20, 21, 23, 24 July.
Toss: England.   Result: MATCH DRAWN.
Debuts: England – W.W. Keeton.

Heavy rain at 1 p.m. on the last day saved England from probable defeat after Bradman had scored his second triple century in successive Tests at Leeds. He batted for 430 minutes, hit two sixes and 43 fours, and added 388 runs with Ponsford (then the highest partnership for any wicket by either side in this series, and still the record for the fourth wicket). Australia's total remains the record for a Leeds Test.

## ENGLAND

| | | | | |
|---|---|--:|---|--:|
| C.F. Walters | c and b Chipperfield | 44 | b O'Reilly | 45 |
| W.W. Keeton | c Oldfield b O'Reilly | 25 | b Grimmett | 12 |
| W.R. Hammond | b Wall | 37 | run out | 20 |
| E.H. Hendren | b Chipperfield | 29 | lbw b O'Reilly | 42 |
| R.E.S. Wyatt* | st Oldfield b Grimmett | 19 | b Grimmett | 44 |
| M. Leyland | lbw b O'Reilly | 16 | not out | 49 |
| L.E.G. Ames† | c Oldfield b Grimmett | 9 | c Brown b Grimmett | 8 |
| J.L. Hopwood | lbw b O'Reilly | 8 | not out | 2 |
| H. Verity | not out | 2 | | |
| T.B. Mitchell | st Oldfield b Grimmett | 9 | | |
| W.E. Bowes | c Ponsford b Grimmett | 0 | | |
| Extras | (LB 2) | 2 | (B 1, LB 6) | 7 |
| **Total** | | **200** | (6 wickets) | **229** |

## AUSTRALIA

| | | |
|---|---|--:|
| W.A. Brown | b Bowes | 15 |
| W.H. Ponsford | hit wkt b Verity | 181 |
| W.A.S. Oldfield† | c Ames b Bowes | 0 |
| W.M. Woodfull* | b Bowes | 0 |
| D.G. Bradman | b Bowes | 304 |
| S.J. McCabe | b Bowes | 27 |
| L.S. Darling | b Bowes | 12 |
| A.G. Chipperfield | c Wyatt b Verity | 1 |
| C.V. Grimmett | run out | 15 |
| W.J. O'Reilly | not out | 11 |
| T.W. Wall | lbw b Verity | 1 |
| Extras | (B 8, LB 9) | 17 |
| **Total** | | **584** |

| AUSTRALIA | O | M | R | W | O | M | R | W |
|---|--:|--:|--:|--:|--:|--:|--:|--:|
| Wall | 18 | 1 | 57 | 1 | 14 | 5 | 36 | 0 |
| McCabe | 4 | 2 | 3 | 0 | 5 | 4 | 5 | 0 |
| Grimmett | 30·4 | 11 | 57 | 4 | 56·5 | 24 | 72 | 3 |
| O'Reilly | 35 | 16 | 46 | 3 | 51 | 25 | 88 | 2 |
| Chipperfield | 18 | 6 | 35 | 2 | 9 | 2 | 21 | 0 |

| ENGLAND | O | M | R | W |
|---|--:|--:|--:|--:|
| Bowes | 50 | 13 | 142 | 6 |
| Hammond | 29 | 5 | 82 | 0 |
| Mitchell | 23 | 1 | 117 | 0 |
| Verity | 46·5 | 15 | 113 | 3 |
| Hopwood | 30 | 7 | 93 | 0 |
| Leyland | 5 | 0 | 20 | 0 |

### FALL OF WICKETS

| | E | A | E |
|---|--:|--:|--:|
| Wkt | 1st | 1st | 2nd |
| 1st | 43 | 37 | 28 |
| 2nd | 85 | 39 | 70 |
| 3rd | 135 | 39 | 87 |
| 4th | 135 | 427 | 152 |
| 5th | 168 | 517 | 190 |
| 6th | 170 | 550 | 213 |
| 7th | 189 | 551 | – |
| 8th | 189 | 557 | – |
| 9th | 200 | 574 | – |
| 10th | 200 | 584 | – |

Umpires: A. Dolphin and J. Hardstaff, sr.

# ENGLAND v AUSTRALIA 1934 (5th Test)

Played at Kennington Oval, London, on 18, 20, 21, 22 August.
Toss: Australia.   Result: AUSTRALIA won by 562 runs.
Debuts: Australia – H.I. Ebeling.

The second wicket partnership of 451 in 316 minutes between Ponsford and Bradman remains the world record for any wicket in Test cricket. Ames retired hurt at 227 for 5 in England's first innings. Woolley, recalled at the age of 47 to make the last Test appearance by a pre-1914 Test player, deputised for Ames in the second innings and conceded 37 byes (still a record) in addition to catching Chipperfield.

## AUSTRALIA

| | | | | |
|---|---|---|---|---|
| W.A. Brown | b Clark | 10 | c Allen b Clark | 1 |
| W.H. Ponsford | hit wkt b Allen | 266 | c Hammond b Clark | 22 |
| D.G. Bradman | c Ames b Bowes | 244 | b Bowes | 77 |
| S.J. McCabe | b Allen | 10 | c Walters b Clark | 70 |
| W.M. Woodfull* | b Bowes | 49 | b Bowes | 13 |
| A.F. Kippax | lbw b Bowes | 28 | c Walters b Clark | 8 |
| A.G. Chipperfield | b Bowes | 3 | c Woolley b Clark | 16 |
| W.A.S. Oldfield† | not out | 42 | c Hammond b Bowes | 0 |
| C.V. Grimmett | c Ames b Allen | 7 | c Hammond b Bowes | 14 |
| H.I. Ebeling | b Allen | 2 | c Allen b Bowes | 41 |
| W.J. O'Reilly | b Clark | 7 | not out | 15 |
| Extras | (B 4, LB 14, W 2, NB 13) | 33 | (B 37, LB 8, W 1, NB 4) | 50 |
| **Total** | | **701** | | **327** |

## ENGLAND

| | | | | |
|---|---|---|---|---|
| C.F. Walters | c Kippax b O'Reilly | 64 | b McCabe | 1 |
| H. Sutcliffe | c Oldfield b Grimmett | 38 | c McCabe b Grimmett | 28 |
| F.E. Woolley | c McCabe b O'Reilly | 4 | c Ponsford b McCabe | 0 |
| W.R. Hammond | c Oldfield b Ebeling | 15 | c and b O'Reilly | 43 |
| R.E.S. Wyatt* | b Grimmett | 17 | (6) c Ponsford b Grimmett | 22 |
| M. Leyland | b Grimmett | 110 | (5) c Brown b Grimmett | 17 |
| L.E.G. Ames† | retired hurt | 33 | absent hurt | – |
| G.O.B. Allen | b Ebeling | 19 | (7) st Oldfield b Grimmett | 26 |
| H. Verity | b Ebeling | 11 | (8) c McCabe b Grimmett | 1 |
| E.W. Clark | not out | 2 | not out | 2 |
| W.E. Bowes | absent ill | – | (9) c Bradman b O'Reilly | 2 |
| Extras | (B 4, LB 3, NB 1) | 8 | (LB 1, NB 2) | 3 |
| **Total** | | **321** | | **145** |

| ENGLAND | O | M | R | W | O | M | R | W | | FALL OF WICKETS | | | |
|---|---|---|---|---|---|---|---|---|---|---|---|---|---|
| Bowes | 38 | 2 | 164 | 4 | 11·3 | 3 | 55 | 5 | | A | E | A | E |
| Allen | 34 | 5 | 170 | 4 | 16 | 2 | 63 | 0 | *Wkt* | *1st* | *1st* | *2nd* | *2nd* |
| Clark | 37·2 | 4 | 110 | 2 | 20 | 1 | 98 | 5 | 1st | 21 | 104 | 13 | 1 |
| Hammond | 12 | 0 | 53 | 0 | 7 | 1 | 18 | 0 | 2nd | 472 | 108 | 42 | 3 |
| Verity | 43 | 7 | 123 | 0 | 14 | 3 | 43 | 0 | 3rd | 488 | 111 | 192 | 67 |
| Wyatt | 4 | 0 | 28 | 0 | | | | | 4th | 574 | 136 | 213 | 89 |
| Leyland | 3 | 0 | 20 | 0 | | | | | 5th | 626 | 142 | 224 | 109 |
| | | | | | | | | | 6th | 631 | 263 | 236 | 122 |
| AUSTRALIA | | | | | | | | | 7th | 638 | 311 | 236 | 138 |
| Ebeling | 21 | 4 | 74 | 3 | 10 | 5 | 15 | 0 | 8th | 676 | 321 | 256 | 141 |
| McCabe | 6 | 1 | 21 | 0 | 5 | 3 | 5 | 2 | 9th | 682 | – | 272 | 145 |
| Grimmett | 49·3 | 13 | 103 | 3 | 26·3 | 10 | 64 | 5 | 10th | 701 | – | 327 | – |
| O'Reilly | 37 | 10 | 93 | 2 | 22 | 9 | 58 | 2 | | | | | |
| Chipperfield | 4 | 0 | 22 | 0 | | | | | | | | | |

Umpires: F. Chester and F. Walden.

# WEST INDIES v ENGLAND 1934-35 (1st Test)

Played at Kensington Oval, Bridgetown, Barbados, on 8, 9, 10 January.
Toss: England.   Result: ENGLAND won by four wickets.
Debuts: West Indies – G.M. Carew, C.M. Christiani, R.S. Grant, L.G. Hylton;
   England – W.E. Hollies, E.R.T. Holmes, J. Iddon, G.A.E. Paine, C.I.J. Smith.

A remarkable match on a 'sticky' pitch, it produced only 309 runs and just one innings was completed. Hammond won the match with a six.

## WEST INDIES

| | | | | |
|---|---|---|---|---|
| C.A. Roach | c Paine b Farnes | 9 | (6) not out | 10 |
| G.M. Carew | c Holmes b Farnes | 0 | | |
| G.A. Headley | run out | 44 | (7) c Paine b Farnes | 0 |
| C.M. Jones | c Leyland b Farnes | 3 | | |
| J.E.D. Sealy | c Paine b Farnes | 0 | | |
| G.C. Grant* | c Hendren b Hollies | 4 | (8) not out | 0 |
| R.S. Grant | c Hammond b Hollies | 5 | (2) c Paine b Smith | 0 |
| L.G. Hylton | st Ames b Paine | 15 | (1) lbw b Smith | 19 |
| C.M. Christiani† | not out | 9 | (5) b Smith | 11 |
| E.E. Achong | st Ames b Paine | 0 | (4) b Smith | 0 |
| E.A. Martindale | c Leyland b Paine | 9 | (3) lbw b Smith | 0 |
| Extras | (LB 2, NB 2) | 4 | (B 4, LB 4, NB 3) | 11 |
| **Total** | | **102** | (6 wickets declared) | **51** |

## ENGLAND

| | | | | |
|---|---|---|---|---|
| R.E.S. Wyatt* | c R.S. Grant b Martindale | 8 | (8) not out | 6 |
| M. Leyland | c and b Martindale | 3 | (5) c R.S. Grant b Martindale | 2 |
| W.R. Hammond | c R.S. Grant b Hylton | 43 | (6) not out | 29 |
| E.H. Hendren | c R.S. Grant b Martindale | 3 | (4) b Martindale | 20 |
| L.E.G. Ames† | lbw b R.S. Grant | 8 | | |
| C.I.J. Smith | c Jones b Hylton | 0 | (2) c Christiani b Martindale | 0 |
| J. Iddon | not out | 14 | | |
| E.R.T. Holmes | c Achong b Hylton | 0 | (3) c G.C. Grant b Martindale | 6 |
| K. Farnes | ) | | (1) c G.C. Grant b Hylton | 5 |
| G.A.E. Paine | ) did not bat | | (7) c R.S. Grant b Martindale | 2 |
| W.E. Hollies | ) | | | |
| Extras | (B 1, NB 1) | 2 | (B 2, NB 3) | 5 |
| **Total** | (7 wickets declared) | **81** | (6 wickets) | **75** |

| ENGLAND | O | M | R | W | O | M | R | W | | FALL OF WICKETS | | | |
|---|---|---|---|---|---|---|---|---|---|---|---|---|---|
| | | | | | | | | | | WI | E | WI | E |
| Farnes | 15 | 4 | 40 | 4 | 9 | 2 | 23 | 1 | Wkt | 1st | 1st | 2nd | 2nd |
| Smith | 7 | 3 | 8 | 0 | 8 | 4 | 16 | 5 | 1st | 1 | 12 | 4 | 3 |
| Hollies | 16 | 4 | 36 | 2 | | | | | 2nd | 11 | 14 | 4 | 7 |
| Paine | 9 | 3 | 14 | 3 | 1 | 1 | 0 | 0 | 3rd | 20 | 28 | 4 | 25 |
| Hammond | | | | | 1 | 0 | 1 | 0 | 4th | 20 | 52 | 40 | 29 |
| | | | | | | | | | 5th | 31 | 54 | 47 | 43 |
| WEST INDIES | | | | | | | | | 6th | 49 | 81 | 51 | 48 |
| Martindale | 9 | 0 | 39 | 3 | 8·3 | 1 | 22 | 5 | 7th | 81 | 81 | – | – |
| Hylton | 7·3 | 3 | 8 | 3 | 8 | 0 | 48 | 1 | 8th | 86 | – | – | – |
| Achong | 6 | 1 | 14 | 0 | | | | | 9th | 88 | – | – | – |
| R.S. Grant | 7 | 0 | 18 | 1 | | | | | 10th | 102 | – | – | – |

Umpires: C.W. Reece and E.L. Ward.

# WEST INDIES v ENGLAND 1934-35 (2nd Test)

Played at Queen's Park Oval, Port-of-Spain, Trinidad, on 24, 25, 26, 28 January.
Toss: England.   Result: WEST INDIES won by 217 runs.
Debuts: England – D.C.H. Townsend.

England, who put West Indies in to bat for the second successive time and virtually reversed their batting order in the second innings, lost their last wicket to the fifth ball of the last possible over. Constantine was cautioned by the umpire in the second innings for excessive use of the short-pitched ball.

## WEST INDIES

| | | | | |
|---|---|---:|---|---:|
| C.M. Christiani† | c Holmes b Smith | 11 | c Farrimond b Smith | 8 |
| C.M. Jones | c Farrimond b Paine | 19 | c Wyatt b Paine | 19 |
| G.A. Headley | c Holmes b Paine | 25 | lbw b Smith | 93 |
| J.E.D. Sealy | b Wyatt | 92 | c Hammond b Leyland | 35 |
| G.C. Grant* | b Smith | 8 | c Hammond b Paine | 23 |
| O.C. Da Costa | b Holmes | 25 | (7) not out | 19 |
| L.N. Constantine | c Hendren b Smith | 90 | (6) c Ames b Paine | 31 |
| R.S. Grant | b Wyatt | 0 | not out | 38 |
| L.G. Hylton | c Hendren b Smith | 8 | | |
| E.E. Achong | lbw b Wyatt | 9 | | |
| E.A. Martindale | not out | 0 | | |
| Extras | (B 2, LB 5, NB 8) | 15 | (B 3, LB 8, W 1, NB 2) | 14 |
| **Total** | | **302** | (6 wickets declared) | **280** |

## ENGLAND

| | | | | |
|---|---|---:|---|---:|
| R.E.S. Wyatt* | c R.S. Grant b Hylton | 15 | (7) c Headley b Constantine | 2 |
| D.C.H. Townsend | lbw b Constantine | 5 | c Da Costa b Achong | 36 |
| W.R. Hammond | c R.S. Grant b Hylton | 1 | (5) b Constantine | 9 |
| L.E.G. Ames | c R.S. Grant b Martindale | 2 | (8) c Achong b Hylton | 6 |
| M. Leyland | lbw b Constantine | 0 | (9) lbw b Constantine | 18 |
| E.H. Hendren | c G.C. Grant b R.S. Grant | 41 | run out | 11 |
| J. Iddon | c Headley b R.S. Grant | 73 | (10) c Christiani b Hylton | 0 |
| E.R.T. Holmes | not out | 85 | (11) not out | 0 |
| C.I.J. Smith | b R.S. Grant | 8 | (4) run out | 3 |
| W. Farrimond† | c Constantine b Sealy | 16 | (1) c Headley b Hylton | 2 |
| G.A.E. Paine | lbw b Sealy | 4 | (3) hit wkt b R.S. Grant | 14 |
| Extras | (B 3, LB 4, NB 1) | 8 | (B 4, LB 2) | 6 |
| **Total** | | **258** | | **107** |

| ENGLAND | O | M | R | W | O | M | R | W | | FALL OF WICKETS | | | |
|---|---:|---:|---:|---:|---:|---:|---:|---:|---|---|---|---|---|
| Smith | 26 | 3 | 100 | 4 | 30 | 9 | 73 | 2 | | WI | E | WI | E |
| Wyatt | 17 | 7 | 33 | 3 | 8 | 2 | 26 | 0 | *Wkt* | *1st* | *1st* | *2nd* | *2nd* |
| Hammond | 14 | 5 | 28 | 0 | 10 | 0 | 17 | 0 | 1st | 32 | 15 | 19 | 14 |
| Paine | 26 | 6 | 85 | 2 | 42 | 10 | 109 | 3 | 2nd | 38 | 19 | 34 | 53 |
| Leyland | 9 | 1 | 31 | 0 | 13 | 3 | 41 | 1 | 3rd | 102 | 23 | 99 | 54 |
| Holmes | 3 | 1 | 10 | 1 | | | | | 4th | 115 | 23 | 163 | 62 |
| | | | | | | | | | 5th | 174 | 23 | 216 | 71 |
| WEST INDIES | | | | | | | | | 6th | 233 | 95 | 225 | 75 |
| Martindale | 17 | 5 | 26 | 1 | 5 | 1 | 5 | 0 | 7th | 233 | 168 | – | 79 |
| Hylton | 23 | 6 | 55 | 2 | 14 | 4 | 25 | 3 | 8th | 253 | 178 | – | 103 |
| Constantine | 19 | 5 | 41 | 2 | 14·5 | 9 | 11 | 3 | 9th | 281 | 240 | – | 103 |
| Achong | 16 | 4 | 27 | 0 | 12 | 5 | 24 | 1 | 10th | 302 | 258 | – | 107 |
| R.S. Grant | 28 | 7 | 68 | 3 | 12 | 4 | 18 | 1 | | | | | |
| Da Costa | 8 | 2 | 23 | 0 | 1 | 1 | 0 | 0 | | | | | |
| Sealy | 6 | 2 | 7 | 2 | 5 | 0 | 16 | 0 | | | | | |
| Headley | 4 | 2 | 3 | 0 | | | | | | | | | |
| Jones | | | | | 2 | 0 | 2 | 0 | | | | | |

Umpires: V. Guillen and A.J. Richardson.

# WEST INDIES v ENGLAND 1934-35 (3rd Test)

Played at Bourda, Georgetown, British Guiana, on 14, 15, 16, 18 February.
Toss: England.   Result: MATCH DRAWN.
Debuts: West Indies – J.M. Neblett, K.L. Wishart.

Rain delayed the start of the match until after lunch. West Indies were set 203 runs to win in less than two hours.

## ENGLAND

| | | | | |
|---|---|---|---|---|
| D.C.H. Townsend | lbw b R.S. Grant | 16 | lbw b Constantine | 7 |
| R.E.S. Wyatt* | c G.C. Grant b Martindale | 21 | b R.S. Grant | |
| C.I.J. Smith | c Headley b Hylton | 25 | (5) b Constantine | |
| G.A.E. Paine | st Christiani b Constantine | 49 | (3) c G. C. Grant b Neblett | 1 |
| W.R. Hammond | run out | 47 | (4) b Constantine | |
| E.H. Hendren | c Martindale b Hylton | 38 | not out | 3 |
| M. Leyland | c Christiani b Hylton | 13 | b R.S. Grant | |
| L.E.G. Ames† | c Christiani b Hylton | 0 | not out | |
| J. Iddon | lbw b Martindale | 0 | | |
| E.R.T. Holmes | b Martindale | 2 | | |
| W.E. Hollies | not out | 1 | | |
| Extras | (B 5, LB 5, NB 4) | 14 | (B 18, LB 3, W 1) | 2 |
| **Total** | | **226** | (6 wickets declared) | **16** |

## WEST INDIES

| | | | | |
|---|---|---|---|---|
| C.M. Jones | lbw b Hollies | 6 | (3) b Paine | |
| K.L. Wishart | run out | 52 | lbw b Wyatt | |
| G.C. Grant* | c Paine b Hollies | 16 | (7) not out | |
| G.A. Headley | lbw b Paine | 53 | | |
| J.E.D. Sealy | c Ames b Hollies | 19 | (4) run out | 3 |
| L.N. Constantine | lbw b Hollies | 7 | (5) st Ames b Paine | |
| J.M. Neblett | not out | 11 | (6) c Hammond b Holmes | |
| R.S. Grant | lbw b Hollies | 2 | | |
| C.M. Christiani† | lbw b Hollies | 0 | (1) not out | 3 |
| L.G. Hylton | b Paine | 6 | | |
| E.A. Martindale | b Hollies | 0 | | |
| Extras | (B 4, LB 7, NB 1) | 12 | (B 9, LB 1, W 4) | 1 |
| **Total** | | **184** | (5 wickets) | **10** |

| WEST INDIES | O | M | R | W | O | M | R | W |
|---|---|---|---|---|---|---|---|---|
| Martindale | 20 | 7 | 47 | 3 | 8 | 3 | 16 | 0 |
| Hylton | 13·2 | 4 | 27 | 4 | 8 | 3 | 18 | 0 |
| Constantine | 22 | 4 | 45 | 1 | 26 | 11 | 32 | 3 |
| Neblett | 20 | 9 | 31 | 0 | 16 | 2 | 44 | 1 |
| R.S. Grant | 26 | 7 | 46 | 1 | 22 | 6 | 28 | 2 |
| Jones | 5 | 4 | 4 | 0 | | | | |
| Sealy | 6 | 2 | 12 | 0 | | | | |
| Headley | 1 | 1 | 0 | 0 | | | | |
| **ENGLAND** | | | | | | | | |
| Smith | 22 | 8 | 37 | 0 | 4 | 2 | 13 | 0 |
| Wyatt | 10 | 5 | 10 | 0 | 4 | 2 | 7 | 1 |
| Hollies | 26 | 7 | 50 | 7 | 5 | 2 | 17 | 0 |
| Paine | 33 | 7 | 63 | 2 | 7 | 0 | 28 | 2 |
| Leyland | 2 | 0 | 12 | 0 | | | | |
| Townsend | | | | | 1 | 0 | 9 | 0 |
| Holmes | | | | | 3 | 1 | 16 | 1 |

| FALL OF WICKETS | | | | |
|---|---|---|---|---|
| | E | WI | E | W |
| Wkt | 1st | 1st | 2nd | 2n |
| 1st | 38 | 18 | 3 | |
| 2nd | 63 | 43 | 39 | 2 |
| 3rd | 72 | 122 | 54 | 7 |
| 4th | 152 | 153 | 60 | 8 |
| 5th | 172 | 157 | 140 | 8 |
| 6th | 209 | 170 | 144 | – |
| 7th | 209 | 173 | – | – |
| 8th | 212 | 173 | – | – |
| 9th | 215 | 183 | – | – |
| 10th | 226 | 184 | – | – |

Umpires: A.J. Richardson and J.G. Blackman.

# WEST INDIES v ENGLAND 1934-35 (4th Test)

Played at Sabina Park, Kingston, Jamaica, on 14, 15, 16, 18 March.
Toss: West Indies.   Result: WEST INDIES won by an innings and 161 runs.
Debuts: West Indies – R.L. Fuller, G.H. Mudie (not 'Moodie').

Headley's innings remained the highest West Indies score against England until L.G. Rowe made 302 in 1973-74 (*Test No. 733*). Wyatt's jaw was fractured by a short-pitched ball from Martindale. His opposite number, G.C. Grant, was forced to retire with an ankle injury in the second innings and handed over the captaincy to Constantine. West Indies were dismissed for what remains their lowest total in any home Test.

## WEST INDIES

| | | |
|---|---|---:|
| . Barrow | b Farnes | 3 |
| C.M. Christiani† | b Paine | 27 |
| G.A. Headley | not out | 270 |
| .E.D. Sealy | b Paine | 91 |
| .N. Constantine | lbw b Paine | 34 |
| G.H. Mudie | c Townsend b Paine | 5 |
| R.L. Fuller | lbw b Hollies | 1 |
| R.S. Grant | c Wyatt b Paine | 77 |
| .G. Hylton | not out | 5 |
| G.C. Grant* | ) did not bat | |
| E.A. Martindale | ) | |
| Extras | (B 8, LB 13, NB 1) | 22 |
| **Total** | (7 wickets declared) | **535** |

## ENGLAND

| | | | | | |
|---|---|---:|---|---|---:|
| R.E.S. Wyatt* | retired hurt | 1 | absent hurt | | – |
| D.C.H. Townsend | c Christiani b Martindale | 8 | b Martindale | | 11 |
| W.R. Hammond | c Hylton b Constantine | 11 | b Martindale | | 34 |
| G.A.E. Paine | lbw b Martindale | 0 | (7) not out | | 10 |
| E.R.T. Holmes | b Martindale | 0 | (6) lbw b Sealy | | 3 |
| L.E.G. Ames† | c Constantine b Mudie | 126 | (5) c R.S. Grant b Constantine | | 17 |
| E.H. Hendren | c Barrow b R.S. Grant | 40 | (4) c Constantine b Mudie | | 11 |
| Iddon | lbw b Mudie | 54 | (1) lbw b Constantine | | 0 |
| C.I.J. Smith | b Constantine | 10 | (8) b Martindale | | 4 |
| K. Farnes | b Constantine | 5 | (9) c Christiani b Martindale | | 0 |
| W.E. Hollies | not out | 1 | (10) c Martindale b Constantine | | 6 |
| Extras | (B 4, LB 6, NB 5) | 15 | (B 4, LB 1, W 2) | | 7 |
| **Total** | | **271** | | | **103** |

| ENGLAND | O | M | R | W | O | M | R | W |
|---|---:|---:|---:|---:|---:|---:|---:|---:|
| Smith | 22 | 2 | 83 | 0 | | | | |
| Farnes | 24 | 4 | 72 | 1 | | | | |
| Wyatt | 5 | 1 | 12 | 0 | | | | |
| Hollies | 46 | 11 | 114 | 1 | | | | |
| Holmes | 8 | 0 | 40 | 0 | | | | |
| Paine | 56 | 12 | 168 | 5 | | | | |
| Iddon | 7 | 1 | 24 | 0 | | | | |
| **WEST INDIES** | | | | | | | | |
| Martindale | 17 | 1 | 56 | 3 | 16 | 5 | 28 | 4 |
| Hylton | 19 | 1 | 59 | 0 | 4 | 1 | 11 | 0 |
| Constantine | 23·2 | 4 | 55 | 3 | 9 | 3 | 13 | 3 |
| Fuller | 6 | 2 | 10 | 0 | 2 | 0 | 2 | 0 |
| R.S. Grant | 16 | 1 | 48 | 1 | 9 | 2 | 19 | 0 |
| Mudie | 17 | 7 | 23 | 2 | 12 | 5 | 17 | 1 |
| G.C. Grant | 1 | 0 | 5 | 0 | | | | |
| Sealy | | | | | 2 | 0 | 6 | 1 |

### FALL OF WICKETS

| Wkt | WI 1st | E 1st | E 2nd |
|---|---:|---:|---:|
| 1st | 5 | 23 | 14 |
| 2nd | 92 | 26 | 18 |
| 3rd | 294 | 26 | 45 |
| 4th | 352 | 26 | 68 |
| 5th | 376 | 95 | 83 |
| 6th | 381 | 252 | 83 |
| 7th | 528 | 265 | 89 |
| 8th | – | 267 | 93 |
| 9th | – | 271 | 103 |
| 10th | – | – | – |

Umpires: E. Knibbs and S.C. Burke.

# ENGLAND v SOUTH AFRICA 1935 (1st Test)

Played at Trent Bridge, Nottingham, on 15, 17, 18 (*no play*) June.
Toss: England.   Result: MATCH DRAWN.
Debuts: England – N.S. Mitchell-Innes; South Africa – R.J. Crisp, A.B.C. Langton, A.D. (Dudley) Nourse, E.A.B. Rowan, D.S. Tomlinson, H.F. Wade.

This was South Africa's first Test at Nottingham. Mitchell-Innes played in his only Test match whilst in his second year at Brasenose College, Oxford.

### ENGLAND

| | | | |
|---|---|---|---|
| H. Sutcliffe | lbw b Langton | 61 | |
| R.E.S. Wyatt* | c Wade b Crisp | 149 | |
| W.R. Hammond | lbw b Vincent | 28 | |
| N.S. Mitchell-Innes | lbw b Mitchell | 5 | |
| M. Leyland | c Mitchell b Crisp | 69 | |
| L.E.G. Ames† | c Viljoen b Vincent | 17 | |
| J. Iddon | c Rowan b Vincent | 29 | |
| M.S. Nichols | not out | 13 | |
| R.W.V. Robins | ) | | |
| H. Verity | ) did not bat | | |
| W.E. Bowes | ) | | |
| Extras | (B 3, LB 10) | 13 | |
| **Total** | (7 wickets declared) | **384** | |

### SOUTH AFRICA

| | | | | | |
|---|---|---|---|---|---|
| I.J. Siedle | b Verity | 59 | c Verity b Nichols | 2 | |
| B. Mitchell | b Nichols | 25 | not out | 8 | |
| E.A.B. Rowan | c Ames b Robins | 20 | not out | 6 | |
| A.D. Nourse | c Hammond b Verity | 4 | | | |
| H.F. Wade* | c Nichols b Verity | 18 | | | |
| H.B. Cameron† | b Nichols | 52 | | | |
| K.G. Viljoen | b Nichols | 13 | | | |
| C.L. Vincent | lbw b Nichols | 0 | | | |
| D.S. Tomlinson | b Nichols | 9 | | | |
| A.B.C. Langton | not out | 0 | | | |
| R.J. Crisp | c Robins b Nichols | 4 | | | |
| Extras | (B 4, LB 10, NB 2) | 16 | (NB 1) | 1 | |
| **Total** | | **220** | (1 wicket) | 17 | |

| SOUTH AFRICA | O | M | R | W | O | M | R | W | | FALL OF WICKETS | | |
|---|---|---|---|---|---|---|---|---|---|---|---|---|
| | | | | | | | | | | E | SA | SA |
| Crisp | 18 | 4 | 49 | 2 | | | | | Wkt | 1st | 1st | 2nd |
| Langton | 39 | 3 | 117 | 1 | | | | | 1st | 118 | 42 | 3 |
| Vincent | 43 | 9 | 101 | 3 | | | | | 2nd | 170 | 98 | – |
| Tomlinson | 10 | 0 | 38 | 0 | | | | | 3rd | 179 | 103 | – |
| Mitchell | 22 | 1 | 66 | 1 | | | | | 4th | 318 | 120 | – |
| | | | | | | | | | 5th | 325 | 174 | – |
| ENGLAND | | | | | | | | | 6th | 355 | 198 | – |
| Bowes | 22 | 9 | 31 | 0 | 4 | 3 | 2 | 0 | 7th | 384 | 198 | – |
| Nichols | 23·5 | 9 | 35 | 6 | 5 | 1 | 14 | 1 | 8th | – | 215 | – |
| Verity | 41 | 18 | 52 | 3 | | | | | 9th | – | 216 | – |
| Robins | 19 | 4 | 65 | 1 | | | | | 10th | – | 220 | – |
| Iddon | 4 | 2 | 3 | 0 | | | | | | | | |
| Leyland | 7 | 2 | 18 | 0 | | | | | | | | |

Umpires: A. Dolphin and J. Hardstaff, sr.

# ENGLAND v SOUTH AFRICA 1935 (2nd Test)

Played at Lord's, London, on 29 June, 1, 2 July.
Toss: South Africa.   Result: SOUTH AFRICA won by 157 runs.
Debuts: Nil.

South Africa gained their first win in England in Sutcliffe's final Test. Both Sutcliffe and Ames batted with a runner in the second innings when England were set 309 runs to win in 4¾ hours. With the exception of Langton's dismissal of Sutcliffe, all the *lbw* decisions in the match were given under the new experimental law which decreed that a batsman could be out *lbw* to a ball pitching outside the off stump, provided that it hit the striker in line with the two wickets and would have hit his stumps.

## SOUTH AFRICA

| | | | | |
|---|---|--:|---|--:|
| B. Mitchell | lbw b Nichols | 30 | not out | 164 |
| J. Siedle | b Mitchell | 6 | c Farrimond b Mitchell | 13 |
| E.A.B. Rowan | c Farrimond b Verity | 40 | lbw b Nichols | 44 |
| A.D. Nourse | b Verity | 3 | b Verity | 2 |
| H.F. Wade* | c Hammond b Langridge | 23 | (7) b Verity | 0 |
| H.B. Cameron† | b Nichols | 90 | (5) c Ames b Mitchell | 3 |
| E.L. Dalton | c and b Langridge | 19 | (6) c Wyatt b Verity | 0 |
| K.C. Balaskas | b Verity | 4 | | |
| A.B.C. Langton | c Holmes b Hammond | 4 | (8) c and b Hammond | 44 |
| R.J. Crisp | not out | 4 | | |
| A.J. Bell | b Hammond | 0 | | |
| Extras | (B 1, LB 1, W 1, NB 2) | 5 | (B 3, LB 5) | 8 |
| **Total** | | **228** | (7 wickets declared) | **278** |

## ENGLAND

| | | | | |
|---|---|--:|---|--:|
| R.E.S. Wyatt* | c Nourse b Dalton | 53 | b Balaskas | 16 |
| H. Sutcliffe | lbw b Bell | 3 | lbw b Langton | 38 |
| M. Leyland | b Balaskas | 18 | b Crisp | 4 |
| W.R. Hammond | b Dalton | 27 | c Cameron b Langton | 27 |
| L.E.G. Ames | b Balaskas | 5 | lbw b Langton | 8 |
| E.R.T. Holmes | c Bell b Balaskas | 10 | b Langton | 8 |
| James Langridge | c Mitchell b Balaskas | 27 | lbw b Balaskas | 17 |
| W. Farrimond† | b Balaskas | 13 | b Crisp | 13 |
| M.S. Nichols | c Cameron b Langton | 10 | not out | 7 |
| H. Verity | lbw b Langton | 17 | c Langton b Balaskas | 8 |
| T.B. Mitchell | not out | 5 | st Cameron b Balaskas | 1 |
| Extras | (B 4, LB 5, W 1) | 10 | (LB 4) | 4 |
| **Total** | | **198** | | **151** |

| ENGLAND | O | M | R | W | O | M | R | W |
|---|--:|--:|--:|--:|--:|--:|--:|--:|
| Nichols | 21 | 5 | 47 | 2 | 18 | 4 | 64 | 1 |
| Wyatt | 4 | 2 | 9 | 0 | 4 | 2 | 2 | 0 |
| Hammond | 5·3 | 3 | 8 | 2 | 14·4 | 4 | 26 | 1 |
| Mitchell | 20 | 3 | 71 | 1 | 33 | 5 | 93 | 2 |
| Verity | 28 | 10 | 61 | 3 | 38 | 16 | 56 | 3 |
| Langridge | 13 | 3 | 27 | 2 | 10 | 4 | 19 | 0 |
| Holmes | | | | | 4 | 2 | 10 | 0 |
| SOUTH AFRICA | | | | | | | | |
| Crisp | 8 | 1 | 32 | 0 | 15 | 4 | 30 | 2 |
| Bell | 6 | 0 | 16 | 1 | 12 | 3 | 21 | 0 |
| Langton | 21·3 | 3 | 58 | 2 | 11 | 3 | 31 | 4 |
| Balaskas | 32 | 8 | 49 | 5 | 27 | 8 | 54 | 4 |
| Dalton | 13 | 1 | 33 | 2 | | | | |
| Mitchell | | | | | 2 | 0 | 11 | 0 |

| | FALL OF WICKETS | | | |
|---|--:|--:|--:|--:|
| | SA | E | SA | E |
| Wkt | *1st* | *1st* | *2nd* | *2nd* |
| 1st | 27 | 5 | 32 | 24 |
| 2nd | 59 | 46 | 136 | 45 |
| 3rd | 62 | 100 | 158 | 89 |
| 4th | 98 | 109 | 169 | 90 |
| 5th | 158 | 116 | 169 | 102 |
| 6th | 187 | 121 | 177 | 111 |
| 7th | 196 | 158 | 278 | 129 |
| 8th | 224 | 161 | – | 141 |
| 9th | 228 | 177 | – | 149 |
| 10th | 228 | 198 | – | 151 |

Umpires: E.J. Smith and F. Walden.

## ENGLAND v SOUTH AFRICA 1935 (3rd Test)

Played at Headingley, Leeds, on 13, 15, 16 July.
Toss: England.   Result: MATCH DRAWN.
Debuts: England – W. Barber, J. Hardstaff, jr, J.M. Sims, D. Smith.

South Africa were set 340 runs to win in just over 4½ hours. Barber took Cameron's wicket with his second ball in Test cricket after the latter's stumps had been hit by a ball from Hammond which did not dislodge a bail.

### ENGLAND

| | | | | | |
|---|---|--:|---|---|--:|
| R.E.S. Wyatt* | c Cameron b Crisp | 0 | (5) | c Vincent b Bell | 44 |
| D. Smith | c Cameron b Vincent | 36 | | b Vincent | 57 |
| W. Barber | c Bell b Langton | 24 | | c Dalton b Vincent | 14 |
| W.R. Hammond | lbw b Vincent | 63 | | not out | 87 |
| A. Mitchell | c Mitchell b Langton | 58 | (1) | c Viljoen b Vincent | 72 |
| J. Hardstaff, jr | c and b Vincent | 10 | | b Bell | 0 |
| L.E.G. Ames† | b Vincent | 0 | | b Bell | 13 |
| M.S. Nichols | lbw b Langton | 4 | | b Vincent | 2 |
| J.M. Sims | b Langton | 12 | | | |
| H. Verity | c Cameron b Crisp | 1 | | | |
| W.E. Bowes | not out | 0 | | | |
| Extras | (B 2, LB 6) | 8 | | (B 1, LB 4) | 5 |
| **Total** | | **216** | | (7 wickets declared) | 29 |

### SOUTH AFRICA

| | | | | | |
|---|---|--:|---|---|--:|
| I.J. Siedle | run out | 33 | | c Hammond b Bowes | 21 |
| B. Mitchell | lbw b Hammond | 8 | | b Hammond | 58 |
| E.A.B. Rowan | c Hammond b Bowes | 62 | | b Bowes | |
| K.G. Viljoen | c Smith b Wyatt | 19 | | b Sims | |
| H. F. Wade* | c Mitchell b Verity | 3 | | not out | 3 |
| H.B. Cameron† | lbw b Nichols | 9 | | st Ames b Barber | 4 |
| E.L. Dalton | b Bowes | 4 | | | |
| C.L. Vincent | c Barber b Verity | 0 | | | |
| A.B.C. Langton | b Nichols | 0 | | | |
| R.J. Crisp | c Hammond b Nichols | 18 | | | |
| A.J. Bell | not out | 3 | | | |
| Extras | (B 8, LB 3, NB 1) | 12 | | (B 14, LB 4, W 1, NB 1) | 20 |
| **Total** | | **171** | | (5 wickets) | 19 |

| SOUTH AFRICA | O | M | R | W | O | M | R | W | FALL OF WICKETS | | | | |
|---|--|--|--|--|--|--|--|--|---|--|--|--|--|
| Crisp | 13·5 | 3 | 26 | 2 | 11 | 1 | 52 | 0 | | E | SA | E | SA |
| Bell | 16 | 3 | 48 | 0 | 14 | 4 | 38 | 3 | *Wkt* | *1st* | *1st* | *2nd* | *2nd* |
| Langton | 26 | 5 | 59 | 4 | 31 | 8 | 95 | 0 | 1st | 0 | 21 | 128 | 52 |
| Vincent | 32 | 12 | 45 | 4 | 23·3 | 3 | 104 | 4 | 2nd | 52 | 65 | 139 | 6 |
| Mitchell | 6 | 0 | 30 | 0 | | | | | 3rd | 78 | 120 | 148 | 9 |
| | | | | | | | | | 4th | 147 | 123 | 277 | 11 |
| ENGLAND | | | | | | | | | 5th | 177 | 141 | 277 | 19 |
| Bowes | 29 | 5 | 62 | 2 | 19 | 9 | 31 | 2 | 6th | 177 | 149 | 291 | – |
| Nichols | 21·4 | 4 | 58 | 3 | 22 | 5 | 65 | 0 | 7th | 188 | 150 | 294 | – |
| Hammond | 12 | 6 | 13 | 1 | 7 | 4 | 10 | 1 | 8th | 215 | 150 | – | – |
| Sims | 9 | 4 | 20 | 0 | 27 | 13 | 48 | 1 | 9th | 216 | 150 | – | – |
| Verity | 12 | 9 | 5 | 2 | 13 | 11 | 4 | 0 | 10th | 216 | 171 | – | – |
| Wyatt | 4 | 3 | 1 | 1 | 6 | 2 | 12 | 0 | | | | | |
| Mitchell | | | | | 1 | 0 | 4 | 0 | | | | | |
| Barber | | | | | 0·2 | 0 | 0 | 1 | | | | | |

Umpires: F. Chester and J. W. Hitch.

# ENGLAND v SOUTH AFRICA 1935 (4th Test)

Played at Old Trafford, Manchester, on 27, 29, 30 July.
Toss: England.   Result: MATCH DRAWN.
Debuts: Nil.

England's declaration at lunch on the third day set South Africa 271 runs at a rate of 72 per hour to win.

## ENGLAND

| | | | | | |
|---|---|---:|---|---|---:|
| D. Smith | c Mitchell b Bell | 35 | lbw b Crisp | | 0 |
| A.H. Bakewell | b Crisp | 63 | b Langton | | 54 |
| W. Barber | c Langton b Bell | 1 | b Vincent | | 44 |
| W.R. Hammond | b Crisp | 29 | not out | | 63 |
| R.E.S. Wyatt* | lbw b Crisp | 3 | (8) not out | | 15 |
| M. Leyland | c Mitchell b Crisp | 53 | (5) c Mitchell b Vincent | | 37 |
| R.W.V. Robins | b Bell | 108 | (6) c Wade b Vincent | | 14 |
| H. Verity | lbw b Langton | 16 | | | |
| M.W. Tate | c Viljoen b Vincent | 34 | (7) b Vincent | | 0 |
| G. Duckworth† | c Nourse b Crisp | 2 | | | |
| W.E. Bowes | not out | 0 | | | |
| Extras | (B 2, LB 9, W 1, NB 1) | 13 | (B 1, LB 1, W 1, NB 1) | | 4 |
| **Total** | | **357** | (6 wickets declared) | | **231** |

## SOUTH AFRICA

| | | | | | |
|---|---|---:|---|---|---:|
| B. Mitchell | c Duckworth b Hammond | 10 | not out | | 48 |
| E.A.B. Rowan | b Bowes | 13 | hit wkt b Robins | | 49 |
| K.G. Viljoen | c Verity b Bowes | 124 | lbw b Robins | | 10 |
| A.D. Nourse | lbw b Verity | 29 | not out | | 53 |
| H.F. Wade* | lbw b Bowes | 16 | | | |
| H.B. Cameron† | c Bowes b Tate | 53 | | | |
| E.L. Dalton | lbw b Robins | 47 | | | |
| C.L. Vincent | not out | 14 | | | |
| A.B.C. Langton | c Bakewell b Bowes | 0 | | | |
| R.J. Crisp | c Verity b Bowes | 3 | | | |
| A.J. Bell | lbw b Tate | 1 | | | |
| Extras | (B 3, LB 5) | 8 | (B 6, LB 1, W 2) | | 9 |
| **Total** | | **318** | (2 wickets) | | **169** |

| SOUTH AFRICA | O | M | R | W | O | M | R | W | | FALL OF WICKETS | | | |
|---|---|---|---|---|---|---|---|---|---|---|---|---|---|
| | | | | | | | | | | E | SA | E | SA |
| Crisp | 26·1 | 1 | 99 | 5 | 11 | 0 | 43 | 1 | *Wkt* | *1st* | *1st* | *2nd* | *2nd* |
| Bell | 26 | 3 | 90 | 3 | 1 | 0 | 3 | 0 | 1st | 71 | 21 | 1 | 67 |
| Vincent | 28 | 4 | 85 | 1 | 26 | 6 | 78 | 4 | 2nd | 77 | 41 | 90 | 103 |
| Langton | 11 | 0 | 59 | 1 | 25 | 2 | 80 | 1 | 3rd | 123 | 91 | 110 | – |
| Mitchell | 1 | 0 | 11 | 0 | | | | | 4th | 132 | 124 | 172 | – |
| Dalton | | | | | 4 | 0 | 23 | 0 | 5th | 141 | 223 | 200 | – |
| ENGLAND | | | | | | | | | 6th | 246 | 288 | 200 | – |
| Bowes | 36 | 7 | 100 | 5 | 15 | 1 | 34 | 0 | 7th | 302 | 311 | – | – |
| Tate | 22·3 | 5 | 67 | 2 | 9 | 2 | 20 | 0 | 8th | 338 | 311 | – | – |
| Hammond | 17 | 2 | 49 | 1 | 5 | 0 | 15 | 0 | 9th | 357 | 315 | – | – |
| Verity | 20 | 4 | 48 | 1 | 20 | 10 | 24 | 0 | 10th | 357 | 318 | – | – |
| Robins | 10 | 0 | 34 | 1 | 19 | 8 | 31 | 2 | | | | | |
| Wyatt | 4 | 1 | 12 | 0 | | | | | | | | | |
| Leyland | | | | | 12 | 4 | 28 | 0 | | | | | |
| Bakewell | | | | | 3 | 0 | 8 | 0 | | | | | |

Umpires: F. Chester and F. Walden.

# ENGLAND v SOUTH AFRICA 1935 (5th Test)

Played at Kennington Oval, London, on 17, 19, 20 August.
Toss: England.   Result: MATCH DRAWN.
Debuts: England – J.C. Clay, H.D. Read.

South Africa won their first rubber in England by drawing this match after being put in to bat on a perfect wicket. The partnership of 137 between Dalton and Langton remains the ninth-wicket record for this series.

## SOUTH AFRICA

| | | | | | |
|---|---|---|---|---|---|
| I.J. Siedle | c Ames b Robins | 35 | b Bowes | | 36 |
| B. Mitchell | c Ames b Read | 128 | b Read | | 9 |
| E.A.B. Rowan | lbw b Robins | 0 | b Bowes | | 7 |
| A.D. Nourse | c Wyatt b Bowes | 32 | b Read | | 34 |
| K.G. Viljoen | c Clay b Read | 60 | st Ames b Robins | | 45 |
| H.B. Cameron† | c Mitchell b Read | 8 | st Ames b Robins | | 42 |
| H.F. Wade* | c Hammond b Bowes | 0 | not out | | 40 |
| E.L. Dalton | c Robins b Read | 117 | not out | | 57 |
| C.L. Vincent | b Robins | 5 | | | |
| A.B.C. Langton | not out | 73 | | | |
| R.J. Crisp | c Ames b Bowes | 0 | | | |
| Extras | (B 6, LB 10, NB 2) | 18 | (B 6, LB 9, NB 2) | | 17 |
| **Total** | | **476** | (6 wickets) | | **287** |

## ENGLAND

| | | |
|---|---|---|
| A.H. Bakewell | c Cameron b Langton | 20 |
| A. Mitchell | b Crisp | 40 |
| R.E.S. Wyatt* | c Cameron b Vincent | 37 |
| W.R. Hammond | st Cameron b Vincent | 65 |
| M. Leyland | st Cameron b Mitchell | 161 |
| L.E.G. Ames† | not out | 148 |
| M.S. Nichols | c Siedle b Langton | 30 |
| R.W.V. Robins | not out | 10 |
| J.C. Clay | ) | |
| W.E. Bowes | ) did not bat | |
| H.D. Read | ) | |
| Extras | (B 5, LB 16, NB 2) | 23 |
| **Total** | (6 wickets declared) | **534** |

| ENGLAND | O | M | R | W | O | M | R | W |
|---|---|---|---|---|---|---|---|---|
| Read | 35 | 13 | 136 | 4 | 10 | 1 | 64 | 2 |
| Nichols | 23 | 3 | 79 | 0 | 5 | 1 | 20 | 0 |
| Bowes | 40·4 | 7 | 112 | 3 | 13 | 2 | 40 | 2 |
| Hammond | 9 | 2 | 25 | 0 | | | | |
| Clay | 14 | 1 | 30 | 0 | 18 | 6 | 45 | 0 |
| Robins | 22 | 3 | 73 | 3 | 17 | 1 | 61 | 2 |
| Wyatt | 2 | 0 | 3 | 0 | 3 | 0 | 25 | 0 |
| Leyland | | | | | 7 | 2 | 15 | 0 |

| SOUTH AFRICA | O | M | R | W |
|---|---|---|---|---|
| Crisp | 28 | 0 | 113 | 1 |
| Langton | 38 | 5 | 124 | 2 |
| Dalton | 16 | 1 | 50 | 0 |
| Vincent | 42 | 5 | 188 | 2 |
| Mitchell | 8 | 0 | 36 | 1 |

FALL OF WICKETS

| Wkt | SA 1st | E 1st | SA 2nd |
|---|---|---|---|
| 1st | 116 | 34 | 16 |
| 2nd | 116 | 98 | 23 |
| 3rd | 164 | 98 | 67 |
| 4th | 234 | 249 | 112 |
| 5th | 248 | 428 | 178 |
| 6th | 254 | 506 | 193 |
| 7th | 312 | – | – |
| 8th | 333 | – | – |
| 9th | 470 | – | – |
| 10th | 476 | – | – |

Umpires: F. Chester and J. Hardstaff, sr.

# SOUTH AFRICA v AUSTRALIA 1935-36 (1st Test)

Played at Kingsmead, Durban, on 14, 16, 17, 18 December.
Toss: South Africa.   Result: AUSTRALIA won by nine wickets.
Debuts: South Africa – F. Nicholson, J.B. Robertson; Australia – L. O'B. Fleetwood-Smith, E.L. McCormick.

South Africa were without H.B. Cameron, their outstanding batsman/wicket-keeper, who died a few weeks after returning from the 1935 tour to England.

## SOUTH AFRICA

| | | | | |
|---|---|---|---|---|
| B. Mitchell | b Fleetwood-Smith | 19 | run out | 19 |
| I.J. Siedle | lbw b O'Reilly | 31 | b Grimmett | 59 |
| E.A.B. Rowan | c and b Grimmett | 66 | b Grimmett | 49 |
| K.G. Viljoen | b Fleetwood-Smith | 4 | b Fleetwood-Smith | 1 |
| A.D. Nourse | b McCormick | 30 | c Fingleton b O'Reilly | 91 |
| H.F. Wade* | b O'Reilly | 31 | lbw b O'Reilly | 11 |
| E.L. Dalton | st Oldfield b Fleetwood-Smith | 4 | c Darling b Grimmett | 5 |
| A.B.C. Langton | b Grimmett | 0 | not out | 12 |
| F. Nicholson† | not out | 16 | b O'Reilly | 0 |
| R.J. Crisp | b Fleetwood-Smith | 35 | b O'Reilly | 16 |
| J.B. Robertson | b O'Reilly | 9 | c Richardson b O'Reilly | 9 |
| Extras | (B 1, LB 2) | 3 | (B 8, LB 1, NB 1) | 10 |
| **Total** | | **248** | | **282** |

## AUSTRALIA

| | | | | |
|---|---|---|---|---|
| W.A. Brown | c Langton b Robertson | 66 | c Crisp b Dalton | 55 |
| J.H.W. Fingleton | c Nicholson b Crisp | 2 | not out | 36 |
| S.J. McCabe | c Rowan b Langton | 149 | not out | 7 |
| L.S. Darling | c Viljoen b Crisp | 60 | | |
| V.Y. Richardson* | b Langton | 2 | | |
| A.G. Chipperfield | b Crisp | 109 | | |
| W.A.S. Oldfield† | lbw b Langton | 0 | | |
| W.J. O'Reilly | c Rowan b Robertson | 11 | | |
| C.V. Grimmett | c Nicholson b Robertson | 15 | | |
| E.L. McCormick | not out | 2 | | |
| L.O'B. Fleetwood-Smith | b Langton | 1 | | |
| Extras | (B 5, LB 2, W 1, NB 4) | 12 | (B 3, LB 1) | 4 |
| **Total** | | **429** | (1 wicket) | **102** |

| AUSTRALIA | O | M | R | W | O | M | R | W |
|---|---|---|---|---|---|---|---|---|
| McCormick | 15 | 4 | 50 | 1 | 6 | 0 | 26 | 0 |
| McCabe | 10 | 1 | 28 | 0 | 2 | 0 | 5 | 0 |
| Grimmett | 28 | 10 | 48 | 2 | 52 | 20 | 83 | 3 |
| O'Reilly | 33·2 | 17 | 55 | 3 | 17 | 5 | 49 | 5 |
| Fleetwood-Smith | 28 | 6 | 64 | 4 | 37 | 7 | 101 | 1 |
| Chipperfield | | | | | 1 | 0 | 8 | 0 |

| SOUTH AFRICA | O | M | R | W | O | M | R | W |
|---|---|---|---|---|---|---|---|---|
| Crisp | 36 | 7 | 87 | 3 | 6 | 1 | 10 | 0 |
| Langton | 48·2 | 10 | 113 | 4 | 9 | 0 | 29 | 0 |
| Robertson | 55 | 11 | 143 | 3 | 13 | 4 | 24 | 0 |
| Dalton | 6 | 0 | 25 | 0 | 1·3 | 0 | 12 | 1 |
| Mitchell | 17 | 2 | 49 | 0 | 7 | 0 | 23 | 0 |

## FALL OF WICKETS

| | SA | A | SA | A |
|---|---|---|---|---|
| Wkt | 1st | 1st | 2nd | 2nd |
| 1st | 45 | 12 | 65 | 93 |
| 2nd | 59 | 173 | 86 | – |
| 3rd | 71 | 269 | 89 | – |
| 4th | 108 | 277 | 207 | – |
| 5th | 168 | 299 | 233 | – |
| 6th | 185 | 299 | 242 | – |
| 7th | 186 | 329 | 242 | – |
| 8th | 187 | 412 | 242 | – |
| 9th | 234 | 428 | 263 | – |
| 10th | 248 | 429 | 282 | – |

Umpires: J.C. Collings and W.J. Routledge.

# SOUTH AFRICA v AUSTRALIA 1935–36 (2nd Test)

Played at Old Wanderers, Johannesburg, on 24, 26, 27, 28 December.
Toss: South Africa.   Result: MATCH DRAWN.
Debuts: South Africa – E.G. Bock, A.W. Briscoe.

A heavy storm ended the match when Australia were 125 runs away from victory with eight wickets in hand. Nourse's 231 was South Africa's highest Test score until 1951 when E.A.B. Rowan made 236 (*Test No. 337*) and it is still the record innings in a Test at Johannesburg.

## SOUTH AFRICA

| | | | | | |
|---|---|---|---|---|---|
| B. Mitchell | c Oldfield b McCormick | 8 | (4) c Oldfield b McCabe | | 45 |
| I.J. Siedle | c Chipperfield b McCormick | 22 | b Grimmett | | 34 |
| E.A.B. Rowan | lbw b Grimmett | 38 | lbw b Grimmett | | 13 |
| A.D. Nourse | b McCormick | 0 | (5) c McCormick b McCabe | | 231 |
| A.W. Briscoe | b O'Reilly | 15 | (6) b McCormick | | 16 |
| H.F. Wade* | b O'Reilly | 0 | (1) lbw b Grimmett | | 30 |
| A.B.C. Langton | c Fingleton b O'Reilly | 7 | (8) b McCormick | | 16 |
| F. Nicholson† | st Oldfield b Grimmett | 27 | (7) lbw Fleetwood-Smith | | 29 |
| R.J. Crisp | b Grimmett | 8 | b O'Reilly | | 35 |
| J.B. Robertson | b O'Reilly | 17 | b McCormick | | 3 |
| E.G. Bock | not out | 9 | not out | | 2 |
| Extras | (LB 6) | 6 | (B 13, LB 19, NB 5) | | 37 |
| **Total** | | **157** | | | **491** |

## AUSTRALIA

| | | | | | |
|---|---|---|---|---|---|
| J.H.W. Fingleton | c and b Langton | 62 | b Mitchell | | 40 |
| W.A. Brown | c Crisp b Robertson | 51 | c Nicholson b Crisp | | 6 |
| S.J. McCabe | c Robertson b Langton | 34 | not out | | 189 |
| L.S. Darling | run out | 42 | not out | | 37 |
| V.Y. Richardson* | b Langton | 2 | | | |
| A.G. Chipperfield | c Rowan b Langton | 0 | | | |
| W.A.S. Oldfield† | c Briscoe b Mitchell | 40 | | | |
| C.V. Grimmett | b Mitchell | 7 | | | |
| W.J. O'Reilly | b Mitchell | 0 | | | |
| E.L. McCormick | b Mitchell | 4 | | | |
| L.O'B. Fleetwood-Smith | not out | 5 | | | |
| Extras | (LB 3) | 3 | (LB 2) | | 2 |
| **Total** | | **250** | (2 wickets) | | **274** |

| AUSTRALIA | O | M | R | W | O | M | R | W | FALL OF WICKETS | | | | |
|---|---|---|---|---|---|---|---|---|---|---|---|---|---|
| | | | | | | | | | | SA | A | SA | A |
| McCormick | 16 | 5 | 36 | 3 | 26 | 3 | 129 | 3 | *Wkt* | *1st* | *1st* | *2nd* | *2nd* |
| O'Reilly | 20·2 | 9 | 54 | 4 | 35·3 | 15 | 91 | 1 | 1st | 11 | 105 | 50 | 17 |
| Grimmett | 15 | 5 | 29 | 3 | 58 | 28 | 111 | 3 | 2nd | 46 | 127 | 89 | 194 |
| McCabe | 6 | 2 | 11 | 0 | 9 | 1 | 30 | 2 | 3rd | 50 | 168 | 90 | – |
| Fleetwood-Smith | 6 | 2 | 21 | 0 | 21 | 5 | 93 | 1 | 4th | 68 | 170 | 219 | – |
| | | | | | | | | | 5th | 70 | 174 | 291 | – |
| SOUTH AFRICA | | | | | | | | | 6th | 78 | 209 | 397 | – |
| Crisp | 15 | 1 | 49 | 0 | 17 | 3 | 62 | 1 | 7th | 112 | 241 | 440 | – |
| Langton | 32 | 6 | 85 | 4 | 22 | 6 | 54 | 0 | 8th | 126 | 241 | 454 | – |
| Mitchell | 7·3 | 0 | 26 | 4 | 15 | 1 | 73 | 1 | 9th | 139 | 242 | 466 | – |
| Bock | 14 | 2 | 49 | 0 | 9 | 0 | 42 | 0 | 10th | 157 | 250 | 491 | – |
| Robertson | 13 | 0 | 38 | 1 | 13 | 3 | 41 | 0 | | | | | |

Umpires: J.C. Collings and R.G.A. Ashman.

# SOUTH AFRICA v AUSTRALIA 1935–36 (3rd Test)

Played at Newlands, Cape Town, on 1 (*no play*), 2, 3, 4 January.
Toss: Australia.   Result: AUSTRALIA won by an innings and 78 runs.
Debuts: Nil.

Grimmett established a new Test record in this match when he overtook S.F. Barnes' total of 189 wickets.

## AUSTRALIA

| | | |
|---|---|---|
| W.A. Brown | c and b Robertson | 121 |
| J.H.W. Fingleton | c Wade b Balaskas | 112 |
| S.J. McCabe | c and b Balaskas | 0 |
| L.S. Darling | lbw b Balaskas | 12 |
| V.Y. Richardson* | lbw b Crisp | 14 |
| A.G. Chipperfield | b Langton | 30 |
| W.A.S. Oldfield† | b Robertson | 8 |
| C.V. Grimmett | not out | 30 |
| W.J. O'Reilly | b Balaskas | 17 |
| E.L. McCormick | not out | 0 |
| L.O'B. Fleetwood-Smith | did not bat | |
| Extras | (B 14, LB 4) | 18 |
| **Total** | (8 wickets declared) | **362** |

## SOUTH AFRICA

| | | | | | |
|---|---|---|---|---|---|
| I. J. Siedle | lbw b Grimmett | 1 | | b Grimmett | 59 |
| H.F. Wade* | c and b McCabe | 0 | | lbw b Fleetwood-Smith | 31 |
| E.A.B. Rowan | b Grimmett | 12 | | c Richardson b O'Reilly | 19 |
| B. Mitchell | c Fingleton b O'Reilly | 14 | (5) | b Grimmett | 0 |
| K.G. Viljoen | st Oldfield b Fleetwood-Smith | 14 | (6) | c O'Reilly b Grimmett | 23 |
| A.D. Nourse | not out | 44 | (4) | c and b Grimmett | 25 |
| F. Nicholson† | b Fleetwood-Smith | 0 | | c and b O'Reilly | 4 |
| A.B.C. Langton | b Grimmett | 3 | | b O'Reilly | 4 |
| R.J. Crisp | b Grimmett | 0 | | c Richardson b O'Reilly | 0 |
| X.C. Balaskas | b Grimmett | 0 | (11) | b Grimmett | 2 |
| J.B. Robertson | run out | 1 | (10) | not out | 12 |
| Extras | (LB 13) | 13 | | (B 1, LB 2) | 3 |
| **Total** | | **102** | | | **182** |

| SOUTH AFRICA | O | M | R | W | O | M | R | W |
|---|---|---|---|---|---|---|---|---|
| Crisp | 14 | 2 | 30 | 1 | | | | |
| Langton | 30 | 2 | 94 | 1 | | | | |
| Robertson | 29 | 8 | 75 | 2 | | | | |
| Balaskas | 38 | 1 | 126 | 4 | | | | |
| Mitchell | 4 | 0 | 19 | 0 | | | | |
| AUSTRALIA | | | | | | | | |
| McCormick | 2 | 1 | 3 | 0 | 2 | 0 | 8 | 0 |
| McCabe | 2 | 1 | 9 | 1 | | | | |
| O'Reilly | 11 | 4 | 24 | 1 | 25 | 15 | 35 | 4 |
| Grimmett | 17 | 4 | 32 | 5 | 36·4 | 17 | 56 | 5 |
| Fleetwood-Smith | 6·2 | 0 | 21 | 2 | 24 | 4 | 80 | 1 |

### FALL OF WICKETS

| | A | SA | SA |
|---|---|---|---|
| Wkt | 1st | 1st | 2nd |
| 1st | 233 | 0 | 87 |
| 2nd | 235 | 12 | 97 |
| 3rd | 251 | 21 | 137 |
| 4th | 259 | 29 | 137 |
| 5th | 299 | 86 | 139 |
| 6th | 313 | 88 | 146 |
| 7th | 313 | 95 | 156 |
| 8th | 361 | 95 | 156 |
| 9th | – | 95 | 174 |
| 10th | – | 102 | 182 |

Umpires: J.C. Collings and R.G.A. Ashman.

# SOUTH AFRICA v AUSTRALIA 1935–36 (4th Test)

Played at Old Wanderers, Johannesburg, on 15, 17 February.
Toss: South Africa.   Result: AUSTRALIA won by an innings and 184 runs.
Debuts: South Africa – E.Q. Davies, R.L. Harvey.

Play continued a few minutes after the scheduled close on the second day to obtain a finish. Grimmett became the first bowler to take 200 Test wickets.

## SOUTH AFRICA

| | | | | |
|---|---|--:|---|--:|
| I.J. Siedle | lbw b Grimmett | 44 | b McCormick | 0 |
| H.F. Wade* | b McCormick | 39 | b McCormick | 2 |
| A.D. Nourse | c Oldfield b McCormick | 3 | (5) b McCormick | 3 |
| K.G. Viljoen | b O'Reilly | 33 | (3) st Oldfield b Grimmett | 7 |
| R.L. Harvey | b O'Reilly | 5 | (6) c Darling b Grimmett | 17 |
| B. Mitchell | st Oldfield b Grimmett | 16 | (4) not out | 48 |
| A.B.C. Langton | lbw b O'Reilly | 7 | (8) lbw b Grimmett | 9 |
| F. Nicholson† | b Grimmett | 0 | (7) b Grimmett | 0 |
| E.P. Nupen | b O'Reilly | 1 | b Grimmett | 6 |
| X.C. Balaskas | lbw b O'Reilly | 0 | c O'Brien b Grimmett | 0 |
| E.Q. Davies | not out | 0 | c Oldfield b Grimmett | 3 |
| Extras | (LB 5, W 4) | 9 | (LB 3) | 3 |
| **Total** | | **157** | | **98** |

## AUSTRALIA

| | | |
|---|---|--:|
| J.H.W. Fingleton | c Langton b Davies | 108 |
| W.A. Brown | lbw b Langton | 34 |
| S.J. McCabe | b Davies | 40 |
| L.P.J. O'Brien | b Balaskas | 59 |
| W.A.S. Oldfield† | c Balaskas b Nupen | 44 |
| L.S. Darling | c Wade b Balaskas | 16 |
| A.G. Chipperfield | lbw b Balaskas | 39 |
| V.Y. Richardson* | b Davies | 21 |
| C.V. Grimmett | lbw b Balaskas | 4 |
| W.J. O'Reilly | not out | 56 |
| E.L. McCormick | c Mitchell b Davies | 13 |
| Extras | (B 1, LB 4) | 5 |
| **Total** | | **439** |

| AUSTRALIA | O | M | R | W | O | M | R | W |
|---|--:|--:|--:|--:|--:|--:|--:|--:|
| McCormick | 11 | 0 | 37 | 2 | 12 | 2 | 28 | 3 |
| McCabe | 5 | 2 | 21 | 0 | 2 | 1 | 1 | 0 |
| Grimmett | 26·4 | 6 | 70 | 3 | 19·5 | 9 | 40 | 7 |
| O'Reilly | 21 | 11 | 20 | 5 | 10 | 3 | 26 | 0 |

| SOUTH AFRICA | O | M | R | W |
|---|--:|--:|--:|--:|
| Davies | 24·4 | 4 | 75 | 4 |
| Langton | 30 | 5 | 88 | 1 |
| Balaskas | 44 | 4 | 165 | 4 |
| Nupen | 14 | 1 | 53 | 1 |
| Mitchell | 14 | 1 | 53 | 0 |

### FALL OF WICKETS

| Wkt | SA 1st | A 1st | SA 2nd |
|---|--:|--:|--:|
| 1st | 81 | 99 | 0 |
| 2nd | 91 | 179 | 5 |
| 3rd | 96 | 184 | 21 |
| 4th | 128 | 260 | 24 |
| 5th | 137 | 282 | 49 |
| 6th | 153 | 333 | 50 |
| 7th | 154 | 352 | 76 |
| 8th | 155 | 368 | 82 |
| 9th | 157 | 370 | 82 |
| 10th | 157 | 439 | 98 |

Umpires: R.G.A. Ashman and J.C. Collings.

# SOUTH AFRICA v AUSTRALIA 1935–36 (5th Test)

Played at Kingsmead, Durban, on 28, 29 February, 2, 3 March.
Toss: South Africa.   Result: AUSTRALIA won by an innings and 6 runs.
Debuts: Nil.

For the third match in succession, Fingleton scored a century (three in consecutive innings), Grimmett took ten or more wickets and Australia won by an innings. Richardson established a Test record, since equalled but never beaten, by holding five catches in the second innings. H.F. Wade captained South Africa in each of his ten Test matches.

## SOUTH AFRICA

| | | | | | |
|---|---|---|---|---|---|
| I.J. Siedle | c Fingleton b Grimmett | 36 | c Brown b Grimmett | | 46 |
| H.F. Wade* | c Richardson b Grimmett | 26 | b O'Reilly | | 25 |
| B. Mitchell | c and b Grimmett | 10 | not out | | 72 |
| A.D. Nourse | lbw b Grimmett | 50 | b O'Reilly | | 41 |
| K.G. Viljoen | c Chipperfield b McCormick | 56 | lbw b Grimmett | | 25 |
| R.L. Harvey | c Oldfield b McCormick | 28 | c Richardson b Grimmett | | 1 |
| A.B.C. Langton | st Oldfield b Grimmett | 1 | b Grimmett | | 3 |
| X.C. Balaskas | st Oldfield b Grimmett | 2 | c Richardson b Grimmett | | 0 |
| R.J. Crisp | b Grimmett | 0 | (11) c Richardson b O'Reilly | | 0 |
| E.A. van der Merwe† | not out | 7 | (9) c Richardson b Grimmett | | 0 |
| E.Q. Davies | b McCormick | 0 | (10) c Richardson b O'Reilly | | 2 |
| Extras | (B 1, LB 5) | 6 | (B 5, LB 7) | | 12 |
| **Total** | | **222** | | | **227** |

## AUSTRALIA

| | | |
|---|---|---|
| J.H.W. Fingleton | b Crisp | 118 |
| W.A. Brown | c Langton b Mitchell | 84 |
| S.J. McCabe | c and b Mitchell | 1 |
| L.P.J. O'Brien | c Van der Merwe b Balaskas | 48 |
| L.S. Darling | lbw b Mitchell | 62 |
| A.G. Chipperfield | c Balaskas b Mitchell | 18 |
| V.Y. Richardson* | b Crisp | 45 |
| W.A.S. Oldfield† | c Crisp b Langton | 29 |
| C.V. Grimmett | c Siedle b Mitchell | 14 |
| W.J. O'Reilly | c Siedle b Langton | 13 |
| E.L. McCormick | not out | 0 |
| Extras | (B 19, LB 3, NB 1) | 23 |
| **Total** | | **455** |

| AUSTRALIA | O | M | R | W | O | M | R | W | | FALL OF WICKETS | | |
|---|---|---|---|---|---|---|---|---|---|---|---|---|
| McCormick | 20·1 | 8 | 37 | 3 | 15 | 1 | 64 | 0 | | SA | A | SA |
| McCabe | 7 | 0 | 20 | 0 | 2 | 0 | 11 | 0 | Wkt | 1st | 1st | 2nd |
| Grimmett | 45 | 18 | 100 | 7 | 48 | 23 | 73 | 6 | 1st | 44 | 162 | 63 |
| O'Reilly | 37 | 15 | 59 | 0 | 40·1 | 18 | 47 | 4 | 2nd | 57 | 164 | 73 |
| Chipperfield | | | | | 8 | 1 | 20 | 0 | 3rd | 124 | 240 | 146 |
| | | | | | | | | | 4th | 125 | 316 | 196 |
| SOUTH AFRICA | | | | | | | | | 5th | 178 | 333 | 206 |
| Davies | 18 | 0 | 54 | 0 | | | | | 6th | 183 | 361 | 212 |
| Crisp | 19 | 2 | 65 | 2 | | | | | 7th | 199 | 423 | 220 |
| Langton | 33 | 9 | 69 | 2 | | | | | 8th | 199 | 433 | 220 |
| Balaskas | 51 | 4 | 157 | 1 | | | | | 9th | 220 | 451 | 227 |
| Mitchell | 25·5 | 2 | 87 | 5 | | | | | 10th | 222 | 455 | 227 |

Umpires: J.C. Collings and W.J. Routledge.

# ENGLAND v INDIA 1936 (1st Test)

Played at Lord's, London, on 27, 29, 30 June.
Toss: England.   Result: ENGLAND won by nine wickets.
Debuts: England – H. Gimblett; India – D.D. Hindlekar, The Maharajkumar of Vizianagram (*who,
    before the 2nd Test, received a knighthood and became Sir Gajapatairaj Vijaya Ananda, The
    Maharajkumar of Vizianagram*).

## INDIA

| | | | | | |
|---|---|---|---|---|---|
| V.M. Merchant | b Allen | 35 | c Duckworth b Allen | | 0 |
| D.D. Hindlekar† | b Robins | 26 | lbw b Robins | | 17 |
| Mushtaq Ali | c Langridge b Allen | 0 | lbw b Allen | | 8 |
| C.K. Nayudu | lbw b Allen | 1 | c Robins b Allen | | 3 |
| S. Wazir Ali | b Allen | 11 | c Verity b Allen | | 4 |
| L. Amar Singh | c Langridge b Robins | 12 | lbw b Verity | | 7 |
| P.E. Palia | c Mitchell b Verity | 11 | c Leyland b Verity | | 16 |
| M. Jahangir Khan | b Allen | 13 | c Duckworth b Verity | | 13 |
| Maharaj Vizianagram* | not out | 19 | c Mitchell b Verity | | 6 |
| C.S. Nayudu | c Wyatt b Robins | 6 | c Hardstaff b Allen | | 2 |
| Mahomed Nissar | st Duckworth b Verity | 9 | not out | | 2 |
| Extras | (B 4) | 4 | (B 4, LB 3, NB 1) | | 8 |
| **Total** | | **147** | | | **93** |

## ENGLAND

| | | | | | |
|---|---|---|---|---|---|
| A. Mitchell | b Amar Singh | 14 | c Merchant b Nissar | | 0 |
| H. Gimblett | c Mushtaq Ali b Amar Singh | 11 | not out | | 67 |
| M.J.L. Turnbull | b Amar Singh | 0 | not out | | 37 |
| M. Leyland | lbw b Amar Singh | 60 | | | |
| R.E.S. Wyatt | c Jahangir Khan b Amar Singh | 0 | | | |
| J. Hardstaff, jr | b Nissar | 2 | | | |
| James Langridge | c Jahangir Khan b C.K. Nayudu | 19 | | | |
| G.O.B. Allen* | c Jahangir Khan b Amar Singh | 13 | | | |
| G. Duckworth† | c Vizianagram b Nissar | 2 | | | |
| R.W.V. Robins | c C.K. Nayudu b Nissar | 0 | | | |
| H. Verity | not out | 2 | | | |
| Extras | (B 4, LB 4, NB 3) | 11 | (B 4) | | 4 |
| **Total** | | **134** | (1 wicket) | | **108** |

| ENGLAND | O | M | R | W | O | M | R | W | FALL OF WICKETS | | | | |
|---|---|---|---|---|---|---|---|---|---|---|---|---|---|
| Allen | 17 | 7 | 35 | 5 | 18 | 1 | 43 | 5 | | I | E | I | E |
| Wyatt | 3 | 2 | 7 | 0 | 7 | 4 | 8 | 0 | Wkt | 1st | 1st | 2nd | 2nd |
| Verity | 18·1 | 5 | 42 | 2 | 16 | 8 | 17 | 4 | 1st | 62 | 16 | 0 | 0 |
| Langridge | 4 | 1 | 9 | 0 | | | | | 2nd | 62 | 16 | 18 | – |
| Robins | 13 | 4 | 50 | 3 | 5 | 1 | 17 | 1 | 3rd | 64 | 30 | 22 | – |
| | | | | | | | | | 4th | 66 | 34 | 28 | – |
| INDIA | | | | | | | | | 5th | 85 | 41 | 39 | – |
| Nissar | 17 | 5 | 36 | 3 | 6 | 3 | 26 | 1 | 6th | 97 | 96 | 45 | – |
| Amar Singh | 25·1 | 11 | 35 | 6 | 16·3 | 6 | 36 | 0 | 7th | 107 | 129 | 64 | – |
| Jahangir Khan | 9 | 0 | 27 | 0 | 10 | 3 | 20 | 0 | 8th | 119 | 132 | 80 | – |
| C.K. Nayudu | 7 | 2 | 17 | 1 | 7 | 2 | 22 | 0 | 9th | 137 | 132 | 90 | – |
| C.S. Nayudu | 3 | 0 | 8 | 0 | | | | | 10th | 147 | 134 | 93 | – |

Umpires: A. Dolphin and F. Walden.

# ENGLAND v INDIA 1936 (2nd Test)

Played at Old Trafford, Manchester, on 25, 27, 28 July.
Toss: India.   Result: MATCH DRAWN.
Debuts: England – A.E. Fagg, L.B. Fishlock, A.R. Gover: India – K.R. Meherhomji,
  C. Ramaswami.

England scored 571 for 8 in only 375 minutes and India's opening partnership of 203 (still their record against England) took just 150 minutes; on the second day 588 runs were scored for the loss of six wickets – this is still the most runs scored in a day of Test cricket.

## INDIA

| | | | | | |
|---|---|---|---|---|---|
| V.M. Merchant | c Hammond b Verity | 33 | lbw b Hammond | | 114 |
| Mushtaq Ali | run out | 13 | c and b Robins | | 112 |
| L. Amar Singh | c Duckworth b Worthington | 27 | (6) not out | | 48 |
| C.K. Nayudu | lbw b Allen | 16 | st Duckworth b Verity | | 34 |
| S. Wazir Ali | c Worthington b Verity | 42 | b Robins | | 4 |
| C. Ramaswami | b Verity | 40 | (3) b Robins | | 60 |
| M. Jahangir Khan | c Duckworth b Allen | 2 | | | |
| C.S. Nayudu | b Verity | 10 | | | |
| Maharaj Vizianagram* | b Robins | 6 | (7) not out | | 0 |
| K.R. Meherhomji† | not out | 0 | | | |
| Mahomed Nissar | c Hardstaff b Robins | 13 | | | |
| Extras | (B 1) | 1 | (B 9, LB 7, NB 2) | | 18 |
| **Total** | | **203** | (5 wickets) | | **390** |

## ENGLAND

| | | |
|---|---|---|
| H. Gimblett | b Nissar | 9 |
| A.E. Fagg | lbw b Mushtaq Ali | 39 |
| W.R. Hammond | b C.K. Nayudu | 167 |
| T.S. Worthington | b C.K. Nayudu b C.S. Nayudu | 87 |
| L.B. Fishlock | b C.K. Nayudu | 6 |
| J. Hardstaff, jr | c and b Amar Singh | 94 |
| G.O.B. Allen* | c Meherhomji b Amar Singh | 1 |
| R.W.V. Robins | c Merchant b Nissar | 76 |
| H. Verity | not out | 66 |
| G. Duckworth† | not out | 10 |
| A.R. Gover | did not bat | |
| Extras | (B 5, LB 9, W 1, NB 1) | 16 |
| **Total** | (8 wickets declared) | **571** |

| ENGLAND | O | M | R | W | O | M | R | W |
|---|---|---|---|---|---|---|---|---|
| Allen | 14 | 3 | 39 | 2 | 19 | 2 | 96 | 0 |
| Gover | 15 | 2 | 39 | 0 | 20 | 2 | 61 | 0 |
| Hammond | 9 | 1 | 34 | 0 | 12 | 2 | 19 | 1 |
| Robins | 9·1 | 1 | 34 | 2 | 29 | 2 | 103 | 3 |
| Verity | 17 | 5 | 51 | 4 | 22 | 8 | 66 | 1 |
| Worthington | 4 | 0 | 15 | 1 | 13 | 4 | 27 | 0 |
| INDIA | | | | | | | | |
| Nissar | 28 | 5 | 125 | 2 | | | | |
| Amar Singh | 41 | 8 | 121 | 2 | | | | |
| C.S. Nayudu | 17 | 1 | 87 | 1 | | | | |
| C.K. Nayudu | 22 | 1 | 84 | 2 | | | | |
| Jahangir Khan | 18 | 5 | 57 | 0 | | | | |
| Mushtaq Ali | 13 | 1 | 64 | 1 | | | | |
| Merchant | 3 | 0 | 17 | 0 | | | | |

### FALL OF WICKETS

| | I | E | I |
|---|---|---|---|
| Wkt | 1st | 1st | 2nd |
| 1st | 18 | 12 | 203 |
| 2nd | 67 | 146 | 279 |
| 3rd | 73 | 273 | 313 |
| 4th | 100 | 289 | 317 |
| 5th | 161 | 375 | 390 |
| 6th | 164 | 376 | – |
| 7th | 181 | 409 | – |
| 8th | 188 | 547 | – |
| 9th | 190 | – | – |
| 10th | 203 | – | – |

Umpires: F. Chester and F. Walden.

# ENGLAND v INDIA 1936 (3rd Test)

Played at Kennington Oval, London, on 15, 17, 18 August.
Toss: England.   Result: ENGLAND won by nine wickets.
Debuts: India – M. Baqa Jilani.

Hammond scored the first double-century against India and, with Worthington, shared in a partnership of 266 which remains England's record for the fourth wicket against India.

## ENGLAND

| | | | | | |
|---|---|--:|---|---|--:|
| C.J. Barnett | lbw b Nayudu | 43 | not out | | 32 |
| A.E. Fagg | c Hussain b Amar Singh | 8 | c Amar Singh b Nissar | | 22 |
| W.R. Hammond | b Nissar | 217 | not out | | 5 |
| M. Leyland | b Nissar | 26 | | | |
| T.S. Worthington | b Nissar | 128 | | | |
| L.B. Fishlock | not out | 19 | | | |
| G.O.B. Allen* | c Hussain b Nissar | 13 | | | |
| H. Verity | c Hussain b Nissar | 4 | | | |
| J.M. Sims | lbw b Amar Singh | 1 | | | |
| W. Voce | not out | 1 | | | |
| G. Duckworth† | did not bat | | | | |
| Extras | (LB 10, NB 1) | 11 | (B 4, NB 1) | | 5 |
| **Total** | (8 wickets declared) | **471** | (1 wicket) | | **64** |

## INDIA

| | | | | | |
|---|---|--:|---|---|--:|
| V.M. Merchant | b Allen | 52 | c Worthington b Allen | | 48 |
| Mushtaq Ali | st Duckworth b Verity | 52 | c Hammond b Allen | | 17 |
| Dilawar Hussain† | st Duckworth b Verity | 35 | lbw b Sims | | 54 |
| C.K. Nayudu | c Allen b Voce | 5 | (6) b Allen | | 81 |
| C. Ramaswami | b Sims | 29 | (8) not out | | 41 |
| S. Wazir Ali | lbw b Sims | 2 | (7) c Duckworth b Allen | | 1 |
| L. Amar Singh | b Verity | 5 | (4) c Sims b Verity | | 44 |
| M. Jahangir Khan | c Fagg b Sims | 9 | (10) c Voce b Allen | | 1 |
| Maharaj Vizianagram* | b Sims | 1 | b Allen | | 1 |
| M. Baqa Jilani | not out | 4 | (5) c Fagg b Allen | | 12 |
| Mahomed Nissar | c Worthington b Sims | 14 | c Voce b Sims | | 0 |
| Extras | (B 8, LB 6) | 14 | (B 3, LB 7, NB 2) | | 12 |
| **Total** | | **222** | | | **312** |

| INDIA | O | M | R | W | O | M | R | W |
|---|--:|--:|--:|--:|--:|--:|--:|--:|
| Nissar | 26 | 1 | 120 | 5 | 7 | 0 | 36 | 1 |
| Amar Singh | 39 | 8 | 102 | 2 | 6 | 0 | 23 | 0 |
| Baqa Jilani | 15 | 4 | 55 | 0 | | | | |
| Nayudu | 24 | 1 | 82 | 1 | | | | |
| Jahangir Khan | 17 | 1 | 65 | 0 | | | | |
| Mushtaq Ali | 2 | 0 | 13 | 0 | | | | |
| Merchant | 6 | 0 | 23 | 0 | | | | |
| **ENGLAND** | | | | | | | | |
| Voce | 20 | 5 | 46 | 1 | 20 | 5 | 40 | 0 |
| Allen | 12 | 3 | 37 | 1 | 20 | 3 | 80 | 7 |
| Hammond | 8 | 2 | 17 | 0 | 7 | 0 | 24 | 0 |
| Verity | 25 | 12 | 30 | 3 | 16 | 6 | 32 | 1 |
| Sims | 18·5 | 1 | 73 | 5 | 25 | 1 | 95 | 2 |
| Leyland | 2 | 0 | 5 | 0 | 3 | 0 | 19 | 0 |
| Worthington | | | | | 2 | 0 | 10 | 0 |

FALL OF WICKETS

| | E | I | I | E |
|---|--:|--:|--:|--:|
| Wkt | 1st | 1st | 2nd | 2nd |
| 1st | 19 | 81 | 64 | 48 |
| 2nd | 93 | 125 | 71 | – |
| 3rd | 156 | 130 | 122 | – |
| 4th | 422 | 185 | 159 | – |
| 5th | 437 | 187 | 212 | – |
| 6th | 455 | 192 | 222 | – |
| 7th | 463 | 195 | 295 | – |
| 8th | 468 | 203 | 307 | – |
| 9th | – | 206 | 309 | – |
| 10th | – | 222 | 312 | – |

Umpires: F. Chester and F. Walden.

# AUSTRALIA v ENGLAND 1936–37 (1st Test)

Played at Woolloongabba, Brisbane, on 4, 5, 7, 8, 9 December.
Toss: England.   Result: ENGLAND won by 322 runs.
Debuts: Australia – C.L. Badcock, R.H. Robinson, M.W. Sievers, F.A. Ward.

Fingleton extended his run of consecutive hundreds to four – only to have it ended by Voce's first ball of the second innings. Australia were dismissed on a rain-affected pitch for their lowest score at home this century.

## ENGLAND

| | | | | | |
|---|---|---|---|---|---|
| T.S. Worthington | c Oldfield b McCormick | 0 | st Oldfield b McCabe | | 8 |
| C.J. Barnett | c Oldfield b O'Reilly | 69 | c Badcock b Ward | | 26 |
| A.E. Fagg | c Oldfield b McCormick | 4 | st Oldfield b Ward | | 27 |
| W.R. Hammond | c Robinson b McCormick | 0 | hit wkt b Ward | | 25 |
| M. Leyland | b Ward | 126 | c Bradman b Ward | | 33 |
| L.E.G. Ames† | c Chipperfield b Ward | 24 | b Sievers | | 9 |
| J. Hardstaff, jr | c McCabe b O'Reilly | 43 | (8) st Oldfield b Ward | | 20 |
| R.W.V. Robins | c sub (W.A. Brown) b O'Reilly | 38 | (9) c Chipperfield b Ward | | 0 |
| G.O.B. Allen* | c McCabe b O'Reilly | 35 | (7) c Fingleton b Sievers | | 68 |
| H. Verity | c Sievers b O'Reilly | 7 | lbw b Sievers | | 19 |
| W. Voce | not out | 4 | not out | | 2 |
| Extras | (B 1, LB 3, NB 4) | 8 | (B 14, LB 4, NB 1) | | 19 |
| **Total** | | **358** | | | **256** |

## AUSTRALIA

| | | | | | |
|---|---|---|---|---|---|
| J.H.W. Fingleton | b Verity | 100 | b Voce | | 0 |
| C.L. Badcock | b Allen | 8 | c Fagg b Allen | | 0 |
| D.G. Bradman* | c Worthington b Voce | 38 | (5) c Fagg b Allen | | 0 |
| S.J. McCabe | c Barnett b Voce | 51 | (6) c Leyland b Allen | | 7 |
| R.H. Robinson | c Hammond b Voce | 2 | (7) c Hammond b Voce | | 3 |
| A.G. Chipperfield | c Ames b Voce | 7 | (8) not out | | 26 |
| M.W. Sievers | b Allen | 8 | (3) c Voce b Allen | | 5 |
| W.A.S. Oldfield† | c Ames b Voce | 6 | (4) b Voce | | 10 |
| W.J. O'Reilly | c Leyland b Voce | 3 | b Allen | | 0 |
| F.A. Ward | c Hardstaff b Allen | 0 | b Voce | | 1 |
| E.L. McCormick | not out | 1 | absent ill | | – |
| Extras | (B 4, LB 1, NB 5) | 10 | (NB 6) | | 6 |
| **Total** | | **234** | | | **58** |

| AUSTRALIA | O | M | R | W | O | M | R | W |
|---|---|---|---|---|---|---|---|---|
| McCormick | 8 | 1 | 26 | 3 | | | | |
| Sievers | 16 | 5 | 42 | 0 | 19·6 | 9 | 29 | 3 |
| O'Reilly | 40·6 | 13 | 102 | 5 | 35 | 15 | 59 | 0 |
| Ward | 36 | 3 | 138 | 2 | 46 | 16 | 102 | 6 |
| Chipperfield | 11 | 3 | 32 | 0 | 10 | 2 | 33 | 0 |
| McCabe | 2 | 0 | 10 | 0 | 6 | 1 | 14 | 1 |
| ENGLAND | | | | | | | | |
| Allen | 16 | 2 | 71 | 3 | 6 | 0 | 36 | 5 |
| Voce | 20·6 | 5 | 41 | 6 | 6·3 | 0 | 16 | 4 |
| Hammond | 4 | 0 | 12 | 0 | | | | |
| Verity | 28 | 11 | 52 | 1 | | | | |
| Robins | 17 | 0 | 48 | 0 | | | | |

FALL OF WICKETS

| | E | A | E | A |
|---|---|---|---|---|
| Wkt | 1st | 1st | 2nd | 2nd |
| 1st | 0 | 13 | 17 | 0 |
| 2nd | 20 | 89 | 50 | 3 |
| 3rd | 20 | 166 | 82 | 7 |
| 4th | 119 | 176 | 105 | 7 |
| 5th | 162 | 202 | 122 | 16 |
| 6th | 252 | 220 | 144 | 20 |
| 7th | 311 | 229 | 205 | 35 |
| 8th | 311 | 231 | 205 | 41 |
| 9th | 343 | 231 | 247 | 58 |
| 10th | 358 | 234 | 256 | – |

Umpires: G. Borwick and J.D. Scott.

## AUSTRALIA v ENGLAND 1936–37 (2nd Test)

Played at Sydney Cricket Ground on 18, 19, 21, 22 December.
Toss: England.   Result: ENGLAND won by an innings and 22 runs.
Debuts: Nil.

The third of Hammond's four double-centuries against Australia took 458 minutes and included 27 fours. His scores in four Tests at Sydney to date were 251, 112, 101, 75* and 231*.

### ENGLAND

| | | |
|---|---|---|
| A.E. Fagg | c Sievers b McCormick | 11 |
| C.J. Barnett | b Ward | 57 |
| W.R. Hammond | not out | 231 |
| M. Leyland | lbw b McCabe | 42 |
| L.E.G. Ames† | c sub (R.H. Robinson) b Ward | 29 |
| G.O.B. Allen* | lbw b O'Reilly | 9 |
| J. Hardstaff, jr | b McCormick | 26 |
| H. Verity | not out | 0 |
| J.M. Sims | ) | |
| R.W.V. Robins | ) did not bat | |
| W. Voce | ) | |
| Extras | (B 8, LB 8, W 1, NB 4) | 21 |
| **Total** | (6 wickets declared) | **426** |

### AUSTRALIA

| | | | | | |
|---|---|---|---|---|---|
| J.H.W. Fingleton | c Verity b Voce | 12 | | b Sims | 73 |
| L.P.J. O'Brien | c Sims b Voce | 0 | | c Allen b Hammond | 17 |
| D.G. Bradman* | c Allen b Voce | 0 | | b Verity | 82 |
| S.J. McCabe | c Sims b Voce | 0 | | lbw b Voce | 93 |
| A.G. Chipperfield | c Sims b Allen | 13 | | b Voce | 21 |
| M.W. Sievers | c Voce b Verity | 4 | (7) | run out | 24 |
| W.A.S. Oldfield† | b Verity | 1 | (8) | c Ames b Voce | 1 |
| W.J. O'Reilly | not out | 37 | (9) | b Hammond | 3 |
| E.L. McCormick | b Allen | 10 | (10) | lbw b Hammond | 0 |
| F.A. Ward | b Allen | 0 | (11) | not out | 1 |
| C.L. Badcock | absent ill | – | (6) | lbw b Allen | 2 |
| Extras | (B 1, LB 1, NB 1) | 3 | | (LB 3, NB 4) | 7 |
| **Total** | | **80** | | | **324** |

| AUSTRALIA | O | M | R | W | O | M | R | W |
|---|---|---|---|---|---|---|---|---|
| McCormick | 20 | 1 | 79 | 2 | | | | |
| Sievers | 16·2 | 4 | 30 | 0 | | | | |
| Ward | 42 | 8 | 132 | 2 | | | | |
| O'Reilly | 41 | 17 | 86 | 1 | | | | |
| Chipperfield | 13 | 2 | 47 | 0 | | | | |
| McCabe | 9 | 1 | 31 | 1 | | | | |
| ENGLAND | | | | | | | | |
| Voce | 8 | 1 | 10 | 4 | 19 | 4 | 66 | 3 |
| Allen | 5·7 | 1 | 19 | 3 | 19 | 4 | 61 | 1 |
| Verity | 3 | 0 | 17 | 2 | 19 | 7 | 55 | 1 |
| Hammond | 4 | 0 | 6 | 0 | 15·7 | 3 | 29 | 3 |
| Sims | 2 | 0 | 20 | 0 | 17 | 0 | 80 | 1 |
| Robins | 1 | 0 | 5 | 0 | 7 | 0 | 26 | 0 |

FALL OF WICKETS

| | E | A | A |
|---|---|---|---|
| Wkt | 1st | 1st | 2nd |
| 1st | 27 | 1 | 38 |
| 2nd | 118 | 1 | 162 |
| 3rd | 247 | 1 | 186 |
| 4th | 351 | 16 | 220 |
| 5th | 368 | 28 | 226 |
| 6th | 424 | 30 | 318 |
| 7th | – | 37 | 319 |
| 8th | – | 80 | 323 |
| 9th | – | 80 | 323 |
| 10th | – | – | 324 |

Umpires: G. Borwick and J.D. Scott.

# AUSTRALIA v ENGLAND 1936–37 (3rd Test)

Played at Melbourne Cricket Ground on 1, 2, 4, 5, 6, 7 January.
Toss: Australia.    Result: AUSTRALIA won by 365 runs.
Debuts: Nil.

Bradman's 270 was the highest score for Australia against England at home; it remains the highest captain's innings in these matches and the highest second innings score. His partnership of 346 with Fingleton is still the highest sixth wicket stand in Test cricket. This match attracted 350,534 spectators – the record attendance for any cricket match.

## AUSTRALIA

| | | | | |
|---|---|---:|---|---:|
| J.H.W. Fingleton | c Sims b Robins | 38 | (6) c Ames b Sims | 136 |
| W.A. Brown | c Ames b Voce | 1 | (5) c Barnett b Voce | 20 |
| D.G. Bradman* | c Robins b Verity | 13 | (7) c Allen b Verity | 270 |
| K.E. Rigg | c Verity b Allen | 16 | lbw b Sims | 47 |
| S.J. McCabe | c Worthington b Voce | 63 | (8) lbw b Allen | 22 |
| L.S. Darling | c Allen b Verity | 20 | (9) b Allen | 0 |
| M.W. Sievers | st Ames b Robins | 1 | (10) not out | 25 |
| W.A.S. Oldfield† | not out | 27 | (11) lbw b Verity | 7 |
| W.J. O'Reilly | c Sims b Hammond | 4 | (1) c and b Voce | 0 |
| F.A. Ward | st Ames b Hammond | 7 | (3) c Hardstaff b Verity | 18 |
| L.O'B. Fleetwood-Smith | did not bat | | (2) c Verity b Voce | 0 |
| Extras | (B 2, LB 6, NB 2) | 10 | (B 6, LB 2, W 1, NB 10) | 19 |
| **Total** | (9 wickets declared) | **200** | | **564** |

## ENGLAND

| | | | | |
|---|---|---:|---|---:|
| T.S. Worthington | c Bradman b McCabe | 0 | c Sievers b Ward | 16 |
| C.J. Barnett | c Darling b Sievers | 11 | lbw b O'Reilly | 23 |
| W.R. Hammond | c Darling b Sievers | 32 | b Sievers | 51 |
| M. Leyland | c Darling b O'Reilly | 17 | not out | 111 |
| J.M. Sims | c Brown b Sievers | 3 | (10) lbw b Fleetwood-Smith | 0 |
| L.E.G. Ames† | b Sievers | 3 | (5) b Fleetwood-Smith | 19 |
| R.W.V. Robins | c O'Reilly b Sievers | 0 | (8) b O'Reilly | 61 |
| J. Hardstaff, jr | b O'Reilly | 3 | (6) c Ward b Fleetwood-Smith | 17 |
| G.O.B. Allen* | not out | 0 | (7) c Sievers b Fleetwood-Smith | 11 |
| H. Verity | c Brown b O'Reilly | 0 | (9) c McCabe b O'Reilly | 11 |
| W. Voce | not out | 0 | c Bradman b Fleetwood-Smith | 0 |
| Extras | (B 5, LB 1, NB 1) | 7 | (LB 3) | 3 |
| **Total** | (9 wickets declared) | **76** | | **323** |

| ENGLAND | O | M | R | W | O | M | R | W |
|---|---|---|---|---|---|---|---|---|
| Voce | 18 | 3 | 49 | 2 | 29 | 2 | 120 | 3 |
| Allen | 12 | 2 | 35 | 1 | 23 | 2 | 84 | 2 |
| Sims | 9 | 1 | 35 | 0 | 23 | 1 | 109 | 2 |
| Verity | 14 | 4 | 24 | 2 | 37·7 | 9 | 79 | 3 |
| Robins | 7 | 0 | 31 | 2 | 11 | 2 | 46 | 0 |
| Hammond | 5·3 | 0 | 16 | 2 | 22 | 3 | 89 | 0 |
| Worthington | | | | | 4 | 0 | 18 | 0 |
| AUSTRALIA | | | | | | | | |
| McCabe | 2 | 1 | 7 | 1 | 8 | 0 | 32 | 0 |
| Sievers | 11·2 | 5 | 21 | 5 | 12 | 2 | 39 | 1 |
| O'Reilly | 12 | 5 | 28 | 3 | 21 | 6 | 65 | 3 |
| Fleetwood-Smith | 3 | 1 | 13 | 0 | 25·6 | 2 | 124 | 5 |
| Ward | | | | | 12 | 1 | 60 | 1 |

## FALL OF WICKETS

| | A | E | A | E |
|---|---|---|---|---|
| Wkt | 1st | 1st | 2nd | 2nd |
| 1st | 7 | 0 | 0 | 29 |
| 2nd | 33 | 14 | 3 | 65 |
| 3rd | 69 | 56 | 38 | 117 |
| 4th | 79 | 68 | 74 | 155 |
| 5th | 122 | 71 | 97 | 179 |
| 6th | 130 | 71 | 443 | 195 |
| 7th | 183 | 76 | 511 | 306 |
| 8th | 190 | 76 | 511 | 322 |
| 9th | 200 | 76 | 549 | 323 |
| 10th | – | – | 564 | 323 |

Umpires: G. Borwick and J.D. Scott.

# AUSTRALIA v ENGLAND 1936–37 (4th Test)

Played at Adelaide Oval on 29, 30 January, 1, 2, 3, 4 February.
Toss: Australia.   Result: AUSTRALIA won by 148 runs.
Debuts: Australia – R.G. Gregory.

For the third time against England, Bradman scored a double-century in two successive Test matches.
Fleetwood-Smith returned the best innings and match analyses of his 10-match Test career.

## AUSTRALIA

| | | | | | |
|---|---|---|---|---|---|
| J.H.W. Fingleton | run out | 10 | lbw b Hammond | | 12 |
| W.A. Brown | c Allen b Farnes | 42 | c Ames b Voce | | 32 |
| K.E. Rigg | c Ames b Farnes | 20 | (5) c Hammond b Farnes | | 7 |
| D.G. Bradman* | b Allen | 26 | (3) c and b Hammond | | 212 |
| S.J. McCabe | c Allen b Robins | 88 | (4) c Wyatt b Robins | | 55 |
| R.G. Gregory | lbw b Hammond | 23 | run out | | 50 |
| A.G. Chipperfield | not out | 57 | c Ames b Hammond | | 31 |
| W.A.S. Oldfield† | run out | 5 | c Ames b Hammond | | 1 |
| W.J. O'Reilly | c Leyland b Allen | 7 | c Hammond b Farnes | | 1 |
| E.L. McCormick | c Ames b Hammond | 4 | b Hammond | | 1 |
| L.O'B. Fleetwood-Smith | b Farnes | 1 | not out | | 4 |
| Extras | (LB 2, NB 3) | 5 | (B 10, LB 15, W 1, NB 1) | | 27 |
| **Total** | | **288** | | | **433** |

## ENGLAND

| | | | | | |
|---|---|---|---|---|---|
| H. Verity | c Bradman b O'Reilly | 19 | b Fleetwood-Smith | | 17 |
| C.J. Barnett | lbw b Fleetwood-Smith | 129 | c Chipperfield b Fleetwood-Smith | | 21 |
| W.R. Hammond | c McCormick b O'Reilly | 20 | (4) b Fleetwood-Smith | | 39 |
| M.Leyland | c Chipperfield b Fleetwood-Smith | 45 | (5) c Chipperfield b Fleetwood-Smith | | 32 |
| R.E.S. Wyatt | c Fingleton b O'Reilly | 3 | (6) c Oldfield b McCabe | | 50 |
| L.E.G. Ames† | b McCormick | 52 | (7) lbw b Fleetwood-Smith | | 0 |
| J. Hardstaff, jr | c and b McCormick | 20 | (3) b O'Reilly | | 43 |
| G.O.B. Allen* | lbw b Fleetwood-Smith | 11 | c Gregory b McCormick | | 9 |
| R.W.V. Robins | c Oldfield b O'Reilly | 10 | b McCormick | | 4 |
| W. Voce | c Rigg b Fleetwood-Smith | 8 | b Fleetwood-Smith | | 1 |
| K. Farnes | not out | 0 | not out | | 7 |
| Extras | (B 6, LB 2, W 1, NB 4) | 13 | (B 12, LB 2, NB 6) | | 20 |
| **Total** | | **330** | | | **243** |

| ENGLAND | O | M | R | W | O | M | R | W |
|---|---|---|---|---|---|---|---|---|
| Voce | 12 | 0 | 49 | 0 | 20 | 2 | 86 | 1 |
| Allen | 16 | 0 | 60 | 2 | 14 | 1 | 61 | 0 |
| Farnes | 20·6 | 1 | 71 | 3 | 24 | 2 | 89 | 2 |
| Hammond | 6 | 0 | 30 | 2 | 15·2 | 1 | 57 | 5 |
| Verity | 16 | 4 | 47 | 0 | 37 | 17 | 54 | 0 |
| Robins | 7 | 1 | 26 | 1 | 6 | 0 | 38 | 1 |
| Barnett | | | | | 5 | 1 | 15 | 0 |
| Leyland | | | | | 2 | 0 | 6 | 0 |
| AUSTRALIA | | | | | | | | |
| McCormick | 21 | 2 | 81 | 2 | 13 | 1 | 43 | 2 |
| McCabe | 9 | 2 | 18 | 0 | 5 | 0 | 15 | 1 |
| Fleetwood-Smith | 41·4 | 10 | 129 | 4 | 30 | 1 | 110 | 6 |
| O'Reilly | 30 | 12 | 51 | 4 | 26 | 8 | 55 | 1 |
| Chipperfield | 9 | 1 | 24 | 0 | | | | |
| Gregory | 3 | 0 | 14 | 0 | | | | |

| FALL OF WICKETS | | | | |
|---|---|---|---|---|
| | A | E | A | E |
| Wkt | 1st | 1st | 2nd | 2nd |
| 1st | 26 | 53 | 21 | 45 |
| 2nd | 72 | 108 | 88 | 50 |
| 3rd | 73 | 190 | 197 | 120 |
| 4th | 136 | 195 | 237 | 149 |
| 5th | 206 | 259 | 372 | 190 |
| 6th | 226 | 299 | 422 | 190 |
| 7th | 249 | 304 | 426 | 225 |
| 8th | 271 | 318 | 427 | 231 |
| 9th | 283 | 322 | 429 | 235 |
| 10th | 288 | 330 | 433 | 243 |

Umpires: G. Borwick and J.D. Scott.

# AUSTRALIA v ENGLAND 1936–37 (5th Test)

Played at Melbourne Cricket Ground on 26, 27 February, 1, 2, 3 March.
Toss: Australia.    Result: AUSTRALIA won by an innings and 200 runs.
Debuts: Nil.

This was the first time that any country had won a Test rubber after losing the first two matches. The five matches attracted 943,000 spectators – the biggest attendance for any Test rubber.

## AUSTRALIA

| | | |
|---|---|---|
| J.H.W. Fingleton | c Voce b Farnes | 17 |
| K.E. Rigg | c Ames b Farnes | 28 |
| D.G. Bradman* | b Farnes | 169 |
| S.J. McCabe | c Farnes b Verity | 112 |
| C.L. Badcock | c Worthington b Voce | 118 |
| R.G. Gregory | c Verity b Farnes | 80 |
| W.A.S. Oldfield† | c Ames b Voce | 21 |
| L.J. Nash | c Ames b Farnes | 17 |
| W.J. O'Reilly | b Voce | 1 |
| E.L. McCormick | not out | 17 |
| L. O'B. Fleetwood-Smith | b Farnes | 13 |
| Extras | (B 1, LB 5, W 1, NB 4) | 11 |
| **Total** | | **604** |

## ENGLAND

| | | | | | |
|---|---|---|---|---|---|
| C.J. Barnett | c Oldfield b Nash | 18 | lbw b O'Reilly | 41 |
| T.S. Worthington | hit wkt b Fleetwood-Smith | 44 | c Bradman b McCormick | 6 |
| J. Hardstaff, jr | c McCormick b O'Reilly | 83 | b Nash | 1 |
| W.R. Hammond | c Nash b O'Reilly | 14 | c Bradman b O'Reilly | 56 |
| M. Leyland | b O'Reilly | 7 | c McCormick b Fleetwood-Smith | 28 |
| R.E.S. Wyatt | c Bradman b O'Reilly | 38 | run out | 9 |
| L.E.G. Ames† | b Nash | 19 | c McCabe b McCormick | 11 |
| G.O.B. Allen* | c Oldfield b Nash | 0 | c Nash b O'Reilly | 7 |
| H. Verity | c Rigg b Nash | 0 | not out | 2 |
| W. Voce | st Oldfield b O'Reilly | 3 | c Badcock b Fleetwood-Smith | 1 |
| K. Farnes | not out | 0 | c Nash b Fleetwood-Smith | 0 |
| Extras | (LB 12, NB 1) | 13 | (LB 3) | 3 |
| **Total** | | **239** | | **165** |

| ENGLAND | O | M | R | W | O | M | R | W | | FALL OF WICKETS | | |
|---|---|---|---|---|---|---|---|---|---|---|---|---|
| Allen | 17 | 0 | 99 | 0 | | | | | | A | E | E |
| Farnes | 28·5 | 5 | 96 | 6 | | | | | Wkt | 1st | 1st | 2nd |
| Voce | 29 | 3 | 123 | 3 | | | | | 1st | 42 | 33 | 9 |
| Hammond | 16 | 1 | 62 | 0 | | | | | 2nd | 54 | 96 | 10 |
| Verity | 41 | 5 | 127 | 1 | | | | | 3rd | 303 | 130 | 70 |
| Worthington | 6 | 0 | 60 | 0 | | | | | 4th | 346 | 140 | 121 |
| Leyland | 3 | 0 | 26 | 0 | | | | | 5th | 507 | 202 | 142 |
| | | | | | | | | | 6th | 544 | 236 | 142 |
| AUSTRALIA | | | | | | | | | 7th | 563 | 236 | 153 |
| McCormick | 13 | 1 | 54 | 0 | 9 | 0 | 33 | 2 | 8th | 571 | 236 | 162 |
| Nash | 17·5 | 1 | 70 | 4 | 7 | 1 | 34 | 1 | 9th | 576 | 239 | 165 |
| O'Reilly | 23 | 7 | 51 | 5 | 19 | 6 | 58 | 3 | 10th | 604 | 239 | 165 |
| Fleetwood-Smith | 18 | 3 | 51 | 1 | 13·2 | 3 | 36 | 3 | | | | |
| McCabe | | | | | 1 | 0 | 1 | 0 | | | | |

Umpires: G. Borwick and J.D. Scott.

## ENGLAND v NEW ZEALAND 1937 (1st Test)

Played at Lord's, London, on 26, 28, 29 June.
Toss: England.   Result: MATCH DRAWN.
Debuts: England – L. Hutton (later Sir Leonard Hutton), J.H. Parks; New Zealand – J. Cowie (*not* '*J.A.*'), M.P. Donnelly, W.A. Hadlee, D.A.R. Moloney, E.W.T. Tindill, W.M. Wallace.

The partnership of 245 between Hammond and Hardstaff is still the highest third wicket stand by either country in this series. When his score reached 23 Hammond passed J.B. Hobbs' record Test aggregate of 5,410.

### ENGLAND

| | | | | |
|---|---|--:|---|--:|
| L. Hutton | b Cowie | 0 | c Vivian b Cowie | 1 |
| J.H. Parks | b Cowie | 22 | b Cowie | 7 |
| J. Hardstaff, jr | c Moloney b Roberts | 114 | c Tindill b Roberts | 64 |
| W.R. Hammond | c Roberts b Vivian | 140 | | |
| E. Paynter | c Dunning b Roberts | 74 | | |
| C.J. Barnett | b Cowie | 5 | (4) not out | 83 |
| L.E.G. Ames† | b Vivian | 5 | (5) c sub (J.R. Lamason) b Roberts | 20 |
| R.W.V. Robins* | c Tindill b Roberts | 18 | (6) not out | 38 |
| W. Voce | c Tindill b Cowie | 27 | | |
| H. Verity | c Cowie b Roberts | 3 | | |
| A.R. Gover | not out | 2 | | |
| Extras | (B 4, LB 9, W 1) | 14 | (B 5, LB 8) | 13 |
| **Total** | | **424** | (4 wickets declared) | **226** |

### NEW ZEALAND

| | | | | |
|---|---|--:|---|--:|
| H.G. Vivian | lbw b Gover | 5 | c Verity b Voce | 11 |
| J.L. Kerr | c Ames b Robins | 31 | (7) not out | 38 |
| W.A. Hadlee | c Verity b Voce | 34 | (2) b Voce | 3 |
| M.L. Page* | c Paynter b Robins | 9 | c and b Robins | 13 |
| W.M. Wallace | lbw b Parks | 52 | lbw b Parks | 56 |
| M.P. Donnelly | lbw b Parks | 0 | (9) c Ames b Voce | 21 |
| D.A.R. Moloney | c and b Verity | 64 | (3) run out | 0 |
| E.W.T. Tindill† | c Hammond b Robins | 8 | lbw b Verity | 3 |
| A.W. Roberts | not out | 66 | (6) c sub (G.E. Hart) b Gover | 17 |
| J.A. Dunning | b Gover | 0 | | |
| J. Cowie | lbw b Voce | 2 | | |
| Extras | (B 4, LB 18, NB 2) | 24 | (B 4, LB 8, W 1) | 13 |
| **Total** | | **295** | (8 wickets) | **175** |

| NEW ZEALAND | O | M | R | W | O | M | R | W | | FALL OF | WICKETS | | |
|---|--:|--:|--:|--:|--:|--:|--:|--:|---|--:|--:|--:|--:|
| Cowie | 41 | 10 | 118 | 4 | 15 | 2 | 49 | 2 | | E | NZ | E | NZ |
| Roberts | 43·3 | 11 | 101 | 4 | 14 | 3 | 73 | 2 | *Wkt* | *1st* | *1st* | *2nd* | *2nd* |
| Dunning | 20 | 3 | 64 | 0 | 9 | 0 | 60 | 0 | 1st | 13 | 9 | 8 | 15 |
| Vivian | 46 | 10 | 106 | 2 | 4 | 0 | 31 | 0 | 2nd | 31 | 36 | 19 | 15 |
| Moloney | 2 | 1 | 9 | 0 | | | | | 3rd | 276 | 66 | 123 | 15 |
| Page | 3 | 0 | 12 | 0 | | | | | 4th | 284 | 131 | 163 | 85 |
| | | | | | | | | | 5th | 302 | 131 | – | 87 |
| ENGLAND | | | | | | | | | 6th | 307 | 147 | – | 143 |
| Gover | 22 | 8 | 49 | 2 | 18 | 7 | 27 | 1 | 7th | 339 | 176 | – | 146 |
| Voce | 24·2 | 2 | 74 | 2 | 18·5 | 8 | 41 | 3 | 8th | 402 | 280 | – | 175 |
| Hammond | 6 | 2 | 12 | 0 | | | | | 9th | 415 | 281 | – | – |
| Robins | 21 | 5 | 58 | 3 | 16 | 3 | 51 | 1 | 10th | 424 | 295 | – | – |
| Verity | 25 | 13 | 48 | 1 | 14 | 7 | 33 | 1 | | | | | |
| Parks | 11 | 3 | 26 | 2 | 10 | 6 | 10 | 1 | | | | | |
| Hutton | 2 | 1 | 4 | 0 | | | | | | | | | |

Umpires: F. Chester and F. Walden.

# ENGLAND v NEW ZEALAND 1937 (2nd Test)

Played at Old Trafford, Manchester, on 24, 26, 27 July.
Toss: England.   Result: ENGLAND won by 130 runs.
Debuts: England – A.W. Wellard; New Zealand – N. Gallichan.

## ENGLAND

| | | | | | |
|---|---|---|---|---|---|
| L. Hutton | c Dunning b Vivian | 100 | c Vivian b Cowie | | 14 |
| C.J. Barnett | c Kerr b Cowie | 62 | lbw b Dunning | | 12 |
| J. Hardstaff, jr | st Tindill b Vivian | 58 | c Tindill b Cowie | | 11 |
| W.R. Hammond | b Gallichan | 33 | c Moloney b Cowie | | 0 |
| E. Paynter | lbw b Cowie | 33 | c Cowie b Vivian | | 7 |
| L.E.G. Ames† | not out | 16 | lbw b Dunning | | 39 |
| A.W. Wellard | b Cowie | 5 | (8) c Wallace b Vivian | | 0 |
| R.W.V. Robins* | b Cowie | 14 | (7) c Moloney b Cowie | | 12 |
| F.R. Brown | b Gallichan | 1 | b Cowie | | 57 |
| C.I.J. Smith | c Kerr b Gallichan | 21 | c and b Cowie | | 27 |
| T.W.J. Goddard | not out | 4 | not out | | 1 |
| Extras | (B 4, LB 7) | 11 | (LB 7) | | 7 |
| **Total** | (9 wickets declared) | **358** | | | **187** |

## NEW ZEALAND

| | | | | | |
|---|---|---|---|---|---|
| H.G. Vivian | b Wellard | 58 | c Ames b Smith | | 50 |
| D.A.R. Moloney | lbw b Smith | 11 | run out | | 20 |
| W.M. Wallace | st Ames b Brown | 23 | b Goddard | | 5 |
| J.L. Kerr | b Wellard | 4 | b Smith | | 3 |
| M.P. Donnelly | lbw b Wellard | 4 | not out | | 37 |
| W.A. Hadlee | hit wkt b Wellard | 93 | (7) b Goddard | | 3 |
| M.L. Page* | c Smith b Hammond | 33 | (6) b Goddard | | 2 |
| E.W.T. Tindill† | b Brown | 6 | lbw b Brown | | 0 |
| N. Gallichan | c Brown b Smith | 30 | c Wellard b Goddard | | 2 |
| J.A. Dunning | not out | 4 | b Goddard | | 3 |
| J. Cowie | st Ames b Brown | 0 | c Wellard b Goddard | | 0 |
| Extras | (B 4, LB 11) | 15 | (B 7, LB 1, NB 1) | | 9 |
| **Total** | | **281** | | | **134** |

| NEW ZEALAND | O | M | R | W | O | M | R | W |
|---|---|---|---|---|---|---|---|---|
| Cowie | 32 | 6 | 73 | 4 | 23·5 | 6 | 67 | 6 |
| Dunning | 28 | 5 | 84 | 0 | 12 | 2 | 35 | 2 |
| Gallichan | 36 | 7 | 99 | 3 | 8 | 4 | 14 | 0 |
| Vivian | 28 | 7 | 75 | 2 | 17 | 5 | 64 | 2 |
| Page | 5 | 0 | 16 | 0 | | | | |
| ENGLAND | | | | | | | | |
| Smith | 22 | 7 | 29 | 2 | 14 | 2 | 34 | 2 |
| Wellard | 30 | 4 | 81 | 4 | 14 | 2 | 30 | 0 |
| Hammond | 15 | 5 | 27 | 1 | 6 | 1 | 18 | 0 |
| Goddard | 18 | 5 | 48 | 0 | 14·4 | 5 | 29 | 6 |
| Brown | 22·4 | 4 | 81 | 3 | 5 | 0 | 14 | 1 |

| FALL OF WICKETS | | | | |
|---|---|---|---|---|
| | E | NZ | E | NZ |
| Wkt | 1st | 1st | 2nd | 2nd |
| 1st | 100 | 19 | 17 | 50 |
| 2nd | 228 | 65 | 29 | 68 |
| 3rd | 231 | 91 | 29 | 73 |
| 4th | 296 | 105 | 46 | 94 |
| 5th | 302 | 119 | 46 | 102 |
| 6th | 307 | 218 | 68 | 104 |
| 7th | 327 | 242 | 75 | 109 |
| 8th | 328 | 268 | 147 | 116 |
| 9th | 352 | 280 | 186 | 134 |
| 10th | – | 281 | 187 | 134 |

Umpires: W. Reeves and E.J. Smith.

# ENGLAND v NEW ZEALAND 1937 (3rd Test)

Played at Kennington Oval, London, on 14, 16, 17 August.
Toss: New Zealand.   Result: MATCH DRAWN.
Debuts: England – D.C.S. Compton, A.D.G. Matthews, C. Washbrook.

Only half an hour's play was possible on the first day.

## NEW ZEALAND

| | | | | | |
|---|---|---|---|---|---|
| H.G. Vivian | c Ames b Gover | 13 | | lbw b Hammond | 57 |
| W.A. Hadlee | b Matthews | 18 | | c Compton b Matthews | 0 |
| W.M. Wallace | run out | 8 | | lbw b Gover | 7 |
| G.L. Weir | c Matthews b Gover | 3 | | c Hutton b Goddard | 8 |
| M.P. Donnelly | c Hutton b Robins | 58 | (6) | c Ames b Hammond | 0 |
| D.A.R. Moloney | b Hammond | 23 | (5) | b Compton | 38 |
| M.L. Page* | c Washbrook b Robins | 53 | | absent hurt | – |
| A.W. Roberts | c Barnett b Gover | 50 | (7) | lbw b Goddard | 9 |
| E.W.T. Tindill† | b Robins | 4 | (8) | not out | 37 |
| J.A. Dunning | c Gover b Robins | 0 | (9) | b Compton | 19 |
| J. Cowie | not out | 4 | (10) | c Robins b Hutton | 2 |
| Extras | (B 2, LB 11, NB 2) | 15 | | (B 4, LB 5, NB 1) | 10 |
| **Total** | | **249** | | | **187** |

## ENGLAND

| | | | | | |
|---|---|---|---|---|---|
| L. Hutton | c and b Vivian | 12 | | | |
| C.J. Barnett | c Hadlee b Cowie | 13 | | c Roberts b Dunning | 21 |
| C. Washbrook | lbw b Vivian | 9 | (1) | not out | 8 |
| D.C.S. Compton | run out | 65 | | | |
| J. Hardstaff, jr | b Cowie | 103 | | | |
| W.R. Hammond | c Wallace b Cowie | 31 | | | |
| L.E.G. Ames† | not out | 6 | | | |
| R.W.V. Robins* | c and b Roberts | 9 | | | |
| A.D.G. Matthews | not out | 2 | | | |
| T.W.J. Goddard | ) did not bat | | | | |
| A.R. Gover | ) | | | | |
| Extras | (B 2, LB 1, W 1) | 4 | | (LB 2) | 2 |
| **Total** | (7 wickets declared) | **254** | | (1 wicket) | **31** |

| ENGLAND | O | M | R | W | O | M | R | W | | FALL OF WICKETS | | | |
|---|---|---|---|---|---|---|---|---|---|---|---|---|---|
| | | | | | | | | | | NZ | E | NZ | E |
| Gover | 28 | 3 | 85 | 3 | 12 | 1 | 42 | 1 | | | | | |
| Matthews | 22 | 6 | 52 | 1 | 8 | 2 | 13 | 1 | *Wkt* | *1st* | *1st* | *2nd* | *2nd* |
| Goddard | 10 | 2 | 25 | 0 | 18 | 8 | 41 | 2 | 1st | 22 | 15 | 4 | 31 |
| Hammond | 7 | 1 | 25 | 1 | 11 | 3 | 19 | 2 | 2nd | 36 | 31 | 19 | – |
| Robins | 14·1 | 2 | 40 | 4 | 11 | 2 | 24 | 0 | 3rd | 42 | 36 | 46 | – |
| Hutton | 2 | 0 | 7 | 0 | 2·4 | 1 | 4 | 1 | 4th | 47 | 161 | 87 | – |
| Compton | | | | | 6 | 0 | 34 | 2 | 5th | 97 | 222 | 94 | – |
| | | | | | | | | | 6th | 145 | 240 | 107 | – |
| NEW ZEALAND | | | | | | | | | 7th | 222 | 249 | 150 | – |
| Cowie | 24 | 5 | 73 | 3 | 4 | 1 | 15 | 0 | 8th | 244 | – | 182 | – |
| Roberts | 15 | 4 | 26 | 1 | 4 | 1 | 9 | 0 | 9th | 244 | – | 187 | – |
| Dunning | 25 | 5 | 89 | 0 | 1·2 | 0 | 5 | 1 | 10th | 249 | – | – | – |
| Vivian | 29 | 5 | 62 | 2 | | | | | | | | | |

Umpires: A. Dolphin and E.J. Smith.

# ENGLAND v AUSTRALIA 1938 (1st Test)

Played at Trent Bridge, Nottingham, on 10, 11, 13, 14 June.
Toss: England.  Result: MATCH DRAWN.
Debuts: England – W.J. Edrich, R.A. Sinfield, D.V.P. Wright; Australia – B.A. Barnett,
A.L. Hassett.

Barnett, 98* at lunch, completed his hundred off the first ball after the interval; it is the nearest that any batsman has come to scoring a century before lunch for England on the first day. This was the only occasion on which four batsmen have scored hundreds in the same innings in this series; Hutton and Compton did so in their first Test against Australia. At 20 years 19 days, Compton remains England's youngest century-maker. Wright bowled Fingleton with his fourth ball in Test cricket.

## ENGLAND

| | | |
|---|---|---:|
| C.J. Barnett | b McCormick | 126 |
| L. Hutton | lbw b Fleetwood-Smith | 100 |
| W.J. Edrich | b O'Reilly | 5 |
| W.R. Hammond* | b O'Reilly | 26 |
| E. Paynter | not out | 216 |
| D.C.S. Compton | c Badcock b Fleetwood-Smith | 102 |
| L.E.G. Ames† | b Fleetwood-Smith | 46 |
| H. Verity | b Fleetwood-Smith | 3 |
| R.A. Sinfield | lbw b O'Reilly | 6 |
| D.V.P. Wright | not out | 1 |
| K. Farnes | did not bat | |
| Extras | (B 1, LB 22, NB 4) | 27 |
| **Total** | **(8 wickets declared)** | **658** |

## AUSTRALIA

| | | | | | |
|---|---|---:|---|---|---:|
| J.H.W. Fingleton | b Wright | 9 | c Hammond b Edrich | | 40 |
| W.A. Brown | c Ames b Farnes | 48 | c Paynter b Verity | | 133 |
| D.G. Bradman* | c Ames b Sinfield | 51 | not out | | 144 |
| S.J. McCabe | c Compton b Verity | 232 | c Hammond b Verity | | 39 |
| F.A. Ward | b Farnes | 2 | (8) not out | | 7 |
| A.L. Hassett | c Hammond b Wright | 1 | (5) c Compton b Verity | | 2 |
| C.L. Badcock | b Wright | 9 | (6) b Wright | | 5 |
| B.A. Barnett† | c Wright b Farnes | 22 | (7) lbw b Sinfield | | 31 |
| W.J. O'Reilly | c Paynter b Farnes | 9 | | | |
| E.L. McCormick | b Wright | 2 | | | |
| L.O'B. Fleetwood-Smith | not out | 5 | | | |
| Extras | (B 10, LB 10, W 1) | 21 | (B 5, LB 16, NB 5) | | 26 |
| **Total** | | **411** | **(6 wickets)** | | **427** |

| AUSTRALIA | O | M | R | W | O | M | R | W |
|---|---:|---:|---:|---:|---:|---:|---:|---:|
| McCormick | 32 | 4 | 108 | 1 | | | | |
| O'Reilly | 56 | 11 | 164 | 3 | | | | |
| McCabe | 21 | 5 | 64 | 0 | | | | |
| Fleetwood-Smith | 49 | 9 | 153 | 4 | | | | |
| Ward | 30 | 2 | 142 | 0 | | | | |
| **ENGLAND** | | | | | | | | |
| Farnes | 37 | 11 | 106 | 4 | 24 | 2 | 78 | 0 |
| Hammond | 19 | 7 | 44 | 0 | 12 | 6 | 15 | 0 |
| Sinfield | 28 | 8 | 51 | 1 | 35 | 8 | 72 | 1 |
| Wright | 39 | 6 | 153 | 4 | 37 | 8 | 85 | 1 |
| Verity | 7·3 | 0 | 36 | 1 | 62 | 27 | 102 | 3 |
| Edrich | | | | | 13 | 2 | 39 | 1 |
| Barnett | | | | | 1 | 0 | 10 | 0 |

### FALL OF WICKETS

| | E | A | A |
|---|---:|---:|---:|
| Wkt | 1st | 1st | 2nd |
| 1st | 219 | 34 | 89 |
| 2nd | 240 | 111 | 259 |
| 3rd | 244 | 134 | 331 |
| 4th | 281 | 144 | 337 |
| 5th | 487 | 151 | 369 |
| 6th | 577 | 194 | 417 |
| 7th | 597 | 263 | – |
| 8th | 626 | 319 | – |
| 9th | – | 334 | – |
| 10th | – | 411 | – |

Umpires: F. Chester and E. Robinson.

# ENGLAND v AUSTRALIA 1938 (2nd Test)

Played at Lord's, London, on 24, 25, 27, 28 June.
Toss: England.   Result: MATCH DRAWN.
Debuts: Nil.

Hammond's 240 is still the highest score for England against Australia at Lord's and the highest by an England captain against Australia. Bradman overtook J.B. Hobbs' record aggregate of 3,636 in this series. Paynter kept wicket and caught Barnett after Ames had fractured a finger. Chipperfield (injured finger) was unable to complete his ninth over.

## ENGLAND

| | | | | | |
|---|---|--:|---|---|--:|
| C.J. Barnett | c Brown b McCormick | 18 | c McCabe b McCormick | | 12 |
| L. Hutton | c Brown b McCormick | 4 | c McCormick b O'Reilly | | 5 |
| W.J. Edrich | b McCormick | 0 | (4) c McCabe b McCormick | | 10 |
| W.R. Hammond* | b McCormick | 240 | (6) c sub (M.G. Waite) b McCabe | | 2 |
| E. Paynter | lbw b O'Reilly | 99 | run out | | 43 |
| D.C.S. Compton | lbw b O'Reilly | 6 | (7) not out | | 76 |
| L.E.G. Ames† | c McCormick b Fleetwood-Smith | 83 | (8) c McCabe b O'Reilly | | 6 |
| H. Verity | b O'Reilly | 5 | (3) b McCormick | | 11 |
| A.W. Wellard | b McCormick b O'Reilly | 4 | b McCabe | | 38 |
| D.V.P. Wright | b Fleetwood-Smith | 6 | not out | | 10 |
| K. Farnes | not out | 5 | | | |
| Extras | (B 1, LB 12, W 1, NB 10) | 24 | (B 12, LB 12, W 1, NB 4) | | 29 |
| **Total** | | **494** | (8 wickets declared) | | **242** |

## AUSTRALIA

| | | | | | |
|---|---|--:|---|---|--:|
| J.H.W. Fingleton | c Hammond b Wright | 31 | c Hammond b Wellard | | 4 |
| W.A. Brown | not out | 206 | b Verity | | 10 |
| D.G. Bradman* | b Verity | 18 | not out | | 102 |
| S.J. McCabe | c Verity b Farnes | 38 | c Hutton b Verity | | 21 |
| A.L. Hassett | lbw b Wellard | 56 | b Wright | | 42 |
| C.L. Badcock | b Wellard | 0 | c Wright b Edrich | | 0 |
| B.A. Barnett† | c Compton b Verity | 8 | c Paynter b Edrich | | 14 |
| A.G. Chipperfield | lbw b Verity | 1 | | | |
| W.J. O'Reilly | b Farnes | 42 | | | |
| E.L. McCormick | c Barnett b Farnes | 0 | | | |
| L.O'B. Fleetwood-Smith | c Barnett b Verity | 7 | | | |
| Extras | (B 1, LB 8, NB 6) | 15 | (B 5, LB 3, W 2, NB 1) | | 11 |
| **Total** | | **422** | (6 wickets) | | **204** |

| AUSTRALIA | O | M | R | W | O | M | R | W |
|---|--:|--:|--:|--:|--:|--:|--:|--:|
| McCormick | 27 | 1 | 101 | 4 | 24 | 5 | 72 | 3 |
| McCabe | 31 | 4 | 86 | 0 | 12 | 1 | 58 | 2 |
| Fleetwood-Smith | 33·5 | 2 | 139 | 2 | 7 | 1 | 30 | 0 |
| O'Reilly | 37 | 6 | 93 | 4 | 29 | 10 | 53 | 2 |
| Chipperfield | 8·4 | 0 | 51 | 0 | | | | |
| ENGLAND | | | | | | | | |
| Farnes | 43 | 6 | 135 | 3 | 13 | 3 | 51 | 0 |
| Wellard | 23 | 2 | 96 | 2 | 9 | 1 | 30 | 1 |
| Wright | 16 | 2 | 68 | 1 | 8 | 0 | 56 | 1 |
| Verity | 35·4 | 9 | 103 | 4 | 13 | 5 | 29 | 2 |
| Edrich | 4 | 2 | 5 | 0 | 5·2 | 0 | 27 | 2 |

### FALL OF WICKETS

| Wkt | E 1st | A 1st | E 2nd | A 2nd |
|---|--:|--:|--:|--:|
| 1st | 12 | 69 | 25 | 8 |
| 2nd | 20 | 101 | 28 | 71 |
| 3rd | 31 | 152 | 43 | 111 |
| 4th | 253 | 276 | 64 | 175 |
| 5th | 271 | 276 | 76 | 180 |
| 6th | 457 | 307 | 128 | 204 |
| 7th | 472 | 308 | 142 | – |
| 8th | 476 | 393 | 216 | – |
| 9th | 483 | 393 | – | – |
| 10th | 494 | 422 | – | – |

Umpires: E.J. Smith and F. Walden.

The 3rd Test at Old Trafford, Manchester, scheduled for 8, 9, 11, 12 July, was abandoned without a ball being bowled (see page 837).

# ENGLAND v AUSTRALIA 1938 (4th Test)

Played at Headingley, Leeds, on 22, 23, 25 July.
Toss: England.   Result: AUSTRALIA won by five wickets.
Debuts: England – W.F.F. Price; Australia – M.G. Waite.

Bradman scored his third hundred in successive Test innings at Leeds.

## ENGLAND

| | | | | | |
|---|---|---|---|---|---|
| W.J. Edrich | b O'Reilly | 12 | st Barnett b Fleetwood-Smith | | 28 |
| C.J. Barnett | c Barnett b McCormick | 30 | c Barnett b McCormick | | 29 |
| J. Hardstaff, jr | run out | 4 | b O'Reilly | | 11 |
| W.R. Hammond* | b O'Reilly | 76 | c Brown b O'Reilly | | 0 |
| E. Paynter | st Barnett b Fleetwood-Smith | 28 | not out | | 21 |
| D.C.S. Compton | b O'Reilly | 14 | c Barnett b O'Reilly | | 15 |
| W.F.F. Price† | c McCabe b O'Reilly | 0 | lbw b Fleetwood-Smith | | 6 |
| H. Verity | not out | 25 | b Fleetwood-Smith | | 0 |
| D.V.P. Wright | c Fingleton b Fleetwood-Smith | 22 | c Waite b Fleetwood-Smith | | 0 |
| K. Farnes | c Fingleton b Fleetwood-Smith | 2 | b O'Reilly | | 7 |
| W.E. Bowes | b O'Reilly | 3 | lbw b O'Reilly | | 0 |
| Extras | (LB 4, NB 3) | 7 | (LB 4, W 1, NB 1) | | 6 |
| **Total** | | **223** | | | **123** |

## AUSTRALIA

| | | | | | |
|---|---|---|---|---|---|
| J.H.W. Fingleton | b Verity | 30 | | lbw b Verity | 9 |
| W.A. Brown | b Wright | 22 | | lbw b Farnes | 9 |
| B.A. Barnett† | c Price b Farnes | 57 | (7) | not out | 15 |
| D.G. Bradman* | b Bowes | 103 | (3) | c Verity b Wright | 16 |
| S.J. McCabe | b Farnes | 1 | (4) | c Barnett b Wright | 15 |
| C.L. Badcock | b Bowes | 4 | | not out | 5 |
| A.L. Hassett | c Hammond b Wright | 13 | (5) | c Edrich b Wright | 33 |
| M.G. Waite | c Price b Farnes | 3 | | | |
| W.J. O'Reilly | c Hammond b Farnes | 2 | | | |
| E.L. McCormick | b Bowes | 0 | | | |
| L.O'B. Fleetwood-Smith | not out | 2 | | | |
| Extras | (B 2, LB 3) | 5 | | (B 4, NB 1) | 5 |
| **Total** | | **242** | | **(5 wickets)** | **107** |

| AUSTRALIA | O | M | R | W | O | M | R | W |
|---|---|---|---|---|---|---|---|---|
| McCormick | 20 | 6 | 46 | 1 | 11 | 4 | 18 | 1 |
| Waite | 18 | 7 | 31 | 0 | 2 | 0 | 9 | 0 |
| O'Reilly | 34·1 | 17 | 66 | 5 | 21·5 | 8 | 56 | 5 |
| Fleetwood-Smith | 25 | 7 | 73 | 3 | 16 | 4 | 34 | 4 |
| McCabe | 1 | 1 | 0 | 0 | | | | |
| ENGLAND | | | | | | | | |
| Farnes | 26 | 3 | 77 | 4 | 11·3 | 4 | 17 | 1 |
| Bowes | 35·4 | 6 | 79 | 3 | 11 | 0 | 35 | 0 |
| Wright | 15 | 4 | 38 | 2 | 5 | 0 | 26 | 3 |
| Verity | 19 | 6 | 30 | 1 | 5 | 2 | 24 | 1 |
| Edrich | 3 | 0 | 13 | 0 | | | | |

### FALL OF WICKETS

| Wkt | E 1st | A 1st | E 2nd | A 2nd |
|---|---|---|---|---|
| 1st | 29 | 28 | 60 | 17 |
| 2nd | 34 | 87 | 73 | 32 |
| 3rd | 88 | 128 | 73 | 50 |
| 4th | 142 | 136 | 73 | 61 |
| 5th | 171 | 145 | 96 | 91 |
| 6th | 171 | 195 | 116 | – |
| 7th | 172 | 232 | 116 | – |
| 8th | 213 | 240 | 116 | – |
| 9th | 215 | 240 | 123 | – |
| 10th | 223 | 242 | 123 | – |

Umpires: F. Chester and E.J. Smith.

# ENGLAND v AUSTRALIA 1938 (5th Test)

Played at Kennington Oval, London, on 20, 22, 23, 24 August.
Toss: England.   Result: ENGLAND won by an innings and 579 runs.
Debuts: England – A. Wood; Australia – S.G. Barnes.

England's total and margin of victory remain records for all Test cricket – as does the 298 runs conceded by Fleetwood-Smith. Hutton's score, length of innings (13 hours 17 minutes), and partnership of 382 with Leyland remain England records against Australia, the partnership being their best for any wicket. Bradman injured his ankle while bowling his third over.

## ENGLAND

| | | |
|---|---|---:|
| L. Hutton | c Hassett b O'Reilly | 364 |
| W.J. Edrich | lbw b O'Reilly | 12 |
| M. Leyland | run out | 187 |
| W.R. Hammond* | lbw b Fleetwood-Smith | 59 |
| E. Paynter | lbw b O'Reilly | 0 |
| D.C.S. Compton | b Waite | 1 |
| J. Hardstaff, jr | not out | 169 |
| A. Wood† | c and b Barnes | 53 |
| H. Verity | not out | 8 |
| K. Farnes | ) did not bat | |
| W.E. Bowes | ) | |
| Extras | (B 22, LB 19, W 1, NB 8) | 50 |
| **Total** | (7 wickets declared) | **903** |

## AUSTRALIA

| | | | | |
|---|---|---:|---|---:|
| W.A. Brown | c Hammond b Leyland | 69 | c Edrich b Farnes | 15 |
| C.L. Badcock | c Hardstaff b Bowes | 0 | b Bowes | 9 |
| S.J. McCabe | c Edrich b Farnes | 14 | c Wood b Farnes | 2 |
| A.L. Hassett | c Compton b Edrich | 42 | lbw b Bowes | 10 |
| S.G. Barnes | b Bowes | 41 | lbw b Verity | 33 |
| B.A. Barnett† | c Wood b Bowes | 2 | b Farnes | 46 |
| M.G. Waite | b Bowes | 8 | c Edrich b Verity | 0 |
| W.J. O'Reilly | c Wood b Bowes | 0 | not out | 7 |
| L.O'B. Fleetwood-Smith | not out | 16 | c Leyland b Farnes | 0 |
| D.G. Bradman* | absent hurt | – | absent hurt | – |
| J.H.W. Fingleton | absent hurt | – | absent hurt | – |
| Extras | (B 4, LB 2, NB 3) | 9 | (B 1) | 1 |
| **Total** | | **201** | | **123** |

| AUSTRALIA | O | M | R | W | O | M | R | W |
|---|---:|---:|---:|---:|---:|---:|---:|---:|
| Waite | 72 | 16 | 150 | 1 | | | | |
| McCabe | 38 | 8 | 85 | 0 | | | | |
| O'Reilly | 85 | 26 | 178 | 3 | | | | |
| Fleetwood-Smith | 87 | 11 | 298 | 1 | | | | |
| Barnes | 38 | 3 | 84 | 1 | | | | |
| Hassett | 13 | 2 | 52 | 0 | | | | |
| Bradman | 2·2 | 1 | 6 | 0 | | | | |
| ENGLAND | | | | | | | | |
| Farnes | 13 | 2 | 54 | 1 | 12·1 | 1 | 63 | 4 |
| Bowes | 19 | 3 | 49 | 5 | 10 | 3 | 25 | 2 |
| Edrich | 10 | 2 | 55 | 1 | | | | |
| Verity | 5 | 1 | 15 | 0 | 7 | 3 | 15 | 2 |
| Leyland | 3·1 | 0 | 11 | 1 | 5 | 0 | 19 | 0 |
| Hammond | 2 | 0 | 8 | 0 | | | | |

| | FALL OF WICKETS | | |
|---|---:|---:|---:|
| | E | A | A |
| Wkt | 1st | 1st | 2nd |
| 1st | 29 | 0 | 15 |
| 2nd | 411 | 19 | 18 |
| 3rd | 546 | 70 | 35 |
| 4th | 547 | 145 | 41 |
| 5th | 555 | 147 | 115 |
| 6th | 770 | 160 | 115 |
| 7th | 876 | 160 | 117 |
| 8th | – | 201 | 123 |
| 9th | – | – | – |
| 10th | – | – | – |

Umpires: F. Chester and F. Walden.

# SOUTH AFRICA v ENGLAND 1938-39 (1st Test)

Played at Old Wanderers, Johannesburg, on 24, 26, 27, 28 December.
Toss: England.   Result: MATCH DRAWN.
Debuts: South Africa – G.E. Bond, N. Gordon, A. Melville, P.G.V. van der Bijl, W.W. Wade;
   England – P.A. Gibb, L.L. Wilkinson, N.W.D. Yardley.

Gibb scored 93 and 106 on his first appearance at Test level, Paynter scored a hundred in each innings and
Goddard took a hat-trick. South Africa achieved a uniquely balanced innings with five fifties and five 'ducks'.

## ENGLAND

| | | | | |
|---|---|---|---|---|
| W.J. Edrich | c Mitchell b Davies | 4 | c Mitchell b Gordon | 10 |
| P.A. Gibb | c Melville b Mitchell | 93 | b Dalton | 106 |
| E. Paynter | b Mitchell | 117 | c Langton b Gordon | 100 |
| W.R. Hammond* | lbw b Gordon | 24 | lbw b Dalton | 58 |
| L.E.G. Ames† | c Wade b Gordon | 42 | not out | 3 |
| N.W.D. Yardley | c and b Mitchell | 7 | | |
| B.H. Valentine | c Wade b Gordon | 97 | | |
| H. Verity | b Dalton | 26 | | |
| L.L. Wilkinson | lbw b Gordon | 2 | | |
| K. Farnes | b Gordon | 0 | | |
| T.W.J. Goddard | not out | 0 | | |
| Extras | (B 3, LB 6, NB 1) | 10 | (B 7, LB 2, W 2, NB 3) | 14 |
| **Total** | | **422** | (4 wickets declared) | **291** |

## SOUTH AFRICA

| | | | | |
|---|---|---|---|---|
| B. Mitchell | b Farnes | 73 | not out | 48 |
| P.G.V. van der Bijl | lbw b Verity | 4 | b Hammond | 38 |
| A. Melville* | c and b Verity | 0 | | |
| A.D. Nourse | c and b Goddard | 73 | (3) not out | 17 |
| N. Gordon | st Ames b Goddard | 0 | | |
| W.W. Wade† | b Goddard | 0 | | |
| K.G. Viljoen | b Wilkinson | 50 | | |
| E.L. Dalton | c Edrich b Verity | 102 | | |
| G.E. Bond | lbw b Wilkinson | 0 | | |
| A.B.C. Langton | not out | 64 | | |
| E.Q. Davies | b Verity | 0 | | |
| Extras | (B 5, LB 18, NB 1) | 24 | (LB 5) | 5 |
| **Total** | | **390** | (1 wicket) | **108** |

| SOUTH AFRICA | O | M | R | W | O | M | R | W | | FALL OF WICKETS | | | |
|---|---|---|---|---|---|---|---|---|---|---|---|---|---|
| Davies | 19 | 0 | 102 | 1 | 14 | 2 | 67 | 0 | | E | SA | E | SA |
| Langton | 27 | 5 | 74 | 0 | 16 | 3 | 64 | 0 | *Wkt* | *1st* | *1st* | *2nd* | *2nd* |
| Gordon | 33·4 | 3 | 103 | 5 | 14 | 0 | 59 | 2 | 1st | 4 | 42 | 38 | 67 |
| Mitchell | 22 | 2 | 75 | 3 | 11 | 1 | 58 | 0 | 2nd | 188 | 44 | 206 | – |
| Dalton | 10 | 1 | 42 | 1 | 6·5 | 0 | 29 | 2 | 3rd | 234 | 160 | 281 | – |
| Bond | 2 | 0 | 16 | 0 | | | | | 4th | 278 | 160 | 291 | – |
| | | | | | | | | | 5th | 292 | 160 | – | – |
| **ENGLAND** | | | | | | | | | 6th | 294 | 173 | – | – |
| Farnes | 23 | 1 | 87 | 1 | 7 | 3 | 17 | 0 | 7th | 378 | 281 | – | – |
| Edrich | 9 | 0 | 44 | 0 | 3 | 0 | 7 | 0 | 8th | 389 | 281 | – | – |
| Verity | 44·1 | 16 | 61 | 4 | 16 | 8 | 17 | 0 | 9th | 415 | 378 | – | – |
| Hammond | 10 | 3 | 27 | 0 | 6 | 3 | 13 | 1 | 10th | 422 | 390 | – | – |
| Wilkinson | 22 | 0 | 93 | 2 | 8 | 3 | 18 | 0 | | | | | |
| Goddard | 27 | 5 | 54 | 3 | 11 | 3 | 31 | 0 | | | | | |

Umpires: R.G.A. Ashman and G.L. Sickler.

# SOUTH AFRICA v ENGLAND 1938–39 (2nd Test)

Played at Newlands, Cape Town, on 31 December, 2, 3, 4 January.
Toss: England.    Result: MATCH DRAWN.
Debuts: Nil.

Hammond and Ames scored 197 runs in 145 minutes; their partnership is still England's highest for the fourth wicket against South Africa.

## ENGLAND

| | | |
|---|---|---|
| L. Hutton | b Gordon | 17 |
| P.A. Gibb | c Wade b Gordon | 58 |
| E. Paynter | lbw b Langton | 1 |
| W.R. Hammond* | b Davies | 181 |
| L.E.G. Ames† | b Gordon | 115 |
| W.J. Edrich | b Gordon | 0 |
| B.H. Valentine | lbw b Gordon | 112 |
| H. Verity | b Langton | 29 |
| D.V.P. Wright | c Nourse b Langton | 33 |
| K. Farnes | not out | 1 |
| T.W.J. Goddard | did not bat | |
| Extras | (LB 9, NB 3) | 12 |
| **Total** | **(9 wickets declared)** | **559** |

## SOUTH AFRICA

| | | | | | |
|---|---|---|---|---|---|
| B. Mitchell | b Wright | 42 | c Ames b Farnes | | 1 |
| P.G.V. van der Bijl | c Valentine b Verity | 37 | hit wkt b Goddard | | 87 |
| E.A.B. Rowan | b Wright | 6 | not out | | 89 |
| A.D. Nourse | lbw b Verity | 120 | not out | | 19 |
| A.W. Briscoe | lbw b Goddard | 2 | | | |
| W.W. Wade† | c Edrich b Verity | 10 | | | |
| A.B.C. Langton | lbw b Goddard | 0 | | | |
| X.C. Balaskas | c Paynter b Verity | 29 | | | |
| A. Melville* | b Verity | 23 | | | |
| N. Gordon | st Ames b Goddard | 0 | | | |
| E.Q. Davies | not out | 0 | | | |
| Extras | (B 2, LB 7, NB 8) | 17 | (B 1, LB 3, NB 1) | | 5 |
| **Total** | | **286** | **(2 wickets)** | | **201** |

| SOUTH AFRICA | O | M | R | W | O | M | R | W | | FALL OF WICKETS | | |
|---|---|---|---|---|---|---|---|---|---|---|---|---|
| Davies | 16 | 1 | 77 | 1 | | | | | | E | SA | SA |
| Langton | 30·7 | 3 | 117 | 3 | | | | | Wkt | 1st | 1st | 2nd |
| Gordon | 40 | 3 | 157 | 5 | | | | | 1st | 29 | 66 | 2 |
| Balaskas | 24 | 0 | 115 | 0 | | | | | 2nd | 30 | 79 | 149 |
| Mitchell | 20 | 0 | 81 | 0 | | | | | 3rd | 139 | 151 | – |
| | | | | | | | | | 4th | 336 | 160 | – |
| ENGLAND | | | | | | | | | 5th | 338 | 176 | – |
| Farnes | 13 | 3 | 37 | 0 | 8 | 1 | 23 | 1 | 6th | 410 | 177 | – |
| Edrich | 5 | 1 | 15 | 0 | 3 | 1 | 5 | 0 | 7th | 504 | 214 | – |
| Goddard | 38 | 15 | 64 | 3 | 11 | 1 | 68 | 1 | 8th | 537 | 283 | – |
| Wright | 26 | 3 | 83 | 2 | 12 | 0 | 62 | 0 | 9th | 559 | 286 | – |
| Verity | 36·6 | 13 | 70 | 5 | 10 | 5 | 13 | 0 | 10th | – | 286 | – |
| Hammond | | | | | 9 | 0 | 25 | 0 | | | | |

Umpires: R.G.A. Ashman and G.L. Sickler.

# SOUTH AFRICA v ENGLAND 1938–39 (3rd Test)

Played at Kingsmead, Durban, on 20, 21, 23 January.
Toss: England.   Result: ENGLAND won by an innings and 13 runs.
Debuts: Nil.

Paynter's 243 is the highest score for either country in this series of Tests. His partnership of 242 with Hammond was scored in less than two hours, the second hundred coming in 42 minutes. Paynter was the first to score double-centuries against both Australia and South Africa.

## ENGLAND

| | | |
|---|---|---|
| L. Hutton | lbw b Gordon | 31 |
| P.A. Gibb | c Wade b Davies | 38 |
| E. Paynter | c Melville b Langton | 243 |
| W.R. Hammond* | c Mitchell b Gordon | 120 |
| L.E.G. Ames† | not out | 27 |
| W.J. Edrich | ) | |
| B.H. Valentine | ) | |
| H. Verity | ) | |
| D.V.P. Wright | ) did not bat | |
| K. Farnes | ) | |
| L.L. Wilkinson | ) | |
| Extras | (B 5, LB 4, NB 1) | 10 |
| **Total** | (4 wickets declared) | **469** |

## SOUTH AFRICA

| | | | | | |
|---|---|---|---|---|---|
| B. Mitchell | c Ames b Edrich | 30 | | c Ames b Farnes | 109 |
| P.G.V. van der Bijl | run out | 28 | | b Verity | 13 |
| E.A.B. Rowan | lbw b Wright | 4 | | c Ames b Hammond | 67 |
| A.D. Nourse | c Hammond b Farnes | 0 | | c Ames b Edrich | 27 |
| K.G. Viljoen | c Hammond b Wright | 2 | | c Hammond b Farnes | 61 |
| E.L. Dalton | b Wilkinson | 12 | (7) | c Hammond b Verity | 8 |
| W.W. Wade† | c Hammond b Farnes | 14 | (8) | lbw b Farnes | 28 |
| A. Melville* | not out | 5 | (6) | b Wilkinson | 10 |
| A.B.C. Langton | c Hutton b Farnes | 0 | | b Wilkinson | 12 |
| N. Gordon | b Farnes | 1 | | c Edrich b Verity | 0 |
| E.Q. Davies | lbw b Wilkinson | 2 | | not out | 2 |
| Extras | (B 1, LB 3, W 1) | 5 | | (B 7, LB 9) | 16 |
| **Total** | | **103** | | | **353** |

| SOUTH AFRICA | O | M | R | W | O | M | R | W |
|---|---|---|---|---|---|---|---|---|
| Davies | 15 | 0 | 106 | 1 | | | | |
| Langton | 23·5 | 0 | 107 | 1 | | | | |
| Gordon | 29 | 0 | 127 | 2 | | | | |
| Mitchell | 8 | 0 | 45 | 0 | | | | |
| Dalton | 13 | 0 | 74 | 0 | | | | |
| ENGLAND | | | | | | | | |
| Farnes | 13 | 1 | 29 | 4 | 28·2 | 8 | 80 | 3 |
| Hammond | 2 | 1 | 2 | 0 | 3 | 0 | 11 | 1 |
| Wright | 12 | 1 | 37 | 2 | 15 | 2 | ·56 | 0 |
| Verity | 8 | 4 | 9 | 0 | 35 | 10 | 71 | 3 |
| Edrich | 4 | 0 | 9 | 1 | 7 | 2 | 16 | 1 |
| Wilkinson | 6·5 | 2 | 12 | 2 | 26 | 4 | 103 | 2 |

FALL OF WICKETS

| Wkt | E 1st | SA 1st | SA 2nd |
|---|---|---|---|
| 1st | 38 | 60 | 46 |
| 2nd | 153 | 61 | 165 |
| 3rd | 395 | 65 | 223 |
| 4th | 469 | 65 | 247 |
| 5th | – | 79 | 282 |
| 6th | – | 87 | 306 |
| 7th | – | 98 | 308 |
| 8th | – | 98 | 345 |
| 9th | – | 100 | 346 |
| 10th | – | 103 | 353 |

Umpires: R.G.A. Ashman and G.L. Sickler.

## SOUTH AFRICA v ENGLAND 1938–39 (4th Test)

Played at Old Wanderers, Johannesburg, on 18, 20, 21 (*no play*), 22 February.
Toss: South Africa.   Result: MATCH DRAWN.
Debuts: South Africa – R.E. Grieveson.

### ENGLAND

| | | | | |
|---|---|---|---|---|
| L. Hutton | b Mitchell | 92 | c Grieveson b Gordon | 3. |
| P.A. Gibb | c Mitchell b Langton | 9 | c Grieveson b Gordon | 4. |
| E. Paynter | c Newson b Langton | 40 | c Grieveson b Newson | 1 |
| W.R. Hammond* | c Newson b Gordon | 1 | not out | 6. |
| L.E.G. Ames† | b Langton | 34 | b Gordon | 1 |
| B.H. Valentine | c Grieveson b Gordon | 11 | not out | 2 |
| W.J. Edrich | lbw b Langton | 6 | | |
| H. Verity | c Rowan b Mitchell | 8 | | |
| K. Farnes | c Grieveson b Newson | 4 | | |
| T.W.J. Goddard | c Van der Bijl b Langton | 8 | | |
| L.L. Wilkinson | not out | 1 | | |
| Extras | (W 1) | 1 | (B 2, LB 6) | 20 |
| **Total** | | **215** | (4 wickets) | **20** |

### SOUTH AFRICA

| | | |
|---|---|---|
| P.G.V. van der Bijl | lbw b Goddard | 31 |
| A. Melville* | c Verity b Wilkinson | 67 |
| E.A.B. Rowan | b Farnes | 85 |
| B. Mitchell | c Ames b Farnes | 63 |
| A.D. Nourse | hit wkt b Verity | 38 |
| A.B.C. Langton | c Hutton b Verity | 6 |
| E.L. Dalton | not out | 20 |
| E.S. Newson | b Hammond | 16 |
| K.G. Viljoen | lbw b Verity | 5 |
| R.E. Grieveson† | ) did not bat | |
| N.Gordon | ) | |
| Extras | (B 5, LB 12, NB 1) | 18 |
| **Total** | (8 wickets declared) | **349** |

| SOUTH AFRICA | O | M | R | W | O | M | R | W | | FALL OF WICKETS | | |
|---|---|---|---|---|---|---|---|---|---|---|---|---|
| | | | | | | | | | | E | SA | E |
| Newson | 13 | 0 | 53 | 1 | 11 | 2 | 22 | 1 | *Wkt* | *1st* | *1st* | *2nd* |
| Langton | 19·2 | 1 | 58 | 5 | 12 | 1 | 49 | 0 | 1st | 18 | 108 | 64 |
| Gordon | 15 | 1 | 47 | 2 | 22 | 4 | 58 | 3 | 2nd | 96 | 108 | 91 |
| Mitchell | 12 | 3 | 37 | 2 | 12 | 1 | 42 | 0 | 3rd | 99 | 224 | 103 |
| Dalton | 5 | 0 | 19 | 0 | 3 | 0 | 24 | 0 | 4th | 159 | 280 | 145 |
| | | | | | | | | | 5th | 187 | 294 | – |
| ENGLAND | | | | | | | | | 6th | 187 | 311 | – |
| Farnes | 26 | 7 | 64 | 2 | | | | | 7th | 197 | 340 | – |
| Edrich | 4 | 0 | 11 | 0 | | | | | 8th | 201 | 349 | – |
| Verity | 37·5 | 10 | 127 | 3 | | | | | 9th | 205 | – | – |
| Goddard | 18 | 2 | 65 | 1 | | | | | 10th | 215 | – | – |
| Wilkinson | 9 | 0 | 45 | 1 | | | | | | | | |
| Hammond | 7 | 1 | 19 | 1 | | | | | | | | |

Umpires: R.G.A. Ashman and G.L. Sickler.

# SOUTH AFRICA v ENGLAND 1938–39 (5th Test)

Played at Kingsmead, Durban, on 3, 4, 6, 7, 8, 9, 10, 11 (*no play*), 13, 14 March.
Toss: South Africa.   Result: MATCH DRAWN.
Debuts: England – R.T.D. Perks.

The most famous Timeless Test, it began when the Editor was 3½ hours old and ended, still undecided, some eleven days later when the tourists had to begin their two-day rail journey back to their ship at Cape Town. It is the longest first-class match ever played (10 days) and produced the highest aggregate (1,981 runs). England's 654 for 5 remains the highest fourth innings total in all first-class cricket.

## SOUTH AFRICA

| | | | | | |
|---|---|---|---|---|---|
| A. Melville* | hit wkt b Wright | 78 | (6) b Farnes | | 103 |
| P.G.V. van der Bijl | b Perks | 125 | c Paynter b Wright | | 97 |
| E.A.B. Rowan | lbw b Perks | 33 | c Edrich b Verity | | 0 |
| B. Mitchell | b Wright | 11 | (1) hit wkt b Verity | | 89 |
| A.D. Nourse | b Perks | 103 | (4) c Hutton b Farnes | | 25 |
| K.G. Viljoen | c Ames b Perks | 0 | (5) b Perks | | 74 |
| E.L. Dalton | c Ames b Farnes | 57 | c and b Wright | | 21 |
| R.E. Grieveson† | b Perks | 75 | b Farnes | | 39 |
| A.B.C. Langton | c Paynter b Verity | 27 | c Hammond b Farnes | | 6 |
| E.S. Newson | c and b Verity | 1 | b Wright | | 3 |
| N. Gordon | not out | 0 | not out | | 7 |
| Extras | (B 2, LB 12, NB 6) | 20 | (B 5, LB 8, NB 4) | | 17 |
| **Total** | | **530** | | | **481** |

## ENGLAND

| | | | | | |
|---|---|---|---|---|---|
| L. Hutton | run out | 38 | b Mitchell | | 55 |
| P.A. Gibb | c Grieveson b Newson | 4 | b Dalton | | 120 |
| E. Paynter | lbw b Langton | 62 | (5) c Grieveson b Gordon | | 75 |
| W.R. Hammond* | st Grieveson b Dalton | 24 | st Grieveson b Dalton | | 140 |
| L.E.G. Ames† | c Dalton b Langton | 84 | (6) not out | | 17 |
| W.J. Edrich | c Rowan b Langton | 1 | (3) c Gordon b Langton | | 219 |
| B.H. Valentine | st Grieveson b Dalton | 26 | not out | | 4 |
| H. Verity | b Dalton | 3 | | | |
| D.V.P. Wright | c Langton b Dalton | 26 | | | |
| K. Farnes | b Newson | 20 | | | |
| R.T.D. Perks | not out | 2 | | | |
| Extras | (B 7, LB 17, W 1, NB 1) | 26 | (B 8, LB 12, W 1, NB 3) | | 24 |
| **Total** | | **316** | (5 wickets) | | **654** |

| ENGLAND | O | M | R | W | O | M | R | W | | FALL OF WICKETS | | | |
|---|---|---|---|---|---|---|---|---|---|---|---|---|---|
| Farnes | 46 | 9 | 108 | 1 | 22·1 | 2 | 74 | 4 | | SA | E | SA | E |
| Perks | 41 | 5 | 100 | 5 | 32 | 6 | 99 | 1 | *Wkt* | *1st* | *1st* | *2nd* | *2nd* |
| Wright | 37 | 6 | 142 | 2 | 32 | 7 | 146 | 3 | 1st | 131 | 9 | 191 | 78 |
| Verity | 55·6 | 14 | 97 | 2 | 40 | 9 | 87 | 2 | 2nd | 219 | 64 | 191 | 358 |
| Hammond | 14 | 4 | 34 | 0 | 9 | 1 | 30 | 0 | 3rd | 236 | 125 | 191 | 447 |
| Edrich | 9 | 2 | 29 | 0 | 6 | 1 | 18 | 0 | 4th | 274 | 169 | 242 | 611 |
| Hutton | | | | | 1 | 0 | 10 | 0 | 5th | 278 | 171 | 346 | 650 |
| | | | | | | | | | 6th | 368 | 229 | 382 | – |
| SOUTH AFRICA | | | | | | | | | 7th | 475 | 245 | 434 | – |
| Newson | 25·6 | 5 | 58 | 2 | 43 | 4 | 91 | 0 | 8th | 522 | 276 | 450 | – |
| Langton | 35 | 12 | 71 | 3 | 56 | 12 | 132 | 1 | 9th | 523 | 305 | 462 | – |
| Gordon | 37 | 7 | 82 | 0 | 55·2 | 10 | 174 | 1 | 10th | 530 | 316 | 481 | – |
| Mitchell | 7 | 0 | 20 | 0 | 37 | 4 | 133 | 1 | | | | | |
| Dalton | 13 | 1 | 59 | 4 | 27 | 3 | 100 | 2 | | | | | |

Umpires: R.G.A. Ashman and G.L. Sickler.

# ENGLAND v WEST INDIES 1939 (1st Test)

Played at Lord's, London, on 24, 26, 27 June.
Toss: West Indies.   Result: ENGLAND won by eight wickets.
Debuts: England – W.H. Copson; West Indies – J.H. Cameron, C.B. Clarke, J.B. Stollmeyer
K.H. Weekes.

Headley was the first to score a hundred in each innings of a Test twice for West Indies.

## WEST INDIES

| | | | | |
|---|---|---|---|---|
| R.S. Grant* | c Compton b Copson | 22 | b Bowes | 2 |
| J.B. Stollmeyer | b Bowes | 59 | c Verity b Copson | |
| G.A. Headley | c Wood b Copson | 106 | c Hutton b Wright | 10 |
| J.E.D. Sealy | c Wood b Wright | 13 | c Wood b Copson | 2 |
| K.H. Weekes | c Gimblett b Copson | 20 | c Wood b Verity | 1 |
| L.N. Constantine | lbw b Copson | 14 | c Hammond b Verity | 1 |
| J.H. Cameron | c Hutton b Bowes | 1 | c and b Wright | |
| I. Barrow† | lbw b Copson | 2 | not out | |
| E.A. Martindale | lbw b Wright | 22 | c Bowes b Wright | |
| L.G. Hylton | not out | 2 | c Hardstaff b Copson | 1 |
| C.B. Clarke | b Bowes | 1 | c and b Copson | |
| Extras | (B 3, LB 9, NB 3) | 15 | (B 6, LB 4, W 1) | 1 |
| **Total** | | **277** | | **22** |

## ENGLAND

| | | | | |
|---|---|---|---|---|
| L. Hutton | c Grant b Hylton | 196 | b Hylton | 1 |
| H. Gimblett | b Cameron | 22 | b Martindale | 2 |
| E. Paynter | c Barrow b Cameron | 34 | not out | 3 |
| W.R. Hammond* | c Grant b Cameron | 14 | not out | 3 |
| D.C.S. Compton | c Stollmeyer b Clarke | 120 | | |
| J. Hardstaff, jr | not out | 3 | | |
| A. Wood† | not out | 0 | | |
| D.V.P. Wright | ) | | | |
| H. Verity | ) did not bat | | | |
| W.H. Copson | ) | | | |
| W.E. Bowes | ) | | | |
| Extras | (B 8, LB 6, W 1) | 15 | (LB 2) | |
| **Total** | (5 wickets declared) | **404** | (2 wickets) | **10** |

| ENGLAND | O | M | R | W | O | M | R | W | | FALL OF WICKETS | | | |
|---|---|---|---|---|---|---|---|---|---|---|---|---|---|
| Bowes | 28·4 | 5 | 86 | 3 | 19 | 7 | 44 | 1 | | WI | E | WI | E |
| Copson | 24 | 2 | 85 | 5 | 16·4 | 2 | 67 | 4 | *Wkt* | *1st* | *1st* | *2nd* | *2nd* |
| Wright | 13 | 1 | 57 | 2 | 17 | 0 | 75 | 3 | 1st | 29 | 49 | 0 | 3 |
| Verity | 16 | 3 | 34 | 0 | 14 | 4 | 20 | 2 | 2nd | 147 | 119 | 42 | 3 |
| Compton | | | | | 3 | 0 | 8 | 0 | 3rd | 180 | 147 | 105 | – |
| | | | | | | | | | 4th | 226 | 395 | 154 | – |
| WEST INDIES | | | | | | | | | 5th | 245 | 402 | 190 | – |
| Martindale | 20 | 2 | 86 | 0 | 7·7 | 0 | 51 | 1 | 6th | 250 | – | 199 | – |
| Hylton | 24 | 4 | 98 | 1 | 7 | 1 | 36 | 1 | 7th | 250 | – | 200 | – |
| Constantine | 13 | 0 | 67 | 0 | 3 | 0 | 11 | 0 | 8th | 261 | – | 204 | – |
| Cameron | 26 | 6 | 66 | 3 | | | | | 9th | 276 | – | 225 | – |
| Clarke | 6 | 0 | 28 | 1 | | | | | 10th | 277 | – | 225 | – |
| Sealy | 3 | 0 | 21 | 0 | | | | | | | | | |
| Grant | 3 | 0 | 23 | 0 | | | | | | | | | |

Umpires: E.J. Smith and F. Walden.

# ENGLAND v WEST INDIES 1939 (2nd Test)

¶ayed at Old Trafford, Mancheter, on 22, 24, 25 July.
oss: West Indies.   Result: MATCH DRAWN.
¶ebuts: West Indies – G.E. Gomez, E.A.V. Williams.

¶ammond bcame the first to hold 100 catches in Test cricket when he caught Headley on the second innings.

## ENGLAND

| | | | | | |
|---|---|---|---|---|---|
| . Hutton | c Martindale b Grant | 13 | c Sealy b Martindale | 17 |
| .E. Fagg | b Hylton | 7 | b Constantine | 32 |
| . Paynter | c Sealy b Clarke | 9 | c Gomez b Martindale | 0 |
| ¹.R. Hammond* | st Sealy b Clarke | 22 | b Constantine | 32 |
| .C.S. Compton | hit wkt b Clarke | 4 | not out | 34 |
| Hardstaff, jr | c Williams b Grant | 76 | c Grant b Constantine | 1 |
| . Wood† | c and b Constantine | 26 | b Constantine | 1 |
| .V.P. Wright | not out | 1 | not out | 0 |
| ¹.E. Bowes | ) | | | |
| ¹.H. Copson | ) did not bat | | | |
| W.J. Goddard | ) | | | |
| Extras | (B 3, LB 2, NB 1) | 6 | (B 8, LB 2, NB 1) | 11 |
| **Total** | (7 wickets declared) | **164** | (6 wickets declared) | **128** |

## WEST INDIES

| | | | | |
|---|---|---|---|---|
| .S. Grant* | c Fagg b Goddard | 47 | c Hardstaff b Bowes | 0 |
| B. Stollmeyer | c and b Goddard | 5 | lbw b Wright | 10 |
| .A. Headley | c Wood b Bowes | 51 | c Hammond b Copson | 5 |
| .E. Gomez | c Wood b Bowes | 0 | b Goddard | 11 |
| E.D. Sealy† | c Hammond b Bowes | 16 | not out | 13 |
| H. Cameron | c Hutton b Bowes | 5 | | |
| .A.V. Williams | b Copson | 1 | | |
| N. Constantine | b Bowes | 0 | | |
| A. Martindale | c Hammond b Copson | 0 | | |
| G. Hylton | lbw b Bowes | 2 | | |
| B. Clarke | not out | 0 | | |
| Extras | (LB 6) | 6 | (LB 3, NB 1) | 4 |
| **Total** | | **133** | (4 wickets) | **43** |

| EST INDIES | O | M | R | W | O | M | R | W |
|---|---|---|---|---|---|---|---|---|
| ¶artindale | 8 | 2 | 10 | 0 | 12 | 2 | 34 | 2 |
| ¶ylton | 11 | 3 | 15 | 1 | 6 | 1 | 18 | 0 |
| ¶arke | 13 | 1 | 59 | 3 | | | | |
| ¶rant | 13·2 | 4 | 16 | 2 | | | | |
| ¶ameron | 3 | 0 | 22 | 0 | | | | |
| ¶onstantine | 7 | 2 | 36 | 1 | 11 | 1 | 42 | 4 |
| ¶illiams | | | | | 9 | 1 | 23 | 0 |
| **NGLAND** | | | | | | | | |
| ¶wes | 17·4 | 4 | 33 | 6 | 5 | 0 | 13 | 1 |
| ¶pson | 9 | 2 | 31 | 2 | 3 | 1 | 2 | 1 |
| ¶oddard | 4 | 0 | 43 | 2 | 4·6 | 1 | 15 | 1 |
| ¶right | 5 | 1 | 20 | 0 | 3 | 0 | 9 | 1 |

### FALL OF WICKETS

| Wkt | E 1st | WI 1st | E 2nd | WI 2nd |
|---|---|---|---|---|
| 1st | 21 | 35 | 26 | 0 |
| 2nd | 34 | 56 | 30 | 11 |
| 3rd | 34 | 56 | 74 | 27 |
| 4th | 53 | 96 | 89 | 43 |
| 5th | 62 | 108 | 113 | – |
| 6th | 150 | 113 | 126 | – |
| 7th | 164 | 124 | – | – |
| 8th | – | 125 | – | – |
| 9th | – | 132 | – | – |
| 10th | – | 133 | – | – |

¶mpires: F. Chester and E.J. Smith.

# ENGLAND v WEST INDIES 1939 (3rd Test)

Played at Kennington Oval, London, on 19, 21, 22 August.
Toss: England.   Result: MATCH DRAWN.
Debuts: England – N. Oldfield; West Indies – T.F. Johnson, V.H. Stollmeyer.

Keeton played on to Johnson's first ball in Test cricket.

## ENGLAND

| | | | | |
|---|---|---|---|---|
| L. Hutton | c and b Johnson | 73 | not out | 16 |
| W.W. Keeton | b Johnson | 0 | b Constantine | 2 |
| N. Oldfield | c Sealy b Constantine | 80 | c Sealy b Johnson | 1 |
| W.R. Hammond* | c Grant b Constantine | 43 | b Clarke | 13 |
| D.C.S. Compton | c Gomez b Martindale | 21 | not out | 1 |
| J. Hardstaff, jr | b Constantine | 94 | | |
| M.S. Nichols | run out | 24 | | |
| A. Wood† | b Constantine | 0 | | |
| D.V.P. Wright | lbw b Constantine | 6 | | |
| T.W.J. Goddard | b Clarke | 0 | | |
| R.T.D. Perks | not out | 1 | | |
| Extras | (B 4, LB 5, NB 1) | 10 | (B 4, LB 5 W 4, NB 1) | 1 |
| **Total** | | **352** | (3 wickets declared) | 36 |

## WEST INDIES

| | | |
|---|---|---|
| R.S. Grant* | c Goddard b Perks | 6 |
| J.B. Stollmeyer | c Perks b Hutton | 59 |
| G.A. Headley | run out | 65 |
| V.H. Stollmeyer | st Wood b Goddard | 96 |
| G.E. Gomez | b Perks | 11 |
| K.H. Weekes | c Hammond b Nichols | 137 |
| J.E.D. Sealy† | c Wright b Nichols | 24 |
| L.N. Constantine | c Wood b Perks | 79 |
| E.A. Martindale | b Perks | 3 |
| C.B. Clarke | b Perks | 2 |
| T.F. Johnson | not out | 9 |
| Extras | (LB 6, NB 1) | 7 |
| **Total** | | **498** |

| WEST INDIES | O | M | R | W | O | M | R | W | FALL OF WICKETS | | | |
|---|---|---|---|---|---|---|---|---|---|---|---|---|
| Martindale | 13 | 0 | 87 | 1 | 10 | 2 | 46 | 0 | | E | WI | E |
| Johnson | 16 | 1 | 53 | 2 | 14 | 2 | 76 | 1 | *Wkt* | *1st* | *1st* | *2nd* |
| Constantine | 17·3 | 2 | 75 | 5 | 20 | 3 | 97 | 1 | 1st | 2 | 15 | 39 |
| Clarke | 21 | 0 | 96 | 1 | 17 | 1 | 78 | 1 | 2nd | 133 | 128 | 77 |
| Grant | 6 | 0 | 31 | 0 | 11 | 1 | 38 | 0 | 3rd | 168 | 134 | 341 |
| Headley | | | | | 4 | 0 | 17 | 0 | 4th | 215 | 164 | – |
| | | | | | | | | | 5th | 244 | 327 | – |
| ENGLAND | | | | | | | | | 6th | 333 | 389 | – |
| Nichols | 34 | 4 | 161 | 2 | | | | | 7th | 333 | 434 | – |
| Perks | 30·5 | 6 | 156 | 5 | | | | | 8th | 345 | 451 | – |
| Wright | 13 | 2 | 53 | 0 | | | | | 9th | 346 | 475 | – |
| Goddard | 12 | 1 | 56 | 1 | | | | | 10th | 352 | 498 | – |
| Hutton | 7 | 0 | 45 | 1 | | | | | | | | |
| Compton | 5 | 1 | 20 | 0 | | | | | | | | |

Umpires: F. Chester and W. Reeves.

# NEW ZEALAND v AUSTRALIA 1945–46 (Only Test)

Played at Basin Reserve, Wellington, on 29, 30 March.
Toss: New Zealand.   Result: AUSTRALIA won by an innings and 103 runs.
Debuts: New Zealand – W.M. Anderson, C. Burke, L.A. Butterfield, D.A.N. McRae, C.G. Rowe,
V.J. Scott; Australia – I.W. Johnson, R.R. Lindwall, C.L. McCool, K.D. Meuleman, K.R. Miller,
D. Tallon, E.R.H. Toshack.

This match was not granted Test status by the I.C.C. until March 1948. New Zealand chose to take first innings on
a rain-affected pitch, were dismissed for their lowest aggregate, and did not meet Australia again in an official
Test until 1973-74.

## NEW ZEALAND

| | | | | | |
|---|---|---|---|---|---|
| W.A. Hadlee* | c Miller b Toshack | 6 | b Miller | | 3 |
| W.M. Anderson | b Lindwall | 4 | b Lindwall | | 1 |
| V.J. Scott | c Barnes b O'Reilly | 14 | c Tallon b Miller | | 4 |
| W.M. Wallace | c Barnes b Toshack | 10 | run out | | 14 |
| R.W.T. Tindill† | b Toshack | 1 | lbw b Toshack | | 13 |
| C.G. Rowe | b O'Reilly | 0 | b O'Reilly | | 0 |
| L.A. Butterfield | lbw b O'Reilly | 0 | lbw b O'Reilly | | 0 |
| D.A.N. McRae | c Hassett b O'Reilly | 0 | (9) c Meuleman b McCool | | 8 |
| C. Burke | lbw b Toshack | 1 | (8) b Toshack | | 3 |
| Cowie | st Tallon b O'Reilly | 2 | c Toshack b O'Reilly | | 0 |
| D.C. Cleverley | not out | 1 | not out | | 1 |
| Extras | (B 3) | 3 | (B 5, NB 2) | | 7 |
| **Total** | | **42** | | | **54** |

## AUSTRALIA

| | | |
|---|---|---|
| W.A. Brown* | c Rowe b Burke | 67 |
| K.D. Meuleman | b Cowie | 0 |
| G. Barnes | b Cowie | 54 |
| K.R. Miller | c Hadlee b Burke | 30 |
| A.L. Hassett | c Tindill b Cowie | 19 |
| C.L. McCool | c Hadlee b Cowie | 7 |
| I.W. Johnson | not out | 7 |
| D. Tallon† | c Scott b Cowie | 5 |
| R.R. Lindwall | c Anderson b Cowie | 0 |
| W.J. O'Reilly | } did not bat | |
| E.R.H. Toshack | } | |
| Extras | (B 5, LB 3, NB 2) | 10 |
| **Total** | (8 wickets declared) | **199** |

| AUSTRALIA | O | M | R | W | O | M | R | W | | FALL OF WICKETS | | |
|---|---|---|---|---|---|---|---|---|---|---|---|---|
| | | | | | | | | | | NZ | A | NZ |
| Lindwall | 8 | 1 | 13 | 1 | 9 | 3 | 16 | 1 | *Wkt* | *1st* | *1st* | *2nd* |
| Toshack | 19 | 13 | 12 | 4 | 10 | 5 | 6 | 2 | 1st | 7 | 9 | 3 |
| O'Reilly | 12 | 5 | 14 | 5 | 7 | 1 | 19 | 3 | 2nd | 15 | 118 | 5 |
| Miller | | | | | 6 | 2 | 6 | 2 | 3rd | 37 | 142 | 12 |
| McCool | | | | | 0·2 | 0 | 0 | 1 | 4th | 37 | 174 | 36 |
| | | | | | | | | | 5th | 37 | 186 | 37 |
| NEW ZEALAND | | | | | | | | | 6th | 37 | 186 | 37 |
| McRae | 14 | 3 | 44 | 0 | | | | | 7th | 37 | 196 | 39 |
| Cowie | 21 | 8 | 40 | 6 | | | | | 8th | 39 | 199 | 41 |
| Cleverley | 15 | 1 | 51 | 0 | | | | | 9th | 40 | – | 42 |
| Butterfield | 13 | 6 | 24 | 0 | | | | | 10th | 42 | – | 54 |
| Burke | 11 | 2 | 30 | 2 | | | | | | | | |

Umpires: R.W. Gourlay and M.F. Pengelly.

# ENGLAND v INDIA 1946 (1st Test)

Played at Lord's, London, on 22, 24, 25 June.
Toss: India.   Result: ENGLAND won by ten wickets.
Debuts: England – A.V. Bedser, J.T. Ikin, T.F. Smailes; India – Gul Mahomed, V.S. Hazare
A.H. Kardar *(Abdul Hafeez Kardar, who played for India as 'Abdul Hafeez' but later took the name of 'Kardar' and appeared for Pakistan as 'A.H. Kardar'. For consistency he is listed throughout thi* book *under the latter name)*, V.M.H. Mankad *(real names Mulvantrai Himmatlal Mankad but wa* known as *'Vinoo'; his son, Ashok, has taken 'Vinoo' as his second name)*, R.S. Modi, S.G. Shinde
*Nawab Iftikhar Ali of Pataudi made his debut for India after appearing in three Tests for England.*

### INDIA

| | | | | | |
|---|---|---|---|---|---|
| V.M. Merchant | c Gibb b Bedser | 12 | | lbw b Ikin | 2 |
| V.M.H. Mankad | b Wright | 14 | | c Hammond b Smailes | 6 |
| L. Amarnath | lbw b Bedser | 0 | (8) | b Smailes | 5 |
| V.S. Hazare | b Bedser | 31 | | c Hammond b Bedser | 3 |
| R.S. Modi | not out | 57 | (3) | lbw b Smailes | 2 |
| Nawab of Pataudi, sr* | c Ikin b Bedser | 9 | | b Wright | 2 |
| Gul Mahomed | b Wright | 1 | | lbw b Wright | |
| A.H. Kardar | b Bowes | 43 | (5) | b Bedser | |
| D.D. Hindlekar† | lbw b Bedser | 3 | | c Ikin b Bedser | 1 |
| C.S. Nayudu | st Gibb b Bedser | 4 | | b Bedser | 1 |
| S.G. Shinde | b Bedser | 10 | | not out | |
| Extras | (B 10, LB 6) | 16 | | (B 10, LB 2, NB 3) | 1 |
| **Total** | | **200** | | | 27 |

### ENGLAND

| | | | | | |
|---|---|---|---|---|---|
| L. Hutton | c Nayudu b Amarnath | 7 | | not out | 2 |
| C. Washbrook | c Mankad b Amarnath | 27 | | not out | 2 |
| D.C.S. Compton | b Amarnath | 0 | | | |
| W.R. Hammond* | b Amarnath | 33 | | | |
| J. Hardstaff, jr | not out | 205 | | | |
| P.A. Gibb† | c Hazare b Mankad | 60 | | | |
| J.T. Ikin | c Hindlekar b Shinde | 16 | | | |
| T.F. Smailes | c Mankad b Amarnath | 25 | | | |
| A.V. Bedser | b Hazare | 30 | | | |
| D.V.P. Wright | b Mankad | 3 | | | |
| W.E. Bowes | lbw b Hazare | 2 | | | |
| Extras | (B 11, LB 8, NB 1) | 20 | | (LB 1, W 1) | |
| **Total** | | **428** | | (0 wickets) | 4 |

| ENGLAND | O | M | R | W | O | M | R | W | | FALL OF WICKETS | | | |
|---|---|---|---|---|---|---|---|---|---|---|---|---|---|
| Bowes | 25 | 7 | 64 | 1 | 4 | 1 | 9 | 0 | | I | E | I | E |
| Bedser | 29·1 | 11 | 49 | 7 | 32·1 | 3 | 96 | 4 | *Wkt* | *1st* | *1st* | *2nd* | *2n* |
| Smailes | 5 | 1 | 18 | 0 | 15 | 2 | 44 | 3 | 1st | 15 | 16 | 67 | – |
| Wright | 17 | 4 | 53 | 2 | 20 | 3 | 68 | 2 | 2nd | 15 | 16 | 117 | – |
| Ikin | | | | | 10 | 1 | 43 | 1 | 3rd | 44 | 61 | 126 | – |
| | | | | | | | | | 4th | 74 | 70 | 129 | – |
| INDIA | | | | | | | | | 5th | 86 | 252 | 174 | – |
| Hazare | 34·4 | 4 | 100 | 2 | 4 | 2 | 7 | 0 | 6th | 87 | 284 | 185 | – |
| Amarnath | 57 | 18 | 118 | 5 | 4 | 0 | 15 | 0 | 7th | 144 | 344 | 190 | – |
| Mahomed | 2 | 0 | 2 | 0 | | | | | 8th | 147 | 416 | 249 | – |
| Mankad | 48 | 11 | 107 | 2 | 4·5 | 1 | 11 | 0 | 9th | 157 | 421 | 263 | – |
| Shinde | 23 | 2 | 66 | 1 | | | | | 10th | 200 | 428 | 275 | – |
| Nayudu | 5 | 1 | 15 | 0 | 4 | 0 | 13 | 0 | | | | | |

Umpires: H.G. Baldwin and J. Smart.

# ENGLAND v INDIA 1946 (2nd Test)

Played at Old Trafford, Manchester, on 20, 22, 23 July.
Toss: India.   Result: MATCH DRAWN.
Debuts: England – R. Pollard; India – C.T. Sarwate, S.W. Sohoni.

Rain prevented play until after lunch on the opening day. India's last pair survived for 13 minutes to earn a draw.

## ENGLAND

| | | | | |
|---|---|---:|---|---:|
| L. Hutton | c Mushtaq Ali b Mankad | 67 | c Hindlekar b Amarnath | 2 |
| C. Washbrook | c Hindlekar b Mankad | 52 | lbw b Mankad | 26 |
| D.C.S. Compton | lbw b Amarnath | 51 | not out | 71 |
| W.R. Hammond* | b Amarnath | 69 | c Kardar b Mankad | 8 |
| J. Hardstaff, jr | c Merchant b Amarnath | 5 | b Amarnath | 0 |
| P.A. Gibb† | b Mankad | 24 | c Modi b Amarnath | 0 |
| J.T. Ikin | c Mankad b Amarnath | 2 | not out | 29 |
| W. Voce | b Mankad | 0 | | |
| R. Pollard | not out | 10 | | |
| A.V. Bedser | lbw b Amarnath | 8 | | |
| D.V.P. Wright | lbw b Mankad | 0 | | |
| Extras | (B 2, LB 4) | 6 | (B 6, LB 10, W 1) | 17 |
| **Total** | | **294** | (5 wickets declared) | **153** |

## INDIA

| | | | | |
|---|---|---:|---|---:|
| V.M. Merchant | c Bedser b Pollard | 78 | c Ikin b Pollard | 0 |
| Mushtaq Ali | b Pollard | 46 | b Pollard | 1 |
| A.H. Kardar | c and b Pollard | 1 | (7) c and b Bedser | 35 |
| V.M.H. Mankad | b Pollard | 0 | (8) c Pollard b Bedser | 5 |
| V.S. Hazare | b Voce | 3 | b Bedser | 44 |
| R.S. Modi | c Ikin b Bedser | 2 | (4) b Bedser | 30 |
| Nawab of Pataudi, sr* | b Pollard | 11 | (3) b Bedser | 4 |
| L. Amarnath | b Bedser | 8 | (6) b Bedser | 3 |
| S.W. Sohoni | c and b Bedser | 3 | not out | 11 |
| C.T. Sarwate | c Ikin b Bedser | 0 | c Gibb b Bedser | 2 |
| D.D. Hindlekar† | not out | 1 | not out | 4 |
| Extras | (B 10, LB 5, NB 2) | 17 | (B 5, LB 8) | 13 |
| **Total** | | **170** | (9 wickets) | **152** |

| INDIA | O | M | R | W | O | M | R | W | | FALL OF WICKETS | | | |
|---|---|---|---|---|---|---|---|---|---|---|---|---|---|
| | | | | | | | | | | E | I | E | I |
| Sohoni | 11 | 1 | 31 | 0 | | | | | | | | | |
| Amarnath | 51 | 17 | 96 | 5 | 30 | 9 | 71 | 3 | Wkt | 1st | 1st | 2nd | 2nd |
| Hazare | 14 | 2 | 48 | 0 | 10 | 3 | 20 | 0 | 1st | 81 | 124 | 7 | 0 |
| Mankad | 46 | 15 | 101 | 5 | 21 | 6 | 45 | 2 | 2nd | 156 | 130 | 48 | 3 |
| Sarwate | 7 | 0 | 12 | 0 | | | | | 3rd | 186 | 130 | 68 | 5 |
| | | | | | | | | | 4th | 193 | 141 | 68 | 79 |
| ENGLAND | | | | | | | | | 5th | 250 | 141 | 84 | 84 |
| Voce | 20 | 3 | 44 | 1 | 6 | 5 | 2 | 0 | 6th | 265 | 146 | – | 87 |
| Bedser | 26 | 9 | 41 | 4 | 25 | 4 | 52 | 7 | 7th | 270 | 156 | – | 113 |
| Pollard | 27 | 16 | 24 | 5 | 25 | 10 | 63 | 2 | 8th | 274 | 168 | – | 132 |
| Wright | 2 | 0 | 12 | 0 | 2 | 0 | 17 | 0 | 9th | 287 | 169 | – | 138 |
| Compton | 4 | 0 | 18 | 0 | 3 | 1 | 5 | 0 | 10th | 294 | 170 | – | – |
| Ikin | 2 | 0 | 11 | 0 | | | | | | | | | |
| Hammond | 1 | 0 | 3 | 0 | | | | | | | | | |

Umpires: F. Chester and G. Beet.

# ENGLAND v INDIA 1946 (3rd Test)

Played at Kennington Oval, London, on 17, 19, 20 (*no play*) August.
Toss: India.   Result: MATCH DRAWN.
Debuts: England – T.G. Evans, T.P.B. Smith.

Playing conditions prevented a start until 5 p.m. on the first day and rain completely washed out the third day
Compton, an Arsenal and England (war-time and Victory internationals) soccer player, ran out Merchant by
kicking the ball into the stumps.

## INDIA

| | | |
|---|---|---:|
| V.M. Merchant | run out | 128 |
| Mushtaq Ali | run out | 59 |
| Nawab of Pataudi, sr* | b Edrich | 9 |
| L. Amarnath | b Edrich | 8 |
| V.S. Hazare | c Compton b Gover | 11 |
| R.S. Modi | b Smith | 27 |
| A.H. Kardar | b Edrich | 1 |
| V. Mankad | b Bedser | 42 |
| S.W. Sohoni | not out | 29 |
| C.S. Nayudu | c Washbrook b Bedser | 4 |
| D.D. Hindlekar† | lbw b Edrich | 3 |
| Extras | (b 1, LB 5, NB 4) | 10 |
| **Total** | | **331** |

## ENGLAND

| | | |
|---|---|---:|
| L. Hutton | lbw b Mankad | 25 |
| C. Washbrook | c Mushtaq Ali b Mankad | 17 |
| L.B. Fishlock | c Merchant b Nayudu | 8 |
| D.C.S. Compton | not out | 24 |
| W.R. Hammond* | not out | 9 |
| W.J. Edrich | ) | |
| James Langridge | ) | |
| T.P.B. Smith | ) did not bat | |
| T.G. Evans† | ) | |
| A.V. Bedser | ) | |
| A.R. Gover | ) | |
| Extras | (B 11, LB 1) | 12 |
| **Total** | (3 wickets) | **95** |

| ENGLAND | O | M | R | W |
|---|---|---|---|---|
| Gover | 21 | 3 | 56 | 1 |
| Bedser | 32 | 6 | 60 | 2 |
| Smith | 21 | 4 | 58 | 1 |
| Edrich | 19·2 | 4 | 68 | 4 |
| Langridge | 29 | 9 | 64 | 0 |
| Compton | 5 | 0 | 15 | 0 |
| | | | | |
| INDIA | | | | |
| Amarnath | 15 | 6 | 30 | 0 |
| Sohoni | 4 | 3 | 2 | 0 |
| Hazare | 2 | 1 | 4 | 0 |
| Mankad | 20 | 7 | 28 | 2 |
| Nayudu | 9 | 2 | 19 | 1 |

### FALL OF WICKETS

| | I | E |
|---|---|---|
| *Wkt* | *1st* | *1st* |
| 1st | 94 | 48 |
| 2nd | 124 | 55 |
| 3rd | 142 | 67 |
| 4th | 162 | – |
| 5th | 225 | – |
| 6th | 226 | – |
| 7th | 272 | – |
| 8th | 313 | – |
| 9th | 325 | – |
| 10th | 331 | – |

Umpires: F. Chester and J. Smart.

# AUSTRALIA v ENGLAND 1946–47 (1st Test)

Played at Woolloongabba, Brisbane, on 29, 30 November 2, 3, 4 December.
Toss: Australia.   Result: AUSTRALIA won by an innings and 332 runs.
Debuts: Australia – A.R. Morris, G.E. Tribe.

Bradman, given not out in response to an appeal for a catch to Ikin at second slip off Voce when 28, added 276 for the third wicket with Hassett in what is still the record partnership for that wicket by either country in this series.

## AUSTRALIA

| | | |
|---|---|---:|
| S.G. Barnes | c Bedser b Wright | 31 |
| A.R. Morris | c Hammond b Bedser | 2 |
| D.G. Bradman* | b Edrich | 187 |
| A.L. Hassett | c Yardley b Bedser | 128 |
| K.R. Miller | lbw b Wright | 79 |
| C.L. McCool | lbw b Wright | 95 |
| I.W. Johnson | lbw b Wright | 47 |
| D. Tallon† | lbw b Edrich | 14 |
| R.R. Lindwall | c Voce b Wright | 31 |
| G.E. Tribe | c Gibb b Edrich | 1 |
| E.R.H. Toshack | not out | 1 |
| Extras | (B 5, LB 11, W 2, NB 11) | 29 |
| **Total** | | **645** |

## ENGLAND

| | | | | | |
|---|---|---:|---|---|---:|
| L. Hutton | b Miller | 7 | c Barnes b Miller | | 0 |
| C. Washbrook | c Barnes b Miller | 6 | c Barnes b Miller | | 13 |
| W.J. Edrich | c McCool b Miller | 16 | lbw b Toshack | | 7 |
| D.C.S. Compton | lbw b Miller | 17 | c Barnes b Toshack | | 15 |
| W.R. Hammond* | lbw b Toshack | 32 | b Toshack | | 23 |
| J.T. Ikin | c Tallon b Miller | 0 | b Tribe | | 32 |
| N.W.D. Yardley | c Tallon b Toshack | 29 | c Hassett b Toshack | | 0 |
| P.A. Gibb† | b Miller | 13 | lbw b Toshack | | 11 |
| W. Voce | not out | 1 | c Hassett b Tribe | | 18 |
| A.V. Bedser | lbw b Miller | 0 | c and b Toshack | | 18 |
| D.V.P. Wright | c Tallon b Toshack | 4 | not out | | 10 |
| Extras | (B 8, LB 3, W 2, NB 3) | 16 | (B 15, LB 7, W 1, NB 2) | | 25 |
| **Total** | | **141** | | | **172** |

| ENGLAND | O | M | R | W | O | M | R | W |
|---|---|---|---|---|---|---|---|---|
| Voce | 28 | 9 | 92 | 0 | | | | |
| Bedser | 41 | 5 | 159 | 2 | | | | |
| Wright | 43·6 | 4 | 167 | 5 | | | | |
| Edrich | 25 | 2 | 107 | 3 | | | | |
| Yardley | 13 | 1 | 47 | 0 | | | | |
| Ikin | 2 | 0 | 24 | 0 | | | | |
| Compton | 6 | 0 | 20 | 0 | | | | |
| AUSTRALIA | | | | | | | | |
| Lindwall | 12 | 4 | 23 | 0 | | | | |
| Miller | 22 | 4 | 60 | 7 | 11 | 3 | 17 | 2 |
| Toshack | 16·5 | 11 | 17 | 3 | 20·7 | 2 | 82 | 6 |
| Tribe | 9 | 2 | 19 | 0 | 12 | 2 | 48 | 2 |
| McCool | 1 | 0 | 5 | 0 | | | | |
| Barnes | 1 | 0 | 1 | 0 | | | | |

## FALL OF WICKETS

| | A | E | E |
|---|---|---|---|
| Wkt | 1st | 1st | 2nd |
| 1st | 9 | 10 | 0 |
| 2nd | 46 | 25 | 13 |
| 3rd | 322 | 49 | 33 |
| 4th | 428 | 56 | 62 |
| 5th | 465 | 56 | 65 |
| 6th | 596 | 121 | 65 |
| 7th | 599 | 134 | 112 |
| 8th | 629 | 136 | 114 |
| 9th | 643 | 136 | 143 |
| 10th | 645 | 141 | 172 |

Umpires: G. Borwick and J.D. Scott.

# AUSTRALIA v ENGLAND 1946–47 (2nd Test)

Played at Sydney Cricket Ground on 13, 14, 16, 17, 18, 19 December.
Toss: England.   Result: AUSTRALIA won by an innings and 33 runs.
Debuts: Australia – F.W. Freer.

Barnes and Bradman established a fifth wicket partnership of 405 which remains the record for all Test cricket.
Barnes took 570 minutes to reach his 200 – the slowest double-century in first-class cricket. His innings lasted 642
minutes and was the longest for Australia until R.B. Simpson scored 311 in 762 minutes in 1964 (*Test No. 564*).
Evans conceded no byes in Australia's total of 659; it is still the highest Test total which does not include a bye.

## ENGLAND

| | | | | | |
|---|---|---|---|---|---|
| L. Hutton | c Tallon b Johnson | 39 | hit wkt b Miller | | 37 |
| C. Washbrook | b Freer | 1 | c McCool b Johnson | | 41 |
| W.J. Edrich | lbw b McCool | 71 | b McCool | | 119 |
| D.C.S. Compton | c Tallon b McCool | 5 | c Bradman b Freer | | 54 |
| W.R. Hammond* | c Tallon b McCool | 1 | c Toshack b McCool | | 37 |
| J.T. Ikin | c Hassett b Johnson | 60 | b Freer | | 17 |
| N.W.D. Yardley | c Tallon b Johnson | 25 | b McCool | | 35 |
| T.P.B. Smith | lbw b Johnson | 4 | c Hassett b Johnson | | 2 |
| T.G. Evans† | b Johnson | 5 | st Tallon b McCool | | 9 |
| A.V. Bedser | b Johnson | 14 | not out | | 3 |
| D.V.P. Wright | not out | 15 | c Tallon b McCool | | 0 |
| Extras | (B 4, LB 11) | 15 | (B 8, LB 6, W 1, NB 2) | | 17 |
| **Total** | | **255** | | | **371** |

## AUSTRALIA

| | | |
|---|---|---|
| S.G. Barnes | c Ikin b Bedser | 234 |
| A.R. Morris | b Edrich | 5 |
| I.W. Johnson | c Washbrook b Edrich | 7 |
| A.L. Hassett | c Compton b Edrich | 34 |
| K.R. Miller | c Evans b Smith | 40 |
| D.G. Bradman* | lbw b Yardley | 234 |
| C.L. McCool | c Hammond b Smith | 12 |
| D. Tallon† | c and b Wright | 30 |
| F.W. Freer | not out | 28 |
| G.E. Tribe | not out | 25 |
| E.R.H. Toshack | did not bat | |
| Extras | (LB 7, W 1, NB 2) | 10 |
| **Total** | (8 wickets declared) | **659** |

| AUSTRALIA | O | M | R | W | O | M | R | W |
|---|---|---|---|---|---|---|---|---|
| Miller | 9 | 2 | 24 | 0 | 11 | 3 | 37 | 1 |
| Freer | 7 | 1 | 25 | 1 | 13 | 2 | 49 | 2 |
| Toshack | 7 | 2 | 6 | 0 | 6 | 1 | 16 | 0 |
| Tribe | 20 | 3 | 70 | 0 | 12 | 0 | 40 | 0 |
| Johnson | 30·1 | 12 | 42 | 6 | 29 | 7 | 92 | 2 |
| McCool | 23 | 2 | 73 | 3 | 32·4 | 4 | 109 | 5 |
| Barnes | | | | | 3 | 0 | 11 | 0 |

| ENGLAND | O | M | R | W |
|---|---|---|---|---|
| Bedser | 46 | 7 | 153 | 1 |
| Edrich | 26 | 3 | 79 | 3 |
| Wright | 46 | 8 | 169 | 1 |
| Smith | 37 | 1 | 172 | 2 |
| Ikin | 3 | 0 | 15 | 0 |
| Compton | 6 | 0 | 38 | 0 |
| Yardley | 9 | 0 | 23 | 1 |

### FALL OF WICKETS

| | E | A | E |
|---|---|---|---|
| Wkt | 1st | 1st | 2nd |
| 1st | 10 | 24 | 49 |
| 2nd | 88 | 37 | 118 |
| 3rd | 97 | 96 | 220 |
| 4th | 99 | 159 | 280 |
| 5th | 148 | 564 | 309 |
| 6th | 187 | 564 | 327 |
| 7th | 197 | 595 | 346 |
| 8th | 205 | 617 | 366 |
| 9th | 234 | – | 369 |
| 10th | 255 | – | 371 |

Umpires: G. Borwick and J.D. Scott.

## AUSTRALIA v ENGLAND 1946–47 (3rd Test)

Played at Melbourne Cricket Ground on 1, 2, 3, 4, 6, 7 January.
Toss: Australia.   Result: MATCH DRAWN.
Debuts: Australia – B. Dooland.

The first drawn Test in Australia since 1881-82.

### AUSTRALIA

| | | | | | |
|---|---|---|---|---|---|
| S.G. Barnes | lbw b Bedser | 45 | c Evans b Yardley | 32 |
| A.R. Morris | lbw b Bedser | 21 | b Bedser | 155 |
| D.G. Bradman* | b Yardley | 79 | c and b Yardley | 49 |
| A.L. Hassett | c Hammond b Wright | 12 | b Wright | 9 |
| K.R. Miller | c Evans b Wright | 33 | c Hammond b Yardley | 34 |
| I.W. Johnson | lbw b Yardley | 0 | (7) run out | 0 |
| C.L. McCool | not out | 104 | (6) c Evans b Bedser | 43 |
| D. Tallon† | c Evans b Edrich | 35 | c and b Wright | 92 |
| R.R. Lindwall | b Bedser | 9 | c Washbrook b Bedser | 100 |
| B. Dooland | c Hammond b Edrich | 19 | c Compton b Wright | 1 |
| E.R.H. Toshack | c Hutton b Edrich | 6 | not out | 2 |
| Extras | (NB 2) | 2 | (B 14, LB 2, NB 3) | 19 |
| **Total** | | **365** | | **536** |

### ENGLAND

| | | | | | |
|---|---|---|---|---|---|
| L. Hutton | c McCool b Lindwall | 2 | c Bradman b Toshack | 40 |
| C. Washbrook | c Tallon b Dooland | 62 | b Dooland | 112 |
| W.J. Edrich | lbw b Lindwall | 89 | lbw b McCool | 13 |
| D.C.S. Compton | lbw b Toshack | 11 | run out | 14 |
| W.R. Hammond* | c and b Dooland | 9 | b Lindwall | 26 |
| J.T. Ikin | c Miller b Dooland | 48 | c Hassett b Miller | 5 |
| N.W.D. Yardley | b McCool | 61 | not out | 53 |
| T.G. Evans† | b McCool | 17 | (9) not out | 0 |
| W. Voce | lbw b Dooland | 0 | | |
| A.V. Bedser | not out | 27 | (8) lbw b Miller | 25 |
| D.V.P. Wright | b Johnson | 10 | | |
| Extras | (B 1, LB 12, NB 2) | 15 | (B 15, LB 6, W 1) | 22 |
| **Total** | | **351** | (7 wickets) | **310** |

| ENGLAND | O | M | R | W | O | M | R | W | | FALL OF WICKETS | | | |
|---|---|---|---|---|---|---|---|---|---|---|---|---|---|
| Voce | 10 | 2 | 40 | 0 | 6 | 1 | 29 | 0 | | A | E | A | E |
| Bedser | 31 | 4 | 99 | 3 | 34·3 | 4 | 176 | 3 | *Wkt* | *1st* | *1st* | *2nd* | *2nd* |
| Wright | 26 | 2 | 124 | 2 | 32 | 3 | 131 | 3 | 1st | 32 | 8 | 68 | 138 |
| Yardley | 20 | 4 | 50 | 2 | 20 | 0 | 67 | 3 | 2nd | 108 | 155 | 159 | 163 |
| Edrich | 10·3 | 2 | 50 | 3 | 18 | 1 | 86 | 0 | 3rd | 143 | 167 | 177 | 186 |
| Hutton | | | | | 3 | 0 | 28 | 0 | 4th | 188 | 176 | 242 | 197 |
| | | | | | | | | | 5th | 188 | 179 | 333 | 221 |
| AUSTRALIA | | | | | | | | | 6th | 192 | 292 | 335 | 249 |
| Lindwall | 20 | 1 | 64 | 2 | 16 | 2 | 59 | 1 | 7th | 255 | 298 | 341 | 294 |
| Miller | 10 | 0 | 34 | 0 | 11 | 0 | 41 | 2 | 8th | 272 | 298 | 495 | – |
| Toshack | 26 | 5 | 88 | 1 | 16 | 5 | 39 | 1 | 9th | 355 | 324 | 511 | – |
| McCool | 19 | 3 | 53 | 2 | 24 | 9 | 41 | 1 | 10th | 365 | 351 | 536 | – |
| Dooland | 27 | 5 | 69 | 4 | 21 | 1 | 84 | 1 | | | | | |
| Johnson | 6·5 | 1 | 28 | 1 | 12 | 4 | 24 | 0 | | | | | |

Umpires: G. Borwick and J.D. Scott.

# AUSTRALIA v ENGLAND 1946–47 (4th Test)

Played at Adelaide Oval on 31 January, 1, 3, 4, 5, 6 February.
Toss: England.   Result: MATCH DRAWN.
Debuts: Australia – M.R. Harvey.

Compton and Morris both scored hundreds in each innings – the only occasion that a batsman on each side has done this in the same Test match. Evans established a world record for all first-class cricket (still unbeaten) by taking 95 minutes to score his first run in the second innings.

## ENGLAND

| | | | | | |
|---|---|---|---|---|---|
| L. Hutton | lbw b McCool | 94 | b Johnson | | 76 |
| C. Washbrook | c Tallon b Dooland | 65 | c Tallon b Lindwall | | 39 |
| W.J. Edrich | c and b Dooland | 17 | c Bradman b Toshack | | 46 |
| W.R. Hammond* | b Toshack | 18 | c Lindwall b Toshack | | 22 |
| D.C.S. Compton | c and b Lindwall | 147 | not out | | 103 |
| J. Hardstaff, jr | b Miller | 67 | b Toshack | | 9 |
| J.T. Ikin | c Toshack b Dooland | 21 | lbw b Toshack | | 1 |
| N.W.D. Yardley | not out | 18 | c Tallon b Lindwall | | 18 |
| A.V. Bedser | b Lindwall | 2 | c Tallon b Miller | | 3 |
| T.G. Evans† | b Lindwall | 0 | not out | | 10 |
| D.V.P. Wright | b Lindwall | 0 | | | |
| Extras | (B 4, LB 5, W 2) | 11 | (B 5, LB 3, W 2, NB 3) | | 13 |
| **Total** | | **460** | (8 wickets declared) | | **340** |

## AUSTRALIA

| | | | | |
|---|---|---|---|---|
| M.R. Harvey | b Bedser | 12 | b Yardley | 31 |
| A.R. Morris | c Evans b Bedser | 122 | not out | 124 |
| D.G. Bradman* | b Bedser | 0 | not out | 56 |
| A.L. Hassett | c Hammond b Wright | 78 | | |
| K.R. Miller | not out | 141 | | |
| I.W. Johnson | lbw b Wright | 52 | | |
| C.L. McCool | c Bedser b Yardley | 2 | | |
| D. Tallon† | b Wright | 3 | | |
| R.R. Lindwall | c Evans b Yardley | 20 | | |
| B. Dooland | c Bedser b Yardley | 29 | | |
| E.R.H. Toshack | run out | 0 | | |
| Extras | (B 16, LB 6, W 2, NB 4) | 28 | (LB 2, NB 2) | 4 |
| **Total** | | **487** | (1 wicket) | **215** |

| AUSTRALIA | O | M | R | W | O | M | R | W |
|---|---|---|---|---|---|---|---|---|
| Lindwall | 23 | 5 | 52 | 4 | 17·1 | 4 | 60 | 2 |
| Miller | 16 | 0 | 45 | 1 | 11 | 0 | 34 | 1 |
| Toshack | 30 | 13 | 59 | 1 | 36 | 6 | 76 | 4 |
| McCool | 29 | 1 | 91 | 1 | 19 | 3 | 41 | 0 |
| Johnson | 22 | 3 | 69 | 0 | 25 | 8 | 51 | 1 |
| Dooland | 33 | 1 | 133 | 3 | 17 | 2 | 65 | 0 |
| ENGLAND | | | | | | | | |
| Bedser | 30 | 6 | 97 | 3 | 15 | 1 | 68 | 0 |
| Edrich | 20 | 3 | 88 | 0 | 7 | 2 | 25 | 0 |
| Wright | 32·4 | 1 | 152 | 3 | 9 | 0 | 49 | 0 |
| Yardley | 31 | 7 | 101 | 3 | 13 | 0 | 69 | 1 |
| Ikin | 2 | 0 | 9 | 0 | | | | |
| Compton | 3 | 0 | 12 | 0 | | | | |

### FALL OF WICKETS

| | E | A | E | A |
|---|---|---|---|---|
| Wkt | 1st | 1st | 2nd | 2nd |
| 1st | 137 | 18 | 100 | 116 |
| 2nd | 173 | 18 | 137 | – |
| 3rd | 196 | 207 | 178 | – |
| 4th | 202 | 222 | 188 | – |
| 5th | 320 | 372 | 207 | – |
| 6th | 381 | 389 | 215 | – |
| 7th | 455 | 396 | 250 | – |
| 8th | 460 | 423 | 255 | – |
| 9th | 460 | 486 | – | – |
| 10th | 460 | 487 | – | – |

Umpires: G. Borwick and J.D. Scott.

# AUSTRALIA v ENGLAND 1946–47 (5th Test)

Played at Sydney Cricket Ground on 28 February, 1 (*no play*), 3, 4, 5 March.
Toss: England.   Result: AUSTRALIA won by five wickets.
Debuts: Australia – R.A. Hamence.

Australia won in the last over of the penultimate day. Hutton, 122 not out on Friday evening, had been hospitalised with tonsillitis and a temperature of 103 degrees by the time play resumed on Monday.

## ENGLAND

| | | | | |
|---|---|---|---|---|
| L. Hutton | retired ill | 122 | absent ill | – |
| C. Washbrook | b Lindwall | 0 | b McCool | 24 |
| W.J. Edrich | c Tallon b Lindwall | 60 | st Tallon b McCool | 24 |
| L.B. Fishlock | b McCool | 14 | (1) lbw b Lindwall | 0 |
| D.C.S. Compton | hit wkt b Lindwall | 17 | (4) c Miller b Toshack | 76 |
| N.W.D. Yardley* | c Miller b Lindwall | 2 | b McCool | 11 |
| J.T. Ikin | b Lindwall | 0 | (5) st Tallon b McCool | 0 |
| T.G. Evans† | b Lindwall | 29 | (7) b Miller | 20 |
| T.P.B. Smith | b Lindwall | 2 | (8) c Tallon b Lindwall | 24 |
| A.V. Bedser | not out | 10 | (9) st Tallon b McCool | 4 |
| D.V.P. Wright | c Tallon b Miller | 7 | (10) not out | 1 |
| Extras | (B 7, LB 8, W 1, NB 1) | 17 | (B 1, LB 1) | 2 |
| **Total** | | **280** | | **186** |

## AUSTRALIA

| | | | | |
|---|---|---|---|---|
| S.G. Barnes | c Evans b Bedser | 71 | c Evans b Bedser | 30 |
| A.R. Morris | lbw b Bedser | 57 | run out | 17 |
| D.G. Bradman* | b Wright | 12 | c Compton b Bedser | 63 |
| A.L. Hassett | c Ikin b Wright | 24 | c Ikin b Wright | 47 |
| K.R. Miller | c Ikin b Wright | 23 | not out | 34 |
| R.A. Hamence | not out | 30 | c Edrich b Wright | 1 |
| C.L. McCool | c Yardley b Wright | 3 | not out | 13 |
| D. Tallon† | c Compton b Wright | 0 | | |
| R.R. Lindwall | c Smith b Wright | 0 | | |
| G.E. Tribe | c Fishlock b Wright | 9 | | |
| E.R.H. Toshack | run out | 5 | | |
| Extras | (B 7, LB 6, NB 6) | 19 | (B 4, LB 1, NB 4) | 9 |
| **Total** | | **253** | (5 wickets) | **214** |

| AUSTRALIA | O | M | R | W | O | M | R | W | | FALL OF WICKETS | | | |
|---|---|---|---|---|---|---|---|---|---|---|---|---|---|
| Lindwall | 22 | 3 | 63 | 7 | 12 | 1 | 46 | 2 | | E | A | E | A |
| Miller | 15·3 | 2 | 31 | 1 | 6 | 1 | 11 | 1 | Wkt | *1st* | *1st* | *2nd* | *2nd* |
| Tribe | 28 | 2 | 95 | 0 | 14 | 0 | 58 | 0 | 1st | 1 | 126 | 0 | 45 |
| Toshack | 16 | 4 | 40 | 0 | 4 | 1 | 14 | 1 | 2nd | 151 | 146 | 42 | 51 |
| McCool | 13 | 0 | 34 | 1 | 21·4 | 5 | 44 | 5 | 3rd | 188 | 146 | 65 | 149 |
| Barnes | | | | | 3 | 0 | 11 | 0 | 4th | 215 | 187 | 65 | 173 |
| | | | | | | | | | 5th | 225 | 218 | 85 | 180 |
| ENGLAND | | | | | | | | | 6th | 225 | 230 | 120 | – |
| Bedser | 27 | 7 | 49 | 2 | 22 | 4 | 75 | 2 | 7th | 244 | 230 | 157 | – |
| Edrich | 7 | 0 | 34 | 0 | 2 | 0 | 14 | 0 | 8th | 269 | 233 | 184 | – |
| Smith | 8 | 0 | 38 | 0 | 2 | 0 | 8 | 0 | 9th | 280 | 245 | 186 | – |
| Wright | 29 | 4 | 105 | 7 | 22 | 1 | 93 | 2 | 10th | – | 253 | – | – |
| Yardley | 5 | 2 | 8 | 0 | 3 | 1 | 7 | 0 | | | | | |
| Compton | | | | | 1·2 | 0 | 8 | 0 | | | | | |

Umpires: G. Borwick and J.D. Scott.

# NEW ZEALAND v ENGLAND 1946–47 (Only Test)

Played at Lancaster Park, Christchurch, on 21, 22, 24 (*no play*), 25 (*no play*) March.
Toss: England.   Result: MATCH DRAWN.
Debuts: New Zealand – T.B. Burtt, R.H. Scott, F.B. Smith, C.A. Snedden, B. Sutcliffe, D.D. Taylor.

For the first time in Test cricket an extra day was added to this match after the third day had been washed out, but rain prevented play on that one too. Hammond was top-scorer in his last innings for England.

## NEW ZEALAND

| | | |
|---|---|---:|
| W.A. Hadlee* | c Bedser b Yardley | 116 |
| B. Sutcliffe | c Evans b Bedser | 58 |
| V.J. Scott | c Hammond b Pollard | 18 |
| W.M. Wallace | c Evans b Bedser | 9 |
| D.D. Taylor | lbw b Bedser | 12 |
| F.B. Smith | b Bedser | 18 |
| E.W.T. Tindill† | b Pollard | 1 |
| R.H. Scott | b Edrich | 18 |
| J. Cowie | b Pollard | 45 |
| T.B. Burtt | not out | 24 |
| C.A. Snedden | did not bat | |
| Extras | (B 10, LB 11, NB 5) | 26 |
| **Total** | (9 wickets declared) | **345** |

## ENGLAND

| | | |
|---|---|---:|
| C. Washbrook | c Smith b Cowie | 2 |
| N.W.D. Yardley | b Cowie | 22 |
| W.J. Edrich | c Taylor b R.H. Scott | 42 |
| D.C.S. Compton | b Cowie | 38 |
| W.R. Hammond* | c Sutcliffe b Cowie | 79 |
| J.T. Ikin | c Tindill b Cowie | 45 |
| T.G. Evans† | not out | 21 |
| T.P.B. Smith | c sub (C. Burke) b Cowie | 1 |
| A.V. Bedser | not out | 8 |
| D.V.P. Wright | ) did not bat | |
| R. Pollard | ) | |
| Extras | (B 5, LB 1, NB 1) | 7 |
| **Total** | (7 wickets declared) | **265** |

| ENGLAND | O | M | R | W |
|---|---|---|---|---|
| Bedser | 39 | 5 | 95 | 4 |
| Pollard | 29·4 | 8 | 73 | 3 |
| Edrich | 11 | 2 | 35 | 1 |
| Wright | 13 | 1 | 61 | 0 |
| Smith | 6 | 0 | 43 | 0 |
| Yardley | 4 | 0 | 12 | 1 |
| NEW ZEALAND | | | | |
| Cowie | 30 | 4 | 83 | 6 |
| R.H. Scott | 23 | 3 | 74 | 1 |
| Burtt | 14 | 1 | 55 | 0 |
| Snedden | 16 | 5 | 46 | 0 |

### FALL OF WICKETS

| Wkt | NZ 1st | E 1st |
|---|---|---|
| 1st | 133 | 2 |
| 2nd | 195 | 46 |
| 3rd | 212 | 79 |
| 4th | 212 | 125 |
| 5th | 234 | 222 |
| 6th | 238 | 241 |
| 7th | 258 | 249 |
| 8th | 281 | – |
| 9th | 345 | – |
| 10th | – | – |

Umpires: O.R. Montgomery and M.F. Pengelly.

# ENGLAND v SOUTH AFRICA 1947 (1st Test)

Played at Trent Bridge, Nottingham, on 7, 9, 10, 11 June.
Toss: South Africa.   Result: MATCH DRAWN.
Debuts: England – C. Cook, H.E. Dollery, J.W. Martin; South Africa – O.C. Dawson, T.A. Harris, J.D. Lindsay, N.B.F. Mann, A.M.B. Rowan, V.I. Smith, L. Tuckett.

Melville was the first South African to score a hundred in each innings of a Test match. Mann opened his Test career with eight consecutive maiden overs. After Hollies and Martin had added 51 for the last wicket in England's second innings, South Africa were left 138 minutes in which to score 227 to win.

## SOUTH AFRICA

| | | | | | |
|---|---|---|---|---|---|
| B. Mitchell | b Bedser | 14 | c Evans b Bedser | | 4 |
| A. Melville* | b Martin | 189 | not out | | 104 |
| K.G. Viljoen | lbw b Edrich | 10 | not out | | 51 |
| A.D. Nourse | b Hollies | 149 | | | |
| O.C. Dawson | st Evans b Hollies | 48 | | | |
| T.A. Harris | c Hutton b Hollies | 60 | | | |
| A.M.B. Rowan | not out | 34 | | | |
| L. Tuckett | lbw b Hollies | 0 | | | |
| N.B.F. Mann | b Bedser | 8 | | | |
| J.D. Lindsay† | b Bedser | 0 | | | |
| V.I. Smith | c Yardley b Hollies | 1 | | | |
| Extras | (B 7, LB 12, W 1) | 20 | (B 1, W 5, NB 1) | | 7 |
| **Total** | | **533** | (1 wicket) | | **166** |

## ENGLAND

| | | | | | |
|---|---|---|---|---|---|
| L. Hutton | lbw b Rowan | 17 | b Tuckett | | 9 |
| C. Washbrook | lbw b Tuckett | 25 | c Lindsay b Rowan | | 59 |
| W.J. Edrich | b Smith | 57 | b Smith | | 50 |
| D.C.S. Compton | c Mitchell b Tuckett | 65 | c Mitchell b Mann | | 163 |
| H.E. Dollery | b Dawson | 9 | c and b Dawson | | 17 |
| N.W.D. Yardley* | lbw b Tuckett | 22 | c Tuckett b Dawson | | 99 |
| T.G. Evans† | st Lindsay b Smith | 2 | c and b Smith | | 74 |
| A.V. Bedser | c Melville b Smith | 7 | c Harris b Smith | | 2 |
| C. Cook | b Tuckett | 0 | c Dawson b Smith | | 4 |
| J.W. Martin | c Lindsay b Tuckett | 0 | (11) b Rowan | | 26 |
| W.E. Hollies | not out | 0 | (10) not out | | 18 |
| Extras | (B 1, LB 2, W 1) | 4 | (B 15, LB 13, W 2) | | 30 |
| **Total** | | **208** | | | **551** |

| ENGLAND | O | M | R | W | O | M | R | W |
|---|---|---|---|---|---|---|---|---|
| Martin | 36 | 4 | 111 | 1 | 9 | 2 | 18 | 0 |
| Bedser | 57·1 | 14 | 106 | 3 | 14 | 3 | 31 | 1 |
| Edrich | 20 | 8 | 56 | 1 | 4 | 0 | 8 | 0 |
| Hollies | 55·2 | 16 | 123 | 5 | 9 | 1 | 33 | 0 |
| Cook | 21 | 4 | 87 | 0 | 9 | 0 | 40 | 0 |
| Yardley | 5 | 0 | 24 | 0 | | | | |
| Compton | 2 | 1 | 6 | 0 | 4 | 0 | 14 | 0 |
| Hutton | | | | | 2 | 0 | 15 | 0 |
| SOUTH AFRICA | | | | | | | | |
| Tuckett | 37 | 9 | 68 | 5 | 47 | 12 | 127 | 1 |
| Dawson | 13 | 2 | 35 | 1 | 25 | 7 | 57 | 2 |
| Rowan | 16 | 6 | 45 | 1 | 43·2 | 8 | 100 | 2 |
| Mann | 20 | 13 | 10 | 0 | 60 | 22 | 94 | 1 |
| Smith | 27·1 | 10 | 46 | 3 | 51 | 15 | 143 | 4 |

## FALL OF WICKETS

| | SA | E | E | SA |
|---|---|---|---|---|
| Wkt | 1st | 1st | 2nd | 2nd |
| 1st | 23 | 40 | 20 | 21 |
| 2nd | 44 | 48 | 116 | – |
| 3rd | 363 | 154 | 133 | – |
| 4th | 384 | 165 | 170 | – |
| 5th | 450 | 198 | 407 | – |
| 6th | 505 | 198 | 434 | – |
| 7th | 505 | 207 | 472 | – |
| 8th | 528 | 208 | 499 | – |
| 9th | 530 | 208 | 500 | – |
| 10th | 533 | 208 | 551 | – |

Umpires: A.R. Coleman and J. Smart.

# ENGLAND v SOUTH AFRICA 1947 (2nd Test)

Played at Lord's, London, on 21, 23, 24, 25 June.
Toss: England.    Result: ENGLAND won by ten wickets.
Debuts: England – G.H. Pope.

Edrich and Compton, in the prime of their halcyon summer in which they aggregated 7,355 runs and 30 centuries in first-class matches, shared a partnership of 370 which remains the record for the third wicket in all Test cricket. Melville scored his fourth hundred in consecutive Test innings spread over eight years.

### ENGLAND

| | | | | |
|---|---|---|---|---|
| L. Hutton | b Rowan | 18 | not out | 13 |
| C. Washbrook | c Tuckett b Dawson | 65 | not out | 13 |
| W.J. Edrich | b Mann | 189 | | |
| D.C.S. Compton | c Rowan b Tuckett | 208 | | |
| C.J. Barnett | b Tuckett | 33 | | |
| N.W.D. Yardley* | c Rowan b Tuckett | 5 | | |
| T.G. Evans† | b Tuckett | 16 | | |
| G.H. Pope | not out | 8 | | |
| A.V. Bedser | b Tuckett | 0 | | |
| D.V.P. Wright | } did not bat | | | |
| W.E. Hollies | } | | | |
| Extras | (B 2, LB 10) | 12 | | |
| **Total** | (8 wickets declared) | **554** | (0 wickets) | **26** |

### SOUTH AFRICA

| | | | | |
|---|---|---|---|---|
| B. Mitchell | st Evans b Compton | 46 | c Edrich b Wright | 80 |
| A. Melville* | c Bedser b Hollies | 117 | b Edrich | 8 |
| K.G. Viljoen | b Wright | 1 | b Edrich | 6 |
| A.D. Nourse | lbw b Wright | 61 | b Edrich | 58 |
| O.C. Dawson | c Barnett b Hollies | 36 | c Edrich b Compton | 33 |
| T.A. Harris | st Evans b Compton | 30 | c Yardley b Compton | 3 |
| A.M.B. Rowan | b Wright | 8 | not out | 38 |
| L. Tuckett | b Wright | 5 | lbw b Wright | 9 |
| N.B.F. Mann | b Wright | 4 | b Wright | 5 |
| J.D. Lindsay† | not out | 7 | c Yardley b Wright | 5 |
| V.I. Smith | c Edrich b Pope | 11 | c Edrich b Wright | 0 |
| Extras | (LB 1) | 1 | (B 3, LB 4) | 7 |
| **Total** | | **327** | | **252** |

| SOUTH AFRICA | O | M | R | W | O | M | R | W | | FALL OF WICKETS | | | |
|---|---|---|---|---|---|---|---|---|---|---|---|---|---|
| Tuckett | 47 | 8 | 115 | 5 | 3 | 0 | 4 | 0 | | E | SA | SA | E |
| Dawson | 33 | 11 | 81 | 1 | 6 | 2 | 6 | 0 | Wkt | 1st | 1st | 2nd | 2nd |
| Mann | 53 | 16 | 99 | 1 | 3·1 | 1 | 16 | 0 | 1st | 75 | 95 | 16 | – |
| Rowan | 65 | 11 | 174 | 1 | | | | | 2nd | 96 | 104 | 28 | – |
| Smith | 17 | 2 | 73 | 0 | | | | | 3rd | 466 | 222 | 120 | – |
| | | | | | | | | | 4th | 515 | 230 | 192 | – |
| ENGLAND | | | | | | | | | 5th | 526 | 290 | 192 | – |
| Edrich | 9 | 1 | 22 | 0 | 13 | 5 | 31 | 3 | 6th | 541 | 300 | 201 | – |
| Bedser | 26 | 1 | 76 | 0 | 14 | 6 | 20 | 0 | 7th | 554 | 302 | 224 | – |
| Pope | 19·2 | 5 | 49 | 1 | 17 | 7 | 36 | 0 | 8th | 554 | 308 | 236 | – |
| Wright | 39 | 10 | 95 | 5 | 32·2 | 6 | 80 | 5 | 9th | – | 309 | 252 | – |
| Hollies | 28 | 10 | 52 | 2 | 20 | 7 | 32 | 0 | 10th | – | 327 | 252 | – |
| Compton | 21 | 11 | 32 | 2 | 32 | 10 | 46 | 2 | | | | | |

Umpires: H.G. Baldwin and D. Davies.

# ENGLAND v SOUTH AFRICA 1947 (3rd Test)

Played at Old Trafford, Manchester, on 5, 7, 8, 9 July.
Toss: South Africa.　Result: ENGLAND won by seven wickets.
Debuts: England – K. Cranston, C. Gladwin; South Africa – D.V. Dyer, J.B. Plimsoll.

Edrich hit 37 runs, including three sixes, off Plimsoll and against the new ball. His stand with Compton, who scored his third successive hundred, added 228 in 196 minutes.

## SOUTH AFRICA

| | | | | |
|---|---|---|---|---|
| A. Melville* | c Hutton b Gladwin | 17 | b Edrich | 59 |
| D.V. Dyer | b Edrich | 62 | b Gladwin | 1 |
| B. Mitchell | run out | 80 | c Hutton b Compton | 6 |
| A.D. Nourse | c Yardley b Cranston | 23 | b Edrich | 115 |
| K.G. Viljoen | c Compton b Edrich | 93 | c Hutton b Wright | 32 |
| O.C. Dawson | b Cranston | 1 | b Edrich | 9 |
| A.M.B. Rowan | lbw b Hollies | 13 | c Evans b Wright | 0 |
| L. Tuckett | b Edrich | 13 | lbw b Edrich | 17 |
| N.B.F. Mann | c Hollies b Gladwin | 8 | c Barnett b Wright | 9 |
| J.D. Lindsay† | not out | 9 | b Hollies | 0 |
| J.B. Plimsoll | c Evans b Edrich | 8 | not out | 8 |
| Extras | (B 3, LB 9) | 12 | (B 5, LB 5, NB 1) | 11 |
| **Total** | | **339** | | **267** |

## ENGLAND

| | | | | |
|---|---|---|---|---|
| L. Hutton | c Lindsay b Plimsoll | 12 | c Dawson b Mann | 24 |
| C. Washbrook | c Nourse b Tuckett | 29 | c Lindsay b Dawson | 40 |
| W.J. Edrich | b Tuckett | 191 | not out | 22 |
| D.C.S. Compton | c Tuckett b Dawson | 115 | hit wkt b Mann | 6 |
| C.J. Barnett | c sub (T.A. Harris) b Mann | 5 | not out | 19 |
| N.W.D. Yardley* | c Melville b Plimsoll | 41 | | |
| K. Cranston | c Dawson b Rowan | 23 | | |
| T.G. Evans† | b Tuckett | 27 | | |
| C. Gladwin | b Tuckett | 16 | | |
| D.V.P. Wright | not out | 4 | | |
| W.E. Hollies | c Nourse b Plimsoll | 5 | | |
| Extras | (B 2, LB 7, NB 1) | 10 | (B 9, LB 8, NB 2) | 19 |
| **Total** | | **478** | (3 wickets) | **130** |

| ENGLAND | O | M | R | W | O | M | R | W | | FALL OF WICKETS | | | |
|---|---|---|---|---|---|---|---|---|---|---|---|---|---|
| Edrich | 35·1 | 9 | 95 | 4 | 22·4 | 4 | 77 | 4 | | SA | E | SA | E |
| Gladwin | 50 | 24 | 58 | 2 | 16 | 6 | 28 | 1 | *Wkt* | *1st* | *1st* | *2nd* | *2nd* |
| Cranston | 34 | 12 | 64 | 2 | | | | | 1st | 32 | 40 | 12 | 63 |
| Barnett | 8 | 3 | 11 | 0 | 5 | 1 | 12 | 0 | 2nd | 125 | 48 | 42 | 80 |
| Wright | 9 | 1 | 30 | 0 | 10 | 2 | 32 | 3 | 3rd | 163 | 276 | 96 | 103 |
| Hollies | 23 | 8 | 42 | 1 | 14 | 4 | 49 | 1 | 4th | 214 | 289 | 217 | – |
| Compton | 7 | 1 | 27 | 0 | 17 | 2 | 58 | 1 | 5th | 215 | 363 | 225 | – |
| | | | | | | | | | 6th | 260 | 415 | 228 | – |
| SOUTH AFRICA | | | | | | | | | 7th | 287 | 439 | 232 | – |
| Tuckett | 50 | 5 | 148 | 4 | 5 | 0 | 26 | 0 | 8th | 298 | 466 | 244 | – |
| Plimsoll | 35·3 | 9 | 128 | 3 | 4 | 0 | 15 | 0 | 9th | 327 | 471 | 244 | – |
| Rowan | 17 | 1 | 63 | 1 | 4 | 0 | 13 | 0 | 10th | 339 | 478 | 267 | – |
| Mann | 35 | 12 | 85 | 1 | 14 | 8 | 19 | 2 | | | | | |
| Dawson | 14 | 2 | 44 | 1 | 9·5 | 2 | 38 | 1 | | | | | |

Umpires: F. Chester and A.R. Coleman.

# ENGLAND v SOUTH AFRICA 1947 (4th Test)

Played at Headingley, Leeds, on 26, 28, 29 July.
Toss: South Africa.   Result: ENGLAND won by ten wickets.
Debuts: England – H.J. Butler, J.A. Young; South Africa – G.M. Fullerton.

Hutton scored a hundred in his first Test at Leeds. Cranston ended South Africa's second innings by taking four wickets in six balls (WOWOWW).

## SOUTH AFRICA

| | | | | | |
|---|---|---|---|---|---|
| A. Melville* | b Edrich | 0 | c Compton b Young | | 30 |
| D.V. Dyer | c Evans b Wright | 9 | c Yardley b Edrich | | 2 |
| B. Mitchell | b Butler | 53 | b Young | | 5 |
| A.D. Nourse | b Butler | 51 | lbw b Butler | | 57 |
| K.G. Viljoen | b Wright | 5 | lbw b Butler | | 29 |
| O.C. Dawson | c Young b Butler | 5 | b Butler | | 17 |
| G.M. Fullerton† | c Cranston b Edrich | 13 | lbw b Cranston | | 13 |
| A.M.B. Rowan | c Yardley b Edrich | 0 | not out | | 21 |
| N.B.F. Mann | c Edrich b Cranston | 29 | c Evans b Cranston | | 0 |
| L. Tuckett | c Evans b Butler | 3 | b Cranston | | 0 |
| V.I. Smith | not out | 0 | b Cranston | | 0 |
| Extras | (LB 5, NB 2) | 7 | (B 4, LB 6) | | 10 |
| **Total** | | **175** | | | **184** |

## ENGLAND

| | | | | |
|---|---|---|---|---|
| L. Hutton | run out | 100 | not out | 32 |
| C. Washbrook | b Mann | 75 | not out | 15 |
| W.J. Edrich | c Melville b Mann | 43 | | |
| D.C.S. Compton | c Mitchell b Mann | 30 | | |
| C.J. Barnett | c Tuckett b Rowan | 6 | | |
| N.W.D. Yardley* | c Nourse b Smith | 36 | | |
| K. Cranston | c Melville b Mann | 3 | | |
| T.G. Evans† | not out | 6 | | |
| J.A. Young | not out | 0 | | |
| D.V.P. Wright | ⎫ did not bat | | | |
| H.J. Butler | ⎭ | | | |
| Extras | (B 8, LB 8, NB 2) | 18 | | |
| **Total** | (7 wickets declared) | **317** | (0 wickets) | **47** |

| ENGLAND | O | M | R | W | O | M | R | W |
|---|---|---|---|---|---|---|---|---|
| Butler | 28 | 15 | 34 | 4 | 24 | 9 | 32 | 3 |
| Edrich | 17 | 4 | 46 | 3 | 14 | 2 | 35 | 1 |
| Young | 17 | 5 | 31 | 0 | 19 | 7 | 54 | 2 |
| Wright | 20 | 9 | 24 | 2 | 14 | 7 | 31 | 0 |
| Cranston | 11·1 | 3 | 24 | 1 | 7 | 3 | 12 | 4 |
| Compton | 4 | 0 | 9 | 0 | 2 | 0 | 10 | 0 |
| SOUTH AFRICA | | | | | | | | |
| Tuckett | 18 | 4 | 48 | 0 | 6 | 1 | 12 | 0 |
| Dawson | 4 | 0 | 12 | 0 | 4 | 1 | 13 | 0 |
| Mann | 50 | 20 | 68 | 4 | 3·4 | 0 | 17 | 0 |
| Smith | 36 | 9 | 82 | 1 | | | | |
| Rowan | 46 | 12 | 89 | 1 | | | | |
| Mitchell | | | | | 2 | 1 | 5 | 0 |

## FALL OF WICKETS

| | SA | E | SA | E |
|---|---|---|---|---|
| Wkt | 1st | 1st | 2nd | 2nd |
| 1st | 1 | 141 | 6 | – |
| 2nd | 23 | 218 | 16 | – |
| 3rd | 113 | 241 | 59 | – |
| 4th | 121 | 253 | 130 | – |
| 5th | 125 | 289 | 139 | – |
| 6th | 130 | 306 | 156 | – |
| 7th | 131 | 316 | 184 | – |
| 8th | 158 | – | 184 | – |
| 9th | 175 | – | 184 | – |
| 10th | 175 | – | 184 | – |

Umpires: F. Chester and J.J. Hills.

# ENGLAND v SOUTH AFRICA 1947 (5th Test)

Played at Kennington Oval, London, on 16, 18, 19, 20 August.
Toss: England.   Result: MATCH DRAWN.
Debuts: England – R. Howorth, J.D.B. Robertson.

Mitchell emulated Melville's feat of the 1st Test by scoring a century in both innings. He was on the field for the entire match bar 8 minutes (12 balls). Howorth dismissed Dyer with his first ball in Test cricket.

## ENGLAND

| | | | | |
|---|---|--:|---|--:|
| L. Hutton | b Mann | 83 | c Tuckett b Mann | 36 |
| C. Washbrook | lbw b Mann | 32 | c Fullerton b Rowan | 43 |
| J.D.B. Robertson | c Melville b Smith | 4 | b Rowan | 30 |
| D.C.S. Compton | c Tuckett b Rowan | 53 | c Nourse b Dawson | 113 |
| N.W.D. Yardley* | b Mann | 59 | c sub (D.W. Begbie) b Mann | 11 |
| K. Cranston | st Fullerton b Rowan | 45 | c Mitchell b Rowan | 0 |
| R. Howorth | c Fullerton b Rowan | 23 | not out | 45 |
| T.G. Evans† | run out | 45 | not out | 39 |
| C. Gladwin | not out | 51 | | |
| D.V.P. Wright | b Mann | 14 | | |
| W.H. Copson | b Dawson | 6 | | |
| Extras | (B 4, LB 7, NB 1) | 12 | (B 6, W 2) | 8 |
| **Total** | | **427** | (6 wickets declared) | **325** |

## SOUTH AFRICA

| | | | | |
|---|---|--:|---|--:|
| B. Mitchell | c Evans b Copson | 120 | not out | 189 |
| D.V. Dyer | c Gladwin b Howorth | 18 | lbw b Wright | 4 |
| K.G. Viljoen | c Evans b Wright | 10 | st Evans b Howorth | 33 |
| A.D. Nourse | c Yardley b Howorth | 10 | b Howorth | 97 |
| A. Melville* | lbw b Cranston | 39 | c Evans b Cranston | 6 |
| O.C. Dawson | lbw b Wright | 55 | c Howorth b Cranston | 0 |
| G.M. Fullerton† | c Howorth b Cranston | 6 | c Evans b Howorth | 14 |
| A.M.B. Rowan | b Howorth | 0 | | |
| N.B.F. Mann | b Copson | 36 | (8) c Hutton b Wright | 10 |
| L. Tuckett | not out | 0 | (9) not out | 40 |
| V.I. Smith | lbw b Copson | 0 | | |
| Extras | (B 3, LB 2, W 1, NB 2) | 8 | (B 12, LB 14, W 4) | 30 |
| **Total** | | **302** | (7 wickets) | **423** |

| SOUTH AFRICA | O | M | R | W | O | M | R | W |
|---|--:|--:|--:|--:|--:|--:|--:|--:|
| Tuckett | 32 | 6 | 82 | 0 | 7 | 0 | 34 | 0 |
| Dawson | 35 | 5 | 80 | 1 | 15 | 1 | 59 | 1 |
| Mann | 64 | 28 | 93 | 4 | 27 | 7 | 102 | 2 |
| Rowan | 38 | 9 | 92 | 3 | 25 | 1 | 95 | 3 |
| Smith | 21 | 0 | 68 | 1 | 3 | 0 | 27 | 0 |
| ENGLAND | | | | | | | | |
| Copson | 27 | 13 | 46 | 3 | 30 | 11 | 66 | 0 |
| Gladwin | 16 | 2 | 39 | 0 | 16 | 5 | 33 | 0 |
| Wright | 29 | 7 | 89 | 2 | 30 | 8 | 103 | 2 |
| Howorth | 39 | 16 | 64 | 3 | 37 | 12 | 85 | 3 |
| Compton | 11 | 4 | 31 | 0 | 4 | 0 | 30 | 0 |
| Cranston | 9 | 2 | 25 | 2 | 21 | 3 | 61 | 2 |
| Hutton | | | | | 2 | 0 | 14 | 0 |
| Yardley | | | | | 1 | 0 | 1 | 0 |

### FALL OF WICKETS

| | E | SA | E | SA |
|---|--:|--:|--:|--:|
| Wkt | 1st | 1st | 2nd | 2nd |
| 1st | 63 | 47 | 73 | 8 |
| 2nd | 80 | 62 | 89 | 48 |
| 3rd | 178 | 78 | 158 | 232 |
| 4th | 178 | 164 | 179 | 247 |
| 5th | 271 | 243 | 180 | 249 |
| 6th | 290 | 253 | 267 | 266 |
| 7th | 322 | 254 | – | 314 |
| 8th | 358 | 293 | – | – |
| 9th | 408 | 302 | – | – |
| 10th | 427 | 302 | – | – |

Umpires: H.G. Baldwin and C. Smart.

# AUSTRALIA v INDIA 1947–48 (1st Test)

Played at Woolloongabba, Brisbane, on 28, 29 November, 1, 2, 3 (*no play*), 4 December.
Toss: Australia.   Result: AUSTRALIA won by an innings and 226 runs.
Debuts: Australia – W.A. Johnston; India – H.R. Adhikari, J.K. Irani, G. Kishenchand,
K.M. Rangnekar.

Brisbane provided its customary sticky pitch for India's first official encounter with Australia.

## AUSTRALIA

| | | |
|---|---|---|
| W.A. Brown | c Irani b Amarnath | 11 |
| A.R. Morris | hit wkt b Sarwate | 47 |
| D.G. Bradman* | hit wkt b Amarnath | 185 |
| A.L. Hassett | c Gul Mahomed b Mankad | 48 |
| K.R. Miller | c Mankad b Amarnath | 58 |
| C.L. McCool | c Sohoni b Amarnath | 10 |
| R.R. Lindwall | st Irani b Mankad | 7 |
| D. Tallon† | not out | 3 |
| I.W. Johnson | c Rangnekar b Mankad | 6 |
| E.R.H. Toshack | not out | 0 |
| W.A. Johnston | did not bat | |
| Extras | (B 5, LB 1, W 1) | 7 |
| **Total** | (8 wickets declared) | **382** |

## INDIA

| | | | | |
|---|---|---|---|---|
| V.M.H. Mankad | c Tallon b Lindwall | 0 | b Lindwall | 7 |
| C.T. Sarwate | c Johnston b Miller | 12 | b Johnston | 26 |
| Gul Mahomed | b Lindwall | 0 | b Toshack | 13 |
| H.R. Adhikari | c McCool b Johnston | 8 | lbw b Toshack | 13 |
| G. Kishenchand | c Tallon b Johnston | 1 | c Bradman b Toshack | 0 |
| V.S. Hazare | c Brown b Toshack | 10 | c Morris b Toshack | 18 |
| L. Amarnath* | c Bradman b Toshack | 22 | b Toshack | 5 |
| K.M. Rangnekar | c Miller b Toshack | 1 | c Hassett b Toshack | 0 |
| S.W. Sohoni | c Miller b Toshack | 2 | c Brown b Miller | 4 |
| C.S. Nayudu | not out | 0 | c Hassett b Lindwall | 6 |
| J.K. Irani† | c Hassett b Toshack | 0 | not out | 2 |
| Extras | (B 1, LB 1) | 2 | (B 3, NB 1) | 4 |
| **Total** | | **58** | | **98** |

| INDIA | O | M | R | W | O | M | R | W | FALL OF WICKETS | | | |
|---|---|---|---|---|---|---|---|---|---|---|---|---|
| Sohoni | 23 | 4 | 81 | 0 | | | | | | A | I | I |
| Amarnath | 39 | 10 | 84 | 4 | | | | | *Wkt* | *1st* | *1st* | *2nd* |
| Mankad | 34 | 3 | 113 | 3 | | | | | 1st | 38 | 0 | 14 |
| Sarwate | 5 | 1 | 16 | 1 | | | | | 2nd | 97 | 0 | 27 |
| Hazare | 11 | 1 | 63 | 0 | | | | | 3rd | 198 | 19 | 41 |
| Nayudu | 3 | 0 | 18 | 0 | | | | | 4th | 318 | 23 | 41 |
| | | | | | | | | | 5th | 344 | 23 | 72 |
| AUSTRALIA | | | | | | | | | 6th | 373 | 53 | 80 |
| Lindwall | 5 | 2 | 11 | 2 | 10·7 | 2 | 19 | 2 | 7th | 373 | 56 | 80 |
| Johnston | 8 | 4 | 17 | 2 | 9 | 6 | 11 | 1 | 8th | 380 | 58 | 89 |
| Miller | 6 | 1 | 26 | 1 | 10 | 2 | 30 | 1 | 9th | – | 58 | 94 |
| Toshack | 2·3 | 1 | 2 | 5 | 17 | 6 | 29 | 6 | 10th | – | 58 | 98 |
| Johnson | | | | | 3 | 1 | 5 | 0 | | | | |

Umpires: G. Borwick and A.N. Barlow.

# AUSTRALIA v INDIA 1947–48 (2nd Test)

Played at Sydney Cricket Ground on 12, 13, 15 (*no play*), 16 (*no play*), 17, 18 (*no play*) December.
Toss: India.   Result: MATCH DRAWN.
Debuts: India – Amir Elahi, D.G. Phadkar.

This was the first Test in Australia to be completely ruined by rain; only ten hours play was possible during the six days. Mankad created Test history by running out non-striker Brown for backing-up. He had rehearsed this successfully when the Indians played an Australian XI.

## INDIA

| | | | | | |
|---|---|---|---|---|---|
| V.M.H. Mankad | c Lindwall | 5 | | b Lindwall | 5 |
| C.T. Sarwate | b Johnston | 0 | (3) | c Johnson b Johnston | 3 |
| Gul Mahomed | c Brown b Miller | 29 | (4) | c Bradman b Johnson | 5 |
| V.S. Hazare | b Miller | 16 | (5) | not out | 13 |
| L. Amarnath* | b Johnson | 25 | (7) | c Morris b Johnson | 14 |
| G. Kishenchand | b Johnson | 44 | (8) | c McCool b Johnston | 0 |
| H.R. Adhikari | lbw b Johnston | 0 | (9) | not out | 0 |
| D.G. Phadkar | c Miller b McCool | 51 | (6) | c Tallon b Miller | 2 |
| C.S. Nayudu | c and b McCool | 6 | | | |
| Amir Elahi | c Miller b McCool | 4 | (2) | c Miller b Johnston | 13 |
| J.K. Irani† | not out | 1 | | | |
| Extras | (B 5, LB 2) | 7 | | (B 3, LB 3) | 6 |
| **Total** | | **188** | | (7 wickets) | **61** |

## AUSTRALIA

| | | |
|---|---|---|
| W.A. Brown | run out | 18 |
| A.R. Morris | lbw b Amarnath | 10 |
| D.G. Bradman* | b Hazare | 13 |
| A.L. Hassett | c Adhikari b Hazare | 6 |
| K.R. Miller | lbw b Phadkar | 17 |
| R.A. Hamence | c Adhikari b Mankad | 25 |
| I.W. Johnson | lbw b Phadkar | 1 |
| C.L. McCool | b Phadkar | 9 |
| R.R. Lindwall | b Hazare | 0 |
| D. Tallon† | c Irani b Hazare | 6 |
| W.A. Johnston | not out | 0 |
| Extras | (B 1, LB 1) | 2 |
| **Total** | | **107** |

| AUSTRALIA | O | M | R | W | O | M | R | W | | FALL OF WICKETS | | |
|---|---|---|---|---|---|---|---|---|---|---|---|---|
| Lindwall | 12 | 3 | 30 | 1 | 5 | 1 | 13 | 1 | | I | A | I |
| Johnston | 17 | 4 | 33 | 2 | 13 | 5 | 15 | 3 | *Wkt* | *1st* | *1st* | *2nd* |
| Miller | 9 | 3 | 25 | 2 | 6 | 2 | 5 | 1 | 1st | 2 | 25 | 17 |
| McCool | 18 | 2 | 71 | 3 | | | | | 2nd | 16 | 30 | 19 |
| Johnson | 14 | 3 | 22 | 2 | 13 | 7 | 22 | 2 | 3rd | 52 | 43 | 26 |
| | | | | | | | | | 4th | 57 | 48 | 29 |
| INDIA | | | | | | | | | 5th | 94 | 86 | 34 |
| Phadkar | 10 | 2 | 14 | 3 | | | | | 6th | 95 | 92 | 53 |
| Amarnath | 14 | 4 | 31 | 1 | | | | | 7th | 165 | 92 | 55 |
| Mankad | 9 | 0 | 31 | 1 | | | | | 8th | 174 | 97 | – |
| Hazare | 13·2 | 3 | 29 | 4 | | | | | 9th | 182 | 105 | – |
| | | | | | | | | | 10th | 188 | 107 | – |

Umpires: G. Borwick and A.N. Barlow.

# AUSTRALIA v INDIA 1947–48 (3rd Test)

Played at Melbourne Cricket Ground on 1, 2, 3, 5 January.
Toss: Australia.   Result: AUSTRALIA won by 233 runs.
Debuts: India – K. Rai Singh, P. Sen.

Bradman added to his considerable collection of records by becoming the first and, as yet, only player to score a hundred in each innings of a Test against India.

## AUSTRALIA

| | | | | | |
|---|---|---|---|---|---|
| S.G. Barnes | b Mankad | 12 | (4) c Sen b Amarnath | | 15 |
| A.R. Morris | b Amarnath | 45 | (5) not out | | 100 |
| D.G. Bradman* | lbw b Phadkar | 132 | (6) not out | | 127 |
| A.L. Hassett | lbw b Mankad | 80 | | | |
| K.R. Miller | lbw b Mankad | 29 | | | |
| R.A. Hamence | st Sen b Amarnath | 25 | | | |
| R.R. Lindwall | b Amarnath | 26 | | | |
| D. Tallon† | c Mankad b Amarnath | 2 | | | |
| B. Dooland | not out | 21 | (2) lbw b Phadkar | | 6 |
| I.W. Johnson | lbw b Mankad | 16 | (1) c Hazare b Amarnath | | 0 |
| W.A. Johnston | run out | 5 | (3) lbw b Amarnath | | 3 |
| Extras | (B 1) | 1 | (B 3, NB 1) | | 4 |
| **Total** | | **394** | (4 wickets declared) | | **255** |

## INDIA

| | | | | |
|---|---|---|---|---|
| V.M.H. Mankad | c Tallon b Johnston | 116 | b Johnston | 13 |
| C.T. Sarwate | c Tallon b Johnston | 36 | b Johnston | 1 |
| Gul Mahomed | c and b Dooland | 12 | c Morris b Johnson | 28 |
| V.S. Hazare | c Tallon b Barnes | 17 | c Barnes b Miller | 10 |
| L. Amarnath* | lbw b Barnes | 0 | b Lindwall | 8 |
| D.G. Phadkar | not out | 55 | c Barnes b Johnston | 13 |
| H.R. Adhikari | st Tallon b Johnson | 26 | c Lindwall b Johnson | 1 |
| K. Rai Singh | c Barnes b Johnson | 2 | c Tallon b Johnston | 24 |
| K.M. Rangnekar | c and b Johnson | 6 | c Hamence b Johnson | 18 |
| P. Sen† | b Johnson | 4 | c Hassett b Johnston | 2 |
| C.S. Nayudu | not out | 4 | c not out | 0 |
| Extras | (B 9, LB 3, NB 1) | 13 | (B 6, LB 1) | 7 |
| **Total** | (9 wickets declared) | **291** | | **125** |

| INDIA | O | M | R | W | O | M | R | W | FALL OF WICKETS | | | | |
|---|---|---|---|---|---|---|---|---|---|---|---|---|---|
| Phadkar | 15 | 1 | 80 | 1 | 10 | 1 | 28 | 1 | | A | I | A | I |
| Amarnath | 21 | 3 | 78 | 4 | 20 | 3 | 52 | 3 | *Wkt* | *1st* | *1st* | *2nd* | *2nd* |
| Hazare | 16·1 | 0 | 62 | 0 | 11 | 1 | 55 | 0 | 1st | 29 | 124 | 1 | 10 |
| Mankad | 37 | 4 | 135 | 4 | 18 | 4 | 74 | 0 | 2nd | 99 | 145 | 11 | 27 |
| Sarwate | 3 | 0 | 16 | 0 | 5 | 0 | 41 | 0 | 3rd | 268 | 188 | 13 | 44 |
| Nayudu | 2 | 0 | 22 | 0 | | | | | 4th | 289 | 188 | 32 | 60 |
| Gul Mahomed | | | | | 1 | 0 | 1 | 0 | 5th | 302 | 198 | – | 60 |
| | | | | | | | | | 6th | 339 | 260 | – | 69 |
| AUSTRALIA | | | | | | | | | 7th | 341 | 264 | – | 100 |
| Lindwall | 12 | 0 | 47 | 0 | 3 | 0 | 10 | 1 | 8th | 352 | 280 | – | 107 |
| Miller | 13 | 2 | 46 | 0 | 7 | 0 | 29 | 1 | 9th | 387 | 284 | – | 125 |
| Johnston | 12 | 0 | 33 | 2 | 10 | 1 | 44 | 4 | 10th | 394 | – | – | 125 |
| Johnson | 14 | 1 | 59 | 4 | 5·7 | 0 | 35 | 4 | | | | | |
| Dooland | 12 | 0 | 68 | 1 | | | | | | | | | |
| Barnes | 6 | 1 | 25 | 2 | | | | | | | | | |

Umpires: A.N. Barlow and H. Elphinston.

# AUSTRALIA v INDIA 1947–48 (4th Test)

Played at Adelaide Oval on 23, 24, 26, 27, 28 January,
Toss: Australia.   Result: AUSTRALIA won by an innings and 16 runs.
Debuts: Australia – R.N. Harvey; India – C.R. Rangachari.

Australia's total of 674 remains the record for any Test in Australia. Hazare became the first batsman to score a hundred in each innings of a Test for India.

## AUSTRALIA

| | | |
|---|---|---|
| S.G. Barnes | lbw b Mankad | 112 |
| A.R. Morris | b Phadkar | 7 |
| D.G. Bradman* | b Hazare | 201 |
| A.L. Hassett | not out | 198 |
| K.R. Miller | b Rangachari | 67 |
| R.N. Harvey | lbw b Rangachari | 13 |
| C.L. McCool | b Phadkar | 27 |
| I.W. Johnson | b Rangachari | 22 |
| R.R. Lindwall | b Rangachari | 2 |
| D. Tallon† | lbw b Mankad | 1 |
| E.R.H. Toshack | lbw b Hazare | 8 |
| Extras | (B 8, LB 6, NB 2) | 16 |
| **Total** | | **674** |

## INDIA

| | | | | | |
|---|---|---|---|---|---|
| V.M.H. Mankad | b McCool | 49 | c Tallon b Lindwall | | 0 |
| C.T. Sarwate | b Miller | 1 | b Toshack | | 11 |
| P. Sen† | b Miller | 0 | (10) not out | | 0 |
| L. Amarnath* | c Bradman b Johnson | 46 | (3) b Lindwall | | 0 |
| V.S. Hazare | lbw b Johnson | 116 | (4) b Lindwall | | 145 |
| Gul Mahomed | st Tallon b Johnson | 4 | (5) b Barnes | | 34 |
| D.G. Phadkar | lbw b Toshack | 123 | (6) lbw b Lindwall | | 14 |
| G. Kishenchand | b Lindwall | 10 | (7) b Lindwall | | 0 |
| H.R. Adhikari | run out | 2 | (8) lbw b Miller | | 51 |
| K.M. Rangnekar | st Tallon b Johnson | 8 | (9) b Lindwall | | 0 |
| C.R. Rangachari | not out | 0 | c McCool b Lindwall | | 0 |
| Extras | (B 11, LB 8, NB 3) | 22 | (B 18, LB 3, NB 1) | | 22 |
| **Total** | | **381** | | | **277** |

| INDIA | O | M | R | W | O | M | R | W |
|---|---|---|---|---|---|---|---|---|
| Phadkar | 15 | 0 | 74 | 2 | | | | |
| Amarnath | 9 | 0 | 42 | 0 | | | | |
| Rangachari | 41 | 5 | 141 | 4 | | | | |
| Mankad | 43 | 8 | 170 | 2 | | | | |
| Sarwate | 22 | 1 | 121 | 0 | | | | |
| Hazare | 21·3 | 1 | 110 | 2 | | | | |
| AUSTRALIA | | | | | | | | |
| Lindwall | 21 | 6 | 61 | 1 | 16·5 | 4 | 38 | 7 |
| Miller | 9 | 1 | 39 | 2 | 9 | 3 | 13 | 1 |
| McCool | 28 | 2 | 102 | 1 | 4 | 0 | 26 | 0 |
| Johnson | 23·1 | 5 | 64 | 4 | 20 | 4 | 54 | 0 |
| Toshack | 18 | 2 | 66 | 1 | 25 | 8 | 73 | 1 |
| Barnes | 9 | 0 | 23 | 0 | 18 | 4 | 51 | 1 |
| Bradman | 1 | 0 | 4 | 0 | | | | |

### FALL OF WICKETS

| | A | I | I |
|---|---|---|---|
| Wkt | 1st | 1st | 2nd |
| 1st | 20 | 6 | 0 |
| 2nd | 256 | 6 | 0 |
| 3rd | 361 | 69 | 33 |
| 4th | 503 | 124 | 99 |
| 5th | 523 | 133 | 139 |
| 6th | 576 | 321 | 139 |
| 7th | 634 | 353 | 271 |
| 8th | 640 | 359 | 273 |
| 9th | 641 | 375 | 273 |
| 10th | 674 | 381 | 277 |

Umpires: G. Borwick and R. Wright.

# AUSTRALIA v INDIA 1947–48 (5th Test)

Played at Melbourne Cricket Ground on 6, 7, 9, 10 February.
Toss: Australia.   Result: AUSTRALIA won by an innings and 177 runs.
Debuts: Australia – L.J. Johnson, S.J.E. Loxton, D.T. Ring.

Bradman retired hurt at 140 for 1. Australia took 16 wickets for 147 runs on the fourth day.

## AUSTRALIA

| | | |
|---|---|---|
| S.G. Barnes | run out | 33 |
| W.A. Brown | run out | 99 |
| D.G. Bradman* | retired hurt | 57 |
| K.R. Miller | c Sen b Phadkar | 14 |
| R.N. Harvey | c Sen b Mankad | 153 |
| S.J.E. Loxton | c Sen b Amarnath | 80 |
| R.R. Lindwall | c Phadkar b Mankad | 35 |
| D. Tallon† | c Sen b Sarwate | 37 |
| L.J. Johnson | not out | 25 |
| D.T. Ring | c Kishenchand b Hazare | 11 |
| W.A. Johnston | not out | 23 |
| Extras | (B 4, LB 4) | 8 |
| **Total** | (8 wickets declared) | **575** |

## INDIA

| | | | | |
|---|---|---|---|---|
| V.M.H. Mankad | c Tallon b Loxton | 111 | c Tallon b Lindwall | 0 |
| C.T. Sarwate | b Lindwall | 0 | lbw b Johnston | 10 |
| H.R. Adhikari | c Tallon b Loxton | 38 | c Bradman b Loxton | 17 |
| V.S. Hazare | lbw b Lindwall | 74 | c and b Johnson | 10 |
| L. Amarnath* | c Barnes b Ring | 12 | (6) c Johnson b Ring | 8 |
| D.G. Phadkar | not out | 56 | (5) lbw b Johnston | 0 |
| Gul Mahomed | c Lindwall b Johnson | 1 | c Barnes b Ring | 4 |
| G. Kishenchand | b Ring | 14 | c Barnes b Johnson | 0 |
| C.S. Nayudu | c Bradman b Ring | 2 | c Brown b Ring | 0 |
| P. Sen† | b Johnson | 13 | b Johnson | 10 |
| C.R. Rangachari | b Johnson | 0 | not out | 0 |
| Extras | (B 6, LB 2, NB 2) | 10 | (B 6, LB 1, NB 1) | 8 |
| **Total** | | **331** | | **67** |

| INDIA | O | M | R | W | O | M | R | W | FALL OF WICKETS | | | |
|---|---|---|---|---|---|---|---|---|---|---|---|---|
| | | | | | | | | | | A | I | I |
| Phadkar | 9 | 0 | 58 | 1 | | | | | Wkt | 1st | 1st | 2nd |
| Amarnath | 23 | 1 | 79 | 1 | | | | | 1st | 48 | 3 | 0 |
| Rangachari | 17 | 1 | 97 | 0 | | | | | 2nd | 182 | 127 | 22 |
| Hazare | 14 | 1 | 63 | 1 | | | | | 3rd | 219 | 206 | 28 |
| Mankad | 33 | 2 | 107 | 2 | | | | | 4th | 378 | 231 | 35 |
| Sarwate | 18 | 1 | 82 | 1 | | | | | 5th | 457 | 257 | 51 |
| Nayudu | 13 | 0 | 77 | 0 | | | | | 6th | 497 | 260 | 51 |
| Adhikari | 1 | 0 | 4 | 0 | | | | | 7th | 527 | 284 | 56 |
| | | | | | | | | | 8th | 544 | 286 | 56 |
| AUSTRALIA | | | | | | | | | 9th | – | 331 | 66 |
| Lindwall | 25 | 5 | 66 | 2 | 3 | 0 | 9 | 1 | 10th | – | 331 | 67 |
| Johnson | 30 | 8 | 66 | 3 | 5·2 | 2 | 8 | 3 | | | | |
| Loxton | 19 | 1 | 61 | 1 | 4 | 1 | 10 | 1 | | | | |
| Johnston | 8 | 4 | 14 | 0 | 7 | 0 | 15 | 2 | | | | |
| Ring | 36 | 8 | 103 | 3 | 5 | 1 | 17 | 3 | | | | |
| Miller | 3 | 0 | 10 | 0 | | | | | | | | |
| Barnes | 2 | 1 | 1 | 0 | | | | | | | | |

Umpires: A.N. Barlow and G.C. Cooper.

# WEST INDIES v ENGLAND 1947–48 (1st Test)

Played at Kensington Oval, Bridgetown, Barbados, on 21, 22, 23, 24, 26 January.
Toss: West Indies.   Result: MATCH DRAWN.
Debuts: West Indies – R.J. Christiani, W. Ferguson, B.B.M. Gaskin, J.D.C. Goddard, P.E. Jones,
  C.L. Walcott, E. de C. Weekes; England – D. Brookes, J.C. Laker, W. Place, G.A. Smithson,
  M.F. Tremlett.

Laker took 7 for 103 in his first Test innings, including a spell of 6 for 25 on the second morning. Williams hit 72
runs in 63 minutes in the second innings, including 6, 6, 4, 4 off his first four balls from Laker. His fifty took 30
minutes and is now the third-fastest in Test cricket. Tropical rain ended play early on the last morning.

## WEST INDIES

| | | | | | |
|---|---|---|---|---|---|
| J.B. Stollmeyer | c Robertson b Ikin | 78 | c Evans b Howorth | | 31 |
| C.L. Walcott† | b Laker | 8 | c Ikin b Howorth | | 16 |
| E. de C. Weekes | c Evans b Tremlett | 35 | b Laker | | 25 |
| G.E. Gomez | b Laker | 86 | st Evans b Howorth | | 0 |
| G.A. Headley* | b Laker | 29 | (11) not out | | 7 |
| R.J. Christiani | lbw b Laker | 1 | lbw b Cranston | | 99 |
| J.D.C. Goddard | b Howorth | 28 | (5) c Ikin b Laker | | 18 |
| E.A.V. Williams | c Ikin b Laker | 2 | (7) c Evans b Howorth | | 72 |
| W. Ferguson | b Laker | 0 | not out | | 56 |
| P.E. Jones | not out | 10 | (8) c Robertson b Howorth | | 7 |
| B.B.M. Gaskin | c Ikin b Laker | 10 | (10) c Brookes b Howorth | | 7 |
| Extras | (LB 4, W 2, NB 3) | 9 | (B 6, LB 4, W 1, NB 2) | | 13 |
| **Total** | | **296** | (9 wickets declared) | | **351** |

## ENGLAND

| | | | | | |
|---|---|---|---|---|---|
| J.D.B. Robertson | lbw b Williams | 80 | not out | | 51 |
| W. Place | c Gomez b Goddard | 12 | (6) not out | | 1 |
| D. Brookes | b Jones | 10 | (2) c Walcott b Goddard | | 7 |
| J. Hardstaff, jr | b Williams | 98 | (5) c Gomez b Goddard | | 0 |
| J.T. Ikin | c Walcott b Williams | 3 | | | |
| G.A. Smithson | c Gomez b Jones | 0 | | | |
| K. Cranston* | run out | 2 | (4) lbw b Gaskin | | 8 |
| R. Howorth | c Goddard b Ferguson | 14 | (3) b Ferguson | | 16 |
| T.G. Evans† | b Jones | 26 | | | |
| J.C. Laker | c Walcott b Jones | 2 | | | |
| M.F. Tremlett | not out | 0 | | | |
| Extras | (B 2, LB 2, W 1, NB 1) | 6 | (LB 3) | | 3 |
| **Total** | | **253** | (4 wickets) | | **86** |

| ENGLAND | O | M | R | W | O | M | R | W | | FALL OF WICKETS | | | |
|---|---|---|---|---|---|---|---|---|---|---|---|---|---|
| Tremlett | 26 | 8 | 49 | 1 | 10 | 0 | 40 | 0 | | WI | E | WI | E |
| Cranston | 15 | 4 | 29 | 0 | 13 | 3 | 31 | 1 | *Wkt* | *1st* | *1st* | *2nd* | *2nd* |
| Laker | 37 | 9 | 103 | 7 | 30 | 12 | 95 | 2 | 1st | 18 | 32 | 46 | 33 |
| Ikin | 16 | 3 | 38 | 1 | 12 | 1 | 48 | 0 | 2nd | 81 | 67 | 69 | 55 |
| Howorth | 30 | 8 | 68 | 1 | 41 | 8 | 124 | 6 | 3rd | 185 | 130 | 71 | 70 |
| | | | | | | | | | 4th | 245 | 153 | 87 | 71 |
| WEST INDIES | | | | | | | | | 5th | 246 | 156 | 144 | – |
| Jones | 25·2 | 6 | 54 | 4 | 9 | 1 | 29 | 0 | 6th | 271 | 176 | 240 | – |
| Gaskin | 11 | 0 | 30 | 0 | 10 | 4 | 15 | 1 | 7th | 273 | 197 | 252 | – |
| Williams | 33 | 15 | 51 | 3 | 9 | 3 | 17 | 0 | 8th | 273 | 250 | 301 | – |
| Goddard | 21 | 6 | 49 | 1 | 14 | 4 | 18 | 2 | 9th | 279 | 252 | 328 | – |
| Ferguson | 14 | 1 | 52 | 1 | 3·4 | 1 | 4 | 1 | 10th | 296 | 253 | – | – |
| Headley | 6 | 1 | 11 | 0 | | | | | | | | | |

Umpires: S.C. Foster and J.H. Walcott.

# WEST INDIES v ENGLAND 1947–48 (2nd Test)

Played at Queen's Park Oval, Port-of-Spain, Trinidad, on 11, 12, 13, 14, 16 February.
Toss: England.   Result: MATCH DRAWN.
Debuts: West Indies – A.G. Ganteaume, F.M.M. Worrell; England – S.C. Griffith, J.H. Wardle.

Griffith was the first player to score his maiden first-class century in his first Test innings; he is still the only one to do so for England.

### ENGLAND

| | | | | | |
|---|---|---|---|---|---|
| J.D.B. Robertson | run out | 2 | c Christiani b Ferguson | | 133 |
| S.C. Griffith | lbw b Worrell | 140 | c Ferguson b Gomez | | 4 |
| J.T. Ikin | b Ferguson | 21 | lbw b Ferguson | | 19 |
| K. Cranston | c and b Ferguson | 7 | c Christiani b Williams | | 6 |
| G.O.B. Allen* | c Walcott b Gaskin | 36 | (6) c Walcott b Williams | | 2 |
| R. Howorth | b Ferguson | 14 | (7) b Ferguson | | 14 |
| T.G. Evans† | c Walcott b Williams | 30 | (8) st Walcott b Ferguson | | 21 |
| G.A. Smithson | c Goddard b Ferguson | 35 | (9) b Ferguson | | 35 |
| J.C. Laker | c Gaskin b Goddard | 55 | (5) c Carew b Williams | | 24 |
| J.H. Wardle | c Worrell b Ferguson | 4 | not out | | 2 |
| H.J. Butler | not out | 15 | b Ferguson | | 0 |
| Extras | (LB 1, NB 2) | 3 | (B 5, LB 3, NB 7) | | 15 |
| **Total** | | **362** | | | **275** |

### WEST INDIES

| | | | | | |
|---|---|---|---|---|---|
| G.M. Carew | lbw b Laker | 107 | (5) not out | | 18 |
| A.G. Ganteaume | c Ikin b Howorth | 112 | | | |
| E. de C.Weekes | b Butler | 36 | (1) c Evans b Butler | | 20 |
| F.M.M. Worrell | c Evans b Cranston | 97 | not out | | 28 |
| C.L. Walcott† | c Butler b Howorth | 20 | (2) lbw b Allen | | 2 |
| G.E. Gomez* | lbw b Laker | 62 | | | |
| R.J. Christiani | c Robertson b Allen | 7 | | | |
| J.D.C. Goddard | not out | 9 | | | |
| E.A.V. Williams | c and b Allen | 31 | (3) b Butler | | 0 |
| W. Ferguson | b Butler | 5 | | | |
| B.B.M. Gaskin | b Butler | 0 | | | |
| Extras | (B 2, LB 4, W 1, NB 4) | 11 | (LB 2, W 1, NB 1) | | 4 |
| **Total** | | **497** | (3 wickets) | | **72** |

| WEST INDIES | O | M | R | W | O | M | R | W |
|---|---|---|---|---|---|---|---|---|
| Gaskin | 37 | 14 | 72 | 1 | 21 | 6 | 41 | 0 |
| Williams | 21 | 8 | 31 | 1 | 27 | 7 | 64 | 3 |
| Ferguson | 39 | 5 | 137 | 5 | 34·2 | 4 | 92 | 6 |
| Goddard | 23·3 | 6 | 64 | 1 | 9 | 4 | 11 | 0 |
| Worrell | 23 | 4 | 55 | 1 | 14 | 2 | 30 | 0 |
| Gomez | | | | | 8 | 2 | 22 | 1 |
| ENGLAND | | | | | | | | |
| Butler | 32 | 4 | 122 | 3 | 8 | 2 | 27 | 2 |
| Allen | 16 | 0 | 82 | 2 | 5 | 0 | 21 | 1 |
| Laker | 36 | 10 | 108 | 2 | | | | |
| Cranston | 7 | 1 | 29 | 1 | 3 | 0 | 18 | 0 |
| Ikin | 20 | 5 | 60 | 0 | | | | |
| Howorth | 32 | 3 | 76 | 2 | 1 | 0 | 2 | 0 |
| Wardle | 3 | 0 | 9 | 0 | | | | |

FALL OF WICKETS

| | E | WI | E | WI |
|---|---|---|---|---|
| Wkt | 1st | 1st | 2nd | 2nd |
| 1st | 5 | 173 | 18 | 3 |
| 2nd | 42 | 226 | 53 | 8 |
| 3rd | 54 | 306 | 62 | 41 |
| 4th | 126 | 341 | 97 | – |
| 5th | 158 | 440 | 122 | – |
| 6th | 201 | 447 | 149 | – |
| 7th | 288 | 454 | 196 | – |
| 8th | 296 | 488 | 270 | – |
| 9th | 306 | 497 | 275 | – |
| 10th | 362 | 497 | 275 | – |

Umpires: B. Henderson and V. Guillen.

# WEST INDIES v ENGLAND 1947–48 (3rd Test)

Played at Bourda, Georgetown, British Guiana, on 3, 4, 5, 6 March.
Toss: West Indies.   Result: WEST INDIES won by seven wickets
Debuts: West Indies – L.R. Pierre, J. Trim.

Hutton had joined the touring team after the 2nd Test. Allen retired injured and was unable to complete his third over.

## WEST INDIES

| | | | | | |
|---|---|---|---|---|---|
| G.M. Carew | b Cranston | 17 | c Allen b Laker | | 8 |
| J.D.C. Goddard* | b Allen | 1 | lbw b Laker | | 3 |
| C.L. Walcott† | lbw b Cranston | 11 | not out | | 31 |
| R.J. Christiani | c Hardstaff b Tremlett | 51 | lbw b Howorth | | 3 |
| F.M.M. Worrell | not out | 131 | | | |
| G.E. Gomez | c Evans b Cranston | 36 | (5) not out | | 25 |
| E.de C. Weekes | b Cranston | 36 | | | |
| E.A.V. Williams | b Laker | 7 | | | |
| W. Ferguson | c Allen b Laker | 2 | | | |
| J. Trim | } did not bat | | | | |
| L.R. Pierre | } | | | | |
| Extras | (LB 1, W 3, NB 1) | 5 | (LB 7, NB 1) | | 8 |
| **Total** | (8 wickets declared) | 297 | (3 wickets) | | 78 |

## ENGLAND

| | | | | | |
|---|---|---|---|---|---|
| L. Hutton | c Williams b Goddard | 31 | b Ferguson | | 24 |
| J.D.B. Robertson | c Ferguson b Goddard | 23 | lbw b Ferguson | | 9 |
| W. Place | c Christiani b Goddard | 1 | b Ferguson | | 15 |
| J. Hardstaff, jr | b Ferguson | 3 | c Christiani b Trim | | 63 |
| J.T. Ikin | c Ferguson b Goddard | 7 | (8) run out | | 24 |
| K. Cranston | st Walcott b Ferguson | 24 | c Christiani b Goddard | | 32 |
| R. Howorth | c Ferguson b Goddard | 4 | (9) lbw b Ferguson | | 2 |
| J.C. Laker | c Walcott b Ferguson | 10 | (10) c Goddard b Williams | | 6 |
| T.G. Evans† | b Trim | 1 | (7) c Goddard b Williams | | 37 |
| M.F. Tremlett | c Christiani b Trim | 0 | (11) not out | | 18 |
| G.O.B. Allen* | not out | 0 | (5) lbw b Ferguson | | 20 |
| Extras | (B 4, LB 1, NB 2) | 7 | (B 4, LB 5, W 1, NB 3) | | 13 |
| **Total** | | 111 | | | 263 |

| ENGLAND | O | M | R | W | O | M | R | W |
|---|---|---|---|---|---|---|---|---|
| Allen | 2·4 | 0 | 5 | 1 | | | | |
| Tremlett | 14 | 4 | 35 | 1 | | | | |
| Cranston | 25 | 5 | 78 | 4 | 2 | 0 | 11 | 0 |
| Laker | 36 | 11 | 94 | 2 | 9 | 1 | 34 | 2 |
| Howorth | 23 | 4 | 58 | 0 | 9 | 0 | 25 | 1 |
| Ikin | 5 | 2 | 22 | 0 | | | | |
| WEST INDIES | | | | | | | | |
| Trim | 10 | 6 | 6 | 2 | 13 | 2 | 38 | 1 |
| Pierre | 2 | 0 | 9 | 0 | 5 | 0 | 19 | 0 |
| Williams | 6 | 0 | 21 | 0 | 24·4 | 12 | 34 | 2 |
| Goddard | 14·2 | 0 | 31 | 5 | 24 | 8 | 43 | 1 |
| Worrell | 2 | 0 | 5 | 0 | | | | |
| Ferguson | 15 | 5 | 23 | 3 | 40 | 6 | 116 | 5 |
| Gomez | 1 | 0 | 9 | 0 | | | | |

### FALL OF WICKETS

| | WI | E | E | WI |
|---|---|---|---|---|
| Wkt | 1st | 1st | 2nd | 2nd |
| 1st | 7 | 59 | 21 | 10 |
| 2nd | 26 | 61 | 51 | 23 |
| 3rd | 48 | 64 | 52 | 26 |
| 4th | 127 | 64 | 137 | – |
| 5th | 224 | 94 | 145 | – |
| 6th | 284 | 96 | 185 | – |
| 7th | 295 | 109 | 226 | – |
| 8th | 297 | 110 | 233 | – |
| 9th | – | 110 | 249 | – |
| 10th | – | 111 | 263 | – |

Umpires: E.S. Gillette and J. Da Silva.

# WEST INDIES v ENGLAND 1947–48 (4th Test)

Played at Sabina Park, Kingston, Jamaica, on 27, 29, 30, 31 March, 1 April.
Toss: England.   Result: WEST INDIES won by ten wickets.
Debuts: West Indies – H.H.H. Johnson, E.S.M. Kentish, K.R. Rickards.

Johnson marked his first appearance in Test cricket at the age of 37 by taking five wickets in each innings. Weekes scored the first of his record run of five hundreds in consecutive innings.

## ENGLAND

| | | | | |
|---|---|---|---|---|
| L. Hutton | b Johnson | 56 | c sub (J.K. Holt) b Goddard | 60 |
| J.D.B. Robertson | lbw b Johnson | 64 | b Johnson | 28 |
| W. Place | st Walcott b Ferguson | 8 | st Walcott b Stollmeyer | 107 |
| J. Hardstaff, jr | c Gomez b Ferguson | 9 | b Johnson | 64 |
| K. Cranston | c Walcott b Johnson | 13 | b Kentish | 36 |
| G.O.B. Allen* | c Walcott b Kentish | 23 | lbw b Johnson | 13 |
| J.T. Ikin | run out | 5 | c Worrell b Stollmeyer | 3 |
| T.G. Evans† | c Weekes b Kentish | 9 | b Johnson | 4 |
| R. Howorth | not out | 12 | st Walcott b Stollmeyer | 1 |
| J.C. Laker | c Walcott b Johnson | 6 | not out | 6 |
| M.F. Tremlett | b Johnson | 0 | c Walcott b Johnson | 2 |
| Extras | (B 12, LB 8, NB 2) | 22 | (B 8, LB 2, NB 2) | 12 |
| **Total** | | **227** | | **336** |

## WEST INDIES

| | | | | |
|---|---|---|---|---|
| J.D.C. Goddard* | c Hutton b Howorth | 17 | not out | 46 |
| J.B. Stollmeyer | lbw b Howorth | 30 | not out | 25 |
| E. de C. Weekes | c Hutton b Ikin | 141 | | |
| F.M.M. Worrell | lbw b Allen | 38 | | |
| G.E. Gomez | b Tremlett | 23 | | |
| K.R. Rickards | b Laker | 67 | | |
| R.J. Christiani | c and b Laker | 14 | | |
| C.L. Walcott† | c Hutton b Tremlett | 45 | | |
| W. Ferguson | c Hardstaff b Laker | 75 | | |
| H.H.H. Johnson | b Howorth | 8 | | |
| E.S.M. Kentish | not out | 1 | | |
| Extras | (B 11, LB 17, NB 3) | 31 | (LB 4, W 1) | 5 |
| **Total** | | **490** | (0 wickets) | **76** |

| WEST INDIES | O | M | R | W | O | M | R | W |
|---|---|---|---|---|---|---|---|---|
| Johnson | 34·5 | 13 | 41 | 5 | 31 | 11 | 55 | 5 |
| Kentish | 21 | 8 | 38 | 2 | 26 | 7 | 68 | 1 |
| Goddard | 19 | 7 | 33 | 0 | 25 | 9 | 38 | 1 |
| Ferguson | 38 | 14 | 53 | 2 | 32 | 7 | 90 | 0 |
| Worrell | 11 | 1 | 25 | 0 | 20 | 3 | 41 | 0 |
| Stollmeyer | 5 | 1 | 15 | 0 | 19 | 7 | 32 | 3 |
| **ENGLAND** | | | | | | | | |
| Allen | 20 | 1 | 83 | 1 | 2 | 0 | 14 | 0 |
| Tremlett | 31 | 1 | 98 | 2 | 1 | 0 | 4 | 0 |
| Howorth | 40 | 10 | 106 | 3 | 4 | 0 | 27 | 0 |
| Laker | 36·4 | 5 | 103 | 3 | 2 | 0 | 11 | 0 |
| Ikin | 19 | 0 | 69 | 1 | 2 | 0 | 15 | 0 |

FALL OF WICKETS

| | E | WI | E | WI |
|---|---|---|---|---|
| Wkt | 1st | 1st | 2nd | 2nd |
| 1st | 129 | 39 | 69 | – |
| 2nd | 132 | 62 | 101 | – |
| 3rd | 147 | 144 | 214 | – |
| 4th | 150 | 204 | 291 | – |
| 5th | 173 | 320 | 316 | – |
| 6th | 185 | 351 | 316 | – |
| 7th | 200 | 358 | 327 | – |
| 8th | 205 | 455 | 327 | – |
| 9th | 221 | 482 | 329 | – |
| 10th | 227 | 490 | 336 | – |

Umpires: S.C. Burke and T.A. Ewart.

# ENGLAND v AUSTRALIA 1948 (1st Test)

Played at Trent Bridge, Nottingham, on 10, 11, 12, 14, 15 June.
Toss: England.   Result: AUSTRALIA won by eight wickets.
Debuts: Nil.

Compton's innings of 184 was spread over three days and was interrupted eleven times by rain, bad light and
scheduled intervals; he was out when he kicked his wicket while trying to hook a bouncer. Young bowled eleven
consecutive maiden overs in a spell of 26-16-14-1.

## ENGLAND

| | | | | | |
|---|---|---|---|---|---|
| L. Hutton | b Miller | 3 | b Miller | | 74 |
| C. Washbrook | c Brown b Lindwall | 6 | c Tallon b Miller | | 1 |
| W.J. Edrich | b Johnston | 18 | c Tallon b Johnson | | 13 |
| D.C.S. Compton | b Miller | 19 | hit wkt b Miller | | 184 |
| J. Hardstaff, jr | c Miller b Johnston | 0 | c Hassett b Toshack | | 43 |
| C.J. Barnett | b Johnston | 8 | c Miller b Johnston | | 6 |
| N.W.D. Yardley* | lbw b Toshack | 3 | c and b Johnston | | 22 |
| T.G. Evans† | c Morris b Johnston | 12 | c Tallon b Johnston | | 50 |
| J.C. Laker | c Tallon b Miller | 63 | b Miller | | 4 |
| A.V. Bedser | c Brown b Johnston | 22 | not out | | 3 |
| J.A. Young | not out | 1 | b Johnston | | 9 |
| Extras | (B 5, LB 5) | 10 | (B 12, LB 17, NB 3) | | 32 |
| **Total** | | **165** | | | **441** |

## AUSTRALIA

| | | | | | |
|---|---|---|---|---|---|
| S.G. Barnes | c Evans b Laker | 62 | not out | | 64 |
| A.R. Morris | b Laker | 31 | b Bedser | | 9 |
| D.G. Bradman* | c Hutton b Bedser | 138 | c Hutton b Bedser | | 0 |
| K.R. Miller | c Edrich b Laker | 0 | | | |
| V.A. Brown | lbw b Yardley | 17 | | | |
| A.L. Hassett | b Bedser | 137 | (4) not out | | 21 |
| I.W. Johnson | b Laker | 21 | | | |
| D. Tallon† | c and b Young | 10 | | | |
| R.R. Lindwall | c Evans b Yardley | 42 | | | |
| W.A. Johnston | not out | 17 | | | |
| E.R.H. Toshack | lbw b Bedser | 19 | | | |
| Extras | (B 9, LB 4, W 1, NB 1) | 15 | (LB 2, W 1, NB 1) | | 4 |
| **Total** | | **509** | (2 wickets) | | **98** |

| AUSTRALIA | O | M | R | W | O | M | R | W |
|---|---|---|---|---|---|---|---|---|
| Lindwall | 13 | 5 | 30 | 1 | | | | |
| Miller | 19 | 8 | 38 | 3 | 44 | 10 | 125 | 4 |
| Johnston | 25 | 11 | 36 | 5 | 59 | 12 | 147 | 4 |
| Toshack | 14 | 8 | 28 | 1 | 33 | 14 | 60 | 1 |
| Johnson | 5 | 1 | 19 | 0 | 42 | 15 | 66 | 1 |
| Morris | 3 | 1 | 4 | 0 | | | | |
| Barnes | | | | | 5 | 2 | 11 | 0 |
| ENGLAND | | | | | | | | |
| Edrich | 18 | 1 | 72 | 0 | 4 | 0 | 20 | 0 |
| Bedser | 44·2 | 12 | 113 | 3 | 14·3 | 4 | 46 | 2 |
| Barnett | 17 | 5 | 36 | 0 | | | | |
| Young | 60 | 28 | 79 | 1 | 10 | 3 | 28 | 0 |
| Laker | 55 | 14 | 138 | 4 | | | | |
| Compton | 5 | 0 | 24 | 0 | | | | |
| Yardley | 17 | 6 | 32 | 2 | | | | |

FALL OF WICKETS

| Wkt | E 1st | A 1st | E 2nd | A 2nd |
|---|---|---|---|---|
| 1st | 9 | 73 | 5 | 38 |
| 2nd | 15 | 121 | 39 | 48 |
| 3rd | 46 | 121 | 150 | – |
| 4th | 46 | 185 | 243 | – |
| 5th | 48 | 305 | 264 | – |
| 6th | 60 | 338 | 321 | – |
| 7th | 74 | 365 | 405 | – |
| 8th | 74 | 472 | 413 | – |
| 9th | 163 | 476 | 423 | – |
| 10th | 165 | 509 | 441 | – |

Umpires: F. Chester and E. Cooke.

# ENGLAND v AUSTRALIA 1948 (2nd Test)

Played at Lord's, London, on 24, 25, 26, 28, 29 June.
Toss: Australia.   Result: AUSTRALIA won by 409 runs.
Debuts: England – A. Coxon.

This was the 14th successive Test against England in which he had batted, that Bradman scored at least one fifty.

## AUSTRALIA

| | | | | | |
|---|---|---:|---|---|---:|
| S.G. Barnes | c Hutton b Coxon | 0 | c Washbrook b Yardley | | 141 |
| A.R. Morris | c Hutton b Coxon | 105 | b Wright | | 62 |
| D.G. Bradman* | c Hutton b Bedser | 38 | c Edrich b Bedser | | 89 |
| A.L. Hassett | b Yardley | 47 | b Yardley | | 0 |
| K.R. Miller | lbw b Bedser | 4 | c Bedser b Laker | | 74 |
| W.A. Brown | lbw b Yardley | 24 | c Evans b Coxon | | 32 |
| I.W. Johnson | c Evans b Edrich | 4 | (8) not out | | 9 |
| D. Tallon† | c Yardley b Bedser | 53 | | | |
| R.R. Lindwall | b Bedser | 15 | (7) st Evans b Laker | | 25 |
| W.A. Johnston | st Evans b Wright | 29 | | | |
| E.R.H. Toshack | not out | 20 | | | |
| Extras | (B 3, LB 7, NB 1) | 11 | (B 22, LB 5, NB 1) | | 28 |
| **Total** | | **350** | (7 wickets declared) | | **460** |

## ENGLAND

| | | | | | |
|---|---|---:|---|---|---:|
| L. Hutton | b Johnson | 20 | c Johnson b Lindwall | | 13 |
| C. Washbrook | c Tallon b Lindwall | 8 | c Tallon b Toshack | | 37 |
| W.J. Edrich | b Lindwall | 5 | c Johnson b Toshack | | 2 |
| D.C.S. Compton | c Miller b Johnston | 53 | c Miller b Johnston | | 29 |
| H.E. Dollery | b Lindwall | 0 | b Lindwall | | 37 |
| N.W.D. Yardley* | b Lindwall | 44 | b Toshack | | 11 |
| A. Coxon | c and b Johnson | 19 | lbw b Toshack | | 0 |
| T.G. Evans† | c Miller b Johnston | 9 | not out | | 24 |
| J.C. Laker | c Tallon b Johnson | 28 | b Lindwall | | 0 |
| A.V. Bedser | b Lindwall | 9 | c Hassett b Johnston | | 9 |
| D.V.P. Wright | not out | 13 | c Lindwall b Toshack | | 4 |
| Extras | (LB 3, NB 4) | 7 | (B 16, LB 4) | | 20 |
| **Total** | | **215** | | | **186** |

| ENGLAND | O | M | R | W | O | M | R | W |
|---|---|---|---|---|---|---|---|---|
| Bedser | 43 | 14 | 100 | 4 | 34 | 6 | 112 | 1 |
| Coxon | 35 | 10 | 90 | 2 | 28 | 3 | 82 | 1 |
| Edrich | 8 | 0 | 43 | 1 | 2 | 0 | 11 | 0 |
| Wright | 21·3 | 8 | 54 | 1 | 19 | 4 | 69 | 1 |
| Laker | 7 | 3 | 17 | 0 | 31·2 | 6 | 111 | 2 |
| Yardley | 15 | 4 | 35 | 2 | 13 | 4 | 36 | 2 |
| Compton | | | | | 3 | 0 | 11 | 0 |
| AUSTRALIA | | | | | | | | |
| Lindwall | 27·4 | 7 | 70 | 5 | 23 | 9 | 61 | 3 |
| Johnston | 22 | 4 | 43 | 2 | 33 | 15 | 62 | 2 |
| Johnson | 35 | 13 | 72 | 3 | 2 | 1 | 3 | 0 |
| Toshack | 18 | 11 | 23 | 0 | 20·1 | 6 | 40 | 5 |

### FALL OF WICKETS

| | A | E | A | E |
|---|---|---|---|---|
| Wkt | 1st | 1st | 2nd | 2nd |
| 1st | 3 | 17 | 122 | 42 |
| 2nd | 87 | 32 | 296 | 52 |
| 3rd | 166 | 46 | 296 | 65 |
| 4th | 173 | 46 | 329 | 106 |
| 5th | 216 | 133 | 416 | 133 |
| 6th | 225 | 134 | 445 | 133 |
| 7th | 246 | 145 | 460 | 141 |
| 8th | 275 | 186 | – | 141 |
| 9th | 320 | 197 | – | 158 |
| 10th | 350 | 215 | – | 186 |

Umpires: C.N. Woolley and D. Davies.

# ENGLAND v AUSTRALIA 1948 (3rd Test)

Played at Old Trafford, Manchester, on 8, 9, 10, 12 (*no play*), 13 July.
Toss: England.   Result: MATCH DRAWN.
Debuts: England – J.F. Crapp, G.M. Emmett.

The selectors omitted Hutton for the first time since he made his debut in 1937 – he had missed one match through injury. Compton (4*) mishooked a ball into his face and retired hurt at 33 for 2; he resumed his innings at 119-5.

## ENGLAND

| | | | | | |
|---|---|---|---|---|---|
| C. Washbrook | b Johnston | 11 | not out | | 85 |
| G.M. Emmett | c Barnes b Lindwall | 10 | c Tallon b Lindwall | | 0 |
| W.J. Edrich | c Tallon b Lindwall | 32 | run out | | 53 |
| D.C.S. Compton | not out | 145 | c Miller b Toshack | | 0 |
| J.F. Crapp | lbw b Lindwall | 37 | not out | | 19 |
| H.E. Dollery | b Johnston | 1 | | | |
| N.W.D. Yardley* | c Johnson b Toshack | 22 | | | |
| T.G. Evans† | c Johnston b Lindwall | 34 | | | |
| A.V. Bedser | run out | 37 | | | |
| R. Pollard | b Toshack | 3 | | | |
| J.A. Young | c Bradman b Johnston | 4 | | | |
| Extras | (B 7, LB 17, NB 3) | 27 | (B 9, LB 7, W 1) | | 17 |
| **Total** | | **363** | (3 wickets declared) | | **174** |

## AUSTRALIA

| | | | | | |
|---|---|---|---|---|---|
| A.R. Morris | c Compton b Bedser | 51 | not out | | 54 |
| I.W. Johnson | c Evans b Bedser | 1 | c Crapp b Young | | 6 |
| D.G. Bradman* | lbw b Pollard | 7 | not out | | 30 |
| A.L. Hassett | c Washbrook b Young | 38 | | | |
| K.R. Miller | lbw b Pollard | 31 | | | |
| S.G. Barnes | retired hurt | 1 | | | |
| S.J.E. Loxton | b Pollard | 36 | | | |
| D. Tallon† | c Evans b Edrich | 18 | | | |
| R.R. Lindwall | c Washbrook b Bedser | 23 | | | |
| W.A. Johnston | c Crapp b Bedser | 3 | | | |
| E.R.H. Toshack | not out | 0 | | | |
| Extras | (B 5, LB 4, NB 3) | 12 | (NB 2) | | 2 |
| **Total** | | **221** | (1 wicket) | | **92** |

| AUSTRALIA | O | M | R | W | O | M | R | W |
|---|---|---|---|---|---|---|---|---|
| Lindwall | 40 | 8 | 99 | 4 | 14 | 4 | 37 | 1 |
| Johnston | 45·5 | 13 | 67 | 3 | 14 | 3 | 34 | 0 |
| Loxton | 7 | 0 | 18 | 0 | 8 | 2 | 29 | 0 |
| Toshack | 41 | 20 | 75 | 2 | 12 | 5 | 26 | 1 |
| Johnson | 38 | 16 | 77 | 0 | 7 | 3 | 16 | 0 |
| Miller | | | | | 14 | 7 | 15 | 0 |
| ENGLAND | | | | | | | | |
| Bedser | 36 | 12 | 81 | 4 | 19 | 12 | 27 | 0 |
| Pollard | 32 | 9 | 53 | 3 | 10 | 8 | 6 | 0 |
| Edrich | 7 | 3 | 27 | 1 | 2 | 0 | 8 | 0 |
| Yardley | 4 | 0 | 12 | 0 | | | | |
| Young | 14 | 5 | 36 | 1 | 21 | 12 | 31 | 1 |
| Compton | | | | | 9 | 3 | 18 | 0 |

### FALL OF WICKETS

| | E | A | E | A |
|---|---|---|---|---|
| Wkt | 1st | 1st | 2nd | 2nd |
| 1st | 22 | 3 | 1 | 10 |
| 2nd | 28 | 13 | 125 | – |
| 3rd | 96 | 82 | 129 | – |
| 4th | 97 | 135 | – | – |
| 5th | 119 | 139 | – | – |
| 6th | 141 | 172 | – | – |
| 7th | 216 | 208 | – | – |
| 8th | 337 | 219 | – | – |
| 9th | 352 | 221 | – | – |
| 10th | 363 | – | – | – |

Umpires: F. Chester and D. Davies.

# ENGLAND v AUSTRALIA 1948 (4th Test)

Played at Headingley, Leeds, on 22, 23, 24. 26, 27 July.
Toss: England.   Result: AUSTRALIA won by seven wickets.
Debuts: Australia – R.A. Saggers.

Harvey became the first Australian left-hander to score a hundred in his first Test against England. Loxton set a record for this series by hitting five sixes in his 93. Bradman's hundred was the last of his 29 in Test matches, 14 as captain, 19 against England, and four in six innings at Leeds – all records which remain unequalled. Australia's 404-3 was the highest fourth innings total to win a Test match until 1975-76 when India scored 406-4 to beat West Indies (*Test No. 775*).

## ENGLAND

| | | | | |
|---|---|---|---|---|
| L. Hutton | b Lindwall | 81 | c Bradman b Johnson | 57 |
| C. Washbrook | c Lindwall b Johnston | 143 | c Harvey b Johnston | 65 |
| W.J. Edrich | c Morris b Johnson | 111 | lbw b Lindwall | 54 |
| A.V. Bedser | c and b Johnson | 79 | (9) c Hassett b Miller | 17 |
| D.C.S. Compton | c Saggers b Lindwall | 23 | (4) c Miller b Johnston | 66 |
| J.F. Crapp | b Toshack | 5 | (5) b Lindwall | 18 |
| N.W.D. Yardley * | b Miller | 25 | (6) c Harvey b Johnston | 7 |
| K. Cranston | b Loxton | 10 | (7) c Saggers b Johnston | 0 |
| T.G. Evans † | c Hassett b Loxton | 3 | (8) not out | 47 |
| J.C. Laker | c Saggers b Loxton | 4 | not out | 15 |
| R. Pollard | not out | 0 | | |
| Extras | (B 2, LB 8, W 1, NB 1) | 12 | (B 4, LB 12, NB 3) | 10 |
| **Total** | | **496** | (8 wickets declared) | **365** |

## AUSTRALIA

| | | | | |
|---|---|---|---|---|
| A.R. Morris | c Cranston b Bedser | 6 | c Pollard b Yardley | 182 |
| A.L. Hassett | c Crapp b Pollard | 13 | c and b Compton | 17 |
| D.G. Bradman* | b Pollard | 33 | not out | 173 |
| K.R. Miller | c Edrich b Yardley | 58 | lbw b Cranston | 12 |
| R.N. Harvey | b Laker | 112 | not out | 4 |
| S.J.E. Loxton | b Yardley | 93 | | |
| I.W. Johnson | c Cranston b Laker | 10 | | |
| R.R. Lindwall | c Crapp b Bedser | 77 | | |
| R.A. Saggers† | st Evans b Laker | 5 | | |
| W.A. Johnston | c Edrich b Bedser | 13 | | |
| E.R.H. Toshack | not out | 12 | | |
| Extras | (B 9, LB 14, NB 3) | 26 | (B 6, LB 9, NB 1) | 16 |
| **Total** | | **458** | (3 wickets) | **404** |

| AUSTRALIA | O | M | R | W | O | M | R | W |
|---|---|---|---|---|---|---|---|---|
| Lindwall | 38 | 10 | 79 | 2 | 26 | 6 | 84 | 2 |
| Miller | 17·1 | 2 | 43 | 1 | 21 | 5 | 53 | 1 |
| Johnston | 38 | 12 | 86 | 1 | 29 | 5 | 95 | 4 |
| Toshack | 35 | 6 | 112 | 1 | | | | |
| Loxton | 26 | 4 | 55 | 3 | 10 | 2 | 29 | 0 |
| Johnson | 33 | 9 | 89 | 2 | 21 | 2 | 85 | 1 |
| Morris | 5 | 0 | 20 | 0 | | | | |
| **ENGLAND** | | | | | | | | |
| Bedser | 31·2 | 4 | 92 | 3 | 21 | 2 | 56 | 0 |
| Pollard | 38 | 6 | 104 | 2 | 22 | 6 | 55 | 0 |
| Cranston | 14 | 1 | 51 | 0 | 7·1 | 0 | 28 | 1 |
| Edrich | 3 | 0 | 19 | 0 | | | | |
| Laker | 30 | 8 | 113 | 3 | 32 | 11 | 93 | 0 |
| Yardley | 17 | 6 | 38 | 2 | 13 | 1 | 44 | 1 |
| Compton | 3 | 0 | 15 | 0 | 14 | 3 | 82 | 1 |
| Hutton | 4 | 1 | 30 | 0 | | | | |

FALL OF WICKETS

| | E | A | E | A |
|---|---|---|---|---|
| Wkt | 1st | 1st | 2nd | 2nd |
| 1st | 168 | 13 | 129 | 57 |
| 2nd | 268 | 65 | 129 | 358 |
| 3rd | 423 | 68 | 232 | 396 |
| 4th | 426 | 189 | 260 | – |
| 5th | 447 | 294 | 277 | – |
| 6th | 473 | 329 | 278 | – |
| 7th | 486 | 344 | 293 | – |
| 8th | 490 | 355 | 330 | – |
| 9th | 496 | 403 | – | – |
| 10th | 496 | 458 | – | – |

Umpires: F. Chester and H.G. Baldwin

# ENGLAND v AUSTRALIA 1948 (5th Test)

Played at Kennington Oval, London, on 14, 16, 17, 18 August.
Toss: England.   Result: AUSTRALIA won by an innings and 149 runs.
Debuts: England – J.G. Dewes, A.J. Watkins.

England were dismissed for their lowest total this century and second-lowest in all Tests. Bradman, playing in his last Test match, was bowled second ball; four runs would have taken his aggregate to 7,000 and his average to 100. Hutton, last out in the first innings, was on the field for all but the last 57 minutes of the match.

## ENGLAND

| | | | | | |
|---|---|---|---|---|---|
| L. Hutton | c Tallon b Lindwall | 30 | c Tallon b Miller | 64 |
| J.G. Dewes | b Miller | 1 | b Lindwall | 10 |
| W.J. Edrich | c Hassett b Johnston | 3 | b Lindwall | 28 |
| D.C.S. Compton | c Morris b Lindwall | 4 | c Lindwall b Johnston | 39 |
| J.F. Crapp | c Tallon b Miller | 0 | b Miller | 9 |
| N.W.D. Yardley* | b Lindwall | 7 | c Miller b Johnston | 9 |
| A.J. Watkins | lbw b Johnston | 0 | c Hassett b Ring | 2 |
| T.G. Evans † | b Lindwall | 1 | b Lindwall | 8 |
| A.V. Bedser | b Lindwall | 0 | b Johnston | 0 |
| J.A. Young | b Lindwall | 0 | not out | 3 |
| W.E. Hollies | not out | 0 | c Morris b Johnston | 0 |
| Extras | (B 6) | 6 | (B 9, LB 4, NB 3) | 16 |
| **Total** | | **52** | | **188** |

## AUSTRALIA

| | | |
|---|---|---|
| S.G. Barnes | c Evans b Hollies | 61 |
| A.R. Morris | run out | 196 |
| D.G. Bradman* | b Hollies | 0 |
| A.L. Hassett | lbw b Young | 37 |
| K.R. Miller | st Evans b Hollies | 5 |
| R.N. Harvey | c Young b Hollies | 17 |
| S.J.E. Loxton | c Evans b Edrich | 15 |
| R.R. Lindwall | c Edrich b Young | 9 |
| D. Tallon † | c Crapp b Hollies | 31 |
| D.T. Ring | c Crapp b Bedser | 9 |
| W.A. Johnston | not out | 0 |
| Extras | (B 4, LB 2, NB 3) | 9 |
| **Total** | | **389** |

| AUSTRALIA | O | M | R | W | O | M | R | W |
|---|---|---|---|---|---|---|---|---|
| Lindwall | 16·1 | 5 | 20 | 6 | 25 | 3 | 50 | 3 |
| Miller | 8 | 5 | 5 | 2 | 15 | 6 | 22 | 2 |
| Johnston | 16 | 4 | 20 | 2 | 27·3 | 12 | 40 | 4 |
| Loxton | 2 | 1 | 1 | 0 | 10 | 2 | 16 | 0 |
| Ring | | | | | 28 | 13 | 44 | 1 |

| ENGLAND | O | M | R | W |
|---|---|---|---|---|
| Bedser | 31·2 | 9 | 61 | 1 |
| Watkins | 4 | 1 | 19 | 0 |
| Young | 51 | 16 | 118 | 2 |
| Hollies | 56 | 14 | 131 | 5 |
| Compton | 2 | 0 | 6 | 0 |
| Edrich | 9 | 1 | 38 | 1 |
| Yardley | 5 | 1 | 7 | 0 |

### FALL OF WICKETS

| Wkt | E 1st | A 1st | E 2nd |
|---|---|---|---|
| 1st | 2 | 117 | 20 |
| 2nd | 10 | 117 | 64 |
| 3rd | 17 | 226 | 125 |
| 4th | 23 | 243 | 153 |
| 5th | 35 | 265 | 164 |
| 6th | 42 | 304 | 167 |
| 7th | 45 | 332 | 178 |
| 8th | 45 | 359 | 181 |
| 9th | 47 | 389 | 188 |
| 10th | 52 | 389 | 188 |

Umpires: H.G. Baldwin and D. Davies.

# INDIA v WEST INDIES 1948–49 (1st Test)

Played at Feroz Shah Kotla, Delhi, on 10, 11, 12, 13, 14 November.
Toss: West Indies.  Result: MATCH DRAWN.
Debuts: India – K.C. Ibrahim, K.K. Tarapore; West Indies – D. St E. Atkinson, F.J. Cameron
A.F. Rae.

This was the first match between India and West Indies, the first Test to be played at Delhi, and the first in India
since 1933-34. West Indies equalled England's performance at Nottingham in 1958 (*Test No. 263*) by scorin
four hundreds in their innings of 631 (their highest total until 1953-54).

## WEST INDIES

| | | |
|---|---|---|
| A.F. Rae | c Sen b Rangachari | 8 |
| J.B. Stollmeyer | lbw b Rangachari | 13 |
| G.A. Headley | b Rangachari | 2 |
| C.L. Walcott† | run out | 152 |
| G.E. Gomez | st Sen b Amarnath | 101 |
| J.D.C. Goddard* | b Mankad | 44 |
| E. de C. Weekes | c Hazare b Mankad | 128 |
| R.J. Christiani | c Hazare b Rangachari | 107 |
| F.J. Cameron | lbw b Sarwate | 2 |
| D.St E. Atkinson | c Sen b Rangachari | 45 |
| P.E. Jones | not out | 1 |
| Extras | (B 20, LB 6) | 28 |
| **Total** | | **631** |

## INDIA

| | | | | |
|---|---|---|---|---|
| V.M.H. Mankad | lbw b Jones | 5 | b Goddard | 1 |
| K.C. Ibrahim | lbw b Gomez | 85 | run out | 4 |
| R.S. Modi | c Rae b Cameron | 63 | b Christiani | 3 |
| L. Amarnath* | c Christiani b Jones | 62 | b Cameron | 3 |
| V.S. Hazare | c Atkinson b Gomez | 18 | b Christiani | |
| D.G. Phadkar | c Weekes b Stollmeyer | 41 | c and b Christiani | |
| H.R. Adhikari | not out | 114 | not out | 2 |
| C.T. Sarwate | st Walcott b Stollmeyer | 37 | not out | 3 |
| P. Sen† | c Walcott b Cameron | 22 | | |
| C.R. Rangachari | c and b Goddard | 0 | | |
| K.K. Tarapore | c Walcott b Jones | 2 | | |
| Extras | (B 1, LB 3, NB 1) | 5 | (B 8, LB 3) | 1 |
| **Total** | | **454** | (6 wickets) | 22 |

| INDIA | O | M | R | W | O | M | R | W | | FALL OF WICKETS | | |
|---|---|---|---|---|---|---|---|---|---|---|---|---|
| Phadkar | 18 | 1 | 61 | 0 | | | | | | WI | I | I |
| Amarnath | 25 | 3 | 73 | 1 | | | | | *Wkt* | *1st* | *1st* | *2nd* |
| Rangachari | 29·4 | 4 | 107 | 5 | | | | | 1st | 15 | 8 | 44 |
| Mankad | 59 | 10 | 176 | 2 | | | | | 2nd | 22 | 129 | 102 |
| Tarapore | 19 | 2 | 72 | 0 | | | | | 3rd | 27 | 181 | 111 |
| Hazare | 17 | 1 | 62 | 0 | | | | | 4th | 294 | 223 | 121 |
| Sarwate | 16 | 0 | 52 | 1 | | | | | 5th | 302 | 249 | 142 |
| | | | | | | | | | 6th | 403 | 309 | 162 |
| WEST INDIES | | | | | | | | | 7th | 521 | 388 | – |
| Jones | 28·4 | 5 | 90 | 3 | 10 | 2 | 32 | 0 | 8th | 524 | 419 | – |
| Gomez | 39 | 14 | 76 | 2 | 10 | 4 | 17 | 0 | 9th | 630 | 438 | – |
| Atkinson | 13 | 3 | 27 | 0 | 5 | 0 | 11 | 0 | 10th | 631 | 454 | – |
| Headley | 2 | 0 | 13 | 0 | 1 | 0 | 5 | 0 | | | | |
| Cameron | 27 | 3 | 74 | 2 | 27 | 10 | 49 | 1 | | | | |
| Stollmeyer | 15 | 0 | 80 | 2 | 10 | 2 | 23 | 0 | | | | |
| Goddar | 30 | 7 | 83 | 1 | 15 | 7 | 18 | 1 | | | | |
| Charistiani | 4 | 0 | 6 | 0 | 23 | 1 | 52 | 3 | | | | |
| Weekes | | | | | 1 | 0 | 2 | 0 | | | | |

Umpires: D.K. Naik and J.R. Patel.

# INDIA v WEST INDIES 1948–49 (2nd Test)

Played at Brabourne Stadium, Bombay, on 9, 10, 11, 12, 13 December.
Toss: West Indies.   Result: MATCH DRAWN.
Debuts: India – P.R. Umrigar.

West Indies recorded their second consecutive total of over 600, Weekes hit his third successive hundred, and India again saved the match after following on. Goddard was taken ill and Stollmeyer assumed the captaincy when he was unable to field.

## WEST INDIES

| | | |
|---|---|---|
| A.F. Rae | c and b Phadkar | 104 |
| J.B. Stollmeyer | b Mankad | 66 |
| C.L. Walcott† | run out | 68 |
| E. de C. Weekes | c Sen b Mankad | 194 |
| G.E. Gomez | c Sen b Hazare | 7 |
| R.J. Christiani | lbw b Mankad | 74 |
| F.J. Cameron | not out | 75 |
| D. St E. Atkinson | not out | 23 |
| D.C. Goddard* | ) | |
| P.E. Jones | ) did not bat | |
| W. Ferguson | ) | |
| Extras | (B 5, LB 5, NB 4) | 18 |
| **Total** | (6 wickets declared) | **629** |

## INDIA

| | | | | | |
|---|---|---|---|---|---|
| V.M.H. Mankad | run out | 21 | c Ferguson b Gomez | | 16 |
| K.C. Ibrahim | run out | 9 | c Goddard b Jones | | 0 |
| R.S. Modi | c Atkinson b Ferguson | 1 | c Gomez b Ferguson | | 112 |
| V.S. Hazare | lbw b Atkinson | 26 | not out | | 134 |
| H.R. Adhikari | lbw b Ferguson | 34 | | | |
| D.G. Phadkar | c Jones b Gomez | 74 | | | |
| L. Amarnath* | c and b Ferguson | 24 | (5) not out | | 58 |
| P.R. Umrigar | c Goddard b Ferguson | 30 | | | |
| Sen† | lbw b Goddard | 19 | | | |
| G. Shinde | st Walcott b Gomez | 13 | | | |
| C.R. Rangachari | not out | 8 | | | |
| Extras | (B 1, LB 5, NB 8) | 14 | (B 11, LB 1, NB 1) | | 13 |
| **Total** | | **273** | (3 wickets) | | **333** |

| INDIA | O | M | R | W | O | M | R | W |
|---|---|---|---|---|---|---|---|---|
| Phadkar | 16 | 5 | 35 | 1 | | | | |
| Rangachari | 34 | 1 | 148 | 0 | | | | |
| Hazare | 42 | 12 | 74 | 1 | | | | |
| Umrigar | 15 | 2 | 51 | 0 | | | | |
| Mankad | 75 | 16 | 202 | 3 | | | | |
| Shinde | 16 | 0 | 68 | 0 | | | | |
| Amarnath | 8 | 1 | 33 | 0 | | | | |
| WEST INDIES | | | | | | | | |
| Jones | 21 | 7 | 34 | 0 | 12 | 2 | 52 | 1 |
| Gomez | 24 | 9 | 32 | 2 | 28 | 12 | 37 | 1 |
| Atkinson | 14 | 5 | 21 | 1 | 13 | 4 | 26 | 0 |
| Ferguson | 57 | 8 | 126 | 4 | 39 | 14 | 105 | 1 |
| Goddard | 12·2 | 7 | 19 | 1 | 3 | 1 | 6 | 0 |
| Cameron | 10 | 3 | 9 | 0 | 27 | 9 | 52 | 0 |
| Stollmeyer | 4 | 0 | 18 | 0 | 4 | 0 | 12 | 0 |
| Christiani | | | | | 6 | 0 | 30 | 0 |

### FALL OF WICKETS

| | WI | I | I |
|---|---|---|---|
| Wkt | 1st | 1st | 2nd |
| 1st | 134 | 27 | 1 |
| 2nd | 206 | 28 | 33 |
| 3rd | 295 | 32 | 189 |
| 4th | 311 | 82 | – |
| 5th | 481 | 116 | – |
| 6th | 574 | 150 | – |
| 7th | – | 229 | – |
| 8th | – | 233 | – |
| 9th | – | 261 | – |
| 10th | – | 273 | – |

Umpires: T.A. Ramachandran and P.K. Sinha.

# INDIA v WEST INDIES 1948–49 (3rd Test)

Played at Eden Gardens, Calcutta, on 31 December, 1, 2, 3, 4 January.
Toss: West Indies.   Result: MATCH DRAWN.
Debuts: India – S. Banerjee, Ghulam Ahmed.

By scoring a hundred in each innings, Weekes extended to five his run of consecutive Test centuries. His record remains unequalled. Christiani deputised as wicket-keeper when Walcott retired ill for a time.

## WEST INDIES

| | | | | |
|---|---|---|---|---|
| A.F. Rae | lbw b Banerjee | 15 | run out | 34 |
| D. St E. Atkinson | b Banerjee | 0 | (10) not out | 5 |
| C.L. Walcott† | c Banerjee b Ghulam Ahmed | 54 | (6) c Amarnath b Mankad | 108 |
| E.De.C. Weekes | c and b Ghulam Ahmed | 162 | c and b Ghulam Ahmed | 101 |
| G.E. Gomez | b Mankad | 26 | (7) b Ghulam Ahmed | 29 |
| G.M. Carew | lbw b Mankad | 11 | (2) b Banerjee | 9 |
| J.D.C. Goddard* | not out | 39 | (5) c Banerjee b Amarnath | 9 |
| R.J. Christiani | c and b Banerjee | 23 | b Amarnath | 22 |
| F.J. Cameron | c Mushtaq Ali b Banerjee | 23 | c and b Mankad | 2 |
| W. Ferguson | b Ghulam Ahmed | 2 | (3) lbw b Mankad | 6 |
| P.E. Jones | b Ghulam Ahmed | 6 | | |
| Extras | (B 1, LB 4) | 5 | (B 6, LB 1, W 1, NB 3) | 11 |
| **Total** | | **366** | (9 wickets declared) | **330** |

## INDIA

| | | | | |
|---|---|---|---|---|
| Mushtaq Ali | c Rae b Goddard | 54 | lbw b Atkinson | 106 |
| K.C. Ibrahim | b Gomez | 1 | c Atkinson b Gomez | 25 |
| R.S. Modi | b Jones | 80 | c Christiani b Goddard | 87 |
| V.S. Hazare | b Gomez | 59 | not out | 58 |
| L. Amarnath* | c Christiani b Gomez | 3 | not out | 34 |
| V.M.H. Mankad | c Ferguson b Goddard | 29 | | |
| H.R. Adhikari | not out | 31 | | |
| C.T. Sarwate | b Goddard | 0 | | |
| P. Sen† | lbw b Ferguson | 1 | | |
| Ghulam Ahmed | st Christiani b Ferguson | 0 | | |
| S. Banerjee | st Christiani b Ferguson | 0 | | |
| Extras | (B 5, LB 6, NB 3) | 14 | (B 12, NB 3) | 15 |
| **Total** | | **272** | (3 wickets) | **32** |

| INDIA | O | M | R | W | O | M | R | W |
|---|---|---|---|---|---|---|---|---|
| Banerjee | 30 | 3 | 120 | 4 | 21 | 0 | 61 | 1 |
| Amarnath | 20 | 6 | 34 | 0 | 23 | 4 | 75 | 2 |
| Hazare | 5 | 0 | 33 | 0 | 11 | 3 | 33 | 0 |
| Ghulam Ahmed | 35·2 | 5 | 94 | 4 | 25 | 0 | 87 | 2 |
| Mankad | 23 | 5 | 74 | 2 | 24·3 | 5 | 68 | 3 |
| Sarwate | 2 | 0 | 6 | 0 | 1 | 0 | 1 | 0 |

| WEST INDIES | O | M | R | W | O | M | R | W |
|---|---|---|---|---|---|---|---|---|
| Jones | 17 | 3 | 48 | 1 | 21 | 5 | 49 | 0 |
| Gomez | 32 | 10 | 65 | 3 | 29 | 10 | 47 | 1 |
| Ferguson | 29 | 8 | 66 | 3 | 9 | 0 | 35 | 0 |
| Goddard | 13 | 3 | 34 | 3 | 23 | 11 | 41 | 1 |
| Cameron | 7 | 2 | 12 | 0 | 30 | 7 | 67 | 0 |
| Atkinson | 9 | 0 | 27 | 0 | 14 | 3 | 42 | 1 |
| Christiani | 2 | 0 | 6 | 0 | 3 | 0 | 12 | 0 |
| Carew | | | | | 3 | 2 | 2 | 0 |
| Walcott | | | | | 3 | 0 | 12 | 0 |
| Weekes | | | | | 1 | 0 | 3 | 0 |

### FALL OF WICKETS

| | WI | I | WI | I |
|---|---|---|---|---|
| Wkt | 1st | 1st | 2nd | 2nd |
| 1st | 1 | 12 | 13 | 84 |
| 2nd | 28 | 77 | 32 | 154 |
| 3rd | 109 | 206 | 104 | 262 |
| 4th | 188 | 206 | 130 | – |
| 5th | 238 | 210 | 181 | – |
| 6th | 284 | 267 | 244 | – |
| 7th | 309 | 267 | 304 | – |
| 8th | 340 | 268 | 321 | – |
| 9th | 342 | 269 | 336 | – |
| 10th | 366 | 272 | – | – |

Umpires: B.J. Mohoni and A.R. Joshi.

# INDIA v WEST INDIES 1948–49 (4th Test)

Played at Chepauk, Madras, on 27, 28, 29, 31 January.
Toss: West Indies.   Result: WEST INDIES won by an innings and 193 runs.
Debuts: India – N.R. Chowdhury, M.R. Rege.

The partnership of 239 by Rae and Stollmeyer remains the highest opening West Indies stand in all Test matches. Weekes was run out when just ten runs short of his sixth successive Test hundred. India, following on for the third time in four Tests, suffered their only defeat of the rubber.

## WEST INDIES

| | | |
|---|---|---|
| A.F. Rae | c Rege b Phadkar | 109 |
| J.B. Stollmeyer | c Sen b Chowdhury | 160 |
| C.L. Walcott† | lbw b Phadkar | 43 |
| E. de C. Weekes | run out | 90 |
| R.J. Christiani | c Modi b Phadkar | 18 |
| J.D.C. Goddard* | c Sen b Phadkar | 24 |
| G.E. Gomez | c Mankad b Phadkar | 50 |
| F.J. Cameron | c Hazare b Phadkar | 48 |
| P.E. Jones | c Ghulam Ahmed b Mankad | 10 |
| J.Trim | c Sen b Phadkar | 9 |
| W. Ferguson | not out | 2 |
| Extras | (B 10, LB 7, NB 2) | 19 |
| **Total** | | **582** |

## INDIA

| | | | | | |
|---|---|---|---|---|---|
| Mushtaq Ali | lbw b Trim | 32 | c Walcott b Jones | 14 |
| M.R. Rege | b Jones | 15 | c Walcott b Jones | 0 |
| R.S. Modi | b Ferguson | 56 | b Gomez | 6 |
| V.S. Hazare | c Goddard b Ferguson | 27 | c Stollmeyer b Trim | 52 |
| L. Amarnath* | hit wkt b Trim | 13 | b Jones | 6 |
| H.R. Adhikari | c Stollmeyer b Jones | 32 | c Walcott b Jones | 1 |
| D.G. Phadkar | c Jones b Goddard | 48 | c Rae b Trim | 10 |
| V.M.H. Mankad | b Trim | 1 | b Trim | 21 |
| P. Sen† | c Stollmeyer b Gomez | 2 | not out | 19 |
| Ghulam Ahmed | b Trim | 5 | c sub (D. St E. Atkinson) b Gomez | 11 |
| N.R. Chowdhury | not out | 3 | c Rae b Gomez | 0 |
| Extras | (B 5, LB 1, NB 5) | 11 | (LB 2, NB 2) | 4 |
| **Total** | | **245** | | **144** |

| INDIA | O | M | R | W | O | M | R | W | FALL OF WICKETS | | | |
|---|---|---|---|---|---|---|---|---|---|---|---|---|
| | | | | | | | | | | WI | I | I |
| Phadkar | 45·3 | 10 | 159 | 7 | | | | | Wkt | 1st | 1st | 2nd |
| Hazare | 12 | 1 | 44 | 0 | | | | | 1st | 239 | 41 | 0 |
| Amarnath | 16 | 4 | 39 | 0 | | | | | 2nd | 319 | 52 | 7 |
| Chowdhury | 37 | 6 | 130 | 1 | | | | | 3rd | 319 | 116 | 29 |
| Mankad | 33 | 4 | 93 | 1 | | | | | 4th | 339 | 136 | 42 |
| Ghulam Ahmed | 32 | 3 | 88 | 0 | | | | | 5th | 420 | 158 | 44 |
| Adhikari | 1 | 0 | 10 | 0 | | | | | 6th | 472 | 220 | 61 |
| WEST INDIES | | | | | | | | | 7th | 532 | 225 | 106 |
| Jones | 16 | 5 | 28 | 2 | 10 | 3 | 30 | 4 | 8th | 551 | 228 | 119 |
| Gomez | 28 | 10 | 60 | 1 | 20·3 | 12 | 35 | 3 | 9th | 565 | 233 | 132 |
| Trim | 27 | 7 | 48 | 4 | 16 | 5 | 28 | 3 | 10th | 582 | 245 | 144 |
| Ferguson | 20 | 2 | 72 | 2 | 11 | 1 | 39 | 0 | | | | |
| Goddard | 8 | 1 | 26 | 1 | 6 | 3 | 8 | 0 | | | | |

Umpires: B.J. Mohoni and A.R. Joshi.

## INDIA v WEST INDIES 1948–49 (5th Test)

Played at Brabourne Stadium, Bombay, on 4, 5, 6, 7, 8 February.
Toss: West Indies.   Result: MATCH DRAWN.
Debuts: India – S.N. Banerjee.

Weekes established a Test record by scoring his seventh consecutive fifty; it remains unequalled. Amarnath kep
wicket after Sen was injured attempting a catch early in the first innings. Needing 361 runs to win in 395 minutes
India fell just six runs short with only one wicket – apart from that of the injured Sen – remaining.

### WEST INDIES

| | | | | | |
|---|---|---|---|---|---|
| A.F. Rae | c Mushtaq Ali b Phadkar | 7 | c Mankad b Phadkar | | 9 |
| J.B. Stollmeyer | c Mankad b Ghulam Ahmed | 85 | b Mankad | | 1 |
| C.L. Walcott† | b Phadkar | 11 | b Phadkar | | 1 |
| E. de C. Weekes | c Mankad b Ghulam Ahmed | 56 | b Hazare | | 4 |
| G.E. Gomez | c Modi b Mankad | 19 | (7) c and b Mankad | | 2 |
| R.J. Christiani | b Banerjee | 40 | lbw b Mankad | | 1 |
| J.D.C. Goddard* | c Amarnath b Mankad | 41 | (8) not out | | 3 |
| F.J. Cameron | c Amarnath b Phadkar | 0 | (9) lbw b Banerjee | | |
| D. St E. Atkinson | c Amarnath b Mankad | 6 | (5) c Amarnath b Banerjee | | |
| P.E. Jones | lbw b Phadkar | 3 | c Amarnath b Banerjee | | |
| J. Trim | not out | 0 | lbw b Banerjee | | 1 |
| Extras | (B 10, LB 5, NB 3) | 18 | (B 4, NB 3) | | |
| **Total** | | **286** | | | **26** |

### INDIA

| | | | | | |
|---|---|---|---|---|---|
| Mushtaq Ali | c Atkinson b Gomez | 28 | c Walcott b Jones | | |
| K.C. Ibrahim | c Atkinson b Gomez | 4 | b Gomez | | |
| R.S. Modi | c Trim b Atkinson | 33 | c Walcott b Goddard | | 8 |
| V.S. Hazare | c Christiani b Atkinson | 40 | (5) b Jones | | 12 |
| H.R. Adhikari | c Walcott b Trim | 5 | (9) c Trim b Jones | | |
| D.G. Phadkar | b Trim | 25 | (7) not out | | 3 |
| L. Amarnath* | b Trim | 19 | (4) b Atkinson | | 3 |
| V.M.H. Mankad | run out | 19 | (6) c Walcott b Jones | | 1 |
| S.N. Banerjee | b Jones | 5 | (8) b Jones | | |
| Ghulam Ahmed | not out | 6 | not out | | |
| P. Sen† | absent hurt | – | | | |
| Extras | (B 6, LB 1, NB 2) | 9 | (B 13, LB 1, NB 11) | | 2 |
| **Total** | | **193** | (8 wickets) | | **35** |

| INDIA | O | M | R | W | O | M | R | W | FALL OF WICKETS | | | | |
|---|---|---|---|---|---|---|---|---|---|---|---|---|---|
| Banerjee | 21 | 2 | 73 | 1 | 24·3 | 6 | 54 | 4 | | WI | I | WI | I |
| Phadkar | 29·2 | 8 | 74 | 4 | 31 | 7 | 82 | 2 | *Wkt* | *1st* | *1st* | *2nd* | *2n* |
| Amarnath | 4 | 2 | 9 | 0 | | | | | 1st | 11 | 10 | 47 | |
| Ghulam Ahmed | 23 | 4 | 58 | 2 | 14 | 3 | 34 | 0 | 2nd | 27 | 37 | 68 | |
| Mankad | 26 | 4 | 54 | 3 | 32 | 8 | 77 | 3 | 3rd | 137 | 109 | 148 | 8 |
| Hazare | 1 | 1 | 0 | 0 | 6 | 1 | 13 | 1 | 4th | 176 | 112 | 152 | 22 |
| WEST INDIES | | | | | | | | | 5th | 190 | 122 | 166 | 27 |
| | | | | | | | | | 6th | 248 | 146 | 192 | 28 |
| Jones | 14·4 | 4 | 31 | 1 | 41 | 8 | 85 | 5 | 7th | 253 | 180 | 228 | 30 |
| Gomez | 21 | 8 | 30 | 2 | 26 | 5 | 55 | 1 | 8th | 281 | 181 | 230 | 32 |
| Trim | 30 | 3 | 69 | 3 | 7 | 0 | 43 | 0 | 9th | 284 | 193 | 240 | – |
| Atkinson | 23 | 2 | 54 | 2 | 3 | 0 | 16 | 1 | 10th | 286 | – | 267 | – |
| Cameron | | | | | 3 | 0 | 15 | 0 | | | | | |
| Goddard | | | | | 27 | 1 | 116 | 1 | | | | | |

Umpires: B.J. Mohoni and A.R. Joshi.

# SOUTH AFRICA v ENGLAND 1948–49 (1st Test)

Played at Kingsmead, Durban, on 16, 17, 18, 20, December.
Toss: South Africa.   Result: ENGLAND won by two wickets.
Debuts: South Africa – D.W. Begie, C.N. McCarthy, O.E. Wynne; England – R.O. Jenkins,
F.G. Mann, R.T. Simpson.

Jenkins took E.A.B. Rowan's wicket with his third ball in Test cricket. England needed eight runs to win from the
last (8-ball) over, bowled by Tuckett, and won with a leg bye off the very last ball.

## SOUTH AFRICA

| | | | | | |
|---|---|---|---|---|---|
| E.A.B. Rowan | c Evans b Jenkins | 7 | c Compton b Jenkins | | 16 |
| O.E. Wynne | c Compton b Bedser | 5 | c Watkins b Wright | | 4 |
| B. Mitchell | c Evans b Bedser | 27 | b Wright | | 19 |
| A.D. Nourse* | c Watkins b Wright | 37 | c and b Bedser | | 32 |
| W.W. Wade† | run out | 8 | b Jenkins | | 63 |
| D.W. Begbie | c Compton b Bedser | 37 | c Mann b Bedser | | 48 |
| O.C. Dawson | b Gladwin | 24 | c Compton b Wright | | 3 |
| A.M.B. Rowan | not out | 5 | b Wright | | 15 |
| L. Tuckett | lbw b Gladwin | 1 | not out | | 3 |
| J.B.F. Mann | c Evans b Gladwin | 4 | c Mann b Compton | | 10 |
| C.N. McCarthy | b Bedser | 0 | b Jenkins | | 0 |
| Extras | (B 3, LB 2, NB 1) | 6 | (B 1, LB 5) | | 6 |
| **Total** | | **161** | | | **219** |

## ENGLAND

| | | | | | |
|---|---|---|---|---|---|
| L. Hutton | c McCarthy b A.M.B. Rowan | 83 | c Dawson b Tuckett | | 5 |
| C. Washbrook | c Wade b Mann | 35 | lbw b Mann | | 25 |
| R.T. Simpson | c Begbie b Mann | 5 | (6) c E.A.B. Rowan b McCarthy | | 0 |
| D.C.S. Compton | c Wade b Mann | 72 | b McCarthy | | 28 |
| A.J. Watkins | c Nourse b A.M.B. Rowan | 9 | b McCarthy | | 4 |
| F.G. Mann* | c E.A.B. Rowan b A.M.B. Rowan | 19 | (3) c Mitchell b McCarthy | | 13 |
| T.G. Evans† | c Wynne b A.M.B. Rowan | 0 | b McCarthy | | 4 |
| R.O. Jenkins | c Mitchell b Mann | 5 | c Wade b McCarthy | | 22 |
| A.V. Bedser | c Tuckett b Mann | 11 | not out | | 1 |
| C. Gladwin | not out | 0 | not out | | 7 |
| D.V.P. Wright | c Tuckett b Mann | 0 | | | |
| Extras | (B 2, LB 12) | 14 | (B 9, LB 10) | | 19 |
| **Total** | | **253** | (8 wickets) | | **128** |

| ENGLAND | O | M | R | W | O | M | R | W | | | | | |
|---|---|---|---|---|---|---|---|---|---|---|---|---|---|
| Bedser | 13·5 | 2 | 39 | 4 | 18 | 5 | 51 | 2 | | FALL OF WICKETS | | | |
| Gladwin | 12 | 3 | 21 | 3 | 7 | 3 | 15 | 0 | | SA | E | SA | E |
| Jenkins | 14 | 3 | 50 | 1 | 22·3 | 6 | 64 | 3 | *Wkt* | *1st* | *1st* | *2nd* | *2nd* |
| Wright | 9 | 3 | 29 | 1 | 26 | 3 | 72 | 4 | 1st | 9 | 84 | 22 | 25 |
| Compton | 2 | 0 | 5 | 0 | 16 | 11 | 11 | 1 | 2nd | 18 | 104 | 22 | 49 |
| Watkins | 3 | 0 | 11 | 0 | | | | | 3rd | 69 | 146 | 67 | 52 |
| | | | | | | | | | 4th | 80 | 172 | 89 | 64 |
| | | | | | | | | | 5th | 99 | 212 | 174 | 64 |
| SOUTH AFRICA | | | | | | | | | 6th | 148 | 212 | 179 | 70 |
| McCarthy | 9 | 2 | 20 | 0 | 12 | 2 | 43 | 6 | 7th | 150 | 221 | 208 | 115 |
| Dawson | 3 | 0 | 16 | 0 | | | | | 8th | 152 | 247 | 208 | 116 |
| Tuckett | 6 | 0 | 36 | 0 | 10 | 0 | 38 | 1 | 9th | 160 | 253 | 219 | – |
| A.M.B. Rowan | 44 | 8 | 108 | 4 | 4 | 0 | 15 | 0 | 10th | 161 | 253 | 219 | – |
| Mann | 37·4 | 14 | 59 | 6 | 2 | 0 | 13 | 1 | | | | | |

Umpires: R.G.A. Ashman and G.L. Sickler.

Test No. 310/71

## SOUTH AFRICA v ENGLAND 1948–49 (2nd Test)

Played at Ellis Park, Johannesburg, on 27, 28, 29, 30 December.
Toss: England.   Result: MATCH DRAWN.
Debuts: Nil.

Hutton and Washbrook scored 359 together in 310 minutes on the first day; it remains England's highes
first-wicket partnership in all Test cricket. The South African selectors dropped E.A.B. Rowan from the team fo
the 4th Test, which they announced at the end of the third day's play. Rowan responded by batting throughout th
last day to save the match.

### ENGLAND

| | | |
|---|---|---:|
| L. Hutton | c Wade b McCarthy | 158 |
| C. Washbrook | c Begbie b McCarthy | 195 |
| J.F. Crapp | c and b Mitchell | 56 |
| D.C.S. Compton | c Mitchell b Mann | 114 |
| A.J. Watkins | c Wade b Mann | 7 |
| F.G. Mann* | c McCarthy b Mann | 7 |
| T.G. Evans† | run out | 18 |
| R.O. Jenkins | c Wade b A.M.B. Rowan | 4 |
| A.V. Bedser | b McCarthy | 12 |
| C. Gladwin | lbw b Dawson | 23 |
| D.V.P. Wright | not out | 1 |
| Extras | (B 3, LB 10) | 13 |
| **Total** | | **608** |

### SOUTH AFRICA

| | | | | |
|---|---|---:|---|---:|
| E.A.B. Rowan | lbw b Bedser | 8 | not out | 15( |
| O.E. Wynne | lbw b Wright | 4 | lbw b Bedser | ´ |
| B. Mitchell | b Gladwin | 86 | c Hutton b Wright | 4( |
| A.D. Nourse* | lbw b Wright | 32 | not out | 5( |
| W.W. Wade† | c Evans b Compton | 85 | | |
| D.W. Begbie | c Watkins b Jenkins | 5 | | |
| O.C. Dawson | c Watkins b Jenkins | 12 | | |
| A.M.B. Rowan | b Wright | 8 | | |
| L. Tuckett | st Evans b Watkins | 38 | | |
| N.B.F. Mann | st Evans b Jenkins | 23 | | |
| C.N. McCarthy | not out | 1 | | |
| Extras | (B 4, LB 7, NB 2) | 13 | (B 9, LB 4, NB 1) | 1( |
| **Total** | | **315** | (2 wickets) | 27( |

| SOUTH AFRICA | O | M | R | W | O | M | R | W |
|---|---|---|---|---|---|---|---|---|
| McCarthy | 26 | 1 | 102 | 3 | | | | |
| Dawson | 16·5 | 3 | 59 | 1 | | | | |
| A.M.B. Rowan | 41 | 4 | 155 | 1 | | | | |
| Tuckett | 12 | 0 | 55 | 0 | | | | |
| Mann | 30 | 2 | 107 | 3 | | | | |
| Begbie | 6 | 0 | 38 | 0 | | | | |
| Mitchell | 18 | 1 | 79 | 1 | | | | |
| **ENGLAND** | | | | | | | | |
| Bedser | 22 | 6 | 42 | 1 | 17 | 4 | 51 | 1 |
| Gladwin | 20 | 6 | 29 | 1 | 16 | 5 | 37 | 0 |
| Jenkins | 21·4 | 3 | 88 | 3 | 19 | 3 | 54 | 0 |
| Wright | 26 | 2 | 104 | 3 | 14 | 3 | 35 | 1 |
| Compton | 10 | 0 | 34 | 1 | 13 | 3 | 31 | 0 |
| Watkins | 5 | 2 | 5 | 1 | 12 | 2 | 48 | 0 |

### FALL OF WICKETS

| Wkt | E 1st | SA 1st | SA 2nd |
|---|---|---|---|
| 1st | 359 | 12 | 15 |
| 2nd | 366 | 17 | 108 |
| 3rd | 516 | 96 | – |
| 4th | 540 | 191 | – |
| 5th | 549 | 204 | – |
| 6th | 550 | 220 | – |
| 7th | 570 | 235 | – |
| 8th | 576 | 273 | – |
| 9th | 602 | 313 | – |
| 10th | 608 | 315 | – |

Umpires: J.V. Hart-Davis and G.L. Sickler.

# SOUTH AFRICA v ENGLAND 1948–49 (3rd Test)

Played at Newlands, Cape Town, on 1, 3, 4, 5 January.
Toss: England.   Result: MATCH DRAWN.
Debuts: South Africa – M.A. Hanley.

South Africa were set 229 runs to win in 125 minutes. Compton (slow left-arm leg-breaks and 'chinamen') took five wickets in an innings for the only time in his 78 Test matches.

## ENGLAND

| | | | | |
|---|---|---:|---|---:|
| L. Hutton | run out | 41 | b Rowan | 87 |
| C. Washbrook | b Rowan | 74 | c Mitchell b McCarthy | 9 |
| J.F. Crapp | c Wynne b Mitchell | 35 | c Wade b McCarthy | 54 |
| D.C.S. Compton | b Rowan | 1 | not out | 51 |
| A.J. Watkins | c Melville b Dawson | 27 | not out | 64 |
| F.G. Mann* | c Mitchell b Hanley | 44 | | |
| T.G. Evans† | b Rowan | 27 | | |
| R.O. Jenkins | c Wynne b Rowan | 1 | | |
| A.V. Bedser | b McCarthy | 16 | | |
| C. Gladwin | not out | 17 | | |
| D.V.P. Wright | c Dawson b Rowan | 11 | | |
| Extras | (B 7, LB 7) | 14 | (B 8, LB 3) | 11 |
| **Total** | | **308** | (3 wickets declared) | **276** |

## SOUTH AFRICA

| | | | | |
|---|---|---:|---|---:|
| O.E. Wynne | c Crapp b Watkins | 50 | c Bedser b Jenkins | 46 |
| A. Melville | b Jenkins | 15 | st Evans b Jenkins | 24 |
| B. Mitchell | b Compton | 120 | (5) not out | 20 |
| A.D. Nourse* | c and b Compton | 112 | st Evans b Jenkins | 34 |
| W.W. Wade† | c Watkins b Compton | 0 | (3) c Evans b Jenkins | 11 |
| D.W. Begbie | run out | 18 | | |
| O.C. Dawson | c Mann b Compton | 25 | (6) not out | 5 |
| A.M.B. Rowan | c Hutton b Gladwin | 2 | | |
| N.B.F. Mann | not out | 10 | | |
| M.A. Hanley | run out | 0 | | |
| C.N. McCarthy | st Evans b Compton | 1 | | |
| Extras | (B 1, NB 2) | 3 | (LB 1, NB 1) | 2 |
| **Total** | | **356** | (4 wickets) | **142** |

| SOUTH AFRICA | O | M | R | W | O | M | R | W |
|---|---:|---:|---:|---:|---:|---:|---:|---:|
| McCarthy | 26 | 2 | 95 | 1 | 20 | 2 | 75 | 2 |
| Dawson | 7 | 2 | 35 | 1 | 13 | 3 | 33 | 0 |
| Rowan | 31·2 | 3 | 80 | 5 | 30 | 5 | 65 | 1 |
| Mann | 3 | 0 | 18 | 0 | 15 | 5 | 27 | 0 |
| Hanley | 6 | 0 | 9 | 1 | 7 | 1 | 34 | 0 |
| ENGLAND | | | | | | | | |
| Bedser | 34 | 5 | 92 | 0 | 7 | 0 | 40 | 0 |
| Gladwin | 30 | 7 | 51 | 1 | 10 | 2 | 27 | 0 |
| Wright | 9 | 0 | 58 | 0 | 2 | 0 | 18 | 0 |
| Jenkins | 11 | 1 | 46 | 1 | 9 | 0 | 48 | 4 |
| Watkins | 10 | 0 | 36 | 1 | | | | |
| Compton | 25·2 | 4 | 70 | 5 | 3 | 1 | 7 | 0 |

FALL OF WICKETS

| Wkt | E 1st | SA 1st | E 2nd | SA 2nd |
|---|---:|---:|---:|---:|
| 1st | 88 | 30 | 11 | 58 |
| 2nd | 149 | 108 | 145 | 83 |
| 3rd | 151 | 298 | 165 | 83 |
| 4th | 152 | 298 | – | 132 |
| 5th | 203 | 303 | – | – |
| 6th | 249 | 342 | – | – |
| 7th | 251 | 344 | – | – |
| 8th | 263 | 349 | – | – |
| 9th | 281 | 349 | – | – |
| 9th | 281 | 349 | – | – |
| 10th | 308 | 356 | – | – |

Umpires: J.V. Hart-Davis and R.G.A. Ashman.

## SOUTH AFRICA v ENGLAND 1948–49 (4th Test)

Played at Ellis Park, Johannesburg. on 12, 14, 15, 16 February.
Toss: England.   Result: MATCH DRAWN.
Debuts: South Africa – L.A. Markham.

South Africa were set 376 runs to win in 270 minutes.

### ENGLAND

| Batsman | Dismissal 1 | | Dismissal 2 | |
|---|---|---|---|---|
| L. Hutton | b Tuckett | 2 | b A.M.B. Rowan | 123 |
| C. Washbrook | c E.A.B. Rowan b McCarthy | 97 | lbw b A.M.B. Rowan | 31 |
| J.F. Crapp | b A.M.B. Rowan | 51 | (5) hit wkt b McCarthy | 25 |
| D.C.S. Compton | c A.M.B. Rowan b Tuckett | 24 | (3) b Markham | 25 |
| A.J. Watkins | hit wkt b McCarthy | 111 | (6) b A.M.B. Rowan | 10 |
| F.G. Mann* | c Wade b McCarthy | 17 | (4) lbw b A.M.B. Rowan | 16 |
| R.O. Jenkins | lbw b Mitchell | 25 | | |
| A.V. Beder | lbw b Tuckett | 1 | (7) b McCarthy | 7 |
| C. Gladwin | b McCarthy | 19 | (8) not out | 7 |
| S.C. Griffith † | c Mitchell b McCarthy | 8 | | |
| J.A. Young | not out | 10 | | |
| Extras | (B 2, LB 12) | 14 | (B 5, LB 11, NB 1) | 17 |
| **Total** | | **379** | (7 wickets declared) | **253** |

### SOUTH AFRICA

| Batsman | Dismissal 1 | | Dismissal 2 | |
|---|---|---|---|---|
| B. Mitchell | c Griffith b Bedser | 2 | c Compton b Gladwin | 6 |
| E.A.B. Rowan | run out | 6 | not out | 86 |
| K.G. Viljoen | run out | 0 | b Watkins | 63 |
| A.D. Nourse * | not out | 129 | b Watkins | 1 |
| W.W. Wade † | lbw b Young | 54 | lbw b Bedser | 27 |
| T.A. Harris | b Bedser | 6 | not out | 1 |
| A.M.B. Rowan | b Gladwin | 12 | | |
| L. Tuckett | b Young | 0 | | |
| L.A. Markham | c Griffith b Jenkins | 20 | | |
| N.B.F. Mann | c Griffith b Gladwin | 14 | | |
| C.N. McCarthy | not out | 0 | | |
| Extras | (B 4, LB 10) | 14 | (B 7, LB 1, NB 2) | 10 |
| **Total** | (9 wickets declared) | **257** | (4 wickets) | **194** |

| SOUTH AFRICA | O | M | R | W | O | M | R | W |
|---|---|---|---|---|---|---|---|---|
| McCarthy | 35·7 | 3 | 114 | 5 | 12·2 | 2 | 50 | 2 |
| Tuckett | 29 | 2 | 109 | 3 | 10 | 0 | 43 | 0 |
| A.M.B. Rowan | 23 | 1 | 70 | 1 | 34 | 10 | 69 | 4 |
| Markham | 5 | 1 | 38 | 0 | 8 | 0 | 34 | 1 |
| Mann | 10 | 3 | 26 | 0 | 7 | 0 | 20 | 0 |
| Mitchell | 3 | 0 | 8 | 1 | 7 | 1 | 20 | 0 |
| **ENGLAND** | | | | | | | | |
| Bedser | 24 | 3 | 81 | 2 | 17 | 0 | 54 | 1 |
| Gladwin | 24 | 7 | 43 | 2 | 16 | 6 | 39 | 1 |
| Jenkins | 8 | 1 | 39 | 1 | 9 | 2 | 26 | 0 |
| Young | 23 | 6 | 52 | 2 | 11 | 6 | 14 | 0 |
| Watkins | 2 | 0 | 9 | 0 | 3 | 0 | 16 | 2 |
| Compton | 4 | 0 | 19 | 0 | 9 | 2 | 35 | 0 |

### FALL OF WICKETS

| Wkt | E 1st | SA 1st | E 2nd | SA 2nd |
|---|---|---|---|---|
| 1st | 3 | 4 | 77 | 23 |
| 2nd | 123 | 4 | 151 | 136 |
| 3rd | 172 | 19 | 186 | 140 |
| 4th | 180 | 125 | 204 | 182 |
| 5th | 213 | 137 | 222 | – |
| 6th | 282 | 156 | 237 | – |
| 7th | 287 | 161 | 253 | – |
| 8th | 316 | 192 | – | – |
| 9th | 346 | 236 | – | – |
| 10th | 379 | – | – | – |

Umpires: J.V. Hart-Davis and R.G.A. Ashman.

# SOUTH AFRICA v ENGLAND 1948–49 (5th Test)

Played at St. George's Park, Port Elizabeth, on 5, 7, 8, 9 March.
Toss: South Africa.   Result: ENGLAND won by three wickets.
Debuts: South Africa – J.E. Cheetham.

Set 172 runs to win in 95 minutes, England won with just one minute remaining for play. Hutton and Washbrook, who hit their first balls for four and six respectively, scored 58 in 27 minutes before Crapp won the match by making ten runs off three successive balls in Mann's final over.

## SOUTH AFRICA

| | | | | |
|---|---|---|---|---|
| B. Mitchell | c Griffith b Bedser | 99 | c Griffith b Bedser | 56 |
| E.A.B. Rowan | c Watkins b Gladwin | 3 | c Jenkins b Young | 37 |
| K.G. Viljoen | b Bedser | 2 | | |
| A.D. Nourse* | c Bedser | 73 | not out | 30 |
| W.W. Wade† | c Compton b Jenkins | 125 | not out | 34 |
| J.E. Cheetham | c and b Bedser | 2 | (3) c Compton b Young | 18 |
| O.C. Dawson | c Gladwin b Jenkins | 20 | | |
| A.M.B. Rowan | not out | 29 | | |
| L. Tuckett | b Jenkins | 2 | | |
| N.B.F. Mann | c Compton b Gladwin | 11 | | |
| C.N. McCarthy | b Gladwin | 3 | | |
| Extras | (B 2, LB 5, NB 3) | 10 | (B 6, LB 5, NB 1) | 12 |
| **Total** | | **379** | (3 wickets declared) | **187** |

## ENGLAND

| | | | | |
|---|---|---|---|---|
| L. Hutton | c Dawson b A.M.B. Rowan | 46 | st Wade b A.M.B. Rowan | 32 |
| C. Washbrook | c Dawson b A.M.B. Rowan | 36 | c A.M.B. Rowan b Mann | 40 |
| J.F. Crapp | c Wade b Mann | 49 | (6) not out | 26 |
| D.C.S Compton | c Wade b Mann | 49 | (3) c Cheetham b A.M.B. Rowan | 42 |
| A.J. Watkins | c A.M.B. Rowan b Mann | 14 | (9) not out | 5 |
| F.G. Mann * | not out | 136 | (4) c Dawson b Mann | 2 |
| R.O. Jenkins | lbw b Mann | 29 | | |
| A.V. Bedser | c Mitchell b A.M.B. Rowan | 33 | (5) c Nourse b A.M.B. Rowan | 1 |
| C. Gladwin | c Dawson b A.M.B. Rowan | 10 | (7) c Tuckett b Mann | 15 |
| S.C. Griffith † | c E.A.B. Rowan b A.M.B. Rowan | 5 | (8) b Mann | 0 |
| J.A. Young | c Wade b McCarthy | 0 | | |
| Extras | (B 11, LB 18, NB 4) | 33 | (B 3, LB 8) | 11 |
| **Total** | | **395** | (7 wickets) | **174** |

| ENGLAND | O | M | R | W | O | M | R | W | FALL OF WICKETS | | | | |
|---|---|---|---|---|---|---|---|---|---|---|---|---|---|
| Bedser | 38 | 9 | 61 | 4 | 16 | 3 | 43 | 1 | | SA | E | SA | E |
| Gladwin | 30·5 | 6 | 70 | 3 | 6 | 2 | 14 | 0 | Wkt | 1st | 1st | 2nd | 2nd |
| Jenkins | 15 | 2 | 53 | 3 | 4 | 0 | 27 | 0 | 1st | 10 | 78 | 101 | 58 |
| Watkins | 5 | 0 | 24 | 0 | | | | | 2nd | 13 | 82 | 101 | 104 |
| Young | 48 | 9 | 122 | 0 | 23 | 9 | 34 | 2 | 3rd | 114 | 96 | 127 | 124 |
| Compton | 7 | 0 | 39 | 0 | 9 | 0 | 57 | 0 | 4th | 264 | 149 | – | 125 |
| SOUTH AFRICA | | | | | | | | | 5th | 282 | 168 | – | 125 |
| McCarthy | 17·4 | 1 | 42 | 2 | 2 | 0 | 20 | 0 | 6th | 330 | 268 | – | 152 |
| Dawson | 3 | 0 | 10 | 0 | | | | | 7th | 336 | 341 | – | 153 |
| Tuckett | 5 | 0 | 22 | 0 | 2 | 0 | 13 | 0 | 8th | 338 | 362 | – | – |
| A.M.B. Rowan | 60 | 9 | 167 | 5 | 10 | 0 | 65 | 3 | 9th | 375 | 390 | – | – |
| Mann | 51 | 18 | 95 | 3 | 9·7 | 0 | 65 | 4 | 10th | 379 | 395 | – | – |
| Mitchell | 5 | 0 | 26 | 0 | | | | | | | | | |

Umpires: D. Collins and R.G.A. Ashman.

# ENGLAND v NEW ZEALAND 1949 (1st Test)

Played at Headingley, Leeds, on 11, 13, 14 June.
Toss: England.   Result: MATCH DRAWN.
Debuts: England – T.E. Bailey, A. Wharton; New Zealand – H.B. Cave, F.L.H. Mooney, G.O. Rabone.

Bailey took Scott's wicket with his eighth ball in Test cricket. Mann scored 49 not out in 25 minutes.

## ENGLAND

| | | | | |
|---|---|---|---|---|
| L. Hutton | c Sutcliffe b Cowie | 101 | c Mooney b Cave | 0 |
| C. Washbrook | c Sutcliffe b Cowie | 10 | not out | 103 |
| W.J. Edrich | c Donnelly b Cowie | 36 | b Cave | 70 |
| D.S.C. Compton | st Mooney b Burtt | 114 | c Mooney b Cave | 26 |
| A. Wharton | lbw b Cowie | 7 | b Sutcliffe | 13 |
| F.G. Mann* | c Scott b Burtt | 38 | not out | 49 |
| T.E. Bailey | c Scott b Cowie | 12 | | |
| T.G. Evans† | c Mooney b Burtt | 27 | | |
| A.V. Bedser | c Donnelly b Burtt | 20 | | |
| J.A. Young | st Mooney b Burtt | 0 | | |
| W.E. Hollies | not out | 0 | | |
| Extras | (B 3, LB 4) | 7 | (B4, LB 2) | 6 |
| **Total** | | **372** | (4 wickets declared) | **267** |

## NEW ZEALAND

| | | | | |
|---|---|---|---|---|
| B. Sutcliffe | c Evans b Young | 32 | c Bedser b Young | 82 |
| V.J. Scott | c Washbrook b Bailey | 1 | c Bedser b Young | 43 |
| W.A. Hadlee* | c Edrich b Bailey | 34 | (4) not out | 13 |
| W.M. Wallace | c Evans b Bailey | 3 | | |
| M.P. Donnelly | c Young b Bailey | 64 | | |
| F.B. Smith | c Compton b Edrich | 96 | (3) not out | 54 |
| G.O. Rabone | c Evans b Edrich | 13 | | |
| F.L.H. Mooney † | c Edrich b Bailey | 46 | | |
| T.B. Burtt | c Bedser b Compton | 7 | | |
| H.B. Cave | c Edrich b Bailey | 2 | | |
| J. Cowie | not out | 26 | | |
| Extras | (B 2, LB 8, NB 7) | 17 | (B 1, LB 2) | 3 |
| **Total** | | **341** | (2 wickets) | **195** |

| NEW ZEALAND | O | M | R | W | O | M | R | W |
|---|---|---|---|---|---|---|---|---|
| Cowie | 43 | 6 | 127 | 5 | | | | |
| Cave | 27 | 5 | 85 | 0 | 26 | 3 | 103 | 3 |
| Rabone | 18 | 7 | 56 | 0 | 17 | 4 | 56 | 0 |
| Burtt | 39·3 | 16 | 97 | 5 | 15 | 2 | 56 | 0 |
| Donnelly | | | | | 5 | 0 | 20 | 0 |
| Sutcliffe | | | | | 4 | 1 | 17 | 1 |
| Scott | | | | | 1 | 0 | 9 | 0 |
| | | | | | | | | |
| ENGLAND | | | | | | | | |
| Bailey | 32·3 | 6 | 118 | 6 | 9 | 0 | 51 | 0 |
| Bedser | 22 | 8 | 56 | 0 | 9 | 1 | 26 | 0 |
| Edrich | 9 | 2 | 18 | 2 | 2 | 0 | 13 | 0 |
| Young | 22 | 6 | 52 | 1 | 14 | 3 | 41 | 2 |
| Hollies | 25 | 6 | 57 | 0 | 11 | 3 | 33 | 0 |
| Compton | 8 | 2 | 23 | 1 | 1 | 0. | 5 | 0 |
| Hutton | | | | | 3 | 0 | 23 | 0 |

### FALL OF WICKETS

| | E | NZ | E | NZ |
|---|---|---|---|---|
| Wkt | 1st | 1st | 2nd | 2nd |
| 1st | 17 | 4 | 0 | 112 |
| 2nd | 92 | 64 | 118 | 147 |
| 3rd | 194 | 69 | 162 | – |
| 4th | 214 | 80 | 201 | – |
| 5th | 273 | 200 | – | – |
| 6th | 322 | 251 | – | – |
| 7th | 330 | 254 | – | – |
| 8th | 353 | 273 | – | – |
| 9th | 367 | 284 | – | – |
| 10th | 372 | 341 | – | – |

Umpires: W.H. Ashdown and D. Davies.

# ENGLAND v NEW ZEALAND 1949 (2nd Test)

Played at Lord's, London, on 25, 27, 28 June.
Toss: England.   Result: MATCH DRAWN.
Debuts: Nil.

Mann created Test match history by declaring on the first day. His declaration was afterwards found to be incorrect as the current experimental law allowing a declaration on the first day of a three-day match did not apply to this Test rubber. No wicket fell in the last 15 minutes and so fortunately England gained no embarrassing advantage. Donnelly remains the only New Zealander to score a double-century against England.

## ENGLAND

| | | | | |
|---|---|---|---|---|
| L. Hutton | b Burtt | 23 | c Cave b Rabone | 66 |
| .D.B. Robertson | c Mooney b Cowie | 26 | c Cave b Rabone | 121 |
| W.J. Edrich | c Donnelly b Cowie | 9 | c Hadlee b Burtt | 31 |
| D.C.S Compton | c Sutcliffe b Burtt | 116 | b Burtt | 6 |
| A.J. Watkins | c Wallace b Burtt | 6 | not out | 49 |
| F.G. Mann* | b Cave | 18 | c Donnelly b Rabone | 17 |
| T.E. Bailey | c Sutcliffe b Rabone | 93 | not out | 6 |
| T.G. Evans† | b Burtt | 5 | | |
| C. Gladwin | run out | 1 | | |
| J.A. Young | not out | 1 | | |
| W.E. Hollies | did not bat | | | |
| Extras | (B 9, LB 2) | 11 | (B 9, LB 1) | 10 |
| **Total** | (9 wickets declared) | **313** | (5 wickets) | **306** |

## NEW ZEALAND

| | | |
|---|---|---|
| B. Sutcliffe | c Compton b Gladwin | 57 |
| V.J. Scott | c Edrich b Compton | 42 |
| W.A. Hadlee* | c Robertson b Hollies | 43 |
| W.M. Wallace | c Evans b Hollies | 2 |
| M.P. Donnelly | c Hutton b Young | 206 |
| F.B. Smith | b Hollies | 23 |
| G.O. Rabone | b Hollies | 25 |
| F.L.H. Mooney† | c Watkins b Young | 33 |
| T.B. Burtt | c Edrich b Hollies | 23 |
| H.B. Cave | c and b Young | 6 |
| J. Cowie | not out | 1 |
| Extras | (B 16, LB 3, W 3, NB 1) | 23 |
| **Total** | | **484** |

| NEW ZEALAND | O | M | R | W | O | M | R | W |
|---|---|---|---|---|---|---|---|---|
| Cowie | 26·1 | 5 | 64 | 2 | 14 | 3 | 39 | 0 |
| Cave | 27 | 2 | 79 | 1 | 7 | 1 | 23 | 0 |
| Rabone | 14 | 5 | 56 | 1 | 28 | 6 | 116 | 3 |
| Burtt | 35 | 7 | 102 | 4 | 37 | 12 | 58 | 2 |
| Sutcliffe | 1 | 0 | 1 | 0 | 16 | 1 | 55 | 0 |
| Wallace | | | | | 1 | 0 | 5 | 0 |
| ENGLAND | | | | | | | | |
| Bailey | 33 | 3 | 136 | 0 | | | | |
| Gladwin | 28 | 5 | 67 | 1 | | | | |
| Edrich | 4 | 0 | 16 | 0 | | | | |
| Hollies | 58 | 18 | 133 | 5 | | | | |
| Compton | 7 | 0 | 33 | 1 | | | | |
| Young | 26·4 | 4 | 65 | 3 | | | | |
| Watkins | 3 | 1 | 11 | 0 | | | | |

### FALL OF WICKETS

| | E | NZ | E |
|---|---|---|---|
| Wkt | 1st | 1st | 2nd |
| 1st | 48 | 89 | 143 |
| 2nd | 59 | 124 | 216 |
| 3rd | 72 | 137 | 226 |
| 4th | 83 | 160 | 226 |
| 5th | 112 | 197 | 252 |
| 6th | 301 | 273 | – |
| 7th | 307 | 351 | – |
| 8th | 307 | 436 | – |
| 9th | 313 | 464 | – |
| 10th | – | 484 | – |

Umpires: F. Chester and W.H. Ashdown.

# ENGLAND v NEW ZEALAND 1949 (3rd Test)

Played at Old Trafford, Manchester, on 23, 25, 26 July.
Toss: England.   Result: MATCH DRAWN.
Debuts: England – D.B. Close, H.L. Jackson; New Zealand – J.R. Reid.

F.R. Brown's first gesture on being appointed captain and recalled to Test cricket after an absence of twelve year
was to send New Zealand in to bat. Close made his debut at the age of 18 years 149 days and remains the younges
to play for England. Simpson scored a century in his first home Test, his last 53 runs coming in just 27 minutes.

## NEW ZEALAND

| | | | | |
|---|---|---|---|---|
| B. Sutcliffe | b Bailey | 9 | lbw b Compton | 10 |
| V.J. Scott | b Bailey | 13 | b Jackson | 1 |
| W.A. Hadlee* | b Bailey | 34 | c Brown b Hollies | 2 |
| W.M. Wallace | c Washbrook b Close | 12 | lbw b Hollies | 1 |
| M.P. Donnelly | lbw b Bailey | 75 | st Evans b Brown | 8 |
| J.R. Reid | lbw b Jackson | 50 | b Bailey | 2 |
| G.O. Rabone | c Brown b Bailey | 33 | not out | 3 |
| F.L.H. Mooney† | b Jackson | 5 | st Evans b Brown | 1 |
| T.B. Burtt | st Evans b Compton | 32 | not out | 2 |
| H.B. Cave | b Bailey | 12 | | |
| J. Cowie | not out | 3 | | |
| Extras | (B 3, LB 9, NB 3) | 15 | (B 2, LB 4, NB 6) | 1 |
| **Total** | | **293** | (7 wickets) | 34 |

## ENGLAND

| | | |
|---|---|---|
| L. Hutton | st Mooney b Burtt | 73 |
| C. Washbrook | c Mooney b Cowies | 44 |
| W.J. Edrich | c Rabone b Burtt | 78 |
| D.C.S. Compton | b Cowies | 25 |
| R.T. Simpson | b Donnelly b Burtt | 103 |
| T.E. Bailey | not out | 72 |
| F.R. Brown* | c Wallace b Burtt | 22 |
| T.G. Evans† | c Mooney b Burtt | 12 |
| D.B. Close | c Rabone b Burtt | 0 |
| W.E. Hollies | c Mooney b Cowie | 0 |
| H.L. Jackson | not out | 7 |
| Extras | (B 2, LB 2) | 4 |
| **Total** | (9 wickets declared) | **440** |

| ENGLAND | O | M | R | W | O | M | R | W | FALL OF WICKETS | | | |
|---|---|---|---|---|---|---|---|---|---|---|---|---|
| Bailey | 30·2 | 5 | 84 | 6 | 16 | 0 | 71 | 1 | | NZ | E | NZ |
| Jackson | 27 | 11 | 47 | 2 | 12 | 3 | 25 | 1 | *Wkt* | *1st* | *1st* | *2nd* |
| Close | 25 | 12 | 39 | 1 | 17 | 2 | 46 | 0 | 1st | 22 | 103 | 24 |
| Hollies | 18 | 8 | 29 | 0 | 26 | 6 | 52 | 2 | 2nd | 23 | 127 | 58 |
| Brown | 18 | 4 | 43 | 0 | 21 | 3 | 71 | 2 | 3rd | 62 | 172 | 109 |
| Compton | 6 | 0 | 28 | 1 | 8 | 0 | 28 | 1 | 4th | 82 | 258 | 187 |
| Edrich | 4 | 1 | 8 | 0 | 5 | 0 | 26 | 0 | 5th | 198 | 363 | 235 |
| Simpson | | | | | 2 | 1 | 9 | 0 | 6th | 205 | 404 | 295 |
| Washbrook | | | | | 2 | 0 | 8 | 0 | 7th | 217 | 419 | 313 |
| Hutton | | | | | 1 | 1 | 0 | 0 | 8th | 269 | 419 | – |
| | | | | | | | | | 9th | 288 | 419 | – |
| NEW ZEALAND | | | | | | | | | 10th | 293 | – | – |
| Cowie | 36 | 8 | 98 | 3 | | | | | | | | |
| Cave | 30 | 4 | 97 | 0 | | | | | | | | |
| Burtt | 45 | 11 | 162 | 6 | | | | | | | | |
| Rabone | 10 | 0 | 43 | 0 | | | | | | | | |
| Sutcliffe | 5 | 0 | 22 | 0 | | | | | | | | |
| Reid | 2 | 0 | 14 | 0 | | | | | | | | |

Umpires: F. Chester and F.S. Lee.

# ENGLAND v NEW ZEALAND 1949 (4th Test)

Played at Kennington Oval, London, 13, 15, 16 August.
Toss: New Zealand.   Result: MATCH DRAWN.
Debuts: New Zealand – G.F. Cresswell.

This rubber, in which all four matches were drawn, proved that three days is too short a period to decide a Test match on good pitches, even in an exceptionally dry summer like 1949. The stand of 147 between Hutton and Simpson remains England's highest first-wicket partnership against New Zealand.

## NEW ZEALAND

| | | | | | |
|---|---|---|---|---|---|
| B. Sutcliffe | c Bedser b Hollies | 88 | | c Brown b Bedser | 54 |
| V.J. Scott | c Edrich b Bedser | 60 | | c Evans b Bedser | 6 |
| J.R. Reid† | lbw b Wright | 5 | (5) | c Wright b Laker | 93 |
| W.M. Wallace | c Edrich b Bedser | 55 | | st Evans b Hollies | 58 |
| M.P. Donnelly | c Edrich b Bailey | 27 | (6) | c Brown b Bedser | 10 |
| W.A. Hadlee* | c Evans b Bedser | 25 | (3) | c Edrich b Hollies | 22 |
| G.O. Rabone | c Evans b Bailey | 18 | | lbw b Laker | 20 |
| T.B. Burtt | c Evans b Bailey | 36 | | c Compton b Laker | 6 |
| H.B. Cave | b Compton | 10 | | not out | 14 |
| J. Cowie | c Hutton b Bedser | 1 | | c Wright b Laker | 4 |
| G.F. Cresswell | not out | 12 | | not out | 0 |
| Extras | (LB 1, W 1, NB 6) | 8 | | (B 10, LB 5, NB 6) | 21 |
| **Total** | | **345** | | (9 wickets declared) | **308** |

## ENGLAND

| | | |
|---|---|---|
| L. Hutton | c Rabone b Cresswell | 206 |
| R.T. Simpson | c Donnelly b Cresswell | 68 |
| W.J. Edrich | c Cave b Cresswell | 100 |
| D.C.S. Compton | c Scott b Cresswell | 13 |
| T.E. Bailey | c Reid b Cowie | 36 |
| F.R. Brown* | c Hadlee b Cresswell | 21 |
| T.G. Evans† | c Donnelly b Cowie | 17 |
| J.C. Laker | c Scott b Cowie | 0 |
| A.V. Bedser | c Reid b Cowie | 0 |
| W.E. Hollies | not out | 1 |
| D.V.P. Wright | lbw b Cresswell | 0 |
| Extras | (B 6, LB 11, NB 3) | 20 |
| **Total** | | **482** |

| ENGLAND | O | M | R | W | O | M | R | W |
|---|---|---|---|---|---|---|---|---|
| Bailey | 26·1 | 7 | 72 | 3 | 11 | 1 | 67 | 0 |
| Bedser | 31 | 6 | 74 | 4 | 23 | 4 | 59 | 3 |
| Edrich | 3 | 0 | 16 | 0 | | | | |
| Wright | 22 | 1 | 93 | 1 | 6 | 0 | 21 | 0 |
| Laker | 3 | 0 | 11 | 0 | 29 | 6 | 78 | 4 |
| Hollies | 20 | 7 | 51 | 1 | 17 | 6 | 30 | 2 |
| Brown | 5 | 1 | 14 | 0 | 10 | 0 | 29 | 0 |
| Compton | 2 | 0 | 6 | 1 | 1 | 0 | 3 | 0 |
| NEW ZEALAND | | | | | | | | |
| Cowie | 28 | 1 | 123 | 4 | | | | |
| Cresswell | 41·2 | 6 | 168 | 6 | | | | |
| Cave | 24 | 4 | 78 | 0 | | | | |
| Burtt | 24 | 2 | 93 | 0 | | | | |

### FALL OF WICKETS

| | NZ | E | NZ |
|---|---|---|---|
| Wkt | 1st | 1st | 2nd |
| 1st | 121 | 147 | 24 |
| 2nd | 134 | 365 | 68 |
| 3rd | 170 | 396 | 115 |
| 4th | 239 | 401 | 131 |
| 5th | 239 | 436 | 188 |
| 6th | 272 | 496 | 276 |
| 7th | 287 | 470 | 283 |
| 8th | 311 | 472 | 299 |
| 9th | 320 | 481 | 308 |
| 10th | 345 | 482 | – |

Umpires: D. Davies and F.S. Lee.

# SOUTH AFRICA v AUSTRALIA 1949–50 (1st Test)

Played at Ellis Park, Johannesburg, on 24, 26, 27, 28 December.
Toss: Australia.   Result: AUSTRALIA won by an innings and 85 runs.
Debuts: South Africa – J.D. Nel, H.J. Tayfield, J.C. Watkins; Australia – J. Moroney (*not 'J.A.R.'*).

Loxton scored his first hundred in Test matches in 135 minutes.

## AUSTRALIA

| | | |
|---|---|---:|
| A.R. Morris | c Tayfield b McCarthy | 0 |
| J. Moroney | run out | 0 |
| K.R. Miller | b Mann | 21 |
| A.L. Hassett* | b Watkins | 112 |
| R.N. Harvey | b Watkins | 34 |
| S.J.E. Loxton | st Wade b Tayfield | 101 |
| C.L. McCool | b Tayfield | 31 |
| I.W. Johnson | c Cheetham b Mann | 66 |
| R.A. Saggers† | lbw b McCarthy | 14 |
| R.R. Lindwall | c Nel b Tayfield | 21 |
| W.A. Johnston | not out | 1 |
| Extras | (B 5, LB 5, W 2) | 12 |
| **Total** | | **413** |

## SOUTH AFRICA

| | | | | |
|---|---|---:|---|---:|
| E.A.B. Rowan | b Miller | 60 | lbw b McCool | 32 |
| O.E. Wynne | lbw b Johnston | 3 | c Saggers b Johnston | 33 |
| J.D. Nel | b Johnson | 4 | c Saggers b Johnston | 14 |
| A.D. Nourse* | c Hassett b Johnson | 0 | c Saggers b Johnson | 36 |
| W.W. Wade† | b Miller | 2 | b Johnston | 11 |
| J.E. Cheetham | lbw b Johnston | 10 | c Hassett b Johnston | 35 |
| J.C. Watkins | c Hassett b Miller | 36 | c Miller b Johnson | 0 |
| H.J. Tayfield | lbw b Miller | 6 | c Miller b Johnson | 0 |
| N.B.F. Mann | b Miller | 0 | lbw b Johnston | 13 |
| V.I. Smith | not out | 1 | c McCool b Johnston | 1 |
| C.N. McCarthy | b Johnson | 0 | not out | 1 |
| Extras | (LB 14, NB 1) | 15 | (B 9, LB 3, W 1, NB 2) | 15 |
| **Total** | | **137** | | **191** |

| SOUTH AFRICA | O | M | R | W | O | M | R | W |
|---|---:|---:|---:|---:|---:|---:|---:|---:|
| McCarthy | 25 | 2 | 90 | 2 | | | | |
| Watkins | 19 | 3 | 56 | 2 | | | | |
| Smith | 13 | 0 | 70 | 0 | | | | |
| Tayfield | 28 | 3 | 93 | 3 | | | | |
| Mann | 28·4 | 4 | 92 | 2 | | | | |
| **AUSTRALIA** | | | | | | | | |
| Lindwall | 10 | 1 | 22 | 0 | 8 | 1 | 25 | 0 |
| Johnston | 12 | 4 | 21 | 2 | 20·1 | 5 | 44 | 6 |
| Miller | 15 | 3 | 40 | 5 | 11 | 1 | 27 | 0 |
| Johnson | 18·2 | 6 | 37 | 3 | 14 | 0 | 54 | 3 |
| Loxton | 1 | 0 | 2 | 0 | 3 | 0 | 11 | 0 |
| McCool | | | | | 9 | 3 | 15 | 1 |

| FALL OF WICKETS | | | |
|---|---:|---:|---:|
| | A | SA | SA |
| *Wkt* | *1st* | *1st* | *2nd* |
| 1st | 0 | 14 | 50 |
| 2nd | 2 | 32 | 83 |
| 3rd | 71 | 40 | 113 |
| 4th | 163 | 47 | 133 |
| 5th | 200 | 82 | 141 |
| 6th | 283 | 112 | 142 |
| 7th | 320 | 122 | 142 |
| 8th | 372 | 122 | 184 |
| 9th | 408 | 133 | 186 |
| 10th | 413 | 137 | 191 |

Umpires: D. Collins and R.G.A. Ashman.

# SOUTH AFRICA v AUSTRALIA 1949–50 (2nd Test)

layed at Newlands, Cape Town, on 31 December, 2, 3, 4 January.
oss: Australia.   Result: AUSTRALIA won by eight wickets.
ebuts: Nil.

ayfield and Mann added 100 runs for the eighth wicket in just an hour.

## AUSTRALIA

| | | | | |
|---|---|---|---|---|
| R. Morris | c Watkins b Tayfield | 42 | c and b Mann | 24 |
| Moroney | c Cheetham b Mann | 87 | lbw b Mann | 19 |
| R. Miller | b Watkins | 58 | (4) not out | 16 |
| L. Hassett* | c and b Mann | 57 | | |
| N. Harvey | c Wade b Mann | 178 | (3) not out | 23 |
| J.E. Loxton | b Tayfield | 35 | | |
| L. McCool | not out | 49 | | |
| W. Johnson | c Watkins b Mann | 0 | | |
| R. Lindwall | not out | 8 | | |
| A. Saggers† | ) did not bat | | | |
| .A. Johnston | ) | | | |
| Extras | (B 8, LB 4) | 12 | (B 5) | 5 |
| **Total** | (7 wickets declared) | **526** | (2 wickets) | **87** |

## SOUTH AFRICA

| | | | | |
|---|---|---|---|---|
| A.B. Rowan | lbw b McCool | 67 | c Harvey b Johnston | 3 |
| E. Wynne | c Johnson b Miller | 13 | c Saggers b Johnston | 10 |
| D. Nel | lbw b Johnson | 38 | c McCool b Johnson | 19 |
| D. Nourse* | c Johnston b Miller | 65 | lbw b McCool | 114 |
| W. Wade† | c Saggers b Loxton | 4 | b Johnston | 11 |
| E. Cheetham | c McCool b Miller | 3 | c Saggers b Lindwall | 27 |
| C. Watkins | st Saggers b McCool | 35 | c Saggers b Lindwall | 9 |
| J. Tayfield | st Saggers b McCool | 15 | b Lindwall | 75 |
| B.F. Mann | b McCool | 16 | b Lindwall | 46 |
| I. Smith | not out | 11 | lbw b Lindwall | 4 |
| N. McCarthy | st Saggers b McCool | 0 | not out | 0 |
| Extras | (B 2, LB 8, W 1) | 11 | (B 3, LB 10, NB 2) | 15 |
| **Total** | | **278** | | **333** |

| )UTH AFRICA | O | M | R | W | O | M | R | W |
|---|---|---|---|---|---|---|---|---|
| cCarthy | 24 | 2 | 98 | 0 | 4 | 1 | 18 | 0 |
| atkins | 12 | 2 | 59 | 1 | 2 | 0 | 10 | 0 |
| ann | 28 | 3 | 105 | 4 | 8 | 1 | 23 | 2 |
| yfield | 37 | 4 | 141 | 2 | 6 | 1 | 31 | 0 |
| nith | 25 | 0 | 111 | 0 | | | | |
| USTRALIA | | | | | | | | |
| ndwall | 12 | 2 | 33 | 0 | 15·4 | 2 | 32 | 5 |
| hnston | 17 | 3 | 53 | 0 | 24 | 2 | 70 | 3 |
| hnson | 12 | 1 | 61 | 1 | 24 | 5 | 91 | 1 |
| iller | 17 | 3 | 54 | 3 | 11 | 0 | 43 | 0 |
| cCool | 11·4 | 1 | 41 | 5 | 21 | 3 | 71 | 1 |
| xton | 6 | 0 | 25 | 1 | 4 | 1 | 6 | 0 |
| arvey | | | | | 3 | 1 | 5 | 0 |

### FALL OF WICKETS

| | A | SA | SA | A |
|---|---|---|---|---|
| Wkt | 1st | 1st | 2nd | 2nd |
| 1st | 68 | 33 | 5 | 37 |
| 2nd | 172 | 92 | 16 | 44 |
| 3rd | 215 | 154 | 61 | – |
| 4th | 276 | 169 | 80 | – |
| 5th | 416 | 194 | 141 | – |
| 6th | 502 | 203 | 159 | – |
| 7th | 502 | 241 | 225 | – |
| 8th | – | 250 | 327 | – |
| 9th | – | 278 | 332 | – |
| 10th | – | 278 | 333 | – |

mpires: D. Collins and R.G.A. Ashman.

# SOUTH AFRICA v AUSTRALIA 1949–50 (3rd Test)

Played at Kingsmead, Durban, on 20, 21, 23, 24 January.
Toss: South Africa.   Result: AUSTRALIA won by five wickets.
Debuts: Nil.

Having dismissed Australia for what remains their lowest total in this series of matches, South Africa did no
enforce the follow on. The pitch took spin from the second day when 18 wickets fell for 146 runs. Australi
needing 336 runs to win in 435 minutes, gained a remarkable victory with 25 minutes to spare.

## SOUTH AFRICA

| | | | | |
|---|---|---|---|---|
| E.A.B. Rowan | c Johnston b Miller | 143 | c Saggers b Lindwall | |
| O.E. Wynne | b Johnston | 18 | b Johnson | 2 |
| J.D. Nel | c and b Johnson | 14 | lbw b Johnston | 2 |
| A.D. Nourse* | c Saggers b Johnston | 66 | c McCool b Johnson | 2 |
| W.W. Wade† | b Lindwall | 24 | b Johnston | |
| N.B.F. Mann | b Johnston | 9 | (9) lbw b Johnson | |
| J.E. Cheetham | c Hassett b Johnston | 4 | (6) c Hassett b Johnson | |
| J.C. Watkins | b Lindwall | 5 | (7) st Saggers b Johnson | |
| H.J. Tayfield | run out | 15 | (8) b Johnston | |
| V.I. Smith | b Lindwall | 1 | b Johnston | |
| C.N. McCarthy | not out | 0 | not out | |
| Extras | (B3, LB 7, NB 2) | 12 | (B 5, LB 1, NB 1) | |
| **Total** | | **311** | | 9 |

## AUSTRALIA

| | | | | |
|---|---|---|---|---|
| A.R. Morris | c Smith b Tayfield | 25 | hit wkt b Tayfield | 4 |
| J. Moroney | b Tayfield | 10 | lbw b Tayfield | 1 |
| I.W. Johnson | lbw b Tayfield | 2 | | |
| K.R. Miller | b Tayfield | 2 | (3) lbw b Mann | |
| A.L. Hassett* | lbw b Tayfield | 2 | (4) lbw b Mann | |
| R.A. Saggers† | c Cheetham b Mann | 2 | | |
| C.L. McCool | lbw b Mann | 1 | not out | 3 |
| R.R. Lindwall | b Mann | 7 | | |
| R.N. Harvey | c and b Tayfield | 2 | (5) not out | 1 |
| S.J.E. Loxton | c Cheetham b Tayfield | 16 | (6) b Mann | |
| W.A. Johnston | not out | 2 | | |
| Extras | (B 3, LB 1) | 4 | (B 7, LB 9, NB 1) | |
| **Total** | | **75** | (5 wickets) | 3. |

| AUSTRALIA | O | M | R | W | O | M | R | W | FALL OF WICKETS |
|---|---|---|---|---|---|---|---|---|---|
| Lindwall | 19 | 3 | 47 | 3 | 4 | 1 | 7 | 1 | |

| | | | | | | | | | | SA | A | SA | A |
|---|---|---|---|---|---|---|---|---|---|---|---|---|---|
| Miller | 24 | 5 | 73 | 1 | 7 | 0 | 12 | 0 | Wkt | 1st | 1st | 2nd | 2n |
| McCool | 13 | 3 | 35 | 0 | | | | | 1st | 32 | 31 | 9 | |
| Johnston | 31·2 | 5 | 75 | 4 | 18·2 | 6 | 39 | 4 | 2nd | 75 | 35 | 51 | |
| Loxton | 6 | 1 | 31 | 0 | | | | | 3rd | 242 | 37 | 85 | |
| Johnson | 16 | 5 | 38 | 1 | 17 | 2 | 34 | 5 | 4th | 264 | 39 | 85 | |
| | | | | | | | | | 5th | 283 | 42 | 88 | 2 |
| SOUTH AFRICA | | | | | | | | | 6th | 289 | 45 | 90 | |
| McCarthy | 6 | 2 | 8 | 0 | 12 | 3 | 32 | 0 | 7th | 293 | 46 | 93 | |
| Watkins | 4 | 1 | 9 | 0 | 6 | 2 | 10 | 0 | 8th | 304 | 53 | 93 | |
| Mann | 10 | 1 | 31 | 3 | 51·6 | 13 | 101 | 3 | 9th | 308 | 63 | 93 | |
| Tayfield | 8·4 | 1 | 23 | 7 | 49 | 5 | 144 | 2 | 10th | 311 | 75 | 99 | |
| Smith | | | | | 5 | 0 | 32 | 0 | | | | | |

Umpires: J.V. Hart-Davis and B.V. Malan.

# SOUTH AFRICA v AUSTRALIA 1949–50 (4th Test)

ayed at Ellis Park, Johnesburg, on 10, 11, 13, 14 February.
oss: Australia.    Result: MATCH DRAWN.
ebuts: South Africa – R.G. Draper, M.G. Melle, P.L. Winslow.

oroney remains the only player to score hundreds in both innings of a Test match between these two countries.

## AUSTRALIA

| | | | | | |
|---|---|---|---|---|---|
| R. Morris | c Fullerton b McCarthy | 111 | c Mann b McCarthy | | 19 |
| Moroney | c Fullerton b Melle | 118 | not out | | 101 |
| R. Miller | c Fullerton b Melle | 84 | (4) not out | | 33 |
| R. Lindwall | b Melle | 5 | | | |
| L. Hassett* | b McCarthy | 53 | | | |
| N. Harvey | not out | 56 | (3) b Melle | | 100 |
| J.E. Loxton | b Melle | 6 | | | |
| L. McCool | st Fullerton b Tayfield | 8 | | | |
| W. Johnson | c sub (J.B. Roothman) b Melle | 3 | | | |
| A. Saggers† | not out | 5 | | | |
| A. Johnston | did not bat | | | | |
| Extras | (B 8, LB 7, NB 1) | 16 | (B 5, LB 1) | | 6 |
| **Total** | (8 wickets declared) | **465** | (2 wickets) | | **259** |

## SOUTH AFRICA

| | | |
|---|---|---|
| A.B. Rowan | b Lindwall | 55 |
| D. Nel | run out | 25 |
| G. Draper | c Saggers b Johnston | 15 |
| D. Nourse* | c Saggers b Lindwall | 5 |
| W. Begbie | c McCool b Miller | 24 |
| L. Winslow | c and b Miller | 19 |
| M. Fullerton† | c Hassett b McCool | 88 |
| J. Tayfield | c Johnson b Miller | 40 |
| B.F. Mann | b Lindwall | 52 |
| G. Melle | lbw b McCool | 14 |
| N. McCarthy | not out | 2 |
| Extras | (B 7, LB 5, NB 1) | 13 |
| **Total** | | **352** |

| OUTH AFRICA | O | M | R | W | O | M | R | W | | FALL OF WICKETS | | | |
|---|---|---|---|---|---|---|---|---|---|---|---|---|---|
| cCarthy | 31 | 4 | 113 | 2 | 13 | 1 | 56 | 1 | | | A | SA | A |
| elle | 33 | 3 | 113 | 5 | 12 | 0 | 58 | 1 | *Wkt* | *1st* | *1st* | *2nd* |
| ayfield | 31 | 4 | 103 | 1 | 14 | 2 | 88 | 0 | 1st | 214 | 84 | 28 |
| ann | 25 | 2 | 85 | 0 | 8 | 1 | 32 | 0 | 2nd | 265 | 86 | 198 |
| egbie | 7 | 0 | 35 | 0 | 3 | 0 | 19 | 0 | 3rd | 273 | 96 | – |
| owan | | | | | 1 | 1 | 0 | 0 | 4th | 382 | 115 | – |
| ourse | | | | | 1 | 1 | 0 | 0 | 5th | 392 | 145 | – |
| | | | | | | | | | 6th | 418 | 148 | – |
| USTRALIA | | | | | | | | | 7th | 437 | 213 | – |
| ndwall | 26 | 3 | 82 | 3 | | | | | 8th | 440 | 307 | – |
| hnston | 29 | 5 | 68 | 1 | | | | | 9th | – | 345 | – |
| iller | 28 | 3 | 75 | 3 | | | | | 10th | – | 352 | – |
| oxton | 10 | 2 | 22 | 0 | | | | | | | | |
| hnson | 18 | 4 | 52 | 0 | | | | | | | | |
| cCool | 7 | 0 | 29 | 2 | | | | | | | | |
| assett | 1 | 0 | 5 | 0 | | | | | | | | |
| arvey | 3 | 0 | 6 | 0 | | | | | | | | |

mpires: D. Collins and D.T. Drew.

# SOUTH AFRICA v AUSTRALIA 1949–50 (5th Test)

Played at St George's Park, Port Elizabeth, on 3, 4, 6 March.
Toss: Australia.   Result: AUSTRALIA won by an innings and 259 runs.
Debuts: Australia – G. Noblet (not 'G.J.').

Australia, having recorded what is still their highest total in South Africa, went on to achieve the largest margin of
victory by either side in these matches. It extended South Africa's run of consecutive Tests without a win to 28

### AUSTRALIA

| | | |
|---|---|---:|
| A.R. Morris | c Winslow b Melle | 157 |
| J. Moroney | c Nourse b Melle | 7 |
| K.R. Miller | c Nourse b Tayfield | 22 |
| R.N. Harvey | b Begbie | 116 |
| A.L. Hassett* | c McCarthy b Mann | 167 |
| S.J.E. Loxton | c Rowan b Mann | 43 |
| C.L. McCool | c Fullerton b Tayfield | 6 |
| I.W. Johnson | not out | 26 |
| R.A. Saggers† | not out | 4 |
| G. Noblet | ) did not bat | |
| W.A. Johnston | ) | |
| Extras | (B 1) | 1 |
| **Total** | (7 wickets declared) | **549** |

### SOUTH AFRICA

| | | | | |
|---|---|---:|---|---:|
| E.A.B. Rowan | b Johnson | 40 | c McCool b Miller | |
| J.D. Nel | b Miller | 0 | lbw b Johnston | |
| R.G. Draper | c Johnston b Miller | 7 | b Johnston | |
| A.D. Nourse* | c McCool b Miller | 37 | b Johnson | 5 |
| D.W. Begbie | c Saggers b Noblet | 1 | b Johnston | |
| P.L. Winslow | lbw b Noblet | 0 | (7) st Saggers b Johnson | 1 |
| G.M. Fullerton† | st Saggers b McCool | 18 | (6) c Saggers b Loxton | 2 |
| H.J. Tayfield | st Saggers b McCool | 6 | st Saggers b McCool | |
| M.G. Melle | b Miller | 1 | (10) c Harvey b McCool | |
| N.B.F. Mann | b Noblet | 41 | (9) lbw b Johnson | |
| C.N. McCarthy | not out | 1 | not out | |
| Extras | (B 5, NB 1) | 6 | (B 3, LB 3) | |
| **Total** | | **158** | | **13** |

| SOUTH AFRICA | O | M | R | W | O | M | R | W |
|---|---|---|---|---|---|---|---|---|
| McCarthy | 29 | 3 | 121 | 0 | | | | |
| Melle | 23 | 2 | 132 | 2 | | | | |
| Tayfield | 25 | 1 | 103 | 2 | | | | |
| Mann | 36 | 4 | 154 | 2 | | | | |
| Begbie | 4 | 0 | 38 | 1 | | | | |
| AUSTRALIA | | | | | | | | |
| Miller | 14 | 3 | 42 | 4 | 8 | 0 | 24 | 1 |
| Johnston | 3 | 0 | 12 | 0 | 6 | 1 | 10 | 3 |
| Noblet | 17·1 | 7 | 21 | 3 | 9 | 2 | 16 | 0 |
| Johnson | 11 | 1 | 48 | 1 | 7 | 1 | 21 | 3 |
| McCool | 5 | 1 | 29 | 2 | 14·2 | 2 | 48 | 2 |
| Loxton | | | | | 4 | 2 | 7 | 1 |

### FALL OF WICKETS

| Wkt | A 1st | SA 1st | SA 2nd |
|---|---|---|---|
| 1st | 16 | 3 | 0 |
| 2nd | 49 | 19 | 3 |
| 3rd | 236 | 71 | 12 |
| 4th | 350 | 84 | 24 |
| 5th | 449 | 84 | 63 |
| 6th | 485 | 95 | 88 |
| 7th | 545 | 104 | 113 |
| 8th | – | 113 | 115 |
| 9th | – | 117 | 126 |
| 10th | – | 158 | 132 |

Umpires: D. Collins and B.V. Malan.

# ENGLAND v WEST INDIES 1950 (1st Test)

Played at Old Trafford, Manchester, on 8, 9, 10, 12 June.
Toss: England.   Result: ENGLAND won by 202 runs.
Debuts: England – R. Berry, G.H.G. Doggart. West Indies – S. Ramadhin, A.L. Valentine.

Valentine took the first eight wickets to fall in his maiden Test; only A.E. Trott and R.A.L. Massie have also taken eight wickets in their first Test innings but neither took the first eight to fall. Hutton retired hurt at 22–0 after being hit on the hand by a ball from Johnson. Thereafter he batted virtually with one hand. Walcott opened the bowling instead of the injured Johnson in the second innings while Christiani kept wicket.

## ENGLAND

| | | | | | |
|---|---|---|---|---|---|
| L. Hutton | b Valentine | 39 | (8) c and b Worrell | | 45 |
| R.T. Simpson | c Goddard b Valentine | 27 | c Weekes b Gomez | | 0 |
| W.J. Edrich | c Gomez b Valentine | 7 | (1) c Weekes b Ramadhin | | 71 |
| G.H.G. Doggart | c Rae b Valentine | 29 | (3) c Goddard b Valentine | | 22 |
| H.E. Dollery | c Gomez b Valentine | 8 | (4) c Gomez b Valentine | | 0 |
| N.W.D. Yardley* | c Gomez b Valentine | 0 | (5) lbw b Gomez | | 25 |
| T.E. Bailey | not out | 82 | (6) run out | | 33 |
| T.G. Evans† | c and b Valentine | 104 | (7) c Worrell b Ramadhin | | 15 |
| J.C. Laker | b Valentine | 4 | c Stollmeyer b Valentine | | 40 |
| W.E. Hollies | c Weekes b Ramadhin | 0 | c Walcott b Worrell | | 3 |
| R. Berry | b Ramadhin | 0 | not out | | 4 |
| Extras | (B 8, LB 3, NB 1) | 12 | (B 17, LB 12, NB 1) | | 30 |
| **Total** | | **312** | | | **288** |

## WEST INDIES

| | | | | | |
|---|---|---|---|---|---|
| A.F. Rae | c Doggart b Berry | 14 | c Doggart b Hollies | | 10 |
| J.B. Stollmeyer | lbw b Hollies | 43 | c sub (P. Hough) b Laker | | 78 |
| F.M.M. Worrell | st Evans b Berry | 15 | st Evans b Hollies | | 28 |
| E. de C. Weekes | c sub (P. Hough) b Bailey | 52 | lbw b Hollies | | 1 |
| C.L. Walcott† | c Evans b Berry | 13 | b Berry | | 9 |
| R.J. Christiani | lbw b Berry | 17 | c Yardley b Hollies | | 6 |
| G.E. Gomez | c Berry b Hollies | 35 | st Evans b Berry | | 8 |
| J.D.C. Goddard* | run out | 7 | not out | | 16 |
| H.H.H. Johnson | c Dollery b Hollies | 8 | b Berry | | 22 |
| S. Ramadhin | not out | 4 | b Berry | | 0 |
| A.L. Valentine | c and b Berry | 0 | c Bailey b Hollies | | 0 |
| Extras | (LB 6, NB 1) | 7 | (B 4, W 1) | | 5 |
| **Total** | | **215** | | | **183** |

| WEST INDIES | O | M | R | W | O | M | R | W | FALL OF WICKETS | | | | |
|---|---|---|---|---|---|---|---|---|---|---|---|---|---|
| | | | | | | | | | | E | WI | E | WI |
| Johnson | 10 | 3 | 18 | 0 | | | | | *Wkt* | *1st* | *1st* | *2nd* | *2nd* |
| Gomez | 10 | 1 | 29 | 0 | 25 | 12 | 47 | 2 | 1st | 31 | 52 | 0 | 32 |
| Valentine | 50 | 14 | 104 | 8 | 56 | 22 | 100 | 3 | 2nd | 74 | 74 | 31 | 68 |
| Ramadhin | 39·3 | 12 | 90 | 2 | 42 | 17 | 77 | 2 | 3rd | 79 | 74 | 43 | 80 |
| Goddard | 15 | 1 | 46 | 0 | 9 | 3 | 12 | 0 | 4th | 83 | 94 | 106 | 113 |
| Worrell | 4 | 1 | 13 | 0 | 5·5 | 1 | 10 | 2 | 5th | 88 | 146 | 131 | 126 |
| Walcott | | | | | 4 | 1 | 12 | 0 | 6th | 249 | 178 | 151 | 141 |
| | | | | | | | | | 7th | 293 | 201 | 200 | 146 |
| ENGLAND | | | | | | | | | 8th | 301 | 211 | 266 | 178 |
| Bailey | 10 | 2 | 28 | 1 | 3 | 1 | 9 | 0 | 9th | 308 | 211 | 284 | 178 |
| Edrich | 2 | 1 | 4 | 0 | 3 | 1 | 10 | 0 | 10th | 312 | 215 | 288 | 183 |
| Hollies | 33 | 13 | 70 | 3 | 35·2 | 11 | 63 | 5 | | | | | |
| Laker | 17 | 5 | 43 | 0 | 14 | 4 | 43 | 1 | | | | | |
| Berry | 31·5 | 13 | 63 | 5 | 26 | 12 | 53 | 4 | | | | | |

Umpires: F. Chester and D. Davies.

# ENGLAND v WEST INDIES 1950 (2nd Test)

Played at Lord's, London, on 24, 26, 27, 28, 29 June.
Toss: West Indies.   Result: WEST INDIES won by 326 runs.
Debuts: England – W.G.A. Parkhouse.

Ramadhin and Valentine, who had each played only two first-class matches before this tour, bowled West Indies to their first win in England. This famous victory introduced Caribbean dancing and calypso singing to the playing area at Lord's.

## WEST INDIES

| | | | | |
|---|---|---|---|---|
| A.F. Rae | c and b Jenkins | 106 | b Jenkings | 24 |
| J.B. Stollmeyer | lbw b Wardle | 20 | b Jenkins | 30 |
| F.M.M. Worrell | b Beder | 52 | c Doggart b Jenkins | 45 |
| E.de C. Weekes | b Bedser | 63 | run out | 63 |
| C.L. Walcott† | st Evans b Jenkins | 14 | (6) not out | 168 |
| G.E. Gomez | st Evans b Jenkins | 1 | (7) c Edrich b Bedser | 70 |
| R.J. Christiani | b Bedser | 33 | (8) not out | 5 |
| J.D.C. Goddard* | b Wardle | 14 | (5) c Evans b Jenkins | 11 |
| P.E. Jones | c Evans b Jenkins | 0 | | |
| S. Ramadhin | not out | 1 | | |
| A.L. Valentine | c Hutton b Jenkins | 5 | | |
| Extras | (B 10, LB 5, W 1, NB 1) | 17 | (LB 8, NB 1) | 9 |
| **Total** | | **326** | (6 wickets declared) | **425** |

## ENGLAND

| | | | | |
|---|---|---|---|---|
| L. Hutton | st Walcott b Valentine | 35 | b Valentine | 10 |
| C. Washbrook | st Walcott b Ramadhin | 36 | b Ramadhin | 114 |
| W.J. Edrich | c Walcott b Ramadhin | 8 | c Jones b Ramadhin | 8 |
| G.H.G. Doggart | lbw b Ramadhin | 0 | b Ramadhin | 25 |
| W.G.A. Parkhouse | b Valentine | 0 | c Goddard b Valentine | 48 |
| N.W.D. Yardley* | b Valentine | 16 | c Weekes b Valentine | 19 |
| T.G. Evans† | b Ramadhin | 8 | c Rae b Ramadhin | 2 |
| R.O. Jenkins | c Walcott b Valentine | 4 | b Ramadhin | 4 |
| J.H. Wardle | not out | 33 | lbw b Worrell | 21 |
| A.V. Bedser | b Ramadhin | 5 | b Ramadhin | 0 |
| R. Berry | c Goddard b Jones | 2 | not out | 0 |
| Extras | (B 2, LB 1, W 1) | 4 | (B 16, LB 7) | 23 |
| **Total** | | **151** | | **274** |

| ENGLAND | O | M | R | W | O | M | R | W |
|---|---|---|---|---|---|---|---|---|
| Bedser | 40 | 14 | 60 | 3 | 44 | 16 | 80 | 1 |
| Edrich | 16 | 4 | 30 | 0 | 13 | 2 | 37 | 0 |
| Jenkins | 35·2 | 6 | 116 | 5 | 59 | 13 | 174 | 4 |
| Wardle | 17 | 6 | 46 | 2 | 30 | 10 | 58 | 0 |
| Berry | 19 | 7 | 45 | 0 | 32 | 15 | 67 | 0 |
| Yardley | 4 | 1 | 12 | 0 | | | | |
| WEST INDIES | | | | | | | | |
| Jones | 8·4 | 2 | 13 | 1 | 7 | 1 | 22 | 0 |
| Worrell | 10 | 4 | 20 | 0 | 22·3 | 9 | 39 | 1 |
| Valentine | 45 | 28 | 48 | 4 | 71 | 47 | 79 | 3 |
| Ramadhin | 43 | 27 | 66 | 5 | 72 | 43 | 86 | 6 |
| Gomez | | | | | 13 | 1 | 25 | 0 |
| Goddard | | | | | 6 | 6 | 0 | 0 |

FALL OF WICKETS

| | WI | E | WI | E |
|---|---|---|---|---|
| Wkt | 1st | 1st | 2nd | 2nd |
| 1st | 37 | 62 | 48 | 28 |
| 2nd | 128 | 74 | 75 | 57 |
| 3rd | 233 | 74 | 108 | 140 |
| 4th | 262 | 75 | 146 | 218 |
| 5th | 273 | 86 | 199 | 228 |
| 6th | 274 | 102 | 410 | 238 |
| 7th | 320 | 110 | – | 245 |
| 8th | 320 | 113 | – | 248 |
| 9th | 320 | 122 | – | 258 |
| 10th | 326 | 151 | – | 274 |

Umpires: D. Davies and F.S. Lee.

# ENGLAND v WEST INDIES 1950 (3rd Test)

Played at Trent Bridge, Nottingham, on 20, 21, 22, 24, 25 July.
Toss: England.   Result: WEST INDIES won by ten wickets.
Debuts: England – D.J. Insole. D. Shackleton.

Worrell's 261 was then the highest score for West Indies in England, and the highest by any batsman in a Nottingham Test. With Weekes he shared a fourth wicket partnership of 283 in 210 minutes. Hutton and Simpson's 212 still stands as England's highest opening partnership against West Indies.

## ENGLAND

| | | | | |
|---|---|---|---|---|
| R.T. Simpson | c Walcott b Johnson | 4 | run out | 94 |
| C. Washbrook | c Stollmeyer b Worrell | 3 | c Worrell b Valentine | 102 |
| W.G.A. Parkhouse | c Weekes b Johnson | 13 | lbw b Goddard | 69 |
| J.G. Dewes | c Gomez b Worrell | 0 | lbw b Valentine | 67 |
| N.W.D. Yardley* | c Goddard b Valentine | 41 | b Ramadhin | 7 |
| D.J. Insole | lbw b Ramadhin | 21 | st Walcott b Ramadhin | 0 |
| T.G. Evans† | b Ramadhin | 32 | c Stollmeyer b Ramadhin | 63 |
| D. Shackleton | b Worrell | 42 | c Weekes b Valentine | 1 |
| R.O Jenkins | b Johnson | 39 | not out | 6 |
| A.V. Bedser | c Stollmeyer b Valentine | 13 | b Ramadhin | 2 |
| W.E. Hollies | not out | 2 | lbw b Ramadhin | 0 |
| Extras | (LB 12, NB 1) | 13 | (B 11, LB 10, W 2, NB 2) | 25 |
| **Total** | | **223** | | **436** |

## WEST INDIES

| | | | | |
|---|---|---|---|---|
| A.F. Rae | st Evans b Yardley | 68 | not out | 46 |
| J.B. Stollmeyer | c and b Jenkins | 46 | not out | 52 |
| R.J. Christiani | lbw b Shackleton | 10 | | |
| F.M.M. Worrell | c Yardley b Bedser | 261 | | |
| E. de C. Weekes | c and b Hollies | 129 | | |
| C.L. Walcott† | b Bedser | 8 | | |
| G.E. Gomez | not out | 19 | | |
| J.D.C. Goddard | c Yardley b Bedser | 0 | | |
| H.H.H. Johnson | c Insol b Bedser | 0 | | |
| S. Ramadhin | b Bedser | 2 | | |
| A.L. Valentine | b Hollies | 1 | | |
| Extras | (B 2, LB 10, NB 2) | 14 | (NB 5) | 5 |
| **Total** | | **558** | (0 wickets) | **103** |

| WEST INDIES | O | M | R | W | O | M | R | W |
|---|---|---|---|---|---|---|---|---|
| Johnson | 25·4 | 5 | 59 | 3 | 30 | 5 | 65 | 0 |
| Worrell | 17 | 4 | 40 | 3 | 19 | 8 | 30 | 0 |
| Gomez | 3 | 1 | 9 | 0 | 11 | 3 | 23 | 0 |
| Goddard | 6 | 3 | 10 | 0 | 12 | 6 | 18 | 1 |
| Ramadhin | 29 | 12 | 49 | 2 | 81·2 | 25 | 135 | 5 |
| Valentine | 18 | 6 | 43 | 2 | 92 | 49 | 140 | 3 |
| **ENGLAND** | | | | | | | | |
| Bedser | 48 | 9 | 127 | 5 | 111 | | 35 | 0 |
| Shackleton | 43 | 7 | 128 | 1 | 6 | 2 | 7 | 0 |
| Yardley | 27 | 3 | 82 | 1 | | | | |
| Jenkins | 13 | 0 | 73 | 1 | 11 | 1 | 46 | 0 |
| Hollies | 43·4 | 8 | 134 | 2 | 7 | 6 | 1 | 0 |
| Simpson | | | | | 1·3 | 0 | 9 | 0 |

### FALL OF WICKETS

| | E | WI | E | WI |
|---|---|---|---|---|
| Wkt | 1st | 1st | 2nd | 2nd |
| 1st | 6 | 77 | 212 | – |
| 2nd | 18 | 95 | 220 | – |
| 3rd | 23 | 238 | 326 | – |
| 4th | 25 | 521 | 346 | – |
| 5th | 75 | 535 | 350 | – |
| 6th | 105 | 537 | 408 | – |
| 7th | 147 | 538 | 410 | – |
| 8th | 174 | 539 | 434 | – |
| 9th | 191 | 551 | 436 | – |
| 10th | 223 | 558 | 436 | – |

Umpires: F. Chester and Harold Elliott.

# ENGLAND v WEST INDIES 1950 (4th Test)

Played at Kennington Oval, London, on 12, 14, 15, 16 August.
Toss: West Indies.   Result: WEST INDIES won by an innings and 56 runs.
Debuts: M.J. Hilton, A.J.W. McIntyre, D.S. Sheppard (*later The Right Reverend D.S. Sheppard, Bishop of Liverpool*).

Hutton scored England's first double-century in a home Test against West Indies and remains the only England player to carry his bat throughout a completed innings against that team. His is the highest score by an England player involved in this feat and he is the only one to achieve it twice for England (also *Test No. 330*).

## WEST INDIES

| | | |
|---|---|---|
| A.F. Rae | b Bedser | 109 |
| J.B. Stollmeyer | lbw b Bailey | 36 |
| F.M.M. Worrell | lbw b Wright | 138 |
| E.de C. Weekes | c Hutton b Wright | 30 |
| C.L. Walcott† | b Wright | 17 |
| G.E. Gomez | c McIntyre b Brown | 74 |
| R.J. Christiani | c McIntyre b Bedser | 11 |
| J.D.C. Goddard* | not out | 58 |
| P.E. Jones | b Wright | 1 |
| S. Ramadhin | c McIntyre b Wright | 3 |
| A.L. Valentine | b Bailey | 9 |
| Extras | (B 5, LB 11, NB 1) | 17 |
| **Total** | | **503** |

## ENGLAND

| | | | | | |
|---|---|---|---|---|---|
| L. Hutton | not out | 202 | c Christiani b Goddard | | 2 |
| R.T. Simpson | c Jones b Valentine | 30 | b Ramadhin | | 16 |
| D.S. Sheppard | b Ramadhin | 11 | c Weekes b Valentine | | 29 |
| D.C.S. Compton | run out | 44 | c Weekes b Valentine | | 11 |
| J.G. Dewes | c Worrell b Valentine | 17 | c Christiani b Valentine | | 3 |
| T.E. Bailey | c Weekes b Goddard | 18 | lbw b Ramadhin | | 12 |
| F.R. Brown* | c Weekes b Valentine | 0 | c Stollmeyer b Valentine | | 15 |
| A.J.W. McIntyre† | c and b Valentine | 4 | c sub (K.B. Trestrail) b Ramadhin | | 0 |
| A.V. Bedser | lbw b Goddard | 0 | c Weekes b Valentine | | 0 |
| M.J. Hilton | b Goddard | 3 | c sub (K.B. Trestrail) b Valentine | | 0 |
| D.V.P. Wright | lbw b Goddard | 4 | not out | | 6 |
| Extras | (B 5, LB 6) | 11 | (B 6, LB 3) | | 9 |
| **Total** | | **344** | | | **103** |

| ENGLAND | O | M | R | W | O | M | R | W |
|---|---|---|---|---|---|---|---|---|
| Bailey | 34·2 | 9 | 84 | 2 | | | | |
| Bedser | 38 | 9 | 75 | 2 | | | | |
| Brown | 21 | 4 | 74 | 1 | | | | |
| Wright | 53 | 16 | 141 | 5 | | | | |
| Hilton | 41 | 12 | 91 | 0 | | | | |
| Compton | 7 | 2 | 21 | 0 | | | | |
| WEST INDIES | | | | | | | | |
| Jones | 23 | 4 | 70 | 0 | | | | |
| Worrell | 20 | 9 | 30 | 0 | | | | |
| Ramadhin | 45 | 23 | 63 | 1 | 26 | 11 | 38 | 3 |
| Valentine | 64 | 21 | 121 | 4 | 26·3 | 10 | 39 | 6 |
| Gomez | 10 | 3 | 24 | 0 | 8 | 4 | 6 | 0 |
| Goddard | 17·4 | 6 | 25 | 4 | 9 | 4 | 11 | 1 |

FALL OF WICKETS

| Wkt | WI 1st | E 1st | E 2nd |
|---|---|---|---|
| 1st | 72 | 73 | 2 |
| 2nd | 244 | 120 | 39 |
| 3rd | 295 | 229 | 50 |
| 4th | 318 | 259 | 56 |
| 5th | 337 | 310 | 79 |
| 6th | 446 | 315 | 83 |
| 7th | 480 | 321 | 83 |
| 8th | 482 | 322 | 83 |
| 9th | 490 | 326 | 85 |
| 10th | 503 | 344 | 103 |

Umpires: F.S. Lee and W.H. Ashdown.

# AUSTRALIA v ENGLAND 1950–51 (1st Test)

Played at Woolloongabba, Brisbane, on 1, 2 (*no play*), 4, 5 December.
Toss: Australia.   Result: AUSTRALIA won by 70 runs.
Debuts: Australia – J.B. Iverson.

Rain provided the traditional Brisbane 'sticky' after England had dismissed Australia on a good batting pitch for only 228. Twenty wickets fell for 102 runs after lunch on the third day, the start of which had been delayed until 1 p.m. Hutton's innings on the last morning was one of the most remarkable in Test cricket.

## AUSTRALIA

| | | | | |
|---|---|---|---|---|
| J. Moroney | c Hutton b Bailey | 0 | lbw b Bailey | 0 |
| A.R. Morris | lbw b Bedser | 25 | c Bailey b Bedser | 0 |
| R.N. Harvey | c Evans b Bedser | 74 | (6) c Simpson b Bedser | 12 |
| K.R. Miller | c McIntyre b Wright | 15 | (7) c Simpson b Bailey | 8 |
| A.L. Hassett* | b Bedser | 8 | lbw b Bailey | 3 |
| S.J.E. Loxton | c Evans b Brown | 24 | (4) c Bailey b Bedser | 0 |
| R.R. Lindwall | c Bedser b Bailey | 41 | (8) not out | 0 |
| D. Tallon† | c Simpson b Brown | 5 | | |
| I.W. Johnson | c Simpson b Bailey | 23 | (3) lbw b Bailey | 8 |
| W.A. Johnston | c Hutton b Bedser | 1 | | |
| J.B. Iverson | not out | 1 | | |
| Extras | (B 5, LB 3, NB 3) | 11 | (NB 1) | 1 |
| **Total** | | **228** | (7 wickets declared) | **32** |

## ENGLAND

| | | | | |
|---|---|---|---|---|
| R.T. Simpson | b Johnston | 12 | b Lindwall | 0 |
| C. Washbrook | c Hassett b Johnston | 19 | c Loxton b Lindwall | 6 |
| T.G. Evans† | c Iverson b Johnston | 16 | (6) c Loxton b Johnston | 5 |
| D.C.S. Compton | c Lindwall b Johnston | 3 | (9) c Loxton b Johnston | 0 |
| J.G. Dewes | c Loxton b Miller | 1 | (3) b Miller | 9 |
| L. Hutton | not out | 8 | (8) not out | 62 |
| A.J.W. McIntyre | b Johnston | 1 | run out | 7 |
| F.R. Brown* | c Tallon b Miller | 4 | (10) c Loxton b Iverson | 17 |
| T.E. Bailey | not out | 1 | (4) c Johnston b Iverson | 7 |
| A.V. Bedser | | | (5) c Harvey b Iverson | 0 |
| D.V.P. Wright | | | c Lindwall b Iverson | 2 |
| Extras | (LB 2, NB 1) | 3 | (B 6, NB 1) | 7 |
| **Total** | (7 wickets declared) | **68** | | **122** |

| ENGLAND | O | M | R | W | O | M | R | W |
|---|---|---|---|---|---|---|---|---|
| Bailey | 12 | 4 | 28 | 3 | 7 | 2 | 22 | 4 |
| Bedser | 16·5 | 4 | 45 | 4 | 6·5 | 2 | 9 | 3 |
| Wright | 16 | 0 | 81 | 1 | | | | |
| Brown | 11 | 0 | 63 | 2 | | | | |
| **AUSTRALIA** | | | | | | | | |
| Lindwall | 1 | 0 | 1 | 0 | 7 | 3 | 21 | 2 |
| Johnston | 11 | 2 | 35 | 5 | 11 | 2 | 30 | 2 |
| Miller | 10 | 1 | 29 | 2 | 7 | 3 | 21 | 1 |
| Iverson | | | | | 13 | 3 | 43 | 4 |

FALL OF WICKETS

| | A | E | A | E |
|---|---|---|---|---|
| *Wkt* | *1st* | *1st* | *2nd* | *2nd* |
| 1st | 0 | 28 | 0 | 0 |
| 2nd | 69 | 49 | 0 | 16 |
| 3rd | 116 | 52 | 0 | 22 |
| 4th | 118 | 52 | 12 | 23 |
| 5th | 129 | 56 | 19 | 23 |
| 6th | 156 | 57 | 31 | 30 |
| 7th | 172 | 67 | 32 | 46 |
| 8th | 219 | – | – | 46 |
| 9th | 226 | – | – | 77 |
| 10th | 228 | – | – | 122 |

Umpires: A.N. Barlow and H. Elphinston.

# AUSTRALIA v ENGLAND 1950–51 (2nd Test)

Played at Melbourne Cricket Ground on 22, 23, 26, 27 December.
Toss: Australia.   Result: AUSTRALIA won by 28 runs.
Debuts: Australia – K.A. Archer.

This match, which included the unusual feature of a two-days interlude for Sunday and Christmas Day, produced a close and tense contest. England, needing to score 179 runs in just over three days to end Australia's long unbeaten run, eventually failed against a fine display by Lindwall, Johnston, and the 'mystery' slow bowler, Iverson.

## AUSTRALIA

| | | | | |
|---|---|---|---|---|
| K.A. Archer | c Bedser b Bailey | 26 | c Bailey b Bedser | 46 |
| A.R. Morris | c Hutton b Bedser | 2 | lbw b Wright | 18 |
| R.N. Harvey | c Evans b Bedser | 42 | run out | 31 |
| K.R. Miller | lbw b Brown | 18 | b Bailey | 14 |
| A.L. Hassett* | b Bailey | 52 | c Bailey b Brown | 19 |
| S.J.E. Loxton | c Evans b Close | 32 | c Evans b Brown | 2 |
| R.R. Lindwall | lbw b Bailey | 8 | c Evans b Brown | 7 |
| D. Tallon† | not out | 7 | lbw b Brown | 0 |
| I.W. Johnson | c Parkhouse b Bedser | 0 | c Close b Bedser | 23 |
| W.A. Johnston | c Hutton b Bedser | 0 | b Bailey | 6 |
| J.B. Iverson | b Bailey | 1 | not out | 0 |
| Extras | (B 4, LB 2) | 6 | (B 10, LB 5) | 15 |
| **Total** | | **194** | | **181** |

## ENGLAND

| | | | | |
|---|---|---|---|---|
| R.T. Simpson | c Johnson b Miller | 4 | b Lindwall | 23 |
| C. Washbrook | lbw b Lindwall | 21 | b Iverson | 8 |
| J.G. Dewes | c Miller b Johnston | 8 | (5) c Harvey b Iverson | 5 |
| L. Hutton | c Tallon b Iverson | 12 | c Lindwall b Johnston | 40 |
| W.G.A. Parkhouse | c Hassett b Miller | 9 | (6) lbw b Johnston | 28 |
| D.B. Close | c Loxton b Iverson | 0 | (7) lbw b Johnston | 1 |
| F.R. Brown* | c Johnson b Iverson | 62 | (8) b Lindwall | 8 |
| T.E. Bailey | b Lindwall | 12 | (3) b Johnson | 0 |
| T.G. Evans† | c Johnson b Iverson | 49 | b Lindwall | 2 |
| A.V. Bedser | not out | 4 | not out | 14 |
| D.V.P. Wright | lbw b Johnston | 2 | lbw b Johnston | 2 |
| Extras | (B 8, LB 6) | 14 | (B 17, LB 2) | 19 |
| **Total** | | **197** | | **150** |

| ENGLAND | O | M | R | W | O | M | R | W |
|---|---|---|---|---|---|---|---|---|
| Bailey | 17·1 | 5 | 40 | 4 | 15 | 3 | 47 | 2 |
| Bedser | 19 | 3 | 37 | 4 | 16·3 | 2 | 43 | 2 |
| Wright | 8 | 0 | 63 | 0 | 9 | 0 | 42 | 1 |
| Brown | 9 | 0 | 28 | 1 | 12 | 2 | 26 | 4 |
| Close | 6 | 1 | 20 | 1 | 1 | 0 | 8 | 0 |
| AUSTRALIA | | | | | | | | |
| Lindwall | 13 | 2 | 46 | 2 | 12 | 1 | 29 | 3 |
| Miller | 13 | 0 | 39 | 2 | 5 | 2 | 16 | 0 |
| Johnston | 9 | 1 | 28 | 2 | 13·7 | 1 | 26 | 4 |
| Iverson | 18 | 3 | 37 | 4 | 20 | 4 | 36 | 2 |
| Johnson | 5 | 1 | 19 | 0 | 13 | 3 | 24 | 1 |
| Loxton | 4 | 1 | 14 | 0 | | | | |

### FALL OF WICKETS

| | A | E | A | E |
|---|---|---|---|---|
| Wkt | 1st | 1st | 2nd | 2nd |
| 1st | 6 | 11 | 43 | 21 |
| 2nd | 67 | 33 | 99 | 22 |
| 3rd | 89 | 37 | 100 | 52 |
| 4th | 93 | 54 | 126 | 82 |
| 5th | 177 | 54 | 131 | 92 |
| 6th | 177 | 61 | 151 | 95 |
| 7th | 192 | 126 | 151 | 122 |
| 8th | 193 | 153 | 156 | 124 |
| 9th | 193 | 194 | 181 | 134 |
| 10th | 194 | 197 | 181 | 150 |

Umpires: G.C. Cooper and R. Wright.

# AUSTRALIA v ENGLAND 1950–51 (3rd Test)

Played at Sydney Cricket Ground on 5, 6, 8, 9 January.
Toss: England.   Result: AUSTRALIA won by an innings and 13 runs.
Debuts: England – J.J. Warr.

England were reduced to three main bowlers after Bailey had had his thumb fractured by a ball from Lindwall and Wright had torn a leg tendon when he was run out. On the third day, Brown bowled 22 eight-ball overs, while Bedser and Warr each sent down 20; all this in great heat and on a good batting pitch.

## ENGLAND

| | | | | |
|---|---|---|---|---|
| L. Hutton | lbw b Miller | 62 | c Tallon b Iverson | 9 |
| C. Washbrook | c Miller b Johnson | 18 | b Iverson | 34 |
| R.T. Simpson | c Loxton b Miller | 49 | c Tallon b Iverson | 0 |
| D.C.S. Compton | b Miller | 0 | c Johnson b Johnston | 23 |
| W.G.A. Parkhouse | c Morris b Johnson | 25 | run out | 15 |
| F.R. Brown* | b Lindwall | 79 | b Iverson | 18 |
| T.E. Bailey | c Tallon b Johnson | 15 | (8) not out | 0 |
| T.G. Evans† | not out | 23 | (7) b Johnson | 14 |
| A.V. Bedser | b Lindwall | 3 | b Iverson | 4 |
| J.J. Warr | b Miller | 4 | b Iverson | 0 |
| D.V.P. Wright | run out | 0 | absent hurt | – |
| Extras | (LB 10, NB 2) | 12 | (B 1, LB 5) | 6 |
| **Total** | | **290** | | **123** |

## AUSTRALIA

| | | |
|---|---|---|
| K.A. Archer | c Evans b Bedser | 48 |
| A.R. Morris | b Bedser | 0 |
| A.L. Hassett* | c Bedser b Brown | 70 |
| R.N. Harvey | b Bedser | 39 |
| K.R. Miller | not out | 145 |
| S.J.E. Loxton | c Bedser b Brown | 17 |
| D. Tallon† | lbw b Bedser | 18 |
| I.W. Johnson | b Brown | 77 |
| R.R. Lindwall | lbw b Brown | 1 |
| W.A. Johnston | run out | 0 |
| J.B. Iverson | run out | 1 |
| Extras | (B 3, LB 7) | 10 |
| **Total** | | **426** |

| AUSTRALIA | O | M | R | W | O | M | R | W |
|---|---|---|---|---|---|---|---|---|
| Lindwall | 16 | 0 | 60 | 2 | 4 | 1 | 12 | 0 |
| Miller | 15·7 | 4 | 37 | 4 | 6 | 2 | 15 | 0 |
| Johnson | 31 | 8 | 94 | 3 | 10 | 2 | 32 | 1 |
| Johnston | 21 | 5 | 50 | 0 | 13 | 6 | 31 | 1 |
| Iverson | 10 | 1 | 25 | 0 | 19·4 | 8 | 27 | 6 |
| Loxton | 5 | 0 | 12 | 0 | | | | |
| ENGLAND | | | | | | | | |
| Bedser | 43 | 4 | 107 | 4 | | | | |
| Warr | 36 | 4 | 142 | 0 | | | | |
| Brown | 44 | 4 | 153 | 4 | | | | |
| Compton | 6 | 1 | 14 | 0 | | | | |

### FALL OF WICKETS

| Wkt | E 1st | A 1st | E 2nd |
|---|---|---|---|
| 1st | 34 | 1 | 32 |
| 2nd | 128 | 122 | 40 |
| 3rd | 128 | 122 | 45 |
| 4th | 137 | 190 | 74 |
| 5th | 187 | 223 | 91 |
| 6th | 258 | 252 | 119 |
| 7th | 267 | 402 | 119 |
| 8th | 281 | 406 | 123 |
| 9th | 286 | 418 | 123 |
| 10th | 290 | 426 | – |

Umpires: A.N. Barlow and H. Elphinston.

# AUSTRALIA v ENGLAND 1950–51 (4th Test)

Played at Adelaide Oval on 2, 3, 5, 6, 7, 8 February.
Toss: Australia.   Result: AUSTRALIA won by 274 runs.
Debuts: Australia – J.W. Burke; England – R. Tattersall.

Hutton became the only England batsman to carry his bat through a complete Test innings twice and the second after R. Abel in 1891-92 (*Test No. 36*) to do so against Australia. Morris (206) made the highest score by an Australian left-hander against England. Burke, aged 20 years 240 days, scored a hundred in his first Test match. Compton captained England on the fifth day after Brown had been injured in a motoring accident the previous night.

## AUSTRALIA

| | | | | | |
|---|---|---|---|---|---|
| K.A. Archer | c Compton b Bedser | 0 | c Bedser b Tattersall | | 32 |
| A.R. Morris | b Tattersall | 206 | run out | | 16 |
| A.L. Hassett* | c Evans b Wright | 43 | lbw b Wright | | 31 |
| R.N. Harvey | b Bedser | 43 | b Brown | | 68 |
| K.R. Miller | c Brown b Wright | 44 | b Wright | | 99 |
| J.W. Burke | b Tattersall | 12 | not out | | 101 |
| I.W. Johnson | c Evans b Bedser | 16 | c Evans b Warr | | 3 |
| R.R. Lindwall | lbw b Wright | 1 | run out | | 31 |
| D. Tallon† | b Tattersall | 1 | c Hutton b Compton | | 5 |
| W.A. Johnston | c Hutton b Wright | 0 | not out | | 9 |
| J.B. Iverson | not out | 0 | | | |
| Extras | (B 2, LB 1, W 1, NB 1) | 5 | (B 7, LB 1) | | 8 |
| **Total** | | **371** | (8 wickets declared) | | **403** |

## ENGLAND

| | | | | | |
|---|---|---|---|---|---|
| L. Hutton | not out | 156 | c sub (S.J.E. Loxton) b Johnston | | 45 |
| C. Washbrook | c Iverson b Lindwall | 2 | lbw b Johnston | | 31 |
| R.T. Simpson | b Johnston | 29 | c Burke b Johnston | | 61 |
| D.C.S. Compton | c Tallon b Lindwall | 5 | c sub (S.J.E. Loxton) b Johnston | | 0 |
| D.S. Sheppard | b Iverson | 9 | lbw b Miller | | 41 |
| F.R. Brown* | b Miller | 16 | absent hurt | | – |
| T.G. Evans† | c Burke b Johnston | 13 | (6) c Johnson b Miller | | 21 |
| A.V. Bedser | lbw b Iverson | 7 | (7) c Morris b Miller | | 0 |
| R. Tattersall | c Harvey b Iverson | 0 | (8) c Morris b Johnson | | 6 |
| J.J. Warr | b Johnston | 0 | (9) b Johnson | | 0 |
| D.V.P. Wright | lbw b Lindwall | 14 | (10) not out | | 0 |
| Extras | (B 15, LB 5, NB 1) | 21 | (B 15, LB 3, W 2, NB 3) | | 23 |
| **Total** | | **272** | | | **228** |

| ENGLAND | O | M | R | W | O | M | R | W | | FALL OF WICKETS | | | |
|---|---|---|---|---|---|---|---|---|---|---|---|---|---|
| Bedser | 26 | 4 | 74 | 3 | 25 | 6 | 62 | 0 | | A | E | A | E |
| Warr | 16 | 2 | 63 | 0 | 21 | 0 | 76 | 1 | *Wkt* | *1st* | *1st* | *2nd* | *2nd* |
| Wright | 25 | 1 | 99 | 4 | 21 | 2 | 109 | 2 | 1st | 0 | 7 | 26 | 74 |
| Tattersall | 25·5 | 5 | 95 | 3 | 27 | 2 | 116 | 1 | 2nd | 95 | 80 | 79 | 90 |
| Brown | 3 | 0 | 24 | 0 | 3 | 1 | 14 | 1 | 3rd | 205 | 96 | 95 | 90 |
| Compton | 1 | 0 | 11 | 0 | 4·6 | 1 | 18 | 1 | 4th | 281 | 132 | 194 | 181 |
| | | | | | | | | | 5th | 310 | 161 | 281 | 221 |
| AUSTRALIA | | | | | | | | | 6th | 357 | 195 | 297 | 221 |
| Lindwall | 13·3 | 0 | 51 | 3 | 10 | 2 | 35 | 0 | 7th | 363 | 206 | 367 | 228 |
| Miller | 13 | 2 | 36 | 1 | 13 | 4 | 27 | 3 | 8th | 366 | 214 | 378 | 228 |
| Johnson | 15 | 2 | 38 | 0 | 25·6 | 6 | 63 | 2 | 9th | 367 | 219 | – | 228 |
| Iverson | 26 | 4 | 68 | 3 | | | | | 10th | 371 | 272 | – | – |
| Johnston | 25 | 4 | 58 | 3 | 27 | 4 | 73 | 4 | | | | | |
| Burke | | | | | 3 | 1 | 7 | 0 | | | | | |

Umpires: A.N. Barlow and A.F. Cocks.

# AUSTRALIA v ENGLAND 1950–51 (5th Test)

Played at Melbourne Cricket Ground on 23, 24 (*no play*), 26, 27, 28 February.
Toss: Australia.   Result: ENGLAND won by eight wickets.
Debuts: Australia – G.B. Hole.

England beat Australia for the first time since 1938 (*Test No. 266*) and ended their record run of 25 consecutive Test matches without defeat (20 wins, 5 draws). Simpson reached his only hundred against Australia on his 31st birthday and went on to score all but ten of a last-wicket partnership of 74 in 55 minutes with Tattersall. Bedser took 30 wickets, average 16·06, in the rubber.

## AUSTRALIA

| | | | | | |
|---|---|---|---|---|---|
| J.W. Burke | c Tattersall b Bedser | 11 | c Hutton b Bedser | | 1 |
| A.R. Morris | lbw b Brown | 50 | lbw b Bedser | | 4 |
| A.L. Hassett* | c Hutton b Brown | 92 | b Wright | | 48 |
| R.N. Harvey | c Evans b Brown | 1 | lbw b Wright | | 52 |
| K.R. Miller | c and b Brown | 7 | c and b Brown | | 0 |
| G.B. Hole | b Bedser | 18 | b Bailey | | 63 |
| I.W. Johnson | lbw b Bedser | 1 | c Brown b Wright | | 0 |
| R.R. Lindwall | c Compton b Bedser | 21 | b Bedser | | 14 |
| D. Tallon† | c Hutton b Bedser | 1 | not out | | 2 |
| W.A. Johnston | not out | 12 | b Bedser | | 1 |
| J.B. Iverson | c Washbrook b Brown | 0 | c Compton b Bedser | | 0 |
| Extras | (B 2, LB 1) | 3 | (B 2, LB 8, W 1, NB 1) | | 12 |
| **Total** | | **217** | | | **197** |

## ENGLAND

| | | | | | |
|---|---|---|---|---|---|
| L. Hutton | b Hole | 79 | not out | | 60 |
| C. Washbrook | c Tallon b Miller | 27 | c Lindwall b Johnston | | 7 |
| R.T. Simpson | not out | 156 | run out | | 15 |
| D.C.S. Compton | c Miller b Lindwall | 11 | not out | | 11 |
| D.S. Sheppard | c Tallon b Miller | 1 | | | |
| F.R. Brown* | b Lindwall | 6 | | | |
| T.G. Evans† | b Miller | 1 | | | |
| A.V. Bedser | b Lindwall | 11 | | | |
| T.E. Bailey | c Johnson b Iverson | 5 | | | |
| D.V.P. Wright | lbw b Iverson | 3 | | | |
| R. Tattersall | b Miller | 10 | | | |
| Extras | (B 9, LB 1) | 10 | (LB 2) | | 2 |
| **Total** | | **320** | (2 wickets) | | **95** |

| ENGLAND | O | M | R | W | O | M | R | W | | FALL OF WICKETS | | | |
|---|---|---|---|---|---|---|---|---|---|---|---|---|---|
| Bedser | 22 | 5 | 46 | 5 | 20·3 | 4 | 59 | 5 | | A | E | A | E |
| Bailey | 9 | 1 | 29 | 0 | 15 | 3 | 32 | 1 | Wkt | 1st | 1st | 2nd | 2nd |
| Brown | 18 | 4 | 49 | 5 | 9 | 1 | 32 | 1 | 1st | 23 | 40 | 5 | 32 |
| Wright | 9 | 1 | 50 | 0 | 15 | 2 | 56 | 3 | 2nd | 111 | 171 | 6 | 62 |
| Tattersall | 11 | 3 | 40 | 0 | 5 | 2 | 6 | 0 | 3rd | 115 | 204 | 87 | – |
| | | | | | | | | | 4th | 123 | 205 | 89 | – |
| AUSTRALIA | | | | | | | | | 5th | 156 | 212 | 142 | – |
| Lindwall | 21 | 1 | 77 | 3 | 2 | 0 | 12 | 0 | 6th | 166 | 213 | 142 | – |
| Miller | 21·7 | 5 | 76 | 4 | 2 | 0 | 5 | 0 | 7th | 184 | 228 | 192 | – |
| Johnston | 12 | 1 | 55 | 0 | 11 | 3 | 36 | 1 | 8th | 187 | 236 | 196 | – |
| Iverson | 20 | 4 | 52 | 2 | 12 | 2 | 32 | 0 | 9th | 216 | 246 | 197 | – |
| Johnson | 11 | 1 | 40 | 0 | 1 | 0 | 1 | 0 | 10th | 217 | 320 | 197 | – |
| Hole | 5 | 0 | 10 | 1 | 1 | 0 | 3 | 0 | | | | | |
| Hassett | | | | | 0·6 | 0 | 4 | 0 | | | | | |

Umpires: A.N. Barlow and H. Elphinston.

# NEW ZEALAND v ENGLAND 1950–51 (1st Test)

Played at Lancaster Park, Christchurch, on 17, 19, 20, 21 March.
Toss: New Zealand.    Result: MATCH DRAWN.
Debuts: New Zealand – J.A. Hayes, A.R. MacGibbon, A.M. Moir; England – J.B. Statham.

A lifeless pitch resulted in 1,013 runs being scored in 22 hours for the loss of 21 wickets. The match provided Statham with the first of his 252 Test wickets and Bailey with his only hundred. Washbrook, given out 'lbw', was recalled after Hadlee had told the umpire that the ball had hit bat before pad.

## NEW ZEALAND

| | | | | |
|---|---|---|---|---|
| B. Sutcliffe | b Statham | 116 | | |
| V.J. Scott | b Bailey | 16 | (5) not out | 10 |
| J.R. Reid | b Wright | 50 | | |
| W.M. Wallace | c Brown b Bedser | 66 | | |
| W.A. Hadlee* | c Brown b Bailey | 50 | | |
| A.R. MacGibbon | lbw b Wright | 4 | (1) c Evans b Simpson | 8 |
| F.L.H. Mooney† | st Evans b Tattersall | 39 | | |
| T.B. Burtt | b Brown | 42 | | |
| A.M. Moir | not out | 0 | (4) not out | 7 |
| J.A. Hayes | ) did not bat | | (2) lbw b Washbrook | 19 |
| G.F. Cresswell | ) | | (3) c Evans b Simpson | 2 |
| Extras | (B 16, LB 16, W 1, NB 1) | 34 | | |
| **Total** | (8 wickets declared) | **417** | (3 wickets) | **46** |

## ENGLAND

| | | |
|---|---|---|
| L. Hutton | b Moir | 28 |
| C. Washbrook | c Mooney b Hayes | 58 |
| R.T. Simpson | c Wallace b Moir | 81 |
| D.C.S. Compton | b Burtt | 79 |
| T.E. Bailey | not out | 134 |
| F.R. Brown* | c Scott b Cresswell | 62 |
| T.G. Evans† | c Hayes b Moir | 19 |
| A.V. Bedser | c Hayes b Moir | 5 |
| R. Tattersall | b Moir | 2 |
| D.V.P. Wright | c MacGibbon b Cresswell | 45 |
| J.B. Statham | b Moir | 9 |
| Extras | (B 20, LB 8) | 28 |
| **Total** | | **550** |

| ENGLAND | O | M | R | W | O | M | R | W | FALL OF WICKETS | | | |
|---|---|---|---|---|---|---|---|---|---|---|---|---|
| | | | | | | | | | | NZ | E | NZ |
| Bedser | 41 | 10 | 83 | 1 | | | | | Wkt | 1st | 1st | 2nd |
| Bailey | 30 | 9 | 51 | 2 | | | | | 1st | 37 | 57 | 9 |
| Statham | 24 | 6 | 47 | 1 | | | | | 2nd | 168 | 108 | 29 |
| Tattersall | 16 | 3 | 48 | 1 | | | | | 3rd | 203 | 237 | 29 |
| Wright | 27 | 2 | 99 | 2 | | | | | 4th | 297 | 264 | – |
| Brown | 15·2 | 3 | 34 | 1 | | | | | 5th | 307 | 356 | – |
| Compton | 4 | 0 | 21 | 0 | 2 | 0 | 10 | 0 | 6th | 335 | 388 | – |
| Washbrook | | | | | 4 | 0 | 25 | 1 | 7th | 415 | 398 | – |
| Simpson | | | | | 4 | 1 | 4 | 2 | 8th | 417 | 406 | – |
| Hutton | | | | | 3 | 0 | 7 | 0 | 9th | – | 523 | – |
| NEW ZEALAND | | | | | | | | | 10th | – | 550 | – |
| Hayes | 43 | 11 | 85 | 1 | | | | | | | | |
| Reid | 10 | 2 | 29 | 0 | | | | | | | | |
| MacGibbon | 27 | 6 | 74 | 0 | | | | | | | | |
| Cresswell | 34 | 10 | 75 | 2 | | | | | | | | |
| Moir | 56·3 | 16 | 155 | 6 | | | | | | | | |
| Burtt | 49 | 23 | 99 | 1 | | | | | | | | |
| Scott | 2 | 0 | 5 | 0 | | | | | | | | |

Umpires: S.B. Tonkinson and E.G. Brook.

# NEW ZEALAND v ENGLAND 1950–51 (2nd Test)

Played at Basin Reserve, Wellington, on 24 (*no play*), 26, 27, 28 March.
Toss: New Zealand.   Result: ENGLAND won by six wickets.
Debuts: Nil.

Torrential rain prevented play until the second morning and an earthquake tested the ground shortly after lunch on the last day. Moir emulated W.W. Armstrong (*Test No. 143*) by bowling two consecutive overs – the last before tea on the fourth day and the first afterwards.

## NEW ZEALAND

| | | | | |
|---|---|---|---|---|
| B. Sutcliffe | c and b Wright | 20 | b Tattersall | 11 |
| V.J. Scott | lbw b Bailey | 0 | (7) c Sheppard b Bedser | 60 |
| J.R. Reid | b Brown | 11 | b Tattersall | 11 |
| W.M. Wallace | b Wright | 15 | (5) c Brown b Bailey | 1 |
| W.A. Hadlee* | lbw b Wright | 15 | (4) c Bailey b Tattersall | 9 |
| A.R. MacGibbon | c Brown b Wright | 20 | lbw b Tattersall | 0 |
| F.L.H. Mooney† | c Compton b Bailey | 3 | (8) b Tattersall | 0 |
| T.B. Burtt | c Parkhouse b Wright | 3 | (2) b Tattersall | 31 |
| A.M. Moir | not out | 26 | c Bedser b Bailey | 26 |
| J.A. Hayes | b Tattersall | 0 | b Bailey | 5 |
| G.F. Cresswell | run out | 0 | not out | 0 |
| Extras | (B 3, LB 5, NB 4) | 12 | (B 30, LB 2, NB 3) | 35 |
| **Total** | | **125** | | **189** |

## ENGLAND

| | | | | |
|---|---|---|---|---|
| L. Hutton | c Reid b Moir | 57 | c Hadlee b Cresswell | 29 |
| R.T. Simpson | b Moir | 6 | b Burtt | 5 |
| W.G.A. Parkhouse | b Burtt | 2 | c and b Burtt | 20 |
| D.S. Sheppard | b Hayes | 3 | (5) not out | 4 |
| D.C.S. Compton | b Burtt | 10 | (4) b Cresswell | 18 |
| F.R. Brown* | b Hayes | 47 | not out | 10 |
| T.E. Bailey | st Mooney b Burtt | 29 | | |
| T.G. Evans† | b Cresswell | 13 | | |
| A.V. Bedser | b Cresswell | 28 | | |
| D.V.P. Wright | not out | 9 | | |
| R. Tattersall | b Cresswell | 1 | | |
| Extras | (B 11, LB 8, NB 3) | 22 | (B 1, LB 4) | 5 |
| **Total** | | **227** | **(4 wickets)** | **91** |

| ENGLAND | O | M | R | W | O | M | R | W | | FALL OF WICKETS | | | |
|---|---|---|---|---|---|---|---|---|---|---|---|---|---|
| Bailey | 11 | 2 | 18 | 2 | 14·2 | 1 | 43 | 3 | | NZ | E | NZ | E |
| Bedser | 19 | 6 | 21 | 0 | 24 | 10 | 34 | 1 | *Wkt* | *1st* | *1st* | *2nd* | *2nd* |
| Brown | 6 | 1 | 10 | 1 | 1 | 0 | 1 | 0 | 1st | 1 | 10 | 25 | 16 |
| Tattersall | 15 | 9 | 16 | 1 | 21 | 6 | 44 | 6 | 2nd | 25 | 31 | 62 | 56 |
| Wright | 19 | 3 | 48 | 5 | 12 | 2 | 32 | 0 | 3rd | 37 | 40 | 76 | 60 |
| | | | | | | | | | 4th | 68 | 69 | 82 | 80 |
| NEW ZEALAND | | | | | | | | | 5th | 69 | 140 | 82 | – |
| Hayes | 20 | 2 | 44 | 2 | | | | | 6th | 83 | 144 | 98 | – |
| Cresswell | 15 | 6 | 18 | 3 | 18 | 8 | 31 | 2 | 7th | 94 | 173 | 105 | – |
| Moir | 28 | 5 | 65 | 2 | 6 | 0 | 19 | 0 | 8th | 102 | 216 | 156 | – |
| Burtt | 27 | 14 | 46 | 3 | 21·2 | 10 | 36 | 2 | 9th | 105 | 218 | 187 | – |
| MacGibbon | 7 | 0 | 32 | 0 | | | | | 10th | 125 | 227 | 189 | – |

Umpires: M.F. Pengelly and J. McLellan.

# ENGLAND v SOUTH AFRICA 1951 (1st Test)

Played at Trent Bridge, Nottingham, on 7, 8, 9, 11, 12 June.
Toss: South Africa.   Result: SOUTH AFRICA won by 71 runs.
Debuts: England – W. Watson; South Africa – G.W.A. Chubb, D.J. McGlew, C.B. van Ryneveld, J.H.B. Waite.

South Africa ended their abortive run of 28 Tests without victory since 1935. Nourse batted in pain for 550 minutes and South Africa's first double-century against England – his thumb had been fractured three weeks earlier. He took no further part in the match after his innings, E.A.B. Rowan taking over as captain. Simpson remains the only Nottinghamshire player to score a hundred for England at Trent Bridge.

## SOUTH AFRICA

| | | | | |
|---|---|---|---|---|
| E.A.B. Rowan | c Evans b Brown | 17 | c Ikin b Bedser | 11 |
| J.H.B. Waite† | run out | 76 | c Ikin b Tattersall | 5 |
| D.J. McGlew | b Brown | 40 | st Evans b Bedser | 5 |
| A.D. Nourse* | run out | 208 | absent hurt | – |
| J.E. Cheetham | c Ikin b Bedser | 31 | b Bedser | 28 |
| G.M. Fullerton | c Compton b Tattersall | 54 | (4) c Brown b Tattersall | 13 |
| C.B. van Ryneveld | lbw b Bedser | 32 | (6) c Hutton b Bedser | 22 |
| A.M.B. Rowan | b Bedser | 2 | (7) c Evans b Bedser | 5 |
| N.B.F. Mann | c Tattersall b Wardle | 1 | (8) b Tattersall | 2 |
| G.W.A. Chubb | not out | 0 | (9) not out | 11 |
| C.N. McCarthy | not out | 1 | (10) b Bedser | 5 |
| Extras | (B 3, LB 17, NB 1) | 21 | (B 4, LB 9, NB 1) | 14 |
| **Total** | (9 wickets declared) | **483** | | **121** |

## ENGLAND

| | | | | |
|---|---|---|---|---|
| L.Hutton | c Waite b A.M.B. Rowan | 63 | c and b A.M.B. Rowan | 11 |
| J.T. Ikin | c McCarthy b Chubb | 1 | b Mann | 33 |
| R.T. Simpson | c Waite b McCarthy | 137 | c and b A.M.B. Rowan | 7 |
| D.C.S. Compton | c Waite b McCarthy | 112 | lbw b AM.B. Rowan | 5 |
| W. Watson | lbw b McCarthy | 57 | lbw b Mann | 5 |
| F.R. Brown* | c Fullerton b Chubb | 29 | (7) c McCarthy b A.M.B. Rowan | 7 |
| T.G. Evans† | c sub (R.A. McLean) b Chubb | 5 | (8) c Van Ryneveld b Mann | 0 |
| J.H. Wardle | c Fullerton b Chubb | 5 | (9) c sub (R.A.McLean) b A.M.B. Rowan | 30 |
| T.E. Bailey | c Fullerton b McCarthy | 3 | (6) c Waite b Mann | 11 |
| A.V. Bedser | not out | 0 | b McCarthy | 0 |
| R. Tattersall | did not bat | | not out | 0 |
| Extras | (B 4, LB 3) | 7 | (LB 5) | 5 |
| **Total** | (9 wickets declared) | **419** | | **114** |

| ENGLAND | O | M | R | W | O | M | R | W | | FALL OF WICKETS | | | |
|---|---|---|---|---|---|---|---|---|---|---|---|---|---|
| Bedser | 63 | 18 | 122 | 3 | 22·4 | 8 | 37 | 6 | | SA | E | SA | E |
| Bailey | 45 | 13 | 102 | 0 | 2 | 0 | 10 | 0 | Wkt | 1st | 1st | 2nd | 2nd |
| Brown | 34 | 11 | 74 | 2 | | | | | 1st | 31 | 4 | 12 | 23 |
| Tattersall | 47 | 20 | 80 | 1 | 23 | 6 | 56 | 3 | 2nd | 107 | 148 | 20 | 41 |
| Wardle | 49 | 21 | 77 | 1 | 4 | 3 | 4 | 0 | 3rd | 189 | 234 | 24 | 57 |
| Compton | 2 | 0 | 7 | 0 | | | | | 4th | 273 | 375 | 52 | 63 |
| | | | | | | | | | 5th | 394 | 382 | 87 | 67 |
| SOUTH AFRICA | | | | | | | | | 6th | 465 | 395 | 98 | 80 |
| McCarthy | 48 | 10 | 104 | 4 | 8 | 1 | 8 | 1 | 7th | 467 | 410 | 103 | 83 |
| Chubb | 46·2 | 12 | 146 | 4 | 6 | 2 | 9 | 0 | 8th | 476 | 419 | 106 | 84 |
| A.M.B. Rowan | 46 | 10 | 101 | 1 | 27·2 | 4 | 68 | 5 | 9th | 482 | 419 | 121 | 110 |
| Mann | 20 | 5 | 51 | 0 | 24 | 16 | 24 | 4 | 10th | – | – | – | 114 |
| Van Ryneveld | 3 | 0 | 10 | 0 | | | | | | | | | |

Umpires: F. Chester and H.G. Baldwin.

# ENGLAND v SOUTH AFRICA 1951 (2nd Test)

Played at Lord's, London, on 21, 22, 23 June.
Toss: England.   Result: ENGLAND won by ten wickets.
Debuts: Nil.

On a rain-affected pitch, Tattersall's off-spin accounted for nine of the fourteen wickets which fell on the second day. The match finished at 2.20 p.m. on the third day.

## ENGLAND

| | | | | |
|---|---|---|---|---|
| Hutton | lbw b McCarthy | 12 | not out | 12 |
| T. Ikin | b Mann | 51 | not out | 4 |
| T. Simpson | lbw b McCarthy | 26 | | |
| .C.S. Compton | lbw b McCarthy | 79 | | |
| . Watson | c McCarthy b Chubb | 79 | | |
| R. Brown* | b Chubb | 1 | | |
| G. Evans† | c Fullerton b McCarthy | 0 | | |
| H. Wardle | lbw b Chubb | 18 | | |
| .V. Bedser | not out | 26 | | |
| B. Statham | b Chubb | 1 | | |
| . Tattersall | b Chubb | 1 | | |
| Extras | (B 8, LB 9) | 17 | | |
| **Total** | | **311** | (0 wickets) | **16** |

## SOUTH AFRICA

| | | | | |
|---|---|---|---|---|
| A.B. Rowan | c Ikin b Tattersall | 24 | c Ikin b Statham | 10 |
| H.B. Waite† | c Hutton b Wardle | 15 | c Compton b Tattersall | 17 |
| J. McGlew | c Evans b Tattersall | 3 | b Tattersall | 2 |
| D. Nourse* | c Watson b Tattersall | 20 | lbw b Wardle | 3 |
| E. Cheetham | c Hutton b Tattersall | 15 | b Statham | 54 |
| M. Fullerton | b Tattersall | 12 | lbw b Bedser | 60 |
| B. van Ryneveld | lbw b Wardle | 0 | c Ikin b Tattersall | 18 |
| M.B. Rowan | c Ikin b Tattersall | 3 | c Brown b Bedser | 10 |
| B.F. Mann | c Brown b Tattersall | 14 | c Brown b Tattersall | 13 |
| W.A. Chubb | c Tattersall b Wardle | 5 | b Tattersall | 3 |
| N. McCarthy | not out | 1 | not out | 2 |
| Extras | (LB 3) | 3 | (B 11, LB 8) | 19 |
| **Total** | | **115** | | **211** |

| SOUTH AFRICA | O | M | R | W | O | M | R | W | FALL OF WICKETS | | | | |
|---|---|---|---|---|---|---|---|---|---|---|---|---|---|
| | | | | | | | | | | E | SA | SA | E |
| cCarthy | 23 | 2 | 76 | 4 | | | | | Wkt | 1st | 1st | 2nd | 2nd |
| hubb | 34·4 | 9 | 77 | 5 | | | | | 1st | 120 | 25 | 21 | – |
| M.B. Rowan | 13 | 1 | 63 | 0 | | | | | 2nd | 89 | 38 | 29 | – |
| ann | 32 | 12 | 51 | 1 | | | | | 3rd | 103 | 47 | 32 | – |
| an Ryneveld | 5 | 0 | 27 | 0 | | | | | 4th | 225 | 72 | 58 | – |
| ourse | | | | | 2 | 0 | 9 | 0 | 5th | 226 | 88 | 152 | – |
| A.B. Rowan | | | | | 1·5 | 0 | 7 | 0 | 6th | 231 | 91 | 160 | – |
| NGLAND | | | | | | | | | 7th | 265 | 91 | 178 | – |
| edser | 8 | 5 | 7 | 0 | 24 | 8 | 53 | 2 | 8th | 299 | 103 | 196 | – |
| atham | 6 | 3 | 7 | 0 | 18 | 6 | 33 | 2 | 9th | 301 | 112 | 200 | – |
| attersall | 28 | 10 | 52 | 7 | 32·2 | 14 | 49 | 5 | 10th | 311 | 115 | 211 | – |
| ardle | 22·5 | 10 | 46 | 3 | 20 | 5 | 44 | 1 | | | | | |
| ompton | | | | | 2 | 0 | 13 | 0 | | | | | |

Umpires: F.S. Lee and Harold Elliott.

Test No. 336/77

# ENGLAND v SOUTH AFRICA 1951 (3rd Test)

Played at Old Trafford, Manchester, on 5, 6 (*no play*), 7, 9, 10 July.
Toss: South Africa.   Result: ENGLAND won by nine wickets.
Debuts: England – T.W. Graveney; South Africa – R.A. McLean.

Although Bedser took full advantage of a pitch livened by heavy rain before the match, England had much t
worst of batting conditions when play resumed on the third day. Chubb, playing in his only Test rubber and in h
41st year, took six of the 21 wickets which made him South Africa's leading wicket-taker. Hutton just miss
scoring his 100th first-class hundred.

## SOUTH AFRICA

| | | | | |
|---|---|---|---|---|
| E.A.B. Rowan | c Brown b Bedser | 0 | c Ikin b Laker | |
| J.H.B. Waite† | c Ikin b Bedser | 1 | b Statham | |
| C.B. van Ryneyeld | lbw b Tattersall | 40 | b Laker | |
| A.D. Nourse* | c Ikin b Bedser | 29 | c Evans b Tattersall | |
| J.E. Cheetham | c Hutton b Bedser | 20 | b Bedser | |
| G.M. Fullerton | c Hutton b Bedser | 0 | c Tattersall b Laker | |
| R.A. McLean | b Laker | 20 | c Ikin b Bedser | |
| A.M.B. Rowan | b Statham | 17 | lbw b Bedser | |
| N.B.F. Mann | b Bedser | 0 | b Bedser | |
| G.W.A. Chubb | not out | 15 | b Bedser | |
| C.N. McCarthy | c Ikin b Bedser | 0 | not out | |
| Extras | (LB 14, NB 2) | 16 | (B 13, LB 10 NB 1) | |
| **Total** | | **158** | | **1** |

## ENGLAND

| | | | | |
|---|---|---|---|---|
| L. Hutton | c Van Ryneveld | | not out | |
| | b A.M.B. Rowan | 27 | | |
| J.T. Ikin | c Cheetham b Chubb | 22 | b Mann | |
| R.T. Simpson | st Waite b Mann | 11 | not out | |
| T.W. Graveney | b A.M.B. Rowan | 15 | | |
| W. Watson | b Chubb | 21 | | |
| F.R. Brown* | c Van Ryneveld b A.M.B. Rowan | 42 | | |
| T.G. Evans† | c Waite b Chubb | 2 | | |
| J.C. Laker | c Nourse b Chubb | 27 | | |
| A.V. Bedser | not out | 30 | | |
| R. Tattersall | c Cheetham b Chubb | 1 | | |
| J.B. Statham | c Cheetham b Chubb | 1 | | |
| Extras | (B 4, LB 8) | 12 | (LB 1, NB 1) | |
| **Total** | | **211** | (1 wicket) | **1** |

| ENGLAND | O | M | R | W | O | M | R | W |
|---|---|---|---|---|---|---|---|---|
| Bedser | 32·3 | 10 | 58 | 7 | 24·2 | 8 | 54 | 5 |
| Statham | 7 | 2 | 8 | 1 | 17 | 3 | 30 | 1 |
| Laker | 27 | 7 | 47 | 1 | 19 | 3 | 42 | 3 |
| Tattersall | 18 | 6 | 29 | 1 | 18 | 3 | 41 | 1 |
| SOUTH AFRICA | | | | | | | | |
| McCarthy | 14 | 4 | 36 | 0 | 19 | 4 | 46 | 0 |
| Chubb | 26·3 | 7 | 51 | 6 | 23 | 6 | 72 | 0 |
| A.M.B. Rowan | 29 | 4 | 75 | 3 | 7 | 1 | 17 | 0 |
| Mann | 16 | 5 | 37 | 1 | 2·3 | 1 | 5 | 1 |

FALL OF WICKETS

| Wkt | SA 1st | E 1st | SA 2nd | |
|---|---|---|---|---|
| 1st | 0 | 30 | 4 | 1 |
| 2nd | 12 | 58 | 19 | |
| 3rd | 66 | 70 | 60 | |
| 4th | 87 | 91 | 145 | |
| 5th | 88 | 127 | 155 | |
| 6th | 105 | 143 | 168 | |
| 7th | 129 | 147 | 181 | |
| 8th | 132 | 200 | 185 | |
| 9th | 143 | 207 | 190 | |
| 10th | 158 | 211 | 191 | |

Umpires: F.S. Lee and H.G. Baldwin.

# ENGLAND v SOUTH AFRICA 1951 (4th Test)

Played at Headingley, Leeds, on 26, 27, 28, 30, 31 (*no play*) July.
Toss: South Africa.   Result: MATCH DRAWN.
Debuts: England – D.V. Brennan, F.A. Lowson, P.B.H. May; South Africa – P.N.F. Mansell.

E.A.B. Rowan's 236 remains South Africa's highest score against England (only E. Paynter with 243 at Durban in 1938–39 has scored more in this series), and his partnership of 198 with Van Ryneveld is still the South African second-wicket record in all Tests. May is the only England batsman to score a hundred in his first Test, that match being at home against South Africa.

## SOUTH AFRICA

| | | | | |
|---|---|---|---|---|
| E.A.B. Rowan | c Bedser b Brown | 236 | not out | 60 |
| H.B. Waite† | lbw b Bedser | 13 | not out | 25 |
| C.B. van Ryneveld | c and b Hilton | 83 | | |
| A.D. Nourse* | lbw b Brown | 13 | | |
| E. Cheetham | b Bedser | 7 | | |
| R.A. McLean | run out | 67 | | |
| P.N.F. Mansell | c Tattersall b Hilton | 90 | | |
| A.M.B. Rowan | b Brown | 9 | | |
| N.B.F. Mann | b Tattersall | 2 | | |
| G.W.A. Chubb | c Lowson b Hilton | 11 | | |
| C.N. McCarthy | not out | 0 | | |
| Extras | (B 1, LB 6) | 7 | (LB 2) | 2 |
| **Total** | | **538** | (0 wickets) | **87** |

## ENGLAND

| | | |
|---|---|---|
| L. Hutton | b Van Ryneveld | 100 |
| F.A. Lowson | c Mansell b A.M.B. Rowan | 58 |
| P.B.H. May | b A.M.B. Rowan | 138 |
| D.C.S. Compton | lbw b A.M.B. Rowan | 25 |
| W. Watson | b Chubb | 32 |
| T.E. Bailey | b Mann | 95 |
| F.R. Brown* | c E.A.B. Rowan b A.M.B. Rowan | 2 |
| A.V. Bedser | b Mann | 8 |
| D.V. Brennan† | b Mann | 16 |
| R. Tattersall | c E.A.B. Rowan b A.M.B. Rowan | 4 |
| M.J. Hilton | not out | 9 |
| Extras | (B 10, LB 7, NB 1) | 18 |
| **Total** | | **505** |

| ENGLAND | O | M | R | W | O | M | R | W | | FALL OF WICKETS | | | |
|---|---|---|---|---|---|---|---|---|---|---|---|---|---|
| Bedser | 58 | 14 | 113 | 2 | 4 | 1 | 5 | 0 | | | SA | E | SA |
| Bailey | 17 | 4 | 48 | 0 | 1 | 0 | 8 | 0 | *Wkt* | | *1st* | *1st* | *2nd* |
| Brown | 38 | 10 | 107 | 3 | 11 | 2 | 26 | 0 | 1st | | 40 | 99 | – |
| Tattersall | 60 | 23 | 83 | 1 | 16 | 9 | 13 | 0 | 2nd | | 238 | 228 | – |
| Hilton | 61·3 | 18 | 176 | 3 | 10 | 5 | 17 | 0 | 3rd | | 267 | 266 | – |
| Compton | 1 | 0 | 4 | 0 | 7 | 1 | 16 | 0 | 4th | | 286 | 345 | – |
| | | | | | | | | | 5th | | 394 | 387 | – |
| SOUTH AFRICA | | | | | | | | | 6th | | 480 | 391 | – |
| McCarthy | 41 | 10 | 81 | 0 | | | | | 7th | | 498 | 400 | – |
| Chubb | 43 | 12 | 99 | 1 | | | | | 8th | | 505 | 432 | – |
| A.M.B. Rowan | 68 | 17 | 174 | 5 | | | | | 9th | | 538 | 445 | – |
| Mann | 60·5 | 23 | 96 | 3 | | | | | 10th | | 538 | 505 | – |
| Mansell | 4 | 0 | 11 | 0 | | | | | | | | | |
| Van Ryneveld | 8 | 0 | 26 | 1 | | | | | | | | | |

Umpires: Harold Elliott and D. Davies.

# ENGLAND v SOUTH AFRICA 1951 (5th Test)

Played at Kennington Oval, London, on 16, 17, 18 August.
Toss: South Africa.   Result: ENGLAND won by four wickets.
Debuts: South Africa – W.R. Endean.

A close match on a pitch which took spin from the start brought England's first win at The Oval since 1938. It als
provided Test cricket with its only instance of a batsman dismissed for obstructing the field; there had been on
four previous instances in first-class cricket and none for 50 years. A ball from A.M.B. Rowan ballooned up fro
the bat or glove and Hutton, in fending it off his wicket with his bat, prevented Endean from making a catch

## SOUTH AFRICA

| | | | | |
|---|---|---|---|---|
| E.A.B. Rowan | c Hutton b Brown | 55 | lbw b Laker | 4 |
| W.R. Endean† | c Brown b Laker | 31 | lbw b Bedser | |
| C.B. van Ryneveld | st Brennan b Laker | 10 | lbw b Laker | |
| A.D. Nourse* | lbw b Brown | 4 | b Laker | |
| J.E. Cheetham | lbw b Laker | 0 | c Hutton b Tattersall | 1 |
| R.A. McLean | c May b Laker | 14 | c Lowson b Laker | |
| P.N.F. Mansell | b Tattersall | 8 | lbw b Laker | |
| A.M.B. Rowan | c Laker b Bedser | 41 | not out | 1 |
| G.W.A. Chubb | b Bedser | 10 | c Hutton b Bedser | |
| M.G. Melle | b Shackleton | 5 | b Laker | |
| C.N. McCarthy | not out | 4 | b Bedser | |
| Extras | (B 11, LB 8, NB 1) | 20 | (B 11, LB 7) | 1 |
| **Total** | | **202** | | 1 |

## ENGLAND

| | | | | |
|---|---|---|---|---|
| L. Hutton | lbw b A.M.B. Rowan | 28 | obstructing the field | 2 |
| F.A. Lowson | c Endean b Melle | 0 | c Van Ryneveld b A.M.B. Rowan | 3 |
| P.B.H. May | b Chubb | 33 | c E.A.B. Rowan b A.M.B. Rowan | |
| D.C.S. Compton | b McCarthy | 73 | c Van Ryneveld b Chubb | 1 |
| W. Watson | run out | 31 | c Endean b Chubb | 1 |
| F.R. Brown* | c Van Ryneveld b A.M.B. Rowan | 1 | lbw b Chubb | 4 |
| J.C. Laker | b Chubb | 6 | not out | 1 |
| D. Shackleton | c Van Ryneveld b Melle | 14 | not out | |
| A.V. Bedser | c Endean b Melle | 2 | | |
| D.V. Brennan† | lbw b Melle | 0 | | |
| R. Tattersall | not out | 0 | | |
| Extras | (LB 4, NB 2) | 6 | (B 5, LB 3, NB 1) | |
| **Total** | | **194** | (6 wickets) | 1 |

| ENGLAND | O | M | R | W | O | M | R | W |
|---|---|---|---|---|---|---|---|---|
| Bedser | 19·3 | 6 | 36 | 2 | 19·5 | 6 | 32 | 3 |
| Shackleton | 15 | 5 | 20 | 1 | 10 | 2 | 19 | 0 |
| Tattersall | 14 | 7 | 26 | 1 | 5 | 1 | 10 | 1 |
| Laker | 37 | 12 | 64 | 4 | 28 | 8 | 55 | 6 |
| Brown | 20 | 10 | 31 | 2 | 13 | 5 | 20 | 0 |
| Compton | 1 | 0 | 5 | 0 | | | | |
| **SOUTH AFRICA** | | | | | | | | |
| McCarthy | 17 | 0 | 45 | 1 | 7 | 0 | 17 | 0 |
| Melle | 10 | 6 | 9 | 4 | 3 | 0 | 8 | 0 |
| A.M.B. Rowan | 27 | 9 | 44 | 2 | 24·1 | 2 | 77 | 2 |
| Chubb | 30 | 5 | 70 | 2 | 28 | 10 | 53 | 3 |
| Van Ryneveld | 3 | 0 | 20 | 0 | | | | |

| FALL OF WICKETS | | | | |
|---|---|---|---|---|
| | SA | E | SA | E |
| Wkt | 1st | 1st | 2nd | 2n |
| 1st | 66 | 2 | 15 | 5 |
| 2nd | 106 | 51 | 35 | 5 |
| 3rd | 106 | 79 | 57 | 8 |
| 4th | 106 | 128 | 84 | 9 |
| 5th | 126 | 134 | 106 | 13 |
| 6th | 131 | 145 | 111 | 15 |
| 7th | 146 | 173 | 116 | – |
| 8th | 175 | 189 | 130 | – |
| 9th | 186 | 190 | 153 | – |
| 10th | 202 | 194 | 154 | – |

Umpires: F. Chester and D. Davies.

# INDIA v ENGLAND 1951–52 (1st Test)

Played at Feroz Shah Kotla, Delhi, on 2, 3, 4, 6, 7 November.
Toss: England.   Result: MATCH DRAWN.
Debuts: India – P.G. Joshi, P. Roy; England – D.B. Carr, N.D. Howard, D. Kenyon, F. Ridgway, R.T. Spooner.

An heroic rearguard action led by Watkins, who batted for nine hours, enabled England to draw a match which India should have won. Merchant and Hazare set a new India record for any wicket against England by adding 211 for the third wicket. Previously published scores of this match give Watkins 138 and Shackleton 20, but the official M.C.C. Scorebook confirms the second innings scores shown here.

## ENGLAND

| | | | | | |
|---|---|---|---|---|---|
| J.D.B. Robertson | lbw b Shinde | 50 | c Phadkar b Mankad | | 22 |
| F.A. Lowson | lbw b Phadkar | 4 | c Phadkar b Mankad | | 68 |
| D. Kenyon | b Shinde | 35 | c Roy b Shinde | | 6 |
| D.B. Carr | c Joshi b Shinde | 14 | (5) c Umrigar b Shinde | | 76 |
| A.J. Watkins | c Joshi b Mankad | 40 | (4) not out | | 137 |
| R.T. Spooner† | hit wkt b Shinde | 11 | b Mankad | | 1 |
| N.D. Howard* | st Joshi b Mankad | 13 | lbw b Mankad | | 9 |
| D. Shackleton | st Joshi b Mankad | 10 | not out | | 21 |
| J.B. Statham | b Shinde | 4 | | | |
| R. Tattersall | not out | 4 | | | |
| F. Ridgway | b Shinde | 15 | | | |
| Extras | (LB 3) | 3 | (B 18, LB 7, W 1, NB 2) | | 28 |
| **Total** | | **203** | (6 wickets) | | **368** |

## INDIA

| | | |
|---|---|---|
| V.M. Merchant | b Statham | 154 |
| P. Roy | lbw b Shackleton | 12 |
| P.R. Umrigar | run out | 21 |
| V.S. Hazare* | not out | 164 |
| D.G. Phadkar | run out | 3 |
| V.M.H. Mankad | c Spooner b Tattersall | 4 |
| R.S. Modi | lbw b Tattersall | 7 |
| H.R. Adhikari | not out | 38 |
| S.G. Shinde | ) | |
| P.G. Joshi† | ) did not bat | |
| N.R. Chowdhury | ) | |
| Extras | (B 12, LB 2, NB 1) | 15 |
| **Total** | (6 wickets declared) | **418** |

| INDIA | O | M | R | W | O | M | R | W | | FALL OF WICKETS | | |
|---|---|---|---|---|---|---|---|---|---|---|---|---|
| | | | | | | | | | | E | I | E |
| Phadkar | 11 | 4 | 26 | 1 | 14 | 3 | 28 | 0 | Wkt | 1st | 1st | 2nd |
| Chowdhury | 18 | 4 | 30 | 0 | 31 | 11 | 45 | 0 | 1st | 9 | 18 | 61 |
| Hazare | 5 | 5 | 0 | 0 | 12 | 4 | 24 | 0 | 2nd | 79 | 64 | 78 |
| Mankad | 33 | 15 | 53 | 3 | 76 | 47 | 58 | 4 | 3rd | 102 | 275 | 116 |
| Shinde | 35·3 | 9 | 91 | 6 | 73 | 26 | 162 | 2 | 4th | 111 | 278 | 274 |
| Umrigar | | | | | 6 | 1 | 8 | 0 | 5th | 153 | 292 | 275 |
| Modi | | | | | 5 | 1 | 14 | 0 | 6th | 161 | 328 | 309 |
| Roy | | | | | 4 | 3 | 1 | 0 | 7th | 175 | – | – |
| ENGLAND | | | | | | | | | 8th | 184 | – | – |
| Statham | 21 | 4 | 49 | 1 | | | | | 9th | 184 | – | – |
| Ridgway | 20 | 1 | 55 | 0 | | | | | 10th | 203 | – | – |
| Watkins | 31 | 7 | 60 | 0 | | | | | | | | |
| Shackleton | 29 | 7 | 76 | 1 | | | | | | | | |
| Tattersall | 53 | 17 | 95 | 2 | | | | | | | | |
| Carr | 16 | 4 | 56 | 0 | | | | | | | | |
| Robertson | 5 | 1 | 12 | 0 | | | | | | | | |

Umpires: M.G. Vijayasarathi and B.J. Mohoni.

# INDIA v ENGLAND 1951–52 (2nd Test)

Played at Brabourne Stadium, Bombay, on 14, 15, 16, 18, 19 December.
Toss: India.    Result: MATCH DRAWN.
Debuts: India – C.D. Gopinath, M.K. Mantri; England – E. Leadbeater.

Hazare scored his second consecutive Test hundred and took his aggregate against England to 325 before he was dismissed by a bowler. Edric Leadbeater, flown out as a replacement for A.E.G. Rhodes, played for England before being capped by his county; he played for Yorkshire and Warwickshire without winning a 1st XI cap.

## INDIA

| | | | | | |
|---|---|--:|---|---|--:|
| P. Roy | c Kenyon b Statham | 140 | | lbw b Ridgway | 0 |
| M.K. Mantri† | c Spooner b Statham | 39 | | c Spooner b Ridgway | 7 |
| P.R. Umrigar | lbw b Leadbeater | 8 | | c Watkins b Statham | 38 |
| V.S. Hazare* | run out | 155 | | c sub (C.J. Poole) b Watkins | 6 |
| L. Amarnath | c Howard b Tattersall | 32 | | c Howard b Watkins | 4 |
| C.T. Sarwate | b Tattersall | 18 | | run out | 16 |
| H.R. Adhikari | c Spooner b Tattersall | 25 | | c Howard b Tattersall | 15 |
| C.D. Gopinath | not out | 50 | | c Leadbeater b Tattersall | 42 |
| S.W. Sohoni | c Robertson b Statham | 6 | (10) | run out | 28 |
| V.M.H. Mankad | b Statham | 0 | (9) | b Watkins | 41 |
| S.G. Shinde | not out | 8 | | not out | 3 |
| Extras | (LB 4) | 4 | | (B 6, LB 2) | 8 |
| **Total** | (9 wickets declared) | **485** | | | **208** |

## ENGLAND

| | | | | | |
|---|---|--:|---|---|--:|
| F.A. Lowson | c Mantri b Sohoni | 5 | | c Sohoni b Gopinath | 22 |
| J.D.B. Robertson | c Amarnath b Mankad | 44 | | | |
| T.W. Graveney | c Adhikari b Shinde | 175 | | not out | 25 |
| R.T. Spooner† | lbw b Hazare | 46 | | not out | 5 |
| D. Kenyon | lbw b Amarnath | 21 | (2) | lbw b Sohoni | 2 |
| A.J. Watkins | c and b Mankad | 80 | | | |
| N.D. Howard* | c Umrigar b Mankad | 20 | | | |
| E. Leadbeater | lbw b Mankad | 2 | | | |
| J.B. Statham | c Mankad b Amarnath | 27 | | | |
| R. Tattersall | not out | 10 | | | |
| F. Ridgway | c and b Amarnath | 5 | | | |
| Extras | (B 10, LB 11) | 21 | | (LB 1) | 1 |
| **Total** | | **456** | | (2 wickets) | **55** |

| ENGLAND | O | M | R | W | O | M | R | W |
|---|--:|--:|--:|--:|--:|--:|--:|--:|
| Statham | 29 | 5 | 96 | 4 | 20 | 11 | 30 | 1 |
| Ridgway | 32 | 5 | 137 | 0 | 16 | 3 | 33 | 2 |
| Watkins | 32 | 2 | 97 | 0 | 13 | 4 | 20 | 3 |
| Leadbeater | 11 | 2 | 38 | 1 | 14·1 | 4 | 62 | 0 |
| Tattersall | 34 | 8 | 112 | 3 | 20 | 6 | 55 | 2 |
| Robertson | 1 | 0 | 1 | 0 | | | | |
| **INDIA** | | | | | | | | |
| Sohoni | 30 | 7 | 72 | 1 | 13 | 5 | 16 | 1 |
| Amarnath | 34·1 | 9 | 61 | 3 | 5 | 1 | 6 | 0 |
| Shinde | 53 | 13 | 151 | 1 | 5 | 0 | 11 | 0 |
| Mankad | 57 | 22 | 91 | 4 | 5 | 1 | 10 | 0 |
| Sarwate | 13 | 2 | 27 | 0 | | | | |
| Hazare | 17 | 5 | 30 | 1 | | | | |
| Umrigar | 3 | 1 | 3 | 0 | | | | |
| Gopinath | | | | | 8 | 2 | 11 | 1 |

### FALL OF WICKETS

| Wkt | I 1st | E 1st | I 2nd | E 2nd |
|---|--:|--:|--:|--:|
| 1st | 75 | 18 | 2 | 3 |
| 2nd | 99 | 79 | 13 | 43 |
| 3rd | 286 | 166 | 24 | – |
| 4th | 368 | 233 | 34 | – |
| 5th | 388 | 381 | 72 | – |
| 6th | 397 | 389 | 77 | – |
| 7th | 460 | 407 | 88 | – |
| 8th | 471 | 408 | 159 | – |
| 9th | 471 | 448 | 177 | – |
| 10th | – | 456 | 208 | – |

Umpires: J.R. Patel and M.M. Naidu.

# INDIA v ENGLAND 1951–52 (3rd Test)

Played at Eden Gardens, Calcutta, on 30, 31 December, 1, 3, 4 January.
Toss: England.   Result: MATCH DRAWN.
Debuts: India – R.V. Divecha, S.P. Gupte, V.L. Manjrekar; England – C.J. Poole.

An uninterrupted match occupying 27½ hours produced only 1,041 runs and, not surprisingly, a draw.

## ENGLAND

| Batsman | Dismissal | R | Dismissal 2 | R2 |
|---|---|---|---|---|
| J.D.B. Robertson | c Phadkar b Divecha | 13 | st Sen b Mankad | 22 |
| R.T. Spooner† | c Sen b Mankad | 71 | b Mankad | 92 |
| T.W. Graveney | c Amarnath b Divecha | 24 | c Sen b Divecha | 21 |
| A.J. Watkins | c Sen b Phadkar | 68 | b Divecha | 2 |
| D. Kenyon | c Manjrekar b Mankad | 3 | b Phadkar | 0 |
| C.J. Poole | c Divecha b Phadkar | 55 | not out | 69 |
| N.D. Howard* | c Amarnath b Mankad | 23 | not out | 20 |
| J.B. Statham | b Phadkar | 1 | | |
| E. Leadbeater | run out | 38 | | |
| F. Ridgway | st Sen b Mankad | 24 | | |
| R. Tattersall | not out | 5 | | |
| Extras | (B 4, LB 1, W 1, NB 11) | 17 | (B 13, LB 6, W 2, NB 5) | 26 |
| Total | | 342 | (5 wickets declared) | 252 |

## INDIA

| Batsman | Dismissal | R | Dismissal 2 | R2 |
|---|---|---|---|---|
| P. Roy | c Spooner b Ridgway | 42 | not out | 31 |
| V.M.H. Mankad | c Tattersall b Leadbeater | 59 | not out | 71 |
| P.R. Umrigar | c Howard b Ridgway | 10 | | |
| V.S. Hazare* | b Tattersall | 2 | | |
| L. Amarnath | b Tattersall | 0 | | |
| D.G. Phadkar | c Leadbeater b Ridgway | 115 | | |
| V.L. Manjrekar | b Tattersall | 48 | | |
| C.D. Gopinath | c Robertson b Ridgway | 19 | | |
| R.V. Divecha | c Watkins b Tattersall | 26 | | |
| S.P. Gupte | c Leadbeater b Statham | 0 | | |
| P. Sen† | not out | 7 | | |
| Extras | (B 3, LB 10, W 1, NB 2) | 16 | (B 1) | 1 |
| Total | | 344 | (0 wickets) | 103 |

| INDIA | O | M | R | W | O | M | R | W |
|---|---|---|---|---|---|---|---|---|
| Phadkar | 38 | 11 | 89 | 3 | 20 | 7 | 27 | 1 |
| Divecha | 33 | 9 | 60 | 2 | 25 | 7 | 55 | 2 |
| Amarnath | 20 | 5 | 35 | 0 | 22 | 5 | 43 | 0 |
| Mankad | 52·5 | 16 | 89 | 4 | 35 | 13 | 64 | 2 |
| Gupte | 13 | 0 | 43 | 0 | 5 | 0 | 14 | 0 |
| Hazare | 3 | 0 | 9 | 0 | 9 | 4 | 11 | 0 |
| Umrigar | | | | | 4 | 1 | 12 | 0 |

| ENGLAND | O | M | R | W | O | M | R | W |
|---|---|---|---|---|---|---|---|---|
| Statham | 27 | 10 | 46 | 1 | 4 | 0 | 8 | 0 |
| Ridgway | 38·1 | 10 | 83 | 4 | 2 | 1 | 8 | 0 |
| Tattersall | 48 | 13 | 104 | 4 | 4 | 2 | 4 | 0 |
| Leadbeater | 15 | 2 | 64 | 1 | 8 | 0 | 54 | 0 |
| Watkins | 21 | 9 | 31 | 0 | | | | |
| Poole | | | | | 5 | 1 | 9 | 0 |
| Robertson | | | | | 5 | 1 | 10 | 0 |
| Graveney | | | | | 1 | 0 | 9 | 0 |

FALL OF WICKETS

| Wkt | E 1st | I 1st | E 2nd | I 2nd |
|---|---|---|---|---|
| 1st | 22 | 72 | 52 | – |
| 2nd | 76 | 90 | 93 | – |
| 3rd | 133 | 93 | 99 | – |
| 4th | 139 | 93 | 102 | – |
| 5th | 246 | 144 | 184 | – |
| 6th | 247 | 220 | – | – |
| 7th | 259 | 272 | – | – |
| 8th | 290 | 320 | – | – |
| 9th | 332 | 327 | – | – |
| 10th | 342 | 344 | – | – |

Umpires: A.R. Joshi and B.J. Mohoni.

# INDIA v ENGLAND 1951–52 (4th Test)

Played at Green Park, Kanpur, on 12, 13, 14 January.
Toss: India. Result: ENGLAND won by eight wickets.
Debuts: Nil.

On a spinners' pitch, England gained a convincing win in only three days through Hilton and Tattersall, the latter taking three wickets with his first eight balls in the match.

## INDIA

| | | | | | |
|---|---|---|---|---|---|
| P. Roy | b Tattersall | 37 | c Ridgway b Hilton | 14 | |
| V.M.H. Mankad | b Tattersall | 19 | c Statham b Hilton | 7 | |
| P.R. Umrigar | b Tattersall | 0 | (5) c Spooner b Robertson | 36 | |
| V.S. Hazare* | c Ridgway b Tattersall | 0 | b Hilton | 0 | |
| D.G. Phadkar | b Tattersall | 8 | (6) lbw b Hilton | 2 | |
| H.R. Adhikari | b Hilton | 6 | (7) c Lowson b Tattersall | 60 | |
| V.L. Manjrekar | c Graveney b Hilton | 6 | (3) c Ridgway b Hilton | 20 | |
| C.S. Nayudu | st Spooner b Hilton | 21 | b Robertson | 0 | |
| P.G. Joshi† | b Tattersall | 4 | (10) run out | 0 | |
| S.G. Shinde | not out | 5 | (9) c Lowson b Tattersall | 14 | |
| Ghulam Ahmed | c Poole b Hilton | 6 | not out | 2 | |
| Extras | (B 8, LB 1) | 9 | (B 2) | 2 | |
| **Total** | | **121** | | **157** | |

## ENGLAND

| | | | | | |
|---|---|---|---|---|---|
| F.A. Lowson | hit wkt b Mankad | 26 | c Adhikari b Ghulam Ahmed | 12 | |
| R.T. Spooner† | b Shinde | 21 | b Mankad | 0 | |
| T.W. Graveney | b Mankad | 6 | not out | 48 | |
| J.D.B. Robertson | lbw b Mankad | 21 | not out | 5 | |
| A.J. Watkins | c Joshi b Ghulam Ahmed | 66 | | | |
| M.J. Hilton | st Joshi b Ghulam Ahmed | 10 | | | |
| C.J. Poole | b Ghulam Ahmed | 19 | | | |
| N.D. Howard* | b Mankad | 1 | | | |
| J.B. Statham | not out | 12 | | | |
| F. Ridgway | b Ghulam Ahmed | 5 | | | |
| R. Tattersall | st Joshi b Ghulam Ahmed | 2 | | | |
| Extras | (B 13, LB 1) | 14 | (B 11) | 11 | |
| **Total** | | **203** | (2 wickets) | **76** | |

| ENGLAND | O | M | R | W | O | M | R | W |
|---|---|---|---|---|---|---|---|---|
| Statham | 6 | 3 | 10 | 0 | | | | |
| Ridgway | 7 | 1 | 16 | 0 | | | | |
| Watkins | 5 | 3 | 6 | 0 | | | | |
| Hilton | 22·5 | 10 | 32 | 4 | 32 | 11 | 61 | 5 |
| Tattersall | 21 | 3 | 48 | 6 | 27·5 | 7 | 77 | 2 |
| Robertson | | | | | 7 | 1 | 17 | 2 |
| INDIA | | | | | | | | |
| Phadkar | 2 | 2 | 0 | 0 | 2 | 0 | 11 | 0 |
| Hazare | 2 | 0 | 5 | 0 | | | | |
| Ghulam Ahmed | 37·1 | 14 | 70 | 5 | 10 | 1 | 10 | 1 |
| Mankad | 35 | 13 | 54 | 4 | 7·2 | 0 | 44 | 1 |
| Shinde | 17 | 4 | 46 | 1 | | | | |
| Nayudu | 2 | 0 | 14 | 0 | | | | |

### FALL OF WICKETS

| | I | E | I | E |
|---|---|---|---|---|
| Wkt | 1st | 1st | 2nd | 2nd |
| 1st | 39 | 46 | 7 | 1 |
| 2nd | 39 | 57 | 37 | 57 |
| 3rd | 39 | 60 | 37 | – |
| 4th | 49 | 103 | 42 | – |
| 5th | 66 | 114 | 44 | – |
| 6th | 76 | 174 | 102 | – |
| 7th | 101 | 181 | 102 | – |
| 8th | 106 | 181 | 142 | – |
| 9th | 110 | 197 | 143 | – |
| 10th | 121 | 203 | 157 | – |

Umpires: J.R. Patel and M.G. Vijayasarathi.

# INDIA v ENGLAND 1951–52 (5th Test)

Played at Chepauk, Madras, on 6, 8, 9, 10 February.
Toss: England.   Result: INDIA won by an innings and 8 runs.
Debuts: Nil.

Playing their 25th official Test match, India gained an emphatic first victory. Mankad's figures of 8 for 55 remain the best by an Indian bowler against England. Because of the death of King George VI on 6 February, the following day was made the rest day.

## ENGLAND

| | | | | | |
|---|---|---|---|---|---|
| F.A. Lowson | b Phadkar | 1 | c Mankad b Phadkar | | 7 |
| R.T. Spooner† | c Phadkar b Hazare | 66 | lbw b Divecha | | 6 |
| T.W. Graveney | st Sen b Mankad | 39 | c Divecha b Ghulam Ahmed | | 25 |
| J.D.B. Robertson | c and b Mankad | 77 | lbw b Ghulam Ahmed | | 56 |
| A.J. Watkins | c Gopinath B Mankad | 9 | c and b Mankad | | 48 |
| C.J. Poole | b Mankad | 15 | c Divecha b Ghulam Ahmed | | 3 |
| D.B. Carr* | st Sen b Mankad | 40 | c Mankad b Ghulam Ahmed | | 5 |
| M.J. Hilton | st Sen b Mankad | 0 | st Sen b Mankad | | 15 |
| J.B. Statham | st Sen b Mankad | 6 | c Gopinath b Mankad | | 9 |
| F. Ridgway | lbw b Mankad | 0 | b Mankad | | 0 |
| R. Tattersall | not out | 2 | not out | | 0 |
| Extras | (B 4, LB 4, NB 3) | 11 | (B 7, LB 2) | | 9 |
| **Total** | | **266** | | | **183** |

## INDIA

| | | |
|---|---|---|
| Mushtaq Ali | st Spooner b Carr | 22 |
| P. Roy | c Watkins b Tattersall | 111 |
| V.S. Hazare* | b Hilton | 20 |
| V.M.H. Mankad | c Watkins b Carr | 22 |
| L. Amarnath | c Spooner b Statham | 31 |
| D.G. Phadkar | b Hilton | 61 |
| P.R. Umrigar | not out | 130 |
| C.D. Gopinath | b Tattersall | 35 |
| R.V. Divecha | c Spooner b Ridgway | 12 |
| P. Sen† | b Watkins | 2 |
| Ghulam Ahmed | not out | 1 |
| Extras | (B 8, LB 2) | 10 |
| **Total** | (9 wickets declared) | **457** |

| INDIA | O | M | R | W | O | M | R | W | FALL OF WICKETS | | | |
|---|---|---|---|---|---|---|---|---|---|---|---|---|
| Phadkar | 16 | 2 | 49 | 1 | 9 | 2 | 17 | 1 | | E | I | E |
| Divecha | 12 | 2 | 27 | 0 | 7 | 1 | 21 | 1 | Wkt | 1st | 1st | 2nd |
| Amarnath | 27 | 6 | 56 | 0 | 3 | 0 | 6 | 0 | 1st | 3 | 53 | 12 |
| Ghulam Ahmed | 18 | 5 | 53 | 0 | 26 | 6 | 77 | 4 | 2nd | 71 | 97 | 15 |
| Mankad | 38·5 | 15 | 55 | 8 | 30·5 | 9 | 53 | 4 | 3rd | 131 | 157 | 68 |
| Hazare | 10 | 5 | 15 | 1 | | | | | 4th | 174 | 191 | 117 |
| | | | | | | | | | 5th | 197 | 216 | 135 |
| ENGLAND | | | | | | | | | 6th | 244 | 320 | 159 |
| Statham | 19 | 3 | 54 | 1 | | | | | 7th | 252 | 413 | 159 |
| Ridgway | 17 | 2 | 47 | 1 | | | | | 8th | 261 | 430 | 178 |
| Tattersall | 39 | 13 | 94 | 2 | | | | | 9th | 261 | 448 | 178 |
| Hilton | 40 | 9 | 100 | 2 | | | | | 10th | 266 | – | 183 |
| Carr | 19 | 2 | 84 | 2 | | | | | | | | |
| Watkins | 14 | 1 | 50 | 1 | | | | | | | | |
| Robertson | 5 | 1 | 18 | 0 | | | | | | | | |

Umpires: B.J. Mohoni and M.G. Vijayasarathi.

# AUSTRALIA v WEST INDIES 1951–52 (1st Test)

Played at Woolloongabba, Brisbane, on 9, 10, 12, 13 November.
Toss: West Indies.   Result: AUSTRALIA won by three wickets.
Debuts: Australia – G.R.A. Langley; West Indies – R.E. Marshall.

Australia narrowly won an intriguing duel with Ramadhin and Valentine whom Goddard bowled for 129·7 overs out of 150·4 (86%) in the match.

## WEST INDIES

| | | | | | |
|---|---|---|---|---|---|
| A.F. Rae | b Lindwall | 0 | lbw b Johnson | | 25 |
| J.B. Stollmeyer | c Langley b Johnston | 8 | st Langley b Johnson | | 10 |
| F.M.M. Worrell | b Johnston | 37 | st Langley b Ring | | 20 |
| E. de C. Weekes | c Langley b Ring | 35 | c Hole b Johnston | | 70 |
| R.J. Christiani | c Ring b Lindwall | 22 | (6) b Ring | | 6 |
| C.L. Walcott† | lbw b Lindwall | 0 | (8) st Langley b Ring | | 4 |
| R.E. Marshall | b Johnson | 28 | (9) c Hassett b Miller | | 30 |
| G.E. Gomez | c Langley b Lindwall | 22 | (7) c Harvey b Ring | | 55 |
| J.D.C. Goddard* | b Miller | 45 | (5) c and b Ring | | 0 |
| S. Ramadhin | not out | 16 | not out | | 2 |
| A.L. Valentine | st Langley b Ring | 2 | c Morris b Ring | | 13 |
| Extras | (LB 1) | 1 | (B 8, LB 2) | | 10 |
| **Total** | | **216** | | | **245** |

## AUSTRALIA

| | | | | | |
|---|---|---|---|---|---|
| K.A. Archer | c Goddard b Valentine | 20 | b Gomez | | 4 |
| A.R. Morris | c Rae b Valentine | 33 | c Gomez b Ramadhin | | 48 |
| A.L. Hassett* | b Ramadhin | 6 | lbw b Ramadhin | | 35 |
| R.N. Harvey | lbw b Valentine | 18 | b Ramadhin | | 42 |
| K.R. Miller | c and b Valentine | 46 | b Valentine | | 4 |
| G.B. Hole | lbw b Valentine | 20 | not out | | 45 |
| R.R. Lindwall | b Gomez | 61 | b Ramadhin | | 29 |
| I.W. Johnson | not out | 16 | b Ramadhin | | 8 |
| D.T. Ring | c Walcott b Gomez | 0 | not out | | 6 |
| G.R.A. Langley† | lbw b Worrell | 0 | | | |
| W.A. Johnston | run out | 2 | | | |
| Extras | (B 4) | 4 | (B 3, LB 11, NB 1) | | 15 |
| **Total** | | **226** | (7 wickets) | | **236** |

| AUSTRALIA | O | M | R | W | O | M | R | W |
|---|---|---|---|---|---|---|---|---|
| Lindwall | 20 | 4 | 62 | 4 | 10 | 0 | 36 | 0 |
| Miller | 14 | 3 | 40 | 1 | 8 | 2 | 19 | 1 |
| Johnston | 17 | 2 | 49 | 2 | 16 | 4 | 41 | 1 |
| Ring | 14 | 2 | 52 | 2 | 16 | 2 | 80 | 6 |
| Johnson | 5 | 1 | 12 | 1 | 18 | 1 | 56 | 2 |
| Hole | | | | | 1 | 0 | 3 | 0 |
| WEST INDIES | | | | | | | | |
| Worrell | 8 | 0 | 38 | 1 | 2 | 1 | 2 | 0 |
| Gomez | 7·5 | 2 | 10 | 2 | 3 | 0 | 12 | 1 |
| Valentine | 25 | 4 | 99 | 5 | 40·7 | 6 | 117 | 1 |
| Ramadhin | 24 | 5 | 75 | 1 | 40 | 9 | 90 | 5 |

### FALL OF WICKETS

| Wkt | WI 1st | A 1st | WI 2nd | A 2nd |
|---|---|---|---|---|
| 1st | 0 | 30 | 23 | 8 |
| 2nd | 18 | 53 | 50 | 69 |
| 3rd | 63 | 80 | 88 | 126 |
| 4th | 92 | 85 | 88 | 143 |
| 5th | 95 | 129 | 96 | 149 |
| 6th | 112 | 188 | 153 | 203 |
| 7th | 150 | 215 | 184 | 225 |
| 8th | 170 | 215 | 229 | – |
| 9th | 207 | 216 | 230 | – |
| 10th | 216 | 226 | 245 | – |

Umpires: A.N. Barlow and H. Elphinston.

# AUSTRALIA v WEST INDIES 1951–52 (2nd Test)

Played at Sydney Cricket Ground on 30 November, 1, 3, 4, 5 December.
Toss: Australia.   Result: AUSTRALIA won by seven wickets.
Debuts: Nil.

Stollmeyer pulled a muscle fielding and batted with a runner in the second innings.

## WEST INDIES

| | | | | |
|---|---|---|---|---|
| A.F. Rae | c Johnson b Johnston | 17 | c Ring b Miller | 9 |
| J.B. Stollmeyer | c Johnson b Lindwall | 36 | b Johnson | 35 |
| F.M.M. Worrell | b Johnson | 64 | c Langley b Lindwall | 20 |
| E. de C. Weekes | b Lindwall | 5 | b Johnson | 56 |
| C.L. Walcott† | c Langley b Ring | 60 | st Langley b Johnson | 10 |
| R.J. Christiani | b Hole | 76 | c Hassett b Miller | 30 |
| G.E. Gomez | lbw b Johnston | 54 | c Miller b Lindwall | 41 |
| J.D.C. Goddard* | c Johnson b Johnston | 33 | not out | 57 |
| P.E. Jones | lbw b Lindwall | 1 | c Miller b Johnston | 7 |
| S. Ramadhin | b Lindwall | 0 | b Johnston | 3 |
| A.L. Valentine | not out | 0 | b Miller | 1 |
| Extras | (B 12, LB 3, NB 1) | 16 | (B 9, LB 12) | 21 |
| **Total** | | **362** | | **290** |

## AUSTRALIA

| | | | | |
|---|---|---|---|---|
| K.A. Archer | c Weekes b Gomez | 11 | lbw b Worrell | 47 |
| A.R. Morris | c Walcott b Jones | 11 | st Walcott b Ramadhin | 30 |
| A.L. Hassett† | c Christiani b Jones | 132 | not out | 46 |
| R.N. Harvey | c Gomez b Goddard | 39 | lbw b Worrell | 1 |
| K.R. Miller | b Valentine | 129 | not out | 6 |
| G.B. Hole | b Valentine | 1 | | |
| R.R. Lindwall | run out | 48 | | |
| I.W. Johnson | c Walcott b Jones | 5 | | |
| D.T. Ring | c Ramadhin b Valentine | 65 | | |
| G.R.A. Langley† | not out | 15 | | |
| W.A. Johnston | b Valentine | 28 | | |
| Extras | (B 12, LB 18, NB 3) | 33 | (B 6, LB 1) | 7 |
| **Total** | | **517** | (3 wickets) | **137** |

| AUSTRALIA | O | M | R | W | O | M | R | W |
|---|---|---|---|---|---|---|---|---|
| Lindwall | 26 | 2 | 66 | 4 | 17 | 3 | 59 | 2 |
| Johnston | 25·4 | 2 | 80 | 3 | 24 | 5 | 61 | 2 |
| Johnson | 14 | 3 | 48 | 1 | 23 | 2 | 78 | 3 |
| Miller | 21 | 3 | 72 | 1 | 13·2 | 2 | 50 | 3 |
| Ring | 17 | 1 | 71 | 1 | 7 | 0 | 21 | 0 |
| Hole | 4 | 1 | 9 | 1 | | | | |
| WEST INDIES | | | | | | | | |
| Jones | 27 | 5 | 68 | 3 | 5 | 1 | 16 | 0 |
| Gomez | 18 | 2 | 47 | 1 | 5 | 1 | 9 | 0 |
| Worrell | 11 | 0 | 60 | 0 | 2 | 0 | 7 | 2 |
| Valentine | 30·5 | 3 | 111 | 4 | 10 | 0 | 45 | 0 |
| Ramadhin | 41 | 7 | 143 | 0 | 12·3 | 1 | 53 | 1 |
| Goddard | 24 | 6 | 55 | 1 | | | | |

FALL OF WICKETS

| Wkt | WI 1st | A 1st | WI 2nd | A 2nd |
|---|---|---|---|---|
| 1st | 33 | 19 | 19 | 49 |
| 2nd | 85 | 27 | 52 | 123 |
| 3rd | 99 | 106 | 102 | 125 |
| 4th | 139 | 341 | 130 | – |
| 5th | 219 | 345 | 141 | – |
| 6th | 286 | 348 | 210 | – |
| 7th | 359 | 372 | 230 | – |
| 8th | 360 | 457 | 246 | – |
| 9th | 360 | 485 | 268 | – |
| 10th | 362 | 517 | 290 | – |

Umpires: A.N. Barlow and H. Elphinston.

# AUSTRALIA v WEST INDIES 1951–52 (3rd Test)

Played at Adelaide Oval on 22, 24, 25 December.
Toss: Australia.   Result: WEST INDIES won by six wickets.
Debuts: West Indies – S.C. Guillen.

Australia, who won the toss and decided to bat on a rain-affected pitch, were dismissed for what is still their lowest total against West Indies. This was the first Test to include play on Christmas Day. Marshall pulled a muscle while fielding and batted with Rae as his runner in the second innings.

## AUSTRALIA

| | | | | |
|---|---|---|---|---|
| J.W. Burke | c Stollmeyer b Worrell | 3 | (9) b Valentine | 15 |
| A.R. Morris* | b Worrell | 1 | (5) b Valentine | 45 |
| R.N. Harvey | c Guillen b Gomez | 10 | (6) c Guillen b Ramadhin | 9 |
| K.R. Miller | c Ramadhin b Worrell | 4 | (7) lbw b Gomez | 35 |
| G.B. Hole | c Worrell b Goddard | 23 | (8) c Weekes b Gomez | 25 |
| R.R. Lindwall | b Worrell | 2 | (10) not out | 8 |
| I.W. Johnson | c Stollmeyer b Worrell | 11 | (1) c Marshall b Valentine | 16 |
| D.T. Ring | c Christiani b Goddard | 5 | (4) run out | 67 |
| G.R.A. Langley† | b Worrell | 5 | (2) b Valentine | 23 |
| G. Noblet | b Goddard | 8 | (3) c Weekes b Valentine | 0 |
| W.A. Johnston | not out | 7 | lbw b Valentine | 0 |
| Extras | (LB 3) | 3 | (B 8, LB 4) | 12 |
| **Total** | | **82** | | **255** |

## WEST INDIES

| | | | | |
|---|---|---|---|---|
| R.E. Marshall | c Burke b Johnston | 14 | c Langley b Ring | 29 |
| J.B. Stollmeyer | b Johnston | 17 | c Miller b Ring | 47 |
| J.D.C. Goddard* | c Langley b Lindwall | 0 | | |
| F.M.M. Worrell | b Miller | 6 | (3) c Noblet b Johnston | 28 |
| E. de C. Weekes | b Johnston | 26 | (4) c and b Ring | 29 |
| G.E. Gomez | c Langley b Johnston | 4 | (5) not out | 46 |
| R.J. Christiani | c Miller b Johnston | 4 | (6) not out | 42 |
| S.C. Guillen† | b Noblet | 9 | | |
| D. St E. Atkinson | c Burke b Johnston | 15 | | |
| S. Ramadhin | not out | 5 | | |
| A.L. Valentine | b Noblet | 0 | | |
| Extras | (LB 5) | 5 | (B 6, LB 5, W 1) | 12 |
| **Total** | | **105** | (4 wickets) | **233** |

| WEST INDIES | O | M | R | W | O | M | R | W |
|---|---|---|---|---|---|---|---|---|
| Gomez | 5 | 3 | 5 | 1 | 7 | 2 | 17 | 2 |
| Worrell | 12·7 | 3 | 38 | 6 | 9 | 2 | 29 | 0 |
| Goddard | 8 | 1 | 36 | 3 | 1 | 0 | 7 | 0 |
| Valentine | | | | | 27·5 | 6 | 102 | 6 |
| Ramadhin | | | | | 25 | 4 | 76 | 1 |
| Marshall | | | | | 5 | 1 | 12 | 0 |
| AUSTRALIA | | | | | | | | |
| Lindwall | 4 | 0 | 18 | 1 | 13 | 1 | 40 | 0 |
| Johnston | 12 | 0 | 62 | 6 | 19 | 4 | 50 | 1 |
| Miller | 5 | 1 | 13 | 1 | 5 | 0 | 12 | 0 |
| Noblet | 3·5 | 0 | 7 | 2 | 13 | 1 | 30 | 0 |
| Ring | | | | | 16·5 | 3 | 62 | 3 |
| Johnson | | | | | 7 | 1 | 27 | 0 |

| | FALL OF WICKETS | | | |
|---|---|---|---|---|
| | A | WI | A | WI |
| *Wkt* | *1st* | *1st* | *2nd* | *2nd* |
| 1st | 4 | 25 | 16 | 72 |
| 2nd | 5 | 26 | 20 | 85 |
| 3rd | 15 | 34 | 81 | 141 |
| 4th | 39 | 44 | 148 | 141 |
| 5th | 41 | 51 | 162 | – |
| 6th | 43 | 55 | 172 | – |
| 7th | 58 | 85 | 227 | – |
| 8th | 62 | 87 | 240 | – |
| 9th | 72 | 101 | 255 | – |
| 10th | 82 | 105 | 255 | – |

Umpires: M.J. McInnes and R. Wright.

# AUSTRALIA v WEST INDIES 1951–52 (4th Test)

Played at Melbourne Cricket Ground on 31 December, 1, 2, 3 January.
Toss: West Indies.   Result: AUSTRALIA won by one wicket.
Debuts: Nil.

Australia's last-wicket pair, Ring and Johnston, scored 38 together to record the fifth – and last – one-wicket win in a Test match.

## WEST INDIES

| | | | | | |
|---|---|---|---|---|---|
| K.R. Rickards | b Miller | 15 | (4) lbw b Johnston | | 22 |
| J.B. Stollmeyer | c Langley b Miller | 7 | lbw b Miller | | 54 |
| F.M.M. Worrell | b Lindwall | 108 | (8) b Johnston | | 30 |
| E. de C. Weekes | c Johnson b Johnston | 1 | (5) lbw b Johnson | | 2 |
| G.E. Gomez | c Langley b Miller | 37 | (7) b Johnston | | 52 |
| R.J. Christiani | run out | 37 | b miller | | 33 |
| J.D.C. Goddard* | b Miller | 21 | (3) lbw b Lindwall | | 0 |
| S.C. Gullen† | not out | 22 | (1) c Johnston b Lindwall | | 0 |
| J. Trim | run out | 0 | run out | | 0 |
| S. Ramadhin | c Langley b Johnston | 1 | run out | | 0 |
| A.L. Valentine | c Lindwall b Miller | 14 | not out | | 1 |
| Extras | (B 2, LB 6, W 1) | 9 | (B 4, LB 5) | | 9 |
| **Total** | | **272** | | | **203** |

## AUSTRALIA

| | | | | | |
|---|---|---|---|---|---|
| J. Moroney | lbw b Ramadhin | 26 | lbw b Ramadin | | 5 |
| A.R. Morris | b Trim | 6 | lbw b Valentine | | 12 |
| A.L. Hassett* | run out | 15 | lbw b Valentine | | 102 |
| R.N. Harvey | c and b Ramadhin | 83 | b Valentine | | 33 |
| K.R. Miller | b Trim | 47 | hit wkt b Valentine | | 2 |
| G.B. Hole | b Valentine | 2 | c Gomez b Worrell | | 13 |
| R.R. Lindwall | lbw b Trim | 13 | c Guillen b Ramadhin | | 29 |
| I.W. Johnson | c Guillen b Trim | 1 | c Guillen b Ramadhin | | 6 |
| D.T. Ring | b Trim | 6 | not out | | 32 |
| G.R.A. Langley† | not out | 0 | lbw b Valentine | | 1 |
| W.A. Johnston | b Gomez | 1 | not out | | 7 |
| Extras | (B 12, LB 4) | 16 | (B 14, LB 4) | | 18 |
| **Total** | | **216** | (9 wickets) | | **260** |

| AUSTRALIA | O | M | R | W | O | M | R | W |
|---|---|---|---|---|---|---|---|---|
| Lindwall | 18 | 2 | 72 | 1 | 17 | 2 | 59 | 2 |
| Miller | 19·3 | 1 | 60 | 5 | 16 | 1 | 49 | 2 |
| Johnston | 20 | 1 | 59 | 2 | 14·3 | 2 | 51 | 3 |
| Ring | 9 | 0 | 43 | 0 | 7 | 1 | 17 | 0 |
| Johnson | 7 | 0 | 23 | 0 | 5 | 0 | 18 | 1 |
| Hole | 2 | 0 | 6 | 0 | | | | |
| WEST INDIES | | | | | | | | |
| Trim | 12 | 2 | 34 | 5 | 10 | 3 | 25 | 0 |
| Gomez | 13·3 | 7 | 25 | 1 | 9 | 1 | 18 | 0 |
| Valentine | 23 | 8 | 50 | 1 | 30 | 9 | 88 | 5 |
| Ramadhin | 17 | 4 | 63 | 2 | 39 | 15 | 93 | 3 |
| Goddard | 8 | 0 | 28 | 0 | | | | |
| Worrell | | | | | 9 | 1 | 18 | 1 |

### FALL OF WICKETS

| | WI | A | WI | A |
|---|---|---|---|---|
| Wkt | 1st | 1st | 2nd | 2nd |
| 1st | 16 | 17 | 0 | 27 |
| 2nd | 29 | 48 | 0 | 93 |
| 3rd | 30 | 49 | 53 | 106 |
| 4th | 102 | 173 | 60 | 109 |
| 5th | 194 | 176 | 97 | 147 |
| 6th | 221 | 208 | 128 | 192 |
| 7th | 237 | 209 | 190 | 218 |
| 8th | 242 | 210 | 194 | 218 |
| 9th | 248 | 215 | 194 | 222 |
| 10th | 272 | 216 | 203 | – |

Umpires: M.J. McInnes and R. Wright.

# AUSTRALIA v WEST INDIES 1951–52 (5th Test)

Played at Sydney Cricket Ground on 25, 26, 28, 29 January.
Toss: Australia.   Result: AUSTRALIA won by 202 runs.
Debuts: Australia – R. Benaud, C.C. McDonald, G.R. Thoms.

On a perfect pitch and with the temperature 105 degrees in the shade, 19 wickets fell for 180 runs on the first day West Indies were dismissed for what is still their lowest total against Australia.

## AUSTRALIA

| | | | | |
|---|---|---|---|---|
| C.C. McDonald | c Worrell b Gomez | 32 | b Ramadhin | 62 |
| G.R. Thoms | b Gomez | 16 | hit wkt b Worrell | 28 |
| A.L. Hassett* | c Guliien b Gomez | 2 | c Worrell b Valentine | 64 |
| R.N. Harvey | b Gomez | 18 | c Guillen b Worrell | 8 |
| K.R. Miller | c Rae b Worrell | 20 | c Weekes b Valentine | 69 |
| G.B. Hole | c Gullen b Worrell | 1 | b Worrell | 62 |
| R. Benaud | c Stollmeyer b Gomez | 3 | c sub (K.R. Rickards) b Worrell | 19 |
| R.R. Lindwall | c Worrell b Gomez | 0 | c Walcott b Gomez | 21 |
| D.T. Ring | c Atkinson b Gomez | 4 | b Gomez | 12 |
| G.R.A. Langley† | c Weekes b Worrell | 6 | b Gomez | 8 |
| W.A. Johnston | not out | 13 | not out | |
| Extras | (LB 1) | 1 | (B 10, LB 8) | 18 |
| **Total** | | **116** | | **377** |

## WEST INDIES

| | | | | |
|---|---|---|---|---|
| A.F. Rae | c Langley b Johnston | 11 | c Harvey b Ring | 25 |
| J.B. Stollmeyer* | lbw b Johnston | 10 | lbw b Lindwall | 104 |
| C.L. Walcott | b Lindwall | 1 | c Langley b Miller | 12 |
| E. de C. Weekes | c Langley b Lindwall | 0 | c Langley b Lindwall | 21 |
| R.J. Christiani | c and b Miller | 7 | (6) c Johnston b Lindwall | 4 |
| F.M.M. Worrell | b Miller | 6 | (5) run out | 18 |
| G.E. Gomez | b Miller | 11 | b Miller | |
| D. St E. Atkinson | b Miller | 6 | hit wkt b Lindwall | |
| S.C. Guillen† | not out | 13 | b Lindwall | 0 |
| S. Ramadhin | b Johnston | 0 | not out | |
| A.L. Valentine | c Langley b Miller | 6 | b Benaud | 0 |
| Extras | (B 3, LB 3, W 1) | 7 | (B 4, LB 11, W 1) | 16 |
| **Total** | | **78** | | **213** |

| AUSTRALIA | O | M | R | W | O | M | R | W | | | | | |
|---|---|---|---|---|---|---|---|---|---|---|---|---|---|
| WEST INDIES | | | | | | | | | FALL OF WICKETS | | | | |
| Worrell | 12·2 | 1 | 42 | 3 | 23 | 2 | 95 | 4 | | A | WI | A | WI |
| Gomez | 18 | 3 | 55 | 7 | 18·2 | 3 | 58 | 3 | *Wkt* | *1st* | *1st* | *2nd* | *2nd* |
| Atkinson | 6 | 2 | 18 | 0 | 8 | 0 | 25 | 0 | 1st | 39 | 17 | 55 | 48 |
| Ramadhin | | | | | 34 | 8 | 102 | 1 | 2nd | 49 | 18 | 138 | 83 |
| Valentine | | | | | 30 | 6 | 79 | 2 | 3rd | 54 | 18 | 152 | 147 |
| | | | | | | | | | 4th | 77 | 34 | 216 | 191 |
| AUSTRALIA | | | | | | | | | 5th | 78 | 34 | 287 | 192 |
| Lindwall | 8 | 1 | 20 | 2 | 21 | 4 | 52 | 5 | 6th | 91 | 51 | 326 | 194 |
| Johnston | 14 | 3 | 25 | 3 | 10 | 2 | 30 | 0 | 7th | 91 | 56 | 347 | 200 |
| Miller | 7·6 | 1 | 26 | 5 | 19 | 2 | 57 | 2 | 8th | 97 | 59 | 353 | 205 |
| Ring | | | | | 13 | 1 | 44 | 1 | 9th | 99 | 60 | 370 | 212 |
| Benaud | | | | | 4·3 | 0 | 14 | 1 | 10th | 116 | 78 | 377 | 213 |

Umpires: H. Elphinston and M.J. McInnes.

# NEW ZEALAND v WEST INDIES 1951–52 (1st Test)

Played at Lancaster Park, Christchurch, on 8, 9, 11, 12 February.
Toss: New Zealand.   Result: WEST INDIES won by five wickets.
Debuts: New Zealand – D.D. Beard, R.W.G. Emery.

The initial meeting between these two sides brought a record Christchurch crowd of 18,000 on the second day.
Guillen, who later played Test cricket for New Zealand, made the highest score of his first-class career to date.

## NEW ZEALAND

| | | | | |
|---|---|--:|---|--:|
| R.W.G. Emery | lbw b Gomez | 5 | c Stollmeyer b Valentine | 28 |
| G.O. Rabone | c Christiani b Ramadhin | 37 | lbw b Goddard | 18 |
| V.J. Scott | lbw b Ramadhin | 45 | b Ramadhin | 29 |
| B. Sutcliffe* | c Stollmeyer b Ramadhin | 45 | (5) b Ramadhin | 36 |
| J.R. Reid | b Ramadhin | 0 | (4) b Valentine | 3 |
| F.B. Smith | c Weekes b Valentine | 9 | b Gomez | 37 |
| F.L.H. Mooney† | not out | 34 | lbw b Gomez | 1 |
| T.B. Burtt | c Christiani b Valentine | 1 | (10) not out | 9 |
| A.M. Moir | c Worrell b Valentine | 15 | lbw b Ramadhin | 5 |
| D.D. Beard | run out | 28 | (8) c Christiani b Worrell | 10 |
| J.A. Hayes | st Guillen b Ramadhin | 1 | b Ramadhin | 2 |
| Extras | (B 15, LB 1) | 16 | (B 10, W 1) | 11 |
| **Total** | | **236** | | **189** |

## WEST INDIES

| | | | | |
|---|---|--:|---|--:|
| J.B. Stollmeyer | c Sutcliffe b Burtt | 23 | c Reid b Beard | 13 |
| R.E. Marshall | c Reid b Moir | 16 | c sub (E.W. Dempster) b Burtt | 26 |
| F.M.M. Worrell | b Hayes | 71 | not out | 62 |
| E. de C. Weekes | b Burtt | 7 | (5) b Moir | 2 |
| C.L. Walcott | b Hayes | 65 | (4) lbw b Burtt | 19 |
| R.J. Christiani | c Scott b Beard | 3 | c Mooney b Hayes | 3 |
| J.D.C. Goddard* | c Reid b Burtt | 26 | | |
| G.E. Gomez | c Mooney b Hayes | 0 | (7) not out | 14 |
| S.C. Guillen† | c and b Burtt | 54 | | |
| S. Ramadhin | b Burtt | 10 | | |
| A.L. Valentine | not out | 0 | | |
| Extras | (B 2, LB 4, NB 6) | 12 | (NB 3) | 3 |
| **Total** | | **287** | (5 wickets) | **142** |

| WEST INDIES | O | M | R | W | O | M | R | W | | FALL OF WICKETS | | | |
|---|--:|--:|--:|--:|--:|--:|--:|--:|---|---|---|---|---|
| Gomez | 28 | 12 | 47 | 1 | 12 | 3 | 25 | 2 | | NZ | WI | NZ | WI |
| Worrell | 11 | 3 | 25 | 0 | 15 | 6 | 24 | 1 | *Wkt* | *1st* | *1st* | *2nd* | *2nd* |
| Ramadhin | 36·4 | 11 | 86 | 5 | 38·2 | 21 | 39 | 4 | 1st | 5 | 42 | 44 | 28 |
| Valentine | 38 | 15 | 51 | 3 | 41 | 19 | 73 | 2 | 2nd | 91 | 42 | 46 | 48 |
| Goddard | 4 | 1 | 8 | 0 | 8 | 3 | 17 | 1 | 3rd | 102 | 57 | 49 | 86 |
| Marshall | 2 | 1 | 3 | 0 | | | | | 4th | 102 | 186 | 118 | 91 |
| | | | | | | | | | 5th | 115 | 189 | 119 | 99 |
| **NEW ZEALAND** | | | | | | | | | 6th | 153 | 189 | 148 | – |
| Hayes | 12 | 2 | 52 | 3 | 12 | 2 | 28 | 1 | 7th | 162 | 189 | 172 | – |
| Reid | 9 | 2 | 25 | 0 | | | | | 8th | 181 | 240 | 172 | – |
| Burtt | 29·2 | 7 | 69 | 5 | 16 | 3 | 37 | 2 | 9th | 231 | 278 | 187 | – |
| Moir | 20 | 1 | 70 | 1 | 18 | 4 | 49 | 1 | 10th | 236 | 287 | 189 | – |
| Rabone | 6 | 1 | 17 | 0 | | | | | | | | | |
| Beard | 21 | 5 | 42 | 1 | 13 | 4 | 25 | 1 | | | | | |

Umpires: M.F. Pengelly and B. Vine.

# NEW ZEALAND v WEST INDIES 1951–52 (2nd Test)

Played at Eden Park, Auckland, on 15, 16, 18, 19 (*no play*) February.
Toss: New Zealand. Result: MATCH DRAWN.
Debuts: New Zealand – J.G. Leggat.

After being put in to bat, West Indies recorded what is still their highest score in New Zealand. Moir made a memorably sporting gesture on the first morning. Rae (9*) fell while backing up but Moir, who was bowling and had had the ball returned to him, allowed the batsman to regain his crease.

## WEST INDIES

| | | |
|---|---|---|
| J.B. Stollmeyer | st Mooney b Beard | 152 |
| A.F. Rae | b Burtt | 99 |
| R.E. Marshall | b Beard | 0 |
| E. de C. Weekes | c Reid b Hayes | 51 |
| F.M.M. Worrell | c Sutcliffe b Emery | 100 |
| C.L. Walcott | lbw b Emery | 115 |
| D. St E. Atkinson | not out | 8 |
| J.D.C. Goddard* | ) | |
| S.C. Guillen† | ) did not bat | |
| S. Ramadhin | ) | |
| A.L. Valentine | ) | |
| Extras | (B 6, LB 10, NB 5) | 21 |
| **Total** | (6 wickets declared) | **546** |

## NEW ZEALAND

| | | | | |
|---|---|---|---|---|
| J.G. Leggat | b Worrell | 0 | not out | 6 |
| R.W.G. Emery | c Guillen b Atkinson | 5 | c Walcott b Atkinson | 8 |
| V.J. Scott | c Stollmeyer b Valentine | 84 | | |
| B. Sutcliffe* | c Worrell b Ramadhin | 20 | (3) not out | 2 |
| J.R. Reid | st Guillen b Valentine | 6 | | |
| G.O. Rabone | b Stollmeyer | 9 | | |
| F.L.H. Mooney† | c Walcott b Stollmeyer | 6 | | |
| A.M. Moir | b Ramadhin | 20 | | |
| T.B. Burtt | c Goddard b Valentine | 1 | | |
| D.D. Beard | c Weekes b Ramadhin | 4 | | |
| J.A. Hayes | not out | 0 | | |
| Extras | (B 4, LB 1) | 5 | (LB 1) | 1 |
| **Total** | | **160** | (1 wicket) | **17** |

| NEW ZEALAND | O | M | R | W | O | M | R | W | | FALL OF WICKETS | | |
|---|---|---|---|---|---|---|---|---|---|---|---|---|
| | | | | | | | | | | WI | NZ | NZ |
| Hayes | 31 | 4 | 106 | 1 | | | | | *Wkt* | *1st* | *1st* | *2nd* |
| Beard | 41 | 9 | 96 | 2 | | | | | 1st | 197 | 0 | 14 |
| Reid | 14 | 4 | 33 | 0 | | | | | 2nd | 202 | 12 | – |
| Burtt | 36 | 4 | 120 | 1 | | | | | 3rd | 317 | 50 | – |
| Moir | 16 | 2 | 69 | 0 | | | | | 4th | 321 | 61 | – |
| Rabone | 15 | 1 | 48 | 0 | | | | | 5th | 510 | 93 | – |
| Emery | 7·4 | 0 | 52 | 2 | | | | | 6th | 546 | 101 | – |
| Sutcliffe | 1 | 0 | 1 | 0 | | | | | 7th | – | 155 | – |
| | | | | | | | | | 8th | – | 155 | – |
| WEST INDIES | | | | | | | | | 9th | – | 160 | – |
| Worrell | 12 | 3 | 20 | 1 | 9 | 3 | 12 | 0 | 10th | – | 160 | – |
| Atkinson | 18 | 3 | 42 | 1 | 8 | 5 | 4 | 1 | | | | |
| Valentine | 34·4 | 21 | 29 | 3 | | | | | | | | |
| Ramadhin | 25 | 12 | 41 | 3 | | | | | | | | |
| Stollmeyer | 6 | 1 | 12 | 2 | | | | | | | | |
| Goddard | 2 | 0 | 11 | 0 | | | | | | | | |

Umpires: T.M. Pearce and J.C. Harris.

# ENGLAND v INDIA 1952 (1st Test)

Played at Headingley, Leeds, on 5, 6, 7, 9, June.
Toss: India.   Result: ENGLAND won by seven wickets.
Debuts: England – F.S. Trueman; India – D.K. Gaekwad, G.S. Ramchand.

The England selectors broke with amateur tradition by appointing Hutton as captain. Hazare and Manjrekar (whose hundred was his first in first-class cricket) shared a partnership of 222 which is still India's highest in all Tests for the fourth wicket. India made Test history by losing four wickets for no runs to the first 14 balls of the second innings, three of them in eight balls from Trueman.

## INDIA

| | | | | | |
|---|---|---|---|---|---|
| P. Roy | st Evans b Jenkins | 19 | | c Compton b Trueman | 0 |
| D.K. Gaekwad | b Bedser | 9 | | c Laker b Bedser | 0 |
| P.R. Umrigar | c Evans b Trueman | 8 | (4) | c and b Jenkins | 9 |
| V.S. Hazare* | c Evans b Bedser | 89 | (6) | b Trueman | 56 |
| V.L. Manjrekar | c Watkins b Trueman | 133 | | b Trueman | 0 |
| D.G. Phadkar | c Watkins b Laker | 12 | (7) | b Bedser | 64 |
| C.D. Gopinath | b Trueman | 0 | (8) | lbw b Jenkins | 8 |
| M.K. Mantri† | not out | 13 | (3) | b Trueman | 0 |
| G.S. Ramchand | c Watkins b Laker | 0 | | st Evans b Jenkins | 0 |
| S.G. Shinde | c May b Laker | 2 | | not out | 7 |
| Ghulam Ahmed | b Laker | 0 | | st Evans b Jenkins | 14 |
| Extras | (B 1, LB 7) | 8 | | (LB 5, W 1, NB 1) | 7 |
| **Total** | | **293** | | | **165** |

## ENGLAND

| | | | | | |
|---|---|---|---|---|---|
| L. Hutton* | c Ramchand b Ghulam Ahmed | 10 | | b Phadkar | 10 |
| R.T. Simpson | c Ramchand b Ghulam Ahmed | 23 | | c Mantri b Ghulam Ahmed | 51 |
| P.B.H. May | b Shinde | 16 | | c Phadkar b Ghulam Ahmed | 4 |
| D.C.S. Compton | c Ramchand b Ghulam Ahmed | 14 | | not out | 35 |
| T.W. Graveney | b Ghulam Ahmed | 71 | | not out | 20 |
| A.J. Watkins | lbw b Ghulam Ahmed | 48 | | | |
| T.G. Evans† | lbw b Hazare | 66 | | | |
| R.O. Jenkins | c Mantri b Ramchand | 38 | | | |
| J.C. Laker | b Phadkar | 15 | | | |
| A.V. Bedser | b Ramchand | 7 | | | |
| F.S. Trueman | not out | 0 | | | |
| Extras | (B 15, LB 11) | 26 | | (B 4, LB 3, NB 1) | 8 |
| **Total** | | **334** | | **(3 wickets)** | **128** |

| ENGLAND | O | M | R | W | O | M | R | W | | FALL OF WICKETS | | | |
|---|---|---|---|---|---|---|---|---|---|---|---|---|---|
| Bedser | 33 | 13 | 38 | 2 | 21 | 9 | 32 | 2 | | I | E | I | E |
| Trueman | 26 | 6 | 89 | 3 | 9 | 1 | 27 | 4 | *Wkt* | *1st* | *1st* | *2nd* | *2nd* |
| Laker | 22·3 | 9 | 39 | 4 | 13 | 4 | 17 | 0 | 1st | 18 | 21 | 0 | 16 |
| Watkins | 11 | 1 | 21 | 0 | 11 | 2 | 32 | 0 | 2nd | 40 | 48 | 0 | 42 |
| Jenkins | 27 | 6 | 78 | 1 | 13 | 2 | 50 | 4 | 3rd | 42 | 62 | 0 | 89 |
| Compton | 7 | 1 | 20 | 0 | | | | | 4th | 264 | 92 | 0 | – |
| | | | | | | | | | 5th | 264 | 182 | 26 | – |
| INDIA | | | | | | | | | 6th | 264 | 211 | 131 | – |
| Phadkar | 24 | 7 | 54 | 1 | 11 | 2 | 21 | 1 | 7th | 291 | 290 | 143 | – |
| Ramchand | 36·2 | 11 | 61 | 2 | 17 | 3 | 43 | 0 | 8th | 291 | 325 | 143 | – |
| Ghulam Ahmed | 63 | 24 | 100 | 5 | 22 | 8 | 37 | 2 | 9th | 293 | 329 | 143 | – |
| Hazare | 20 | 9 | 22 | 1 | 3 | 0 | 11 | 0 | 10th | 293 | 334 | 165 | – |
| Shinde | 22 | 5 | 71 | 1 | 2 | 0 | 8 | 0 | | | | | |

Umpires: H.G. Baldwin and Harold Elliott.

# ENGLAND v INDIA 1952 (2nd Test)

Played at Lord's, London, on 19, 20, 21, 23, 24 June.
Toss: India.    Result: ENGLAND won by eight wickets.
Debuts: Nil.

Evans became the first England wicket-keeper to make a hundred dismissals when he stumped Shinde, and he narrowly missed scoring a century before lunch, being 98* at the interval on the third day. Mankad's 184 remains the highest innings for India in England; he scored 256 runs and bowled 97 overs in the match. His partnership of 211 with Hazare equalled India's third-wicket record against England.

## INDIA

| | | | | |
|---|---|---|---|---|
| V.M.H. Mankad | c Watkins b Trueman | 72 | b Laker | 184 |
| P. Roy | c and b Bedser | 35 | b Bedser | 0 |
| P.R. Umrigar | b Trueman | 5 | (7) b Trueman | 14 |
| V.S. Hazare* | not out | 69 | c Laker b Bedser | 49 |
| V.L. Manjrekar | lbw b Bedser | 5 | b Laker | 1 |
| D.G. Phadkar | b Watkins | 8 | b Laker | 16 |
| H.R. Adhikari | lbw b Watkins | 0 | (3) b Trueman | 16 |
| G.S. Ramchand | b Trueman | 18 | (9) b Trueman | 42 |
| M.K. Mantri† | b Trueman | 1 | (8) c Compton b Laker | 5 |
| S.G. Shinde | st Evans b Watkins | 5 | c Hutton b Truemann | 14 |
| Ghulam Ahmed | b Jenkins | 0 | not out | 1 |
| Extras | (B 7, NB 10) | 17 | (B 29, LB 3, NB 4) | 36 |
| **Total** | | **235** | | **378** |

## ENGLAND

| | | | | |
|---|---|---|---|---|
| L. Hutton* | c Mantri b Hazare | 150 | not out | 39 |
| R.T. Simpson | b Mankad | 53 | run out | 2 |
| P.B.H. May | c Mantri b Mankad | 74 | c Roy b Ghulam Ahmed | 26 |
| D.C.S. Compton | lbw b Hazare | 6 | not out | 4 |
| T.W. Graveney | c Mantri b Ghulam Ahmed | 73 | | |
| A.J. Watkins | b Mankad | 0 | | |
| T.G. Evans† | c and b Ghulam Ahmed | 104 | | |
| R.O. Jenkins | st Mantri b Mankad | 21 | | |
| J.C. Laker | not out | 23 | | |
| A.V. Bedser | c Ramchand b Mankad | 3 | | |
| F.S. Trueman | b Ghulam Ahmed | 17 | | |
| Extras | (B 8, LB 5) | 13 | (B 4, LB 4) | 8 |
| **Total** | | **537** | (2 wickets) | **79** |

| ENGLAND | O | M | R | W | O | M | R | W | | FALL OF WICKETS | | | |
|---|---|---|---|---|---|---|---|---|---|---|---|---|---|
| Bedser | 33 | 8 | 62 | 2 | 36 | 13 | 60 | 2 | | I | E | I | E |
| Trueman | 25 | 3 | 72 | 4 | 27 | 4 | 110 | 4 | Wkt | 1st | 1st | 2nd | 2nd |
| Jenkins | 7·3 | 1 | 26 | 1 | 10 | 1 | 40 | 0 | 1st | 106 | 106 | 7 | 8 |
| Laker | 12 | 5 | 21 | 0 | 39 | 15 | 102 | 4 | 2nd | 116 | 264 | 59 | 71 |
| Watkins | 17 | 7 | 37 | 3 | 8 | 0 | 20 | 0 | 3rd | 118 | 272 | 270 | – |
| Compton | | | | | 2 | 0 | 10 | 0 | 4th | 126 | 292 | 272 | – |
| | | | | | | | | | 5th | 135 | 292 | 289 | – |
| INDIA | | | | | | | | | 6th | 139 | 451 | 312 | – |
| Phadkar | 27 | 8 | 44 | 0 | | | | | 7th | 167 | 468 | 314 | – |
| Ramchand | 29 | 8 | 67 | 0 | 1 | 0 | 5 | 0 | 8th | 180 | 506 | 323 | – |
| Hazare | 24 | 4 | 53 | 2 | 1 | 1 | 0 | 0 | 9th | 221 | 514 | 377 | – |
| Mankad | 73 | 24 | 196 | 5 | 24 | 12 | 35 | 0 | 10th | 235 | 537 | 378 | – |
| Ghulam Ahmed | 43·4 | 12 | 106 | 3 | 23·2 | 9 | 31 | 1 | | | | | |
| Shinde | 6 | 0 | 43 | 0 | | | | | | | | | |
| Umrigar | 4 | 0 | 15 | 0 | | | | | | | | | |

Umpires: F. Chester and F.S. Lee.

# ENGLAND v INDIA 1952 (3rd Test)

Played at Old Trafford, Manchester, on 17, 18, 19 July.
Toss: England.   Result: ENGLAND won by an innings and 207 runs.
Debuts: England – G.A.R. Lock.

India equalled their lowest Test score to date and became the second team after England in 1894-95 (*Test No. 45*) to be dismissed twice in a day; 22 wickets fell on the third day. Trueman's analysis of 8 for 31 remains the best in Tests between England and India. When Lock held a stunning catch at short leg to dismiss Mankad it was the first time he had touched a ball in a Test match.

## ENGLAND

| | | |
|---|---|---|
| L. Hutton* | c Sen b Divecha | 104 |
| D.S. Sheppard | lbw b Ramchand | 34 |
| J.T. Ikin | c Divecha b Ghulam Ahmed | 29 |
| P.B.H. May | c Sen b Mankad | 69 |
| T.W. Graveney | lbw b Divecha | 14 |
| A.J. Watkins | c Phadkar b Mankad | 4 |
| T.G. Evans† | c and b Ghulam Ahmed | 71 |
| J.C. Laker | c Sen b Divecha | 0 |
| A.V. Bedser | c Phadkar b Ghulam Ahmed | 17 |
| G.A.R. Lock | not out | 1 |
| F.S. Trueman | did not bat | |
| Extras | (B 2, LB 2) | 4 |
| **Total** | (9 wickets declared) | **347** |

## INDIA

| | | | | | |
|---|---|---|---|---|---|
| V.M.H. Mankad | c Lock b Bedser | 4 | lbw b Bedser | 6 |
| P. Roy | c Hutton b Trueman | 0 | c Laker b Trueman | 0 |
| H.R. Adhikari | c Graveney b Trueman | 0 | c May b Lock | 27 |
| V.S. Hazare* | b Bedser | 16 | c Ikin b Lock | 16 |
| P.R. Umrigar | b Trueman | 4 | c Watkins b Bedser | 3 |
| D.G. Phadkar | c Sheppard b Trueman | 0 | b Bedser | 5 |
| V.L. Manjrekar | c Ikin b Trueman | 22 | c Evans b Bedser | 0 |
| R.V. Divecha | b Trueman | 4 | b Bedser | 2 |
| G.S. Ramchand | c Graveney b Trueman | 2 | c Watkins b Lock | 1 |
| P. Sen† | c Lock b Trueman | 4 | not out | 13 |
| Ghulam Ahmed | not out | 1 | c Ikin b Lock | 0 |
| Extras | (LB 1) | 1 | (B 8, NB 1) | 9 |
| **Total** | | **58** | | **82** |

| INDIA | O | M | R | W | O | M | R | W | | FALL OF WICKETS | | |
|---|---|---|---|---|---|---|---|---|---|---|---|---|
| Phadkar | 22 | 10 | 30 | 0 | | | | | | E | I | I |
| Divecha | 45 | 12 | 102 | 3 | | | | | Wkt | 1st | 1st | 2nd |
| Ramchand | 33 | 7 | 78 | 1 | | | | | 1st | 78 | 4 | 7 |
| Mankad | 28 | 9 | 67 | 2 | | | | | 2nd | 133 | 4 | 7 |
| Ghulam Ahmed | 9 | 3 | 43 | 3 | | | | | 3rd | 214 | 5 | 55 |
| Hazare | 7 | 3 | 23 | 0 | | | | | 4th | 248 | 17 | 59 |
| | | | | | | | | | 5th | 252 | 17 | 66 |
| ENGLAND | | | | | | | | | 6th | 284 | 45 | 66 |
| Bedser | 11 | 4 | 19 | 2 | 15 | 6 | 27 | 5 | 7th | 292 | 51 | 66 |
| Trueman | 8·4 | 2 | 31 | 8 | 8 | 5 | 9 | 1 | 8th | 336 | 53 | 67 |
| Laker | 2 | 0 | 7 | 0 | | | | | 9th | 347 | 53 | 77 |
| Watkins | | | | | 4 | 3 | 1 | 0 | 10th | – | 58 | 82 |
| Lock | | | | | 9·3 | 2 | 36 | 4 | | | | |

Umpires: F.S. Lee and D. Davies.

# ENGLAND v INDIA 1952 (4th Test)

Played at Kennington Oval, London, on 14, 15, 16 (*no play*), 18, 19 (*no play*) August.
Toss: England.   Result: MATCH DRAWN.
Debuts: Nil.

Hutton and Sheppard shared England's highest opening partnership against India to date. Only 56 runs came before lunch on the first day, Mankad conceding only a single in his first 13 overs. India achieved another dismal Test record by losing their first five wickets for six runs. Rain reduced play by almost two-thirds, only ten hours 35 minutes being possible.

## ENGLAND

| | | |
|---|---|---:|
| L. Hutton* | c Phadkar b Ramchand | 86 |
| D.S. Sheppard | lbw b Divecha | 119 |
| J.T. Ikin | c Sen b Phadkar | 53 |
| P.B.H. May | c Manjrekar b Mankad | 17 |
| T.W. Graveney | c Divecha b Ghulam Ahmed | 13 |
| W. Watson | not out | 18 |
| T.G. Evans† | c Phadkar b Mankad | 1 |
| J.C. Laker | not out | 6 |
| A.V. Bedser | ) | |
| G.A.R. Lock | ) did not bat | |
| F.S. Trueman | ) | |
| Extras | (B 10, LB 2, NB 1) | 13 |
| **Total** | (6 wickets declared) | **326** |

## INDIA

| | | |
|---|---|---:|
| V.M.H. Mankad | c Evans b Trueman | 5 |
| P. Roy | c Lock b Trueman | 0 |
| H.R. Adhikari | c Trueman b Bedser | 0 |
| V.S. Hazare* | c May b Trueman | 38 |
| V.L. Manjrekar | c Ikin b Bedser | 1 |
| P.R. Umrigar | b Bedser | 0 |
| D.G. Phadkar | b Trueman | 17 |
| R.V. Divecha | b Bedser | 16 |
| G.S. Ramchand | c Hutton b Bedser | 5 |
| P. Sen† | b Trueman | 9 |
| Ghulam Ahmed | not out | 2 |
| Extras | (LB 3, NB 2) | 5 |
| **Total** | | **98** |

| INDIA | O | M | R | W |
|---|---|---|---|---|
| Divecha | 33 | 9 | 60 | 1 |
| Phadkar | 32 | 8 | 61 | 1 |
| Ramchand | 14 | 2 | 50 | 1 |
| Mankad | 48 | 23 | 88 | 2 |
| Ghulam Ahmed | 24 | 1 | 54 | 1 |
| Hazare | 3 | 3 | 0 | 0 |
| ENGLAND | | | | |
| Bedser | 14·5 | 4 | 41 | 5 |
| Trueman | 16 | 4 | 48 | 5 |
| Lock | 6 | 5 | 1 | 0 |
| Laker | 2 | 0 | 3 | 0 |

FALL OF WICKETS

| | E | I |
|---|---|---|
| Wkt | 1st | 1st |
| 1st | 143 | 0 |
| 2nd | 261 | 5 |
| 3rd | 273 | 5 |
| 4th | 293 | 6 |
| 5th | 304 | 6 |
| 6th | 307 | 64 |
| 7th | – | 71 |
| 8th | – | 78 |
| 9th | – | 94 |
| 10th | – | 98 |

Umpires: F. Chester and Harold Elliott.

# INDIA v PAKISTAN 1952–53 (1st Test)

Played at Feroz Shah Kotla, Delhi, on 16, 17, 18 October.
Toss: India.   Result: INDIA won by an innings and 70 runs.
Debuts: Pakistan – all except A.H. Kardar and Amir Elahi who had previously appeared for India,
   Kardar playing as 'Abdul Hafeez'.

Mankad's innings and match analysis in Pakistan's first official Test established new records for India. Adhikari and Ghulam Ahmed added 109 for the tenth wicket. It was the fifth century partnership for the last wicket in Tests and remains the only one by India.

## INDIA

| | | |
|---|---|---:|
| V.M.H. Mankad | b Khan | 11 |
| P. Roy | b Khan | 7 |
| V.S. Hazare | b Amir Elahi | 76 |
| V.L. Manjrekar | c Nazar b Amir Elahi | 23 |
| L. Amarnath* | c Khan b Fazal | 9 |
| P.R. Umrigar | lbw b Kardar | 25 |
| Gul Mahomed | c Hanif b Amir Elahi | 24 |
| H.R. Adhikari | not out | 81 |
| G.S. Ramchand | c Imtiaz b Fazal | 13 |
| P. Sen† | c Nazar b Kardar | 25 |
| Ghulam Ahmed | b Amir Elahi | 50 |
| Extras | (B 28) | 28 |
| **Total** | | **372** |

## PAKISTAN

| | | | | | |
|---|---|---:|---|---|---:|
| Nazar Mohammad | run out | 27 | b Mankad | | 7 |
| Hanif Mohammad† | c Ramchand b Mankad | 51 | b Amarnath | | 1 |
| Israr Ali | b Mankad | 1 | lbw b Mankad | | 9 |
| Imtiaz Ahmed | lbw b Mankad | 0 | lbw b Ghulam Ahmed | | 41 |
| Maqsood Ahmed | c Roy b Mankad | 15 | c Adhikari b Mankad | | 5 |
| A.H. Kardar* | c Roy b Mankad | 4 | not out | | 43 |
| Anwar Hussain | c and b Mankad | 4 | lbw b Ghulam Ahmed | | 4 |
| Waqar Hassan | lbw b Mankad | 8 | c Gul Mahomed b Ghulam Ahmed | 5 |
| Fazal Mahmood | not out | 21 | c and b Ghulam Ahmed | | 27 |
| Khan Mohammad | c Ramchand b Mankad | 0 | st Sen b Mankad | | 5 |
| Amir Elahi | c Gul Mahomed b Ghulam Ahmed | 9 | c Ramchand b Mankad | | 0 |
| Extras | (B 9, LB 1) | 10 | (B 5) | | 5 |
| **Total** | | **150** | | | **152** |

| PAKISTAN | O | M | R | W | O | M | R | W |
|---|---|---|---|---|---|---|---|---|
| Khan Mohammad | 20 | 5 | 52 | 2 | | | | |
| Maqsood | 6 | 1 | 13 | 0 | | | | |
| Fazal | 40 | 13 | 92 | 2 | | | | |
| Amir Elahi | 39·4 | 4 | 134 | 4 | | | | |
| Kardar | 34 | 12 | 53 | 2 | | | | |
| **INDIA** | | | | | | | | |
| Ramchand | 14 | 7 | 24 | 0 | 6 | 1 | 21 | 0 |
| Amarnath | 13· | 9 | 10 | 0 | 5 | 2 | 12 | 1 |
| Mankad | 47 | 27 | 52 | 8 | 24·2 | 3 | 79 | 5 |
| Ghulam Ahmed | 22·3 | 6 | 51 | 1 | 23 | 7 | 35 | 4 |
| Hazare | 6 | 5 | 3 | 0 | | | | |
| Gul Mahomed | 2 | 2 | 0 | 0 | | | | |

FALL OF WICKETS

| | I | P | P |
|---|---|---|---|
| Wkt | 1st | 1st | 2nd |
| 1st | 19 | 64 | 2 |
| 2nd | 26 | 65 | 17 |
| 3rd | 67 | 65 | 42 |
| 4th | 76 | 97 | 48 |
| 5th | 110 | 102 | 73 |
| 6th | 180 | 111 | 79 |
| 7th | 195 | 112 | 87 |
| 8th | 229 | 129 | 121 |
| 9th | 263 | 129 | 152 |
| 10th | 372 | 150 | 152 |

Umpires: M.G. Vijayasarathi and B.J. Mohoni.

# INDIA v PAKISTAN 1952–53 (2nd Test)

Played at University Ground, Lucknow, on 23, 24, 25, 26 October.
Toss: India.   Result: PAKISTAN won by an innings and 43 runs.
Debuts: India – H.G. Gaekwad, S. Nyalchand; Pakistan – Mahmood Hussain, Zulfiqar Ahmed.

The first Test played at Lucknow (on jute matting) brought Pakistan's first victory in only their second match. Nazar Mohammad scored Pakistan's first century, carried his bat through a completed innings, and became the first player to be on the field for an entire Test match.

## INDIA

| | | | | | |
|---|---|---|---|---|---|
| P. Roy | lbw b Fazal | 30 | | c Imtiaz b Mahmood | 2 |
| D.K. Gaekwad | b Maqsood | 6 | | c Nazar b Fazal | 32 |
| Gul Mahomed | lbw b Maqsood | 0 | (6) | b Fazal | 2 |
| V.L. Manjrekar | b Fazal | 3 | | lbw b Fazal | 3 |
| G. Kishenchand | lbw b Fazal | 0 | (3) | c Nazar b Fazal | 20 |
| P.R. Umrigar | b Mahmood | 15 | (5) | lbw b Fazal | 32 |
| L. Amarnath* | c Zulfiqar b Mahmood | 10 | | not out | 61 |
| P.G. Joshi† | b Mahmood | 9 | (9) | b Amir Elahi | 15 |
| H.G. Gaekwad | b Fazal | 14 | (8) | b Fazal | 8 |
| S. Nyalchand | not out | 6 | (11) | lbw b Fazal | 1 |
| Ghulam Ahmed | c Hanif b Fazal | 8 | (10) | c sub (Israr Ali) b Amir Elahi | 0 |
| Extras | (B 5) | 5 | | (B 5, NB 1) | 6 |
| **Total** | | **106** | | | **182** |

## PAKISTAN

| | | |
|---|---|---|
| Nazar Mohammad | not out | 124 |
| Hanif Mohammad† | c Umrigar b Ghulam Ahmed | 34 |
| Waqar Hassan | lbw b Amarnath | 23 |
| Imtiaz Ahmed | lbw b Amarnath | 0 |
| Maqsood Ahmed | lbw b Nyalchand | 41 |
| A.H. Kardar* | c Ghulam Ahmed b Nyalchand | 16 |
| Anwar Hussain | b Nyalchand | 5 |
| Fazal Mahmood | c Joshi b Gul Mahomed | 29 |
| Zulfiqar Ahmed | lbw b Ghulam Ahmed | 34 |
| Mahmood Hussain | b Ghulam Ahmed | 13 |
| Amir Elahi | b Gul Mahomed | 4 |
| Extras | (B 4, LB 3, NB 1) | 8 |
| **Total** | | **331** |

| PAKISTAN | O | M | R | W | O | M | R | W |
|---|---|---|---|---|---|---|---|---|
| Mahmood Hussain | 23 | 7 | 35 | 3 | 19 | 5 | 57 | 1 |
| Kardar | 3 | 2 | 2 | 0 | 13 | 5 | 15 | 0 |
| Fazal | 24·1 | 8 | 52 | 5 | 27·3 | 11 | 42 | 7 |
| Maqsood | 5 | 1 | 12 | 2 | 5 | 0 | 25 | 0 |
| Amir Elahi | | | | | 7 | 1 | 20 | 2 |
| Zulfiqar | | | | | 5 | 1 | 17 | 0 |

| INDIA | O | M | R | W |
|---|---|---|---|---|
| Amarnath | 40 | 18 | 74 | 2 |
| Umrigar | 1 | 0 | 1 | 0 |
| Nyalchand | 64 | 33 | 97 | 3 |
| H.G. Gaekwad | 37 | 21 | 47 | 0 |
| Ghulam Ahmed | 45 | 19 | 83 | 3 |
| Gul Mahomed | 7·3 | 2 | 21 | 2 |

### FALL OF WICKETS

| | I | P | I |
|---|---|---|---|
| Wkt | 1st | 1st | 2nd |
| 1st | 17 | 63 | 4 |
| 2nd | 17 | 118 | 27 |
| 3rd | 20 | 120 | 43 |
| 4th | 22 | 167 | 73 |
| 5th | 55 | 194 | 77 |
| 6th | 65 | 201 | 103 |
| 7th | 68 | 239 | 115 |
| 8th | 85 | 302 | 170 |
| 9th | 93 | 318 | 170 |
| 10th | 106 | 331 | 182 |

Umpires: B.J. Mohoni and J.R. Patel.

# INDIA v PAKISTAN 1952–53 (3rd Test)

Played at Brabourne Stadium, Bombay, on 13, 14, 15, 16 November.
Toss: Pakistan.   Result: INDIA won by ten wickets.
Debuts: India – M.L. Apte, H.T. Dani, V. Rajindernath; Pakistan – Wazir Mohammad.

Mankad completed the Test 'double' of 1,000 runs and 100 wickets in his 23rd match. This remains the record for the fastest 'double' in Tests.

## PAKISTAN

| | | | | |
|---|---|--:|---|--:|
| Nazar Mohammad | b Amarnath | 4 | c Umrigar b Dani | 0 |
| Hanif Mohammad† | b Mankad | 15 | c sub (G.S. Ramchand) b Mankad | 96 |
| A.H. Kardar* | c Dani b Amarnath | 20 | (5) lbw b Mankad | 3 |
| Imtiaz Ahmed | b Amarnath | 0 | c Adhikari b Gupte | 28 |
| Maqsood Ahmed | c Umrigar b Amarnath | 6 | (6) c Hazare b Mankad | 9 |
| Wazir Mohammad | c and b Mankad | 8 | (7) lbw b Mankad | 4 |
| Waqar Hassan | st Rajindernath b Mankad | 81 | (3) c Hazare b Mankad | 65 |
| Fazal Mahmood | c Amarnath b Hazare | 33 | st Rajindernath b Gupte | 0 |
| Israr Ali | b Gupte | 10 | st Rajindernath b Gupte | 5 |
| Mahmood Hussain | st Rajindernath b Gupte | 2 | not out | 21 |
| Amir Elahi | not out | 0 | run out | 1 |
| Extras | (B 5, LB 2) | 7 | (B 4, LB 6) | 10 |
| **Total** | | **186** | | **242** |

## INDIA

| | | | | |
|---|---|--:|---|--:|
| V.M.H. Mankad | c Nazar b Kardar | 41 | not out | 35 |
| M.L. Apte | c Imtiaz b Mahmood | 30 | not out | 10 |
| R.S. Modi | b Mahmood | 32 | | |
| V.S. Hazare | not out | 146 | | |
| P.R. Umrigar | b Mahmood | 102 | | |
| H.R. Adhikari | not out | 31 | | |
| L. Amarnath* | ) | | | |
| H.T. Dani | ) | | | |
| V. Rajindernath† | ) did not bat | | | |
| S.P. Gupte | ) | | | |
| Ghulam Ahmed | ) | | | |
| Extras | (B 1, LB 4) | 5 | | |
| **Total** | (4 wickets declared) | **387** | (0 wickets) | **45** |

| INDIA | O | M | R | W | O | M | R | W | | FALL OF WICKETS | | | |
|---|--:|--:|--:|--:|--:|--:|--:|--:|---|---|---|---|---|
| Amarnath | 21 | 10 | 40 | 4 | 18 | 9 | 25 | 0 | | P | I | P | I |
| Dani | 4 | 2 | 10 | 0 | 6 | 3 | 9 | 1 | Wkt | 1st | 1st | 2nd | 2nd |
| Hazare | 7 | 1 | 21 | 1 | 6 | 2 | 13 | 0 | 1st | 10 | 55 | 1 | – |
| Mankad | 25 | 11 | 52 | 3 | 65 | 31 | 72 | 5 | 2nd | 40 | 103 | 166 | – |
| Ghulam Ahmed | 7 | 1 | 14 | 0 | 21 | 8 | 36 | 0 | 3rd | 40 | 122 | 171 | – |
| Gupte | 9 | 1 | 42 | 2 | 33·2 | 10 | 77 | 3 | 4th | 44 | 305 | 183 | – |
| | | | | | | | | | 5th | 56 | – | 201 | – |
| PAKISTAN | | | | | | | | | 6th | 60 | – | 215 | – |
| Mahmood Hussain | 35 | 5 | 121 | 3 | 6 | 2 | 21 | 0 | 7th | 143 | – | 215 | – |
| Fazal | 39 | 10 | 111 | 0 | 7·2 | 2 | 22 | 0 | 8th | 174 | – | 215 | – |
| Maqsood | 7 | 2 | 20 | 0 | | | | | 9th | 182 | – | 232 | – |
| Kardar | 14 | 2 | 54 | 1 | 2 | 1 | 2 | 0 | 10th | 186 | – | 242 | – |
| Amir Elahi | 14 | 0 | 65 | 0 | | | | | | | | | |
| Israr Ali | 3 | 1 | 11 | 0 | | | | | | | | | |

Umpires: M.G. Vijayasarathi and J.R. Patel.

# INDIA v PAKISTAN 1952–53 (4th Test)

Played at Chepauk, Madras, on 28, 29, 30 (*no play*) November, 1 (*no play*) December.
Toss: Pakistan.   Result: MATCH DRAWN.
Debuts: India – E.S. Maka.

This was the first Test in India to be seriously interrupted by rain. Zulfiqar Ahmed and Amir Elahi added 104 for the last wicket. It was the sixth century last-wicket partnership in Tests, the second of this rubber, and it remains the only one scored against India.

## PAKISTAN

| | | |
|---|---|---:|
| Nazar Mohammad | run out | 13 |
| Hanif Mohammad | lbw b Divecha | 22 |
| Waqar Hassan | st Maka b Mankad | 49 |
| Imtiaz Ahmed† | c Maka b Divecha | 6 |
| A.H. Kardar* | b Ramchand | 79 |
| Maqsood Ahmed | c sub (D.H. Shodhan) b Mankad | 1 |
| Anwar Hussain | run out | 17 |
| Fazal Mahmood | c Maka b Phadkar | 30 |
| Zulifqar Ahmed | not out | 63 |
| Mahmood Hussain | b Phadkar | 0 |
| Amir Elahi | b Amarnath | 47 |
| Extras | (B 9, LB 7, NB 1) | 17 |
| **Total** | | **344** |

## INDIA

| | | |
|---|---|---:|
| V.M.H. Mankad | b Fazal | 7 |
| M.L. Apte | c Maqsood b Kardar | 42 |
| V.S. Hazare | c Zulfiqar b Mahmood | 1 |
| C.D. Gopinath | c Nazar b Mahmood | 0 |
| P.R. Umrigar | c Nazar b Fazal | 62 |
| L. Amarnath* | c Imtiaz b Kardar | 14 |
| D.G. Phadkar | not out | 18 |
| G.S. Ramchand | not out | 25 |
| R.V. Divecha | ) | |
| E.S. Maka | ) did not bat | |
| S.P. Gupte | ) | |
| Extras | (B 4, NB 2) | 6 |
| **Total** | (6 wickets) | **175** |

| INDIA | O | M | R | W |
|---|---|---|---|---|
| Phadkar | 19 | 3 | 61 | 2 |
| Divecha | 19 | 4 | 36 | 2 |
| Ramchand | 20 | 3 | 66 | 1 |
| Amarnath | 6·5 | 3 | 9 | 1 |
| Mankad | 35 | 3 | 113 | 2 |
| Gupte | 5 | 2 | 14 | 0 |
| Hazare | 6 | 0 | 28 | 0 |
| **PAKISTAN** | | | | |
| Mahmood Hussain | 22 | 4 | 70 | 2 |
| Fazal | 27 | 11 | 52 | 2 |
| Maqsood | 4 | 1 | 10 | 0 |
| Kardar | 21 | 7 | 37 | 2 |

### FALL OF WICKETS

| | P | I |
|---|---|---|
| Wkt | 1st | 1st |
| 1st | 26 | 21 |
| 2nd | 46 | 28 |
| 3rd | 73 | 30 |
| 4th | 111 | 104 |
| 5th | 115 | 132 |
| 6th | 195 | 134 |
| 7th | 195 | – |
| 8th | 240 | – |
| 9th | 240 | – |
| 10th | 344 | – |

Umpires: P.K. Sinha and N.D. Nagarwalla.

# INDIA v PAKISTAN 1952–53 (5th Test)

Played at Eden Gardens, Calcutta, on 12, 13, 14, 15 December.
Toss: India.   Result: MATCH DRAWN.
Debuts: India – D.H. Shodhan.

Shodhan, a left-hander, became the first player to score a hundred in the first innings of his first Test for India, L. Amarnath having done so in the second innings (*Test No. 230*). The match ended with a intriguing declaration by Kardar which set India to score 97 runs in 15 minutes.

## PAKISTAN

| | | | | |
|---|---|---|---|---|
| Nazar Mohammad | c Amarnath b Ghulam Ahmed | 55 | lbw b Mankad | 47 |
| Hanif Mohammad | c Ramchand b Phadkar | 56 | b Ramchand | 12 |
| Waqar Hassan | lbw b Phadkar | 29 | b Ramchand | 97 |
| Imtiaz Ahmed† | c Gaekwad b Phadkar | 57 | b Mankad | 13 |
| A.H. Kardar* | b Phadkar | 7 | c Ramchand b Ghulam Ahmed | 1 |
| Maqsood Ahmed | c Manjrekar b Amarnath | 17 | c Shodhan b Ghulam Ahmed | 8 |
| Anwar Hussain | lbw b Phadkar | 9 | c Mankad b Ghulam Ahmed | 3 |
| Fazal Mahmood | c Mankad b Ramchand | 5 | not out | 28 |
| Zulifqar Ahmed | not out | 6 | not out | 5 |
| Mahmood Hussain | st Sen b Ramchand | 5 | | |
| Amir Elahi | c Sen b Ramchand | 4 | | |
| Extras | (B 3, LB 3, NB 1) | 7 | (B 14, LB 6, NB 2) | 22 |
| **Total** | | **257** | (7 wickets declared) | **236** |

## INDIA

| | | | | |
|---|---|---|---|---|
| P. Roy | c Zulifqar b Amir Elahi | 29 | not out | 8 |
| D.K. Gaekwad | b Mahmood | 21 | not out | 20 |
| V.M.H. Mankad | lbw b Fazal | 35 | | |
| V.L. Manjrekar | c Fazal b Mahmood | 29 | | |
| P.R. Umrigar | c Kardar b Fazal | 22 | | |
| D.G. Phadkar | c Imtiaz b Kardar | 57 | | |
| L. Amarnath* | c Maqsood b Fazal | 11 | | |
| D.H. Shodhan | c Imtiaz b Fazal | 110 | | |
| G.S. Ramchand | b Mahmood | 25 | | |
| P. Sen† | b Anwar | 13 | | |
| Ghulam Ahmed | not out | 20 | | |
| Extras | (B 7, LB 16, LB 2) | 25 | | |
| **Total** | | **397** | (0 wickets) | **28** |

| INDIA | O | M | R | W | O | M | R | W |
|---|---|---|---|---|---|---|---|---|
| Phadkar | 32 | 10 | 72 | 5 | 21 | 8 | 30 | 0 |
| Ramchand | 13 | 6 | 20 | 3 | 16 | 3 | 43 | 2 |
| Amarnath | 21 | 7 | 31 | 1 | 3 | 2 | 1 | 0 |
| Mankad | 28 | 7 | 78 | 0 | 41 | 18 | 68 | 2 |
| Ghulam Ahmed | 22 | 6 | 49 | 1 | 33 | 11 | 56 | 3 |
| Shodhan | | | | | 2 | 1 | 6 | 0 |
| Roy | | | | | 2 | 1 | 4 | 0 |
| Manjrekar | | | | | 2 | 0 | 6 | 0 |
| PAKISTAN | | | | | | | | |
| Mahmood Hussain | 46 | 11 | 114 | 3 | | | | |
| Fazal | 64 | 19 | 141 | 4 | | | | |
| Maqsood | 8 | 2 | 20 | 0 | | | | |
| Amir Elahi | 6 | 0 | 29 | 1 | | | | |
| Kardar | 15 | 3 | 43 | 1 | | | | |
| Anwar | 5 | 1 | 25 | 1 | 1 | 0 | 4 | 0 |
| Nazar | | | | | 2 | 1 | 4 | 0 |
| Hanif | | | | | 2 | 0 | 10 | 0 |
| Waqar | | | | | 1 | 0 | 10 | 0 |

### FALL OF WICKETS

| | P | I | P | I |
|---|---|---|---|---|
| Wkt | 1st | 1st | 2nd | 2nd |
| 1st | 94 | 37 | 18 | – |
| 2nd | 128 | 87 | 96 | – |
| 3rd | 169 | 99 | 126 | – |
| 4th | 185 | 135 | 131 | – |
| 5th | 215 | 157 | 141 | – |
| 6th | 233 | 179 | 152 | – |
| 7th | 240 | 265 | 216 | – |
| 8th | 242 | 319 | – | – |
| 9th | 253 | 357 | – | – |
| 10th | 257 | 397 | – | – |

Umpires: M.G. Vijayasarathi and J.R. Patel.

# AUSTRALIA v SOUTH AFRICA 1952–53 (1st Test)

Played at Woolloongabba, Brisbane, on 5, 6, 8, 9, 10 December.
Toss: Australia.   Result: AUSTRALIA won by 96 runs.
Debuts: South Africa – K.J. Funston, A.R.A. Murray.

This match was played during a Brisbane heat-wave. Miller was confined to bed with a throat infection during South Africa's second innings.

## AUSTRALIA

| Batsman | Dismissal 1 | Score | Dismissal 2 | Score |
|---|---|---|---|---|
| C.C. McDonald | c and b Watkins | 27 | st Waite b Tayfield | 17 |
| A.R. Morris | lbw b Watkins | 29 | c Melle b Tayfield | 58 |
| R.N. Harvey | c sub (G.A.S. Innes) b Melle | 109 | (4) run out | 52 |
| A.L. Hassett* | c Waite b Watkins | 55 | (3) c McGlew b Melle | 17 |
| K.R. Miller | b Watkins | 3 | lbw b Tayfield | 3 |
| G.B. Hole | c Tayfield b Melle | 8 | lbw b Melle | 42 |
| R.R. Lindwall | lbw b Melle | 5 | not out | 38 |
| G.R.A. Langley† | c Tayfield b Melle | 17 | b Watkins | 27 |
| D.T. Ring | c Mansell b Melle | 13 | b Melle | 4 |
| I.W. Johnson | lbw b Melle | 7 | lbw b Watkins | 13 |
| W.A. Johnston | not out | 1 | c McGlew b Tayfield | 0 |
| Extras | (B 1, LB 3, NB 2) | 6 | (B 2, LB 4) | 6 |
| **Total** | | **280** | | **277** |

## SOUTH AFRICA

| Batsman | Dismissal 1 | Score | Dismissal 2 | Score |
|---|---|---|---|---|
| D.J. McGlew | c Johnson b Miller | 9 | lbw b Lindwall | 69 |
| J.H.B. Waite† | lbw b Ring | 39 | st Langley b Johnson | 14 |
| W.R. Endean | c Langley b Ring | 14 | lbw b Lindwall | 12 |
| K.J. Funston | b Ring | 33 | c Langley b Johnston | 65 |
| R.A. McLean | c Miller b Johnson | 13 | b Lindwall | 38 |
| J.E. Cheetham* | c Langley b Lindwall | 26 | b Johnston | 18 |
| J.C. Watkins | c Miller b Ring | 25 | hit wkt b Johnson | 1 |
| P.N.F. Mansell | c Lindwall b Ring | 31 | b Lindwall | 4 |
| A.R.A. Murray | lbw b Johnston | 18 | not out | 11 |
| H.J. Tayfield | lbw b Ring | 3 | c Langley b Johnson | 1 |
| M.G. Melle | not out | 7 | b Lindwall | 4 |
| Extras | (B 3) | 3 | (B 2, NB 1) | 3 |
| **Total** | | **221** | | **240** |

| SOUTH AFRICA | O | M | R | W | O | M | R | W |
|---|---|---|---|---|---|---|---|---|
| Melle | 20·5 | 0 | 71 | 6 | 26 | 2 | 95 | 3 |
| Watkins | 24 | 8 | 41 | 4 | 26 | 13 | 47 | 2 |
| Murray | 14 | 1 | 63 | 0 | 13 | 7 | 13 | 0 |
| Tayfield | 15 | 3 | 59 | 0 | 33·3 | 5 | 116 | 4 |
| Mansell | 8 | 0 | 40 | 0 | | | | |
| **AUSTRALIA** | | | | | | | | |
| Lindwall | 12 | 0 | 48 | 1 | 30 | 8 | 60 | 5 |
| Miller | 10 | 0 | 46 | 1 | | | | |
| Johnston | 7·6 | 2 | 21 | 1 | 26 | 5 | 62 | 2 |
| Ring | 21 | 2 | 72 | 6 | 17 | 3 | 58 | 0 |
| Johnson | 12 | 3 | 31 | 1 | 30 | 7 | 52 | 3 |
| Hole | | | | | 3 | 0 | 5 | 0 |
| Harvey | | | | | 1 | 1 | 0 | 0 |

### FALL OF WICKETS

| Wkt | A 1st | SA 1st | A 2nd | SA 2nd |
|---|---|---|---|---|
| 1st | 55 | 13 | 48 | 20 |
| 2nd | 56 | 39 | 75 | 57 |
| 3rd | 211 | 88 | 115 | 153 |
| 4th | 216 | 103 | 123 | 170 |
| 5th | 231 | 113 | 160 | 209 |
| 6th | 237 | 153 | 198 | 210 |
| 7th | 252 | 177 | 246 | 215 |
| 8th | 272 | 195 | 251 | 226 |
| 9th | 273 | 211 | 276 | 227 |
| 10th | 280 | 221 | 277 | 240 |

Umpires: R. Wright and H. Elphinston.

# AUSTRALIA v SOUTH AFRICA 1952–53 (2nd Test)

Played at Melbourne Cricket Ground on 24, 26, 27, 29, 30 December.
Toss: South Africa.   Result: SOUTH AFRICA won by 82 runs.
Debuts: Nil.

South Africa gained their first win against Australia since 1910-11; it was only their second in 31 Tests in this series. Tayfield's match analysis of 13 for 165 remains the best for South Africa in all Test matches. Miller completed the Test 'double' of 1,000 runs and 100 wickets in his 33rd Test.

## SOUTH AFRICA

| | | | | | |
|---|---|---|---|---|---|
| D.J. McGlew | b Lindwall | 46 | st Langley b Ring | | 13 |
| J.H.B. Waite† | c Lindwall b Miller | 0 | c Hole b Miller | | 62 |
| W.R. Endean | c Benaud b Lindwall | 2 | not out | | 162 |
| K.J. Funston | c Ring b Miller | 9 | run out | | 26 |
| R.A. McLean | c Lindwall b Ring | 27 | lbw b Miller | | 42 |
| J.E. Cheetham* | c Johnston b Miller | 15 | lbw b Johnston | | 6 |
| J.C. Watkins | c Langley b Benaud | 19 | b Johnston | | 3 |
| P.N.F. Mansell | b Lindwall | 24 | b Miller | | 18 |
| A.R.A. Murray | c Johnston b Benaud | 51 | st Langley b Ring | | 23 |
| H.J. Tayfield | c Langley b Miller | 23 | lbw b Lindwall | | 22 |
| M.G. Melle | not out | 4 | b Lindwall | | 0 |
| Extras | (B 4, LB 3) | 7 | (B 1, LB 5, W 4, NB 1) | | 11 |
| **Total** | | **227** | | | **388** |

## AUSTRALIA

| | | | | | |
|---|---|---|---|---|---|
| C.C. McDonald | c sub (E.R.H. Fuller) b Mansell | 82 | c Mansell b Murray | | 23 |
| A.R. Morris | c and b Tayfield | 43 | c Watkins b Melle | | 1 |
| R.N. Harvey | c Cheetham b Tayfield | 11 | (4) c Watkins b Tayfield | | 60 |
| A.L. Hassett* | c Melle b Mansell | 18 | (3) lbw b Tayfield | | 21 |
| K.R. Miller | c Endean b Tayfield | 52 | b Tayfield | | 31 |
| G.B. Hole | c Waite b Mansell | 13 | (7) b Tayfield | | 25 |
| R. Benaud | b Tayfield | 5 | (8) c Melle b Tayfield | | 45 |
| R.R. Lindwall | run out | 1 | (9) b Melle | | 19 |
| D.T. Ring | c McGlew b Tayfield | 14 | (10) c Melle b Tayfield | | 53 |
| G.R.A. Langley† | not out | 2 | (6) b Tayfield | | 4 |
| W.A. Johnston | lbw b Tayfield | 0 | not out | | 0 |
| Extras | (NB 2) | 2 | (B 1, LB 6, NB 1) | | 8 |
| **Total** | | **243** | | | **290** |

| AUSTRALIA | O | M | R | W | O | M | R | W | | FALL OF WICKETS | | | |
|---|---|---|---|---|---|---|---|---|---|---|---|---|---|
| Lindwall | 14 | 2 | 29 | 3 | 31·5 | 4 | 87 | 2 | | SA | A | SA | A |
| Miller | 21 | 3 | 62 | 4 | 22 | 5 | 51 | 3 | *Wkt* | *1st* | *1st* | *2nd* | *2nd* |
| Johnston | 12 | 2 | 37 | 0 | 31 | 9 | 77 | 2 | 1st | 2 | 84 | 23 | 3 |
| Ring | 18 | 1 | 72 | 1 | 31 | 5 | 115 | 2 | 2nd | 9 | 98 | 134 | 34 |
| Benaud | 6·6 | 1 | 20 | 2 | 6 | 0 | 23 | 0 | 3rd | 27 | 155 | 196 | 76 |
| Hole | | | | | 7 | 0 | 24 | 0 | 4th | 63 | 158 | 261 | 131 |
| | | | | | | | | | 5th | 93 | 188 | 284 | 139 |
| SOUTH AFRICA | | | | | | | | | 6th | 112 | 211 | 290 | 148 |
| Melle | 14 | 0 | 73 | 0 | 11 | 2 | 39 | 2 | 7th | 126 | 219 | 317 | 181 |
| Watkins | 6 | 1 | 15 | 0 | 10 | 2 | 34 | 0 | 8th | 156 | 239 | 353 | 216 |
| Murray | 3 | 1 | 11 | 0 | 23 | 7 | 59 | 1 | 9th | 207 | 243 | 388 | 277 |
| Tayfield | 29·4 | 9 | 84 | 6 | 37·1 | 13 | 81 | 7 | 10th | 227 | 243 | 388 | 290 |
| Mansell | 19 | 3 | 58 | 3 | 14 | 2 | 69 | 0 | | | | | |

Umpires: H. Elphinston and M.J. McInnes.

# AUSTRALIA v SOUTH AFRICA 1952–53 (3rd Test)

Played at Sydney Cricket Ground on 9, 10, 12, 13 January.
Toss: South Africa.   Result: AUSTRALIA won by an innings and 38 runs.
Debuts: Nil.

Harvey became the first Australian to score 1,000 runs against South Africa; it was only his eighth Test against them. His stand of 168 with Miller remains Australia's highest for the fourth wicket in this series. Tayfield fractured his left thumb fielding a drive by Miller.

## SOUTH AFRICA

| | | | | |
|---|---|---|---|---|
| D.J. McGlew | run out | 24 | c Langley b Lindwall | 9 |
| J.H.B. Waite† | c Morris b Johnston | 32 | c Hole b Lindwall | 0 |
| W.R. Endean | b Lindwall | 18 | lbw b Miller | 71 |
| K.J. Funston | b Ring | 56 | c Hole b Miller | 16 |
| R.A. McLean | b Lindwall | 0 | (6) c Benaud b Lindwall | 65 |
| J.E. Cheetham* | c Johnston b Miller | 5 | (5) c Morris b Lindwall | 5 |
| A.R.A. Murray | c sub (J.H. de Courcy) b Miller | 4 | c Hole b Benaud | 17 |
| J.C. Watkins | c sub (J.H. de Courcy) b Miller | 17 | c Miller b Johnston | 48 |
| P.N.F. Mansell | b Lindwall | 8 | c Hole b Benaud | 0 |
| H.J. Tayfield | not out | 3 | absent hurt | – |
| M.G. Melle | c Langley b Lindwall | 1 | (10) not out | 0 |
| Extras | (B 1, LB 3, W 1) | 5 | (LB 1) | 1 |
| **Total** | | **173** | | **232** |

## AUSTRALIA

| | | |
|---|---|---|
| C.C. McDonald | c Endean b Tayfield | 67 |
| A.R. Morris | b Watkins | 18 |
| A.L. Hassett* | c Funston b Murray | 2 |
| R.N. Harvey | c Watkins b Murray | 190 |
| K.R. Miller | lbw b Tayfield | 55 |
| G.B. Hole | run out | 5 |
| R. Benaud | lbw b Melle | 0 |
| D.T. Ring | b Tayfield | 58 |
| R.R. Lindwall | b Murray | 1 |
| G.R.A. Langley† | c Mansell b Murray | 20 |
| W.A. Johnston | not out | 7 |
| Extras | (B 3, LB 12, W 1, NB 4) | 20 |
| **Total** | | **443** |

| AUSTRALIA | O | M | R | W | O | M | R | W |
|---|---|---|---|---|---|---|---|---|
| Lindwall | 14·2 | 1 | 40 | 4 | 20 | 3 | 72 | 4 |
| Miller | 17 | 1 | 48 | 3 | 18 | 6 | 33 | 2 |
| Johnston | 18 | 5 | 46 | 1 | 14·6 | 0 | 51 | 1 |
| Ring | 12 | 4 | 23 | 1 | 12 | 1 | 54 | 0 |
| Hole | 2 | 0 | 11 | 0 | | | | |
| Benaud | | | | | 5 | 1 | 21 | 2 |
| SOUTH AFRICA | | | | | | | | |
| Melle | 23 | 3 | 98 | 1 | | | | |
| Watkins | 12 | 5 | 16 | 1 | | | | |
| Murray | 51·2 | 11 | 169 | 4 | | | | |
| Tayfield | 38 | 9 | 94 | 3 | | | | |
| Mansell | 7 | 0 | 46 | 0 | | | | |

| FALL OF WICKETS | SA | A | SA |
|---|---|---|---|
| Wkt | 1st | 1st | 2nd |
| 1st | 54 | 40 | 9 |
| 2nd | 65 | 49 | 10 |
| 3rd | 83 | 162 | 60 |
| 4th | 83 | 330 | 68 |
| 5th | 115 | 344 | 167 |
| 6th | 142 | 350 | 167 |
| 7th | 144 | 374 | 232 |
| 8th | 156 | 379 | 232 |
| 9th | 172 | 425 | 232 |
| 10th | 173 | 443 | – |

Umpires: H. Elphinston and M.J. McInnes.

# AUSTRALIA v SOUTH AFRICA 1952–53 (4th Test)

Played at Adelaide Oval, on 24, 26, 27, 28, 29 January.
Toss: Australia.   Result: MATCH DRAWN.
Debuts: South Africa – E.R.H. Fuller.

South Africa saved the follow on by seven runs and, set 377 runs in 4¼ hours for victory, forced a draw. The second-wicket partnership of 275 between McDonald and Hassett remains Australia's highest for any wicket against South Africa. Lindwall (damaged leg tendon) and Miller (pulled ligament in the back) were unable to bowl in the second innings.

## AUSTRALIA

| | | | | | |
|---|---|--:|---|---|--:|
| C.C. McDonald | st Waite b Tayfield | 154 | | b Mansell | 15 |
| A.R. Morris | c Endean b Fuller | 1 | | c Endean b Melle | 77 |
| A.L. Hassett* | c McGlew b Mansell | 163 | | | |
| R.N. Harvey | c Tayfield b Fuller | 84 | (3) | c Endean b Watkins | 116 |
| K.R. Miller | c Waite b Tayfield | 9 | | | |
| G.B. Hole | c and b Mansell | 59 | (4) | not out | 6 |
| R. Benaud | b Melle | 6 | (5) | not out | 18 |
| D.T. Ring | c McLean b Tayfield | 28 | | | |
| R.R. Lindwall | lbw b Tayfield | 2 | | | |
| G.R.A. Langley† | not out | 5 | | | |
| W.A. Johnston | run out | 11 | | | |
| Extras | (B 1, LB 7) | 8 | | (B 1) | 1 |
| **Total** | | **530** | | (3 wickets declared) | **233** |

## SOUTH AFRICA

| | | | | | |
|---|---|--:|---|---|--:|
| D.J. McGlew | c Hole b Johnston | 26 | | c Langley b Johnston | 54 |
| W.R. Endean | c Langley b Benaud | 56 | (4) | b Harvey | 17 |
| R.A. McLean | c Hassett b Ring | 11 | | c Hole b Benaud | 17 |
| J.H.B. Waite† | c Hole b Benaud | 44 | (2) | b Hole | 20 |
| K.J. Funston | c and b Benaud | 92 | | lbw b Johnston | 17 |
| J.C. Watkins | b Benaud | 76 | | b Morris | 21 |
| J.E. Cheetham* | b Johnston | 6 | | not out | 13 |
| P.N.F. Mansell | c Hole b Johnston | 33 | | not out | 2 |
| H.J. Tayfield | b Johnston | 16 | | | |
| E.R.H. Fuller | c and b Johnston | 0 | | | |
| M.G. Melle | not out | 9 | | | |
| Extras | (B 12, LB 4, NB 2) | 18 | | (B 16) | 16 |
| **Total** | | **387** | | (6 wickets) | **177** |

| SOUTH AFRICA | O | M | R | W | O | M | R | W |
|---|--:|--:|--:|--:|--:|--:|--:|--:|
| Melle | 26 | 1 | 105 | 1 | 10 | 1 | 50 | 1 |
| Fuller | 25 | 2 | 119 | 2 | 3 | 0 | 12 | 0 |
| Tayfield | 44 | 6 | 142 | 4 | 14 | 1 | 65 | 0 |
| Mansell | 32 | 1 | 113 | 2 | 7 | 0 | 40 | 1 |
| McGlew | 2 | 0 | 9 | 0 | 1 | 0 | 7 | 0 |
| Watkins | 6 | 1 | 34 | 0 | 12 | 1 | 58 | 1 |
| AUSTRALIA | | | | | | | | |
| Lindwall | 13 | 0 | 47 | 0 | | | | |
| Johnston | 49·3 | 17 | 110 | 5 | 24 | 4 | 67 | 2 |
| Miller | 2·1 | 1 | 1 | 0 | | | | |
| Ring | 30 | 8 | 88 | 1 | 11 | 3 | 25 | 0 |
| Benaud | 44 | 9 | 118 | 4 | 14 | 5 | 28 | 1 |
| Hole | 3 | 1 | 5 | 0 | 9 | 4 | 17 | 1 |
| Harvey | | | | | 7 | 2 | 9 | 1 |
| Morris | | | | | 5 | 0 | 11 | 1 |
| Hassett | | | | | 1 | 0 | 1 | 0 |
| McDonald | | | | | 1 | 0 | 3 | 0 |

| | FALL OF WICKETS | | | |
|---|--:|--:|--:|--:|
| | A | SA | A | SA |
| Wkt | 1st | 1st | 2nd | 2nd |
| 1st | 2 | 62 | 42 | 81 |
| 2nd | 277 | 79 | 199 | 95 |
| 3rd | 356 | 100 | 209 | 109 |
| 4th | 387 | 208 | – | 127 |
| 5th | 439 | 270 | – | 158 |
| 6th | 448 | 296 | – | 166 |
| 7th | 494 | 350 | – | – |
| 8th | 505 | 374 | – | – |
| 9th | 517 | 378 | – | – |
| 10th | 530 | 387 | – | – |

Umpires: M.J. McInnes and R. Wright.

# AUSTRALIA v SOUTH AFRICA 1952–53 (5th Test)

Played at Melbourne Cricket Ground on 6, 7, 9, 10, 11, 12 February.
Toss: Australia.   Result: SOUTH AFRICA won by six wickets.
Debuts: Australia – R.G. Archer, I.D. Craig; South Africa – H.J. Keith.

At 17 years 239 days Craig became the youngest Australian to play Test cricket – a record he still holds. South Africa achieved the third instance in Test cricket of a side winning in face of a first innings total of over 500, and so squared the rubber.

## AUSTRALIA

| | | | | | |
|---|---|---|---|---|---|
| C.C. McDonald | c McLean b Mansell | 41 | c Watkins b Fuller | | 11 |
| A.R. Morris | run out | 99 | lbw b Tayfield | | 44 |
| R.N. Harvey | c Cheetham b Fuller | 205 | b Fuller | | 7 |
| A.L. Hassett* | run out | 40 | c Endean b Mansell | | 30 |
| I.D. Craig | c Keith b Fuller | 53 | c Endean b Tayfield | | 47 |
| R.G. Archer | c Waite b Fuller | 18 | c Watkins b Tayfield | | 0 |
| R. Benaud | c and b Tayfield | 20 | c Watkins b Fuller | | 30 |
| D.T. Ring | b Tayfield | 14 | c Endean b Mansell | | 0 |
| G.R.A. Langley† | b Murray | 2 | not out | | 26 |
| W.A. Johnston | c Endean b Tayfield | 12 | c Cheetham b Fuller | | 5 |
| G. Noblet | not out | 13 | b Fuller | | 1 |
| Extras | (LB 3) | 3 | (B 7, LB 1) | | 8 |
| **Total** | | **520** | | | **209** |

## SOUTH AFRICA

| | | | | | |
|---|---|---|---|---|---|
| W.R. Endean | c Langley b Johnston | 16 | b Johnston | | 70 |
| J.H.B. Waite† | run out | 64 | c Archer b Noblet | | 18 |
| J.C. Watkins | b Archer | 92 | b Ring | | 50 |
| K.J. Funston | lbw b Johnston | 16 | b Benaud | | 35 |
| H.J. Keith | b Johnston | 10 | not out | | 40 |
| R.A. McLean | lbw b Noblet | 81 | not out | | 76 |
| J.E. Cheetham* | c McDonald b Johnston | 66 | | | |
| P.N.F. Mansell | lbw b Johnston | 52 | | | |
| A.R.A. Murray | c and b Johnston | 17 | | | |
| H.J. Tayfield | c Benaud b Ring | 17 | | | |
| E.R.H. Fuller | not out | 0 | | | |
| Extras | (B 1, LB 3) | 4 | (B 2, LB 6) | | 8 |
| **Total** | | **435** | (4 wickets) | | **297** |

| SOUTH AFRICA | O | M | R | W | O | M | R | W | | FALL OF WICKETS | | | |
|---|---|---|---|---|---|---|---|---|---|---|---|---|---|
| Fuller | 19 | 4 | 74 | 3 | 30·2 | 4 | 66 | 5 | | A | SA | A | SA |
| Watkins | 23 | 3 | 72 | 0 | 14 | 4 | 33 | 0 | *Wkt* | *1st* | *1st* | *2nd* | *2nd* |
| Tayfield | 35·4 | 4 | 129 | 3 | 32 | 8 | 73 | 3 | 1st | 122 | 31 | 36 | 42 |
| Murray | 25 | 3 | 84 | 1 | | | | | 2nd | 166 | 129 | 44 | 124 |
| Mansell | 22 | 0 | 114 | 1 | 8 | 3 | 29 | 2 | 3rd | 269 | 189 | 70 | 174 |
| Keith | 9 | 0 | 44 | 0 | | | | | 4th | 417 | 189 | 128 | 191 |
| | | | | | | | | | 5th | 450 | 239 | 129 | – |
| AUSTRALIA | | | | | | | | | 6th | 459 | 290 | 152 | – |
| Noblet | 30 | 6 | 65 | 1 | 24 | 9 | 44 | 1 | 7th | 490 | 401 | 152 | – |
| Archer | 33 | 4 | 97 | 1 | 5 | 0 | 23 | 0 | 8th | 493 | 402 | 187 | – |
| Johnston | 46 | 8 | 152 | 6 | 38 | 7 | 114 | 1 | 9th | 495 | 435 | 193 | – |
| Ring | 19·1 | 1 | 62 | 1 | 13 | 2 | 55 | 1 | 10th | 520 | 435 | 209 | – |
| Benaud | 15 | 3 | 55 | 0 | 15 | 4 | 41 | 1 | | | | | |
| Hassett | | | | | 0·5 | 0 | 12 | 0 | | | | | |

Umpires: R. Wright and M.J. McInnes.

# WEST INDIES v INDIA 1952–53 (1st Test)

Played at Queen's Park Oval, Port-of-Spain, Trinidad, on 21, 22, 23, 24, 27, 28 January.
Toss: India.   Result: MATCH DRAWN.
Debuts: West Indies – A.P. Binns, F.M. King, B.H. Pairaudeau; India – C.V. Gadkari.

Played on an easy-paced jute matting pitch, this match had reached only the halfway stage at the end of the fourth day. Needing 274 to win in 160 minutes West Indies settled for batting practice. Weekes scored the first double-century for West Indies in this series of Tests, Pairaudeau scored a hundred on debut, and they shared together a partnership of 219 which was a fifth-wicket record for West Indies in all Tests to date and remains the record against India. A record Caribbean crowd of 22,000 watched the third day.

## INDIA

| | | | | | |
|---|---|---|---|---|---|
| V.M.H. Mankad | lbw b King | 2 | (9) | b Ramadhin | 10 |
| M.L. Apte | c Binns b Stollmeyer | 64 | | b Valentine | 52 |
| G.S. Ramchand | c Stollmeyer b Ramadhin | 61 | | c Binns b Walcott | 17 |
| V.S. Hazare* | c Worrell b Valentine | 29 | | c and b Walcott | 0 |
| P.R. Umrigar | c Binns b Valentine | 130 | | b Worrell | 69 |
| D.G. Phadkar | b Gomez | 30 | | c Walcott b Worrell | 65 |
| D.K. Gaekwad | c Worrell b Stollmeyer | 43 | | lbw b King | 24 |
| D.H. Shodhan | c Worrell b Gomez | 45 | | b Ramadhin | 11 |
| C.V. Gadkari | c Walcott b Gomes | 7 | (10) | not out | 11 |
| P.G. Joshi† | c Binns b King | 3 | (1) | run out | 32 |
| S.P. Gupte | not out | 0 | | c Rae b Ramadhin | 1 |
| Extras | (LB 2, NB 1) | 3 | | (LB 1, NB 1) | 2 |
| **Total** | | **417** | | | **294** |

## WEST INDIES

| | | | | | |
|---|---|---|---|---|---|
| A.F. Rae | b Ramchand | 1 | | not out | 63 |
| J.B. Stollmeyer* | c Phadkar b Gupte | 33 | | not out | 76 |
| F.M.M. Worrell | b Gupte | 18 | | | |
| E. de C. Weekes | c Gadkari b Gupte | 207 | | | |
| C.L. Walcott | c Ramchand b Mankad | 47 | | | |
| B.H. Pairaudeau | st Joshi b Gupte | 115 | | | |
| G.E. Gomez | c Mankad b Gupte | 0 | | | |
| A.P. Binns† | run out | 2 | | | |
| F.M. King | lbw b Gupte | 0 | | | |
| S. Ramadhin | not out | 5 | | | |
| A.L. Valentine | st Joshi b Gupte | 0 | | | |
| Extras | (B 5, LB 1, W 2, NB 2) | 10 | | (B 1, LB 1 W 1) | 3 |
| **Total** | | **438** | | (0 wickets) | **142** |

| WEST INDIES | O | M | R | W | O | M | R | W |
|---|---|---|---|---|---|---|---|---|
| King | 41·1 | 10 | 75 | 2 | 24 | 12 | 35 | 1 |
| Gomez | 42 | 12 | 84 | 3 | 18 | 5 | 51 | 0 |
| Ramadhin | 37 | 13 | 107 | 1 | 24·5 | 7 | 58 | 3 |
| Valentine | 56 | 28 | 92 | 2 | 28 | 13 | 47 | 1 |
| Stollmeyer | 16 | 2 | 56 | 2 | 11 | 1 | 47 | 0 |
| Worrell | | | | | 20 | 4 | 32 | 2 |
| Walcott | | | | | 16 | 10 | 12 | 2 |
| Weekes | | | | | 2 | 0 | 10 | 0 |
| **INDIA** | | | | | | | | |
| Phadkar | 13 | 4 | 38 | 0 | 9 | 4 | 12 | 0 |
| Ramchand | 22 | 7 | 56 | 1 | 13 | 2 | 31 | 0 |
| Gupte | 66 | 15 | 162 | 7 | 2 | 1 | 2 | 0 |
| Mankad | 63 | 16 | 129 | 1 | 12 | 1 | 32 | 0 |
| Hazare | 12 | 1 | 30 | 0 | | | | |
| Shodhan | 1 | 0 | 1 | 0 | 7 | 2 | 19 | 0 |
| Gadkari | 5 | 0 | 12 | 0 | 9 | 3 | 25 | 0 |
| Umrigar | | | | | 2 | 0 | 14 | 0 |
| Gaekwad | | | | | 1 | 0 | 4 | 0 |

### FALL OF WICKETS

| Wkt | I 1st | WI 1st | I 2nd | WI 2nd |
|---|---|---|---|---|
| 1st | 16 | 3 | 55 | – |
| 2nd | 110 | 36 | 90 | – |
| 3rd | 157 | 89 | 90 | – |
| 4th | 158 | 190 | 106 | – |
| 5th | 210 | 409 | 237 | – |
| 6th | 328 | 409 | 238 | – |
| 7th | 379 | 413 | 257 | – |
| 8th | 412 | 419 | 273 | – |
| 9th | 417 | 438 | 291 | – |
| 10th | 417 | 438 | 294 | – |

Umpires: C. John and E.N. Lee Kow.

# WEST INDIES v INDIA 1952–53 (2nd Test)

Played at Kensington Oval, Bridgetown, Barbados, on 7, 9, 10, 11, 12 February.
Toss: West Indies.   Result: WEST INDIES won by 142 runs.
Debuts: West Indies – R.A. Legall.

### WEST INDIES

| | | | | | |
|---|---|---|---|---|---|
| B.H. Pairaudeau | c Joshi b Hazare | 43 | | lbw b Phadkar | 0 |
| J.B. Stollmeyer* | c Mankad b Gupte | 32 | | c Gupte b Mankad | 54 |
| F.M.M. Worrell | lbw b Mankad | 24 | | b Phadkar | 7 |
| E. de C. Weekes | c Joshi b Hazare | 47 | | b Mankad | 15 |
| C.L. Walcott | lbw b Phadkar | 98 | (6) | b Phadkar | 34 |
| R.J. Christiani | st Joshi b Gupte | 4 | (7) | st Joshi b Gupte | 33 |
| G.E. Gomez | c Gaekwad b Gupte | 0 | (5) | lbw b Phadkar | 35 |
| R.A. Legall† | c Ramchand b Mankad | 23 | | b Gupte | 1 |
| F.M. King | lbw b Mankad | 0 | | c Manjekar b Ramchand | 19 |
| S. Ramadhin | not out | 16 | | b Phadkar | 12 |
| A.L. Valentine | b Phadkar | 6 | | not out | 0 |
| Extras | (LB 3) | 3 | | (B 6, LB 11, W 1) | 18 |
| **Total** | | **296** | | | **228** |

### INDIA

| | | | | | |
|---|---|---|---|---|---|
| P. Roy | c Worrell b King | 1 | (3) | c Legall b Valentine | 22 |
| M.L. Apte | c Worrell b Valentine | 64 | | b King | 9 |
| V.L. Manjrekar | lbw b Ramadhin | 25 | (6) | not out | 32 |
| V.S. Hazare* | c Weekes b King | 63 | (7) | b Ramadhin | 0 |
| P.R. Umrigar | c Christiani b Valentine | 56 | | b Ramadhin | 6 |
| G.S. Ramchand | b Ramadhin | 17 | (4) | b Ramadhin | 34 |
| D.K. Gaekwad | c and b Valentine | 0 | | absent hurt | — |
| D.G. Phadkar | b Worrell | 17 | | c Valentine b Ramadhin | 8 |
| P.G. Joshi† | c Worrell b Valentine | 0 | | c Worrell b Valentine | 0 |
| S.P. Gupte | run out | 2 | | lbw b Ramadhin | 5 |
| V.M.H. Mankad | not out | 0 | (1) | b Gomez | 3 |
| Extras | (B 2, LB 5, NB 1) | 8 | | (B 8, LB 2) | 10 |
| **Total** | | **253** | | | **129** |

| INDIA | O | M | R | W | O | M | R | W | | FALL OF WICKETS | | | |
|---|---|---|---|---|---|---|---|---|---|---|---|---|---|
| | | | | | | | | | | WI | I | WI | I |
| Phadkar | 11·4 | 2 | 24 | 2 | 29·3 | 4 | 64 | 5 | Wkt | 1st | 1st | 2nd | 2nd |
| Ramchand | 9 | 1 | 32 | 0 | 4 | 1 | 9 | 1 | 1st | 52 | 6 | 0 | 9 |
| Gupte | 41 | 10 | 99 | 3 | 36 | 12 | 82 | 2 | 2nd | 81 | 44 | 25 | 13 |
| Mankad | 46 | 15 | 125 | 3 | 19 | 3 | 54 | 2 | 3rd | 123 | 156 | 47 | 70 |
| Hazare | 9 | 2 | 13 | 2 | 2 | 1 | 1 | 0 | 4th | 168 | 164 | 105 | 72 |
| | | | | | | | | | 5th | 173 | 204 | 138 | 89 |
| WEST INDIES | | | | | | | | | 6th | 177 | 205 | 175 | 89 |
| King | 28 | 7 | 66 | 2 | 9 | 3 | 18 | 1 | 7th | 222 | 242 | 190 | 107 |
| Gomez | 17 | 9 | 27 | 0 | 5 | 2 | 9 | 1 | 8th | 222 | 243 | 205 | 110 |
| Ramadhin | 30 | 13 | 59 | 2 | 24·5 | 11 | 26 | 5 | 9th | 280 | 251 | 228 | 129 |
| Worrell | 13 | 4 | 25 | 1 | 6 | 0 | 13 | 0 | 10th | 296 | 253 | 228 | – |
| Valentine | 41 | 21 | 58 | 4 | 35 | 16 | 53 | 2 | | | | | |
| Stollmeyer | 5 | 2 | 10 | 0 | | | | | | | | | |

Umpires: H.B. de C. Jordan and F. Walcott.

# WEST INDIES v INDIA 1952–53 (3rd Test)

Played at Queen's Park Oval, Port-of-Spain, Trinidad, on 19, 20, 21, 23, 24, 25 February.
Toss: India.    Result: MATCH DRAWN.
Debuts: India – J.M. Ghorpade.

Originally scheduled for Georgetown, this Test had to be transferred because of serious flooding in British Guiana. Weekes scored his sixth hundred in eight Tests against India. Manjrekar kept wicket in both innings after Maka had fractured two bones in his hand while batting.

## INDIA

| | | | | | |
|---|---|---|---|---|---|
| P. Roy | c Weekes b Worrell | 49 | c sub (N. Asgarali) b Gomez | | 0 |
| M.L. Apte | b Gomez | 0 | not out | | 163 |
| G.S. Ramchand | c Legall b King | 62 | c Weekes b King | | 1 |
| V.S. Hazare* | c Rae b Worrell | 11 | (6) lbw b Worrell | | 24 |
| P.R. Umrigar | c Gomez b King | 61 | st Legall b Valentine | | 67 |
| V.L. Manjrekar | c Weekes b King | 3 | (4) Legall b Worrell | | 2 |
| V.M.H. Mankad | lbw b King | 17 | (8) run out | | 96 |
| D.G. Phadkar | c Pairaudeau b King | 13 | | | |
| J.M. Ghorpade | c Walcott b Valentine | 35 | (7) run out | | 0 |
| E.S. Maka† | retired hurt | 2 | | | |
| S.P. Gupte | not out | 17 | | | |
| Extras | (LB 5, W 2, NB 2) | 9 | (LB 4, W 3, NB 2) | | 9 |
| **Total** | | **279** | (7 wickets declared) | | **362** |

## WEST INDIES

| | | | | | |
|---|---|---|---|---|---|
| A.F. Rae | c sub (C.V. Gadkari) b Gupte | 15 | | | |
| B.H. Pairaudeau | b Ramchand | 8 | c Ghorpade b Gupte | | 29 |
| C.L. Walcott | st Manjrekar b Gupte | 30 | | | |
| E. de C. Weekes | run out | 161 | not out | | 55 |
| F.M.M. Worrell | b Gupte | 31 | (3) c Manjrekar b Ramchand | | 2 |
| G.E. Gomez | c Hazare b Phadkar | 15 | | | |
| R.A. Legall† | run out | 17 | | | |
| J.B. Stollmeyer* | not out | 20 | (1) not out | | 104 |
| F.M. King | c sub (C.V. Gadkari) b Gupte | 12 | | | |
| S. Ramadhin | c Manjrekar b Phadkar | 1 | | | |
| A.L. Valentine | c Ghorpade b Gupte | 0 | | | |
| Extras | (B 3, W 2) | 5 | (B 1, LB 1) | | 2 |
| **Total** | | **315** | (2 wickets) | | **192** |

| WEST INDIES | O | M | R | W | O | M | R | W |
|---|---|---|---|---|---|---|---|---|
| King | 31 | 9 | 74 | 5 | 22 | 9 | 29 | 1 |
| Gomez | 16 | 5 | 26 | 1 | 46·1 | 20 | 42 | 1 |
| Worrell | 26 | 9 | 47 | 2 | 31 | 7 | 62 | 2 |
| Valentine | 37·2 | 18 | 62 | 1 | 50 | 17 | 105 | 1 |
| Ramadhin | 21 | 7 | 61 | 0 | 28 | 13 | 47 | 0 |
| Stollmeyer | | | | | 15 | 3 | 54 | 0 |
| Walcott | | | | | 7 | 2 | 13 | 0 |
| Weekes | | | | | 1 | 0 | 1 | 0 |
| INDIA | | | | | | | | |
| Phadkar | 43 | 14 | 85 | 2 | 7 | 5 | 7 | 0 |
| Ramchand | 15 | 3 | 48 | 1 | 20 | 3 | 61 | 1 |
| Gupte | 48 | 14 | 107 | 5 | 7 | 0 | 19 | 1 |
| Mankad | 33 | 16 | 47 | 0 | | | | |
| Hazare | 2 | 0 | 6 | 0 | 2 | 0 | 12 | 0 |
| Ghorpade | 5 | 0 | 17 | 0 | 11 | 0 | 53 | 0 |
| Roy | | | | | 6 | 0 | 35 | 0 |
| Apte | | | | | 1 | 0 | 3 | 0 |

FALL OF WICKETS

| | I | WI | I | WI |
|---|---|---|---|---|
| Wkt | 1st | 1st | 2nd | 2nd |
| 1st | 6 | 12 | 1 | 47 |
| 2nd | 87 | 41 | 4 | 65 |
| 3rd | 117 | 82 | 10 | – |
| 4th | 124 | 178 | 145 | – |
| 5th | 136 | 215 | 209 | – |
| 6th | 177 | 281 | 209 | – |
| 7th | 211 | 286 | 362 | – |
| 8th | 225 | 299 | – | – |
| 9th | 279 | 304 | – | – |
| 10th | – | 315 | – | – |

Umpires: C. John and E.N. Lee Kow.

# WEST INDIES v INDIA 1952–53 (4th Test)

Played at Bourda, Georgetown, British Guiana, on 11, 12, 13, 14, 16, 17 March.
Toss: India.   Result: MATCH DRAWN.
Debuts: West Indies – R. Miller, G.L. Wight.

Another slow-scoring match much interrupted by rain produced only 793 runs from over 19 hours of cricket. Although the umpires ruled that play was impossible on the second day, a crowd demonstration resulted in the officials ordering the restart of play for the final hour.

## INDIA

| | | | | |
|---|---|---:|---|---:|
| P. Roy | lbw b Valentine | 28 | c Worrell b Valentine | 48 |
| M.L. Apte | lbw b Ramadhin | 30 | hit wkt b Stollmeyer | 30 |
| G.S. Ramchand | run out | 0 | b Valentine | 2 |
| V.L. Manjrekar | run out | 0 | (6) b Valentine | 31 |
| P.R. Umrigar | c Walcott b Valentine | 1 | not out | 40 |
| V.S. Hazare* | c Walcott b Valentine | 30 | (4) lbw b King | 9 |
| V.M.H. Mankad | c Legall b Valenine | 66 | not out | 20 |
| D.G. Phadkar | c Legall b Valentine | 30 | | |
| C.V. Gadkari | not out | 50 | | |
| P.G. Joshi† | lbw b Ramadhin | 7 | | |
| S.P. Gupte | run out | 12 | | |
| Extras | (B 4, LB 2, NB 2) | 8 | (B 4, LB 5, W 1) | 10 |
| **Total** | | **262** | (5 wickets) | **190** |

## WEST INDIES

| | | |
|---|---|---:|
| B.H. Pairaudeau | b Ramchand | 2 |
| J.B. Stollmeyer* | lbw b Mankad | 13 |
| F.M.M. Worrell | b Mankad | 56 |
| E. de C.Weekes | lbw b Ramchand | 86 |
| C.L. Walcott | lbw b Hazare | 125 |
| G.L. Wight | b Mankad | 21 |
| R.A. Legall† | lbw b Gupte | 8 |
| R. Miller | c Apte b Gupte | 23 |
| F.M. King | b Gupte | 2 |
| S. Ramadhin | not out | 6 |
| A.L. Valentine | c Hazare b Gupte | 13 |
| Extras | (B 4, LB 4, W 1) | 9 |
| **Total** | | **364** |

| WEST INDIES | O | M | R | W | O | M | R | W | FALL OF WICKETS | | | |
|---|---|---|---|---|---|---|---|---|---|---|---|---|
| King | 6 | 3 | 4 | 0 | 17 | 6 | 32 | 1 | | I | WI | I |
| Miller | 16 | 8 | 28 | 0 | | | | | *Wkt* | *1st* | *1st* | *2nd* |
| Valentine | 53·5 | 20 | 127 | 5 | 34 | 14 | 71 | 3 | 1st | 47 | 2 | 66 |
| Ramadhin | 41 | 18 | 74 | 2 | 26 | 14 | 39 | 0 | 2nd | 47 | 44 | 72 |
| Stollmeyer | 1 | 0 | 1 | 0 | 8 | 2 | 15 | 1 | 3rd | 56 | 101 | 91 |
| Walcott | 3 | 0 | 8 | 0 | | | | | 4th | 62 | 231 | 117 |
| Worrell | 4 | 1 | 12 | 0 | 13 | 2 | 23 | 0 | 5th | 64 | 302 | 161 |
| | | | | | | | | | 6th | 120 | 311 | – |
| INDIA | | | | | | | | | 7th | 183 | 343 | – |
| Ramchand | 17 | 4 | 48 | 2 | | | | | 8th | 211 | 345 | – |
| Hazare | 12 | 3 | 22 | 1 | | | | | 9th | 236 | 345 | – |
| Gadkari | 3 | 1 | 8 | 0 | | | | | 10th | 262 | 364 | – |
| Gupte | 56·2 | 19 | 122 | 4 | | | | | | | | |
| Mankad | 68 | 23 | 155 | 3 | | | | | | | | |

Umpires: A.B. Rollox and E.S. Gillette.

# WEST INDIES v INDIA 1952–53 (5th Test)

Played at Sabina Park, Kingston, Jamaica, on 28, 30, 31 March, 1, 2, 4 April.
Toss: India.   Result: MATCH DRAWN.
Debuts: West Indies – A.P.H. Scott.

Needing 181 runs in 145 minutes for victory, West Indies settled for a draw after losing both openers cheaply. Worrell's 237 remains the highest score for West Indies in a home Test against India. The partnership of 237 in 255 minutes between Roy and Manjrekar is still India's highest for the second wicket in all Tests.

## INDIA

| | | | | | |
|---|---|---|---|---|---|
| P. Roy | c Legall b King | 85 | | lbw b Valentine | 150 |
| M.L. Apte | run out | 15 | | lbw b Valentine | 33 |
| G.S. Ramchand | lbw b Valentine | 22 | (7) | c Pairaudeau b Valentine | 33 |
| V.S. Hazare* | c Valentine b King | 16 | | c Weekes b Valentine | 12 |
| P.R. Umrigar | b Valentine | 117 | | c Weekes b King | 13 |
| V.L. Manjrekar† | c Weekes b Valentine | 43 | (3) | c Weekes b Gomez | 118 |
| V.M.H. Mankad | lbw b Valentine | 6 | (6) | c Weekes b Gomez | 9 |
| C.V. Gadkari | c Legall b Valentine | 0 | | c Stollmeyer b Gomez | 0 |
| D.M. Ghorpade | c Legall b Gomez | 4 | | b King | 24 |
| S.P. Gupte | not out | 0 | (11) | b Gomez | 8 |
| D.H. Shodhan | absent ill | – | (10) | not out | 15 |
| Extras | (B 1, W 3) | 4 | | (B 18, LB 10, W 1) | 29 |
| **Total** | | **312** | | | **444** |

## WEST INDIES

| | | | | |
|---|---|---|---|---|
| B.H. Pairaudeau | b Gupte | 58 | run out | 2 |
| J.B. Stollmeyer* | b Mankad | 13 | b Ramchand | 9 |
| F.M.M. Worrell | c Hazare b Mankad | 237 | c Apte b Mankad | 23 |
| E. de C. Weekes | c Gadkari b Gupte | 109 | c Ghorpade b Ramchand | 36 |
| C.L. Walcott | c Gadkari b Mankad | 118 | not out | 5 |
| R.J. Christiani | lbw b Mankad | 4 | not out | 1 |
| G.E. Gomez | c Hazare b Mankad | 12 | | |
| R.A. Legall† | c sub (D.K. Gaekwad) b Gupte | 1 | | |
| F.M. King | st Manjrekar b Gupte | 0 | | |
| A.P.H. Scott | c and b Gupte | 5 | | |
| A.L. Valentine | not out | 4 | | |
| Extras | (B 7, LB 4, W 4) | 15 | (B 15, W 1) | 16 |
| **Total** | | **576** | (4 wickets) | **92** |

| WEST INDIES | O | M | R | W | O | M | R | W |
|---|---|---|---|---|---|---|---|---|
| King | 34 | 13 | 64 | 2 | 26 | 6 | 83 | 2 |
| Gomez | 28 | 13 | 40 | 1 | 47 | 25 | 72 | 4 |
| Worrell | 16 | 6 | 31 | 0 | 6 | 2 | 17 | 0 |
| Scott | 31 | 7 | 88 | 0 | 13 | 2 | 52 | 0 |
| Valentine | 27·5 | 9 | 64 | 5 | 67 | 22 | 149 | 4 |
| Stollmeyer | 4 | 0 | 20 | 0 | 11 | 3 | 28 | 0 |
| Walcott | 1 | 0 | 1 | 0 | 8 | 2 | 14 | 0 |
| INDIA | | | | | | | | |
| Ramchand | 36 | 9 | 84 | 0 | 15 | 6 | 33 | 2 |
| Hazare | 17 | 2 | 47 | 0 | 2 | 1 | 1 | 0 |
| Gupte | 65·1 | 14 | 180 | 5 | 8 | 2 | 16 | 0 |
| Mankad | 82 | 17 | 228 | 5 | 22 | 11 | 26 | 1 |
| Ghorpade | 6 | 1 | 22 | 0 | | | | |

### FALL OF WICKETS

| | I | WI | I | WI |
|---|---|---|---|---|
| Wkt | 1st | 1st | 2nd | 2nd |
| 1st | 30 | 36 | 80 | 11 |
| 2nd | 57 | 133 | 317 | 15 |
| 3rd | 80 | 330 | 327 | 82 |
| 4th | 230 | 543 | 346 | 91 |
| 5th | 277 | 554 | 360 | – |
| 6th | 295 | 554 | 360 | – |
| 7th | 295 | 567 | 368 | – |
| 8th | 312 | 567 | 408 | – |
| 9th | 312 | 569 | 431 | – |
| 10th | – | 576 | 444 | – |

Umpires: T.A. Ewart and S.C. Burke.

# NEW ZEALAND v SOUTH AFRICA 1952–53 (1st Test)

Played at Basin Reserve, Wellington, on 6, 7, 9, 10 March.
Toss: South Africa.   Result: SOUTH AFRICA won by an innings and 180 runs.
Debuts: New Zealand – R.W. Blair, F.E. Fisher, E.M. Meuli, L.S.M. Miller.

McGlew, whose 255* was the highest score for South Africa in Tests, then became the second player after Nazar Mohammad to be on the field throughout a Test match. The Pakistani had achieved this feat in the previous October (*Test No. 356*). The partnership of 246 between McGlew and Murray established a new seventh-wicket record, since beaten, for all Test cricket.

## SOUTH AFRICA

| | | |
|---|---|---:|
| D.J. McGlew | not out | 255 |
| J.H.B. Waite† | c Mooney b Blair | 35 |
| J.C. Watkins | c Reid b Blair | 14 |
| K.J. Funston | b Fisher | 2 |
| W.R. Endean | c Mooney b Blair | 41 |
| R.A. McLean | b Blair | 5 |
| J.E. Cheetham* | b Burtt | 17 |
| A.R.A. Murray | st Mooney b Burtt | 109 |
| P.N.F. Mansell | run out | 10 |
| H.J. Tayfield | not out | 27 |
| E.R.H. Fuller | did not bat | |
| Extras | (B 5, LB 4) | 9 |
| **Total** | (8 wickets declared) | **524** |

## NEW ZEALAND

| | | | | | |
|---|---|---:|---|---|---:|
| B. Sutcliffe | c McGlew b Watkins | 62 | | b Murray | 33 |
| J.G. Leggat | c Fuller b Tayfield | 22 | | c Endean b Watkins | 47 |
| F.E. Fisher | b Fuller | 9 | (9) | c Waite b Watkins | 14 |
| W.M. Wallace* | c Waite b Murray | 4 | (3) | b Tayfield | 2 |
| E.M. Meuli | c Endean b Murray | 15 | (4) | b Fuller | 23 |
| L.S.M. Miller | c Endean b Tayfield | 17 | (5) | c Waite b Watkins | 13 |
| J.R. Reid | b Murray | 1 | (6) | c Waite b Murray | 9 |
| F.L.H. Mooney† | not out | 27 | (7) | b Tayfield | 9 |
| A.M. Moir | run out | 1 | (8) | c Fuller b Watkins | 0 |
| T.B. Burtt | lbw b Fuller | 10 | | lbw b Tayfield | 0 |
| R.W. Blair | b Fuller | 0 | | not out | 6 |
| Extras | (B 3, NB 1) | 4 | | (B 16) | 16 |
| **Total** | | **172** | | | **172** |

| NEW ZEALAND | O | M | R | W | O | M | R | W |
|---|---:|---:|---:|---:|---:|---:|---:|---:|
| Blair | 36 | 4 | 98 | 4 | | | | |
| Fisher | 34 | 6 | 78 | 1 | | | | |
| Reid | 24 | 8 | 36 | 0 | | | | |
| Burtt | 44 | 7 | 140 | 2 | | | | |
| Moir | 35 | 4 | 159 | 0 | | | | |
| Sutcliffe | 1 | 0 | 4 | 0 | | | | |
| SOUTH AFRICA | | | | | | | | |
| Fuller | 19·4 | 7 | 29 | 3 | 27 | 8 | 43 | 1 |
| Watkins | 27 | 17 | 29 | 1 | 23·5 | 14 | 22 | 4 |
| Tayfield | 38 | 15 | 53 | 2 | 32 | 12 | 42 | 3 |
| Mansell | 11 | 3 | 27 | 0 | 13 | 2 | 30 | 0 |
| Murray | 28 | 15 | 30 | 3 | 23 | 16 | 19 | 2 |

| | FALL OF WICKETS | | |
|---|---:|---:|---:|
| | SA | NZ | NZ |
| *Wkt* | *1st* | *1st* | *2nd* |
| 1st | 83 | 71 | 43 |
| 2nd | 92 | 91 | 46 |
| 3rd | 177 | 96 | 109 |
| 4th | 187 | 98 | 121 |
| 5th | 189 | 127 | 137 |
| 6th | 238 | 131 | 141 |
| 7th | 484 | 134 | 142 |
| 8th | 494 | 135 | 162 |
| 9th | – | 172 | 162 |
| 10th | – | 172 | 172 |

Umpires: J. McLellan and R.G. Currie

# NEW ZEALAND v SOUTH AFRICA 1952–53 (2nd Test)

Played at Eden Park, Auckland, on 13, 14, 16, 17 March.
Toss: South Africa.   Result: MATCH DRAWN.
Debuts: New Zealand – M.E. Chapple, E.W. Dempster, M.B. Poore.

## SOUTH AFRICA

| | | | | | |
|---|---|---|---|---|---|
| D.J. McGlew | c Chapple b Dempster | 18 | | b Reid | 50 |
| J.H.B. Waite† | c Mooney b Blair | 72 | | b Poore | 26 |
| J.C. Watkins | c Reid b Blair | 30 | | c Sutcliffe b Poore | 12 |
| K.J. Funston | c Dempster b Poore | 13 | (5) | b Rabone | 17 |
| W.R. Endean | st Mooney b Rabone | 116 | (6) | not out | 47 |
| J.E. Cheetham* | run out | 54 | (7) | not out | 10 |
| R.A. McLean | c Reid b Rabone | 0 | (4) | c Rabone b MacGibbon | 20 |
| A.R.A. Murray | b Reid | 6 | | | |
| P.N.F. Mansell | not out | 30 | | | |
| H.J. Tayfield | b Rabone | 9 | | | |
| E.R.H. Fuller | c Mooney b Poore | 17 | | | |
| Extras | (B 7, LB 2, NB 3) | 12 | | (B 6, LB 6, W 4, NB 2) | 18 |
| **Total** | | **377** | | (5 wickets declared) | **200** |

## NEW ZEALAND

| | | | | |
|---|---|---|---|---|
| B. Sutcliffe | c Waite b Tayfield | 45 | run out | 10 |
| M.E. Chapple | c Cheetham b Tayfield | 22 | c McGlew b Watkins | 7 |
| G.O. Rabone | run out | 29 | not out | 6 |
| M.B. Poore | b Mansell | 45 | not out | 8 |
| W.M. Wallace* | c Mansell b Tayfield | 23 | | |
| L.S.M. Miller | c Waite b Murray | 44 | | |
| F.L.H. Mooney† | c Endean b Tayfield | 2 | | |
| J.R. Reid | c Waite b Watkins | 7 | | |
| A.R. MacGibbon | c Murray b Watkins | 2 | | |
| E.W. Dempster | c Funston b Tayfield | 14 | | |
| R.W. Blair | not out | 0 | | |
| Extras | (B 7, LB 5) | 12 | | |
| **Total** | | **245** | (2 wickets) | **31** |

| NEW ZEALAND | O | M | R | W | O | M | R | W |
|---|---|---|---|---|---|---|---|---|
| Blair | 30 | 6 | 64 | 2 | 11 | 3 | 26 | 0 |
| MacGibbon | 28 | 6 | 72 | 0 | 16 | 6 | 17 | 1 |
| Reid | 22 | 3 | 55 | 1 | 13 | 5 | 21 | 1 |
| Dempster | 39 | 9 | 84 | 1 | 13 | 4 | 29 | 0 |
| Rabone | 24 | 4 | 62 | 3 | 17 | 4 | 46 | 1 |
| Poore | 19 | 8 | 28 | 2 | 8 | 1 | 43 | 2 |
| SOUTH AFRICA | | | | | | | | |
| Fuller | 37 | 13 | 60 | 0 | 8 | 1 | 14 | 0 |
| Watkins | 38 | 20 | 51 | 2 | 8 | 3 | 12 | 1 |
| Murray | 31 | 16 | 29 | 1 | | | | |
| Tayfield | 46·2 | 19 | 62 | 5 | 2·3 | 0 | 5 | 0 |
| Mansell | 18 | 9 | 29 | 1 | 1 | 1 | 0 | 0 |
| Cheetham | 1 | 0 | 2 | 0 | | | | |

| FALL OF WICKETS | | | | |
|---|---|---|---|---|
| | SA | NZ | SA | NZ |
| Wkt | 1st | 1st | 2nd | 2nd |
| 1st | 39 | 54 | 62 | 16 |
| 2nd | 78 | 70 | 80 | 20 |
| 3rd | 124 | 141 | 116 | – |
| 4th | 139 | 152 | 124 | – |
| 5th | 269 | 175 | 173 | – |
| 6th | 274 | 185 | – | – |
| 7th | 308 | 203 | – | – |
| 8th | 330 | 207 | – | – |
| 9th | 340 | 245 | – | – |
| 10th | 377 | 245 | – | – |

Umpires: J.C. Harris and T.M. Pearce.

# ENGLAND v AUSTRALIA 1953 (1st Test)

Played at Trent Bridge, Nottingham, on 11, 12, 13, 15 ( *no play*), 16 June.
Toss: Australia.   Result: MATCH DRAWN.
Debuts: Australia – A.K. Davidson, J.C. Hill.

Australia lost their last seven first innings wickets for 12 runs to Bedser, Bailey and the new ball. Bedser's match analysis of 14 for 99, still the record for a Nottingham Test, was the best by an England bowler since 1934. With two days left, England needed 187 to win with nine wickets in hand, but rain prevented further play until 4.30 p.m. on the final afternoon.

## AUSTRALIA

| | | | | |
|---|---|--:|---|--:|
| G.B. Hole | b Bedser | 0 | b Bedser | 5 |
| A.R. Morris | lbw b Bedser | 67 | b Tattersall | 60 |
| A.L. Hassett* | b Bedser | 115 | c Hutton b Bedser | 5 |
| R.N. Harvey | c Compton b Bedser | 0 | c Graveney b Bedser | 2 |
| K.R. Miller | c Bailey b Wardle | 55 | c Kenyon b Bedser | 5 |
| R. Benaud | c Evans b Bailey | 3 | b Bedser | 0 |
| A.K. Davidson | b Bedser | 4 | c Graveney b Tattersall | 6 |
| D. Tallon† | b Bedser | 0 | c Simpson b Tattersall | 15 |
| R.R. Lindwall | c Evans b Bailey | 0 | c Tattersall b Bedser | 12 |
| J.C. Hill | b Bedser | 0 | c Tattersall b Bedser | 4 |
| W.A. Johnston | not out | 0 | not out | 4 |
| Extras | (B 2, LB 2, NB 1) | 5 | (LB 5) | 5 |
| **Total** | | **249** | | **123** |

## ENGLAND

| | | | | |
|---|---|--:|---|--:|
| L. Hutton* | c Benaud b Davidson | 43 | not out | 60 |
| D. Kenyon | c Hill b Lindwall | 8 | c Hassett b Hill | 16 |
| R.T. Simpson | lbw b Lindwall | 0 | not out | 28 |
| D.C.S. Compton | c Morris b Lindwall | 0 | | |
| T.W. Graveney | c Benaud b Hill | 22 | | |
| P.B.H. May | c Tallon b Hill | 9 | | |
| T.E. Bailey | lbw b Hill | 13 | | |
| T.G. Evans† | c Tallon b Davidson | 8 | | |
| J.H. Wardle | not out | 29 | | |
| A.V. Bedser | lbw b Lindwall | 2 | | |
| R. Tattersall | b Lindwall | 2 | | |
| Extras | (B 5, LB 3) | 8 | (B 8, LB 4, W 2, NB 2) | 16 |
| **Total** | | **144** | (1 wicket) | **120** |

| ENGLAND | O | M | R | W | O | M | R | W |
|---|--:|--:|--:|--:|--:|--:|--:|--:|
| Bedser | 38·3 | 16 | 55 | 7 | 17·2 | 7 | 44 | 7 |
| Bailey | 44 | 14 | 75 | 2 | 5 | 1 | 28 | 0 |
| Wardle | 35 | 16 | 55 | 1 | 12 | 3 | 24 | 0 |
| Tattersall | 23 | 5 | 59 | 0 | 5 | 0 | 22 | 3 |
| **AUSTRALIA** | | | | | | | | |
| Lindwall | 20·4 | 2 | 57 | 5 | 16 | 4 | 37 | 0 |
| Johnston | 18 | 7 | 22 | 0 | 18 | 9 | 14 | 0 |
| Hill | 19 | 8 | 35 | 3 | 12 | 3 | 26 | 1 |
| Davidson | 15 | 7 | 22 | 2 | 5 | 1 | 7 | 0 |
| Benaud | | | | | 5 | 0 | 15 | 0 |
| Morris | | | | | 2 | 0 | 5 | 0 |

### FALL OF WICKETS

| | A | E | A | E |
|---|--:|--:|--:|--:|
| Wkt | 1st | 1st | 2nd | 2nd |
| 1st | 2 | 17 | 28 | 26 |
| 2nd | 124 | 17 | 44 | – |
| 3rd | 128 | 17 | 50 | – |
| 4th | 237 | 76 | 64 | – |
| 5th | 244 | 82 | 68 | – |
| 6th | 244 | 92 | 81 | – |
| 7th | 246 | 107 | 92 | – |
| 8th | 247 | 121 | 106 | – |
| 9th | 248 | 136 | 115 | – |
| 10th | 249 | 144 | 123 | – |

Umpires: D. Davies and Harold Elliott.

# ENGLAND v AUSTRALIA 1953 (2nd Test)

Played at Lord's, London, on 25, 26, 27, 29, 30 June.
Toss: Australia.   Result: MATCH DRAWN.
Debuts: Nil.

Hassett, who scored his second hundred in successive Tests, retired with cramp when 101* (Australia 201 for 2) and resumed at 280 for 6. The final day saw one of the classic rearguard actions of Test cricket, with Watson (109 in 346 minutes on debut against Australia) and Bailey (71 in 257 minutes) saving England from defeat with a fifth wicket partnership of 163 which lasted from 12.42 p.m. to 5.50 p.m. (40 minutes before the close).

### AUSTRALIA

| | | | | |
|---|---|---:|---|---:|
| A.L. Hassett* | c Bailey b Bedser | 104 | c Evans b Statham | 3 |
| A.R. Morris | st Evans b Bedser | 30 | c Statham b Compton | 89 |
| R.N. Harvey | lbw b Bedser | 59 | (4) b Bedser | 21 |
| K.R. Miller | b Wardle | 25 | (3) b Wardle | 109 |
| G.B. Hole | c Compton b Wardle | 13 | lbw b Brown | 47 |
| R. Benaud | lbw b Wardle | 0 | c Graveney b Bedser | 5 |
| A.K. Davidson | c Statham b Bedser | 76 | c and b Brown | 15 |
| D.T. Ring | lbw b Wardle | 18 | lbw b Brown | 7 |
| R.R. Lindwall | b Statham | 9 | b Bedser | 50 |
| G.R.A. Langley† | c Watson b Bedser | 1 | b Brown | 9 |
| W.A. Johnston | not out | 3 | not out | 0 |
| Extras | (B 4, LB 4) | 8 | (B 8, LB 5) | 13 |
| **Total** | | **346** | | **368** |

### ENGLAND

| | | | | |
|---|---|---:|---|---:|
| L. Hutton* | c Hole b Johnston | 145 | c Hole b Lindwall | 5 |
| D. Kenyon | c Davidson b Lindwall | 3 | c Hassett b Lindwall | 2 |
| T.W. Graveney | b Lindwall | 78 | c Langley b Johnston | 2 |
| D.C.S. Compton | c Hole b Benaud | 57 | lbw b Johnston | 33 |
| W. Watson | st Langley b Johnston | 4 | c Hole b Ring | 109 |
| T.E. Bailey | c and b Miller | 2 | c Benaud b Ring | 71 |
| F.R. Brown | c Langley b Lindwall | 22 | c Hole b Benaud | 28 |
| T.G. Evans† | b Lindwall | 0 | not out | 11 |
| J.H. Wardle | b Davidson | 23 | not out | 0 |
| A.V. Bedser | b Lindwall | 1 | | |
| J.B. Statham | not out | 17 | | |
| Extras | (B 11, LB 1, W 1, NB 7) | 20 | (B 7, LB 6, W 2, NB 6) | 21 |
| **Total** | | **372** | (7 wickets) | **282** |

| ENGLAND | O | M | R | W | O | M | R | W |
|---|---|---|---|---|---|---|---|---|
| Bedser | 42·4 | 8 | 105 | 5 | 31·5 | 8 | 77 | 3 |
| Statham | 28 | 7 | 48 | 1 | 15 | 3 | 40 | 1 |
| Brown | 25 | 7 | 53 | 0 | 27 | 4 | 82 | 4 |
| Bailey | 16 | 2 | 55 | 0 | 10 | 4 | 24 | 0 |
| Wardle | 29 | 8 | 77 | 4 | 46 | 18 | 111 | 1 |
| Compton | | | | | 3 | 0 | 21 | 1 |
| AUSTRALIA | | | | | | | | |
| Lindwall | 23 | 4 | 66 | 5 | 19 | 3 | 26 | 2 |
| Miller | 25 | 6 | 57 | 1 | 17 | 8 | 17 | 0 |
| Johnston | 35 | 11 | 91 | 2 | 29 | 10 | 70 | 2 |
| Ring | 14 | 2 | 43 | 0 | 29 | 5 | 84 | 2 |
| Benaud | 19 | 4 | 70 | 1 | 17 | 6 | 51 | 1 |
| Davidson | 10·5 | 2 | 25 | 1 | 14 | 5 | 13 | 0 |
| Hole | | | | | 1 | 1 | 0 | 0 |

FALL OF WICKETS

| | A | E | A | E |
|---|---|---|---|---|
| *Wkt* | *1st* | *1st* | *2nd* | *2nd* |
| 1st | 65 | 9 | 3 | 6 |
| 2nd | 190 | 177 | 168 | 10 |
| 3rd | 225 | 279 | 227 | 12 |
| 4th | 229 | 291 | 235 | 73 |
| 5th | 240 | 301 | 248 | 236 |
| 6th | 280 | 328 | 296 | 246 |
| 7th | 291 | 328 | 305 | 282 |
| 8th | 330 | 332 | 308 | – |
| 9th | 331 | 341 | 362 | – |
| 10th | 346 | 372 | 368 | – |

Umpires: F.S. Lee and H.G. Baldwin.

# ENGLAND v AUSTRALIA 1953 (3rd Test)

Played at Old Trafford, Manchester, on 9, 10, 11, 13 ( *no play*), 14, July.
Toss: Australia.   Result: MATCH DRAWN.
Debuts: Australia – J.H. De Courcy.

Rain restricted playing time to 13 hours 50 minutes, the last half hour of which saw Wardle induce a startling collapse against the turning ball.

## AUSTRALIA

| | | | | | |
|---|---|---|---|---|---|
| A.L. Hassett* | b Bailey | 26 | | c Bailey b Bedser | 8 |
| A.R. Morris | b Bedser | 1 | | c Hutton b Laker | 0 |
| K.R. Miller | b Bedser | 17 | | st Evans b Laker | 6 |
| R.N. Harvey | c Evans b Bedser | 122 | (7) | b Wardle | 0 |
| G.B. Hole | c Evans b Bedser | 66 | (4) | c Evans b Bedser | 2 |
| J.H. de Courcy | lbw b Wardle | 41 | (5) | st Evans b Wardle | 8 |
| A.K. Davidson | st Evans b Laker | 15 | (6) | not out | 4 |
| R.G. Archer | c Compton b Bedser | 5 | | lbw b Wardle | 0 |
| R.R. Lindwall | c Edrich b Waadle | 1 | | b Wardle | 4 |
| J.C. Hill | not out | 8 | | not out | 0 |
| G.R.A. Langley† | c Edrich b Wardle | 8 | | | |
| Extras | (B 6, LB 1, NB 1) | 8 | | (LB 3) | 3 |
| **Total** | | **318** | | (8 wickets) | 35 |

## ENGLAND

| | | |
|---|---|---|
| L. Hutton* | lbw b Lindwall | 66 |
| W.J. Edrich | c Hole b Hill | 6 |
| T.W. Graveney | c De Courcy b Miller | 5 |
| D.C.S. Compton | c Langley b Archer | 45 |
| J.H. Wardle | b Lindwall | 5 |
| W. Watson | b Davidson | 16 |
| R.T. Simpson | c Langley b Davidson | 31 |
| T.E. Bailey | c Hole b Hill | 27 |
| T.G. Evans† | not out | 44 |
| J.C. Laker | lbw b Hill | 5 |
| A.V. Bedser | b Morris | 10 |
| Extras | (B 8, LB 8) | 16 |
| **Total** | | **276** |

| ENGLAND | O | M | R | W | O | M | R | W | | FALL OF WICKETS | | |
|---|---|---|---|---|---|---|---|---|---|---|---|---|
| | | | | | | | | | Wkt | A 1st | E 1st | A 2nd |
| Bedser | 45 | 10 | 115 | 5 | 4 | 1 | 14 | 2 | 1st | 15 | 19 | 8 |
| Bailey | 26 | 4 | 83 | 1 | | | | | 2nd | 48 | 32 | 12 |
| Wardle | 28·3 | 10 | 70 | 3 | 5 | 2 | 7 | 4 | 3rd | 48 | 126 | 18 |
| Laker | 17 | 3 | 42 | 1 | 9 | 5 | 11 | 2 | 4th | 221 | 126 | 18 |
| | | | | | | | | | 5th | 256 | 149 | 31 |
| AUSTRALIA | | | | | | | | | 6th | 285 | 149 | 31 |
| Lindwall | 20 | 8 | 30 | 2 | | | | | 7th | 290 | 209 | 31 |
| Archer | 15 | 8 | 12 | 1 | | | | | 8th | 291 | 231 | 35 |
| Hill | 35 | 7 | 97 | 3 | | | | | 9th | 302 | 243 | – |
| Miller | 24 | 11 | 38 | 1 | | | | | 10th | 318 | 276 | – |
| Davidson | 20 | 4 | 60 | 2 | | | | | | | | |
| Harvey | 3 | 2 | 2 | 0 | | | | | | | | |
| Hole | 2 | 0 | 16 | 0 | | | | | | | | |
| Morris | 1 | 0 | 5 | 1 | | | | | | | | |

Umpires: D. Davies and Harold Elliott.

# ENGLAND v AUSTRALIA 1953 (4th Test)

Played at Headingley, Leeds, on 23, 24, 25, 27, 28 July.
Toss: Australia.    Result: MATCH DRAWN.
Debuts: Nil.

England, put in to bat by Australia for the first time since 1909, scored only 142 runs off 96 overs on the opening day, which rain shortened by 25 minutes. Simpson retired hurt with a severely bruised elbow in the first innings. Bedser set a world Test record when he dismissed Langley and passed C.V. Grimmett's total of 216 wickets. Lock opened the bowling with Bedser in the second innings when Australia needed 177 runs in 115 minutes.

## ENGLAND

| | | | | | |
|---|---|---|---|---|---|
| L. Hutton* | b Lindwall | 0 | c Langley b Archer | 25 |
| W.J. Edrich | lbw b Miller | 10 | c De Courcy b Lindwall | 64 |
| T.W. Graveney | c Benaud b Miller | 55 | b Lindwall | 3 |
| D.C.S. Compton | c Davidson b Lindwall | 0 | lbw b Lindwall | 61 |
| W. Watson | b Lindwall | 24 | c Davidson b Miller | 15 |
| R.T. Simpson | c Langley b Lindwall | 15 | c De Courcy b Miller | 0 |
| T.E. Bailey | run out | 7 | c Hole b Davidson | 38 |
| T.G. Evans† | lbw b Lindwall | 25 | c Lindwall b Miller | 1 |
| J.C. Laker | c Lindwall b Archer | 10 | c Benaud b Davidson | 48 |
| G.A.R. Lock | b Davidson | 9 | c Morris b Miller | 8 |
| A.V. Bedser | not out | 0 | not out | 3 |
| Extras | (B 8, LB 4) | 12 | (B 1, LB 8) | 9 |
| **Total** | | **167** | | **275** |

## AUSTRALIA

| | | | | | |
|---|---|---|---|---|---|
| A.L. Hassett* | c Lock b Bedser | 37 | b Lock | 4 |
| A.R. Morris | c Lock b Bedser | 10 | st Evans b Laker | 38 |
| R.N. Harvey | lbw b Bailey | 71 | (4) lbw b Bedser | 34 |
| K.R. Miller | c Edrich b Bailey | 5 | | |
| G.B. Hole | c Lock b Bedser | 53 | (3) c Graveney b Bailey | 33 |
| J.H. de Courcy | lbw b Lock | 10 | not out | 13 |
| R. Benaud | b Bailey | 7 | | |
| A.K. Davidson | c Evans b Bedser | 2 | (5) not out | 17 |
| R.G. Archer | not out | 31 | | |
| R.R. Lindwall | b Bedser | 9 | | |
| G.R.A. Langley† | c Hutton b Bedser | 17 | | |
| Extras | (B 4, LB 8, W 2) | 14 | (B 3, LB 4, W 1) | 8 |
| **Total** | | **266** | (4 wickets) | **147** |

| AUSTRALIA | O | M | R | W | O | M | R | W | | FALL OF WICKETS | | | |
|---|---|---|---|---|---|---|---|---|---|---|---|---|---|
| Lindwall | 35 | 10 | 54 | 5 | 54 | 19 | 104 | 3 | | E | A | E | A |
| Miller | 28 | 13 | 39 | 2 | 47 | 19 | 63 | 4 | Wkt | 1st | 1st | 2nd | 2nd |
| Davidson | 20·4 | 7 | 23 | 1 | 29·3 | 15 | 36 | 2 | 1st | 0 | 27 | 57 | 27 |
| Archer | 18 | 4 | 27 | 1 | 25 | 12 | 31 | 1 | 2nd | 33 | 70 | 62 | 54 |
| Benaud | 8 | 1 | 12 | 0 | 19 | 8 | 26 | 0 | 3rd | 36 | 84 | 139 | 111 |
| Hole | | | | | 3 | 1 | 6 | 0 | 4th | 98 | 168 | 167 | 117 |
| | | | | | | | | | 5th | 108 | 183 | 171 | – |
| ENGLAND | | | | | | | | | 6th | 110 | 203 | 182 | – |
| Bedser | 28·5 | 2 | 95 | 6 | 17 | 1 | 65 | 1 | 7th | 133 | 203 | 239 | – |
| Bailey | 22 | 4 | 71 | 3 | 6 | 1 | 9 | 1 | 8th | 149 | 208 | 244 | – |
| Lock | 23 | 9 | 53 | 1 | 8 | 1 | 48 | 1 | 9th | 167 | 218 | 258 | – |
| Laker | 9 | 1 | 33 | 0 | 2 | 0 | 17 | 1 | 10th | 167 | 266 | 275 | – |

Umpires: F. Chester and F.S. Lee.

# ENGLAND v AUSTRALIA 1953 (5th Test)

Played at Kennington Oval, London, on 15, 17, 18, 19 August.
Toss: Australia.   Result: ENGLAND won by eight wickets.
Debuts: Nil.

By winning this six-day Test, England regained the Ashes after Australia had held them for the record period of 18 years 362 days. Hutton became the only captain to win an England v Australia rubber after losing the toss in all five Tests. Bedser, who dismissed Morris for the 18th time in 20 Tests, beat M.W. Tate's record by taking 39 wickets in a rubber against Australia.

## AUSTRALIA

| | | | | | |
|---|---|---|---|---|---|
| A.L. Hassett* | c Evans b Bedser | 53 | | lbw b Laker | 10 |
| A.R. Morris | lbw b Bedser | 16 | | lbw b Lock | 26 |
| K.R. Miller | lbw b Bailey | 1 | (5) | c Trueman b Laker | 0 |
| R.N. Harvey | c Hutton b Trueman | 36 | | b Lock | 1 |
| G.B. Hole | c Evans b Trueman | 37 | (3) | lbw b Laker | 17 |
| J.H. de Courcy | c Evans b Trueman | 5 | | run out | 4 |
| R.G. Archer | c and b Bedser | 10 | | c Edrich b Lock | 49 |
| A.K. Davidson | c Edrich b Laker | 22 | | b Lock | 21 |
| R.R. Lindwall | c Evans b Trueman | 62 | | c Compton b Laker | 12 |
| G.R.A. Langley† | c Edrich b Lock | 18 | | c Trueman b Lock | 2 |
| W.A. Johnston | not out | 9 | | not out | 6 |
| Extras | (B 4, NB 2) | 6 | | (B 11, LB 3) | 14 |
| **Total** | | **275** | | | **162** |

## ENGLAND

| | | | | |
|---|---|---|---|---|
| L. Hutton* | b Johnston | 82 | run out | 17 |
| W.J. Edrich | lbw b Lindwall | 21 | not out | 55 |
| P.B.H. May | c Archer b Johnston | 39 | c Davidson b Miller | 37 |
| D.C.S. Compton | c Langley b Lindwall | 16 | not out | 22 |
| T.W. Graveney | c Miller b Lindwall | 4 | | |
| T.E. Bailey | b Archer | 64 | | |
| T.G. Evans† | run out | 28 | | |
| J.C. Laker | c Langley b Miller | 1 | | |
| G.A.R. Lock | c Davidson b Lindwall | 4 | | |
| F.S. Trueman | b Johnston | 10 | | |
| A.V. Bedser | not out | 22 | | |
| Extras | (B 9, LB 5, W 1) | 15 | (LB 1) | 1 |
| **Total** | | **306** | **(2 wickets)** | **132** |

| ENGLAND | O | M | R | W | O | M | R | W | | FALL OF WICKETS | | | |
|---|---|---|---|---|---|---|---|---|---|---|---|---|---|
| Bedser | 29 | 3 | 88 | 3 | 11 | 2 | 24 | 0 | | A | E | A | E |
| Trueman | 24·3 | 3 | 86 | 4 | 2 | 1 | 4 | 0 | Wkt | 1st | 1st | 2nd | 2nd |
| Bailey | 14 | 3 | 42 | 1 | | | | | 1st | 38 | 37 | 23 | 24 |
| Lock | 9 | 2 | 19 | 1 | 21 | 9 | 45 | 5 | 2nd | 41 | 137 | 59 | 88 |
| Laker | 5 | 0 | 34 | 1 | 16·5 | 2 | 75 | 4 | 3rd | 107 | 154 | 60 | – |
| | | | | | | | | | 4th | 107 | 167 | 61 | – |
| AUSTRALIA | | | | | | | | | 5th | 118 | 170 | 61 | – |
| Lindwall | 32 | 7 | 70 | 4 | 21 | 5 | 46 | 0 | 6th | 160 | 210 | 85 | – |
| Miller | 34 | 12 | 65 | 1 | 11 | 3 | 24 | 1 | 7th | 160 | 225 | 135 | – |
| Johnston | 45 | 16 | 94 | 3 | 29 | 14 | 52 | 0 | 8th | 207 | 237 | 140 | – |
| Davidson | 10 | 1 | 26 | 0 | | | | | 9th | 245 | 262 | 144 | – |
| Archer | 10·3 | 2 | 25 | 1 | 1 | 1 | 0 | 0 | 10th | 275 | 306 | 162 | – |
| Hole | 11 | 6 | 11 | 0 | | | | | | | | | |
| Hassett | | | | | 1 | 0 | 4 | 0 | | | | | |
| Morris | | | | | 0·5 | 0 | 5 | 0 | | | | | |

Umpires: D. Davies and F.S. Lee.

# SOUTH AFRICA v NEW ZEALAND 1953–54 (1st Test)

Played at Kingsmead, Durban, on 11, 12, 14, 15 December.
Toss: South Africa.   Result: SOUTH AFRICA won by an innings and 58 runs.
Debuts: South Africa – N.A.T. Adcock; New Zealand – G.W.F. Overton.

South Africa overcame strong resistance from Rabone – he batted for 9¾ hours in the match – to gain their first home win for 23 years.

## SOUTH AFRICA

| | | |
|---|---|---:|
| D.J. McGlew | b MacGibbon | 84 |
| J.H.B. Waite† | b Overton | 43 |
| W.R. Endean | b MacGibbon | 6 |
| K.J. Funston | lbw b Reid | 39 |
| R.A. McLean | c Chapple b Blair | 101 |
| J.C. Watkins | c Mooney b MacGibbon | 29 |
| J.E. Cheetham* | b Rabone | 17 |
| C.B. van Ryneveld | not out | 68 |
| H.J. Tayfield | b Overton | 28 |
| A.R.A. Murray | b Blair | 0 |
| N.A.T. Adcock | did not bat | |
| Extras | (B 10, LB 8, W 1, NB 3) | 22 |
| **Total** | (9 wickets declared) | **437** |

## NEW ZEALAND

| | | | | | |
|---|---|---:|---|---|---:|
| B. Sutcliffe | c Waite b Tayfield | 20 | | c Endean b Tayfield | 16 |
| G.O. Rabone* | lbw b Tayfield | 107 | (5) | b Adcock | 68 |
| M.E. Chapple | b Tayfield | 1 | (2) | c Funston b Watkins | 1 |
| J.R. Reid | b Tayfield | 6 | (3) | c Funston b Watkins | 0 |
| L.S.M. Miller | lbw b Van Ryneveld | 13 | (6) | lbw b Murray | 18 |
| M.B. Poore | c Cheetham b Tayfield | 32 | (7) | st Waite b Van Ryneveld | 1 |
| F.L.H. Mooney† | b Watkins | 9 | (4) | c Waite b Adcock | 7 |
| A.R. MacGibbon | st Waite b Van Ryneveld | 21 | | c Watkins b Tayfield | 19 |
| E.W. Dempster | not out | 7 | | c McGlew b Adcock | 0 |
| R.W. Blair | b Tayfield | 2 | | st Waite b Tayfield | 6 |
| G.W.F. Overton | b Van Ryneveld | 2 | | not out | 3 |
| Extras | (B 9, LB 1) | 10 | | (B 6, LB 3, NB 1) | 10 |
| **Total** | | **230** | | | **149** |

| NEW ZEALAND | O | M | R | W | O | M | R | W |
|---|---|---|---|---|---|---|---|---|
| Blair | 22 | 2 | 104 | 2 | | | | |
| Reid | 16 | 2 | 49 | 1 | | | | |
| Overton | 27 | 8 | 92 | 2 | | | | |
| MacGibbon | 27 | 4 | 73 | 3 | | | | |
| Poore | 5 | 0 | 30 | 0 | | | | |
| Dempster | 10 | 1 | 36 | 0 | | | | |
| Rabone | 8 | 0 | 31 | 1 | | | | |
| SOUTH AFRICA | | | | | | | | |
| Adcock | 19 | 3 | 52 | 0 | 14 | 4 | 38 | 3 |
| Watkins | 15 | 5 | 28 | 1 | 14 | 7 | 16 | 2 |
| Murray | 7 | 5 | 9 | 0 | 7 | 4 | 8 | 1 |
| Tayfield | 36 | 17 | 62 | 6 | 26·1 | 12 | 35 | 3 |
| Van Ryneveld | 28·6 | 6 | 69 | 3 | 21 | 9 | 42 | 1 |

| FALL OF WICKETS | | | |
|---|---|---|---|
| | SA | NZ | NZ |
| *Wkt* | *1st* | *1st* | *2nd* |
| 1st | 113 | 39 | 6 |
| 2nd | 140 | 53 | 15 |
| 3rd | 143 | 75 | 24 |
| 4th | 278 | 100 | 36 |
| 5th | 294 | 162 | 85 |
| 6th | 335 | 181 | 103 |
| 7th | 337 | 215 | 125 |
| 8th | 422 | 215 | 125 |
| 9th | 437 | 219 | 146 |
| 10th | – | 230 | 149 |

Umpires: A.N. McCabe and B.V. Malan.

# SOUTH AFRICA v NEW ZEALAND 1953–54 (2nd Test)

Played at Ellis Park, Johannesburg, on 24, 26, 28, 29 December.
Toss: South Africa.   Result: SOUTH AFRICA won by 132 runs.
Debuts: South Africa – D.E.J. Ironside; New Zealand – J.E.F. Beck.

Sutcliffe and Miller both retired hurt to hospital before scoring, struck on the head and chest respectively by balls from Adcock. Both resumed their innings, Sutcliffe hitting seven sixes in his 80 not out, scored out of 106 runs in 112 minutes. Blair, who, on the second morning, learnt of the death of his fiancée in a train disaster in New Zealand, helped Sutcliffe score 33 runs in ten minutes, including four sixes and a single off one Tayfield over. Sutcliffe became the first New Zealander to score 1,000 runs in Test cricket.

## SOUTH AFRICA

| | | | | |
|---|---|---|---|---|
| D.J. McGlew | c Reid b MacGibbon | 13 | b MacGibbon | 8 |
| A.R.A. Murray | c Chapple b Blair | 7 | (9) c Blair b Overton | 13 |
| W.R. Endean | c Sutcliffe b Reid | 93 | c sub (I.B. Leggat) b Reid | 1 |
| K.J. Funston | lbw b Overton | 0 | c Overton b MacGibbon | 11 |
| R.A. McLean | c Blair b Overton | 27 | (7) lbw b Reid | 36 |
| C.B. van Ryneveld | b Blair | 65 | (8) c Reid b MacGibbon | 17 |
| J.E. Cheetham* | c Mooney b MacGibbon | 20 | (6) c Sutcliffe b Reid | 1 |
| H.J. Tayfield | not out | 20 | (5) b Reid | 34 |
| J.H.B. Waite† | c Mooney b MacGibbon | 0 | (2) c Reid b MacGibbon | 5 |
| D.E.J. Ironside | b Reid | 13 | not out | 11 |
| N.A.T. Adcock | run out | 0 | c Poore b Overton | 6 |
| Extras | (B 3, LB 2, NB 8) | 13 | (LB 3, NB 2) | 5 |
| **Total** | | **271** | | **148** |

## NEW ZEALAND

| | | | | |
|---|---|---|---|---|
| G.O. Rabone* | c Endean b Ironside | 1 | c Van Ryneveld b Adcock | 22 |
| M.E. Chapple | b Adcock | 8 | c Waite b Ironside | 22 |
| M.B. Poore | b Adcock | 15 | b Adcock | 1 |
| B. Sutcliffe | not out | 80 | c Endean b Murray | 10 |
| J.R. Reid | c Endean b Adcock | 3 | (6) c Funston b Ironside | 1 |
| L.S.M. Miller | b Ironside | 14 | (7) c Waite b Adcock | 0 |
| J.E.F. Beck | c Waite b Murray | 16 | (8) c Endean b Ironside | 7 |
| F.L.H. Mooney† | b Ironside | 35 | (5) c Funston b Adcock | 10 |
| A.R. MacGibbon | c Endean b Ironside | 0 | not out | 11 |
| G.W.F. Overton | c Murray b Ironside | 0 | (11) run out | 2 |
| R.W. Blair | st Waite b Tayfield | 6 | (10) b Adcock | 4 |
| Extras | (B 3, LB 4, NB 2) | 9 | (B 3, LB 5, NB 2) | 10 |
| **Total** | | **187** | | **100** |

| NEW ZEALAND | O | M | R | W | O | M | R | W |
|---|---|---|---|---|---|---|---|---|
| Blair | 17 | 4 | 50 | 2 | 5 | 0 | 14 | 0 |
| Reid | 18 | 3 | 63 | 2 | 16 | 5 | 34 | 4 |
| Overton | 20 | 4 | 68 | 2 | 12·2 | 1 | 33 | 2 |
| MacGibbon | 22 | 5 | 61 | 3 | 20 | 2 | 62 | 4 |
| Rabone | 3 | 0 | 16 | 0 | | | | |
| SOUTH AFRICA | | | | | | | | |
| Adcock | 14 | 2 | 44 | 3 | 19 | 4 | 43 | 5 |
| Ironside | 19 | 4 | 51 | 5 | 20·5 | 10 | 37 | 3 |
| Murray | 12 | 3 | 30 | 1 | 8 | 3 | 10 | 1 |
| Tayfield | 8·2 | 2 | 53 | 1 | | | | |

### FALL OF WICKETS

| | SA | NZ | SA | NZ |
|---|---|---|---|---|
| Wkt | 1st | 1st | 2nd | 2nd |
| 1st | 13 | 5 | 11 | 35 |
| 2nd | 37 | 9 | 13 | 38 |
| 3rd | 43 | 23 | 24 | 58 |
| 4th | 100 | 35 | 37 | 75 |
| 5th | 168 | 59 | 44 | 76 |
| 6th | 226 | 82 | 67 | 76 |
| 7th | 244 | 138 | 112 | 76 |
| 8th | 244 | 146 | 122 | 84 |
| 9th | 271 | 154 | 138 | 89 |
| 10th | 271 | 187 | 148 | 100 |

Umpires: D.T. Drew and C.D. Coote.

# SOUTH AFRICA v NEW ZEALAND 1953–54 (3rd Test)

Played at Newlands, Cape Town, on 1, 2, 4, 5 January.
Toss: New Zealand.   Result: MATCH DRAWN.
Debuts: South Africa – R.J. Westcott; New Zealand – W. Bell, I.B. Leggat.

New Zealand recorded their highest total and enforced the follow on for the first time in any Test match. The partnership of 174 between Reid, who batted 196 minutes, and Beck, a 19-year-old who batted 224 minutes, set a record, subsequently twice beaten, for New Zealand's seventh wicket, and is their highest for any wicket against South Africa. Rabone's figures of 6 for 68 remain New Zealand's best analysis in a Test in South Africa.

## NEW ZEALAND

| | | |
|---|---|---:|
| G.O. Rabone* | lbw b Van Ryneveld | 56 |
| M.E. Chapple | c Waite b Van Ryneveld | 76 |
| M.B. Poore | c McGlew b Adcock | 44 |
| B. Sutcliffe | c Waite b Ironside | 66 |
| J.R. Reid | b Murray | 135 |
| J.E.F. Beck | run out | 99 |
| F.L.H. Mooney† | b Ironside | 4 |
| A.R. MacGibbon | c McGlew b Ironside | 8 |
| E.W. Dempster | c Endean b Ironside | 0 |
| I.B. Leggat | c McGlew b Tayfield | 0 |
| W. Bell | not out | 0 |
| Extras | (B 14, LB 3) | 17 |
| **Total** | | **505** |

## SOUTH AFRICA

| | | | | |
|---|---|---:|---|---:|
| D.J. McGlew | c Sutcliffe b MacGibbon | 86 | c Chapple b Poore | 28 |
| J.H.B. Waite† | lbw b MacGibbon | 8 | st Mooney b Rabone | 16 |
| R.J. Westcott | c Leggat b MacGibbon | 2 | b Dempster | 62 |
| W.R. Endean | c Sutcliffe b MacGibbon | 33 | not out | 34 |
| R.A. McLean | c Mooney b Rabone | 9 | not out | 18 |
| C.B. van Ryneveld | c Mooney b Rabone | 23 | | |
| J.E. Cheetham* | b Rabone | 89 | | |
| A.R.A. Murray | lbw b Rabone | 6 | | |
| H.J. Tayfield | c Leggat b Rabone | 34 | | |
| D.E.J. Ironside | c MacGibbon b Rabone | 10 | | |
| N.A.T. Adcock | not out | 8 | | |
| Extras | (B 6, LB 6, NB 6) | 18 | (B 1) | 1 |
| **Total** | | **326** | (3 wickets) | **159** |

| SOUTH AFRICA | O | M | R | W | O | M | R | W | | FALL OF WICKETS | | |
|---|---|---|---|---|---|---|---|---|---|---|---|---|
| | | | | | | | | | | NZ | SA | SA |
| Adcock | 29 | 3 | 105 | 1 | | | | | *Wkt* | *1st* | *1st* | *2nd* |
| Ironside | 46·3 | 16 | 117 | 4 | | | | | 1st | 126 | 17 | 26 |
| Murray | 34 | 8 | 93 | 1 | | | | | 2nd | 145 | 23 | 57 |
| Tayfield | 33 | 10 | 80 | 1 | | | | | 3rd | 239 | 82 | 139 |
| Van Ryneveld | 23 | 1 | 93 | 2 | | | | | 4th | 271 | 101 | – |
| | | | | | | | | | 5th | 445 | 172 | – |
| NEW ZEALAND | | | | | | | | | 6th | 472 | 180 | – |
| MacGibbon | 33 | 13 | 71 | 4 | 8 | 4 | 15 | 0 | 7th | 490 | 204 | – |
| Reid | 20 | 7 | 48 | 0 | 4 | 1 | 8 | 0 | 8th | 505 | 299 | – |
| Leggat | 3 | 0 | 6 | 0 | | | | | 9th | 505 | 313 | – |
| Bell | 18 | 5 | 77 | 0 | 6 | 2 | 22 | 0 | 10th | 505 | 326 | – |
| Rabone | 38·7 | 10 | 68 | 6 | 10 | 6 | 16 | 1 | | | | |
| Dempster | 8 | 3 | 19 | 0 | 6 | 0 | 24 | 1 | | | | |
| Sutcliffe | 5 | 1 | 13 | 0 | 7 | 0 | 33 | 0 | | | | |
| Poore | 2 | 0 | 6 | 0 | 12 | 1 | 39 | 1 | | | | |
| Chapple | | | | | 1 | 0 | 1 | 0 | | | | |

Umpires: D. Collins and S. Collins.

# SOUTH AFRICA v NEW ZEALAND 1953–54 (4th Test)

Played at Ellis Park, Johannesburg, on 29, 30 January, 1, 2 February.
Toss: New Zealand.   Result: SOUTH AFRICA won by nine wickets.
Debuts: Nil.

South Africa won their first home rubber since beating England one-nil in 1930-31. In one first innings spell, Tayfield's off-spin accounted for five wickets for no runs in 32 balls. New Zealand's 79 remains the lowest score by either country in this series.

## SOUTH AFRICA

| | | | | |
|---|---|---|---|---|
| D.J. McGlew | lbw b MacGibbon | 61 | not out | 6 |
| R.J. Westcott | c Chapple b Overton | 43 | lbw b MacGibbon | 1 |
| J.C. Watkins | c Mooney b MacGibbon | 6 | | |
| W.R. Endean | c Sutcliffe b Overton | 7 | | |
| R.A. McLean | c Sutcliffe b Overton | 0 | | |
| C.B. van Ryneveld | c Mooney b Blair | 11 | | |
| J.E. Cheetham* | run out | 29 | (3) not out | 16 |
| J.H.B. Waite† | run out | 52 | | |
| H.J. Tayfield | c Reid b Blair | 19 | | |
| D.E.J. Ironside | not out | 3 | | |
| N.A.T. Adcock | b Blair | 0 | | |
| Extras | (B 3, LB 5, NB 4) | 12 | (NB 2) | 2 |
| **Total** | | **243** | (1 wicket) | 25 |

## NEW ZEALAND

| | | | | |
|---|---|---|---|---|
| F.L.H. Mooney† | run out | 23 | b Adcock | 2 |
| M.E. Chapple | c Waite b Ironside | 4 | (4) c sub (K.J. Funston) b Watkins | 42 |
| M.B. Poore | c and b Tayfield | 18 | c Endean b Adcock | 0 |
| B. Sutcliffe* | c McLean b Tayfield | 0 | (6) b Adcock | 23 |
| J.R. Reid | c Waite b Tayfield | 0 | c Ironside b Tayfield | 26 |
| L.S.M. Miller | b Tayfield | 0 | (7) c Waite b Tayfield | 0 |
| J.E.F. Beck | b Tayfield | 0 | (8) b Adcock | 21 |
| E.W. Dempster | not out | 21 | (2) c Waite b Watkins | 47 |
| A.R. MacGibbon | st Waite b Ironside | 10 | b Adcock | 8 |
| R.W. Blair | b Tayfield | 1 | not out | 5 |
| G.W.F. Overton | b Adcock | 0 | c Van Ryneveld b Ironside | 1 |
| Extras | (LB 1, NB 1) | 2 | (B 5, LB 6, NB 2) | 13 |
| **Total** | | **79** | | **188** |

| NEW ZEALAND | O | M | R | W | O | M | R | W | | FALL OF WICKETS | | | |
|---|---|---|---|---|---|---|---|---|---|---|---|---|---|
| Blair | 19 | 4 | 42 | 3 | 3 | 0 | 6 | 0 | | SA | NZ | NZ | SA |
| Reid | 21 | 3 | 67 | 0 | | | | | Wkt | 1st | 1st | 2nd | 2nd |
| MacGibbon | 26 | 6 | 57 | 2 | 3 | 0 | 16 | 1 | 1st | 104 | 14 | 4 | 4 |
| Overton | 32 | 10 | 65 | 3 | | | | | 2nd | 112 | 34 | 8 | — |
| Miller | | | | | 0·2 | 0 | 1 | 0 | 3rd | 122 | 34 | 79 | — |
| | | | | | | | | | 4th | 122 | 34 | 113 | — |
| SOUTH AFRICA | | | | | | | | | 5th | 125 | 42 | 139 | — |
| Adcock | 11·3 | 1 | 27 | 1 | 26 | 8 | 45 | 5 | 6th | 139 | 42 | 141 | — |
| Ironside | 14 | 5 | 20 | 2 | 23·1 | 6 | 50 | 1 | 7th | 174 | 46 | 168 | — |
| Watkins | 7 | 1 | 17 | 0 | 12 | 4 | 13 | 2 | 8th | 227 | 69 | 182 | — |
| Tayfield | 14 | 7 | 13 | 6 | 29 | 12 | 48 | 2 | 9th | 243 | 76 | 183 | — |
| Van Ryneveld | | | | | 2 | 0 | 19 | 0 | 10th | 243 | 79 | 188 | — |

Umpires: B.V. Malan and D.T. Drew.

# SOUTH AFRICA v NEW ZEALAND 1953–54 (5th Test)

Played at St George's Park, Port Elizabeth, on 5, 6, 8, 9 February.
Toss: New Zealand.    Result: SOUTH AFRICA won by five wickets.
Debuts: Nil.

## NEW ZEALAND

| | | | | | |
|---|---|---|---|---|---|
| F.L.H. Mooney† | c Tayfield b Murray | 24 | c Van Ryneveld b Adcock | | 9 |
| M.E. Chapple | c Waite b Watkins | 18 | lbw b Murray | | 8 |
| M.B. Poore | c Waite b Adcock | 41 | c Waite b Van Ryneveld | | 18 |
| B. Sutcliffe* | c Waite b Watkins | 38 | c and b Van Ryneveld | | 52 |
| J.R. Reid | b Adcock | 19 | run out | | 73 |
| L.S.M. Miller | c Endean b Adcock | 0 | (9) c Waite b Adcock | | 2 |
| J.E.F. Beck | b Adcock | 48 | (6) b Tayfield | | 12 |
| E.W. Dempster | c and b Watkins | 16 | (7) st Waite b Van Ryneveld | | 1 |
| A.R. MacGibbon | b Watkins | 7 | (8) c Adcock b Watkins | | 14 |
| R.W. Blair | c Murray b Tayfield | 8 | st Waite b Van Ryneveld | | 8 |
| W. Bell | not out | 0 | not out | | 21 |
| Extras | (LB 1, W 1, NB 5) | 7 | (LB 3, NB 1) | | 4 |
| **Total** | | **226** | | | **222** |

## SOUTH AFRICA

| | | | | | |
|---|---|---|---|---|---|
| D.J. McGlew | b Bell | 27 | run out | | 38 |
| R.J. Westcott | lbw b Reid | 29 | b MacGibbon | | 11 |
| J.E. Cheetham* | c Sutcliffe b MacGibbon | 42 | (7) not out | | 13 |
| K.J. Funston | lbw b Reid | 10 | (3) c Mooney b MacGibbon | | 0 |
| W.R. Endean | c Reid b MacGibbon | 32 | (4) c and b Bell | | 87 |
| J.C. Watkins | b Reid | 13 | (5) b Reid | | 45 |
| C.B. van Ryneveld | lbw b Blair | 40 | (6) not out | | 10 |
| J.H.B. Waite† | not out | 20 | | | |
| H.J. Tayfield | c Sutcliffe b Blair | 2 | | | |
| A.R.A. Murray | lbw b Reid | 7 | | | |
| N.A.T. Adcock | b MacGibbon | 5 | | | |
| Extras | (B 3, LB 1, NB 6) | 10 | (B 5, LB 4, NB 2) | | 11 |
| **Total** | | **237** | (5 wickets) | | **215** |

| SOUTH AFRICA | O | M | R | W | O | M | R | W | | FALL OF WICKETS | | | |
|---|---|---|---|---|---|---|---|---|---|---|---|---|---|
| Adcock | 19 | 1 | 86 | 4 | 19 | 1 | 45 | 2 | | NZ | SA | NZ | SA |
| Watkins | 16 | 6 | 34 | 4 | 14 | 6 | 21 | 1 | Wkt | 1st | 1st | 2nd | 2nd |
| Tayfield | 29·3 | 15 | 35 | 1 | 17 | 5 | 51 | 1 | 1st | 24 | 40 | 13 | 44 |
| Van Ryneveld | 7 | 1 | 15 | 0 | 20·6 | 1 | 67 | 4 | 2nd | 64 | 69 | 17 | 46 |
| Murray | 21 | 4 | 49 | 1 | 17 | 7 | 34 | 1 | 3rd | 99 | 89 | 77 | 81 |
| NEW ZEALAND | | | | | | | | | 4th | 141 | 140 | 122 | 188 |
| Blair | 16 | 4 | 39 | 2 | 7 | 0 | 15 | 0 | 5th | 146 | 146 | 161 | 198 |
| MacGibbon | 22·1 | 2 | 55 | 3 | 10 | 0 | 44 | 2 | 6th | 146 | 173 | 166 | – |
| Reid | 32 | 16 | 51 | 4 | 15 | 2 | 64 | 1 | 7th | 176 | 207 | 181 | – |
| Bell | 28 | 6 | 82 | 1 | 9·3 | 0 | 54 | 1 | 8th | 188 | 209 | 189 | – |
| Dempster | | | | | 5 | 0 | 27 | 0 | 9th | 226 | 224 | 193 | – |
| Mooney | | | | | 1 | 1 | 0 | 0 | 10th | 226 | 237 | 222 | – |

Umpires: D. Collins and F.R.W. Payne.

# WEST INDIES v ENGLAND 1953–54 (1st Test)

Played at Sabina Park, Kingston, Jamaica, on 15, 16, 18, 19, 20, 21 January.
Toss: West Indies.    Result: WEST INDIES won by 140 runs.
Debuts: West Indies – M. Frederick, J.K. Holt, jr, C.A. McWatt; England – A.E. Moss.

Stollmeyer evoked much criticism for not enforcing the follow on. Lock became the second bowler after E. Jones in 1897-98 to be no-balled for throwing in a Test match. Physical attacks were made on the wife and son of umpire Burke who upheld an appeal against Holt when the local player was six runs short of a century in his first Test.

## WEST INDIES

| | | | | | |
|---|---|---|---|---|---|
| M. Frederick | c Graveney b Statham | 0 | lbw b Statham | | 30 |
| J.B. Stollmeyer* | lbw b Statham | 60 | c Evans b Bailey | | 8 |
| J.K. Holt | lbw b Statham | 94 | lbw b Moss | | 1 |
| E. de C. Weekes | b Moss | 55 | not out | | 90 |
| C.L. Walcott | b Lock | 65 | c Bailey b Lock | | 25 |
| G.A. Headley | c Graveney b Lock | 16 | b Lock | | 1 |
| G.E. Gomez | not out | 47 | lbw b Statham | | 3 |
| C.A. McWatt† | b Lock | 54 | not out | | 36 |
| S. Ramadhin | lbw b Trueman | 7 | | | |
| E.S.M. Kentish | b Statham | 0 | | | |
| A.L. Valentine | b Trueman | 0 | | | |
| Extras | (B 9, LB 4, W 1, NB 5) | 19 | (B 10, LB 4, NB 1) | | 15 |
| **Total** | | **417** | (6 wickets declared) | | **209** |

## ENGLAND

| | | | | | |
|---|---|---|---|---|---|
| W. Watson | b Gomez | 3 | c and b Stollmeyer | | 116 |
| L. Hutton* | b Valentine | 24 | lbw b Gomez | | 56 |
| P.B.H. May | c Headley b Ramadhin | 31 | c McWatt b Kentish | | 69 |
| D.C.S. Compton | lbw b Valentine | 12 | (5) b Ramadhin | | 2 |
| T.W. Graveney | lbw b Ramadhin | 16 | (4) c Weekes b Kentish | | 34 |
| T.E. Bailey | not out | 28 | not out | | 15 |
| T.G. Evans† | c Kentish b Valentine | 10 | b Kentish | | 0 |
| G.A.R. Lock | b Ramadhin | 4 | b Kentish | | 0 |
| J.B. Statham | b Ramadhin | 8 | lbw b Ramadhin | | 1 |
| F.S. Trueman | c McWatt b Gomez | 18 | b Kentish | | 1 |
| A.E. Moss | b Gomez | 0 | run out | | 16 |
| Extras | (B 9, LB 2, W 1, NB 4) | 16 | (B 4, LB 1, NB 1) | | 6 |
| **Total** | | **170** | | | **316** |

| ENGLAND | O | M | R | W | O | M | R | W | | FALL OF WICKETS | | | |
|---|---|---|---|---|---|---|---|---|---|---|---|---|---|
| Statham | 36 | 6 | 90 | 4 | 17 | 2 | 50 | 2 | | WI | E | WI | E |
| Trueman | 34·4 | 8 | 107 | 2 | 6 | 0 | 32 | 0 | Wkt | 1st | 1st | 2nd | 2nd |
| Moss | 26 | 5 | 84 | 1 | 10 | 0 | 30 | 1 | 1st | 6 | 4 | 28 | 130 |
| Bailey | 16 | 4 | 36 | 0 | 20 | 4 | 46 | 1 | 2nd | 140 | 49 | 31 | 220 |
| Lock | 41 | 14 | 76 | 3 | 14 | 2 | 36 | 2 | 3rd | 216 | 73 | 46 | 277 |
| Compton | 2 | 1 | 5 | 0 | | | | | 4th | 234 | 79 | 92 | 282 |
| | | | | | | | | | 5th | 286 | 94 | 94 | 282 |
| WEST INDIES | | | | | | | | | 6th | 316 | 105 | 119 | 282 |
| Kentish | 14 | 5 | 23 | 0 | 29 | 11 | 49 | 5 | 7th | 404 | 117 | – | 282 |
| Gomez | 9·2 | 3 | 16 | 3 | 30 | 9 | 63 | 1 | 8th | 415 | 135 | – | 283 |
| Ramadhin | 35 | 14 | 65 | 4 | 35·3 | 12 | 88 | 2 | 9th | 416 | 165 | – | 285 |
| Valentine | 31 | 10 | 30 | 3 | 25 | 6 | 71 | 0 | 10th | 417 | 170 | – | 316 |
| Headley | | | | | 5 | 0 | 23 | 0 | | | | | |
| Walcott | | | | | 2 | 1 | 4 | 0 | | | | | |
| Stollmeyer | | | | | 3 | 0 | 12 | 1 | | | | | |

Umpires: P. Burke and T.A. Ewart.

# WEST INDIES v ENGLAND 1953–54 (2nd Test)

Played at Kensington Oval, Bridgetown, Barbados, on 6, 8, 9, 10, 11, 12 February.
Toss: West Indies.   Result: WEST INDIES won by 181 runs.
Debuts: England – C.H. Palmer.

Walcott recorded his only double-century in Tests in an innings lasting 6½ hours. On the third day England scored only 128 runs from 114 overs.

## WEST INDIES

| | | | | | |
|---|---|---|---|---|---|
| J.K. Holt | c Graveney b Bailey | 11 | c and b Statham | | 166 |
| J.B. Stollmeyer* | run out | 0 | run out | | 28 |
| F.M.M. Worrell | b Statham | 0 | not out | | 76 |
| C.L. Walcott | st Evans b Laker | 220 | not out | | 17 |
| B.H. Pairaudeau | c Hutton b Laker | 71 | | | |
| G.E. Gomez | lbw b Statham | 7 | | | |
| D. St E. Atkinson | c Evans b Laker | 53 | | | |
| C.A. McWatt† | lbw b Lock | 11 | | | |
| S. Ramadhin | b Statham | 1 | | | |
| F.M. King | b Laker | 5 | | | |
| A.L. Valentine | not out | 0 | | | |
| Extras | (LB 2, NB 2) | 4 | (B 4, NB 1) | | 5 |
| **Total** | | **383** | (2 wickets declared) | | **292** |

## ENGLAND

| | | | | | |
|---|---|---|---|---|---|
| L. Hutton* | c Ramadhin b Valentine | 72 | c Worrell b Ramadhin | | 77 |
| W. Watson | st McWatt b Ramadhin | 6 | c McWatt b King | | 0 |
| P.B.H. May | c King b Ramadhin | 7 | c Walcott b Gomez | | 62 |
| D.C.S. Compton | c King b Valentine | 13 | lbw b Stollmeyer | | 93 |
| T.W. Graveney | c and b Ramadhin | 15 | not out | | 64 |
| C.H. Palmer | c Walcott b Ramadhin | 22 | c Gomez b Atkinson | | 0 |
| T.E. Bailey | c McWatt b Atkinson | 28 | c sub (C.C. Hunte) b Stollmeyer | | 4 |
| T.G. Evans† | b Gomez | 10 | b Ramadhin | | 5 |
| J.C. Laker | c Gomez b Atkinson | 1 | lbw b Ramadhin | | 0 |
| G.A.R. Lock | not out | 0 | b King | | 0 |
| J.B. Statham | c Holt b Valentine | 3 | b Gomez | | 0 |
| Extras | (B 2, LB 1, NB 1) | 4 | (B 6, LB 1, W 1) | | 8 |
| **Total** | | **181** | | | **313** |

| ENGLAND | O | M | R | W | O | M | R | W | | FALL OF WICKETS | | | |
|---|---|---|---|---|---|---|---|---|---|---|---|---|---|
| Statham | 27 | 6 | 90 | 3 | 15 | 1 | 49 | 1 | | | WI | E | WI | E |
| Bailey | 22 | 6 | 63 | 1 | 12 | 1 | 48 | 0 | | *Wkt* | *1st* | *1st* | *2nd* | *2nd* |
| Lock | 41 | 9 | 116 | 1 | 33 | 7 | 100 | 0 | | 1st | 11 | 35 | 51 | 1 |
| Laker | 30·1 | 6 | 81 | 4 | 30 | 13 | 62 | 0 | | 2nd | 11 | 45 | 273 | 108 |
| Compton | 5 | 0 | 29 | 0 | 1 | 0 | 13 | 0 | | 3rd | 25 | 70 | – | 181 |
| Palmer | | | | | 5 | 1 | 15 | 0 | | 4th | 190 | 107 | – | 258 |
| | | | | | | | | | | 5th | 226 | 119 | – | 259 |
| WEST INDIES | | | | | | | | | | 6th | 319 | 158 | – | 264 |
| King | 14 | 6 | 28 | 0 | 18 | 6 | 56 | 2 | | 7th | 352 | 176 | – | 281 |
| Gomez | 13 | 8 | 10 | 1 | 13·4 | 3 | 28 | 2 | | 8th | 372 | 176 | – | 281 |
| Worrell | 9 | 2 | 21 | 0 | 1 | 0 | 10 | 0 | | 9th | 378 | 177 | – | 300 |
| Atkinson | 9 | 7 | 5 | 2 | 23 | 10 | 35 | 1 | | 10th | 383 | 181 | – | 313 |
| Ramadhin | 53 | 30 | 50 | 4 | 37 | 17 | 71 | 3 | | | | | | |
| Valentine | 51·5 | 30 | 61 | 3 | 39 | 18 | 87 | 0 | | | | | | |
| Stollmeyer | 1 | 0 | 2 | 0 | 6 | 1 | 14 | 2 | | | | | | |
| Walcott | | | | | 2 | 0 | 4 | 0 | | | | | | |

Umpires: H. Walcott and H.B. de C. Jordan.

# WEST INDIES v ENGLAND 1953–54 (3rd Test)

Played at Bourda, Georgetown, British Guiana, on 24, 25, 26, 27 February, 1, 2 March.
Toss: England.   Result: ENGLAND won by nine wickets.
Debuts: Nil.

Valentine took his hundredth Test wicket at the age of 23 years 302 days. The partnership of 99 between McWatt and Holt remains the West Indies record for the eighth wicket against England. When it was ended with a run out, sections of the crowd hurled bottles and other missiles on to the playing area.

## ENGLAND

| | | | | |
|---|---|---|---|---|
| W. Watson | b Ramadhin | 12 | (3) not out | 27 |
| L. Hutton* | c Worrell b Ramadhin | 169 | | |
| P.B.H. May | lbw b Atkinson | 12 | (2) b Atkinson | 12 |
| D.C.S. Compton | c Stollmeyer b Atkinson | 64 | | |
| T.W. Graveney | b Ramadhin | 0 | (1) not out | 33 |
| J.H. Wardle | b Ramadhin | 38 | | |
| T.E. Bailey | c Weekes b Ramadhin | 49 | | |
| T.G. Evans† | lbw b Atkinson | 19 | | |
| J.C. Laker | b Valentine | 27 | | |
| G.A.R. Lock | b Ramadhin | 13 | | |
| J.B. Statham | not out | 10 | | |
| Extras | (B 20, NB 2) | 22 | (B 3) | 3 |
| **Total** | | **435** | **(1 wicket)** | **75** |

## WEST INDIES

| | | | | |
|---|---|---|---|---|
| F.M.M. Worrell | c Evans b Statham | 0 | (3) c Evans b Statham | 2 |
| J.B. Stollmeyer* | b Statham | 2 | c Compton b Laker | 44 |
| E. de C. Weekes | b Lock | 94 | (4) c Graveney b Bailey | 38 |
| C.L. Walcott | b Statham | 4 | (5) lbw b Laker | 26 |
| R.J. Christiani | c Watson b Laker | 25 | (6) b Bailey | 11 |
| G.E. Gomez | b Statham | 8 | (7) c Graveney b Wardle | 35 |
| D. St E. Atkinson | c and b Lock | 0 | (8) b Wardle | 18 |
| C.A. McWatt† | run out | 54 | (9) not out | 9 |
| J.K. Holt | not out | 48 | (1) b Lock | 64 |
| S. Ramadhin | b Laker | 0 | b Statham | 1 |
| A.L. Valentine | run out | 0 | b Wardle | 0 |
| Extras | (B 8, LB 7, W 1) | 16 | (B 2, LB 4, NB 2) | 8 |
| **Total** | | **251** | | **256** |

| WEST INDIES | O | M | R | W | O | M | R | W | | FALL OF WICKETS | | | |
|---|---|---|---|---|---|---|---|---|---|---|---|---|---|
| Gomez | 32 | 6 | 75 | 0 | 5 | 1 | 15 | 0 | | E | WI | WI | E |
| Worrell | 15 | 4 | 33 | 0 | | | | | *Wkt* | *1st* | *1st* | *2nd* | *2nd* |
| Ramadhin | 67 | 34 | 113 | 6 | 4 | 0 | 7 | 0 | 1st | 33 | 1 | 79 | 18 |
| Valentine | 44 | 18 | 109 | 1 | | | | | 2nd | 76 | 12 | 96 | – |
| Atkinson | 58 | 27 | 78 | 3 | 7 | 0 | 34 | 1 | 3rd | 226 | 16 | 120 | – |
| Stollmeyer | 2 | 1 | 3 | 0 | | | | | 4th | 227 | 78 | 168 | – |
| Walcott | 2 | 0 | 2 | 0 | 2 | 0 | 6 | 0 | 5th | 306 | 132 | 186 | – |
| Weekes | | | | | 1·1 | 0 | 8 | 0 | 6th | 321 | 134 | 200 | – |
| Christiani | | | | | 1 | 0 | 2 | 0 | 7th | 350 | 139 | 245 | – |
| | | | | | | | | | 8th | 390 | 238 | 246 | – |
| ENGLAND | | | | | | | | | 9th | 412 | 240 | 251 | – |
| Statham | 27 | 6 | 64 | 4 | 22 | 3 | 86 | 2 | 10th | 435 | 251 | 256 | – |
| Bailey | 5 | 0 | 13 | 0 | 22 | 9 | 41 | 2 | | | | | |
| Laker | 21 | 11 | 32 | 2 | 36 | 18 | 56 | 2 | | | | | |
| Wardle | 22 | 4 | 60 | 0 | 12·3 | 4 | 24 | 3 | | | | | |
| Compton | 3 | 1 | 6 | 0 | | | | | | | | | |
| Lock | 27·5 | 7 | 60 | 2 | 25 | 11 | 41 | 1 | | | | | |

Umpires: E.S. Gillette and B. Menzies.

# WEST INDIES v ENGLAND 1953–54 (4th Test)

Played at Queen's Park Oval, Port-of-Spain, Trinidad, on 17, 18, 19, 20, 22, 23 March.
Toss: West Indies.   Result: MATCH DRAWN.
Debuts: Nil.

No Test had been finished on this ground since the jute matting pitch was put down in 1934. This match produced 1,528 runs for the loss of 25 wickets and yet another draw. The West Indies total of 681 for 8 remains their highest at home against England and a record for any Trinidad Test. Weekes and Worrell shared a stand of 338 which is still the West Indies third-wicket record in all Tests. W. Ferguson kept wicket in the second innings and held two catches.

## WEST INDIES

| | | | | |
|---|---|---|---|---|
| J.K. Holt | c Compton b Trueman | 40 | c sub (K.G. Suttle) b Trueman | 1 |
| J.B. Stollmeyer* | c and b Compton | 41 | | |
| E. de C. Weekes | c Bailey b Lock | 206 | c sub (A.E. Moss) b Lock | 56 |
| F.M.M. Worrell | b Lock | 167 | not out | 51 |
| C.L. Walcott | c and b Laker | 124 | | |
| B.H. Pairaudeau | run out | 0 | (1) hit wkt b Bailey | 5 |
| D. St E. Atkinson | c Graveney b Compton | 74 | (6) not out | 53 |
| C.A. McWatt* | b Laker | 4 | | |
| W. Ferguson | not out | 8 | (2) b Bailey | 44 |
| S. Ramadhin | } did not bat | | | |
| F.M. King | } | | | |
| Extras | (B 6, LB 4, W 4, NB 3) | 17 | (LB 2) | 2 |
| **Total** | (8 wickets declared) | **681** | (4 wickets declared) | **212** |

## ENGLAND

| | | | | |
|---|---|---|---|---|
| L. Hutton* | c Ferguson b King | 44 | (4) not out | 30 |
| T.E. Bailey | c Weekes b Ferguson | 46 | | |
| P.B.H. May | c Pairaudeau b King | 135 | c Worrell b McWatt | 16 |
| D.C.S. Compton | c and b Ramadhin | 133 | | |
| W. Watkins | c Atkinson b Walcott | 4 | (1) c Ferguson b Worrell | 32 |
| T.W. Graveney | c and b Walcott | 92 | (5) not out | 0 |
| R.T. Spooner† | b Walcott | 19 | (2) c Ferguson b Ramadhin | 16 |
| J.C. Laker | retired hurt | 7 | | |
| G.A.R. Lock | lbw b Worrell | 10 | | |
| F.S. Trueman | lbw b King | 19 | | |
| J.B. Statham | not out | 6 | | |
| Extras | (B 10, LB 5, W 7) | 22 | (LB 4) | 4 |
| **Total** | | **537** | (3 wickets) | **98** |

| ENGLAND | O | M | R | W | O | M | R | W |
|---|---|---|---|---|---|---|---|---|
| Statham | 9 | 0 | 31 | 0 | | | | |
| Trueman | 33 | 3 | 131 | 1 | 15 | 5 | 23 | 1 |
| Bailey | 32 | 7 | 104 | 0 | 12 | 2 | 20 | 2 |
| Laker | 50 | 8 | 154 | 2 | | | | |
| Lock | 63 | 14 | 178 | 2 | 10 | 2 | 40 | 1 |
| Compton | 8·4 | 1 | 40 | 2 | 7 | 0 | 51 | 0 |
| Graveney | 3 | 0 | 26 | 0 | 5 | 0 | 33 | 0 |
| Hutton | | | | | 6 | 0 | 43 | 0 |

| WEST INDIES | O | M | R | W | O | M | R | W |
|---|---|---|---|---|---|---|---|---|
| King | 48·2 | 16 | 97 | 3 | | | | |
| Worrell | 20 | 2 | 58 | 1 | 9 | 1 | 29 | 1 |
| Ramadhin | 34 | 13 | 74 | 1 | 7 | 4 | 6 | 1 |
| Atkinson | 32 | 12 | 60 | 0 | 4 | 0 | 12 | 0 |
| Ferguson | 47 | 7 | 155 | 1 | | | | |
| Stollmeyer | 6 | 2 | 19 | 0 | | | | |
| Walcott | 34 | 18 | 52 | 3 | | | | |
| Weekes | | | | | 5 | 1 | 28 | 0 |
| McWatt | | | | | 4 | 2 | 16 | 1 |
| Pairaudeau | | | | | 1 | 0 | 3 | 0 |

## FALL OF WICKETS

| Wkt | WI 1st | E 1st | WI 2nd | E 2nd |
|---|---|---|---|---|
| 1st | 78 | 73 | 19 | 52 |
| 2nd | 92 | 135 | 20 | 52 |
| 3rd | 430 | 301 | 72 | 83 |
| 4th | 517 | 314 | 111 | – |
| 5th | 540 | 424 | – | – |
| 6th | 627 | 493 | – | – |
| 7th | 641 | 496 | – | – |
| 8th | 681 | 510 | – | – |
| 9th | – | 537 | – | – |
| 10th | – | – | – | – |

Umpires: K. Woods and E.E. Achong.

# WEST INDIES v ENGLAND 1953–54 (5th Test)

Played at Sabina Park, Kingston, Jamaica, on 30, 31 March, 1, 2, 3 April.
Toss: West Indies.   Result: ENGLAND won by nine wickets.
Debuts: West Indies – G. St A. Sobers.

West Indies suffered their first defeat at Sabina Park after Hutton had scored the first double-century by an England captain in an overseas Test, and Bailey had returned what was then England's best analysis against West Indies. England thus squared the rubber after being two matches down and in spite of losing the toss four times. Sobers took the first of his 235 Test wickets when he dismissed his eventual biographer.

## WEST INDIES

| | | | | |
|---|---|--:|---|--:|
| J.K. Holt | c Lock b Bailey | 0 | c Lock b Trueman | 8 |
| J.B. Stollmeyer* | c Evans b Bailey | 9 | lbw b Trueman | 64 |
| E. de C. Weekes | b Bailey | 0 | b Wardle | 3 |
| F.M.M. Worrell | c Wardle b Trueman | 4 | c Graveney b Trueman | 29 |
| C.L. Walcott | c Laker b Lock | 50 | c Graveney b Laker | 116 |
| D. St E. Atkinson | lbw b Bailey | 21 | (7) c Watson b Bailey | 40 |
| G.E. Gomez | c Watson b Bailey | 4 | (6) lbw b Laker | 22 |
| C.A. McWatt† | c Lock b Bailey | 22 | c Wardle b Laker | 8 |
| G. St A. Sobers | not out | 14 | c Compton b Lock | 26 |
| F.M. King | b Bailey | 9 | (11) not out | 10 |
| S. Ramadhin | lbw b Trueman | 4 | (10) c and b Laker | 10 |
| Extras | (LB 1, NB 1) | 2 | (B 4, LB 3, W 1, NB 2) | 10 |
| **Total** | | **139** | | **346** |

## ENGLAND

| | | | | |
|---|---|--:|---|--:|
| L. Hutton* | c McWatt b Walcott | 205 | | |
| T.E. Bailey | c McWatt b Sobers | 23 | | |
| P.B.H. May | c sub (B.H. Pairaudeau) b Ramadhin | 30 | not out | 40 |
| D.C.S. Compton | hit wkt b King | 31 | | |
| W. Watson | c McWatt b King | 4 | (2) not out | 20 |
| T.W. Graveney | lbw b Atkinson | 11 | (1) b King | 0 |
| T.G. Evans† | c Worrell b Ramadhin | 28 | | |
| J.H. Wardle | c Holt b Sobers | 66 | | |
| G.A.R. Lock | b Sobers | 4 | | |
| J.C. Laker | b Sobers | 9 | | |
| F.S. Trueman | not out | 0 | | |
| Extras | (LB 3) | 3 | (B 12) | 12 |
| **Total** | | **414** | (1 wicket) | **72** |

| ENGLAND | O | M | R | W | O | M | R | W |
|---|---|---|---|---|---|---|---|---|
| Bailey | 16 | 7 | 34 | 7 | 25 | 11 | 54 | 1 |
| Trueman | 15·4 | 4 | 39 | 2 | 29 | 7 | 88 | 3 |
| Wardle | 10 | 1 | 20 | 0 | 39 | 14 | 83 | 1 |
| Lock | 15 | 6 | 31 | 1 | 27 | 16 | 40 | 1 |
| Laker | 4 | 1 | 13 | 0 | 50 | 27 | 71 | 4 |
| WEST INDIES | | | | | | | | |
| King | 26 | 12 | 45 | 2 | 4 | 1 | 21 | 1 |
| Gomez | 25 | 8 | 56 | 0 | | | | |
| Atkinson | 41 | 15 | 82 | 1 | 3 | 0 | 8 | 0 |
| Ramadhin | 29 | 9 | 71 | 2 | 3 | 0 | 14 | 0 |
| Sobers | 28·5 | 9 | 75 | 4 | 1 | 0 | 6 | 0 |
| Walcott | 11 | 5 | 26 | 1 | | | | |
| Worrell | 11 | 0 | 34 | 0 | 4 | 0 | 8 | 0 |
| Stollmeyer | 5 | 0 | 22 | 0 | | | | |
| Weekes | | | | | 0·5 | 0 | 3 | 0 |

FALL OF WICKETS

| Wkt | WI 1st | E 1st | WI 2nd | E 2nd |
|---|---|---|---|---|
| 1st | 0 | 43 | 26 | 0 |
| 2nd | 2 | 104 | 38 | – |
| 3rd | 13 | 152 | 102 | – |
| 4th | 13 | 160 | 123 | – |
| 5th | 65 | 179 | 191 | – |
| 6th | 75 | 287 | 273 | – |
| 7th | 110 | 392 | 293 | – |
| 8th | 115 | 401 | 306 | – |
| 9th | 133 | 406 | 326 | – |
| 10th | 139 | 414 | 346 | – |

Umpires: P. Burke and T.A. Ewart.

# ENGLAND v PAKISTAN 1954 (1st Test)

Played at Lord's, London, on 10 (*no play*), 11 (*no play*), 12 (*no play*), 14, 15 June.
Toss: England.   Result: MATCH DRAWN.
Debuts: Pakistan – Alimuddin, Khalid Wazir, Shujauddin.

Play in Pakistan's first official Test against England could not begin until 3.45 p.m. on the fourth day. Pakistan's total of 87 remains their lowest in any Test and occupied 235 minutes. Hanif took 340 minutes to score 59 runs in the match. Khan Mohammad bowled all five of his victims, including Hutton with his first ball.

## PAKISTAN

| | | | | | |
|---|---|---|---|---|---|
| Hanif Mohammad | b Tattersall | 20 | lbw b Laker | 39 |
| Alimuddin | c Edrich b Wardle | 19 | b Bailey | 0 |
| Waqar Hassan | c Compton b Wardle | 9 | c Statham b Compton | 53 |
| Maqsood Ahmed | st Evans b Wardle | 0 | not out | 29 |
| Imtiaz Ahmed† | b Laker | 12 | | |
| A.H. Kardar* | b Statham | 2 | | |
| Fazal Mahmood | b Wardle | 5 | | |
| Khalid Wazir | b Statham | 3 | | |
| Khan Mohammad | b Statham | 0 | | |
| Zulfiqar Ahmed | b Statham | 11 | | |
| Shujauddin | not out | 0 | | |
| Extras | (B 4, LB 1, NB 1) | 6 | | |
| **Total** | | **87** | (3 wickets) | **121** |

## ENGLAND

| | | |
|---|---|---|
| L. Hutton* | b Khan | 0 |
| R.T. Simpson | lbw b Fazal | 40 |
| P.B.H. May | b Khan | 27 |
| D.C.S. Compton | b Fazal | 0 |
| W.J. Edrich | b Khan | 4 |
| J.H. Wardle | c Maqsood b Fazal | 3 |
| T.G. Evans† | b Khan | 25 |
| T.E. Bailey | b Khan | 3 |
| J.C. Laker | not out | 13 |
| J.B. Statham | b Fazal | 0 |
| R. Tattersall | did not bat | |
| Extras | (B 2) | 2 |
| **Total** | (9 wickets declared) | **117** |

| ENGLAND | O | M | R | W | O | M | R | W |
|---|---|---|---|---|---|---|---|---|
| Statham | 13 | 6 | 18 | 4 | 5 | 2 | 17 | 0 |
| Bailey | 3 | 2 | 1 | 0 | 6 | 2 | 13 | 1 |
| Wardle | 30·5 | 22 | 33 | 4 | 8 | 6 | 6 | 0 |
| Tattersall | 15 | 8 | 12 | 1 | 10 | 1 | 27 | 0 |
| Laker | 22 | 12 | 17 | 1 | 10·2 | 5 | 22 | 1 |
| Compton | | | | | 13 | 2 | 36 | 1 |
| PAKISTAN | | | | | | | | |
| Fazal | 16 | 2 | 54 | 4 | | | | |
| Khan | 15 | 3 | 61 | 5 | | | | |

FALL OF WICKETS

| Wkt | P 1st | E 1st | P 2nd |
|---|---|---|---|
| 1st | 24 | 9 | 0 |
| 2nd | 42 | 55 | 71 |
| 3rd | 43 | 59 | 121 |
| 4th | 57 | 72 | – |
| 5th | 67 | 75 | – |
| 6th | 67 | 79 | – |
| 7th | 71 | 85 | – |
| 8th | 71 | 110 | – |
| 9th | 87 | 117 | – |
| 10th | 87 | – | – |

Umpires: D. Davies and T.J. Bartley.

# ENGLAND v PAKISTAN 1954 (2nd Test)

Played at Trent Bridge, Nottingham, on 1, 2, 3, 5 July.
Toss: Pakistan.   Result: ENGLAND won by an innings and 129 runs.
Debuts: England – R. Appleyard; Pakistan – M.E.Z. Ghazali, Khalid Hassan (*aged 16 years 352 days — then the youngest Test cricketer*), Mohammad Aslam.

England recorded their highest total against Pakistan. Compton reached his 200 in 245 minutes and batted 290 minutes for his highest Test innings which included a six and 33 fours; it remains the Test record for Trent Bridge and the highest innings for either country in this series. His stand of 192 in 105 minutes with Bailey is still England's highest for the fifth wicket against Pakistan. Appleyard took a wicket with his second ball in Test cricket.

## PAKISTAN

| | | | | |
|---|---|---|---|---|
| Hanif Mohammad | lbw b Appleyard | 19 | c Evans b Bedser | 51 |
| Alimuddin | b Statham | 4 | b Statham | 18 |
| Waqar Hassan | b Appleyard | 7 | c Evans b Statham | 7 |
| Maqsood Ahmed | c Evans b Appleyard | 6 | c Statham b Appleyard | 69 |
| Imtiaz Ahmed† | b Appleyard | 11 | lbw b Wardle | 33 |
| A.H. Kardar* | c Compton b Bedser | 28 | c Graveney b Wardle | 4 |
| Fazal Mahmood | c Sheppard b Bedser | 14 | b Statham | 36 |
| M.E.Z. Ghazali | b Statham | 18 | c Statham b Bedser | 14 |
| Mohammad Aslam | b Wardle | 16 | c Sheppard b Appleyard | 18 |
| Khalid Hassan | c May b Appleyard | 10 | (11) not out | 7 |
| Khan Mohammad | not out | 13 | (10) c Compton b Wardle | 8 |
| Extras | (B 9, LB 1, NB 1) | 11 | (B 4, LB 3) | 7 |
| **Total** | | **157** | | **272** |

## ENGLAND

| | | |
|---|---|---|
| D.S. Sheppard* | c Imtiaz b Khan | 37 |
| R.T. Simpson | b Khalid | 101 |
| P.B.H. May | b Khan | 0 |
| D.C.S. Compton | b Khalid | 278 |
| T.W. Graveney | c Maqsood b Kardar | 84 |
| T.E. Bailey | not out | 36 |
| T.G. Evans† | b Khan | 4 |
| J.H. Wardle | not out | 14 |
| A.V. Bedser | ) | |
| J.B. Statham | ) did not bat | |
| R. Appleyard | ) | |
| Extras | (B 2, LB 1, NB 1) | 4 |
| **Total** | (6 wickets declared) | **558** |

| ENGLAND | O | M | R | W | O | M | R | W | | FALL OF WICKETS | | | |
|---|---|---|---|---|---|---|---|---|---|---|---|---|---|
| Bedser | 21 | 8 | 30 | 2 | 30 | 11 | 83 | 2 | | | P | E | P |
| Statham | 18 | 3 | 38 | 2 | 20 | 3 | 66 | 3 | Wkt | 1st | 1st | 2nd |
| Appleyard | 17 | 5 | 51 | 5 | 30·4 | 8 | 72 | 2 | 1st | 26 | 98 | 69 |
| Bailey | 3 | 0 | 18 | 0 | | | | | 2nd | 37 | 102 | 70 |
| Wardle | 6 | 3 | 9 | 1 | 32 | 17 | 44 | 3 | 3rd | 43 | 185 | 95 |
| | | | | | | | | | 4th | 50 | 339 | 164 |
| PAKISTAN | | | | | | | | | 5th | 55 | 531 | 168 |
| Fazal | 47 | 7 | 148 | 0 | | | | | 6th | 86 | 536 | 189 |
| Khan | 40 | 3 | 155 | 3 | | | | | 7th | 111 | – | 216 |
| Kardar | 28 | 4 | 110 | 1 | | | | | 8th | 121 | – | 242 |
| Khalid Hassan | 21 | 1 | 116 | 2 | | | | | 9th | 138 | – | 254 |
| Maqsood | 3 | 0 | 25 | 0 | | | | | 10th | 157 | – | 272 |

Umpires: F. Chester and T.W. Spencer.

# ENGLAND v PAKISTAN 1954 (3rd Test)

Played at Old Trafford, Manchester, on 22, 23 (*no play*), 24, 26 (*no play*), 27 (*no play*) July.
Toss: England.   Result: MATCH DRAWN.
Debuts: England – J.E. McConnon, J.M. Parks.

Rain allowed play on only two days – 10¾ hours in all. McConnon began his short Test career with 3 for 12 in six overs and held four catches.

## ENGLAND

| | | | |
|---|---|---:|---|
| D.S. Sheppard* | b Fazal | 13 | |
| T.E. Bailey | run out | 42 | |
| P.B.H. May | c Imtiaz b Shujauddin | 14 | |
| D.C.S. Compton | c Imtiaz b Shujauddin | 93 | |
| T.W. Graveney | st Imtiaz b Shujauddin | 65 | |
| J.M. Parks | b Fazal | 15 | |
| T.G. Evans† | c Hanif b Fazal | 31 | |
| J.H. Wardle | c Waqar b Fazal | 54 | |
| A.V. Bedser | not out | 22 | |
| J.E. McConnon | not out | 5 | |
| J.B. Statham | did not bat | | |
| Extras | (B 1, LB 4) | 5 | |
| **Total** | (8 wickets declared) | **359** | |

## PAKISTAN

| | | | | | |
|---|---|---:|---|---:|---:|
| Hanif Mohammad | c Wardle b McConnon | 32 | c Sheppard b Wardle | 1 | |
| Imtiaz Ahmed† | c McConnon b Wardle | 13 | | | |
| Waqar Hassan | c and b McConnon | 11 | | | |
| Maqsood Ahmed | c Wardle b McConnon | 4 | | | |
| A.H. Kardar* | b Wardle | 9 | (4) not out | 0 | |
| M.E.Z. Ghazali | c Sheppard b Wardle | 0 | (5) c Wardle b Bedser | 0 | |
| Wazir Mohammad | c McConnon b Bedser | 5 | (3) c Parks b Bedser | 7 | |
| Fazal Mahmood | c Compton b Bedser | 9 | | | |
| Khalid Wazir | c McConnon b Wardle | 2 | (6) not out | 9 | |
| Shujauddin | not out | 0 | (2) c Graveney b Bedser | 1 | |
| Mahmood Hussain | b Bedser | 0 | | | |
| Extras | (B 4, NB 1) | 5 | (B 2, LB 4, NB 1) | 7 | |
| **Total** | | **90** | (4 wickets) | 25 | |

| PAKISTAN | O | M | R | W | O | M | R | W | | FALL OF WICKETS | | |
|---|---:|---:|---:|---:|---:|---:|---:|---:|---|---|---|---|
| Fazal | 42 | 14 | 107 | 4 | | | | | | E | P | P |
| Mahmood Hussain | 27 | 5 | 88 | 0 | | | | | *Wkt* | *1st* | *1st* | *2nd* |
| Shujauddin | 48 | 12 | 127 | 3 | | | | | 1st | 20 | 26 | 1 |
| Ghazali | 8 | 1 | 18 | 0 | | | | | 2nd | 57 | 58 | 8 |
| Maqsood | 4 | 0 | 14 | 0 | | | | | 3rd | 97 | 63 | 10 |
| | | | | | | | | | 4th | 190 | 66 | 10 |
| AUSTRALIA | | | | | | | | | 5th | 217 | 66 | – |
| Statham | 4 | 0 | 11 | 0 | | | | | 6th | 261 | 77 | – |
| Bedser | 15·5 | 4 | 36 | 3 | 8 | 5 | 9 | 3 | 7th | 293 | 80 | – |
| Wardle | 24 | 16 | 19 | 4 | 7 | 2 | 9 | 1 | 8th | 348 | 87 | – |
| McConnon | 13 | 5 | 19 | 3 | | | | | 9th | – | 89 | – |
| | | | | | | | | | 10th | – | 90 | – |

Umpires: F. Chester and F.S. Lee.

# ENGLAND v PAKISTAN 1954 (4th Test)

Played at Kennington Oval, London, on 12, 13 (*no play*), 14, 16, 17 August.
Toss: Pakistan.   Result: PAKISTAN won by 24 runs.
Debuts: England – P.J. Loader, F.H. Tyson.

Pakistan gained their first and only victory against England and so squared the rubber. In doing so they became the first country to win a Test in their first rubber in England. Evans beat W.A.S. Oldfield's world record of 130 dismissals when he caught Kardar. England recorded their lowest total against Pakistan and Fazal claimed the best Pakistan analysis in a Test in England.

## PAKISTAN

| | | | | | |
|---|---|---|---|---|---|
| Hanif Mohammad | lbw b Statham | 0 | | c Graveney b Wardle | 19 |
| Alimuddin | b Tyson | 10 | (7) | lbw b Wardle | 0 |
| Waqar Hasan | b Loader | 7 | | run out | 9 |
| Maqsood Ahmed | b Tyson | 0 | | c Wardle b McConnon | 4 |
| Imtiaz Ahmed† | c Evans b Tyson | 23 | | c Wardle b Tyson | 12 |
| A.H. Kardar* | c Evans b Statham | 36 | | c and b Wardle | 17 |
| Wazir Mohammad | run out | 0 | (8) | not out | 42 |
| Fazal Mahmood | c Evans b Loader | 0 | (9) | b Wardle | 6 |
| Shujauddin | not out | 16 | (2) | c May b Wardle | 12 |
| Zulfiqar Ahmed | c Compton b Loader | 16 | | c May b Wardle | 34 |
| Mahmood Hussain | b Tyson | 23 | | c Statham b Wardle | 6 |
| Extras | (NB 2) | 2 | | (B 3) | 3 |
| **Total** | | **133** | | | **164** |

## ENGLAND

| | | | | | |
|---|---|---|---|---|---|
| L. Hutton* | c Imtiaz b Fazal | 14 | | c Imtiaz b Fazal | 5 |
| R.T. Simpson | c Kardar b Mahmood | 2 | | c and b Zulfiqar | 27 |
| P.B.H. May | c Kardar b Fazal | 26 | | c Kardar b Fazal | 53 |
| D.C.S. Compton | c Imtiaz b Fazal | 53 | | c Imtiaz b Fazal | 29 |
| T.W. Graveney | c Hanif b Fazal | 1 | (6) | lbw b Shujauddin | 0 |
| T.G. Evans† | c Maqsood b Mahmood | 0 | (5) | b Fazal | 3 |
| J.H. Wardle | c Imtiaz b Fazal | 8 | | c Shujauddin b Fazal | 9 |
| F.H. Tyson | c Imtiaz b Fazal | 3 | | c Imtiaz b Fazal | 3 |
| J.E. McConnon | c Fazal b Mahmood | 11 | (10) | run out | 2 |
| J.B. Statham | c Shujauddin b Mahmood | 1 | (11) | not out | 2 |
| P.J Loader | not out | 8 | (9) | c Waqar b Mahmood | 5 |
| Extras | (LB 1, W 1, NB 1) | 3 | | (LB 2, NB 3) | 5 |
| **Total** | | **130** | | | **143** |

| ENGLAND | O | M | R | W | O | M | R | W | | FALL OF WICKETS | | | |
|---|---|---|---|---|---|---|---|---|---|---|---|---|---|
| Statham | 11 | 5 | 26 | 2 | 18 | 7 | 37 | 0 | | P | E | P | E |
| Tyson | 13·4 | 3 | 35 | 4 | 9 | 2 | 22 | 1 | Wkt | 1st | 1st | 2nd | 2nd |
| Loader | 18 | 5 | 35 | 3 | 16 | 6 | 26 | 0 | 1st | 0 | 6 | 19 | 15 |
| McConnon | 9 | 2 | 35 | 0 | 14 | 5 | 20 | 1 | 2nd | 10 | 26 | 38 | 66 |
| Wardle | | | | | 35 | 16 | 56 | 7 | 3rd | 10 | 56 | 43 | 109 |
| | | | | | | | | | 4th | 26 | 63 | 54 | 115 |
| PAKISTAN | | | | | | | | | 5th | 51 | 69 | 63 | 116 |
| Fazal | 30 | 16 | 53 | 6 | 30 | 11 | 46 | 6 | 6th | 51 | 92 | 73 | 121 |
| Mahmood Hussain | 21·3 | 6 | 58 | 4 | 14 | 4 | 32 | 1 | 7th | 51 | 106 | 76 | 131 |
| Zulfiqar | 5 | 2 | 8 | 0 | 14 | 2 | 35 | 1 | 8th | 77 | 115 | 82 | 138 |
| Shujauddin | 3 | 0 | 8 | 0 | 10 | 1 | 25 | 1 | 9th | 106 | 116 | 140 | 138 |
| | | | | | | | | | 10th | 133 | 130 | 164 | 143 |

Umpires: F.S. Lee and D. Davies.

# AUSTRALIA v ENGLAND 1954–55 (1st Test)

Played at Woolloongabba, Brisbane, on 26, 27, 29, 30 November, 1 December.
Toss: England.    Result: AUSTRALIA won by an innings and 154 runs.
Debuts: Australia – L.E. Favell; England – K.V. Andrew, M.C. Cowdrey.

Hutton was the first England captain to put the opposition in to bat in Australia since J.W.H.T. Douglas (1911-12) and Australia's total was the highest in response to this action in a Test match. England took the field without a slow bowler for only the second time (also *Test No. 221*). Compton fractured a bone in his left hand on the fencing while fielding.

## AUSTRALIA

| | | |
|---|---|---|
| L.E. Favell | c Cowdrey b Statham | 23 |
| A.R. Morris | c Cowdrey b Bailey | 153 |
| K.R. Miller | b Bailey | 49 |
| R.N. Harvey | c Bailey b Bedser | 162 |
| G.B. Hole | run out | 57 |
| R. Benaud | c May b Tyson | 34 |
| R.G. Archer | c Bedser b Statham | 0 |
| R.R. Lindwall | not out | 64 |
| G.R.A. Langley† | b Bailey | 16 |
| I.W. Johnson* | not out | 24 |
| W.A. Johnston | did not bat | |
| Extras | (B 11, LB 7, NB 1) | 19 |
| **Total** | (8 wickets declared) | **601** |

## ENGLAND

| | | | | | |
|---|---|---|---|---|---|
| L. Hutton* | c Langley b Lindwall | 4 | lbw b Miller | | 13 |
| R.T. Simpson | b Miller | 2 | run out | | 9 |
| W.J Edrich | c Langley b Archer | 15 | b Johnston | | 88 |
| P.B.H May | b Lindwall | 1 | lbw b Lindwall | | 44 |
| M.C. Cowdrey | c Hole b Johnston | 40 | b Benaud | | 10 |
| T.E. Bailey | b Johnston | 88 | c Langley b Lindwall | | 23 |
| F.H. Tyson | b Johnson | 7 | not out | | 37 |
| A.V. Bedser | b Johnson | 5 | c Archer b Johnson | | 5 |
| K.V. Andrew† | b Lindwall | 6 | b Johnson | | 5 |
| J.B. Statham | b Johnson | 11 | (11) c Harvey b Benaud | | 14 |
| D.C.S. Compton | not out | 2 | (10) c Langley b Benaud | | 0 |
| Extras | (B 3, LB 6) | 9 | (B 7, LB 2) | | 9 |
| **Total** | | **190** | | | **257** |

| ENGLAND | O | M | R | W | O | M | R | W |
|---|---|---|---|---|---|---|---|---|
| Bedser | 37 | 4 | 131 | 1 | | | | |
| Statham | 34 | 2 | 123 | 2 | | | | |
| Tyson | 29 | 1 | 160 | 1 | | | | |
| Bailey | 26 | 1 | 140 | 3 | | | | |
| Edrich | 3 | 0 | 28 | 0 | | | | |
| AUSTRALIA | | | | | | | | |
| Lindwall | 14 | 4 | 27 | 3 | 17 | 3 | 50 | 2 |
| Miller | 11 | 5 | 19 | 1 | 12 | 2 | 30 | 1 |
| Archer | 4 | 1 | 14 | 1 | 15 | 4 | 28 | 0 |
| Johnson | 19 | 5 | 46 | 3 | 17 | 5 | 38 | 2 |
| Benaud | 12 | 5 | 28 | 0 | 8·1 | 1 | 43 | 3 |
| Johnston | 16·1 | 5 | 47 | 2 | 21 | 8 | 59 | 1 |

## FALL OF WICKETS

| | A | E | E |
|---|---|---|---|
| Wkt | 1st | 1st | 2nd |
| 1st | 51 | 4 | 22 |
| 2nd | 123 | 10 | 23 |
| 3rd | 325 | 11 | 147 |
| 4th | 456 | 25 | 163 |
| 5th | 463 | 107 | 181 |
| 6th | 464 | 132 | 220 |
| 7th | 545 | 141 | 231 |
| 8th | 572 | 156 | 242 |
| 9th | – | 181 | 243 |
| 10th | – | 190 | 257 |

Umpires: M.J. McInnes and C. Hoy.

# AUSTRALIA v ENGLAND 1954–55 (2nd Test)

Played at Sydney Cricket Ground on 17, 18, 20, 21, 22 December.
Toss: Australia. Result: ENGLAND won by 38 runs.
Debuts: Nil.

Tyson, having been knocked unconscious by a Lindwall bouncer, bowled with great speed and stamina to win a palpitating victory for England. He was only the fourth fast bowler this century to take ten wickets in an England v Australia Test – Larwood, Farnes and Voce being the others. Statham, bowling into a very strong wind, gave him splendid support.

## ENGLAND

| | | | | | |
|---|---|---|---|---|---|
| L. Hutton* | c Davidson b Johnston | 30 | c Benaud b Johnston | | 28 |
| T.E. Bailey | b Lindwall | 0 | c Langley b Archer | | 6 |
| P.B.H. May | c Johnston b Archer | 5 | b Lindwall | | 104 |
| T.W. Graveney | c Favell b Johnston | 21 | c Langley b Johnston | | 0 |
| M.C. Cowdrey | c Langley b Davidson | 23 | c Archer b Benaud | | 54 |
| W.J. Edrich | c Benaud b Archer | 10 | b Archer | | 29 |
| F.H. Tyson | b Lindwall | 0 | b Lindwall | | 9 |
| T.G. Evans† | c Langley b Archer | 3 | c Lindwall b Archer | | 4 |
| J.H. Wardle | c Burke b Johnson | 35 | lbw b Lindwall | | 8 |
| R. Appleyard | c Hole b Davidson | 8 | not out | | 19 |
| J.B. Statham | not out | 14 | c Langley b Johnston | | 25 |
| Extras | (LB 5) | 5 | (LB 6, NB 4) | | 10 |
| **Total** | | **154** | | | **296** |

## AUSTRALIA

| | | | | | |
|---|---|---|---|---|---|
| L.E. Favell | c Graveney b Bailey | 26 | c Edrich b Tyson | | 16 |
| A.R. Morris* | c Hutton b Bailey | 12 | lbw b Statham | | 10 |
| J.W. Burke | c Graveney b Bailey | 44 | b Tyson | | 14 |
| R.N. Harvey | c Cowdrey b Tyson | 12 | not out | | 92 |
| G.B. Hole | b Tyson | 12 | b Tyson | | 0 |
| R. Denaud | lbw b Statham | 20 | c Tyson b Appleyard | | 12 |
| R.G. Archer | c Hutton b Tyson | 49 | b Tyson | | 6 |
| A.K. Davidson | b Statham | 20 | c Evans b Statham | | 5 |
| R.R. Lindwall | c Evans b Tyson | 19 | b Tyson | | 8 |
| G.R.A. Langley† | b Bailey | 5 | b Statham | | 0 |
| W.A. Johnston | not out | 0 | c Evans b Tyson | | 11 |
| Extras | (B 5, LB 2, NB 2) | 9 | (LB 7, NB 3) | | 10 |
| **Total** | | **228** | | | **184** |

| AUSTRALIA | O | M | R | W | O | M | R | W |
|---|---|---|---|---|---|---|---|---|
| Lindwall | 17 | 3 | 47 | 2 | 31 | 10 | 69 | 3 |
| Archer | 12 | 7 | 12 | 3 | 22 | 9 | 53 | 3 |
| Davidson | 12 | 3 | 34 | 2 | 13 | 2 | 52 | 0 |
| Johnston | 13·3 | 1 | 56 | 3 | 19·3 | 2 | 70 | 3 |
| Benaud | | | | | 19 | 3 | 42 | 1 |
| AUSTRALIA | | | | | | | | |
| Statham | 18 | 1 | 83 | 2 | 19 | 6 | 45 | 3 |
| Bailey | 17·4 | 3 | 59 | 4 | 6 | 0 | 21 | 0 |
| Tyson | 13 | 2 | 45 | 4 | 18·4 | 1 | 85 | 6 |
| Appleyard | 7 | 1 | 32 | 0 | 6 | 1 | 12 | 1 |
| Wardle | | | | | 4 | 2 | 11 | 0 |

FALL OF WICKETS

| Wkt | E 1st | A 1st | E 2nd | A 2nd |
|---|---|---|---|---|
| 1st | 14 | 18 | 18 | 27 |
| 2nd | 19 | 65 | 55 | 34 |
| 3rd | 58 | 100 | 55 | 77 |
| 4th | 63 | 104 | 171 | 77 |
| 5th | 84 | 122 | 222 | 102 |
| 6th | 85 | 141 | 232 | 122 |
| 7th | 88 | 193 | 239 | 127 |
| 8th | 99 | 213 | 249 | 136 |
| 9th | 111 | 224 | 250 | 145 |
| 10th | 154 | 228 | 296 | 184 |

Umpires: M.J. McInnes and R. Wright.

# AUSTRALIA v ENGLAND 1954–55 (3rd Test)

Played at Melbourne Cricket Ground on 31 December, 1, 3, 4, 5 January.
Toss: England.   Result: ENGLAND won by 128 runs.
Debuts: Australia – L.V. Maddocks.

Cowdrey, the fiftieth England batsman to score a hundred against Australia, made his runs out of the lowest total to contain a century in this series to share that record with Bradman (103* out of 191 in 1932-33 – *Test No. 221*).
Australia's last eight second-innings wickets fell for 36 runs, Tyson taking 6 for 16 in 51 balls to finish with an exceptional analysis for a fast bowler in this long series.

## ENGLAND

| | | | | |
|---|---|---|---|---|
| L. Hutton* | c Hole b Miller | 12 | lbw b Archer | 42 |
| W.J. Edrich | c Lindwall b Miller | 4 | b Johnston | 13 |
| P.B.H. May | c Benaud b Lindwall | 0 | b Johnston | 91 |
| M.C. Cowdrey | b Johnson | 102 | b Benaud | 7 |
| D.C.S. Compton | c Harvey b Miller | 14 | c Maddocks b Archer | 23 |
| T.E. Bailey | c Maddocks b Johnston | 30 | not out | 24 |
| T.G. Evans† | lbw b Archer | 20 | c Maddocks b Miller | 22 |
| J.H. Wardle | b Archer | 0 | b Johnson | 38 |
| F.H. Tyson | b Archer | 6 | c Harvey b Johnston | 6 |
| J.B. Statham | b Archer | 3 | c Favell b Johnston | 0 |
| R. Appleyard | not out | 1 | b Johnston | 6 |
| Extras | (B 9) | 9 | (B 2, LB 4, W 1) | 7 |
| **Total** | | **191** | | **279** |

## AUSTRALIA

| | | | | | |
|---|---|---|---|---|---|
| L.E. Favell | lbw b Statham | 25 | | b Appleyard | 30 |
| A.R. Morris | lbw b Tyson | 3 | | c Cowdrey b Tyson | 4 |
| K.R. Miller | c Evans b Statham | 7 | (5) | c Edrich b Tyson | 6 |
| R.N. Harvey | b Appleyard | 31 | | c Evans b Tyson | 11 |
| G.B. Hole | b Tyson | 11 | (6) | c Evans b Statham | 5 |
| R. Benaud | c sub (J.V. Wilson) b Appleyard | 15 | (3) | b Tyson | 22 |
| R.G. Archer | b Wardle | 23 | | b Statham | 15 |
| L.V. Maddocks† | c Evans b Statham | 47 | | b Tyson | 0 |
| R.R. Lindwall | b Statham | 13 | | lbw b Tyson | 0 |
| I.W. Johnson* | not out | 33 | | not out | 4 |
| W.A. Johnston | b Statham | 11 | | c Evans b Tyson | 0 |
| Extras | (B 7, LB 3, NB 2) | 12 | | (B 1, LB 13) | 14 |
| **Total** | | **231** | | | **111** |

| AUSTRALIA | O | M | R | W | O | M | R | W |
|---|---|---|---|---|---|---|---|---|
| Lindwall | 13 | 0 | 59 | 1 | 18 | 3 | 52 | 0 |
| Miller | 11 | 8 | 14 | 3 | 18 | 6 | 35 | 1 |
| Archer | 13·6 | 4 | 33 | 4 | 24 | 7 | 50 | 2 |
| Benaud | 7 | 0 | 30 | 0 | 8 | 2 | 25 | 1 |
| Johnston | 12 | 6 | 26 | 1 | 24·5 | 2 | 85 | 5 |
| Johnson | 11 | 3 | 20 | 1 | 8 | 2 | 25 | 1 |
| **ENGLAND** | | | | | | | | |
| Tyson | 21 | 2 | 68 | 2 | 12·3 | 1 | 27 | 7 |
| Statham | 16·3 | 0 | 60 | 5 | 11 | 1 | 38 | 2 |
| Bailey | 9 | 1 | 33 | 0 | 3 | 0 | 14 | 0 |
| Appleyard | 11 | 3 | 38 | 2 | 4 | 1 | 17 | 1 |
| Wardle | 6 | 0 | 20 | 1 | 1 | 0 | 1 | 0 |

### FALL OF WICKETS

| | E | A | E | A |
|---|---|---|---|---|
| Wkt | 1st | 1st | 2nd | 2nd |
| 1st | 14 | 15 | 40 | 23 |
| 2nd | 21 | 38 | 96 | 57 |
| 3rd | 29 | 43 | 128 | 77 |
| 4th | 41 | 65 | 173 | 86 |
| 5th | 115 | 92 | 185 | 87 |
| 6th | 169 | 115 | 211 | 97 |
| 7th | 181 | 134 | 257 | 98 |
| 8th | 181 | 151 | 273 | 98 |
| 9th | 190 | 205 | 273 | 110 |
| 10th | 191 | 231 | 279 | 111 |

Umpires: M.J. McInnes and C. Hoy.

# AUSTRALIA v ENGLAND 1954–55 (4th Test)

Played at Adelaide Oval on 28, 29, 31 January, 1, 2 February.
Toss: Australia.   Result: ENGLAND won by five wickets.
Debuts: Nil.

England won their first rubber in Australia since the 'bodyline' tour of 1932-33 and so retained the Ashes.

## AUSTRALIA

| | | | | |
|---|---|---:|---|---:|
| C.C. McDonald | c May b Appleyard | 48 | b Statham | 29 |
| A.R. Morris | c Evans b Tyson | 25 | c and b Appleyard | 16 |
| J.W. Burke | c May b Tyson | 18 | b Appleyard | 5 |
| R.N. Harvey | c Edrich b Bailey | 25 | b Appleyard | 7 |
| K.R. Miller | c Bailey b Appleyard | 44 | b Statham | 14 |
| R. Benaud | c May b Appleyard | 15 | (7) lbw b Tyson | 1 |
| L.V. Maddocks† | run out | 69 | (6) lbw b Statham | 2 |
| R.G. Archer | c May b Tyson | 21 | c Evans b Tyson | 3 |
| A.K. Davidson | c Evans b Bailey | 5 | lbw b Wardle | 23 |
| I.W. Johnson* | c Statham b Bailey | 41 | (11) not out | 3 |
| W.A. Johnston | not out | 0 | (10) c Appleyard b Tyson | 3 |
| Extras | (B 3, LB 7, NB 2) | 12 | (B 4, LB 1) | 5 |
| **Total** | | **323** | | **111** |

## ENGLAND

| | | | | |
|---|---|---:|---|---:|
| L. Hutton* | c Davidson b Johnston | 80 | c Davidson b Miller | 5 |
| W.J. Edrich | b Johnson | 21 | b Miller | 0 |
| P.B.H. May | c Archer b Benaud | 1 | c Miller b Johnston | 26 |
| M.C. Cowdrey | c Maddocks b Davison | 79 | c Archer b Miller | 4 |
| D.C.S. Compton | lbw b Miller | 44 | not out | 34 |
| T.E. Bailey | c Davidson b Johnston | 38 | lbw b Johnston | 15 |
| T.G. Evans† | c Maddocks b Benaud | 37 | not out | 6 |
| J.H. Wardle | c and b Johnson | 23 | | |
| F.H. Tyson | c Burke b Benaud | 1 | | |
| R. Appleyard | not out | 10 | | |
| J.B. Statham | c Maddocks b Benaud | 0 | | |
| Extras | (B 1, LB 2, NB 4) | 7 | (B 3, LB 4) | 7 |
| **Total** | | **341** | (5 wickets) | **97** |

| ENGLAND | O | M | R | W | O | M | R | W | | FALL OF WICKETS | | | |
|---|---|---|---|---|---|---|---|---|---|---|---|---|---|
| Tyson | 26·1 | 4 | 85 | 3 | 15 | 2 | 47 | 3 | | A | E | A | E |
| Statham | 19 | 4 | 70 | 0 | 12 | 1 | 38 | 3 | *Wkt* | *1st* | *1st* | *2nd* | *2nd* |
| Bailey | 12 | 3 | 39 | 3 | | | | | 1st | 59 | 60 | 24 | 3 |
| Appleyard | 23 | 7 | 58 | 3 | 12 | 7 | 13 | 3 | 2nd | 86 | 63 | 40 | 10 |
| Wardle | 19 | 5 | 59 | 0 | 4·2 | 1 | 8 | 1 | 3rd | 115 | 162 | 54 | 18 |
| | | | | | | | | | 4th | 129 | 232 | 69 | 49 |
| AUSTRALIA | | | | | | | | | 5th | 175 | 232 | 76 | 90 |
| Miller | 11 | 4 | 34 | 1 | 10·4 | 2 | 40 | 3 | 6th | 182 | 283 | 77 | – |
| Archer | 3 | 0 | 12 | 0 | 4 | 0 | 13 | 0 | 7th | 212 | 321 | 79 | – |
| Johnson | 36 | 17 | 46 | 2 | | | | | 8th | 229 | 323 | 83 | – |
| Davidson | 25 | 8 | 55 | 1 | 2 | 0 | 7 | 0 | 9th | 321 | 336 | 101 | – |
| Johnston | 27 | 11 | 60 | 2 | 8 | 2 | 20 | 2 | 10th | 323 | 341 | 111 | – |
| Benaud | 36·6 | 6 | 120 | 4 | 6 | 2 | 10 | 0 | | | | | |
| Burke | 2 | 0 | 7 | 0 | | | | | | | | | |

Umpires: M.J. McInnes and R. Wright.

# AUSTRALIA v ENGLAND 1954–55 (5th Test)

Played at Sydney Cricket Ground on 25 (*no play*), 26(*no play*), 28 (*no play*) February, 1, 2, 3 March.
Toss: Australia. Result: MATCH DRAWN.
Debuts: Australia - P.J.P. Burge, W.J. Watson.

Incessant heavy rain wrought havoc in New South Wales and delayed the start of this match until 2 p.m. on the fourth day. Graveney became the hundredth player to score a century in this series of Tests. Bailey allowed himself to be bowled to give Lindwall 100 wickets in Australia-England Tests. Lindwall acknowledged this gesture by dismissing Bailey for a 'pair' four years later in the latter's last Test.

## ENGLAND

| | | |
|---|---|---:|
| L. Hutton* | c Burge b Lindwall | 6 |
| T.W. Graveney | c and b Johnson | 111 |
| P.B.H. May | c Davidson b Benaud | 79 |
| M.C. Cowdrey | c Maddocks b Johnson | 0 |
| D.C.S. Compton | c and b Johnson | 84 |
| T.E. Bailey | b Lindwall | 72 |
| T.G. Evans† | c McDonald b Lindwall | 10 |
| J.H. Wardle | not out | 5 |
| F.H. Tyson | ) | |
| R. Appleyard | ) did not bat | |
| J.B. Statham | ) | |
| Extras | (B 1, LB 3) | 4 |
| **Total** | (7 wickets declared) | **371** |

## AUSTRALIA

| | | | | | |
|---|---|---:|---|---|---:|
| W.J. Watson | b Wardle | 18 | c Graveney b Statham | | 3 |
| C.C. McDonald | c May b Appleyard | 72 | c Evans b Graveney | | 37 |
| L.E. Favell | b Tyson | 1 | c Graveney b Wardle | | 9 |
| R.N. Harvey | c and b Tyson | 13 | c and b Wardle | | 1 |
| K.R. Miller | run out | 19 | b Wardle | | 28 |
| P.J.P. Burge | c Appleyard b Wardle | 17 | not out | | 18 |
| R. Benaud | b Wardle | 7 | b Hutton | | 22 |
| L.V. Maddocks† | c Appleyard b Wardle | 32 | | | |
| A.K. Davidson | c Evans b Wardle | 18 | | | |
| I.W. Johnson† | run out | 11 | | | |
| R.R. Lindwall | not out | 2 | | | |
| Extras | (B 10, LB 1) | 11 | | | |
| **Total** | | **221** | (6 wickets) | | **118** |

| AUSTRALIA | O | M | R | W | O | M | R | W |
|---|---|---|---|---|---|---|---|---|
| Lindwall | 20·6 | 5 | 77 | 3 | | | | |
| Miller | 15 | 1 | 71 | 0 | | | | |
| Davidson | 19 | 3 | 72 | 0 | | | | |
| Johnson | 20 | 5 | 68 | 3 | | | | |
| Benaud | 20 | 4 | 79 | 1 | | | | |
| **ENGLAND** | | | | | | | | |
| Tyson | 11 | 1 | 46 | 2 | 5 | 2 | 20 | 0 |
| Statham | 9 | 1 | 31 | 0 | 5 | 0 | 11 | 1 |
| Appleyard | 16 | 2 | 54 | 1 | | | | |
| Wardle | 24·4 | 6 | 79 | 5 | 12 | 1 | 51 | 3 |
| Graveney | | | | | 6 | 0 | 34 | 1 |
| Hutton | | | | | 0·6 | 0 | 2 | 1 |

### FALL OF WICKETS

| Wkt | E 1st | A 1st | A 2nd |
|---|---|---|---|
| 1st | 6 | 52 | 14 |
| 2nd | 188 | 53 | 27 |
| 3rd | 188 | 85 | 29 |
| 4th | 196 | 129 | 67 |
| 5th | 330 | 138 | 87 |
| 6th | 359 | 147 | 118 |
| 7th | 371 | 157 | – |
| 8th | – | 202 | – |
| 9th | – | 217 | – |
| 10th | – | 221 | – |

Umpires: M.J. McInnes and R. Wright.

# PAKISTAN v INDIA 1954–55 (1st Test)

Played at Dacca Stadium on 1, 2, 3, 4 January.
Toss: Pakistan. Result: MATCH DRAWN.
Debuts: India – P.H. Punjabi, N.S. Tamhane.

The first official Test in Pakistan established the defensive nature of the cricket played in this series. At the end of four days only 710 runs had been scored from 387·3 overs; a scoring rate of 1·83 runs per over.

## PAKISTAN

| | | | | | |
|---|---|---|---|---|---|
| Hanif Mohammad | c Tamhane b Ghulam Ahmed | 41 | c Umrigar b Phadkar | | 14 |
| Alimuddin | c Phadkar b Ghulam Ahmed | 7 | c sub (P. Bhandari) b Gupte | | 51 |
| Waqar Hassan | c and b Ghulam Ahmed | 52 | st Tamhane b Gupte | | 51 |
| Maqsood Ahmed | c Tamhane b Ghulam Ahmed | 11 | c Mantri b Gupte | | 16 |
| Wazir Mohammad | c Phadkar b Gupte | 23 | (8) run out | | 0 |
| Imtiaz Ahmed† | b Phadkar | 54 | (5) c Umrigar b Gupte | | 5 |
| A.H. Kardar* | b Ramchand | 29 | (6) c Mantri b Phadkar | | 3 |
| Shujauddin | st Tamhane b Mankad | 25 | (7) run out | | 1 |
| Fazal Mahmood | c Tamhane b Ramchand | 0 | not out | | 15 |
| Mahmood Hussain | b Ghulam Ahmed | 9 | c Punjabi b Gupte | | 0 |
| Khan Mohammad | not out | 4 | run out | | 0 |
| Extras | (LB 2) | 2 | (LB 2) | | 2 |
| **Total** | | **257** | | | **158** |

## INDIA

| | | | | |
|---|---|---|---|---|
| P. Roy | b Mahmood | 0 | not out | 67 |
| P.H. Punjabi | b Khan | 26 | lbw b Khan | 3 |
| M.K. Mantri | b Mahmood | 0 | c Imtiaz b Khan | 2 |
| V.L. Manjrekar | b Khan | 18 | not out | 74 |
| P.R. Umrigar | c Kardar b Mahmood | 32 | | |
| G.S. Ramchand | c Imtiaz b Mahmood | 37 | | |
| D.G. Phadkar | c Imtiaz b Mahmood | 11 | | |
| V.M.H. Mankad* | c Imtiaz b Mahmood | 2 | | |
| N.S. Tamhane† | b Khan | 5 | | |
| Ghulam Ahmed | b Khan | 2 | | |
| S.P. Gupte | not out | 1 | | |
| Extras | (B 7, LB 5, NB 2) | 14 | (B 1) | 1 |
| **Total** | | **148** | (2 wickets) | **147** |

| INDIA | O | M | R | W | O | M | R | W | | FALL OF WICKETS | | | |
|---|---|---|---|---|---|---|---|---|---|---|---|---|---|
| Phadkar | 18 | 11 | 24 | 1 | 28·2 | 11 | 57 | 2 | | P | I | P | I |
| Ramchand | 15 | 7 | 19 | 2 | 19 | 10 | 30 | 0 | *Wkt* | *1st* | *1st* | *2nd* | *2nd* |
| Gupte | 46 | 14 | 79 | 1 | 6 | 0 | 18 | 5 | 1st | 21 | 17 | 24 | 15 |
| Ghulam Ahmed | 45 | 8 | 109 | 5 | | | | | 2nd | 74 | 19 | 116 | 17 |
| Mankad | 12·2 | 3 | 24 | 1 | 18 | 6 | 34 | 0 | 3rd | 88 | 45 | 122 | – |
| Umrigar | | | | | 15 | 8 | 17 | 0 | 4th | 125 | 56 | 137 | – |
| | | | | | | | | | 5th | 157 | 115 | 139 | – |
| PAKISTAN | | | | | | | | | 6th | 207 | 129 | 140 | – |
| Fazal | 25 | 19 | 18 | 0 | 23 | 11 | 34 | 0 | 7th | 227 | 131 | 140 | – |
| Mahmood Hussain | 27 | 6 | 67 | 6 | 7 | 2 | 21 | 0 | 8th | 227 | 143 | 148 | – |
| Khan | 26·5 | 12 | 42 | 4 | 12 | 5 | 18 | 2 | 9th | 240 | 145 | 156 | – |
| Shujauddin | 4 | 2 | 7 | 0 | 14 | 6 | 25 | 0 | 10th | 257 | 148 | 158 | – |
| Maqsood | | | | | 3 | 1 | 4 | 0 | | | | | |
| Kardar | | | | | 12 | 3 | 17 | 0 | | | | | |
| Hanif | | | | | 5 | 1 | 15 | 0 | | | | | |
| Alimuddin | | | | | 5 | 0 | 12 | 0 | | | | | |
| Imtiaz | | | | | 1 | 1 | 0 | 0 | | | | | |

Umpires: Daud Khan and Idris Beg.

# PAKISTAN v INDIA 1954–55 (2nd Test)

Played at Dring Stadium, Bahawalpur, on 15, 16, 17, 18 January.
Toss: India.    Result: MATCH DRAWN.
Debuts: Nil.

Hanif recorded the highest score for Pakistan in a home Test against India. A run rate of under two per over resulted in only two innings being completed in the four days.

## INDIA

| | | | | | |
|---|---|---|---|---|---|
| P. Roy | b Fazal | 0 | c Kardar b Khan | | 78 |
| P.H. Punjabi | b Khan | 18 | c Maqsood b Mahmood | | 33 |
| V.M.H. Mankad* | c Imtiaz b Fazal | 6 | c Imtiaz b Fazal | | 1 |
| V.L. Manjrekar | c Mahmood b Khan | 50 | c Imtiaz b Fazal | | 59 |
| P.R. Umrigar | b Khan | 20 | | | |
| G.S. Ramchand | b Mahmood | 53 | | | |
| C.V. Gadkari | lbw b Khan | 2 | (6) not out | | 4 |
| C.D. Gopinath | c Waqar b Fazal | 0 | (5) c Maqsood b Khan | | 8 |
| N.S. Tamhane† | not out | 54 | (7) not out | | 12 |
| S.P. Gupte | b Khan | 15 | | | |
| Ghulam Ahmed | b Fazal | 8 | | | |
| Extras | (LB 4, NB 5) | 9 | (B 12, LB 1, NB 1) | | 14 |
| **Total** | | **235** | (5 wickets) | | **209** |

## PAKISTAN

| | | |
|---|---|---|
| Hanif Mohammad | c Gadkari b Umrigar | 142 |
| Alimuddin | b Ghulam Ahmed | 64 |
| Waqar Hassan | c Gupte b Umrigar | 48 |
| Maqsood Ahmed | c Gadkari b Umrigar | 10 |
| Imtiaz Ahmed† | st Tamhane b Gupte | 3 |
| A.H. Kardar* | c Punjabi b Umrigar | 13 |
| Fazal Mahmood | b Umrigar | 9 |
| Mahmood Hussain | c Gadkari b Umrigar | 0 |
| Shujauddin | run out | 7 |
| Wazir Mohammad | not out | 4 |
| Khan Mohammad | not out | 1 |
| Extras | (B 6, LB 5) | 11 |
| **Total** | (9 wickets declared) | **312** |

| PAKISTAN | O | M | R | W | O | M | R | W | | FALL OF WICKETS | | | |
|---|---|---|---|---|---|---|---|---|---|---|---|---|---|
| Fazal | 52·5 | 23 | 86 | 4 | 28 | 6 | 58 | 2 | | | I | P | I |
| Mahmood Hussain | 25 | 6 | 56 | 1 | 17 | 3 | 47 | 1 | *Wkt* | *1st* | *1st* | *2nd* |
| Khan | 33 | 7 | 74 | 5 | 22 | 6 | 50 | 2 | 1st | 0 | 127 | 58 |
| Shujauddin | 9 | 4 | 10 | 0 | 8 | 6 | 2 | 0 | 2nd | 16 | 220 | 62 |
| Maqsood | | | | | 7 | 3 | 19 | 0 | 3rd | 61 | 226 | 185 |
| Kardar | | | | | 7 | 0 | 19 | 0 | 4th | 93 | 229 | 189 |
| | | | | | | | | | 5th | 95 | 250 | 193 |
| INDIA | | | | | | | | | 6th | 100 | 286 | – |
| Ramchand | 13 | 5 | 26 | 0 | | | | | 7th | 107 | 286 | – |
| Umrigar | 58 | 25 | 74 | 6 | | | | | 8th | 189 | 301 | – |
| Gupte | 17 | 8 | 49 | 1 | | | | | 9th | 205 | 307 | – |
| Ghulam Ahmed | 36 | 4 | 63 | 1 | | | | | 10th | 235 | – | – |
| Mankad | 40 | 19 | 89 | 0 | | | | | | | | |

Umpires: Idris Beg and Shujauddin.

# PAKISTAN v INDIA 1954–55 (3rd Test)

Played at Bagh-i-Jinnah, Lahore, on 29, 30, 31 January, 1 February.
Toss: Pakistan.    Result: MATCH DRAWN.
Debuts: Pakistan – Miran Bux.

## PAKISTAN

| | | | | | |
|---|---|---|---|---|---|
| Hanif Mohammad | c Tamhane b Gupte | 12 | (6) not out | | 0 |
| Alimuddin | run out | 38 | b Mankad | | 58 |
| Waqar Hassan | c Mankad b Gupte | 9 | c Tamhane b Mankad | | 12 |
| Maqsood Ahmed | st Tamhane b Gupte | 99 | c Punjabi b Mankad | | 15 |
| A.H. Kardar* | c Ramchand b Mankad | 44 | | | |
| Wazir Mohammad | lbw b Mankad | 55 | | | |
| Imtiaz Ahmed† | run out | 55 | (5) c Tamhane b Gupte | | 9 |
| Shujauddin | c Mankad b Ghulam | 3 | (1) c sub (P. Bhandari) b Gupte | | 40 |
| Fazal Mahmood | st Tamhane b Gupte | 12 | | | |
| Mahmood Hussain | b Gupte | 0 | | | |
| Miran Bux | not out | 1 | | | |
| Extras | | 0 | (B 2) | | 2 |
| **Total** | | **328** | (5 wickets declared) | | **136** |

## INDIA

| | | | | | |
|---|---|---|---|---|---|
| P. Roy | b Mahmood | 23 | c Imtiaz b Kardar | | 23 |
| P.H. Punjabi | b Miran Bux | 27 | c Maqsood b Kardar | | 1 |
| C.V. Gadkari | b Fazal | 13 | not out | | 27 |
| V.L. Manjrekar | b Miran Bux | 0 | not out | | 22 |
| P.R. Umrigar | c Hanif b Mahmood | 78 | | | |
| G.S. Ramchand | c Maqsood b Fazal | 12 | | | |
| C.D. Gopinath | c Fazal b Shujauddin | 41 | | | |
| V.M.H. Mankad* | c Imtiaz b Mahmood | 33 | | | |
| N.S. Tamhane† | c Imtiaz b Mahmood | 0 | | | |
| Ghulam Ahmed | c Imtiaz b Fazal | 0 | | | |
| S.P. Gupte | not out | 0 | | | |
| Extras | (B 12, LB 10, NB 2) | 24 | (NB 1) | | 1 |
| **Total** | | **251** | (2 wickets) | | **74** |

| INDIA | O | M | R | W | O | M | R | W |
|---|---|---|---|---|---|---|---|---|
| Umrigar | 14 | 4 | 23 | 0 | | | | |
| Ramchand | 10 | 5 | 12 | 0 | 6 | 1 | 20 | 0 |
| Ghulam Ahmed | 46 | 11 | 95 | 1 | 14 | 2 | 47 | 0 |
| Gupte | 73·5 | 32 | 33 | 5 | 36·3 | 22 | 34 | 2 |
| Mankad | 44 | 25 | 65 | 2 | 28 | 17 | 33 | 3 |
| **PAKISTAN** | | | | | | | | |
| Mahmood Hussain | 26·1 | 6 | 70 | 4 | 1 | 0 | 1 | 0 |
| Fazal | 47 | 24 | 62 | 3 | 1 | 0 | 2 | 0 |
| Miran Bux | 48 | 20 | 82 | 2 | | | | |
| Shujauddin | 7 | 1 | 13 | 1 | 6 | 1 | 20 | 0 |
| Maqsood | | | | | 4 | 2 | 4 | 0 |
| Kardar | | | | | 12 | 3 | 20 | 2 |
| Alimuddin | | | | | 3 | 0 | 12 | 0 |
| Hanif | | | | | 3 | 0 | 9 | 0 |
| Wazir | | | | | 2 | 0 | 5 | 0 |

### FALL OF WICKETS

| | P | I | P | I |
|---|---|---|---|---|
| Wkt | 1st | 1st | 2nd | 2nd |
| 1st | 32 | 52 | 83 | 3 |
| 2nd | 55 | 56 | 109 | 40 |
| 3rd | 62 | 58 | 112 | – |
| 4th | 198 | 91 | 135 | – |
| 5th | 202 | 117 | 136 | – |
| 6th | 286 | 179 | – | – |
| 7th | 302 | 243 | – | – |
| 8th | 327 | 243 | – | – |
| 9th | 327 | 251 | – | – |
| 10th | 328 | 251 | – | – |

Umpires: Idris Beg and Shujauddin.

# PAKISTAN v INDIA 1954–55 (4th Test)

Played at Gymkhana Ground, Peshawar, on 13, 14, 15, 16 February.
Toss: Pakistan.    Result: MATCH DRAWN.
Debuts: Nil.

The run rate declined to 1·61 per over, with 638 runs accruing from 395·3 overs. India never threatened to score the 126 runs needed for victory in the final hour of this saga.

## PAKISTAN

| | | | | | |
|---|---|---:|---|---|---:|
| Hanif Mohammad | c Phadkar b Gupte | 13 | c and b Mankad | | 21 |
| Alimuddin | c Ramchand | 0 | lbw b Ghulam Ahmed | | 4 |
| Waqar Hassan | c and b Gupte | 43 | lbw b Gupte | | 16 |
| Maqsood Ahmed | c Punjabi b Phadkar | 31 | (5) c and b Mankad | | 44 |
| Imtiaz Ahmed† | b Phadkar | 0 | (6) c Punjabi b Mankad | | 69 |
| Wazir Mohammad | hit wkt b Mankad | 34 | (4) b Mankad | | 0 |
| A.H. Kardar* | b Gupte | 11 | b Phadkar | | 0 |
| Shujauddin | c Tamhane b Gupte | 37 | run out | | 11 |
| Khan Mohammad | c Mankad b Ghulam Ahmed | 4 | c sub (P. Bhandari) b Mankad | | 3 |
| Mahmood Hussain | not out | 5 | st Tamhane b Phadkar | | 2 |
| Miran Bux | lbw b Gupte | 0 | not out | | 0 |
| Extras | (B 5, LB 4, NB 1) | 10 | (B 8, LB 4) | | 12 |
| **Total** | | **188** | | | **182** |

## INDIA

| | | | | | |
|---|---|---:|---|---|---:|
| P. Roy | run out | 16 | not out | | 13 |
| P.H. Punjabi | b Khan | 16 | b Hanif | | 6 |
| P.R. Umrigar | run out | 108 | not out | | 3 |
| V.L. Manjrekar | run out | 32 | | | |
| C.V. Gadkari | c Maqsood b Mahmood | 15 | | | |
| G.S. Ramchand | c Shujauddin b Khan | 18 | | | |
| V.M.H. Mankad* | not out | 3 | | | |
| N.S. Tamhane† | run out | 0 | | | |
| D.G. Phadkar | b Khan | 13 | | | |
| S.P. Gupte | c Waqar b Mahmood | 2 | | | |
| Ghulam Ahmed | b Khan | 8 | | | |
| Extras | (B 5, LB 4, W 1, NB 4) | 14 | (NB 1) | | 1 |
| **Total** | | **245** | (1 wicket) | | **23** |

| INDIA | O | M | R | W | O | M | R | W |
|---|---|---|---|---|---|---|---|---|
| Phadkar | 24 | 14 | 19 | 2 | 18 | 2 | 42 | 2 |
| Ramchand | 7 | 2 | 13 | 1 | 2 | 1 | 3 | 0 |
| Gupte | 41·3 | 22 | 63 | 5 | 35 | 16 | 52 | 1 |
| Mankad | 61 | 34 | 71 | 1 | 54 | 26 | 64 | 5 |
| Ghulam Ahmed | 13 | 7 | 12 | 1 | 13 | 9 | 9 | 1 |
| **PAKISTAN** | | | | | | | | |
| Khan | 36 | 14 | 79 | 4 | 4 | 0 | 10 | 0 |
| Mahmood Hussain | 38 | 11 | 78 | 2 | 2 | 1 | 2 | 0 |
| Miran Bux | 8 | 2 | 30 | 0 | 2 | 0 | 3 | 0 |
| Kardar | 19 | 6 | 34 | 0 | 1 | 1 | 0 | 0 |
| Maqsood | 7 | 3 | 10 | 0 | 6 | 2 | 6 | 0 |
| Hanif | | | | | 4 | 3 | 1 | 1 |

## FALL OF WICKETS

| Wkt | P 1st | I 1st | P 2nd | I 2nd |
|---|---|---|---|---|
| 1st | 2 | 30 | 10 | 19 |
| 2nd | 31 | 44 | 50 | – |
| 3rd | 81 | 135 | 68 | – |
| 4th | 81 | 182 | 70 | – |
| 5th | 96 | 210 | 153 | – |
| 6th | 111 | 218 | 156 | – |
| 7th | 171 | 219 | 176 | – |
| 8th | 176 | 232 | 177 | – |
| 9th | 188 | 235 | 182 | – |
| 10th | 188 | 245 | 182 | – |

Umpires: Shujauddin and Idris Beg.

# PAKISTAN v INDIA 1954–55 (5th Test)

Played at National Stadium, Karachi, on 26, 27, 28 February, 1 March.
Toss: Pakistan.    Result: MATCH DRAWN.
Debuts: India – P. Bhandari, J.M. Patel.

A heavy thunderstorm restricted play to less than two hours on the third day. Alimuddin and Kardar shared a fifth-wicket partnership of 155 in even time – it provided the fastest scoring of the rubber and remains Pakistan's record for that wicket against India.

## PAKISTAN

| | | | | |
|---|---|--:|---|--:|
| Hanif Mohammad | c Tamhane b Phadkar | 2 | (3) c Tamhane b Umrigar | 28 |
| Alimuddin | c Tamhane b Ramchand | 7 | not out | 103 |
| Waqar Hassan | c Umrigar b Ramchand | 12 | (7) not out | 1 |
| Maqsood Ahmed | c Tamhane b Ramchand | 22 | c Bhandari b Umrigar | 2 |
| Imtiaz Ahmed† | c Ramchand b Patel | 37 | run out | 1 |
| Wazir Mohammad | c Phadkar b Patel | 23 | | |
| A.H. Kardar* | c Tamhane b Ramchand | 14 | (6) st Tamhane b Gupte | 93 |
| Shujauddin | c Mankad b Ramchand | 0 | (1) b Ramchand | 8 |
| Fazal Mahmood | lbw b Patel | 3 | | |
| Khan Mohammad | not out | 15 | | |
| Mahmood Hussain | c Phadkar b Ramchand | 14 | | |
| Extras | (B 10, NB 3) | 13 | (B 1, LB 3, NB 1) | 5 |
| **Total** | | **162** | (5 wickets declared) | **241** |

## INDIA

| | | | | |
|---|---|--:|---|--:|
| P. Roy | c Kardar b Khan | 37 | lbw b Maqsood | 16 |
| P.H. Punjabi | lbw b Khan | 12 | c Imtiaz b Fazal | 22 |
| P.R. Umrigar | b Fazal | 16 | not out | 14 |
| V.L. Manjrekar | c Kardar b Khan | 14 | | |
| V.M.H. Mankad* | c Maqsood b Fazal | 6 | | |
| G.S. Ramchand | c Hanif b Fazal | 15 | (4) not out | 12 |
| N.S. Tamhane† | b Fazal | 9 | | |
| P. Bhandari | b Khan | 19 | | |
| D.G. Phadkar | not out | 6 | | |
| J.M. Patel | lbw b Khan | 0 | | |
| S.P. Gupte | c Shujauddin | 1 | | |
| Extras | (LB 7, NB 3) | 10 | (B 1, LB 1, NB 3) | 5 |
| **Total** | | **145** | (2 wickets) | **69** |

| INDIA | O | M | R | W | O | M | R | W | FALL OF WICKETS | | | | |
|---|--:|--:|--:|--:|--:|--:|--:|--:|---|---|---|---|---|
| Phadkar | 10 | 6 | 7 | 1 | 34 | 6 | 95 | 0 | | P | I | P | I |
| Ramchand | 28 | 10 | 49 | 6 | 11 | 4 | 27 | 1 | *Wkt* | *1st* | *1st* | *2nd* | *2nd* |
| Patel | 33 | 12 | 49 | 3 | 7 | 1 | 23 | 0 | 1st | 2 | 22 | 25 | 34 |
| Gupte | 15 | 4 | 24 | 0 | 6 | 0 | 24 | 1 | 2nd | 19 | 45 | 69 | 49 |
| Mankad | 5 | 0 | 16 | 0 | 1 | 0 | 3 | 0 | 3rd | 37 | 68 | 77 | – |
| Umrigar | 5 | 3 | 4 | 0 | 27 | 6 | 64 | 2 | 4th | 66 | 89 | 81 | – |
| | | | | | | | | | 5th | 88 | 95 | 236 | – |
| PAKISTAN | | | | | | | | | 6th | 119 | 110 | – | – |
| Khan | 28 | 5 | 73 | 5 | 7 | 5 | 4 | 0 | 7th | 119 | 131 | – | – |
| Mahmood Hussain | 7 | 0 | 14 | 0 | 3 | 0 | 16 | 0 | 8th | 122 | 144 | – | – |
| Fazal | 28·3 | 7 | 48 | 5 | 11 | 4 | 21 | 1 | 9th | 135 | 144 | – | – |
| Hanif | | | | | 6 | 1 | 18 | 0 | 10th | 162 | 145 | – | – |
| Maqsood | | | | | 5 | 2 | 5 | 1 | | | | | |

Umpires: Masood Salahuddin and Daud Khan.

# NEW ZEALAND v ENGLAND 1954–55 (1st Test)

Played at Carisbrook, Dunedin, on 11, 12, 14 (*no play*), 15 (*no play*), 16 March.
Toss: England.   Result: ENGLAND won by eight wickets.
Debuts: New Zealand – I.A. Colquhoun, S.N. McGregor, L. Watt (*not 'L.A.'*).

The first day of Test cricket in Dunedin produced only 125 runs in 271 minutes. Even so, a record crowd of 16,000 was attracted to the Carisbrook Ground on the following day. England needed only 50 of the last 90 minutes to score the 49 runs required to win a match reduced to one of three days by rain.

## NEW ZEALAND

| | | | | |
|---|---|---|---|---|
| G.O. Rabone* | st Evans b Wardle | 18 | lbw b Wardle | 7 |
| M.E. Chapple | b Statham | 0 | (3) b Statham | 20 |
| B. Sutcliffe | c Statham b Bailey | 74 | (2) run out | 35 |
| J.R. Reid | b Statham | 4 | b Tyson | 28 |
| S.N. McGregor | b Tyson | 2 | c Cowdrey b Appleyard | 8 |
| L. Watt | b Tyson | 0 | b Appleyard | 2 |
| H.B. Cave | b Tyson | 1 | b Tyson | 1 |
| A.M. Moir | b Statham | 7 | (9) lbw b Tyson | 10 |
| R.W. Blair | b Statham | 0 | (10) b Wardle | 3 |
| A.R. MacGibbon | c Evans b Bailey | 7 | (8) b Tyson | 0 |
| I.A. Colquhoun† | not out | 0 | not out | 1 |
| Extras | (B 5, LB 4, NB 3) | 12 | (B 7, LB 10) | 17 |
| **Total** | | **125** | | **132** |

## ENGLAND

| | | | | |
|---|---|---|---|---|
| L. Hutton* | c Colquhoun b Reid | 11 | c Colquhoun b Blair | 3 |
| T.W. Graveney | b Cave | 41 | not out | 32 |
| P.B.H. May | b MacGibbon | 10 | b MacGibbon | 13 |
| M.C. Cowdrey | lbw b Reid | 42 | not out | 0 |
| R.T. Simpson | b Cave | 21 | | |
| T.E. Bailey | lbw b Reid | 0 | | |
| T.G. Evans† | b Reid | 0 | | |
| J.H. Wardle | not out | 32 | | |
| F.H. Tyson | c McGregor b MacGibbon | 16 | | |
| R. Appleyard | not out | 0 | | |
| J.B. Statham | did not bat | | | |
| Extras | (B 13, LB 17, NB 6) | 36 | (LB 1) | 1 |
| **Total** | (8 wickets declared) | **209** | (2 wickets) | **49** |

| ENGLAND | O | M | R | W | O | M | R | W | | FALL OF WICKETS | | | |
|---|---|---|---|---|---|---|---|---|---|---|---|---|---|
| Tyson | 19 | 7 | 23 | 3 | 12 | 6 | 16 | 4 | | NZ | E | NZ | E |
| Statham | 17 | 9 | 24 | 4 | 15 | 5 | 30 | 1 | *Wkt* | *1st* | *1st* | *2nd* | *2nd* |
| Bailey | 12·2 | 6 | 19 | 2 | 8 | 4 | 9 | 0 | 1st | 3 | 60 | 24 | 22 |
| Wardle | 26 | 15 | 31 | 1 | 14·3 | 4 | 41 | 2 | 2nd | 63 | 71 | 68 | 47 |
| Appleyard | 7 | 3 | 16 | 0 | 7 | 2 | 19 | 2 | 3rd | 68 | 101 | 75 | – |
| NEW ZEALAND | | | | | | | | | 4th | 72 | 150 | 96 | – |
| Blair | 8 | 1 | 29 | 0 | 4 | 0 | 20 | 1 | 5th | 76 | 152 | 98 | – |
| MacGibbon | 24·5 | 11 | 39 | 2 | 7·2 | 2 | 16 | 1 | 6th | 86 | 152 | 103 | – |
| Reid | 27 | 11 | 36 | 4 | 4 | 2 | 12 | 0 | 7th | 103 | 156 | 103 | – |
| Cave | 24 | 15 | 27 | 2 | | | | | 8th | 113 | 208 | 123 | – |
| Moir | 9 | 1 | 42 | 0 | | | | | 9th | 122 | – | 126 | – |
| | | | | | | | | | 10th | 125 | – | 132 | – |

Umpires: R.G. Currie and S.B. Tonkinson.

# NEW ZEALAND v ENGLAND 1954–55 (2nd Test)

Played at Eden Park, Auckland, on 25, 26, 28 March.
Toss: New Zealand.    Result: ENGLAND won by an innings and 20 runs.
Debuts: Nil.

England dismissed New Zealand in 104 minutes for the lowest total in all Test cricket. The previous lowest was 30 – inflicted twice by England upon South Africa (1895–96 and 1924). Tyson and Statham brought their aggregate of Test wickets for the tour of Australasia to 69 (Tyson 39, Statham 30). Appleyard took three wickets in four balls in the second innings and twice during the match was on a hat-trick. Hutton was top-scorer in his last innings for England.

## NEW ZEALAND

| | | | | |
|---|---|---|---|---|
| B. Sutcliffe | c Bailey b Statham | 49 | b Wardle | 11 |
| J.G. Leggat | lbw b Tyson | 4 | c Hutton b Tyson | 1 |
| M.B. Poore | c Evans b Tyson | 0 | b Tyson | 0 |
| J.R. Reid | c Statham b Wardle | 73 | b Statham | 1 |
| G.O. Rabone* | c Evans b Statham | 29 | (6) lbw b Statham | 7 |
| S.N. McGregor | not out | 15 | (5) c May b Appleyard | 1 |
| H.B. Cave | c Bailey b Appleyard | 6 | c Graveney b Appleyard | 5 |
| A.R. MacGibbon | b Appleyard | 9 | lbw b Appleyard | 0 |
| I.A. Colquhoun† | c sub (J.V. Wilson) b Appleyard | 0 | c Graveney b Appleyard | 0 |
| A.M. Moir | lbw b Statham | 0 | not out | 0 |
| J.A. Hayes | b Statham | 0 | b Statham | 0 |
| Extras | (B 3, LB 6, W 4, NB 2) | 15 | | |
| **Total** | | **200** | | **26** |

## ENGLAND

| | | |
|---|---|---|
| R.T. Simpson | c and b Moir | 23 |
| T.W. Graveney | c Rabone b Hayes | 13 |
| P.B.H. May | b Hayes | 48 |
| M.C. Cowdrey | b Moir | 22 |
| L. Hutton* | b MacGibbon | 53 |
| T.E. Bailey | c Colquhoun b Cave | 18 |
| T.G. Evans† | c Reid b Moir | 0 |
| J.H. Wardle | c Reid b Moir | 0 |
| F.H. Tyson | not out | 27 |
| R. Appleyard | c Colquhoun b Hayes | 6 |
| J.B. Statham | c Reid b Moir | 13 |
| Extras | (B 12, LB 3, NB 8) | 23 |
| **Total** | | **246** |

| ENGLAND | O | M | R | W | O | M | R | W |
|---|---|---|---|---|---|---|---|---|
| Tyson | 11 | 2 | 41 | 2 | 7 | 2 | 10 | 2 |
| Statham | 17·4 | 7 | 28 | 4 | 9 | 3 | 9 | 3 |
| Bailey | 13 | 2 | 34 | 0 | | | | |
| Appleyard | 16 | 4 | 38 | 3 | 6 | 3 | 7 | 4 |
| Wardle | 31 | 19 | 44 | 1 | 5 | 5 | 0 | 1 |
| NEW ZEALAND | | | | | | | | |
| Hayes | 23 | 7 | 71 | 3 | | | | |
| MacGibbon | 20 | 7 | 33 | 1 | | | | |
| Reid | 25 | 15 | 28 | 0 | | | | |
| Cave | 24 | 10 | 25 | 1 | | | | |
| Moir | 25·1 | 3 | 62 | 5 | | | | |
| Rabone | 2 | 0 | 4 | 0 | | | | |

FALL OF WICKETS

| Wkt | NZ 1st | E 1st | NZ 2nd |
|---|---|---|---|
| 1st | 13 | 21 | 6 |
| 2nd | 13 | 56 | 8 |
| 3rd | 76 | 112 | 9 |
| 4th | 154 | 112 | 14 |
| 5th | 171 | 163 | 14 |
| 6th | 189 | 164 | 22 |
| 7th | 199 | 164 | 22 |
| 8th | 199 | 201 | 22 |
| 9th | 200 | 218 | 26 |
| 10th | 200 | 246 | 26 |

Umpires: J. McLellan and J.C. Harries.

# WEST INDIES v AUSTRALIA 1954–55 (1st Test)

Played at Sabina Park, Kingston, Jamaica, on 26, 28, 29, 30, 31 March.
Toss: Australia.   Result: AUSTRALIA won by nine wickets.
Debuts: West Indies – G.L. Gibbs, O.G. Smith.

Australia won their first Test match in the Caribbean with a day to spare. O.G. 'Collie' Smith scored a hundred in his first Test match. At 20 years 330 days he was exactly 100 days older than G.A. Headley, the youngest West Indies century-maker, had been when he scored 176 against England in the 1929-30 rubber.

## AUSTRALIA

| | | | | |
|---|---|---|---|---|
| C.C. McDonald | st Binns b Valentine | 50 | (3) not out | 7 |
| A.R. Morris | lbw b Valentine | 65 | c Gibbs b Weekes | 1 |
| R.N. Harvey | b Walcott | 133 | | |
| K.R. Miller | lbw b Walcott | 147 | | |
| R.R. Lindwall | lbw b Ramadhin | 10 | | |
| P.J.P. Burge | c and b Atkinson | 14 | | |
| L.V. Maddocks† | b Valentine | 1 | (1) not not | 12 |
| R. Benaud | b Walcott | 46 | | |
| R.G. Archer | c Walcott b Holt | 24 | | |
| I.W. Johnson* | not out | 18 | | |
| W.A. Johnston | not out | 0 | | |
| Extras | (B 3, LB 3, W 1) | 7 | | |
| **Total** | (9 wickets declared) | **515** | (1 wicket) | **20** |

## WEST INDIES

| | | | | |
|---|---|---|---|---|
| J.K. Holt | c Benaud b Lindwall | 31 | c Maddocks b Benaud | 60 |
| G.L. Gibbs | lbw b Archer | 12 | b Johnston | 0 |
| A.P. Binns† | c Burge b Archer | 0 | (7) lbw b Miller | 0 |
| E. de C. Weekes | run out | 19 | c and b Benaud | 1 |
| C.L. Walcott | c Benaud b Miller | 108 | c Archer b Lindwall | 39 |
| F.M.M. Worrell | b Johnston | 9 | (8) b Archer | 9 |
| O.G. Smith | lbw b Lindwall | 44 | (3) c Harvey b Miller | 104 |
| D. St E. Atkinson* | c Harvey b Miller | 1 | (6) c Benaud b Miller | 30 |
| F.M. King | c Maddocks b Lindwall | 4 | b Lindwall | 21 |
| S. Ramadhin | not out | 12 | c Lindwall b Archer | 3 |
| A.L. Valentine | b Lindwall | 0 | not out | 2 |
| Extras | (B 14, LB 2, NB 3) | 19 | (B 5, NB 1) | 6 |
| **Total** | | **259** | | **275** |

| WEST INDIES | O | M | R | W | O | M | R | W | | FALL OF WICKETS | | | |
|---|---|---|---|---|---|---|---|---|---|---|---|---|---|
| | | | | | | | | | | A | WI | WI | A |
| King | 28 | 7 | 122 | 0 | 2 | 0 | 10 | 0 | Wkt | 1st | 1st | 2nd | 2nd |
| Worrell | 7 | 2 | 13 | 0 | | | | | 1st | 102 | 27 | 20 | 6 |
| Atkinson | 23 | 9 | 46 | 1 | | | | | 2nd | 137 | 27 | 122 | – |
| Ramadhin | 46 | 12 | 112 | 1 | | | | | 3rd | 361 | 56 | 132 | – |
| Valentine | 54 | 20 | 113 | 3 | | | | | 4th | 391 | 75 | 209 | – |
| Smith | 11 | 0 | 27 | 0 | | | | | 5th | 417 | 101 | 213 | – |
| Walcott | 26 | 9 | 50 | 3 | | | | | 6th | 430 | 239 | 213 | – |
| Gibbs | 3 | 1 | 5 | 0 | 1 | 0 | 2 | 0 | 7th | 435 | 240 | 239 | – |
| Holt | 3 | 0 | 20 | 1 | | | | | 8th | 475 | 243 | 253 | – |
| Weekes | | | | | 2·2 | 0 | 8 | 1 | 9th | 506 | 253 | 270 | – |
| AUSTRALIA | | | | | | | | | 10th | – | 259 | 275 | – |
| Lindwall | 24 | 6 | 61 | 4 | 16·1 | 3 | 63 | 2 | | | | | |
| Archer | 19 | 8 | 39 | 2 | 12 | 3 | 44 | 2 | | | | | |
| Johnston | 23 | 4 | 75 | 1 | 16 | 3 | 54 | 1 | | | | | |
| Benaud | 19 | 7 | 29 | 0 | 23 | 7 | 44 | 2 | | | | | |
| Miller | 16 | 5 | 36 | 2 | 28 | 9 | 62 | 3 | | | | | |
| Harvey | | | | | 1 | 0 | 2 | 0 | | | | | |

Umpires: P. Burke and T.A. Ewart.

# WEST INDIES v AUSTRALIA 1954–55 (2nd Test)

Played at Queen's Park Oval, Port-of-Spain, Trinidad, on 11, 12, 13, 14, 15, 16 April.
Toss: West Indies.   Result: MATCH DRAWN.
Debuts: West Indies – L.S. Butler.

This was the first Trinidad Test match to be played on a turf pitch and it yielded 1,255 runs and only 23 wickets. Rain restricted play to 85 minutes on the first day. Walcott became the third West Indian after G.A. Headley and E. de C. Weekes to score a hundred in both innings of a Test. His partnership of 242 with Weekes set a record, since beaten, for any West Indies wicket against Australia.

## WEST INDIES

| | | | | |
|---|---|---|---|---|
| J.K. Holt | c Johnston b Lindwall | 25 | lbw b Archer | 21 |
| J.B. Stollmeyer* | b Lindwall | 14 | b Johnson | 42 |
| C.L. Walcott | st Langley b Benaud | 126 | c Watson b Archer | 110 |
| E. de C. Weekes | c Johnson b Benaud | 139 | not out | 87 |
| O.G. Smith | b Benaud | 0 | c Langley b Archer | 0 |
| G. St A. Sobers | c Langley b Lindwall | 47 | not out | 8 |
| C.A. McWatt† | c Benaud b Miller | 4 | | |
| F.M. King | b Lindwall | 2 | | |
| S. Ramadhin | b Lindwall | 0 | | |
| L.S. Butler | c Johnson b Lindwall | 16 | | |
| A.L. Valentine | not out | 4 | | |
| Extras | (B 1, LB 3, NB 1) | 5 | (LB 3, NB 2) | 5 |
| **Total** | | **382** | (4 wickets) | **273** |

## AUSTRALIA

| | | |
|---|---|---|
| C.C. McDonald | c Walcott b Valentine | 110 |
| A.R. Morris | c King b Butler | 111 |
| R.N. Harvey | lbw b King | 133 |
| W.J. Watson | lbw b Ramadhin | 27 |
| R. Benaud | c Walcott b Ramadhin | 5 |
| K.R. Miller | run out | 3 |
| R.G. Archer | c McWatt b Valentine | 84 |
| I.W. Johnson* | c McWatt b Butler | 66 |
| R.R. Lindwall | not out | 37 |
| G.R.A. Langley† | c King b Walcott | 9 |
| W.A. Johnston | not out | 1 |
| Extras | (B 5, LB 6, W 1, NB 2) | 14 |
| **Total** | (9 wickets declared) | **600** |

| AUSTRALIA | O | M | R | W | O | M | R | W |
|---|---|---|---|---|---|---|---|---|
| Lindwall | 24·5 | 3 | 95 | 6 | 17 | 0 | 70 | 0 |
| Miller | 28 | 8 | 96 | 1 | 11 | 0 | 52 | 0 |
| Archer | 9 | 0 | 42 | 0 | 8 | 1 | 37 | 3 |
| Johnston | 7 | 2 | 29 | 0 | 7 | 0 | 31 | 0 |
| Johnson | 19 | 5 | 72 | 0 | 7 | 2 | 26 | 1 |
| Benaud | 17 | 3 | 43 | 3 | 12 | 2 | 52 | 0 |
| **WEST INDIES** | | | | | | | | |
| Butler | 40 | 7 | 151 | 2 | | | | |
| King | 37 | 7 | 98 | 1 | | | | |
| Holt | 1 | 1 | 0 | 0 | | | | |
| Ramadhin | 32 | 8 | 90 | 2 | | | | |
| Valentine | 49 | 12 | 133 | 2 | | | | |
| Walcott | 19 | 5 | 45 | 1 | | | | |
| Sobers | 3 | 1 | 10 | 0 | | | | |
| Smith | 15 | 1 | 48 | 0 | | | | |
| Stollmeyer | 5 | 0 | 11 | 0 | | | | |

FALL OF WICKETS

| Wkt | WI 1st | A 1st | WI 2nd |
|---|---|---|---|
| 1st | 39 | 191 | 40 |
| 2nd | 40 | 259 | 103 |
| 3rd | 282 | 328 | 230 |
| 4th | 282 | 336 | 236 |
| 5th | 323 | 345 | – |
| 6th | 355 | 439 | – |
| 7th | 360 | 529 | – |
| 8th | 360 | 570 | – |
| 9th | 361 | 594 | – |
| 10th | 382 | – | – |

Umpires: E.N. Lee Kow and H.B. de C. Jordan.

# WEST INDIES v AUSTRALIA 1954–55 (3rd Test)

Played at Bourda, Georgetown, British Guiana, on 26, 27, 28, 29 April.
Toss: West Indies.   Result: AUSTRALIA won by eight wickets.
Debuts: West Indies – C.C. Depeiza, N.E. Marshall.

Australia won in the first over after lunch on the fourth day after Johnson's off-breaks had established a record innings analysis for a Georgetown Test.

## WEST INDIES

| | | | | | |
|---|---|---|---|---|---|
| J.K. Holt | c and b Miller | 12 | | c Langley b Miller | 6 |
| J.B. Stollmeyer* | c Archer b Miller | 16 | | c and b Johnson | 17 |
| C.L. Walcott | c and b Archer | 8 | | hit wkt b Lindwall | 73 |
| E. de C. Weekes | c Archer b Benaud | 81 | | c Langley b Johnson | 0 |
| F.M.M. Worrell | c Johnson b Archer | 9 | | hit wkt b Benaud | 56 |
| G. St A. Sobers | c Watson b Johnson | 12 | (8) | b Johnson | 11 |
| D. St E. Atkinson | b Lindwall | 13 | | st Langley b Johnson | 16 |
| C.C. Depeiza† | not out | 16 | (6) | st Langley b Johnson | 13 |
| N.E. Marshall | b Benaud | 0 | | c sub (L.E. Favell) b Johnson | 8 |
| S. Ramadhin | c Archer b Benaud | 0 | | st Langley b Johnson | 2 |
| F.M. King | c Langley b Benaud | 13 | | not out | 0 |
| Extras | (B 1, LB 1) | 2 | | (B 1, LB 2, NB 2) | 5 |
| **Total** | | **182** | | | **207** |

## AUSTRALIA

| | | | | | |
|---|---|---|---|---|---|
| C.C. McDonald | b Atkinson | 61 | | b Atkinson | 31 |
| A.R. Morris | c Sobers b Atkinson | 44 | | c Walcott b Marshall | 38 |
| R.N. Harvey | c Holt b Ramadhin | 38 | | not out | 41 |
| W.J. Watson | c and b Ramadhin | 6 | | not out | 22 |
| K.R. Miller | c Depeiza b Sobers | 33 | | | |
| R. Benaud | c sub (O.G. Smith) b Marshall | 68 | | | |
| R.G. Archer | st Depeiza b Sobers | 2 | | | |
| I.W. Johnson* | c Stollmeyer b Sobers | 0 | | | |
| R.R. Lindwall | b Atkinson | 2 | | | |
| G.R.A. Langley† | not out | 1 | | | |
| W.A. Johnston | absent hurt | – | | | |
| Extras | (LB 2) | 2 | | (NB 1) | 1 |
| **Total** | | **257** | | (2 wickets) | **133** |

| AUSTRALIA | O | M | R | W | O | M | R | W |
|---|---|---|---|---|---|---|---|---|
| Lindwall | 12 | 0 | 44 | 1 | 18 | 1 | 54 | 1 |
| Miller | 9 | 1 | 33 | 2 | 9 | 3 | 18 | 1 |
| Archer | 10 | 0 | 46 | 2 | 12 | 3 | 43 | 0 |
| Johnson | 9 | 1 | 42 | 1 | 22·2 | 10 | 44 | 7 |
| Benaud | 3·5 | 1 | 15 | 4 | 14 | 3 | 43 | 1 |
| WEST INDIES | | | | | | | | |
| King | 12 | 1 | 37 | 0 | 3 | 0 | 10 | 0 |
| Worrell | 9 | 2 | 17 | 0 | 7 | 2 | 20 | 0 |
| Ramadhin | 26 | 9 | 55 | 2 | 9 | 1 | 29 | 0 |
| Atkinson | 37 | 13 | 85 | 3 | 15·5 | 5 | 32 | 1 |
| Marshall | 33·3 | 16 | 40 | 1 | 13 | 6 | 22 | 1 |
| Stollmeyer | 1 | 0 | 1 | 0 | | | | |
| Sobers | 16 | 10 | 20 | 3 | 11 | 4 | 19 | 0 |

### FALL OF WICKETS

| Wkt | WI 1st | A 1st | WI 2nd | A 2nd |
|---|---|---|---|---|
| 1st | 23 | 71 | 25 | 70 |
| 2nd | 30 | 135 | 25 | 70 |
| 3rd | 42 | 147 | 25 | – |
| 4th | 52 | 161 | 150 | – |
| 5th | 83 | 215 | 162 | – |
| 6th | 124 | 231 | 175 | – |
| 7th | 156 | 231 | 186 | – |
| 8th | 156 | 238 | 204 | – |
| 9th | 160 | 257 | 204 | – |
| 10th | 182 | – | 207 | – |

Umpires: E.N. Lee Kow and E.S. Gillette.

# WEST INDIES v AUSTRALIA 1954–55 (4th Test)

Played at Kensington Oval, Bridgetown, Bardados, on 14, 16, 17, 18, 19, 20 May.
Toss: Australia.   Result: MATCH DRAWN.
Debuts: West Indies – D.T. Dewdney.

Australia's total of 668 remains the highest of any Barbados Test match and the partnership of 206 between Miller and Archer is still the highest for the sixth wicket in this series. Both records were overshadowed by the batting of Atkinson and Depeiza, who set a new world first-class record of 348 for the seventh wicket after six wickets had fallen for 146. Atkinson was the first to score a double century and take five wickets in an innings of the same Test.

## AUSTRALIA

| | | | | | |
|---|---|---|---|---|---|
| C.C. McDonald | run out | 46 | b Smith | | 17 |
| L.E. Favell | c Weekes b Atkinson | 72 | run out | | 53 |
| R.N. Harvey | c Smith b Worrell | 74 | c Valentine b Smith | | 27 |
| W.J. Watson | c Depeiza b Dewdney | 30 | b Atkinson | | 0 |
| K.R. Miller | c Depeiza b Dewdney | 137 | lbw b Atkinson | | 10 |
| R. Benaud | c Walcott b Dewdney | 1 | b Sobers | | 5 |
| R.G. Archer | b Worrell | 98 | lbw b Atkinson | | 28 |
| R.R. Lindwall | c Valentine b Atkinson | 118 | (9) b Atkinson | | 10 |
| I.W. Johnson* | b Dewdney | 23 | (8) c Holt b Smith | | 57 |
| G.R.A. Langley† | b Sobers | 53 | not out | | 28 |
| J.C. Hill | not out | 8 | c Weekes b Atkinson | | 1 |
| Extras | (B 1, LB 2, W 4, NB 1) | 8 | (B 9, LB 4) | | 13 |
| **Total** | | **668** | | | **249** |

## WEST INDIES

| | | | | |
|---|---|---|---|---|
| J.K. Holt | b Lindwall | 22 | lbw b Hill | 49 |
| G. St A. Sobers | c Hill b Johnson | 43 | lbw b Archer | 11 |
| C.L. Walcott | c Langley b Benaud | 15 | b Benaud | 83 |
| E. de C. Weekes | c Langley b Miller | 44 | run out | 6 |
| F.M.M. Worrell | run out | 16 | c Archer b Miller | 34 |
| O.G. Smith | c Langley b Miller | 2 | b Lindwall | 11 |
| D. St E. Atkinson* | c Archer b Johnson | 219 | not out | 20 |
| C.C. Depeiza† | b Benaud | 122 | not out | 11 |
| S. Ramadhin | c and b Benaud | 10 | | |
| D.T. Dewdney | b Johnson | 0 | | |
| A.L. Valentine | not out | 2 | | |
| Extras | (B 5, LB 4, W 2, NB 4) | 15 | (B 6, LB 2, W 1) | 9 |
| **Total** | | **510** | **(6 wickets)** | **234** |

| WEST INDIES | O | M | R | W | O | M | R | W | | FALL OF WICKETS | | | |
|---|---|---|---|---|---|---|---|---|---|---|---|---|---|
| Worrell | 40 | 7 | 120 | 2 | 7 | 0 | 25 | 0 | | | A | WI | A | WI |
| Dewdney | 33 | 5 | 125 | 4 | 10 | 4 | 23 | 0 | *Wkt* | *1st* | *1st* | *2nd* | *2nd* |
| Walcott | 26 | 10 | 57 | 0 | | | | | 1st | 108 | 52 | 71 | 38 |
| Valentine | 31 | 9 | 87 | 0 | 6 | 1 | 16 | 0 | 2nd | 126 | 69 | 72 | 67 |
| Ramadhin | 24 | 3 | 84 | 0 | 2 | 0 | 10 | 0 | 3rd | 226 | 105 | 73 | 81 |
| Atkinson | 48 | 14 | 108 | 2 | 36·2 | 16 | 56 | 5 | 4th | 226 | 142 | 87 | 154 |
| Smith | 22 | 8 | 49 | 0 | 34 | 12 | 71 | 3 | 5th | 233 | 143 | 107 | 193 |
| Sobers | 11·5 | 6 | 30 | 1 | 14 | 3 | 35 | 1 | 6th | 439 | 147 | 119 | 207 |
| | | | | | | | | | 7th | 483 | 494 | 151 | – |
| AUSTRALIA | | | | | | | | | 8th | 562 | 504 | 177 | – |
| Lindwall | 25 | 3 | 96 | 1 | 8 | 1 | 39 | 1 | 9th | 623 | 504 | 241 | – |
| Miller | 22 | 2 | 113 | 2 | 21 | 3 | 66 | 1 | 10th | 668 | 510 | 249 | – |
| Archer | 15 | 4 | 44 | 0 | 7 | 1 | 11 | 1 | | | | | |
| Johnson | 35 | 13 | 77 | 3 | 14 | 4 | 30 | 0 | | | | | |
| Hill | 24 | 9 | 71 | 0 | 11 | 2 | 44 | 1 | | | | | |
| Benaud | 31·1 | 6 | 73 | 3 | 11 | 3 | 35 | 1 | | | | | |
| Harvey | 4 | 0 | 16 | 0 | | | | | | | | | |
| Watson | 1 | 0 | 5 | 0 | | | | | | | | | |

Umpires: E.N. Lee Kow and H.B. de C. Jordan.

# WEST INDIES v AUSTRALIA 1954–55 (5th Test)

Played at Sabina Park, Kingston, Jamaica, on 11, 13, 14, 15, 16, 17 June.
Toss: West Indies.   Result: AUSTRALIA won by an innings and 82 runs.
Debuts: West Indies – H.A. Furlonge.

Australia's total was then the highest by a country other than England and remains unique in including five centuries, Benaud's taking only 78 minutes. Walcott is the only batsman to score a hundred in each innings of a Test twice in the same rubber; nor has any batsman equalled his feat of scoring five centuries in a Test rubber.

## WEST INDIES

| | | | | | |
|---|---|---|---|---|---|
| J.K. Holt | c Langley b Miller | 4 | | c Langley b Benaud | 21 |
| H.A. Furlonge | c Benaud b Lindwall | 4 | | c sub (A.K. Davidson) b Miller | 28 |
| C.L. Walcott | c Langley b Miller | 155 | (4) | c Langley b Lindwall | 110 |
| E. de C. Weekes | b Benaud | 56 | (9) | not out | 36 |
| F.M.M. Worrell | c Langley b Lindwall | 61 | (7) | b Johnson | 12 |
| O.G. Smith | c Langley b Miller | 29 | | c and b Benaud | 16 |
| G. St A. Sobers | not out | 35 | (5) | c Favell b Lindwall | 64 |
| D. St E. Atkinson* | run out | 8 | | c Langley b Archer | 4 |
| C.C. Depeiza† | c Langley b Miller | 0 | (3) | b Miller | 7 |
| F.M. King | b Miller | 0 | | c Archer b Johnson | 6 |
| D.T. Dewdney | b Miller | 2 | | lbw b Benaud | 0 |
| Extras | (LB 2, W 1) | 3 | | (B 8, LB 6, W 1) | 15 |
| **Total** | | **357** | | | **319** |

## AUSTRALIA

| | | |
|---|---|---|
| C.C. McDonald | b Worrell | 127 |
| L.E. Favell | c Weekes b King | 0 |
| A.R. Morris | lbw b Dewdney | 7 |
| R.N. Harvey | c Atkinson b Smith | 204 |
| K.R. Miller | c Worrell b Atkinson | 109 |
| R.G. Archer | c Depeiza b Sobers | 128 |
| R.R. Lindwall | c Depeiza b King | 10 |
| R. Benaud | c Worrell b Smith | 121 |
| I.W. Johnson* | not out | 27 |
| G.R.A. Langley† | did not bat | |
| W.A. Johnston | | |
| Extras | (B 8, LB 7, W 9, NB 1) | 25 |
| **Total** | (8 wickets declared) | **758** |

| AUSTRALIA | O | M | R | W | O | M | R | W |
|---|---|---|---|---|---|---|---|---|
| Lindwall | 12 | 2 | 64 | 2 | 19 | 6 | 51 | 2 |
| Miller | 25·2 | 3 | 107 | 6 | 19 | 3 | 58 | 2 |
| Archer | 11 | 1 | 39 | 0 | 27 | 6 | 73 | 1 |
| Benaud | 24 | 5 | 75 | 1 | 29·5 | 10 | 76 | 3 |
| Johnson | 22 | 7 | 69 | 0 | 23 | 10 | 46 | 2 |
| WEST INDIES | | | | | | | | |
| Dewdney | 24 | 4 | 115 | 1 | | | | |
| King | 31 | 1 | 126 | 2 | | | | |
| Atkinson | 55 | 20 | 132 | 1 | | | | |
| Smith | 52·4 | 17 | 145 | 2 | | | | |
| Worrell | 45 | 10 | 116 | 1 | | | | |
| Sobers | 38 | 12 | 99 | 1 | | | | |

### FALL OF WICKETS

| Wkt | WI 1st | A 1st | WI 2nd |
|---|---|---|---|
| 1st | 5 | 0 | 47 |
| 2nd | 13 | 7 | 60 |
| 3rd | 95 | 302 | 65 |
| 4th | 204 | 373 | 244 |
| 5th | 268 | 593 | 244 |
| 6th | 327 | 597 | 268 |
| 7th | 341 | 621 | 273 |
| 8th | 347 | 758 | 283 |
| 9th | 347 | – | 289 |
| 10th | 357 | – | 319 |

Umpires: P. Burke and T.A. Ewart.

# ENGLAND v SOUTH AFRICA 1955 (1st Test)

Played at Trent Bridge, Nottingham, on 9, 10, 11, 13 June.
Toss: England.   Result: ENGLAND won by an innings and 5 runs.
Debuts: England – K.F. Barrington; South Africa – T.L. Goddard.

Hutton, chosen as captain for all five Tests, stood down because of lumbago. Evans became the first wicket-keeper to make 150 dismissals in Test matches when he caught Fuller. Tyson ended the match with a spell of 5 for 5 in 7·3 overs; it brought his tally of Test wickets to 52 from nine matches.

## ENGLAND

| | | |
|---|---|---|
| D. Kenyon | lbw b Goddard | 87 |
| T.W. Graveney | c Waite b Adcock | 42 |
| P.B.H. May* | c McGlew b Smith | 83 |
| D.C.S. Compton | lbw b Adcock | 27 |
| K.F. Barrington | c Waite b Fuller | 0 |
| T.E. Bailey | lbw b Goddard | 49 |
| T.G. Evans† | c Goddard b Fuller | 12 |
| J.H. Wardle | lbw b Tayfield | 2 |
| F.H. Tyson | c McLean b Tayfield | 0 |
| J.B. Statham | c Waite b Fuller | 20 |
| R. Appleyard | not out | 0 |
| Extras | (B 6, LB 6) | 12 |
| **Total** | | **334** |

## SOUTH AFRICA

| | | | | | |
|---|---|---|---|---|---|
| D.J. McGlew | c Evans b Wardle | 68 | | c May b Bailey | 51 |
| T.L. Goddard | lbw b Statham | 12 | | run out | 32 |
| J.H.B. Waite† | run out | 0 | | c Compton b Tyson | 3 |
| W.R. Endean | lbw b Tyson | 0 | | c Graveney b Bailey | 6 |
| R.A. McLean | b Tyson | 13 | | c Graveney b Tyson | 16 |
| P.L. Winslow | c May b Appleyard | 2 | (7) | b Tyson | 3 |
| J.E. Cheetham* | c Graveney b Wardle | 54 | (6) | b Tyson | 5 |
| H.J. Tayfield | c Bailey b Appleyard | 11 | | b Tyson | 0 |
| E.R.H. Fuller | b Wardle | 15 | | c Evans b Wardle | 6 |
| V.I. Smith | c May b Wardle | 0 | | not out | 2 |
| N.A.T. Adcock | not out | 1 | | b Tyson | 6 |
| Extras | (B 1, LB 2, NB 2) | 5 | | (B 8, LB 4, W 4, NB 2) | 18 |
| **Total** | | **181** | | | **148** |

| SOUTH AFRICA | O | M | R | W | O | M | R | W |
|---|---|---|---|---|---|---|---|---|
| Adcock | 36 | 9 | 74 | 2 | | | | |
| Goddard | 36·4 | 18 | 61 | 2 | | | | |
| Fuller | 29 | 5 | 59 | 3 | | | | |
| Tayfield | 37 | 11 | 66 | 2 | | | | |
| Smith | 30 | 9 | 62 | 1 | | | | |
| ENGLAND | | | | | | | | |
| Statham | 25 | 5 | 47 | 1 | 10 | 4 | 16 | 0 |
| Tyson | 24 | 5 | 51 | 2 | 21·3 | 7 | 28 | 6 |
| Bailey | 5 | 2 | 8 | 0 | 17 | 8 | 21 | 2 |
| Appleyard | 28 | 9 | 46 | 2 | 19 | 4 | 32 | 0 |
| Wardle | 32 | 23 | 24 | 4 | 29 | 17 | 33 | 1 |

### FALL OF WICKETS

| Wkt | E 1st | SA 1st | SA 2nd |
|---|---|---|---|
| 1st | 91 | 15 | 73 |
| 2nd | 166 | 17 | 83 |
| 3rd | 228 | 19 | 101 |
| 4th | 233 | 35 | 108 |
| 5th | 252 | 55 | 131 |
| 6th | 285 | 149 | 132 |
| 7th | 294 | 156 | 132 |
| 8th | 298 | 174 | 135 |
| 9th | 334 | 180 | 141 |
| 10th | 334 | 181 | 148 |

Umpires: F.S. Lee and T.J. Bartley.

# ENGLAND v SOUTH AFRICA 1955 (2nd Test)

Played at Lord's, London, on 23, 24, 25, 27 June.
Toss: England.   Result: ENGLAND won by 71 runs.
Debuts: England – F.J. Titmus; South Africa – P.S. Heine.

Compton emulated Hobbs, Bradman, Hammond and Hutton by scoring his 5,000th run in Test cricket. Tayfield overtook C.L. Vincent's South African Test record of 84 wickets. May scored a hundred on his first appearance as England's captain at Lord's.

## ENGLAND

| | | | | |
|---|---|---|---|---|
| D. Kenyon | b Adcodk | 1 | lbw b Goddard | 2 |
| T.W. Graveney | c Waite b Heine | 15 | c Heine b Goddard | 60 |
| P.B.H. May* | c Tayfield b Heine | 0 | hit wkt b Heine | 112 |
| D.C.S. Compton | c Keith b Heine | 20 | c Mansell b Goddard | 69 |
| K.F. Barrington | b Heine | 34 | c McLean b Tayfield | 18 |
| T.E. Bailey | lbw b Goddard | 13 | c Adcock b Tayfield | 22 |
| T.G. Evans† | c Waite b Heine | 20 | c and b Tayfield | 14 |
| F.J. Titmus | lbw b Goddard | 4 | (9) c Waite b Adcock | 16 |
| J.H. Wardle | c Tayfield b Goddard | 20 | (8) c Heine b Tayfield | 4 |
| J.B. Statham | c McLean b Goddard | 0 | b Tayfield | 11 |
| F.S. Trueman | not out | 2 | not out | 6 |
| Extras | (B 2, LB 2) | 4 | (B 15, LB 2, NB 2) | 19 |
| **Total** | | **133** | | **353** |

## SOUTH AFRICA

| | | | | |
|---|---|---|---|---|
| D.J. McGlew | c Evans b Statham | 0 | lbw b Statham | 0 |
| T.L. Goddard | c Evans b Trueman | 0 | c Evans b Statham | 10 |
| J.E. Cheetham* | lbw b Bailey | 13 | retired hurt | 3 |
| W.R. Endean | lbw b Wardle | 48 | (5) c Evans b Statham | 28 |
| R.A. McLean | b Statham | 142 | (6) b Statham | 8 |
| J.H.B. Waite† | c Evans b Trueman | 8 | (8) lbw b Statham | 9 |
| H.J. Keith | c Titmus b Wardle | 57 | c Graveney b Statham | 5 |
| P.N.F. Mansell | c Graveney b Wardle | 2 | (9) c Kenyon b Wardle | 16 |
| H.J. Tayfield | b Titmus | 21 | (4) c Evans b Statham | 3 |
| P.S. Heine | st Evans b Wardle | 2 | c Kenyon b Wardle | 14 |
| N.A.T. Adcock | not out | 0 | not out | 0 |
| Extras | (B 6, LB 1, NB 4) | 11 | (B 11, LB 3, NB 1) | 15 |
| **Total** | | **304** | | **111** |

| SOUTH AFRICA | O | M | R | W | O | M | R | W |
|---|---|---|---|---|---|---|---|---|
| Heine | 25 | 7 | 60 | 5 | 29 | 5 | 87 | 1 |
| Adcock | 8 | 3 | 10 | 1 | 25 | 5 | 64 | 1 |
| Goddard | 21·2 | 8 | 59 | 4 | 55 | 23 | 96 | 3 |
| Tayfield | | | | | 38·5 | 12 | 80 | 5 |
| Mansell | | | | | 2 | 0 | 7 | 0 |
| ENGLAND | | | | | | | | |
| Statham | 27 | 9 | 49 | 2 | 29 | 12 | 39 | 7 |
| Trueman | 16 | 2 | 73 | 2 | 19 | 2 | 39 | 0 |
| Bailey | 16 | 2 | 56 | 1 | | | | |
| Wardle | 29 | 10 | 65 | 4 | 9·4 | 4 | 18 | 2 |
| Titmus | 14 | 3 | 50 | 1 | | | | |

### FALL OF WICKETS

| Wkt | E 1st | SA 1st | E 2nd | SA 2nd |
|---|---|---|---|---|
| 1st | 7 | 0 | 9 | 0 |
| 2nd | 8 | 7 | 141 | 17 |
| 3rd | 30 | 51 | 237 | 40 |
| 4th | 45 | 101 | 277 | 54 |
| 5th | 82 | 138 | 285 | 63 |
| 6th | 98 | 247 | 302 | 75 |
| 7th | 111 | 259 | 306 | 78 |
| 8th | 111 | 302 | 336 | 111 |
| 9th | 111 | 304 | 336 | 111 |
| 10th | 133 | 304 | 353 | – |

Umpires: F. Chester and L.H. Gray.

# ENGLAND v SOUTH AFRICA 1955 (3rd Test)

Played at Old Trafford, Manchester, on 7, 8, 9, 11, 12 July.
Toss: England.   Result: SOUTH AFRICA won by three wickets.
Debuts: Nil.

Needing 145 runs to win in 135 minutes, South Africa gained their third victory in England with nine balls to spare. It was England's first defeat at Manchester since 1902. Evans fractured his right-hand little finger in two places (Graveney deputised as wicket-keeper) but hit powerfully in a last-wicket stand of 48 with Bailey which almost saved the match for England. Winslow reached his hundred with a straight drive over the sight-screen. McGlew retired with a damaged hand when 77*, shortly after the fall of the first wicket, and resumed at 457 for 7.

## ENGLAND

| | | | | | |
|---|---|---:|---|---|---:|
| D. Kenyon | c Waite b Heine | 5 | c Waite b Heine | | 1 |
| T.W. Graveney | c Tayfield b Adcock | 0 | b Adcock | | 1 |
| P.B.H. May* | c Mansell b Goddard | 34 | b Mansell | | 117 |
| D.C.S. Compton | c Waite b Adcock | 158 | c Mansell b Heine | | 71 |
| M.C. Cowdrey | c Mansell b Tayfield | 1 | c Goddard b Heine | | 50 |
| T.E. Bailey | c Waite b Adcock | 44 | (7) not out | | 38 |
| F.J. Titmus | lbw b Heine | 0 | (8) c Mansell b Adcock | | 19 |
| T.G. Evans† | c Keith b Heine | 0 | (11) c McLean b Tayfield | | 36 |
| G.A.R. Lock | not out | 19 | (6) c McGlew b Adcock | | 17 |
| F.H. Tyson | b Goddard | 2 | (9) b Heine | | 8 |
| A.V. Bedser | lbw b Goddard | 1 | (10) c Waite b Heine | | 3 |
| Extras | (B 13, LB 6, W 1) | 20 | (B 13, LB 5, W 2) | | 20 |
| **Total** | | **284** | | | **381** |

## SOUTH AFRICA

| | | | | | |
|---|---|---:|---|---|---:|
| D.J. McGlew* | not out | 104 | b Tyson | | 48 |
| T.L. Goddard | c Graveney b Tyson | 62 | c May b Bedser | | 8 |
| H.J. Keith | c Graveney b Bailey | 38 | b Bedser | | 0 |
| P.N.F. Mansell | lbw b Lock | 7 | (6) lbw b Tyson | | 4 |
| W.R. Endean | c Evans b Lock | 5 | (8) c Titmus b Lock | | 2 |
| R.A. McLean | b Tyson | 3 | (4) run out | | 50 |
| J.H.B. Waite† | c Kenyon b Bedser | 113 | not out | | 10 |
| P.L. Winslow | lbw b Bedser | 108 | (5) b Tyson | | 16 |
| H.J. Tayfield | b Tyson | 28 | not out | | 1 |
| P.S. Heine | not out | 22 | | | |
| N.A.T. Adcock | did not bat | | | | |
| Extras | (B 15, LB 12, W 1, NB 3) | 31 | (B 2, LB 2, W 1, NB 1) | | 6 |
| **Total** | (8 wickets declared) | **521** | (7 wickets) | | **145** |

| SOUTH AFRICA | O | M | R | W | O | M | R | W | FALL OF WICKETS | | | | |
|---|---:|---:|---:|---:|---:|---:|---:|---:|---|---:|---:|---:|---:|
| Heine | 24 | 4 | 71 | 3 | 32 | 8 | 86 | 5 | | E | SA | E | SA |
| Adcock | 28 | 5 | 52 | 3 | 28 | 12 | 48 | 3 | *Wkt* | *1st* | *1st* | *2nd* | *2nd* |
| Tayfield | 35 | 15 | 57 | 1 | 51·5 | 21 | 102 | 1 | 1st | 2 | 147 | 2 | 18 |
| Goddard | 27 | 10 | 52 | 3 | 47 | 21 | 92 | 0 | 2nd | 22 | 171 | 2 | 23 |
| Mansell | 6 | 2 | 13 | 0 | 15 | 3 | 33 | 1 | 3rd | 70 | 179 | 126 | 95 |
| Keith | 6 | 2 | 19 | 0 | | | | | 4th | 75 | 182 | 234 | 112 |
| | | | | | | | | | 5th | 219 | 245 | 270 | 129 |
| ENGLAND | | | | | | | | | 6th | 234 | 416 | 274 | 132 |
| Bedser | 31 | 2 | 92 | 2 | 10 | 1 | 61 | 2 | 7th | 242 | 457 | 304 | 135 |
| Tyson | 44 | 5 | 124 | 3 | 13·3 | 2 | 55 | 3 | 8th | 271 | 494 | 325 | – |
| Bailey | 37 | 8 | 102 | 1 | | | | | 9th | 280 | – | 333 | – |
| Lock | 64 | 24 | 121 | 2 | 7 | 2 | 23 | 1 | 10th | 284 | – | 381 | – |
| Titmus | 19 | 7 | 51 | 0 | | | | | | | | | |

Umpires: F.S. Lee and D. Davies.

# ENGLAND v SOUTH AFRICA 1955 (4th Test)

Played at Headingley, Leeds, on 21, 22, 23, 25, 26 July.
Toss: South Africa.   Result: SOUTH AFRICA won by 224 runs.
Debuts: Nil.

Despite losing Adcock with a broken bone in his left foot, South Africa gained an unprecedented second victory in a rubber in England. McGlew and Goddard shared a record opening partnership for South Africa in England. England's first innings contained a record six 'lbw's' (since equalled).

## SOUTH AFRICA

| | | | | |
|---|---|---:|---|---:|
| D.J. McGlew* | c McIntyre b Loader | 23 | c May b Wardle | 133 |
| T.L. Goddard | b Loader | 9 | c McIntyre b Wardle | 74 |
| H.J. Keith | c McIntyre b Loader | 0 | b Wardle | 73 |
| P.N.F. Mansell | b Bailey | 1 | (8) lbw b Bailey | 1 |
| R.A. McLean | c May b Loader | 41 | (4) c Lowson b Wardle | 3 |
| J.H.B. Waite† | run out | 2 | (7) c McIntyre b Lock | 32 |
| P.L. Winslow | b Statham | 8 | (5) c Lock b Statham | 19 |
| W.R. Endean | b Statham | 41 | (6) not out | 116 |
| H.J. Tayfield | not out | 25 | lbw b Statham | 14 |
| P.S. Heine | b Lock | 14 | b Bailey | 10 |
| N.A.T. Adcock | lbw b Statham | 0 | b Bailey | 6 |
| Extras | (LB 4, NB 4) | 8 | (B 8, LB 6, W 1, NB 4) | 19 |
| **Total** | | **171** | | **500** |

## ENGLAND

| | | | | |
|---|---|---:|---|---:|
| T.E. Bailey | lbw b Heine | 9 | (6) c and b Tayfield | 8 |
| F.A. Lowson | lbw b Goddard | 5 | b Goddard | 0 |
| P.B.H. May* | b Tayfield | 47 | lbw b Tayfield | 97 |
| G.A.R. Lock | lbw b Goddard | 17 | (9) c Mansell b Goddard | 7 |
| D.C.S. Compton | c Mansell b Tayfield | 61 | c Waite b Goddard | 26 |
| T.W. Graveney | lbw b Heine | 10 | (1) c McLean b Tayfield | 36 |
| D.J. Insole | lbw b Heine | 3 | (4) c Keith b Goddard | 47 |
| A.J.W. McIntyre† | lbw b Heine | 3 | (7) c Heine b Tayfield | 4 |
| J.H. Wardle | c Goddard b Tayfield | 24 | (8) c Heine b Tayfield | 21 |
| J.B. Statham | b Tayfield | 4 | hit wkt b Goddard | 3 |
| P.J. Loader | not out | 0 | not out | 0 |
| Extras | (B 5, LB 2, W 1) | 8 | (B 1, LB 6) | 7 |
| **Total** | | **191** | | **256** |

| ENGLAND | O | M | R | W | O | M | R | W |
|---|---|---|---|---|---|---|---|---|
| Statham | 20·2 | 7 | 35 | 3 | 40 | 10 | 129 | 2 |
| Loader | 19 | 7 | 52 | 4 | 29 | 9 | 67 | 0 |
| Bailey | 16 | 7 | 23 | 1 | 40·5 | 11 | 97 | 3 |
| Wardle | 9 | 1 | 33 | 0 | 57 | 22 | 100 | 4 |
| Lock | 6 | 1 | 20 | 1 | 42 | 13 | 88 | 1 |
| **SOUTH AFRICA** | | | | | | | | |
| Heine | 29·5 | 11 | 70 | 4 | 14 | 2 | 33 | 0 |
| Adcock | 4 | 3 | 4 | 0 | | | | |
| Goddard | 25 | 12 | 39 | 2 | 62 | 37 | 69 | 5 |
| Tayfield | 31 | 14 | 70 | 4 | 47·1 | 15 | 94 | 5 |
| Mansell | | | | | 19 | 2 | 53 | 0 |

### FALL OF WICKETS

| Wkt | SA 1st | E 1st | SA 2nd | E 2nd |
|---|---|---|---|---|
| 1st | 33 | 15 | 176 | 3 |
| 2nd | 33 | 23 | 265 | 59 |
| 3rd | 34 | 53 | 269 | 160 |
| 4th | 34 | 117 | 303 | 204 |
| 5th | 38 | 152 | 311 | 210 |
| 6th | 63 | 152 | 387 | 215 |
| 7th | 98 | 161 | 400 | 239 |
| 8th | 154 | 186 | 439 | 246 |
| 9th | 170 | 191 | 468 | 256 |
| 10th | 171 | 191 | 500 | 256 |

Umpires: F. Chester and T.J. Bartley.

# ENGLAND v SOUTH AFRICA 1955 (5th Test)

Played at Kennington Oval, London, on 13, 15, 16, 17 August.
Toss: England.   Result: ENGLAND won by 92 runs.
Debuts: Nil.

This was the first rubber in England to produce five definite results, England winning this deciding match at 5.15 p.m. on the fourth day. On the third day Tayfield had bowled unchanged from 12.30 to 6.30 p.m., five hours of play during which he bowled 52 overs for 54 runs and four wickets.

## ENGLAND

|  | | | | |
|---|---|---|---|---|
| J.T. Ikin | c Waite b Heine | 17 | c Goddard b Heine | 0 |
| D.B. Close | c Mansell b Goddard | 32 | b Goddard | 15 |
| P.B.H. May* | c Goddard b Fuller | 3 | (4) not out | 89 |
| D.C.S. Compton | c Waite b Goddard | 30 | (5) c Waite b Fuller | 30 |
| W. Watson | c Mansell b Tayfield | 25 | (6) b Fuller | 3 |
| T.W. Graveney | c Fuller b Goddard | 13 | (3) b Tayfield | 42 |
| T.E. Bailey | c Heine b Tayfield | 0 | lbw b Tayfield | 1 |
| R.T. Spooner† | b Tayfield | 0 | b Tayfield | 0 |
| J.C. Laker | c and b Goddard | 2 | b Tayfield | 12 |
| G.A.R. Lock | c McLean b Goddard | 18 | lbw b Heine | 1 |
| J.B. Statham | not out | 4 | lbw b Tayfield | 0 |
| Extras | (B 2, LB 5) | 7 | (B 4, LB 6, NB 1) | 11 |
| **Total** | | **151** | | **204** |

## SOUTH AFRICA

|  | | | | |
|---|---|---|---|---|
| D.J. McGlew | c Spooner b Statham | 30 | lbw b Lock | 19 |
| T.L. Goddard | lbw b Bailey | 8 | c Graveney b Lock | 20 |
| H.J. Keith | b Lock | 5 | c May b Lock | 0 |
| W.R. Endean | c Ikin b Lock | 0 | lbw b Laker | 0 |
| R.A. McLean | b Lock | 1 | lbw b Laker | 0 |
| J.H.B. Waite† | c Lock b Laker | 28 | b Laker | 60 |
| J.E. Cheetham* | not out | 12 | lbw b Laker | 9 |
| P.N.F. Mansell | lbw b Laker | 6 | c Watson b Lock | 0 |
| H.J. Tayfield | b Statham | 4 | not out | 10 |
| E.R.H. Fuller | c Spooner b Lock | 5 | run out | 10 |
| P.S. Heine | run out | 5 | c Graveney b Laker | 1 |
| Extras | (LB 7, NB 1) | 8 | (LB 1) | 1 |
| **Total** | | **112** | | **151** |

| SOUTH AFRICA | O | M | R | W | O | M | R | W |
|---|---|---|---|---|---|---|---|---|
| Heine | 21 | 3 | 43 | 1 | 25 | 6 | 44 | 2 |
| Goddard | 22·4 | 9 | 31 | 5 | 19 | 10 | 29 | 1 |
| Fuller | 27 | 11 | 31 | 1 | 20 | 3 | 36 | 2 |
| Tayfield | 19 | 7 | 39 | 3 | 53·4 | 29 | 60 | 5 |
| Mansell | | | | | 6 | 0 | 24 | 0 |
| **ENGLAND** | | | | | | | | |
| Statham | 15 | 3 | 31 | 2 | 11 | 4 | 17 | 0 |
| Bailey | 5 | 1 | 6 | 1 | 6 | 1 | 15 | 0 |
| Lock | 22 | 11 | 39 | 4 | 33 | 14 | 62 | 4 |
| Laker | 23 | 13 | 28 | 2 | 37·4 | 18 | 56 | 5 |

### FALL OF WICKETS

| | E | SA | E | SA |
|---|---|---|---|---|
| Wkt | 1st | 1st | 2nd | 2nd |
| 1st | 51 | 22 | 5 | 28 |
| 2nd | 59 | 29 | 30 | 28 |
| 3rd | 69 | 31 | 95 | 29 |
| 4th | 105 | 33 | 157 | 33 |
| 5th | 117 | 77 | 165 | 59 |
| 6th | 117 | 77 | 166 | 88 |
| 7th | 118 | 86 | 170 | 118 |
| 8th | 123 | 91 | 188 | 118 |
| 9th | 130 | 98 | 197 | 144 |
| 10th | 151 | 112 | 204 | 151 |

Umpires: D. Davies and T.J. Bartley.

# PAKISTAN v NEW ZEALAND 1955–56 (1st Test)

Played at National Stadium, Karachi, on 13, 14, 16, 17 October.
Toss: New Zealand.   Result: PAKISTAN won by an innings and 1 run.
Debuts: New Zealand – J.C. Alabaster, P.G.Z. Harris, T.G. McMahon.

Zulfiqar Ahmed's off-spin on a matting pitch laid on grass provided – at the earliest possible opportunity – the first instance of a bowler taking ten wickets in a Test match between these two countries.

## NEW ZEALAND

| | | | | | |
|---|---|---|---|---|---|
| J.G. Leggat | c Imtiaz b Fazal | 16 | | lbw b Zulfiqar | 39 |
| B. Sutcliffe | c Kardar b Zulfiqar | 15 | | b Shujauddin | 17 |
| M.B. Poore | st Imtiaz b Zulfiqar | 43 | | b Shujauddin | 0 |
| J.R. Reid | c Khan b Kardar | 10 | (5) | c Waqar b Zulfiqar | 11 |
| P.G.Z. Harris | c Wazir b Kardar | 7 | (6) | run out | 21 |
| S.N. McGregor | c Alimuddin b Shujauddin | 10 | (4) | lbw b Shujauddin | 0 |
| H.B. Cave* | b Kardar | 0 | | c sub (Agha Saadat) b Zulfiqar | 21 |
| J.C. Alabaster | c sub (Agha Saadat) b Zulfiqar | 14 | | b Zulfiqar | 8 |
| A.R. MacGibbon | b Zulfiqar | 33 | | c Hanif b Zulfiqar | 0 |
| A.M. Moir | c Khan b Zulfiqar | 10 | | c Alimuddin b Zulfiqar | 2 |
| T.G. McMahon† | not out | 0 | | not out | 0 |
| Extras | (B 4, LB 2) | 6 | | (B 1, LB 4) | 5 |
| **Total** | | **164** | | | **124** |

## PAKISTAN

| | | |
|---|---|---|
| Hanif Mohammad | c McGregor b Cave | 5 |
| Alimuddin | c MacGibbon b Moir | 28 |
| Waqar Hassan | c McMahon b Cave | 17 |
| Maqsood Ahmed | b MacGibbon | 2 |
| Imtiaz Ahmed† | c McMahon b MacGibbon | 64 |
| A.H. Kardar* | run out | 22 |
| Wazir Mohammad | c and b Cave | 43 |
| Shujauddin | b MacGibbon | 47 |
| Zulfiqar Ahmed | b MacGibbon | 10 |
| Fazal Mahmood | not out | 34 |
| Khan Mohammad | run out | 5 |
| Extras | (B 4, LB 1, NB 7) | 12 |
| **Total** | | **289** |

| PAKISTAN | O | M | R | W | O | M | R | W | FALL OF WICKETS | | | |
|---|---|---|---|---|---|---|---|---|---|---|---|---|
| | | | | | | | | | | NZ | P | NZ |
| Fazal | 31 | 12 | 46 | 1 | 13 | 3 | 33 | 0 | Wkt | 1st | 1st | 2nd |
| Khan | 23 | 9 | 27 | 0 | 13 | 3 | 33 | 0 | 1st | 18 | 5 | 27 |
| Zulfiqar | 37·2 | 19 | 37 | 5 | 46·3 | 21 | 42 | 6 | 2nd | 50 | 25 | 27 |
| Kardar | 31 | 10 | 35 | 3 | 27 | 15 | 22 | 0 | 3rd | 71 | 32 | 27 |
| Shujauddin | 11 | 7 | 13 | 1 | 22 | 12 | 22 | 3 | 4th | 95 | 74 | 42 |
| | | | | | | | | | 5th | 95 | 140 | 79 |
| NEW ZEALAND | | | | | | | | | 6th | 95 | 144 | 109 |
| MacGibbon | 37·1 | 8 | 98 | 4 | | | | | 7th | 114 | 222 | 118 |
| Cave | 24 | 6 | 56 | 3 | | | | | 8th | 129 | 240 | 120 |
| Reid | 30 | 17 | 34 | 0 | | | | | 9th | 163 | 251 | 122 |
| Moir | 37 | 9 | 87 | 1 | | | | | 10th | 164 | 289 | 124 |
| Poore | 2 | 0 | 2 | 0 | | | | | | | | |

Umpires: Shujauddin and Idris Beg.

# PAKISTAN v NEW ZEALAND 1955–56 (2nd Test)

Played at Bagh-e-Jinnah, Lahore, on 26, 27, 29, 30, 31 October.
Toss: New Zealand.   Result: PAKISTAN won by four wickets.
Debuts: New Zealand – N.S. Harford, E.C. Petrie.

Pakistan won with 18 minutes to spare after compiling their highest total in any Test so far. First Waqar Hassan and then Imtiaz Ahmed established a new record score for their country, Imtiaz hitting Pakistan's first double-century in an innings lasting 680 minutes and containing 28 fours. His partnership of 308 with Waqar remains Pakistan's highest for the seventh wicket in all Tests.

## NEW ZEALAND

| | | | | | |
|---|---|---|---|---|---|
| B. Sutcliffe | c Waqar b Khan | 4 | lbw b Shujauddin | | 25 |
| M.B. Poore | c Alimuddin b Khan | 6 | c Imtiaz b Zulfiqar | | 9 |
| P.G.Z. Harris | run out | 28 | b Shujauddin | | 11 |
| S.N. McGregor | lbw b Kardar | 111 | c Imtiaz b Khan | | 43 |
| J.R. Reid | c Maqsood b Khan | 5 | b Kardar | | 86 |
| N.S. Harford | c Maqsood b Khan | 93 | (7) c Khan b Zulfiqar | | 64 |
| A.R. MacGibbon | lbw b Zulfiqar | 61 | (6) c Wazir b Kardar | | 40 |
| E.C. Petrie† | b Kardar | 0 | c Hanif b Kardar | | 7 |
| H.B. Cave* | c and b Zulfiqar | 14 | c Alimuddin b Zulfiqar | | 17 |
| A.M. Moir | b Mahmood | 8 | not out | | 11 |
| J.A. Hayes | not out | 0 | lbw b Zulfiqar | | 0 |
| Extras | (B 4, LB 10, NB 4) | 18 | (B 6, LB 5, NB 4) | | 15 |
| **Total** | | **348** | | | **328** |

## PAKISTAN

| | | | | | |
|---|---|---|---|---|---|
| Hanif Mohammad | hit wkt b Hayes | 10 | lbw b Reid | | 33 |
| Alimuddin | c Sutcliffe b MacGibbon | 4 | c MacGibbon b Reid | | 37 |
| Shujauddin | b Moir | 29 | (7) not out | | 1 |
| Waqar Hassan | c Petrie b MacGibbon | 189 | (5) c MacGibbon b Hayes | | 17 |
| Wazir Mohammad | lbw b Moir | 0 | (8) not out | | 2 |
| A.H. Kardar* | b Moir | 2 | c Reid b Hayes | | 11 |
| Khan Mohammad | run out | 10 | | | |
| Imtiaz Ahmed† | b Moir | 209 | (3) c Cave b Reid | | 0 |
| Maqsood Ahmed | c Cave b Reid | 33 | (4) c McGregor b Reid | | 8 |
| Zulfiqar Ahmed | not out | 21 | | | |
| Mahmood Hussain | c MacGibbon b Sutcliffe | 32 | | | |
| Extras | (B 3, LB 7, NB 12) | 22 | (B 2, LB 4, NB 2) | | 8 |
| **Total** | | **561** | (6 wickets) | | **117** |

| PAKISTAN | O | M | R | W | O | M | R | W | | FALL OF WICKETS | | | |
|---|---|---|---|---|---|---|---|---|---|---|---|---|---|
| Khan | 34 | 10 | 78 | 4 | 18 | 6 | 26 | 1 | | NZ | P | NZ | P |
| Mahmood Hussain | 31·5 | 4 | 67 | 1 | 21 | 6 | 47 | 0 | Wkt | 1st | 1st | 2nd | 2nd |
| Shujauddin | 43 | 11 | 84 | 0 | 38 | 12 | 79 | 2 | 1st | 8 | 11 | 34 | 45 |
| Zulfiqar | 35 | 13 | 71 | 2 | 43·2 | 10 | 114 | 4 | 2nd | 13 | 23 | 43 | 49 |
| Maqsood | 3 | 1 | 4 | 0 | | | | | 3rd | 48 | 84 | 60 | 80 |
| Kardar | 14 | 5 | 26 | 2 | 38 | 15 | 47 | 3 | 4th | 76 | 84 | 148 | 93 |
| | | | | | | | | | 5th | 226 | 87 | 224 | 107 |
| NEW ZEALAND | | | | | | | | | 6th | 267 | 111 | 237 | 115 |
| Hayes | 37 | 12 | 107 | 1 | 8·5 | 2 | 25 | 2 | 7th | 267 | 419 | 252 | – |
| MacGibbon | 40 | 7 | 135 | 2 | 5 | 0 | 20 | 0 | 8th | 333 | 482 | 293 | – |
| Reid | 35 | 13 | 82 | 1 | 8 | 2 | 38 | 4 | 9th | 348 | 517 | 324 | – |
| Cave | 30 | 6 | 84 | 0 | 5 | 0 | 26 | 0 | 10th | 348 | 561 | 328 | – |
| Moir | 39 | 13 | 114 | 4 | | | | | | | | | |
| Poore | 3 | 0 | 13 | 0 | | | | | | | | | |
| Sutcliffe | 1·3 | 0 | 4 | 1 | | | | | | | | | |

Umpires: Daud Khan and Idris Beg.

# PAKISTAN v NEW ZEALAND 1955–56 (3rd Test)

Played at Dacca Stadium on 7 (*no play*), 8 (*no play*), 9, 11, 12 November.
Toss: New Zealand.   Result: MATCH DRAWN.
Debuts: Pakistan – Agha Saadat Ali, Wallis Mathias; New Zealand – J.W. Guy.

Incessant drizzle prevented play until the third day. On a wet coir matting pitch laid on grass, New Zealand were bowled out in a humid atmosphere for the lowest total in any Pakistan-New Zealand Test.

## NEW ZEALAND

| | | | | | |
|---|---|---|---|---|---|
| J.G. Leggat | b Khan | 1 | c Agha Saadat b Fazal | | 1 |
| B. Sutcliffe | b Fazal | 3 | c Imtiaz b Khan | | 17 |
| M.B. Poore | b Fazal | 0 | c Agha Saadat b Kardar | | 18 |
| S.N. McGregor | b Khan | 7 | c Imtiaz b Zulfiqar | | 4 |
| J.R. Reid | c Imtiaz b Khan | 9 | b Kardar | | 12 |
| N.S. Harford | c Imtiaz b Fazal | 0 | c Hanif b Khan | | 1 |
| J.W. Guy | st Imtiaz b Zulfiqar | 11 | not out | | 8 |
| A.R. MacGibbon | not out | 29 | not out | | 7 |
| E.C. Petrie† | lbw b Khan | 6 | | | |
| H.B. Cave* | c Agha Saadat b Khan | 0 | | | |
| A.M. Moir | c Shujauddin b Khan | 0 | | | |
| Extras | (LB 4) | 4 | (LB 1) | | 1 |
| **Total** | | **70** | (6 wickets) | | **69** |

## PAKISTAN

| | | |
|---|---|---|
| Alimuddin | b Reid | 5 |
| Hanif Mohammad | c Reid b Cave | 103 |
| Waqar Hassan | lbw b Reid | 8 |
| Shujauddin | c Guy b Cave | 3 |
| Imtiaz Ahmed† | b Cave | 11 |
| A.H. Kardar* | b MacGibbon | 14 |
| W. Mathias | not out | 41 |
| Agha Saadat Ali | not out | 8 |
| Fazal Mahmood | ) | |
| Zulfiqar Ahmed | ) did not bat | |
| Khan Mohammad | ) | |
| Extras | (LB 1, NB 1) | 2 |
| **Total** | (6 wickets declared) | **195** |

| PAKISTAN | O | M | R | W | O | M | R | W |
|---|---|---|---|---|---|---|---|---|
| Fazal | 20 | 7 | 34 | 3 | 6 | 3 | 12 | 1 |
| Khan | 16·2 | 6 | 21 | 6 | 30 | 19 | 20 | 2 |
| Zulfiqar | 3 | 1 | 11 | 1 | 16 | 8 | 13 | 1 |
| Kardar | | | | | 28 | 17 | 21 | 2 |
| Shujauddin | | | | | 9 | 8 | 1 | 0 |
| Hanif | | | | | 1 | 0 | 1 | 0 |

| NEW ZEALAND | O | M | R | W |
|---|---|---|---|---|
| MacGibbon | 20 | 4 | 64 | 1 |
| Cave | 20 | 4 | 45 | 3 |
| Reid | 30 | 10 | 67 | 2 |
| Moir | 6 | 1 | 17 | 0 |

### FALL OF WICKETS

| Wkt | NZ 1st | P 1st | NZ 2nd |
|---|---|---|---|
| 1st | 1 | 22 | 12 |
| 2nd | 4 | 30 | 22 |
| 3rd | 9 | 37 | 32 |
| 4th | 15 | 55 | 51 |
| 5th | 20 | 86 | 52 |
| 6th | 26 | 182 | 56 |
| 7th | 54 | – | – |
| 8th | 64 | – | – |
| 9th | 68 | – | – |
| 10th | 70 | – | – |

Umpires: Daud Khan and Idris Beg.

# INDIA v NEW ZEALAND 1955–56 (1st Test)

Played at Fateh Maidan, Hyderabad, on 19, 20, 22, 23, 24 November.
Toss: India.    Result: MATCH DRAWN.
Debuts: India – A.G. Kripal Singh, N.V. Swamy.

The first Test between these two countries was also the first to be staged at Hyderabad where a turf pitch had recently been laid. It proved a perfect batting surface as India made their highest Test total so far and Umrigar reached India's first double-century; his partnership of 238 with Manjrekar remains India's third-wicket record in all Tests. Kripal Singh scored a hundred in his first Test and Guy made one in his second.

## INDIA

| | | |
|---|---|---|
| V.M.H. Mankad | c Alabaster b MacGibbon | 30 |
| P. Roy | c Petrie b Hayes | 0 |
| P.R. Umrigar | c Petrie b Hayes | 223 |
| V.L. Manjrekar | c MacGibbon b Hayes | 118 |
| A.G. Kripal Singh | not out | 100 |
| G.S. Ramchand | not out | 12 |
| D.G. Phadkar | ) | |
| N.V. Swamy | ) | |
| N.S. Tamhane† | ) did not bat | |
| S.P. Gupte | ) | |
| Ghulam Ahmed* | ) | |
| Extras | (B 8, LB 4, NB 3) | 15 |
| **Total** | (4 wickets declared) | **498** |

## NEW ZEALAND

| | | | | |
|---|---|---|---|---|
| B. Sutcliffe | c Umrigar b Gupte | 17 | not out | 137 |
| E.C. Petrie† | b Gupte | 15 | lbw b Gupte | 4 |
| J.W. Guy | c Ghulam Ahmed b Mankad | 102 | c Ghulam Ahmed b Mankad | 21 |
| J.R. Reid | lbw b Ramchand | 54 | not out | 45 |
| S.M. McGregor | st Tamhane b Gupte | 19 | | |
| N.S. Harford | lbw b Gupte | 4 | | |
| A.R. MacGibbon | c Kripal Singh b Ghulam Ahmed | 59 | | |
| M.B. Poore | lbw b Gupte | 23 | | |
| H.B. Cave* | st Tamhane b Gupte | 14 | | |
| J.C. Alabaster | lbw b Gupte | 11 | | |
| J.A. Hayes | not out | 1 | | |
| Extras | (B 2, LB 5) | 7 | (B 2, LB 2, NB 1) | 5 |
| **Total** | | **326** | (2 wickets) | **212** |

| NEW ZEALAND | O | M | R | W | O | M | R | W | | FALL OF WICKETS | | |
|---|---|---|---|---|---|---|---|---|---|---|---|---|
| Hayes | 26 | 5 | 91 | 3 | | | | | | I | NZ | NZ |
| MacGibbon | 43·1 | 15 | 102 | 1 | | | | | *Wkt* | *1st* | *1st* | *2nd* |
| Reid | 16 | 2 | 63 | 0 | | | | | 1st | 1 | 27 | 42 |
| Cave | 41 | 20 | 59 | 0 | | | | | 2nd | 48 | 36 | 104 |
| Alabaster | 31 | 5 | 96 | 0 | | | | | 3rd | 286 | 119 | – |
| Poore | 9 | 2 | 36 | 0 | | | | | 4th | 457 | 154 | – |
| Sutcliffe | 9 | 1 | 36 | 0 | | | | | 5th | – | 166 | – |
| | | | | | | | | | 6th | – | 253 | – |
| INDIA | | | | | | | | | 7th | – | 292 | – |
| Phadkar | 25 | 11 | 34 | 0 | 12 | 5 | 24 | 0 | 8th | – | 305 | – |
| Swamy | 8 | 2 | 15 | 0 | 10 | 3 | 30 | 0 | 9th | – | 325 | – |
| Gupte | 76·4 | 35 | 128 | 7 | 18 | 7 | 28 | 1 | 10th | – | 326 | – |
| Ghulam Ahmed | 39 | 15 | 56 | 1 | 13 | 2 | 36 | 0 | | | | |
| Mankad | 36 | 16 | 48 | 1 | 25 | 7 | 75 | 1 | | | | |
| Ramchand | 20 | 12 | 33 | 1 | 14 | 7 | 14 | 0 | | | | |
| Kripal Singh | 1 | 0 | 5 | 0 | | | | | | | | |
| Umrigar | 4 | 4 | 0 | 0 | | | | | | | | |

Umpires: M.G. Vijayasarathi and J.R. Patel.

# INDIA v NEW ZEALAND 1955–56 (2nd Test)

Played at Brabourne Stadium, Bombay, on 2, 3, 4, 6, 7 December.
Toss: India.   Result: INDIA won by an innings and 27 runs.
Debuts: India – N.J. Contractor, V.L. Mehra, S.R. Patil.

Mankad scored India's second double-century and equalled Umrigar's record score set in the previous Test. Reid (bruised ankle) batted with a runner in both innings.

## INDIA

| | | |
|---|---|---:|
| V.M.H. Mankad | c sub (T.G. McMahon) b Poore | 223 |
| V.L. Mehra | c Harris b Hayes | 10 |
| P.R. Umrigar* | b Cave | 15 |
| V.L. Manjrekar | c Alabaster b Cave | 0 |
| A.G. Kripal Singh | b Cave | 63 |
| G.S. Ramchand | b MacGibbon | 22 |
| N.J. Contractor | c Petrie b MacGibbon | 16 |
| D.G. Phadkar | not out | 37 |
| N.S. Tamhane† | b Poore | 10 |
| S.R. Patil | not out | 14 |
| S.P. Gupte | did not bat | |
| Extras | (LB 3, NB 8) | 11 |
| **Total** | (8 wickets declared) | **421** |

## NEW ZEALAND

| | | | | |
|---|---|---:|---|---:|
| B. Sutcliffe | c Gupte b Ramchand | 73 | c Mankad b Gupte | 37 |
| E.C. Petrie† | lbw b Gupte | 4 | c Gupte b Phadkar | 4 |
| J.W. Guy | c Gupte b Ramchand | 23 | lbw b Gupte | 2 |
| J.R. Reid | lbw b Patil | 39 | c Phadkar b Patil | 4 |
| P.G.Z. Harris | lbw b Gupte | 19 | c Tamhane b Mankad | 7 |
| A.R. MacGibbon | c Mankad b Phadkar | 46 | c Patil b Gupte | 24 |
| M.B. Poore | c Umrigar b Phadkar | 17 | b Mankad | 0 |
| H.B. Cave* | run out | 12 | c Umrigar b Mankad | 21 |
| A.M. Moir | lbw b Gupte | 0 | c Manjrekar b Gupte | 28 |
| J.C. Alabaster | b Mankad | 16 | b Gupte | 4 |
| J.A. Hayes | not out | 0 | not out | 0 |
| Extras | (B 3, LB 2, W 4) | 9 | (B 1, LB 4) | 5 |
| **Total** | | **258** | | **136** |

| NEW ZEALAND | O | M | R | W | O | M | R | W |
|---|---|---|---|---|---|---|---|---|
| Hayes | 26 | 4 | 79 | 1 | | | | |
| MacGibbon | 23 | 6 | 56 | 2 | | | | |
| Cave | 48 | 23 | 77 | 3 | | | | |
| Reid | 3 | 1 | 6 | 0 | | | | |
| Alabaster | 25 | 4 | 83 | 0 | | | | |
| Moir | 12 | 2 | 51 | 0 | | | | |
| Poore | 19 | 3 | 49 | 2 | | | | |
| Sutcliffe | 2 | 0 | 9 | 0 | | | | |
| **INDIA** | | | | | | | | |
| Phadkar | 28 | 10 | 53 | 2 | 6 | 4 | 5 | 1 |
| Patil | 14 | 3 | 36 | 1 | 9 | 4 | 15 | 1 |
| Gupte | 51 | 26 | 83 | 3 | 32·4 | 19 | 45 | 5 |
| Ramchand | 31 | 15 | 48 | 2 | 6 | 4 | 9 | 0 |
| Mankad | 10·1 | 3 | 29 | 1 | 24 | 8 | 57 | 3 |

## FALL OF WICKETS

| | I | NZ | NZ |
|---|---|---|---|
| *Wkt* | *1st* | *1st* | *2nd* |
| 1st | 36 | 21 | 13 |
| 2nd | 61 | 94 | 22 |
| 3rd | 63 | 133 | 33 |
| 4th | 230 | 156 | 45 |
| 5th | 281 | 166 | 67 |
| 6th | 347 | 218 | 68 |
| 7th | 365 | 231 | 86 |
| 8th | 377 | 232 | 117 |
| 9th | – | 258 | 136 |
| 10th | – | 258 | 136 |

Umpires: M.G. Vijayasarathi and B.J. Mohoni.

# INDIA v NEW ZEALAND 1955–56 (3rd Test)

Played at Feroz Shah Kotla, Delhi, on 16, 17, 18, 20, 21 December.
Toss: New Zealand.   Result: MATCH DRAWN.
Debuts: India – R.G. Nadkarni, G.R. Sunderam.

Sutcliffe's 230* remains the record score in a Test at Delhi and was then the highest for New Zealand in any Test. His unfinished partnership of 222 with Reid is still New Zealand's highest for the third wicket. India reached a total of 500 for the first time in Test cricket.

## NEW ZEALAND

| | | | | | |
|---|---|---|---|---|---|
| J.G. Leggat | c Manjrekar b Gupte | 37 | not out | | 50 |
| B. Sutcliffe | not out | 230 | | | |
| J.W. Guy | c Mehra b Sunderam | 52 | not out | | 10 |
| J.R. Reid | not out | 119 | | | |
| S.N. McGregor | ) | | (2) c Tamhane b Manjrekar | | 49 |
| A.R. MacGibbon | ) | | | | |
| M.B. Poore | ) | | | | |
| H.B. Cave* | ) did not bat | | | | |
| J.C. Alabaster | ) | | | | |
| T.G. McMahon† | ) | | | | |
| J.A. Hayes | ) | | | | |
| Extras | (B 7, LB 5) | 12 | (B 3) | | 3 |
| **Total** | (2 wickets declared) | **450** | (1 wicket) | | **112** |

## INDIA

| | | |
|---|---|---|
| V.L. Mehra | c McMahon b Hayes | 32 |
| N.J. Contractor | b Reid | 62 |
| P.R. Umrigar* | b MacGibbon | 18 |
| V.L. Manjrekar | c McMahon b Cave | 177 |
| A.G. Kripal Singh | b Hayes | 36 |
| G.S. Ramchand | st McMahon b Poore | 72 |
| R.G. Nadkarni | not out | 68 |
| P. Bhandari | b MacGibbon | 39 |
| N.S. Tamhane† | ) | |
| G.R. Sunderam | ) did not bat | |
| S.P. Gupte | ) | |
| Extras | (B 16, LB 4, NB 7) | 27 |
| **Total** | (7 wickets declared) | **531** |

| INDIA | O | M | R | W | O | M | R | W | | FALL OF WICKETS | | |
|---|---|---|---|---|---|---|---|---|---|---|---|---|
| | | | | | | | | | | NZ | I | NZ |
| Sunderam | 39 | 5 | 99 | 1 | 3 | 0 | 8 | 0 | *Wkt* | *1st* | *1st* | *2nd* |
| Ramchand | 38 | 11 | 82 | 0 | 3 | 0 | 11 | 0 | 1st | 98 | 68 | 101 |
| Gupte | 39 | 10 | 98 | 1 | 6 | 1 | 22 | 0 | 2nd | 228 | 111 | – |
| Nadkarni | 54 | 13 | 132 | 0 | 3 | 1 | 10 | 0 | 3rd | – | 119 | – |
| Bhandari | 6 | 0 | 27 | 0 | 7 | 2 | 12 | 0 | 4th | – | 208 | – |
| Manjrekar | | | | | 20 | 13 | 16 | 1 | 5th | – | 335 | – |
| Kripal Singh | | | | | 7 | 3 | 10 | 0 | 6th | – | 458 | – |
| Contractor | | | | | 6 | 1 | 17 | 0 | 7th | – | 531 | – |
| Mehra | | | | | 3 | 0 | 3 | 0 | 8th | – | – | – |
| | | | | | | | | | 9th | – | – | – |
| NEW ZEALAND | | | | | | | | | 10th | – | – | – |
| MacGibbon | 59·5 | 16 | 121 | 2 | | | | | | | | |
| Cave | 50 | 28 | 68 | 1 | | | | | | | | |
| Hayes | 44 | 9 | 105 | 2 | | | | | | | | |
| Reid | 41 | 14 | 86 | 1 | | | | | | | | |
| Alabaster | 29 | 9 | 90 | 0 | | | | | | | | |
| Poore | 15 | 4 | 26 | 1 | | | | | | | | |
| Sutcliffe | 3 | 0 | 8 | 0 | | | | | | | | |

Umpires: D.D. Desai and N.D. Nagarwalla.

# INDIA v NEW ZEALAND 1955–56 (4th Test)

Played at Eden Gardens, Calcutta, on 28, 29, 31 December, 1, 2 January.
Toss: India.   Result: MATCH DRAWN.
Debuts: India – C.T. Patankar.

India's total of 132 was then the lowest by any country against New Zealand.

## INDIA

| | | | | |
|---|---|---|---|---|
| V.M.H. Mankad | c McMahon b Reid | 25 | c MacGibbon b Reid | 17 |
| N.J. Contractor | b Hayes | 6 | b Hayes | 61 |
| P. Roy | b Hayes | 28 | lbw b Cave | 100 |
| V.L. Manjrekar | c Reid b Cave | 1 | c MacGibbon b Reid | 90 |
| P.R. Umrigar* | run out | 1 | b MacGibbon | 15 |
| G.S. Ramchand | b Reid | 1 | not out | 106 |
| J.M. Ghorpade | b Alabaster | 39 | c Sutcliffe b Cave | 4 |
| D.G. Phadkar | run out | 0 | b Hayes | 17 |
| C.T. Patankar† | b Reid | 13 | not out | 1 |
| G.R. Sunderam | not out | 3 | | |
| S.P. Gupte | b Alabaster | 4 | | |
| Extras | (B 4, LB 2, NB 5) | 11 | (B 9, LB 10, NB 8) | 27 |
| **Total** | | **132** | (7 wickets declared) | **438** |

## NEW ZEALAND

| | | | | |
|---|---|---|---|---|
| J.G. Leggat | c Patankar b Sundaram | 8 | c Mankad b Phadkar | 7 |
| B. Sutcliffe | c Patankar b Ramchand | 25 | lbw b Gupte | 5 |
| J.W. Guy | lbw b Gupte | 91 | b Phadkar | 0 |
| J.R. Reid | b Sunderam | 120 | (5) b Mankad | 5 |
| S.N. McGregor | b Gupte | 6 | (4) b Mankad | 29 |
| A.R. MacGibbon | st Patankar b Gupte | 23 | (7) not out | 21 |
| N.S. Harford | c Mankad b Ramchand | 25 | (6) c Phadkar b Gupte | 1 |
| H.B. Cave* | c Umrigar b Gupte | 5 | not out | 4 |
| J.C. Alabaster | c Patankar b Gupte | 18 | | |
| J.A. Hayes | b Gupte | 1 | | |
| T.G. McMahon† | not out | 1 | | |
| Extras | (B 7, LB 3, NB 3) | 13 | (LB 2, NB 1) | 3 |
| **Total** | | **336** | (6 wickets) | **75** |

| NEW ZEALAND | O | M | R | W | O | M | R | W | FALL OF WICKETS | | | | |
|---|---|---|---|---|---|---|---|---|---|---|---|---|---|
| Hayes | 14 | 3 | 38 | 2 | 30 | 4 | 67 | 2 | | I | NZ | I | NZ |
| MacGibbon | 13 | 3 | 27 | 0 | 43 | 16 | 92 | 1 | *Wkt* | *1st* | *1st* | *2nd* | *2nd* |
| Cave | 14 | 6 | 29 | 1 | 57 | 26 | 85 | 2 | 1st | 13 | 25 | 40 | 8 |
| Reid | 16 | 9 | 19 | 3 | 45 | 21 | 87 | 2 | 2nd | 41 | 55 | 119 | 9 |
| Alabaster | 2·3 | 0 | 8 | 2 | 27 | 7 | 52 | 0 | 3rd | 42 | 239 | 262 | 37 |
| Sutcliffe | | | | | 7 | 0 | 28 | 0 | 4th | 47 | 255 | 287 | 42 |
| | | | | | | | | | 5th | 49 | 262 | 331 | 47 |
| INDIA | | | | | | | | | 6th | 87 | 300 | 370 | 55 |
| Phadkar | 35 | 9 | 76 | 0 | 4 | 1 | 11 | 2 | 7th | 88 | 310 | 424 | – |
| Sunderam | 21 | 6 | 46 | 2 | 3 | 1 | 13 | 0 | 8th | 125 | 318 | – | – |
| Gupte | 33·5 | 7 | 90 | 6 | 14 | 7 | 30 | 2 | 9th | 125 | 333 | – | – |
| Ramchand | 37 | 15 | 64 | 2 | 1 | 0 | 4 | 0 | 10th | 132 | 336 | – | – |
| Mankad | 1 | 0 | 9 | 0 | 12 | 8 | 14 | 2 | | | | | |
| Ghorpade | 1 | 0 | 17 | 0 | | | | | | | | | |
| Umrigar | 17 | 7 | 21 | 0 | | | | | | | | | |

Umpires: D.D. Desai and S.K. Ganguli.

# INDIA v NEW ZEALAND 1955–56 (5th Test)

Played at Corporation Stadium, Madras, on 6, 7, 8, 10, 11 January.
Toss: India.   Result: INDIA won by an innings and 109 runs.
Debuts: Nil.

Mankad and Roy scored 413 for the first wicket to set the present record for all Test matches. It beat the 359 by Hutton and Washbrook in 1948-49 (*Test No. 310*) and, until 1977-78, was the highest first-wicket stand in Indian first-class cricket. Mankad's 231 remains the highest score for India and the highest in any Madras Test. India's total was also a new record.

## INDIA

| | | |
|---|---|---|
| V.M.H. Mankad | c Cave b Moir | 231 |
| P. Roy | b Poore | 173 |
| P.R. Umrigar* | not out | 79 |
| G.S. Ramchand | lbw b MacGibbon | 21 |
| V.L. Manjrekar | not out | 0 |
| A.G. Kripal Singh | ) | |
| N.J. Contractor | ) | |
| D.G. Phadkar | ) did not bat | |
| N.S. Tamhane† | ) | |
| J.M. Patel | ) | |
| S.P. Gupte | ) | |
| Extras | (B 18, LB 11, NB 4) | 33 |
| **Total** | (3 wickets declared) | **537** |

## NEW ZEALAND

| | | | | | |
|---|---|---|---|---|---|
| J.G. Leggat | lbw b Phadkar | 31 | | c Tamhane b Mankad | 61 |
| B. Sutcliffe | c Umrigar b Patel | 47 | | c and b Gupte | 40 |
| J.R. Reid | b Patel | 44 | (4) | c Umrigar b Gupte | 63 |
| J.W. Guy | c Umrigar b Gupte | 3 | (3) | st Tamhane b Gupte | 9 |
| S.N. McGregor | c Phadkar b Gupte | 10 | (6) | c Gupte b Mankad | 12 |
| A.R. MacGibbon | c Phadkar b Gupte | 0 | (7) | lbw b Patel | 0 |
| M.B. Poore | lbw b Gupte | 15 | (5) | b Mankad | 1 |
| A.M. Moir | c Umrigar b Patel | 30 | | c Ramchand b Mankad | 1 |
| H.B. Cave* | c Roy b Gupte | 9 | | not out | 22 |
| T.G. McMahon† | not out | 4 | | b Gupte | 0 |
| J.A. Hayes | absent ill | – | | absent ill | – |
| Extras | (B 4, LB 10, NB 2) | 16 | | (B 1, LB 8, NB 1) | 10 |
| **Total** | | **209** | | | **219** |

| NEW ZEALAND | O | M | R | W | O | M | R | W |
|---|---|---|---|---|---|---|---|---|
| Hayes | 31 | 2 | 94 | 0 | | | | |
| MacGibbon | 38 | 9 | 97 | 1 | | | | |
| Cave | 44 | 16 | 94 | 0 | | | | |
| Reid | 7 | 3 | 10 | 0 | | | | |
| Moir | 26 | 1 | 114 | 1 | | | | |
| Poore | 31 | 5 | 95 | 1 | | | | |
| India | | | | | | | | |
| Phadkar | 15 | 4 | 25 | 1 | 28 | 13 | 33 | 0 |
| Ramchand | 4 | 3 | 1 | 0 | 8 | 5 | 10 | 0 |
| Gupte | 49 | 26 | 72 | 5 | 36·3 | 14 | 73 | 4 |
| Patel | 45 | 23 | 63 | 3 | 18 | 7 | 28 | 1 |
| Mankad | 19 | 10 | 32 | 0 | 40 | 14 | 65 | 4 |

### FALL OF WICKETS

| | I | NZ | NZ |
|---|---|---|---|
| Wkt | 1st | 1st | 2nd |
| 1st | 413 | 75 | 89 |
| 2nd | 449 | 109 | 114 |
| 3rd | 537 | 121 | 116 |
| 4th | – | 141 | 117 |
| 5th | – | 144 | 147 |
| 6th | – | 145 | 148 |
| 7th | – | 190 | 151 |
| 8th | – | 201 | 219 |
| 9th | – | 209 | 219 |
| 10th | – | – | – |

Umpires: M.G. Vijayasarathi and A.R. Joshi.

# NEW ZEALAND v WEST INDIES 1955–56 (1st Test)

Played at Carisbrook, Dunedin, on 3, 4, 6 February.
Toss: New Zealand.   Result: WEST INDIES won by an innings and 71 runs.
Debuts: New Zealand – A.F. Lissette.

New Zealand were dismissed for what is still the lowest score in this series of Tests. Ramadhin took his hundredth Test wicket when he dismissed Leggat. When King pulled a muscle as he ran in to bowl the first ball of his ninth over, the umpire ruled that the over had not begun and the bowling was continued from the same end.

## NEW ZEALAND

| | | | | | |
|---|---|---|---|---|---|
| B. Sutcliffe | b Valentine | 9 | c Binns b Valentine | | 48 |
| J.G. Leggat | c Sobers b Atkinson | 3 | lbw b Ramadhin | | 17 |
| J.W. Guy | c Goddard b Ramadhin | 23 | st Binns b Smith | | 0 |
| J.R. Reid | b Ramadhin | 10 | run out | | 23 |
| S.N. McGregor | run out | 0 | b Smith | | 11 |
| J.E.F. Beck | b Valentine | 7 | lbw b Atkinson | | 66 |
| R.W. Blair | c Binns b Ramadhin | 0 | c Depeiza b Smith | | 0 |
| A.M. Moir | not out | 15 | c Binns b Ramadhin | | 20 |
| H.B. Cave* | b Ramadhin | 0 | c Pairaudeau b Valentine | | 0 |
| T.G. McMahon† | c Binns b Ramadhin | 0 | b Ramadhin | | 2 |
| A.F. Lissette | lbw b Ramadhin | 0 | not out | | 1 |
| Extras | (B 5, LB 2) | 7 | (B 19, LB 1) | | 20 |
| **Total** | | **74** | | | **208** |

## WEST INDIES

| | | |
|---|---|---|
| B.H. Pairaudeau | c Lissette b Blair | 0 |
| A.P. Binns† | b Lissette | 10 |
| G. St A. Sobers | run out | 27 |
| E. de C. Weekes | c McMahon b Cave | 123 |
| O.G. Smith | b Blair | 64 |
| D. St E. Atkinson* | c McMahon b Cave | 0 |
| C.C. Depeiza | b Lissette | 14 |
| J.D.C. Goddard | not out | 48 |
| S. Ramadhin | b Blair | 44 |
| A.L. Valentine | lbw b Blair | 2 |
| F.M. King | absent hurt | – |
| Extras | (B 9, LB 10, NB 2) | 21 |
| **Total** | | **353** |

| WEST INDIES | O | M | R | W | O | M | R | W | | FALL OF WICKETS | | |
|---|---|---|---|---|---|---|---|---|---|---|---|---|
| | | | | | | | | | | NZ | WI | NZ |
| King | 8 | 2 | 11 | 0 | | | | | *Wkt* | *1st* | *1st* | *2nd* |
| Atkinson | 7 | 5 | 2 | 1 | 13 | 5 | 25 | 1 | 1st | 3 | 0 | 61 |
| Depeiza | 2 | 0 | 3 | 0 | 3 | 0 | 12 | 0 | 2nd | 36 | 30 | 65 |
| Valentine | 24 | 13 | 28 | 2 | 36 | 17 | 51 | 2 | 3rd | 36 | 72 | 73 |
| Ramadhin | 21·2 | 13 | 23 | 6 | 36·2 | 17 | 58 | 3 | 4th | 43 | 234 | 108 |
| Smith | | | | | 18 | 7 | 42 | 3 | 5th | 54 | 234 | 108 |
| Sobers | | | | | 4 | 4 | 0 | 0 | 6th | 54 | 236 | 108 |
| NEW ZEALAND | | | | | | | | | 7th | 54 | 272 | 198 |
| Blair | 22·5 | 5 | 90 | 4 | | | | | 8th | 62 | 347 | 201 |
| Cave | 26 | 12 | 47 | 2 | | | | | 9th | 70 | 353 | 207 |
| Reid | 17 | 3 | 43 | 0 | | | | | 10th | 74 | – | 208 |
| Lissette | 28 | 11 | 73 | 2 | | | | | | | | |
| Moir | 19 | 3 | 79 | 0 | | | | | | | | |

Umpires: A.E. Jelley and L.G. Clark.

# NEW ZEALAND v WEST INDIES 1955–56 (2nd Test)

Played at Lancaster Park, Christchurch, on 18, 20, 21 February.
Toss: West Indies.   Result: WEST INDIES won by an innings and 64 runs.
Debuts: New Zealand – I.M. Sinclair, S.C. Guillen.

Guillen made his debut for New Zealand after appearing in five Tests for West Indies. Weekes scored his second consecutive Test hundred to bring his run in first-class matches on the tour to five centuries in successive innings. He was out for 43 and 56 against Central Districts in the tourists' next match.

## WEST INDIES

| | | |
|---|---|---:|
| H.A. Furlonge | lbw b Blair | 0 |
| B.H. Pairaudeau | b Reid | 13 |
| G. St A. Sobers | b Lissette | 25 |
| E. de C. Weekes | b Sinclair | 103 |
| O.G. Smith | c Reid b MacGibbon | 11 |
| C.C. Depeiza† | b Reid | 4 |
| D. St E. Atkinson* | c and b Reid | 85 |
| J.D.C. Goddard | not out | 83 |
| S. Ramadhin | b MacGibbon | 33 |
| D.T. Dewdney | run out | 3 |
| A.L. Valentine | run out | 1 |
| Extras | (B 9, LB 8, W 1, NB 7) | 25 |
| **Total** | | **386** |

## NEW ZEALAND

| | | | | | |
|---|---|---:|---|---|---:|
| B. Sutcliffe | st Depeiza b Ramadhin | 26 | | st Depeiza b Smith | 10 |
| S.N. McGregor | b Dewdney | 19 | | c Depeiza b Valentine | 17 |
| L.S.M. Miller | c Goddard b Ramadhin | 7 | | c Weekes b Ramadhin | 31 |
| J.R. Reid* | b Valentine | 28 | (5) | b Smith | 40 |
| J.W. Guy | c and b Ramadhin | 3 | (6) | b Valentine | 4 |
| J.E.F. Beck | lbw b Ramadhin | 4 | (4) | st Depeiza b Smith | 13 |
| S.C. Guillen† | b Valentine | 15 | | c and b Smith | 0 |
| A.R. MacGibbon | not out | 31 | | hit wkt b Valentine | 34 |
| I.M. Sinclair | b Ramadhin | 7 | | c Goddard b Valentine | 0 |
| R.W. Blair | b Smith | 2 | | c Sobers b Valentine | 9 |
| A.F. Lissette | b Smith | 0 | | not out | 1 |
| Extras | (B 14, LB 2) | 16 | | (B 4, LB 1) | 5 |
| **Total** | | **158** | | | **164** |

| NEW ZEALAND | O | M | R | W | O | M | R | W | | FALL OF WICKETS | | |
|---|---:|---:|---:|---:|---:|---:|---:|---:|---|---:|---:|---:|
| Blair | 27 | 5 | 66 | 1 | | | | | | WI | NZ | NZ |
| MacGibbon | 33 | 9 | 81 | 2 | | | | | Wkt | 1st | 1st | 2nd |
| Reid | 24 | 7 | 68 | 3 | | | | | 1st | 0 | 39 | 22 |
| Lissette | 20 | 5 | 51 | 1 | | | | | 2nd | 28 | 50 | 62 |
| Sinclair | 30·5 | 9 | 79 | 1 | | | | | 3rd | 72 | 67 | 62 |
| Sutcliffe | 2 | 0 | 16 | 0 | | | | | 4th | 109 | 85 | 115 |
| | | | | | | | | | 5th | 163 | 90 | 120 |
| WEST INDIES | | | | | | | | | 6th | 169 | 113 | 120 |
| Dewdney | 16 | 5 | 31 | 1 | 8 | 2 | 20 | 0 | 7th | 312 | 121 | 120 |
| Atkinson | 10 | 3 | 16 | 0 | 3 | 0 | 6 | 0 | 8th | 361 | 140 | 121 |
| Ramadhin | 26 | 10 | 46 | 5 | 9 | 1 | 26 | 1 | 9th | 368 | 156 | 133 |
| Valentine | 22 | 9 | 48 | 2 | 22·4 | 11 | 32 | 5 | 10th | 386 | 158 | 164 |
| Smith | 1·5 | 1 | 1 | 2 | 18 | 4 | 75 | 4 | | | | |

Umpires: J. Cowie and W.J.C. Gwynne.

# NEW ZEALAND v WEST INDIES 1955–56 (3rd Test)

Played at Basin Reserve, Wellington, on 3, 5, 6, 7 March.
Toss: West Indies.   Result: WEST INDIES won by nine wickets.
Debuts: New Zealand – R.T. Barber.

Weekes scored his third hundred in consecutive Test innings. New Zealand narrowly averted a third successive innings defeat thanks to some enterprising batting by Taylor who had been recalled to Test cricket after an interval of nine years.

## WEST INDIES

| | | | | |
|---|---|--:|---|--:|
| B.H. Pairaudeau | c MacGibbon b Cave | 68 | c Sinclair b MacGibbon | 8 |
| G. St A. Sobers | c Barber b Reid | 27 | | |
| J.D.C. Goddard | c Beard b MacGibbon | 16 | not out | 0 |
| E. de C. Weekes | c Guillen b Cave | 156 | | |
| O.G. Smith | lbw b MacGibbon | 1 | | |
| D. St E. Atkinson* | run out | 60 | | |
| A.P. Binns† | lbw b Beard | 27 | (2) not out | 5 |
| S. Ramadhin | c Beard b Reid | 15 | | |
| F.M. King | not out | 13 | | |
| D.T. Dewdney | run out | 2 | | |
| A.L. Valentine | c McGregor b Reid | 2 | | |
| Extras | (B 9, LB 3, NB 5) | 17 | | |
| **Total** | | **404** | (1 wicket) | **13** |

## NEW ZEALAND

| | | | | |
|---|---|--:|---|--:|
| L.S.M. Miller | c and b King | 16 | c Binns b Dewdney | 7 |
| S.N. McGregor | c Weekes b Smith | 5 | c Binns b Atkinson | 41 |
| A.R. MacGibbon | c Goddard b Valentine | 3 | b Atkinson | 36 |
| D.D. Taylor | run out | 43 | c Pairaudeau b Atkinson | 77 |
| J.R. Reid* | b Ramadhin | 1 | b Atkinson | 5 |
| J.E.F. Beck | lbw b Sobers | 55 | b Smith | 6 |
| R.T. Barber | b Ramadhin | 12 | c Goddard b Ramadhin | 5 |
| S.C. Guillen† | b Smith | 36 | c Goddard b Dewdney | 0 |
| D.D. Beard | not out | 17 | c Binns b Atkinson | 5 |
| H.B. Cave | b Atkinson | 0 | c and b Sobers | 5 |
| I.M. Sinclair | lbw b Atkinson | 0 | not out | 18 |
| Extras | (B 11, LB 9) | 20 | (B 2, NB 1) | 3 |
| **Total** | | **208** | | **208** |

| NEW ZEALAND | O | M | R | W | O | M | R | W |
|---|--:|--:|--:|--:|--:|--:|--:|--:|
| MacGibbon | 24 | 4 | 75 | 2 | 3 | 1 | 6 | 1 |
| Cave | 37 | 10 | 96 | 2 | | | | |
| Beard | 34 | 9 | 90 | 1 | 2·2 | 0 | 7 | 0 |
| Reid | 32·5 | 8 | 85 | 3 | | | | |
| Sinclair | 8 | 0 | 41 | 0 | | | | |
| **WEST INDIES** | | | | | | | | |
| Dewdney | 11 | 3 | 26 | 0 | 17 | 3 | 54 | 2 |
| King | 9 | 3 | 18 | 1 | | | | |
| Smith | 29 | 15 | 27 | 2 | 14 | 7 | 23 | 1 |
| Ramadhin | 30 | 11 | 63 | 2 | 21 | 10 | 33 | 1 |
| Valentine | 35 | 20 | 31 | 1 | 15 | 9 | 18 | 0 |
| Atkinson | 12·2 | 2 | 20 | 2 | 31 | 12 | 66 | 5 |
| Sobers | 14 | 11 | 3 | 1 | 8·5 | 4 | 11 | 1 |

### FALL OF WICKETS

| Wkt | WI 1st | NZ 1st | NZ 2nd | WI 2nd |
|---|--:|--:|--:|--:|
| 1st | 72 | 23 | 16 | 12 |
| 2nd | 117 | 23 | 82 | – |
| 3rd | 117 | 27 | 93 | – |
| 4th | 119 | 28 | 99 | – |
| 5th | 239 | 104 | 121 | – |
| 6th | 345 | 116 | 141 | – |
| 7th | 387 | 176 | 142 | – |
| 8th | 387 | 205 | 180 | – |
| 9th | 391 | 208 | 185 | – |
| 10th | 404 | 208 | 208 | – |

Umpires: W.J.C. Gwynne and L.G. Clark.

# NEW ZEALAND v WEST INDIES 1955–56 (4th Test)

Played at Eden Park, Auckland, on 9, 10, 12, 13 March.
Toss: New Zealand.   Result: NEW ZEALAND won by 190 runs.
Debuts: West Indies – A.T. Roberts.

Shortly after tea on the fourth day, Guillen stumped Valentine off Cave's bowling to dismiss West Indies for their (then) lowest total, and to bring New Zealand their first win in any official Test match. They had waited 26 years and 45 matches for this success. Roberts was the first St Vincent Islander to represent West Indies.

## NEW ZEALAND

| | | | | | |
|---|---|---|---|---|---|
| S.N. McGregor | c Smith b Dewdney | 2 | c Binns b Atkinson | | 5 |
| L.S.M. Miller | c Weekes b Valentine | 47 | c Weekes b Atkinson | | 25 |
| A.R. MacGibbon | b Smith | 9 | c Weekes b Atkinson | | 35 |
| D.D. Taylor | lbw b Valentine | 11 | c Valentine b Atkinson | | 16 |
| J.R. Reid* | hit wkt b Dewdney | 84 | c Binns b Atkinson | | 12 |
| J.E.F. Beck | c Sobers b Ramadhin | 38 | lbw b Atkinson | | 2 |
| S.C. Guillen† | run out | 6 | st Binns b Valentine | | 41 |
| M.E. Chapple | c Atkinson b Dewdney | 3 | lbw b Ramadhin | | 1 |
| D.D. Beard | c Binns b Dewdney | 31 | not out | | 6 |
| H.B. Cave | c Smith b Dewdney | 11 | (11) not out | | 0 |
| J.C. Alabaster | not out | 1 | (10) b Atkinson | | 5 |
| Extras | (B 7, LB 5) | 12 | (B 4, LB 5) | | 9 |
| **Total** | | **255** | (9 wickets declared) | | **157** |

## WEST INDIES

| | | | | | |
|---|---|---|---|---|---|
| H.A. Furlonge | c Guillen b Cave | 64 | c MacGibbon b Beard | | 3 |
| B.H. Pairaudeau | c MacGibbon b Cave | 9 | b Cave | | 3 |
| G. St A. Sobers | c Guillen b MacGibbon | 1 | (6) run out | | 1 |
| E. de C. Weekes | c Guillen b MacGibbon | 5 | c McGregor b Alabaster | | 31 |
| O.G. Smith | b Beard | 2 | b Cave | | 0 |
| D. St E. Atkinson* | b Reid | 28 | (3) c Chapple b Cave | | 10 |
| A.T. Roberts | b MacGibbon | 28 | b Beard | | 0 |
| A.P. Binns† | lbw b MacGibbon | 0 | b Alabaster | | 20 |
| S. Ramadhin | b Cave | 3 | c Miller b Beard | | 0 |
| A.L. Valentine | c Taylor b Cave | 0 | st Guillen b Cave | | 5 |
| D.T. Dewdney | not out | 0 | not out | | 4 |
| Extras | (B 1, LB 3, NB 1) | 5 | | | |
| **Total** | | **145** | | | **77** |

| WEST INDIES | O | M | R | W | O | M | R | W | | FALL OF WICKETS | | | |
|---|---|---|---|---|---|---|---|---|---|---|---|---|---|
| Dewdney | 19·5 | 11 | 21 | 5 | 12 | 5 | 22 | 0 | | NZ | WI | NZ | WI |
| Atkinson | 32 | 14 | 45 | 0 | 40 | 21 | 53 | 7 | *Wkt* | *1st* | *1st* | *2nd* | *2nd* |
| Valentine | 41 | 20 | 46 | 2 | 6 | 0 | 29 | 1 | 1st | 9 | 25 | 14 | 4 |
| Ramadhin | 23 | 8 | 41 | 1 | 18 | 6 | 26 | 1 | 2nd | 45 | 32 | 61 | 16 |
| Smith | 31 | 19 | 55 | 1 | 4 | 0 | 18 | 0 | 3rd | 66 | 46 | 66 | 16 |
| Sobers | 20 | 7 | 35 | 0 | | | | | 4th | 87 | 59 | 91 | 16 |
| | | | | | | | | | 5th | 191 | 94 | 100 | 18 |
| NEW ZEALAND | | | | | | | | | 6th | 203 | 139 | 101 | 22 |
| MacGibbon | 21 | 5 | 44 | 4 | 6 | 1 | 16 | 0 | 7th | 205 | 140 | 109 | 68 |
| Cave | 27·3 | 17 | 22 | 4 | 13·1 | 9 | 21 | 4 | 8th | 210 | 145 | 146 | 68 |
| Reid | 18 | 5 | 48 | 1 | 6 | 2 | 14 | 0 | 9th | 250 | 145 | 155 | 68 |
| Beard | 9 | 4 | 20 | 1 | 15 | 7 | 22 | 3 | 10th | 255 | 145 | – | 77 |
| Alabaster | 3 | 1 | 6 | 0 | 5 | 4 | 4 | 2 | | | | | |

Umpires: J.C. Harris and T.M. Pearce.

# ENGLAND v AUSTRALIA 1956 (1st Test)

Played at Trent Bridge, Nottingham, on 7, 8 (*no play*), 9, 11, 12 June.
Toss: England.   Result: MATCH DRAWN.
Debuts: England – P.E. Richardson.

More than twelve hours of play was lost to rain and even two declarations by England could not force a result. Left 258 runs to win in four hours on the final day, Australia settled for survival. Richardson was the first batsman to score fifty in each innings of his first England–Australia Test without reaching a hundred in either of them. Davidson fell while bowling his tenth over and was carried off with a chipped ankle bone.

## ENGLAND

| | | | | |
|---|---|---|---|---|
| P.E. Richardson | c Langley b Miller | 81 | c Langley b Archer | 73 |
| M.C. Cowdrey | c Miller b Davidson | 25 | c Langley b Miller | 81 |
| T.W. Graveney | c Archer b Johnson | 8 | (4) not out | 10 |
| P.B.H. May* | c Langley b Miller | 73 | | |
| W. Watson | lbw b Archer | 0 | (3) c Langley b Miller | 8 |
| T.E. Bailey | c Miller b Archer | 14 | | |
| T.G. Evans† | c Langley b Miller | 0 | (5) not out | 8 |
| J.C. Laker | not out | 9 | | |
| G.A.R. Lock | lbw b Miller | 0 | | |
| R. Appleyard | not out | 1 | | |
| A.E. Moss | did not bat | | | |
| Extras | (B 5, LB 1) | 6 | (B 4, LB 1, W 2, NB 1) | 8 |
| **Total** | (8 wickets declared) | **217** | (3 wickets declared) | **188** |

## AUSTRALIA

| | | | | |
|---|---|---|---|---|
| C.C. McDonald | lbw b Lock | 1 | c Lock b Laker | 6 |
| J.W. Burke | c Lock b Laker | 11 | not out | 58 |
| R.N. Harvey | lbw b Lock | 64 | b Lock | 3 |
| P.J.P. Burge | c sub (J.M. Parks) b Lock | 7 | (5) not out | 35 |
| K.R. Miller | lbw b Laker | 0 | (4) lbw b Laker | 4 |
| R.G. Archer | c Lock b Appleyard | 33 | | |
| R. Benaud | b Appleyard | 17 | | |
| I. W. Johnson* | c Bailey b Laker | 12 | | |
| R.R. Lindwall | c Bailey b Laker | 0 | | |
| G.R.A. Langley† | not out | 0 | | |
| A.K. Davidson | absent hurt | – | | |
| Extras | (LB 3) | 3 | (B 10, LB 3, NB 1) | 14 |
| **Total** | | **148** | (3 wickets) | **120** |

| AUSTRALIA | O | M | R | W | O | M | R | W |
|---|---|---|---|---|---|---|---|---|
| Lindwall | 15 | 4 | 43 | 0 | | | | |
| Miller | 33 | 5 | 69 | 4 | 19 | 2 | 58 | 2 |
| Davidson | 9·4 | 1 | 22 | 1 | | | | |
| Archer | 31 | 10 | 51 | 2 | 9 | 0 | 46 | 1 |
| Johnson | 14 | 7 | 26 | 1 | 12 | 2 | 29 | 0 |
| Burke | 1 | 1 | 0 | 0 | 3 | 1 | 6 | 0 |
| Benaud | | | | | 18 | 4 | 41 | 0 |
| ENGLAND | | | | | | | | |
| Moss | 4 | 3 | 1 | 0 | | | | |
| Bailey | 3 | 1 | 8 | 0 | 9 | 3 | 16 | 0 |
| Laker | 29·1 | 11 | 58 | 4 | 30 | 19 | 29 | 2 |
| Lock | 36 | 16 | 61 | 3 | 22 | 11 | 23 | 1 |
| Appleyard | 11 | 4 | 17 | 2 | 19 | 6 | 32 | 0 |
| Graveney | | | | | 6 | 3 | 6 | 0 |

FALL OF WICKETS

| Wkt | E 1st | A 1st | E 2nd | A 2nd |
|---|---|---|---|---|
| 1st | 53 | 10 | 151 | 13 |
| 2nd | 72 | 12 | 163 | 18 |
| 3rd | 180 | 33 | 178 | 41 |
| 4th | 181 | 36 | – | – |
| 5th | 201 | 90 | – | – |
| 6th | 203 | 110 | – | – |
| 7th | 213 | 148 | – | – |
| 8th | 214 | 148 | – | – |
| 9th | – | 148 | – | – |
| 10th | – | – | – | – |

Umpires: T.J. Bartley and J.S. Buller.

# ENGLAND v AUSTRALIA 1956 (2nd Test)

Played at Lord's, London, on 21, 22, 23, 25, 26 June.
Toss: Australia.   Result: AUSTRALIA won by 185 runs.
Debuts: Australia – W.P.A. Crawford, K.D. Mackay.

Australia gained their first victory in England since 1948. McDonald and Burke's stand of 137 was the highest by Australia against England since 1930. Langley established a world Test record (which still stands) when he made his ninth dismissal of the match. Miller took ten wickets in the Test for the only time in his 55-match career. Crawford pulled a muscle behind his thigh and was unable to complete his first spell in Test cricket.

## AUSTRALIA

| | | | | |
|---|---|---|---|---|
| C.C. McDonald | c Trueman b Bailey | 78 | c Cowdrey b Bailey | 26 |
| J.W. Burke | st Evans b Laker | 65 | c Graveney b Trueman | 16 |
| R.N. Harvey | c Evans b Bailey | 0 | c Bailey b Trueman | 10 |
| P.J.P. Burge | b Statham | 21 | b Trueman | 14 |
| K.R. Miller | b Trueman | 28 | (7) c Evans b Trueman | 30 |
| K.D. Mackay | c Bailey b Laker | 38 | (5) c Evans b Statham | 31 |
| R.G. Archer | b Wardle | 28 | (6) c Evans b Bailey | 1 |
| R. Benaud | b Statham | 5 | c Evans b Trueman | 97 |
| I.W. Johnson* | c Evans b Trueman | 6 | lbw b Bailey | 17 |
| G.R.A. Langley† | c Bailey b Laker | 14 | not out | 7 |
| W.P.A. Crawford | not out | 0 | lbw b Bailey | 0 |
| Extras | (LB 2) | 2 | (B 2, LB 2, NB 4) | 8 |
| **Total** | | **285** | | **257** |

## ENGLAND

| | | | | |
|---|---|---|---|---|
| P.E. Richardson | c Langley b Miller | 9 | c Langley b Archer | 21 |
| M.C. Cowdrey | c Benaud b Mackay | 23 | lbw b Benaud | 27 |
| T.W. Graveney | b Miller | 5 | c Langley b Miller | 18 |
| P.B.H. May* | b Benaud | 63 | (5) c Langley b Miller | 53 |
| W. Watson | c Benaud b Miller | 6 | (4) b Miller | 18 |
| T.E. Bailey | b Miller | 32 | c Harvey b Archer | 18 |
| T.G. Evans† | st Langley b Benaud | 0 | c Langley b Miller | 20 |
| J.C. Laker | b Archer | 12 | c Langley b Archer | 4 |
| J.H. Wardle | c Langley b Archer | 0 | b Miller | 0 |
| F.S. Trueman | c Langley b Miller | 7 | b Archer | 2 |
| J.B. Statham | not out | 0 | not out | 0 |
| Extras | (LB 14) | 14 | (LB 5) | 5 |
| **Total** | | **171** | | **186** |

| ENGLAND | O | M | R | W | O | M | R | W | | | FALL OF WICKETS | | |
|---|---|---|---|---|---|---|---|---|---|---|---|---|---|
| | | | | | | | | | | A | E | A | E |
| Statham | 35 | 9 | 70 | 2 | 26 | 5 | 59 | 1 | Wkt | 1st | 1st | 2nd | 2nd |
| Trueman | 28 | 6 | 54 | 2 | 28 | 2 | 90 | 5 | 1st | 137 | 22 | 36 | 35 |
| Bailey | 34 | 12 | 72 | 2 | 24·5 | 8 | 64 | 4 | 2nd | 137 | 32 | 47 | 59 |
| Laker | 29·1 | 10 | 47 | 3 | 7 | 3 | 17 | 0 | 3rd | 151 | 60 | 69 | 89 |
| Wardle | 20 | 7 | 40 | 1 | 7 | 2 | 19 | 0 | 4th | 185 | 87 | 70 | 91 |
| AUSTRALIA | | | | | | | | | 5th | 196 | 128 | 79 | 142 |
| Miller | 34·1 | 9 | 72 | 5 | 36 | 12 | 80 | 5 | 6th | 249 | 128 | 112 | 175 |
| Crawford | 4·5 | 2 | 4 | 0 | | | | | 7th | 255 | 161 | 229 | 180 |
| Archer | 23 | 9 | 47 | 2 | 31·2 | 8 | 71 | 4 | 8th | 265 | 161 | 243 | 184 |
| Mackay | 11 | 3 | 15 | 1 | | | | | 9th | 285 | 170 | 257 | 184 |
| Benaud | 9 | 2 | 19 | 2 | 28 | 14 | 27 | 1 | 10th | 285 | 171 | 257 | 186 |
| Johnson | | | | | 4 | 2 | 3 | 0 | | | | | |

Umpires: F.S. Lee and E. Davies.

# ENGLAND v AUSTRALIA 1956 (3rd Test)

Played at Headingley, Leeds, on 12, 13, 14 (*no play*), 16, 17 July.
Toss: England.   Result: ENGLAND won by an innings and 42 runs.
Debuts: England – A.S.M. Oakman.

Washbrook, who had not played Test cricket since the 1950-51 Australasian tour, was recalled to the England team at the age of 41 and whilst a selector. He joined May with the score 17 for 3 and their partnership of 187 in 287 minutes proved to be the turning point of the rubber. May became the first England batsman to score five consecutive fifties against Australia.

## ENGLAND

| | | |
|---|---|---|
| P.E. Richardson | c Maddocks b Archer | 5 |
| M.C. Cowdrey | c Maddocks b Archer | 0 |
| A.S.M. Oakman | b Archer | 4 |
| P.B.H. May* | c Lindwall b Johnson | 101 |
| C. Washbrook | lbw b Benaud | 98 |
| G.A.R. Lock | c Miller b Benaud | 21 |
| D.J. Insole | c Mackay b Benaud | 5 |
| T.E. Bailey | not out | 33 |
| T.G. Evans† | b Lindwall | 40 |
| J.C. Laker | b Lindwall | 5 |
| F.S. Trueman | c and b Lindwall | 0 |
| Extras | (B 4, LB 9) | 13 |
| **Total** | | **325** |

## AUSTRALIA

| | | | | | |
|---|---|---|---|---|---|
| C.C. McDonald | c Evans b Trueman | 2 | | b Trueman | 6 |
| J.W. Burke | lbw b Lock | 41 | | b Laker | 16 |
| R.N. Harvey | c Trueman b Lock | 11 | | c and b Lock | 69 |
| P.J.P. Burge | lbw b Laker | 2 | (5) | lbw b Laker | 5 |
| K.D. Mackay | c Bailey b Laker | 2 | (8) | b Laker | 2 |
| K.R. Miller | b Laker | 41 | (4) | c Trueman b Laker | 26 |
| R.G. Archer | b Laker | 4 | (9) | c Washbrook b Lock | 1 |
| R. Benaud | c Oakman b Laker | 30 | (6) | b Laker | 1 |
| L.V. Maddocks† | c Trueman b Lock | 0 | (10) | lbw b Lock | 0 |
| I.W. Johnson* | c Richardson b Lock | 0 | (7) | c Oakman b Laker | 3 |
| R.R. Lindwall | not out | 0 | | not out | 0 |
| Extras | (B 4, LB 6) | 10 | | (B 7, LB 4) | 11 |
| **Total** | | **143** | | | **140** |

| AUSTRALIA | O | M | R | W | O | M | R | W |
|---|---|---|---|---|---|---|---|---|
| Lindwall | 33·4 | 11 | 67 | 3 | | | | |
| Archer | 50 | 24 | 68 | 3 | | | | |
| Mackay | 13 | 3 | 29 | 0 | | | | |
| Benaud | 42 | 9 | 89 | 3 | | | | |
| Johnson | 29 | 8 | 59 | 1 | | | | |
| ENGLAND | | | | | | | | |
| Trueman | 8 | 2 | 19 | 1 | 11 | 3 | 21 | 1 |
| Bailey | 7 | 2 | 15 | 0 | 7 | 2 | 13 | 0 |
| Laker | 29 | 10 | 58 | 5 | 41·3 | 21 | 55 | 6 |
| Lock | 27·1 | 11 | 41 | 4 | 40 | 23 | 40 | 3 |

### FALL OF WICKETS

| Wkt | E 1st | A 1st | A 2nd |
|---|---|---|---|
| 1st | 2 | 2 | 10 |
| 2nd | 8 | 40 | 45 |
| 3rd | 17 | 59 | 108 |
| 4th | 204 | 59 | 120 |
| 5th | 226 | 63 | 128 |
| 6th | 243 | 69 | 136 |
| 7th | 248 | 142 | 138 |
| 8th | 301 | 143 | 140 |
| 9th | 321 | 143 | 140 |
| 10th | 325 | 143 | 140 |

Umpires: J.S. Buller and D. Davies.

# ENGLAND v AUSTRALIA 1956 (4th Test)

Played at Old Trafford, Manchester, on 26, 27, 28, 30, 31 July.
Toss: England.   Result: ENGLAND won by an innings and 170 runs.
Debuts: Nil.

'Laker's Match', in which the Yorkshire-born Surrey offspinner broke several major bowling records with his match analysis of 19 for 90, all taken from the Stretford End: most wickets in any first-class match; only instance of ten wickets in a Test innings; only instance of ten wickets in a season twice – also 10 for 88 for Surrey v Australians; 39 wickets in the rubber equalling A.V. Bedser's record for England–Australia matches with a game to play. Not since 1905 had England twice beaten Australia in a home rubber, nor indeed finished a Test against them at Manchester.

## ENGLAND

| | | |
|---|---|---:|
| P.E. Richardson | c Maddocks b Benaud | 104 |
| M.C. Cowdrey | c Maddocks b Lindwall | 80 |
| Rev.D.S. Sheppard | b Archer | 113 |
| P.B.H. May* | c Archer b Benaud | 43 |
| T.E. Bailey | b Johnson | 20 |
| C. Washbrook | lbw b Johnson | 6 |
| A.S.M. Oakman | c Archer b Johnson | 10 |
| T.G. Evans† | st Maddocks b Johnson | 47 |
| J.C. Laker | run out | 3 |
| G.A.R. Lock | not out | 25 |
| J.B. Statham | c Maddocks b Lindwall | 0 |
| Extras | (B 2, LB 5, W 1) | 8 |
| **Total** | | **459** |

## AUSTRALIA

| | | | | | |
|---|---|---:|---|---|---:|
| C.C. McDonald | c Lock b Laker | 32 | | c Oakman b Laker | 89 |
| J.W. Burke | c Cowdrey b Lock | 22 | | c Lock b Laker | 33 |
| R.N. Harvey | b Laker | 0 | | c Cowdrey b Laker | 0 |
| I.D. Craig | lbw b Laker | 8 | | lbw b Laker | 38 |
| K.R. Miller | c Oakman b Laker | 6 | (6) | b Laker | 0 |
| K.D. Mackay | c Oakman b Laker | 0 | (5) | c Oakman b Laker | 0 |
| R.G. Archer | st Evans b Laker | 6 | | c Oakman b Laker | 0 |
| R. Benaud | c Statham b Laker | 0 | | b Laker | 18 |
| R.R. Lindwall | not out | 6 | | c Lock b Laker | 8 |
| L.V. Maddocks† | b Laker | 4 | (11) | lbw b Laker | 2 |
| I.W. Johnson* | b Laker | 0 | (10) | not out | 1 |
| Extras | | 0 | | (B 12, LB 4) | 16 |
| **Total** | | **84** | | | **205** |

| AUSTRALIA | O | M | R | W | O | M | R | W | | FALL OF WICKETS | | |
|---|---|---|---|---|---|---|---|---|---|---|---|---|
| | | | | | | | | | | E | A | A |
| Lindwall | 21·3 | 6 | 63 | 2 | | | | | Wkt | 1st | 1st | 2nd |
| Miller | 21 | 6 | 41 | 0 | | | | | 1st | 174 | 48 | 28 |
| Archer | 22 | 6 | 73 | 1 | | | | | 2nd | 195 | 48 | 55 |
| Johnson | 47 | 10 | 151 | 4 | | | | | 3rd | 288 | 62 | 114 |
| Benaud | 47 | 17 | 123 | 2 | | | | | 4th | 321 | 62 | 124 |
| | | | | | | | | | 5th | 327 | 62 | 130 |
| ENGLAND | | | | | | | | | 6th | 339 | 73 | 130 |
| Statham | 6 | 3 | 6 | 0 | 16 | 10 | 15 | 0 | 7th | 401 | 73 | 181 |
| Bailey | 4 | 3 | 4 | 0 | 20 | 8 | 31 | 0 | 8th | 417 | 78 | 198 |
| Laker | 16·4 | 4 | 37 | 9 | 51·2 | 23 | 53 | 10 | 9th | 458 | 84 | 203 |
| Lock | 14 | 3 | 37 | 1 | 55 | 30 | 69 | 0 | 10th | 459 | 84 | 205 |
| Oakman | | | | | 8 | 3 | 21 | 0 | | | | |

Umpires: F.S. Lee and E. Davies.

# ENGLAND v AUSTRALIA 1956 (5th Test)

Played at Kennington Oval, London, on 23, 24, 25, 27 (*no play*), 28 August.
Toss: England.　　Result: MATCH DRAWN.
Debuts: Nil.

Exactly the same amount of time, 12 hours 20 minutes, was lost to rain as in the 1st Test – with the same result. The selectors completed their hat-trick of successful recalls, Compton, minus his right knee-cap, top-scoring with 94 to follow the achievements of Washbrook and Sheppard in the previous two Tests. Laker extended his record haul to 46 wickets in the rubber. Harvey kept wicket when Langley retired to hospital after being struck on the forehead by a ball from Archer.

## ENGLAND

| | | | | |
|---|---|--:|---|--:|
| P.E. Richardson | c Langley b Miller | 37 | c Langley b Lindwall | 34 |
| M.C. Cowdrey | c Langley b Lindwall | 0 | c Benaud b Davidson | 8 |
| Rev.D.S. Sheppard | c Archer b Miller | 24 | c Archer b Miller | 62 |
| P.B.H. May* | not out | 83 | not out | 37 |
| D.C.S. Compton | c Davidson b Archer | 94 | not out | 35 |
| G.A.R. Lock | c Langley b Archer | 0 | | |
| C. Washbrook | lbw b Archer | 0 | | |
| T.G. Evans† | lbw b Miller | 0 | | |
| J.C. Laker | c Archer b Miller | 4 | | |
| F.H. Tyson | c Davidson b Archer | 3 | | |
| J.B. Statham | b Archer | 0 | | |
| Extras | (W2) | 2 | (B 3, LB 3) | 6 |
| **Total** | | **247** | (3 wickets declared) | **182** |

## AUSTRALIA

| | | | | |
|---|---|--:|---|--:|
| C.C. McDonald | c Lock b Tyson | 3 | lbw b Statham | 0 |
| J.W. Burke | b Laker | 8 | lbw b Laker | 1 |
| R.N. Harvey | c May b Lock | 39 | c May b Lock | 1 |
| I.D. Craig | c Statham b Lock | 2 | c Lock b Laker | 7 |
| I.W. Johnson* | b Laker | 12 | (6) c Lock b Laker | 10 |
| A.K. Davidson | c May b Laker | 8 | | |
| K.R. Miller | c Washbrook b Statham | 61 | (5) not out | 7 |
| R.G. Archer | c Tyson b Laker | 9 | (7) not out | 0 |
| R. Benaud | b Statham | 32 | | |
| R.R. Lindwall | not out | 22 | | |
| G.R.A. Langley† | lbw b Statham | 0 | | |
| Extras | (B 6) | 6 | (B 1) | 1 |
| **Total** | | **202** | (5 wickets) | **27** |

| AUSTRALIA | O | M | R | W | O | M | R | W |
|---|--:|--:|--:|--:|--:|--:|--:|--:|
| Lindwall | 18 | 5 | 36 | 1 | 12 | 3 | 29 | 1 |
| Miller | 40 | 7 | 91 | 4 | 22 | 3 | 56 | 1 |
| Davidson | 5 | 1 | 16 | 0 | 5 | 0 | 18 | 1 |
| Archer | 28·2 | 7 | 53 | 5 | 13 | 3 | 42 | 0 |
| Johnson | 9 | 2 | 28 | 0 | 4 | 1 | 7 | 0 |
| Benaud | 9 | 2 | 21 | 0 | 1 | 0 | 10 | 0 |
| Burke | | | | | 4 | 2 | 14 | 0 |
| **ENGLAND** | | | | | | | | |
| Statham | 21 | 8 | 33 | 3 | 2 | 1 | 1 | 1 |
| Tyson | 14 | 5 | 34 | 1 | | | | |
| Laker | 32 | 12 | 80 | 4 | 18 | 14 | 8 | 3 |
| Lock | 25 | 10 | 49 | 2 | 18·1 | 11 | 17 | 1 |

### FALL OF WICKETS

| Wkt | E 1st | A 1st | E 2nd | A 2nd |
|---|--:|--:|--:|--:|
| 1st | 1 | 3 | 17 | 0 |
| 2nd | 53 | 17 | 100 | 1 |
| 3rd | 66 | 20 | 108 | 5 |
| 4th | 222 | 35 | – | 10 |
| 5th | 222 | 47 | – | 27 |
| 6th | 222 | 90 | – | – |
| 7th | 223 | 111 | – | – |
| 8th | 231 | 154 | – | – |
| 9th | 243 | 202 | – | – |
| 10th | 247 | 202 | – | – |

Umpires: D. Davies and T.J. Bartley.

# PAKISTAN v AUSTRALIA 1956–57 (Only Test)

Played at National Stadium, Karachi, on 11, 12, 13, 15, 17 October.
Toss: Australia.   Result: PAKISTAN won by nine wickets.
Debuts: Nil. *Gul Mahomed made his only appearance for Pakistan after playing in eight Tests for India.*

Pakistan won their first victory against Australia at the earliest possible opportunity. Played on matting, this match produced the slowest day of Test cricket, the two sides combining to score only 95 runs on the first day. Australia's 80 remains the lowest total in any Karachi Test and Fazal's 13 for 114 is still Pakistan's best match analysis and the record for any Karachi Test match. Lindwall took his 200th Test wicket.

## AUSTRALIA

| | | | | |
|---|---|---|---|---|
| C.C. McDonald | c Imtiaz b Fazal | 17 | b Fazal | 3 |
| J.W. Burke | c Mathias b Fazal | 4 | c Mathias b Fazal | 10 |
| R.N. Harvey | lbw b Fazal | 2 | b Fazal | 4 |
| I.D. Craig | c Imtiaz b Fazal | 0 | lbw b Fazal | 18 |
| K.R. Miller | c Wazir b Fazal | 21 | b Khan | 11 |
| R.G. Archer | c Imtiaz b Khan | 10 | c Fazal b Khan | 27 |
| R. Benaud | c Waqar b Fazal | 4 | b Fazal | 56 |
| A.K. Davidson | c Kardar b Khan | 3 | c Imtiaz b Khan | 37 |
| R.R. Lindwall | c Mathias b Khan | 2 | lbw b Fazal | 0 |
| I.W. Johnson* | not out | 13 | b Fazal | 0 |
| G.R.A. Langley† | c Waqar b Khan | 1 | not out | 13 |
| Extras | (LB 2, NB 1) | 3 | (LB 2, NB 6) | 8 |
| **Total** | | **80** | | **187** |

## PAKISTAN

| | | | | |
|---|---|---|---|---|
| Hanif Mohammad | c Langley b Miller | 0 | c Harvey b Davidson | 5 |
| Alimuddin | c Lindwall b Archer | 10 | not out | 34 |
| Gul Mahomed | b Davidson | 12 | not out | 27 |
| Imtiaz Ahmed† | c McDonald b Benaud | 15 | | |
| Waqar Hassan | c Langley b Miller | 6 | | |
| Wazir Mohammad | c and b Johnson | 67 | | |
| A.H. Kardar* | lbw b Johnson | 69 | | |
| W. Mathias | b Johnson | 0 | | |
| Fazal Mahmood | not out | 10 | | |
| Zulfiqar Ahmed | c Langley b Lindwall | 0 | | |
| Khan Mohammad | b Johnson | 3 | | |
| Extras | (B 5, LB 2) | 7 | (LB 1, NB 2) | 3 |
| **Total** | | **199** | (1 wicket) | **69** |

| PAKISTAN | O | M | R | W | O | M | R | W | FALL OF WICKETS | | | | |
|---|---|---|---|---|---|---|---|---|---|---|---|---|---|
| Fazal | 27 | 11 | 34 | 6 | 48 | 17 | 80 | 7 | | A | P | A | P |
| Khan | 26·1 | 9 | 43 | 4 | 40·5 | 13 | 69 | 3 | *Wkt* | *1st* | *1st* | *2nd* | *2nd* |
| Zulfiqar | | | | | 9 | 1 | 18 | 0 | 1st | 19 | 3 | 6 | 7 |
| Kardar | | | | | 12 | 5 | 12 | 0 | 2nd | 23 | 15 | 10 | – |
| | | | | | | | | | 3rd | 24 | 25 | 23 | – |
| AUSTRALIA | | | | | | | | | 4th | 43 | 35 | 46 | – |
| Lindwall | 27 | 8 | 42 | 1 | 16 | 8 | 22 | 0 | 5th | 48 | 70 | 47 | – |
| Miller | 17 | 5 | 40 | 2 | 12 | 4 | 18 | 0 | 6th | 52 | 174 | 111 | – |
| Archer | 4 | 0 | 18 | 1 | 3·5 | 3 | 1 | 0 | 7th | 56 | 174 | 141 | – |
| Davidson | 6 | 4 | 6 | 1 | 9 | 5 | 9 | 1 | 8th | 65 | 189 | 141 | – |
| Benaud | 17 | 5 | 36 | 1 | | | | | 9th | 76 | 190 | 143 | – |
| Johnson | 20·3 | 3 | 50 | 4 | 7·5 | 2 | 16 | 0 | 10th | 80 | 199 | 187 | – |

Umpires: Idris Beg and Daud Khan.

# INDIA v AUSTRALIA 1956–57 (1st Test)

Played at Corporation Stadium, Madras, on 19, 20, 22, 23 October.
Toss: India.    Result: AUSTRALIA won by an innings and 5 runs.
Debuts: Nil.

Returning to a turf pitch, Australia won their first Test in India with more than a day to spare.

## INDIA

| | | | | | |
|---|---|---|---|---|---|
| V.M.H. Mankad | c McDonald b Benaud | 27 | c Langley b Lindwall | | 11 |
| P. Roy | c Harvey b Benaud | 13 | c Harvey b Lindwall | | 9 |
| P.R. Umrigar* | c Craig b Benaud | 31 | c Langley b Lindwall | | 25 |
| V.L. Manjrekar | lbw b Benaud | 41 | (5) b Crawford | | 16 |
| G.S. Ramchand | b Crawford | 0 | (6) lbw b Johnson | | 28 |
| H.R. Adhikari | c Burke b Crawford | 5 | (7) lbw b Lindwall | | 0 |
| A.G. Kripal Singh | c Harvey b Crawford | 13 | (8) not out | | 20 |
| N.S. Tamhane† | not out | 9 | (4) c Crawford b Benaud | | 5 |
| J.M. Patel | c Johnson b Benaud | 3 | b Lindwall | | 0 |
| Ghulam Ahmed | c Harvey b Benaud | 11 | c Burge b Lindwall | | 13 |
| S.P. Gupte | c McDonald b Benaud | 4 | b Lindwall | | 8 |
| Extras | (LB 4) | 4 | (B 10, LB 5, NB 3) | | 18 |
| **Total** | | **161** | | | **153** |

## AUSTRALIA

| | | |
|---|---|---|
| C.C. McDonald | st Tamhane b Mankad | 29 |
| J.W. Burke | c Tamhane b Gupte | 10 |
| R.N. Harvey | b Mankad | 37 |
| I.D. Craig | c Ramchand b Mankad | 40 |
| P.J.P. Burge | lbw b Patel | 35 |
| K.D. Mackay | c Tamhane b Ghulam Ahmed | 29 |
| R. Benaud | b Ghulam Ahmed | 6 |
| R.R. Lindwall | c Adhikari b Gupte | 8 |
| I.W. Johnson* | c Roy b Gupte | 73 |
| W.P.A. Crawford | st Tamhane b Mankad | 34 |
| G.R.A. Langley† | not out | 10 |
| Extras | (B 5, LB 3) | 8 |
| **Total** | | **319** |

| AUSTRALIA | O | M | R | W | O | M | R | W | | FALL OF WICKETS | | |
|---|---|---|---|---|---|---|---|---|---|---|---|---|
| Lindwall | 9 | 1 | 15 | 0 | 22·5 | 9 | 43 | 7 | | I | A | I |
| Crawford | 26 | 8 | 32 | 3 | 12 | 6 | 18 | 1 | *Wkt* | *1st* | *1st* | *2nd* |
| Benaud | 29·3 | 10 | 72 | 7 | 20 | 5 | 59 | 1 | 1st | 41 | 12 | 18 |
| Mackay | 20 | 9 | 25 | 0 | | | | | 2nd | 44 | 58 | 22 |
| Johnson | 15 | 10 | 13 | 0 | 9 | 5 | 15 | 1 | 3rd | 97 | 97 | 39 |
| **INDIA** | | | | | | | | | 4th | 98 | 152 | 63 |
| Ramchand | 5 | 1 | 12 | 0 | | | | | 5th | 106 | 186 | 99 |
| Umrigar | 4 | 0 | 17 | 0 | | | | | 6th | 134 | 186 | 100 |
| Gupte | 28·3 | 6 | 89 | 3 | | | | | 7th | 134 | 198 | 113 |
| Ghulam Ahmed | 38 | 17 | 67 | 2 | | | | | 8th | 137 | 200 | 119 |
| Mankad | 45 | 15 | 90 | 4 | | | | | 9th | 151 | 287 | 143 |
| Patel | 14 | 3 | 36 | 1 | | | | | 10th | 161 | 319 | 153 |

Umpires: M.G. Vijayasarathi and D.D. Desai.

# INDIA v AUSTRALIA 1956–57 (2nd Test)

Played at Brabourne Stadium, Bombay, on 26, 27, 29, 30, 31 October.
Toss: India.   Result: MATCH DRAWN.
Debuts: Australia – J.W. Rutherford, J.W. Wilson.

Crawford retired because of a muscular injury on the first day. Umrigar batted six hours for 78 in India's successful rearguard action after Harvey had scored 140 in just over four hours (73 overs).

## INDIA

| | | | | | |
|---|---|---|---|---|---|
| V.M.H. Mankad | c Burge b Lindwall | 0 | | c Burke b Benaud | 16 |
| P. Roy | c Burge b Crawford | 31 | | c Maddocks b Benaud | 79 |
| P.R. Umrigar* | b Crawford | 8 | | c and b Lindwall | 78 |
| V.L. Manjrekar | c Harvey b Benaud | 55 | | b Rutherford | 30 |
| J.M. Ghorpade | b Crawford | 0 | | | |
| G.S. Ramchand | c sub (C.C. McDonald) b Mackay | 109 | | c Maddocks b Wilson | 16 |
| D.G. Phadkar | c Maddocks b Benaud | 1 | | not out | 3 |
| H.R. Adhikari | c Davidson b Mackay | 33 | (5) | not out | 22 |
| N.S. Tamhane† | c Harvey b Davidson | 5 | | | |
| J.M. Patel | c Maddocks b Mackay | 6 | | | |
| S.P. Gupte | not out | 0 | | | |
| Extras | (LB 1, NB 2) | 3 | | (B 1, LB 1, NB 4) | 6 |
| **Total** | | **251** | | **(5 wickets)** | **250** |

## AUSTRALIA

| | | |
|---|---|---|
| J.W. Burke | c Umrigar b Mankad | 161 |
| J.W. Rutherford | c Tamhane b Gupte | 30 |
| R.N. Harvey | c sub (R.G. Nadkarni) b Patel | 140 |
| P.J.P. Burge | c Patel b Gupte | 83 |
| K.D. Mackay | c Roy b Patel | 26 |
| A.K. Davidson | lbw b Ramchand | 16 |
| R. Benaud | c sub (R.G. Nadkarni) b Gupte | 2 |
| R.R. Lindwall* | not out | 48 |
| L.V. Maddocks† | not out | 8 |
| W.P.A. Crawford | ) did not bat | |
| J.W. Wilson | ) | |
| Extras | (B 2, LB 4, NB 3) | 9 |
| **Total** | **(7 wickets declared)** | **523** |

| AUSTRALIA | O | M | R | W | O | M | R | W |
|---|---|---|---|---|---|---|---|---|
| Lindwall | 22 | 7 | 60 | 1 | 23 | 9 | 40 | 1 |
| Crawford | 12 | 3 | 28 | 3 | 13 | 4 | 24 | 0 |
| Davidson | 9 | 1 | 24 | 1 | 14 | 9 | 18 | 0 |
| Benaud | 25 | 6 | 54 | 2 | 42 | 15 | 98 | 2 |
| Mackay | 14·2 | 5 | 27 | 3 | 17 | 6 | 22 | 0 |
| Wilson | 15 | 6 | 39 | 0 | 21 | 11 | 25 | 1 |
| Burke | 2 | 0 | 12 | 0 | 2 | 0 | 6 | 0 |
| Rutherford | 1 | 0 | 4 | 0 | 5 | 2 | 11 | 1 |
| INDIA | | | | | | | | |
| Phadkar | 39 | 9 | 92 | 0 | | | | |
| Ramchand | 18 | 2 | 78 | 1 | | | | |
| Patel | 39 | 10 | 111 | 2 | | | | |
| Gupte | 38 | 13 | 115 | 3 | | | | |
| Mankad | 46 | 9 | 118 | 1 | | | | |

### FALL OF WICKETS

| | I | A | I |
|---|---|---|---|
| Wkt | 1st | 1st | 2nd |
| 1st | 0 | 57 | 31 |
| 2nd | 18 | 261 | 121 |
| 3rd | 74 | 398 | 191 |
| 4th | 74 | 432 | 217 |
| 5th | 130 | 459 | 242 |
| 6th | 140 | 462 | – |
| 7th | 235 | 470 | – |
| 8th | 240 | – | – |
| 9th | 251 | – | – |
| 10th | 251 | – | – |

Umpires: B.J. Mohoni and A.R. Joshi.

# INDIA v AUSTRALIA 1956–57 (3rd Test)

Played at Eden Gardens, Calcutta, on 2, 3, 5, 6 November.
Toss: India.    Result: AUSTRALIA won by 94 runs.
Debuts: Nil.

Spin bowlers took all but four of the 39 wickets which fell on a pitch that encouraged them from the start, and enabled Australia to win a low-scoring match with a day and a half to spare. Benaud's match analysis of 11 for 105 remains the best in any Test match in Calcutta.

## AUSTRALIA

| | | | | | |
|---|---|---|---|---|---|
| C.C. McDonald | b Ghulam Ahmed | 3 | lbw b Ramchand | 0 |
| J.W. Burke | c Manjrekar b Ghulam Ahmed | 10 | c Contractor b Ghulam Ahmed | 2 |
| R.N. Harvey | c Tamhane b Ghulam Ahmed | 7 | c Umrigar b Mankad | 69 |
| I.D. Craig | c Tamhane b Gupte | 36 | b Ghulam Ahmed | 6 |
| P.J.P. Burge | c Ramchand b Ghulam Ahmed | 58 | c Ramchand b Ghulam Ahmed | 22 |
| K.D. Mackay | lbw b Mankad | 5 | hit wkt b Mankad | 27 |
| R. Benaud | b Ghulam Ahmed | 24 | b Gupte | 21 |
| R.R. Lindwall | b Ghulam Ahmed | 8 | c Tamhane b Mankad | 28 |
| I.W. Johnson* | c Ghulam Ahmed b Mankad | 1 | st Tamhane b Mankad | 5 |
| W.P.A. Crawford | c Contractor b Ghulam Ahmed | 18 | not out | 1 |
| G.R.A. Langley† | not out | 1 | | |
| Extras | (B 6) | 6 | (B 6, LB 2) | 8 |
| **Total** | | **177** | (9 wickets declared) | **189** |

## INDIA

| | | | | | |
|---|---|---|---|---|---|
| P. Roy | b Lindwall | 13 | lbw b Burke | 24 |
| N.J. Contractor | lbw b Benaud | 22 | b Johnson | 20 |
| P.R. Umrigar* | c Burge b Johnson | 5 | c Burke b Benaud | 28 |
| V.L. Manjrekar | c Harvey b Benaud | 33 | c Harvey b Benaud | 22 |
| V.M.H. Mankad | lbw b Benaud | 4 | c Harvey b Benaud | 24 |
| G.S. Ramchand | st Langley b Benaud | 2 | b Burke | 3 |
| A.G. Kripal Singh | c Mackay b Benaud | 14 | b Benaud | 0 |
| P. Bhandari | lbw b Lindwall | 17 | c Harvey b Burke | 2 |
| N.S. Tamhane† | b Benaud | 5 | b Benaud | 0 |
| Ghulam Ahmed | c Mackay b Lindwall | 10 | b Burke | 0 |
| S.P. Gupte | not out | 1 | not out | 0 |
| Extras | (B 7, LB 1, NB 2) | 10 | (B 5, LB 5, NB 3) | 13 |
| **Total** | | **136** | | **136** |

| INDIA | O | M | R | W | O | M | R | W | | FALL OF WICKETS | | | |
|---|---|---|---|---|---|---|---|---|---|---|---|---|---|
| Ramchand | 2 | 1 | 1 | 0 | 2 | 1 | 6 | 1 | | A | I | A | I |
| Umrigar | 16 | 3 | 30 | 0 | 20 | 9 | 21 | 0 | Wkt | 1st | 1st | 2nd | 2nd |
| Ghulam Ahmed | 20·3 | 6 | 49 | 7 | 29 | 5 | 81 | 3 | 1st | 6 | 15 | 0 | 44 |
| Gupte | 23 | 11 | 35 | 1 | 7 | 1 | 24 | 1 | 2nd | 22 | 20 | 9 | 50 |
| Mankad | 25 | 4 | 56 | 2 | 9·4 | 1 | 49 | 4 | 3rd | 25 | 76 | 27 | 94 |
| | | | | | | | | | 4th | 93 | 80 | 59 | 99 |
| AUSTRALIA | | | | | | | | | 5th | 106 | 82 | 122 | 102 |
| Lindwall | 25·2 | 12 | 32 | 3 | 12 | 7 | 9 | 0 | 6th | 141 | 98 | 149 | 121 |
| Crawford | 3 | 3 | 0 | 0 | 2 | 1 | 1 | 0 | 7th | 152 | 99 | 159 | 134 |
| Johnson | 12 | 2 | 27 | 1 | 14 | 5 | 23 | 1 | 8th | 157 | 115 | 188 | 136 |
| Benaud | 29 | 10 | 52 | 6 | 24·2 | 6 | 53 | 5 | 9th | 163 | 135 | 189 | 136 |
| Harvey | 1 | 1 | 0 | 0 | | | | | 10th | 177 | 136 | – | 136 |
| Burke | 8 | 3 | 15 | 0 | 17 | 4 | 37 | 4 | | | | | |

Umpires: G. Ayling and B.J. Mohoni.

## SOUTH AFRICA v ENGLAND 1956–57 (1st Test)

Played at New Wanderers, Johannesburg, on 24, 26, 27, 28, 29 December.
Toss: England.   Result: ENGLAND won by 131 runs.
Debuts: South Africa – A.I. Taylor.

This was the first Test match to be played on the New Wanderers ground and it attracted the highest attendance (100,000) for any match in South Africa so far. Richardson took 488 minutes to reach what was then the slowest century in Test cricket. South Africa's total of 72 was their lowest in a home Test since 1898–99.

### ENGLAND

| | | | | | |
|---|---|--:|---|---|--:|
| P.E. Richardson | lbw b Goddard | 117 | | lbw b Adcock | 10 |
| T.E. Bailey | c Waite b Heine | 16 | | c Endean b Heine | 10 |
| D.C.S. Compton | c Keith b Goddard | 5 | | c and b Tayfield | 32 |
| P.B.H. May* | c Goddard b Adcock | 6 | (6) | c Endean b Heine | 14 |
| M.C. Cowdrey | c Goddard b Heine | 59 | (7) | c Goddard b Adcock | 6 |
| D.J. Insole | c Waite b Van Ryneveld | 1 | (5) | c Waite b Goddard | 29 |
| T.G. Evans† | c Keith b Adcock | 20 | (8) | c Heine b Tayfield | 30 |
| F.H. Tyson | b Adcock | 22 | (9) | c Watkins b Adcock | 2 |
| J.H. Wardle | not out | 6 | (4) | lbw b Heine | 0 |
| J.C. Laker | c Goddard b Adcock | 0 | | not out | 3 |
| J.B. Statham | c Waite b Goddard | 0 | | lbw b Tayfield | 2 |
| Extras | (B 4, LB 9, NB 3) | 16 | | (B 8, LB 1, NB 3) | 12 |
| **Total** | | **268** | | | **150** |

### SOUTH AFRICA

| | | | | | |
|---|---|--:|---|---|--:|
| A.I. Taylor | st Evans b Wardle | 12 | | c Insole b Bailey | 6 |
| T.L. Goddard | c Cowdrey b Statham | 49 | | c Insole b Bailey | 5 |
| H.J. Keith | c Cowdrey b Bailey | 42 | | c Evans b Bailey | 2 |
| W.R. Endean | c Cowdrey b Laker | 18 | (5) | b Statham | 3 |
| R.A. McLean | lbw b Bailey | 0 | (6) | c Insole b Bailey | 6 |
| J.C. Watkins | c Insole b Wardle | 9 | (7) | b Laker | 8 |
| C.B. van Ryneveld* | c Bailey b Statham | 10 | (8) | run out | 16 |
| J.H.B. Waite† | c Evans b Bailey | 17 | (4) | b Statham | 0 |
| H.J. Tayfield | b Wardle | 24 | | c Evans b Bailey | 2 |
| P.S. Heine | not out | 13 | | run out | 17 |
| N.A.T. Adcock | b Statham | 17 | | not out | 0 |
| Extras | (B 1, LB 3) | 4 | | (B 2, LB 3, NB 2) | 7 |
| **Total** | | **215** | | | **72** |

| SOUTH AFRICA | O | M | R | W | O | M | R | W |
|---|--:|--:|--:|--:|--:|--:|--:|--:|
| Heine | 31 | 5 | 89 | 2 | 19 | 7 | 41 | 3 |
| Adcock | 20 | 6 | 36 | 4 | 13 | 1 | 33 | 3 |
| Goddard | 28·5 | 9 | 51 | 3 | 14 | 7 | 14 | 1 |
| Watkins | 11 | 3 | 23 | 0 | 3 | 0 | 10 | 0 |
| Tayfield | 20 | 4 | 30 | 0 | 17·6 | 5 | 40 | 3 |
| Van Ryneveld | 8 | 2 | 23 | 1 | | | | |
| ENGLAND | | | | | | | | |
| Statham | 24·1 | 4 | 71 | 3 | 13 | 4 | 22 | 2 |
| Tyson | 9 | 1 | 22 | 0 | | | | |
| Wardle | 20 | 4 | 52 | 3 | 3 | 0 | 18 | 0 |
| Laker | 21 | 10 | 33 | 1 | 2 | 1 | 5 | 1 |
| Bailey | 15 | 5 | 33 | 3 | 15·4 | 6 | 20 | 5 |

### FALL OF WICKETS

| | E | SA | E | SA |
|---|--:|--:|--:|--:|
| Wkt | 1st | 1st | 2nd | 2nd |
| 1st | 28 | 54 | 11 | 6 |
| 2nd | 37 | 92 | 37 | 10 |
| 3rd | 48 | 112 | 37 | 11 |
| 4th | 169 | 112 | 84 | 20 |
| 5th | 170 | 126 | 100 | 25 |
| 6th | 205 | 141 | 107 | 36 |
| 7th | 259 | 141 | 126 | 40 |
| 8th | 263 | 176 | 145 | 44 |
| 9th | 263 | 194 | 147 | 71 |
| 10th | 268 | 215 | 150 | 72 |

Umpires: W. Marais and J.H. McMenamin.

# SOUTH AFRICA v ENGLAND 1956–57 (2nd Test)

Played at Newlands, Cape Town, on 1, 2, 3, 4, 5 January.
Toss: England.   Result: ENGLAND won by 312 runs.
Debuts: Nil.

The only 'handled ball' dismissal in Test cricket occurred on the fifth day; Endean padded away a ball from Laker pitched outside the off stump and, as it deflected upwards and towards the stumps, he diverted it with his hand. Endean was involved in Test cricket's other unique dismissal when Hutton was given out 'obstructing the field' in 1951 (*Test No. 338*).

## ENGLAND

| | | | | |
|---|---|---|---|---|
| P.E. Richardson | lbw b Heine | 45 | c Endean b Goddard | 44 |
| T.E. Bailey | c Waite b Tayfield | 34 | b Heine | 28 |
| D.C.S. Compton | c McLean b Tayfield | 58 | c and b Goddard | 64 |
| P.B.H. May* | c Waite b Tayfield | 8 | c Waite b Heine | 15 |
| M.C. Cowdrey | lbw b Adcock | 101 | c Waite b Tayfield | 61 |
| D.J. Insole | c Goddard b Adcock | 29 | (7) not out | 3 |
| T.G. Evans† | c McGlew b Goddard | 62 | (6) c Endean b Goddard | 1 |
| J.H. Wardle | st Waite b Tayfield | 3 | | |
| J.C. Laker | b Adcock | 0 | | |
| P.J. Loader | c Keith b Tayfield | 10 | | |
| J.B. Statham | not out | 2 | | |
| Extras | (B 6, LB 6, NB 5) | 17 | (LB 2, NB 2) | 4 |
| **Total** | | **369** | **(6 wickets declared)** | **220** |

## SOUTH AFRICA

| | | | | |
|---|---|---|---|---|
| D.J. McGlew | c Cowdrey b Laker | 14 | b Wardle | 7 |
| T.L. Goddard | c Evans b Loader | 18 | c Bailey b Wardle | 26 |
| H.J. Keith | c Evans b Loader | 14 | c May b Wardle | 4 |
| C.B. van Ryneveld* | b Wardle | 25 | (7) not out | 0 |
| H.J. Tayfield | run out | 5 | (10) c Evans b Wardle | 4 |
| R.A. McLean | c May b Statham | 42 | (5) lbw b Laker | 22 |
| J.H.B. Waite† | c Evans b Wardle | 49 | (6) c Cowdrey b Wardle | 2 |
| W.R. Endean | b Wardle | 17 | (4) handled ball | 3 |
| J.C. Watkins | not out | 7 | (8) c and b Wardle | 0 |
| P.S. Heine | b Wardle | 0 | (9) b Wardle | 0 |
| N.A.T. Adcock | c Evans b Wardle | 11 | b Laker | 1 |
| Extras | (B 1, LB 1, NB 1) | 3 | (LB 2, NB 1) | 3 |
| **Total** | | **205** | | **72** |

| SOUTH AFRICA | O | M | R | W | O | M | R | W |
|---|---|---|---|---|---|---|---|---|
| Heine | 19 | 0 | 78 | 1 | 21 | 1 | 67 | 2 |
| Adcock | 22·2 | 2 | 54 | 3 | 3 | 0 | 8 | 0 |
| Tayfield | 53 | 21 | 130 | 5 | 12 | 4 | 33 | 1 |
| Goddard | 38 | 12 | 74 | 1 | 17·5 | 1 | 62 | 3 |
| van Ryneveld | 3 | 0 | 16 | 0 | | | | |
| Watkins | | | | | 10 | 2 | 46 | 0 |
| ENGLAND | | | | | | | | |
| Statham | 16 | 0 | 38 | 1 | 8 | 2 | 12 | 0 |
| Loader | 21 | 5 | 33 | 2 | 7 | 2 | 11 | 0 |
| Laker | 28 | 8 | 65 | 1 | 14·1 | 9 | 7 | 2 |
| Bailey | 11 | 5 | 13 | 0 | | | | |
| Wardle | 23·6 | 9 | 53 | 5 | 19 | 3 | 36 | 7 |
| Compton | | | | | 2 | 1 | 3 | 0 |

### FALL OF WICKETS

| | E | SA | E | SA |
|---|---|---|---|---|
| Wkt | 1st | 1st | 2nd | 2nd |
| 1st | 76 | 23 | 74 | 21 |
| 2nd | 88 | 39 | 74 | 28 |
| 3rd | 116 | 48 | 109 | 42 |
| 4th | 183 | 63 | 196 | 56 |
| 5th | 233 | 110 | 208 | 67 |
| 6th | 326 | 126 | 220 | 67 |
| 7th | 334 | 178 | – | 67 |
| 8th | 335 | 191 | – | 67 |
| 9th | 346 | 191 | – | 71 |
| 10th | 369 | 205 | – | 72 |

Umpires: D. Collins and V. Costello.

# SOUTH AFRICA v ENGLAND 1956–57 (3rd Test)

Played at Kingsmead, Durban, on 25, 26, 28, 29, 30 January.
Toss: England.   Result: MATCH DRAWN.
Debuts: South Africa – A.J. Pithey.

In the second innings, Bailey retired hurt at 48 for 1, a bone in his right hand fractured by a short ball from Heine. He resumed at 167 for 5 with his hand in plaster and scored three more runs in 55 minutes. Tayfield's analysis of 8 for 69 was the best by a South African bowler in Tests and his spell of 137 balls without conceding a run remains a record for all first-class cricket.

## ENGLAND

| | | | | |
|---|---|---|---|---|
| P.E. Richardson | lbw b Adcock | 68 | b Van Ryneveld | 32 |
| T.E. Bailey | c Keith b Adcock | 80 | c Van Ryneveld b Tayfield | 18 |
| D.C.S. Compton | b Heine | 16 | c Keith b Tayfield | 19 |
| P.B.H. May* | c Goddard b Tayfield | 2 | (5) lbw b Tayfield | 2 |
| M.C. Cowdrey | lbw b Goddard | 6 | (6) lbw b Heine | 24 |
| D.J. Insole | b Van Ryneveld | 13 | (4) not out | 110 |
| T.G. Evans† | st Waite b Van Ryneveld | 0 | c Waite b Tayfield | 10 |
| J.H. Wardle | b Heine | 13 | c Waite b Tayfield | 8 |
| J.C. Laker | not out | 0 | c Goddard b Tayfield | 6 |
| P.J. Loader | c Waite b Adcock | 1 | lbw b Tayfield | 3 |
| J.B. Statham | b Adcock | 6 | c Van Ryneveld b Tayfield | 9 |
| Extras | (B 2, LB 4, W 5, NB 2) | 13 | (B 8, LB 4, NB 1) | 13 |
| **Total** | | **218** | | **254** |

## SOUTH AFRICA

| | | | | |
|---|---|---|---|---|
| A.J. Pithey | st Evans b Wardle | 25 | b Statham | 0 |
| T.L. Goddard | lbw b Statham | 69 | c Cowdrey b Wardle | 18 |
| H.J. Keith | c Evans b Loader | 6 | c sub (G.A.R. Lock) b Laker | 22 |
| W.R. Endean | c sub (G.A.R. Lock) b Wardle | 5 | c and b Laker | 26 |
| R.A. McLean | c Insole b Bailey | 100 | b Wardle | 4 |
| K.J. Funston | b Wardle | 19 | b Loader | 44 |
| J.H.B. Waite† | b Statham | 12 | (8) not out | 1 |
| C.B. van Ryneveld* | c Cowdrey b Loader | 16 | (7) not out | 14 |
| H.J. Tayfield | not out | 20 | | |
| P.S. Heine | b Wardle | 6 | | |
| N.A.T. Adcock | lbw b Wardle | 3 | | |
| Extras | (LB 2) | 2 | (B 5, LB 6, NB 2) | 13 |
| **Total** | | **283** | (6 wickets) | **142** |

| SOUTH AFRICA | O | M | R | W | O | M | R | W | | FALL OF WICKETS | | | |
|---|---|---|---|---|---|---|---|---|---|---|---|---|---|
| Heine | 16 | 2 | 65 | 2 | 22 | 3 | 58 | 1 | | E | SA | E | SA |
| Adcock | 15·3 | 3 | 39 | 4 | 21 | 8 | 39 | 0 | *Wkt* | *1st* | *1st* | *2nd* | *2nd* |
| Goddard | 25 | 11 | 42 | 1 | 13 | 5 | 26 | 0 | 1st | 115 | 65 | 45 | 0 |
| Tayfield | 24 | 17 | 21 | 1 | 37·7 | 14 | 69 | 8 | 2nd | 148 | 76 | 77 | 39 |
| Van Ryneveld | 14 | 4 | 38 | 2 | 14 | 2 | 49 | 1 | 3rd | 151 | 81 | 79 | 45 |
| | | | | | | | | | 4th | 163 | 145 | 144 | 49 |
| ENGLAND | | | | | | | | | 5th | 186 | 199 | 167 | 124 |
| Statham | 22 | 4 | 56 | 2 | 11 | 0 | 32 | 1 | 6th | 186 | 225 | 192 | 124 |
| Loader | 25 | 6 | 79 | 2 | 8 | 2 | 21 | 1 | 7th | 202 | 241 | 203 | – |
| Bailey | 17 | 3 | 38 | 1 | | | | | 8th | 210 | 264 | 220 | – |
| Wardle | 20·2 | 6 | 61 | 5 | 20 | 7 | 42 | 2 | 9th | 212 | 279 | 230 | – |
| Laker | 12 | 1 | 47 | 0 | 18 | 7 | 29 | 2 | 10th | 218 | 283 | 254 | – |
| Compton | | | | | 1 | 0 | 5 | 0 | | | | | |

Umpires: W. Marais and B.V. Malan.

# SOUTH AFRICA v ENGLAND 1956-57 (4th Test)

Played at New Wanderers, Johannesburg, on 15, 16, 18, 19, 20 February.
Toss: South Africa.   Result: SOUTH AFRICA won by 17 runs.
Debuts: South Africa – C.A.R. Duckworth.

South Africa gained their first win against England at home since 1930-31; it was their first home win on a turf pitch in this series. Tayfield remains the only South African to take nine wickets in a Test innings, or 13 in a match. He bowled throughout the last day, sending down 35 eight-ball overs in 4 hours 50 minutes, and had Loader caught by his brother, Arthur, who was substituting for Funston.

## SOUTH AFRICA

| | | | | |
|---|---|---|---|---|
| A.J. Pithey | c Wardle b Bailey | 10 | b Laker | 18 |
| T.L. Goddard | b Bailey | 67 | c Evans b Bailey | 49 |
| J.H.B. Waite† | c Evans b Statham | 61 | (7) c Cowdrey b Statham | 17 |
| K.J. Funston | c Evans b Bailey | 20 | (3) run out | 23 |
| R.A. McLean | run out | 93 | (4) c Cowdrey b Statham | 0 |
| C.A.R. Duckworth | c Wardle b Loader | 13 | b Wardle | 3 |
| W.R. Endean | b Statham | 13 | (5) c Insole b Bailey | 2 |
| C.B. van Ryneveld* | c Cowdrey b Laker | 36 | c and b Statham | 12 |
| H.J. Tayfield | c Bailey b Wardle | 10 | not out | 12 |
| P.S. Heine | not out | 1 | c Insole b Wardle | 0 |
| N.A.T. Adcock | lbw b Wardle | 6 | run out | 1 |
| Extras | (LB 8, W 1, NB 1) | 10 | (B 4, LB 1) | 5 |
| **Total** | | **340** | | **142** |

## ENGLAND

| | | | | |
|---|---|---|---|---|
| P.E. Richardson | c Tayfield b Heine | 11 | b Tayfield | 39 |
| T.E. Bailey | c Waite b Adcock | 13 | c Endean b Tayfield | 1 |
| D.J. Insole | run out | 47 | c Tayfield b Goddard | 68 |
| P.B.H. May* | b Adcock | 61 | (5) c Endean b Tayfield | 0 |
| D.C.S. Compton | c Pithey b Heine | 42 | (6) c Goddard b Tayfield | 1 |
| M.C. Cowdrey | c Goddard b Tayfield | 8 | (4) c and b Tayfield | 55 |
| T.G. Evans† | c Endean b Tayfield | 7 | (8) b Tayfield | 8 |
| J.H. Wardle | c Goddard b Tayfield | 16 | (7) c Waite b Tayfield | 22 |
| J.C. Laker | lbw b Tayfield | 17 | c Duckworth b Tayfield | 5 |
| P.J. Loader | c Endean b Goddard | 13 | c sub (A. Tayfield) b Tayfield | 7 |
| J.B. Statham | not out | 12 | not out | 4 |
| Extras | (LB 1, NB 3) | 4 | (B 1, LB 3) | 4 |
| **Total** | | **251** | | **214** |

| ENGLAND | O | M | R | W | O | M | R | W | | FALL OF WICKETS | | | |
|---|---|---|---|---|---|---|---|---|---|---|---|---|---|
| Statham | 23 | 5 | 81 | 2 | 13 | 1 | 37 | 3 | | | SA | E | SA | E |
| Loader | 23 | 3 | 78 | 1 | 13 | 3 | 33 | 0 | *Wkt* | *1st* | *1st* | *2nd* | *2nd* |
| Bailey | 21 | 3 | 54 | 3 | 13 | 4 | 12 | 2 | 1st | 22 | 25 | 62 | 10 |
| Wardle | 19·6 | 4 | 68 | 2 | 14 | 4 | 29 | 2 | 2nd | 134 | 40 | 91 | 65 |
| Laker | 15 | 3 | 49 | 1 | 7 | 1 | 26 | 1 | 3rd | 151 | 131 | 94 | 147 |
| | | | | | | | | | 4th | 172 | 135 | 95 | 148 |
| SOUTH AFRICA | | | | | | | | | 5th | 238 | 152 | 97 | 156 |
| Adcock | 21 | 5 | 52 | 2 | 8 | 1 | 22 | 0 | 6th | 251 | 160 | 104 | 186 |
| Heine | 23 | 6 | 54 | 2 | 8 | 1 | 21 | 0 | 7th | 309 | 176 | 129 | 196 |
| Goddard | 25·2 | 15 | 22 | 1 | 25 | 5 | 54 | 1 | 8th | 328 | 213 | 130 | 199 |
| Tayfield | 37 | 15 | 79 | 4 | 37 | 11 | 113 | 9 | 9th | 333 | 227 | 131 | 208 |
| Van Ryneveld | 8 | 0 | 40 | 0 | | | | | 10th | 340 | 251 | 142 | 214 |

Umpires: B.V. Malan and J.H. McMenamin.

## SOUTH AFRICA v ENGLAND 1956-57 (5th Test)

Played at St. George's Park, Port Elizabeth, on 1, 2, 4, 5 March.
Toss: South Africa.    Result: SOUTH AFRICA won by 58 runs.
Debuts: Nil.

Evans conceded only one bye on a recently relaid pitch where the ball frequently kept low or 'shot'. Waite tore fibres in his shoulder diving to stop a 'shooter' towards the end of the first innings and Endean took over as wicket-keeper after the first few overs of the second innings. Tayfield's 37 wickets in this rubber still stands as the South African record against any country.

### SOUTH AFRICA

| | | | | | |
|---|---|---|---|---|---|
| A.J. Pithey | c Evans b Bailey | 15 | | b Laker | 6 |
| T.L. Goddard | lbw b Bailey | 2 | | c Evans b Tyson | 30 |
| J.H.B. Waite† | c Evans b Loader | 3 | (9) | not out | 7 |
| K.J. Funston | b Bailey | 3 | | b Lock | 24 |
| W.R. Endean | lbw b Tyson | 70 | (3) | b Tyson | 1 |
| R.A. McLean | c Evans b Lock | 23 | | b Bailey | 19 |
| C.B. van Ryneveld* | c Tyson b Loader | 24 | (5) | lbw b Tyson | 13 |
| C.A.R. Duckworth | lbw b Laker | 6 | (7) | b Tyson | 6 |
| H.J. Tayfield | b Loader | 4 | (8) | c Evans b Tyson | 10 |
| P.S. Heine | b Tyson | 4 | | c Evans b Tyson | 4 |
| N.A.T. Adcock | not out | 0 | | b Bailey | 3 |
| Extras | (LB 1, NB 9) | 10 | | (B 1, LB 7, NB 3) | 11 |
| **Total** | | **164** | | | **134** |

### ENGLAND

| | | | | | |
|---|---|---|---|---|---|
| P.E. Richardson | lbw b Adcock | 0 | | b Adcock | 3 |
| T.E. Bailey | b Heine | 41 | | c McLean b Tayfield | 18 |
| D.C.S. Compton | b Adcock | 0 | (6) | c Endean b Tayfield | 5 |
| P.B.H. May* | c Duckworth b Goddard | 24 | (3) | lbw b Goddard | 21 |
| D.J. Insole | lbw b Heine | 4 | | c Duckworth b Tayfield | 8 |
| M.C. Cowdrey | c Waite b Adcock | 3 | (4) | c Van Ryneveld b Tayfield | 8 |
| T.G. Evans† | b Heine | 5 | | c Endean b Heine | 21 |
| G.A.R. Lock | b Adcock | 14 | | c Goddard b Tayfield | 12 |
| F.H. Tyson | c and b Heine | 1 | | c Tayfield b Goddard | 23 |
| J.C. Laker | b Goddard | 6 | | not out | 3 |
| P.J. Loader | not out | 0 | | c McLean b Tayfield | 0 |
| Extras | (B 8, LB 4) | 12 | | (B 5, LB 3) | 8 |
| **Total** | | **110** | | | **130** |

| ENGLAND | O | M | R | W | O | M | R | W |
|---|---|---|---|---|---|---|---|---|
| Loader | 20 | 3 | 35 | 3 | 4 | 3 | 1 | 0 |
| Bailey | 25 | 12 | 23 | 3 | 24·7 | 5 | 39 | 2 |
| Tyson | 17 | 6 | 38 | 2 | 23 | 7 | 40 | 6 |
| Laker | 14 | 1 | 37 | 1 | 14 | 5 | 26 | 1 |
| Lock | 11 | 5 | 21 | 1 | 15 | 6 | 17 | 1 |
| SOUTH AFRICA | | | | | | | | |
| Heine | 15 | 6 | 22 | 4 | 11 | 3 | 22 | 1 |
| Adcock | 11·3 | 4 | 20 | 4 | 7 | 2 | 10 | 1 |
| Tayfield | 22 | 8 | 43 | 0 | 24·3 | 6 | 78 | 6 |
| Goddard | 13 | 8 | 13 | 2 | 16 | 8 | 12 | 2 |

### FALL OF WICKETS

| | SA | E | SA | E |
|---|---|---|---|---|
| Wkt | 1st | 1st | 2nd | 2nd |
| 1st | 4 | 1 | 20 | 15 |
| 2nd | 15 | 1 | 21 | 41 |
| 3rd | 21 | 55 | 65 | 53 |
| 4th | 41 | 77 | 98 | 57 |
| 5th | 78 | 78 | 99 | 71 |
| 6th | 143 | 86 | 105 | 72 |
| 7th | 155 | 89 | 111 | 99 |
| 8th | 155 | 97 | 123 | 127 |
| 9th | 163 | 110 | 129 | 129 |
| 10th | 164 | 110 | 134 | 130 |

Umpires: W. Marais and V. Costello.

# ENGLAND v WEST INDIES 1957 (1st Test)

Played at Edgbaston, Birmingham, on 30, 31 May, 1, 3, 4 June.
Toss: England.   Result: MATCH DRAWN.
Debuts: West Indies – R. Gilchrist, R.B. Kanhai.

Birmingham's first Test for 28 years brought a host of records. May's 285* remains the highest score by an England captain and the highest in any Edgbaston Test. His stand of 411 is still England's highest for any wicket and the Test record for the fourth wicket. Ramadhin bowled most balls (588) in any first-class innings and the most in any Test match (774); both records still stand. Smith scored a hundred in his first Test against England.

## ENGLAND

| | | | | |
|---|---|---|---|---|
| P.E. Richardson | c Walcott b Ramadhin | 47 | c sub (N.R. Asgarali) b Ramadhin | 34 |
| D.B. Close | c Kanhai b Gilchrist | 15 | c Weekes b Gilchrist | 42 |
| D.J. Insole | b Ramadhin | 20 | b Ramadhin | 0 |
| P.B.H. May* | c Weekes b Ramadhin | 30 | not out | 285 |
| M.C. Cowdrey | c Gilchrist b Ramadhin | 4 | c sub (N.R. Asgarali) b Smith | 154 |
| T.E. Bailey | b Ramadhin | 1 | | |
| G.A.R. Lock | b Ramadhin | 0 | | |
| T.G. Evans† | b Gilchrist | 14 | (6) not out | 29 |
| J.C. Laker | b Ramadhin | 7 | | |
| F.S. Trueman | not out | 29 | | |
| J.B. Statham | b Atkinson | 13 | | |
| Extras | (B 3, LB 3) | 6 | (B 23, LB 16) | 39 |
| **Total** | | **186** | (4 wickets declared) | **583** |

## WEST INDIES

| | | | | |
|---|---|---|---|---|
| B.H. Pairaudeau | b Trueman | 1 | b Trueman | 7 |
| R.B. Kanhai† | lbw b Statham | 42 | c Close b Trueman | 1 |
| C.L. Walcott | c Evans b Laker | 90 | (6) c Lock b Laker | 1 |
| E. de C. Weekes | b Trueman | 9 | c Trueman b Lock | 33 |
| G. St A. Sobers | c Bailey b Statham | 53 | (3) c Cowdrey b Lock | 14 |
| O.G. Smith | lbw b Laker | 161 | (7) lbw b Laker | 5 |
| F.M.M. Worrell | b Statham | 81 | (5) c May b Lock | 0 |
| J.D.C. Goddard* | c Lock b Laker | 24 | not out | 0 |
| D. St E. Atkinson | c Statham b Laker | 1 | not out | 4 |
| S. Ramadhin | not out | 5 | | |
| R. Gilchrist | run out | 0 | | |
| Extras | (B 1, LB 6) | 7 | (B 7) | 7 |
| **Total** | | **474** | (7 wickets) | **72** |

| WEST INDIES | O | M | R | W | O | M | R | W |
|---|---|---|---|---|---|---|---|---|
| Worrell | 9 | 1 | 27 | 0 | | | | |
| Gilchrist | 27 | 4 | 74 | 2 | 26 | 2 | 67 | 1 |
| Ramadhin | 31 | 16 | 49 | 7 | 98 | 35 | 179 | 2 |
| Atkinson | 12·4 | 3 | 30 | 1 | 72 | 29 | 137 | 0 |
| Sobers | | | | | 30 | 4 | 77 | 0 |
| Smith | | | | | 26 | 4 | 72 | 1 |
| Goddard | | | | | 6 | 2 | 12 | 0 |
| ENGLAND | | | | | | | | |
| Statham | 39 | 4 | 114 | 3 | 2 | 0 | 6 | 0 |
| Trueman | 30 | 4 | 99 | 2 | 5 | 3 | 7 | 2 |
| Bailey | 34 | 11 | 80 | 0 | | | | |
| Laker | 54 | 17 | 119 | 4 | 24 | 20 | 13 | 2 |
| Lock | 34·4 | 15 | 55 | 0 | 27 | 19 | 31 | 3 |
| Close | | | | | 2 | 1 | 8 | 0 |

### FALL OF WICKETS

| Wkt | E 1st | WI 1st | E 2nd | WI 2nd |
|---|---|---|---|---|
| 1st | 32 | 4 | 63 | 1 |
| 2nd | 61 | 83 | 65 | 9 |
| 3rd | 104 | 120 | 113 | 25 |
| 4th | 115 | 183 | 524 | 27 |
| 5th | 116 | 197 | – | 43 |
| 6th | 118 | 387 | – | 66 |
| 7th | 121 | 466 | – | 68 |
| 8th | 130 | 469 | – | – |
| 9th | 150 | 474 | – | – |
| 10th | 186 | 474 | – | – |

Umpires: C.S. Elliott and E. Davies.

# ENGLAND v WEST INDIES 1957 (2nd Test)

Played at Lord's, London, on 20, 21, 22 June.
Toss: West Indies.   Result: ENGLAND won by an innings and 36 runs.
Debuts: England – D.V. Smith; West Indies – N.R. Asgarali.

Bailey's analysis of 7 for 44, returned in his 50th Test match, was the best for England in a home Test against West Indies (equalled by F.S. Trueman in 1963). Bailey's eleven wickets equalled England's match record for any West Indies Test.

## WEST INDIES

| | | | | | |
|---|---|---:|---|---|---:|
| N.R. Asgarali | lbw b Trueman | 0 | (4) c Trueman b Wardle | | 26 |
| R.B. Kanhai† | c Cowdrey b Bailey | 34 | (1) c Bailey b Statham | | 0 |
| C.L. Walcott | lbw b Bailey | 14 | c Trueman b Bailey | | 21 |
| G. St A. Sobers | c May b Statham | 17 | (5) c May b Bailey | | 66 |
| E. de C.Weekes | c Evans b Bailey | 13 | (6) c Evans b Bailey | | 90 |
| F.M.M. Worrell | c Close b Bailey | 12 | (7) c Evans b Trueman | | 10 |
| O.G. Smith | c Graveney b Bailey | 25 | (2) lbw b Statham | | 5 |
| J.D.C. Goddard* | c Cowdrey b Bailey | 1 | c Evans b Trueman | | 21 |
| S. Ramadhin | b Trueman | 0 | c Statham b Bailey | | 0 |
| R. Gilchrist | c and b Bailey | 4 | not out | | 11 |
| A.L. Valentine | not out | 0 | b Statham | | 1 |
| Extras | (B 2, LB 1, W 4) | 7 | (B 4, LB 6) | | 10 |
| **Total** | | **127** | | | **261** |

## ENGLAND

| | | |
|---|---|---:|
| P.E. Richardson | b Gilchrist | 76 |
| D.V. Smith | lbw b Worrell | 8 |
| T.W. Graveney | lbw b Gilchrist | 0 |
| P.B.H. May* | c Kanhai b Gilchrist | 0 |
| M.C. Cowdrey | c Walcott b Sobers | 152 |
| T.E. Bailey | b Worrell | 1 |
| D.B. Close | c Kanhai b Goddard | 32 |
| T.G. Evans† | b Sobers | 82 |
| J.H. Wardle | c Sobers b Ramadhin | 11 |
| F.S. Trueman | not out | 36 |
| J.B. Statham | b Gilchrist | 7 |
| Extras | (B 7, LB 11, W 1) | 19 |
| **Total** | | **424** |

| ENGLAND | O | M | R | W | O | M | R | W | | FALL OF WICKETS | | |
|---|---|---|---|---|---|---|---|---|---|---|---|---|
| Statham | 18 | 3 | 46 | 1 | 29·1 | 9 | 71 | 3 | | WI | E | WI |
| Trueman | 12·3 | 2 | 30 | 2 | 23 | 5 | 73 | 2 | *Wkt* | *1st* | *1st* | *2nd* |
| Bailey | 21 | 8 | 44 | 7 | 22 | 6 | 54 | 4 | 1st | 7 | 25 | 0 |
| Wardle | | | | | 22 | 5 | 53 | 1 | 2nd | 34 | 34 | 17 |
| | | | | | | | | | 3rd | 55 | 34 | 32 |
| WEST INDIES | | | | | | | | | 4th | 79 | 129 | 80 |
| Worrell | 42 | 7 | 114 | 2 | | | | | 5th | 85 | 134 | 180 |
| Gilchrist | 36·3 | 7 | 115 | 4 | | | | | 6th | 118 | 192 | 203 |
| Ramadhin | 22 | 5 | 83 | 1 | | | | | 7th | 120 | 366 | 233 |
| Valentine | 3 | 0 | 20 | 0 | | | | | 8th | 123 | 379 | 241 |
| Goddard | 13 | 1 | 45 | 1 | | | | | 9th | 127 | 387 | 256 |
| Sobers | 7 | 0 | 28 | 2 | | | | | 10th | 127 | 424 | 261 |

Umpires: C.S. Elliott and E. Davies.

# ENGLAND v WEST INDIES 1957 (3rd Test)

Played at Trent Bridge, Nottingham, on 4, 5, 6, 8, 9 July.
Toss: England.   Result: MATCH DRAWN.
Debuts: England – D.W. Richardson.

England's partnership of 266 between Richardson and Graveney, whose highest first-class score took 475 minutes and included 30 fours, remains their highest for the second wicket against West Indies. Worrell was the first to carry his bat through a completed West Indies innings and his stand of 55 with Ramadhin, who batted with a runner, is still the West Indies tenth-wicket record against England. Worrell was on the field for the first 20½ hours of the match.

## ENGLAND

| | | | | |
|---|---|---|---|---|
| P.E. Richardson | c Walcott b Atkinson | 126 | c Kanhai b Gilchrist | 11 |
| D.V. Smith | c Kanhai b Worrell | 1 | not out | 16 |
| T.W. Graveney | b Smith | 258 | not out | 28 |
| P.B.H. May* | lbw b Smith | 104 | | |
| M.C. Cowdrey | run out | 55 | | |
| D.W. Richardson | b Sobers | 33 | | |
| T.G. Evans† | not out | 26 | | |
| T.E. Bailey | not out | 3 | | |
| J.C. Laker | ) | | | |
| F.S. Trueman | ) did not bat | | | |
| J.B. Statham | ) | | | |
| Extras | (B 1, LB 10, W 1, NB 1) | 13 | (B 7, LB 2) | 9 |
| **Total** | (6 wickets declared) | **619** | (1 wicket) | **64** |

## WEST INDIES

| | | | | |
|---|---|---|---|---|
| F.M.M. Worrell | not out | 191 | b Statham | 16 |
| G. St A. Sobers | b Laker | 47 | lbw b Trueman | 9 |
| C.L. Walcott | c and b Laker | 17 | c Evans b Laker | 7 |
| R.B. Kanhai† | c Evans b Bailey | 42 | c Evans b Trueman | 28 |
| E. de C.Weekes | b Trueman | 33 | b Statham | 3 |
| O.G. Smith | c Evans b Trueman | 2 | b Trueman | 168 |
| D. St E. Atkinson | c Evans b Trueman | 4 | c Evans b Statham | 46 |
| J.D.C. Goddard* | c May b Trueman | 0 | c Evans b Statham | 61 |
| R. Gilchrist | c D.W. Richardson b Laker | 1 | (10) b Statham | 0 |
| A.L. Valentine | b Trueman | 1 | (11) not out | 2 |
| S. Ramadhin | b Statham | 19 | (9) b Trueman | 15 |
| Extras | (B 5, LB 10) | 15 | (B 2, LB 10) | 12 |
| **Total** | | **372** | | **367** |

| WEST INDIES | O | M | R | W | O | M | R | W | | FALL OF WICKETS | | | |
|---|---|---|---|---|---|---|---|---|---|---|---|---|---|
| Worrell | 21 | 4 | 79 | 1 | 7 | 1 | 27 | 0 | | E | WI | WI | E |
| Gilchrist | 29 | 3 | 118 | 0 | 7 | 0 | 21 | 1 | *Wkt* | *1st* | *1st* | *2nd* | *2nd* |
| Atkinson | 40 | 7 | 99 | 1 | 1 | 0 | 1 | 0 | 1st | 14 | 87 | 22 | 13 |
| Ramadhin | 38 | 5 | 95 | 0 | | | | | 2nd | 280 | 120 | 30 | – |
| Valentine | 23 | 4 | 68 | 0 | | | | | 3rd | 487 | 229 | 39 | – |
| Sobers | 21 | 6 | 60 | 1 | | | | | 4th | 510 | 295 | 56 | – |
| Goddard | 15 | 5 | 26 | 0 | 1 | 0 | 2 | 0 | 5th | 573 | 297 | 89 | – |
| Smith | 25 | 5 | 61 | 2 | | | | | 6th | 609 | 305 | 194 | – |
| Walcott | | | | | 1 | 0 | 4 | 0 | 7th | – | 305 | 348 | – |
| | | | | | | | | | 8th | – | 314 | 352 | – |
| ENGLAND | | | | | | | | | 9th | – | 317 | 365 | – |
| Statham | 28·4 | 9 | 78 | 1 | 41·2 | 12 | 118 | 5 | 10th | – | 372 | 367 | – |
| Trueman | 30 | 8 | 63 | 5 | 35 | 5 | 80 | 4 | | | | | |
| Laker | 62 | 27 | 101 | 3 | 43 | 14 | 98 | 1 | | | | | |
| Bailey | 28 | 9 | 77 | 1 | 12 | 3 | 22 | 0 | | | | | |
| Smith | 12 | 1 | 38 | 0 | 12 | 5 | 23 | 0 | | | | | |
| Graveney | | | | | 5 | 2 | 14 | 0 | | | | | |

Umpires: F.S. Lee and J.S. Buller.

# ENGLAND v WEST INDIES 1957 (4th Test)

Played at Headingley, Leeds, on 25, 26, 27 July.
Toss: West Indies.   Result: ENGLAND won by an innings and 5 runs.
Debuts: West Indies – F.C.M. Alexander.

West Indies last four first-innings wickets fell in consecutive balls, Trueman bowling Smith with the last ball of an over before Loader dismissed Goddard, Ramadhin and Gilchrist to complete the first hat-trick for England in a home Test since 1899. Evans became the first wicket-keeper to make 200 dismissals in Tests when he caught Smith.

## WEST INDIES

| | | | | |
|---|---|---|---|---|
| F.M.M. Worrell | b Loader | 29 | c Cowdrey b Trueman | 7 |
| G. St A. Sobers | c Lock b Loader | 4 | run out | 29 |
| R.B. Kanhai | lbw b Laker | 47 | lbw b Loader | 0 |
| E. de C.Weekes | b Loader | 0 | c Cowdrey b Trueman | 14 |
| C.L. Walcott | c Cowdrey b Laker | 38 | c Sheppard b Loader | 35 |
| O.G. Smith | b Trueman | 15 | c Evans b Smith | 8 |
| B.H. Pairaudeau | b Trueman | 6 | c Trueman b Loader | 6 |
| J.D.C. Goddard* | b Loader | 1 | c Loader b Lock | 4 |
| F.C.M. Alexander† | not out | 0 | b Laker | 11 |
| S. Ramadhin | c Trueman b Loader | 0 | run out | 6 |
| R. Gilchrist | b Loader | 0 | not out | 6 |
| Extras | (LB 2) | 2 | (LB 5, NB 1) | 6 |
| **Total** | | **142** | | **132** |

## ENGLAND

| | | |
|---|---|---|
| P.E. Richardson | c Alexander b Worrell | 10 |
| D.V. Smith | b Worrell | 0 |
| T.W. Graveney | b Gilchrist | 22 |
| P.B.H. May* | c Alexander b Sobers | 69 |
| M.C. Cowdrey | c Weekes b Worrell | 68 |
| Rev. D.S. Sheppard | c Walcott b Worrell | 68 |
| T.G. Evans† | b Worrell | 10 |
| G.A.R. Lock | b Gilchrist | 20 |
| J.C. Laker | c Alexander b Worrell | 1 |
| F.S. Trueman | not out | 2 |
| P.J. Loader | c Pairaudeau b Worrell | 1 |
| Extras | (B 2, LB 5, W 1) | 8 |
| **Total** | | **279** |

| ENGLAND | O | M | R | W | O | M | R | W |
|---|---|---|---|---|---|---|---|---|
| Trueman | 17 | 4 | 33 | 2 | 11 | 0 | 42 | 2 |
| Loader | 20·3 | 9 | 36 | 6 | 14 | 2 | 50 | 3 |
| Smith | 17 | 6 | 24 | 0 | 4 | 1 | 12 | 1 |
| Laker | 17 | 4 | 24 | 2 | 6·2 | 1 | 16 | 1 |
| Lock | 14 | 6 | 23 | 0 | 1 | 0 | 6 | 1 |
| WEST INDIES | | | | | | | | |
| Worrell | 38·2 | 9 | 70 | 7 | | | | |
| Gilchrist | 27 | 3 | 71 | 2 | | | | |
| Sobers | 32 | 9 | 79 | 1 | | | | |
| Ramadhin | 19 | 5 | 34 | 0 | | | | |
| Smith | 8 | 1 | 17 | 0 | | | | |

### FALL OF WICKETS

| | WI | E | WI |
|---|---|---|---|
| Wkt | 1st | 1st | 2nd |
| 1st | 16 | 1 | 40 |
| 2nd | 42 | 12 | 40 |
| 3rd | 42 | 42 | 49 |
| 4th | 112 | 136 | 56 |
| 5th | 125 | 227 | 71 |
| 6th | 139 | 239 | 92 |
| 7th | 142 | 264 | 103 |
| 8th | 142 | 272 | 113 |
| 9th | 142 | 278 | 123 |
| 10th | 142 | 279 | 132 |

Umpires: J.S. Buller and D. Davies.

# ENGLAND v WEST INDIES 1957 (5th Test)

Played at Kennington Oval, London, on 22, 23, 24 August.
Toss: England.   Result: ENGLAND won by an innings and 237 runs.
Debuts: Nil.

Dismissed for what are still their two lowest totals against England, West Indies were beaten in three days for the third time in this rubber, the match ending at 2.30 p.m. Walcott took over the captaincy when Goddard was taken ill with influenza at the end of the first day.

## ENGLAND

| | | |
|---|---|---|
| P.E. Richardson | b Smith | 107 |
| Rev.D.S. Sheppard | c and b Goddard | 40 |
| T.W. Graveney | b Ramadhin | 164 |
| P.B.H. May* | c Worrell b Smith | 1 |
| M.C. Cowdrey | b Ramadhin | 2 |
| T.E. Bailey | run out | 0 |
| T.G. Evans† | c Weekes b Dewdney | 40 |
| G.A.R. Lock | c Alexander b Sobers | 17 |
| F.S. Trueman | b Ramadhin | 22 |
| J.C. Laker | not out | 10 |
| P.J. Loader | lbw b Ramadhin | 0 |
| Extras | (B 1, LB 8) | 9 |
| **Total** | | **412** |

## WEST INDIES

| | | | | | |
|---|---|---|---|---|---|
| F.M.M. Worrell | c Lock b Loader | 4 | (4) c Cowdrey b Lock | | 0 |
| N.R. Asgarali | c Cowdrey b Lock | 29 | b Lock | | 7 |
| G. St A. Sobers | b Lock | 39 | b Lock | | 42 |
| C.L. Walcott | b Laker | 5 | (5) not out | | 19 |
| E. de C. Weekes | c Trueman b Laker | 0 | (6) b Lock | | 0 |
| O.G. Smith | c May b Laker | 7 | (7) c Sheppard b Lock | | 0 |
| R.B. Kanhai | not out | 4 | (1) c Evans b Trueman | | 8 |
| F.C.M. Alexander† | b Lock | 0 | b Laker | | 0 |
| D.T. Dewdney | b Lock | 0 | st Evans b Lock | | 1 |
| S. Ramadhin | c Trueman b Lock | 0 | b Laker | | 2 |
| J.D.C. Goddard* | absent ill | – | absent ill | | – |
| Extras | (NB 1) | 1 | (B 4, LB 2, NB 1) | | 7 |
| **Total** | | **89** | | | **86** |

| WEST INDIES | O | M | R | W | O | M | R | W | FALL OF WICKETS | | | |
|---|---|---|---|---|---|---|---|---|---|---|---|---|
| Worrell | 11 | 3 | 26 | 0 | | | | | | E | WI | WI |
| Dewdney | 15 | 2 | 43 | 1 | | | | | *Wkt* | *1st* | *1st* | *2nd* |
| Ramadhin | 53·3 | 12 | 107 | 4 | | | | | 1st | 92 | 7 | 10 |
| Sobers | 44 | 6 | 111 | 1 | | | | | 2nd | 238 | 68 | 39 |
| Goddard | 23 | 10 | 43 | 1 | | | | | 3rd | 242 | 73 | 43 |
| Smith | 30 | 4 | 73 | 2 | | | | | 4th | 255 | 73 | 69 |
| **ENGLAND** | | | | | | | | | 5th | 256 | 85 | 69 |
| Trueman | 5 | 1 | 9 | 0 | 5 | 2 | 19 | 1 | 6th | 322 | 89 | 69 |
| Loader | 7 | 4 | 12 | 1 | 3 | 2 | 2 | 0 | 7th | 366 | 89 | 70 |
| Laker | 23 | 12 | 39 | 3 | 17 | 4 | 38 | 2 | 8th | 399 | 89 | 75 |
| Lock | 21·4 | 12 | 28 | 5 | 16 | 7 | 20 | 6 | 9th | 412 | 89 | 86 |
| | | | | | | | | | 10th | 412 | – | – |

Umpires: E. Davies and F.S. Lee.

# SOUTH AFRICA v AUSTRALIA 1957-58 (1st Test)

Played at New Wanderers, Johannesburg, on 23, 24, 26, 27, 28 December.
Toss: South Africa.   Result: MATCH DRAWN.
Debuts: Australia – A.T.W. Grout, L.F. Kline, I. Meckiff, R.B. Simpson.

McGlew and Goddard opened the rubber with what is still South Africa's highest first-wicket partnership against Australia. Playing his first match, Grout set a world Test record (since equalled) by holding six catches in an innings.

## SOUTH AFRICA

| | | | | | |
|---|---|---|---|---|---|
| D.J. McGlew* | c Simpson b Meckiff | 108 | | c Simpson b Meckiff | 6 |
| T.L. Goddard | b Meckiff | 90 | | c Grout b Davidson | 5 |
| J.D. Nel | b Meckiff | 4 | | c Grout b Davidson | 7 |
| J.H.B. Waite† | c Burge b Benaud | 115 | | c Grout b Burke | 59 |
| W.R. Endean | lbw b Meckiff | 50 | (6) | c Meckiff b Davidson | 77 |
| R.A. McLean | b Meckiff | 50 | (5) | c Grout b Davidson | 0 |
| K.J. Funston | lbw b Mackay | 12 | | b Meckiff | 27 |
| H.J. Tayfield | b Davidson | 18 | | c Grout b Meckiff | 3 |
| P.S. Heine | b Mackay | 7 | | c Grout b Davidson | 2 |
| V.J. Smith | not out | 2 | | not out | 1 |
| N.A.T. Adcock | did not bat | | | c Simpson b Davidson | 0 |
| Extras | (B 8, LB 4, W 1, NB 1) | 14 | | (B 5, LB 7, W 1, NB 1) | 14 |
| **Total** | (9 wickets declared) | **470** | | | **201** |

## AUSTRALIA

| | | | | | |
|---|---|---|---|---|---|
| C.C. McDonald | c Tayfield b Smith | 75 | | st Waite b Smith | 25 |
| J.W. Burke | c Waite b Heine | 16 | | retired hurt | 10 |
| K.D. Mackay | c Waite b Heine | 3 | | not out | 65 |
| I.D. Craig* | b Heine | 14 | | b Tayfield | 17 |
| P.J.P. Burge | c Waite b Heine | 0 | | b Tayfield | 14 |
| R.B. Simpson | lbw b Tayfield | 60 | | not out | 23 |
| R. Benaud | c Heine b Adcock | 122 | | | |
| A.K. Davidson | c sub (E.R.H. Fuller) b Heine | 24 | | | |
| A.T.W. Grout† | c Endean b Tayfield | 21 | | | |
| I. Meckiff | c Smith b Heine | 11 | | | |
| L.F. Kline | not out | 6 | | | |
| Extras | (B 4, LB 11, NB 1) | 16 | | (B 6, LB 2) | 8 |
| **Total** | | **368** | | (3 wickets) | **162** |

| AUSTRALIA | O | M | R | W | O | M | R | W |
|---|---|---|---|---|---|---|---|---|
| Davidson | 32 | 4 | 115 | 1 | 17·4 | 4 | 34 | 6 |
| Meckiff | 31 | 3 | 125 | 5 | 26 | 3 | 52 | 3 |
| Mackay | 20·6 | 3 | 54 | 2 | 11 | 1 | 29 | 0 |
| Benaud | 27 | 7 | 115 | 1 | 2 | 0 | 15 | 0 |
| Kline | 20 | 6 | 47 | 0 | 8 | 2 | 18 | 0 |
| Burke | | | | | 14 | 3 | 39 | 1 |
| SOUTH AFRICA | | | | | | | | |
| Heine | 14·2 | 3 | 58 | 6 | 8 | 2 | 17 | 0 |
| Adcock | 23 | 3 | 106 | 1 | 3 | 0 | 11 | 0 |
| Goddard | 16 | 5 | 57 | 0 | 12 | 6 | 24 | 0 |
| Tayfield | 29 | 9 | 101 | 2 | 33 | 12 | 70 | 2 |
| Smith | 9 | 2 | 30 | 1 | 16 | 8 | 25 | 1 |
| McGlew | | | | | 1 | 0 | 7 | 0 |

FALL OF WICKETS

| Wkt | SA 1st | A 1st | SA 2nd | A 2nd |
|---|---|---|---|---|
| 1st | 176 | 34 | 6 | 44 |
| 2nd | 182 | 40 | 19 | 85 |
| 3rd | 237 | 56 | 19 | 118 |
| 4th | 341 | 62 | 19 | – |
| 5th | 412 | 151 | 148 | – |
| 6th | 436 | 177 | 193 | – |
| 7th | 461 | 244 | 196 | – |
| 8th | 465 | 313 | 199 | – |
| 9th | 470 | 355 | 199 | – |
| 10th | – | 368 | 201 | – |

Umpires: J.H. McMenamin and A. Birkett.

# SOUTH AFRICA v AUSTRALIA 1957-58 (2nd Test)

Played at Newlands, Cape Town, on 31 December, 1, 2, 3 January.
Toss: Australia.    Result: AUSTRALIA won by an innings and 141 runs.
Debuts: Nil.

Burke batted 578 minutes for his highest Test score. Meckiff left the field with a pulled shoulder muscle after bowling four balls on the third day. Kline ended the match soon after lunch on the fourth day when he did the hat-trick, dismissing Fuller, Tayfield and Adcock.

## AUSTRALIA

| | | |
|---|---|---|
| C.C. McDonald | c Waite b Fuller | 99 |
| J.W. Burke | b Tayfield | 189 |
| R.N. Harvey | c Goddard b Adcock | 15 |
| I.D. Craig* | b Goddard | 0 |
| K.D. Mackay | lbw b Tayfield | 63 |
| R. Benaud | c McGlew b Tayfield | 33 |
| A.K. Davidson | c and b Tayfield | 21 |
| R.B. Simpson | c Funston b Tayfield | 3 |
| A.T.W. Grout† | run out | 0 |
| I. Meckiff | not out | 11 |
| L.F. Kline | lbw b Fuller | 5 |
| Extras | (B 1, LB 6, NB 3) | 10 |
| **Total** | | **449** |

## SOUTH AFRICA

| | | | | |
|---|---|---|---|---|
| D.J. McGlew | c Mackay b Davidson | 30 | c McDonald b Davidson | 0 |
| T.L. Goddard | lbw b Benaud | 29 | not out | 56 |
| R.J. Westcott | c Simpson b Davidson | 0 | c Davidson b Benaud | 18 |
| J.H.B. Waite† | c Simpson b Kline | 7 | c Benaud b Davidson | 8 |
| R.A. McLean | c Harvey b Kline | 38 | c Burke b Benaud | 2 |
| W.R. Endean | c Davidson b Burke | 21 | b Benaud | 5 |
| K.J. Funston | c and b Benaud | 2 | b Benaud | 8 |
| C.B. van Ryneveld* | b Benaud | 43 | c Burke b Benaud | 1 |
| E.R.H. Fuller | c Harvey b Benaud | 5 | c Benaud b Kline | 0 |
| H.J. Tayfield | c Benaud b Kline | 21 | lbw b Kline | 0 |
| N.A.T. Adcock | not out | 0 | c Simpson b Kline | 0 |
| Extras | (B 6, LB 5, W 1, NB 1) | 13 | (LB 1) | 1 |
| **Total** | | **209** | | **99** |

| SOUTH AFRICA | O | M | R | W | O | M | R | W |
|---|---|---|---|---|---|---|---|---|
| Adcock | 27 | 5 | 80 | 1 | | | | |
| Goddard | 29 | 9 | 57 | 1 | | | | |
| Fuller | 34·2 | 3 | 125 | 2 | | | | |
| Tayfield | 51 | 18 | 120 | 5 | | | | |
| Westcott | 4 | 0 | 22 | 0 | | | | |
| Van Ryneveld | 7 | 0 | 35 | 0 | | | | |
| AUSTRALIA | | | | | | | | |
| Meckiff | 5·4 | 1 | 18 | 0 | | | | |
| Davidson | 18 | 5 | 31 | 2 | 15 | 6 | 18 | 2 |
| Benaud | 35 | 6 | 95 | 4 | 21 | 6 | 49 | 5 |
| Kline | 19·1 | 5 | 29 | 3 | 10·4 | 2 | 18 | 3 |
| Burke | 9 | 2 | 23 | 1 | 6 | 4 | 7 | 0 |
| Mackay | | | | | 5 | 3 | 6 | 0 |

### FALL OF WICKETS

| | A | SA | SA |
|---|---|---|---|
| Wkt | 1st | 1st | 2nd |
| 1st | 190 | 61 | 0 |
| 2nd | 215 | 61 | 56 |
| 3rd | 220 | 70 | 69 |
| 4th | 350 | 103 | 74 |
| 5th | 399 | 118 | 80 |
| 6th | 408 | 121 | 88 |
| 7th | 412 | 146 | 98 |
| 8th | 412 | 164 | 99 |
| 9th | 434 | 209 | 99 |
| 10th | 449 | 209 | 99 |

Umpires: V. Costello and D. Collins.

# SOUTH AFRICA v AUSTRALIA 1957–58 (3rd Test)

Played at Kingsmead, Durban, on 24, 25, 27, 28, 29 January.
Toss: Australia.   Result: MATCH DRAWN.
Debuts: Australia – R.A. Gaunt.

Gaunt bowled Westcott during his first over in Test cricket. McGlew took nine hours five minutes to reach the slowest century then in Test cricket, his 105 lasting a further 30 minutes. His third-wicket partnership of 231 with Goddard was the highest so far for any South African wicket against Australia.

## AUSTRALIA

| | | | | | |
|---|---|---|---|---|---|
| C.C. McDonald | c Goddard b Adcock | 28 | lbw b Tayfield | | 33 |
| J.W. Burke | c Waite b Adcock | 2 | b Goddard | | 83 |
| R.N. Harvey | c Waite b Adcock | 6 | b Adcock | | 68 |
| I.D. Craig* | b Goddard | 52 | c Goddard b Tayfield | | 0 |
| R.B. Simpson | b Goddard | 17 | (8) c Tayfield b Van Ryneveld | | 4 |
| K.D. Mackay | hit wkt b Adcock | 32 | (5) not out | | 52 |
| R. Benaud | lbw b Adcock | 5 | (6) b Van Ryneveld | | 20 |
| A.K. Davidson | c Waite b Heine | 12 | (7) c McGlew b Tayfield | | 4 |
| A.T.W. Grout† | b Heine | 2 | not out | | 3 |
| L.F. Kline | c Goddard b Adcock | 0 | | | |
| R.A. Gaunt | not out | 0 | | | |
| Extras | (NB 7) | 7 | (B 19, LB 5, NB 1) | | 25 |
| **Total** | | **163** | (7 wickets) | | **292** |

## SOUTH AFRICA

| | | |
|---|---|---|
| D.J. McGlew | c Grout b Gaunt | 105 |
| R.J. Westcott | b Gaunt | 0 |
| W.R. Endean | c Simpson b Benaud | 15 |
| J.H.B. Waite† | b Davidson | 134 |
| T.L. Goddard | lbw b Davidson | 45 |
| K.J. Funston | c Grout b Mackay | 27 |
| C.B. van Ryneveld* | not out | 32 |
| R.A. McLean | c Grout b Benaud | 11 |
| H.J. Tayfield | st Grout b Benaud | 0 |
| P.S. Heine | c Burke b Benaud | 7 |
| N.A.T. Adcock | c Grout b Benaud | 0 |
| Extras | (B 2, LB 5, NB 1) | 8 |
| **Total** | | **384** |

| SOUTH AFRICA | O | M | R | W | O | M | R | W |
|---|---|---|---|---|---|---|---|---|
| Heine | 17·4 | 4 | 30 | 2 | 14 | 1 | 40 | 0 |
| Adcock | 18 | 2 | 43 | 6 | 15 | 1 | 34 | 1 |
| Goddard | 23 | 12 | 25 | 2 | 42 | 18 | 62 | 1 |
| Tayfield | 21 | 7 | 41 | 0 | 59 | 24 | 94 | 3 |
| Van Ryneveld | 3 | 0 | 17 | 0 | 17 | 1 | 37 | 2 |

| AUSTRALIA | O | M | R | W |
|---|---|---|---|---|
| Davidson | 34 | 8 | 62 | 2 |
| Gaunt | 27 | 2 | 87 | 2 |
| Mackay | 35 | 5 | 77 | 1 |
| Benaud | 50·7 | 13 | 114 | 5 |
| Kline | 17 | 6 | 36 | 0 |

## FALL OF WICKETS

| | A | SA | A |
|---|---|---|---|
| Wkt | 1st | 1st | 2nd |
| 1st | 13 | 6 | 92 |
| 2nd | 19 | 28 | 170 |
| 3rd | 54 | 259 | 179 |
| 4th | 87 | 259 | 221 |
| 5th | 131 | 313 | 261 |
| 6th | 142 | 356 | 274 |
| 7th | 161 | 371 | 289 |
| 8th | 163 | 371 | – |
| 9th | 163 | 383 | – |
| 10th | 163 | 384 | – |

Umpires: V. Costello and W. Marais.

# SOUTH AFRICA v AUSTRALIA 1957–58 (4th Test)

Played at New Wanderers, Johannesburg, on 7, 8, 10, 11, 12 February.
Toss: Australia.   Result: AUSTRALIA won by ten wickets.
Debuts: South Africa – C.G. de V. Burger.

Australia won immediately after lunch on the fifth day, South Africa being handicapped on the first day when Adcock retired at lunch with influenza and Heine's bowling was restricted by a damaged ankle.

## AUSTRALIA

| | | | | |
|---|---|---|---|---|
| C.C. McDonald | lbw b Tayfield | 26 | not out | 1 |
| J.W. Burke | c Waite b Heine | 81 | not out | 0 |
| R.N. Harvey | c Waite b Goddard | 5 | | |
| R. Benaud | c Endean b Heine | 100 | | |
| I.D. Craig* | b Heine | 3 | | |
| A.T.W. Grout† | lbw b Adcock | 7 | | |
| K.D. Mackay | not out | 83 | | |
| R.B. Simpson | c Waite b Adcock | 6 | | |
| A.K. Davidson | c Burger b Heine | 62 | | |
| I. Meckiff | c Endean b Heine | 26 | | |
| L.F. Kline | c Waite b Heine | 1 | | |
| Extras | (LB 1) | 1 | | |
| **Total** | | **401** | (0 wickets) | **1** |

## SOUTH AFRICA

| | | | | |
|---|---|---|---|---|
| D.J. McGlew | c Grout b Meckiff | 1 | c Simpson b Benaud | 70 |
| W.R. Endean | lbw b Davidson | 22 | c Simpson b Benaud | 38 |
| H.J. Tayfield | lbw b Benaud | 27 | (9) st Grout b Kline | 0 |
| T.L. Goddard | c and b Meckiff | 9 | (3) c Simpson b Benaud | 0 |
| K.J. Funston | c Craig b Kline | 70 | (4) not out | 64 |
| R.A. McLean | c Grout b Davidson | 9 | (5) c Grout b Davidson | 0 |
| C.G. de V. Burger | st Grout b Kline | 21 | c McDonald b Kline | 1 |
| J.H.B. Waite† | lbw b Benaud | 12 | (6) c Grout b Benaud | 10 |
| P.S. Heine | c and b Benaud | 24 | (10) c Meckiff b Benaud | 1 |
| N.A.T. Adcock | b Benaud | 0 | (11) run out | 3 |
| C.B. van Ryneveld* | not out | 0 | (8) lbw b Kline | 0 |
| Extras | (B 3, W 2, NB 3) | 8 | (LB 8, W 2, NB 1) | 11 |
| **Total** | | **203** | | **198** |

| SOUTH AFRICA | O | M | R | W | O | M | R | W |
|---|---|---|---|---|---|---|---|---|
| Heine | 37·5 | 6 | 96 | 6 | | | | |
| Adcock | 17 | 3 | 37 | 2 | | | | |
| Goddard | 43 | 10 | 136 | 1 | | | | |
| Tayfield | 49 | 17 | 107 | 1 | | | | |
| Van Ryneveld | 3 | 0 | 24 | 0 | | | | |
| McLean | | | | | 0·4 | 0 | 1 | 0 |
| AUSTRALIA | | | | | | | | |
| Meckiff | 21 | 3 | 38 | 2 | 13 | 2 | 24 | 0 |
| Davidson | 19 | 2 | 39 | 2 | 20 | 4 | 44 | 1 |
| Mackay | 11 | 5 | 11 | 0 | | | | |
| Benaud | 20·2 | 0 | 70 | 4 | 41 | 8 | 84 | 5 |
| Kline | 9 | 1 | 37 | 2 | 16 | 6 | 27 | 3 |
| Burke | | | | | 15 | 10 | 8 | 0 |

### FALL OF WICKETS

| Wkt | A 1st | SA 1st | SA 2nd | A 2nd |
|---|---|---|---|---|
| 1st | 43 | 17 | 78 | – |
| 2nd | 52 | 27 | 78 | – |
| 3rd | 210 | 46 | 147 | – |
| 4th | 213 | 104 | 148 | – |
| 5th | 222 | 115 | 161 | – |
| 6th | 222 | 166 | 180 | – |
| 7th | 234 | 166 | 180 | – |
| 8th | 315 | 186 | 182 | – |
| 9th | 393 | 194 | 183 | – |
| 10th | 401 | 203 | 198 | – |

Umpires: J. McMenamin and A. Birkett.

# SOUTH AFRICA v AUSTRALIA 1957–58 (5th Test)

Played at St George's Park, Port Elizabeth, on 28 February, 1, 3, 4 March.
Toss: South Africa.    Result: AUSTRALIA won by eight wickets.
Debuts: South Africa – P.R. Carlstein.

Australia won their third victory of the rubber and with a day to spare. It extended their unbeaten run of Test matches in the Union to 21. Benaud took his hundredth Test wicket to complete the Test 'double' in his 32nd match.

## SOUTH AFRICA

| | | | | | |
|---|---|---|---|---|---|
| D.J. McGlew | c Simpson b Davidson | 14 | (7) b Benaud | 20 |
| T.L. Goddard | c Harvey b Meckiff | 17 | lbw b Benaud | 33 |
| W.R. Endean | c McDonald b Davidson | 2 | (1) c Simpson b Davidson | 23 |
| J.H.B. Waite† | c Harvey b Davidson | 17 | (3) b Davidson | 0 |
| K.J. Funston | c Grout b Davidson | 20 | (4) c Simpson b Davidson | 4 |
| C.B. van Ryneveld* | c Burke b Kline | 26 | b Benaud | 5 |
| C.G. de V. Burger | lbw b Kline | 3 | (8) not out | 37 |
| P.R. Carlstein | c and b Kline | 32 | (9) lbw b Benaud | 1 |
| H.J. Tayfield | c Burke b Kline | 66 | (5) c Grout b Davidson | 2 |
| P.S. Heine | lbw b Benaud | 3 | lbw b Benaud | 15 |
| N.A.T. Adcock | not out | 3 | b Davidson | 0 |
| Extras | (B 4, LB 5, NB 2) | 11 | (B 2, LB 2) | 4 |
| **Total** | | **214** | | **144** |

## AUSTRALIA

| | | | | | |
|---|---|---|---|---|---|
| C.C. McDonald | c Waite b Adcock | 58 | c Tayfield b Adcock | 4 |
| J.W. Burke | c Endean b Adcock | 8 | | |
| R.N. Harvey | lbw b Heine | 15 | c and b Tayfield | 22 |
| I.D. Craig* | c Endean b Tayfield | 17 | | |
| R. Benaud | c and b Goddard | 43 | (4) not out | 6 |
| R.B. Simpson | c Carlstein b Tayfield | 23 | | |
| K.D. Mackay | not out | 77 | | |
| A.K. Davidson | lbw b Heine | 4 | | |
| A.T.W. Grout† | c Endean b Goddard | 25 | (2) not out | 35 |
| I. Meckiff | c Waite b Heine | 8 | | |
| L.F. Kline | c Goddard b Tayfield | 0 | | |
| Extras | (B 2, LB 4, NB 7) | 13 | (B 1) | 1 |
| **Total** | | **291** | (2 wickets) | **68** |

| AUSTRALIA | O | M | R | W | O | M | R | W |
|---|---|---|---|---|---|---|---|---|
| Davidson | 20 | 6 | 44 | 4 | 26·1 | 8 | 38 | 5 |
| Meckiff | 18 | 4 | 76 | 1 | 16 | 8 | 20 | 0 |
| Benaud | 12 | 2 | 34 | 1 | 33 | 14 | 82 | 5 |
| Mackay | 11 | 3 | 16 | 0 | | | | |
| Kline | 13·6 | 3 | 33 | 4 | | | | |
| SOUTH AFRICA | | | | | | | | |
| Heine | 30 | 3 | 68 | 3 | 3 | 0 | 12 | 0 |
| Adcock | 24 | 1 | 81 | 2 | 4 | 0 | 18 | 1 |
| Goddard | 23 | 9 | 48 | 2 | 1 | 0 | 8 | 0 |
| Tayfield | 30·3 | 12 | 81 | 3 | 4 | 1 | 25 | 1 |
| Van Ryneveld | | | | | 0·4 | 0 | 4 | 0 |

### FALL OF WICKETS

| Wkt | SA 1st | A 1st | SA 2nd | A 2nd |
|---|---|---|---|---|
| 1st | 28 | 13 | 55 | 4 |
| 2nd | 30 | 37 | 55 | 53 |
| 3rd | 36 | 124 | 63 | – |
| 4th | 57 | 145 | 63 | – |
| 5th | 86 | 194 | 70 | – |
| 6th | 96 | 199 | 70 | – |
| 7th | 105 | 239 | 97 | – |
| 8th | 191 | 265 | 99 | – |
| 9th | 198 | 278 | 131 | – |
| 10th | 214 | 291 | 144 | – |

Umpires: V. Costello and W. Marais.

# WEST INDIES v PAKISTAN 1957-58 (1st Test)

Played at Kensington Oval, Bridgetown, Barbados, on 17, 18, 20, 21, 22, 23 January.
Toss: West Indies. Result: MATCH DRAWN.
Debuts: West Indies – E. St E. Atkinson, C.C. Hunte; Pakistan – Haseeb Ahsan, Nasim-ul-Ghani, Saeed Ahmed.

In the first meeting of these teams, Nasim-ul-Ghani, aged 16 years 248 days, became the youngest Test player so far. Hanif, in what remains the longest first-class innings (16 hours 10 minutes), scored the then second-highest score in Test cricket. Hutton had scored 27 more runs in 173 fewer minutes in 1938. Hanif shared in four century-partnerships during the innings which is still Pakistan's highest in all Test matches. Hunte scored a hundred on debut.

## WEST INDIES

| | | | | |
|---|---|---|---|---|
| C.C. Hunte | c Imtiaz b Fazal | 142 | not out | 11 |
| R.B. Kanhai | c Mathias b Fazal | 27 | not out | 17 |
| G. St A. Sobers | c Mathias b Mahmood | 52 | | |
| E. de C. Weekes | c Imtiaz b Mahmood | 197 | | |
| C.L. Walcott | c Mathias b Kardar | 43 | | |
| O.G. Smith | c Mathias b Alimuddin | 78 | | |
| D. St E. Atkinson | b Mahmood | 4 | | |
| E. St E. Atkinson | b Fazal | 0 | | |
| F.C.M. Alexander*† | b Mahmood | 9 | | |
| A.L. Valentine | not out | 5 | | |
| R. Gilchrist | did not bat | | | |
| Extras | (B 9, LB 4, W 3, NB 6) | 22 | | |
| **Total** | (9 wickets declared) | **579** | (0 wickets) | **28** |

## PAKISTAN

| | | | | |
|---|---|---|---|---|
| Hanif Mohammad | b E. St E. Atkinson | 17 | c Alexander b D. St E. Atkinson | 337 |
| Imtiaz Ahmed† | lbw b Gilchrist | 20 | lbw b Gilchrist | 91 |
| Alimuddin | c Weekes b Gilchrist | 3 | c Alexander b Sobers | 37 |
| Saeed Ahmed | st Alexander b Smith | 13 | c Alexander b Smith | 65 |
| Wazir Mohammad | lbw b Valentine | 4 | c Alexander b E. St E. Atkinson | 35 |
| W. Mathias | c Alexander b Smith | 17 | lbw b E. St E. Atkinson | 17 |
| A.H. Kardar* | c D. St E. Atkinson b Smith | 4 | not out | 23 |
| Fazal Mahmood | b Gilchrist | 4 | b Valentine | 19 |
| Nasim-ul-Ghani | run out | 11 | b Valentine | 0 |
| Mahmood Hussain | b Gilchrist | 3 | not out | 0 |
| Haseeb Ahsan | not out | 1 | | |
| Extras | (B 4, LB 5) | 9 | (B 19, LB 7, NB 7) | 33 |
| **Total** | | **106** | (8 wickets declared) | **657** |

| PAKISTAN | O | M | R | W | O | M | R | W |
|---|---|---|---|---|---|---|---|---|
| Fazal | 62 | 21 | 145 | 3 | 2 | 1 | 3 | 0 |
| Mahmood Hussain | 41·2 | 4 | 153 | 4 | | | | |
| Kardar | 32 | 4 | 107 | 1 | 3 | 1 | 13 | 0 |
| Haseeb | 21 | 0 | 84 | 0 | | | | |
| Nasim | 14 | 1 | 51 | 0 | | | | |
| Alimuddin | 2 | 0 | 17 | 1 | | | | |
| Hanif | | | | | 3 | 1 | 10 | 0 |
| Saeed | | | | | 2 | 2 | 0 | 0 |
| Wazir | | | | | 1 | 0 | 2 | 0 |
| **WEST INDIES** | | | | | | | | |
| Gilchrist | 15 | 4 | 32 | 4 | 41 | 5 | 121 | 1 |
| E. St E. Atkinson | 8 | 0 | 27 | 1 | 49 | 5 | 136 | 2 |
| Smith | 13 | 4 | 23 | 3 | 61 | 30 | 93 | 1 |
| Valentine | 6·2 | 1 | 15 | 1 | 39 | 8 | 109 | 2 |
| D. St E. Atkinson | | | | | 62 | 35 | 61 | 1 |
| Sobers | | | | | 57 | 25 | 94 | 1 |
| Walcott | | | | | 10 | 5 | 10 | 0 |

### FALL OF WICKETS

| | WI | P | P | WI |
|---|---|---|---|---|
| Wkt | 1st | 1st | 2nd | 2nd |
| 1st | 122 | 35 | 152 | – |
| 2nd | 209 | 39 | 264 | – |
| 3rd | 266 | 44 | 418 | – |
| 4th | 356 | 53 | 539 | – |
| 5th | 541 | 81 | 598 | – |
| 6th | 551 | 84 | 626 | – |
| 7th | 556 | 91 | 649 | – |
| 8th | 570 | 93 | 649 | – |
| 9th | 579 | 96 | – | – |
| 10th | – | 106 | – | – |

Umpires: H. Walcott and H.B. de C. Jordan.

# WEST INDIES v PAKISTAN 1957-58 (2nd Test)

Played at Queen's Park Oval, Port-of-Spain, Trinidad, on 5, 6, 7, 8, 10, 11 February.
Toss: West Indies.   Result: WEST INDIES won by 120 runs.
Debuts: West Indies – L.R. Gibbs, E.D.A. St J. McMorris, I.S. Madray.

West Indies gained the first victory in this new series. Waqar Hassan was the first of 309 wickets to fall to the off-spin of Gibbs.

## WEST INDIES

| | | | | |
|---|---|---|---|---|
| C.C. Hunte | c Imtiaz b Fazal | 8 | c Kardar b Nasim | 37 |
| E.D.A. St J. McMorris | b Kardar | 13 | lbw b Fazal | 16 |
| G. St A. Sobers | b Nasim | 52 | (6) lbw b Fazal | 80 |
| E. de C. Weekes | run out | 78 | (5) b Nasim | 24 |
| R.B. Kanhai | c Mathias b Mahmood | 96 | (3) c Mathias b Mahmood | 5 |
| O.G. Smith | c Kardar b Mahmood | 41 | (7) c Waqar b Fazal | 51 |
| F.C.M. Alexander*† | c Imtiaz b Nasim | 26 | (4) run out | 57 |
| I.S. Madray | lbw b Fazal | 1 | lbw b Mahmood | 0 |
| L.R. Gibbs | c Kardar b Nasim | 2 | b Nasim | 22 |
| R. Gilchrist | run out | 0 | b Fazal | 7 |
| D.T. Dewdney | not out | 0 | not out | 5 |
| Extras | (B 5, LB 2, NB 1) | 8 | (B 4, LB 2, NB 2) | 8 |
| **Total** | | **325** | | **312** |

## PAKISTAN

| | | | | |
|---|---|---|---|---|
| Hanif Mahammad | c Gibbs b Smith | 30 | c Sobers b Gilchrist | 81 |
| Alimuddin | b Gilchrist | 9 | b Gilchrist | 0 |
| Imtiaz Ahmed† | lbw b Smith | 39 | (4) b Sobers | 18 |
| Saeed Ahmed | lbw b Smith | 11 | (3) c Alexander b Sobers | 64 |
| W. Mathias | b Dewdney | 73 | (6) c Weekes b Dewdney | 10 |
| Nasim-ul-Ghani | c Alexander b Gilchrist | 0 | (11) b Gibbs | 0 |
| Wazir Mohammad | c Weekes b Gilchrist | 0 | (5) b Gilchrist | 0 |
| Waqar Hasan | c Weekes b Gibbs | 17 | (7) st Alexander b Gibbs | 28 |
| A.H. Kardar* | st Alexander b Smith | 4 | b Gibbs | 24 |
| Fazal Mahmood | c Madray b Sobers | 60 | (8) b Gilchrist | 0 |
| Mahmood Hussain | not out | 19 | (10) not out | 1 |
| Extras | (B 13, LB 5, NB 2) | 20 | (B 1, LB 5, NB 3) | 9 |
| **Total** | | **282** | | **235** |

| PAKISTAN | O | M | R | W | O | M | R | W | | FALL OF WICKETS | | | |
|---|---|---|---|---|---|---|---|---|---|---|---|---|---|
| Mahmood Hussain | 36 | 6 | 128 | 2 | 37 | 4 | 132 | 2 | | WI | P | WI | P |
| Fazal | 50 | 24 | 76 | 2 | 51 | 21 | 89 | 4 | *Wkt* | *1st* | *1st* | *2nd* | *2nd* |
| Kardar | 32 | 13 | 71 | 1 | 9 | 2 | 19 | 0 | 1st | 11 | 21 | 38 | 1 |
| Nasim | 13·1 | 3 | 42 | 3 | 33·2 | 11 | 64 | 3 | 2nd | 51 | 66 | 51 | 131 |
| | | | | | | | | | 3rd | 129 | 90 | 71 | 159 |
| WEST INDIES | | | | | | | | | 4th | 177 | 91 | 105 | 161 |
| Gilchrist | 21 | 4 | 67 | 3 | 19 | 5 | 61 | 4 | 5th | 276 | 104 | 206 | 180 |
| Dewdney | 17 | 3 | 50 | 1 | 18 | 8 | 29 | 1 | 6th | 302 | 116 | 255 | 180 |
| Smith | 25 | 7 | 71 | 4 | 19 | 7 | 31 | 0 | 7th | 307 | 150 | 277 | 180 |
| Sobers | 5·3 | 1 | 14 | 1 | 22 | 8 | 41 | 2 | 8th | 325 | 155 | 277 | 222 |
| Madray | 6 | 0 | 22 | 0 | 13 | 5 | 32 | 0 | 9th | 325 | 226 | 288 | 235 |
| Gibbs | 12 | 2 | 38 | 1 | 13·5 | 6 | 32 | 3 | 10th | 325 | 282 | 312 | 235 |

Umpires: E.L. Lloyd and E.N. Lee Kow.

# WEST INDIES v PAKISTAN 1957-58 (3rd Test)

Played at Sabina Park, Kingston, Jamaica, on 26, 27, 28, February, 1, 3, 4 March.
Toss: Pakistan.   Result: WEST INDIES won by an innings and 174 runs.
Debuts: Nil.

Garfield St Aubrun Sobers, aged 21, recorded the highest score in Test cricket, hitting 38 fours and batting for 10 hours 14 minutes (3 hours 3 minutes less than Hutton, whose record he beat by one run). His stand of 446 with Hunte for the second wicket remains the second-highest for any wicket in Test matches. It was Sobers' first three-figure score in a Test. West Indies compiled the third-highest total in a Test against an attack containing only two uninjured specialist bowlers.

## PAKISTAN

| | | | | | |
|---|---|---|---|---|---|
| Hanif Mohammad | c Alexander b Gilchrist | 3 | | b Gilchrist | 13 |
| Imtiaz Ahmed† | c Alexander b Gilchrist | 122 | | lbw b Dewdney | 0 |
| Saeed Ahmed | c Weekes b Smith | 52 | | c Gilchrist b Gibbs | 44 |
| W. Mathias | b Dewdney | 77 | | c Alexander b Atkinson | 19 |
| Alimuddin | c Alexander b Atkinson | 15 | | b Gibbs | 30 |
| A.H. Kardar* | c Sobers b Atkinson | 15 | (7) | lbw b Dewdney | 57 |
| Wazir Mohammad | c Walcott b Dewdney | 2 | (6) | lbw b Atkinson | 106 |
| Fazal Mahmood | c Alexander b Atkinson | 6 | | c Alexander b Atkinson | 0 |
| Nasim-ul-Ghani | b Atkinson | 5 | | absent hurt | – |
| Mahmood Hussain | b Atkinson | 20 | | absent hurt | – |
| Khan Mohammad | not out | 3 | (9) | not out | 0 |
| Extras | (LB 5, NB 3) | 8 | | (B o 16, LB 3) | 19 |
| **Total** | | **328** | | | **288** |

## WEST INDIES

| | | |
|---|---|---|
| C.C. Hunte | run out | 260 |
| R.B. Kanhai | c Imtiaz b Fazal | 25 |
| G. St A. Sobers | not out | 365 |
| E. de C.Weekes | c Hanif b Fazal | 39 |
| C.L. Walcott | not out | 88 |
| O.G. Smith | ) | |
| F.C.M. Alexander*† | ) | |
| L.R. Gibbs | ) did not bat | |
| E. St E. Atkinson | ) | |
| R. Gilchrist | ) | |
| D.T. Dewdney· | ) | |
| Extras | (B 2, LB 7, W 4) | 13 |
| **Total** | (3 wickets declared) | **790** |

| WEST INDIES | O | M | R | W | O | M | R | W | | FALL OF WICKETS | | |
|---|---|---|---|---|---|---|---|---|---|---|---|---|
| | | | | | | | | | | P | WI | P |
| Gilchrist | 25 | 3 | 106 | 2 | 12 | 3 | 65 | 1 | *Wkt* | *1st* | *1st* | *2nd* |
| Dewdney | 26 | 4 | 88 | 2 | 19·3 | 2 | 51 | 2 | 1st | 4 | 87 | 8 |
| Atkinson | 21 | 7 | 42 | 5 | 18 | 6 | 36 | 3 | 2nd | 122 | 533 | 20 |
| Gibbs | 7 | 0 | 32 | 0 | 21 | 6 | 46 | 2 | 3rd | 223 | 602 | 57 |
| Smith | 18 | 3 | 39 | 1 | 8 | 2 | 20 | 0 | 4th | 249 | – | 105 |
| Sobers | 5 | 1 | 13 | 0 | 15 | 4 | 41 | 0 | 5th | 287 | – | 120 |
| Weekes | | | | | 3 | 1 | 10 | 0 | 6th | 291 | – | 286 |
| **PAKISTAN** | | | | | | | | | 7th | 299 | – | 286 |
| Mahmood Hussain | 0·5 | 0 | 2 | 0 | | | | | 8th | 301 | – | 288 |
| Fazal | 85·2 | 20 | 247 | 2 | | | | | 9th | 317 | – | – |
| Khan | 54 | 5 | 259 | 0 | | | | | 10th | 328 | – | – |
| Nasim | 15 | 3 | 39 | 0 | | | | | | | | |
| Kardar | 37 | 2 | 141 | 0 | | | | | | | | |
| Wallis | 4 | 0 | 20 | 0 | | | | | | | | |
| Alimuddin | 4 | 0 | 34 | 0 | | | | | | | | |
| Hanif | 2 | 0 | 11 | 0 | | | | | | | | |
| Saeed | 6 | 0 | 24 | 0 | | | | | | | | |

Umpires: P. Burke and T.A. Ewart.

## WEST INDIES v PAKISTAN 1957–58 (4th Test)

Played at Bourda, Georgetown, British Guiana, on 13, 14, 15, 17, 18, 19 March.
Toss: Pakistan.    Result: WEST INDIES won by eight wickets.
Debuts: Pakistan – S.F. Rehman.

Sobers scored a hundred in each innings to bring his aggregate in his last three innings against Pakistan to 599 runs for once out. He put on 269 for the second wicket with Walcott. Fazal, struck on the knee while batting, broke down after four overs in the final innings.

### PAKISTAN

| | | | | | |
|---|---|---|---|---|---|
| Alimuddin | b Smith | 30 | lbw b Smith | | 41 |
| Imtiaz Ahmed† | c Walcott b Smith | 32 | b Gibbs | | 7 |
| Saeed Ahmed | b Gibbs | 150 | run out | | 12 |
| Hanif Mohammad | b Gilchrist | 79 | c Madray b Gilchrist | | 14 |
| Wazir Mohammad | lbw b Gilchrist | 7 | not out | | 97 |
| W. Mathias | b Gilchrist | 16 | lbw b Gibbs | | 18 |
| A.H. Kardar* | b Smith | 26 | c Smith b Gibbs | | 56 |
| Fazal Mahmood | c Gibbs b Gilchrist | 39 | c Alexander b Gibbs | | 31 |
| S.F. Rehman | b Gibbs | 8 | run out | | 2 |
| Nasim-ul-Ghani | b Dewdney | 13 | c and b Gibbs | | 22 |
| Haseeb Ahsan | not out | 0 | b Gilchrist | | 0 |
| Extras | (B 2, LB 2, W 2, NB 2) | 8 | (B 8, LB 4, W 1, NB 5) | | 18 |
| **Total** | | **408** | | | **318** |

### WEST INDIES

| | | | | | |
|---|---|---|---|---|---|
| C.C. Hunte | b Fazal | 5 | b Rehman | | 114 |
| G. St A. Sobers | b Nasim | 125 | (3) not out | | 109 |
| C.L. Walcott | run out | 145 | | | |
| E. de C. Weekes | c Rehman b Nasim | 41 | not out | | 16 |
| O.G. Smith | c sub (Ijaz Butt) b Haseeb | 27 | | | |
| R.B. Kanhai | st Imtiaz b Nasim | 24 | (2) c Mathias b Haseeb | | 62 |
| F.C.M. Alexander*† | c Mathias b Haseeb | 2 | | | |
| I.S. Madray | c Fazal b Nasim | 2 | | | |
| L.R. Gibbs | run out | 11 | | | |
| R. Gilchrist | c Alimuddin | 12 | | | |
| D.T. Dewdney | not out | 0 | | | |
| Extras | (B 4, LB 9, W 1, NB 2) | 16 | (B 12, LB 1, W 2, NB 1) | | 16 |
| **Total** | | **410** | (2 wickets) | | **317** |

| WEST INDIES | O | M | R | W | O | M | R | W | | FALL OF WICKETS | | | |
|---|---|---|---|---|---|---|---|---|---|---|---|---|---|
| Gilchrist | 28 | 3 | 102 | 4 | 19·1 | 3 | 66 | 2 | | P | WI | P | WI |
| Dewdney | 16·1 | 1 | 79 | 1 | 11 | 3 | 30 | 0 | *Wkt* | *1st* | *1st* | *2nd* | *2nd* |
| Gibbs | 30 | 12 | 56 | 2 | 42 | 12 | 80 | 5 | 1st | 60 | 11 | 22 | 125 |
| Sobers | 16 | 2 | 47 | 0 | 17 | 6 | 32 | 0 | 2nd | 69 | 280 | 44 | 260 |
| Smith | 25 | 2 | 74 | 3 | 44 | 12 | 80 | 1 | 3rd | 205 | 297 | 62 | – |
| Madray | 10 | 0 | 42 | 0 | 6 | 1 | 12 | 0 | 4th | 221 | 336 | 102 | – |
| | | | | | | | | | 5th | 249 | 361 | 130 | – |
| PAKISTAN | | | | | | | | | 6th | 337 | 370 | 224 | – |
| Fazal | 25 | 5 | 74 | 1 | 4 | 2 | 12 | 0 | 7th | 349 | 384 | 263 | – |
| Kardar | 6 | 1 | 24 | 0 | 2 | 0 | 10 | 0 | 8th | 365 | 389 | 265 | – |
| Nasim | 41·4 | 11 | 116 | 5 | 28 | 4 | 76 | 0 | 9th | 408 | 410 | 304 | – |
| Haseeb | 44 | 10 | 124 | 2 | 41 | 7 | 151 | 1 | 10th | 408 | 410 | 318 | – |
| Rehman | 17 | 1 | 56 | 0 | 17 | 2 | 43 | 1 | | | | | |
| Wazir | | | | | 1 | 0 | 8 | 0 | | | | | |
| Saeed | | | | | 0·1 | 0 | 1 | 0 | | | | | |

Umpires: E.S. Gillette and C.P. Kippins.

# WEST INDIES v PAKISTAN 1957–58 (5th Test)

Played at Queen's Park Oval, Port-of-Spain, Trinidad, on 26, 27, 28, 29, 31 March.
Toss: West Indies.   Result: PAKISTAN won by an innings and 1 run.
Debuts: West Indies – J.O. Taylor.

Pakistan completed their first win against West Indies before lunch on the penultimate day. Gilchrist sprained an ankle early in the Pakistan innings but his fellow fast bowler, Taylor, took five wickets in his first match.

## WEST INDIES

| | | | | |
|---|---|---|---|---|
| C.C. Hunte | c Hanif b Fazal | 0 | c Fazal b Nasim | 45 |
| R.B. Kanhai | c Imtiaz b Khan | 0 | b Haseeb | 43 |
| G. St A. Sobers | c Kardar b Fazal | 14 | b Nasim | 27 |
| E. de C. Weekes | c Imtiaz b Khan | 51 | b Haseeb | 9 |
| C.L. Walcott | st Imtiaz b Nasim | 47 | c Wazir b Nasim | 62 |
| O.G. Smith | lbw b Fazal | 86 | st Imtiaz b Nasim | 0 |
| F.C.M. Alexander*† | b Fazal | 38 | b Nasim | 1 |
| E. St E. Atkinson | c Hanif b Fazal | 0 | b Fazal | 19 |
| L.R. Gibbs | lbw b Fazal | 14 | c Mathias b Fazal | 2 |
| J.O. Taylor | not out | 4 | st Imtiaz b Nasim | 0 |
| R. Gilchrist | c Kardar b Nasim | 9 | not out | 2 |
| Extras | (B 5) | 5 | (B 12, LB 4, NB 1) | 17 |
| **Total** | | **268** | | **227** |

## PAKISTAN

| | | |
|---|---|---|
| Imtiaz Ahmed† | b Taylor | 15 |
| Alimuddin | b Gibbs | 21 |
| Saeed Ahmed | c Alexander b Taylor | 97 |
| Wazir Mohammad | b Gibbs | 189 |
| Hanif Mohammad | b Taylor | 54 |
| W. Mathias | b Atkinson | 4 |
| A.H. Kardar* | c Walcott b Gibbs | 44 |
| Fazal Mahmood | b Taylor | 0 |
| Nasim-ul-Ghani | c Alexander b Gibbs | 15 |
| Khan Mohammad | not out | 26 |
| Haseeb Ahsan | b Taylor | 2 |
| Extras | (B 14, LB 10, W 1, NB 4) | 29 |
| **Total** | | **496** |

| PAKISTAN | O | M | R | W | O | M | R | W |
|---|---|---|---|---|---|---|---|---|
| Fazal | 32 | 10 | 83 | 6 | 9 | 1 | 35 | 2 |
| Khan | 25 | 8 | 79 | 2 | 2 | 0 | 19 | 0 |
| Nasim | 22·1 | 6 | 53 | 2 | 30·5 | 9 | 67 | 6 |
| Haseeb | 14 | 2 | 48 | 0 | 24 | 3 | 89 | 2 |

| WEST INDIES | O | M | R | W |
|---|---|---|---|---|
| Gilchrist | 7 | 2 | 16 | 0 |
| Taylor | 36·5 | 6 | 109 | 5 |
| Atkinson | 31 | 3 | 66 | 1 |
| Smith | 23 | 4 | 63 | 0 |
| Gibbs | 41 | 9 | 108 | 4 |
| Sobers | 34 | 6 | 95 | 0 |
| Walcott | 2 | 0 | 6 | 0 |
| Weekes | 3 | 1 | 4 | 0 |

### FALL OF WICKETS

| | WI | P | WI |
|---|---|---|---|
| Wkt | 1st | 1st | 2nd |
| 1st | 0 | 22 | 71 |
| 2nd | 2 | 69 | 115 |
| 3rd | 48 | 238 | 130 |
| 4th | 78 | 392 | 140 |
| 5th | 141 | 407 | 141 |
| 6th | 219 | 407 | 162 |
| 7th | 219 | 408 | 219 |
| 8th | 249 | 463 | 223 |
| 9th | 254 | 478 | 225 |
| 10th | 268 | 496 | 227 |

Umpires: E.L. Lloyd and G. Williams.

# ENGLAND v NEW ZEALAND 1958 (1st Test)

Played at Edgbaston, Birmingham, on 5, 6, 7, 9 June.
Toss: England.    Result: ENGLAND won by 205 runs.
Debuts: England – M.J.K. Smith; New Zealand – J.W. D'Arcy, T. Meale, W.R. Playle.

England won at 2.48 p.m. on the fourth day. Harford was struck in the face by a lifting ball from Trueman in the second innings and retired hurt for a time.

## ENGLAND

| | | | | |
|---|---|---:|---|---:|
| P.E. Richardson | lbw b MacGibbon | 4 | c Cave b MacGibbon | 100 |
| M.J.K. Smith | lbw b MacGibbon | 0 | c Petrie b MacGibbon | 7 |
| T.W. Graveney | c Alabaster b Hayes | 7 | c Petrie b Cave | 19 |
| P.B.H. May* | c Petrie b MacGibbon | 84 | c Petrie b MacGibbon | 11 |
| M.C. Cowdrey | b MacGibbon | 81 | c Reid b Hayes | 70 |
| T.E. Bailey | c Petrie b Alabaster | 2 | not out | 6 |
| T.G. Evans† | c Petrie b MacGibbon | 2 | c Reid b Cave | 0 |
| G.A.R. Lock | lbw b Alabaster | 4 | | |
| F.S. Trueman | b Alabaster | 0 | | |
| J.C. Laker | not out | 11 | | |
| P.J. Loader | b Alabaster | 17 | | |
| Extras | (LB 3, W 4, NB 2) | 9 | (B 1, LB 1) | 2 |
| **Total** | | **221** | (6 wickets declared) | **215** |

## NEW ZEALAND

| | | | | |
|---|---|---:|---|---:|
| L.S.M. Miller | lbw b Trueman | 7 | b Trueman | 8 |
| J.W. D'Arcy | c Evans b Trueman | 19 | c Trueman b Loader | 25 |
| N.S. Harford | b Bailey | 9 | (4) c Graveney b Loader | 23 |
| J.R. Reid* | b Bailey | 7 | (6) b Bailey | 13 |
| W.R. Playle | b Trueman | 4 | (3) c Bailey b Loader | 8 |
| T. Meale | lbw b Trueman | 7 | (5) c Smith b Lock | 10 |
| A.R. MacGibbon | c Evans b Laker | 5 | (8) c Cowdrey b Laker | 26 |
| E.C. Petrie† | lbw b Loader | 1 | (10) not out | 5 |
| J.C. Alabaster | b Trueman | 9 | c Laker b Lock | 11 |
| H.B. Cave | not out | 12 | (7) b Bailey | 1 |
| J.A. Hayes | run out | 14 | c Bailey b Lock | 5 |
| Extras | | | (LB 1, W 1) | 2 |
| **Total** | | **94** | | **137** |

| NEW ZEALAND | O | M | R | W | O | M | R | W |
|---|---|---|---|---|---|---|---|---|
| Hayes | 15 | 2 | 57 | 1 | 20 | 3 | 51 | 1 |
| MacGibbon | 27 | 11 | 64 | 5 | 24 | 8 | 41 | 3 |
| Cave | 12 | 2 | 29 | 0 | 28·2 | 9 | 70 | 2 |
| Reid | 6 | 3 | 16 | 0 | 9 | 2 | 18 | 0 |
| Alabaster | 15·5 | 4 | 46 | 4 | 15 | 7 | 33 | 0 |
| ENGLAND | | | | | | | | |
| Trueman | 21 | 8 | 31 | 5 | 17 | 5 | 33 | 1 |
| Loader | 21·3 | 6 | 37 | 1 | 23 | 11 | 40 | 3 |
| Bailey | 20 | 9 | 17 | 2 | 20 | 9 | 23 | 2 |
| Lock | 2 | 2 | 0 | 0 | 8·3 | 3 | 25 | 3 |
| Laker | 5 | 2 | 9 | 1 | 9 | 4 | 14 | 1 |

FALL OF WICKETS

| | E | NZ | E | NZ |
|---|---|---|---|---|
| Wkt | 1st | 1st | 2nd | 2nd |
| 1st | 4 | 12 | 24 | 19 |
| 2nd | 11 | 21 | 71 | 42 |
| 3rd | 29 | 39 | 94 | 49 |
| 4th | 150 | 43 | 198 | 64 |
| 5th | 153 | 46 | 214 | 93 |
| 6th | 172 | 54 | 215 | 94 |
| 7th | 185 | 59 | – | 95 |
| 8th | 191 | 67 | – | 123 |
| 9th | 191 | 68 | – | 131 |
| 10th | 221 | 94 | – | 137 |

Umpires: J.S. Buller and C.S. Elliott.

# ENGLAND v NEW ZEALAND 1958 (2nd Test)

Played at Lord's, London, on 19, 20, 21 June.
Toss: England.    Result: ENGLAND won by an innings and 148 runs.
Debuts: Nil.

New Zealand, trapped on a pitch affected by rain after England's innings, were dismissed for the then lowest total in a Lord's Test and beaten by 3.30 p.m. on the third day. Flags were flown at half-mast on the first day in tribute to the memory of D.R. Jardine who had died in Switzerland.

## ENGLAND

| | | |
|---|---|---|
| P.E. Richardson | c Petrie b Hayes | 36 |
| M.J.K. Smith | c Petrie b Hayes | 47 |
| T.W. Graveney | c Petrie b Alabaster | 37 |
| P.B.H. May* | c Alabaster b MacGibbon | 19 |
| M.C. Cowdrey | b Hayes | 65 |
| T.E. Bailey | c Petrie b Reid | 17 |
| T.G. Evans† | c Hayes b MacGibbon | 11 |
| G.A.R. Lock | not out | 23 |
| F.S. Trueman | b Hayes | 8 |
| J.C. Laker | c Blair b MacGibbon | 1 |
| P.J. Loader | c Playle b MacGibbon | 4 |
| Extras | (LB 1) | 1 |
| **Total** | | **269** |

## NEW ZEALAND

| | | | | |
|---|---|---|---|---|
| L.S.M. Miller | lbw b Trueman | 4 | c Trueman b Loader | 0 |
| J.W. D'Arcy | c Trueman b Laker | 14 | c Bailey b Trueman | 33 |
| W.R. Playle | c Graveney b Laker | 1 | b Loader | 3 |
| N.S. Harford | c and b Laker | 0 | c May b Lock | 3 |
| J.R. Reid* | c Loader b Lock | 6 | c Cowdrey b Trueman | 5 |
| B. Sutcliffe | b Lock | 18 | b Bailey | 0 |
| A.R. MacGibbon | c May b Lock | 2 | c May b Lock | 7 |
| J.C. Alabaster | c and b Lock | 0 | b Laker | 5 |
| E.C. Petrie† | c Trueman b Laker | 0 | not out | 4 |
| R.W. Blair | not out | 0 | b Lock | 0 |
| J.A. Hayes | c Cowdrey b Lock | 1 | c and b Lock | 14 |
| Extras | (LB 1) | 1 | | |
| **Total** | | **47** | | **74** |

| NEW ZEALAND | O | M | R | W | O | M | R | W | FALL OF WICKETS | | | |
|---|---|---|---|---|---|---|---|---|---|---|---|---|
| Hayes | 22 | 5 | 36 | 4 | | | | | | E | NZ | NZ |
| MacGibbon | 36·4 | 11 | 86 | 4 | | | | | *Wkt* | *1st* | *1st* | *2nd* |
| Blair | 25 | 6 | 57 | 0 | | | | | 1st | 54 | 4 | 11 |
| Reid | 24 | 12 | 41 | 1 | | | | | 2nd | 113 | 12 | 21 |
| Alabaster | 16 | 6 | 48 | 1 | | | | | 3rd | 139 | 12 | 34 |
| | | | | | | | | | 4th | 141 | 19 | 41 |
| ENGLAND | | | | | | | | | 5th | 201 | 25 | 44 |
| Trueman | 4 | 1 | 6 | 1 | 11 | 6 | 24 | 2 | 6th | 222 | 31 | 44 |
| Loader | 4 | 2 | 6 | 0 | 9 | 6 | 7 | 2 | 7th | 237 | 34 | 56 |
| Laker | 12 | 6 | 13 | 4 | 13 | 8 | 24 | 1 | 8th | 259 | 46 | 56 |
| Lock | 11·3 | 7 | 17 | 5 | 12·3 | 8 | 12 | 4 | 9th | 260 | 46 | 56 |
| Bailey | 1 | 0 | 4 | 0 | 5 | 1 | 7 | 1 | 10th | 269 | 47 | 74 |

Umpires: C.S. Elliott and D. Davies.

467

# ENGLAND v NEW ZEALAND 1958 (3rd Test)

Played at Headingley, Leeds, on 3 (*no play*), 4 (*no play*), 5, 7, 8 July.
Toss: New Zealand.   Result: ENGLAND won by an innings and 71 runs.
Debuts: England – C.A. Milton; New Zealand – J.T. Sparling.

England again won inside three days, there being no play on the first two. They omitted Richardson to try out possible opening partners for him on the forthcoming tour to Australia. Milton (Association Football) opened with his fellow double-international Smith (Rugby Union) and became the first Gloucestershire player since W.G. Grace in 1880 to score a hundred for England in his first Test. He was the first England player to be on the field throughout a Test match.

### NEW ZEALAND

| | | | | | |
|---|---|---|---|---|---|
| L.S.M. Miller | c Smith b Laker | 26 | lbw b Lock | | 18 |
| J.W. D'Arcy | c Smith b Trueman | 11 | b Lock | | 6 |
| N.S. Harford | c Cowdrey b Laker | 0 | lbw b Lock | | 0 |
| B. Sutcliffe | b Laker | 6 | lbw b Lock | | 0 |
| J.R. Reid* | b Lock | 3 | c Trueman b Laker | | 13 |
| W.R. Playle | c Milton b Lock | 0 | b Laker | | 18 |
| A.R. MacGibbon | b Laker | 3 | lbw b Lock | | 39 |
| J.T. Sparling† | not out | 9 | c May b Lock | | 18 |
| E.C. Petrie† | c Cowdrey b Lock | 5 | b Lock | | 3 |
| H.B. Cave | c Milton b Laker | 2 | c Cowdrey b Laker | | 2 |
| J.A. Hayes | c Evans b Lock | 1 | not out | | 0 |
| Extras | (LB 1) | 1 | (B 6, LB 6) | | 12 |
| **Total** | | **67** | | | **129** |

### ENGLAND

| | | |
|---|---|---|
| M.J.K. Smith | c Reid b MacGibbon | 3 |
| C.A. Milton | not out | 104 |
| T.W. Graveney | c and b Sparling | 31 |
| P.B.H. May* | not out | 113 |
| M.C. Cowdrey | ) | |
| T.E. Bailey | ) | |
| T.G. Evans† | ) | |
| G.A.R. Lock | ) did not bat | |
| F.S. Trueman | ) | |
| J.C. Laker | ) | |
| P.J. Loader | ) | |
| Extras | (B 5, LB 8, W 1, NB 2) | 16 |
| **Total** | (2 wickets declared) | **267** |

| ENGLAND | O | M | R | W | O | M | R | W | | FALL OF WICKETS | | | |
|---|---|---|---|---|---|---|---|---|---|---|---|---|---|
| Trueman | 11 | 5 | 18 | 1 | 14 | 6 | 22 | 0 | | | NZ | E | NZ |
| Loader | 5 | 2 | 10 | 0 | 13 | 7 | 14 | 0 | Wkt | | 1st | 1st | 2nd |
| Bailey | 3 | 0 | 7 | 0 | 3 | 2 | 3 | 0 | 1st | | 37 | 7 | 23 |
| Laker | 22 | 11 | 17 | 5 | 36 | 23 | 27 | 3 | 2nd | | 37 | 73 | 23 |
| Lock | 18·1 | 13 | 14 | 4 | 35·2 | 20 | 51 | 7 | 3rd | | 37 | – | 24 |
| | | | | | | | | | 4th | | 40 | – | 32 |
| NEW ZEALAND | | | | | | | | | 5th | | 46 | – | 42 |
| Hayes | 13 | 4 | 30 | 0 | | | | | 6th | | 46 | – | 88 |
| MacGibbon | 27 | 8 | 47 | 1 | | | | | 7th | | 49 | – | 121 |
| Reid | 26 | 7 | 54 | 0 | | | | | 8th | | 59 | – | 124 |
| Sparling | 23 | 2 | 78 | 1 | | | | | 9th | | 66 | – | 129 |
| Cave | 13 | 4 | 42 | 0 | | | | | 10th | | 67 | – | 129 |

Umpires: F.S. Lee and J.S. Buller.

# ENGLAND v NEW ZEALAND 1958 (4th Test)

Played at Old Trafford, Manchester, on 24, 25, 26, 28, 29 July.
Toss: New Zealand.   Result: ENGLAND won by an innings and 13 runs.
Debuts: England – E.R. Dexter, R. Illingworth, R. Subba Row.

England became the first team to win the first four Tests of a rubber in England – in spite of the loss of over eight hours to rain on the third and fourth days. Reid kept wicket on Friday and Saturday after Petrie had edged a hook on to his left ear while batting against Trueman. Lock's 29th wicket of this rubber was his hundredth in Tests.

## NEW ZEALAND

| | | | | |
|---|---|---|---|---|
| B. Sutcliffe | b Statham | 41 | b Statham | 28 |
| J.W. D'Arcy | lbw b Trueman | 1 | c Subba Row b Lock | 8 |
| N.S. Harford | lbw b Statham | 2 | b Illingworth | 4 |
| J.R. Reid* | c Trueman b Lock | 14 | c Watson b Lock | 8 |
| W.R. Playle | lbw b Illingworth | 15 | lbw b Lock | 1 |
| A.R. MacGibbon | c Evans b Statham | 66 | lbw b Lock | 1 |
| J.T. Sparling | c Evans b Statham | 50 | c and b Lock | 2 |
| E.C. Petrie† | retired hurt | 45 | c Statham b Illingworth | 9 |
| A.M. Moir | not out | 21 | c Evans b Lock | 12 |
| J.A. Hayes | b Trueman | 4 | not out | 5 |
| R.W. Blair | b Trueman | 2 | b Lock | 0 |
| Extras | (B 4, LB 2) | 6 | (B 5, LB 2) | 7 |
| **Total** | | **267** | | **85** |

## ENGLAND

| | | |
|---|---|---|
| P.E. Richardson | st Reid b Sparling | 74 |
| W. Watson | c MacGibbon b Moir | 66 |
| T.W. Graveney | c sub (J.C. Alabaster) b MacGibbon | 25 |
| P.B.H. May* | c Playle b MacGibbon | 101 |
| R. Subba Row | c Petrie b Blair | 9 |
| E.R. Dexter | lbw b Reid | 52 |
| T.G. Evans† | c Blair b Reid | 3 |
| R. Illingworth | not out | 3 |
| G.A.R. Lock | lbw b MacGibbon | 7 |
| F.S. Trueman | b Reid | 5 |
| J.B. Statham | did not bat | |
| Extras | (B 13, LB 4, W 1, NB 2) | 20 |
| **Total** | (9 wickets declared) | **365** |

| ENGLAND | O | M | R | W | O | M | R | W |
|---|---|---|---|---|---|---|---|---|
| Trueman | 29·5 | 4 | 67 | 3 | 2 | 1 | 11 | 0 |
| Statham | 33 | 10 | 71 | 4 | 9 | 4 | 12 | 1 |
| Dexter | 5 | 0 | 23 | 0 | | | | |
| Lock | 33 | 12 | 61 | 1 | 24 | 11 | 35 | 7 |
| Illingworth | 28 | 9 | 39 | 1 | 17 | 9 | 20 | 2 |

| NEW ZEALAND | O | M | R | W |
|---|---|---|---|---|
| Hayes | 19 | 4 | 51 | 0 |
| MacGibbon | 34 | 8 | 86 | 3 |
| Blair | 27 | 5 | 68 | 1 |
| Moir | 17 | 3 | 47 | 1 |
| Sparling | 21 | 7 | 46 | 1 |
| Reid | 11·3 | 2 | 47 | 3 |

FALL OF WICKETS

| | NZ | E | NZ |
|---|---|---|---|
| Wkt | 1st | 1st | 2nd |
| 1st | 15 | 126 | 36 |
| 2nd | 22 | 180 | 36 |
| 3rd | 62 | 193 | 46 |
| 4th | 62 | 248 | 49 |
| 5th | 117 | 330 | 49 |
| 6th | 166 | 337 | 51 |
| 7th | 227 | 351 | 60 |
| 8th | 257 | 360 | 78 |
| 9th | 267 | 365 | 80 |
| 10th | – | – | 85 |

Umpires: E. Davies and W.E. Phillipson.

# ENGLAND v NEW ZEALAND 1958 (5th Test)

Played at Kennington Oval, London, on 21, 22, 23 (*no play*), 25 (*no play*), 26 August.
Toss: New Zealand.   Result: MATCH DRAWN.
Debuts: Nil.

Rain frustrated England's attempt to win all five Tests of a rubber in England for the first time – only twelve hours of play was possible over the five days. Sparling ducked into a short-pitched ball from Trueman which bounced lower than he expected and he took no further part in the match. Lock's figures of 34 wickets at 7.47 runs each for the rubber are easily the record for this series.

## NEW ZEALAND

| | | | | | |
|---|---|---|---|---|---|
| L.S.M. Miller | c Lock b Laker | 25 | c Evans b Statham | | 4 |
| J.W. D'Arcy | c Milton b Bailey | 9 | c and b Lock | | 10 |
| T. Meale | c Lock b Trueman | 1 | c Cowdrey b Laker | | 3 |
| B. Sutcliffe | c Watson b Trueman | 11 | not out | | 18 |
| J.R. Reid* | b Lock | 27 | not out | | 51 |
| W.R. Playle | b Statham | 6 | | | |
| A.R. MacGibbon | b Bailey | 26 | | | |
| J.T. Sparling | retired hurt | 0 | | | |
| E.C. Petrie† | c Milton b Lock | 8 | | | |
| A.M. Moir | not out | 41 | | | |
| R.W. Blair | run out | 3 | | | |
| Extras | (LB 4) | 4 | (B 2, LB 3) | | 5 |
| **Total** | | **161** | (3 wickets) | | **91** |

## ENGLAND

| | | |
|---|---|---|
| P.E. Richardson | b Blair | 28 |
| C.A. Milton | lbw b MacGibbon | 36 |
| W. Watson | b MacGibbon | 10 |
| P.B.H. May* | c Petrie b Blair | 9 |
| M.C. Cowdrey | c Playle b Reid | 25 |
| T.E. Bailey | c Petrie b MacGibbon | 14 |
| T.G. Evans† | c Petrie b MacGibbon | 12 |
| G.A.R. Lock | c Reid b Moir | 25 |
| J.C. Laker | c Blair b Reid | 15 |
| F.S. Trueman | not out | 39 |
| J.B. Statham | did not bat | |
| Extras | (B 2, LB 4) | 6 |
| **Total** | (9 wickets declared) | **219** |

| ENGLAND | O | M | R | W | O | M | R | W | | FALL OF WICKETS | | |
|---|---|---|---|---|---|---|---|---|---|---|---|---|
| Trueman | 16 | 3 | 41 | 2 | 6 | 5 | 3 | 0 | | NZ | E | NZ |
| Statham | 18 | 6 | 21 | 1 | 7 | 0 | 26 | 1 | *Wkt* | *1st* | *1st* | *2nd* |
| Bailey | 14 | 3 | 32 | 2 | | | | | 1st | 19 | 39 | 9 |
| Laker | 14 | 3 | 44 | 1 | 20 | 10 | 25 | 1 | 2nd | 24 | 62 | 17 |
| Lock | 13 | 6 | 19 | 2 | 18 | 11 | 20 | 1 | 3rd | 40 | 85 | 21 |
| Milton | | | | | 4 | 2 | 12 | 0 | 4th | 46 | 87 | – |
| | | | | | | | | | 5th | 55 | 109 | – |
| NEW ZEALAND | | | | | | | | | 6th | 93 | 125 | – |
| Blair | 26 | 5 | 85 | 2 | | | | | 7th | 105 | 162 | – |
| MacGibbon | 27 | 4 | 65 | 4 | | | | | 8th | 132 | 162 | – |
| Reid | 7·5 | 2 | 11 | 2 | | | | | 9th | 161 | 219 | – |
| Moir | 8 | 1 | 52 | 1 | | | | | 10th | – | – | – |

Umpires: F.S. Lee and E. Davies.

# INDIA v WEST INDIES 1958-59 (1st Test)

Played at Brabourne Stadium, Bombay, on 28, 29, 30 November, 2, 3 December.
Toss: West Indies.   Result: MATCH DRAWN.
Debuts: India – C.G. Borde, G.M. Guard, M.S. Hardikar; West Indies – B.F. Butcher, W.W. Hall.

Sobers and Butcher each had leg injuries and batted with a runner during their unfinished fifth-wicket partnership of 134. Gupte's leg-breaks acquired their hundredth wicket in Test matches. Kanhai's two catches were taken while keeping wicket in the second innings.

## WEST INDIES

| | | | | |
|---|---|--:|---|--:|
| J.K. Holt | c Tamhane b Ramchand | 16 | c Hardikar b Guard | 24 |
| C.C. Hunte | c Guard b Ramchand | 0 | c Nadkarni b Guard | 10 |
| G.St A. Sobers | c and b Guard | 25 | not out | 142 |
| R.B. Kanhai | lbw b Hardikar | 66 | c Roy b Gupte | 22 |
| O.G. Smith | c Ramchand b Nadkarni | 63 | c Roy b Gupte | 58 |
| B.F. Butcher | lbw b Gupte | 28 | not out | 64 |
| F.C.M. Alexander*† | st Tamhane b Gupte | 5 | | |
| E. St E. Atkinson | b Gupte | 1 | | |
| S. Ramadhin | c Nadkarni b Gupte | 9 | | |
| W.W. Hall | not out | 12 | | |
| R. Gilchrist | b Nadkarni | 1 | | |
| Extras | (B 1) | 1 | (LB 3) | 3 |
| **Total** | | **227** | **(4 wickets declared)** | **323** |

## INDIA

| | | | | |
|---|---|--:|---|--:|
| P. Roy | b Hall | 18 | c and b Hall | 90 |
| N.J. Contractor | c Atkinson b Hall | 0 | run out | 6 |
| P.R. Umrigar* | b Gilchrist | 55 | b Gilchrist | 36 |
| V.L. Manjrekar | c Sobers b Hall | 0 | c Kanhai b Gilchrist | 23 |
| R.G. Nadkarni | b Atkinson | 2 | c Kanhai b Atkinson | 7 |
| G.S. Ramchand | c Alexander b Atkinson | 48 | not out | 67 |
| M.S. Hardikar | lbw b Gilchrist | 0 | not out | 32 |
| C.G. Borde | run out | 7 | | |
| N.S. Tamhane* | not out | 9 | | |
| G.M. Guard | b Gilchrist | 4 | | |
| S.P. Gupte | c Sobers b Gilchrist | 1 | | |
| Extras | (B 3, LB 5) | 8 | (B 19, LB 2, NB 7) | 28 |
| **Total** | | **152** | **(5 wickets)** | **289** |

| INDIA | O | M | R | W | O | M | R | W |
|---|--:|--:|--:|--:|--:|--:|--:|--:|
| Guard | 15 | 7 | 19 | 1 | 17 | 2 | 69 | 2 |
| Ramchand | 12 | 2 | 31 | 2 | 10 | 3 | 22 | 0 |
| Umrigar | 3 | 0 | 12 | 0 | 9 | 0 | 22 | 0 |
| Gupte | 33 | 9 | 86 | 4 | 35 | 4 | 111 | 2 |
| Borde | 10 | 1 | 29 | 0 | 16 | 3 | 31 | 0 |
| Nadkarni | 21·1 | 7 | 40 | 2 | 15 | 3 | 29 | 0 |
| Hardikar | 7 | 5 | 9 | 1 | 10 | 2 | 36 | 0 |
| WEST INDIES | | | | | | | | |
| Gilchrist | 23·2 | 8 | 39 | 4 | 41 | 13 | 75 | 2 |
| Hall | 14 | 4 | 35 | 3 | 30 | 10 | 72 | 1 |
| Atkinson | 19 | 10 | 21 | 2 | 29 | 11 | 56 | 1 |
| Ramadhin | 9 | 0 | 30 | 0 | 11 | 4 | 20 | 0 |
| Sobers | 3 | 0 | 19 | 0 | 3 | 0 | 8 | 0 |
| Smith | | | | | 18 | 4 | 30 | 0 |

FALL OF WICKETS

| | WI | I | WI | I |
|---|--:|--:|--:|--:|
| *Wkt* | *1st* | *1st* | *2nd* | *2nd* |
| 1st | 2 | 0 | 27 | 27 |
| 2nd | 36 | 37 | 37 | 88 |
| 3rd | 50 | 37 | 70 | 136 |
| 4th | 118 | 40 | 189 | 159 |
| 5th | 172 | 120 | – | 204 |
| 6th | 200 | 120 | – | – |
| 7th | 202 | 132 | – | – |
| 8th | 206 | 138 | – | – |
| 9th | 226 | 148 | – | – |
| 10th | 227 | 152 | – | – |

Umpires: M.G. Vijayasarathi and J.R. Patel.

# INDIA v WEST INDIES 1958-59 (2nd Test)

Played at Green Park, Kanpur, on 12, 13, 14, 16, 17 December.
Toss: West Indies.　Result: WEST INDIES won by 203 runs.
Debuts: India – V.B. Ranjane; West Indies – J.S. Solomon.

Gupte (leg-breaks) became the first Indian to take nine wickets in an innings of a Test match. West Indies won with 78 minutes to spare after Hall had taken eleven wickets in his second Test and Sobers had scored his fifth hundred in five matches. Run out for 198 after batting for 340 minutes and hitting 28 fours, Sobers set a sixth-wicket partnership record for this series by adding 163 with Solomon.

## WEST INDIES

| | | | | | |
|---|---|---|---|---|---|
| J.K. Holt | lbw b Gupte | 31 | | c Borde b Ramchand | 0 |
| C.C. Hunte | c Borde b Gupte | 29 | | c and b Umrigar | 0 |
| G. St A. Sobers | c Hardikar b Gupte | 4 | (4) | run out | 198 |
| R.B. Kanhai | b Gupte | 0 | (3) | c Tamhane b Gupte | 41 |
| O.G. Smith | c and b Gupte | 20 | | run out | 7 |
| B.F. Butcher | b Gupte | 2 | | c Tamhane b Ramchand | 60 |
| J.S. Solomon | lbw b Gupte | 45 | | run out | 86 |
| F.C.M. Alexander*† | c Hardikar b Gupte | 70 | | not out | 45 |
| L.R. Gibbs | b Ranjane | 16 | | | |
| W.W. Hall | c Tamhane b Gupte | 0 | | | |
| J.O. Taylor | not out | 0 | | | |
| Extras | (B 1, LB 2, NB 2) | 5 | | (LB 6) | 6 |
| **Total** | | **222** | | (7 wickets declared) | **443** |

## INDIA

| | | | | | |
|---|---|---|---|---|---|
| P. Roy | lbw b Sobers | 46 | | run out | 45 |
| N.J. Contractor | lbw b Sobers | 41 | | b Taylor | 50 |
| P.R. Umrigar | c Holt b Hall | 57 | | c Smith b Hall | 34 |
| V.L. Manjrekar | lbw b Taylor | 30 | | run out | 31 |
| C.G. Borde | c Alexander b Hall | 0 | | c Alexander b Taylor | 13 |
| G.S. Ramchand | c Alexander b Hall | 4 | | b Hall | 0 |
| M.S. Hardikar | b Hall | 13 | | b Hall | 11 |
| N.S. Tamhane† | c Holt b Hall | 0 | | c Solomon b Hall | 20 |
| V.B. Ranjane | b Taylor | 3 | | b Taylor | 12 |
| Ghulam Ahmed* | not out | 0 | | b Hall | 0 |
| S.P. Gupte | b Hall | 0 | | not out | 8 |
| Extras | (LB 17, NB 11) | 28 | | (B 4, LB 1, NB 11) | 16 |
| **Total** | | **222** | | | **240** |

| INDIA | O | M | R | W | O | M | R | W | | FALL OF WICKETS | | | |
|---|---|---|---|---|---|---|---|---|---|---|---|---|---|
| | | | | | | | | | | WI | I | WI | I |
| Ranjane | 18 | 6 | 35 | 1 | | | | | *Wkt* | *1st* | *1st* | *2nd* | *2nd* |
| Ramchand | 10 | 3 | 22 | 0 | 40 | 6 | 114 | 2 | 1st | 55 | 93 | 0 | 99 |
| Gupte | 34·3 | 11 | 102 | 9 | 23 | 2 | 121 | 1 | 2nd | 63 | 118 | 0 | 107 |
| Ghulam Ahmed | 10 | 3 | 29 | 0 | 30 | 8 | 81 | 0 | 3rd | 65 | 182 | 73 | 173 |
| Borde | 13 | 4 | 29 | 0 | 5 | 0 | 15 | 0 | 4th | 74 | 184 | 83 | 178 |
| Umrigar | | | | | 28 | 4 | 96 | 1 | 5th | 76 | 191 | 197 | 182 |
| Hardikar | | | | | 1 | 0 | 10 | 0 | 6th | 88 | 210 | 360 | 194 |
| | | | | | | | | | 7th | 188 | 211 | 443 | 204 |
| WEST INDIES | | | | | | | | | 8th | 220 | 222 | – | 227 |
| Hall | 28·4 | 4 | 50 | 6 | 32 | 12 | 76 | 5 | 9th | 222 | 222 | – | 227 |
| Taylor | 18 | 7 | 38 | 2 | 30·1 | 11 | 68 | 3 | 10th | 222 | 222 | – | 240 |
| Gibbs | 21 | 8 | 28 | 0 | 9 | 4 | 33 | 0 | | | | | |
| Sobers | 24 | 4 | 62 | 2 | 21 | 10 | 29 | 0 | | | | | |
| Smith | 8 | 1 | 14 | 0 | 6 | 0 | 12 | 0 | | | | | |
| Solomon | 2 | 1 | 2 | 0 | 3 | 2 | 6 | 0 | | | | | |

Umpires: J.R. Patel and Mahomed Yunus.

# INDIA v WEST INDIES 1958-59 (3rd Test)

Played at Eden Gardens, Calcutta, on 31 December, 1, 3, 4 January.
Toss: West Indies.   Result: WEST INDIES won by an innings and 336 runs.
Debuts: India – R.B. Kenny, R. Surendranath.

Kanhai scored his maiden Test century and went on to record what is still the highest score in any Test in India in 6½ hours with 42 fours. Sobers' hundred was his sixth in ten innings in six Tests, and his third of this rubber.

## WEST INDIES

| | | |
|---|---|---|
| J.K. Holt | c Contractor b Surendranath | 5 |
| C.C. Hunte | c Surendranath b Gupte | 23 |
| R.B. Kanhai | c Umrigar b Surendranath | 256 |
| O.G. Smith | b Umrigar | 34 |
| B.F. Butcher | lbw b Ghulam Ahmed | 103 |
| G. St A. Sobers | not out | 106 |
| J.S. Solomon | not out | 69 |
| F.C.M. Alexander*† | ) | |
| S. Ramadhin | ) did not bat | |
| W.W. Hall | ) | |
| R. Gilchrist | ) | |
| Extras | (B 8, LB 9, NB 1) | 18 |
| **Total** | (5 wickets declared) | **614** |

## INDIA

| | | | | |
|---|---|---|---|---|
| P. Roy | c Solomon b Gilchrist | 11 | c Alexander b Hall | 0 |
| N.J. Contractor | lbw b Ramadhin | 4 | b Gilchrist | 6 |
| J.M. Ghorpade | c Alexander b Gilchrist | 7 | (6) b Sobers | 16 |
| R.B. Kenny | c Alexander b Hall | 16 | (5) b Hall | 0 |
| P.R. Umrigar | not out | 44 | (3) c Alexander b Hall | 2 |
| V.L. Manjrekar | b Hall | 0 | (4) not out | 58 |
| D.G. Phadkar | c Sobers b Gilchrist | 3 | b Gilchrist | 35 |
| N.S. Tamhane† | c Sobers b Hall | 0 | (9) b Gilchrist | 0 |
| R. Surendranath | run out | 8 | (8) c Alexander b Gilchrist | 3 |
| Ghulam Ahmed* | lbw b Sobers | 4 | b Gilchrist | 0 |
| S.P. Gupte | b Ramadhin | 12 | b Gilchrist | 15 |
| Extras | (B 2, LB 8, W 1, NB 4) | 15 | (B 3, NB 16) | 19 |
| **Total** | | **124** | | **154** |

| INDIA | O | M | R | W | O | M | R | W | | FALL OF WICKETS | | |
|---|---|---|---|---|---|---|---|---|---|---|---|---|
| Phadkar | 43 | 6 | 173 | 0 | | | | | | WI | I | I |
| Surendranath | 46 | 8 | 168 | 2 | | | | | *Wkt* | *1st* | *1st* | *2nd* |
| Gupte | 39 | 8 | 119 | 1 | | | | | 1st | 12 | 24 | 5 |
| Ghulam Ahmed | 16·1 | 1 | 52 | 1 | | | | | 2nd | 72 | 26 | 7 |
| Umrigar | 16 | 1 | 62 | 1 | | | | | 3rd | 180 | 52 | 10 |
| Ghorpade | 2 | 0 | 22 | 0 | | | | | 4th | 397 | 52 | 17 |
| | | | | | | | | | 5th | 454 | 52 | 44 |
| WEST INDIES | | | | | | | | | 6th | – | 57 | 115 |
| Gilchrist | 23 | 13 | 18 | 3 | 21 | 7 | 55 | 6 | 7th | – | 58 | 131 |
| Hall | 15 | 6 | 31 | 3 | 18 | 5 | 55 | 3 | 8th | – | 89 | 131 |
| Ramadhin | 16·5 | 8 | 27 | 2 | 8 | 3 | 14 | 0 | 9th | – | 99 | 131 |
| Smith | 2 | 1 | 1 | 0 | | | | | 10th | – | 124 | 154 |
| Sobers | 6 | 0 | 32 | 1 | 2 | 0 | 11 | 1 | | | | |

Umpires: Mahomed Yunus and N.D. Nagarwalla.

# INDIA v WEST INDIES 1958-59 (4th Test)

Played at Corporation Stadium, Madras, on 21, 22, 24, 25, 26 January.
Toss: West Indies.   Result: WEST INDIES won by 295 runs.
Debuts: India – A.K. Sengupta.

Umrigar resigned the captaincy shortly before the start of this match following a disagreement with the Indian selectors. Mankad was appointed in his place but illness prevented him from taking part after the first innings in what proved to be his final Test. Butcher scored his second consecutive hundred and Kanhai missed his by a fraction of a run.

### WEST INDIES

| | | | | | |
|---|---|---|---|---|---|
| C.C. Hunte | b Mankad | 32 | c Surendranath b Gupte | | 30 |
| J.K. Holt | lbw b Gupte | 63 | not out | | 81 |
| R.B. Kanhai | run out | 99 | lbw b Gupte | | 14 |
| G. St A. Sobers | c Gupte b Mankad | 29 | c Joshi b Borde | | 9 |
| O.G. Smith | b Mankad | 0 | c Joshi b Gupte | | 5 |
| B.F. Butcher | b Ramchand | 142 | lbw b Gupte | | 16 |
| J.S. Solomon | lbw b Borde | 43 | not out | | 8 |
| F.C.M. Alexander*† | run out | 11 | | | |
| E. St E. Atkinson | not out | 29 | | | |
| W.W. Hall | lbw b Mankad | 25 | | | |
| R. Gilchrist | c Roy b Borde | 7 | | | |
| Extras | (B 8, LB 11, NB 1) | 20 | (B 5) | | 5 |
| **Total** | | **500** | (5 wickets declared) | | **168** |

### INDIA

| | | | | | |
|---|---|---|---|---|---|
| P. Roy | b Sobers | 49 | c Kanhai b Hall | | 16 |
| A.K. Sengupta | c Sobers b Hall | 1 | (4) c Alexander b Gilchrist | | 8 |
| P.G. Joshi† | c Alexander b Gilchrist | 17 | (8) c Alexander b Hall | | 3 |
| N.J. Contractor | run out | 22 | (2) c Alexander b Gilchrist | | 3 |
| P.R. Umrigar | c Alexander b Hall | 4 | (3) b Sobers | | 29 |
| G.S. Ramchand | c Gilchrist b Atkinson | 30 | b Gilchrist | | 1 |
| A.G. Kripal Singh | c Hall b Sobers | 53 | c Alexander b Hall | | 9 |
| V.M.H. Mankad* | b Gilchrist | 4 | absent ill | | – |
| C.G. Borde | c Smith b Sobers | 0 | (5) c Butcher b Sobers | | 56 |
| R. Surendranath | lbw b Sobers | 0 | (9) c Hunte b Smith | | 8 |
| S.P. Gupte | not out | 0 | (10) not out | | 2 |
| Extras | (B 14, LB 5, NB 23) | 42 | (B 5, LB 4, NB 7) | | 16 |
| **Total** | | **222** | | | **151** |

| INDIA | O | M | R | W | O | M | R | W |
|---|---|---|---|---|---|---|---|---|
| Ramchand | 22 | 5 | 45 | 1 | 6 | 2 | 13 | 0 |
| Surendranath | 26 | 5 | 77 | 0 | 7 | 3 | 13 | 0 |
| Umrigar | 8 | 2 | 16 | 0 | 11 | 3 | 25 | 0 |
| Gupte | 58 | 15 | 166 | 1 | 30 | 6 | 78 | 4 |
| Mankad | 38 | 6 | 95 | 4 | | | | |
| Borde | 27 | 2 | 80 | 2 | 22 | 11 | 34 | 1 |
| Kripal Singh | 2 | 1 | 1 | 0 | | | | |
| **WEST INDIES** | | | | | | | | |
| Gilchrist | 18 | 9 | 44 | 2 | 17 | 9 | 36 | 3 |
| Hall | 22 | 7 | 57 | 2 | 23 | 8 | 49 | 3 |
| Atkinson | 15 | 6 | 31 | 1 | 9 | 5 | 7 | 0 |
| Sobers | 18·1 | 8 | 26 | 4 | 18 | 8 | 39 | 2 |
| Smith | 5 | 0 | 22 | 0 | 3 | 1 | 4 | 1 |

FALL OF WICKETS

| Wkt | WI 1st | I 1st | WI 2nd | I 2nd |
|---|---|---|---|---|
| 1st | 61 | 11 | 70 | 11 |
| 2nd | 152 | 60 | 108 | 19 |
| 3rd | 206 | 102 | 123 | 45 |
| 4th | 206 | 121 | 130 | 97 |
| 5th | 248 | 131 | 150 | 98 |
| 6th | 349 | 135 | – | 114 |
| 7th | 384 | 147 | – | 118 |
| 8th | 453 | 221 | – | 149 |
| 9th | 489 | 222 | – | 151 |
| 10th | 500 | 222 | – | – |

Umpires: M.G. Vijayasarathi and A.R. Joshi.

# INDIA v WEST INDIES 1958-59 (5th Test)

Played at Feroz Shah Kotla, Delhi, on 6, 7, 8, 10, 11 February.
Toss: India.   Result: MATCH DRAWN.
Debuts: India – R.B. Desai.

West Indies scored the highest total in any Test match in India. They would have needed only 47 runs to gain their fourth successive win in this rubber, but Borde batted until the last possible over before hitting his wicket when just four runs short of becoming the second Indian to score a hundred in each innings of a Test.

## INDIA

| Player | Dismissal | Score | 2nd innings | Score |
|---|---|---|---|---|
| P. Roy | c Solomon b Gilchrist | 1 | c Holt b Smith | 58 |
| N.J. Contractor | lbw b Hall | 92 | run out | 4 |
| P.R. Umrigar | b Hall | 76 | absent hurt | – |
| V.L. Manjrekar | c Alexander b Hall | 6 | (10) not out | 0 |
| C.G. Borde | c Alexander b Smith | 109 | (4) hit wkt b Gilchrist | 96 |
| D.K. Gaekwad | c Holt b Gilchrist | 6 | (3) c Hunte b Smith | 52 |
| H.R. Adhikari* | c Alexander b Smith | 63 | (5) c sub (J.O. Taylor) b Smith | 40 |
| V.M.H. Mankad | c sub (L.R. Gibbs) b Gilchrist | 21 | (6) b Smith | 0 |
| N.S. Tamhane† | c Gilchrist b Smith | 3 | (7) hit wkt b Smith | 5 |
| S.P. Gupte | b Hall | 5 | (8) b Gilchrist | 0 |
| R.B. Desai | not out | 2 | (9) b Gilchrist | 5 |
| Extras | (B 6, LB 15, NB 10) | 31 | (B 2, LB 6, NB 7) | 15 |
| **Total** | | **415** | | **275** |

## WEST INDIES

|  |  |  |
|---|---|---|
| C.C. Hunte | lbw b Adhikari | 92 |
| J.K. Holt | c Roy b Desai | 123 |
| R.B. Kanhai | lbw b Desai | 40 |
| B.F. Butcher | lbw b Adhikari | 71 |
| O.G. Smith | c Tamhane b Desai | 100 |
| J.S. Solomon | not out | 100 |
| G. St A. Sobers | c Tamhane b Desai | 44 |
| F.C.M. Alexander*† | run out | 25 |
| E.St E. Atkinson | c and b Adhikari | 37 |
| W.W. Hall | not out | 0 |
| R. Gilchrist | did not bat | |
| Extras | (B 2, LB 8, W 1, NB 1) | 12 |
| **Total** | (8 wickets declared) | **644** |

| WEST INDIES | O | M | R | W | O | M | R | W |
|---|---|---|---|---|---|---|---|---|
| Gilchrist | 30·3 | 8 | 90 | 3 | 24·2 | 6 | 62 | 3 |
| Hall | 26 | 4 | 66 | 4 | 13 | 5 | 39 | 0 |
| Atkinson | 14 | 4 | 44 | 0 | 1 | 0 | 4 | 0 |
| Smith | 40 | 7 | 94 | 3 | 42 | 19 | 90 | 5 |
| Sobers | 24 | 3 | 66 | 0 | | | | |
| Solomon | 7 | 2 | 24 | 0 | 21 | 9 | 44 | 0 |
| Butcher | | | | | 6 | 1 | 17 | 0 |
| Hunte | | | | | 4 | 2 | 4 | 0 |
| INDIA | | | | | | | | |
| Desai | 49 | 10 | 169 | 4 | | | | |
| Roy | 2 | 0 | 12 | 0 | | | | |
| Mankad | 55 | 12 | 167 | 0 | | | | |
| Gupte | 60 | 16 | 144 | 0 | | | | |
| Adhikari | 26 | 2 | 68 | 3 | | | | |
| Gaekwad | 1 | 0 | 8 | 0 | | | | |
| Contractor | 4 | 1 | 11 | 0 | | | | |
| Borde | 17 | 3 | 53 | 0 | | | | |

### FALL OF WICKETS

| Wkt | I 1st | WI 1st | I 2nd |
|---|---|---|---|
| 1st | 6 | 159 | 5 |
| 2nd | 143 | 244 | 98 |
| 3rd | 170 | 263 | 135 |
| 4th | 208 | 390 | 243 |
| 5th | 242 | 455 | 247 |
| 6th | 376 | 524 | 260 |
| 7th | 399 | 565 | 264 |
| 8th | 407 | 635 | 274 |
| 9th | 413 | – | 275 |
| 10th | 415 | – | – |

Umpires: S.K. Ganguli and N.D. Nagarwalla.

## AUSTRALIA v ENGLAND 1958-59 (1st Test)

Played at Woolloongabba, Brisbane, on 5, 6, 8, 9, 10 December.
Toss: England.   Result: AUSTRALIA won by eight wickets.
Debuts: Australia – N.C. O'Neill.

Bailey batted 357 minutes before reaching his fifty and this remains the slowest recorded half-century in all first-class cricket. His innings of 68 endured for 458 minutes at an average of slightly less than nine runs per hour. Out of 425 balls bowled to him, Bailey scored off 40: 4 fours, 3 threes, 10 twos and 23 singles.

### ENGLAND

| | | | | |
|---|---|---|---|---|
| P.E. Richardson | c Mackay b Davidson | 11 | c and b Benaud | 8 |
| C.A. Milton | b Meckiff | 5 | c Grout b Davidson | 17 |
| T.W. Graveney | c Grout b Davidson | 19 | (4) run out | 36 |
| P.B.H. May* | c Grout b Meckiff | 26 | (5) lbw b Benaud | |
| M.C. Cowdrey | c Kline b Meckiff | 13 | (6) c Kline b Meckiff | 28 |
| T.E. Bailey | st Grout b Benaud | 27 | (3) b Mackay | 68 |
| T.G. Evans† | c Burge b Davidson | 4 | lbw b Davidson | 4 |
| G.A.R. Lock | c Davidson b Benaud | 5 | b Meckiff | |
| J.C. Laker | c Burke b Benaud | 13 | b Benaud | 13 |
| J.B. Statham | c Grout b Mackay | 2 | c McDonald b Benaud | |
| P.J. Loader | not out | 6 | not out | 8 |
| Extras | (LB 1, W 1, NB 1) | 3 | (B 10, LB 4) | 14 |
| **Total** | | **134** | | **198** |

### AUSTRALIA

| | | | | |
|---|---|---|---|---|
| C.C. McDonald | c Graveney b Bailey | 42 | c Statham b Laker | 1 |
| J.W. Burke | c Evans b Loader | 20 | not out | 28 |
| R.N. Harvey | lbw b Loader | 14 | c Milton b Lock | 23 |
| N.C. O'Neill | c Graveney b Bailey | 34 | not out | 71 |
| P.J.P. Burge | c Cowdrey b Bailey | 2 | | |
| K.D. Mackay | c Evans b Laker | 16 | | |
| R. Benaud* | lbw b Loader | 16 | | |
| A.K. Davidson | lbw b Laker | 25 | | |
| A.T.W. Grout† | b Statham | 2 | | |
| I. Meckiff | b Loader | 5 | | |
| L.F. Kline | not out | 4 | | |
| Extras | (B 4, LB 1, NB 1) | 6 | (B 2, LB 3, NB 5) | 10 |
| **Total** | | **186** | (2 wickets) | **147** |

| AUSTRALIA | O | M | R | W | O | M | R | W | | FALL OF WICKETS | | | |
|---|---|---|---|---|---|---|---|---|---|---|---|---|---|
| Davidson | 16 | 4 | 36 | 3 | 28 | 12 | 30 | 2 | | E | A | E | A |
| Meckiff | 17 | 5 | 33 | 3 | 19 | 7 | 30 | 2 | *Wkt* | *1st* | *1st* | *2nd* | *2nd* |
| Mackay | 8 | 1 | 16 | 1 | 9 | 6 | 7 | 1 | 1st | 16 | 55 | 28 | 20 |
| Benaud | 18·4 | 9 | 46 | 3 | 39·2 | 10 | 66 | 4 | 2nd | 16 | 65 | 34 | 58 |
| Kline | | | | | 14 | 4 | 34 | 0 | 3rd | 62 | 88 | 96 | – |
| Burke | | | | | 10 | 5 | 17 | 0 | 4th | 75 | 94 | 102 | – |
| ENGLAND | | | | | | | | | 5th | 79 | 122 | 153 | – |
| Statham | 20 | 2 | 57 | 1 | 6 | 1 | 13 | 0 | 6th | 83 | 136 | 161 | – |
| Loader | 19 | 4 | 56 | 4 | 9 | 1 | 27 | 0 | 7th | 92 | 162 | 169 | – |
| Bailey | 13 | 2 | 35 | 3 | 5 | 1 | 21 | 0 | 8th | 112 | 165 | 190 | – |
| Laker | 10·1 | 3 | 15 | 2 | 17 | 3 | 39 | 1 | 9th | 116 | 178 | 198 | – |
| Lock | 10 | 4 | 17 | 0 | 14·7 | 5 | 37 | 1 | 10th | 134 | 186 | 198 | – |

Umpires: M.J. McInnes and C. Hoy.

# AUSTRALIA v ENGLAND 1958-59 (2nd Test)

Played at Melbourne Cricket Ground on 31 December, 1, 2, 3, 5 January.
Toss: England.   Result: AUSTRALIA won by eight wickets.
Debuts: Nil.

Davidson took the wickets of Richardson, Watson and Graveney with the first, fourth and fifth balls of his second over. May scored the first hundred by an England captain in Australia since A.C. MacLaren in 1901-02, and Harvey scored Australia's first hundred against England for eleven Tests. England's total of 87 was their lowest in Australia since 1903-04.

## ENGLAND

| | | | | |
|---|---|---|---|---|
| P.E. Richardson | c Grout b Davidson | 3 | c Harvey b Meckiff | 2 |
| T.E. Bailey | c Benaud b Meckiff | 48 | c Burke b Meckiff | 14 |
| W. Watson | b Davidson | 0 | c Davidson | 7 |
| T.W. Graveney | lbw b Davidson | 0 | c Davidson b Meckiff | 3 |
| P.B.H. May* | b Meckiff | 113 | c Davidson b Meckiff | 17 |
| M.C. Cowdrey | c Grout b Davidson | 44 | c Grout b Meckiff | 12 |
| T.G. Evans† | c Davidson b Meckiff | 4 | run out | 11 |
| G.A.R. Lock | st Grout b Benaud | 5 | c and b Davidson | 6 |
| C. Laker | not out | 22 | c Harvey b Davidson | 3 |
| J.B. Statham | b Davidson | 13 | not out | 8 |
| J.J. Loader | b Davidson | 1 | b Meckiff | 0 |
| Extras | (B 1, LB 2, W 3) | 6 | (B 1, LB 1, NB 2) | 4 |
| **Total** | | **259** | | **87** |

## AUSTRALIA

| | | | | |
|---|---|---|---|---|
| C.C. McDonald | c Graveney b Statham | 47 | lbw b Statham | 5 |
| J.W. Burke | b Statham | 3 | not out | 18 |
| R.N. Harvey | b Loader | 167 | (4) not out | 7 |
| N.C. O'Neill | c Evans b Statham | 37 | | |
| K.D. Mackay | c Evans b Statham | 18 | | |
| R.B. Simpson | lbw b Loader | 0 | | |
| R. Benaud* | lbw b Statham | 0 | | |
| A.K. Davidson | b Statham | 24 | | |
| A.T.W. Grout† | c May b Loader | 8 | (3) st Evans b Laker | 12 |
| Meckiff | b Statham | 0 | | |
| L.F. Kline | not out | 1 | | |
| Extras | (LB 3) | 3 | | |
| **Total** | | **308** | (2 wickets) | **42** |

| AUSTRALIA | O | M | R | W | O | M | R | W |
|---|---|---|---|---|---|---|---|---|
| Davidson | 25·5 | 7 | 64 | 6 | 15 | 2 | 41 | 3 |
| Meckiff | 24 | 4 | 69 | 3 | 15·2 | 3 | 38 | 6 |
| Mackay | 9 | 2 | 16 | 0 | | | | |
| Benaud | 29 | 7 | 61 | 1 | 1 | 0 | 4 | 0 |
| Kline | 11 | 2 | 43 | 0 | | | | |
| **ENGLAND** | | | | | | | | |
| Statham | 28 | 6 | 57 | 7 | 5 | 1 | 11 | 1 |
| Loader | 27·2 | 4 | 97 | 3 | 5 | 1 | 13 | 0 |
| Bailey | 16 | 0 | 50 | 0 | | | | |
| Laker | 12 | 1 | 47 | 0 | 4 | 1 | 7 | 1 |
| Lock | 17 | 2 | 54 | 0 | 3·1 | 1 | 11 | 0 |

### FALL OF WICKETS

| | E | A | E | A |
|---|---|---|---|---|
| Wkt | 1st | 1st | 2nd | 2nd |
| 1st | 7 | 11 | 3 | 6 |
| 2nd | 7 | 137 | 14 | 26 |
| 3rd | 7 | 255 | 21 | – |
| 4th | 92 | 257 | 27 | – |
| 5th | 210 | 261 | 44 | – |
| 6th | 218 | 262 | 57 | – |
| 7th | 218 | 295 | 71 | – |
| 8th | 233 | 300 | 75 | – |
| 9th | 253 | 300 | 80 | – |
| 10th | 259 | 308 | 87 | – |

Umpires: M.J. McInnes and R. Wright.

# AUSTRALIA v ENGLAND 1958-59 (3rd Test)

Played at Sydney Cricket Ground on 9, 10, 12, 13, 14, 15 January.
Toss: England.   Result: MATCH DRAWN.
Debuts: Australia – K.N. Slater; England – R. Swetman.

Set to score 150 runs in 110 minutes on a wearing pitch, Australia were content to draw. Cowdrey's hundred took 362 minutes and was the slowest for either country in Australia-England Tests until R.A. Woolmer took 394 minutes to reach his century at The Oval in 1975 (*Test No. 763*). Rain delayed the start of play on the second day until 4.15 p.m.

## ENGLAND

| | | | | |
|---|---|--:|---|--:|
| T.E. Bailey | lbw b Meckiff | 8 | c sub (R.B. Simpson) b Benaud | 25 |
| C.A. Milton | c Meckiff b Davidson | 8 | c Davidson b Benaud | 8 |
| T.W. Graveney | c Harvey b Benaud | 33 | lbw b Davidson | 22 |
| P.B.H. May* | c Mackay b Slater | 42 | b Burke | 92 |
| M.C. Cowdrey | c Harvey b Benaud | 34 | not out | 100 |
| E.R. Dexter | lbw b Slater | 1 | c Grout b Benaud | 11 |
| R. Swetman† | c Mackay b Benaud | 41 | lbw b Burke | 5 |
| G.A.R. Lock | lbw b Mackay | 21 | (9) not out | 11 |
| F.S. Trueman | c Burke b Benaud | 18 | (8) st Grout b Benaud | 0 |
| J.C. Laker | c Harvey b Benaud | 2 | | |
| J.B. Statham | not out | 0 | | |
| Extras | (B 4, LB 5, W 2) | 11 | (B 11, LB 1, W 1) | 13 |
| **Total** | | **219** | (7 wickets declared) | **287** |

## AUSTRALIA

| | | | | |
|---|---|--:|---|--:|
| C.C. McDonald | c Graveney b Lock | 40 | b Laker | 16 |
| J.W. Burke | c Lock b Laker | 12 | b Laker | 7 |
| R.N. Harvey | b Laker | 7 | not out | 18 |
| N.C. O'Neill | c Swetman b Laker | 77 | not out | 7 |
| L.E. Favell | c Cowdrey b Lock | 54 | | |
| K.D. Mackay | b Trueman | 57 | | |
| R. Benaud* | b Laker | 6 | | |
| A.K. Davidson | lbw b Lock | 71 | | |
| A.T.W. Grout† | c Statham b Laker | 14 | | |
| K.N. Slater | not out | 1 | | |
| I. Meckiff | b Lock | 2 | | |
| Extras | (B 5, LB 10, NB 1) | 16 | (B 6) | 6 |
| **Total** | | **357** | (2 wickets) | **54** |

| AUSTRALIA | O | M | R | W | O | M | R | W |
|---|--:|--:|--:|--:|--:|--:|--:|--:|
| Davidson | 12 | 3 | 21 | 1 | 33 | 11 | 65 | 1 |
| Meckiff | 15 | 2 | 45 | 1 | 3 | 1 | 7 | 0 |
| Benaud | 33·4 | 10 | 83 | 5 | 33 | 7 | 94 | 4 |
| Slater | 14 | 4 | 40 | 2 | 18 | 5 | 61 | 0 |
| Mackay | 8 | 3 | 19 | 1 | 11 | 2 | 21 | 0 |
| Burke | | | | | 11 | 3 | 26 | 2 |
| ENGLAND | | | | | | | | |
| Statham | 16 | 2 | 48 | 0 | 2 | 0 | 6 | 0 |
| Trueman | 18 | 3 | 37 | 1 | 4 | 1 | 9 | 0 |
| Lock | 43·2 | 9 | 130 | 4 | 11 | 4 | 23 | 0 |
| Laker | 46 | 9 | 107 | 5 | 8 | 3 | 10 | 2 |
| Bailey | 5 | 0 | 19 | 0 | | | | |

### FALL OF WICKETS

| | E | A | E | A |
|---|--:|--:|--:|--:|
| Wkt | 1st | 1st | 2nd | 2nd |
| 1st | 19 | 26 | 30 | 22 |
| 2nd | 23 | 52 | 37 | 33 |
| 3rd | 91 | 87 | 64 | – |
| 4th | 97 | 197 | 246 | – |
| 5th | 98 | 199 | 262 | – |
| 6th | 155 | 208 | 269 | – |
| 7th | 194 | 323 | 270 | – |
| 8th | 200 | 353 | – | – |
| 9th | 202 | 355 | – | – |
| 10th | 219 | 357 | – | – |

Umpires: M.J. McInnes and C. Hoy.

# AUSTRALIA v ENGLAND 1958-59 (4th Test)

Played at Adelaide Oval on 30, 31 January, 2, 3, 4, 5 February.
Toss: England.   Result: AUSTRALIA won by ten wickets.
Debuts: Australia – G.F. Rorke.

McDonald, almost bowled first ball of the match by Statham, became the fiftieth Australian to score a hundred against England. He pulled a thigh muscle when 137*, retired hurt 149* at lunch with Australia 268 for 1, and resumed his innings with a runner at 407 for 7. Evans re-fractured a little finger and, after continuing to keep wicket throughout the first day, handed over to Graveney for the rest of the match. Australia regained the Ashes after a period of five years 170 days.

## AUSTRALIA

| | | | | |
|---|---|---|---|---|
| C.C. McDonald | b Trueman | 170 | | |
| J.W. Burke | c Cowdrey b Bailey | 66 | not out | 16 |
| R.N. Harvey | run out | 41 | | |
| N.C. O'Neill | b Statham | 56 | | |
| L.E. Favell | b Statham | 4 | (1) not out | 15 |
| K.D. Mackay | c Evans b Statham | 4 | | |
| R. Benaud* | b Trueman | 46 | | |
| A.K. Davidson | c Bailey b Tyson | 43 | | |
| A.T.W. Grout† | lbw b Trueman | 9 | | |
| R.R. Lindwall | b Trueman | 19 | | |
| G.F. Rorke | not out | 2 | | |
| Extras | (B 2, LB 8, W 4, NB 2) | 16 | (B 4, LB 1) | 5 |
| **Total** | | **476** | (0 wickets) | **36** |

## ENGLAND

| | | | | |
|---|---|---|---|---|
| P.E. Richardson | lbw b Lindwall | 4 | lbw b Benaud | 43 |
| T.E. Bailey | b Davidson | 4 | (6) c Grout b Lindwall | 6 |
| P.B.H. May* | b Benaud | 37 | lbw b Rorke | 59 |
| M.C. Cowdrey | b Rorke | 84 | b Lindwall | 8 |
| T.W. Graveney | c Benaud b Rorke | 41 | not out | 53 |
| W. Watson | b Rorke | 25 | (2) c Favell b Benaud | 40 |
| F.S. Trueman | c Grout b Benaud | 0 | c Grout b Davidson | 0 |
| G.A.R. Lock | c Grout b Benaud | 2 | b Rorke | 9 |
| F.H. Tyson | c and b Benaud | 0 | c Grout b Benaud | 33 |
| T.G. Evans† | c Burke b Benaud | 4 | (11) c Benaud b Davidson | 0 |
| J.B. Statham | not out | 36 | (10) c O'Neill b Benaud | 2 |
| Extras | (LB 2, NB 1) | 3 | (B 5, LB 5, W 3, NB 4) | 17 |
| **Total** | | **240** | | **270** |

| ENGLAND | O | M | R | W | O | M | R | W |
|---|---|---|---|---|---|---|---|---|
| Statham | 23 | 0 | 83 | 3 | 4 | 0 | 11 | 0 |
| Trueman | 30·1 | 6 | 90 | 4 | 3 | 1 | 3 | 0 |
| Tyson | 28 | 1 | 100 | 1 | | | | |
| Bailey | 22 | 2 | 91 | 1 | | | | |
| Lock | 25 | 0 | 96 | 0 | 2 | 0 | 8 | 0 |
| Cowdrey | | | | | 1·3 | 0 | 9 | 0 |
| AUSTRALIA | | | | | | | | |
| Davidson | 12 | 0 | 49 | 1 | 8·3 | 3 | 17 | 2 |
| Lindwall | 15 | 0 | 66 | 1 | 26 | 6 | 70 | 2 |
| Rorke | 18·1 | 7 | 23 | 3 | 34 | 7 | 78 | 2 |
| Benaud | 27 | 6 | 91 | 5 | 29 | 10 | 82 | 4 |
| O'Neill | 2 | 1 | 8 | 0 | | | | |
| Burke | | | | | 4 | 2 | 6 | 0 |

### FALL OF WICKETS

| | A | E | E | A |
|---|---|---|---|---|
| Wkt | 1st | 1st | 2nd | 2nd |
| 1st | 171 | 7 | 89 | – |
| 2nd | 276 | 11 | 110 | – |
| 3rd | 286 | 74 | 125 | – |
| 4th | 294 | 170 | 177 | – |
| 5th | 369 | 173 | 198 | – |
| 6th | 388 | 180 | 199 | – |
| 7th | 407 | 184 | 222 | – |
| 8th | 445 | 184 | 268 | – |
| 9th | 473 | 188 | 270 | – |
| 10th | 476 | 240 | 270 | – |

Umpires: M.J. McInnes and R. Wright.

# AUSTRALIA v ENGLAND 1958-59 (5th Test)

Played at Melbourne Cricket Ground on 13, 14, 16, 17, 18 February.
Toss: Australia.   Result: AUSTRALIA won by nine wickets.
Debuts: England – J.B. Mortimore.

McDonald scored his second consecutive hundred after being given not out when 12 after a bail had been dislodged as he glanced Trueman to the boundary. Bailey, playing in his final Test match, was dismissed for a 'pair' by the bowler to whom he had sacrificed his wicket (Lindwall's 100th against England) four years earlier (*Test No. 395*). During this match Lindwall broke C.V. Grimmett's Australian record of 216 Test wickets.

## ENGLAND

| | | | | |
|---|---|---|---|---|
| P.E. Richardson | c and b Benaud | 68 | lbw b Benaud | 2 |
| T.E. Bailey | c Davidson b Lindwall | 0 | b Lindwall | |
| P.B.H. May* | c Benaud b Meckiff | 11 | c Harvey b Lindwall | |
| M.C. Cowdrey | c Lindwall b Davidson | 22 | run out | 4 |
| T.W. Graveney | c McDonald b Benaud | 19 | c Harvey b Davidson | 5 |
| E.R. Dexter | c Lindwall b Meckiff | 0 | c Grout b Davidson | |
| R. Swetman† | c Grout b Davidson | 1 | lbw b Lindwall | |
| J.B. Mortimore | not out | 44 | b Rorke | 1 |
| F.S Trueman | c and b Benaud | 21 | b Rorke | 3 |
| F.H. Tyson | c Grout b Benaud | 9 | c Grout b Rorke | |
| J.C. Laker | c Harvey b Davidson | 2 | not out | |
| Extras | (B 4, W 4) | 8 | (B 9, LB 3, W 2) | 1 |
| **Total** | | **205** | | **21** |

## AUSTRALIA

| | | | | |
|---|---|---|---|---|
| C.C. McDonald | c Cowdrey b Laker | 133 | not out | 5 |
| J.W. Burke | c Trueman b Tyson | 16 | lbw b Tyson | 1 |
| R.N. Harvey | c Swetman b Trueman | 13 | not out | |
| N.C. O'Neill | c Cowdrey b Trueman | 0 | | |
| K.D. Mackay | c Graveney b Laker | 23 | | |
| A.K. Davidson | b Mortimore | 17 | | |
| R. Benaud* | c Swetman b Laker | 64 | | |
| A.T.W. Grout† | c Trueman b Laker | 74 | | |
| R.R. Lindwall | c Cowdrey b Trueman | 0 | | |
| I. Meckiff | c and b Trueman | 2 | | |
| G.F. Rorke | not out | 0 | | |
| Extras | (B 5, LB 4) | 9 | (LB 4) | |
| **Total** | | **351** | (1 wicket) | **6** |

| AUSTRALIA | O | M | R | W | O | M | R | W |
|---|---|---|---|---|---|---|---|---|
| Davidson | 12·5 | 2 | 38 | 3 | 21 | 1 | 95 | 2 |
| Lindwall | 14 | 2 | 36 | 1 | 11 | 2 | 37 | 3 |
| Meckiff | 15 | 2 | 57 | 2 | 4 | 0 | 13 | 0 |
| Rorke | 6 | 1 | 23 | 0 | 12·4 | 2 | 41 | 3 |
| Benaud | 17 | 5 | 43 | 4 | 6 | 1 | 14 | 1 |
| **ENGLAND** | | | | | | | | |
| Trueman | 25 | 0 | 92 | 4 | 6·7 | 0 | 45 | 0 |
| Tyson | 20 | 1 | 73 | 1 | 6 | 0 | 20 | 1 |
| Bailey | 14 | 2 | 43 | 0 | | | | |
| Laker | 30·5 | 4 | 93 | 4 | | | | |
| Mortimore | 11 | 1 | 41 | 1 | | | | |

### FALL OF WICKETS

| Wkt | E 1st | A 1st | E 2nd | A 2n |
|---|---|---|---|---|
| 1st | 0 | 41 | 0 | 6 |
| 2nd | 13 | 83 | 12 | – |
| 3rd | 61 | 83 | 78 | |
| 4th | 109 | 154 | 105 | – |
| 5th | 112 | 207 | 131 | – |
| 6th | 124 | 209 | 142 | – |
| 7th | 128 | 324 | 158 | – |
| 8th | 191 | 327 | 172 | – |
| 9th | 203 | 329 | 182 | – |
| 10th | 205 | 351 | 214 | – |

Umpires: R. Wright and L. Townsend.

# PAKISTAN v WEST INDIES 1958-59 (1st Test)

Played at National Stadium, Karachi, on 20, 21, 22, 24, 25 February.
Toss: Pakistan.    Result: PAKISTAN won by ten wickets.
Debuts: Pakistan – Antao D'Souza, Ijaz Butt.

Fazal Mahmood began his Test captaincy by putting Pakistan's newest visitors in to bat on a matting pitch. Hanif and Saeed shared a record Pakistan second-wicket partnership of 178 (subsequently beaten). Fazal became the first bowler to take 100 wickets for Pakistan when he had Sobers 'lbw' for the second time in the match. Hanif took no further part in the rubber after injuring his knee in the second innings; he had played in Pakistan's first 24 Test matches.

## WEST INDIES

| | | | | | |
|---|---|---|---|---|---|
| C.C. Hunte | c Imtiaz b Fazal | 0 | lbw b Fazal | | 21 |
| J.K. Holt | lbw b Nasim | 29 | c Ijaz Butt b Fazal | | 2 |
| R.B. Kanhai | c Hanif b Nasim | 33 | c Imtiaz b Mahmood | | 12 |
| G.St A. Sobers | lbw b Fazal | 0 | (6) lbw b Fazal | | 14 |
| O.G. Smith | st Imtiaz b Nasim | 0 | lbw b Mahmood | | 11 |
| B.F. Butcher | not out | 45 | (4) c Imitiaz b Nasim | | 61 |
| J.S. Solomon | c Hanif b D'Souza | 14 | run out | | 66 |
| F.C.M. Alexander*† | b D'Souza | 0 | lbw b Shujauddin | | 16 |
| L.R. Gibbs | b Nasim | 5 | b Shujauddin | | 21 |
| W.W. Hall | b Fazal | 7 | st Imtiaz b Shujauddin | | 4 |
| J.O. Taylor | b Fazal | 0 | not out | | 0 |
| Extras | (B 3, NB 10) | 13 | (LB 7, NB 10) | | 17 |
| **Total** | | **146** | | | **245** |

## PAKISTAN

| | | | | | |
|---|---|---|---|---|---|
| Hanif Mohammad | c Alexander b Smith | 103 | retired hurt | | 5 |
| Ijaz Butt | c Alexander b Hall | 14 | not out | | 41 |
| Saeed Ahmed | run out | 78 | not out | | 33 |
| Imtiaz Ahmed† | lbw b Smith | 31 | | | |
| Wazir Mohammad | st Alexander b Gibbs | 23 | | | |
| W. Mathias | b Hall | 16 | | | |
| Fazal Mahmood* | c Alexander b Hall | 0 | | | |
| Shujauddin | run out | 1 | | | |
| Nasim-ul-Ghani | b Gibbs | 11 | | | |
| Mahmood Hussain | b Gibbs | 1 | | | |
| A. D'Souza | not out | 3 | | | |
| Extras | (B 9, LB 3, W 1, NB 10) | 23 | (NB 9) | | 9 |
| **Total** | | **304** | (0 wickets) | | **88** |

| PAKISTAN | O | M | R | W | O | M | R | W | | FALL OF WICKETS | | | |
|---|---|---|---|---|---|---|---|---|---|---|---|---|---|
| Fazal | 22 | 9 | 35 | 4 | 36 | 9 | 89 | 3 | | WI | P | WI | P |
| Mahmood Hussain | 8 | 3 | 13 | 0 | 26 | 10 | 59 | 2 | *Wkt* | *1st* | *1st* | *2nd* | *2nd* |
| D'Souza | 14 | 0 | 50 | 2 | 13 | 5 | 28 | 0 | 1st | 0 | 33 | 12 | – |
| Nasim | 16 | 5 | 35 | 4 | 25 | 16 | 34 | 1 | 2nd | 62 | 211 | 34 | – |
| Shujauddin | | | | | 13 | 7 | 18 | 3 | 3rd | 64 | 214 | 55 | – |
| | | | | | | | | | 4th | 65 | 263 | 84 | – |
| WEST INDIES | | | | | | | | | 5th | 69 | 284 | 109 | – |
| Hall | 30 | 7 | 57 | 3 | 8 | 1 | 35 | 0 | 6th | 104 | 287 | 140 | – |
| Taylor | 21 | 7 | 43 | 0 | 6 | 2 | 15 | 0 | 7th | 104 | 289 | 189 | – |
| Gibbs | 38·2 | 13 | 92 | 3 | 7 | 4 | 8 | 0 | 8th | 117 | 290 | 233 | – |
| Sobers | 40 | 24 | 45 | 0 | 9 | 5 | 12 | 0 | 9th | 145 | 291 | 241 | – |
| Smith | 27 | 14 | 36 | 2 | 3 | 2 | 9 | 0 | 10th | 146 | 304 | 245 | – |
| Solomon | 4 | 1 | 8 | 0 | | | | | | | | | |
| Holt | | | | | 1 | 1 | 0 | 0 | | | | | |

Umpires: Daud Khan and Murrawat Hussain.

# PAKISTAN v WEST INDIES 1958–59 (2nd Test)

Played at Dacca Stadium on 6, 7, 8 March.
Toss: West Indies.   Result: PAKISTAN won by 41 runs.
Debuts: Nil.

Fazal Mahmood's first innings analysis of 6 for 34 remains the best for either country in this series in Pakistan, and he is the only bowler to take ten wickets in Tests between these two countries. His match analysis of 12 for 100 i the record for any Test at Dacca. The match aggregate of 537 runs is the lowest for any completed Wes Indies-Pakistan Test and West Indies' innings of 76 remains the lowest total by either side.

## PAKISTAN

| | | | | |
|---|---|---|---|---|
| Ijaz Butt | b Hall | 2 | b Ramadhin | 2 |
| Alimuddin | c and b Hall | 6 | c Smith b Atkinson | 0 |
| Saeed Ahmed | c Alexander b Hall | 6 | lbw b Ramadhin | 22 |
| Imtiaz Ahmed† | b Ramadhin | 3 | c Smith b Atkinson | 4 |
| Wazir Mohammad | b Hall | 1 | c Alexander b Atkinson | 4 |
| W. Mathias | c Atkinson b Gibbs | 64 | b Atkinson | 45 |
| Shujauddin | b Atkinson | 26 | b Hall | 17 |
| Fazal Mahmood* | c Alexander b Ramadhin | 12 | (9) not out | 7 |
| Nasim-ul-Ghani | run out | 7 | (8) b Hall | 0 |
| Mahmood Hussain | b Ramadhin | 4 | b Hall | 2 |
| Haseeb Ahsan | not out | 4 | b Hall | 0 |
| Extras | (B 5, LB 2, NB 3) | 10 | (B 9, LB 4, W 1, NB 8) | 22 |
| **Total** | | **145** | | **144** |

## WEST INDIES

| | | | | |
|---|---|---|---|---|
| J.K. Holt | b Mahmood | 4 | c Imtiaz b Fazal | 5 |
| R.B. Kanhai | c Wazir b Fazal | 4 | (3) lbw b Fazal | 8 |
| G. St A. Sobers | lbw b Fazal | 29 | (5) c Fazal b Mahmood | 45 |
| F.C.M. Alexander*† | st Imtiaz b Nasim | 14 | (2) c Imtiaz b Fazal | 18 |
| B.F. Butcher | c Shujauddin b Fazal | 11 | (4) b Fazal | 8 |
| O.G. Smith | c Nasim b Fazal | 0 | b Fazal | 39 |
| J.S. Solomon | c Imtiaz b Nasim | 0 | c Mahmood b Fazal | 8 |
| E. St E. Atkinson | c Mathias b Fazal | 0 | (9) lbw b Mahmood | 20 |
| L.R. Gibbs | st Imtiaz b Nasim | 0 | (8) b Mahmood | 0 |
| W.W. Hall | c Mathias b Fazal | 0 | lbw b Mahmood | 6 |
| S. Ramadhin | not out | 0 | not out | 4 |
| Extras | (B 5, LB 3, NB 6) | 14 | (LB 5, NB 6) | 11 |
| **Total** | | **76** | | **172** |

| WEST INDIES | O | M | R | W | O | M | R | W |
|---|---|---|---|---|---|---|---|---|
| Hall | 13 | 5 | 28 | 4 | 16·5 | 2 | 49 | 4 |
| Atkinson | 10 | 2 | 22 | 1 | 22 | 9 | 42 | 4 |
| Ramadhin | 23·3 | 6 | 45 | 3 | 15 | 9 | 10 | 2 |
| Gibbs | 21 | 8 | 33 | 1 | 6 | 0 | 17 | 0 |
| Sobers | 8 | 4 | 7 | 0 | 3 | 2 | 4 | 0 |
| **PAKISTAN** | | | | | | | | |
| Fazal | 18·3 | 9 | 34 | 6 | 27 | 10 | 66 | 6 |
| Mahmood Hussain | 10 | 1 | 21 | 1 | 19·5 | 1 | 48 | 4 |
| Nasim | 7 | 5 | 4 | 3 | 8 | 2 | 34 | 0 |
| Haseeb | 1 | 0 | 3 | 0 | | | | |
| Shujauddin | | | | | 6 | 2 | 13 | 0 |

| FALL OF WICKETS | | | | |
|---|---|---|---|---|
| | P | WI | P | WI |
| Wkt | 1st | 1st | 2nd | 2nd |
| 1st | 6 | 4 | 2 | 12 |
| 2nd | 15 | 19 | 33 | 31 |
| 3rd | 18 | 56 | 40 | 35 |
| 4th | 22 | 65 | 54 | 48 |
| 5th | 22 | 68 | 71 | 113 |
| 6th | 108 | 71 | 130 | 134 |
| 7th | 126 | 72 | 130 | 141 |
| 8th | 130 | 74 | 131 | 150 |
| 9th | 139 | 74 | 139 | 159 |
| 10th | 145 | 76 | 144 | 172 |

Umpires: Saeed Ahmed and Munawar Hussain.

# PAKISTAN v WEST INDIES 1958–59 (3rd Test)

Played at Bagh-i-Jinnah, Lahore, 26, 28, 29, 30, 31 March.
Toss: West Indies.   Result: WEST INDIES won by an innings and 156 runs.
Debuts: Pakistan – Mushtaq Mohammad; West Indies – M.R. Bynoe.

This was Pakistan's first defeat in a Test at home. Mushtaq Mohammad made his first appearance in Test cricket at the age of 15 years 124 days and remains the youngest ever to do so. Kanhai's 217 is still the highest score for either side in this series in Pakistan, and his partnership of 162 with Sobers remains their best third-wicket stand against Pakistan. Hall became the first West Indies bowler to take a Test hat-trick when he dismissed Mushtaq, Fazal and Nasim in the first innings. Kanhai kept wicket in the second innings, Alexander's three catches being taken in the field.

### WEST INDIES

| | | |
|---|---|---:|
| F.C.M. Alexander*† | lbw b Fazal | 21 |
| M.R. Bynoe | c Mahmood b Fazal | 1 |
| R.B. Kanhai | c and b Shujauddin | 217 |
| G. St A. Sobers | b Nasim | 72 |
| O.G. Smith | c Waqar b Saeed | 31 |
| B.F. Butcher | run out | 8 |
| J.S. Solomon | c Mathias b Mahmood | 56 |
| E. St E. Atkinson | c Mathias b Nasim | 20 |
| L.R. Gibbs | c Saeed b Nasim | 18 |
| S. Ramadhin | not out | 4 |
| W.W. Hall | b Shujauddin | 0 |
| Extras | (B 7, LB 8, NB 6) | 21 |
| **Total** | | **469** |

### PAKISTAN

| | | | | |
|---|---|---:|---|---:|
| Ijaz Butt | not out | 47 | c Gibbs b Atkinson | 2 |
| Imtiaz Ahmed† | run out | 40 | c Gibbs b Atkinson | 1 |
| Saeed Ahmed | c Gibbs b Smith | 27 | c Kanhai b Atkinson | 33 |
| Waqar Hassan | b Gibbs | 41 | c Alexander b Gibbs | 28 |
| W. Mathias | b Hall | 14 | c Alexander b Ramadhin | 9 |
| Shujauddin | b Hall | 1 | (7) c and b Ramadhin | 0 |
| Wazir Mohammad | run out | 11 | (6) c Alexander b Ramadhin | 0 |
| Mushtaq Mohammad | lbw b Hall | 14 | b Ramadhin | 4 |
| Fazal Mahmood* | c Sobers b Hall | 0 | b Gibbs | 14 |
| Nasim-ul-Ghani | b Hall | 0 | not out | 6 |
| Mahmood Hussain | c Sobers b Atkinson | 0 | c Bynoe b Gibbs | 1 |
| Extras | (B 1, LB 3, NB 10) | 14 | (B 2, LB 2, NB 2) | 6 |
| **Total** | | **209** | | **104** |

| PAKISTAN | O | M | R | W | O | M | R | W | FALL OF WICKETS | | | |
|---|---|---|---|---|---|---|---|---|---|---|---|---|
| Fazal | 40 | 10 | 109 | 2 | | | | | | WI | P | P |
| Mahmood Hussain | 28 | 4 | 99 | 1 | | | | | *Wkt* | *1st* | *1st* | *2nd* |
| Nasim | 30 | 6 | 106 | 3 | | | | | 1st | 11 | 70 | 4 |
| Shujauddin | 34·3 | 7 | 81 | 2 | | | | | 2nd | 38 | 75 | 5 |
| Mushtaq | 6 | 0 | 34 | 0 | | | | | 3rd | 200 | 98 | 55 |
| Saeed | 11 | 1 | 19 | 1 | | | | | 4th | 290 | 105 | 72 |
| | | | | | | | | | 5th | 307 | 160 | 73 |
| WEST INDIES | | | | | | | | | 6th | 407 | 180 | 73 |
| Hall | 24 | 2 | 87 | 5 | 9 | 1 | 31 | 0 | 7th | 426 | 208 | 78 |
| Atkinson | 14·2 | 1 | 40 | 1 | 12 | 8 | 15 | 3 | 8th | 463 | 208 | 97 |
| Ramadhin | 22 | 9 | 41 | 0 | 10 | 4 | 25 | 4 | 9th | 464 | 208 | 97 |
| Smith | 7 | 3 | 11 | 1 | 2 | 1 | 4 | 0 | 10th | 469 | 209 | 104 |
| Gibbs | 12 | 5 | 16 | 1 | 9·5 | 3 | 14 | 3 | | | | |
| Sobers | | | | | 6 | 1 | 9 | 0 | | | | |

Umpires: Akhtar Hussain and Munawar Hussain.

## NEW ZEALAND v ENGLAND 1958–59 (1st Test)

Played at Lancaster Park, Christchurch, on 27, 28 February, 2 March.
Toss: England.   Result: ENGLAND won by an innings and 99 runs.
Debuts: New Zealand – B.A. Bolton, R.M. Harris, K.W. Hough.

Petrie, struck near his eye by a ball from Moir, retired for a time and Reid kept wicket. Later Petrie became
Trueman's hundredth Test wicket. A record ground attendance of 20,000 watched the second day.

### ENGLAND

| P.E. Richardson | c Petrie b Blair | 8 |
|---|---|---|
| W. Watson | c Petrie b Blair | 10 |
| T.W. Graveney | lbw b Hough | 42 |
| P.B.H. May* | c Hough b Moir | 71 |
| M.C. Cowdrey | b Hough | 15 |
| E.R. Dexter | b Reid | 141 |
| J.B. Mortimore | c and b Moir | 11 |
| R. Swetman† | b Hough | 9 |
| F.S. Trueman | lbw b Reid | 21 |
| G.A.R. Lock | b Reid | 15 |
| F.H. Tyson | not out | 6 |
| Extras | (B 12, LB 13) | 25 |
| **Total** | | **374** |

### NEW ZEALAND

| R.M. Harris | c Lock b Tyson | 6 | b Trueman | 13 |
|---|---|---|---|---|
| B.A. Bolton | c Swetman b Lock | 33 | c May b Mortimore | 26 |
| J.W. Guy | c Trueman b Lock | 3 | c Lock b Tyson | 56 |
| J.R. Reid* | b Tyson | 40 | c Cowdrey b Lock | 1 |
| B. Sutcliffe | c Lock b Tyson | 0 | c Trueman b Lock | 12 |
| S.N. McGregor | c Lock b Mortimore | 0 | lbw b Lock | 6 |
| J.T. Sparling | st Swetman b Lock | 12 | b Tyson | 0 |
| A.M. Moir | c Graveney b Lock | 0 | c Swetman b Lock | 1 |
| E.C. Petrie† | lbw b Trueman | 8 | not out | 2 |
| R.W. Blair | lbw b Lock | 0 | c Trueman b Lock | 2 |
| K.W. Hough | not out | 31 | b Lock | 7 |
| Extras | (B 5, LB 4) | 9 | (B 1, LB 5, NB 1) | 7 |
| **Total** | | **142** | | **133** |

| NEW ZEALAND | O | M | R | W | O | M | R | W |
|---|---|---|---|---|---|---|---|---|
| Blair | 31 | 5 | 89 | 2 | | | | |
| Hough | 39 | 11 | 96 | 3 | | | | |
| Moir | 36 | 9 | 83 | 2 | | | | |
| Reid | 18·1 | 9 | 34 | 3 | | | | |
| Sparling | 16 | 7 | 38 | 0 | | | | |
| Sutcliffe | 2 | 0 | 9 | 0 | | | | |
| ENGLAND | | | | | | | | |
| Trueman | 10·5 | 3 | 39 | 1 | 8 | 2 | 20 | 1 |
| Tyson | 14 | 4 | 23 | 3 | 14 | 6 | 23 | 2 |
| Lock | 26 | 15 | 31 | 5 | 28·2 | 13 | 53 | 6 |
| Mortimore | 22 | 8 | 40 | 1 | 21 | 10 | 27 | 1 |
| Dexter | | | | | 1 | 0 | 3 | 0 |

| | FALL OF WICKETS | | |
|---|---|---|---|
| | E | NZ | NZ |
| Wkt | 1st | 1st | 2nd |
| 1st | 13 | 22 | 37 |
| 2nd | 30 | 33 | 68 |
| 3rd | 98 | 83 | 79 |
| 4th | 126 | 83 | 101 |
| 5th | 171 | 86 | 117 |
| 6th | 197 | 101 | 119 |
| 7th | 224 | 101 | 120 |
| 8th | 305 | 102 | 121 |
| 9th | 367 | 102 | 123 |
| 10th | 374 | 142 | 133 |

Umpires: J. Cowie and E.W.T. Tindill.

# NEW ZEALAND v ENGLAND 1958–59 (2nd Test)

Played at Eden Park, Auckland, on 14, 16, 17 (*no play*), 18 (*no play*) March.
Toss: England.    Result: MATCH DRAWN.
Debuts: Nil.

The first two days were played in blustery conditions with the bails frequently being blown off, and the last two were completely ruined by rain.

## NEW ZEALAND

| | | |
|---|---|---:|
| B.A. Bolton | run out | 0 |
| R.M. Harris | c Swetman b Dexter | 12 |
| S.N. McGregor | hit wkt b Trueman | 1 |
| J.W. Guy | b Dexter | 1 |
| B. Sutcliffe | b Lock | 61 |
| J.R. Reid* | b Dexter | 3 |
| J.T. Sparling | c Swetman b Trueman | 25 |
| A.M. Moir | c Graveney b Trueman | 10 |
| E.C. Petrie† | c Trueman b Lock | 13 |
| R.W. Blair | c Cowdrey b Tyson | 22 |
| K.W. Hough | not out | 24 |
| Extras | (B 7, LB 1, NB 1) | 9 |
| **Total** | | **181** |

## ENGLAND

| | | |
|---|---|---:|
| P.E. Richardson | c Bolton b Moir | 67 |
| W. Watson | b Hough | 11 |
| T.W. Graveney | b Moir | 46 |
| P.B.H. May* | not out | 124 |
| M.C. Cowdrey | b Hough | 5 |
| E.R. Dexter | c Petrie b Moir | 1 |
| J.B. Mortimore | b Hough | 9 |
| R. Swetman† | run out | 17 |
| F.S. Trueman | not out | 21 |
| G.A.R. Lock | } did not bat | |
| F.H. Tyson | | |
| Extras | (B 4, LB 6) | 10 |
| **Total** | (7 wickets) | **311** |

| ENGLAND | O | M | R | W |
|---|---|---|---|---|
| Trueman | 26 | 12 | 46 | 3 |
| Tyson | 20 | 9 | 50 | 1 |
| Dexter | 19 | 8 | 23 | 3 |
| Lock | 20·3 | 12 | 29 | 2 |
| Mortimore | 4 | 1 | 24 | 0 |
| NEW ZEALAND | | | | |
| Blair | 27 | 6 | 69 | 0 |
| Hough | 38 | 12 | 79 | 3 |
| Reid | 4 | 1 | 19 | 0 |
| Sparling | 20 | 6 | 48 | 0 |
| Moir | 27 | 14 | 84 | 3 |
| Sutcliffe | 1 | 0 | 2 | 0 |

### FALL OF WICKETS

| | NZ | E |
|---|---|---|
| *Wkt* | *1st* | *1st* |
| 1st | 3 | 26 |
| 2nd | 6 | 94 |
| 3rd | 11 | 165 |
| 4th | 16 | 182 |
| 5th | 41 | 183 |
| 6th | 98 | 223 |
| 7th | 116 | 261 |
| 8th | 125 | – |
| 9th | 157 | – |
| 10th | 181 | – |

Umpires: J. Cowie and R.W.R. Shortt.

# ENGLAND v INDIA 1959 (1st Test)

Played at Trent Bridge, Nottingham, on 4, 5, 6, 8 June.
Toss: England.   Result: ENGLAND won by an innings and 59 runs.
Debuts: England – T. Greenhough, M.J. Horton, K. Taylor.

Borde's left-hand little finger was fractured by a ball from Trueman. England won at 3.30 p.m. on the fourth day. Nadkarni was unable to complete his 29th over after a drive from Statham had severely bruised his left hand. May gave no chances in scoring the last of his 13 Test hundreds.

## ENGLAND

| | | |
|---|---|---|
| C.A. Milton | b Surendranath | 9 |
| K. Taylor | lbw b Gupte | 24 |
| M.C. Cowdrey | c Borde b Surendranath | 5 |
| P.B.H. May* | c Joshi b Gupte | 106 |
| K.F. Barrington | b Nadkarni | 56 |
| M.J. Horton | c Nadkarni b Desai | 58 |
| T.G. Evans† | c Umrigar b Nadkarni | 73 |
| F.S. Trueman | b Borde | 28 |
| J.B. Statham | not out | 29 |
| T. Greenhough | c Gaekwad b Gupte | 0 |
| A.E. Moss | c Roy b Gupte | 11 |
| Extras | (B 15, LB 7, W 1) | 23 |
| **Total** | | **422** |

## INDIA

| | | | | | |
|---|---|---|---|---|---|
| P. Roy | b Trueman | 54 | | c Trueman b Greenhough | 49 |
| N.J. Contractor | c Barrington b Greenhough | 15 | | c Cowdrey b Statham | 0 |
| P.R. Umrigar | b Trueman | 21 | | b Statham | 20 |
| V.L. Manjrekar | lbw b Trueman | 17 | | lbw b Greenhough | 44 |
| C.G. Borde | retired hurt | 15 | | absent hurt | – |
| D.K. Gaekwad* | c Evans b Statham | 33 | (5) | c Horton b Statham | 31 |
| R.G. Nadkarni | lbw b Trueman | 15 | (6) | b Statham | 1 |
| P.G. Joshi† | lbw b Moss | 21 | (7) | lbw b Trueman | 1 |
| S.P. Gupte | c Taylor b Moss | 2 | (8) | c May b Statham | 8 |
| R. Surendranath | not out | 4 | (9) | not out | 1 |
| R.B. Desai | b Statham | 0 | (10) | c May b Trueman | 1 |
| Extras | (B 5, NB 4) | 9 | | (NB 1) | 1 |
| **Total** | | **206** | | | **157** |

| INDIA | O | M | R | W | O | M | R | W |
|---|---|---|---|---|---|---|---|---|
| Desai | 33 | 7 | 127 | 1 | | | | |
| Surendranath | 24 | 8 | 59 | 2 | | | | |
| Gupte | 38·1 | 11 | 102 | 4 | | | | |
| Nadkarni | 28·1 | 15 | 48 | 2 | | | | |
| Borde | 20 | 4 | 63 | 1 | | | | |
| **ENGLAND** | | | | | | | | |
| Statham | 23·5 | 11 | 46 | 2 | 21 | 10 | 31 | 5 |
| Trueman | 24 | 9 | 45 | 4 | 22·3 | 10 | 44 | 2 |
| Moss | 24 | 11 | 33 | 2 | 12 | 7 | 13 | 0 |
| Greenhough | 26 | 7 | 58 | 1 | 23 | 5 | 48 | 2 |
| Horton | 5 | 0 | 15 | 0 | 19 | 11 | 20 | 0 |

### FALL OF WICKETS

| Wkt | E 1st | I 1st | I 2nd |
|---|---|---|---|
| 1st | 17 | 34 | 8 |
| 2nd | 29 | 85 | 52 |
| 3rd | 60 | 95 | 85 |
| 4th | 185 | 126 | 124 |
| 5th | 221 | 158 | 140 |
| 6th | 327 | 190 | 143 |
| 7th | 358 | 198 | 147 |
| 8th | 389 | 206 | 156 |
| 9th | 390 | 206 | 157 |
| 10th | 422 | – | – |

Umpires: J.S. Buller and W.E. Phillipson.

# ENGLAND v INDIA 1959 (2nd Test)

Played at Lord's, London, on 18, 19, 20 June.
Toss: India.   Result: ENGLAND won by eight wickets.
Debuts: India – M.L. Jaisimha.

England won shortly after tea on the third day. Contractor played the highest innings of the match, batting part of the time with a runner after a ball from Statham had fractured one of his ribs. Roy, captain in the absence of Gaekwad through bronchitis, became Statham's 150th Test wicket. In the last of his 91 Test appearances, Evans took his record total of Test dismissals to 219, including 46 stumpings.

## INDIA

| | | | | | |
|---|---|---|---|---|---|
| P. Roy* | c Evans b Statham | 15 | | c May b Trueman | 0 |
| N.J. Contractor | b Greenhough | 81 | (8) | not out | 11 |
| P.R. Umrigar | b Statham | 1 | | c Horton b Trueman | 0 |
| V.L. Manjrekar | lbw b Trueman | 12 | (5) | lbw b Statham | 61 |
| M.M. Ghorpade | lbw b Greenhough | 41 | (4) | c Evans b Statham | 22 |
| A.G. Kripal Singh | b Greenhough | 0 | | b Statham | 41 |
| M.L. Jaisimha | lbw b Greenhough | 1 | (2) | lbw b Moss | 8 |
| P.G. Joshi† | b Horton | 4 | (7) | b Moss | 6 |
| R. Surendranath | b Greenhough | 0 | | run out | 0 |
| S.P. Gupte | c May b Horton | 0 | | st Evans b Greenhough | 7 |
| R.B. Desai | not out | 2 | | b Greenhough | 5 |
| Extras | (LB 11) | 11 | | (LB 4) | 4 |
| **Total** | | **168** | | | **165** |

## ENGLAND

| | | | | |
|---|---|---|---|---|
| C.A. Milton | c Surendranath b Desai | 14 | c Joshi b Desai | 3 |
| K. Taylor | c Gupte b Desai | 6 | lbw b Surendranath | 3 |
| M.C. Cowdrey | c Joshi b Desai | 34 | not out | 63 |
| P.B.H. May* | b Surendranath | 9 | not out | 33 |
| K.F. Barrington | c sub (V.M. Muddiah) b Desai | 80 | | |
| M.J. Horton | b Desai | 2 | | |
| T.G. Evans† | b Surendranath | 0 | | |
| F.S. Trueman | lbw b Gupte | 7 | | |
| J.B. Statham | c Surendranath b Gupte | 38 | | |
| A.E. Moss | b Surendranath | 26 | | |
| T. Greenhough | not out | 0 | | |
| Extras | (B 5, LB 4, W 1) | 10 | (B 5, LB 1) | 6 |
| **Total** | | **226** | (2 wickets) | **108** |

| ENGLAND | O | M | R | W | O | M | R | W | | FALL OF WICKETS | | | |
|---|---|---|---|---|---|---|---|---|---|---|---|---|---|
| Trueman | 16 | 4 | 40 | 1 | 21 | 3 | 55 | 2 | | I | E | I | E |
| Statham | 16 | 6 | 27 | 2 | 17 | 7 | 45 | 3 | Wkt | 1st | 1st | 2nd | 2nd |
| Moss | 14 | 5 | 31 | 0 | 23 | 10 | 30 | 2 | 1st | 32 | 9 | 0 | 8 |
| Greenhough | 16 | 4 | 35 | 5 | 18·1 | 8 | 31 | 2 | 2nd | 40 | 26 | 0 | 12 |
| Horton | 15·4 | 7 | 24 | 2 | | | | | 3rd | 61 | 35 | 22 | – |
| INDIA | | | | | | | | | 4th | 144 | 69 | 42 | – |
| Desai | 31·4 | 8 | 89 | 5 | 7 | 1 | 29 | 1 | 5th | 152 | 79 | 131 | – |
| Surendranath | 30 | 17 | 46 | 3 | 11 | 2 | 32 | 1 | 6th | 158 | 80 | 140 | – |
| Umrigar | 1 | 1 | 0 | 0 | 1 | 0 | 8 | 0 | 7th | 163 | 100 | 147 | – |
| Gupte | 19 | 2 | 62 | 2 | 6 | 2 | 21 | 0 | 8th | 163 | 184 | 147 | – |
| Kripal Singh | 3 | 0 | 19 | 0 | 1 | 1 | 0 | 0 | 9th | 164 | 226 | 159 | – |
| Jaisimha | | | | | 1 | 0 | 8 | 0 | 10th | 168 | 226 | 165 | – |
| Roy | | | | | 0·2 | 0 | 4 | 0 | | | | | |

Umpires: E. Davies and C.S. Elliott.

# ENGLAND v INDIA 1959 (3rd Test)

Played at Headingley, Leeds, on 2, 3, 4 July.
Toss: India.   Result: ENGLAND won by an innings and 173 runs.
Debuts: England – G. Pullar, H.J. Rhodes; India – A.L. Apte.

May, who missed the next match, equalled F.E. Woolley's world record of 52 consecutive Test appearances
Rhodes dismissed Roy and Borde with his fourth and twelfth balls in Test cricket. The opening partnership of 146
between Parkhouse and Pullar set a new England record against India. England won the rubber shortly before
5 p.m. on the third day.

## INDIA

| | | | | | |
|---|---|---|---|---|---|
| P. Roy | c Swetman b Rhodes | 2 | c Swetman b Trueman | 20 |
| A.L. Apte | b Moss | 8 | c Close b Moss | 7 |
| J.M. Ghorpade | c Swetman b Trueman | 8 | lbw b Trueman | 0 |
| C.G. Borde | c Swetman b Rhodes | 0 | c May b Close | 41 |
| P.R. Umrigar | c Trueman b Moss | 29 | c Trueman b Mortimore | 39 |
| D.K. Gaekwad* | c Cowdrey b Rhodes | 25 | c and b Close | 8 |
| R.G. Nadkarni | c Parkhouse b Rhodes | 27 | c Barrington b Close | 11 |
| N.S. Tamhane† | c Moss b Trueman | 20 | not out | 9 |
| R. Surendranath | c Close b Trueman | 5 | c Cowdrey b Mortimore | 1 |
| S.P. Gupte | c Swetman b Close | 21 | c and b Close | 1 |
| R.B. Desai | not out | 7 | c Cowdrey b Mortimore | 8 |
| Extras | (LB 4, NB 5) | 9 | (LB 4) | 4 |
| **Total** | | **161** | | **149** |

## ENGLAND

| | | |
|---|---|---|
| W.G.A. Parkhouse | c Tamhane b Desai | 78 |
| G. Pullar | c Borde b Nadkarni | 75 |
| M.C. Cowdrey | c Ghorpade b Gupte | 160 |
| P.B.H. May* | b Desai | 2 |
| K.F. Barrington | c Tamhane b Nadkarni | 80 |
| D.B. Close | b Gupte | 27 |
| J.B. Mortimore | b Gupte | 7 |
| R. Swetman† | not out | 19 |
| F.S. Trueman | c Desai b Gupte | 17 |
| A.E. Moss | } did not bat | |
| H.J. Rhodes | } | |
| Extras | (B 13, LB 5) | 18 |
| **Total** | (8 wickets declared) | **483** |

| ENGLAND | O | M | R | W | O | M | R | W | | FALL OF WICKETS | | |
|---|---|---|---|---|---|---|---|---|---|---|---|---|
| Trueman | 15 | 6 | 30 | 3 | 10 | 1 | 29 | 2 | | I | E | I |
| Moss | 22 | 11 | 30 | 2 | 6 | 3 | 10 | 1 | *Wkt* | *1st* | *1st* | *2nd* |
| Rhodes | 18·5 | 3 | 50 | 4 | 10 | 2 | 35 | 0 | 1st | 10 | 146 | 16 |
| Mortimore | 8 | 3 | 24 | 0 | 18·4 | 6 | 36 | 3 | 2nd | 10 | 180 | 19 |
| Close | 5 | 1 | 18 | 1 | 11 | 0 | 35 | 4 | 3rd | 11 | 186 | 38 |
| | | | | | | | | | 4th | 23 | 379 | 107 |
| INDIA | | | | | | | | | 5th | 75 | 432 | 115 |
| Desai | 38 | 10 | 111 | 2 | | | | | 6th | 75 | 439 | 121 |
| Surendranath | 32 | 11 | 84 | 0 | | | | | 7th | 103 | 453 | 138 |
| Gupte | 44·3 | 13 | 111 | 4 | | | | | 8th | 112 | 483 | 139 |
| Umrigar | 24 | 8 | 44 | 0 | | | | | 9th | 141 | – | 140 |
| Borde | 14 | 1 | 51 | 0 | | | | | 10th | 161 | – | 149 |
| Nadkarni | 22 | 2 | 64 | 2 | | | | | | | | |

Umpires: F.S. Lee and W.E. Phillipson.

# ENGLAND v INDIA 1959 (4th Test)

Played at Old Trafford, Manchester, on 23, 24, 25, 27, 28 July.
Toss: England.   Result: ENGLAND won by 171 runs.
Debuts: India – Abbas Ali Baig.

Baig, an Oxford University Freshman who had scored a hundred against Middlesex on his first appearance for the tourists in their previous match, remains the only Indian to score a hundred in his first Test, that match being in England. At 20 years 131 days he is still the youngest to score a hundred for India. Pullar was the first Lancashire player to score a hundred for England at Old Trafford.

## ENGLAND

| | | | | | |
|---|---|---|---|---|---|
| W.G.A. Parkhouse | c Roy b Surendranath | 17 | | c Contractor b Nadkarni | 49 |
| G. Pullar | c Joshi b Surendranath | 131 | | c Joshi b Gupte | 14 |
| M.C. Cowdrey* | c Joshi b Nadkarni | 67 | (5) | c Borde b Gupte | 9 |
| M.J.K. Smith | c Desai b Borde | 100 | | c Desai b Gupte | 9 |
| K.F. Barrington | lbw b Surendranath | 87 | (6) | lbw b Nadkarni | 46 |
| E.R. Dexter | c Roy b Surendranath | 13 | (3) | c Umrigar b Gupte | 45 |
| R. Illingworth | c Gaekwad b Desai | 21 | | not out | 47 |
| J.B. Mortimore | c Contractor b Gupte | 29 | (9) | c Nadkarni b Borde | 7 |
| R. Swetman† | c Joshi b Gupte | 9 | (10) | not out | 21 |
| F.S. Trueman | b Surendranath | 0 | (8) | c Baig b Borde | 8 |
| H.J. Rhodes | not out | 0 | | | |
| Extras | (B 7, LB 7, W 2) | 16 | | (B 9, LB 1) | 10 |
| **Total** | | **490** | | (8 wickets declared) | **265** |

## INDIA

| | | | | |
|---|---|---|---|---|
| P. Roy | c Smith b Rhodes | 15 | c Illingworth b Dexter | 21 |
| N.J. Contractor | c Swetman b Rhodes | 23 | c Barrington b Rhodes | 56 |
| A.A. Baig | c Cowdrey b Illingworth | 26 | run out | 112 |
| D.K. Gaekwad* | lbw b Trueman | 5 | c Illingworth b Rhodes | 0 |
| P.R. Umrigar | b Rhodes | 2 | c Illingworth b Barrington | 118 |
| C.G. Borde | c and b Barrington | 75 | c Swetman b Mortimore | 3 |
| R.G. Nadkarni | b Barrington | 31 | lbw b Trueman | 28 |
| P.G. Joshi† | run out | 5 | b Illingworth | 5 |
| R. Surendranath | b Illingworth | 11 | c Trueman b Barrington | 4 |
| S.P. Gupte | not out | 4 | b Trueman | 8 |
| R.B. Desai | b Barrington | 5 | not out | 7 |
| Extras | (LB 1, W 4, NB 1) | 6 | (B 8, LB 5, NB 1) | 14 |
| **Total** | | **208** | | **376** |

| INDIA | O | M | R | W | O | M | R | W |
|---|---|---|---|---|---|---|---|---|
| Desai | 39 | 7 | 129 | 1 | 8 | 2 | 14 | 0 |
| Surendranath | 47·1 | 17 | 115 | 5 | 8 | 5 | 15 | 0 |
| Umrigar | 19 | 3 | 47 | 0 | 7 | 3 | 4 | 0 |
| Gupte | 28 | 8 | 98 | 2 | 26 | 6 | 76 | 4 |
| Nadkarni | 28 | 14 | 47 | 1 | 30 | 6 | 93 | 2 |
| Borde | 13 | 1 | 38 | 1 | 11 | 1 | 53 | 2 |
| ENGLAND | | | | | | | | |
| Trueman | 15 | 4 | 29 | 1 | 23·1 | 6 | 75 | 2 |
| Rhodes | 18 | 3 | 72 | 3 | 28 | 2 | 87 | 2 |
| Dexter | 3 | 0 | 3 | 0 | 12 | 2 | 33 | 1 |
| Illingworth | 16 | 10 | 16 | 2 | 39 | 13 | 63 | 1 |
| Mortimore | 13 | 6 | 46 | 0 | 16 | 6 | 29 | 1 |
| Barrington | 14 | 3 | 36 | 3 | 27 | 4 | 75 | 2 |

## FALL OF WICKETS

| Wkt | E 1st | I 1st | E 2nd | I 2nd |
|---|---|---|---|---|
| 1st | 33 | 23 | 44 | 35 |
| 2nd | 164 | 54 | 100 | 144 |
| 3rd | 262 | 70 | 117 | 146 |
| 4th | 371 | 72 | 132 | 180 |
| 5th | 417 | 78 | 136 | 243 |
| 6th | 440 | 124 | 196 | 321 |
| 7th | 454 | 154 | 209 | 334 |
| 8th | 490 | 199 | 219 | 358 |
| 9th | 490 | 199 | – | 361 |
| 10th | 490 | 208 | – | 376 |

Umpires: J.S. Buller and C.S. Elliott.

# ENGLAND v INDIA 1959 (5th Test)

Played at Kennington Oval, London, on 20, 21, 22, 24 August.
Toss: India.    Result: ENGLAND won by an innings and 27 runs.
Debuts: Nil.

England won before lunch on the fourth day and for the first time gained five victories in a series. It was also the first time that this had been achieved in England, the only other instances so far being by Australia at home – against England in 1920-21 and against South Africa in 1931-32. The partnership of 169 between Subba Row and Smith remains England's highest for the third wicket against India.

## INDIA

| | | | | | |
|---|---|---|---|---|---|
| P. Roy | b Statham | 3 | lbw b Statham | | 0 |
| N.J. Contractor | c Illingworth b Dexter | 22 | c Trueman b Statham | | 25 |
| A.A. Baig | c Cowdrey b Trueman | 23 | c Cowdrey b Statham | | 4 |
| R.G. Nadkarni | c Swetman b Trueman | 6 | lbw b Illingworth | | 76 |
| C.G. Borde | b Greenhough | 0 | run out | | 6 |
| D.K. Gaekwad* | c Barrington b Dexter | 11 | c Swetman b Greenhough | | 15 |
| J.M. Ghorpade | b Greenhough | 5 | b Greenhough | | 24 |
| N.S. Tamhane† | c Swetman b Statham | 32 | b Trueman | | 9 |
| R. Surendranath | c Illingworth b Trueman | 27 | not out | | 17 |
| S.P. Gupte | b Trueman | 2 | c Greenhough b Trueman | | 5 |
| R.B. Desai | not out | 3 | c Swetman b Trueman | | 0 |
| Extras | (B 1, LB 4, NB 1) | 6 | (B 4, LB 6, NB 3) | | 13 |
| **Total** | | **140** | | | **194** |

## ENGLAND

| | | |
|---|---|---|
| G. Pullar | c Tamhane b Surendranath | 22 |
| R. Subba Row | c Tamhane b Desai | 94 |
| M.C. Cowdrey* | c Borde b Surendranath | 6 |
| M.J.K. Smith | b Desai | 98 |
| K.F. Barrington | c sub (M.L. Jaisimha) b Gupte | 8 |
| E.R. Dexter | c Tamhane b Surendranath | 0 |
| R. Illingworth | c Gaekwad b Nadkarni | 50 |
| R. Swetman† | c Baig b Surendranath | 65 |
| F.S. Trueman | st Tamhane b Nadkarni | 1 |
| J.B. Statham | not out | 3 |
| T. Greenhough | c Contractor b Surendranath | 2 |
| Extras | (B 3, LB 8, W 1) | 12 |
| **Total** | | **361** |

| ENGLAND | O | M | R | W | O | M | R | W |
|---|---|---|---|---|---|---|---|---|
| Trueman | 17 | 6 | 24 | 4 | 14 | 4 | 30 | 3 |
| Statham | 16·3 | 6 | 24 | 2 | 18 | 4 | 50 | 3 |
| Dexter | 16 | 7 | 24 | 2 | 7 | 1 | 11 | 0 |
| Greenhough | 29 | 11 | 36 | 2 | 27 | 12 | 47 | 2 |
| Illingworth | 1 | 0 | 2 | 0 | 29 | 10 | 43 | 1 |
| Barrington | 6 | 0 | 24 | 0 | | | | |
| INDIA | | | | | | | | |
| Desai | 33 | 5 | 103 | 2 | | | | |
| Surendranath | 51·3 | 25 | 75 | 5 | | | | |
| Gupte | 38 | 9 | 119 | 1 | | | | |
| Nadkarni | 25 | 11 | 52 | 2 | | | | |

### FALL OF WICKETS

| | I | E | I |
|---|---|---|---|
| Wkt | 1st | 1st | 2nd |
| 1st | 12 | 38 | 5 |
| 2nd | 43 | 52 | 17 |
| 3rd | 49 | 221 | 44 |
| 4th | 50 | 232 | 70 |
| 5th | 67 | 233 | 106 |
| 6th | 72 | 235 | 159 |
| 7th | 74 | 337 | 163 |
| 8th | 132 | 347 | 173 |
| 9th | 134 | 358 | 188 |
| 10th | 140 | 361 | 194 |

Umpires: F.S. Lee and E. Davies.

# PAKISTAN v AUSTRALIA 1959–60 (1st Test)

Played at Dacca Stadium on 13, 14, 15, 17, 18 November.
Toss: Australia.   Result: AUSTRALIA won by eight wickets.
Debuts: Pakistan – D.A. Sharpe.

Australia gained their first win in Pakistan. The match was played on matting after heavy rain had made it impossible to use the new grass pitch.

## PAKISTAN

| | | | | |
|---|---|---|---|---|
| Hanif Mohammad | b Mackay | 66 | b Benaud | 19 |
| Ijaz Butt | c Grout b Davidson | 0 | b Mackay | 20 |
| Saeed Ahmed | c Harvey b Davidson | 37 | b Mackay | 15 |
| W. Mathias | c and b Benaud | 4 | lbw b Mackay | 1 |
| D.A. Sharpe | run out | 56 | lbw b Mackay | 35 |
| Wazir Mohammad | c Meckiff b Benaud | 0 | lbw b Benaud | 5 |
| Imtiaz Ahmed† | b Davidson | 13 | b Mackay | 4 |
| Israr Ali | st Grout b Benaud | 7 | (9) b Benaud | 1 |
| Shujauddin | not out | 2 | (8) not out | 16 |
| Fazal Mahmood* | b Benaud | 1 | c and b Mackay | 4 |
| Nasim-ul-Ghani | b Davidson | 5 | c McDonald b Benaud | 0 |
| Extras | (B 5, LB 1, NB 3) | 9 | (B 7, LB 5, NB 2) | 14 |
| **Total** | | **200** | | **134** |

## AUSTRALIA

| | | | | |
|---|---|---|---|---|
| C.C. McDonald | lbw b Fazal | 19 | not out | 44 |
| L.E. Favell | b Israr | 0 | c and b Israr | 4 |
| R.N. Harvey | b Fazal | 96 | b Fazal | 30 |
| N.C. O'Neill | b Nasim | 2 | not out | 26 |
| P.J.P. Burge | c Imtiaz b Nasim | 0 | | |
| R. Benaud* | lbw b Nasim | 16 | | |
| K.D. Mackay | b Fazal | 7 | | |
| A.K. Davidson | lbw b Israr | 4 | | |
| A.T.W. Grout† | not out | 66 | | |
| R.R. Lindwall | lbw b Fazal | 4 | | |
| I. Meckiff | b Fazal | 2 | | |
| Extras | (LB 9) | 9 | (B 3, LB 3, NB 2) | 8 |
| **Total** | | **225** | (2 wickets) | **112** |

| AUSTRALIA | O | M | R | W | O | M | R | W |
|---|---|---|---|---|---|---|---|---|
| Davidson | 23·5 | 7 | 42 | 4 | 11 | 3 | 23 | 0 |
| Meckiff | 10 | 2 | 33 | 0 | 3 | 1 | 8 | 0 |
| Lindwall | 15 | 1 | 31 | 0 | 2 | 0 | 5 | 0 |
| Benaud | 38 | 10 | 69 | 4 | 39·3 | 26 | 42 | 4 |
| Mackay | 19 | 12 | 16 | 1 | 45 | 27 | 42 | 6 |
| PAKISTAN | | | | | | | | |
| Fazal | 35·5 | 11 | 71 | 5 | 20·1 | 4 | 52 | 1 |
| Israr | 23 | 5 | 85 | 2 | 9 | 0 | 20 | 1 |
| Nasim | 17 | 4 | 51 | 3 | 10 | 2 | 16 | 0 |
| Shujauddin | 3 | 0 | 9 | 0 | 8 | 4 | 12 | 0 |
| Saeed | | | | | 1 | 0 | 4 | 0 |

| | FALL OF WICKETS | | | |
|---|---|---|---|---|
| | P | A | P | A |
| Wkt | 1st | 1st | 2nd | 2nd |
| 1st | 3 | 0 | 32 | 12 |
| 2nd | 75 | 51 | 57 | 65 |
| 3rd | 82 | 53 | 62 | – |
| 4th | 145 | 53 | 68 | – |
| 5th | 146 | 112 | 81 | – |
| 6th | 170 | 134 | 94 | – |
| 7th | 184 | 143 | 117 | – |
| 8th | 191 | 151 | 128 | – |
| 9th | 193 | 189 | 133 | – |
| 10th | 200 | 225 | 134 | – |

Umpires: Saeed Ahmed and A.A. Qureshi.

# PAKISTAN v AUSTRALIA 1959–60 (2nd Test)

Played at Lahore (*now Gaddafi*) Stadium on 21, 22, 23, 25, 26 November.
Toss: Pakistan.    Result: AUSTRALIA won by seven wickets.
Debuts: Pakistan – Mohammad Munaf; Australia – G.B. Stevens.

This was the first Test match to be played at Lahore Stadium with its turf pitch. Previous Tests in Lahore had been staged on matting at the Bagh-i-Jinnah Ground (formerly Lawrence Gardens). Australia required 122 runs in just under even time and, with just twelve minutes to spare, became the first country to win a rubber in Pakistan.

## PAKISTAN

| | | | | | |
|---|---|---|---|---|---|
| Hanif Mohammad | c Grout b Meckiff | 49 | (5) b Kline | | 18 |
| Imtiaz Ahmed*† | b Davidson | 18 | c O'Neill b Kline | | 54 |
| Saeed Ahmed | c Grout b Meckiff | 17 | st Grout b Kline | | 166 |
| Alimuddin | b Meckiff | 8 | (1) b Kline | | 7 |
| D.A. Sharpe | c Grout b Kline | 12 | (6) st Grout b Kline | | 1 |
| Waqar Hassan | c Grout b Davidson | 12 | (7) b Kline | | 4 |
| Shujauddin | b Benaud | 17 | (4) lbw b O'Neill | | 45 |
| Israr Ali | lbw b Benaud | 0 | (10) not out | | 0 |
| Nasim-ul-Ghani | c Stevens b Davidson | 6 | (8) b Benaud | | 15 |
| Mohammad Munaf | c Grout b Davidson | 5 | (9) c Davidson b Kline | | 19 |
| Haseeb Ahsan | not out | 0 | c Grout b Benaud | | 4 |
| Extras | (B 1, LB 1) | 2 | (B 31, LB 2) | | 33 |
| **Total** | | **146** | | | **366** |

## AUSTRALIA

| | | | | | |
|---|---|---|---|---|---|
| C.C. McDonald | c Imtiaz b Haseeb | 42 | | | |
| G.B. Stevens | c Imtiaz b Munaf | 9 | c Alimuddin b Munaf | | 8 |
| R.N. Harvey | lbw b Munaf | 43 | b Munaf | | 37 |
| N.C. O'Neill | st Imtiaz b Shujauddin | 134 | not out | | 43 |
| L.E. Favell | b Israr | 32 | (1) b Israr | | 4 |
| A.T.W. Grout† | lbw b Nasim | 12 | | | |
| R. Benaud* | b Haseeb | 29 | (5) not out | | 21 |
| A.K. Davidson | c Imtiaz b Israr | 47 | | | |
| K.D. Mackay | c Imtiaz b Haseeb | 26 | | | |
| L.F. Kline | not out | 0 | | | |
| I. Meckiff | did not bat | | | | |
| Extras | (B 5, LB 5, NB 7) | 17 | (B 6, LB 4) | | 10 |
| **Total** | (9 wickets declared) | **391** | (3 wickets) | | **123** |

| AUSTRALIA | O | M | R | W | O | M | R | W | FALL OF WICKETS | | | |
|---|---|---|---|---|---|---|---|---|---|---|---|---|
| | | | | | | | | | | P | A | P | A |
| Davidson | 19 | 2 | 48 | 4 | 35 | 9 | 56 | 0 | | P | A | P | A |
| Meckiff | 19 | 7 | 45 | 3 | 22 | 4 | 44 | 0 | Wkt | 1st | 1st | 2nd | 2nd |
| Benaud | 16 | 6 | 36 | 2 | 54·4 | 22 | 92 | 2 | 1st | 39 | 27 | 45 | 13 |
| Kline | 12 | 6 | 15 | 1 | 44 | 21 | 75 | 7 | 2nd | 56 | 83 | 87 | 15 |
| O'Neill | | | | | 13 | 5 | 37 | 1 | 3rd | 92 | 114 | 256 | 77 |
| Mackay | | | | | 6 | 1 | 21 | 0 | 4th | 109 | 213 | 312 | – |
| Harvey | | | | | 5 | 2 | 8 | 0 | 5th | 115 | 247 | 319 | – |
| | | | | | | | | | 6th | 120 | 310 | 324 | – |
| PAKISTAN | | | | | | | | | 7th | 121 | 311 | 325 | – |
| Munaf | 31 | 8 | 100 | 2 | 10 | 2 | 38 | 2 | 8th | 126 | 391 | 362 | – |
| Israr | 13 | 5 | 29 | 2 | 5 | 1 | 20 | 1 | 9th | 142 | 391 | 362 | – |
| Nasim | 21 | 3 | 72 | 1 | 3·3 | 0 | 18 | 0 | 10th | 146 | – | 366 | – |
| Shujauddin | 20 | 2 | 58 | 1 | 3 | 0 | 16 | 0 | | | | | |
| Haseeb | 33·3 | 8 | 115 | 3 | 4 | 0 | 21 | 0 | | | | | |

Umpires: Saeed Ahmed and A.A. Qureshi.

# PAKISTAN v AUSTRALIA 1959–60 (3rd Test)

Played at National Stadium, Karachi, on 4, 5, 6, 8, 9 December.
Toss: Pakistan.   Result: MATCH DRAWN.
Debuts: Pakistan – Intikhab Alam, Munir Malik.

Dwight D. Eisenhower became the first President of the United States of America to see Test cricket when he attended the fourth day of this match. It remains the second slowest day's play in Test history with Pakistan scoring 104 for 5. On a similar matting pitch on the same ground three years earlier, these countries had combined to produce only 95 runs in a full day. Intikhab became the first Pakistan bowler to take a wicket with his first ball in Test cricket when he bowled McDonald.

## PAKISTAN

| | | | | | |
|---|---|---|---|---|---|
| Hanif Mohammad | lbw b Lindwall | 51 | (4) not out | | 101 |
| Imtiaz Ahmed† | b Davidson | 18 | c Harvey b Davidson | | 9 |
| Saeed Ahmed | c Harvey b Lindwall | 91 | c Harvey b Davidson | | 8 |
| Shujauddin | c O'Neill b Benaud | 5 | (6) c Favell b Mackay | | 4 |
| D.A. Sharpe | c Burge b Benaud | 4 | c Mackay b Lindwall | | 26 |
| Ijaz Butt | c Grout b Benaud | 58 | (1) run out | | 8 |
| W. Mathias | c Favell b Mackay | 43 | c Davidson b Benaud | | 13 |
| Intikhab Alam | run out | 0 | c Burge b Mackay | | 6 |
| Fazal Mahmood* | c Harvey b Benaud | 7 | c Benaud b Davidson | | 11 |
| Mohammad Munaf | not out | 4 | not out | | 4 |
| Munir Malik | st Grout b Benaud | 0 | | | |
| Extras | (LB 3, NB 3) | 6 | (LB 2, NB 2) | | 4 |
| **Total** | | **287** | (8 wickets declared) | | **194** |

## AUSTRALIA

| | | | | | |
|---|---|---|---|---|---|
| C.C. McDonald | b Intikhab | 19 | lbw b Munir | | 30 |
| G.B. Stevens | c Mathias b Fazal | 13 | c Imtiaz b Intikhab | | 28 |
| A.T.W. Grout† | c and b Intikhab | 20 | | | |
| K.D. Mackay | c Ijaz Butt b Fazal | 40 | | | |
| R.N. Harvey | c Imtiaz b Fazal | 54 | (3) not out | | 13 |
| N.C. O'Neill | b Munir | 6 | (4) not out | | 7 |
| L.E. Favell | c Sharpe b Fazal | 10 | | | |
| P.J.P. Burge | c Sharpe b Munaf | 12 | | | |
| R. Benaud* | c Imtiaz b Munir | 18 | | | |
| A.K. Davidson | not out | 39 | | | |
| R.R. Lindwall | c Imtiaz b Fazal | 23 | | | |
| Extras | (LB 1, NB 2) | 3 | (LB 3, NB 2) | | 5 |
| **Total** | | **257** | (2 wickets) | | **83** |

| AUSTRALIA | O | M | R | W | O | M | R | W |
|---|---|---|---|---|---|---|---|---|
| Davidson | 26 | 5 | 59 | 1 | 34 | 8 | 70 | 3 |
| Lindwall | 25 | 6 | 72 | 2 | 17 | 10 | 14 | 1 |
| Benaud | 49·5 | 17 | 93 | 5 | 26 | 13 | 48 | 1 |
| Mackay | 27 | 8 | 53 | 1 | 32·4 | 11 | 58 | 2 |
| O'Neill | 4 | 1 | 4 | 0 | | | | |
| PAKISTAN | | | | | | | | |
| Fazal | 30·2 | 12 | 74 | 5 | 10 | 5 | 16 | 0 |
| Munaf | 8 | 0 | 42 | 1 | 3 | 0 | 10 | 0 |
| Intikhab | 19 | 4 | 49 | 2 | 6 | 1 | 13 | 1 |
| Munir | 22 | 5 | 76 | 2 | 9 | 1 | 24 | 1 |
| Shujauddin | 3 | 0 | 13 | 0 | 2 | 1 | 9 | 0 |
| Saeed | | | | | 3 | 0 | 6 | 0 |

FALL OF WICKETS

| Wkt | P 1st | A 1st | P 2nd | A 2nd |
|---|---|---|---|---|
| 1st | 36 | 29 | 11 | 54 |
| 2nd | 124 | 33 | 25 | 76 |
| 3rd | 143 | 82 | 25 | – |
| 4th | 149 | 106 | 78 | – |
| 5th | 181 | 122 | 91 | – |
| 6th | 265 | 145 | 124 | – |
| 7th | 267 | 174 | 159 | – |
| 8th | 276 | 184 | 179 | – |
| 9th | 287 | 207 | – | – |
| 10th | 287 | 257 | – | – |

Umpires: Saeed Ahmed and Munawar Hussain.

# INDIA v AUSTRALIA 1959–60 (1st Test)

Played at Feroz Shah Kotla, Delhi, on 12, 13, 14, 16 December.
Toss: India.    Result: AUSTRALIA won by an innings and 127 runs.
Debuts: India – V.M. Muddiah.

Spectators reacted to Australia's comprehensive win with more than a day to spare by throwing bottles on to the field and jostling the umpires. It was only the second Test to be finished in six matches played at Delhi. Benaud achieved the unique Test analysis of 3 for 0.

## INDIA

| | | | | |
|---|---|---|---|---|
| P. Roy | c Grout b Davidson | 0 | c Benaud b Kline | 99 |
| N.J. Contractor | b Davidson | 41 | c Favell b Benaud | 34 |
| P.R. Umrigar | c Grout b Davidson | 0 | (5) c Favell b Kline | 32 |
| A.A. Baig | b Rorke | 9 | (3) run out | 5 |
| C.G. Borde | c Grout b Meckiff | 14 | (4) c Davidson b Benaud | 0 |
| G.S. Ramchand* | c Grout b Kline | 20 | c Davidson b Kline | 6 |
| R.G. Nadkarni | b Rorke | 1 | lbw b Benaud | 7 |
| P.G. Joshi† | b Benaud | 15 | c Davidson b Kline | 8 |
| R. Surendranath | not out | 24 | c Davidson b Benaud | 0 |
| V.M. Muddiah | lbw b Benaud | 0 | not out | 0 |
| R.B. Desai | c O'Neill b Benaud | 0 | c Meckiff b Benaud | 0 |
| Extras | (B 6, LB 2, NB 3) | 11 | (B 8, LB 5, NB 2) | 15 |
| **Total** | | **135** | | **206** |

## AUSTRALIA

| | | |
|---|---|---|
| C.C. McDonald | b Surendranath | 20 |
| L. Favell | b Surendranath | 39 |
| R.N. Harvey | lbw b Nadkarni | 114 |
| N.C. O'Neill | run out | 39 |
| K.D. Mackay | c Joshi b Umrigar | 78 |
| A.K. Davidson | c Baig b Desai | 25 |
| R. Benaud* | c Borde b Umrigar | 20 |
| A.T.W. Grout† | b Umrigar | 42 |
| L.F. Kline | c and b Ramchand | 14 |
| I. Meckiff | not out | 45 |
| G.F. Rorke | c sub (B.K. Kunderan) b Umrigar | 7 |
| Extras | (B 11, LB 13, NB 1) | 25 |
| **Total** | | **468** |

| AUSTRALIA | O | M | R | W | O | M | R | W | | FALL OF WICKETS | | |
|---|---|---|---|---|---|---|---|---|---|---|---|---|
| Davidson | 14 | 9 | 22 | 3 | 14 | 5 | 16 | 0 | | I | A | I |
| Meckiff | 17 | 4 | 52 | 1 | 14 | 3 | 33 | 0 | *Wkt* | *1st* | *1st* | *2nd* |
| Rorke | 14 | 5 | 30 | 2 | 7 | 3 | 5 | 0 | 1st | 4 | 53 | 121 |
| Kline | 9 | 3 | 15 | 1 | 24 | 12 | 42 | 4 | 2nd | 8 | 64 | 132 |
| Benaud | 3·4 | 3 | 0 | 3 | 46 | 18 | 76 | 5 | 3rd | 32 | 143 | 132 |
| Mackay | 1 | 0 | 1 | 0 | | | | | 4th | 66 | 275 | 172 |
| O'Neill | 1 | 0 | 4 | 0 | 5 | 0 | 19 | 0 | 5th | 69 | 318 | 187 |
| Harvey | | | | | 1 | 1 | 0 | 0 | 6th | 70 | 353 | 192 |
| | | | | | | | | | 7th | 100 | 398 | 202 |
| INDIA | | | | | | | | | 8th | 131 | 402 | 206 |
| Desai | 34·3 | 3 | 123 | 1 | | | | | 9th | 135 | 443 | 206 |
| Surendranath | 38 | 8 | 101 | 2 | | | | | 10th | 135 | 468 | 206 |
| Borde | 15 | 3 | 49 | 0 | | | | | | | | |
| Muddiah | 13 | 4 | 32 | 0 | | | | | | | | |
| Nadkarni | 20 | 6 | 62 | 1 | | | | | | | | |
| Ramchand | 7 | 1 | 27 | 1 | | | | | | | | |
| Umrigar | 15·3 | 1 | 49 | 4 | | | | | | | | |

Umpires: Mohammad Yunus and S.K. Ganguli.

# INDIA v AUSTRALIA 1959–60 (2nd Test)

Played at Green Park, Kanpur, on 19, 20, 21, 23, 24 December.
Toss: India.   Result: INDIA won by 119 runs.
Debuts: Australia – B.N. Jarman.

Jasu Patel exploited a newly-laid turf pitch with his off-spin to return what is still India's best analysis in Test cricket. S.P. Gupte had taken 9 for 102 against West Indies on the same ground the previous season. Patel remains the only Indian bowler to take 14 wickets in a Test match. This was India's first success in ten Tests against Australia since 1947. Australia's second innings total is their lowest in any Test against India.

## INDIA

| | | | | | |
|---|---|---|---|---|---|
| P. Roy | c Harvey b Benaud | 17 | c Benaud b Davidson | | 8 |
| N.J. Contractor | c Jarman b Benaud | 24 | c Harvey b Davidson | | 74 |
| P.R. Umrigar | c Davidson b Kline | 6 | c Rorke b Davidson | | 14 |
| A.A. Baig | b Davidson | 19 | c Harvey b Benaud | | 36 |
| C.G. Borde | c Kline b Davidson | 20 | c O'Neill b Meckiff | | 44 |
| G.S. Ramchand* | c Mackay b Benaud | 24 | b Harvey | | 5 |
| R.B. Kenny | b Davidson | 0 | c Jarman b Davidson | | 51 |
| R.G. Nadkarni | c Harvey b Davidson | 25 | lbw b Davidson | | 46 |
| N.S. Tamhane† | b Benaud | 1 | c Harvey b Davidson | | 0 |
| J.M. Patel | c Kline b Davidson | 4 | (11) b Davidson | | 0 |
| R. Surendranath | not out | 8 | (10) not out | | 4 |
| Extras | (LB 2, NB 2) | 4 | (B 7, LB 2) | | 9 |
| **Total** | | **152** | | | **291** |

## AUSTRALIA

| | | | | | |
|---|---|---|---|---|---|
| C.C. McDonald | b Patel | 53 | st Tamhane b Patel | | 34 |
| G.B. Stevens | c and b Patel | 25 | c Kenny b Patel | | 7 |
| R.N. Harvey | b Patel | 51 | c Nadkarni b Umrigar | | 25 |
| N.C. O'Neill | b Borde | 16 | c Nadkarni b Umrigar | | 5 |
| K.D. Mackay | lbw b Patel | 0 | lbw b Umrigar | | 0 |
| A.K. Davidson | b Patel | 41 | b Patel | | 8 |
| R. Benaud* | b Patel | 7 | c Ramchand b Patel | | 0 |
| B.N. Jarman† | lbw b Patel | 1 | b Umrigar | | 0 |
| L.F. Kline | b Patel | 9 | b Patel | | 0 |
| I. Meckiff | not out | 1 | not out | | 14 |
| G.F. Rorke | c Baig b Patel | 0 | absent ill | | – |
| Extras | (B 9, LB 2, NB 4) | 15 | (B 5, LB 7) | | 12 |
| **Total** | | **219** | | | **105** |

| AUSTRALIA | O | M | R | W | O | M | R | W | | | | | |
|---|---|---|---|---|---|---|---|---|---|---|---|---|---|
| Davidson | 20·1 | 7 | 31 | 5 | 57·3 | 23 | 93 | 7 | | FALL OF WICKETS | | | |
| Meckiff | 8 | 2 | 15 | 0 | 18 | 4 | 37 | 1 | *Wkt* | *1st* | *1st* | *2nd* | *2nd* |
| Benaud | 25 | 8 | 63 | 4 | 38 | 15 | 81 | 1 | 1st | 38 | 71 | 32 | 12 |
| Rorke | 2 | 1 | 3 | 0 | | | | | 2nd | 47 | 128 | 72 | 49 |
| Kline | 15 | 7 | 36 | 1 | 7 | 3 | 14 | 0 | 3rd | 51 | 149 | 121 | 59 |
| Mackay | | | | | 10 | 5 | 14 | 0 | 4th | 77 | 159 | 147 | 61 |
| Harvey | | | | | 12 | 3 | 31 | 1 | 5th | 112 | 159 | 153 | 78 |
| O'Neill | | | | | 2 | 0 | 12 | 0 | 6th | 112 | 174 | 214 | 78 |
| | | | | | | | | | 7th | 126 | 186 | 286 | 79 |
| INDIA | | | | | | | | | 8th | 128 | 216 | 286 | 84 |
| Surendranath | 4 | 0 | 13 | 0 | 4 | 2 | 4 | 0 | 9th | 141 | 219 | 291 | 105 |
| Ramchand | 6 | 3 | 14 | 0 | 3 | 0 | 7 | 0 | 10th | 152 | 219 | 291 | – |
| Patel | 35·5 | 16 | 69 | 9 | 25·4 | 7 | 55 | 5 | | | | | |
| Umrigar | 15 | 1 | 40 | 0 | 25 | 11 | 27 | 4 | | | | | |
| Borde | 15 | 1 | 61 | 1 | | | | | | | | | |
| Nadkarni | 2 | 0 | 7 | 0 | | | | | | | | | |

Umpires: S.K. Ganguli and A.R. Joshi.

# INDIA v AUSTRALIA 1959–60 (3rd Test)

Played at Brabourne Stadium, Bombay, on 1, 2, 3, 5, 6 January.
Toss: India.   Result: MATCH DRAWN.
Debuts: India – S.A. Durani (*not A.S. Durrani*), B.K. Kunderan (*not B.K. Kunderam*).

Patel, hero of the previous Test, was taken ill on the morning of the match and his replacement, Durani, was unable to bowl because of a cut finger. Umrigar (back strain) took no part in the last two days' play. India declared leaving Australia 25 minutes in which to score 129 runs. The partnership of 207 between Harvey and O'Neill remains the highest for the third-wicket by either country in this series.

## INDIA

| | | | | |
|---|---|---|---|---|
| P. Roy | b Davidson | 6 | b Meckiff | 57 |
| N.J. Contractor | c Benaud b Meckiff | 108 | b Lindwall | 43 |
| P.R. Umrigar | c Harvey b Davidson | 0 | | |
| A.A. Baig | c Grout b Davidson | 50 | (5) c Mackay b Lindwall | 58 |
| C.G. Borde | b Meckiff | 26 | (4) b Meckiff | 1 |
| G.S. Ramchand* | lbw b Meckiff | 0 | | |
| R.B. Kenny | b Meckiff | 20 | (6) not out | 55 |
| B.K. Kunderan† | lbw b Lindwall | 19 | (3) hit wkt b Meckiff | 2 |
| R.G. Nadkarni | not out | 18 | (7) not out | 1 |
| S.A. Durani | c Stevens b Benaud | 18 | | |
| G.M. Guard | c Benaud b Davidson | 7 | | |
| Extras | (B 9, LB 4, NB 4) | 17 | (LB 9) | 9 |
| **Total** | | **289** | (5 wickets declared) | **226** |

## AUSTRALIA

| | | | | |
|---|---|---|---|---|
| C.C. McDonald | b Nadkarni | 36 | | |
| G.B. Stevens | b Nadkarni | 22 | | |
| R.N. Harvey | b Nadkarni | 102 | | |
| N.C. O'Neill | c sub (M.M. Sood) b Borde | 163 | | |
| L.E. Favell | b Nadkarni | 1 | | |
| A.T.W. Grout† | b Nadkarni | 31 | (1) not out | 22 |
| R. Benaud* | lbw b Nadkarni | 14 | (3) not out | 12 |
| A.K. Davidson | not out | 9 | | |
| K.D. Mackay | b Borde | 1 | | |
| R.R. Lindwall | not out | 1 | | |
| I. Meckiff | did not bat | – | (2) b Roy | 0 |
| Extras | (B 4, LB 3) | 7 | | |
| **Total** | (8 wickets declared) | **387** | (1 wicket) | **34** |

| AUSTRALIA | O | M | R | W | O | M | R | W | | FALL OF WICKETS | | | |
|---|---|---|---|---|---|---|---|---|---|---|---|---|---|
| | | | | | | | | | | I | A | I | A |
| Davidson | 34·5 | 9 | 62 | 4 | 14 | 4 | 25 | 0 | Wkt | 1st | 1st | 2nd | 2nd |
| Lindwall | 23 | 7 | 56 | 1 | 23 | 7 | 56 | 2 | 1st | 21 | 60 | 95 | 4 |
| Mackay | 6 | 3 | 11 | 0 | 6 | 4 | 6 | 0 | 2nd | 21 | 63 | 99 | – |
| Meckiff | 38 | 12 | 79 | 4 | 28 | 8 | 67 | 3 | 3rd | 154 | 270 | 111 | – |
| Benaud | 41 | 24 | 64 | 1 | 24 | 10 | 36 | 0 | 4th | 199 | 282 | 112 | – |
| O'Neill | | | | | 3 | 1 | 16 | 0 | 5th | 199 | 358 | 221 | – |
| Harvey | | | | | 3 | 1 | 11 | 0 | 6th | 203 | 376 | – | – |
| INDIA | | | | | | | | | 7th | 229 | 379 | – | – |
| Guard | 33 | 7 | 93 | 0 | 1 | 0 | 1 | 0 | 8th | 246 | 380 | – | – |
| Ramchand | 35 | 13 | 85 | 0 | | | | | 9th | 272 | – | – | – |
| Umrigar | 8 | 2 | 19 | 0 | | | | | 10th | 289 | – | – | – |
| Nadkarni | 51 | 11 | 105 | 6 | | | | | | | | | |
| Borde | 13 | 1 | 78 | 2 | | | | | | | | | |
| Roy | | | | | 2 | 0 | 6 | 1 | | | | | |
| Contractor | | | | | 2 | 1 | 5 | 0 | | | | | |
| Baig | | | | | 2 | 0 | 13 | 0 | | | | | |
| Durani | | | | | 1 | 0 | 9 | 0 | | | | | |

Umpires: N.D. Nagarwalla and H.E. Choudhury.

# INDIA v AUSTRALIA 1959–60 (4th Test)

Played at Corporation Stadium, Madras, on 13, 14, 15, 17 January.
Toss: Australia.   Result: AUSTRALIA won by an innings and 55 runs.
Debuts: India – A.G. Milkha Singh, M.M. Sood.

Australia's second victory by an innings in the rubber was completed with 40 minutes of the penultimate day to spare. Davidson took his hundredth Test wicket when he bowled Sood.

## AUSTRALIA

| | | |
|---|---|---:|
| C.C. McDonald | b Patel | 16 |
| L.E. Favell | st Kunderan b Nadkarni | 101 |
| R.N. Harvey | b Desai | 11 |
| N.C. O'Neill | b Desai | 40 |
| P.J.P. Burge | b Desai | 35 |
| K.D. Mackay | st Kunderan b Patel | 89 |
| A.K. Davidson | lbw b Nadkarni | 6 |
| A.T.W. Grout† | c Milkha Singh b Nadkarni | 2 |
| R. Benaud* | b Borde | 25 |
| I. Meckiff | c Roy b Desai | 8 |
| L.F. Kline | not out | 0 |
| Extras | (B 3, LB 5, NB 1) | 9 |
| **Total** | | **342** |

## INDIA

| | | | | | |
|---|---|---:|---|---|---:|
| P. Roy | c Grout b Davidson | 1 | | c O'Neill b Meckiff | 3 |
| B.K. Kunderan† | b Benaud | 71 | (4) | b Benaud | 33 |
| R.B. Kenny | b Mackay | 33 | | c Grout b Meckiff | 1 |
| N.J. Contractor | c Kline b Benaud | 7 | (2) | c Meckiff b Kline | 41 |
| C.G. Borde | c Grout b Kline | 3 | | c Davidson b Benaud | 1 |
| G.S. Ramchand* | c Harvey b Benaud | 13 | (8) | st Grout b Benaud | 22 |
| A.G. Milkha Singh | b Davidson | 16 | (6) | b Harvey | 9 |
| R.G. Nadkarni | c Kline b Benaud | 3 | (7) | run out | 18 |
| M.M. Sood | st Grout b Davidson | 0 | | b Davidson | 3 |
| R.B. Desai | c McDonald b Benaud | 0 | | not out | 0 |
| J.M. Patel | not out | 0 | | c Kline b Davidson | 0 |
| Extras | (B 1, NB 1) | 2 | | (B 4, LB 2, NB 1) | 7 |
| **Total** | | **149** | | | **138** |

| INDIA | O | M | R | W | O | M | R | W |
|---|---|---|---|---|---|---|---|---|
| Desai | 41 | 10 | 93 | 4 | | | | |
| Ramchand | 15 | 6 | 26 | 0 | | | | |
| Nadkarni | 44 | 15 | 75 | 3 | | | | |
| Patel | 37 | 12 | 84 | 2 | | | | |
| Borde | 16 | 1 | 55 | 1 | | | | |
| **AUSTRALIA** | | | | | | | | |
| Davidson | 19 | 6 | 36 | 3 | 19 | 7 | 33 | 2 |
| Meckiff | 7 | 4 | 21 | 0 | 22 | 10 | 33 | 2 |
| Benaud | 32·1 | 14 | 43 | 5 | 35 | 19 | 43 | 3 |
| Kline | 15 | 8 | 21 | 1 | 12 | 5 | 13 | 1 |
| Harvey | 1 | 0 | 9 | 0 | 13 | 7 | 8 | 1 |
| Mackay | 3 | 0 | 17 | 1 | 4 | 3 | 1 | 0 |

### FALL OF WICKETS

| | A | I | I |
|---|---|---|---|
| Wkt | 1st | 1st | 2nd |
| 1st | 58 | 20 | 7 |
| 2nd | 77 | 95 | 11 |
| 3rd | 147 | 111 | 54 |
| 4th | 197 | 114 | 62 |
| 5th | 216 | 130 | 78 |
| 6th | 239 | 130 | 100 |
| 7th | 249 | 145 | 127 |
| 8th | 308 | 148 | 138 |
| 9th | 329 | 149 | 138 |
| 10th | 342 | 149 | 138 |

Umpires: M.G. Vijayasarathi and N.D. Sane.

## INDIA v AUSTRALIA 1959–60 (5th Test)

Played at Eden Gardens, Calcutta, on 23, 24, 25, 27, 28 January.
Toss: India.    Result: MATCH DRAWN.
Debuts: Nil.

Left to score 203 runs in 150 minutes, Australia were content to draw and take the rubber by two matches to one. After O'Neill had scored Australia's first century in a Calcutta Test, Lindwall, in his final match, took his record Australian total of Test wickets to 228 – just eight short of the current world record held by A.V. Bedser. Jaisimha batted on each of the five days.

### INDIA

| | | | | |
|---|---|---|---|---|
| B.K. Kunderan† | b Mackay | 12 | b Davidson | 0 |
| N.J. Contractor | b Benaud | 36 | c Davidson b Benaud | 30 |
| P. Roy | c Grout b Davidson | 33 | lbw b Benaud | 39 |
| R.G. Nadkarni | c Burge b Lindwall | 2 | (6) c Grout b Lindwall | 29 |
| R.B. Kenny | c Grout b Lindwall | 7 | (8) c Grout b Mackay | 62 |
| C.D. Gopinath | b Benaud | 39 | (5) c Grout b Benaud | 0 |
| C.G. Borde | b Benaud | 6 | b Meckiff | 50 |
| G.S. Ramchand* | b Davidson | 12 | (9) b Benaud | 9 |
| M.L. Jaisimha | not out | 20 | (4) b Mackay | 74 |
| R.B. Desai | c Grout b Davidson | 17 | not out | 17 |
| J.M. Patel | run out | 0 | c Benaud b Davidson | 12 |
| Extras | (B 5, LB 1, W 1, NB 3) | 10 | (B 11, LB 4, NB 2) | 17 |
| **Total** | | **194** | | **339** |

### AUSTRALIA

| | | | | |
|---|---|---|---|---|
| L.E. Favell | b Desai | 26 | not out | 62 |
| A.T.W. Grout† | b Patel | 50 | | |
| R.N. Harvey | c Jaisimha b Patel | 17 | c and b Contractor | 36 |
| N.C. O'Neill | c Kunderan b Desai | 113 | | |
| P.J.P. Burge | b Desai | 60 | | |
| C.C. McDonald | lbw b Borde | 27 | (2) run out | 6 |
| K.D. Mackay | b Patel | 18 | | |
| R.R. Lindwall | c Kunderan b Desai | 10 | | |
| A.K. Davidson | b Borde | 4 | | |
| R. Benaud* | c and b Borde | 3 | (4) not out | 10 |
| I. Meckiff | not out | 0 | | |
| Extras | (LB 3) | 3 | (B 1, LB 5, NB 1) | 7 |
| **Total** | | **331** | (2 wickets) | **121** |

| AUSTRALIA | O | M | R | W | O | M | R | W | | FALL OF WICKETS | | | |
|---|---|---|---|---|---|---|---|---|---|---|---|---|---|
| | | | | | | | | | | I | A | I | A |
| Davidson | 16 | 2 | 37 | 3 | 36·2 | 13 | 76 | 2 | Wkt | 1st | 1st | 2nd | 2nd |
| Meckiff | 17 | 5 | 28 | 0 | 21 | 2 | 41 | 1 | 1st | 30 | 76 | 0 | 20 |
| Mackay | 11 | 5 | 16 | 1 | 21 | 7 | 36 | 2 | 2nd | 59 | 76 | 67 | 104 |
| Lindwall | 16 | 6 | 44 | 2 | 20 | 3 | 66 | 1 | 3rd | 71 | 116 | 78 | – |
| Benaud | 29·3 | 12 | 59 | 3 | 48 | 23 | 103 | 4 | 4th | 83 | 266 | 78 | – |
| | | | | | | | | | 5th | 112 | 273 | 123 | – |
| INDIA | | | | | | | | | 6th | 131 | 299 | 206 | – |
| Desai | 36 | 4 | 111 | 4 | 11 | 4 | 18 | 0 | 7th | 142 | 323 | 289 | – |
| Ramchand | 10 | 1 | 37 | 0 | 3 | 2 | 4 | 0 | 8th | 158 | 325 | 294 | – |
| Patel | 26 | 2 | 104 | 3 | 7 | 1 | 15 | 0 | 9th | 194 | 328 | 316 | – |
| Nadkarni | 22 | 10 | 36 | 0 | 7 | 4 | 10 | 0 | 10th | 194 | 331 | 339 | – |
| Borde | 13·1 | 4 | 23 | 3 | 13 | 1 | 45 | 0 | | | | | |
| Jaisimha | 4 | 0 | 17 | 0 | 6 | 2 | 13 | 0 | | | | | |
| Contractor | | | | | 5 | 1 | 9 | 1 | | | | | |

Umpires: S.K. Ganguli and A.R. Joshi.

# WEST INDIES v ENGLAND 1959–60 (1st Test)

Played at Kensington Oval, Bridgetown, Barbados, on 6, 7, 8, 9, 11, 12 January.
Toss: England. Result: MATCH DRAWN.
Debuts: West Indies – R.G. Scarlett, C.D. Watson; England – D.A. Allen.

Worrell (682 minutes) and Sobers (647 minutes) played the two then longest innings against England and their partnership of 399 in 570 minutes remains the West Indies record for any wicket against England, the West Indies fourth-wicket record in all Tests, and the highest fourth-wicket stand by any country against England. Earlier Alexander had set a West Indies record by holding five catches in an innings and McMorris had been run out off a no-ball.

## ENGLAND

| | | | | | |
|---|---|---|---|---|---|
| G. Pullar | run out | 65 | not out | | 46 |
| M.C. Cowdrey | c Sobers b Watson | 30 | not out | | 16 |
| K.F. Barrington | c Alexander b Ramadhin | 128 | | | |
| P.B.H. May* | c Alexander b Hall | 1 | | | |
| M.J.K. Smith | c Alexander b Scarlett | 39 | | | |
| E.R. Dexter | not out | 136 | | | |
| R. Illingworth | b Ramadhin | 5 | | | |
| R. Swetman† | c Alexander b Worrell | 45 | | | |
| F.S. Trueman | c Alexander b Ramadhin | 3 | | | |
| D.A. Allen | lbw b Watson | 10 | | | |
| A.E. Moss | b Watson | 4 | | | |
| Extras | (B 4, LB 6, NB 6) | 16 | (B 7, LB 1, W 1) | | 9 |
| **Total** | | **482** | (0 wickets) | | **71** |

## WEST INDIES

| | | |
|---|---|---|
| C.C. Hunte | c Swetman b Barrington | 42 |
| E.D.A. St J. McMorris | run out | 0 |
| R.B. Kanhai | b Trueman | 40 |
| G. St A. Sobers | b Trueman | 226 |
| F.M.M. Worrell | not out | 197 |
| B.F. Butcher | c Trueman b Dexter | 13 |
| W.W. Hall | lbw b Trueman | 14 |
| F.C.M. Alexander*† | c Smith b Trueman | 3 |
| R.G. Scarlett | lbw b Dexter | 7 |
| C.D. Watson | } did not bat | |
| S. Ramadhin | | |
| Extras | (B 8, LB 7, W 1, NB 5) | 21 |
| **Total** | (8 wickets declared) | **563** |

| WEST INDIES | O | M | R | W | O | M | R | W |
|---|---|---|---|---|---|---|---|---|
| Hall | 40 | 9 | 98 | 1 | 6 | 2 | 9 | 0 |
| Watson | 32·4 | 6 | 121 | 3 | 8 | 1 | 19 | 0 |
| Worrell | 15 | 2 | 39 | 1 | | | | |
| Ramadhin | 54 | 22 | 109 | 3 | 7 | 2 | 11 | 0 |
| Scarlett | 26 | 9 | 46 | 1 | 10 | 4 | 12 | 0 |
| Sobers | 21 | 3 | 53 | 0 | | | | |
| Hunte | | | | | 7 | 2 | 9 | 0 |
| Kanhai | | | | | 4 | 3 | 2 | 0 |
| ENGLAND | | | | | | | | |
| Trueman | 47 | 15 | 93 | 4 | | | | |
| Moss | 47 | 14 | 116 | 0 | | | | |
| Dexter | 37·4 | 11 | 85 | 2 | | | | |
| Illingworth | 47 | 9 | 106 | 0 | | | | |
| Allen | 43 | 12 | 82 | 0 | | | | |
| Barrington | 18 | 3 | 60 | 1 | | | | |

FALL OF WICKETS

| | E | WI | E |
|---|---|---|---|
| Wkt | 1st | 1st | 2nd |
| 1st | 50 | 6 | – |
| 2nd | 153 | 68 | – |
| 3rd | 162 | 102 | – |
| 4th | 251 | 501 | – |
| 5th | 291 | 521 | – |
| 6th | 303 | 544 | – |
| 7th | 426 | 556 | – |
| 8th | 439 | 563 | – |
| 9th | 478 | – | – |
| 10th | 482 | – | – |

Umpires: H.B. de C. Jordan and J. Roberts.

# WEST INDIES v ENGLAND 1959–60 (2nd Test)

Played at Queen's Park Oval, Port-of-Spain, Trinidad, on 28, 29, 30 January, 1, 2, 3 February.
Toss: England.   Result: ENGLAND won by 256 runs.
Debuts: West Indies – C.K. Singh.

A dramatic match which was marred when sections of the crowd of 30,000 – a record for any sporting event in the West Indies – threw bottles, rioted, and brought play to a premature close when Singh was run out soon after tea on the third day. Earlier Hall and Watson had been warned by umpires Lloyd and Lee Kow respectively for intimidatory bowling (Law 46). Barrington scored his second hundred in only his second innings against West Indies. England won with 110 minutes to spare after setting West Indies 501 runs to win in ten hours.

## ENGLAND

| | | | | |
|---|---|---|---|---|
| G. Pullar | c Alexander b Watson | 17 | c Worrell b Ramadhin | 28 |
| M.C. Cowdrey | b Hall | 18 | c Alexander b Watson | 5 |
| K.F. Barrington | c Alexander b Hall | 121 | c Alexander b Hall | 49 |
| P.B.H. May* | c Kanhai b Watson | 0 | c and b Singh | 28 |
| E.R. Dexter | c and b Singh | 77 | b Hall | 0 |
| M.J.K. Smith | c Worrell b Ramadhin | 108 | lbw b Watson | 12 |
| R. Illingworth | b Ramadhin | 10 | not out | 41 |
| R. Swetman† | lbw b Watson | 1 | lbw b Singh | 0 |
| F.S. Trueman | lbw b Ramadhin | 7 | c Alexander b Watson | 37 |
| D.A. Allen | not out | 10 | c Alexander b Hall | 16 |
| J.B. Statham | b Worrell | 1 | | |
| Extras | (LB 3, W 1, NB 8) | 12 | (B 6, LB 2, W 4, NB 2) | 14 |
| **Total** | | **382** | (9 wickets declared) | **230** |

## WEST INDIES

| | | | | |
|---|---|---|---|---|
| C.C. Hunte | c Trueman b Statham | 8 | c Swetman b Allen | 47 |
| J.S. Solomon | run out | 23 | c Swetman b Allen | 9 |
| R.B. Kanhai | lbw b Trueman | 5 | c Smith b Dexter | 110 |
| G. St A. Sobers | c Barrington b Trueman | 0 | lbw b Trueman | 31 |
| F.M.M. Worrell | c Swetman b Trueman | 9 | lbw b Statham | 0 |
| B.F. Butcher | lbw b Statham | 9 | lbw b Statham | 9 |
| F.C.M. Alexander *† | lbw b Trueman | 28 | c Trueman b Allen | 7 |
| S. Ramadhin | b Trueman | 23 | lbw b Dexter | 0 |
| C.K. Singh | run out | 0 | c and b Barrington | 11 |
| W.W. Hall | b Statham | 4 | not out | 0 |
| C.D. Watson | not out | 0 | c Allen b Barrington | 0 |
| Extras | (LB 2, W 1) | 3 | (B 11, LB 6, W 2, NB 1) | 20 |
| **Total** | | **112** | | **244** |

| WEST INDIES | O | M | R | W | O | M | R | W | | FALL OF WICKETS | | | |
|---|---|---|---|---|---|---|---|---|---|---|---|---|---|
| Hall | 33 | 9 | 92 | 2 | 23·4 | 4 | 50 | 3 | | E | WI | E | WI |
| Watson | 31 | 5 | 100 | 3 | 19 | 6 | 57 | 3 | *Wkt* | *1st* | *1st* | *2nd* | *2nd* |
| Worrell | 11·5 | 3 | 2 | 1 | 12 | 5 | 27 | 0 | 1st | 37 | 22 | 18 | 29 |
| Singh | 23 | 6 | 59 | 1 | 8 | 3 | 28 | 2 | 2nd | 42 | 31 | 79 | 107 |
| Ramadhin | 35 | 12 | 61 | 3 | 28 | 8 | 54 | 1 | 3rd | 57 | 31 | 97 | 158 |
| Sobers | 3 | 0 | 16 | 0 | | | | | 4th | 199 | 45 | 101 | 159 |
| Solomon | 7 | 0 | 19 | 0 | | | | | 5th | 276 | 45 | 122 | 188 |
| ENGLAND | | | | | | | | | 6th | 307 | 73 | 133 | 222 |
| Trueman | 21 | 11 | 35 | 5 | 19 | 9 | 44 | 1 | 7th | 308 | 94 | 133 | 222 |
| Statham | 19·3 | 8 | 42 | 3 | 25 | 12 | 44 | 2 | 8th | 343 | 98 | 201 | 244 |
| Allen | 5 | 0 | 9 | 0 | 31 | 13 | 57 | 3 | 9th | 378 | 108 | 230 | 244 |
| Barrington | 16 | 10 | 15 | 0 | 25·5 | 13 | 34 | 2 | 10th | 382 | 112 | – | 244 |
| Illingworth | 7 | 3 | 8 | 0 | 28 | 14 | 38 | 0 | | | | | |
| Dexter | | | | | 6 | 3 | 7 | 2 | | | | | |

Umpires: E.N. Lee Kow and E.L. Lloyd.

# WEST INDIES v ENGLAND 1959–60 (3rd Test)

Played at Sabina Park, Kingston, Jamaica, on 17, 18, 19, 20, 22, 23 February.
Toss: England.   Result: MATCH DRAWN.
Debuts: West Indies – S.M. Nurse.

England failed to take a wicket on the third day, McMorris (65*) retiring with a contused lung at 189 for 2 after being hit on the chest by a ball from Statham; he resumed his innings at 329 for 6. After England's last wicket had survived for 45 minutes on the final morning, West Indies required 230 to square the rubber in 245 minutes. At tea their target had become 115 in 90 minutes with six wickets left. They gave up the chase when Kanhai was sixth out and England failed to take the remaining wickets during the subsequent 45 minutes. Six England batsmen were 'lbw' in the second innings, equalling the Test record which they had set in 1955 (*Test No. 411*).

### ENGLAND

| | | | | |
|---|---|---|---|---|
| G. Pullar | c Sobers b Hall | 19 | lbw b Ramadhin | 66 |
| M.C. Cowdrey | c Scarlett b Ramadhin | 114 | c Alexander b Scarlett | 97 |
| K.F. Barrington | c Alexander b Watson | 16 | lbw b Solomon | 4 |
| P.B.H. May* | c Hunte b Hall | 9 | b Hall | 45 |
| E.R. Dexter | c Alexander b Hall | 25 | b Watson | 16 |
| M.J.K. Smith | b Hall | 0 | lbw b Watson | 10 |
| R. Illingworth | c Alexander b Hall | 17 | b Ramadhin | 6 |
| R. Swetman† | b Hall | 0 | lbw b Watson | 5 |
| F.S. Trueman | c Solomon b Ramadhin | 17 | lbw b Watson | 4 |
| D.A. Allen | not out | 30 | not out | 17 |
| J.B. Statham | b Hall | 13 | lbw b Ramadhin | 12 |
| Extras | (LB 4, W 10, NB 3) | 17 | (B 8, LB 10, W 3, NB 2) | 23 |
| **Total** | | **277** | | **305** |

### WEST INDIES

| | | | | |
|---|---|---|---|---|
| C.C. Hunte | c Illingworth b Statham | 7 | b Trueman | 40 |
| E.D.A. St J. McMorris | b Barrington | 73 | b Trueman | 1 |
| R.B. Kanhai | run out | 18 | b Trueman | 57 |
| G. St A. Sobers | lbw b Trueman | 147 | run out | 19 |
| S.M. Nurse | c Smith b Illingworth | 70 | b Trueman | 11 |
| J.S. Solomon | c Swetman b Allen | 8 | (8) not out | 10 |
| R.G. Scarlett | c Statham b Illingworth | 6 | (6) lbw b Statham | 12 |
| F.C.M. Alexander*† | b Trueman | 0 | (7) not out | 7 |
| S. Ramadhin | b Statham | 5 | | |
| C.D. Watson | b Statham | 3 | | |
| W.W. Hall | not out | 0 | | |
| Extras | (B 6, LB 7, W 1, NB 2) | 16 | (B 9, LB 3, W 6) | 18 |
| **Total** | | **353** | (6 wickets) | **175** |

| WEST INDIES | O | M | R | W | O | M | R | W | | FALL OF WICKETS | | | |
|---|---|---|---|---|---|---|---|---|---|---|---|---|---|
| Hall | 31·2 | 8 | 69 | 7 | 26 | 5 | 93 | 1 | | E | WI | E | WI |
| Watson | 29 | 7 | 74 | 1 | 27 | 8 | 62 | 4 | *Wkt* | *1st* | *1st* | *2nd* | *2nd* |
| Ramadhin | 28 | 3 | 78 | 2 | 28·3 | 14 | 38 | 3 | 1st | 28 | 12 | 177 | 11 |
| Scarlett | 10 | 4 | 13 | 0 | 28 | 12 | 51 | 1 | 2nd | 54 | 56 | 177 | 48 |
| Sobers | 2 | 0 | 14 | 0 | 8 | 2 | 18 | 0 | 3rd | 68 | 299 | 190 | 86 |
| Solomon | 4 | 1 | 12 | 0 | 6 | 1 | 20 | 1 | 4th | 113 | 329 | 211 | 111 |
| | | | | | | | | | 5th | 113 | 329 | 239 | 140 |
| ENGLAND | | | | | | | | | 6th | 165 | 329 | 258 | 152 |
| Statham | 32·1 | 8 | 76 | 3 | 18 | 6 | 45 | 1 | 7th | 170 | 341 | 269 | – |
| Trueman | 33 | 10 | 82 | 2 | 18 | 4 | 54 | 4 | 8th | 215 | 347 | 269 | – |
| Dexter | 12 | 3 | 38 | 0 | | | | | 9th | 245 | 350 | 280 | – |
| Allen | 28 | 10 | 57 | 1 | 9 | 4 | 19 | 0 | 10th | 277 | 353 | 305 | – |
| Barrington | 21 | 7 | 38 | 1 | 4 | 4 | 0 | 0 | | | | | |
| Illingworth | 30 | 13 | 46 | 2 | 13 | 4 | 35 | 0 | | | | | |
| Cowdrey | | | | | 1 | 0 | 4 | 0 | | | | | |

Umpires: P. Burke and E.N. Lee Kow.

# WEST INDIES v ENGLAND 1959–60 (4th Test)

Played at Bourda, Georgetown, British Guiana, on 9, 10, 11, 12, 14, 15 March.
Toss: England.　Result: MATCH DRAWN.
Debuts: Nil.

Rain delayed the start by 75 minutes. Barrington, struck above the elbow by Hall on the first day, retired at 161 for three after 20 minutes' batting on the second, and resumed at 219 for 7. After Sobers had scored his third hundred of the rubber, West Indies declared with a lead of 107, eight hours of play left, and Watson (torn ankle ligaments) unable to bowl. Subba Row scored his first Test hundred under the handicap of a chipped knuckle.

## ENGLAND

| | | | | |
|---|---|--:|---|--:|
| G. Pullar | c Alexander b Hall | 33 | lbw b Worrell | 47 |
| M.C. Cowdrey* | c Alexander b Hall | 65 | st Alexander b Singh | 27 |
| R. Subba Row | c Alexander b Sobers | 27 | (4) lbw b Worrell | 100 |
| K.F. Barrington | c Walcott b Sobers | 27 | (7) c Walcott b Worrell | 0 |
| E.R. Dexter | c Hunte b Hall | 39 | (3) c Worrell b Walcott | 110 |
| M.J.K. Smith | b Hall | 0 | (5) c Scarlett b Sobers | 23 |
| R. Illingworth | b Sobers | 4 | (6) c Kanhai b Worrell | 9 |
| R. Swetman† | lbw b Watson | 4 | (9) c Hall b Singh | 3 |
| D.A. Allen | c Alexander b Hall | 55 | (8) not out | 1 |
| F.S. Trueman | b Hall | 6 | | |
| J.B. Statham | not out | 20 | | |
| Extras | (B 5, LB 2, W 2, NB 6) | 15 | (B 6, LB 4, NB 4) | 14 |
| **Total** | | **295** | (8 wickets) | **334** |

## WEST INDIES

| | | |
|---|---|--:|
| C.C. Hunte | c Trueman b Allen | 39 |
| E.D.A. St J. McMorris | c Swetman b Statham | 35 |
| R.B. Kanhai | c Dexter b Trueman | 55 |
| G. St A. Sobers | st Swetman b Allen | 145 |
| C.L. Walcott | b Trueman | 9 |
| F.M.M. Worrell | b Allen | 38 |
| F.C.M. Alexander*† | run out | 33 |
| R.G. Scarlett | not out | 29 |
| C.K. Singh | b Trueman | 0 |
| W.W. Hall | not out | 1 |
| C.D. Watson | did not bat | |
| Extras | (B 4, LB 12, NB 2) | 18 |
| **Total** | (8 wickets declared) | **402** |

| WEST INDIES | O | M | R | W | O | M | R | W | | FALL OF WICKETS | | |
|---|--:|--:|--:|--:|--:|--:|--:|--:|---|--:|--:|--:|
| Hall | 30·2 | 8 | 90 | 6 | 18 | 1 | 79 | 0 | | E | WI | E |
| Watson | 20 | 2 | 56 | 1 | | | | | *Wkt* | *1st* | *1st* | *2nd* |
| Worrell | 16 | 9 | 22 | 0 | 31 | 12 | 49 | 4 | 1st | 73 | 67 | 40 |
| Scarlett | 22 | 11 | 24 | 0 | 38 | 13 | 63 | 0 | 2nd | 121 | 77 | 110 |
| Singh | 12 | 4 | 29 | 0 | 41·2 | 22 | 50 | 2 | 3rd | 152 | 192 | 258 |
| Sobers | 19 | 1 | 59 | 3 | 12 | 1 | 36 | 1 | 4th | 161 | 212 | 320 |
| Walcott | | | | | 9 | 0 | 43 | 1 | 5th | 169 | 333 | 322 |
| | | | | | | | | | 6th | 175 | 338 | 322 |
| ENGLAND | | | | | | | | | 7th | 219 | 393 | 331 |
| Trueman | 40 | 6 | 116 | 3 | | | | | 8th | 258 | 398 | 334 |
| Statham | 36 | 8 | 79 | 1 | | | | | 9th | 268 | – | – |
| Illingworth | 43 | 11 | 72 | 0 | | | | | 10th | 295 | – | – |
| Barrington | 6 | 2 | 22 | 0 | | | | | | | | |
| Allen | 42 | 11 | 75 | 3 | | | | | | | | |
| Dexter | 5 | 0 | 20 | 0 | | | | | | | | |

Umpires: E.N. Lee Kow and C.P. Kippins.

# WEST INDIES v ENGLAND 1959–60 (5th Test)

Played at Queen's Park Oval, Port-of-Spain, Trinidad, on 25, 26, 28, 29, 30, 31 March.
Toss: England.   Result: MATCH DRAWN.
Debuts: West Indies – C.C. Griffith.

England won their fifth toss of the rubber – the only time that this has been achieved by a side with a change of captain. Barrington (23*) retired hurt at 256 for 3 in the last over of the first day after twice being hit on the knuckles by Hall. Although fit to resume immediately the next morning, he had to wait until the fall of the fourth wicket as the umpires ruled, quite correctly, that a new batsman must go in. Hunte (12*) retired hurt at 24 for 1 when he edged a hook at Trueman into his ear. Smith and Parks (a late addition to the touring party) added 197 to set the present record for England's seventh wicket. West Indies were set 406 to win at 140 runs per hour.

## ENGLAND

| | | | | |
|---|---|---|---|---|
| G. Pullar | c Sobers b Griffith | 10 | c and b Sobers | 54 |
| M.C. Cowdrey* | c Alexander b Sobers | 119 | c Worrell b Hall | 0 |
| E.R. Dexter | c and b Sobers | 76 | (4) run out | 47 |
| R. Subba Row | c Hunte b Hall | 22 | (5) lbw b Ramadhin | 13 |
| K.F. Barrington | c Alexander b Ramadhin | 69 | (6) c McMorris b Sobers | 6 |
| M.J.K. Smith | b Ramadhin | 20 | (7) c Alexander b Hunte | 96 |
| J.M. Parks† | c and b Sobers | 43 | (8) not out | 101 |
| R. Illingworth | c Sobers b Ramadhin | 0 | | |
| D.A. Allen | c sub (S.M. Nurse) b Ramadhin | 7 | (3) run out | 25 |
| F.S. Trueman | not out | 10 | (9) not out | 2 |
| A.E. Moss | b Watson | 1 | | |
| Extras | (B 7, NB 9) | 16 | (B 2, LB 3, NB 1) | 6 |
| **Total** | | **393** | (7 wickets declared) | **350** |

## WEST INDIES

| | | | | |
|---|---|---|---|---|
| C.C. Hunte | not out | 72 | st Parks b Illingworth | 36 |
| E.D.A. St J. McMorris | run out | 13 | lbw b Moss | 2 |
| F.C.M. Alexander*† | b Allen | 26 | (7) not out | 4 |
| G. St A. Sobers | b Moss | 92 | (6) not out | 49 |
| C.L. Walcott | st Parks b Allen | 53 | (4) c Parks b Barrington | 22 |
| F.M.M. Worrell | b Trueman | 15 | (5) c Trueman b Pullar | 61 |
| R.B. Kanhai | b Moss | 6 | (3) c Trueman b Illingworth | 34 |
| S. Ramadhin | c Cowdrey b Dexter | 13 | | |
| W.W. Hall | b Trueman | 29 | | |
| C.C. Griffith | not out | 5 | | |
| C.D. Watson | did not bat | | | |
| Extras | (B 6, LB 4, NB 4) | 14 | (LB 1) | 1 |
| **Total** | (8 wickets declared) | **338** | (5 wickets) | **209** |

| WEST INDIES | O | M | R | W | O | M | R | W | | FALL OF WICKETS | | | |
|---|---|---|---|---|---|---|---|---|---|---|---|---|---|
| | | | | | | | | | | E | WI | E | WI |
| Hall | 24 | 3 | 83 | 1 | 4 | 0 | 16 | 1 | *Wkt* | *1st* | *1st* | *2nd* | *2nd* |
| Griffith | 15 | 2 | 62 | 1 | 9 | 1 | 40 | 0 | 1st | 19 | 26 | 3 | 11 |
| Watson | 18·2 | 3 | 52 | 1 | 14 | 1 | 52 | 0 | 2nd | 210 | 103 | 69 | 72 |
| Ramadhin | 34 | 13 | 73 | 4 | 34 | 9 | 67 | 1 | 3rd | 215 | 190 | 102 | 75 |
| Worrell | 8 | 1 | 29 | 0 | 22 | 5 | 44 | 0 | 4th | 268 | 216 | 136 | 107 |
| Sobers | 20 | 1 | 75 | 3 | 29 | 6 | 84 | 2 | 5th | 317 | 227 | 145 | 194 |
| Walcott | 4 | 2 | 3 | 0 | 7 | 2 | 24 | 0 | 6th | 350 | 230 | 148 | – |
| Hunte | | | | | 5 | 1 | 17 | 1 | 7th | 350 | 263 | 345 | – |
| ENGLAND | | | | | | | | | 8th | 374 | 328 | – | – |
| Trueman | 37·3 | 6 | 103 | 2 | 5 | 1 | 22 | 0 | 9th | 388 | – | – | – |
| Moss | 34 | 3 | 94 | 2 | 4 | 0 | 16 | 1 | 10th | 393 | – | – | – |
| Allen | 24 | 1 | 61 | 2 | 15 | 2 | 57 | 0 | | | | | |
| Illingworth | 12 | 4 | 25 | 0 | 16 | 3 | 53 | 2 | | | | | |
| Dexter | 4 | 1 | 20 | 1 | | | | | | | | | |
| Barrington | 8 | 0 | 21 | 0 | 8 | 2 | 27 | 1 | | | | | |
| Subba Row | | | | | 1 | 0 | 2 | 0 | | | | | |
| Smith | | | | | 1 | 0 | 15 | 0 | | | | | |
| Pullar | | | | | 1 | 0 | 1 | 1 | | | | | |
| Cowdrey | | | | | 1 | 0 | 15 | 0 | | | | | |

Umpires: H.B. de C. Jordan and C.P. Kippins.

# ENGLAND v SOUTH AFRICA 1960 (1st Test)

Played at Edgbaston, Birmingham, on 9, 10, 11, 13, 14 June.
Toss: England.   Result: ENGLAND won by 100 runs.
Debuts: England – R.W. Barber, P.M. Walker; South Africa – J.P. Fellows-Smith, G.M. Griffin,
S.O'Linn.

England included five county captains in Cowdrey, Dexter, Subba Row, Smith and Barber, but no Surrey player
for the first time in a home Test since 1949 (*Test No. 316*). Pullar cracked a bone in his left wrist when he fended
off an Adcock bouncer in the first innings. He came in last and played one ball single-handed in the second
innings. England won with four hours to spare.

## ENGLAND

| | | | | | |
|---|---|---|---|---|---|
| G. Pullar | c McLean b Goddard | 37 | (11) not out | | 1 |
| M.C. Cowdrey* | c Waite b Adcock | 3 | (1) b Adcock | | 0 |
| E.R. Dexter | b Tayfield | 52 | b Adcock | | 26 |
| R. Subba Row | c Waite b Griffin | 56 | (2) c Waite b Tayfield | | 32 |
| M.J.K. Smith | c Waite b Adcock | 54 | (4) c O'Linn b Tayfield | | 28 |
| J.M. Parks† | c Waite b Adcock | 35 | (5) b Griffin | | 4 |
| R. Illingworth | b Tayfield | 1 | (6) c Waite b Adcock | | 16 |
| R.W. Barber | lbw b Adcock | 5 | (7) c McLean b Tayfield | | 4 |
| P.M. Walker | c Goddard b Adcock | 9 | (8) c Goddard b Griffin | | 37 |
| F.S. Trueman | b Tayfield | 11 | (9) b Tayfield | | 25 |
| J.B. Statham | not out | 14 | (10) c McLean b Griffin | | 22 |
| Extras | (B 4, LB 9, NB 2) | 15 | (B 2, LB 4, NB 2) | | 8 |
| **Total** | | **292** | | | **203** |

## SOUTH AFRICA

| | | | | |
|---|---|---|---|---|
| D.J. McGlew* | c Parks b Trueman | 11 | c Parks b Statham | 5 |
| T.L. Goddard | c Smith b Statham | 10 | c Walker b Statham | 0 |
| A.J. Pithey | lbw b Statham | 6 | b Illingworth | 17 |
| R.A. McLean | c Statham b Trueman | 21 | lbw b Trueman | 68 |
| J.H.B. Waite† | b Illingworth | 58 | not out | 56 |
| P.R. Carstein | lbw b Trueman | 4 | b Trueman | 10 |
| S. O'Linn | c Cowdrey b Illingworth | 42 | lbw b Barber | 12 |
| J.P. Fellows-Smith | lbw b Illingworth | 18 | lbw b Illingworth | 5 |
| G.M. Griffin | b Trueman | 6 | (10) c Walker b Trueman | 14 |
| H.J. Tayfield | run out | 6 | (9) b Illingworth | 3 |
| N.A.T. Adcock | not out | 1 | b Statham | 7 |
| Extras | (B 2, NB 1) | 3 | (B 7, LB 5) | 12 |
| **Total** | | **186** | | **209** |

| SOUTH AFRICA | O | M | R | W | O | M | R | W | | FALL OF WICKETS | | | |
|---|---|---|---|---|---|---|---|---|---|---|---|---|---|
| | | | | | | | | | | E | SA | E | SA |
| Adcock | 41·5 | 14 | 62 | 5 | 28 | 8 | 57 | 3 | Wkt | 1st | 1st | 2nd | 2nd |
| Griffin | 21 | 3 | 61 | 1 | 21 | 4 | 44 | 3 | 1st | 19 | 11 | 0 | 4 |
| Goddard | 33 | 17 | 47 | 1 | 10 | 5 | 32 | 0 | 2nd | 80 | 21 | 42 | 5 |
| Tayfield | 50 | 19 | 93 | 3 | 27 | 12 | 62 | 4 | 3rd | 100 | 40 | 69 | 58 |
| Fellows-Smith | 5 | 1 | 14 | 0 | | | | | 4th | 196 | 52 | 74 | 120 |
| | | | | | | | | | 5th | 225 | 61 | 112 | 132 |
| ENGLAND | | | | | | | | | 6th | 2 4 | 146 | 112 | 156 |
| Statham | 28 | 8 | 67 | 2 | 18 | 5 | 41 | 3 | 7th | 255 | 168 | 118 | 161 |
| Trueman | 24·5 | 4 | 58 | 4 | 22 | 4 | 58 | 3 | 8th | 262 | 179 | 163 | 167 |
| Dexter | 1 | 0 | 4 | 0 | 6 | 4 | 4 | 0 | 9th | 275 | 179 | 202 | 200 |
| Barber | 6 | 0 | 26 | 0 | 10 | 2 | 29 | 1 | 10th | 292 | 186 | 203 | 209 |
| Illingworth | 17 | 11 | 15 | 3 | 24 | 6 | 57 | 3 | | | | | |
| Walker | 6 | 1 | 13 | 0 | 4 | 2 | 8 | 0 | | | | | |

Umpires: J.G. Langridge and W.E. Phillipson.

# ENGLAND v SOUTH AFRICA 1960 (2nd Test)

Played at Lord's, London, on 23, 24, 25, 27 June.
Toss: England.   Result: ENGLAND won by an innings and 73 runs.
Debuts: South Africa – C. Wesley.

Griffin became the first bowler to take a hat-trick for South Africa when he dismissed Smith with the last ball of one over and Walker and Trueman with the first two balls of his next. It was also the first hat-trick in a Test at Lord's. Griffin was called eleven times by umpire Lee for throwing during England's innings; it was the first instance in a Test in England and only the third in all Tests.

## ENGLAND

| | | |
|---|---|---:|
| M.C. Cowdrey* | c McLean b Griffin | 4 |
| R. Subba Row | lbw b Adcock | 90 |
| E.R. Dexter | c McLean b Adcock | 56 |
| K.F. Barrington | lbw b Goddard | 24 |
| M.J.K. Smith | c Waite b Griffin | 99 |
| J.M. Parks† | c Fellows-Smith b Adcock | 3 |
| P.M. Walker | b Griffin | 52 |
| R. Illingworth | not out | 0 |
| F.S. Trueman | b Griffin | 0 |
| J.B. Statham | not out | 2 |
| A.E.Moss | did not bat | |
| Extras | (B 6, LB 14, W 1, NB 11) | 32 |
| **Total** | (8 wickets declared) | **362** |

## SOUTH AFRICA

| | | | | |
|---|---|---:|---|---:|
| D.J. McGlew* | lbw b Statham | 15 | b Statham | 17 |
| T.L. Goddard | b Statham | 19 | c Parks b Statham | 24 |
| S. O'Linn | c Walker b Moss | 18 | lbw b Trueman | 8 |
| R.A. McLean | c Cowdrey b Statham | 15 | c Parks b Trueman | 13 |
| J.H.B. Waite† | c Parks b Statham | 3 | lbw b Statham | 0 |
| P.R. Carlstein | c Cowdrey b Moss | 12 | c Parks b Moss | 6 |
| C. Wesley | c Parks b Statham | 11 | b Dexter | 35 |
| J.P. Fellows-Smith | c Parks b Moss | 29 | not out | 27 |
| H.J. Tayfield | c Smith b Moss | 12 | b Dexter | 4 |
| G.M. Griffin | b Statham | 5 | b Statham | 0 |
| N.A.T. Adcock | not out | 8 | b Statham | 2 |
| Extras | (LB 4, NB 1) | 5 | (NB 1) | 1 |
| **Total** | | **152** | | **137** |

| SOUTH AFRICA | O | M | R | W | O | M | R | W |
|---|---|---|---|---|---|---|---|---|
| Adcock | 36 | 11 | 70 | 3 | | | | |
| Griffin | 30 | 7 | 87 | 4 | | | | |
| Goddard | 31 | 6 | 96 | 1 | | | | |
| Tayfield | 27 | 9 | 64 | 0 | | | | |
| Fellows-Smith | 5 | 0 | 13 | 0 | | | | |
| ENGLAND | | | | | | | | |
| Statham | 20 | 5 | 63 | 6 | 21 | 6 | 34 | 5 |
| Trueman | 13 | 2 | 49 | 0 | 17 | 5 | 44 | 2 |
| Moss | 10·3 | 0 | 35 | 4 | 14 | 1 | 41 | 1 |
| Illingworth | | | | | 1 | 1 | 0 | 0 |
| Dexter | | | | | 4 | 0 | 17 | 2 |

## FALL OF WICKETS

| Wkt | E 1st | SA 1st | SA 2nd |
|---|---|---|---|
| 1st | 7 | 33 | 26 |
| 2nd | 103 | 48 | 49 |
| 3rd | 165 | 56 | 49 |
| 4th | 220 | 69 | 50 |
| 5th | 227 | 78 | 63 |
| 6th | 347 | 88 | 72 |
| 7th | 360 | 112 | 126 |
| 8th | 360 | 132 | 132 |
| 9th | – | 138 | 133 |
| 10th | – | 152 | 137 |

Umpires: J.S. Buller and F.S. Lee.

# ENGLAND v SOUTH AFRICA 1960 (3rd Test)

Played at Trent Bridge, Nottingham, on 7, 8, 9, 11 July.
Toss: England.   Result: ENGLAND won by eight wickets.
Debuts: South Africa – J.E. Pothecary.

Waite dislocated his left-hand little finger during England's first innings and O'Linn took over as wicket-keeper, in which position he caught Barrington and Walker. South Africa's total of 88 remains the lowest in any Test at Trent Bridge. McGlew, run out after colliding with the bowler (Moss), was recalled by Cowdrey but umpire Elliott refused to change his decision. Wesley was dismissed first ball in both innings.

## ENGLAND

| | | | | |
|---|---|---|---|---|
| R. Subba Row | b Tayfield | 30 | not out | 16 |
| M.C. Cowdrey* | c Fellows-Smith b Goddard | 67 | lbw b Goddard | 27 |
| E.R. Dexter | b Adcock | 3 | c Adcock b Goddard | 0 |
| K.F. Barrington | c O'Linn b Goddard | 80 | not out | 1 |
| M.J.K. Smith | lbw b Goddard | 0 | | |
| J.M. Parks† | run out | 16 | | |
| R. Illingworth | c and b Tayfield | 37 | | |
| P.M. Walker | c O'Linn b Tayfield | 30 | | |
| F.S. Trueman | b Goddard | 15 | | |
| J.B. Statham | b Goddard | 2 | | |
| A.E. Moss | not out | 3 | | |
| Extras | (B 2, LB 2) | 4 | (B 4, LB 1) | 5 |
| **Total** | | **287** | (2 wickets) | **49** |

## SOUTH AFRICA

| | | | | |
|---|---|---|---|---|
| D.J. McGlew* | c Parks b Trueman | 0 | run out | 45 |
| T.L. Goddard | run out | 16 | b Trueman | 0 |
| S. O'Linn | c Walker b Trueman | 1 | (5) c Cowdrey b Moss | 98 |
| R.A. McLean | b Statham | 11 | c Parks b Trueman | 0 |
| P.R. Carlstein | c Walker b Statham | 2 | (6) c Cowdrey b Statham | 19 |
| C. Wesley | c Subba Row b Statham | 0 | (7) c Parks b Statham | 0 |
| J.P. Fellows-Smith | not out | 31 | (3) c Illingworth b Trueman | 15 |
| J.H.B. Waite† | c Trueman b Moss | 1 | lbw b Moss | 60 |
| H.J. Tayfield | b Trueman | 11 | c Parks b Moss | 6 |
| J.E. Pothecary | b Trueman | 7 | c Parks b Trueman | 3 |
| N.A.T. Adcock | b Trueman | 0 | not out | 1 |
| Extras | (B 4, LB 4) | 8 | | |
| **Total** | | **88** | | **247** |

| SOUTH AFRICA | O | M | R | W | O | M | R | W | FALL OF WICKETS | | | | |
|---|---|---|---|---|---|---|---|---|---|---|---|---|---|
| Adcock | 30 | 2 | 86 | 1 | 7·4 | 2 | 16 | 0 | | E | SA | SA | E |
| Pothecary | 20 | 5 | 42 | 0 | 2 | 0 | 15 | 0 | *Wkt* | *1st* | *1st* | *2nd* | *2nd* |
| Fellows-Smith | 5 | 0 | 17 | 0 | | | | | 1st | 57 | 0 | 1 | 48 |
| Goddard | 42 | 17 | 80 | 5 | 5 | 1 | 13 | 2 | 2nd | 82 | 12 | 23 | 48 |
| Tayfield | 28·3 | 11 | 58 | 3 | | | | | 3rd | 129 | 31 | 23 | – |
| | | | | | | | | | 4th | 129 | 33 | 91 | – |
| ENGLAND | | | | | | | | | 5th | 154 | 33 | 122 | – |
| Trueman | 14·3 | 6 | 27 | 5 | 22 | 3 | 77 | 4 | 6th | 229 | 44 | 122 | – |
| Statham | 14 | 5 | 27 | 3 | 26 | 3 | 71 | 2 | 7th | 241 | 49 | 231 | – |
| Moss | 10 | 3 | 26 | 1 | 15·4 | 3 | 36 | 3 | 8th | 261 | 68 | 242 | – |
| Illingworth | | | | | 19 | 9 | 33 | 0 | 9th | 267 | 82 | 245 | – |
| Barrington | | | | | 3 | 1 | 5 | 0 | 10th | 287 | 88 | 247 | – |
| Dexter | | | | | 6 | 2 | 12 | 0 | | | | | |
| Walker | | | | | 3 | 0 | 13 | 0 | | | | | |

Umpires: C.S. Elliott and F.S. Lee.

# ENGLAND v SOUTH AFRICA 1960 (4th Test)

Played at Old Trafford, Manchester, on 21 (*no play*), 22 (*no play*), 23, 25, 26 July.
Toss: England.   Result: MATCH DRAWN.
Debuts: England – D.E.V. Padgett.

Manchester's total of blank days of Test cricket was brought to 23 (out of 48 lost on all English grounds) when rain prevented a start until the third day. Goddard ended England's first innings with a spell of 3 for 0 in 56 balls. On the final afternoon England fielded substitutes for Subba Row (fractured thumb), Barrington (pulled thigh muscle) and Statham (tonsillitis). This was England's 16th consecutive Test without a defeat – then their longest unbeaten run.

## ENGLAND

| | | | | | |
|---|---|--:|---|---|--:|
| G. Pullar | b Pothecary | 12 | | c and b Pothecary | 9 |
| R. Subba Row | lbw b Adcock | 27 | | | |
| E.R. Dexter | b Pothecary | 38 | | c McLean b Pothecary | 22 |
| M.C. Cowdrey* | c Waite b Adcock | 20 | (2) | b Adcock | 25 |
| K.F. Barrington | b Goddard | 76 | (7) | c Waite b Goddard | 35 |
| D.E.V. Padgett | c Wesley b Pothecary | 5 | (5) | c Waite b Adcock | 2 |
| J.M. Parks† | lbw b Goddard | 36 | (6) | c and b Goddard | 20 |
| R. Illingworth | not out | 22 | (4) | c McLean b Adcock | 5 |
| D.A. Allen | lbw b Goddard | 0 | (8) | not out | 14 |
| F.S. Trueman | c Tayfield b Adcock | 10 | (9) | not out | 14 |
| J.B. Statham | b Adcock | 0 | | | |
| Extras | (B 8, LB 6) | 14 | | (B 1, LB 5, NB 1) | 7 |
| **Total** | | **260** | | (7 wickets declared) | **153** |

## SOUTH AFRICA

| | | | | | |
|---|---|--:|---|---|--:|
| D.J. McGlew* | c Subba Row b Trueman | 32 | | not out | 26 |
| T.L. Goddard | c Parks b Statham | 8 | | not out | 16 |
| A.J. Pithey | c Parks b Statham | 7 | | | |
| P.R. Carlstein | b Trueman | 11 | | | |
| R.A. McLean | b Allen | 109 | | | |
| J.H.B. Waite† | b Statham | 11 | | | |
| S. O'Linn | c sub (M.J. Hilton) b Allen | 27 | | | |
| C. Wesley | c Trueman b Allen | 3 | | | |
| H.J. Tayfield | c Trueman b Allen | 4 | | | |
| J.E. Pothecary | b Trueman | 12 | | | |
| N.A.T. Adcock | not out | 0 | | | |
| Extras | (B 1, LB 4) | 5 | | (B 3, NB 1) | 4 |
| **Total** | | **229** | | (0 wickets) | **46** |

| SOUTH AFRICA | O | M | R | W | O | M | R | W | FALL OF WICKETS | | | | |
|---|--:|--:|--:|--:|--:|--:|--:|--:|---|--:|--:|--:|--:|
| Adcock | 23 | 5 | 66 | 4 | 27 | 9 | 59 | 3 | | E | SA | E | SA |
| Pothecary | 28 | 3 | 85 | 3 | 32 | 10 | 61 | 2 | *Wkt* | *1st* | *1st* | *2nd* | *2nd* |
| Goddard | 24 | 16 | 26 | 3 | 16 | 5 | 26 | 2 | 1st | 27 | 25 | 23 | – |
| Tayfield | 18 | 3 | 69 | 0 | | | | | 2nd | 85 | 33 | 41 | – |
| | | | | | | | | | 3rd | 108 | 57 | 63 | – |
| ENGLAND | | | | | | | | | 4th | 113 | 62 | 65 | – |
| Statham | 22 | 11 | 32 | 3 | 4 | 2 | 3 | 0 | 5th | 134 | 92 | 71 | – |
| Trueman | 20 | 2 | 58 | 3 | 6 | 1 | 10 | 0 | 6th | 197 | 194 | 101 | – |
| Dexter | 17 | 5 | 41 | 0 | | | | | 7th | 239 | 198 | 134 | – |
| Allen | 19·5 | 6 | 58 | 4 | 7 | 4 | 5 | 0 | 8th | 239 | 202 | – | – |
| Illingworth | 11 | 2 | 35 | 0 | 5 | 3 | 6 | 0 | 9th | 260 | 225 | – | – |
| Pullar | | | | | 1 | 0 | 6 | 0 | 10th | 260 | 229 | – | – |
| Padgett | | | | | 2 | 0 | 8 | 0 | | | | | |
| Cowdrey | | | | | 1 | 0 | 4 | 0 | | | | | |

Umpires: J.G. Langridge and N. Oldfield.

# ENGLAND v SOUTH AFRICA 1960 (5th Test)

Played at Kennington Oval, London, on 18, 19, 20, 22, 23 August.
Toss: England.   Result: MATCH DRAWN.
Debuts: South Africa – A.H. McKinnon.

For the second consecutive rubber England won all five tosses – a unique run. When he stumped Pullar, Waite became the first South African to complete the wicket-keeper's double of 1,000 runs and 100 dismissals in Test cricket; W.A.S. Oldfield (Australia) and T.G. Evans (England) were then the only others to achieve this double. The opening partnership of 290 between Pullar and Cowdrey was England's third-highest in all Tests and the fourth-highest by all countries.

## ENGLAND

| Batsman | Dismissal 1 | R | Dismissal 2 | R |
|---|---|---|---|---|
| G. Pullar | c Goddard b Pothecary | 59 | st Waite b McKinnon | 175 |
| M.C. Cowdrey* | b Adcock | 11 | lbw b Goddard | 155 |
| E.R. Dexter | b Adcock | 28 | b Tayfield | 16 |
| K.F. Barrington | lbw b Pothecary | 1 | c Carlstein b McKinnon | 10 |
| M.J.K. Smith | b Adcock | 0 | (6) c Goddard b Tayfield | 11 |
| D.E.V. Padgett | c Waite b Pothecary | 13 | (7) run out | 31 |
| J.M. Parks† | c Waite b Pothecary | 23 | (5) c Waite b Adcock | 17 |
| D.A. Allen | lbw b Adcock | 0 | not out | 12 |
| F.S. Trueman | lbw b Adcock | 0 | b Goddard | 24 |
| J.B. Statham | not out | 13 | c Pothecary b Goddard | 4 |
| T. Greenhough | b Adcock | 2 | | |
| Extras | (B 3, LB 2) | 5 | (B 14, LB 9, W 1) | 24 |
| **Total** | | **155** | (9 wickets declared) | **479** |

## SOUTH AFRICA

| Batsman | Dismissal 1 | R | Dismissal 2 | R |
|---|---|---|---|---|
| D.J. McGlew* | c Smith b Greenhough | 22 | c Allen b Statham | 16 |
| T.L. Goddard | c Cowdrey b Statham | 99 | c Cowdrey b Statham | 28 |
| J.P. Fellows-Smith | c Smith b Dexter | 35 | c Parks b Trueman | 6 |
| R.A. McLean | lbw b Dexter | 0 | (5) not out | 32 |
| J.H.B. Waite† | c Trueman b Dexter | 87 | (6) not out | 1 |
| S. O'Linn | b Trueman | 55 | | |
| P.R. Carlstein | b Greenhough | 42 | (4) lbw b Trueman | 13 |
| J.E. Pothecary | run out | 4 | | |
| H.J. Tayfield | not out | 46 | | |
| A.H. McKinnon | run out | 22 | | |
| N.A.T. Adcock | b Trueman | 1 | | |
| Extras | (B 6, LB 7, NB 3) | 16 | (W 1) | 1 |
| **Total** | | **419** | (4 wickets) | **97** |

| SOUTH AFRICA | O | M | R | W | O | M | R | W |
|---|---|---|---|---|---|---|---|---|
| Adcock | 31·3 | 10 | 65 | 6 | 38 | 8 | 106 | 1 |
| Pothecary | 29 | 9 | 58 | 4 | 27 | 5 | 93 | 0 |
| Goddard | 14 | 6 | 25 | 0 | 27 | 6 | 69 | 3 |
| McKinnon | 2 | 1 | 2 | 0 | 24 | 7 | 62 | 2 |
| Tayfield | | | | | 37 | 14 | 108 | 2 |
| Fellows-Smith | | | | | 4 | 0 | 17 | 0 |
| ENGLAND | | | | | | | | |
| Trueman | 31·1 | 4 | 93 | 2 | 10 | 0 | 34 | 2 |
| Statham | 38 | 8 | 96 | 1 | 12 | 1 | 57 | 2 |
| Dexter | 30 | 5 | 79 | 3 | 0·2 | 0 | 0 | 0 |
| Greenhough | 44 | 17 | 99 | 2 | 5 | 2 | 3 | 0 |
| Allen | 28 | 15 | 36 | 0 | 2 | 1 | 2 | 0 |

### FALL OF WICKETS

| Wkt | E 1st | SA 1st | E 2nd | SA 2nd |
|---|---|---|---|---|
| 1st | 27 | 44 | 290 | 21 |
| 2nd | 89 | 107 | 339 | 30 |
| 3rd | 90 | 107 | 362 | 52 |
| 4th | 95 | 222 | 373 | 89 |
| 5th | 107 | 252 | 387 | – |
| 6th | 125 | 326 | 412 | – |
| 7th | 130 | 330 | 447 | – |
| 8th | 130 | 374 | 475 | – |
| 9th | 142 | 412 | 479 | – |
| 10th | 155 | 419 | – | – |

Umpires: C.S. Elliott and W.E. Phillipson.

# INDIA v PAKISTAN 1960–61 (1st Test)

Played at Brabourne Stadium, Bombay, on 2, 3, 4, 6, 7 December.
Toss: Pakistan.   Result: MATCH DRAWN.
Debuts: India – R.F. Surti; Pakistan – Javed Burki, Mohammad Farooq.

The partnership of 246 between Hanif and Saeed was a Pakistan second-wicket record in all Tests (since beaten). Mohammad Farooq took the wickets of Roy and Baig in his second over in Test cricket. Joshi and Desai added 149 to establish the present ninth-wicket record for India in all Tests.

## PAKISTAN

| | | | | |
|---|---|---|---|---|
| Hanif Mohammad | run out | 160 | c Umrigar b Desai | 0 |
| Imtiaz Ahmed† | b Desai | 19 | c Roy b Nadkarni | 69 |
| Saeed Ahmed | st Joshi b Gupte | 121 | c and b Gupte | 41 |
| Mushtaq Mohammad | lbw b Gupte | 6 | lbw b Nadkarni | 19 |
| W. Mathias | c Nadkarni b Desai | 0 | not out | 6 |
| Javed Burki | lbw b Gupte | 7 | not out | 13 |
| Nasim-ul-Ghani | c Joshi b Desai | 4 | | |
| Fazal Mahmood* | c Joshi b Gupte | 1 | | |
| Mahmood Hussain | c Desai b Nadkarni | 23 | | |
| Mohammad Farooq | not out | 2 | | |
| Haseeb Ahsan | c Contractor b Nadkarni | 0 | | |
| Extras | (B 6, LB 1) | 7 | (B 16, LB 1, NB 1) | 18 |
| **Total** | | **350** | (4 wickets) | **166** |

## INDIA

| | | |
|---|---|---|
| P. Roy | c Mahmood b Farooq | 23 |
| N.J. Contractor* | c Burki b Farooq | 62 |
| A.A. Baig | c Hanif b Farooq | 1 |
| V.L. Manjrekar | b Mahmood | 73 |
| P.R. Umrigar | c sub (Zafar Altaf) b Mahmood | 33 |
| C.G. Borde | lbw b Mahmood | 41 |
| R.G. Nadkarni | c Burki b Mahmood | 34 |
| R.F. Surti | c Nasim b Farooq | 11 |
| P.G. Joshi† | not out | 52 |
| R.B. Desai | b Mahmood | 85 |
| S.P. Gupte | did not bat | |
| Extras | (B 14, LB 11, NB 9) | 34 |
| **Total** | (9 wickets declared) | **449** |

| INDIA | O | M | R | W | O | M | R | W | | FALL OF WICKETS | | |
|---|---|---|---|---|---|---|---|---|---|---|---|---|
| Desai | 36 | 6 | 116 | 3 | 8 | 2 | 27 | 1 | | P | I | P |
| Surti | 9 | 0 | 37 | 0 | 8 | 1 | 21 | 0 | *Wkt* | *1st* | *1st* | *2nd* |
| Umrigar | 17 | 2 | 46 | 0 | | | | | 1st | 55 | 56 | 0 |
| Nadkarni | 37·4 | 14 | 75 | 2 | 15 | 10 | 9 | 2 | 2nd | 301 | 58 | 80 |
| Gupte | 31 | 15 | 43 | 4 | 25 | 10 | 46 | 1 | 3rd | 302 | 121 | 142 |
| Borde | 6 | 1 | 26 | 0 | 16 | 4 | 25 | 0 | 4th | 303 | 206 | 147 |
| Contractor | 1 | 1 | 0 | 0 | 7 | 2 | 16 | 0 | 5th | 318 | 207 | – |
| Roy | | | | | 1 | 0 | 4 | 0 | 6th | 319 | 289 | – |
| | | | | | | | | | 7th | 321 | 296 | – |
| PAKISTAN | | | | | | | | | 8th | 331 | 300 | – |
| Mahmood Hussain | 51·4 | 10 | 129 | 5 | | | | | 9th | 349 | 449 | – |
| Fazal | 6 | 2 | 5 | 0 | | | | | 10th | 350 | – | – |
| Farooq | 46 | 7 | 139 | 4 | | | | | | | | |
| Nasim | 41 | 19 | 74 | 0 | | | | | | | | |
| Haseeb | 31 | 10 | 68 | 0 | | | | | | | | |
| Mushtaq | 1 | 1 | 0 | 0 | | | | | | | | |

Umpires: A.R. Joshi and S.K. Ganguli.

# INDIA v PAKISTAN 1960–61 (2nd Test)

Played at Green Park, Kanpur, on 16, 17, 18, 20, 21 December.
Toss: Pakistan.   Result: MATCH DRAWN.
Debuts: Nil.

This match produced a daily average run rate of 155 and India did not complete their first innings until just before lunch on the fifth day. Jaisimha batted 500 minutes for 99 and made only five scoring strokes in the entire pre-lunch session on the third day.

## PAKISTAN

| | | | | |
|---|---|---|---|---|
| Hanif Mohammad | c Contractor b Umrigar | 5 | c Jaisimha b Muddiah | 19 |
| Imtiaz Ahmed† | b Gupte | 20 | c Contractor b Muddiah | 16 |
| Saeed Ahmed | c Tamhane b Desai | 32 | b Gupte | 4 |
| Javed Burki | run out | 79 | not out | 48 |
| W. Mathias | lbw b Desai | 37 | not out | 46 |
| Alimuddin | c Nadkarni b Umrigar | 24 | | |
| Mushtaq Mohammad | c Umrigar b Muddiah | 13 | | |
| Nasim-ul-Ghani | not out | 70 | | |
| Fazal Mahmood* | lbw b Umrigar | 16 | | |
| Mahmood Hussain | c Borde b Umrigar | 7 | | |
| Haseeb Ahsan | c Tamhane b Gupte | 13 | | |
| Extras | (B 13, LB 6) | 19 | (B 2, LB 5) | 7 |
| **Total** | | **335** | (3 wickets) | **140** |

## INDIA

| | | |
|---|---|---|
| N.J. Contractor* | b Haseeb | 47 |
| M.L. Jaisimha | run out | 99 |
| A.A. Baig | b Haseeb | 13 |
| V.L. Manjrekar | c Nasim b Fazal | 52 |
| P.R. Umrigar | c Burki b Mahmood | 115 |
| C.G. Borde | c Fazal b Nasim | 0 |
| R.G. Nadkarni | b Haseeb | 16 |
| R.B. Desai | b Haseeb | 14 |
| N.S. Tamhane† | c Mathias b Haseeb | 3 |
| V.M. Muddiah | b Mahmood | 11 |
| S.P. Gupte | not out | 1 |
| Extras | (B 20, LB 1, NB 12) | 33 |
| **Total** | | **404** |

| INDIA | O | M | R | W | O | M | R | W | | FALL OF WICKETS | | |
|---|---|---|---|---|---|---|---|---|---|---|---|---|
| Desai | 30 | 6 | 54 | 2 | 4 | 1 | 3 | 0 | | P | I | P |
| Umrigar | 55 | 23 | 71 | 4 | 3 | 0 | 10 | 0 | *Wkt* | *1st* | *1st* | *2nd* |
| Gupte | 42·4 | 14 | 84 | 2 | 17 | 6 | 29 | 1 | 1st | 21 | 71 | 31 |
| Muddiah | 22 | 6 | 62 | 1 | 18 | 7 | 40 | 2 | 2nd | 29 | 92 | 42 |
| Nadkarni | 32 | 24 | 23 | 0 | 7 | 4 | 6 | 0 | 3rd | 93 | 182 | 42 |
| Borde | 6 | 2 | 16 | 0 | 10 | 0 | 36 | 0 | 4th | 174 | 258 | – |
| Contractor | 1 | 0 | 6 | 0 | | | | | 5th | 177 | 263 | – |
| Jaisimha | | | | | 3 | 0 | 5 | 0 | 6th | 214 | 294 | – |
| Manjrekar | | | | | 1 | 0 | 2 | 0 | 7th | 240 | 334 | – |
| Baig | | | | | 1 | 0 | 2 | 0 | 8th | 293 | 342 | – |
| PAKISTAN | | | | | | | | | 9th | 305 | 403 | – |
| Mahmood Hussain | 44·5 | 1 | 101 | 2 | | | | | 10th | 335 | 404 | – |
| Fazal | 36 | 14 | 37 | 1 | | | | | | | | |
| Nasim | 55 | 17 | 109 | 1 | | | | | | | | |
| Haseeb | 56 | 15 | 121 | 5 | | | | | | | | |
| Mushtaq | 2 | 1 | 3 | 0 | | | | | | | | |

Umpires: A.R. Joshi and S.K. Ganguli.

# INDIA v PAKISTAN 1960–61 (3rd Test)

Played at Eden Gardens, Calcutta, on 30, 31 December, 1, 3, 4, January.
Toss: Pakistan.    Result: MATCH DRAWN.
Debuts: Nil.

Rain on the third day and drying operations on the fourth reduced play by 4½ hours. Pakistan set India 267 to win in three hours.

## PAKISTAN

| | | | | | |
|---|---|---|---|---|---|
| Hanif Mohammad | c Baig b Desai | 56 | not out | | 63 |
| Imtiaz Ahmed† | b Surendranath | 9 | b Desai | | 9 |
| Saeed Ahmed | c Nadkarni b Surendranath | 41 | lbw b Surendranath | | 13 |
| Javed Burki | lbw b Borde | 48 | run out | | 42 |
| W. Mathias | c Umrigar b Desai | 8 | | | |
| Mushtaq Mohammad | c Jaisimha b Borde | 61 | | | |
| Nasim-ul-Ghani | b Surendranath | 0 | | | |
| Intikhab Alam | c Tamhane b Surendranath | 56 | (5) not out | | 11 |
| Fazal Mahmood* | lbw b Borde | 8 | | | |
| Mahmood Hussain | b Borde | 4 | | | |
| Haseeb Ahsan | not out | 1 | | | |
| Extras | (B 6, LB 3) | 9 | (B 3, LB 5) | | 8 |
| **Total** | | **301** | (3 wickets declared) | | **146** |

## INDIA

| | | | | | |
|---|---|---|---|---|---|
| N.J. Contractor* | b Intikhab | 25 | c Fazal b Haseeb | | 12 |
| M.L. Jaisimha | c Mathias b Mahmood | 28 | c Mathias b Intikhab | | 26 |
| A.A. Baig | b Intikhab | 19 | b Haseeb | | 1 |
| P.R. Umrigar | c Imtiaz b Mahmood | 1 | (5) b Intikhab | | 4 |
| V.L. Manjrekar | b Fazal | 29 | (4) not out | | 45 |
| C.G. Borde | c Imtiaz b Fazal | 44 | not out | | 23 |
| R.G. Nadkarni | c Imtiaz b Fazal | 1 | | | |
| R.B. Desai | b Haseeb | 14 | | | |
| N.S. Tamhane† | c Intikhab b Fazal | 0 | | | |
| R. Surendranath | not out | 5 | | | |
| S.P. Gupte | b Fazal | 0 | | | |
| Extras | (B 10, LB 3, NB 1) | 14 | (B 3, LB 9, NB 4) | | 16 |
| **Total** | | **180** | (4 wickets) | | **127** |

| INDIA | O | M | R | W | O | M | R | W |
|---|---|---|---|---|---|---|---|---|
| Desai | 35 | 3 | 118 | 2 | 16 | 4 | 37 | 1 |
| Surendranath | 46 | 19 | 93 | 4 | 18 | 2 | 51 | 1 |
| Umrigar | 6 | 2 | 15 | 0 | 7 | 2 | 14 | 0 |
| Gupte | 18 | 5 | 41 | 0 | 1 | 1 | 0 | 0 |
| Borde | 16·2 | 7 | 21 | 4 | | | | |
| Nadkarni | 6 | 5 | 4 | 0 | 7 | 0 | 36 | 0 |
| PAKISTAN | | | | | | | | |
| Mahmood Hussain | 31 | 12 | 56 | 2 | 8 | 3 | 9 | 0 |
| Fazal | 25·3 | 12 | 26 | 5 | 12 | 5 | 19 | 0 |
| Intikhab | 24 | 11 | 35 | 2 | 15 | 2 | 33 | 2 |
| Nasim | 12 | 5 | 32 | 0 | 2 | 1 | 5 | 0 |
| Haseeb | 7 | 1 | 17 | 1 | 14 | 6 | 25 | 2 |
| Saeed | | | | | 1 | 0 | 2 | 0 |
| Mushtaq | | | | | 3 | 1 | 9 | 0 |
| Hanif | | | | | 1 | 0 | 6 | 0 |
| Burki | | | | | 1 | 0 | 3 | 0 |

### FALL OF WICKETS

| Wkt | P 1st | I 1st | P 2nd | I 2nd |
|---|---|---|---|---|
| 1st | 12 | 59 | 15 | 47 |
| 2nd | 84 | 83 | 34 | 47 |
| 3rd | 135 | 83 | 116 | 48 |
| 4th | 164 | 85 | – | 65 |
| 5th | 185 | 145 | – | – |
| 6th | 186 | 147 | – | – |
| 7th | 274 | 174 | – | – |
| 8th | 296 | 175 | – | – |
| 9th | 296 | 180 | – | – |
| 10th | 301 | 180 | – | – |

Umpires: S.K. Ganguli and B. Satyaji Rao.

# INDIA v PAKISTAN 1960–61 (4th Test)

Played at Corporation Stadium, Madras, on 13, 14, 15, 17, 18 January.
Toss: Pakistan.   Result: MATCH DRAWN.
Debuts: India – B.P. Gupte.

India's total of 539 for 9 declared remains their highest in any Test match. The main contributions came from Borde, whose innings of 177* is the highest for either country in this series, and Umrigar; their stand of 177 set a new Indian fifth-wicket record. Earlier Hanif and Imtiaz had established a Pakistan first-wicket record for all Tests of 162. A fire gutted the eastern section of the stands and ended play 20 minutes prematurely on the fourth day.

## PAKISTAN

| | | | | |
|---|---|---|---|---|
| Hanif Mohammad | c Kunderan b Surendranath | 62 | | |
| Imtiaz Ahmed† | b Desai | 135 | not out | 20 |
| Saeed Ahmed | c Kunderan b Desai | 103 | not out | 38 |
| Javed Burki | c Contractor b Borde | 19 | | |
| W. Mathias | lbw b Umrigar | 49 | | |
| Mushtaq Mohammad | not out | 41 | | |
| Nasim-ul-Ghani | c Kunderan b Umrigar | 5 | | |
| Intikhab Alam | c Kunderan b Desai | 13 | | |
| Fazal Mahmood* | lbw b Desai | 4 | | |
| Mahmood Hussain | ) did not bat | | | |
| Haseeb Ahsan | ) | | | |
| Extras | (B 12, LB 3, NB 2) | 17 | (NB 1) | 1 |
| **Total** | (8 wickets declared) | **448** | (0 wickets) | **59** |

## INDIA

| | | |
|---|---|---|
| M.L. Jaisimha | c Intikhab b Mahmood | 32 |
| N.J. Contractor* | c Intikhab b Haseeb | 81 |
| D.K. Gaekwad | c and b Haseeb | 9 |
| V.L. Manjrekar | b Haseeb | 30 |
| P.R. Umrigar | b Haseeb | 117 |
| C.G. Borde | not out | 177 |
| A.G. Milkha Singh | c Fazal b Haseeb | 18 |
| B.K. Kunderan† | b Haseeb | 12 |
| R.B. Desai | st Imtiaz b Nasim | 18 |
| R. Surendranath | st Imtiaz b Nasim | 6 |
| B.P. Gupte | not out | 17 |
| Extras | (B 10, LB 7, NB 5) | 22 |
| **Total** | (9 wickets declared) | **539** |

| INDIA | O | M | R | W | O | M | R | W | FALL OF WICKETS | | | |
|---|---|---|---|---|---|---|---|---|---|---|---|---|
| Desai | 28·5 | 4 | 66 | 4 | 3 | 0 | 14 | 0 | | P | I | P |
| Surendranath | 38 | 10 | 99 | 1 | 3 | 2 | 8 | 0 | Wkt | 1st | 1st | 2nd |
| Gupte | 30 | 9 | 97 | 0 | 5 | 0 | 19 | 0 | 1st | 162 | 84 | – |
| Umrigar | 53 | 24 | 64 | 2 | | | | | 2nd | 252 | 102 | – |
| Borde | 33 | 4 | 105 | 1 | | | | | 3rd | 322 | 146 | – |
| Jaisimha | | | | | 3 | 0 | 8 | 0 | 4th | 338 | 164 | – |
| Manjrekar | | | | | 2 | 0 | 6 | 0 | 5th | 408 | 341 | – |
| Contractor | | | | | 1 | 0 | 1 | 0 | 6th | 420 | 396 | – |
| Milkha Singh | | | | | 1 | 0 | 2 | 0 | 7th | 444 | 416 | – |
| | | | | | | | | | 8th | 448 | 447 | – |
| PAKISTAN | | | | | | | | | 9th | – | 476 | – |
| Mahmood Hussain | 37 | 12 | 86 | 1 | | | | | 10th | – | – | – |
| Fazal | 43 | 22 | 66 | 0 | | | | | | | | |
| Haseeb | 84 | 19 | 202 | 6 | | | | | | | | |
| Intikhab | 17 | 5 | 40 | 0 | | | | | | | | |
| Nasim | 46 | 12 | 123 | 2 | | | | | | | | |

Umpires: S. Pan and S.K. Raghunatha Rao.

# INDIA v PAKISTAN 1960–61 (5th Test)

Played at Feroz Shah Kotla, Delhi, on 8, 9, 11, 12, 13 February.
Toss: India.   Result: MATCH DRAWN.
Debuts: India – V.V. Kumar.

India and Pakistan achieved their twelfth successive draw in their last match to date. After many abortive attempts to continue the series in the intervening years, an Indian tour of Pakistan has been scheduled to start in October 1978. It will include three Test matches.

## INDIA

| | | | | |
|---|---|---|---|---|
| M.L. Jaisimha | b Farooq | 27 | not out | 14 |
| N.J. Contractor* | c and b Intikhab | 92 | | |
| R.F. Surti | c Imtiaz b Fazal | 64 | | |
| V.L. Manjrekar | c Mathias b Hazeeb | 18 | | |
| P.R. Umrigar | b Fazal | 112 | | |
| C.G. Borde | c Imtiaz b Farooq | 45 | | |
| A.G. Milkha Singh | b Mahmood | 35 | | |
| R.G. Nadkarni | b Fazal | 21 | | |
| B.K. Kunderan† | not out | 12 | (2) not out | 1 |
| R.B. Desai | b Mahmood | 3 | | |
| V.V. Kumar | b Mahmood | 6 | | |
| Extras | (B 6, LB 13, NB 9) | 28 | (NB 1) | 1 |
| **Total** | | **463** | (0 wickets) | **16** |

## PAKISTAN

| | | | | |
|---|---|---|---|---|
| Hanif Mohammad | c Milkha Singh b Desai | 1 | b Desai | 44 |
| Imtiaz Ahmed† | b Kumar | 25 | lbw b Nadkarni | 53 |
| Saeed Ahmed | c Umrigar b Nadkarni | 36 | c sub (D.N. Sardesai) b Nadkarni | 31 |
| Javed Burki | c Manjrekar b Desai | 61 | c and b Kumar | 8 |
| W. Mathias | c Nadkarni b Kumar | 10 | c Borde b Nadkarni | 2 |
| Mushtaq Mohammad | c Kumar b Desai | 101 | lbw b Desai | 22 |
| Intikhab Alam | b Desai | 0 | b Kumar | 10 |
| Fazal Mahmood*, | c Nadkarni b Jumar | 13 | lbw b Desai | 18 |
| Mahmood Hussain | lbw b Kumar | 20 | b Nadkarni | 35 |
| Haseeb Ahsan | b Kumar | 5 | b Desai | 6 |
| Mohammad Farooq | not out | 0 | not out | 14 |
| Extras | (B 8, LB 1, W 1, NB 4) | 14 | (B 2, LB 5) | 7 |
| **Total** | | **286** | | **250** |

| PAKISTAN | O | M | R | W | O | M | R | W |
|---|---|---|---|---|---|---|---|---|
| Mahmood Hussain | 40 | 9 | 115 | 3 | 1 | 0 | 7 | 0 |
| Fazal | 38 | 8 | 86 | 3 | | | | |
| Farooq | 29 | 2 | 101 | 2 | 1 | 0 | 8 | 0 |
| Haseeb | 17 | 5 | 57 | 1 | | | | |
| Intikhab | 34 | 6 | 76 | 1 | | | | |
| INDIA | | | | | | | | |
| Desai | 28 | 5 | 102 | 4 | 27 | 3 | 88 | 4 |
| Surti | 11 | 1 | 38 | 0 | 7 | 0 | 34 | 0 |
| Nadkarni | 34 | 24 | 24 | 1 | 52·4 | 38 | 43 | 4 |
| Kumar | 37·5 | 21 | 64 | 5 | 36 | 17 | 68 | 2 |
| Borde | 10 | 3 | 30 | 0 | 2 | 0 | 2 | 0 |
| Umrigar | 5 | 1 | 14 | 0 | 3 | 2 | 8 | 0 |

FALL OF WICKETS

| Wkt | I 1st | P 1st | P 2nd | I 2nd |
|---|---|---|---|---|
| 1st | 43 | 10 | 83 | – |
| 2nd | 150 | 60 | 107 | – |
| 3rd | 201 | 78 | 126 | – |
| 4th | 324 | 89 | 131 | – |
| 5th | 338 | 225 | 142 | – |
| 6th | 401 | 229 | 165 | – |
| 7th | 439 | 254 | 189 | – |
| 8th | 441 | 265 | 196 | – |
| 9th | 453 | 281 | 212 | – |
| 10th | 463 | 286 | 250 | – |

Umpires: I. Gopalakrishnan and S.K. Raghunatha Rao.

# AUSTRALIA v WEST INDIES 1960–61 (1st Test)

Played at Woolloongabba, Brisbane, on 9, 10, 12, 13, 14 December.
Toss: West Indies.   Result: MATCH TIED.
Debuts: West Indies – P.D. Lashley, C.W. Smith.

Chronologically, and including the matches abandoned to Manchester's summers of 1890 and 1938, this was the 500th game of Test cricket. It produced the only tie when Australia, requiring 233 runs to win in 310 minutes, lost their last wicket to a run out off the seventh ball of the final over and with the scores level. Davidson became the first and, so far, only player to complete the match double of 100 runs and ten wickets in a Test. Sobers, who hit his tenth hundred, scored his 3,000th run in Tests.

## WEST INDIES

| | | | | | |
|---|---|---|---|---|---|
| C.C. Hunte | c Benaud b Davidson | 24 | c Simpson b Mackay | | 39 |
| C.W. Smith | c Grout b Davidson | 7 | c O'Neill b Davidson | | 6 |
| R.B. Kanhai | c Grout b Davidson | 15 | c Grout b Davidson | | 54 |
| G. St A. Sobers | c Kline b Meckiff | 132 | b Davidson | | 14 |
| F.M.M. Worrell* | c Grout b Davidson | 65 | c Grout b Davidson | | 65 |
| J.S. Solomon | hit wkt b Simpson | 65 | lbw b Simpson | | 47 |
| P.D. Lashley | c Grout b Kline | 19 | b Davidson | | 0 |
| F.C.M. Alexander† | c Davidson b Kline | 60 | b Benaud | | 5 |
| S. Ramadhin | c Harvey b Davidson | 12 | c Harvey b Simpson | | 6 |
| W.W. Hall | st Grout b Kline | 50 | b Davidson | | 18 |
| A.L. Valentine | not out | 0 | not out | | 7 |
| Extras | (LB 3, W 1) | 4 | (B 14, LB 7, W 2) | | 23 |
| **Total** | | **453** | | | **284** |

## AUSTRALIA

| | | | | | |
|---|---|---|---|---|---|
| C.C. McDonald | c Hunte b Sobers | 57 | b Worrell | | 16 |
| R.B. Simpson | b Ramadhin | 92 | c sub (L.R. Gibbs) b Hall | | 0 |
| R.N. Harvey | b Valentine | 15 | c Sobers b Hall | | 5 |
| N.C. O'Neill | c Valentine b Hall | 181 | c Alexander b Hall | | 26 |
| L.E. Favell | run out | 45 | c Solomon b Hall | | 7 |
| K.D. Mackay | b Sobers | 35 | b Ramadhin | | 28 |
| A.K. Davidson | c Alexander b Hall | 44 | run out | | 80 |
| R. Benaud* | lbw b Hall | 10 | c Alexander b Hall | | 52 |
| A.T.W. Grout† | lbw b Hall | 4 | run out | | 2 |
| I. Meckiff | run out | 4 | run out | | 2 |
| L.F. Kline | not out | 3 | not out | | 0 |
| Extras | (B 2, LB 8, W 1, NB 4) | 15 | (B 2, LB 9, NB 3) | | 14 |
| **Total** | | **505** | | | **232** |

| AUSTRALIA | O | M | R | W | O | M | R | W | FALL OF WICKETS | | | | |
|---|---|---|---|---|---|---|---|---|---|---|---|---|---|
| | | | | | | | | | | WI | A | WI | A |
| Davidson | 30 | 2 | 135 | 5 | 24·6 | 4 | 87 | 6 | *Wkt* | *1st* | *1st* | *2nd* | *2nd* |
| Meckiff | 18 | 0 | 129 | 1 | 4 | 1 | 19 | 0 | 1st | 23 | 84 | 13 | 1 |
| Mackay | 3 | 0 | 15 | 0 | 21 | 7 | 52 | 1 | 2nd | 42 | 138 | 88 | 7 |
| Benaud | 24 | 3 | 93 | 0 | 31 | 6 | 69 | 1 | 3rd | 65 | 194 | 114 | 49 |
| Simpson | 8 | 0 | 25 | 1 | 7 | 2 | 18 | 2 | 4th | 239 | 278 | 127 | 49 |
| Kline | 17·6 | 6 | 52 | 3 | 4 | 0 | 14 | 0 | 5th | 243 | 381 | 210 | 57 |
| O'Neill | | | | | 1 | 0 | 2 | 0 | 6th | 283 | 469 | 210 | 92 |
| | | | | | | | | | 7th | 347 | 484 | 241 | 226 |
| WEST INDIES | | | | | | | | | 8th | 366 | 489 | 250 | 228 |
| Hall | 29·3 | 1 | 140 | 4 | 17·7 | 3 | 63 | 5 | 9th | 452 | 496 | 253 | 232 |
| Worrell | 30 | 0 | 93 | 0 | 16 | 3 | 41 | 1 | 10th | 453 | 505 | 284 | 232 |
| Sobers | 32 | 0 | 115 | 2 | 8 | 0 | 30 | 0 | | | | | |
| Valentine | 24 | 6 | 82 | 1 | 10 | 4 | 27 | 0 | | | | | |
| Ramadhin | 15 | 1 | 60 | 1 | 17 | 3 | 57 | 1 | | | | | |

Umpires: C. Hoy and C.J. Egar.

# AUSTRALIA v WEST INDIES 1960–61 (2nd Test)

Played at Melbourne Cricket Ground on 30, 31 December, 2, 3 January.
Toss: Australia.   Result: AUSTRALIA won by seven wickets.
Debuts: Australia – J.W. Martin, F.M. Misson.

Although rain ended the second day's play shortly after lunch, Australia won with over a day to spare. Misson took Hunte's wicket with his second ball in Test cricket. In the second innings, Solomon was out when his cap fell on to the wicket as he was playing defensively. Martin, playing in his first Test, took the wickets of Kanhai, Sobers and Worrell in four balls.

## AUSTRALIA

| | | | | |
|---|---|---|---|---|
| I.C. McDonald | c Watson b Hall | 15 | c Sobers b Hall | 13 |
| R.B. Simpson | c Alexander b Hall | 49 | not out | 27 |
| R.N. Harvey | c Sobers b Worrell | 12 | c Alexander b Hall | 0 |
| N.C. O'Neill | c Sobers b Worrell | 40 | lbw b Watson | 0 |
| L.E. Favell | c Nurse b Sobers | 51 | not out | 24 |
| K.D. Mackay | b Ramadhin | 74 | | |
| A.K. Davidson | b Hall | 35 | | |
| R. Benaud* | b Hall | 2 | | |
| A.T.W. Grout† | b Watson | 5 | | |
| J.W. Martin | b Valentine | 55 | | |
| F.M. Misson | not out | 0 | | |
| Extras | (LB 7, W 1, NB 2) | 10 | (B 4, LB 1, NB 1) | 6 |
| **Total** | | **348** | (3 wickets) | **70** |

## WEST INDIES

| | | | | |
|---|---|---|---|---|
| C.C. Hunte | c Simpson b Misson | 1 | c Grout b O'Neill | 110 |
| J.S. Solomon | c Grout b Davidson | 0 | hit wkt b Benaud | 4 |
| S.M. Nurse | c Grout b Davidson | 70 | run out | 3 |
| R.B. Kanhai | c Harvey b Davidson | 84 | c Misson b Martin | 25 |
| G. St A. Sobers | c Simpson b Benaud | 9 | c Simpson b Martin | 0 |
| F.M.M. Worrell* | b Misson | 0 | c Simpson b Martin | 0 |
| F.C.M. Alexander† | c Favell b Davidson | 5 | c Grout b Davidson | 72 |
| S. Ramadhin | b Davidson | 0 | st Grout b Benaud | 3 |
| W.W. Hall | b Davidson | 5 | b Davidson | 4 |
| C.D. Watson | c McDonald b Benaud | 4 | run out | 5 |
| A.L. Valentine | not out | 1 | not out | 0 |
| Extras | (NB 2) | 2 | (B 2, LB 2, W 1, NB 2) | 7 |
| **Total** | | **181** | | **233** |

| WEST INDIES | O | M | R | W | O | M | R | W | | FALL OF WICKETS | | | |
|---|---|---|---|---|---|---|---|---|---|---|---|---|---|
| Hall | 12 | 2 | 51 | 4 | 9·4 | 0 | 32 | 2 | | A | WI | WI | A |
| Watson | 12 | 1 | 73 | 1 | 9 | 1 | 32 | 1 | *Wkt* | *1st* | *1st* | *2nd* | *2nd* |
| Sobers | 17 | 1 | 88 | 1 | | | | | 1st | 35 | 1 | 40 | 27 |
| Worrell | 9 | 0 | 50 | 2 | | | | | 2nd | 60 | 1 | 51 | 27 |
| Valentine | 11·1 | 1 | 55 | 1 | | | | | 3rd | 105 | 124 | 97 | 30 |
| Ramadhin | 5 | 0 | 21 | 1 | | | | | 4th | 155 | 139 | 99 | – |
| | | | | | | | | | 5th | 189 | 142 | 99 | – |
| AUSTRALIA | | | | | | | | | 6th | 242 | 160 | 186 | – |
| Davidson | 22 | 4 | 53 | 6 | 15·4 | 2 | 51 | 2 | 7th | 244 | 160 | 193 | – |
| Misson | 11 | 0 | 36 | 2 | 12 | 3 | 36 | 0 | 8th | 251 | 166 | 206 | – |
| Benaud | 27·2 | 10 | 58 | 2 | 20 | 3 | 49 | 2 | 9th | 348 | 177 | 222 | – |
| Martin | 8 | 1 | 32 | 0 | 20 | 3 | 56 | 3 | 10th | 348 | 181 | 233 | – |
| Simpson | 1 | 1 | 0 | 0 | 8 | 0 | 24 | 0 | | | | | |
| O'Neill | | | | | 5 | 1 | 10 | 1 | | | | | |

Umpires: C. Hoy and C.J. Egar.

## AUSTRALIA v WEST INDIES 1960–61 (3rd Test)

Played at Sydney Cricket Ground on 13, 14, 16, 17, 18 January.
Toss: West Indies.  Result: WEST INDIES won by 222 runs.
Debuts: Nil.

West Indies drew level in the rubber before lunch on the fifth day. Gibbs took the wickets of Mackay, Martin an[d] Grout in four balls. Alexander's hundred remained the only one of his first-class career.

### WEST INDIES

|  | |  | | |
|---|---|---|---|---|
| C.C. Hunte | c Simpson b Meckiff | 34 | c O'Neill b Davidson | |
| C.W. Smith | c Simpson b Davidson | 16 | c Simpson b Benaud | 5 |
| R.B. Kanhai | c Grout b Davidson | 21 | c Martin b Davidson | |
| G.St A. Sobers | c and b Davidson | 168 | c Grout b Davidson | |
| F.M.M. Worrell* | c Davidson b Benaud | 22 | lbw b Benaud | 8 |
| S.M. Nurse | c Simpson b Benaud | 43 | c and b Mackay | 1 |
| J.S. Solomon | c Simpson b Benaud | 14 | c Harvey b Benaud | |
| F.C.M. Alexander† | c Harvey b Benaud | 0 | lbw b Mackay | 10 |
| L.R. Gibbs | c Grout b Davidson | 0 | st Grout b Benaud | 1 |
| W.W. Hall | c Grout b Davidson | 10 | b Mackay | 2 |
| A.L. Valentine | not out | 0 | not out | 1 |
| Extras | (B 6, LB 4, W 1) | 11 | (B 4, LB 7, W 1) | 1 |
| **Total** | | **339** | | **32** |

### AUSTRALIA

|  | |  | | |
|---|---|---|---|---|
| C.C. McDonald | b Valentine | 34 | c Alexander b Valentine | 2 |
| R.B. Simpson | c Kanhai b Hall | 10 | b Sobers | 1 |
| R.N. Harvey | c Sobers b Hall | 9 | c Sobers b Gibbs | 8 |
| N.C. O'Neill | b Sobers | 71 | c Sobers b Gibbs | 7 |
| L.E. Favell | c Worrell b Valentine | 16 | b Gibbs | |
| K.D. Mackay | c Solomon b Gibbs | 39 | c Nurse b Gibbs | |
| A.K. Davidson | c Worrell b Valentine | 16 | (10) b Valentine | |
| R. Benaud* | c and b Valentine | 3 | (7) c and b Valentine | 2 |
| J.W. Martin | c Solomon b Gibbs | 0 | (8) b Valentine | |
| A.T.W. Grout† | c Hunte b Gibbs | 0 | (9) b Gibbs | |
| I. Meckiff | not out | 0 | not out | |
| Extras | (B 1, LB 2, NB 1) | 4 | (B 3, LB 6) | |
| **Total** | | **202** | | **24** |

| AUSTRALIA | O | M | R | W | O | M | R | W |
|---|---|---|---|---|---|---|---|---|
| Davidson | 21·6 | 4 | 80 | 5 | 8 | 1 | 33 | 3 |
| Meckiff | 13 | 1 | 74 | 1 | 5 | 2 | 12 | 0 |
| Mackay | 14 | 1 | 40 | 0 | 31·4 | 5 | 75 | 3 |
| Benaud | 23 | 3 | 86 | 4 | 44 | 14 | 113 | 4 |
| Martin | 8 | 1 | 37 | 0 | 10 | 0 | 65 | 0 |
| Simpson | 2 | 0 | 11 | 0 | 4 | 0 | 16 | 0 |
| WEST INDIES | | | | | | | | |
| Hall | 13 | 0 | 53 | 2 | 8 | 0 | 35 | 0 |
| Worrell | 9 | 4 | 18 | 0 | 4 | 0 | 7 | 0 |
| Gibbs | 23 | 6 | 46 | 3 | 26 | 5 | 66 | 5 |
| Valentine | 24·2 | 6 | 67 | 4 | 25·2 | 7 | 86 | 4 |
| Sobers | 5 | 2 | 14 | 1 | 9 | 1 | 38 | 1 |

FALL OF WICKETS

| Wkt | WI 1st | A 1st | WI 2nd | A 2nd |
|---|---|---|---|---|
| 1st | 48 | 17 | 10 | 27 |
| 2nd | 68 | 40 | 20 | 83 |
| 3rd | 89 | 65 | 22 | 19 |
| 4th | 152 | 105 | 123 | 197 |
| 5th | 280 | 155 | 144 | 197 |
| 6th | 329 | 194 | 159 | 202 |
| 7th | 329 | 200 | 166 | 209 |
| 8th | 329 | 200 | 240 | 220 |
| 9th | 329 | 202 | 309 | 234 |
| 10th | 339 | 202 | 326 | 241 |

Umpires: C. Hoy and C.J. Egar.

# AUSTRALIA v WEST INDIES 1960–61 (4th Test)

Played at Adelaide Oval on 27, 28, 30, 31 January, 1 February.
Toss: West Indies.   Result: MATCH DRAWN.
Debuts: Australia – D.E. Hoare.

After Hoare had taken Hunte's wicket in his second over of Test cricket, Kanhai scored a century in 126 minutes. Gibbs achieved the first hat-trick in this series when he dismissed Mackay, Grout and Misson; it remains the only hat-trick in an Adelaide Test. Kanhai became the first West Indian to score a hundred in each innings of a Test in Australia, his second hundred taking 150 minutes, before becoming Benaud's 200th Test wicket. Mackay and Kline earned Australia a draw when their tenth-wicket partnership survived the final 100 minutes of the match.

## WEST INDIES

| | | | | |
|---|---|--:|---|--:|
| C.C. Hunte | lbw b Hoare | 6 | run out | 79 |
| C.W. Smith | c and b Benaud | 28 | c Hoare b Mackay | 46 |
| R.B. Kanhai | c Simpson b Benaud | 117 | lbw b Benaud | 115 |
| G. St A. Sobers | b Benaud | 1 | run out | 20 |
| F.M.M. Worrell* | c Misson b Hoare | 71 | c Burge b Mackay | 53 |
| S.M. Nurse | c and b Misson | 49 | c Simpson b Benaud | 5 |
| J.S. Solomon | c and b Benaud | 22 | (8) not out | 16 |
| F.C.M. Alexander† | not out | 63 | (7) not out | 87 |
| L.R. Gibbs | b Misson | 18 | | |
| W.W. Hall | c Hoare b Benaud | 5 | | |
| A.L. Valentine | lbw b Misson | 0 | | |
| Extras | (B 3, LB 3, W 5, NB 2) | 13 | (B 2, LB 6, W 2, NB 1) | 11 |
| **Total** | | **393** | (6 wickets declared) | **432** |

## AUSTRALIA

| | | | | |
|---|---|--:|---|--:|
| C.C. McDonald | c Hunte b Gibbs | 71 | run out | 2 |
| L.E. Favell | c Alexander b Worrell | 1 | c Alexander b Hall | 4 |
| N.C. O'Neill | c Alexander b Sobers | 11 | c and b Sobers | 65 |
| R.B. Simpson | c Alexander b Hall | 85 | c Alexander b Hall | 3 |
| P.J.P. Burge | b Sobers | 45 | c Alexander b Valentine | 49 |
| R. Benaud* | c Solomon b Gibbs | 77 | c and b Sobers | 17 |
| K.D. Mackay | lbw b Gibbs | 29 | not out | 62 |
| A.T.W. Grout† | c Sobers b Gibbs | 0 | lbw b Worrell | 42 |
| F.M. Misson | b Gibbs | 0 | c Solomon b Worrell | 1 |
| D.E. Hoare | b Sobers | 35 | b Worrell | 0 |
| L.F. Kline | not out | 0 | not out | 15 |
| Extras | (B 2, LB 3, NB 7) | 12 | (B 9, LB 1, NB 3) | 13 |
| **Total** | | **366** | (9 wickets) | **273** |

| AUSTRALIA | O | M | R | W | O | M | R | W |
|---|--:|--:|--:|--:|--:|--:|--:|--:|
| Hoare | 16 | 0 | 68 | 2 | 13 | 0 | 88 | 0 |
| Misson | 17·5 | 2 | 79 | 3 | 28 | 3 | 106 | 0 |
| Mackay | 2 | 0 | 11 | 0 | 12 | 0 | 72 | 2 |
| Benaud | 27 | 5 | 96 | 5 | 27 | 3 | 107 | 2 |
| Kline | 21 | 3 | 109 | 0 | 12 | 2 | 48 | 0 |
| Simpson | 5 | 0 | 17 | 0 | | | | |
| WEST INDIES | | | | | | | | |
| Hall | 22 | 3 | 85 | 1 | 13 | 4 | 61 | 2 |
| Worrell | 7 | 0 | 34 | 1 | 17 | 9 | 27 | 3 |
| Sobers | 24 | 3 | 64 | 3 | 39 | 11 | 87 | 2 |
| Gibbs | 35·6 | 4 | 97 | 5 | 28 | 13 | 44 | 0 |
| Valentine | 21 | 4 | 74 | 0 | 20 | 7 | 40 | 1 |
| Solomon | | | | | 3 | 2 | 1 | 0 |

### FALL OF WICKETS

| | WI | A | WI | A |
|---|--:|--:|--:|--:|
| Wkt | 1st | 1st | 2nd | 2nd |
| 1st | 12 | 9 | 66 | 6 |
| 2nd | 83 | 45 | 229 | 7 |
| 3rd | 91 | 119 | 263 | 31 |
| 4th | 198 | 213 | 270 | 113 |
| 5th | 271 | 221 | 275 | 129 |
| 6th | 288 | 281 | 388 | 144 |
| 7th | 316 | 281 | – | 203 |
| 8th | 375 | 281 | – | 207 |
| 9th | 392 | 366 | – | 207 |
| 10th | 393 | 366 | – | – |

Umpires: C. Hoy and C.J. Egar.

# AUSTRALIA v WEST INDIES 1960–61 (5th Test)

Played at Melbourne Cricket Ground on 10, 11, 13, 14, 15 February.
Toss: Australia.   Result: AUSTRALIA won by two wickets.
Debuts: Nil.

The most enterprising and exciting rubber of recent times ended late on the penultimate day (it was a six-day match) when Australia's ninth-wicket pair scampered a bye. The second day was watched by 90,800 – the world record attendance for any day's cricket. Sobers bowled unchanged for 41 eight-ball overs in the first innings during the course of which Davidson scored his 1,000th run and completed the Test 'double' in his 34th match.

## WEST INDIES

| | | | | |
|---|---|---:|---|---:|
| C.W. Smith | c O'Neill b Misson | 11 | lbw b Davidson | 3 |
| C.C. Hunte | c Simpson b Davidson | 31 | c Grout b Davidson | 5 |
| R.B. Kanhai | c Harvey b Benaud | 38 | c Misson b Benaud | 3 |
| G. St A. Sobers | c Grout b Simpson | 64 | (5) c Grout b Simpson | 2 |
| F.M.M. Worrell* | c Grout b Martin | 10 | (7) c Grout b Davidson | |
| P.D. Lashley | c Misson b Benaud | 41 | (8) lbw b Martin | 1 |
| F.C.M. Alexander† | c McDonald b Misson | 11 | (6) c Mackay b Davidson | 7 |
| J.S. Solomon | run out | 45 | (4) run out | 3 |
| L.R. Gibbs | c Burge b Misson | 11 | c O'Neill b Simpson | 8 |
| W.W. Hall | b Misson | 21 | c Grout b Davidson | 2 |
| A.L. Valentine | not out | 0 | not out | |
| Extras | (B 4, LB 4, W 1) | 9 | (B 5, LB 8, W 1) | 1 |
| **Total** | | **292** | | **32** |

## AUSTRALIA

| | | | | |
|---|---|---:|---|---:|
| R.B. Simpson | c Gibbs b Sobers | 75 | b Gibbs | 9 |
| C.C. McDonald | lbw b Sobers | 91 | c Smith b Gibbs | 1 |
| N.C. O'Neill | b Gibbs | 10 | (4) c Alexander b Worrell | 4 |
| P.J.P. Burge | c Sobers b Gibbs | 68 | (5) b Valentine | 5 |
| K.D. Mackay | c Alexander b Hall | 19 | (8) not out | |
| R.N. Harvey | c Alexander b Sobers | 5 | c Smith b Worrell | 1 |
| A.K. Davidson | c Alexander b Sobers | 24 | c Sobers b Worrell | 1 |
| R. Benaud* | b Gibbs | 3 | (3) b Valentine | |
| J.W. Martin | c Kanhai b Sobers | 15 | (10) not out | |
| F.M. Misson | not out | 12 | | |
| A.T.W. Grout† | c Hunte b Gibbs | 14 | (9) c Smith b Valentine | |
| Extras | (B 4, LB 8, NB 8) | 20 | (B 3, LB 9, NB 3) | 1 |
| **Total** | | **356** | (8 wickets) | **25** |

| AUSTRALIA | O | M | R | W | O | M | R | W | | FALL OF WICKETS | | | |
|---|---|---|---|---|---|---|---|---|---|---|---|---|---|
| Davidson | 27 | 4 | 89 | 1 | 24·7 | 4 | 84 | 5 | | WI | A | WI | A |
| Misson | 14 | 3 | 58 | 4 | 10 | 1 | 58 | 0 | *Wkt* | *1st* | *1st* | *2nd* | *2nd* |
| Mackay | 1 | 0 | 1 | 0 | 10 | 2 | 21 | 0 | 1st | 18 | 146 | 54 | 5 |
| Benaud | 21·7 | 5 | 55 | 2 | 23 | 4 | 53 | 1 | 2nd | 75 | 181 | 103 | 7 |
| Martin | 8 | 0 | 29 | 1 | 10 | 1 | 36 | 1 | 3rd | 81 | 181 | 135 | 15 |
| Simpson | 18 | 3 | 51 | 1 | 18 | 4 | 55 | 2 | 4th | 107 | 244 | 173 | 17 |
| | | | | | | | | | 5th | 200 | 260 | 201 | 20 |
| WEST INDIES | | | | | | | | | 6th | 204 | 309 | 218 | 23 |
| Hall | 15 | 1 | 56 | 1 | 5 | 0 | 40 | 0 | 7th | 221 | 309 | 262 | 24 |
| Worrell | 11 | 2 | 44 | 0 | 31 | 16 | 43 | 3 | 8th | 235 | 319 | 295 | 25 |
| Sobers | 44 | 7 | 120 | 5 | 13 | 2 | 32 | 0 | 9th | 290 | 335 | 304 | – |
| Gibbs | 38·4 | 18 | 74 | 4 | 41 | 19 | 68 | 2 | 10th | 292 | 356 | 321 | – |
| Valentine | 13 | 3 | 42 | 0 | 21·7 | 4 | 60 | 3 | | | | | |

Umpires: C. Hoy and C.J. Egar.

# ENGLAND v AUSTRALIA 1961 (1st Test)

Played at Edgbaston, Birmingham, on 8, 9, 10, 12, 13 June.
Toss: England.   Result: MATCH DRAWN.
Debuts: England – J.T. Murray; Australia – W.M. Lawry.

Harvey's 20th hundred in Test matches was Australia's first at Birmingham, their only previous Tests there being in 1902 and 1909. Earlier Mackay had taken the wickets of Barrington, Smith and Subba Row in four balls. On the final day Subba Row became the twelfth England player to score a hundred in his first Test against Australia. Curiously this list includes the first four batsmen of Indian descent to play for England.

## ENGLAND

| | | | | |
|---|---|---|---|---|
| G. Pullar | b Davidson | 17 | c Grout b Misson | 28 |
| R. Subba Row | c Simpson b Mackay | 59 | b Misson | 112 |
| E.R. Dexter | c Davidson b Mackay | 10 | st Grout b Simpson | 180 |
| M.C. Cowdrey* | b Misson | 13 | b Mackay | 14 |
| K.F. Barrington | c Misson b Mackay | 21 | not out | 48 |
| M.J.K. Smith | c Lawry b Mackay | 0 | not out | 1 |
| R. Illingworth | c Grout b Benaud | 15 | | |
| J.T. Murray† | c Davidson b Benaud | 16 | | |
| D.A. Allen | run out | 11 | | |
| F.S. Trueman | c Burge b Benaud | 20 | | |
| J.B. Statham | not out | 7 | | |
| Extras | (B 3, LB 3) | 6 | (LB 18) | 18 |
| **Total** | | **195** | (4 wickets) | **401** |

## AUSTRALIA

| | | |
|---|---|---|
| W.M. Lawry | c Murray b Illingworth | 57 |
| C.C. McDonald | c Illingworth b Statham | 22 |
| R.N. Harvey | lbw b Allen | 114 |
| N.C. O'Neill | b Statham | 82 |
| P.J.P. Burge | lbw b Allen | 25 |
| R.B. Simpson | c and b Trueman | 76 |
| A.K. Davidson | c and b Illingworth | 22 |
| K.D. Mackay | c Barrington b Statham | 64 |
| R. Benaud* | not out | 36 |
| A.T.W. Grout† | c Dexter b Trueman | 5 |
| F.M. Misson | did not bat | |
| Extras | (B 8, LB 4, NB 1) | 13 |
| **Total** | (9 wickets declared) | **516** |

| AUSTRALIA | O | M | R | W | O | M | R | W |
|---|---|---|---|---|---|---|---|---|
| Davidson | 26 | 6 | 70 | 1 | 31 | 10 | 60 | 0 |
| Misson | 15 | 6 | 47 | 1 | 28 | 6 | 82 | 2 |
| Mackay | 29 | 10 | 57 | 4 | 41 | 13 | 87 | 1 |
| Benaud | 14·3 | 8 | 15 | 3 | 20 | 4 | 67 | 0 |
| Simpson | | | | | 34 | 12 | 87 | 1 |
| ENGLAND | | | | | | | | |
| Trueman | 36·5 | 1 | 136 | 2 | | | | |
| Statham | 43 | 6 | 147 | 3 | | | | |
| Illingworth | 44 | 12 | 110 | 2 | | | | |
| Allen | 24 | 4 | 88 | 2 | | | | |
| Dexter | 5 | 1 | 22 | 0 | | | | |

| | FALL OF WICKETS | | | |
|---|---|---|---|---|
| | E | A | E | |
| Wkt | 1st | 1st | 2nd | |
| 1st | 36 | 47 | 93 | |
| 2nd | 53 | 106 | 202 | |
| 3rd | 88 | 252 | 239 | |
| 4th | 121 | 299 | 400 | |
| 5th | 121 | 322 | – | |
| 6th | 122 | 381 | – | |
| 7th | 153 | 469 | – | |
| 8th | 156 | 501 | – | |
| 9th | 181 | 516 | – | |
| 10th | 195 | – | – | |

Umpires: J.S. Buller and F.S. Lee.

# ENGLAND v AUSTRALIA 1961 (2nd Test)

Played at Lord's, London, on 22, 23, 24, 26 June.
Toss: England.   Result: AUSTRALIA won by five wickets.
Debuts: Australia – G.D. McKenzie.

England won their twelfth consecutive toss, Cowdrey setting a Test record by winning nine in succession. Statham took his 200th wicket for England when he bowled McDonald. Grout made his hundredth dismissal when he caught Murray. Australia's win, completed at 2.50 p.m. on the fourth day, ended England's then longest unbeaten run of 18 matches starting with the Christchurch Test of 1958-59 (*No. 472*). It was England's first defeat at home since the corresponding fixture in 1956 (*Test No. 426*).

## ENGLAND

| | | | | | |
|---|---|---|---|---|---|
| G. Pullar | b Davidson | 11 | c Grout b Misson | | 42 |
| R. Subba Row | lbw b Mackay | 48 | c Grout b Davidson | | 8 |
| E.R. Dexter | c McKenzie b Misson | 27 | b McKenzie | | 17 |
| M.C. Cowdrey* | c Grout b McKenzie | 16 | c Mackay b Misson | | 7 |
| P.B.H. May | c Grout b Davidson | 17 | c Grout b McKenzie | | 22 |
| K.F. Barrington | c Mackay b Davidson | 4 | lbw b Davidson | | 66 |
| R. Illingworth | b Misson | 13 | c Harvey b Simpson | | 0 |
| J.T. Murray† | lbw b Mackay | 18 | c Grout b McKenzie | | 25 |
| G.A.R. Lock | c Grout b Davidson | 5 | b McKenzie | | 1 |
| F.S. Trueman | b Davidson | 25 | c Grout b McKenzie | | 0 |
| J.B. Statham | not out | 11 | not out | | 2 |
| Extras | (LB 9, W 2) | 11 | (B 1, LB 10, W 1) | | 12 |
| **Total** | | **206** | | | **202** |

## AUSTRALIA

| | | | | | |
|---|---|---|---|---|---|
| W.M. Lawry | c Murray b Dexter | 130 | c Murray b Statham | | 1 |
| C.C. McDonald | b Statham | 4 | c Illingworth b Trueman | | 14 |
| R.B. Simpson | c Illingworth b Trueman | 0 | (6) c Illingworth b Statham | | 15 |
| R.N. Harvey* | c Barrington b Trueman | 27 | (3) c Murray b Trueman | | 4 |
| N.C. O'Neill | b Dexter | 1 | (4) b Statham | | 0 |
| P.J.P. Burge | c Murray b Statham | 46 | (5) not out | | 37 |
| A.K. Davidson | lbw b Trueman | 6 | not out | | 0 |
| K.D. Mackay | c Barrington b Illingworth | 54 | | | |
| A.T.W. Grout† | lbw b Dexter | 0 | | | |
| G.D. McKenzie | b Trueman | 34 | | | |
| F.M. Misson | not out | 25 | | | |
| Extras | (B 1, LB 12) | 13 | | | |
| **Total** | | **340** | (5 wickets) | | **71** |

| AUSTRALIA | O | M | R | W | O | M | R | W | FALL OF WICKETS | | | | |
|---|---|---|---|---|---|---|---|---|---|---|---|---|---|
| Davidson | 24·3 | 6 | 42 | 5 | 24 | 8 | 50 | 2 | | E | A | E | A |
| McKenzie | 26 | 7 | 81 | 1 | 29 | 13 | 37 | 5 | *Wkt* | *1st* | *1st* | *2nd* | *2nd* |
| Misson | 16 | 4 | 48 | 2 | 17 | 2 | 66 | 2 | 1st | 26 | 5 | 33 | 15 |
| Mackay | 12 | 3 | 24 | 2 | 8 | 6 | 5 | 0 | 2nd | 87 | 6 | 63 | 15 |
| Simpson | | | | | 19 | 10 | 32 | 1 | 3rd | 87 | 81 | 67 | 19 |
| | | | | | | | | | 4th | 111 | 88 | 80 | 19 |
| ENGLAND | | | | | | | | | 5th | 115 | 183 | 127 | 58 |
| Statham | 44 | 10 | 89 | 2 | 10·5 | 3 | 31 | 3 | 6th | 127 | 194 | 144 | – |
| Trueman | 34 | 3 | 118 | 4 | 10 | 0 | 40 | 2 | 7th | 156 | 238 | 191 | – |
| Dexter | 24 | 7 | 56 | 3 | | | | | 8th | 164 | 238 | 199 | – |
| Lock | 26 | 13 | 48 | 0 | | | | | 9th | 167 | 291 | 199 | – |
| Illingworth | 11·3 | 5 | 16 | 1 | | | | | 10th | 206 | 340 | 202 | – |

Umpires: C.S. Elliott and W.E. Philipson.

# ENGLAND v AUSTRALIA 1961 (3rd Test)

Played at Headingley, Leeds, on 6, 7, 8, July.
Toss: Australia.　　Result: ENGLAND won by eight wickets.
Debuts: Nil.

England recalled Jackson for his first Test for twelve years and lost the toss for the first time in 13 matches. Australia bowled 70 balls while England's total stayed at 239, before Lock scored 30 off 20 balls with seven fours in 19 minutes. Trueman had a spell of 5 for 0 in 24 balls in the second innings.

## AUSTRALIA

| | | | | |
|---|---|---|---|---|
| C.C. McDonald | st Murray b Lock | 54 | b Jackson | 1 |
| W.M. Lawry | lbw b Lock | 28 | c Murray b Allen | 28 |
| R.N. Harvey | c Lock b Trueman | 73 | c Dexter b Trueman | 53 |
| N.C. O'Neill | c Cowdrey b Trueman | 27 | c Cowdrey b Trueman | 19 |
| P.J.P. Burge | c Cowdrey b Jackson | 5 | lbw b Allen | 0 |
| K.D. Mackay | lbw b Jackson | 6 | (9) c Murray b Trueman | 0 |
| R.B. Simpson | lbw b Trueman | 2 | (6) b Trueman | 3 |
| A.K. Davidson | not out | 22 | (7) c Cowdrey b Trueman | 7 |
| R. Benaud* | b Trueman | 0 | (8) b Trueman | 0 |
| A.T.W. Grout† | c Murray b Trueman | 3 | c and b Jackson | 7 |
| G.D. McKenzie | b Allen | 8 | not out | 0 |
| Extras | (B 7, LB 2) | 9 | (LB 2) | 2 |
| **Total** | | **237** | | **120** |

## ENGLAND

| | | | | |
|---|---|---|---|---|
| G. Pullar | b Benaud | 53 | not out | 26 |
| R. Subba Row | lbw b Davidson | 35 | b Davidson | 6 |
| M.C. Cowdrey | c Grout b McKenzie | 93 | c Grout b Benaud | 22 |
| P.B.H. May* | c and b Davidson | 26 | not out | 8 |
| E.R. Dexter | b Davidson | 28 | | |
| K.F. Barrington | c Simpson b Davidson | 6 | | |
| J.T. Murray† | b McKenzie | 6 | | |
| F.S. Trueman | c Burge b Davidson | 4 | | |
| G.A.R. Lock | lbw b McKenzie | 30 | | |
| D.A. Allen | not out | 5 | | |
| H.L. Jackson | run out | 8 | | |
| Extras | (LB 5) | 5 | | |
| **Total** | | **299** | (2 wickets) | **62** |

| ENGLAND | O | M | R | W | O | M | R | W | | FALL OF WICKETS | | | |
|---|---|---|---|---|---|---|---|---|---|---|---|---|---|
| Trueman | 22 | 5 | 58 | 5 | 15·5 | 5 | 30 | 6 | | A | E | A | E |
| Jackson | 31 | 11 | 57 | 2 | 13 | 5 | 26 | 2 | *Wkt* | *1st* | *1st* | *2nd* | *2nd* |
| Allen | 28 | 12 | 45 | 1 | 14 | 6 | 30 | 2 | 1st | 65 | 59 | 4 | 14 |
| Lock | 29 | 5 | 68 | 2 | 10 | 1 | 32 | 0 | 2nd | 113 | 145 | 49 | 45 |
| | | | | | | | | | 3rd | 187 | 190 | 99 | – |
| AUSTRALIA | | | | | | | | | 4th | 192 | 223 | 102 | – |
| Davidson | 47 | 23 | 63 | 5 | 11 | 6 | 17 | 1 | 5th | 196 | 239 | 102 | – |
| McKenzie | 27 | 4 | 64 | 3 | 5 | 0 | 15 | 0 | 6th | 203 | 248 | 105 | – |
| Mackay | 22 | 4 | 34 | 0 | 1 | 0 | 8 | 0 | 7th | 203 | 252 | 109 | – |
| Benaud | 39 | 15 | 86 | 1 | 6 | 1 | 22 | 1 | 8th | 204 | 286 | 109 | – |
| Simpson | 14 | 5 | 47 | 0 | | | | | 9th | 208 | 291 | 120 | – |
| | | | | | | | | | 10th | 237 | 299 | 120 | – |

Umpires: J.S. Buller and J.G. Langridge.

# ENGLAND v AUSTRALIA 1961 (4th Test)

Played at Old Trafford, Manchester, on 27, 28, 29, 31 July, 1 August.
Toss: Australia.   Result: AUSTRALIA won by 54 runs.
Debuts: England – J.A. Flavell; Australia - B.C. Booth.

Rain delayed the start until 2.40 p.m. on the first day and brought the total of time lost in post-war Tests at Manchester to 103 hours. Simpson ended England's first innings with a spell of 4 for 2 in 26 balls. Davidson scored 20 runs (604046) off one over from Allen and shared in a last-wicket partnership of 98 with McKenzie. Murray took seven catches to equal T.G. Evans' England record against Australia set in 1956 at Lord's. Benaud bowled his side to victory on the last afternoon with a spell of 5 for 12 in 25 balls.

## AUSTRALIA

| | | | | |
|---|---|---|---|---|
| W.M. Lawry | lbw b Statham | 74 | c Trueman b Allen | 102 |
| R.B. Simpson | c Murray b Statham | 4 | c Murray b Flavell | 51 |
| R.N. Harvey | c Subba Row b Statham | 19 | c Murray b Dexter | 35 |
| N.C. O'Neill | hit wkt b Trueman | 11 | c Murray b Statham | 67 |
| P.J.P. Burge | b Flavell | 15 | c Murray b Dexter | 23 |
| B.C. Booth | c Close b Statham | 46 | lbw b Dexter | 9 |
| K.D. Mackay | c Murray b Statham | 11 | c Close b Allen | 18 |
| A.K. Davidson | c Barrington b Dexter | 0 | not out | 77 |
| R. Benaud* | b Dexter | 2 | lbw b Allen | 1 |
| A.T.W. Grout† | c Murray b Dexter | 2 | c Statham b Allen | 0 |
| G.D. McKenzie | not out | 1 | b Flavell | 32 |
| Extras | (B 4, LB 1) | 5 | (B 6, LB 9, W 2) | 17 |
| **Total** | | **190** | | **432** |

## ENGLAND

| | | | | |
|---|---|---|---|---|
| G. Pullar | b Davidson | 63 | c O'Neill b Davidson | 26 |
| R. Subba Row | c Simpson b Davidson | 2 | b Benaud | 49 |
| E.R. Dexter | c Davidson b McKenzie | 16 | c Grout b Benaud | 76 |
| P.B.H. May* | c Simpson b Davidson | 95 | b Benaud | 0 |
| D.B. Close | lbw b McKenzie | 33 | c O'Neill b Benaud | 8 |
| K.F. Barrington | c O'Neill b Simpson | 78 | lbw b Mackay | 5 |
| J.T. Murray† | c Grout b Mackay | 24 | c Simpson b Benaud | 4 |
| D.A. Allen | c Booth b Simpson | 42 | c Simpson b Benaud | 10 |
| F.S. Trueman | c Harvey b Simpson | 3 | c Benaud b Simpson | 8 |
| J.B. Statham | c Mackay b Simpson | 4 | b Davidson | 8 |
| J.A. Flavell | not out | 0 | not out | 0 |
| Extras | (B 2, LB 4, W 1) | 7 | (B 5. W 2) | 7 |
| **Total** | | **367** | | **201** |

| ENGLAND | O | M | R | W | O | M | R | W |  | FALL OF WICKETS | | | |
|---|---|---|---|---|---|---|---|---|---|---|---|---|---|
| Trueman | 14 | 1 | 55 | 1 | 32 | 6 | 92 | 0 | | A | E | A | E |
| Statham | 21 | 3 | 53 | 5 | 44 | 9 | 106 | 1 | Wkt | 1st | 1st | 2nd | 2nd |
| Flavell | 22 | 8 | 61 | 1 | 29·4 | 4 | 65 | 2 | 1st | 8 | 3 | 113 | 40 |
| Dexter | 6·4 | 2 | 16 | 3 | 20 | 4 | 61 | 3 | 2nd | 51 | 43 | 175 | 150 |
| Allen | | | | | 38 | 25 | 58 | 4 | 3rd | 89 | 154 | 210 | 150 |
| Close | | | | | 8 | 1 | 33 | 0 | 4th | 106 | 212 | 274 | 158 |
| | | | | | | | | | 5th | 150 | 212 | 290 | 163 |
| AUSTRALIA | | | | | | | | | 6th | 174 | 272 | 296 | 171 |
| Davidson | 39 | 11 | 70 | 3 | 14·4 | 1 | 50 | 2 | 7th | 185 | 358 | 332 | 171 |
| McKenzie | 38 | 11 | 106 | 2 | 4 | 1 | 20 | 0 | 8th | 185 | 362 | 334 | 189 |
| Mackay | 40 | 9 | 81 | 1 | 13 | 7 | 33 | 1 | 9th | 189 | 367 | 334 | 193 |
| Benaud | 35 | 15 | 80 | 0 | 32 | 11 | 70 | 6 | 10th | 190 | 367 | 432 | 201 |
| Simpson | 11·4 | 4 | 23 | 4 | 8 | 4 | 21 | 1 | | | | | |

Umpires: J.G. Langridge and W.E. Phillipson.

# ENGLAND v AUSTRALIA 1961 (5th Test)

Played at Kennington Oval, London, on 17, 18, 19, 21, 22 August.
Toss: England.    Result: MATCH DRAWN.
Debuts: Nil.

Rain interrupted play on the third and fourth days. Subba Row scored a hundred in his last Test against Australia, having also scored one in his first (*Test No. 507*). Murray's total of 18 dismissals was a new England record for a home rubber and Grout's 21 dismissals set a new record for a rubber in this series.

## ENGLAND

| | | | | | |
|---|---|---|---|---|---|
| G. Pullar | b Davidson | 8 | | c Grout b Mackay | 13 |
| R. Subba Row | lbw b Gaunt | 12 | | c and b Benaud | 137 |
| M.C. Cowdrey | c Grout b Davidson | 0 | (5) | c Benaud b Mackay | 3 |
| P.B.H. May* | c Lawry b Benaud | 71 | | c O'Neill b Mackay | 33 |
| E.R. Dexter | c Grout b Gaunt | 24 | (3) | c Gaunt b Mackay | 0 |
| K.F. Barrington | c Grout b Gaunt | 53 | | c O'Neill b Benaud | 83 |
| J.T. Murray† | c O'Neill b Mackay | 27 | | c Grout b Benaud | 40 |
| G.A.R. Lock | c Grout b Mackay | 3 | | c Benaud b Mackay | 0 |
| D.A. Allen | not out | 22 | | not out | 42 |
| J.B. Statham | b Davidson | 18 | | not out | 9 |
| J.A. Flavell | c Simpson b Davidson | 14 | | | |
| Extras | (B 1, LB 2, W 1) | 4 | | (B 6, LB 3, W 1) | 10 |
| **Total** | | **256** | | (8 wickets) | **370** |

## AUSTRALIA

| | | |
|---|---|---|
| W.M. Lawry | c Murray b Statham | 0 |
| R.B. Simpson | b Allen | 40 |
| R.N. Harvey | lbw b Flavell | 13 |
| N.C. O'Neill | c sub (M.J. Stewart) b Allen | 117 |
| P.J.P. Burge | b Allen | 181 |
| B.C. Booth | c Subba Row b Lock | 71 |
| K.D. Mackay | c Murray b Flavell | 5 |
| A.K. Davidson | lbw b Statham | 17 |
| R. Benaud* | b Allen | 6 |
| A.T.W. Grout† | not out | 30 |
| R.A. Gaunt | b Statham | 3 |
| Extras | (B 10, LB 1) | 11 |
| **Total** | | **494** |

| AUSTRALIA | O | M | R | W | O | M | R | W |
|---|---|---|---|---|---|---|---|---|
| Davidson | 34·1 | 8 | 83 | 4 | 29 | 7 | 67 | 0 |
| Gaunt | 24 | 3 | 53 | 3 | 22 | 7 | 33 | 0 |
| Benaud | 17 | 4 | 35 | 1 | 51 | 18 | 113 | 3 |
| Mackay | 39 | 14 | 75 | 2 | 68 | 21 | 121 | 5 |
| Simpson | 4 | 2 | 6 | 0 | 2 | 0 | 13 | 0 |
| O'Neill | | | | | 4 | 1 | 13 | 0 |
| Harvey | | | | | 1 | 1 | 0 | 0 |
| | | | | | | | | |
| ENGLAND | | | | | | | | |
| Statham | 38·5 | 10 | 75 | 3 | | | | |
| Flavell | 31 | 5 | 105 | 2 | | | | |
| Dexter | 24 | 2 | 68 | 0 | | | | |
| Allen | 30 | 6 | 133 | 4 | | | | |
| Lock | 42 | 14 | 102 | 1 | | | | |

## FALL OF WICKETS

| | E | A | E |
|---|---|---|---|
| Wkt | 1st | 1st | 2nd |
| 1st | 18 | 0 | 33 |
| 2nd | 20 | 15 | 33 |
| 3rd | 20 | 88 | 83 |
| 4th | 67 | 211 | 90 |
| 5th | 147 | 396 | 262 |
| 6th | 193 | 401 | 283 |
| 7th | 199 | 441 | 283 |
| 8th | 202 | 455 | 355 |
| 9th | 238 | 472 | – |
| 10th | 256 | 494 | – |

Umpires: C.S. Elliott and F.S. Lee.

# PAKISTAN v ENGLAND 1961–62 (1st Test)

Played at Lahore Stadium on 21, 22, 24, 25, 26 Ocober.
Toss: Pakistan.   Result: ENGLAND won by 5 wickets.
Debuts: Pakistan – Afaq Hussain; England – A. Brown, W.E. Russell, D.W. White.

England's first official Test in Pakistan – and the first match between the two countries since Pakistan's memorable win at The Oval in 1954 – brought the only result in twelve such contests in Pakistan to date. Barrington and Burki both scored hundreds on debut in this particular series. White took the wickets of Imtiaz and Hanif with his 11th and 16th balls in Test cricket. Javed Burki and Mushtaq shared a partnership of 153 which remains Pakistan's highest for the fourth wicket against England. This three-match rubber was continued after the five-Test rubber in India.

## PAKISTAN

| | | | | | |
|---|---|---|---|---|---|
| Hanif Mohammad | b White | 19 | c Murray b Brown | 17 |
| Imtiaz Ahmed*† | c Murray b White | 4 | b Dexter | 12 |
| Saeed Ahmed | c Murray b Barber | 74 | c Murray b Brown | 0 |
| Javed Burki | c Murray b Allen | 138 | c Allen b Barber | 15 |
| Mushtaq Mohammad | run out | 76 | c Pullar b Allen | 23 |
| W. Mathias | c Smith b Barber | 3 | lbw b Allen | 32 |
| Intikhab Alam | b Barber | 24 | b Barber | 17 |
| Mohammad Munaf | b Allen | 7 | c Dexter b Brown | 12 |
| Mahmood Hussain | b White | 14 | b Allen | 7 |
| Afaq Hussain | not out | 10 | not out | 35 |
| Haseeb Ahsan | not out | 7 | c Smith b Barber | 14 |
| Extras | (B 4, LB 3, NB 4) | 11 | (B 9, LB 2, NB 5) | 16 |
| **Total** | (9 wickets declared) | **387** | | **200** |

## ENGLAND

| | | | | | |
|---|---|---|---|---|---|
| P.E. Richardson | c Afaq b Munaf | 4 | c Imtiaz b Intikhab | 48 |
| G. Pullar | c Mahmood b Munaf | 0 | b Munaf | 0 |
| K.F. Barrington | run out | 139 | lbw b Mahmood | 6 |
| M.J.K. Smith | run out | 99 | c Afaq b Haseeb | 34 |
| E.R. Dexter* | hit wkt b Afaq | 20 | not out | 66 |
| W.E. Russell | b Intikhab | 34 | b Intikhab | 0 |
| R.W. Barber | st Imtiaz b Haseeb | 6 | not out | 39 |
| J.T. Murray† | b Munaf | 4 | | |
| D.A. Allen | lbw b Munaf | 40 | | |
| D.W. White | b Saeed | 0 | | |
| A. Brown | not out | 3 | | |
| Extras | (B 21, LB 1, NB 9) | 31 | (B 10, LB 4, NB 2) | 16 |
| **Total** | | **380** | (5 wickets) | **209** |

| ENGLAND | O | M | R | W | O | M | R | W | | FALL OF WICKETS | | | |
|---|---|---|---|---|---|---|---|---|---|---|---|---|---|
| White | 22 | 3 | 65 | 3 | 12 | 2 | 42 | 0 | | P | E | P | E |
| Brown | 15·5 | 3 | 44 | 0 | 14 | 4 | 27 | 3 | Wkt | 1st | 1st | 2nd | 2nd |
| Dexter | 7 | 1 | 26 | 0 | 7 | 2 | 10 | 1 | 1st | 17 | 2 | 33 | 1 |
| Barber | 40 | 4 | 124 | 3 | 20·5 | 6 | 54 | 3 | 2nd | 24 | 21 | 33 | 17 |
| Allen | 33 | 14 | 67 | 2 | 22 | 13 | 51 | 3 | 3rd | 162 | 213 | 33 | 86 |
| Russell | 19 | 9 | 25 | 0 | | | | | 4th | 315 | 275 | 69 | 108 |
| Barrington | 6 | 0 | 25 | 0 | | | | | 5th | 324 | 294 | 93 | 108 |
| | | | | | | | | | 6th | 324 | 306 | 113 | – |
| PAKISTAN | | | | | | | | | 7th | 327 | 322 | 138 | – |
| Mahmood Hussain | 25 | 8 | 35 | 0 | 12 | 3 | 30 | 1 | 8th | 365 | 361 | 146 | – |
| Munaf | 31·1 | 15 | 42 | 4 | 15 | 1 | 54 | 1 | 9th | 369 | 362 | 148 | – |
| Intikhab | 48 | 6 | 118 | 1 | 16 | 3 | 37 | 2 | 10th | – | 380 | 200 | – |
| Afaq | 23 | 6 | 40 | 1 | 5 | 0 | 21 | 0 | | | | | |
| Haseeb | 36 | 7 | 95 | 1 | 9 | 0 | 42 | 1 | | | | | |
| Saeed | 11 | 3 | 19 | 1 | 2 | 0 | 9 | 0 | | | | | |

Umpires: Shujauddin and Saeed Ahmed.

# INDIA v ENGLAND 1961–62 (1st Test)

Played at Brabourne Stadium, Bombay on 11, 12, 14, 15, 16 November.
Toss: England.   Result: MATCH DRAWN.
Debuts: England – D.R. Smith.

The partnership of 159 in 170 minutes between Richardson and Pullar remains England's highest for the first wicket against India. Kunderan became Lock's 2,000th wicket in first-class matches. India were set 297 runs to win in 245 minutes.

## ENGLAND

| | | | | | |
|---|---|---|---|---|---|
| P.E. Richardson | c Kunderan b Borde | 71 | c Kripal Singh b Durani | | 43 |
| G. Pullar | st Kunderan b Borde | 83 | | | |
| K.F. Barrington | not out | 151 | not out | | 52 |
| M.J.K. Smith | c Kunderan b Ranjane | 36 | b Durani | | 0 |
| E.R. Dexter* | b Durani | 85 | c sub (D.N. Sardesai) b Ranjane | | 27 |
| R.W. Barber | st Kunderan b Borde | 19 | (2) run out | | 31 |
| J.T. Murray† | c sub (D.N. Sardesai) b Ranjane | 8 | (6) b Desai | | 2 |
| D.A. Allen | c Kunderan b Ranjane | 0 | | | |
| G.A.R. Lock | b Ranjane | 23 | (7) not out | | 22 |
| D.R. Smith | } did not bat | | | | |
| A. Brown | | | | | |
| Extras | (B 7, LB 15, NB 2) | 24 | (B 3, LB 4) | | 7 |
| **Total** | (8 wickets declared) | **500** | (5 wickets declared) | | **184** |

## INDIA

| | | | | |
|---|---|---|---|---|
| N.J. Contractor* | b Allen | 19 | c Allen b D.R. Smith | 1 |
| M.L. Jaisimha | c Barrington b Dexter | 56 | c Barber b M.J.K. Smith | 51 |
| V.L. Manjrekar | c Lock b Barber | 68 | lbw b Lock | 84 |
| A.G. Milkha Singh | c Brown b Allen | 2 | c Allen b Richardson | 12 |
| C.G. Borde | b D.R. Smith | 69 | not out | 12 |
| S.A. Durani | c Barber b Allen | 71 | c and b Richardson | 0 |
| A.G. Kripal Singh | not out | 38 | not out | 13 |
| B.K. Kunderan† | lbw b Lock | 5 | | |
| R.B. Desai | c Richardson b Lock | 1 | | |
| V.B. Ranjane | c Barber b Lock | 16 | | |
| V.V. Kumar | b Lock | 0 | | |
| Extras | (B 33, LB 4, NB 8) | 45 | (B 4 LB 2, NB 1) | 7 |
| **Total** | | **390** | (5 wickets) | **180** |

| INDIA | O | M | R | W | O | M | R | W |
|---|---|---|---|---|---|---|---|---|
| Desai | 32 | 4 | 85 | 0 | 13 | 2 | 39 | 1 |
| Ranjane | 21 | 2 | 76 | 4 | 13 | 1 | 53 | 1 |
| Kripal Singh | 33 | 9 | 64 | 0 | 14 | 3 | 33 | 0 |
| Kumar | 27 | 8 | 70 | 0 | | | | |
| Durani | 30 | 5 | 91 | 1 | 11 | 1 | 28 | 2 |
| Borde | 30 | 5 | 90 | 3 | 7 | 1 | 24 | 0 |
| ENGLAND | | | | | | | | |
| D.R. Smith | 31 | 12 | 54 | 1 | 7 | 2 | 18 | 1 |
| Brown | 19 | 2 | 64 | 0 | 5 | 0 | 15 | 0 |
| Dexter | 12 | 4 | 25 | 1 | 4 | 0 | 15 | 0 |
| Barber | 22 | 5 | 74 | 1 | 13 | 2 | 42 | 0 |
| Lock | 45 | 22 | 74 | 4 | 16 | 9 | 33 | 1 |
| Allen | 39 | 21 | 54 | 3 | 11 | 5 | 12 | 0 |
| Barrington | | | | | 3 | 0 | 18 | 0 |
| M.J.K. Smith | | | | | 8 | 3 | 10 | 1 |
| Richardson | | | | | 6 | 3 | 10 | 2 |

## FALL OF WICKETS

| Wkt | E 1st | I 1st | E 2nd | I 2nd |
|---|---|---|---|---|
| 1st | 159 | 80 | 74 | 5 |
| 2nd | 164 | 121 | 93 | 136 |
| 3rd | 228 | 140 | 93 | 140 |
| 4th | 389 | 173 | 144 | 162 |
| 5th | 434 | 315 | 147 | 162 |
| 6th | 458 | 341 | – | – |
| 7th | 458 | 356 | – | – |
| 8th | 500 | 358 | – | – |
| 9th | – | 383 | – | – |
| 10th | – | 390 | – | – |

Umpires: S.K. Ganguli and A.R. Joshi.

# INDIA v ENGLAND 1961-62 (2nd Test)

Played at Green Park, Kanpur, on 1, 2, 3, 5, 6 December.
Toss: India.   Result: MATCH DRAWN.
Debuts: India – F.M. Engineer, D.N. Sardesai; England – B.R. Knight.

In the course of his eleventh Test hundred Umrigar became the first Indian to score 3,000 runs in Test cricket. Gupte took four wickets for six runs in 18 balls.

## INDIA

| | | |
|---|---|---:|
| M.L. Jaisimha | c Richardson b Lock | 70 |
| N.J. Contractor* | b Knight | 17 |
| V.L. Manjrekar | c Knight b Allen | 96 |
| S.A. Durani | c Lock b Dexter | 37 |
| P.R. Umrigar | not out | 147 |
| C.G. Borde | b Dexter | 21 |
| D.N. Sardesai | hit wkt b Lock | 28 |
| A.G. Kripal Singh | b Knight | 7 |
| F.M. Engineer† | st Murray b Lock | 33 |
| V.B. Ranjane | ) did not bat | |
| S.P. Gupte | ) | |
| Extras | (B 2, LB 7, NB 2) | 11 |
| **Total** | (8 wickets declared) | **467** |

## ENGLAND

| | | | | |
|---|---|---:|---|---:|
| P.E. Richardson | c Engineer b Gupte | 22 | c Umrigar b Borde | 48 |
| G. Pullar | c Sardesai b Gupte | 46 | c Contractor b Durani | 119 |
| K.F. Barrington | b Gupte | 21 | run out | 172 |
| M.J.K. Smith | c and b Gupte | 0 | lbw b Gupte | 0 |
| E.R. Dexter* | c Kripal Singh b Gupte | 2 | not out | 126 |
| R.W. Barber | not out | 69 | run out | 10 |
| J.T. Murray† | b Borde | 2 | not out | 9 |
| B.R. Knight | c and b Borde | 12 | | |
| D.A. Allen | c Engineer b Borde | 12 | | |
| G.A.R. Lock | c and b Durani | 49 | | |
| D.R. Smith | lbw b Ranjane | 0 | | |
| Extras | (B 6, LB 2, NB 1) | 9 | (B 4, LB 7, NB 2) | 13 |
| **Total** | | **244** | (5 wickets) | **497** |

| ENGLAND | O | M | R | W | O | M | R | W |
|---|---|---|---|---|---|---|---|---|
| D.R. Smith | 44 | 11 | 111 | 0 | | | | |
| Knight | 36 | 11 | 80 | 2 | | | | |
| Dexter | 31 | 5 | 84 | 2 | | | | |
| Lock | 44 | 15 | 93 | 3 | | | | |
| Allen | 43 | 17 | 88 | 1 | | | | |
| **INDIA** | | | | | | | | |
| Ranjane | 21·3 | 9 | 38 | 1 | 18 | 1 | 61 | 0 |
| Umrigar | 6 | 1 | 11 | 0 | 19 | 6 | 53 | 0 |
| Gupte | 40 | 12 | 90 | 5 | 33 | 8 | 89 | 1 |
| Kripal Singh | 1 | 0 | 5 | 0 | 36 | 7 | 78 | 0 |
| Durani | 16 | 6 | 36 | 1 | 53 | 15 | 139 | 1 |
| Borde | 22 | 6 | 55 | 3 | 16 | 4 | 44 | 1 |
| Jaisimha | | | | | 6 | 1 | 8 | 0 |
| Contractor | | | | | 2 | 0 | 9 | 0 |
| Sardesai | | | | | 1 | 0 | 3 | 0 |

## FALL OF WICKETS

| Wkt | I 1st | E 1st | E 2nd |
|---|---|---|---|
| 1st | 41 | 29 | 94 |
| 2nd | 150 | 87 | 233 |
| 3rd | 193 | 87 | 234 |
| 4th | 261 | 95 | 440 |
| 5th | 293 | 100 | 459 |
| 6th | 368 | 104 | – |
| 7th | 414 | 128 | – |
| 8th | 467 | 162 | – |
| 9th | – | 243 | – |
| 10th | – | 244 | – |

Umpires: Mohammed Yunus and V.S. Roy.

# INDIA v ENGLAND 1961–62 (3rd Test)

Played at Feroz Shah Kotla, Delhi, on 13, 14, 16, 17 (*no play*), 18 (*no play*) December.
Toss: India.   Result: MATCH DRAWN.
Debuts: India – The Nawab Mansur Ali of Pataudi. *After the Indian Government abolished royal titles, Pataudi assumed the name of 'Mansur Ali Khan'. He is shown throughout this book as 'Nawab of Pataudi, jr'.*

For only the second time in India, rain interrupted a Test match and, as had happened when Pakistan played at Madras in 1952-53 (*Test No. 358*), the last two days were abandoned. Barrington scored his fourth hundred in consecutive Tests and his partnership of 164 with Pullar remains England's highest for the second wicket in India. Manjrekar's 189 not out was India's highest score against England so far.

## INDIA

| | | |
|---|---|---|
| M.L. Jaisimha | c and b D.R. Smith | 127 |
| N.J. Contractor* | c Pullar b Lock | 39 |
| V.L. Manjrekar | not out | 189 |
| Nawab of Pataudi, jr | c Richardson b Allen | 13 |
| P.R. Umrigar | lbw b Allen | 22 |
| C.G. Borde | b Barber | 45 |
| S.A. Durani | b Allen | 18 |
| F.M. Engineer† | lbw b Allen | 1 |
| A.G. Kripal Singh | run out | 2 |
| R.B. Desai | lbw b Knight | 5 |
| S.P. Gupte | b Knight | 0 |
| Extras | (B 2, LB 2, NB 1) | 5 |
| **Total** | | **466** |

## ENGLAND

| | | |
|---|---|---|
| P.E. Richardson | lbw b Desai | 1 |
| G. Pullar | c Manjrekar b Kripal Singh | 89 |
| K.F. Barrington | not out | 113 |
| M.J.K. Smith | b Gupte | 2 |
| E.R. Dexter* | not out | 45 |
| R.W. Barber | ) | |
| J.T. Murray† | ) | |
| B.R. Knight | ) | |
| D.A. Allen | ) did not bat | |
| G.A.R. Lock | ) | |
| D.R. Smith | ) | |
| Extras | (B 5, NB 1) | 6 |
| **Total** | (3 wickets) | **256** |

| ENGLAND | O | M | R | W |
|---|---|---|---|---|
| D.R. Smith | 30 | 11 | 66 | 1 |
| Knight | 24·3 | 5 | 72 | 2 |
| Allen | 47 | 18 | 87 | 4 |
| Barber | 25 | 3 | 103 | 1 |
| Dexter | 2 | 0 | 11 | 0 |
| Lock | 40 | 15 | 83 | 1 |
| Barrington | 9 | 1 | 39 | 0 |
| INDIA | | | | |
| Desai | 28 | 5 | 57 | 1 |
| Jaisimha | 11 | 2 | 28 | 0 |
| Gupte | 36 | 14 | 78 | 1 |
| Durani | 13 | 3 | 38 | 0 |
| Kripal Singh | 12 | 4 | 27 | 1 |
| Borde | 10 | 4 | 19 | 0 |
| Umrigar | 4 | 1 | 3 | 0 |

### FALL OF WICKETS

| | I | E |
|---|---|---|
| Wkt | 1st | 1st |
| 1st | 121 | 2 |
| 2nd | 199 | 166 |
| 3rd | 244 | 177 |
| 4th | 276 | – |
| 5th | 408 | – |
| 6th | 443 | – |
| 7th | 451 | – |
| 8th | 455 | – |
| 9th | 462 | – |
| 10th | 466 | – |

Umpires: S. Kumaraswamy and B. Satyaji Rao.

**Test No. 516/28**

# INDIA v ENGLAND 1961–62 (4th Test)

Played at Eden Gardens, Calcutta, on 30, 31 December, 1, 3, 4 January.
Toss: India.   Result: INDIA won by 187 runs.
Debuts: England – G. Millman, P.H. Parfitt.

India gained their second win against England in 28 matches and ended a run of nine drawn Tests in India when England failed to score 421 runs in 490 minutes.

## INDIA

| Batsman | 1st innings | | 2nd innings | |
|---|---|---|---|---|
| N.J. Contractor* | b Smith | 4 | st Millman b Allen | 11 |
| V.L. Mehra | c Parfitt b Lock | 62 | (11) not out | - |
| V.L. Manjrekar | b Allen | 24 | st Millman b Lock | 2? |
| Nawab of Pataudi, jr | c Lock b Allen | 64 | c Millman b Lock | 3? |
| P.R. Umrigar | c Smith b Allen | 36 | (6) b Allen | 3( |
| M.L. Jaisimha | c Millman b Smith | 37 | (2) b Lock | 3( |
| C.G. Borde | run out | 68 | (8) c Barrington b Allen | 61 |
| S.A. Durani | b Allen | 43 | (7) c Parfitt b Lock | ( |
| F.M. Engineer† | c Parfitt b Lock | 12 | (5) c Millman b Allen | ( |
| R.B. Desai | not out | 13 | (9) c Parfitt b Knight | 29 |
| V.B. Ranjane | c Barber b Allen | 7 | (10) c Lock b Knight | ( |
| Extras | (B 2, LB 6, NB 2) | 10 | (LB 3, NB 1) | 4 |
| **Total** | | **380** | | **252** |

## ENGLAND

| Batsman | 1st innings | | 2nd innings | |
|---|---|---|---|---|
| P.E. Richardson | c Contractor b Borde | 62 | b Umrigar | 42 |
| W.E. Russell | b Ranjane | 10 | b Ranjane | 9 |
| K.F. Barrington | b Durani | 14 | c Durani b Desai | 3 |
| P.H. Parfitt | c sub (G. Kasturirangan) b Borde | 21 | (6) lbw b Umrigar | 46 |
| E.R. Dexter* | b Borde | 57 | (4) lbw b Durani | 62 |
| R.W. Barber | b Borde | 12 | (5) c Jaisimha b Durani | 6 |
| B.R. Knight | st Engineer b Durani | 12 | not out | 39 |
| D.A. Allen | b Durani | 15 | c Manjrekar b Desai | 7 |
| G. Millman† | c Engineer b Durani | 0 | b Ranjane | 4 |
| G.A.R. Lock | not out | 2 | run out | 1 |
| D.R. Smith | b Durani | 0 | c Manjrekar b Durani | 2 |
| Extras | (B 1, LB 2, NB 4) | 7 | (B 1, LB 11) | 12 |
| **Total** | | **212** | | **233** |

| ENGLAND | O | M | R | W | O | M | R | W |
|---|---|---|---|---|---|---|---|---|
| Smith | 31 | 10 | 60 | 2 | 3 | 0 | 15 | 0 |
| Knight | 18 | 3 | 61 | 0 | 7 | 2 | 18 | 2 |
| Dexter | 29 | 7 | 83 | 0 | | | | |
| Allen | 34 | 13 | 67 | 5 | 43·2 | 16 | 95 | 4 |
| Lock | 36 | 19 | 63 | 2 | 46 | 15 | 111 | 4 |
| Barber | 3 | 0 | 17 | 0 | 2 | 0 | 9 | 0 |
| Russell | 5 | 0 | 19 | 0 | | | | |
| INDIA | | | | | | | | |
| Desai | 10 | 1 | 34 | 0 | 17 | 4 | 32 | 2 |
| Ranjane | 21 | 3 | 59 | 1 | 14 | 3 | 31 | 2 |
| Durani | 23·2 | 8 | 47 | 5 | 33·2 | 12 | 66 | 3 |
| Borde | 25 | 8 | 65 | 4 | 22 | 10 | 46 | 0 |
| Umrigar | | | | | 30 | 10 | 46 | 2 |

### FALL OF WICKETS

| Wkt | I 1st | E 1st | I 2nd | E 2nd |
|---|---|---|---|---|
| 1st | 6 | 26 | 39 | 20 |
| 2nd | 50 | 69 | 55 | 27 |
| 3rd | 145 | 91 | 102 | 92 |
| 4th | 185 | 130 | 119 | 101 |
| 5th | 194 | 155 | 119 | 129 |
| 6th | 259 | 181 | 119 | 195 |
| 7th | 314 | 208 | 192 | 208 |
| 8th | 355 | 209 | 233 | 217 |
| 9th | 357 | 212 | 233 | 224 |
| 10th | 380 | 212 | 252 | 233 |

Umpires: H.E. Choudhury and S.K. Ragunatha Rao.

# INDIA v ENGLAND 1961–62 (5th Test)

Played at Corporation Stadium, Madras, on 10, 11, 13, 14, 15 January.
Toss: India.   Result: INDIA won by 128 runs.
Debuts: India – E.A.S. Prasanna.

India won their first rubber against England and only their third against any country with this second victory in successive matches. Engineer, who began the second day's play by scoring 16 (404224) off Knight's opening over, and Nadkarni shared India's first century partnership for the eighth wicket. Three years later, on the same ground against New Zealand, the same batsmen shared India's only other hundred partnership (143) for that wicket.

## INDIA

| | | | | | |
|---|---|---|---|---|---|
| M.L. Jaisimha | b Knight | 12 | | c Millman b Lock | 10 |
| N.J. Contractor* | b Barber | 86 | | c Parfitt b D.R. Smith | 3 |
| V.L. Manjrekar | c Lock b Parfitt | 13 | | run out | 85 |
| Nawab of Pataudi, jr | c Lock b Knight | 103 | | c M.J.K. Smith b Lock | 10 |
| P.R. Umrigar | c Millman b Allen | 2 | | c and b Allen | 11 |
| C.G. Borde | b Lock | 31 | (7) | c Dexter b Parfitt | 7 |
| S.A. Durani | b Allen | 21 | (8) | c Millman b Lock | 9 |
| R.G. Nadkarni | b Allen | 63 | (9) | c Parfitt b Lock | 1 |
| F.M. Engineer† | b Dexter | 65 | (10) | not out | 15 |
| R.B. Desai | lbw b Barber | 13 | (6) | c Parfitt b Lock | 12 |
| E.A.S. Prasanna | not out | 9 | | c Dexter b Lock | 17 |
| Extras | (B 4, LB 6) | 10 | | (B 6, LB 4) | 10 |
| **Total** | | **428** | | | **190** |

## ENGLAND

| | | | | |
|---|---|---|---|---|
| P.E. Richardson | c Contractor b Desai | 13 | c Jaisimha b Desai | 2 |
| R.W. Barber | lbw b Borde | 16 | b Durani | 21 |
| K.F. Barrington | c Manjrekar b Durani | 20 | lbw b Nadkarni | 48 |
| E.R. Dexter* | b Borde | 2 | c Nadkarni b Borde | 3 |
| M.J.K. Smith | c Umrigar b Durani | 73 | c Borde b Durani | 15 |
| P.H. Parfitt | c Prasanna b Durani | 25 | c Contractor b Durani | 33 |
| B.R. Knight | c Nadkarni b Durani | 19 | c Engineer b Durani | 33 |
| D.A. Allen | b Durani | 34 | c Umrigar b Borde | 21 |
| G. Millman† | not out | 32 | c Contractor b Prasanna | 14 |
| G.A.R. Lock | c Borde b Durani | 0 | c Nadkarni b Borde | 11 |
| D.R. Smith | b Nadkarni | 34 | not out | 2 |
| Extras | (B 1, LB 12) | 13 | (B 2, LB 4) | 6 |
| **Total** | | **281** | | **209** |

| ENGLAND | O | M | R | W | O | M | R | W | FALL OF WICKETS | | | | |
|---|---|---|---|---|---|---|---|---|---|---|---|---|---|
| D.R. Smith | 9 | 1 | 20 | 0 | 7 | 0 | 15 | 1 | | I | E | I | E |
| Knight | 14 | 2 | 62 | 2 | 4 | 0 | 12 | 0 | *Wkt* | *1st* | *1st* | *2nd* | *2nd* |
| Lock | 40 | 13 | 106 | 1 | 39·3 | 16 | 65 | 6 | 1st | 27 | 18 | 15 | 2 |
| Allen | 51·3 | 20 | 116 | 3 | 33 | 11 | 64 | 1 | 2nd | 74 | 41 | 30 | 32 |
| Parfitt | 11 | 2 | 22 | 1 | 11 | 3 | 24 | 1 | 3rd | 178 | 45 | 50 | 41 |
| Barber | 14 | 0 | 70 | 2 | | | | | 4th | 193 | 54 | 80 | 86 |
| Dexter | 5 | 0 | 22 | 1 | | | | | 5th | 245 | 134 | 99 | 90 |
| | | | | | | | | | 6th | 273 | 180 | 122 | 155 |
| INDIA | | | | | | | | | 7th | 277 | 189 | 146 | 164 |
| Desai | 12 | 1 | 56 | 1 | 4 | 0 | 16 | 1 | 8th | 378 | 226 | 150 | 194 |
| Jaisimha | 5 | 0 | 18 | 0 | | | | | 9th | 398 | 226 | 158 | 202 |
| Durani | 36 | 9 | 105 | 6 | 34 | 12 | 72 | 4 | 10th | 428 | 281 | 190 | 209 |
| Borde | 30 | 9 | 58 | 2 | 25·3 | 8 | 59 | 3 | | | | | |
| Prasanna | 9 | 2 | 20 | 0 | 11 | 3 | 19 | 1 | | | | | |
| Umrigar | 12 | 6 | 11 | 0 | 6 | 1 | 12 | 0 | | | | | |
| Nadkarni | 6·1 | 6 | 0 | 1 | 12 | 3 | 25 | 1 | | | | | |

Umpires: S. Pan and I. Gopalakrishnan.

# PAKISTAN v ENGLAND 1961–62 (2nd Test)

Played at Dacca Stadium, on 19, 20, 21, 23, 24 January.
Toss: Pakistan.    Result: MATCH DRAWN.
Debuts: Nil.

Hanif, who batted for 893 minutes in the match, became the only Pakistan batsman to score a hundred in each innings of a Test match. Only 175 runs were scored from 111 overs on the first day. The opening partnerships of 198 by Pullar and Barber and 122 by Hanif and Alimuddin remain the highest for each country in this series.

## PAKISTAN

| | | | | | |
|---|---|---|---|---|---|
| Hanif Mohammad | c Lock b Allen | 111 | | b Allen | 104 |
| Alimuddin | c Smith b Lock | 7 | | c Dexter b Richardson | 50 |
| Saeed Ahmed | b Knight | 69 | | c Parfitt b Lock | 13 |
| Javed Burki | c and b Lock | 140 | | c Knight b Lock | 0 |
| Intikhab Alam | c Barrington b Lock | 18 | (9) | b Lock | 5 |
| Mushtaq Mohammad | b Allen | 26 | (5) | c and b Allen | 6 |
| Imtiaz Ahmed*† | b Lock | 0 | (6) | hit wkt b Allen | 0 |
| Nasim-ul-Ghani | not out | 15 | | c Richardson b Allen | 12 |
| Shujauddin | ) | | (7) | b Lock | 0 |
| Mohammad Munaf | ) did not bat | | | b Allen | 12 |
| A. D'Souza | ) | | | not out | 7 |
| Extras | (B 4, LB 3) | 7 | | (B 5, LB 1, NB 1) | 7 |
| **Total** | (7 wickets declared) | **393** | | | **216** |

## ENGLAND

| | | | | | |
|---|---|---|---|---|---|
| G. Pullar | c and b D'Souza | 165 | | not out | 8 |
| R.W. Barber | lbw b Nasim | 86 | | | |
| K.F. Barrington | b D'Souza | 84 | | | |
| M.J.K. Smith | lbw b D'Souza | 10 | | | |
| E.R. Dexter* | b Munaf | 12 | | | |
| P.E. Richardson | c D'Souza b Nasim | 19 | (2) | not out | 21 |
| P.H. Parfitt | c and b Shujauddin | 9 | | | |
| B.R. Knight | b D'Souza | 10 | | | |
| D.A. Allen | b Shujauddin | 0 | | | |
| G. Millman† | not out | 3 | | | |
| G.A.R. Lock | c Hanif b Shujauddin | 4 | | | |
| Extras | (B 16, LB 15, NB 6) | 37 | | (B 2, LB 6, NB 1) | 9 |
| **Total** | | **439** | | (0 wickets) | **38** |

| ENGLAND | O | M | R | W | O | M | R | W | | FALL OF WICKETS | | | |
|---|---|---|---|---|---|---|---|---|---|---|---|---|---|
| Knight | 29 | 13 | 52 | 1 | 14 | 6 | 19 | 0 | | P | E | P | E |
| Dexter | 28 | 12 | 34 | 0 | 5 | 4 | 1 | 0 | *Wkt* | *1st* | *1st* | *2nd* | *2nd* |
| Lock | 73 | 24 | 155 | 4 | 42 | 23 | 70 | 4 | 1st | 14 | 198 | 122 | – |
| Allen | 40·3 | 13 | 94 | 2 | 23·1 | 11 | 30 | 5 | 2nd | 127 | 345 | 137 | – |
| Barrington | 11 | 1 | 39 | 0 | 21 | 13 | 17 | 0 | 3rd | 283 | 358 | 137 | – |
| Barber | 11 | 8 | 12 | 0 | | | | | 4th | 344 | 373 | 158 | – |
| Parfitt | | | | | 8 | 3 | 14 | 0 | 5th | 361 | 386 | 158 | – |
| Richardson | | | | | 12 | 5 | 28 | 1 | 6th | 365 | 414 | 159 | – |
| Pullar | | | | | 9 | 3 | 30 | 0 | 7th | 393 | 418 | 184 | – |
| | | | | | | | | | 8th | – | 422 | 191 | – |
| PAKISTAN | | | | | | | | | 9th | – | 432 | 201 | – |
| Munaf | 30 | 5 | 55 | 1 | | | | | 10th | – | 439 | 216 | – |
| D'Souza | 46 | 13 | 94 | 4 | | | | | | | | | |
| Shujauddin | 34 | 10 | 73 | 3 | | | | | | | | | |
| Nasim | 50 | 19 | 119 | 2 | 3 | 3 | 0 | 0 | | | | | |
| Intikhab | 9 | 0 | 43 | 0 | 5 | 0 | 16 | 0 | | | | | |
| Saeed | 12 | 3 | 18 | 0 | 4 | 2 | 2 | 0 | | | | | |
| Burki | | | | | 2 | 1 | 3 | 0 | | | | | |
| Hanif | | | | | 2 | 0 | 8 | 0 | | | | | |

Umpires: Daud Khan and Shujauddin.

# PAKISTAN v ENGLAND 1961–62 (3rd Test)

Played at National Stadium, Karachi, on 2, 3, 4, 6, 7 February.
Toss: Pakistan.   Result: MATCH DRAWN.
Debuts: Nil.

White, who pulled a muscle and was unable to complete his third over, took the wicket of Imtiaz with his first ball. Dexter batted for 495 minutes for England's only double century in Pakistan and shared in a record fourth-wicket partnership of 188 with Parfitt.

## PAKISTAN

| | | | | | |
|---|---|---|---|---|---|
| Hanif Mohammad | c Dexter b Lock | 67 | | c Dexter b Knight | 89 |
| Imtiaz Ahmed*† | b White | 0 | (5) | c Smith b Dexter | 86 |
| Saeed Ahmed | c Millman b Knight | 16 | | c and b Barber | 19 |
| Javed Burki | c Millman b Dexter | 3 | | c Millman b Dexter | 44 |
| Mushtaq Mohammad | lbw b Knight | 14 | (6) | b Lock | 41 |
| Alimuddin | c Lock b Knight | 109 | (2) | c Parfitt b Barber | 53 |
| Shujauddin | c Parfitt b Allen | 15 | | c Lock b Barber | 5 |
| Nasim-ul-Ghani | b Barber | 3 | | not out | 41 |
| Fazal Mahmood | b Knight | 12 | | b Dexter | 0 |
| A. D'Souza | b Dexter | 3 | | not out | 10 |
| Haseeb Ahsan | not out | 4 | | | |
| Extras | (B 2, LB 1, NB 4) | 7 | | (B 8, LB 2, NB 6) | 16 |
| **Total** | | **253** | | (8 wickets) | **404** |

## ENGLAND

| | | |
|---|---|---|
| P.E. Richardson | c Alimuddin b Nasim | 26 |
| G. Pullar | c Alimuddin b Nasim | 60 |
| E.R. Dexter* | c Saeed b D'Souza | 205 |
| M.J.K. Smith | c Imtiaz b Nasim | 56 |
| P.H. Parfitt | c Saeed b D'Souza | 111 |
| R.W. Barber | st Imtiaz b Haseeb | 23 |
| B.R. Knight | c Imtiaz b D'Souza | 6 |
| D.A. Allen | c Imtiaz b D'Souza | 1 |
| G. Millman† | c Nasim b Haseeb | 0 |
| G.A.R. Lock | not out | 0 |
| D.W. White | b D'Souza | 0 |
| Extras | (B 7, LB 11, NB 1) | 19 |
| **Total** | | **507** |

| ENGLAND | O | M | R | W | O | M | R | W |
|---|---|---|---|---|---|---|---|---|
| Knight | 19 | 4 | 66 | 4 | 17 | 3 | 43 | 1 |
| White | 2·4 | 0 | 12 | 1 | | | | |
| Dexter | 18·2 | 4 | 48 | 2 | 32 | 9 | 86 | 3 |
| Allen | 27 | 14 | 51 | 1 | 35 | 19 | 42 | 0 |
| Barber | 14 | 1 | 44 | 1 | 41 | 7 | 117 | 3 |
| Lock | 14 | 8 | 25 | 1 | 37 | 16 | 86 | 1 |
| Parfitt | | | | | 3 | 2 | 4 | 0 |
| Richardson | | | | | 2 | 1 | 10 | 0 |

| PAKISTAN | O | M | R | W |
|---|---|---|---|---|
| Fazal | 63 | 23 | 98 | 0 |
| D'Souza | 57·5 | 16 | 112 | 5 |
| Nasim | 45 | 10 | 125 | 3 |
| Haseeb | 36 | 7 | 68 | 2 |
| Shujauddin | 27 | 5 | 63 | 0 |
| Saeed | 3 | 0 | 12 | 0 |
| Mushtaq | 2 | 0 | 10 | 0 |

### FALL OF WICKETS

| | P | E | P |
|---|---|---|---|
| Wkt | 1st | 1st | 2nd |
| 1st | 2 | 77 | 91 |
| 2nd | 25 | 107 | 129 |
| 3rd | 36 | 250 | 211 |
| 4th | 56 | 438 | 227 |
| 5th | 148 | 493 | 256 |
| 6th | 183 | 497 | 337 |
| 7th | 196 | 502 | 373 |
| 8th | 245 | 503 | 383 |
| 9th | 248 | 507 | – |
| 10th | 253 | 507 | – |

Umpires: Shujauddin and Daud Khan.

# SOUTH AFRICA v NEW ZEALAND 1961–62 (1st Test)

Played at Kingsmead, Durban, on 8, 9, 11, 12 December.
Toss: South Africa.   Result: SOUTH AFRICA won by 30 runs.
Debuts: South Africa – E.J. Barlow, K.C. Bland, H.D. Bromfield, M.K. Elgie, G.B. Lawrence,
P.M. Pollock, K.A. Walter; New Zealand – G.A. Bartlett, P.T. Barton, F.J. Cameron, A.E. Dick,
R.C. Motz.

Elgie represented Scotland at Rugby Union football. McGlew became the fourth South African after
A.B. Tancred, J.W. Zulch and T.L. Goddard to carry his bat through a completed Test innings. He remains the
only South African to score a century while doing so and 292 is the highest of the four innings totals involved.

## SOUTH AFRICA

| | | | | | |
|---|---|---:|---|---|---:|
| D.J. McGlew* | not out | 127 | b Motz | | 5 |
| E.J. Barlow | b Motz | 15 | c Dick b Motz | | 10 |
| J.H.B. Waite† | c Dick b Bartlett | 25 | c sub (G.T. Dowling) b Cameron | | 63 |
| R.A. McLean | b Alabaster | 63 | c Bartlett b Motz | | 0 |
| K.C. Bland | c Reid b Cameron | 5 | run out | | 30 |
| M.K. Elgie | b Motz | 1 | st Dick b Alabaster | | 0 |
| S. O'Linn | lbw b Cameron | 8 | c Sparling b Alabaster | | 6 |
| P.M. Pollock | c Dick b Cameron | 0 | c Dick b Cameron | | 15 |
| G.B. Lawrence | c Sparling b Alabaster | 16 | lbw b Alabaster | | 0 |
| K.A. Walter | c Dick b Alabaster | 0 | c Dick b Cameron | | 1 |
| H.D. Bromfield | lbw b Alabaster | 0 | not out | | 0 |
| Extras | (B 11, LB 6, W 1, NB 14) | 32 | (B 2, LB 4, W 5, NB 8) | | 19 |
| **Total** | | **292** | | | **149** |

## NEW ZEALAND

| | | | | | |
|---|---|---:|---|---|---:|
| J.W. Guy | c Walter b Pollock | 8 | c Bromfield b Pollock | | 1 |
| J.T. Sparling | c Waite b Pollock | 13 | c Waite b Walter | | 10 |
| P.T. Barton | c Elgie b Lawrence | 54 | c Waite b Pollock | | 23 |
| S.N. McGregor | c Barlow b Walter | 20 | c Walter b Bromfield | | 55 |
| J.R. Reid* | c Pollock b Lawrence | 13 | (6) c Waite b Pollock | | 16 |
| P.G.Z. Harris | c Elgie b Walter | 74 | (5) lbw b Pollock | | 0 |
| A.E. Dick† | c Waite b Pollock | 3 | c Waite b Pollock | | 2 |
| R.C. Motz | c McGlew b Walter | 0 | (9) b Bromfield | | 10 |
| G.A Bartlett | c Pollock b Walter | 40 | (8) c O'Linn b Bromfield | | 23 |
| J.C. Alabaster | lbw b Lawrence | 2 | c Bromfield b Pollock | | 8 |
| F.J. Cameron | not out | 0 | not out | | 1 |
| Extras | (B 1, LB 1, NB 16) | 18 | (B 1, LB 1, NB 15) | | 17 |
| **Total** | | **245** | | | **166** |

| NEW ZEALAND | O | M | R | W | O | M | R | W | | FALL OF WICKETS | | | |
|---|---|---|---|---|---|---|---|---|---|---|---|---|---|
| | | | | | | | | | | SA | NZ | SA | NZ |
| Motz | 23 | 3 | 64 | 2 | 20 | 1 | 51 | 3 | *Wkt* | *1st* | *1st* | *2nd* | *2nd* |
| Bartlett | 9 | 3 | 39 | 1 | 9 | 3 | 11 | 0 | 1st | 20 | 20 | 17 | 7 |
| Cameron | 27 | 5 | 60 | 3 | 15·2 | 1 | 32 | 3 | 2nd | 82 | 33 | 38 | 23 |
| Reid | 11 | 1 | 38 | 0 | | | | | 3rd | 185 | 63 | 38 | 53 |
| Alabaster | 17·5 | 2 | 59 | 4 | 17 | 6 | 36 | 3 | 4th | 216 | 89 | 110 | 53 |
| Sparling | 1 | 1 | 0 | 0 | | | | | 5th | 233 | 150 | 113 | 100 |
| SOUTH AFRICA | | | | | | | | | 6th | 253 | 153 | 129 | 102 |
| Pollock | 22 | 3 | 61 | 3 | 20·3 | 8 | 38 | 6 | 7th | 263 | 162 | 137 | 137 |
| Walter | 25·3 | 6 | 63 | 4 | 16 | 5 | 34 | 1 | 8th | 286 | 235 | 137 | 150 |
| Lawrence | 29 | 6 | 63 | 3 | 25 | 8 | 40 | 0 | 9th | 292 | 245 | 144 | 162 |
| Barlow | 8 | 3 | 17 | 0 | | | | | 10th | 292 | 245 | 149 | 166 |
| Bromfield | 15 | 5 | 23 | 0 | 18 | 4 | 37 | 3 | | | | | |

Umpires: D.R. Fell and W.P. Anderson.

# SOUTH AFRICA v NEW ZEALAND 1961–62 (2nd Test)

Played at New Wanderers, Johannesburg, on 26, 27, 28, 29 December.
Toss: South Africa.   Result: MATCH DRAWN.
Debuts: New Zealand – G.T. Dowling.

Rain allowed only 79 minutes of play on the first day. Lawrence, a 6ft 5in tall fast bowler, remains the only player to take eight wickets in an innings in matches between these two countries. New Zealand were set to score 278 runs in four hours.

## SOUTH AFRICA

| | | | | | |
|---|---|---:|---|---|---:|
| D.J. McGlew* | lbw b Motz | 5 | | run out | 38 |
| E.J. Barlow | c Reid b Motz | 47 | | c Dick b Motz | 45 |
| J.H.B. Waite† | c Dick b Cameron | 101 | (6) | c Dick b Bartlett | 4 |
| R.A. McLean | c Bartlett b Cameron | 2 | | c and b Motz | 45 |
| K.C. Bland | c Barton b Cameron | 0 | | c McGregor b Motz | 24 |
| S. O'Linn | b Cameron | 17 | (7) | not out | 5 |
| M.K. Elgie | b Bartlett | 56 | (3) | b Motz | 0 |
| P.M. Pollock | run out | 37 | | not out | 1 |
| G.B. Lawrence | c Guy b Bartlett | 22 | | | |
| K.A. Walter | c Barton b Cameron | 10 | | | |
| H.D. Bromfield | not out | 11 | | | |
| Extras | (B 3, LB 9, NB 1, W 1) | 14 | | (B 8, LB 4, NB 4) | 16 |
| **Total** | | **322** | | **(6 wickets declared)** | **178** |

## NEW ZEALAND

| | | | | |
|---|---|---:|---|---:|
| S.N. McGregor | c Walter b Lawrence | 13 | c Bromfield b Walter | 11 |
| G.T. Dowling | run out | 74 | c Waite b Pollock | 58 |
| P.T. Barton | c Waite b Lawrence | 10 | c Waite b Lawrence | 11 |
| J.R. Reid* | lbw b Lawrence | 39 | not out | 75 |
| J.W. Guy | c Waite b Lawrence | 9 | b Pollock | 0 |
| P.G.Z. Harris | c Elgie b Lawrence | 0 | not out | 9 |
| A.E. Dick† | b Bromfield | 16 | | |
| G.A. Bartlett | c Waite b Lawrence | 31 | | |
| R.C. Motz | c Waite b Lawrence | 3 | | |
| J.C. Alabaster | c Barlow b Lawrence | 17 | | |
| F.J. Cameron | not out | 1 | | |
| Extras | (B 1, LB 6, NB 3) | 10 | (LB 1) | 1 |
| **Total** | | **223** | **(4 wickets)** | **165** |

| NEW ZEALAND | O | M | R | W | O | M | R | W |
|---|---|---|---|---|---|---|---|---|
| Motz | 27 | 4 | 70 | 2 | 17 | 2 | 68 | 4 |
| Bartlett | 21 | 2 | 82 | 2 | 13 | 1 | 44 | 1 |
| Cameron | 36·2 | 9 | 83 | 5 | 13 | 1 | 50 | 0 |
| Reid | 9 | 2 | 33 | 0 | | | | |
| Alabaster | 10 | 2 | 40 | 0 | | | | |
| SOUTH AFRICA | | | | | | | | |
| Pollock | 20 | 4 | 49 | 0 | 14 | 6 | 18 | 2 |
| Walter | 23 | 4 | 62 | 0 | 18 | 5 | 38 | 1 |
| Lawrence | 30·3 | 12 | 53 | 8 | 22 | 4 | 45 | 1 |
| Barlow | 3 | 0 | 15 | 0 | 3 | 2 | 5 | 0 |
| Bromfield | 16 | 6 | 34 | 1 | 7 | 0 | 30 | 0 |
| Elgie | | | | | 4 | 0 | 28 | 0 |

| FALL OF WICKETS | | | | |
|---|---|---|---|---|
| | SA | NZ | SA | NZ |
| Wkt | 1st | 1st | 2nd | 2nd |
| 1st | 25 | 18 | 85 | 22 |
| 2nd | 99 | 41 | 85 | 49 |
| 3rd | 102 | 107 | 92 | 120 |
| 4th | 102 | 132 | 168 | 124 |
| 5th | 159 | 132 | 169 | – |
| 6th | 188 | 163 | 177 | – |
| 7th | 259 | 167 | – | – |
| 8th | 287 | 187 | – | – |
| 9th | 296 | 216 | – | – |
| 10th | 322 | 223 | – | – |

Umpires: W.P. Anderson and H.C. Kidson.

# SOUTH AFRICA v NEW ZEALAND 1961–62 (3rd Test)

Played at Newlands, Cape Town, on 1, 2, 3, 4 January.
Toss: New Zealand.   Result: NEW ZEALAND won by 72 runs.
Debuts: South Africa – S.F. Burke, W.S. Farrer.

New Zealand, who did not enforce the follow on, gained their first Test victory against South Africa and only their second in all Test matches. Playing in his first Test, Burke (fast-medium) took 11 for 196 and remains the only bowler from either country to take ten wickets in a Test in this series. McGlew retired hurt when 11* and resumed at 100 for 3 in the second innings.

## NEW ZEALAND

| | | | | |
|---|---|---|---|---|
| S.N. McGregor | b Burke | 68 | run out | 20 |
| G.T. Dowling | lbw b Lawrence | 0 | c Barlow b Burke | 12 |
| J.T. Sparling | c Elgie b Burke | 19 | c Waite b Burke | 9 |
| J.R. Reid* | c Bromfield b McKinnon | 92 | c Bromfield b Burke | 14 |
| P.G.Z. Harris | st Waite b Bromfield | 101 | c Bland b Burke | 30 |
| M.E. Chapple | c Waite b Burke | 69 | b Burke | 33 |
| A.E. Dick† | c Waite b Burke | 4 | (8) not out | 50 |
| G.A. Bartlett | c Waite b Burke | 12 | (7) st Waite b McKinnon | 29 |
| R.C. Motz | b Burke | 0 | c Barlow b Bromfield | 4 |
| J.C. Alabaster | c Farrer b Bromfield | 1 | st Waite b McKinnon | 4 |
| F.J. Cameron | not out | 2 | not out | 10 |
| Extras | (LB 8, NB 9) | 17 | (B 1) | 1 |
| **Total** | | **385** | (9 wickets declared) | **212** |

## SOUTH AFRICA

| | | | | |
|---|---|---|---|---|
| D.J. McGlew* | c Bartlett b Motz | 14 | c Dick b Bartlett | 63 |
| E.J. Barlow | c Harris b Alabaster | 51 | c Reid b Alabaster | 16 |
| W.S. Farrer | c Dick b Alabaster | 11 | c Dowling b Alabaster | 20 |
| J.H.B. Waite† | c Chapple b Cameron | 33 | lbw b Alabaster | 21 |
| R.A. McLean | c Dick b Cameron | 20 | c Harris b Bartlett | 113 |
| K.C. Bland | b Alabaster | 32 | lbw b Reid | 42 |
| M.K. Elgie | c Chapple b Alabaster | 6 | c Harris b Cameron | 12 |
| S.F. Burke | c Dick b Cameron | 0 | c Motz b Sparling | 12 |
| G.B. Lawrence | c Reid b Cameron | 4 | c Harris b Reid | 0 |
| A.H. McKinnon | not out | 9 | b Alabaster | 4 |
| H.D. Bromfield | lbw b Cameron | 1 | not out | 0 |
| Extras | (B 6, LB 2, NB 1) | 9 | (B 14, LB 13, W 4, NB 1) | 32 |
| **Total** | | **190** | | **335** |

| SOUTH AFRICA | O | M | R | W | O | M | R | W |
|---|---|---|---|---|---|---|---|---|
| Burke | 53·5 | 19 | 128 | 6 | 27·1 | 10 | 68 | 5 |
| Lawrence | 23 | 7 | 46 | 1 | | | | |
| McKinnon | 19 | 6 | 42 | 1 | 17 | 7 | 32 | 2 |
| Barlow | 9 | 0 | 40 | 0 | 20 | 2 | 53 | 0 |
| Bromfield | 46 | 11 | 94 | 2 | 24 | 3 | 58 | 1 |
| Elgie | 7 | 2 | 18 | 0 | | | | |
| NEW ZEALAND | | | | | | | | |
| Motz | 11 | 2 | 30 | 1 | 24 | 9 | 69 | 0 |
| Cameron | 24·4 | 10 | 48 | 5 | 26 | 14 | 42 | 1 |
| Alabaster | 21 | 4 | 61 | 4 | 50 | 12 | 119 | 4 |
| Bartlett | 5 | 1 | 17 | 0 | 22 | 8 | 40 | 2 |
| Sparling | 6 | 1 | 22 | 0 | 6 | 3 | 12 | 1 |
| Chapple | 1 | 0 | 3 | 0 | | | | |
| Reid | | | | | 14·2 | 8 | 21 | 2 |

### FALL OF WICKETS

| | NZ | SA | NZ | SA |
|---|---|---|---|---|
| Wkt | 1st | 1st | 2nd | 2nd |
| 1st | 15 | 36 | 28 | 27 |
| 2nd | 59 | 67 | 40 | 54 |
| 3rd | 116 | 85 | 44 | 100 |
| 4th | 209 | 124 | 61 | 201 |
| 5th | 357 | 157 | 106 | 273 |
| 6th | 367 | 164 | 127 | 315 |
| 7th | 369 | 165 | 158 | 317 |
| 8th | 369 | 173 | 159 | 331 |
| 9th | 370 | 185 | 163 | 335 |
| 10th | 385 | 190 | – | 335 |

Umpires: D. Collins and J. Warner.

# SOUTH AFRICA v NEW ZEALAND 1961–62 (4th Test)

Played at New Wanderers, Johannesburg, on 2, 3, 5 February.
Toss: New Zealand.   Result: SOUTH AFRICA won by an innings and 51 runs.
Debuts: South Africa – H.R. Lance.

South Africa won at 4.35 pm on the third day.

## NEW ZEALAND

| | | | | | |
|---|---|---:|---|---|---:|
| S.N. McGregor | c Waite b Lance | 21 | | c McLean b Heine | 0 |
| G.T. Dowling | lbw b Lawrence | 14 | | b Adcock | 0 |
| P.T. Barton | b Adcock | 22 | (7) | c Waite b Lance | 9 |
| J.R. Reid* | c Bland b Lawrence | 60 | (5) | c McGlew b Heine | 142 |
| P.G.Z. Harris | c Lawrence b Adcock | 4 | (3) | b Adcock | 46 |
| M.E. Chapple | c Lawrence b Lance | 11 | (4) | lbw b Lawrence | 9 |
| A.E. Dick† | b Lawrence | 16 | (6) | c McLean b Lawrence | 1 |
| G.A. Bartlett | c Waite b Lawrence | 0 | | c Waite b Lawrence | 33 |
| J.C. Alabaster | c Bromfield b Lance | 2 | | c Waite b Lawrence | 3 |
| R.C. Motz | not out | 10 | | lbw b Adcock | 0 |
| F.J. Cameron | lbw b Lawrence | 2 | | not out | 0 |
| Extras | (LB 1, NB 1) | 2 | | (LB 2, NB 4) | 6 |
| **Total** | | **164** | | | **249** |

## SOUTH AFRICA

| | | |
|---|---|---:|
| D.J. McGlew* | run out | 120 |
| E.J. Barlow | c Dick b Reid | 67 |
| J.H.B. Waite† | c Dick b Alabaster | 9 |
| R.A. McLean | lbw b Motz | 78 |
| W.S. Farrer | c Bartlett b Alabaster | 40 |
| K.C. Bland | lbw b Reid | 28 |
| H.R. Lance | c Dick b Reid | 7 |
| G.B. Lawrence | c Harris b Motz | 39 |
| P.S. Heine | c Dick b Alabaster | 31 |
| N.A.T. Adcock | b Motz | 17 |
| H.D. Bromfield | not out | 4 |
| Extras | (B 1, LB 11, NB 7 W 5) | 24 |
| **Total** | | **464** |

| SOUTH AFRICA | O | M | R | W | O | M | R | W |
|---|---|---|---|---|---|---|---|---|
| Heine | 12 | 2 | 45 | 0 | 24 | 5 | 78 | 2 |
| Adcock | 10 | 4 | 23 | 2 | 24 | 12 | 40 | 3 |
| Lawrence | 16·1 | 3 | 52 | 5 | 22·2 | 10 | 57 | 4 |
| Lance | 13 | 6 | 30 | 3 | 13 | 0 | 50 | 1 |
| Bromfield | 2 | 0 | 12 | 0 | 5 | 2 | 18 | 0 |
| NEW ZEALAND | | | | | | | | |
| Motz | 26·2 | 2 | 86 | 3 | | | | |
| Cameron | 30 | 6 | 84 | 0 | | | | |
| Bartlett | 18 | 1 | 57 | 0 | | | | |
| Alabaster | 31 | 4 | 143 | 3 | | | | |
| Reid | 16 | 3 | 55 | 3 | | | | |
| Chapple | 3 | 0 | 15 | 0 | | | | |

### FALL OF WICKETS

| Wkt | NZ 1st | SA 1st | NZ 2nd |
|---|---|---|---|
| 1st | 36 | 134 | 0 |
| 2nd | 40 | 170 | 23 |
| 3rd | 76 | 282 | 38 |
| 4th | 94 | 282 | 70 |
| 5th | 130 | 351 | 84 |
| 6th | 150 | 363 | 138 |
| 7th | 150 | 367 | 222 |
| 8th | 150 | 422 | 244 |
| 9th | 157 | 445 | 245 |
| 10th | 164 | 464 | 249 |

Umpires: G. Parry and H.C. Kidson.

# SOUTH AFRICA v NEW ZEALAND 1961–62 (5th Test)

Played at St George's Park, Port Elizabeth, on 16, 17, 19, 20 February.
Toss: New Zealand.   Result: NEW ZEALAND won by 40 runs.
Debuts: Nil.

New Zealand won two Tests to square a rubber for the first time. Their last three second-innings wickets fell to successive balls from Lawrence (two) and Pollock.

## NEW ZEALAND

| | | | | | |
|---|---|---|---|---|---|
| G.T. Dowling | lbw b Adcock | 2 | | lbw b Lawrence | 78 |
| J.T. Sparling | c Lance b Pollock | 3 | | c Bromfield b Pollock | 4 |
| P.T. Barton | c Bromfield b Lance | 109 | (4) | lbw b Pollock | 2 |
| J.R. Reid* | b Adcock | 26 | (5) | c Bromfield b Lance | 69 |
| S.N. McGregor | b Pollock | 10 | (6) | b Lawrence | 24 |
| P.G.Z. Harris | c McGlew b Bromfield | 7 | (3) | c Bland b Adcock | 13 |
| A.E. Dick† | c Waite b Pollock | 46 | | lbw b Lance | 1 |
| G.A. Bartlett | hit wkt b Adcock | 29 | | c Barlow b Lawrence | 18 |
| J.C. Alabaster | lbw b Lawrence | 24 | | c Adcock b Lawrence | 7 |
| R.C. Motz | c McLean b Lawrence | 2 | | c Waite b Pollock | 0 |
| F.J. Cameron | not out | 1 | | not out | 0 |
| Extras | (B 1, LB 7, NB 8) | 16 | | (B 4, LB 6, NB 2) | 12 |
| **Total** | | **275** | | | **228** |

## SOUTH AFRICA

| | | | | | |
|---|---|---|---|---|---|
| E.J. Barlow | c Dowling b Motz | 20 | | b Reid | 59 |
| G.B. Lawrence | c Dick b Alabaster | 43 | (8) | b Alabaster | 17 |
| J.H.B. Waite† | c Dowling b Cameron | 0 | (4) | c Dowling b Reid | 7 |
| W.S. Farrer | c Dick b Motz | 7 | (2) | lbw b Cameron | 10 |
| R.A. McLean | c McGregor b Bartlett | 25 | | b Alabaster | 10 |
| K.C. Bland | lbw b Bartlett | 12 | | lbw b Reid | 32 |
| H.R. Lance | st Dick b Reid | 9 | | c Dick b Reid | 9 |
| D.J. McGlew* | not out | 28 | (3) | run out | 26 |
| P.M. Pollock | lbw b Motz | 8 | | not out | 54 |
| N.A.T. Adcock | c Dowling b Reid | 5 | | b Motz | 24 |
| H.D. Bromfield | c Dick b Alabaster | 21 | | c McGregor b Cameron | 0 |
| Extras | (LB 6, NB 6) | 12 | | (B 6, LB 3, NB 14, W 2) | 25 |
| **Total** | | **190** | | | **273** |

| SOUTH AFRICA | O | M | R | W | O | M | R | W | | FALL OF WICKETS | | | |
|---|---|---|---|---|---|---|---|---|---|---|---|---|---|
| Adcock | 27 | 11 | 60 | 3 | 21 | 11 | 25 | 1 | | NZ | SA | NZ | SA |
| Pollock | 28 | 9 | 63 | 3 | 24·1 | 5 | 70 | 3 | *Wkt* | *1st* | *1st* | *2nd* | *2nd* |
| Lawrence | 26·2 | 7 | 71 | 2 | 28 | 5 | 85 | 4 | 1st | 4 | 34 | 4 | 57 |
| Lance | 14 | 4 | 50 | 1 | 8 | 0 | 36 | 2 | 2nd | 20 | 39 | 37 | 101 |
| Bromfield | 16 | 7 | 15 | 1 | 2 | 2 | 0 | 0 | 3rd | 82 | 65 | 50 | 117 |
| | | | | | | | | | 4th | 108 | 92 | 175 | 125 |
| NEW ZEALAND | | | | | | | | | 5th | 115 | 112 | 185 | 133 |
| Cameron | 11 | 2 | 46 | 1 | 18 | 6 | 48 | 2 | 6th | 180 | 115 | 192 | 142 |
| Bartlett | 8 | 4 | 10 | 2 | 9 | 3 | 26 | 0 | 7th | 225 | 125 | 216 | 193 |
| Motz | 14 | 7 | 33 | 3 | 20 | 11 | 34 | 1 | 8th | 269 | 137 | 228 | 199 |
| Alabaster | 25·4 | 7 | 63 | 2 | 52 | 23 | 96 | 2 | 9th | 272 | 143 | 228 | 259 |
| Reid | 14 | 6 | 26 | 2 | 45 | 27 | 44 | 4 | 10th | 275 | 190 | 228 | 273 |

Umpires: G. Parry and G.D. Gibbon.

# WEST INDIES v INDIA 1961–62 (1st Test)

Played at Queen's Park Oval, Port-of-Spain, Trinidad, on 16, 17, 19, 20 February.
Toss: India.   Result: WEST INDIES won by ten wickets.
Debuts: West Indies – J.L. Hendriks, S.C. Stayers.

C.W. Smith kept wicket for the remainder of the match after Hendriks fractured a finger on the first day. India were dismissed for their lowest total (so far) after Hall had taken the wickets of Contractor, Manjrekar and Sardesai in four balls.

## INDIA

| | | | | |
|---|---|---|---|---|
| N.J. Contractor* | c Sobers b Hall | 10 | b Hall | 6 |
| V.L. Mehra | c Hendriks b Hall | 0 | b Stayers | 8 |
| V.L. Manjrekar | b Stayers | 19 | hit wkt b Hall | 0 |
| D.N. Sardesai | c Solomon b Stayers | 16 | c Smith b Hall | 2 |
| P.R. Umrigar | c Sobers b Watson | 2 | c sub (W.V. Rodriguez) b Sobers | 23 |
| C.G. Borde | c Gibbs b Stayers | 16 | b Sobers | 27 |
| S.A. Durani | c and b Sobers | 56 | c Worrell b Sobers | 7 |
| R.F. Surti | st Smith b Sobers | 57 | c sub (W.V. Rodriguez) b Sobers | 0 |
| R.G. Nadkarni | run out | 2 | not out | 12 |
| F. M. Engineer† | c sub (W.V. Rodriguez) b Gibbs | 3 | c and b Gibbs | 2 |
| R.B. Desai | not out | 4 | c Kanhai b Gibbs | 2 |
| Extras | (B 11, LB 5, NB 2) | 18 | (LB 4, W 1, NB 4) | 9 |
| **Total** | | **203** | | **98** |

## WEST INDIES

| | | | | |
|---|---|---|---|---|
| C.C. Hunte | c and b Durani | 58 | not out | 10 |
| C.W. Smith | c Umrigar b Desai | 12 | not out | 4 |
| R.B. Kanhai | c and b Borde | 24 | | |
| G. St A. Sobers | b Umrigar | 40 | | |
| F.M.M. Worrell* | c Surti b Durani | 0 | | |
| J.S. Solomon | c Engineer b Desai | 43 | | |
| S.C. Stayers | c Borde b Durani | 4 | | |
| J.L. Hendriks† | c Durani b Borde | 64 | | |
| L.R. Gibbs | c Durani b Umrigar | 0 | | |
| W.W. Hall | not out | 37 | | |
| C.D. Watson | c Contractor b Durani | 0 | | |
| Extras | (B 4, LB 3) | 7 | (NB 1) | 1 |
| **Total** | | **289** | (0 wickets) | **15** |

| WEST INDIES | O | M | R | W | O | M | R | W | FALL OF WICKETS | | | |
|---|---|---|---|---|---|---|---|---|---|---|---|---|
| Hall | 20 | 6 | 38 | 2 | 8 | 3 | 11 | 3 | | I | WI | I | WI |
| Watson | 12 | 4 | 20 | 1 | 4 | 2 | 6 | 0 | Wkt | 1st | 1st | 2nd | 2nd |
| Stayers | 18 | 1 | 65 | 3 | 8 | 4 | 20 | 1 | 1st | 7 | 13 | 6 | – |
| Gibbs | 14 | 4 | 34 | 1 | 7·5 | 1 | 16 | 2 | 2nd | 32 | 67 | 6 | – |
| Sobers | 9·3 | 1 | 28 | 2 | 15 | 7 | 22 | 4 | 3rd | 38 | 136 | 8 | – |
| Worrell | | | | | 8 | 2 | 14 | 0 | 4th | 45 | 139 | 35 | – |
| | | | | | | | | | 5th | 76 | 140 | 56 | – |
| | | | | | | | | | 6th | 89 | 148 | 70 | – |
| INDIA | | | | | | | | | 7th | 170 | 212 | 70 | – |
| Desai | 13 | 3 | 46 | 2 | 1 | 0 | 5 | 0 | 8th | 186 | 217 | 91 | – |
| Umrigar | 35 | 8 | 77 | 2 | | | | | 9th | 194 | 287 | 96 | – |
| Durani | 35·2 | 9 | 82 | 4 | | | | | 10th | 203 | 289 | 98 | – |
| Borde | 25 | 4 | 65 | 2 | | | | | | | | | |
| Nadkarni | 3 | 2 | 1 | 0 | | | | | | | | | |
| Surti | 2 | 0 | 11 | 0 | 0·4 | 0 | 9 | 0 | | | | | |

Umpires: H.B. de C. Jordan and B. Jacelon.

## WEST INDIES v INDIA 1961–62 (2nd Test)

Played at Sabina Park, Kingston, Jamaica, on 7, 8, 9, 10, 12 March.
Toss: India.   Result: WEST INDIES won by an innings and 18 runs.
Debuts: West Indies – I. Mendonça, W.V. Rodriguez.

Play was interrupted for five minutes on the third day when spectators threw bottles on to the field after Solomon was run out. McMorris and Kanhai added 255 to set a West Indies record for the second wicket against India. Hall took his hundredth Test wicket in 20 matches.

### INDIA

| | | | | |
|---|---|---|---|---|
| M.L. Jaisimha | c Gibbs b Stayers | 28 | b Hall | 11 |
| N.J. Contractor* | c Mendonça b Hall | 1 | b Hall | 9 |
| R.F. Surti | lbw b Sobers | 35 | lbw b Hall | 26 |
| V.L. Manjrekar | c Sobers b Gibbs | 13 | (6) lbw b Sobers | 19 |
| P.R. Umrigar | lbw b Sobers | 50 | c Sobers b Gibbs | 32 |
| C.G. Borde | b Hall | 93 | (7) c McMorris b Hall | 0 |
| S.A. Durani | lbw b Hall | 17 | (8) b Gibbs | 0 |
| R.G. Nadkarni | not out | 78 | (4) c Mendonça b Gibbs | 35 |
| F.M. Engineer† | st Mendonça b Gibbs | 53 | c Hunte b Hall | 40 |
| R.B. Desai | c Gibbs b Sobers | 0 | c Mendonça b Hall | 20 |
| E.A.S. Prasanna | c Mendonça b Sobers | 6 | not out | 1 |
| Extras | (B 14, LB 5, NB 2) | 21 | (B 18, LB 4, NB 2, W 1) | 25 |
| **Total** | | **395** | | **218** |

### WEST INDIES

| | | |
|---|---|---|
| C.C. Hunte | c Contractor b Desai | 9 |
| E.D.A. St J. McMorris | b Prasanna | 125 |
| R.B. Kanhai | c Umrigar b Prasanna | 138 |
| W.V. Rodriguez | c Umrigar b Prasanna | 3 |
| G. St A. Sobers | c Desai b Durani | 153 |
| J.S. Solomon | run out | 9 |
| F.M.M. Worrell* | b Durani | 58 |
| I. Mendonça† | b Nadkarni | 78 |
| S.C. Stayers | not out | 35 |
| L.R. Gibbs | ) did not bat | |
| W.W. Hall | ) | |
| Extras | (B 7, LB 15, W 1) | 23 |
| **Total** | (8 wickets declared) | **631** |

| WEST INDIES | O | M | R | W | O | M | R | W | | FALL OF WICKETS | | |
|---|---|---|---|---|---|---|---|---|---|---|---|---|
| Hall | 28 | 4 | 79 | 3 | 20·5 | 5 | 49 | 6 | | I | WI | I |
| Stayers | 23 | 4 | 76 | 1 | 10 | 0 | 25 | 0 | Wkt | 1st | 1st | 2nd |
| Worrell | 9 | 1 | 35 | 0 | 10 | 1 | 26 | 0 | 1st | 14 | 16 | 16 |
| Gibbs | 33 | 9 | 69 | 2 | 26 | 8 | 44 | 3 | 2nd | 44 | 271 | 46 |
| Sobers | 39 | 8 | 75 | 4 | 17 | 3 | 41 | 1 | 3rd | 79 | 282 | 50 |
| Rodriguez | 7 | 0 | 37 | 0 | 1 | 0 | 8 | 0 | 4th | 89 | 293 | 116 |
| Solomon | 2 | 0 | 3 | 0 | | | | | 5th | 183 | 320 | 137 |
| | | | | | | | | | 6th | 234 | 430 | 138 |
| INDIA | | | | | | | | | 7th | 263 | 557 | 141 |
| Desai | 20 | 6 | 84 | 1 | | | | | 8th | 357 | 631 | 157 |
| Surti | 19 | 2 | 73 | 0 | | | | | 9th | 358 | – | 205 |
| Borde | 31 | 6 | 93 | 0 | | | | | 10th | 395 | – | 218 |
| Durani | 70 | 14 | 173 | 2 | | | | | | | | |
| Nadkarni | 25·4 | 9 | 57 | 1 | | | | | | | | |
| Prasanna | 50 | 14 | 122 | 3 | | | | | | | | |
| Contractor | 2 | 0 | 6 | 0 | | | | | | | | |

Umpires: O. Davies and R. Cole.

# WEST INDIES v INDIA 1961–62 (3rd Test)

Played at Kensington Oval, Bridgetown, Barbados, on 23, 24, 26, 27, 28 March.
Toss: West Indies.　Result: WEST INDIES won by an innings and 30 runs.
Debuts: West Indies – D.W. Allan.

The Nawab of Pataudi led India in place of the injured N.J. Contractor and, at 21 years 77 days, became the youngest Test captain. Contractor, whose skull had been fractured by a ball from C.C. Griffith in the tourists' previous match against Barbados, underwent an emergency brain operation and played no further Test cricket. In the final session of this match, Gibbs achieved the outstanding analysis of 15·3–14–6–8.

## INDIA

| | | | | | |
|---|---|---|---|---|---|
| M.L. Jaisimha | c Allan b Hall | 41 | lbw b Stayers | 0 |
| D.N. Sardesai | c McMorris b Gibbs | 31 | c Sobers b Gibbs | 60 |
| R.F. Surti | lbw b Worrell | 7 | lbw b Stayers | 36 |
| V.L. Manjrekar | c Worrell b Hall | 8 | c Worrell b Gibbs | 51 |
| P.R. Umrigar | c Allan b Hall | 8 | c Allan b Gibbs | 10 |
| Nawab of Pataudi, jr* | c and b Valentine | 48 | c Sobers b Gibbs | 0 |
| C.G. Borde | c Allan b Sobers | 19 | c Worrell b Gibbs | 8 |
| R.G. Nadkarni | b Stayers | 22 | not out | 2 |
| F.M. Engineer† | c Worrell b Sobers | 12 | st Allan b Gibbs | 0 |
| S.A. Durani | not out | 48 | c Hunte b Gibbs | 5 |
| R.B. Desai | b Worrell | 12 | c Sobers b Gibbs | 1 |
| Extras | (NB 2) | 2 | (B 8, LB 3, W 2, NB 1) | 14 |
| **Total** | | **258** | | **187** |

## WEST INDIES

| | | |
|---|---|---|
| C.C. Hunte | c Engineer b Surti | 59 |
| E. D.A. St J. McMorris | c Engineer b Durani | 39 |
| R.B. Kanhai | run out | 89 |
| G. St A. Sobers | c Engineer b Nadkarni | 42 |
| J.S. Solomon | c Desai b Durani | 96 |
| L.R. Gibbs | b Borde | 7 |
| F.M.M. Worrell* | b Umrigar | 77 |
| S.C. Stayers | c Umrigar b Nadkarni | 7 |
| W.W. Hall | lbw b Umrigar | 3 |
| D.W. Allan† | not out | 40 |
| A.L. Valentine | b Borde | 4 |
| Extras | (LB 5, NB 7) | 12 |
| **Total** | | **475** |

| WEST INDIES | O | M | R | W | O | M | R | W | | FALL OF WICKETS | | |
|---|---|---|---|---|---|---|---|---|---|---|---|---|
| | | | | | | | | | | I | WI | I |
| Hall | 22 | 4 | 64 | 3 | 10 | 3 | 17 | 0 | Wkt | 1st | 1st | 2nd |
| Stayers | 11 | 0 | 81 | 1 | 18 | 8 | 24 | 2 | 1st | 56 | 67 | 0 |
| Worrell | 7·1 | 3 | 12 | 2 | 27 | 18 | 16 | 0 | 2nd | 76 | 152 | 60 |
| Gibbs | 16 | 7 | 25 | 1 | 53·3 | 37 | 38 | 8 | 3rd | 82 | 226 | 158 |
| Valentine | 17 | 7 | 28 | 1 | 29 | 19 | 26 | 0 | 4th | 89 | 255 | 159 |
| Sobers | 16 | 2 | 46 | 2 | 17 | 10 | 14 | 0 | 5th | 112 | 282 | 159 |
| Solomon | | | | | 29 | 17 | 33 | 0 | 6th | 153 | 378 | 174 |
| Kanhai | | | | | 2 | 1 | 5 | 0 | 7th | 171 | 394 | 177 |
| | | | | | | | | | 8th | 188 | 399 | 177 |
| INDIA | | | | | | | | | 9th | 229 | 454 | 183 |
| Desai | 19 | 7 | 25 | 0 | | | | | 10th | 258 | 475 | 187 |
| Surti | 29 | 6 | 80 | 1 | | | | | | | | |
| Durani | 45 | 13 | 123 | 2 | | | | | | | | |
| Nadkarni | 67 | 28 | 92 | 2 | | | | | | | | |
| Borde | 31·3 | 4 | 89 | 2 | | | | | | | | |
| Jaisimha | 1 | 0 | 6 | 0 | | | | | | | | |
| Umrigar | 49 | 27 | 48 | 2 | | | | | | | | |

Umpires: H.B. de C. Jordan and J. Roberts.

# WEST INDIES v INDIA 1961–62 (4th Test)

Played at Queen's Park Oval, Port-of-Spain, Trinidad, on 4, 5, 6, 7, 9 April.
Toss: West Indies.   Result: WEST INDIES won by seven wickets.
Debuts: Nil.

Umrigar's innings of 172 not out – out of 230 in 248 minutes – was India's highest against West Indies until 1970-71.

## WEST INDIES

| | | | | | |
|---|---|---:|---|---|---:|
| C.C. Hunte | b Umrigar | 28 | c Kunderan b Durani | | 30 |
| E.D.A. St J. McMorris | c Sardesai b Nadkarni | 50 | b Durani | | 56 |
| R.B. Kanhai | lbw b Umrigar | 139 | c Nadkarni b Durani | | 20 |
| S.M. Nurse | c and b Durani | 1 | not out | | 46 |
| G. St A. Sobers | lbw b Jaisimha | 19 | not out | | 16 |
| W.V. Rodriguez | b Umrigar | 50 | | | |
| I. Mendonça† | b Umrigar | 3 | | | |
| L.R. Gibbs | lbw b Nadkarni | 15 | | | |
| F.M.M. Worrell* | not out | 73 | | | |
| S.C. Stayers | c Surti b Umrigar | 12 | | | |
| W.W. Hall | not out | 50 | | | |
| Extras | (LB 4) | 4 | (B 3, LB 1, NB 4) | | 8 |
| **Total** | (9 wickets declared) | **444** | (3 wickets) | | **176** |

## INDIA

| | | | | | |
|---|---|---:|---|---|---:|
| D.N. Sardesai | b Hall | 0 | (9) c Worrell b Gibbs | | 0 |
| V.L. Mehra | b Hall | 14 | b Hall | | 62 |
| R.F. Surti | c Nurse b Hall | 0 | (7) c Mendonça b Gibbs | | 2 |
| V.L. Manjrekar | c Mendonça b Hall | 4 | c Nurse b Sobers | | 13 |
| M.L. Jaisimha | c Mendonça b Hall | 10 | (1) c Mendonça b Stayers | | 15 |
| P.R. Umrigar | st Mendonça b Sobers | 56 | not out | | 172 |
| Nawab of Pataudi, jr* | c Sobers b Rodriguez | 47 | (5) c Kanhai b Sobers | | 1 |
| C.G. Borde | c Nurse b Rodriguez | 42 | c Sobers b Gibbs | | 13 |
| S.A. Durani | c Worrell b Rodriguez | 12 | (3) c Rodriguez b Sobers | | 104 |
| R.G. Nadkarni | c Rodriguez b Sobers | 1 | run out | | 23 |
| B.K. Kunderan† | not out | 4 | c Rodriguez b Gibbs | | 4 |
| Extras | (B 1, LB 4, NB 2) | 7 | (B 9, LB 3, NB 1) | | 13 |
| **Total** | | **197** | | | **422** |

| INDIA | O | M | R | W | O | M | R | W | | FALL OF WICKETS | | | |
|---|---|---|---|---|---|---|---|---|---|---|---|---|---|
| Surti | 26 | 4 | 81 | 0 | 21 | 7 | 48 | 0 | | WI | I | I | WI |
| Jaisimha | 18 | 4 | 61 | 1 | 4 | 1 | 5 | 0 | *Wkt* | *1st* | *1st* | *2nd* | *2nd* |
| Umrigar | 56 | 24 | 107 | 5 | 16 | 8 | 17 | 0 | 1st | 50 | 0 | 19 | 93 |
| Durani | 18 | 4 | 54 | 1 | 31 | 13 | 64 | 3 | 2nd | 169 | 0 | 163 | 100 |
| Borde | 23 | 4 | 68 | 0 | 1 | 1 | 0 | 0 | 3rd | 174 | 9 | 190 | 132 |
| Nadkarni | 35 | 14 | 69 | 2 | 28 | 13 | 34 | 0 | 4th | 212 | 25 | 192 | – |
| | | | | | | | | | 5th | 258 | 30 | 221 | – |
| WEST INDIES | | | | | | | | | 6th | 265 | 124 | 236 | – |
| Hall | 9 | 3 | 20 | 5 | 18 | 3 | 74 | 1 | 7th | 292 | 144 | 278 | – |
| Stayers | 8 | 1 | 23 | 0 | 10 | 2 | 50 | 1 | 8th | 316 | 169 | 278 | – |
| Gibbs | 19 | 5 | 48 | 0 | 56·1 | 18 | 112 | 4 | 9th | 346 | 175 | 371 | – |
| Sobers | 25 | 6 | 48 | 2 | 47 | 14 | 116 | 3 | 10th | – | 197 | 422 | – |
| Rodriguez | 19·3 | 2 | 51 | 3 | 9 | 1 | 47 | 0 | | | | | |
| Worrell | | | | | 3 | 0 | 10 | 0 | | | | | |

Umpires: H.B. de C. Jordan and B. Jacelon.

# WEST INDIES v INDIA 1961–62 (5th Test)

Played at Sabina Park, Kingston, Jamaica, on 13, 14, 16, 17, 18 April.
Toss: West Indies.   Result: WEST INDIES won by 123 runs.
Debuts: West Indies – L.A. King.

West Indies won the rubber by five victories to none and so emulated Australia (v England in 1920-21 and v South Africa in 1931-32) and England (v India in 1959).

## WEST INDIES

| | | | | |
|---|---|---|---|---|
| C.C. Hunte | c Kunderan b Ranjane | 1 | c Kunderan b Surti | 0 |
| E.D.A. St J. McMorris | lbw b Durani | 37 | hit wkt b Borde | 42 |
| R.B. Kanhai | c and b Ranjane | 44 | (9) Ranjane | 41 |
| J.S. Solomon | b Durani | 0 | (3) b Surti | 0 |
| G. St A. Sobers | c Manjrekar b Ranjane | 104 | (4) c Kunderan b Surti | 50 |
| F.M.M. Worrell* | lbw b Ranjane | 26 | (5) not out | 98 |
| W.W. Hall | c Kunderan b Nadkarni | 20 | (10) lbw b Ranjane | 10 |
| D.W. Allan † | c sub (E.A.S. Prasanna) b Borde | 1 | (6) lbw b Durani | 2 |
| L.R. Gibbs | lbw b Nadkarni | 3 | (7) lbw b Durani | 0 |
| L.A. King | b Nadkarni | 0 | (8) c Nadkarni b Durani | 13 |
| A.L. Valentine | not out | 7 | lbw b Nadkarni | 7 |
| Extras | (B 4, LB 2, NB 4) | 10 | (B 4, LB 5, NB 11) | 20 |
| **Total** | | **253** | | **283** |

## INDIA

| | | | | |
|---|---|---|---|---|
| M.L. Jaisimha | c Sobers b King | 6 | lbw b King | 6 |
| V.L. Mehra | c Allan b King | 8 | c Allan b Sobers | 39 |
| S.A. Durani | c Allan b King | 6 | lbw b King | 4 |
| V.L. Manjrekar | c Solomon b King | 0 | (5) lbw b Sobers | 40 |
| Nawab of Pataudi,jr* | c Kanhai b Hall | 14 | (6) b Sobers | 4 |
| C.G. Borde | c Hall b King | 0 | (4) b Sobers | 26 |
| R.G. Nadkarni | b Gibbs | 61 | (9) c Allan b Hall | 0 |
| R.F. Surti | b Gibbs | 41 | st Allan b Sobers | 42 |
| P.R. Umrigar | lbw b Gibbs | 32 | (7) b Hall | 60 |
| B.K. Kunderan† | c McMorris b Valentine | 2 | b Hall | 1 |
| V.B. Ranjane | not out | 0 | not out | 0 |
| Extras | (LB 6, NB 2) | 8 | (B 11, LB 1, NB 1) | 13 |
| **Total** | | **178** | | **235** |

| INDIA | O | M | R | W | O | M | R | W |
|---|---|---|---|---|---|---|---|---|
| Ranjane | 19·2 | 2 | 72 | 4 | 28 | 3 | 81 | 2 |
| Surti | 6 | 0 | 25 | 0 | 18 | 3 | 56 | 3 |
| Nadkarni | 17 | 3 | 50 | 3 | 9 | 3 | 13 | 1 |
| Durani | 18 | 6 | 56 | 2 | 12 | 3 | 48 | 3 |
| Borde | 12 | 2 | 33 | 1 | 21 | 5 | 65 | 1 |
| Jaisimha | 4 | 0 | 7 | 0 | | | | |
| **WEST INDIES** | | | | | | | | |
| Hall | 11 | 3 | 26 | 1 | 20·5 | 3 | 47 | 3 |
| King | 19 | 4 | 46 | 5 | 13 | 3 | 18 | 2 |
| Worrell | 5 | 0 | 8 | 0 | | | | |
| Gibbs | 14·2 | 2 | 38 | 3 | 25 | 2 | 66 | 0 |
| Valentine | 12 | 4 | 32 | 1 | 14 | 9 | 28 | 0 |
| Sobers | 6 | 1 | 20 | 0 | 32 | 9 | 63 | 5 |

### FALL OF WICKETS

| Wkt | WI 1st | I 1st | WI 2nd | I 2nd |
|---|---|---|---|---|
| 1st | 2 | 11 | 1 | 15 |
| 2nd | 64 | 22 | 1 | 21 |
| 3rd | 64 | 22 | 75 | 77 |
| 4th | 93 | 26 | 118 | 80 |
| 5th | 140 | 26 | 138 | 86 |
| 6th | 174 | 40 | 138 | 135 |
| 7th | 201 | 112 | 154 | 218 |
| 8th | 218 | 171 | 234 | 219 |
| 9th | 218 | 178 | 248 | 230 |
| 10th | 253 | 178 | 283 | 235 |

Umpires: O. Davies and D. Sang Hue.

# ENGLAND v PAKISTAN 1962 (1st Test)

Played at Edgbaston, Birmingham, on 31 May, 1, 2, 4 June.
Toss: England.   Result: ENGLAND won by an innings and 24 runs.
Debuts: Nil.

England won with over a day and half to spare after scoring their highest total for five years. The unbroken partnership of 153 between Parfitt and Allen remains England's highest for the sixth wicket against Pakistan.

### ENGLAND

| | | |
|---|---|---:|
| G. Pullar | b D'Souza | 22 |
| M.C. Cowdrey | c Imtiaz b Intikhab | 159 |
| E.R. Dexter* | c Burki b Intikhab | 72 |
| T.W. Graveney | c Ijaz Butt b Mahmood | 97 |
| K.F. Barrington | lbw b Mahmood | 9 |
| P.H. Parfitt | not out | 101 |
| D.A. Allen | not out | 79 |
| G. Millman† | ) | |
| G.A.R. Lock | ) did not bat | |
| F.S. Trueman | ) | |
| J.B. Statham | ) | |
| Extras | (LB 5) | 5 |
| **Total** | (5 wickets declared) | **544** |

### PAKISTAN

| | | | | | |
|---|---|---:|---|---|---:|
| Hanif Mohammad | c Millman b Allen | 47 | | c Cowdrey b Allen | 31 |
| Ijaz Butt | c Lock b Statham | 10 | | c Trueman b Allen | 33 |
| Saeed Ahmed | c Graveney b Trueman | 5 | (5) | c Parfitt b Lock | 65 |
| Mushtaq Mohammad | c Cowdrey b Lock | 63 | | c Millman b Allen | 8 |
| Javed Burki* | c Barrington b Allen | 13 | (6) | b Statham | 19 |
| Imtiaz Ahmed† | b Trueman | 39 | (3) | c Graveney b Lock | 46 |
| W. Mathias | b Statham | 21 | | b Statham | 4 |
| Nasim-ul-Ghani | b Statham | 0 | | c Parfitt b Trueman | 35 |
| Intikhab Alam | b Lock | 16 | | c Cowdrey b Lock | 0 |
| Mahmood Hussain | b Statham | 0 | | c Graveney b Trueman | 22 |
| A. D'Souza | not out | 23 | | not out | 9 |
| Extras | (B 8, LB 1) | 9 | | (B 1, LB 1) | 2 |
| **Total** | | **246** | | | **274** |

| PAKISTAN | O | M | R | W | O | M | R | W |
|---|---|---|---|---|---|---|---|---|
| Mahmood Hussain | 43 | 14 | 130 | 2 | | | | |
| D'Souza | 46 | 9 | 161 | 1 | | | | |
| Intikhab | 25 | 2 | 117 | 2 | | | | |
| Nasim | 30 | 7 | 109 | 0 | | | | |
| Saeed | 2 | 0 | 22 | 0 | | | | |

| ENGLAND | O | M | R | W | O | M | R | W |
|---|---|---|---|---|---|---|---|---|
| Statham | 21 | 9 | 54 | 4 | 19 | 6 | 32 | 2 |
| Trueman | 13 | 3 | 59 | 2 | 24 | 5 | 70 | 2 |
| Dexter | 12 | 6 | 23 | 0 | 7 | 2 | 16 | 0 |
| Allen | 32 | 16 | 62 | 2 | 36 | 16 | 73 | 3 |
| Lock | 19 | 8 | 37 | 2 | 36 | 14 | 80 | 3 |
| Parfitt | 2 | 1 | 2 | 0 | | | | |
| Barrington | 2 | 2 | 0 | 0 | | | | |
| Cowdrey | | | | | 1 | 0 | 1 | 0 |

### FALL OF WICKETS

| | E | P | P |
|---|---|---|---|
| Wkt | 1st | 1st | 2nd |
| 1st | 31 | 11 | 60 |
| 2nd | 197 | 30 | 77 |
| 3rd | 304 | 108 | 119 |
| 4th | 330 | 144 | 127 |
| 5th | 391 | 146 | 187 |
| 6th | – | 202 | 199 |
| 7th | – | 206 | 207 |
| 8th | – | 206 | 207 |
| 9th | – | 206 | 257 |
| 10th | – | 246 | 274 |

Umpires: J.S. Buller and C.S. Elliott.

# ENGLAND v PAKISTAN 1962 (2nd Test)

Played at Lord's, London, on 21, 22, 23 June.
Toss: Pakistan.   Result: ENGLAND won by nine wickets.
Debuts: England – L.J. Coldwell, M.J. Stewart.

Trueman took his 200th wicket in 47 Test matches when he dismissed Javed Burki and later shared with Graveney in a record ninth-wicket partnership against Pakistan which added 76 runs. Nasim became the first Pakistan batsman to score a Test hundred in England. His fifth-wicket partnership of 197 with Javed Burki was then Pakistan's record for that wicket in all Tests and remains so against England. Nasim was promoted two places as 'night-watchman' and scored his maiden hundred in first-class cricket.

## PAKISTAN

| | | | | | |
|---|---|---|---|---|---|
| Hanif Mohammad | c Cowdrey b Trueman | 13 | lbw b Coldwell | | 24 |
| Imtiaz Ahmed† | b Coldwell | 1 | (7) c Trueman b Coldwell | | 33 |
| Saeed Ahmed | b Dexter | 10 | b Coldwell | | 20 |
| Javed Burki* | c Dexter b Trueman | 5 | (5) lbw b Coldwell | | 101 |
| Mustaq Mohammad | c Cowdrey b Trueman | 7 | (4) c Millman b Trueman | | 18 |
| Alimuddin | b Coldwell | 9 | (2) c Graveney b Allen | | 10 |
| W. Mathias | b Trueman | 15 | (8) c Graveney b Trueman | | 1 |
| Nasim-ul-Ghani | c Millman b Trueman | 17 | (6) c Graveney b Coldwell | | 101 |
| Mahmood Hussain | c Cowdrey b Coldwell | 1 | b Coldwell | | 20 |
| A. D'Souza | not out | 6 | not out | | 12 |
| Mohammad Farooq | c Stewart b Trueman | 13 | b Trueman | | 1 |
| Extras | (B 1, LB 2) | 3 | (B 6, LB 4, W 4) | | 14 |
| **Total** | | **100** | | | **355** |

## ENGLAND

| | | | | |
|---|---|---|---|---|
| M.J. Stewart | c Imtiaz b D'Souza | 39 | not out | 34 |
| M.C. Cowdrey | c D'Souza b Farooq | 41 | c Imtiaz b D'Souza | 20 |
| E.R. Dexter* | c Imtiaz b Farooq | 65 | not out | 32 |
| T.W. Graveney | b D'Souza | 153 | | |
| K.F. Barrington | c Imtiaz b Farooq | 0 | | |
| D.A. Allen | lbw b Farooq | 2 | | |
| P.H. Parfitt | b Mahmood | 16 | | |
| G. Millman† | c Hanif b Mahmood | 7 | | |
| G.A.R. Lock | c Mathias b Saeed | 7 | | |
| F.S. Trueman | lbw b Saeed | 29 | | |
| L.J. Coldwell | not out | 0 | | |
| Extras | (B 1, LB 5, NB 5) | 11 | | |
| **Total** | | **370** | (1 wicket) | **86** |

| ENGLAND | O | M | R | W | O | M | R | W | FALL OF WICKETS | | | | |
|---|---|---|---|---|---|---|---|---|---|---|---|---|---|
| Trueman | 17·4 | 6 | 31 | 6 | 33·3 | 6 | 85 | 3 | | P | E | P | E |
| Coldwell | 14 | 2 | 25 | 3 | 41 | 13 | 85 | 6 | *Wkt* | *1st* | *1st* | *2nd* | *2nd* |
| Dexter | 12 | 3 | 41 | 1 | 15 | 4 | 44 | 0 | 1st | 2 | 59 | 36 | 36 |
| Allen | | | | | 15 | 6 | 41 | 1 | 2nd | 23 | 137 | 36 | – |
| Lock | | | | | 14 | 1 | 78 | 0 | 3rd | 25 | 168 | 57 | – |
| Barrington | | | | | 1 | 0 | 8 | 0 | 4th | 31 | 168 | 77 | – |
| | | | | | | | | | 5th | 36 | 184 | 274 | – |
| PAKISTAN | | | | | | | | | 6th | 51 | 221 | 299 | – |
| Mahmood Hussain | 40 | 9 | 106 | 2 | | | | | 7th | 77 | 247 | 300 | – |
| Farooq | 19 | 4 | 70 | 4 | 7 | 1 | 37 | 0 | 8th | 78 | 290 | 333 | – |
| D'Souza | 35·4 | 3 | 147 | 2 | 7 | 0 | 29 | 1 | 9th | 78 | 366 | 354 | – |
| Nasim | 2 | 0 | 15 | 0 | | | | | 10th | 100 | 370 | 355 | – |
| Saeed | 5 | 1 | 21 | 2 | 2 | 0 | 12 | 0 | | | | | |
| Mushtaq | | | | | 1 | 0 | 8 | 0 | | | | | |

Umpires: J.S. Buller and N. Oldfield.

# ENGLAND v PAKISTAN 1962 (3rd Test)

Played at Headingley, Leeds, on 5, 6, 7 July.
Toss: Pakistan.   Result: ENGLAND won by an innings and 117 runs.
Debuts: Pakistan – Javed Akhtar (*his first match in England*).

Cowdrey ended his run of nine consecutive successes with the toss in Test matches. Parfitt and Allen shared what is still England's highest eighth-wicket partnership against Pakistan (99). For the fifth successive Test at Leeds, the match ended within three days' actual play. Pakistan were without Imtiaz Ahmed for the first time in 40 matches since their elevation to full Test status in 1952.

## ENGLAND

| | | |
|---|---|---|
| M.J. Stewart | lbw b Munir | 86 |
| M.C. Cowdrey* | c Saeed b Mahmood | 7 |
| E.R. Dexter | b Mahmood | 20 |
| T.W. Graveney | c Ijaz Butt b Munir | 37 |
| K.F. Barrington | c Mushtaq b Farooq | 1 |
| P.H. Parfitt | c and b Nasim | 119 |
| F.J. Titmus | c and b Munir | 2 |
| J.T. Murray† | c and b Nasim | 29 |
| D.A. Allen | c Ijaz Butt b Munir | 62 |
| F.S. Trueman | lbw b Munir | 20 |
| J.B. Statham | not out | 26 |
| Extras | (B 6, LB 9, W 1, NB 3) | 19 |
| **Total** | | **428** |

## PAKISTAN

| | | | | | |
|---|---|---|---|---|---|
| Alimuddin | c Barrington b Titmus | 50 | | c Titmus b Allen | 60 |
| Ijaz Butt† | b Trueman | 1 | | b Trueman | 6 |
| Saeed Ahmed | c Trueman b Statham | 16 | (5) | c Cowdrey b Statham | 54 |
| Mushtaq Mohammad | c Murray b Dexter | 27 | | c Trueman b Allen | 8 |
| Hanif Mohammad | b Statham | 9 | (6) | c Barrington b Allen | 4 |
| Javed Burki* | b Trueman | 1 | (7) | c Murray b Statham | 21 |
| Nasim-ul-Ghani | c Graveney b Titmus | 5 | (3) | lbw b Statham | 19 |
| Mahmood Hussain | not out | 0 | | c and b Dexter | 0 |
| Munir Malik | b Dexter | 3 | | b Statham | 4 |
| Javed Akhtar | b Dexter | 2 | | not out | 2 |
| Mohammad Farooq | c Statham b Dexter | 8 | | c Statham b Trueman | 0 |
| Extras | (B 8, NB 1) | 9 | | (LB 2) | 2 |
| **Total** | | **131** | | | **180** |

| PAKISTAN | O | M | R | W | O | M | R | W |
|---|---|---|---|---|---|---|---|---|
| Farooq | 28 | 8 | 74 | 1 | | | | |
| Mahmood Hussain | 25 | 5 | 87 | 2 | | | | |
| Munir | 49 | 11 | 128 | 5 | | | | |
| Javed Akhtar | 16 | 5 | 52 | 0 | | | | |
| Nasim | 14 | 2 | 68 | 2 | | | | |
| ENGLAND | | | | | | | | |
| Trueman | 23 | 6 | 55 | 2 | 10·4 | 3 | 33 | 2 |
| Statham | 20 | 9 | 40 | 2 | 20 | 3 | 50 | 4 |
| Dexter | 9·1 | 3 | 10 | 4 | 8 | 1 | 24 | 1 |
| Allen | 9 | 6 | 14 | 0 | 24 | 11 | 47 | 3 |
| Titmus | 4 | 1 | 3 | 2 | 11 | 2 | 20 | 0 |
| Barrington | | | | | 1 | 0 | 4 | 0 |

FALL OF WICKETS

| | E | P | P |
|---|---|---|---|
| Wkt | 1st | 1st | 2nd |
| 1st | 7 | 13 | 10 |
| 2nd | 43 | 51 | 40 |
| 3rd | 108 | 72 | 57 |
| 4th | 117 | 88 | 130 |
| 5th | 177 | 118 | 136 |
| 6th | 180 | 118 | 163 |
| 7th | 247 | 118 | 178 |
| 8th | 346 | 121 | 179 |
| 9th | 377 | 123 | 179 |
| 10th | 428 | 131 | 180 |

Umpires: J.G. Langridge and W.E. Phillipson.

# ENGLAND v PAKISTAN 1962 (4th Test)

Played at Trent Bridge, Nottingham, on 26 (*no play*), 27, 28, 30, 31 July.
Toss: Pakistan.   Result: MATCH DRAWN.
Debuts: Pakistan – Shahid Mahmood.

After a blank first day, rain reduced play to 195 minutes on the fourth day. Parfitt's hundred was his sixth in seven successive first-class innings against Pakistani bowling and his third in three innings against the tourists within a week. Statham exceeded R.R. Lindwall's record aggregate of Test wickets by a fast bowler (228) when he dismissed Imtiaz.

## ENGLAND

| | | |
|---|---|---|
| G. Pullar | lbw b Munir | 5 |
| Rev. D.S. Sheppard | c Imtiaz b Intikhab | 83 |
| E.R. Dexter* | c Burki b Fazal | 85 |
| T.W. Graveney | c Intikhab b Fazal | 114 |
| P.H. Parfitt | not out | 101 |
| B.R. Knight | c Saeed b Fazal | 14 |
| F.J. Titmus | not out | 11 |
| J.T. Murray† | ) | |
| F.S. Trueman | ) did not bat | |
| G.A.R. Lock | ) | |
| J.B. Statham | ) | |
| Extras | (LB 13, NB 2) | 15 |
| **Total** | (5 wickets declared) | **428** |

## PAKISTAN

| | | | | |
|---|---|---|---|---|
| Hanif Mohammad | c Titmus b Trueman | 0 | c and b Trueman | 3 |
| Shahid Mahmood | c Graveney b Trueman | 16 | (7) c Statham b Dexter | 9 |
| Mushtaq Mohammad | c Lock b Knight | 55 | not out | 100 |
| Javed Burki* | c Murray b Knight | 19 | c sub (C.J. Poole) b Titmus | 28 |
| Saeed Ahmed | c Murray b Statham | 43 | c Trueman b Lock | 64 |
| Imtiaz Ahmed† | lbw b Trueman | 15 | lbw b Statham | 1 |
| Alimuddin | b Trueman | 0 | (2) c Murray b Statham | 11 |
| Nasim-ul-Ghani | c Murray b Knight | 41 | not out | 0 |
| Intikhab Alam | c Murray b Statham | 14 | | |
| Fazal Mahmood | lbw b Knight | 2 | | |
| Munir Malik | not out | 0 | | |
| Extras | (B 2, LB 10, NB 2) | 14 | | |
| **Total** | | **219** | (6 wickets) | **216** |

| PAKISTAN | O | M | R | W | O | M | R | W |
|---|---|---|---|---|---|---|---|---|
| Fazal | 60 | 15 | 130 | 3 | | | | |
| Munir | 34 | 4 | 130 | 1 | | | | |
| Nasim | 20·2 | 1 | 76 | 0 | | | | |
| Intikhab | 14 | 3 | 49 | 1 | | | | |
| Shahid | 6 | 1 | 23 | 0 | | | | |
| Saeed | 2 | 0 | 5 | 0 | | | | |
| **ENGLAND** | | | | | | | | |
| Trueman | 24 | 3 | 71 | 4 | 19 | 5 | 35 | 1 |
| Statham | 18·1 | 5 | 55 | 2 | 22 | 8 | 47 | 2 |
| Knight | 17 | 1 | 38 | 4 | 21 | 6 | 48 | 0 |
| Lock | 14 | 5 | 19 | 0 | 15 | 4 | 27 | 1 |
| Titmus | 13 | 2 | 22 | 0 | 16 | 7 | 29 | 1 |
| Dexter | | | | | 7 | 0 | 25 | 1 |
| Parfitt | | | | | 1 | 0 | 5 | 0 |

### FALL OF WICKETS

| | E | P | P |
|---|---|---|---|
| Wkt | 1st | 1st | 2nd |
| 1st | 11 | 0 | 4 |
| 2nd | 172 | 39 | 22 |
| 3rd | 185 | 95 | 78 |
| 4th | 369 | 98 | 185 |
| 5th | 388 | 120 | 187 |
| 6th | – | 120 | 216 |
| 7th | – | 171 | – |
| 8th | – | 213 | – |
| 9th | – | 217 | – |
| 10th | – | 219 | – |

Umpires: F.S. Lee and W.E. Phillipson.

# ENGLAND v PAKISTAN 1962 (5th Test)

Played at Kennington Oval, London, on 16, 17, 18, 20 August.
Toss: England.   Result: ENGLAND won by ten wickets.
Debuts: England – J.D.F. Larter.

Cowdrey, who scored the highest of his 22 Test hundreds, and Dexter shared what is still England's highest second-wicket partnership against Pakistan (248). Imtiaz became the second batsman after Hanif Mohammad to score 2,000 runs for Pakistan. Larter (6ft 7½in tall) took nine wickets in his first Test match.

## ENGLAND

| | | | | |
|---|---|---|---|---|
| Rev. D.S. Sheppard | c Fazal b Nasim | 57 | not out | 9 |
| M.C. Cowdrey | c Hanif b Fazal | 182 | | |
| E.R. Dexter* | b Fazal | 172 | | |
| K.F. Barrington | not out | 50 | | |
| P.H. Parfitt | c Imtiaz b D'Souza | 3 | | |
| B.R. Knight | b D'Souza | 3 | | |
| R. Illingworth | not out | 2 | | |
| J.T. Murray† | ) | | (2) not out | 14 |
| D.A. Allen | ) did not bat | | | |
| L.J. Coldwell | ) | | | |
| J.D.F. Larter | ) | | | |
| Extras | (B 4, LB 5, NB 2) | 11 | (B 4) | 4 |
| **Total** | (5 wickets declared) | **480** | (0 wickets) | **27** |

## PAKISTAN

| | | | | |
|---|---|---|---|---|
| Ijaz Butt | c Cowdrey b Larter | 10 | run out | 6 |
| Imtiaz Ahmed† | c Murray b Knight | 49 | c Cowdrey b Larter | 98 |
| Mushtaq Mohammad | lbw b Larter | 43 | b Illingworth | 72 |
| Javed Burki* | b Larter | 3 | (6) c Parfitt b Knight | 42 |
| Saeed Ahmed | c Parfitt b Allen | 21 | c Knight b Allen | 4 |
| Hanif Mohammad | b Larter | 46 | (4) c Dexter b Larter | 0 |
| W. Mathias | c Murray b Larter | 0 | run out | 48 |
| A. D'Souza | c Parfitt b Coldwell | 1 | (10) not out | 2 |
| Nasim-ul-Ghani | c Murray b Coldwell | 5 | (8) b Coldwell | 24 |
| Intikhab Alam | not out | 3 | (9) b Larter | 12 |
| Fazal Mahmood | b Coldwell | 0 | b Larter | 5 |
| Extras | (NB 2) | 2 | (B 4, LB 5, NB 1) | 10 |
| **Total** | | **183** | | **323** |

| PAKISTAN | O | M | R | W | O | M | R | W | | FALL OF WICKETS | | | |
|---|---|---|---|---|---|---|---|---|---|---|---|---|---|
| Fazal | 49 | 9 | 192 | 2 | 4 | 1 | 10 | 0 | | E | P | P | E |
| D'Souza | 42 | 9 | 116 | 2 | 3 | 1 | 8 | 0 | Wkt | 1st | 1st | 2nd | 2nd |
| Intikhab | 38 | 5 | 109 | 0 | | | | | 1st | 117 | 11 | 34 | – |
| Javed Burki | 1 | 0 | 12 | 0 | 1 | 0 | 2 | 0 | 2nd | 365 | 93 | 171 | – |
| Nasim | 9 | 1 | 39 | 1 | | | | | 3rd | 441 | 102 | 171 | – |
| Saeed | 1 | 0 | 1 | 0 | | | | | 4th | 444 | 115 | 180 | – |
| Mushtaq | | | | | 0·3 | 0 | 3 | 0 | 5th | 452 | 165 | 186 | – |
| | | | | | | | | | 6th | – | 168 | 250 | – |
| ENGLAND | | | | | | | | | 7th | – | 175 | 294 | – |
| Coldwell | 28 | 11 | 53 | 3 | 23 | 4 | 60 | 1 | 8th | – | 179 | 316 | – |
| Larter | 25 | 4 | 57 | 5 | 21·1 | 0 | 88 | 4 | 9th | – | 183 | 316 | – |
| Allen | 22 | 9 | 33 | 1 | 27 | 14 | 52 | 1 | 10th | – | 183 | 323 | – |
| Knight | 9 | 5 | 11 | 1 | 11 | 3 | 33 | 1 | | | | | |
| Illingworth | 13 | 5 | 27 | 0 | 21 | 9 | 54 | 1 | | | | | |
| Dexter | | | | | 6 | 1 | 16 | 0 | | | | | |
| Barrington | | | | | 2 | 0 | 10 | 0 | | | | | |

Umpires: F.S. Lee and C.S. Elliott.

# AUSTRALIA v ENGLAND 1962-63 (1st Test)

Played at Woolloongabba, Brisbane, on 30 November, 1, 3, 4, 5 December.
Toss: Australia.   Result: MATCH DRAWN.
Debuts: England – A.C. Smith.

Six playing hours per day were scheduled for the first time in Test matches in Australia. England were set 378 runs to win at 63 per hour. Fourteen fifties were scored in the match, equalling the record for this series set at Leeds in 1948 (*Test No. 302*).

### AUSTRALIA

| | | | | |
|---|---|--:|---|--:|
| W.M. Lawry | c Smith b Trueman | 5 | c Sheppard b Titmus | 98 |
| R.B. Simpson | c Trueman b Dexter | 50 | c Smith b Dexter | 71 |
| N.C. O'Neill | c Statham b Trueman | 19 | lbw b Statham | 56 |
| R.N. Harvey | b Statham | 39 | c Statham b Dexter | 57 |
| P.J.P. Burge | c Dexter b Trueman | 6 | not out | 47 |
| B.C. Booth | c Dexter b Titmus | 112 | not out | 19 |
| A.K. Davidson | c Trueman b Barrington | 23 | | |
| K.D. Mackay | not out | 86 | | |
| R. Benaud* | c Smith b Knight | 51 | | |
| G.D. McKenzie | c and b Knight | 4 | | |
| B.N. Jarman† | c Barrington b Knight | 2 | | |
| Extras | (B 5, LB 1, NB 1) | 7 | (B 4, LB 10) | 14 |
| **Total** | | **404** | (4 wickets declared) | **362** |

### ENGLAND

| | | | | |
|---|---|--:|---|--:|
| G. Pullar | c and b Benaud | 33 | c and b Davidson | 56 |
| Rev. D.S. Sheppard | c McKenzie b Benaud | 31 | c Benaud b Davidson | 53 |
| E.R. Dexter* | b Benaud | 70 | b McKenzie | 99 |
| M.C. Cowdrey | c Lawry b Simpson | 21 | c and b Benaud | 9 |
| K.F. Barrington | c Burge b Benaud | 78 | c McKenzie b Davidson | 23 |
| A.C. Smith† | c Jarman b McKenzie | 21 | | |
| P.H. Parfitt | c Davidson b Benaud | 80 | (6) c Jarman b McKenzie | 4 |
| F.J. Titmus | c Simpson b Benaud | 21 | (7) not out | 3 |
| B.R. Knight | c Davidson b McKenzie | 0 | (8) not out | 4 |
| F.S. Trueman | c Jarman b McKenzie | 19 | | |
| J.B. Statham | not out | 8 | | |
| Extras | (B 4, LB 2, W 1) | 7 | (B 15, LB 10, NB 2) | 27 |
| **Total** | | **389** | (6 wickets) | **278** |

| ENGLAND | O | M | R | W | O | M | R | W |
|---|--:|--:|--:|--:|--:|--:|--:|--:|
| Trueman | 18 | 0 | 76 | 3 | 15 | 0 | 59 | 0 |
| Statham | 16 | 1 | 75 | 1 | 16 | 1 | 67 | 1 |
| Knight | 17·5 | 2 | 65 | 3 | 14 | 1 | 63 | 0 |
| Titmus | 33 | 8 | 91 | 1 | 26 | 3 | 81 | 1 |
| Dexter | 10 | 0 | 46 | 1 | 16 | 0 | 78 | 2 |
| Barrington | 12 | 3 | 44 | 1 | | | | |
| AUSTRALIA | | | | | | | | |
| Davidson | 21 | 4 | 77 | 0 | 20 | 6 | 43 | 3 |
| McKenzie | 25·3 | 2 | 78 | 3 | 20 | 4 | 61 | 2 |
| Mackay | 28 | 7 | 55 | 0 | 7 | 0 | 28 | 0 |
| Benaud | 42 | 12 | 115 | 6 | 27 | 7 | 71 | 1 |
| Simpson | 18 | 6 | 52 | 1 | 7 | 0 | 48 | 0 |
| O'Neill | 1 | 0 | 5 | 0 | 2 | 2 | 0 | 0 |

### FALL OF WICKETS

| | A | E | A | E |
|---|--:|--:|--:|--:|
| Wkt | *1st* | *1st* | *2nd* | *2nd* |
| 1st | 5 | 62 | 136 | 114 |
| 2nd | 46 | 65 | 216 | 135 |
| 3rd | 92 | 145 | 241 | 191 |
| 4th | 101 | 169 | 325 | 257 |
| 5th | 140· | 220 | – | 257 |
| 6th | 194 | 297 | – | 261 |
| 7th | 297 | 361 | – | – |
| 8th | 388 | 362 | – | – |
| 9th | 392 | 362 | – | – |
| 10th | 404 | 389 | – | – |

Umpires: C.J. Egar and E. Wykes.

# AUSTRALIA v ENGLAND 1962–63 (2nd Test)

Played at Melbourne Cricket Ground on 29, 31 December, 1, 2, 3 January.
Toss: Australia.   Result: ENGLAND won by seven wickets.
Debuts: Nil.

England won their first Test in Australia since 1954-55 and with 75 minutes to spare. On the last day they scored
226 runs for the loss of only two wickets – both being run out.

## AUSTRALIA

| | | | | | |
|---|---|---|---|---|---|
| W.M. Lawry | b Trueman | 52 | b Dexter | 5? |
| R.B. Simpson | c Smith b Coldwell | 38 | b Trueman | 14 |
| N.C. O'Neill | c Graveney b Statham | 19 | c Cowdrey b Trueman | ( |
| R.N. Harvey | b Coldwell | 0 | run out | 1( |
| P.J.P. Burge | lbw b Titmus | 23 | b Statham | 14 |
| B.C. Booth | c Barrington b Titmus | 27 | c Trueman b Statham | 10? |
| A.K. Davidson | c Smith b Trueman | 40 | c Smith b Titmus | 1? |
| K.D. Mackay | lbw b Titmus | 49 | lbw b Trueman | ? |
| R. Benaud* | c Barrington b Titmus | 36 | c Cowdrey b Trueman | ? |
| G.D. McKenzie | b Trueman | 16 | b Trueman | ( |
| B.N. Jarman† | not out | 10 | not out | 1? |
| Extras | (B 2, LB 4) | 6 | (B 4, LB 5) | ? |
| **Total** | | **316** | | **24?** |

## ENGLAND

| | | | | | |
|---|---|---|---|---|---|
| Rev. D.S. Sheppard | lbw b Davidson | 0 | run out | 113 |
| G. Pullar | b Davidson | 11 | c Jarman b McKenzie | ? |
| E.R. Dexter* | c Simpson b Benaud | 93 | run out | 52 |
| M.C. Cowdrey | c Burge b McKenzie | 113 | not out | 58 |
| K.F. Barrington | lbw b McKenzie | 35 | not out | ( |
| T.W. Graveney | run out | 41 | | |
| F.J. Titmus | c Jarman b Davidson | 15 | | |
| A.C. Smith† | not out | 6 | | |
| F.S. Trueman | c O'Neill b Davidson | 6 | | |
| J.B. Statham | b Davidson | 1 | | |
| L.J. Coldwell | c Benaud b Davidson | 1 | | |
| Extras | (B 4, LB 4, NB 1) | 9 | (B 5, LB 3, NB 1) | ? |
| **Total** | | **331** | (3 wickets) | **23?** |

| ENGLAND | O | M | R | W | O | M | R | W |
|---|---|---|---|---|---|---|---|---|
| Trueman | 23 | 1 | 83 | 3 | 20 | 1 | 62 | 5 |
| Statham | 22 | 2 | 83 | 1 | 23 | 1 | 52 | 2 |
| Coldwell | 17 | 2 | 58 | 2 | 25 | 2 | 60 | 0 |
| Barrington | 6 | 0 | 23 | 0 | 5 | 0 | 22 | 0 |
| Dexter | 6 | 1 | 10 | 0 | 9 | 2 | 18 | 1 |
| Titmus | 15 | 2 | 43 | 4 | 14 | 4 | 25 | 1 |
| Graveney | 3 | 1 | 10 | 0 | | | | |
| AUSTRALIA | | | | | | | | |
| Davidson | 23·1 | 4 | 75 | 6 | 19 | 2 | 53 | 0 |
| McKenzie | 29 | 3 | 95 | 2 | 20 | 3 | 58 | 1 |
| Mackay | 6 | 2 | 17 | 0 | 9 | 0 | 34 | 0 |
| Benaud | 18 | 3 | 82 | 1 | 14 | 1 | 69 | 0 |
| Simpson | 7 | 1 | 34 | 0 | 2 | 0 | 10 | 0 |
| O'Neill | 5 | 1 | 19 | 0 | | | | |
| Booth | | | | | 0·2 | 0 | 4 | 0 |

FALL OF WICKETS

| Wkt | A 1st | E 1st | A 2nd | E 2nd |
|---|---|---|---|---|
| 1st | 62 | 0 | 30 | 5 |
| 2nd | 111 | 19 | 30 | 129 |
| 3rd | 112 | 194 | 46 | 233 |
| 4th | 112 | 254 | 69 | – |
| 5th | 155 | 255 | 161 | – |
| 6th | 164 | 292 | 193 | – |
| 7th | 237 | 315 | 212 | – |
| 8th | 289 | 324 | 228 | – |
| 9th | 294 | 327 | 228 | – |
| 10th | 316 | 331 | 248 | – |

Umpires: C.J. Egar and W. Smyth.

# AUSTRALIA v ENGLAND 1962–63 (3rd Test)

Played at Sydney Cricket Ground on 11, 12, 14, 15 January.
Toss: England.   Result: AUSTRALIA won by eight wickets.
Debuts: Australia – C.E.J. Guest, B.K. Shepherd.

Australia squared the rubber at 2.15 p.m. on the fourth day. Parfitt kept wicket after Murray injured his shoulder when he caught Lawry. On the second day Titmus took four wickets for five runs in 58 balls.

## ENGLAND

| | | | | |
|---|---|--:|---|--:|
| G. Pullar | c Benaud b Simpson | 53 | b Davidson | 0 |
| Rev. D.S. Sheppard | c McKenzie b Davidson | 3 | c Simpson b Davidson | 12 |
| E.R. Dexter* | c Lawry b Benaud | 32 | c Simpson b Davidson | 11 |
| M.C. Cowdrey | c Jarman b Simpson | 85 | c Simpson b Benaud | 8 |
| K.F. Barrington | lbw b Davidson | 35 | b McKenzie | 21 |
| P.H. Parfitt | c Lawry b Simpson | 0 | c O'Neill b McKenzie | 28 |
| F.J. Titmus | b Davidson | 32 | c Booth b O'Neill | 6 |
| J.T. Murray† | lbw b Davidson | 0 | not out | 3 |
| F.S. Trueman | b Simpson | 32 | c Jarman b McKenzie | 9 |
| J.B. Statham | c Benaud b Simpson | 0 | b Davidson | 2 |
| L.J. Coldwell | not out | 2 | c Shepherd b Davidson | 0 |
| Extras | (LB 3, W 2) | 5 | (B 2, LB 2) | 4 |
| **Total** | | **279** | | **104** |

## AUSTRALIA

| | | | | |
|---|---|--:|---|--:|
| W.M. Lawry | c Murray b Coldwell | 8 | b Trueman | 8 |
| R.B. Simpson | b Titmus | 91 | not out | 34 |
| R.N. Harvey | c Barrington b Titmus | 64 | lbw b Trueman | 15 |
| B.C. Booth | c Trueman b Titmus | 16 | not out | 5 |
| N.C. O'Neill | b Titmus | 3 | | |
| B.K. Shepherd | not out | 71 | | |
| B.N. Jarman† | run out | 0 | | |
| A.K. Davidson | c Trueman b Titmus | 15 | | |
| R. Benaud* | c and b Titmus | 15 | | |
| G.D. McKenzie | lbw b Titmus | 4 | | |
| C.E.J. Guest | b Statham | 11 | | |
| Extras | (B 10, LB 11) | 21 | (B 5) | 5 |
| **Total** | | **319** | (2 wickets) | **67** |

| AUSTRALIA | O | M | R | W | O | M | R | W |
|---|--:|--:|--:|--:|--:|--:|--:|--:|
| Davidson | 24·5 | 7 | 54 | 4 | 10·6 | 2 | 25 | 5 |
| McKenzie | 15 | 3 | 52 | 0 | 14 | 3 | 26 | 3 |
| Guest | 16 | 0 | 51 | 0 | 2 | 0 | 8 | 0 |
| Benaud | 16 | 2 | 60 | 1 | 19 | 10 | 29 | 1 |
| Simpson | 15 | 3 | 57 | 5 | 4 | 2 | 5 | 0 |
| O'Neill | | | | | 7 | 5 | 7 | 1 |
| **ENGLAND** | | | | | | | | |
| Trueman | 20 | 2 | 68 | 0 | 6 | 1 | 20 | 2 |
| Statham | 21·2 | 2 | 67 | 1 | 3 | 0 | 15 | 0 |
| Coldwell | 15 | 1 | 41 | 1 | | | | |
| Titmus | 37 | 14 | 79 | 7 | | | | |
| Barrington | 8 | 0 | 43 | 0 | | | | |
| Dexter | | | | | 3·2 | 0 | 27 | 0 |

### FALL OF WICKETS

| | E | A | E | A |
|---|--:|--:|--:|--:|
| Wkt | 1st | 1st | 2nd | 2nd |
| 1st | 4 | 14 | 0 | 28 |
| 2nd | 65 | 174 | 20 | 54 |
| 3rd | 132 | 177 | 25 | – |
| 4th | 201 | 187 | 37 | – |
| 5th | 203 | 212 | 53 | – |
| 6th | 221 | 216 | 71 | – |
| 7th | 221 | 242 | 90 | – |
| 8th | 272 | 274 | 100 | – |
| 9th | 272 | 280 | 104 | – |
| 10th | 279 | 319 | 104 | – |

Umpires: W. Smyth and L.P. Rowan.

# AUSTRALIA v ENGLAND 1962–63 (4th Test)

Played at Adelaide Oval on 25, 26, 28, 29, 30 January.
Toss: Australia.   Result: MATCH DRAWN.
Debuts: Nil.

Rain reduced play by three hours on the third day. Barrington became the second batsman after J. Darling in 1897-98 (*Test No. 55*) to reach a hundred in this series of Tests with a six. Statham overtook A.V. Bedser's world record of 236 Test wickets. Davidson pulled a hamstring and was unable to complete his fourth over.

## AUSTRALIA

| | | | | | |
|---|---|---|---|---|---|
| W.M. Lawry | b Illingworth | 10 | c Graveney b Trueman | | 16 |
| R.B. Simpson | c Smith b Statham | 0 | c Smith b Dexter | | 71 |
| R.N. Harvey | c Statham b Dexter | 154 | c Barrington b Statham | | 6 |
| B.C. Booth | c Cowdrey b Titmus | 34 | c Smith b Dexter | | 77 |
| N.C. O'Neill | c Cowdrey b Dexter | 100 | c Cowdrey b Trueman | | 23 |
| A.K. Davidson | b Statham | 46 | (10) b Statham | | 2 |
| B.K. Shepherd | c Trueman b Statham | 10 | (6) c Titmus b Dexter | | 13 |
| K.D. Mackay | c Smith b Trueman | 1 | (7) c Graveney b Trueman | | 3 |
| R. Benaud* | b Dexter | 16 | (8) c Barrington b Trueman | | 48 |
| G.D. McKenzie | c Sheppard b Titmus | 15 | (9) c Smith b Statham | | 13 |
| A.T.W. Grout† | not out | 1 | not out | | 16 |
| Extras | (LB 5, W 1) | 6 | (B 1, LB 4) | | 5 |
| **Total** | | **393** | | | **293** |

## ENGLAND

| | | | | | |
|---|---|---|---|---|---|
| G. Pullar | b McKenzie | 9 | c Simpson b McKenzie | | 3 |
| Rev. D.S. Sheppard | st Grout b Benaud | 30 | c Grout b Mackay | | 1 |
| K.F. Barrington | b Simpson | 63 | not out | | 132 |
| M.C. Cowdrey | c Grout b McKenzie | 13 | run out | | 32 |
| E.R. Dexter* | c Grout b McKenzie | 61 | c Simpson b Benaud | | 10 |
| T.W. Graveney | c Booth b McKenzie | 22 | not out | | 36 |
| F.J. Titmus | not out | 59 | | | |
| R. Illingworth | c Grout b McKenzie | 12 | | | |
| A.C. Smith† | c Lawry b Mackay | 13 | | | |
| F.S. Trueman | c Benaud b Mackay | 38 | | | |
| J.B. Statham | b Mackay | 1 | | | |
| Extras | (B 5, LB 5) | 10 | (B 4, W 5) | | 9 |
| **Total** | | **331** | (4 wickets) | | **223** |

| ENGLAND | O | M | R | W | O | M | R | W |
|---|---|---|---|---|---|---|---|---|
| Trueman | 19 | 1 | 54 | 1 | 23·3 | 3 | 60 | 4 |
| Statham | 21 | 5 | 66 | 3 | 21 | 2 | 71 | 3 |
| Illingworth | 20 | 3 | 85 | 1 | 5 | 1 | 23 | 0 |
| Dexter | 23 | 1 | 94 | 3 | 17 | 0 | 65 | 3 |
| Titmus | 20·1 | 2 | 88 | 2 | 24 | 5 | 69 | 0 |
| AUSTRALIA | | | | | | | | |
| Davidson | 3·4 | 0 | 30 | 0 | | | | |
| McKenzie | 33 | 3 | 89 | 5 | 14 | 0 | 64 | 1 |
| Mackay | 27·6 | 8 | 80 | 3 | 8 | 2 | 13 | 1 |
| Benaud | 18 | 3 | 82 | 1 | 15 | 3 | 38 | 1 |
| Simpson | 8 | 1 | 40 | 1 | 10 | 1 | 50 | 0 |
| O'Neill | | | | | 8 | 0 | 49 | 0 |
| Lawry | | | | | 1 | 1 | 0 | 0 |
| Harvey | | | | | 1 | 1 | 0 | 0 |

FALL OF WICKETS

| Wkt | A 1st | E 1st | A 2nd | E 2nd |
|---|---|---|---|---|
| 1st | 2 | 17 | 27 | 2 |
| 2nd | 16 | 84 | 37 | 4 |
| 3rd | 101 | 117 | 170 | 98 |
| 4th | 295 | 119 | 175 | 122 |
| 5th | 302 | 165 | 199 | – |
| 6th | 331 | 226 | 205 | – |
| 7th | 336 | 246 | 228 | – |
| 8th | 366 | 275 | 254 | – |
| 9th | 383 | 327 | 258 | – |
| 10th | 393 | 331 | 293 | – |

Umpires: C.J. Egar and A. Mackley.

# AUSTRALIA v ENGLAND 1962–63 (5th Test)

Played at Sydney Cricket Ground on 15, 16, 18, 19, 20 February.
Toss: England.    Result: MATCH DRAWN.
Debuts: Australia – N.J.N. Hawke.

For the first time a five-match series in Australia ended with the sides level. Dexter's aggregate of 481 remains the record by an England captain in a rubber in Australia.

## ENGLAND

| | | | | | |
|---|---|--:|---|---|--:|
| Rev. D.S. Sheppard | c and b Hawke | 19 | | c Harvey b Benaud | 68 |
| M.C. Cowdrey | c Harvey b Davidson | 2 | (5) | c Benaud b Davidson | 53 |
| K.F. Barrington | c Harvey b Benaud | 101 | | c Grout b McKenzie | 94 |
| E.R. Dexter* | c Simpson b O'Neill | 47 | | st Grout b Benaud | 6 |
| T.W. Graveney | c Harvey b McKenzie | 14 | (6) | c and b Davidson | 3 |
| R. Illingworth | c Grout b Davidson | 27 | (2) | c Hawke b Benaud | 18 |
| F.J. Titmus | c Grout b Hawke | 34 | | not out | 12 |
| F.S. Trueman | c Harvey b Benaud | 30 | | c Harvey b McKenzie | 8 |
| A.C. Smith† | b Simpson | 6 | | c Simpson b Davidson | 1 |
| D.A. Allen | c Benaud b Davidson | 14 | | | |
| J.B. Statham | not out | 17 | | | |
| Extras | (B 4, LB 6) | 10 | | (B 1, LB 4) | 5 |
| **Total** | | **321** | | (8 wickets declared) | **268** |

## AUSTRALIA

| | | | | | |
|---|---|--:|---|---|--:|
| W.M. Lawry | c Smith b Trueman | 11 | | not out | 45 |
| R.B. Simpson | c Trueman b Titmus | 32 | | b Trueman | 0 |
| B.C. Booth | b Titmus | 11 | (5) | b Allen | 0 |
| N.C. O'Neill | c Graveney b Allen | 73 | | c Smith b Allen | 17 |
| P.J.P. Burge | lbw b Titmus | 103 | (6) | not out | 52 |
| R.N. Harvey | c sub (P.H. Parfitt) b Statham | 22 | (3) | b Allen | 28 |
| A.K. Davidson | c Allen b Dexter | 15 | | | |
| R. Benaud* | c Graveney b Allen | 57 | | | |
| G.D. McKenzie | c and b Titmus | 0 | | | |
| N.J.N. Hawke | c Graveney b Titmus | 14 | | | |
| A.T.W. Grout† | not out | 0 | | | |
| Extras | (B 6, LB 5) | 11 | | (B 4, LB 6) | 10 |
| **Total** | | **349** | | (4 wickets) | **152** |

| AUSTRALIA | O | M | R | W | O | M | R | W |
|---|--:|--:|--:|--:|--:|--:|--:|--:|
| Davidson | 25·6 | 4 | 43 | 3 | 28 | 1 | 80 | 3 |
| McKenzie | 27 | 4 | 57 | 1 | 8 | 0 | 39 | 2 |
| Hawke | 20 | 1 | 51 | 2 | 9 | 0 | 38 | 0 |
| Benaud | 34 | 9 | 71 | 2 | 30 | 8 | 71 | 3 |
| Simpson | 18 | 4 | 51 | 1 | 4 | 0 | 22 | 0 |
| O'Neill | 10 | 0 | 38 | 1 | | | | |
| Harvey | | | | | 3 | 0 | 13 | 0 |
| ENGLAND | | | | | | | | |
| Trueman | 11 | 0 | 33 | 1 | 3 | 0 | 6 | 1 |
| Statham | 18 | 1 | 76 | 1 | 4 | 1 | 8 | 0 |
| Dexter | 7 | 1 | 24 | 1 | 4 | 1 | 11 | 0 |
| Titmus | 47·2 | 9 | 103 | 5 | 20 | 7 | 37 | 0 |
| Allen | 43 | 15 | 87 | 2 | 19 | 11 | 26 | 3 |
| Illingworth | 5 | 1 | 15 | 0 | 10 | 5 | 8 | 0 |
| Barrington | | | | | 8 | 3 | 22 | 0 |
| Graveney | | | | | 4 | 0 | 24 | 0 |

### FALL OF WICKETS

| | E | A | E | A |
|---|--:|--:|--:|--:|
| Wkt | 1st | 1st | 2nd | 2nd |
| 1st | 5 | 28 | 40 | 0 |
| 2nd | 39 | 50 | 137 | 39 |
| 3rd | 129 | 71 | 145 | 70 |
| 4th | 177 | 180 | 239 | 70 |
| 5th | 189 | 231 | 247 | – |
| 6th | 224 | 271 | 249 | – |
| 7th | 276 | 299 | 257 | – |
| 8th | 286 | 303 | 268 | – |
| 9th | 293 | 347 | – | – |
| 10th | 321 | 349 | – | – |

Umpires: C.J. Egar and L.P. Rowan.

# NEW ZEALAND v ENGLAND 1962–63 (1st Test)

Played at Eden Park, Auckland, on 23, 25, 26, 27 February.
Toss: England.   Result: ENGLAND won by an innings and 215 runs.
Debuts: New Zealand – B.W. Sinclair, B.W. Yuile.

England scored their highest total against New Zealand (subsequently bettered), 240 of the runs coming in a partnership between Parfitt and Knight which is still England's highest for the sixth wicket against all countries. An umpiring error allowed Sparling to bowl eleven balls (excluding no balls and wides) in his sixth over. The match ended after 66 minutes of play on the last day.

## ENGLAND

| | | |
|---|---|---|
| Rev. D.S. Sheppard | c Dick b Cameron | 12 |
| R. Illingworth | c Reid b Cameron | 20 |
| K.F. Barrington | c Playle b Cameron | 126 |
| E.R. Dexter* | c Barton b Yuile | 7 |
| M.C. Cowdrey | c Barton b Cameron | 86 |
| P.H. Parfitt | not out | 131 |
| B.R. Knight | b Alabaster | 125 |
| F.J. Titmus | st Dick b Sparling | 26 |
| J.T. Murray† | not out | 9 |
| J.D.F. Larter | ) did not bat | |
| L.J. Coldwell | ) | |
| Extras | (B 18, LB 1, NB 1) | 20 |
| **Total** | (7 wickets declared) | **562** |

## NEW ZEALAND

| | | | | | |
|---|---|---|---|---|---|
| G.T. Dowling | b Coldwell | 3 | | b Illingworth | 14 |
| W.R. Playle | c Dexter b Larter | 0 | | c Dexter b Coldwell | 4 |
| P.T. Barton | c Sheppard b Larter | 3 | | lbw b Titmus | 16 |
| J.R. Reid* | b Titmus | 59 | (6) | not out | 21 |
| B.W. Sinclair | c Coldwell b Titmus | 24 | | b Larter | 2 |
| J.T. Sparling | c Murray b Larter | 3 | (4) | c Barrington b Illingworth | 0 |
| A.E. Dick† | run out | 29 | | c Illingworth b Larter | 0 |
| B.W. Yuile | run out | 64 | | lbw b Larter | 1 |
| R.C. Motz | c Murray b Knight | 60 | | c and b Illingworth | 20 |
| J.C. Alabaster | b Knight | 2 | | c Titmus b Illingworth | 0 |
| F.J. Cameron | not out | 0 | | b Larter | 1 |
| Extras | (B 5, LB 3, W 1, NB 2) | 11 | | (B 2, LB 8) | 10 |
| **Total** | | **258** | | | **89** |

| NEW ZEALAND | O | M | R | W | O | M | R | W |
|---|---|---|---|---|---|---|---|---|
| Motz | 42 | 12 | 98 | 0 | | | | |
| Cameron | 43 | 7 | 118 | 4 | | | | |
| Alabaster | 40 | 6 | 130 | 1 | | | | |
| Yuile | 21 | 4 | 77 | 1 | | | | |
| Reid | 28 | 8 | 67 | 0 | | | | |
| Sparling | 12 | 2 | 52 | 1 | | | | |
| ENGLAND | | | | | | | | |
| Coldwell | 27 | 9 | 66 | 1 | 5 | 2 | 4 | 1 |
| Larter | 26 | 12 | 51 | 3 | 14·1 | 3 | 26 | 4 |
| Knight | 10·4 | 2 | 23 | 2 | 10 | 2 | 13 | 0 |
| Titmus | 25 | 9 | 44 | 2 | 6 | 5 | 2 | 1 |
| Barrington | 12 | 4 | 38 | 0 | | | | |
| Dexter | 9 | 4 | 20 | 0 | | | | |
| Illingworth | 1 | 0 | 5 | 0 | 18 | 7 | 34 | 4 |

## FALL OF WICKETS

| | E | NZ | NZ |
|---|---|---|---|
| Wkt | 1st | 1st | 2nd |
| 1st | 24 | 0 | 15 |
| 2nd | 45 | 7 | 42 |
| 3rd | 63 | 7 | 42 |
| 4th | 229 | 62 | 42 |
| 5th | 258 | 71 | 46 |
| 6th | 498 | 109 | 46 |
| 7th | 535 | 161 | 56 |
| 8th | – | 256 | 83 |
| 9th | – | 258 | 83 |
| 10th | – | 258 | 89 |

Umpires: R.W.R. Shortt and J.M. Brown.

# NEW ZEALAND v ENGLAND 1962–63 (2nd Test)

Played at Basin Reserve, Wellington, on 1, 2, 4 March.
Toss: England.   Result: ENGLAND won by an innings and 47 runs.
Debuts: New Zealand – B.D. Morrison, M.J.F. Shrimpton.

Cowdrey and Smith shared an unbroken partnership of 163 to set a world Test record for the ninth wicket. It remains the England record for that wicket and has been bettered only by the partnership of 190 between Asif Iqbal and Intikhab Alam for Pakistan v England at The Oval in 1967 (*Test No. 623*).

## NEW ZEALAND

| | | | | |
|---|---|---|---|---|
| G.T. Dowling | c Smith b Trueman | 12 | c Knight b Trueman | 2 |
| W.R. Playle | c Smith b Knight | 23 | c and b Illingworth | 65 |
| P.T. Barton | c Cowdrey b Trueman | 0 | c Barrington b Knight | 3 |
| J.R. Reid* | c Smith b Knight | 0 | c Barrington b Titmus | 9 |
| B.W. Sinclair | b Trueman | 4 | c and b Barrington | 36 |
| M.J.F. Shrimpton | lbw b Knight | 28 | c Parfitt b Barrington | 10 |
| A.E. Dick† | c Sheppard b Trueman | 7 | not out | 8 |
| B.W. Yuile | c Illingworth b Titmus | 13 | b Titmus | 0 |
| R.W. Blair | not out | 64 | c Larter b Titmus | 5 |
| B.D. Morrison | run out | 10 | c Larter b Titmus | 0 |
| F.J. Cameron | lbw b Barrington | 12 | lbw b Barrington | 0 |
| Extras | (B 13, LB 5, NB 3) | 21 | (B 13, LB 4, NB 2) | 19 |
| **Total** | | **194** | | **187** |

## ENGLAND

| | | |
|---|---|---|
| Rev. D.S. Sheppard | b Blair | 0 |
| R. Illingworth | c Morrison b Blair | 46 |
| K.F. Barrington | c Dick b Reid | 76 |
| E.R. Dexter* | b Morrison | 31 |
| P.H. Parfitt | c Dick b Morrison | 0 |
| B.R. Knight | c Dick b Cameron | 31 |
| F.J. Titmus | run out | 33 |
| M.C. Cowdrey | not out | 128 |
| F.S. Trueman | b Cameron | 3 |
| A.C. Smith† | not out | 69 |
| J.D.F. Larter | did not bat | |
| Extras | (B 3, LB 6, NB 2) | 11 |
| **Total** | (8 wickets declared) | **428** |

| ENGLAND | O | M | R | W | O | M | R | W | | FALL OF WICKETS | | |
|---|---|---|---|---|---|---|---|---|---|---|---|---|
| | | | | | | | | | | NZ | E | NZ |
| Trueman | 20 | 5 | 46 | 4 | 18 | 7 | 27 | 1 | *Wkt* | *1st* | *1st* | *2nd* |
| Larter | 14 | 2 | 52 | 0 | 7 | 1 | 18 | 0 | 1st | 32 | 0 | 15 |
| Knight | 21 | 8 | 32 | 3 | 4 | 1 | 7 | 1 | 2nd | 32 | 77 | 18 |
| Titmus | 18 | 3 | 40 | 1 | 3 | 1 | 50 | 4 | 3rd | 35 | 125 | 41 |
| Barrington | 2·3 | 1 | 1 | 1 | 11 | 3 | 32 | 3 | 4th | 40 | 125 | 122 |
| Dexter | 1 | 0 | 2 | 0 | | | | | 5th | 61 | 173 | 126 |
| Illingworth | | | | | 2 | 1 | 34 | 1 | 6th | 74 | 197 | 158 |
| | | | | | | | | | 7th | 96 | 258 | 159 |
| NEW ZEALAND | | | | | | | | | 8th | 129 | 265 | 171 |
| Blair | 33 | 11 | 81 | 2 | | | | | 9th | 150 | – | 179 |
| Morrison | 31 | 5 | 129 | 2 | | | | | 10th | 194 | – | 187 |
| Cameron | 43 | 16 | 98 | 2 | | | | | | | | |
| Reid | 32 | 8 | 73 | 1 | | | | | | | | |
| Yuile | 10 | 1 | 36 | 0 | | | | | | | | |

Umpires: D.P. Dumbleton and W.T. Martin.

# NEW ZEALAND v ENGLAND 1962–63 (3rd Test)

Played at Lancaster Park, Christchurch, on 15, 16, 18, 19 March.
Toss: New Zealand.   Result: ENGLAND won by seven wickets.
Debuts: Nil.

Knight completed England's 3-0 victory in this rubber by hitting 14 runs (6, 4, 4) off successive balls from Alabaster. Trueman overtook J.B. Statham's world record of 242 Test wickets and ended his 56th Test with an aggregate of 250.

## NEW ZEALAND

| | | | | |
|---|---|---|---|---|
| G.T. Dowling | c Dexter b Titmus | 40 | c Smith b Larter | 22 |
| W.R. Playle | c Barrington b Trueman | 0 | c Smith b Trueman | 3 |
| B.W. Sinclair | hit wkt b Trueman | 44 | lbw b Larter | 0 |
| J.R. Reid* | c Parfitt b Knight | 74 | b Titmus | 100 |
| P.T. Barton | c Smith b Knight | 11 | lbw b Knight | 12 |
| M.J.F. Shrimpton | c Knight b Trueman | 31 | b Titmus | 8 |
| A.E. Dick† | b Trueman | 16 | c Parfitt b Titmus | 1 |
| R.C. Motz | c Parfitt b Trueman | 7 | b Larter | 3 |
| R.W. Blair | c Parfitt b Trueman | 0 | b Titmus | 0 |
| J.C. Alabaster | not out | 20 | c Parfitt b Trueman | 1 |
| F.J. Cameron | c Smith b Trueman | 1 | not out | 0 |
| Extras | (B 1, LB 9, W 3, NB 9) | 22 | (LB 7, NB 2) | 9 |
| **Total** | | **266** | | **159** |

## ENGLAND

| | | | | |
|---|---|---|---|---|
| Rev. D.S. Sheppard | b Cameron | 42 | b Alabaster | 31 |
| R. Illingworth | c Dick b Cameron | 2 | | |
| K.F. Barrington | lbw b Motz | 47 | (2) c Reid b Blair | 45 |
| E.R. Dexter* | b Alabaster | 46 | | |
| M.C. Cowdrey | c Motz b Blair | 43 | (3) not out | 35 |
| P.H. Parfitt | lbw b Reid | 4 | (4) c Shrimpton b Alabaster | 31 |
| B.R. Knight | b Blair | 32 | (5) not out | 20 |
| F.J. Titmus | c Dick b Motz | 4 | | |
| F.S. Trueman | c Reid b Alabaster | 11 | | |
| A.C. Smith† | not out | 2 | | |
| J.D.F. Larter | b Motz | 2 | | |
| Extras | (B 4, LB 6, W 5, NB 3) | 18 | (B 9, NB 2) | 11 |
| **Total** | | **253** | (3 wickets) | **173** |

| ENGLAND | O | M | R | W | O | M | R | W |
|---|---|---|---|---|---|---|---|---|
| Trueman | 30·2 | 9 | 75 | 7 | 19·4 | 8 | 16 | 2 |
| Larter | 21 | 5 | 59 | 0 | 23 | 8 | 32 | 3 |
| Knight | 23 | 5 | 39 | 2 | 10 | 3 | 38 | 1 |
| Titmus | 30 | 13 | 45 | 1 | 21 | 8 | 46 | 4 |
| Dexter | 9 | 3 | 8 | 0 | 10 | 2 | 18 | 0 |
| Barrington | 5 | 0 | 18 | 0 | | | | |
| NEW ZEALAND | | | | | | | | |
| Motz | 19·5 | 3 | 68 | 3 | 20 | 6 | 33 | 0 |
| Cameron | 24 | 6 | 47 | 2 | 12 | 3 | 38 | 0 |
| Blair | 24 | 12 | 42 | 2 | 12 | 3 | 34 | 1 |
| Alabaster | 20 | 6 | 47 | 2 | 15·3 | 5 | 57 | 2 |
| Reid | 8 | 1 | 31 | 1 | | | | |

### FALL OF WICKETS

| | NZ | E | NZ | E |
|---|---|---|---|---|
| Wkt | 1st | 1st | 2nd | 2nd |
| 1st | 3 | 11 | 16 | 70 |
| 2nd | 83 | 87 | 17 | 96 |
| 3rd | 98 | 103 | 66 | 149 |
| 4th | 128 | 186 | 91 | – |
| 5th | 195 | 188 | 129 | – |
| 6th | 234 | 210 | 133 | – |
| 7th | 235 | 225 | 151 | – |
| 8th | 235 | 244 | 154 | – |
| 9th | 251 | 250 | 159 | – |
| 10th | 266 | 253 | 159 | – |

Umpires: L.C. Johnston and W.T. Martin.

# ENGLAND v WEST INDIES 1963 (1st Test)

Played at Old Trafford, Manchester, on 6, 7, 8, 10 June.
Toss: West Indies.   Result: WEST INDIES won by ten wickets.
Debuts: England – J.H. Edrich; West Indies – M.C. Carew, D.L. Murray.

West Indies gained their first victory in a Test at Old Trafford. Following their 5-0 defeat of India in 1961-62, this win gave West Indies six consecutive Test victories for the first time. Hunte's 182 not out was then the highest score against England at Manchester. For the first time in England three players from the same county, Stewart, Edrich and Barrington of Surrey, occupied the first three places in England's batting order.

## WEST INDIES

| | | | | |
|---|---|---|---|---|
| C.C. Hunte | c Titmus b Allen | 182 | not out | 1 |
| M.C. Carew | c Andrew b Trueman | 16 | not out | 0 |
| R.B. Kanhai | run out | 90 | | |
| B.F. Butcher | lbw b Trueman | 22 | | |
| G. St A. Sobers | c Edrich b Allen | 64 | | |
| J.S. Solomon | lbw b Titmus | 35 | | |
| F.M.M. Worrell* | not out | 74 | | |
| D.L. Murray† | not out | 7 | | |
| W.W. Hall | ) | | | |
| C.C. Griffith | ) did not bat | | | |
| L.R. Gibbs | ) | | | |
| Extras | (B 3, LB 7, NB 1) | 11 | | |
| **Total** | (6 wickets declared) | **501** | (0 wickets) | **1** |

## ENGLAND

| | | | | |
|---|---|---|---|---|
| M.J. Stewart | c Murray b Gibbs | 37 | c Murray b Gibbs | 87 |
| J.H. Edrich | c Murray b Hall | 20 | c Hunte b Worrell | 38 |
| K.F. Barrington | c Murray b Hall | 16 | (4) b Gibbs | 8 |
| M.C. Cowdrey | b Hall | 4 | (5) c Hunte b Gibbs | 12 |
| E.R. Dexter* | c Worrell b Sobers | 73 | (6) c Murray b Gibbs | 35 |
| D.B. Close | c Hunte b Gibbs | 30 | (7) c Sobers b Gibbs | 32 |
| F.J. Titmus | c Sobers b Gibbs | 0 | (8) b Sobers | 17 |
| D.A. Allen | c Sobers b Gibbs | 5 | (9) b Gibbs | 1 |
| F.S. Trueman | c Worrell b Sobers | 5 | (10) not out | 29 |
| K.V. Andrew† | not out | 3 | (3) c Murray b Sobers | 15 |
| J.B. Statham | b Gibbs | 0 | b Griffith | 7 |
| Extras | (B 2, LB 7, NB 3) | 12 | (B 10, LB 4, NB 1) | 15 |
| **Total** | | **205** | | **296** |

| ENGLAND | O | M | R | W | O | M | R | W | FALL OF WICKETS | | | | |
|---|---|---|---|---|---|---|---|---|---|---|---|---|---|
| Trueman | 40 | 7 | 95 | 2 | | | | | | WI | E | E | WI |
| Statham | 37 | 6 | 121 | 0 | | | | | Wkt | 1st | 1st | 2nd | 2nd |
| Titmus | 40 | 13 | 105 | 1 | | | | | 1st | 37 | 34 | 93 | – |
| Close | 10 | 2 | 31 | 0 | | | | | 2nd | 188 | 61 | 131 | – |
| Allen | 57 | 22 | 122 | 2 | 0·1 | 0 | 1 | 0 | 3rd | 239 | 67 | 160 | – |
| Dexter | 12 | 4 | 16 | 0 | | | | | 4th | 359 | 108 | 165 | – |
| | | | | | | | | | 5th | 398 | 181 | 186 | – |
| WEST INDIES | | | | | | | | | 6th | 479 | 190 | 231 | – |
| Hall | 17 | 4 | 51 | 3 | 14 | 0 | 39 | 0 | 7th | – | 192 | 254 | – |
| Griffith | 21 | 4 | 37 | 0 | 8·5 | 4 | 11 | 1 | 8th | – | 202 | 256 | – |
| Gibbs | 29·3 | 9 | 59 | 5 | 46 | 16 | 98 | 6 | 9th | – | 202 | 268 | – |
| Sobers | 22 | 11 | 34 | 2 | 37 | 4 | 122 | 2 | 10th | – | 205 | 296 | – |
| Worrell | 1 | 0 | 12 | 0 | 4 | 2 | 11 | 1 | | | | | |

Umpires: C.S. Elliott and J.G. Langridge.

# ENGLAND v WEST INDIES 1963 (2nd Test)

Played at Lord's, London, on 20, 21, 22, 24, 25 June.
Toss: West Indies.　Result: MATCH DRAWN.
Debuts: Nil.

This was one of the most dramatic of cricket matches with any of the four results possible as the last ball was being bowled. England needed six runs to win with their last pair together as Allen played Hall's final ball defensively to draw the match. His partner, Cowdrey, had his fractured left arm in plaster and intended to bat left-handed, but using only his right arm, had he been called upon to face the bowling. Hall bowled throughout the 200 minutes of play possible after rain had delayed the start of the last day. Shackleton ended West Indies' first innings by taking three wickets in four balls.

## WEST INDIES

| | | | | |
|---|---|---|---|---|
| C.C. Hunte | c Close b Trueman | 44 | c Cowdrey b Shackleton | 7 |
| E.D.A. St J. McMorris | lbw b Trueman | 16 | c Cowdrey b Trueman | 8 |
| G. St A. Sobers | c Cowdrey b Allen | 42 | (5) c Parks b Trueman | 8 |
| R.B. Kanhai | c Edrich b Trueman | 73 | (3) c Cowdrey b Shackleton | 21 |
| B.F. Butcher | c Barrington b Trueman | 14 | (4) lbw b Shackleton | 133 |
| J.S. Solomon | lbw b Shackleton | 56 | c Stewart b Allen | 5 |
| F.M.M. Worrell* | b Trueman | 0 | c Stewart b Trueman | 33 |
| D.L. Murray† | c Cowdrey b Trueman | 20 | c Parks b Trueman | 2 |
| W.W. Hall | not out | 25 | c Parks b Trueman | 2 |
| C.C. Griffith | c Cowdrey b Shackleton | 0 | b Shackleton | 1 |
| L.R. Gibbs | c Stewart b Shackleton | 0 | not out | 1 |
| Extras | (B 10, LB 1) | 11 | (B 5, LB 2, NB 1) | 8 |
| **Total** | | **301** | | **229** |

## ENGLAND

| | | | | |
|---|---|---|---|---|
| M.J. Stewart | c Kanhai b Griffith | 2 | c Solomon b Hall | 17 |
| J.H. Edrich | c Murray b Griffith | 0 | c Murray b Hall | 8 |
| E.R. Dexter* | lbw b Sobers | 70 | b Gibbs | 2 |
| K.F. Barrington | c Sobers b Worrell | 80 | c Murray b Griffith | 60 |
| M.C. Cowdrey | b Gibbs | 4 | not out | 19 |
| D.B. Close | c Murray b Griffith | 9 | c Murray b Griffith | 70 |
| J.M. Parks† | b Worrell | 35 | lbw b Griffith | 17 |
| F.J. Titmus | not out | 52 | c McMorris b Hall | 11 |
| F.S. Trueman | b Hall | 10 | c Murray b Hall | 0 |
| D.A. Allen | lbw b Griffith | 2 | not out | 4 |
| D. Shackleton | b Griffith | 8 | run out | 4 |
| Extras | (B 8, LB 8, NB 9) | 25 | (B 5, LB 8, NB 3) | 16 |
| **Total** | | **297** | (9 wickets) | **228** |

| ENGLAND | O | M | R | W | O | M | R | W | | FALL OF WICKETS | | | |
|---|---|---|---|---|---|---|---|---|---|---|---|---|---|
| Trueman | 44 | 16 | 100 | 6 | 26 | 9 | 52 | 5 | | WI | E | WI | E |
| Shackleton | 50·2 | 22 | 93 | 3 | 34 | 14 | 72 | 4 | *Wkt* | *1st* | *1st* | *2nd* | *2nd* |
| Dexter | 20 | 6 | 41 | 0 | | | | | 1st | 51 | 2 | 15 | 15 |
| Close | 9 | 3 | 21 | 0 | | | | | 2nd | 64 | 20 | 15 | 27 |
| Allen | 10 | 3 | 35 | 1 | 21 | 7 | 50 | 1 | 3rd | 127 | 102 | 64 | 31 |
| Titmus | | | | | 17 | 3 | 47 | 0 | 4th | 145 | 115 | 84 | 130 |
| | | | | | | | | | 5th | 219 | 151 | 104 | 158 |
| WEST INDIES | | | | | | | | | 6th | 219 | 206 | 214 | 203 |
| Hall | 18 | 2 | 65 | 1 | 40 | 9 | 93 | 4 | 7th | 263 | 235 | 224 | 203 |
| Griffith | 26 | 6 | 91 | 5 | 30 | 7 | 59 | 3 | 8th | 297 | 271 | 226 | 219 |
| Sobers | 18 | 4 | 45 | 1 | 4 | 1 | 4 | 0 | 9th | 297 | 274 | 228 | 228 |
| Gibbs | 27 | 9 | 59 | 1 | 17 | 7 | 56 | 1 | 10th | 301 | 297 | 229 | – |
| Worrell | 13 | 6 | 12 | 2 | | | | | | | | | |

Umpires: J.S. Buller and W.E. Phillipson.

# ENGLAND v WEST INDIES 1963 (3rd Test)

Played at Edgbaston, Birmingham, on 4, 5, 6, 8, 9 July.
Toss: England.   Result: ENGLAND won by 217 runs.
Debuts: England – P.J. Sharpe.

Rain curtailed play on each of the first three days. England's victory maintained their unbeaten run at Edgbaston. Trueman's match analysis of 12 for 119 remains the best by any bowler in a Birmingham Test. His last six wickets were taken in a 24-ball spell which cost him just one scoring stroke for four runs by Gibbs.

## ENGLAND

| | | | | | |
|---|---|---|---|---|---|
| P.E. Richardson | b Hall | 2 | | c Murray b Griffith | 14 |
| M.J. Stewart | lbw b Sobers | 39 | | c Murray b Griffith | 27 |
| E.R. Dexter* | b Sobers | 29 | (5) | st Murray b Gibbs | 57 |
| K.F. Barrington | b Sobers | 9 | (3) | b Sobers | 1 |
| D.B. Close | lbw b Sobers | 55 | (4) | c Sobers b Griffith | 13 |
| P.J. Sharpe | c Kanhai b Gibbs | 23 | | not out | 85 |
| J.M. Parks† | c Murray b Sobers | 12 | | c Sobers b Gibbs | 5 |
| F.J. Titmus | c Griffith b Hall | 27 | | b Gibbs | 0 |
| F.S. Trueman | b Griffith | 4 | | c Gibbs b Sobers | 1 |
| G.A.R. Lock | b Griffith | 1 | | b Gibbs | 56 |
| D. Shackleton | not out | 6 | | | |
| Extras | (LB 6, NB 3) | 9 | | (B 9, LB 9, NB 1) | 19 |
| **Total** | | **216** | | (9 wickets declared) | **278** |

## WEST INDIES

| | | | | | |
|---|---|---|---|---|---|
| C.C. Hunte | b Trueman | 18 | | c Barrington b Trueman | 5 |
| M.C. Carew | c and b Trueman | 40 | | lbw b Shackleton | 1 |
| R.B. Kanhai | c Lock b Shackleton | 32 | | c Lock b Trueman | 38 |
| B.F. Butcher | lbw b Dexter | 15 | | b Dexter | 14 |
| J.S. Solomon | lbw b Dexter | 0 | (6) | c Parks b Trueman | 14 |
| G. St A. Sobers | b Trueman | 19 | (5) | c Sharpe b Shackleton | 9 |
| F.M.M. Worrell* | b Dexter | 1 | | c Parks b Trueman | 0 |
| D.L. Murray† | not out | 20 | | c Parks b Trueman | 3 |
| W.W. Hall | c Sharpe b Dexter | 28 | | b Trueman | 0 |
| C.C. Griffith | lbw b Trueman | 5 | | lbw b Trueman | 0 |
| L.R. Gibbs | b Trueman | 0 | | not out | 4 |
| Extras | (LB 7, W 1) | 8 | | (LB 2, W 1) | 3 |
| **Total** | | **186** | | | **91** |

| WEST INDIES | O | M | R | W | O | M | R | W | | FALL OF WICKETS | | | |
|---|---|---|---|---|---|---|---|---|---|---|---|---|---|
| Hall | 16·4 | 2 | 56 | 2 | 16 | 1 | 47 | 0 | | E | WI | E | WI |
| Griffith | 21 | 5 | 48 | 2 | 28 | 7 | 55 | 3 | *Wkt* | *1st* | *1st* | *2nd* | *2nd* |
| Sobers | 31 | 10 | 60 | 5 | 27 | 4 | 80 | 2 | 1st | 2 | 42 | 30 | 2 |
| Worrell | 14 | 5 | 15 | 0 | 8 | 3 | 28 | 0 | 2nd | 50 | 79 | 31 | 10 |
| Gibbs | 16 | 7 | 28 | 1 | 26·2 | 4 | 49 | 4 | 3rd | 72 | 108 | 60 | 38 |
| | | | | | | | | | 4th | 89 | 109 | 69 | 64 |
| ENGLAND | | | | | | | | | 5th | 129 | 128 | 170 | 78 |
| Trueman | 26 | 5 | 75 | 5 | 14·3 | 2 | 44 | 7 | 6th | 172 | 130 | 184 | 80 |
| Shackleton | 21 | 9 | 60 | 1 | 17 | 4 | 37 | 2 | 7th | 187 | 130 | 184 | 86 |
| Lock | 2 | 1 | 5 | 0 | | | | | 8th | 194 | 178 | 189 | 86 |
| Dexter | 20 | 5 | 38 | 4 | 3 | 1 | 7 | 1 | 9th | 200 | 186 | 278 | 86 |
| | | | | | | | | | 10th | 216 | 186 | – | 91 |

Umpires: C.S. Elliott and L.H. Gray.

## ENGLAND v WEST INDIES 1963 (4th Test)

Played at Headingley, Leeds, on 25, 26, 27, 29 July.
Toss: West Indies.   Result: WEST INDIES won by 221 runs.
Debuts: England – J.B. Bolus.

West Indies gained their first Test victory at Headingley at 2.30 p.m. on the fourth day.

### WEST INDIES

| | | | | | |
|---|---|---|---|---|---|
| C.C. Hunte | c Parks b Trueman | 22 | | b Trueman | 4 |
| E.D.A. St J. McMorris | c Barrington b Shackleton | 11 | | lbw b Trueman | 1 |
| R.B. Kanhai | b Lock | 92 | | lbw b Shackleton | 44 |
| B.F. Butcher | c Parks b Dexter | 23 | | c Dexter b Shackleton | 78 |
| G. St A. Sobers | c and b Lock | 102 | | c Sharpe b Titmus | 52 |
| J.S. Solomon | c Stewart b Trueman | 62 | | c Titmus b Shackleton | 16 |
| D.L. Murray† | lbw b Titmus | 34 | (8) | c Lock b Titmus | 2 |
| F.M.M. Worrell* | c Close b Lock | 25 | (7) | c Parks b Titmus | 0 |
| W.W. Hall | c Shackleton b Trueman | 15 | | c Trueman b Titmus | 7 |
| C.C. Griffith | c Stewart b Trueman | 1 | | not out | 12 |
| L.R. Gibbs | not out | 0 | | c Sharpe b Lock | 6 |
| Extras | (B 4, LB 5, W 1) | 10 | | (LB 7) | 7 |
| **Total** | | **397** | | | **229** |

### ENGLAND

| | | | | | |
|---|---|---|---|---|---|
| M.J. Stewart | c Gibbs b Griffith | 2 | | b Sobers | 0 |
| J.B. Bolus | c Hunte b Hall | 14 | | c Gibbs b Sobers | 43 |
| E.R. Dexter* | b Griffith | 8 | | lbw b Griffith | 10 |
| K.F. Barrington | c Worrell b Gibbs | 25 | | lbw b Sobers | 32 |
| D.B. Close | b Griffith | 0 | | c Solomon b Griffith | 56 |
| P.J. Sharpe | c Kanhai b Griffith | 0 | | c Kanhai b Gibbs | 13 |
| J.M. Parks† | c Gibbs b Griffith | 22 | | lbw b Gibbs | 57 |
| F.J. Titmus | lbw b Gibbs | 33 | | st Murray b Gibbs | 5 |
| F.S. Trueman | c Hall b Gibbs | 4 | | c Griffith b Gibbs | 5 |
| G.A.R. Lock | b Griffith | 53 | | c Murray b Griffith | 1 |
| D. Shackleton | not out | 1 | | not out | 1 |
| Extras | (B 4, LB 6, NB 2) | 12 | | (B 3, LB 5) | 8 |
| **Total** | | **174** | | | **231** |

| ENGLAND | O | M | R | W | O | M | R | W |
|---|---|---|---|---|---|---|---|---|
| Trueman | 46 | 10 | 117 | 4 | 13 | 1 | 46 | 2 |
| Shackleton | 42 | 10 | 88 | 1 | 26 | 2 | 63 | 3 |
| Dexter | 23 | 4 | 68 | 1 | 2 | 0 | 15 | 0 |
| Titmus | 25 | 5 | 60 | 1 | 19 | 2 | 44 | 4 |
| Lock | 28·4 | 9 | 54 | 3 | 7·1 | 0 | 54 | 1 |
| WEST INDIES | | | | | | | | |
| Hall | 13 | 2 | 61 | 1 | 5 | 1 | 12 | 0 |
| Griffith | 21 | 5 | 36 | 6 | 18 | 5 | 45 | 3 |
| Gibbs | 14 | 2 | 50 | 3 | 37·4 | 12 | 76 | 4 |
| Sobers | 6 | 1 | 15 | 0 | 32 | 5 | 90 | 3 |

### FALL OF WICKETS

| Wkt | WI 1st | E 1st | WI 2nd | E 2nd |
|---|---|---|---|---|
| 1st | 28 | 13 | 1 | 0 |
| 2nd | 42 | 19 | 20 | 23 |
| 3rd | 71 | 32 | 85 | 82 |
| 4th | 214 | 32 | 181 | 95 |
| 5th | 287 | 34 | 186 | 130 |
| 6th | 348 | 69 | 188 | 199 |
| 7th | 355 | 87 | 196 | 221 |
| 8th | 379 | 93 | 206 | 224 |
| 9th | 389 | 172 | 212 | 225 |
| 10th | 397 | 174 | 229 | 231 |

Umpires: W.E. Phillipson and J.G. Langridge.

# ENGLAND v WEST INDIES 1963 (5th Test)

Played at Kennington Oval, London, 22, 23, 24, 26 August.
Toss: England.    Result: WEST INDIES won by eight wickets.
Debuts: Nil.

West Indies won the Wisden Trophy by three Tests to one. Although a bruised ankle bone limited his second-innings spell to one over, Trueman set a new record for this series by taking 34 wickets. Murray made 24 dismissals in his first Test rubber. Close kept wicket on the second morning.

## ENGLAND

| | | | | |
|---|---|---|---|---|
| J.B. Bolus | c Murray b Sobers | 33 | c Gibbs b Sobers | 15 |
| J.H. Edrich | c Murray b Sobers | 25 | c Murray b Griffith | 12 |
| E.R. Dexter* | c and b Griffith | 29 | c Murray b Sobers | 27 |
| K.F. Barrington | c Sobers b Gibbs | 16 | b Griffith | 28 |
| D.B. Close | b Griffith | 46 | lbw b Sobers | 4 |
| P.J. Sharpe | c Murray b Griffith | 63 | c Murray b Hall | 83 |
| J.M. Parks† | c Kanhai b Griffith | 19 | lbw b Griffith | 23 |
| F.S. Trueman | b Griffith | 19 | c Sobers b Hall | 5 |
| G.A.R. Lock | hit wkt b Griffith | 4 | b Hall | 0 |
| J.B. Statham | b Hall | 8 | b Hall | 14 |
| D. Shackleton | not out | 0 | not out | 0 |
| Extras | (B 4, LB 2, NB 7) | 13 | (B 5, LB 3, NB 4) | 12 |
| **Total** | | **275** | | **223** |

## WEST INDIES

| | | | | |
|---|---|---|---|---|
| C.C. Hunte | c Parks b Shackleton | 80 | not out | 108 |
| W.V. Rodriguez | c Lock b Statham | 5 | c Lock b Dexter | 28 |
| R.B. Kanhai | b Lock | 30 | c Bolus b Lock | 77 |
| B.F. Butcher | run out | 53 | not out | 31 |
| G. St A. Sobers | run out | 26 | | |
| J.S. Solomon | c Trueman b Statham | 16 | | |
| F.M.M. Worrell* | b Statham | 9 | | |
| D.L. Murray† | c Lock b Trueman | 5 | | |
| W.W. Hall | b Trueman | 2 | | |
| C.C. Griffith | not out | 13 | | |
| L.R. Gibbs | b Trueman | 4 | | |
| Extras | (LB 3) | 3 | (B 4, LB 7) | 11 |
| **Total** | | **246** | (2 wickets) | **255** |

| WEST INDIES | O | M | R | W | O | M | R | W | | FALL OF WICKETS | | | |
|---|---|---|---|---|---|---|---|---|---|---|---|---|---|
| Hall | 22·2 | 2 | 71 | 1 | 16 | 3 | 39 | 4 | | E | WI | E | WI |
| Griffith | 27 | 4 | 71 | 6 | 23 | 7 | 66 | 3 | *Wkt* | *1st* | *1st* | *2nd* | *2nd* |
| Sobers | 21 | 4 | 44 | 2 | 33 | 6 | 77 | 3 | 1st | 59 | 10 | 29 | 78 |
| Gibbs | 27 | 7 | 50 | 1 | 9 | 1 | 29 | 0 | 2nd | 64 | 72 | 31 | 191 |
| Worrell | 5 | 0 | 26 | 0 | | | | | 3rd | 103 | 152 | 64 | – |
| | | | | | | | | | 4th | 115 | 185 | 69 | – |
| ENGLAND | | | | | | | | | 5th | 216 | 198 | 121 | – |
| Trueman | 26·1 | 2 | 65 | 3 | 1 | 1 | 0 | 0 | 6th | 224 | 214 | 173 | – |
| Statham | 22 | 3 | 68 | 3 | 22 | 2 | 54 | 0 | 7th | 254 | 221 | 196 | – |
| Shackleton | 21 | 5 | 37 | 1 | 32 | 7 | 68 | 0 | 8th | 258 | 225 | 196 | – |
| Lock | 29 | 6 | 65 | 1 | 25 | 8 | 52 | 1 | 9th | 275 | 233 | 218 | – |
| Dexter | 6 | 1 | 8 | 0 | 9 | 1 | 34 | 1 | 10th | 275 | 246 | 223 | – |
| Close | | | | | 6 | 0 | 36 | 0 | | | | | |

Umpires: J.S. Buller and A.E.G. Rhodes.

# AUSTRALIA v SOUTH AFRICA 1963–64 (1st Test)

Played at Woolloongabba, Brisbane, on 6, 7, 9 (*no play*), 10, 11 December.
Toss: Australia.   Result: MATCH DRAWN.
Debuts: Australia – A.N. Connolly. T.R. Veivers; South Africa – D.T. Lindsay, J.T. Partridge,
   D.B. Pithey, R.G. Pollock, M.A. Seymour, P.L. van der Merwe.

Torrential rain ended play soon after lunch on the last day. Meckiff announced his retirement from all classes of
cricket after being no-balled for throwing four times in his only over by umpire Egar. Barlow remains the only
South African to score a hundred in his first Test against Australia.

## AUSTRALIA

| | | | | | |
|---|---|---|---|---|---|
| W.M. Lawry | c R.G. Pollock b Barlow | 43 | not out | | 87 |
| R.B. Simpson | c Waite b P.M. Pollock | 12 | c sub (K.C. Bland) b Partridge | | 34 |
| N.C. O'Neill | c Barlow b P.M. Pollock | 82 | not out | | 19 |
| P.J.P. Burge | run out | 13 | | | |
| B.C. Booth | c Barlow b P.M. Pollock | 169 | | | |
| R. Benaud* | lbw b Goddard | 43 | | | |
| G.D. McKenzie | c P.M. Pollock b Goddard | 39 | | | |
| T.R. Veivers | c Goddard b P.M. Pollock | 14 | | | |
| A.T.W. Grout† | c Seymour b P.M. Pollock | 6 | | | |
| I. Meckiff | b P.M. Pollock | 7 | | | |
| A.N. Connolly | not out | 1 | | | |
| Extras | (B 1, LB 5) | 6 | (LB 4) | | 4 |
| **Total** | | **435** | (1 wicket declared) | | **144** |

## SOUTH AFRICA

| | | | | | |
|---|---|---|---|---|---|
| T.L.Goddard* | c Meckiff b Benaud | 52 | not out | | 8 |
| E.J. Barlow | b Benaud | 114 | c Simpson b McKenzie | | 0 |
| P.R. Carlstein | c and b Benaud | 0 | not out | | 1 |
| R.G. Pollock | b McKenzie | 25 | | | |
| D.T. Lindsay | lbw b Benaud | 17 | | | |
| J.H.B. Waite† | lbw b Connolly | 66 | | | |
| P.L. van der Merwe | b O'Neill | 17 | | | |
| D.B. Pithey | c Meckiff b Veivers | 18 | | | |
| P.M. Pollock | lbw b Benaud | 8 | | | |
| M.A. Seymour | b Simpson | 10 | | | |
| J.T. Partridge | not out | 3 | | | |
| Extras | (B 3, LB 5, NB 8) | 16 | (B 4) | | 4 |
| **Total** | | **346** | (1 wicket) | | **13** |

| SOUTH AFRICA | O | M | R | W | O | M | R | W | | FALL OF WICKETS | | | |
|---|---|---|---|---|---|---|---|---|---|---|---|---|---|
| | | | | | | | | | | A | SA | A | SA |
| P.M. Pollock | 22·6 | 0 | 95 | 6 | 6 | 0 | 26 | 0 | Wkt | 1st | 1st | 2nd | 2nd |
| Partridge | 25 | 3 | 87 | 0 | 17 | 1 | 50 | 1 | 1st | 39 | 74 | 83 | 1 |
| Goddard | 24 | 6 | 52 | 2 | 7 | 0 | 34 | 0 | 2nd | 73 | 78 | – | – |
| Barlow | 9 | 0 | 71 | 1 | | | | | 3rd | 88 | 120 | – | – |
| Seymour | 11 | 0 | 39 | 0 | | | | | 4th | 208 | 157 | – | – |
| Pithey | 23 | 6 | 85 | 0 | 5 | 0 | 30 | 0 | 5th | 310 | 239 | – | – |
| AUSTRALIA | | | | | | | | | 6th | 394 | 272 | – | – |
| McKenzie | 23 | 1 | 88 | 1 | 3·3 | 1 | 3 | 1 | 7th | 415 | 321 | -- | – |
| Meckiff | 1 | 0 | 8 | 0 | | | | | 8th | 427 | 325 | – | – |
| Connolly | 19 | 4 | 46 | 1 | 1 | 0 | 2 | 0 | 9th | 434 | 335 | – | – |
| Veivers | 34 | 15 | 48 | 1 | | | | | 10th | 435 | 346 | – | – |
| Benaud | 33 | 10 | 68 | 5 | 2 | 1 | .4 | 0 | | | | | |
| Simpson | 18·5 | 5 | 52 | 1 | | | | | | | | | |
| O'Neill | 7 | 0 | 20 | 1 | | | | | | | | | |

Umpires: C.J. Egar and L.P. Rowan.

# AUSTRALIA v SOUTH AFRICA 1963–64 (2nd Test)

Played at Melbourne Cricket Ground on 1, 2, 3, 4, 6 January.
Toss: Australia.    Result: AUSTRALIA won by eight wickets.
Debuts: Australia – I.R. Redpath.

Simpson, in his first Test as captain, put South Africa in to bat and made the winning hit on the morning of the fifth day. Barlow became the only South African to score hundreds in his first two Tests against Australia. Lawry and Redpath recorded Australia's highest opening partnership (219) in any home Test. It was beaten by Lawry and Simpson when they scored 244 against England in 1965-66 (*Test No. 600*). South Africa provided the third instance of a side playing two pairs of brothers in the same Test (also *Test Nos. 134 and 232*). Injuries prevented P.M. Pollock and Seymour from bowling in the second innings.

## SOUTH AFRICA

| | | | | | |
|---|---|---|---|---|---|
| T.L. Goddard* | c Grout b McKenzie | 17 | lbw b Hawke | | 8 |
| E.J. Barlow | c Connolly b McKenzie | 109 | run out | | 54 |
| A.J. Pithey | lbw b Connolly | 21 | c Grout b Connolly | | 76 |
| R.G. Pollock | c Simpson b McKenzie | 16 | c Martin b Connolly | | 2 |
| J.H.B. Waite† | c Grout b Hawke | 14 | b McKenzie | | 77 |
| P.L. van der Merwe | st Grout b Martin | 14 | c Grout b Martin | | 31 |
| K.C. Bland | run out | 50 | c and b Martin | | 22 |
| D.B. Pithey | c Grout b McKenzie | 0 | c Martin b Hawke | | 4 |
| P.M. Pollock | c Simpson b Martin | 14 | (10) b Hawke | | 0 |
| M.A. Seymour | not out | 7 | (11) not out | | 11 |
| J.T. Partridge | run out | 9 | (9) b McKenzie | | 12 |
| Extras | (LB 3) | 3 | (B 2, LB 3, W 2, NB 2) | | 9 |
| **Total** | | **274** | | | **306** |

## AUSTRALIA

| | | | | | |
|---|---|---|---|---|---|
| W.M. Lawry | c sub (P.R. Carlstein) b Partridge | 157 | b Partridge | | 20 |
| I.R. Redpath | b Partridge | 97 | c Van der Merwe b Barlow | | 25 |
| R.B. Simpson* | b P.M. Pollock | 0 | not out | | 55 |
| P.J.P. Burge | c Bland b P.M. Pollock | 23 | not out | | 26 |
| B.K. Shepherd | c D.B. Pithey b Barlow | 96 | | | |
| A.T.W. Grout† | c Waite b P.M. Pollock | 3 | | | |
| T.R. Veivers | c Waite b Partridge | 19 | | | |
| G.D. McKenzie | c Partridge b Seymour | 2 | | | |
| N.J.N. Hawke | b Barlow | 24 | | | |
| J.W. Martin | c D.B. Pithey b Partridge | 17 | | | |
| A.N. Connolly | not out | 0 | | | |
| Extras | (B 1, LB 2, NB 6) | 9 | (B 5, LB 2, W 1, NB 2) | | 10 |
| **Total** | | **447** | (2 wickets) | | **136** |

| AUSTRALIA | O | M | R | W | O | M | R | W |
|---|---|---|---|---|---|---|---|---|
| McKenzie | 19 | 1 | 82 | 4 | 25 | 1 | 81 | 2 |
| Hawke | 20 | 2 | 77 | 1 | 19 | 1 | 53 | 3 |
| Connolly | 18 | 2 | 62 | 1 | 18 | 2 | 49 | 2 |
| Martin | 16 | 3 | 44 | 2 | 27 | 4 | 83 | 2 |
| Veivers | 5 | 1 | 6 | 0 | | | | |
| Simpson | | | | | 12 | 2 | 31 | 0 |
| SOUTH AFRICA | | | | | | | | |
| P.M. Pollock | 20·5 | 1 | 98 | 3 | | | | |
| Partridge | 34 | 4 | 108 | 4 | 17 | 1 | 49 | 1 |
| Bland | 11 | 2 | 35 | 0 | 2 | 0 | 6 | 0 |
| Goddard | 21 | 2 | 70 | 0 | 1 | 1 | 0 | 0 |
| D.B. Pithey | 5 | 1 | 20 | 0 | 6 | 0 | 18 | 0 |
| Seymour | 19 | 2 | 56 | 1 | | | | |
| Barlow | 7 ·6 | 0 | 51 | 2 | 11 | 0 | 49 | 1 |
| Van der Merwe | | | | | 0·1 | 0 | 4 | 0 |

## FALL OF WICKETS

| Wkt | SA 1st | A 1st | SA 2nd | A 2nd |
|---|---|---|---|---|
| 1st | 26 | 219 | 35 | 33 |
| 2nd | 74 | 222 | 83 | 75 |
| 3rd | 100 | 270 | 85 | – |
| 4th | 129 | 291 | 213 | – |
| 5th | 179 | 301 | 233 | – |
| 6th | 201 | 340 | 273 | – |
| 7th | 201 | 357 | 282 | – |
| 8th | 256 | 413 | 282 | – |
| 9th | 256 | 439 | 282 | – |
| 10th | 274 | 447 | 306 | – |

Umpires: C.J. Egar and L.P. Rowan.

# AUSTRALIA v SOUTH AFRICA 1963–64 (3rd Test)

Played at Sydney Cricket Ground on 10, 11, 13, 14, 15 January.
Toss: Australia.   Result: MATCH DRAWN.
Debuts: South Africa – C.G. Halse.

Australia set South Africa to score 409 runs in 430 minutes. Australia's partnership of 160 between Benaud and McKenzie remains their highest for the seventh wicket against South Africa. R.G. Pollock, aged 19 years 318 days, became the youngest South African to score a hundred in Test cricket – a record he still holds.

## AUSTRALIA

| | | | | |
|---|---|---:|---|---:|
| R.B. Simpson* | c Goddard b P.M. Pollock | 58 | lbw b Halse | 31 |
| W.M. Lawry | b Partridge | 23 | c R.G. Pollock b Goddard | 89 |
| N.C. O'Neill | c Goddard b Halse | 3 | c Barlow b Partridge | 88 |
| P.J.P. Burge | b Partridge | 36 | c Waite b P.M. Pollock | 13 |
| B.C. Booth | b Partridge | 75 | b Partridge | 16 |
| B.K. Shepherd | c Waite b P.M. Pollock | 0 | c Waite b Partridge | 11 |
| R. Benaud | c Bland b P.M. Pollock | 43 | c D.B. Pithey b P.M. Pollock | 90 |
| G.D. McKenzie | c Goddard b Partridge | 3 | c Van der Merwe b Partridge | 76 |
| N.J.N. Hawke | c Goddard b P.M. Pollock | 2 | not out | 6 |
| A.T.W. Grout† | c Partridge b P.M. Pollock | 1 | c Bland b Partridge | 8 |
| A.N. Connolly | not out | 3 | | |
| Extras | (B 5, LB 6, W 1, NB 1) | 13 | (B 8, LB 8, W 1, NB 5) | 22 |
| **Total** | | **260** | (9 wickets declared) | **450** |

## SOUTH AFRICA

| | | | | |
|---|---|---:|---|---:|
| T.L. Goddard* | c Connolly b Benaud | 80 | lbw b Simpson | 84 |
| E.J. Barlow | c Grout b Connolly | 6 | c Simpson b Hawke | 35 |
| A.J. Pithey | c Grout b Hawke | 9 | (6) not out | 53 |
| R.G. Pollock | c McKenzie b Connolly | 122 | c Grout b Hawke | 42 |
| J.H.B. Waite† | b McKenzie | 8 | | |
| P.L. van der Merwe | b McKenzie | 0 | (7) not out | 13 |
| K.C. Bland | c McKenzie b Benaud | 51 | (5) c Benaud b O'Neill | 85 |
| D.B. Pithey | c Lawry b Benaud | 10 | (3) b McKenzie | 7 |
| P.M. Pollock | c Grout b Hawke | 1 | | |
| J.T. Partridge | b McKenzie | 7 | | |
| C.G. Halse | not out | 1 | | |
| Extras | (B 3, LB 4) | 7 | (B 2, LB 5) | 7 |
| **Total** | | **302** | (5 wickets) | **326** |

| SOUTH AFRICA | O | M | R | W | O | M | R | W |
|---|---:|---:|---:|---:|---:|---:|---:|---:|
| P.M. Pollock | 18 | 2 | 83 | 5 | 24 | 0 | 129 | 2 |
| Partridge | 19·6 | 2 | 88 | 4 | 32·5 | 4 | 123 | 5 |
| Goddard | 10 | 1 | 24 | 0 | 11 | 3 | 20 | 1 |
| Halse | 11 | 1 | 36 | 1 | 15 | 2 | 58 | 1 |
| Bland | 2 | 0 | 7 | 0 | 1 | 0 | 7 | 0 |
| Barlow | 2 | 0 | 9 | 0 | 1 | 0 | 5 | 0 |
| D.B. Pithey | | | | | 16 | 1 | 86 | 0 |
| **AUSTRALIA** | | | | | | | | |
| McKenzie | 19 | 2 | 70 | 3 | 14 | 2 | 61 | 1 |
| Connolly | 19 | 2 | 66 | 2 | 13 | 0 | 41 | 0 |
| Hawke | 18 | 1 | 56 | 2 | 19 | 5 | 43 | 2 |
| Simpson | 9 | 2 | 32 | 0 | 23 | 8 | 48 | 1 |
| Benaud | 24·1 | 4 | 55 | 3 | 30 | 8 | 61 | 0 |
| O'Neill | 3 | 0 | 16 | 0 | 16 | 1 | 59 | 1 |
| Booth | | | | | 1 | 0 | 3 | 0 |
| Shepherd | | | | | 1 | 0 | 3 | 0 |

### FALL OF WICKETS

| Wkt | A 1st | SA 1st | A 2nd | SA 2nd |
|---|---:|---:|---:|---:|
| 1st | 59 | 10 | 58 | 57 |
| 2nd | 66 | 58 | 198 | 67 |
| 3rd | 108 | 137 | 235 | 141 |
| 4th | 128 | 162 | 235 | 201 |
| 5th | 129 | 162 | 259 | 291 |
| 6th | 229 | 244 | 264 | – |
| 7th | 238 | 277 | 424 | – |
| 8th | 248 | 278 | 436 | – |
| 9th | 256 | 300 | 450 | – |
| 10th | 260 | 302 | – | – |

Umpires: C.J. Egar and L.P. Rowan.

# AUSTRALIA v SOUTH AFRICA 1963–64 (4th Test)

Played at Adelaide Oval on 24, 25, 27, 28, 29 January.
Toss: Australia.    Result: SOUTH AFRICA won by ten wickets.
Debuts: Nil.

South Africa completed an emphatic victory before lunch on the fifth day after scoring their highest total against Australia so far; it remains their highest in Australia. Barlow became the third South African after G.A. Faulkner and A.D. Nourse to score a double-century against Australia. His third-wicket partnership of 341 with R.G. Pollock remains South Africa's highest for any wicket in all Test cricket. Grout beat W.A.S. Oldfield's Australian Test record of 130 dismissals when he caught Pithey.

## AUSTRALIA

| Batsman | Dismissal | Score | 2nd Dismissal | 2nd Score |
|---|---|---|---|---|
| R.B. Simpson* | b Goddard | 78 | c Lindsay b Halse | 34 |
| W.M. Lawry | c Partridge b P.M. Pollock | 14 | c Goddard b P.M. Pollock | 38 |
| N.C. O'Neill | c Goddard b P.M. Pollock | 0 | c Partridge b Halse | 66 |
| P.J.P. Burge | c Halse b P.M. Pollock | 91 | run out | 20 |
| B.C. Booth | c Lindsay b Goddard | 58 | lbw b P.M. Pollock | 24 |
| B.K. Shepherd | lbw b Goddard | 70 | c Lindsay b Barlow | 78 |
| R. Benaud | b Partridge | 7 | b Barlow | 34 |
| G.D. McKenzie | c Lindsay b Goddard | 12 | c and b Barlow | 4 |
| A.T.W. Grout† | c P.M. Pollock b Goddard | 0 | (10) c Pithey b Halse | 23 |
| N.J.N. Hawke | not out | 0 | (9) c Carlstein b Seymour | 0 |
| R.A. Gaunt | run out | 1 | not out | 2 |
| Extras | (B 1, LB 8, NB 5) | 14 | (LB 4, W 1, NB 3) | 8 |
| **Total** | | **345** | | **331** |

## SOUTH AFRICA

| Batsman | Dismissal | Score | 2nd Dismissal | 2nd Score |
|---|---|---|---|---|
| T.L. Goddard* | b Hawke | 34 | not out | 34 |
| E.J. Barlow | lbw b Hawke | 201 | not out | 47 |
| A.J. Pithey | c Grout b Hawke | 0 | | |
| R.G. Pollock | b Hawke | 175 | | |
| K.C. Bland | c Grout b Gaunt | 33 | | |
| P.R. Carlstein | c Benaud b Gaunt | 37 | | |
| D.T. Lindsay† | b Simpson | 41 | | |
| P.M. Pollock | c Benaud b Hawke | 21 | | |
| M.A. Seymour | c Simpson b Hawke | 3 | | |
| J.T. Partridge | b McKenzie | 6 | | |
| C.G. Halse | not out | 19 | | |
| Extras | (B 7, LB 8, W 3, NB 7) | 25 | (W 1) | 1 |
| **Total** | | **595** | (0 wickets) | **82** |

| SOUTH AFRICA | O | M | R | W | O | M | R | W |
|---|---|---|---|---|---|---|---|---|
| P.M. Pollock | 21 | 1 | 96 | 3 | 14 | 1 | 73 | 2 |
| Partridge | 22 | 4 | 76 | 1 | 17 | 3 | 76 | 0 |
| Halse | 13 | 1 | 54 | 0 | 13·3 | 0 | 50 | 3 |
| Goddard | 24·6 | 4 | 60 | 5 | 21 | 3 | 64 | 0 |
| Seymour | 12 | 2 | 38 | 0 | 19 | 1 | 54 | 1 |
| Bland | 1 | 0 | 7 | 0 | | | | |
| Barlow | | | | | 5 | 2 | 6 | 3 |
| **AUSTRALIA** | | | | | | | | |
| Gaunt | 24 | 2 | 115 | 2 | 4 | 0 | 22 | 0 |
| McKenzie | 30·1 | 2 | 156 | 1 | 4 | 0 | 22 | 0 |
| Hawke | 39 | 5 | 139 | 6 | 6 | 0 | 20 | 0 |
| Benaud | 20 | 1 | 101 | 0 | 3 | 1 | 17 | 0 |
| Simpson | 10 | 1 | 59 | 1 | | | | |

### FALL OF WICKETS

| Wkt | A 1st | SA 1st | A 2nd | SA 2nd |
|---|---|---|---|---|
| 1st | 35 | 70 | 72 | – |
| 2nd | 37 | 70 | 81 | – |
| 3rd | 141 | 411 | 125 | – |
| 4th | 225 | 437 | 178 | – |
| 5th | 279 | 500 | 210 | – |
| 6th | 290 | 501 | 301 | – |
| 7th | 333 | 559 | 301 | – |
| 8th | 333 | 568 | 302 | – |
| 9th | 344 | 575 | 310 | – |
| 10th | 345 | 595 | 331 | – |

Umpires: C.J. Egar and L.P. Rowan.

# AUSTRALIA v SOUTH AFRICA 1963–64 (5th Test)

Played at Sydney Cricket Ground on 7, 8, 10, 11, 12 February.
Toss: South Africa.    Result: MATCH DRAWN.
Debuts: Nil.

South Africa were left to score 171 runs in 85 minutes to win the rubber after Veivers and Hawke had frustrated them with a last-wicket partnership of 45 in 75 minutes.

## AUSTRALIA

| | | | | | |
|---|---|---|---|---|---|
| W.M. Lawry | b Halse | 13 | | c Waite b P.M. Pollock | 12 |
| R.B. Simpson* | c Lindsay b Partridge | 28 | | lbw b Partridge | 31 |
| N.C. O'Neill | b P.M. Pollock | 21 | (7) | b P.M. Pollock | 6 |
| P.J.P. Burge | b Partridge | 56 | | c Partridge b Seymour | 39 |
| B.C. Booth | not out | 102 | (3) | c sub (P.R. Carlstein) b Seymour | 87 |
| B.K. Shepherd | lbw b Partridge | 1 | | c Bland b Goddard | 12 |
| R. Benaud | b Goddard | 11 | (5) | c sub (P.R. Carlstein) b Seymour | 3 |
| T.R. Veivers | b Partridge | 43 | | c Barlow b Goddard | 39 |
| G.D. McKenzie | b Partridge | 0 | | c Bland b P.M. Pollock | 0 |
| N.J.N. Hawke | c Lindsay b Partridge | 0 | (11) | not out | 16 |
| A.T.W. Grout† | c Waite b Partridge | 29 | (10) | c Barlow b Partridge | 14 |
| Extras | (LB 2, NB 5) | 7 | | (B 5, LB 4, NB 2) | 11 |
| **Total** | | **311** | | | **270** |

## SOUTH AFRICA

| | | | | | |
|---|---|---|---|---|---|
| T.L. Goddard* | c Grout b Veivers | 93 | | not out | 44 |
| E.J. Barlow | c Benaud b O'Neill | 5 | | not out | 32 |
| A.J. Pithey | c Grout b McKenzie | 49 | | | |
| R.G. Pollock | c and b Veivers | 17 | | | |
| K.C. Bland | c Booth b Benaud | 126 | | | |
| J.H.B. Waite† | c Simpson b McKenzie | 19 | | | |
| D.T. Lindsay | c sub (A.N. Connolly) b Benaud | 65 | | | |
| P.M. Pollock | c Lawry b Benaud | 6 | | | |
| M.A. Seymour | c Benaud b McKenzie | 0 | | | |
| J.T. Partridge | lbw b Benaud | 6 | | | |
| C.G. Halse | not out | 10 | | | |
| Extras | (B 4, LB 4, W 1, NB 6) | 15 | | | |
| **Total** | | **411** | | (0 wickets) | **76** |

| SOUTH AFRICA | O | M | R | W | O | M | R | W |
|---|---|---|---|---|---|---|---|---|
| P.M. Pollock | 22 | 5 | 75 | 1 | 11 | 1 | 35 | 3 |
| Partridge | 31·1 | 6 | 91 | 7 | 32 | 5 | 85 | 2 |
| Halse | 14 | 3 | 40 | 1 | 7 | 0 | 22 | 0 |
| Goddard | 16 | 1 | 67 | 1 | 24·7 | 10 | 29 | 2 |
| Barlow | 9 | 1 | 31 | 0 | 1 | 0 | 8 | 0 |
| Seymour | | | | | 38 | 9 | 80 | 3 |
| AUSTRALIA | | | | | | | | |
| McKenzie | 37 | 4 | 110 | 3 | 4 | 0 | 16 | 0 |
| Hawke | 22 | 4 | 69 | 0 | 4 | 0 | 16 | 0 |
| O'Neill | 2 | 0 | 2 | 1 | | | | |
| Benaud | 49 | 10 | 118 | 4 | 8 | 2 | 25 | 0 |
| Veivers | 35 | 5 | 97 | 2 | 8 | 0 | 19 | 0 |

FALL OF WICKETS

| | A | SA | A | SA |
|---|---|---|---|---|
| Wkt | 1st | 1st | 2nd | 2nd |
| 1st | 42 | 18 | 29 | – |
| 2nd | 44 | 142 | 49 | – |
| 3rd | 103 | 157 | 132 | – |
| 4th | 142 | 182 | 152 | – |
| 5th | 144 | 223 | 181 | – |
| 6th | 179 | 341 | 189 | – |
| 7th | 263 | 365 | 207 | – |
| 8th | 263 | 368 | 209 | – |
| 9th | 265 | 389 | 225 | – |
| 10th | 311 | 411 | 270 | – |

Umpires: C.J. Egar and L.P. Rowan.

# INDIA v ENGLAND 1963–64 (1st Test)

Played at Corporation Stadium, Madras, on 10, 11, 12, 14, 15 January.
Toss: India.   Result: MATCH DRAWN.
Debuts: England – D. Wilson.

England, set to score 29 runs in 265 minutes on a dusting pitch and with several players suffering from stomach indispositions, did well to finish 52 runs short of victory and with five wickets intact. Kunderan scored 170 not out off 91 overs in 330 minutes on the first day and went on to record India's highest score against England (subsequently beaten in this rubber). Nadkarni bowled 21 consecutive maiden overs to establish the record for all first-class cricket. His spell of 131 balls without conceding a run has been beaten only by H.J. Tayfield (137 balls, 16 eight-ball maidens) in *Test No. 436*.

## INDIA

| | | | | |
|---|---|---|---|---|
| V.L. Mehra | c Parks b Titmus | 17 | run out | 26 |
| B.K. Kunderan† | b Titmus | 192 | lbw b Titmus | 38 |
| D.N. Sardesai | b Titmus | 65 | (4) st Parks b Mortimore | 2 |
| V.L. Manjrekar | c Smith b Knight | 108 | (7) run out | 0 |
| Nawab of Pataudi, jr* | lbw b Titmus | 0 | (6) c Bolus b Titmus | 18 |
| S.A. Durani | lbw b Titmus | 8 | (5) c Parks b Mortimore | 3 |
| M.L. Jaisimha | lbw b Wilson | 51 | (3) b Titmus | 35 |
| A.G. Kripal Singh | not out | 2 | b Wilson | 10 |
| C.G. Borde | not out | 8 | not out | 11 |
| R.G. Nadkarni | ) did not bat | | c Parks b Titmus | 7 |
| V.B. Ranjane | ) | | | |
| Extras | (B 1, LB 5) | 6 | (LB 2) | 2 |
| **Total** | (7 wickets declared) | **457** | (9 wickets declared) | **152** |

## ENGLAND

| | | | | |
|---|---|---|---|---|
| J.B. Bolus | lbw b Durani | 88 | st Kunderan b Borde | 22 |
| M.J.K. Smith* | c Kunderan b Ranjane | 3 | c Kunderan b Nadkarni | 57 |
| P.J. Sharpe | lbw b Borde | 27 | (7) not out | 31 |
| D. Wilson | c Manjrekar b Durani | 42 | | |
| K.F. Barrington | c and b Borde | 80 | | |
| B.R. Knight | b Durani | 6 | (4) c Kunderan b Kripal Singh | 7 |
| J.M. Parks† | b Borde | 27 | (3) c Kunderan b Nadkarni | 30 |
| F.J. Titmus | c Pataudi b Kripal Singh | 14 | (6) b Kripal Singh | 10 |
| J.B. Mortimore | c and b Borde | 0 | (5) not out | 73 |
| M.J. Stewart | st Kunderan b Borde | 15 | | |
| J.D.F. Larter | not out | 2 | | |
| Extras | (B 6, LB 5, NB 2) | 13 | (B 6, LB 2, NB 3) | 11 |
| **Total** | | **317** | (5 wickets) | **241** |

| ENGLAND | O | M | R | W | O | M | R | W |
|---|---|---|---|---|---|---|---|---|
| Larter | 19 | 2 | 62 | 0 | 11 | 3 | 33 | 0 |
| Knight | 27 | 7 | 73 | 1 | 7 | 1 | 22 | 0 |
| Wilson | 24 | 6 | 67 | 1 | 4 | 2 | 2 | 1 |
| Titmus | 50 | 14 | 116 | 5 | 19·5 | 4 | 46 | 4 |
| Mortimore | 38 | 7 | 110 | 0 | 15 | 3 | 41 | 2 |
| Barrington | 4 | 0 | 23 | 0 | 2 | 0 | 6 | 0 |
| INDIA | | | | | | | | |
| Ranjane | 16 | 2 | 46 | 1 | 2 | 0 | 14 | 0 |
| Jaisimha | 7 | 3 | 16 | 0 | 4 | 2 | 8 | 0 |
| Borde | 67·4 | 30 | 88 | 5 | 22 | 7 | 44 | 1 |
| Durani | 43 | 13 | 97 | 3 | 21 | 8 | 64 | 0 |
| Nadkarni | 32 | 27 | 5 | 0 | 6 | 4 | 6 | 2 |
| Kripal Singh | 25 | 10 | 52 | 1 | 26 | 7 | 66 | 2 |
| Manjrekar | | | | | 3 | 0 | 3 | 0 |
| Mehra | | | | | 1 | 0 | 2 | 0 |
| Sardesai | | | | | 1 | 0 | 14 | 0 |
| Pataudi | | | | | 1 | 0 | 9 | 0 |

### FALL OF WICKETS

| | I | E | I | E |
|---|---|---|---|---|
| Wkt | 1st | 1st | 2nd | 2nd |
| 1st | 85 | 12 | 59 | 67 |
| 2nd | 228 | 49 | 77 | 105 |
| 3rd | 323 | 116 | 82 | 120 |
| 4th | 323 | 235 | 100 | 123 |
| 5th | 343 | 251 | 104 | 155 |
| 6th | 431 | 263 | 106 | – |
| 7th | 447 | 287 | 125 | – |
| 8th | – | 287 | 135 | – |
| 9th | – | 314 | 152 | – |
| 10th | – | 317 | – | – |

Umpires: I. Gopalakrishnan and S.K. Banerjee.

## INDIA v ENGLAND 1963–64 (2nd Test)

Played at Brabourne Stadium, Bombay, on 21, 22, 23, 25, 26 January.
Toss: India.   Result: MATCH DRAWN.
Debuts: India – B.S. Chandrasekhar, Rajinder Pal; England – J.G. Binks, I.J. Jones, J.S.E. Price.

A superb performance by England earned the touring team a draw after they had been deprived of the services of Barrington (fractured finger), Edrich, Sharpe and Mortimore (stomach disorders). Barrington and Stewart (who retired from the match with dysentery at tea on the first day) took no further part in the tour. England's ten-man team comprised two specialist batsmen, two wicket-keepers, four fast-medium bowlers and two spinners. The partnership of 153 by Borde and Durani remains the highest for the seventh wicket by either side in this series.

### INDIA

| | | | | | |
|---|---|---|---|---|---|
| V.L. Mehra | lbw b Knight | 9 | | lbw b Titmus | 35 |
| B.K. Kunderan† | c Wilson b Price | 29 | | c Titmus b Price | 16 |
| D.N. Sardesai | b Price | 12 | | run out | 66 |
| V.L. Manjrekar | c Binks b Titmus | 0 | (8) not out | 43 |
| Nawab of Pataudi, jr* | c Titmus b Knight | 10 | (4) b Price | 0 |
| M.L. Jaisimha | c Price b Titmus | 23 | (5) c Larter b Knight | 66 |
| C.G. Borde | c Binks b Wilson | 84 | | c Smith b Titmus | 7 |
| S.A. Durani | c Binks b Price | 90 | (6) c Knight b Titmus | 3 |
| R.G. Nadkarni | not out | 26 | | lbw b Knight | 0 |
| Rajinder Pal | lbw b Larter | 3 | | not out | 3 |
| B.S. Chandrasekhar | b Larter | 0 | | | |
| Extras | (B 2, LB 9, NB 3) | 14 | | (LB 4, W 1, NB 5) | 10 |
| **Total** | | **300** | | (8 wickets declared) | **249** |

### ENGLAND

| | | | | | |
|---|---|---|---|---|---|
| J.B. Bolus | c Chandrasekhar b Durani | 25 | | c Pataudi b Durani | 57 |
| M.J.K. Smith* | c Borde b Chandrasekhar | 46 | (4) not out | 31 |
| J.M. Parks | run out | 1 | (5) not out | 40 |
| B.R. Knight | b Chandrasekhar | 12 | | | |
| F.J. Titmus | not out | 84 | | | |
| D. Wilson | c and b Durani | 1 | (3) c Pataudi b Chandrasekhar | 2 |
| J.G. Binks† | b Chandrasekhar | 10 | (2) c Borde b Jaisimha | 55 |
| J.S.E. Price | b Chandrasekhar | 32 | | | |
| J.D.F. Larter | c Borde b Durani | 0 | | | |
| I.J. Jones | run out | 5 | | | |
| M.J. Stewart | absent ill | – | | | |
| Extras | (B 4, LB 7, NB 6 ) | 17 | | (B 12, LB 7, W 1, NB 1) | 21 |
| **Total** | | **233** | | (3 wickets) | **206** |

| ENGLAND | O | M | R | W | O | M | R | W | | FALL OF WICKETS | | | |
|---|---|---|---|---|---|---|---|---|---|---|---|---|---|
| Knight | 20 | 3 | 53 | 2 | 13 | 2 | 28 | 2 | | I | E | I | E |
| Larter | 10·3 | 2 | 35 | 2 | 5 | 0 | 13 | 0 | Wkt | 1st | 1st | 2nd | 2nd |
| Jones | 13 | 0 | 48 | 0 | 11 | 1 | 31 | 0 | 1st | 20 | 42 | 23 | 125 |
| Price | 19 | 2 | 66 | 3 | 17 | 1 | 47 | 2 | 2nd | 55 | 48 | 104 | 127 |
| Titmus | 36 | 17 | 56 | 2 | 46 | 18 | 79 | 3 | 3rd | 56 | 82 | 107 | 134 |
| Wilson | 15 | 5 | 28 | 1 | 23 | 10 | 41 | 0 | 4th | 58 | 91 | 140 | – |
| | | | | | | | | | 5th | 75 | 98 | 152 | – |
| INDIA | | | | | | | | | 6th | 99 | 116 | 180 | – |
| Rajinder Pal | 11 | 4 | 19 | 0 | 2 | 0 | 3 | 0 | 7th | 252 | 184 | 231 | – |
| Jaisimha | 3 | 1 | 9 | 0 | 22 | 9 | 36 | 1 | 8th | 284 | 185 | 231 | – |
| Durani | 38 | 15 | 59 | 3 | 29 | 12 | 35 | 1 | 9th | 300 | 233 | – | – |
| Borde | 34 | 12 | 54 | 0 | 37 | 12 | 38 | 0 | 10th | 300 | – | – | – |
| Chandrasekhar | 40 | 16 | 67 | 4 | 22 | 5 | 40 | 1 | | | | | |
| Nadkarni | 4 | 2 | 8 | 0 | 14 | 11 | 3 | 0 | | | | | |
| Sardesai | | | | | 3 | 2 | 6 | 0 | | | | | |
| Mehra | | | | | 2 | 1 | 1 | 0 | | | | | |
| Pataudi | | | | | 3 | 0 | 23 | 0 | | | | | |

Umpires: H.E. Choudhury and A.M. Mamsa.

# INDIA v ENGLAND 1963–64 (3rd Test)

Played at Eden Gardens, Calcutta, on 29, 30 January, 1, 2, 3 February.
Toss: India.   Result: MATCH DRAWN.
Debuts: Nil.

Reinforced by the arrival of Cowdrey and Parfitt, England achieved a first-innings lead of 26. India did not begin their second innings until the fourth day and the match never promised a definite result. 150 minutes of play was lost on the third day when the umpires decided that a shower of rain had rendered the ground unfit.

## INDIA

| | | | | |
|---|---|---|---|---|
| M.L. Jaisimha | c Binks b Price | 33 | c Larter b Titmus | 129 |
| B.K. Kunderan† | c Binks b Price | 23 | lbw b Wilson | 27 |
| D.N. Sardesai | c Binks b Larter | 54 | c and b Parfitt | 36 |
| V.L. Manjrekar | c and b Price | 25 | b Parfitt | 16 |
| R.F. Surti | b Price | 0 | | |
| C.G. Borde | c Cowdrey b Wilson | 21 | c Parks b Titmus | 8 |
| Nawab of Pataudi, jr* | c Binks b Wilson | 2 | (5) c Smith b Larter | 31 |
| S.A. Durani | c Binks b Price | 8 | (7) c Cowdrey b Larter | 25 |
| R.G. Nadkarni | not out | 43 | (8) not out | 10 |
| R.B. Desai | lbw b Titmus | 11 | (9) not out | 2 |
| B.S. Chandrasekhar | c Cowdrey b Knight | 16 | | |
| Extras | (LB 1, NB 4) | 5 | (B 7, LB 5, NB 4) | 16 |
| **Total** | | **241** | (7 wickets declared) | **300** |

## ENGLAND

| | | | | |
|---|---|---|---|---|
| J.B. Bolus | c and b Durani | 39 | c Jaisimha b Borde | 35 |
| J.G. Binks† | c Desai b Durani | 13 | b Durani | 13 |
| M.J.K. Smith* | c Jaisimha b Borde | 19 | not out | 75 |
| M.C. Cowdrey | c Pataudi b Desai | 107 | not out | 13 |
| J.M. Parks | lbw b Nadkarni | 30 | | |
| P.H. Parfitt | c and b Desai | 4 | | |
| D. Wilson | st Kunderan b Chandrasekhar | 1 | | |
| B.R. Knight | c Manjrekar b Nadkarni | 13 | | |
| F.J. Titmus | b Desai | 26 | | |
| J.S.E. Price | not out | 1 | | |
| J.D.F. Larter | c Manjrekar b Desai | 0 | | |
| Extras | (B 6, LB 5, NB 3) | 14 | (B 9) | 9 |
| **Total** | | **267** | (2 wickets) | **145** |

| ENGLAND | O | M | R | W | O | M | R | W |
|---|---|---|---|---|---|---|---|---|
| Knight | 13·2 | 5 | 39 | 1 | 4 | 0 | 33 | 0 |
| Price | 23 | 4 | 73 | 5 | 7 | 0 | 31 | 0 |
| Larter | 18 | 4 | 61 | 1 | 8 | 0 | 27 | 2 |
| Titmus | 15 | 4 | 46 | 1 | 46 | 23 | 67 | 2 |
| Wilson | 16 | 10 | 17 | 2 | 21 | 7 | 55 | 1 |
| Parfitt | | | | | 34 | 16 | 71 | 2 |

| INDIA | O | M | R | W | O | M | R | W |
|---|---|---|---|---|---|---|---|---|
| Desai | 22·5 | 3 | 62 | 4 | 5 | 0 | 12 | 0 |
| Surti | 6 | 2 | 8 | 0 | | | | |
| Jaisimha | 4 | 1 | 10 | 0 | 13 | 5 | 32 | 0 |
| Durani | 22 | 7 | 59 | 2 | 8 | 3 | 15 | 1 |
| Borde | 31 | 14 | 40 | 1 | 15 | 5 | 39 | 1 |
| Chandrasekhar | 21 | 5 | 36 | 1 | 8 | 2 | 20 | 0 |
| Nadkarni | 42 | 24 | 38 | 2 | | | | |
| Pataudi | | | | | 3 | 1 | 8 | 0 |
| Sardesai | | | | | 3 | 0 | 10 | 0 |

## FALL OF WICKETS

| | I | E | I | E |
|---|---|---|---|---|
| Wkt | 1st | 1st | 2nd | 2nd |
| 1st | 47 | 40 | 80 | 30 |
| 2nd | 61 | 74 | 161 | 87 |
| 3rd | 103 | 77 | 217 | – |
| 4th | 103 | 158 | 218 | – |
| 5th | 150 | 175 | 237 | – |
| 6th | 158 | 193 | 272 | – |
| 7th | 169 | 214 | 289 | – |
| 8th | 169 | 258 | – | – |
| 9th | 190 | 267 | – | – |
| 10th | 241 | 267 | – | – |

Umpires: S. Roy and M.V. Nagendra.

# INDIA v ENGLAND 1963–64 (4th Test)

Played at Feroz Shah Kotla, Delhi, on 8, 9, 11, 12, 13 February.
Toss: India.   Result: MATCH DRAWN.
Debuts: India – Hanumant Singh.

Hanumant Singh became the third Indian after L. Amarnath and A.A. Baig to score a hundred against England in his first Test match; he remains the only one to do so in his first innings. Pataudi scored India's only double-century against England; his unbroken partnership of 190 with Borde remains India's highest for the fifth wicket against England and against all countries in India.

## INDIA

| | | | | | |
|---|---|--:|---|---|--:|
| M.L. Jaisimha | b Titmus | 47 | st Parks b Parfitt | | 50 |
| B.K. Kunderan† | b Titmus | 40 | lbw b Price | | 100 |
| D.N. Sardesai | c Parks b Mortimore | 44 | b Wilson | | 4 |
| Nawab of Pataudi, jr* | b Titmus | 13 | not out | | 203 |
| Hanumant Singh | c and b Mortimore | 105 | c Mortimore b Wilson | | 23 |
| C.G. Borde | b Price | 26 | not out | | 67 |
| S.A. Durani | c Smith b Wilson | 16 | | | |
| A.G. Kripal Singh | b Mortimore | 0 | | | |
| R.G. Nadkarni | run out | 34 | | | |
| R.B. Desai | not out | 14 | | | |
| B.S. Chandrasekhar | run out | 0 | | | |
| Extras | (LB 3, NB 2) | 5 | (B 5, LB 9, NB 2) | | 16 |
| **Total** | | **344** | (4 wickets) | | **463** |

## ENGLAND

| | | |
|---|---|--:|
| J.B. Bolus | lbw b Kripal Singh | 58 |
| J.H. Edrich | c and b Kripal Singh | 41 |
| M.J.K. Smith* | c Pataudi b Kripal Singh | 37 |
| D. Wilson | c Pataudi b Chandrasekhar | 6 |
| P.H. Parfitt | c Kunderan b Durani | 67 |
| M.C. Cowdrey | lbw b Nadkarni | 151 |
| J.M. Parks† | c sub (P.C. Poddar) | |
| | b Chandrasekhar | 32 |
| B.R. Knight | c Desai b Nadkarni | 21 |
| J.B. Mortimore | c Hanumant b Nadkarni | 21 |
| F.J. Titmus | not out | 4 |
| J.S.E. Price | b Chandrasekhar | 0 |
| Extras | (B 8, LB 3, NB 2) | 13 |
| **Total** | | **451** |

| ENGLAND | O | M | R | W | O | M | R | W | | FALL OF WICKETS | | |
|---|--:|--:|--:|--:|--:|--:|--:|--:|---|--:|--:|--:|
| Price | 23 | 3 | 71 | 1 | 9 | 1 | 36 | 1 | | I | E | I |
| Knight | 11 | 0 | 46 | 0 | 8 | 1 | 47 | 0 | Wkt | 1st | 1st | 2nd |
| Wilson | 22 | 9 | 41 | 1 | 41 | 17 | 74 | 2 | 1st | 81 | 101 | 74 |
| Titmus | 49 | 15 | 100 | 3 | 43 | 12 | 105 | 0 | 2nd | 90 | 114 | 101 |
| Mortimore | 38 | 13 | 74 | 3 | 32 | 11 | 52 | 0 | 3rd | 116 | 134 | 226 |
| Parfitt | 5 | 2 | 7 | 0 | 19 | 3 | 81 | 1 | 4th | 201 | 153 | 273 |
| Smith | | | | | 13 | 0 | 52 | 0 | 5th | 267 | 268 | – |
| | | | | | | | | | 6th | 283 | 354 | – |
| INDIA | | | | | | | | | 7th | 283 | 397 | – |
| Desai | 9 | 2 | 23 | 0 | | | | | 8th | 307 | 438 | – |
| Jaisimha | 4 | 0 | 14 | 0 | | | | | 9th | 344 | 451 | – |
| Kripal Singh | 36 | 13 | 90 | 3 | | | | | 10th | 344 | 451 | – |
| Chandrasekhar | 34·3 | 11 | 79 | 3 | | | | | | | | |
| Borde | 12 | 2 | 42 | 0 | | | | | | | | |
| Durani | 33 | 5 | 93 | 1 | | | | | | | | |
| Nadkarni | 57 | 30 | 97 | 3 | | | | | | | | |

Umpires: S. Pan and B. Satyaji Rao.

# INDIA v ENGLAND 1963–64 (5th Test)

Played at Green Park, Kanpur, on 15, 16, 18, 19, 20 February.
Toss: India.    Result: MATCH DRAWN.
Debuts: Nil.

Pataudi won the toss for the fifth time in the rubber. England's total remains their highest in India. With the match devoid of interest, Durani reached his first fifty in 29 minutes against the bowling of Cowdrey and Parks. It was one minute slower than the fastest Test fifty which J.T. Brown scored for England against Australia in 1894-95 (*Test No. 46*). Kunderan (525) became the first wicket-keeper to score 500 runs in a Test rubber.

## ENGLAND

| | | |
|---|---|---|
| J.B. Bolus | c Hanumant b Nadkarni | 67 |
| J.H. Edrich | c Pataudi b Borde | 35 |
| M.J.K. Smith* | c Borde b Gupte | 38 |
| B.R. Knight | c Manjrekar b Jaisimha | 127 |
| P.H. Parfitt | lbw b Jaisimha | 121 |
| M.C. Cowdrey | lbw b Pataudi | 38 |
| J.M. Parks† | not out | 51 |
| J.B. Mortimore | b Chandrasekhar | 19 |
| F.J. Titmus | c and b Nadkarni | 5 |
| D. Wilson | not out | 18 |
| J.S.E. Price | did not bat | |
| Extras | (B 29, LB 9, NB 2) | 40 |
| **Total** | **(8 wickets declared)** | **559** |

## INDIA

| | | | | |
|---|---|---|---|---|
| M.L. Jaisimha | c Parks b Titmus | 5 | c Cowdrey b Titmus | 5 |
| B.K. Kunderan | b Price | 5 | lbw b Parfitt | 55 |
| V.L. Manjrekar | c and b Titmus | 33 | | |
| D.N. Sardesai | c Mortimore b Parfitt | 79 | c Edrich b Parks | 87 |
| Hanumant Singh | c Parks b Titmus | 24 | | |
| Nawab of Pataudi, jr* | b Titmus | 31 | | |
| C.G. Borde | b Titmus | 0 | | |
| S.A. Durani | b Mortimore | 16 | (5) not out | 61 |
| R.G. Nadkarni | not out | 52 | (3) not out | 122 |
| B.P. Gupte | c and b Titmus | 8 | | |
| B.S. Chandrasekhar | b Price | 3 | | |
| Extras | (B 5, LB 1, NB 4) | 10 | (B 5, LB 11, NB 1) | 17 |
| **Total** | | **266** | **(3 wickets)** | **347** |

| INDIA | O | M | R | W | O | M | R | W |
|---|---|---|---|---|---|---|---|---|
| Jaisimha | 19 | 4 | 54 | 2 | | | | |
| Durani | 25 | 8 | 49 | 0 | | | | |
| Chandrasekhar | 36 | 7 | 97 | 1 | | | | |
| Gupte | 40 | 9 | 115 | 1 | | | | |
| Borde | 23 | 4 | 73 | 1 | | | | |
| Nadkarni | 57 | 22 | 121 | 2 | | | | |
| Pataudi | 3 | 1 | 10 | 1 | | | | |
| ENGLAND | | | | | | | | |
| Price | 16·1 | 5 | 32 | 2 | 10 | 2 | 27 | 0 |
| Knight | 1 | 0 | 4 | 0 | 2 | 0 | 12 | 0 |
| Titmus | 60 | 37 | 73 | 6 | 34 | 12 | 59 | 1 |
| Mortimore | 48 | 31 | 39 | 1 | 23 | 14 | 28 | 0 |
| Wilson | 27 | 9 | 47 | 0 | 19 | 10 | 26 | 0 |
| Parfitt | 30 | 12 | 61 | 1 | 27 | 7 | 68 | 1 |
| Edrich | | | | | 4 | 1 | 17 | 0 |
| Bolus | | | | | 3 | 0 | 16 | 0 |
| Parks | | | | | 6 | 0 | 43 | 1 |
| Cowdrey | | | | | 5 | 0 | 34 | 0 |

## FALL OF WICKETS

| | E | I | I |
|---|---|---|---|
| Wkt | 1st | 1st | 2nd |
| 1st | 63 | 9 | 17 |
| 2nd | 134 | 17 | 126 |
| 3rd | 174 | 96 | 270 |
| 4th | 365 | 135 | – |
| 5th | 458 | 182 | – |
| 6th | 474 | 182 | – |
| 7th | 520 | 188 | – |
| 8th | 531 | 229 | – |
| 9th | – | 245 | – |
| 10th | – | 266 | – |

Umpires: S. Bhattacharya and S.K. Raghunatha Rao.

# NEW ZEALAND v SOUTH AFRICA 1963–64 (1st Test)

Played at Basin Reserve, Wellington, on 21, 22, 24, 25 February.
Toss: South Africa.   Result: MATCH DRAWN.
Debuts: New Zealand – S.G. Gedye, J.T. Ward.

Anti-apartheid demonstrators damaged the pitch but failed to prevent the match from starting on time. New Zealand made no attempt to score 268 runs in four hours.

## SOUTH AFRICA

| | | | | | |
|---|---|---|---|---|---|
| T.L. Goddard* | b Cameron | 24 | b Reid | | 40 |
| E.J. Barlow | b Cameron | 22 | c Ward b Cameron | | 92 |
| A.J. Pithey | c Chapple b Motz | 31 | | | |
| W.S. Farrer | b Reid | 30 | (3) not out | | 38 |
| K.C. Bland | c Ward b Blair | 40 | (4) not out | | 46 |
| J.H.B. Waite† | b Blair | 30 | | | |
| D.T. Lindsay | b Cameron | 27 | | | |
| P.L. van der Merwe | b Motz | 44 | | | |
| D.B. Pithey | b Blair | 7 | | | |
| P.M. Pollock | c Dowling b Reid | 24 | | | |
| J.T. Partridge | not out | 2 | | | |
| Extras | (B 9, LB 3, NB 9) | 21 | (B 2) | | 2 |
| **Total** | | **302** | (2 wickets declared) | | **218** |

## NEW ZEALAND

| | | | | | |
|---|---|---|---|---|---|
| G.T. Dowling | b Pollock | 1 | lbw b Bland | | 32 |
| S.G. Gedye | lbw b Pollock | 10 | c Van der Merwe b Pollock | | 52 |
| B.W. Sinclair | lbw b D.B. Pithey | 44 | b Bland | | 0 |
| J.R. Reid* | c Barlow b Partridge | 16 | b Goddard | | 12 |
| S.N. McGregor | b D.B. Pithey | 39 | lbw b Van der Merwe | | 24 |
| J.T. Sparling | lbw b Pollock | 49 | c Van der Merwe b Pollock | | 1 |
| M.E. Chapple | c Goddard b Partridge | 59 | not out | | 0 |
| R.C. Motz | c D.B. Pithey b Pollock | 2 | not out | | 0 |
| J.T. Ward† | b Pollock | 5 | | | |
| R.W. Blair | b Pollock | 5 | | | |
| F.J. Cameron | not out | 1 | | | |
| Extras | (B 10, LB 5, NB 7) | 22 | (B 6, LB 7, NB 3, W 1) | | 17 |
| **Total** | | **253** | (6 wickets) | | **138** |

| NEW ZEALAND | O | M | R | W | O | M | R | W | FALL OF WICKETS | | | |
|---|---|---|---|---|---|---|---|---|---|---|---|---|
| | | | | | | | | | | SA | NZ | SA | NZ |
| Motz | 25 | 3 | 68 | 2 | 15 | 2 | 53 | 0 | *Wkt* | *1st* | *1st* | *2nd* | *2nd* |
| Cameron | 30 | 13 | 58 | 3 | 19 | 6 | 60 | 1 | 1st | 41 | 14 | 117 | 64 |
| Blair | 41 | 10 | 86 | 3 | 11 | 0 | 48 | 0 | 2nd | 56 | 17 | 143 | 64 |
| Reid | 29·5 | 12 | 47 | 2 | 21 | 8 | 55 | 1 | 3rd | 97 | 49 | – | 79 |
| Sparling | 6 | 1 | 22 | 0 | | | | | 4th | 121 | 112 | – | 134 |
| SOUTH AFRICA | | | | | | | | | 5th | 189 | 148 | – | 136 |
| Pollock | 31·5 | 9 | 47 | 6 | 16 | 4 | 31 | 2 | 6th | 198 | 234 | – | 138 |
| Partridge | 45 | 24 | 50 | 2 | 14 | 8 | 10 | 0 | 7th | 233 | 242 | – | – |
| Goddard | 38 | 21 | 42 | 0 | 16 | 10 | 11 | 1 | 8th | 257 | 243 | – | – |
| Barlow | 11 | 0 | 38 | 0 | 2 | 1 | 13 | 0 | 9th | 292 | 252 | – | – |
| D.B. Pithey | 24 | 11 | 53 | 2 | 14 | 3 | 34 | 0 | 10th | 302 | 253 | – | – |
| Bland | 3 | 2 | 1 | 0 | 9 | 3 | 16 | 2 | | | | | |
| Van der Merwe | | | | | 5 | 4 | 6 | 1 | | | | | |

Umpires: W.T. Martin and D.P. Dumbleton.

# NEW ZEALAND v SOUTH AFRICA 1963–64 (2nd Test)

Played at Carisbrook, Dunedin, on 28 (*no play*), 29 February, 2, 3 March.
Toss: New Zealand.   Result: MATCH DRAWN.
Debuts: New Zealand – W.P. Bradburn.

Rain allowed only four hours of play on the first two days. New Zealand failed to score 65 runs in the final 26 minutes of the match.

### NEW ZEALAND

| | | | | | |
|---|---|---|---|---|---|
| S.G. Gedye | c Waite b Partridge | 6 | | b D.B. Pithey | 25 |
| W.P. Bradburn | b Pollock | 32 | | lbw b D.B. Pithey | 14 |
| B.W. Sinclair | c Lindsay b Goddard | 52 | | lbw b Goddard | 11 |
| J.R. Reid* | b Pollock | 2 | (7) | c Bland b D.B. Pithey | 2 |
| S.N. McGregor | run out | 3 | (4) | run out | 11 |
| J.T. Sparling | b Pollock | 1 | (5) | b D.B. Pithey | 1 |
| M.E. Chapple | c Farrer b D.B. Pithey | 37 | (6) | b D.B. Pithey | 7 |
| A.E. Dick† | c D.B. Pithey b Partridge | 3 | | lbw b D.B. Pithey | 22 |
| R.C. Motz | c D.B. Pithey b Partridge | 3 | | lbw b Pollock | 0 |
| R.W. Blair | b Partridge | 0 | | not out | 26 |
| F.J. Cameron | not out | 1 | | b Pollock | 8 |
| Extras | (B 3, LB 3, NB 3) | 9 | | (LB 7, NB 4) | 11 |
| **Total** | | **149** | | | **138** |

### SOUTH AFRICA

| | | | | | |
|---|---|---|---|---|---|
| T.L. Goddard* | c Dick b Reid | 63 | | | |
| E.J. Barlow | b Reid | 49 | | hit wkt b Cameron | 13 |
| A.J. Pithey | run out | 1 | | | |
| W.S. Farrer | run out | 39 | | | |
| K.C. Bland | lbw b Reid | 1 | (1) | not out | 16 |
| J.H.B. Waite† | c Sparling b Reid | 4 | | | |
| D.T. Lindsay | c Motz b Reid | 20 | (3) | b Blair | 1 |
| P.L. van der Merwe | c Sinclair b Reid | 8 | (4) | b Blair | 0 |
| D.B. Pithey | c Bradburn b Sparling | 9 | (5) | not out | 8 |
| P.M. Pollock | b Cameron | 6 | | | |
| J.T. Partridge | not out | 8 | | | |
| Extras | (B 6, LB 4, NB 5) | 15 | | (LB 4) | 4 |
| **Total** | | **223** | | (3 wickets) | **42** |

| SOUTH AFRICA | O | M | R | W | O | M | R | W |
|---|---|---|---|---|---|---|---|---|
| Pollock | 27 | 13 | 53 | 3 | 10·5 | 2 | 25 | 2 |
| Partridge | 34 | 15 | 51 | 4 | 5 | 4 | 3 | 0 |
| Bland | 9 | 4 | 9 | 0 | | | | |
| Goddard | 17 | 14 | 10 | 1 | 26 | 10 | 29 | 1 |
| Barlow | 3 | 0 | 11 | 0 | | | | |
| D.B. Pithey | 4 | 1 | 6 | 1 | 35 | 11 | 58 | 6 |
| Van der Merwe | | | | | 8 | 3 | 12 | 0 |
| **NEW ZEALAND** | | | | | | | | |
| Motz | 6 | 1 | 23 | 0 | | | | |
| Cameron | 17·2 | 3 | 40 | 1 | 4 | 0 | 22 | 1 |
| Blair | 13 | 3 | 35 | 0 | 3 | 0 | 16 | 2 |
| Reid | 35 | 15 | 60 | 6 | | | | |
| Chapple | 27 | 14 | 41 | 0 | | | | |
| Sparling | 7 | 2 | 9 | 1 | | | | |

### FALL OF WICKETS

| Wkt | NZ 1st | SA 1st | NZ 2nd | SA 2nd |
|---|---|---|---|---|
| 1st | 11 | 117 | 38 | 18 |
| 2nd | 62 | 124 | 42 | 23 |
| 3rd | 64 | 124 | 63 | 25 |
| 4th | 98 | 130 | 64 | – |
| 5th | 100 | 134 | 67 | – |
| 6th | 100 | 158 | 72 | – |
| 7th | 132 | 168 | 73 | – |
| 8th | 142 | 185 | 79 | – |
| 9th | 148 | 209 | 111 | – |
| 10th | 149 | 223 | 138 | – |

Umpires: D.C. Burns and H.B. Cassie.

# NEW ZEALAND v SOUTH AFRICA 1963–64 (3rd Test)

Played at Eden Park, Auckland, on 13, 14, 16, 17 March.
Toss: New Zealand.   Result: MATCH DRAWN.
Debuts: New Zealand – R.S. Cunis.

New Zealand, set to score 309 runs in 313 minutes, managed to avoid defeat when the last ten minutes of play was lost to rain. Sinclair's 138 was the highest score for New Zealand in any home Test match. The Pollock and Pithey brothers provided the first instance of two pairs of brothers in one team in a Test in New Zealand.

## SOUTH AFRICA

| | | | | |
|---|---|---|---|---|
| T.L. Goddard* | c Sinclair b Cameron | 73 | c McGregor b Blair | 33 |
| E.J. Barlow | c Shrimpton b Blair | 61 | b Blair | 58 |
| A.J. Pithey | c Bradburn b Blair | 13 | | |
| R.G. Pollock | b Reid | 30 | c Sinclair b Cunis | 23 |
| K.C. Bland | lbw b Cameron | 83 | not out | 21 |
| J.H.B. Waite | c Dick b Cameron | 28 | (3) c Sinclair b Blair | 41 |
| D.T. Lindsay† | b Blair | 37 | (6) b Cunis | 1 |
| W.S. Farrer | lbw b Reid | 21 | (7) not out | 5 |
| D.B. Pithey | c Dick b Blair | 1 | | |
| P.M. Pollock | c and b Reid | 2 | | |
| J.T. Partridge | not out | 0 | | |
| Extras | (B 2, LB 16, NB 4) | 22 | (LB 17, NB 1) | 18 |
| **Total** | | **371** | (5 wickets declared) | **200** |

## NEW ZEALAND

| | | | | |
|---|---|---|---|---|
| S.G. Gedye | c Lindsay b Partridge | 18 | b Partridge | 55 |
| W.P. Bradburn | b Partridge | 2 | c Lindsay b D.B. Pithey | 14 |
| B.W. Sinclair | c A.J. Pithey b Barlow | 138 | c Partridge b D.B. Pithey | 19 |
| J.R. Reid* | c Lindsay b Partridge | 19 | b Goddard | 37 |
| S.N. McGregor | hit wkt b P.M. Pollock | 62 | c Barlow b D.B. Pithey | 29 |
| M.J.F. Shrimpton | lbw b Barlow | 0 | b Goddard | 0 |
| M.E. Chapple | b Partridge | 4 | lbw b Goddard | 20 |
| A.E. Dick† | b P.M. Pollock | 1 | not out | 4 |
| R.W. Blair | b Partridge | 0 | b Goddard | 0 |
| R.S. Cunis | lbw b Partridge | 0 | not out | 4 |
| F.J. Cameron | not out | 0 | | |
| Extras | (B 4, LB 7, NB 8) | 19 | (B 3, LB 2, NB 4) | 9 |
| **Total** | | **263** | (8 wickets) | **191** |

| NEW ZEALAND | O | M | R | W | O | M | R | W | | FALL OF WICKETS | | | |
|---|---|---|---|---|---|---|---|---|---|---|---|---|---|
| Cunis | 21 | 2 | 80 | 0 | 17·4 | 0 | 47 | 2 | | SA | NZ | SA | NZ |
| Cameron | 39 | 8 | 107 | 3 | 13 | 1 | 39 | 0 | *Wkt* | *1st* | *1st* | *2nd* | *2nd* |
| Reid | 29·5 | 12 | 77 | 3 | 13 | 2 | 39 | 0 | 1st | 115 | 7 | 92 | 49 |
| Blair | 36 | 8 | 85 | 4 | 21 | 2 | 57 | 3 | 2nd | 149 | 34 | 105 | 89 |
| | | | | | | | | | 3rd | 158 | 76 | 165 | 95 |
| SOUTH AFRICA | | | | | | | | | 4th | 202 | 247 | 187 | 145 |
| P.M. Pollock | 28·3 | 13 | 60 | 2 | 16 | 3 | 42 | 0 | 5th | 256 | 247 | 190 | 145 |
| Partridge | 40 | 10 | 86 | 6 | 24 | 8 | 47 | 1 | 6th | 339 | 260 | – | 180 |
| Goddard | 26 | 17 | 32 | 0 | 17 | 9 | 18 | 4 | 7th | 357 | 262 | – | 182 |
| D.B. Pithey | 12 | 3 | 33 | 0 | 25 | 13 | 40 | 3 | 8th | 362 | 263 | – | 185 |
| Barlow | 12 | 5 | 20 | 2 | 16 | 8 | 19 | 0 | 9th | 371 | 263 | – | – |
| Bland | 13 | 6 | 13 | 0 | | | | | 10th | 371 | 263 | – | – |
| R.G. Pollock | | | | | 3 | 0 | 16 | 0 | | | | | |

Umpires: J.M.A. Brown and E.C.A. MacKintosh.

# ENGLAND v AUSTRALIA 1964 (1st Test)

Played at Trent Bridge, Nottingham, on 4, 5, 6 *(no play)*, 8, 9 June.
Toss: England.   Result: MATCH DRAWN.
Debuts: England – G. Boycott; Australia – G.E. Corling.

Rain interrupted every day except the fourth, a total of 14¾ hours being lost. Titmus, who improvised as an opening batsman after Edrich had reported unfit shortly before the start, escaped being run out when Grout declined to break the wicket after the batsman had collided with the bowler in responding to a call for a quick single. Boycott fractured a finger when fielding and was unable to bat in the second innings. Australia were set to score 242 runs in 195 minutes but rain ended the match after 45 minutes.

## ENGLAND

| | | | | | |
|---|---|---|---|---|---|
| G. Boycott | c Simpson b Corling | 48 | | | |
| F.J. Titmus | c Redpath b Hawke | 16 | | lbw b McKenzie | 17 |
| E.R. Dexter* | c Grout b Hawke | 9 | (1) | c O'Neill b McKenzie | 68 |
| M.C. Cowdrey | b Hawke | 32 | (3) | b McKenzie | 33 |
| K.F. Barrington | c Lawry b Veivers | 22 | (4) | lbw b Corling | 33 |
| P.J. Sharpe | not out | 35 | | c and b Veivers | 1 |
| J.M. Parks† | c Booth b Veivers | 15 | (5) | c Hawke b Veivers | 19 |
| F.S. Trueman | c Simpson b Veivers | 0 | (7) | c Grout b McKenzie | 4 |
| D.A. Allen | c Grout b McKenzie | 21 | (8) | lbw b McKenzie | 3 |
| L.J. Coldwell | not out | 0 | | not out | 0 |
| J.A. Flavell | did not bat | | (9) | c Booth b Corling | 7 |
| Extras | (B 5, LB 11, NB 2) | 18 | | (B 2, LB 2, W 1, NB 3) | 8 |
| **Total** | (8 wickets declared) | **216** | | (9 wickets declared) | **193** |

## AUSTRALIA

| | | | | | |
|---|---|---|---|---|---|
| W.M. Lawry | c Barrington b Coldwell | 11 | | run out | 3 |
| I.R. Redpath | b Trueman | 6 | | c Parks b Flavell | 2 |
| N.C. O'Neill | b Allen | 26 | | retired hurt | 24 |
| P.J.P. Burge | lbw b Trueman | 31 | | not out | 4 |
| B.C. Booth | run out | 0 | | not out | 6 |
| R.B. Simpson* | c Barrington b Titmus | 50 | | | |
| T.R. Veivers | c Trueman b Flavell | 8 | | | |
| G.D. McKenzie | c Parks b Coldwell | 4 | | | |
| N.J.N. Hawke | not out | 10 | | | |
| A.T.W. Grout† | c Parks b Coldwell | 13 | | | |
| G.E. Corling | b Trueman | 3 | | | |
| Extras | (LB 1, NB 5) | 6 | | (NB 1) | 1 |
| **Total** | | **168** | | (2 wickets) | **40** |

| AUSTRALIA | O | M | R | W | O | M | R | W |
|---|---|---|---|---|---|---|---|---|
| McKenzie | 28 | 7 | 53 | 1 | 24 | 5 | 53 | 5 |
| Corling | 23 | 7 | 38 | 1 | 15·5 | 4 | 54 | 2 |
| Hawke | 35 | 15 | 68 | 3 | 19 | 5 | 53 | 0 |
| Veivers | 16 | 2 | 39 | 3 | 8 | 0 | 25 | 2 |
| **ENGLAND** | | | | | | | | |
| Trueman | 20·3 | 3 | 58 | 3 | 5 | 0 | 28 | 0 |
| Coldwell | 22 | 3 | 48 | 3 | | | | |
| Allen | 16 | 8 | 22 | 1 | | | | |
| Flavell | 16 | 3 | 28 | 1 | 4·2 | 0 | 11 | 1 |
| Titmus | 4 | 1 | 6 | 1 | | | | |

### FALL OF WICKETS

| | E | A | E | A |
|---|---|---|---|---|
| *Wkt* | *1st* | *1st* | *2nd* | *2nd* |
| 1st | 38 | 8 | 90 | 3 |
| 2nd | 70 | 37 | 95 | 25 |
| 3rd | 90 | 57 | 147 | – |
| 4th | 135 | 61 | 174 | – |
| 5th | 141 | 91 | 179 | – |
| 6th | 164 | 118 | 180 | – |
| 7th | 165 | 137 | 186 | – |
| 8th | 212 | 141 | 187 | – |
| 9th | – | 165 | 193 | – |
| 10th | – | 168 | – | – |

Umpires: J.S. Buller and C.S. Elliott.

# ENGLAND v AUSTRALIA 1964 (2nd Test)

Played at Lord's, London, on 18 *(no play)*, 19 *(no play)*, 20, 22, 23 June.
Toss: England.   Result: MATCH DRAWN.
Debuts: England – N. Gifford.

Over half the possible playing time was lost to rain which prevented a start until the third day and ended the match just before 2.30 on the fifth afternoon.

## AUSTRALIA

| | | | | |
|---|---|---|---|---|
| W.M. Lawry | b Trueman | 4 | c Dexter b Gifford | 20 |
| I.R. Redpath | c Parfitt b Coldwell | 30 | lbw b Titmus | 36 |
| N.C. O'Neill | c Titmus b Dexter | 26 | c Parfitt b Trueman | 22 |
| P.J.P. Burge | lbw b Dexter | 1 | c Parfitt b Titmus | 59 |
| B.C. Booth | lbw b Trueman | 14 | not out | 2 |
| R.B. Simpson* | c Parfitt b Trueman | 0 | not out | 15 |
| T.R. Veivers | b Gifford | 54 | | |
| G.D. McKenzie | b Trueman | 10 | | |
| A.T.W. Grout† | c Dexter b Gifford | 14 | | |
| N.J.N. Hawke | not out | 5 | | |
| G.E. Corling | b Trueman | 0 | | |
| Extras | (B 8, LB 5, NB 5) | 18 | (B 8, LB 4, NB 2) | 14 |
| **Total** | | **176** | (4 wickets) | **168** |

## ENGLAND

| | | |
|---|---|---|
| E.R. Dexter* | b McKenzie | 2 |
| J.H. Edrich | c Redpath b McKenzie | 120 |
| M.C. Cowdrey | c Burge b Hawke | 10 |
| K.F. Barrington | lbw b McKenzie | 5 |
| P.H. Parfitt | lbw b Corling | 20 |
| P.J. Sharpe | lbw b Hawke | 35 |
| J.M. Parks† | c Simpson b Hawke | 12 |
| F.J. Titmus | b Corling | 15 |
| F.S. Trueman | b Corling | 8 |
| N. Gifford | c Hawke b Corling | 5 |
| L.J. Coldwell | not out | 6 |
| Extras | (LB 7, NB 1) | 8 |
| **Total** | | **246** |

| ENGLAND | O | M | R | W | O | M | R | W |
|---|---|---|---|---|---|---|---|---|
| Trueman | 25 | 8 | 48 | 5 | 18 | 6 | 52 | 1 |
| Coldwell | 23 | 7 | 51 | 1 | 19 | 4 | 59 | 0 |
| Gifford | 12 | 6 | 14 | 2 | 17 | 9 | 17 | 1 |
| Dexter | 7 | 1 | 16 | 2 | 3 | 0 | 5 | 0 |
| Titmus | 17 | 6 | 29 | 0 | 17 | 7 | 21 | 2 |
| AUSTRALIA | | | | | | | | |
| McKenzie | 26 | 8 | 69 | 3 | | | | |
| Corling | 27·3 | 9 | 60 | 4 | | | | |
| Hawke | 16 | 4 | 41 | 3 | | | | |
| Veivers | 9 | 4 | 17 | 0 | | | | |
| Simpson | 21 | 8 | 51 | 0 | | | | |

### FALL OF WICKETS

| Wkt | A 1st | E 1st | A 2nd |
|---|---|---|---|
| 1st | 8 | 2 | 35 |
| 2nd | 46 | 33 | 76 |
| 3rd | 58 | 42 | 143 |
| 4th | 84 | 83 | 148 |
| 5th | 84 | 138 | – |
| 6th | 88 | 170 | – |
| 7th | 132 | 227 | – |
| 8th | 163 | 229 | – |
| 9th | 167 | 235 | – |
| 10th | 176 | 246 | – |

Umpires: J.F. Crapp and J.S. Buller.

# ENGLAND v AUSTRALIA 1964 (3rd Test)

Played at Headingley, Leeds, on 2, 3, 4, 6 July.
Toss: England.   Result: AUSTRALIA won by seven wickets.
Debuts: Australia – R.M. Cowper.

Australia achieved the only victory of the rubber and so retained the Ashes. Dexter took the second new ball when Australia's first innings total was 187 for 7, and, after struggling against the off-spin of Titmus, Burge (then 88 not out) took his score to 160 and added a further 202 runs. The first seven overs of the new ball conceded 42 runs. In the second innings Titmus, who took the new ball in the absence of the injured Flavell, conceded only 12 runs in his first 24 overs.

## ENGLAND

| | | | | |
|---|---|---:|---|---:|
| G. Boycott | c Simpson b Corling | 38 | c Simpson b Corling | 4 |
| J.H. Edrich | c Veivers b McKenzie | 3 | c Grout b McKenzie | 32 |
| E.R. Dexter* | c Grout b McKenzie | 66 | (5) c Redpath b Veivers | 17 |
| K.F. Barrington | b McKenzie | 29 | lbw b Veivers | 85 |
| P.H. Parfitt | b Hawke | 32 | (3) c Redpath b Hawke | 6 |
| K. Taylor | c Grout b Hawke | 9 | (8) b Veivers | 15 |
| J.M. Parks† | c Redpath b Hawke | 68 | (6) c Booth b McKenzie | 23 |
| F.J. Titmus | c Burge b McKenzie | 3 | (9) c Cowper b Corling | 14 |
| F.S. Trueman | c Cowper b Hawke | 4 | (10) not out | 12 |
| N. Gifford | not out | 1 | (7) b McKenzie | 1 |
| J.A. Flavell | c Redpath b Hawke | 5 | c Simpson b Corling | 5 |
| Extras | (LB 9, NB 1) | 10 | (B 6, LB 6, W 1, NB 2) | 15 |
| **Total** | | **268** | | **229** |

## AUSTRALIA

| | | | | |
|---|---|---:|---|---:|
| W.M. Lawry | run out | 78 | c Gifford b Trueman | 1 |
| R.B. Simpson* | b Gifford | 24 | c Barrington b Titmus | 30 |
| I.R. Redpath | b Gifford | 20 | not out | 58 |
| P.J.P. Burge | c sub (A. Rees) b Trueman | 160 | b Titmus | 8 |
| B.C. Booth | st Parks b Titmus | 4 | not out | 12 |
| R.M. Cowper | b Trueman | 2 | | |
| T.R. Veivers | c Parks b Titmus | 8 | | |
| G.D. McKenzie | b Titmus | 0 | | |
| N.J.N. Hawke | c Parfitt b Trueman | 37 | | |
| A.T.W. Grout† | lbw b Titmus | 37 | | |
| G.E. Corling | not out | 2 | | |
| Extras | (B 1, LB 8, W 2, NB 6) | 17 | (B 1, LB 1) | 2 |
| **Total** | | **389** | (3 wickets) | **111** |

| AUSTRALIA | O | M | R | W | O | M | R | W | | FALL OF WICKETS | | | |
|---|---|---|---|---|---|---|---|---|---|---|---|---|---|
| McKenzie | 26 | 7 | 74 | 4 | 28 | 8 | 53 | 3 | | E | A | E | A |
| Hawke | 31·3 | 11 | 75 | 5 | 13 | 1 | 28 | 1 | *Wkt* | *1st* | *1st* | *2nd* | *2nd* |
| Corling | 24 | 7 | 50 | 1 | 17·5 | 6 | 52 | 3 | 1st | 17 | 50 | 13 | 3 |
| Veivers | 17 | 3 | 35 | 0 | 30 | 12 | 70 | 3 | 2nd | 74 | 124 | 88 | 45 |
| Simpson | 5 | 0 | 24 | 0 | 1 | 0 | 11 | 0 | 3rd | 129 | 129 | 145 | 64 |
| | | | | | | | | | 4th | 138 | 154 | 156 | – |
| ENGLAND | | | | | | | | | 5th | 163 | 157 | 169 | – |
| Trueman | 24·3 | 2 | 98 | 3 | 7 | 0 | 28 | 1 | 6th | 215 | 178 | 184 | – |
| Flavell | 29 | 5 | 97 | 0 | | | | | 7th | 232 | 178 | 192 | – |
| Gifford | 34 | 15 | 62 | 2 | 20 | 5 | 47 | 0 | 8th | 260 | 283 | 199 | – |
| Dexter | 19 | 5 | 40 | 0 | 3 | 0 | 9 | 0 | 9th | 263 | 372 | 212 | – |
| Titmus | 50 | 24 | 69 | 4 | 27 | 19 | 25 | 2 | 10th | 268 | 389 | 229 | – |
| Taylor | 2 | 0 | 6 | 0 | | | | | | | | | |

Umpires: W.F.F. Price and C.S. Elliott.

# ENGLAND v AUSTRALIA 1964 (4th Test)

Played at Old Trafford, Manchester, on 23, 24, 25, 27, 28 July.
Toss: Australia.   Result: MATCH DRAWN.
Debuts: England – T.W. Cartwright, F.E. Rumsey.

Australia's total of 656 for 8 declared remains the highest in any Manchester Test. Simpson scored his maiden Test hundred in his 52nd innings; his 311 is still the highest score in an Old Trafford Test and the highest by an Australian captain. Only Bradman (334 in *Test No. 196*) has made a higher score for Australia. His innings lasted 762 minutes and remains the longest against England and the third-longest in all first-class cricket. His partnership of 201 with Lawry set a new Australian first-wicket record against England. Barrington's tenth Test hundred was his first in England and his score of 256 remains England's highest at Manchester. Veivers established a record for this series by bowling 571 balls in an innings, including a spell of 51 overs unchanged. Only S. Ramadhin (588 balls in *Test No. 439*) has bowled more overs in a first-class innings.

## AUSTRALIA

| | | | | |
|---|---|---|---|---|
| W.M. Lawry | run out | 106 | not out | 0 |
| R.B. Simpson* | c Parks b Price | 311 | not out | 4 |
| I.R. Redpath | lbw b Cartwright | 19 | | |
| N.C. O'Neill | b Price | 47 | | |
| P.J.P. Burge | c Price b Cartwright | 34 | | |
| B.C. Booth | c and b Price | 98 | | |
| T.R. Veivers | c Edrich b Rumsey | 22 | | |
| A.T.W. Grout† | c Dexter b Rumsey | 0 | | |
| G.D. McKenzie | not out | 0 | | |
| N.J.N. Hawke | } did not bat | | | |
| G.E. Corling | } | | | |
| Extras | (B 1, LB 9, NB 9) | 19 | | |
| **Total** | (8 wickets declared) | **656** | (0 wickets) | |

## ENGLAND

| | | |
|---|---|---|
| G. Boycott | b McKenzie | 58 |
| J.H. Edrich | c Redpath b McKenzie | .6 |
| E.R. Dexter* | b Veivers | 174 |
| K.F. Barrington | lbw b McKenzie | 256 |
| P.H. Parfitt | c Grout b McKenzie | 12 |
| J.M. Parks† | c Hawke b Veivers | 60 |
| F.J. Titmus | c Simpson b McKenzie | 9 |
| J.B. Mortimore | c Burge b McKenzie | 12 |
| T.W. Cartwright | b McKenzie | 4 |
| J.S.E. Price | b Veivers | 1 |
| F.E. Rumsey | not out | 3 |
| Extras | (B 5, LB 11) | 16 |
| **Total** | | **611** |

| ENGLAND | O | M | R | W | O | M | R | W | | FALL OF WICKETS | | |
|---|---|---|---|---|---|---|---|---|---|---|---|---|
| | | | | | | | | | | A | E | A |
| Rumsey | 35·5 | 4 | 99 | 2 | | | | | Wkt | 1st | 1st | 2nd |
| Price | 45 | 4 | 183 | 3 | | | | | 1st | 201 | 15 | – |
| Cartwright | 77 | 32 | 118 | 2 | | | | | 2nd | 233 | 126 | – |
| Titmus | 44 | 14 | 100 | 0 | 1 | 1 | 0 | 0 | 3rd | 318 | 372 | – |
| Dexter | 4 | 0 | 12 | 0 | | | | | 4th | 382 | 417 | – |
| Mortimore | 49 | 13 | 122 | 0 | | | | | 5th | 601 | 560 | – |
| Boycott | 1 | 0 | 3 | 0 | | | | | 6th | 646 | 589 | – |
| Barrington | | | | | 1 | 0 | 4 | 0 | 7th | 652 | 594 | – |
| | | | | | | | | | 8th | 656 | 602 | – |
| AUSTRALIA | | | | | | | | | 9th | – | 607 | – |
| McKenzie | 60 | 15 | 153 | 7 | | | | | 10th | – | 611 | – |
| Corling | 46 | 11 | 96 | 0 | | | | | | | | |
| Hawke | 63 | 28 | 95 | 0 | | | | | | | | |
| Simpson | 19 | 4 | 59 | 0 | | | | | | | | |
| Veivers | 95·1 | 36 | 155 | 3 | | | | | | | | |
| O'Neill | 10 | 0 | 37 | 0 | | | | | | | | |

Umpires: J.S. Buller and W.F.F. Price.

# ENGLAND v AUSTRALIA 1964 (5th Test)

Played at Kennington Oval, London, on 13, 14, 15, 17, 18 (*no play*) August.
Toss: England.    Result: MATCH DRAWN.
Debuts: Nil.

Trueman became the first bowler to take 300 wickets in Test matches when he had Hawke caught by Cowdrey at first slip on the third afternoon. Barrington scored his 4,000th run in Test cricket during the first innings and Cowdrey his 5,000th during the second.

## ENGLAND

| | | | | | |
|---|---|---|---|---|---|
| G. Boycott | b Hawke | 30 | c Redpath b Simpson | | 113 |
| R.W. Barber | b Hawke | 24 | lbw b McKenzie | | 29 |
| E.R. Dexter* | c Booth b Hawke | 23 | c Simpson b McKenzie | | 25 |
| M.C. Cowdrey | c Grout b McKenzie | 20 | (5) not out | | 93 |
| K.F. Barrington | c Simpson b Hawke | 47 | (6) not out | | 54 |
| P.H. Parfitt | b McKenzie | 3 | | | |
| J.M. Parks† | c Simpson b Corling | 10 | | | |
| F.J. Titmus | c Grout b Hawke | 8 | (4) b McKenzie | | 56 |
| F.S. Trueman | c Redpath b Hawke | 14 | | | |
| T.W. Cartwright | c Grout b McKenzie | 0 | | | |
| J.S.E. Price | not out | 0 | | | |
| Extras | (LB 3) | 3 | (B 6, LB 4, NB 1) | | 11 |
| **Total** | | **182** | (4 wickets) | | **381** |

## AUSTRALIA

| | | |
|---|---|---|
| R.B. Simpson* | c Dexter b Cartwright | 24 |
| W.M. Lawry | c Trueman b Dexter | 94 |
| N.C. O'Neill | c Parfitt b Cartwright | 11 |
| P.J.P. Burge | lbw b Titmus | 25 |
| B.C. Booth | c Trueman b Price | 74 |
| I.R. Redpath | b Trueman | 45 |
| A.T.W. Grout† | b Cartwright | 20 |
| T.R. Veivers | not out | 67 |
| G.D. McKenzie | c Cowdrey b Trueman | 0 |
| N.J.N. Hawke | c Cowdrey b Trueman | 14 |
| G.E. Corling | c Parfitt b Trueman | 0 |
| Extras | (B 4, LB 1) | 5 |
| **Total** | | **379** |

| AUSTRALIA | O | M | R | W | O | M | R | W |
|---|---|---|---|---|---|---|---|---|
| McKenzie | 26 | 6 | 87 | 3 | 38 | 5 | 112 | 3 |
| Corling | 14 | 2 | 32 | 1 | 25 | 4 | 65 | 0 |
| Hawke | 25·4 | 8 | 47 | 6 | 39 | 8 | 89 | 0 |
| Veivers | 6 | 1 | 13 | 0 | 47 | 15 | 90 | 0 |
| Simpson | | | | | 14 | 7 | 14 | 1 |
| ENGLAND | | | | | | | | |
| Trueman | 33·3 | 6 | 87 | 4 | | | | |
| Price | 21 | 2 | 67 | 1 | | | | |
| Cartwright | 62 | 23 | 110 | 3 | | | | |
| Titmus | 42 | 20 | 51 | 1 | | | | |
| Barber | 6 | 1 | 23 | 0 | | | | |
| Dexter | 13 | 1 | 36 | 1 | | | | |

| FALL OF WICKETS | | | |
|---|---|---|---|
| | E | A | E |
| Wkt | 1st | 1st | 2nd |
| 1st | 44 | 45 | 80 |
| 2nd | 61 | 57 | 120 |
| 3rd | 82 | 96 | 200 |
| 4th | 111 | 202 | 255 |
| 5th | 117 | 245 | – |
| 6th | 141 | 279 | – |
| 7th | 160 | 343 | – |
| 8th | 173 | 343 | – |
| 9th | 174 | 367 | – |
| 10th | 182 | 379 | – |

Umpires: C.S. Elliott and J.F. Crapp.

## INDIA v AUSTRALIA 1964–65 (1st Test)

Played at Corporation Stadium, Madras, on 2, 3, 4, 6, 7 October.
Toss: Australia.   Result: AUSTRALIA won by 139 runs.
Debuts: India – K.S. Indrajitsinhji.

Australia won their third consecutive Test at Madras. They completed their victory with 109 minutes to spare after India had been left to score 332 runs in 390 minutes. Pataudi's 128 not out remains the highest score by an Indian captain against Australia. He emulated his father by scoring a hundred in his first innings against Australia (*see Test No. 220*).

### AUSTRALIA

| | | | | |
|---|---|--:|---|--:|
| W.M. Lawry | b Nadkarni | 62 | c sub (R.F. Surti) b Nadkarni | 41 |
| R.B. Simpson* | st Indrajitsinhji b Durani | 30 | run out | 77 |
| N.C. O'Neill | b Durani | 40 | b Nadkarni | 0 |
| P.J.P. Burge | b Nadkarni | 20 | lbw b Nadkarni | 60 |
| B.C. Booth | lbw b Nadkarni | 8 | c Indrajitsinhji b Durani | 29 |
| J.W. Martin | c Indrajitsinhji b Kripal Singh | 20 | (8) c Nadkarni b Ranjane | 39 |
| I.R. Redpath | c Hanumant b Nadkarni | 10 | (6) c Indrajitsinhji b Nadkarni | 0 |
| T.R. Veivers | b Kripal Singh | 0 | (7) c Pataudi b Nadkarni | 74 |
| G.D. McKenzie | not out | 8 | c Sardesai b Ranjane | 27 |
| A.T.W. Grout† | c Jaisimha b Nadkarni | 0 | c Hanumant b Nadkarni | 12 |
| N.J.N. Hawke | b Kripal Singh | 0 | not out | 1 |
| Extras | (LB 6, NB 7) | 13 | (B 15, LB 11, NB 11) | 37 |
| **Total** | | **211** | | **397** |

### INDIA

| | | | | |
|---|---|--:|---|--:|
| M.L. Jaisimha | lbw b McKenzie | 29 | b McKenzie | 0 |
| K.S. Indrajitsinhji† | c Grout b Hawke | 4 | b Hawke | 0 |
| D.N. Sardesai | b McKenzie | 0 | c Redpath b Martin | 14 |
| V.L. Manjrekar | c Grout b Martin | 33 | c Simpson b O'Neill | 40 |
| Hanumant Singh | c Grout b Martin | 0 | (6) c O'Neill b Veivers | 94 |
| Nawab of Pataudi, jr* | not out | 128 | (7) b McKenzie | 1 |
| C.G. Borde | c Simpson b McKenzie | 49 | (8) b McKenzie | 0 |
| S.A. Durani | c Grout b McKenzie | 5 | (10) c O'Neill b Veivers | 10 |
| R.G. Nadkarni | lbw b Hawke | 3 | c Simpson b Hawke | 20 |
| A.G. Kripal Singh | b McKenzie | 0 | (5) b McKenzie | 1 |
| V.B. Ranjane | c Redpath b McKenzie | 2 | not out | 0 |
| Extras | (B 13, LB 9, NB 1) | 23 | (B 11, LB 2) | 13 |
| **Total** | | **276** | | **193** |

| INDIA | O | M | R | W | O | M | R | W |
|---|--:|--:|--:|--:|--:|--:|--:|--:|
| Ranjane | 7 | 0 | 30 | 0 | 12 | 1 | 53 | 2 |
| Jaisimha | 4 | 1 | 13 | 0 | 9 | 2 | 13 | 0 |
| Durani | 21 | 5 | 68 | 2 | 40 | 9 | 102 | 1 |
| Kripal Singh | 18 | 5 | 43 | 3 | 38 | 13 | 91 | 0 |
| Borde | 4 | 2 | 13 | 0 | 5 | 2 | 10 | 0 |
| Nadkarni | 18 | 6 | 31 | 5 | 54·4 | 21 | 91 | 6 |
| **AUSTRALIA** | | | | | | | | |
| McKenzie | 32·3 | 8 | 58 | 6 | 20 | 9 | 33 | 4 |
| Hawke | 33 | 13 | 55 | 2 | 17 | 7 | 26 | 2 |
| Redpath | 2 | 1 | 1 | 0 | | | | |
| Simpson | 12 | 3 | 23 | 0 | 5 | 3 | 9 | 0 |
| Martin | 26 | 11 | 63 | 2 | 16 | 4 | 43 | 1 |
| Booth | 10 | 4 | 14 | 0 | 3 | 0 | 10 | 0 |
| Veivers | 10 | 2 | 20 | 0 | 10 | 4 | 18 | 2 |
| O'Neill | 7 | 3 | 19 | 0 | 9 | 3 | 41 | 1 |

### FALL OF WICKETS

| | A | I | A | I |
|---|--:|--:|--:|--:|
| Wkt | 1st | 1st | 2nd | 2nd |
| 1st | 66 | 12 | 91 | 0 |
| 2nd | 127 | 13 | 91 | 0 |
| 3rd | 139 | 55 | 175 | 23 |
| 4th | 161 | 56 | 228 | 24 |
| 5th | 174 | 76 | 232 | 117 |
| 6th | 203 | 218 | 237 | 130 |
| 7th | 203 | 232 | 301 | 130 |
| 8th | 203 | 249 | 374 | 168 |
| 9th | 209 | 256 | 392 | 191 |
| 10th | 211 | 276 | 397 | 193 |

Umpires: S. Roy and M.V. Nagendra.

# INDIA v AUSTRALIA 1964–65 (2nd Test)

Played at Brabourne Stadium, Bombay, on 10, 11, 12, 14, 15 October.
Toss: Australia.    Result: INDIA won by two wickets.
Debuts: Nil.

India gained their first victory against Australia at Bombay and with only two wickets and half an hour to spare.
O'Neill was taken ill with stomach pains soon after the start.

## AUSTRALIA

| | | | | |
|---|---|--:|---|--:|
| W.M. Lawry | c Indrajitsinhji b Durani | 16 | lbw b Chandrasekhar | 68 |
| R.B. Simpson* | b Chandrasekhar | 27 | c Hanumant b Surti | 20 |
| B.C. Booth | b Chandrasekhar | 1 | (5) st Indrajitsinhji b Nadkarni | 74 |
| P.J.P. Burge | c Chandrasekhar b Borde | 80 | b Chandrasekhar | 0 |
| R.M. Cowper | lbw b Nadkarni | 20 | (3) c Indrajitsinhji b Nadkarni | 81 |
| T.R. Veivers | c Borde b Chandrasekhar | 67 | lbw b Chandrasekhar | 0 |
| B.N. Jarman† | c Durani b Surti | 78 | b Chandrasekhar | 0 |
| J.W. Martin | c Nadkarni b Chandrasekhar | 0 | c Surti b Nadkarni | 16 |
| G.D. McKenzie | b Nadkarni | 17 | c Surti b Nadkarni | 4 |
| A.N. Connolly | not out | 0 | not out | 0 |
| N.C. O'Neill | absent ill | – | absent ill | – |
| Extras | (B 7, LB 4, NB 3) | 14 | (B 4, NB 7) | 11 |
| **Total** | | **320** | | **274** |

## INDIA

| | | | | |
|---|---|--:|---|--:|
| D.N. Sardesai | c Simpson b Connolly | 3 | lbw b McKenzie | 56 |
| M.L. Jaisimha | b Veivers | 66 | c Jarman b Connolly | 0 |
| S.A. Durani | c Jarman b Simpson | 12 | c Cowper b Simpson | 31 |
| V.L. Manjrekar | c Cowper b Veivers | 59 | (8) c Simpson b Connolly | 39 |
| Hanumant Singh | b Veivers | 4 | (6) b McKenzie | 11 |
| Nawab of Pataudi,jr* | c McKenzie b Veivers | 86 | (7) c Burge b Connolly | 53 |
| C.G. Borde | c Simpson b Martin | 4 | (9) not out | 30 |
| R.F. Surti | c Jarman b Connolly | 21 | (5) c Booth b Veivers | 10 |
| R.G. Nadkarni | c Jarman b Martin | 34 | (4) c Simpson b Veivers | 0 |
| K.S. Indrajitsinhji† | c sub (I.R. Redpath) b Connolly | 23 | not out | 3 |
| B.S. Chandrasekhar | not out | 1 | | |
| Extras | (B 4, LB 8, NB 6) | 18 | (B 15, LB 8) | 23 |
| **Total** | | **341** | (8 wickets) | **256** |

| INDIA | O | M | R | W | O | M | R | W | FALL OF WICKETS | | | | |
|---|--:|--:|--:|--:|--:|--:|--:|--:|---|--:|--:|--:|--:|
| | | | | | | | | | | A | I | A | I |
| Surti | 18 | 1 | 70 | 1 | 21 | 5 | 77 | 1 | Wkt | *1st* | *1st* | *2nd* | *2nd* |
| Jaisimha | 8 | 1 | 20 | 0 | 11 | 4 | 18 | 0 | 1st | 35 | 7 | 59 | 4 |
| Durani | 20 | 5 | 78 | 1 | 15 | 3 | 48 | 0 | 2nd | 36 | 30 | 121 | 70 |
| Chandrasekhar | 26 | 10 | 50 | 4 | 30 | 11 | 73 | 4 | 3rd | 53 | 142 | 121 | 71 |
| Nadkarni | 24·5 | 6 | 65 | 2 | 20·4 | 10 | 33 | 4 | 4th | 142 | 149 | 246 | 99 |
| Borde | 7 | 0 | 23 | 1 | 2 | 0 | 14 | 0 | 5th | 146 | 181 | 247 | 113 |
| | | | | | | | | | 6th | 297 | 188 | 247 | 122 |
| AUSTRALIA | | | | | | | | | 7th | 303 | 255 | 257 | 215 |
| McKenzie | 22 | 2 | 49 | 0 | 21 | 6 | 43 | 2 | 8th | 304 | 293 | 265 | 224 |
| Connolly | 22·3 | 5 | 66 | 3 | 18 | 8 | 24 | 3 | 9th | 320 | 331 | 274 | – |
| Martin | 34 | 11 | 72 | 2 | 14 | 2 | 35 | 0 | 10th | – | 341 | – | – |
| Simpson | 13 | 1 | 40 | 1 | 24 | 12 | 34 | 1 | | | | | |
| Veivers | 48 | 20 | 68 | 4 | 43·4 | 12 | 82 | 2 | | | | | |
| Cowper | 13 | 3 | 28 | 0 | 4 | 0 | 14 | 0 | | | | | |
| Booth | | | | | 4 | 3 | 1 | 0 | | | | | |

Umpires: H.E. Chowdhury and S.K. Raghunatha Rao.

# INDIA v AUSTRALIA 1964–65 (3rd Test)

Played at Eden Gardens, Calcutta, on 17, 18, 20, 21 (*no play*), 22 (*no play*) October.
Toss: India.   Result: MATCH DRAWN.
Debuts: Australia – R.H.D. Sellers.

## AUSTRALIA

| | | | | |
|---|---|---|---|---|
| W.M. Lawry | b Durani | 50 | not out | 47 |
| R.B. Simpson* | lbw b Surti | 67 | c Hanumant b Surti | 71 |
| R.M. Cowper | c Nadkarni b Durani | 4 | not out | 14 |
| P.J.P. Burge | c Hanumant b Durani | 4 | | |
| B.C. Booth | b Durani | 0 | | |
| I.R. Redpath | not out | 32 | | |
| T.R. Veivers | c Pataudi b Durani | 2 | | |
| B.N. Jarman† | b Durani | 1 | | |
| G.D. McKenzie | st Indrajitsinhji b Surti | 0 | | |
| R.H.D. Sellers | b Surti | 0 | | |
| A.N. Connolly | c Hanumant b Chandrasekhar | 0 | | |
| Extras | (B 1, LB 8, NB 5) | 14 | (B 6, NB 5) | 11 |
| **Total** | | **174** | (1 wicket) | **143** |

## INDIA

| | | |
|---|---|---|
| D.N. Sardesai | c Veivers b Booth | 42 |
| M.L. Jaisimha | c Booth b Simpson | 57 |
| S.A. Durani | c Simpson b Veivers | 12 |
| V.L. Manjrekar | lbw b Veivers | 9 |
| Hanumant Singh | c Burge b Veivers | 5 |
| Nawab of Pataudi,jr* | b Simpson | 2 |
| R.G. Nadkarni | b McKenzie | 24 |
| C.G. Borde | not out | 68 |
| R.F. Surti | c Sellers b Simpson | 9 |
| K.S. Indrajitsinhji† | st Jarman b Booth | 2 |
| B.S. Chandrasekhar | b Simpson | 1 |
| Extras | (B 4) | 4 |
| **Total** | | **235** |

| INDIA | O | M | R | W | O | M | R | W | | FALL OF WICKETS | | |
|---|---|---|---|---|---|---|---|---|---|---|---|---|
| Surti | 21 | 7 | 38 | 3 | 10 | 2 | 37 | 1 | | A | I | A |
| Jaisimha | 5 | 3 | 2 | 0 | 2 | 1 | 4 | 0 | Wkt | 1st | 1st | 2nd |
| Durani | 28 | 11 | 73 | 6 | 18 | 3 | 59 | 0 | 1st | 97 | 60 | 115 |
| Chandrasekhar | 28·5 | 15 | 39 | 1 | 8 | 3 | 27 | 0 | 2nd | 104 | 97 | – |
| Nadkarni | 2 | 0 | 8 | 0 | 8 | 6 | 5 | 0 | 3rd | 109 | 119 | – |
| | | | | | | | | | 4th | 109 | 127 | – |
| AUSTRALIA | | | | | | | | | 5th | 145 | 129 | – |
| McKenzie | 13 | 1 | 31 | 1 | | | | | 6th | 165 | 133 | – |
| Connolly | 8 | 4 | 10 | 0 | | | | | 7th | 167 | 166 | – |
| Veivers | 52 | 18 | 81 | 3 | | | | | 8th | 167 | 187 | – |
| Sellers | 5 | 1 | 17 | 0 | | | | | 9th | 169 | 196 | – |
| Booth | 18 | 10 | 33 | 2 | | | | | 10th | 174 | 235 | – |
| Cowper | 6 | 0 | 14 | 0 | | | | | | | | |
| Simpson | 28 | 12 | 45 | 4 | | | | | | | | |

Umpires: S. Pan and B. Satyaji Rao.

# PAKISTAN v AUSTRALIA 1964–65 (Only Test)

Played at National Stadium, Karachi, on 24, 25, 27, 28, 29 October.
Toss: Pakistan.   Results: MATCH DRAWN.
Debuts: Pakistan – Abdul Kadir, Asif Iqbal (*who played Ranji Trophy cricket for Hyderabad as 'A.I. Razvi'*), Khalid Ibadulla (*who played for Warwickshire, Tasmania and Otago as 'K. Ibadulla'*), Majid Jahangir Khan (*who has appeared as 'Majid Jahangir' and as 'M.J. Khan' for Cambridge University and Glamorgan; he is shown throughout this book as 'Majid Khan'*), Pervez Sajjad, Shafqat Rana.

Khalid Ibadulla became the first Pakistan batsman to score a hundred in his first Test match and he equalled Saeed Ahmed's record score of 166 (*Test No. 480*) for Pakistan against Australia. His partnership of 249 with Abdul Kadir set a new Pakistan record for any wicket and remains their first wicket record in all Tests. Simpson is the only batsman to score a hundred in each innings of a Test in Pakistan. Australia were set to score 342 runs in 290 minutes.

## PAKISTAN

| | | | | |
|---|---|---|---|---|
| Khalid Ibadulla | c Grout b McKenzie | 166 | c Redpath b McKenzie | 3 |
| Abdul Kadir† | run out | 95 | hit wkt b Veivers | 26 |
| Saeed Ahmed | c Redpath b Martin | 7 | (4) c sub (R.H.D. Sellers) b Martin | 35 |
| Javed Burki | hit wkt b McKenzie | 8 | (5) c Grout b Cowper | 62 |
| Hanif Mohammad* | c and b McKenzie | 2 | (6) c McKenzie b Booth | 40 |
| Shafqat Rana | c Grout b McKenzie | 0 | (7) lbw b McKenzie | 24 |
| Nasim-ul-Ghani | c Redpath b Hawke | 15 | (8) c Grout b Veivers | 22 |
| Majid Khan | lbw b Martin | 0 | | |
| Intikhab Alam | c Grout b McKenzie | 53 | not out | 21 |
| Asif Iqbal | c Booth b McKenzie | 41 | (3) c and b Simpson | 36 |
| Pervez Sajjad | not out | 3 | | |
| Extras | (B 9, LB 12, NB 3) | 24 | (B 1, LB 6, NB 3) | 10 |
| **Total** | | **414** | (8 wickets declared) | **279** |

## AUSTRALIA

| | | | | |
|---|---|---|---|---|
| W.M. Lawry | hit wkt b Majid | 7 | c Ibadulla b Majid | 22 |
| R.B. Simpson* | c Pervez b Saeed | 153 | c Ibadulla b Nasim | 115 |
| I.R. Redpath | lbw b Intikhab | 19 | not out | 40 |
| P.J.P. Burge | c Majid b Pervez | 54 | not out | 28 |
| B.C. Booth | c Asif b Majid | 15 | | |
| R.M. Cowper | b Asif | 16 | | |
| T.R. Veivers | st Kadir b Saeed | 25 | | |
| J.W. Martin | b Asif | 26 | | |
| A.T.W. Grout† | c Asif b Saeed | 0 | | |
| G.D. McKenzie | lbw b Intikhab | 2 | | |
| N.J.N. Hawke | not out | 8 | | |
| Extras | (B 12, LB 8, NB 7) | 27 | (LB 14, NB 8) | 22 |
| **Total** | | **352** | (2 wickets) | **227** |

| AUSTRALIA | O | M | R | W | O | M | R | W | | FALL OF WICKETS | | | |
|---|---|---|---|---|---|---|---|---|---|---|---|---|---|
| McKenzie | 30 | 9 | 69 | 6 | 25 | 5 | 62 | 2 | | P | A | P | A |
| Hawke | 20 | 2 | 84 | 1 | 6 | 2 | 20 | 0 | Wkt | 1st | 1st | 2nd | 2nd |
| Martin | 36 | 11 | 106 | 2 | 17 | 4 | 42 | 1 | 1st | 249 | 10 | 13 | 54 |
| Veivers | 16 | 5 | 33 | 0 | 30 | 16 | 44 | 2 | 2nd | 266 | 78 | 65 | 173 |
| Simpson | 30 | 8 | 69 | 0 | 20 | 5 | 47 | 1 | 3rd | 284 | 194 | 81 | – |
| Booth | 5 | 2 | 15 | 0 | 13 | 4 | 18 | 1 | 4th | 296 | 228 | 118 | – |
| Redpath | 1 | 0 | 14 | 0 | | | | | 5th | 296 | 257 | 202 | – |
| Cowper | | | | | 11 | 3 | 36 | 1 | 6th | 301 | 315 | 224 | – |
| PAKISTAN | | | | | | | | | 7th | 302 | 315 | 236 | – |
| Majid | 30 | 9 | 55 | 2 | 16 | 3 | 42 | 1 | 8th | 334 | 315 | 236 | – |
| Asif | 23·5 | 5 | 68 | 2 | 12 | 4 | 28 | 0 | 9th | 383 | 320 | – | – |
| Pervez | 22 | 5 | 52 | 1 | 8 | 2 | 17 | 0 | 10th | 414 | 352 | – | – |
| Intikhab | 28 | 5 | 83 | 2 | 16 | 3 | 48 | 0 | | | | | |
| Nasim | 4 | 0 | 17 | 0 | 12 | 3 | 24 | 1 | | | | | |
| Saeed | 19 | 5 | 41 | 3 | 13 | 6 | 28 | 0 | | | | | |
| Ibadulla | 7 | 3 | 9 | 0 | 2 | 0 | 14 | 0 | | | | | |
| Burki | | | | | 2 | 1 | 3 | 0 | | | | | |
| Shafqat | | | | | 1 | 0 | 1 | 0 | | | | | |

Umpires: Shujauddin and Daud Khan.

# AUSTRALIA v PAKISTAN 1964–65 (Only Test)

Played at Melbourne Cricket Ground on 4, 5, 7, 8 December.
Toss: Australia.   Result: MATCH DRAWN.
Debuts: Australia – I.M. Chappell, D.J. Sincock; Pakistan – Arif Butt, Farooq Hamid, Mohammad Ilyas.

Hanif, captaining Pakistan in their first Test in Australia, made top score in both innings and kept wicket throughout in place of Abdul Kadir, who was injured while batting.

### PAKISTAN

| | | | | | |
|---|---|---|---|---|---|
| Abdul Kadir† | c Chappell b McKenzie | 0 | (7) | c Jarman b Hawke | 35 |
| Mohammad Ilyas | run out | 6 | | lbw b McKenzie | 3 |
| Saeed Ahmed | c Chappell b Hawke | 80 | | c Chappell b McKenzie | 24 |
| Javed Burki | c Simpson b McKenzie | 29 | | b Hawke | 47 |
| Hanif Mohammad* | c McKenzie b Sincock | 104 | | st Jarman b Veivers | 93 |
| Nasim-ul-Ghani | b McKenzie | 27 | | b Sincock | 10 |
| Asif Iqbal | c McKenzie b Hawke | 1 | (8) | c Jarman b Hawke | 15 |
| Intikhab Alam | c Shepherd b Hawke | 13 | (9) | c Simpson b Hawke | 61 |
| Afaq Hussain | not out | 8 | (10) | not out | 13 |
| Arif Butt | c Chappell b Sincock | 7 | (1) | c Jarman b McKenzie | 12 |
| Farooq Hamid | b Sincock | 0 | | b McKenzie | 3 |
| Extras | (B 4, LB 4, W 3, NB 1) | 12 | | (B 5, LB 2, W 2, NB 1) | 10 |
| **Total** | | **287** | | | **326** |

### AUSTRALIA

| | | | | | |
|---|---|---|---|---|---|
| R.B. Simpson* | b Arif | 47 | | c Hanif b Arif | 1 |
| W.M. Lawry | c Hanif b Arif | 41 | | run out | 19 |
| I.M. Chappell | c Hanif b Farooq | 11 | | | |
| B.K. Shepherd | c sub (Ghulam Abbas) b Asif | 55 | (3) | not out | 43 |
| B.C. Booth | c Hanif b Arif | 57 | | | |
| R.M. Cowper | c Intikhab b Saeed | 83 | | | |
| T.R. Veivers | c Hanif b Arif | 88 | (4) | not out | 16 |
| B.N. Jarman† | b Asif | 33 | | | |
| D.J. Sincock | b Arif | 7 | | | |
| G.D. McKenzie | b Arif | 1 | | | |
| N.J.N. Hawke | not out | 1 | | | |
| Extras | (B 6, LB 3, W 1, NB 14) | 24 | | (B 2, LB 4, W 2, NB 1) | 9 |
| **Total** | | **448** | | (2 wickets) | **88** |

| AUSTRALIA | O | M | R | W | O | M | R | W | | FALL OF WICKETS | | | |
|---|---|---|---|---|---|---|---|---|---|---|---|---|---|
| McKenzie | 22 | 5 | 66 | 3 | 24·4 | 1 | 74 | 4 | | P | A | P | A |
| Hawke | 21 | 1 | 69 | 3 | 21 | 2 | 72 | 4 | *Wkt* | *1st* | *1st* | *2nd* | *2nd* |
| Sincock | 17·6 | 0 | 67 | 3 | 28 | 5 | 102 | 1 | 1st | 0 | 81 | 6 | 12 |
| Simpson | 9 | 1 | 21 | 0 | | | | | 2nd | 18 | 105 | 37 | 55 |
| Chappell | 15 | 2 | 49 | 0 | 11 | 2 | 31 | 0 | 3rd | 112 | 105 | 46 | – |
| Veivers | 3 | 2 | 3 | 0 | 12 | 4 | 37 | 1 | 4th | 127 | 200 | 130 | – |
| | | | | | | | | | 5th | 225 | 233 | 152 | – |
| | | | | | | | | | 6th | 226 | 372 | 198 | – |
| PAKISTAN | | | | | | | | | 7th | 255 | 418 | 229 | – |
| Farooq | 19 | 1 | 82 | 1 | 4 | 0 | 25 | 0 | 8th | 275 | 434 | 267 | – |
| Asif | 19 | 1 | 90 | 2 | 2 | 0 | 25 | 0 | 9th | 287 | 446 | 323 | – |
| Arif | 21·3 | 1 | 89 | 6 | 5·5 | 0 | 29 | 1 | 10th | 287 | 448 | 326 | – |
| Afaq | 9 | 1 | 45 | 0 | | | | | | | | | |
| Intikhab | 10 | 0 | 51 | 0 | | | | | | | | | |
| Saeed | 10 | 0 | 31 | 1 | | | | | | | | | |
| Nasim | 4 | 0 | 36 | 0 | | | | | | | | | |

Umpires: C.J. Egar and W. Smyth.

# SOUTH AFRICA v ENGLAND 1964–65 (1st Test)

Played at Kingsmead, Durban, on 4, 5, 7, 8 December.
Toss: England.   Result: ENGLAND won by an innings and 104 runs.
Debuts: South Africa – G.D. Varnals; England – N.I. Thomson.

England's victory, gained shortly after lunch on the penultimate day, ended a run of twelve consecutive matches without a win – their longest sequence without a success. The unbroken partnership of 206 between Barrington and Parks remains the sixth-wicket record for this series. Barrington's hundred was his eleventh for England and his tenth overseas. He became the first to score a Test hundred in all seven Test-playing countries.

## ENGLAND

| | | |
|---|---|---|
| G. Boycott | lbw b Partridge | 73 |
| R.W. Barber | b Goddard | 74 |
| E.R. Dexter | c and b Seymour | 28 |
| K.F. Barrington | not out | 148 |
| P.H. Parfitt | c Goddard b Partridge | 0 |
| M.J.K. Smith* | c Lindsay b Partridge | 35 |
| J.M. Parks† | not out | 108 |
| F.J. Titmus | ) | |
| D.A. Allen | ) did not bat | |
| N.I. Thomson | ) | |
| J.S.E. Price | ) | |
| Extras | (B 2, LB 1, NB 16) | 19 |
| **Total** | (5 wickets declared) | **485** |

## SOUTH AFRICA

| | | | | | |
|---|---|---|---|---|---|
| T.L. Goddard* | c Smith b Price | 8 | c Thomson b Titmus | 15 |
| E.J. Barlow | b Thomson | 2 | c Barrington b Price | 0 |
| A.J. Pithey | b Allen | 15 | c Dexter b Allen | 43 |
| R.G. Pollock | b Titmus | 5 | c Smith b Titmus | 0 |
| K.C. Bland | c Barber b Allen | 26 | c Barber b Titmus | 68 |
| D.T. Lindsay† | c Price b Barber | 38 | c Dexter b Titmus | 10 |
| R.A. McLean | c Smith b Allen | 30 | c Smith b Allen | 9 |
| G.D. Varnals | b Allen | 3 | c Parks b Thomson | 11 |
| M.A. Seymour | not out | 15 | b Titmus | 36 |
| P.M. Pollock | c Dexter b Barber | 3 | not out | 18 |
| J.T. Partridge | b Allen | 6 | run out | 1 |
| Extras | (B 4) | 4 | (B 9, LB 6) | 15 |
| **Total** | | **155** | | **226** |

| SOUTH AFRICA | O | M | R | W | O | M | R | W | | FALL OF WICKETS | | |
|---|---|---|---|---|---|---|---|---|---|---|---|---|
| | | | | | | | | | | E | SA | SA |
| P.M. Pollock | 33 | 11 | 80 | 0 | | | | | *Wkt* | *1st* | *1st* | *2nd* |
| Partridge | 45 | 14 | 85 | 3 | | | | | 1st | 120 | 10 | 4 |
| Barlow | 20 | 5 | 36 | 0 | | | | | 2nd | 169 | 10 | 28 |
| Seymour | 46 | 4 | 144 | 1 | | | | | 3rd | 205 | 19 | 28 |
| Goddard | 32 | 8 | 79 | 1 | | | | | 4th | 206 | 54 | 123 |
| R.G. Pollock | 10 | 1 | 32 | 0 | | | | | 5th | 279 | 67 | 142 |
| Bland | 4 | 1 | 10 | 0 | | | | | 6th | – | 120 | 145 |
| ENGLAND | | | | | | | | | 7th | – | 130 | 157 |
| Price | 6 | 2 | 19 | 1 | 9 | 7 | 7 | 1 | 8th | – | 131 | 178 |
| Thomson | 15 | 5 | 23 | 1 | 13 | 6 | 25 | 1 | 9th | – | 142 | 225 |
| Titmus | 20 | 9 | 20 | 1 | 45·5 | 19 | 66 | 5 | 10th | – | 155 | 226 |
| Allen | 19·5 | 5 | 41 | 5 | 47 | 15 | 99 | 2 | | | | |
| Barber | 14 | 1 | 48 | 2 | 6 | 2 | 8 | 0 | | | | |
| Parfitt | | | | | 2 | 0 | 6 | 0 | | | | |

Umpires: H.C. Kidson and J.G. Draper.

# SOUTH AFRICA v ENGLAND 1964–65 (2nd Test)

Played at New Wanderers, Johannesburg, on 23, 24, 26, 28, 29 December.
Toss: England.   Result: MATCH DRAWN.
Debuts: Nil.

England again enforced the follow-on and Barrington scored his second hundred in consecutive innings. Rain and bad light prevented play after tea on the fifth day.

### ENGLAND

| | | |
|---|---|---|
| G. Boycott | c Lindsay b P.M. Pollock | 4 |
| R.W. Barber | b Seymour | 97 |
| E.R. Dexter | c Lindsay b R.G. Pollock | 172 |
| K.F. Barrington | c R.G. Pollock b P.M. Pollock | 121 |
| P.H. Parfitt | c Goddard b Partridge | 52 |
| M.J.K. Smith* | c McLean b Goodard | 25 |
| J.M. Parks† | lbw b R.G. Pollock | 26 |
| F.J. Titmus | b P.M. Pollock | 2 |
| D.A. Allen | lbw b P.M. Pollock | 2 |
| N.I. Thomson | not out | 27 |
| J.S.E. Price | b P.M. Pollock | 0 |
| Extras | (LB 3) | 3 |
| **Total** | | **531** |

### SOUTH AFRICA

| | | | | |
|---|---|---|---|---|
| T.L. Goddard* | b Titmus | 40 | c Smith b Allen | 5( |
| E.J. Barlow | c Price b Titmus | 71 | c Smith b Allen | 1 |
| A.J. Pithey | b Allen | 85 | c Dexter b Allen | |
| R.G. Pollock | c Smith b Titmus | 12 | (5) b Allen | 5 |
| K.C. Bland | c Thomson b Price | 29 | (6) not out | 144 |
| R.A. McLean | lbw b Barber | 12 | (4) b Titmus | 24 |
| G.D. Varnals | b Price | 21 | c Parks b Dexter | 23 |
| D.T. Lindsay† | b Thomson | 10 | not out | 4 |
| M.A. Seymour | run out | 2 | | |
| P.M. Pollock | c Smith b Titmus | 20 | | |
| J.T. Partridge | not out | 13 | | |
| Extras | (LB 2) | 2 | (B 4, LB 8, NB 3) | 1 |
| **Total** | | **317** | (6 wickets) | 33 |

| SOUTH AFRICA | O | M | R | W | O | M | R | W |
|---|---|---|---|---|---|---|---|---|
| P.M. Pollock | 38·3 | 10 | 129 | 5 | | | | |
| Partridge | 40 | 10 | 106 | 1 | | | | |
| Goddard | 31 | 8 | 90 | 1 | | | | |
| Seymour | 35 | 10 | 109 | 1 | | | | |
| Barlow | 8 | 2 | 33 | 0 | | | | |
| R.G. Pollock | 11 | 1 | 50 | 2 | | | | |
| Bland | 3 | 0 | 11 | 0 | | | | |
| ENGLAND | | | | | | | | |
| Price | 32 | 11 | 66 | 2 | 15 | 3 | 49 | 0 |
| Thomson | 23 | 8 | 47 | 1 | 16 | 5 | 36 | 0 |
| Titmus | 39·5 | 15 | 73 | 4 | 45 | 18 | 101 | 1 |
| Dexter | 4 | 0 | 16 | 0 | 8 | 0 | 33 | 1 |
| Allen | 39 | 19 | 45 | 1 | 49 | 17 | 87 | 4 |
| Barrington | 4 | 0 | 29 | 0 | | | | |
| Barber | 14 | 1 | 33 | 1 | 2 | 0 | 12 | 0 |
| Parfitt | 4 | 2 | 6 | 0 | | | | |
| Boycott | | | | | 5 | 3 | 3 | 0 |

FALL OF WICKETS

| Wkt | E 1st | SA 1st | SA 2nd |
|---|---|---|---|
| 1st | 10 | 78 | 50 |
| 2nd | 146 | 139 | 74 |
| 3rd | 337 | 153 | 75 |
| 4th | 419 | 211 | 109 |
| 5th | 467 | 231 | 196 |
| 6th | 477 | 271 | 320 |
| 7th | 484 | 271 | – |
| 8th | 490 | 282 | – |
| 9th | 526 | 285 | – |
| 10th | 531 | 317 | – |

Umpires: H.C. Kidson and L.M. Baxter.

# SOUTH AFRICA v ENGLAND 1964–65 (3rd Test)

Played at Newlands, Cape Town, on 1, 2, 4, 5, 6 January.
Toss: South Africa.   Result: MATCH DRAWN.
Debuts: South Africa – G.G. Hall.

South Africa won their first toss in eight Tests against England. Barrington 'walked' after being given not out.

## SOUTH AFRICA

| | | | | | |
|---|---|---|---|---|---|
| T.L. Goddard* | b Titmus | 40 | | c Parfitt b Price | 6 |
| E.J. Barlow | c Parks b Thomson | 138 | | c Parks b Dexter | 78 |
| A.J. Pithey | c Barber b Allen | 154 | | c Parks b Thomson | 2 |
| R.G. Pollock | c Parks b Allen | 31 | (5) | b Boycott | 73 |
| K.C. Bland | run out | 78 | (6) | b Boycott | 64 |
| D.T. Lindsay† | lbw b Thomson | 2 | (7) | b Barrington | 50 |
| G.D. Varnals | c Smith b Titmus | 19 | (4) | c Smith b Parfitt | 20 |
| S.F. Burke | not out | 10 | | c Barber b Boycott | 20 |
| P.M. Pollock | ) | | | lbw b Barrington | 7 |
| H.D. Bromfield | ) did not bat | | | not out | 12 |
| G.G. Hall | ) | | | b Barrington | 0 |
| Extras | (B 5, LB 11, W 1, NB 12) | 29 | | (B 1, LB 9, W 1, NB 3) | 14 |
| **Total** | (7 wickets declared) | **501** | | | **346** |

## ENGLAND

| | | | | | |
|---|---|---|---|---|---|
| G. Boycott | c Barlow b Bromfield | 15 | | not out | 1 |
| R.W. Barber | lbw b Goddard | 58 | | | |
| E.R. Dexter | c and b Bromfield | 61 | | | |
| K.F. Barrington | c Lindsay b P.M. Pollock | 49 | (2) | not out | 14 |
| P.H. Parfitt | b Hall | 44 | | | |
| M.J.K. Smith* | c Goddard b Bromfield | 121 | | | |
| J.M. Parks† | c Lindsay b Barlow | 59 | | | |
| F.J. Titmus | c Lindsay b P.M. Pollock | 4 | | | |
| D.A. Allen | c Barlow b Bromfield | 22 | | | |
| N.I. Thomson | c R.G. Pollock b Bromfield | 0 | | | |
| J.S.E. Price | not out | 0 | | | |
| Extras | (B 2, LB 5, NB 2) | 9 | | | |
| **Total** | | **442** | | (0 wickets) | **15** |

| ENGLAND | O | M | R | W | O | M | R | W | | FALL OF WICKETS | | | |
|---|---|---|---|---|---|---|---|---|---|---|---|---|---|
| | | | | | | | | | | SA | E | SA | E |
| Price | 34 | 6 | 133 | 0 | 11 | 4 | 19 | 1 | Wkt | 1st | 1st | 2nd | 2nd |
| Thomson | 45 | 19 | 89 | 2 | 14 | 4 | 31 | 1 | 1st | 80 | 72 | 10 | – |
| Titmus | 50·2 | 11 | 133 | 2 | 6 | 2 | 21 | 0 | 2nd | 252 | 80 | 13 | – |
| Dexter | 2 | 0 | 10 | 0 | 17 | 3 | 64 | 1 | 3rd | 313 | 170 | 86 | – |
| Allen | 40 | 14 | 79 | 2 | 17 | 6 | 27 | 0 | 4th | 430 | 206 | 144 | – |
| Parfitt | 8 | 0 | 28 | 0 | 19 | 4 | 74 | 1 | 5th | 439 | 243 | 231 | – |
| Barber | | | | | 1 | 0 | 2 | 0 | 6th | 470 | 360 | 256 | – |
| Boycott | | | | | 20 | 5 | 47 | 3 | 7th | 501 | 368 | 310 | – |
| Smith | | | | | 11 | 1 | 43 | 0 | 8th | – | 438 | 331 | – |
| Barrington | | | | | 3·1 | 1 | 4 | 3 | 9th | – | 440 | 334 | – |
| | | | | | | | | | 10th | – | 442 | 346 | – |
| SOUTH AFRICA | | | | | | | | | | | | | |
| P.M. Pollock | 39 | 14 | 89 | 2 | | | | | | | | | |
| Burke | 29 | 8 | 61 | 0 | | | | | | | | | |
| Bromfield | 57·2 | 26 | 88 | 5 | | | | | | | | | |
| Hall | 31 | 7 | 94 | 1 | | | | | | | | | |
| Goddard | 37 | 13 | 64 | 1 | | | | | | | | | |
| Barlow | 12 | 3 | 37 | 1 | | | | | | | | | |
| Bland | | | | | 2 | 0 | 3 | 0 | | | | | |
| R.G. Pollock | | | | | 2 | 1 | 5 | 0 | | | | | |
| Pithey | | | | | 2 | 0 | 5 | 0 | | | | | |
| Varnals | | | | | 2 | 1 | 2 | 0 | | | | | |

Umpires: V. Costello and J.E. Warner.

# SOUTH AFRICA v ENGLAND 1964–65 (4th Test)

Played at New Wanderers, Johannesburg, on 22, 23, 25, 26, 27 January.
Toss: England.   Result: MATCH DRAWN.
Debuts: Nil.

England elected to field in South Africa for the first time since 1930-31 (*Test No. 208*). Rain caused the loss of 195 minutes of play during the first two days. The partnership of 157 between Pithey and Waite remains South Africa's highest for the fifth wicket against England. Goddard scored his first Test hundred in his 62nd innings. In the first innings, Van der Merwe (leg slip) threw down the wicket after the ball had been tossed to him by the wicket-keeper. The batsman, Smith, who had gone down the pitch 'gardening', was given out by the umpire Kidson but was recalled after Goddard had asked for the appeal to be revoked. Barber fractured a finger when fielding and was unable to bat in the second innings.

## SOUTH AFRICA

| | | | | | |
|---|---|---|---|---|---|
| T.L. Goddard* | run out | 60 | | c Barber b Price | 112 |
| E.J. Barlow | c and b Cartwright | 96 | | c Barber b Titmus | 42 |
| K.C. Bland | c Parks b Price | 55 | (5) | not out | 38 |
| A.J. Pithey | c Cartwright b Titmus | 95 | (3) | b Cartwright | 39 |
| R.G. Pollock | c Parks b Price | 4 | (4) | not out | 65 |
| J.H.B. Waite† | run out | 64 | | | |
| P.L. van der Merwe | not out | 5 | | | |
| P.M. Pollock | not out | 0 | | | |
| H.D. Bromfield | ) | | | | |
| A.K. McKinnon | ) did not bat | | | | |
| J.T. Partridge | ) | | | | |
| Extras | (LB 7, NB 4) | 11 | | (LB 7, NB 4) | 11 |
| **Total** | (6 wickets declared) | **390** | | (3 wickets declared) | **307** |

## ENGLAND

| | | | | | |
|---|---|---|---|---|---|
| G. Boycott | c Barlow b Partridge | 5 | | not out | 76 |
| R.W. Barber | lbw b McKinnon | 61 | | | |
| E.R. Dexter | c Waite b Goddard | 38 | | c R.G. Pollock b P.M. Pollock | 0 |
| K.F. Barrington | c Waite b Barlow | 93 | | c Bromfield b McKinnon | 11 |
| P.H. Parfitt | not out | 122 | | c Barlow b McKinnon | 22 |
| M.J.K. Smith* | c R.G. Pollock b McKinnon | 42 | | b Bromfield | 8 |
| J.M. Parks† | c Barlow b Partridge | 0 | | c R.G. Pollock b McKinnon | 10 |
| F.J. Titmus | lbw b McKinnon | 1 | (2) | c Van der Merwe b P.M. Pollock | 13 |
| T.W. Cartwright | b McKinnon | 9 | (8) | not out | 8 |
| N.I. Thomson | c Barlow b P.M. Pollock | 3 | | | |
| J.S.E. Price | c Bromfield b P.M. Pollock | 0 | | | |
| Extras | (B 1, LB 5, W 1, NB 3) | 10 | | (LB 5) | 5 |
| **Total** | | **384** | | (6 wickets) | **153** |

| ENGLAND | O | M | R | W | O | M | R | W |
|---|---|---|---|---|---|---|---|---|
| Price | 17 | 1 | 68 | 2 | 14 | 1 | 56 | 1 |
| Thomson | 31 | 3 | 91 | 0 | 19 | 4 | 43 | 0 |
| Cartwright | 55 | 18 | 97 | 1 | 24 | 6 | 99 | 1 |
| Dexter | 6 | 0 | 30 | 0 | | | | |
| Titmus | 29 | 2 | 68 | 1 | 31 | 4 | 98 | 1 |
| Boycott | 8 | 1 | 25 | 0 | | | | |
| SOUTH AFRICA | | | | | | | | |
| P.M. Pollock | 15·2 | 4 | 42 | 2 | 11 | 3 | 27 | 2 |
| Partridge | 30 | 6 | 92 | 2 | 7 | 4 | 10 | 0 |
| Barlow | 18 | 5 | 34 | 1 | | | | |
| Goddard | 16 | 4 | 35 | 1 | 6 | 4 | 5 | 0 |
| McKinnon | 51 | 13 | 128 | 4 | 35 | 17 | 44 | 3 |
| R.G. Pollock | 4 | 0 | 12 | 0 | 11 | 2 | 35 | 0 |
| Bromfield | 13 | 4 | 31 | 0 | 17 | 8 | 27 | 1 |

FALL OF WICKETS

| Wkt | SA 1st | E 1st | SA 2nd | E 2nd |
|---|---|---|---|---|
| 1st | 134 | 7 | 65 | 21 |
| 2nd | 189 | 78 | 180 | 21 |
| 3rd | 222 | 144 | 211 | 33 |
| 4th | 226 | 244 | – | 80 |
| 5th | 383 | 333 | – | 107 |
| 6th | 389 | 333 | – | 124 |
| 7th | – | 338 | – | – |
| 8th | – | 350 | – | – |
| 9th | – | 374 | – | – |
| 10th | – | 384 | – | – |

Umpires: H.C. Kidson and L.M. Baxter.

# SOUTH AFRICA v. ENGLAND 1964–65 (5th Test)

Played at St. George's Park, Port Elizabeth, on 12, 13, 15, 16, 17 February.
Toss: South Africa.   Result: MATCH DRAWN.
Debuts: South Africa – M.J. Macaulay; England – K.E. Palmer.

England's thirteenth draw in fifteen matches secured a 1-0 victory in the rubber. With Price, Brown and Cartwright injured, England called upon Palmer who had been coaching in Johannesburg. R.G. Pollock became the second player after G.A. Headley to score three hundreds before attaining the age of 21. Rain restricted play to 19·2 overs after lunch on the fifth day, England having been set to score 246 runs at 65 per hour.

## SOUTH AFRICA

| | | | | | |
|---|---|---|---|---|---|
| T.L. Goddard* | c Boycott b Allen | 61 | c Boycott b Thomson | | 13 |
| E.J. Barlow | c Parfitt b Boycott | 69 | b Titmus | | 47 |
| K.C. Bland | c Parfitt b Titmus | 48 | c and b Thomson | | 22 |
| R.G. Pollock | c and b Allen | 137 | not out | | 77 |
| A.J. Pithey | c Barrington b Allen | 23 | | | |
| J.H.B. Waite† | run out | 6 | | | |
| P.L. van der Merwe | c Barrington b Palmer | 66 | | | |
| P.M. Pollock | c Titmus b Thomson | 18 | | | |
| M.J. Macaulay | b Titmus | 21 | (5) c Titmus b Boycott | | 12 |
| A.H. McKinnon | run out | 27 | (6) not out | | 0 |
| H.D. Bromfield | not out | 1 | | | |
| Extras | (B 10, LB 11, NB 4) | 25 | (B 1, LB 4, NB 2) | | 7 |
| **Total** | | **502** | (4 wickets declared) | | **178** |

## ENGLAND

| | | | | | |
|---|---|---|---|---|---|
| G. Boycott | c Van der Merwe b Bromfield | 117 | c Waite b Macaulay | | 7 |
| J.T. Murray | lbw b Macaulay | 4 | not out | | 8 |
| F.J. Titmus | b P.M. Pollock | 12 | | | |
| E.R. Dexter | run out | 40 | (3) not out | | 5 |
| K.F. Barrington | c Van der Merwe b Goddard | 72 | | | |
| N.I. Thomson | c Barlow b McKinnon | 39 | | | |
| M.J.K. Smith* | c Waite b Barlow | 26 | | | |
| P.H. Parfitt | lbw b Barlow | 0 | | | |
| J.M. Parks† | c Waite b Barlow | 35 | | | |
| D.A. Allen | not out | 38· | | | |
| K.E. Palmer | lbw b Goddard | 10 | | | |
| Extras | (B 7, LB 14, W 2, NB 19) | 42 | (B 7, LB 2) | | 9 |
| **Total** | | **435** | (1 wicket) | | **29** |

| ENGLAND | O | M | R | W | O | M | R | W | | FALL OF WICKETS | | | |
|---|---|---|---|---|---|---|---|---|---|---|---|---|---|
| Thomson | 47 | 7 | 128 | 1 | 25 | 7 | 55 | 2 | | | SA | E | SA | E |
| Palmer | 35 | 6 | 113 | 1 | 28 | 1 | 76 | 0 | *Wkt* | *1st* | *1st* | *2nd* | *2nd* |
| Boycott | 26 | 7 | 69 | 1 | 2 | 0 | 13 | 1 | 1st | 114 | 28 | 30 | 17 |
| Titmus | 37·1 | 7 | 87 | 2 | 5 | 0 | 27 | 1 | 2nd | 171 | 52 | 69 | – |
| Allen | 44 | 13 | 80 | 3 | | | | | 3rd | 185 | 115 | 124 | – |
| | | | | | | | | | 4th | 268 | 272 | 171 | – |
| SOUTH AFRICA | | | | | | | | | 5th | 276 | 277 | – | – |
| P.M. Pollock | 27 | 8 | 71 | 1 | 5·2 | 1 | 7 | 0 | 6th | 389 | 346 | – | – |
| Macaulay | 37 | 13 | 63 | 1 | 9 | 4 | 10 | 1 | 7th | 447 | 346 | – | – |
| Goddard | 35·5 | 18 | 34 | 2 | 5 | 3 | 3 | 0 | 8th | 455 | 346 | – | – |
| McKinnon | 46 | 17 | 99 | 1 | | | | | 9th | 498 | 410 | – | – |
| Barlow | 22 | 2 | 55 | 3 | | | | | 10th | 502 | 435 | – | – |
| Bromfield | 33 | 14 | 57 | 1 | | | | | | | | | |
| R.G. Pollock | 7 | 3 | 14 | 0 | | | | | | | | | |

Umpires: H.C. Kidson and L.M. Baxter.

# NEW ZEALAND v PAKISTAN 1964–65 (1st Test)

Played at Basin Reserve, Wellington, on 22, 23, 25, 26 January.
Toss: Pakistan.   Result: MATCH DRAWN.
Debuts: New Zealand – R.O. Collinge, B.E. Congdon; Pakistan – Naushad Ali.

Only two hours of play was possible on the first day. New Zealand's last six wickets fell for the addition of just five runs, the last four falling in five balls. Pakistan, set to score 259 runs in 188 minutes, lost seven wickets for 104 before their eighth-wicket pair played out the last 34 minutes.

## NEW ZEALAND

| | | | | | |
|---|---|---|---|---|---|
| S.G. Gedye | b Asif | 1 | b Arif | | 26 |
| G.T. Dowling | c Burki b Pervez | 29 | b Arif | | 19 |
| B.W. Sinclair | c Nasim b Saeed | 65 | c Saeed b Pervez | | 17 |
| B.E. Congdon | c Naushad b Asif | 42 | b Asif | | 30 |
| J.R. Reid* | b Arif | 97 | c Saeed b Pervez | | 14 |
| S.N. McGregor | lbw b Asif | 11 | not out | | 37 |
| B.W. Yuile | b Asif | 4 | (8) run out | | 7 |
| A.E. Dick† | b Arif | 1 | | | |
| R.C. Motz | b Asif | 0 | (7) b Arif | | 13 |
| R.O. Collinge | not out | 0 | | | |
| F.J. Cameron | lbw b Arif | 0 | | | |
| Extras | (B 2, LB 14) | 16 | (B 12, LB 3, NB 1) | | 16 |
| **Total** | | **266** | (7 wickets declared) | | **179** |

## PAKISTAN

| | | | | | |
|---|---|---|---|---|---|
| Naushad Ali† | run out | 11 | c and b Motz | | 3 |
| Mohammad Ilyas | b Collinge | 13 | c Reid b Motz | | 4 |
| Saeed Ahmed | c Congdon b Motz | 11 | c Yuile b Collinge | | 4 |
| Javed Burki | b Motz | 0 | c Dick b Collinge | | 0 |
| Hanif Mohammad* | b Collinge | 5 | b Collinge | | 25 |
| Abdul Kadir | c and b Motz | 46 | b Motz | | 0 |
| Nasim-ul-Ghani | b Cameron | 16 | c Dowling b Reid | | 23 |
| Asif Iqbal | c Sinclair b Yuile | 30 | not out | | 52 |
| Intikhab Alam | b Motz | 28 | not out | | 13 |
| Arif Butt | b Yuile | 20 | | | |
| Pervez Sajjad | not out | 1 | | | |
| Extras | (B 2, LB 4) | 6 | (B 8, LB 6, W 1, NB 1) | | 16 |
| **Total** | | **187** | (7 wickets) | | **140** |

| PAKISTAN | O | M | R | W | O | M | R | W | FALL OF WICKETS | | | | |
|---|---|---|---|---|---|---|---|---|---|---|---|---|---|
| | | | | | | | | | | NZ | P | NZ | P |
| Arif | 22·2 | 10 | 46 | 3 | 29 | 10 | 62 | 3 | Wkt | 1st | 1st | 2nd | 2nd |
| Asif | 25 | 11 | 48 | 5 | 20·4 | 6 | 33 | 1 | 1st | 1 | 26 | 35 | 3 |
| Pervez | 24 | 7 | 48 | 1 | 25 | 5 | 61 | 2 | 2nd | 82 | 26 | 62 | 8 |
| Intikhab | 17 | 6 | 35 | 0 | 5 | 1 | 7 | 0 | 3rd | 114 | 26 | 83 | 10 |
| Saeed | 16 | 7 | 40 | 1 | 1 | 1 | 0 | 0 | 4th | 223 | 41 | 102 | 17 |
| Nasim | 3 | 1 | 5 | 0 | | | | | 5th | 261 | 47 | 140 | 19 |
| Ilyas | 7 | 1 | 28 | 0 | | | | | 6th | 261 | 64 | 156 | 64 |
| | | | | | | | | | 7th | 266 | 114 | 179 | 104 |
| NEW ZEALAND | | | | | | | | | 8th | 266 | 144 | – | – |
| Collinge | 17 | 6 | 51 | 2 | 13 | 3 | 43 | 3 | 9th | 266 | 179 | – | – |
| Cameron | 19 | 11 | 33 | 1 | 8 | 5 | 10 | 0 | 10th | 266 | 187 | – | – |
| Motz | 20 | 9 | 45 | 4 | 15 | 6 | 34 | 3 | | | | | |
| Yuile | 26 | 16 | 28 | 2 | 8 | 2 | 21 | 0 | | | | | |
| Reid | 13 | 6 | 24 | 0 | 8 | 3 | 16 | 1 | | | | | |

Umpires: D.E.A. Copps and W.T. Martin.

# NEW ZEALAND v PAKISTAN 1964–65 (2nd Test)

Played at Eden Park, Auckland, on 29, 30 January, 1, 2 February.
Toss: Pakistan.   Result: MATCH DRAWN.
Debuts: New Zealand – R.W. Morgan.

Pakistan scored only 161 for 8 off 131 overs, including 71 maidens, on the first day. New Zealand needed 220 runs to win in four hours. Pervez took four wickets for no runs in ten balls.

## PAKISTAN

| | | | | |
|---|---|--:|---|--:|
| Naushad Ali† | b Yuile | 14 | c Yuile b Reid | 8 |
| Abdul Kadir | c and b Yuile | 12 | b Collinge | 58 |
| Saeed Ahmed | c Dick b Yuile | 17 | c Dick b Cameron | 16 |
| Javed Burki | c sub (S.G. Gedye) b Cameron | 63 | c Congdon b Collinge | 15 |
| Nasim-ul-Ghani | c Dowling b Yuile | 2 | lbw b Cameron | 14 |
| Hanif Mohammad* | b Collinge | 27 | c Congdon b Collinge | 27 |
| Mohammad Ilyas | lbw b Cameron | 10 | lbw b Reid | 36 |
| Asif Iqbal | c Morgan b Collinge | 3 | b Cameron | 0 |
| Intikhab Alam | lbw b Cameron | 45 | c Morgan b Cameron | 7 |
| Arif Butt | b Cameron | 20 | c Dick b Cameron | 0 |
| Pervez Sajjad | not out | 2 | not out | 0 |
| Extras | (B 5, LB 4, NB 2) | 11 | (B 9, LB 8, NB 9) | 26 |
| **Total** | | **226** | | **207** |

## NEW ZEALAND

| | | | | |
|---|---|--:|---|--:|
| G.T. Dowling | lbw b Asif | 0 | c Asif b Nasim | 62 |
| B.E. Congdon | b Asif | 9 | c Intikhab b Pervez | 42 |
| R.W. Morgan | b Pervez | 66 | b Asif | 5 |
| J.R. Reid* | run out | 52 | b Pervez | 11 |
| S.N. McGregor | c Hanif b Saeed | 1 | c Saeed b Pervez | 0 |
| P.G.Z. Harris | c Hanif b Asif | 1 | b Pervez | 0 |
| B.W. Yuile | b Asif | 0 | (8) not out | 30 |
| A.E. Dick† | b Saeed | 19 | (9) not out | 3 |
| R.C. Motz | c Naushad b Asif | 31 | (7) c Intikhab b Pervez | 0 |
| R.O. Collinge | b Arif | 13 | | |
| F.J. Cameron | not out | 5 | | |
| Extras | (B 7, LB 8, NB 2) | 17 | (B 6, LB 2, NB 5) | 13 |
| **Total** | | **214** | (7 wickets) | **166** |

| NEW ZEALAND | O | M | R | W | O | M | R | W | | FALL OF WICKETS | | | |
|---|--:|--:|--:|--:|--:|--:|--:|--:|---|---|---|---|---|
| Collinge | 28 | 8 | 57 | 2 | 22·1 | 9 | 41 | 3 | | P | NZ | P | NZ |
| Motz | 12 | 4 | 15 | 0 | 6 | 1 | 15 | 0 | *Wkt* | *1st* | *1st* | *2nd* | *2nd* |
| Cameron | 26 | 11 | 36 | 4 | 23 | 11 | 34 | 5 | 1st | 19 | 9 | 25 | 68 |
| Yuile | 54 | 38 | 43 | 4 | 30 | 15 | 39 | 0 | 2nd | 44 | 25 | 51 | 82 |
| Reid | 20 | 14 | 26 | 0 | 19 | 7 | 52 | 2 | 3rd | 70 | 101 | 75 | 102 |
| Harris | 7 | 2 | 14 | 0 | | | | | 4th | 99 | 113 | 95 | 102 |
| Morgan | 7 | 3 | 24 | 0 | | | | | 5th | 129 | 125 | 139 | 102 |
| **PAKISTAN** | | | | | | | | | 6th | 151 | 127 | 197 | 102 |
| Arif | 17·4 | 4 | 43 | 1 | 6 | 1 | 19 | 0 | 7th | 156 | 148 | 200 | 150 |
| Asif | 27 | 6 | 52 | 5 | 18 | 4 | 40 | 1 | 8th | 159 | 195 | 207 | – |
| Intikhab | 29 | 10 | 52 | 0 | 15 | 7 | 17 | 0 | 9th | 211 | 195 | 207 | – |
| Pervez | 15 | 4 | 35 | 1 | 25 | 7 | 42 | 5 | 10th | 226 | 214 | 207 | – |
| Saeed | 10 | 4 | 15 | 2 | 9 | 3 | 14 | 0 | | | | | |
| Ilyas | | | | | 2 | 0 | 12 | 0 | | | | | |
| Nasim | | | | | 5 | 2 | 9 | 1 | | | | | |

Umpires: R.W.R. Shortt and E.C.A. MacKintosh.

# NEW ZEALAND v PAKISTAN 1964-65 (3rd Test)

Played at Lancaster Park, Christchurch, on 12, 13, 15, 16 February.
Toss: Pakistan.   Result: MATCH DRAWN.
Debuts: New Zealand – P.B. Truscott; Pakistan – Mufasir-ul-Haq.

Rain ended the first day's play at 3.21 p.m. Sinclair, who was struck in the face by a ball from Mufasir in the first innings, retired hurt and resumed his innings at the fall of sixth wicket. New Zealand were set to score 314 runs in 243 minutes.

## PAKISTAN

| | | | | |
|---|---|---|---|---|
| Khalid Ibadulla | c Ward b Cameron | 28 | b Collinge | 9 |
| Naushad Ali† | c Truscott b Motz | 12 | c Collinge b Yuile | 20 |
| Javed Burki | b Collinge | 4 | (4) b Collinge | 12 |
| Saeed Ahmed | c Ward b Cameron | 1 | (3) lbw b Reid | 87 |
| Hanif Mohammad* | c and b Collinge | 10 | not out | 100 |
| Mohammad Ilyas | st Ward b Yuile | 88 | b Yuile | 13 |
| Nasim-ul-Ghani | b Motz | 5 | b Collinge | 12 |
| Asif Iqbal | c Motz b Yuile | 3 | c Bartlett b Cameron | 20 |
| Intikhab Alam | c Sinclair b Yuile | 27 | c Reid b Yuile | 15 |
| Pervez Sajjad | b Motz | 9 | not out | 0 |
| Mufasir-ul-Haq | not out | 8 | | |
| Extras | (LB 4, NB 7) | 11 | (B 9, LB 6, W 1, NB 5) | 21 |
| **Total** | | **206** | (8 wickets declared) | **309** |

## NEW ZEALAND

| | | | | |
|---|---|---|---|---|
| B.E. Congdon | b Mufasir | 21 | c Hanif b Asif | 8 |
| P.B. Truscott | lbw b Asif | 3 | c and b Asif | 26 |
| B.W. Sinclair | c Naushad b Intikhab | 46 | (6) not out | 7 |
| R.W. Morgan | c Nasim b Mufasir | 19 | (3) c and b Mufasir | 97 |
| J.R. Reid* | b Asif | 27 | (4) c Ilyas b Intikhab | 28 |
| B.W. Yuile | c Hanif b Nasim | 7 | (5) c Ilyas b Pervez | 42 |
| G.A. Bartlett | b Pervez | 1 | not out | 4 |
| R.C. Motz | c Naushad b Pervez | 21 | | |
| J.T. Ward† | c Naushad b Asif | 2 | | |
| R.O. Collinge | c Hanif b Asif | 32 | | |
| F.J. Cameron | not out | 8 | | |
| Extras | (B 3, LB 3, W 1, NB 8) | 15 | (B 7, NB 4) | 11 |
| **Total** | | **202** | (5 wickets) | **223** |

| NEW ZEALAND | O | M | R | W | O | M | R | W | | | | | |
|---|---|---|---|---|---|---|---|---|---|---|---|---|---|
| Bartlett | 18 | 6 | 47 | 0 | 14·3 | 2 | 46 | 0 | | | | | |
| Collinge | 12 | 3 | 23 | 2 | 17 | 3 | 50 | 3 | | | | | |
| Cameron | 24 | 15 | 29 | 2 | 14 | 2 | 61 | 1 | | | | | |
| Motz | 18 | 4 | 48 | 3 | 17 | 7 | 43 | 0 | | | | | |
| Yuile | 11 | 3 | 48 | 3 | 20 | 9 | 64 | 3 | | | | | |
| Reid | | | | | 11 | 5 | 24 | 1 | | | | | |

| | | | | | | | | | | | | | |
|---|---|---|---|---|---|---|---|---|---|---|---|---|---|

## FALL OF WICKETS

| Wkt | P 1st | NZ 1st | P 2nd | NZ 2nd |
|---|---|---|---|---|
| 1st | 36 | 7 | 27 | 18 |
| 2nd | 41 | 34 | 58 | 41 |
| 3rd | 42 | 76 | 97 | 98 |
| 4th | 62 | 81 | 159 | 179 |
| 5th | 66 | 83 | 199 | 219 |
| 6th | 78 | 112 | 222 | – |
| 7th | 81 | 129 | 254 | – |
| 8th | 132 | 137 | 300 | – |
| 9th | 160 | 178 | – | – |
| 10th | 206 | 202 | – | – |

| PAKISTAN | O | M | R | W | O | M | R | W |
|---|---|---|---|---|---|---|---|---|
| Asif | 25·5 | 9 | 46 | 4 | 16 | 6 | 29 | 2 |
| Mufasir | 29 | 11 | 50 | 2 | 8 | 1 | 34 | 1 |
| Ibadulla | 9 | 5 | 17 | 0 | 3 | 0 | 12 | 0 |
| Pervez | 21 | 6 | 53 | 2 | 21 | 8 | 33 | 1 |
| Intikhab | 7 | 1 | 17 | 1 | 21 | 6 | 60 | 1 |
| Nasim | 4 | 3 | 3 | 1 | 3 | 1 | 5 | 0 |
| Saeed | 3 | 2 | 1 | 0 | 8 | 1 | 25 | 0 |
| Ilyas | | | | | 3 | 0 | 14 | 0 |

Umpires: W.T. Martin and F.R. Goodall.

# INDIA v NEW ZEALAND 1964–65 (1st Test)

Played at Corporation Stadium, Madras, on 27, 28 February, 1, 2 March.
Toss: India.   Result: MATCH DRAWN.
Debuts: India – S. Venkataraghavan; New Zealand – T.W. Jarvis, V. Pollard.

The partnership of 143 between Nadkarni and Engineer (whose 90 was scored in 115 minutes) remains India's highest eight-wicket stand against all countries. Jarvis batted for 125 minutes for nine runs in the first innings. Sardesai retired hurt after being struck on the knee in Motz's opening over with the score 1-0. Manjrekar scored his seventh Test hundred in his final Test innings.

## INDIA

| | | | | | |
|---|---|---|---|---|---|
| D.N. Sardesai | b Pollard | 22 | retired hurt | | 0 |
| M.L. Jaisimha | c Morgan b Motz | 51 | c Collinge b Yuile | | 49 |
| V.L. Manjrekar | c Dowling b Pollard | 19 | not out | | 102 |
| C.G. Borde | c Reid b Motz | 68 | b Pollard | | 20 |
| Nawab of Pataudi, jr* | b Motz | 9 | | | |
| Hanumant Singh | c Ward b Pollard | 0 | | | |
| S.A. Durani | b Reid | 34 | | | |
| R.G. Nadkarni | c Collinge b Yuile | 75 | | | |
| F.M. Engineer† | c Pollard b Yuile | 90 | | | |
| R.F. Surti | not out | 9 | (5) not out | | 17 |
| S. Venkataraghavan | b Collinge | 4 | | | |
| Extras | (B 10, LB 1, NB 5) | 16 | (B 3, LB 1, NB 7) | | 11 |
| **Total** | | **397** | (2 wickets declared) | | **199** |

## NEW ZEALAND

| | | | | |
|---|---|---|---|---|
| T.W. Jarvis | b Durani | 9 | not out | 40 |
| G.T. Dowling | b Venkataraghavan | 29 | not out | 21 |
| B.W. Sinclair | b Venkataraghavan | 30 | | |
| J.R. Reid* | lbw b Nadkarni | 42 | | |
| R.W. Morgan | lbw b Durani | 39 | | |
| B. Sutcliffe | b Surti | 56 | | |
| B.W. Yuile | c Nadkarni b Durani | 0 | | |
| V. Pollard | c Venkataraghavan b Jaisimha | 3 | | |
| R.C. Motz | b Nadkarni | 11 | | |
| J.T. Ward† | not out | 35 | | |
| R.O. Collinge | lbw b Borde | 34 | | |
| Extras | (B 8, LB 10, W 3, NB 6) | 27 | (NB 1) | 1 |
| **Total** | | **315** | (0 wickets) | **62** |

| NEW ZEALAND | O | M | R | W | O | M | R | W |
|---|---|---|---|---|---|---|---|---|
| Collinge | 22·5 | 5 | 55 | 1 | 9 | 2 | 29 | 0 |
| Motz | 30 | 6 | 87 | 3 | 19 | 1 | 57 | 0 |
| Reid | 30 | 11 | 70 | 1 | | | | |
| Yuile | 20 | 7 | 62 | 2 | 11·1 | 0 | 53 | 1 |
| Pollard | 34 | 16 | 90 | 3 | 14 | 4 | 32 | 1 |
| Morgan | 7 | 2 | 17 | 0 | 5 | 2 | 17 | 0 |
| **INDIA** | | | | | | | | |
| Jaisimha | 12 | 4 | 30 | 1 | 4 | 2 | 8 | 0 |
| Surti | 33 | 12 | 55 | 1 | 1 | 0 | 10 | 0 |
| Durani | 45 | 23 | 53 | 3 | 1 | 0 | 4 | 0 |
| Venkataraghavan | 48 | 23 | 90 | 2 | | | | |
| Nadkarni | 36 | 21 | 42 | 2 | | | | |
| Borde | 5 | 2 | 18 | 1 | | | | |
| Pataudi | | | | | 3 | 2 | 9 | 0 |
| Hanumant Singh | | | | | 6 | 0 | 19 | 0 |
| Manjrekar | | | | | 6 | 4 | 11 | 0 |

### FALL OF WICKETS

| | I | NZ | I | NZ |
|---|---|---|---|---|
| Wkt | 1st | 1st | 2nd | 2nd |
| 1st | 51 | 38 | 88 | – |
| 2nd | 94 | 58 | 130 | – |
| 3rd | 94 | 119 | – | – |
| 4th | 107 | 139 | – | – |
| 5th | 114 | 200 | – | – |
| 6th | 202 | 200 | – | – |
| 7th | 232 | 227 | – | – |
| 8th | 375 | 227 | – | – |
| 9th | 378 | 254 | – | – |
| 10th | 397 | 315 | – | – |

Umpires: S.K. Raghunatha Rao and Mohammad Yunus.

# INDIA v NEW ZEALAND 1964–65 (2nd Test)

Played at Eden Gardens, Calcutta, on 5, 6, 7, 8 March.
Toss: New Zealand.    Result: MATCH DRAWN.
Debuts: New Zealand – B.R. Taylor, G.E. Vivian.

Vivian, aged 19 years 6 days, made his first-class debut in this match. Taylor became the second New Zealander after J.E. Mills to score a hundred on his first appearance in Test cricket. He batted for 158 minutes, hit three sixes and 14 fours, and added 163 runs with Sutcliffe in New Zealand's (then) highest seventh-wicket partnership in all Tests. It was Taylor's first hundred in first-class cricket. He remains the only player to score a century and take five wickets in an innings in his first Test. Morgan kept wicket in the second innings.

## NEW ZEALAND

| | | | | |
|---|---|---|---|---|
| G.T. Dowling | lbw b Venkataraghavan | 27 | c Engineer b Gupte | 23 |
| B.E. Congdon | b Desai | 9 | c Borde b Desai | 0 |
| R.W. Morgan | c Engineer b Desai | 20 | (4) b Durani | 33 |
| J.R. Reid* | c Borde b Venkataraghavan | 82 | (5) lbw b Venkataraghavan | 11 |
| B. Sutcliffe | not out | 151 | (6) c Hanumant b Venkataraghavan | 6 |
| B.W. Yuile | b Gupte | 1 | (3) lbw b Venkataraghavan | 21 |
| V. Pollard | c Jaisimha b Desai | 31 | b Jaisimha | 43 |
| B.R. Taylor | c Kunderan b Nadkarni | 105 | (10) not out | 0 |
| G.E. Vivian | b Desai | 1 | c Jaisimha b Nadkarni | 43 |
| R.C. Motz | lbw b Venkataraghavan | 21 | (8) c Nadkarni b Durani | 0 |
| J.T. Ward† | not out | 1 | | |
| Extras | (B 10, LB 3) | 13 | (B 10, NB 1) | 11 |
| **Total** | (9 wickets declared) | **462** | (9 wickets declared) | **191** |

## INDIA

| | | | | |
|---|---|---|---|---|
| M.L. Jaisimha | b Motz | 22 | c Morgan b Congdon | 0 |
| B.K. Kunderan | b Congdon | 36 | not out | 12 |
| F.M. Engineer† | c Pollard b Taylor | 10 | c Pollard b Dowling | 45 |
| C.G. Borde | c Pollard b Taylor | 62 | | |
| R.G. Nadkarni | b Taylor | 0 | | |
| Nawab of Pataudi, jr* | c Ward b Taylor | 153 | | |
| Hanumant Singh | c sub (T.W. Jarvis) b Yuile | 31 | | |
| S.A. Durani | c sub (T.W. Jarvis) b Yuile | 20 | (4) b Vivian | 23 |
| R.B. Desai | c Ward b Yuile | 0 | | |
| S. Venkataraghavan | b Taylor | 7 | (5) not out | 0 |
| B.P. Gupte | not out | 3 | | |
| Extras | (B 23, LB 2, NB 11) | 36 | (B 11, LB 1) | 12 |
| **Total** | | **380** | (3 wickets) | **92** |

| INDIA | O | M | R | W | O | M | R | W | | FALL OF WICKETS | | | |
|---|---|---|---|---|---|---|---|---|---|---|---|---|---|
| Desai | 33 | 6 | 128 | 4 | 12 | 6 | 32 | 1 | | NZ | I | NZ | I |
| Jaisimha | 20 | 6 | 73 | 0 | 15·1 | 12 | 21 | 1 | *Wkt* | *1st* | *1st* | *2nd* | *2nd* |
| Durani | 15 | 3 | 49 | 0 | 18 | 10 | 34 | 2 | 1st | 13 | 45 | 4 | 3 |
| Nadkarni | 35 | 12 | 59 | 1 | 7 | 4 | 14 | 1 | 2nd | 37 | 61 | 37 | 52 |
| Gupte | 16 | 3 | 54 | 1 | 22 | 7 | 64 | 1 | 3rd | 138 | 100 | 61 | 92 |
| Venkataraghavan | 41 | 18 | 86 | 3 | 17 | 11 | 15 | 3 | 4th | 139 | 101 | 83 | – |
| | | | | | | | | | 5th | 152 | 211 | 97 | – |
| NEW ZEALAND | | | | | | | | | 6th | 233 | 301 | 103 | – |
| Motz | 21 | 3 | 74 | 1 | | | | | 7th | 396 | 357 | 103 | – |
| Taylor | 23·5 | 2 | 86 | 5 | | | | | 8th | 407 | 357 | 184 | – |
| Congdon | 18 | 5 | 49 | 1 | 5 | 0 | 33 | 1 | 9th | 450 | 371 | 191 | – |
| Pollard | 15 | 1 | 50 | 0 | | | | | 10th | – | 380 | – | – |
| Vivian | 12 | 3 | 37 | 0 | 3 | 0 | 14 | 1 | | | | | |
| Reid | 2 | 1 | 5 | 0 | | | | | | | | | |
| Yuile | 14 | 3 | 43 | 3 | | | | | | | | | |
| Dowling | | | | | 6 | 2 | 19 | 1 | | | | | |
| Sutcliffe | | | | | 3 | 2 | 14 | 0 | | | | | |

Umpires: S.K. Ganguli and A.R. Joshi.

# INDIA v NEW ZEALAND 1964–65 (3rd Test)

Played at Brabourne Stadium, Bombay, on 12, 13, 14, 15 March.
Toss: New Zealand.   Result: MATCH DRAWN.
Debuts: Nil.

India were dismissed for their lowest total in any home Test and the lowest by any side in a Test in Bombay. Sardesai and Hanumant Singh added 193 in 181 minutes in an unbroken partnership which remains India's record for the sixth wicket against all countries. New Zealand were set to score 255 in 150 minutes.

## NEW ZEALAND

| | | | | |
|---|---|---|---|---|
| G.T. Dowling | b Desai | 129 | c Engineer b Jaisimha | 0 |
| B.E. Congdon | c Engineer b Desai | 3 | c Hanumant b Durani | 14 |
| B.W. Sinclair | b Desai | 9 | c Venkataraghavan b Desai | 0 |
| R.W. Morgan | b Chandrasekhar | 71 | b Chandrasekhar | 11 |
| B. Sutcliffe | run out | 4 | (6) c Durani b Chandrasekhar | 1 |
| V. Pollard | c Jaisimha b Desai | 26 | (7) c Borde b Duran | 4 |
| J.R. Reid* | lbw b Desai | 22 | (5) c Borde b Chandrasekhar | 10 |
| B.R. Taylor | c Hanumant b Desai | 8 | b Venkataraghavan | 21 |
| B.W. Yuile | lbw b Durani | 2 | not out | 8 |
| R.C. Motz | not out | 5 | | |
| J.T. Ward† | b Durani | 0 | (10) not out | 4 |
| Extras | (B 4, LB 13, NB 1) | 18 | (B 5, NB 2) | 7 |
| **Total** | | **297** | (8 wickets) | **80** |

## INDIA

| | | | | |
|---|---|---|---|---|
| D.N. Sardesai | c Ward b Motz | 4 | not out | 200 |
| M.L. Jaisimha | c Ward b Taylor | 4 | (4) c Ward b Pollard | 47 |
| S.A. Durani | c Morgan b Taylor | 4 | c Ward b Taylor | 6 |
| C.G. Borde | c Ward b Taylor | 25 | (5) c Yuile b Taylor | 109 |
| Hanumant Singh | hit wkt b Taylor | 0 | (7) not out | 75 |
| Nawab of Pataudi, jr* | c Ward b Congdon | 9 | b Motz | 3 |
| R.G. Nadkarni | lbw b Congdon | 7 | | |
| F.M. Engineer† | run out | 17 | (2) c Reid b Taylor | 6 |
| R.B. Desai | c Reid b Motz | 0 | | |
| S. Venkataraghavan | c Congdon b Taylor | 7 | | |
| B.S. Chandrasekhar | not out | 4 | | |
| Extras | (LB 4, NB 3) | 7 | (B 4, LB 5, W 1, NB 7) | 17 |
| **Total** | | **88** | (5 wickets declared) | **463** |

| INDIA | O | M | R | W | O | M | R | W | | FALL OF WICKETS | | | |
|---|---|---|---|---|---|---|---|---|---|---|---|---|---|
| | | | | | | | | | | NZ | I | I | NZ |
| Desai | 25 | 9 | 56 | 6 | 9 | 5 | 18 | 1 | Wkt | 1st | 1st | 2nd | 2nd |
| Jaisimha | 17 | 6 | 53 | 0 | 6 | 5 | 4 | 1 | 1st | 13 | 4 | 8 | 0 |
| Chandrasekhar | 23 | 6 | 76 | 1 | 14 | 7 | 25 | 3 | 2nd | 31 | 8 | 18 | 0 |
| Durani | 20·2 | 10 | 26 | 2 | 7 | 2 | 16 | 2 | 3rd | 165 | 13 | 107 | 18 |
| Venkataraghavan | 32 | 13 | 46 | 0 | 7 | 3 | 10 | 1 | 4th | 170 | 23 | 261 | 34 |
| Nadkarni | 12 | 7 | 22 | 0 | | | | | 5th | 227 | 38 | 270 | 37 |
| NEW ZEALAND | | | | | | | | | 6th | 256 | 48 | – | 45 |
| Motz | 15 | 4 | 30 | 2 | 29·4 | 11 | 63 | 1 | 7th | 276 | 71 | – | 46 |
| Taylor | 7·3 | 2 | 26 | 5 | 29 | 5 | 76 | 3 | 8th | 281 | 76 | – | 76 |
| Congdon | 9 | 5 | 21 | 2 | 17 | 6 | 44 | 0 | 9th | 297 | 77 | – | – |
| Pollard | 2 | 1 | 4 | 0 | 29 | 6 | 95 | 1 | 10th | 297 | 88 | – | – |
| Yuile | | | | | 25 | 8 | 76 | 0 | | | | | |
| Morgan | | | | | 18 | 3 | 54 | 0 | | | | | |
| Reid | | | | | 3 | 1 | 8 | 0 | | | | | |
| Sutcliffe | | | | | 4 | 0 | 30 | 0 | | | | | |

Umpires: M.V. Nagendra and S. Roy.

# INDIA v NEW ZEALAND 1964–65 (4th Test)

Played at Feroz Shah Kotla, Delhi, on 19, 20, 21, 22 March.
Toss: New Zealand.    Result: INDIA won by seven wickets.
Debuts: India – V. Subramanya.

Needing to score 70 runs in an hour, India won with 13 minutes to spare and so gained a 1–0 victory in the rubber. Venkataraghavan's innings analysis of 8 for 72 and match figures of 12 for 152 remain the best performances by a bowler from either country in this series. Congdon caught Hanumant Singh while keeping wicket after Ward had been injured.

## NEW ZEALAND

| | | | | |
|---|---|--:|---|--:|
| G.T Dowling | lbw b Venkateraghavan | 7 | lbw b Subramanya | 0 |
| T.W. Jarvis | b Venkataraghavan | 34 | b Venkataraghavan | 77 |
| R.W. Morgan | lbw b Venkataraghavan | 82 | c Venkataraghavan b Desai | 4 |
| B.E. Congdon | c Chandrasakhar | | | |
| | b Venkataraghavan | 48 | b Chandrasekhar | 7 |
| J.R. Reid* | b Chandrasekhar | 9 | b Venkataraghavan | 22 |
| B. Sutcliffe | b Venkataraghavan | 2 | c Engineer b Chandrasekhar | 54 |
| B.R. Taylor | c Borde b Chandrasekhar | 21 | c Sardesai b Venkataraghavan | 3 |
| V. Pollard | b Venkataraghavan | 27 | c Engineer b Subramanya | 6 |
| J.T. Ward† | lbw b Venkataraghavan | 11 | (11) run out | 0 |
| R.O. Collinge | not out | 4 | (9) c Engineer b Venkataraghavan | 54 |
| F.J. Cameron | b Venkataraghavan | 0 | (10) not out | 27 |
| Extras | (B 8, LB 6, NB 3) | 17 | (B 15, LB 1, NB 2) | 18 |
| **Total** | | **262** | | **272** |

## INDIA

| | | | | |
|---|---|--:|---|--:|
| D.N. Sardesai | c Jarvis b Morgan | 106 | not out | 28 |
| M.L. Jaisimha | c Dowling b Reid | 10 | (3) run out | 1 |
| Hanumant Singh | c Congdon b Collinge | 82 | (5) not out | 7 |
| C.G. Borde | c Jarvis b Cameron | 87 | | |
| Nawab of Pataudi, jr* | b Collinge | 113 | (4) b Reid | 29 |
| V. Subramanya | b Taylor | 9 | | |
| F.M. Engineer† | b Collinge | 5 | (2) b Taylor | 2 |
| R.G. Nadkarni | not out | 14 | | |
| R.B. Desai | b Collinge | 7 | | |
| S. Venkataraghavan | ) | | | |
| B.S. Chandrasekhar | ) did not bat | | | |
| Extras | (B 23, LB 4, W 1, NB 4) | 32 | (LB 4, NB 2) | 6 |
| **Total** | (8 wickets declared) | **465** | (3 wickets) | **73** |

| INDIA | O | M | R | W | O | M | R | W | | FALL OF WICKETS | | | |
|---|--:|--:|--:|--:|--:|--:|--:|--:|---|---|---|---|---|
| | | | | | | | | | | NZ | I | NZ | I |
| Desai | 9 | 2 | 36 | 0 | 18 | 3 | 35 | 1 | | 1st | 1st | 2nd | 2nd |
| Jaisimha | 5 | 2 | 12 | 0 | 1 | 0 | 2 | 0 | Wkt | 1st | 1st | 2nd | 2nd |
| Subramanya | 5 | 2 | 3 | 0 | 16 | 5 | 32 | 2 | 1st | 27 | 56 | 1 | 9 |
| Venkataraghavan | 51·1 | 26 | 72 | 8 | 61·2 | 30 | 80 | 4 | 2nd | 54 | 179 | 10 | 13 |
| Chandrasekhar | 37 | 14 | 96 | 2 | 34 | 14 | 95 | 2 | 3rd | 108 | 240 | 22 | 65 |
| Nadkarni | 16 | 8 | 21 | 0 | 19 | 13 | 10 | 0 | 4th | 117 | 378 | 68 | – |
| Hanumant Singh | 2 | 0 | 5 | 0 | | | | | 5th | 130 | 414 | 172 | – |
| | | | | | | | | | 6th | 157 | 421 | 178 | – |
| NEW ZEALAND | | | | | | | | | 7th | 194 | 457 | 179 | – |
| Taylor | 18 | 4 | 57 | 1 | 4 | 0 | 31 | 1 | 8th | 256 | 465 | 213 | – |
| Collinge | 20·4 | 4 | 89 | 4 | | | | | 9th | 260 | – | 264 | – |
| Reid | 24 | 4 | 89 | 1 | 1 | 0 | 3 | 1 | 10th | 262 | – | 272 | – |
| Cameron | 26 | 5 | 86 | 1 | 4 | 0 | 29 | 0 | | | | | |
| Morgan | 15 | 1 | 68 | 1 | | | | | | | | | |
| Pollard | 10 | 1 | 44 | 0 | | | | | | | | | |
| Sutcliffe | | | | | 0·1 | 0 | 4 | 0 | | | | | |

Umpires: B. Satyaji Rao and S. Pan.

# WEST INDIES v AUSTRALIA 1964–65 (1st Test)

Played at Sabina Park, Kingston, Jamaica, on 3, 4, 5, 6, 8 March.
Toss: West Indies.   Result: WEST INDIES won by 179 runs.
Debuts: West Indies – A.W. White; Australia – L.C. Mayne, P.I. Philpott, G. Thomas.

This result represented West Indies' first home win against Australia and it was the first time that they had led Australia in any rubber. Captaining West Indies for the first time, Sobers took his 100th Test wicket when he dismissed Philpott and became the only player to complete a double of 4,000 runs and 100 wickets in Tests.

## WEST INDIES

| | | | | |
|---|---|---|---|---|
| C.C. Hunte | c Grout b Philpott | 41 | c Simpson b Mayne | 81 |
| S.M. Nurse | c Grout b Hawke | 15 | run out | 17 |
| R.B. Kanhai | c Philpott b McKenzie | 17 | c and b Philpott | 16 |
| B.F. Butcher | b Mayne | 39 | c Booth b Philpott | 71 |
| G. St A. Sobers* | lbw b Simpson | 30 | (6) c Simpson b Philpott | 27 |
| J.S. Solomon | c Grout b Mayne | 0 | (7) c Grout b Mayne | 76 |
| J.L. Hendriks† | b Philpott | 11 | (8) b O'Neill | 30 |
| A.W. White | not out | 57 | (9) st Grout b Philpott | 3 |
| W.W. Hall | b Hawke | 9 | (10) b Mayne | 16 |
| C.C. Griffith | b Mayne | 6 | (11) not out | 1 |
| L.R. Gibbs | b Mayne | 6 | (5) b Mayne | 5 |
| Extras | (B 4, LB 3, W 1) | 8 | (B 20, LB 7, W 1, NB 2) | 30 |
| **Total** | | **239** | | **373** |

## AUSTRALIA

| | | | | |
|---|---|---|---|---|
| W.M. Lawry | lbw b Hall | 19 | b Griffith | 17 |
| R.B. Simpson* | c Kanhai b Hall | 11 | c Hendriks b Hall | 16 |
| R.M. Cowper | c Nurse b Hall | 26 | (4) lbw b Hall | 2 |
| N.C. O'Neill | c Butcher b White | 40 | (5) c Nurse b Gibbs | 22 |
| B.C. Booth | b Griffith | 2 | (6) b Griffith | 56 |
| G. Thomas | b Griffith | 23 | (7) b Hall | 15 |
| P.I. Philpott | c White b Hall | 22 | (8) c Kanhai b Sobers | 9 |
| N.J.N. Hawke | not out | 45 | (3) b Solomon | 33 |
| A.T.W. Grout† | c Nurse b Hall | 5 | lbw b Hall | 2 |
| G.D. McKenzie | b White | 0 | c Hill b White | 20 |
| L.C. Mayne | b Sobers | 9 | not out | 11 |
| Extras | (B 2, LB 8, NB 5) | 15 | (NB 13) | 13 |
| **Total** | | **217** | | **216** |

| AUSTRALIA | O | M | R | W | O | M | R | W | | FALL OF WICKETS | | | |
|---|---|---|---|---|---|---|---|---|---|---|---|---|---|
| McKenzie | 20 | 2 | 70 | 1 | 33 | 7 | 56 | 0 | | | WI | A | WI | A |
| Hawke | 14 | 4 | 47 | 2 | 18 | 5 | 25 | 0 | *Wkt* | *1st* | *1st* | *2nd* | *2nd* |
| Mayne | 17·2 | 2 | 43 | 4 | 23·4 | 5 | 56 | 4 | 1st | 48 | 32 | 50 | 39 |
| Philpott | 14 | 2 | 56 | 2 | 47 | 10 | 109 | 4 | 2nd | 70 | 39 | 78 | 40 |
| Simpson | 4 | 2 | 15 | 1 | 15 | 2 | 36 | 0 | 3rd | 82 | 42 | 194 | 43 |
| Cowper | | | | | 9 | 1 | 27 | 0 | 4th | 149 | 80 | 211 | 75 |
| O'Neill | | | | | 7 | 0 | 34 | 1 | 5th | 149 | 96 | 226 | 144 |
| | | | | | | | | | 6th | 149 | 136 | 247 | 167 |
| WEST INDIES | | | | | | | | | 7th | 181 | 176 | 311 | 180 |
| Hall | 24 | 0 | 60 | 5 | 19 | 5 | 45 | 4 | 8th | 211 | 192 | 314 | 184 |
| Griffith | 20 | 2 | 59 | 2 | 14 | 3 | 36 | 2 | 9th | 229 | 193 | 372 | 192 |
| Sobers | 20·4 | 7 | 30 | 1 | 17 | 2 | 64 | 1 | 10th | 239 | 217 | 373 | 216 |
| Gibbs | 16 | 8 | 19 | 0 | 9 | 1 | 21 | 1 | | | | | |
| White | 15 | 4 | 34 | 2 | 14·5 | 8 | 14 | 1 | | | | | |
| Solomon | | | | | 5 | 0 | 23 | 1 | | | | | |

Umpires: D. Sang Hue and O. Davies.

# WEST INDIES v AUSTRALIA 1964–65 (2nd Test)

Played at Queen's Park Oval, Port-of-Spain, Trinidad, on 26, 27, 29, 30, 31 March, 1 April.
Toss: Australia.   Result: MATCH DRAWN.
Debuts: West Indies – B.A. Davis.

Simpson was only the second captain to invite the West Indies to bat in a Test in the Caribbean, R.E.S. Wyatt having done so twice in 1930-31. Cowper and Booth added 225 runs for the third wicket after O'Neill had retired hurt at 63 for 2 (struck on the left arm while protecting his head from a Griffith bouncer).

## WEST INDIES

| | | | | |
|---|---|---|---|---|
| C.C. Hunte | c Simpson b McKenzie | 89 | b Philpott | 53 |
| B.A. Davis | c Simpson b McKenzie | 54 | c Simpson b O'Neill | 58 |
| R.B. Kanhai | c Grout b Cowper | 27 | c McKenzie b Philpott | 53 |
| B.F. Butcher | run out | 117 | c Thomas b Mayne | 47 |
| G. St A. Sobers* | run out | 69 | lbw b Simpson | 24 |
| J.S. Solomon | not out | 31 | c Booth b Simpson | 48 |
| J.L. Hendriks† | c Philpott b O'Neill | 2 | c Grout b Hawke | 22 |
| A.W. White | c Grout b Philpott | 7 | lbw b Hawke | 4 |
| W.W. Hall | c Booth b O'Neill | 4 | c Mayne b Simpson | 37 |
| C.C. Griffith | b O'Neill | 12 | not out | 18 |
| L.R. Gibbs | st Grout b O'Neill | 1 | c Booth b Simpson | 1 |
| Extras | (B 4, LB 9, W 2, NB 1) | 16 | (B 11, LB 8, NB 2) | 21 |
| **Total** | | **429** | | **386** |

## AUSTRALIA

| | | |
|---|---|---|
| W.M. Lawry | c Davis b Griffith | 1 |
| R.B. Simpson* | b Griffith | 30 |
| R.M. Cowper | run out | 143 |
| N.C. O'Neill | c Sobers b Hall | 36 |
| B.C. Booth | c Handriks b Griffith | 117 |
| G. Thomas | c Hendriks b Hall | 61 |
| P.I. Philpott | c Sobers b Gibbs | 19 |
| N.J.N. Hawke | c Hall b Sobers | 39 |
| A.T.W. Grout† | c Hendriks b Sobers | 35 |
| G.D. McKenzie | c Butcher b Sobers | 13 |
| L.C. Mayne | not out | 1 |
| Extras | (B 8, LB 3, NB 10) | 21 |
| **Total** | | **516** |

| AUSTRALIA | O | M | R | W | O | M | R | W | | FALL OF WICKETS | | | |
|---|---|---|---|---|---|---|---|---|---|---|---|---|---|
| McKenzie | 36 | 9 | 94 | 2 | 21 | 5 | 62 | 0 | | | WI | A | WI |
| Hawke | 23 | 4 | 50 | 0 | 21 | 4 | 42 | 2 | *Wkt* | *1st* | *1st* | *2nd* |
| Mayne | 17 | 0 | 65 | 0 | 11 | 2 | 37 | 1 | 1st | 116 | 15 | 91 |
| Philpott | 36 | 10 | 82 | 1 | 28 | 4 | 57 | 2 | 2nd | 164 | 60 | 166 |
| Booth | 2 | 0 | 5 | 0 | 5 | 1 | 14 | 0 | 3rd | 205 | 288 | 166 |
| Simpson | 8 | 1 | 28 | 0 | 36·5 | 5 | 83 | 4 | 4th | 365 | 306 | 236 |
| Cowper | 12 | 1 | 48 | 1 | 1 | 0 | 5 | 0 | 5th | 372 | 372 | 266 |
| O'Neill | 17·4 | 3 | 41 | 4 | 24 | 6 | 65 | 1 | 6th | 380 | 415 | 323 |
| | | | | | | | | | 7th | 393 | 431 | 327 |
| WEST INDIES | | | | | | | | | 8th | 404 | 489 | 328 |
| Hall | 35 | 6 | 104 | 2 | | | | | 9th | 425 | 511 | 382 |
| Griffith | 33 | 5 | 81 | 3 | | | | | 10th | 429 | 516 | 386 |
| Sobers | 27·5 | 5 | 75 | 3 | | | | | | | | |
| Gibbs | 66 | 22 | 129 | 1 | | | | | | | | |
| White | 52 | 15 | 104 | 0 | | | | | | | | |
| Hunte | 2 | 1 | 2 | 0 | | | | | | | | |

Umpires: C.Z. Bain and R. Gosein.

# WEST INDIES v AUSTRALIA 1964–65 (3rd Test)

Played at Bourda, Georgetown, British Guiana, on 14, 15, 17, 19, 20 April.
Toss: West Indies.   Result: WEST INDIES won by 212 runs.
Debuts: Nil.

G.E. Gomez, the former West Indies all rounder who was currently a Test selector, was appointed as umpire after C.P. Kippins had withdrawn on the eve of the match. Kippins had done so only at the insistance of the British Guiana Umpires' Association who objected to the appointment of Jordan of Barbados. Gomez held an umpiring certificate although he had not previously officiated in a first-class match. Gibbs, who took his 100th Test wicket during the match, completed West Indies' second victory of the rubber with the second ball bowled on the fifth day. Hawke's match analysis of 10 for 115 is the record for any Test at Georgetown.

## WEST INDIES

| | | | | |
|---|---|---|---|---|
| C.C. Hunte | c McKenzie b Philpott | 31 | c Grout b Hawke | 38 |
| B.A. Davis | b Hawke | 28 | b McKenzie | 17 |
| R.B. Kanhai | b Hawke | 89 | b McKenzie | 0 |
| B.F. Butcher | run out | 49 | b Hawke | 18 |
| S.M. Nurse | c and b Hawke | 42 | st Grout b Philpott | 6 |
| G. St A. Sobers* | c Grout b Hawke | 45 | c Simpson b Philpott | 42 |
| J.S. Solomon | c Grout b Hawke | 0 | c Simpson b Philpott | 17 |
| J.L. Hendriks† | not out | 31 | c Grout b Hawke | 2 |
| W.W. Hall | c Mayne b Hawke | 7 | not out | 20 |
| C.C. Griffith | lbw b O'Neill | 19 | c Thomas b Philpott | 13 |
| L.R. Gibbs | b O'Neill | 2 | b Hawke | 1 |
| Extras | (B 7, LB 1, W 1, NB 3) | 12 | (LB 3, W 1, NB 2) | 6 |
| **Totals** | | **355** | | **180** |

## AUSTRALIA

| | | | | |
|---|---|---|---|---|
| R.B. Simpson* | b Sobers | 7 | b Griffith | 23 |
| W.M. Lawry | run out | 20 | b Gibbs | 22 |
| R.M. Cowper | c Hendriks b Gibbs | 41 | st Hendriks b Gibbs | 30 |
| N.C. O'Neill | b Griffith | 27 | c Sobers b Gibbs | 16 |
| P.I. Philpott | c Butcher b Sobers | 5 | (8) c Sobers b Gibbs | 6 |
| B.C. Booth | c Sobers b Gibbs | 37 | (5) c Hendriks b Gibbs | 0 |
| G. Thomas | b Hall | 8 | (6) st Hendriks b Solomon | 5 |
| N.J.N. Hawke | c Sobers b Hall | 0 | (7) c Hendriks b Sobers | 14 |
| A.T.W. Grout† | run out | 19 | b Sobers | 8 |
| G.D. McKenzie | not out | 3 | b Gibbs | 6 |
| L.C. Mayne | b Gibbs | 5 | not out | 0 |
| Extras | (LB 1, NB 6) | 7 | (B 4, LB 4, NB 6) | 14 |
| **Total** | | **179** | | **144** |

| AUSTRALIA | O | M | R | W | O | M | R | W |
|---|---|---|---|---|---|---|---|---|
| McKenzie | 23 | 2 | 92 | 0 | 21 | 7 | 53 | 2 |
| Hawke | 32 | 8 | 72 | 6 | 20·4 | 7 | 43 | 4 |
| Mayne | 12 | 1 | 54 | 0 | 2 | 1 | 6 | 0 |
| Philpott | 26 | 5 | 75 | 1 | 16 | 3 | 49 | 4 |
| O'Neill | 6·2 | 1 | 26 | 2 | 1 | 0 | 4 | 0 |
| Simpson | 7 | 1 | 23 | 0 | 17 | 9 | 19 | 0 |
| Cowper | 1 | 0 | 1 | 0 | | | | |
| WEST INDIES | | | | | | | | |
| Hall | 13 | 2 | 43 | 2 | 2 | 1 | 1 | 0 |
| Sobers | 12 | 2 | 38 | 2 | 19 | 7 | 39 | 2 |
| Griffith | 14 | 2 | 40 | 1 | 6 | 1 | 30 | 1 |
| Gibbs | 25·5 | 9 | 51 | 3 | 22·2 | 9 | 29 | 6 |
| Solomon | | | | | 9 | 2 | 31 | 1 |

### FALL OF WICKETS

| Wkt | WI 1st | A 1st | WI 2nd | A 2nd |
|---|---|---|---|---|
| 1st | 56 | 11 | 31 | 31 |
| 2nd | 68 | 68 | 31 | 88 |
| 3rd | 203 | 71 | 62 | 91 |
| 4th | 210 | 85 | 69 | 104 |
| 5th | 290 | 116 | 125 | 109 |
| 6th | 290 | 127 | 129 | 115 |
| 7th | 297 | 130 | 146 | 130 |
| 8th | 309 | 170 | 146 | 130 |
| 9th | 353 | 171 | 176 | 144 |
| 10th | 355 | 179 | 180 | 144 |

Umpires: H.B. de C. Jordan and G.E. Gomez.

# WEST INDIES v AUSTRALIA 1964–65 (4th Test)

Played at Kensington Oval, Bridgetown, Barbados, on 5, 6, 7, 8, 10, 11 May.
Toss: Australia.    Result: MATCH DRAWN.
Debuts: Nil.

Lawry and Simpson, who batted throughout the first day to score 263, became the first opening pair to score double centuries in the same Test innings. Their stand of 382 remains Australia's highest first-wicket partnership and was only 31 runs short of the world Test record set by V.M.H. Mankad and P. Roy in 1955-56 (*Test No. 420*). Hunte retired hurt in the first innings when he was hit in the face attempting to hook Hawke and Lawry retired hurt at 139 in the second innings. Set to score 253 runs in 270 minutes, West Indies finished eleven runs short with five wickets in hand. Nurse kept wicket in the second innings. Hendriks retired after being struck on the head by a steeply lifting ball from McKenzie.

### AUSTRALIA

| | | | | | |
|---|---|---|---|---|---|
| W.M. Lawry | c Sobers b Solomon | 210 | retired hurt | | 58 |
| R.B. Simpson* | b Hall | 201 | c Nurse b Sobers | | 5 |
| R.M. Cowper | b Sobers | 102 | c and b Hall | | 4 |
| N.C. O'Neill | c Kanhai b Gibbs | 51 | not out | | 74 |
| B.C. Booth | b Gibbs | 5 | c Sobers b Gibbs | | 17 |
| G. Thomas | not out | 27 | b Gibbs | | 1 |
| B.K. Shepherd | lbw b Hall | 4 | | | |
| N.J.N. Hawke | not out | 8 | | | |
| P.I. Philpott | ) | | | | |
| A.T.W. Grout† | ) did not bat | | | | |
| G.D. McKenzie | ) | | | | |
| Extras | (B 10, LB 12, W 2, NB 18) | 42 | (B 11, LB 3, W 1, NB 1) | | 16 |
| **Totals** | (6 wickets declared) | **650** | (4 wickets declared) | | **175** |

### WEST INDIES

| | | | | | |
|---|---|---|---|---|---|
| C.C. Hunte | c Simpson b McKenzie | 75 | c Grout b McKenzie | | 31 |
| B.A. Davis | b McKenzie | 8 | c sub (D.J. Sincock) b Philpott | | 68 |
| R.B. Kanhai | c Hawke b McKenzie | 129 | lbw b McKenzie | | 1 |
| B.F. Butcher | c Simpson b O'Neill | 9 | c Booth b Philpott | | 27 |
| S.M. Nurse | c Simpson b Hawke | 201 | (6) lbw b Hawke | | 0 |
| G. St A. Sobers* | c Grout b McKenzie | 55 | (5) not out | | 34 |
| J.S. Solomon | c McKenzie b Hawke | 1 | not out | | 6 |
| J.L. Hendriks† | retired hurt | 4 | | | |
| W.W. Hall | c Simpson b Hawke | 3 | | | |
| C.C. Griffith | run out | 54 | | | |
| L.R. Gibbs | not out | 3 | | | |
| Extras | (B 13, LB 12, W 1, NB 5) | 31 | (B 19, LB 3, W 2, NB 1) | | 25 |
| **Total** | | **573** | (5 wickets) | | **242** |

| WEST INDIES | O | M | R | W | O | M | R | W | FALL OF WICKETS | | | | |
|---|---|---|---|---|---|---|---|---|---|---|---|---|---|
| Hall | 27 | 3 | 117 | 2 | 8 | 0 | 31 | 1 | | A | WI | A | WI |
| Griffith | 35 | 3 | 131 | 0 | 7 | 0 | 38 | 0 | *Wkt* | *1st* | *1st* | *2nd* | *2nd* |
| Sobers | 37 | 7 | 143 | 1 | 20 | 11 | 29 | 1 | 1st | 382 | 13 | 7 | 145 |
| Gibbs | 73 | 17 | 168 | 2 | 18·2 | 3 | 61 | 2 | 2nd | 522 | 99 | 13 | 146 |
| Solomon | 14 | 1 | 42 | 1 | | | | | 3rd | 583 | 299 | 160 | 183 |
| Hunte | 3 | 1 | 7 | 0 | | | | | 4th | 604 | 445 | 175 | 216 |
| | | | | | | | | | 5th | 615 | 448 | – | 217 |
| AUSTRALIA | | | | | | | | | 6th | 631 | 453 | – | – |
| McKenzie | 47 | 11 | 114 | 4 | 24 | 6 | 60 | 2 | 7th | – | 474 | – | – |
| Hawke | 49 | 11 | 135 | 3 | 15 | 4 | 37 | 1 | 8th | – | 539 | – | – |
| Philpott | 45 | 17 | 102 | 0 | 24 | 7 | 74 | 2 | 9th | – | 573 | – | – |
| O'Neill | 26 | 13 | 60 | 1 | | | | | 10th | – | – | – | – |
| Simpson | 15 | 3 | 44 | 0 | 9 | 4 | 15 | 0 | | | | | |
| Cowper | 21 | 6 | 64 | 0 | 8 | 4 | 19 | 0 | | | | | |
| Booth | 6 | 2 | 17 | 0 | 5 | 1 | 12 | 0 | | | | | |
| Shepherd | 3 | 1 | 6 | 0 | | | | | | | | | |

Umpires: H.B. de C. Jordan and C.P. Kippins.

# WEST INDIES v AUSTRALIA 1964–65 (5th Test)

Played at Queen's Park Oval, Port-of-Spain, Trinidad, on 14, 15, 17 May.
Toss: West Indies.   Result: AUSTRALIA won by ten wickets.
Debuts: Nil.

Although defeated by ten wickets and with three days to spare in this match, West Indies gained their first victory in a rubber against Australia. Hunte was the second batsman after F.M.M. Worrell (*Test No. 441*) to carry his bat through a completed West Indies innings. McKenzie ended the second innings by bowling Hall, Griffith and Gibbs with four consecutive balls.

## WEST INDIES

| | | | | |
|---|---|---|---|---|
| C.C. Hunte | c Grout b Hawke | 1 | not out | 60 |
| B.A. Davis | c McKenzie b Hawke | 4 | lbw b Hawke | 8 |
| R.B. Kanhai | c Hawke b Cowper | 121 | b Hawke | 9 |
| B.F. Butcher | lbw b Hawke | 2 | c Cowper b Sincock | 26 |
| S.M. Nurse | b McKenzie | 9 | lbw b Hawke | 1 |
| G. St A. Sobers* | b Sincock | 18 | b McKenzie | 8 |
| W.V. Rodriguez | c and b Sincock | 9 | st Grout b Sincock | 1 |
| D.W. Allan† | run out | 11 | c Cowper b McKenzie | 7 |
| W.W. Hall | b Philpott | 29 | b McKenzie | 8 |
| C.C. Griffith | c Sincock b Philpott | 11 | b McKenzie | 0 |
| L.R. Gibbs | not out | 0 | b McKenzie | 0 |
| Extras | (B 4, LB 2, W 2, NB 1) | 9 | (B 2, W 1) | 3 |
| **Total** | | **224** | | **131** |

## AUSTRALIA

| | | | | |
|---|---|---|---|---|
| W.M. Lawry | c Allan b Griffith | 3 | not out | 18 |
| R.B. Simpson* | b Griffith | 72 | not out | 34 |
| R.M. Cowper | lbw b Sobers | 69 | | |
| B.C. Booth | lbw b Griffith | 0 | | |
| G. Thomas | c Allan b Griffith | 38 | | |
| B.K. Shepherd | c sub (C.A. Davis) b Gibbs | 38 | | |
| N.J.N. Hawke | b Griffith | 3 | | |
| P.I. Philpott | b Gibbs | 10 | | |
| A.T.W. Grout† | c Griffith b Gibbs | 14 | | |
| D.J. Sincock | not out | 17 | | |
| G.D. McKenzie | b Griffith | 8 | | |
| Extras | (B 12, LB 3, W 1, NB 6) | 22 | (B 4, W 1, NB 6) | 11 |
| **Total** | | **294** | (0 wickets) | **63** |

| AUSTRALIA | O | M | R | W | O | M | R | W |
|---|---|---|---|---|---|---|---|---|
| McKenzie | 14 | 0 | 43 | 1 | 17 | 7 | 33 | 5 |
| Hawke | 13 | 3 | 42 | 3 | 13 | 2 | 31 | 3 |
| Sincock | 15 | 1 | 79 | 2 | 18 | 0 | 64 | 2 |
| Philpott | 7·3 | 0 | 25 | 2 | | | | |
| Cowper | 6 | 0 | 26 | 1 | | | | |
| WEST INDIES | | | | | | | | |
| Hall | 14 | 2 | 46 | 0 | 4 | 0 | 7 | 0 |
| Griffith | 20 | 6 | 46 | 6 | 6 | 0 | 19 | 0 |
| Gibbs | 44 | 17 | 71 | 3 | 4 | 2 | 7 | 0 |
| Rodriguez | 13 | 2 | 44 | 0 | 1 | 0 | 8 | 0 |
| Sobers | 37 | 13 | 65 | 1 | 2 | 0 | 7 | 0 |
| Kanhai | | | | | 1 | 0 | 4 | 0 |

### FALL OF WICKETS

| Wkt | WI 1st | A 1st | WI 2nd | A 2nd |
|---|---|---|---|---|
| 1st | 2 | 5 | 12 | – |
| 2nd | 18 | 143 | 22 | – |
| 3rd | 26 | 143 | 63 | – |
| 4th | 64 | 167 | 66 | – |
| 5th | 100 | 222 | 87 | – |
| 6th | 114 | 230 | 92 | – |
| 7th | 162 | 248 | 103 | – |
| 8th | 202 | 261 | 131 | – |
| 9th | 217 | 270 | 131 | – |
| 10th | 224 | 294 | 131 | – |

Umpires: H.B.de C. Jordan and C.P. Kippins.

# PAKISTAN v NEW ZEALAND 1964–65 (1st Test)

Played at Rawalpindi Club Ground, on 27, 28, 30 March.
Toss: Pakistan.   Result: PAKISTAN won by an innings and 64 runs.
Debuts: Pakistan – Salahuddin.

The first Test to be played at Rawalpindi brought Pakistan their first home win for six years and with over a day to spare. Reid made his 53rd consecutive appearance beating the Test record held jointly by F.E. Woolley and P.B.H. May. Salahuddin made his debut at the age of 18 years 41 days. New Zealand's second innings lasted 173 minutes.

## NEW ZEALAND

| | | | | | |
|---|---|---|---|---|---|
| G.T. Dowling | b Farooq | 5 | | b Majid | 0 |
| T.W. Jarvis | c Naushad b Asif | 4 | | c Majid b Salahuddin | 17 |
| B.W. Sinclair | b Farooq | 22 | | c Salahuddin b Pervez | 21 |
| J.R. Reid* | b Salahuddin | 4 | (6) | c Asif b Farooq | 0 |
| R.W. Morgan | c Farooq b Salahuddin | 0 | (4) | b Pervez | 6 |
| B. Sutcliffe | b Pervez | 7 | (8) | b Pervez | 0 |
| B.R. Taylor | b Pervez | 76 | (9) | not out | 7 |
| A.E. Dick† | b Pervez | 0 | (7) | b Farooq | 0 |
| V. Pollard | lbw b Pervez | 15 | (10) | c Hanif b Pervez | 0 |
| B.W. Yuile | not out | 11 | (5) | run out | 1 |
| R.O. Collinge | c Ilyas b Intikhab | 15 | | c Asif b Farooq | 8 |
| Extras | (B 1, LB 7, NB 8) | 16 | | (B 6, LB 10, NB 3) | 19 |
| **Total** | | **175** | | | **79** |

## PAKISTAN

| | | |
|---|---|---|
| Mohammad Ilyas | c Pollard b Reid | 56 |
| Naushad Ali† | b Reid | 2 |
| Saeed Ahmed | b Taylor | 68 |
| Javed Burki | b Collinge | 6 |
| Asif Iqbal | b Taylor | 51 |
| Hanif Mohammad* | b Pollard | 16 |
| Majid Khan | b Collinge | 11 |
| Salahuddin | not out | 34 |
| Intikhab Alam | c Yuile b Reid | 1 |
| Pervez Sajjad | c Dick b Taylor | 18 |
| Mohammad Farooq | c Dowling b Morgan | 47 |
| Extras | (B 5, LB 3) | 8 |
| **Total** | | **318** |

| PAKISTAN | O | M | R | W | O | M | R | W | | FALL OF WICKETS | | |
|---|---|---|---|---|---|---|---|---|---|---|---|---|
| | | | | | | | | | | NZ | P | NZ |
| Asif | 4 | 1 | 7 | 1 | 4 | 3 | 4 | 0 | | | | |
| Majid | 4 | 2 | 11 | 0 | 5 | 2 | 9 | 1 | *Wkt* | *1st* | *1st* | *2nd* |
| Farooq | 16 | 3 | 57 | 2 | 12 | 3 | 25 | 3 | 1st | 5 | 13 | 3 |
| Salahuddin | 15 | 5 | 36 | 2 | 11 | 5 | 16 | 1 | 2nd | 24 | 127 | 42 |
| Pervez | 16 | 5 | 42 | 4 | 12 | 8 | 5 | 4 | 3rd | 34 | 135 | 57 |
| Intikhab | 1·5 | 0 | 6 | 1 | 3 | 2 | 1 | 0 | 4th | 39 | 145 | 58 |
| | | | | | | | | | 5th | 39 | 177 | 59 |
| NEW ZEALAND | | | | | | | | | 6th | 91 | 215 | 59 |
| Collinge | 21 | 9 | 36 | 2 | | | | | 7th | 91 | 217 | 59 |
| Taylor | 15 | 3 | 38 | 3 | | | | | 8th | 143 | 220 | 59 |
| Pollard | 22 | 6 | 80 | 1 | | | | | 9th | 148 | 253 | 59 |
| Reid | 34 | 18 | 80 | 3 | | | | | 10th | 175 | 318 | 79 |
| Yuile | 16 | 5 | 42 | 0 | | | | | | | | |
| Morgan | 8·3 | 1 | 34 | 1 | | | | | | | | |

Umpires: Shujauddin and Q.D. Butt.

# PAKISTAN v NEW ZEALAND 1964–65 (2nd Test)

Played at Lahore Stadium on 2, 3, 4, 6, 7 April.
Toss: New Zealand.   Result: MATCH DRAWN.
Debuts: Nil.

Hanif and Majid added 217 – still Pakistan's highest sixth wicket partnership in all Tests – after New Zealand had elected to bowl on a rain-affected pitch. Hanif's highest score in a home Test took 445 minutes and included 33 fours. New Zealand fielded three substitutes on the final day, Jarvis, Dowling and Dick being unfit. Reid kept wicket until tea when Congdon took over. In stumping Pervez Sajjad, he became the second substitute fielder to make a stumping in a Test match – the first being N.C. Tufnell for England in South Africa in 1909-10 (*Test No. 107*).

## PAKISTAN

| | | | | |
|---|---|---|---|---|
| Mohammad Ilyas | c Dick b Cameron | 17 | c sub (R.C. Motz) b Taylor | 4 |
| Naushad Ali† | c Collinge b Cameron | 9 | b Cameron | 29 |
| Saeed Ahmed | b Pollard | 23 | (8) c and b Sutcliffe | 4 |
| Salahuddin | c Dick b Taylor | 23 | (3) b Cameron | 25 |
| Javed Burki | c Dick b Cameron | 10 | (4) c Reid b Sinclair | 14 |
| Hanif Mohammad* | not out | 203 | | |
| Majid Khan | c Reid b Taylor | 80 | (5) c Reid b Sutcliffe | 44 |
| Asif Iqbal | lbw b Cameron | 4 | (6) c Sutcliffe b Pollard | 43 |
| Intikhab Alam | not out | 10 | (7) not out | 5 |
| Pervez Sajjad | ) did not bat | | (9) st sub (B.E. Congdon) b Sinclair | 16 |
| Mohammad Farooq | ) | | (10) not out | 0 |
| Extras | (B 2, LB 3, NB 1) | 6 | (B 6, LB 3, NB 1) | 10 |
| **Total** | (7 wickets declared) | **385** | (8 wickets declared) | **194** |

## NEW ZEALAND

| | | |
|---|---|---|
| G.T. Dowling | c Naushad b Farooq | 83 |
| T.W. Jarvis | b Salahuddin | 53 |
| B.W. Sinclair | c Hanif b Intikhab | 130 |
| J.R. Reid* | lbw b Majid | 88 |
| R.W. Morgan | c Majid b Farooq | 50 |
| B. Sutcliffe | b Asif | 23 |
| B.R. Taylor | not out | 25 |
| V. Pollard | not out | 8 |
| A.E. Dick† | ) did not bat | |
| F.J. Cameron | ) | |
| R.O. Collinge | ) | |
| Extras | (B 5, LB 8, NB 7) | 20 |
| **Total** | (6 wickets declared) | **482** |

| NEW ZEALAND | O | M | R | W | O | M | R | W | FALL OF WICKETS | | | |
|---|---|---|---|---|---|---|---|---|---|---|---|---|
| Collinge | 27 | 6 | 85 | 0 | 11 | 4 | 11 | 0 | | P | NZ | P |
| Cameron | 44 | 12 | 90 | 4 | 11 | 5 | 15 | 2 | *Wkt* | *1st* | *1st* | *2nd* |
| Reid | 9 | 3 | 21 | 0 | | | | | 1st | 14 | 136 | 5 |
| Pollard | 42 | 20 | 76 | 1 | 19 | 6 | 41 | 1 | 2nd | 45 | 164 | 61 |
| Morgan | 17 | 8 | 46 | 0 | 8 | 1 | 32 | 0 | 3rd | 49 | 342 | 74 |
| Taylor | 28 | 9 | 61 | 2 | 7 | 3 | 15 | 1 | 4th | 62 | 391 | 99 |
| Sinclair | | | | | 10 | 3 | 32 | 2 | 5th | 121 | 439 | 169 |
| Sutcliffe | | | | | 11 | 4 | 38 | 2 | 6th | 338 | 469 | 169 |
| | | | | | | | | | 7th | 362 | – | 173 |
| PAKISTAN | | | | | | | | | 8th | – | – | 194 |
| Asif | 33 | 12 | 85 | 1 | | | | | 9th | – | – | – |
| Majid | 24 | 3 | 57 | 1 | | | | | 10th | – | – | – |
| Farooq | 41 | 12 | 71 | 2 | | | | | | | | |
| Pervez | 43 | 18 | 72 | 0 | | | | | | | | |
| Salahuddin | 33 | 8 | 76 | 1 | | | | | | | | |
| Intikhab | 33 | 5 | 92 | 1 | | | | | | | | |
| Saeed | 1 | 0 | 1 | 0 | | | | | | | | |
| Ilyas | 1 | 0 | 8 | 0 | | | | | | | | |

Umpires: Shujauddin and Akhtar Hussain.

# PAKISTAN v NEW ZEALAND 1964–65 (3rd Test)

Played at National Stadium, Karachi, on 9, 10, 11, 13, 14 April.
Toss: New Zealand.   Result: PAKISTAN won by eight wickets.
Debuts: Nil.

Pakistan, needing 205 runs in 330 minutes to win the rubber 2-0, reached their objective in only 205 minutes.

## NEW ZEALAND

| | | | | |
|---|---|---|---|---|
| T.W. Jarvis | lbw b Salahuddin | 27 | b Asif | 0 |
| A.E. Dick† | c Naushad b Asif | 33 | b Majid | 2 |
| B.W. Sinclair | c Majid b Farooq | 24 | lbw b Farooq | 14 |
| J.R. Reid* | b Asif | 128 | c Majid b Salahuddin | 76 |
| R.W. Morgan | lbw b Saeed | 13 | c Salahuddin b Pervez | 25 |
| B.E. Congdon | c sub (Masood-ul-Hasan) b Intikhab | 17 | (8) b Intikhab | 57 |
| B.R. Taylor | c Pervez b Intikhab | 6 | c Hanif b Intikhab | 3 |
| V. Pollard | b Farooq | 1 | (9) b Salahuddin | 4 |
| R.C. Motz | b Intikhab | 0 | (10) lbw b Intikhab | 2 |
| B. Sutcliffe | not out | 13 | (6) c Majid b Intikhab | 18 |
| F.J. Cameron | c Naushad b Asif | 9 | not out | 10 |
| Extras | (LB 2, NB 12) | 14 | (B 1, LB 3, NB 8) | 12 |
| **Total** | | **285** | | **223** |

## PAKISTAN

| | | | | |
|---|---|---|---|---|
| Mohammad Ilyas | lbw b Motz | 20 | st Dick b Reid | 126 |
| Naushad Ali† | c Taylor b Motz | 9 | c sub (G.E. Vivian) b Pollard | 39 |
| Saeed Ahmed | b Cameron | 172 | not out | 19 |
| Javed Burki | c Morgan b Pollard | 29 | not out | 4 |
| Hanif Mohammad* | b Reid | 1 | | |
| Majid Khan | run out | 12 | | |
| Salahuddin | not out | 11 | | |
| Asif Iqbal | lbw b Cameron | 4 | | |
| Intikhab Alam | c Dick b Congdon | 3 | | |
| Pervez Sajjad | not out | 8 | | |
| Mohammad Farooq | did not bat | | | |
| Extras | (B 17, LB 12, NB 9) | 38 | (B 8, LB 2, W 1, NB 3) | 14 |
| **Total** | (8 wickets declared) | **307** | (2 wickets) | **202** |

| PAKISTAN | O | M | R | W | O | M | R | W | | FALL OF WICKETS | | | |
|---|---|---|---|---|---|---|---|---|---|---|---|---|---|
| Asif | 11 | 3 | 35 | 3 | 14 | 7 | 29 | 1 | | NZ | P | NZ | P |
| Majid | 20 | 1 | 63 | 0 | 8 | 0 | 30 | 1 | *Wkt* | *1st* | *1st* | *2nd* | *2nd* |
| Farooq | 21 | 5 | 59 | 2 | 17 | 5 | 41 | 1 | 1st | 50 | 21 | 0 | 121 |
| Salahuddin | 6 | 4 | 3 | 1 | 26 | 5 | 56 | 2 | 2nd | 76 | 84 | 10 | 198 |
| Pervez | 11 | 4 | 29 | 0 | 8 | 3 | 16 | 1 | 3rd | 123 | 198 | 45 | – |
| Intikhab | 24 | 6 | 53 | 3 | 26·4 | 10 | 39 | 4 | 4th | 167 | 201 | 93 | – |
| Saeed | 10 | 3 | 29 | 1 | | | | | 5th | 206 | 248 | 129 | – |
| | | | | | | | | | 6th | 220 | 286 | 133 | – |
| NEW ZEALAND | | | | | | | | | 7th | 226 | 290 | 151 | – |
| Motz | 22 | 11 | 35 | 2 | | | | | 8th | 233 | 297 | 157 | – |
| Comeron | 28 | 7 | 70 | 2 | 11 | 3 | 29 | 0 | 9th | 268 | – | 160 | – |
| Pollard | 27 | 13 | 41 | 1 | 18 | 3 | 52 | 1 | 10th | 285 | – | 223 | – |
| Taylor | 15 | 2 | 54 | 0 | 14 | 3 | 43 | 0 | | | | | |
| Morgan | 13 | 2 | 31 | 0 | 7 | 2 | 31 | 0 | | | | | |
| Reid | 10 | 5 | 28 | 1 | 1 | 0 | 6 | 1 | | | | | |
| Congdon | 6 | 3 | 10 | 1 | 9 | 2 | 27 | 0 | | | | | |

Umpires: Shujauddin and Daud Khan.

# ENGLAND v NEW ZEALAND 1965 (1st Test)

Played at Edgbaston, Birmingham, on 27, 28, 29, 31 May, 1 June.
Toss: England.   Result: ENGLAND won by nine wickets.
Debuts: Nil.

England maintained their unbeaten record at Birmingham, this being their seventh win in eleven Tests. Barrington's innings occupied 437 minutes and resulted in his omission from the next Test; his score remained at 85 for 62 minutes while 20 overs were bowled. Sutcliffe retired hurt after being hit on the right ear by a Trueman bouncer, came back for the last two minutes before lunch but was unfit to continue afterwards. Congdon retired in the second innings after edging a sweep against Barber into his face but he resumed at 105 for 2. The partnership of 104 between Sutcliffe and Pollard remains New Zealand's highest for the seventh wicket against England. This match was played in miserably cold weather; twice on the second day hot drinks were brought on to the field.

## ENGLAND

| | | | | | |
|---|---|--:|---|---|--:|
| G. Boycott | c Dick b Motz | 23 | not out | | 44 |
| R.W. Barber | b Motz | 31 | c sub (G.E. Vivian) b Morgan | | 51 |
| E.R. Dexter | c Dick b Motz | 57 | not out | | 0 |
| K.F. Barrington | c Dick b Collinge | 137 | | | |
| M.C. Cowdrey | b Collinge | 85 | | | |
| M.J.K. Smith* | lbw b Collinge | 0 | | | |
| J.M. Parks† | c Cameron b Reid | 34 | | | |
| F.J. Titmus | c Congdon b Motz | 13 | | | |
| T.W. Cartwright | b Motz | 4 | | | |
| F.S. Trueman | c Pollard b Cameron | 3 | | | |
| F.E. Rumsey | not out | 21 | | | |
| Extras | (B 10, LB 6, NB 11) | 27 | (NB 1) | | 1 |
| **Total** | | **435** | (1 wicket) | | **96** |

## NEW ZEALAND

| | | | | | |
|---|---|--:|---|---|--:|
| G.T. Dowling | b Titmus | 32 | b Barber | | 41 |
| B.F. Congdon | c Smith b Titmus | 24 | b Titmus | | 47 |
| B.W. Sinclair | b Titmus | 14 | st Parks b Barber | | 2 |
| J.R. Reid* | b Trueman | 2 | c Barrington b Titmus | | 44 |
| B.Sutcliffe | retired hurt | 4 | (7) c Titmus b Dexter | | 53 |
| R.W. Morgan | c Parks b Barber | 22 | (5) lbw b Trueman | | 43 |
| A.E. Dick† | c Titmus b Cartwright | · 0 | (6) b Barber | | 42 |
| V. Pollard | lbw b Titmus | 4 | not out | | 81 |
| R.C. Motz | c Trueman b Cartwright | 0 | c and b Barber | | 21 |
| R.O. Collinge | c Dexter b Barber | 4 | c Parks b Trueman | | 9 |
| F.J. Cameron | not out | 4 | b Trueman | | 0 |
| Extras | (B 1, LB 1, NB 4) | 6 | (B 17, LB 11, NB 2) | | 30 |
| **Total** | | **116** | | | **413** |

| NEW ZEALAND | O | M | R | W | O | M | R | W |
|---|--:|--:|--:|--:|--:|--:|--:|--:|
| Collinge | 29·4 | 8 | 63 | 3 | 5 | 1 | 14 | 0 |
| Cameron | 43 | 10 | 117 | 1 | 3 | 0 | 11 | 0 |
| Motz | 43 | 14 | 108 | 5 | 13 | 3 | 34 | 0 |
| Pollard | 18 | 4 | 60 | 0 | 1 | 0 | 5 | 0 |
| Congdon | 7 | 2 | 17 | 0 | 2 | 1 | 6 | 0 |
| Reid | 16 | 5 | 43 | 1 | 5 | 2 | 7 | 0 |
| Morgan | | | | | 1·5 | 0 | 18 | 1 |
| ENGLAND | | | | | | | | |
| Rumsey | 9 | 2 | 22 | 0 | 17 | 5 | 32 | 0 |
| Trueman | 18 | 3 | 49 | 1 | 32·4 | 8 | 79 | 3 |
| Titmus | 26 | 17 | 18 | 4 | 59 | 30 | 85 | 2 |
| Cartwright | 7 | 3 | 14 | 2 | 12 | 6 | 12 | 0 |
| Barber | 3 | 2 | 7 | 2 | 45 | 15 | 132 | 4 |
| Barrington | | | | | 5 | 0 | 25 | 0 |
| Dexter | | | | | 5 | 1 | 18 | 1 |

FALL OF WICKETS

| Wkt | E 1st | NZ 1st | NZ 2nd | E 2nd |
|---|--:|--:|--:|--:|
| 1st | 54 | 54 | 72 | 92 |
| 2nd | 76 | 63 | 105 | – |
| 3rd | 164 | 67 | 131 | – |
| 4th | 300 | 86 | 145 | – |
| 5th | 300 | 97 | 220 | – |
| 6th | 335 | 104 | 249 | – |
| 7th | 368 | 105 | 353 | – |
| 8th | 391 | 108 | 386 | – |
| 9th | 394 | 115 | 413 | – |
| 10th | 435 | – | 413 | – |

Umpires: C.S. Elliott and W.F.F. Price.

# ENGLAND v NEW ZEALAND 1965 (2nd Test)

Played at Lord's, London, on 17, 18, 19, 21, 22 June.
Toss: New Zealand.   Result: ENGLAND won by seven wickets.
Debuts: England – J.A. Snow.

England won with just 15 minutes to spare after rain had claimed over five hours of play during the last two days. In his 67th and final Test match Frederick Sewards Trueman took his total of Test wickets to 307 – an aggregate which remained unbeaten until 31st January, 1976, when L.R. Gibbs overtook it in his 79th match (*Test No. 769*).

## NEW ZEALAND

| | | | | | |
|---|---|---|---|---|---|
| B.E. Congdon | lbw b Rumsey | 0 | | lbw b Titmus | 26 |
| G.T. Dowling | lbw b Rumsey | 12 | | b Parfitt | 66 |
| B.W. Sinclair | b Rumsey | 1 | | c Parks b Barber | 72 |
| J.R. Reid* | c Parks b Snow | 21 | | b Titmus | 22 |
| R.W. Morgan | c Parfitt b Rumsey | 0 | | lbw b Rumsey | 35 |
| V. Pollard | c and b Titmus | 55 | | run out | 55 |
| A.E. Dick† | b Snow | 7 | | c Parks b Snow | 3 |
| B.R. Taylor | b Trueman | 51 | | c Smith b Snow | 0 |
| R.C. Motz | c Parks b Titmus | 11 | (10) | c Snow b Barber | 8 |
| R.O. Collinge | b Trueman | 7 | (9) | c Parks b Barber | 21 |
| F.J. Cameron | not out | 3 | | not out | 9 |
| Extras | (B 3, LB 2, NB 2) | 7 | | (B 8, LB 12, NB 10) | 30 |
| **Total** | | **175** | | | **347** |

## ENGLAND

| | | | | | |
|---|---|---|---|---|---|
| G. Boycott | c Dick b Motz | 14 | | lbw b Motz | 76 |
| P.W. Barber | c Dick b Motz | 13 | | b Motz | 34 |
| E.R. Dexter | c Dick b Taylor | 62 | (4) | not out | 80 |
| M.C. Cowdrey | c sub (T.W. Jarvis) b Collinge | ·119 | (5) | not out | 4 |
| P.H. Parfitt | c Dick b Cameron | 11 | | | |
| M.J.K. Smith* | c sub (T.W. Jarvis) b Taylor | 44 | | | |
| J.M. Parks† | b Collinge | 2 | | | |
| F.J. Titmus | run out | 13 | (3) | c Dick b Motz | 1 |
| F.S. Trueman | b Collinge | 3 | | | |
| F.F. Rumsey | b Collinge | 3 | | | |
| J.A. Snow | not out | 2 | | | |
| Extras | (B 1, LB 7, W 1, NB 12) | 21 | | (B 9, LB 5, NB 9) | 23 |
| **Total** | | **307** | | **(3 wickets)** | **218** |

| ENGLAND | O | M | R | W | O | M | R | W |
|---|---|---|---|---|---|---|---|---|
| Rumsey | 13 | 4 | 25 | 4 | 26 | 10 | 42 | 1 |
| Trueman | 19·5 | 8 | 40 | 2 | 26 | 4 | 69 | 0 |
| Dexter | 8 | 2 | 27 | 0 | | | | |
| Snow | 11 | 2 | 27 | 2 | 24 | 4 | 53 | 2 |
| Titmus | 15 | 7 | 25 | 2 | 39 | 12 | 71 | 2 |
| Barber | 8 | 2 | 24 | 0 | 28 | 10 | 57 | 3 |
| Parfitt | | | | | 5 | 2 | 25 | 1 |
| NEW ZEALAND | | | | | | | | |
| Collinge | 28·2 | 4 | 85 | 4 | 15 | 1 | 43 | 0 |
| Motz | 20 | 1 | 62 | 2 | 19 | 5 | 45 | 3 |
| Taylor | 25 | 4 | 66 | 2 | 10 | 0 | 53 | 0 |
| Cameron | 19 | 6 | 40 | 1 | 13 | 0 | 39 | 0 |
| Morgan | 8 | 1 | 33 | 0 | 3 | 0 | 11 | 0 |
| Reid | | | | | 0 | 0·5 | 0 | 4 |

| | FALL OF WICKETS | | | |
|---|---|---|---|---|
| | NZ | E | NZ | E |
| Wkt | 1st | 1st | 2nd | 2nd |
| 1st | 0 | 18 | 59 | 64 |
| 2nd | 4 | 38 | 149 | 70 |
| 3rd | 24 | 131 | 196 | 196 |
| 4th | 28 | 166 | 206 | – |
| 5th | 49 | 271 | 253 | – |
| 6th | 62 | 285 | 258 | – |
| 7th | 154 | 292 | 259 | – |
| 8th | 160 | 300 | 293 | – |
| 9th | 171 | 302 | 303 | – |
| 10th | 175 | 307 | 347 | – |

Umpires: J.S. Buller and W.E. Phillipson.

# ENGLAND v NEW ZEALAND 1965 (3rd Test)

Played at Headingley, Leeds, on 8, 9, 10, 12, 13 July.
Toss: England.    Result: ENGLAND won by an innings and 187 runs.
Debuts: Nil.

Edrich scored England's only triple century since 1938, his 310 not out being the highest score by an Englishman in first-class cricket at Leeds. He batted for 532 minutes and hit five sixes and 52 fours – the highest number of boundaries in any Test innings. He was on the field throughout the match. His partnership of 369 in 339 minutes with Barrington remains the highest for any wicket by either country in this series. Titmus took the wickets of Yuile, Taylor, Motz and Collinge for no runs in his 21st over (WOWWOW). England completed their third victory of the rubber after 16 minutes on the fifth morning – just before rain waterlogged the ground.

## ENGLAND

| | | |
|---|---|---:|
| R.W. Barber | c Ward b Taylor | 13 |
| J.H. Edrich | not out | 310 |
| K.F. Barrington | c Ward b Motz | 163 |
| M.C. Cowdrey | b Taylor | 13 |
| P.H. Parfitt | b Collinge | 32 |
| M.J.K. Smith* | not out | 2 |
| J.M. Parks† | ) | |
| R. Illingworth | ) | |
| F.J. Titmus | ) did not bat | |
| F.E. Rumsey | ) | |
| J.D.F. Larter | ) | |
| Extras | (B 4, LB 8, NB 1) | 13 |
| **Total** | (4 wickets declared) | **546** |

## NEW ZEALAND

| | | | | | |
|---|---|---:|---|---|---:|
| G.T. Dowling | c Parks b Larter | 5 | b Rumsey | | 41 |
| B.E. Congdon | c Parks b Rumsey | 13 | b Rumsey | | 1 |
| B.W. Sinclair | c Smith b Larter | 13 | lbw b Larter | | 29 |
| J.R. Reid* | lbw b Illingworth | 54 | c Barrington b Rumsey | | 5 |
| R.W. Morgan | b Illingworth | 1 | (6) b Titmus | | 21 |
| V. Pollard | run out | 33 | (5) c Cowdrey b Larter | | 53 |
| B.W. Yuile | b Larter | 46 | c Cowdrey b Titmus | | 12 |
| B.R. Taylor | c Parks b Illingworth | 9 | c and b Titmus | | 0 |
| R.C. Motz | c Barber b Illingworth | 3 | c Barrington b Titmus | | 0 |
| J.T. Ward† | not out | 0 | (11) not out | | 2 |
| R.O. Collinge | b Larter | 8 | (10) b Titmus | | 0 |
| Extras | (B 5, LB 2, W 2) | 8 | (NB 2) | | 2 |
| **Total** | | **193** | | | **166** |

| NEW ZEALAND | O | M | R | W | O | M | R | W |
|---|---:|---:|---:|---:|---:|---:|---:|---:|
| Motz | 41 | 8 | 140 | 1 | | | | |
| Taylor | 40 | 8 | 140 | 2 | | | | |
| Collinge | 32 | 7 | 87 | 1 | | | | |
| Yuile | 17 | 5 | 80 | 0 | | | | |
| Morgan | 6 | 0 | 28 | 0 | | | | |
| Pollard | 11 | 2 | 46 | 0 | | | | |
| Congdon | 4 | 0 | 12 | 0 | | | | |
| ENGLAND | | | | | | | | |
| Rumsey | 24 | 6 | 59 | 1 | 15 | 5 | 49 | 3 |
| Larter | 28·1 | 6 | 66 | 4 | 22 | 10 | 54 | 2 |
| Illingworth | 28 | 14 | 42 | 4 | 7 | 0 | 28 | 0 |
| Titmus | 6 | 2 | 16 | 0 | 26 | 17 | 19 | 5 |
| Barber | 2 | 0 | 2 | 0 | 14 | 7 | 14 | 0 |

### FALL OF WICKETS

| | E | NZ | NZ |
|---|---:|---:|---:|
| Wkt | 1st | 1st | 2nd |
| 1st | 13 | 15 | 4 |
| 2nd | 382 | 19 | 67 |
| 3rd | 407 | 53 | 75 |
| 4th | 516 | 61 | 86 |
| 5th | – | 100 | 111 |
| 6th | – | 153 | 158 |
| 7th | – | 165 | 158 |
| 8th | – | 173 | 158 |
| 9th | – | 181 | 158 |
| 10th | – | 193 | 166 |

Umpires: C.S. Elliott and J.F. Crapp.

# ENGLAND v SOUTH AFRICA 1965 (1st Test)

Played at Lord's, London on 22, 23, 24, 26, 27 July.
Toss: South Africa.   Result: MATCH DRAWN.
Debuts: England – D.J. Brown; South Africa – A. Bacher, J.T. Botten, R. Dumbrill.

Needing 191 runs to win in 235 minutes, England were never on terms with the required scoring rate. With seven wickets down and Edrich unable to resume his innings after being hit on the side of the head by a ball from P.M. Pollock, England did well to draw this 100th match between the two countries. Bland ran out Barrington and Parks with two outstanding pieces of fielding which culminated in direct hits on the stumps.

## SOUTH AFRICA

| Batsman | Dismissal 1 | R | Dismissal 2 | R |
|---|---|---|---|---|
| E.J. Barlow | c Barber b Rumsey | 1 | c Parks b Brown | 52 |
| H.R. Lance | c and b Brown | 28 | c Titmus b Brown | 9 |
| D.T. Lindsay† | c Titmus b Rumsey | 40 | c Parks b Larter | 22 |
| R.G. Pollock | c Barrington b Titmus | 56 | b Brown | 5 |
| K.C. Bland | b Brown | 39 | c Edrich b Barber | 70 |
| A. Bacher | lbw b Titmus | 4 | b Titmus | 37 |
| P.L. van der Merwe* | c Barrington b Rumsey | 17 | c Barrington b Rumsey | 31 |
| R. Dumbrill | b Barber | 3 | c Cowdrey b Rumsey | 2 |
| J.T. Botten | b Brown | 33 | b Rumsey | 0 |
| P.M. Pollock | st Parks b Barber | 34 | not out | 14 |
| H.D. Bromfield | not out | 9 | run out | 0 |
| Extras | (LB 14, NB 2) | 16 | (B 4, LB 2) | 6 |
| **Total** | | **280** | | **248** |

## ENGLAND

| Batsman | Dismissal 1 | R | Dismissal 2 | R |
|---|---|---|---|---|
| G. Boycott | c Barlow b Botten | 31 | c and b Dumbrill | 28 |
| R.W. Barber | b Bromfield | 56 | c Lindsay b P.M. Pollock | 12 |
| J.H. Edrich | lbw b P.M. Pollock | 0 | retired hurt | 7 |
| K.F. Barrington | run out | 91 | lbw b Dumbrill | 18 |
| M.C. Cowdrey | b Dumbrill | 29 | lbw b P.M. Pollock | 37 |
| M.J.K. Smith* | c Lindsay b Botten | 26 | c Lindsay b Dumbrill | 13 |
| J.M. Parks† | run out | 32 | c Van der Merwe b Dumbrill | 7 |
| F.J. Titmus | c P.M. Pollock b Bromfield | 59 | not out | 9 |
| D.J. Brown | c Bromfield b Dumbrill | 1 | c Barlow b R.G. Pollock | 5 |
| F.E. Rumsey | b Dumbrill | 3 | not out | 0 |
| J.D.F. Larter | not out | 0 | | |
| Extras | (B 1, LB 4, W 1, NB 4) | 10 | (LB 7, W 1, NB 1) | 9 |
| **Total** | | **338** | (7 wickets) | **145** |

| ENGLAND | O | M | R | W | O | M | R | W |
|---|---|---|---|---|---|---|---|---|
| Larter | 26 | 10 | 47 | 0 | 17 | 2 | 67 | 1 |
| Rumsey | 30 | 9 | 84 | 3 | 21 | 8 | 49 | 3 |
| Brown | 24 | 9 | 44 | 3 | 21 | 11 | 30 | 3 |
| Titmus | 29 | 10 | 59 | 2 | 26 | 13 | 36 | 1 |
| Barber | 10·3 | 3 | 30 | 2 | 25 | 5 | 60 | 1 |
| SOUTH AFRICA | | | | | | | | |
| P.M. Pollock | 39 | 12 | 91 | 1 | 20 | 6 | 52 | 2 |
| Botten | 33 | 11 | 65 | 2 | 12 | 6 | 25 | 0 |
| Barlow | 19 | 6 | 31 | 0 | 9 | 1 | 25 | 0 |
| Bromfield | 25·2 | 5 | 71 | 2 | 5 | 4 | 4 | 0 |
| Dumbrill | 24 | 11 | 31 | 3 | 18 | 8 | 30 | 4 |
| Lance | 5 | 0 | 18 | 0 | | | | |
| R.G. Pollock | 5 | 1 | 21 | 0 | 4 | 4 | 0 | 1 |

## FALL OF WICKETS

| Wkt | SA 1st | E 1st | SA 2nd | E 2nd |
|---|---|---|---|---|
| 1st | 1 | 82 | 55 | 23 |
| 2nd | 60 | 88 | 62 | 70 |
| 3rd | 75 | 88 | 68 | 79 |
| 4th | 155 | 144 | 120 | 113 |
| 5th | 170 | 240 | 170 | 121 |
| 6th | 170 | 240 | 216 | 135 |
| 7th | 178 | 294 | 230 | 140 |
| 8th | 212 | 314 | 230 | – |
| 9th | 241 | 338 | 247 | – |
| 10th | 280 | 338 | 248 | – |

Umpires: J.S. Buller and A.E.G. Rhodes.

# ENGLAND v SOUTH AFRICA 1965 (2nd Test)

Played at Trent Bridge, Nottingham, on 5, 6, 7, 9 August.
Toss: South Africa.   Result: SOUTH AFRICA won by 94 runs.
Debuts: Nil.

This was England's first defeat in 15 matches under Smith's captaincy. It was brought about mainly by the performances of the Pollock brothers, Graeme scoring 184 runs and Peter taking 10 for 87 in 48 overs. The former received 145 balls in the first innings, scoring 125 out of 160 with 21 boundaries; the last 91 of his runs were made off 90 balls in 70 minutes while his partner, Van der Merwe, scored 10. Cartwright (fractured thumb) was unable to bowl in the second innings.

## SOUTH AFRICA

| | | | | | |
|---|---|---|---|---|---|
| E.J. Barlow | c Cowdrey b Cartwright | 19 | (4) b Titmus | | 76 |
| H.R. Lance | lbw b Cartwright | 7 | c Barber b Snow | | 0 |
| D.T. Lindsay† | c Parks b Cartwright | 0 | (1) c Cowdrey b Larter | | 9 |
| R.G. Pollock | c Cowdrey b Cartwright | 125 | (5) c Titmus b Larter | | 59 |
| K.C. Bland | st Parks b Titmus | 1 | (6) b Snow | | 10 |
| A. Bacher | b Snow | 12 | (3) lbw b Larter | | 67 |
| P.L. van der Merwe* | run out | 38 | c Parfitt b Larter | | 4 |
| R. Dumbrill | c Parfitt b Cartwright | 30 | b Snow | | 13 |
| J.T. Botten | c Parks b Larter | 10 | b Larter | | 18 |
| P.M. Pollock | c Larter b Cartweight | 15 | not out | | 12 |
| A.H. McKinnon | not out | 8 | b Titmus | | 9 |
| Extras | (LB 4) | 4 | (B 4, LB 5, NB 3) | | 12 |
| **Total** | | **269** | | | **289** |

## ENGLAND

| | | | | | |
|---|---|---|---|---|---|
| G. Boycott | c Lance b P.M. Pollock | 0 | b McKinnon | | 16 |
| R.W. Barber | c Bacher b Dumbrill | 41 | c Lindsay b P.M. Pollock | | 1 |
| K.F. Barrington | b P.M. Pollock | 1 | (5) c Lindsay b P.M. Pollock | | 1 |
| F.J. Titmus | c R.G. Pollock b McKinnon | 20 | (3) c Lindsay b McKinnon | | 4 |
| M.C. Cowdrey | c Lindsay b Botten | 105 | (6) st Lindsay b McKinnon | | 20 |
| P.H. Parfitt | c Dumbrill b P.M. Pollock | 18 | (7) b P.M. Pollock | | 86 |
| M.J.K. Smith* | b P.M. Pollock | 32 | (8) lbw b R.G. Pollock | | 24 |
| J.M. Parks† | c and b Botten | 6 | (9) not out | | 44 |
| J.A. Snow | run out | 3 | (4) b Botten | | 0 |
| J.D.F. Larter | b P.M. Pollock | 2 | (11) c Van der Merwe b P.M. Pollock | 10 |
| T.W. Cartwright | not out | 1 | (10) lbw b P.M. Pollock | | 0 |
| Extras | (B 1, LB 3. W 1, NB 6) | 11 | (LB 5, W 2, NB 11) | | 18 |
| **Total** | | **240** | | | **224** |

| ENGLAND | O | M | R | W | O | M | R | W | FALL OF WICKETS | | | | |
|---|---|---|---|---|---|---|---|---|---|---|---|---|---|
| Larter | 17 | 6 | 25 | 1 | 29 | 7 | 68 | 5 | | SA | E | SA | E |
| Snow | 22 | 6 | 63 | 1 | 33 | 6 | 83 | 3 | Wkt | 1st | 1st | 2nd | 2nd |
| Cartwright | 31·3 | 9 | 94 | 6 | | | | | 1st | 16 | 0 | 2 | 1 |
| Titmus | 22 | 8 | 44 | 1 | 19·4 | 5 | 46 | 2 | 2nd | 16 | 8 | 35 | 10 |
| Barber | 9 | 3 | 39 | 0 | 3 | 0 | 20 | 0 | 3rd | 42 | 63 | 134 | 10 |
| Boycott | | | | | 26 | 10 | 60 | 0 | 4th | 43 | 67 | 193 | 13 |
| | | | | | | | | | 5th | 80 | 133 | 228 | 41 |
| SOUTH AFRICA | | | | | | | | | 6th | 178 | 225 | 232 | 59 |
| P.M. Pollock | 23·5 | 8 | 53 | 5 | 24 | 15 | 34 | 5 | 7th | 221 | 229 | 243 | 114 |
| Botten | 23 | 5 | 60 | 2 | 19 | 5 | 58 | 1 | 8th | 242 | 236 | 265 | 207 |
| McKinnon | 28 | 11 | 54 | 1 | 27 | 12 | 50 | 3 | 9th | 252 | 238 | 269 | 207 |
| Dumbrill | 18 | 3 | 60 | 1 | 16 | 4 | 40 | 0 | 10th | 269 | 240 | 289 | 224 |
| R.G. Pollock | 1 | 0 | 2 | 0 | 5 | 2 | 4 | 1 | | | | | |
| Barlow | | | | | 7 | 1 | 20 | 0 | | | | | |

Umpires: C.S. Elliott and J.F. Crapp.

# ENGLAND v SOUTH AFRICA 1965 (3rd Test)

Played at Kennington Oval, London, on 26, 27, 28, 30, 31 August.
Toss: England.   Result: MATCH DRAWN.
Debuts: England – K. Higgs.

England needed 91 runs to win with 70 minutes left when heavy rain ensured that South Africa won their second rubber in England, the first being in 1935. Higgs took the wicket of Lindsay with his 16th ball in Test cricket. Recalled after an interval of two years and 20 Tests, Statham took seven wickets in his final match to bring his tally to 252 wickets in 70 Tests – an aggregate at the time exceeded only by F.S. Trueman (307).

## SOUTH AFRICA

| | | | | | |
|---|---|--:|---|---|--:|
| E.J. Barlow | lbw b Statham | 18 | b Statham | | 18 |
| D.T. Lindsay† | lbw b Higgs | 4 | b Brown | | 17 |
| A. Bacher | lbw b Higgs | 28 | c Smith b Statham | | 70 |
| R.G. Pollock | b Titmus | 12 | run out | | 34 |
| K.C. Bland | lbw b Statham | 39 | c Titmus b Higgs | | 127 |
| H.R. Lance | lbw b Statham | 69 | b Higgs | | 53 |
| P.L. van der Merwe* | c Barrington b Higgs | 20 | b Higgs | | 0 |
| R. Dumbrill | c Smith b Higgs | 14 | c Barrington b Brown | | 36 |
| J.T. Botten | c Cowdrey b Statham | 0 | b Titmus | | 4 |
| P.M. Pollock | b Statham | 3 | not out | | 9 |
| A.H. McKinnon | not out | 0 | b Higgs | | 14 |
| Extras | (NB 1) | 1 | (B 1, LB 7, NB 2) | | 10 |
| **Total** | | **208** | | | **392** |

## ENGLAND

| | | | | | |
|---|---|--:|---|---|--:|
| R.W. Barber | st Lindsay b McKinnon | 40 | c and b P.M. Pollock | | 22 |
| W.E. Russell | lbw b P.M. Pollock | 0 | c Bacher b McKinnon | | 70 |
| K.F. Barrington | b Botten | 18 | (4) lbw b P.M. Pollock | | 73 |
| M.C. Cowdrey | c Barlow b P.M. Pollock | 58 | (5) not out | | 78 |
| P.H. Parfitt | c and b McKinnon | 24 | (3) lbw b Botten | | 46 |
| M.J.K. Smith* | lbw b P.M. Pollock | 7 | not out | | 10 |
| D.J. Brown | c Dumbrill b McKinnon | 0 | | | |
| J.M. Parks† | c Bland b Botten | 42 | | | |
| F.J. Titmus | not out | 2 | | | |
| K. Higgs | b P.M. Pollock | 2 | | | |
| J.B. Statham | b P.M. Pollock | 0 | | | |
| Extras | (LB 6, W 3) | 9 | (LB 6, NB 3) | | 9 |
| **Total** | | **202** | (4 wickets) | | **308** |

| ENGLAND | O | M | R | W | O | M | R | W |
|---|--:|--:|--:|--:|--:|--:|--:|--:|
| Statham | 24·2 | 11 | 40 | 5 | 29 | 1 | 105 | 2 |
| Brown | 22 | 4 | 63 | 0 | 23 | 3 | 63 | 2 |
| Higgs | 24 | 4 | 47 | 4 | 41·1 | 10 | 96 | 4 |
| Titmus | 26 | 12 | 57 | 1 | 27 | 3 | 74 | 1 |
| Barber | | | | | 13 | 1 | 44 | 0 |
| SOUTH AFRICA | | | | | | | | |
| P.M. Pollock | 25·1 | 7 | 43 | 5 | 32·2 | 7 | 93 | 2 |
| Botten | 27 | 6 | 56 | 2 | 24 | 4 | 73 | 1 |
| Barlow | 11 | 1 | 27 | 0 | 6 | 1 | 22 | 0 |
| Dumbrill | 6 | 2 | 11 | 0 | 9 | 1 | 30 | 0 |
| McKinnon | 27 | 11 | 50 | 3 | 31 | 7 | 70 | 1 |
| Lance | 2 | 0 | 6 | 0 | 2 | 0 | 11 | 0 |

### FALL OF WICKETS

| Wkt | SA 1st | E 1st | SA 2nd | E 2nd |
|---|--:|--:|--:|--:|
| 1st | 21 | 1 | 28 | 39 |
| 2nd | 23 | 42 | 61 | 138 |
| 3rd | 60 | 76 | 123 | 144 |
| 4th | 86 | 125 | 164 | 279 |
| 5th | 109 | 141 | 260 | – |
| 6th | 156 | 142 | 260 | – |
| 7th | 196 | 198 | 343 | – |
| 8th | 197 | 198 | 367 | – |
| 9th | 207 | 200 | 371 | – |
| 10th | 208 | 202 | 392 | – |

Umpires: J.S. Buller and W.F.F. Price.

# AUSTRALIA v ENGLAND 1965–66 (1st Test)

Played at Woolloongabba, Brisbane, on 10, 11 (*no play*), 13, 14, 15 December.
Toss: Australia.   Result: MATCH DRAWN.
Debuts: Australia – P.J. Allan, K.D. Walters.

Rain restricted play on the first day to 111 minutes and washed out the second completely. Lawry, having survived a confident appeal for a catch at the wicket off Brown's seventh ball of the innings, batted 419 minutes and hit 23 fours. Walters was the fifth Australian to score a hundred in the first innings of his first Test; all five instances have been against England. At 19 years 357 days, Walters was the third-youngest Australian after R.N. Harvey and A. Jackson to score a Test hundred. Russell, who began the match with a fractured thumb, split the webbing of his right hand when fielding.

## AUSTRALIA

| | | | |
|---|---|---:|---|
| W.M. Lawry | c Parks b Higgs | 166 | |
| I.R. Redpath | b Brown | 17 | |
| R.M. Cowper | c Barrington b Brown | 22 | |
| P.J.P. Burge | b Brown | 0 | |
| B.C. Booth* | c and b Titmus | 16 | |
| K.D. Walters | c Parks b Higgs | 155 | |
| T.R. Veivers | not out | 56 | |
| N.J.N. Hawke | not out | 6 | |
| P.I. Philpott | ) | | |
| A.T.W. Grout† | ) did not bat | | |
| P.J. Allan | ) | | |
| Extras | (LB 2, NB 3) | 5 | |
| **Total** | **(6 wickets declared)** | **443** | |

## ENGLAND

| | | | | | |
|---|---|---:|---|---|---:|
| R.W. Barber | c Walters b Hawke | 5 | c Veivers b Walters | | 34 |
| G. Boycott | b Philpott | 45 | not out | | 63 |
| J.H. Edrich | c Lawry b Philpott | 32 | c Veivers b Philpott | | 37 |
| K.F. Barrington | b Hawke | 53 | c Booth b Cowper | | 38 |
| M.J.K. Smith* | b Allan | 16 | not out | | 10 |
| J.M. Parks† | c Redpath b Philpott | 52 | | | |
| F.J. Titmus | st Grout b Philpott | 60 | | | |
| D.A. Allen | c Cowper b Walters | 3 | | | |
| D.J. Brown | b Philpott | 3 | | | |
| K. Higgs | lbw b Allan | 4 | | | |
| W.E. Russell | not out | 0 | | | |
| Extras | (B 4, NB 3) | 7 | (B 2, LB 2) | | 4 |
| **Total** | | **280** | **(3 wickets)** | | **186** |

| ENGLAND | O | M | R | W | O | M | R | W |
|---|---|---|---|---|---|---|---|---|
| Brown | 21 | 4 | 71 | 3 | | | | |
| Higgs | 30 | 6 | 102 | 2 | | | | |
| Titmus | 38 | 9 | 99 | 1 | | | | |
| Allen | 39 | 12 | 108 | 0 | | | | |
| Barber | 5 | 0 | 42 | 0 | | | | |
| Boycott | 4 | 0 | 16 | 0 | | | | |
| **AUSTRALIA** | | | | | | | | |
| Allan | 21 | 6 | 58 | 2 | 3 | 0 | 25 | 0 |
| Hawke | 16 | 7 | 44 | 2 | 10 | 2 | 16 | 0 |
| Walters | 10 | 1 | 25 | 1 | 5 | 1 | 22 | 1 |
| Philpott | 28·1 | 3 | 90 | 5 | 14 | 1 | 62 | 1 |
| Cowper | 7 | 4 | 7 | 0 | 6 | 0 | 20 | 1 |
| Veivers | 11 | 1 | 49 | 0 | 12 | 0 | 37 | 0 |

| FALL OF WICKETS | | | |
|---|---|---|---|
| | A | E | E |
| Wkt | 1st | 1st | 2nd |
| 1st | 51 | 5 | 46 |
| 2nd | 90 | 75 | 114 |
| 3rd | 90 | 86 | 168 |
| 4th | 125 | 115 | – |
| 5th | 312 | 191 | – |
| 6th | 431 | 221 | – |
| 7th | – | 232 | – |
| 8th | – | 253 | – |
| 9th | – | 272 | – |
| 10th | – | 280 | – |

Umpires: C.J. Egar and L.P. Rowan.

## AUSTRALIA v ENGLAND 1965–66 (2nd Test)

Played at Melbourne Cricket Ground on 30, 31 December, 1, 3, 4 January.
Toss: Australia.   Result: MATCH DRAWN.
Debuts: Nil.

Simpson, Australia's appointed captain, had recovered from the fractured wrist which prevented him from playing in the 1st Test. For a variety of reasons both sides had a complete change of opening bowlers for this match. Boycott and Barber scored 98 in 77 minutes for England's first wicket. Cowdrey's hundred was his fourth against Australia and his third at Melbourne. McKenzie bowled 35·5 overs but earlier in the innings retired after bowling five balls of an over. On the fourth day Barrington deputised for Parks (stomach upset) from the start of the innings until tea and caught Simpson. Parks returned after the interval but rain ended play after nine minutes. Parks missed a vital stumping chance off Barber when Burge was 34 and Australia 204 for 4 in the second innings.

### AUSTRALIA

| | | | | | |
|---|---|---|---|---|---|
| R.B. Simpson* | c Edrich b Allen | 59 | | c Barrington b Knight | 67 |
| W.M. Lawry | c Cowdrey b Allen | 88 | | c Smith b Barber | 78 |
| P.J.P. Burge | b Jones | 5 | (4) | c Edrich b Boycott | 120 |
| R.M. Cowper | c Titmus b Jones | 99 | (3) | lbw b Jones | 5 |
| B.C. Booth | lbw b Jones | 23 | | b Allen | 10 |
| K.D. Walters | c Parks b Knight | 22 | | c and b Barrington | 115 |
| T.R. Veivers | run out | 19 | | st Parks b Boycott | 3 |
| P.I. Philpott | b Knight | 10 | | b Knight | 2 |
| A.T.W. Grout† | c Barber b Knight | 11 | | c Allen b Barrington | 16 |
| G.D. McKenzie | not out | 12 | | run out | 2 |
| A.N. Connolly | c Parks b Knight | 0 | | not out | 0 |
| Extras | (B 2, LB 7, NB 1) | 10 | | (B 1, LB 3, W 1 NB 3) | 8 |
| **Total** | | **358** | | | **426** |

### ENGLAND

| | | | | |
|---|---|---|---|---|
| G. Boycott | c McKenzie b Walters | 51 | not out | 5 |
| R.W. Barber | c Grout b McKenzie | 48 | not out | 0 |
| J.H. Edrich | c and b Veivers | 109 | | |
| K.F. Barrington | c Burge b Veivers | 63 | | |
| M.C. Cowdrey | c Connolly b Cowper | 104 | | |
| M.J.K. Smith* | c Grout b McKenzie | 41 | | |
| J.M. Parks† | c Cowper b McKenzie | 71 | | |
| B.R. Knight | c Simpson b McKenzie | 1 | | |
| F.J. Titmus | not out | 56 | | |
| D.A. Allen | c Grout b Connolly | 2 | | |
| I.J. Jones | b McKenzie | 1 | | |
| Extras | (B 4, LB 5, W 2) | 11 | | |
| **Total** | | **558** | (0 wickets) | **5** |

| ENGLAND | O | M | R | W | O | M | R | W |
|---|---|---|---|---|---|---|---|---|
| Jones | 24 | 4 | 92 | 3 | 20 | 1 | 92 | 1 |
| Knight | 26·5 | 2 | 84 | 4 | 21 | 4 | 61 | 2 |
| Titmus | 31 | 7 | 93 | 0 | 22 | 6 | 43 | 0 |
| Allen | 20 | 4 | 55 | 2 | 18 | 3 | 48 | 1 |
| Barber | 6 | 1 | 24 | 0 | 17 | 0 | 87 | 1 |
| Barrington | | | | | 7·4 | 0 | 47 | 2 |
| Boycott | | | | | 9 | 0 | 32 | 2 |
| Smith | | | | | 2 | 0 | 8 | 0 |
| AUSTRALIA | | | | | | | | |
| McKenzie | 35·2 | 3 | 134 | 5 | 1 | 0 | 2 | 0 |
| Connolly | 37 | 5 | 125 | 1 | 1 | 0 | 3 | 0 |
| Philpott | 30 | 2 | 133 | 0 | | | | |
| Walters | 10 | 2 | 32 | 1 | | | | |
| Simpson | 16 | 4 | 61 | 0 | | | | |
| Veivers | 12 | 3 | 46 | 2 | | | | |
| Cowper | 3 | 0 | 16 | 1 | | | | |

### FALL OF WICKETS

| | A | E | A | E |
|---|---|---|---|---|
| Wkt | 1st | 1st | 2nd | 2nd |
| 1st | 93 | 98 | 120 | – |
| 2nd | 109 | 110 | 141 | – |
| 3rd | 203 | 228 | 163 | – |
| 4th | 262 | 333 | 176 | – |
| 5th | 297 | 409 | 374 | – |
| 6th | 318 | 443 | 382 | – |
| 7th | 330 | 447 | 385 | – |
| 8th | 342 | 540 | 417 | – |
| 9th | 352 | 551 | 426 | – |
| 10th | 358 | 558 | 426 | – |

Umpires: C.J. Egar and W. Smyth.

# AUSTRALIA v ENGLAND 1965–66 (3rd Test)

Played at Sydney Cricket Ground on 7, 8, 10, 11 January.
Toss: England.   Result: ENGLAND won by an innings and 93 runs.
Debuts: Nil.

England beat Australia for the first time in eleven matches since the 2nd Test at Melbourne in 1962-63. The opening partnership of 234 in 240 minutes between Boycott and Barber was England's third-highest against Australia. Barber reached his only Test hundred in 200 minutes. He batted 291 minutes, faced 272 balls and hit 19 fours in making his highest score in first-class cricket; it remains the highest score by an England batsman on the first day of a Test against Australia. Edrich completed his second successive Test hundred with a six. Titmus scored his 1,000th run and completed the 'double' in his 40th Test. Brown took the wickets of Sincock, Hawke and Grout with the second, seventh, and eighth balls of his first over with the second new ball.

## ENGLAND

| | | |
|---|---|---|
| G. Boycott | c and b Philpott | 84 |
| R.W. Barber | b Hawke | 185 |
| J.H. Edrich | c and b Philpott | 103 |
| K.F. Barrington | c McKenzie b Hawke | 1 |
| M.C. Cowdrey | c Grout b Hawke | 0 |
| M.J.K. Smith* | c Grout b Hawke | 6 |
| D.J. Brown | c Grout b Hawke | 1 |
| J.M. Parks† | c Grout b Hawke | 13 |
| F.J. Titmus | c Grout b Walters | 14 |
| D.A. Allen | not out | 50 |
| I.J. Jones | b Hawke | 16 |
| Extras | (B 3, LB 8, W 2, NB 2) | 15 |
| **Total** | | **488** |

## AUSTRALIA

| | | | | | |
|---|---|---|---|---|---|
| W.M. Lawry | c Parks b Jones | 0 | | c Cowdrey b Brown | 33 |
| G. Thomas | c Titmus b Brown | 51 | | c Cowdrey b Titmus | 25 |
| R.M. Cowper | st Parks b Allen | 60 | | c Boycott b Titmus | 0 |
| P.J.P. Burge | c Parks b Brown | 6 | | run out | 1 |
| B.C. Booth* | c Cowdrey b Jones | 8 | | b Allen | 27 |
| D.J. Sincock | c Parks b Brown | 29 | (7) | c Smith b Allen | 27 |
| K.D. Walters | st Parks b Allen | 23 | (6) | not out | 35 |
| N.J.N. Hawke | c Barber b Brown | 0 | (9) | c Smith b Titmus | 2 |
| A.T.W. Grout† | b Brown | 0 | (10) | c Smith b Allen | 3 |
| G.D. McKenzie | c Cowdrey b Barber | 24 | (11) | c Barber b Titmus | 12 |
| P.I. Philpott | not out | 5 | (8) | lbw b Allen | 5 |
| Extras | (B 7, LB 8) | 15 | | (B 3, LB 1) | 4 |
| **Total** | | **221** | | | **174** |

| AUSTRALIA | O | M | R | W | O | M | R | W |
|---|---|---|---|---|---|---|---|---|
| McKenzie | 25 | 2 | 113 | 0 | | | | |
| Hawke | 33·7 | 6 | 105 | 7 | | | | |
| Walters | 10 | 1 | 38 | 1 | | | | |
| Philpott | 28 | 3 | 86 | 2 | | | | |
| Sincock | 20 | 1 | 98 | 0 | | | | |
| Cowper | 6 | 1 | 33 | 0 | | | | |
| ENGLAND | | | | | | | | |
| Jones | 20 | 6 | 51 | 2 | 7 | 0 | 35 | 0 |
| Brown | 17 | 1 | 63 | 5 | 11 | 2 | 32 | 1 |
| Boycott | 3 | 1 | 8 | 0 | | | | |
| Titmus | 23 | 8 | 40 | 0 | 17·3 | 4 | 40 | 4 |
| Barber | 2·1 | 1 | 2 | 1 | 5 | 0 | 16 | 0 |
| Allen | 19 | 5 | 42 | 2 | 20 | 8 | 47 | 4 |

FALL OF WICKETS

| | E | A | A |
|---|---|---|---|
| Wkt | 1st | 1st | 2nd |
| 1st | 234 | 0 | 46 |
| 2nd | 303 | 81 | 50 |
| 3rd | 309 | 91 | 51 |
| 4th | 309 | 105 | 86 |
| 5th | 317 | 155 | 86 |
| 6th | 328 | 174 | 119 |
| 7th | 358 | 174 | 131 |
| 8th | 395 | 174 | 135 |
| 9th | 433 | 203 | 140 |
| 10th | 488 | 221 | 174 |

Umpires: C.J. Egar and L.P. Rowan.

# AUSTRALIA v ENGLAND 1965–66 (4th Test)

Played at Adelaide Oval on 28, 29, 31 January, 1 February.
Toss: England.   Result: AUSTRALIA won by an innings and 9 runs.
Debuts: Australia – K.R. Stackpole.

Australia's opening partnership of 244 in 260 minutes between Simpson and Lawry remains their highest for the first wicket against England and against all opponents in Australia. Simpson batted for 547 minutes and hit a six and 18 fours. Barrington, in his final Test appearance at Adelaide, extended his unique run of success by scoring his tenth consecutive fifty in first-class matches on that ground: 104, 52, 52*, 63, 132* (in 1962-63); 69, 51, 63, 60, 102 (in 1965-66).

## ENGLAND

| | | | | |
|---|---|--:|---|--:|
| G. Boycott | c Chappell b Hawke | 22 | lbw b McKenzie | 12 |
| R.W. Barber | b McKenzie | 0 | c Grout b Hawke | 19 |
| J.H. Edrich | c Simpson b McKenzie | 5 | c Simpson b Hawke | 1 |
| K.F. Barrington | lbw b Walters | 60 | c Chappell b Hawke | 102 |
| M.C. Cowdrey | run out | 38 | c Grout b Stackpole | 35 |
| M.J.K. Smith* | b Veivers | 29 | c McKenzie b Stackpole | 5 |
| J.M. Parks† | c Stackpole b McKenzie | 49 | run out | 16 |
| F.J. Titmus | lbw b McKenzie | 33 | c Grout b Hawke | 53 |
| D.A. Allen | c Simpson b McKenzie | 2 | not out | 5 |
| D.J. Brown | c Thomas b McKenzie | 1 | c and b Hawke | 0 |
| I.J. Jones | not out | 0 | c Lawry b Veivers | 8 |
| Extras | (LB 2) | 2 | (LB 2, NB 8) | 10 |
| **Total** | | **241** | | **266** |

## AUSTRALIA

| | | |
|---|---|--:|
| R.B. Simpson* | c Titmus b Jones | 225 |
| W.M. Lawry | b Titmus | 119 |
| G. Thomas | b Jones | 52 |
| T.R. Veivers | c Parks b Jones | 1 |
| P.J.P. Burge | c Parks b Jones | 27 |
| K.D. Walters | c Parks b Brown | 0 |
| I.M. Chappell | c Edrich b Jones | 17 |
| K.R. Stackpole | c Parks b Jones | 43 |
| N.J.N. Hawke | not out | 20 |
| A.T.W. Grout† | b Titmus | 4 |
| G.D. McKenzie | lbw b Titmus | 1 |
| Extras | (B 4, LB 3) | 7 |
| **Total** | | **516** |

| AUSTRALIA | O | M | R | W | O | M | R | W |
|---|--:|--:|--:|--:|--:|--:|--:|--:|
| McKenzie | 21·7 | 4 | 48 | 6 | 18 | 4 | 53 | 1 |
| Hawke | 23 | 2 | 69 | 1 | 21 | 6 | 54 | 5 |
| Walters | 14 | 0 | 50 | 1 | 9 | 0 | 47 | 0 |
| Stackpole | 5 | 0 | 30 | 0 | 14 | 3 | 33 | 2 |
| Chappell | 4 | 1 | 18 | 0 | 22 | 4 | 53 | 0 |
| Veivers | 13 | 3 | 24 | 1 | 3·7 | 0 | 16 | 1 |
| ENGLAND | | | | | | | | |
| Jones | 29 | 3 | 118 | 6 | | | | |
| Brown | 28 | 4 | 109 | 1 | | | | |
| Boycott | 7 | 3 | 33 | 0 | | | | |
| Titmus | 37 | 6 | 116 | 3 | | | | |
| Allen | 21 | 1 | 103 | 0 | | | | |
| Barber | 4 | 0 | 30 | 0 | | | | |

### FALL OF WICKETS

| Wkt | E 1st | A 1st | E 2nd |
|---|--:|--:|--:|
| 1st | 7 | 244 | 23 |
| 2nd | 25 | 331 | 31 |
| 3rd | 33 | 333 | 32 |
| 4th | 105 | 379 | 114 |
| 5th | 150 | 383 | 123 |
| 6th | 178 | 425 | 163 |
| 7th | 210 | 480 | 244 |
| 8th | 212 | 501 | 253 |
| 9th | 222 | 506 | 257 |
| 10th | 241 | 516 | 266 |

Umpires: C.J. Egar and L.P. Rowan.

## AUSTRALIA v ENGLAND 1965–66 (5th Test)

Played at Melbourne Cricket Ground on 11, 12, 14, 15 (*no play*), 16 February.
Toss: England.    Result: MATCH DRAWN.
Debuts: Nil.

Cowper scored Australia's only triple hundred in a home Test. He hit 20 fours and batted for 727 minutes to record the longest first-class innings in Australia, the longest innings against England overseas, and the fourth-longest innings in all first-class cricket. Barrington hit his 122nd ball for six to complete his second consecutive Test hundred in 148 minutes. He was the first to reach a hundred with a six twice in Tests between England and Australia (also *Test No. 538*).

### ENGLAND

| | | | | |
|---|---|---|---|---|
| G. Boycott | c Stackpole b McKenzie | 17 | lbw b McKenzie | 1 |
| R.W. Barber | run out | 17 | b McKenzie | 20 |
| J.H. Edrich | c McKenzie b Walters | 85 | b McKenzie | 3 |
| K.F. Barrington | c Grout b Walters | 115 | not out | 32 |
| M.C. Cowdrey | c Grout b Walters | 79 | not out | 11 |
| M.J.K. Smith* | c Grout b Walters | 0 | | |
| J.M. Parks† | run out | 89 | | |
| F.J. Titmus | not out | 42 | | |
| B.R. Knight | c Grout b Hawke | 13 | | |
| D.J. Brown | c and b Chappell | 12 | | |
| I.J. Jones | not out | 4 | | |
| Extras | (B 9, LB 2, NB 1) | 12 | (LB 2) | 2 |
| **Total** | (9 wickets declared) | **485** | (3 wickets) | **69** |

### AUSTRALIA

| | | |
|---|---|---|
| W.M. Lawry | c Edrich b Jones | 108 |
| R.B. Simpson* | b Brown | 4 |
| G. Thomas | c Titmus b Jones | 19 |
| R.M. Cowper | b Knight | 307 |
| K.D. Walters | c and b Barber | 60 |
| I.M. Chappell | c Parks b Jones | 19 |
| K.R. Stackpole | b Knight | 9 |
| T.R. Veivers | b Titmus | 4 |
| N.J.N. Hawke | not out | 0 |
| A.T.W. Grout† | ) did not bat | |
| G.D. McKenzie | ) | |
| Extras | (B 6, LB 5, NB 2) | 13 |
| **Total** | (8 wickets declared) | **543** |

| AUSTRALIA | O | M | R | W | O | M | R | W |
|---|---|---|---|---|---|---|---|---|
| McKenzie | 26 | 5 | 100 | 1 | 6 | 2 | 17 | 3 |
| Hawke | 35 | 5 | 109 | 1 | 4 | 1 | 22 | 0 |
| Walters | 19 | 3 | 53 | 4 | 2 | 0 | 16 | 0 |
| Simpson | 5 | 1 | 20 | 0 | | | | |
| Stackpole | 10 | 2 | 43 | 0 | 3 | 0 | 10 | 0 |
| Veivers | 15 | 3 | 78 | 0 | | | | |
| Chappell | 17 | 4 | 70 | 1 | 2 | 0 | 20 | 0 |
| ENGLAND | | | | | | | | |
| Brown | 31 | 3 | 134 | 1 | | | | |
| Jones | 29 | 1 | 145 | 3 | | | | |
| Knight | 36·2 | 4 | 105 | 2 | | | | |
| Titmus | 42 | 12 | 86 | 1 | | | | |
| Barber | 16 | 0 | 60 | 1 | | | | |

FALL OF WICKETS

| Wkt | E 1st | A 1st | E 2nd |
|---|---|---|---|
| 1st | 36 | 15 | 6 |
| 2nd | 41 | 36 | 21 |
| 3rd | 219 | 248 | 34 |
| 4th | 254 | 420 | – |
| 5th | 254 | 481 | – |
| 6th | 392 | 532 | – |
| 7th | 419 | 543 | – |
| 8th | 449 | 543 | – |
| 9th | 474 | – | – |
| 10th | – | – | – |

Umpires: C.J. Egar and L.P. Rowan.

# NEW ZEALAND v ENGLAND 1965–66 (1st Test)

Played at Lancaster Park, Christchurch on 25, 26, 28 February, 1 March.
Toss: England.   Result: MATCH DRAWN.
Debuts: New Zealand – G.P. Bilby, N. Puna.

Cowdrey became the second non-wicket-keeper after W.R. Hammond to hold 100 catches in Test cricket when he caught Chapple at second slip.

## ENGLAND

| | | | | | |
|---|---|---|---|---|---|
| G. Boycott | c Petrie b Motz | 4 | run out | | 4 |
| W.E. Russell | b Motz | 30 | b Bartlett | | 25 |
| J.H. Edrich | c Bartlett b Motz | 2 | lbw b Cunis | | 2 |
| M.C. Cowdrey | c Bilby b Cunis | 0 | c Pollard b Motz | | 21 |
| M.J.K. Smith* | c Puna b Pollard | 54 | c Bilby b Puna | | 87 |
| P.H. Parfitt | c Congdon b Bartlett | 54 | not out | | 46 |
| J.M. Parks† | c Petrie b Chapple | 30 | not out | | 4 |
| D.A. Allen | c Chapple b Bartlett | 88 | | | |
| D.J. Brown | b Cunis | 44 | | | |
| K. Higgs | not out | 8 | | | |
| I.J. Jones | b Bartlett | 0 | | | |
| Extras | (B 6, LB 6, NB 16) | 28 | (B 4, LB 1, NB 7) | | 12 |
| **Total** | | **342** | (5 wickets declared) | | **201** |

## NEW ZEALAND

| | | | | | |
|---|---|---|---|---|---|
| G.P. Bilby | c Parks b Higgs | 28 | c Parks b Brown | | 3 |
| M.J.F. Shrimpton | c Parks b Brown | 11 | c Smith b Allen | | 13 |
| B.E. Congdon | c Smith b Jones | 104 | c Cowdrey b Higgs | | 4 |
| B.W. Sinclair | c and b Higgs | 23 | c Parks b Higgs | | 0 |
| V. Pollard | lbw b Higgs | 23 | not out | | 6 |
| M.E. Chapple* | c Cowdrey b Jones | 15 | (7) c Parks b Higgs | | 0 |
| G.A. Bartlett | c Parks b Brown | 0 | (8) c Brown b Parfitt | | 0 |
| E.C. Petrie† | c Parks b Brown | 55 | (6) lbw b Higgs | | 1 |
| R.C. Motz | c Parks b Jones | 58 | c Russell b Parfitt | | 2 |
| R.S. Cunis | not out | 8 | not out | | 16 |
| N. Puna | c Smith b Jones | 1 | | | |
| Extras | (B 7, LB 13, NB 1) | 21 | (B 2, LB 1) | | 3 |
| **Total** | | **347** | (8 wickets) | | **48** |

| NEW ZEALAND | O | M | R | W | O | M | R | W | | FALL OF WICKETS | | | |
|---|---|---|---|---|---|---|---|---|---|---|---|---|---|
| Motz | 31 | 9 | 83 | 3 | 20 | 6 | 38 | 1 | | E | NZ | E | NZ |
| Bartlett | 33·2 | 6 | 63 | 3 | 14 | 2 | 44 | 1 | Wkt | 1st | 1st | 2nd | 2nd |
| Cunis | 31 | 9 | 63 | 2 | 19 | 3 | 58 | 1 | 1st | 19 | 39 | 18 | 5 |
| Puna | 18 | 6 | 54 | 0 | 14 | 6 | 49 | 1 | 2nd | 28 | 41 | 32 | 19 |
| Chapple | 9 | 3 | 24 | 1 | | | | | 3rd | 47 | 112 | 48 | 21 |
| Pollard | 5 | 1 | 27 | 1 | | | | | 4th | 47 | 181 | 68 | 21 |
| | | | | | | | | | 5th | 160 | 202 | 193 | 22 |
| ENGLAND | | | | | | | | | 6th | 160 | 203 | – | 22 |
| Brown | 30 | 3 | 80 | 3 | 4 | 2 | 6 | 1 | 7th | 209 | 237 | – | 22 |
| Jones | 28·4 | 9 | 71 | 4 | 7 | 3 | 13 | 0 | 8th | 316 | 326 | – | 32 |
| Higgs | 30 | 6 | 51 | 3 | 9 | 7 | 5 | 4 | 9th | 342 | 344 | – | – |
| Allen | 40 | 14 | 80 | 0 | 19 | 15 | 8 | 1 | 10th | 342 | 347 | – | – |
| Boycott | 12 | 6 | 30 | 0 | | | | | | | | | |
| Parfitt | 3 | 0 | 14 | 0 | 6 | 3 | 5 | 2 | | | | | |
| Parks | | | | | 3 | 1 | 8 | 0 | | | | | |

Umpires: W.T. Martin and F.R. Goodall.

# NEW ZEALAND v ENGLAND 1965–66 (2nd Test)

Played at Carisbrook, Dunedin, on 4, 5, 7, 8 March.
Toss: New Zealand.    Result: MATCH DRAWN.
Debuts: Nil.

Motz hit 22 runs (064066) off Allen's 26th over to establish the record for the most runs by one batsman off a six-ball over in Test matches. Rain restricted play to 3¼ hours on the first day and to just over two hours on the third.

## NEW ZEALAND

| | | | | |
|---|---|---|---|---|
| G.P. Bilby | c Murray b Jones | 3 | c Parfitt b Higgs | 21 |
| M.J.F. Shrimpton | c Boycott b Higgs | 38 | (6) b Allen | 0 |
| B.E. Congdon | c Murray b Jones | 0 | b Parfitt | 19 |
| B.W. Sinclair* | b Knight | 33 | c Knight b Jones | 39 |
| V. Pollard | c Murray b Higgs | 8 | (2) b Higgs | 2 |
| R.W. Morgan | c Murray b Higgs | 0 | (5) c Smith b Allen | 3 |
| G.A. Bartlett | c Parfitt b Allen | 6 | c Knight b Allen | 4 |
| E.C. Petrie† | c Smith b Jones | 28 | not out | 13 |
| R.C. Motz | c Higgs b Knight | 57 | b Jones | 1 |
| R.S. Cunis | c Boycott b Allen | 8 | lbw b Allen | 9 |
| N. Puna | not out | 3 | not out | 18 |
| Extras | (B 4, LB 4) | 8 | (B 10, LB 6, NB 2) | 18 |
| **Total** | | **192** | (9 wickets) | **147** |

## ENGLAND

| | | |
|---|---|---|
| G. Boycott | b Bartlett | 5 |
| W.E. Russell | b Motz | 11 |
| J.H. Edrich | c Bilby b Cunis | 36 |
| M.C. Cowdrey | not out | 89 |
| M.J.K. Smith* | c Pollard b Bartlett | 20 |
| P.H. Parfitt | c Pollard b Puna | 4 |
| J.T. Murray† | c Sinclair b Puna | 50 |
| B.R. Knight | c Bartlett b Motz | 12 |
| D.A. Allen | b Cunis | 9 |
| K. Higgs | not out | 0 |
| I.J. Jones | did not bat | |
| Extras | (B 4, LB 6, NB 8) | 18 |
| **Total** | (8 wickets declared) | **254** |

| ENGLAND | O | M | R | W | O | M | R | W | | FALL OF WICKETS | | |
|---|---|---|---|---|---|---|---|---|---|---|---|---|
| Jones | 26 | 11 | 46 | 3 | 15 | 4 | 32 | 2 | | NZ | E | NZ |
| Higgs | 20 | 6 | 29 | 3 | 13 | 7 | 12 | 2 | Wkt | 1st | 1st | 2nd |
| Knight | 32 | 14 | 41 | 2 | 3 | 1 | 3 | 0 | 1st | 4 | 9 | 8 |
| Allen | 27·4 | 9 | 68 | 2 | 33 | 17 | 46 | 4 | 2nd | 6 | 32 | 27 |
| Parfitt | | | | | 17 | 6 | 30 | 1 | 3rd | 66 | 72 | 66 |
| Edrich | | | | | 1 | 0 | 6 | 0 | 4th | 83 | 103 | 75 |
| | | | | | | | | | 5th | 83 | 119 | 75 |
| NEW ZEALAND | | | | | | | | | 6th | 92 | 200 | 79 |
| Motz | 32 | 7 | 76 | 2 | | | | | 7th | 100 | 213 | 100 |
| Bartlett | 29 | 4 | 70 | 2 | | | | | 8th | 170 | 241 | 102 |
| Cunis | 28 | 7 | 49 | 2 | | | | | 9th | 181 | – | 112 |
| Puna | 14 | 2 | 40 | 2 | | | | | 10th | 192 | – | – |
| Pollard | 1 | 0 | 1 | 0 | | | | | | | | |

Umpires: W.T. Martin and W.J.C. Gwynne.

# NEW ZEALAND v ENGLAND 1965–66 (3rd Test)

Played at Eden Park, Auckland, on 11, 12, 14, 15 March.
Toss: New Zealand.   Result: MATCH DRAWN.
Debuts: Nil.

England needed 204 runs to win in 4½ hours. Edrich was taken ill with appendicitis after the first day and operated upon before the start of the second. Brown severely strained his back and was unable to complete his ninth over.

## NEW ZEALAND

| | | | | | |
|---|---|--:|---|---|--:|
| T.W. Jarvis | c Parks b Jones | 39 | | c Parks b Jones | 0 |
| M.J.F. Shrimpton | b Brown | 6 | | lbw b Brown | 0 |
| B.E. Congdon | lbw b Higgs | 64 | | run out | 23 |
| B.W. Sinclair* | c Russell b Jones | 114 | | b Higgs | 9 |
| R.W. Morgan | c Smith b Allen | 5 | | lbw b Knight | 25 |
| V. Pollard | c Knight b Allen | 2 | | c Parks b Jones | 25 |
| E.C. Petrie† | c Smith b Higgs | 12 | (8) | b Higgs | 6 |
| R.C. Motz | c Jones b Allen | 16 | (7) | c Smith b Jones | 14 |
| B.R. Taylor | b Allen | 18 | | b Higgs | 6 |
| R.S. Cunis | not out | 6 | | c sub (J.T. Murray) b Allen | 8 |
| N. Puna | c Russell b Allen | 7 | | not out | 2 |
| Extras | (B 1, LB 4, NB 2) | 7 | | (B 2, LB 7, NB 2) | 11 |
| **Total** | | **296** | | | **129** |

## ENGLAND

| | | | | | |
|---|---|--:|---|---|--:|
| P.H. Parfitt | b Taylor | 3 | | b Taylor | 30 |
| W.E. Russell | lbw b Motz | 56 | | c Petrie b Taylor | 1 |
| M.C. Cowdrey | run out | 59 | | lbw b Puna | 27 |
| M.J.K. Smith* | b Taylor | 18 | | lbw b Cunis | 30 |
| J.M. Parks† | lbw b Taylor | 38 | | not out | 45 |
| B.R. Knight | c Taylor b Pollard | 25 | | not out | 13 |
| D.A. Allen | not out | 7 | | | |
| D.J. Brown | b Pollard | 0 | | | |
| K. Higgs | c Petrie b Pollard | 0 | | | |
| I.J. Jones | b Cunis | 0 | | | |
| J.H. Edrich | absent ill | – | | | |
| Extras | (B 11, LB 3, NB 2) | 16 | | (B 4, LB 4, NB 5) | 13 |
| **Total** | | **222** | | (4 wickets) | **159** |

| ENGLAND | O | M | R | W | O | M | R | W |
|---|--:|--:|--:|--:|--:|--:|--:|--:|
| Brown | 18 | 6 | 32 | 1 | 8·1 | 3 | 8 | 1 |
| Jones | 21 | 4 | 52 | 2 | 25 | 9 | 28 | 3 |
| Higgs | 28 | 13 | 33 | 2 | 28 | 11 | 27 | 3 |
| Allen | 47·5 | 12 | 123 | 5 | 23·3 | 7 | 34 | 1 |
| Knight | 16 | 7 | 40 | 0 | 18 | 9 | 21 | 1 |
| Parfitt | 2 | 0 | 9 | 0 | | | | |
| NEW ZEALAND | | | | | | | | |
| Motz | 15 | 4 | 42 | 1 | 16 | 1 | 32 | 0 |
| Taylor | 21 | 6 | 46 | 3 | 12 | 4 | 20 | 2 |
| Cunis | 25·5 | 8 | 45 | 1 | 18 | 5 | 33 | 1 |
| Puna | 22 | 2 | 70 | 0 | 12 | 4 | 27 | 1 |
| Pollard | 5 | 2 | 3 | 3 | 14 | 3 | 30 | 0 |
| Shrimpton | | | | | 2 | 1 | 1 | 0 |
| Jarvis | | | | | 1 | 0 | 3 | 0 |

FALL OF WICKETS

| | NZ | E | NZ | E |
|---|--:|--:|--:|--:|
| Wkt | 1st | 1st | 2nd | 2nd |
| 1st | 22 | 3 | 0 | 0 |
| 2nd | 99 | 121 | 0 | 50 |
| 3rd | 142 | 128 | 20 | 79 |
| 4th | 153 | 175 | 48 | 112 |
| 5th | 189 | 195 | 68 | — |
| 6th | 237 | 215 | 88 | — |
| 7th | 262 | 215 | 109 | — |
| 8th | 264 | 219 | 118 | — |
| 9th | 288 | 222 | 121 | — |
| 10th | 296 | — | 129 | — |

Umpires: W.T. Martin and R.W.R. Shortt.

# ENGLAND v WEST INDIES 1966 (1st Test)

Played at Old Trafford, Manchester, on 2, 3, 4 June.
Toss: West Indies.   Result: WEST INDIES won by an innings and 40 runs.
Debuts: England – C. Milburn; West Indies – D.A.J. Holford.

Hunte square cut the first ball of the rubber for four runs. England were beaten in three days for the first time since 1938 (*Test No. 265*) and it was their first such defeat in a five-day Test. The weather was hot throughout.

## WEST INDIES

| | | |
|---|---|---|
| C.C. Hunte | c Smith b Higgs | 135 |
| E.D.A. St J. McMorris | c Russell b Higgs | 11 |
| R.B. Kanhai | b Higgs | 0 |
| B.F. Butcher | c Parks b Titmus | 44 |
| S.M. Nurse | b Titmus | 49 |
| G. St A. Sobers* | c Cowdrey b Titmus | 161 |
| D.A.J. Holford | c Smith b Allen | 32 |
| D.W. Allan† | lbw b Titmus | 1 |
| C.C. Griffith | lbw b Titmus | 30 |
| W.W. Hall | b Allen | 1 |
| L.R. Gibbs | not out | 1 |
| Extras | (B 8, LB 10, NB 1) | 19 |
| **Total** | | **484** |

## ENGLAND

| | | | | | |
|---|---|---|---|---|---|
| C. Milburn | run out | 0 | b Gibbs | | 94 |
| W.E. Russell | c Sobers b Gibbs | 26 | b Griffith | | 20 |
| K.F. Barrington | c and b Griffith | 5 | c Nurse b Holford | | 30 |
| M.C. Cowdrey | c and b Gibbs | 12 | c Butcher b Sobers | | 69 |
| M.J.K. Smith* | c Butcher b Gibbs | 5 | b Gibbs | | 6 |
| J.M. Parks† | c Nurse b Holford | 43 | c and b Sobers | | 11 |
| F.J. Titmus | b Holford | 15 | c Butcher b Sobers | | 12 |
| D.A. Allen | c Sobers b Gibbs | 37 | c Allan b Gibbs | | 1 |
| D.J. Brown | b Gibbs | 14 | c Sobers b Gibbs | | 10 |
| K. Higgs | c Sobers b Holford | 1 | st Allan b Gibbs | | 5 |
| I.J. Jones | not out | 0 | not out | | 0 |
| Extras | (B 1, LB 4, NB 4) | 9 | (B 11, LB 1, NB 7) | | 19 |
| **Total** | | **167** | | | **277** |

| ENGLAND | O | M | R | W | O | M | R | W | | FALL OF WICKETS | | | |
|---|---|---|---|---|---|---|---|---|---|---|---|---|---|
| Jones | 28 | 6 | 100 | 0 | | | | | | | WI | E | E |
| Brown | 28 | 4 | 84 | 0 | | | | | | Wkt | 1st | 1st | 2nd |
| Higgs | 31 | 5 | 94 | 3 | | | | | | 1st | 38 | 11 | 53 |
| Allen | 31·1 | 8 | 104 | 2 | | | | | | 2nd | 42 | 24 | 142 |
| Titmus | 35 | 10 | 83 | 5 | | | | | | 3rd | 116 | 42 | 166 |
| | | | | | | | | | | 4th | 215 | 48 | 184 |
| WEST INDIES | | | | | | | | | | 5th | 283 | 65 | 203 |
| Hall | 14 | 6 | 43 | 0 | 5 | 0 | 28 | 0 | | 6th | 410 | 85 | 217 |
| Griffith | 10 | 3 | 28 | 1 | 6 | 1 | 25 | 1 | | 7th | 411 | 143 | 218 |
| Sobers | 7 | 1 | 16 | 0 | 42 | 11 | 87 | 3 | | 8th | 471 | 153 | 268 |
| Gibbs | 28·1 | 13 | 37 | 5 | 41 | 16 | 69 | 5 | | 9th | 482 | 163 | 276 |
| Holford | 15 | 4 | 34 | 3 | 14 | 2 | 49 | 1 | | 10th | 484 | 167 | 277 |

Umpires: J.S. Buller and C.S. Elliott.

# ENGLAND v WEST INDIES 1966 (2nd Test)

Played at Lord's, London, on 16, 17, 18, 20, 21 June.
Toss: West Indies.   Result: MATCH DRAWN.
Debuts: England – B.L. D'Oliveira.

England needed to score 284 runs in 240 minutes. The unbroken partnership of 274 between Sobers and his cousin, Holford, remains the highest for West Indies' sixth wicket in all Tests. Milburn and Graveney recorded England's highest fifth-wicket partnership against West Indies (130 unbroken). Both Holford and Milburn scored hundreds in their second Test match. Parks made his 100th dismissal as a wicket-keeper and completed the double of 1,000 runs and 100 dismissals when he caught Kanhai.

## WEST INDIES

| | | | | |
|---|---|---|---|---|
| C.C. Hunte | c Parks b Higgs | 18 | c Milburn b Knight | 13 |
| M.C. Carew | c Parks b Higgs | 2 | c Knight b Higgs | 0 |
| R.B. Kanhai | c Titmus b Higgs | 25 | c Parks b Knight | 40 |
| B.F. Butcher | c Milburn b Knight | 49 | lbw b Higgs | 3 |
| S.M. Nurse | b D'Oliveira | 64 | c Parks b D'Oliveira | 35 |
| G. St A. Sobers* | lbw b Knight | 46 | not out | 163 |
| D.A.J. Holford | b Jones | 26 | not out | 105 |
| D.W. Allan† | c Titmus b Higgs | 13 | | |
| C.C. Griffith | lbw b Higgs | 5 | | |
| W.W. Hall | not out | 8 | | |
| L.R. Gibbs | c Parks b Higgs | 4 | | |
| Extras | (B 2, LB 7) | 9 | (LB 8, NB 2) | 10 |
| **Total** | | **269** | (5 wickets declared) | **369** |

## ENGLAND

| | | | | |
|---|---|---|---|---|
| G. Boycott | c Griffith b Gibbs | 60 | c Allan b Griffith | 25 |
| C. Milburn | lbw b Hall | 6 | not out | 126 |
| T.W. Graveney | c Allan b Hall | 96 | (6) not out | 30 |
| K.F. Barrington | b Sobers | 19 | (3) b Griffith | 5 |
| M.C. Cowdrey* | c Gibbs b Hall | 9 | (4) c Allan b Hall | 5 |
| J.M. Parks† | lbw b Carew | 91 | (5) b Hall | 0 |
| B.L. D'Oliveira | run out | 27 | | |
| B.R. Knight | b Griffith | 6 | | |
| F.J. Titmus | c Allan b Hall | 6 | | |
| K. Higgs | c Holford b Gibbs | 13 | | |
| I.J. Jones | not out | 0 | | |
| Extras | (B 7, LB 10, NB 5) | 22 | (B 4, LB 2) | 6 |
| **Totals** | | **355** | (4 wickets) | **197** |

| ENGLAND | O | M | R | W | O | M | R | W |
|---|---|---|---|---|---|---|---|---|
| Jones | 21 | 3 | 64 | 1 | 25 | 2 | 95 | 0 |
| Higgs | 33 | 9 | 91 | 6 | 34 | 5 | 82 | 2 |
| Knight | 21 | 0 | 63 | 2 | 30 | 3 | 106 | 2 |
| Titmus | 5 | 0 | 18 | 0 | 19 | 3 | 30 | 0 |
| D'Oliveira | 14 | 5 | 24 | 1 | 25 | 7 | 46 | 1 |
| WEST INDIES | | | | | | | | |
| Sobers | 39 | 12 | 89 | 1 | 8 | 4 | 8 | 0 |
| Hall | 36 | 2 | 106 | 4 | 14 | 1 | 65 | 2 |
| Griffith | 28 | 4 | 79 | 1 | 11 | 2 | 43 | 2 |
| Gibbs | 37·3 | 18 | 48 | 2 | 13 | 4 | 40 | 0 |
| Carew | 3 | 0 | 11 | 1 | | | | |
| Holford | | | | | 9 | 1 | 35 | 0 |

### FALL OF WICKETS

| Wkt | WI 1st | E 1st | WI 2nd | E 2nd |
|---|---|---|---|---|
| 1st | 8 | 8 | 2 | 37 |
| 2nd | 42 | 123 | 22 | 43 |
| 3rd | 53 | 164 | 25 | 67 |
| 4th | 119 | 198 | 91 | 67 |
| 5th | 205 | 203 | 95 | – |
| 6th | 213 | 251 | – | – |
| 7th | 252 | 266 | – | – |
| 8th | 252 | 296 | – | – |
| 9th | 261 | 355 | – | – |
| 10th | 269 | 355 | – | – |

Umpires: J.S. Buller and W.F.F. Price.

# ENGLAND v WEST INDIES 1966 (3rd Test)

Played at Trent Bridge, Nottingham, on 30 June, 1, 2, 4, 5 July.
Toss: West Indies.   Result: WEST INDIES won by 139 runs.
Debuts: England – D.L. Underwood.

England, needing to score 393 runs in 389 minutes, were all out at 4.14 p.m. Graveney scored his third hundred in consecutive Test appearances at Nottingham. Butcher, who batted for 461 minutes and hit 22 fours, shared in century partnerships for three successive wickets.

## WEST INDIES

| | | | | | |
|---|---|---:|---|---|---:|
| C.C. Hunte | lbw b Higgs | 9 | c Graveney b D'Oliveira | | 12 |
| P.D. Lashley | c Parks b Snow | 49 | lbw b D'Oliveira | | 23 |
| R.B. Kanhai | c Underwood b Higgs | 32 | c Cowdrey b Higgs | | 63 |
| B.F. Butcher | b Snow | 5 | not out | | 209 |
| S.M. Nurse | c Illingworth b Snow | 93 | lbw b Higgs | | 53 |
| G. St A. Sobers* | c Parks b Snow | 3 | c Underwood b Higgs | | 94 |
| D.A.J. Holford | lbw b D'Oliveira | 11 | not out | | 17 |
| J.L. Hendriks† | b D'Oliveira | 2 | | | |
| C.C. Griffith | c Cowdrey b Higgs | 14 | | | |
| W.W. Hall | b Higgs | 12 | | | |
| L.R. Gibbs | not out | 0 | | | |
| Extras | (B 3, LB 2) | 5 | (LB 6, W 5) | | 11 |
| **Total** | | **235** | (5 wickets declared) | | **482** |

## ENGLAND

| | | | | | |
|---|---|---:|---|---|---:|
| G. Boycott | lbw b Sobers | 0 | c Sobers b Griffith | | 71 |
| C. Milburn | c Sobers b Hall | 7 | c Griffith b Hall | | 12 |
| W.E. Russell | b Hall | 4 | c Sobers b Gibbs | | 11 |
| T.W. Graveney | c Holford b Sobers | 109 | c Hendriks b Griffith | | 32 |
| M.C. Cowdrey* | c Hendriks b Griffith | 96 | c Sobers b Gibbs | | 32 |
| J.M. Parks† | c Butcher b Sobers | 11 | c Lashley b Hall | | 7 |
| B.L. D'Oliveira | b Hall | 76 | lbw b Griffith | | 54 |
| R. Illingworth | c Lashley b Griffith | 0 | c Lashley b Sobers | | 4 |
| K. Higgs | c Lashley b Sobers | 5 | c Sobers b Gibbs | | 4 |
| J.A. Snow | b Hall | 0 | b Griffith | | 3 |
| D.L. Underwood | not out | 12 | not out | | 10 |
| Extras | (LB 2, NB 3) | 5 | (B 8, LB 2, NB 3) | | 13 |
| **Total** | | **325** | | | **253** |

| ENGLAND | O | M | R | W | O | M | R | W |
|---|---:|---:|---:|---:|---:|---:|---:|---:|
| Snow | 25 | 7 | 82 | 4 | 38 | 10 | 117 | 0 |
| Higgs | 25·4 | 3 | 71 | 4 | 38 | 6 | 109 | 3 |
| D'Oliveira | 30 | 14 | 51 | 2 | 34 | 8 | 77 | 2 |
| Underwood | 2 | 1 | 5 | 0 | 43 | 15 | 86 | 0 |
| Illingworth | 8 | 1 | 21 | 0 | 25 | 7 | 82 | 0 |

| WEST INDIES | O | M | R | W | O | M | R | W |
|---|---:|---:|---:|---:|---:|---:|---:|---:|
| Sobers | 49 | 12 | 90 | 4 | 31 | 6 | 71 | 1 |
| Hall | 34·3 | 8 | 105 | 4 | 16 | 3 | 52 | 2 |
| Griffith | 20 | 5 | 62 | 2 | 13·3 | 3 | 34 | 4 |
| Gibbs | 23 | 9 | 40 | 0 | 48 | 16 | 83 | 3 |
| Holford | 8 | 2 | 23 | 0 | | | | |

### FALL OF WICKETS

| Wkt | WI 1st | E 1st | WI 2nd | E 2nd |
|---|---:|---:|---:|---:|
| 1st | 19 | 0 | 29 | 32 |
| 2nd | 68 | 10 | 65 | 71 |
| 3rd | 80 | 13 | 175 | 125 |
| 4th | 140 | 182 | 282 | 132 |
| 5th | 144 | 221 | 455 | 142 |
| 6th | 180 | 238 | – | 176 |
| 7th | 190 | 247 | – | 181 |
| 8th | 215 | 255 | – | 222 |
| 9th | 228 | 260 | – | 240 |
| 10th | 235 | 325 | – | 253 |

Umpires: C.S. Elliott and A. Jepson.

# ENGLAND v WEST INDIES 1966 (4th Test)

Played at Headingley, Leeds, on 4, 5, 6, 8 August.
Toss: West Indies.   Result: WEST INDIES won by an innings and 55 runs.
Debuts: Nil.

West Indies retained the Wisden Trophy, completing their third victory of the rubber at 3.07 p.m. on the fourth day. Sobers scored his third hundred of the rubber and hit 103 runs between lunch and tea on the second day. His highest Test innings in England took 240 minutes, included 24 fours and took him past 5,000 runs in Tests, 2,000 runs against England, 500 runs in the rubber and 1,000 runs for the tour. His partnership of 265 in 240 minutes with Nurse remains the West Indies fifth-wicket record in all Tests.

## WEST INDIES

| | | |
|---|---|---:|
| C.C. Hunte | lbw b Snow | 48 |
| P.D. Lashley | b Higgs | 9 |
| R.B. Kanhai | c Graveney b Underwood | 45 |
| B.F. Butcher | c Parks b Higgs | 38 |
| S.M. Nurse | c Titmus b Snow | 137 |
| G. St A. Sobers* | b Barber | 174 |
| D.A.J. Holford | b Higgs | 24 |
| C.C. Griffith | b Higgs | 0 |
| J.L. Hendriks† | not out | 9 |
| W.W. Hall | b Snow | 1 |
| L.R. Gibbs | not out | 2 |
| Extras | (B 1, LB 12) | 13 |
| **Total** | (9 wickets declared) | **500** |

## ENGLAND

| | | | | | |
|---|---|---:|---|---|---:|
| G. Boycott | c Holford b Hall | 12 | | c Hendriks b Lashley | 14 |
| R.W. Barber | c Hendriks b Griffith | 6 | | b Sobers | 55 |
| C. Milburn | not out | 29 | (7) | b Gibbs | 42 |
| T.W. Graveney | b Hall | 8 | | b Gibbs | 19 |
| M.C. Cowdrey* | b Hall | 17 | | lbw b Gibbs | 12 |
| B.L. D'Oliveira | c Hall b Griffith | 88 | (3) | c Butcher b Sobers | 7 |
| J.M. Parks† | lbw b Sobers | 2 | (6) | c Nurse b Gibbs | 16 |
| F.J. Titmus | c Hendriks b Sobers | 6 | | b Gibbs | 22 |
| K. Higgs | c Nurse b Sobers | 49 | | c Hunte b Sobers | 7 |
| D.L. Underwood | c Gibbs b Sobers | 0 | | c Kanhai b Gibbs | 0 |
| J.A. Snow | c Holford b Sobers | 0 | | not out | 0 |
| Extras | (B 12, LB 11) | 23 | | (B 8, LB 1, NB 2) | 11 |
| **Total** | | **240** | | | **205** |

| ENGLAND | O | M | R | W | O | M | R | W | | FALL OF WICKETS | | |
|---|---|---|---|---|---|---|---|---|---|---|---|---|
| Snow | 42 | 6 | 146 | 3 | | | | | | | WI | E | E |
| Higgs | 43 | 11 | 94 | 4 | | | | | Wkt | 1st | 1st | 2nd |
| D'Oliveira | 19 | 3 | 52 | 0 | | | | | 1st | 37 | 10 | 28 |
| Titmus | 22 | 7 | 59 | 0 | | | | | 2nd | 102 | 18 | 70 |
| Underwood | 24 | 9 | 81 | 1 | | | | | 3rd | 122 | 42 | 84 |
| Barber | 14 | 2 | 55 | 1 | | | | | 4th | 154 | 49 | 109 |
| | | | | | | | | | 5th | 419 | 63 | 129 |
| WEST INDIES | | | | | | | | | 6th | 467 | 83 | 133 |
| Hall | 17 | 5 | 47 | 3 | 8 | 2 | 24 | 0 | 7th | 467 | 179 | 184 |
| Griffith | 12 | 2 | 37 | 2 | 12 | 0 | 52 | 0 | 8th | 489 | 238 | 205 |
| Sobers | 19·3 | 4 | 41 | 5 | 20·1 | 5 | 39 | 3 | 9th | 491 | 240 | 205 |
| Gibbs | 20 | 5 | 49 | 0 | 19 | 6 | 39 | 6 | 10th | – | 240 | 205 |
| Holford | 10 | 3 | 43 | 0 | 9 | 0 | 39 | 0 | | | | |
| Lashley | | | | | 3 | 2 | 1 | 1 | | | | |

Umpires: J.S. Buller and C.S. Elliott.

# ENGLAND v WEST INDIES 1966 (5th Test)

Played at Kennington Oval, London, on 18, 19, 20, 22 August.
Toss: West Indies.   Result: ENGLAND won by an innings and 34 runs.
Debuts: England – D.L. Amiss.

Sobers won the toss for the fifth time in the rubber. England's last three wickets added a record 361 runs and for the first time in Test cricket the last three batsmen scored one hundred and two fifties. The partnership of 217 in 235 minutes between Graveney and Murray remains England's highest for the eighth wicket against West Indies and second-highest in all Tests. Higgs and Snow each scored their maiden fifties in first-class cricket and their partnership of 128 in 140 minutes was only two runs short of the England tenth-wicket record by R.E. Foster and W. Rhodes against Australia in 1903–04 (*Test No. 78*).

## WEST INDIES

| | | | | | |
|---|---|---|---|---|---|
| C.C. Hunte | b Higgs | 1 | c Murray b Snow | | 7 |
| E.D.A. St J. McMorris | b Snow | 14 | c Murray b Snow | | 1 |
| R.B. Kanhai | c Graveney b Illingworth | 104 | b D'Oliveira | | 15 |
| B.F. Butcher | c Illingworth b Close | 12 | c Barber b Illingworth | | 60 |
| S.M. Nurse | c Graveney b D'Oliveira | 0 | c Edrich b Barber | | 70 |
| G. St A. Sobers* | c Graveney b Barber | 81 | (7) c Close b Snow | | 0 |
| D.A.J. Holford | c D'Oliveira b Illingworth | 5 | (6) run out | | 7 |
| J.L. Hendriks† | b Barber | 0 | b Higgs | | 0 |
| C.C. Griffith | c Higgs b Barber | 4 | not out | | 29 |
| W.W. Hall | not out | 30 | c D'Oliveira b Illingworth | | 17 |
| L.R. Gibbs | c Murray b Snow | 12 | c and b Barber | | 3 |
| Extras | (B 1, LB 3, NB 1) | 5 | (B 1, LB 14, NB 1) | | 16 |
| **Total** | | **268** | | | **225** |

## ENGLAND

| | | |
|---|---|---|
| G. Boycott | b Hall | 4 |
| R.W. Barber | c Nurse b Sobers | 36 |
| J.H. Edrich | c Hendriks b Sobers | 35 |
| T.W. Graveney | run out | 165 |
| D.L. Amiss | lbw b Hall | 17 |
| B.L. D'Oliveira | b Hall | 4 |
| D.B. Close* | run out | 4 |
| R. Illingworth | c Hendriks b Griffith | 3 |
| J.T. Murray† | lbw b Sobers | 112 |
| K. Higgs | c and b Holford | 63 |
| J.A. Snow | not out | 59 |
| Extras | (B 8, LB 14, NB 3) | 25 |
| **Total** | | **527** |

| ENGLAND | O | M | R | W | O | M | R | W |
|---|---|---|---|---|---|---|---|---|
| Snow | 20·5 | 1 | 66 | 2 | 13 | 5 | 40 | 3 |
| Higgs | 17 | 4 | 52 | 1 | 15 | 6 | 18 | 1 |
| D'Oliveira | 21 | 7 | 35 | 1 | 17 | 4 | 44 | 1 |
| Close | 9 | 2 | 21 | 1 | 3 | 1 | 7 | 0 |
| Barber | 15 | 3 | 49 | 3 | 22·1 | 2 | 78 | 2 |
| Illingworth | 15 | 7 | 40 | 2 | 15 | 9 | 22 | 2 |

| WEST INDIES | O | M | R | W |
|---|---|---|---|---|
| Hall | 31 | 8 | 85 | 3 |
| Griffith | 32 | 7 | 78 | 1 |
| Sobers | 54 | 23 | 104 | 3 |
| Holford | 25·5 | 1 | 79 | 1 |
| Gibbs | 44 | 16 | 115 | 0 |
| Hunte | 13 | 2 | 41 | 0 |

### FALL OF WICKETS

| | WI | E | WI |
|---|---|---|---|
| Wkt | 1st | 1st | 2nd |
| 1st | 1 | 6 | 5 |
| 2nd | 56 | 72 | 12 |
| 3rd | 73 | 85 | 50 |
| 4th | 74 | 126 | 107 |
| 5th | 196 | 130 | 137 |
| 6th | 218 | 150 | 137 |
| 7th | 218 | 166 | 142 |
| 8th | 223 | 383 | 168 |
| 9th | 223 | 399 | 204 |
| 10th | 268 | 527 | 225 |

Umpires: J.S. Buller and C.S. Elliott.

# INDIA v WEST INDIES 1966–67 (1st Test)

Played at Brabourne Stadium, Bombay, on 13, 14, 15, 17, 18 December.
Toss: India.   Result: WEST INDIES won by six wickets.
Debuts: India – A.L. Wadekar; West Indies – C.H. Lloyd.

Chandrasekhar's match analysis of 11 for 235 is the record for any Test in Bombay.

## INDIA

| | | | | |
|---|---|---|---|---|
| D.N. Sardesai | b Hall | 6 | b Sobers | 26 |
| M.L. Jaisimha | c Hendriks b Griffith | 4 | c Bynoe b Sobers | 44 |
| A.A. Baig | b Hall | 0 | c and b Holford | 42 |
| C.G. Borde | c Hendriks b Sobers | 121 | c Sobers b Gibbs | 12 |
| Nawab of Pataudi, jr* | b Holford | 44 | (6) b Gibbs | 51 |
| A.L. Wadekar | c Gibbs b Sobers | 8 | (5) c Sobers b Holford | 4 |
| S.A. Durani | b Sobers | 55 | c Hendriks b Gibbs | 17 |
| R.G. Nadkarni | c Sobers b Griffith | 9 | lbw b Holford | 0 |
| B.K. Kunderan† | lbw b Griffith | 6 | b Griffith | 79 |
| S. Venkataraghavan | not out | 36 | lbw b Gibbs | 26 |
| B.S. Chandrasekhar | c Gibbs b Holford | 2 | not out | 2 |
| Extras | (LB 3, NB 2) | 5 | (B 8, NB 5) | 13 |
| **Total** | | **296** | | **316** |

## WEST INDIES

| | | | | |
|---|---|---|---|---|
| C.C. Hunte | b Durani | 101 | c sub (R.F. Surti) b Chandrasekhar | 40 |
| M.R. Bynoe | c Venkataraghavan b Chandrasekhar | 2 | c Wadekar b Chandrasekhar | 5 |
| R.B. Kanhai | c Baig b Chandrasekhar | 24 | | |
| B.F. Butcher | b Chandrasekhar | 16 | (3) lbw b Chandrasekhar | 11 |
| C.H. Lloyd | c Kunderan b Chandrasekhar | 82 | not out | 78 |
| G. St A. Sobers* | b Venkataraghavan | 50 | not out | 53 |
| D.A.J. Holford | b Chandrasekhar | 80 | | |
| J.L. Hendriks† | b Chandrasekhar | 48 | | |
| C.C. Griffith | b Chandrasekhar | 12 | | |
| W.W. Hall | lbw b Venkataraghavan | 1 | | |
| L.R. Gibbs | not out | 1 | (4) c Wadekar b Chandrasekhar | 5 |
| Extras | (LB 2, NB 2) | 4 | | |
| **Total** | | **421** | **(4 wickets)** | **192** |

| WEST INDIES | O | M | R | W | O | M | R | W | | FALL OF WICKETS | | | |
|---|---|---|---|---|---|---|---|---|---|---|---|---|---|
| Hall | 19 | 4 | 54 | 2 | 10 | 3 | 10 | 0 | | I | WI | I | WI |
| Griffith | 21 | 6 | 63 | 3 | 11 | 4 | 53 | 1 | *Wkt* | *1st* | *1st* | *2nd* | *2nd* |
| Sobers | 25 | 9 | 46 | 3 | 27 | 6 | 79 | 2 | 1st | 10 | 12 | 74 | 11 |
| Gibbs | 25 | 8 | 60 | 0 | 24·5 | 3 | 67 | 4 | 2nd | 10 | 52 | 92 | 25 |
| Holford | 19·4 | 2 | 68 | 2 | 39 | 7 | 94 | 3 | 3rd | 14 | 82 | 119 | 51 |
| | | | | | | | | | 4th | 107 | 192 | 124 | 90 |
| INDIA | | | | | | | | | 5th | 138 | 242 | 141 | – |
| Jaisimha | 2 | 0 | 5 | 0 | 1 | 0 | 3 | 0 | 6th | 240 | 295 | 192 | – |
| Wadekar | 1 | 0 | 5 | 0 | 0·1 | 0 | 4 | 0 | 7th | 242 | 378 | 193 | – |
| Chandrasekhar | 61·5 | 17 | 157 | 7 | 31 | 7 | 78 | 4 | 8th | 253 | 402 | 217 | – |
| Venkataraghavan | 52 | 17 | 120 | 2 | 19 | 2 | 65 | 0 | 9th | 260 | 409 | 312 | – |
| Durani | 30 | 6 | 83 | 1 | 13 | 4 | 42 | 0 | 10th | 296 | 421 | 316 | – |
| Nadkarni | 15 | 5 | 47 | 0 | | | | | | | | | |

Umpires: B. Satyaji Rao and A.M. Mamsa.

# INDIA v WEST INDIES 1966–67 (2nd Test)

Played at Eden Gardens, Calcutta, on 31 December, 1 (*no play*), 3, 4, 5 January.
Toss: West Indies.   Result: WEST INDIES won by an innings and 45 runs.
Debuts: India – B.S. Bedi.

The second day's play was abandoned after a riot had prevented it from being started. The authorities had oversold the seating accommodation and disappointed spectators invaded the ground, clashed with police and set fire to several stands. West Indies gained their second victory at Calcutta after less than 18 hours of play.

## WEST INDIES

| | | |
|---|---|---|
| C.C. Hunte | run out | 43 |
| M.R. Bynoe | run out | 19 |
| R.B. Kanhai | c Pataudi b Surti | 90 |
| B.F. Butcher | c Pataudi b Bedi | 35 |
| C.H. Lloyd | c Kunderan b Bedi | 5 |
| S.M. Nurse | c Surti b Jaisimha | 56 |
| G. St A. Sobers* | c Jaisimha b Chandrasekhar | 70 |
| J.L. Hendriks† | b Surti | 5 |
| W.W. Hall | c Subramanya b Chandrasekhar | 35 |
| L.R. Gibbs | lbw b Chandrasekhar | 1 |
| C.C. Griffith | not out | 9 |
| Extras | (B 7, LB 11, NB 4) | 22 |
| **Total** | | **390** |

## INDIA

| | | | | |
|---|---|---|---|---|
| B.K. Kunderan† | b Hall | 39 | lbw b Hall | 4 |
| M.L. Jaisimha | b Gibbs | 37 | c and b Gibbs | 31 |
| R.F. Surti | lbw b Sobers | 16 | c Griffith b Sobers | 31 |
| C.G. Borde | run out | 10 | b Lloyd | 28 |
| Nawab of Pataudi, jr* | c Griffith b Gibbs | 2 | c Griffith b Lloyd | 2 |
| Hanumant Singh | c Bynoe b Gibbs | 4 | b Sobers | 37 |
| V. Subramanya | c Hendriks b Gibbs | 12 | run out | 17 |
| S. Venkataraghavan | b Sobers | 18 | (9) c Hendriks b Sobers | 2 |
| A.A. Baig | b Gibbs | 4 | (8) b Gibbs | 6 |
| B.S. Bedi | st Hendriks b Sobers | 5 | c Bynoe b Sobers | 0 |
| B.S. Chandrasekhar | not out | 3 | not out | 1 |
| Extras | (B 12, LB 1, NB 4) | 17 | (B 14, LB 2, NB 3) | 19 |
| **Total** | | **167** | | **178** |

| INDIA | O | M | R | W | O | M | R | W |
|---|---|---|---|---|---|---|---|---|
| Surti | 30 | 3 | 106 | 2 | | | | |
| Subramanya | 6 | 1 | 9 | 0 | | | | |
| Chandrasekhar | 46 | 11 | 107 | 3 | | | | |
| Bedi | 36 | 11 | 92 | 2 | | | | |
| Venkataraghavan | 14 | 3 | 43 | 0 | | | | |
| Jaisimha | 6 | 2 | 11 | 1 | | | | |
| **WEST INDIES** | | | | | | | | |
| Sobers | 28·5 | 16 | 42 | 3 | 20 | 2 | 56 | 4 |
| Griffith | 6 | 3 | 14 | 0 | 5 | 4 | 4 | 0 |
| Gibbs | 37 | 17 | 51 | 5 | 30·4 | 8 | 36 | 2 |
| Hall | 6 | 0 | 32 | 1 | 7 | 0 | 35 | 1 |
| Lloyd | 4 | 2 | 4 | 0 | 14 | 5 | 23 | 2 |
| Nurse | 4 | 1 | 7 | 0 | | | | |
| Hunte | | | | | 1 | 0 | 5 | 0 |

## FALL OF WICKETS

| | WI | I | I |
|---|---|---|---|
| Wkt | 1st | 1st | 2nd |
| 1st | 43 | 60 | 4 |
| 2nd | 76 | 98 | 62 |
| 3rd | 133 | 100 | 89 |
| 4th | 154 | 117 | 105 |
| 5th | 259 | 119 | 108 |
| 6th | 272 | 128 | 155 |
| 7th | 290 | 139 | 170 |
| 8th | 362 | 157 | 176 |
| 9th | 371 | 161 | 176 |
| 10th | 390 | 167 | 178 |

Umpires: I. Gopalakrishnan and S. Pan.

# INDIA v WEST INDIES 1966–67 (3rd Test)

Played at Chepauk, Madras, 13, 14, 15, 17, 18 January.
Toss: India.    Result: MATCH DRAWN.
Debuts: Nil.

Engineer was six runs short of becoming the first Indian batsman to score a Test match hundred before lunch. His partnership of 129 with Sardesai was a first-wicket record against West Indies. India came close to their first win in this series when West Indies, needing 322 for victory in 4½ hours, lost their seventh wicket at 193.

## INDIA

| | | | | |
|---|---|---|---|---|
| D.N. Sardesai | c Hendriks b Gibbs | 28 | lbw b Hall | 0 |
| F.M. Engineer† | c Kanhai b Sobers | 109 | c Butcher b Hall | 24 |
| A.L. Wadekar | c Hendriks b Gibbs | 0 | c Sobers b Gibbs | 67 |
| C.G. Borde | c Kanhai b Hunte | 125 | c Lloyd b Gibbs | 49 |
| Nawab of Pataudi, jr* | b Hall | 40 | c Sobers b Gibbs | 5 |
| Hanumant Singh | c Kanhai b Griffith | 7 | b Griffith | 50 |
| V. Subramanya | c Sobers b Hall | 17 | c Lloyd b Griffith | 61 |
| R.F. Surti | not out | 50 | c Hendriks b Griffith | 8 |
| E.A.S. Prasanna | b Bynoe | 1 | c Sobers b Gibbs | 24 |
| B.S. Bedi | c Griffith b Gibbs | 11 | c Nurse b Griffith | 8 |
| B.S. Chandrasekhar | c Hendriks b Sobers | 1 | not out | 10 |
| Extras | (B 4, LB 2, NB 9) | 15 | (LB 13, W 1, NB 3) | 17 |
| **Total** | | **404** | | **323** |

## WEST INDIES

| | | | | |
|---|---|---|---|---|
| C.C. Hunte | c Subramanya b Chandrasekhar | 49 | c Surti b Prasanna | 26 |
| M.R. Bynoe | lbw b Chandrasekhar | 48 | c Surti b Bedi | 36 |
| R.B. Kanhai | c Borde b Surti | 77 | c Pataudi b Bedi | 36 |
| B.F. Butcher | b Prasanna | 0 | c Surti b Prasanna | 24 |
| C.H. Lloyd | b Surti | 38 | b Bedi | 24 |
| S.M. Nurse | b Chandrasekhar | 26 | lbw b Bedi | 0 |
| G. St A. Sobers* | c Engineer b Chandrasekhar | 95 | not out | 74 |
| J.L. Hendriks† | c Engineer b Surti | 0 | lbw b Prasanna | 9 |
| C.C. Griffith | c Surti b Bedi | 27 | not out | 40 |
| W.W. Hall | b Prasanna | 31 | | |
| L.R. Gibbs | not out | 1 | | |
| Extras | (B 5, LB 6, NB 3) | 14 | (NB 1) | 1 |
| **Total** | | **406** | (7 wickets) | **270** |

| WEST INDIES | O | M | R | W | O | M | R | W | | FALL OF WICKETS | | | |
|---|---|---|---|---|---|---|---|---|---|---|---|---|---|
| Hall | 19 | 1 | 68 | 2 | 12 | 2 | 67 | 2 | | I | WI | I | WI |
| Griffith | 23 | 4 | 96 | 1 | 14 | 2 | 61 | 4 | *Wkt* | *1st* | *1st* | *2nd* | *2nd* |
| Sobers | 27·2 | 7 | 69 | 2 | 27 | 11 | 58 | 0 | 1st | 129 | 99 | 0 | 63 |
| Gibbs | 46 | 10 | 87 | 3 | 40·4 | 13 | 96 | 4 | 2nd | 131 | 114 | 45 | 71 |
| Lloyd | 13 | 2 | 39 | 0 | 12 | 3 | 24 | 0 | 3rd | 145 | 115 | 107 | 118 |
| Hunte | 10 | 2 | 25 | 1 | | | | | 4th | 239 | 194 | 123 | 130 |
| Bynoe | 5 | 4 | 5 | 1 | | | | | 5th | 257 | 246 | 192 | 131 |
| | | | | | | | | | 6th | 292 | 246 | 245 | 166 |
| INDIA | | | | | | | | | 7th | 377 | 251 | 266 | 193 |
| Surti | 19 | 2 | 68 | 3 | 9 | 1 | 27 | 0 | 8th | 382 | 324 | 281 | – |
| Subramanya | 7 | 1 | 21 | 0 | 7 | 3 | 14 | 0 | 9th | 403 | 404 | 297 | – |
| Chandrasekhar | 46 | 15 | 130 | 4 | 12 | 2 | 41 | 0 | 10th | 404 | 406 | 323 | – |
| Bedi | 19 | 3 | 55 | 1 | 28 | 7 | 81 | 4 | | | | | |
| Prasanna | 41 | 11 | 118 | 2 | 37 | 9 | 106 | 3 | | | | | |

Umpires: S. Roy and S.K. Raghunatha Rao.

# SOUTH AFRICA v AUSTRALIA 1966–67 (1st Test)

Played at New Wanderers, Johannesburg, on 23, 24, 26, 27, 28 December.
Toss: South Africa.   Result: SOUTH AFRICA won by 233 runs.
Debuts: Australia – D.A. Renneberg, H.B. Taber.

South Africa gained their first home victory against Australia at the 22nd attempt and 64 years after this series began. South Africa's total of 620 was then their highest in Tests and it remains the third-highest second innings total in all Test matches. Lindsay's 182 was his first Test hundred; it took 274 minutes and included five sixes. He then equalled the world Test wicket-keeping record of six dismissals in an innings. His partnership of 221 with Van der Merwe remains the highest for South Africa's seventh wicket against Australia. Taber made eight dismissals in the first Test match he had ever attended.

## SOUTH AFRICA

| | | | | |
|---|---|--:|---|--:|
| T.L. Goddard | c Taber b Hawke | 5 | c Simpson b Hawke | 13 |
| E.J. Barlow | c Taber b McKenzie | 13 | c Taber b Renneberg | 50 |
| A. Bacher | c Cowper b McKenzie | 5 | run out | 63 |
| R.G. Pollock | c McKenzie b Renneberg | 5 | b Cowper | 90 |
| K.C. Bland | lbw b McKenzie | 0 | c Simpson b Chappell | 32 |
| H.R. Lance | hit wkt b McKenzie | 44 | c Simpson b McKenzie | 70 |
| D.T. Lindsay† | c Taber b Renneberg | 69 | c Chappell b Stackpole | 182 |
| P.L. van der Merwe* | c Taber b Simpson | 19 | c Chappell b Simpson | 76 |
| R. Dumbrill | c Chappell b Simpson | 19 | c Taber b Chappell | 29 |
| P.M. Pollock | c Taber b McKenzie | 6 | st Taber b Simpson | 2 |
| A.H. McKinnon | not out | 0 | not out | 0 |
| Extras | (B 11, W 3) | 14 | (B 7, LB 5, W 1) | 13 |
| **Total** | | **199** | | **620** |

## AUSTRALIA

| | | | | |
|---|---|--:|---|--:|
| R.B. Simpson* | c Goddard b P.M. Pollock | 65 | run out | 48 |
| W.M. Lawry | c Lindsay b Goddard | 98 | b Mckinnon | 27 |
| I.R. Redpath | c Lindsay b Barlow | 41 | c Van der Merwe b Barlow | 21 |
| R.M. Cowper | c Lindsay b Barlow | 0 | c Lindsay b Goddard | 1 |
| K.R. Stackpole | c Lindsay b Barlow | 0 | b Goddard | 9 |
| I.M. Chappell | c Lindsay b Goddard | 37 | c Lindsay b Dumbrill | 34 |
| T.R. Veivers | b Lance | 18 | b Goddard | 55 |
| H.B. Taber† | c Lindsay b McKinnon | 13 | b Goddard | 7 |
| G.D. McKenzie | run out | 16 | c sub (M.J. Procter) b Goddard | 34 |
| N.J.N. Hawke | not out | 18 | c sub (M.J. Procter) b Goddard | 13 |
| D.A. Renneberg | c Goddard b McKinnon | 9 | not out | 2 |
| Extras | (LB 5, W 2, NB 3) | 10 | (LB 6, W 2, NB 2) | 10 |
| **Total** | | **325** | | **261** |

| AUSTRALIA | O | M | R | W | O | M | R | W |
|---|--:|--:|--:|--:|--:|--:|--:|--:|
| McKenzie | 21·5 | 6 | 46 | 5 | 39 | 4 | 118 | 1 |
| Hawke | 8 | 1 | 25 | 1 | 14·2 | 1 | 46 | 1 |
| Renneberg | 16 | 3 | 54 | 2 | 32 | 8 | 96 | 1 |
| Chappell | 2 | 0 | 16 | 0 | 21 | 3 | 91 | 2 |
| Veivers | 9 | 1 | 13 | 0 | 18 | 3 | 59 | 0 |
| Cowper | 6 | 0 | 21 | 0 | 16 | 2 | 56 | 1 |
| Simpson | 4 | 1 | 10 | 2 | 16·1 | 3 | 66 | 2 |
| Stackpole | | | | | 21 | 6 | 75 | 1 |
| SOUTH AFRICA | | | | | | | | |
| P.M. Pollock | 25 | 6 | 74 | 1 | 18 | 3 | 33 | 0 |
| Dumbrill | 18 | 3 | 55 | 0 | 16 | 6 | 43 | 1 |
| Goddard | 26 | 11 | 39 | 2 | 32·5 | 14 | 53 | 6 |
| Lance | 17 | 6 | 35 | 1 | 3 | 0 | 6 | 0 |
| McKinnon | 27·2 | 9 | 73 | 2 | 30 | 14 | 64 | 1 |
| Barlow | 17 | 3 | 39 | 3 | 15 | 1 | 47 | 1 |
| R.G. Pollock | | | | | 3 | 1 | 5 | 0 |

| FALL OF WICKETS | | | | |
|---|--:|--:|--:|--:|
| | SA | A | SA | A |
| Wkt | 1st | 1st | 2nd | 2nd |
| 1st | 14 | 118 | 29 | 62 |
| 2nd | 31 | 204 | 87 | 97 |
| 3rd | 31 | 207 | 178 | 98 |
| 4th | 35 | 207 | 228 | 110 |
| 5th | 41 | 218 | 268 | 112 |
| 6th | 151 | 267 | 349 | 183 |
| 7th | 156 | 267 | 570 | 210 |
| 8th | 190 | 294 | 614 | 212 |
| 9th | 199 | 299 | 620 | 248 |
| 10th | 199 | 325 | 620 | 261 |

Umpires: H.C. Kidson and L.M. Baxter.

# SOUTH AFRICA v AUSTRALIA 1966–67 (2nd Test)

Played at Newlands, Cape Town, on 31 December, 2, 3, 4, 5 January.
Toss: Australia.   Result: AUSTRALIA won by six wickets.
Debuts: Australia – G.D. Watson.

Australia completed their win with 24 minutes to spare. Simpson's sixth Test hundred was his first against South Africa and his 50th in first-class cricket. R.G. Pollock scored his first hundred off 139 balls in 193 minutes; his innings of 209 in 350 minutes is the highest in any Test at Cape Town. The Pollocks' partnership of 85 remains the highest for the ninth wicket by either side in this series.

## AUSTRALIA

| | | | | |
|---|---|---|---|---|
| R.B. Simpson* | c Lance b Barlow | 153 | c Goddard b P.M. Pollock | 18 |
| W.M. Lawry | lbw b P.M. Pollock | 10 | c P.M. Pollock b Goddard | 39 |
| I.R. Redpath | lbw b McKinnon | 54 | not out | 69 |
| R.M. Cowper | c Van der Merwe b Lance | 36 | c Lindsay b Goddard | 4 |
| I.M. Chappell | c Lindsay b Goddard | 49 | b McKinnon | 7 |
| T.R. Veivers | lbw b P.M. Pollock | 30 | not out | 35 |
| K.R. Stackpole | c Lindsay b Barlow | 134 | | |
| G.D. Watson | c Lance b Barlow | 50 | | |
| G.D. McKenzie | c and b Barlow | 11 | | |
| H.B. Taber† | not out | 2 | | |
| D.A. Renneberg | b Barlow | 2 | | |
| Extras | (B 2, LB 7, W 2) | 11 | (LB 5, NB 3) | 8 |
| **Total** | | **542** | (4 wickets) | **180** |

## SOUTH AFRICA

| | | | | |
|---|---|---|---|---|
| T.L. Goddard | c Stackpole b McKenzie | 7 | lbw b Simpson | 37 |
| E.J. Barlow | c Redpath b McKenzie | 19 | run out | 17 |
| A. Bacher | b McKenzie | 0 | c Simpson b McKenzie | 4 |
| R.G. Pollock | c Taber b Simpson | 209 | b Simpson | 4 |
| H.R. Lance | c Simpson b Chappell | 2 | run out | 53 |
| D.T. Lindsay† | c and b Renneberg | 5 | c Simpson b Cowper | 81 |
| P.L. van der Merwe* | c Cowper b Simpson | 50 | lbw b Chappell | 18 |
| D.B. Pithey | c Taber b McKenzie | 4 | c Redpath b Renneberg | 55 |
| R. Dumbrill | c Chappell b McKenzie | 6 | (10) b McKenzie | 1 |
| P.M. Pollock | c Stackpole b Veivers | 41 | (9) not out | 75 |
| A.H. McKinnon | not out | 6 | b McKenzie | 8 |
| Extras | (LB 4) | 4 | (B 5, LB 9) | 14 |
| **Total** | | **353** | | **367** |

| SOUTH AFRICA | O | M | R | W | O | M | R | W | | FALL OF WICKETS | | | |
|---|---|---|---|---|---|---|---|---|---|---|---|---|---|
| P.M. Pollock | 22 | 4 | 84 | 2 | 12 | 2 | 42 | 1 | | A | SA | SA | A |
| Dumbrill | 11 | 2 | 36 | 0 | | | | | *Wkt* | *1st* | *1st* | *2nd* | *2nd* |
| Goddard | 42 | 15 | 79 | 1 | 29·1 | 10 | 67 | 2 | 1st | 21 | 12 | 45 | 49 |
| Barlow | 33·3 | 9 | 85 | 5 | 2 | 1 | 1 | 0 | 2nd | 138 | 12 | 60 | 81 |
| Pithey | 22 | 5 | 59 | 0 | | | | | 3rd | 216 | 41 | 60 | 98 |
| McKinnon | 38 | 16 | 93 | 1 | 22 | 5 | 62 | 1 | 4th | 310 | 66 | 64 | 119 |
| Lance | 20 | 1 | 95 | 1 | | | | | 5th | 316 | 85 | 183 | – |
| | | | | | | | | | 6th | 368 | 197 | 211 | – |
| AUSTRALIA | | | | | | | | | 7th | 496 | 242 | 245 | – |
| McKenzie | 33 | 10 | 65 | 5 | 39·3 | 11 | 67 | 3 | 8th | 537 | 258 | 331 | – |
| Renneberg | 18 | 6 | 51 | 1 | 24 | 2 | 63 | 1 | 9th | 538 | 343 | 345 | – |
| Watson | 11 | 2 | 27 | 0 | | | | | 10th | 542 | 353 | 367 | – |
| Chappell | 13 | 4 | 51 | 1 | 39 | 17 | 71 | 1 | | | | | |
| Simpson | 24 | 9 | 59 | 2 | 39 | 12 | 99 | 2 | | | | | |
| Veivers | 8·1 | 2 | 32 | 1 | 7 | 2 | 21 | 0 | | | | | |
| Cowper | 6 | 0 | 28 | 0 | 10 | 2 | 21 | 1 | | | | | |
| Stackpole | 14 | 2 | 36 | 0 | 8 | 4 | 11 | 0 | | | | | |

Umpires: H.C. Kidson and G. Goldman.

# SOUTH AFRICA v AUSTRALIA 1966–67 (3rd Test)

Played at Kingsmead, Durban, on 20, 21, 23, 24, 25 January.
Toss: Australia.    Result: SOUTH AFRICA won by eight wickets.
Debuts: South Africa – M.J. Procter, P.H.J. Trimborn.

South Africa completed their second home win against Australia soon after tea on the fifth day after Simpson had become the first captain since 1930–31 to elect to field in a Durban Test. Barlow was out to the first ball of the match. In the first innings, Lawry retired hurt to have ten stitches inserted in a head wound caused by a lifting ball from P.M. Pollock, but returned to make top score.

## SOUTH AFRICA

| | | | | |
|---|---|---|---|---|
| E.J. Barlow | c and b McKenzie | 0 | c Redpath b McKenzie | 22 |
| T.L. Goddard | b Cowper | 19 | c Taber b Cowper | 33 |
| A. Bacher | c Taber b McKenzie | 47 | not out | 60 |
| R.G. Pollock | c Redpath b Cowper | 2 | not out | 67 |
| H.R. Lance | c Taber b Cowper | 13 | | |
| D.T. Lindsay† | c Chappell b Hawke | 137 | | |
| M.J. Procter | b Renneberg | 1 | | |
| P.L. van der Merwe* | run out | 42 | | |
| D.B. Pithey | b Hawke | 15 | | |
| P.M. Pollock | not out | 12 | | |
| P.H.J. Trimborn | run out | 2 | | |
| Extras | (B 3, LB 2, NB 5) | 10 | (LB 2, NB 1) | 3 |
| **Total** | | **300** | (2 wickets) | **185** |

## AUSTRALIA

| | | | | |
|---|---|---|---|---|
| R.B. Simpson* | c Lindsay b Procter | 6 | lbw b Trimborn | 94 |
| W.M. Lawry | c Lindsay b Barlow | 44 | c Lindsay b Lance | 34 |
| I.R. Redpath | c Barlow b Goddard | 7 | c Barlow b P.M. Pollock | 80 |
| R.M. Cowper | c Goddard b Trimborn | 19 | c Lindsay b Lance | 40 |
| K.R. Stackpole | c Lindsay b Barlow | 24 | (7) c R.G. Pollock b P.M. Pollock | 35 |
| T.R. Veivers | b Goddard | 6 | c Lindsay b Procter | 0 |
| I.M. Chappell | run out | 5 | (5) c R.G. Pollock b Procter | 25 |
| G.D. McKenzie | lbw b Procter | 17 | b Procter | 8 |
| H.B. Taber† | c Bacher b Barlow | 4 | (10) c Trimborn b Procter | 0 |
| N.J.N. Hawke | not out | 9 | (9) b Goddard | 5 |
| D.A. Renneberg | b Procter | 0 | not out | 0 |
| Extras | (LB 1, NB 5) | 6 | (B 4, LB 4, NB 5) | 13 |
| **Total** | | **147** | | **334** |

| AUSTRALIA | O | M | R | W | O | M | R | W |
|---|---|---|---|---|---|---|---|---|
| McKenzie | 31 | 7 | 93 | 2 | 20 | 7 | 36 | 1 |
| Hawke | 18 | 1 | 69 | 2 | 14 | 6 | 22 | 0 |
| Renneberg | 21 | 4 | 58 | 1 | 11 | 1 | 27 | 0 |
| Cowper | 37 | 14 | 57 | 3 | 17 | 9 | 29 | 1 |
| Redpath | 4 | 0 | 13 | 0 | | | | |
| Simpson | | | | | 4 | 0 | 21 | 0 |
| Chappell | | | | | 7 | 0 | 39 | 0 |
| Stackpole | | | | | 2 | 0 | 8 | 0 |
| SOUTH AFRICA | | | | | | | | |
| P.M. Pollock | 13 | 4 | 35 | 0 | 19 | 5 | 58 | 2 |
| Procter | 14 | 4 | 27 | 3 | 29·1 | 7 | 71 | 4 |
| Trimborn | 14 | 3 | 35 | 1 | 28 | 9 | 47 | 1 |
| Goddard | 17 | 6 | 26 | 2 | 27 | 15 | 23 | 1 |
| Barlow | 11 | 4 | 18 | 3 | 14 | 5 | 28 | 0 |
| Pithey | | | | | 28 | 12 | 55 | 0 |
| Lance | | | | | 15 | 4 | 39 | 2 |

### FALL OF WICKETS

| | SA | A | A | SA |
|---|---|---|---|---|
| Wkt | 1st | 1st | 2nd | 2nd |
| 1st | 0 | 14 | 94 | 52 |
| 2nd | 53 | 37 | 159 | 58 |
| 3rd | 57 | 45 | 224 | – |
| 4th | 83 | 74 | 266 | – |
| 5th | 90 | 88 | 266 | – |
| 6th | 94 | 96 | 317 | – |
| 7th | 197 | 132 | 320 | – |
| 8th | 286 | 137 | 334 | – |
| 9th | 287 | 137 | 334 | – |
| 10th | 300 | 147 | 334 | – |

Umpires: H.C. Kidson and J.G. Draper.

# SOUTH AFRICA v AUSTRALIA 1966–67 (4th Test)

Played at New Wanderers, Johannesburg, on 3, 4, 6, 7 (*no play*), 8 February.
Toss: Australia.   Result: MATCH DRAWN.
Debuts: South Arica – J.H. du Preez.

A rain storm allowed only three balls to be bowled after tea on the final day when two wickets separated Australia from an innings defeat. Lindsay's third hundred of the rubber was reached in 107 minutes and he went on to exceed B.K. Kunderan's 526 runs against England in 1963–64 to set the present record aggregate for a wicket-keeper in any rubber.

## AUSTRALIA

| | | | | | |
|---|---|---|---|---|---|
| W.M. Lawry | c Bacher b Trimborn | 17 | | b Procter | 2 |
| R.B. Simpson* | c Du Preez b Goddard | 24 | | c Bacher b Procter | 28 |
| I.R. Redpath | c Lindsay b Barlow | 14 | (4) | c Trimborn b P.M. Pollock | 46 |
| R.M. Cowper | c Trimborn b Procter | 25 | (5) | b Du Preez | 16 |
| I.M. Chappell | lbw b Goddard | 0 | (6) | not out | 13 |
| K.R. Stackpole | b Goddard | 4 | (7) | c Goddard b Du Preez | 5 |
| T.R. Veivers | c Lindsay b Procter | 19 | (8) | c Lindsay b Goddard | 21 |
| G.D. Watson | c Lance b Procter | 17 | (9) | b Goddard | 0 |
| G.D. McKenzie | c R.G. Pollock b Procter | 11 | (10) | not out | 0 |
| H.B. Taber† | c Trimborn b P.M. Pollock | 4 | (3) | lbw b Goddard | 14 |
| D.A. Renneberg | not out | 0 | | | |
| Extras | (LB 6, W 1, NB 1) | 8 | | (LB 2, NB 1) | 3 |
| **Total** | | **143** | | **(8 wickets)** | **148** |

## SOUTH AFRICA

| | | |
|---|---|---|
| T.L. Goddard | c Stackpole b Renneberg | 47 |
| E.J. Barlow | c Taber b Renneberg | 4 |
| A. Bacher | c Taber b Watson | 22 |
| R.G. Pollock | c Taber b Cowper | 22 |
| H.R. Lance | lbw b Watson | 30 |
| D.T. Lindsay† | c Simpson b Renneberg | 131 |
| M.J. Procter | lbw b Simpson | 16 |
| P.L. van der Merwe* | c Taber b Renneberg | 12 |
| J.H. du Preez | c Simpson b Renneberg | 0 |
| P.M. Pollock | not out | 34 |
| P.H.J. Trimborn | not out | 11 |
| Extras | (LB 3) | 3 |
| **Total** | **(9 wickets declared)** | **332** |

| SOUTH AFRICA | O | M | R | W | O | M | R | W | | FALL OF WICKETS | | |
|---|---|---|---|---|---|---|---|---|---|---|---|---|
| P.M. Pollock | 12·1 | 3 | 21 | 1 | 14 | 6 | 24 | 1 | | A | SA | A |
| Procter | 18 | 7 | 32 | 4 | 17 | 6 | 38 | 2 | *Wkt* | *1st* | *1st* | *2nd* |
| Goddard | 19 | 6 | 36 | 3 | 16·3 | 9 | 23 | 3 | 1st | 33 | 8 | 11 |
| Trimborn | 10 | 3 | 21 | 1 | 7 | 3 | 14 | 0 | 2nd | 59 | 39 | 41 |
| Barlow | 11 | 6 | 25 | 1 | 7 | 3 | 20 | 0 | 3rd | 59 | 86 | 58 |
| Du Preez | | | | | 14 | 6 | 22 | 2 | 4th | 59 | 120 | 94 |
| Lance | | | | | 3 | 1 | 4 | 0 | 5th | 69 | 177 | 116 |
| | | | | | | | | | 6th | 103 | 210 | 125 |
| AUSTRALIA | | | | | | | | | 7th | 108 | 266 | 148 |
| McKenzie | 39 | 7 | 96 | 0 | | | | | 8th | 139 | 272 | 148 |
| Renneberg | 25 | 3 | 97 | 5 | | | | | 9th | 139 | 299 | – |
| Watson | 20 | 4 | 67 | 2 | | | | | 10th | 143 | – | – |
| Cowper | 15 | 7 | 36 | 1 | | | | | | | | |
| Simpson | 6 | 0 | 33 | 1 | | | | | | | | |

Umpires: H.C. Kidson and J.G. Draper.

# SOUTH AFRICA v AUSTRALIA 1966–67 (5th Test)

Played at St George's Park, Port Elizabeth, on 24, 25, 27, 28 February.
Toss: South Africa.   Result: SOUTH AFRICA won by seven wickets.
Debuts: Nil.

South Africa won their first rubber against Australia when Lance completed this third victory with a six over mid-wicket on the fourth afternoon. P.M. Pollock became the fourth (and youngest) South African to take a hundred Test wickets when he dismissed Redpath in the second innings. Lindsay established a record for any Test rubber by holding 24 catches; although Marsh held 26 in the six-match rubber between Australia and England in 1975–76, Lindsay still retains the record for a five-match rubber.

## AUSTRALIA

| | | | | | |
|---|---|---|---|---|---|
| R.B. Simpson* | c Lindsay b P.M. Pollock | 12 | lbw b Goddard | | 35 |
| W.M. Lawry | run out | 0 | c Bacher b Barlow | | 25 |
| I.M. Chappell | c Bacher b Procter | 11 | lbw b Goddard | | 15 |
| I.R. Redpath | c Du Preez b P.M. Pollock | 26 | lbw b P.M. Pollock | | 28 |
| R.M. Cowper | c Lindsay b Trimborn | 60 | b Barlow | | 54 |
| K.R. Stackpole | c R.G. Pollock b Goddard | 24 | c Lindsay b Trimborn | | 19 |
| J.W. Martin | lbw b Goddard | 0 | c Lindsay b Goddard | | 20 |
| G.D. Watson | c Barlow b Goddard | 0 | b P.M. Pollock | | 9 |
| G.D. McKenzie | c Trimborn b Du Preez | 14 | c R.G. Pollock b Trimborn | | 29 |
| H.B. Taber† | c Bacher b Procter | 20 | c Goddard b Trimborn | | 30 |
| D.A. Renneberg | not out | 0 | not out | | 0 |
| Extras | (W 1, NB 5) | 6 | (LB 2, W 1, NB 11) | | 14 |
| **Total** | | **173** | | | **278** |

## SOUTH AFRICA

| | | | | | |
|---|---|---|---|---|---|
| T.L. Goddard | c Taber b McKenzie | 74 | c Taber b McKenzie | | 59 |
| E.J. Barlow | lbw b McKenzie | 46 | c Chappell b McKenzie | | 15 |
| A. Bacher | c Taber b McKenzie | 3 | c Martin b Chappell | | 40 |
| R.G. Pollock | b Cowper | 105 | not out | | 33 |
| H.R. Lance | c Renneberg b Simpson | 21 | not out | | 28 |
| D.T. Lindsay† | c Redpath b McKenzie | 1 | | | |
| M.J. Procter | hit wkt b McKenzie | 0 | | | |
| P.L. van der Merwe* | lbw b Watson | 8 | | | |
| P.M. Pollock | c Lawry b Cowper | 13 | | | |
| J.H. du Preez | lbw b Cowper | 0 | | | |
| P.H.J. Trimborn | not out | 0 | | | |
| Extras | (B 1, LB 3, W 1) | 5 | (LB 1, W 2, NB 1) | | 4 |
| **Total** | | **276** | (3 wickets) | | **179** |

| SOUTH AFRICA | O | M | R | W | O | M | R | W | | FALL OF WICKETS | | | |
|---|---|---|---|---|---|---|---|---|---|---|---|---|---|
| P.M. Pollock | 17 | 2 | 57 | 2 | 15 | 0 | 42 | 2 | | A | SA | A | SA |
| Procter | 15·1 | 3 | 36 | 2 | 16 | 3 | 59 | 0 | *Wkt* | *1st* | *1st* | *2nd* | *2nd* |
| Trimborn | 18 | 4 | 37 | 1 | 10·1 | 4 | 12 | 3 | 1st | 4 | 112 | 50 | 28 |
| Goddard | 10 | 3 | 13 | 3 | 36 | 12 | 63 | 3 | 2nd | 17 | 124 | 74 | 109 |
| Barlow | 4 | 2 | 9 | 0 | 15 | 3 | 52 | 2 | 3rd | 27 | 125 | 79 | 118 |
| Lance | 8 | 4 | 15 | 0 | 5 | 2 | 7 | 0 | 4th | 89 | 175 | 144 | – |
| Du Preez | 2 | 2 | 0 | 1 | 8 | 4 | 29 | 0 | 5th | 137 | 201 | 166 | – |
| | | | | | | | | | 6th | 137 | 201 | 207 | – |
| AUSTRALIA | | | | | | | | | 7th | 137 | 201 | 207 | – |
| McKenzie | 35 | 13 | 65 | 5 | 17 | 5 | 38 | 2 | 8th | 137 | 271 | 229 | – |
| Renneberg | 19 | 6 | 44 | 0 | 12 | 1 | 38 | 0 | 9th | 173 | 271 | 268 | – |
| Watson | 18 | 4 | 58 | 1 | 3 | 0 | 10 | 0 | 10th | 173 | 276 | 278 | – |
| Cowper | 19·3 | 9 | 27 | 3 | 12 | 4 | 26 | 0 | | | | | |
| Martin | 17 | 1 | 64 | 0 | 5 | 0 | 25 | 0 | | | | | |
| Simpson | 8 | 2 | 13 | 1 | 5 | 0 | 10 | 0 | | | | | |
| Chappell | | | | | 7·1 | 2 | 28 | 1 | | | | | |

Umpires: H.C. Kidson and J.G. Draper.

# ENGLAND v INDIA 1967 (1st Test)

Played at Headingley, Leeds, on 8, 9, 10, 12, 13 June.
Toss: England.   Result: ENGLAND won by six wickets.
Debuts: England – R.N.S. Hobbs; India – S. Guha, R. Saxena.

India, without a victory in any first-class match on the tour so far, lost the services of two key bowlers (Surti – bruised knee, Bedi – leg strain) from the first afternoon. Following on 386 in arrears, India retaliated with their highest total against England and took the match to 2.59 on the fifth afternoon. Boycott's 246 not out was scored off 555 balls in 573 minutes and included a six and 29 fours; it remains the highest innings by either side in this series and he shared in hundred partnerships for three successive wickets. His first hundred occupied 341 minutes (316 balls) and he was excluded from the next Test as a disciplinary measure. England's total was their highest at Leeds. The stand of 168 between Engineer and Wadekar was the first hundred partnership of the tour and was then India's highest for the second wicket against England.

## ENGLAND

| | | | | |
|---|---|---:|---|---:|
| J.H. Edrich | c Engineer b Surti | 1 | c Wadekar b Chandrasekhar | 22 |
| G. Boycott | not out | 246 | | |
| K.F. Barrington | run out | 93 | (2) c Engineer b Chandrasekhar | 46 |
| T.W. Graveney | c sub (S. Venkataraghavan) | | | |
| | b Chandrasekhar | 59 | (3) b Chandrasekhar | 14 |
| B.L. D'Oliveira | c sub (V. Subramanya) | | | |
| | b Chandrasekhar | 109 | (4) not out | 24 |
| D.B. Close* | not out | 22 | | |
| J.T. Murray† | ) | | (5) c sub (V. Subramanya) b Prasanna | 4 |
| R. Illingworth | ) | | (6) not out | 12 |
| K. Higgs | ) did not bat | | | |
| J.A. Snow | ) | | | |
| R.N.S. Hobbs | ) | | | |
| Extras | (B 8, LB 12) | 20 | (B 3, LB 1) | 4 |
| **Total** | (4 wickets declared) | **550** | (4 wickets) | **126** |

## INDIA

| | | | | |
|---|---|---:|---|---:|
| F.M. Engineer† | c and b Illingworth | 42 | c and b Close | 87 |
| R. Saxena | b D'Oliveira | 9 | (7) b Snow | 16 |
| A.L. Wadekar | run out | 0 | c Close b Illingworth | 91 |
| C.G. Borde | b Snow | 8 | b Illingworth | 33 |
| Hanumant Singh | c D'Oliveira b Illingworth | 9 | c D'Oliveira b Illingworth | 73 |
| Nawab of Pataudi, jr* | c Barrington b Hobbs | 64 | b Illingworth | 148 |
| E.A.S. Prasanna | c Murray b Illingworth | 0 | (8) lbw b Close | 19 |
| S. Guha | b Snow | 4 | (9) b Higgs | 1 |
| R.F. Surti | c and b Hobbs | 22 | (2) c Murray b Snow | 5 |
| B.S. Bedi | lbw b Hobbs | 0 | c Snow b Hobbs | 14 |
| B.S. Chandrasekhar | not out | 0 | not out | 0 |
| Extras | (LB 6) | 6 | (B 10, LB 13) | 23 |
| **Total** | | **164** | | **510** |

| INDIA | O | M | R | W | O | M | R | W | | FALL OF WICKETS | | | |
|---|---:|---:|---:|---:|---:|---:|---:|---:|---|---|---|---|---|
| Guha | 43 | 10 | 105 | 0 | 5 | 0 | 10 | 0 | | E | I | I | E |
| Surti | 11 | 2 | 25 | 1 | | | | | Wkt | 1st | 1st | 2nd | 2nd |
| Chandrasekhar | 45 | 9 | 121 | 2 | 19 | 8 | 50 | 3 | 1st | 7 | 39 | 5 | 58 |
| Bedi | 15 | 8 | 32 | 0 | | | | | 2nd | 146 | 40 | 173 | 78 |
| Prasanna | 59 | 8 | 187 | 0 | 21·3 | 5 | 54 | 1 | 3rd | 253 | 59 | 217 | 87 |
| Pataudi | 4 | 1 | 13 | 0 | | | | | 4th | 505 | 59 | 228 | 92 |
| Wadekar | 1 | 0 | 9 | 0 | 2 | 0 | 8 | 0 | 5th | – | 81 | 362 | – |
| Hanumant Singh | 3 | 0 | 27 | 0 | | | | | 6th | – | 81 | 388 | – |
| Saxena | 2 | 0 | 11 | 0 | | | | | 7th | – | 92 | 448 | – |
| | | | | | | | | | 8th | – | 151 | 469 | – |
| ENGLAND | | | | | | | | | 9th | – | 151 | 506 | – |
| Snow | 17 | 7 | 34 | 2 | 41 | 11 | 108 | 2 | 10th | – | 164 | 510 | – |
| Higgs | 14 | 8 | 19 | 0 | 24 | 3 | 71 | 1 | | | | | |
| D'Oliveira | 9 | 4 | 29 | 1 | 11 | 5 | 22 | 0 | | | | | |
| Hobbs | 22·2 | 9 | 45 | 3 | 45·2 | 13 | 100 | 1 | | | | | |
| Illingworth | 22 | 11 | 31 | 3 | 58 | 26 | 100 | 4 | | | | | |
| Close | 3 | 3 | 0 | 0 | 21 | 5 | 48 | 2 | | | | | |
| Barrington | | | | | 9 | 1 | 38 | 0 | | | | | |

Umpires: C.S. Elliott and H. Yarnold.

# ENGLAND v INDIA 1967 (2nd Test)

Played at Lord's, London, on 22, 23, 24, 26 June.
Toss: India.    Result: ENGLAND won by an innings and 124 runs.
Debuts: Nil.

Although over six hours of play were lost to rain and bad light on the second and third days, England completed their innings victory at 3.08 on the fourth afternoon. Murray's six catches in the first innings equalled the Test record held jointly by A.T.W. Grout and D.T. Lindsay. Sardesai retired hurt (when 9 and with India's total 22 for 1) after being struck on the right hand by a ball from Snow. He resumed at 102 for 6 but X-ray examinations subsequently revealed a fracture and he did not bat in the second innings.

## INDIA

| | | | | | |
|---|---|---|---|---|---|
| D.N. Sardesai | c Murray b Illingworth | 28 | absent hurt | | – |
| F.M. Engineer† | c Murray b Brown | 8 | c Amiss b Snow | | 8 |
| A.L. Wadekar | c Illingworth b D'Oliveira | 57 | b Illingworth | | 19 |
| C.G. Borde | b Snow | 0 | c Snow b Close | | 1 |
| Nawab of Pataudi, jr* | c Murray b Brown | 5 | c Graveney b Close | | 5 |
| R.F. Surti | c Murray b D'Oliveira | 6 | c D'Oliveira b Illingworth | | 0 |
| V. Subramanya | c Murray b Brown | 0 | c Edrich b Illingworth | | 1 |
| B.K. Kunderan | c Murray b Snow | 20 | (1) lbw b Illingworth | | 47 |
| E.A.S. Prasanna | run out | 17 | (8) c D'Oliveira b Illingworth | | 0 |
| B.S. Bedi | c Amiss b Snow | 5 | (9) b Illingworth | | 11 |
| B.S. Chandrasekhar | not out | 2 | (10) not out | | 3 |
| Extras | (B 2, LB 2) | 4 | (B 11, LB 4) | | 15 |
| **Total** | | **152** | | | **110** |

## ENGLAND

| | | |
|---|---|---|
| J.H. Edrich | c and b Surti | 12 |
| K.F. Barrington | b Chandrasekhar | 97 |
| D.L. Amiss | b Chandrasekhar | 29 |
| T.W. Graveney | st Engineer b Bedi | 151 |
| B.L. D'Oliveira | c and b Chandrasekhar | 33 |
| D.B. Close* | c Borde b Prasanna | 7 |
| J.T. Murray† | b Chandrasekhar | 7 |
| R. Illingworth | lbw b Chandrasekhar | 4 |
| R.N.S. Hobbs | b Bedi | 7 |
| D.J. Brown | c Pataudi b Bedi | 5 |
| J.A. Snow | not out | 8 |
| Extras | (B 5, LB 18, W 1, NB 2) | 26 |
| **Total** | | **386** |

| ENGLAND | O | M | R | W | O | M | R | W | FALL OF WICKETS | | | |
|---|---|---|---|---|---|---|---|---|---|---|---|---|
| Snow | 20·4 | 5 | 49 | 3 | 8 | 4 | 12 | 1 | | I | E | I |
| Brown | 18 | 3 | 61 | 3 | 5 | 2 | 10 | 0 | *Wkt* | *1st* | *1st* | *2nd* |
| D'Oliveira | 15 | 6 | 38 | 2 | | | | | 1st | 12 | 46 | 8 |
| Illingworth | 2 | 2 | 0 | 1 | 22·3 | 12 | 29 | 6 | 2nd | 24 | 107 | 60 |
| Hobbs | | | | | 6 | 1 | 16 | 0 | 3rd | 29 | 185 | 67 |
| Close | | | | | 15 | 5 | 28 | 2 | 4th | 45 | 307 | 79 |
| | | | | | | | | | 5th | 58 | 334 | 80 |
| INDIA | | | | | | | | | 6th | 102 | 359 | 86 |
| Surti | 31 | 10 | 67 | 1 | | | | | 7th | 112 | 365 | 90 |
| Subramanya | 7 | 1 | 20 | 0 | | | | | 8th | 144 | 372 | 101 |
| Chandrasekhar | 53 | 9 | 127 | 5 | | | | | 9th | 145 | 372 | 110 |
| Bedi | 31·2 | 13 | 68 | 3 | | | | | 10th | 152 | 386 | – |
| Prasanna | 32 | 5 | 78 | 1 | | | | | | | | |

Umpires: J.S. Buller and A. Jepson.

# ENGLAND v INDIA 1967 (3rd Test)

Played at Edgbaston, Birmingham, on 13, 14, 15 July.
Toss: England.   Result: ENGLAND won by 132 runs.
Debuts: Nil.

England achieved their third win in this three-match rubber at 6.18 on the third evening after 20 wickets had fallen on the second day. Murray and Hobbs shared a partnership of 57 which is still England's highest for the tenth wicket against India.

## ENGLAND

| Batsman | Dismissal 1 | R | Dismissal 2 | R |
|---|---|---|---|---|
| G. Boycott | st Engineer b Bedi | 25 | b Subramanya | 6 |
| C. Milburn | c Wadekar b Chandrasekhar | 40 | b Bedi | 15 |
| K.F. Barrington | c Wadekar b Prasanna | 75 | c Kunderan b Chandrasekhar | 13 |
| T.W. Graveney | c Venkataraghavan b Chandrasekhar | 10 | c Subramanya b Prasanna | 17 |
| D.L. Amiss | c Wadekar b Venkataraghavan | 5 | c Wadekar b Prasanna | 45 |
| D.B. Close* | c Subramanya b Prasanna | 26 | c Chandrasekhar b Prasanna | 47 |
| J.T. Murray† | c Subramanya b Chandrasekhar | 77 | b Bedi | 4 |
| R. Illingworth | c Wadekar b Prasanna | 2 | c Pataudi b Prasanna | 10 |
| D.J. Brown | run out | 3 | not out | 29 |
| J.A. Snow | c Engineer b Bedi | 10 | c Borde b Chandrasekhar | 9 |
| R.N.S. Hobbs | not out | 15 | c Prasanna b Chandrasekhar | 2 |
| Extras | (B 5, LB 5) | 10 | (B 4, LB 2) | 6 |
| Total | | 298 | | 203 |

## INDIA

| Batsman | Dismissal 1 | R | Dismissal 2 | R |
|---|---|---|---|---|
| F.M. Engineer† | c Graveney b Brown | 23 | c Barrington b Hobbs | 28 |
| B.K. Kunderan | b Brown | 2 | c Murray b Close | 33 |
| A.L. Wadekar | c Amiss b Snow | 5 | c Boycott b Illingworth | 70 |
| C.G. Borde | b Snow | 8 | b Illingworth | 10 |
| Nawab of Pataudi, jr* | b Brown | 0 | c Hobbs b Close | 47 |
| Hanumant Singh | c Amiss b Illingworth | 15 | c Milburn b Illingworth | 6 |
| V. Subramanya | b Hobbs | 10 | c Milburn b Illingworth | 4 |
| S. Venkataraghavan | not out | 19 | c Hobbs b Close | 17 |
| E.A.S. Prasanna | b Illingworth | 1 | b Hobbs | 15 |
| B.S. Bedi | c and b Hobbs | 1 | not out | 15 |
| B.S. Chandrasekhar | st Murray b Hobbs | 0 | c Boycott b Close | 22 |
| Extras | (B 4, LB 2, NB 2) | 8 | (B 5, LB 5) | 10 |
| Total | | 92 | | 277 |

| INDIA | O | M | R | W | O | M | R | W |
|---|---|---|---|---|---|---|---|---|
| Subramanya | 10 | 2 | 28 | 0 | 4 | 0 | 22 | 1 |
| Kunderan | 4 | 0 | 13 | 0 | | | | |
| Bedi | 27 | 6 | 76 | 2 | 24 | 9 | 60 | 2 |
| Chandrasekhar | 32 | 8 | 94 | 3 | 20·5 | 6 | 43 | 3 |
| Venkataraghavan | 13 | 3 | 26 | 1 | 2 | 1 | 4 | 0 |
| Prasanna | 20 | 5 | 51 | 3 | 24 | 9 | 60 | 4 |
| Pataudi | | | | | 2 | 0 | 8 | 0 |

| ENGLAND | O | M | R | W | O | M | R | W |
|---|---|---|---|---|---|---|---|---|
| Snow | 12 | 3 | 28 | 2 | 14 | 0 | 33 | 0 |
| Brown | 11 | 6 | 17 | 3 | 2 | 1 | 1 | 0 |
| Illingworth | 7 | 4 | 14 | 2 | 43 | 13 | 92 | 4 |
| Hobbs | 6·3 | 1 | 25 | 3 | 32 | 10 | 73 | 2 |
| Close | | | | | 21·4 | 7 | 68 | 4 |

### FALL OF WICKETS

| Wkt | E 1st | I 1st | E 2nd | I 2nd |
|---|---|---|---|---|
| 1st | 63 | 9 | 6 | 48 |
| 2nd | 67 | 18 | 32 | 91 |
| 3rd | 89 | 35 | 34 | 102 |
| 4th | 112 | 35 | 66 | 185 |
| 5th | 182 | 41 | 144 | 201 |
| 6th | 183 | 66 | 149 | 203 |
| 7th | 186 | 72 | 149 | 207 |
| 8th | 191 | 73 | 179 | 226 |
| 9th | 241 | 82 | 193 | 240 |
| 10th | 298 | 92 | 203 | 277 |

Umpires: W.F.F. Price and A.E. Fagg.

# ENGLAND v PAKISTAN 1967 (1st Test)

Played at Lord's, London, on 27, 28, 29, 31 July, 1 August.
Toss: England.   Result: MATCH DRAWN.
Debuts: Pakistan – Salim Altaf, Wasim Bari.

Five wickets fell for nine runs after Barrington and Graveney had established England's third-wicket record against Pakistan with a partnership of 201 in 223 minutes. Hanif's 187 not out, scored off 556 balls in 542 minutes, included 21 fours, was then Pakistan's highest score against England, and represented 55% of their total. His partnership of 130 in 191 minutes with Asif is still Pakistan's record for the eighth wicket against all countries. Set 257 runs in 210 minutes, Pakistan scored only 88 in 165 minutes off 62 overs, 32 of which were maidens. Rain claimed 3 hours 37 minutes of the match.

## ENGLAND

| | | | | |
|---|---|---|---|---|
| C. Milburn | c Wasim b Asif | 3 | c Asif b Majid | 32 |
| W.E. Russell | b Intikhab | 43 | b Majid | 12 |
| K.F. Barrington | c Wasim b Asif | 148 | b Intikhab | 14 |
| T.W. Graveney | b Salim | 81 | c Ibadulla b Asif | 30 |
| B.L. D'Oliveira | c Intikhab b Mushtaq | 59 | not out | 81 |
| D.B. Close* | c sub (Ghulam Abbas) b Salim | 4 | st Wasim b Nasim | 36 |
| J.T. Murray† | b Salim | 0 | c and b Nasim | 0 |
| R. Illingworth | b Asif | 4 | c and b Nasim | 9 |
| K. Higgs | lbw b Mushtaq | 14 | c Hanif b Intikhab | 1 |
| J.A. Snow | b Mushtaq | 0 | c Hanif b Mushtaq | 7 |
| R.N.S. Hobbs | not out | 1 | not out | 1 |
| Extras | (LB 5, NB 7) | 12 | (B 12, LB 5, NB 1) | 18 |
| **Total** | | **369** | (9 wickets declared) | **241** |

## PAKISTAN

| | | | | |
|---|---|---|---|---|
| Khalid Ibadulla | b Higgs | 8 | c Close b Illingworth | 32 |
| Javed Burki | lbw b Higgs | 31 | c and b Barrington | 13 |
| Mushtaq Mohammad | c Murray b Higgs | 4 | (4) not out | 30 |
| Hanif Mohammad* | not out | 187 | | |
| Majid Khan | c and b Hobbs | 5 | (3) c Close b Barrington | 5 |
| Nasim-ul-Ghani | c D'Oliveira b Snow | 2 | | |
| Saeed Ahmed | c Graveney b Snow | 6 | (5) not out | 6 |
| Intikhab Alam | lbw b Illingworth | 17 | | |
| Asif Iqbal | c Barrington b Illingworth | 76 | | |
| Wasim Bari† | c Close b Barrington | 13 | | |
| Salim Altaf | c Milburn b Snow | 2 | | |
| Extras | (B 1, LB 2) | 3 | (B 1, LB 1) | 2 |
| **Total** | | **354** | (3 wickets) | **88** |

| PAKISTAN | O | M | R | W | O | M | R | W | FALL OF WICKETS | | | | |
|---|---|---|---|---|---|---|---|---|---|---|---|---|---|
| Salim | 33 | 6 | 74 | 3 | 0·3 | 0 | 4 | 0 | | E | P | E | P |
| Asif | 28 | 10 | 76 | 3 | 21 | 5 | 50 | 1 | Wkt | 1st | 1st | 2nd | 2nd |
| Ibadulla | 3 | 0 | 5 | 0 | | | | | 1st | 5 | 19 | 33 | 27 |
| Majid | 11 | 2 | 28 | 0 | 10 | 1 | 32 | 2 | 2nd | 82 | 25 | 48 | 39 |
| Nasim | 12 | 1 | 36 | 0 | 13 | 3 | 32 | 3 | 3rd | 283 | 67 | 76 | 77 |
| Intikhab | 29 | 3 | 86 | 1 | 30 | 7 | 70 | 2 | 4th | 283 | 76 | 95 | – |
| Mushtaq | 11·3 | 3 | 23 | 3 | 16 | 4 | 35 | 1 | 5th | 287 | 91 | 199 | – |
| Saeed | 11 | 3 | 29 | 0 | | | | | 6th | 287 | 99 | 201 | – |
| ENGLAND | | | | | | | | | 7th | 292 | 139 | 215 | – |
| Snow | 45·1 | 11 | 120 | 3 | 4 | 2 | 6 | 0 | 8th | 352 | 269 | 220 | – |
| Higgs | 39 | 12 | 81 | 3 | 6 | 3 | 6 | 0 | 9th | 354 | 310 | 239 | – |
| D'Oliveira | 15 | 7 | 17 | 0 | | | | | 10th | 369 | 354 | – | – |
| Illingworth | 31 | 14 | 48 | 2 | 15 | 11 | 10 | 1 | | | | | |
| Hobbs | 35 | 16 | 46 | 1 | 16 | 9 | 28 | 0 | | | | | |
| Barrington | 11 | 1 | 29 | 1 | 13 | 2 | 23 | 2 | | | | | |
| Close | 6 | 3 | 10 | 0 | 8 | 5 | 13 | 0 | | | | | |

Umpire: C.S. Elliott and A. Jepson.

# ENGLAND v PAKISTAN 1967 (2nd Test)

Played at Trent Bridge, Nottingham, on 10, 11, 12, 14 (*no play*), 15 August.
Toss: Pakistan.   Result: ENGLAND won by ten wickets.
Debuts: England – G.G. Arnold, A.P.E. Knott; Pakistan – Niaz Ahmed.

Barrington reached his hundred off 344 balls and altogether batted for 409 minutes. The Nottingham Fire Brigade pumped 100,000 gallons of water off the ground after a violent thunderstorm soon after 5 p.m. on the first day had transformed the playing area into a lake. Play was able to restart at 12.45 p.m. on the second day. Alan Bull, a young recruit to the Nottinghamshire playing staff who was not destined to play in a first-class match, fielded substitute for D'Oliveira and caught Asif at long on. This was Hanif's first defeat in ten Tests as captain.

## PAKISTAN

| | | | | |
|---|---|---|---|---|
| Khalid Ibadulla | c Knott b Higgs | 2 | c Knott b Close | 5 |
| Javed Burki | lbw b Arnold | 1 | c Knott b Higgs | 3 |
| Saeed Ahmed | c Knott b Arnold | 44 | c Arnold b Underwood | 68 |
| Mushtaq Mohammad | b Higgs | 29 | (6) lbw b Underwood | 0 |
| Hanif Mohammad* | c Titmus b Underwood | 16 | c Knott b Higgs | 4 |
| Majid Khan | lbw b D'Oliveira | 17 | (7) c Close b Underwood | 5 |
| Asif Iqbal | b Higgs | 18 | (8) c sub (A. Bull) b Titmus | 5 |
| Nasim-ul-Ghani | run out | 11 | (4) c Close b Titmus | 6 |
| Intikhab Alam | c Knott b Arnold | 0 | c Knott b Underwood | 16 |
| Wasim Bari† | b Higgs | 0 | c Barrington b Underwood | 3 |
| Niaz Ahmed | not out | 0 | not out | 1 |
| Extras | (LB 1, NB 1) | 2 | (LB 1, NB 1) | 2 |
| **Total** | | **140** | | **114** |

## ENGLAND

| | | | | |
|---|---|---|---|---|
| G. Boycott | b Asif | 15 | not out | 1 |
| M.C. Cowdrey | c Majid b Nasim | 14 | not out | 2 |
| K.F. Barrington | not out | 109 | | |
| T.W. Graveney | c Niaz b Ibadulla | 28 | | |
| B.L. D'Oliveira | run out | 7 | | |
| D.B. Close* | c Wasim b Niaz | 41 | | |
| F.J. Titmus | lbw b Asif | 13 | | |
| A.P.E. Knott† | c Hanif b Mushtaq | 0 | | |
| G.G. Arnold | lbw b Niaz | 14 | | |
| K. Higgs | not out | 0 | | |
| D.L. Underwood | did not bat | | | |
| Extras | (B 3, LB 3, W 1, NB 4) | 11 | | |
| **Total** | (8 wickets declared) | **252** | (0 wickets) | **3** |

| ENGLAND | O | M | R | W | O | M | R | W | | FALL OF WICKETS | | | |
|---|---|---|---|---|---|---|---|---|---|---|---|---|---|
| Arnold | 17 | 5 | 35 | 3 | 5 | 3 | 5 | 0 | | P | E | P | E |
| Higgs | 19 | 12 | 35 | 4 | 6 | 1 | 8 | 2 | Wkt | 1st | 1st | 2nd | 2nd |
| D'Oliveira | 18 | 9 | 27 | 1 | | | | | 1st | 3 | 21 | 4 | – |
| Close | 3 | 0 | 12 | 0 | 4 | 1 | 11 | 1 | 2nd | 21 | 31 | 35 | – |
| Titmus | 7 | 3 | 12 | 0 | 23 | 11 | 36 | 2 | 3rd | 65 | 75 | 60 | – |
| Underwood | 5 | 2 | 17 | 1 | 26 | 8 | 52 | 5 | 4th | 82 | 92 | 71 | – |
| | | | | | | | | | 5th | 104 | 187 | 76 | – |
| PAKISTAN | | | | | | | | | 6th | 116 | 213 | 89 | – |
| Asif | 39 | 10 | 72 | 2 | | | | | 7th | 140 | 214 | 93 | – |
| Niaz | 37 | 10 | 72 | 2 | | | | | 8th | 140 | 251 | 99 | – |
| Nasim | 8 | 2 | 20 | 1 | | | | | 9th | 140 | – | 113 | – |
| Saeed | 2 | 2 | 0 | 0 | 1 | 1 | 0 | 0 | 10th | 140 | – | 114 | – |
| Intikhab | 7 | 2 | 19 | 0 | | | | | | | | | |
| Ibadulla | 32 | 13 | 42 | 1 | | | | | | | | | |
| Mushtaq | 9·3 | 3 | 16 | 1 | 1·1 | 0 | 3 | 0 | | | | | |

Umpires: J.S. Buller and W.F.F. Price.

# ENGLAND v PAKISTAN 1967 (3rd Test)

Played at Kennington Oval, London, on 24, 25, 26, 28 August.
Toss: England.   Result: ENGLAND won by eight wickets.
Debuts: Pakistan – Ghulam Abbas.

Barrington's 19th Test hundred was his third in successive Tests and his first in a Test on his county ground. He thus became the first to score a Test hundred on each of England's six current Test grounds. It was his 52nd score of 50 or more and equalled L. Hutton's world Test record. Asif's 146 off 244 balls in 200 minutes included two sixes and 21 fours. His partnership of 190 in 170 minutes with Intikhab remains the highest for the ninth wicket in all Test cricket. England won at 5.11 on the fourth evening.

## PAKISTAN

| | | | | | |
|---|---|---|---|---|---|
| Hanif Mohammad* | b Higgs | 3 | (5) c Knott b Higgs | | 18 |
| Mohammad Ilyas | b Arnold | 2 | c Cowdrey b Higgs | | 1 |
| Saeed Ahmed | b Arnold | 38 | c Knott b Higgs | | 0 |
| Majid Khan | c Knott b Arnold | 6 | b Higgs | | 0 |
| Mashtaq Mohammad | lbw b Higgs | 66 | (7) c D'Oliveira b Underwood | | 17 |
| Javed Burki | c D'Oliveira b Titmus | 27 | (8) b Underwood | | 7 |
| Ghulam Abbas | c Underwood b Titmus | 12 | (6) c Knott b Higgs | | 0 |
| Asif Iqbal | c Close b Arnold | 26 | (9) st Knott b Close | | 146 |
| Intikhab Alam | b Higgs | 20 | (10) b Titmus | | 51 |
| Wasim Bari† | c Knott b Arnold | 1 | (1) b Titmus | | 12 |
| Salim Altaf | not out | 7 | not out | | 0 |
| Extras | (B 5, LB 2, NB 1) | 8 | (B 1, LB 1, NB 1) | | 3 |
| **Total** | | **216** | | | **255** |

## ENGLAND

| | | | | | |
|---|---|---|---|---|---|
| M.C. Cowdrey | c Mushtaq b Majid | 16 | c Intikhab b Asif | | 9 |
| D.B. Close* | c Wasim b Asif | 6 | b Asif | | 8 |
| K.F. Barrington | c Wasim b Salim | 142 | not out | | 13 |
| T.W. Graveney | c Majid b Intikhab | 77 | | | |
| D.L. Amiss | c Saeed b Asif | 26 | (4) not out | | 3 |
| B.L. D'Oliveira | c Mushtaq b Asif | 3 | | | |
| F.J. Titmus | c sub (Niaz Ahmed) b Mushtaq | 65 | | | |
| A.P.E. Knott† | c Ilyas b Mushtaq | 28 | | | |
| G.G. Arnold | c Majid b Mushtaq | 59 | | | |
| K. Higgs | b Mushtaq | 7 | | | |
| D.L. Underwood | not out | 2 | | | |
| Extras | (LB 4, NB 5) | 9 | (NB 1) | | 1 |
| **Total** | | **440** | (2 wickets) | | **34** |

| ENGLAND | O | M | R | W | O | M | R | W | | FALL OF WICKETS | | | |
|---|---|---|---|---|---|---|---|---|---|---|---|---|---|
| Arnold | 29 | 9 | 58 | 5 | 17 | 5 | 49 | 0 | | P | E | P | E |
| Higgs | 29 | 10 | 61 | 3 | 20 | 7 | 58 | 5 | Wkt | 1st | 1st | 2nd | 2nd |
| D'Oliveira | 17 | 6 | 41 | 0 | | | | | 1st | 3 | 16 | 1 | 17 |
| Close | 5 | 1 | 15 | 0 | 1 | 0 | 4 | 1 | 2nd | 5 | 35 | 5 | 20 |
| Titmus | 13 | 6 | 21 | 2 | 29·1 | 8 | 64 | 2 | 3rd | 17 | 176 | 5 | – |
| Underwood | 9 | 5 | 12 | 0 | 26 | 12 | 48 | 2 | 4th | 74 | 270 | 26 | – |
| Barrington | | | | | 8 | 2 | 29 | 0 | 5th | 138 | 276 | 26 | – |
| | | | | | | | | | 6th | 155 | 276 | 41 | – |
| PAKISTAN | | | | | | | | | 7th | 182 | 323 | 53 | – |
| Salim | 40 | 14 | 94 | 1 | 2 | 1 | 8 | 0 | 8th | 188 | 416 | 65 | – |
| Asif | 42 | 19 | 66 | 3 | 4 | 1 | 14 | 2 | 9th | 194 | 437 | 255 | – |
| Majid | 10 | 0 | 29 | 1 | | | | | 10th | 216 | 440 | 255 | – |
| Mushtaq | 26·4 | 7 | 80 | 4 | | | | | | | | | |
| Saeed | 21 | 5 | 69 | 0 | 2 | 0 | 7 | 0 | | | | | |
| Intikhab | 28 | 3 | 93 | 1 | | | | | | | | | |
| Hanif | | | | | 0·2 | 0 | 4 | 0 | | | | | |

Umpires: W.F.F. Price and H. Yarnold.

# AUSTRALIA v INDIA 1967–68 (1st Test)

Played at Adelaide Oval on 23, 25, 26, 27, 28 December.
Toss: Australia.   Result: AUSTRALIA won by 146 runs.
Debuts: Australia – J.W. Gleeson, A.P. Sheahan; India – S. Abid Ali, U.N. Kulkarni.

In his first match Abid Ali (6 for 55) achieved India's best innings analysis in a Test in Australia.

## AUSTRALIA

| | | | | |
|---|---|---|---|---|
| R.B. Simpson* | c and b Abid Ali | 55 | b Surti | 103 |
| W.M. Lawry | c Engineer b Abid Ali | 42 | c Engineer b Kulkarni | 0 |
| A.P. Sheahan | lbw b Prasanna | 81 | lbw b Prasanna | 35 |
| R.M. Cowper | c Engineer b Abid Ali | 92 | b Abid Ali | 108 |
| I.R. Redpath | c Borde b Prasanna | 0 | (7) lbw b Surti | 34 |
| I.M. Chappell | c Borde b Prasanna | 2 | (5) b Surti | 13 |
| B.N. Jarman† | b Abid Ali | 34 | (6) c and b Surti | 17 |
| G.D. McKenzie | c Borde b Abid Ali | 5 | run out | 28 |
| J.W. Gleeson | lbw b Abid Ali | 1 | not out | 18 |
| A.N. Connolly | not out | 7 | c sub (R.B. Desai) b Surti | 0 |
| D.A. Renneberg | b Chandrasekhar | 1 | run out | 0 |
| Extras | (B 2, LB 10, NB 3) | 15 | (B 5, LB 6, NB 2) | 13 |
| **Total** | | **335** | | **369** |

## INDIA

| | | | | |
|---|---|---|---|---|
| F.M. Engineer† | c Jarman b McKenzie | 89 | run out | 19 |
| D.N. Sardesai | c Redpath b Renneberg | 1 | c Jarman b Renneberg | 11 |
| A.L. Wadekar | st Jarman b Connolly | 28 | c Jarman b Renneberg | 0 |
| C.G. Borde* | lbw b Gleeson | 69 | b Renneberg | 12 |
| R.F. Surti | b Simpson | 70 | c Redpath b Gleeson | 53 |
| R.G. Nadkarni | lbw b Gleeson | 3 | (8) b McKenzie | 15 |
| S. Abid Ali | c and b Connolly | 33 | (6) lbw b Renneberg | 33 |
| V. Subramanya | b Connolly | 7 | (7) run out | 75 |
| E.A.S. Prasanna | c Lawry b McKenzie | 1 | not out | 18 |
| U.N. Kulkarni | lbw b Connolly | 0 | (11) c Chappell b Renneberg | 2 |
| B.S. Chandrasekhar | not out | 1 | (10) c Simpson b Gleeson | 0 |
| Extras | (NB 5) | 5 | (B 3, LB 8, NB 2) | 13 |
| **Total** | | **307** | | **251** |

| INDIA | O | M | R | W | O | M | R | W | | FALL OF WICKETS | | | |
|---|---|---|---|---|---|---|---|---|---|---|---|---|---|
| Kulkarni | 5 | 0 | 25 | 0 | 4 | 1 | 12 | 1 | | A | I | A | I |
| Surti | 7 | 0 | 30 | 0 | 20·1 | 6 | 74 | 5 | *Wkt* | *1st* | *1st* | *2nd* | *2nd* |
| Abid Ali | 17 | 2 | 55 | 6 | 16 | 2 | 61 | 1 | 1st | 99 | 19 | 0 | 24 |
| Nadkarni | 17 | 2 | 68 | 0 | 9·4 | 3 | 24 | 0 | 2nd | 109 | 80 | 61 | 24 |
| Chandrasekhar | 27·1 | 3 | 72 | 1 | 13 | 1 | 67 | 0 | 3rd | 227 | 129 | 233 | 46 |
| Prasanna | 17 | 2 | 60 | 3 | 25 | 2 | 109 | 1 | 4th | 227 | 250 | 263 | 49 |
| Subramanya | 2 | 0 | 10 | 0 | 1 | 0 | 9 | 0 | 5th | 235 | 259 | 263 | 104 |
| | | | | | | | | | 6th | 311 | 272 | 295 | 159 |
| AUSTRALIA | | | | | | | | | 7th | 319 | 287 | 322 | 209 |
| McKenzie | 15 | 1 | 70 | 2 | 17 | 2 | 91 | 1 | 8th | 324 | 288 | 364 | 232 |
| Renneberg | 6 | 0 | 45 | 1 | 14·2 | 2 | 39 | 5 | 9th | 330 | 291 | 365 | 236 |
| Connolly | 12·4 | 1 | 54 | 4 | 3 | 0 | 21 | 0 | 10th | 335 | 307 | 369 | 251 |
| Gleeson | 13 | 4 | 36 | 2 | 16 | 4 | 38 | 2 | | | | | |
| Chappell | 10 | 1 | 41 | 0 | 5 | 0 | 24 | 0 | | | | | |
| Simpson | 12 | 2 | 42 | 1 | 5 | 0 | 25 | 0 | | | | | |
| Cowper | 3 | 0 | 14 | 0 | | | | | | | | | |

Umpires: C.J. Egar and L.P. Rowan.

# AUSTRALIA v INDIA 1967–68 (2nd Test)

Played at Melbourne Cricket Ground on 30 December, 1, 2, 3 January.
Toss: India.    Result: AUSTRALIA won by an innings and 4 runs.
Debuts: Nil.

Batting for the first time in a first-class match in Australia, the Nawab of Pataudi achieved a match aggregate of 160 runs despite his limited vision and the added handicap of a damaged hamstring muscle. The partnership of 191 between Simpson and Lawry is still the highest for the first wicket by either side in this series. Simpson, who was captaining Australia for a record 29th time, became the third Australian to score 4,000 runs in Tests.

## INDIA

| | | | | | |
|---|---|---|---|---|---|
| D.N. Sardesai | b McKenzie | 1 | b McKenzie | | 5 |
| F.M. Engineer† | c Connolly b McKenzie | 9 | c Chappell b Renneberg | | 42 |
| S. Abid Ali | c Jarman b McKenzie | 4 | (8) lbw b Cowper | | 21 |
| A.L. Wadekar | c Connolly b McKenzie | 6 | (3) c Sheahan b Simpson | | 99 |
| R.F. Surti | lbw b Simpson | 30 | (4) c Jarman b McKenzie | | 43 |
| C.G. Borde | c Redpath b McKenzie | 0 | c Redpath b Renneberg | | 6 |
| Nawab of Pataudi, jr* | c Jarman b Renneberg | 75 | c Redpath b Simpson | | 85 |
| V. Subramanya | b McKenzie | 5 | (9) lbw b McKenzie | | 10 |
| E.A.S. Prasanna | c Chappell b Renneberg | 14 | (5) c Chappell b Simpson | | 21 |
| R.B. Desai | not out | 13 | c Simpson b Connolly | | 14 |
| B.S. Chandrasekhar | c Jarman b McKenzie | 0 | not out | | 0 |
| Extras | (B 8, LB 2, NB 6) | 16 | (B 1, LB 4, NB 1) | | 6 |
| **Total** | | **173** | | | **352** |

## AUSTRALIA

| | | |
|---|---|---|
| R.B. Simpson* | b Surti | 109 |
| W.M. Lawry | st Engineer b Prasanna | 100 |
| A.P. Sheahan | c Engineer b Surti | 24 |
| R.M. Cowper | b Prasanna | 12 |
| I.M. Chappell | c Wadekar b Surti | 151 |
| I.R. Redpath | run out | 26 |
| B.N. Jarman† | b Prasanna | 65 |
| G.D. McKenzie | c sub (B.S. Bedi) b Prasanna | 0 |
| J.W. Gleeson | c Borde b Prasanna | 13 |
| A.N. Connolly | c sub (B.S. Bedi) b Prasanna | 5 |
| D.A. Renneberg | not out | 8 |
| Extras | (B 3, LB 10, NB 3) | 16 |
| **Total** | | **529** |

| AUSTRALIA | O | M | R | W | O | M | R | W |
|---|---|---|---|---|---|---|---|---|
| McKenzie | 21·4 | 2 | 66 | 7 | 19 | 2 | 85 | 3 |
| Renneberg | 15 | 4 | 37 | 2 | 14 | 1 | 98 | 2 |
| Connolly | 13 | 3 | 33 | 0 | 11·7 | 2 | 48 | 1 |
| Gleeson | 5 | 0 | 9 | 0 | 14 | 5 | 37 | 0 |
| Chappell | 1 | 0 | 7 | 0 | 4 | 0 | 14 | 0 |
| Simpson | 2 | 0 | 5 | 1 | 14 | 3 | 44 | 3 |
| Cowper | | | | | 8 | 2 | 20 | 1 |
| **INDIA** | | | | | | | | |
| Desai | 12 | 0 | 63 | 0 | | | | |
| Surti | 29·3 | 4 | 150 | 3 | | | | |
| Abid Ali | 20 | 0 | 106 | 0 | | | | |
| Chandrasekhar | 7 | 0 | 35 | 0 | | | | |
| Prasanna | 34 | 6 | 141 | 6 | | | | |
| Subramanya | 3 | 0 | 18 | 0 | | | | |

### FALL OF WICKETS

| | I | A | I |
|---|---|---|---|
| Wkt | 1st | 1st | 2nd |
| 1st | 2 | 191 | 11 |
| 2nd | 10 | 233 | 66 |
| 3rd | 18 | 246 | 182 |
| 4th | 25 | 274 | 194 |
| 5th | 25 | 329 | 217 |
| 6th | 47 | 463 | 227 |
| 7th | 72 | 463 | 276 |
| 8th | 146 | 500 | 292 |
| 9th | 162 | 508 | 346 |
| 10th | 173 | 529 | 352 |

Umpires: C.J. Egar and L.P. Rowan.

# AUSTRALIA v INDIA 1967–68 (3rd Test)

Played at Woolloongabba, Brisbane, on 19, 20, 22, 23, 24 January.
Toss: India.   Result: AUSTRALIA won by 39 runs.
Debuts: Australia – E.W. Freeman.

Jaisimha scored 74 and 101 on his first-class debut in Australia only a few days after arriving from India. Freeman's first scoring stroke in Test cricket was a six over mid-wicket off Prasanna. He then took the wickets of Engineer and Abid Ali in the course of his first ten balls.

## AUSTRALIA

| | | | | | |
|---|---|---|---|---|---|
| W.M. Lawry* | c Bedi b Nadkarni | 64 | c Engineer b Surti | | 45 |
| I.R. Redpath | c Wadekar b Prasanna | 41 | lbw b Prasanna | | 79 |
| R.M. Cowper | b Nadkarni | 51 | b Surti | | 25 |
| A.P. Sheahan | st Engineer b Surti | 58 | c Surti b Bedi | | 26 |
| I.M. Chappell | b Surti | 17 | b Prasanna | | 27 |
| K.D. Walters | c Wadekar b Kulkarni | 93 | not out | | 62 |
| B.N. Jarman† | lbw b Prasanna | 2 | c and b Prasanna | | 9 |
| E.W. Freeman | b Surti | 18 | c Surti b Prasanna | | 8 |
| J.W. Gleeson | run out | 15 | c Abid Ali b Surti | | 1 |
| A.N. Connolly | c Pataudi b Kulkarni | 14 | b Prasanna | | 0 |
| D.A. Renneberg | not out | 0 | c Surti b Prasanna | | 0 |
| Extras | (B 1, LB 1, NB 4) | 6 | (B 1, LB 10, NB 1) | | 12 |
| **Total** | | **379** | | | **294** |

## INDIA

| | | | | | |
|---|---|---|---|---|---|
| F.M. Engineer† | c Gleeson b Freeman | 2 | c Jarman b Renneberg | | 0 |
| S. Abid Ali | c Redpath b Freeman | 2 | c Jarman b Connolly | | 47 |
| A.L. Wadekar | c Jarman b Renneberg | 1 | c Connolly b Cowper | | 11 |
| R.F. Surti | c Cowper b Chappell | 52 | b Cowper | | 64 |
| Nawab of Pataudi, jr* | lbw b Freeman | 74 | b Walters | | 48 |
| M.L. Jaisimha | c Lawry b Cowper | 74 | c Gleeson b Cowper | | 101 |
| C.G. Borde | c and b Connolly | 12 | c Redpath b Cowper | | 63 |
| R.G. Nadkarni | b Cowper | 17 | lbw b Gleeson | | 2 |
| E.A.S. Prasanna | c Walters b Cowper | 24 | b Gleeson | | 4 |
| B.S. Bedi | not out | 2 | c Lawry b Gleeson | | 0 |
| U.N. Kulkarni | c Cowper b Connolly | 7 | not out | | 1 |
| Extras | (B 6, LB 4, NB 2) | 12 | (B 4, LB 6, NB 4) | | 14 |
| **Total** | | **279** | | | **355** |

| INDIA | O | M | R | W | O | M | R | W | | FALL OF WICKETS | | | |
|---|---|---|---|---|---|---|---|---|---|---|---|---|---|
| Kulkarni | 8·2 | 1 | 37 | 2 | 4 | 0 | 22 | 0 | | A | I | A | I |
| Surti | 26 | 2 | 102 | 3 | 16 | 4 | 59 | 3 | Wkt | 1st | 1st | 2nd | 2nd |
| Prasanna | 38 | 6 | 114 | 2 | 33·4 | 9 | 104 | 6 | 1st | 76 | 2 | 116 | 17 |
| Bedi | 23 | 4 | 71 | 0 | 14 | 4 | 44 | 1 | 2nd | 148 | 5 | 136 | 48 |
| Abid Ali | 2 | 0 | 9 | 0 | 1 | 0 | 6 | 0 | 3rd | 160 | 9 | 162 | 61 |
| Nadkarni | 14 | 5 | 34 | 2 | 15 | 5 | 47 | 0 | 4th | 215 | 137 | 196 | 154 |
| Jaisimha | 1 | 0 | 6 | 0 | | | | | 5th | 239 | 139 | 240 | 191 |
| | | | | | | | | | 6th | 250 | 165 | 266 | 310 |
| AUSTRALIA | | | | | | | | | 7th | 277 | 209 | 284 | 313 |
| Renneberg | 10 | 1 | 40 | 1 | 7 | 0 | 43 | 1 | 8th | 323 | 268 | 293 | 323 |
| Freeman | 21 | 1 | 56 | 3 | 8 | 2 | 29 | 0 | 9th | 378 | 270 | 294 | 333 |
| Walters | 6 | 0 | 22 | 0 | 11 | 2 | 33 | 1 | 10th | 379 | 279 | 294 | 355 |
| Connolly | 15 | 4 | 43 | 2 | 18 | 6 | 51 | 1 | | | | | |
| Gleeson | 15 | 7 | 20 | 0 | 21 | 6 | 50 | 3 | | | | | |
| Cowper | 15 | 5 | 31 | 3 | 39·6 | 8 | 104 | 4 | | | | | |
| Chappell | 18 | 4 | 55 | 1 | 5 | 1 | 31 | 0 | | | | | |

Umpires: C.J. Egar and L.P. Rowan.

# AUSTRALIA v INDIA 1967–68 (4th Test)

Played at Sydney Cricket Ground on 26, 27, 29, 30, 31 January.
Toss: India.    Result: AUSTRALIA won by 144 runs.
Debuts: Australia – L.R. Joslin.

This was India's seventh consecutive defeat, Australia's four victories in this rubber following three by England in 1967. Pataudi decided to field first for the second Test in succession. Simpson, playing in what was intended to be his final Test, achieved his best bowling figures and held his 99th catch.

## AUSTRALIA

| | | | | |
|---|---|---|---|---|
| W.M. Lawry* | c Engineer b Prasanna | 66 | c sub (V. Subramanya) b Nadkarni | 52 |
| R.M. Cowper | b Abid Ali | 32 | st Engineer b Prasanna | 165 |
| A.P. Sheahan | c and b Bedi | 72 | (4) c Wadekar b Jaisimha | 22 |
| K.D. Walters | not out | 94 | (5) run out | 5 |
| L.R. Joslin | c Wadekar b Prasanna | 7 | (6) c Abid Ali b Bedi | 2 |
| R.B. Simpson | b Bedi | 7 | (3) run out | 20 |
| I.M. Chappell | run out | 0 | lbw b Prasanna | 2 |
| B.N. Jarman† | c Engineer b Surti | 4 | run out | 5 |
| E.W. Freeman | lbw b Kulkarni | 11 | c sub (R. Saxena) b Prasanna | 8 |
| N.J.N. Hawke | c Engineer b Kulkarni | 1 | c Abid Ali b Prasanna | 4 |
| J.W. Gleeson | lbw b Prasanna | 14 | not out | 4 |
| Extras | (B 2, LB 4, NB 3) | 9 | (B 1, LB 1, NB 1) | 3 |
| **Total** | | **317** | | **292** |

## INDIA

| | | | | |
|---|---|---|---|---|
| F.M. Engineer† | c Chappell b Walters | 17 | c Simpson b Gleeson | 37 |
| S. Abid Ali | hit wkt b Gleeson | 78 | c Simpson b Cowper | 81 |
| A.L. Wadekar | c and b Cowper | 49 | lbw b Cowper | 18 |
| R.F. Surti | b Simpson | 29 | c Chappell b Simpson | 26 |
| Nawab of Pataudi, jr* | c Simpson b Freeman | 51 | c Chappell b Simpson | 6 |
| M.L. Jaisimha | c Jarman b Simpson | 0 | c Gleeson b Cowper | 13 |
| R.G. Nadkarni | c Sheahan b Simpson | 0 | (8) c Sheahan b Simpson | 6 |
| E.A.S. Prasanna | c Cowper b Freeman | 26 | (9) b Simpson | 0 |
| C.G. Borde | lbw b Freeman | 0 | (7) c Simpson b Cowper | 4 |
| B.S. Bedi | c Simpson b Freeman | 8 | b Simpson | 2 |
| U.N. Kulkarni | not out | 1 | not out | 1 |
| Extras | (B 4, LB 2, NB 3) | 9 | (LB 3) | 3 |
| **Total** | | **268** | | **197** |

| INDIA | O | M | R | W | O | M | R | W | | FALL OF WICKETS | | | |
|---|---|---|---|---|---|---|---|---|---|---|---|---|---|
| Kulkarni | 17 | 0 | 73 | 2 | 8 | 0 | 31 | 0 | | A | I | A | I |
| Surti | 11 | 1 | 64 | 1 | 8 | 1 | 49 | 0 | Wkt | 1st | 1st | 2nd | 2nd |
| Abid Ali | 15 | 1 | 58 | 1 | 2 | 0 | 7 | 0 | 1st | 61 | 56 | 111 | 83 |
| Jaisimha | 2 | 0 | 9 | 0 | 1 | 0 | 2 | 1 | 2nd | 136 | 111 | 166 | 120 |
| Bedi | 21 | 4 | 42 | 2 | 21 | 5 | 66 | 1 | 3rd | 219 | 178 | 222 | 145 |
| Prasanna | 20·6 | 5 | 62 | 3 | 29·3 | 4 | 96 | 4 | 4th | 228 | 178 | 240 | 164 |
| Nadkarni | | | | | 16 | 3 | 38 | 1 | 5th | 239 | 184 | 243 | 175 |
| | | | | | | | | | 6th | 242 | 184 | 260 | 180 |
| AUSTRALIA | | | | | | | | | 7th | 256 | 236 | 271 | 193 |
| Hawke | 18 | 2 | 51 | 0 | 6 | 2 | 22 | 0 | 8th | 275 | 236 | 278 | 193 |
| Freeman | 18·1 | 2 | 86 | 4 | 4 | 0 | 26 | 0 | 9th | 277 | 267 | 286 | 195 |
| Walters | 4 | 0 | 20 | 1 | 3 | 1 | 11 | 0 | 10th | 317 | 268 | 292 | 197 |
| Gleeson | 12 | 3 | 40 | 1 | 12 | 4 | 27 | 1 | | | | | |
| Cowper | 12 | 5 | 21 | 1 | 25·6 | 12 | 49 | 4 | | | | | |
| Simpson | 20 | 10 | 38 | 3 | 23 | 5 | 59 | 5 | | | | | |
| Chappell | 1 | 0 | 3 | 0 | | | | | | | | | |

Umpires: C.J. Egar and L.P. Rowan.

# WEST INDIES v ENGLAND 1967–68 (1st Test)

Played at Queen's Park Oval, Port-of-Spain, Trinidad, on 19, 20, 22, 23, 24 January.
Toss: England.   Result: MATCH DRAWN.
Debuts: West Indies – G.S. Camacho.

England's total was their second-highest in the West Indies. Barrington reached his hundred with a six; it was his fourth century in consecutive Tests. Lloyd became the fourth West Indies batsman to score a hundred in his first match against England. West Indies followed on for the first time in their 14 matches under the captaincy of Sobers. Brown dismissed Butcher, Murray and Griffith in the last over before tea but Hall partnered Sobers throughout the final session and avoided the possibility of an innings defeat. Their unbroken partnership of 63 remains the West Indies record for the ninth wicket against England.

## ENGLAND

| | | |
|---|---|---:|
| G. Boycott | lbw b Holford | 68 |
| J.H. Edrich | c Murray b Gibbs | 25 |
| M.C. Cowdrey* | c Murray b Griffith | 72 |
| K.F. Barrington | c Griffith b Gibbs | 143 |
| T.W. Graveney | b Gibbs | 118 |
| J.M. Parks† | lbw b Sobers | 42 |
| B.L. D'Oliveira | b Griffith | 32 |
| F.J. Titmus | lbw b Griffith | 15 |
| D.J. Brown | not out | 22 |
| R.N.S. Hobbs | c Butcher b Griffith | 2 |
| I.J. Jones | c Murray b Griffith | 2 |
| Extras | (B 8, LB 11, W 1, NB 7) | 27 |
| **Total** | | **568** |

## WEST INDIES

| | | | | | |
|---|---|---:|---|---|---:|
| S.M. Nurse | c Graveney b Titmus | 41 | | b Titmus | 42 |
| G.S. Camacho | c Graveney b Brown | 22 | | c Graveney b Barrington | 43 |
| R.B. Kanhai | c Cowdrey b D'Oliveira | 85 | (4) | c and b Hobbs | 37 |
| B.F. Butcher | lbw b Brown | 14 | (3) | lbw b Brown | 52 |
| C.H. Lloyd | b Jones | 118 | | c Titmus b Jones | 2 |
| G. St A. Sobers* | c Graveney b Barrington | 17 | (7) | not out | 33 |
| D.A.J. Holford | run out | 4 | (6) | b Titmus | 1 |
| D.L. Murray† | c D'Oliveira b Hobbs | 16 | | lbw b Brown | 0 |
| C.C. Griffith | c Parks b Jones | 18 | | b Brown | 0 |
| W.W. Hall | not out | 10 | | not out | 26 |
| L.R. Gibbs | b Jones | 1 | | | |
| Extras | (B 4, LB 6, NB 7) | 17 | | (LB 5, NB 2) | 7 |
| **Total** | | **363** | | **(8 wickets)** | **243** |

| WEST INDIES | O | M | R | W | O | M | R | W |
|---|---:|---:|---:|---:|---:|---:|---:|---:|
| Hall | 28 | 5 | 92 | 0 | | | | |
| Sobers | 26 | 5 | 83 | 1 | | | | |
| Griffith | 29·5 | 13 | 69 | 5 | | | | |
| Gibbs | 63 | 15 | 147 | 3 | | | | |
| Holford | 43 | 1 | 121 | 1 | | | | |
| Lloyd | 8 | 3 | 17 | 0 | | | | |
| Camacho | 3 | 1 | 12 | 0 | | | | |
| ENGLAND | | | | | | | | |
| Brown | 22 | 3 | 65 | 2 | 14 | 4 | 27 | 3 |
| Jones | 19 | 5 | 63 | 3 | 15 | 3 | 32 | 1 |
| D'Oliveira | 27 | 13 | 49 | 1 | 5 | 2 | 21 | 0 |
| Titmus | 34 | 9 | 91 | 1 | 27 | 13 | 42 | 2 |
| Hobbs | 15 | 1 | 34 | 1 | 13 | 2 | 44 | 1 |
| Barrington | 18 | 6 | 44 | 1 | 15 | 0 | 69 | 1 |
| Cowdrey | | | | | 1 | 0 | 1 | 0 |

### FALL OF WICKETS

| | E | WI | WI |
|---|---:|---:|---:|
| Wkt | 1st | 1st | 2nd |
| 1st | 80 | 50 | 70 |
| 2nd | 110 | 102 | 100 |
| 3rd | 244 | 124 | 164 |
| 4th | 432 | 240 | 167 |
| 5th | 471 | 290 | 178 |
| 6th | 511 | 294 | 180 |
| 7th | 527 | 329 | 180 |
| 8th | 554 | 352 | 180 |
| 9th | 566 | 357 | – |
| 10th | 568 | 363 | – |

Umpires: H.B. de C. Jordan and R. Gosein.

# WEST INDIES v ENGLAND 1967–68 (2nd Test)

Played at Sabina Park, Kingston, Jamaica, on 8, 9, 10, 12, 13, 14 February.
Toss: England.    Result: MATCH DRAWN.
Debuts: Nil.

West Indies followed on for the second Test running after Snow dismissed Sobers first ball for the second time in successive innings in which he had bowled to him. Butcher's second innings dismissal in mid-afternoon on the fourth day sparked off a bottle-throwing riot with West Indies 204 for 5 and needing 29 runs to avoid an innings defeat. Play resumed after tea and it was agreed that the 75 minutes lost would be played on an extra (sixth) day.

## ENGLAND

| | | | | |
|---|---|---|---|---|
| G. Boycott | b Hall | 17 | b Sobers | 0 |
| J.H. Edrich | c Kanhai b Sobers | 96 | b Hall | 6 |
| M.C. Cowdrey* | c Murray b Gibbs | 101 | lbw b Sobers | 0 |
| K.F. Barrington | c and b Holford | 63 | lbw b Griffith | 13 |
| T.W. Graveney | b Hall | 30 | c Griffith b Gibbs | 21 |
| J.M. Parks† | c Sobers b Holford | 3 | lbw b Gibbs | 3 |
| B.L. D'Oliveira | st Murray b Holford | 0 | not out | 13 |
| F.J. Titmus | lbw b Hall | 19 | c Camacho b Gibbs | 4 |
| D.J. Brown | c Murray b Hall | 14 | b Sobers | 0 |
| J.A. Snow | b Griffith | 10 | | |
| I.J. Jones | not out | 0 | | |
| Extras | (B 12, LB 7, NB 4) | 23 | (B 8) | 8 |
| **Total** | | **376** | (8 wickets) | **68** |

## WEST INDIES

| | | | | |
|---|---|---|---|---|
| G.S. Camacho | b Snow | 5 | b D'Oliveira | 25 |
| D.L. Murray† | c D'Oliveira b Brown | 0 | (8) lbw b Brown | 14 |
| R.B. Kanhai | c Graveney b Snow | 26 | c Edrich b Jones | 36 |
| S.M. Nurse | b Jones | 22 | (2) b Snow | 73 |
| C.H. Lloyd | not out | 34 | b Brown | 7 |
| G. St A. Sobers* | lbw b Snow | 0 | not out | 113 |
| B.F. Butcher | c Parks b Snow | 21 | (4) c Parks b D'Oliveira | 25 |
| D.A.J. Holford | c Parks b Snow | 6 | (7) lbw b Titmus | 35 |
| C.C. Griffith | c D'Oliveira b Snow | 8 | lbw b Jones | 14 |
| W.W. Hall | b Snow | 0 | c Parks b Jones | 0 |
| L.R. Gibbs | c Parks b Jones | 0 | not out | 1 |
| Extras | (B 12, LB 5, W 1, NB 3) | 21 | (B 33, LB 10, NB 5) | 48 |
| **Total** | | **143** | (9 wickets declared) | **391** |

| WEST INDIES | O | M | R | W | O | M | R | W | | FALL OF WICKETS | | | |
|---|---|---|---|---|---|---|---|---|---|---|---|---|---|
| Hall | 27 | 5 | 63 | 4 | 3 | 2 | 3 | 1 | | E | WI | WI | E |
| Griffith | 31·2 | 7 | 72 | 1 | 5 | 2 | 13 | 1 | *Wkt* | *1st* | *1st* | *2nd* | *2nd* |
| Sobers | 31 | 11 | 56 | 1 | 16·5 | 7 | 33 | 3 | 1st | 49 | 5 | 102 | 0 |
| Gibbs | 47 | 18 | 91 | 1 | 14 | 11 | 11 | 3 | 2nd | 178 | 5 | 122 | 0 |
| Holford | 33 | 10 | 71 | 3 | | | | | 3rd | 279 | 51 | 164 | 19 |
| | | | | | | | | | 4th | 310 | 80 | 174 | 19 |
| ENGLAND | | | | | | | | | 5th | 318 | 80 | 204 | 38 |
| Brown | 13 | 1 | 34 | 1 | 33 | 9 | 65 | 2 | 6th | 318 | 120 | 314 | 51 |
| Snow | 21 | 7 | 49 | 7 | 27 | 4 | 91 | 1 | 7th | 351 | 126 | 351 | 61 |
| Jones | 14·1 | 4 | 39 | 2 | 30 | 4 | 90 | 3 | 8th | 352 | 143 | 388 | 68 |
| D'Oliveira | | | | | 32 | 12 | 51 | 2 | 9th | 376 | 142 | 388 | – |
| Titmus | | | | | 7 | 2 | 32 | 1 | 10th | 376 | 143 | – | – |
| Barrington | | | | | 6 | 1 | 14 | 0 | | | | | |

Umpires: D. Sang Hue and H.B. de C. Jordan.

## WEST INDIES v ENGLAND 1967–68 (3rd Test)

Played at Kensington Oval, Bridgetown, Barbados, on 29 February, 1, 2, 4, 5 March.
Toss: West Indies.   Result: MATCH DRAWN.
Debuts: England – P.I. Pocock.

### WEST INDIES

| | | | | | |
|---|---|---|---|---|---|
| S.M. Nurse | c Cowdrey b Brown | 26 | c Parks b Snow | | 19 |
| G.S. Camacho | c Graveney b Barrington | 57 | lbw b Snow | | 18 |
| R.B. Kanhai | c Parks b Snow | 12 | lbw b Snow | | 12 |
| B.F. Butcher | lbw b Snow | 86 | run out | | 60 |
| C.H. Lloyd | c and b Pocock | 20 | not out | | 113 |
| G. St A. Sobers* | c Jones b Snow | 68 | b Brown | | 19 |
| D.A.J. Holford | c Graveney b Snow | 0 | | | |
| D.L. Murray† | c Parks b Brown | 27 | (7) c Snow b Pocock | | 18 |
| C.C. Griffith | not out | 16 | (8) not out | | 8 |
| W.W. Hall | c Barrington b Snow | 2 | | | |
| L.R. Gibbs | b Jones | 14 | | | |
| Extras | (B 1, LB 14, NB 6) | 21 | (B 8, LB 3, NB 6) | | 17 |
| **Total** | | **349** | (6 wickets) | | **284** |

### ENGLAND

| | | |
|---|---|---|
| J.H. Edrich | c Murray b Griffith | 146 |
| G. Boycott | lbw b Sobers | 90 |
| M.C. Cowdrey* | c Sobers b Griffith | 1 |
| K.F. Barrington | c Butcher b Hall | 17 |
| T.W. Graveney | c Sobers b Gibbs | 55 |
| J.M. Parks† | lbw b Gibbs | 0 |
| B.L. D'Oliveira | b Hall | 51 |
| D.J. Brown | b Griffith | 1 |
| J.A. Snow | c Nurse b Gibbs | 37 |
| P.I. Pocock | b Sobers | 6 |
| I.J. Jones | not out | 1 |
| Extras | (B 16, LB 9, NB 19) | 44 |
| **Total** | | **449** |

| ENGLAND | O | M | R | W | O | M | R | W | FALL OF WICKETS | | | |
|---|---|---|---|---|---|---|---|---|---|---|---|---|
| | | | | | | | | | | WI | E | WI |
| Brown | 32 | 10 | 66 | 2 | 11 | 0 | 61 | 1 | *Wkt* | *1st* | *1st* | *2nd* |
| Snow | 35 | 11 | 86 | 5 | 10 | 2 | 39 | 3 | 1st | 54 | 172 | 38 |
| D'Oliveira | 19 | 5 | 36 | 0 | 4 | 0 | 19 | 0 | 2nd | 67 | 174 | 49 |
| Pocock | 28 | 11 | 55 | 1 | 13 | 0 | 78 | 1 | 3rd | 163 | 210 | 79 |
| Jones | 21·1 | 3 | 56 | 1 | 11 | 3 | 53 | 0 | 4th | 198 | 319 | 180 |
| Barrington | 8 | 1 | 29 | 1 | 4 | 0 | 17 | 0 | 5th | 252 | 319 | 217 |
| | | | | | | | | | 6th | 252 | 349 | 274 |
| WEST INDIES | | | | | | | | | 7th | 315 | 354 | – |
| Sobers | 41 | 10 | 76 | 2 | | | | | 8th | 315 | 411 | – |
| Hall | 32 | 8 | 98 | 2 | | | | | 9th | 319 | 439 | – |
| Griffith | 24 | 6 | 71 | 3 | | | | | 10th | 349 | 449 | – |
| Gibbs | 47·5 | 16 | 98 | 3 | | | | | | | | |
| Holford | 32 | 9 | 52 | 0 | | | | | | | | |
| Lloyd | 3 | 0 | 10 | 0 | | | | | | | | |
| Nurse | 1 | 1 | 0 | 0 | | | | | | | | |

Umpires: H.B. de C. Jordan and D. Sang Hue.

# WEST INDIES v ENGLAND 1967–68 (4th Test)

Played at Queen's Park Oval, Port-of-Spain, Trinidad, on 14, 15, 16, 18, 19 March.
Toss: West Indies.   Result: ENGLAND won by seven wickets.
Debuts: Nil.

Butcher, whose leg-breaks had been allowed only one spell of six overs in his previous 31 Test matches, took five wickets for 15 runs in a spell of ten overs. Carew set a West Indies record by bowling 16 consecutive maidens. England, set to score 215 runs in 165 minutes, won with three minutes to spare.

## WEST INDIES

| | | | | |
|---|---|---|---|---|
| G.S. Camacho | c Knott b Brown | 87 | c Graveney b Snow | 31 |
| M.C. Carew | c Lock b Brown | 36 | not out | 40 |
| S.M. Nurse | c Edrich b Barrington | 136 | run out | 9 |
| R.B. Kanhai | c Barrington b Lock | 153 | not out | 2 |
| C.H. Lloyd | b Jones | 43 | | |
| G. St A. Sobers* | c Jones b Brown | 48 | | |
| B.F. Butcher | not out | 7 | | |
| W.V. Rodriguez | b Jones | 0 | | |
| D.L. Murray† | not out | 5 | | |
| C.C. Griffith | ) did not bat | | | |
| L.R. Gibbs | ) | | | |
| Extras | (LB 6, NB 5) | 11 | (B 1, LB 7, NB 2) | 10 |
| **Total** | (7 wickets declared) | **526** | (2 wickets declared) | **92** |

## ENGLAND

| | | | | | |
|---|---|---|---|---|---|
| J.H. Edrich | c Lloyd b Carew | 32 | | b Rodriguez | 29 |
| G. Boycott | c Nurse b Rodriguez | 62 | | not out | 80 |
| M.C. Cowdrey* | c Murray b Butcher | 148 | | c Sobers b Gibbs | 71 |
| K.F. Barrington | lbw b Gibbs | 48 | | | |
| T.W. Graveney | c Murray b Rodriguez | 8 | (4) | b Gibbs | 2 |
| B.L. D'Oliveira | b Rodriguez | 0 | (5) | not out | 12 |
| A.P.E. Knott† | not out | 69 | | | |
| J.A. Snow | b Butcher | 0 | | | |
| D.J. Brown | c Murray b Butcher | 0 | | | |
| G.A.R. Lock | lbw b Butcher | 3 | | | |
| I.J. Jones | b Butcher | 1 | | | |
| Extras | (B 13, LB 11, W 2, NB 7) | 33 | | (B 11, LB 6, NB 4) | 21 |
| **Total** | | **404** | | (3 wickets) | **215** |

| ENGLAND | O | M | R | W | O | M | R | W |
|---|---|---|---|---|---|---|---|---|
| Brown | 27 | 2 | 107 | 3 | 10 | 2 | 33 | 0 |
| Snow | 20 | 3 | 68 | 0 | 9 | 0 | 29 | 1 |
| Jones | 29 | 1 | 108 | 2 | 11 | 2 | 20 | 0 |
| D'Oliveira | 15 | 2 | 62 | 0 | | | | |
| Lock | 32 | 3 | 129 | 1 | | | | |
| Barrington | 10 | 2 | 41 | 1 | | | | |
| WEST INDIES | | | | | | | | |
| Sobers | 36 | 8 | 87 | 0 | 14 | 0 | 48 | 0 |
| Griffith | 3 | 1 | 7 | 0 | | | | |
| Gibbs | 57 | 24 | 68 | 1 | 16·4 | 1 | 76 | 2 |
| Rodriguez | 35 | 4 | 145 | 3 | 10 | 1 | 34 | 1 |
| Carew | 25 | 18 | 23 | 1 | 7 | 2 | 19 | 0 |
| Butcher | 13·4 | 2 | 34 | 5 | 5 | 1 | 17 | 0 |
| Lloyd | 4 | 2 | 7 | 0 | | | | |
| Nurse | 2 | 2 | 0 | 0 | | | | |

### FALL OF WICKETS

| | WI | E | WI | E |
|---|---|---|---|---|
| Wkt | 1st | 1st | 2nd | 2nd |
| 1st | 119 | 86 | 66 | 55 |
| 2nd | 142 | 112 | 88 | 173 |
| 3rd | 415 | 245 | – | 182 |
| 4th | 421 | 260 | – | – |
| 5th | 506 | 260 | – | – |
| 6th | 513 | 373 | – | – |
| 7th | 514 | 377 | – | – |
| 8th | – | 377 | – | – |
| 9th | – | 381 | – | – |
| 10th | – | 404 | – | – |

Umpires: D. Sang Hue and R. Gosein.

# WEST INDIES v ENGLAND 1967–68 (5th Test)

Played at Bourda, Georgetown, Guyana, on 28, 29, 30 March, 1, 2, 3 April.
Toss: West Indies.    Result: MATCH DRAWN.
Debuts: Nil.

Sobers became the first to score 6,000 runs in Tests for West Indies. Pocock batted for 82 minutes before scoring his first run – the second-longest instance in Test cricket. His partnership of 109 with Lock, who made his highest Test score on his final appearance for England, remains the highest for the ninth wicket in this series. Snow took 27 wickets in the rubber (in only four Tests) to beat England's previous best in the West Indies – 21 by F.S. Trueman in 1959–60.

## WEST INDIES

| | | | | | |
|---|---|---|---|---|---|
| S.M. Nurse | c Knott b Snow | 17 | | lbw b Snow | 49 |
| G.S. Camacho | c and b Jones | 14 | | c Graveney b Snow | 26 |
| R.B. Kanhai | c Edrich b Pocock | 150 | | c Edrich b Jones | 22 |
| B.F. Butcher | run out | 18 | (6) | c Lock b Pocock | 18 |
| G. St A. Sobers* | c Cowdrey b Barrington | 152 | | not out | 95 |
| C.H. Lloyd | b Lock | 31 | (4) | c Knott b Snow | 1 |
| D.A.J. Holford | lbw b Snow | 1 | (8) | b Lock | 3 |
| D.L. Murray† | c Knott b Lock | 8 | (7) | c Boycott b Pocock | 16 |
| L.A. King | b Snow | 8 | | b Snow | 20 |
| W.W. Hall | not out | 5 | | b Snow | 7 |
| L.R. Gibbs | b Snow | 1 | | b Snow | 0 |
| Extras | (LB 3, W 2, NB 4) | 9 | | (B 1, LB 2, W 1, NB 3) | 7 |
| **Total** | | **414** | | | **264** |

## ENGLAND

| | | | | | |
|---|---|---|---|---|---|
| J.H. Edrich | c Murray b Sobers | 0 | | c Gibbs b Sobers | 6 |
| G. Boycott | c Murray b Hall | 116 | | b Gibbs | 30 |
| M.C. Cowdrey* | lbw b Sobers | 59 | | lbw b Gibbs | 82 |
| T.W. Graveney | c Murray b Hall | 27 | | c Murray b Gibbs | 0 |
| K.F. Barrington | c Kanhai b Sobber | 4 | | c Lloyd b Gibbs | 0 |
| B.L. D'Oliveira | c Nurse b Holford | 27 | | c and b Gibbs | 2 |
| A.P.E. Knott† | lbw b Holford | 7 | | not out | 73 |
| J.A. Snow | b Gibbs | 0 | | lbw b Sobers | 1 |
| G.A.R. Lock | b King | 89 | | c King b Sobers | 2 |
| P.I. Pocock | c and b King | 13 | | c Lloyd b Gibbs | 0 |
| I.J. Jones | not out | 0 | | not out | 0 |
| Extras | (B 12, LB 14, NB 3) | 29 | | (B 9, W 1) | 10 |
| **Total** | | **371** | | (9 wickets) | **206** |

| ENGLAND | O | M | R | W | O | M | R | W |
|---|---|---|---|---|---|---|---|---|
| Snow | 27·4 | 2 | 82 | 4 | 15·2 | 0 | 60 | 6 |
| Jones | 31 | 5 | 114 | 1 | 17 | 1 | 81 | 1 |
| D'Oliveira | 8 | 1 | 27 | 0 | 8 | 0 | 28 | 0 |
| Pocock | 38 | 11 | 78 | 1 | 17 | 1 | 66 | 2 |
| Lock | 28 | 7 | 61 | 2 | 9 | 1 | 22 | 1 |
| Barrington | 18 | 4 | 43 | 1 | | | | |
| WEST INDIES | | | | | | | | |
| Sobers | 37 | 15 | 72 | 3 | 31 | 16 | 53 | 3 |
| Hall | 19 | 3 | 71 | 2 | 13 | 6 | 26 | 0 |
| King | 38·2 | 11 | 79 | 2 | 9 | 1 | 11 | 0 |
| Holford | 31 | 10 | 54 | 2 | 17 | 9 | 37 | 0 |
| Gibbs | 33 | 9 | 59 | 1 | 40 | 20 | 60 | 6 |
| Butcher | 5 | 3 | 7 | 0 | 10 | 7 | 9 | 0 |

FALL OF WICKETS

| | WI | E | WI | E |
|---|---|---|---|---|
| Wkt | 1st | 1st | 2nd | 2nd |
| 1st | 29 | 13 | 78 | 33 |
| 2nd | 35 | 185 | 84 | 37 |
| 3rd | 72 | 185 | 86 | 37 |
| 4th | 322 | 194 | 133 | 39 |
| 5th | 385 | 240 | 171 | 41 |
| 6th | 387 | 252 | 201 | 168 |
| 7th | 399 | 257 | 216 | 198 |
| 8th | 400 | 259 | 252 | 200 |
| 9th | 412 | 368 | 264 | 206 |
| 10th | 414 | 371 | 264 | — |

Umpires: H.B. de C. Jordan and C.P. Kippins.

# NEW ZEALAND v INDIA 1967–68 (1st Test)

Played at Carisbrook, Dunedin, on 15, 16, 17, 19, 20 February.
Toss: New Zealand.   Result: INDIA won by five wickets.
Debuts: New Zealand – M.G. Burgess, R.I. Harford, B.A.G. Murray.

India's first Test in New Zealand brought them their first victory outside the sub-continent. The partnership of 155 between Dowling and Congdon remains New Zealand's highest for the second wicket against all countries. All India's batsmen reached double figures in the first innings – the seventh instance in Test matches and the second by India. Desai continued batting after his jaw had been fractured by a ball from Motz and his partnership of 57 with Bedi remains the highest for India's tenth wicket against New Zealand. In the second innings, Motz's 22 included two sixes and was scored off five balls from Prasanna.

## NEW ZEALAND

| | | | | | |
|---|---|---|---|---|---|
| B.A.G. Murray | lbw b Desai | 17 | b Prasanna | | 54 |
| G.T. Dowling | lbw b Abid Ali | 143 | c Borde b Nadkarni | | 10 |
| B.E. Congdon | b Nadkarni | 58 | c Engineer b Prasanna | | 8 |
| B.W. Sinclair* | c Wadekar b Bedi | 0 | run out | | 8 |
| V. Pollard | b Abid Ali | 20 | (7) c Abid Ali b Bedi | | 15 |
| M.G. Burgess | b Nadkarni | 50 | run out | | 39 |
| B.W. Yuile | run out | 4 | (5) b Prasanna | | 2 |
| B.R. Taylor | c Engineer b Abid Ali | 7 | (9) c Engineer b Prasanna | | 14 |
| R.C. Motz | c Surti b Desai | 10 | (8) c sub (R. Saxena) b Prasanna | | 22 |
| J.C. Alabaster | c Prasanna b Abid Ali | 34 | not out | | 13 |
| R.I. Harford† | not out | 0 | lbw b Prasanna | | 6 |
| Extras | (LB 5, NB 2) | 7 | (B 6, LB 6, NB 5) | | 17 |
| **Total** | | **350** | | | **208** |

## INDIA

| | | | | | |
|---|---|---|---|---|---|
| S. Abid Ali | c Sinclair b Taylor | 21 | run out | | 10 |
| F.M. Engineer† | b Motz | 63 | c and b Alabaster | | 29 |
| A.L. Wadekar | c Harford b Alabaster | 80 | c Murray b Alabaster | | 71 |
| R.F. Surti | c Harford b Motz | 28 | b Alabaster | | 44 |
| E.A.S. Prasanna | b Motz | 23 | | | |
| Nawab of Pataudi, jr* | b Alabaster | 24 | (5) c and b Taylor | | 11 |
| M.L. Jaisimha | c Yuile b Alabaster | 17 | (6) not out | | 11 |
| C.G. Borde | c Pollard b Motz | 21 | (7) not out | | 15 |
| R.G. Nadkarni | lbw b Taylor | 12 | | | |
| R.B. Desai | not out | 32 | | | |
| B.S. Bedi | c Yuile b Motz | 22 | | | |
| Extras | (B 2, LB 6, NB 8) | 16 | (B 1, LB 8) | | 9 |
| **Total** | | **359** | (5 wickets) | | **200** |

| INDIA | O | M | R | W | O | M | R | W |
|---|---|---|---|---|---|---|---|---|
| Desai | 21 | 3 | 61 | 2 | 7 | 1 | 15 | 0 |
| Surti | 11 | 1 | 51 | 0 | 4 | 1 | 3 | 0 |
| Abid Ali | 15 | 6 | 26 | 4 | 19 | 9 | 22 | 0 |
| Bedi | 37 | 10 | 90 | 1 | 22 | 11 | 44 | 1 |
| Nadkarni | 36·3 | 19 | 31 | 2 | 12 | 7 | 13 | 1 |
| Prasanna | 37 | 14 | 84 | 0 | 40 | 11 | 94 | 6 |
| NEW ZEALAND | | | | | | | | |
| Motz | 34 | 7 | 86 | 5 | 11 | 2 | 39 | 0 |
| Taylor | 19 | 1 | 66 | 2 | 24 | 5 | 51 | 1 |
| Alabaster | 24 | 6 | 66 | 3 | 22 | 9 | 48 | 3 |
| Pollard | 19 | 5 | 55 | 0 | 10 | 1 | 30 | 0 |
| Yuile | 28 | 9 | 70 | 0 | 5 | 1 | 17 | 0 |
| Congdon | | | | | 1·4 | 1 | 6 | 0 |
| Burgess | | | | | 1 | 1 | 0 | 0 |

### FALL OF WICKETS

| | NZ | I | NZ | I |
|---|---|---|---|---|
| Wkt | 1st | 1st | 2nd | 2nd |
| 1st | 45 | 39 | 33 | 30 |
| 2nd | 200 | 118 | 57 | 49 |
| 3rd | 201 | 192 | 83 | 152 |
| 4th | 243 | 215 | 91 | 163 |
| 5th | 246 | 224 | 92 | 169 |
| 6th | 252 | 258 | 120 | – |
| 7th | 264 | 279 | 142 | – |
| 8th | 281 | 300 | 187 | – |
| 9th | 350 | 302 | 191 | – |
| 10th | 350 | 359 | 208 | – |

Umpires: D.E.A. Copps and W.T. Martin.

# NEW ZEALAND v INDIA 1967–68 (2nd Test)

Played at Lancaster Park, Christchurch, on 22, 23, 24, 26, 27 February.
Toss: India.   Result: NEW ZEALAND won by six wickets.
Debuts: New Zealand – K. Thomson.

New Zealand gained their fourth victory in 81 official Test matches and their first against India. Their second total of over 500 owed much to their captain, Dowling, who batted for 556 minutes, faced 519 balls, hit five sixes, a five, and 28 fours, and set a new record (beaten by G.M. Turner in *Test No. 696*) for the highest Test innings by a New Zealander. His partnerships of 126 with Murray, 103 with Burgess, and 119 with Thomson are still New Zealand's highest against India for the first, fourth and fifth wickets respectively.

## NEW ZEALAND

| | | | | |
|---|---|---:|---|---:|
| B.A.G. Murray | b Abid Ali | 74 | b Abid Ali | 0 |
| G.T. Dowling* | st Engineer b Prasanna | 239 | lbw b Bedi | 5 |
| B.E. Congdon | c Wadekar b Bedi | 28 | not out | 61 |
| V. Pollard | c Jaisimha b Bedi | 1 | c Jaisimha b Prasanna | 9 |
| M.G. Burgess | c Pataudi b Nadkarni | 26 | lbw b Bedi | 1 |
| K. Thomson | c Wadekar b Bedi | 69 | not out | 0 |
| G.A. Bartlett | c Wadekar b Bedi | 22 | | |
| R.C. Motz | c sub (R. Saxena) b Bedi | 1 | | |
| R.O. Collinge | c Pataudi b Nadkarni | 11 | | |
| J.C. Alabaster | c Wadekar b Bedi | 1 | | |
| R.I. Harford† | not out | 0 | | |
| Extras | (B 1, LB 13, W 1, NB 15) | 30 | (B 8, LB 1, NB 3) | 12 |
| **Total** | | **502** | (4 wickets) | **88** |

## INDIA

| | | | | |
|---|---|---:|---|---:|
| S. Abid Ali | c and b Motz | 7 | c Harford b Alabaster | 16 |
| F.M. Engineer† | c Congdon b Motz | 12 | c Burgess b Bartlett | 63 |
| A.L. Wadekar | b Motz | 15 | c Murray b Alabaster | 8 |
| R.F. Surti | c Pollard b Motz | 67 | lbw b Pollard | 45 |
| Nawab of Pataudi, jr* | c Murray b Pollard | 52 | b Bartlett | 47 |
| M.L. Jaisimha | c Murray b Collinge | 1 | (7) run out | 15 |
| C.G. Borde | lbw b Motz | 57 | (6) b Bartlett | 33 |
| R.G. Nadkarni | c Harford b Collinge | 32 | b Bartlett | 29 |
| E.A.S. Prasanna | c Dowling b Motz | 7 | c Pollard b Bartlett | 7 |
| B.S. Bedi | c Congdon b Collinge | 3 | c Murray b Bartlett | 5 |
| U.N. Kulkarni | not out | 0 | not out | 1 |
| Extras | (B 5, LB 8, NB 22) | 35 | (B 2, LB 11, NB 19) | 32 |
| **Total** | | **288** | | **301** |

| INDIA | O | M | R | W | O | M | R | W | | FALL OF | WICKETS | | |
|---|---|---|---|---|---|---|---|---|---|---|---|---|---|
| Kulkarni | 13 | 3 | 38 | 0 | | | | | | NZ | I | I | NZ |
| Surti | 20 | 3 | 65 | 0 | 2·4 | 1 | 3 | 0 | Wkt | 1st | 1st | 2nd | 2nd |
| Abid Ali | 18 | 4 | 40 | 1 | 3 | 0 | 13 | 1 | 1st | 126 | 7 | 56 | 0 |
| Nadkarni | 66 | 34 | 114 | 2 | 8 | 3 | 11 | 0 | 2nd | 208 | 30 | 82 | 30 |
| Bedi | 47·3 | 11 | 127 | 6 | 17 | 9 | 21 | 2 | 3rd | 214 | 50 | 107 | 70 |
| Prasanna | 19 | 2 | 83 | 1 | 8 | 1 | 18 | 1 | 4th | 317 | 153 | 186 | 79 |
| Jaisimha | 3 | 1 | 5 | 0 | 2 | 0 | 10 | 0 | 5th | 436 | 154 | 230 | – |
| | | | | | | | | | 6th | 471 | 179 | 231 | – |
| NEW ZEALAND | | | | | | | | | 7th | 473 | 270 | 264 | – |
| Collinge | 18·2 | 6 | 43 | 3 | 22 | 4 | 79 | 0 | 8th | 498 | 281 | 278 | – |
| Motz | 21 | 6 | 63 | 6 | 14 | 5 | 37 | 0 | 9th | 502 | 287 | 300 | – |
| Bartlett | 14 | 1 | 52 | 0 | 16·5 | 5 | 38 | 6 | 10th | 502 | 288 | 301 | – |
| Alabaster | 15 | 7 | 36 | 0 | 31 | 13 | 63 | 2 | | | | | |
| Pollard | 24 | 7 | 59 | 1 | 15 | 2 | 52 | 1 | | | | | |

Umpires: F.R. Goodall and R.W.R. Shortt.

# NEW ZEALAND v INDIA 1967–68 (3rd Test)

Played at Basin Reserve, Wellington, on 29 February, 1, 2, 4 March.
Toss: New Zealand.   Result: INDIA won by eight wickets.
Debuts: Nil.

Wadekar's innings of 143, his only hundred in Test matches, is still India's highest score in New Zealand.

## NEW ZEALAND

| Batsman | Dismissal 1 | Runs | Dismissal 2 | Runs |
|---|---|---|---|---|
| G.T. Dowling* | c Wadekar b Surti | 15 | c Abid Ali b Nadkarni | 14 |
| B.A.G. Murray | run out | 10 | c Pataudi b Nadkarni | 22 |
| B.E. Congdon | c Wadekar b Surti | 4 | c Jaisimha b Bedi | 51 |
| M.G. Burgess | c Surti b Prasanna | 66 | (5) c Pataudi b Nadkarni | 60 |
| K. Thomson | b Surti | 25 | (6) c Wadekar b Nadkarni | 0 |
| V. Pollard | c Engineer b Nadkarni | 24 | (4) c Abid Ali b Nadkarni | 1 |
| B.R. Taylor | st Engineer b Prasanna | 17 | c Subramanya b Prasanna | 28 |
| R.C. Motz | c Surti b Prasanna | 5 | c Subramanya b Prasanna | 9 |
| R.O. Collinge | c Wadekar b Prasanna | 5 | c sub (R. Saxena) b Nadkarni | 5 |
| J.C. Alabaster | not out | 3 | not out | 2 |
| R.I. Harford† | c Engineer b Prasanna | 1 | c Subramanya b Prasanna | 0 |
| Extras | (B 2, NB 9) | 11 | (B 5, LB 2) | 7 |
| **Total** | | **186** | | **199** |

## INDIA

| Batsman | Dismissal 1 | Runs | Dismissal 2 | Runs |
|---|---|---|---|---|
| S. Abid Ali | c Harford b Collinge | 11 | c Harford b Murray | 36 |
| F.M. Engineer† | run out | 44 | c Harford b Thomson | 18 |
| A.L. Wadekar | c Harford b Collinge | 143 | not out | 5 |
| R.F. Surti | c Congdon b Taylor | 10 | not out | 0 |
| Nawab of Pataudi, jr* | c Harford b Taylor | 30 | | |
| C.G. Borde | c Harford b Collinge | 10 | | |
| M.L. Jaisimha | c Harford b Alabaster | 20 | | |
| R.G. Nadkarni | c Murray b Alabaster | 3 | | |
| V. Subramanya | not out | 32 | | |
| E.A.S. Prasanna | b Taylor | 1 | | |
| B.S. Bedi | run out | 8 | | |
| Extras | (LB 8, NB 7) | 15 | | |
| **Total** | | **327** | (2 wickets) | **59** |

| INDIA | O | M | R | W | O | M | R | W |
|---|---|---|---|---|---|---|---|---|
| Surti | 22 | 6 | 44 | 3 | 8 | 1 | 31 | 0 |
| Abid Ali | 8 | 0 | 31 | 0 | | | | |
| Jaisimha | 22 | 11 | 34 | 0 | 5 | 1 | 10 | 0 |
| Bedi | 2 | 0 | 12 | 0 | 16 | 5 | 42 | 1 |
| Nadkarni | 17 | 8 | 22 | 1 | 30 | 12 | 43 | 6 |
| Prasanna | 18·2 | 6 | 32 | 5 | 20·2 | 3 | 56 | 3 |
| Subramanya | | | | | 2 | 1 | 10 | 0 |
| **NEW ZEALAND** | | | | | | | | |
| Collinge | 18 | 3 | 65 | 3 | 2 | 0 | 7 | 0 |
| Motz | 20 | 5 | 62 | 0 | 3 | 0 | 21 | 0 |
| Taylor | 27·1 | 9 | 59 | 3 | | | | |
| Alabaster | 18 | 2 | 64 | 2 | 1 | 0 | 8 | 0 |
| Pollard | 25 | 6 | 62 | 0 | 1 | 0 | 7 | 0 |
| Thomson | | | | | 3·3 | 1 | 9 | 1 |
| Burgess | | | | | 2 | 0 | 7 | 0 |
| Murray | | | | | 1 | 1 | 0 | 1 |

### FALL OF WICKETS

| Wkt | NZ 1st | I 1st | NZ 2nd | I 2nd |
|---|---|---|---|---|
| 1st | 24 | 18 | 35 | 43 |
| 2nd | 30 | 78 | 42 | 57 |
| 3rd | 33 | 97 | 49 | – |
| 4th | 88 | 163 | 135 | – |
| 5th | 154 | 186 | 148 | – |
| 6th | 155 | 256 | 179 | – |
| 7th | 160 | 268 | 192 | – |
| 8th | 169 | 295 | 193 | – |
| 9th | 182 | 296 | 199 | – |
| 10th | 186 | 327 | 199 | – |

Umpires: D.E.A. Copps and W.T. Martin.

## NEW ZEALAND v INDIA 1967–68 (4th Test)

Played at Eden Park, Auckland, on 7, 8, 9, 11, 12 March.
Toss: New Zealand.   Result: INDIA won by 272 runs.
Debuts: Nil.

Eight hours and 20 minutes of playing time were lost on the first two days. New Zealand, set 374 runs in 290 minutes, were all out 15 minutes after tea. This is the only rubber in which India have won three matches.

### INDIA

| | | | | |
|---|---|---|---|---|
| F.M. Engineer† | c Bartlett b Motz | 44 | c and b Alabaster | 48 |
| S. Abid Ali | c Dowling b Motz | 1 | c Murray b Taylor | 22 |
| A.L. Wadekar | c Ward b Bartlett | 5 | b Taylor | 1 |
| R.F. Surti | c Pollard b Bartlett | 28 | c Burgess b Bartlett | 99 |
| Nawab of Pataudi, jr* | c Pollard b Motz | 51 | lbw b Pollard | 6 |
| C.G. Borde | c Alabaster b Pollard | 41 | not out | 65 |
| M.L. Jaisimha | c Pollard b Alabaster | 19 | not out | 1 |
| V. Subramanya | run out | 3 | | |
| R.G. Nadkarni | c Burgess b Bartlett | 21 | | |
| E.A.S. Prasanna | not out | 3 | | |
| B.S. Bedi | c Murray b Motz | 0 | | |
| Extras | (B 9, LB 3, W 2, NB 22) | 36 | (B 6, LB 4, NB 9) | 19 |
| **Total** | | **252** | (5 wickets declared) | **261** |

### NEW ZEALAND

| | | | | |
|---|---|---|---|---|
| G.T. Dowling* | c Engineer b Surti | 8 | b Bedi | 37 |
| B.A.G. Murray | c Engineer b Surti | 17 | c Jaisimha b Surti | 3 |
| B.E. Congdon | c Abid Ali b Nadkarni | 27 | c Surti b Nadkarni | 3 |
| M.G. Burgess | c Subramanya b Prasanna | 11 | c Bedi b Surti | 18 |
| B.W. Sinclair | b Bedi | 20 | b Prasanna | 12 |
| V. Pollard | run out | 3 | b Bedi | 0 |
| G.A. Bartlett | c Wadekar b Prasanna | 0 | (8) b Prasanna | 11 |
| B.R. Taylor | c Abid Ali b Bedi | 7 | (9) b Prasanna | 0 |
| R.C. Motz | c and b Prasanna | 18 | (10) c Engineer b Bedi | 6 |
| J.T. Ward† | not out | 10 | (7) b Prasanna | 5 |
| J.C. Alabaster | c Bedi b Prasanna | 6 | not out | 0 |
| Extras | (B 4, NB 9) | 13 | (B 3, LB 2, NB 1) | 6 |
| **Total** | | **140** | | **101** |

| NEW ZEALAND | O | M | R | W | O | M | R | W |
|---|---|---|---|---|---|---|---|---|
| Motz | 26·4 | 12 | 51 | 4 | 16 | 4 | 44 | 0 |
| Bartlett | 26 | 11 | 66 | 3 | 15 | 1 | 40 | 1 |
| Taylor | 17 | 4 | 49 | 0 | 22 | 4 | 60 | 2 |
| Pollard | 8 | 4 | 9 | 1 | 21 | 8 | 42 | 1 |
| Alabaster | 13 | 0 | 41 | 1 | 22 | 4 | 56 | 1 |
| INDIA | | | | | | | | |
| Surti | 10 | 2 | 32 | 2 | 11 | 2 | 30 | 2 |
| Jaisimha | 7 | 3 | 14 | 0 | 3 | 1 | 5 | 0 |
| Nadkarni | 14 | 6 | 16 | 1 | 2 | 1 | 1 | 1 |
| Prasanna | 28·1 | 11 | 44 | 4 | 27 | 15 | 40 | 4 |
| Bedi | 17 | 8 | 21 | 2 | 17·4 | 11 | 14 | 3 |
| Subramanya | 1 | 1 | 0 | 0 | 1 | 0 | 5 | 0 |

### FALL OF WICKETS

| | I | NZ | I | NZ |
|---|---|---|---|---|
| Wkt | 1st | 1st | 2nd | 2nd |
| 1st | 6 | 30 | 43 | 1 |
| 2nd | 13 | 33 | 48 | 1 |
| 3rd | 69 | 67 | 112 | 5 |
| 4th | 132 | 74 | 127 | 7 |
| 5th | 175 | 77 | 253 | 7 |
| 6th | 215 | 88 | – | 7 |
| 7th | 226 | 103 | – | 9 |
| 8th | 244 | 106 | – | 9 |
| 9th | 251 | 124 | – | 10 |
| 10th | 252 | 140 | – | 10 |

Umpires: D.E.A. Copps and W.T. Martin.

## ENGLAND v AUSTRALIA 1968 (1st Test)

Played at Old Trafford, Manchester, on 6, 7, 8, 10, 11 June.
Toss: Australia.   Result: AUSTRALIA won by 159 runs.
Debuts: Nil.

Australia won at 1.02 p.m. on the fifth day.

### AUSTRALIA

| | | | | | |
|---|---|---|---|---|---|
| W.M. Lawry* | c Boycott b Barber | 81 | c Pocock b D'Oliveira | | 16 |
| I.R. Redpath | lbw b Snow | 8 | lbw b Snow | | 8 |
| R.M. Cowper | b Snow | 0 | c and b Pocock | | 37 |
| K.D. Walters | lbw b Barber | 81 | lbw b Pocock | | 86 |
| A.P. Sheahan | c D'Oliveira b Snow | 88 | c Graveney b Pocock | | 8 |
| I.M. Chappell | run out | 73 | c Knott b Pocock | | 9 |
| B.N. Jarman† | c and b Higgs | 12 | b Pocock | | 41 |
| N.J.N. Hawke | c Knott b Snow | 5 | c Edrich b Pocock | | 0 |
| G.D. McKenzie | c Cowdrey b D'Oliveira | 0 | c Snow b Barber | | 0 |
| J.W. Gleeson | c Knott b Higgs | 0 | run out | | 2 |
| A.N. Connolly | not out | 0 | not out | | 2 |
| Extras | (LB 7, NB 2) | 9 | (B 2, LB 9) | | 11 |
| **Total** | | **357** | | | **220** |

### ENGLAND

| | | | | | |
|---|---|---|---|---|---|
| J.H. Edrich | run out | 49 | c Jarman b Cowper | | 38 |
| G. Boycott | c Jarman b Cowper | 35 | c Redpath b McKenzie | | 11 |
| M.C. Cowdrey* | c Lawry b McKenzie | 4 | c Jarman b McKenzie | | 11 |
| T.W. Graveney | c McKenzie b Cowper | 2 | c Jarman b Gleeson | | 33 |
| D.L. Amiss | c Cowper b McKenzie | 0 | b Cowper | | 0 |
| R.W. Barber | c Sheahan b McKenzie | 20 | c Cowper b Hawke | | 46 |
| B.L. D'Oliveira | b Connolly | 9 | not out | | 87 |
| A.P.E. Knott† | c McKenzie b Cowper | 5 | lbw b Connolly | | 4 |
| J.A. Snow | not out | 18 | c Lawry b Connolly | | 2 |
| K. Higgs | lbw b Cowper | 2 | c Jarman b Gleeson | | 0 |
| P.I. Pocock | c Redpath b Gleeson | 6 | lbw b Gleeson | | 10 |
| Extras | (B 9, LB 3, W 3) | 15 | (B 5, LB 6) | | 11 |
| **Total** | | **165** | | | **253** |

| ENGLAND | O | M | R | W | O | M | R | W |
|---|---|---|---|---|---|---|---|---|
| Snow | 34 | 5 | 97 | 4 | 17 | 2 | 51 | 1 |
| Higgs | 35·3 | 11 | 80 | 2 | 23 | 8 | 41 | 0 |
| D'Oliveira | 25 | 11 | 38 | 1 | 5 | 3 | 7 | 1 |
| Pocock | 25 | 5 | 77 | 0 | 33 | 10 | 79 | 6 |
| Barber | 11 | 0 | 56 | 2 | 10 | 1 | 31 | 1 |
| AUSTRALIA | | | | | | | | |
| McKenzie | 28 | 11 | 33 | 3 | 18 | 3 | 52 | 2 |
| Hawke | 15 | 7 | 18 | 0 | 8 | 4 | 15 | 1 |
| Connolly | 28 | 15 | 26 | 1 | 13 | 4 | 35 | 2 |
| Gleeson | 6·3 | 2 | 21 | 1 | 30 | 14 | 44 | 3 |
| Cowper | 26 | 11 | 48 | 4 | 39 | 12 | 82 | 2 |
| Chappell | 1 | 0 | 4 | 0 | 2 | 0 | 14 | 0 |

### FALL OF WICKETS

| | A | E | A | E |
|---|---|---|---|---|
| *Wkt* | *1st* | *1st* | *2nd* | *2nd* |
| 1st | 29 | 86 | 24 | 13 |
| 2nd | 29 | 87 | 24 | 25 |
| 3rd | 173 | 89 | 106 | 91 |
| 4th | 174 | 90 | 122 | 91 |
| 5th | 326 | 97 | 140 | 105 |
| 6th | 341 | 120 | 211 | 185 |
| 7th | 351 | 137 | 211 | 214 |
| 8th | 353 | 137 | 214 | 218 |
| 9th | 357 | 144 | 214 | 219 |
| 10th | 357 | 165 | 220 | 253 |

Umpires: J.S. Buller and C.S. Elliott.

# ENGLAND v AUSTRALIA 1968 (2nd Test)

Played at Lord's, London, on 20, 21, 22, 24, 25 June.
Toss: England.   Result: MATCH DRAWN.
Debuts: Nil.

After England had won their 103rd toss against Australia, rain reduced the playing time in this 200th match of the original series of Tests by over half, a total of 15 hours 3 minutes being lost, although some play was possible on each of the five days. Barrington (damaged finger) retired hurt at 271 for 5 when 61* and resumed at 330 for 6. Australia's total of 78 was their lowest since South Africa dismissed them for 75 in 1949-50 (*Test No. 320*). Cowdrey overtook W.R. Hammond's world Test record of 110 catches when he caught Gleeson at 1st slip. Knight took his 1,000th first-class wicket when he dismissed Sheahan. Jarman, who had fractured his right index finger when keeping wicket, retired after being hit on the same finger by the first ball he received.

## ENGLAND

| | | | |
|---|---|---|---|
| J.H. Edrich | c Cowper b McKenzie | | 7 |
| G. Boycott | c Sheahan b McKenzie | | 49 |
| C. Milburn | c Walters b Gleeson | | 83 |
| M.C. Cowdrey* | c Cowper b McKenzie | | 45 |
| K.F. Barrington | c Jarman b Connolly | | 75 |
| T.W. Graveney | c Jarman b Connolly | | 14 |
| B.R. Knight | not out | | 27 |
| A.P.E. Knott† | run out | | 33 |
| J.A. Snow | not out | | 0 |
| D.J. Brown | ) did not bat | | |
| D.L. Underwood | ) | | |
| Extras | (B 7, LB 5, W 1, NB 5) | | 18 |
| **Total** | (7 wickets declared) | | **351** |

## AUSTRALIA

| | | | | | | |
|---|---|---|---|---|---|---|
| W.M. Lawry* | c Knott b Brown | 0 | | c Brown b Snow | | 28 |
| I.R. Redpath | c Cowdrey b Brown | 4 | | b Underwood | | 53 |
| R.M. Cowper | c Graveney b Snow | 8 | | c Underwood b Barrington | | 32 |
| K.D. Walters | c Knight b Brown | 26 | | b Underwood | | 0 |
| A.P. Sheahan | c Knott b Knight | 6 | | not out | | 0 |
| I.M. Chappell | lbw b Knight | 7 | | not out | | 12 |
| N.J.N. Hawke | c Cowdrey b Knight | 2 | | | | |
| G.D. McKenzie | b Brown | 5 | | | | |
| J.W. Gleeson | c Cowdrey b Brown | 14 | | | | |
| B.N. Jarman† | retired hurt | 0 | | | | |
| A.N. Connolly | not out | 0 | | | | |
| Extras | (LB 2, NB 4) | 6 | | (NB 2) | | 2 |
| **Total** | | **78** | | (4 wickets) | | **127** |

| AUSTRLIA | O | M | R | W | O | M | R | W | | FALL OF WICKETS | | |
|---|---|---|---|---|---|---|---|---|---|---|---|---|
| McKenzie | 45 | 18 | 111 | 3 | | | | | | E | A | A |
| Hawke | 35 | 7 | 82 | 0 | | | | | *Wkt* | *1st* | *1st* | *2nd* |
| Connolly | 26·3 | 8 | 55 | 2 | | | | | 1st | 10 | 1 | 66 |
| Walters | 3 | 2 | 2 | 0 | | | | | 2nd | 142 | 12 | 93 |
| Cowper | 8 | 2 | 40 | 0 | | | | | 3rd | 147 | 23 | 97 |
| Gleeson | 27 | 11 | 43 | 1 | | | | | 4th | 244 | 46 | 115 |
| | | | | | | | | | 5th | 271 | 52 | – |
| ENGLAND | | | | | | | | | 6th | 330 | 58 | – |
| Snow | 9 | 5 | 14 | 1 | 12 | 5 | 30 | 1 | 7th | 351 | 63 | – |
| Brown | 14 | 5 | 42 | 5 | 19 | 9 | 40 | 0 | 8th | – | 78 | – |
| Knight | 10·4 | 5 | 16 | 3 | 16 | 9 | 35 | 0 | 9th | – | 78 | – |
| Underwood | | | | | 18 | 15 | 8 | 2 | 10th | – | – | – |
| Barrington | | | | | 2 | 0 | 12 | 1 | | | | |

Umpires: J.S. Buller and A.E. Fagg.

# ENGLAND v AUSTRALIA 1968 (3rd Test)

Played at Edgbaston, Birmingham, on 11 (*no play*), 12, 13, 15, 16 July.
Toss: England.   Result: MATCH DRAWN.
Debuts: Nil.

Cowdrey celebrated his becoming the first to appear in 100 Test matches by scoring his 21st hundred for England. He pulled a muscle in his left leg and used Boycott as his runner when he had scored 58. Two runs later he became the second batsman after W.R. Hammond to score 7,000 runs in Test cricket. Graveney assumed the captaincy when Cowdrey was unable to field. After scoring Australia's first six runs, Lawry retired when his right-hand little finger was fractured by a ball in Snow's opening over. McKenzie deputised as captain when Australia fielded again. Rain ended the match at 12.30 p.m. when Australia needed 262 runs to win in 270 minutes.

## ENGLAND

| | | | | |
|---|---|---:|---|---:|
| J.H. Edrich | c Taber b Freeman | 88 | c Cowper b Freeman | 64 |
| G. Boycott | lbw b Gleeson | 36 | c Taber b Connolly | 31 |
| M.C. Cowdrey* | b Freeman | 104 | | |
| K.F. Barrington | lbw b Freeman | 0 | | |
| T.W. Graveney | b Connolly | 96 | (3) not out | 39 |
| B.R. Knight | c Chappell b Connolly | 6 | (4) b Connolly | 1 |
| A.P.E. Knott† | b McKenzie | 4 | (5) not out | 4 |
| R. Illingworth | lbw b Gleeson | 27 | | |
| D.J. Brown | b Connolly | 0 | | |
| J.A. Snow | c Connolly b Freeman | 19 | | |
| D.L. Underwood | not out | 14 | | |
| Extras | (B 4, LB 6, W 1, NB 4) | 15 | (LB 2, NB 1) | 3 |
| **Total** | | **409** | (3 wickets declared) | **142** |

## AUSTRALIA

| | | | | |
|---|---|---:|---|---:|
| W.M. Lawry* | retired hurt | 6 | | |
| I.R. Redpath | b Brown | 0 | lbw b Snow | 22 |
| R.M. Cowper | b Snow | 57 | (1) not out | 25 |
| I.M. Chappell | b Knight | 71 | (3) not out | 18 |
| K.D. Walters | c and b Underwood | 46 | | |
| A.P. Sheahan | b Underwood | 4 | | |
| H.B. Taber† | c Barrington b Illingworth | 16 | | |
| E.W. Freeman | b Illingworth | 6 | | |
| G.D. McKenzie | not out | 0 | | |
| J.W. Gleeson | c Illingworth b Underwood | 3 | | |
| A.N. Connolly | b Illingworth | 0 | | |
| Extras | (B 1, LB 10, NB 2) | 13 | (LB 1, NB 2) | 3 |
| **Total** | | **222** | (1 wicket) | **68** |

| AUSTRALIA | O | M | R | W | O | M | R | W | | | | | |
|---|---|---|---|---|---|---|---|---|---|---|---|---|---|
| McKenzie | 47 | 14 | 115 | 1 | 18 | 1 | 57 | 0 | | | | | |
| Freeman | 30·5 | 8 | 78 | 4 | 9 | 2 | 23 | 1 | | | | | |
| Connolly | 35 | 8 | 84 | 3 | 15 | 3 | 59 | 2 | | | | | |
| Gleeson | 46 | 19 | 84 | 2 | | | | | | | | | |
| Cowper | 7 | 1 | 25 | 0 | | | | | | | | | |
| Walters | 7 | 3 | 8 | 0 | | | | | | | | | |

FALL OF WICKETS

| Wkt | E 1st | A 1st | E 2nd | A 2nd |
|---|---|---|---|---|
| 1st | 80 | 10 | 57 | 44 |
| 2nd | 188 | 121 | 131 | – |
| 3rd | 189 | 165 | 134 | – |
| 4th | 282 | 176 | – | – |
| 5th | 293 | 213 | – | – |
| 6th | 323 | 213 | – | – |
| 7th | 374 | 219 | – | – |
| 8th | 374 | 222 | – | – |
| 9th | 376 | 222 | – | – |
| 10th | 409 | – | – | – |

| ENGLAND | O | M | R | W | O | M | R | W |
|---|---|---|---|---|---|---|---|---|
| Snow | 17 | 3 | 46 | 1 | 9 | 1 | 32 | 1 |
| Brown | 13 | 2 | 44 | 1 | 6 | 1 | 15 | 0 |
| Knight | 14 | 2 | 34 | 1 | | | | |
| Underwood | 25 | 9 | 48 | 3 | 8 | 4 | 14 | 0 |
| Illingworth | 22 | 10 | 37 | 3 | 5·2 | 2 | 4 | 0 |

Umpires: C.S. Elliott and H. Yarnold.

# ENGLAND v AUSTRALIA 1968 (4th Test)

Played at Headingley, Leeds, on 25, 26, 27, 29, 30 July.
Toss: Australia.   Result: MATCH DRAWN.
Debuts: England – K.W.R. Fletcher, R.M. Prideaux; Australia – R.J. Inverarity.

With Cowdrey and Lawry both injured, Graveney and Jarman were called upon to make their only appearances as Test captains. Australia retained the Ashes when England failed to score 326 runs in 295 minutes. Underwood's score of 45 not out is the highest by an England No. 11 against Australia.

## AUSTRALIA

| | | | | |
|---|---|---|---|---|
| R.J. Inverarity | b Snow | 8 | lbw b Illingworth | 34 |
| R.M. Cowper | b Snow | 27 | st Knott b Illingworth | 5 |
| I.R. Redpath | b Illingworth | 92 | c Edrich b Snow | 48 |
| K.D. Walters | c Barrington b Underwood | 42 | c Graveney b Snow | 56 |
| I.M. Chappell | b Brown | 65 | c Barrington b Underwood | 81 |
| A.P. Sheahan | c Knott b Snow | 38 | st Knott b Illingworth | 31 |
| B.N. Jarman*† | c Dexter b Brown | 10 | st Knott b Illingworth | 4 |
| E.W. Freeman | b Underwood | 21 | b Illingworth | 10 |
| G.D. McKenzie | lbw b Underwood | 5 | c Snow b Illingworth | 10 |
| J.W. Gleeson | not out | 2 | c Knott b Underwood | 7 |
| A.N. Connolly | c Graveney b Underwood | 0 | not out | 0 |
| Extras | (LB 4, NB 1) | 5 | (B 13, LB 8, NB 5) | 26 |
| **Total** | | **315** | | **312** |

## ENGLAND

| | | | | |
|---|---|---|---|---|
| J.H. Edrich | c Jarman b McKenzie | 62 | c Jarman b Connolly | 65 |
| R.M. Prideaux | c Freeman b Gleeson | 64 | b McKenzie | 2 |
| E.R. Dexter | b McKenzie | 10 | b Connolly | 38 |
| T.W. Graveney* | c Cowper b Connolly | 37 | c and b Cowper | 41 |
| K.F. Barrington | b Connolly | 49 | not out | 46 |
| K.W.R. Fletcher | c Jarman b Connolly | 0 | not out | 23 |
| A.P.E. Knott† | lbw b Freeman | 4 | | |
| R. Illingworth | c Gleeson b Connolly | 6 | | |
| J.A. Snow | b Connolly | 0 | | |
| D.J. Brown | b Cowper | 14 | | |
| D.L. Underwood | not out | 45 | | |
| Extras | (B 1, LB 7, NB 3) | 11 | (LB 7, NB 8) | 15 |
| **Total** | | **302** | (4 wickets) | **230** |

| ENGLAND | O | M | R | W | O | M | R | W | | FALL OF WICKETS | | | |
|---|---|---|---|---|---|---|---|---|---|---|---|---|---|
| Snow | 35 | 3 | 98 | 3 | 24 | 3 | 51 | 2 | | A | E | A | E |
| Brown | 35 | 4 | 99 | 2 | 27 | 5 | 79 | 0 | Wkt | 1st | 1st | 2nd | 2nd |
| Illingworth | 29 | 15 | 47 | 1 | 51 | 22 | 87 | 6 | 1st | 10 | 123 | 28 | 4 |
| Underwood | 27·4 | 13 | 41 | 4 | 45·1 | 22 | 52 | 2 | 2nd | 104 | 136 | 81 | 81 |
| Dexter | 7 | 0 | 25 | 0 | 1 | 0 | 3 | 0 | 3rd | 152 | 141 | 119 | 134 |
| Barrington | | | | | 6 | 1 | 14 | 0 | 4th | 188 | 209 | 198 | 168 |
| | | | | | | | | | 5th | 248 | 215 | 273 | – |
| AUSTRALIA | | | | | | | | | 6th | 267 | 235 | 281 | – |
| McKenzie | 39 | 20 | 61 | 2 | 25 | 2 | 65 | 1 | 7th | 307 | 237 | 283 | – |
| Freeman | 22 | 6 | 60 | 1 | 6 | 1 | 25 | 0 | 8th | 309 | 241 | 296 | – |
| Gleeson | 25 | 5 | 68 | 1 | 11 | 4 | 26 | 0 | 9th | 315 | 241 | 311 | – |
| Connolly | 39 | 13 | 72 | 5 | 31 | 10 | 68 | 2 | 10th | 315 | 302 | 312 | – |
| Cowper | 18 | 10 | 24 | 1 | 5 | 0 | 22 | 1 | | | | | |
| Chappell | 4 | 1 | 6 | 0 | 5 | 3 | 6 | 0 | | | | | |
| Inverarity | | | | | 1 | 0 | 3 | 0 | | | | | |

Umpires: J.S. Buller and A.E. Fagg.

# ENGLAND v AUSTRALIA 1968 (5th Test)

Played at Kennington Oval, London, on 22, 23, 24, 26, 27 August.
Toss: England.   Result: ENGLAND won by 226 runs.
Debuts: Australia – A.A. Mallett.

England won with just five minutes to spare when Inverarity padded up to a ball from Underwood after batting throughout Australia's 250-minute innings. Rain brought the players in to lunch a minute early on the final day. During the interval a freak storm completely flooded the playing area but the sun's reappearance, combined with heroic efforts by a groundstaff reinforced with volunteers from the crowd, enabled play to resume at 4.45 p.m. with Australia's score 86 for 5. Until D'Oliveira bowled Jarman at 5.24 p.m. they seemed to have saved the match. Cowdrey brought Underwood back to bowl the next over from the pavilion end and Mallett and McKenzie fell to the first and sixth balls. Gleeson survived until 5.48 p.m. Seven minutes later Inverarity made his fatal lapse and England had taken five wickets and bowled 20·3 overs in the last hour of play. Earlier Mallett had dismissed Cowdrey with his fifth ball in Test cricket.

## ENGLAND

| | | | | | |
|---|---|---|---|---|---|
| J.H. Edrich | b Chappell | 164 | c Lawry b Mallett | | 17 |
| C. Milburn | b Connolly | 8 | c Lawry b Connolly | | 18 |
| E.R. Dexter | b Gleeson | 21 | b Connolly | | 28 |
| M.C. Cowdrey* | lbw b Mattett | 16 | b Mallett | | 35 |
| T.W. Graveney | c Redpath b McKenzie | 63 | run out | | 12 |
| B.L. D'Oliveira | c Inverarity b Mallett | 158 | c Gleeson b Connolly | | 9 |
| A.P.E. Knott† | c Jarman b Mallett | 28 | run out | | 34 |
| R. Illingworth | lbw b Connolly | 8 | b Gleeson | | 10 |
| J.A. Snow | run out | 4 | c Sheahan b Gleeson | | 13 |
| D.L. Underwood | not out | 9 | not out | | 1 |
| D.J. Brown | c Sheahan b Gleeson | 2 | b Connolly | | 1 |
| Extras | (B 1, LB 11, W 1) | 13 | (LB 3) | | 3 |
| **Total** | | **494** | | | **181** |

## AUSTRALIA

| | | | | | |
|---|---|---|---|---|---|
| W.M. Lawry* | c Knott b Snow | 135 | c Milburn b Brown | | 4 |
| R.J. Inverarity | c Milburn b Snow | 1 | lbw b Underwood | | 56 |
| I.R. Redpath | c Cowdrey b Snow | 67 | lbw b Underwood | | 8 |
| I.M. Chappell | c Knott b Brown | 10 | lbw b Underwood | | 2 |
| K.D. Walters | c Knott b Brown | 5 | c Knott b Underwood | | 1 |
| A.P. Sheahan | b Illingworth | 14 | c Snow b Illingworth | | 24 |
| B.N. Jarman† | st Knott b Illingworth | 0 | b D'Oliveira | | 21 |
| G.D. McKenzie | b Brown | 12 | (9) c Brown b Underwood | | 0 |
| A.A. Mallett | not out | 43 | (8) c Brown b Underwood | | 0 |
| J.W. Gleeson | c Dexter b Underwood | 19 | b Underwood | | 5 |
| A.N. Connolly | b Underwood | 3 | not out | | 0 |
| Extras | (B 4, LB 7, NB 4) | 15 | (LB 4) | | 4 |
| **Total** | | **324** | | | **125** |

| AUSTRALIA | O | M | R | W | O | M | R | W |
|---|---|---|---|---|---|---|---|---|
| McKenzie | 40 | 8 | 87 | 1 | 4 | 0 | 14 | 0 |
| Connolly | 57 | 12 | 127 | 2 | 22·4 | 2 | 65 | 4 |
| Walters | 6 | 2 | 17 | 0 | | | | |
| Gleeson | 41·2 | 8 | 109 | 2 | 7 | 2 | 22 | 2 |
| Mallett | 36 | 11 | 87 | 3 | 25 | 4 | 77 | 2 |
| Chappell | 21 | 5 | 54 | 1 | | | | |
| **ENGLAND** | | | | | | | | |
| Snow | 35 | 12 | 67 | 3 | 11 | 5 | 22 | 0 |
| Brown | 22 | 5 | 63 | 3 | 8 | 3 | 19 | 1 |
| Illingworth | 48 | 15 | 87 | 2 | 28 | 18 | 29 | 1 |
| Underwood | 54·3 | 21 | 89 | 2 | 31·3 | 19 | 50 | 7 |
| D'Oliveira | 4 | 2 | 3 | 0 | 5 | 4 | 1 | 1 |

### FALL OF WICKETS

| Wkt | E 1st | A 1st | E 2nd | A 2nd |
|---|---|---|---|---|
| 1st | 28 | 7 | 23 | 4 |
| 2nd | 84 | 136 | 53 | 13 |
| 3rd | 113 | 151 | 67 | 19 |
| 4th | 238 | 161 | 90 | 29 |
| 5th | 359 | 185 | 114 | 65 |
| 6th | 421 | 188 | 126 | 110 |
| 7th | 458 | 237 | 149 | 110 |
| 8th | 468 | 269 | 179 | 110 |
| 9th | 489 | 302 | 179 | 120 |
| 10th | 494 | 324 | 181 | 125 |

Umpires: C.S. Elliott and A.E. Fagg.

# AUSTRALIA v WEST INDIES 1968–69 (1st Test)

Played at Woolloongabba, Brisbane, on 6, 7, 8, 10 December.
Toss: West Indies.   Result: WEST INDIES won by 125 runs.
Debuts: Nil.

West Indies gained their first victory in a Brisbane Test with a day and five minutes to spare. Chappell and Lloyd scored hundreds on their first appearances in this series. The partnership of 165 between Carew and Kanhai remains the highest for West Indies' second wicket against Australia.

## WEST INDIES

| | | | | |
|---|---|---|---|---|
| G.S. Camacho | b Gleeson | 6 | c Redpath b Connolly | 40 |
| M.C. Carew | run out | 83 | (8) not out | 71 |
| R.B. Kanhai | c Gleeson b Mallett | 94 | c Inverarity b Gleeson | 29 |
| S.M. Nurse | c Jarman b McKenzie | 25 | (2) c Mallett b Gleeson | 16 |
| B.F. Butcher | c Chappell b Connolly | 22 | (4) b Gleeson | 1 |
| G. St A. Sobers* | c Jarman b Connolly | 2 | c Jarman b Gleeson | 36 |
| C.H. Lloyd | c Jarman b Connolly | 7 | (5) lbw b McKenzie | 129 |
| D.A.J. Holford | c Jarman b Gleeson | 6 | (7) c Jarman b McKenzie | 4 |
| J.L. Hendriks† | not out | 15 | c Jarman b Chappell | 10 |
| C.C. Griffith | c Sheahan b Connolly | 8 | b Gleeson | 1 |
| L.R. Gibbs | b McKenzie | 17 | c Inverarity b Chappell | 0 |
| Extras | (B 1, LB 6, NB 4) | 11 | (B 4, LB 10, NB 2) | 16 |
| **Total** | | **296** | | **353** |

## AUSTRALIA

| | | | | |
|---|---|---|---|---|
| I.R. Redpath | c Hendriks b Sobers | 0 | c Lloyd b Sobers | 18 |
| W.M. Lawry* | c Sobers b Lloyd | 105 | b Gibbs | 9 |
| I.M. Chappell | c Sobers b Lloyd | 117 | c sub (C.A. Davis) b Sobers | 50 |
| K.R. Stackpole | c Holford b Gibbs | 1 | b Sobers | 32 |
| A.P. Sheahan | c Nurse b Holford | 14 | b Gibbs | 34 |
| R.J. Inverarity | c Holford b Gibbs | 5 | c Kanhai b Gibbs | 9 |
| B.N. Jarman† | c Sobers b Gibbs | 17 | st Hendriks b Sobers | 4 |
| G.D. McKenzie | c Gibbs b Holford | 4 | not out | 38 |
| A.A. Mallett | b Gibbs | 6 | lbw b Carew | 19 |
| J.W. Gleeson | not out | 1 | c sub (C.A. Davis) b Sobers | 10 |
| A.N. Connolly | lbw b Gibbs | 0 | c Holford b Sobers | 0 |
| Extras | (B 7, LB 1, NB 6) | 14 | (B 9, LB 7, NB 1) | 17 |
| **Total** | | **284** | | **240** |

| AUSTRALIA | O | M | R | W | O | M | R | W |
|---|---|---|---|---|---|---|---|---|
| McKenzie | 21 | 5 | 55 | 2 | 16 | 2 | 55 | 2 |
| Connolly | 19 | 5 | 60 | 4 | 21 | 1 | 75 | 1 |
| Gleeson | 28 | 7 | 72 | 2 | 33 | 5 | 122 | 5 |
| Mallett | 14 | 2 | 54 | 1 | 4 | 0 | 32 | 0 |
| Chappell | 4 | 0 | 10 | 0 | 6 | 0 | 21 | 2 |
| Stackpole | 9 | 3 | 34 | 0 | 7 | 1 | 32 | 0 |
| WEST INDIES | | | | | | | | |
| Sobers | 14 | 5 | 30 | 1 | 33·6 | 12 | 73 | 6 |
| Griffith | 12 | 1 | 47 | 0 | | | | |
| Gibbs | 39·4 | 7 | 88 | 5 | 30 | 6 | 82 | 3 |
| Holford | 25 | 6 | 88 | 2 | 14 | 1 | 31 | 0 |
| Lloyd | 8 | 1 | 17 | 2 | 2 | 0 | 7 | 0 |
| Carew | | | | | 9 | 1 | 30 | 1 |

| FALL OF WICKETS | | | | |
|---|---|---|---|---|
| | WI | A | WI | A |
| Wkt | 1st | 1st | 2nd | 2nd |
| 1st | 23 | 0 | 48 | 27 |
| 2nd | 188 | 217 | 92 | 29 |
| 3rd | 192 | 220 | 92 | 66 |
| 4th | 241 | 246 | 137 | 137 |
| 5th | 243 | 255 | 165 | 161 |
| 6th | 247 | 257 | 178 | 165 |
| 7th | 250 | 263 | 298 | 165 |
| 8th | 258 | 283 | 331 | 220 |
| 9th | 267 | 284 | 350 | 238 |
| 10th | 296 | 284 | 353 | 240 |

Umpires: C.J. Egar and L.P. Rowan.

# AUSTRALIA v WEST INDIES 1968–69 (2nd Test)

Played at Melbourne Cricket Ground on 26, 27, 28, 30 December.
Toss: Australia.   Result: AUSTRALIA won by an innings and 30 runs.
Debuts: West Indies – C.A. Davis, R.M. Edwards, R.C. Fredericks.

Australia won in the last over of the fourth (penultimate) day. McKenzie's analysis of 8 for 71 remains the best for either side in this series. Chappell scored the 1,000th hundred in Test cricket and made the same score as C. Bannerman achieved in the first Test match of all. His partnership of 298 in 310 minutes with Lawry is still the highest for the second wicket in this series. Lawry's 205 took 440 minutes and included a six and 12 fours.

## WEST INDIES

| | | | | | |
|---|---|--:|---|---|--:|
| G.S. Camacho | c Chappell b McKenzie | 0 | | lbw b Gleeson | 11 |
| R.C. Fredericks | c Redpath b McKenzie | 76 | | c Freeman b Gleeson | 47 |
| M.C. Carew | c Gleeson b McKenzie | 7 | (8) | b Stackpole | 33 |
| S.M. Nurse | c Jarman b Freeman | 22 | (5) | c Stackpole b Gleeson | 74 |
| B.F. Butcher | lbw b Gleeson | 42 | (7) | c Jarman b McKenzie | 0 |
| G. St A. Sobers* | b McKenzie | 19 | | lbw b McKenzie | 67 |
| R.B. Kanhai | c Sheahan b McKenzie | 5 | (4) | c Redpath b Freeman | 4 |
| C.A. Davis | b McKenzie | 18 | (9) | c Redpath b Gleeson | 10 |
| J.L. Hendriks† | c Chappell b McKenzie | 0 | (10) | c Redpath b Gleeson | 3 |
| R.M. Edwards | not out | 9 | (3) | run out | 21 |
| L.R. Gibbs | b McKenzie | 0 | | not out | 0 |
| Extras | (B 1, LB 1) | 2 | | (B 7, LB 3) | 10 |
| **Total** | | **200** | | | **280** |

## AUSTRALIA

| | | |
|---|---|--:|
| I.R. Redpath | c Hendriks b Edwards | 7 |
| W.M. Lawry* | c Carew b Davis | 205 |
| I.M. Chappell | b Sobers | 165 |
| K.D. Walters | c Camacho b Sobers | 76 |
| K.R. Stackpole | b Gibbs | 15 |
| A.P. Sheahan | c and b Sobers | 18 |
| B.N. Jarman† | c Butcher b Gibbs | 12 |
| E.W. Freeman | c Carew b Gibbs | 2 |
| G.D. McKenzie | b Sobers | 1 |
| J.W. Gleeson | b Gibbs | 0 |
| A.N. Connolly | not out | 3 |
| Extras | (LB 4, NB 2) | 6 |
| **Total** | | **510** |

| AUSTRALIA | O | M | R | W | O | M | R | W | FALL OF WICKETS | | | |
|---|--:|--:|--:|--:|--:|--:|--:|--:|---|--:|--:|--:|
| McKenzie | 28 | 5 | 71 | 8 | 20 | 2 | 88 | 2 | | WI | A | WI |
| Connolly | 12 | 2 | 34 | 0 | 19 | 7 | 35 | 0 | *Wkt* | *1st* | *1st* | *2nd* |
| Freeman | 7 | 0 | 32 | 1 | 11 | 1 | 31 | 1 | 1st | 0 | 14 | 23 |
| Gleeson | 25 | 8 | 49 | 1 | 26·4 | 9 | 61 | 5 | 2nd | 14 | 312 | 76 |
| Stackpole | 1 | 0 | 12 | 0 | 13 | 9 | 19 | 1 | 3rd | 42 | 435 | 85 |
| Chappell | | | | | 9 | 1 | 36 | 0 | 4th | 135 | 453 | 85 |
| | | | | | | | | | 5th | 158 | 488 | 219 |
| WEST INDIES | | | | | | | | | 6th | 170 | 501 | 219 |
| Sobers | 33·3 | 4 | 97 | 4 | | | | | 7th | 177 | 505 | 243 |
| Edwards | 26 | 1 | 128 | 1 | | | | | 8th | 177 | 506 | 264 |
| Davis | 24 | 0 | 94 | 1 | | | | | 9th | 200 | 506 | 278 |
| Gibbs | 43 | 8 | 139 | 4 | | | | | 10th | 200 | 510 | 280 |
| Carew | 10 | 2 | 46 | 0 | | | | | | | | |

Umpires: C.J. Egar and L.P. Rowan.

# AUSTRALIA v WEST INDIES 1968–69 (3rd Test)

Played at Sydney Cricket Ground on 3, 4, 5, 7, 8 January.
Toss: West Indies.   Result: AUSTRALIA won by ten wickets.
Debuts: Nil.

The partnership of 73 between Gleeson and Connolly remains the highest for the tenth wicket by either side in this series.

## WEST INDIES

| | | | | | |
|---|---|---|---|---|---|
| R.C. Fredericks | c Chappell b McKenzie | 26 | | c Redpath b Connolly | 43 |
| M.C. Carew | c Jarman b McKenzie | 30 | | c Jarman b Freeman | 10 |
| R.B. Kanhai | b McKenzie | 17 | | c Chappell b McKenzie | 69 |
| B.F. Butcher | b Stackpole | 28 | | c and b Gleeson | 101 |
| S.M. Nurse | c Redpath b Connolly | 3 | | c Stackpole b McKenzie | 17 |
| G. St A. Sobers* | b Freeman | 49 | | c Chappell b Gleeson | 36 |
| C.H. Lloyd | c Jarman b Freeman | 50 | | c Stackpole b Freeman | 13 |
| J.L. Hendriks† | c Stackpole b Freeman | 4 | (9) | c Connolly b Gleeson | 22 |
| R.M. Edwards | b Connolly | 10 | (8) | b Freeman | 0 |
| W.W. Hall | c Gleeson b McKenzie | 33 | | st Jarman b Gleeson | 5 |
| L.R. Gibbs | not out | 1 | | not out | 1 |
| Extras | (B 2, LB 10, NB 1) | 13 | | (LB 3, NB 4) | 7 |
| **Total** | | **264** | | | **324** |

## AUSTRALIA

| | | | | | |
|---|---|---|---|---|---|
| W.M. Lawry* | c Carew b Edwards | 29 | | | |
| K.R. Stackpole | c Gibbs b Hall | 58 | | not out | 21 |
| I.M. Chappell | c Kanhai b Gibbs | 33 | | | |
| I.R. Redpath | st Hendriks b Carew | 80 | | | |
| K.D. Walters | b Gibbs | 118 | | | |
| A.P. Sheahan | c Lloyd b Hall | 47 | (1) | not out | 21 |
| B.N. Jarman† | c Fredericks b Hall | 0 | | | |
| E.W. Freeman | b Edwards | 76 | | | |
| G.D. McKenzie | run out | 10 | | | |
| J.W. Gleeson | not out | 42 | | | |
| A.N. Connolly | run out | 37 | | | |
| Extras | (B 5, LB 11, W 1) | 17 | | | |
| **Total** | | **547** | | (0 wickets) | **42** |

| AUSTRALIA | O | M | R | W | O | M | R | W | | FALL OF WICKETS | | | |
|---|---|---|---|---|---|---|---|---|---|---|---|---|---|
| McKenzie | 22·1 | 3 | 85 | 4 | 24 | 2 | 80 | 2 | | WI | A | WI | A |
| Connolly | 16 | 1 | 54 | 2 | 23 | 7 | 54 | 1 | *Wkt* | *1st* | *1st* | *2nd* | *2nd* |
| Freeman | 13 | 2 | 57 | 3 | 15 | 3 | 59 | 3 | 1st | 49 | 68 | 20 | – |
| Walters | 2 | 1 | 3 | 0 | | | | | 2nd | 72 | 95 | 123 | – |
| Gleeson | 18 | 7 | 45 | 0 | 26 | 5 | 91 | 4 | 3rd | 79 | 153 | 127 | – |
| Stackpole | 4 | 2 | 7 | 1 | 5 | 0 | 33 | 0 | 4th | 85 | 235 | 168 | – |
| | | | | | | | | | 5th | 143 | 345 | 243 | – |
| WEST INDIES | | | | | | | | | 6th | 181 | 349 | 263 | – |
| Hall | 26 | 2 | 113 | 3 | 2 | 0 | 8 | 0 | 7th | 216 | 387 | 264 | – |
| Edwards | 25 | 1 | 139 | 2 | 1 | 0 | 7 | 0 | 8th | 217 | 418 | 318 | – |
| Sobers | 21 | 4 | 109 | 0 | | | | | 9th | 236 | 474 | 323 | – |
| Gibbs | 37·6 | 6 | 124 | 2 | | | | | 10th | 264 | 547 | 324 | – |
| Carew | 12 | 1 | 45 | 1 | 2 | 0 | 9 | 0 | | | | | |
| Lloyd | | | | | 2 | 0 | 8 | 0 | | | | | |
| Kanhai | | | | | 1 | 0 | 10 | 0 | | | | | |

Umpires: C.J. Egar and L.P. Rowan.

# AUSTRALIA v WEST INDIES 1968–69 (4th Test)

Played at Adelaide Oval on 24, 25, 27, 28, 29 January.
Toss: West Indies.   Result: MATCH DRAWN.
Debuts: Nil.

Although drawn, this match produced the most exciting finish of the rubber. Australia's tenth-wicket pair, Sheahan and Connolly, survived the last 26 balls – 16 of them bowled with a new ball by Sobers and Griffith. At the end of the highest scoring Test match in Australia only 20 runs and one wicket separated the two sides. West Indies 616 remains their highest score against Australia and the highest second-innings total in any Test in that country. The partnership of 122 between Holford and Hendriks is the highest for the West Indies' ninth wicket against any country and the record by either side in this series. Redpath, the non-striker, was run out by the bowler, Griffith, without a warning for backing-up before the ball had been bowled. W.A. Brown fell victim to a similar action by V.M.H. Mankad in *Test No. 291*. Nurse kept wicket after lunch in the second innings instead of Hendriks who had a sore foot.

## WEST INDIES

| | | | | | |
|---|---|---|---|---|---|
| R.C. Fredericks | lbw b Connolly | 17 | c Chappell b Connolly | | 23 |
| M.C. Carew | c Chappell b Gleeson | 36 | c Chappell b Connolly | | 90 |
| R.B. Kanhai | lbw b Connolly | 11 | b Connolly | | 80 |
| B.F. Butcher | c Chappell b Gleeson | 52 | c Sheahan b McKenzie | | 118 |
| S.M. Nurse | c and b McKenzie | 5 | (6) lbw b Gleeson | | 40 |
| G. St A. Sobers* | b Freeman | 110 | (7) c Walters b Connolly | | 52 |
| C.H. Lloyd | c Lawry b Gleeson | 10 | (8) c Redpath b Connolly | | 42 |
| D.A.J. Holford | c McKenzie b Freeman | 6 | (9) c Stackpole b McKenzie | | 80 |
| C.C. Griffith | b Freeman | 7 | (5) run out | | 24 |
| J.L. Hendriks† | not out | 10 | not out | | 37 |
| L.R. Gibbs | c Connolly b Freeman | 4 | b McKenzie | | 1 |
| Extras | (B 5, LB 2, NB 1) | 8 | (B 5, LB 12, NB 12) | | 29 |
| **Total** | | **276** | | | **616** |

## AUSTRALIA

| | | | | | |
|---|---|---|---|---|---|
| W.M. Lawry* | c Butcher b Sobers | 62 | c sub (C.A. Davis) b Sobers | | 89 |
| K.R. Stackpole | c Hendriks b Holford | 62 | c Hendriks b Gibbs | | 50 |
| I.M. Chappell | c Sobers b Gibbs | 76 | lbw b Griffith | | 96 |
| I.R. Redpath | lbw b Carew | 45 | run out | | 9 |
| K.D. Walters | c and b Griffith | 110 | run out | | 50 |
| A.P. Sheahan | b Gibbs | 51 | not out | | 11 |
| E.W. Freeman | lbw b Griffith | 33 | run out | | 1 |
| B.N. Jarman† | c Hendriks b Gibbs | 3 | run out | | 4 |
| G.D. McKenzie | c Nurse b Holford | 59 | c sub (G.S. Camacho) b Gibbs | | 4 |
| J.W. Gleeson | b Gibbs | 17 | lbw b Griffith | | 0 |
| A.N. Connolly | not out | 1 | not out | | 6 |
| Extras | (B 3, LB 6, NB 5) | 14 | (B 8, LB 10, NB 1) | | 19 |
| **Total** | | **533** | (9 wickets) | | **339** |

| AUSTRALIA | O | M | R | W | O | M | R | W |
|---|---|---|---|---|---|---|---|---|
| McKenzie | 14 | 1 | 51 | 1 | 22·2 | 4 | 90 | 3 |
| Connolly | 13 | 3 | 61 | 2 | 34 | 7 | 122 | 5 |
| Freeman | 10·3 | 0 | 52 | 4 | 18 | 3 | 96 | 0 |
| Gleeson | 25 | 5 | 91 | 3 | 35 | 2 | 176 | 1 |
| Stackpole | 3 | 1 | 13 | 0 | 12 | 3 | 44 | 0 |
| Chappell | | | | | 14 | 0 | 50 | 0 |
| Walters | | | | | 1 | 0 | 6 | 0 |
| Redpath | | | | | 1 | 0 | 3 | 0 |
| **WEST INDIES** | | | | | | | | |
| Sober | 28 | 4 | 106 | 1 | 22 | 1 | 107 | 1 |
| Griffith | 22 | 4 | 94 | 2 | 19 | 2 | 73 | 2 |
| Holford | 18·5 | 0 | 118 | 2 | 15 | 1 | 53 | 0 |
| Gibbs | 43 | 8 | 145 | 4 | 26 | 7 | 79 | 2 |
| Carew | 9 | 3 | 30 | 1 | 2 | 0 | 8 | 0 |
| Lloyd | 6 | 0 | 26 | 0 | | | | |

### FALL OF WICKETS

| | WI | A | WI | A |
|---|---|---|---|---|
| Wkt | 1st | 1st | 2nd | 2nd |
| 1st | 21 | 89 | 35 | 86 |
| 2nd | 39 | 170 | 167 | 185 |
| 3rd | 89 | 248 | 240 | 215 |
| 4th | 107 | 254 | 304 | 304 |
| 5th | 199 | 345 | 376 | 315 |
| 6th | 215 | 424 | 404 | 318 |
| 7th | 228 | 429 | 476 | 322 |
| 8th | 261 | 465 | 492 | 333 |
| 9th | 264 | 529 | 614 | 333 |
| 10th | 276 | 533 | 616 | – |

Umpires: C.J. Egar and L.P. Rowan.

# AUSTRALIA v WEST INDIES 1968–69 (5th Test)

Played at Sydney Cricket Ground on 14, 15, 16, 18, 19, 20 February.
Toss: West Indies.   Result: AUSTRALIA won by 382 runs.
Debuts: Nil.

Australia gained the biggest victory by a runs margin in this series in a match played over six days because the rubber had not been decided. Australia's total of 619 remains the highest by any side being put in to bat in a Test match and is also Australia's highest in a home Test against West Indies. Walters became the first to score a double-century and a century in the same Test; his score of 242 is the highest for either side in this series and the highest for Australia at Sydney. He was the second Australian after J. Ryder to score six fifties in consecutive innings and the first to score four hundreds in a rubber against West Indies. His partnership of 336 with Lawry, who batted for 487 minutes, remains the highest for the fourth wicket in this series. Hendriks conceded no byes in the first innings – only T.G. Evans has prevented any byes in a larger Test innings (*Test No. 280*).

## AUSTRALIA

| | | | | | |
|---|---|---|---|---|---|
| W.M. Lawry* | b Griffith | 151 | c Fredericks b Griffith | | 17 |
| K.R. Stackpole | b Hall | 20 | c Carew b Hall | | 6 |
| I.M. Chappell | lbw b Sobers | 1 | c Hendriks b Hall | | 10 |
| I.R. Redpath | c Nurse b Sobers | 0 | c Sobers b Gibbs | | 132 |
| K.D. Walters | b Gibbs | 242 | c Fredericks b Gibbs | | 103 |
| A.P. Sheahan | c Fredericks b Griffith | 27 | c Hendriks b Sobers | | 34 |
| E.W. Freeman | c Hendriks b Griffith | 56 | c Carew b Sobers | | 15 |
| G.D. McKenzie | b Gibbs | 19 | c Carew b Sobers | | 40 |
| H.B. Taber† | lbw b Hall | 48 | not out | | 15 |
| J.W. Gleeson | c Hendriks b Hall | 45 | not out | | 5 |
| A.N. Connolly | not out | 1 | | | |
| Extras | (LB 2, W 1, NB 6) | 9 | (B 4, LB 6, W 1, NB 6) | | 17 |
| **Total** | | **619** | (8 wickets declared) | | **394** |

## WEST INDIES

| | | | | | |
|---|---|---|---|---|---|
| R.C. Fredericks | c Taber b Connolly | 39 | c Taber b McKenzie | | 0 |
| M.C. Carew | c Taber b Freeman | 64 | b Connolly | | 3 |
| R.B. Kanhai | c Taber b Connolly | 44 | c Connolly b McKenzie | | 18 |
| G. St A. Sobers* | c Taber b Connolly | 13 | (5) c Redpath b Gleeson | | 113 |
| B.F. Butcher | c Sheahan b McKenzie | 10 | (4) c Gleeson b Stackpole | | 31 |
| C.H. Lloyd | b McKenzie | 53 | c Freeman b Stackpole | | 11 |
| S.M. Nurse | c Stackpole b Connolly | 9 | b Gleeson | | 137 |
| J.L. Hendriks† | c Taber b McKenzie | 1 | c Stackpole b McKenzie | | 16 |
| C.C. Griffith | c Freeman b Gleeson | 27 | b Gleeson | | 15 |
| W.W. Hall | b Gleeson | 1 | c Sheahan b Chappell | | 0 |
| L.R. Gibbs | not out | 4 | not out | | 0 |
| Extras | (B 2, LB 4, NB 8) | 14 | (B 1, LB 5, NB 2) | | 8 |
| **Total** | | **279** | | | **352** |

| WEST INDIES | O | M | R | W | O | M | R | W | | FALL OF WICKETS | | | |
|---|---|---|---|---|---|---|---|---|---|---|---|---|---|
| Hall | 35·7 | 3 | 157 | 3 | 12 | 0 | 47 | 2 | | A | WI | A | WI |
| Griffith | 37 | 1 | 175 | 3 | 14 | 0 | 41 | 1 | Wkt | 1st | 1st | 2nd | 2nd |
| Sobers | 28 | 4 | 94 | 2 | 26 | 3 | 117 | 3 | 1st | 43 | 100 | 21 | 0 |
| Gibbs | 40 | 8 | 133 | 2 | 33 | 2 | 133 | 2 | 2nd | 51 | 154 | 36 | 10 |
| Carew | 10 | 2 | 44 | 0 | 5 | 0 | 26 | 0 | 3rd | 51 | 159 | 40 | 30 |
| Lloyd | 2 | 1 | 7 | 0 | 2 | 0 | 13 | 0 | 4th | 387 | 179 | 250 | 76 |
| | | | | | | | | | 5th | 435 | 179 | 301 | 102 |
| AUSTRALIA | | | | | | | | | 6th | 453 | 190 | 329 | 220 |
| McKenzie | 22·6 | 2 | 90 | 3 | 16 | 1 | 93 | 3 | 7th | 483 | 193 | 329 | 284 |
| Connolly | 17 | 2 | 61 | 4 | 18 | 4 | 72 | 1 | 8th | 543 | 257 | 388 | 351 |
| Freeman | 12 | 2 | 48 | 1 | 2 | 0 | 16 | 0 | 9th | 614 | 259 | – | 352 |
| Gleeson | 19 | 8 | 53 | 2 | 15·2 | 1 | 84 | 3 | 10th | 619 | 279 | – | 352 |
| Chappell | 6 | 1 | 13 | 0 | 6 | 0 | 22 | 1 | | | | | |
| Stackpole | | | | | 7 | 0 | 57 | 2 | | | | | |

Umpires: C.J. Egar and L.P. Rowan.

# PAKISTAN v ENGLAND 1968–69 (1st Test)

Played at Lahore Stadium on 21, 22, 23, 24 February.
Toss: England.   Result: MATCH DRAWN.
Debuts: Pakistan – Aftab Gul, Asif Masood; England – R.M.H. Cottam.

Cowdrey's 22nd and last Test hundred equalled the England record held by W.R. Hammond. It was made in a match frequently interrupted by crowd invasions of the playing area and by minor riots and skirmishes. Pakistan were set to score 323 runs in 295 minutes. Graveney captained England throughout the final innings when Cowdrey went to hospital for treatment to a jarred nerve in the right forearm.

## ENGLAND

| | | | | | |
|---|---|---|---|---|---|
| J.H. Edrich | c Asif Masood b Intikhab | 54 | c Majid b Asif Masood | | 8 |
| R.M. Prideaux | c Shafqat b Asif Masood | 9 | b Majid | | 5 |
| M.C. Cowdrey* | c Wasim b Majid | 100 | c Wasim b Asif Masood | | 12 |
| T.W. Graveney | c Asif Iqbal b Intikhab | 13 | run out | | 12 |
| K.W.R. Fletcher | c Intikhab b Saeed | 20 | b Majid | | 83 |
| B.L. D'Oliveira | c Ilyas b Intikhab | 26 | c Mushtaq b Saeed | | 5 |
| A.P.E. Knott† | lbw b Saeed | 52 | b Asif Masood | | 30 |
| D.L. Underwood | c Intikhab b Saeed | 0 | c Aftab b Mushtaq | | 6 |
| D.J. Brown | b Saeed | 7 | not out | | 44 |
| P.I. Pocock | b Intikhab | 12 | b Saeed | | 1 |
| R.M.H. Cottam | not out | 4 | | | |
| Extras | (B 4, LB 2, NB 3) | 9 | (B 6, LB 9, NB 4) | | 19 |
| **Total** | | **306** | (9 wickets declared) | | **225** |

## PAKISTAN

| | | | | | |
|---|---|---|---|---|---|
| Mohammad Ilyas | lbw b Brown | 0 | c Fletcher b Brown | | 1 |
| Aftab Gul | c D'Oliveira b Brown | 12 | c Pocock b Underwood | | 29 |
| Saeed Ahmed* | c Knott b D'Oliveira | 18 | b Cottam | | 39 |
| Asif Iqbal | c D'Oliveira b Cottam | 70 | c and b Cottam | | 0 |
| Mushtaq Mohammad | c Fletcher b Cottam | 4 | not out | | 34 |
| Hanif Mohammad | b Brown | 7 | (7) not out | | 23 |
| Majid Khan | c Pocock b Underwood | 18 | (6) c Pocock b Brown | | 68 |
| Shafqat Rana | c Knott b Cottam | 30 | | | |
| Intikhab Alam | c D'Oliveira b Pocock | 12 | | | |
| Wasim Bari† | not out | 14 | | | |
| Asif Masood | b Cottam | 11 | | | |
| Extras | (B 8, LB 4, NB 1) | 13 | (B 3, LB 5, NB 1) | | 9 |
| **Total** | | **209** | (5 wickets) | | **203** |

| PAKISTAN | O | M | R | W | O | M | R | W |
|---|---|---|---|---|---|---|---|---|
| Asif Masood | 21 | 5 | 59 | 1 | 25 | 4 | 68 | 3 |
| Asif Iqbal | 4 | 2 | 11 | 0 | | | | |
| Majid | 18 | 8 | 25 | 1 | 20 | 5 | 41 | 2 |
| Intikhab | 40·1 | 8 | 117 | 4 | 15 | 5 | 29 | 0 |
| Saeed | 20 | 5 | 64 | 4 | 15·5 | 3 | 44 | 2 |
| Mushtaq | 14 | 6 | 15 | 0 | 9 | 1 | 24 | 1 |
| Shafqat | 2 | 0 | 6 | 0 | | | | |
| ENGLAND | | | | | | | | |
| Brown | 14 | 0 | 43 | 3 | 15 | 4 | 47 | 2 |
| Cottam | 22·2 | 5 | 50 | 4 | 13 | 1 | 35 | 2 |
| D'Oliveira | 8 | 2 | 28 | 1 | | | | |
| Underwood | 16 | 4 | 36 | 1 | 19 | 8 | 29 | 1 |
| Pocock | 10 | 3 | 39 | 1 | 16 | 4 | 41 | 0 |
| Fletcher | | | | | 8 | 2 | 31 | 0 |
| Graveney | | | | | 6 | 0 | 11 | 0 |
| Prideaux | | | | | 2 | 2 | 0 | 0 |

### FALL OF WICKETS

| Wkt | E 1st | P 1st | E 2nd | P 2nd |
|---|---|---|---|---|
| 1st | 41 | 0 | 8 | 6 |
| 2nd | 92 | 32 | 25 | 71 |
| 3rd | 113 | 32 | 41 | 71 |
| 4th | 182 | 52 | 46 | 156 |
| 5th | 219 | 72 | 68 | 156 |
| 6th | 246 | 119 | 136 | – |
| 7th | 257 | 145 | 151 | – |
| 8th | 287 | 176 | 201 | – |
| 9th | 294 | 187 | 225 | – |
| 10th | 306 | 209 | – | – |

Umpires: Shujauddin and Munawar Hussain.

# PAKISTAN v ENGLAND 1968–69 (2nd Test)

Played at Dacca Stadium on 28 February, 1, 2, 3, March.
Toss: Pakistan.   Result: MATCH DRAWN.
Debuts: Nil.

The only riot-free match of this rubber was played in front of crowds controlled by the student leaders of East Pakistan and without either police or army presence.

## PAKISTAN

| | | | | | |
|---|---|---|---|---|---|
| Mohammad Ilyas | c Knott b Snow | 20 | | c Snow b Cottam | 21 |
| Salahuddin | c Brown b Snow | 6 | | lbw b Underwood | 5 |
| Saeed Ahmed* | b Brown | 19 | (5) | c Knott b Underwood | 33 |
| Asif Iqbal | b Brown | 44 | (3) | b Underwood | 16 |
| Mushtaq Mohammad | c Cottam b Snow | 52 | (4) | c D'Oliveira b Underwood | 31 |
| Majid Khan | c Knott b Brown | 27 | | not out | 49 |
| Hanif Mohammad | lbw b Snow | 8 | | lbw b Underwood | 8 |
| Intikhab Alam | lbw b Underwood | 25 | | not out | 19 |
| Wasim Bari† | c Knott b Cottam | 14 | | | |
| Niaz Ahmed | not out | 16 | | | |
| Pervez Sajjad | b Cottam | 2 | | | |
| Extras | (B 4, LB 4, NB 5) | 13 | | (LB 5, NB 8) | 13 |
| **Total** | | **246** | | (6 wickets declared) | **195** |

## ENGLAND

| | | | | | |
|---|---|---|---|---|---|
| J.H. Edrich | c Mushtaq b Intikhab | 24 | | not out | 12 |
| R.M. Prideaux | c Hanif b Pervez | 4 | | not out | 18 |
| T.W. Graveney | b Pervez | 46 | | | |
| K.W.R. Fletcher | c Hanif b Saeed | 16 | | | |
| M.C. Cowdrey* | lbw b Pervez | 7 | | | |
| B.L. D'Oliveira | not out | 114 | | | |
| A.P.E. Knott† | c and b Pervez | 2 | | | |
| D.J. Brown | c Hanif b Saeed | 4 | | | |
| J.A. Snow | c Majid b Niaz | 9 | | | |
| D.L. Underwood | c Ilyas b Mushtaq | 22 | | | |
| R.M.H. Cottam | c Hanif b Saeed | 4 | | | |
| Extras | (B 14, LB 8) | 22 | | (B 2, NB 1) | 3 |
| **Total** | | **274** | | (0 wickets) | **33** |

| ENGLAND | O | M | R | W | O | M | R | W |
|---|---|---|---|---|---|---|---|---|
| Snow | 25 | 5 | 70 | 4 | 12 | 7 | 15 | 0 |
| Brown | 23 | 8 | 51 | 3 | 6 | 1 | 18 | 0 |
| Underwood | 27 | 13 | 45 | 1 | 44 | 15 | 94 | 5 |
| Cottam | 27·1 | 6 | 52 | 2 | 30 | 17 | 43 | 1 |
| D'Oliveira | 8 | 1 | 15 | 0 | 9 | 2 | 12 | 0 |
| PAKISTAN | | | | | | | | |
| Niaz | 10 | 4 | 20 | 1 | 2 | 0 | 2 | 0 |
| Majid | 11 | 4 | 15 | 0 | | | | |
| Pervez | 37 | 8 | 75 | 4 | 3 | 2 | 1 | 0 |
| Saeed | 37·4 | 15 | 59 | 3 | 3 | 2 | 4 | 0 |
| Intikhab | 26 | 7 | 65 | 1 | 4 | 0 | 19 | 0 |
| Mushtaq | 11 | 3 | 18 | 1 | | | | |
| Asif | | | | | 4 | 2 | 2 | 0 |
| Hanif | | | | | 3 | 2 | 1 | 0 |
| Ilyas | | | | | 1 | 0 | 1 | 0 |

### FALL OF WICKETS

| Wkt | P 1st | E 1st | P 2nd | E 2nd |
|---|---|---|---|---|
| 1st | 16 | 17 | 8 | – |
| 2nd | 39 | 61 | 48 | – |
| 3rd | 55 | 96 | 50 | – |
| 4th | 123 | 100 | 97 | – |
| 5th | 168 | 113 | 129 | – |
| 6th | 184 | 117 | 147 | – |
| 7th | 186 | 130 | – | – |
| 8th | 211 | 170 | – | – |
| 9th | 237 | 236 | – | – |
| 10th | 246 | 274 | – | – |

Umpires: Shujauddin and Gulzar.

# PAKISTAN v ENGLAND 1968–69 (3rd Test)

Played at National Stadium, Karachi, on 6, 7, 8 March.
Toss: England.   Result: MATCH DRAWN – abandoned because of rioting.
Debuts: Pakistan – Sarfraz Nawaz.

Rioting compelled the abandonment of this match on the penultimate morning. The playing area was invaded when Knott needed four runs for his first hundred in Test cricket. Earlier Milburn, who had joined the M.C.C. team from Western Australia where he had been playing in the Sheffield Shield, reached his hundred off 163 balls. It was his first innings in Pakistan and his last in Test cricket. Within a few weeks he had lost his left eye as a result of a car accident near Northampton.

## ENGLAND

| | | |
|---|---|---:|
| C. Milburn | c Wasim b Asif Masood | 139 |
| J.H. Edrich | c Saeed b Intikhab | 32 |
| T.W. Graveney | c Asif Iqbal b Intikhab | 105 |
| M.C. Cowdrey* | c Hanif b Intikhab | 14 |
| K.W.R. Fletcher | b Mushtaq | 38 |
| B.L. D'Oliveira | c Aftab b Mushtaq | 16 |
| A.P.E. Knott† | not out | 96 |
| J.A. Snow | b Asif Masood | 9 |
| D.J. Brown | not out | 25 |
| D.L. Underwood | ) did not bat | |
| R.N.S. Hobbs | ) | |
| Extras | (B 5, LB 12, NB 11) | 28 |
| **Total** | (7 wickets) | **502** |

## PAKISTAN

Aftab Gul
Hanif Mohamad
Mushtaq Mohammad
Asif Iqbal
Saeed Ahmed*
Majid Khan
Shafqat Rana
Intikhab Alam
Wasim Bari†
Asif Masood
Sarfraz Nawaz

| PAKISTAN | O | M | R | W |
|---|---|---|---|---|
| Asif Masood | 28 | 2 | 94 | 2 |
| Majid | 20 | 5 | 51 | 0 |
| Sarfraz | 34 | 6 | 78 | 0 |
| Intikhab | 48 | 4 | 129 | 3 |
| Saeed | 22 | 5 | 53 | 0 |
| Mushtaq | 23·1 | 5 | 69 | 2 |

Umpires: Shujauddin and Daud Khan.

FALL OF WICKETS
E

| Wkt | 1st |
|---|---|
| 1st | 78 |
| 2nd | 234 |
| 3rd | 286 |
| 4th | 309 |
| 5th | 360 |
| 6th | 374 |
| 7th | 427 |
| 8th | – |
| 9th | – |
| 10th | – |

# NEW ZEALAND v WEST INDIES 1968–69 (1st Test)

Played at Eden Park, Auckland, on 27, 28, February, 1, 3 March.
Toss: West Indies.   Result: WEST INDIES won by five wickets.
Debuts: New Zealand – B.F. Hastings, B.D. Milburn, G.M. Turner.

West Indies won with three of the fifteen mandatory last-hour overs to spare. Taylor batted only 86 minutes for New Zealand's first hundred against West Indies which he reached with a six; it remains the fifth-fastest century in Test cricket. His 124 – New Zealand's highest score against West Indies in a home Test – took only 110 minutes and included five sixes and 14 fours. It was his second hundred in both first-class and Test cricket. His fifty took 30 minutes and remains the third-fastest in a Test match. The partnership of 174 between Nurse and Butcher took only 142 minutes and is still the highest for the third wicket by either side in this series.

## NEW ZEALAND

| | | | | | |
|---|---|---|---|---|---|
| G.T. Dowling* | c Hendriks b Edwards | 18 | b Edwards | | 71 |
| G.M. Turner | c Sobers b Hall | 0 | b Edwards | | 40 |
| B.E. Congdon | c Sobers b Gibbs | 85 | lbw b Edwards | | 7 |
| B.F. Hastings | c Hendriks b Sobers | 21 | c Gibbs b Holford | | 31 |
| M.G. Burgess | c Hendriks b Sobers | 11 | c Fredericks b Holford | | 30 |
| V. Pollard | c and b Gibbs | 4 | (7) not out | | 51 |
| B.W. Yuile | c Lloyd b Holford | 20 | (8) c Hendriks b Gibbs | | 1 |
| B.R. Taylor | c Fredericks b Edwards | 124 | (6) c Gibbs b Holford | | 9 |
| R.C. Motz | c Hall b Edwards | 13 | lbw b Sobers | | 23 |
| R.S. Cunis | c Fredericks b Gibbs | 13 | not out | | 20 |
| B.D. Milburn† | not out | 4 | | | |
| Extras | (B 5, LB 2, NB 3) | 10 | (B 3, LB 2, NB 9) | | 14 |
| **Total** | | **323** | (8 wickets declared) | | **297** |

## WEST INDIES

| | | | | | |
|---|---|---|---|---|---|
| R.C. Fredericks | b Motz | 6 | c Turner b Pollard | | 23 |
| M.C. Carew | c Burgess b Yuile | 109 | c Hastings b Cunis | | 38 |
| S.M. Nurse | c Turner b Pollard | 95 | c Yuile b Motz | | 168 |
| C.H. Lloyd | lbw b Yuile | 3 | (5) run out | | 14 |
| B.F. Butcher | c Hastings b Yuile | 0 | (4) not out | | 78 |
| G. St A. Sobers* | c Milburn b Pollard | 11 | lbw b Taylor | | 0 |
| D.A.J. Holford | c Burgess b Taylor | 18 | not out | | 4 |
| J.L. Hendriks† | c Dowling b Taylor | 15 | | | |
| R.M. Edwards | c Milburn b Motz | 2 | | | |
| W.W. Hall | b Motz | 1 | | | |
| L.R. Gibbs | not out | 0 | | | |
| Extras | (B 2, LB 9, NB 5) | 16 | (B 12, LB 10, NB 1) | | 23 |
| **Total** | | **276** | (5 wickets) | | **348** |

| WEST INDIES | O | M | R | W | O | M | R | W | | FALL OF WICKETS | | | |
|---|---|---|---|---|---|---|---|---|---|---|---|---|---|
| | | | | | | | | | | NZ | WI | NZ | WI |
| Hall | 8 | 1 | 34 | 1 | 8·2 | 4 | 8 | 0 | *Wkt* | *1st* | *1st* | *2nd* | *2nd* |
| Edwards | 16 | 2 | 58 | 3 | 24 | 4 | 71 | 3 | 1st | 8 | 25 | 112 | 50 |
| Gibbs | 25·4 | 3 | 96 | 3 | 35 | 9 | 69 | 1 | 2nd | 28 | 197 | 122 | 122 |
| Sobers | 19 | 1 | 87 | 2 | 30 | 7 | 79 | 1 | 3rd | 92 | 212 | 131 | 296 |
| Holford | 5 | 1 | 38 | 1 | 15 | 1 | 56 | 3 | 4th | 122 | 212 | 185 | 320 |
| NEW ZEALAND | | | | | | | | | 5th | 135 | 225 | 200 | 320 |
| Motz | 19 | 3 | 70 | 3 | 12 | 0 | 85 | 1 | 6th | 152 | 249 | 200 | – |
| Taylor | 16·7 | 2 | 48 | 2 | 11 | 1 | 54 | 1 | 7th | 232 | 269 | 201 | – |
| Cunis | 9 | 2 | 36 | 0 | 20 | 1 | 80 | 1 | 8th | 275 | 272 | 235 | – |
| Yuile | 15 | 2 | 64 | 3 | 14 | 2 | 58 | 0 | 9th | 315 | 274 | – | – |
| Pollard | 20 | 5 | 42 | 2 | 12 | 1 | 48 | 1 | 10th | 323 | 276 | – | – |

Umpires: E.C.A. MacKintosh and R.W.R. Shortt.

# NEW ZEALAND v WEST INDIES 1968–69 (2nd Test)

Played at Basin Reserve, Wellington, on 7, 8, 10, 11 March.
Toss: New Zealand.   Result: NEW ZEALAND won by six wickets.
Debuts: Nil.

New Zealand gained their fifth Test victory and their first at Wellington. The match ended at 2.26 p.m. on the last day. Motz passed J.R. Reid's New Zealand record of 85 wickets when he dismissed Griffith. Gibbs became the first West Indies bowler to take 200 Test wickets.

## WEST INDIES

| | | | | |
|---|---|---:|---|---:|
| R.C. Fredericks | c Milburn b Motz | 15 | c Hastings b Motz | 2 |
| M.C. Carew | c Taylor b Motz | 17 | run out | 1 |
| S.M. Nurse | b Motz | 21 | c Congdon b Cunis | 16 |
| B.F. Butcher | lbw b Motz | 50 | lbw b Yuile | 59 |
| C.H. Lloyd | c Milburn b Cunis | 44 | b Cunis | 1 |
| G. St A. Sobers* | c Morgan b Motz | 20 | c Pollard b Cunis | 39 |
| D.A.J. Holford | lbw b Cunis | 1 | b Yuile | 12 |
| J.L. Hendriks† | not out | 54 | b Motz | 5 |
| C.C. Griffith | c Congdon b Motz | 31 | b Yuile | 4 |
| R.M. Edwards | run out | 22 | run out | 1 |
| L.R. Gibbs | c Milburn b Yuile | 2 | not out | 1 |
| Extras | (B 3, LB 6, W 1, NB 10) | 20 | (NB 7) | 7 |
| **Total** | | **297** | | **148** |

## NEW ZEALAND

| | | | | |
|---|---|---:|---|---:|
| G.T. Dowling* | c Gibbs b Griffith | 21 | c Hendriks b Griffith | 23 |
| G.M. Turner | c Sobers b Edwards | 74 | c Griffith b Edwards | 1 |
| B.E. Congdon | c Sobers b Carew | 52 | c Griffith b Edwards | 4 |
| B.F. Hastings | c Hendriks b Edwards | 8 | not out | 62 |
| V. Pollard | c Hendriks b Griffith | 9 | | |
| R.W. Morgan | c Gibbs b Edwards | 0 | not out | 16 |
| B.W. Yuile | c Hendriks b Sobers | 33 | (5) lbw b Gibbs | 37 |
| B.R. Taylor | c Holford b Griffith | 33 | | |
| R.G. Motz | c Gibbs b Edwards | 18 | | |
| R.S. Cunis | lbw b Edwards | 5 | | |
| B.D. Milburn† | not out | 4 | | |
| Extras | (LB 7, NB 18) | 25 | (B 13, LB 4, W 1, NB 5) | 23 |
| **Total** | | **282** | (4 wickets) | **166** |

| NEW ZEALAND | O | M | R | W | O | M | R | W |
|---|---|---|---|---|---|---|---|---|
| Motz | 18 | 2 | 69 | 6 | 13 | 3 | 44 | 2 |
| Taylor | 14 | 1 | 67 | 0 | 6 | 0 | 36 | 0 |
| Cunis | 18 | 4 | 76 | 2 | 12 | 2 | 36 | 3 |
| Yuile | 9·4 | 4 | 27 | 1 | 6·4 | 0 | 25 | 3 |
| Pollard | 2 | 0 | 19 | 0 | | | | |
| Morgan | 4 | 0 | 19 | 0 | | | | |
| WEST INDIES | | | | | | | | |
| Griffith | 26 | 2 | 92 | 3 | 15 | 6 | 29 | 1 |
| Edwards | 24·7 | 5 | 84 | 5 | 11 | 2 | 42 | 2 |
| Sobers | 9 | 2 | 22 | 1 | 8 | 2 | 22 | 0 |
| Gibbs | 14 | 3 | 41 | 0 | 14·5 | 3 | 50 | 1 |
| Carew | 10 | 3 | 18 | 1 | | | | |

### FALL OF WICKETS

| | WI | NZ | WI | NZ |
|---|---|---|---|---|
| Wkt | 1st | 1st | 2nd | 2nd |
| 1st | 27 | 41 | 2 | 20 |
| 2nd | 58 | 137 | 17 | 32 |
| 3rd | 67 | 152 | 36 | 39 |
| 4th | 130 | 169 | 38 | 113 |
| 5th | 174 | 169 | 92 | – |
| 6th | 177 | 194 | 116 | – |
| 7th | 181 | 224 | 140 | – |
| 8th | 241 | 262 | 140 | – |
| 9th | 287 | 270 | 144 | – |
| 10th | 297 | 282 | 148 | – |

Umpires: E.C.A. MacKintosh and R.W.R. Shortt.

# NEW ZEALAND v WEST INDIES 1968–69 (3rd Test)

Played at Lancaster Park, Christchurch, on 13, 14, 15, 17 March.
Toss: West Indies.   Result: MATCH DRAWN.
Debuts: Nil.

Making his final appearance in Test cricket, Nurse batted for 476 minutes and hit a six and 34 fours in the highest innings in any Test at Christchurch. It also remains the highest score for West Indies against New Zealand. Motz took the wickets of Lloyd, Sobers and Holford in six balls.

## WEST INDIES

| | | |
|---|---|---|
| R.C. Fredericks | c Turner b Motz | 4 |
| M.C. Carew | c Turner b Pollard | 91 |
| S.M. Nurse | st Milburn b Yuile | 258 |
| B.F. Butcher | lbw b Motz | 29 |
| C.H. Lloyd | c Yuile b Motz | 3 |
| G. St A. Sobers* | b Motz | 0 |
| D.A.J. Holford | b Motz | 0 |
| J.L. Hendriks† | c Milburn b Taylor | 10 |
| C.C. Griffith | c Pollard b Taylor | 8 |
| R.M. Edwards | st Milburn b Yuile | 0 |
| L.R. Gibbs | not out | 0 |
| Extras | (B 4, LB 9, NB 1) | 14 |
| **Total** | | **417** |

## NEW ZEALAND

| | | | | | |
|---|---|---|---|---|---|
| G.T. Dowling* | lbw b Edwards | 23 | | lbw b Sobers | 76 |
| G.M. Turner | b Gibbs | 30 | | c Holford b Sobers | 38 |
| B.W. Yuile | lbw b Carew | 17 | (7) | b Griffith | 20 |
| B.E. Congdon | b Gibbs | 42 | (3) | b Sobers | 43 |
| B.F. Hastings | b Holford | 0 | (4) | not out | 117 |
| M.G. Burgess | b Edwards | 26 | (5) | c Sobers b Holford | 2 |
| V. Pollard | b Holford | 21 | (6) | b Carew | 44 |
| B.R. Taylor | not out | 43 | | not out | 0 |
| R.C. Motz | c Fredericks b Holford | 6 | | | |
| R.S. Cunis | c Carew b Holford | 0 | | | |
| B.D. Milburn† | c Holford b Gibbs | 0 | | | |
| Extras | (B 5, LB 3, W 1) | 9 | | (B 10, LB 14, NB 3) | 27 |
| **Total** | | **217** | | (6 wickets) | **367** |

| NEW ZEALAND | O | M | R | W | O | M | R | W | | FALL OF WICKETS | | |
|---|---|---|---|---|---|---|---|---|---|---|---|---|
| Motz | 27 | 3 | 113 | 5 | | | | | | WI | NZ | NZ |
| Cunis | 22 | 2 | 93 | 0 | | | | | *Wkt* | *1st* | *1st* | *2nd* |
| Taylor | 14·4 | 0 | 63 | 2 | | | | | 1st | 16 | 55 | 115 |
| Pollard | 18 | 6 | 64 | 1 | | | | | 2nd | 247 | 63 | 128 |
| Yuile | 20 | 5 | 70 | 2 | | | | | 3rd | 326 | 95 | 203 |
| | | | | | | | | | 4th | 340 | 117 | 210 |
| WEST INDIES | | | | | | | | | 5th | 350 | 119 | 320 |
| Sobers | 8 | 3 | 21 | 0 | 31 | 8 | 70 | 3 | 6th | 350 | 160 | 363 |
| Griffith | 5 | 2 | 15 | 0 | 13·4 | 1 | 55 | 1 | 7th | 382 | 182 | – |
| Edwards | 15 | 4 | 30 | 2 | 21 | 6 | 67 | 0 | 8th | 413 | 200 | – |
| Gibbs | 24·3 | 6 | 64 | 3 | 19 | 4 | 42 | 0 | 9th | 417 | 216 | – |
| Holford | 20 | 5 | 66 | 4 | 25 | 5 | 82 | 1 | 10th | 417 | 217 | – |
| Carew | 8 | 2 | 12 | 1 | 9 | 4 | 24 | 1 | | | | |

Umpires: E.C.A. MacKintosh and W.T. Martin.

# ENGLAND v WEST INDIES 1969 (1st Test)

Played at Old Trafford, Manchester, on 12, 13, 14, 16, 17 June.
Toss: England.   Result: ENGLAND won by ten wickets.
Debuts: West Indies – M.L.C. Foster, V.A. Holder, J.N. Shepherd.

England's win, completed at 12.02 p.m. on the fifth day, was their first at Old Trafford since they beat India there in 1959.

## ENGLAND

| | | | | |
|---|---|---|---|---|
| G. Boycott | lbw b Shepherd | 128 | not out | 1 |
| J.H. Edrich | run out | 58 | not out | 9 |
| P.J. Sharpe | b Gibbs | 2 | | |
| T.W. Graveney | b Holder | 75 | | |
| B.L. D'Oliveira | c Hendriks b Shepherd | 57 | | |
| A.P.E. Knott† | c Gibbs b Shepherd | 0 | | |
| R. Illingworth* | c and b Gibbs | 21 | | |
| B.R. Knight | lbw b Shepherd | 31 | | |
| D.J. Brown | b Sobers | 15 | | |
| D.L. Underwood | not out | 11 | | |
| J.A. Snow | b Shepherd | 0 | | |
| Extras | (B 5, LB 9, W 1) | 15 | (LB 1, NB 1) | 2 |
| **Total** | | **413** | (0 wickets) | **12** |

## WEST INDIES

| | | | | |
|---|---|---|---|---|
| R.C. Fredericks | c Graveney b Snow | 0 | c Illingworth b Underwood | 64 |
| M.C. Carew | b Brown | 1 | c Sharpe b D'Oliveira | 44 |
| B.F. Butcher | lbw b Snow | 31 | lbw b Knight | 48 |
| C.A. Davis | c D'Oliveira b Brown | 34 | c Underwood b Illingworth | 24 |
| G. St A. Sobers* | c Edrich b Brown | 10 | c Sharpe b Knight | 48 |
| C.H. Lloyd | b Snow | 32 | c Knott b Brown | 13 |
| M.L.C. Foster | st Knott b Underwood | 4 | lbw b Brown | 3 |
| J.N. Shepherd | c Illingworth b Snow | 9 | lbw b Snow | 13 |
| J.L. Hendriks† | c Edrich b Brown | 1 | not out | 5 |
| V.A. Holder | run out | 19 | lbw b Brown | 0 |
| L.R. Gibbs | not out | 1 | b Snow | 0 |
| Extras | (LB 3, NB 2) | 5 | (B 4, LB 8, NB 1) | 13 |
| **Total** | | **147** | | **275** |

| WEST INDIES | O | M | R | W | O | M | R | W | | FALL OF WICKETS | | | |
|---|---|---|---|---|---|---|---|---|---|---|---|---|---|
| Sobers | 27 | 7 | 78 | 1 | 2 | 1 | 1 | 0 | | E | WI | WI | E |
| Holder | 38 | 11 | 93 | 1 | 2·5 | 1 | 9 | 0 | Wkt | 1st | 1st | 2nd | 2nd |
| Shepherd | 58·5 | 19 | 104 | 5 | | | | | 1st | 112 | 0 | 92 | – |
| Gibbs | 60 | 22 | 96 | 2 | | | | | 2nd | 121 | 5 | 138 | – |
| Davis | 1 | 0 | 1 | 0 | | | | | 3rd | 249 | 58 | 180 | – |
| Carew | 11 | 3 | 19 | 0 | | | | | 4th | 307 | 72 | 202 | – |
| Foster | 2 | 0 | 7 | 0 | | | | | 5th | 314 | 83 | 234 | – |
| | | | | | | | | | 6th | 343 | 92 | 256 | – |
| ENGLAND | | | | | | | | | 7th | 365 | 119 | 258 | – |
| Snow | 15 | 2 | 54 | 4 | 22·3 | 4 | 76 | 2 | 8th | 390 | 126 | 273 | – |
| Brown | 13 | 1 | 39 | 4 | 22 | 3 | 59 | 3 | 9th | 411 | 139 | 274 | – |
| Knight | 2 | 0 | 11 | 0 | 12 | 3 | 15 | 2 | 10th | 413 | 147 | 275 | – |
| Illingworth | 6 | 2 | 23 | 0 | 30 | 12 | 52 | 1 | | | | | |
| Underwood | 12 | 6 | 15 | 1 | 19 | 11 | 31 | 1 | | | | | |
| D'Oliveira | | | | | 9 | 2 | 29 | 1 | | | | | |

Umpires: J.S. Buller and C.S. Elliott.

# ENGLAND v WEST INDIES 1969 (2nd Test)

Played at Lord's, London, on 26, 27, 28, 30 June, 1 July.
Toss: West Indies.   Result: MATCH DRAWN.
Debuts: England – J.H. Hampshire; West Indies – T.M. Findlay, G.C. Shillingford.

England were set to score 332 runs in 240 minutes plus 20 overs. Hampshire became the first England batsman to score a hundred in his first Test, that match being at Lord's. His 107 took 288 minutes, came off 258 balls and included 15 fours. In England's first innings, Gibbs assumed the captaincy when Sobers left the field at 241 for 6 because of a strained thigh. It was only the second time in 75 Tests that the latter had required a substitute. In the second innings Sobers batted with Camacho as his runner throughout but later in the same day bowled 29 overs when England batted again.

## WEST INDIES

| | | | | | |
|---|---|---|---|---|---|
| R.C. Fredericks | c Hampshire b Knight | 63 | c Hampshire b Illingworth | 60 |
| G.S. Camacho | c Sharpe b Snow | 67 | b D'Oliveira | 45 |
| C.A. Davis | c Knott b Brown | 103 | c Illingworth b D'Oliveira | 0 |
| B.F. Butcher | c Hampshire b Brown | 9 | b Illingworth | 24 |
| G. St A. Sobers* | run out | 29 | (7) not out | 50 |
| C.H. Lloyd | c Illingworth b Brown | 18 | (5) c Knott b Snow | 70 |
| J.N. Shepherd | c Edrich b Snow | 32 | (6) c Sharpe b Illingworth | 11 |
| T.M. Findlay† | b Snow | 23 | c Sharpe b Knight | 11 |
| V.A. Holder | lbw b Snow | 6 | run out | 7 |
| L.R. Gibbs | not out | 18 | b Knight | 5 |
| G.C. Shillingford | c Knott b Snow | 3 | | |
| Extras | (B 5, LB 4) | 9 | (B 4, LB 7, NB 1) | 12 |
| **Total** | | **380** | (9 wickets declared) | **295** |

## ENGLAND

| | | | | | |
|---|---|---|---|---|---|
| G. Boycott | c Findlay b Shepherd | 23 | c Butcher b Shillingford | 106 |
| J.H. Edrich | c Fredericks b Holder | 7 | c Camacho b Holder | 1 |
| P.H. Parfitt | c Davis b Sobers | 4 | c Findlay b Shepherd | 39 |
| B.L. D'Oliveira | c Shepherd b Sobers | 0 | c Fredericks b Gibbs | 18 |
| P.J. Sharpe | b Holder | 11 | c Davis b Sobers | 86 |
| J.H. Hampshire | lbw b Shepherd | 107 | run out | 5 |
| A.P.E. Knott† | b Shillingford | 53 | (8) b Shillingford | 11 |
| R. Illingworth* | c and b Gibbs | 113 | (7) not out | 9 |
| B.R. Knight | lbw b Shillingford | 0 | not out | 1 |
| D.J. Brown | c Findlay b Shepherd | 1 | | |
| J.A. Snow | not out | 9 | | |
| Extras | (B 1, LB 5, NB 10) | 16 | (B 9, LB 5, NB 5) | 19 |
| **Total** | | **344** | (7 wickets) | **295** |

| ENGLAND | O | M | R | W | O | M | R | W |
|---|---|---|---|---|---|---|---|---|
| Snow | 39 | 5 | 114 | 5 | 22 | 4 | 69 | 1 |
| Brown | 38 | 8 | 99 | 3 | 9 | 3 | 25 | 0 |
| Knight | 38 | 11 | 65 | 1 | 27·5 | 6 | 78 | 2 |
| D'Oliveira | 26 | 10 | 46 | 0 | 15 | 2 | 45 | 2 |
| Illingworth | 16 | 4 | 39 | 0 | 27 | 9 | 66 | 3 |
| Parfitt | 1 | 0 | 8 | 0 | | | | |

| WEST INDIES | O | M | R | W | O | M | R | W |
|---|---|---|---|---|---|---|---|---|
| Sobers | 26 | 12 | 57 | 2 | 29 | 8 | 72 | 1 |
| Holder | 38 | 16 | 83 | 2 | 11 | 4 | 36 | 1 |
| Shillingford | 19 | 4 | 53 | 2 | 13 | 4 | 30 | 2 |
| Shepherd | 43 | 14 | 74 | 3 | 12 | 3 | 45 | 1 |
| Gibbs | 27·4 | 9 | 53 | 1 | 41 | 14 | 93 | 1 |
| Davis | 1 | 0 | 2 | 0 | | | | |
| Butcher | 3 | 1 | 6 | 0 | | | | |

## FALL OF WICKETS

| Wkt | WI 1st | E 1st | WI 2nd | E 2nd |
|---|---|---|---|---|
| 1st | 106 | 19 | 73 | 1 |
| 2nd | 151 | 37 | 73 | 94 |
| 3rd | 167 | 37 | 128 | 137 |
| 4th | 217 | 37 | 135 | 263 |
| 5th | 247 | 61 | 191 | 271 |
| 6th | 324 | 189 | 232 | 272 |
| 7th | 336 | 249 | 263 | 292 |
| 8th | 343 | 250 | 280 | – |
| 9th | 376 | 261 | 295 | – |
| 10th | 380 | 344 | – | – |

Umpires: J.S. Buller and A.E. Fagg.

# ENGLAND v WEST INDIES 1969 (3rd Test)

Played at Headingley, Leeds, on 10, 11, 12, 14, 15 July.
Toss: England.   Result: ENGLAND won by 30 runs.
Debuts: Nil.

England completed their second win in the three-match rubber at 12.16 p.m. on the fifth day and so retained the Wisden Trophy.

## ENGLAND

| | | | | | |
|---|---|---|---|---|---|
| G. Boycott | lbw b Sobers | 12 | c Findlay b Sobers | | 0 |
| J.H. Edrich | lbw b Shepherd | 79 | lbw b Sobers | | 15 |
| P.J. Sharpe | c Findlay b Holder | 6 | lbw b Sobers | | 15 |
| J.H. Hampshire | c Findlay b Holder | 1 | lbw b Shillingford | | 22 |
| B.L. D'Oliveira | c Sobers b Shepherd | 48 | c Sobers b Davis | | 39 |
| A.P.E. Knott† | c Findlay b Sobers | 44 | c Findlay b Sobers | | 31 |
| R. Illingworth* | b Shepherd | 1 | c Lloyd b Holder | | 19 |
| B.R. Knight | c Fredericks b Gibbs | 7 | c Holder b Gibbs | | 27 |
| D.L. Underwood | c Findlay b Holder | 4 | b Sobers | | 16 |
| D.J. Brown | b Holder | 12 | b Shillingford | | 34 |
| J.A. Snow | not out | 1 | not out | | 15 |
| Extras | (B 4, LB 3, NB 1) | 8 | (LB 5, W 1, NB 1) | | 7 |
| **Total** | | **223** | | | **240** |

## WEST INDIES

| | | | | | |
|---|---|---|---|---|---|
| R.C. Fredericks | lbw b Knight | 11 | c Sharpe b Snow | | 6 |
| G.S. Camacho | c Knott b Knight | 4 | c Hampshire b Underwood | | 71 |
| C.A. Davis | c Underwood b Knight | 18 | c and b Underwood | | 29 |
| B.F. Butcher | b Snow | 35 | c Knott b Underwood | | 91 |
| G. St A. Sobers* | c Sharpe b Knight | 13 | (6) b Knight | | 0 |
| C.H. Lloyd | c Snow b Brown | 27 | (5) c Knott b Illingworth | | 23 |
| T.M. Findlay† | lbw b D'Oliveira | 1 | b Knight | | 16 |
| V.A. Holder | b Snow | 35 | (9) c Sharpe b Brown | | 13 |
| L.R. Gibbs | not out | 6 | (10) c Knott b Brown | | 4 |
| G.C. Shillingford | c Knott b Brown | 3 | (11) not out | | 5 |
| J.N. Shepherd | absent hurt | – | (8) c Knott b Underwood | | 0 |
| Extras | (LB 7, NB 1) | 8 | (LB 11, NB 3) | | 14 |
| **Total** | | **161** | | | **272** |

| WEST INDIES | O | M | R | W | O | M | R | W |
|---|---|---|---|---|---|---|---|---|
| Sobers | 21 | 1 | 68 | 2 | 40 | 18 | 42 | 5 |
| Holder | 26 | 7 | 48 | 4 | 33 | 13 | 66 | 1 |
| Shillingford | 7 | 0 | 21 | 0 | 20·4 | 4 | 56 | 2 |
| Gibbs | 19 | 6 | 33 | 1 | 21 | 6 | 42 | 1 |
| Shepherd | 24 | 8 | 43 | 3 | | | | |
| Davis | 1 | 0 | 2 | 0 | 17 | 8 | 27 | 1 |
| **ENGLAND** | | | | | | | | |
| Snow | 20 | 4 | 50 | 2 | 21 | 7 | 43 | 1 |
| Brown | 7·3 | 2 | 13 | 2 | 21 | 8 | 53 | 2 |
| Knight | 22 | 5 | 63 | 4 | 18·2 | 4 | 47 | 2 |
| D'Oliveira | 15 | 8 | 27 | 1 | 10 | 3 | 22 | 0 |
| Illingworth | | | | | 14 | 5 | 38 | 1 |
| Underwood | | | | | 22 | 12 | 55 | 4 |

### FALL OF WICKETS

| | E | WI | E | WI |
|---|---|---|---|---|
| *Wkt* | *1st* | *1st* | *2nd* | *2nd* |
| 1st | 30 | 17 | 0 | 8 |
| 2nd | 52 | 37 | 23 | 69 |
| 3rd | 64 | 46 | 42 | 177 |
| 4th | 140 | 80 | 58 | 219 |
| 5th | 165 | 88 | 102 | 224 |
| 6th | 167 | 91 | 147 | 228 |
| 7th | 182 | 151 | 147 | 228 |
| 8th | 199 | 153 | 171 | 251 |
| 9th | 217 | 161 | 203 | 255 |
| 10th | 223 | – | 240 | 270 |

Umpires: C.S. Elliott and A.E. Fagg.

# ENGLAND v NEW ZEALAND 1969 (1st Test)

Played at Lord's, London, on 24, 25, 26, 28 July.
Toss: England.   Result: ENGLAND won by 230 runs.
Debuts: England – A. Ward; New Zealand – D.R. Hadlee, H.J. Howarth, K.J. Wadsworth.

England won at 6.00 on the fourth evening. Effectively they won with 30 minutes to spare as rain would have prevented any play on the fifth day. Turner was the first to carry his bat throughout a completed innings for New Zealand. At 22 years 63 days he remains the youngest player to achieve this feat in a Test. He batted for 253 minutes, faced 226 balls and hit five fours. Underwood's analysis of 7 for 32 is still the best for either country in this series.

## ENGLAND

| | | | | |
|---|---|---:|---|---:|
| G. Boycott | c Congdon b Motz | 0 | c Turner b Pollard | 47 |
| J.H. Edrich | c Motz b Taylor | 16 | c Wadsworth b Hadlee | 115 |
| P.J. Sharpe | c Turner b Taylor | 20 | c Congdon b Howarth | 46 |
| K.W.R. Fletcher | b Motz | 9 | b Howarth | 7 |
| B.L. D'Oliveira | run out | 37 | c Wadsworth b Taylor | 12 |
| A.P.E. Knott† | c and b Hadlee | 8 | lbw b Howarth | 10 |
| R. Illingworth* | c Wadsworth b Howarth | 53 | c Wadsworth b Taylor | 0 |
| B.R. Knight | c Hadlee b Pollard | 29 | b Motz | 49 |
| D.J. Brown | not out | 11 | c Wadsworth b Taylor | 7 |
| D.L. Underwood | c Pollard b Howarth | 1 | b Motz | 4 |
| A. Ward | b Taylor | 0 | not out | 19 |
| Extras | (B 1, LB 3, W 1, NB 1) | 6 | (B 4, LB 15, NB 5) | 24 |
| **Total** | | **190** | | **340** |

## NEW ZEALAND

| | | | | |
|---|---|---:|---|---:|
| G.T. Dowling* | c Illingworth b Underwood | 41 | c Knott b Ward | 4 |
| G.M. Turner | c Knott b Ward | 5 | not out | 43 |
| B.E. Congdon | c Sharpe b Ward | 41 | c Fletcher b Underwood | 17 |
| B.F. Hastings | c Ward b Illingworth | 23 | c Knott b Underwood | 0 |
| V. Pollard | c Ward b Underwood | 8 | lbw b Underwood | 0 |
| M.G. Burgess | lbw b Illingworth | 10 | lbw b Underwood | 6 |
| K.J. Wadsworth† | lbw b Illingworth | 14 | (8) b Underwood | 5 |
| B.R. Taylor | c Brown b Illingworth | 3 | (7) b Underwood | 0 |
| R.C. Motz | b Underwood | 15 | c Knott b Underwood | 23 |
| D.R. Hadlee | c Illingworth b Underwood | 1 | c Sharpe b D'Oliveira | 19 |
| H.J. Howarth | not out | 0 | b Ward | 4 |
| Extras | (B 4, LB 4) | 8 | (B 5, LB 4, NB 1) | 10 |
| **Total** | | **169** | | **131** |

| NEW ZEALAND | O | M | R | W | O | M | R | W |
|---|---|---|---|---|---|---|---|---|
| Motz | 19 | 5 | 46 | 2 | 39·4 | 17 | 78 | 2 |
| Hadlee | 14 | 2 | 48 | 1 | 16 | 5 | 43 | 1 |
| Taylor | 13·5 | 4 | 35 | 3 | 25 | 4 | 62 | 3 |
| Howarth | 19 | 9 | 24 | 2 | 49 | 20 | 102 | 3 |
| Pollard | 9 | 1 | 31 | 1 | 8 | 2 | 20 | 1 |
| Burgess | | | | | 3 | 0 | 11 | 0 |
| ENGLAND | | | | | | | | |
| Brown | 12 | 5 | 17 | 0 | 5 | 3 | 6 | 0 |
| Ward | 14 | 2 | 49 | 2 | 10·5 | 0 | 48 | 2 |
| Underwood | 29·3 | 16 | 38 | 4 | 31 | 18 | 32 | 7 |
| Knight | 10 | 3 | 20 | 0 | 3 | 1 | 5 | 0 |
| Illingworth | 22 | 8 | 37 | 4 | 18 | 9 | 24 | 0 |
| D'Oliveira | | | | | 8 | 3 | 6 | 1 |

### FALL OF WICKETS

| | E | NZ | E | NZ |
|---|---|---|---|---|
| Wkt | 1st | 1st | 2nd | 2nd |
| 1st | 0 | 14 | 125 | 5 |
| 2nd | 27 | 76 | 199 | 27 |
| 3rd | 47 | 92 | 234 | 45 |
| 4th | 47 | 101 | 243 | 45 |
| 5th | 63 | 126 | 259 | 67 |
| 6th | 113 | 137 | 259 | 67 |
| 7th | 158 | 146 | 259 | 73 |
| 8th | 186 | 150 | 284 | 101 |
| 9th | 188 | 168 | 300 | 126 |
| 10th | 190 | 169 | 340 | 131 |

Umpires: J.S. Buller and A. Jepson.

# ENGLAND v NEW ZEALAND 1969 (2nd Test)

Played at Trent Bridge, Nottingham, on 7, 8, 9, 11, 12 August.
Toss: New Zealand.   Result: MATCH DRAWN.
Debuts: Nil.

Eleven hours 48 minutes of playing time were lost in this match which was abandoned at 4.35 p.m. on the final afternoon. The third-wicket partnership of 150 between Congdon and Hastings was then the highest for any New Zealand wicket in a Test in England.

## NEW ZEALAND

| | | | | |
|---|---|---|---|---|
| G.T. Dowling* | b Ward | 18 | b Illingworth | 22 |
| B.A.G. Murray | c Knight b D'Oliveira | 23 | not out | 40 |
| B.E. Congdon | c Knott b Illingworth | 66 | not out | 1 |
| B.F. Hastings | c Sharpe b Illingworth | 83 | | |
| V. Pollard | c Fletcher b Underwood | 8 | | |
| M.G. Burgess | c Knight b Ward | 2 | | |
| K.J. Wadsworth† | c D'Oliveira b Ward | 21 | | |
| D.R. Hadlee | not out | 35 | | |
| R.O. Collinge | c Knott b Knight | 19 | | |
| R.C. Motz | b Ward | 1 | | |
| H.J. Howarth | b Knight | 3 | | |
| Extras | (B 1, LB 12, NB 2) | 15 | (LB 1, NB 2) | 3 |
| **Total** | | **294** | (1 wicket) | **66** |

## ENGLAND

| | | |
|---|---|---|
| G. Boycott | b Motz | 0 |
| J.H. Edrich | b Hadlee | 155 |
| P.J. Sharpe | c and b Howarth | 111 |
| K.W.R. Fletcher | b Hadlee | 31 |
| B.L. D'Oliveira | c and b Hadlee | 45 |
| A.P.E. Knott† | c Burgess b Motz | 15 |
| R. Illingworth* | lbw b Collinge | 33 |
| B.R. Knight | not out | 18 |
| D.L. Underwood | c Collinge b Hadlee | 16 |
| J.A. Snow | not out | 4 |
| A. Ward | did not bat | |
| Extras | (B 6, LB 12, W 1, NB 4) | 23 |
| **Total** | (8 wicket declared) | **451** |

| ENGLAND | O | M | R | W | O | M | R | W |
|---|---|---|---|---|---|---|---|---|
| Snow | 24 | 4 | 61 | 0 | 6 | 2 | 19 | 0 |
| Ward | 23 | 3 | 61 | 4 | 3 | 0 | 14 | 0 |
| Knight | 18·5 | 4 | 44 | 2 | 4 | 0 | 14 | 0 |
| D'Oliveira | 25 | 9 | 40 | 1 | 5 | 0 | 8 | 0 |
| Underwood | 22 | 8 | 44 | 1 | 3 | 1 | 5 | 0 |
| Illingworth | 12 | 4 | 15 | 2 | 2 | 0 | 3 | 1 |
| Fletcher | 3 | 1 | 14 | 0 | | | | |

| NEW ZEALAND | O | M | R | W |
|---|---|---|---|---|
| Motz | 36 | 5 | 97 | 2 |
| Collinge | 29 | 6 | 88 | 1 |
| Hadlee | 25 | 3 | 88 | 4 |
| Howarth | 41 | 14 | 89 | 1 |
| Pollard | 10 | 2 | 26 | 0 |
| Burgess | 14 | 4 | 40 | 0 |

### FALL OF WICKETS

| Wkt | NZ 1st | E 1st | NZ 2nd |
|---|---|---|---|
| 1st | 47 | 2 | 61 |
| 2nd | 53 | 251 | – |
| 3rd | 203 | 301 | – |
| 4th | 206 | 314 | – |
| 5th | 212 | 344 | – |
| 6th | 229 | 408 | – |
| 7th | 244 | 408 | – |
| 8th | 280 | 441 | – |
| 9th | 285 | – | – |
| 10th | 294 | – | – |

Umpires: C.S. Elliott and A.E.G. Rhodes.

# ENGLAND v NEW ZEALAND 1969 (3rd Test)

Played at Kennington Oval, London, on 21, 22, 23, 25, 26 August.
Toss: New Zealand.　Result: ENGLAND won by eight wickets.
Debuts: England – M.H. Denness.

England completed their second win in this rubber at 2.30 on the fifth afternoon. When he dismissed Sharpe, Motz became the first bowler to take 100 wickets in Test matches for New Zealand. Underwood's match analysis of 12 for 101 remains the best against New Zealand in England and was the series record until 1970–71 when he took 12 for 97 at Christchurch (*Test No. 685*).

## NEW ZEALAND

| | | | | | |
|---|---|---|---|---|---|
| B.A.G. Murray | b Snow | 2 | c and b Underwood | | 5 |
| G.M. Turner | c Sharpe b Underwood | 53 | b Underwood | | 25 |
| B.E. Congdon | c Sharpe b Underwood | 24 | c Knott b Ward | | 30 |
| G.T. Dowling* | c Edrich b Illingworth | 14 | lbw b Snow | | 30 |
| B.F. Hastings | b Illingworth | 21 | c Knott b Ward | | 61 |
| V. Pollard | st Knott b Illingworth | 13 | c Denness b Underwood | | 9 |
| B.R. Taylor | c Denness b Underwood | 0 | st Knott b Underwood | | 4 |
| K.J. Wadsworth† | c Arnold b Underwood | 2 | c Knott b Snow | | 10 |
| R.C. Motz | c Arnold b Underwood | 16 | c Denness b Underwood | | 11 |
| R.S. Cunis | c Illingworth b Underwood | 0 | lbw b Underwood | | 7 |
| H.J. Howarth | not out | 0 | not out | | 4 |
| Extras | (NB 5) | 5 | (B 3, LB 11, NB 19) | | 33 |
| **Total** | | **150** | | | **229** |

## ENGLAND

| | | | | | |
|---|---|---|---|---|---|
| J.H. Edrich | b Howarth | 68 | c Wadsworth b Cunis | | 22 |
| G. Boycott | b Cunis | 46 | b Cunis | | 8 |
| M.H. Denness | c Wadsworth b Cunis | 2 | not out | | 55 |
| P.J. Sharpe | lbw b Motz | 48 | not out | | 45 |
| B.L. D'Oliveira | c Cunis b Howarth | 1 | | | |
| A.P.E. Knott† | c Murray b Taylor | 21 | | | |
| R. Illingworth* | c Wadsworth b Taylor | 4 | | | |
| G.G. Arnold | b Taylor | 1 | | | |
| D.L. Underwood | lbw b Taylor | 3 | | | |
| J.A. Snow | not out | 21 | | | |
| A. Ward | c Turner b Cunis | 21 | | | |
| Extras | (LB 5, NB 1) | 6 | (B 2, LB 4, NB 2) | | 8 |
| **Total** | | **242** | (2 wickets) | | **138** |

| ENGLAND | O | M | R | W | O | M | R | W |
|---|---|---|---|---|---|---|---|---|
| Arnold | 8 | 2 | 13 | 0 | 10 | 3 | 17 | 0 |
| Snow | 10 | 4 | 22 | 1 | 21 | 4 | 52 | 2 |
| Ward | 5 | 0 | 10 | 0 | 18 | 10 | 28 | 2 |
| Illingworth | 32·3 | 13 | 55 | 3 | 15 | 9 | 20 | 0 |
| Underwood | 26 | 12 | 41 | 6 | 38·3 | 15 | 60 | 6 |
| D'Oliveira | 1 | 0 | 4 | 0 | 14 | 9 | 19 | 0 |
| NEW ZEALAND | | | | | | | | |
| Motz | 19 | 6 | 54 | 1 | 9·3 | 1 | 35 | 0 |
| Taylor | 21 | 9 | 47 | 4 | 4 | 0 | 11 | 0 |
| Cunis | 19 | 3 | 49 | 3 | 11 | 3 | 36 | 2 |
| Howarth | 34 | 14 | 66 | 2 | 23 | 10 | 32 | 0 |
| Pollard | 5 | 1 | 20 | 0 | 5 | 1 | 16 | 0 |

### FALL OF WICKETS

| | NZ | E | NZ | E |
|---|---|---|---|---|
| Wkt | 1st | 1st | 2nd | 2nd |
| 1st | 3 | 88 | 22 | 19 |
| 2nd | 77 | 118 | 39 | 56 |
| 3rd | 90 | 118 | 88 | – |
| 4th | 96 | 131 | 124 | – |
| 5th | 118 | 174 | 153 | – |
| 6th | 119 | 180 | 159 | – |
| 7th | 123 | 188 | 200 | – |
| 8th | 150 | 192 | 206 | – |
| 9th | 150 | 202 | 224 | – |
| 10th | 150 | 242 | 229 | – |

Umpires: A.E. Fagg and T.W. Spencer.

# INDIA v NEW ZEALAND 1969–70 (1st Test)

Played at Brabourne Stadium, Bombay, on 25, 26, 27, 28, 30 September.
Toss: India.   Result: INDIA won by 60 runs.
Debuts: India – C.P.S. Chauhan, A.V. Mankad, A.M. Pai.

Serious rioting in Ahmedabad prevented that city from staging its first Test match. Transferred to Bombay at short notice, it was played on an under-prepared pitch. New Zealand's total of 127 was then the lowest in any Test at Bombay and is still their lowest in India.

## INDIA

| | | | | | |
|---|---|---|---|---|---|
| S. Abid Ali | c Congdon b Hadlee | 3 | run out | | 27 |
| C.P.S. Chauhan | c Murray b Cunis | 18 | c Wadsworth b Burgess | | 34 |
| A.L. Wadekar | c Congdon b Cunis | 49 | c Wadsworth b Taylor | | 40 |
| R.F. Surti | c Hastings b Congdon | 6 | b Hadlee | | 1 |
| Nawab of Pataudi, jr* | c Congdon b Hadlee | 18 | c Howarth b Taylor | | 67 |
| Hanumant Singh | c Wadsworth b Hadlee | 1 | c Wadsworth b Hadlee | | 13 |
| A.V. Mankad | not out | 19 | (8) c and b Howarth | | 29 |
| F.M. Engineer† | run out | 20 | (7) b Taylor | | 9 |
| A.M. Pai | b Congdon | 1 | b Howarth | | 9 |
| E.A.S. Prasanna | c Turner b Congdon | 12 | not out | | 17 |
| B.S. Bedi | lbw b Taylor | 4 | c Wadsworth b Hadlee | | 4 |
| Extras | (NB 5) | 5 | (LB 4, NB 6) | | 10 |
| **Total** | | **156** | | | **260** |

## NEW ZEALAND

| | | | | | |
|---|---|---|---|---|---|
| G.M. Turner | c Surti b Prasanna | 24 | c Surti b Prasanna | | 5 |
| B.A.G. Murray | c Chauhan b Pai | 17 | c Surti b Prasanna | | 11 |
| G.T. Dowling* | c Surti b Prasanna | 32 | (4) not out | | 36 |
| B.E. Congdon | c Wadekar b Bedi | 78 | (5) c Surti b Bedi | | 4 |
| B.F. Hastings | b Abid Ali | 11 | (6) c Wadekar b Bedi | | 7 |
| M.G. Burgess | c Abid Ali b Pai | 10 | (7) c and b Bedi | | 0 |
| K.J. Wadsworth† | c Wadekar b Bedi | 14 | (8) c Pataudi b Prasanna | | 13 |
| H.J. Howarth | c Bedi b Prasanna | 1 | (11) c Engineer b Bedi | | 3 |
| B.R. Taylor | c Mankad b Prasanna | 21 | c Abid Ali b Bedi | | 9 |
| D.R. Hadlee | not out | 0 | c Pataudi b Prasanna | | 21 |
| R.S. Cunis | run out | 2 | (3) c Wadekar b Bedi | | 12 |
| Extras | (B 8, LB 5, NB 6) | 19 | (LB 1, NB 5) | | 6 |
| **Total** | | **229** | | | **127** |

| NEW ZEALAND | O | M | R | W | O | M | R | W | | | | | |
|---|---|---|---|---|---|---|---|---|---|---|---|---|---|
| Taylor | 12·2 | 2 | 37 | 1 | 18 | 8 | 30 | 3 | | | | | |
| Hadlee | 11 | 7 | 17 | 3 | 25·2 | 7 | 57 | 3 | | | | | |
| Cunis | 14 | 5 | 31 | 2 | 22 | 6 | 50 | 0 | | | | | |
| Congdon | 15 | 3 | 33 | 3 | 6 | 1 | 14 | 0 | | | | | |
| Howarth | 14 | 5 | 33 | 0 | 45 | 21 | 69 | 2 | | | | | |
| Burgess | | | | | 20 | 9 | 30 | 1 | | | | | |

**FALL OF WICKETS**

| Wkt | I 1st | NZ 1st | I 2nd | NZ 2nd |
|---|---|---|---|---|
| 1st | 4 | 27 | 44 | 10 |
| 2nd | 34 | 78 | 105 | 31 |
| 3rd | 45 | 97 | 105 | 31 |
| 4th | 99 | 125 | 111 | 35 |
| 5th | 99 | 165 | 151 | 49 |
| 6th | 102 | 203 | 165 | 49 |
| 7th | 131 | 204 | 229 | 76 |
| 8th | 132 | 227 | 233 | 88 |
| 9th | 151 | 227 | 243 | 115 |
| 10th | 156 | 229 | 260 | 127 |

| INDIA | O | M | R | W | O | M | R | W |
|---|---|---|---|---|---|---|---|---|
| Pai | 17 | 4 | 29 | 2 | 2 | 1 | 2 | 0 |
| Abid Ali | 11 | 1 | 23 | 1 | 2 | 1 | 1 | 0 |
| Surti | 6 | 2 | 10 | 0 | 2 | 1 | 2 | 0 |
| Bedi | 37 | 19 | 51 | 2 | 30·5 | 16 | 42 | 6 |
| Prasanna | 46·3 | 16 | 97 | 4 | 33 | 13 | 74 | 4 |

Umpires: A.M. Mamsa and B. Satyaji Rao.

# INDIA v NEW ZEALAND 1969–70 (2nd Test)

Played at Vidarbha C.A. Ground, Nagpur, on 3, 4, 5, 7, 8 October.
Toss: New Zealand.   Result: NEW ZEALAND won by 167 runs.
Debuts: India – A. Roy.

New Zealand gained their first success in India in the only Test match to be played at Nagpur, and after just 40 minutes' play on the fifth morning. Howarth's match analysis of 9 for 100 remains New Zealand's best in India.

## NEW ZEALAND

| | | | | | |
|---|---|---|---|---|---|
| G.T. Dowling* | lbw b Venkataraghavan | 69 | | c Engineer b Venkataraghavan | 18 |
| B.A.G. Murray | c Abid Ali b Prasanna | 30 | | lbw b Abid Ali | 2 |
| B.E. Congdon | c Engineer b Bedi | 64 | (4) | c Abid Ali b Bedi | 7 |
| M.G. Burgess | lbw b Prasanna | 89 | (5) | c Chauhan b Venkataraghavan | 12 |
| G.M. Turner | c Surti b Bedi | 2 | (3) | c Chauhan b Venkataraghavan | 57 |
| V. Pollard | c Wadekar b Abid Ali | 10 | | c Wadekar b Prasanna | 29 |
| B.W. Yuile | b Bedi | 9 | | b Prasanna | 10 |
| K.J. Wadsworth† | c and b Bedi | 1 | | lbw b Venkataraghavan | 5 |
| D.R. Hadlee | c Chauhan b Venkataraghavan | 26 | | c and b Venkataraghavan | 32 |
| R.S. Cunis | lbw b Venkataraghavan | 7 | | c Chauhan b Venkataraghavan | 2 |
| H.J. Howarth | not out | 0 | | not out | 17 |
| Extras | (B 4, LB 6, NB 2) | 12 | | (B 12, LB 8, NB 3) | 23 |
| **Total** | | **319** | | | **214** |

## INDIA

| | | | | | |
|---|---|---|---|---|---|
| S. Abid Ali | c Dowling b Pollard | 63 | | c Congdon b Cunis | 0 |
| C.P.S. Chauhan | c Turner b Yuile | 14 | | c Congdon b Howarth | 19 |
| A.L. Wadekar | b Burgess | 32 | | c and b Howarth | 23 |
| R.F. Surti | b Howarth | 26 | | c Murray b Howarth | 0 |
| S. Venkataraghavan | c Turner b Burgess | 0 | (8) | lbw b Burgess | 4 |
| Nawab of Pataudi, jr* | c Wadsworth b Burgess | 7 | (5) | lbw b Howarth | 28 |
| A.V. Mankad | c and b Howarth | 10 | (6) | c Congdon b Pollard | 7 |
| A. Roy | b Pollard | 48 | (7) | c and b Howarth | 2 |
| F.M. Engineer† | b Howarth | 40 | | st Wadsworth b Pollard | 19 |
| E.A.S. Prasanna | lbw b Howarth | 3 | | b Pollard | 0 |
| B.S. Bedi | not out | 0 | | not out | 5 |
| Extras | (B 4, LB 7, NB 3) | 14 | | (B 2) | 2 |
| **Total** | | **257** | | | **109** |

| INDIA | O | M | R | W | O | M | R | W | | FALL OF WICKETS | | | |
|---|---|---|---|---|---|---|---|---|---|---|---|---|---|
| Surti | 9 | 3 | 27 | 0 | 3 | 0 | 3 | 0 | | NZ | I | NZ | I |
| Abid Ali | 12 | 2 | 31 | 1 | 9 | 4 | 7 | 1 | Wkt | 1st | 1st | 2nd | 2nd |
| Venkataraghavan | 31 | 9 | 59 | 3 | 30·1 | 8 | 74 | 6 | 1st | 74 | 55 | 5 | 1 |
| Bedi | 45 | 18 | 98 | 4 | 32 | 13 | 46 | 1 | 2nd | 123 | 95 | 41 | 44 |
| Prasanna | 33 | 10 | 92 | 2 | 31 | 10 | 61 | 2 | 3rd | 206 | 139 | 59 | 44 |
| | | | | | | | | | 4th | 208 | 143 | 79 | 49 |
| NEW ZEALAND | | | | | | | | | 5th | 244 | 145 | 144 | 60 |
| Hadlee | 12 | 2 | 32 | 0 | 5 | 2 | 14 | 0 | 6th | 284 | 150 | 146 | 79 |
| Cunis | 15 | 6 | 45 | 0 | 4 | 2 | 8 | 1 | 7th | 286 | 161 | 152 | 84 |
| Pollard | 19·2 | 6 | 36 | 2 | 11·5 | 4 | 21 | 3 | 8th | 288 | 234 | 168 | 102 |
| Howarth | 30 | 5 | 66 | 4 | 23 | 11 | 34 | 5 | 9th | 316 | 243 | 171 | 104 |
| Yuile | 15 | 6 | 41 | 1 | 3 | 1 | 8 | 0 | 10th | 319 | 257 | 214 | 109 |
| Burgess | 8 | 4 | 23 | 3 | 6 | 0 | 18 | 1 | | | | | |
| Congdon | | | | | 3 | 1 | 4 | 0 | | | | | |

Umpires: S. Pan and V. Rajagopal.

# INDIA v NEW ZEALAND 1969–70 (3rd Test)

Played at Lal Bahadur Stadium, Hyderabad, on 15, 16 (*no play*), 18, 19, 20.
Toss: New Zealand.    Result: MATCH DRAWN.
Debuts: India – A. Gandotra, E.D. Solkar.

New Zealand's attempt to win their first Test rubber was frustrated by the weather, the crowd and by the umpires, who forgot to arrange for the pitch to be cut on the rest day. Dowling, quite correctly, refused to allow the error to be compounded when the umpires wanted it cut on the third morning. Batting on a pitch unmown for three days, India were dismissed for the lowest total in a Test at Hyderabad. Rioting prevented New Zealand from starting their innings on the third evening. Their declaration set India 268 to win on the final day (5½ hours). At 2.26 p.m., after 190 minutes of play, heavy rain brought the teams off with New Zealand just three wickets short of an historic victory. Little effort was made to restart play, even though sun baked the ground from 3.00 p.m.

## NEW ZEALAND

| | | | | | |
|---|---|---:|---|---|---:|
| G.T. Dowling* | run out | 42 | lbw b Abid Ali | | 60 |
| B.A.G. Murray | c Jaisimha b Prasanna | 80 | lbw b Prasanna | | 26 |
| G.M. Turner | c Indrajitsinhji b Bedi | 2 | (9) not out | | 15 |
| B.E. Congdon | c Pataudi b Prasanna | 3 | (3) c Prasanna b Venkataraghavan | | 18 |
| B.F. Hastings | c Venkataraghavan b Prasanna | 2 | (4) c Venkataraghavan b Prasanna | | 21 |
| M.G. Burgess | lbw b Bedi | 2 | (5) b Abid Ali | | 3 |
| B.R. Taylor | c Gandotra b Prasanna | 16 | b Venkataraghavan | | 18 |
| D.R. Hadlee | c Pataudi b Prasanna | 1 | b Abid Ali | | 0 |
| K.J. Wadsworth† | run out | 14 | (6) lbw b Prasanna | | 5 |
| R.S. Cunis | c Solkar b Abid Ali | 7 | not out | | 0 |
| H.J. Howarth | not out | 5 | | | |
| Extras | (LB 7) | 7 | (B 6, LB 3) | | 9 |
| **Total** | | **181** | (8 wickets declared) | | **175** |

## INDIA

| | | | | | |
|---|---|---:|---|---|---:|
| S. Abid Ali | b Taylor | 4 | c Howarth b Taylor | | 5 |
| K.S. Indrajitsinhji† | lbw b Cunis | 7 | c Dowling b Cunis | | 12 |
| A.L. Wadekar | c Congdon b Hadlee | 9 | c Wadsworth b Hadlee | | 14 |
| M.L. Jaisimha | c Hastings b Cunis | 0 | c Taylor b Hadlee | | 0 |
| Nawab of Pataudi, jr* | c Murray b Hadlee | 0 | lbw b Cunis | | 9 |
| A. Roy | c Wadsworth b Hadlee | 0 | c Wadsworth b Hadlee | | 4 |
| A. Gandotra | c Wadsworth b Howarth | 18 | b Cunis | | 15 |
| E.D. Solkar | c Murray b Cunis | 0 | not out | | 13 |
| S. Venkataraghavan | not out | 25 | not out | | 2 |
| E.A.S. Prasanna | b Hadlee | 2 | | | |
| B.S. Bedi | c Dowling b Congdon | 20 | | | |
| Extras | (B 1, LB 3) | 4 | (LB 2) | | 2 |
| **Total** | | **89** | (7 wickets) | | **76** |

| INDIA | O | M | R | W | O | M | R | W | FALL OF WICKETS | | | | |
|---|---|---|---|---|---|---|---|---|---|---|---|---|---|
| Jaisimha | 4 | 0 | 13 | 0 | 4 | 2 | 2 | 0 | | NZ | I | NZ | I |
| Abid Ali | 12·1 | 5 | 17 | 1 | 27 | 7 | 47 | 3 | *Wkt* | *1st* | *1st* | *2nd* | *2nd* |
| Venkataraghavan | 17 | 5 | 33 | 0 | 16 | 3 | 40 | 2 | 1st | 106 | 5 | 45 | 10 |
| Bedi | 34 | 14 | 52 | 2 | 9 | 2 | 19 | 0 | 2nd | 122 | 21 | 86 | 20 |
| Solkar | 3 | 1 | 8 | 0 | | | | | 3rd | 128 | 21 | 127 | 21 |
| Prasanna | 29 | 13 | 51 | 5 | 26 | 7 | 58 | 3 | 4th | 132 | 21 | 133 | 34 |
| | | | | | | | | | 5th | 133 | 21 | 141 | 44 |
| NEW ZEALAND | | | | | | | | | 6th | 135 | 27 | 141 | 50 |
| Hadlee | 17 | 5 | 30 | 4 | 10·4 | 2 | 31 | 3 | 7th | 136 | 28 | 144 | 66 |
| Taylor | 10 | 2 | 20 | 1 | 8 | 2 | 18 | 1 | 8th | 158 | 46 | 175 | – |
| Cunis | 14 | 7 | 12 | 3 | 12 | 5 | 12 | 3 | 9th | 166 | 49 | – | – |
| Congdon | 3·2 | 1 | 7 | 1 | 5 | 3 | 4 | 0 | 10th | 181 | 89 | – | – |
| Howarth | 9 | 2 | 12 | 1 | 5 | 2 | 4 | 0 | | | | | |
| Burgess | 1 | 0 | 4 | 0 | 6 | 3 | 5 | 0 | | | | | |

Umpires: M.V. Nagendra and S. Bhattacharya.

## PAKISTAN v NEW ZEALAND 1969–70 (1st Test)

Played at National Stadium, Karachi, on 24, 25, 26, 27 October.
Toss: Pakistan.   Result: MATCH DRAWN.
Debuts: Pakistan – Mohammad Nazir, Sadiq Mohammad, Mohammad Younis Ahmed, Zaheer Abbas.

New Zealand needed to score 230 runs in 195 minutes. This match provided the third instance of three brothers playing in the same Test, with the Mohammads emulating the Graces (*Test No. 4*) and the Hearnes (*No. 38*). The Pakistan family is alone in providing Test cricket with four brothers (Wazir, Hanif, Mushtaq and Sadiq) and a fifth, Raees, was 12th man in an official Test. This was Hanif's last appearance in Test cricket; he played in all but two of Pakistan's first 57 official matches. The partnership of 100 between Yuile and Hadlee remains the highest for the eighth wicket in this series. Mohammad Nazir's analysis of 7 for 99 in his first Test was the record for this series in Pakistan until Pervez improved upon it in the next match.

### PAKISTAN

| | | | | | |
|---|---|---|---|---|---|
| Hanif Mohammad | c Yuile b Howarth | 22 | lbw b Yuile | | 35 |
| Sadiq Mohammad | b Howarth | 69 | run out | | 37 |
| Younis Ahmed | c Dowling b Howarth | 8 | (5) c Dowling b Cunis | | 62 |
| Mushtaq Mohammad | b Yuile | 14 | c Murray b Howarth | | 19 |
| Zaheer Abbas | c Murray b Yuile | 12 | (6) c Burgess b Hadlee | | 27 |
| Asif Iqbal | st Wadsworth b Howarth | 22 | (3) c Hastings b Yuile | | 0 |
| Intikhab Alam* | c Congdon b Howarth | 0 | (8) c Yuile b Cunis | | 47 |
| Wasim Bari† | c Murray b Hadlee | 15 | (7) c Congdon b Howarth | | 19 |
| Mohammad Nazir | not out | 29 | not out | | 17 |
| Pervez Sajjad | b Hadlee | 0 | | | |
| Asif Masood | c Howarth b Hadlee | 17 | | | |
| Extras | (B 2, LB 10) | 12 | (B 13, LB 7) | | 20 |
| **Total** | | **220** | (8 wickets declared) | | **283** |

### NEW ZEALAND

| | | | | | |
|---|---|---|---|---|---|
| G.T. Dowling* | b Nazir | 40 | lbw b Pervez | | 3 |
| B.A.G. Murray | c Hanif b Nazir | 50 | c Asif Iqbal b Pervez | | 6 |
| B.E. Congdon | c Sadiq b Pervez | 20 | c Sadiq b Pervez | | 2 |
| B.F. Hastings | b Nazir | 22 | b Pervez | | 9 |
| M.G. Burgess | b Nazir | 21 | c Asif Iqbal b Pervez | | 45 |
| V. Pollard | b Nazir | 2 | not out | | 28 |
| B.W. Yuile | not out | 47 | not out | | 5 |
| K.J. Wadsworth† | st Wasim b Pervez | 0 | | | |
| D.R. Hadlee | lbw b Mushtaq | 56 | | | |
| R.S. Cunis | b Nazir | 5 | | | |
| H.J. Howarth | b Nazir | 0 | | | |
| Extras | (B 6, LB 3, NB 2) | 11 | (B 12, LB 2) | | 14 |
| **Total** | | **274** | (5 wickets) | | **112** |

| NEW ZEALAND | O | M | R | W | O | M | R | W |
|---|---|---|---|---|---|---|---|---|
| Hadlee | 17·2 | 5 | 27 | 3 | 16 | 5 | 31 | 1 |
| Cunis | 11 | 5 | 18 | 0 | 15·4 | 4 | 38 | 2 |
| Congdon | 8 | 5 | 14 | 0 | | | | |
| Howarth | 33 | 10 | 80 | 5 | 31 | 13 | 60 | 2 |
| Pollard | 15 | 5 | 34 | 0 | 31 | 11 | 50 | 0 |
| Yuile | 13 | 3 | 35 | 2 | 35 | 13 | 70 | 2 |
| Burgess | | | | | 6 | 1 | 14 | 0 |
| PAKISTAN | | | | | | | | |
| Asif Masood | 3 | 0 | 18 | 0 | 2 | 1 | 7 | 0 |
| Asif Iqbal | 3 | 0 | 12 | 0 | 2 | 0 | 2 | 0 |
| Intikhab | 13 | 3 | 51 | 0 | 5 | 1 | 18 | 0 |
| Nazir | 30·1 | 3 | 99 | 7 | 14 | 5 | 15 | 0 |
| Pervez | 31 | 7 | 71 | 2 | 24 | 12 | 33 | 5 |
| Mushtaq | 5 | 0 | 12 | 1 | 12 | 5 | 20 | 0 |
| Sadiq | | | | | 2 | 0 | 2 | 0 |
| Hanif | | | | | 2 | 1 | 1 | 0 |

### FALL OF WICKETS

| Wkt | P | NZ | P | NZ |
|---|---|---|---|---|
| | *1st* | *1st* | *2nd* | *2nd* |
| 1st | 55 | 92 | 75 | 9 |
| 2nd | 78 | 99 | 75 | 10 |
| 3rd | 111 | 125 | 83 | 11 |
| 4th | 121 | 139 | 133 | 44 |
| 5th | 135 | 144 | 183 | 92 |
| 6th | 142 | 163 | 195 | – |
| 7th | 153 | 164 | 244 | – |
| 8th | 191 | 264 | 283 | – |
| 9th | 191 | 273 | – | – |
| 10th | 220 | 274 | – | – |

Umpires: Idris Beg and Munawar Hussain.

# PAKISTAN v NEW ZEALAND 1969–70 (2nd Test)

Played at Lahore Stadium on 30, 31 October, 1, 2 November.
Toss: Pakistan.   Result: NEW ZEALAND won by five wickets.
Debuts: Nil.

New Zealand's first win against Pakistan came after they had dismissed the home side for what is still their lowest total in this series. Pervez Sajjad's innings analysis of 7 for 74 and match analysis of 9 for 112 remain the records for any Test at Lahore.

## PAKISTAN

| | | | | | |
|---|---|---|---|---|---|
| Sadiq Mohammad | b Congdon | 16 | | c and b Howarth | 17 |
| Salahuddin | c Wadsworth b Taylor | 2 | | b Taylor | 11 |
| Younis Ahmed | b Hadlee | 0 | (5) | c Murray b Pollard | 19 |
| Mushtaq Mohammad | c Wadsworth b Pollard | 25 | | c Yuile b Howarth | 1 |
| Shafqat Rana | c Murray b Congdon | 4 | (6) | c Hastings b Hadlee | 95 |
| Asif Iqbal | c Murray b Pollard | 20 | (3) | c Congdon b Yuile | 22 |
| Intikhab Alam* | c Dowling b Howarth | 6 | | b Pollard | 11 |
| Wasim Bari† | c Burgess b Pollard | 7 | | c Murray b Hadlee | 11 |
| Salim Altaf | c Hastings b Howarth | 1 | | lbw b Hadlee | 0 |
| Mohammad Nazir | c Wadsworth b Howarth | 12 | | not out | 4 |
| Pervez Sajjad | not out | 6 | | lbw b Taylor | 2 |
| Extras | (B 9, LB 6) | 15 | | (B 4, LB 9, NB 2) | 15 |
| **Total** | | **114** | | | **208** |

## NEW ZEALAND

| | | | | |
|---|---|---|---|---|
| G.T. Dowling* | b Salim | 10 | c Salahuddin b Pervez | 9 |
| B.A.G. Murray | c Shafqat b Pervez | 90 | c Asif b Pervez | 8 |
| B.E. Congdon | lbw b Pervez | 22 | c Shafqat b Nazir | 5 |
| B.F. Hastings | not out | 80 | c Mushtaq b Nazir | 16 |
| M.G. Burgess | c Mushtaq b Pervez | 0 | not out | 29 |
| V. Pollard | c Wasim b Pervez | 11 | st Wasim b Nazir | 0 |
| B.W. Yuile | c Asif b Pervez | 2 | not out | 4 |
| D.R. Hadlee | c and b Pervez | 0 | | |
| B.R. Taylor | b Pervez | 0 | | |
| K.J. Wadsworth† | b Salim | 13 | | |
| H.J. Howarth | b Salim | 4 | | |
| Extras | (B 1, LB 6, NB 2) | 9 | (B 4, LB 5, NB 2) | 11 |
| **Total** | | **241** | (5 wickets) | **82** |

| NEW ZEALAND | O | M | R | W | O | M | R | W | | FALL OF WICKETS | | | |
|---|---|---|---|---|---|---|---|---|---|---|---|---|---|
| | | | | | | | | | | P | NZ | P | NZ |
| Hadlee | 7 | 3 | 10 | 1 | 17 | 4 | 27 | 3 | *Wkt* | *1st* | *1st* | *2nd* | *2nd* |
| Taylor | 9 | 3 | 12 | 1 | 19·5 | 7 | 27 | 2 | 1st | 8 | 20 | 30 | 19 |
| Congdon | 10 | 4 | 15 | 2 | 8 | 4 | 17 | 0 | 2nd | 13 | 61 | 48 | 28 |
| Howarth | 21·4 | 13 | 35 | 23 | 26 | 7 | 63 | 2 | 3rd | 33 | 162 | 56 | 29 |
| Pollard | 20 | 7 | 27 | 3 | 20 | 7 | 32 | 2 | 4th | 39 | 162 | 66 | 66 |
| Yuile | | | | | 14 | 6 | 16 | 1 | 5th | 70 | 184 | 85 | 78 |
| Burgess | | | | | 1 | 0 | 11 | 0 | 6th | 83 | 186 | 117 | – |
| | | | | | | | | | 7th | 87 | 188 | 194 | – |
| PAKISTAN | | | | | | | | | 8th | 90 | 188 | 194 | – |
| Salim | 17 | 3 | 33 | 3 | 4 | 0 | 12 | 0 | 9th | 100 | 230 | 205 | – |
| Asif | 4 | 0 | 6 | 0 | 2 | 1 | 2 | 0 | 10th | 114 | 241 | 208 | – |
| Pervez | 40 | 15 | 74 | 7 | 14 | 6 | 38 | 2 | | | | | |
| Nazir | 36 | 15 | 54 | 0 | 12·3 | 4 | 19 | 3 | | | | | |
| Mushtaq | 8 | 1 | 34 | 0 | | | | | | | | | |
| Intikhab | 10 | 2 | 31 | 0 | | | | | | | | | |

Umpires: Akhtar Hussain and Omer Khan.

# PAKISTAN v NEW ZEALAND 1969–70 (3rd Test)

Played at Dacca Stadium on 8, 9, 10, 11 November.
Toss: New Zealand.    Result: MATCH DRAWN.
Debuts: Pakistan – Aftab Baloch.

This result gave New Zealand their first victory in a Test rubber; they had waited for 40 years. New Zealand's record ninth-wicket partnership against Pakistan of 96 between Burgess and Cunis left the home side to score 184 runs in 2½ hours. Bad light stopped play with 90 minutes left but minor rioting and an invasion of the playing area caused the match to be abandoned 65 minutes before the scheduled close.

## NEW ZEALAND

| | | | | | |
|---|---|---|---|---|---|
| B.A.G. Murray | b Asif | 7 | c Asif b Intikhab | | 2 |
| G.M. Turner | c Shafqat b Pervez | 110 | c Intikhab b Pervez | | 26 |
| G.T. Dowling* | c Asif b Intikhab | 15 | c Wasim b Intikhab | | 2 |
| B.E. Congdon | c Pervez b Intikhab | 6 | b Pervez | | 0 |
| B.F. Hastings | b Intikhab | 22 | b Pervez | | 3 |
| M.G. Burgess | c Wasim b Pervez | 59 | not out | | 119 |
| V. Pollard | c Shafqat b Intikhab | 2 | b Intikhab | | 11 |
| D.R. Hadlee | c Burki b Intikhab | 16 | lbw b Intikhab | | 0 |
| K.J. Wadsworth† | c Wasim b Salim | 7 | c Aftab Gul b Pervez | | 0 |
| R.S. Cunis | lbw b Salim | 0 | b Shafqat | | 23 |
| H.J. Howarth | not out | 0 | c Wasim b Intikhab | | 2 |
| Extras | (B 14, LB 11, NB 4) | 29 | (B 2, LB 8, NB 2) | | 12 |
| **Total** | | **273** | | | **200** |

## PAKISTAN

| | | | | | |
|---|---|---|---|---|---|
| Aftab Gul | c and b Howarth | 30 | b Cunis | | 5 |
| Sadiq Mohammad | c Turner b Pollard | 21 | b Cunis | | 3 |
| Javed Burki | c Turner b Howarth | 22 | not out | | 17 |
| Shafqat Rana | run out | 65 | (5) c Dowling b Cunis | | 3 |
| Aftab Baloch | lbw b Pollard | 25 | | | |
| Asif Iqbal | c Wadsworth b Howarth | 92 | (4) b Cunis | | 16 |
| Intikhab Alam* | b Howarth | 20 | (6) not out | | 3 |
| Wasim Bari† | not out | 6 | | | |
| Salim Altaf | ) | | | | |
| Mohammad Nazir | ) did not bat | | | | |
| Pervez Sajjad | ) | | | | |
| Extras | (B 6, LB 3) | 9 | (B 1, LB 3) | | 4 |
| **Total** | (7 wickets declared) | **290** | (4 wickets) | | **51** |

| PAKISTAN | O | M | R | W | O | M | R | W | | FALL OF WICKETS | | | |
|---|---|---|---|---|---|---|---|---|---|---|---|---|---|
| Salim | 19·3 | 6 | 27 | 2 | 11 | 4 | 18 | 0 | | NZ | P | NZ | P |
| Asif | 13 | 4 | 22 | 1 | 7 | 2 | 8 | 0 | *Wkt* | *1st* | *1st* | *2nd* | *2nd* |
| Pervez | 48 | 20 | 66 | 2 | 34 | 11 | 60 | 4 | 1st | 13 | 53 | 12 | 7 |
| Intikhab | 56 | 26 | 91 | 5 | 39·4 | 13 | 91 | 5 | 2nd | 67 | 55 | 14 | 12 |
| Nazir | 30 | 15 | 38 | 0 | 3 | 1 | 3 | 0 | 3rd | 99 | 81 | 17 | 40 |
| Sadiq | | | | | 2 | 1 | 4 | 0 | 4th | 147 | 150 | 25 | 46 |
| Baloch | | | | | 2 | 0 | 2 | 0 | 5th | 226 | 201 | 70 | – |
| Shafqat | | | | | 3 | 1 | 2 | 1 | 6th | 241 | 277 | 92 | – |
| | | | | | | | | | 7th | 251 | 290 | 92 | – |
| NEW ZEALAND | | | | | | | | | 8th | 271 | – | 101 | – |
| Hadlee | 17 | 2 | 41 | 0 | 7 | 0 | 17 | 0 | 9th | 272 | – | 197 | – |
| Cunis | 23 | 5 | 65 | 0 | 7 | 0 | 21 | 4 | 10th | 273 | – | 200 | – |
| Congdon | 14 | 2 | 41 | 0 | | | | | | | | | |
| Howarth | 33·1 | 8 | 85 | 4 | | | | | | | | | |
| Pollard | 14 | 2 | 49 | 2 | 1 | 0 | 9 | 0 | | | | | |

Umpires: Shujauddin and Daud Khan.

# INDIA v AUSTRALIA 1969–70 (1st Test)

Played at Brabourne Stadium, Bombay, on 4, 5, 7, 8, 9 November.
Toss: India.　Result: AUSTRALIA won by eight wickets.
Debuts: Nil.

Australia gained their first Test victory at Bombay soon after lunch on the fifth day. The omission of S. Venkataraghavan from India's side caused such a public outcry that S. Guha agreed to stand down from the selected team. The partnership of 146 between Mankad and Pataudi remains India's highest for the fourth wicket against Australia. Stackpole became the second Australian after D.G. Bradman to score a hundred in his first Test against India. On the fourth day, the last hour of play endured through a riot resulting from Venkataraghavan's second innings dismissal.

## INDIA

| | | | | |
|---|---|---|---|---|
| D.N. Sardesai | b McKenzie | 20 | c Taber b Gleeson | 3 |
| F.M. Engineer† | c Redpath b McKenzie | 19 | c McKenzie b Mallett | 28 |
| A.V. Mankad | b McKenzie | 74 | b Gleeson | 8 |
| C.G. Borde | c Chappell b McKenzie | 2 | c Redpath b Gleeson | 18 |
| Nawab of Pataudi, jr* | c Lawry b Gleeson | 95 | c Stackpole b Gleeson | 0 |
| A.L. Wadekar | lbw b Connolly | 9 | c McKenzie b Stackpole | 46 |
| R.F. Surti | st Taber b Gleeson | 4 | lbw b Connolly | 13 |
| S. Abid Ali | c Stackpole b McKenzie | 3 | lbw b Connolly | 2 |
| S. Venkataraghavan | c Taber b Connolly | 2 | c Taber b Connolly | 9 |
| E.A.S. Prasanna | not out | 12 | b Mallett | 3 |
| B.S. Bedi | c McKenzie b Gleeson | 7 | not out | 1 |
| Extras | (B 15, LB 4, NB 5) | 24 | (B 4, NB 2) | 6 |
| **Total** | | **271** | | **137** |

## AUSTRALIA

| | | | | |
|---|---|---|---|---|
| W.M. Lawry* | b Prasanna | 25 | b Surti | 2 |
| K.R. Stackpole | c Surti b Prasanna | 103 | lbw b Surti | 11 |
| I.M. Chappell | b Prasanna | 31 | not out | 31 |
| K.D. Walters | c Venkataraghavan b Bedi | 48 | not out | 22 |
| I.R. Redpath | c Wadekar b Venkataraghavan | 77 | | |
| A.P. Sheahan | lbw b Venkataraghavan | 14 | | |
| G.D. McKenzie | c Borde b Prasanna | 16 | | |
| H.B. Taber† | c Surti b Bedi | 5 | | |
| A.A. Mallett | not out | 10 | | |
| J.W. Gleeson | c Borde b Prasanna | 0 | | |
| A.N. Connolly | c sub (E.D. Solkar) b Bedi | 8 | | |
| Extras | (B 4, NB 4) | 8 | (B 1) | 1 |
| **Total** | | **345** | (2 wickets) | **67** |

| AUSTRALIA | O | M | R | W | O | M | R | W | FALL OF WICKETS | | | | |
|---|---|---|---|---|---|---|---|---|---|---|---|---|---|
| McKenzie | 29 | 7 | 69 | 5 | 16 | 4 | 33 | 0 | | I | A | I | A |
| Connolly | 31 | 11 | 55 | 2 | 20 | 10 | 20 | 3 | *Wkt* | *1st* | *1st* | *2nd* | *2nd* |
| Gleeson | 35·4 | 18 | 52 | 3 | 32 | 17 | 56 | 4 | 1st | 39 | 81 | 19 | 8 |
| Walters | 6 | 0 | 13 | 0 | | | | | 2nd | 40 | 164 | 37 | 13 |
| Mallett | 30 | 19 | 43 | 0 | 21 | 9 | 22 | 2 | 3rd | 42 | 167 | 55 | – |
| Stackpole | 3 | 1 | 8 | 0 | 1·2 | 1 | 0 | 1 | 4th | 188 | 285 | 56 | – |
| Chappell | 1 | 0 | 7 | 0 | | | | | 5th | 239 | 297 | 59 | – |
| | | | | | | | | | 6th | 245 | 322 | 87 | – |
| INDIA | | | | | | | | | 7th | 246 | 322 | 89 | – |
| Abid Ali | 18 | 3 | 52 | 0 | 3 | 0 | 14 | 0 | 8th | 249 | 337 | 114 | – |
| Surti | 9 | 2 | 23 | 0 | 4 | 1 | 9 | 2 | 9th | 252 | 337 | 125 | – |
| Venkataraghavan | 31 | 11 | 67 | 2 | 1 | 0 | 2 | 0 | 10th | 271 | 345 | 137 | – |
| Bedi | 62·4 | 33 | 74 | 3 | 9 | 5 | 11 | 0 | | | | | |
| Prasanna | 49 | 19 | 121 | 5 | 9 | 3 | 20 | 0 | | | | | |
| Mankad | | | | | 0·5 | 0 | 10 | 0 | | | | | |

Umpires: S. Pan and I. Gopalakrishnan.

# INDIA v AUSTRALIA 1969–70 (2nd Test)

Played at Green Park, Kanpur, on 15, 16, 18, 19, 20 November.
Toss: India.    Result: MATCH DRAWN.
Debuts: India – G.R. Viswanath.

Viswanath became the sixth batsman to score a hundred on his Test debut for India and the first to do so against Australia. His innings of 137, scored in 354 minutes and including 25 fours, is India's highest against Australia in a home Test.

## INDIA

| | | | | |
|---|---|---|---|---|
| F.M. Engineer† | c and b Stackpole | 77 | c Gleeson b Connolly | 21 |
| A.V. Mankad | c and b Mallett | 64 | b McKenzie | 68 |
| A.L. Wadekar | c Mallett b Connolly | 27 | c Chappell b Connolly | 12 |
| G.R. Viswanath | c Redpath b Connolly | 0 | lbw b Mallett | 137 |
| Nawab of Pataudi, jr* | c Redpath b McKenzie | 38 | lbw b McKenzie | 0 |
| A. Gandotra | c Taber b Connolly | 13 | c Chappell b Gleeson | 8 |
| E.D. Solkar | b Connolly | 44 | c Taber b McKenzie | 35 |
| S. Venkataraghavan | run out | 17 | not out | 20 |
| S. Guha | lbw b Mallett | 6 | not out | 1 |
| E.A.S. Prasanna | c McKenzie b Mallett | 22 | | |
| B.S. Bedi | not out | 1 | | |
| Extras | (LB 5, NB 6) | 22 | (LB 1, NB 9) | 10 |
| **Total** | | **320** | (7 wickets declared) | **312** |

## AUSTRALIA

| | | | | |
|---|---|---|---|---|
| K.R. Stackpole | run out | 40 | not out | 37 |
| W.M. Lawry* | c Solkar b Venkataraghavan | 14 | not out | 56 |
| I.M. Chappell | lbw b Prasanna | 16 | | |
| K.D. Walters | b Bedi | 53 | | |
| I.R. Redpath | c Guha b Solkar | 70 | | |
| A.P. Sheahan | c Engineer b Guha | 114 | | |
| A.A. Mallett | b Venkataraghavan | 4 | | |
| G.D. McKenzie | lbw b Prasanna | 0 | | |
| H.B. Taber† | c Viswanath b Venkataraghavan | 1 | | |
| J.W. Gleeson | b Guha | 13 | | |
| A.N. Connolly | not out | 7 | | |
| Extras | (B 4, LB 7, NB 5) | 16 | (NB 2) | 2 |
| **Total** | | **348** | (0 wickets) | **95** |

| AUSTRALIA | O | M | R | W | O | M | R | W |
|---|---|---|---|---|---|---|---|---|
| McKenzie | 25 | 7 | 70 | 1 | 34 | 13 | 63 | 3 |
| Connolly | 36 | 13 | 91 | 4 | 36 | 7 | 69 | 2 |
| Gleeson | 29 | 5 | 79 | 0 | 35 | 11 | 74 | 1 |
| Mallett | 51·5 | 30 | 58 | 3 | 36 | 18 | 62 | 1 |
| Stackpole | 2 | 1 | 4 | 1 | 7 | 1 | 21 | 0 |
| Walters | 2 | 1 | 7 | 0 | 3 | 1 | 7 | 0 |
| Lawry | | | | | 1 | 0 | 6 | 0 |
| INDIA | | | | | | | | |
| Guha | 21·2 | 6 | 55 | 2 | 5 | 1 | 7 | 0 |
| Solkar | 19 | 7 | 44 | 1 | 12 | 3 | 37 | 0 |
| Bedi | 49 | 21 | 82 | 1 | 3 | 1 | 8 | 0 |
| Prasanna | 39 | 18 | 71 | 2 | 15 | 6 | 17 | 0 |
| Venkataraghavan | 37 | 16 | 76 | 3 | 4 | 1 | 11 | 0 |
| Viswanath | 1 | 0 | 4 | 0 | 1 | 0 | 4 | 0 |
| Pataudi | | | | | 1 | 0 | 4 | 0 |
| Mankad | | | | | 1 | 1 | 0 | 0 |
| Gandotra | | | | | 1 | 0 | 5 | 0 |
| Wadekar | | | | | 1 | 1 | 0 | 0 |

### FALL OF WICKETS

| Wkt | I 1st | A 1st | I 2nd | A 2nd |
|---|---|---|---|---|
| 1st | 111 | 48 | 43 | – |
| 2nd | 167 | 56 | 94 | – |
| 3rd | 171 | 93 | 125 | – |
| 4th | 171 | 140 | 125 | – |
| 5th | 197 | 271 | 147 | – |
| 6th | 239 | 287 | 257 | – |
| 7th | 285 | 290 | 306 | – |
| 8th | 287 | 297 | – | – |
| 9th | 315 | 331 | – | – |
| 10th | 320 | 348 | – | – |

Umpires: B. Satyaji Rao and A.M. Mamsa.

# INDIA v AUSTRALIA 1969–70 (3rd Test)

Played at Feroz Shah Kotla, Delhi, on 28, 29, 30 November, 2 December.
Toss: Australia.    Result: INDIA won by seven wickets.
Debuts: Nil.

India gained their third victory against Australia and with more than a day to spare. Australia's total of 107 is the lowest in any Test at Delhi. Lawry, who batted for 195 minutes, became the sixth Australian to carry his bat through a completed innings and the second batsman after Nazar Mohammad of Pakistan (*Test No. 356*) to do so against India. Prasanna took his 100th Test wicket when he dismissed Sheahan.

## AUSTRALIA

| | | | | |
|---|---|--:|---|--:|
| K.R. Stackpole | st Engineer b Bedi | 61 | b Prasanna | 9 |
| W.M. Lawry* | b Guha | 6 | not out | 49 |
| I.M. Chappell | b Bedi | 138 | c Solkar b Bedi | 0 |
| K.D. Walters | c Solkar b Prasanna | 4 | b Bedi | 0 |
| I.R. Redpath | c Bedi b Prasanna | 6 | b Bedi | 4 |
| A.P. Sheahan | b Bedi | 4 | c Venkataraghavan b Prasanna | 15 |
| H.B. Taber† | st Engineer b Bedi | 46 | c and b Prasanna | 7 |
| A.A. Mallett | b Venkataraghavan | 2 | (9) c Venkataraghavan b Prasanna | 0 |
| G.D. McKenzie | lbw b Prasanna | 20 | (8) lbw b Bedi | 7 |
| J.W. Gleeson | c Solkar b Prasanna | 1 | c Viswanath b Bedi | 1 |
| A.N. Connolly | not out | 4 | c and b Prasanna | 11 |
| Extras | (B 2, LB 1, NB 1) | 4 | (B 4) | 4 |
| **Total** | | **296** | | **107** |

## INDIA

| | | | | |
|---|---|--:|---|--:|
| F.M. Engineer† | b Connolly | 38 | c McKenzie b Mallett | 6 |
| A.V. Mankad | c Walters b Mallett | 97 | b Mallett | 7 |
| A.L. Wadekar | c and b Stackpole | 22 | (4) not out | 91 |
| G.R. Viswanath | b Gleeson | 29 | (5) not out | 44 |
| S. Venkataraghavan | c Walters b Mallett | 0 | | |
| Nawab of Pataudi, jr* | c Chappell b Mallett | 8 | | |
| A. Roy | c Taber b Mallett | 0 | | |
| E.D. Solkar | not out | 13 | | |
| S. Guha | b Mallett | 0 | | |
| E.A.S. Prasanna | lbw b Gleeson | 1 | | |
| B.S. Bedi | b Mallett | 6 | (3) b Connolly | 20 |
| Extras | (B 3, LB 1, NB 5) | 9 | (B 9, LB 2, NB 2) | 13 |
| **Total** | | **223** | (3 wickets) | **181** |

| INDIA | O | M | R | W | O | M | R | W | | FALL OF WICKETS | | | |
|---|--:|--:|--:|--:|--:|--:|--:|--:|---|--:|--:|--:|--:|
| Guha | 14 | 0 | 47 | 1 | 2 | 0 | 7 | 0 | | A | I | A | I |
| Solkar | 11 | 1 | 43 | 0 | 1 | 1 | 0 | 0 | Wkt | 1st | 1st | 2nd | 2nd |
| Bedi | 42 | 15 | 71 | 4 | 23 | 11 | 37 | 5 | 1st | 33 | 85 | 15 | 13 |
| Prasanna | 38·4 | 9 | 111 | 4 | 24·2 | 10 | 42 | 5 | 2nd | 100 | 124 | 16 | 18 |
| Venkataraghavan | 14 | 4 | 20 | 1 | 8 | 2 | 17 | 0 | 3rd | 105 | 176 | 16 | 61 |
| | | | | | | | | | 4th | 117 | 177 | 24 | – |
| AUSTRALIA | | | | | | | | | 5th | 133 | 197 | 61 | – |
| McKenzie | 12 | 4 | 22 | 0 | 13·4 | 5 | 19 | 0 | 6th | 251 | 202 | 81 | – |
| Connolly | 20 | 4 | 43 | 1 | 16 | 5 | 35 | 1 | 7th | 260 | 207 | 88 | – |
| Gleeson | 34 | 14 | 62 | 2 | 12 | 5 | 24 | 0 | 8th | 283 | 207 | 89 | – |
| Mallett | 32·3 | 10 | 64 | 6 | 29 | 10 | 60 | 2 | 9th | 291 | 208 | 92 | – |
| Stackpole | 10 | 4 | 23 | 1 | 8 | 4 | 13 | 0 | 10th | 296 | 223 | 107 | – |
| Chappell | | | | | 2 | 0 | 17 | 0 | | | | | |

Umpires: I. Gopalakrishnan and S. Roy.

# INDIA v AUSTRALIA 1969–70 (4th Test)

Played at Eden Gardens, Calcutta, on 12, 13, 14, 16 December.
Toss: Australia.   Result: AUSTRALIA won by ten wickets.
Debuts: Nil.

Australia completed this convincing victory with more than a day to spare. Bad light claimed 2½ hours of playing time on the first three days and a minor riot caused a 15-minute interruption on the fourth.

## INDIA

| | | | | |
|---|---|--:|---|--:|
| F.M. Engineer† | c Stackpole b McKenzie | 0 | c Redpath b Freeman | 10 |
| A.V. Mankad | c Stackpole b McKenzie | 9 | c Taber b McKenzie | 20 |
| A.L. Wadekar | c Freeman b McKenzie | 0 | lbw b Freeman | 62 |
| G.R. Viswanath | c Taber b Mallett | 54 | b Freeman | 3 |
| Nawab of Pataudi, jr* | c Chappell b Mallett | 15 | (6) c Connolly b Mallett | 1 |
| A. Roy | c Taber b McKenzie | 18 | (7) c Sheahan b Connolly | 19 |
| E.D. Solkar | c Taber b McKenzie | 42 | (5) lbw b Connolly | 21 |
| S. Venkataraghavan | c Stackpole b Mallett | 24 | b Connolly | 0 |
| E.A.S. Prasanna | run out | 26 | c Stackpole b Freeman | 0 |
| S. Guha | b McKenzie | 4 | (11) not out | 1 |
| B.S. Bedi | not out | 9 | (10) c Chappell b Connolly | 7 |
| Extras | (B 5, LB 1, W 1, NB 4) | 11 | (B 6, LB 4, NB 5) | 15 |
| **Total** | | **212** | | **161** |

## AUSTRALIA

| | | | | |
|---|---|--:|---|--:|
| W.M. Lawry* | c Solkar b Bedi | 35 | not out | 17 |
| K.R. Stackpole | run out | 41 | not out | 25 |
| I.M. Chappell | c Wadekar b Bedi | 99 | | |
| K.D. Walters | st Engineer b Bedi | 56 | | |
| I.R. Redpath | c Wadekar b Bedi | 0 | | |
| A.P. Sheahan | run out | 32 | | |
| E.W. Freeman | c Prasanna b Bedi | 29 | | |
| H.B. Taber† | b Bedi | 2 | | |
| G.D. McKenzie | c Pataudi b Bedi | 0 | | |
| A.A. Mallett | not out | 2 | | |
| A.N. Connolly | c Guha b Solkar | 31 | | |
| Extras | (B 4, LB 2, NB 2) | 8 | | |
| **Total** | | **335** | (0 wickets) | **42** |

| AUSTRALIA | O | M | R | W | O | M | R | W | | FALL OF WICKETS | | | |
|---|--:|--:|--:|--:|--:|--:|--:|--:|---|---|---|---|---|
| | | | | | | | | | | I | A | I | A |
| McKenzie | 33·4 | 12 | 67 | 6 | 18 | 4 | 34 | 1 | *Wkt* | *1st* | *1st* | *2nd* | *2nd* |
| Freeman | 17 | 6 | 43 | 0 | 26 | 7 | 54 | 4 | 1st | 0 | 65 | 29 | – |
| Connolly | 17 | 5 | 27 | 0 | 16·1 | 3 | 31 | 4 | 2nd | 0 | 84 | 31 | – |
| Mallett | 27 | 9 | 55 | 3 | 17 | 5 | 27 | 1 | 3rd | 22 | 185 | 40 | – |
| Stackpole | 2 | 0 | 9 | 0 | | | | | 4th | 64 | 185 | 90 | – |
| | | | | | | | | | 5th | 103 | 257 | 93 | – |
| INDIA | | | | | | | | | 6th | 103 | 279 | 141 | – |
| Guha | 19 | 5 | 55 | 0 | 3 | 1 | 25 | 0 | 7th | 154 | 302 | 141 | – |
| Solkar | 9·1 | 1 | 28 | 1 | | | | | 8th | 178 | 302 | 142 | – |
| Prasanna | 49 | 15 | 116 | 0 | | | | | 9th | 184 | 302 | 159 | – |
| Venkataraghavan | 16 | 6 | 30 | 0 | | | | | 10th | 212 | 335 | 161 | – |
| Bedi | 50 | 19 | 98 | 7 | | | | | | | | | |
| Wadekar | | | | | 2 | 0 | 17 | 0 | | | | | |

Umpires: S. Pan and J. Reuben.

# INDIA v AUSTRALIA 1969–70 (5th Test)

Played at Chepauk, Madras, on 24, 25, 27, 28 December.
Toss: Australia.   Result: AUSTRALIA won by 77 runs.
Debuts: India – M. Amarnath.

Australia won this six-day match an hour after lunch on the fourth afternoon and so gained a 3-1 victory in the rubber.

## AUSTRALIA

| | | | | |
|---|---|---|---|---|
| K.R. Stackpole | c Solkar b Venkataraghavan | 37 | b Amarnath | 4 |
| W.M. Lawry* | c Bedi b Prasanna | 33 | b Prasanna | 2 |
| I.M. Chappell | b Prasanna | 4 | b Amarnath | 5 |
| K.D. Walters | c Venkataraghavan b Bedi | 102 | c Solkar b Prasanna | 1 |
| A.P. Sheahan | c Solkar b Prasanna | 1 | (6) st Engineer b Prasanna | 8 |
| I.R. Redpath | c Engineer b Prasanna | 33 | (5) lbw b Prasanna | 63 |
| H.B. Taber† | lbw b Venkataraghavan | 10 | c Solkar b Prasanna | 0 |
| G.D. McKenzie | lbw b Venkataraghavan | 2 | lbw b Venkataraghavan | 24 |
| L.C. Mayne | c Chauhan b Venkataraghavan | 10 | c Viswanath b Prasanna | 13 |
| A.A. Mallett | not out | 2 | not out | 11 |
| A.N. Connolly | c and b Solkar | 11 | c Engineer b Venkataraghavan | 8 |
| Extras | (B 11, LB 2) | 13 | (B 8, LB 5, NB 1) | 14 |
| **Total** | | **258** | | **153** |

## INDIA

| | | | | |
|---|---|---|---|---|
| C.P.S. Chauhan | c Chappell b Mallett | 19 | c Redpath b McKenzie | 1 |
| A.V. Mankad | c Taber b Mayne | 0 | c Redpath b McKenzie | 10 |
| A.L. Wadekar | c Chappell b Mallett | 12 | c Stackpole b Mayne | 55 |
| G.R. Viswanath | b Mallett | 6 | c Redpath b Mallett | 59 |
| F.M. Engineer† | c Connolly b Mallett | 32 | c and b McKenzie | 3 |
| Nawab of Pataudi, jr* | c Sheahan b McKenzie | 59 | c Chappell b Mallett | 4 |
| E.D. Solkar | c Taber b Mallett | 11 | c and b Mallett | 12 |
| M. Amarnath | not out | 16 | c Taber b Mayne | 0 |
| S. Venkataraghavan | run out | 2 | b Mallett | 13 |
| E.A.S. Prasanna | c Chappell b McKenzie | 0 | c McKenzie b Mallett | 5 |
| B.S. Bedi | absent ill | – | not out | 0 |
| Extras | (LB 5, NB 1) | 6 | (LB 4, NB 5) | 9 |
| **Total** | | **163** | | **171** |

| INDIA | O | M | R | W | O | M | R | W | | FALL OF WICKETS | | | |
|---|---|---|---|---|---|---|---|---|---|---|---|---|---|
| Amarnath | 7 | 0 | 21 | 0 | 24 | 11 | 31 | 2 | | A | I | A | I |
| Solkar | 8·2 | 5 | 8 | 1 | 4 | 2 | 2 | 0 | Wkt | 1st | 1st | 2nd | 2nd |
| Bedi | 26 | 10 | 45 | 1 | 9 | 5 | 6 | 0 | 1st | 60 | 0 | 4 | 3 |
| Prasanna | 40 | 13 | 100 | 4 | 31 | 14 | 74 | 6 | 2nd | 69 | 30 | 12 | 12 |
| Venkataraghavan | 34 | 13 | 71 | 4 | 12·5 | 2 | 26 | 2 | 3rd | 78 | 33 | 15 | 114 |
| | | | | | | | | | 4th | 82 | 40 | 16 | 119 |
| AUSTRALIA | | | | | | | | | 5th | 184 | 96 | 24 | 135 |
| McKenzie | 16·4 | 8 | 19 | 2 | 24 | 9 | 45 | 3 | 6th | 219 | 128 | 24 | 142 |
| Mayne | 7 | 2 | 21 | 1 | 18 | 8 | 32 | 2 | 7th | 225 | 158 | 57 | 144 |
| Connolly | 14 | 5 | 26 | 0 | 9 | 4 | 18 | 0 | 8th | 243 | 163 | 107 | 159 |
| Mallett | 25 | 7 | 91 | 5 | 29·2 | 12 | 53 | 5 | 9th | 245 | 163 | 140 | 169 |
| Stackpole | | | | | 5 | 2 | 14 | 0 | 10th | 258 | – | 153 | 171 |

Umpires: I. Gopalakrishnan and B. Satyaji Rao.

# SOUTH AFRICA v AUSTRALIA 1969–70 (1st Test)

Played at Newlands, Cape Town, on 22, 23, 24, 26, 27 January.
Toss: South Africa.   Result: SOUTH AFRICA won by 170 runs.
Debuts: South Africa – G.A. Chevalier, D. Gamsy, B.L. Irvine, B.A. Richards.

South Africa beat Australia at Newlands for the first time, having lost all six previous encounters dating back to 1902–03. Barlow's fifth Test hundred was his fourth against Australia. Chevalier took the wicket of Sheahan with his fifth ball in Test cricket.

## SOUTH AFRICA

| | | | | | |
|---|---|---|---|---|---|
| B.A Richards | b Connolly | 29 | c Taber b Connolly | 32 |
| T.L. Goddard | c Taber b Walters | 16 | c Lawry b Mallett | 17 |
| A. Bacher* | lbw b Connolly | 57 | lbw b Gleeson | 16 |
| R.G. Pollock | c Chappell b Walters | 49 | c Walters b Connolly | 50 |
| E.J. Barlow | c Chappell b Gleeson | 127 | c Taber b Gleeson | 16 |
| B.L. Irvine | c Gleeson b Mallett | 42 | c Walters b Connolly | 19 |
| M.J. Procter | b Mallett | 22 | c Taber b Connolly | 48 |
| D. Gamsy† | not out | 30 | c Taber b Gleeson | 2 |
| P.M. Pollock | lbw b Mallett | 1 | b Gleeson | 25 |
| M.A. Seymour | c Lawry b Mallett | 0 | c Lawry b Connolly | 0 |
| G.A. Chevalier | c Chappell b Mallett | 0 | not out | 0 |
| Extras | (B 2, LB 5, NB 2) | 9 | (B 1, LB 4, NB 2) | 7 |
| **Total** | | **382** | | **232** |

## AUSTRALIA

| | | | | | |
|---|---|---|---|---|---|
| K.R. Stackpole | c Barlow b Procter | 19 | c Barlow b Goddard | 29 |
| W.M. Lawry* | b P.M. Pollock | 2 | lbw b Procter | 83 |
| I.M. Chappell | c Chevalier b P.M. Pollock | 0 | b Chevalier | 13 |
| K.D. Walters | c Irvine b P.M. Pollock | 73 | c Irvine b Procter | 4 |
| I.R. Redpath | c Barlow b Procter | 0 | not out | 47 |
| A.P. Sheahan | c Barlow b Chevalier | 8 | b Seymour | 16 |
| H.B. Taber† | lbw b Seymour | 11 | lbw b Procter | 15 |
| G.D. McKenzie | c R.G. Pollock b P.M. Pollock | 5 | (9) c R.G. Pollock b Chevalier | 19 |
| A.A. Mallett | c Goddard b Chevalier | 19 | (8) c P.M. Pollock b Procter | 5 |
| J.W. Gleeson | b Goddard | 17 | b Richards | 10 |
| A.N. Connolly | not out | 0 | b Chevalier | 25 |
| Extras | (B 1, NB 9) | 10 | (B 7, LB 2, NB 5) | 14 |
| **Total** | | **164** | | **280** |

| AUSTRALIA | O | M | R | W | O | M | R | W |
|---|---|---|---|---|---|---|---|---|
| McKenzie | 30 | 8 | 74 | 0 | 8 | 0 | 29 | 0 |
| Connolly | 29 | 12 | 62 | 2 | 26 | 10 | 47 | 5 |
| Walters | 8 | 1 | 19 | 2 | | | | |
| Gleeson | 45 | 17 | 92 | 1 | 30 | 11 | 70 | 4 |
| Mallett | 55·1 | 16 | 126 | 5 | 32 | 10 | 79 | 1 |
| SOUTH AFRICA | | | | | | | | |
| Procter | 12 | 4 | 30 | 2 | 17 | 4 | 47 | 4 |
| P.M. Pollock | 12 | 4 | 20 | 4 | 18 | 12 | 19 | 0 |
| Goddard | 19·4 | 9 | 29 | 1 | 32 | 12 | 66 | 1 |
| Chevalier | 11 | 2 | 32 | 2 | 31·1 | 9 | 68 | 3 |
| Seymour | 11 | 2 | 28 | 1 | 19 | 6 | 40 | 1 |
| Barlow | 1 | 0 | 15 | 0 | 6 | 2 | 14 | 0 |
| Richards | | | | | 6 | 1 | 12 | 1 |

### FALL OF WICKETS

| | SA | A | SA | A |
|---|---|---|---|---|
| Wkt | 1st | 1st | 2nd | 2nd |
| 1st | 21 | 5 | 52 | 75 |
| 2nd | 96 | 5 | 52 | 130 |
| 3rd | 111 | 38 | 91 | 131 |
| 4th | 187 | 39 | 121 | 136 |
| 5th | 281 | 58 | 147 | 161 |
| 6th | 323 | 92 | 171 | 188 |
| 7th | 363 | 123 | 187 | 198 |
| 8th | 364 | 134 | 222 | 228 |
| 9th | 374 | 164 | 226 | 239 |
| 10th | 382 | 164 | 232 | 280 |

Umpires: G. Goldman and W.W. Wade.

# SOUTH AFRICA v AUSTRALIA 1969–70 (2nd Test)

Played at Kingsmead, Durban, on 5, 6, 7, 9 February.
Toss: South Africa.   Result: SOUTH AFRICA won by an innings and 129 runs.
Debuts: South Africa – A.J. Traicos.

South Africa's first victory against Australia was achieved by an innings margin with over a day to spare. It remains their largest margin of victory in a home Test. South Africa's total is their highest in all Test cricket. R.G. Pollock batted for 417 minutes; his innings of 274 included a five and 43 fours and is the highest score for South Africa in Test matches (beating D.J. McGlew's 255* in *Test No. 370*). It is also the record score by any batsman in a Test in South Africa. His partnership of 200 with Lance is South Africa's highest for the sixth wicket in any Test. Richards reached his first Test hundred off 116 balls.

## SOUTH AFRICA

| | | |
|---|---|---|
| B.A. Richards | b Freeman | 140 |
| T.L. Goddard | c Lawry b Gleeson | 17 |
| A. Bacher* | b Connolly | 9 |
| R.G. Pollock | c and b Stackpole | 274 |
| E.J. Barlow | lbw b Freeman | 1 |
| B.L. Irvine | b Gleeson | 13 |
| H.R. Lance | st Taber b Gleeson | 61 |
| M.J. Procter | c Connolly b Stackpole | 32 |
| D. Gamsy† | lbw b Connolly | 7 |
| P.M. Pollock | not out | 36 |
| A.J. Traicos | not out | 5 |
| Extras | (B 1, LB 3, NB 23) | 27 |
| **Total** | (9 wickets declared) | **622** |

## AUSTRALIA

| | | | | | |
|---|---|---|---|---|---|
| K.R. Stackpole | c Gamsy b Goddard | 27 | lbw b Traicos | 71 |
| W.M. Lawry* | lbw b Barlow | 15 | c Gamsy b Goddard | 14 |
| I.M. Chappell | c Gamsy b Barlow | 0 | c Gamsy b P.M. Pollock | 14 |
| K.D. Walters | c Traicos b Barlow | 4 | c R.G. Pollock b Traicos | 74 |
| I.R. Redpath | c Richards b Procter | 4 | not out | 74 |
| A.P. Sheahan | c Traicos b Goddard | 62 | c Barlow b Procter | 4 |
| E.W. Freeman | c Traicos b P.M. Pollock | 5 | b Barlow | 18 |
| H.B. Taber† | c and b P.M. Pollock | 6 | c Lance b Barlow | 0 |
| G.D. McKenzie | c Traicos b Procter | 1 | lbw b Barlow | 4 |
| J.W. Gleeson | not out | 4 | c Gamsy b Procter | 24 |
| A.N. Connolly | c Bacher b Traicos | 14 | lbw b Procter | 0 |
| Extras | (LB 5, NB 10) | 15 | (B 9, LB 8, NB 22) | 39 |
| **Total** | | **157** | | **336** |

| AUSTRALIA | O | M | R | W | O | M | R | W |
|---|---|---|---|---|---|---|---|---|
| McKenzie | 25·5 | 3 | 92 | 0 | | | | |
| Connolly | 33 | 7 | 104 | 2 | | | | |
| Freeman | 28 | 4 | 120 | 2 | | | | |
| Gleeson | 51 | 9 | 160 | 3 | | | | |
| Walters | 9 | 0 | 44 | 0 | | | | |
| Stackpole | 21 | 2 | 75 | 2 | | | | |
| SOUTH AFRICA | | | | | | | | |
| Procter | 11 | 2 | 39 | 2 | 18·5 | 5 | 62 | 3 |
| P.M. Pollock | 10 | 3 | 31 | 2 | 21·3 | 4 | 45 | 1 |
| Goddard | 7 | 4 | 10 | 2 | 17 | 7 | 30 | 1 |
| Barlow | 10 | 3 | 24 | 3 | 31 | 10 | 63 | 3 |
| Traicos | 8·2 | 3 | 27 | 1 | 30 | 8 | 70 | 2 |
| Lance | 2 | 0 | 11 | 0 | 7 | 4 | 11 | 0 |
| Richards | | | | | 3 | 1 | 8 | 0 |
| R.G. Pollock | | | | | 3 | 1 | 8 | 0 |

### FALL OF WICKETS

| Wkt | SA 1st | A 1st | A 2nd |
|---|---|---|---|
| 1st | 88 | 44 | 65 |
| 2nd | 126 | 44 | 83 |
| 3rd | 229 | 44 | 151 |
| 4th | 231 | 48 | 208 |
| 5th | 281 | 56 | 222 |
| 6th | 481 | 79 | 264 |
| 7th | 558 | 100 | 264 |
| 8th | 575 | 114 | 268 |
| 9th | 580 | 139 | 336 |
| 10th | – | 157 | 336 |

Umpires: J.G. Draper and C.M.P. Coetzee.

# SOUTH AFRICA v AUSTRALIA 1969–70 (3rd Test)

Played at New Wanderers, Johannesburg, on 19, 20, 21, 23, 24 February.
Toss: South Africa.    Result: SOUTH AFRICA won by 307 runs.
Debuts: Nil.

South Africa's victory remained their record by a runs margin in all Tests for just one match. Freeman was run out when his runner, Sheahan, attempted an impossible second run. Goddard took his 123rd wicket with his final ball in Test cricket.

## SOUTH AFRICA

| | | | | |
|---|---|---|---|---|
| B.A. Richards | c Taber b Connolly | 65 | c Taber b Mayne | 35 |
| T.L. Goddard | c Walters b Connolly | 6 | (9) c Taber b Connolly | 2 |
| A. Bacher* | lbw b Mayne | 30 | b Connolly | 15 |
| R.G. Pollock | c Taber b Freeman | 52 | b Freeman | 87 |
| E.J. Barlow | st Taber b Gleeson | 6 | (2) c Lawry b Gleeson | 110 |
| B.L. Irvine | c Stackpole b Gleeson | 79 | (5) c Lawry b Gleeson | 73 |
| H.R. Lance | run out | 8 | lbw b Gleeson | 30 |
| D.T. Lindsay† | c Stackpole b Gleeson | 0 | (6) b Gleeson | 6 |
| M.J. Procter | c Chappell b Walters | 22 | (8) not out | 36 |
| P.M. Pollock | c Taber b Walters | 0 | c Taber b Gleeson | 1 |
| A.J. Traicos | not out | 1 | lbw b Mayne | 0 |
| Extras | (LB 7, W 1, NB 2) | 10 | (LB 8, NB 5) | 13 |
| **Total** | | **279** | | **408** |

## AUSTRALIA

| | | | | |
|---|---|---|---|---|
| K.R. Stackpole | c Lindsay b Procter | 5 | c Lindsay b Procter | 1 |
| W.M. Lawry* | c Lindsay b P.M. Pollock | 1 | c R.G. Pollock b Barlow | 17 |
| I.R. Redpath | lbw b Procter | 0 | b Goddard | 66 |
| I.M. Chappell | c Lance b Goddard | 34 | b Barlow | 0 |
| K.D. Walters | c Procter b P.M. Pollock | 64 | b Procter | 15 |
| A.P. Sheahan | b P.M. Pollock | 44 | b Procter | 0 |
| E.W. Freeman | c Goddard b P.M. Pollock | 10 | run out | 18 |
| L.C. Mayne | run out | 0 | c Procter b Traicos | 2 |
| H.B. Taber† | not out | 26 | not out | 18 |
| J.W. Gleeson | b Procter | 0 | b Goddard | 0 |
| A.N. Connolly | c Richards b P.M. Pollock | 3 | c Richards b Goddard | 36 |
| Extras | (LB 4, W 1, NB 10) | 15 | (W 2, NB 3) | 5 |
| **Total** | | **202** | | **178** |

| AUSTRALIA | O | M | R | W | O | M | R | W | | FALL OF WICKETS | | | |
|---|---|---|---|---|---|---|---|---|---|---|---|---|---|
| Mayne | 26 | 5 | 83 | 1 | 18·3 | 1 | 77 | 2 | | SA | A | SA | A |
| Connolly | 30 | 10 | 49 | 2 | 32 | 6 | 83 | 2 | *Wkt* | *1st* | *1st* | *2nd* | *2nd* |
| Freeman | 20 | 4 | 60 | 1 | 19 | 4 | 77 | 1 | 1st | 56 | 7 | 76 | 11 |
| Gleeson | 21·4 | 2 | 61 | 3 | 45 | 15 | 125 | 5 | 2nd | 85 | 7 | 102 | 43 |
| Walters | 5 | 1 | 16 | 2 | 7 | 1 | 33 | 0 | 3rd | 141 | 12 | 241 | 43 |
| SOUTH AFRICA | | | | | | | | | 4th | 162 | 109 | 269 | 73 |
| Procter | 21 | 5 | 48 | 3 | 14 | 8 | 24 | 3 | 5th | 170 | 112 | 275 | 73 |
| P.M. Pollock | 23·2 | 10 | 39 | 5 | 15 | 4 | 56 | 0 | 6th | 194 | 139 | 349 | 122 |
| Barlow | 12 | 5 | 31 | 0 | 7 | 3 | 17 | 2 | 7th | 194 | 140 | 372 | 124 |
| Goddard | 26 | 10 | 41 | 1 | 24·5 | 16 | 27 | 3 | 8th | 238 | 194 | 375 | 126 |
| Lance | 3 | 1 | 5 | 0 | | | | | 9th | 246 | 195 | 380 | 126 |
| Traicos | 6 | 3 | 23 | 0 | 17 | 4 | 49 | 1 | 10th | 279 | 202 | 408 | 178 |

Umpires: C.M.P. Coetzee and A.J. Warner.

# SOUTH AFRICA v AUSTRALIA 1969–70 (4th Test)

Played at St George's Park, Port Elizabeth, on 5, 6, 7, 9, 10 March.
Toss: South Africa.   Result: SOUTH AFRICA won by 323 runs.
Debuts: Nil.

South Africa won the last of their 172 Test matches prior to excommunication by their record margin of runs. It was the first time that they had won every match in a rubber of more than two matches and the first time they had won four matches in a rubber against Australia. Connolly took his 100th Test wicket when he dismissed Traicos. Richards (508 runs, average 72·57) is the only batsman to score 500 runs in his first rubber for South Africa. P.M. Pollock pulled a hamstring muscle and was unable to complete his last over in Test cricket.

## SOUTH AFRICA

| | | | | |
|---|---|--:|---|--:|
| B.A. Richards | c Taber b Connolly | 81 | c Chappell b Mayne | 126 |
| E.J. Barlow | c McKenzie b Connolly | 73 | c Stackpole b Walters | 27 |
| A. Bacher* | run out | 17 | hit wkt b McKenzie | 73 |
| R.G. Pollock | c Taber b Gleeson | 1 | b Mayne | 4 |
| B.L. Irvine | c Redpath b Gleeson | 25 | c Gleeson b Mayne | 102 |
| D.T. Lindsay† | c Taber b Connolly | 43 | b Connolly | 60 |
| H.R. Lance | b Mayne | 21 | run out | 19 |
| M.J. Procter | c Taber b Connolly | 26 | c Mayne b Gleeson | 23 |
| P.M. Pollock | not out | 4 | not out | 7 |
| P.H.J. Trimborn | b Connolly | 0 | | |
| A.J. Traicos | c Taber b Connolly | 2 | | |
| Extras | (B 4, LB 3, NB 11) | 18 | (LB 9, NB 20) | 29 |
| **Total** | | **311** | (8 wickets declared) | **470** |

## AUSTRALIA

| | | | | |
|---|---|--:|---|--:|
| K.R. Stackpole | c Barlow b Procter | 15 | b Procter | 20 |
| W.M. Lawry* | c Lindsay b Lance | 18 | c Lindsay b Barlow | 43 |
| I.R. Redpath | c Trimborn b Procter | 55 | c Barlow b Procter | 37 |
| I.M. Chappell | c Procter b Trimborn | 17 | c Trimborn b Barlow | 14 |
| K.D. Walters | c Lindsay b Trimborn | 1 | b Procter | 23 |
| A.P. Sheahan | c Procter b P.M. Pollock | 67 | c Lindsay b Trimborn | 46 |
| H.B. Taber† | lbw b Barlow | 3 | not out | 30 |
| L.C. Mayne | b Procter | 13 | c Lindsay b Procter | 12 |
| G.D. McKenzie | c Barlow b P.M. Pollock | 0 | c Lindsay b Procter | 2 |
| J.W. Gleeson | c Lindsay b P.M. Pollock | 8 | b Procter | 0 |
| A.N. Connolly | not out | 2 | c Bacher b Trimborn | 3 |
| Extras | (LB 3, W 1, NB 9) | 13 | (LB 2, NB 14) | 16 |
| **Total** | | **212** | | **246** |

| AUSTRALIA | O | M | R | W | O | M | R | W |
|---|--:|--:|--:|--:|--:|--:|--:|--:|
| McKenzie | 27 | 7 | 66 | 0 | 20 | 3 | 72 | 1 |
| Mayne | 27 | 4 | 71 | 1 | 29 | 6 | 83 | 3 |
| Connolly | 28·2 | 9 | 47 | 6 | 36 | 3 | 130 | 1 |
| Walters | 9 | 1 | 19 | 0 | 5 | 2 | 14 | 1 |
| Gleeson | 32 | 9 | 90 | 2 | 30·2 | 5 | 142 | 1 |
| Redpath | | | | | 1 | 1 | 0 | 0 |
| **SOUTH AFRICA** | | | | | | | | |
| P.M. Pollock | 14 | 2 | 46 | 3 | 1·1 | 0 | 2 | 0 |
| Procter | 25·1 | 11 | 30 | 3 | 24 | 11 | 73 | 6 |
| Barlow | 9 | 1 | 27 | 1 | 18 | 3 | 66 | 2 |
| Lance | 8 | 1 | 32 | 1 | 10 | 4 | 18 | 0 |
| Trimborn | 17 | 1 | 47 | 2 | 20·2 | 4 | 44 | 2 |
| Traicos | 3 | 1 | 17 | 0 | 14 | 5 | 21 | 0 |
| Richards | | | | | 3 | 1 | 6 | 0 |

FALL OF WICKETS

| | SA | A | SA | A |
|---|--:|--:|--:|--:|
| Wkt | 1st | 1st | 2nd | 2nd |
| 1st | 157 | 27 | 73 | 22 |
| 2nd | 158 | 46 | 199 | 98 |
| 3rd | 159 | 80 | 213 | 116 |
| 4th | 183 | 82 | 279 | 130 |
| 5th | 208 | 152 | 367 | 189 |
| 6th | 259 | 177 | 440 | 207 |
| 7th | 294 | 191 | 440 | 234 |
| 8th | 305 | 195 | 470 | 243 |
| 9th | 305 | 208 | – | 243 |
| 10th | 311 | 212 | – | 246 |

Umpires: C.M.P. Coetzee and A.J. Warner.

# AUSTRALIA v ENGLAND 1970–71 (1st Test)

Played at Woolloongabba, Brisbane, on 27, 28, 29 November, 1, 2 December.
Toss: Australia. Result: MATCH DRAWN.
Debuts: Australia – T.J. Jenner, R.W. Marsh, A.L. Thomson; England – B.W. Luckhurst,
K. Shuttleworth.

Stackpole, favoured by a run out decision when he had scored 18, became the first to score a double century in an Australia v England Test at Brisbane; only Bradman (twice) has played a higher innings there. Stackpole batted for 440 minutes and hit a six and 25 fours. Australia's last seven first innings wickets fell for 15 runs in 47 minutes – Underwood claiming those of Redpath, Sheahan and Walters in seven balls without conceding a run. Cowdrey passed W.R. Hammond's world Test record aggregate of 7,249 runs when he had scored 22.

## AUSTRALIA

| | | | | | |
|---|---|---|---|---|---|
| W.M. Lawry* | c Knott b Snow | 4 | c Snow b Fletcher | | 84 |
| K.R. Stackpole | c Knott b Snow | 207 | c Knott b Shuttleworth | | 8 |
| I.M. Chappell | run out | 59 | st Knott b Illingworth | | 10 |
| K.D. Walters | b Underwood | 112 | c Luckhurst b Snow | | 7 |
| I.R. Redpath | c Illingworth b Underwood | 22 | c and b Underwood | | 28 |
| A.P. Sheahan | c Knott b Underwood | 0 | c Shuttleworth b Snow | | 36 |
| R.W. Marsh† | b Snow | 9 | b Shuttleworth | | 14 |
| T.J. Jenner | c Cowdrey b Snow | 0 | c Boycott b Shuttleworth | | 2 |
| G.D. McKenzie | not out | 3 | b Shuttleworth | | 1 |
| J.W. Gleeson | c Cowdrey b Snow | 0 | b Shuttleworth | | 6 |
| A.L. Thomson | b Snow | 0 | not out | | 4 |
| Extras | (B 7, LB 4, NB 6) | 17 | (B 4, LB 3, NB 7) | | 14 |
| **Total** | | **433** | | | **214** |

## ENGLAND

| | | | | |
|---|---|---|---|---|
| G. Boycott | c Marsh b Gleeson | 37 | c and b Jenner | 16 |
| B.W. Luckhurst | run out | 74 | not out | 20 |
| A.P.E. Knott† | c Lawry b Walters | 73 | | |
| J.H. Edrich | c Chappell b Jenner | 79 | | |
| M.C. Cowdrey | c Chappell b Gleeson | 28 | | |
| K.W.R. Fletcher | c Marsh b McKenzie | 34 | | |
| B.L. D'Oliveira | c Sheahan b McKenzie | 57 | | |
| R. Illingworth* | c Marsh b Thomson | 8 | | |
| J.A. Snow | c Marsh b Walters | 34 | | |
| D.L. Underwood | not out | 2 | | |
| K. Shuttleworth | c Lawry b Walters | 7 | | |
| Extras | (B 2, LB 7, NB 22) | 31 | (LB 3) | 3 |
| **Total** | | **464** | (1 wicket) | **39** |

| ENGLAND | O | M | R | W | O | M | R | W | | FALL OF WICKETS | | | |
|---|---|---|---|---|---|---|---|---|---|---|---|---|---|
| Snow | 32·3 | 6 | 114 | 6 | 20 | 3 | 48 | 2 | | A | E | A | E |
| Shuttleworth | 27 | 6 | 81 | 0 | 17·5 | 2 | 47 | 5 | *Wkt* | *1st* | *1st* | *2nd* | *2nd* |
| D'Oliveira | 16 | 2 | 63 | 0 | 7 | 5 | 7 | 0 | 1st | 12 | 92 | 30 | 39 |
| Illingworth | 11 | 1 | 47 | 0 | 18 | 11 | 19 | 1 | 2nd | 163 | 136 | 47 | – |
| Underwood | 28 | 6 | 101 | 3 | 20 | 10 | 23 | 1 | 3rd | 372 | 245 | 64 | – |
| Cowdrey | 1 | 0 | 10 | 0 | 2 | 0 | 8 | 0 | 4th | 418 | 284 | 137 | – |
| Fletcher | | | | | 9 | 1 | 48 | 1 | 5th | 418 | 336 | 152 | – |
| | | | | | | | | | 6th | 421 | 346 | 193 | – |
| AUSTRALIA | | | | | | | | | 7th | 422 | 371 | 199 | – |
| McKenzie | 28 | 5 | 90 | 2 | 3 | 0 | 6 | 0 | 8th | 433 | 449 | 201 | – |
| Thomson | 43 | 8 | 136 | 1 | 4 | 0 | 20 | 0 | 9th | 433 | 456 | 208 | – |
| Gleeson | 42 | 15 | 97 | 2 | | | | | 10th | 433 | 464 | 214 | – |
| Jenner | 24 | 5 | 86 | 1 | 4·6 | 2 | 9 | 1 | | | | | |
| Stackpole | 4 | 0 | 12 | 0 | 4 | 3 | 1 | 0 | | | | | |
| Walters | 5·5 | 0 | 12 | 3 | | | | | | | | | |

Umpires: L.P. Rowan and T.F. Brooks.

# AUSTRALIA v ENGLAND 1970–71 (2nd Test)

Played at W.A.C.A. Ground, Perth, on 11, 12, 13, 15, 16 December.
Toss: Australia.    Result: MATCH DRAWN.
Debuts: Australia – G.S. Chappell; England – P. Lever.

Perth's first Test match attracted nearly 85,000 spectators and produced receipts approaching £50,000. Luckhurst, his thumb damaged early in his innings, scored a hundred in his second Test. G.S. Chappell became the sixth Australian to score a hundred in his first Test innings. When Australia were asked to score 245 runs in 145 minutes, Lawry managed only six runs in the first 68 minutes; the second of them was his 5,000th in Test cricket and the third was his 2,000th against England.

## ENGLAND

| | | | | | |
|---|---|---|---|---|---|
| G. Boycott | c McKenzie b Gleeson | 70 | | st Marsh b Gleeson | 50 |
| B.W. Luckhurst | b McKenzie | 131 | | c Stackpole b Walters | 19 |
| J.H. Edrich | run out | 47 | | not out | 115 |
| A.P.E. Knott† | c Stackpole b Thomson | 24 | (8) | not out | 30 |
| K.W.R. Fletcher | b Walters | 22 | (4) | lbw b Gleeson | 0 |
| M.C. Cowdrey | c and b G.S. Chappell | 40 | (5) | c Marsh b Thomson | 1 |
| B.L. D'Oliveira | c Stackpole b Thomson | 8 | (6) | b Gleeson | 31 |
| R. Illingworth* | b McKenzie | 34 | (7) | c Marsh b Stackpole | 29 |
| J.A. Snow | not out | 4 | | | |
| K. Shuttleworth | b McKenzie | 2 | | | |
| P. Lever | b McKenzie | 2 | | | |
| Extras | (LB 8, W 1, NB 4) | 13 | | (B 2, LB 3, NB 7) | 12 |
| **Total** | | **397** | | (6 wickets declared) | **287** |

## AUSTRALIA

| | | | | | |
|---|---|---|---|---|---|
| W.M. Lawry* | c Illingworth b Snow | 0 | | not out | 38 |
| K.R. Stackpole | c Lever b Snow | 5 | | c sub (J.H. Hampshire) b Snow | 0 |
| I.M. Chappell | c Knott b Snow | 50 | | c sub (J.H. Hampshire) b Snow | 17 |
| K.D. Walters | c Knott b Lever | 7 | | b Lever | 8 |
| I.R. Redpath | c and b Illingworth | 171 | | not out | 26 |
| A.P. Sheahan | run out | 2 | | | |
| G.S. Chappell | c Luckhurst b Shuttleworth | 108 | | | |
| R.W. Marsh† | c D'Oliveira b Shuttleworth | 44 | | | |
| G.D. McKenzie | c Lever b D'Oliveira | 7 | | | |
| J.W. Gleeson | c Knott b Snow | 15 | | | |
| A.L. Thomson | not out | 12 | | | |
| Extras | (B 5, LB 4, NB 10) | 19 | | (B 4, LB 4, NB 3) | 11 |
| **Total** | | **440** | | (3 wickets) | **100** |

| AUSTRALIA | O | M | R | W | O | M | R | W | FALL OF WICKETS | | | | |
|---|---|---|---|---|---|---|---|---|---|---|---|---|---|
| McKenzie | 31·4 | 4 | 66 | 4 | 18 | 2 | 50 | 0 | | E | A | E | A |
| Thomson | 24 | 4 | 118 | 2 | 25 | 3 | 71 | 1 | *Wkt* | *1st* | *1st* | *2nd* | *2nd* |
| G.S. Chappell | 24 | 4 | 54 | 1 | 4 | 1 | 17 | 0 | 1st | 171 | 5 | 60 | 0 |
| Gleeson | 32 | 10 | 78 | 1 | 32 | 11 | 68 | 3 | 2nd | 243 | 8 | 98 | 20 |
| Walters | 11 | 1 | 35 | 1 | 7 | 1 | 26 | 1 | 3rd | 281 | 17 | 98 | 40 |
| Stackpole | 11 | 2 | 33 | 0 | 15 | 3 | 43 | 1 | 4th | 291 | 105 | 101 | – |
| | | | | | | | | | 5th | 310 | 107 | 152 | – |
| ENGLAND | | | | | | | | | 6th | 327 | 326 | 209 | – |
| Snow | 33·5 | 3 | 143 | 4 | 9 | 4 | 17 | 2 | 7th | 389 | 393 | – | – |
| Shuttleworth | 28 | 4 | 105 | 2 | 3 | 1 | 9 | 0 | 8th | 389 | 408 | – | – |
| Lever | 21 | 3 | 78 | 1 | 5 | 2 | 10 | 1 | 9th | 393 | 426 | – | – |
| D'Oliveira | 17 | 1 | 41 | 1 | 4 | 2 | 5 | 0 | 10th | 397 | 440 | – | – |
| Illingworth | 13 | 2 | 43 | 1 | 4 | 2 | 12 | 0 | | | | | |
| Boycott | 1 | 0 | 7 | 0 | | | | | | | | | |
| Fletcher | 1 | 0 | 4 | 0 | 4 | 0 | 18 | 0 | | | | | |
| Cowdrey | | | | | 3 | 0 | 18 | 0 | | | | | |

Umpires: L.P. Rowan and T.F. Brooks.

**The 3rd Test at Melbourne Cricket Ground, scheduled for 31 December, 1, 2, 4, 5 January was abandoned on the third day without a ball being bowled (see page 837).**

# AUSTRALIA v ENGLAND 1970–71 (4th Test)

Played at Sydney Cricket Ground on 9, 10, 11, 13, 14 January.
Toss: England.   Result: ENGLAND won by 299 runs.
Debuts: England – R.G.D. Willis.

England achieved their largest victory against Australia by a runs margin since 1936–37 (*Test No. 255*). Lawry carried his bat through a completed Test innings – the first Australian to do so at Sydney and the second after W.M. Woodfull to achieve this feat twice.

## ENGLAND

| | | | | |
|---|---|---|---|---|
| G. Boycott | c Gleeson b Connolly | 77 | not out | 142 |
| B.W. Luckhurst | lbw b Gleeson | 38 | c I.M. Chappell b McKenzie | 5 |
| J.H. Edrich | c Gleeson b G.S. Chappell | 55 | run out | 12 |
| K.W.R. Fletcher | c Walters b Mallett | 23 | c Stackpole b Mallett | 8 |
| B.L. D'Oliveira | c Connolly b Mallett | 0 | c I.M. Chappell b G.S. Chappell | 56 |
| R. Illingworth* | b Gleeson | 25 | st Marsh b Mallett | 53 |
| A.P.E. Knott† | st Marsh b Mallett | 6 | not out | 21 |
| J.A. Snow | c Lawry b Gleeson | 37 | | |
| P. Lever | c Connolly b Mallett | 36 | | |
| D.L. Underwood | c G.S. Chappell b Gleeson | 0 | | |
| R.G.D. Willis | not out | 15 | | |
| Extras | (B 5, LB 2, W 1, NB 12) | 20 | (B 9, LB 4, NB 9) | 22 |
| **Total** | | **332** | (5 wickets declared) | **319** |

## AUSTRALIA

| | | | | |
|---|---|---|---|---|
| W.M. Lawry* | c Edrich b Lever | 9 | not out | 60 |
| I.M. Chappell | c Underwood b Snow | 12 | c D'Oliveira b Snow | 0 |
| I.R. Redpath | c Fletcher b D'Oliveira | 64 | c Edrich b Snow | 6 |
| K.D. Walters | c Luckhurst b Illingworth | 55 | c Knott b Lever | 3 |
| G.S. Chappell | c and b Underwood | 15 | b Snow | 2 |
| K.R. Stackpole | c Boycott b Underwood | 33 | c Lever b Snow | 30 |
| R.W. Marsh† | c D'Oliveira b Underwood | 8 | c Willis b Snow | 0 |
| A.A. Mallett | b Underwood | 4 | c Knott b Willis | 6 |
| G.D. McKenzie | not out | 11 | retired hurt | 6 |
| J.W. Gleeson | c Fletcher b D'Oliveira | 0 | b Snow | 0 |
| A.N. Connolly | b Lever | 14 | c Knott b Snow | 0 |
| Extras | (NB 11) | 11 | (B 2, NB 1) | 3 |
| **Total** | | **236** | | **116** |

| AUSTRALIA | O | M | R | W | O | M | R | W | FALL OF WICKETS | | | | |
|---|---|---|---|---|---|---|---|---|---|---|---|---|---|
| McKenzie | 15 | 3 | 74 | 0 | 15 | 0 | 65 | 1 | | E | A | E | A |
| Connolly | 13 | 2 | 43 | 1 | 14 | 1 | 38 | 0 | *Wkt* | *1st* | *1st* | *2nd* | *2nd* |
| Gleeson | 29 | 7 | 83 | 4 | 23 | 4 | 54 | 0 | 1st | 116 | 14 | 7 | 1 |
| G.S. Chappell | 11 | 4 | 30 | 1 | 15 | 5 | 24 | 1 | 2nd | 130 | 38 | 35 | 11 |
| Mallett | 16·7 | 5 | 40 | 4 | 19 | 1 | 85 | 2 | 3rd | 201 | 137 | 48 | 14 |
| Walters | 3 | 1 | 11 | 0 | 2 | 0 | 14 | 0 | 4th | 205 | 160 | 181 | 21 |
| Stackpole | 7 | 2 | 31 | 0 | 6 | 1 | 17 | 0 | 5th | 208 | 189 | 276 | 66 |
| | | | | | | | | | 6th | 219 | 199 | – | 66 |
| ENGLAND | | | | | | | | | 7th | 262 | 208 | – | 86 |
| Snow | 14 | 6 | 23 | 1 | 17·5 | 5 | 40 | 7 | 8th | 291 | 208 | – | 116 |
| Willis | 9 | 2 | 26 | 0 | 3 | 2 | 1 | 1 | 9th | 291 | 219 | – | 116 |
| Lever | 8·6 | 1 | 31 | 2 | 11 | 1 | 24 | 1 | 10th | 332 | 236 | – | – |
| Underwood | 22 | 7 | 66 | 4 | 8 | 2 | 17 | 0 | | | | | |
| Illingworth | 14 | 3 | 59 | 1 | 9 | 5 | 9 | 0 | | | | | |
| D'Oliveira | 9 | 2 | 20 | 2 | 7 | 3 | 16 | 0 | | | | | |
| Fletcher | | | | | 1 | 0 | 6 | 0 | | | | | |

Umpires: L.P. Rowan and T.F. Brooks.

# AUSTRALIA v ENGLAND 1970–71 (5th Test)

Played at Melbourne Cricket Ground on 21, 22, 23, 25, 26 January.
Toss: Australia.    Result: MATCH DRAWN.
Debuts: Australia – J.R.F. Duncan, K.J. O'Keeffe.

This additional Test match was arranged after the 3rd Test had been abandoned without a ball being bowled; it replaced the touring team's four-day return match with Victoria and a one-day game at Euroa. Lawry's declaration temporarily deprived Marsh of the opportunity of becoming the first Australian wicket-keeper to score a Test hundred. Luckhurst scored his second hundred of the rubber despite fracturing his left little finger early in his innings. The third day produced receipts of £25,070 – then a world record.

## AUSTRALIA

| | | | | |
|---|---|---|---|---|
| K.R. Stackpole | c Lever b D'Oliveira | 30 | c Knott b Willis | 18 |
| W.M. Lawry* | c Snow b Willis | 56 | c sub (K. Shuttleworth) b Snow | 42 |
| I.M. Chappell | c Luckhurst b Snow | 111 | b Underwood | 30 |
| I.R. Redpath | b Snow | 72 | c Knott b Snow | 5 |
| K.D. Walters | b Underwood | 55 | not out | 39 |
| G.S. Chappell | c Edrich b Willis | 3 | not out | 20 |
| R.W. Marsh† | not out | 92 | | |
| K.J. O'Keeffe | c Luckhurst b Illingworth | 27 | | |
| J.W. Gleeson | c Cowdrey b Willis | 5 | | |
| J.R.F. Duncan | c Edrich b Illingworth | 3 | | |
| A.L. Thomson | not out | 0 | | |
| Extras | (B 10, LB 17, NB 12) | 39 | (B 8, LB 3, NB 4) | 15 |
| **Total** | (9 wickets declared) | **493** | (4 wickets declared) | **169** |

## ENGLAND

| | | | | |
|---|---|---|---|---|
| G. Boycott | c Redpath b Thomson | 12 | not out | 76 |
| B.W. Luckhurst | b Walters | 109 | | |
| J.H. Edrich | c Marsh b Thomson | 9 | (2) not out | 74 |
| M.C. Cowdrey | c and b Gleeson | 13 | | |
| B.L. D'Oliveira | c Marsh b Thomson | 117 | | |
| R. Illingworth* | c Redpath b Gleeson | 41 | | |
| A.P.E. Knott† | lbw b Stackpole | 19 | | |
| J.A. Snow | b I.M. Chappell | 1 | | |
| P. Lever | run out | 19 | | |
| D.L. Underwood | c and b Gleeson | 5 | | |
| R.G.D. Willis | not out | 5 | | |
| Extras | (B 17, LB 14, NB 11) | 42 | (B 1, LB 8, NB 2) | 11 |
| **Total** | | **392** | (0 wickets) | **161** |

| ENGLAND | O | M | R | W | O | M | R | W | | FALL OF WICKETS | | | |
|---|---|---|---|---|---|---|---|---|---|---|---|---|---|
| Snow | 29 | 6 | 94 | 2 | 12 | 4 | 21 | 2 | | A | E | A | E |
| Lever | 25 | 6 | 79 | 0 | 12 | 1 | 53 | 0 | *Wkt* | *1st* | *1st* | *2nd* | *2nd* |
| D'Oliveira | 22 | 6 | 71 | 1 | | | | | 1st | 64 | 40 | 51 | – |
| Willis | 20 | 5 | 73 | 3 | 10 | 1 | 42 | 1 | 2nd | 266 | 64 | 84 | – |
| Underwood | 19 | 4 | 78 | 1 | 12 | 0 | 38 | 1 | 3rd | 269 | 88 | 91 | – |
| Illingworth | 13 | 0 | 59 | 2 | | | | | 4th | 310 | 228 | 132 | – |
| | | | | | | | | | 5th | 314 | 306 | – | – |
| AUSTRALIA | | | | | | | | | 6th | 374 | 340 | – | – |
| Thomson | 34 | 5 | 110 | 3 | 11 | 5 | 26 | 0 | 7th | 471 | 354 | – | – |
| Duncan | 14 | 4 | 30 | 0 | | | | | 8th | 477 | 362 | – | – |
| G.S. Chappell | 8 | 0 | 21 | 0 | 5 | 0 | 19 | 0 | 9th | 480 | 379 | – | – |
| O'Keeffe | 31 | 11 | 71 | 0 | 19 | 3 | 45 | 0 | 10th | – | 392 | – | – |
| Gleeson | 25 | 7 | 60 | 3 | 3 | 1 | 18 | 0 | | | | | |
| Stackpole | 17·5 | 4 | 41 | 1 | 13 | 2 | 28 | 0 | | | | | |
| Walters | 5 | 2 | 7 | 1 | 7 | 1 | 14 | 0 | | | | | |
| I.M. Chappell | 3 | 0 | 10 | 1 | | | | | | | | | |

Umpires: L.P. Rowan and M.G. O'Connell.

# AUSTRALIA v ENGLAND 1970–71 (6th Test)

Played at Adelaide Oval on 29, 30 January, 1, 2, 3 February.
Toss: England.    Result: MATCH DRAWN.
Debuts: Australia – D.K. Lillee.

After deciding not to enforce the follow-on, England set Australia to score 469 runs in 500 minutes. Boycott and Edrich became the third opening pair to share century partnerships in both innings of a Test against Australia; the others were J.B. Hobbs and H. Sutcliffe, and L. Hutton and C. Washbrook (twice). Lillee took five wickets in his first Test innings.

## ENGLAND

| | | | | |
|---|---|---|---|---|
| G. Boycott | run out | 58 | not out | 119 |
| J.H. Edrich | c Stackpole b Lillee | 130 | b Thomson | 40 |
| K.W.R. Fletcher | b Thomson | 80 | b Gleeson | 5 |
| A.P.E. Knott† | c Redpath b Lillee | 7 | | |
| B.L. D'Oliveira | c Marsh b G.S. Chappell | 47 | (4) c Walters b Thomson | 5 |
| J.H. Hampshire | c Lillee b G.S. Chappell | 55 | (5) lbw b Thomson | 3 |
| R. Illingworth* | b Lillee | 24 | (6) not out | 48 |
| J.A. Snow | b Lillee | 38 | | |
| P. Lever | b Thomson | 5 | | |
| D.L. Underwood | not out | 1 | | |
| R.G.D. Willis | c Walters b Lillee | 4 | | |
| Extras | (B 1, LB 5, W 4, NB 11) | 21 | (LB 4, W 1, NB 8) | 13 |
| **Total** | | **470** | (4 wickets declared) | **233** |

## AUSTRALIA

| | | | | |
|---|---|---|---|---|
| K.R. Stackpole | b Underwood | 87 | b Snow | 136 |
| W.M. Lawry* | c Knott b Snow | 10 | c Knott b Willis | 21 |
| I.M. Chappell | c Knott b Lever | 28 | c Willis b Underwood | 104 |
| I.R. Redpath | c Lever b Illingworth | 9 | not out | 21 |
| K.D. Walters | c Knott b Lever | 8 | not out | 36 |
| G.S. Chappell | c Edrich b Lever | 0 | | |
| R.W. Marsh† | c Knott b Willis | 28 | | |
| A.A. Mallett | c Illingworth b Snow | 28 | | |
| J.W. Gleeson | c Boycott b Willis | 16 | | |
| D.K. Lillee | c Boycott b Lever | 10 | | |
| A.L. Thomson | not out | 6 | | |
| Extras | (LB 2, NB 3) | 5 | (B 2, LB 3, NB 5) | 10 |
| **Total** | | **235** | (3 wickets) | **328** |

| AUSTRALIA | O | M | R | W | O | M | R | W |
|---|---|---|---|---|---|---|---|---|
| Thomson | 29·7 | 6 | 94 | 2 | 19 | 2 | 79 | 3 |
| Lillee | 28·3 | 0 | 84 | 5 | 7 | 0 | 40 | 0 |
| Walters | 9 | 2 | 29 | 0 | 3 | 0 | 5 | 0 |
| G.S. Chappell | 18 | 1 | 54 | 2 | 5 | 0 | 27 | 0 |
| Gleeson | 19 | 1 | 78 | 0 | 16 | 1 | 69 | 1 |
| Mallett | 20 | 1 | 63 | 0 | 1 | 1 | 0 | 0 |
| Stackpole | 12 | 2 | 47 | 0 | | | | |
| ENGLAND | | | | | | | | |
| Snow | 21 | 4 | 73 | 2 | 17 | 3 | 60 | 1 |
| Lever | 17·1 | 2 | 49 | 4 | 17 | 4 | 49 | 0 |
| Underwood | 21 | 6 | 45 | 1 | 35 | 7 | 85 | 1 |
| Willis | 12 | 3 | 49 | 2 | 13 | 1 | 48 | 1 |
| Illingworth | 5 | 2 | 14 | 1 | 14 | 7 | 32 | 0 |
| D'Oliveira | | | | | 15 | 4 | 28 | 0 |
| Fletcher | | | | | 4 | 0 | 16 | 0 |

## FALL OF WICKETS

| | E | A | E | A |
|---|---|---|---|---|
| Wkt | 1st | 1st | 2nd | 2nd |
| 1st | 107 | 61 | 103 | 65 |
| 2nd | 276 | 117 | 128 | 267 |
| 3rd | 289 | 131 | 143 | 271 |
| 4th | 289 | 141 | 151 | – |
| 5th | 385 | 145 | – | – |
| 6th | 402 | 163 | – | – |
| 7th | 458 | 180 | – | – |
| 8th | 465 | 219 | – | – |
| 9th | 465 | 221 | – | – |
| 10th | 470 | 235 | – | – |

Umpires: T.F. Brooks and M.G. O'Connell.

# AUSTRALIA v ENGLAND 1970–71 (7th Test)

Played at Sydney Cricket Ground on 12, 13, 14, 16, 17 February.
Toss: Australia.   Result: ENGLAND won by 62 runs.
Debuts: Australia – A.R. Dell, K.H. Eastwood.

England regained the Ashes at 12.36 p.m. on the fifth day of this six-day Test after the longest rubber in Test history. Chappell emulated P.S. McDonnell, G. Giffen and R.B. Simpson when he invited the opposition to bat in his first Test as Australia's captain. Crowd disturbances around 5.00 p.m. on the second day, after Snow had hit Jenner on the head with a short-pitched ball, led to Illingworth leading the England team off the field. They returned when the playing area had been cleared of missiles. In the second innings Snow fractured and dislocated his right little finger when he collided with the fencing in trying to catch Stackpole. Knott's total of 24 dismissals remains the England record for any rubber. No 'lbw' appeal was upheld against an Australian batsman in the entire rubber.

## ENGLAND

| | | | | | |
|---|---|---|---|---|---|
| J.H. Edrich | c G.S. Chappell b Dell | 30 | c I.M. Chappell b O'Keeffe | 57 |
| B.W. Luckhurst | c Redpath b Walters | 0 | c Lillee b O'Keeffe | 59 |
| K.W.R. Fletcher | c Stackpole b O'Keeffe | 33 | c Stackpole b Eastwood | 20 |
| J.H. Hampshire | c Marsh b Lillee | 10 | c I.M. Chappell b O'Keeffe | 24 |
| B.L. D'Oliveira | b Dell | 1 | c I.M. Chappell b Lillee | 47 |
| R. Illingworth* | b Jenner | 42 | lbw b Lillee | 29 |
| A.P.E. Knott† | c Stackpole b O'Keeffe | 27 | b Dell | 15 |
| J.A. Snow | b Jenner | 7 | c Stackpole b Dell | 20 |
| P. Lever | c Jenner b O'Keeffe | 4 | c Redpath b Jenner | 17 |
| D.L. Underwood | not out | 8 | c Marsh b Dell | 0 |
| R.G.D. Willis | b Jenner | 11 | not out | 2 |
| Extras | (B 4, LB 4, W 1, NB 2) | 11 | (B 3, LB 3, NB 6) | 12 |
| **Total** | | **184** | | **302** |

## AUSTRALIA

| | | | | | |
|---|---|---|---|---|---|
| K.H. Eastwood | c Knott b Lever | 5 | b Snow | 0 |
| K.R. Stackpole | b Snow | 6 | b Illingworth | 67 |
| R.W. Marsh† | c Willis b Lever | 4 | (7) b Underwood | 16 |
| I.M. Chappell* | b Willis | 25 | (3) c Knott b Lever | 6 |
| I.R. Redpath | c and b Underwood | 59 | (4) c Hampshire b Illingworth | 14 |
| K.D. Walters | st Knott b Underwood | 42 | (5) c D'Oliveira b Willis | 1 |
| G.S. Chappell | b Willis | 65 | (6) st Knott b Illingworth | 30 |
| K.J. O'Keeffe | c Knott b Illingworth | 3 | c sub (K. Shuttleworth) b D'Oliveira | 12 |
| T.J. Jenner | b Lever | 30 | c Fletcher b Underwood | 4 |
| D.K. Lillee | c Knott b Willis | 6 | c Hampshire b D'Oliveira | 0 |
| A.R. Dell | not out | 3 | not out | 3 |
| Extras | (LB 5, W 1, NB 10) | 16 | (B 2, NB 5) | 7 |
| **Total** | | **264** | | **160** |

| AUSTRALIA | O | M | R | W | O | M | R | W |
|---|---|---|---|---|---|---|---|---|
| Lillee | 13 | 5 | 32 | 1 | 14 | 0 | 43 | 2 |
| Dell | 16 | 8 | 32 | 2 | 26·7 | 3 | 65 | 3 |
| Walters | 4 | 0 | 10 | 1 | 5 | 0 | 18 | 0 |
| G.S. Chappell | 3 | 0 | 9 | 0 | | | | |
| Jenner | 16 | 3 | 42 | 3 | 21 | 5 | 39 | 1 |
| O'Keeffe | 24 | 8 | 48 | 3 | 26 | 8 | 96 | 3 |
| Eastwood | | | | | 5 | 0 | 21 | 1 |
| Stackpole | | | | | 3 | 1 | 8 | 0 |
| ENGLAND | | | | | | | | |
| Snow | 18 | 2 | 68 | 1 | 2 | 1 | 7 | 1 |
| Lever | 14·6 | 3 | 43 | 3 | 12 | 2 | 23 | 1 |
| D'Oliveira | 12 | 2 | 24 | 0 | 5 | 1 | 15 | 2 |
| Willis | 12 | 1 | 58 | 3 | 9 | 1 | 32 | 1 |
| Underwood | 16 | 3 | 39 | 2 | 13·6 | 5 | 28 | 2 |
| Illingworth | 11 | 3 | 16 | 1 | 20 | 7 | 39 | 3 |
| Fletcher | | | | | 1 | 0 | 9 | 0 |

FALL OF WICKETS

| | E | A | E | A |
|---|---|---|---|---|
| Wkt | 1st | 1st | 2nd | 2nd |
| 1st | 5 | 11 | 94 | 0 |
| 2nd | 60 | 13 | 130 | 22 |
| 3rd | 68 | 32 | 158 | 71 |
| 4th | 69 | 66 | 165 | 82 |
| 5th | 98 | 147 | 234 | 96 |
| 6th | 145 | 162 | 251 | 131 |
| 7th | 156 | 178 | 276 | 142 |
| 8th | 165 | 235 | 298 | 154 |
| 9th | 165 | 239 | 299 | 154 |
| 10th | 184 | 264 | 302 | 160 |

Umpires: L.P. Rowan and T.F. Brooks.

# WEST INDIES v INDIA 1970–71 (1st Test)

Played at Sabina Park, Kingston, Jamaica, on 18 (*no play*), 19, 20, 22, 23 February.
Toss: West Indies.   Result: MATCH DRAWN.
Debuts: West Indies – A.G. Barrett, J.M. Noreiga; India – K. Jayantilal, P. Krishnamurthy.

Because of rain this match began 35 minutes after the scheduled start on the second day. Sardesai batted for just over eight hours and hit a six and 17 fours in scoring India's first double century against West Indies. His partnerships of 137 with Solkar and 122 with Prasanna are still India's best against West Indies for the sixth and ninth wickets respectively. India enforced the follow-on after gaining a first innings lead against West Indies for the first time in 24 Tests dating back to 1948–49.

## INDIA

| | | |
|---|---|---|
| S. Abid Ali | c Camacho b Shillingford | 6 |
| K. Jayantilal | c Sobers b Shillingford | 5 |
| A.L. Wadekar* | c Fredericks b Holder | 8 |
| D.N. Sardesai | c Findlay b Holder | 212 |
| S.A. Durani | b Barrett | 13 |
| M.L. Jaisimha | b Holder | 3 |
| E.D. Solkar | b Sobers | 61 |
| S. Venkataraghavan | c Findlay b Sobers | 4 |
| P. Krishnamurthy† | b Noreiga | 10 |
| E.A.S. Prasanna | b Holder | 25 |
| B.S. Bedi | not out | 5 |
| Extras | (B 9, LB 6, NB 20) | 35 |
| **Total** | | **387** |

## WEST INDIES

| | | | | | |
|---|---|---|---|---|---|
| R.C. Fredericks | c Abid Ali b Prasanna | 45 | c Krishnamurthy b Bedi | | 16 |
| G.S. Camacho | c Wadekar b Prasanna | 35 | c Abid Ali b Venkataraghavan | | 12 |
| R.B. Kanhai | c sub (D. Govindraj) b Venkataraghavan | 56 | not out | | 158 |
| C.H. Lloyd | run out | 15 | run out | | 57 |
| G. St A. Sobers* | c Abid Ali b Prasanna | 44 | c Krishnamurthy b Solkar | | 93 |
| M.C. Carew | c Wadekar b Prasanna | 3 | | | |
| A.G. Barrett | c Solkar b Venkataraghavan | 2 | (6) c Abid Ali b Solkar | | 4 |
| T.M. Findlay† | b Bedi | 6 | (7) not out | | 30 |
| V.A. Holder | b Venkataraghavan | 7 | | | |
| G.C. Shillingford | b Bedi | 0 | | | |
| J.M. Noreiga | not out | 0 | | | |
| Extras | (B 4) | 4 | (B 9, LB 5, NB 1) | | 15 |
| **Total** | | **217** | (5 wickets) | | **385** |

| WEST INDIES | O | M | R | W | O | M | R | W |
|---|---|---|---|---|---|---|---|---|
| Holder | 27·4 | 9 | 60 | 4 | | | | |
| Shillingford | 26 | 2 | 70 | 2 | | | | |
| Sobers | 30 | 8 | 57 | 2 | | | | |
| Noreiga | 31 | 7 | 69 | 1 | | | | |
| Barrett | 35 | 6 | 86 | 1 | | | | |
| Lloyd | 4 | 1 | 7 | 0 | | | | |
| Carew | 5 | 2 | 3 | 0 | | | | |
| INDIA | | | | | | | | |
| Abid Ali | 9 | 2 | 30 | 0 | 5 | 2 | 11 | 0 |
| Solkar | 2 | 0 | 9 | 0 | 22 | 4 | 56 | 2 |
| Bedi | 31·5 | 12 | 63 | 2 | 24 | 5 | 63 | 1 |
| Prasanna | 33 | 12 | 65 | 4 | 21 | 5 | 72 | 0 |
| Venkataraghavan | 18 | 5 | 46 | 3 | 37 | 8 | 94 | 1 |
| Durani | | | | | 14 | 0 | 42 | 0 |
| Jaisimha | | | | | 13 | 1 | 32 | 0 |

## FALL OF WICKETS

| | I | WI | WI |
|---|---|---|---|
| Wkt | 1st | 1st | 2nd |
| 1st | 10 | 73 | 18 |
| 2nd | 13 | 90 | 32 |
| 3rd | 36 | 119 | 147 |
| 4th | 66 | 183 | 320 |
| 5th | 75 | 202 | 326 |
| 6th | 212 | 203 | – |
| 7th | 222 | 205 | – |
| 8th | 260 | 217 | – |
| 9th | 382 | 217 | – |
| 10th | 387 | 217 | – |

Umpires: D. Sang Hue and R. Gosein.

# WEST INDIES v INDIA 1970–71 (2nd Test)

Played at Queen's Park Oval, Port-of-Spain, Trinidad, on 6, 7, 9, 10 March.
Toss: West Indies.   Result: INDIA won by seven wickets.
Debuts: India – S.M. Gavaskar.

India gained their first victory against West Indies at their 25th attempt and with over a day to spare. Gavaskar completed a memorable debut by hitting the winning boundary. West Indies were dismissed for their lowest total against India and it is still their lowest for this series in a home Test. Fredericks was bowled by the first ball of the match. Noreiga, a 34-year-old offspinner playing in his second Test match, became the first bowler to take nine wickets in an innings for West Indies. His analysis is the record for a Test in Trinidad. Davis, 33* overnight, was struck over his right eye while batting in the nets before the start of the fourth day's play when West Indies were 150 for 1, and was taken to hospital to have the wound stitched. He resumed at the fall of the fifth wicket.

## WEST INDIES

| | | | | | |
|---|---|---|---|---|---|
| R.C. Fredericks | b Abid Ali | 0 | run out | | 80 |
| G.S. Camacho | c Solkar b Bedi | 18 | (6) b Venkataraghavan | | 3 |
| R.B. Kanhai | c Solkar b Prasanna | 37 | (2) c Venkataraghavan b Bedi | | 27 |
| C.H. Lloyd | b Abid Ali | 7 | c Wadekar b Durani | | 15 |
| C.A. Davis | not out | 71 | (3) not out | | 74 |
| G. St A. Sobers* | b Venkataraghavan | 29 | (5) b Durani | | 0 |
| A.G. Barrett | c Solkar b Prasanna | 8 | b Venkataraghavan | | 19 |
| T.M. Findlay† | c Bedi | 1 | c Solkar b Venkataraghavan | | 0 |
| V.A. Holder | c Krishnamurthy b Bedi | 14 | b Venkataraghavan | | 14 |
| G.C. Shillingford | c Solkar b Prasanna | 25 | c Durani b Venkataraghavan | | 1 |
| J.M. Noreiga | b Prasanna | 0 | c Solkar b Bedi | | 2 |
| Extras | (B 2, LB 2) | 4 | (B 18, LB 7, NB 1) | | 26 |
| **Total** | | **214** | | | **261** |

## INDIA

| | | | | | |
|---|---|---|---|---|---|
| A.V. Mankad | b Shillingford | 44 | c sub (S.A. Gomes) b Barrett | | 29 |
| S.M. Gavaskar | c Lloyd b Noreiga | 65 | not out | | 67 |
| S.A. Durani | c and b Noreiga | 9 | b Barrett | | 0 |
| D.N. Sardesai | c Shillingford b Noreiga | 112 | c Findlay b Barrett | | 3 |
| A.L. Wadekar* | c Kanhai b Noreiga | 0 | | | |
| E.D. Solkar | c and b Noreiga | 55 | | | |
| S. Abid Ali | c Shillingford b Noreiga | 20 | (5) not out | | 21 |
| S. Venkataraghavan | st Findlay b Noreiga | 5 | | | |
| P. Krishnamurthy† | c sub (S.A. Gomes) b Noreiga | 0 | | | |
| E.A.S. Prasanna | not out | 10 | | | |
| B.S. Bedi | c Holder b Noreiga | 4 | | | |
| Extras | (B 18, LB 2, NB 8) | 28 | (B 2, LB 2, NB 1) | | 5 |
| **Total** | | **352** | (3 wickets) | | **125** |

| INDIA | O | M | R | W | O | M | R | W | | FALL OF WICKETS | | | |
|---|---|---|---|---|---|---|---|---|---|---|---|---|---|
| Abid Ali | 20 | 4 | 54 | 2 | 5 | 2 | 3 | 0 | | WI | I | WI | I |
| Solkar | 3 | 0 | 12 | 0 | 7 | 2 | 19 | 0 | Wkt | 1st | 1st | 2nd | 2nd |
| Gavaskar | 1 | 0 | 9 | 0 | | | | | 1st | 0 | 68 | 73 | 74 |
| Bedi | 16 | 5 | 46 | 3 | 29·5 | 11 | 50 | 2 | 2nd | 42 | 90 | 150 | 74 |
| Prasanna | 19·5 | 3 | 54 | 4 | 16 | 5 | 47 | 0 | 3rd | 62 | 186 | 152 | 84 |
| Venkataraghavan | 13 | 0 | 35 | 1 | 36 | 11 | 95 | 5 | 4th | 62 | 186 | 169 | – |
| Durani | | | | | 17 | 8 | 21 | 2 | 5th | 108 | 300 | 169 | – |
| | | | | | | | | | 6th | 132 | 330 | 218 | – |
| WEST INDIES | | | | | | | | | 7th | 133 | 337 | 222 | – |
| Holder | 19 | 8 | 37 | 0 | 2 | 0 | 12 | 0 | 8th | 161 | 337 | 254 | – |
| Shillingford | 20 | 3 | 45 | 1 | 6 | 2 | 13 | 0 | 9th | 214 | 342 | 256 | – |
| Sobers | 28 | 7 | 65 | 0 | 15 | 5 | 16 | 0 | 10th | 214 | 352 | 261 | – |
| Noreiga | 49·4 | 16 | 95 | 9 | 18 | 4 | 36 | 0 | | | | | |
| Barrett | 37 | 13 | 65 | 0 | 8·4 | 0 | 43 | 3 | | | | | |
| Davis | 3 | 1 | 11 | 0 | | | | | | | | | |
| Lloyd | 1 | 0 | 6 | 0 | | | | | | | | | |

Umpires: R. Gosein and S. Ishmael.

# WEST INDIES v INDIA 1970–71 (3rd Test)

Played at Bourda, Georgetown, Guyana, on 19, 20, 21, 23, 24 March.
Toss: West Indies.　Result: MATCH DRAWN.
Debuts: West Indies – K.D. Boyce, D.M. Lewis.

India were left 90 minutes in which to score 295 runs to win. Gavaskar scored his first Test hundred in his second match. Sobers scored 99 runs between lunch and tea on the fifth day, taking his score from 9* to 108*. When he had scored 54 in that innings he became the third player after W.R. Hammond and M.C. Cowdrey to score 7,000 runs in official Tests.

## WEST INDIES

| | | | | |
|---|---|---|---|---|
| R.C. Fredericks | c Abid Ali b Venkataraghavan | 47 | lbw b Solkar | 5 |
| M.C. Carew | c Mankad b Durani | 41 | c Durani b Bedi | 45 |
| R.B. Kanhai | c Krishnamurthy b Bedi | 25 | | |
| C.H. Lloyd | run out | 60 | c Krishnamurthy b Bedi | 9 |
| C.A. Davis | lbw b Solkar | 34 | (3) not out | 125 |
| G. St A. Sobers* | c Venkataraghavan b Bedi | 4 | (5) not out | 108 |
| D.M. Lewis† | not out | 81 | | |
| K.D. Boyce | c Gavaskar b Venkataraghavan | 9 | | |
| G.C. Shillingford | c Bedi b Venkataraghavan | 5 | | |
| L.R. Gibbs | run out | 25 | | |
| J.M. Noreiga | run out | 9 | | |
| Extras | (B 11, LB 9, NB 3) | 23 | (B 5, LB 6, NB 4) | 15 |
| **Total** | | **363** | (3 wickets declared) | **307** |

## INDIA

| | | | | |
|---|---|---|---|---|
| A.V. Mankad | b Noreiga | 40 | not out | 53 |
| S.M. Gavaskar | c Carew b Sobers | 116 | not out | 64 |
| A.L. Wadekar* | b Sobers | 16 | | |
| G.R. Viswanath | b Boyce | 50 | | |
| S.A. Durani | lbw b Sobers | 2 | | |
| D.N. Sardesai | run out | 45 | | |
| E.D. Solkar | run out | 16 | | |
| S. Abid Ali | not out | 50 | | |
| S. Venkataraghavan | lbw b Shillingford | 12 | | |
| P. Krishnamurthy† | run out | 0 | | |
| B.S. Bedi | lbw b Boyce | 2 | | |
| Extras | (B 5, LB 6, W 1, NB 15) | 27 | (B 4, W 1, NB 1) | 6 |
| **Total** | | **376** | (0 wickets) | **123** |

| INDIA | O | M | R | W | O | M | R | W |
|---|---|---|---|---|---|---|---|---|
| Abid Ali | 13·2 | 5 | 42 | 0 | 14 | 2 | 55 | 0 |
| Solkar | 17 | 3 | 34 | 1 | 16 | 4 | 43 | 1 |
| Venkataraghavan | 59 | 14 | 128 | 3 | 20 | 10 | 47 | 0 |
| Bedi | 55 | 18 | 85 | 2 | 26 | 9 | 55 | 2 |
| Durani | 14 | 3 | 51 | 1 | 16 | 2 | 47 | 0 |
| Mankad | | | | | 5 | 0 | 33 | 0 |
| Wadekar | | | | | 3 | 0 | 12 | 0 |
| **WEST INDIES** | | | | | | | | |
| Boyce | 20·4 | 5 | 47 | 2 | 2 | 0 | 12 | 0 |
| Shillingford | 21 | 2 | 76 | 1 | 2 | 0 | 13 | 0 |
| Sobers | 43 | 15 | 72 | 3 | 5 | 1 | 14 | 0 |
| Gibbs | 39 | 17 | 61 | 0 | 1 | 0 | 4 | 0 |
| Noreiga | 42 | 9 | 91 | 1 | 10 | 0 | 30 | 0 |
| Carew | 2 | 0 | 2 | 0 | | | | |
| Lloyd | | | | | 3 | 0 | 20 | 0 |
| Fredericks | | | | | 4 | 0 | 9 | 0 |
| Davis | | | | | 3 | 0 | 15 | 0 |

FALL OF WICKETS

| | WI | I | WI | I |
|---|---|---|---|---|
| *Wkt* | *1st* | *1st* | *2nd* | *2nd* |
| 1st | 78 | 72 | 11 | – |
| 2nd | 119 | 116 | 114 | – |
| 3rd | 135 | 228 | 137 | – |
| 4th | 213 | 244 | – | – |
| 5th | 226 | 246 | – | – |
| 6th | 231 | 278 | – | – |
| 7th | 246 | 339 | – | – |
| 8th | 256 | 370 | – | – |
| 9th | 340 | 374 | – | – |
| 10th | 363 | 376 | – | – |

Umpires: C.P. Kippins and R. Gosein.

# WEST INDIES v INDIA 1970–71 (4th Test)

Played at Kensington Oval, Bridgetown, Barbados, on 1, 2, 3, 5, 6 April.
Toss: India.   Result: MATCH DRAWN
Debuts: West Indies – Inshan Ali, U.G. Dowe.

Sobers scored his third hundred in successive first-class innings against India, having made 135 for Barbados in the intervening match. He took his 200th wicket in official Tests when he dismissed Viswanath in the first innings and became the second player after R. Benaud to score over 2,000 runs and take 200 wickets in Test cricket. Sardesai shared record India partnerships for this series of 186 with Solkar and 62 with Bedi for the seventh and tenth wickets respectively. His stand with Solkar remains India's highest for the seventh wicket against all countries.

## WEST INDIES

| | | | | | |
|---|---|---|---|---|---|
| R.C. Fredericks | b Abid Ali | 1 | b Venkataraghavan | | 48 |
| D.M. Lewis† | b Bedi | 88 | b Abid Ali | | 14 |
| R.B. Kanhai | c Mankad b Venkataraghavan | 85 | c Krishnamurthy b Solkar | | 11 |
| C.A. Davis | c Venkataraghavan b Abid Ali | 79 | (8) not out | | 22 |
| G. St A. Sobers* | not out | 178 | c Bedi b Abid Ali | | 9 |
| C.H. Lloyd | c Mankad b Bedi | 19 | (4) c Venkataraghavan b Abid Ali | | 43 |
| M.L.C. Foster | not out | 36 | not out | | 24 |
| J.N. Shepherd | ) | | (6) c Solkar b Venkataraghavan | | 3 |
| Inshan Ali | ) | | | | |
| V.A. Holder | ) did not bat | | | | |
| U.G. Dowe | ) | | | | |
| Extras | (B 10, LB 4, NB 1) | 15 | (B 2, LB 3, NB 1) | | 6 |
| **Total** | (5 wickets declared) | **501** | (6 wickets declared) | | **180** |

## INDIA

| | | | | | |
|---|---|---|---|---|---|
| A.V. Mankad | c Lewis b Holder | 6 | c Shepherd b Ali | | 8 |
| S.M. Gavaskar | c Holder b Dowe | 1 | not out | | 117 |
| P. Krishnamurthy† | c Ali b Dowe | 1 | | | |
| A.L. Wadekar* | c Lewis b Sobers | 28 | (3) c Lloyd b Sobers | | 17 |
| G.R. Viswanath | c Lewis b Sobers | 25 | (4) c Shepherd b Sobers | | 0 |
| D.N. Sardesai | lbw b Holder | 150 | c Fredericks b Shepherd | | 24 |
| M.L. Jaisimha | b Dowe | 0 | (5) lbw b Dowe | | 17 |
| E.D. Solkar | c Lewis b Dowe | 65 | (7) not out | | 10 |
| S. Abid Ali | run out | 9 | | | |
| S. Venkataraghavan | b Shepherd | 12 | | | |
| B.S. Bedi | not out | 20 | | | |
| Extras | (B 6, LB 6, NB 18) | 30 | (B 2, LB 8, W 1, NB 17) | | 28 |
| **Total** | | **347** | (5 wickets) | | **221** |

| INDIA | O | M | R | W | O | M | R | W | | | FALL OF WICKETS | | | |
|---|---|---|---|---|---|---|---|---|---|---|---|---|---|---|
| Abid Ali | 31 | 1 | 127 | 2 | 21 | 3 | 70 | 3 | | | WI | I | WI | I |
| Solkar | 19 | 4 | 40 | 0 | 14 | 0 | 73 | 1 | | *Wkt* | *1st* | *1st* | *2nd* | *2nd* |
| Jaisimha | 10 | 2 | 32 | 0 | | | | | | 1st | 4 | 2 | 17 | 35 |
| Bedi | 54 | 15 | 124 | 2 | 1 | 0 | 6 | 0 | | 2nd | 170 | 5 | 36 | 71 |
| Venkataraghavan | 57 | 12 | 163 | 1 | 7 | 0 | 25 | 2 | | 3rd | 179 | 20 | 112 | 79 |
| | | | | | | | | | | 4th | 346 | 64 | 126 | 132 |
| WEST INDIES | | | | | | | | | | 5th | 394 | 69 | 132 | 192 |
| Holder | 25·4 | 7 | 70 | 2 | 8 | 4 | 13 | 0 | | 6th | – | 70 | 133 | – |
| Dowe | 23 | 7 | 69 | 4 | 11 | 5 | 22 | 1 | | 7th | – | 256 | – | – |
| Shepherd | 24 | 4 | 54 | 1 | 20 | 7 | 36 | 1 | | 8th | – | 269 | – | – |
| Sobers | 20 | 9 | 34 | 2 | 23 | 8 | 31 | 2 | | 9th | – | 285 | – | – |
| Ali | 20 | 4 | 60 | 1 | 18 | 1 | 65 | 1 | | 10th | – | 347 | – | – |
| Foster | 11 | 3 | 28 | 0 | 14 | 7 | 10 | 0 | | | | | | |
| Davis | 2 | 0 | 2 | 0 | 3 | 2 | 1 | 0 | | | | | | |
| Lloyd | | | | | 4 | 0 | 13 | 0 | | | | | | |
| Fredericks | | | | | 1 | 0 | 1 | 0 | | | | | | |
| Kanhai | | | | | 1 | 0 | 1 | 0 | | | | | | |

Umpires: H.B. de C. Jordan and D. Sang Hue.

# WEST INDIES v INDIA 1970–71 (5th Test)

Played at Queen's Park Oval, Port-of-Spain, Trinidad, on 13, 14, 15, 17, 18, 19 April.
Toss: India.    Result: MATCH DRAWN.
Debuts: Nil.

After rain had extended the lunch interval by 20 minutes, West Indies needed to score 262 runs in 155 minutes. This draw gave India their first victory in a rubber against West Indies. Gavaskar became the second batsman after K.D. Walters to score a century and a double century in the same Test, the second Indian after V.S. Hazare to score hundreds in both innings of a Test, and the third Indian after Hazare and P.R. Umrigar to score three hundreds in successive Test innings. His aggregate of 774 (average 154·80) remains the India record for a rubber against West Indies and the world record for any batsman playing in his first rubber. His innings of 220 made in 505 minutes with 22 fours, is India's highest against West Indies, their highest in any first-class match in the Caribbean, and the highest in any Test in Trinidad; he was suffering from severe toothache throughout it. He is the only Indian to score four hundreds in a rubber.

## INDIA

| | | | | |
|---|---|---|---|---|
| S. Abid Ali | c Davis b Sobers | 10 | lbw b Sobers | 3 |
| S.M. Gavaskar | c Lewis b Holford | 124 | b Shepherd | 220 |
| A.L. Wadekar* | c Sobers b Shepherd | 28 | c Shepherd b Noreiga | 54 |
| D.N. Sardesai | c Lewis b Holford | 75 | c and b Foster | 21 |
| G.R. Viswanath | c Lewis b Shepherd | 22 | b Sobers | 38 |
| M.L. Jaisimha | c Carew b Dowe | 0 | lbw b Shepherd | 23 |
| E.D. Solkar | c sub (R.C. Fredericks) b Dowe | 3 | c Sobers b Noreiga | 14 |
| S. Venkataraghavan | c Carew b Shepherd | 51 | b Noreiga | 21 |
| P. Krishnamurthy† | c Lewis b Noreiga | 20 | c sub (S.A. Gomes) b Noreiga | 2 |
| E.A.S. Prasanna | c Lloyd b Holford | 16 | not out | 10 |
| B.S. Bedi | not out | 1 | c Sobers b Noreiga | 5 |
| Extras | (LB 1, NB 9) | 10 | (B 6, LB 8, NB 2) | 16 |
| **Total** | | **360** | | **427** |

## WEST INDIES

| | | | | |
|---|---|---|---|---|
| M.C. Carew | c Wadekar b Prasanna | 28 | run out | 4 |
| D.M. Lewis† | c Krishnamurthy b Bedi | 72 | (9) not out | 4 |
| R.B. Kanhai | run out | 13 | (4) b Abid Ali | 21 |
| C.A. Davis | c Solkar b Venkataraghavan | 105 | (8) c Viswanath b Venkataraghavan | 19 |
| C.H. Lloyd | c Venkataraghavan b Prasanna | 6 | (3) c Wadekar b Venkataraghavan | 64 |
| G. St A. Sobers* | b Prasanna | 132 | (5) b Abid Ali | 0 |
| M.L.C. Foster | b Abid Ali | 99 | (6) run out | 18 |
| D.A.J. Holford | st Krishnamurthy b Venkataraghavan | 44 | (7) c Bedi b Solkar | 9 |
| J.N. Shepherd | c Abid Ali b Venkataraghavan | 0 | (2) c and b Abid Ali | 9 |
| U.G. Dowe | lbw b Venkataraghavan | 3 | not out | 0 |
| J.M. Noreiga | not out | 0 | | |
| Extras | (B 14, LB 8, NB 2) | 24 | (B 9, LB 8) | 17 |
| **Total** | | **526** | (8 wickets) | **165** |

| WEST INDIES | O | M | R | W | O | M | R | W |
|---|---|---|---|---|---|---|---|---|
| Sobers | 13 | 3 | 30 | 1 | 42 | 14 | 82 | 2 |
| Dowe | 29 | 1 | 99 | 2 | 22 | 2 | 55 | 0 |
| Shepherd | 35 | 7 | 78 | 3 | 24 | 8 | 45 | 2 |
| Davis | 10 | 0 | 28 | 0 | 10 | 2 | 12 | 0 |
| Noreiga | 16 | 3 | 43 | 1 | 53·4 | 8 | 129 | 5 |
| Holford | 28·3 | 5 | 68 | 3 | 27 | 3 | 63 | 0 |
| Foster | 2 | 0 | 4 | 0 | 12 | 4 | 10 | 1 |
| Carew | | | | | 7 | 2 | 15 | 0 |
| INDIA | | | | | | | | |
| Abid Ali | 31 | 7 | 58 | 1 | 15 | 1 | 73 | 3 |
| Solkar | 11 | 1 | 35 | 0 | 13 | 1 | 40 | 1 |
| Bedi | 71 | 19 | 163 | 1 | 2 | 1 | 1 | 0 |
| Prasanna | 65 | 15 | 146 | 3 | 5 | 0 | 23 | 0 |
| Venkataraghavan | 37·3 | 6 | 100 | 4 | 5 | 1 | 11 | 2 |
| Jaisimha | 1 | 1 | 0 | 0 | | | | |

## FALL OF WICKETS

| | I | WI | I | WI |
|---|---|---|---|---|
| Wkt | 1st | 1st | 2nd | 2nd |
| 1st | 26 | 52 | 11 | 0 |
| 2nd | 68 | 94 | 159 | 16 |
| 3rd | 190 | 142 | 194 | 50 |
| 4th | 238 | 153 | 293 | 50 |
| 5th | 239 | 330 | 374 | 101 |
| 6th | 247 | 424 | 377 | 114 |
| 7th | 296 | 517 | 409 | 152 |
| 8th | 335 | 522 | 412 | 161 |
| 9th | 354 | 523 | 413 | – |
| 10th | 360 | 526 | 427 | – |

Umpires: D. Sang Hue and R. Gosein.

# NEW ZEALAND v ENGLAND 1970–71 (1st Test)

Played at Lancaster Park, Christchurch, on 25, 26, 27 February, 1 March.
Toss: New Zealand.   Result: ENGLAND won by eight wickets.
Debuts: England – R.W. Taylor.

New Zealand were dismissed for the lowest total in any Test at Christchurch and their third-lowest against England. Underwood took his 1,000th first-class wicket when he dismissed Shrimpton in the second innings. His match analysis of 12 for 97 is the record for any Test at Christchurch. C.S. Elliott, in New Zealand on a Churchill Fellowship, was invited to umpire by the New Zealand Cricket Council.

## NEW ZEALAND

| | | | | |
|---|---|---|---|---|
| G.T. Dowling* | c Edrich b Underwood | 13 | c Luckhurst b Lever | 1 |
| B.A.G. Murray | c Taylor b Shuttleworth | 1 | b Shuttleworth | 1 |
| B.E. Congdon | c Taylor b Shuttleworth | 1 | b Underwood | 55 |
| R.W. Morgan | c Luckhurst b Shuttleworth | 6 | (5) b Underwood | 0 |
| M.J.F. Shrimpton | c Fletcher b Underwood | 0 | (6) c Illingworth b Underwood | 8 |
| G.M. Turner | b Underwood | 11 | (4) b Underwood | 76 |
| V. Pollard | b Wilson | 18 | lbw b Underwood | 34 |
| K.J. Wadsworth† | c Fletcher b Underwood | 0 | c Fletcher b Wilson | 1 |
| R.S. Cunis | b Underwood | 0 | b Shuttleworth | 35 |
| H.J. Howarth | st Taylor b Underwood | 0 | c Illingworth b Underwood | 25 |
| R.O. Collinge | not out | 3 | not out | 7 |
| Extras | (B 9, LB 1, W 1, NB 1) | 12 | (B 6, LB 3, W 1, NB 1) | 11 |
| **Total** | | **65** | | **254** |

## ENGLAND

| | | | | |
|---|---|---|---|---|
| B.W. Luckhurst | c Wadsworth b Collinge | 10 | not out | 29 |
| J.H. Edrich | lbw b Cunis | 12 | c Wadsworth b Collinge | 2 |
| K.W.R. Fletcher | b Collinge | 4 | c Howarth b Collinge | 2 |
| J.H. Hampshire | c Turner b Howarth | 40 | not out | 51 |
| B.L. D'Oliveira | b Shrimpton | 100 | | |
| R. Illingworth* | b Shrimpton | 36 | | |
| R.W. Taylor† | st Wadsworth b Howarth | 4 | | |
| D. Wilson | c Murray b Howarth | 5 | | |
| P. Lever | b Howarth | 4 | | |
| K. Shuttleworth | b Shrimpton | 5 | | |
| D.L. Underwood | not out | 0 | | |
| Extras | (B 1, LB 9, NB 1) | 11 | (B 1, LB 4) | 5 |
| **Total** | | **231** | (2 wickets) | **89** |

| ENGLAND | O | M | R | W | O | M | R | W | | FALL OF WICKETS | | | |
|---|---|---|---|---|---|---|---|---|---|---|---|---|---|
| Lever | 5 | 4 | 1 | 0 | 15 | 3 | 30 | 1 | | NZ | E | NZ | E |
| Shuttleworth | 8 | 1 | 14 | 3 | 12 | 1 | 27 | 2 | *Wkt* | *1st* | *1st* | *2nd* | *2nd* |
| D'Oliveira | 3 | 1 | 2 | 0 | | | | | 1st | 4 | 20 | 1 | 3 |
| Underwood | 11·6 | 7 | 12 | 6 | 32·3 | 7 | 85 | 6 | 2nd | 7 | 26 | 6 | 11 |
| Illingworth | 6 | 3 | 12 | 0 | 17 | 5 | 45 | 0 | 3rd | 19 | 31 | 83 | – |
| Wilson | 4 | 2 | 12 | 1 | 21 | 6 | 56 | 1 | 4th | 28 | 95 | 83 | – |
| | | | | | | | | | 5th | 33 | 188 | 99 | – |
| NEW ZEALAND | | | | | | | | | 6th | 54 | 213 | 151 | – |
| Collinge | 12 | 2 | 39 | 2 | 7 | 2 | 20 | 2 | 7th | 54 | 220 | 152 | – |
| Cunis | 13 | 2 | 44 | 1 | 8 | 0 | 17 | 0 | 8th | 62 | 224 | 209 | – |
| Howarth | 19 | 7 | 46 | 4 | 4 | 0 | 17 | 0 | 9th | 62 | 231 | 231 | – |
| Pollard | 9 | 3 | 45 | 0 | 3 | 1 | 9 | 0 | 10th | 65 | 231 | 254 | – |
| Shrimpton | 11·5 | 0 | 35 | 3 | 3 | 0 | 21 | 0 | | | | | |
| Congdon | 3 | 0 | 11 | 0 | | | | | | | | | |

Umpires: C.S. Elliott and W.T. Martin.

# NEW ZEALAND v ENGLAND 1970–71 (2nd Test)

Played at Eden Park, Auckland, on 5, 6, 7, 8 March.
Toss: New Zealand.    Result: MATCH DRAWN.
Debuts: New Zealand – M.G. Webb.

New Zealand were unable to include either B.A.G. Murray or V. Pollard in their team as neither would play on a Sunday. Burgess scored his second hundred in successive Test innings and shared with Shrimpton a New Zealand fifth-wicket record partnership against England of 141. Knott narrowly missed becoming the first wicket-keeper to score a hundred in each innings of a Test. His partnership of 149 with Lever remains the highest for the seventh wicket in this series.

## ENGLAND

| | | | | | |
|---|---|---|---|---|---|
| J.H. Edrich | c Morgan b Webb | 1 | | c Burgess b Collinge | 24 |
| B.W. Luckhurst | c Dowling b Cunis | 14 | | c Wadsworth b Webb | 15 |
| M.C. Cowdrey | c Congdon b Cunis | 54 | (6) | b Collinge | 45 |
| J.H. Hampshire | c Turner b Cunis | 9 | (3) | c Wadsworth b Cunis | 0 |
| B.L. D'Oliveira | c Morgan b Congdon | 58 | (9) | b Collinge | 5 |
| R. Illingworth* | c Wadsworth b Cunis | 0 | (4) | c Turner b Collinge | 22 |
| A.P.E. Knott† | b Collinge | 101 | (5) | b Cunis | 96 |
| P. Lever | c Wadsworth b Cunis | 64 | (7) | lbw b Howarth | 0 |
| K. Shuttleworth | c Wadsworth b Cunis | 0 | (8) | c Wadsworth b Morgan | 11 |
| R.G.D. Willis | c Burgess b Collinge | 7 | | lbw b Cunis | 3 |
| D.L. Underwood | not out | 1 | | not out | 8 |
| Extras | (B 1, LB 4, NB 7) | 12 | | (B 5, LB 3) | 8 |
| **Total** | | **321** | | | **237** |

## NEW ZEALAND

| | | | | | |
|---|---|---|---|---|---|
| G.M. Turner | c and b Underwood | 65 | | not out | 8 |
| G.T. Dowling* | c and b Underwood | 53 | | not out | 31 |
| B.E. Congdon | b Underwood | 0 | | | |
| R.W. Morgan | c and b Underwood | 8 | | | |
| M.G. Burgess | c Edrich b Willis | 104 | | | |
| M.J.F. Shrimpton | lbw b Underwood | 46 | | | |
| K.J. Wadsworth† | c Hampshire b Willis | 16 | | | |
| R.S. Cunis | not out | 5 | | | |
| H.J. Howarth | not out | 2 | | | |
| R.O. Collinge | ) did not bat | | | | |
| M.G. Webb | ) | | | | |
| Extras | (B 7, LB 4, NB 3) | 14 | | (LB 1) | 1 |
| **Total** | (7 wickets declared) | **313** | | (0 wickets) | **40** |

| NEW ZEALAND | O | M | R | W | O | M | R | W |
|---|---|---|---|---|---|---|---|---|
| Webb | 18 | 0 | 94 | 1 | 11 | 0 | 50 | 1 |
| Collinge | 18·6 | 5 | 51 | 2 | 19 | 6 | 41 | 4 |
| Cunis | 24 | 4 | 76 | 6 | 21·7 | 5 | 52 | 3 |
| Howarth | 7 | 0 | 41 | 0 | 21 | 8 | 37 | 1 |
| Congdon | 2 | 0 | 18 | 1 | | | | |
| Shrimpton | 3 | 0 | 29 | 0 | 6 | 0 | 33 | 0 |
| Morgan | | | | | 6 | 0 | 16 | 1 |
| ENGLAND | | | | | | | | |
| Lever | 19 | 3 | 43 | 0 | 2 | 0 | 6 | 0 |
| Shuttleworth | 17 | 3 | 49 | 0 | 4 | 0 | 12 | 0 |
| Willis | 14 | 2 | 54 | 2 | 6 | 1 | 15 | 0 |
| Underwood | 38 | 12 | 108 | 5 | 2 | 2 | 0 | 0 |
| Illingworth | 18 | 4 | 45 | 0 | | | | |
| Luckhurst | | | | | 2 | 0 | 6 | 0 |

## FALL OF WICKETS

| | E | NZ | E | NZ |
|---|---|---|---|---|
| *Wkt* | *1st* | *1st* | *2nd* | *2nd* |
| 1st | 8 | 91 | 26 | – |
| 2nd | 38 | 91 | 27 | – |
| 3rd | 59 | 121 | 62 | – |
| 4th | 111 | 142 | 67 | – |
| 5th | 111 | 283 | 143 | – |
| 6th | 145 | 302 | 152 | – |
| 7th | 294 | 307 | 177 | – |
| 8th | 297 | – | 199 | – |
| 9th | 317 | – | 218 | – |
| 10th | 321 | – | 237 | – |

Umpires: E.C.A. MacKintosh and R.W.R. Shortt.

# ENGLAND v PAKISTAN 1971 (1st Test)

Played at Edgbaston, Birmingham on 3, 4, 5, 7, 8 June.
Toss: Pakistan.   Result: MATCH DRAWN.
Debuts: Pakistan – Imran Khan.

Following-on for the first time against Pakistan, England (184 for 3) were still 71 runs behind the highest total ever made in a Test at Edgbaston when rain eventually allowed the fifth day's play to start at 5.06 p.m. Bad light ended the match with 3·1 of a mandatory 18 overs still to be bowled. Zaheer scored Pakistan's first double century against England and his partnership of 291 with Mushtaq is still Pakistan's record for the second wicket in all first-class cricket. His score of 274 remains the highest for Pakistan against England and the highest by any batsman playing his first innings against England. Pakistan's total is the highest by either country in this series, as is the partnership of 159 between Knott and Lever for the seventh wicket. Aftab (0*) retired at 1 for 0 after being struck on the head by Ward's third ball of the innings. He resumed at 469 for 5.

## PAKISTAN

| | | |
|---|---|---:|
| Aftab Gul | b D'Oliveira | 28 |
| Sadiq Mohammad | c and b Lever | 17 |
| Zaheer Abbas | c Luckhurst b Illingworth | 274 |
| Mushtaq Mohammad | c Cowdrey b Illingworth | 100 |
| Majid Khan | c Lever b Illingworth | 35 |
| Asif Iqbal | not out | 104 |
| Intikhab Alam* | c Underwood b D'Oliveira | 9 |
| Imran Khan | run out | 5 |
| Wasim Bari † | not out | 4 |
| Asif Masood | ) did not bat | |
| Pervez Sajjad | ) | |
| Extras | (B 6, LB 14, NB 12) | 32 |
| **Total** | (7 wickets declared) | **608** |

## ENGLAND

| | | | | |
|---|---|---:|---|---:|
| J.H. Edrich | c Zaheer b Asif Masood | 0 | c Wasim b Asif Masood | 15 |
| B.W. Luckhurst | c Sadiq b Pervez | 35 | not out | 108 |
| M.C. Cowdrey | b Asif Masood | 16 | b Asif Masood | 34 |
| D.L. Amiss | b Asif Masood | 4 | c Pervez b Asif Masood | 22 |
| B.L. D'Oliveira | c Mushtaq b Intikhab | 73 | c Mushtaq b Asif Iqbal | 22 |
| R. Illingworth* | b Intikhab | 1 | c Wasim b Asif Masood | 1 |
| A.P.E. Knott† | b Asif Masood | 116 | not out | 4 |
| P. Lever | c Pervez b Asif Masood | 47 | | |
| K. Shuttleworth | c Imran b Pervez | 21 | | |
| D.L. Underwood | not out | 9 | | |
| A. Ward | c Mushtaq b Pervez | 0 | | |
| Extras | (B 16, LB 6, W 3, NB 6) | 31 | (B 4, LB 5, W 6, NB 8) | 23 |
| **Total** | | **353** | (5 wickets) | **229** |

| ENGLAND | O | M | R | W | O | M | R | W | | FALL OF WICKETS | | | |
|---|---:|---:|---:|---:|---:|---:|---:|---:|---|---|---:|---:|---:|
| Ward | 29 | 3 | 115 | 0 | | | | | | | P | E | E |
| Lever | 38 | 7 | 126 | 1 | | | | | Wkt | 1st | 1st | 2nd |
| Shuttleworth | 23 | 2 | 83 | 0 | | | | | 1st | 68 | 0 | 34 |
| D'Oliveira | 38 | 17 | 78 | 2 | | | | | 2nd | 359 | 29 | 114 |
| Underwood | 41 | 13 | 102 | 0 | | | | | 3rd | 441 | 46 | 169 |
| Illingworth | 26 | 5 | 72 | 3 | | | | | 4th | 456 | 112 | 218 |
| PAKISTAN | | | | | | | | | 5th | 469 | 127 | 221 |
| Asif Masood | 34 | 6 | 111 | 5 | 23·5 | 7 | 49 | 4 | 6th | 567 | 148 | – |
| Imran | 23 | 9 | 36 | 0 | 5 | 0 | 19 | 0 | 7th | 581 | 307 | – |
| Majid | 4 | 1 | 8 | 0 | | | | | 8th | – | 324 | – |
| Intikhab | 31 | 13 | 82 | 2 | 20 | 8 | 52 | 0 | 9th | – | 351 | – |
| Pervez | 15·5 | 6 | 46 | 3 | 14 | 4 | 27 | 0 | 10th | – | 353 | – |
| Mushtaq | 13 | 3 | 39 | 0 | 8 | 2 | 23 | 0 | | | | |
| Asif Iqbal | | | | | 20 | 6 | 36 | 1 | | | | |

Umpires: C.S. Elliott and T.W. Spencer.

# ENGLAND v PAKISTAN 1971 (2nd Test)

Played at Lord's, London, on 17, 18, 19 *(no play)*, 21, 22 June.
Toss: England.   Result: MATCH DRAWN.
Debuts: England – R.A. Hutton.

Rain claimed 17 hours 17 minutes of playing time during the match; play started at 3.30 p.m. on the first day, at 2.30 p.m. on the fourth, not at all on the third, and there was only 23 minutes of cricket on the second. Price dismissed Wasim Bari and Asif Masood with successive balls but was denied the chance of a hat-trick by Pervez's illness. Luckhurst shared in century opening partnerships in both innings.

## ENGLAND

| | | | | |
|---|---|---:|---|---:|
| G. Boycott | not out | 121 | | |
| B.W. Luckhurst | c Wasim b Salim | 46 | (1) not out | 53 |
| J.H. Edrich | c Asif Masood b Pervez | 37 | | |
| D.L. Amiss | not out | 19 | | |
| R.A. Hutton | ) | | (2) not out | 58 |
| B.L. D'Oliveira | ) | | | |
| R. Illingworth* | ) | | | |
| A.P.E. Knott† | ) did not bat | | | |
| P. Lever | ) | | | |
| N. Gifford | ) | | | |
| J.S.E. Price | ) | | | |
| Extras | (B 6, LB 2, W 5, NB 5) | 18 | (B 1, LB 1, NB 4) | 6 |
| **Total** | (2 wickets declared) | **241** | (0 wickets) | **117** |

## PAKISTAN

| | | |
|---|---|---:|
| Aftab Gul | c Knott b Hutton | 33 |
| Sadiq Mohammad | c Knott b D'Oliveira | 28 |
| Zaheer Abbas | c Hutton b Lever | 40 |
| Mushtaq Mohammad | c Amiss b Hutton | 2 |
| Asif Iqbal | c Knott b Gifford | 9 |
| Majid Khan | c Edrich b Price | 9 |
| Intikhab Alam* | c Gifford b Lever | 18 |
| Wasim Bari† | c Knott b Price | 0 |
| Salim Altaf | not out | 0 |
| Asif Masood | b Price | 0 |
| Pervez Sajjad | absent ill | – |
| Extras | (LB 5, W 1, NB 3) | 9 |
| **Total** | | **148** |

| PAKISTAN | O | M | R | W | O | M | R | W | FALL OF WICKETS | | | |
|---|---|---|---|---|---|---|---|---|---|---|---|---|
| Asif Masood | 21 | 3 | 60 | 0 | 3 | 1 | 3 | 0 | | E | P | E |
| Salim | 19 | 5 | 42 | 1 | 5 | 2 | 11 | 0 | *Wkt* | *1st* | *1st* | *2nd* |
| Asif Iqbal | 13 | 2 | 24 | 0 | 4 | 1 | 11 | 0 | 1st | 124 | 57 | – |
| Majid | 4 | 0 | 16 | 0 | 6 | 2 | 7 | 0 | 2nd | 205 | 66 | – |
| Intikhab | 20 | 2 | 64 | 0 | 9 | 1 | 26 | 0 | 3rd | – | 97 | – |
| Pervez | 6 | 2 | 17 | 1 | | | | | 4th | – | 117 | – |
| Mushtaq | | | | | 11 | 3 | 31 | 0 | 5th | – | 119 | – |
| Sadiq | | | | | 5 | 1 | 17 | 0 | 6th | – | 146 | – |
| Aftab | | | | | 1 | 0 | 4 | 0 | 7th | – | 148 | – |
| Zaheer | | | | | 1 | 0 | 1 | 0 | 8th | – | 148 | – |
| | | | | | | | | | 9th | – | 148 | – |
| ENGLAND | | | | | | | | | 10th | – | – | – |
| Price | 11·4 | 5 | 29 | 3 | | | | | | | | |
| Lever | 16 | 3 | 38 | 2 | | | | | | | | |
| Gifford | 12 | 6 | 13 | 1 | | | | | | | | |
| Illingworth | 7 | 6 | 1 | 0 | | | | | | | | |
| Hutton | 16 | 5 | 36 | 2 | | | | | | | | |
| D'Oliveira | 10 | 5 | 22 | 1 | | | | | | | | |

Umpires: A.E. Fagg and A.E.G. Rhodes.

# ENGLAND v PAKISTAN 1971 (3rd Test)

Played at Headingley, Leeds, on 8, 9, 10, 12, 13 July.
Toss: England.   Result: ENGLAND won by 25 runs.
Debuts: Nil.

England won the rubber at 3.49 on the fifth afternoon when Pakistan narrowly failed to score 231 runs in 385 minutes. Boycott's tenth Test hundred was his third in successive innings. Only 159 runs were scored off 107.4 overs on the third day (Pakistan 142 for 6, England 17 for 1) – the slowest full day of Test cricket in England. Wasim Bari equalled the Test record by holding eight catches in the match, which ended when Lever took three wickets in four balls.

## ENGLAND

| | | | | | |
|---|---|---|---|---|---|
| G. Boycott | c Wasim b Intikhab | 112 | c Mushtaq b Asif Masood | 13 |
| B.W. Luckhurst | c Wasim b Salim | 0 | c Wasim b Asif Masood | 0 |
| J.H. Edrich | c Wasim b Asif Masood | 2 | c Mashtaq b Intikhab | 33 |
| D.L. Amiss | c Wasim b Pervez | 23 | c and b Saeed | 56 |
| B.L. D'Oliveira | b Intikhab | 74 | c Wasim b Salim | 72 |
| A.P.E. Knott† | b Asif Masood | 10 | c Zaheer b Intikhab | 7 |
| R. Illingworth* | b Asif Iqbal | 20 | c Wasim b Salim | 45 |
| R.A. Hutton | c Sadiq b Asif Iqbal | 28 | c Zaheer b Intikhab | 4 |
| R.N.S. Hobbs | c Wasim b Asif Iqbal | 6 | b Salim | 0 |
| P. Lever | c Salim b Intikhab | 19 | b Salim | 8 |
| N. Gifford | not out | 3 | not out | 2 |
| Extras | (B 5, LB 5, NB 9) | 19 | (B 6, LB 11, W 2, NB 5) | 24 |
| **Total** | | **316** | | **264** |

## PAKISTAN

| | | | | | |
|---|---|---|---|---|---|
| Aftab Gul | b Gifford | 27 | c Hobbs b Illingworth | 18 |
| Sadiq Mohammad | c Knott b Gifford | 28 | c and b D'Oliveira | 91 |
| Zaheer Abbas | c Edrich b Lever | 72 | c Luckhurst b Illingworth | 0 |
| Mushtaq Mohammad | c Knott b Hutton | 57 | c Edrich b Illingworth | 5 |
| Saeed Ahmed | c Knott b D'Oliveira | 22 | c D'Oliveira b Gifford | 5 |
| Asif Iqbal | c Hutton b D'Oliveira | 14 | st Knott b Gifford | 33 |
| Intikhab Alam* | c Hobbs b D'Oliveira | 17 | c Hutton b D'Oliveira | 4 |
| Wasim Bari† | c Edrich b Gifford | 63 | c Knott b Lever | 10 |
| Salim Altaf | c Knott b Hutton | 22 | not out | 8 |
| Asif Masood | c and b Hutton | 0 | c Knott b Lever | 1 |
| Pervez Sajjad | not out | 9 | lbw b Lever | 0 |
| Extras | (B 6, LB 11, W 1, NB 1) | 19 | (B 17, LB 9, W 1, NB 3) | 30 |
| **Total** | | **350** | | **205** |

| PAKISTAN | O | M | R | W | O | M | R | W |
|---|---|---|---|---|---|---|---|---|
| Asif Masood | 18 | 2 | 75 | 2 | 20 | 7 | 46 | 2 |
| Salim | 20·1 | 4 | 46 | 1 | 14·3 | 9 | 11 | 4 |
| Asif Iqbal | 13 | 2 | 37 | 3 | | | | |
| Pervez | 20 | 2 | 65 | 1 | 16 | 3 | 46 | 0 |
| Intikhab | 27·1 | 12 | 51 | 3 | 36 | 10 | 91 | 3 |
| Saeed | 4 | 0 | 13 | 0 | 15 | 4 | 30 | 1 |
| Mushtaq | 3 | 1 | 10 | 0 | 6 | 1 | 16 | 0 |
| ENGLAND | | | | | | | | |
| Lever | 31 | 9 | 65 | 1 | 3·3 | 1 | 10 | 3 |
| Hutton | 41 | 8 | 72 | 3 | 6 | 0 | 18 | 0 |
| Gifford | 53·4 | 26 | 69 | 3 | 34 | 14 | 51 | 2 |
| Illingworth | 28 | 14 | 31 | 0 | 26 | 11 | 58 | 3 |
| Hobbs | 20 | 5 | 48 | 0 | 4 | 0 | 22 | 0 |
| D'Oliveira | 36 | 18 | 46 | 3 | 15 | 7 | 16 | 2 |

### FALL OF WICKETS

| | E | P | E | P |
|---|---|---|---|---|
| Wkt | 1st | 1st | 2nd | 2nd |
| 1st | 4 | 54 | 0 | 25 |
| 2nd | 10 | 69 | 21 | 25 |
| 3rd | 74 | 198 | 112 | 54 |
| 4th | 209 | 198 | 120 | 65 |
| 5th | 234 | 223 | 142 | 160 |
| 6th | 234 | 249 | 248 | 184 |
| 7th | 283 | 256 | 252 | 187 |
| 8th | 286 | 313 | 252 | 203 |
| 9th | 294 | 313 | 262 | 205 |
| 10th | 316 | 350 | 264 | 205 |

Umpires: A.E. Fagg and D.J. Constant.

# ENGLAND v INDIA 1971 (1st Test)

Played at Lord's, London, on 22, 23, 24, 26, 27 July.
Toss: England.    Result: MATCH DRAWN.
Debuts: Nil.

Rain prevented play after tea on the fifth day when India wanted 38 runs with two wickets left to win their first Test in England. 304 minutes were lost during the match. Snow made his highest score in first-class cricket but was excluded from the next Test as a disciplinary measure for colliding with Gavaskar as the latter was completing a fast single in the second innings.

## ENGLAND

| | | | | |
|---|---|---|---|---|
| G. Boycott | c Engineer b Abid Ali | 3 | c Wadekar b Venkataraghavan | 33 |
| B.W. Luckhurst | c Solkar b Chandrasekhar | 30 | b Solkar | 1 |
| J.H. Edrich | c Venkataraghavan b Bedi | 18 | c Engineer b Bedi | 62 |
| D.L. Amiss | c Engineer b Bedi | 9 | run out | 0 |
| B.L. D'Oliveira | c Solkar b Chandrasekhar | 4 | b Bedi | 30 |
| A.P.E. Knott† | c Wadekar b Venkataraghavan | 67 | c Wadekar b Chandrasekhar | 24 |
| R. Illingworth* | c Engineer b Bedi | 33 | c Wadekar b Venkataraghavan | 20 |
| R.A. Hutton | b Venkataraghavan | 20 | b Chandrasekhar | 0 |
| J.A. Snow | c Abid Ali b Chandrasekhar | 73 | c Chandrasekhar b Venkataraghavan | 9 |
| N. Gifford | b Bedi | 17 | not out | 7 |
| J.S.E. Price | not out | 5 | c Abid Ali b Venkataraghavan | 0 |
| Extras | (B 8, LB 12, NB 5) | 25 | (LB 5) | 5 |
| **Total** | | **304** | | **191** |

## INDIA

| | | | | |
|---|---|---|---|---|
| A.V. Mankad | c Gifford b Snow | 1 | c Knott b Snow | 5 |
| S.M. Gavaskar | c Amiss b Price | 4 | c Edrich b Gifford | 53 |
| A.L. Wadekar* | c Illingworth b Gifford | 85 | c Boycott b Price | 5 |
| D.N. Sardesai | c Illingworth b Gifford | 25 | (6) b Illingworth | 1 |
| G.R. Viswanath | c Knott b Hutton | 68 | c Amiss b Gifford | 9 |
| F.M. Engineer† | c Illingworth b Hutton | 28 | (4) st Knott b Gifford | 35 |
| E.D. Solkar | c Knott b Gifford | 67 | not out | 6 |
| S. Abid Ali | c Luckhurst b Snow | 6 | c Snow b Illingworth | 14 |
| S. Venkataraghavan | c Hutton b Price | 11 | c Hutton b Gifford | 7 |
| B.S. Bedi | c Price b Gifford | 0 | not out | 2 |
| B.S. Chandrasekhar | not out | 0 | | |
| Extras | (B 7, LB 9, NB 2) | 18 | (LB 7, NB 1) | 8 |
| **Total** | | **313** | (8 wickets) | **145** |

| INDIA | O | M | R | W | O | M | R | W | | FALL OF WICKETS | | | |
|---|---|---|---|---|---|---|---|---|---|---|---|---|---|
| Abid Ali | 15 | 3 | 38 | 1 | 9 | 1 | 20 | 0 | | E | I | E | I |
| Solkar | 8 | 3 | 17 | 0 | 6 | 3 | 13 | 1 | *Wkt* | *1st* | *1st* | *2nd* | *2nd* |
| Venkataraghavan | 28 | 8 | 44 | 2 | 30·5 | 11 | 52 | 4 | 1st | 18 | 1 | 4 | 8 |
| Chandrasekhar | 49 | 10 | 110 | 3 | 23 | 7 | 60 | 2 | 2nd | 46 | 29 | 65 | 21 |
| Bedi | 39·3 | 18 | 70 | 4 | 30 | 13 | 41 | 2 | 3rd | 56 | 108 | 70 | 87 |
| | | | | | | | | | 4th | 61 | 125 | 117 | 101 |
| ENGLAND | | | | | | | | | 5th | 71 | 175 | 145 | 108 |
| Price | 25 | 9 | 46 | 2 | 4 | 0 | 26 | 1 | 6th | 161 | 267 | 153 | 114 |
| Snow | 31 | 9 | 64 | 2 | 8 | 0 | 23 | 1 | 7th | 183 | 279 | 153 | 135 |
| Hutton | 24 | 8 | 38 | 2 | 3 | 0 | 12 | 0 | 8th | 223 | 302 | 174 | 142 |
| Gifford | 45·3 | 14 | 84 | 4 | 19 | 4 | 43 | 4 | 9th | 294 | 311 | 189 | – |
| D'Oliveira | 15 | 7 | 20 | 0 | | | | | 10th | 304 | 313 | 191 | – |
| Illingworth | 25 | 12 | 43 | 0 | 16 | 2 | 33 | 2 | | | | | |

Umpires: C.S. Elliott and D.J. Constant.

# ENGLAND v INDIA 1971 (2nd Test)

Played at Old Trafford, Manchester, on 5, 6, 7, 9, 10 *(no play)* August.
Toss: England.   Result: MATCH DRAWN.
Debuts: England – J.A. Jameson.

Rain, which began at 10.30 the previous night, caused the fifth day's play to be abandoned and rescued India from probable defeat after they had been left to score 420 runs in 475 minutes. Lever batted 227 minutes for his highest score in first-class cricket and shared with Illingworth in the highest eighth-wicket partnership by either country in this series. Gifford fractured his thumb while fielding and was unable to bowl in the match. This result extended to 26 England's unbroken run of official Tests without defeat since the Manchester Test against Australia in 1968. This is still the record, beating Australia's run of 25 matches from Wellington 1945-46 to Adelaide 1950-51.

## ENGLAND

| | | | | |
|---|---|---|---|---|
| B.W. Luckhurst | c Viswanath b Bedi | 78 | st Engineer b Solkar | 101 |
| J.A. Jameson | c Gavaskar b Abid Ali | 15 | run out | 28 |
| J.H. Edrich | c Engineer b Abid Ali | 0 | b Bedi | 59 |
| K.W.R. Fletcher | lbw b Abid Ali | 1 | not out | 28 |
| B.L. D'Oliveira | c Gavaskar b Abid Ali | 12 | not out | 23 |
| A.P.E. Knott† | b Venkatarashavan | 41 | | |
| R. Illingworth* | c Gavaskar b Venkataraghavan | 107 | | |
| R.A. Hutton | c and b Venkataraghavan | 15 | | |
| P. Lever | not out | 88 | | |
| N. Gifford | c Engineer b Solkar | 8 | | |
| J.S.E. Price | run out | 0 | | |
| Extras | (B 6, LB 12, W 1, NB 2) | 21 | (LB 5, NB 1) | 6 |
| **Total** | | **386** | (3 wickets declared) | **245** |

## INDIA

| | | | | |
|---|---|---|---|---|
| A.V. Mankad | c Knott b Lever | 8 | b Price | 7 |
| S.M. Gavaskar | c Knott b Price | 57 | c Knott b Hutton | 24 |
| A.L. Wadekar* | c Knott b Hutton | 12 | b Price | 9 |
| D.N. Sardesai | b Lever | 14 | not out | 13 |
| G.R. Viswanath | b Lever | 10 | not out | 8 |
| F.M. Engineer† | c Edrich b Lever | 22 | | |
| E.D. Solkar | c Hutton b D'Oliveira | 50 | | |
| S. Abid Ali | b D'Oliveira | 0 | | |
| S. Venkataraghavan | c Knott b Lever | 20 | | |
| B.S. Bedi | b Price | 8 | | |
| B.S. Chandrasekhar | not out | 4 | | |
| Extras | (B 1, LB 4, NB 2) | 7 | (LB 2, NB 2) | 4 |
| **Total** | | **212** | (3 wickets) | **65** |

| INDIA | O | M | R | W | O | M | R | W |
|---|---|---|---|---|---|---|---|---|
| Abid Ali | 32·4 | 5 | 64 | 4 | 26 | 2 | 95 | 0 |
| Solkar | 21 | 5 | 46 | 1 | 5 | 0 | 23 | 1 |
| Chandrasekhar | 30 | 6 | 90 | 0 | 2 | 0 | 5 | 0 |
| Bedi | 40 | 10 | 72 | 1 | 5 | 0 | 21 | 1 |
| Venkataraghavan | 35 | 9 | 89 | 3 | 16 | 3 | 58 | 0 |
| Gavaskar | 2 | 0 | 4 | 0 | 12 | 3 | 37 | 0 |
| **ENGLAND** | | | | | | | | |
| Price | 22 | 7 | 44 | 2 | 10 | 3 | 30 | 2 |
| Lever | 26 | 4 | 70 | 5 | 7 | 3 | 14 | 0 |
| D'Oliveira | 24 | 11 | 40 | 2 | 3 | 2 | 1 | 0 |
| Hutton | 14 | 3 | 35 | 1 | 7 | 1 | 16 | 1 |
| Illingworth | 7 | 2 | 16 | 0 | | | | |

FALL OF WICKETS

| | E | I | E | I |
|---|---|---|---|---|
| Wkt | 1st | 1st | 2nd | 2nd |
| 1st | 21 | 19 | 44 | 9 |
| 2nd | 21 | 52 | 167 | 22 |
| 3rd | 25 | 90 | 212 | 50 |
| 4th | 41 | 103 | – | – |
| 5th | 116 | 104 | – | – |
| 6th | 168 | 163 | – | – |
| 7th | 187 | 164 | – | – |
| 8th | 355 | 194 | – | – |
| 9th | 384 | 200 | – | – |
| 10th | 386 | 212 | – | – |

Umpires: A.E. Fagg and T.W. Spencer.

# ENGLAND v INDIA 1971 (3rd Test)

Played at Kennington Oval, London, on 19, 20 *(no play)*, 21, 23, 24 August.
Toss: England.    Result: INDIA won by four wickets.
Debuts: Nil.

Abid Ali cut Luckhurst to the boundary at 2.42 on the fifth afternoon to give India her first victory in 22 Tests in England dating back to 1932. It ended England's record run by any country of 26 official matches without defeat. The partnership of 103 in 66 minutes between Knott and Hutton remains England's highest for the seventh wicket against India. England's total of 101 is still their lowest against India. Chandrasekhar's second innings analysis of 6 for 36 was the second-best for India in England, L. Amar Singh taking 6 for 35 at Lord's in 1936 *(Test No. 252)*.

## ENGLAND

| | | | | |
|---|---|---|---|---|
| B.W. Luckhurst | c Gavaskar b Solkar | 1 | c Venkataraghavan b Chandrasekhar | 33 |
| J.A. Jameson | run out | 82 | run out | 16 |
| J.H. Edrich | c Engineer b Bedi | 41 | b Chandrasekhar | 0 |
| K.W.R. Fletcher | c Gavaskar b Bedi | 1 | c Solkar b Chandrasekhar | 0 |
| B.L. D'Oliveira | c Mankad b Chandrasekhar | 2 | c sub (K. Jayantilal) b Venkataraghavan | 17 |
| A.P.E. Knott† | c and b Solkar | 90 | c Solkar b Venkataraghavan | 1 |
| R. Illingworth* | b Chandrasekhar | 11 | c and b Chandrasekhar | 4 |
| R.A. Hutton | b Venkataraghavan | 81 | not out | 13 |
| J.A. Snow | c Engineer b Solkar | 3 | c and b Chandrasekhar | 0 |
| D.L. Underwood | c Wadekar b Venkataraghavan | 22 | c Mankad b Bedi | 11 |
| J.S.E. Price | not out | 1 | lbw b Chandrasekhar | 3 |
| Extras | (B 4, LB 15, W 1) | 20 | (LB 3) | 3 |
| **Total** | | **355** | | **101** |

## INDIA

| | | | | |
|---|---|---|---|---|
| S.M. Gavaskar | b Snow | 6 | lbw b Snow | 0 |
| A.V. Mankad | b Price | 10 | c Hutton b Underwood | 11 |
| A.L. Wadekar* | c Hutton b Illingworth | 48 | run out | 45 |
| D.N. Sardesai | b Illingworth | 54 | c Knott b Underwood | 40 |
| G.R. Viswanath | b Illingworth | 0 | c Knott b Luckhurst | 33 |
| E.D. Solkar | c Fletcher b D'Oliveira | 44 | c and b Underwood | 1 |
| F.M. Engineer† | c Illingworth b Snow | 59 | not out | 28 |
| S. Abid Ali | b Illingworth | 26 | not out | 4 |
| S. Venkataraghavan | lbw b Underwood | 24 | | |
| B.S. Bedi | c D'Oliveira b Illingworth | 2 | | |
| B.S. Chandrasekhar | not out | 0 | | |
| Extras | (B 6, LB 4, NB 1) | 11 | (B 6, LB 5, NB 1) | 12 |
| **Total** | | **284** | (6 wickets) | **174** |

| INDIA | O | M | R | W | O | M | R | W | | FALL OF WICKETS | | | |
|---|---|---|---|---|---|---|---|---|---|---|---|---|---|
| Abid Ali | 12 | 2 | 47 | 0 | 3 | 1 | 5 | 0 | | E | I | E | I |
| Solkar | 15 | 4 | 28 | 3 | 3 | 1 | 10 | 0 | Wkt | 1st | 1st | 2nd | 2nd |
| Gavaskar | 1 | 0 | 1 | 0 | | | | | 1st | 5 | 17 | 23 | 2 |
| Bedi | 36 | 5 | 120 | 2 | 1 | 0 | 1 | 1 | 2nd | 111 | 21 | 24 | 37 |
| Chandrasekhar | 24 | 6 | 76 | 2 | 18·1 | 3 | 38 | 6 | 3rd | 135 | 114 | 24 | 76 |
| Venkataraghavan | 20·4 | 3 | 63 | 2 | 20 | 4 | 44 | 2 | 4th | 139 | 118 | 49 | 124 |
| | | | | | | | | | 5th | 143 | 125 | 54 | 134 |
| ENGLAND | | | | | | | | | 6th | 175 | 222 | 65 | 170 |
| Snow | 24 | 5 | 68 | 2 | 11 | 7 | 14 | 1 | 7th | 278 | 230 | 72 | – |
| Price | 15 | 2 | 51 | 1 | 5 | 0 | 10 | 0 | 8th | 284 | 278 | 72 | – |
| Hutton | 12 | 2 | 30 | 0 | | | | | 9th | 352 | 284 | 96 | – |
| D'Oliveira | 7 | 5 | 5 | 1 | 9 | 3 | 17 | 0 | 10th | 355 | 284 | 101 | – |
| Illingworth | 34·3 | 12 | 70 | 5 | 36 | 15 | 40 | 0 | | | | | |
| Underwood | 25 | 6 | 49 | 1 | 38 | 14 | 72 | 3 | | | | | |
| Luckhurst | | | | | 2 | 0 | 9 | 1 | | | | | |

Umpires: C.S. Elliott and A.E.G. Rhodes.

# WEST INDIES v NEW ZEALAND 1971–72 (1st Test)

Played at Sabina Park, Kingston, Jamaica, on 16, 17, 18, 19, 21 February.
Toss: West Indies.   Result: MATCH DRAWN.
Debuts: West Indies – L.G. Rowe.

Lawrence George Rowe, a 23-year-old right-handed batsman playing in the town of his birth, became the first player to score hundreds in both innings of his first Test match. He was the first player to score a double century in this series and the third after K.D. Walters and S.M. Gavaskar to score a century and a double century in the same Test. Rowe's 214 was scored in 427 minutes and included a six and 19 fours. His partnership of 269 with Fredericks remains the highest for any West Indies wicket against New Zealand. Turner carried his bat throughout New Zealand's innings for the highest score by any batsman achieving this feat in a Test. It was the second time he had carried his bat in a Test. He batted for 572 minutes and hit a five and 26 fours. His partnership of 220 with Wadsworth was a new record for New Zealand overseas and is still New Zealand's highest for the sixth wicket in all Tests. Rowe and Turner had both scored double centuries in their last first-class innings before this match. New Zealand were asked to score 341 runs in 310 minutes.

## WEST INDIES

| | | | | | |
|---|---|---|---|---|---|
| R.C. Fredericks | c and b Howarth | 163 | b Congdon | | 33 |
| M.C. Carew | lbw b Congdon | 43 | b Congdon | | 22 |
| L.G. Rowe | c Dowling b Howarth | 214 | not out | | 100 |
| C.A. Davis | c Turner b Cunis | 31 | b Howarth | | 41 |
| M.L.C. Foster | not out | 28 | not out | | 13 |
| G. St A. Sobers* | not out | 13 | | | |
| D.A.J. Holford | ) | | | | |
| T.M. Findlay† | ) | | | | |
| L.R. Gibbs | ) did not bat | | | | |
| G.C. Shillingford | ) | | | | |
| U.G. Dowe | ) | | | | |
| Extras | (B 1, LB 11, NB 4) | 16 | (B 9) | | 9 |
| **Total** | ( 4 wickets declared) | **508** | (3 wickets declared) | | **218** |

## NEW ZEALAND

| | | | | | |
|---|---|---|---|---|---|
| G.T. Dowling* | lbw b Dowe | 4 | b Holford | | 23 |
| G.M. Turner | not out | 223 | b Holford | | 21 |
| T.W. Jarvis | b Shillingford | 7 | (6) lbw b Holford | | 0 |
| M.G. Burgess | b Dowe | 15 | c and b Dowe | | 101 |
| B.E. Congdon | c and b Holford | 11 | (3) run out | | 16 |
| B.F. Hastings | c Sobers b Gibbs | 16 | (5) b Holford | | 13 |
| K.J. Wadsworth† | c Fredericks b Dowe | 78 | not out | | 36 |
| R.S. Cunis | c Findlay b Shillingford | 0 | not out | | 13 |
| H.J. Howarth | lbw b Holford | 16 | | | |
| J.C. Alabaster | c Dowe b Gibbs | 2 | | | |
| M.G. Webb | lbw b Shillingford | 0 | | | |
| Extras | (B 9, LB 1, NB 4) | 14 | (B 5, LB 6, NB 2) | | 13 |
| **Total** | | **386** | (6 wickets) | | **236** |

| NEW ZEALAND | O | M | R | W | O | M | R | W |
|---|---|---|---|---|---|---|---|---|
| Webb | 25 | 4 | 86 | 0 | 5 | 1 | 34 | 0 |
| Cunis | 34 | 3 | 118 | 1 | 20·4 | 2 | 87 | 0 |
| Congdon | 23 | 2 | 55 | 1 | 11 | 2 | 45 | 2 |
| Alabaster | 25 | 4 | 110 | 0 | | | | |
| Howarth | 44 | 6 | 108 | 2 | 17 | 6 | 43 | 1 |
| Burgess | 2 | 0 | 15 | 0 | | | | |
| WEST INDIES | | | | | | | | |
| Dowe | 29 | 5 | 75 | 3 | 13 | 3 | 46 | 1 |
| Shillingford | 26·5 | 8 | 63 | 3 | 11 | 2 | 32 | 0 |
| Sobers | 11 | 3 | 20 | 0 | 13 | 5 | 16 | 0 |
| Holford | 44 | 18 | 64 | 2 | 33 | 12 | 55 | 4 |
| Gibbs | 45 | 9 | 94 | 2 | 21 | 8 | 42 | 0 |
| Foster | 14 | 8 | 20 | 0 | 9 | 5 | 12 | 0 |
| Fredericks | 4 | 1 | 5 | 0 | 4 | 0 | 14 | 0 |
| Carew | 9 | 0 | 29 | 0 | 4 | 1 | 6 | 0 |
| Davis | 5 | 3 | 2 | 0 | | | | |

FALL OF WICKETS

| | WI | NZ | WI | NZ |
|---|---|---|---|---|
| Wkt | 1st | 1st | 2nd | 2nd |
| 1st | 78 | 4 | 44 | 50 |
| 2nd | 347 | 25 | 57 | 51 |
| 3rd | 428 | 48 | 155 | 96 |
| 4th | 488 | 75 | – | 131 |
| 5th | – | 108 | – | 135 |
| 6th | – | 328 | – | 214 |
| 7th | – | 329 | – | – |
| 8th | – | 361 | – | – |
| 9th | – | 364 | – | – |
| 10th | – | 386 | – | – |

Umpires: D. Sang Hue and J. Gayle.

# WEST INDIES v NEW ZEALAND 1971–72 (2nd Test)

Played at Queen's Park Oval, Port-of-Spain, Trinidad, on 9, 10, 11, 12, 14 March.
Toss: West Indies.   Result: MATCH DRAWN.
Debuts: Nil.

Dowling's declaration left West Indies 170 minutes in which to score 296, with a minimum of 20 overs to be bowled in the last hour. Congdon's partnership of 136 with Cunis remains New Zealand's highest for the eighth wicket in all Tests, and his stand of 139 with Turner in the second innings is their highest for the second wicket in this series.

## NEW ZEALAND

| | | | | | |
|---|---|---|---|---|---|
| G.T. Dowling* | c Carew b Sobers | 8 | c Holder b Gibbs | | 10 |
| G.M. Turner | c Carew b Sobers | 2 | b Sobers | | 95 |
| B.E. Congdon | not out | 166 | c Holford b Ali | | 82 |
| M.G. Burgess | c Findlay b Holder | 32 | not out | | 62 |
| B.F. Hastings | c Rowe b Ali | 3 | not out | | 29 |
| G.E. Vivian | lbw b Holder | 0 | | | |
| K.J. Wadsworth† | c and b Holford | 7 | | | |
| B.R. Taylor | b Foster | 46 | | | |
| R.S. Cunis | c and b Holder | 51 | | | |
| H.J. Howarth | lbw b Holder | 0 | | | |
| J.C. Alabaster | c Carew b Ali | 18 | | | |
| Extras | (B 6, NB 9) | 15 | (B 3, NB 7) | | 10 |
| **Total** | | **348** | (3 wickets declared) | | **288** |

## WEST INDIES

| | | | | | |
|---|---|---|---|---|---|
| R.C. Fredericks | c Wadsworth b Howarth | 69 | c Hastings b Taylor | | 31 |
| M.C. Carew | lbw b Taylor | 4 | c Vivian b Taylor | | 28 |
| L.G. Rowe | b Congdon | 22 | c and b Howarth | | 1 |
| C.A. Davis | c Turner b Howarth | 90 | not out | | 29 |
| M.L.C. Foster | b Howarth | 23 | c Burgess b Taylor | | 3 |
| G. St A. Sobers* | c Wadsworth b Congdon | 19 | b Alabaster | | 9 |
| D.A.J. Holford | lbw b Congdon | 14 | not out | | 9 |
| T.M. Findlay† | b Taylor | 16 | | | |
| Inshan Ali | c Burgess b Taylor | 25 | | | |
| V.A. Holder | b Taylor | 30 | | | |
| L.R. Gibbs | not out | 3 | | | |
| Extras | (B 12, LB 9, W 1, NB 4) | 26 | (B 8, W 1, NB 2) | | 11 |
| **Total** | | **341** | (5 wickets) | | **121** |

| WEST INDIES | O | M | R | W | O | M | R | W | | FALL OF WICKETS | | | |
|---|---|---|---|---|---|---|---|---|---|---|---|---|---|
| Holder | 32 | 13 | 60 | 4 | 15 | 5 | 17 | 0 | | | NZ | WI | NZ | WI |
| Sobers | 26 | 7 | 40 | 2 | 20 | 3 | 54 | 1 | *Wkt* | *1st* | *1st* | *2nd* | *2nd* |
| Gibbs | 29 | 6 | 64 | 0 | 35 | 14 | 67 | 1 | 1st | 5 | 18 | 35 | 59 |
| Ali | 46·5 | 10 | 92 | 2 | 33 | 8 | 60 | 1 | 2nd | 16 | 65 | 174 | 66 |
| Holford | 22 | 6 | 45 | 1 | 17 | 2 | 50 | 0 | 3rd | 66 | 143 | 218 | 68 |
| Davis | 3 | 1 | 9 | 0 | 4 | 2 | 5 | 0 | 4th | 77 | 200 | – | 73 |
| Foster | 9 | 5 | 12 | 1 | 7 | 2 | 9 | 0 | 5th | 78 | 239 | – | 95 |
| Carew | 3 | 0 | 8 | 0 | 5 | 0 | 10 | 0 | 6th | 99 | 245 | – | – |
| Fredericks | 5 | 3 | 3 | 0 | 4 | 2 | 6 | 0 | 7th | 168 | 270 | – | – |
| | | | | | | | | | 8th | 304 | 281 | – | – |
| NEW ZEALAND | | | | | | | | | 9th | 307 | 327 | – | – |
| Cunis | 22 | 5 | 67 | 0 | 5 | 0 | 33 | 0 | 10th | 348 | 341 | – | – |
| Taylor | 20·1 | 9 | 41 | 4 | 12 | 2 | 26 | 3 | | | | | |
| Howarth | 53 | 17 | 102 | 3 | 20 | 8 | 36 | 1 | | | | | |
| Congdon | 39 | 19 | 56 | 3 | 1 | 1 | 0 | 0 | | | | | |
| Alabaster | 21 | 7 | 49 | 0 | 4 | 2 | 5 | 1 | | | | | |
| Vivian | | | | | 4 | 2 | 10 | 0 | | | | | |

Umpires: D. Sang Hue and R. Gosein.

# WEST INDIES v NEW ZEALAND 1971–72 (3rd Test)

Played at Kensington Oval, Bridgetown, Barbados, on 23, 24, 25, 26, 28 March.
Toss: West Indies.    Result: MATCH DRAWN.
Debuts: Nil.

Taylor's innings analysis of 7 for 74 and match figures of 9 for 182 are the best for New Zealand in this series. West Indies recorded their lowest total in a home Test against New Zealand. The partnership of 175 between Congdon and Hastings was New Zealand's highest for the fourth wicket in all Tests and remains the record by either side in this series – as does the sixth-wicket stand of 254 which Davis and Sobers shared in 363 minutes. West Indies scored their highest second innings total in any home Test. Sobers passed M.C. Cowdrey's world record aggregate of 7,459 when he had scored 11 in the second innings. Cowdrey subsequently scored a further 165 runs against Australia in 1974-75, but the record has remained with Sobers since this match.

## WEST INDIES

| | | | | | |
|---|---|---|---|---|---|
| R.C. Fredericks | c Hastings b Cunis | 5 | lbw b Cunis | | 28 |
| M.C. Carew | c Morgan b Taylor | 1 | c Turner b Howarth | | 45 |
| L.G. Rowe | c Wadsworth bTaylor | 0 | lbw b Congdon | | 51 |
| C.A. Davis | c Jarvis b Taylor | 1 | (5) run out | | 183 |
| G. St A. Sobers* | c Wadsworth b Congdon | 35 | (7) c Vivian b Taylor | | 142 |
| M.L.C. Foster | c Wadsworth b Taylor | 22 | lbw b Taylor | | 4 |
| D.A.J. Holford | c Wadsworth b Taylor | 3 | (8) c Wadsworth b Congdon | | 50 |
| T.M. Findlay† | not out | 44 | (4) c Morgan b Howarth | | 9 |
| Inshan Ali | b Taylor | 3 | not out | | 12 |
| V.A. Holder | b Congdon | 3 | not out | | 16 |
| G.C. Shillingford | c Morgan b Taylor | 15 | | | |
| Extras | (NB 1) | 1 | (B 6, LB 9, W 1, NB 8) | | 24 |
| **Total** | | **133** | (8 wickets) | | **564** |

## NEW ZEALAND

| | | |
|---|---|---|
| G.M. Turner | c Holford b Holder | 21 |
| T.W. Jarvis | lbw b Shillingford | 26 |
| B.E. Congdon* | lbw b Holder | 126 |
| M.G. Burgess | c Fredericks b Sobers | 19 |
| B.F. Hastings | lbw b Sobers | 105 |
| R.W. Morgan | c Fredericks b Ali | 2 |
| G.E. Vivian | b Sobers | 38 |
| K.J. Wadsworth† | not out | 15 |
| B.R. Taylor | lbw b Sobers | 0 |
| R.S. Cunis | c Findlay b Holder | 27 |
| H.J. Howarth | b Shillingford | 8 |
| Extras | (LB 13, NB 22) | 35 |
| **Total** | | **422** |

| NEW ZEALAND | O | M | R | W | O | M | R | W |
|---|---|---|---|---|---|---|---|---|
| Cunis | 10 | 3 | 26 | 1 | 38 | 8 | 130 | 1 |
| Taylor | 20·3 | 6 | 74 | 7 | 33 | 3 | 108 | 2 |
| Congdon | 16 | 3 | 26 | 2 | 31 | 7 | 66 | 2 |
| Howarth | 3 | 1 | 6 | 0 | 74 | 24 | 138 | 2 |
| Morgan | | | | | 30 | 8 | 78 | 0 |
| Vivian | | | | | 8 | 2 | 20 | 0 |

| WEST INDIES | O | M | R | W |
|---|---|---|---|---|
| Holder | 40 | 13 | 91 | 3 |
| Sobers | 29 | 6 | 64 | 4 |
| Shillingford | 24·2 | 7 | 65 | 2 |
| Davis | 10 | 3 | 19 | 0 |
| Ali | 35 | 11 | 81 | 1 |
| Holford | 9 | 0 | 20 | 0 |
| Foster | 14 | 2 | 40 | 0 |
| Fredericks | 2 | 0 | 7 | 0 |

### FALL OF WICKETS

| Wkt | WI 1st | NZ 1st | WI 2nd |
|---|---|---|---|
| 1st | 6 | 54 | 48 |
| 2nd | 6 | 68 | 91 |
| 3rd | 6 | 112 | 105 |
| 4th | 12 | 287 | 163 |
| 5th | 44 | 293 | 171 |
| 6th | 52 | 356 | 425 |
| 7th | 83 | 369 | 518 |
| 8th | 99 | 369 | 544 |
| 9th | 102 | 412 | – |
| 10th | 133 | 422 | – |

Umpires: H.B. de C. Jordan and C.P. Kippins.

# WEST INDIES v NEW ZEALAND 1971–72 (4th Test)

Played at Bourda, Georgetown, Guyana, on 6, 7, 8, 9, 11 April.
Toss: West Indies.    Result: MATCH DRAWN.
Debuts: West Indies – G.A. Greenidge, A.B. Howard, A.I. Kallicharran.

West Indies declared on the third day after Kallicharran had completed his hundred on debut. The innings, which lasted 522 minutes, had been suspended for 16 minutes when bottles had been thrown on to the playing area after Lloyd's dismissal. New Zealand declared after batting for 780 minutes and reaching what was then their highest total in any Test; it remains the highest total in a Test at Georgetown. Turner's score of 259 is the highest for New Zealand in all Tests (beating G.T. Dowling's 239 in *Test No. 634*), the highest in any Test in Guyana and the record for either side in this series. He batted for 704 minutes and hit 22 fours. In his previous innings he had compiled the identical score against Guyana on the same ground. His partnership of 387 in 540 minutes with Jarvis remains the highest first-wicket partnership by New Zealand batsmen in all first-class cricket and the record for any wicket by either side in this series.

## WEST INDIES

| | | | | |
|---|---|---|---|---|
| R.C. Fredericks | c Turner b Cunis | 41 | not out | 42 |
| G.A. Greenidge | c Wadsworth b Taylor | 50 | not out | 35 |
| L.G. Rowe | b Congdon | 31 | | |
| C.H. Lloyd | run out | 43 | | |
| C.A. Davis | c Wadsworth b Taylor | 28 | | |
| A.I. Kallicharran | not out | 100 | | |
| G. St A. Sobers* | c Burgess b Taylor | 5 | | |
| D.A.J. Holford | lbw b Congdon | 28 | | |
| T.M. Findlay† | not out | 15 | | |
| V.A. Holder | } did not bat | | | |
| A.B. Howard | | | | |
| Extras | (B 10, LB 5, W 1, NB 8) | 24 | (B 4, LB 2, W 1, NB 2) | 9 |
| **Total** | (7 wickets declared) | **365** | (0 wickets) | **86** |

## NEW ZEALAND

| | | |
|---|---|---|
| G.M. Turner | lbw b Howard | 259 |
| T.W. Jarvis | c Greenidge b Holford | 182 |
| B.E. Congdon* | not out | 61 |
| M.G. Burgess | b Howard | 8 |
| B.F. Hastings | not out | 18 |
| R.W. Morgan | ) | |
| G.E. Vivian | ) | |
| K.J. Wadsworth† | ) did not bat | |
| B.R. Taylor | ) | |
| R.S. Cunis | ) | |
| H.J. Howarth | ) | |
| Extras | (LB 11, NB 4) | 15 |
| **Total** | (3 wickets declared) | **543** |

| NEW ZEALAND | O | M | R | W | O | M | R | W |
|---|---|---|---|---|---|---|---|---|
| Cunis | 24 | 5 | 61 | 1 | 5 | 2 | 13 | 0 |
| Taylor | 37 | 7 | 105 | 3 | 6 | 3 | 9 | 0 |
| Congdon | 33 | 7 | 86 | 2 | | | | |
| Howarth | 38 | 10 | 79 | 0 | 9 | 3 | 12 | 0 |
| Vivian | 3 | 0 | 10 | 0 | 3 | 0 | 16 | 0 |
| Morgan | | | | | 9 | 3 | 10 | 0 |
| Burgess | | | | | 5 | 3 | 12 | 0 |
| Turner | | | | | 2 | 1 | 5 | 0 |
| Jarvis | | | | | 1 | 1 | 0 | 0 |

| WEST INDIES | O | M | R | W |
|---|---|---|---|---|
| Holder | 24 | 8 | 39 | 0 |
| Sobers | 42 | 15 | 76 | 0 |
| Lloyd | 36 | 11 | 74 | 0 |
| Howard | 62 | 16 | 140 | 2 |
| Holford | 54 | 24 | 78 | 1 |
| Greenidge | 14 | 4 | 34 | 0 |
| Davis | 25 | 8 | 42 | 0 |
| Kallicharran | 6 | 1 | 17 | 0 |
| Rowe | 5 | 0 | 28 | 0 |

FALL OF WICKETS

| | WI | NZ | WI |
|---|---|---|---|
| Wkt | 1st | 1st | 2nd |
| 1st | 79 | 387 | – |
| 2nd | 103 | 482 | – |
| 3rd | 160 | 496 | – |
| 4th | 178 | – | – |
| 5th | 237 | – | – |
| 6th | 244 | – | – |
| 7th | 305 | – | – |
| 8th | – | – | – |
| 9th | – | – | – |
| 10th | – | – | – |

Umpires: H.B. de C. Jordan and C.P. Kippins.

# WEST INDIES v NEW ZEALAND 1971–72 (5th Test)

Played at Queen's Park Oval, Port-of-Spain, Trinidad, on 20, 21, 22, 23, 25, 26 April.
Toss: West Indies.   Result: MATCH DRAWN.
Debuts: West Indies – R.R. Jumadeen.

Sobers became the first captain to win all five tosses in a rubber twice; he had been equally successful in England in 1966. Kallicharran was the second batsman after Rowe to score hundreds in his first two innings in Test cricket: Rowe had done so in his first match *(Test No. 693)*. West Indies did not enforce the follow on and New Zealand were eventually left 605 minutes in which to score 401 to win the rubber. Wadsworth and Taylor batted out the last 106 minutes to earn a draw.

## WEST INDIES

| | | | | |
|---|---|---|---|---|
| R.C. Fredericks | run out | 60 | c Turner b Taylor | 15 |
| G.A. Greenidge | c Hastings b Howarth | 38 | c Wadsworth b Taylor | 21 |
| A.I. Kallicharran | c Wadsworth b Cunis | 101 | c Vivian b Taylor | 18 |
| C.A. Davis | c Hastings b Morgan | 40 | c Taylor b Howarth | 23 |
| C.H. Lloyd | c Howarth b Taylor | 18 | c Congdon b Howarth | 5 |
| T.M. Findlay† | b Congdon | 9 | (7) lbw b Howarth | 6 |
| D.A.J. Holford | retired hurt | 46 | (9) run out | 25 |
| G. St A. Sobers* | c Hastings b Howarth | 28 | (6) b Taylor | 2 |
| Inshan Ali | c Wadsworth b Taylor | 0 | (8) lbw b Taylor | 16 |
| V.A. Holder | c and b Taylor | 12 | b Cunis | 42 |
| R.R. Jumadeen | not out | 3 | not out | 2 |
| Extras | (B 2, LB 6, NB 5) | 13 | (B 5, LB 12, NB 2) | 19 |
| **Total** | | **368** | | **194** |

## NEW ZEALAND

| | | | | |
|---|---|---|---|---|
| G.M. Turner | b Holder | 1 | c Findlay b Holder | 50 |
| T.W. Jarvis | c Sobers b Ali | 40 | lbw b Ali | 22 |
| B.E. Congdon* | c Findlay b Lloyd | 11 | b Sobers | 58 |
| M.G. Burgess | b Ali | 5 | c Greenidge b Ali | 6 |
| R.S. Cunis | c Findlay b Ali | 2 | | |
| B.F. Hastings | c Findlay b Jumadeen | 27 | (5) c Lloyd b Holder | 11 |
| G.E. Vivian | b Sobers | 24 | (6) lbw b Holder | 4 |
| B.R. Taylor | b Sobers | 26 | (9) not out | 42 |
| R.W. Morgan | c Holder b Ali | 4 | (8) b Holder | 2 |
| K.J. Wadsworth† | st Findlay b Ali | 1 | (7) not out | 40 |
| H.J. Howarth | not out | 0 | | |
| Extras | (B 3, LB 6, NB 12) | 21 | (B 2, LB 1, W 1, NB 14) | 18 |
| **Total** | | **162** | (7 wickets) | **253** |

| NEW ZEALAND | O | M | R | W | O | M | R | W | | FALL OF WICKETS | | | |
|---|---|---|---|---|---|---|---|---|---|---|---|---|---|
| Cunis | 20 | 5 | 61 | 1 | 4·2 | 0 | 21 | 1 | | WI | NZ | WI | NZ |
| Taylor | 19·4 | 1 | 74 | 3 | 24 | 8 | 41 | 5 | *Wkt* | *1st* | *1st* | *2nd* | *2nd* |
| Congdon | 31 | 6 | 73 | 1 | 15 | 2 | 39 | 0 | 1st | 92 | 18 | 35 | 62 |
| Howarth | 51 | 17 | 109 | 2 | 29 | 8 | 70 | 3 | 2nd | 107 | 39 | 48 | 105 |
| Morgan | 7 | 0 | 38 | 1 | 2 | 1 | 4 | 0 | 3rd | 208 | 51 | 66 | 122 |
| | | | | | | | | | 4th | 265 | 53 | 73 | 157 |
| WEST INDIES | | | | | | | | | 5th | 265 | 86 | 90 | 157 |
| Holder | 16 | 1 | 37 | 1 | 26 | 12 | 41 | 4 | 6th | 312 | 106 | 90 | 181 |
| Sobers | 11 | 5 | 17 | 2 | 29 | 12 | 45 | 1 | 7th | 348 | 142 | 97 | 188 |
| Lloyd | 3 | 0 | 10 | 1 | | | | | 8th | 360 | 150 | 123 | – |
| Ali | 26·4 | 8 | 59 | 5 | 51 | 16 | 99 | 2 | 9th | 368 | 162 | 179 | – |
| Jumadeen | 19 | 9 | 18 | 1 | 45 | 22 | 46 | 0 | 10th | – | 162 | 194 | – |
| Greenidge | | | | | 1 | 0 | 2 | 0 | | | | | |
| Fredericks | | | | | 2 | 1 | 2 | 0 | | | | | |
| Kallicharran | | | | | 1 | 1 | 0 | 0 | | | | | |

Umpires: D. Sang Hue and R. Gosein.

# ENGLAND v AUSTRALIA 1972 (1st Test)

Played at Old Trafford, Manchester, on 8, 9, 10, 12, 13 June.
Toss: England.   Result: ENGLAND won by 89 runs.
Debuts: England – A.W. Greig; Australia – D.J. Colley, B.C. Francis.

At 3.12 on the fifth afternoon England gained their first victory in the first Test of a home series against Australia since 1930. Illingworth won the toss on his 40th birthday. Soon after the start, which had been delayed 90 minutes because of a wet outfield, Boycott was struck above the left elbow by a ball from Lillee. He retired (3*) at lunch when England were 13 for 1 and resumed at 118 for 4. Greig was top scorer in both innings of his first official Test. England lost their last four second innings wickets to the first six deliveries with the second new ball, including those of Illingworth, Snow and Gifford to four balls from Lillee. Marsh, who equalled the series record with five catches in the second innings, scored 91 off 111 balls in 123 minutes and hit four sixes and nine fours. His partnership of 104 in 82 minutes with Gleeson was Australia's highest for the ninth wicket in all Tests outside Australia.

## ENGLAND

| | | | | | |
|---|---|---:|---|---|---:|
| G. Boycott | c Stackpole b Gleeson | 8 | lbw b Gleeson | | 47 |
| J.H. Edrich | run out | 49 | c Marsh b Watson | | 26 |
| B.W. Luckhurst | b Colley | 14 | c Marsh b Colley | | 0 |
| M.J.K. Smith | lbw b Lillee | 10 | c Marsh b Lillee | | 34 |
| B.L. D'Oliveira | b G.S. Chappell | 23 | c Watson b Lillee | | 37 |
| A.W. Greig | lbw b Colley | 57 | b G.S. Chappell | | 62 |
| A.P.E. Knott† | c Marsh b Lillee | 18 | c Marsh b Lillee | | 1 |
| R. Illingworth* | not out | 26 | c I.M. Chappell b Lillee | | 14 |
| J.A. Snow | b Colley | 3 | lbw b Lillee | | 0 |
| N. Gifford | run out | 15 | c Marsh b Lillee | | 0 |
| G.G. Arnold | c Francis b Gleeson | 1 | not out | | 0 |
| Extras | (B 10, LB 9, W 2, NB 4) | 25 | (B 4, LB 8, NB 1) | | 13 |
| **Total** | | **249** | | | **234** |

## AUSTRALIA

| | | | | | |
|---|---|---:|---|---|---:|
| K.R. Stackpole | lbw b Arnold | 53 | b Greig | | 67 |
| B.C. Francis | lbw b D'Oliveira | 27 | lbw b Snow | | 6 |
| I.M. Chappell* | c Smith b Greig | 0 | c Knott b Snow | | 7 |
| G.S. Chappell | c Greig b Snow | 24 | c D'Oliveira b Arnold | | 23 |
| G.D. Watson | c Knott b Arnold | 2 | c and b Snow | | 0 |
| K.D. Walters | c Illingworth b Snow | 17 | b Greig | | 20 |
| R.J. Inverarity | c Knott b Arnold | 4 | c Luckhurst b D'Oliveira | | 3 |
| R.W. Marsh† | c Edrich b Arnold | 8 | c Knott b Greig | | 91 |
| D.J. Colley | b Snow | 1 | c Greig b Snow | | 4 |
| J.W. Gleeson | b Snow | 0 | b Greig | | 30 |
| D.K. Lillee | not out | 1 | not out | | 0 |
| Extras | (B 1, LB 4) | 5 | (W 1) | | 1 |
| **Total** | | **142** | | | **252** |

| AUSTRALIA | O | M | R | W | O | M | R | W |
|---|---:|---:|---:|---:|---:|---:|---:|---:|
| Lillee | 29 | 14 | 40 | 2 | 30 | 8 | 66 | 6 |
| Colley | 33 | 3 | 83 | 3 | 23 | 3 | 68 | 1 |
| G.S. Chappell | 16 | 6 | 28 | 1 | 21·2 | 6 | 42 | 1 |
| Walters | 5 | 1 | 7 | 0 | | | | |
| Watson | 4 | 2 | 8 | 0 | 5 | 0 | 29 | 1 |
| Gleeson | 24·4 | 10 | 45 | 2 | 7 | 3 | 16 | 1 |
| Inverarity | 9 | 3 | 13 | 0 | | | | |
| ENGLAND | | | | | | | | |
| Snow | 20 | 7 | 41 | 4 | 27 | 2 | 87 | 4 |
| Arnold | 25 | 4 | 62 | 4 | 20 | 2 | 59 | 1 |
| Greig | 7 | 1 | 21 | 1 | 19·2 | 7 | 53 | 4 |
| D'Oliveira | 6 | 1 | 13 | 1 | 16 | 4 | 23 | 1 |
| Gifford | | | | | 3 | 0 | 29 | 0 |

### FALL OF WICKETS

| | E | A | E | A |
|---|---:|---:|---:|---:|
| Wkt | 1st | 1st | 2nd | 2nd |
| 1st | 50 | 68 | 60 | 9 |
| 2nd | 86 | 69 | 65 | 31 |
| 3rd | 99 | 91 | 81 | 77 |
| 4th | 118 | 99 | 140 | 78 |
| 5th | 127 | 119 | 182 | 115 |
| 6th | 190 | 124 | 192 | 120 |
| 7th | 200 | 134 | 234 | 136 |
| 8th | 209 | 137 | 234 | 147 |
| 9th | 243 | 137 | 234 | 251 |
| 10th | 249 | 142 | 234 | 252 |

Umpires: C.S. Elliott and T.W. Spencer.

# ENGLAND v AUSTRALIA 1972 (2nd Test)

Played at Lord's, London, on 22, 23, 24, 26 June.
Toss: England.   Result: AUSTRALIA won by eight wickets.
Debuts: Australia – R. Edwards, R.A.L. Massie.

Australia won what has become known as 'Massie's Match' at 2.34 on the fourth afternoon. Robert Arnold Lockyer Massie, a 25-year-old Western Australian from Perth, returned match figures of 16 for 137 on his first appearance in Test cricket. His analysis remains the record for any bowler in his first Test and for any Test at Lord's; only J.C. Laker and S.F. Barnes have taken more wickets in a Test. Only two other bowlers, A.E. Trott and A.L. Valentine, have taken eight wickets in an innings in their first Test. In 1970 the right-arm fast-medium swing bowling of Massie produced figures of 3 for 166 in two matches for Northamptonshire Second Eleven and he was not offered a contract by the county.

## ENGLAND

| | | | | | |
|---|---|---|---|---|---|
| G. Boycott | b Massie | 11 | b Lillee | | 6 |
| J.H. Edrich | lbw b Lillee | 10 | c Marsh b Massie | | 6 |
| B.W. Luckhurst | b Lillee | 1 | c Marsh b Lillee | | 4 |
| M.J.K. Smith | b Massie | 34 | c Edwards b Massie | | 30 |
| B.L. D'Oliveira | lbw b Massie | 32 | c G.S. Chappell b Massie | | 3 |
| A.W. Greig | c Marsh b Massie | 54 | c I.M. Chappell b Massie | | 3 |
| A.P.E. Knott† | c Colley b Massie | 43 | c G.S. Chappell b Massie | | 12 |
| R. Illingworth* | lbw b Massie | 30 | c Stackpole b Massie | | 12 |
| J.A. Snow | b Massie | 37 | c Marsh b Massie | | 0 |
| N. Gifford | c Marsh b Massie | 3 | not out | | 16 |
| J.S.E. Price | not out | 4 | c G.S. Chappell b Massie | | 19 |
| Extras | (LB 6, W 1, NB 6) | 13 | (W 1, NB 4) | | 5 |
| **Total** | | **272** | | | **116** |

## AUSTRALIA

| | | | | |
|---|---|---|---|---|
| K.R. Stackpole | c Gifford b Price | 5 | not out | 57 |
| B.C. Francis | b Snow | 0 | c Knott b Price | 9 |
| I.M. Chappell* | c Smith b Snow | 56 | c Luckhurst b D'Oliveira | 6 |
| G.S. Chappell | b D'Oliveira | 131 | not out | 7 |
| K.D. Walters | c Illingworth b Snow | 1 | | |
| R. Edwards | c Smith b Illingworth | 28 | | |
| J.W. Gleeson | c Knott b Greig | 1 | | |
| R.W. Marsh† | c Greig b Snow | 50 | | |
| D.J. Colley | c Greig b Price | 25 | | |
| R.A.L. Massie | c Knott b Snow | 0 | | |
| D.K. Lillee | not out | 2 | | |
| Extras | (LB 7, NB 2) | 9 | (LB 2) | 2 |
| **Total** | | **308** | (2 wickets) | **81** |

| AUSTRALIA | O | M | R | W | O | M | R | W | FALL OF WICKETS | | | | |
|---|---|---|---|---|---|---|---|---|---|---|---|---|---|
| Lillee | 28 | 3 | 90 | 2 | 21 | 6 | 50 | 2 | | E | A | E | A |
| Massie | 32·5 | 7 | 84 | 8 | 27·2 | 9 | 53 | 8 | Wkt | 1st | 1st | 2nd | 2nd |
| Colley | 16 | 2 | 42 | 0 | 7 | 1 | 8 | 0 | 1st | 22 | 1 | 12 | 20 |
| G.S. Chappell | 6 | 1 | 18 | 0 | | | | | 2nd | 23 | 7 | 16 | 51 |
| Gleeson | 9 | 1 | 25 | 0 | | | | | 3rd | 28 | 82 | 18 | – |
| | | | | | | | | | 4th | 84 | 84 | 25 | – |
| ENGLAND | | | | | | | | | 5th | 97 | 190 | 31 | – |
| Snow | 32 | 13 | 57 | 5 | 8 | 2 | 15 | 0 | 6th | 193 | 212 | 52 | – |
| Price | 26·1 | 5 | 87 | 2 | 7 | 0 | 28 | 1 | 7th | 200 | 250 | 74 | – |
| Greig | 29 | 6 | 74 | 1 | 3 | 0 | 17 | 0 | 8th | 260 | 290 | 74 | – |
| D'Oliveira | 17 | 5 | 48 | 1 | 8 | 3 | 14 | 1 | 9th | 265 | 290 | 81 | – |
| Gifford | 11 | 4 | 20 | 0 | | | | | 10th | 272 | 308 | 116 | – |
| Illingworth | 7 | 2 | 13 | 1 | | | | | | | | | |
| Luckhurst | | | | | 0·5 | 0 | 5 | 0 | | | | | |

Umpires: A.E. Fagg and D.J. Constant.

# ENGLAND v AUSTRALIA 1972 (3rd Test)

Played at Trent Bridge, Nottingham, on 13, 14, 15, 17, 18 July.
Toss: England.   Result: MATCH DRAWN.
Debuts: Nil.

England were set 451 runs in 569 minutes after Illingworth had become the first England captain to invite the opposition to bat in a Test at Trent Bridge. For the second time in the rubber Marsh equalled the series record by holding five catches in an innings.

## AUSTRALIA

| | | | | | |
|---|---|---|---|---|---|
| K.R. Stackpole | c Parfitt b Greig | 114 | c Luckhurst b Snow | | 12 |
| B.C. Francis | c Smith b Lever | 10 | | | |
| I.M. Chappell* | c Knott b Snow | 34 | lbw b Illingworth | | 50 |
| G.S. Chappell | c Parfitt b Snow | 26 | b Snow | | 72 |
| K.D. Walters | c Parfitt b Snow | 2 | c Gifford b Snow | | 7 |
| R. Edwards | c Knott b Snow | 13 | (2) not out | | 170 |
| R.W. Marsh† | c D'Oliveira b Gifford | 41 | (6) not out | | 7 |
| D.J. Colley | c Greig b D'Oliveira | 54 | | | |
| R.A.L. Massie | c Parfitt b Snow | 0 | | | |
| J.W. Gleeson | not out | 6 | | | |
| D.K. Lillee | c Knott b Greig | 0 | | | |
| Extras | (B 4, LB 6, NB 5) | 15 | (LB 4, W 1, NB 1) | | 6 |
| **Total** | | **315** | (4 wickets declared) | | **324** |

## ENGLAND

| | | | | | |
|---|---|---|---|---|---|
| B.W. Luckhurst | lbw b Lillee | 23 | c G.S. Chappell b I.M. Chappell | | 96 |
| J.H. Edrich | c Marsh b Colley | 37 | b Massie | | 15 |
| P.H. Parfitt | b Massie | 0 | b Lillee | | 46 |
| M.J.K. Smith | b Lillee | 17 | lbw b Lillee | | 15 |
| B.L. D'Oliveira | lbw b Lillee | 29 | not out | | 50 |
| N. Gifford | c Marsh b Massie | 16 | | | |
| A.W. Greig | c Marsh b Massie | 7 | (6) not out | | 36 |
| A.P.E. Knott† | c Marsh b Massie | 0 | | | |
| R. Illingworth* | not out | 24 | | | |
| J.A. Snow | c Marsh b Lillee | 6 | | | |
| P. Lever | c Walters b Colley | 9 | | | |
| Extras | (B 5, LB 2, W 1, NB 13) | 21 | (B 17, LB 9, W 4, NB 2) | | 32 |
| **Total** | | **189** | (4 wickets) | | **290** |

| ENGLAND | O | M | R | W | O | M | R | W | | FALL OF WICKETS | | | |
|---|---|---|---|---|---|---|---|---|---|---|---|---|---|
| Snow | 31 | 8 | 92 | 5 | 24 | 1 | 94 | 3 | | A | E | A | E |
| Lever | 26 | 8 | 61 | 1 | 19 | 3 | 76 | 0 | *Wkt* | *1st* | *1st* | *2nd* | *2nd* |
| Greig | 38·4 | 9 | 88 | 2 | 12 | 1 | 46 | 0 | 1st | 16 | 55 | 15 | 50 |
| D'Oliveira | 18 | 5 | 41 | 1 | 7 | 0 | 12 | 0 | 2nd | 98 | 60 | 139 | 167 |
| Gifford | 5 | 1 | 18 | 1 | 15 | 1 | 49 | 0 | 3rd | 157 | 74 | 285 | 200 |
| Illingworth | | | | | 15 | 4 | 41 | 1 | 4th | 165 | 111 | 295 | 201 |
| | | | | | | | | | 5th | 189 | 133 | – | – |
| AUSTRALIA | | | | | | | | | 6th | 227 | 145 | – | – |
| Lillee | 29 | 15 | 35 | 4 | 25 | 10 | 40 | 2 | 7th | 289 | 145 | – | – |
| Massie | 30 | 10 | 43 | 4 | 36 | 13 | 49 | 1 | 8th | 298 | 155 | – | – |
| Colley | 23·3 | 5 | 68 | 2 | 19 | 6 | 43 | 0 | 9th | 315 | 166 | – | – |
| Gleeson | 6 | 1 | 22 | 0 | 30 | 13 | 49 | 0 | 10th | 315 | 189 | – | – |
| I.M.Chappell | | | | | 12 | 5 | 26 | 1 | | | | | |
| G.S.Chappell | | | | | 9 | 4 | 16 | 0 | | | | | |
| Stackpole | | | | | 17 | 7 | 35 | 0 | | | | | |

Umpires: A.E.G. Rhodes and T.W. Spencer.

# ENGLAND v AUSTRALIA 1972 (4th Test)

Played at Headingley, Leeds, on 27, 28, 29 July.
Toss: Australia.    Result: ENGLAND won by nine wickets.
Debuts: Nil.

England won on the third evening with two days and 86 minutes to spare. The pitch took spin from the first morning and was the subject of much criticism. It had been flooded by a freak storm the previous weekend and the weather had prevented the use of a heavy roller; it was also grassless – the result, apparently, of an attack by a fungus called fuserium.

## AUSTRALIA

| | | | | |
|---|---|---|---|---|
| K.R. Stackpole | c Knott b Underwood | 52 | lbw b Underwood | 28 |
| R. Edwards | c Knott b Snow | 0 | c Knott b Arnold | 0 |
| I.M. Chappell* | c and b Illingworth | 26 | c Knott b Arnold | 0 |
| G.S. Chappell | lbw b Underwood | 12 | c D'Oliveira b Underwood | 13 |
| A.P. Sheahan | c Illingworth b Underwood | 0 | not out | 41 |
| K.D. Walters | b Illingworth | 4 | c Parfitt b Underwood | 3 |
| R.W. Marsh† | c Illingworth b Underwood | 1 | c Knott b Underwood | 1 |
| R.J. Inverarity | not out | 26 | c Illingworth b Underwood | 0 |
| A.A. Mallett | lbw b Snow | 20 | b Illingworth | 9 |
| R.A.L. Massie | b Arnold | 0 | (11) b Illingworth | 18 |
| D.K. Lillee | c Greig b Arnold | 0 | (10) b Underwood | 7 |
| Extras | (LB 2, NB 3) | 5 | (LB 12, NB 4) | 16 |
| **Total** | | **146** | | **136** |

## ENGLAND

| | | | | |
|---|---|---|---|---|
| B.W. Luckhurst | c G.S. Chappell b Mallett | 18 | not out | 12 |
| J.H. Edrich | c I.M. Chappell b Mallett | 45 | lbw b Lillee | 4 |
| P.H. Parfitt | c Marsh b Lillee | 2 | not out | 0 |
| K.W.R. Fletcher | lbw b Mallett | 5 | | |
| B.L. D'Oliveira | b Mallett | 12 | | |
| A.W. Greig | c G.S. Chappell b Inverarity | 24 | | |
| A.P.E. Knott† | st Marsh b Mallett | 0 | | |
| R. Illingworth* | lbw b Lillee | 57 | | |
| J.A. Snow | st Marsh b Inverarity | 48 | | |
| D.L. Underwood | c I.M. Chappell b Inverarity | 5 | | |
| G.G. Arnold | not out | 1 | | |
| Extras | (B 19, LB 15, W 4, NB 8) | 46 | (LB 3, NB 2) | 5 |
| **Total** | | **263** | (1 wicket) | **21** |

| ENGLAND | O | M | R | W | O | M | R | W |
|---|---|---|---|---|---|---|---|---|
| Arnold | 9·5 | 2 | 28 | 2 | 6 | 1 | 17 | 2 |
| Snow | 13 | 5 | 11 | 2 | 10 | 2 | 26 | 0 |
| Greig | 10 | 1 | 25 | 0 | | | | |
| Illingworth | 21 | 11 | 32 | 2 | 19·1 | 5 | 32 | 2 |
| Underwood | 31 | 16 | 37 | 4 | 21 | 6 | 45 | 6 |
| D'Oliveira | 2 | 1 | 8 | 0 | | | | |
| AUSTRALIA | | | | | | | | |
| Lillee | 26·1 | 10 | 39 | 2 | 5 | 2 | 7 | 1 |
| Massie | 14 | 4 | 34 | 0 | | | | |
| Mallett | 52 | 20 | 114 | 5 | 5 | 1 | 9 | 0 |
| Inverarity | 33 | 19 | 26 | 3 | | | | |
| I.M. Chappell | 3 | 2 | 1 | 0 | | | | |
| G.S. Chappell | 2 | 0 | 3 | 0 | | | | |

### FALL OF WICKETS

| | A | E | A | E |
|---|---|---|---|---|
| Wkt | 1st | 1st | 2nd | 2nd |
| 1st | 10 | 43 | 5 | 7 |
| 2nd | 79 | 52 | 7 | – |
| 3rd | 93 | 66 | 31 | – |
| 4th | 93 | 76 | 51 | – |
| 5th | 97 | 108 | 63 | – |
| 6th | 98 | 108 | 69 | – |
| 7th | 98 | 128 | 69 | – |
| 8th | 145 | 232 | 93 | – |
| 9th | 146 | 246 | 111 | – |
| 10th | 146 | 263 | 136 | – |

Umpires: C.S. Elliott and D.J. Constant.

# ENGLAND v AUSTRALIA 1972 (5th Test)

Played at Kennington Oval, London, on 10, 11, 12, 14, 15, 16 August.
Toss: England.   Result: AUSTRALIA won by five wickets.
Debuts: England – B. Wood.

Australia won at 2.49 on the sixth afternoon and so squared the rubber. Lillee dismissed Parfitt, Illingworth and Snow to take three wickets in four balls for the second time in the rubber. His 31 wickets in this rubber is the record for Australia in England. The Chappells provided the first instance in Test cricket of brothers each scoring hundreds in the same innings. Marsh's 23 dismissals established a new record for Australia in a rubber against England.

## ENGLAND

| | | | | |
|---|---|---|---|---|
| B. Wood | c Marsh b Watson | 26 | lbw b Massie | 90 |
| J.H. Edrich | lbw b Lillee | 8 | b Lillee | 18 |
| P.H. Parfitt | b Lillee | 51 | b Lillee | 18 |
| J.H. Hampshire | c Inverarity b Mallett | 42 | c I.M. Chappell b Watson | 20 |
| B.L. D'Oliveira | c G.S. Chappell b Mallett | 4 | c I.M. Chappell b Massie | 43 |
| A.W. Greig | c Stackpole b Mallett | 16 | c Marsh b Lillee | 29 |
| R. Illingworth* | c G.S. Chappell b Lillee | 0 | lbw b Lillee | 31 |
| A.P.E. Knott† | c Marsh b Lillee | 92 | b Lillee | 63 |
| J.A. Snow | c Marsh b Lillee | 3 | c Stackpole b Mallett | 14 |
| G.G. Arnold | b Inverarity | 22 | lbw b Mallett | 4 |
| D.L. Underwood | not out | 3 | not out | 0 |
| Extras | (LB 8, W 1, NB 8) | 17 | (B 11, LB 8, NB 7) | 26 |
| **Total** | | **284** | | **356** |

## AUSTRALIA

| | | | | |
|---|---|---|---|---|
| G.D. Watson | c Knott b Arnold | 13 | lbw b Arnold | 6 |
| K.R. Stackpole | b Snow | 18 | c Knott b Greig | 79 |
| I.M. Chappell* | c Snow b Arnold | 118 | c sub (R.G.D. Willis) b Underwood | 37 |
| G.S. Chappell | c Greig b Illingworth | 113 | lbw b Underwood | 16 |
| R. Edwards | b Underwood | 79 | lbw b Greig | 1 |
| A.P. Sheahan | c Hampshire b Underwood | 5 | not out | 44 |
| R.W. Marsh† | b Underwood | 0 | not out | 43 |
| R.J. Inverarity | c Greig b Underwood | 28 | | |
| A.A. Mallett | run out | 5 | | |
| R.A.L. Massie | b Arnold | 4 | | |
| D.K. Lillee | not out | 0 | | |
| Extras | (LB 8, W 1, NB 7) | 16 | (LB 6, NB 10) | 16 |
| **Total** | | **399** | **(5 wickets)** | **242** |

| AUSTRALIA | O | M | R | W | O | M | R | W |
|---|---|---|---|---|---|---|---|---|
| Lillee | 24·2 | 7 | 58 | 5 | 32·2 | 8 | 123 | 5 |
| Massie | 27 | 5 | 69 | 0 | 32 | 10 | 77 | 2 |
| Watson | 12 | 4 | 23 | 1 | 19 | 8 | 32 | 1 |
| Mallett | 23 | 4 | 80 | 3 | 23 | 7 | 66 | 2 |
| G.S. Chappell | 2 | 0 | 18 | 0 | | | | |
| Inverarity | 4 | 0 | 19 | 1 | 15 | 4 | 32 | 0 |
| **ENGLAND** | | | | | | | | |
| Arnold | 35 | 11 | 87 | 3 | 15 | 5 | 26 | 1 |
| Snow | 34·5 | 5 | 111 | 1 | 6 | 1 | 21 | 0 |
| Greig | 18 | 9 | 25 | 0 | 25·3 | 10 | 49 | 2 |
| D'Oliveira | 9 | 4 | 17 | 0 | | | | |
| Underwood | 38 | 16 | 90 | 4 | 35 | 11 | 94 | 2 |
| Illingworth | 17 | 4 | 53 | 1 | 8·5 | 2 | 26 | 0 |
| Parfitt | | | | | 2 | 0 | 10 | 0 |

### FALL OF WICKETS

| | E | A | E | A |
|---|---|---|---|---|
| Wkt | 1st | 1st | 2nd | 2nd |
| 1st | 25 | 24 | 56 | 16 |
| 2nd | 50 | 34 | 81 | 132 |
| 3rd | 133 | 235 | 114 | 136 |
| 4th | 142 | 296 | 194 | 137 |
| 5th | 145 | 310 | 205 | 171 |
| 6th | 145 | 310 | 270 | – |
| 7th | 159 | 383 | 271 | – |
| 8th | 181 | 387 | 333 | – |
| 9th | 262 | 399 | 356 | – |
| 10th | 284 | 399 | 356 | – |

Umpires: A.E. Fagg and A.E.G. Rhodes.

# INDIA v ENGLAND 1972–73 (1st Test)

Played at Feroz Shah Kotla, Delhi, on 20, 21, 23, 24, 25 December.
Toss: India.   Result: ENGLAND won by six wickets.
Debuts: India – R.D. Parkar; England – A.R. Lewis.

Lewis captained England in his first Test and shared with Greig an unbroken fifth wicket partnership of 101 which, shortly after lunch on Christmas Day, took England to their first victory in Delhi and their first in India since 1951-52. Chandrasekhar achieved his best innings analysis in Test matches. Bedi took his 100th Test wicket when he dismissed Fletcher.

## INDIA

| | | | | |
|---|---|---|---|---|
| S.M. Gavaskar | c Greig b Arnold | 12 | c Greig b Underwood | 8 |
| R.D. Parkar | c Pocock b Arnold | 4 | lbw b Arnold | 35 |
| A.L. Wadekar* | b Arnold | 3 | st Knott b Pocock | 24 |
| D.N. Sardesai | b Arnold | 12 | c Greig b Underwood | 10 |
| G.R. Viswanath | c Knott b Greig | 27 | b Underwood | 3 |
| E.D. Solkar | c Knott b Greig | 20 | c sub (G.R.J. Roope) b Arnold | 75 |
| F.M. Engineer† | b Cottam | 15 | c Knott b Underwood | 63 |
| S. Abid Ali | c Greig b Cottam | 58 | c Fletcher b Pocock | 0 |
| S. Venkataraghavan | c Greig b Arnold | 17 | b Pocock | 0 |
| B.S. Bedi | not out | 4 | b Arnold | 2 |
| B.S. Chandrasekhar | b Arnold | 0 | not out | 1 |
| Extras | (LB 1) | 1 | (B 8, LB 2, NB 2) | 12 |
| **Total** | | **173** | | **233** |

## ENGLAND

| | | | | |
|---|---|---|---|---|
| B. Wood | c Venkataraghavan b Chandrasekhar | 19 | c Solkar b Bedi | 45 |
| D.L. Amiss | st Engineer b Bedi | 46 | c Chandrasekhar b Bedi | 9 |
| K.W.R. Fletcher | b Chandrasekhar | 2 | c Wadekar b Bedi | 0 |
| M.H. Denness | c Engineer b Bedi | 16 | c Viswanath b Chandrasekhar | 35 |
| A.R. Lewis* | lbw b Chandrasekhar | 0 | not out | 70 |
| A.W. Greig | not out | 68 | not out | 40 |
| A.P.E. Knott† | c Solkar b Chandrasekhar | 4 | | |
| G.G. Arnold | c Abid Ali b Chandrasekhar | 12 | | |
| P.I. Pocock | lbw b Chandrasekhar | 0 | | |
| D.L. Underwood | c Solkar b Chandrasekhar | 6 | | |
| R.M.H. Cottam | c Abid Ali b Chandrasekhar | 3 | | |
| Extras | (B 4, LB 17, NB 3) | 24 | (LB 9) | 9 |
| **Total** | | **200** | (4 wickets) | **208** |

| ENGLAND | O | M | R | W | O | M | R | W |
|---|---|---|---|---|---|---|---|---|
| Arnold | 23·4 | 7 | 45 | 6 | 20·4 | 6 | 46 | 3 |
| Cottam | 23 | 5 | 66 | 2 | 7 | 1 | 18 | 0 |
| Greig | 23 | 8 | 32 | 2 | 6 | 1 | 16 | 0 |
| Pocock | 6 | 1 | 13 | 0 | 33 | 7 | 72 | 3 |
| Underwood | 9 | 1 | 16 | 0 | 30 | 13 | 56 | 4 |
| Wood | | | | | 2 | 0 | 13 | 0 |
| INDIA | | | | | | | | |
| Abid Ali | 9 | 5 | 13 | 0 | 4 | 2 | 6 | 0 |
| Solkar | 3 | 0 | 8 | 0 | 3 | 0 | 13 | 0 |
| Bedi | 47 | 23 | 59 | 2 | 39 | 20 | 50 | 3 |
| Chandrasekhar | 41·5 | 18 | 79 | 8 | 24 | 7 | 70 | 1 |
| Venkataraghavan | 8 | 2 | 17 | 0 | 16 | 0 | 47 | 0 |
| Sardesai | | | | | 1·5 | 0 | 12 | 0 |
| Gavaskar | | | | | 1 | 0 | 1 | 0 |

### FALL OF WICKETS

| | I | E | I | E |
|---|---|---|---|---|
| Wkt | 1st | 1st | 2nd | 2nd |
| 1st | 7 | 61 | 26 | 18 |
| 2nd | 15 | 69 | 59 | 20 |
| 3rd | 20 | 71 | 82 | 76 |
| 4th | 43 | 71 | 86 | 107 |
| 5th | 59 | 119 | 103 | – |
| 6th | 80 | 123 | 206 | – |
| 7th | 123 | 152 | 207 | – |
| 8th | 169 | 160 | 211 | – |
| 9th | 169 | 180 | 215 | – |
| 10th | 173 | 200 | 233 | – |

Umpires: B. Satyaji Rao and M.V. Nagendra.

## INDIA v ENGLAND 1972–73 (2nd Test)

Played at Eden Gardens, Calcutta, on 30, 31 December, 1, 3, 4 January.
Toss:India.   Result: INDIA won by 28 runs.
Debuts: England – C.M. Old.

India won in the first over after lunch on the fifth day. Durani (strained thigh) batted with Gavaskar as his runner in the second innings. Engineer captained India on the field for most of the match after Wadekar had been taken ill with influenza.

### INDIA

| | | | | | |
|---|---|---|---|---|---|
| S.M. Gavaskar | c Old b Underwood | 18 | | lbw b Old | 2 |
| R.D. Parkar | c Knott b Old | 26 | | c Fletcher b Old | 15 |
| A.L. Wadekar* | run out | 44 | (7) | lbw b Greig | 0 |
| G.R. Viswanath | c Wood b Cottam | 3 | | c Fletcher b Old | 34 |
| S.A. Durani | b Greig | 4 | (3) | c Fletcher b Greig | 53 |
| E.D. Solkar | b Old | 19 | | c Knott b Greig | 6 |
| F.M. Engineer† | b Underwood | 75 | (5) | c Knott b Underwood | 17 |
| S. Abid Ali | b Cottam | 3 | | c Amiss b Old | 3 |
| E.A.S. Prasanna | lbw b Cottam | 6 | | b Greig | 0 |
| B.S. Bedi | run out | 0 | | not out | 9 |
| B.S. Chandrasekhar | not out | 1 | | b Greig | 1 |
| Extras | (LB 3, NB 8) | 11 | | (B 8, LB 2, NB 5) | 15 |
| **Total** | | **210** | | | **155** |

### ENGLAND

| | | | | | |
|---|---|---|---|---|---|
| B. Wood | b Bedi | 11 | | b Abid Ali | 1 |
| D.L. Amiss | c Solkar b Chandrasekhar | 11 | | c Engineer b Bedi | 1 |
| K.W.R. Fletcher | c Gavaskar b Prasanna | 16 | | lbw b Bedi | 5 |
| M.H. Denness | c Solkar b Chandrasekhar | 21 | | lbw b Chandrasekhar | 32 |
| A.R. Lewis* | lbw b Bedi | 4 | | c Solkar b Bedi | 3 |
| A.W. Greig | c sub (S. Venkataraghavan) b Prasanna | 29 | | lbw b Chandrasekhar | 67 |
| A.P.E. Knott† | st Engineer b Chandrasekhar | 35 | | c Durani b Chandrasekhar | 2 |
| C.M. Old | not out | 33 | | not out | 17 |
| P.I. Pocock | b Prasanna | 3 | | c and b Bedi | 5 |
| D.L. Underwood | c Solkar b Chandrasekhar | 0 | | c Wadekar b Bedi | 4 |
| R.M.H. Cottam | lbw b Chandrasekhar | 3 | | lbw b Chandrasekhar | 13 |
| Extras | (LB 4, NB 4) | 8 | | (B 6, LB 5, NB 2) | 13 |
| **Total** | | **174** | | | **163** |

| ENGLAND | O | M | R | W | O | M | R | W |
|---|---|---|---|---|---|---|---|---|
| Old | 26 | 7 | 72 | 2 | 21 | 6 | 43 | 4 |
| Cottam | 23 | 6 | 45 | 3 | 5 | 0 | 18 | 0 |
| Underwood | 20·4 | 11 | 43 | 2 | 14 | 4 | 36 | 1 |
| Pocock | 19 | 10 | 26 | 0 | 8 | 1 | 19 | 0 |
| Greig | 9 | 1 | 13 | 1 | 19·5 | 9 | 24 | 5 |
| INDIA | | | | | | | | |
| Abid Ali | 4 | 1 | 4 | 0 | 8 | 2 | 12 | 1 |
| Solkar | 3 | 1 | 5 | 0 | 1 | 1 | 0 | 0 |
| Bedi | 26 | 7 | 59 | 2 | 40 | 12 | 63 | 5 |
| Chandrasekhar | 26·2 | 5 | 65 | 5 | 29 | 14 | 42 | 4 |
| Prasanna | 16 | 4 | 33 | 3 | 9 | 0 | 19 | 0 |
| Durani | | | | | 4 | 1 | 14 | 0 |

### FALL OF WICKETS

| Wkt | I 1st | E 1st | I 2nd | E 2nd |
|---|---|---|---|---|
| 1st | 29 | 18 | 2 | 3 |
| 2nd | 68 | 37 | 33 | 8 |
| 3rd | 78 | 47 | 104 | 11 |
| 4th | 99 | 56 | 112 | 17 |
| 5th | 100 | 84 | 133 | 114 |
| 6th | 163 | 117 | 133 | 119 |
| 7th | 176 | 144 | 135 | 123 |
| 8th | 192 | 153 | 135 | 130 |
| 9th | 192 | 154 | 147 | 138 |
| 10th | 210 | 174 | 155 | 163 |

Umpires: A.M. Mamsa and J. Reuben.

# INDIA v ENGLAND 1972–73 (3rd Test)

Played at Chepauk, Madras, on 12, 13, 14, 16, 17 January.
Toss: England.   Result: INDIA won by four wickets.
Debuts: Nil.

India won shortly before lunch on the fifth day. Chandrasekhar took his 100th wicket in Test matches when he dismissed Amiss in the second innings. The Nawab of Pataudi had been stripped of his royal title by the Indian government since making his last appearance in Test cricket in 1969. Although he played in this and the 1974-75 rubber against West Indies as 'Mansur Ali Khan', he is given his original title throughout to avoid confusion.

## ENGLAND

| | | | | |
|---|---|---|---|---|
| B. Wood | c Engineer b Bedi | 20 | c sub (R.D. Parkar) b Bedi | 5 |
| D.L. Amiss | c Solkar b Chandrasekhar | 15 | c Engineer b Chandrasekhar | 8 |
| A.P.E. Knott† | c Pataudi b Bedi | 10 | c Chandrasekhar b Bedi | 13 |
| M.H. Denness | b Prasanna | 17 | c Solkar b Prasanna | 76 |
| K.W.R. Fletcher | not out | 97 | c Chauhan b Bedi | 21 |
| A.W. Greig | lbw b Chandrasekhar | 17 | c Solkar b Durani | 5 |
| A.R. Lewis* | c Solkar b Chandrasekhar | 4 | c Chauhan b Bedi | 11 |
| C.M. Old | c Durani b Chandrasekhar | 4 | c Bedi b Prasanna | 9 |
| G.G. Arnold | c Solkar b Prasanna | 17 | c Wadekar b Prasanna | 0 |
| N. Gifford | lbw b Chandrasekhar | 19 | not out | 3 |
| P.I. Pocock | lbw b Chandrasekhar | 2 | c Wadekar b Prasanna | 0 |
| Extras | (B 8, LB 11, NB 1) | 20 | (B 2, LB 3, NB 3) | 8 |
| **Total** | | **242** | | **159** |

## INDIA

| | | | | |
|---|---|---|---|---|
| C.P.S. Chauhan | c Knott b Arnold | 0 | c Knott b Pocock | 11 |
| S.M. Gavaskar | c Greig b Gifford | 20 | (8) not out | 0 |
| A.L. Wadekar* | c Wood b Pocock | 44 | c Greig b Old | 0 |
| S.A. Durani | c and b Gifford | 38 | lbw b Pocock | 38 |
| Nawab of Pataudi, jr | c sub (R.W. Tolchard) b Pocock | 73 | (6) not out | 14 |
| G.R. Viswanath | c Old b Pocock | 37 | (5) b Pocock | 0 |
| F.M. Engineer† | c Wood b Gifford | 31 | (2) lbw b Old | 10 |
| E.D. Solkar | b Pocock | 10 | (7) c Denness b Pocock | 7 |
| E.A.S. Prasanna | lbw b Arnold | 37 | | |
| B.S. Bedi | b Arnold | 5 | | |
| B.S. Chandrasekhar | not out | 3 | | |
| Extras | (B 6, LB 3, NB 9) | 18 | (LB 1, NB 5) | 6 |
| **Total** | | **316** | (6 wickets) | **86** |

| INDIA | O | M | R | W | O | M | R | W | FALL OF WICKETS | | | | |
|---|---|---|---|---|---|---|---|---|---|---|---|---|---|
| Solkar | 2 | 0 | 13 | 0 | 2 | 2 | 0 | 0 | | E | I | E | I |
| Gavaskar | 1 | 0 | 6 | 0 | | | | | *Wkt* | *1st* | *1st* | *2nd* | *2nd* |
| Bedi | 30 | 9 | 66 | 2 | 43 | 24 | 38 | 4 | 1st | 33 | 4 | 14 | 11 |
| Chandrasekhar | 38·5 | 9 | 90 | 6 | 35 | 9 | 69 | 1 | 2nd | 47 | 28 | 14 | 11 |
| Prasanna | 15 | 3 | 47 | 2 | 10 | 5 | 16 | 4 | 3rd | 52 | 89 | 30 | 44 |
| Pataudi | | | | | 1 | 0 | 4 | 0 | 4th | 69 | 155 | 77 | 51 |
| Durani | | | | | 15 | 5 | 24 | 1 | 5th | 98 | 220 | 97 | 67 |
| | | | | | | | | | 6th | 106 | 224 | 126 | 78 |
| ENGLAND | | | | | | | | | 7th | 110 | 247 | 152 | – |
| Arnold | 23·1 | 12 | 34 | 3 | 4 | 1 | 11 | 0 | 8th | 151 | 288 | 152 | – |
| Old | 20 | 4 | 51 | 0 | 9 | 3 | 19 | 2 | 9th | 234 | 303 | 159 | – |
| Gifford | 34 | 15 | 64 | 3 | 7·5 | 2 | 22 | 0 | 10th | 242 | 316 | 159 | – |
| Greig | 12 | 1 | 35 | 0 | | | | | | | | | |
| Pocock | 46 | 15 | 114 | 4 | 13 | 3 | 28 | 4 | | | | | |

Umpires: A.M. Mamsa and M.V. Nagendra.

# INDIA v ENGLAND 1972–73 (4th Test)

Played at Green Park, Kanpur, on 25, 27, 28, 29, 30 January.
Toss: India.    Result: MATCH DRAWN.
Debuts: England – J. Birkenshaw, G.R.J. Roope.

Lewis batted for 267 minutes and hit a six and 16 fours in his innings of 125. It was the first hundred by an England batsman for ten Test matches. Gifford fractured his left-hand little finger when fielding before lunch on the first day and took no further part in the match.

## INDIA

| | | | | |
|---|---|--:|---|--:|
| C.P.S. Chauhan | c Old b Underwood | 22 | c Roope b Arnold | 1 |
| S.M. Gavaskar | c Greig b Birkenshaw | 69 | c sub (B. Wood) b Underwood | 24 |
| A.L. Wadekar* | c Fletcher b Greig | 90 | c and b Underwood | 9 |
| G.R. Viswanath | c Denness b Old | 25 | not out | 75 |
| Nawab of Pataudi, jr | lbw b Arnold | 54 | | |
| E.D. Solkar | b Underwood | 10 | c Greig b Birkenshaw | 26 |
| F.M. Engineer† | b Underwood | 15 | (5) c Old b Birkenshaw | 2 |
| S. Abid Ali | b Old | 41 | (7) b Greig | 36 |
| E.A.S. Prasanna | c Knott b Old | 0 | (8) not out | 2 |
| B.S. Bedi | not out | 4 | | |
| B.S. Chandrasekhar | b Old | 0 | | |
| Extras | (B 1, LB 9, NB 17) | 27 | (B 5, LB 4, NB 2) | 11 |
| **Total** | | **357** | (6 wickets) | **186** |

## ENGLAND

| | | |
|---|---|--:|
| M.H. Denness | c Abid Ali b Chandrasekhar | 31 |
| G.R.J. Roope | c Abid Ali b Chandrasekhar | 11 |
| A.P.E. Knott† | c Gavaskar b Prasanna | 40 |
| A.R. Lewis* | b Abid Ali | 125 |
| K.W.R. Fletcher | c Chandrasekhar b Bedi | 58 |
| A.W. Greig | c Chauhan b Bedi | 8 |
| J. Birkenshaw | c Abid Ali b Chandrasekhar | 64 |
| C.M. Old | lbw b Chandrasekhar | 4 |
| G.G. Arnold | b Bedi | 45 |
| D.L. Underwood | not out | 0 |
| N. Gifford | absent hurt | – |
| Extras | (B 1, LB 8, W 1, NB 1) | 11 |
| **Total** | | **397** |

| ENGLAND | O | M | R | W | O | M | R | W | | FALL OF WICKETS | | |
|---|--:|--:|--:|--:|--:|--:|--:|--:|---|--:|--:|--:|
| Arnold | 35 | 10 | 72 | 1 | 7 | 3 | 15 | 1 | | I | E | I |
| Old | 24 | 5 | 69 | 4 | 11 | 3 | 28 | 0 | *Wkt* | *1st* | *1st* | *2nd* |
| Underwood | 51 | 20 | 90 | 3 | 26 | 11 | 46 | 2 | 1st | 85 | 37 | 8 |
| Greig | 29 | 11 | 40 | 1 | 10 | 7 | 6 | 1 | 2nd | 109 | 48 | 33 |
| Gifford | 8 | 2 | 17 | 0 | | | | | 3rd | 179 | 118 | 36 |
| Birkenshaw | 20 | 6 | 42 | 1 | 25 | 5 | 66 | 2 | 4th | 265 | 262 | 39 |
| Roope | | | | | 5 | 1 | 14 | 0 | 5th | 292 | 274 | 103 |
| | | | | | | | | | 6th | 296 | 288 | 181 |
| INDIA | | | | | | | | | 7th | 326 | 301 | – |
| Abid Ali | 22 | 3 | 55 | 1 | | | | | 8th | 345 | 397 | – |
| Solkar | 5 | 0 | 14 | 0 | | | | | 9th | 357 | 397 | – |
| Bedi | 68·5 | 15 | 134 | 3 | | | | | 10th | 357 | – | – |
| Chandrasekhar | 41 | 12 | 86 | 4 | | | | | | | | |
| Prasanna | 34 | 4 | 87 | 1 | | | | | | | | |
| Viswanath | 2 | 0 | 10 | 0 | | | | | | | | |

Umpires: J. Reuben and M.V. Gothoskar.

# INDIA v ENGLAND 1972–73 (5th Test)

Played at Brabourne Stadium, Bombay, on 6, 7, 8, 10, 11 February.
Toss: India.    Result: MATCH DRAWN.
Debuts: Nil.

India won the rubber 2-1 when England were unable to score 203 runs in 90 minutes. Viswanath became the first of six Indian batsman who scored a hundred on Test debut to reach a second century for their country. His partnership of 192 with Engineer is still India's highest for the second wicket against England. Fletcher and Greig shared a partnership of 254 which remains England's highest for the fifth wicket in all Test matches. In the second innings Pataudi batted 95 minutes for five runs and did not score for the last 65 minutes of his innings. Chandrasekhar took 35 wickets in this rubber to set a new record for India against all countries.

## INDIA

| | | | | |
|---|---|---|---|---|
| F.M. Engineer† | c Roope b Birkenshaw | 121 | b Underwood | 66 |
| S.M. Gavaskar | b Old | 4 | c and b Underwood | 67 |
| A.L. Wadekar* | c Old b Birkenshaw | 87 | (6) not out | 11 |
| S.A. Durani | c Underwood b Pocock | 73 | (3) c Knott b Pocock | 37 |
| Nawab of Pataudi, jr | b Underwood | 1 | b Pocock | 5 |
| G.R. Viswanath | b Arnold | 113 | (4) c Knott b Greig | 48 |
| E.D. Solkar | c Denness b Old | 6 | not out | 6 |
| S. Abid Ali | c Roope b Arnold | 15 | | |
| S. Venkataraghavan | not out | 11 | | |
| B.S. Bedi | b Arnold | 0 | | |
| B.S. Chandrasekhar | c Fletcher b Old | 3 | | |
| Extras | (B 4, LB 4, NB 6) | 14 | (LB 4) | 4 |
| **Total** | | **448** | (5 wickets declared) | **244** |

## ENGLAND

| | | | | |
|---|---|---|---|---|
| A.R. Lewis* | b Abid Ali | 0 | (4) not out | 17 |
| G.R.J. Roope | c Abid Ali b Chandrasekhar | 10 | not out | 26 |
| A.P.E. Knott† | lbw b Chandrasekhar | 56 | b Chandrasekhar | 8 |
| D.L. Underwood | c Abid Ali b Bedi | 9 | | |
| K.W.R. Fletcher | lbw b Bedi | 113 | | |
| A.W. Greig | lbw b Chandrasekhar | 148 | | |
| M.H. Denness | c Venkataraghavan b Bedi | 29 | | |
| J. Birkenshaw | b Chandrasekhar | 36 | (1) b Bedi | 12 |
| C.M. Old | c and b Venkataraghavan | 28 | | |
| G.G. Arnold | lbw b Chandrasekhar | 27 | | |
| P.I. Pocock | not out | 0 | | |
| Extras | (B 13, LB 5, NB 6) | 24 | (B 3, LB 1) | 4 |
| **Total** | | **480** | (2 wickets) | **67** |

| ENGLAND | O | M | R | W | O | M | R | W |
|---|---|---|---|---|---|---|---|---|
| Arnold | 21 | 3 | 64 | 3 | 3 | 0 | 13 | 0 |
| Old | 21·2 | 2 | 78 | 3 | 3 | 1 | 11 | 0 |
| Underwood | 26 | 6 | 100 | 1 | 38 | 16 | 70 | 2 |
| Greig | 22 | 7 | 62 | 0 | 13 | 7 | 19 | 1 |
| Pocock | 25 | 7 | 63 | 1 | 27 | 5 | 75 | 2 |
| Birkenshaw | 23 | 2 | 67 | 2 | 12 | 1 | 52 | 0 |
| INDIA | | | | | | | | |
| Abid Ali | 15 | 2 | 60 | 1 | | | | |
| Solkar | 4 | 0 | 16 | 0 | 2 | 0 | 4 | 0 |
| Bedi | 69 | 20 | 138 | 3 | 10 | 4 | 25 | 1 |
| Chandrasekhar | 46·1 | 8 | 135 | 5 | 9 | 1 | 26 | 1 |
| Durani | 4 | 0 | 21 | 0 | | | | |
| Venkataraghavan | 25 | 1 | 86 | 1 | 5 | 1 | 8 | 0 |
| Gavaskar | | | | | 2 | 2 | 0 | 0 |
| Pataudi | | | | | 1 | 1 | 0 | 0 |

## FALL OF WICKETS

| | I | E | I | E |
|---|---|---|---|---|
| Wkt | 1st | 1st | 2nd | 2nd |
| 1st | 25 | 0 | 135 | 23 |
| 2nd | 217 | 38 | 136 | 37 |
| 3rd | 220 | 67 | 198 | – |
| 4th | 221 | 79 | 227 | – |
| 5th | 371 | 333 | 233 | – |
| 6th | 395 | 381 | – | – |
| 7th | 427 | 397 | – | – |
| 8th | 435 | 442 | – | – |
| 9th | 439 | 479 | – | – |
| 10th | 448 | 480 | – | – |

Umpires: J. Reuben and M.V. Gothoskar.

# AUSTRALIA v PAKISTAN 1972–73 (1st Test)

Played at Adelaide Oval on 22, 23, 24, 26, 27 December.
Toss: Pakistan.   Result: AUSTRALIA won by an innings and 114 runs.
Debuts: Australia – J. Benaud; Pakistan – Talat Ali.

Australia's first win against Pakistan in a home Test was gained off the 14th ball of the fifth morning. I.M. Chappell's highest Test innings remains the record individual score by either side in this series, as does Australia's total of 585 which included three century partnerships. Marsh, playing in his first Test against Pakistan, became the first Australia wicket-keeper to score a Test hundred. Mallett's analysis of 8 for 59 is the record for either team in this series. Talat Ali, his right thumb fractured by a ball from Lillee, batted one-handed in the second innings to take the match into the last day.

## PAKISTAN

| | | | | | |
|---|---|---|---|---|---|
| Sadiq Mohammad | c G.S. Chappell b Massie | 11 | | c and b Mallett | 81 |
| Talat Ali | retired hurt | 7 | (11) | c Edwards b Mallett | 0 |
| Zaheer Abbas | c Marsh b Lillee | 7 | | c Marsh b O'Keeffe | 0 |
| Majid Khan | c Sheahan b Massie | 11 | | c I.M. Chappell b Mallett | 11 |
| Mushtaq Mohammad | c G.S. Chappell b Lillee | 3 | | lbw b Mallett | 32 |
| Saeed Ahmed | c Marsh b Massie | 36 | (2) | lbw b Mallett | 39 |
| Asif Iqbal | c Marsh b Massie | 16 | (6) | c G.S. Chappell b Mallett | 0 |
| Intikhab Alam* | c Edwards b Lillee | 64 | (7) | c G.S. Chappell b Lillee | 30 |
| Wasim Bari† | c Redpath b Mallett | 72 | (8) | c O'Keeffe b Mallett | 0 |
| Salim Altaf | not out | 17 | (9) | not out | 9 |
| Asif Masood | c Marsh b Lillee | 0 | (10) | c Marsh b Mallett | 1 |
| Extras | (B 4, LB 3, W 4, NB 2) | 13 | | (B 3, LB 4, W 1, NB 3) | 11 |
| **Total** | | **257** | | | **214** |

## AUSTRALIA

| | | |
|---|---|---|
| A.P. Sheahan | b Asif Masood | 44 |
| I.R. Redpath | c Wasim b Asif Masood | 2 |
| I.M. Chappell* | c Asif Iqbal b Majid | 196 |
| G.S. Chappell | lbw b Salim | 28 |
| R. Edwards | lbw b Asif Masood | 89 |
| J. Benaud | lbw b Salim | 24 |
| R.W. Marsh† | b Mushtaq | 118 |
| K.J. O'Keeffe | b Mushtaq | 40 |
| A.A. Mallett | c sub (Sarfraz Nawaz) b Majid | 0 |
| D.K. Lillee | c Saeed b Mushtaq | 14 |
| R.A.L. Massie | not out | 12 |
| Extras | (B 2, LB 12, NB 4) | 18 |
| **Total** | | **585** |

| AUSTRALIA | O | M | R | W | O | M | R | W | | FALL OF WICKETS | | | |
|---|---|---|---|---|---|---|---|---|---|---|---|---|---|
| | | | | | | | | | | | P | A | P |
| Lillee | 20·3 | 7 | 49 | 4 | 15 | 3 | 53 | 1 | | | | | |
| Massie | 24 | 3 | 70 | 4 | 9 | 3 | 26 | 0 | | Wkt | 1st | 1st | 2nd |
| G.S. Chappell | 11 | 2 | 29 | 0 | 4 | 0 | 21 | 0 | | 1st | 30 | 3 | 88 |
| Mallett | 12 | 3 | 52 | 1 | 23·6 | 6 | 59 | 8 | | 2nd | 30 | 103 | 89 |
| O'Keeffe | 8 | 1 | 44 | 0 | 14 | 1 | 44 | 1 | | 3rd | 33 | 158 | 111 |
| | | | | | | | | | | 4th | 74 | 330 | 162 |
| PAKISTAN | | | | | | | | | | 5th | 95 | 390 | 162 |
| Asif Masood | 19 | 1 | 110 | 3 | | | | | | 6th | 104 | 413 | 182 |
| Salim | 25 | 1 | 83 | 2 | | | | | | 7th | 208 | 533 | 182 |
| Asif Iqbal | 14 | 0 | 76 | 0 | | | | | | 8th | 255 | 534 | 211 |
| Intikhab | 18 | 2 | 115 | 0 | | | | | | 9th | 257 | 566 | 214 |
| Saeed | 3 | 0 | 28 | 0 | | | | | | 10th | – | 585 | 214 |
| Majid | 20 | 1 | 88 | 2 | | | | | | | | | |
| Mushtaq | 11·2 | 0 | 67 | 3 | | | | | | | | | |

Umpires: M.G. O'Connell and N. Townsend.

# AUSTRALIA v PAKISTAN 1972–73 (2nd Test)

Played at Melbourne Cricket Ground on 29, 30 December, 1, 2, 3 January.
Toss: Australia.   Result: AUSTRALIA won by 92 runs.
Debuts: Australia – J.R. Thomson, M.H.N. Walker.

Pakistan scored their highest total of the series. Majid's first Test hundred, scored in his 20th innings and eight years after his debut, remains Pakistan's highest score in a Test in Australia. Benaud's hundred in his second Test included 93 before lunch on the fourth day after being told that he had not been selected for the next Test. His second-wicket partnership of 233 with Sheahan is Australia's highest for any wicket in this series.

## AUSTRALIA

| | | | | |
|---|---|---|---|---|
| I.R. Redpath | c Saeed b Intikhab | 135 | c Wasim b Salim | 6 |
| A.P. Sheahan | run out | 23 | c Sarfraz b Asif Masood | 127 |
| I.M. Chappell* | c Wasim b Sarfraz | 66 | (4) st Wasim b Majid | 9 |
| G.S. Chappell | not out | 116 | (5) run out | 62 |
| J. Benaud | c Sarfraz b Intikhab | 13 | (3) c Wasim b Salim | 142 |
| R.W. Marsh† | c Wasim b Sarfraz | 74 | c Asif Iqbal b Asif Masood | 3 |
| K.J. O'Keeffe | ) | | b Sarfraz | 24 |
| A.A. Mallett | ) | | c Wasim b Sarfraz | 8 |
| M.H.N. Walker | ) did not bat | | run out | 11 |
| J.R. Thomson | ) | | not out | 19 |
| D.K. Lillee | ) | | c Mushtaq b Intikhab | 2 |
| Extras | (B 1, LB 6, NB 7) | 14 | (LB 3, NB 9) | 12 |
| **Total** | (5 wickets declared) | **441** | | **425** |

## PAKISTAN

| | | | | |
|---|---|---|---|---|
| Sadiq Mohammad | lbw b Lillee | 137 | c Marsh b Walker | 5 |
| Saeed Ahmed | c G.S. Chappell b Walker | 50 | c Mallett b Lillee | 6 |
| Zaheer Abbas | run out | 51 | run out | 25 |
| Majid Khan | c Marsh b Walker | 158 | c Marsh b Lillee | 47 |
| Mushtaq Mohammad | c Marsh b O'Keeffe | 60 | run out | 13 |
| Asif Iqbal | c Lillee b Mallett | 7 | c Redpath b Walker | 37 |
| Intikhab Alam* | c Sheahan b Mallett | 68 | c I.M. Chappell b Mallett | 48 |
| Wasim Bari† | b Mallett | 7 | b Walker | 0 |
| Salim Altaf | not out | 13 | b O'Keeffe | 10 |
| Sarfraz Nawaz | not out | 0 | run out | 8 |
| Asif Masood | did not bat | | not out | 1 |
| Extras | (B 12, LB 7, W 1, NB 3) | 23 | | |
| **Total** | (8 wickets declared) | **574** | | **200** |

| PAKISTAN | O | M | R | W | O | M | R | W | | FALL OF WICKETS | | | |
|---|---|---|---|---|---|---|---|---|---|---|---|---|---|
| Asif Masood | 17 | 0 | 97 | 0 | 12 | 0 | 100 | 2 | | A | P | A | P |
| Salim | 9 | 0 | 49 | 0 | 14 | 0 | 50 | 2 | *Wkt* | *1st* | *1st* | *2nd* | *2nd* |
| Sarfraz | 22·5 | 4 | 100 | 2 | 22 | 2 | 99 | 2 | 1st | 60 | 128 | 18 | 11 |
| Intikhab | 16 | 0 | 101 | 2 | 15·6 | 3 | 70 | 1 | 2nd | 183 | 323 | 251 | 15 |
| Majid | 21 | 2 | 80 | 0 | 17 | 1 | 61 | 1 | 3rd | 273 | 395 | 288 | 80 |
| Mushtaq | | | | | 7 | 0 | 33 | 0 | 4th | 295 | 416 | 298 | 83 |
| | | | | | | | | | 5th | 441 | 429 | 305 | 128 |
| AUSTRALIA | | | | | | | | | 6th | – | 519 | 375 | 138 |
| Lillee | 16·6 | 1 | 90 | 1 | 11 | 1 | 59 | 2 | 7th | – | 541 | 391 | 138 |
| Thomson | 17 | 1 | 100 | 0 | 2 | 0 | 10 | 0 | 8th | – | 572 | 392 | 161 |
| Walker | 24 | 1 | 112 | 2 | 14 | 3 | 39 | 3 | 9th | – | – | 418 | 181 |
| Mallett | 38 | 4 | 124 | 3 | 17·5 | 3 | 56 | 1 | 10th | – | – | 425 | 200 |
| O'Keeffe | 23 | 1 | 94 | 1 | 9 | 4 | 10 | 1 | | | | | |
| I.M. Chappell | 5 | 0 | 21 | 0 | 3 | 0 | 16 | 0 | | | | | |
| Redpath | 1 | 0 | 10 | 0 | | | | | | | | | |
| G.S. Chappell | | | | | 1 | 0 | 10 | 0 | | | | | |

Umpires: J.R. Collins and P.R. Enright.

# AUSTRALIA v PAKISTAN 1972–73 (3rd Test)

Played at Sydney Cricket Ground on 6, 7, 8, 10, 11 January.
Toss: Pakistan.   Result: AUSTRALIA won by 52 runs.
Debuts: Australia – J.R. Watkins.

Australia gained a remarkable victory to win the rubber 3-0. Pakistan needed to score only 159 runs in their second innings, despite a record ninth-wicket partnership of 83 in 150 minutes between Watkins and Massie. Walker, who took five wickets for three runs with his last 30 balls, and Lillee, restricted by a vertebral injury, bowled unchanged throughout the 138 minutes of play on the final day to dismiss Pakistan for their lowest score in this series.

## AUSTRALIA

| Player | 1st innings | | 2nd innings | |
|---|---|---|---|---|
| K.R. Stackpole | c Wasim b Sarfraz | 28 | c Intikhab b Salim | 9 |
| I.R. Redpath | run out | 79 | c Nasim b Sarfraz | 18 |
| I.M. Chappell* | lbw b Sarfraz | 43 | c Wasim b Sarfraz | 27 |
| G.S. Chappell | b Majid | 30 | (6) lbw b Sarfraz | 6 |
| R. Edwards | c Wasim b Salim | 69 | (4) lbw b Salim | 3 |
| K.D. Walters | b Asif Iqbal | 19 | (5) lbw b Salim | 6 |
| R.W. Marsh† | c Wasim b Salim | 15 | c Zaheer b Salim | 0 |
| M.H.N. Walker | c Majid b Sarfraz | 5 | c Mushtaq b Sarfraz | 16 |
| J.R. Watkins | not out | 3 | c Zaheer b Intikhab | 36 |
| D.K. Lillee | b Sarfraz | 2 | (11) not out | 0 |
| R.A.L. Massie | b Salim | 2 | (10) c Sadiq b Mushtaq | 42 |
| Extras | (B 18, LB 8, W 4, NB 9) | 39 | (B 10, LB 3, NB 8) | 21 |
| **Total** | | **334** | | **184** |

## PAKISTAN

| Player | 1st innings | | 2nd innings | |
|---|---|---|---|---|
| Sadiq Mohammad | c G.S. Chappell b Lillee | 30 | c Edwards b Massie | 6 |
| Nasim-ul-Ghani | c Redpath c G.S. Chappell | 64 | b Lillee | 5 |
| Zaheer Abbas | c Marsh b Massie | 14 | c Redpath b Lillee | 47 |
| Majid Khan | b Massie | 0 | lbw b Walker | 12 |
| Mushtaq Mohammad | c Walker b G.S. Chappell | 121 | c Marsh b Lillee | 15 |
| Asif Iqbal | c Marsh b G.S. Chappell | 65 | c Marsh b Walker | 5 |
| Intikhab Alam* | c Marsh b Massie | 9 | c Watkins b Walker | 8 |
| Wasim Bari† | b G.S. Chappell | 1 | c Edwards b Walker | 0 |
| Salim Altaf | c Marsh b Walker | 12 | c Massie b Walker | 0 |
| Sarfraz Nawaz | b G.S. Chappell | 12 | c Redpath b Walker | 1 |
| Asif Masood | not out | 1 | not out | 3 |
| Extras | (B 12, LB 10, W 6, NB 3) | 31 | (LB 2, W 1, NB 1) | 4 |
| **Total** | | **360** | | **106** |

| PAKISTAN | O | M | R | W | O | M | R | W |
|---|---|---|---|---|---|---|---|---|
| Asif Masood | 18 | 1 | 81 | 0 | 3 | 0 | 15 | 0 |
| Salim | 21·5 | 3 | 71 | 3 | 20 | 5 | 60 | 4 |
| Sarfraz | 19 | 3 | 53 | 4 | 21 | 7 | 56 | 4 |
| Majid | 18 | 1 | 66 | 1 | | | | |
| Intikhab | 2 | 0 | 13 | 0 | 4 | 2 | 9 | 1 |
| Asif Iqbal | 2 | 0 | 11 | 1 | 2 | 0 | 10 | 0 |
| Mushtaq | | | | | 3·1 | 0 | 13 | 1 |
| AUSTRALIA | | | | | | | | |
| Lillee | 10 | 2 | 34 | 1 | 23 | 5 | 68 | 3 |
| Massie | 28 | 6 | 123 | 3 | 7 | 4 | 19 | 1 |
| Walker | 16 | 2 | 65 | 1 | 16 | 8 | 15 | 6 |
| G.S. Chappell | 18·6 | 5 | 61 | 5 | | | | |
| Walters | 9 | 3 | 25 | 0 | | | | |
| Watkins | 6 | 1 | 21 | 0 | | | | |
| I.M. Chappell | 1 | 1 | 0 | 0 | | | | |

## FALL OF WICKETS

| Wkt | A 1st | P 1st | A 2nd | P 2nd |
|---|---|---|---|---|
| 1st | 56 | 56 | 29 | 7 |
| 2nd | 138 | 79 | 31 | 11 |
| 3rd | 196 | 83 | 34 | 52 |
| 4th | 220 | 131 | 44 | 83 |
| 5th | 271 | 270 | 70 | 88 |
| 6th | 315 | 279 | 73 | 93 |
| 7th | 324 | 280 | 94 | 95 |
| 8th | 327 | 336 | 101 | 95 |
| 9th | 329 | 349 | 184 | 103 |
| 10th | 334 | 360 | 184 | 106 |

Umpires: T.F. Brooks and J.R. Collins.

# NEW ZEALAND v PAKISTAN 1972–73 (1st Test)

Played at Basin Reserve, Wellington, on 2, 3, 4, 5 February.
Toss: Pakistan.   Result: MATCH DRAWN.
Debuts: New Zealand – R.J. Hadlee, J.M. Parker; Pakistan – Wasim Hasan Raja.

New Zealand were asked to score 323 runs to win in 121 minutes. Wasim Bari was taken to hospital after being hit in the face by a bouncer from Collinge. Parker fractured a bone in his hand while fielding and was unable to bat in his first Test.

## PAKISTAN

| | | | | | |
|---|---|---|---|---|---|
| Sadiq Mohammad | c sub (D.R. O'Sullivan) b Hadlee | 166 | c Congdon b Howarth | | 68 |
| Talat Ali | c Turner b Collinge | 6 | lbw b Taylor | | 2 |
| Zaheer Abbas | c Hadlee b Taylor | 2 | c Wadsworth b Collinge | | 8 |
| Majid Khan | c Congdon b Taylor | 79 | c Burgess b Howarth | | 79 |
| Asif Iqbal | c and b Hadlee | 39 | c Hastings b Howarth | | 23 |
| Wasim Raja | c Congdon b Taylor | 10 | c sub (D.R. O'Sullivan) b Howarth | | 41 |
| Intikhab Alam* | run out | 16 | not out | | 53 |
| Wasim Bari† | retired hurt | 13 | | | |
| Salim Altaf | c Howarth b Taylor | 14 | (8) not out | | 6 |
| Sarfraz Nawaz | c Wadsworth b Collinge | 0 | | | |
| Pervez Sajjad | not out | 1 | | | |
| Extras | (B 1, LB 5, NB 5) | 11 | (B 4, LB 2, NB 4) | | 10 |
| **Total** | | **357** | (6 wickets declared) | | **290** |

## NEW ZEALAND

| | | | | | |
|---|---|---|---|---|---|
| G.M. Turner | c Intikhab b Sarfraz | 43 | not out | | 49 |
| T.W. Jarvis | c Majid b Sarfraz | 0 | c Majid b Salim | | 0 |
| B.E. Congdon* | run out | 19 | c and b Salim | | 0 |
| B.F. Hastings | c Majid b Sarfraz | 72 | c Wasim Bari b Salim | | 0 |
| M.G. Burgess | c and b Intikhab | 79 | not out | | 21 |
| B.R. Taylor | c Zaheer b Majid | 5 | | | |
| K.J. Wadsworth† | c Asif b Sarfraz | 28 | | | |
| R.J. Hadlee | c Asif b Salim | 46 | | | |
| H.J. Howarth | not out | 3 | | | |
| R.O. Collinge | b Salim | 0 | | | |
| J.M. Parker | absent hurt | – | | | |
| Extras | (B 9, LB 9, NB 12) | 30 | (LB 1, W 1, NB 6) | | 8 |
| **Total** | | **325** | (3 wickets) | | **78** |

| NEW ZEALAND | O | M | R | W | O | M | R | W | | FALL OF WICKETS | | | |
|---|---|---|---|---|---|---|---|---|---|---|---|---|---|
| Hadlee | 18 | 0 | 84 | 2 | 7 | 0 | 28 | 0 | | | P | NZ | P | NZ |
| Collinge | 20 | 1 | 63 | 2 | 13 | 1 | 50 | 1 | *Wkt* | *1st* | *1st* | *2nd* | *2nd* |
| Taylor | 24·4 | 1 | 110 | 4 | 11 | 2 | 63 | 1 | 1st | 20 | 4 | 20 | 1 |
| Howarth | 25 | 6 | 73 | 0 | 31 | 7 | 99 | 4 | 2nd | 26 | 55 | 35 | 1 |
| Congdon | 3 | 0 | 16 | 0 | 9 | 0 | 40 | 0 | 3rd | 197 | 88 | 129 | 11 |
| | | | | | | | | | 4th | 271 | 216 | 177 | – |
| PAKISTAN | | | | | | | | | 5th | 308 | 221 | 202 | – |
| Salim | 16·4 | 3 | 70 | 2 | 6 | 1 | 15 | 3 | 6th | 308 | 261 | 255 | – |
| Sarfraz | 29 | 5 | 126 | 4 | 5 | 1 | 15 | 0 | 7th | 334 | 302 | – | – |
| Asif | 2 | 1 | 6 | 0 | | | | | 8th | 342 | 325 | – | – |
| Intikhab | 13 | 1 | 55 | 1 | 3 | 0 | 11 | 0 | 9th | 357 | 325 | – | – |
| Pervez | 5 | 0 | 19 | 0 | 4 | 1 | 5 | 0 | 10th | – | – | – | – |
| Majid | 9 | 2 | 19 | 1 | | | | | | | | | |
| Wasim Raja | | | | | 4 | 0 | 10 | 0 | | | | | |
| Sadiq | | | | | 3 | 0 | 13 | 0 | | | | | |
| Talat | | | | | 1 | 0 | 1 | 0 | | | | | |

Umpires: W.T. Martin and E.C.A. MacKintosh.

# NEW ZEALAND v PAKISTAN 1972–73 (2nd Test)

Played at Carisbrook, Dunedin, on 7, 8, 9, 10 February.
Toss: Pakistan.   Result: PAKISTAN won by an innings and 166 runs.
Debuts: New Zealand – D.R. O'Sullivan.

Pakistan gained their first victory in New Zealand after 55 minutes of play on the fourth morning. Their total of 507 is the highest by either country in this series in New Zealand. Mushtaq batted 383 minutes and hit 20 fours in scoring Pakistan's first double century in New Zealand. His partnership of 350 in 275 minutes with Asif Iqbal remains Pakistan's highest for any wicket in all Test matches and their highest for the fourth wicket in all first-class cricket. Mushtaq was the second player after D. St E. Atkinson *(Test No. 406)* to score a double century and take five wickets in an innings in the same Test. Intikhab (11 for 130) returned the best match analysis for any Test in Dunedin.

## PAKISTAN

| | | |
|---|---|---|
| Sadiq Mohammad | b Hadlee | 61 |
| Zaheer Abbas | c Wadsworth b Hadlee | 15 |
| Majid Khan | c and b Taylor | 26 |
| Mushtaq Mohammad | c Wadsworth b Congdon | 201 |
| Asif Iqbal | c Hastings b Taylor | 175 |
| Wasim Raja | not out | 8 |
| Intikhab Alam* | c Pollard b Howarth | 3 |
| Wasim Bari† | not out | 2 |
| Salim Altaf | ) | |
| Sarfraz Nawaz | ) did not bat | |
| Pervez Sajjad | ) | |
| Extras | (LB 13, NB 3) | 16 |
| **Total** | (6 wickets declared) | **507** |

## NEW ZEALAND

| | | | | | |
|---|---|---|---|---|---|
| G.M. Turner | c Mushtaq b Intikhab | 37 | | c Mushtaq b Intikhab | 24 |
| T.W. Jarvis | c Mushtaq b Sarfraz | 7 | | c Wasim Bari b Mushtaq | 39 |
| B.E. Congdon* | c Wasim Bari b Intikhab | 35 | | c Majid b Mushtaq | 7 |
| B.F. Hastings | c Sarfraz b Intikhab | 4 | | b Mushtaq | 9 |
| M.G. Burgess | b Intikhab | 10 | | c Pervez b Intikhab | 4 |
| V. Pollard | c Sarfraz b Intikhab | 3 | | b Intikhab | 61 |
| B.R. Taylor | c Sarfraz b Intikhab | 0 | (8) | run out | 3 |
| K.J. Wadsworth† | b Mushtaq | 45 | (7) | c Majid b Intikhab | 17 |
| D.R. Hadlee | st Wasim Bari b Intikhab | 1 | | c Majid b Mushtaq | 0 |
| D.R. O'Sullivan | c Wasim Raja b Mushtaq | 4 | | b Mushtaq | 1 |
| H.J. Howarth | not out | 4 | | not out | 7 |
| Extras | (B 1, LB 2, NB 3) | 6 | | (B 5, LB 7, NB 1) | 13 |
| **Total** | | **156** | | | **185** |

| NEW ZEALAND | O | M | R | W | O | M | R | W |
|---|---|---|---|---|---|---|---|---|
| Hadlee | 24 | 3 | 100 | 2 | | | | |
| Taylor | 22 | 3 | 91 | 2 | | | | |
| Congdon | 17 | 1 | 72 | 1 | | | | |
| Howarth | 29 | 6 | 83 | 1 | | | | |
| Pollard | 13 | 2 | 64 | 0 | | | | |
| O'Sullivan | 18 | 2 | 81 | 0 | | | | |
| PAKISTAN | | | | | | | | |
| Salim | 5 | 0 | 23 | 0 | 4 | 2 | 11 | 0 |
| Sarfraz | 5 | 0 | 20 | 1 | 4 | 0 | 16 | 0 |
| Intikhab | 21 | 3 | 52 | 7 | 18·4 | 2 | 78 | 4 |
| Pervez | 17 | 5 | 40 | 0 | 3 | 0 | 10 | 0 |
| Mushtaq | 3·5 | 1 | 15 | 2 | 18 | 2 | 49 | 5 |
| Wasim Raja | | | | | 2 | 0 | 8 | 0 |

### FALL OF WICKETS

| | P | NZ | NZ |
|---|---|---|---|
| Wkt | 1st | 1st | 2nd |
| 1st | 23 | 15 | 48 |
| 2nd | 81 | 73 | 57 |
| 3rd | 126 | 84 | 78 |
| 4th | 476 | 87 | 87 |
| 5th | 500 | 99 | 91 |
| 6th | 504 | 99 | 127 |
| 7th | – | 104 | 150 |
| 8th | – | 116 | 159 |
| 9th | – | 139 | 169 |
| 10th | – | 156 | 185 |

Umpires: D.E.A. Copps and R.W.R. Shortt.

# NEW ZEALAND v PAKISTAN 1972–73 (3rd Test)

Played at Eden Park, Auckland, on 16, 17, 18, 19 February.
Toss: Pakistan.   Result MATCH DRAWN.
Debuts: New Zealand – R.E. Redmond.

Pakistan won their first Test rubber away from their own country. Redmond became the third New Zealander after J.E. Mills and B.R. Taylor to score a hundred in his first Test; all three were left-handed. This was Redmond's only appearance in Test cricket. His innings of 107, New Zealand's first hundred in a home Test against Pakistan, took 145 minutes and included a five and 20 fours. Hastings and Collinge set the present world Test record for the tenth wicket with their partnership of 151 runs in 155 minutes; it beat the 130 added by R.E. Foster and W. Rhodes against Australia in 1903-04 (*Test No. 78*). During this match Taylor became the second bowler after R.C. Motz to take 100 Test wickets for New Zealand. His next wicket gave him the New Zealand record. Wadsworth became New Zealand's most successful wicket-keeper when he passed A.E. Dick's record of 51 Test match dismissals.

## PAKISTAN

| | | | | | |
|---|---|---|---|---|---|
| Sadiq Mohammad | c Wadsworth b Collinge | 33 | c Hadlee b Taylor | | 38 |
| Zaheer Abbas | c Turner b Taylor | 10 | c Turner b Taylor | | 0 |
| Majid Khan | c Wadsworth b Taylor | 110 | c Wadsworth b Howarth | | 33 |
| Mushtaq Mohammad | c Hastings b Congdon | 61 | b Howarth | | 52 |
| Asif Iqbal | b Taylor | 34 | (6) lbw b Congdon | | 39 |
| Wasim Raja | c Wadsworth b Collinge | 1 | (7) b Collinge | | 49 |
| Intikhab Alam* | c Wadsworth b Taylor | 34 | (8) b Howarth | | 2 |
| Wasim Bari† | c and b Howarth | 30 | (9) lbw b Hadlee | | 27 |
| Salim Altaf | not out | 53 | (5) lbw b Congdon | | 11 |
| Sarfraz Nawaz | c Wadsworth b Howarth | 2 | c Taylor b Collinge | | 4 |
| Pervez Sajjad | lbw b Congdon | 24 | not out | | 8 |
| Extras | (B 1, LB 3, NB 6) | 10 | (B 3, LB 3, NB 2) | | 8 |
| **Total** | | **402** | | | **271** |

## NEW ZEALAND

| | | | | | |
|---|---|---|---|---|---|
| R.E. Redmond | c Mushtaq b Pervez | 107 | c Intikhab b Wasim Raja | | 56 |
| G.M. Turner | c Sarfraz b Intikhab | 58 | b Wasim Raja | | 24 |
| B.E. Congdon* | b Intikhab | 24 | not out | | 6 |
| B.F. Hastings | b Wasim Raja | 110 | (5) not out | | 4 |
| M.G. Burgess | b Intikhab | 2 | (4) c Mushtaq b Wasim Raja | | 1 |
| T.W. Jarvis | lbw b Intikhab | 0 | | | |
| K.J. Wadsworth† | c Sadiq b Intikhab | 6 | | | |
| B.R. Taylor | c Majid b Pervez | 2 | | | |
| D.R. Hadlee | b Intikhab | 0 | | | |
| H.J. Howarth | c Majid b Mushtaq | 8 | | | |
| R.O. Collinge | not out | 68 | | | |
| Extras | (B 8, LB 6, NB 3) | 17 | (B 1) | | 1 |
| **Total** | | **402** | (3 wickets) | | **92** |

| NEW ZEALAND | O | M | R | W | O | M | R | W |
|---|---|---|---|---|---|---|---|---|
| Collinge | 24 | 2 | 72 | 2 | 7 | 2 | 19 | 2 |
| Hadlee | 18 | 3 | 100 | 0 | 5·7 | 0 | 35 | 1 |
| Taylor | 32 | 9 | 86 | 4 | 19 | 5 | 66 | 2 |
| Howarth | 32 | 5 | 86 | 2 | 31 | 11 | 99 | 3 |
| Congdon | 11·5 | 0 | 48 | 2 | 16 | 3 | 44 | 2 |
| PAKISTAN | | | | | | | | |
| Salim | 20 | 1 | 58 | 0 | 4 | 0 | 17 | 0 |
| Sarfraz | 16 | 1 | 85 | 0 | 4 | 0 | 13 | 0 |
| Intikhab | 30 | 4 | 127 | 6 | | | | |
| Majid | 3 | 0 | 30 | 0 | 3 | 0 | 11 | 0 |
| Pervez | 15 | 3 | 50 | 2 | | | | |
| Mushtaq | 5 | 0 | 26 | 1 | | | | |
| Wasim Raja | 1·6 | 0 | 9 | 1 | 8 | 2 | 32 | 3 |
| Sadiq | | | | | 5 | 1 | 18 | 0 |

### FALL OF WICKETS

| | P | NZ | P | NZ |
|---|---|---|---|---|
| *Wkt* | *1st* | *1st* | *2nd* | *2nd* |
| 1st | 43 | 159 | 4 | 80 |
| 2nd | 43 | 180 | 61 | 81 |
| 3rd | 147 | 203 | 71 | 87 |
| 4th | 233 | 205 | 116 | – |
| 5th | 238 | 205 | 159 | – |
| 6th | 267 | 225 | 203 | – |
| 7th | 295 | 235 | 206 | – |
| 8th | 342 | 236 | 238 | – |
| 9th | 354 | 251 | 242 | – |
| 10th | 402 | 402 | 271 | – |

Umpires: W.T. Martin and E.C.A. MacKintosh.

## WEST INDIES v AUSTRALIA 1972–73 (1st Test)

Played at Sabina Park, Kingston, Jamaica, on 16, 17, 18, 20, 21 February.
Toss: Australia.    Result: MATCH DRAWN.
Debuts: Australia – J.R. Hammond.

Foster scored a hundred in his first Test against Australia and with Kanhai shared a partnership of 210 which remains the West Indies fifth-wicket record for this series. For the first time since 1954-55, West Indies were without G. St A. Sobers. His 85 consecutive appearances constitute the record unbroken run for a Test cricketer, as do his 39 successive matches as captain.

### AUSTRALIA

| | | | | | |
|---|---|---:|---|---|---:|
| K.R. Stackpole | b Foster | 44 | c Rowe b Holder | | 142 |
| I.R. Redpath | b Gibbs | 46 | c Kanhai b Gibbs | | 60 |
| I.M. Chappell* | c Dowe b Ali | 19 | not out | | 38 |
| G.S. Chappell | c Kallicharran b Gibbs | 42 | not out | | 14 |
| R. Edwards | c and b Gibbs | 63 | | | |
| K.D. Walters | c Kanhai b Gibbs | 72 | | | |
| R.W. Marsh† | hit wkt b Dowe | 97 | | | |
| K.J. O'Keeffe | not out | 19 | | | |
| M.H.N. Walker | ) | | | | |
| J.R. Hammond | ) did not bat | | | | |
| D.K. Lillee | ) | | | | |
| Extras | (B 6, LB 12, W 1, NB 7) | 26 | (LB 2, NB 4) | | 6 |
| **Total** | (7 wickets declared) | **428** | (2 wickets declared) | | **260** |

### WEST INDIES

| | | | | | |
|---|---|---:|---|---|---:|
| R.C. Fredericks | c O'Keeffe b Walker | 31 | c Marsh b G.S. Chappell | | 21 |
| G.A. Greenidge | b Walker | 0 | | | |
| L.G. Rowe | c Stackpole b Walker | 76 | c G.S. Chappell b Hammond | | 4 |
| A.I. Kallicharran | c Marsh b Hammond | 50 | not out | | 7 |
| R.B. Kanhai* | c Marsh b Hammond | 84 | | | |
| M.L.C. Foster | b Walker | 125 | (5) not out | | 18 |
| T.M. Findlay† | c Marsh b Walker | 12 | (2) c Marsh b G.S. Chappell | | 13 |
| Inshan Ali | c Marsh b Walker | 10 | | | |
| V.A. Holder | lbw b Hammond | 12 | | | |
| L.R. Gibbs | c O'Keeffe b Hammond | 5 | | | |
| U.G. Dowe | not out | 5 | | | |
| Extras | (LB 9, NB 9) | 18 | (B 1, W 1, NB 2) | | 4 |
| **Total** | | **428** | (3 wickets) | | **67** |

| WEST INDIES | O | M | R | W | O | M | R | W | | | FALL OF WICKETS | | |
|---|---|---|---|---|---|---|---|---|---|---|---|---|---|
| Holder | 26 | 5 | 55 | 0 | 19 | 5 | 34 | 1 | | | A | WI | A | WI |
| Dowe | 21 | 3 | 96 | 1 | 21 | 4 | 72 | 0 | Wkt | 1st | 1st | 2nd | 2nd |
| Foster | 44 | 18 | 84 | 1 | 22 | 7 | 71 | 0 | 1st | 66 | 6 | 161 | 35 |
| Gibbs | 41 | 14 | 85 | 4 | 15 | 4 | 40 | 1 | 2nd | 106 | 49 | 230 | 36 |
| Ali | 25 | 5 | 82 | 1 | 4 | 0 | 28 | 0 | 3rd | 128 | 165 | – | 42 |
| Fredericks | | | | | 1 | 0 | 9 | 0 | 4th | 179 | 165 | – | – |
| | | | | | | | | | 5th | 271 | 375 | – | – |
| AUSTRALIA | | | | | | | | | 6th | 365 | 385 | – | – |
| Lillee | 26 | 4 | 112 | 0 | 6 | 1 | 20 | 0 | 7th | 428 | 400 | – | – |
| Walker | 39 | 10 | 114 | 6 | 6 | 3 | 8 | 0 | 8th | – | 417 | – | – |
| Hammond | 28·5 | 5 | 79 | 4 | 10 | 4 | 17 | 1 | 9th | – | 423 | – | – |
| O'Keeffe | 18 | 1 | 71 | 0 | | | | | 10th | – | 428 | – | – |
| I.M. Chappell | 11 | 3 | 30 | 0 | | | | | | | | | |
| G.S. Chappell | 2 | 0 | 4 | 0 | 10 | 4 | 18 | 2 | | | | | |
| Walters | | | | | 1 | 1 | 0 | 0 | | | | | |

Umpires: D. Sang Hue and R. Gosein.

# WEST INDIES v AUSTRALIA 1972–73 (2nd Test)

Played at Kensington Oval, Bridgetown, Barbados, on 9, 10, 11, 13, 14 March.
Toss: Australia.   Result: MATCH DRAWN.
Debuts: West Indies – E.T. Willett.

This was the 15th drawn match out of the last 17 Tests played in the West Indies. Australia did not begin their second innings until the last session of the fourth day. The partnership of 165 between Kanhai and Murray is the West Indies sixth-wicket record for this series.

## AUSTRALIA

| | | | | |
|---|---|--:|---|--:|
| K.R. Stackpole | c Kanhai b Holder | 1 | b Foster | 53 |
| I.R. Redpath | c Kanhai b Boyce | 6 | c Greenidge b Gibbs | 20 |
| I.M. Chappell* | run out | 72 | not out | 106 |
| G.S. Chappell | c Murray b Holder | 106 | | |
| R. Edwards | c Murray b Boyce | 15 | | |
| K.D. Walters | c Kanhai b Gibbs | 1 | (4) not out | 102 |
| R.W. Marsh† | c Rowe b Willett | 78 | | |
| K.J. O'Keeffe | b Willett | 21 | | |
| J.R. Hammond | lbw b Boyce | 0 | | |
| T.J. Jenner | not out | 10 | | |
| M.H.N. Walker | b Gibbs | 0 | | |
| Extras | (NB 14) | 14 | (B 1, LB 6, NB 12) | 19 |
| **Total** | | **324** | (2 wickets declared) | **300** |

## WEST INDIES

| | | | | |
|---|---|--:|---|--:|
| R.C. Fredericks | lbw b Hammond | 98 | not out | 22 |
| G.A. Greenidge | lbw b Walker | 9 | not out | 10 |
| L.G. Rowe | c Stackpole b Walker | 16 | | |
| A.I. Kallicharran | b Walker | 14 | | |
| R.B. Kanhai* | lbw b I.M. Chappell | 105 | | |
| M.L.C. Foster | b Jenner | 12 | | |
| D.L. Murray† | c Redpath b Jenner | 90 | | |
| K.D. Boyce | lbw b Walker | 10 | | |
| E.T. Willett | c Stackpole b Jenner | 0 | | |
| V.A. Holder | b Walker | 1 | | |
| L.R. Gibbs | not out | 0 | | |
| Extras | (B 13, LB 5, W 4, NB 14) | 36 | (LB 2, W 1, NB 1) | 4 |
| **Total** | | **391** | (0 wickets) | **36** |

| WEST INDIES | O | M | R | W | O | M | R | W | | FALL OF WICKETS | | | |
|---|--:|--:|--:|--:|--:|--:|--:|--:|---|--:|--:|--:|--:|
| Holder | 21 | 5 | 49 | 2 | 21 | 5 | 52 | 0 | | A | WI | A | WI |
| Boyce | 22 | 5 | 68 | 3 | 18 | 4 | 54 | 0 | *Wkt* | *1st* | *1st* | *2nd* | *2nd* |
| Foster | 15 | 4 | 35 | 0 | 13 | 4 | 29 | 1 | 1st | 2 | 19 | 79 | – |
| Willett | 37 | 11 | 79 | 2 | 28 | 15 | 45 | 0 | 2nd | 19 | 77 | 108 | – |
| Gibbs | 36 | 9 | 79 | 2 | 25 | 10 | 55 | 1 | 3rd | 148 | 118 | – | – |
| Fredericks | | | | | 1 | 0 | 3 | 0 | 4th | 189 | 162 | – | – |
| Greenidge | | | | | 7 | 0 | 24 | 0 | 5th | 194 | 179 | – | – |
| Kanhai | | | | | 6·1 | 1 | 19 | 0 | 6th | 218 | 344 | – | – |
| | | | | | | | | | 7th | 264 | 385 | – | – |
| AUSTRALIA | | | | | | | | | 8th | 283 | 386 | – | – |
| Hammond | 31 | 9 | 114 | 1 | 4 | 1 | 10 | 0 | 9th | 320 | 391 | – | – |
| Walker | 51·4 | 20 | 97 | 5 | 4 | 3 | 1 | 0 | 10th | 324 | 391 | – | – |
| G.S. Chappell | 22 | 11 | 37 | 0 | | | | | | | | | |
| Jenner | 28 | 9 | 65 | 3 | | | | | | | | | |
| O'Keeffe | 10 | 3 | 18 | 0 | 6 | 2 | 15 | 0 | | | | | |
| Walters | 2 | 0 | 7 | 0 | | | | | | | | | |
| I.M. Chappell | 8 | 3 | 17 | 1 | | | | | | | | | |
| Stackpole | | | | | 5 | 3 | 6 | 0 | | | | | |

Umpires: D. Sang Hue and H.B. de C. Jordan.

# WEST INDIES v AUSTRALIA 1972–73 (3rd Test)

Played at Queen's Park Oval, Port-of-Spain, Trinidad, on 23, 24, 25, 27, 28 March.
Toss: Australia.    Result: AUSTRALIA won by 44 runs.
Debuts: Nil.

Walters scored 100 runs (out of 130) between lunch and tea on the first day. Rowe fell while fielding on the first evening, damaged ligaments in his right ankle, and took no further part in the rubber.

## AUSTRALIA

| | | | | | |
|---|---|---|---|---|---|
| K.R. Stackpole | c Foster b Boyce | 0 | | c Fredericks b Boyce | 18 |
| I.R. Redpath | run out | 66 | | c Kanhai b Willett | 44 |
| G.S. Chappell | c Kallicharran b Gibbs | 56 | (4) | c and b Gibbs | 1 |
| K.D. Walters | c Fredericks b Ali | 112 | (5) | c Gibbs b Willett | 32 |
| R. Edwards | lbw b Boyce | 12 | (6) | b Gibbs | 14 |
| I.M. Chappell* | c and b Ali | 8 | (3) | c Fredericks b Willett | 97 |
| R.W. Marsh† | b Ali | 14 | | b Ali | 8 |
| K.J. O'Keeffe | run out | 37 | | c Kallicharran b Gibbs | 7 |
| T.J. Jenner | lbw b Gibbs | 2 | | b Gibbs | 6 |
| M.H.N. Walker | b Gibbs | 0 | (11) | not out | 23 |
| J.R. Hammond | not out | 2 | (10) | c Kanhai b Gibbs | 19 |
| Extras | (B 10, LB 7, NB 6) | 23 | | (B 5, LB 7) | 12 |
| **Total** | | **332** | | | **281** |

## WEST INDIES

| | | | | | |
|---|---|---|---|---|---|
| R.C. Fredericks | c I.M. Chappell b Jenner | 16 | | c Redpath b Stackpole | 76 |
| M.L.C. Foster | lbw b Jenner | 25 | (6) | c G.S. Chappell b O'Keeffe | 34 |
| A.I. Kallicharran | c G.S. Chappell b Jenner | 53 | | c Marsh b Walker | 91 |
| C.H. Lloyd | c and b G.S. Chappell | 20 | (5) | c Stackpole b O'Keeffe | 15 |
| R.B. Kanhai* | c Redpath b O'Keeffe | 56 | (4) | b G.S. Chappell | 14 |
| D.L. Murray† | lbw b Hammond | 40 | (2) | c Redpath b Walker | 7 |
| K.D. Boyce | c Marsh b O'Keeffe | 12 | | c I.M. Chappell b O'Keeffe | 11 |
| Inshan Ali | c Marsh b Walker | 15 | | b Walker | 2 |
| E.T. Willett | not out | 4 | | b O'Keeffe | 0 |
| L.R. Gibbs | c O'Keeffe b Jenner | 6 | | not out | 0 |
| L.G. Rowe | absent hurt | – | | absent hurt | – |
| Extras | (B 17, LB 11, W 1, NB 4) | 33 | | (B 19, LB 13, NB 7) | 39 |
| **Total** | | **280** | | | **289** |

| WEST INDIES | O | M | R | W | O | M | R | W |
|---|---|---|---|---|---|---|---|---|
| Boyce | 18 | 4 | 54 | 2 | 10 | 1 | 41 | 1 |
| Lloyd | 7 | 3 | 13 | 0 | 3 | 1 | 11 | 0 |
| Gibbs | 38 | 11 | 79 | 3 | 45 | 14 | 102 | 5 |
| Willett | 19 | 3 | 62 | 0 | 28 | 15 | 33 | 3 |
| Ali | 41·1 | 11 | 89 | 3 | 21 | 2 | 82 | 1 |
| Foster | 6 | 2 | 12 | 0 | | | | |
| AUSTRALIA | | | | | | | | |
| Walker | 30 | 8 | 55 | 1 | 25 | 6 | 43 | 3 |
| Hammond | 7 | 3 | 7 | 1 | 6 | 3 | 12 | 0 |
| Jenner | 38·3 | 7 | 98 | 4 | 15 | 2 | 46 | 0 |
| O'Keeffe | 28 | 10 | 62 | 2 | 24·1 | 5 | 57 | 4 |
| G.S. Chappell | 14 | 8 | 16 | 1 | 32 | 10 | 65 | 1 |
| Stackpole | 2 | 0 | 8 | 0 | 11 | 4 | 27 | 1 |
| I.M. Chappell | 2 | 1 | 1 | 0 | | | | |

FALL OF WICKETS

| Wkt | A 1st | WI 1st | A 2nd | WI 2nd |
|---|---|---|---|---|
| 1st | 1 | 33 | 31 | 39 |
| 2nd | 108 | 44 | 96 | 141 |
| 3rd | 181 | 100 | 99 | 177 |
| 4th | 240 | 149 | 156 | 219 |
| 5th | 257 | 206 | 185 | 268 |
| 6th | 262 | 230 | 208 | 274 |
| 7th | 312 | 265 | 231 | 281 |
| 8th | 321 | 267 | 231 | 288 |
| 9th | 321 | 280 | 248 | 289 |
| 10th | 332 | – | 281 | – |

Umpires: D. Sang Hue and R. Gosein.

# WEST INDIES v AUSTRALIA 1972–73 (4th Test)

Played at Bourda, Georgetown, Guyana, on 6, 7, 8, 10, 11 April.
Toss: West Indies.    Result: AUSTRALIA won by ten wickets.
Debuts: Nil.

Australia won their second rubber in the West Indies after 20 minutes of play on the fifth morning. West Indies were dismissed for their second-lowest total in a home Test – they scored only 103 against England at Kingston in 1934-35 *(Test No. 241)*.

## WEST INDIES

| | | | | |
|---|---|---|---|---|
| R.C. Fredericks | c I.M. Chappell b Walters | 30 | c Marsh b Hammond | 6 |
| G.A. Greenidge | b Walters | 22 | b Hammond | 24 |
| A.I. Kallicharran | run out | 13 | c Walker b Hammond | 8 |
| C.H. Lloyd | b Hammond | 178 | c Marsh b Hammond | 3 |
| R.B. Kanhai* | c O'Keeffe b Hammond | 57 | lbw b Walker | 23 |
| C.A. Davis | lbw b Walker | 5 | c Marsh b Walker | 16 |
| D.L. Murray† | c I.M. Chappell b Hammond | 1 | c Marsh b Walker | 3 |
| K.D. Boyce | c Edwards b Walters | 23 | c G.S. Chappell b Walters | 10 |
| E.T. Willett | lbw b Walters | 12 | not out | 3 |
| V.A. Holder | not out | 9 | b Walters | 3 |
| L.R. Gibbs | b Walters | 1 | b Walker | 7 |
| Extras | (B 5, LB 6, W 2, NB 2) | 15 | (LB 3) | 3 |
| **Total** | | **366** | | **109** |

## AUSTRALIA

| | | | | |
|---|---|---|---|---|
| K.R. Stackpole | lbw b Boyce | 1 | not out | 76 |
| I.R. Redpath | c Fredericks b Holder | 22 | not out | 57 |
| I.M. Chappell* | b Gibbs | 109 | | |
| G.S. Chappell | b Willett | 51 | | |
| K.D. Walters | c Murray b Gibbs | 81 | | |
| R. Edwards | c Murray b Boyce | 13 | | |
| R.W. Marsh† | lbw b Willett | 23 | | |
| K.J. O'Keeffe | b Gibbs | 5 | | |
| T.J. Jenner | c Kallicharran b Boyce | 10 | | |
| J.R. Hammond | run out | 1 | | |
| M.H.N. Walker | not out | 2 | | |
| Extras | (B 9, LB 7, W 4, NB 3) | 23 | (LB 2) | 2 |
| **Total** | | **341** | (0 wickets) | **135** |

| AUSTRALIA | O | M | R | W | O | M | R | W |
|---|---|---|---|---|---|---|---|---|
| Hammond | 33 | 6 | 110 | 3 | 16 | 4 | 38 | 4 |
| Walker | 38 | 11 | 77 | 1 | 23·3 | 4 | 45 | 4 |
| G.S. Chappell | 16 | 4 | 56 | 0 | | | | |
| Walters | 18·2 | 1 | 66 | 5 | 13 | 3 | 23 | 2 |
| O'Keeffe | 8 | 1 | 27 | 0 | | | | |
| Jenner | 7 | 0 | 15 | 0 | | | | |
| I.M. Chappell | 1 | 1 | 0 | 0 | | | | |
| WEST INDIES | | | | | | | | |
| Holder | 35 | 6 | 64 | 1 | 7 | 2 | 21 | 0 |
| Boyce | 24·4 | 6 | 69 | 3 | 8 | 1 | 33 | 0 |
| Davis | 6 | 0 | 15 | 0 | 3 | 2 | 5 | 0 |
| Willett | 27 | 3 | 88 | 2 | 6 | 2 | 20 | 0 |
| Gibbs | 36 | 15 | 67 | 3 | 5 | 4 | 9 | 0 |
| Lloyd | 7 | 1 | 15 | 0 | 5 | 1 | 15 | 0 |
| Kanhai | | | | | 5 | 1 | 15 | 0 |
| Greenidge | | | | | 4 | 0 | 15 | 0 |

### FALL OF WICKETS

| | WI | A | WI | A |
|---|---|---|---|---|
| *Wkt* | *1st* | *1st* | *2nd* | *2nd* |
| 1st | 55 | 5 | 12 | – |
| 2nd | 56 | 36 | 30 | – |
| 3rd | 90 | 157 | 39 | – |
| 4th | 277 | 229 | 42 | – |
| 5th | 307 | 262 | 77 | – |
| 6th | 310 | 306 | 82 | – |
| 7th | 337 | 316 | 91 | – |
| 8th | 347 | 334 | 95 | – |
| 9th | 356 | 336 | 100 | – |
| 10th | 366 | 341 | 109 | – |

Umpires: D. Sang Hue and C.P. Kippins.

# AUSTRALIA v WEST INDIES 1972–73 (5th Test)

Played at Queen's Park Oval, Port-of-Spain, Trinidad, on 21, 22, 23, 25, 26 April.
Toss: Australia.   Result: MATCH DRAWN.
Debuts: Nil.

West Indies were asked to score 319 runs in 270 minutes. Rain curtailed the second day by 175 minutes and ended play on the third day 25 minutes before tea. In this match, Gibbs became the first bowler to bowl 20,000 balls in Test cricket. He and Walker each took 26 wickets in the rubber to set the present records for this series in the West Indies.

## AUSTRALIA

| | | | | | |
|---|---|---|---|---|---|
| I.R. Redpath | c Fredericks b Gibbs | 36 | c Boyce b Foster | | 24 |
| R. Edwards | c Fredericks b Jumadeen | 74 | c Kallicharran b Ali | | 14 |
| I.M. Chappell* | c Kallicharran b Ali | 56 | c Kallicharran b Gibbs | | 37 |
| G.S. Chappell | c Fredericks b Gibbs | 41 | c Fredericks b Gibbs | | 31 |
| K.D. Walters | c Fredericks b Gibbs | 70 | c Murray b Gibbs | | 27 |
| J. Benaud | c and b Ali | 8 | c Davis b Ali | | 36 |
| R.W. Marsh† | c Ali b Jumadeen | 56 | not out | | 21 |
| K.J. O'Keeffe | b Ali | 37 | c Lloyd b Gibbs | | 0 |
| T.J. Jenner | not out | 27 | not out | | 11 |
| J.R. Hammond | not out | 6 | | | |
| M.H.N. Walker | did not bat | | | | |
| Extras | (B 5, LB 1, NB 2) | 8 | (B 13, LB 2, W 1, NB 1) | | 17 |
| **Total** | (8 wickets declared) | **419** | (7 wickets declared) | | **218** |

## WEST INDIES

| | | | | | |
|---|---|---|---|---|---|
| R.C. Fredericks | c Edwards b Jenner | 73 | c Marsh b Hammond | | 8 |
| M.L.C. Foster | c Marsh b Walker | 29 | c I.M. Chappell b Walker | | 19 |
| C.A. Davis | c Marsh b Walker | 25 | b Benaud | | 24 |
| A.I. Kallicharran | c Hammond b Jenner | 32 | c O'Keeffe b Benaud | | 26 |
| R.B. Kanhai* | b Jenner | 3 | (6) not out | | 16 |
| C.H. Lloyd | c Redpath b Walker | 59 | (7) not out | | 22 |
| D.L. Murray† | c Marsh b Walker | 34 | (5) c I.M. Chappell b Jenner | | 7 |
| K.D. Boyce | b Jenner | 31 | | | |
| Inshan Ali | c G.S. Chappell b Walker | 0 | | | |
| R.R. Jumadeen | not out | 11 | | | |
| L.R. Gibbs | c Hammond b Jenner | 6 | | | |
| Extras | (B 6, LB 4, W 1, NB 5) | 16 | (B 10, NB 3) | | 13 |
| **Total** | | **319** | (5 wickets) | | **135** |

| WEST INDIES | O | M | R | W | O | M | R | W |
|---|---|---|---|---|---|---|---|---|
| Boyce | 10 | 3 | 21 | 0 | | | | |
| Lloyd | 12 | 6 | 19 | 0 | 3 | 0 | 16 | 0 |
| Davis | 5 | 0 | 22 | 0 | 5 | 0 | 16 | 0 |
| Gibbs | 52 | 15 | 114 | 3 | 32 | 12 | 66 | 4 |
| Jumadeen | 40 | 8 | 89 | 2 | 18 | 5 | 32 | 0 |
| Ali | 44 | 4 | 124 | 3 | 19 | 2 | 68 | 2 |
| Foster | 8 | 3 | 15 | 0 | 3 | 1 | 3 | 1 |
| Fredericks | 2 | 0 | 7 | 0 | | | | |
| AUSTRALIA | | | | | | | | |
| Hammond | 21 | 4 | 76 | 0 | 15 | 8 | 25 | 1 |
| Walker | 37 | 10 | 75 | 5 | 17 | 8 | 24 | 1 |
| G.S. Chappell | 7 | 2 | 21 | 0 | 6 | 2 | 11 | 0 |
| Walters | 3 | 2 | 5 | 0 | | | | |
| Jenner | 32·2 | 9 | 90 | 5 | 17 | 7 | 33 | 1 |
| O'Keeffe | 11 | 1 | 36 | 0 | 10 | 5 | 17 | 0 |
| Benaud | | | | | 4 | 1 | 12 | 2 |

| FALL OF WICKETS | | | | |
|---|---|---|---|---|
| | A | WI | A | WI |
| Wkt | 1st | 1st | 2nd | 2nd |
| 1st | 50 | 48 | 37 | 25 |
| 2nd | 159 | 88 | 49 | 30 |
| 3rd | 169 | 151 | 101 | 81 |
| 4th | 280 | 171 | 114 | 86 |
| 5th | 281 | 180 | 157 | 96 |
| 6th | 293 | 270 | 195 | – |
| 7th | 379 | 271 | 197 | – |
| 8th | 395 | 271 | – | – |
| 9th | – | 303 | – | – |
| 10th | – | 319 | – | – |

Umpires: D. Sang Hue and R. Gosein.

# PAKISTAN v ENGLAND 1972–73 (1st Test)

Played at Lahore (Gaddafi) Stadium on 2, 3, 4, 6, 7 March.
Toss: England.    Result: MATCH DRAWN.
Debuts: Nil.

Pakistan were left 145 minutes in which to score 240 runs. Amiss scored the first of his eleven Test hundreds in his 22nd innings.

## ENGLAND

| | | | | | |
|---|---|---|---|---|---|
| M.H. Denness | lbw b Salim | 50 | c Wasim Bari b Intikhab | 68 |
| D.L. Amiss | b Salim | 112 | c Mushtaq b Intikhab | 16 |
| G.R.J. Roope | c Wasim Bari b Pervez | 15 | st Wasim Bari b Intikhab | 0 |
| A.R. Lewis* | b Wasim Raja | 29 | b Salim | 74 |
| K.W.R. Fletcher | c Wasim Bari b Pervez | 55 | c Majid b Intikhab | 12 |
| A.W. Greig | c Majid b Sarfraz | 41 | c Talat b Mushtaq | 72 |
| A.P.E. Knott† | c Wasim Bari b Mushtaq | 29 | c Majid b Mushtaq | 34 |
| C.M. Old | b Pervez | 0 | not out | 17 |
| G.G. Arnold | c Sarfraz b Mushtaq | 0 | not out | 3 |
| D.L. Underwood | not out | 5 | | |
| P.I. Pocock | c Talat b Mushtaq | 5 | | |
| Extras | (LB 11, NB 3) | 14 | (B 6, LB 3, NB 1) | 10 |
| **Total** | | **355** | (7 wickets declared) | **306** |

## PAKISTAN

| | | | | | |
|---|---|---|---|---|---|
| Sadiq Mohammad | c Roope b Greig | 119 | c Roope b Greig | 9 |
| Talat Ali | c Greig b Arnold | 35 | c and b Pocock | 57 |
| Majid Khan* | run out | 32 | c and b Greig | 43 |
| Mushtaq Mohammad | b Underwood | 66 | not out | 5 |
| Asif Iqbal | c Denness b Arnold | 102 | | |
| Intikhab Alam | b Underwood | 3 | | |
| Wasim Raja | c Roope b Greig | 23 | (5) not out | 6 |
| Salim Altaf | not out | 11 | | |
| Wasim Bari† | b Underwood | 7 | | |
| Sarfraz Nawaz | b Greig | 8 | | |
| Pervez Sajjad | lbw b Greig | 4 | | |
| Extras | (B 1, LB 6, NB 5) | 12 | (LB 4) | 4 |
| **Total** | | **422** | (3 wickets) | **124** |

| PAKISTAN | O | M | R | W | O | M | R | W | FALL OF WICKETS | | | | |
|---|---|---|---|---|---|---|---|---|---|---|---|---|---|
| Salim | 28 | 3 | 80 | 2 | 11 | 2 | 24 | 1 | | E | P | E | P |
| Sarfraz | 31 | 14 | 51 | 1 | 17 | 7 | 41 | 0 | Wkt | 1st | 1st | 2nd | 2nd |
| Wasim Raja | 21 | 0 | 69 | 1 | 14 | 7 | 36 | 0 | 1st | 105 | 99 | 63 | 9 |
| Pervez | 23 | 9 | 58 | 3 | 23 | 9 | 37 | 0 | 2nd | 147 | 155 | 63 | 102 |
| Intikhab | 32 | 14 | 62 | 0 | 35 | 10 | 80 | 4 | 3rd | 201 | 222 | 108 | 114 |
| Mushtaq | 8·3 | 1 | 21 | 3 | 16 | 2 | 66 | 2 | 4th | 219 | 294 | 154 | – |
| Majid | | | | | 3 | 1 | 12 | 0 | 5th | 286 | 310 | 203 | – |
| | | | | | | | | | 6th | 333 | 383 | 282 | – |
| ENGLAND | | | | | | | | | 7th | 333 | 391 | 287 | – |
| Arnold | 43 | 10 | 95 | 2 | 4 | 1 | 12 | 0 | 8th | 334 | 404 | – | – |
| Old | 27 | 2 | 98 | 0 | | | | | 9th | 345 | 413 | – | – |
| Underwood | 35 | 15 | 58 | 3 | 13 | 5 | 38 | 0 | 10th | 355 | 422 | – | – |
| Pocock | 24 | 6 | 73 | 0 | 15 | 3 | 42 | 1 | | | | | |
| Greig | 29·2 | 5 | 86 | 4 | 6 | 0 | 28 | 2 | | | | | |

Umpires: Shujauddin and Daud Khan.

# PAKISTAN v ENGLAND 1972–73 (2nd Test)

Played at Niaz Stadium, Hyderabad, on 16, 17, 18, 20, 21 March.
Toss: England.    Result: MATCH DRAWN.
Debuts: Nil.

Hyderabad's first Test match provided Pakistan with their highest total in a home Test against England. Mushtaq and Intikhab shared a partnership of 145 which remains the highest for Pakistan's sixth wicket against England. Mushtaq's 157 is the highest score against England in Pakistan. Intikhab's only Test hundred included four sixes and 15 fours. Mohammad Aslam Khokhar, who made his debut as a Test umpire in this match, played in one Test (*Test No. 388*) as 'Mohammad Aslam'.

## ENGLAND

| | | | | | |
|---|---|---|---|---|---|
| M.H. Denness | b Salim | 8 | c Mushtaq b Salim | | 0 |
| D.L. Amiss | st Wasim b Mushtaq | 158 | c Sadiq b Intikhab | | 0 |
| K.W.R. Fletcher | c Zaheer b Intikhab | 78 | c Asif b Intikhab | | 21 |
| A.R. Lewis* | c Wasim b Mushtaq | 7 | c Pervez b Intikhab | | 21 |
| G.R.J. Roope | st Wasim b Intikhab | 27 | b Mushtaq | | 18 |
| A.W. Greig | b Mushtaq | 36 | c Wasim b Asif | | 64 |
| A.P.E. Knott† | c Nazir b Mushtaq | 71 | not out | | 63 |
| G.G. Arnold | c Wasim b Intikhab | 8 | not out | | 19 |
| N. Gifford | b Intikhab | 24 | | | |
| D.L. Underwood | not out | 20 | | | |
| P.I. Pocock | b Pervez | 33 | | | |
| Extras | (B 2, LB 11, NB 4) | 17 | (B 1, LB 5, NB 6) | | 12 |
| **Total** | | **487** | (6 wickets) | | **218** |

## PAKISTAN

| | | |
|---|---|---|
| Sadiq Mohammad | c Knott b Pocock | 30 |
| Talat Ali | c Fletcher b Gifford | 22 |
| Majid Khan* | c Knott b Pocock | 17 |
| Mushtaq Mohammad | lbw b Gifford | 157 |
| Zaheer Abbas | c Roope b Pocock | 24 |
| Asif Iqbal | c Roope b Pocock | 68 |
| Intikhab Alam | b Arnold | 138 |
| Salim Altaf | c Gifford b Pocock | 2 |
| Wasim Bari† | c Pocock b Gifford | 48 |
| Mohammad Nazir | not out | 22 |
| Pervez Sajjad | not out | 10 |
| Extras | (B 14, LB 10, NB 7) | 31 |
| **Total** | (9 wickets declared) | **569** |

| PAKISTAN | O | M | R | W | O | M | R | W | | FALL OF WICKETS | | |
|---|---|---|---|---|---|---|---|---|---|---|---|---|
| | | | | | | | | | | E | P | E |
| Salim | 29 | 10 | 63 | 1 | 10 | 1 | 40 | 1 | *Wkt* | *1st* | *1st* | *2nd* |
| Asif | 11 | 5 | 31 | 0 | 1 | 0 | 3 | 1 | 1st | 22 | 53 | 0 |
| Intikhab | 65 | 17 | 137 | 4 | 19 | 5 | 44 | 3 | 2nd | 190 | 66 | 0 |
| Nazir | 36 | 9 | 84 | 0 | 16 | 3 | 41 | 0 | 3rd | 250 | 77 | 34 |
| Pervez | 21·2 | 5 | 56 | 1 | 11 | 5 | 11 | 0 | 4th | 259 | 139 | 52 |
| Mushtaq | 35 | 10 | 93 | 4 | 20 | 5 | 42 | 1 | 5th | 319 | 292 | 77 |
| Sadiq | 3 | 1 | 6 | 0 | 3 | 0 | 14 | 0 | 6th | 343 | 437 | 189 |
| Majid | | | | | 2 | 0 | 4 | 0 | 7th | 364 | 449 | – |
| Talat | | | | | 1 | 0 | 1 | 0 | 8th | 428 | 514 | – |
| Zaheer | | | | | 1 | 0 | 1 | 0 | 9th | 432 | 553 | – |
| | | | | | | | | | 10th | 487 | – | – |
| ENGLAND | | | | | | | | | | | | |
| Arnold | 24 | 2 | 78 | 1 | | | | | | | | |
| Greig | 13 | 2 | 39 | 0 | | | | | | | | |
| Pocock | 52 | 9 | 169 | 5 | | | | | | | | |
| Gifford | 52 | 16 | 111 | 3 | | | | | | | | |
| Underwood | 48 | 15 | 119 | 0 | | | | | | | | |
| Fletcher | 3 | 0 | 22 | 0 | | | | | | | | |

Umpires: Shujauddin and Mohammad Aslam Khokhar.

# PAKISTAN v ENGLAND 1972–73 (3rd Test)

Played at National Stadium, Karachi, on 24, 25, 27, 28, 29 March.
Toss: Pakistan.    Result: MATCH DRAWN.
Debuts: Nil.

This match and the rubber were left drawn when play was abandoned 45 minutes early because of a dust storm. Sundry riots and crowd incursions lost nearly two hours of playing time earlier in the match. Amiss failed by one run to score his third hundred in successive Tests. His aggregate of 406 (average 81·20) is England's highest in a rubber in Pakistan; his previous 12 Test matches produced only 348 runs (average 18·31). Amiss was one of three batsmen to be out for 99 in the match – a unique record in Test cricket. Pakistan's total of 199 is their lowest in a home Test against England.

## PAKISTAN

| | | | | | |
|---|---|--:|---|---|--:|
| Sadiq Mohammad | c Denness b Gifford | 89 | (6) b Gifford | | 1 |
| Talat Ali | c Amiss b Gifford | 33 | b Gifford | | 39 |
| Majid Khan* | c Amiss b Pocock | 99 | (1) b Gifford | | 23 |
| Mushtaq Mohammad | run out | 99 | (5) c Denness b Birkenshaw | | 0 |
| Asif Iqbal | c and b Pocock | 6 | (4) c Fletcher b Gifford | | 36 |
| Intikhab Alam | c and b Birkenshaw | 61 | (7) c Greig b Birkenshaw | | 0 |
| Zaheer Abbas | not out | 22 | (3) c Knott b Gifford | | 4 |
| Wasim Bari† | not out | 17 | c Denness b Birkenshaw | | 41 |
| Salim Altaf | ) | | c Knott b Birkenshaw | | 13 |
| Sarfraz Nawaz | ) did not bat | | not out | | 33 |
| Asif Masood | ) | | c Gifford b Birkenshaw | | 0 |
| Extras | (B 4, LB 9, NB 6) | 19 | (LB 4, NB 5) | | 9 |
| **Total** | (6 wickets declared) | **445** | | | **199** |

## ENGLAND

| | | | | | |
|---|---|--:|---|---|--:|
| B. Wood | c Sarfraz b Asif Masood | 3 | c Asif Masood b Salim | | 5 |
| D.L. Amiss | c Sarfraz b Intikhab | 99 | not out | | 21 |
| K.W.R. Fletcher | c Talat b Intikhab | 54 | not out | | 1 |
| M.H. Denness | lbw b Asif Masood | 47 | | | |
| A.R. Lewis* | c Asif Iqbal b Intikhab | 88 | | | |
| P.I. Pocock | c Sarfraz b Mushtaq | 4 | | | |
| A.W. Greig | b Majid | 48 | | | |
| A.P.E. Knott† | b Majid | 2 | | | |
| J. Birkenshaw | c Majid b Mushtaq | 21 | | | |
| G.G. Arnold | c Mushtaq b Intikhab | 2 | | | |
| N. Gifford | not out | 4 | | | |
| Extras | (B 3, LB 3, NB 8) | 14 | (NB 3) | | 3 |
| **Total** | | **386** | (1 wicket) | | **30** |

| ENGLAND | O | M | R | W | O | M | R | W | | FALL OF WICKETS | | | |
|---|--:|--:|--:|--:|--:|--:|--:|--:|---|---|---|---|---|
| Arnold | 19 | 2 | 69 | 0 | 15 | 2 | 52 | 0 | | P | E | P | E |
| Greig | 20 | 1 | 76 | 0 | 10 | 2 | 26 | 0 | *Wkt* | *1st* | *1st* | *2nd* | *2nd* |
| Pocock | 38 | 7 | 93 | 2 | | | | | 1st | 79 | 13 | 39 | 27 |
| Gifford | 46 | 12 | 99 | 2 | 29 | 9 | 55 | 5 | 2nd | 176 | 143 | 51 | – |
| Birkenshaw | 31 | 5 | 89 | 1 | 18·3 | 5 | 57 | 5 | 3rd | 297 | 182 | 105 | – |
| | | | | | | | | | 4th | 307 | 220 | 106 | – |
| PAKISTAN | | | | | | | | | 5th | 389 | 323 | 106 | – |
| Salim | 15 | 3 | 38 | 0 | 5 | 1 | 16 | 1 | 6th | 413 | 331 | 106 | – |
| Asif Masood | 21 | 4 | 41 | 2 | 4 | 1 | 11 | 0 | 7th | – | 370 | 108 | – |
| Intikhab | 39 | 8 | 105 | 4 | | | | | 8th | – | 373 | 129 | – |
| Sarfraz | 25 | 3 | 64 | 0 | 1 | 1 | 0 | 0 | 9th | – | 381 | 198 | – |
| Mushtaq | 34·3 | 9 | 73 | 2 | | | | | 10th | – | 386 | 199 | – |
| Majid | 22 | 5 | 51 | 2 | | | | | | | | | |

Umpires: Daud Khan and Mohammad Aslam Khokhar.

# ENGLAND v NEW ZEALAND 1973 (1st Test)

Played at Trent Bridge, Nottingham, on 7, 8, 9, 11, 12 June.
Toss: England.   Result: ENGLAND won by 38 runs.
Debuts: Nil.

England won at 3.33 on the fifth afternoon after New Zealand had scored the second-highest total in the fourth innings of any Test match; it was then the highest fourth innings total by a losing team in Test cricket. The partnership between Congdon, who scored New Zealand's first century in England since 1949, and Pollard, whose hundred was his first in 56 innings in 30 Tests, shared a partnership of 177 which was then New Zealand's highest for the fifth wicket in all Tests and which remains their record for that wicket against England. New Zealand's first innings was the highest in all Test matches in which extras have made the largest contribution. The partnership of 59 by Knott and Gifford remains the record for the tenth wicket by either side in this series.

## ENGLAND

|  |  |  |  |  |
|---|---|---|---|---|
| G. Boycott | lbw b Taylor | 51 | run out | 1 |
| D.L. Amiss | c Wadsworth b Taylor | 42 | not out | 138 |
| G.R.J. Roope | lbw b D.R. Hadlee | 28 | c Wadsworth b Collinge | 2 |
| A.R. Lewis | c Wadsworth b Taylor | 2 | c Wadsworth b Taylor | 2 |
| K.W.R. Fletcher | lbw b D.R. Hadlee | 17 | b D.R. Hadlee | 8 |
| A.W. Greig | c Parker b Collinge | 2 | lbw b Collinge | 139 |
| R. Illingworth* | b D.R. Hadlee | 8 | c Parker b Pollard | 3 |
| A.P.E. Knott† | b Congdon | 49 | c Hastings b Pollard | 2 |
| J.A. Snow | b D.R. Hadlee | 8 | b R.J. Hadlee | 7 |
| G.G. Arnold | c Wadsworth b Taylor | 1 | not out | 10 |
| N. Gifford | not out | 25 | | |
| Extras | (LB 10, NB 7) | 17 | (B 4, LB 6, NB 3) | 13 |
| **Total** | | **250** | (8 wickets declared) | **325** |

## NEW ZEALAND

|  |  |  |  |  |
|---|---|---|---|---|
| G.M. Turner | c Roope b Greig | 11 | c Roope b Arnold | 9 |
| J.M. Parker | c Knott b Greig | 2 | c Illingworth b Snow | 6 |
| B.E. Congdon* | run out | 9 | b Arnold | 176 |
| B.F. Hastings | c Roope b Arnold | 3 | lbw b Arnold | 11 |
| M.G. Burgess | c Knott b Arnold | 0 | c Knott b Arnold | 26 |
| V. Pollard | not out | 16 | lbw b Greig | 116 |
| K.J. Wadsworth† | c Knott b Greig | 0 | c Roope b Arnold | 46 |
| B.R. Taylor | c Knott b Snow | 19 | lbw b Snow | 11 |
| D.R. Hadlee | b Snow | 0 | hit wkt b Greig | 14 |
| R.J. Hadlee | b Snow | 0 | not out | 4 |
| R.O. Collinge | b Greig | 17 | b Greig | 0 |
| Extras | (B 8, LB 6, NB 6) | 20 | (LB 13, W 1, NB 7) | 21 |
| **Total** | | **97** | | **440** |

| NEW ZEALAND | O | M | R | W | O | M | R | W |
|---|---|---|---|---|---|---|---|---|
| Collinge | 27 | 6 | 62 | 1 | 24 | 7 | 43 | 2 |
| R.J. Hadlee | 26 | 5 | 64 | 0 | 19 | 3 | 79 | 1 |
| Taylor | 29 | 7 | 53 | 4 | 23 | 3 | 87 | 1 |
| D.R. Hadlee | 19 | 6 | 42 | 4 | 13 | 2 | 51 | 1 |
| Congdon | 6·4 | 1 | 12 | 1 | 9 | 1 | 28 | 0 |
| Pollard | | | | | 9 | 3 | 24 | 2 |

| ENGLAND | O | M | R | W | O | M | R | W |
|---|---|---|---|---|---|---|---|---|
| Snow | 13 | 5 | 21 | 3 | 43 | 10 | 104 | 2 |
| Arnold | 18 | 8 | 23 | 2 | 53 | 15 | 131 | 5 |
| Greig | 10·4 | 0 | 33 | 4 | 45·1 | 10 | 101 | 3 |
| Roope | | | | | 9 | 2 | 17 | 0 |
| Gifford | | | | | 17 | 7 | 35 | 0 |
| Illingworth | | | | | 21 | 7 | 31 | 0 |

### FALL OF WICKETS

| | E | NZ | E | NZ |
|---|---|---|---|---|
| Wkt | 1st | 1st | 2nd | 2nd |
| 1st | 92 | 24 | 2 | 16 |
| 2nd | 106 | 31 | 8 | 16 |
| 3rd | 108 | 34 | 11 | 68 |
| 4th | 140 | 34 | 24 | 130 |
| 5th | 147 | 45 | 234 | 307 |
| 6th | 161 | 45 | 241 | 402 |
| 7th | 162 | 71 | 263 | 414 |
| 8th | 184 | 72 | 311 | 431 |
| 9th | 191 | 72 | – | 440 |
| 10th | 250 | 97 | – | 440 |

Umpires: A.E.G. Rhodes and D.J. Constant.

# ENGLAND v NEW ZEALAND 1973 (2nd Test)

Played at Lord's, London, on 21, 22, 23, 25, 26 June.
Toss: New Zealand.    Result: MATCH DRAWN.
Debuts: Nil.

New Zealand scored their highest total in all Tests after winning the toss for the first time in ten matches. This was the first instance of three batsmen scoring hundreds in the same innings for New Zealand. The partnerships of 190 between Congdon and Hastings and 117 between Burgess and Pollard remain New Zealand's highest against England for the third and sixth wickets respectively. A stand of 92 in 87 minutes between Fletcher, who batted 379 minutes and hit two sixes and 21 fours, and Arnold saved England from their first defeat in this series.

## ENGLAND

| | | | | | |
|---|---|---|---|---|---|
| G. Boycott | c Parker b Collinge | 61 | c and b Howarth | | 92 |
| D.L. Amiss | c Howarth b Hadlee | 9 | c and b Howarth | | 53 |
| G.R.J. Roope | lbw b Howarth | 56 | c Parker b Taylor | | 51 |
| K.W.R. Fletcher | c Hastings b Howarth | 25 | c Taylor b Collinge | | 178 |
| A.W. Greig | c Howarth b Collinge | 63 | c Wadsworth b Hadlee | | 12 |
| R. Illingworth* | c Collinge b Hadlee | 3 | c Turner b Howarth | | 22 |
| A.P.E. Knott† | b Hadlee | 0 | c Congdon b Howarth | | 0 |
| C.M. Old | b Howarth | 7 | c Congdon b Pollard | | 7 |
| J.A. Snow | b Taylor | 2 | c Hastings b Pollard | | 0 |
| G.G. Arnold | not out | 8 | not out | | 23 |
| N. Gifford | c Wadsworth b Collinge | 8 | not out | | 2 |
| Extras | (LB 1, W 1, NB 9) | 11 | (B 8, LB 3, NB 12) | | 23 |
| **Total** | | **253** | (9 wickets) | | **463** |

## NEW ZEALAND

| | | |
|---|---|---|
| G.M. Turner | c Greig b Arnold | 4 |
| J.M. Parker | c Knott b Snow | 3 |
| B.E. Congdon* | c Knott b Old | 175 |
| B.F. Hastings | lbw b Snow | 86 |
| H.J. Howarth | hit wkt b Old | 17 |
| M.G. Burgess | b Snow | 105 |
| V.Pollard | not out | 105 |
| K.J. Wadsworth† | c Knott b Old | 27 |
| B.R. Taylor | b Old | 11 |
| D.R. Hadlee | c Fletcher b Old | 6 |
| R.O. Collinge | did not bat | |
| Extras | (LB 5, NB 7) | 12 |
| **Total** | (9 wickets declared) | **551** |

| NEW ZEALAND | O | M | R | W | O | M | R | W | | FALL OF WICKETS | | |
|---|---|---|---|---|---|---|---|---|---|---|---|---|
| Collinge | 31 | 8 | 69 | 3 | 19 | 4 | 41 | 1 | | E | NZ | E |
| Taylor | 19 | 1 | 54 | 1 | 34 | 10 | 90 | 1 | Wkt | 1st | 1st | 2nd |
| Hadlee | 26 | 4 | 70 | 3 | 25 | 2 | 79 | 1 | 1st | 24 | 5 | 112 |
| Congdon | 5 | 2 | 7 | 0 | 8 | 3 | 22 | 0 | 2nd | 116 | 10 | 185 |
| Howarth | 25 | 6 | 42 | 3 | 70 | 24 | 144 | 4 | 3rd | 148 | 200 | 250 |
| Pollard | | | | | 39 | 11 | 61 | 2 | 4th | 165 | 249 | 274 |
| Hastings | | | | | 1 | 0 | 3 | 0 | 5th | 171 | 330 | 335 |
| ENGLAND | | | | | | | | | 6th | 175 | 447 | 339 |
| Snow | 38 | 4 | 109 | 3 | | | | | 7th | 195 | 523 | 352 |
| Arnold | 41 | 6 | 108 | 1 | | | | | 8th | 217 | 535 | 368 |
| Old | 41·5 | 7 | 113 | 5 | | | | | 9th | 237 | 551 | 460 |
| Roope | 6 | 1 | 15 | 0 | | | | | 10th | 253 | – | – |
| Gifford | 39 | 6 | 107 | 0 | | | | | | | | |
| Illingworth | 39 | 12 | 87 | 0 | | | | | | | | |

Umpires: A.E. Fagg and T.W. Spencer.

# ENGLAND v NEW ZEALAND 1973 (3rd Test)

Played at Headingley, Leeds, on 5, 6, 7, 9, 10 July.
Toss: New Zealand.　Result: ENGLAND won by an innings and one run.
Debuts: Nil.

England won after 13 minutes (21 balls) of play on the fifth morning. Turner narrowly missed becoming the first batsman to carry his bat through a completed Test innings on three occasions; he was last out after batting for 274 minutes in the second innings. Rain prevented any play after lunch on the second day.

## NEW ZEALAND

| | | | | | |
|---|---|---|---|---|---|
| G.M. Turner | lbw b Old | 11 | lbw b Snow | | 81 |
| J.M. Parker | c Knott b Arnold | 8 | c Knott b Arnold | | 4 |
| B.E. Congdon* | c Knott b Arnold | 0 | c Knott b Arnold | | 2 |
| B.F. Hastings | lbw b Arnold | 18 | b Old | | 10 |
| M.G. Burgess | c Roope b Old | 87 | lbw b Old | | 18 |
| V. Pollard | c Boycott b Old | 62 | c Roope b Arnold | | 3 |
| K.J. Wadsworth† | b Old | 8 | b Arnold | | 5 |
| B.R. Taylor | c Fletcher b Greig | 20 | c Roope b Snow | | 1 |
| D.R. Hadlee | b Snow | 34 | lbw b Snow | | 0 |
| R.O. Collinge | b Snow | 5 | b Arnold | | 0 |
| H.J. Howarth | not out | 8 | not out | | 15 |
| Extras | (B 5, LB 7, W 1, NB 2) | 15 | (B 1, LB 2) | | 3 |
| **Total** | | **276** | | | **142** |

## ENGLAND

| | | |
|---|---|---|
| G. Boycott | c Parker b Congdon | 115 |
| D.L. Amiss | lbw b Collinge | 8 |
| G.R.J. Roope | c Turner b Collinge | 18 |
| K.W.R. Fletcher | c Howarth b Collinge | 81 |
| A.W. Greig | c Howarth b Congdon | 0 |
| R. Illingworth* | lbw b Taylor | 65 |
| A.P.E. Knott† | c Wadsworth b Taylor | 21 |
| C.M. Old | lbw b Collinge | 34 |
| J.A. Snow | c Howarth b Collinge | 6 |
| G.G. Arnold | c Wadsworth b Hadlee | 26 |
| D.L. Underwood | not out | 20 |
| Extras | (B 5, LB 16, W 1, NB 3) | 25 |
| **Total** | | **419** |

| ENGLAND | O | M | R | W | O | M | R | W |
|---|---|---|---|---|---|---|---|---|
| Snow | 21·4 | 4 | 52 | 2 | 19·3 | 4 | 34 | 3 |
| Arnold | 27 | 8 | 62 | 3 | 22 | 11 | 27 | 5 |
| Old | 20 | 4 | 71 | 4 | 14 | 1 | 41 | 2 |
| Underwood | 11 | 4 | 27 | 0 | 7 | 2 | 14 | 0 |
| Greig | 13 | 4 | 29 | 1 | 6 | 1 | 22 | 0 |
| Illingworth | 6 | 0 | 20 | 0 | 2 | 1 | 1 | 0 |

| NEW ZEALAND | O | M | R | W |
|---|---|---|---|---|
| Collinge | 34 | 7 | 74 | 5 |
| Taylor | 31 | 3 | 111 | 2 |
| Hadlee | 23·1 | 2 | 98 | 1 |
| Congdon | 32 | 10 | 54 | 2 |
| Howarth | 18 | 6 | 44 | 0 |
| Pollard | 7 | 4 | 13 | 0 |

### FALL OF WICKETS

| Wkt | NZ 1st | E 1st | NZ 2nd |
|---|---|---|---|
| 1st | 24 | 23 | 16 |
| 2nd | 24 | 71 | 20 |
| 3rd | 24 | 190 | 39 |
| 4th | 78 | 190 | 85 |
| 5th | 184 | 280 | 88 |
| 6th | 202 | 300 | 94 |
| 7th | 215 | 339 | 95 |
| 8th | 227 | 346 | 97 |
| 9th | 233 | 365 | 106 |
| 10th | 276 | 419 | 142 |

Umpires: C.S. Elliott and H.D. Bird.

# ENGLAND v WEST INDIES 1973 (1st Test)

Played at Kennington Oval, London, on 26, 27, 28, 30, 31 July.
Toss: West Indies.   Result: WEST INDIES won by 158 runs.
Debuts: England – F.C. Hayes; West Indies – R.G.A. Headley, B.D. Julien.

West Indies won at 2.26 on the fifth afternoon to end a run of 20 Test matches without a victory. Hayes scored a hundred in his first Test after batting for exactly four hours and hitting 12 fours. Boyce's match analysis of 11 for 147 was then the best for West Indies in this series.

## WEST INDIES

| | | | | | |
|---|---|--:|---|---|--:|
| R.C. Fredericks | lbw b Arnold | 35 | | c Hayes b Arnold | 3 |
| R.G.A. Headley | lbw b Greig | 8 | | b Arnold | 42 |
| R.B. Kanhai* | b Greig | 10 | | c Knott b Snow | 0 |
| C.H. Lloyd | lbw b Arnold | 132 | | c Greig b Snow | 14 |
| A.I. Kallicharran | c Knott b Arnold | 80 | | b Illingworth | 80 |
| D.L. Murray† | c Roope b Arnold | 28 | (7) | c Roope b Underwood | 4 |
| G. St A. Sobers | run out | 10 | (6) | c Underwood b Snow | 51 |
| B.D. Julien | lbw b Arnold | 11 | | b Illingworth | 23 |
| K.D. Boyce | b Underwood | 72 | | b Illingworth | 9 |
| Inshan Ali | c Boycott b Underwood | 15 | | not out | 5 |
| L.R. Gibbs | not out | 1 | | c Knott b Arnold | 3 |
| Extras | (B 1, LB 2, NB 10) | 13 | | (B 2, LB 13, NB 6) | 21 |
| **Total** | | **415** | | | **255** |

## ENGLAND

| | | | | | |
|---|---|--:|---|---|--:|
| G. Boycott | c Murray b Julien | 97 | | c and b Gibbs | 30 |
| D.L. Amiss | b Boyce | 29 | | c Kanhai b Boyce | 15 |
| G.R.J. Roope | b Boyce | 9 | | c and b Gibbs | 31 |
| F.C. Hayes | c Lloyd b Sobers | 16 | | not out | 106 |
| K.W.R. Fletcher | c Lloyd b Julien | 11 | | c Kallicharran b Gibbs | 5 |
| A.W. Greig | c Sobers b Boyce | 38 | | c Gibbs b Ali | 0 |
| R. Illingworth* | lbw b Sobers | 27 | (8) | b Boyce | 40 |
| A.P.E. Knott† | not out | 4 | (9) | lbw b Boyce | 5 |
| J.A. Snow | b Boyce | 0 | (11) | b Boyce | 1 |
| G.G. Arnold | c Kallicharran b Boyce | 4 | | c Headley b Boyce | 4 |
| D.L. Underwood | c Headley b Sobers | 0 | (7) | lbw b Boyce | 7 |
| Extras | (B 2, LB 7, W 2, NB 11) | 22 | | (LB 5, W 1, NB 5) | 11 |
| **Total** | | **257** | | | **255** |

| ENGLAND | O | M | R | W | O | M | R | W | | FALL OF WICKETS | | | |
|---|--:|--:|--:|--:|--:|--:|--:|--:|---|--:|--:|--:|--:|
| | | | | | | | | | | WI | E | WI | E |
| Snow | 31 | 8 | 71 | 0 | 18 | 4 | 62 | 3 | *Wkt* | *1st* | *1st* | *2nd* | *2nd* |
| Arnold | 39 | 10 | 113 | 5 | 18·1 | 7 | 49 | 3 | 1st | 33 | 50 | 9 | 36 |
| Greig | 30·3 | 6 | 81 | 2 | 8 | 1 | 22 | 0 | 2nd | 47 | 95 | 31 | 66 |
| Roope | 6 | 1 | 26 | 0 | | | | | 3rd | 64 | 134 | 52 | 91 |
| Underwood | 23·3 | 8 | 68 | 2 | 19 | 5 | 51 | 1 | 4th | 272 | 163 | 117 | 97 |
| Illingworth | 15 | 3 | 43 | 0 | 24 | 8 | 50 | 3 | 5th | 275 | 185 | 177 | 107 |
| | | | | | | | | | 6th | 297 | 247 | 184 | 136 |
| WEST INDIES | | | | | | | | | 7th | 309 | 247 | 215 | 229 |
| Sobers | 22·1 | 13 | 27 | 3 | 11 | 3 | 22 | 0 | 8th | 346 | 247 | 232 | 239 |
| Boyce | 22 | 4 | 70 | 5 | 21·1 | 4 | 77 | 6 | 9th | 405 | 257 | 252 | 253 |
| Julien | 20 | 6 | 49 | 2 | 17 | 4 | 35 | 0 | 10th | 415 | 257 | 255 | 255 |
| Gibbs | 23 | 8 | 37 | 0 | 33 | 9 | 61 | 3 | | | | | |
| Ali | 11 | 3 | 52 | 0 | 23 | 6 | 49 | 1 | | | | | |

Umpires: T.W. Spencer and D.J. Constant.

# ENGLAND v WEST INDIES 1973 (2nd Test)

Played at Edgbaston, Birmingham, on 9, 10, 11, 13, 14 August.
Toss: West Indies.   Result: MATCH DRAWN.
Debuts: Nil.

England needed to score 325 runs to win in 227 minutes. Boycott retired because of bruised ribs when 54* at 105 for 0, resumed at 249 for 6 but retired after being hit on the arm first ball by Holder at the same total, and resumed again at 299 for 8. A.S.M. Oakman, a former first-class umpire, deputised for the first over of the third day, when A.E. Fagg refused to umpire because of dissent shown by Kanhai when he did not uphold an appeal against Boycott for a catch by Murray on the second afternoon.

## WEST INDIES

| | | | | |
|---|---|---|---|---|
| R.C. Fredericks | c Amiss b Underwood | 150 | c Knott b Arnold | 12 |
| R.G.A. Headley | b Old | 1 | c Knott b Old | 11 |
| R.B. Kanhai* | c Greig b Arnold | 2 | c Arnold b Illingworth | 54 |
| C.H. Lloyd | lbw b Old | 15 | c Knott b Underwood | 94 |
| A.I. Kallicharran | c Hayes b Arnold | 34 | b Underwood | 4 |
| G. St A. Sobers | b Old | 21 | b Arnold | 74 |
| D.L. Murray† | b Underwood | 25 | hit wkt b Arnold | 15 |
| B.D. Julien | c Greig b Arnold | 54 | b Greig | 11 |
| K.D. Boyce | lbw b Illingworth | 12 | c Knott b Arnold | 0 |
| V.A. Holder | c Boycott b Underwood | 6 | c Luckhurst b Greig | 10 |
| L.R. Gibbs | not out | 1 | not out | 3 |
| Extras | (LB 2, W 1, NB 3) | 6 | (LB 10, NB 4) | 14 |
| **Total** | | **327** | | **302** |

## ENGLAND

| | | | | |
|---|---|---|---|---|
| G. Boycott | not out | 56 | | |
| D.L. Amiss | c Murray b Julien | 56 | not out | 86 |
| B.W. Luckhurst | lbw b Sobers | 12 | (1) c Murray b Lloyd | 42 |
| F.C. Hayes | c Kallicharran b Holder | 29 | (3) lbw b Lloyd | 0 |
| A.W. Greig | c Fredericks b Julien | 27 | | |
| A.P.E. Knott† | b Holder | 0 | | |
| K.W.R. Fletcher | c Holder b Sobers | 52 | (4) not out | 44 |
| R. Illingworth* | lbw b Holder | 27 | | |
| C.M. Old | run out | 0 | | |
| G.G. Arnold | c Kallicharran b Sobers | 24 | | |
| D.L. Underwood | c Murray b Gibbs | 2 | | |
| Extras | (B 4, LB 1, NB 15) | 20 | (B 8, NB 2) | 10 |
| **Total** | | **305** | (2 wickets) | **182** |

| ENGLAND | O | M | R | W | O | M | R | W |
|---|---|---|---|---|---|---|---|---|
| Arnold | 37 | 13 | 74 | 3 | 20 | 1 | 43 | 4 |
| Old | 30 | 3 | 86 | 3 | 14 | 0 | 65 | 1 |
| Greig | 26 | 3 | 84 | 0 | 7·4 | 0 | 35 | 2 |
| Illingworth | 32 | 19 | 37 | 1 | 26 | 6 | 67 | 1 |
| Underwood | 24·3 | 10 | 40 | 3 | 32 | 9 | 66 | 2 |
| Luckhurst | | | | | 4 | 2 | 12 | 0 |
| WEST INDIES | | | | | | | | |
| Holder | 44 | 16 | 83 | 3 | 7 | 1 | 17 | 0 |
| Sobers | 30 | 6 | 62 | 3 | 7 | 1 | 21 | 0 |
| Boyce | 19 | 2 | 48 | 0 | | | | |
| Julien | 26 | 8 | 55 | 2 | 18 | 3 | 32 | 0 |
| Gibbs | 35·4 | 21 | 32 | 1 | 12 | 2 | 32 | 0 |
| Lloyd | 2 | 0 | 5 | 0 | 12 | 3 | 26 | 2 |
| Fredericks | | | | | 4 | 0 | 23 | 0 |
| Kanhai | | | | | 7 | 1 | 21 | 0 |

| | FALL OF WICKETS | | | |
|---|---|---|---|---|
| | WI | E | WI | E |
| Wkt | 1st | 1st | 2nd | 2nd |
| 1st | 14 | 119 | 24 | 96 |
| 2nd | 17 | 139 | 42 | 100 |
| 3rd | 39 | 191 | 136 | – |
| 4th | 93 | 191 | 152 | – |
| 5th | 128 | 197 | 197 | – |
| 6th | 242 | 249 | 247 | – |
| 7th | 280 | 249 | 283 | – |
| 8th | 302 | 299 | 283 | – |
| 9th | 325 | 302 | 293 | – |
| 10th | 327 | 305 | 302 | – |

Umpires: A.E. Fagg and H.D. Bird.

# ENGLAND v WEST INDIES 1973 (3rd Test)

Played at Lord's, London, on 23, 24, 25, 27 August.
Toss: West Indies.   Result: WEST INDIES won by an innings and 226 runs.
Debuts: Nil.

West Indies gained their largest margin of victory against England after scoring what was then their highest total in England. The match ended at 2.56 on the fourth afternoon. Sobers (132*) retired at 528 for 6 because of a stomach disorder after sharing an unbroken partnership of 155 in 113 minutes with Julien; it remains the West Indies record for the seventh wicket against England. He resumed at 604 for 7 and altogether batted for 288 minutes (227 balls) and hit 19 fours; it was his 26th and last hundred in official Tests – only Bradman (29) has scored more. Earlier Kanhai, during the last of his 15 centuries, had become the second batsman after Sobers to score 6,000 runs for West Indies. Julien reached his first hundred in first-class cricket off 127 balls. A bomb alert at 2.42 on the third afternoon resulted in 89 minutes being lost but an hour of this time was subsequently made up.

## WEST INDIES

| | | |
|---|---|---|
| R.C. Fredericks | c Underwood b Willis | 51 |
| D.L. Murray† | b Willis | 4 |
| R.B. Kanhai* | c Greig b Willis | 157 |
| C.H. Lloyd | c and b Willis | 63 |
| A.I. Kallicharran | c Arnold b Illingworth | 14 |
| G. St A. Sobers | not out | 150 |
| M.L.C. Foster | c Willis b Greig | 9 |
| B.D. Julien | c and b Greig | 121 |
| K.D. Boyce | c Amiss b Greig | 36 |
| V.A. Holder | not out | 23 |
| L.R. Gibbs | did not bat | |
| Extras | (B 1, LB 14, W 1, NB 8) | 24 |
| **Total** | (8 wickets declared) | **652** |

## ENGLAND

| | | | | | |
|---|---|---|---|---|---|
| G. Boycott | c Kanhai b Holder | 4 | | c Kallicharran b Boyce | 15 |
| D.L. Amiss | c Sobers b Holder | 35 | | c Sobers b Boyce | 10 |
| B.W. Luckhurst | c Murray b Boyce | 1 | (4) | c Sobers b Julien | 12 |
| F.C. Hayes | c Fredericks b Holder | 8 | (5) | c Holder b Boyce | 0 |
| K.W.R. Fletcher | c Sobers b Gibbs | 68 | (6) | not out | 86 |
| A.W. Greig | c Sobers b Boyce | 44 | (7) | lbw b Julien | 13 |
| R. Illingworth* | c Sobers b Gibbs | 0 | (8) | c Kanhai b Gibbs | 13 |
| A.P.E. Knott† | c Murray b Boyce | 21 | (3) | c Murray b Boyce | 5 |
| G.G. Arnold | c Murray b Boyce | 5 | | c Fredericks b Gibbs | 1 |
| R.G.D. Willis | not out | 5 | | c Fredericks b Julien | 0 |
| D.L. Underwood | c Gibbs b Holder | 12 | | b Gibbs | 14 |
| Extras | (B 6, LB 4, W 3, NB 17) | 30 | | (B 9, W 1, NB 14) | 24 |
| **Total** | | **233** | | | **193** |

| ENGLAND | O | M | R | W | O | M | R | W |
|---|---|---|---|---|---|---|---|---|
| Arnold | 35 | 6 | 111 | 0 | | | | |
| Willis | 35 | 3 | 118 | 4 | | | | |
| Greig | 33 | 2 | 180 | 3 | | | | |
| Underwood | 34 | 6 | 105 | 0 | | | | |
| Illingworth | 31·4 | 3 | 114 | 1 | | | | |
| **WEST INDIES** | | | | | | | | |
| Holder | 15 | 3 | 56 | 4 | 14 | 4 | 18 | 0 |
| Boyce | 20 | 7 | 50 | 4 | 16 | 5 | 49 | 4 |
| Julien | 11 | 4 | 26 | 0 | 18 | 2 | 69 | 3 |
| Gibbs | 18 | 3 | 39 | 2 | 13·3 | 3 | 26 | 3 |
| Sobers | 8 | 0 | 30 | 0 | 4 | 1 | 7 | 0 |
| Foster | 1 | 0 | 2 | 0 | | | | |

## FALL OF WICKETS

| | WI | E | E |
|---|---|---|---|
| Wkt | 1st | 1st | 2nd |
| 1st | 8 | 5 | 32 |
| 2nd | 87 | 7 | 38 |
| 3rd | 225 | 29 | 42 |
| 4th | 256 | 97 | 49 |
| 5th | 339 | 176 | 63 |
| 6th | 373 | 176 | 87 |
| 7th | 604 | 187 | 132 |
| 8th | 610 | 205 | 143 |
| 9th | – | 213 | 146 |
| 10th | – | 233 | 193 |

Umpires: C.S. Elliott and H.D. Bird.

# AUSTRALIA v NEW ZEALAND 1973–74 (1st Test)

Played at Melbourne Cricket Ground on 29, 30 December, 1, 2 January.
Toss: Australia.　Result: AUSTRALIA won by an innings and 25 runs.
Debuts: Australia – I.C. Davis, G.J. Gilmour; New Zealand – B. Andrews, J.F.M. Morrison.

Remarkably this was New Zealand's first official Test in Australia, the only previous match in this series being played at Wellington in 1945–46 when Australia won in two days. Stackpole scored the first hundred of the series and Wadsworth became the first New Zealander to score a fifty against Australia. Turner fractured a finger on his right-hand for the second time on the tour when he was hit by a ball from Dell.

## AUSTRALIA

| | | |
|---|---|---:|
| K.R. Stackpole | c Parker b Shrimpton | 122 |
| A.P. Sheahan | c Wadswoth b D.R. Hadlee | 28 |
| I.M. Chappell* | c R.J. Hadlee b Shrimpton | 54 |
| G.S. Chappell | c Wadsworth b Congdon | 60 |
| K.D. Walters | c Wadsworth b D.R. Hadlee | 79 |
| I.C. Davis | c Wadsworth b D.R. Hadlee | 15 |
| R.W. Marsh† | c Parker b D.R. Hadlee | 6 |
| K.J. O'Keeffe | not out | 40 |
| G.J. Gilmour | b Congdon | 52 |
| A.A. Mallett | } did not bat | |
| A.R. Dell | } | |
| Extras | (LB 4, W 1, NB 1) | 6 |
| **Total** | (8 wickets declared) | **462** |

## NEW ZEALAND

| | | | | | |
|---|---|---:|---|---|---:|
| G.M. Turner | c Gilmour b Dell | 6 | absent hurt | | – |
| J.M. Parker | c I.M. Chappell b O'Keeffe | 27 | c I.M. Chappell b Walters | | 23 |
| M.J.F. Shrimpton | c Marsh b Gilmour | 16 | b Walters | | 22 |
| B.F. Hastings | b O'Keeffe | 1 | c Marsh b Mallett | | 22 |
| B.E. Congdon* | st Marsh b Mallett | 31 | c Marsh b Mallett | | 14 |
| J.F.M. Morrison | c Marsh b Gilmour | 44 | (1) c Marsh b Walters | | 16 |
| K.J. Wadsworth† | c G.S. Chappell b Gilmour | 80 | (6) c Stackpole b Mallett | | 30 |
| R.J. Hadlee | c Marsh b Gilmour | 9 | (7) c I.M. Chappell b O'Keeffe | | 6 |
| D.R. Hadlee | run out | 2 | (8) c and b O'Keeffe | | 37 |
| D.R. O'Sullivan | c Davis b Mallett | 6 | (9) c and b Mallett | | 8 |
| B. Andrews | not out | 0 | (10) not out | | 5 |
| Extras | (B 8, LB 5, NB 2) | 15 | (B 8, LB 9) | | 17 |
| **Total** | | **237** | | | **200** |

| NEW ZEALAND | O | M | R | W | O | M | R | W | | FALL OF WICKETS | | |
|---|---|---|---|---|---|---|---|---|---|---|---|---|
| | | | | | | | | | | A | NZ | NZ |
| R.J. Hadlee | 25 | 4 | 104 | 0 | | | | | *Wkt* | *1st* | *1st* | *2nd* |
| Andrews | 19 | 2 | 100 | 0 | | | | | 1st | 75 | 19 | 37 |
| D.R. Hadlee | 20 | 2 | 102 | 4 | | | | | 2nd | 203 | 47 | 54 |
| O'Sullivan | 22 | 3 | 80 | 0 | | | | | 3rd | 212 | 51 | 83 |
| Shrimpton | 7 | 0 | 39 | 2 | | | | | 4th | 304 | 56 | 109 |
| Congdon | 8·5 | 1 | 31 | 2 | | | | | 5th | 345 | 100 | 113 |
| AUSTRALIA | | | | | | | | | 6th | 363 | 189 | 134 |
| Dell | 22 | 7 | 54 | 1 | 5 | 0 | 9 | 0 | 7th | 381 | 215 | 150 |
| Gilmour | 22 | 4 | 75 | 4 | 3 | 0 | 16 | 0 | 8th | 462 | 230 | 188 |
| G.S. Chappell | 4 | 2 | 4 | 0 | 7 | 3 | 18 | 0 | 9th | – | 237 | 200 |
| Mallett | 16·7 | 2 | 46 | 2 | 24 | 4 | 63 | 4 | 10th | – | 237 | – |
| O'Keeffe | 14 | 4 | 40 | 2 | 29·6 | 12 | 51 | 2 | | | | |
| I.M. Chappell | 1 | 0 | 3 | 0 | | | | | | | | |
| Walters | | | | | 13 | 4 | 26 | 3 | | | | |

Umpires: T.F. Brooks and J.R. Collins.

# AUSTRALIA v NEW ZEALAND 1973–74 (2nd Test)

Played at Sydney Cricket Ground on 5, 6, 7 (*no play*), 9, 10 (*no play*) January.
Toss: Australia.   Result: MATCH DRAWN.
Debuts: New Zealand – J.V. Coney.

Australia were 425 runs behind with eight second innings wickets left when rain prevented any play on the fifth day. Parker scored New Zealand's first hundred of the series. A groin injury prevented Walker from bowling in the second innings when Morrison scored a hundred in his second Test match.

## NEW ZEALAND

| | | | | | |
|---|---|---|---|---|---|
| J.M. Parker | c Marsh b Walker | 108 | c Marsh b G.S. Chappell | | 11 |
| J.F.M. Morrison | c G.S. Chappell b Walters | 28 | c Davis b I.M. Chappell | | 117 |
| M.J.F. Shrimpton | b Walters | 0 | c and b Walters | | 28 |
| B.E. Congdon* | c Marsh b Walters | 4 | b Gilmour | | 17 |
| B.F. Hastings | c Marsh b Walker | 16 | b G.S. Chappell | | 83 |
| J.V. Coney | c Stackpole b O'Keeffe | 45 | (7) c Davis b G.S. Chappell | | 11 |
| K.J. Wadsworth† | c Marsh b Walters | 54 | (6) c G.S. Chappell b Gilmour | | 2 |
| D.R. Hadlee | c and b G.S. Chappell | 14 | (9) not out | | 18 |
| R.J. Hadlee | c I.M. Chappell b G.S. Chappell | 17 | (8) run out | | 1 |
| D.R. O'Sullivan | not out | 3 | lbw b Gilmour | | 1 |
| B. Andrews | c Marsh b Gilmour | 17 | | | |
| Extras | (B 2, NB 4) | 6 | (B 4, LB 11, W 1) | | 16 |
| **Total** | | **312** | (9 wickets declared) | | **305** |

## AUSTRALIA

| | | | | |
|---|---|---|---|---|
| A.P. Sheahan | c Coney b Andrews | 7 | not out | 14 |
| K.R. Stackpole | c Morrison b R.J. Hadlee | 8 | lbw b R.J. Hadlee | 2 |
| I.M. Chappell* | c Hastings b D.R. Hadlee | 45 | lbw b R.J. Hadlee | 6 |
| G.S. Chappell | c Coney b Andrews | 0 | not out | 8 |
| K.D. Walters | c Coney b D.R. Hadlee | 41 | | |
| I.C. Davis | c Andrews b R.J. Hadlee | 29 | | |
| R.W. Marsh† | c Wadsworth b D.R. Hadlee | 10 | | |
| K.J. O'Keeffe | c Wadsworth b R.J. Hadlee | 9 | | |
| G.J. Gilmour | c Wadsworth b Congdon | 3 | | |
| A.A. Mallett | lbw b R.J. Hadlee | 0 | | |
| M.H.N. Walker | not out | 2 | | |
| Extras | (LB 5, NB 3) | 8 | | |
| **Total** | | **162** | (2 wickets) | **30** |

| AUSTRALIA | O | M | R | W | O | M | R | W | | FALL OF WICKETS | | | |
|---|---|---|---|---|---|---|---|---|---|---|---|---|---|
| Gilmour | 18·6 | 3 | 70 | 1 | 21·2 | 1 | 70 | 3 | | NZ | A | NZ | A |
| Walker | 22 | 2 | 71 | 2 | | | | | Wkt | 1st | 1st | 2nd | 2nd |
| G.S. Chappll | 19 | 2 | 76 | 2 | 16 | 3 | 54 | 3 | 1st | 78 | 20 | 23 | 10 |
| Walters | 11 | 0 | 39 | 4 | 11 | 0 | 54 | 1 | 2nd | 78 | 20 | 94 | 22 |
| Mallett | 8 | 0 | 30 | 0 | 14 | 1 | 65 | 0 | 3rd | 90 | 21 | 120 | – |
| O'Keeffe | 8 | 2 | 20 | 1 | 10 | 0 | 40 | 0 | 4th | 113 | 98 | 244 | – |
| I.M. Chappell | | | | | 3 | 0 | 6 | 1 | 5th | 193 | 115 | 255 | – |
| | | | | | | | | | 6th | 221 | 133 | 276 | – |
| NEW ZEALAND | | | | | | | | | 7th | 268 | 150 | 282 | – |
| R.J. Hadlee | 9·4 | 2 | 33 | 4 | 4·3 | 0 | 16 | 2 | 8th | 292 | 157 | 292 | – |
| Andrews | 9 | 1 | 40 | 2 | 4 | 0 | 14 | 0 | 9th | 293 | 160 | 305 | – |
| D.R. Hadlee | 13 | 3 | 52 | 3 | | | | | 10th | 312 | 162 | – | – |
| Congdon | 13 | 2 | 29 | 1 | | | | | | | | | |

Umpires: M.G. O'Connell and P.R. Enright.

# AUSTRALIA v NEW ZEALAND 1973–74 (3rd Test)

Played at Adelaide Oval on 26, 27, 28, 30 (*no play*), 31 January.
Toss: Australia.   Result: AUSTRALIA won by an innings and 57 runs.
Debuts: Australia – G. Dymock, A.G. Hurst, A.J. Woodcock; New Zealand – B.L. Cairns.

Australia gained their third victory by an innings margin in four matches against New Zealand. A blank fourth day and stoppages amounting to 95 minutes on the fifth extended the match until 5.02 on the final evening. The partnership of 168 between Marsh and O'Keeffe was an Australian record, subsequently beaten, in all Tests, improving on the one of 165 between C. Hill and H. Trumble against England in 1897-98 (*Test No. 56*). Dymock took the wicket of Parker with his second ball in Test cricket.

### AUSTRALIA

| | | |
|---|---|---:|
| K.R. Stackpole | c Parker b D.R. Hadlee | 15 |
| A.J. Woodcock | c Coney b Cairns | 27 |
| I.M. Chappell* | c R.J. Hadlee b Cairns | 22 |
| G.S. Chappell | b Congdon | 42 |
| K.D. Walters | b O'Sullivan | 94 |
| I.C. Davis | c Congdon b O'Sullivan | 15 |
| R.W. Marsh† | st Wadsworth b O'Sullivan | 132 |
| K.J. O'Keeffe | lbw b R.J.Hadlee | 85 |
| A.A. Mallett | c Wadsworth b O'Sullivan | 11 |
| A.G. Hurst | c Hastings b O'Sullivan | 16 |
| G. Dymock | not out | 0 |
| Extras | (B 3, LB 6, NB 9) | 18 |
| **Total** | | **477** |

### NEW ZEALAND

| | | | | |
|---|---|---:|---|---:|
| J.M. Parker | c Marsh b Dymock | 0 | c I.M. Chappell b Dymock | 22 |
| G.M. Turner | lbw b Hurst | 20 | c O'Keeffe b Dymock | 34 |
| J.F.M. Morrison | c I.M. Chappell b O'Keeffe | 40 | c I.M. Chappell b O'Keeffe | 4 |
| B.F. Hastings | c Woodcock b O'Keeffe | 23 | c Stackpole b Dymock | 7 |
| B.E. Congdon* | run out | 13 | not out | 71 |
| J.V. Coney | c Marsh b Dymock | 8 | b Dymock | 17 |
| K.J. Wadsworth† | lbw b I.M. Chappell | 48 | c Marsh b O'Keeffe | 16 |
| D.R. Hadlee | c G.S. Chappell b Mallett | 29 | c G.S. Chappell b Mallett | 0 |
| R.J. Hadlee | c I.M. Chappell b Mallett | 20 | c Marsh b O'Keeffe | 15 |
| D.R. O'Sullivan | b O'Keeffe | 2 | c I.M. Chappell b Dymock | 4 |
| B.L.Cairns | not out | 4 | c I.M. Chappell b Mallett | 0 |
| Extras | (B 4, LB 4, NB 3) | 11 | (B 2, LB 8, NB 2) | 12 |
| **Total** | | **218** | | **202** |

| NEW ZEALAND | O | M | R | W | O | M | R | W |
|---|---|---|---|---|---|---|---|---|
| R.J. Hadlee | 28 | 3 | 102 | 1 | | | | |
| D.R. Hadlee | 21 | 2 | 76 | 1 | | | | |
| Cairns | 21 | 4 | 73 | 2 | | | | |
| O'Sullivan | 35·5 | 4 | 148 | 5 | | | | |
| Congdon | 15 | 1 | 60 | 1 | | | | |
| **AUSTRALIA** | | | | | | | | |
| Hurst | 19 | 3 | 56 | 1 | 10 | 2 | 17 | 0 |
| Dymock | 19 | 5 | 44 | 2 | 27 | 7 | 58 | 5 |
| Walters | 1 | 0 | 2 | 0 | 3 | 0 | 17 | 0 |
| Mallett | 23 | 6 | 46 | 2 | 21·5 | 9 | 47 | 2 |
| O'Keeffe | 24·3 | 9 | 55 | 3 | 28 | 12 | 51 | 3 |
| I.M. Chappell | 1 | 0 | 4 | 1 | | | | |

FALL OF WICKETS

| Wkt | A 1st | NZ 1st | NZ 2nd |
|---|---|---|---|
| 1st | 21 | 1 | 56 |
| 2nd | 67 | 35 | 65 |
| 3rd | 73 | 84 | 65 |
| 4th | 173 | 89 | 73 |
| 5th | 221 | 107 | 105 |
| 6th | 232 | 110 | 130 |
| 7th | 400 | 176 | 143 |
| 8th | 452 | 209 | 170 |
| 9th | 472 | 214 | 197 |
| 10th | 477 | 218 | 202 |

Umpires: J.R. Collins and P.R. Enright.

# WEST INDIES v ENGLAND 1973–74 (1st Test)

Played at Queen's Park Oval, Port-of-Spain, Trinidad, on 2, 3, 5, 6, 7 February.
Toss: West Indies.   Result: WEST INDIES won by seven wickets.
Debuts: Nil.

This result ended a run of 22 home Tests without victory for West Indies and an unbeaten run of 13 Tests in the West Indies for England. When Julien played the last ball of the second day down the pitch, Greig picked it up and, seeing Kallicharran (142*) out of his ground, threw down the bowler's stumps and appealed. Kallicharran was given 'run out' by umpire Sang Hue. After a lengthy off-the-field conference between the captains, administrators, and umpires, the appeal was withdrawn in the interests of the rubber. When he bowled Greig, Gibbs became the first bowler to take 250 Test wickets for West Indies.

## ENGLAND

| | | | | |
|---|---|---|---|---|
| G. Boycott | c Julien b Boyce | 6 | c Fredericks b Gibbs | 93 |
| D.L. Amiss | c Murray b Sobers | 6 | lbw b Sobers | 174 |
| M.H. Denness* | b Julien | 9 | run out | 44 |
| F.C. Hayes | c Fredericks b Sobers | 12 | b Sobers | 8 |
| K.W.R. Fletcher | b Julien | 4 | c Rowe b Sobers | 0 |
| A.W. Greig | c Murray b Boyce | 37 | b Gibbs | 20 |
| A.P.E. Knott† | b Boyce | 7 | c Rowe b Gibbs | 21 |
| C.M. Old | c Fredericks b Ali | 11 | c and b Gibbs | 3 |
| P.I. Pocock | b Boyce | 2 | c Fredericks b Gibbs | 0 |
| D.L. Underwood | not out | 10 | c Kanhai b Gibbs | 9 |
| R.G.D. Willis | b Gibbs | 6 | not out | 0 |
| Extras | (B 1, LB 8, NB 12) | 21 | (B 5, LB 5, NB 10) | 20 |
| **Total** | | **131** | | **392** |

## WEST INDIES

| | | | | |
|---|---|---|---|---|
| R.C. Fredericks | c Knott b Old | 5 | not out | 65 |
| L.G. Rowe | c Knott b Willis | 13 | c Hayes b Pocock | 5 |
| A.I. Kallicharran | c Underwood b Pocock | 158 | c Greig b Underwood | 21 |
| C.H. Lloyd | c Denness b Old | 18 | c Hayes b Underwood | 0 |
| R.B. Kanhai* | b Pocock | 8 | not out | 39 |
| G. St A. Sobers | c Denness b Underwood | 23 | | |
| D.L. Murray† | c Fletcher b Pocock | 19 | | |
| B.D. Julien | not out | 86 | | |
| K.D. Boyce | c Boycott b Pocock | 26 | | |
| Inshan Ali | c Knott b Pocock | 9 | | |
| L.R. Gibbs | b Old | 2 | | |
| Extras | (B 3, LB 6, NB 16) | 25 | (LB 1, NB 1) | 2 |
| **Total** | | **392** | (3 wickets) | **132** |

| WEST INDIES | O | M | R | W | O | M | R | W |
|---|---|---|---|---|---|---|---|---|
| Boyce | 19 | 4 | 42 | 4 | 10 | 1 | 36 | 0 |
| Julien | 12 | 5 | 14 | 2 | 15 | 2 | 48 | 0 |
| Sobers | 14 | 3 | 37 | 2 | 34 | 15 | 54 | 3 |
| Gibbs | 3 | 1 | 5 | 1 | 57·2 | 15 | 108 | 6 |
| Ali | 7 | 5 | 12 | 1 | 37 | 5 | 99 | 0 |
| Fredericks | | | | | 10 | 2 | 24 | 0 |
| Lloyd | | | | | 3 | 1 | 3 | 0 |
| ENGLAND | | | | | | | | |
| Willis | 19 | 5 | 52 | 1 | 4 | 1 | 6 | 0 |
| Old | 20·4 | 2 | 89 | 3 | 3 | 0 | 18 | 0 |
| Greig | 17 | 3 | 60 | 0 | 2 | 1 | 4 | 0 |
| Pocock | 43 | 12 | 110 | 5 | 16 | 6 | 49 | 1 |
| Underwood | 23 | 8 | 56 | 1 | 12 | 2 | 48 | 2 |
| Fletcher | | | | | 0·5 | 0 | 5 | 0 |

### FALL OF WICKETS

| Wkt | E 1st | WI 1st | E 2nd | WI 2nd |
|---|---|---|---|---|
| 1st | 6 | 14 | 209 | 15 |
| 2nd | 22 | 27 | 328 | 77 |
| 3rd | 23 | 63 | 338 | 77 |
| 4th | 30 | 106 | 338 | – |
| 5th | 71 | 147 | 349 | – |
| 6th | 90 | 196 | 366 | – |
| 7th | 100 | 296 | 378 | – |
| 8th | 108 | 324 | 378 | – |
| 9th | 116 | 373 | 391 | – |
| 10th | 131 | 392 | 392 | – |

Umpires: D. Sang Hue and R. Gosein.

# WEST INDIES v ENGLAND 1973–74 (2nd Test)

Played at Sabina Park, Kingston, Jamaica, on 16, 17, 19, 20, 21 February.
Toss: England.    Result: MATCH DRAWN.
Debuts: Nil.

The partnership of 206 between Fredericks and Rowe remains the first-wicket record for West Indies against England. Sobers became the first batsman to score 8,000 runs in Tests. Amiss batted 570 minutes, received 563 balls and hit a six and 40 fours in the highest innings of his first-class career (to date). Only an unbeaten innings lasting 53 minutes by Willis prevented his becoming the fourth batsman to carry his bat through a completed innings for England; his 262* would have been the highest score by anyone achieving this feat in Test cricket. This innings gave Amiss a Test aggregate of 1,356 within a period of twelve months. Pocock scored four singles off 88 balls in 83 minutes in the second innings.

## ENGLAND

| | | | | | |
|---|---|---|---|---|---|
| G. Boycott | c Kanhai b Sobers | 68 | c Murray b Boyce | | 5 |
| D.L. Amiss | c Kanhai b Barrett | 27 | not out | | 262 |
| J.A. Jameson | st Murray b Gibbs | 23 | c Rowe b Barrett | | 38 |
| F.C. Hayes | c Boyce b Sobers | 10 | run out | | 0 |
| M.H. Denness* | c Fredericks b Boyce | 67 | c Rowe b Barrett | | 28 |
| A.W. Greig | c Fredericks b Barrett | 45 | b Gibbs | | 14 |
| A.P.E. Knott† | c Murray b Barrett | 39 | (8) run out | | 6 |
| C.M. Old | c Murray b Julien | 2 | (9) b Barrett | | 19 |
| D.L. Underwood | c Fredericks b Sobers | 24 | (7) c Murray b Sobers | | 12 |
| P.I. Pocock | c Gibbs b Julien | 23 | c sub (V.A. Holder) b Boyce | | 4 |
| R.G.D. Willis | not out | 6 | not out | | 3 |
| Extras | (LB 7, NB 12) | 19 | (B 10, LB 11, W 1, NB 19) | | 41 |
| **Total** | | **353** | (9 wickets) | | **432** |

## WEST INDIES

| | | |
|---|---|---|
| R.C. Fredericks | b Old | 94 |
| L.G. Rowe | lbw b Willis | 120 |
| A.I. Kallicharran | c Denness b Old | 93 |
| C.H. Lloyd | b Jameson | 49 |
| R.B. Kanhai* | c Willis b Greig | 39 |
| G. St A. Sobers | c Willis b Greig | 57 |
| B.D. Julien | c Denness b Greig | 66 |
| K.D. Boyce | c Greig b Willis | 8 |
| D.L. Murray† | not out | 6 |
| A.G. Barrett | lbw b Willis | 0 |
| L.R. Gibbs | not out | 6 |
| Extras | (B 16, LB 18, NB 11) | 45 |
| **Total** | (9 wickets declared) | **583** |

| WEST INDIES | O | M | R | W | O | M | R | W | FALL OF WICKETS | | | |
|---|---|---|---|---|---|---|---|---|---|---|---|---|
| Boyce | 19 | 2 | 52 | 1 | 21 | 4 | 70 | 2 | | E | WI | E |
| Julien | 18 | 3 | 40 | 2 | 13 | 3 | 36 | 0 | *Wkt* | *1st* | *1st* | *2nd* |
| Sobers | 33 | 11 | 65 | 3 | 34 | 13 | 73 | 1 | 1st | 68 | 206 | 32 |
| Barrett | 39 | 16 | 86 | 3 | 54 | 24 | 87 | 3 | 2nd | 104 | 226 | 102 |
| Gibbs | 40 | 16 | 78 | 1 | 44 | 15 | 82 | 1 | 3rd | 133 | 338 | 107 |
| Fredericks | 4 | 0 | 11 | 0 | 6 | 1 | 17 | 0 | 4th | 134 | 401 | 176 |
| Lloyd | 4 | 2 | 2 | 0 | 3 | 1 | 5 | 0 | 5th | 224 | 439 | 217 |
| Kanhai | | | | | 3 | 1 | 8 | 0 | 6th | 278 | 551 | 258 |
| Rowe | | | | | 2 | 1 | 1 | 0 | 7th | 286 | 563 | 271 |
| Kallicharran | | | | | 3 | 0 | 12 | 0 | 8th | 322 | 567 | 343 |
| | | | | | | | | | 9th | 333 | 574 | 392 |
| ENGLAND | | | | | | | | | 10th | 353 | — | — |
| Willis | 24 | 5 | 97 | 3 | | | | | | | | |
| Old | 23 | 6 | 72 | 2 | | | | | | | | |
| Pocock | 57 | 14 | 152 | 0 | | | | | | | | |
| Underwood | 36 | 12 | 98 | 0 | | | | | | | | |
| Greig | 49 | 14 | 102 | 3 | | | | | | | | |
| Jameson | 7 | 2 | 17 | 1 | | | | | | | | |

Umpires: D. Sang Hue and H.B. de C. Jordan.

# WEST INDIES v ENGLAND 1973–74 (3rd Test)

Played at Kensington Oval, Bridgetown, Barbados, on 6, 7, 9, 10, 11 March.
Toss: West Indies.   Result: MATCH DRAWN.
Debuts: West Indies – A.M.E. Roberts.

Roberts was the first Antiguan to play Test cricket. Greig and Knott shared an England sixth-wicket record partnership for this series of 163. Rowe batted for 612 minutes, received 430 balls, and hit a six and 36 fours in scoring the first triple century for West Indies against England. His previous ten first-class hundreds had all been scored at Sabina Park. His partnership of 249 with Kallicharran remains the highest for the second wicket by West Indies in this series. Greig became the first to score a century and take five wickets in an innings of the same Test for England. The match produced 99 calls of 'no ball' (runs being scored off 20 of them) – a record for Test cricket. West Indies bowlers were responsible for 47 such infringements.

## ENGLAND

| | | | | | |
|---|---|---|---|---|---|
| M.H. Denness* | c Murray b Sobers | 24 | lbw b Holder | | 0 |
| D.L. Amiss | b Julien | 12 | c Julien b Roberts | | 4 |
| J.A. Jameson | c Fredericks b Julien | 3 | lbw b Roberts | | 9 |
| G. Boycott | c Murray b Julien | 10 | c Kanhai b Sobers | | 13 |
| K.W.R. Fletcher | c Murray b Julien | 37 | not out | | 129 |
| A.W. Greig | c Sobers b Julien | 148 | c Roberts b Gibbs | | 25 |
| A.P.E. Knott† | b Gibbs | 87 | lbw b Lloyd | | 67 |
| C.M. Old | c Murray b Roberts | 1 | b Lloyd | | 0 |
| G.G. Arnold | b Holder | 12 | not out | | 2 |
| P.I. Pocock | c Lloyd b Gibbs | 18 | | | |
| R.G.D. Willis | not out | 10 | | | |
| Extras | (LB 5, NB 28) | 33 | (B 7, LB 5, NB 16) | | 28 |
| **Total** | | **395** | (7 wickets) | | **277** |

## WEST INDIES

| | | |
|---|---|---|
| R.C. Fredericks | b Greig | 32 |
| L.G. Rowe | c Arnold b Greig | 302 |
| A.I. Kallicharran | b Greig | 119 |
| C.H. Lloyd | c Fletcher b Greig | 8 |
| V.A. Holder | c and b Greig | 8 |
| R.B. Kanhai* | b Arnold | 18 |
| G. St A. Sobers | c Greig b Willis | 0 |
| D.L. Murray† | not out | 53 |
| B.D. Julien | c Willis b Greig | 1 |
| A.M.E. Roberts | not out | 9 |
| L.R. Gibbs | did not bat | |
| Extras | (B 3, LB 8, NB 35) | 46 |
| **Total** | (8 wickets declared) | **596** |

| WEST INDIES | O | M | R | W | O | M | R | W |
|---|---|---|---|---|---|---|---|---|
| Holder | 27 | 6 | 68 | 1 | 15 | 6 | 37 | 1 |
| Roberts | 33 | 8 | 75 | 1 | 17 | 4 | 49 | 2 |
| Julien | 26 | 9 | 57 | 5 | 11 | 4 | 21 | 0 |
| Sobers | 18 | 4 | 57 | 1 | 35 | 21 | 55 | 1 |
| Gibbs | 33·4 | 10 | 91 | 2 | 28·3 | 15 | 40 | 1 |
| Lloyd | 4 | 2 | 9 | 0 | 12 | 4 | 13 | 2 |
| Fredericks | 3 | 0 | 5 | 0 | 6 | 2 | 24 | 0 |
| Rowe | | | | | 1 | 0 | 5 | 0 |
| Kallicharran | | | | | 1 | 0 | 5 | 0 |
| ENGLAND | | | | | | | | |
| Arnold | 26 | 5 | 91 | 1 | | | | |
| Willis | 26 | 4 | 100 | 1 | | | | |
| Greig | 46 | 2 | 164 | 6 | | | | |
| Old | 28 | 4 | 102 | 0 | | | | |
| Pocock | 28 | 4 | 93 | 0 | | | | |

### FALL OF WICKETS

| Wkt | E 1st | WI 1st | E 2nd |
|---|---|---|---|
| 1st | 28 | 126 | 4 |
| 2nd | 34 | 375 | 8 |
| 3rd | 53 | 390 | 29 |
| 4th | 68 | 420 | 40 |
| 5th | 130 | 465 | 106 |
| 6th | 293 | 466 | 248 |
| 7th | 306 | 551 | 248 |
| 8th | 344 | 556 | – |
| 9th | 371 | – | – |
| 10th | 395 | – | – |

Umpires: D. Sang Hue and S.E. Parris.

# WEST INDIES v ENGLAND 1973–74 (4th Test)

Played at Bourda, Georgetown, Guyana, on 22, 23, 24, 26 *(no play)*, 27 March.
Toss: England.   Result: MATCH DRAWN.
Debuts: Nil.

Rain and poor drainage accounted for 13 hours and 26 minutes of playing time being lost. Amiss was the first England batsman to score three hundreds in a rubber against West Indies.

### ENGLAND

| | | |
|---|---|---:|
| G. Boycott | b Julien | 15 |
| D.L. Amiss | c Murray b Boyce | 118 |
| M.H. Denness* | b Barrett | 42 |
| K.W.R. Fletcher | c Murray b Julien | 41 |
| A.W. Greig | b Boyce | 121 |
| F.C. Hayes | c and b Gibbs | 6 |
| A.P.E. Knott† | c Julien b Gibbs | 61 |
| J. Birkenshaw | c Murray b Fredericks | 0 |
| C.M. Old | c Kanhai b Boyce | 14 |
| G.G. Arnold | run out | 1 |
| D.L. Underwood | not out | 7 |
| Extras | (B 1, LB 13, NB 8) | 22 |
| **Total** | | **448** |

### WEST INDIES

| | | |
|---|---|---:|
| R.C. Fredericks | c and b Greig | 98 |
| L.G. Rowe | b Greig | 28 |
| A.I. Kallicharran | b Birkenshaw | 6 |
| R.B. Kanhai* | b Underwood | 44 |
| C.H. Lloyd | not out | 7 |
| M.L.C. Foster | ) | |
| D.L. Murray† | ) | |
| B.D. Julien | ) did not bat | |
| K.D. Boyce | ) | |
| A.G. Barrett | ) | |
| L.R. Gibbs | ) | |
| Extras | (B 6, LB 4, NB 5) | 15 |
| **Total** | (4 wickets) | **198** |

| WEST INDIES | O | M | R | W |
|---|---|---|---|---|
| Boyce | 27·4 | 6 | 70 | 3 |
| Julien | 36 | 10 | 96 | 2 |
| Lloyd | 19 | 5 | 27 | 0 |
| Foster | 16 | 5 | 32 | 0 |
| Gibbs | 37 | 5 | 102 | 2 |
| Barrett | 31 | 6 | 87 | 1 |
| Fredericks | 5 | 2 | 12 | 1 |
| **ENGLAND** | | | | |
| Arnold | 10 | 5 | 17 | 0 |
| Old | 13 | 3 | 32 | 0 |
| Underwood | 17·5 | 4 | 36 | 1 |
| Greig | 24 | 8 | 57 | 2 |
| Birkenshaw | 22 | 7 | 41 | 1 |

### FALL OF WICKETS

| Wkt | E 1st | WI 1st |
|---|---|---|
| 1st | 41 | 73 |
| 2nd | 128 | 90 |
| 3rd | 228 | 179 |
| 4th | 244 | 198 |
| 5th | 257 | – |
| 6th | 376 | – |
| 7th | 377 | – |
| 8th | 410 | – |
| 9th | 428 | – |
| 10th | 448 | – |

Umpires: D. Sang Hue and C.A. Vyfhuis.

# WEST INDIES v ENGLAND 1973–74 (5th Test)

Played at Queen's Park Oval, Port-of-Spain, Trinidad, on 30, 31 March, 2, 3, 4, 5 April.
Toss: England.    Result: ENGLAND won by 26 runs.
Debuts: Nil.

England won this six-day Test with an hour to spare and so squared the rubber. Sobers, playing in the last of his 93 Test matches, became the first bowler to take 100 wickets for West Indies against England when he dismissed Amiss. Gibbs became the second to do so when he bowled Boycott, who failed by just one run to be the first to score a hundred in both innings for England in this series. Greig's innings analysis of 8 for 86 and match analysis of 13 for 156 are the best by an England bowler against West Indies. His match figures are also a record for any Test in Trinidad. Kanhai caught Amiss when he kept wicket for part of the first day after Murray had sustained a cut head.

## ENGLAND

| | | | | | |
|---|---|---|---|---|---|
| G. Boycott | c Murray b Julien | 99 | b Gibbs | | 112 |
| D.L. Amiss | c Kanhai b Sobers | 44 | b Lloyd | | 16 |
| M.H. Denness* | c Fredericks b Ali | 13 | run out | | 4 |
| K.W.R. Fletcher | c Kanhai b Gibbs | 6 | b Julien | | 45 |
| A.W. Greig | lbw b Gibbs | 19 | (6) c Fredericks b Julien | | 1 |
| F.C. Hayes | c Rowe b Ali | 24 | (7) lbw b Julien | | 0 |
| A.P.E. Knott† | not out | 33 | (8) lbw b Sobers | | 44 |
| J. Birkenshaw | c Lloyd b Julien | 8 | (9) c Gibbs b Ali | | 7 |
| G.G. Arnold | run out | 6 | (10) b Sobers | | 13 |
| P.I. Pocock | c Lloyd b Ali | 0 | (5) c Kallicharran b Boyce | | 5 |
| D.L. Underwood | b Gibbs | 4 | not out | | 1 |
| Extras | (B 2, LB 3, NB 6) | 11 | (LB 4, NB 11) | | 15 |
| **Total** | | **267** | | | **263** |

## WEST INDIES

| | | | | | |
|---|---|---|---|---|---|
| R.C. Fredericks | c Fletcher b Pocock | 67 | run out | | 36 |
| L.G. Rowe | c Boycott b Greig | 123 | lbw b Birkenshaw | | 25 |
| A.I. Kallicharran | c and b Pocock | 0 | c Fletcher b Greig | | 0 |
| C.H. Lloyd | c Knott b Greig | 52 | c and b Greig | | 13 |
| G. St A. Sobers | c Birkenshaw b Greig | 0 | (6) b Underwood | | 20 |
| R.B. Kanhai* | c and b Greig | 2 | (5) c Fletcher b Greig | | 7 |
| D.L. Murray† | c Pocock b Greig | 2 | c Fletcher b Greig | | 33 |
| B.D. Julien | c Birkenshaw b Greig | 17 | c Denness b Pocock | | 2 |
| K.D. Boyce | c Pocock b Greig | 19 | not out | | 34 |
| Inshan Ali | lbw b Greig | 5 | c Underwood b Greig | | 15 |
| L.R. Gibbs | not out | 0 | b Arnold | | 1 |
| Extras | (B 11, LB 4, NB 3) | 18 | (B 9, LB 2, NB 2) | | 13 |
| **Total** | | **305** | | | **199** |

| WEST INDIES | O | M | R | W | O | M | R | W | | FALL OF WICKETS | | | |
|---|---|---|---|---|---|---|---|---|---|---|---|---|---|
| Boyce | 10 | 3 | 14 | 0 | 12 | 3 | 40 | 1 | | E | WI | E | WI |
| Julien | 21 | 8 | 35 | 2 | 22 | 7 | 31 | 3 | *Wkt* | *1st* | *1st* | *2nd* | *2nd* |
| Sobers | 31 | 16 | 44 | 1 | 24·2 | 9 | 36 | 2 | 1st | 83 | 110 | 39 | 63 |
| Ali | 35 | 12 | 86 | 3 | 34 | 12 | 51 | 1 | 2nd | 114 | 122 | 44 | 64 |
| Gibbs | 34·3 | 10 | 70 | 3 | 50 | 15 | 85 | 1 | 3rd | 133 | 224 | 145 | 65 |
| Lloyd | 4 | 2 | 7 | 0 | 7 | 4 | 5 | 1 | 4th | 165 | 224 | 169 | 84 |
| | | | | | | | | | 5th | 204 | 226 | 174 | 85 |
| ENGLAND | | | | | | | | | 6th | 212 | 232 | 176 | 135 |
| Arnold | 8 | 0 | 27 | 0 | 5·3 | 1 | 13 | 1 | 7th | 244 | 270 | 213 | 138 |
| Greig | 36·1 | 10 | 86 | 8 | 33 | 7 | 70 | 5 | 8th | 257 | 300 | 226 | 166 |
| Pocock | 31 | 7 | 86 | 2 | 25 | 7 | 60 | 1 | 9th | 260 | 300 | 258 | 197 |
| Underwood | 34 | 12 | 57 | 0 | 15 | 7 | 19 | 1 | 10th | 267 | 305 | 263 | 199 |
| Birkenshaw | 8 | 1 | 31 | 0 | 10 | 1 | 24 | 1 | | | | | |

Umpires: D. Sang Hue and S. Ishmael.

# NEW ZEALAND v AUSTRALIA 1973–74 (1st Test)

Played at Basin Reserve, Wellington, on 1, 2, 3, 5, 6 March.
Toss: Australia.   Result: MATCH DRAWN.
Debuts: Nil.

Gregory Stephen Chappell set the present record for the most runs in a Test match by scoring 380 to beat the 375 (325 and 50) by A. Sandham at Kingston in 1929-30 *(Test No. 193)*. He was the fourth batsman after K.D. Walters, S.M. Gavaskar and L.G. Rowe to score a double century and a century in the same Test match. He batted for 410 minutes and his highest innings in first-class cricket included a six and 30 fours. With Ian Michael Chappell he provided only the second instance in all first-class cricket of brothers each scoring a hundred in both innings of a match; R.E. and W.L. Foster were the first to achieve this feat, for Worcestershire against Hampshire at Worcester in 1899. The Chappells' partnership of 264 remains the highest for any wicket by either country in this series. New Zealand's record fourth-wicket partnership of 229 between Congdon and Hastings is also their highest for any wicket against Australia. Congdon's 132 and the total of 484 are both New Zealand records for this series. The match aggregate of 1,455 is the highest for any Test in New Zealand.

## AUSTRALIA

| | | | | | |
|---|---|---|---|---|---|
| K.R. Stackpole | b Webb | 10 | b Collinge | | 27 |
| I.R. Redpath | c Coney b Hadlee | 19 | c Howarth b Congdon | | 93 |
| I.M. Chappell* | c Wadsworth b Webb | 145 | c Hadlee b Howarth | | 121 |
| G.S. Chappell | not out | 247 | c Wadsworth b Collinge | | 133 |
| I.C. Davis | c Wadsworth b Hadlee | 16 | c Wadsworth b Howarth | | 8 |
| K.D. Walters | c Howarth b Collinge | 32 | c Morrison b Hadlee | | 8 |
| R.W. Marsh† | lbw b Congdon | 22 | c Collinge b Congdon | | 17 |
| K.J. O'Keeffe | ) | | c Howarth b Congdon | | 2 |
| M.H.N. Walker | ) did not bat | | not out | | 22 |
| A.A. Mallett | ) | | not out | | 4 |
| G. Dymock | ) | | | | |
| Extras | (B 1, LB 4, NB 15) | 20 | (B 4, LB 4, W 1, NB 16) | | 25 |
| **Total** | (6 wickets declared) | **511** | (8 wickets) | | **460** |

## NEW ZEALAND

| | | |
|---|---|---|
| G.M. Turner | c Redpath b O'Keeffe | 79 |
| J.M. Parker | lbw b Walker | 10 |
| J.F.M. Morrison | b Walker | 66 |
| B.E. Congdon* | c Davis b Mallett | 132 |
| B.F. Hastings | c I.M. Chappell b Dymock | 101 |
| J.V. Coney | c G.S. Chappell b Walker | 13 |
| K.J. Wadsworth† | b Dymock | 5 |
| D.R. Hadlee | c Davis b O'Keeffe | 9 |
| R.O. Collinge | run out | 2 |
| H.J. Howarth | not out | 29 |
| M.G. Webb | c O'Keeffe b Dymock | 12 |
| Extras | (B 10, LB 5, NB 11) | 26 |
| **Total** | | **484** |

| NEW ZEALAND | O | M | R | W | O | M | R | W |
|---|---|---|---|---|---|---|---|---|
| Webb | 21 | 1 | 114 | 2 | 19 | 0 | 93 | 0 |
| Collinge | 24 | 3 | 103 | 1 | 19 | 3 | 60 | 2 |
| Hadlee | 27 | 7 | 107 | 2 | 21 | 2 | 106 | 1 |
| Howarth | 21 | 0 | 113 | 0 | 25 | 3 | 97 | 2 |
| Congdon | 12·5 | 0 | 54 | 1 | 13 | 1 | 60 | 3 |
| Coney | | | | | 2 | 0 | 13 | 0 |
| Hastings | | | | | 2 | 0 | 6 | 0 |

| AUSTRALIA | O | M | R | W |
|---|---|---|---|---|
| Walker | 41 | 11 | 107 | 3 |
| Dymock | 35 | 7 | 77 | 3 |
| Walters | 8 | 1 | 39 | 0 |
| Mallett | 41 | 8 | 117 | 1 |
| O'Keeffe | 33 | 9 | 83 | 2 |
| G.S. Chappell | 7 | 0 | 27 | 0 |
| I.M. Chappell | 4 | 0 | 8 | 0 |

### FALL OF WICKETS

| Wkt | A 1st | NZ 1st | A 2nd |
|---|---|---|---|
| 1st | 13 | 28 | 67 |
| 2nd | 55 | 136 | 208 |
| 3rd | 319 | 169 | 294 |
| 4th | 359 | 398 | 318 |
| 5th | 431 | 409 | 359 |
| 6th | 511 | 423 | 414 |
| 7th | – | 423 | 433 |
| 8th | – | 430 | 433 |
| 9th | – | 437 | – |
| 10th | – | 484 | – |

Umpires: D.E.A. Copps and F.R. Goodall.

# NEW ZEALAND v AUSTRALIA 1973–74 (2nd Test)

Played at Lancaster Park, Christchurch, on 8, 9, 10, 12, 13 March.
Toss: New Zealand.    Result: NEW ZEALAND won by five wickets.
Debuts: Nil.

When Wadsworth hit the winning boundary after 92 minutes of play on the fifth morning, New Zealand gained their first success in this series and their eighth in 113 official Tests. They had beaten every country except England. Turner became the first to score a hundred in each innings of a Test for New Zealand.

## AUSTRALIA

| | | | | | |
|---|---|---|---|---|---|
| K.R. Stackpole | b Collinge | 4 | c Wadsworth b Collinge | | 9 |
| I.R. Redpath | c and b Collinge | 71 | c Howarth b R.J. Hadlee | | 58 |
| I.M. Chappell* | b R.J. Hadlee | 20 | b Collinge | | 1 |
| G.S. Chappell | c Howarth b Congdon | 25 | c Coney b R.J. Hadlee | | 6 |
| I.C. Davis | lbw b R.J. Hadlee | 5 | c Congdon b R.J. Hadlee | | 50 |
| K.D. Walters | b R.J. Hadlee | 6 | lbw b D.R. Hadlee | | 65 |
| R.W. Marsh† | b Congdon | 38 | c and b D.R. Hadlee | | 4 |
| K.J. O'Keeffe | c Wadsworth b Congdon | 3 | not out | | 23 |
| M.H.N. Walker | not out | 18 | c Howarth b D.R. Hadlee | | 4 |
| A.A. Mallett | b Collinge | 1 | (11) c Wadsworth b R.J. Hadlee | | 11 |
| G. Dymock | c Congdon b D.R. Hadlee | 13 | (10) c Wadsworth b D.R. Hadlee | | 0 |
| Extras | (B 1, LB 6, NB 12) | 19 | (B 16, LB 4, NB 8) | | 28 |
| **Total** | | **223** | | | **259** |

## NEW ZEALAND

| | | | | |
|---|---|---|---|---|
| G.M. Turner | c Stackpole b G.S. Chappell | 101 | not out | 110 |
| J.M. Parker | lbw b Dymock | 18 | c Marsh b Walker | 26 |
| J.F.M. Morrison | c Marsh b G.S. Chappell | 12 | lbw b Walker | 0 |
| B.E. Congdon* | c I.M. Chappell b Walker | 8 | run out | 2 |
| B.F. Hastings | c Marsh b Walker | 19 | b Mallett | 46 |
| J.V. Coney | c Marsh b Dymock | 15 | c Marsh b G.S. Chappell | 14 |
| K.J. Wadsworth† | c Marsh b Mallett | 24 | not out | 9 |
| D.R. Hadlee | c Marsh b Dymock | 11 | | |
| R.J. Hadlee | lbw b Walker | 23 | | |
| H.J. Howarth | c I.M. Chappell b Walker | 0 | | |
| R.O. Collinge | not out | 1 | | |
| Extras | (B 4, LB 8, NB 11) | 23 | (B 4, LB 14, NB 5) | 23 |
| **Total** | | **255** | (5 wickets) | **230** |

| NEW ZEALAND | O | M | R | W | O | M | R | W | | FALL OF WICKETS | | | |
|---|---|---|---|---|---|---|---|---|---|---|---|---|---|
| R.J. Hadlee | 14 | 2 | 59 | 3 | 18·4 | 3 | 71 | 4 | | A | NZ | A | NZ |
| Collinge | 21 | 4 | 70 | 3 | 9 | 0 | 37 | 2 | *Wkt* | *1st* | *1st* | *2nd* | *2nd* |
| D.R. Hadlee | 12·2 | 2 | 42 | 1 | 20 | 2 | 75 | 4 | 1st | 8 | 59 | 12 | 51 |
| Congdon | 11 | 2 | 33 | 3 | 9 | 3 | 26 | 0 | 2nd | 45 | 90 | 26 | 55 |
| Howarth | | | | | 11 | 2 | 22 | 0 | 3rd | 101 | 104 | 33 | 62 |
| | | | | | | | | | 4th | 120 | 136 | 139 | 177 |
| AUSTRALIA | | | | | | | | | 5th | 128 | 171 | 142 | 206 |
| Walker | 19·6 | 5 | 60 | 4 | 28 | 10 | 50 | 2 | 6th | 181 | 213 | 160 | – |
| Dymock | 24 | 6 | 59 | 3 | 25 | 5 | 84 | 0 | 7th | 190 | 220 | 232 | – |
| Walters | 7 | 1 | 34 | 0 | | | | | 8th | 194 | 241 | 238 | – |
| G.S. Chappell | 20 | 2 | 76 | 2 | 17·6 | 5 | 38 | 1 | 9th | 196 | 242 | 239 | – |
| Mallett | 3 | 1 | 3 | 1 | 13 | 4 | 35 | 1 | 10th | 223 | 255 | 259 | – |

Umpires: J.B.R. Hastie and R.L. Monteith.

# NEW ZEALAND v AUSTRALIA 1973–74 (3rd Test)

Played at Eden Park, Auckland, on 22, 23, 24 March.
Toss: New Zealand.   Result: AUSTRALIA won by 297 runs.
Debuts: Nil.

Australia's victory on the third evening squared the rubber with two days to spare. Stackpole was out to the first ball of the match. A record Auckland crowd of 35,000 saw Redpath become the first player to carry his bat through a completed innings of a Test in New Zealand. He batted for 348 minutes and hit 20 fours. Marsh made his 100th dismissal in Test matches when he caught Congdon.

## AUSTRALIA

| | | | | | |
|---|---|---|---|---|---|
| K.R. Stackpole | c Parker b R.J. Hadlee | 0 | c Congdon b Collinge | | 0 |
| I.R. Redpath | c Wadsworth b Collinge | 13 | not out | | 159 |
| I.M. Chappell* | c Turner b Collinge | 37 | lbw b Collinge | | 35 |
| G.S. Chappell | c Howarth b Collinge | 0 | c Wadsworth b Howarth | | 38 |
| I.C. Davis | c Hastings b Collinge | 0 | c Parker b Howarth | | 5 |
| K.D. Walters | not out | 104 | c Parker b Congdon | | 5 |
| R.W. Marsh† | c Hastings b Collinge | 45 | c R.J. Hadlee b Howarth | | 47 |
| K.J. O'Keeffe | c Morrison b Congdon | 0 | c Burgess b Collinge | | 32 |
| G.J. Gilmour | c Morrison b Congdon | 1 | b R.J. Hadlee | | 4 |
| M.H.N. Walker | c Burgess b Congdon | 7 | b R.J. Hadlee | | 0 |
| A.A. Mallett | c Turner b Congdon | 7 | c Parker b Collinge | | 6 |
| Extras | (B 4, LB 1, NB 2) | 7 | (B 4, LB 4, W 1, NB 6) | | 15 |
| **Total** | | **221** | | | **346** |

## NEW ZEALAND

| | | | | | |
|---|---|---|---|---|---|
| G.M. Turner | c G.S. Chappell b Mallett | 41 | c I.M. Chappell b Walker | | 72 |
| J.M. Parker | lbw b Gilmour | 11 | c Marsh b Gilmour | | 34 |
| J.F.M. Morrison | c Marsh b Walker | 9 | c Marsh b Gilmour | | 0 |
| B.E. Congdon* | lbw b Gilmour | 4 | c Marsh b Walker | | 4 |
| B.F. Hastings | b Gilmour | 0 | lbw b Walker | | 1 |
| M.G. Burgess | c Marsh b Gilmour | 7 | c Stackpole b Walker | | 6 |
| K.J. Wadsworth† | c Marsh b Gilmour | 0 | c G.S. Chappell b Mallett | | 21 |
| H.J. Howarth | c Gilmour b Mallett | 0 | (10) not out | | 3 |
| D.R. Hadlee | b Mallett | 4 | (8) c Walters b Mallett | | 4 |
| R.J. Hadlee | c I.M. Chappell b Mallett | 13 | (9) b O'Keeffe | | 1 |
| R.O. Collinge | not out | 8 | c I.M. Chappell b O'Keeffe | | 4 |
| Extras | (B 4, LB 1, NB 10) | 15 | (B 3, LB 2, NB 3) | | 8 |
| **Total** | | **112** | | | **158** |

| NEW ZEALAND | O | M | R | W | O | M | R | W | | | | | |
|---|---|---|---|---|---|---|---|---|---|---|---|---|---|
| R.J. Hadlee | 9 | 1 | 45 | 1 | 9 | 1 | 50 | 2 | | | | | |
| Collinge | 18 | 4 | 82 | 5 | 16·4 | 0 | 84 | 4 | | | | | |
| D.R. Hadlee | 9 | 0 | 41 | 0 | 7 | 0 | 48 | 0 | | | | | |
| Congdon | 10·2 | 0 | 46 | 4 | 19 | 1 | 66 | 1 | | | | | |
| Howarth | | | | | 28 | 5 | 83 | 3 | | | | | |

### FALL OF WICKETS

| Wkt | A 1st | NZ 1st | A 2nd | NZ 2nd |
|---|---|---|---|---|
| 1st | 0 | 16 | 2 | 107 |
| 2nd | 32 | 28 | 69 | 107 |
| 3rd | 37 | 34 | 118 | 112 |
| 4th | 37 | 40 | 132 | 115 |
| 5th | 64 | 62 | 143 | 116 |
| 6th | 150 | 62 | 230 | 127 |
| 7th | 154 | 63 | 315 | 145 |
| 8th | 162 | 72 | 330 | 147 |
| 9th | 191 | 102 | 330 | 147 |
| 10th | 221 | 112 | 346 | 158 |

| AUSTRALIA | O | M | R | W | O | M | R | W |
|---|---|---|---|---|---|---|---|---|
| Walker | 10 | 4 | 11 | 1 | 19 | 8 | 39 | 4 |
| Gilmour | 15 | 3 | 64 | 5 | 16 | 0 | 52 | 2 |
| Mallett | 5·2 | 0 | 22 | 4 | 13 | 6 | 51 | 2 |
| O'Keeffe | | | | | 5 | 1 | 8 | 2 |

Umpires: D.E.A. Copps and W.R.C. Gardiner.

# ENGLAND v INDIA 1974 (1st Test)

Played at Old Trafford, Manchester, on 6, 7, 8, 10, 11 June.
Toss: England. Result: ENGLAND won by 113 runs.
Debuts: England – M. Hendrick (not 'M.J.'); India – S. Madan Lal (full name: Madan Lal Sharma),
B.P. Patel.

England won at 5.19 on the fifth evening with 15·5 of the mandatory last 20 overs in hand. Rain claimed five
hours 38 minutes of playing time. This was the first match to be played under regulations providing for an hour's
extension of play on any of the first four days of a Test in England when more than one hour of that day's playing
time had been lost for any reason other than the normal intervals. This regulation was invoked on the first and
third days, play continuing until 7.30 p.m.

## ENGLAND

| | | | | |
|---|---|---|---|---|
| G. Boycott | lbw b Abid Ali | 10 | c Engineer b Solkar | 6 |
| D.L. Amiss | c Madan Lal b Chandrasekhar | 56 | c Gavaskar b Bedi | 47 |
| J.H. Edrich | b Abid Ali | 7 | (4) not out | 100 |
| M.H. Denness* | b Bedi | 26 | (5) not out | 45 |
| K.W.R. Fletcher | not out | 123 | | |
| D.L. Underwood | c Solkar b Bedi | 7 | (3) c Engineer b Abid Ali | 9 |
| A.W. Greig | c Engineer b Madan Lal | 53 | | |
| A.P.E. Knott† | lbw b Madan Lal | 0 | | |
| C.M. Old | c Engineer b Chandrasekhar | 12 | | |
| R.G.D. Willis | lbw b Abid Ali | 24 | | |
| M. Hendrick | did not bat | | | |
| Extras | (B 1, LB 7, W 1, NB 1) | 10 | (B 4, LB 2) | 6 |
| **Total** | (9 wickets declared) | **328** | (3 wickets declared) | **213** |

## INDIA

| | | | | |
|---|---|---|---|---|
| S.M. Gavaskar | run out | 101 | c Hendrick b Old | 58 |
| E.D. Solkar | c Willis b Hendrick | 7 | c Hendrick b Underwood | 19 |
| S. Venkataraghavan | b Willis | 3 | (9) not out | 5 |
| A.L. Wadekar* | c Hendrick b Old | 6 | (3) c Knott b Greig | 14 |
| G.R. Viswanath | b Underwood | 40 | (4) c Knott b Old | 50 |
| B.P. Patel | c Knott b Willis | 5 | (5) c Knott b Old | 3 |
| F.M. Engineer† | b Willis | 0 | (6) c Knott b Hendrick | 12 |
| S. Madan Lal | b Hendrick | 2 | (7) hit wkt b Willis | 7 |
| S. Abid Ali | c Knott b Hendrick | 71 | (8) c Boycott b Greig | 4 |
| B.S. Bedi | b Willis | 0 | b Old | 0 |
| B.S. Chandrasekhar | not out | 0 | st Knott b Greig | 0 |
| Extras | (B 3, LB 3, Nb 5) | 11 | (B 1, LB 2, NB 7) | 10 |
| **Total** | | **246** | | **182** |

| INDIA | O | M | R | W | O | M | R | W | | FALL OF WICKETS | | | |
|---|---|---|---|---|---|---|---|---|---|---|---|---|---|
| | | | | | | | | | | E | I | E | I |
| Abid Ali | 30·3 | 6 | 79 | 3 | 11 | 2 | 31 | 1 | Wkt | 1st | 1st | 2nd | 2nd |
| Solkar | 13 | 4 | 33 | 0 | 7 | 0 | 24 | 1 | 1st | 18 | 22 | 13 | 32 |
| Madan Lal | 31 | 11 | 56 | 2 | 12 | 2 | 39 | 0 | 2nd | 28 | 25 | 30 | 68 |
| Venkataraghavan | 5 | 1 | 8 | 0 | 9 | 1 | 17 | 0 | 3rd | 90 | 32 | 104 | 103 |
| Bedi | 43 | 14 | 87 | 2 | 20 | 2 | 58 | 1 | 4th | 104 | 105 | – | 111 |
| Chandrasekhar | 21 | 4 | 55 | 2 | 11 | 2 | 38 | 0 | 5th | 127 | 129 | – | 139 |
| ENGLAND | | | | | | | | | 6th | 231 | 135 | – | 157 |
| Willis | 24 | 3 | 64 | 4 | 12 | 5 | 33 | 1 | 7th | 231 | 143 | – | 165 |
| Old | 16 | 0 | 46 | 1 | 16 | 7 | 20 | 4 | 8th | 265 | 228 | – | 180 |
| Hendrick | 20 | 4 | 57 | 3 | 17 | 1 | 39 | 1 | 9th | 328 | 228 | – | 180 |
| Underwood | 19 | 7 | 50 | 1 | 15 | 4 | 45 | 1 | 10th | – | 246 | – | 182 |
| Greig | 5 | 1 | 18 | 0 | 25·1 | 8 | 35 | 3 | | | | | |

Umpires: H.D. Bird and D.J. Constant.

# ENGLAND v INDIA 1974 (2nd Test)

Played at Lord's, London, on 20, 21, 22, 24 June.
Toss: England.   Result: ENGLAND won by an innings and 285 runs.
Debuts: England – D. Lloyd.

England gained their second-largest margin of victory in all Tests at 12.39 p.m. on the fourth day. England's total of 629, scored in 650 minutes, remains their highest against India, their highest at Lord's, and their highest in all post-war Tests. The partnership of 221 in 226 minutes between Amiss and Edrich is England's highest for the second wicket in this series and in all Tests at Lord's. Bedi became the first bowler to concede 200 runs in a Test at Lord's. India were dismissed in 77 minutes in their second innings for their lowest total in Test cricket and the lowest total in all Test matches at Lord's.

## ENGLAND

| | | |
|---|---|---:|
| D.L. Amiss | lbw b Prasanna | 188 |
| D.Lloyd | c Solkar b Prasanna | 46 |
| J.H. Edrich | lbw b Bedi | 96 |
| M.H. Denness* | c sub (S. Venkataraghavan) b Bedi | 118 |
| K.W.R. Fletcher | c Solkar b Bedi | 15 |
| A.W. Greig | c and b Abid Ali | 106 |
| A.P.E. Knott† | c and b Bedi | 26 |
| C.M. Old | b Abid Ali | 3 |
| G.G. Arnold | b Bedi | 5 |
| D.L. Underwood | c Solkar b Bedi | 9 |
| M. Hendrick | not out | 1 |
| Extras | (B 8, LB 4, W 2, NB 2) | 16 |
| **Total** | | **629** |

## INDIA

| | | | | |
|---|---|---:|---|---:|
| S.M. Gavaskar | c Knott b Old | 49 | lbw b Arnold | 5 |
| F.M. Engineer† | c Denness b Old | 86 | lbw b Arnold | 0 |
| A.L. Wadekar* | c Underwood b Hendrick | 18 | b Old | 3 |
| G.R. Viswanath | b Underwood | 52 | c Knott b Arnold | 5 |
| B.P. Patel | c Fletcher b Greig | 1 | c Knott b Arnold | 1 |
| E.D. Solkar | c Underwood b Hendrick | 43 | not out | 18 |
| S. Abid Ali | c Arnold b Old | 14 | c Knott b Old | 3 |
| S. Madan Lal | c Knott b Old | 0 | c Hendrick b Old | 2 |
| E.A.S. Prasanna | c Denness b Hendrick | 0 | b Old | 5 |
| B.S. Bedi | b Arnold | 14 | b Old | 0 |
| B.S. Chandrasekhar | not out | 2 | absent hurt | – |
| Extras | (B 4, LB 7, NB 12) | 23 | | |
| **Total** | | **302** | | **42** |

| INDIA | O | M | R | W | O | M | R | W | | FALL OF WICKETS | | |
|---|---:|---:|---:|---:|---:|---:|---:|---:|---|---|---|---|
| Abid Ali | 22 | 2 | 79 | 2 | | | | | | E | I | I |
| Solkar | 6 | 2 | 16 | 0 | | | | | Wkt | 1st | 1st | 2nd |
| Madan Lal | 30 | 6 | 93 | 0 | | | | | 1st | 116 | 131 | 2 |
| Bedi | 64·2 | 8 | 226 | 6 | | | | | 2nd | 337 | 149 | 5 |
| Chandrasekhar | 9·3 | 1 | 33 | 0 | | | | | 3rd | 339 | 183 | 12 |
| Prasanna | 51 | 6 | 166 | 2 | | | | | 4th | 369 | 188 | 14 |
| | | | | | | | | | 5th | 571 | 250 | 25 |
| ENGLAND | | | | | | | | | 6th | 591 | 280 | 28 |
| Arnold | 24·5 | 6 | 81 | 1 | 8 | 1 | 19 | 4 | 7th | 604 | 281 | 30 |
| Old | 21 | 6 | 67 | 4 | 8 | 3 | 21 | 5 | 8th | 611 | 286 | 42 |
| Hendrick | 18 | 4 | 46 | 3 | 1 | 0 | 2 | 0 | 9th | 624 | 286 | 42 |
| Greig | 21 | 4 | 63 | 1 | | | | | 10th | 629 | 302 | – |
| Underwood | 15 | 10 | 18 | 1 | | | | | | | | |
| Lloyd | 2 | 0 | 4 | 0 | | | | | | | | |

Umpires: A.E. Fagg and T.W. Spencer.

# ENGLAND v INDIA 1974 (3rd Test)

Played at Edgbaston, Birmingham, on 4 (*no play*), 5, 6, 8 July.
Toss: India.   Result: ENGLAND won by an innings and 78 runs.
Debuts: India – S.S. Naik.

England won at 4.10 on the fourth afternoon in spite of a blank first day. It was the third time that a side had won a Test after losing only two wickets in the match; the other instances were both by England, against South Africa at Lord's in 1924 and against New Zealand at Leeds in 1958. Gavaskar was out to the first ball of the match, umpire Alley being called upon to make a decision about his first ball in Test cricket. Lloyd batted for 448 minutes, received 396 balls and hit 17 fours in making the highest score of his first-class career (to date). He was on the field throughout his second Test match. Edrich, who took his Test aggregate past 4,000 runs in the previous match, was not called upon to bat.

## INDIA

| | | | | |
|---|---|---|---|---|
| S.M. Gavaskar | c Knott b Arnold | 0 | Knott b Old | 4 |
| S.S. Naik | b Arnold | 4 | lbw b Greig | 77 |
| A.L. Wadekar* | c Knott b Hendrick | 36 | (4) lbw b Old | 5 |
| G.R. Viswanath | b Hendrick | 28 | (5) c Greig b Hendrick | 25 |
| A.V. Mankad | c Knott b Arnold | 14 | (6) hit wkt b Old | 43 |
| F.M. Engineer† | not out | 64 | (7) lbw b Hendrick | 33 |
| E.D. Solkar | lbw b Old | 3 | (8) c Edrich b Arnold | 8 |
| S. Abid Ali | run out | 6 | (3) b Arnold | 3 |
| S. Venkataraghavan | b Underwood | 0 | c Lloyd b Greig | 5 |
| E.A.S. Prasanna | c Greig b Hendrick | 0 | b Hendrick | 4 |
| B.S. Bedi | c Old b Hendrick | 0 | not out | 1 |
| Extras | (B 1, LB 1, NB 8) | 10 | (LB 3, NB 5) | 8 |
| **Total** | | **165** | | **216** |

## ENGLAND

| | | |
|---|---|---|
| D.L. Amiss | c Mankad b Prasanna | 79 |
| D. Lloyd | not out | 214 |
| M.H. Denness* | c and b Bedi | 100 |
| K.W.R. Fletcher | not out | 51 |
| J.H. Edrich | ) | |
| A.W. Greig | ) | |
| A.P.E. Knott† | ) | |
| C.M. Old | ) did not bat | |
| G.G. Arnold | ) | |
| D.L. Underwood | ) | |
| M. Hendrick | ) | |
| Extras | (B 4, LB 5, W 1, NB 5) | 15 |
| **Total** | (2 wickets declared) | **459** |

| ENGLAND | O | M | R | W | O | M | R | W |
|---|---|---|---|---|---|---|---|---|
| Arnold | 14 | 3 | 43 | 3 | 19 | 3 | 61 | 2 |
| Old | 13 | 0 | 43 | 1 | 15 | 3 | 52 | 3 |
| Hendrick | 14·2 | 1 | 28 | 4 | 14·4 | 4 | 43 | 3 |
| Greig | 3 | 0 | 11 | 0 | 16 | 3 | 49 | 2 |
| Underwood | 15 | 3 | 30 | 1 | 3 | 1 | 3 | 0 |
| INDIA | | | | | | | | |
| Abid Ali | 18 | 2 | 63 | 0 | | | | |
| Solkar | 18 | 5 | 52 | 0 | | | | |
| Bedi | 45 | 4 | 152 | 1 | | | | |
| Venkataraghavan | 23 | 1 | 71 | 0 | | | | |
| Prasanna | 35 | 4 | 101 | 1 | | | | |
| Gavaskar | 1 | 0 | 5 | 0 | | | | |

FALL OF WICKETS

| | I | E | I |
|---|---|---|---|
| Wkt | 1st | 1st | 2nd |
| 1st | 0 | 157 | 6 |
| 2nd | 17 | 368 | 12 |
| 3rd | 62 | – | 21 |
| 4th | 81 | – | 59 |
| 5th | 115 | – | 146 |
| 6th | 129 | – | 172 |
| 7th | 153 | – | 183 |
| 8th | 156 | – | 196 |
| 9th | 165 | – | 211 |
| 10th | 165 | – | 216 |

Umpires: C.S. Elliott and W.E. Alley.

# ENGLAND v PAKISTAN 1974 (1st Test)

Played at Headingley, Leeds, on 25, 26, 27, 29, 30 (*no play*) July.
Toss: Pakistan.　Result: MATCH DRAWN.
Debuts: Pakistan – Shafiq Ahmed.

This was England's 500th official Test, excluding the three abandoned without a ball being bowled. England needed to score 44 runs with four wickets in hand when rain ended the match prematurely. If England had reached their target of 282 runs, they would have scored their highest fourth innings total to win a Test at home. The partnership of 62 between Sarfraz and Asif Masood remains the highest for the tenth wicket by either side in this series. A bomb alert at 11.50 on the first morning caused play to be suspended for 14 minutes.

## PAKISTAN

| | | | | | |
|---|---|---|---|---|---|
| Sadiq Mohammad | c Lloyd b Hendrick | 28 | c Greig b Old | | 12 |
| Shafiq Ahmed | b Old | 7 | c Greig b Arnold | | 18 |
| Majid Khan | c and b Greig | 75 | c Knott b Arnold | | 4 |
| Mushtaq Mohammad | c Fletcher b Underwood | 6 | c Greig b Hendrick | | 43 |
| Zaheer Abbas | c Knott b Hendrick | 48 | c Knott b Greig | | 19 |
| Asif Iqbal | c Knott b Arnold | 14 | b Old | | 8 |
| Intikhab Alam* | c Knott b Arnold | 3 | lbw b Old | | 10 |
| Imran Khan | c Greig b Old | 23 | c Greig b Hendrick | | 31 |
| Wasim Bari† | c Denness b Old | 2 | b Hendrick | | 3 |
| Sarfraz Nawaz | b Arnold | 53 | c Fletcher b Arnold | | 2 |
| Asif Masood | not out | 4 | not out | | 2 |
| Extras | (LB 5, W 2, NB 15) | 22 | (LB 14, W 1, NB 12) | | 27 |
| **Total** | | **285** | | | **179** |

## ENGLAND

| | | | | | |
|---|---|---|---|---|---|
| D.L. Amiss | c Sadiq b Sarfraz | 13 | lbw b Sarfraz | | 8 |
| D. Lloyd | c Sadiq b Asif Masood | 48 | c Wasim b Sarfraz | | 9 |
| J.H. Edrich | c Asif Iqbal b Asif Masood | 9 | c Sadiq b Imran | | 70 |
| M.H. Denness* | b Asif Masood | 9 | c Sarfraz b Intikhab | | 44 |
| K.W.R. Fletcher | lbw b Sarfraz | 11 | not out | | 67 |
| A.W. Greig | c Wasim b Imran | 37 | c Majid b Sarfraz | | 12 |
| A.P.E. Knott† | c Wasim b Asif Iqbal | 35 | c Majid b Sarfraz | | 5 |
| C.M. Old | c Asif Masood b Imran | 0 | not out | | 10 |
| G.G. Arnold | c Intikhab b Sarfraz | 1 | | | |
| D.L. Underwood | run out | 9 | | | |
| M. Hendrick | not out | 1 | | | |
| Extras | (B 1, LB 3, W 4, NB 2) | 10 | (B 4, LB 3, W 1, NB 5) | | 13 |
| **Total** | | **183** | (6 wickets) | | **238** |

| ENGLAND | O | M | R | W | O | M | R | W | | FALL OF WICKETS | | | |
|---|---|---|---|---|---|---|---|---|---|---|---|---|---|
| Arnold | 31·5 | 8 | 67 | 3 | 23·1 | 11 | 36 | 3 | | P | E | P | E |
| Old | 21 | 4 | 65 | 3 | 17 | 0 | 54 | 3 | *Wkt* | *1st* | *1st* | *2nd* | *2nd* |
| Hendrick | 26 | 4 | 91 | 2 | 18 | 6 | 39 | 3 | 1st | 12 | 25 | 24 | 17 |
| Underwood | 12 | 6 | 26 | 1 | 1 | 1 | 0 | 0 | 2nd | 60 | 69 | 35 | 22 |
| Greig | 11 | 4 | 14 | 1 | 9 | 3 | 23 | 1 | 3rd | 70 | 79 | 38 | 94 |
| | | | | | | | | | 4th | 170 | 84 | 83 | 174 |
| PAKISTAN | | | | | | | | | 5th | 182 | 100 | 97 | 198 |
| Asif Masood | 16 | 3 | 50 | 3 | 19 | 2 | 63 | 0 | 6th | 189 | 172 | 115 | 213 |
| Sarfraz | 22 | 4 | 51 | 3 | 36 | 14 | 56 | 4 | 7th | 198 | 172 | 154 | – |
| Imran | 21 | 1 | 55 | 2 | 29 | 7 | 55 | 1 | 8th | 209 | 172 | 168 | – |
| Mushtaq | 1 | 1 | 0 | 0 | 4 | 1 | 8 | 0 | 9th | 223 | 182 | 177 | – |
| Intikhab | 6 | 2 | 14 | 0 | 14 | 4 | 25 | 1 | 10th | 285 | 183 | 179 | – |
| Asif Iqbal | 6 | 3 | 3 | 1 | 5 | 1 | 18 | 0 | | | | | |

Umpires: A.E. Fagg and T.W. Spencer.

# ENGLAND v PAKISTAN 1974 (2nd Test)

Played at Lord's, London, on 8, 9, 10, 12, 13 (*no play*) August.
Toss: Pakistan.    Result: MATCH DRAWN.
Debuts: Nil.

England needed 60 runs to win when rain caused the final day to be abandoned for the second Test in succession. Underwood's second innings analysis of 8 for 51 included a spell of 6 for 2 off 51 balls. He was the first bowler to take eight wickets in an innings and ten wickets in a match for either country in this series. Water had seeped under the covers during an overnight storm. The total time lost in this match was 13 hours and 11 minutes.

## PAKISTAN

| | | | | | |
|---|---|---|---|---|---|
| Sadiq Mohammad | lbw b Hendrick | 40 | lbw b Arnold | | 43 |
| Majid Khan | c Old b Greig | 48 | lbw b Underwood | | 19 |
| Zaheer Abbas | c Hendrick b Underwood | 1 | c Greig b Underwood | | 1 |
| Mushtaq Mohammad | c Greig b Underwood | 0 | c Denness b Greig | | 76 |
| Wasim Raja | c Greig b Underwood | 24 | c Lloyd b Underwood | | 53 |
| Asif Iqbal | c Amiss b Underwood | 2 | c Greig b Underwood | | 0 |
| Intikhab Alam* | b Underwood | 5 | (8) b Underwood | | 0 |
| Imran Khan | c Hendrick b Greig | 4 | (7) c Lloyd b Underwood | | 0 |
| Wasim Bari† | lbw b Greig | 4 | (10) lbw b Underwood | | 1 |
| Sarfraz Nawaz | not out | 0 | (9) c Lloyd b Underwood | | 1 |
| Asif Masood | did not bat | | not out | | 17 |
| Extras | (NB 2) | 2 | (LB 8, NB 7) | | 15 |
| **Total** | (9 wickets declared) | **130** | | | **226** |

## ENGLAND

| | | | | |
|---|---|---|---|---|
| D.L. Amiss | c Sadiq b Asif Masood | 2 | not out | 14 |
| D. Lloyd | c Zaheer b Sarfraz | 23 | not out | 12 |
| J.H. Edrich | c Sadiq b Intikhab | 40 | | |
| M.H. Denness* | b Imran | 20 | | |
| K.W.R. Fletcher | lbw b Imran | 8 | | |
| A.W. Greig | run out | 9 | | |
| A.P.E. Knott† | c Wasim Bari b Asif Masood | 83 | | |
| C.M. Old | c Wasim Bari b Mushtaq | 41 | | |
| G.G. Arnold | c Wasim Bari b Asif Masood | 10 | | |
| D.L. Underwood | not out | 12 | | |
| M. Hendrick | c Imran b Intikhab | 6 | | |
| Extras | (LB 14, W 1, NB 1) | 16 | (NB 1) | 1 |
| **Total** | | **270** | (0 wickets) | **27** |

| ENGLAND | O | M | R | W | O | M | R | W |
|---|---|---|---|---|---|---|---|---|
| Arnold | 8 | 1 | 32 | 0 | 15 | 3 | 37 | 1 |
| Old | 5 | 0 | 17 | 0 | 14 | 1 | 39 | 0 |
| Hendrick | 9 | 2 | 36 | 1 | 15 | 4 | 29 | 0 |
| Underwood | 14 | 8 | 20 | 5 | 34·5 | 17 | 51 | 8 |
| Greig | 8·5 | 4 | 23 | 3 | 19 | 6 | 55 | 1 |
| PAKISTAN | | | | | | | | |
| Asif Masood | 25 | 10 | 47 | 3 | 4 | 0 | 9 | 0 |
| Sarfraz | 22 | 8 | 42 | 1 | 3 | 0 | 7 | 0 |
| Intikhab | 26 | 4 | 80 | 2 | 1 | 1 | 0 | 0 |
| Wasim Raja | 2 | 0 | 8 | 0 | | | | |
| Mushtaq | 7 | 3 | 16 | 1 | | | | |
| Imran | 18 | 2 | 48 | 2 | | | | |
| Asif Iqbal | 5 | 0 | 13 | 0 | | | | |
| Majid | | | | | 2 | 0 | 10 | 0 |

### FALL OF WICKETS

| | P | E | P | E |
|---|---|---|---|---|
| Wkt | 1st | 1st | 2nd | 2nd |
| 1st | 71 | 2 | 55 | – |
| 2nd | 91 | 52 | 61 | – |
| 3rd | 91 | 90 | 77 | – |
| 4th | 91 | 94 | 192 | – |
| 5th | 103 | 100 | 192 | – |
| 6th | 111 | 118 | 200 | – |
| 7th | 116 | 187 | 200 | – |
| 8th | 130 | 231 | 206 | – |
| 9th | 130 | 254 | 208 | – |
| 10th | – | 270 | 226 | – |

Umpires: C.S. Elliott and D.J. Constant.

## ENGLAND v PAKISTAN 1974 (3rd Test)

Played at Kennington Oval, London, on 22, 23, 24, 26, 27 August.
Toss: Pakistan.    Result: MATCH DRAWN.
Debuts: Nil.

The first four days of play, during which only 74 minutes were lost to rain, produced 1,038 runs and only 13 wickets. Pakistan batted for 670 minutes, Zaheer's second double-century innings taking 545 minutes (410 balls) and including 22 fours. His partnership of 172 in 202 minutes with Mushtaq was then Pakistan's highest for the third wicket in all Tests. England saved the follow-on at 6.19 on the fourth evening. Fletcher took 458 minutes to reach his hundred and set a new record for the slowest first-class century in England. His innings lasted 513 minutes, he faced 377 balls and hit ten fours. Intikhab took his 100th Test wicket and became the first to complete the Test 'double' of 100 wickets and 1,000 runs for Pakistan, when he bowled Knott.

### PAKISTAN

| | | | | |
|---|---|---:|---|---:|
| Sadiq Mohammad | c Old b Willis | 21 | c and b Arnold | 4 |
| Majid Khan | b Underwood | 98 | c Denness b Old | 18 |
| Zaheer Abbas | b Underwood | 240 | c Knott b Arnold | 15 |
| Mushtaq Mohammad | b Arnold | 76 | b Underwood | 8 |
| Asif Iqbal | c and b Greig | 29 | | |
| Wasim Raja | C Denness b Greig | 28 | (5) not out | 30 |
| Imran Khan | c Knott b Willis | 24 | (6) not out | 10 |
| Intikhab Alam* | not out | 32 | | |
| Sarfraz Nawaz | not out | 14 | | |
| Wasim Bari† | } did not bat | | | |
| Asif Masood | } | | | |
| Extras | (B 6, LB 18, NB 14) | 38 | (B 5, NB 4) | 9 |
| **Total** | (7 wickets declared) | **600** | (4 wickets) | **94** |

### ENGLAND

| | | |
|---|---|---:|
| D.L. Amiss | c Majid b Intikhab | 183 |
| D. Lloyd | c Sadiq b Sarfraz | 4 |
| D.L. Underwood | lbw b Wasim Raja | 43 |
| J.H. Edrich | c Wasim Bari b Intikhab | 25 |
| M.H. Denness* | c Imran b Asif Masood | 18 |
| K.W.R. Fletcher | run out | 122 |
| A.W. Greig | b Intikhab | 32 |
| A.P.E. Knott† | b Intikhab | 9 |
| C.M. Old | lbw b Intikhab | 65 |
| G.G. Arnold | c Wasim Bari b Mushtaq | 2 |
| R.G.D. Willis | not out | 1 |
| Extras | (B 8, LB 13, NB 20) | 41 |
| **Total** | | **545** |

| ENGLAND | O | M | R | W | O | M | R | W | | FALL OF WICKETS | | |
|---|---|---|---|---|---|---|---|---|---|---|---|---|
| Arnold | 37 | 5 | 106 | 1 | 6 | 0 | 22 | 2 | | P | E | P |
| Willis | 28 | 3 | 102 | 2 | 7 | 1 | 27 | 0 | Wkt | 1st | 1st | 2nd |
| Old | 29·3 | 3 | 143 | 0 | 2 | 0 | 6 | 1 | 1st | 66 | 14 | 8 |
| Underwood | 44 | 14 | 106 | 2 | 8 | 2 | 15 | 1 | 2nd | 166 | 143 | 33 |
| Greig | 25 | 5 | 92 | 2 | 7 | 1 | 15 | 0 | 3rd | 338 | 209 | 41 |
| Lloyd | 2 | 0 | 13 | 0 | | | | | 4th | 431 | 244 | 68 |
| | | | | | | | | | 5th | 503 | 383 | – |
| PAKISTAN | | | | | | | | | 6th | 550 | 401 | – |
| Asif Masood | 40 | 13 | 66 | 1 | | | | | 7th | 550 | 531 | – |
| Sarfraz | 38 | 8 | 103 | 1 | | | | | 8th | – | 539 | – |
| Intikhab | 51·4 | 14 | 116 | 5 | | | | | 9th | – | 539 | – |
| Imran | 44 | 16 | 100 | 0 | | | | | 10th | – | 545 | – |
| Mushtaq | 29 | 12 | 51 | 1 | | | | | | | | |
| Wasim Raja | 23 | 6 | 68 | 1 | | | | | | | | |

Umpires: H.D. Bird and W.E. Alley.

# INDIA v WEST INDIES 1974–75 (1st Test)

Played at Karnataka C.A. Ground, Bangalore, on 22, 23, 24, 26, 27 November.
Toss: India.   Result: WEST INDIES won by 267 runs.
Debuts: India – H.S. Kanitkar; West Indies – C.G. Greenidge, I.V.A. Richards.

West Indies won the first Test to be played at Bangalore, completing their victory before lunch on the fifth day. Pataudi (dislocated finger) and Engineer (hit over the eye) had suffered their injuries while fielding, Kanitkar deputised as wicket-keeper during the second innings. Unseasonal rain delayed the start on the first day until 20 minutes before lunch and no play was possible on the second until after the interval. Fredericks retired with a sprained ankle when the first innings score was 38 for 0. Greenidge became the first West Indies player to score a hundred on his Test debut, that match being overseas. Lloyd reached his hundred off 85 balls with a six and 18 fours. India's total of 118 is their lowest against West Indies in a home Test. Bedi's run of 30 consecutive Test appearances for India was ended when he was banned from selection for this match by the President of the Indian Board of Control as a disciplinary measure for giving a live television interview during India's tour of England in 1974.

## WEST INDIES

| | | | | | |
|---|---|--:|---|---|--:|
| R.C. Fredericks | c Patel b Venkataraghavan | 23 | | | |
| C.G. Greenidge | run out | 93 | | c Gavaskar b Venkataraghavan | 107 |
| A.I. Kallicharran | c Engineer b Prasanna | 124 | | lbw b Prasanna | 29 |
| I.V.A. Richards | c Prasanna b Chandrasekhar | 4 | | c Abid Ali b Chandrasekhar | 3 |
| C.H. Lloyd* | c Abid Ali b Venkataraghavan | 30 | | c Solkar b Chandrasekhar | 163 |
| D.L. Murray† | c Solkar b Venkataraghavan | 0 | (1) | lbw b Abid Ali | 0 |
| K.D. Boyce | b Chandrasekhar | 4 | (6) | c Pataudi b Venkataraghavan | 4 |
| A.G. Barrett | c Patel b Chandrasekhar | 2 | | not out | 5 |
| V.A. Holder | b Chandrasekhar | 0 | (7) | not out | 26 |
| L.R. Gibbs | c Solkar b Venkataraghavan | 2 | | | |
| A.M.E. Roberts | not out | 0 | | | |
| Extras | (B 5, LB 1, NB 1) | 7 | | (LB 15, NB 4) | 19 |
| **Total** | | **289** | | (6 wickets declared) | **356** |

## INDIA

| | | | | | |
|---|---|--:|---|---|--:|
| S.M. Gavaskar | c Richards b Holder | 14 | | c Murray b Boyce | 0 |
| F.M. Engineer† | c Richards b Roberts | 3 | | absent hurt | – |
| H.S. Kanitkar | st Murray b Barrett | 65 | (2) | c Kallicharran b Holder | 18 |
| G.R. Viswanath | lbw b Gibbs | 29 | | b Holder | 22 |
| Nawab of Pataudi, jr* | c Lloyd b Holder | 22 | | absent hurt | – |
| B.P. Patel | c Murray b Holder | 2 | (5) | lbw b Roberts | 22 |
| E.D. Solkar | run out | 14 | (3) | c Murray b Boyce | 15 |
| S. Abid Ali | run out | 49 | (6) | c sub (D. A. Murray) b Boyce | 1 |
| S. Venkataraghavan | b Roberts | 1 | (7) | lbw b Roberts | 7 |
| E.A.S. Prasanna | c Kallicharran b Roberts | 23 | (8) | not out | 12 |
| B.S. Chandrasekhar | not out | 5 | (9) | b Roberts | 0 |
| Extras | (B 4, LB 8, W 4, NB 17) | 33 | | (B 1, LB 5, NB 15) | 21 |
| **Total** | | **260** | | | **118** |

| INDIA | O | M | R | W | O | M | R | W | | FALL OF WICKETS | | | |
|---|--:|--:|--:|--:|--:|--:|--:|--:|---|---|---|---|---|
| Abid Ali | 8 | 1 | 21 | 0 | 19 | 1 | 92 | 1 | | WI | I | WI | I |
| Solkar | 7 | 1 | 28 | 0 | 2 | 0 | 7 | 0 | *Wkt* | *1st* | *1st* | *2nd* | *2nd* |
| Chandrasekhar | 28 | 5 | 112 | 4 | 23 | 3 | 102 | 2 | 1st | 177 | 23 | 5 | 5 |
| Prasanna | 22·2 | 4 | 46 | 1 | 18 | 3 | 57 | 1 | 2nd | 181 | 23 | 71 | 25 |
| Venkataraghavan | 30 | 8 | 75 | 4 | 21 | 4 | 79 | 2 | 3rd | 230 | 112 | 75 | 54 |
| | | | | | | | | | 4th | 236 | 154 | 282 | 69 |
| WEST INDIES | | | | | | | | | 5th | 245 | 157 | 301 | 71 |
| Roberts | 22 | 5 | 65 | 3 | 10·5 | 4 | 24 | 3 | 6th | 255 | 163 | 340 | 96 |
| Holder | 20·5 | 7 | 37 | 3 | 10 | 3 | 18 | 2 | 7th | 255 | 197 | – | 118 |
| Gibbs | 15 | 4 | 39 | 1 | 1 | 0 | 1 | 0 | 8th | 264 | 199 | – | 118 |
| Boyce | 12 | 1 | 51 | 0 | 13 | 3 | 43 | 3 | 9th | 289 | 241 | – | – |
| Barrett | 14 | 3 | 35 | 1 | 8 | 3 | 11 | 0 | 10th | 289 | 260 | – | – |

Umpires: M.V. Nagendra and J. Reuben.

# INDIA v WEST INDIES 1974–75 (2nd Test)

Played at Feroz Shah Kotla, Delhi, on 11, 12, 14, 15 December.
Toss: India.   Result: WEST INDIES won by an innings and 17 runs.
Debuts: India – P. Sharma.

West Indies won after an hour's play on the fourth day. Richards batted for five hours and hit 6 sixes and 20 fours in his second Test match. His partnership of 124 with Boyce is the highest for the eighth wicket by either side in this series.

## INDIA

| | | | | |
|---|---|---|---|---|
| S.S. Naik | lbw b Boyce | 48 | b Julien | 6 |
| F.M. Engineer† | b Julien | 17 | b Gibbs | 75 |
| H.S. Kanitkar | lbw b Roberts | 8 | b Gibbs | 20 |
| G.R. Viswanath | c Murray b Julien | 32 | c Lloyd b Gibbs | 39 |
| P. Sharma | c Julien b Willett | 54 | run out | 49 |
| B.P. Patel | c Kallicharran b Willett | 11 | c and b Roberts | 29 |
| E.D. Solkar | c Lloyd b Gibbs | 1 | c Kallicharran b Gibbs | 8 |
| S. Abid Ali | c Boyce b Gibbs | 8 | run out | 4 |
| S. Venkataraghavan* | c Greenidge b Roberts | 13 | c Richards b Gibbs | 5 |
| E.A.S. Prasanna | not out | 8 | not out | 0 |
| B.S. Bedi | b Roberts | 0 | c Greenidge b Gibbs | 0 |
| Extras | (B 1, LB 3, NB 16) | 20 | (B 5, LB 8, W 1, NB 7) | 21 |
| **Total** | | **220** | | **256** |

## WEST INDIES

| | | |
|---|---|---|
| C.G. Greenidge | c Engineer b Prasanna | 31 |
| D.L. Murray† | c Patel b Solkar | 0 |
| E.T. Willett | b Prasanna | 26 |
| A.I. Kallicharran | c Patel b Bedi | 44 |
| I.V.A. Richards | not out | 192 |
| C.H. Lloyd* | lbw b Solkar | 71 |
| R.C. Fredericks | c Engineer b Venkataraghavan | 5 |
| B.D. Julien | c Bedi b Prasanna | 45 |
| K.D. Boyce | c Patel b Prasanna | 68 |
| L.R. Gibbs | run out | 6 |
| A.M.E. Roberts | run out | 2 |
| Extras | (B 2, LB 1) | 3 |
| **Total** | | **493** |

| WEST INDIES | O | M | R | W | O | M | R | W | | FALL OF WICKETS | | |
|---|---|---|---|---|---|---|---|---|---|---|---|---|
| | | | | | | | | | | I | WI | I |
| Roberts | 17·3 | 3 | 51 | 3 | 16 | 6 | 43 | 1 | | | | |
| Boyce | 11 | 2 | 41 | 1 | 3 | 0 | 10 | 0 | Wkt | 1st | 1st | 2nd |
| Julien | 16 | 3 | 38 | 2 | 9 | 2 | 33 | 1 | 1st | 36 | 2 | 9 |
| Gibbs | 29 | 17 | 40 | 2 | 40·5 | 17 | 76 | 6 | 2nd | 51 | 50 | 81 |
| Willett | 13 | 3 | 30 | 2 | 26 | 9 | 61 | 0 | 3rd | 104 | 73 | 103 |
| Fredericks | | | | | 2 | 0 | 12 | 0 | 4th | 132 | 123 | 204 |
| | | | | | | | | | 5th | 164 | 243 | 214 |
| INDIA | | | | | | | | | 6th | 173 | 248 | 246 |
| Abid Ali | 7 | 0 | 47 | 0 | | | | | 7th | 189 | 320 | 249 |
| Solkar | 13 | 3 | 43 | 2 | | | | | 8th | 196 | 444 | 252 |
| Bedi | 53 | 13 | 146 | 1 | | | | | 9th | 220 | 467 | 256 |
| Prasanna | 34 | 7 | 147 | 4 | | | | | 10th | 220 | 493 | 256 |
| Venkataraghavan | 34 | 6 | 107 | 1 | | | | | | | | |

Umpires: B. Satyaji Rao and M.V. Gothoskar.

# INDIA v WEST INDIES 1974–75 (3rd Test)

Played at Eden Gardens, Calcutta, on 27, 28, 29, 31 December, 1 January.
Toss: India.   Result: INDIA won by 85 runs.
Debuts: India – A.D. Gaekwad, K.D. Ghavri.

At five minutes before lunch on the fifth day India beat West Indies in a home Test for the first time in 16 attempts. This success ended a run of five successive Test defeats. Naik was out to the first ball of the match. Viswanath's innings of 139, scored in 6¼ hours and including 22 fours, is India's highest score against West Indies in a home Test.

## INDIA

| | | | | |
|---|---|---|---|---|
| S.S. Naik | c Murray b Roberts | 0 | c Fredericks b Roberts | 6 |
| F.M. Engineer† | c Lloyd b Roberts | 24 | c Lloyd b Willett | 61 |
| P. Sharma | b Julien | 6 | run out | 9 |
| G.R. Viswanath | lbw b Gibbs | 52 | b Holder | 139 |
| Nawab of Pataudi, jr* | b Roberts | 36 | c Holder b Willett | 8 |
| A.D. Gaekwad | c Murray b Fredericks | 36 | c Greenidge b Gibbs | 4 |
| S. Madan Lal | c Murray b Holder | 48 | b Roberts | 15 |
| K.D. Ghavri | b Holder | 3 | b Roberts | 27 |
| E.A.S. Prasanna | c Greenidge b Roberts | 17 | lbw b Holder | 2 |
| B.S. Bedi | b Roberts | 0 | c Julien b Holder | 5 |
| B.S. Chandrasekhar | not out | 4 | not out | 7 |
| Extras | (LB 1, NB 6) | 7 | (B 3, LB 13, NB 17) | 33 |
| **Total** | | **233** | | **316** |

## WEST INDIES

| | | | | |
|---|---|---|---|---|
| R.C. Fredericks | c Viswanath b Madan Lal | 100 | b Bedi | 21 |
| C.G. Greenidge | c Bedi b Madan Lal | 20 | lbw b Ghavri | 3 |
| A.I. Kallicharran | c Pataudi b Madan Lal | 0 | c Viswanath b Chandrasekhar | 57 |
| I.V.A. Richards | run out | 15 | b Madan Lal | 47 |
| C.H. Lloyd* | c Engineer b Bedi | 19 | b Chandrasekhar | 28 |
| D.L. Murray† | run out | 24 | lbw b Bedi | 13 |
| B.D. Julien | c Viswanath b Bedi | 19 | lbw b Chandrasekhar | 7 |
| E.T. Willett | b Ghavri | 13 | not out | 16 |
| V.A. Holder | b Chandrasekhar | 2 | run out | 0 |
| L.R. Gibbs | not out | 6 | c Prasanna b Bedi | 3 |
| A.M.E. Roberts | lbw b Madan Lal | 1 | b Bedi | 6 |
| Extras | (B 6, LB 11, NB 4) | 21 | (B 8, LB 10, NB 5) | 23 |
| **Total** | | **240** | | **224** |

| WEST INDIES | O | M | R | W | O | M | R | W |
|---|---|---|---|---|---|---|---|---|
| Roberts | 19·3 | 6 | 50 | 5 | 31 | 6 | 88 | 3 |
| Julien | 12 | 1 | 57 | 1 | 17 | 8 | 29 | 0 |
| Holder | 16 | 3 | 48 | 2 | 27·2 | 5 | 61 | 3 |
| Fredericks | 9 | 4 | 24 | 1 | 1 | 0 | 1 | 0 |
| Gibbs | 17 | 6 | 34 | 1 | 37 | 17 | 53 | 1 |
| Willett | 7 | 3 | 13 | 0 | 30 | 14 | 51 | 2 |
| **INDIA** | | | | | | | | |
| Ghavri | 7 | 1 | 28 | 1 | 7 | 0 | 18 | 1 |
| Madal Lal | 16·1 | 5 | 22 | 4 | 6 | 1 | 23 | 1 |
| Bedi | 25 | 8 | 68 | 2 | 26·2 | 13 | 52 | 4 |
| Chandrasekhar | 22 | 6 | 80 | 1 | 20 | 3 | 66 | 3 |
| Prasanna | 11 | 4 | 21 | 0 | 25 | 12 | 42 | 0 |

### FALL OF WICKETS

| | I | WI | I | WI |
|---|---|---|---|---|
| Wkt | 1st | 1st | 2nd | 2nd |
| 1st | 0 | 42 | 19 | 5 |
| 2nd | 23 | 42 | 46 | 41 |
| 3rd | 32 | 66 | 120 | 125 |
| 4th | 94 | 115 | 138 | 163 |
| 5th | 169 | 189 | 152 | 178 |
| 6th | 169 | 212 | 192 | 186 |
| 7th | 180 | 219 | 283 | 198 |
| 8th | 224 | 221 | 301 | 203 |
| 9th | 224 | 235 | 303 | 213 |
| 10th | 233 | 240 | 316 | 224 |

Umpires: J. Reuben and H.P. Sharma.

# INDIA v WEST INDIES 1974–75 (4th Test)

Played at Chepauk, Madras, on 11, 12, 14, 15 January.
Toss: India.    Result: INDIA won by 100 runs.
Debuts: Nil.

India drew level in the rubber 45 minutes after lunch on the fourth day after dismissing West Indies for their two lowest totals of this series. Roberts was the first bowler to take twelve wickets in a Test for West Indies and his analysis of 12 for 121 in this match is the record for this series. His first innings analysis of 7 for 64 is the best for West Indies in India.

## INDIA

| | | | | |
|---|---|---|---|---|
| F.M. Engineer† | c Greenidge b Julien | 14 | b Holder | 28 |
| E.D. Solkar | c Kallicharran b Julien | 4 | c Kallicharran b Julien | 15 |
| A.D. Gaekwad | lbw b Roberts | 7 | (7) run out | 80 |
| G.R. Viswanath | not out | 97 | c Murray b Roberts | 46 |
| Nawab of Pataudi, jr* | lbw b Roberts | 6 | lbw b Roberts | 4 |
| A.V. Mankad | c Fredericks b Roberts | 19 | (3) b Boyce | 20 |
| S. Madan Lal | b Roberts | 0 | (8) c Murray b Roberts | 5 |
| K.D. Ghavri | b Roberts | 12 | (9) not out | 35 |
| E.A.S. Prasanna | c Murray b Roberts | 0 | (6) lbw b Boyce | 0 |
| B.S. Bedi | b Gibbs | 14 | c Murray b Roberts | 0 |
| B.S. Chandrasekhar | c Lloyd b Roberts | 1 | b Roberts | 0 |
| Extras | (B 1, LB 6, NB 9) | 16 | (B 12, LB 3, NB 8) | 23 |
| **Total** | | **190** | | **256** |

## WEST INDIES

| | | | | |
|---|---|---|---|---|
| R.C. Fredericks | c Solkar b Ghavri | 14 | c Solkar b Prasanna | 19 |
| C.G. Greenidge | c Prasanna b Bedi | 14 | b Chandrasekhar | 17 |
| A.I. Kallicharran | c Viswanath b Bedi | 17 | (4) run out | 51 |
| V.A. Holder | hit wkt b Bedi | 0 | (10) c Viswanath b Bedi | 4 |
| I.V.A. Richards | c Chandrasekhar b Prasanna | 50 | c Engineer b Prasanna | 2 |
| C.H. Lloyd* | c Viswanath b Prasanna | 39 | st Engineer b Prasanna | 7 |
| D.L. Murray† | c Engineer b Prasanna | 8 | c Solkar b Bedi | 18 |
| B.D. Julien | c and b Prasanna | 2 | not out | 14 |
| K.D. Boyce | c Bedi b Prasanna | 0 | lbw b Prasanna | 4 |
| L.R. Gibbs | not out | 14 | (3) c Solkar b Chandrasekhar | 3 |
| A.M.E. Roberts | lbw b Chandrasekhar | 17 | lbw b Bedi | 0 |
| Extras | (B 7, LB 10) | 17 | (B 14, LB 1) | 15 |
| **Total** | | **192** | | **154** |

| WEST INDIES | O | M | R | W | O | M | R | W | | FALL OF WICKETS | | | |
|---|---|---|---|---|---|---|---|---|---|---|---|---|---|
| | | | | | | | | | | I | WI | I | WI |
| Roberts | 20·5 | 5 | 64 | 7 | 21·4 | 6 | 57 | 5 | *Wkt* | *1st* | *1st* | *2nd* | *2nd* |
| Julien | 6 | 2 | 12 | 2 | 13 | 4 | 31 | 1 | 1st | 21 | 20 | 40 | 32 |
| Boyce | 11 | 3 | 40 | 0 | 15 | 4 | 61 | 2 | 2nd | 24 | 35 | 65 | 45 |
| Holder | 9 | 1 | 26 | 0 | 24 | 8 | 40 | 1 | 3rd | 30 | 35 | 73 | 62 |
| Gibbs | 12 | 1 | 32 | 1 | 26 | 11 | 36 | 0 | 4th | 41 | 70 | 85 | 65 |
| Fredericks | | | | | 5 | 2 | 8 | 0 | 5th | 74 | 138 | 85 | 85 |
| | | | | | | | | | 6th | 76 | 155 | 178 | 125 |
| INDIA | | | | | | | | | 7th | 117 | 160 | 188 | 133 |
| Ghavri | 6 | 0 | 25 | 1 | 2 | 0 | 13 | 0 | 8th | 117 | 160 | 256 | 138 |
| Madan Lal | 2 | 0 | 7 | 0 | 2 | 0 | 5 | 0 | 9th | 169 | 165 | 256 | 152 |
| Prasanna | 23 | 6 | 70 | 5 | 24 | 8 | 41 | 4 | 10th | 190 | 192 | 256 | 154 |
| Bedi | 19 | 7 | 40 | 3 | 19 | 8 | 29 | 3 | | | | | |
| Chandrasekhar | 9·2 | 1 | 33 | 1 | 20 | 6 | 51 | 2 | | | | | |

Umpires: B. Satyaji Rao and M.S. Sivasankariah.

# INDIA v WEST INDIES 1974–75 (5th Test)

Played at Wankhede Stadium, Bombay, on 23, 24, 25, 27, 28, 29 January.
Toss: West Indies.   Result: WEST INDIES won by 201 runs.
Debuts: Nil.

West Indies gained their victory 72 minutes after lunch on the final afternoon of this six-day Test to win their fourth rubber in four visits to India. This was the first Test match to be played at the new stadium named after the president of the Bombay Cricket Association. Bombay thus equalled Johannesburg in playing Test cricket on three different grounds. Lloyd's innings of 242* is the highest on any of them; he batted for 429 minutes and hit 4 sixes and 19 fours. His partnership of 250 with Murray is the record for the sixth wicket in this series. Police brutality involving a young spectator, when Lloyd reached his double century, resulted in rioting and the loss of 90 minutes of play after tea on the second day. Roberts, with 32 wickets in the rubber, set a new record for this series.

## WEST INDIES

| | | | | |
|---|---|---|---|---|
| R.C. Fredericks | c Solkar b Bedi | 104 | b Ghavri | 37 |
| C.G. Greenidge | c Engineer b Ghavri | 32 | c Patel b Bedi | 54 |
| A.I. Kallicharran | c Viswanath b Ghavri | 98 | not out | 34 |
| C.H. Lloyd* | not out | 242 | c Patel b Ghavri | 37 |
| V.A. Holder | c Chandrasekhar b Ghavri | 5 | | |
| I.V.A. Richards | c Engineer b Chandrasekhar | 1 | (5) not out | 39 |
| D.L. Murray† | c Patel b Ghavri | 91 | | |
| B.D. Julien | not out | 6 | | |
| A.G. Barrett | ) | | | |
| L.R. Gibbs | ) did not bat | | | |
| A.M.E. Roberts | ) | | | |
| Extras | (B 12, LB 10, NB 3) | 25 | (LB 4) | 4 |
| **Total** | (6 wickets declared) | **604** | (3 wickets declared) | **205** |

## INDIA

| | | | | |
|---|---|---|---|---|
| S.M. Gavaskar | b Gibbs | 86 | c Fredericks b Roberts | 8 |
| F.M. Engineer† | c Richards b Julien | 0 | b Julien | 0 |
| E.D. Solkar | b Barrett | 102 | lbw b Holder | 25 |
| E.A.S. Prasanna | c Murray b Gibbs | 4 | (5) b Holder | 1 |
| G.R. Viswanath | c Fredericks b Gibbs | 95 | (4) b Holder | 17 |
| A.D. Gaekwad | c Richards b Gibbs | 51 | b Gibbs | 42 |
| B.P. Patel | b Gibbs | 5 | (8) not out | 73 |
| B.S. Bedi | lbw b Roberts | 13 | (10) c Julien b Holder | 13 |
| Nawab of Pataudi, jr* | b Gibbs | 9 | (7) lbw b Gibbs | 9 |
| K.D. Ghavri | c Kallicharran b Gibbs | 9 | (9) c Murray b Holder | 1 |
| B.S. Chandrasekhar | not out | 0 | c Murray b Holder | 0 |
| Extras | (B 16, LB 9, W 1, NB 6) | 32 | (LB 3, NB 10) | 13 |
| **Total** | | **406** | | **202** |

| INDIA | O | M | R | W | O | M | R | W | | FALL OF WICKETS | | | |
|---|---|---|---|---|---|---|---|---|---|---|---|---|---|
| Ghavri | 35 | 8 | 140 | 4 | 17 | 1 | 92 | 2 | | WI | I | WI | I |
| Solkar | 16 | 2 | 57 | 0 | 6 | 2 | 14 | 0 | *Wkt* | *1st* | *1st* | *2nd* | *2nd* |
| Prasanna | 45 | 5 | 149 | 0 | 5 | 0 | 28 | 0 | 1st | 81 | 0 | 75 | 2 |
| Chandrasekhar | 35 | 3 | 135 | 1 | | | | | 2nd | 194 | 168 | 105 | 17 |
| Bedi | 30 | 4 | 98 | 1 | 11 | 2 | 66 | 1 | 3rd | 298 | 180 | 149 | 46 |
| Gaekwad | | | | | 1 | 0 | 1 | 0 | 4th | 323 | 238 | – | 56 |
| | | | | | | | | | 5th | 341 | 359 | – | 59 |
| WEST INDIES | | | | | | | | | 6th | 591 | 373 | – | 89 |
| Roberts | 31·1 | 6 | 79 | 1 | 18 | 4 | 64 | 1 | 7th | – | 374 | – | 161 |
| Julien | 19 | 8 | 34 | 1 | 7 | 2 | 16 | 1 | 8th | – | 392 | – | 167 |
| Holder | 23 | 8 | 46 | 0 | 20·1 | 6 | 39 | 6 | 9th | – | 406 | – | 188 |
| Gibbs | 59 | 20 | 98 | 7 | 23 | 10 | 45 | 2 | 10th | – | 406 | – | 202 |
| Barrett | 35 | 10 | 85 | 1 | 7 | 2 | 18 | 0 | | | | | |
| Fredericks | 7 | 0 | 22 | 0 | 2 | 0 | 7 | 0 | | | | | |
| Richards | 7 | 2 | 10 | 0 | | | | | | | | | |

Umpires: M.V. Nagendra and J. Reuban.

# AUSTRALIA v ENGLAND 1974–75 (1st Test)

Played at Woolloongabba, Brisbane, on 29, 30 November, 1, 3, 4 December.
Toss: Australia.    Result: AUSTRALIA won by 166 runs.
Debuts: Australia – W.J. Edwards.

With 80 minutes of the last day to spare, Australia completed their fifth victory in eight post-war Tests against England at Brisbane. Knott overtook the world Test record of 173 catches by T.G. Evans when he caught R. Edwards in the second innings. Greig's hundred was the first for England at Brisbane since 1936–37.

## AUSTRALIA

| | | | | |
|---|---|---:|---|---:|
| I.R. Redpath | b Willis | 5 | b Willis | 25 |
| W.J. Edwards | c Amiss b Hendrick | 4 | c Knott b Willis | 5 |
| I.M. Chappell* | c Greig b Willis | 90 | c Fletcher b Underwood | 11 |
| G.S. Chappell | c Fletcher b Underwood | 58 | b Underwood | 71 |
| R. Edwards | c Knott b Underwood | 32 | c Knott b Willis | 53 |
| K.D. Walters | c Lever b Willis | 3 | not out | 62 |
| R.W. Marsh† | c Denness b Hendrick | 14 | not out | 46 |
| T.J. Jenner | c Lever b Willis | 12 | | |
| D.K. Lillee | c Knott b Greig | 15 | | |
| M.H.N. Walker | not out | 41 | | |
| J.R. Thomson | run out | 23 | | |
| Extras | (LB 4, NB 8) | 12 | (B 1, LB 7, W 1, NB 6) | 15 |
| **Total** | | **309** | (5 wickets declared) | **288** |

## ENGLAND

| | | | | |
|---|---|---:|---|---:|
| D.L. Amiss | c Jenner b Thomson | 7 | c Walters b Thomson | 25 |
| B.W. Luckhurst | c Marsh b Thomson | 1 | c I.M. Chappell b Lillee | 3 |
| J.H. Edrich | c I.M. Chappell b Thomson | 48 | b Thomson | 6 |
| M.H. Denness* | lbw b Walker | 6 | c Walters b Thomson | 27 |
| K.W.R. Fletcher | b Lillee | 17 | c G.S. Chappell b Jenner | 19 |
| A.W. Greig | c Marsh b Lillee | 110 | b Thomson | 2 |
| A.P.E. Knott† | c Jenner b Walker | 12 | b Thomson | 19 |
| P. Lever | c I.M. Chappell b Walker | 4 | c Redpath b Lillee | 14 |
| D.L. Underwood | c Redpath b Walters | 25 | c Walker b Jenner | 30 |
| R.G.D. Willis | not out | 13 | not out | 3 |
| M. Hendrick | c Redpath b Walker | 4 | b Thomson | 0 |
| Extras | (B 5, LB 2, W 3, NB 8) | 18 | (B 8, LB 3, W 2, NB 5) | 18 |
| **Total** | | **265** | | **166** |

| ENGLAND | O | M | R | W | O | M | R | W |
|---|---|---|---|---|---|---|---|---|
| Willis | 21·5 | 3 | 56 | 4 | 15 | 3 | 45 | 3 |
| Lever | 16 | 1 | 53 | 0 | 18 | 4 | 58 | 0 |
| Hendrick | 19 | 3 | 64 | 2 | 13 | 2 | 47 | 0 |
| Greig | 16 | 2 | 70 | 1 | 13 | 2 | 60 | 0 |
| Underwood | 20 | 6 | 54 | 2 | 26 | 6 | 63 | 2 |
| AUSTRALIA | | | | | | | | |
| Lillee | 23 | 6 | 73 | 2 | 12 | 2 | 25 | 2 |
| Thomson | 21 | 5 | 59 | 3 | 17·5 | 3 | 46 | 6 |
| Walker | 24·5 | 2 | 73 | 4 | 9 | 4 | 32 | 0 |
| Walters | 6 | 1 | 18 | 1 | 2 | 2 | 0 | 0 |
| Jenner | 6 | 1 | 24 | 0 | 16 | 5 | 45 | 2 |

### FALL OF WICKETS

| Wkt | A 1st | E 1st | A 2nd | E 2nd |
|---|---|---|---|---|
| 1st | 7 | 9 | 15 | 18 |
| 2nd | 10 | 10 | 39 | 40 |
| 3rd | 110 | 33 | 59 | 44 |
| 4th | 197 | 57 | 173 | 92 |
| 5th | 202 | 130 | 190 | 94 |
| 6th | 205 | 162 | – | 94 |
| 7th | 228 | 168 | – | 115 |
| 8th | 229 | 226 | – | 162 |
| 9th | 257 | 248 | – | 163 |
| 10th | 309 | 265 | – | 166 |

Umpires: T.F. Brooks and R.C. Bailhache.

# AUSTRALIA v ENGLAND 1974–75 (2nd Test)

Played at W.A.C.A. Ground, Perth, on 13, 14, 15, 17 December.
Toss: Australia.    Result: AUSTRALIA won by nine wickets.
Debuts: Nil.

Australia's first win against England in Perth was gained with a day and 50 minutes to spare. Hand fractures sustained by Amiss and Edrich in the first Test resulted in Cowdrey making his first Test appearance since June 1971 just four days after arriving in Australia. This was his sixth tour of that continent, equalling the record of J. Briggs. Walters scored 100 runs between tea and the close of play on the second day; he took his score to 103* with a six off the last ball of the session. G.S. Chappell set the present record (seven) for the most catches by a non-wicket-keeper in a Test match. He was the third after S.J.E. Loxton and R.N. Harvey to hold four in an England innings in this series. Lloyd retired at 52 for 0 in the second innings, after being hit in the stomach by a ball from Thomson, and resumed at 106 for 2.

## ENGLAND

| | | | | | |
|---|---|---|---|---|---|
| D. Lloyd | c G.S. Chappell b Thomson | 49 | c G.S. Chappell b Walker | | 35 |
| B.W. Luckhurst | c Mallett b Walker | 27 | (7) c Mallett b Lillee | | 23 |
| M.C. Cowdrey | b Thomson | 22 | (2) lbw b Thomson | | 41 |
| A.W. Greig | c Mallett b Walker | 23 | c G.S. Chappell b Thomson | | 32 |
| K.W.R. Fletcher | c Redpath b Lillee | 4 | c Marsh b Thomson | | 0 |
| M.H. Denness* | c G.S. Chappell b Lillee | 2 | (3) c Redpath b Thomson | | 20 |
| A.P.E. Knott† | c Redpath b Walters | 51 | (6) c G.S. Chappell b Lillee | | 18 |
| F.J. Titmus | c Redpath b Walters | 10 | c G.S. Chappell b Mallett | | 61 |
| C.M. Old | c G.S. Chappell b I.M. Chappell | 7 | c Thomson b Mallett | | 43 |
| G.G. Arnold | run out | 1 | c Mallett b Thomson | | 4 |
| R.G.D. Willis | not out | 4 | not out | | 0 |
| Extras | (W 3, NB 5) | 8 | (LB 4, W 1, NB 11) | | 16 |
| **Total** | | **208** | | | **293** |

## AUSTRALIA

| | | | | |
|---|---|---|---|---|
| I.R. Redpath | st Knott b Titmus | 41 | not out | 12 |
| W.J. Edwards | c Lloyd b Greig | 30 | lbw b Arnold | 0 |
| I.M. Chappell* | c Knott b Arnold | 25 | not out | 11 |
| G.S. Chappell | c Greig b Willis | 62 | | |
| R. Edwards | b Arnold | 115 | | |
| K.D. Walters | c Fletcher b Willis | 103 | | |
| R.W. Marsh† | c Lloyd b Titmus | 41 | | |
| M.H.N. Walker | c Knott b Old | 19 | | |
| D.K. Lillee | b Old | 11 | | |
| A.A. Mallett | c Knott b Old | 0 | | |
| J.R. Thomson | not out | 11 | | |
| Extras | (B 7, LB 14, NB 2) | 23 | | |
| **Total** | | **481** | (1 wicket) | **23** |

| AUSTRALIA | O | M | R | W | O | M | R | W | | FALL OF WICKETS | | | |
|---|---|---|---|---|---|---|---|---|---|---|---|---|---|
| Lillee | 16 | 4 | 48 | 2 | 22 | 5 | 59 | 2 | | E | A | E | A |
| Thomson | 15 | 6 | 45 | 2 | 25 | 4 | 93 | 5 | *Wkt* | *1st* | *1st* | *2nd* | *2nd* |
| Walker | 20 | 5 | 49 | 2 | 24 | 7 | 76 | 1 | 1st | 44 | 64 | 62 | 4 |
| Mallett | 10 | 3 | 35 | 0 | 11·1 | 4 | 32 | 2 | 2nd | 99 | 101 | 106 | – |
| Walters | 2·3 | 0 | 13 | 2 | 9 | 4 | 17 | 0 | 3rd | 119 | 113 | 124 | – |
| I.M. Chappell | 2 | 0 | 10 | 1 | | | | | 4th | 128 | 192 | 124 | – |
| | | | | | | | | | 5th | 132 | 362 | 154 | – |
| ENGLAND | | | | | | | | | 6th | 132 | 416 | 156 | – |
| Willis | 22 | 0 | 91 | 2 | 2 | 0 | 8 | 0 | 7th | 194 | 449 | 219 | – |
| Arnold | 27 | 1 | 129 | 2 | 1·7 | 0 | 15 | 1 | 8th | 201 | 462 | 285 | – |
| Old | 22·6 | 3 | 85 | 3 | | | | | 9th | 202 | 462 | 293 | – |
| Greig | 9 | 0 | 69 | 1 | | | | | 10th | 208 | 481 | 293 | – |
| Titmus | 28 | 3 | 84 | 2 | | | | | | | | | |

Umpires: T.F. Brooks and R.C. Bailhache.

# AUSTRALIA v ENGLAND 1974–75 (3rd Test)

Played at Melbourne Cricket Ground on 26, 27, 28, 30, 31 December.
Toss: Australia.   Result: MATCH DRAWN.
Debuts: Nil.

Australia, needing to score 246 runs to win, were 4 for no wicket when the last day began. Amiss took his aggregate of runs in Test cricket in 1974 to 1,379 – just two runs short of the record for a calendar year which R.B. Simpson had set in 1964. Hendrick damaged a hamstring muscle and was unable to complete his third over.

## ENGLAND

| | | | | | |
|---|---|---|---|---|---|
| D.L. Amiss | c Walters b Lillee | 4 | c I.M. Chappell b Mallett | | 90 |
| D. Lloyd | c Mallett b Thomson | 14 | c and b Mallett | | 44 |
| M.C. Cowdrey | lbw b Thomson | 35 | c G.S. Chappell b Lillee | | 8 |
| J.H. Edrich | c Marsh b Mallett | 49 | c Marsh b Thomson | | 4 |
| M.H. Denness* | c Marsh b Mallett | 8 | c I.M. Chappell b Thomson | | 2 |
| A.W. Greig | run out | 28 | c G.S. Chappell b Lillee | | 60 |
| A.P.E. Knott† | b Thomson | 52 | c Marsh b Thomson | | 4 |
| F.J. Titmus | c Mallett b Lillee | 10 | b Mallett | | 0 |
| D.L. Underwood | c Marsh b Walker | 9 | c I.M. Chappell b Mallett | | 4 |
| R.G.D. Willis | c Walters b Thomson | 13 | b Thomson | | 15 |
| M. Hendrick | not out | 8 | not out | | 0 |
| Extras | (LB 2, W 1, NB 9) | 12 | (B 2, LB 9, W 2) | | 13 |
| **Total** | | **242** | | | **244** |

## AUSTRALIA

| | | | | | |
|---|---|---|---|---|---|
| I.R. Redpath | c Knott b Greig | 55 | run out | | 39 |
| W.J. Edwards | c Denness b Willis | 29 | lbw b Greig | | 0 |
| G.S. Chappell | c Greig b Willis | 2 | (4) lbw b Titmus | | 61 |
| R. Edwards | c Cowdrey b Titmus | 1 | (5) c Lloyd b Titmus | | 10 |
| K.D. Walters | c Lloyd b Greig | 36 | (6) c Denness b Greig | | 32 |
| I.M. Chappell* | lbw b Willis | 36 | (3) lbw b Willis | | 0 |
| R.W. Marsh† | c Knott b Titmus | 44 | c Knott b Greig | | 40 |
| M.H.N. Walker | c Knott b Willis | 30 | not out | | 23 |
| D.K. Lillee | not out | 2 | c Denness b Greig | | 14 |
| A.A. Mallett | run out | 0 | not out | | 0 |
| J.R. Thomson | b Willis | 2 | | | |
| Extras | (B 2, LB 2) | 4 | (B 6, LB 9, NB 4) | | 19 |
| **Total** | | **241** | (8 wickets) | | **238** |

| AUSTRALIA | O | M | R | W | O | M | R | W |
|---|---|---|---|---|---|---|---|---|
| Lillee | 20 | 2 | 70 | 2 | 17 | 3 | 55 | 2 |
| Thomson | 22·4 | 4 | 72 | 4 | 17 | 1 | 71 | 4 |
| Walker | 24 | 10 | 36 | 1 | 11 | 0 | 45 | 0 |
| Walters | 7 | 2 | 15 | 0 | | | | |
| Mallett | 15 | 3 | 37 | 2 | 24 | 6 | 60 | 4 |
| **ENGLAND** | | | | | | | | |
| Willis | 21·7 | 4 | 61 | 5 | 14 | 2 | 56 | 1 |
| Hendrick | 2·6 | 1 | 8 | 0 | | | | |
| Underwood | 22 | 6 | 62 | 0 | 19 | 7 | 43 | 0 |
| Greig | 24 | 2 | 63 | 2 | 18 | 2 | 56 | 4 |
| Titmus | 22 | 11 | 43 | 2 | 29 | 10 | 64 | 2 |

FALL OF WICKETS

| Wkt | E 1st | A 1st | E 2nd | A 2nd |
|---|---|---|---|---|
| 1st | 4 | 65 | 115 | 4 |
| 2nd | 34 | 67 | 134 | 5 |
| 3rd | 110 | 68 | 152 | 106 |
| 4th | 110 | 121 | 156 | 126 |
| 5th | 141 | 126 | 158 | 121 |
| 6th | 157 | 173 | 165 | 171 |
| 7th | 176 | 237 | 178 | 208 |
| 8th | 213 | 237 | 182 | 235 |
| 9th | 232 | 238 | 238 | – |
| 10th | 242 | 241 | 244 | – |

Umpires: T.F. Brooks and R.C. Bailhache.

# AUSTRALIA v ENGLAND 1974–75 (4th Test)

Played at Sydney Cricket Ground on 4, 5, 6, 8, 9 January.
Toss: Australia.　Result: AUSTRALIA won by 171 runs.
Debuts: Australia – R.B. McCosker.

With 4·3 of the mandatory last 15 overs to spare, Mallett had Arnold caught at short-leg to regain the Ashes which had been lost three years and 326 days previously. It was Mallett's 100th wicket in 23 Tests. Arnold took his 100th wicket in 29 Tests when he dismissed G.S. Chappell. The partnership of 220 between Redpath and G.S. Chappell is a record for the second wicket against England in Australia. In the second innings Edrich retired at 70 for 2 after being hit in the ribs by his first ball (from Lillee) and he resumed at 156 for 6.

## AUSTRALIA

| | | | | |
|---|---|---|---|---|
| I.R. Redpath | hit wkt b Titmus | 33 | c sub (C.M. Old) b Underwood | 105 |
| R.B. McCosker | c Knott b Greig | 80 | | |
| I.M. Chappell* | c Knott b Arnold | 53 | (2) c Lloyd b Willis | 5 |
| G.S. Chappell | c Greig b Arnold | 84 | (3) c Lloyd b Arnold | 144 |
| R. Edwards | b Greig | 15 | not out | 17 |
| K.D. Walters | lbw b Arnold | 1 | (4) b Underwood | 5 |
| R.W. Marsh† | b Greig | 30 | (6) not out | 7 |
| M.H.N. Walker | c Greig b Arnold | 30 | | |
| D.K. Lillee | b Arnold | 8 | | |
| A.A. Mallett | lbw b Greig | 31 | | |
| J.R. Thomson | not out | 24 | | |
| Extras | (LB 4, W 1, NB 11) | 16 | (LB 2, W 1, NB 3) | 6 |
| **Total** | | **405** | (4 wickets declared) | **289** |

## ENGLAND

| | | | | |
|---|---|---|---|---|
| D.L. Amiss | c Mallett b Walker | 12 | c Marsh b Lillee | 37 |
| D. Lloyd | c Thomson b Lillee | 19 | c G.S. Chappell b Thomson | 26 |
| M.C. Cowdrey | c McCosker b Thomson | 22 | c I.M. Chappell b Walker | 1 |
| J.H. Edrich* | c Marsh b Walters | 50 | not out | 33 |
| K.W.R. Fletcher | c Redpath b Walker | 24 | c Redpath b Thomson | 11 |
| A.W. Greig | c G.S. Chappell b Thomson | 9 | st Marsh b Mallett | 54 |
| A.P.E. Knott† | b Thomson | 82 | c Redpath b Mallett | 10 |
| F.J. Titmus | c Marsh b Walters | 22 | c Thomson b Mallett | 4 |
| D.L. Underwood | c Walker b Lillee | 27 | c and b Walker | 5 |
| R.G.D. Willis | b Thomson | 2 | b Lillee | 12 |
| G.G. Arnold | not out | 3 | c G.S. Chappell b Mallett | 14 |
| Extras | (B 15, LB 7, W 1) | 23 | (B 13, LB 3, NB 5) | 21 |
| **Total** | | **295** | | **228** |

| ENGLAND | O | M | R | W | O | M | R | W | FALL OF WICKETS | | | | |
|---|---|---|---|---|---|---|---|---|---|---|---|---|---|
| Willis | 18 | 2 | 80 | 0 | 11 | 1 | 52 | 1 | | A | E | A | E |
| Arnold | 29 | 7 | 86 | 5 | 22 | 3 | 78 | 1 | *Wkt* | *1st* | *1st* | *2nd* | *2nd* |
| Greig | 22·7 | 2 | 104 | 4 | 12 | 1 | 64 | 0 | 1st | 96 | 36 | 15 | 68 |
| Underwood | 13 | 3 | 54 | 0 | 12 | 1 | 65 | 2 | 2nd | 142 | 46 | 235 | 70 |
| Titmus | 16 | 2 | 65 | 1 | 7·3 | 2 | 24 | 0 | 3rd | 199 | 69 | 242 | 74 |
| AUSTRALIA | | | | | | | | | 4th | 251 | 108 | 280 | 103 |
| Lillee | 19·1 | 2 | 66 | 2 | 21 | 5 | 65 | 2 | 5th | 255 | 123 | – | 136 |
| Thomson | 19 | 3 | 74 | 4 | 23 | 7 | 74 | 2 | 6th | 305 | 180 | – | 156 |
| Walker | 23 | 2 | 77 | 2 | 16 | 5 | 46 | 2 | 7th | 310 | 240 | – | 158 |
| Mallett | 1 | 0 | 8 | 0 | 16·5 | 9 | 21 | 4 | 8th | 332 | 273 | – | 175 |
| Walters | 7 | 2 | 26 | 2 | | | | | 9th | 368 | 285 | – | 201 |
| I.M. Chappell | 4 | 0 | 21 | 0 | 3 | 2 | 1 | 0 | 10th | 405 | 295 | – | 228 |

Umpires: T.F. Brooks and R.C. Bailhache.

# AUSTRALIA v ENGLAND 1974–75 (5th Test)

Played at Adelaide Oval on 25 (*no play*), 26, 27, 29, 30 January.
Toss: England.    Result: AUSTRALIA won by 163 runs.
Debuts: Nil.

Australia's fourth victory in the rubber was gained with two hours and 40 minutes to spare, despite the loss of the first day after overnight rain had seeped under the covers. Knott became the second wicket-keeper after T.G. Evans to make 200 dismissals in Test cricket, when he caught I.M. Chappell in the first innings. Later Knott scored the second hundred by a wicket-keeper in this series, L.E.G. Ames having scored the first in 1934 (*Test No. 234*). Underwood's match analysis of 11 for 215 was England's best in Australia since 1928–29. Thomson tore fibres in his right shoulder when playing tennis on the rest day and was unable to bowl in the second innings. His total of 33 wickets in the rubber was Australia's third-highest in this series (A.A. Mailey 36 in 1920-21, G. Giffen 34 in 1894-95). Cowdrey's 42nd appearance against Australia beat the record previously held jointly by W. Rhodes and J.B. Hobbs.

## AUSTRALIA

| | | | | | |
|---|---|---|---|---|---|
| I.R. Redpath | c Greig b Underwood | 21 | b Underwood | | 52 |
| R.B. McCosker | c Cowdrey b Underwood | 35 | c Knott b Arnold | | 11 |
| I.M. Chappell* | c Knott b Underwood | 0 | c Knott b Underwood | | 41 |
| G.S. Chappell | lbw b Underwood | 5 | c Greig b Underwood | | 18 |
| K.D. Walters | c Willis b Underwood | 55 | not out | | 71 |
| R.W. Marsh† | c Greig b Underwood | 6 | c Greig b Underwood | | 55 |
| T.J. Jenner | b Underwood | 74 | not out | | 14 |
| M.H.N. Walker | run out | 41 | | | |
| D.K. Lillee | b Willis | 26 | | | |
| A.A. Mallett | not out | 23 | | | |
| J.R. Thomson | b Arnold | 5 | | | |
| Extras | (B 4, LB 4, NB 5) | 13 | (LB 4, NB 6) | | 10 |
| **Total** | | **304** | (5 wickets declared) | | **272** |

## ENGLAND

| | | | | | |
|---|---|---|---|---|---|
| D.L. Amiss | c I.M. Chappell b Lillee | 0 | c Marsh b Lillee | | 0 |
| D. Lloyd | c Marsh b Lillee | 4 | c Walters b Walker | | 5 |
| M.C. Cowdrey | c Walker b Thomson | 26 | c Mallett b Lillee | | 3 |
| M.H. Denness* | c Marsh b Thomson | 51 | c Jenner b Lillee | | 14 |
| K.W.R. Fletcher | c I.M. Chappell b Thomson | 40 | lbw b Lillee | | 63 |
| A.W. Greig | c Marsh b Lille | 19 | lbw b Walker | | 20 |
| A.P.E. Knott† | c Lillee b Mallett | 5 | not out | | 106 |
| F.J. Titmus | c G.S. Chappell b Mallett | 11 | lbw b Jenner | | 20 |
| D.L. Underwood | c Lillee b Mallett | 0 | c I.M. Chappell b Mallett | | 0 |
| G.G. Arnold | b Lillee | 0 | b Mallett | | 0 |
| R.G.D. Willis | not out | 11 | b Walker | | 3 |
| Extras | (LB 2, NB 3) | 5 | (B 3, LB 3, NB 1) | | 7 |
| **Total** | | **172** | | | **241** |

| ENGLAND | O | M | R | W | O | M | R | W |
|---|---|---|---|---|---|---|---|---|
| Willis | 10 | 0 | 46 | 1 | 5 | 0 | 27 | 0 |
| Arnold | 12·2 | 3 | 42 | 1 | 20 | 1 | 71 | 1 |
| Underwood | 29 | 3 | 113 | 7 | 26 | 5 | 102 | 4 |
| Greig | 10 | 0 | 63 | 0 | 2 | 0 | 9 | 0 |
| Titmus | 7 | 1 | 27 | 0 | 13 | 1 | 53 | 0 |
| AUSTRALIA | | | | | | | | |
| Lillee | 12·5 | 2 | 49 | 4 | 14 | 3 | 69 | 4 |
| Thomson | 15 | 1 | 58 | 3 | | | | |
| Walker | 5 | 1 | 18 | 0 | 20 | 3 | 89 | 3 |
| Jenner | 5 | 0 | 28 | 0 | 15 | 4 | 39 | 1 |
| Mallett | 9 | 4 | 14 | 3 | 25 | 10 | 36 | 2 |
| I.M. Chappell | | | | | 1 | 0 | 1 | 0 |

### FALL OF WICKETS

| | A | E | A | E |
|---|---|---|---|---|
| Wkt | 1st | 1st | 2nd | 2nd |
| 1st | 52 | 2 | 16 | 0 |
| 2nd | 52 | 19 | 92 | 8 |
| 3rd | 58 | 66 | 128 | 10 |
| 4th | 77 | 90 | 133 | 33 |
| 5th | 84 | 130 | 245 | 70 |
| 6th | 164 | 147 | – | 144 |
| 7th | 241 | 155 | – | 212 |
| 8th | 259 | 156 | – | 213 |
| 9th | 295 | 161 | – | 217 |
| 10th | 304 | 172 | – | 241 |

Umpires: T.F. Brooks and R.C. Bailhache.

# AUSTRALIA v ENGLAND 1974–75 (6th Test)

Played at Melbourne Cricket Ground on 8, 9, 10, 12, 13 February.
Toss: Australia.   Result: ENGLAND won by an innings and 4 runs.
Debuts: Nil.

England gained their solitary success in this rubber 35 minutes after lunch on the the fifth day. Denness made the highest score by an England captain in Australia, his 188 improving upon A.E. Stoddart's 173 in 1894–95 (*Test No. 43*). Lillee bruised his right foot and left the field after bowling six overs. In the last of his record 114 Test appearances, Cowdrey extended his aggregate to 7,624; only G. St A. Sobers (8,032) has scored more runs in official Tests. His total of 22 hundreds has been exceeded by D.G. Bradman (29) and Sobers (26), and equalled by W.R. Hammond. Cowdrey's total of 120 catches remains the record by a fielder in Test cricket.

## AUSTRALIA

| | | | | |
|---|---|---:|---|---:|
| R. Redpath | c Greig b Lever | 1 | c Amiss b Greig | 83 |
| R.B. McCosker | c Greig b Lever | 0 | c Cowdrey b Arnold | 76 |
| I.M. Chappell* | c Knott b Old | 65 | c Knott b Greig | 50 |
| G.S. Chappell | c Denness b Lever | 1 | b Lever | 102 |
| R. Edwards | c Amiss b Lever | 0 | c Knott b Arnold | 18 |
| K.D. Walters | c Edrich b Old | 12 | b Arnold | 3 |
| R.W. Marsh† | b Old | 29 | c Denness b Lever | 1 |
| M.H.N. Walker | not out | 20 | c and b Greig | 17 |
| D.K. Lillee | c Knott b Lever | 12 | (11) not out | 0 |
| A.A. Mallett | b Lever | 7 | (9) c Edrich b Greig | 0 |
| G. Dymock | c Knott b Greig | 0 | (10) c Knott b Lever | 0 |
| Extras | (B 2, LB 1, NB 2) | 5 | (B 9, LB 5, W 4, NB 5) | 23 |
| **Total** | | **152** | | **373** |

## ENGLAND

| | | |
|---|---|---:|
| D.L. Amiss | lbw b Lillee | 0 |
| M.C. Cowdrey | c Marsh b Walker | 7 |
| J.H. Edrich | c I.M. Chappell b Walker | 70 |
| M.H. Denness* | c and b Walker | 188 |
| K.W.R. Fletcher | c Redpath b Walker | 146 |
| A.W. Greig | c sub (T.J. Jenner) b Walker | 89 |
| A.P.E. Knott† | c Marsh b Walker | 5 |
| C.M. Old | b Dymock | 0 |
| D.L. Underwood | b Walker | 11 |
| G.G. Arnold | c Marsh b Walker | 0 |
| P. Lever | not out | 6 |
| Extras | (B 4, LB 2, NB 1) | 7 |
| **Total** | | **529** |

| ENGLAND | O | M | R | W | O | M | R | W | | FALL OF WICKETS | | |
|---|---:|---:|---:|---:|---:|---:|---:|---:|---|---|---|---|
| Arnold | 6 | 2 | 24 | 0 | 23 | 6 | 83 | 3 | | A | E | A |
| Lever | 11 | 2 | 38 | 6 | 16 | 1 | 65 | 3 | *Wkt* | *1st* | *1st* | *2nd* |
| Old | 11 | 0 | 50 | 3 | 18 | 1 | 75 | 0 | 1st | 0 | 4 | 111 |
| Greig | 8·7 | 1 | 35 | 1 | 31·7 | 7 | 88 | 4 | 2nd | 5 | 18 | 215 |
| Underwood | | | | | 18 | 5 | 39 | 0 | 3rd | 19 | 167 | 248 |
| | | | | | | | | | 4th | 23 | 359 | 289 |
| AUSTRALIA | | | | | | | | | 5th | 50 | 507 | 297 |
| Lillee | 6 | 2 | 17 | 1 | | | | | 6th | 104 | 507 | 306 |
| Walker | 42·2 | 7 | 143 | 8 | | | | | 7th | 115 | 508 | 367 |
| Dymock | 39 | 6 | 130 | 1 | | | | | 8th | 141 | 514 | 373 |
| Walters | 23 | 3 | 86 | 0 | | | | | 9th | 149 | 514 | 373 |
| Mallett | 29 | 8 | 96 | 0 | | | | | 10th | 152 | 529 | 373 |
| I.M. Chappell | 12 | 1 | 50 | 0 | | | | | | | | |

Umpires: T.F. Brooks and R.C. Bailhache.

# PAKISTAN v WEST INDIES 1974–75 (1st Test)

Played at Lahore (Gaddafi) Stadium on 15, 16, 17, 19, 20 February.
Toss: West Indies.    Result: MATCH DRAWN.
Debuts: Pakistan – Agha Zahid; West Indies – L. Baichan.

This first meeting between these countries since March 1959 was left drawn when Baichan batted throughout the fifth day and shared a match-saving partnership with his captain. He was the ninth West Indies player to score a hundred in his first Test match and the first overseas batsman to do so in Pakistan. The innings and match analyses by Roberts are the best for West Indies in Pakistan. Mushtaq played the highest Test innings against West Indies in Pakistan.

### PAKISTAN

| | | | | |
|---|---|---|---|---|
| Majid Khan | c Murray b Roberts | 2 | b Roberts | 17 |
| Agha Zahid | c Gibbs b Roberts | 14 | lbw b Roberts | 1 |
| Zaheer Abbas | c Murray b Roberts | 18 | lbw b Holder | 33 |
| Mushtaq Mohammad | c Murray b Gibbs | 27 | b Holder | 123 |
| Asif Iqbal | c Lloyd b Roberts | 25 | b Roberts | 52 |
| Wasim Raja | c Fredericks b Boyce | 13 | b Holder | 35 |
| Aftab Baloch | c Holder b Boyce | 12 | not out | 60 |
| Intikhab Alam* | b Gibbs | 29 | c Gibbs b Roberts | 19 |
| Wasim Bari† | lbw b Boyce | 8 | not out | 1 |
| Sarfraz Nawaz | c Richards b Roberts | 1 | | |
| Asif Masood | not out | 30 | | |
| Extras | (B 1, LB 3, NB 16) | 20 | (B 4, LB 5, NB 23) | 32 |
| **Total** | | **199** | (7 wickets declared) | 37? |

### WEST INDIES

| | | | | |
|---|---|---|---|---|
| R.C. Fredericks | lbw b Sarfraz | 44 | lbw b Sarfraz | 14 |
| L. Baichan | c Majid b Sarfraz | 20 | not out | 105 |
| A.I. Kallicharran | not out | 92 | c Wasim Bari b Intikhab | 44 |
| I.V.A. Richards | b Asif Masood | 7 | lbw b Intikhab | 0 |
| C.H. Lloyd* | b Sarfraz | 8 | c Wasim Bari b Asif Masood | 8? |
| D.L. Murray† | run out | 10 | not out | 1 |
| B.D. Julien | b Sarfraz | 2 | | |
| K.D. Boyce | lbw b Sarfraz | 13 | | |
| V.A. Holder | lbw b Intikhab | 4 | | |
| A.M.E. Roberts | lbw b Sarfraz | 0 | | |
| L.R. Gibbs | lbw b Asif Masood | 0 | | |
| Extras | (B 6, LB 5, NB 3) | 14 | (B 1, LB 4, NB 6) | 1? |
| **Total** | | **214** | (4 wickets) | 25? |

| WEST INDIES | O | M | R | W | O | M | R | W |
|---|---|---|---|---|---|---|---|---|
| Roberts | 23 | 5 | 66 | 5 | 26 | 4 | 121 | 4 |
| Julien | 2 | 1 | 4 | 0 | 15 | 4 | 53 | 0 |
| Holder | 13 | 4 | 33 | 0 | 19·6 | 5 | 69 | 3 |
| Boyce | 15 | 1 | 55 | 3 | 14 | 4 | 47 | 0 |
| Gibbs | 6·4 | 0 | 21 | 2 | 20 | 4 | 51 | 0 |
| PAKISTAN | | | | | | | | |
| Asif Masood | 19·5 | 0 | 63 | 2 | 17 | 2 | 70 | 1 |
| Sarfraz | 27 | 1 | 89 | 6 | 20 | 3 | 71 | 1 |
| Asif Iqbal | 2 | 0 | 16 | 0 | | | | |
| Wasim Raja | 4 | 1 | 15 | 0 | 4 | 0 | 10 | 0 |
| Intikhab | 9 | 2 | 17 | 1 | 18 | 3 | 61 | 2 |
| Mushtaq | | | | | 6 | 0 | 20 | 0 |
| Baloch | | | | | 4 | 0 | 15 | 0 |

FALL OF WICKETS

| Wkt | P 1st | WI 1st | P 2nd | WI 2n? |
|---|---|---|---|---|
| 1st | 2 | 66 | 8 | 3? |
| 2nd | 35 | 83 | 53 | 8? |
| 3rd | 40 | 92 | 58 | 8? |
| 4th | 92 | 105 | 137 | 25? |
| 5th | 98 | 141 | 214 | – |
| 6th | 117 | 156 | 330 | – |
| 7th | 130 | 199 | 370 | – |
| 8th | 140 | 212 | – | – |
| 9th | 142 | 213 | – | – |
| 10th | 199 | 214 | – | – |

Umpires: Amanullah Khan and Shakoor Rana.

# PAKISTAN v WEST INDIES 1974–75 (2nd Test)

Played at National Stadium, Karachi, on 1, 2, 3, 5, 6 March.
Toss: Pakistan.   Result: MATCH DRAWN.
Debuts: Pakistan – Liaquat Ali (*not Liaqat*).

Rioting, which followed spectator intrusions when Wasim Raja completed his hundred, caused 2½ hours to be lost on the second day. As West Indies eventually had only 25 minutes in which to score 170 for victory, this interruption greatly influenced the result of the match. The partnership of 128 between Wasim Raja and Wasim Bari is the highest by either side for the seventh wicket in this series. Both sides scored their highest totals of the series for matches played in Pakistan. Sadiq, unable to turn his head after being hit in the neck when fielding, batted in pain for 315 minutes. Wasim Raja, whose ankle was put in plaster after he had damaged ligaments when fielding, was unable to survive sufficiently long to allow Sadiq to reach his hundred.

## PAKISTAN

| | | | | | |
|---|---|---|---|---|---|
| Majid Khan | c Baichan b Gibbs | 100 | run out | | 18 |
| Sadiq Mohammad | c Murray b Roberts | 27 | (7) not out | | 98 |
| Zaheer Abbas | c Murray b Gibbs | 18 | (2) c Fredericks b Roberts | | 2 |
| Mushtaq Mohammad | c Murray b Holder | 5 | (3) c Kallicharran b Boyce | | 1 |
| Asif Iqbal | c Boyce b Holder | 3 | (4) c Holder b Julien | | 77 |
| Wasim Raja | not out | 107 | (11) b Gibbs | | 1 |
| Intikhab Alam* | c Fredericks b Julien | 34 | (5) c Richards b Fredericks | | 6 |
| Wasim Bari† | c Baichan b Roberts | 58 | (6) run out | | 0 |
| Sarfraz Nawaz | b Gibbs | 0 | (8) run out | | 15 |
| Asif Masood | not out | 5 | (9) c Julien b Gibbs | | 0 |
| Liaquat Ali | did not bat | | (10) c and b Richards | | 12 |
| Extras | (B 1, LB 16, NB 32) | 49 | (B 6, LB 6, NB 14) | | 26 |
| **Total** | (8 wickets declared) | **406** | | | **256** |

## WEST INDIES

| | | | | |
|---|---|---|---|---|
| R.C. Fredericks | c Liaquat b Intikhab | 77 | not out | 0 |
| L. Baichan | c Wasim Bari b Intikhab | 36 | not out | 0 |
| A.I. Kallicharran | c Zaheer b Sarfraz | 115 | | |
| I.V.A. Richards | lbw b Mushtaq | 10 | | |
| C.H. Lloyd* | c Sadiq b Asif Masood | 73 | | |
| D.L. Murray† | c Majid b Intikhab | 19 | | |
| B.D. Julien | b Asif Masood | 101 | | |
| K.D. Boyce | run out | 2 | | |
| V.A. Holder | lbw b Liaquat | 29 | | |
| A.M.E. Roberts | run out | 6 | | |
| L.R. Gibbs | not out | 4 | | |
| Extras | (B 1, LB 2, NB 18) | 21 | (NB 1) | 1 |
| **Total** | | **493** | (0 wickets) | **1** |

| WEST INDIES | O | M | R | W | O | M | R | W | FALL OF WICKETS | | | | |
|---|---|---|---|---|---|---|---|---|---|---|---|---|---|
| Roberts | 25 | 3 | 81 | 2 | 16 | 0 | 54 | 1 | | P | WI | P | WI |
| Julien | 11 | 0 | 51 | 1 | 16 | 7 | 37 | 1 | *Wkt* | *1st* | *1st* | *2nd* | *2nd* |
| Holder | 19 | 2 | 66 | 2 | 6 | 3 | 19 | 0 | 1st | 94 | 95 | 2 | – |
| Boyce | 12 | 1 | 60 | 0 | 3 | 0 | 15 | 1 | 2nd | 144 | 136 | 11 | – |
| Fredericks | 1 | 0 | 10 | 0 | 12 | 3 | 39 | 1 | 3rd | 167 | 151 | 61 | – |
| Gibbs | 26 | 4 | 89 | 3 | 37·1 | 19 | 49 | 2 | 4th | 170 | 290 | 88 | – |
| Richards | | | | | 9 | 2 | 17 | 1 | 5th | 178 | 336 | 90 | – |
| | | | | | | | | | 6th | 246 | 391 | 148 | – |
| PAKISTAN | | | | | | | | | 7th | 374 | 399 | 212 | – |
| Asif Masood | 15·2 | 2 | 76 | 2 | | | | | 8th | 393 | 449 | 213 | – |
| Sarfraz | 21 | 1 | 106 | 1 | | | | | 9th | – | 474 | 253 | – |
| Liaquat | 19 | 1 | 90 | 1 | | | | | 10th | – | 493 | 256 | – |
| Intikhab | 28 | 1 | 122 | 3 | | | | | | | | | |
| Mushtaq | 15 | 4 | 56 | 1 | | | | | | | | | |
| Wasim Raja | 4·7 | 0 | 22 | 0 | | | | | | | | | |
| Zaheer | | | | | 1 | 1 | 0 | 0 | | | | | |

Umpires: Amanullah Khan and Mahboob Shah.

# NEW ZEALAND v ENGLAND 1974–75 (1st Test)

Played at Eden Park, Auckland, on 20, 21, 22, 23, 25 February.
Toss: England.   Result: ENGLAND won by an innings and 83 runs.
Debuts: New Zealand – E.J. Chatfield, G.P. Howarth.

The match ended after 47 minutes of play on the fifth morning when Chatfield deflected a bouncer from Lever into his left temple and collapsed unconscious with a hairline fracture of the skull. Chatfield's heart stopped beating for several seconds and only heart massage and mouth-to-mouth resuscitation by Bernard Thomas, the M.C.C. physiotherapist, saved his life. England's total is the highest by either country in this series. Wood, who arrived three days earlier after a 63-hour flight from the West Indies, was out first ball. Denness (414 minutes, 25 fours) and Fletcher (443 minutes, 30 fours) added 266 runs to set a new record for the fourth wicket in this series. Greig took his 100th wicket in 37 official Tests when he dismissed Howarth and became the third player after W. Rhodes and T.E. Bailey to score 2,000 runs and take 100 wickets for England.

## ENGLAND

| | | |
|---|---|---:|
| D.L. Amiss | c Wadsworth b Hadlee | 19 |
| B. Wood | c Parker b Hadlee | 0 |
| J.H. Edrich | c Congdon b H.J. Howarth | 64 |
| M.H. Denness* | c Parker b Congdon | 181 |
| K.W.R. Fletcher | c Hadlee b Congdon | 216 |
| A.W. Greig | b G.P. Howarth | 51 |
| A.P.E. Knott† | not out | 29 |
| C.M. Old | not out | 9 |
| D.L. Underwood | ) | |
| G.G. Arnold | ) did not bat | |
| P. Lever | ) | |
| Extras | (B 2, LB 14, NB 8) | 24 |
| **Total** | **(6 wickets declared)** | **593** |

## NEW ZEALAND

| | | | | | |
|---|---|---:|---|---|---:|
| J.F.M. Morrison | c Amiss b Greig | 58 | | c Fletcher b Greig | 58 |
| G.M. Turner | c Amiss b Arnold | 8 | | c Knott b Lever | 2 |
| J.M. Parker | c Knott b Underwood | 121 | (5) | c Edrich b Greig | 13 |
| B.E. Congdon* | c Old b Greig | 2 | (3) | b Underwood | 18 |
| B.F. Hastings | c Knott b Old | 13 | (4) | c Amiss b Lever | 0 |
| G.P. Howarth | c Wood b Greig | 6 | | not out | 51 |
| K.J. Wadsworth† | lbw b Underwood | 58 | | c Fletcher b Underwood | 6 |
| D.R. Hadlee | c sub (B.W. Luckhurst) b Underwood | 22 | | c Edrich b Greig | 1 |
| H.J. Howarth | c Fletcher b Greig | 9 | | b Greig | 4 |
| R.O. Collinge | not out | 0 | | c Fletcher b Greig | 0 |
| E.J. Chatfield | c Fletcher b Greig | 0 | | retired hurt | 13 |
| Extras | (B 5, LB 4, NB 20) | 29 | | (LB 6, NB 12) | 18 |
| **Total** | | **326** | | | **184** |

| NEW ZEALAND | O | M | R | W | O | M | R | W |
|---|---:|---:|---:|---:|---:|---:|---:|---:|
| Collinge | 24 | 6 | 75 | 0 | | | | |
| Hadlee | 20 | 2 | 102 | 2 | | | | |
| Chatfield | 19 | 2 | 95 | 0 | | | | |
| Congdon | 30 | 3 | 115 | 2 | | | | |
| H.J. Howarth | 46 | 9 | 135 | 1 | | | | |
| G.P. Howarth | 14 | 1 | 47 | 1 | | | | |
| ENGLAND | | | | | | | | |
| Arnold | 20 | 4 | 69 | 1 | 6 | 1 | 31 | 0 |
| Lever | 20 | 4 | 75 | 0 | 11·5 | 0 | 37 | 2 |
| Greig | 26 | 4 | 98 | 5 | 15 | 3 | 51 | 5 |
| Underwood | 16 | 6 | 38 | 3 | 25 | 9 | 47 | 2 |
| Old | 7 | 3 | 17 | 1 | | | | |

**FALL OF WICKETS**

| Wkt | E 1st | NZ 1st | NZ 2nd |
|---|---:|---:|---:|
| 1st | 4 | 9 | 3 |
| 2nd | 36 | 125 | 42 |
| 3rd | 153 | 131 | 46 |
| 4th | 419 | 166 | 99 |
| 5th | 497 | 173 | 102 |
| 6th | 578 | 285 | 131 |
| 7th | – | 315 | 134 |
| 8th | – | 326 | 140 |
| 9th | – | 326 | 140 |
| 10th | – | 326 | – |

Umpires: D.E.A. Copps and W.R.C. Gardiner.

# NEW ZEALAND v ENGLAND 1974–75 (2nd Test)

Played at Lancaster Park, Christchurch, on 28 February *(no play)*, 1 *(no play)*, 2, 3, 4, 5 *(no play)* March.
Toss: England.    Result: MATCH DRAWN.
Debuts: Nil.

To compensate for the loss of the first two days to rain, play began, after an early lunch, on the scheduled rest day. Morrison was out to the first ball of the match.

## NEW ZEALAND

| | | |
|---|---|---:|
| J.F.M. Morrison | c Hendrick b Arnold | 0 |
| G.M. Turner | lbw b Arnold | 98 |
| B.E. Congdon* | c Wood b Hendrick | 38 |
| B.F. Hastings | c Wood b Lever | 0 |
| J.M. Parker | c Edrich b Greig | 41 |
| G.P. Howarth | b Underwood | 11 |
| K.J. Wadsworth† | c Lever b Greig | 58 |
| D.R. Hadlee | c Greig b Arnold | 22 |
| B.L. Cairns | c and b Hendrick | 39 |
| H.J. Howarth | lbw b Underwood | 9 |
| R.O. Collinge | not out | 0 |
| Extras | (B 3, LB 9, W 1, NB 13) | 26 |
| **Total** | | **342** |

## ENGLAND

| | | |
|---|---|---:|
| D.L. Amiss | not out | 164 |
| B. Wood | c Wadsworth b Hadlee | 33 |
| J.H. Edrich | c Hadlee b H.J. Howarth | 11 |
| M.H. Denness* | not out | 59 |
| K.W.R. Fletcher | ) | |
| A.W. Greig | ) | |
| A.P.E. Knott† | ) | |
| D.L. Underwood | ) did not bat | |
| G.G. Arnold | ) | |
| P. Lever | ) | |
| M. Hendrick | ) | |
| Extras | (LB 3, NB 2) | 5 |
| **Total** | (2 wickets) | **272** |

| ENGLAND | O | M | R | W |
|---|---|---|---|---|
| Arnold | 25 | 5 | 80 | 3 |
| Lever | 18 | 2 | 66 | 1 |
| Hendrick | 20 | 2 | 89 | 2 |
| Underwood | 13·5 | 3 | 35 | 2 |
| Greig | 9 | 1 | 27 | 2 |
| Wood | 4 | 0 | 19 | 0 |
| **NEW ZEALAND** | | | | |
| Collinge | 19 | 3 | 63 | 0 |
| Hadlee | 19 | 2 | 61 | 1 |
| Cairns | 13 | 5 | 44 | 0 |
| Congdon | 7 | 2 | 27 | 0 |
| H.J. Howarth | 18 | 5 | 53 | 1 |
| G.P. Howarth | 7 | 0 | 19 | 0 |

### FALL OF WICKETS

| | NZ | E |
|---|---|---|
| *Wkt* | *1st* | *1st* |
| 1st | 0 | 80 |
| 2nd | 64 | 121 |
| 3rd | 66 | – |
| 4th | 181 | – |
| 5th | 208 | – |
| 6th | 212 | – |
| 7th | 267 | – |
| 8th | 318 | – |
| 9th | 338 | – |
| 10th | 342 | – |

Umpires: D.E.A. Copps and W.R.C. Gardiner.

# ENGLAND v AUSTRALIA 1975 (1st Test)

Played at Edgbaston, Birmingham, on 10, 11, 12, 14 July.
Toss: England.   Result: AUSTRALIA won by an innings and 85 runs.
Debuts: England – G.A. Gooch; Australia – A. Turner.

This four-match rubber was played after the first Prudential World Cup competition. Australia's victory, completed at 3.05 on the fourth afternoon, was the first by any visiting country in a Test at Edgbaston. Denness became the first England captain to elect to field in a Birmingham Test. A thunderstorm at 2.55 on the second afternoon, after England had batted for one over, provided the Australian bowlers with a rain-affected pitch. A.S.M. Oakman, formerly a first-class umpire, deputised for H.D. Bird (injured back) after tea on the third day. T.W. Spencer took his place on the fourth day.

## AUSTRALIA

| | | |
|---|---|---|
| R.B. McCosker | b Arnold | 59 |
| A. Turner | c Denness b Snow | 37 |
| I.M. Chappell* | c Fletcher b Snow | 52 |
| G.S. Chappell | lbw b Old | 0 |
| R. Edwards | c Gooch b Old | 56 |
| K.D. Walters | c Old b Greig | 14 |
| R.W. Marsh† | c Fletcher b Arnold | 61 |
| M.H.N. Walker | c Knott b Snow | 7 |
| J.R. Thomson | c Arnold b Underwood | 49 |
| D.K. Lillee | c Knott b Arnold | 3 |
| A.A. Mallett | not out | 3 |
| Extras | (B 1, LB 8, NB 9) | 18 |
| **Total** | | **359** |

## ENGLAND

| | | | | |
|---|---|---|---|---|
| J.H. Edrich | lbw b Lillee | 34 | c Marsh b Walker | 5 |
| D.L. Amiss | c Thomson b Lillee | 4 | c sub (G.J. Gilmour) b Thomson | 5 |
| K.W.R. Fletcher | c Mallett b Walker | 6 | Walters b Lillee | 51 |
| M.H. Denness* | c G.S. Chappell b Walker | 3 | b Thomson | 8 |
| G.A. Gooch | c Marsh b Walker | 0 | c Marsh b Thomson | 0 |
| A.W. Greig | c Marsh b Walker | 8 | c Marsh b Walker | 7 |
| A.P.E. Knott† | b Lillee | 14 | c McCosker b Thomson | 38 |
| D.L. Underwood | b Lillee | 10 | (10) b Mallett | 3 |
| C.M. Old | c G.S. Chappell b Walker | 13 | (8) c Walters b Lillee | 7 |
| J.A. Snow | lbw b Lillee | 0 | (9) c Marsh b Thomson | 34 |
| G.G. Arnold | not out | 0 | not out | 6 |
| Extras | (LB 3, W 5, NB 1) | 9 | (LB 5, W 2, NB 2) | 9 |
| **Total** | | **101** | | **173** |

| ENGLAND | O | M | R | W | O | M | R | W |
|---|---|---|---|---|---|---|---|---|
| Arnold | 33 | 3 | 91 | 3 | | | | |
| Snow | 33 | 6 | 86 | 3 | | | | |
| Old | 33 | 7 | 111 | 2 | | | | |
| Greig | 15 | 2 | 43 | 1 | | | | |
| Underwood | 7 | 3 | 10 | 1 | | | | |
| AUSTRALIA | | | | | | | | |
| Lillee | 15 | 8 | 15 | 5 | 20 | 8 | 45 | 2 |
| Thomson | 10 | 3 | 21 | 0 | 18 | 8 | 38 | 5 |
| Walker | 17·3 | 5 | 48 | 5 | 24 | 9 | 47 | 2 |
| Mallett | 3 | 1 | 8 | 0 | 13·2 | 6 | 34 | 1 |

### FALL OF WICKETS

| | A | E | E |
|---|---|---|---|
| Wkt | 1st | 1st | 2nd |
| 1st | 80 | 9 | 7 |
| 2nd | 126 | 24 | 18 |
| 3rd | 135 | 46 | 20 |
| 4th | 161 | 46 | 52 |
| 5th | 186 | 54 | 90 |
| 6th | 265 | 75 | 100 |
| 7th | 286 | 78 | 122 |
| 8th | 332 | 87 | 151 |
| 9th | 343 | 97 | 167 |
| 10th | 359 | 101 | 173 |

Umpires: A.E. Fagg and H.D. Bird.

# ENGLAND v AUSTRALIA 1975 (2nd Test)

Played at Lord's, London, on 31 July, 1, 2, 4, 5 August.
Toss: England.   Result: MATCH DRAWN.
Debuts: England – D.S. Steele, R.A. Woolmer.

Australia needed to score 484 runs in 500 minutes to win. Edrich batted 538 minutes, faced 420 balls and hit 21 fours in the highest and last of his seven three-figure innings against Australia. Thomson bowled 28 no balls and six wides in the match. The first streaker (naked spectator) to intrude upon the field of play during a Test in England hurdled over both sets of stumps at 3.20 on the fourth afternoon.

## ENGLAND

| | | | | | |
|---|---|---|---|---|---|
| B. Wood | lbw b Lillee | 6 | c Marsh b Thomson | 52 |
| J.H. Edrich | lbw b Lillee | 9 | c Thomson b Mallett | 175 |
| D.S. Steele | b Thomson | 50 | c and b Walters | 45 |
| D.L. Amiss | lbw b Lillee | 0 | c G.S. Chappell b Lillee | 10 |
| G.A. Gooch | c Marsh b Lillee | 6 | b Mallett | 31 |
| A.W. Greig* | c I.M. Chappell b Walker | 96 | c Walters b I.M. Chappell | 41 |
| A.P.E. Knott† | lbw b Thomson | 69 | not out | 22 |
| R.A. Woolmer | c Turner b Mallett | 33 | b Mallett | 31 |
| J.A. Snow | c Walker b Mallett | 11 | | |
| D.L. Underwood | not out | 0 | | |
| P. Lever | lbw b Walker | 4 | | |
| Extras | (B 3, LB 1, W 4, NB 23) | 31 | (LB 18, W 2, NB 9) | 29 |
| **Total** | | **315** | (7 wickets declared) | **436** |

## AUSTRALIA

| | | | | | |
|---|---|---|---|---|---|
| R.B. McCosker | c and b Lever | 29 | lbw b Steele | 79 |
| A. Turner | lbw b Snow | 9 | c Gooch b Greig | 21 |
| I.M. Chappell* | c Knott b Snow | 2 | lbw b Greig | 86 |
| G.S. Chappell | lbw b Snow | 4 | not out | 73 |
| R. Edwards | lbw b Woolmer | 99 | not out | 52 |
| K.D. Walters | c Greig b Lever | 2 | | |
| R.W. Marsh† | c Amiss b Greig | 3 | | |
| M.H.N. Walker | b Snow | 5 | | |
| J.R. Thomson | b Underwood | 17 | | |
| D.K. Lillee | not out | 73 | | |
| A.A. Mallett | lbw b Steele | 14 | | |
| Extras | (LB 5, NB 6) | 11 | (B 4, NB 14) | 18 |
| **Total** | | **268** | (3 wickets) | **329** |

| AUSTRALIA | O | M | R | W | O | M | R | W |
|---|---|---|---|---|---|---|---|---|
| Lillee | 20 | 4 | 84 | 4 | 33 | 10 | 80 | 1 |
| Thomson | 24 | 7 | 92 | 2 | 29 | 8 | 73 | 1 |
| Walker | 21·4 | 7 | 52 | 2 | 37 | 8 | 95 | 0 |
| Mallett | 22 | 4 | 56 | 2 | 36·4 | 10 | 127 | 3 |
| I.M. Chappell | | | | | 10 | 2 | 26 | 1 |
| Walters | | | | | 2 | 0 | 6 | 1 |
| ENGLAND | | | | | | | | |
| Snow | 21 | 4 | 66 | 4 | 19 | 3 | 82 | 0 |
| Lever | 15 | 0 | 83 | 2 | 20 | 5 | 55 | 0 |
| Woolmer | 13 | 5 | 31 | 1 | 3 | 1 | 3 | 0 |
| Greig | 15 | 5 | 47 | 1 | 26 | 6 | 82 | 2 |
| Underwood | 13 | 5 | 29 | 1 | 31 | 14 | 64 | 0 |
| Steele | 0·4 | 0 | 1 | 1 | 9 | 4 | 19 | 1 |
| Wood | | | | | 1 | 0 | 6 | 0 |

### FALL OF WICKETS

| Wkt | E 1st | A 1st | E 2nd | A 2nd |
|---|---|---|---|---|
| 1st | 10 | 21 | 111 | 50 |
| 2nd | 29 | 29 | 215 | 169 |
| 3rd | 31 | 37 | 249 | 222 |
| 4th | 49 | 54 | 315 | – |
| 5th | 145 | 56 | 380 | – |
| 6th | 222 | 64 | 387 | – |
| 7th | 288 | 81 | 436 | – |
| 8th | 309 | 133 | – | – |
| 9th | 310 | 199 | – | – |
| 10th | 315 | 268 | – | – |

Umpires: T.W. Spencer and W.E. Alley.

# ENGLAND v AUSTRALIA 1975 (3rd Test)

Played at Headingley, Leeds, on 14, 15, 16, 18, 19 (*no play*) August.
Toss: England.   Result: MATCH DRAWN.
Debuts: England – P.H. Edmonds.

This match was abandoned as a draw after vandals, campaigning for the release from prison of a convicted criminal, sabotaged the rugby ground end of the pitch with knives and oil. Rain, which fell from noon to 4.00 p.m., would probably have produced the same result. The day should have started with Australia needing 225 runs to win with seven wickets to fall, and with McCosker five runs short of his first Test hundred. Edmonds took five wickets, including those of I.M. Chappell and Edwards with successive balls, in his first Test innings. In the second innings of his 57th match, Underwood became the fourth bowler after A.V. Bedser, F.S. Trueman, and J.B. Statham to take 200 wickets in official Tests for England.

## ENGLAND

| | | | | | |
|---|---|---|---|---|---|
| B. Wood | lbw b Gilmour | 9 | | lbw b Walker | 25 |
| J.H. Edrich | c Mallett b Thomson | 62 | | b Mallett | 35 |
| D.S. Steele | c Walters b Thomson | 73 | | c G.S. Chappell b Gilmour | 92 |
| J.H. Hampshire | lbw b Gilmour | 14 | (7) | c G.S. Chappell b Thomson | 0 |
| K.W.R. Fletcher | c Mallett b Lillee | 8 | (4) | c G.S. Chappell b Lillee | 14 |
| A.W. Greig* | run out | 51 | (5) | c and b Mallett | 49 |
| A.P.E. Knott† | lbw b Gilmour | 14 | (8) | c Thomson b Lillee | 31 |
| P.H. Edmonds | not out | 13 | (9) | c sub (A. Turner) b Gilmour | 8 |
| C.M. Old | b Gilmour | 5 | (6) | st Marsh b Mallett | 10 |
| J.A. Snow | c Walters b Gilmour | 0 | | c Marsh b Gilmour | 9 |
| D.L. Underwood | c G.S. Chappell b Gilmour | 0 | | not out | 0 |
| Extras | (B 4, LB 15, W 11, NB 9) | 39 | | (B 5, LB 2, W 2, NB 9) | 18 |
| **Total** | | **288** | | | **291** |

## AUSTRALIA

| | | | | | |
|---|---|---|---|---|---|
| R.B. McCosker | c Hampshire b Old | 0 | | not out | 95 |
| R.W. Marsh† | b Snow | 25 | | b Underwood | 12 |
| I.M. Chappell* | b Edmonds | 35 | | lbw b Old | 62 |
| G.S. Chappell | c Underwood b Edmonds | 13 | | c Steele b Edmonds | 12 |
| R. Edwards | lbw b Edmonds | 0 | | | |
| K.D. Walters | lbw b Edmonds | 19 | (5) | not out | 25 |
| G.J. Gilmour | c Greig b Underwood | 6 | | | |
| M.H.N. Walker | c Old b Edmonds | 0 | | | |
| J.R. Thomson | c Steele b Snow | 16 | | | |
| D.K. Lillee | b Snow | 11 | | | |
| A.A. Mallett | not out | 1 | | | |
| Extras | (LB 5, W 1, NB 3) | 9 | | (B 4, LB 8, NB 2) | 14 |
| **Total** | | **135** | | (3 wickets) | **220** |

| AUSTRALIA | O | M | R | W | O | M | R | W | | FALL OF WICKETS | | | |
|---|---|---|---|---|---|---|---|---|---|---|---|---|---|
| Lillee | 28 | 12 | 53 | 1 | 20 | 5 | 48 | 2 | | E | A | E | A |
| Thomson | 22 | 8 | 53 | 2 | 20 | 6 | 67 | 1 | *Wkt* | *1st* | *1st* | *2nd* | *2nd* |
| Gilmour | 31·2 | 10 | 85 | 6 | 20 | 5 | 72 | 3 | 1st | 25 | 8 | 55 | 55 |
| Walker | 18 | 4 | 54 | 0 | 15 | 4 | 36 | 1 | 2nd | 137 | 53 | 70 | 161 |
| I.M. Chappell | 2 | 0 | 4 | 0 | | | | | 3rd | 159 | 78 | 103 | 174 |
| Mallett | | | | | 19 | 4 | 50 | 3 | 4th | 189 | 78 | 197 | – |
| | | | | | | | | | 5th | 213 | 81 | 209 | – |
| ENGLAND | | | | | | | | | 6th | 268 | 96 | 210 | – |
| Snow | 18·5 | 7 | 22 | 3 | 15 | 6 | 21 | 0 | 7th | 269 | 104 | 272 | – |
| Old | 11 | 3 | 30 | 1 | 17 | 5 | 61 | 1 | 8th | 284 | 107 | 276 | – |
| Greig | 3 | 0 | 14 | 0 | 9 | 3 | 20 | 0 | 9th | 284 | 128 | 285 | – |
| Wood | 5 | 2 | 10 | 0 | | | | | 10th | 288 | 135 | 291 | – |
| Underwood | 19 | 12 | 22 | 1 | 15 | 4 | 40 | 1 | | | | | |
| Edmonds | 20 | 7 | 28 | 5 | 17 | 4 | 64 | 1 | | | | | |

Umpires: A.E. Fagg and D.J. Constant.

# ENGLAND v AUSTRALIA 1975 (4th Test)

Played at Kennington Oval, London, on 28, 29, 30 August, 1, 2, 3 September.
Toss: Australia.    Result: MATCH DRAWN.
Debuts: Nil.

Following on 341 runs behind on the first innings, England scored their highest second innings total against Australia. The innings lasted 886 minutes. Woolmer took 394 minutes to reach his hundred, the slowest century of the series (previously 362 minutes by M.C. Cowdrey in 1958–59 in *Test No. 466*).

## AUSTRALIA

| | | | | |
|---|---|---|---|---|
| R.B. McCosker | c Roope b Old | 127 | not out | 25 |
| A. Turner | c Steele b Old | 2 | c Woolmer b Greig | 8 |
| I.M. Chappell* | c Greig b Woolmer | 192 | | |
| G.S. Chappell | c Knott b Old | 0 | not out | 4 |
| R. Edwards | c Edrich b Snow | 44 | (3) c Old b Underwood | 2 |
| K.D. Walters | b Underwood | 65 | | |
| R.W. Marsh† | c and b Greig | 32 | | |
| M.H.N. Walker | c Steele b Greig | 13 | | |
| J.R. Thomson | c Old b Greig | 0 | | |
| D.K. Lillee | not out | 28 | | |
| A.A. Mallett | not out | 5 | | |
| Extras | (LB 5, W 2, NB 17) | 24 | (LB 1) | 1 |
| **Total** | (9 wickets declared) | **532** | (2 wickets) | **40** |

## ENGLAND

| | | | | |
|---|---|---|---|---|
| B. Wood | b Walker | 32 | lbw b Thomson | 22 |
| J.H. Edrich | lbw b Walker | 12 | b Lillee | 96 |
| D.S. Steele | b Lillee | 39 | c Marsh b Lillee | 66 |
| G.R.J. Roope | c Turner b Walker | 0 | b Lillee | 77 |
| R.A. Woolmer | c Mallett b Thomson | 5 | lbw b Walters | 149 |
| A.W. Greig* | c Marsh b Lillee | 17 | c Marsh b Lillee | 15 |
| A.P.E. Knott† | lbw b Walker | 9 | c Marsh b Walters | 64 |
| P.H. Edmonds | c Marsh b Thomson | 4 | (9) run out | 7 |
| C.M. Old | not out | 25 | (8) c I.M. Chappell b Walters | 0 |
| J.A. Snow | c G.S. Chappell b Thomson | 30 | c and b Walters | 0 |
| D.L. Underwood | c G.S. Chappell b Thomson | 0 | not out | 3 |
| Extras | (LB 3, W 3, NB 12) | 18 | (B 2, LB 15, W 5, NB 17) | 39 |
| **Total** | | **191** | | **538** |

| ENGLAND | O | M | R | W | O | M | R | W | FALL OF WICKETS | | | | |
|---|---|---|---|---|---|---|---|---|---|---|---|---|---|
| | | | | | | | | | | A | E | E | A |
| Old | 28 | 7 | 74 | 3 | 2 | 0 | 7 | 0 | *Wkt* | *1st* | *1st* | *2nd* | *2nd* |
| Snow | 27 | 4 | 74 | 1 | 2 | 1 | 4 | 0 | 1st | 7 | 45 | 77 | 22 |
| Woolmer | 18 | 3 | 38 | 1 | | | | | 2nd | 284 | 78 | 202 | 33 |
| Edmonds | 38 | 7 | 118 | 0 | 6·1 | 2 | 14 | 0 | 3rd | 286 | 83 | 209 | – |
| Underwood | 44 | 13 | 96 | 1 | 2 | 0 | 5 | 1 | 4th | 356 | 96 | 331 | – |
| Greig | 24 | 5 | 107 | 3 | 5 | 2 | 9 | 1 | 5th | 396 | 103 | 371 | – |
| Steele | 2 | 1 | 1 | 0 | | | | | 6th | 441 | 125 | 522 | – |
| | | | | | | | | | 7th | 477 | 131 | 522 | – |
| AUSTRALIA | | | | | | | | | 8th | 477 | 147 | 535 | – |
| Lillee | 19 | 7 | 44 | 2 | 52 | 18 | 91 | 4 | 9th | 501 | 190 | 533 | – |
| Thomson | 22·1 | 7 | 50 | 4 | 30 | 9 | 63 | 1 | 10th | – | 191 | 538 | – |
| Walker | 25 | 7 | 63 | 4 | 46 | 15 | 91 | 0 | | | | | |
| Mallett | 3 | 1 | 16 | 0 | 64 | 31 | 95 | 0 | | | | | |
| I.M. Chappell | | | | | 17 | 6 | 52 | 0 | | | | | |
| Walters | | | | | 10·5 | 3 | 34 | 4 | | | | | |
| G.S. Chappell | | | | | 12 | 2 | 53 | 0 | | | | | |
| Edwards | | | | | 2 | 0 | 20 | 0 | | | | | |

Umpires: T.W. Spencer and H.D. Bird.

# AUSTRALIA v WEST INDIES 1975–76 (1st Test)

Played at Woolloongabba, Brisbane, on 28, 29, 30 November, 2 December.
Toss: West Indies.   Result: AUSTRALIA won by eight wickets.
Debuts: West Indies – M.A. Holding.

G.S. Chappell became the first player to score hundreds in both innings of his first Test as captain. He was the first Australian to achieve this feat twice in Test cricket having done so against New Zealand in 1973–74 (*Test No. 736*). He also made the winning hit with a day and 38 minutes to spare. Lillee took his 100th wicket in his 22nd Test when he dismissed Richards. The partnership of 198 between Rowe and Kallicharran is the highest for the fourth wicket by West Indies in this series.

## WEST INDIES

| | | | | | |
|---|---|---|---|---|---|
| R.C. Fredericks | c Marsh b Gilmour | 46 | c Marsh b Gilmour | | 7 |
| C.G. Greenidge | lbw b Lillee | 0 | c McCosker b Gilmour | | 0 |
| L.G. Rowe | run out | 28 | (4) c I.M. Chappell b Jenner | | 107 |
| A.I. Kallicharran | c Turner b Lillee | 4 | (5) b Mallett | | 101 |
| I.V.A. Richards | c Gilmour b Lillee | 0 | (7) run out | | 12 |
| C.H. Lloyd* | c Marsh b Gilmour | 7 | c Redpath b Jenner | | 0 |
| D.L. Murray† | c Mallett b Gilmour | 66 | (8) c and b Mallett | | 55 |
| M.A. Holding | c G.S. Chappell b Gilmour | 34 | (3) c Turner b Lillee | | 19 |
| Inshan Ali | c Redpath b Thomson | 12 | b Lillee | | 24 |
| A.M.E. Roberts | c I.M. Chappell b Mallett | 3 | lbw b Lillee | | 3 |
| L.R. Gibbs | not out | 11 | not out | | 4 |
| Extras | (LB 1, NB 2) | 3 | (B 4, LB 15, W 5, NB 14) | | 38 |
| **Total** | | **214** | | | **370** |

## AUSTRALIA

| | | | | | |
|---|---|---|---|---|---|
| I.R. Redpath | run out | 39 | | | |
| A. Turner | b Roberts | 81 | b Gibbs | | 26 |
| I.M. Chappell | lbw b Gibbs | 41 | not out | | 74 |
| G.S. Chappell* | c Greenidge b Roberts | 123 | not out | | 109 |
| R.B. McCosker | c Kallicharran b Ali | 1 | (1) c Murray b Roberts | | 2 |
| R.W. Marsh† | c Murray b Gibbs | 48 | | | |
| G.J. Gilmour | c Lloyd b Gibbs | 13 | | | |
| T.J. Jenner | not out | 6 | | | |
| D.K. Lillee | b Roberts | 1 | | | |
| J.R. Thomson | lbw b Gibbs | 4 | | | |
| A.A. Mallett | c Fredericks b Gibbs | 0 | | | |
| Extras | (LB 5, NB 4) | 9 | (B 5, LB 2, NB 1) | | 8 |
| **Total** | | **366** | (2 wickets) | | **219** |

| AUSTRALIA | O | M | R | W | O | M | R | W | | FALL OF WICKETS | | | |
|---|---|---|---|---|---|---|---|---|---|---|---|---|---|
| Lillee | 11 | 0 | 84 | 3 | 16 | 3 | 72 | 3 | | WI | A | WI | A |
| Thomson | 10 | 0 | 69 | 1 | 18 | 3 | 89 | 0 | *Wkt* | *1st* | *1st* | *2nd* | *2nd* |
| Gilmour | 12 | 1 | 42 | 4 | 11 | 4 | 26 | 2 | 1st | 3 | 99 | 6 | 7 |
| Jenner | 4 | 1 | 15 | 0 | 20 | 2 | 75 | 2 | 2nd | 63 | 142 | 12 | 60 |
| Mallett | 0·5 | 0 | 1 | 1 | 21·4 | 6 | 70 | 2 | 3rd | 70 | 178 | 50 | – |
| | | | | | | | | | 4th | 70 | 195 | 248 | – |
| | | | | | | | | | 5th | 81 | 317 | 248 | – |
| WEST INDIES | | | | | | | | | 6th | 99 | 350 | 269 | – |
| Roberts | 25 | 2 | 85 | 3 | 14 | 2 | 47 | 1 | 7th | 171 | 354 | 275 | – |
| Holding | 20 | 4 | 81 | 0 | 10 | 0 | 46 | 0 | 8th | 199 | 361 | 346 | – |
| Gibbs | 38 | 7 | 102 | 5 | 20 | 8 | 48 | 1 | 9th | 199 | 366 | 348 | – |
| Ali | 17 | 1 | 67 | 1 | 10 | 0 | 57 | 0 | 10th | 214 | 366 | 370 | – |
| Lloyd | 6 | 1 | 22 | 0 | | | | | | | | | |
| Fredericks | | | | | 2 | 0 | 12 | 0 | | | | | |
| Kallicharran | | | | | 0·2 | 0 | 1 | 0 | | | | | |

Umpires: T.F. Brooks and R.C. Bailhache.

# AUSTRALIA v WEST INDIES 1975–76 (2nd Test)

Played at W.A.C.A. Ground, Perth, on 12, 13, 14, 16 December.
Toss: Australia.   Result: WEST INDIES won by an innings and 87 runs.
Debuts: Nil.

West Indies won their first Test match in Perth and, at 12.29 p.m. on the fourth day, gained their first victory by an innings in this series. I.M. Chappell became the fourth Australian after D.G. Bradman, R.N. Harvey and W.M. Lawry to score 5,000 runs in Test cricket. Playing in his 75th Test, Gibbs became the second bowler after F.S. Trueman to take 300 wickets. West Indies scored the highest total in a Perth Test and their second-highest in this series. Fredericks batted 212 minutes and scored 169 runs off 145 balls with a six and 27 fours. He reached 50 in 45 minutes off 33 balls and 100 in 116 minutes off 71 balls. Kallicharran retired when 46* (at 271 for 3) to spend a night in hospital after fracturing his nose attempting to hook a bouncer from Lillee. He resumed at 522 for 7. Lloyd took his score from 42* to 140* before lunch on the third day. Australia's total of 169 is the lowest in a Test at Perth. Roberts achieved the best analysis for West Indies against Australia.

## AUSTRALIA

| | | | | | |
|---|---|---:|---|---|---:|
| R.B. McCosker | lbw b Roberts | 0 | c Rowe b Roberts | | 13 |
| A. Turner | c Gibbs b Roberts | 23 | c Murray b Roberts | | 0 |
| I.M. Chappell | b Holding | 156 | c sub (C.G. Greenidge) b Roberts | | 20 |
| G.S. Chappell* | c Murray b Julien | 13 | c Rowe b Roberts | | 43 |
| I.R. Redpath | c Murray b Julien | 33 | lbw b Roberts | | 0 |
| R.W. Marsh† | c Julien b Boyce | 23 | c Murray b Roberts | | 39 |
| G.J. Gilmour | c Julien b Gibbs | 45 | c Fredericks b Roberts | | 3 |
| M.H.N. Walker | c Richards b Holding | 1 | c sub (C.G. Greenidge) b Julien | | 3 |
| D.K. Lillee | not out | 12 | c Lloyd b Julien | | 4 |
| J.R. Thomson | b Holding | 0 | b Julien | | 9 |
| A.A. Mallett | b Holding | 0 | not out | | 18 |
| Extras | (B 12, LB 5, NB 6) | 23 | (B 13, LB 2, NB 2) | | 17 |
| **Total** | | **329** | | | **169** |

## WEST INDIES

| | | |
|---|---|---:|
| R.C. Fredericks | c G.S. Chappell b Lillee | 169 |
| B.D. Julien | c Mallett b Gilmour | 25 |
| L.G. Rowe | c Marsh b Thomson | 19 |
| A.I. Kallicharran | c I.M. Chappell b Walker | 57 |
| I.V.A. Richards | c Gilmour b Thomson | 12 |
| C.H. Lloyd* | b Gilmour | 149 |
| D.L. Murray† | c Marsh b Lillee | 63 |
| M.A. Holding | c Marsh b Thomson | 0 |
| K.D. Boyce | not out | 49 |
| A.M.E. Roberts | b Walker | 0 |
| L.R. Gibbs | run out | 13 |
| Extras | (B 2, LB 16, NB 11) | 29 |
| **Total** | | **585** |

| WEST INDIES | O | M | R | W | O | M | R | W | | FALL OF WICKETS | | |
|---|---|---|---|---|---|---|---|---|---|---|---|---|
| Roberts | 13 | 1 | 65 | 2 | 14 | 3 | 54 | 7 | | A | WI | A |
| Boyce | 12 | 2 | 53 | 1 | 2 | 0 | 8 | 0 | *Wkt* | *1st* | *1st* | *2nd* |
| Holding | 18·7 | 1 | 88 | 4 | 10·6 | 1 | 53 | 0 | 1st | 0 | 91 | 0 |
| Julien | 12 | 0 | 51 | 2 | 10·1 | 1 | 32 | 3 | 2nd | 37 | 134 | 25 |
| Gibbs | 14 | 4 | 49 | 1 | 3 | 1 | 3 | 0 | 3rd | 70 | 258 | 45 |
| Fredericks | | | | | 1 | 0 | 2 | 0 | 4th | 149 | 297 | 45 |
| | | | | | | | | | 5th | 189 | 461 | 124 |
| AUSTRALIA | | | | | | | | | 6th | 277 | 461 | 128 |
| Lillee | 20 | 0 | 123 | 2 | | | | | 7th | 285 | 522 | 132 |
| Thomson | 17 | 0 | 128 | 3 | | | | | 8th | 329 | 548 | 142 |
| Gilmour | 14 | 0 | 103 | 2 | | | | | 9th | 329 | 548 | 146 |
| Walker | 17 | 1 | 99 | 2 | | | | | 10th | 329 | 585 | 169 |
| Mallett | 26 | 4 | 103 | 0 | | | | | | | | |
| I.M. Chappell | 1·4 | 1 | 0 | 0 | | | | | | | | |

Umpires: M.G. O'Connell and R.R. Ledwidge.

# AUSTRALIA v WEST INDIES 1975–76 (3rd Test)

Played at Melbourne Cricket Ground on 26, 27, 28, 30 December.
Toss: Australia.   Result: AUSTRALIA won by eight wickets.
Debuts: Australia – G.J. Cosier.

Australia won at 5.11 on the fourth evening. I.M. Chappell became the first Australian to hold 100 catches in Test cricket when he caught Rowe at first slip. Cosier was the seventh batsman to score a hundred in his first Test innings for Australia and the first to achieve the feat in this series. Fredericks batted with a runner in the second innings.

## WEST INDIES

| | | | | |
|---|---|---|---|---|
| R.C. Fredericks | c McCosker b Thomson | 59 | b G.S. Chappell | 26 |
| C.G. Greenidge | c Marsh b Thomson | 3 | c Marsh b Walker | 8 |
| L.G. Rowe | c I.M. Chappell b Thomson | 0 | c Marsh b Lillee | 8 |
| A.I. Kallicharran | c Marsh b Thomson | 20 | c Marsh b Lillee | 32 |
| I.V.A. Richards | b Lillee | 41 | c Marsh b Thomson | 36 |
| C.H. Lloyd* | c G.S. Chappell b Thomson | 2 | c Lillee b Mallett | 102 |
| D.L. Murray† | c Walker b Lillee | 24 | c Marsh b Lillee | 22 |
| B.D. Julien | c Mallett b Lillee | 18 | b Walker | 27 |
| V.A. Holder | b Walker | 24 | run out | 15 |
| A.M.E. Roberts | c Marsh b Lillee | 6 | c Mallett b I.M. Chappell | 5 |
| L.R. Gibbs | not out | 0 | not out | 5 |
| Extras | (LB 4, W 1, NB 22) | 27 | (B 8, LB 4, NB 14) | 26 |
| **Total** | | **224** | | **312** |

## AUSTRALIA

| | | | | |
|---|---|---|---|---|
| I.R. Redpath | b Roberts | 102 | (3) c sub (K.D. Boyce) b Julien | 9 |
| A. Turner | b Roberts | 21 | b Roberts | 7 |
| R.B. McCosker | c Murray b Julien | 4 | (1) not out | 22 |
| I.M. Chappell | c Kallicharran b Gibbs | 35 | not out | 13 |
| G.S. Chappell* | c Murray b Julien | 52 | | |
| G.J. Cosier | c Kallicharran b Roberts | 109 | | |
| R.W. Marsh† | c and b Gibbs | 56 | | |
| M.H.N. Walker | c Murray b Roberts | 1 | | |
| D.K. Lillee | c Richards b Holder | 25 | | |
| J.R. Lillee | c Richards b Holder | 25 | | |
| J.R. Thomson | lbw b Julien | 44 | | |
| A.A. Mallett | not out | 3 | | |
| Extras | (B 5, LB 6, NB 22) | 33 | (LB 1, NB 3) | 4 |
| **Total** | | **485** | (2 wickets) | **55** |

| AUSTRALIA | O | M | R | W | O | M | R | W | FALL OF WICKETS | | | | |
|---|---|---|---|---|---|---|---|---|---|---|---|---|---|
| Lillee | 14 | 2 | 56 | 4 | 15 | 1 | 70 | 3 | | WI | A | WI | A |
| Thomson | 11 | 1 | 62 | 5 | 9 | 0 | 51 | 1 | *Wkt* | *1st* | *1st* | *2nd* | *2nd* |
| Walker | 13 | 1 | 46 | 1 | 19 | 1 | 74 | 2 | 1st | 22 | 49 | 14 | 23 |
| Cosier | 4 | 0 | 15 | 0 | | | | | 2nd | 22 | 61 | 48 | 36 |
| Mallett | 5 | 1 | 18 | 0 | 14 | 0 | 61 | 1 | 3rd | 91 | 151 | 48 | – |
| G.S. Chappell | | | | | 7 | 1 | 23 | 1 | 4th | 103 | 188 | 99 | – |
| I.M. Chappell | | | | | 5·2 | 3 | 7 | 1 | 5th | 108 | 302 | 151 | – |
| | | | | | | | | | 6th | 167 | 390 | 229 | – |
| WEST INDIES | | | | | | | | | 7th | 172 | 392 | 278 | – |
| Roberts | 32 | 2 | 126 | 4 | 3 | 0 | 19 | 1 | 8th | 199 | 415 | 288 | – |
| Holder | 27 | 2 | 123 | 1 | | | | | 9th | 218 | 471 | 297 | – |
| Julien | 28·3 | 5 | 120 | 3 | 3 | 0 | 13 | 1 | 10th | 224 | 485 | 312 | – |
| Gibbs | 30 | 9 | 81 | 2 | | | | | | | | | |
| Richards | 1 | 0 | 2 | 0 | | | | | | | | | |
| Greenidge | | | | | 1 | 1 | 0 | 0 | | | | | |
| Rowe | | | | | 1 | 0 | 6 | 0 | | | | | |
| Kallicharran | | | | | 0·7 | 0 | 13 | 0 | | | | | |

Umpires: R.C. Bailhache and J.R. Collins.

# AUSTRALIA v WEST INDIES 1975–76 (4th Test)

Played at Sydney Cricket Ground on 3, 4, 5, 7 January.
Toss: Australia.   Result: AUSTRALIA won by seven wickets.
Debuts: Australia – G.N. Yallop.

At 4.45 on the fourth afternoon Australia took a 3–1 lead in the six-match series and retained the Frank Worrell Trophy. Three West Indies players retired hurt during the first innings: Julien (7*) fractured his right thumb at 15 for 0 and resumed batting one-handed at 259 for 6; Lloyd (0*) was struck on the jaw at 166 for 3 and resumed at 233 for 5; and Holding (2*) was hit in the face at 286 for 6 and resumed at 321 for 7. The umpires ruled that Holding, who had retired hurt off the last ball of the day, could not resume at the start of the next morning, but allowed Julien, who had also retired hurt, to resume instead. The Law allows an injured player to resume his innings 'only on the fall of a wicket'. Walker, playing his 24th Test, took his 100th wicket when he dismissed Roberts in the first innings. Murray, who scored his 1,000th run in this Test, became the first West Indies player to make 100 dismissals and complete the wicket-keeper's 'double' when he caught Turner.

## WEST INDIES

| | | | | |
|---|---|---|---|---|
| R.C. Fredericks | c I.M. Chappell b Thomson | 48 | c Turner b Gilmour | 24 |
| B.D. Julien | not out | 46 | (9) lbw b Walker | 8 |
| A.I. Kallicharran | c Redpath b Thomson | 9 | (2) c Walker b Thomson | 7 |
| L.G. Rowe | b Walker | 67 | c Marsh b Thomson | 7 |
| I.V.A. Richards | c I.M. Chappell b G.S. Chappell | 44 | (3) c Thomson b Gilmour | 2 |
| C.H. Lloyd* | c Turner b Walker | 51 | c Marsh b Thomson | 19 |
| D.L. Murray† | c Thomson b Walker | 32 | b Thomson | 50 |
| K.D. Boyce | c and b Mallett | 16 | c Redpath b Thomson | 0 |
| M.A. Holding | hit wkt b Thomson | 2 | (5) b Thomson | 9 |
| A.M.E. Roberts | c Marsh b Walker | 4 | b Walker | 2 |
| L.R. Gibbs | c Marsh b G.S. Chappell | 5 | not out | 0 |
| Extras | (B 5, LB 14, W 9, NB 3) | 31 | | |
| **Total** | | **355** | | **128** |

## AUSTRALIA

| | | | | |
|---|---|---|---|---|
| I.R. Redpath | c Murray b Holding | 25 | b Boyce | 28 |
| A. Turner | c Lloyd b Boyce | 53 | c Murray b Holding | 15 |
| G.N. Yallop | c Murray b Julien | 16 | not out | 16 |
| I.M. Chappell | c Murray b Holding | 4 | c sub (C.G. Greenidge) b Kallicharran | 9 |
| G.S. Chappell* | not out | 182 | not out | 6 |
| G.J. Cosier | b Holding | 28 | | |
| R.W. Marsh† | c Gibbs b Julien | 38 | | |
| G.J. Gilmour | run out | 20 | | |
| M.H.N. Walker | c Lloyd b Roberts | 8 | | |
| J.R. Thomson | c Richards b Roberts | 0 | | |
| A.A. Mallett | lbw b Roberts | 13 | | |
| Extras | (B 3, LB 8, W 2, NB 5) | 18 | (LB 4, W 4) | 8 |
| **Total** | | **405** | (3 wickets) | **82** |

| AUSTRALIA | O | M | R | W | O | M | R | W | | FALL OF WICKETS | | | |
|---|---|---|---|---|---|---|---|---|---|---|---|---|---|
| | | | | | | | | | | WI | A | WI | A |
| Thomson | 25 | 5 | 117 | 3 | 15 | 4 | 50 | 6 | *Wkt* | *1st* | *1st* | *2nd* | *2nd* |
| Gilmour | 13 | 2 | 54 | 0 | 12 | 4 | 40 | 2 | 1st | 44 | 70 | 23 | 45 |
| Walker | 21 | 8 | 70 | 4 | 9·3 | 3 | 31 | 2 | 2nd | 87 | 93 | 32 | 51 |
| Cosier | 3 | 1 | 13 | 0 | | | | | 3rd | 160 | 103 | 33 | 67 |
| Mallett | 13 | 4 | 50 | 1 | 1 | 0 | 2 | 0 | 4th | 213 | 103 | 47 | – |
| G.S. Chappell | 4·2 | 0 | 10 | 2 | 2 | 0 | 5 | 0 | 5th | 233 | 202 | 52 | – |
| I.M. Chappell | 1 | 0 | 10 | 0 | | | | | 6th | 259 | 319 | 95 | – |
| | | | | | | | | | 7th | 321 | 348 | 95 | – |
| WEST INDIES | | | | | | | | | 8th | 321 | 377 | 120 | – |
| Roberts | 20·6 | 3 | 94 | 3 | 4 | 1 | 12 | 0 | 9th | 346 | 377 | 126 | – |
| Holding | 21 | 2 | 79 | 3 | 7 | 0 | 33 | 1 | 10th | 355 | 405 | 128 | – |
| Boyce | 16 | 1 | 75 | 1 | 4 | 0 | 14 | 1 | | | | | |
| Gibbs | 18 | 3 | 52 | 0 | 1 | 0 | 4 | 0 | | | | | |
| Julien | 15 | 2 | 87 | 2 | | | | | | | | | |
| Kallicharran | | | | | 2 | 1 | 7 | 1 | | | | | |
| Richards | | | | | 0·1 | 0 | 4 | 0 | | | | | |

Umpires: T.F. Brooks and R.R. Ledwidge.

# AUSTRALIA v WEST INDIES 1975–76 (5th Test)

Played at Adelaide Oval on 23, 24, 26, 27, 28 January.
Toss: Australia.    Result: AUSTRALIA won by 190 runs.
Debuts: Nil.

Australia won the rubber at 11.43 on the fifth morning. Redpath, playing his 117th innings in 65 Tests, hit the only two sixes of his Test career. Gibbs (78 Tests) equalled the world record of F.S. Trueman (67 Tests) when he dismissed Mallett to take his 307th wicket.

## AUSTRALIA

| | | | | |
|---|---|---|---|---|
| I.R. Redpath | b Gibbs | 103 | c Lloyd b Gibbs | 65 |
| A. Turner | b Boyce | 26 | c Richards b Gibbs | 136 |
| G.N. Yallop | c Richards b Holder | 47 | lbw b Holder | 43 |
| I.M. Chappell | lbw b Holder | 42 | run out | 23 |
| G.S. Chappell* | c Richards b Holder | 4 | not out | 48 |
| G.J. Cosier | c Murray b Holder | 37 | | |
| R.W. Marsh† | b Roberts | 24 | (6) c Murray b Holder | 1 |
| G.J. Gilmour | c Holding b Gibbs | 95 | (7) c Fredericks b Holder | 0 |
| A.A. Mallett | c Fredericks b Holding | 5 | (8) c Murray b Gibbs | 11 |
| J.R. Thomson | c Murray b Holder | 6 | | |
| D.K. Lillee | not out | 16 | | |
| Extras | (B 1, LB 9, W 1, NB 2) | 13 | (LB 7, NB 11) | 18 |
| **Total** | | **418** | (7 wickets declared) | **345** |

## WEST INDIES

| | | | | |
|---|---|---|---|---|
| R.C. Fredericks | lbw b Gilmour | 0 | lbw b Lillee | 10 |
| I.V.A. Richards | c Yallop b Thomson | 30 | b Lillee | 101 |
| L.G. Rowe | run out | 7 | c G.S. Chappell b Thomson | 15 |
| A.I. Kallicharran | lbw b Thomson | 76 | c Redpath b Mallett | 67 |
| C.H. Lloyd* | lbw b Lillee | 6 | b Mallett | 5 |
| D.L. Murray† | c Mallett b Lillee | 18 | c Marsh b Thomson | 6 |
| K.D. Boyce | not out | 95 | c sub (M.H.N. Walker) b Mallett | 69 |
| M.A. Holding | c Mallett b Thomson | 8 | c I.M. Chappell b Gilmour | 10 |
| V.A. Holder | lbw b Thomson | 0 | c Marsh b Gilmour | 7 |
| A.M.E. Roberts | c Redpath b I.M. Chappell | 17 | c and b Gilmour | 0 |
| L.R. Gibbs | b Gilmour | 3 | not out | 0 |
| Extras | (LB 1, NB 13) | 14 | (B 1, LB 2, W 1, NB 5) | 9 |
| **Total** | | **274** | | **299** |

| WEST INDIES | O | M | R | W | O | M | R | W |
|---|---|---|---|---|---|---|---|---|
| Roberts | 12 | 1 | 54 | 1 | 4 | 0 | 24 | 0 |
| Holding | 22 | 3 | 126 | 1 | 14 | 0 | 55 | 0 |
| Boyce | 7 | 0 | 40 | 1 | 5 | 0 | 22 | 0 |
| Holder | 21 | 1 | 108 | 5 | 23 | 2 | 115 | 3 |
| Gibbs | 26 | 4 | 77 | 2 | 32·5 | 5 | 106 | 3 |
| Fredericks | | | | | 1 | 0 | 5 | 0 |
| AUSTRALIA | | | | | | | | |
| Gilmour | 8·2 | 1 | 37 | 2 | 10·4 | 1 | 44 | 3 |
| Thomson | 11 | 0 | 68 | 4 | 13 | 2 | 66 | 2 |
| Lillee | 10 | 0 | 68 | 2 | 14 | 0 | 64 | 2 |
| Cosier | 5 | 0 | 23 | 0 | | | | |
| Mallett | 5 | 0 | 37 | 0 | 20 | 3 | 91 | 3 |
| I.M. Chappell | 2 | 0 | 23 | 1 | 1 | 0 | 4 | 0 |
| G.S. Chappell | 1 | 0 | 4 | 0 | 5 | 0 | 21 | 0 |

### FALL OF WICKETS

| Wkt | A 1st | WI 1st | A 2nd | WI 2nd |
|---|---|---|---|---|
| 1st | 43 | 0 | 148 | 23 |
| 2nd | 171 | 21 | 253 | 55 |
| 3rd | 190 | 50 | 261 | 182 |
| 4th | 199 | 78 | 302 | 189 |
| 5th | 259 | 110 | 318 | 212 |
| 6th | 272 | 149 | 318 | 216 |
| 7th | 327 | 171 | 345 | 265 |
| 8th | 355 | 171 | – | 285 |
| 9th | 362 | 239 | – | 299 |
| 10th | 418 | 274 | – | 299 |

Umpires: T.F. Brooks and M.G. O'Connell.

# AUSTRALIA v WEST INDIES 1975–76 (6th Test)

Played at Melbourne Cricket Ground on 31 January, 1, 2, 4, 5 February.
Toss: Australia.   Result: AUSTRALIA won by 165 runs.
Debuts: Nil.

Australia won at 12.02 p.m. on the fifth day. West Indies lost five matches in a rubber for the first time. Gibbs became the leading wicket-taker in Test cricket when he had Redpath caught on the long-on boundary at 5.25 on the first evening and passed F.S. Trueman's record of 307 wickets. Gibbs ended his Test career with 309 wickets, average 29·09, in this his 79th match. Trueman bowled 15,178 balls; Gibbs took his 308th wicket with his 26,853rd ball. Marsh made 26 dismissals in the six-match rubber to equal the record set by J.H.B. Waite for South Africa in the five-match rubber against New Zealand in 1961–62.

## AUSTRALIA

| | | | | |
|---|---|---|---|---|
| I.R. Redpath | c Holding b Gibbs | 101 | c sub (C.G. Greenidge) b Holder | 70 |
| A. Turner | c Gibbs b Holder | 30 | lbw b Boyce | 21 |
| R.B. McCosker | b Boyce | 21 | not out | 109 |
| I.M. Chappell | b Holder | 1 | c Holder b Boyce | 31 |
| G.S. Chappell* | c Boyce b Fredericks | 68 | not out | 54 |
| G.N. Yallop | c Holding b Boyce | 57 | | |
| R.W. Marsh† | b Holding | 7 | | |
| G.J. Gilmour | lbw b Gibbs | 9 | | |
| A.A. Mallett | lbw b Boyce | 16 | | |
| J.R. Thomson | lbw b Holder | 0 | | |
| D.K. Lillee | not out | 19 | | |
| Extras | (B 4, LB 11, NB 7) | 22 | (B 5, LB 9, NB 1) | 15 |
| Total | | 351 | (3 wickets declared) | 300 |

## WEST INDIES

| | | | | |
|---|---|---|---|---|
| R.C. Fredericks | c Thomson b Gilmour | 22 | b Thomson | 6 |
| I.V.A. Richards | c Marsh b Lillee | 50 | c G.S. Chappell b Lillee | 98 |
| L. Baichan | c G.S. Chappell b Gilmour | 3 | b Thomson | 20 |
| A.I. Kallicharran | b Gilmour | 4 | c McCosker b Lillee | 44 |
| C.H. Lloyd* | c Redpath b Lillee | 37 | not out | 91 |
| L.G. Rowe | c Marsh b Gilmour | 6 | c Redpath b Mallett | 6 |
| D.L. Murray† | c Marsh b Lillee | 1 | c Marsh b Lillee | 5 |
| K.D. Boyce | lbw b Gilmour | 0 | c G.S. Chappell b Mallett | 11 |
| M.A. Holding | b Lillee | 9 | c Gilmour b Mallett | 4 |
| V.A. Holder | not out | 14 | b Thomson | 22 |
| L.R. Gibbs | c Marsh b Lillee | 2 | c Marsh b Thomson | 0 |
| Extras | (LB 5, W 1, NB 6) | 12 | (B 6, LB 10, NB 3) | 19 |
| Total | | 160 | | 326 |

| WEST INDIES | O | M | R | W | O | M | R | W | FALL OF WICKETS | | | | |
|---|---|---|---|---|---|---|---|---|---|---|---|---|---|
| Boyce | 17·2 | 1 | 75 | 3 | 19 | 2 | 74 | 2 | | A | WI | A | WI |
| Holding | 16 | 4 | 51 | 1 | 1 | 0 | 2 | 0 | *Wkt* | *1st* | *1st* | *2nd* | *2nd* |
| Holder | 20 | 2 | 86 | 3 | 18 | 0 | 81 | 1 | 1st | 44 | 44 | 53 | 6 |
| Lloyd | 7 | 2 | 20 | 0 | 4 | 1 | 14 | 0 | 2nd | 92 | 49 | 132 | 53 |
| Fredericks | 6 | 0 | 29 | 1 | 3 | 1 | 14 | 0 | 3rd | 96 | 53 | 190 | 170 |
| Gibbs | 24 | 4 | 68 | 2 | 26 | 3 | 62 | 0 | 4th | 220 | 99 | – | 175 |
| Richards | | | | | 7 | 0 | 38 | 0 | 5th | 250 | 110 | – | 186 |
| | | | | | | | | | 6th | 261 | 113 | – | 199 |
| AUSTRALIA | | | | | | | | | 7th | 277 | 118 | – | 226 |
| Thomson | 9 | 0 | 51 | 0 | 12·5 | 0 | 80 | 4 | 8th | 317 | 140 | – | 238 |
| Lillee | 11·3 | 0 | 63 | 5 | 18 | 1 | 112 | 3 | 9th | 323 | 151 | – | 326 |
| Gilmour | 10 | 3 | 34 | 5 | 7 | 1 | 26 | 0 | 10th | 351 | 160 | – | 326 |
| G.S. Chappell | | | | | 2 | 0 | 6 | 0 | | | | | |
| I.M. Chappell | | | | | 2 | 0 | 10 | 0 | | | | | |
| Mallett | | | | | 13 | 1 | 73 | 3 | | | | | |

Umpires: T.F. Brooks and M.G. O'Connell.

# NEW ZEALAND v INDIA 1975–76 (1st Test)

Played at Eden Park, Auckland, on 24, 25, 26, 28 January.
Toss: New Zealand.   Result: INDIA won by eight wickets.
Debuts: India – S. Amarnath, S.M.H. Kirmani, D.B. Vengsarkar.

India's second victory in successive Tests at Auckland was completed at 2.08 on the fourth afternoon, with more than a day and a half to spare. Surinder Amarnath became the seventh Indian to score a hundred in his first Test innings and the first to achieve the feat for India in New Zealand. He was also the first to emulate his father by scoring a hundred in his first Test, Lala Amarnath having scored 118 in the second innings of India's first home Test in 1933–34 (*Test No. 230*). His partnership of 203 with Gavaskar is the highest for the second wicket by either side in this series. Prasanna's analysis of 8 for 76 is the best in any Auckland Test. His country's total of 414, his match figures of 11 for 140 and his second innings analysis are all Indian records for Tests in New Zealand. Gavaskar led India in B.S. Bedi's absence (leg injury).

## NEW ZEALAND

| | | | | | |
|---|---|---|---|---|---|
| J.F.M. Morrison | c and b Chandrasekhar | 46 | c Viswanath b Prasanna | | 23 |
| G.M. Turner* | c Gavaskar b Chandrasekhar | 23 | c Madan Lal b Prasanna | | 13 |
| B.E. Congdon | c Madan Lal b Prasanna | 54 | c Gavaskar b Prasanna | | 54 |
| J.M. Parker | b Chandrasekhar | 17 | c Vengsarkar b Prasanna | | 70 |
| B.F. Hastings | lbw b Prasanna | 8 | b Prasanna | | 1 |
| M.G. Burgess | c Prasanna b Venkataraghavan | 31 | lbw b Chandrasekhar | | 6 |
| K.J. Wadsworth† | c Gavaskar b Prasanna | 41 | b Chandrasekhar | | 19 |
| D.R. Hadlee | b Chandrasekhar | 24 | c Vengsarkar b Prasanna | | 0 |
| D.R. O'Sullivan | c S. Amarnath b Chandrasekhar | 0 | c S. Amarnath b Prasanna | | 1 |
| H.J. Howarth | c and b Chandrasekhar | 0 | (11) not out | | 1 |
| R.O. Collinge | not out | 3 | (10) c S. Amarnath b Prasanna | | 13 |
| Extras | (B 5, LB 12, NB 2) | 19 | (B 4, LB 8, NB 2) | | 14 |
| **Total** | | **266** | | | **215** |

## INDIA

| | | | | |
|---|---|---|---|---|
| S.M. Gavaskar* | c Turner b Howarth | 116 | not out | 35 |
| D.B. Vengsarkar | lbw b Collinge | 7 | c Turner b Howarth | 6 |
| S. Amarnath | c sub (G.N. Edwards) b Hadlee | 124 | lbw b Howarth | 9 |
| G.R. Viswanath | c Wadsworth b Hadlee | 0 | not out | 11 |
| B.P. Patel | c Morrison b Congdon | 10 | | |
| S. Venkataraghavan | c Congdon b Howarth | 1 | | |
| M. Amarnath | b Congdon | 64 | | |
| S. Madan Lal | c Turner b Congdon | 27 | | |
| S.M.H. Kirmani† | b Congdon | 14 | | |
| E.A.S. Prasanna | not out | 25 | | |
| B.S. Chandrasekhar | b Congdon | 0 | | |
| Extras | (B 13, LB 9, NB 4) | 26 | (B 7, NB 3) | 10 |
| **Total** | | **414** | (2 wickets) | **71** |

| INDIA | O | M | R | W | O | M | R | W | | FALL OF WICKETS | | | |
|---|---|---|---|---|---|---|---|---|---|---|---|---|---|
| | | | | | | | | | | NZ | I | NZ | I |
| Madan Lal | 5 | 0 | 14 | 0 | 4 | 4 | 0 | 0 | | 1st | 1st | 2nd | 2nd |
| M. Amarnath | 4 | 1 | 16 | 0 | 2 | 0 | 8 | 0 | Wkt | | | | |
| Chandrasekhar | 30 | 6 | 94 | 6 | 22·2 | 2 | 85 | 2 | 1st | 38 | 16 | 32 | 38 |
| Venkataraghavan | 24 | 4 | 59 | 1 | 19 | 8 | 32 | 0 | 2nd | 110 | 220 | 39 | 56 |
| Prasanna | 24 | 5 | 64 | 3 | 23 | 5 | 76 | 8 | 3rd | 144 | 220 | 161 | – |
| | | | | | | | | | 4th | 145 | 270 | 169 | – |
| NEW ZEALAND | | | | | | | | | 5th | 155 | 270 | 180 | – |
| Collinge | 19 | 3 | 61 | 1 | 2 | 0 | 14 | 0 | 6th | 211 | 275 | 180 | – |
| Hadlee | 18 | 3 | 71 | 2 | 3 | 0 | 15 | 0 | 7th | 263 | 368 | 180 | – |
| Congdon | 26·7 | 3 | 65 | 5 | | | | | 8th | 263 | 369 | 182 | – |
| Howarth | 29 | 6 | 97 | 2 | 5·2 | 3 | 15 | 2 | 9th | 263 | 414 | 214 | – |
| O'Sullivan | 29 | 4 | 94 | 0 | 4 | 1 | 17 | 0 | 10th | 266 | 414 | 215 | – |

Umpires: D.E.A. Copps and R.L. Monteith.

# NEW ZEALAND v INDIA 1975–76 (2nd Test)

Played at Lancaster Park, Christchurch, on 5, 6, 7 *(no play)*, 8, 9, 10 February.
Toss: India.   Result: MATCH DRAWN.
Debuts: New Zealand – A.D.G. Roberts.

When the third day (Saturday) was lost to rain, the scheduled rest day (Monday) became a playing day under the tour regulations. Kirmani equalled the Test match wicket-keeping record of six dismissals in an innings, shared by A.T.W. Grout, D.T. Lindsay and J.T. Murray. During his third hundred in four Test innings at Christchurch (he scored 98 in the other one), Turner became the first to score 1,000 runs in a season of first-class cricket in New Zealand.

## INDIA

| | | | | |
|---|---|---|---|---|
| S.M. Gavaskar | c Burgess b Collinge | 22 | c Howarth b D.R. Hadlee | 71 |
| D.B. Vengsarkar | c Wadsworth b Collinge | 16 | c Wadsworth b R.J. Hadlee | 30 |
| S. Amarnath | b Collinge | 11 | c Wadsworth b Collinge | 21 |
| G.R. Viswanath | c Turner b D.R. Hadlee | 83 | c Wadsworth b Roberts | 79 |
| B.P. Patel | c Burgess b Collinge | 8 | c Morrison b Parker | 7 |
| M. Amarnath | lbw b Congdon | 45 | c Wadsworth b Howarth | 30 |
| S. Madan Lal | c Wadsworth b D.R. Hadlee | 5 | not out | 4 |
| S.M.H. Kirmani† | lbw b Collinge | 27 | not out | 1 |
| E.A.S. Prasanna | c Roberts b D.R. Hadlee | 1 | | |
| B.S. Bedi* | c Howarth b Collinge | 30 | | |
| B.S. Chandrasekhar | not out | 2 | | |
| Extras | (B 6, LB 4, NB 10) | 20 | (B 2, LB 3, W 1, NB 6) | 12 |
| **Total** | | **270** | (6 wickets) | **255** |

## NEW ZEALAND

| | | |
|---|---|---|
| J.F.M. Morrison | lbw b Madan Lal | 31 |
| G.M. Turner* | c Kirmani b M. Amarnath | 117 |
| B.E. Congdon | st Kirmani b Bedi | 58 |
| J.M. Parker | c Bedi b M. Amarnath | 44 |
| M.G. Burgess | c and b Madan Lal | 31 |
| A.D.G. Roberts | lbw b Madan Lal | 17 |
| K.J. Wadsworth† | c Kirmani b Madan Lal | 29 |
| D.R. Hadlee | c Kirmani b Madan Lal | 10 |
| R.J. Hadlee | c Kirmani b M. Amarnath | 33 |
| R.O. Collinge | c Kirmani b M. Amarnath | 0 |
| H.J. Howarth | not out | 8 |
| Extras | (B 8, LB 14, LB 3) | 25 |
| **Total** | | **403** |

| NEW ZEALAND | O | M | R | W | O | M | R | W | FALL OF WICKETS | | | |
|---|---|---|---|---|---|---|---|---|---|---|---|---|
| Collinge | 16·6 | 0 | 63 | 6 | 14 | 1 | 36 | 1 | | I | NZ | I |
| R.J. Hadlee | 12 | 1 | 75 | 0 | 14 | 2 | 64 | 1 | *Wkt* | *1st* | *1st* | *2nd* |
| D.R. Hadlee | 16 | 0 | 76 | 3 | 12 | 1 | 52 | 1 | 1st | 32 | 56 | 60 |
| Congdon | 16 | 3 | 36 | 1 | 5 | 2 | 5 | 0 | 2nd | 41 | 170 | 97 |
| Howarth | | | | | 22 | 7 | 48 | 1 | 3rd | 52 | 254 | 138 |
| Parker | | | | | 5 | 2 | 24 | 1 | 4th | 98 | 260 | 175 |
| Roberts | | | | | 5 | 1 | 12 | 1 | 5th | 196 | 293 | 250 |
| Burgess | | | | | 2 | 1 | 2 | 0 | 6th | 204 | 325 | 250 |
| | | | | | | | | | 7th | 204 | 347 | – |
| INDIA | | | | | | | | | 8th | 206 | 360 | – |
| Madan Lal | 43 | 9 | 134 | 5 | | | | | 9th | 258 | 361 | – |
| M. Amarnath | 25·1 | 5 | 63 | 4 | | | | | 10th | 270 | 403 | – |
| Chandrasekhar | 15 | 2 | 60 | 0 | | | | | | | | |
| Bedi | 33 | 7 | 59 | 1 | | | | | | | | |
| Prasanna | 16 | 1 | 62 | 0 | | | | | | | | |

Umpires: D.E.A. Copps and W.R.C. Gardiner.

## NEW ZEALAND v INDIA 1975–76 (3rd Test)

Played at Basin Reserve, Wellington, on 13, 14, 15, 17 February.
Toss: India.   Result: NEW ZEALAND won by an innings and 33 runs.
Debuts: Nil.

New Zealand won this six-day match at 2.31 on the fourth afternoon to gain their ninth Test victory and their first by an innings. The partnership of 116 between Patel and Kirmani is India's highest for the seventh wicket in this series. On the third day, Bedi was confined to bed with a chill, Mohinder Amarnath (migraine) retired after starting his 19th over, and Gavaskar was taken to hospital for surgery after being hit on the right cheekbone. In the second innings, India were dismissed for the lowest total by either country in this series. Richard John Hadlee returned the best innings (7 for 23) and match (11 for 58) analyses by a New Zealand bowler in Test cricket. They are also the records for any Test at Wellington.

### INDIA

| | | | | |
|---|---|---|---|---|
| S.M. Gavaskar | c Wadsworth b R.J. Hadlee | 22 | absent hurt | – |
| D.B. Vengsarkar | c Wadsworth b R.J. Hadlee | 20 | c Turner b Collinge | 4 |
| S. Amarnath | c Roberts b R.J. Hadlee | 2 | (1) c Burgess b R.J. Hadlee | 27 |
| G.R. Viswanath | c Turner b D.R. Hadlee | 4 | (3) c Congdon b R.J. Hadlee | 20 |
| B.P. Patel | c Congdon b Cairns | 81 | (4) c Wadsworth b R.J. Hadlee | 3 |
| M. Amarnath | lbw b Collinge | 26 | (5) c Roberts b D.R. Hadlee | 13 |
| S. Madan Lal | b D.R. Hadlee | 3 | not out | 2 |
| S.M.H. Kirmani† | c Wadsworth b R.J. Hadlee | 49 | (6) c Burgess b R.J. Hadlee | 1 |
| E.A.S. Prasanna | not out | 0 | (8) b R.J. Hadlee | 0 |
| B.S. Bedi* | run out | 2 | (9) b R.J. Hadlee | 2 |
| B.S. Chandrasekhar | b Cairns | 0 | (10) b R.J. Hadlee | 0 |
| Extras | (LB 8, NB 3) | 11 | (B 5, LB 2, NB 2) | 9 |
| **Total** | | **220** | | **81** |

### NEW ZEALAND

| | | |
|---|---|---|
| G.M. Turner* | st Kirmani b Bedi | 64 |
| J.F.M. Morrison | c Kirmani b Madan Lal | 12 |
| B.E. Congdon | c Viswanath b Chandrasekhar | 52 |
| J.M. Parker | c Gavaskar b Bedi | 5 |
| M.G. Burgess | lbw b Madan Lal | 95 |
| A.D.G. Roberts | c Kirmani b Chandrasekhar | 0 |
| K.J. Wadsworth† | c Gavaskar b Bedi | 10 |
| B.L. Cairns | c sub (E.D. Solkar) b M. Amarnath | 47 |
| R.J. Hadlee | c Prasanna b Madan Lal | 12 |
| D.R. Hadlee | c Kirmani b Chandrasekhar | 13 |
| R.O. Collinge | not out | 5 |
| Extras | (LB 15, NB 4) | 19 |
| **Total** | | **334** |

| NEW ZEALAND | O | M | R | W | O | M | R | W |
|---|---|---|---|---|---|---|---|---|
| Collinge | 12 | 1 | 33 | 1 | 5 | 0 | 21 | 1 |
| Cairns | 20·7 | 2 | 57 | 2 | 4 | 1 | 9 | 0 |
| D.R. Hadlee | 18 | 1 | 51 | 2 | 9 | 2 | 19 | 1 |
| R.J. Hadlee | 14 | 1 | 35 | 4 | 8·3 | 0 | 23 | 7 |
| Congdon | 9 | 1 | 33 | 0 | | | | |

| INDIA | O | M | R | W |
|---|---|---|---|---|
| M. Amarnath | 18·2 | 2 | 60 | 1 |
| Madan Lal | 38 | 4 | 116 | 3 |
| Bedi | 27 | 6 | 63 | 3 |
| Chandrasekhar | 22·5 | 2 | 55 | 3 |
| Prasanna | 8 | 2 | 21 | 0 |

### FALL OF WICKETS

| Wkt | I 1st | NZ 1st | I 2nd |
|---|---|---|---|
| 1st | 40 | 55 | 10 |
| 2nd | 46 | 103 | 46 |
| 3rd | 47 | 117 | 62 |
| 4th | 50 | 155 | 75 |
| 5th | 92 | 155 | 77 |
| 6th | 101 | 180 | 77 |
| 7th | 217 | 270 | 77 |
| 8th | 218 | 301 | 79 |
| 9th | 220 | 324 | 81 |
| 10th | 220 | 334 | – |

Umpires: W.R.C. Gardiner and R.L. Monteith.

# WEST INDIES v INDIA 1975–76 (1st Test)

Played at Kensington Oval, Bridgetown, Barbados, on 10, 11, 13 March.
Toss: India.   Result. WEST INDIES won by an innings and 97 runs.
Debuts: Nil.

West Indies won with two days and 12 minutes to spare to end a run of six drawn Tests at Bridgetown. They gained their largest margin of victory against India in a home Test. The partnership of 220 between Richards and Kallicharran is the highest for the third wicket by either side in this series. Lloyd, playing in his 50th Test match, scored his tenth hundred for West Indies.

## INDIA

| | | | | | |
|---|---|---|---|---|---|
| S.M. Gavaskar | lbw b Roberts | 37 | c Jumadeen b Roberts | | 1 |
| P. Sharma | c Fredericks b Holding | 6 | c Murray b Holding | | 1 |
| A.D. Gaekwad | c Murray b Julien | 16 | c Murray b Roberts | | 14 |
| G.R. Viswanath | c Rowe b Holford | 11 | lbw b Roberts | | 62 |
| S. Amarnath | c Richards b Holford | 0 | b Jumadeen | | 8 |
| M. Amarnath | b Holding | 26 | c Rowe b Jumadeen | | 25 |
| S. Madan Lal | b Holford | 45 | not out | | 55 |
| S.M.H. Kirmani† | b Roberts | 8 | lbw b Holford | | 15 |
| E.A.S. Prasanna | c Richards b Holford | 3 | absent hurt | | – |
| B.S. Bedi* | c Julien b Holford | 0 | (9) c Murray b Jumadeen | | 10 |
| B.S. Chandrasekhar | not out | 1 | (10) b Holding | | 0 |
| Extras | (B 2, LB 7, NB 15) | 24 | (B 7, LB 3, NB 13) | | 23 |
| **Total** | | **177** | | | **214** |

## WEST INDIES

| | | |
|---|---|---|
| R.C. Fredericks | c M. Amarnath b Chandrasekhar | 54 |
| L.G. Rowe | lbw b Chandrasekhar | 30 |
| I.V.A. Richards | c Kirmani b M. Amarnath | 142 |
| A.I. Kallicharran | c Viswanath b M. Amarnath | 93 |
| C.H. Lloyd* | st Kirmani b Bedi | 102 |
| D.L. Murray† | b Bedi | 27 |
| D.A.J. Holford | c Kirmani b Chandrasekhar | 9 |
| B.D. Julien | not out | 13 |
| M.A. Holding | lbw b Chandrasekhar | 0 |
| A.M.E. Roberts | c S. Amarnath b Bedi | 0 |
| R.R. Jumadeen | did not bat | |
| Extras | (B 7, LB 7, NB 4) | 18 |
| **Total** | (9 wickets declared) | **488** |

| WEST INDIES | O | M | R | W | O | M | R | W | | FALL OF WICKETS | | |
|---|---|---|---|---|---|---|---|---|---|---|---|---|
| Roberts | 11 | 2 | 48 | 2 | 14 | 4 | 51 | 3 | | I | WI | I |
| Holding | 15 | 10 | 24 | 2 | 13 | 6 | 22 | 2 | *Wkt* | *1st* | *1st* | *2nd* |
| Julien | 15 | 5 | 46 | 1 | 4 | 2 | 8 | 0 | 1st | 51 | 58 | 4 |
| Holford | 8·1 | 1 | 23 | 5 | 17 | 1 | 52 | 1 | 2nd | 57 | 108 | 9 |
| Jumadeen | 5 | 1 | 12 | 0 | 24 | 7 | 57 | 3 | 3rd | 74 | 328 | 40 |
| Fredericks | | | | | 1 | 0 | 1 | 0 | 4th | 74 | 337 | 66 |
| | | | | | | | | | 5th | 103 | 417 | 117 |
| INDIA | | | | | | | | | 6th | 133 | 446 | 146 |
| Madan Lal | 16 | 1 | 61 | 0 | | | | | 7th | 162 | 482 | 182 |
| M. Amarnath | 12 | 2 | 53 | 2 | | | | | 8th | 171 | 483 | 213 |
| Bedi | 43·5 | 8 | 113 | 3 | | | | | 9th | 176 | 488 | 214 |
| Chandrasekhar | 39 | 5 | 163 | 4 | | | | | 10th | 177 | – | – |
| Prasanna | 24 | 2 | 66 | 0 | | | | | | | | |
| Gaekwad | 4 | 0 | 14 | 0 | | | | | | | | |

Umpires: D. Sang Hue and S.E. Parris.

# WEST INDIES v INDIA 1975–76 (2nd Test)

Played at Queen's Park Oval, Port-of-Spain, Trinidad, on 24 *(no play)*, 25, 27, 28, 29 March.
Toss: India.   Result: MATCH DRAWN.
Debuts: Nil.

The partnership of 204 between Gavaskar and Patel is India's highest for the fifth wicket against all countries. Gavaskar scored his third hundred in successive Test innings at Queen's Park Oval. Richards, who had strained a thigh muscle when fielding, retired hurt at 34 for 2 after facing five balls, and resumed at 112 for 4.

## WEST INDIES

| | | | | | |
|---|---|---|---|---|---|
| R.C. Fredericks | b Madan Lal | 0 | lbw b Venkataraghavan | | 8 |
| L.G. Rowe | b M. Amarnath | 4 | b Venkataraghavan | | 47 |
| I.V.A. Richards | b Bedi | 130 | (4) run out | | 20 |
| A.I. Kallicharran | c Madan Lal b Bedi | 17 | (5) c Venkataraghavan | | |
| | | | b Chandrasekhar | | 12 |
| C.H. Lloyd* | b Chandrasekhar | 7 | (6) c M. Amarnath b Bedi | | 70 |
| D.L. Murray† | c Kirmani b Bedi | 46 | (7) c Vengsarkar b Bedi | | 9 |
| B.D. Julien | run out | 28 | (8) not out | | 12 |
| D.A.J. Holford | b Bedi | 4 | (9) b Bedi | | 0 |
| M.A. Holding | c Viswanath b Bedi | 1 | (3) b Chandrasekhar | | 3 |
| A.M.E. Roberts | c Vengsarkar b Chandrasekhar | 1 | not out | | 4 |
| R.R. Jumadeen | not out | 1 | | | |
| Extras | (LB 1, NB 1) | 2 | (B 14, LB 15, NB 1) | | 30 |
| **Total** | | **241** | (8 wickets) | | **215** |

## INDIA

| | | |
|---|---|---|
| S.M. Gavaskar | c Murray b Holding | 156 |
| D.B. Vengsarkar | c Murray b Roberts | 0 |
| M. Amarnath | c Murray b Jumadeen | 19 |
| G.R. Viswanath | c Murray b Holding | 21 |
| S. Amarnath | c Rowe b Jumadeen | 21 |
| B.P. Patel | not out | 115 |
| S. Madan Lal | not out | 33 |
| S. Venkataraghavan | ) | |
| S.M.H. Kirmani† | ) did not bat | |
| B.S. Bedi* | ) | |
| B.S. Chandrasekhar | ) | |
| Extras | (B 11, LB 10, LB 16) | 37 |
| **Total** | (5 wickets declared) | **402** |

| INDIA | O | M | R | W | O | M | R | W | FALL OF WICKETS | | | |
|---|---|---|---|---|---|---|---|---|---|---|---|---|
| | | | | | | | | | | WI | I | WI |
| Madan Lal | 9 | 3 | 16 | 1 | 4 | 2 | 2 | 0 | *Wkt* | *1st* | *1st* | *2nd* |
| M. Amarnath | 5 | 1 | 13 | 1 | 3 | 0 | 11 | 0 | 1st | 0 | 1 | 23 |
| Chandrasekhar | 21 | 2 | 64 | 2 | 40 | 16 | 68 | 2 | 2nd | 4 | 35 | 30 |
| Bedi | 34 | 11 | 82 | 5 | 36 | 18 | 44 | 3 | 3rd | 39 | 77 | 52 |
| Venkataraghavan | 28 | 5 | 64 | 0 | 41 | 19 | 60 | 2 | 4th | 52 | 126 | 112 |
| | | | | | | | | | 5th | 174 | 330 | 137 |
| WEST INDIES | | | | | | | | | 6th | 212 | – | 185 |
| Roberts | 28 | 6 | 77 | 1 | | | | | 7th | 236 | – | 188 |
| Holding | 27 | 8 | 68 | 2 | | | | | 8th | 238 | – | 194 |
| Julien | 30 | 7 | 63 | 0 | | | | | 9th | 239 | – | – |
| Jumadeen | 42 | 12 | 79 | 2 | | | | | 10th | 241 | – | – |
| Richards | 6 | 0 | 17 | 0 | | | | | | | | |
| Holford | 20 | 5 | 51 | 0 | | | | | | | | |
| Lloyd | 3 | 0 | 10 | 0 | | | | | | | | |

Umpires: D. Sang Hue and R. Gosein.

# WEST INDIES v INDIA 1975–76 (3rd Test)

Played at Queen's Park Oval, Port-of-Spain, Trinidad, on 7, 8, 10, 11, 12 April.
Toss: West Indies.   Result: INDIA won by six wickets.
Debuts: West Indies – Imtiaz Ali, A.L. Padmore.

This match, scheduled for Georgetown, had to be moved to Trinidad because of incessant rain in Guyana. India achieved one of Test cricket's most remarkable victories; set to score 403 runs to win in a minimum of 595 minutes, India reached their target with seven of the mandatory last 20 overs to spare. Their total of 406 for 4 remains the highest in the fourth innings to win a Test match. There has been only one other instance of a side scoring over 400 in the fourth innings to win a Test: Australia scored 404 for 3 at Leeds in 1938 (*Test No. 302*). The partnership of 159 between Amarnath and Viswanath is India's highest for the third wicket against West Indies.

## WEST INDIES

| | | | | |
|---|---|--:|---|--:|
| R.C. Fredericks | c Amarnath b Chandrasekhar | 27 | c Solkar b Chandrasekhar | 25 |
| L.G. Rowe | c Viswanath b Chandrasekhar | 18 | c Kirmani b Venkataraghavan | 27 |
| I.V.A. Richards | c Chandrasekhar b Bedi | 177 | c Solkar b Venkataraghavan | 23 |
| A.I. Kallicharran | b Chandrasekhar | 0 | not out | 103 |
| C.H. Lloyd* | c Gaekwad b Chandrasekhar | 68 | c Viswanath b Chandrasekhar | 36 |
| D.L. Murray† | b Chandrasekhar | 11 | c Solkar b Bedi | 25 |
| B.D. Julien | c Viswanath b Bedi | 47 | c Kirmani b Venkataraghavan | 6 |
| M.A. Holding | lbw b Bedi | 1 | not out | 17 |
| Imtiaz Ali | not out | 1 | | |
| A.L. Padmore | c Gavaskar b Bedi | 0 | | |
| R.R. Jumadeen | lbw b Chandrasekhar | 0 | | |
| Extras | (LB 7, NB 2) | 9 | (B 1, LB 7, NB 1) | 9 |
| **Total** | | **359** | (6 wickets declared) | **271** |

## INDIA

| | | | | |
|---|---|--:|---|--:|
| S.M. Gavaskar | lbw b Holding | 26 | c Murray b Jumadeen | 102 |
| A.D. Gaekwad | c Murray b Julien | 6 | c Kallicharran b Jumadeen | 28 |
| M. Amarnath | st Murray b Padmore | 25 | run out | 85 |
| G.R. Viswanath | b Ali | 41 | run out | 112 |
| E.D. Solkar | b Holding | 13 | | |
| B.P. Patel | c Fredericks b Holding | 29 | (5) not out | 49 |
| S. Madan Lal | c Richards b Holding | 42 | (6) not out | 1 |
| S. Venkataraghavan | b Ali | 13 | | |
| S.M.H. Kirmani† | lbw b Holding | 12 | | |
| B.S. Bedi* | b Holding | 0 | | |
| B.S. Chandrasekhar | not out | 0 | | |
| Extras | (B 11, LB 6, W 4) | 21 | (B 8, LB 12, W 1, NB 8) | 29 |
| **Total** | | **228** | (4 wickets) | **406** |

| INDIA | O | M | R | W | O | M | R | W |
|---|--:|--:|--:|--:|--:|--:|--:|--:|
| Madan Lal | 6 | 1 | 22 | 0 | 11 | 2 | 14 | 0 |
| Amarnath | 5 | 0 | 26 | 0 | 11 | 3 | 19 | 0 |
| Solkar | 9 | 2 | 40 | 0 | | | | |
| Bedi | 30 | 11 | 73 | 4 | 25 | 3 | 76 | 1 |
| Chandrasekhar | 32·2 | 8 | 120 | 6 | 27 | 5 | 88 | 2 |
| Venkataraghavan | 27 | 7 | 69 | 0 | 30·3 | 5 | 65 | 3 |
| **WEST INDIES** | | | | | | | | |
| Julien | 13 | 4 | 35 | 1 | 13 | 3 | 52 | 0 |
| Holding | 26·4 | 3 | 65 | 6 | 21 | 1 | 82 | 0 |
| Lloyd | 1 | 0 | 1 | 0 | 6 | 1 | 22 | 0 |
| Padmore | 29 | 11 | 36 | 1 | 47 | 10 | 98 | 0 |
| Imtiaz Ali | 17 | 7 | 37 | 2 | 17 | 3 | 52 | 0 |
| Jumadeen | 16 | 7 | 33 | 0 | 41 | 13 | 70 | 2 |
| Fredericks | | | | | 2 | 1 | 1 | 0 |

### FALL OF WICKETS

| Wkt | WI 1st | I 1st | WI 2nd | I 2nd |
|---|--:|--:|--:|--:|
| 1st | 45 | 22 | 41 | 69 |
| 2nd | 50 | 50 | 78 | 177 |
| 3rd | 52 | 86 | 81 | 336 |
| 4th | 176 | 112 | 162 | 392 |
| 5th | 227 | 147 | 214 | – |
| 6th | 334 | 182 | 230 | – |
| 7th | 357 | 203 | – | – |
| 8th | 358 | 225 | – | – |
| 9th | 358 | 227 | – | – |
| 10th | 359 | 228 | – | – |

Umpires: R. Gosein and C.F. Vyfhuis.

# WEST INDIES v INDIA 1975–76 (4th Test)

Played at Sabina Park, Kingston, Jamaica, on 21, 22, 24, 25 April.
Toss: West Indies.   Result: WEST INDIES won by ten wickets.
Debuts: West Indies – W.W. Daniel.

West Indies won this six-day Test with over two days to spare and so gained a 2–1 victory in the rubber. The recently relaid pitch, with its unpredictable bounce which differed vastly at each end, encouraged a surfeit of short-pitched bowling, particularly from Holding. Three batsmen were injured in the first innings and took no further part in the match: Viswanath was dismissed by a ball that fractured and dislocated his right middle finger, Gaekwad was struck on the left ear and spent two days in hospital, and Patel had three stitches inserted in a cut in his mouth. Bedi declared his first innings closed as a protest against the intimidatory bowling. At the time it was thought that he also declared his second innings closed for the same reason. He later denied this, stating that neither he nor Chandrasekhar was fit to bat because of hand injuries sustained when fielding. India's second innings total, albeit with five men absent, is their lowest in the West Indies and the lowest in any Test at Kingston. All 17 members of the touring party fielded at some stage during the match; Surinder Amarnath, who fielded as substitute for much of the first innings, was operated on for appendicitis on the fourth day.

## INDIA

| | | | | |
|---|---|---|---|---|
| S.M. Gavaskar | b Holding | 66 | c Julien b Holding | 2 |
| A.D. Gaekwad | retired hurt | 81 | absent hurt | – |
| M. Amarnath | c Julien b Holding | 39 | st Murray b Jumadeen | 60 |
| G.R. Viswanath | c Julien b Holding | 8 | absent hurt | – |
| D.B. Vengsarkar | b Holding | 39 | (2) lbw b Jumadeen | 21 |
| B.P. Patel | retired hurt | 14 | absent hurt | – |
| S. Madan Lal | lbw b Daniel | 5 | (4) b Holding | 8 |
| S. Venkataraghavan | lbw b Daniel | 9 | (5) b Holding | 0 |
| S.M.H. Kirmani† | not out | 0 | (6) not out | 0 |
| B.S. Bedi* | ) did not bat | | absent hurt | – |
| B.S. Chandrasekhar | ) | | absent hurt | – |
| Extras | (B 6, LB 6, W 12, NB 21) | 45 | (NB 6) | 6 |
| **Total** | (6 wickets declared) | **306** | | **97** |

## WEST INDIES

| | | | | |
|---|---|---|---|---|
| R.C. Fredericks | run out | 82 | not out | 6 |
| L.G. Rowe | st Kirmani b Bedi | 47 | not out | 6 |
| I.V.A. Richards | b Chandrasekhar | 64 | | |
| A.I. Kallicharran | b Chandrasekhar | 12 | | |
| C.H. Lloyd* | c and b Chandrasekhar | 0 | | |
| D.L. Murray† | c sub (E.D. Solkar) | | | |
| | b Chandrasekhar | 71 | | |
| B.D. Julien | b Chandrasekhar | 5 | | |
| M.A. Holding | c sub (P. Sharma) b Bedi | 55 | | |
| V.A. Holder | not out | 36 | | |
| R.R. Jumadeen | c Gavaskar b Venkataraghavan | 3 | | |
| W.W. Daniel | c Amarnath b Venkataraghavan | 11 | | |
| Extras | (B 1, LB 2, NB 2) | 5 | (NB 1) | 1 |
| **Total** | | **391** | | **13** |

| WEST INDIES | O | M | R | W | O | M | R | W | FALL OF WICKETS | | | | |
|---|---|---|---|---|---|---|---|---|---|---|---|---|---|
| | | | | | | | | | | I | WI | I | WI |
| Holding | 28 | 7 | 82 | 4 | 7·2 | 0 | 35 | 3 | | I | WI | I | WI |
| Daniel | 20·2 | 7 | 52 | 2 | 3 | 0 | 12 | 0 | Wkt | 1st | 1st | 2nd | 2nd |
| Julien | 23 | 10 | 53 | 0 | 3 | 0 | 13 | 0 | 1st | 136 | 105 | 5 | – |
| Holder | 27 | 4 | 58 | 0 | 6 | 2 | 12 | 0 | 2nd | 205 | 186 | 68 | – |
| Jumadeen | 3 | 1 | 8 | 0 | 7 | 3 | 19 | 2 | 3rd | 216 | 197 | 97 | – |
| Fredericks | 3 | 1 | 8 | 0 | | | | | 4th | 280 | 206 | 97 | – |
| | | | | | | | | | 5th | 306 | 209 | 97 | – |
| INDIA | | | | | | | | | 6th | 306 | 217 | – | – |
| Madan Lal | 7 | 1 | 25 | 0 | 1 | 0 | 5 | 0 | 7th | – | 324 | – | – |
| Amarnath | 8 | 1 | 28 | 0 | | | | | 8th | – | 345 | – | – |
| Chandrasekhar | 42 | 7 | 153 | 5 | | | | | 9th | – | 352 | – | – |
| Bedi | 32 | 10 | 68 | 2 | | | | | 10th | – | 391 | – | – |
| Venkataraghavan | 51·3 | 12 | 112 | 2 | | | | | | | | | |
| Vengsarkar | | | | | 0·5 | 0 | 7 | 0 | | | | | |

Umpires: D. Sang Hue and R. Gosein.

# ENGLAND v WEST INDIES 1976 (1st Test)

Played at Trent Bridge, Nottingham, on 3, 4, 5, 7, 8 June.
Toss: West Indies.   Result: MATCH DRAWN.
Debuts: England – J.M. Brearley; West Indies – H.A. Gomes.

England needed to score 339 runs in 315 minutes to win. Richards scored his fifth Test hundred of 1976 and took his Test aggregate for the calendar year past 1,000 runs. He batted for 438 minutes, faced 313 balls, and hit 4 sixes and 31 fours. Both Richards and Steele scored hundreds in their first innings in this series. Knott, playing in his 74th Test, became the first to hold 200 catches when he dismissed Julien. Edrich scored his 5,000th run in 76 Tests. In the second innings, the umpires refused to allow the West Indies' twelfth man, C.L. King, to act as runner for Greenidge (injured leg). Gomes took his place for Greenidge's last ten runs.

## WEST INDIES

| | | | | |
|---|---|---|---|---|
| R.C. Fredericks | c Hendrick b Greig | 42 | b Snow | 15 |
| C.G. Greenidge | c Edrich b Hendrick | 22 | c and b Old | 23 |
| I.V.A. Richards | c Greig b Underwood | 232 | lbw b Snow | 63 |
| A.I. Kallicharran | c Steele b Underwood | 97 | (6) not out | 29 |
| C.H. Lloyd* | c Hendrick b Underwood | 16 | (4) c Brearley b Snow | 21 |
| B.D. Julien | c Knott b Old | 21 | (5) c Hendrick b Snow | 13 |
| H.A. Gomes | c Close b Underwood | 0 | | |
| D.L. Murray† | c Close b Snow | 19 | | |
| V.A. Holder | not out | 19 | | |
| A.M.E. Roberts | b Old | 1 | | |
| W.W. Daniel | c Knott b Old | 4 | | |
| Extras | (LB 12, W 1, NB 8) | 21 | (LB 6, W 2, NB 4) | 12 |
| **Total** | | **494** | (5 wickets declared) | **176** |

## ENGLAND

| | | | | |
|---|---|---|---|---|
| J.H. Edrich | c Murray b Daniel | 37 | not out | 76 |
| J.M. Brearley | c Richards b Julien | 0 | c Murray b Holder | 17 |
| D.S. Steele | c Roberts b Daniel | 106 | c Julien b Roberts | 6 |
| D.B. Close | c Murray b Daniel | 2 | not out | 36 |
| R.A. Woolmer | lbw b Julien | 82 | | |
| A.W. Greig* | b Roberts | 0 | | |
| A.P.E. Knott† | c sub (C.L. King) b Holder | 9 | | |
| C.M. Old | b Daniel | 33 | | |
| J.A. Snow | not out | 20 | | |
| D.L. Underwood | c Murray b Holder | 0 | | |
| M. Hendrick | c Daniel b Fredericks | 5 | | |
| Extras | (B 5, LB 1, W 3, NB 29) | 38 | (B 9, W 2, NB 10) | 21 |
| **Total** | | **332** | (2 wickets) | **156** |

| ENGLAND | O | M | R | W | O | M | R | W | FALL OF WICKETS | | | | |
|---|---|---|---|---|---|---|---|---|---|---|---|---|---|
| | | | | | | | | | | WI | E | WI | E |
| Snow | 31 | 5 | 123 | 1 | 11 | 2 | 53 | 4 | Wkt | 1st | 1st | 2nd | 2nd |
| Hendrick | 24 | 7 | 59 | 1 | 7 | 2 | 22 | 0 | 1st | 36 | 0 | 33 | 38 |
| Old | 34·3 | 7 | 80 | 3 | 10 | 0 | 64 | 1 | 2nd | 105 | 98 | 77 | 55 |
| Greig | 27 | 4 | 82 | 1 | 1 | 0 | 16 | 0 | 3rd | 408 | 105 | 109 | – |
| Woolmer | 10 | 2 | 47 | 0 | | | | | 4th | 423 | 226 | 124 | – |
| Underwood | 27 | 8 | 82 | 4 | 7 | 3 | 9 | 0 | 5th | 432 | 229 | 176 | – |
| **WEST INDIES** | | | | | | | | | 6th | 432 | 255 | – | – |
| Roberts | 34 | 15 | 53 | 1 | 9 | 3 | 20 | 1 | 7th | 458 | 278 | – | – |
| Julien | 34 | 9 | 75 | 2 | 16 | 8 | 19 | 0 | 8th | 481 | 279 | – | – |
| Holder | 25 | 5 | 66 | 2 | 12 | 6 | 12 | 1 | 9th | 488 | 318 | – | – |
| Daniel | 23 | 8 | 53 | 4 | 10 | 2 | 20 | 0 | 10th | 494 | 332 | – | – |
| Fredericks | 8·4 | 2 | 24 | 1 | 9 | 1 | 21 | 0 | | | | | |
| Richards | 3 | 1 | 8 | 0 | 3 | 1 | 7 | 0 | | | | | |
| Gomes | 4 | 1 | 8 | 0 | 9 | 1 | 18 | 0 | | | | | |
| Lloyd | 3 | 1 | 7 | 0 | | | | | | | | | |
| Kallicharran | | | | | 10 | 3 | 18 | 0 | | | | | |

Umpires: T.W. Spencer and H.D. Bird.

# ENGLAND v WEST INDIES 1976 (2nd Test)

Played at Lord's, London, on 17, 18, 19 *(no play)*, 21, 22 June.
Toss: England.   Result: MATCH DRAWN.
Debuts: Nil.

West Indies needed 323 runs to win in a minimum of 294 minutes. Lloyd claimed the last half hour when West Indies were 210 for 2 with 11 overs left but wanted to end the match when he was out (233 for 4) with 6·5 overs left. Greig insisted on continuing into the last of the mandatory 20 overs of the final hour and captured two more wickets. Wood (10*) retired at 19 for 0 after twice being struck on the right hand by balls from Roberts in the second innings, and resumed at 207 for 6.

## ENGLAND

| | | | | | |
|---|---|---|---|---|---|
| B. Wood | c Murray b Roberts | 6 | c Murray b Holding | | 30 |
| J.M. Brearley | b Roberts | 40 | b Holding | | 13 |
| D.S. Steele | lbw b Roberts | 7 | (4) c Jumadeen b Roberts | | 64 |
| D.B. Close | c Holder b Jumadeen | 60 | (5) c and b Holder | | 46 |
| R.A. Woolmer | c Murray b Holding | 38 | (6) c Murray b Roberts | | 29 |
| A.W. Greig* | c Lloyd b Roberts | 6 | (7) c Gomes b Holder | | 20 |
| A.P.E. Knott† | b Holder | 17 | (8) lbw b Roberts | | 4 |
| C.M. Old | b Holder | 19 | (9) run out | | 13 |
| J.A. Snow | b Roberts | 0 | (10) not out | | 6 |
| D.L. Underwood | b Holder | 31 | (11) b Roberts | | 2 |
| P.I. Pocock | not out | 0 | (3) c Jumadeen b Roberts | | 3 |
| Extras | (B 7, LB 5, W 5, NB 9) | 26 | (B 7, LB 7, NB 10) | | 24 |
| **Total** | | **250** | | | **254** |

## WEST INDIES

| | | | | | |
|---|---|---|---|---|---|
| R.C. Fredericks | c Snow b Old | 0 | c Greig b Old | | 138 |
| C.G. Greenidge | c Snow b Underwood | 84 | c Close b Pocock | | 22 |
| H.A. Gomes | c Woolmer b Snow | 11 | (7) b Underwood | | 0 |
| A.I. Kallicharran | c Old b Snow | 0 | (3) b Greig | | 34 |
| C.H. Lloyd* | c Knott b Underwood | 50 | (4) b Greig | | 33 |
| D.L. Murray† | b Snow | 2 | not out | | 7 |
| B.D. Julien | lbw b Snow | 3 | (5) b Underwood | | 1 |
| M.A. Holding | b Underwood | 0 | | | |
| V.A. Holder | c Woolmer b Underwood | 12 | (8) not out | | 0 |
| A.M.E. Roberts | b Underwood | 16 | | | |
| R.R. Jumadeen | not out | 0 | | | |
| Extras | (B 2, NB 2) | 4 | (B 3, LB 2, NB 1) | | 6 |
| **Total** | | **182** | (6 wickets) | | **241** |

| WEST INDIES | O | M | R | W | O | M | R | W | FALL OF WICKETS | | | | |
|---|---|---|---|---|---|---|---|---|---|---|---|---|---|
| Roberts | 23 | 6 | 60 | 5 | 29·5 | 10 | 63 | 5 | | E | WI | E | WI |
| Holding | 19 | 4 | 52 | 1 | 27 | 10 | 56 | 2 | *Wkt* | *1st* | *1st* | *2nd* | *2nd* |
| Julien | 23 | 6 | 54 | 0 | 13 | 5 | 20 | 0 | 1st | 15 | 0 | 29 | 41 |
| Holder | 18·4 | 7 | 35 | 3 | 19 | 2 | 50 | 2 | 2nd | 31 | 28 | 29 | 154 |
| Jumadeen | 12 | 4 | 23 | 1 | 16 | 4 | 41 | 0 | 3rd | 115 | 40 | 112 | 230 |
| | | | | | | | | | 4th | 153 | 139 | 169 | 233 |
| ENGLAND | | | | | | | | | 5th | 161 | 141 | 186 | 238 |
| Old | 10 | 0 | 58 | 1 | 14 | 4 | 46 | 1 | 6th | 188 | 145 | 207 | 238 |
| Snow | 19 | 3 | 68 | 4 | 7 | 2 | 22 | 0 | 7th | 196 | 146 | 215 | – |
| Underwood | 18·4 | 7 | 39 | 5 | 24·3 | 8 | 73 | 2 | 8th | 197 | 153 | 245 | – |
| Pocock | 3 | 0 | 13 | 0 | 27 | 9 | 52 | 1 | 9th | 249 | 178 | 249 | – |
| Greig | | | | | 14 | 3 | 42 | 2 | 10th | 250 | 182 | 254 | – |

Umpires: H.D. Bird and D.J. Constant.

# ENGLAND v WEST INDIES 1976 (3rd Test)

Played at Old Trafford, Manchester, on 8, 9, 10, 12, 13 July.
Toss: West Indies.   Result: WEST INDIES won by 425 runs.
Debuts: England – M.W.W. Selvey; West Indies – C.L. King.

West Indies won at 11.12 on the fifth morning; it was their largest victory by a runs margin in this series. Selvey took a wicket with his sixth ball in Test Cricket and 3 for 6 in his first 20 balls. Greenidge scored 63·5% of his side's total in the first innings; only C. Bannerman, who scored 67·3% in *Test No. 1*, has exceeded this contribution in a Test match. Greenidge was the second West Indies batsman after G.A. Headley to score a hundred in each innings of a Test in this series. England's 71 is the lowest total by either side in this series; only Australia (seven occasions) had dismissed England for a lower total. West Indies' second innings provided the first instance of century stands for the first three wickets against England. Underwood emulated R. Peel and R.W. Blair by being dismissed for a 'pair' three times in Test matches. Extras were the main contributor to England's second innings (fourth instance) and to their match aggregate (unique at Test level). West Indies' second innings included the Test record for leg byes in an innings.

## WEST INDIES

| | | | | | |
|---|---|---|---|---|---|
| R.C. Fredericks | c Underwood b Selvey | 0 | hit wkt b Hendrick | | 50 |
| C.G. Greenidge | b Underwood | 134 | b Selvey | | 101 |
| I.V.A. Richards | b Selvey | 4 | lbw b Pocock | | 135 |
| A.I. Kallicharran | b Selvey | 0 | (5) c Close b Pocock | | 20 |
| C.H. Lloyd* | c Hayes b Hendrick | 2 | (4) c Underwood b Selvey | | 43 |
| C.L. King | c Greig b Underwood | 32 | not out | | 14 |
| D.L. Murray† | c Greig b Hendrick | 1 | not out | | 7 |
| M.A. Holding | b Selvey | 3 | | | |
| A.M.E. Roberts | c Steele b Pocock | 6 | | | |
| A.L. Padmore | not out | 8 | | | |
| W.W. Daniel | lbw b Underwood | 10 | | | |
| Extras | (LB 8, NB 3) | 11 | (B 5, LB 30, W 1, NB 5) | | 41 |
| **Total** | | **211** | (5 wickets declared) | | **411** |

## ENGLAND

| | | | | | |
|---|---|---|---|---|---|
| J.H. Edrich | c Murray b Roberts | 8 | b Daniel | | 24 |
| D.B. Close | lbw b Daniel | 2 | b Roberts | | 20 |
| D.S. Steele | lbw b Roberts | 20 | c Roberts b Holding | | 15 |
| P.I. Pocock | c Kallicharran b Holding | 7 | (10) c King b Daniel | | 3 |
| R.A. Woolmer | c Murray b Holding | 3 | (4) lbw b Roberts | | 0 |
| F.C. Hayes | c Lloyd b Roberts | 0 | (5) c Greenidge b Roberts | | 18 |
| A.W. Greig* | b Daniel | 9 | (6) b Holding | | 3 |
| A.P.E. Knott† | c Greenidge b Holding | 1 | (7) c Fredericks b Roberts | | 14 |
| D.L. Underwood | b Holding | 0 | (8) c King b Roberts | | 0 |
| M.W.W. Selvey | not out | 2 | (9) c Greenidge b Roberts | | 4 |
| M. Hendrick | b Holding | 0 | not out | | 0 |
| Extras | (B 8, NB 11) | 19 | (B 4, LB 1, NB 20) | | 25 |
| **Total** | | **71** | | | **126** |

| ENGLAND | O | M | R | W | O | M | R | W | | FALL OF WICKETS | | | |
|---|---|---|---|---|---|---|---|---|---|---|---|---|---|
| Hendrick | 14 | 1 | 48 | 2 | 24 | 4 | 63 | 1 | | WI | E | WI | E |
| Selvey | 17 | 4 | 41 | 4 | 26 | 3 | 111 | 2 | *Wkt* | *1st* | *1st* | *2nd* | *2nd* |
| Greig | 8 | 1 | 24 | 0 | 2 | 0 | 8 | 0 | 1st | 1 | 9 | 116 | 54 |
| Woolmer | 3 | 0 | 22 | 0 | | | | | 2nd | 15 | 36 | 224 | 60 |
| Underwood | 24 | 5 | 55 | 3 | 35 | 9 | 90 | 0 | 3rd | 19 | 46 | 356 | 60 |
| Pocock | 4 | 2 | 10 | 1 | 27 | 4 | 98 | 2 | 4th | 26 | 48 | 385 | 80 |
| | | | | | | | | | 5th | 137 | 48 | 388 | 94 |
| WEST INDIES | | | | | | | | | 6th | 154 | 65 | – | 112 |
| Roberts | 12 | 4 | 22 | 3 | 20·5 | 8 | 37 | 6 | 7th | 167 | 66 | – | 112 |
| Holding | 14·5 | 7 | 17 | 5 | 23 | 15 | 24 | 2 | 8th | 193 | 67 | – | 118 |
| Daniel | 6 | 2 | 13 | 2 | 17 | 8 | 39 | 2 | 9th | 193 | 71 | – | 124 |
| Padmore | | | | | 3 | 2 | 1 | 0 | 10th | 211 | 71 | – | 126 |

Umpires: W.E. Alley and W.L. Budd.

# ENGLAND v WEST INDIES 1976 (4th Test)

Played at Headingley, Leeds, on 22, 23, 24, 26, 27 July.
Toss: West Indies.   Result: WEST INDIES won by 55 runs.
Debuts: England – J.C. Balderstone, P. Willey.

West Indies won at 12.22 p.m. on the fifth day and so retained the Wisden Trophy. Richards' first run took his aggregate for 1976 past R.B. Simpson's record of 1,381 set in 1964. His dismissal gave Knott his 219th wicket to equal T.G. Evans' Test record. Greenidge scored his third hundred in successive innings against England, and became the first to do so since A.R. Morris in 1946–47. West Indies scored 437 for 9 on the first day. Snow took his 200th wicket in 49 Tests when he bowled Roberts; he was the fifth England bowler to achieve this feat. Knott's hundred included a seven (one, plus two overthrows, plus four boundary overthrows). Roberts took his 100th wicket in 19 Tests when he dismissed Steele. His is the fastest 100 Test wickets in terms of time: two years and 142 days. Murray's five catches in the second innings equalled the West Indies record set by F.C.M. Alexander in 1959–60 (*Test No. 487*).

## WEST INDIES

| | | | | |
|---|---|---|---|---|
| R.C. Fredericks | b Willis | 109 | b Snow | 6 |
| C.G. Greenidge | c Ward b Snow | 115 | lbw b Ward | 6 |
| I.V.A. Richards | c Knott b Willis | 66 | b Willis | 38 |
| L.G. Rowe | c Greig b Woolmer | 50 | run out | 6 |
| C.H. Lloyd* | c Steele b Ward | 18 | b Ward | 29 |
| C.L. King | c Hayes b Ward | 0 | c Greig b Snow | 58 |
| D.L. Murray† | c Willis b Snow | 33 | b Willis | 18 |
| M.A. Holding | b Snow | 2 | (9) lbw b Willis | 4 |
| V.A. Holder | c Hayes b Willis | 1 | (8) b Willis | 5 |
| A.M.E. Roberts | b Snow | 19 | b Willis | 3 |
| W.W. Daniel | not out | 4 | not out | 0 |
| Extras | (B 1, LB 15, W 2, NB 15) | 33 | (B 4, LB 6, W 1, NB 12) | 23 |
| **Total** | | **450** | | **196** |

## ENGLAND

| | | | | |
|---|---|---|---|---|
| R.A. Woolmer | c Greenidge b Holder | 18 | lbw b Holder | 37 |
| D.S. Steele | b Holding | 4 | c Murray b Roberts | 0 |
| F.C. Hayes | c Murray b Daniel | 7 | c Richards b Roberts | 0 |
| J.C. Balderstone | c Murray b Roberts | 35 | c Murray b Roberts | 4 |
| P. Willey | lbw b Roberts | 36 | c Roberts b Holding | 45 |
| A.W. Greig* | c Lloyd b Daniel | 116 | not out | 76 |
| A.P.E. Knott† | c Daniel b Holder | 116 | (8) c Murray b Daniel | 2 |
| J.A. Snow | c Fredericks b Holder | 20 | (9) c Greenidge b Daniel | 8 |
| D.L. Underwood | c Lloyd b King | 1 | (7) c Murray b Daniel | 0 |
| A. Ward | lbw b Roberts | 0 | c Murray b Holding | 0 |
| R.G.D. Willis | not out | 0 | lbw b Holding | 0 |
| Extras | (B 2, LB 7, W 2, NB 23) | 34 | (B 12, LB 5, W 7, NB 8) | 32 |
| **Total** | | **387** | | **204** |

| ENGLAND | O | M | R | W | O | M | R | W | FALL OF WICKETS | | | |
|---|---|---|---|---|---|---|---|---|---|---|---|---|
| | | | | | | | | | | WI | E | WI | E |
| Willis | 20 | 2 | 71 | 3 | 15·3 | 6 | 42 | 5 | | | | | |
| Snow | 18·4 | 3 | 77 | 4 | 20 | 1 | 80 | 2 | *Wkt* | *1st* | *1st* | *2nd* | *2nd* |
| Underwood | 18 | 2 | 80 | 0 | | | | | 1st | 192 | 4 | 13 | 5 |
| Ward | 15 | 0 | 103 | 2 | 9 | 2 | 25 | 2 | 2nd | 287 | 24 | 23 | 12 |
| Greig | 10 | 2 | 57 | 0 | | | | | 3rd | 330 | 32 | 60 | 23 |
| Woolmer | 6 | 0 | 25 | 1 | 7 | 0 | 26 | 0 | 4th | 370 | 80 | 72 | 80 |
| Willey | 1 | 0 | 4 | 0 | | | | | 5th | 370 | 169 | 121 | 140 |
| | | | | | | | | | 6th | 413 | 321 | 178 | 148 |
| WEST INDIES | | | | | | | | | 7th | 421 | 364 | 184 | 150 |
| Roberts | 35 | 7 | 102 | 3 | 18 | 8 | 41 | 3 | 8th | 423 | 367 | 188 | 158 |
| Holding | 8 | 2 | 14 | 1 | 14 | 1 | 44 | 3 | 9th | 433 | 379 | 193 | 204 |
| Daniel | 29 | 7 | 102 | 2 | 13 | 0 | 60 | 3 | 10th | 450 | 387 | 196 | 204 |
| Holder | 30·3 | 13 | 73 | 3 | 11 | 3 | 27 | 1 | | | | | |
| King | 26 | 6 | 56 | 1 | | | | | | | | | |
| Fredericks | 3 | 1 | 5 | 0 | | | | | | | | | |
| Lloyd | 2 | 1 | 1 | 0 | | | | | | | | | |

Umpires: T.W. Spencer and D.J. Constant.

# ENGLAND v WEST INDIES 1976 (5th Test)

Played at Kennington Oval, London, on 12, 13, 14, 16, 17 August.
Toss: West Indies. Result: WEST INDIES won by 231 runs.
Debuts: England – G. Miller.

West Indies won the rubber 3–0 at 4.20 on the fifth afternoon after setting England to score 435 runs in a minimum of 380 minutes. Their highest total against England was scored in 650 minutes and included hundred partnerships for three successive wickets. Richards (472 minutes, 386 balls, 38 fours) made the highest of the series in England to bring his record total of runs in a calendar year to 1,710. His aggregate of 829 runs is the fourth highest in any Test rubber and a record for the West Indies. Playing in his 78th match, Knott beat T.G. Evans' world Test record of 219 dismissals in 91 Tests when he stumped Rowe. Holding's analysis of 8 for 92 is the best by a West Indies bowler against England. He became the first West Indian to take more than twelve wickets in a Test against any country when he achieved match figures of 14 for 149. The umpires suspended play for nine minutes on the third evening when several dozen spectators invaded the field of play after Greig had been dismissed.

## WEST INDIES

| | | | | |
|---|---|---|---|---|
| R.C. Fredericks | c Balderstone b Miller | 71 | not out | 86 |
| C.G. Greenidge | lbw b Willis | 0 | not out | 85 |
| I.V.A. Richards | b Greig | 291 | | |
| L.G. Rowe | st Knott b Underwood | 70 | | |
| C.H. Lloyd* | c Knott b Greig | 84 | | |
| C.L. King | c Selvey b Balderstone | 63 | | |
| D.L. Murray† | c and b Underwood | 36 | | |
| V.A. Holder | not out | 13 | | |
| M.A. Holding | b Underwood | 32 | | |
| A.M.E. Roberts | ) did not bat | | | |
| W.W. Daniel | ) | | | |
| Extras | (B 1, LB 17, NB 9) | 27 | (B 4, LB 1, W 1, NB 5) | 11 |
| **Total** | (8 wickets declared) | **687** | (0 wickets declared) | **182** |

## ENGLAND

| | | | | |
|---|---|---|---|---|
| R.A. Woolmer | lbw b Holding | 8 | c Murray b Holding | 30 |
| D.L. Amiss | b Holding | 203 | c Greenidge b Holding | 16 |
| D.S. Steele | lbw b Holding | 44 | c Murray b Holder | 42 |
| J.C. Balderstone | b Holding | 0 | b Holding | 0 |
| P. Willey | c Fredericks b King | 33 | c Greenidge b Holder | 1 |
| A.W. Greig* | b Holding | 12 | b Holding | 1 |
| D.L. Underwood | b Holding | 4 | (9) c Lloyd b Roberts | 2 |
| A.P.E. Knott† | b Holding | 50 | (7) b Holding | 57 |
| G. Miller | c sub (B.D. Julien) b Holder | 36 | (8) b Richards | 24 |
| M.W.W. Selvey | b Holding | 0 | not out | 4 |
| R.G.D. Willis | not out | 5 | lbw b Holding | 0 |
| Extras | (B 8, LB 11, NB 21) | 40 | (B 15, LB 3, W 8) | 26 |
| **Total** | | **435** | | **203** |

| ENGLAND | O | M | R | W | O | M | R | W |
|---|---|---|---|---|---|---|---|---|
| Willis | 15 | 3 | 73 | 1 | 7 | 0 | 48 | 0 |
| Selvey | 15 | 0 | 67 | 0 | 9 | 1 | 44 | 0 |
| Underwood | 60·5 | 15 | 165 | 3 | 9 | 2 | 38 | 0 |
| Woolmer | 9 | 0 | 44 | 0 | 5 | 0 | 30 | 0 |
| Miller | 27 | 4 | 106 | 1 | | | | |
| Balderstone | 16 | 0 | 80 | 1 | | | | |
| Greig | 34 | 5 | 96 | 2 | 2 | 0 | 11 | 0 |
| Willey | 3 | 0 | 11 | 0 | | | | |
| Steele | 3 | 0 | 18 | 0 | | | | |
| WEST INDIES | | | | | | | | |
| Roberts | 27 | 4 | 102 | 0 | 13 | 4 | 37 | 1 |
| Holding | 33 | 9 | 92 | 8 | 20·4 | 6 | 57 | 6 |
| Holder | 27·5 | 7 | 75 | 1 | 14 | 5 | 29 | 2 |
| Daniel | 10 | 1 | 30 | 0 | | | | |
| Fredericks | 11 | 2 | 36 | 0 | 12 | 5 | 33 | 0 |
| Richards | 14 | 4 | 30 | 0 | 11 | 6 | 11 | 1 |
| King | 7 | 3 | 30 | 1 | 6 | 2 | 9 | 0 |
| Lloyd | | | | | 2 | 1 | 1 | 0 |

### FALL OF WICKETS

| Wkt | WI 1st | E 1st | WI 2nd | E 2nd |
|---|---|---|---|---|
| 1st | 5 | 47 | – | 49 |
| 2nd | 159 | 147 | – | 54 |
| 3rd | 350 | 151 | – | 64 |
| 4th | 524 | 279 | – | 77 |
| 5th | 547 | 303 | – | 78 |
| 6th | 640 | 323 | – | 148 |
| 7th | 642 | 342 | – | 196 |
| 8th | 687 | 411 | – | 196 |
| 9th | – | 411 | – | 202 |
| 10th | – | 435 | – | 203 |

Umpires: W.E. Alley and H.D. Bird.

# PAKISTAN v NEW ZEALAND 1976–77 (1st Test)

Played at Lahore (Gaddafi) Stadium on 9, 10, 11, 13 October.
Toss: Pakistan.   Result: PAKISTAN won by six wickets.
Debuts: Pakistan – Javed Miandad; New Zealand – R.W. Anderson, W.K. Lees, P.J. Petherick.

Pakistan won with a day and three hours to spare. Javed Miandad became the second batsman after Khalid
Ibadulla to score a hundred in his first innings for Pakistan. His partnership of 281 with Asif Iqbal is the highest
for the fifth wicket by Pakistan in all Test matches. Petherick's offspin dismissed Miandad, Wasim Raja and
Intikhab in successive balls. It was the second hat-trick by a bowler playing in his first Test: M.J.C. Allom also
achieved the feat on his debut in 1929–30 (*Test No. 186*). The partnership of 183 between Burgess and
Anderson, who scored 92 in his first Test, is New Zealand's highest for the fifth wicket against all countries.

## PAKISTAN

| | | | | | |
|---|---|---|---|---|---|
| Majid Khan | c Lees b Hadlee | 23 | c Turner b Collinge | | 21 |
| Sadiq Mohammad | c Burgess b Hadlee | 5 | c Parker b Howarth | | 38 |
| Zaheer Abbas | b Burgess | 15 | c Morrison b Petherick | | 15 |
| Mushtaq Mohammad* | b Hadlee | 4 | (5) c Morrison b Petherick | | 5 |
| Javed Miandad | c Hadlee b Petherick | 163 | (4) not out | | 25 |
| Asif Iqbal | b Hadlee | 166 | not out | | 1 |
| Wasim Raja | c and b Petherick | 0 | | | |
| Intikhab Alam | c Howarth b Petherick | 0 | | | |
| Imran Khan | c Burgess b Hadlee | 29 | | | |
| Sarfraz Nawaz | lbw b O'Sullivan | 4 | | | |
| Wasim Bari† | not out | 2 | | | |
| Extras | (B 1, LB 2, NB 3) | 6 | | | |
| **Total** | | **417** | (4 wickets) | | **105** |

## NEW ZEALAND

| | | | | | |
|---|---|---|---|---|---|
| J.F.M. Morrison | c Wasim Bari b Sarfraz | 3 | c Zaheer b Sarfraz | | 0 |
| G.M. Turner* | c Wasim Raja b Sarfraz | 8 | b Imran | | 1 |
| G.P. Howarth | c and b Intikhab | 38 | c Sadiq b Sarfraz | | 0 |
| J.M. Parker | c Wasim Bari b Imran | 9 | lbw b Imran | | 22 |
| M.G. Burgess | b Imran | 17 | b Intikhab | | 111 |
| R.W. Anderson | c Mushtaq b Intikhab | 14 | c Majid b Mushtaq | | 92 |
| W.K. Lees† | st Wasim Bari b Intikhab | 8 | c Mushtaq b Imran | | 42 |
| R.J. Hadlee | c Wasim Raja b Mushtaq | 27 | c Majid b Miandad | | 42 |
| D.R. O'Sullivan | c Miandad b Mushtaq | 8 | (11) not out | | 23 |
| R.O. Collinge | c Wasim Bari b Intikhab | 8 | (9) b Imran | | 0 |
| P.J. Petherick | not out | 1 | (10) c Mushtaq b Sarfraz | | 1 |
| Extras | (B 1, LB 4, NB 11) | 16 | (B 4, LB 11, NB 11) | | 26 |
| **Total** | | **157** | | | **360** |

| NEW ZEALAND | O | M | R | W | O | M | R | W | | FALL OF WICKETS | | | |
|---|---|---|---|---|---|---|---|---|---|---|---|---|---|
| Collinge | 14 | 0 | 81 | 0 | 6 | 0 | 30 | 1 | | | P | NZ | NZ | P |
| Hadlee | 19 | 0 | 121 | 5 | 5 | 0 | 36 | 0 | | Wkt | 1st | 1st | 2nd | 2nd |
| Burgess | 4 | 1 | 20 | 1 | | | | | | 1st | 22 | 9 | 1 | 49 |
| O'Sullivan | 25·5 | 3 | 86 | 1 | | | | | | 2nd | 33 | 26 | 1 | 74 |
| Petherick | 18 | 1 | 103 | 3 | 4·7 | 2 | 26 | 2 | | 3rd | 44 | 64 | 1 | 74 |
| Howarth | | | | | 3 | 0 | 13 | 1 | | 4th | 55 | 72 | 62 | 96 |
| | | | | | | | | | | 5th | 336 | 99 | 245 | – |
| PAKISTAN | | | | | | | | | | 6th | 336 | 105 | 245 | – |
| Sarfraz | 13 | 5 | 33 | 2 | 18 | 1 | 69 | 3 | | 7th | 336 | 106 | 306 | – |
| Imran | 15 | 1 | 57 | 2 | 21 | 4 | 59 | 4 | | 8th | 408 | 146 | 306 | – |
| Asif | 2 | 0 | 10 | 0 | | | | | | 9th | 413 | 149 | 315 | – |
| Intikhab | 16·4 | 6 | 35 | 4 | 26 | 4 | 85 | 1 | | 10th | 417 | 157 | 360 | – |
| Mushtaq | 3 | 0 | 6 | 2 | 13 | 2 | 56 | 1 | | | | | | |
| Wasim Raja | | | | | 7 | 0 | 31 | 0 | | | | | | |
| Miandad | | | | | 7·4 | 1 | 34 | 1 | | | | | | |

Umpires: Amanullah Khan and Shujauddin.

# PAKISTAN v NEW ZEALAND 1976–77 (2nd Test)

Played at Niaz Stadium, Hyderabad, on 23, 24, 25, 27 October.
Toss: Pakistan.   Result: PAKISTAN won by ten wickets.
Debuts: Pakistan – Farrukh Zaman.

A boundary off the bowling of the wicket-keeper gave Pakistan victory in their first match against New Zealand at Hyderabad soon after tea on the penultimate day. Sadiq (56*) retired with cramp in his leg at 136 for 0 and resumed at 384 for 4. Sadiq and Mushtaq Mohammad became the second pair of brothers after G.S. and I.M. Chappell to score hundreds in the same Test match.

## PAKISTAN

| | | | | |
|---|---|---|---|---|
| Sadiq Mohammad | not out | 103 | | |
| Majid Khan | st Lees b O'Sullivan | 98 | | |
| Zaheer Abbas | lbw b Roberts | 11 | | |
| Javed Miandad | c sub (N.M. Parker) b Cairns | 25 | | |
| Mushtaq Mohammad* | run out | 101 | | |
| Asif Iqbal | st Lees b Petherick | 73 | | |
| Imran Khan | c Turner b O'Sullivan | 13 | | |
| Intikhab Alam | lbw b Hadlee | 4 | | |
| Sarfraz Nawaz | c Turner b Petherick | 10 | (1) not out | 4 |
| Wasim Bari† | not out | 13 | (2) not out | 0 |
| Farrukh Zaman | did not bat | | | |
| Extras | (B 18, LB 2, NB 2) | 22 | | |
| **Total** | (8 wickets declared) | **473** | (0 wickets) | **4** |

## NEW ZEALAND

| | | | | |
|---|---|---|---|---|
| G.M. Turner* | c Wasim b Imran | 49 | b Sarfraz | 2 |
| G.P. Howarth | b Sarfraz | 0 | c Miandad b Mushtaq | 23 |
| J.M. Parker | c Miandad b Imran | 7 | c Mushtaq b Miandad | 82 |
| A.D.G. Roberts | c Wasim b Sarfraz | 8 | b Miandad | 33 |
| M.G. Burgess | c Wasim b Imran | 33 | c sub (Wasim Raja) b Intikhab | 21 |
| R.W. Anderson | b Intikhab | 30 | c Zaheer b Intikhab | 4 |
| W.K. Lees† | lbw b Intikhab | 15 | c sub (Mohsin Khan) b Miandad | 29 |
| B.L. Cairns | c Majid b Miandad | 18 | lbw b Intikhab | 3 |
| R.J. Hadlee | not out | 28 | c Wasim b Intikhab | 0 |
| D.R. O'Sullivan | b Miandad | 4 | b Sarfraz | 23 |
| P.J. Petherick | b Sarfraz | 0 | not out | 12 |
| Extras | (B 13, LB 8, NB 6) | 27 | (B 15, LB 2, NB 5) | 22 |
| **Total** | | **219** | | **254** |

| NEW ZEALAND | O | M | R | W | O | M | R | W |
|---|---|---|---|---|---|---|---|---|
| Hadlee | 19 | 1 | 77 | 1 | | | | |
| Cairns | 26 | 7 | 101 | 1 | | | | |
| Roberts | 8 | 1 | 23 | 1 | | | | |
| Petherick | 36 | 5 | 158 | 2 | | | | |
| O'Sullivan | 39 | 10 | 92 | 2 | | | | |
| Lees | | | | | 0·5 | 0 | 4 | 0 |
| PAKISTAN | | | | | | | | |
| Sarfraz | 17·6 | 4 | 53 | 3 | 10·4 | 1 | 45 | 2 |
| Imran | 15 | 4 | 41 | 3 | 16 | 1 | 53 | 0 |
| Intikhab | 20 | 7 | 51 | 2 | 20 | 7 | 44 | 4 |
| Farrukh | 6 | 1 | 8 | 0 | 4 | 1 | 7 | 0 |
| Miandad | 8 | 1 | 20 | 2 | 19 | 2 | 74 | 3 |
| Mushtaq | 7 | 2 | 19 | 0 | 9 | 4 | 9 | 1 |
| Majid | | | | | 2 | 2 | 0 | 0 |

FALL OF WICKETS

| Wkt | P 1st | NZ 1st | NZ 2nd | P 2nd |
|---|---|---|---|---|
| 1st | 164 | 5 | 5 | – |
| 2nd | 176 | 27 | 70 | – |
| 3rd | 220 | 38 | 147 | – |
| 4th | 384 | 101 | 158 | – |
| 5th | 387 | 111 | 171 | – |
| 6th | 410 | 161 | 190 | – |
| 7th | 415 | 178 | 193 | – |
| 8th | 427 | 200 | 193 | – |
| 9th | – | 208 | 223 | – |
| 10th | – | 219 | 254 | – |

Umpires: Amanullah Khan and Shakoor Rana.

# PAKISTAN v NEW ZEALAND 1976–77 (3rd Test)

Played at National Stadium, Karachi, on 30, 31 October, 1, 3, 4 November.
Toss: Pakistan.   Result: MATCH DRAWN.
Debuts: Pakistan – Shahid Israr, Sikander Bakht; New Zealand – N.M. Parker.

This match produced the highest aggregate of runs for any Test in the Indian sub-continent: 1,585. Pakistan's total of 565 is the highest by either country in this series. Majid reached his hundred in 113 minutes before lunch on the first day and was 108* at the interval. Only three others – V.T. Trumper, C.G. Macartney and D.G. Bradman, all Australians playing against England – have scored a hundred before lunch on the first day of a Test match. Javed Miandad, who batted for 410 minutes and hit two sixes and 29 fours, is the youngest to score a double century in Test cricket (19 years and 141 days). Lees made New Zealand's highest score against Pakistan and his partnership of 186 with Hadlee is the highest for New Zealand's seventh wicket in all Test matches. In the first innings, Imran was banned from bowling after being warned by both umpires for bowling too many short-pitched balls.

## PAKISTAN

| | | | | |
|---|---|---|---|---|
| Sadiq Mohammad | c Burgess b Hadlee | 34 | c Lees b Collinge | 31 |
| Majid Khan | c Burgess b Collinge | 112 | run out | 50 |
| Zaheer Abbas | b O'Sullivan | 3 | c Lees b O'Sullivan | 16 |
| Javed Miandad | c Hadlee b Collinge | 206 | (5) st Lees b O'Sullivan | 85 |
| Mushtaq Mohammad* | c Lees b Hadlee | 107 | (6) not out | 67 |
| Asif Iqbal | c Lees b Hadlee | 12 | (4) st Lees b Roberts | 30 |
| Imran Khan | c O'Sullivan b Hadlee | 59 | not out | 4 |
| Intikhab Alam | lbw b O'Sullivan | 0 | | |
| Sarfraz Nawaz | lbw b Cairns | 15 | | |
| Shahid Israr† | not out | 7 | | |
| Sikander Bakht | did not bat | | | |
| Extras | (B 3, LB 5, NB 2) | 10 | (LB 4, NB 3) | 7 |
| **Total** | (9 wickets declared) | **565** | (5 wickets declared) | **290** |

## NEW ZEALAND

| | | | | |
|---|---|---|---|---|
| N.M. Parker | c Shahid b Sarfraz | 2 | c Imran b Intikhab | 40 |
| J.F.M. Morrison | b Sarfraz | 4 | c Mushtaq b Sikander | 31 |
| J.M. Parker* | c Majid b Imran | 24 | c Sadiq b Miandad | 16 |
| A.D.G. Roberts | b Imran | 39 | b Sikander | 45 |
| M.G. Burgess | c Miandad b Sarfraz | 44 | c Majid b Miandad | 1 |
| R.W. Anderson | lbw b Imran | 8 | lbw b Imran | 30 |
| W.K. Lees† | b Sikander | 152 | c Asif b Imran | 46 |
| R.J. Hadlee | c Shahid b Intikhab | 87 | not out | 30 |
| B.L. Cairns | not out | 52 | not out | 9 |
| D.R. O'Sullivan | c Mushtaq b Intikhab | 1 | | |
| R.O. Collinge | b Intikhab | 3 | | |
| Extras | (B 12, LB 7, NB 33) | 52 | (B 4, LB 5, NB 5) | 14 |
| **Total** | | **468** | (7 wickets) | **262** |

| NEW ZEALAND | O | M | R | W | O | M | R | W |
|---|---|---|---|---|---|---|---|---|
| Collinge | 21 | 1 | 141 | 2 | 12 | 0 | 88 | 1 |
| Hadlee | 20·2 | 1 | 138 | 4 | 12 | 0 | 75 | 0 |
| Cairns | 28 | 2 | 142 | 1 | | | | |
| O'Sullivan | 35 | 6 | 131 | 2 | 17 | 0 | 96 | 2 |
| Morrison | 1 | 0 | 3 | 0 | 2 | 0 | 6 | 0 |
| Roberts | | | | | 4·4 | 2 | 18 | 1 |
| PAKISTAN | | | | | | | | |
| Sarfraz | 20 | 1 | 84 | 3 | | | | |
| Imran | 24·6 | 4 | 107 | 3 | 21·6 | 1 | 104 | 2 |
| Sikander | 16 | 3 | 68 | 1 | 8 | 2 | 38 | 2 |
| Intikhab | 20·7 | 5 | 76 | 3 | 17 | 5 | 42 | 1 |
| Mushtaq | 6 | 2 | 30 | 0 | 6 | 2 | 9 | 0 |
| Miandad | 10 | 3 | 34 | 0 | 17 | 4 | 45 | 2 |
| Majid | 5 | 2 | 17 | 0 | 9 | 4 | 6 | 0 |
| Sadiq | 1 | 1 | 0 | 0 | 1 | 0 | 4 | 0 |

### FALL OF WICKETS

| | P | NZ | P | NZ |
|---|---|---|---|---|
| Wkt | 1st | 1st | 2nd | 2nd |
| 1st | 147 | 5 | 76 | 43 |
| 2nd | 151 | 10 | 88 | 90 |
| 3rd | 161 | 78 | 117 | 91 |
| 4th | 413 | 93 | 137 | 93 |
| 5th | 427 | 104 | 275 | 140 |
| 6th | 524 | 195 | – | 200 |
| 7th | 525 | 381 | – | 241 |
| 8th | 548 | 433 | – | – |
| 9th | 565 | 434 | – | – |
| 10th | – | 468 | – | – |

Umpires: Shujauddin and Shakoor Rana.

# INDIA v NEW ZEALAND 1976–77 (1st Test)

Played at Wankhede Stadium, Bombay, on 10, 11, 13, 14, 15 November.
Toss: India.     Result: INDIA won by 162 runs.
Debuts: Nil.

The partnership of 105 between Kirmani and Bedi is India's highest for the ninth wicket against New Zealand.

## INDIA

| | | | | | |
|---|---|---|---|---|---|
| S.M. Gavaskar | c Cairns b Petherick | 119 | c Burgess b Hadlee | | 14 |
| A.D. Gaekwad | lbw b O'Sullivan | 42 | | | |
| M. Amarnath | c O'Sullivan b Hadlee | 45 | (2) c Roberts b Collinge | | 30 |
| G.R. Viswanath | b Petherick | 10 | (3) st Lees b Petherick | | 39 |
| B.P. Patel | b Cairns | 4 | (4) c sub (R.W. Anderson) b Collinge | 82 |
| A.V. Mankad | c and b Hadlee | 16 | (5) not out | | 27 |
| S. Madan Lal | c N.M. Parker b Hadlee | 8 | (6) not out | | 8 |
| S.M.H. Kirmani† | c J.M. Parker b Petherick | 88 | | | |
| S. Venkataraghavan | c Turner b Hadlee | 3 | | | |
| B.S. Bedi* | c J.M. Parker b Cairns | 36 | | | |
| B.S. Chandrasekhar | not out | 20 | | | |
| Extras | (B 2, LB 1, NB 5) | 8 | (LB 1, NB 1) | | 2 |
| **Total** | | **399** | (4 wickets declared) | | **202** |

## NEW ZEALAND

| | | | | |
|---|---|---|---|---|
| G.M. Turner* | c Amarnath b Venkataraghavan | 65 | c Gavaskar b Madan Lal | 6 |
| N.M. Parker | c Kirmani b Chandrasekhar | 9 | c Amarnath b Chandrasekhar | 14 |
| J.M. Parker | run out | 104 | b Bedi | 7 |
| M.G. Burgess | c sub (K.D. Ghavri) b Bedi | 42 | c Gavaskar b Bedi | 0 |
| A.D.G. Roberts | lbw b Chandrasekhar | 2 | c Mankad b Bedi | 16 |
| W.K. Lees† | c Kirmani b Chandrasekhar | 7 | b Venkataraghavan | 42 |
| R.J. Hadlee | c Kirmani b Venkataraghavan | 17 | c Patel b Bedi | 7 |
| B.L. Cairns | b Chandrasekhar | 12 | st Kirmani b Venkataraghavan | 1 |
| D.R. O'Sullivan | c Venkataraghavan b Bedi | 3 | (10) not out | 7 |
| R.O. Collinge | c Kirmani b Venkataraghavan | 26 | (9) c Madan Lal b Bedi | 36 |
| P.J. Petherick | not out | 0 | c Amarnath b Chandrasekhar | 1 |
| Extras | (B 1, LB 6, NB 4) | 11 | (B 4) | 4 |
| **Total** | | **298** | | **141** |

| NEW ZEALAND | O | M | R | W | O | M | R | W | | FALL OF WICKETS | | | |
|---|---|---|---|---|---|---|---|---|---|---|---|---|---|
| Collinge | 15 | 5 | 41 | 0 | 12 | 2 | 45 | 2 | | I | NZ | I | NZ |
| Hadlee | 29 | 5 | 95 | 4 | 16 | 0 | 76 | 1 | *Wkt* | *1st* | *1st* | *2nd* | *2nd* |
| Cairns | 34 | 8 | 76 | 2 | | | | | 1st | 120 | 37 | 24 | 6 |
| Roberts | 6 | 0 | 27 | 0 | 6 | 1 | 13 | 0 | 2nd | 188 | 143 | 63 | 25 |
| O'Sullivan | 27 | 9 | 62 | 1 | 10 | 6 | 21 | 0 | 3rd | 218 | 220 | 118 | 27 |
| Petherick | 31·5 | 6 | 90 | 3 | 14 | 4 | 45 | 1 | 4th | 218 | 228 | 175 | 27 |
| | | | | | | | | | 5th | 239 | 238 | – | 50 |
| INDIA | | | | | | | | | 6th | 241 | 239 | – | 64 |
| Madan Lal | 9 | 2 | 27 | 0 | 6 | 0 | 13 | 1 | 7th | 247 | 267 | – | 67 |
| Amarnath | 13 | 3 | 33 | 0 | 3 | 0 | 9 | 0 | 8th | 252 | 267 | – | 132 |
| Bedi | 50·3 | 22 | 71 | 2 | 33 | 18 | 27 | 5 | 9th | 357 | 298 | – | 136 |
| Chandrasekhar | 44 | 13 | 77 | 4 | 19·2 | 5 | 59 | 2 | 10th | 399 | 298 | – | 141 |
| Venkataraghavan | 37 | 11 | 79 | 3 | 19 | 9 | 29 | 2 | | | | | |

Umpires: J. Reuben and B. Satyaji Rao.

# INDIA v NEW ZEALAND 1976–77 (2nd Test)

Played at Green Park, Kanpur, on 18, 19, 20, 21, 23 November.
Toss: India.   Result: MATCH DRAWN.
Debuts: New Zealand – G.B. Troup.

New Zealand's eighth-wicket pair survived for the final two hours of the match to earn a draw. India's total of 524 is the highest in Test cricket in which no batsman has scored a century. It provided the eighth instance of all eleven batsmen reaching double figures in a Test innings. Six batsmen reached fifty in the innings to equal the Test record.

## INDIA

| | | | | | |
|---|---|---|---|---|---|
| S.M. Gavaskar | b O'Sullivan | 66 | b Hadlee | | 15 |
| A.D. Gaekwad | c Lees b Hadlee | 43 | not out | | 77 |
| M. Amarnath | b O'Sullivan | 70 | c N.M. Parker b Hadlee | | 8 |
| G.R. Viswanath | lbw b Roberts | 68 | not out | | 103 |
| B.P. Patel | b Petherick | 13 | | | |
| A.V. Mankad | lbw b Troup | 50 | | | |
| S.M.H. Kirmani† | c Turner b O'Sullivan | 64 | | | |
| K.D. Ghavri | c Troup b Petherick | 37 | | | |
| S. Venkataraghavan | c and b Petherick | 27 | | | |
| B.S. Bedi* | not out | 50 | | | |
| B.S. Chandrasekhar | not out | 10 | | | |
| Extras | (B 17, LB 4, W 1, NB 4) | 26 | (LB 4, NB 1) | | 5 |
| **Total** | (9 wickets declared) | **524** | (2 wickets declared) | | **208** |

## NEW ZEALAND

| | | | | | |
|---|---|---|---|---|---|
| G.M. Turner* | c Viswanath b Bedi | 113 | c Venkataraghavan b Bedi | | 35 |
| G.P. Howarth | c Kirmani b Ghavri | 19 | (6) c Mankad b Venkataraghavan | | 4 |
| J.M. Parker | c Ghavri b Bedi | 34 | lbw b Bedi | | 17 |
| M.G. Burgess | c Ghavri b Bedi | 54 | lbw b Venkataraghavan | | 24 |
| A.D.G. Roberts | not out | 84 | c Mankad b Chandrasekhar | | 9 |
| N.M. Parker | lbw b Venkataraghavan | 6 | (2) lbw b Chandrasekhar | | 18 |
| W.K. Lees† | b Chandrasekhar | 3 | not out | | 49 |
| R.J. Hadlee | b Chandrasekhar | 0 | c Venkataraghavan b Bedi | | 10 |
| D.R. O'Sullivan | c Chandrasekhar b Venkataraghavan | 15 | not out | | 23 |
| G.B. Troup | c Amarnath b Venkataraghavan | 0 | | | |
| P.J. Petherick | c Kirmani b Chandrasekhar | 13 | | | |
| Extras | (LB 9) | 9 | (LB 4) | | 4 |
| **Total** | | **350** | (7 wickets) | | **193** |

| NEW ZEALAND | O | M | R | W | O | M | R | W |
|---|---|---|---|---|---|---|---|---|
| Hadlee | 29 | 2 | 121 | 1 | 15 | 1 | 56 | 2 |
| Troup | 20 | 3 | 69 | 1 | 10 | 0 | 47 | 0 |
| Roberts | 19 | 5 | 53 | 1 | | | | |
| O'Sullivan | 50 | 14 | 125 | 3 | 16 | 1 | 49 | 0 |
| Petherick | 45 | 12 | 109 | 3 | 11 | 0 | 51 | 0 |
| Howarth | 5 | 0 | 21 | 0 | | | | |
| INDIA | | | | | | | | |
| Ghavri | 12 | 3 | 16 | 1 | 6 | 2 | 35 | 0 |
| Amarnath | 5 | 0 | 23 | 0 | 4 | 2 | 5 | 0 |
| Bedi | 41 | 12 | 80 | 3 | 40 | 23 | 42 | 3 |
| Chandrasekhar | 36·5 | 6 | 102 | 3 | 33 | 15 | 61 | 2 |
| Venkataraghavan | 48 | 9 | 120 | 3 | 34 | 20 | 46 | 2 |

FALL OF WICKETS

| | I | NZ | I | NZ |
|---|---|---|---|---|
| Wkt | 1st | 1st | 2nd | 2nd |
| 1st | 79 | 54 | 23 | 43 |
| 2nd | 193 | 118 | 45 | 59 |
| 3rd | 196 | 224 | – | 86 |
| 4th | 217 | 225 | – | 97 |
| 5th | 312 | 241 | – | 110 |
| 6th | 341 | 250 | – | 114 |
| 7th | 413 | 250 | – | 134 |
| 8th | 450 | 291 | – | – |
| 9th | 493 | 298 | – | – |
| 10th | – | 350 | – | – |

Umpires: M.V. Nagendra and M.S. Sivasankariah.

# INDIA v NEW ZEALAND 1976–77 (3rd Test)

Played at Chepauk, Madras, on 26 (*no play*), 27, 28, 30 November, 1, 2 December.
Toss: India.   Result: INDIA won by 216 runs.
Debuts: Nil.

Heavy rain, which had flooded the ground, prevented a start until 11.15 on the second morning.

## INDIA

| | | | | | |
|---|---|---|---|---|---|
| S.M. Gavaskar | b Cairns | 2 | st Lees b O'Sullivan | 43 |
| A.D. Gaekwad | c Parker b Cairns | 0 | b Hadlee | 11 |
| M. Amarnath | c Petherick b Cairns | 21 | c Morrison b Hadlee | 55 |
| G.R. Viswanath | c Lees b Hadlee | 87 | st Lees b O'Sullivan | 17 |
| B.P. Patel | run out | 33 | not out | 40 |
| A.V. Mankad | b Cairns | 14 | c Burgess b Petherick | 21 |
| S.M.H. Kirmani† | lbw b Petherick | 44 | | |
| K.D. Ghavri | c Petherick b Hadlee | 8 | | |
| S. Venkataraghavan | c sub (R.O. Collinge) b Cairns | 64 | | |
| B.S. Bedi* | c Cairns b Hadlee | 5 | | |
| B.S. Chandrasekhar | not out | 1 | | |
| Extras | (B 7, LB 8, W 1, NB 3) | 19 | (B 11, LB 2, NB 1) | 14 |
| **Total** | | **298** | (5 wickets declared) | **201** |

## NEW ZEALAND

| | | | | | |
|---|---|---|---|---|---|
| G.M. Turner* | c Kirmani b Chandrasekhar | 37 | c Amarnath b Chandrasekhar | 5 |
| J.F.M. Morrison | c Kirmani b Ghavri | 7 | c Chandrasekhar b Ghavri | 1 |
| J.M. Parker | c Patel b Ghavri | 9 | c Kirmani b Chandrasekhar | 38 |
| M.G. Burgess | b Bedi | 40 | run out | 15 |
| A.D.G. Roberts | c Venkataraghavan b Chandrasekhar | 1 | c Gavaskar b Bedi | 0 |
| G.P. Howarth | c Venkataraghavan b Bedi | 3 | c Chandrasekhar b Bedi | 18 |
| W.K. Lees† | c Venkataraghavan b Bedi | 9 | c sub (S. Madan Lal) b Bedi | 21 |
| R.J. Hadlee | c Gaekwad b Bedi | 21 | c Amarnath b Bedi | 5 |
| B.L. Cairns | c Mankad b Bedi | 5 | not out | 8 |
| D.R. O'Sullivan | c Venkataraghavan b Chandrasekhar | 0 | c Patel b Chandrasekhar | 21 |
| P.J. Petherick | not out | 0 | lbw b Venkataraghavan | 1 |
| Extras | (B 1, LB 2, NB 5) | 8 | (B 7, LB 1, NB 2) | 10 |
| **Total** | | **140** | | **143** |

| NEW ZEALAND | O | M | R | W | O | M | R | W |
|---|---|---|---|---|---|---|---|---|
| Hadlee | 21 | 7 | 37 | 3 | 17 | 3 | 52 | 2 |
| Cairns | 33·1 | 11 | 55 | 5 | 16 | 2 | 49 | 0 |
| Roberts | 17 | 5 | 32 | 0 | 2 | 0 | 4 | 0 |
| O'Sullivan | 34 | 9 | 69 | 0 | 20 | 3 | 70 | 2 |
| Petherick | 25 | 5 | 77 | 1 | 6·5 | 0 | 12 | 1 |
| Howarth | 3 | 1 | 9 | 0 | | | | |
| INDIA | | | | | | | | |
| Ghavri | 13 | 3 | 32 | 2 | 8 | 4 | 14 | 1 |
| Amarnath | 8 | 3 | 17 | 0 | 3 | 1 | 6 | 0 |
| Bedi | 16·4 | 4 | 48 | 5 | 22 | 12 | 22 | 4 |
| Chandrasekhar | 16 | 5 | 28 | 3 | 20 | 3 | 64 | 3 |
| Venkataraghavan | 2 | 0 | 7 | 0 | 14 | 8 | 27 | 1 |

## FALL OF WICKETS

| | I | NZ | I | NZ |
|---|---|---|---|---|
| *Wkt* | *1st* | *1st* | *2nd* | *2nd* |
| 1st | 0 | 17 | 33 | 2 |
| 2nd | 3 | 37 | 86 | 21 |
| 3rd | 60 | 91 | 118 | 50 |
| 4th | 137 | 99 | 142 | 53 |
| 5th | 167 | 101 | 201 | 79 |
| 6th | 167 | 103 | – | 85 |
| 7th | 181 | 133 | – | 103 |
| 8th | 255 | 133 | – | 114 |
| 9th | 276 | 136 | – | 142 |
| 10th | 298 | 140 | – | 143 |

Umpires: Mohammad Ghouse and K.B. Ramaswami.

# INDIA v ENGLAND 1976–77 (1st Test)

Played at Feroz Shah Kotla, Delhi, on 17, 18, 19, 21, 22 December.
Toss: England.   Result: ENGLAND won by an innings and 25 runs.
Debuts: England – G.D. Barlow, J.K. Lever.

This was England's first victory by an innings in India and only their fifth success in 24 Tests there. Amiss reached his hundred with a six and made England's highest score in a Test in India. Gavaskar became the first Indian to score 1,000 runs in a calendar year, taking his aggregate for 1976 to 1,024. Lever was the sixth Englishman to take ten wickets in his first Test; only A.E. Trott, A.L. Valentine and R.A.L. Massie have achieved better figures than his 7 for 46 in their first Test innings. Bedi became the fourth player after R. Peel, R.W. Blair and D.L. Underwood to be dismissed for a 'pair' three times in Test matches.

## ENGLAND

| | | |
|---|---|---|
| D.L. Amiss | c Sharma b Venkataraghavan | 179 |
| J.M. Brearley | run out | 5 |
| G.D. Barlow | c Amarnath b Bedi | 0 |
| R.A. Woolmer | lbw b Chandrasekhar | 4 |
| K.W.R. Fletcher | b Chandrasekhar | 8 |
| A.W. Greig* | lbw b Venkataraghavan | 25 |
| A.P.E. Knott† | st Kirmani b Bedi | 75 |
| C.M. Old | c Viswanath b Bedi | 15 |
| J.K. Lever | c Bedi b Chandrasekhar | 53 |
| R.G.D. Willis | c Venkataraghavan b Bedi | 1 |
| D.L. Underwood | not out | 7 |
| Extras | (B 1, LB 5, W 1, NB 2) | 9 |
| **Total** | | **381** |

## INDIA

| | | | | | |
|---|---|---|---|---|---|
| S.M. Gavaskar | c Willis b Lever | 38 | c Woolmer b Underwood | | 71 |
| A.D. Gaekwad | lbw b Lever | 20 | b Willis | | 11 |
| M. Amarnath | lbw b Lever | 0 | (6) c sub (D.W. Randall) b Underwood | 24 |
| G.R. Viswanath | lbw b Lever | 3 | c Knott b Greig | | 18 |
| S. Venkataraghavan | b Lever | 0 | (9) c Knott b Lever | | 4 |
| B.P. Patel | c Knott b Lever | 33 | (5) c and b Underwood | | 14 |
| P. Sharma | c Willis b Underwood | 4 | (3) c Fletcher b Underwood | | 29 |
| S.M.H. Kirmani† | b Lever | 13 | (7) c Lever b Greig | | 10 |
| K.D. Ghavri | not out | 3 | (8) not out | | 35 |
| B.S. Bedi* | c Greig b Old | 0 | b Lever | | 0 |
| B.S. Chandrasekhar | b Old | 0 | b Lever | | 0 |
| Extras | (LB 4, W 1, NB 3) | 8 | (B 3, LB 8, NB 7) | | 18 |
| **Total** | | **122** | | | **234** |

| INDIA | O | M | R | W | O | M | R | W | FALL OF WICKETS | | | |
|---|---|---|---|---|---|---|---|---|---|---|---|---|
| | | | | | | | | | | E | I | I |
| Ghavri | 14 | 3 | 50 | 0 | | | | | Wkt | 1st | 1st | 2nd |
| Amarnath | 8 | 2 | 12 | 0 | | | | | 1st | 34 | 43 | 20 |
| Bedi | 59 | 22 | 92 | 4 | | | | | 2nd | 34 | 43 | 110 |
| Chandrasekhar | 32·5 | 6 | 117 | 3 | | | | | 3rd | 51 | 49 | 133 |
| Venkataraghavan | 34 | 6 | 94 | 2 | | | | | 4th | 65 | 49 | 153 |
| Gaekwad | 1 | 0 | 1 | 0 | | | | | 5th | 125 | 96 | 163 |
| Sharma | 3 | 0 | 6 | 0 | | | | | 6th | 226 | 99 | 182 |
| | | | | | | | | | 7th | 263 | 103 | 190 |
| ENGLAND | | | | | | | | | 8th | 357 | 121 | 226 |
| Old | 12·5 | 0 | 28 | 2 | 4 | 2 | 6 | 0 | 9th | 363 | 122 | 226 |
| Willis | 7 | 3 | 21 | 0 | 9 | 3 | 24 | 1 | 10th | 381 | 122 | 234 |
| Lever | 23 | 6 | 46 | 7 | 13·4 | 6 | 24 | 3 | | | | |
| Underwood | 9 | 3 | 19 | 1 | 44 | 15 | 78 | 4 | | | | |
| Greig | | | | | 40 | 11 | 84 | 2 | | | | |

Umpires: J. Reuben and M.V. Nagendra.

# INDIA v ENGLAND 1976–77 (2nd Test)

Played at Eden Gardens, Calcutta, on 1, 2, 3, 5, 6 January.
Toss: India.   Result: ENGLAND won by ten wickets.
Debuts: England – D.W. Randall, R.W. Tolchard.

England won successive Tests in India for the first time; it was also their first victory in six Tests in Calcutta. Greig reached his hundred in 415 minutes, the fourth-slowest ever for England. When he had made 3, he scored his 3,000th run in 49 Tests and became the first to achieve a double of 3,000 runs and 100 wickets for England.

## INDIA

| | | | | |
|---|---|---|---|---|
| S.M. Gavaskar | c Old b Willis | 0 | b Underwood | 18 |
| A.D. Gaekwad | b Lever | 32 | c Tolchard b Greig | 8 |
| P. Sharma | c Greig b Lever | 9 | c Knott b Willis | 20 |
| G.R. Viswanath | c Tolchard b Underwood | 35 | c Lever b Greig | 3 |
| B.P. Patel | hit wkt b Willis | 21 | lbw b Old | 56 |
| E.D. Solkar | c Greig b Willis | 2 | c Knott b Willis | 3 |
| S. Madan Lal | c Knott b Old | 17 | c Brearley b Old | 16 |
| S.M.H. Kirmani† | not out | 25 | b Old | 0 |
| E.A.S. Prasanna | b Willis | 2 | c Brearley b Underwood | 13 |
| B.S. Bedi* | c Lever b Old | 1 | b Underwood | 18 |
| B.S. Chandrasekhar | b Willis | 1 | not out | 4 |
| Extras | (LB 2, NB 8) | 10 | (B 2, LB 4, NB 16) | 22 |
| **Total** | | **155** | | **181** |

## ENGLAND

| | | | | |
|---|---|---|---|---|
| D.L. Amiss | c Kirmani b Prasanna | 35 | not out | 7 |
| G.D. Barlow | c Kirmani b Madan Lal | 4 | not out | 7 |
| J.M. Brearley | c Solkar b Bedi | 5 | | |
| D.W. Randall | lbw b Prasanna | 37 | | |
| R.W. Tolchard | b Bedi | 67 | | |
| A.W. Greig* | lbw b Prasanna | 103 | | |
| A.P.E. Knott† | c Gavaskar b Bedi | 2 | | |
| C.M. Old | c Madan Lal b Prasanna | 52 | | |
| J.K. Lever | c Gravaskar b Bedi | 2 | | |
| D.L. Underwood | c Gavaskar b Bedi | 4 | | |
| R.G.D. Willis | not out | 0 | | |
| Extras | (B 5, LB 5) | 10 | (LB 1, NB 1) | 2 |
| **Total** | | **321** | (0 wickets) | **16** |

| ENGLAND | O | M | R | W | O | M | R | W | FALL OF WICKETS | | | | |
|---|---|---|---|---|---|---|---|---|---|---|---|---|---|
| Willis | 20 | 3 | 27 | 5 | 13 | 1 | 32 | 2 | | I | E | I | E |
| Lever | 22 | 2 | 57 | 2 | 3 | 0 | 12 | 0 | *Wkt* | *1st* | *1st* | *2nd* | *2nd* |
| Underwood | 13 | 5 | 24 | 1 | 32·5 | 18 | 50 | 3 | 1st | 1 | 7 | 31 | – |
| Old | 20 | 5 | 57 | 2 | 12 | 4 | 38 | 3 | 2nd | 23 | 14 | 33 | – |
| Greig | | | | | 10 | 0 | 27 | 2 | 3rd | 65 | 81 | 36 | – |
| | | | | | | | | | 4th | 92 | 90 | 60 | – |
| INDIA | | | | | | | | | 5th | 99 | 232 | 70 | – |
| Madan Lal | 17 | 4 | 25 | 1 | 1 | 0 | 3 | 0 | 6th | 106 | 234 | 97 | – |
| Solkar | 6 | 1 | 15 | 0 | | | | | 7th | 136 | 298 | 97 | – |
| Bedi | 64 | 25 | 110 | 5 | 1·4 | 0 | 6 | 0 | 8th | 147 | 307 | 146 | – |
| Chandrasekhar | 33 | 9 | 66 | 0 | | | | | 9th | 149 | 321 | 171 | – |
| Prasanna | 57·4 | 16 | 93 | 4 | 1 | 0 | 5 | 0 | 10th | 155 | 321 | 181 | – |
| Sharma | 1 | 0 | 2 | 0 | | | | | | | | | |

Umpires: B. Satyaji Rao and H.P. Sharma.

# INDIA v ENGLAND 1976–77 (3rd Test)

Played at Chepauk, Madras, on 14, 15, 16, 18, 19 January.
Toss: England.   Result: ENGLAND won by 200 runs.
Debuts: Nil.

England won their first rubber in India since 1933-34. It was the first time that India had lost the first three matches in any home rubber. Bedi, playing in his 51st match, became the first bowler to take 200 wickets in Tests for India when he dismissed Greig. In the first innings, Tolchard (1*) retired at 33 for 3 after being hit on the back of his right hand by a ball from Amarnath, and resumed at 209 for 7. India's second total of 83 is the lowest by any side in a Test match in India. Vengsarkar, struck on the hand by his first ball from Willis, retired at the tea interval.

## ENGLAND

| | | | | | |
|---|---|---|---|---|---|
| D.L. Amiss | lbw b Madan Lal | 4 | | c Amarnath b Chandrasekhar | 46 |
| R.A. Woolmer | c Gavaskar b Madan Lal | 22 | | lbw b Prasanna | 16 |
| J.M. Brearley | c and b Prasanna | 59 | (4) | b Chandrasekhar | 29 |
| D.W. Randall | run out | 2 | (5) | c Kirmani b Chandrasekhar | 0 |
| R.W. Tolchard | not out | 8 | (9) | not out | 10 |
| A.W. Greig* | c Viswanath b Bedi | 54 | | lbw b Prasanna | 41 |
| A.P.E. Knott† | c Viswanath b Bedi | 45 | | c Patel b Prasanna | 11 |
| J.K. Lever | c Kirmani b Bedi | 23 | (3) | c Amarnath b Chandrasekhar | 2 |
| C.M. Old | c Amarnath b Bedi | 2 | (8) | c Chandrasekhar b Prasanna | 4 |
| D.L. Underwood | b Prasanna | 23 | | st Kirmani b Chandrasekhar | 8 |
| R.G.D. Willis | run out | 7 | | not out | 4 |
| Extras | (B 5, LB 8) | 13 | | (B 14) | 14 |
| **Total** | | **262** | | (9 wickets declared) | **185** |

## INDIA

| | | | | | |
|---|---|---|---|---|---|
| S.M. Gavaskar | c Brearley b Old | 39 | | c Woolmer b Underwood | 24 |
| M. Amarnath | b Old | 0 | (3) | c Woolmer b Underwood | 12 |
| G.R. Viswanath | c Knott b Lever | 9 | (4) | c Brearley b Underwood | 6 |
| A.V. Mankad | b Lever | 0 | (7) | c Old b Lever | 4 |
| B.P. Patel | b Underwood | 32 | (6) | c Old b Willis | 4 |
| D.B. Vengsarkar | c Randall b Lever | 8 | (2) | retired hurt | 1 |
| S. Madan Lal | c Underwood b Willis | 12 | (9) | c Knott b Willis | 6 |
| S.M.H. Kirmani† | c Brearley b Lever | 27 | | c Brearley b Willis | 1 |
| E.A.S. Prasanna | c and b Underwood | 13 | (5) | c Brearley b Underwood | 0 |
| B.S. Bedi* | c sub (G.D. Barlow) b Lever | 5 | | not out | 11 |
| B.S. Chandrasekhar | not out | 1 | | b Lever | 6 |
| Extras | (LB 1, NB 17) | 18 | | (B 5, LB 1, NB 2) | 8 |
| **Total** | | **164** | | | **83** |

| INDIA | O | M | R | W | O | M | R | W | | FALL OF WICKETS | | | |
|---|---|---|---|---|---|---|---|---|---|---|---|---|---|
| Madan Lal | 21 | 5 | 43 | 2 | 9 | 2 | 15 | 0 | | E | I | E | I |
| Amarnath | 14 | 3 | 26 | 0 | 7 | 2 | 18 | 0 | Wkt | 1st | 1st | 2nd | 2nd |
| Chandrasekhar | 25 | 4 | 63 | 0 | 20·5 | 4 | 50 | 5 | 1st | 14 | 5 | 39 | 40 |
| Bedi | 38·5 | 16 | 72 | 4 | 13 | 3 | 33 | 0 | 2nd | 29 | 17 | 54 | 45 |
| Prasanna | 27 | 11 | 45 | 2 | 22 | 5 | 55 | 4 | 3rd | 31 | 17 | 83 | 45 |
| | | | | | | | | | 4th | 142 | 69 | 83 | 54 |
| ENGLAND | | | | | | | | | 5th | 162 | 86 | 124 | 54 |
| Willis | 19 | 5 | 46 | 1 | 13 | 4 | 18 | 3 | 6th | 201 | 114 | 135 | 57 |
| Old | 13 | 4 | 19 | 2 | 5 | 1 | 11 | 0 | 7th | 209 | 115 | 141 | 66 |
| Lever | 19·5 | 2 | 59 | 5 | 6·5 | 0 | 18 | 2 | 8th | 228 | 151 | 169 | 71 |
| Woolmer | 1 | 0 | 2 | 0 | | | | | 9th | 253 | 161 | 180 | 83 |
| Greig | 4 | 1 | 4 | 0 | | | | | 10th | 262 | 164 | – | – |
| Underwood | 17 | 9 | 16 | 2 | 14 | 7 | 28 | 4 | | | | | |

Umpires: J. Reuben and M.S. Sivasankariah.

# INDIA v ENGLAND 1976–77 (4th Test)

Played at Karnataka C.A. Ground on 28, 29, 30 January, 1, 2 February.
Toss: India.   Result: INDIA won by 140 runs.
Debuts: India – Yajurvindra Singh.

This was England's first Test match in Bangalore. On only one previous occasion in all Test matches has England's fourth wicket fallen for eight runs or less; against Australia in 1903-04 (*Test No. 82*) their first four wickets fell for five runs. Playing in his first Test match, Yajurvindra Singh equalled the innings and match catching records for non-wicket-keepers; his five catches in the first innings equalled V.Y. Richardson's feat in 1935-36 (*Test No. 251*), and his seven in the match enabled him to share G.S. Chappell's record set in 1974–75 (*Test No. 751*).

## INDIA

| | | | | |
|---|---|--:|---|--:|
| S.M. Gavaskar | c Underwood b Lever | 4 | c Brearley b Underwood | 50 |
| A.D. Gaekwad | c Tolchard b Greig | 39 | b Old | 9 |
| S. Amarnath | b Greig | 63 | c Tolchard b Willis | 14 |
| G.R. Viswanath | c Brearley b Underwood | 13 | (7) not out | 79 |
| B.P. Patel | c Randall b Willis | 23 | (4) c Knott b Underwood | 17 |
| Yajurvindra Singh | c Knott b Willis | 8 | (5) c Fletcher b Underwood | 15 |
| S.M.H. Kirmani† | b Willis | 52 | (8) c Randall b Underwood | 21 |
| K.D. Ghavri | c Knott b Willis | 16 | (9) c Amiss b Lever | 12 |
| E.A.S. Prasanna | c Greig b Willis | 6 | (6) c Old b Willis | 12 |
| B.S. Bedi* | not out | 8 | run out | 15 |
| B.S. Chandrasekhar | c Knott b Willis | 1 | not out | 0 |
| Extras | (B 8, LB 6, NB 6) | 20 | (B 1, LB 6, NB 8) | 15 |
| **Total** | | **253** | (9 wickets declared) | **259** |

## ENGLAND

| | | | | |
|---|---|--:|---|--:|
| D.L. Amiss | c Yajurvindra b Chandrasekhar | 82 | c Yajurvindra b Ghavri | 0 |
| J.M. Brearley | c Viswanath b Chandrasekhar | 4 | c Gaekwad b Bedi | 4 |
| K.W.R. Fletcher | c Yajurvindra b Prasanna | 10 | c Yajurvindra b Chandrasekhar | 1 |
| D.W. Randall | c Yajurvindra b Prasanna | 10 | c Gaekwad b Bedi | 0 |
| R.W. Tolchard | b Chandrasekhar | 0 | lbw b Chandrasekhar | 14 |
| A.W. Greig* | c Yajurvindra b Chandrasekhar | 2 | st Kirmani b Bedi | 31 |
| A.P.E. Knott† | b Bedi | 29 | not out | 81 |
| C.M. Old | lbw b Prasanna | 9 | lbw b Chandrasekhar | 13 |
| J.K. Lever | not out | 20 | c Ghavri b Bedi | 11 |
| D.L. Underwood | c Yajurvindra b Chandrasekhar | 12 | c Patel b Bedi | 10 |
| R.G.D. Willis | lbw b Chandrasekhar | 7 | st Kirmani b Bedi | 0 |
| Extras | (B 3, LB 5, NB 2) | 10 | (B 5, LB 6, NB 1) | 12 |
| **Total** | | **195** | | **177** |

| ENGLAND | O | M | R | W | O | M | R | W |
|---|--:|--:|--:|--:|--:|--:|--:|--:|
| Willis | 17 | 2 | 53 | 6 | 18 | 2 | 47 | 2 |
| Lever | 17 | 2 | 48 | 1 | 9 | 1 | 28 | 1 |
| Old | 12 | 0 | 43 | 0 | 10 | 4 | 19 | 1 |
| Underwood | 21 | 7 | 45 | 1 | 31 | 8 | 76 | 4 |
| Greig | 18 | 5 | 44 | 2 | 23 | 2 | 74 | 0 |
| INDIA | | | | | | | | |
| Ghavri | 13 | 3 | 31 | 0 | 4 | 1 | 4 | 1 |
| Yajurvindra Singh | 1 | 0 | 2 | 0 | | | | |
| Bedi | 23 | 11 | 29 | 1 | 21·3 | 4 | 71 | 6 |
| Chandrasekhar | 31·2 | 7 | 76 | 6 | 15 | 3 | 55 | 3 |
| Prasanna | 28 | 10 | 47 | 3 | 15 | 5 | 35 | 0 |
| Gavaskar | | | | | 2 | 2 | 0 | 0 |

### FALL OF WICKETS

| | I | E | I | E |
|---|--:|--:|--:|--:|
| Wkt | 1st | 1st | 2nd | 2nd |
| 1st | 9 | 13 | 31 | 0 |
| 2nd | 102 | 34 | 80 | 7 |
| 3rd | 124 | 64 | 82 | 7 |
| 4th | 134 | 65 | 104 | 8 |
| 5th | 153 | 67 | 124 | 35 |
| 6th | 170 | 137 | 154 | 61 |
| 7th | 236 | 146 | 189 | 105 |
| 8th | 240 | 154 | 223 | 148 |
| 9th | 249 | 175 | 257 | 166 |
| 10th | 253 | 195 | – | 177 |

Umpires: M.V. Nagendra and Mohammad Ghouse.

# INDIA v ENGLAND 1976–77 (5th Test)

Played at Wankhede Stadium, Bombay, on 11, 12, 14, 15, 16 February.
Toss: India.   Result: MATCH DRAWN.
Debuts: Nil.

India used only one ball in England's first innings which lasted 154 overs. Underwood took 29 wickets in the rubber to equal F.S. Trueman's record for England against India set in 1952.

## INDIA

| | | | | |
|---|---|---|---|---|
| S.M. Gavaskar | c and b Underwood | 108 | c Willis b Underwood | 42 |
| A.D. Gaekwad | c Tolchard b Lever | 21 | st Knott b Underwood | 25 |
| S. Amarnath | b Underwood | 40 | run out | 63 |
| G.R. Viswanath | c and b Lever | 4 | (5) c Lever b Greig | 5 |
| B.P. Patel | st Knott b Greig | 83 | (4) c Fletcher b Underwood | 3 |
| Yajurvindra Singh | b Greig | 6 | run out | 21 |
| S.M.H. Kirmani† | c Knott b Underwood | 8 | c Greig b Underwood | 10 |
| K.D. Ghavri | lbw b Greig | 25 | c Fletcher b Underwood | 8 |
| E.A.S. Prasanna | b Underwood | 9 | not out | 0 |
| B.S. Bedi* | not out | 20 | lbw b Lever | 3 |
| B.S. Chandrasekhar | b Lever | 3 | b Lever | 4 |
| Extras | (LB 9, NB 2) | 11 | (B 4, LB 1, NB 3) | 8 |
| **Total** | | **338** | | **192** |

## ENGLAND

| | | | | |
|---|---|---|---|---|
| D.L. Amiss | c Viswanath b Bedi | 50 | c Viswanath b Bedi | 14 |
| J.M. Brearley | st Kirmani b Prasanna | 91 | c Yajurvindra b Prasanna | 18 |
| D.W. Randall | c Gaekwad b Prasanna | 22 | c Kirmani b Ghavri | 15 |
| K.W.R. Fletcher | c Viswanath b Chandrasekhar | 14 | not out | 58 |
| A.W. Greig* | b Prasanna | 76 | c Bedi b Ghavri | 10 |
| A.P.E. Knott† | b Chandrasekhar | 24 | b Ghavri | 1 |
| R.W. Tolchard | st Kirmani b Prasanna | 4 | c Gavaskar b Ghavri | 26 |
| J.K. Lever | c Gavaskar b Bedi | 7 | c Patel b Ghavri | 4 |
| D.L. Underwood | b Bedi | 7 | | |
| M.W.W. Selvey | not out | 5 | | |
| R.G.D. Willis | c Gavaskar b Bedi | 0 | | |
| Extras | (B 1, LB 13, NB 3) | 17 | (B 2, LB 3, NB 1) | 6 |
| **Total** | | **317** | (7 wickets) | **152** |

| ENGLAND | O | M | R | W | O | M | R | W |
|---|---|---|---|---|---|---|---|---|
| Willis | 13 | 1 | 52 | 0 | 6 | 1 | 15 | 0 |
| Lever | 17·4 | 4 | 42 | 3 | 17·4 | 6 | 46 | 2 |
| Selvey | 15 | 1 | 80 | 0 | | | | |
| Underwood | 38 | 13 | 89 | 4 | 33 | 10 | 84 | 5 |
| Greig | 22 | 6 | 64 | 3 | 14 | 3 | 39 | 1 |
| INDIA | | | | | | | | |
| Ghavri | 12 | 2 | 31 | 0 | 15 | 6 | 33 | 5 |
| Gavaskar | 2 | 0 | 2 | 0 | 1 | 1 | 0 | 0 |
| Bedi | 56 | 20 | 109 | 4 | 21 | 5 | 52 | 1 |
| Chandrasekhar | 32 | 7 | 85 | 2 | 4 | 0 | 25 | 0 |
| Prasanna | 52 | 20 | 73 | 4 | 30 | 12 | 36 | 1 |

## FALL OF WICKETS

| Wkt | I 1st | E 1st | I 2nd | E 2nd |
|---|---|---|---|---|
| 1st | 52 | 146 | 68 | 34 |
| 2nd | 115 | 175 | 72 | 38 |
| 3rd | 122 | 180 | 80 | 86 |
| 4th | 261 | 206 | 92 | 112 |
| 5th | 267 | 247 | 136 | 113 |
| 6th | 273 | 256 | 156 | 148 |
| 7th | 289 | 290 | 182 | 152 |
| 8th | 303 | 300 | 185 | – |
| 9th | 321 | 312 | 188 | – |
| 10th | 338 | 317 | 192 | – |

Umpires: B. Satyaji Rao and H.P. Sharma.

# AUSTRALIA v PAKISTAN 1976–77 (1st Test)

Played at Adelaide Oval on 24, 26, 27, 28, 29 December.
Toss: Pakistan.   Result: MATCH DRAWN.
Debuts: Pakistan – Iqbal Qasim, Mudassar Nazar.

Australia's seventh-wicket pair needed to score 56 runs to win the match when the first of the mandatory last 15 overs began. They were content with a draw and finished 24 runs short of their target. Thomson, attempting to catch Zaheer off his own bowling, collided with Turner (short leg) and dislocated his collar bone. He took no further part in the rubber.

## PAKISTAN

| | | | | |
|---|---|---|---|---|
| Majid Khan | c McCosker b Thomson | 15 | lbw b Lillee | 47 |
| Mudassar Nazar | c Marsh b Gilmour | 13 | c Marsh b O'Keeffe | 22 |
| Zaheer Abbas | c Walters b O'Keeffe | 85 | c Davis b Lillee | 101 |
| Mushtaq Mohammad* | c McCosker b Thomson | 18 | c Marsh b Lillee | 37 |
| Javed Miandad | b O'Keeffe | 15 | b Gilmour | 54 |
| Asif Iqbal | c Marsh b O'Keeffe | 0 | not out | 152 |
| Imran Khan | b Chappell | 48 | b O'Keeffe | 5 |
| Salim Altaf | c Davis b Chappell | 16 | c Turner b Lillee | 21 |
| Wasim Bari† | run out | 21 | lbw b Lillee | 0 |
| Sarfraz Nawaz | c Marsh b Lillee | 29 | c Lillee b O'Keeffe | 0 |
| Iqbal Qasim | not out | 1 | run out | 4 |
| Extras | (LB 6, NB 5) | 11 | (B 14, LB 1, NB 8) | 23 |
| **Total** | | **272** | | **466** |

## AUSTRALIA

| | | | | |
|---|---|---|---|---|
| I.C. Davis | c Mushtaq b Miandad | 105 | b Sarfraz | 0 |
| A. Turner | c Zaheer b Imran | 33 | c Sarfraz b Miandad | 48 |
| R.B. McCosker | b Mushtaq | 65 | c Wasim b Qasim | 42 |
| G.S. Chappell* | c Zaheer b Miandad | 52 | c Mushtaq b Qasim | 70 |
| K.D. Walters | c Miandad b Sarfraz | 107 | c Wasim b Qasim | 51 |
| G.J. Cosier | c Asif b Miandad | 33 | (7) not out | 25 |
| R.W. Marsh† | b Mushtaq | 36 | (8) not out | 13 |
| G.J. Gilmour | c Qasim b Mushtaq | 3 | (6) b Qasim | 5 |
| K.J. O'Keeffe | not out | 3 | | |
| D.K. Lillee | c Majid b Mushtaq | 0 | | |
| J.R. Thomson | absent hurt | – | | |
| Extras | (LB 4, NB 13) | 17 | (B 1, LB 3, NB 3) | 7 |
| **Total** | | **454** | **(6 wickets)** | **261** |

| AUSTRALIA | O | M | R | W | O | M | R | W | FALL OF WICKETS | | | | |
|---|---|---|---|---|---|---|---|---|---|---|---|---|---|
| Lillee | 19 | 1 | 104 | 1 | 47·7 | 10 | 163 | 5 | | P | A | P | A |
| Thomson | 8·5 | 2 | 34 | 2 | | | | | *Wkt* | *1st* | *1st* | *2nd* | *2nd* |
| Gilmour | 14·2 | 1 | 55 | 1 | 14 | 1 | 67 | 1 | 1st | 19 | 63 | 58 | 0 |
| Walters | 3 | 0 | 12 | 0 | 2 | 1 | 5 | 0 | 2nd | 56 | 188 | 92 | 92 |
| O'Keeffe | 19 | 5 | 42 | 3 | 53 | 12 | 166 | 3 | 3rd | 98 | 244 | 182 | 100 |
| Chappell | 7 | 2 | 14 | 2 | 11 | 3 | 31 | 0 | 4th | 140 | 278 | 236 | 201 |
| Cosier | | | | | 5 | 1 | 11 | 0 | 5th | 152 | 366 | 293 | 219 |
| PAKISTAN | | | | | | | | | 6th | 157 | 445 | 298 | 228 |
| Sarfraz | 24 | 3 | 75 | 1 | 8 | 1 | 24 | 1 | 7th | 220 | 451 | 368 | – |
| Salim | 15 | 0 | 71 | 0 | | | | | 8th | 221 | 451 | 378 | – |
| Imran | 22 | 2 | 92 | 1 | 5 | 0 | 25 | 0 | 9th | 271 | 454 | 379 | – |
| Qasim | 14 | 0 | 56 | 0 | 30 | 6 | 84 | 4 | 10th | 272 | – | 466 | – |
| Miandad | 25 | 3 | 85 | 3 | 21 | 6 | 71 | 1 | | | | | |
| Mushtaq | 19·4 | 2 | 58 | 4 | 9 | 1 | 50 | 0 | | | | | |

Umpires: M.G. O'Connell and R.C. Bailhache.

# AUSTRALIA v PAKISTAN 1976–77 (2nd Test)

Played at Melbourne Cricket Ground on 1, 2, 3, 5, 6 January.
Toss: Australia.   Result: AUSTRALIA won by 348 runs.
Debuts: Nil.

In the first innings Australia achieved their highest partnerships against Pakistan for the first, fifth and eighth wickets: 134 by Davis and Turner; 171 by G.S. Chappell and Cosier; and 118 by Cosier and O'Keeffe. Lillee's match figures of 10 for 135 are the best by an Australian bowler in Tests against Pakistan.

## AUSTRALIA

| | | | | |
|---|---|---|---|---|
| I.C. Davis | c Imran b Asif Iqbal | 56 | c Asif Iqbal b Qasim | 88 |
| A. Turner | b Asif Iqbal | 82 | lbw b Imran | 5 |
| R.B. McCosker | lbw b Asif Iqbal | 0 | st Wasim b Qasim | 105 |
| G.S. Chappell* | c Wasim b Qasim | 121 | c and b Imran | 67 |
| K.D. Walters | st Wasim b Qasim | 42 | b Imran | 0 |
| G.J. Cosier | c Asif Masood b Majid | 168 | b Imran | 8 |
| R.W. Marsh† | lbw b Qasim | 2 | st Wasim b Qasim | 13 |
| G.J. Gilmour | st Wasim b Qasim | 0 | not out | 7 |
| K.J. O'Keeffe | not out | 28 | | |
| D.K. Lillee | ) did not bat | | (9) b Imran | 6 |
| M.H.N. Walker | ) | | | |
| Extras | (B 3, LB 7, W 1, NB 7) | 18 | (B 2, LB 11, NB 3) | 16 |
| **Total** | (8 wickets declared) | **517** | (8 wickets declared) | **315** |

## PAKISTAN

| | | | | |
|---|---|---|---|---|
| Majid Khan | c Marsh b Lillee | 76 | b Lillee | 35 |
| Sadiq Mohammad | c McCosker b O'Keeffe | 105 | c Walters b Gilmour | 0 |
| Zaheer Abbas | b Gilmour | 90 | lbw b Walker | 58 |
| Mushtaq Mohammad* | lbw b Lillee | 9 | c Chappell b Lillee | 4 |
| Javed Miandad | lbw b Lillee | 5 | c Turner b O'Keeffe | 10 |
| Asif Iqbal | c sub (K.J. Hughes) b Gilmour | 35 | lbw b Lillee | 6 |
| Imran Khan | c Marsh b Lillee | 5 | c and b O'Keeffe | 28 |
| Salim Altaf | c Chappell b Lillee | 0 | b O'Keeffe | 0 |
| Wasim Bari† | lbw b Lillee | 0 | c Walker b O'Keeffe | 2 |
| Iqbal Qasim | run out | 1 | c Marsh b Lillee | 1 |
| Asif Masood | not out | 0 | not out | 0 |
| Extras | (LB 2, NB 5) | 7 | (B 1, LB 6) | 7 |
| **Total** | | **333** | | **151** |

| PAKISTAN | O | M | R | W | O | M | R | W | | FALL OF WICKETS | | | |
|---|---|---|---|---|---|---|---|---|---|---|---|---|---|
| Imran | 22 | 0 | 115 | 0 | 25·5 | 2 | 122 | 5 | | A | P | A | P |
| Salim | 17 | 2 | 117 | 0 | 6 | 1 | 28 | 0 | *Wkt* | *1st* | *1st* | *2nd* | *2nd* |
| Asif Masood | 13 | 1 | 79 | 0 | | | | | 1st | 134 | 113 | 6 | 4 |
| Asif Iqbal | 16 | 3 | 52 | 3 | | | | | 2nd | 134 | 241 | 182 | 86 |
| Miandad | 2 | 0 | 15 | 0 | | | | | 3rd | 151 | 270 | 223 | 99 |
| Qasim | 21 | 5 | 111 | 4 | 25 | 2 | 119 | 3 | 4th | 227 | 285 | 226 | 104 |
| Majid | 1·6 | 0 | 10 | 1 | 2 | 0 | 12 | 0 | 5th | 398 | 292 | 244 | 120 |
| Mushtaq | | | | | 3 | 0 | 18 | 0 | 6th | 400 | 303 | 301 | 124 |
| | | | | | | | | | 7th | 400 | 303 | 301 | 128 |
| AUSTRALIA | | | | | | | | | 8th | 517 | 303 | 315 | 136 |
| Lillee | 23 | 4 | 82 | 6 | 14 | 1 | 53 | 4 | 9th | – | 332 | – | 145 |
| Gilmour | 16·1 | 2 | 78 | 2 | 3 | 0 | 19 | 1 | 10th | – | 333 | – | 151 |
| Walker | 22 | 1 | 93 | 0 | 9 | 2 | 34 | 1 | | | | | |
| O'Keeffe | 21 | 4 | 63 | 1 | 18·1 | 5 | 38 | 4 | | | | | |
| Cosier | 2 | 0 | 10 | 0 | | | | | | | | | |

Umpires: T.F. Brooks and M.G. O'Connell.

# AUSTRALIA v PAKISTAN 1976–77 (3rd Test)

Played at Sydney Cricket Ground on 14, 15, 16, 18 January.
Toss: Australia.   Result: PAKISTAN won by eight wickets.
Debuts: Pakistan – Haroon Rashid.

Pakistan gained their first Test victory in Australia and only their second of this series. Imran Khan, with 6 for 63 in the second innings and 12 for 165 in the match, set new records for Pakistan in Australia. The partnership of 115 by Asif Iqbal and Javed Miandad is Pakistan's highest for the sixth wicket against Australia. Australia's total of 180 is their lowest against Pakistan in a home Test.

## AUSTRALIA

| | | | | |
|---|---|---|---|---|
| I.C. Davis | b Sarfraz | 20 | c Haroon b Imran | 25 |
| A. Turner | c Wasim b Sarfraz | 0 | c Majid b Sarfraz | 11 |
| R.B. McCosker | c Mushtaq b Imran | 8 | c Wasim b Imran | 8 |
| G.S. Chappell* | c Zaheer b Imran | 28 | c Wasim b Sarfraz | 5 |
| K.D. Walters | c Wasim b Imran | 2 | c Wasim b Imran | 38 |
| G.J. Cosier | c Wasim b Imran | 50 | c Wasim b Sarfraz | 4 |
| R.W. Marsh† | c and b Imran | 14 | run out | 41 |
| G.J. Gilmour | c Miandad b Sarfraz | 32 | c Zaheer b Imran | 0 |
| K.J. O'Keeffe | c Asif b Imran | 1 | c Haroon b Imran | 7 |
| D.K. Lillee | lbw b Miandad | 14 | c Zaheer b Imran | 27 |
| M.H.N. Walker | not out | 34 | not out | 3 |
| Extras | (B 5, NB 3) | 8 | (B 7, NB 4) | 11 |
| **Total** | | **211** | | **180** |

## PAKISTAN

| | | | | |
|---|---|---|---|---|
| Majid Khan | c Marsh b Walker | 48 | not out | 26 |
| Sadiq Mohammad | c Cosier b Walker | 25 | c Marsh b Lillee | 0 |
| Zaheer Abbas | c Turner b Lillee | 5 | c Walters b Lillee | 4 |
| Mushtaq Mohammad* | c Turner b Lillee | 9 | not out | 0 |
| Haroon Rashid | c Marsh b Gilmour | 57 | | |
| Asif Iqbal | b Gilmour | 120 | | |
| Javed Miandad | c Walters b Walker | 64 | | |
| Imran Khan | c Turner b Gilmour | 0 | | |
| Sarfraz Nawaz | c Turner b Walker | 13 | | |
| Wasim Bari† | c Walters b Lillee | 5 | | |
| Iqbal Qasim | not out | 0 | | |
| Extras | (B 6, LB 6, NB 2) | 14 | (B 1, NB 1) | 2 |
| **Total** | | **360** | (2 wickets) | **32** |

| PAKISTAN | O | M | R | W | O | M | R | W | | FALL OF WICKETS | | | |
|---|---|---|---|---|---|---|---|---|---|---|---|---|---|
| Sarfraz | 16 | 4 | 42 | 3 | 15 | 3 | 77 | 3 | | A | P | A | P |
| Imran | 26 | 6 | 102 | 6 | 19·7 | 3 | 63 | 6 | Wkt | 1st | 1st | 2nd | 2nd |
| Asif | 15 | 5 | 53 | 0 | | | | | 1st | 3 | 42 | 32 | 1 |
| Mushtaq | 2 | 1 | 2 | 0 | | | | | 2nd | 26 | 51 | 41 | 22 |
| Qasim | 4 | 3 | 2 | 0 | 2 | 1 | 2 | 0 | 3rd | 28 | 77 | 51 | – |
| Miandad | 1·2 | 0 | 2 | 1 | 5 | 0 | 27 | 0 | 4th | 38 | 111 | 61 | – |
| | | | | | | | | | 5th | 100 | 205 | 75 | – |
| AUSTRALIA | | | | | | | | | 6th | 125 | 320 | 99 | – |
| Lillee | 22·3 | 0 | 114 | 3 | 4 | 0 | 24 | 2 | 7th | 138 | 322 | 99 | – |
| Gilmour | 16 | 1 | 81 | 3 | | | | | 8th | 146 | 339 | 115 | – |
| Walker | 29 | 4 | 112 | 4 | 3·2 | 1 | 6 | 0 | 9th | 159 | 360 | 177 | – |
| Walters | 4 | 1 | 7 | 0 | | | | | 10th | 211 | 360 | 180 | – |
| O'Keeffe | 11 | 2 | 32 | 0 | | | | | | | | | |

Umpires: T.F. Brooks and R.R. Ledwidge.

## NEW ZEALAND v AUSTRALIA 1976–77 (1st Test)

Played at Lancaster Park, Christchurch, on 18, 19, 20, 22, 23 February.
Toss: New Zealand.   Result: MATCH DRAWN.
Debuts: New Zealand – G.N. Edwards.

New Zealand were set to score 350 runs in 390 minutes. Congdon (297 minutes) and D.R. Hadlee (52 minutes) earned a draw after the final hour had begun with their total at 260 for 8. Australia's 552 and Walters' score of 250 are records for this series. Walters batted for 394 minutes and hit 2 sixes and 30 fours in the highest and last of his 14 Test hundreds. His partnership of 217 in 187 minutes with Gilmour is Australia's highest for the seventh wicket against all countries.

### AUSTRALIA

| | | | | |
|---|---|---|---|---|
| A. Turner | b Chatfield | 3 | lbw b D.R. Hadlee | 20 |
| I.C. Davis | c G.P. Howarth b R.J. Hadlee | 34 | c Lees b R.J. Hadlee | 22 |
| R.B. McCosker | c Parker b D.R. Hadlee | 37 | not out | 77 |
| G.S. Chappell* | c Turner b R.J. Hadlee | 44 | c Parker b H.J. Howarth | 0 |
| G.J. Cosier | b R.J. Hadlee | 23 | run out | 2 |
| K.D. Walters | c H.J. Howarth b D.R. Hadlee | 250 | not out | 20 |
| R.W. Marsh† | c Parker b H.J. Howarth | 2 | | |
| G.J. Gilmour | b Chatfield | 101 | | |
| K.J. O'Keeffe | run out | 8 | | |
| D.K. Lillee | c R.J. Hadlee b Chatfield | 19 | | |
| M.H.N. Walker | not out | 10 | | |
| Extras | (B 7, LB 10, NB 4) | 21 | (LB 10, NB 3) | 13 |
| **Total** | | **552** | (4 wickets declared) | **154** |

### NEW ZEALAND

| | | | | |
|---|---|---|---|---|
| G.M. Turner* | c Turner b O'Keeffe | 15 | c and b O'Keeffe | 36 |
| G.P. Howarth | c Marsh b O'Keeffe | 42 | c Marsh b Gilmour | 28 |
| B.E. Congdon | c Gilmour b Walker | 23 | not out | 107 |
| J.M. Parker | c Marsh b O'Keeffe | 34 | c McCosker b Walker | 21 |
| M.G. Burgess | c Marsh b Walker | 66 | c McCosker b Walker | 39 |
| G.N. Edwards | c Gilmour b O'Keeffe | 34 | c Marsh b Walker | 15 |
| W.K. Lees† | c Marsh b Lillee | 14 | c Marsh b Lillee | 3 |
| R.J. Hadlee | c Marsh b O'Keeffe | 3 | (9) c Cosier b Walker | 15 |
| H.J. Howarth | b Walker | 61 | (8) b Lillee | 0 |
| D.R. Hadlee | not out | 37 | not out | 8 |
| E.J. Chatfield | b Lillee | 5 | | |
| Extras | (LB 9, W 2, NB 12) | 23 | (LB 12, W 1, NB 8) | 21 |
| **Total** | | **357** | (8 wickets) | **293** |

| NEW ZEALAND | O | M | R | W | O | M | R | W | | FALL OF WICKETS | | | |
|---|---|---|---|---|---|---|---|---|---|---|---|---|---|
| R.J. Hadlee | 29 | 1 | 155 | 3 | 13 | 4 | 41 | 1 | | A | NZ | A | NZ |
| Chatfield | 31 | 4 | 125 | 3 | 11 | 1 | 34 | 0 | *Wkt* | *1st* | *1st* | *2nd* | *2nd* |
| D.R. Hadlee | 24·5 | 1 | 130 | 2 | 8 | 0 | 28 | 1 | 1st | 9 | 60 | 37 | 70 |
| Congdon | 7 | 0 | 27 | 0 | 1 | 0 | 1 | 0 | 2nd | 76 | 65 | 70 | 70 |
| H.J. Howarth | 19 | 2 | 94 | 1 | 10 | 0 | 37 | 1 | 3rd | 78 | 91 | 68 | 128 |
| | | | | | | | | | 4th | 112 | 189 | 82 | 218 |
| AUSTRALIA | | | | | | | | | 5th | 205 | 193 | – | 238 |
| Lillee | 31·2 | 6 | 119 | 2 | 18 | 1 | 70 | 2 | 6th | 208 | 220 | – | 245 |
| Gilmour | 10 | 0 | 48 | 0 | 10 | 0 | 48 | 1 | 7th | 425 | 223 | – | 245 |
| Walker | 26 | 7 | 66 | 3 | 25 | 4 | 65 | 4 | 8th | 454 | 265 | – | 260 |
| O'Keeffe | 28 | 5 | 101 | 5 | 20 | 4 | 56 | 1 | 9th | 504 | 338 | – | – |
| Chappell | | | | | 11 | 0 | 33 | 0 | 10th | 552 | 357 | – | – |

Umpires: D.E.A. Copps and F.R. Goodall.

# NEW ZEALAND v AUSTRALIA 1976–77 (2nd Test)

Played at Eden Park, Auckland, on 25, 26, 27 February, 1 March.
Toss: Australia.    Result: AUSTRALIA won by ten wickets.
Debuts: Nil.

Australia gained their fifth victory in nine Tests against New Zealand and with almost two days to spare. Lillee took his 150th wicket in 31 Tests. His match figures of 11 for 123 are the record for this series and for all Tests at Auckland.

## NEW ZEALAND

| | | | | |
|---|---|---|---|---|
| G.M. Turner* | c Marsh b Walker | 4 | c Walters b Lillee | 23 |
| G.P. Howarth | c McCosker b Lillee | 59 | c Turner b Lillee | 2 |
| B.E. Congdon | c Marsh b Lillee | 25 | c McCosker b Lillee | 1 |
| J.M. Parker | c Cosier b Lillee | 20 | c Turner b Walker | 5 |
| M.G. Burgess | c Marsh b Walters | 1 | b Walker | 38 |
| G.N. Edwards† | c Lillee b Gilmour | 51 | c Marsh b Lillee | 0 |
| R.J. Hadlee | c McCosker b Lillee | 44 | b Chappell | 81 |
| B.L. Cairns | b Chappell | 2 | c Lillee b Walker | 7 |
| H.J. Howarth | b Walker | 5 | lbw b Lillee | 6 |
| P.J. Petherick | c Marsh b Lillee | 4 | b Lillee | 1 |
| E.J. Chatfield | not out | 0 | not out | 4 |
| Extras | (LB 7, NB 7) | 14 | (B 4, LB 2, NB 1) | 7 |
| **Total** | | **229** | | **175** |

## AUSTRALIA

| | | | | |
|---|---|---|---|---|
| I.C. Davis | b Chatfield | 13 | not out | 6 |
| A. Turner | c Edwards b Cairns | 30 | not out | 20 |
| R.B. McCosker | c Edwards b Cairns | 84 | | |
| G.S. Chappell* | run out | 58 | | |
| G.J. Cosier | c and b Cairns | 21 | | |
| K.D. Walters | c Hadlee b Chatfield | 16 | | |
| R.W. Marsh† | lbw b Hadlee | 4 | | |
| G.J. Gilmour | b Chatfield | 64 | | |
| K.J. O'Keeffe | c Congdon b Hadlee | 32 | | |
| D.K. Lillee | not out | 23 | | |
| M.H.N. Walker | c Turner b Chatfield | 9 | | |
| Extras | (B 9, LB 9, NB 5) | 23 | (LB 1, NB 1) | 2 |
| **Total** | | **377** | (0 wickets) | **28** |

| AUSTRALIA | O | M | R | W | O | M | R | W | | FALL OF WICKETS | | | |
|---|---|---|---|---|---|---|---|---|---|---|---|---|---|
| | | | | | | | | | | NZ | A | NZ | A |
| Lillee | 17·3 | 4 | 51 | 5 | 15·7 | 2 | 72 | 6 | *Wkt* | *1st* | *1st* | *2nd* | *2nd* |
| Walker | 24 | 6 | 60 | 2 | 17 | 4 | 70 | 3 | 1st | 6 | 31 | 10 | – |
| Gilmour | 7 | 0 | 56 | 1 | 1 | 0 | 11 | 0 | 2nd | 63 | 56 | 12 | – |
| Chappell | 13 | 4 | 28 | 1 | 9 | 4 | 15 | 1 | 3rd | 112 | 171 | 23 | – |
| Walters | 4 | 1 | 20 | 1 | | | | | 4th | 113 | 202 | 31 | – |
| O'Keeffe | 1 | 1 | 0 | 0 | | | | | 5th | 121 | 217 | 31 | – |
| | | | | | | | | | 6th | 177 | 221 | 136 | – |
| NEW ZEALAND | | | | | | | | | 7th | 202 | 245 | 162 | – |
| Hadlee | 28 | 2 | 147 | 2 | 2 | 0 | 11 | 0 | 8th | 211 | 338 | 163 | – |
| Chatfield | 27·1 | 1 | 100 | 4 | 1·5 | 0 | 15 | 0 | 9th | 228 | 364 | 169 | – |
| Cairns | 28 | 9 | 69 | 3 | | | | | 10th | 229 | 377 | 175 | – |
| Congdon | 5 | 1 | 8 | 0 | | | | | | | | | |
| H.J. Howarth | 5 | 1 | 16 | 0 | | | | | | | | | |
| Petherick | 4 | 2 | 14 | 0 | | | | | | | | | |

Umpires: D.E.A. Copps and W.R.C. Gardiner.

# WEST INDIES v PAKISTAN 1976–77 (1st Test)

Played at Kensington Oval, Bridgetown, Barbados, on 18, 19, 20, 22, 23 February.
Toss: Pakistan.    Result: MATCH DRAWN.
Debuts: West Indies – C.E.H. Croft, J. Garner.

West Indies, needing 306 for victory, came close to losing their first Test at Bridgetown since 1934-35. Their last three batsmen survived the final twenty mandatory overs plus 15 minutes. The partnership of 133 between Wasim Raja and Wasim Bari is Pakistan's highest for the tenth wicket in all Tests. West Indies conceded 68 extras in the second innings – the record for any Test innings.

## PAKISTAN

| | | | | |
|---|---|---|---|---|
| Majid Khan | b Garner | 88 | c Garner b Croft | 28 |
| Sadiq Mohammad | c Croft b Garner | 37 | c Garner b Croft | 9 |
| Haroon Rashid | c Kallicharran b Foster | 33 | b Roberts | 39 |
| Mushtaq Mohammad* | c Murray b Croft | 0 | c Murray b Roberts | 6 |
| Asif Iqbal | c Murray b Croft | 36 | b Croft | 0 |
| Javed Miandad | lbw b Garner | 2 | c Greenidge b Croft | 1 |
| Wasim Raja | not out | 117 | c Garner b Foster | 71 |
| Imran Khan | c Garner b Roberts | 20 | c Fredericks b Garner | 1 |
| Salim Altaf | lbw b Garner | 19 | b Garner | 2 |
| Sarfraz Nawaz | c Kallicharran b Foster | 38 | c Murray b Roberts | 6 |
| Wasim Bari† | lbw b Croft | 10 | not out | 60 |
| Extras | (B 5, LB 6, W 1, NB 23) | 35 | (B 29, LB 11, NB 28) | 68 |
| **Total** | | **435** | | **291** |

## WEST INDIES

| | | | | |
|---|---|---|---|---|
| R.C. Fredericks | c and b Sarfraz | 24 | b Sarfraz | 52 |
| C.G. Greenidge | c Majid b Imran | 47 | c Wasim Raja b Sarfraz | 2 |
| I.V.A. Richards | c Salim b Sarfraz | 32 | c Sadiq b Sarfraz | 92 |
| A.I. Kallicharran | c Sarfraz b Imran | 17 | c Wasim Bari b Salim | 9 |
| C.H. Lloyd* | c Sadiq b Salim | 157 | c Wasim Bari b Imran | 11 |
| M.L.C. Foster | b Sarfraz | 15 | b Sarfraz | 4 |
| D.L. Murray† | c Mushtaq b Imran | 52 | c Wasim Bari b Salim | 20 |
| J. Garner | b Miandad | 43 | b Salim | 0 |
| A.M.E. Roberts | c Wasim Bari b Salim | 4 | not out | 9 |
| C.E.H. Croft | not out | 1 | (11) not out | 5 |
| V.A. Holder | absent hurt | – | (10) b Imran | 6 |
| Extras | (B 2, LB 6, NB 21) | 29 | (B 1, LB 8, W 1, NB 31) | 41 |
| **Total** | | **421** | (9 wickets) | **251** |

| WEST INDIES | O | M | R | W | O | M | R | W | | FALL OF WICKETS | | | |
|---|---|---|---|---|---|---|---|---|---|---|---|---|---|
| Roberts | 30 | 3 | 124 | 1 | 25 | 5 | 66 | 3 | | P | WI | P | WI |
| Croft | 31·4 | 6 | 85 | 3 | 15 | 3 | 47 | 4 | *Wkt* | *1st* | *1st* | *2nd* | *2nd* |
| Holder | 4 | 0 | 13 | 0 | | | | | 1st | 72 | 59 | 29 | 12 |
| Garner | 37 | 7 | 130 | 4 | 17 | 4 | 60 | 2 | 2nd | 148 | 91 | 68 | 142 |
| Foster | 27 | 13 | 41 | 2 | 8 | 2 | 34 | 1 | 3rd | 149 | 120 | 102 | 166 |
| Richards | 3 | 1 | 3 | 0 | 2 | 0 | 16 | 0 | 4th | 186 | 134 | 103 | 179 |
| Fredericks | 1 | 0 | 4 | 0 | | | | | 5th | 207 | 183 | 108 | 185 |
| | | | | | | | | | 6th | 233 | 334 | 113 | 206 |
| PAKISTAN | | | | | | | | | 7th | 271 | 404 | 126 | 210 |
| Imran | 28 | 3 | 147 | 3 | 32 | 16 | 58 | 2 | 8th | 335 | 418 | 146 | 217 |
| Sarfraz | 29 | 3 | 125 | 3 | 34 | 10 | 79 | 4 | 9th | 408 | 421 | 158 | 237 |
| Salim | 21 | 3 | 70 | 2 | 21 | 7 | 33 | 3 | 10th | 435 | – | 291 | – |
| Miandad | 10·4 | 3 | 22 | 1 | 11 | 4 | 31 | 0 | | | | | |
| Mushtaq | 5 | 0 | 27 | 0 | | | | | | | | | |
| Majid | 1 | 0 | 1 | 0 | 1 | 0 | 1 | 0 | | | | | |
| Asif | | | | | 1 | 0 | 8 | 0 | | | | | |

Umpires: D. Sang Hue and R. Gosein.

# WEST INDIES v PAKISTAN 1976–77 (2nd Test)

Played at Queen's Park Oval, Port-of-Spain, Trinidad, on 4, 5, 6, 8, 9 March.
Toss: Pakistan.    Result: WEST INDIES won by six wickets.
Debuts: West Indies – I.T. Shillingford.

Croft, playing in his second match, achieved the best analysis by a West Indies fast bowler in Test cricket. In that innings, Sadiq (0*) retired at 6 for 0 after being hit on the arm by a ball from Croft and resumed at 112 for 5. Wasim Raja was top scorer in both innings for the second Test in succession.

## PAKISTAN

| Batsman | Dismissal 1 | Score 1 | Dismissal 2 | Score 2 |
|---|---|---|---|---|
| Majid Khan | lbw b Garner | 47 | c Kallicharran b Jumadeen | 54 |
| Sadiq Mohammad | c and b Croft | 17 | c Kallicharran b Garner | 81 |
| Haroon Rashid | c Lloyd b Croft | 4 | lbw b Fredericks | 7 |
| Mushtaq Mohammad* | c Richards b Croft | 9 | c Greenidge b Roberts | 21 |
| Asif Iqbal | c Murray b Croft | 0 | b Garner | 12 |
| Wasim Raja | b Croft | 65 | c Garner b Croft | 84 |
| Imran Khan | c Fredericks b Jumadeen | 1 | (8) c Murray b Roberts | 35 |
| Intikhab Alam | b Croft | 0 | (9) b Garner | 12 |
| Wasim Bari† | c Murray b Croft | 21 | (10) c Fredericks b Roberts | 2 |
| Salim Altaf | b Croft | 1 | (11) not out | 0 |
| Iqbal Qasim | not out | 0 | (7) b Roberts | 4 |
| Extras | (B 3, LB 3, NB 9) | 15 | (B 13, LB 4, NB 11) | 28 |
| **Total** | | **180** | | **340** |

## WEST INDIES

| Batsman | Dismissal 1 | Score 1 | Dismissal 2 | Score 2 |
|---|---|---|---|---|
| R.C. Fredericks | c Sadiq b Mushtaq | 120 | c Asif b Wasim Raja | 57 |
| C.G. Greenidge | b Salim | 5 | c Wasim Bari b Imran | 70 |
| I.V.A. Richards | b Salim | 4 | b Imran | 30 |
| A.I. Kallicharran | c Wasim Bari b Intikhab | 37 | not out | 11 |
| I.T. Shillingford | lbw b Mushtaq | 39 | c Wasim Bari b Imran | 2 |
| C.H. Lloyd* | c Haroon b Intikhab | 22 | not out | 23 |
| D.L. Murray† | b Mushtaq | 10 | | |
| J. Garner | lbw b Imran | 36 | | |
| A.M.E. Roberts | b Mushtaq | 4 | | |
| C.E.H. Croft | not out | 23 | | |
| R.R. Jumadeen | lbw b Imran | 0 | | |
| Extras | (B 5, LB 11) | 16 | (B 1, LB 11, W 1) | 13 |
| **Total** | | **316** | (4 wickets) | **206** |

| WEST INDIES | O | M | R | W | O | M | R | W |
|---|---|---|---|---|---|---|---|---|
| Roberts | 17 | 2 | 34 | 0 | 26 | 4 | 85 | 4 |
| Croft | 18·5 | 7 | 29 | 8 | 25 | 3 | 66 | 1 |
| Garner | 16 | 1 | 47 | 1 | 20·1 | 6 | 48 | 3 |
| Jumadeen | 16 | 3 | 55 | 1 | 35 | 13 | 72 | 1 |
| Fredericks | | | | | 6 | 2 | 14 | 1 |
| Richards | | | | | 12 | 4 | 27 | 0 |
| **PAKISTAN** | | | | | | | | |
| Imran | 21 | 5 | 50 | 2 | 24 | 8 | 59 | 3 |
| Salim | 18 | 3 | 44 | 2 | 21 | 3 | 58 | 0 |
| Intikhab | 29 | 6 | 90 | 2 | 2 | 1 | 6 | 0 |
| Majid | 8 | 3 | 9 | 0 | | | | |
| Qasim | 10 | 2 | 26 | 0 | 13 | 6 | 30 | 0 |
| Mushtaq | 20 | 7 | 50 | 4 | 9 | 1 | 27 | 0 |
| Wasim Raja | 10 | 1 | 31 | 0 | 5 | 1 | 13 | 1 |

### FALL OF WICKETS

| Wkt | P 1st | WI 1st | P 2nd | WI 2nd |
|---|---|---|---|---|
| 1st | 10 | 18 | 123 | 97 |
| 2nd | 21 | 22 | 155 | 159 |
| 3rd | 21 | 102 | 167 | 166 |
| 4th | 103 | 183 | 181 | 170 |
| 5th | 112 | 216 | 223 | – |
| 6th | 150 | 243 | 239 | – |
| 7th | 154 | 258 | 315 | – |
| 8th | 159 | 270 | 334 | – |
| 9th | 161 | 316 | 340 | – |
| 10th | 180 | 316 | 340 | – |

Umpires: D. Sang Hue and R. Gosein.

# WEST INDIES v PAKISTAN 1976–77 (3rd Test)

Played at Bourda, Georgetown, Guyana, on 18, 19, 20, 22, 23 March.
Toss: West Indies.   Result: MATCH DRAWN.
Debuts: Nil.

Lloyd tore a hamstring muscle after only 20 minutes of play on the first day and Murray assumed the West Indies' captaincy on the field. Sadiq retired at 60 for 0 after being hit on the jaw when attempting a hook against Roberts. Majid and Zaheer added a further 159 to set a new first wicket record for Pakistan in this series. A bottle-throwing incident caused play to be suspended for 20 minutes on the second day.

## PAKISTAN

| | | | | | |
|---|---|---|---|---|---|
| Majid Khan | c Murray b Roberts | 23 | c Greenidge b Roberts | | 167 |
| Sadiq Mohammad | c Murray b Garner | 12 | lbw b Croft | | 48 |
| Zaheer Abbas | b Garner | 0 | c Fredericks b Croft | | 80 |
| Haroon Rashid | c Murray b Croft | 32 | (5) c and b Garner | | 60 |
| Mushtaq Mohammad* | c Murray b Julien | 41 | (4) b Roberts | | 19 |
| Asif Iqbal | c and b Croft | 15 | (7) lbw b Garner | | 35 |
| Wasim Raja | c and b Croft | 5 | (8) b Garner | | 0 |
| Imran Khan | c Shillingford b Roberts | 47 | (9) lbw b Roberts | | 35 |
| Sarfraz Nawaz | c Kallicharran b Garner | 6 | (10) c Kallicharran b Fredericks | | 25 |
| Wasim Bari† | c Murray b Garner | 1 | (11) not out | | 25 |
| Salim Altaf | not out | 0 | (6) lbw b Garner | | 6 |
| Extras | (LB 5, NB 7) | 12 | (B 13, LB 7, W 1, NB 19) | | 40 |
| **Total** | | **194** | | | **540** |

## WEST INDIES

| | | | | |
|---|---|---|---|---|
| R.C. Fredericks | c Majid b Sarfraz | 5 | not out | 52 |
| C.G. Greenidge | b Majid | 91 | c Haroon b Imran | 96 |
| I.V.A. Richards | lbw b Imran | 50 | | |
| A.I. Kallicharran | lbw b Imran | 72 | | |
| I.T. Shillingford | c Haroon b Sarfraz | 120 | | |
| B.D. Julien | b Salim | 5 | | |
| D.L. Murray† | c Zaheer b Majid | 42 | | |
| J. Garner | b Majid | 4 | | |
| C.H. Lloyd* | c Imran b Majid | 14 | | |
| A.M.E. Roberts | not out | 20 | | |
| C.E.H. Croft | b Mushtaq | 6 | | |
| Extras | (B 1, LB 9, W 3, NB 6) | 19 | (LB 5, NB 1) | 6 |
| **Total** | | **448** | (1 wicket) | **154** |

| WEST INDIES | O | M | R | W | O | M | R | W | FALL OF WICKETS | | | | |
|---|---|---|---|---|---|---|---|---|---|---|---|---|---|
| Roberts | 16·3 | 3 | 49 | 2 | 45 | 6 | 174 | 3 | | P | WI | P | WI |
| Croft | 15 | 3 | 60 | 3 | 35 | 7 | 119 | 2 | *Wkt* | *1st* | *1st* | *2nd* | *2nd* |
| Garner | 16 | 4 | 48 | 4 | 39 | 8 | 100 | 4 | 1st | 36 | 11 | 219 | 154 |
| Julien | 9 | 2 | 25 | 1 | 28 | 3 | 63 | 0 | 2nd | 40 | 94 | 304 | – |
| Richards | | | | | 5 | 0 | 11 | 0 | 3rd | 46 | 193 | 311 | – |
| Fredericks | | | | | 11·3 | 2 | 33 | 1 | 4th | 96 | 244 | 381 | – |
| | | | | | | | | | 5th | 125 | 255 | 404 | – |
| PAKISTAN | | | | | | | | | 6th | 133 | 378 | 417 | – |
| Imran | 31 | 6 | 119 | 2 | 12·5 | 0 | 79 | 1 | 7th | 143 | 390 | 417 | – |
| Sarfraz | 45 | 16 | 105 | 2 | 9 | 0 | 58 | 0 | 8th | 174 | 422 | 471 | – |
| Salim | 29 | 6 | 71 | 1 | | | | | 9th | 188 | 422 | 491 | – |
| Asif | 4 | 1 | 15 | 0 | | | | | 10th | 194 | 448 | 540 | – |
| Mushtaq | 29·3 | 7 | 74 | 1 | | | | | | | | | |
| Majid | 24 | 9 | 45 | 4 | 3 | 0 | 11 | 0 | | | | | |

Umpires: C.A. Vyfhuis and C. Paynter.

# WEST INDIES v PAKISTAN 1976–77 (4th Test)

Played at Queen's Park Oval, Port-of-Spain, on 1, 2, 3, 5, 6 April.
Toss: West Indies.   Result: PAKISTAN won by 266 runs.
Debuts: Nil.

Pakistan drew level in the rubber with their second victory in the West Indies. Mushtaq became the second all-rounder after G. St A. Sobers to score a hundred and take five wickets in an innings of the same Test on two occasions.

## PAKISTAN

| | | | | | |
|---|---|---|---|---|---|
| Majid Khan | c Murray b Croft | 92 | c Murray b Croft | | 16 |
| Sadiq Mohammad | c Lloyd b Roberts | 0 | b Ali | | 24 |
| Zaheer Abbas | b Roberts | 14 | lbw b Garner | | 9 |
| Haroon Rashid | c Kallicharran b Ali | 11 | lbw b Garner | | 11 |
| Mushtaq Mohammad* | c Greenidge b Richards | 121 | c Fredericks b Roberts | | 56 |
| Asif Iqbal | c Ali b Roberts | 11 | c and b Ali | | 10 |
| Wasim Raja | c and b Ali | 28 | b Garner | | 70 |
| Imran Khan | c Greenidge b Ali | 1 | c and b Croft | | 30 |
| Sarfraz Nawaz | c Richards b Croft | 29 | c Lloyd b Croft | | 51 |
| Wasim Bari† | not out | 5 | not out | | 2 |
| Iqbal Qasim | b Richards | 2 | | | |
| Extras | (B 4, LB 8, NB 15) | 27 | (B 8, LB 11, NB 3) | | 22 |
| **Total** | | **341** | (9 wickets declared) | | **301** |

## WEST INDIES

| | | | | | |
|---|---|---|---|---|---|
| R.C. Fredericks | b Imran | 41 | c Majid b Qasim | | 17 |
| C.G. Greenidge | b Qasim | 32 | c Majid b Sarfraz | | 11 |
| I.V.A. Richards | b Imran | 4 | st Wasim Bari b Mushtaq | | 33 |
| A.I. Kallicharran | c Sarfraz b Mushtaq | 11 | c Asif b Mushtaq | | 45 |
| I.T. Shillingford | st Wasim Bari b Mushtaq | 15 | c Qasim b Mushtaq | | 23 |
| J. Garner | c Qasim b Mushtaq | 0 | (8) b Sarfraz | | 0 |
| C.H. Lloyd* | lbw b Imran | 22 | (6) b Sarfraz | | 17 |
| D.L. Murray† | lbw b Imran | 0 | (7) c Sadiq b Wasim Raja | | 30 |
| A.M.E. Roberts | c Qasim b Mushtaq | 6 | c Majid b Wasim Raja | | 35 |
| Inshan Ali | c Qasim b Mushtaq | 4 | c Sadiq b Wasim Raja | | 0 |
| C.E.H. Croft | not out | 0 | not out | | 0 |
| Extras | (B 11, LB 2, NB 6) | 19 | (B 7, LB 1, NB 3) | | 11 |
| **Total** | | **154** | | | **222** |

| WEST INDIES | O | M | R | W | O | M | R | W |
|---|---|---|---|---|---|---|---|---|
| Roberts | 25 | 2 | 82 | 3 | 20 | 2 | 56 | 1 |
| Croft | 21 | 4 | 56 | 2 | 22·5 | 6 | 79 | 3 |
| Garner | 24 | 6 | 55 | 0 | 23 | 4 | 71 | 3 |
| Inshan Ali | 32 | 9 | 86 | 3 | 20 | 2 | 73 | 2 |
| Richards | 18·3 | 6 | 34 | 2 | | | | |
| Fredericks | 1 | 0 | 1 | 0 | | | | |
| PAKISTAN | | | | | | | | |
| Imran | 21 | 6 | 64 | 4 | 21 | 5 | 46 | 0 |
| Sarfraz | 10 | 4 | 17 | 0 | 19 | 10 | 21 | 3 |
| Qasim | 13 | 6 | 26 | 1 | 20 | 6 | 50 | 1 |
| Mushtaq | 10·5 | 3 | 28 | 5 | 31 | 9 | 69 | 3 |
| Wasim Raja | 1 | 1 | 0 | 0 | 3·5 | 1 | 22 | 3 |
| Majid | | | | | 10 | 8 | 3 | 0 |

| FALL OF WICKETS | | | | |
|---|---|---|---|---|
| | P | WI | P | WI |
| *Wkt* | *1st* | *1st* | *2nd* | *2nd* |
| 1st | 1 | 73 | 25 | 24 |
| 2nd | 19 | 77 | 46 | 42 |
| 3rd | 51 | 82 | 58 | 82 |
| 4th | 159 | 106 | 74 | 126 |
| 5th | 191 | 106 | 95 | 148 |
| 6th | 246 | 122 | 211 | 154 |
| 7th | 252 | 125 | 213 | 154 |
| 8th | 320 | 144 | 286 | 196 |
| 9th | 331 | 154 | 301 | 196 |
| 10th | 341 | 154 | – | 222 |

Umpires: R. Gosein and C.A. Vyfhuis.

## WEST INDIES v PAKISTAN 1976–77 (5th Test)

Played at Sabina Park, Kingston, Jamaica, on 15, 16, 17, 19, 20 April.
Toss: West Indies.   Result: WEST INDIES won by 140 runs.
Debuts: Nil.

Soon after the start of the fifth day's play West Indies won their second rubber against Pakistan. Wasim Bari, who became the first wicket-keeper to make 100 dismissals for Pakistan, retired after being hit in the face attempting a hook against Croft. Majid kept wicket for part of the second innings and held four catches. Croft emulated A.L. Valentine by taking 33 wickets in his first rubber.

### WEST INDIES

| | | | | |
|---|---|---|---|---|
| R.C. Fredericks | c and b Imran | 6 | c Majid b Wasim Raja | 83 |
| C.G. Greenidge | c Wasim Bari b Sikander | 100 | c Majid b Sikander | 82 |
| I.V.A. Richards | c Wasim Bari b Imran | 5 | b Wasim Raja | 7 |
| C.H. Lloyd* | c Zaheer b Imran | 22 | c Asif b Wasim Raja | 48 |
| A.I. Kallicharran | c Wasim Bari b Imran | 34 | c Majid b Sikander | 22 |
| C.L. King | c Wasim Bari b Sikander | 41 | c Majid b Sikander | 3 |
| D.L. Murray† | c Sikander b Imran | 31 | c Wasim Bari b Imran | 33 |
| D.A.J. Holford | c Majid b Imran | 2 | c Wasim Bari b Sarfraz | 37 |
| J. Garner | c Mushtaq b Sarfraz | 9 | c Sadiq b Imran | 0 |
| A.M.E. Roberts | b Sarfraz | 7 | c Wasim Bari b Sarfraz | 2 |
| C.E.H. Croft | not out | 6 | not out | 12 |
| Extras | (LB 9, NB 8) | 17 | (B 13, LB 7, NB 10) | 30 |
| **Total** | | **280** | | **359** |

### PAKISTAN

| | | | | |
|---|---|---|---|---|
| Majid Khan | c Richards b Croft | 11 | c Fredericks b Croft | 4 |
| Sadiq Mohammad | b Roberts | 3 | c Greenidge b Croft | 14 |
| Zaheer Abbas | lbw b Roberts | 28 | c Richards b Croft | 0 |
| Haroon Rashid | c Greenidge b Croft | 72 | c Greenidge b Garner | 31 |
| Mushtaq Mohammad* | c Lloyd b Garner | 24 | b Garner | 17 |
| Asif Iqbal | c Kallicharran b Holford | 5 | st Murray b Holford | 135 |
| Wasim Raja | c King b Holford | 13 | c Fredericks b Holford | 64 |
| Imran Khan | c and b Croft | 23 | c Lloyd b Holford | 22 |
| Sarfraz Nawaz | c Holford b Croft | 8 | b Garner | 9 |
| Wasim Bari† | retired hurt | 0 | run out | 0 |
| Sikander Bakht | not out | 1 | not out | 0 |
| Extras | (LB 1, NB 9) | 10 | (B 3, NB 2) | 5 |
| **Total** | | **198** | | **301** |

| PAKISTAN | O | M | R | W | O | M | R | W | | FALL OF WICKETS | | | |
|---|---|---|---|---|---|---|---|---|---|---|---|---|---|
| Imran | 18 | 2 | 90 | 6 | 27·2 | 3 | 78 | 2 | | WI | P | WI | P |
| Sarfraz | 24·3 | 5 | 81 | 2 | 27 | 6 | 93 | 2 | *Wkt* | *1st* | *1st* | *2nd* | *2nd* |
| Sikander | 12 | 0 | 71 | 2 | 16 | 3 | 55 | 3 | 1st | 6 | 11 | 182 | 5 |
| Asif | 4 | 1 | 6 | 0 | | | | | 2nd | 22 | 26 | 182 | 9 |
| Mushtaq | 7 | 2 | 15 | 0 | 11 | 3 | 38 | 0 | 3rd | 56 | 47 | 193 | 32 |
| Wasim Raja | | | | | 21 | 5 | 65 | 3 | 4th | 146 | 106 | 252 | 51 |
| | | | | | | | | | 5th | 200 | 122 | 260 | 138 |
| | | | | | | | | | 6th | 229 | 140 | 269 | 253 |
| WEST INDIES | | | | | | | | | 7th | 252 | 174 | 335 | 289 |
| Roberts | 14 | 4 | 36 | 2 | 18 | 6 | 57 | 0 | 8th | 254 | 190 | 343 | 296 |
| Croft | 13·3 | 1 | 49 | 4 | 20 | 5 | 86 | 3 | 9th | 268 | 198 | 345 | 301 |
| Garner | 9 | 1 | 57 | 1 | 18·2 | 0 | 72 | 3 | 10th | 280 | – | 359 | 301 |
| Holford | 16 | 3 | 40 | 2 | 18 | 3 | 69 | 3 | | | | | |
| King | 4 | 2 | 6 | 0 | 3 | 0 | 12 | 0 | | | | | |

Umpires: D. Sang Hue and R. Gosein.

# AUSTRALIA v ENGLAND 1976–77 (Centenary Test)

Played at Melbourne Cricket Ground on 12, 13, 14, 16, 17 March.
Toss: England.   Result: AUSTRALIA won by 45 runs.
Debuts: Australia – D.W. Hookes.

At 5.12 p.m. on the fifth day, Australia exactly repeated their margin of victory in the first ever Test played on the same ground 100 years earlier. The brainchild of Hans Ebeling (*Test No. 237*), this celebration match, for which the Ashes were not at stake, attracted by courtesy of the Victoria C.A. and allied sponsors, the largest gathering of international cricketers in history. Underwood became the fourth bowler to take 250 Test wickets when he dismissed Chappell. Marsh, who surpassed A.T.W. Grout's Australian record of 187 Test dismissals when he caught Lever, became the first Australian wicket-keeper to score a hundred in this series. Knott set a new England record of 85 dismissals against Australia when he caught Cosier. Randall (174 off 353 balls in 446 minutes with 21 fours) recorded the second-highest innings by a debutant in this series. England's total of 417 was the highest for any fourth innings in this series.

## AUSTRALIA

| | | | | | |
|---|---|---|---|---|---|
| I.C. Davis | lbw b Lever | 5 | | c Knott b Greig | 68 |
| R.B. McCosker | b Willis | 4 | (10) | c Greig b Old | 25 |
| G.J. Cosier | c Fletcher b Lever | 10 | (4) | c Knott b Lever | 4 |
| G.S. Chappell* | b Underwood | 40 | (3) | b Old | 2 |
| D.W. Hookes | c Greig b Old | 17 | (6) | c Fletcher b Underwood | 56 |
| K.D. Walters | c Greig b Willis | 4 | (5) | c Knott b Greig | 66 |
| R.W. Marsh† | c Knott b Old | 28 | | not out | 110 |
| G.J. Gilmour | c Greig b Old | 4 | | b Lever | 16 |
| K.J. O'Keeffe | c Brearley b Underwood | 0 | (2) | c Willis b Old | 14 |
| D.K. Lillee | not out | 10 | (9) | c Amiss b Old | 25 |
| M.H.N. Walker | b Underwood | 2 | | not out | 8 |
| Extras | (B 4, LB 2, NB 8) | 14 | | (LB 10, NB 15) | 25 |
| **Total** | | **138** | | (9 wickets declared) | **419** |

## ENGLAND

| | | | | | |
|---|---|---|---|---|---|
| R.A. Woolmer | c Chappell b Lillee | 9 | | lbw b Walker | 12 |
| J.M. Brearley | c Hookes b Lillee | 12 | | lbw b Lillee | 43 |
| D.L. Underwood | c Chappell b Walker | 7 | (10) | b Lillee | 7 |
| D.W. Randall | c Marsh b Lillee | 4 | (3) | c Cosier b O'Keeffe | 174 |
| D.L. Amiss | c O'Keeffe b Walker | 4 | (4) | b Chappell | 64 |
| K.W.R. Fletcher | c Marsh b Walker | 4 | (5) | c Marsh b Lillee | 1 |
| A.W. Greig* | b Walker | 18 | (6) | c Cosier b O'Keeffe | 41 |
| A.P.E. Knott† | lbw b Lillee | 15 | (7) | lbw b Lillee | 42 |
| C.M. Old | c Marsh b Lillee | 3 | (8) | c Chappell b Lillee | 2 |
| J.K. Lever | c Marsh b Lillee | 11 | (9) | lbw b O'Keeffe | 4 |
| R.G.D. Willis | not out | 1 | | not out | 5 |
| Extras | (B 2, LB 2, W 1, NB 2) | 7 | | (B 8, LB 4, W 3, NB 7) | 22 |
| **Total** | | **95** | | | **417** |

| ENGLAND | O | M | R | W | O | M | R | W |
|---|---|---|---|---|---|---|---|---|
| Lever | 12 | 1 | 36 | 2 | 21 | 1 | 95 | 2 |
| Willis | 8 | 0 | 33 | 2 | 22 | 0 | 91 | 0 |
| Old | 12 | 4 | 39 | 3 | 27·6 | 2 | 104 | 4 |
| Underwood | 11·6 | 2 | 16 | 3 | 12 | 2 | 38 | 1 |
| Greig | | | | | 14 | 3 | 66 | 2 |
| AUSTRALIA | | | | | | | | |
| Lillee | 13·3 | 2 | 26 | 6 | 34·4 | 7 | 139 | 5 |
| Walker | 15 | 3 | 54 | 4 | 22 | 4 | 83 | 1 |
| O'Keeffe | 1 | 0 | 4 | 0 | 33 | 6 | 108 | 3 |
| Gilmour | 5 | 3 | 4 | 0 | 4 | 0 | 29 | 0 |
| Chappell | | | | | 16 | 7 | 29 | 1 |
| Walters | | | | | 3 | 2 | 7 | 0 |

### FALL OF WICKETS

| Wkt | A 1st | E 1st | A 2nd | E 2nd |
|---|---|---|---|---|
| 1st | 11 | 19 | 33 | 28 |
| 2nd | 13 | 30 | 40 | 113 |
| 3rd | 23 | 34 | 53 | 279 |
| 4th | 45 | 40 | 132 | 290 |
| 5th | 51 | 40 | 187 | 346 |
| 6th | 102 | 61 | 244 | 369 |
| 7th | 114 | 65 | 277 | 380 |
| 8th | 117 | 78 | 353 | 385 |
| 9th | 136 | 86 | 407 | 410 |
| 10th | 138 | 95 | – | 417 |

Umpires: T.F. Brooks and M.G. O'Connell.

# ENGLAND v AUSTRALIA 1977 (1st Test)

Played at Lord's, London, on 16, 17, 18, 20, 21 June.
Toss: England.   Result: MATCH DRAWN.
Debuts: Australia – L.S. Pascoe *(born L.S. Durtanovich)*, R.D. Robinson, C.S. Serjeant.

Staged at Lord's as a Jubilee Test to commemorate 25 years of the reign of Queen Elizabeth II, this match produced record receipts for any cricket match in Britain (£220,384) and a total attendance of 101,050. Marsh set a new Australian catching record for this series (70) when he dismissed Old. Australia needed to score 226 runs in a minimum of 165 minutes. Old took his 100th wicket in 32 Tests when he dismissed Robinson. Five hours 43 minutes were lost to rain.

## ENGLAND

| | | | | | |
|---|---|---|---|---|---|
| D.L. Amiss | b Thomson | 4 | b Thomson | | 0 |
| J.M. Brearley* | c Robinson b Thomson | 9 | c Robinson b O'Keeffe | | 49 |
| R.A. Woolmer | run out | 79 | c Chappell b Pascoe | | 120 |
| D.W. Randall | c Chappell b Walker | 53 | (7) c McCosker b Thomson | | 0 |
| A.W. Greig | b Pascoe | 5 | (4) c O'Keeffe b Pascoe | | 91 |
| G.D. Barlow | c McCosker b Walker | 1 | (5) lbw b Pascoe | | 5 |
| A.P.E. Knott† | c Walters b Thomson | 8 | (6) c Walters b Walker | | 8 |
| C.M. Old | c Marsh b Walker | 9 | c Walters b Walker | | 0 |
| J.K. Lever | b Pascoe | 8 | c Marsh b Thomson | | 3 |
| D.L. Underwood | not out | 11 | not out | | 12 |
| R.G.D. Willis | b Thomson | 17 | c Marsh b Thomson | | 0 |
| Extras | (B 1, LB 3, W 1, NB 7) | 12 | (B 5, LB 9, W 1, NB 2) | | 17 |
| **Total** | | **216** | | | **305** |

## AUSTRALIA

| | | | | | |
|---|---|---|---|---|---|
| R.D. Robinson | b Lever | 11 | c Woolmer b Old | | 4 |
| R.B. McCosker | b Old | 23 | b Willis | | 1 |
| G.S. Chappell* | c Old b Willis | 66 | c Lever b Old | | 24 |
| C.S. Serjeant | c Knott b Willis | 81 | (6) c Amiss b Underwood | | 3 |
| K.D. Walters | c Brearley b Willis | 53 | c sub (A.G.E. Ealham) | | |
| | | | b Underwood | | 10 |
| D.W. Hookes | c Brearley b Old | 11 | (4) c and b Willis | | 50 |
| R.W. Marsh† | lbw b Willis | 1 | not out | | 6 |
| K.J. O'Keeffe | c sub (A.G.E. Ealham) b Willis | 12 | not out | | 8 |
| M.H.N. Walker | c Knott b Willis | 4 | | | |
| J.R. Thomson | b Willis | 6 | | | |
| L.S. Pascoe | not out | 3 | | | |
| Extras | (LB 7, W 1, NB 17) | 25 | (NB 8) | | 8 |
| **Total** | | **296** | (6 wickets) | | **114** |

| AUSTRALIA | O | M | R | W | O | M | R | W |
|---|---|---|---|---|---|---|---|---|
| Thomson | 20·5 | 5 | 41 | 4 | 24·4 | 3 | 86 | 4 |
| Pascoe | 23 | 7 | 53 | 2 | 26 | 2 | 96 | 3 |
| Walker | 30 | 6 | 66 | 3 | 35 | 13 | 56 | 2 |
| O'Keeffe | 10 | 3 | 32 | 0 | 15 | 7 | 26 | 1 |
| Chappell | 3 | 0 | 12 | 0 | 12 | 2 | 24 | 0 |
| ENGLAND | | | | | | | | |
| Willis | 30·1 | 7 | 78 | 7 | 10 | 1 | 40 | 2 |
| Lever | 19 | 5 | 61 | 1 | 5 | 2 | 4 | 0 |
| Underwood | 25 | 6 | 42 | 0 | 10 | 3 | 16 | 2 |
| Old | 35 | 10 | 70 | 2 | 14 | 0 | 46 | 2 |
| Woolmer | 5 | 1 | 20 | 0 | | | | |

### FALL OF WICKETS

| | E | A | E | A |
|---|---|---|---|---|
| Wkt | 1st | 1st | 2nd | 2nd |
| 1st | 12 | 25 | 0 | 5 |
| 2nd | 13 | 51 | 132 | 5 |
| 3rd | 111 | 135 | 224 | 48 |
| 4th | 121 | 238 | 263 | 64 |
| 5th | 134 | 256 | 286 | 71 |
| 6th | 155 | 264 | 286 | 102 |
| 7th | 171 | 265 | 286 | – |
| 8th | 183 | 284 | 286 | – |
| 9th | 189 | 290 | 305 | – |
| 10th | 216 | 296 | 305 | – |

Umpires: H.D. Bird and W.L. Budd.

# ENGLAND v AUSTRALIA 1977 (2nd Test)

Played at Old Trafford, Manchester, on 7, 8, 9, 11, 12 July.
Toss: Australia.   Result: ENGLAND won by nine wickets.
Debuts: Australia – R.J. Bright.

England completed their victory at 12.34 p.m. on the fifth day. Remarkably, considering the venue, no time was lost to rain or bad light during the match. Woolmer scored his second successive hundred in the rubber and Chappell recorded the last of his 14 Test centuries.

## AUSTRALIA

| | | | | | |
|---|---|---|---|---|---|
| R.B. McCosker | c Old b Willis | 2 | c Underwood b Willis | 0 |
| I.C. Davis | c Knott b Old | 34 | c Lever b Willis | 12 |
| G.S. Chappell* | c Knott b Greig | 44 | b Underwood | 112 |
| C.S. Serjeant | lbw b Lever | 14 | c Woolmer b Underwood | 8 |
| K.D. Walters | c Greig b Miller | 88 | lbw b Greig | 10 |
| D.W. Hookes | c Knott b Lever | 5 | c Brearley b Miller | 28 |
| R.W. Marsh† | c Amiss b Miller | 36 | c Randall b Underwood | 1 |
| R.J. Bright | c Greig b Lever | 12 | c and b Underwood | 0 |
| K.J. O'Keeffe | c Knott b Willis | 12 | not out | 24 |
| M.H.N. Walker | b Underwood | 9 | c Greig b Underwood | 6 |
| J.R. Thomson | not out | 14 | c Randall b Underwood | 1 |
| Extras | (LB 15, NB 12) | 27 | (LB 1, W 1, NB 14) | 16 |
| **Total** | | **297** | | **218** |

## ENGLAND

| | | | | | |
|---|---|---|---|---|---|
| D.L. Amiss | c Chappell b Walker | 11 | not out | 28 |
| J.M. Brearley* | c Chappell b Thomson | 6 | c Walters b O'Keeffe | 44 |
| R.A. Woolmer | c Davis b O'Keeffe | 137 | not out | 0 |
| D.W. Randall | lbw b Bright | 79 | | |
| A.W. Greig | c and b Walker | 76 | | |
| A.P.E. Knott† | c O'Keeffe b Thomson | 39 | | |
| G. Miller | c Marsh b Thomson | 6 | | |
| C.M. Old | c Marsh b Walker | 37 | | |
| J.K. Lever | b Bright | 10 | | |
| D.L. Underwood | b Bright | 10 | | |
| R.G.D. Willis | not out | 1 | | |
| Extras | (B 9, LB 9, NB 7) | 25 | (LB 3, NB 7) | 10 |
| **Total** | | **437** | (1 wicket) | **82** |

| ENGLAND | O | M | R | W | O | M | R | W | FALL OF WICKETS | | | | |
|---|---|---|---|---|---|---|---|---|---|---|---|---|---|
| Willis | 21 | 8 | 45 | 2 | 16 | 2 | 56 | 2 | | A | E | A | E |
| Lever | 25 | 8 | 60 | 3 | 4 | 1 | 11 | 0 | Wkt | 1st | 1st | 2nd | 2nd |
| Old | 20 | 3 | 57 | 1 | 8 | 1 | 26 | 0 | 1st | 4 | 19 | 0 | 75 |
| Underwood | 20·2 | 7 | 53 | 1 | 32·5 | 13 | 66 | 6 | 2nd | 80 | 23 | 30 | – |
| Greig | 13 | 4 | 37 | 1 | 12 | 6 | 19 | 1 | 3rd | 96 | 165 | 74 | – |
| Miller | 10 | 3 | 18 | 2 | 9 | 2 | 24 | 1 | 4th | 125 | 325 | 92 | – |
| | | | | | | | | | 5th | 140 | 348 | 146 | – |
| AUSTRALIA | | | | | | | | | 6th | 238 | 366 | 147 | – |
| Thomson | 38 | 11 | 73 | 3 | 8 | 2 | 24 | 0 | 7th | 246 | 377 | 147 | – |
| Walker | 54 | 15 | 131 | 3 | 7 | 0 | 17 | 0 | 8th | 272 | 404 | 202 | – |
| Bright | 35·1 | 12 | 69 | 3 | 5 | 2 | 6 | 0 | 9th | 272 | 435 | 212 | – |
| O'Keeffe | 36 | 11 | 114 | 1 | 9·1 | 4 | 25 | 1 | 10th | 297 | 437 | 218 | – |
| Chappell | 6 | 1 | 25 | 0 | | | | | | | | | |

Umpires: T.W. Spencer and W.E. Alley.

# ENGLAND v AUSTRALIA 1977 (3rd Test)

Played at Trent Bridge, Nottingham, on 28, 29, 30 July, 1, 2 August.
Toss: Australia.    Result: ENGLAND won by seven wickets.
Debuts: England – I.T. Botham.

At 4.42 p.m. on the fifth day, England gained their first win against Australia at Nottingham since 1930. Boycott returned to Test cricket after a self-imposed exile of 30 matches and scored his 13th hundred in official Tests; it was his 98th century in first-class cricket. Knott became the first wicket-keeper to score 4,000 runs in Test matches and his innings of 135 was the highest by a 'keeper in this series. His partnership of 215 with Boycott equalled England's sixth-wicket record against Australia. Boycott became the second player after M.L. Jaisimha to bat on each day of a five-day Test.

## AUSTRALIA

| | | | | |
|---|---|---|---|---|
| R.B. McCosker | c Brearley b Hendrick | 51 | c Brearley b Willis | 107 |
| I.C. Davis | c Botham b Underwood | 33 | c Greig b Willis | 9 |
| G.S. Chappell* | b Botham | 19 | b Hendrick | 27 |
| D.W. Hookes | c Hendrick b Willis | 17 | lbw b Hendrick | 42 |
| K.D. Walters | c Hendrick b Botham | 11 | c Randall b Greig | 28 |
| R.D. Robinson | c Brearley b Greig | 11 | lbw b Underwood | 34 |
| R.W. Marsh† | lbw b Botham | 0 | c Greig b Willis | 0 |
| K.J. O'Keeffe | not out | 48 | not out | 21 |
| M.H.N. Walker | c Hendrick b Botham | 0 | b Willis | 17 |
| J.R. Thomson | c Knott b Botham | 21 | b Willis | 0 |
| L.S. Pascoe | c Greig b Hendrick | 20 | c Hendrick b Underwood | 0 |
| Extras | (B 4, LB 2, NB 6) | 12 | (B 1, LB 5, W 1, NB 17) | 24 |
| **Total** | | **243** | | **309** |

## ENGLAND

| | | | | |
|---|---|---|---|---|
| J.M. Brearley* | c Hookes b Pascoe | 15 | b Walker | 81 |
| G. Boycott | c McCosker b Thomson | 107 | not out | 80 |
| R.A. Woolmer | lbw b Pascoe | 0 | | |
| D.W. Randall | run out | 13 | (5) not out | 19 |
| A.W. Greig | b Thomson | 11 | (4) b Walker | 0 |
| G. Miller | c Robinson b Pascoe | 13 | | |
| A.P.E. Knott† | c Davis b Thomson | 135 | (3) c O'Keeffe b Walker | 2 |
| I.T. Botham | b Walker | 25 | | |
| D.L. Underwood | b Pascoe | 7 | | |
| M. Hendrick | b Walker | 1 | | |
| R.G.D. Willis | not out | 2 | | |
| Extras | (B 9, LB 7, W 3, NB 16) | 35 | (B 2, LB 2, W 1, NB 2) | 7 |
| **Total** | | **364** | (3 wickets) | **189** |

| ENGLAND | O | M | R | W | O | M | R | W | | FALL OF WICKETS | | | |
|---|---|---|---|---|---|---|---|---|---|---|---|---|---|
| Willis | 15 | 0 | 58 | 1 | 26 | 6 | 88 | 5 | | A | E | A | E |
| Hendrick | 21·2 | 6 | 46 | 2 | 32 | 14 | 56 | 2 | Wkt | 1st | 1st | 2nd | 2nd |
| Botham | 20 | 5 | 74 | 5 | 25 | 5 | 60 | 0 | 1st | 79 | 34 | 18 | 154 |
| Greig | 15 | 4 | 35 | 1 | 9 | 2 | 24 | 1 | 2nd | 101 | 34 | 60 | 156 |
| Underwood | 11 | 5 | 18 | 1 | 27 | 15 | 49 | 2 | 3rd | 131 | 52 | 154 | 158 |
| Miller | | | | | 5 | 2 | 5 | 0 | 4th | 133 | 64 | 204 | – |
| Woolmer | | | | | 3 | 0 | 3 | 0 | 5th | 153 | 82 | 240 | – |
| | | | | | | | | | 6th | 153 | 297 | 240 | – |
| AUSTRALIA | | | | | | | | | 7th | 153 | 326 | 270 | – |
| Thomson | 31 | 6 | 103 | 3 | 16 | 6 | 34 | 0 | 8th | 155 | 357 | 307 | – |
| Pascoe | 32 | 10 | 80 | 4 | 22 | 6 | 43 | 0 | 9th | 196 | 357 | 308 | – |
| Walker | 39·2 | 12 | 79 | 2 | 24 | 8 | 40 | 3 | 10th | 243 | 364 | 309 | – |
| Chappell | 8 | 0 | 19 | 0 | | | | | | | | | |
| O'Keeffe | 11 | 4 | 43 | 0 | 19·2 | 2 | 65 | 0 | | | | | |
| Walters | 3 | 0 | 5 | 0 | | | | | | | | | |

Umpires: H.D. Bird and D.J. Constant.

# ENGLAND v AUSTRALIA 1977 (4th Test)

Played at Headingley, Leeds, on 11, 12, 13, 15 August.
Toss: England.   Result: ENGLAND won by an innings and 85 runs.
Debuts: Nil.

England regained the Ashes at 4.39 on the fourth afternoon when Marsh skied a drive to cover, Randall, who turned a somersault after completing the catch. At 5.49 p.m. on the first day, Boycott became the first batsman to score his 100th first-class hundred during a Test match. Australia were dismissed for their lowest total in a Leeds Test. Knott made his 250th dismissal in 88 Tests (Davis) and Willis took his 100th wicket in 28 Tests (Thomson).

## ENGLAND

| | | |
|---|---|---:|
| J.M. Brearley* | c Marsh b Thomson | 0 |
| G. Boycott | c Chappell b Pascoe | 191 |
| R.A. Woolmer | c Chappell b Thomson | 37 |
| D.W. Randall | lbw b Pascoe | 20 |
| A.W. Greig | b Thomson | 43 |
| G.R.J. Roope | c Walters b Thomson | 34 |
| A.P.E. Knott† | lbw b Bright | 57 |
| I.T. Botham | b Bright | 0 |
| D.L. Underwood | c Bright b Pascoe | 6 |
| M. Hendrick | c Robinson b Pascoe | 4 |
| R.G.D. Willis | not out | 5 |
| Extras | (B 5, LB 9, W 3, NB 22) | 39 |
| **Total** | | **436** |

## AUSTRALIA

| | | | | |
|---|---|---:|---|---:|
| R.B. McCosker | run out | 27 | c Knott b Greig | 12 |
| I.C. Davis | lbw b Hendrick | 0 | c Knott b Greig | 19 |
| G.S. Chappell* | c Brearley b Hendrick | 4 | c Greig b Willis | 36 |
| D.W. Hookes | lbw b Botham | 24 | lbw b Hendrick | 21 |
| K.D. Walters | c Hendrick b Botham | 4 | lbw b Woolmer | 15 |
| R.D. Robinson | c Greig b Hendrick | 20 | b Hendrick | 20 |
| R.W. Marsh† | c Knott b Botham | 2 | c Randall b Hendrick | 63 |
| R.J. Bright | not out | 9 | c Greig b Hendrick | 5 |
| M.H.N. Walker | c Knott b Botham | 7 | b Willis | 30 |
| J.R. Thomson | b Botham | 0 | b Willis | 0 |
| L.S. Pascoe | b Hendrick | 0 | not out | 0 |
| Extras | (LB 3, W 1, NB 2) | 6 | (B 1, LB 4, W 4, NB 18) | 27 |
| **Total** | | **103** | | **248** |

| AUSTRALIA | O | M | R | W | O | M | R | W |
|---|---:|---:|---:|---:|---:|---:|---:|---:|
| Thomson | 34 | 7 | 113 | 4 | | | | |
| Walker | 48 | 21 | 97 | 0 | | | | |
| Pascoe | 34·4 | 10 | 91 | 4 | | | | |
| Walters | 3 | 1 | 5 | 0 | | | | |
| Bright | 26 | 9 | 66 | 2 | | | | |
| Chappell | 10 | 2 | 25 | 0 | | | | |
| **ENGLAND** | | | | | | | | |
| Willis | 5 | 0 | 35 | 0 | 14 | 7 | 32 | 3 |
| Hendrick | 15·3 | 2 | 41 | 4 | 22·5 | 6 | 54 | 4 |
| Botham | 11 | 3 | 21 | 5 | 17 | 3 | 47 | 0 |
| Greig | | | | | 20 | 7 | 64 | 2 |
| Woolmer | | | | | 8 | 4 | 8 | 1 |
| Underwood | | | | | 8 | 3 | 16 | 0 |

### FALL OF WICKETS

| | E | A | A |
|---|---:|---:|---:|
| Wkt | 1st | 1st | 2nd |
| 1st | 0 | 8 | 31 |
| 2nd | 82 | 26 | 35 |
| 3rd | 105 | 52 | 63 |
| 4th | 201 | 57 | 97 |
| 5th | 275 | 66 | 130 |
| 6th | 398 | 77 | 167 |
| 7th | 398 | 87 | 179 |
| 8th | 412 | 100 | 244 |
| 9th | 422 | 100 | 245 |
| 10th | 436 | 103 | 248 |

Umpires: W.E. Alley and W.L. Budd.

Test No. 808/230

# ENGLAND v AUSTRALIA 1977 (5th Test)

Played at Kennington Oval, London, on 25 (*no play*), 26, 27, 29, 30 August.
Toss: Australia.    Result: MATCH DRAWN.
Debuts: Australia – K.J. Hughes, M.F. Malone.

This match, in which 11 hours and 51 minutes were lost because of rain and a waterlogged ground, probably marked the end of the Test careers of four England and eight Australian players contracted to World Series Cricket. Three of those players had uninterrupted Test careers of over 50 matches (Greig 58, Marsh 52 and Chappell 51), while Knott had achieved an England record of 65 consecutive appearances. Thomson took his 100th wicket in 22 Tests; Malone celebrated his only Test cap with five first innings wickets and his highest first-class score; and Boycott achieved the highest average for a rubber in this series (147·33) and scored his 5000th run in official Tests.

## ENGLAND

| | | | | |
|---|---|---:|---|---:|
| J.M. Brearley* | c Marsh b Malone | 39 | c Serjeant b Thomson | 4 |
| G. Boycott | c McCosker b Walker | 39 | not out | 25 |
| R.A. Woolmer | lbw b Thomson | 15 | c Marsh b Malone | 6 |
| D.W. Randall | c Marsh b Malone | 3 | not out | 20 |
| A.W. Greig | c Bright b Malone | 0 | | |
| G.R.J. Roope | b Thomson | 38 | | |
| A.P.E. Knott† | c McCosker b Malone | 6 | | |
| J.K. Lever | lbw b Malone | 3 | | |
| D.L. Underwood | b Thomson | 20 | | |
| M. Hendrick | b Thomson | 15 | | |
| R.G.D. Willis | not out | 24 | | |
| Extras | (LB 6, W 1, NB 5) | 12 | (W 2) | 2 |
| **Total** | | **214** | (2 wickets) | **57** |

## AUSTRALIA

| | | |
|---|---|---:|
| C.S. Serjeant | lbw b Willis | 0 |
| R.B. McCosker | lbw b Willis | 32 |
| G.S. Chappell* | c and b Underwood | 39 |
| K.J. Hughes | c Willis b Hendrick | 1 |
| D.W. Hookes | c Knott b Greig | 85 |
| K.D. Walters | b Willis | 4 |
| R.W. Marsh† | lbw b Hendrick | 57 |
| R.J. Bright | lbw b Willis | 16 |
| M.H.N. Walker | not out | 78 |
| M.F. Malone | b Lever | 46 |
| J.R. Thomson | b Willis | 17 |
| Extras | (B 1, LB 6, NB 3) | 10 |
| **Total** | | **385** |

| AUSTRALIA | O | M | R | W | O | M | R | W |
|---|---|---|---|---|---|---|---|---|
| Thomson | 23·2 | 3 | 87 | 4 | 5 | 1 | 22 | 1 |
| Malone | 47 | 20 | 63 | 5 | 10 | 4 | 14 | 1 |
| Walker | 28 | 11 | 51 | 1 | 8 | 2 | 14 | 0 |
| Bright | 3 | 2 | 1 | 0 | 3 | 2 | 5 | 0 |
| ENGLAND | | | | | | | | |
| Willis | 29·3 | 5 | 102 | 5 | | | | |
| Hendrick | 37 | 5 | 93 | 2 | | | | |
| Lever | 22 | 6 | 61 | 1 | | | | |
| Underwood | 35 | 9 | 102 | 1 | | | | |
| Greig | 8 | 2 | 17 | 1 | | | | |

### FALL OF WICKETS

| | E | A | E |
|---|---|---|---|
| Wkt | 1st | 1st | 2nd |
| 1st | 86 | 0 | 5 |
| 2nd | 88 | 54 | 16 |
| 3rd | 104 | 67 | – |
| 4th | 104 | 84 | – |
| 5th | 106 | 104 | – |
| 6th | 122 | 184 | – |
| 7th | 130 | 236 | – |
| 8th | 169 | 252 | – |
| 9th | 174 | 352 | – |
| 10th | 214 | 385 | – |

Umpires: T.W. Spencer and D.J. Constant.

*820*

# AUSTRALIA v INDIA 1977–78 (1st Test)

Played at Wooloongabba, Brisbane, on 2, 3, 4, 6 December.
Toss: Australia.   Result: AUSTRALIA won by 16 runs.
Debuts: Australia – W.M. Clark, P.A. Hibbert, A.L. Mann, A.D. Ogilvie, S.J. Rixon, P.M. Toohey.

Australia achieved the eighth-narrowest victory by a runs margin in Test cricket. With 12 of the players who appeared against England in 1977 having defected to World Series Cricket, Australia recalled Simpson to play his first Test since 1967-68.

## AUSTRALIA

| | | | | | |
|---|---|---|---|---|---|
| P.A. Hibbert | c Kirmani b Amarnath | 13 | lbw b Madan Lal | | 2 |
| G.J. Cosier | c Madan Lal b Amarnath | 19 | c Prasanna b Madan Lal | | 0 |
| A.D. Ogilvie | c Viswanath b Bedi | 5 | b Chandrasekhar | | 46 |
| C.S. Serjeant | c Gavaskar b Bedi | 0 | b Amarnath | | 0 |
| R.B. Simpson* | c Gavaskar b Bedi | 7 | c Viswanath b Amarnath | | 89 |
| P.M. Toohey | st Kirmani b Bedi | 82 | c Bedi b Chandrasekhar | | 57 |
| A.L. Mann | lbw b Madan Lal | 19 | c Amarnath b Madan Lal | | 29 |
| S.J. Rixon† | c Amarnath b Bedi | 9 | c Kirmani b Madan Lal | | 6 |
| W.M. Clark | c Gavaskar b Chandrasekhar | 4 | b Madan Lal | | 12 |
| J.R. Thomson | b Chandrasekhar | 3 | not out | | 41 |
| A.G. Hurst | not out | 0 | run out | | 26 |
| Extras | (B 3, LB 1, W 1) | 5 | (B 6, LB 11, NB 2) | | 19 |
| **Total** | | **166** | | | **327** |

## INDIA

| | | | | | | |
|---|---|---|---|---|---|---|
| S.M. Gavaskar | c Cosier b Clark | 3 | | c Rixon b Clark | | 113 |
| D.B. Vengsarkar | hit wkt b Thomson | 48 | | b Clark | | 1 |
| M. Amarnath | lbw b Clark | 0 | | c Rixon b Thomson | | 47 |
| G.R. Viswanath | c Hurst b Mann | 45 | | c Ogilvie b Thomson | | 35 |
| B.P. Patel | c Serjeant b Clark | 13 | | lbw b Thomson | | 3 |
| A.V. Mankad | c Rixon b Thomson | 0 | | b Hurst | | 21 |
| S. Madan Lal | b Clark | 4 | (8) | c Rixon b Clark | | 2 |
| S.M.H. Kirmani† | c Ogilvie b Thomson | 11 | (7) | c Serjeant b Hurst | | 55 |
| E.A.S. Prasanna | c Thomson b Mann | 23 | | c Hibbert b Clark | | 8 |
| B.S. Bedi* | not out | 2 | | not out | | 26 |
| B.S. Chandrasekhar | lbw b Mann | 0 | | c Rixon b Thomson | | 0 |
| Extras | (NB 4) | 4 | | (LB 6, NB 7) | | 13 |
| **Total** | | **153** | | | | **324** |

| INDIA | O | M | R | W | O | M | R | W | | FALL OF WICKETS | | | |
|---|---|---|---|---|---|---|---|---|---|---|---|---|---|
| Madan Lal | 10 | 3 | 27 | 1 | 19 | 2 | 72 | 5 | | A | I | A | I |
| Amarnath | 13 | 4 | 43 | 2 | 8 | 1 | 24 | 2 | Wkt | 1st | 1st | 2nd | 2nd |
| Bedi | 13·7 | 3 | 55 | 5 | 18·5 | 2 | 71 | 0 | 1st | 24 | 11 | 0 | 7 |
| Prasanna | 4 | 2 | 2 | 0 | 20 | 4 | 59 | 0 | 2nd | 33 | 15 | 6 | 88 |
| Chandrasekhar | 6 | 1 | 34 | 2 | 26 | 6 | 82 | 2 | 3rd | 33 | 90 | 7 | 147 |
| | | | | | | | | | 4th | 43 | 108 | 100 | 151 |
| AUSTRALIA | | | | | | | | | 5th | 49 | 110 | 184 | 196 |
| Thomson | 16 | 1 | 54 | 3 | 19·7 | 1 | 76 | 4 | 6th | 90 | 112 | 233 | 243 |
| Clark | 18 | 5 | 46 | 4 | 26 | 1 | 101 | 4 | 7th | 107 | 119 | 237 | 251 |
| Hurst | 7 | 0 | 31 | 0 | 15 | 3 | 50 | 2 | 8th | 112 | 149 | 246 | 275 |
| Cosier | 3 | 1 | 6 | 0 | 5 | 1 | 10 | 0 | 9th | 132 | 151 | 277 | 318 |
| Mann | 6 | 0 | 12 | 3 | 15 | 3 | 52 | 0 | 10th | 166 | 153 | 327 | 324 |
| Simpson | | | | | 4 | 0 | 22 | 0 | | | | | |

Umpires: T.F. Brooks and M.G. O'Connell.

# AUSTRALIA v INDIA 1977–78 (2nd Test)

Played at W.A.C.A. Ground, Perth, on 16, 17, 18, 20, 21 December.
Toss: India.    Result: AUSTRALIA won by two wickets.
Debuts: Australia – J. Dyson, J.B. Gannon.

Australia scored the highest fourth innings total to win a Test in Australia and achieved the victory by a narrow margin for the second match running. India reached 400 for the first time in this series. Simpson, leading Australia for a record 31st time, took his 100th catch in 54 Tests – the fifth fielder to achieve this aggregate and in the fewest matches. Mann became the first 'night-watchman' to score a hundred in a Test match. Simpson's 176 and Bedi's match analysis of 11 for 194 set new records for Tests in Perth.

## INDIA

| | | | | |
|---|---|--:|---|--:|
| S.M. Gavaskar | c Rixon b Clark | 4 | b Clark | 127 |
| C.P.S. Chauhan | c Gannon b Simpson | 88 | c Ogilvie b Thomson | 32 |
| M. Amarnath | c Gannon b Thomson | 90 | c Rixon b Simpson | 100 |
| G.R. Viswanath | b Thomson | 38 | c Rixon b Clark | 1 |
| D.B. Vengsarkar | c Rixon b Clark | 49 | c Hughes b Gannon | 9 |
| B.P. Patel | c Rixon b Thomson | 3 | b Gannon | 27 |
| S.M.H. Kirmani† | c Rixon b Thomson | 38 | lbw b Gannon | 2 |
| S. Venkataraghavan | c Simpson b Gannon | 37 | c Hughes b Gannon | 14 |
| S. Madan Lal | b Gannon | 43 | b Thomson | 3 |
| B.S. Bedi* | b Gannon | 3 | not out | 0 |
| B.S. Chandrasekhar | not out | 0 | not out | 0 |
| Extras | (B 1, NB 8) | 9 | (B 1, LB 4, NB 10) | 15 |
| **Total** | | **402** | (9 wickets declared) | **330** |

## AUSTRALIA

| | | | | |
|---|---|--:|---|--:|
| J. Dyson | c Patel b Bedi | 53 | c Vengsarkar b Bedi | 4 |
| C.S. Serjeant | c Kirmani b Madan Lal | 13 | c Kirmani b Madan Lal | 12 |
| A.D. Ogilvie | b Bedi | 27 | (4) b Bedi | 47 |
| P.M. Toohey | st Kirmani b Bedi | 0 | (5) c Amarnath b Bedi | 83 |
| R.B. Simpson* | c Vengsarkar b Venkataraghavan | 176 | (6) run out | 39 |
| S.J. Rixon† | c Kirmani b Amarnath | 50 | (8) lbw b Bedi | 23 |
| K.J. Hughes | c Patel b Bedi | 28 | lbw b Madan Lal | 0 |
| A.L. Mann | c Vengsarkar b Bedi | 7 | (3) c Kirmani b Bedi | 105 |
| W.M. Clark | c Patel b Chandrasekhar | 15 | not out | 5 |
| J.R. Thomson | c Amarnath b Venkataraghavan | 0 | not out | 6 |
| J.B. Gannon | not out | 0 | | |
| Extras | (LB 25) | 25 | (B 8, LB 10) | 18 |
| **Total** | | **394** | (8 wickets) | **342** |

| AUSTRALIA | O | M | R | W | O | M | R | W | | FALL OF WICKETS | | | |
|---|--:|--:|--:|--:|--:|--:|--:|--:|---|--:|--:|--:|--:|
| | | | | | | | | | | I | A | I | A |
| Thomson | 24 | 1 | 101 | 4 | 21·5 | 3 | 65 | 2 | Wkt | 1st | 1st | 2nd | 2nd |
| Clark | 17 | 0 | 95 | 2 | 18 | 1 | 83 | 2 | 1st | 14 | 19 | 47 | 13 |
| Gannon | 16·6 | 1 | 84 | 3 | 18 | 2 | 77 | 4 | 2nd | 163 | 61 | 240 | 33 |
| Mann | 11 | 0 | 63 | 0 | 8 | 0 | 49 | 0 | 3rd | 224 | 65 | 244 | 172 |
| Simpson | 11 | 0 | 50 | 1 | 8 | 2 | 41 | 1 | 4th | 229 | 149 | 283 | 195 |
| INDIA | | | | | | | | | 5th | 235 | 250 | 287 | 295 |
| Madan Lal | 15 | 1 | 54 | 1 | 11 | 0 | 44 | 2 | 6th | 311 | 321 | 289 | 296 |
| Amarnath | 16 | 2 | 57 | 1 | 3 | 0 | 22 | 0 | 7th | 319 | 341 | 327 | 330 |
| Chandrasekhar | 33·6 | 6 | 114 | 1 | 15 | 0 | 67 | 0 | 8th | 383 | 388 | 328 | 330 |
| Bedi | 31 | 6 | 89 | 5 | 30·2 | 6 | 105 | 5 | 9th | 391 | 388 | 330 | – |
| Venkataraghavan | 23 | 4 | 55 | 2 | 28 | 9 | 86 | 0 | 10th | 402 | 394 | – | – |

Umpires: R.C. Bailhache and R.A. French.

# AUSTRALIA v INDIA 1977–78 (3rd Test)

Played at Melbourne Cricket Ground on 30, 31 December, 2, 3, 4 January.
Toss: India.    Result: INDIA won by 222 runs.
Debuts: Nil.

India gained their first victory in Australia. Chandrasekhar took his 200th wicket in 48 Tests, three matches fewer than Bedi who is the only other Indian to achieve this total. Chandrasekhar also became the first to be dismissed for a 'pair' in Test cricket on four occasions.

## INDIA

| | | | | |
|---|---|---|---|---|
| S.M. Gavaskar | c Rixon b Thomson | 0 | c Serjeant b Gannon | 118 |
| C.P.S. Chauhan | c Mann b Clark | 0 | run out | 20 |
| M. Amarnath | c Simpson b Clark | 72 | (7) b Cosier | 41 |
| G.R. Viswanath | c Rixon b Thomson | 59 | lbw b Clark | 54 |
| D.B. Vengsarkar | c Simpson b Thomson | 37 | c Cosier b Clark | 6 |
| A.V. Mankad | c Clark b Gannon | 44 | b Clark | 38 |
| S.M.H. Kirmani† | lbw b Simpson | 29 | (3) c Thomson b Mann | 29 |
| K.D. Ghavri | c Rixon b Gannon | 6 | c Simpson b Clark | 6 |
| E.A.S. Prasanna | b Clark | 0 | c Rixon b Gannon | 11 |
| B.S. Bedi* | not out | 2 | not out | 12 |
| B.S. Chandrasekhar | b Clark | 0 | lbw b Cosier | 0 |
| Extras | (LB 3, NB 4) | 7 | (LB 1, NB 7) | 8 |
| **Total** | | **256** | | **343** |

## AUSTRALIA

| | | | | |
|---|---|---|---|---|
| J. Dyson | b Ghavri | 0 | lbw b Bedi | 12 |
| G.J. Cosier | c Chauhan b Chandrasekhar | 67 | b Chandrasekhar | 34 |
| A.D. Ogilvie | lbw b Ghavri | 6 | c Chauhan b Bedi | 0 |
| C.S. Serjeant | b Chandrasekhar | 85 | b Chandrasekhar | 17 |
| R.B. Simpson* | c Mankad b Chandrasekhar | 2 | lbw b Chandrasekhar | 4 |
| P.M. Toohey | c Viswanath b Bedi | 14 | c Chauhan b Chandrasekhar | 14 |
| A.L. Mann | c Gavaskar b Bedi | 11 | c Gavaskar b Chandrasekhar | 18 |
| S.J. Rixon† | lbw b Chandrasekhar | 11 | c and b Chandrasekhar | 12 |
| W.M. Clark | lbw b Chandrasekhar | 3 | c Ghavri b Bedi | 33 |
| J.R. Thomson | c Ghavri b Chandrasekhar | 0 | c and b Bedi | 7 |
| J.B. Gannon | not out | 0 | not out | 3 |
| Extras | (B 6, LB 7, NB 1) | 14 | (B 6, LB 4) | 10 |
| **Total** | | **213** | | **164** |

| AUSTRALIA | O | M | R | W | O | M | R | W | | FALL OF WICKETS | | | |
|---|---|---|---|---|---|---|---|---|---|---|---|---|---|
| Thomson | 16 | 2 | 78 | 3 | 18 | 4 | 47 | 0 | | I | A | I | A |
| Clark | 19·2 | 2 | 73 | 4 | 29 | 3 | 96 | 4 | *Wkt* | *1st* | *1st* | *2nd* | *2nd* |
| Gannon | 14 | 2 | 47 | 2 | 22 | 4 | 88 | 2 | 1st | 0 | 0 | 40 | 42 |
| Cosier | 12 | 3 | 25 | 0 | 12·7 | 2 | 58 | 2 | 2nd | 0 | 18 | 89 | 42 |
| Simpson | 3 | 1 | 11 | 1 | 3 | 0 | 22 | 0 | 3rd | 105 | 122 | 187 | 52 |
| Mann | 5 | 1 | 15 | 0 | 4 | 0 | 24 | 1 | 4th | 174 | 124 | 198 | 60 |
| | | | | | | | | | 5th | 180 | 166 | 265 | 77 |
| INDIA | | | | | | | | | 6th | 234 | 178 | 286 | 98 |
| Ghavri | 9 | 0 | 37 | 2 | 4 | 0 | 29 | 0 | 7th | 254 | 202 | 294 | 115 |
| Gavaskar | 2 | 0 | 7 | 0 | | | | | 8th | 254 | 211 | 315 | 122 |
| Bedi | 15 | 2 | 71 | 2 | 16·1 | 5 | 58 | 4 | 9th | 256 | 211 | 343 | 151 |
| Chandrasekhar | 14·1 | 2 | 52 | 6 | 20 | 3 | 52 | 6 | 10th | 256 | 213 | 343 | 164 |
| Prasanna | 10 | 1 | 32 | 0 | 8 | 4 | 5 | 0 | | | | | |
| Amarnath | | | | | 3 | 0 | 10 | 0 | | | | | |

Umpires: M.G. O'Connell and R.A. French.

# AUSTRALIA v INDIA 1977–78 (4th Test)

Played at Sydney Cricket Ground on 7, 8, 9, 11, 12 January.
Toss: Australia.   Result: INDIA won by an innings and 2 runs.
Debuts: Nil.

India gained their first victory by an innings margin against Australia. It was also the first time since England's tour in 1954-55 that Australia had lost successive home Tests.

## AUSTRALIA

| | | | | | |
|---|---|---|---|---|---|
| J. Dyson | lbw b Chandrasekhar | 26 | c and b Chandrasekhar | | 6 |
| G.J. Cosier | b Amarnath | 17 | b Bedi | | 68 |
| P.M. Toohey | run out | 4 | (6) c sub (S. Madan Lal) b Ghavri | | 85 |
| C.S. Serjeant | c Ghavri b Bedi | 4 | b Prasanna | | 1 |
| R.B. Simpson* | c Kirmani b Chandrasekhar | 38 | lbw b Prasanna | | 33 |
| K.J. Hughes | b Bedi | 17 | (3) c Vengsarkar b Bedi | | 19 |
| A.L. Mann | b Bedi | 0 | c and b Prasanna | | 0 |
| S.J. Rixon† | lbw b Chandrasekhar | 17 | c Viswanath b Chandrasekhar | | 11 |
| W.M. Clark | c Gavaskar b Chandrasekhar | 0 | b Prasanna | | 10 |
| J.R. Thomson | not out | 1 | b Ghavri | | 16 |
| J.B. Gannon | c Amarnath b Prasanna | 0 | not out | | 0 |
| Extras | (LB 5, NB 2) | 7 | (B 5, LB 6, NB 3) | | 14 |
| **Total** | | **131** | | | **263** |

## INDIA

| | | |
|---|---|---|
| S.M. Gavaskar | c Rixon b Thomson | 49 |
| C.P.S. Chauhan | c Mann b Clark | 42 |
| M. Amarnath | c Gannon b Clark | 9 |
| G.R. Viswanath | b Thomson | 79 |
| D.B. Vengsarkar | c Rixon b Cosier | 48 |
| A.V. Mankad | b Thomson | 16 |
| S.M.H. Kirmani† | b Cosier | 42 |
| K.D. Ghavri | c Serjeant b Thomson | 64 |
| E.A.S. Prasanna | not out | 25 |
| B.S. Bedi* | not out | 1 |
| B.S. Chandrasekhar | did not bat | |
| Extras | (LB 9, NB 12) | 21 |
| **Total** | (8 wickets declared) | **396** |

| INDIA | O | M | R | W | O | M | R | W | | FALL OF WICKETS | | |
|---|---|---|---|---|---|---|---|---|---|---|---|---|
| | | | | | | | | | | A | I | A |
| Ghavri | 7 | 1 | 25 | 0 | 12·7 | 3 | 42 | 2 | Wkt | 1st | 1st | 2nd |
| Amarnath | 7 | 4 | 6 | 1 | 5 | 3 | 9 | 0 | 1st | 29 | 97 | 26 |
| Bedi | 13 | 3 | 49 | 3 | 28 | 8 | 62 | 2 | 2nd | 34 | 102 | 87 |
| Chandrasekhar | 15 | 3 | 30 | 4 | 24 | 3 | 85 | 2 | 3rd | 46 | 116 | 88 |
| Prasanna | 7·4 | 2 | 14 | 1 | 29 | 11 | 51 | 4 | 4th | 61 | 241 | 106 |
| | | | | | | | | | 5th | 84 | 261 | 171 |
| AUSTRALIA | | | | | | | | | 6th | 84 | 263 | 171 |
| Thomson | 27 | 8 | 83 | 4 | | | | | 7th | 125 | 344 | 194 |
| Clark | 21 | 3 | 66 | 2 | | | | | 8th | 125 | 395 | 221 |
| Gannon | 20 | 4 | 65 | 0 | | | | | 9th | 130 | – | 257 |
| Mann | 20 | 0 | 101 | 0 | | | | | 10th | 131 | – | 263 |
| Simpson | 4 | 0 | 34 | 0 | | | | | | | | |
| Cosier | 9 | 1 | 26 | 2 | | | | | | | | |

Umpires: T.F. Brooks and R.C. Bailhache.

# AUSTRALIA v INDIA 1977–78 (5th Test)

Played at Adelaide Oval on 28, 29, 30 January, 1, 2, 3 February.
Toss: Australia.   Result: AUSTRALIA won by 47 runs.
Debuts: Australia – I.W. Callen, W.M. Darling, G.M. Wood, B. Yardley.

Australia won the rubber 3-2 after India had achieved the second-highest fourth innings total in Test cricket. India's 445 also represented their highest total against Australia and the highest by any side in the fourth innings to lose a Test match. Bedi set a new record for either country by taking 31 wickets in the rubber.

## AUSTRALIA

| | | | | | |
|---|---|---|---|---|---|
| G.M. Wood | st Kirmani b Chandrasekhar | 39 | c Vengsarkar b Bedi | | 8 |
| W.M. Darling | c Vengsarkar b Chandrasekhar | 65 | b Bedi | | 56 |
| G.N. Yallop | c Gavaskar b Amarnath | 121 | b Bedi | | 24 |
| P.M. Toohey | c Gavaskar b Chandrasekhar | 60 | c Kirmani b Prasanna | | 10 |
| R.B. Simpson* | c Viswanath b Ghavri | 100 | lbw b Ghavri | | 51 |
| G.J. Cosier | b Ghavri | 1 | st Kirmani b Bedi | | 34 |
| S.J. Rixon† | b Bedi | 32 | run out | | 13 |
| B. Yardley | c and b Ghavri | 22 | c Vengsarkar b Ghavri | | 26 |
| J.R. Thomson | c Ghavri b Chandrasekhar | 24 | (11) c Amarnath b Ghavri | | 3 |
| W.M. Clark | b Chandrasekhar | 0 | (9) lbw b Ghavri | | 1 |
| I.W. Callen | not out | 22 | (10) not out | | 4 |
| Extras | (B 4, LB 14, NB 1) | 19 | (B 5, LB 15, W 3, NB 3) | | 26 |
| **Total** | | **505** | | | **256** |

## INDIA

| | | | | | |
|---|---|---|---|---|---|
| S.M. Gavaskar | c Toohey b Thomson | 7 | c Rixon b Callen | | 29 |
| C.P.S. Chauhan | c Cosier b Clark | 15 | c Wood b Yardley | | 32 |
| M. Amarnath | c Cosier b Thomson | 0 | c Callen b Yardley | | 86 |
| G.R. Viswanath | c Rixon b Callen | 89 | c Simpson b Clark | | 73 |
| D.B. Vengsarkar | c Rixon b Callen | 44 | c Toohey b Yardley | | 78 |
| A.D. Gaekwad | c Rixon b Callen | 27 | c and b Yardley | | 12 |
| S.M.H. Kirmani† | run out | 48 | b Clark | | 51 |
| K.D. Ghavri | c Simpson b Clark | 3 | c sub (K.J. Hughes) b Callen | | 23 |
| E.A.S. Prasanna | not out | 15 | not out | | 10 |
| B.S. Bedi* | c sub (K.J. Hughes) b Clark | 6 | c Cosier b Callen | | 16 |
| B.S. Chandrasekhar | c and b Clark | 2 | c Rixon b Simpson | | 2 |
| Extras | (B 4, LB 1, NB 8) | 13 | (B 6, LB 11, NB 16) | | 33 |
| **Total** | | **269** | | | **445** |

| INDIA | O | M | R | W | O | M | R | W | | FALL OF WICKETS | | | |
|---|---|---|---|---|---|---|---|---|---|---|---|---|---|
| Ghavri | 22 | 2 | 93 | 3 | 10·5 | 2 | 45 | 4 | | A | I | A | I |
| Amarnath | 12 | 0 | 45 | 1 | 4 | 0 | 12 | 0 | Wkt | 1st | 1st | 2nd | 2nd |
| Bedi | 34 | 1 | 127 | 1 | 20 | 3 | 53 | 4 | 1st | 89 | 23 | 17 | 40 |
| Prasanna | 10 | 1 | 48 | 0 | 34 | 7 | 68 | 1 | 2nd | 110 | 23 | 84 | 79 |
| Chandrasekhar | 29·4 | 0 | 136 | 5 | 14 | 0 | 52 | 0 | 3rd | 230 | 23 | 95 | 210 |
| Gaekwad | 5 | 0 | 37 | 0 | | | | | 4th | 334 | 159 | 107 | 256 |
| | | | | | | | | | 5th | 337 | 166 | 172 | 323 |
| AUSTRALIA | | | | | | | | | 6th | 406 | 216 | 210 | 348 |
| Thomson | 3·3 | 1 | 12 | 2 | | | | | 7th | 450 | 226 | 214 | 415 |
| Clark | 20·7 | 6 | 62 | 4 | 29 | 6 | 79 | 2 | 8th | 457 | 249 | 240 | 417 |
| Callen | 22 | 0 | 83 | 3 | 33 | 5 | 108 | 3 | 9th | 458 | 263 | 248 | 442 |
| Cosier | 4 | 3 | 4 | 0 | 13 | 6 | 21 | 0 | 10th | 505 | 269 | 256 | 445 |
| Yardley | 23 | 6 | 62 | 0 | 43 | 6 | 134 | 4 | | | | | |
| Simpson | 9 | 0 | 33 | 0 | 23·4 | 6 | 70 | 1 | | | | | |

Umpires: M.G. O'Connell and R.A. French.

# PAKISTAN v ENGLAND 1977–78 (1st Test)

Played at Lahore (Gaddafi) Stadium on 14, 15, 16, 18, 19 December.
Toss: Pakistan.   Result: MATCH DRAWN.
Debuts: Pakistan – Abdul Qadir; England – G.A. Cope, B.C. Rose.

Mudassar took 557 minutes to reach his hundred and record the slowest century in all first-class cricket. His innings lasted 575 minutes.

## PAKISTAN

| | | | | |
|---|---|---|---|---|
| Mudassar Nazar | c and b Miller | 114 | c Taylor b Willis | 26 |
| Sadiq Mohammad | lbw b Miller | 18 | b Lever | 1 |
| Shafiq Ahmed | c Rose b Old | 0 | lbw b Willis | 7 |
| Haroon Rashid | c and b Lever | 122 | not out | 45 |
| Javed Miandad | c Taylor b Lever | 71 | not out | 19 |
| Wasim Raja | st Taylor b Cope | 24 | | |
| Abdul Qadir | lbw b Cope | 11 | | |
| Wasim Bari*† | c Cope b Miller | 17 | | |
| Sarfraz Nawaz | b Cope | 0 | | |
| Iqbal Qasim | not out | 8 | | |
| Liaquat Ali | not out | 0 | | |
| Extras | (B 1, LB 4, NB 17) | 22 | (NB 8) | 8 |
| **Total** | (9 wickets declared) | **407** | (3 wickets) | **106** |

## ENGLAND

| | | |
|---|---|---|
| G. Boycott | b Qasim | 63 |
| J.M. Brearley* | run out | 23 |
| B.C. Rose | lbw b Sarfraz | 1 |
| D.W. Randall | c Qasim b Liaquat | 19 |
| G.R.J. Roope | b Qasim | 19 |
| G. Miller | not out | 98 |
| C.M. Old | c Mudassar b Qasim | 2 |
| R.W. Taylor† | b Sarfraz | 32 |
| G.A. Cope | lbw b Sarfraz | 0 |
| J.K. Lever | c Wasim Bari b Sarfraz | 0 |
| R.G.D. Willis | c Qasim b Qadir | 14 |
| Extras | (B 2, LB 8, NB 7) | 17 |
| **Total** | | **288** |

| ENGLAND | O | M | R | W | O | M | R | W | | FALL OF WICKETS | | |
|---|---|---|---|---|---|---|---|---|---|---|---|---|
| | | | | | | | | | | P | E | P |
| Willis | 17 | 3 | 67 | 0 | 7 | 0 | 34 | 2 | Wkt | 1st | 1st | 2nd |
| Lever | 16 | 1 | 47 | 2 | 3 | 0 | 13 | 1 | 1st | 48 | 53 | 15 |
| Old | 21 | 7 | 63 | 1 | 4 | 0 | 18 | 0 | 2nd | 49 | 55 | 40 |
| Miller | 37 | 10 | 102 | 3 | 10 | 4 | 24 | 0 | 3rd | 229 | 96 | 45 |
| Cope | 39 | 6 | 102 | 3 | 3 | 0 | 7 | 0 | 4th | 329 | 127 | – |
| Boycott | 3 | 0 | 4 | 0 | | | | | 5th | 356 | 148 | – |
| Randall | | | | | 1 | 0 | 2 | 0 | 6th | 378 | 162 | – |
| | | | | | | | | | 7th | 387 | 251 | – |
| PAKISTAN | | | | | | | | | 8th | 387 | 251 | – |
| Sarfraz | 34 | 11 | 68 | 4 | | | | | 9th | 403 | 253 | – |
| Liaquat | 27 | 11 | 43 | 1 | | | | | 10th | – | 288 | – |
| Qadir | 32·7 | 7 | 82 | 1 | | | | | | | | |
| Qasim | 32 | 12 | 57 | 3 | | | | | | | | |
| Wasim Raja | 10 | 2 | 21 | 0 | | | | | | | | |

Umpires: Amanullah Khan and Mohammad Aslam Khokhar.

# PAKISTAN v ENGLAND 1977-78 (2nd Test)

Played at Niaz Stadium, Hyderabad, on 2, 3, 4, 6, 7 January.
Toss: Pakistan.    Result: MATCH DRAWN.
Debuts: Nil.

Haroon reached his hundred with his sixth six; it was his second century in successive Tests. Brearley claimed the optional last half-hour of the match to allow Boycott to complete his 15th hundred in official Tests. Qadir's analysis of 6 for 44 is a record for any Test at Hyderabad and the best for Pakistan against England.

| PAKISTAN | | | | | |
|---|---|---|---|---|---|
| Mudassar Nazar | c Edmonds b Cope | 27 | c Taylor b Willis | | 66 |
| Sadiq Mohammad | c Taylor b Willis | 9 | c Edmonds b Cope | | 22 |
| Shafiq Ahmed | c Miller b Edmonds | 13 | (6) not out | | 27 |
| Haroon Rashid | c and b Edmonds | 108 | c Brearley b Cope | | 35 |
| Javed Miandad | not out | 88 | not out | | 61 |
| Wasim Raja | c Brearley b Edmonds | 0 | (3) c Edmonds b Willis | | 24 |
| Abdul Qadir | c Brearley b Cope | 4 | | | |
| Wasim Bari*† | run out | 10 | | | |
| Iqbal Qasim | c Roope b Willis | 0 | | | |
| Liaquat Ali | c Edmonds b Lever | 0 | | | |
| Sikander Bakht | run out | 3 | | | |
| Extras | (B 4, LB 7, NB 2) | 13 | (B 13, LB 11) | | 24 |
| **Total** | | **275** | (4 wickets declared) | | **259** |

| ENGLAND | | | | | |
|---|---|---|---|---|---|
| G. Boycott | run out | 79 | not out | | 100 |
| J.M. Brearley* | c Wasim Bari b Qasim | 17 | c sub (Hasan Jamil) b Wasim Raja | | 74 |
| B.C. Rose | b Qadir | 27 | | | |
| D.W. Randall | c and b Qadir | 7 | | | |
| G.R.J. Roope | c and b Qadir | 1 | | | |
| G. Miller | c Wasim Bari b Qasim | 5 | | | |
| R.W. Taylor† | b Qadir | 0 | | | |
| P.H. Edmonds | c Wasim Bari b Qadir | 4 | | | |
| G.A. Cope | c Sadiq b Wasim Raja | 22 | | | |
| J.K. Lever | b Qadir | 4 | (3) not out | | 0 |
| R.G.D. Willis | not out | 8 | | | |
| Extras | (B 10, LB 6, W 1) | 17 | (B 4, LB 7, NB 1) | | 12 |
| **Total** | | **191** | (1 wicket) | | **186** |

| ENGLAND | O | M | R | W | O | M | R | W |
|---|---|---|---|---|---|---|---|---|
| Willis | 16 | 2 | 40 | 2 | 11 | 2 | 26 | 2 |
| Lever | 16·6 | 7 | 41 | 1 | 20 | 2 | 62 | 0 |
| Edmonds | 24 | 2 | 75 | 3 | 30 | 6 | 95 | 0 |
| Cope | 14 | 6 | 49 | 2 | 24 | 9 | 42 | 2 |
| Miller | 9 | 0 | 57 | 0 | 2 | 0 | 8 | 0 |
| Roope | | | | | 1 | 0 | 2 | 0 |
| PAKISTAN | | | | | | | | |
| Sikander | 16 | 4 | 35 | 0 | 10 | 3 | 22 | 0 |
| Liaquat | 6 | 0 | 18 | 0 | 4 | 1 | 14 | 0 |
| Qasim | 34 | 11 | 54 | 2 | 24·4 | 6 | 42 | 0 |
| Miandad | 5 | 0 | 21 | 0 | 4 | 0 | 10 | 0 |
| Qadir | 24 | 8 | 44 | 6 | 27 | 5 | 72 | 0 |
| Wasim Raja | 1·6 | 0 | 2 | 1 | 12 | 5 | 14 | 1 |

| FALL OF WICKETS | | | | |
|---|---|---|---|---|
| | P | E | P | E |
| Wkt | 1st | 1st | 2nd | 2nd |
| 1st | 14 | 40 | 55 | 185 |
| 2nd | 40 | 123 | 116 | – |
| 3rd | 101 | 137 | 117 | – |
| 4th | 213 | 139 | 189 | – |
| 5th | 213 | 142 | – | – |
| 6th | 222 | 142 | – | – |
| 7th | 247 | 146 | – | – |
| 8th | 248 | 152 | – | – |
| 9th | 249 | 157 | – | – |
| 10th | 275 | 191 | – | – |

Umpires: Shujauddin and Mahboob Shah.

# PAKISTAN v ENGLAND 1977–78 (3rd Test)

Played at National Stadium, Karachi, on 18, 19, 20, 22, 23 January.
Toss: England.   Result: MATCH DRAWN.
Debuts: Pakistan – Mohsin Khan; England – M.W. Gatting.

The sides achieved their eleventh successive draw in Pakistan. Edmonds returned the best innings analysis for either side in this series. The six 'lbw' decisions in England's first innings equalled the Test record.

## ENGLAND

| | | | | |
|---|---|---|---|---|
| G. Boycott* | b Qasim | 31 | c Miandad b Sikander | 56 |
| B.C. Rose | c Miandad b Sarfraz | 10 | c Haroon b Qadir | 18 |
| D.W. Randall | lbw b Qasim | 23 | b Sikander | 55 |
| G.R.J. Roope | lbw b Sikander | 56 | not out | 33 |
| M.W. Gatting | lbw b Qadir | 5 | lbw b Qasim | 6 |
| G. Miller | c Mudassar b Wasim Raja | 11 | c Wasim Bari b Qasim | 3 |
| R.W. Taylor† | lbw b Qadir | 36 | not out | 18 |
| P.H. Edmonds | lbw b Qadir | 6 | | |
| G.A. Cope | b Qasim | 18 | | |
| J.K. Lever | not out | 33 | | |
| R.G.D. Willis | lbw b Qadir | 5 | | |
| Extras | (B 3, LB 21, NB 8) | 32 | (B 9, LB 6, W 3, NB 15) | 33 |
| **Total** | | **266** | (5 wickets) | **222** |

## PAKISTAN

| | | |
|---|---|---|
| Mudassar Nazar | c sub (I.T. Botham) b Edmonds | 76 |
| Shafiq Ahmed | c sub (I.T. Botham) b Willis | 10 |
| Mohsin Khan | c Willis b Cope | 44 |
| Haroon Rashid | c Taylor b Edmonds | 27 |
| Javed Miandad | c Roope b Edmonds | 23 |
| Wasim Raja | c Gatting b Edmonds | 47 |
| Abdul Qadir | c Roope b Edmonds | 21 |
| Wasim Bari*† | lbw b Miller | 6 |
| Sarfraz Nawaz | c Gatting b Edmonds | 0 |
| Iqbal Qasim | b Edmonds | 8 |
| Sikander Bakht | not out | 7 |
| Extras | (B 2, LB 3, NB 7) | 12 |
| **Total** | | **281** |

| PAKISTAN | O | M | R | W | O | M | R | W | FALL OF WICKETS | | | |
|---|---|---|---|---|---|---|---|---|---|---|---|---|
| | | | | | | | | | | E | P | E |
| Sarfraz | 15 | 6 | 27 | 1 | 28 | 7 | 57 | 0 | *Wkt* | *1st* | *1st* | *2nd* |
| Sikander | 15 | 4 | 39 | 1 | 17 | 4 | 40 | 2 | 1st | 17 | 33 | 35 |
| Qasim | 40 | 20 | 56 | 3 | 29 | 11 | 51 | 2 | 2nd | 69 | 121 | 125 |
| Qadir | 40·1 | 9 | 81 | 4 | 8 | 2 | 26 | 1 | 3rd | 72 | 167 | 148 |
| Wasim Raja | 13 | 3 | 31 | 1 | | | | | 4th | 85 | 170 | 162 |
| Mudassar | | | | | 1 | 0 | 1 | 0 | 5th | 107 | 230 | 171 |
| Miandad | | | | | 2 | 0 | 5 | 0 | 6th | 189 | 243 | – |
| Shafiq | | | | | 1 | 0 | 1 | 0 | 7th | 197 | 263 | – |
| Wasim Bari | | | | | 1 | 0 | 2 | 0 | 8th | 203 | 263 | – |
| Haroon | | | | | 1 | 0 | 3 | 0 | 9th | 232 | 269 | – |
| Mohsin | | | | | 1 | 0 | 3 | 0 | 10th | 266 | 281 | – |
| | | | | | | | | | | | | |
| ENGLAND | | | | | | | | | | | | |
| Willis | 8 | 1 | 23 | 1 | | | | | | | | |
| Lever | 12 | 4 | 32 | 0 | | | | | | | | |
| Edmonds | 33 | 7 | 66 | 7 | | | | | | | | |
| Cope | 28 | 8 | 77 | 1 | | | | | | | | |
| Miller | 14 | 0 | 71 | 1 | | | | | | | | |

Umpires: Amanullah Khan and Shakoor Rana.

# NEW ZEALAND v ENGLAND 1977–78 (1st Test)

Played at Basin Reserve, Wellington, on 10, 11, 12, 14, 15 February.
Toss: England.　Result: NEW ZEALAND won by 72 runs.
Debuts: New Zealand – S.L. Boock, J.G. Wright.

New Zealand beat England for the first time in 48 matches dating back to 1929-30. England's total of 64 was their lowest since 1948 and their lowest against all countries except Australia. Collinge took his 100th wicket in 32 Tests.

## NEW ZEALAND

| | | | | |
|---|---|---|---|---|
| J.G. Wright | lbw b Botham | 55 | c Roope b Willis | 19 |
| R.W. Anderson | c Taylor b Old | 28 | lbw b Old | 26 |
| G.P. Howarth | c Botham b Old | 13 | c Edmonds b Willis | 21 |
| M.G. Burgess* | b Willis | 9 | c Boycott b Botham | 6 |
| B.E. Congdon | c Taylor b Old | 44 | c Roope b Willis | 0 |
| J.M. Parker | c Rose b Willis | 16 | c Edmonds b Willis | 4 |
| W.K. Lees† | c Taylor b Old | 1 | lbw b Hendrick | 11 |
| R.J. Hadlee | not out | 27 | c Boycott b Willis | 2 |
| D.R. Hadlee | c Taylor b Old | 1 | c Roope b Botham | 2 |
| R.O. Collinge | b Old | 1 | c Edmonds b Hendrick | 6 |
| S.L. Boock | b Botham | 4 | not out | 0 |
| Extras | (B 12, LB 3, W 1, NB 13) | 29 | (B 2, LB 9, W 2, NB 13) | 26 |
| **Total** | | **228** | | **123** |

## ENGLAND

| | | | | |
|---|---|---|---|---|
| B.C. Rose | c Lees b Collinge | 21 | not out | 5 |
| G. Boycott* | c Congdon b Collinge | 77 | b Collinge | 1 |
| G. Miller | b Boock | 24 | c Anderson b Collinge | 4 |
| R.W. Taylor† | c and b Collinge | 8 | (7) run out | 0 |
| D.W. Randall | c Burgess b R.J. Hadlee | 4 | (4) lbw b Collinge | 9 |
| G.R.J. Roope | c Lees b R.J. Hadlee | 37 | (5) c Lees b R.J. Hadlee | 0 |
| I.T. Botham | c Burgess b R.J. Hadlee | 7 | (6) c Boock b R.J. Hadlee | 19 |
| C.M. Old | b R.J. Hadlee | 10 | lbw b R.J. Hadlee | 9 |
| P.H. Edmonds | lbw b Congdon | 4 | c Parker b R.J. Hadlee | 11 |
| M. Hendrick | lbw b Congdon | 0 | c Parker b R.J. Hadlee | 0 |
| R.G.D. Willis | not out | 6 | c Howarth b R.J. Hadlee | 3 |
| Extras | (LB 4, NB 13) | 17 | (NB 3) | 3 |
| **Total** | | **215** | | **64** |

| ENGLAND | O | M | R | W | O | M | R | W |
|---|---|---|---|---|---|---|---|---|
| Willis | 25 | 7 | 65 | 2 | 15 | 2 | 32 | 5 |
| Hendrick | 17 | 2 | 46 | 0 | 10 | 2 | 16 | 2 |
| Old | 30 | 11 | 54 | 6 | 9 | 2 | 32 | 1 |
| Edmonds | 3 | 1 | 7 | 0 | 1 | 0 | 4 | 0 |
| Botham | 12·6 | 2 | 27 | 2 | 9·3 | 3 | 13 | 2 |
| NEW ZEALAND | | | | | | | | |
| R.J. Hadlee | 28 | 5 | 74 | 4 | 13·3 | 4 | 26 | 6 |
| Collinge | 18 | 5 | 42 | 3 | 13 | 5 | 35 | 3 |
| D.R. Hadlee | 21 | 5 | 47 | 0 | 1 | 1 | 0 | 0 |
| Boock | 10 | 5 | 21 | 1 | | | | |
| Congdon | 17·4 | 11 | 14 | 2 | | | | |

### FALL OF WICKETS

| | NZ | E | NZ | E |
|---|---|---|---|---|
| Wkt | 1st | 1st | 2nd | 2nd |
| 1st | 42 | 39 | 54 | 2 |
| 2nd | 96 | 89 | 82 | 8 |
| 3rd | 114 | 108 | 93 | 18 |
| 4th | 152 | 126 | 93 | 18 |
| 5th | 191 | 183 | 98 | 38 |
| 6th | 193 | 188 | 99 | 38 |
| 7th | 194 | 203 | 104 | 53 |
| 8th | 196 | 205 | 116 | 53 |
| 9th | 208 | 206 | 123 | 63 |
| 10th | 228 | 215 | 123 | 64 |

Umpires: W.R.C. Gardiner and R.L. Monteith.

# NEW ZEALAND v ENGLAND 1977–78 (2nd Test)

Played at Lancaster Park, Christchurch, on 24, 25, 26, 28 February, 1 March.
Toss: England.   Result: ENGLAND won by 174 runs.
Debuts: England – C.T. Radley.

Botham became the second England player after A.W. Greig (*Test No. 733*) to score a hundred and take five wickets in an innings of the same Test.

## ENGLAND

| | | | | |
|---|---|---|---|---|
| B.C. Rose | c Howarth b Chatfield | 11 | c Lees b Collinge | 7 |
| G. Boycott* | lbw b Collinge | 8 | run out | 26 |
| D.W. Randall | c Burgess b Hadlee | 0 | run out | 13 |
| G.R.J. Roope | c Burgess b Hadlee | 50 | (6) not out | 9 |
| G. Miller | c Congdon b Collinge | 89 | | |
| C.T. Radley | c Lees b Hadlee | 15 | | |
| I.T. Botham | c Lees b Boock | 103 | (4) not out | 30 |
| R.W. Taylor† | run out | 45 | | |
| C.M. Old | b Hadlee | 8 | (5) b Collinge | 1 |
| P.H. Edmonds | c Lees b Collinge | 50 | | |
| R.G.D. Willis | not out | 6 | | |
| Extras | (B 14, LB 9, NB 10) | 33 | (B 4, LB 3, NB 3) | 10 |
| **Total** | | **418** | (4 wickets declared) | **96** |

## NEW ZEALAND

| | | | | |
|---|---|---|---|---|
| J.G. Wright | c and b Edmonds | 4 | c Roope b Willis | 0 |
| R.W. Anderson | b Edmonds | 62 | b Willis | 15 |
| G.P. Howarth | c Edmonds b Willis | 5 | c Edmonds b Old | 1 |
| M.G. Burgess* | c Roope b Botham | 29 | not out | 6 |
| B.E. Congdon | lbw b Botham | 20 | c Botham b Willis | 0 |
| J.M. Parker | not out | 53 | c Botham b Edmonds | 16 |
| W.K. Lees† | c Miller b Botham | 0 | b Willis | 0 |
| R.J. Hadlee | b Edmonds | 1 | c Botham b Edmonds | 39 |
| R.O. Collinge | c Edmonds b Botham | 32 | c Miller b Botham | 0 |
| S.L. Boock | c Taylor b Edmonds | 2 | c Taylor b Botham | 0 |
| E.J. Chatfield | c Edmonds b Botham | 3 | lbw b Botham | 6 |
| Extras | (B 4, LB 1, NB 19) | 24 | (LB 6, NB 16) | 22 |
| **Total** | | **235** | | **105** |

| NEW ZEALAND | O | M | R | W | O | M | R | W |
|---|---|---|---|---|---|---|---|---|
| Hadlee | 43 | 10 | 147 | 4 | 6 | 1 | 17 | 0 |
| Collinge | 26·5 | 6 | 89 | 3 | 9 | 2 | 29 | 2 |
| Chatfield | 37 | 8 | 94 | 1 | 5 | 0 | 22 | 0 |
| Congdon | 18 | 11 | 14 | 0 | 2 | 0 | 18 | 0 |
| Boock | 21 | 11 | 41 | 1 | | | | |
| ENGLAND | | | | | | | | |
| Willis | 20 | 5 | 45 | 1 | 7 | 2 | 14 | 4 |
| Old | 14 | 4 | 55 | 0 | 7 | 4 | 9 | 1 |
| Botham | 24·7 | 6 | 73 | 5 | 7 | 1 | 38 | 3 |
| Edmonds | 34 | 11 | 8 | 4 | 6 | 2 | 22 | 2 |

FALL OF WICKETS

| Wkt | E 1st | NZ 1st | E 2nd | NZ 2nd |
|---|---|---|---|---|
| 1st | 15 | 37 | 25 | 2 |
| 2nd | 18 | 52 | 47 | 14 |
| 3rd | 26 | 82 | 67 | 19 |
| 4th | 127 | 119 | 74 | 25 |
| 5th | 128 | 148 | – | 25 |
| 6th | 288 | 151 | – | 59 |
| 7th | 294 | 153 | – | 81 |
| 8th | 305 | 211 | – | 90 |
| 9th | 375 | 216 | – | 95 |
| 10th | 418 | 235 | – | 105 |

Umpires: F.R. Goodall and R.L. Monteith.

# NEW ZEALAND v ENGLAND 1977–78 (3rd Test)

Played at Eden Park, Auckland, on 4, 5, 6, 8, 9, 10 March.
Toss: New Zealand.   Result: MATCH DRAWN.
Debuts: Nil.

Howarth became the second batsman after G.M. Turner (*Test No. 737*) to score a hundred in each innings of a Test for New Zealand. Radley, playing in his second Test, took 487 minutes to reach his hundred. Collinge passed B.R. Taylor's New Zealand record of 111 Test wickets.

## NEW ZEALAND

| | | | | | |
|---|---|---|---|---|---|
| J.G. Wright | c Taylor b Lever | 4 | c Taylor b Edmonds | | 25 |
| R.W. Anderson | c Gatting b Botham | 17 | c Botham b Miller | | 55 |
| G.P. Howarth | c Roope b Willis | 122 | b Miller | | 102 |
| M.G. Burgess* | c Randall b Botham | 50 | c Taylor b Edmonds | | 17 |
| B.E. Congdon | c Miller b Botham | 5 | c Roope b Lever | | 20 |
| J.M. Parker | lbw b Botham | 14 | (7) not out | | 47 |
| G.N. Edwards† | lbw b Lever | 55 | (6) c Randall b Lever | | 54 |
| R.J. Hadlee | c Roope b Botham | 1 | b Miller | | 10 |
| B.L. Cairns | b Lever | 11 | lbw b Edmonds | | 20 |
| R.O. Collinge | not out | 5 | not out | | 12 |
| S.L. Boock | c Edmonds b Willis | 1 | | | |
| Extras | (B 5, LB 10, NB 15) | 30 | (B 6, LB 4, NB 10) | | 20 |
| **Total** | | **315** | (8 wickets) | | **382** |

## ENGLAND

| | | |
|---|---|---|
| G. Boycott* | c Burgess b Collinge | 54 |
| D.W. Randall | lbw b Hadlee | 30 |
| C.T. Radley | c Wright b Collinge | 158 |
| G.R.J. Roope | c Burgess b Boock | 68 |
| M.W. Gatting | b Boock | 0 |
| I.T. Botham | c Edwards b Collinge | 53 |
| R.W. Taylor† | b Boock | 16 |
| G. Miller | lbw b Collinge | 15 |
| P.H. Edmonds | b Boock | 8 |
| J.K. Lever | c and b Boock | 1 |
| R.G.D. Willis | not out | 0 |
| Extras | (B 6, LB 6, W 4, NB 10) | 26 |
| **Total** | | **429** |

| ENGLAND | O | M | R | W | O | M | R | W | | FALL OF WICKETS | | |
|---|---|---|---|---|---|---|---|---|---|---|---|---|
| | | | | | | | | | | NZ | E | NZ |
| Willis | 26·6 | 8 | 57 | 2 | 10 | 3 | 42 | 0 | *Wkt* | *1st* | *1st* | *2nd* |
| Lever | 34 | 5 | 96 | 3 | 17 | 4 | 59 | 2 | 1st | 12 | 52 | 69 |
| Botham | 34 | 4 | 109 | 5 | 13 | 1 | 51 | 0 | 2nd | 32 | 115 | 98 |
| Edmonds | 10 | 2 | 23 | 0 | 45 | 15 | 107 | 3 | 3rd | 113 | 254 | 125 |
| Miller | 1 | 1 | 0 | 0 | 30 | 10 | 99 | 3 | 4th | 129 | 258 | 185 |
| Gatting | | | | | 1 | 0 | 1 | 0 | 5th | 182 | 355 | 272 |
| Roope | | | | | 1 | 0 | 2 | 0 | 6th | 278 | 396 | 287 |
| Randall | | | | | 1 | 0 | 1 | 0 | 7th | 285 | 418 | 305 |
| | | | | | | | | | 8th | 302 | 427 | 350 |
| NEW ZEALAND | | | | | | | | | 9th | 314 | 428 | – |
| Hadlee | 31 | 6 | 107 | 1 | | | | | 10th | 315 | 429 | – |
| Collinge | 38 | 9 | 98 | 4 | | | | | | | | |
| Cairns | 33 | 9 | 63 | 0 | | | | | | | | |
| Congdon | 26 | 8 | 68 | 0 | | | | | | | | |
| Boock | 28·3 | 4 | 67 | 5 | | | | | | | | |

Umpires: W.R.C. Gardiner and J.B.R. Hastie.

# WEST INDIES v AUSTRALIA 1977–78 (1st Test)

Played at Queen's Park Oval, Port-of-Spain, Trinidad, on 3, 4, 5 March.
Toss: West Indies.   Result: WEST INDIES won by an innings and 106 runs.
Debuts: West Indies – R.A. Austin, D.L. Haynes, D.R. Parry; Australia – J.D. Higgs.

West Indies, who retained their World Series cricketers, beat Australia with more than two days to spare.
Australia's first innings total of 90 was the lowest in any Test at Port-of-Spain.

## AUSTRALIA

| | | | | |
|---|---|---|---|---|
| G.M. Wood | c Haynes b Croft | 2 | lbw b Roberts | 32 |
| C.S. Serjeant | c Murray b Croft | 3 | lbw b Garner | 40 |
| G.N. Yallop | c Richards b Croft | 2 | b Roberts | 81 |
| P.M. Toohey | b Garner | 20 | absent hurt | – |
| R.B. Simpson* | lbw b Garner | 0 | b Parry | 14 |
| G.J. Cosier | c Greenidge b Croft | 46 | (4) lbw b Garner | 19 |
| S.J. Rixon† | run out | 1 | (6) c Parry b Roberts | 0 |
| B. Yardley | c Murray b Roberts | 2 | (7) not out | 7 |
| J.R. Thomson | c Austin b Roberts | 0 | (8) b Parry | 4 |
| W.M. Clark | b Garner | 0 | (9) b Roberts | 0 |
| J.D. Higgs | not out | 0 | (10) b Roberts | 2 |
| Extras | (B 4, LB 6, NB 4) | 14 | (B 5, LB 2, W 1, NB 2) | 10 |
| **Total** | | **90** | | **209** |

## WEST INDIES

| | | |
|---|---|---|
| C.G. Greenidge | b Yardley | 43 |
| D.L. Haynes | c Rixon b Higgs | 61 |
| I.V.A. Richards | lbw b Thomson | 39 |
| A.I. Kallicharran | b Yardley | 127 |
| C.H. Lloyd* | b Thomson | 86 |
| R.A. Austin | c sub (T.J. Laughlin) b Thomson | 2 |
| D.L. Murray† | c Rixon b Higgs | 21 |
| D.R. Parry | b Yardley | 0 |
| A.M.E. Roberts | st Rixon b Higgs | 7 |
| J. Garner | c Cosier b Higgs | 0 |
| C.E.H. Croft | not out | 4 |
| Extras | (LB 9, NB 6) | 15 |
| **Total** | | **405** |

| WEST INDIES | O | M | R | W | O | M | R | W |
|---|---|---|---|---|---|---|---|---|
| Roberts | 12 | 4 | 26 | 2 | 16·2 | 3 | 56 | 5 |
| Croft | 9·1 | 5 | 15 | 4 | 13 | 1 | 55 | 0 |
| Garner | 14 | 6 | 35 | 3 | 17 | 5 | 39 | 2 |
| Parry | | | | | 17 | 1 | 49 | 2 |
| **AUSTRALIA** | | | | | | | | |
| Thomson | 21 | 6 | 84 | 3 | | | | |
| Clark | 16 | 3 | 41 | 0 | | | | |
| Higgs | 24·5 | 3 | 91 | 4 | | | | |
| Simpson | 16 | 2 | 65 | 0 | | | | |
| Yardley | 19 | 1 | 64 | 3 | | | | |
| Cosier | 13 | 2 | 45 | 0 | | | | |

### FALL OF WICKETS

| | A | WI | A |
|---|---|---|---|
| Wkt | 1st | 1st | 2nd |
| 1st | 7 | 87 | 59 |
| 2nd | 10 | 143 | 90 |
| 3rd | 16 | 143 | 149 |
| 4th | 23 | 313 | 194 |
| 5th | 45 | 324 | 194 |
| 6th | 75 | 385 | 194 |
| 7th | 75 | 385 | 200 |
| 8th | 84 | 391 | 201 |
| 9th | 90 | 391 | 209 |
| 10th | 90 | 405 | – |

Umpires: D. Sang Hue and R. Gosein.

# WEST INDIES v AUSTRALIA 1977–78 (2nd Test)

Played at Kensington Oval, Bridgetown, Barbados, on 17, 18, 19 March.
Toss: West Indies.   Result: WEST INDIES won by nine wickets.
Debuts: Nil.

West Indies beat Australia at Bridgetown for the first time and completed their second successive victory inside three days.

## AUSTRALIA

| | | | | | |
|---|---|---|---|---|---|
| W.M. Darling | c Richards b Croft | 4 | c Murray b Croft | | 8 |
| G.M. Wood | lbw b Croft | 69 | run out | | 56 |
| G.N. Yallop | c Austin b Croft | 47 | c Lloyd b Garner | | 14 |
| C.S. Serjeant | c Murray b Parry | 4 | c Murray b Roberts | | 2 |
| R.B. Simpson* | c Murray b Croft | 9 | (7) c Murray b Roberts | | 17 |
| G.J. Cosier | c Murray b Roberts | 1 | (5) c Croft b Roberts | | 8 |
| S.J. Rixon† | lbw b Garner | 16 | (6) c Lloyd b Roberts | | 0 |
| B. Yardley | b Garner | 74 | b Garner | | 43 |
| J.R. Thomson | b Garner | 12 | c Richards b Garner | | 11 |
| W.M. Clark | b Garner | 0 | lbw b Garner | | 0 |
| J.D. Higgs | not out | 4 | not out | | 0 |
| Extras | (B 3, LB 4, NB 3) | 10 | (B 1, LB 8, NB 10) | | 19 |
| **Total** | | **250** | | | **178** |

## WEST INDIES

| | | | | | |
|---|---|---|---|---|---|
| C.G. Greenidge | c Cosier b Thomson | 8 | not out | | 80 |
| D.L. Haynes | c Rixon b Higgs | 66 | c Yardley b Higgs | | 55 |
| I.V.A. Richards | c Clark b Thomson | 23 | | | |
| A.I. Kallicharran | c Yardley b Thomson | 8 | | | |
| C.H. Lloyd* | c Serjeant b Clark | 42 | | | |
| R.A. Austin | c Serjeant b Clark | 20 | | | |
| D.L. Murray† | c Darling b Thomson | 60 | | | |
| D.R. Parry | c Serjeant b Simpson | 27 | (3) not out | | 3 |
| A.M.E. Roberts | lbw b Thomson | 4 | | | |
| J. Garner | not out | 5 | | | |
| C.E.H. Croft | lbw b Thomson | 3 | | | |
| Extras | (LB 3, NB 19) | 22 | (LB 2, W 1) | | 3 |
| **Total** | | **288** | (1 wicket) | | **141** |

| WEST INDIES | O | M | R | W | O | M | R | W | FALL OF WICKETS | | | | |
|---|---|---|---|---|---|---|---|---|---|---|---|---|---|
| Roberts | 18 | 2 | 79 | 1 | 18 | 5 | 50 | 4 | | A | WI | A | WI |
| Croft | 18 | 3 | 47 | 4 | 15 | 4 | 53 | 1 | *Wkt* | *1st* | *1st* | *2nd* | *2nd* |
| Garner | 16·1 | 2 | 65 | 4 | 15 | 3 | 56 | 4 | 1st | 13 | 15 | 21 | 131 |
| Parry | 12 | 4 | 44 | 1 | | | | | 2nd | 105 | 56 | 62 | – |
| Austin | 1 | 0 | 5 | 0 | | | | | 3rd | 116 | 71 | 69 | – |
| | | | | | | | | | 4th | 134 | 154 | 80 | – |
| AUSTRALIA | | | | | | | | | 5th | 135 | 172 | 95 | – |
| Thomson | 13 | 1 | 77 | 6 | 6 | 1 | 22 | 0 | 6th | 149 | 198 | 99 | – |
| Clark | 24 | 3 | 77 | 2 | 7 | 0 | 27 | 0 | 7th | 161 | 263 | 154 | – |
| Cosier | 9 | 4 | 24 | 0 | | | | | 8th | 216 | 269 | 167 | – |
| Higgs | 16 | 4 | 46 | 1 | 13 | 4 | 34 | 1 | 9th | 216 | 282 | 173 | – |
| Simpson | 7 | 1 | 30 | 1 | | | | | 10th | 250 | 288 | 178 | – |
| Yardley | 2 | 0 | 12 | 0 | 10·5 | 2 | 55 | 0 | | | | | |

Umpires: R. Gosein and S.E. Parris.

# WEST INDIES v AUSTRALIA 1977–78 (3rd Test)

Played at Bourda, Georgetown, Guyana, on 31 March, 1, 2, 4, 5 April.
Toss: West Indies.   Result: AUSTRALIA won by three wickets.
Debuts: West Indies – S. Clarke, A.T. Greenidge, D.A. Murray, N. Phillip, S. Shivnarine, A.B. Williams; Australia – T.J. Laughlin.

A pre-match dispute between the West Indies Board of Control and their captain, C.H. Lloyd, over team selection resulted in all the World Series cricketers withdrawing from the team. Australia's 362 for 7 was the third-highest total to win any Test. Williams scored a hundred on debut.

## WEST INDIES

| | | | | |
|---|---|--:|---|--:|
| A.T. Greenidge | lbw b Thomson | 56 | b Clark | 11 |
| A.B. Williams | lbw b Clark | 10 | c Serjeant b Clark | 100 |
| H.A. Gomes | b Clark | 4 | (5) c Simpson b Yardley | 101 |
| A.I. Kallicharran* | b Thomson | 0 | (6) b Yardley | 22 |
| I.T. Shillingford | c Clark b Laughlin | 3 | (7) c and b Thomson | 16 |
| D.A. Murray† | c Ogilvie b Clark | 21 | (3) lbw b Simpson | 16 |
| S. Shivnarine | c Rixon b Thomson | 53 | (8) b Cosier | 63 |
| N. Phillip | c Yardley b Simpson | 15 | (9) st Rixon b Yardley | 4 |
| V.A. Holder | c Laughlin b Clark | 1 | (10) lbw b Clark | 31 |
| D.R. Parry | not out | 21 | (4) lbw b Clark | 51 |
| S. Clarke | b Thomson | 6 | not out | 5 |
| Extras | (LB 2, NB 13) | 15 | (B 4, LB 5, NB 10) | 19 |
| **Total** | | **205** | | **439** |

## AUSTRALIA

| | | | | |
|---|---|--:|---|--:|
| W.M. Darling | c Greenidge b Phillip | 15 | c Williams b Clarke | 0 |
| G.M. Wood | lbw b Holder | 50 | run out | 126 |
| A.D. Ogilvie | c and b Phillip | 4 | lbw b Clarke | 0 |
| G.J. Cosier | lbw b Clarke | 9 | (6) b Phillip | 0 |
| C.S. Serjeant | b Clarke | 0 | c sub (S.F.A. Bacchus) b Phillip | 124 |
| R.B. Simpson* | run out | 67 | (4) c Murray b Clarke | 4 |
| T.J. Laughlin | c Greenidge b Parry | 21 | (8) c and b Parry | 24 |
| S.J. Rixon† | c Holder b Phillip | 54 | (7) not out | 39 |
| B. Yardley | b Clarke | 33 | not out | 15 |
| J.R. Thomson | c and b Phillip | 3 | | |
| W.M. Clark | not out | 2 | | |
| Extras | (LB 12, W 1, NB 15) | 28 | (B 8, LB 4, W 2, NB 16) | 30 |
| **Total** | | **286** | (7 wickets) | **362** |

| AUSTRALIA | O | M | R | W | O | M | R | W |
|---|--:|--:|--:|--:|--:|--:|--:|--:|
| Thomson | 16·2 | 1 | 56 | 4 | 20 | 2 | 83 | 1 |
| Clark | 24 | 6 | 65 | 4 | 34·4 | 4 | 124 | 4 |
| Laughlin | 10 | 4 | 34 | 1 | 7 | 1 | 33 | 0 |
| Cosier | 2 | 1 | 1 | 0 | 6 | 1 | 14 | 1 |
| Simpson | 8 | 1 | 34 | 1 | 19 | 4 | 70 | 1 |
| Yardley | | | | | 30 | 6 | 96 | 3 |
| **WEST INDIES** | | | | | | | | |
| Phillip | 18 | 0 | 75 | 4 | 19 | 2 | 65 | 2 |
| Holder | 17 | 1 | 40 | 1 | 20 | 3 | 55 | 0 |
| Clarke | 22 | 3 | 58 | 3 | 27 | 5 | 83 | 3 |
| Gomes | 3 | 0 | 8 | 0 | | | | |
| Parry | 15 | 2 | 39 | 1 | 17 | 1 | 61 | 1 |
| Shivnarine | 8 | 0 | 38 | 0 | 18 | 2 | 68 | 0 |

## FALL OF WICKETS

| Wkt | WI 1st | A 1st | WI 2nd | A 2nd |
|---|--:|--:|--:|--:|
| 1st | 31 | 28 | 36 | 11 |
| 2nd | 36 | 36 | 95 | 13 |
| 3rd | 48 | 77 | 172 | 22 |
| 4th | 77 | 85 | 199 | 273 |
| 5th | 84 | 90 | 249 | 279 |
| 6th | 130 | 142 | 285 | 290 |
| 7th | 165 | 237 | 355 | 338 |
| 8th | 166 | 256 | 369 | – |
| 9th | 193 | 268 | 431 | – |
| 10th | 205 | 286 | 439 | – |

Umpires: R. Gosein and C.A. Vyfhuis.

# WEST INDIES v AUSTRALIA 1977–78 (4th Test)

Played at Queen's Park Oval, Port-of-Spain, Trinidad, on 15, 16, 17, 18 April.
Toss: Australia.   Result: WEST INDIES won by 198 runs.
Debuts: West Indies – S.F.A. Bacchus.

This win, with over a day to spare, gave West Indies victory against Australia for the second time in four home rubbers.

## WEST INDIES

| | | | | | |
|---|---|---|---|---|---|
| A.T. Greenidge | c Wood b Clark | 6 | c Thomson b Yardley | 69 |
| A.B. Williams | c Yallop b Higgs | 87 | c Yallop b Simpson | 24 |
| D.A. Murray† | c Wood b Yardley | 4 | lbw b Clark | 4 |
| H.A. Gomes | c Simpson b Clark | 30 | c Simpson b Higgs | 14 |
| A.I. Kallicharran* | c Yallop b Clark | 92 | c and b Clark | 27 |
| S.F.A. Bacchus | b Higgs | 9 | c Wood b Yardley | 7 |
| S. Shivnarine | c Simpson b Thomson | 10 | c Serjeant b Simpson | 11 |
| D.R. Parry | st Rixon b Higgs | 22 | c Serjeant b Yardley | 65 |
| N. Phillip | c Rixon b Thomson | 3 | c Wood b Yardley | 46 |
| V.A. Holder | b Thomson | 7 | b Simpson | 0 |
| R.R. Jumadeen | not out | 0 | not out | 2 |
| Extras | (B 7, LB 1, W 2, NB 12) | 22 | (B 1, LB 13, NB 7) | 21 |
| **Total** | | **292** | | **290** |

## AUSTRALIA

| | | | | | |
|---|---|---|---|---|---|
| G.M. Wood | c Murray b Phillip | 16 | lbw b Holder | 17 |
| W.M. Darling | c Jumadeen b Holder | 10 | b Phillip | 6 |
| P.M. Toohey | c Williams b Parry | 40 | c Bacchus b Jumadeen | 17 |
| G.N. Yallop | c Murray b Jumadeen | 75 | c Kallicharran b Parry | 18 |
| C.S. Serjeant | st Murray b Jumadeen | 49 | c Bacchus b Jumadeen | 4 |
| R.B. Simpson* | lbw b Holder | 36 | lbw b Jumadeen | 6 |
| S.J. Rixon† | c Murray b Holder | 21 | not out | 13 |
| B. Yardley | c Williams b Holder | 22 | b Parry | 3 |
| J.R. Thomson | b Holder | 0 | b Parry | 1 |
| W.M. Clark | b Holder | 4 | b Parry | 0 |
| J.D. Higgs | not out | 0 | b Parry | 4 |
| Extras | (B 4, LB 2, NB 11) | 17 | (LB 2, NB 3) | 5 |
| **Toal** | | **290** | | **94** |

| AUSTRALIA | O | M | R | W | O | M | R | W | | FALL OF WICKETS | | | |
|---|---|---|---|---|---|---|---|---|---|---|---|---|---|
| Thomson | 23 | 8 | 64 | 3 | 15 | 1 | 76 | 0 | | WI | A | WI | A |
| Clark | 24 | 6 | 65 | 3 | 21 | 4 | 62 | 2 | *Wkt* | *1st* | *1st* | *2nd* | *2nd* |
| Yardley | 18 | 5 | 48 | 1 | 30·2 | 15 | 40 | 4 | 1st | 7 | 23 | 36 | 9 |
| Higgs | 16·5 | 2 | 53 | 3 | 21 | 7 | 46 | 1 | 2nd | 16 | 43 | 51 | 42 |
| Simpson | 15 | 4 | 40 | 0 | 14 | 2 | 45 | 3 | 3rd | 111 | 92 | 79 | 44 |
| | | | | | | | | | 4th | 166 | 193 | 134 | 60 |
| WEST INDIES | | | | | | | | | 5th | 185 | 204 | 151 | 72 |
| Phillip | 17 | 0 | 73 | 1 | 7 | 0 | 24 | 1 | 6th | 242 | 254 | 151 | 76 |
| Holder | 13 | 4 | 28 | 6 | 11 | 3 | 16 | 1 | 7th | 258 | 275 | 204 | 80 |
| Jumadeen | 24 | 4 | 83 | 2 | 15 | 3 | 34 | 3 | 8th | 262 | 275 | 273 | 86 |
| Parry | 30 | 5 | 77 | 1 | 10·4 | 4 | 15 | 5 | 9th | 291 | 289 | 280 | 88 |
| Shivnarine | 6 | 1 | 12 | 0 | | | | | 10th | 292 | 290 | 290 | 94 |

Umpires: R. Gosein and C.A. Vyfhuis.

# WEST INDIES v AUSTRALIA 1977–78 (5th Test)

Played at Sabina Park, Kingston, Jamaica, on 28, 29, 30 April, May 2, 3.
Toss: Australia.   Result: MATCH DRAWN.
Debuts: Nil.

Australia were denied a probable victory when spectators rioted and invaded the field after Holder had been given out ten minutes before the close of the fifth day's play. Although 38 balls of the mandatory last 20 overs remained, attempts to complete the match on the following day were thwarted by the refusal of umpire Gosein to officiate.

## AUSTRALIA

| | | | | | |
|---|---|---|---|---|---|
| G.M. Wood | c Parry b Phillip | 16 | c Bacchus b Jumadeen | | 90 |
| A.D. Ogilvie | c Shivnarine b Holder | 0 | st Murray b Parry | | 43 |
| P.M. Toohey | c Williams b Holder | 122 | st Murray b Jumadeen | | 97 |
| G.N. Yallop | c sub (H.G. Gordon) b Shivnarine | 57 | not out | | 23 |
| C.S. Serjeant | b Holder | 26 | not out | | 32 |
| R.B. Simpson* | c Murray b Foster | 46 | | | |
| T.J. Laughlin | c sub (H.G. Gordon) b Jumadeen | 35 | | | |
| S.J. Rixon† | not out | 13 | | | |
| B. Yardley | b Jumadeen | 7 | | | |
| J.R. Thomson | c Murray b Jumadeen | 4 | | | |
| J.D. Higgs | c Foster b Jumadeen | 0 | | | |
| Extras | (LB 5, W 1, NB 11) | 17 | (B 5, LB 8, NB 7) | | 20 |
| **Total** | | **343** | (3 wickets declared) | | **305** |

## WEST INDIES

| | | | | | |
|---|---|---|---|---|---|
| A.B. Williams | c Serjeant b Laughlin | 17 | c Wood b Yardley | | 19 |
| S.F.A. Bacchus | c Yardley b Thomson | 5 | c Simpson b Thomson | | 21 |
| D.A. Murray† | c Wood b Laughlin | 12 | (6) b Yardley | | 10 |
| H.A. Gomes | b Thomson | 115 | (3) c Rixon b Higgs | | 1 |
| A.I. Kallicharran* | c Ogilvie b Laughlin | 6 | lbw b Higgs | | 126 |
| M.L.C. Foster | c Rixon b Laughlin | 8 | (4) run out | | 5 |
| S. Shivnarine | st Rixon b Higgs | 53 | c Yallop b Yardley | | 27 |
| D.R. Parry | lbw b Higgs | 4 | c Serjeant b Yardley | | 0 |
| N. Phillip | c Rixon b Simpson | 26 | not out | | 26 |
| V.A. Holder | lbw b Laughlin | 24 | c Rixon b Higgs | | 6 |
| R.R. Jumadeen | not out | 4 | not out | | 0 |
| Extras | (LB 1, NB 5) | 6 | (B 14, LB 1, NB 2) | | 17 |
| **Total** | | **280** | (9 wickets) | | **258** |

| WEST INDIES | O | M | R | W | O | M | R | W |
|---|---|---|---|---|---|---|---|---|
| Phillip | 32 | 5 | 90 | 1 | 17 | 1 | 64 | 0 |
| Holder | 31 | 8 | 68 | 3 | 18 | 2 | 41 | 0 |
| Parry | 5 | 0 | 15 | 0 | 18 | 3 | 60 | 1 |
| Jumadeen | 38·4 | 6 | 72 | 4 | 23 | 2 | 90 | 2 |
| Foster | 32 | 10 | 68 | 1 | 7 | 1 | 22 | 0 |
| Shivnarine | 9 | 2 | 13 | 1 | 3 | 1 | 8 | 0 |
| **AUSTRALIA** | | | | | | | | |
| Thomson | 22 | 4 | 61 | 2 | 15 | 1 | 53 | 1 |
| Laughlin | 25·4 | 4 | 101 | 5 | 10 | 1 | 34 | 0 |
| Yardley | 14 | 4 | 27 | 0 | 29 | 17 | 35 | 4 |
| Simpson | 10 | 0 | 38 | 1 | 11 | 4 | 44 | 0 |
| Higgs | 19 | 3 | 47 | 2 | 28·4 | 10 | 67 | 3 |
| Yallop | | | | | 3 | 1 | 8 | 0 |

### FALL OF WICKETS

| Wkt | A 1st | WI 1st | A 2nd | WI 2nd |
|---|---|---|---|---|
| 1st | 0 | 13 | 65 | 42 |
| 2nd | 38 | 28 | 245 | 43 |
| 3rd | 171 | 41 | 246 | 43 |
| 4th | 217 | 47 | – | 59 |
| 5th | 266 | 63 | – | 88 |
| 6th | 308 | 159 | – | 179 |
| 7th | 324 | 173 | – | 181 |
| 8th | 335 | 219 | – | 242 |
| 9th | 343 | 276 | – | 258 |
| 10th | 343 | 280 | – | – |

Umpires: R. Gosein and W. Malcolm.

# ABANDONED TEST MATCHES

Three Test matches, all of them in the series between England and Australia, have been abandoned without a ball being bowled. These matches are excluded from the team and individual Test records which follow.

## 3rd Test 1890

At Old Trafford, Manchester, on 25, 26, 27 August. No toss.

ENGLAND
W.G. Grace*, A.E. Stoddart, W.W. Read, G. MacGregor†, G.A. Lohmann, J.M. Read, W. Attewell,
W. Gunn, A. Shrewsbury, J. Briggs, A. Mold (or F.H. Sugg).

AUSTRALIA
W.L. Murdoch*, G.H.S. Trott, J.E. Barrett, C.T.B. Turner, J.J. Ferris, J.J. Lyons, J.M. Blackham†,
P.C. Charlton, S.E. Gregory, K.E. Burn, H. Trumble.

## 3rd Test 1938

At Old Trafford, Manchester, on 8, 9, 11, 12 July. No toss.

ENGLAND
(From) W.R. Hammond*, C.J. Barnett, L. Hutton, W.J. Edrich, E. Paynter, D.C.S. Compton,
J. Hardstaff jr, P.A. Gibb†, M.S. Nichols, T.F. Smailes, H. Verity, D.V.P. Wright, T.W.J. Goddard.

AUSTRALIA
(From) D.G. Bradman*, S.J. McCabe, C.L. Badcock, S.G. Barnes, B.A. Barnett†, W.A. Brown,
A.G. Chipperfield, J.H.W. Fingleton, L.O'B. Fleetwood-Smith, A.L. Hassett, E.L. McCormick,
W.J. O'Reilly, M.G. Waite, C.W. Walker, F.A. Ward, E.S. White.

Umpires: W. Reeves and A. Dolphin.

## 3rd Test 1970-71

At Melbourne Cricket Ground on 31 December, 1, 2, 4, 5 January.
Toss: England

AUSTRALIA
W.M. Lawry*, K.R. Stackpole, I.M. Chappell, K.D. Walters, I.R. Redpath, G.S. Chappell, R.W. Marsh†,
A.A. Mallett, G.D. McKenzie, J.W. Gleeson, A.N. Connolly.

ENGLAND
G. Boycott, B.W. Luckhurst, J.H. Edrich, M.C. Cowdrey, B.L. D'Oliveira, R. Illingworth*, A.P.E. Knott†,
J.A. Snow, K. Shuttleworth, P. Lever, D.L. Underwood.

Umpires: L.P. Rowan and T.F. Brooks.

England won the toss on the first day and elected to field before rain prevented a start and eventually caused the match to be abandoned on the third day. This decision was taken by a conference of members of the Australian Board of Control, led by Sir Donald Bradman, and the M.C.C. manager, D.G. Clark, and two visiting M.C.C. officials, Sir Cyril Hawker and G.O.B. Allen. The touring schedule was rearranged to include an additional Test at Melbourne on 21, 22, 23, 25, 26 January.

# Test Match Records 1876-77 to 1977-78

# RESULTS SUMMARY

## RESULTS SUMMARY OF ALL TEST MATCHES, 1876-78 to1977-78
### *(824 MATCHES)*

| | | Tests | E | A | SA | WI | NZ | I | P | Tied | Drawn |
|---|---|---|---|---|---|---|---|---|---|---|---|
| England | v Australia | 230 | 74 | 88 | – | – | – | – | – | – | 68 |
| | v South Africa | 102 | 46 | – | 18 | – | – | – | – | – | 38 |
| | v West Indies | 71 | 21 | – | – | 22 | – | – | – | – | 28 |
| | v New Zealand | 50 | 24 | – | – | – | 1 | – | – | – | 25 |
| | v India | 53 | 25 | – | – | – | – | 7 | – | – | 21 |
| | v Pakistan | 30 | 9 | – | – | – | – | – | 1 | – | 20 |
| Australia | v South Africa | 53 | – | 29 | 11 | – | – | – | – | – | 13 |
| | v West Indies | 46 | – | 25 | – | 10 | – | – | – | 1 | 10 |
| | v New Zealand | 9 | – | 5 | – | – | 1 | – | – | – | 3 |
| | v India | 30 | – | 19 | – | – | – | 5 | – | – | 6 |
| | v Pakistan | 12 | – | 6 | – | – | – | – | 2 | – | 4 |
| South Africa | v New Zealand | 17 | – | – | 9 | – | 2 | – | – | – | 6 |
| West Indies | v New Zealand | 14 | – | – | – | 5 | 2 | – | – | – | 7 |
| | v India | 37 | – | – | – | 17 | – | 4 | – | – | 16 |
| | v Pakistan | 15 | – | – | – | 6 | – | – | 4 | – | 5 |
| New Zealand | v.India | 22 | – | – | – | – | 3 | 10 | – | – | 9 |
| | v Pakistan | 18 | – | – | – | – | 1 | – | 7 | – | 10 |
| India | v Pakistan | 15 | – | – | – | – | – | 2 | 1 | – | 12 |
| | | 824 | 199 | 172 | 38 | 60 | 10 | 28 | 15 | 1 | 301 |

| | Tests | Won | Lost | Drawn | Tied | Toss Won |
|---|---|---|---|---|---|---|
| England | 536 | 199 | 137 | 200 | – | 264 |
| Australia | 380 | 172 | 103 | 104 | 1 | 187 |
| South Africa | 172 | 38 | 77 | 57 | – | 80 |
| West Indies | 183 | 60 | 56 | 66 | 1 | 100 |
| New Zealand | 130 | 10 | 60 | 60 | – | 62 |
| India | 157 | 28 | 65 | 64 | – | 80 |
| Pakistan | 90 | 15 | 24 | 51 | – | 51 |

# RESULTS SUMMARIES BY GROUNDS OF EACH SERIES

*ENGLAND v AUSTRALIA — IN ENGLAND*

| | | Won by | | | Oval | | | Manchester | | | Lord's | | | Nottingham | | | Leeds | | | Birmingham | | | Sheffield | | |
|---|---|---|---|---|---|---|---|---|---|---|---|---|---|---|---|---|---|---|---|---|---|---|---|---|---|
| | Tests | E. | A. | Drawn | E. | A. | Drawn | E. | A. | Drawn | E. | A. | Drawn | E. | A. | Drawn | E. | A. | Drawn | E. | A. | Drawn | E. | A. | Drawn |
| 1880 | 1 | 1 | – | – | 1 | – | – | – | – | – | – | – | – | – | – | – | – | – | – | – | – | – | – | – | – |
| 1882 | 1 | – | 1 | – | – | 1 | – | – | – | – | – | – | – | – | – | – | – | – | – | – | – | – | – | – | – |
| 1884 | 3 | 1 | – | 2 | – | – | 1 | – | – | 1 | 1 | – | – | – | – | – | – | – | – | – | – | – | – | – | – |
| 1886 | 3 | 3 | – | – | 1 | – | – | 1 | – | – | 1 | – | – | – | – | – | – | – | – | – | – | – | – | – | – |
| 1888 | 3 | 2 | 1 | – | 1 | – | – | 1 | – | – | – | 1 | – | – | – | – | – | – | – | – | – | – | – | – | – |
| 1890 | 2 | 2 | – | – | 1 | – | – | – | – | – | 1 | – | – | – | – | – | – | – | – | – | – | – | – | – | – |
| 1893 | 3 | 1 | – | 2 | 1 | – | – | – | – | 1 | – | – | 1 | – | – | – | – | – | – | – | – | – | – | – | – |
| 1896 | 3 | 2 | 1 | – | 1 | – | – | – | 1 | – | 1 | – | – | – | – | – | – | – | – | – | – | – | – | – | – |
| 1899 | 5 | – | 1 | 4 | – | – | 1 | – | – | 1 | – | 1 | – | – | – | 1 | – | – | 1 | – | – | – | – | – | – |
| 1902 | 5 | 1 | 2 | 2 | 1 | – | – | – | 1 | – | – | – | 1 | – | – | – | – | – | – | – | – | 1 | – | 1 | – |
| 1905 | 5 | 2 | – | 3 | – | – | 1 | 1 | – | – | – | – | 1 | 1 | – | – | – | – | 1 | – | – | – | – | – | – |
| 1909 | 5 | 1 | 2 | 2 | – | – | 1 | – | – | 1 | – | 1 | – | – | – | – | – | 1 | – | 1 | – | – | – | – | – |
| 1912 | 3 | 1 | – | 2 | 1 | – | – | – | – | 1 | – | – | 1 | – | – | – | – | – | – | – | – | – | – | – | – |
| 1921 | 5 | – | 3 | 2 | – | – | 1 | – | – | 1 | – | 1 | – | – | 1 | – | – | 1 | – | – | – | – | – | – | – |
| 1926 | 5 | 1 | – | 4 | 1 | – | – | – | – | 1 | – | – | 1 | – | – | 1 | – | – | 1 | – | – | – | – | – | – |
| 1930 | 5 | 1 | 2 | 2 | – | 1 | – | – | – | 1 | – | 1 | – | 1 | – | – | – | – | 1 | – | – | – | – | – | – |
| 1934 | 5 | 1 | 2 | 2 | – | 1 | – | – | – | 1 | 1 | – | – | – | 1 | – | – | – | 1 | – | – | – | – | – | – |
| 1938 | 4 | 1 | 1 | 2 | 1 | – | – | – | – | – | – | – | 1 | – | – | 1 | – | 1 | – | – | – | – | – | – | – |
| 1948 | 5 | – | 4 | 1 | – | 1 | – | – | – | 1 | – | 1 | – | – | 1 | – | – | 1 | – | – | – | – | – | – | – |
| 1953 | 5 | 1 | – | 4 | 1 | – | – | – | – | 1 | – | – | 1 | – | – | 1 | – | – | 1 | – | – | – | – | – | – |
| 1956 | 5 | 2 | 1 | 2 | – | – | 1 | 1 | – | – | – | 1 | – | – | – | 1 | 1 | – | – | – | – | – | – | – | – |
| 1961 | 5 | 1 | 2 | 2 | – | – | 1 | – | 1 | – | – | 1 | – | – | – | – | 1 | – | – | – | – | 1 | – | – | – |
| 1964 | 5 | – | 1 | 4 | – | – | 1 | – | – | 1 | – | – | 1 | – | – | 1 | – | 1 | – | – | – | – | – | – | – |
| 1968 | 5 | 1 | 1 | 3 | 1 | – | – | – | 1 | – | – | – | 1 | – | – | – | – | – | 1 | – | – | 1 | – | – | – |
| 1972 | 5 | 2 | 2 | 1 | – | 1 | – | 1 | – | – | – | 1 | – | – | – | 1 | 1 | – | – | – | – | – | – | – | – |
| 1975 | 4 | – | 1 | 3 | – | – | 1 | – | – | – | – | – | 1 | – | – | – | – | – | 1 | – | 1 | – | – | – | – |
| 1977 | 5 | 3 | – | 2 | – | – | 1 | 1 | – | – | – | – | 1 | 1 | – | – | 1 | – | – | – | – | – | – | – | – |
| | 110 | 31 | 28 | 51 | 12 | 5 | 10 | 6 | 4 | 12 | 5 | 9 | 11 | 3 | 3 | 7 | 4 | 5 | 8 | 1 | 1 | 3 | – | 1 | – |

# RESULTS SUMMARIES BY GROUNDS OF EACH SERIES – continued

### ENGLAND v AUSTRALIA — IN AUSTRALIA

| | | Won by | | | Melbourne | | | Sydney | | | Adelaide | | | Brisbane | | | Perth | | |
|---|---|---|---|---|---|---|---|---|---|---|---|---|---|---|---|---|---|---|---|
| | Tests | E. | A. | Drawn | E. | A. | Drawn | E. | A. | Drawn | E. | A. | Drawn | E. | A. | Drawn | E. | A. | Drawn |
| 1876-77 | 2 | 1 | 1 | – | 1 | 1 | – | – | – | – | – | – | – | – | – | – | – | – | – |
| 1878-79 | 1 | – | 1 | – | – | 1 | – | – | – | – | – | – | – | – | – | – | – | – | – |
| 1881-82 | 4 | – | 2 | 2 | – | – | 2 | – | 2 | – | – | – | – | – | – | – | – | – | – |
| 1882-83 | 4 | 2 | 2 | – | 1 | 1 | – | 1 | 1 | – | – | – | – | – | – | – | – | – | – |
| 1884-85 | 5 | 3 | 2 | – | 2 | – | – | – | 2 | – | 1 | – | – | – | – | – | – | – | – |
| 1886-87 | 2 | 2 | – | – | – | – | – | 2 | – | – | – | – | – | – | – | – | – | – | – |
| 1887-88 | 1 | 1 | – | – | – | – | – | 1 | – | – | – | – | – | – | – | – | – | – | – |
| 1891-92 | 3 | 1 | 2 | – | – | 1 | – | – | 1 | – | 1 | – | – | – | – | – | – | – | – |
| 1894-95 | 5 | 3 | 2 | – | 2 | – | – | 1 | 1 | – | – | 1 | – | – | – | – | – | – | – |
| 1897-98 | 5 | 1 | 4 | – | – | 2 | – | 1 | 1 | – | – | 1 | – | – | – | – | – | – | – |
| 1901-02 | 5 | 1 | 4 | – | – | 2 | – | 1 | 1 | – | – | 1 | – | – | – | – | – | – | – |
| 1903-04 | 5 | 3 | 2 | – | 1 | 1 | – | 2 | – | – | – | 1 | – | – | – | – | – | – | – |
| 1907-08 | 5 | 1 | 4 | – | 1 | 1 | – | – | 2 | – | – | 1 | – | – | – | – | – | – | – |
| 1911-12 | 5 | 4 | 1 | – | 2 | – | – | 1 | 1 | – | 1 | – | – | – | – | – | – | – | – |
| 1920-21 | 5 | – | 5 | – | – | 2 | – | – | 2 | – | – | 1 | – | – | – | – | – | – | – |
| 1924-25 | 5 | 1 | 4 | – | 1 | 1 | – | – | 2 | – | – | 1 | – | – | – | – | – | – | – |
| 1928-29 | 5 | 4 | 1 | – | 1 | 1 | – | 1 | – | – | 1 | – | – | 1 | – | – | – | – | – |
| 1932-33 | 5 | 4 | 1 | – | – | 1 | – | 2 | – | – | 1 | – | – | 1 | – | – | – | – | – |
| 1936-37 | 5 | 2 | 3 | – | – | 2 | – | 1 | – | – | – | 1 | – | 1 | – | – | – | – | – |
| 1946-47 | 5 | – | 3 | 2 | – | – | 1 | – | 2 | – | – | – | 1 | – | 1 | – | – | – | – |
| 1950-51 | 5 | 1 | 4 | – | 1 | 1 | – | – | 1 | – | – | 1 | – | – | 1 | – | – | – | – |
| 1954-55 | 5 | 3 | 1 | 1 | 1 | – | – | 1 | – | 1 | 1 | – | – | – | 1 | – | – | – | – |
| 1958-59 | 5 | – | 4 | 1 | – | 2 | – | – | – | 1 | – | 1 | – | – | 1 | – | – | – | – |
| 1962-63 | 5 | 1 | 1 | 3 | 1 | – | – | – | 1 | 1 | – | – | 1 | – | – | 1 | – | – | – |
| 1965-66 | 5 | 1 | 1 | 3 | – | – | 2 | 1 | – | – | – | 1 | – | – | – | 1 | – | – | – |
| 1970-71 | 6 | 2 | – | 4 | – | – | 1 | 2 | – | – | – | – | 1 | – | – | 1 | – | – | 1 |
| 1974-75 | 6 | 1 | 4 | 1 | 1 | – | 1 | – | 1 | – | – | 1 | – | – | 1 | – | – | 1 | – |
| 1976-77 | 1 | 1 | – | – | – | 1 | – | – | – | – | – | – | – | – | – | – | – | – | – |
| **Totals** | 120 | 43 | 60 | 17 | 16 | 21 | 7 | 18 | 21 | 3 | 6 | 12 | 3 | 3 | 5 | 3 | – | 1 | 1 |
| | 230 | 74 | 88 | 68 | | | | | | | | | | | | | | | |

*The matches abandoned without a ball being bowled at Manchester in 1890 and 1938 and at Melbourne in 1970-71 are excluded from these tables.*

# RESULTS SUMMARIES BY GROUNDS OF EACH SERIES – continued

## ENGLAND v SOUTH AFRICA — IN ENGLAND

| | | Won by | | | Lord's | | | Leeds | | | Oval | | | Birmingham | | | Manchester | | | Nottingham | | |
|---|---|---|---|---|---|---|---|---|---|---|---|---|---|---|---|---|---|---|---|---|---|---|
| | Tests | E. | S.A. | Drawn | E. | S.A. | Drawn | E. | S.A. | Drawn | E. | S.A. | Drawn | E. | S.A. | Drawn | E. | S.A. | Drawn | E. | S.A. | Drawn |
| 1907 | 3 | 1 | – | 2 | – | – | 1 | 1 | – | – | – | – | 1 | – | – | – | – | – | – | – | – | – |
| 1912 | 3 | 3 | – | – | 1 | – | – | 1 | – | – | 1 | – | – | – | – | – | – | – | – | – | – | – |
| 1924 | 5 | 3 | – | 2 | 1 | – | – | 1 | – | – | – | – | 1 | 1 | – | – | – | – | 1 | – | – | – |
| 1929 | 5 | 2 | – | 3 | – | – | 1 | 1 | – | – | – | – | 1 | – | – | 1 | 1 | – | – | – | – | – |
| 1935 | 5 | – | 1 | 4 | – | 1 | – | – | – | 1 | – | – | 1 | – | – | – | – | – | 1 | – | – | 1 |
| 1947 | 5 | 3 | – | 2 | 1 | – | – | 1 | – | – | – | – | 1 | – | – | – | 1 | – | – | – | – | 1 |
| 1951 | 5 | 3 | 1 | 1 | 1 | – | – | – | – | 1 | 1 | – | – | – | – | – | 1 | – | – | – | 1 | – |
| 1955 | 5 | 3 | 2 | – | 1 | – | – | – | 1 | – | 1 | – | – | – | – | – | – | 1 | – | 1 | – | – |
| 1960 | 5 | 3 | – | 2 | 1 | – | – | – | – | – | – | – | 1 | 1 | – | – | – | – | 1 | 1 | – | – |
| 1965 | 3 | – | 1 | 2 | – | – | 1 | – | – | – | – | – | 1 | – | – | – | – | – | – | – | 1 | – |
| | 44 | 21 | 5 | 18 | 6 | 1 | 3 | 5 | 1 | 2 | 3 | – | 7 | 2 | – | 1 | 3 | 1 | 3 | 2 | 2 | 2 |

## ENGLAND v SOUTH AFRICA — IN SOUTH AFRICA

| | | Won by | | | Port Elizabeth | | | Capetown | | | Johannesburg | | | Durban | | |
|---|---|---|---|---|---|---|---|---|---|---|---|---|---|---|---|---|
| | Tests | E. | S.A. | Drawn | E. | S.A. | Drawn | E. | S.A. | Drawn | E. | S.A. | Drawn | E. | S.A. | Drawn |
| 1888-89 | 2 | 2 | – | – | 1 | – | – | 1 | – | – | – | – | – | – | – | – |
| 1891-92 | 1 | 1 | – | – | – | – | – | 1 | – | – | – | – | – | – | – | – |
| 1895-96 | 3 | 3 | – | – | 1 | – | – | 1 | – | – | 1 | – | – | – | – | – |
| 1898-99 | 2 | 2 | – | – | – | – | – | 1 | – | – | 1 | – | – | – | – | – |
| 1905-06 | 5 | 1 | 4 | – | – | – | – | 1 | 1 | – | – | 3 | – | – | – | – |
| 1909-10 | 5 | 2 | 3 | – | – | – | – | 1 | 1 | – | 1 | 1 | – | – | 1 | – |
| 1913-14 | 5 | 4 | – | 1 | 1 | – | – | – | – | – | 2 | – | – | 1 | – | 1 |
| 1922-23 | 5 | 2 | 1 | 2 | – | – | – | 1 | – | – | – | 1 | 1 | 1 | – | 1 |
| 1927-28 | 5 | 2 | 2 | 1 | – | – | – | 1 | – | – | 1 | – | 1 | – | 2 | – |
| 1930-31 | 5 | – | 1 | 4 | – | – | – | – | – | 1 | – | 1 | 1 | – | – | 2 |
| 1938-39 | 5 | 1 | – | 4 | – | – | – | – | – | 1 | – | – | 2 | 1 | – | 1 |
| 1948-49 | 5 | 2 | – | 3 | 1 | – | – | – | – | 1 | – | – | 2 | 1 | – | – |
| 1956-57 | 5 | 2 | 2 | 1 | – | 1 | – | 1 | – | – | 1 | 1 | – | – | – | 1 |
| 1964-65 | 5 | 1 | – | 4 | – | – | 1 | – | – | 1 | – | – | 2 | 1 | – | – |
| | 58 | 25 | 13 | 20 | 4 | 1 | 1 | 9 | 2 | 4 | 7 | 7 | 9 | 5 | 3 | 6 |
| Totals | 102 | 46 | 18 | 38 | | | | | | | | | | | | |

# RESULTS SUMMARIES BY GROUNDS OF EACH SERIES – *continued*

## ENGLAND *v* WEST INDIES — IN ENGLAND

| | | Won by | | | Lord's | | | Manchester | | | Oval | | | Nottingham | | | Birmingham | | | Leeds | | |
|---|---|---|---|---|---|---|---|---|---|---|---|---|---|---|---|---|---|---|---|---|---|---|
| | Tests | E. | W.I. | Drawn | E. | W.I. | Drawn | E. | W.I. | Drawn | E. | W.I. | Drawn | E. | W.I. | Drawn | E. | W.I. | Drawn | E. | W.I. | Drawn |
| 1928 | 3 | 3 | – | – | 1 | – | – | 1 | – | – | 1 | – | – | – | – | – | – | – | – | – | – | – |
| 1933 | 3 | 2 | – | 1 | 1 | – | – | – | – | 1 | 1 | – | – | – | – | – | – | – | – | – | – | – |
| 1939 | 3 | 1 | – | 2 | 1 | – | – | – | – | 1 | – | – | 1 | – | – | – | – | – | – | – | – | – |
| 1950 | 4 | 1 | 3 | – | – | 1 | – | 1 | – | – | – | 1 | – | – | 1 | – | – | – | – | – | – | – |
| 1957 | 5 | 3 | – | 2 | 1 | – | – | – | – | – | 1 | – | – | – | – | 1 | – | – | 1 | 1 | – | – |
| 1963 | 5 | 1 | 3 | 1 | – | – | 1 | – | 1 | – | – | 1 | – | – | – | – | 1 | – | – | – | 1 | – |
| 1966 | 5 | 1 | 3 | 1 | – | – | 1 | – | 1 | – | 1 | – | – | – | 1 | – | – | – | – | – | 1 | – |
| 1969 | 3 | 2 | – | 1 | – | – | 1 | 1 | – | – | – | – | – | – | – | – | – | – | – | 1 | – | – |
| 1973 | 3 | – | 2 | 1 | – | 1 | – | – | – | – | – | 1 | – | – | – | – | – | – | 1 | – | – | – |
| 1976 | 5 | – | 3 | 2 | – | – | 1 | – | 1 | – | – | 1 | – | – | – | 1 | – | – | – | – | 1 | – |
| | 39 | 14 | 14 | 11 | 4 | 2 | 4 | 3 | 3 | 2 | 4 | 4 | 1 | – | 2 | 2 | 1 | – | 2 | 2 | 3 | – |

## ENGLAND *v* WEST INDIES — IN WEST INDIES

| | | Won by | | | Bridgetown | | | Port-of-Spain | | | Georgetown | | | Kingston | | |
|---|---|---|---|---|---|---|---|---|---|---|---|---|---|---|---|---|---|
| | Tests | E. | W.I. | Drawn | E. | W.I. | Drawn | E. | W.I. | Drawn | E. | W.I. | Drawn | E. | W.I. | Drawn |
| 1929-30 | 4 | 1 | 1 | 2 | – | – | 1 | 1 | – | – | – | 1 | – | – | – | 1 |
| 1934-35 | 4 | 1 | 2 | 1 | 1 | – | – | – | 1 | – | – | – | 1 | – | 1 | – |
| 1947-48 | 4 | – | 2 | 2 | – | – | 1 | – | – | 1 | – | 1 | – | – | 1 | – |
| 1953-54 | 5 | 2 | 2 | 1 | – | 1 | – | – | – | 1 | 1 | – | – | 1 | 1 | – |
| 1959-60 | 5 | 1 | – | 4 | – | – | 1 | 1 | – | 1 | – | – | 1 | – | – | 1 |
| 1967-68 | 5 | 1 | – | 4 | – | – | 1 | 1 | – | 1 | – | – | 1 | – | – | 1 |
| 1973-74 | 5 | 1 | 1 | 3 | – | – | 1 | 1 | 1 | – | – | – | 1 | – | – | 1 |
| | 32 | 7 | 8 | 17 | 1 | 1 | 5 | 4 | 2 | 4 | 1 | 2 | 4 | 1 | 3 | 4 |

| Totals | Tests | E. | W.I. | Drawn |
|---|---|---|---|---|
| | 71 | 21 | 22 | 28 |

# RESULTS SUMMARIES BY GROUNDS OF EACH SERIES – continued

## ENGLAND v NEW ZEALAND — IN ENGLAND

| | | Won by | | | Lord's | | | Oval | | | Manchester | | | Leeds | | | Birmingham | | | Nottingham | | |
|---|---|---|---|---|---|---|---|---|---|---|---|---|---|---|---|---|---|---|---|---|---|---|
| | Tests | E. | N.Z. | Drawn | E. | N.Z. | Drawn | E. | N.Z. | Drawn | E. | N.Z. | Drawn | E. | N.Z. | Drawn | E. | N.Z. | Drawn | E. | N.Z. | Drawn |
| 1931 | 3 | 1 | – | 2 | – | – | 1 | 1 | – | – | – | – | 1 | – | – | – | – | – | – | – | – | – |
| 1937 | 3 | 1 | – | 2 | – | – | 1 | – | – | 1 | 1 | – | – | – | – | – | – | – | – | – | – | – |
| 1949 | 4 | – | – | 4 | – | – | 1 | – | – | 1 | – | – | 1 | – | – | 1 | – | – | – | – | – | – |
| 1958 | 5 | 4 | – | 1 | 1 | – | – | – | – | 1 | 1 | – | – | 1 | – | – | 1 | – | – | – | – | – |
| 1965 | 3 | 3 | – | – | 1 | – | – | – | – | – | – | – | – | 1 | – | – | 1 | – | – | – | – | – |
| 1969 | 3 | 2 | – | 1 | 1 | – | – | 1 | – | – | – | – | – | – | – | – | – | – | – | – | – | 1 |
| 1973 | 3 | 2 | – | 1 | – | – | 1 | – | – | – | – | – | – | 1 | – | – | – | – | – | 1 | – | – |
| | 24 | 13 | – | 11 | 3 | – | 4 | 2 | – | 3 | 2 | – | 2 | 3 | – | 1 | 2 | – | – | 1 | – | 1 |

## ENGLAND v NEW ZEALAND — IN NEW ZEALAND

| | | Won by | | | Christchurch | | | Wellington | | | Auckland | | | Dunedin | | |
|---|---|---|---|---|---|---|---|---|---|---|---|---|---|---|---|---|
| | Tests | E. | N.Z. | Drawn | E. | N.Z. | Drawn | E. | N.Z. | Drawn | E. | N.Z. | Drawn | E. | N.Z. | Drawn |
| 1929-30 | 4 | 1 | – | 3 | 1 | – | – | – | – | 1 | – | – | 2 | – | – | – |
| 1932-33 | 2 | – | – | 2 | – | – | 1 | – | – | – | – | – | 1 | – | – | – |
| 1946-47 | 1 | – | – | 1 | – | – | 1 | – | – | – | – | – | – | – | – | – |
| 1950-51 | 2 | 1 | – | 1 | – | – | 1 | 1 | – | – | – | – | – | – | – | – |
| 1954-55 | 2 | 2 | – | – | – | – | – | – | – | – | 1 | – | – | 1 | – | – |
| 1958-59 | 2 | 1 | – | 1 | 1 | – | – | – | – | – | – | – | 1 | – | – | – |
| 1962-63 | 3 | 3 | – | – | 1 | – | – | 1 | – | – | 1 | – | – | – | – | – |
| 1965-66 | 3 | – | – | 3 | – | – | 1 | – | – | – | – | – | 1 | – | – | 1 |
| 1970-71 | 2 | 1 | – | 1 | 1 | – | – | – | – | – | – | – | 1 | – | – | – |
| 1974-75 | 2 | 1 | – | 1 | – | – | 1 | – | – | – | 1 | – | – | – | – | – |
| 1977-78 | 3 | 1 | 1 | 1 | 1 | – | – | – | 1 | – | – | – | 1 | – | – | – |
| | 26 | 11 | 1 | 14 | 5 | – | 5 | 2 | 1 | 1 | 3 | – | 7 | 1 | – | 1 |
| Totals | 50 | 24 | 1 | 25 | | | | | | | | | | | | |

# RESULTS SUMMARIES BY GROUNDS OF EACH SERIES – continued

## ENGLAND v INDIA — IN ENGLAND

| | | Won by | | | Lord's | | | Manchester | | | Oval | | | Leeds | | | Nottingham | | | Birmingham | | |
|---|---|---|---|---|---|---|---|---|---|---|---|---|---|---|---|---|---|---|---|---|---|---|
| | Tests | E. | I. | Drawn | E. | I. | Drawn | E. | I. | Drawn | E. | I. | Drawn | E. | I. | Drawn | E. | I. | Drawn | E. | I. | Drawn |
| 1932 | 1 | 1 | — | — | 1 | — | — | — | — | — | — | — | — | — | — | — | — | — | — | — | — | — |
| 1936 | 3 | 2 | — | 1 | 1 | — | — | — | — | 1 | 1 | — | — | — | — | — | — | — | — | — | — | — |
| 1946 | 3 | 1 | — | 2 | 1 | — | — | — | — | 1 | — | — | 1 | — | — | — | — | — | — | — | — | — |
| 1952 | 4 | 3 | — | 1 | 1 | — | — | 1 | — | — | — | — | 1 | 1 | — | — | — | — | — | — | — | — |
| 1959 | 5 | 5 | — | — | 1 | — | — | 1 | — | — | 1 | — | — | 1 | — | — | 1 | — | — | — | — | — |
| 1967 | 3 | 3 | — | — | 1 | — | — | — | — | — | — | — | — | 1 | — | — | — | — | — | 1 | — | — |
| 1971 | 3 | — | 1 | 2 | — | — | 1 | — | — | 1 | — | 1 | — | — | — | — | — | — | — | — | — | — |
| 1974 | 3 | 3 | — | — | 1 | — | — | 1 | — | — | — | — | — | — | — | — | — | — | — | 1 | — | — |
| | 25 | 18 | 1 | 6 | 7 | — | 1 | 3 | — | 3 | 2 | 1 | 2 | 3 | — | — | 1 | — | — | 2 | — | — |

## ENGLAND v INDIA — IN INDIA

| | | Won by | | | Bombay | | | Calcutta | | | Madras | | | Delhi | | | Kanpur | | | Bangalore | | |
|---|---|---|---|---|---|---|---|---|---|---|---|---|---|---|---|---|---|---|---|---|---|---|
| | Tests | E. | I. | Drawn | E. | I. | Drawn | E. | I. | Drawn | E. | I. | Drawn | E. | I. | Drawn | E. | I. | Drawn | E. | I. | Drawn |
| 1933-34 | 3 | 2 | — | 1 | 1 | — | — | — | — | 1 | 1 | — | — | — | — | — | — | — | — | — | — | — |
| 1951-52 | 5 | 1 | 1 | 3 | — | — | 1 | — | — | 1 | — | 1 | — | — | — | 1 | 1 | — | — | — | — | — |
| 1961-62 | 5 | — | 2 | 3 | — | — | 1 | — | 1 | — | — | 1 | — | — | — | 1 | — | — | 1 | — | — | — |
| 1963-64 | 5 | — | — | 5 | — | — | 1 | — | — | 1 | — | — | 1 | — | — | 1 | — | — | 1 | — | — | — |
| 1972-73 | 5 | 1 | 2 | 2 | — | — | 1 | — | 1 | — | — | 1 | — | 1 | — | — | — | — | 1 | — | — | — |
| 1976-77 | 5 | 3 | 1 | 1 | — | — | 1 | 1 | — | — | 1 | — | — | 1 | — | — | — | — | — | — | 1 | — |
| | 28 | 7 | 6 | 15 | 1 | — | 5 | 1 | 2 | 3 | 2 | 3 | 1 | 2 | — | 3 | 1 | — | 3 | — | 1 | — |
| Totals | 53 | 25 | 7 | 21 | | | | | | | | | | | | | | | | | | |

# RESULTS SUMMARIES BY GROUNDS OF EACH SERIES – *continued*

## ENGLAND v PAKISTAN — IN ENGLAND

| | Won by | | | | Lord's | | | Nottingham | | | Manchester | | | Oval | | | Birmingham | | | Leeds | | |
|---|---|---|---|---|---|---|---|---|---|---|---|---|---|---|---|---|---|---|---|---|---|---|
| | Tests | E. | P. | Drawn | E. | P. | Drawn | E. | P. | Drawn | E. | P. | Drawn | E. | P. | Drawn | E. | P. | Drawn | E. | P. | Drawn |
| 1954 | 4 | 1 | 1 | 2 | – | – | 1 | 1 | – | – | – | – | 1 | – | 1 | – | – | – | – | – | – | – |
| 1962 | 5 | 4 | – | 1 | 1 | – | – | – | – | 1 | – | – | – | 1 | – | – | 1 | – | – | 1 | – | – |
| 1967 | 3 | 2 | – | 1 | – | – | 1 | 1 | – | – | – | – | – | 1 | – | – | – | – | – | – | – | – |
| 1971 | 3 | 1 | – | 2 | – | – | 1 | – | – | – | – | – | – | – | – | – | – | – | 1 | 1 | – | – |
| 1974 | 3 | – | – | 3 | – | – | 1 | – | – | – | – | – | – | – | – | 1 | – | – | – | – | – | 1 |
| | 18 | 8 | 1 | 9 | 1 | – | 4 | 2 | – | 1 | – | – | 1 | 2 | 1 | 1 | 1 | – | 1 | 2 | – | 1 |

## ENGLAND v PAKISTAN — IN PAKISTAN

| | Won by | | | | Lahore | | | Dacca | | | Karachi | | | Hyderabad | | |
|---|---|---|---|---|---|---|---|---|---|---|---|---|---|---|---|---|
| | Tests | E. | P. | Drawn | E. | P. | Drawn | E. | P. | Drawn | E. | P. | Drawn | E. | P. | Drawn |
| 1961-62 | 3 | 1 | – | 2 | 1 | – | – | – | – | 1 | – | – | 1 | – | – | – |
| 1968-69 | 3 | – | – | 3 | – | – | 1 | – | – | 1 | – | – | 1 | – | – | – |
| 1972-73 | 3 | – | – | 3 | – | – | 1 | – | – | – | – | – | 1 | – | – | 1 |
| 1977-78 | 3 | – | – | 3 | – | – | 1 | – | – | – | – | – | 1 | – | – | 1 |
| | 12 | 1 | – | 11 | 1 | – | 3 | – | – | 2 | – | – | 4 | – | – | 2 |
| **Totals** | 30 | 9 | 1 | 20 | | | | | | | | | | | | |

## AUSTRALIA v SOUTH AFRICA — IN AUSTRALIA

| | Won by | | | | Sydney | | | Melbourne | | | Adelaide | | | Brisbane | | |
|---|---|---|---|---|---|---|---|---|---|---|---|---|---|---|---|---|
| | Tests | A. | S.A. | Drawn | A. | S.A. | Drawn | A. | S.A. | Drawn | A. | S.A. | Drawn | A. | S.A. | Drawn |
| 1910-11 | 5 | 4 | 1 | – | 2 | – | – | 2 | – | – | – | 1 | – | – | – | – |
| 1931-32 | 5 | 5 | – | – | 1 | – | – | 2 | – | – | 1 | – | – | 1 | – | – |
| 1952-53 | 5 | 2 | 2 | 1 | 1 | – | – | – | 2 | – | – | – | 1 | 1 | – | – |
| 1963-64 | 5 | 1 | 1 | 3 | – | – | 2 | 1 | – | – | – | 1 | – | – | – | 1 |
| | 20 | 12 | 4 | 4 | 4 | – | 2 | 5 | 2 | – | 1 | 2 | 1 | 2 | – | 1 |

# RESULTS SUMMARIES BY GROUNDS OF EACH SERIES – continued

## AUSTRALIA v SOUTH AFRICA — IN SOUTH AFRICA

| | Won by | | | | Johannesburg | | | Cape Town | | | Durban | | | Port Elizabeth | | |
|---|---|---|---|---|---|---|---|---|---|---|---|---|---|---|---|---|
| | Tests | A. | S.A. | Drawn | A. | S.A. | Drawn | A. | S.A. | Drawn | A. | S.A. | Drawn | A. | S.A. | Drawn |
| 1902-03 | 3 | 2 | – | 1 | 1 | – | 1 | 1 | – | – | – | – | – | – | – | – |
| 1921-22 | 3 | 1 | – | 2 | 1 | – | – | – | – | 1 | – | – | 1 | – | – | – |
| 1935-36 | 5 | 4 | – | 1 | 2 | – | – | 1 | – | – | 1 | – | 1 | – | – | – |
| 1949-50 | 5 | 4 | – | 1 | 1 | – | 1 | 1 | – | – | 1 | – | – | 1 | – | – |
| 1957-58 | 5 | 3 | – | 2 | 1 | – | 1 | 1 | – | – | – | – | 1 | 1 | – | – |
| 1966-67 | 5 | 1 | 3 | 1 | – | 1 | 1 | 1 | – | – | – | 1 | – | – | 1 | – |
| 1969-70 | 4 | – | 4 | – | – | 1 | – | – | 1 | – | – | 1 | – | – | 1 | – |
| | 30 | 15 | 7 | 8 | 6 | 2 | 4 | 5 | 1 | 1 | 2 | 2 | 3 | 2 | 2 | – |

## AUSTRALIA v SOUTH AFRICA — IN ENGLAND

| | Won by | | | | Manchester | | | Lord's | | | Nottingham | | |
|---|---|---|---|---|---|---|---|---|---|---|---|---|---|
| | Tests | A. | S.A. | Drawn | A. | S.A. | Drawn | A. | S.A. | Drawn | A. | S.A. | Drawn |
| 1912 | 3 | 2 | – | 1 | 1 | – | – | 1 | – | – | – | – | 1 |

| | Tests | A. | S.A. | Drawn |
|---|---|---|---|---|
| Totals | 53 | 29 | 11 | 13 |

## AUSTRALIA v WEST INDIES — IN AUSTRALIA

| | Won by | | | | | Adelaide | | | Sydney | | | Brisbane | | | | Melbourne | | | Perth | | |
|---|---|---|---|---|---|---|---|---|---|---|---|---|---|---|---|---|---|---|---|---|---|
| | Tests | A. | W.I. | Drawn | Tied | A. | W.I. | Drawn | A. | W.I. | Drawn | A. | W.I. | Drawn | Tied | A. | W.I. | Drawn | A. | W.I. | Drawn |
| 1930-31 | 5 | 4 | 1 | – | – | 1 | – | – | 1 | 1 | – | 1 | – | – | – | 1 | – | – | – | – | – |
| 1951-52 | 5 | 4 | 1 | – | – | – | 1 | – | 2 | – | – | 1 | – | – | – | 1 | – | – | – | – | – |
| 1960-61 | 5 | 2 | 1 | 1 | 1 | – | – | 1 | – | 1 | – | – | – | – | 1 | 2 | – | – | – | – | – |
| 1968-69 | 5 | 3 | 1 | 1 | – | – | – | 1 | 2 | – | – | – | 1 | – | – | 1 | – | – | – | – | – |
| 1975-76 | 6 | 5 | 1 | – | – | 1 | – | – | 1 | – | – | 1 | – | – | – | 2 | – | – | – | 1 | – |
| | 26 | 18 | 5 | 2 | 1 | 2 | 1 | 2 | 6 | 2 | – | 3 | 1 | – | 1 | 7 | – | – | – | 1 | – |

# RESULTS SUMMARIES BY GROUNDS OF EACH SERIES – continued

## AUSTRALIA v WEST INDIES — IN WEST INDIES

| | | Won by | | | | Kingston | | | Port-of-Spain | | | Georgetown | | | Bridgetown | | |
|---|---|---|---|---|---|---|---|---|---|---|---|---|---|---|---|---|---|
| | Tests | A. | W.I. | Drawn | Tied | A. | W.I. | Drawn | A. | W.I. | Drawn | A. | W.I. | Drawn | A. | W.I. | Drawn |
| 1954-55 | 5 | 3 | – | 2 | – | 2 | – | – | – | – | 1 | 1 | – | – | – | – | 1 |
| 1964-65 | 5 | 1 | 2 | 2 | – | – | 1 | – | 1 | – | 1 | – | 1 | – | – | – | 1 |
| 1972-73 | 5 | 2 | – | 3 | – | – | – | 1 | 1 | – | 1 | 1 | – | – | – | – | 1 |
| 1977-78 | 5 | 1 | 3 | 1 | – | – | – | 1 | – | 2 | – | 1 | – | – | – | 1 | – |
| Totals | 20 | 7 | 5 | 8 | – | 2 | 1 | 2 | 2 | 2 | 3 | 3 | 1 | – | – | 1 | 3 |
| | 46 | 25 | 10 | 10 | 1 | | | | | | | | | | | | |

## AUSTRALIA v NEW ZEALAND — IN AUSTRALIA

| | | Won by | | | Melbourne | | | Sydney | | | Adelaide | | |
|---|---|---|---|---|---|---|---|---|---|---|---|---|---|
| | Tests | A. | N.Z. | Drawn | A. | N.Z. | Drawn | A. | N.Z. | Drawn | A. | N.Z. | Drawn |
| 1973-74 | 3 | 2 | – | 1 | 1 | – | – | – | – | 1 | 1 | – | – |

## AUSTRALIA v NEW ZEALAND — IN NEW ZEALAND

| | | Won by | | | Wellington | | | Christchurch | | | Auckland | | |
|---|---|---|---|---|---|---|---|---|---|---|---|---|---|
| | Tests | A. | N.Z. | Drawn | A. | N.Z. | Drawn | A. | N.Z. | Drawn | A. | N.Z. | Drawn |
| 1945-46 | 1 | 1 | – | – | 1 | – | – | – | – | – | – | – | – |
| 1973-74 | 3 | 1 | 1 | 1 | – | – | 1 | – | 1 | – | 1 | – | – |
| 1976-77 | 2 | 1 | – | 1 | – | – | – | – | – | 1 | 1 | – | – |
| Totals | 6 | 3 | 1 | 2 | 1 | – | 1 | – | 1 | 1 | 2 | – | – |
| | 9 | 5 | 1 | 3 | | | | | | | | | |

# RESULTS SUMMARIES BY GROUNDS OF EACH SERIES – continued

## AUSTRALIA v INDIA – IN AUSTRALIA

| | | Won by | | | Brisbane | | | Sydney | | | Melbourne | | | Adelaide | | | Perth | | |
| --- | --- | --- | --- | --- | --- | --- | --- | --- | --- | --- | --- | --- | --- | --- | --- | --- | --- | --- | --- |
| | Tests | A. | I. | Drawn | A. | I. | Drawn | A. | I. | Drawn | A. | I. | Drawn | A. | I. | Drawn | A. | I. | Drawn |
| 1947-48 | 5 | 4 | – | 1 | 1 | – | – | – | – | 1 | 2 | – | – | 1 | – | – | – | – | – |
| 1967-68 | 4 | 4 | – | – | 1 | – | – | 1 | – | – | 1 | – | – | 1 | – | – | – | – | – |
| 1977-78 | 5 | 3 | 2 | – | 1 | – | – | – | 1 | – | – | 1 | – | 1 | – | – | 1 | – | – |
| | 14 | 11 | 2 | 1 | 3 | – | – | 1 | 1 | 1 | 3 | 1 | – | 3 | – | – | 1 | – | – |

## AUSTRALIA v INDIA – IN INDIA

| | | Won by | | | Madras | | | Bombay | | | Calcutta | | | Delhi | | | Kanpur | | |
| --- | --- | --- | --- | --- | --- | --- | --- | --- | --- | --- | --- | --- | --- | --- | --- | --- | --- | --- | --- |
| | Tests | A. | I. | Drawn | A. | I. | Drawn | A. | I. | Drawn | A. | I. | Drawn | A. | I. | Drawn | A. | I. | Drawn |
| 1956-57 | 3 | 2 | – | 1 | 1 | – | – | – | – | 1 | 1 | – | – | – | – | – | – | – | – |
| 1959-60 | 5 | 2 | 1 | 2 | 1 | – | – | – | – | 1 | – | – | 1 | 1 | – | – | – | 1 | – |
| 1964-65 | 3 | 1 | 1 | 1 | 1 | – | – | – | 1 | – | – | – | 1 | – | – | – | – | – | – |
| 1969-70 | 5 | 3 | 1 | 1 | 1 | – | – | 1 | – | – | 1 | – | – | – | 1 | – | – | – | 1 |
| Totals | 16 | 8 | 3 | 5 | 4 | – | – | 1 | 1 | 2 | 2 | – | 2 | 1 | 1 | – | – | 1 | 1 |
| Totals | 30 | 19 | 5 | 6 | | | | | | | | | | | | | | | |

## AUSTRALIA v PAKISTAN – IN AUSTRALIA

| | | Won by | | | Melbourne | | | Adelaide | | | Sydney | | |
| --- | --- | --- | --- | --- | --- | --- | --- | --- | --- | --- | --- | --- | --- |
| | Tests | A. | P. | Drawn | A. | P. | Drawn | A. | P. | Drawn | A. | P. | Drawn |
| 1964-65 | 1 | – | – | 1 | – | – | 1 | – | – | – | – | – | – |
| 1972-73 | 3 | 3 | – | – | 1 | – | – | 1 | – | – | 1 | – | – |
| 1976-77 | 3 | 1 | 1 | 1 | 1 | – | – | – | – | 1 | – | 1 | – |
| | 7 | 4 | 1 | 2 | 2 | – | 1 | 1 | – | 1 | 1 | 1 | – |

# RESULTS SUMMARIES BY GROUNDS OF EACH SERIES – continued

## AUSTRALIA v PAKISTAN — IN PAKISTAN

| | | Won by | | | Karachi | | | Dacca | | | Lahore | | |
|---|---|---|---|---|---|---|---|---|---|---|---|---|---|
| | Tests | A. | P. | Drawn | A. | P. | Drawn | A. | P. | Drawn | A. | P. | Drawn |
| 1956-57 | 1 | – | 1 | – | – | 1 | – | – | – | – | – | – | – |
| 1959-60 | 3 | 2 | – | 1 | – | – | 1 | 1 | – | – | 1 | – | – |
| 1964-65 | 1 | – | – | 1 | – | – | 1 | – | – | – | – | – | – |
| | 5 | 2 | 1 | 2 | – | 1 | 2 | 1 | – | – | 1 | – | – |
| Totals | 12 | 6 | 2 | 4 | | | | | | | | | |

## SOUTH AFRICA v NEW ZEALAND — IN SOUTH AFRICA

| | | Won by | | | Durban | | | Johannesburg | | | Cape Town | | | Port Elizabeth | | |
|---|---|---|---|---|---|---|---|---|---|---|---|---|---|---|---|---|
| | Tests | S.A. | N.Z. | Drawn | S.A. | N.Z. | Drawn | S.A. | N.Z. | Drawn | S.A. | N.Z. | Drawn | S.A. | N.Z. | Drawn |
| 1953-54 | 5 | 4 | – | 1 | 1 | – | – | 2 | – | – | – | – | 1 | 1 | – | – |
| 1961-62 | 5 | 2 | 2 | 1 | 1 | – | – | 1 | – | 1 | – | 1 | – | – | 1 | – |
| | 10 | 6 | 2 | 2 | 2 | – | – | 3 | – | 1 | – | 1 | 1 | 1 | 1 | – |

## SOUTH AFRICA v NEW ZEALAND — IN NEW ZEALAND

| | | Won by | | | Christchurch | | | Wellington | | | Auckland | | | Dunedin | | |
|---|---|---|---|---|---|---|---|---|---|---|---|---|---|---|---|---|
| | Tests | S.A. | N.Z. | Drawn | S.A. | N.Z. | Drawn | S.A. | N.Z. | Drawn | S.A. | N.Z. | Drawn | S.A. | N.Z. | Drawn |
| 1931-32 | 2 | 2 | – | – | 1 | – | – | 1 | – | – | – | – | – | – | – | – |
| 1952-53 | 2 | 1 | – | 1 | – | – | – | 1 | – | – | – | – | 1 | – | – | – |
| 1963-64 | 3 | – | – | 3 | – | – | 1 | – | – | 1 | – | – | 1 | – | – | 1 |
| | 7 | 3 | – | 4 | 1 | – | 1 | 2 | – | 1 | – | – | 2 | – | – | 1 |
| Totals | 17 | 9 | 2 | 6 | | | | | | | | | | | | |

# RESULTS SUMMARIES BY GROUNDS OF EACH SERIES – *continued*

## WEST INDIES v NEW ZEALAND – IN WEST INDIES

| | Kingston | | | Port-of-Spain | | | Bridgetown | | | Georgetown | | | | Won by | | |
|---|---|---|---|---|---|---|---|---|---|---|---|---|---|---|---|---|
| | W.I. | N.Z. | Drawn | W.I. | N.Z. | Drawn | W.I. | N.Z. | Drawn | W.I. | N.Z. | Drawn | Tests | W.I. | N.Z. | Drawn |
| 1971-72 | - | - | 1 | - | - | 2 | - | - | 1 | - | - | 1 | 5 | - | - | 5 |
| Totals | | | | | | | | | | | | | 14 | 5 | 2 | 7 |

## WEST INDIES v NEW ZEALAND – IN NEW ZEALAND

| | Christchurch | | | Auckland | | | Dunedin | | | Wellington | | | | Won by | | |
|---|---|---|---|---|---|---|---|---|---|---|---|---|---|---|---|---|
| | W.I. | N.Z. | Drawn | W.I. | N.Z. | Drawn | W.I. | N.Z. | Drawn | W.I. | N.Z. | Drawn | Tests | W.I. | N.Z. | Drawn |
| 1951-52 | 1 | - | - | - | - | 1 | - | - | - | - | - | - | 2 | 1 | - | 1 |
| 1955-56 | 1 | - | - | 1 | - | - | - | 1 | - | 1 | - | - | 4 | 3 | 1 | - |
| 1968-69 | - | - | 1 | - | 1 | - | - | - | - | 1 | - | - | 3 | 1 | 1 | 1 |
| | 2 | - | 1 | 1 | 1 | 1 | - | 1 | - | 2 | - | - | 9 | 5 | 2 | 2 |

## WEST INDIES v INDIA – IN WEST INDIES

| | Port-of-Spain | | | Bridgetown | | | Georgetown | | | Kingston | | | | Won by | | |
|---|---|---|---|---|---|---|---|---|---|---|---|---|---|---|---|---|
| | W.I. | I. | Drawn | W.I. | I. | Drawn | W.I. | I. | Drawn | W.I. | I. | Drawn | Tests | W.I. | I. | Drawn |
| 1952-53 | - | - | 2 | 1 | - | - | - | - | 1 | - | - | 1 | 5 | 1 | - | 4 |
| 1961-62 | 2 | - | - | 1 | - | - | - | - | - | 2 | - | - | 5 | 5 | - | - |
| 1970-71 | - | 1 | 2 | - | - | 1 | - | - | - | - | - | 1 | 5 | - | 1 | 4 |
| 1975-76 | - | 1 | - | 1 | - | 1 | - | - | - | 1 | - | - | 4 | 2 | 1 | 1 |
| | 2 | 2 | 4 | 3 | - | 2 | - | - | 1 | 3 | - | 2 | 19 | 8 | 2 | 9 |

# RESULTS SUMMARIES BY GROUNDS OF EACH SERIES – *continued*

## *WEST INDIES v INDIA — IN INDIA*

| | Delhi | | | Bombay | | | Calcutta | | | Madras | | | Kanpur | | | Bangalore | | |
|---|---|---|---|---|---|---|---|---|---|---|---|---|---|---|---|---|---|---|
| | W.I. | I. | Drawn | W.I. | I. | Drawn | W.I. | I. | Drawn | W.I. | I. | Drawn | W.I. | I. | Drawn | W.I. | I. | Drawn |
| 1948-49 | – | – | 1 | – | – | 2 | – | – | 1 | 1 | – | – | – | – | – | – | – | – |
| 1958-59 | – | – | 1 | 1 | – | – | 1 | – | – | – | – | 1 | 1 | – | – | – | – | – |
| 1966-67 | – | – | – | 1 | – | – | 1 | – | – | 1 | – | – | – | – | – | – | – | – |
| 1974-75 | 1 | – | – | 1 | – | – | – | 1 | – | – | 1 | – | – | – | – | 1 | – | – |
| | 1 | – | 2 | 2 | – | 3 | 2 | 1 | 1 | 2 | 1 | 1 | 1 | – | – | 1 | – | – |

| | Tests | Won by W.I. | I. | Drawn |
|---|---|---|---|---|
| 1948-49 | 5 | 1 | – | 4 |
| 1958-59 | 5 | 3 | – | 2 |
| 1966-67 | 3 | 2 | – | 1 |
| 1974-75 | 5 | 3 | 2 | – |
| | 18 | 9 | 2 | 7 |
| Totals | 37 | 17 | 4 | 16 |

## *WEST INDIES v PAKISTAN — IN WEST INDIES*

| | Bridgetown | | | Port-of-Spain | | | Kingston | | | Georgetown | | |
|---|---|---|---|---|---|---|---|---|---|---|---|---|
| | W.I. | P. | Drawn | W.I. | P. | Drawn | W.I. | P. | Drawn | W.I. | P. | Drawn |
| 1957-58 | – | – | 1 | 1 | 1 | – | 1 | – | – | 1 | – | – |
| 1976-77 | – | – | 1 | 1 | 1 | – | 1 | – | – | – | – | 1 |
| | – | – | 2 | 2 | 2 | – | 2 | – | – | 1 | – | 1 |

| | Tests | Won by W.I. | P. | Drawn |
|---|---|---|---|---|
| 1957-58 | 5 | 3 | 1 | 1 |
| 1976-77 | 5 | 2 | 1 | 2 |
| | 10 | 5 | 2 | 3 |

## *WEST INDIES v PAKISTAN — IN PAKISTAN*

| | Karachi | | | Dacca | | | Lahore | | |
|---|---|---|---|---|---|---|---|---|---|
| | W.I. | P. | Drawn | W.I. | P. | Drawn | W.I. | P. | Drawn |
| 1958-59 | – | 1 | – | 1 | 1 | – | – | – | – |
| 1974-75 | – | – | 1 | – | – | – | – | – | 1 |
| | – | 1 | 1 | 1 | 1 | – | – | – | 1 |

| | Tests | Won by W.I. | P. | Drawn |
|---|---|---|---|---|
| 1958-59 | 3 | 1 | 2 | – |
| 1974-75 | 2 | – | – | 2 |
| | 5 | 1 | 2 | 2 |
| Totals | 15 | 6 | 4 | 5 |

# RESULTS SUMMARIES BY GROUNDS OF EACH SERIES – continued

## NEW ZEALAND v INDIA – IN NEW ZEALAND

| | | Won by | | | Dunedin | | | Christchurch | | | Wellington | | | Auckland | | |
|---|---|---|---|---|---|---|---|---|---|---|---|---|---|---|---|---|
| | Tests | N.Z. | I. | Drawn | N.Z. | I. | Drawn | N.Z. | I. | Drawn | N.Z. | I. | Drawn | N.Z. | I. | Drawn |
| 1967-68 | 4 | 1 | 3 | – | – | 1 | – | 1 | – | – | – | 1 | – | – | 1 | – |
| 1975-76 | 3 | 1 | 1 | 1 | – | – | – | – | – | 1 | – | 1 | – | 1 | – | – |
| | 7 | 2 | 4 | 1 | – | 1 | – | 1 | – | 1 | – | 2 | – | 1 | 1 | – |

## NEW ZEALAND v INDIA – IN INDIA

| | | Won by | | | Hyderabad | | | Bombay | | | Delhi | | | Calcutta | | | Madras | | | Nagpur | | | Kanpur | | |
|---|---|---|---|---|---|---|---|---|---|---|---|---|---|---|---|---|---|---|---|---|---|---|---|---|---|---|
| | Tests | N.Z. | I. | Drawn | N.Z. | I. | Drawn | N.Z. | I. | Drawn | N.Z. | I. | Drawn | N.Z. | I. | Drawn | N.Z. | I. | Drawn | N.Z. | I. | Drawn | N.Z. | I. | Drawn |
| 1955-56 | 5 | – | 2 | 3 | – | – | 1 | – | – | 1 | – | 1 | – | – | – | 1 | – | 1 | – | – | – | – | – | – | – |
| 1964-65 | 4 | – | 1 | 3 | – | – | – | – | – | 1 | – | 1 | – | – | – | 1 | – | – | 1 | – | – | – | – | – | – |
| 1969-70 | 3 | 1 | 1 | 1 | – | – | 1 | – | 1 | – | – | – | – | – | – | – | – | – | – | 1 | – | – | – | – | – |
| 1976-77 | 3 | – | 2 | 1 | – | – | – | – | 1 | – | – | – | – | – | – | – | – | 1 | – | – | – | – | – | – | 1 |
| | 15 | 1 | 6 | 8 | – | – | 2 | – | 2 | 2 | – | 2 | – | – | – | 2 | – | 2 | 1 | 1 | – | – | – | – | 1 |
| Totals | 22 | 3 | 10 | 9 | | | | | | | | | | | | | | | | | | | | | |

## NEW ZEALAND v PAKISTAN – IN NEW ZEALAND

| | | Won by | | | Wellington | | | Auckland | | | Christchurch | | | Dunedin | | |
|---|---|---|---|---|---|---|---|---|---|---|---|---|---|---|---|---|---|
| | Tests | N.Z. | P. | Drawn | N.Z. | P. | Drawn | N.Z. | P. | Drawn | N.Z. | P. | Drawn | N.Z. | P. | Drawn |
| 1964-65 | 3 | – | – | 3 | – | – | 1 | – | – | 1 | – | – | 1 | – | – | – |
| 1972-73 | 3 | – | 1 | 2 | – | – | 1 | – | 1 | – | – | – | – | – | – | 1 |
| | 6 | – | 1 | 5 | – | – | 2 | – | 1 | 1 | – | – | 1 | – | – | 1 |

854

# RESULTS SUMMARIES BY GROUNDS OF EACH SERIES – continued

## NEW ZEALAND v PAKISTAN — IN PAKISTAN

| | Karachi | | | Lahore | | | Dacca | | | Rawalpindi | | | Hyderabad | | |
|---|---|---|---|---|---|---|---|---|---|---|---|---|---|---|---|
| | N.Z. | P. | Drawn | N.Z. | P. | Drawn | N.Z. | P. | Drawn | N.Z. | P. | Drawn | N.Z. | P. | Drawn |
| 1955-56 | – | 1 | – | – | 1 | – | – | 1 | – | – | – | – | – | – | – |
| 1964-65 | – | – | 1 | – | – | 1 | – | – | – | – | 1 | – | – | – | – |
| 1969-70 | – | – | 1 | 1 | – | – | – | – | 1 | – | – | – | – | – | – |
| 1976-77 | – | 1 | – | – | – | 1 | – | – | – | – | – | – | – | 1 | – |
| | – | 2 | 2 | 1 | – | 3 | – | 1 | 1 | – | 1 | – | – | 1 | – |

| | | Won by | | |
|---|---|---|---|---|
| | Tests | N.Z. | P. | Drawn |
| 1955-56 | 3 | – | 2 | 1 |
| 1964-65 | 3 | – | 1 | 2 |
| 1969-70 | 3 | 1 | – | 2 |
| 1976-77 | 3 | – | 2 | 1 |
| | 12 | 1 | 5 | 6 |
| Totals | 18 | 1 | 7 | 10 |

## INDIA v PAKISTAN — IN INDIA

| | Delhi | | | Lucknow | | | Bombay | | | Madras | | | Calcutta | | | Kanpur | | |
|---|---|---|---|---|---|---|---|---|---|---|---|---|---|---|---|---|---|---|
| | I. | P. | Drawn | I. | P. | Drawn | I. | P. | Drawn | I. | P. | Drawn | I. | P. | Drawn | I. | P. | Drawn |
| 1952-53 | 1 | – | – | – | 1 | – | 1 | – | – | – | – | 1 | – | – | 1 | – | – | – |
| 1960-61 | – | – | 1 | – | – | – | – | – | 1 | – | – | 1 | – | – | 1 | – | – | 1 |
| | 1 | – | 1 | – | 1 | – | 1 | – | 1 | – | – | 2 | – | – | 2 | – | – | 1 |

| | | Won by | | |
|---|---|---|---|---|
| | Tests | I. | P. | Drawn |
| 1952-53 | 5 | 2 | 1 | 2 |
| 1960-61 | 5 | – | – | 5 |
| | 10 | 2 | 1 | 7 |

## INDIA v PAKISTAN — IN PAKISTAN

| | Dacca | | | Bahawalpur | | | Lahore | | | Peshawar | | | Karachi | | |
|---|---|---|---|---|---|---|---|---|---|---|---|---|---|---|---|
| | I. | P. | Drawn | I. | P. | Drawn | I. | P. | Drawn | I. | P. | Drawn | I. | P. | Drawn |
| 1954-55 | – | – | 1 | – | – | 1 | – | – | 1 | – | – | 1 | – | – | 1 |

| | | Won by | | |
|---|---|---|---|---|
| | Tests | I. | P. | Drawn |
| 1954-55 | 5 | – | – | 5 |
| Totals | 15 | 2 | 1 | 12 |

# THE GROUNDS
## A GUIDE TO THE TEST MATCH GROUNDS

Official Test matches have been played on 48 grounds and at 40 centres – if the two London grounds are counted as separate centres. London is the only city to have two grounds in regular current use for Test cricket but six others have staged Test matches on more than one ground; Johannesburg and Bombay have used three, while Brisbane, Durban, Madras and Lahore have each played Tests on two different grounds.

Where any of these six centres appears in this Records section, the exact ground is denoted by an indicator number (e.g. Bombay[3]). This number refers to the key included in the following tables and which is summarised in the Key to Test Match Grounds on page 10.

| Test Match Centre | No. of Tests | Year of First Test | Grounds |
|---|---|---|---|
| **ENGLAND** (263) | | | |
| Birmingham | 17 | 1902 | Edgbaston |
| Leeds | 40 | 1899 | Headingley |
| Lord's, London | 66 | 1884 | Lord's Cricket Ground |
| Manchester | 49† | 1884 | Old Trafford |
| Nottingham | 30 | 1899 | Trent Bridge |
| Oval, London | 60 | 1880 | Kennington Oval |
| Sheffield | 1 | 1902 | Bramall Lane |
| | | | |
| **AUSTRALIA** (190) | | | |
| Adelaide | 36 | 1884 | Adelaide Oval |
| Brisbane | 22 | 1928 | [1]Exhibition Ground (1928-29 to 1930-31) |
| | | | [2]Woolloongabba (1931-32 to date) |
| Melbourne | 66‡ | 1877 | Melbourne Cricket Ground |
| Perth | 4 | 1970 | Western Australia Cricket Association (W.A.C.A.) Ground |
| Sydney | 62 | 1882 | Sydney Cricket Ground (No. 1) |
| | | | |
| **SOUTH AFRICA** (98) | | | |
| Cape Town | 24 | 1889 | Newlands |
| Durban | 23 | 1910 | [1]Lord's (1909-10 to 1921-22) |
| | | | [2]Kingsmead (1922-23 to date) |
| Johannesburg | 39 | 1896 | [1]Old Wanderers (1895-96 to 1938-39) |
| | | | [2]Ellis Park (1947-48 to 1953-54) |
| | | | [3]New Wanderers (1956-57 to date) |
| Port Elizabeth | 12 | 1889 | St George's Park |
| | | | |
| **WEST INDIES** (86) | | | |
| Bridgetown | 18 | 1930 | Kensington Oval |
| Georgetown | 16 | 1930 | Bourda |
| Kingston | 21 | 1930 | Sabina Park |
| Port-of-Spain | 31 | 1930 | Queen's Park Oval |
| | | | |
| **NEW ZEALAND** (61) | | | |
| Auckland | 21 | 1930 | Eden Park |
| Christchurch | 19 | 1930 | Lancaster Park |
| Dunedin | 6 | 1955 | Carisbrook |
| Wellington | 15 | 1930 | Basin Reserve |
| | | | |
| **INDIA** (87) | | | |
| Bangalore | 2 | 1974 | Karnataka Cricket Association Ground |
| Bombay | 21 | 1933 | [1]Gymkhana (1933-34 only) |
| | | | [2]Brabourne Stadium (1948-49 to 1972-73) |
| | | | [3]Wankhede Stadium (1974-75 to date) |
| Calcutta | 18 | 1934 | Eden Gardens |

| Test Match Centre | No. of Tests | Year of First Test | Grounds |
|---|---|---|---|
| Delhi | 14 | 1948 | Feroz Shah Kotla |
| Hyderabad | 2 | 1955 | Fateh Maidan (Lal Bahadur Stadium) |
| Kanpur | 9 | 1952 | Green Park (Modi Stadium) |
| Lucknow | 1 | 1952 | University Ground |
| Madras | 19 | 1934 | [1]Chepauk (1933-34 to 1952-53, and 1966-67 to date) [2]Corporation (Nehru) Stadium (1955-56 to 1964-65) |
| Nagpur | 1 | 1969 | Vidarbha Cricket Association Ground |
| *PAKISTAN* (39) | | | |
| Bahawalpur | 1 | 1955 | Dring Stadium |
| Dacca | 7 | 1955 | Dacca Stadium |
| Hyderabad | 3 | 1973 | Niaz Stadium |
| Karachi | 14 | 1955 | National Stadium |
| Lahore | 12 | 1955 | [1]Lawrence Gardens (Bagh-i-Jinnah) (1954-55 to 1958-59) [2]Lahore (Gaddafi) Stadium (1959-60 to date) |
| Peshawar | 1 | 1955 | Gymkhana |
| Rawalpindi | 1 | 1965 | Club |

*The 1890 and 1938 Tests at Manchester and the 1970-71 Third Test at Melbourne, all abandoned without a ball being bowled, are excluded from these figures.*

# RECORD TOTALS FOR EACH TEST MATCH CENTRE

| Centre | Highest Total | | | Lowest Total | | |
|---|---|---|---|---|---|---|
| Birmingham | 608-7d | Pakistan v England | 1971 | 30 | S. Africa v England | 1924 |
| Leeds | 584 | Australia v England | 1934 | 67 | N. Zealand v England | 1958 |
| Lord's | 729-6d | Australia v England | 1930 | 42 | India v England | 1974 |
| Manchester | 656-8d | Australia v England | 1964 | 58 | India v England | 1952 |
| Nottingham | 658-8d | England v Australia | 1938 | 88 | S. Africa v England | 1960 |
| Oval | 903-7d | England v Australia | 1938 | 44 | Australia v England | 1896 |
| Sheffield | 289 | Australia v England | 1902 | 145 | England v Australia | 1902 |
| Adelaide | 674 | Australia v India | 1947-48 | 82 | Australia v W. Indies | 1951-52 |
| Brisbane | 645 | Australia v England | 1946-47 | 58 | Australia v England | 1936-37 |
| | | | | 58 | India v Australia | 1947-48 |
| Melbourne | 604 | Australia v England | 1936-37 | 36 | S. Africa v Australia | 1931-32 |
| Perth | 585 | W. Indies v Australia | 1975-76 | 169 | Australia v W. Indies | 1975-76 |
| Sydney | 659-8d | Australia v England | 1946-47 | 42 | Australia v England | 1887-88 |
| Cape Town | 559-9d | England v S. Africa | 1938-39 | 35 | S. Africa v England | 1898-99 |
| Durban | 654-5 | England v S. Africa | 1938-39 | 75 | Australia v S. Africa | 1949-50 |
| Johannesburg | 620 | S. Africa v Australia | 1966-67 | 72 | S. Africa v England | 1956-57 |
| Port Elizabeth | 549-7d | Australia v S. Africa | 1949-50 | 30 | S. Africa v England | 1895-96 |
| Bridgetown | 668 | Australia v W. Indies | 1954-55 | 102 | W. Indies v England | 1934-35 |
| Georgetown | 543-3d | N. Zealand v W. Indies | 1971-72 | 109 | W. Indies v Australia | 1972-73 |
| Kingston | 849 | England v W. Indies | 1929-30 | 97† | India v W. Indies | 1975-76 |
| Port-of-Spain | 681-8d | W. Indies v England | 1953-54 | 90 | Australia v W. Indies | 1977-78 |
| Auckland | 593-6d | England v N. Zealand | 1974-75 | 26 | N. Zealand v England | 1954-55 |
| Christchurch | 560-8d | England v N. Zealand | 1932-33 | 65 | N. Zealand v England | 1970-71 |
| Dunedin | 507-6d | Pakistan v N. Zealand | 1972-73 | 74 | N. Zealand v W. Indies | 1955-56 |
| Wellington | 524-8d | S. Africa v N. Zealand | 1952-53 | 42 | N. Zealand v Australia | 1945-46 |
| Bangalore | 356-6d | W. Indies v India | 1974-75 | 118 | India v W. Indies | 1974-75 |
| Bombay | 629-6d | W. Indies v India | 1948-49 | 88 | India v N. Zealand | 1964-65 |
| Calcutta | 614-5d | W. Indies v India | 1958-59 | 124 | India v W. Indies | 1958-59 |
| Delhi | 644-8d | W. Indies v India | 1958-59 | 107 | Australia v India | 1969-70 |
| Hyderabad | 498-4d | India v N. Zealand | 1955-56 | 89 | India v N. Zealand | 1969-70 |
| Kanpur | 559-8d | England v India | 1963-64 | 105 | Australia v India | 1959-60 |
| Lucknow | 331 | Pakistan v India | 1952-53 | 106 | India v Pakistan | 1952-53 |
| Madras | 582 | W. Indies v India | 1948-49 | 83 | India v England | 1976-77 |
| Nagpur | 319 | N. Zealand v India | 1969-70 | 109 | India v N. Zealand | 1969-70 |
| Bahawalpur | 312-9d | Pakistan v India | 1954-55 | 235 | India v Pakistan | 1954-55 |
| Dacca | 439 | England v Pakistan | 1961-62 | 70 | N. Zealand v Pakistan | 1955-56 |
| Hyderabad | 569-9d | Pakistan v England | 1972-73 | 191 | England v Pakistan | 1977-78 |
| Karachi | 565-9d | Pakistan v N. Zealand | 1976-77 | 80 | Australia v Pakistan | 1956-57 |
| Lahore | 561 | Pakistan v N. Zealand | 1955-56 | 104 | Pakistan v W. Indies | 1958-59 |
| Peshawar | 245 | India v Pakistan | 1954-55 | 182 | Pakistan v India | 1954-55 |
| Rawalpindi | 318 | Pakistan v England | 1964-65 | 79 | N. Zealand v Pakistan | 1964-65 |

† Five men were absent hurt. The second lowest total at Kingston is 103 by England in 1934-35.

# HIGHEST INDIVIDUAL SCORE FOR EACH TEST MATCH CENTRE

| | | | | |
|---|---|---|---|---|
| Birmingham | 285* | P.B.H. May | England v West Indies | 1957 |
| Leeds | 334 | D.G. Bradman | Australia v England | 1930 |
| Lord's | 254 | D.G. Bradman | Australia v England | 1930 |
| Manchester | 311 | R.B. Simpson | Australia v England | 1964 |
| Nottingham | 278 | D.C.S. Compton | England v Pakistan | 1954 |
| Oval | 364 | L. Hutton | England v Australia | 1938 |
| Sheffield | 119 | C. Hill | Australia v England | 1902 |
| Adelaide | 299* | D.G. Bradman | Australia v South Africa | 1931-32 |
| Brisbane | 226 | D.G. Bradman | Australia v South Africa | 1931-32 |
| Melbourne | 307 | R.M. Cowper | Australia v England | 1965-66 |
| Perth | 176 | R.B. Simpson | Australia v India | 1977-78 |
| Sydney | 287 | R.E. Foster | England v Australia | 1903-04 |
| Cape Town | 209 | R.G. Pollock | South Africa v Australia | 1966-67 |
| Durban | 274 | R.G. Pollock | South Africa v Australia | 1969-70 |
| Johannesburg | 231 | A.D. Nourse | South Africa v Australia | 1935-36 |
| Port Elizabeth | 167 | A.L. Hassett | Australia v South Africa | 1949-50 |
| Bridgetown | 337 | Hanif Mohammad | Pakistan v West Indies | 1957-58 |
| Georgetown | 259 | G.M. Turner | New Zealand v West Indies | 1971-72 |
| Kingston | 365* | G.St A. Sobers | West Indies v Pakistan | 1957-58 |
| Port-of-Spain | 220 | S.M. Gavaskar | India v West Indies | 1970-71 |
| Auckland | 336* | W.R. Hammond | England v New Zealand | 1932-33 |
| Christchurch | 258 | S.M. Nurse | West Indies v New Zealand | 1968-69 |
| Dunedin | 201 | Mushtaq Mohammad | Pakistan v New Zealand | 1972-73 |
| Wellington | 255* | D.J. McGlew | South Africa v New Zealand | 1952-53 |
| Bangalore | 163 | C.H. Lloyd | West Indies v India | 1974-75 |
| Bombay | 242* | C.H. Lloyd | West Indies v India | 1974-75 |
| Calcutta | 256 | R.B. Kanhai | West Indies v India | 1958-59 |
| Delhi | 230* | B. Sutcliffe | New Zealand v India | 1955-56 |
| Hyderabad | 223 | P.R. Umrigar | India v New Zealand | 1955-56 |
| Kanpur | 198 | G.St A. Sobers | West Indies v India | 1958-59 |
| Lucknow | 124* | Nazar Mohammad | Pakistan v India | 1952-53 |
| Madras | 231 | V.M.H. Mankad | India v New Zealand | 1955-56 |
| Nagpur | 89 | M.G. Burgess | New Zealand v India | 1969-70 |
| Bahawalpur | 142 | Hanif Mohammad | Pakistan v India | 1954-55 |
| Dacca | 165 | G. Pullar | England v Pakistan | 1961-62 |
| Hyderabad | 158 | D.L. Amiss | England v Pakistan | 1972-73 |
| Karachi | 206 | Javed Miandad | Pakistan v New Zealand | 1976-77 |
| Lahore | 217 | R.B. Kanhai | West Indies v Pakistan | 1958-59 |
| Peshawar | 108 | P.R. Umrigar | India v Pakistan | 1954-55 |
| Rawalpindi | 76 | B.R. Taylor | New Zealand v Pakistan | 1964-65 |

# BEST INNINGS BOWLING ANALYSIS FOR EACH TEST MATCH CENTRE

| | | | | |
|---|---|---|---|---|
| Birmingham | 7-17 | W. Rhodes | England v Australia | 1902 |
| Leeds | 8-59 | C. Blythe | England v South Africa | 1907 |
| Lord's | 8-43 | H. Verity | England v Australia | 1934 |
| Manchester | 10-53 | J.C. Laker | England v Australia | 1956 |
| Nottingham | 8-107 | B.J.T. Bosanquet | England v Australia | 1905 |
| Oval | 8-29 | S.F. Barnes | England v South Africa | 1912 |
| Sheffield | 6-49 | S.F. Barnes | England v Australia | 1902 |
| | | | | |
| Adelaide | 8-43 | A.E. Trott | Australia v England | 1894-95 |
| Brisbane | 7-60 | K.R. Miller | Australia v England | 1946-47 |
| Melbourne | 9-121 | A.A. Mailey | Australia v England | 1920-21 |
| Perth | 7-54 | A.M.E. Roberts | West Indies v Australia | 1975-76 |
| Sydney | 8-35 | G.A. Lohmann | England v Australia | 1886-87 |
| | | | | |
| Cape Town | 8-11 | J. Briggs | England v South Africa | 1888-89 |
| Durban | 8-69 | H.J. Tayfield | South Africa v England | 1956-57 |
| Johannesburg | 9-28 | G.A. Lohmann | England v South Africa | 1895-96 |
| Port Elizabeth | 8-7 | G.A. Lohmann | England v South Africa | 1895-96 |
| | | | | |
| Bridgetown | 8-38 | L.R. Gibbs | West Indies v India | 1961-62 |
| Georgetown | 7-44 | I.W. Johnson | Australia v West Indies | 1954-55 |
| Kingston | 7-34 | T.E. Bailey | England v West Indies | 1953-54 |
| Port-of-Spain | 9-95 | J.M. Noreiga | West Indies v India | 1970-71 |
| | | | | |
| Auckland | 8-76 | E.A.S. Prasanna | India v New Zealand | 1975-76 |
| Christchurch | 7-75 | F.S. Trueman | England v New Zealand | 1962-63 |
| Dunedin | 7-52 | Intikhab Alam | Pakistan v New Zealand | 1972-73 |
| Wellington | 7-23 | R.J. Hadlee | New Zealand v India | 1975-76 |
| | | | | |
| Bangalore | 6-53 | R.G.D. Willis | England v India | 1976-77 |
| Bombay | 7-98 | L.R. Gibbs | West Indies v India | 1974-75 |
| Calcutta | 7-49 | Ghulam Ahmed | India v Australia | 1956-57 |
| Delhi | 8-52 | V.M.H. Mankad | India v Pakistan | 1952-53 |
| Hyderabad | 7-128 | S.P. Gupte | India v New Zealand | 1955-56 |
| Kanpur | 9-69 | J.M. Patel | India v Australia | 1959-60 |
| Lucknow | 7-42 | Fazal Mahmood | Pakistan v India | 1952-53 |
| Madras | 8-55 | V.M.H. Mankad | India v England | 1951-52 |
| Nagpur | 6-74 | S. Venkataraghavan | India v New Zealand | 1969-70 |
| | | | | |
| Bahawalpur | 6-74 | P.R. Umrigar | India v Pakistan | 1954-55 |
| Dacca | 6-21 | Khan Mohammad | Pakistan v New Zealand | 1955-56 |
| Hyderabad | 6-44 | Abdul Qadir | Pakistan v England | 1977-78 |
| Karachi | 7-66 | P.H. Edmonds | England v Pakistan | 1977-78 |
| Lahore | 7-74 | Pervez Sajjad | Pakistan v New Zealand | 1969-70 |
| Peshawar | 5-63 | S.P. Gupte | India v Pakistan | 1954-55 |
| Rawalpindi | 4-5 | Pervez Sajjad | Pakistan v New Zealand | 1964-65 |

# BEST MATCH BOWLING FIGURES FOR EACH
## TEST MATCH CENTRE

| Birmingham | 12-119 | F.S. Trueman | England v West Indies | 1963 |
|---|---|---|---|---|
| Leeds | 15-99 | C. Blythe | England v South Africa | 1907 |
| Lord's | 16-137 | R.A.L. Massie | Australia v England | 1972 |
| Manchester | 19-90 | J.C. Laker | England v Australia | 1956 |
| Nottingham | 14-99 | A.V. Bedser | England v Australia | 1953 |
| Oval | 14-90 | F.R. Spofforth | Australia v England | 1882 |
| Sheffield | 11-103 | M.A. Noble | Australia v England | 1902 |

| Adelaide | 14-199 | C.V. Grimmett | Australia v South Africa | 1931-32 |
|---|---|---|---|---|
| Brisbane | 11-31 | E.R.H. Toshack | Australia v India | 1947-48 |
| Melbourne | 15-124 | W. Rhodes | England v Australia | 1903-04 |
| Perth | 10-194 | B.S. Bedi | India v Australia | 1977-78 |
| Sydney | 12-87 | C.T.B. Turner | Australia v England | 1887-88 |

| Cape Town | 15-28 | J. Briggs | England v South Africa | 1888-89 |
|---|---|---|---|---|
| Durban | 14-144 | S.F. Barnes | England v South Africa | 1913-14 |
| Johannesburg | 17-159 | S.F. Barnes | England v South Africa | 1913-14 |
| Port Elizabeth | 15-45 | G.A. Lohmann | England v South Africa | 1895-96 |

| Bridgetown | 10-195 | G.T.S. Stevens | England v West Indies | 1929-30 |
|---|---|---|---|---|
| Georgetown | 10-115 | N.J.N. Hawke | Australia v West Indies | 1964-65 |
| Kingston | 10-96 | H.H.H. Johnson | West Indies v England | 1947-48 |
| Port-of-Spain | 13-156 | A.W. Greig | England v West Indies | 1973-74 |

| Auckland | 11-123 | D.K. Lillee | Australia v New Zealand | 1976-77 |
|---|---|---|---|---|
| Christchurch | 12-97 | D.L. Underwood | England v New Zealand | 1970-71 |
| Dunedin | 11-130 | Intikhab Alam | Pakistan v New Zealand | 1972-73 |
| Wellington | 11-58 | R.J. Hadlee | New Zealand v India | 1975-76 |

| Bangalore | 9-131 | B.S. Chandrasekhar | India v England | 1976-77 |
|---|---|---|---|---|
| Bombay | 11-235 | B.S. Chandrasekhar | India v West Indies | 1966-67 |
| Calcutta | 11-105 | R. Benaud | Australia v India | 1956-57 |
| Delhi | 13-131 | V.M.H. Mankad | India v Pakistan | 1952-53 |
| Hyderabad | 8-109 | E.A.S. Prasanna | India v New Zealand | 1969-70 |
| Kanpur | 14-124 | J.M. Patel | India v Australia | 1959-60 |
| Lucknow | 12-94 | Fazal Mahmood | Pakistan v India | 1952-53 |
| Madras | 12-108 | V.M.H. Mankad | India v England | 1951-52 |
| Nagpur | 9-100 | H.J. Howarth | New Zealand v India | 1969-70 |

| Bahawalpur | 7-124 | Khan Mohammad | Pakistan v India | 1954-55 |
|---|---|---|---|---|
| Dacca | 12-100 | Fazal Mahmood | Pakistan v West Indies | 1958-59 |
| Hyderabad | 7-181 | Intikhab Alam | Pakistan v England | 1972-73 |
| Karachi | 13-114 | Fazal Mahmood | Pakistan v Australia | 1956-57 |
| Lahore | 9-112 | Pervez Sajjad | Pakistan v New Zealand | 1969-70 |
| Peshawar | 6-115 | S.P. Gupte | India v Pakistan | 1954-55 |
| Rawalpindi | 8-47 | Pervez Sajjad | Pakistan v New Zealand | 1964-65 |

# TEAM RECORDS
## HIGHEST INNINGS TOTALS

| | | | |
|---|---|---|---|
| 903-7d | England v Australia | Oval | 1938 |
| 849 | England v West Indies | Kingston | 1929-30 |
| 790-3d | West Indies v Pakistan | Kingston | 1957-58 |
| 758-8d | Australia v West Indies | Kingston | 1954-55 |
| 729-6d | Australia v England | Lord's | 1930 |
| 701 | Australia v England | Oval | 1934 |
| 695 | Australia v England | Oval | 1930 |
| 687-8d | West Indies v England | Oval | 1976 |
| 681-8d | West Indies v England | Port-of-Spain | 1953-54 |
| 674 | Australia v India | Adelaide | 1947-48 |
| 668 | Australia v West Indies | Bridgetown | 1954-55 |
| 659-8d | Australia v England | Sydney | 1946-47 |
| 658-8d | England v Australia | Nottingham | 1938 |
| 657-8d | Pakistan v West Indies | Bridgetown | 1957-58 |
| 656-8d | Australia v England | Manchester | 1964 |
| 654-5 | England v South Africa | Durban² | 1938-39 |
| 652-8d | West Indies v England | Lord's | 1973 |
| 650-6d | Australia v West Indies | Bridgetown | 1964-65 |
| 645 | Australia v England | Brisbane² | 1946-47 |
| 644-8d | West Indies v India | Delhi | 1958-59 |
| 636 | England v Australia | Sydney | 1928-29 |
| 631-8d | West Indies v India | Kingston | 1961-62 |
| 631 | West Indies v India | Delhi | 1948-49 |
| 629-6d | West Indies v India | Bombay² | 1948-49 |
| 629 | England v India | Lord's | 1974 |
| 627-9d | England v Australia | Manchester | 1934 |
| 622-9d | South Africa v Australia | Durban² | 1969-70 |
| 620 | South Africa v Australia | Johannesburg³ | 1966-67 |
| 619-6d | England v West Indies | Nottingham | 1957 |
| 619 | Australia v West Indies | Sydney | 1968-69 |
| 616 | West Indies v Australia | Adelaide | 1968-69 |
| 614-5d | West Indies v India | Calcutta | 1958-59 |
| 611 | England v Australia | Manchester | 1964 |
| 608-7d | Pakistan v England | Birmingham | 1971 |
| 608 | England v South Africa | Johannesburg² | 1948-49 |
| 604-6d | West Indies v India | Bombay³ | 1974-75 |
| 604 | Australia v England | Melbourne | 1936-37 |
| 601-8d | Australia v England | Brisbane² | 1954-55 |
| 600-7d | Pakistan v England | Oval | 1974 |
| 600-9d | Australia v West Indies | Port-of-Spain | 1954-55 |
| 600 | Australia v England | Melbourne | 1924-25 |

*The highest innings totals by New Zealand and India are:*

| | | | |
|---|---|---|---|
| 551-9d | New Zealand v England | Lord's | 1973 |
| 539-9d | India v Pakistan | Madras² | 1960-61 |

## HIGHEST SECOND INNINGS TOTALS
### (First innings in brackets)

| | | | | |
|---|---|---|---|---|
| 657-8d | (106) | Pakistan v West Indies | Bridgetown | 1957-58 |
| 654-5 | (316) | England v South Africa | Durban² | 1938-39 |
| 620 | (199) | South Africa v Australia | Johannesburg³ | 1966-67 |
| 616 | (276) | West Indies v Australia | Adelaide | 1968-69 |
| 583-4d | (186) | England v West Indies | Birmingham | 1957 |
| 582 | (354) | Australia v England | Adelaide | 1920-21 |
| 581 | (267) | Australia v England | Sydney | 1920-21 |
| 578 | (328) | Australia v South Africa | Melbourne | 1910-11 |
| 564-8 | (133) | West Indies v New Zealand | Bridgetown | 1971-72 |
| 564 | (200-9d) | Australia v England | Melbourne | 1936-37 |
| 554 | (198) | Australia v South Africa | Melbourne | 1931-32 |
| 551 | (208) | England v South Africa | Nottingham | 1947 |

# HIGHEST FOURTH INNINGS TOTALS

*TO WIN*

| | | | |
|---|---|---|---|
| 406-4 | India v West Indies | Port-of-Spain | 1975-76 |
| 404-3 | Australia v England | Leeds | 1948 |
| 362-7 | Australia v West Indies | Georgetown | 1977-78 |
| 348-5 | West Indies v New Zealand | Auckland | 1968-69 |
| 342-8 | Australia v India | Perth | 1977-78 |
| 336-5 | Australia v South Africa | Durban² | 1949-50 |
| 332-7 | England v Australia | Melbourne | 1928-29 |
| 317-2 | West Indies v Pakistan | Georgetown | 1957-58 |
| 315-6 | Australia v England | Adelaide | 1901-02 |

*TO DRAW*

| | | | | Runs set in 4th innings |
|---|---|---|---|---|
| 654-5 | England v South Africa | Durban² | 1938-39 | 696 |
| 423-7 | South Africa v England | Oval | 1947 | 451 |
| 408-5 | West Indies v England | Kingston | 1929-30 | 836 |
| 355-8 | India v West Indies | Bombay² | 1948-49 | 361 |
| 339-9 | Australia v West Indies | Adelaide | 1968-69 | 360 |
| 329-3 | Australia v England | Lord's | 1975 | 484 |
| 328-3 | Australia v England | Adelaide | 1970-71 | 469 |
| 326-5 | South Africa v Australia | Sydney | 1963-64 | 409 |
| 325-3 | India v West Indies | Calcutta | 1948-49 | 431 |
| 310-7 | England v Australia | Melbourne | 1946-47 | 551 |
| 308-4 | England v South Africa | Oval | 1965 | 399 |

*TO LOSE*

| | | | | Losing Margin |
|---|---|---|---|---|
| 445 | India v Australia | Adelaide | 1977-78 | 47 |
| 440 | New Zealand v England | Nottingham | 1973 | 38 |
| 417 | England v Australia | Melbourne | 1976-77 | 45 |
| 411 | England v Australia | Sydney | 1924-25 | 193 |
| 376 | India v England | Manchester | 1959 | 171 |
| 370 | England v Australia | Adelaide | 1920-21 | 119 |
| 363 | England v Australia | Adelaide | 1924-25 | 11 |
| 355 | India v Australia | Brisbane² | 1967-68 | 39 |
| 352 | West Indies v Australia | Sydney | 1968-69 | 382 |
| 339 | Australia v South Africa | Adelaide | 1910-11 | 38 |
| 336 | Australia v England | Adelaide | 1928-29 | 12 |
| 335 | Australia v England | Nottingham | 1930 | 93 |
| 335 | South Africa v New Zealand | Cape Town | 1961-62 | 72 |
| 333 | Australia v England | Melbourne | 1894-95 | 94 |
| 327 | England v West Indies | Georgetown | 1929-30 | 289 |
| 326 | West Indies v Australia | Melbourne | 1975-76 | 165 |
| 324 | India v Australia | Brisbane² | 1977-78 | 16 |
| 323 | England v Australia | Melbourne | 1936-37 | 365 |
| 316 | England v West Indies | Kingston | 1953-54 | 140 |
| 313 | England v West Indies | Bridgetown | 1953-54 | 181 |
| 304 | South Africa v England | Johannesburg¹ | 1913-14 | 91 |
| 301 | Pakistan v West Indies | Kingston | 1976-77 | 140 |

# HIGHEST MATCH AGGREGATES

| Runs | Wkts | | | | Days Played |
|------|------|---|---|---|---|
| *BOTH SIDES* | | | | | |
| 1981 | 35 | South Africa v England | Durban² | 1938-39 | 10* |
| 1815 | 34 | West Indies v England | Kingston | 1929-30 | 9† |
| 1764 | 39 | Australia v West Indies | Adelaide | 1968-69 | 5 |
| 1753 | 40 | Australia v England | Adelaide | 1920-21 | 6 |
| 1723 | 31 | England v Australia | Leeds | 1948 | 5 |
| 1661 | 36 | West Indies v Australia | Bridgetown | 1954-55 | 6 |
| 1646 | 40 | Australia v South Africa | Adelaide | 1910-11 | 6 |
| 1644 | 38 | Australia v West Indies | Sydney | 1968-69 | 6 |
| 1640 | 24 | West Indies v Australia | Bridgetown | 1964-65 | 6 |
| 1640 | 33 | Australia v Pakistan | Melbourne | 1972-73 | 5 |
| 1619 | 40 | Australia v England | Melbourne | 1924-25 | 7 |
| 1611 | 40 | Australia v England | Sydney | 1924-25 | 7 |
| 1601 | 29 | England v Australia | Lord's | 1930 | 4 |
| 1585 | 31 | Pakistan v New Zealand | Karachi | 1976-77 | 5 |
| 1562 | 37 | Australia v England | Melbourne | 1946-47 | 6 |
| 1554 | 35 | Australia v England | Melbourne | 1928-29 | 8 |
| 1541 | 35 | Australia v England | Sydney | 1903-04 | 6 |
| 1528 | 24 | West Indies v England | Port-of-Spain | 1953-54 | 6 |
| 1514 | 40 | Australia v England | Sydney | 1894-95 | 6 |
| 1507 | 28 | England v West Indies | Oval | 1976 | 5 |
| 1502 | 29 | Australia v England | Adelaide | 1946-47 | 6 |

*\*No play on one day        †No play on two days*

| Runs | Wkts | | | | |
|------|------|---|---|---|---|
| *ONE SIDE* | | | | | |
| 1121 | 19 | England v West Indies | Kingston | | 1929-30 |
| 1028 | 20 | Australia v England | Oval | | 1934 |
| 1013 | 18 | Australia v West Indies | Sydney | | 1968-69 |
| 1011 | 20 | South Africa v England | Durban² | | 1938-39 |

# LOWEST INNINGS TOTALS

| | | | |
|---|---|---|---|
| 26 | New Zealand v England | Auckland | 1954-55 |
| 30 | South Africa v England | Port Elizabeth | 1895-96 |
| 30 | South Africa v England | Birmingham | 1924 |
| 35 | South Africa v England | Cape Town | 1898-99 |
| 36 | Australia v England | Birmingham | 1902 |
| 36 | South Africa v Australia | Melbourne | 1931-32 |
| 42 | Australia v England | Sydney | 1887-88 |
| 42 | New Zealand v Australia | Wellington | 1945-46 |
| 42 | India v England | Lord's | 1974 |
| 43 | South Africa v England | Cape Town | 1888-89 |
| 44 | Australia v England | Oval | 1896 |
| 45 | England v Australia | Sydney | 1886-87 |
| 45 | South Africa v Australia | Melbourne | 1931-32 |
| 47 | South Africa v England | Cape Town | 1888-89 |
| 47 | New Zealand v England | Lord's | 1958 |
| 52 | England v Australia | Oval | 1948 |
| 53 | England v Australia | Lord's | 1888 |
| 53 | Australia v England | Lord's | 1896 |
| 54 | New Zealand v Australia | Wellington | 1945-46 |
| 58 | South Africa v England | Lord's | 1912 |
| 58 | Australia v England | Brisbane² | 1936-37 |
| 58 | India v Australia | Brisbane² | 1947-48 |
| 58 | India v England | Manchester | 1952 |
| 60 | Australia v England | Lord's | 1888 |

*The lowest innings totals by Pakistan and West Indies are:*

| | | | |
|---|---|---|---|
| 87 | Pakistan v England | Lord's | 1954 |
| 76 | West Indies v Pakistan | Dacca | 1958-59 |

*The following innings closed at a low total:*

| | | | |
|---|---|---|---|
| 32-7d | Australia v England | Brisbane² | 1950-51 |
| 35-8 | Australia v England | Manchester | 1953 |
| 48-8 | New Zealand v England | Christchurch | 1965-66 |
| 51-6d | West Indies v England | Bridgetown | 1934-35 |

## DISMISSED FOR UNDER 100 IN BOTH INNINGS

| | | | |
|---|---|---|---|
| 42 & 82 | Australia v England | Sydney | 1887-88 |
| 53 & 62 | England v Australia | Lord's | 1888 |
| 81 & 70 | Australia v England | Manchester | 1888 |
| 47 & 43 | South Africa v England | Cape Town | 1888-89 |
| 97 & 83 | South Africa v England | Cape Town | 1891-92 |
| 65 & 72 | England v Australia | Sydney | 1894-95 |
| 93 & 30 | South Africa v England | Port Elizabeth | 1895-96 |
| 95 & 93 | South Africa v England | Oval | 1912 |
| 36 & 45 | South Africa v Australia | Melbourne | 1931-32 |
| 42 & 54 | New Zealand v Australia | Wellington | 1945-46 |
| 58 & 98 | India v Australia | Brisbane[2] | 1947-48 |
| 58 & 82 | India v England | Manchester | 1952 |
| 89 & 86 | West Indies v England | Oval | 1957 |
| 47 & 74 | New Zealand v England | Lord's | 1958 |

## LOWEST MATCH AGGREGATES
### (Completed match)

| Runs | Wkts | | | | | Days Played |
|---|---|---|---|---|---|---|
| 234 | 29 | Australia v South Africa | Melbourne | 1931-32 | | 3† |
| 291 | 40 | England v Australia | Lord's | 1888 | | 2 |
| 295 | 28 | New Zealand v Australia | Wellington | 1945-46 | | 2 |
| 309 | 29 | West Indies v England | Bridgetown | 1934-35 | | 3 |
| 323 | 30 | England v Australia | Manchester | 1888 | | 2 |
| 363 | 40 | England v Australia | Oval | 1882 | | 2 |
| 374 | 40 | Australia v England | Sydney | 1887-88 | | 5 |
| 378 | 30 | England v South Africa | Oval | 1912 | | 2 |
| 382 | 30 | South Africa v England | Cape Town | 1888-89 | | 2 |
| 389 | 38 | England v Australia | Oval | 1890 | | 2 |
| 390 | 30 | England v New Zealand | Lord's | 1958 | | 3 |
| 392 | 40 | England v Australia | Oval | 1896 | | 3 |

†No play on one day

## LARGEST MARGINS OF VICTORY

| | | | |
|---|---|---|---|
| Inns and 579 runs | England v Australia | Oval | 1938 |
| Inns and 336 runs | West Indies v India | Calcutta | 1958-59 |
| Inns and 332 runs | Australia v England | Brisbane[2] | 1946-47 |
| Inns and 285 runs | England v India | Lord's | 1974 |
| Inns and 259 runs | Australia v South Africa | Port Elizabeth | 1949-50 |
| Inns and 237 runs | England v West Indies | Oval | 1957 |
| Inns and 230 runs | England v Australia | Adelaide | 1891-92 |
| Inns and 226 runs | Australia v India | Brisbane[2] | 1947-48 |
| Inns and 226 runs | West Indies v England | Lord's | 1973 |
| Inns and 225 runs | England v Australia | Melbourne | 1911-12 |
| Inns and 217 runs | England v Australia | Oval | 1886 |
| Inns and 217 runs | Australia v West Indies | Brisbane[1] | 1930-31 |
| Inns and 215 runs | England v New Zealand | Auckland | 1962-63 |
| Inns and 207 runs | England v India | Manchester | 1952 |
| Inns and 202 runs | England v South Africa | Cape Town | 1888-89 |
| Inns and 200 runs | Australia v England | Melbourne | 1936-37 |
| | | | |
| 675 runs | England v Australia | Brisbane[1] | 1928-29 |
| 562 runs | Australia v England | Oval | 1934 |
| 530 runs | Australia v South Africa | Melbourne | 1910-11 |
| 425 runs | West Indies v England | Manchester | 1976 |
| 409 runs | Australia v England | Lord's | 1948 |
| 382 runs | Australia v England | Adelaide | 1894-95 |
| 382 runs | Australia v West Indies | Sydney | 1968-69 |
| 377 runs | Australia v England | Sydney | 1920-21 |
| 365 runs | Australia v England | Melbourne | 1936-37 |
| 348 runs | Australia v Pakistan | Melbourne | 1976-77 |
| 338 runs | England v Australia | Adelaide | 1932-33 |

| | | | |
|---|---|---|---|
| 326 runs | West Indies v England | Lord's | 1950 |
| 323 runs | South Africa v Australia | Port Elizabeth | 1969-70 |
| 322 runs | England v Australia | Brisbane[2] | 1936-37 |
| 312 runs | England v South Africa | Cape Town | 1956-57 |
| 308 runs | Australia v England | Melbourne | 1907-08 |
| 307 runs | Australia v England | Sydney | 1924-25 |
| 307 runs | South Africa v Australia | Johannesburg[3] | 1969-70 |

## VICTORY LOSING FEWEST WICKETS

*TWO WICKETS*

| | | |
|---|---|---|
| England (531-2d) v South Africa (273 & 240) | Lord's | 1924 |
| England (267-2d) v New Zealand (67 & 129) | Leeds | 1958 |
| England (459-2d) v India (165 & 216) | Birmingham | 1974 |

## RESULTS BY NARROW MARGINS

*TIE*

| | | |
|---|---|---|
| Australia v West Indies | Brisbane[2] | 1960-61 |

*WON BY ONE WICKET*

| | | | 10th Wicket Partnership |
|---|---|---|---|
| England v Australia | Oval | 1902 | 15* |
| South Africa v England | Johannesburg[1] | 1905-06 | 48* |
| England v Australia | Melbourne | 1907-08 | 39* |
| England v South Africa | Cape Town | 1922-23 | 5* |
| Australia v West Indies | Melbourne | 1951-52 | 38* |
| | | | (*unbroken) |

*WON BY TWO WICKETS*

| | | |
|---|---|---|
| England v Australia | Oval | 1890 |
| Australia v England | Sydney | 1907-08 |
| England v South Africa | Durban[2] | 1948-49 |
| Australia v West Indies | Melbourne | 1960-61 |
| India v Australia | Bombay[2] | 1964-65 |
| Australia v India | Perth | 1977-78 |

*LESS THAN TWENTY RUNS*

| | | | |
|---|---|---|---|
| 3 | Australia v England | Manchester | 1902 |
| 6 | Australia v England | Sydney | 1884-85 |
| 7 | Australia v England | Oval | 1882 |
| 10 | England v Australia | Sydney | 1894-95 |
| 11 | Australia v England | Adelaide | 1924-25 |
| 12 | England v Australia | Adelaide | 1928-29 |
| 13 | England v Australia | Sydney | 1886-87 |
| 16 | Australia v India | Brisbane[2] | 1977-78 |
| 17 | South Africa v England | Johannesburg[3] | 1956-57 |
| 19 | South Africa v England | Johannesburg[1] | 1909-10 |

*England won the Durban[2] Test of the 1948-49 rubber by two wickets, scoring a leg-bye off the last possible ball of the match.*

*At Port-of-Spain in 1934-35, West Indies took England's last second innings wicket with the fifth ball of the last possible over to win by 217 runs.*

## VICTORY AFTER FOLLOWING-ON

| | | |
|---|---|---|
| England (325 & 437) beat Australia (586 & 166) by 10 runs | Sydney | 1894-95 |

# LONGEST MATCHES

| 10 days | South Africa v England | Durban[2] | 1938-39 |
|---|---|---|---|
| 9 days | West Indies v England | Kingston | 1929-30 |
| 8 days | Australia v England | Melbourne | 1928-29 |

## MATCHES COMPLETED IN TWO DAYS

| | | |
|---|---|---|
| England (101 & 77) v Australia (63 & 122) | Oval | 1882 |
| England (53 & 62) v Australia (116 & 60) | Lord's | 1888 |
| England (317) v Australia (80 & 100) | Oval | 1888 |
| England (172) v Australia (81 & 70) | Manchester | 1888 |
| South Africa (84 & 129) v England (148 & 67-2) | Port Elizabeth | 1888-89 |
| South Africa (47 & 43) v England (292) | Cape Town | 1888-89 |
| England (100 & 95-8) v Australia (92 & 102) | Oval | 1890 |
| South Africa (93 & 30) v England (185 & 226) | Port Elizabeth | 1895-96 |
| South Africa (115 & 117) v England (265) | Cape Town | 1895-96 |
| England (176 & 14-0) v South Africa (95 & 93) | Oval | 1912 |
| Australia (448) v South Africa (265 & 95) | Manchester | 1912 |
| England (112 & 147) v Australia (232 & 30-0) | Nottingham | 1921 |
| Australia (328-8d) v West Indies (99 & 107) | Melbourne | 1930-31 |
| South Africa (157 & 98) v Australia (439) | Johannesburg[1] | 1935-36 |
| New Zealand (42 & 54) v Australia (199-8d) | Wellington | 1945-46 |

## COMPLETE SIDE DISMISSED TWICE IN A DAY

| | | | |
|---|---|---|---|
| England (65 & 72) v Australia | Sydney | 1894-95 | 3rd day |
| India (58 & 82) v England | Manchester | 1952 | 3rd day |

## MOST RUNS IN ONE DAY

### BY ONE TEAM

| | | | | |
|---|---|---|---|---|
| 503-2 | England v South Africa | Lord's | 1924 | 2nd day |
| 494-6 | Australia v South Africa | Sydney | 1910-11 | 1st day |
| 475-2 | Australia v England | Oval | 1934 | 1st day |
| 471-8 | England v India | Oval | 1936 | 1st day |
| 458-3 | Australia v England | Leeds | 1930 | 1st day |
| 455-1 | Australia v England | Leeds | 1934 | 2nd day |

### BY BOTH TEAMS

| | | | | |
|---|---|---|---|---|
| 588-6 | England (398-6) v India (190-0) | Manchester | 1936 | 2nd day |
| 522-2 | England (503-2) v South Africa (19-0) | Lord's | 1924 | 2nd day |
| 508-8 | England (221-2) v South Africa (287-6) | Oval | 1935 | 3rd day |
| 496-4 | England (437-4) v Pakistan (59-0) | Nottingham | 1954 | 2nd day |
| 473-4 | England (264-1) v South Africa (209-3) | Oval | 1929 | 3rd day |
| 471-9 | England (244-2) v Australia (277-7) | Oval | 1921 | 3rd day |
| 469-7 | England (366-3) v West Indies (103-4) | Oval | 1939 | 3rd day |
| 464-11 | Australia (448) v South Africa (16-1) | Manchester | 1912 | 1st day |
| 458-12 | Australia (155-5) v West Indies (303-7) | Sydney | 1968-69 | 5th day |

## LEAST RUNS IN A FULL DAY'S PLAY

| | | | |
|---|---|---|---|
| 95 | Australia (80) v Pakistan (15-2) | Karachi | 1956-57 |
| 104 | Pakistan (104-5) v Australia | Karachi | 1959-60 |
| 106 | England (92-2 to 198 out) v Australia | Brisbane[2] | 1958-59 |
| 112 | Australia (138-6 to 187 out) v Pakistan (63-1) | Karachi | 1956-57 |
| 117 | India (117-5) v Australia | Madras[2] | 1956-57 |
| 119 | South Africa (7-0 to 126-2) v Australia | Johannesburg[3] | 1957-58 |
| 120 | India (15-0 to 135-8) v Australia | Calcutta | 1956-57 |

# BATSMEN'S MATCHES

*(Over 60 runs per wicket)*

| Runs/Wkt | Runs-Wkts | | | |
|---|---|---|---|---|
| 109.3 | (1093-10) | India v New Zealand | Delhi | 1955-56 |
| 99.4 | (994-10) | West Indies v New Zealand | Georgetown | 1971-72 |
| 70.6 | (1271-18) | England v Australia | Manchester | 1964 |
| 68-3 | (1640-24) | West Indies v Australia | Bridgetown | 1964-65 |
| 66.9 | (1406-21) | West Indies v Pakistan | Kingston | 1957-58 |
| 65.3 | (1307-20) | England v Australia | Manchester | 1934 |
| 65.0 | (1235-19) | India v West Indies | Bombay[2] | 1948-49 |
| 64.7 | (1036-16) | India v New Zealand | Hyderabad | 1955-56 |
| 63.6 | (1528-24) | West Indies v England | Port-of-Spain | 1953-54 |
| 62.3 | (1496-24) | England v Australia | Nottingham | 1938 |
| 62.0 | (1116-18) | West Indies v England | Bridgetown | 1959-60 |
| 61.5 | (1046-17) | India v Pakistan | Madras[2] | 1960-61 |
| 60.6 | (1455-24) | New Zealand v Australia | Wellington | 1973-74 |

## HIGHEST SCORES FOR EACH BATTING POSITION

| No. | | | | | |
|---|---|---|---|---|---|
| 1 | 364 | L. Hutton | England v Australia | Oval | 1938 |
| 2 | 325 | A. Sandham | England v West Indies | Kingston | 1929-30 |
| 3 | 365* | G.St A. Sobers | West Indies v Pakistan | Kingston | 1957-58 |
| 4 | 307 | R.M. Cowper | Australia v England | Melbourne | 1965-66 |
| 5 | 304 | D.G. Bradman | Australia v England | Leeds | 1934 |
| 6 | 250 | K.D. Walters | Australia v New Zealand | Christchurch | 1976-77 |
| 7 | 270 | D.G. Bradman | Australia v England | Melbourne | 1936-37 |
| 8 | 209 | Imtiaz Ahmed | Pakistan v New Zealand | Lahore[1] | 1955-56 |
| 9 | 160 | C. Hill | Australia v England | Adelaide | 1907-08 |
| 10 | 117 | W.W. Read | England v Australia | Oval | 1884 |
| 11 | 68* | R.O. Collinge | New Zealand v Pakistan | Auckland | 1972-73 |

## HIGHEST SCORE REACHED AT THE FALL OF EACH WICKET

| | | | | |
|---|---|---|---|---|
| 1st | 413 | India (537-3d) v New Zealand | Madras[2] | 1955-56 |
| 2nd | 533 | West Indies (790-3d) v Pakistan | Kingston | 1957-58 |
| 3rd | 602 | West Indies (790-3d) v Pakistan | Kingston | 1957-58 |
| 4th | 667 | England (849) v West Indies | Kingston | 1929-30 |
| 5th | 720 | England (849) v West Indies | Kingston | 1929-30 |
| 6th | 770 | England (903-7d) v Australia | Oval | 1938 |
| 7th | 876 | England (903-7d) v Australia | Oval | 1938 |
| 8th | 813 | England (849) v West Indies | Kingston | 1929-30 |
| 9th | 821 | England (849) v West Indies | Kingston | 1929-30 |
| 10th | 849 | England (849) v West Indies | Kingston | 1929-30 |

## LOWEST SCORE REACHED AT THE FALL OF EACH WICKET

| | | | | |
|---|---|---|---|---|
| 1st | 0 | | | |
| 2nd | 0 | | | |
| 3rd | 0 | (Australia (32-7d) v England | Brisbane[2] | 1950-51 |
| | | (India (165) v England | Leeds | 1952 |
| 4th | 0 | India (165) v England | Leeds | 1952 |
| 5th | 6 | India (98) v England | Oval | 1952 |
| 6th | 7 | Australia (70) v England | Manchester | 1888 |
| 7th | 18 | Australia (60) v England | Lord's | 1888 |
| 8th | 22 | New Zealand (26) v England | Auckland | 1954-55 |
| 9th | 26 | New Zealand (26) v England | Auckland | 1954-55 |
| 10th | 26 | New Zealand (26) v England | Auckland | 1954-55 |

# MOST HUNDREDS IN AN INNINGS

| | | | |
|---|---|---|---|
| 5 | Australia v West Indies | Kingston | 1954-55 |
| 4 | England v Australia | Nottingham | 1938 |
| 4 | West Indies v India | Delhi | 1948-49 |

# MOST HUNDREDS IN A MATCH (BOTH TEAMS)

| | | | |
|---|---|---|---|
| 7 | England (4) v Australia (3) | Nottingham | 1938 |
| 7 | West Indies (2) v Australia (5) | Kingston | 1954-55 |

# MOST HUNDREDS IN A RUBBER (ONE TEAM)

| | | Tests | |
|---|---|---|---|
| 12 | Australia v West Indies | 5 | 1954-55 |
| 11 | England v South Africa | 5 | 1938-39 |
| 11 | West Indies v India | 5 | 1948-49 |
| 11 | Australia v South Africa | 5 | 1949-50 |

# MOST HUNDREDS IN A RUBBER (BOTH TEAMS)

| | | Tests | |
|---|---|---|---|
| 21 | West Indies (9) v Australia (12) | 5 | 1954-55 |
| 17 | Australia (9) v England (8) | 5 | 1928-29 |
| 17 | South Africa (6) v England (11) | 5 | 1938-39 |
| 16 | India (5) v West Indies (11) | 5 | 1948-49 |
| 16 | Australia (10) v West Indies (6) | 5 | 1968-69 |
| 16 | Australia (10) v West Indies (6) | 6 | 1975-76 |
| 15 | Australia (10) v England (5) | 5 | 1946-47 |

# TEAM UNCHANGED THROUGHOUT A RUBBER

| Tests | | Venue | |
|---|---|---|---|
| 5 | England v Australia | Australia | 1884-85 |
| 5 | South Africa v England | South Africa | 1905-06 |
| 4 | England v Australia | Australia | 1881-82 |
| 3 | Australia v England | England | 1884 |
| 3 | Australia v England | England | 1893 |
| 3 | Pakistan v New Zealand | Pakistan | 1964-65 |
| 3 | India v England | England | 1971 |

# MOST PLAYERS ENGAGED BY ONE SIDE IN A RUBBER

| | | Venue | |
|---|---|---|---|
| 30 in 5 Tests | England v Australia | England | 1921 |
| 28 in 5 Tests | Australia v England | Australia | 1884-85 |
| 27 in 4 Tests | West Indies v England | West Indies | 1929-30 |
| 26 in 5 Tests | India v Pakistan | India | 1952-53 |
| 25 in 4 Tests | England v West Indies | England | 1950 |
| 25 in 5 Tests | England v Australia | England | 1909 |
| 25 in 5 Tests | England v South Africa | England | 1935 |

*South Africa used 20 players in the 3-match rubber of 1895-96 against England in South Africa.*

# MOST CONSECUTIVE WINS

| | | |
|---|---|---|
| 8 | Australia | Sydney 1920-21 to Leeds 1921 |
| 7 | England | Melbourne 1884-85 to Sydney 1887-88 |
| 7 | England | Lord's 1928 to Adelaide 1928-29 |
| 6 | England | Oval 1888 to Oval 1890 |
| 6 | England | Leeds 1957 to Manchester 1958 |
| 6 | West Indies | Port-of-Spain 1961-62 to Manchester 1963 |

# MOST CONSECUTIVE DEFEATS

| | | |
|---|---|---|
| 8 | South Africa | Port Elizabeth 1888-89 to Cape Town 1898-99 |
| 8 | England | Sydney 1920-21 to Leeds 1921 |
| 7 | Australia | Melbourne 1884-85 to Sydney 1887-88 |
| 7 | England | Lord's 1950 to Adelaide 1950-51 |
| 7 | India | Leeds 1967 to Sydney 1967-68 |
| 6 | South Africa | Melbourne 1910-11 to Lord's 1912 |
| 6 | New Zealand | Johannesburg[2] 1953-54 to Lahore[1] 1955-56 |
| 6 | India | Nottingham 1959 to Delhi 1959-60 |

# MOST CONSECUTIVE MATCHES WITHOUT DEFEAT

| | | |
|---|---|---|
| 26 | England | Lord's 1968 to Manchester 1971 |
| 25 | Australia | Wellington 1945-46 to Adelaide 1950-51 |
| 18 | England | Christchurch 1958-59 to Birmingham 1961 |
| 17 | Australia | Madras[2] 1956-57 to Delhi 1959-60 |
| 16 | Australia | Sydney 1920-21 to Adelaide 1924-25 |
| 15 | England | Melbourne 1910-11 to Port Elizabeth 1913-14 |
| 15 | Pakistan | Wellington 1972-73 to Adelaide 1976-77 |
| 13 | India | Port-of-Spain 1952-53 to Madras[2] 1955-56 |
| 13 | Australia | Oval 1972 to Wellington 1973-74 |
| 12 | England | Oval 1938 to Oval 1946 |
| 12 | Pakistan | Manchester 1954 to Bridgetown 1957-58 |
| 12 | England | Oval 1966 to Georgetown 1967-68 |

# MOST CONSECUTIVE MATCHES WITHOUT VICTORY

| | | |
|---|---|---|
| 44 | New Zealand | Christchurch 1929-30 to Wellington 1955-56 |
| 28 | South Africa | Leeds 1935 to Port Elizabeth 1949-50 |
| 24 | India | Lord's 1932 to Kanpur 1951-52 |
| 23 | New Zealand | Auckland 1962-63 to Dunedin 1967-68 |
| 22 | Pakistan | Lahore[1] 1958-59 to Christchurch 1964-65 |
| 20 | West Indies | Wellington 1968-69 to Port-of-Spain 1972-73 |
| 18 | New Zealand | Dacca 1969-70 to Wellington 1973-74 |
| 16 | South Africa | Melbourne 1910-11 to Cape Town 1921-22 |
| 16 | Pakistan | Lord's 1967 to Wellington 1972-73 |
| 14 | India | Madras[2] 1956-57 to Delhi 1959-60 |
| 13 | India | Madras[1] 1952-53 to Hyderabad 1955-56 |
| 12 | South Africa | Cape Town 1922-23 to Durban[2] 1927-28 |
| 12 | England | Leeds 1963 to Oval 1964 |

# WINNING EVERY TEST IN A RUBBER

*(Minimum: 4 Matches)*

| | | Venue | Tests |
|---|---|---|---|
| 1920-21 | Australia v England | Australia | 5 |
| 1931-32 | Australia v South Africa | Australia | 5 |
| 1959 | England v India | England | 5 |
| 1961-62 | West Indies v India | West Indies | 5 |
| 1967-68 | Australia v India | Australia | 4 |
| 1969-70 | South Africa v Australia | South Africa | 4 |

# EACH BATSMAN REACHING DOUBLE FIGURES IN AN INNINGS

|  |  | Venue | Lowest Score |
|---|---|---|---|
| 1894-95 | England (475) v Australia | Melbourne | 11 |
| 1905-06 | South Africa (385) v England | Johannesburg[1] | 10 |
| 1928-29 | England (636) v Australia | Sydney | 11 |
| 1931-32 | South Africa (358) v Australia | Melbourne | 10* |
| 1947-48 | Australia (575-9d) v India | Melbourne | 11 |
| 1952-53 | India (397) v Pakistan | Calcutta | 11 |
| 1967-68 | India (359) v New Zealand | Dunedin | 12 |
| 1976-77 | India (524-9d) v New Zealand | Kanpur | 10* |

## NO BATSMAN ACHIEVING DOUBLE FIGURES IN A COMPLETED INNINGS

| | | |
|---|---|---|
| South Africa (30 – highest score 7) v England | Birmingham | 1924 |

## EXTRAS BEING HIGHEST SCORER IN A COMPLETED INNINGS

|  | Total | Highest Score | Extras | Opponents |  |  |
|---|---|---|---|---|---|---|
| South Africa | 58 | 13 | 17 | England | Lord's | 1912 |
| South Africa | 30 | 7 | 11 | England | Birmingham | 1924 |
| New Zealand | 97 | 19 | 20 | England | Nottingham | 1973 |
| England | 126 | 24 | 25 | West Indies | Manchester | 1976 |

# UNUSUAL DISMISSALS

**HANDLED BALL**

| | | | |
|---|---|---|---|
| W.R. Endean (3) | SA v E | Cape Town | 1956-57 |

**HIT THE BALL TWICE**
No instance

**OBSTRUCTING THE FIELD**

| | | | |
|---|---|---|---|
| L. Hutton (27) | E v SA | Oval | 1951 |

**RUN OUT BY THE BOWLER**
(while backing up before the ball had been bowled)

| | | | |
|---|---|---|---|
| W.A. Brown (18) by V.M.H. Mankad | A v I | Sydney | 1947-48 |
| I.R. Redpath (9) by C.C. Griffith | A v WI | Adelaide | 1968-69 |
| D.W. Randall (13) by E.J. Chatfield | E v NZ | Christchurch | 1977-78 |

**STUMPED BY A SUBSTITUTE**

| | | | |
|---|---|---|---|
| N.C. Tufnell (sub for H. Strudwick) st S.J. Snooke | E v SA | Durban[1] | 1909-10 |
| B.E. Congdon (sub for A.E. Dick) st Pervez Sajjad | NZ v P | Lahore[2] | 1964-65 |

# PLAYERS' RECORDS — BATTING
## 2000 RUNS IN TESTS

### ENGLAND

| | M | I | Runs | Opponents A | SA | WI | NZ | I | P |
|---|---|---|---|---|---|---|---|---|---|
| M.C. Cowdrey | 114 | 188 | **7624** | 2433 | 1021 | 1751 | 1133 | 653 | 633 |
| W.R. Hammond | 85 | 140 | **7249** | 2852 | 2188 | 639 | 1015 | 555 | — |
| L. Hutton | 79 | 138 | **6971** | 2428 | 1564 | 1661 | 777 | 522 | 19 |
| K.F. Barrington | 82 | 131 | **6806** | 2111 | 989 | 1042 | 594 | 1355 | 715 |
| D.C.S. Compton | 78 | 131 | **5807** | 1842 | 2205 | 592 | 510 | 205 | 453 |
| G. Boycott | 72 | 125 | **5516** | 1924 | 373 | 1542 | 757 | 329 | 591 |
| J.B. Hobbs | 61 | 102 | **5410** | 3636 | 1562 | 212 | — | — | — |
| J.H. Edrich | 77 | 127 | **5138** | 2644 | 7 | 792 | 840 | 494 | 361 |
| T.W. Graveney | 79 | 123 | **4882** | 1075 | 234 | 1532 | 293 | 805 | 943 |
| H. Sutcliffe | 54 | 84 | **4555** | 2741 | 1336 | 206 | 250 | 22 | — |
| P.B.H. May | 66 | 106 | **4537** | 1566 | 906 | 986 | 603 | 356 | 120 |
| E.R. Dexter | 62 | 102 | **4502** | 1358 | 585 | 866 | 477 | 467 | 749 |
| A.P.E. Knott | 89 | 138 | **4175** | 1504 | — | 958 | 352 | 685 | 676 |
| D.L. Amiss | 50 | 88 | **3612** | 305 | — | 1130 | 433 | 965 | 779 |
| A.W. Greig | 58 | 93 | **3599** | 1303 | — | 795 | 267 | 883 | 351 |
| E.H. Hendren | 51 | 83 | **3525** | 1740 | 876 | 909 | — | — | — |
| F.E. Woolley | 64 | 98 | **3283** | 1664 | 1354 | — | 235 | 30 | — |
| K.W.R. Fletcher | 52 | 85 | **2975** | 661 | — | 528 | 578 | 622 | 586 |
| M. Leyland | 41 | 65 | **2764** | 1705 | 936 | 37 | — | 86 | — |
| C. Washbrook | 37 | 66 | **2569** | 996 | 938 | 255 | 234 | 146 | — |
| B.L. D'Oliveira | 44 | 70 | **2484** | 865 | — | 555 | 258 | 254 | 552 |
| W.J. Edrich | 39 | 63 | **2440** | 1184 | 792 | 94 | 366 | — | 4 |
| T.G. Evans | 91 | 133 | **2439** | 783 | 511 | 625 | 142 | 315 | 63 |
| L.E.G. Ames | 47 | 72 | **2434** | 675 | 530 | 748 | 410 | 71 | — |
| W. Rhodes | 58 | 98 | **2325** | 1706 | 568 | 51 | — | — | — |
| T.E. Bailey | 61 | 91 | **2290** | 875 | 552 | 343 | 439 | — | 81 |
| M.J.K. Smith | 50 | 78 | **2278** | 248 | 561 | 319 | 312 | 639 | 199 |
| P.E. Richardson | 34 | 56 | **2061** | 526 | 369 | 427 | 317 | 304 | 118 |

### AUSTRALIA

| | M | I | Runs | Opponents E | SA | WI | NZ | I | P |
|---|---|---|---|---|---|---|---|---|---|
| D.G. Bradman | 52 | 80 | **6996** | 5028 | 806 | 447 | — | 715 | — |
| R.N. Harvey | 79 | 137 | **6149** | 2416 | 1625 | 1054 | — | 775 | 279 |
| W.M. Lawry | 67 | 123 | **5234** | 2233 | 985 | 1035 | — | 892 | 89 |
| I.M. Chappell | 72 | 130 | **5187** | 1986 | 288 | 1539 | 486 | 536 | 352 |
| K.D. Walters | 68 | 116 | **4960** | 1981 | 258 | 1196 | 720 | 540 | 265 |
| R.B. Simpson | 62 | 111 | **4869** | 1405 | 980 | 1043 | — | 1125 | 316 |
| I.R. Redpath | 66 | 120 | **4737** | 1512 | 791 | 1247 | 413 | 475 | 299 |
| G.S. Chappell | 51 | 90 | **4097** | 1807 | — | 1044 | 661 | — | 585 |
| A.R. Morris | 46 | 79 | **3533** | 2080 | 792 | 452 | — | 209 | — |
| C. Hill | 49 | 89 | **3412** | 2660 | 752 | — | — | — | — |
| V.T. Trumper | 48 | 89 | **3163** | 2263 | 900 | — | — | — | — |
| C.C. McDonald | 47 | 83 | **3107** | 1043 | 786 | 880 | — | 224 | 174 |
| A.L. Hassett | 43 | 69 | **3073** | 1572 | 748 | 402 | 19 | 332 | — |
| K.R. Miller | 55 | 87 | **2958** | 1511 | 399 | 801 | 30 | 185 | 32 |
| W.W. Armstrong | 50 | 84 | **2863** | 2172 | 691 | — | — | — | — |
| K.R. Stackpole | 43 | 80 | **2807** | 1164 | 441 | 600 | 197 | 368 | 37 |
| N.C. O'Neill | 42 | 69 | **2779** | 1072 | 285 | 788 | — | 416 | 218 |
| S.J. McCabe | 39 | 62 | **2748** | 1922 | 621 | 205 | — | — | — |
| W. Bardsley | 41 | 66 | **2469** | 1487 | 982 | — | — | — | — |
| R.W. Marsh | 52 | 82 | **2396** | 1207 | — | 533 | 327 | — | 329 |
| W.M. Woodfull | 35 | 54 | **2300** | 1684 | 421 | 195 | — | — | — |
| P.J.P. Burge | 42 | 68 | **2290** | 1179 | 331 | 229 | — | 457 | 94 |
| S.E. Gregory | 58 | 100 | **2282** | 2193 | 89 | — | — | — | — |
| R. Benaud | 63 | 97 | **2201** | 767 | 684 | 462 | — | 144 | 144 |
| C.G. Macartney | 35 | 55 | **2131** | 1640 | 491 | — | — | — | — |
| W.H. Ponsford | 29 | 48 | **2122** | 1558 | 97 | 467 | — | — | — |
| R.M. Cowper | 27 | 46 | **2061** | 686 | 255 | 417 | — | 604 | 99 |

## SOUTH AFRICA

| | M | I | Runs | *Opponents* E | A | NZ | | |
|---|---|---|---|---|---|---|---|---|
| B. Mitchell | 42 | 80 | **3471** | 2732 | 573 | 166 | | |
| A.D. Nourse | 34 | 62 | **2960** | 2037 | 923 | — | | |
| H.W. Taylor | 42 | 76 | **2936** | 2287 | 640 | 9 | | |
| E.J. Barlow | 30 | 57 | **2516** | 742 | 1149 | 625 | | |
| T.L. Goddard | 41 | 78 | **2516** | 1193 | 1090 | 233 | | |
| D.J. McGlew | 34 | 64 | **2440** | 736 | 604 | 1100 | | |
| J.H.B. Waite | 50 | 86 | **2405** | 923 | 839 | 643 | | |
| R.G. Pollock | 23 | 41 | **2256** | 750 | 1453 | 53 | | |
| A.W. Nourse | 45 | 83 | **2234** | 1415 | 819 | — | | |
| R.A. McLean | 40 | 73 | **2120** | 1068 | 480 | 572 | | |

## WEST INDIES

| | M | I | Runs | *Opponents* E | A | NZ | I | P |
|---|---|---|---|---|---|---|---|---|
| G. St A. Sobers | 93 | 160 | **8032** | 3214 | 1510 | 404 | 1920 | 984 |
| R.B. Kanhai | 79 | 137 | **6227** | 2267 | 1694 | — | 1693 | 573 |
| C.H. Lloyd | 65 | 113 | **4594** | 1313 | 1209 | 131 | 1441 | 500 |
| E. de C. Weekes | 48 | 81 | **4455** | 1313 | 714 | 478 | 1495 | 455 |
| R.C. Fredericks | 59 | 109 | **4334** | 1369 | 1069 | 537 | 767 | 592 |
| F.M.M. Worrell | 51 | 87 | **3860** | 1979 | 918 | 233 | 730 | — |
| C.L. Walcott | 44 | 74 | **3798** | 1391 | 914 | 199 | 909 | 385 |
| A.I. Kallicharran | 45 | 76 | **3331** | 789 | 1123 | 219 | 691 | 509 |
| C.C. Hunte | 44 | 78 | **3245** | 1005 | 927 | — | 670 | 643 |
| B.F. Butcher | 44 | 78 | **3104** | 1373 | 810 | 216 | 572 | 133 |
| S.M. Nurse | 29 | 54 | **2523** | 1016 | 820 | 558 | 129 | — |
| I.V.A. Richards | 28 | 47 | **2500** | 829 | 488 | — | 909 | 274 |
| G.A. Headley | 22 | 40 | **2190** | 1852 | 336 | — | 2 | — |
| J.B. Stollmeyer | 32 | 56 | **2159** | 858 | 417 | 188 | 696 | — |

## NEW ZEALAND

| | M | I | Runs | *Opponents* E | A | SA | WI | I | P |
|---|---|---|---|---|---|---|---|---|---|
| J.R. Reid | 58 | 108 | **3428** | 953 | — | 914 | 212 | 691 | 658 |
| B.E. Congdon | 58 | 108 | **3374** | 1069 | 456 | — | 764 | 713 | 372 |
| G.M. Turner | 39 | 70 | **2920** | 510 | 541 | — | 855 | 583 | 431 |
| B. Sutcliffe | 42 | 76 | **2727** | 1049 | — | 455 | 196 | 885 | 142 |
| G.T. Dowling | 39 | 77 | **2306** | 517 | — | 271 | 277 | 964 | 277 |
| M.G. Burgess | 41 | 75 | **2291** | 475 | 157 | — | 317 | 725 | 617 |

## INDIA

| | M | I | Runs | *Opponents* E | A | WI | NZ | P |
|---|---|---|---|---|---|---|---|---|
| P.R. Umrigar | 59 | 94 | **3631** | 770 | 227 | 1372 | 351 | 911 |
| S.M. Gavaskar | 37 | 71 | **3226** | 979 | 450 | 1272 | 525 | — |
| V.L. Manjrekar | 55 | 92 | **3208** | 1181 | 377 | 569 | 507 | 574 |
| G.R. Viswanath | 43 | 82 | **3154** | 868 | 807 | 958 | 521 | — |
| C.G. Borde | 55 | 97 | **3061** | 746 | 502 | 870 | 613 | 330 |
| Nawab of Pataudi, jr | 46 | 83 | **2793** | 946 | 829 | 352 | 666 | — |
| F.M. Engineer | 46 | 87 | **2611** | 1113 | 449 | 465 | 584 | — |
| P. Roy | 43 | 79 | **2442** | 620 | 432 | 717 | 301 | 372 |
| V.S. Hazare | 30 | 52 | **2192** | 803 | 429 | 737 | — | 223 |
| A.L. Wadekar | 37 | 71 | **2113** | 840 | 548 | 230 | 495 | — |
| V.M.H. Mankad | 44 | 72 | **2109** | 618 | 388 | 397 | 526 | 180 |
| M.L. Jaisimha | 39 | 71 | **2056** | 852 | 434 | 276 | 268 | 226 |
| D.N. Sardesai | 30 | 55 | **2001** | 674 | 156 | 811 | 360 | — |

## PAKISTAN

| | M | I | Runs | *Opponents* E | A | WI | NZ | I |
|---|---|---|---|---|---|---|---|---|
| Hanif Mohammad | 55 | 97 | **3915** | 1039 | 548 | 736 | 622 | 970 |
| Mushtaq Mohammad | 49 | 88 | **3283** | 1554 | 321 | 488 | 657 | 263 |
| Saeed Ahmed | 41 | 78 | **2991** | 791 | 611 | 707 | 422 | 460 |
| Asif Iqbal | 45 | 77 | **2748** | 822 | 536 | 416 | 974 | — |
| Majid Khan | 37 | 64 | **2651** | 720 | 486 | 667 | 778 | — |
| Sadiq Mohammad | 31 | 57 | **2120** | 610 | 400 | 370 | 740 | — |
| Imtiaz Ahmed | 41 | 72 | **2079** | 488 | 131 | 423 | 284 | 753 |

# HIGHEST BATTING AVERAGES

*(Qualification: 15 innings)*

| | Country | Tests | I | NO | Runs | HS | Avge | 100 | 50 |
|---|---|---|---|---|---|---|---|---|---|
| D.G. Bradman | Australia | 52 | 80 | 10 | 6996 | 334 | **99.94** | 29 | 13 |
| Javed Miandad | Pakistan | 10 | 17 | 4 | 917 | 206 | **70.53** | 2 | 6 |
| C.S. Dempster | New Zealand | 10 | 15 | 4 | 723 | 136 | **65.72** | 2 | 5 |
| S.G. Barnes | Australia | 13 | 19 | 2 | 1072 | 234 | **63.05** | 3 | 5 |
| R.G. Pollock | South Africa | 23 | 41 | 4 | 2256 | 274 | **60.97** | 7 | 11 |
| G.A. Headley | West Indies | 22 | 40 | 4 | 2190 | 270* | **60.83** | 10 | 5 |
| H. Sutcliffe | England | 54 | 84 | 9 | 4555 | 194 | **60.73** | 16 | 23 |
| E. Paynter | England | 20 | 31 | 5 | 1540 | 243 | **59.23** | 4 | 7 |
| K.F. Barrington | England | 82 | 131 | 15 | 6806 | 256 | **58.67** | 20 | 35 |
| E. de C. Weekes | West Indies | 48 | 81 | 5 | 4455 | 207 | **58.61** | 15 | 19 |
| K.S. Duleepsinhji | England | 12 | 19 | 2 | 995 | 173 | **58.52** | 3 | 5 |
| W.R. Hammond | England | 85 | 140 | 16 | 7249 | 336* | **58.45** | 22 | 24 |
| G. St A. Sobers | West Indies | 93 | 160 | 21 | 8032 | 365* | **57.78** | 26 | 30 |
| J.B. Hobbs | England | 61 | 102 | 7 | 5410 | 211 | **56.94** | 15 | 28 |
| C.A.G. Russell | England | 10 | 18 | 2 | 910 | 140 | **56.87** | 5 | 2 |
| C.L. Walcott | West Indies | 44 | 74 | 7 | 3798 | 220 | **56.68** | 15 | 14 |
| L. Hutton | England | 79 | 138 | 15 | 6971 | 364 | **56.67** | 19 | 33 |
| I.V.A. Richards | West Indies | 28 | 47 | 2 | 2500 | 291 | **55.55** | 8 | 8 |
| E. Tyldesley | England | 14 | 20 | 2 | 990 | 122 | **55.00** | 3 | 6 |
| C.A. Davis | West Indies | 15 | 29 | 5 | 1301 | 183 | **54.20** | 4 | 4 |
| A.D. Nourse | South Africa | 34 | 62 | 7 | 2960 | 231 | **53.81** | 9 | 14 |
| G.S. Chappell | Australia | 51 | 90 | 13 | 4097 | 247* | **53.20** | 14 | 20 |
| A. Melville | South Africa | 11 | 19 | 2 | 894 | 189 | **52.58** | 4 | 3 |
| C.F. Walters | England | 11 | 18 | 3 | 784 | 102 | **52.26** | 1 | 7 |
| J. Ryder | Australia | 20 | 32 | 5 | 1394 | 201* | **51.62** | 3 | 9 |
| G. Boycott | England | 72 | 125 | 17 | 5516 | 246* | **51.07** | 15 | 32 |
| D.C.S. Compton | England | 78 | 131 | 15 | 5807 | 278 | **50.06** | 17 | 28 |

# HIGHEST AGGREGATES IN A RUBBER

| | | | M | I | NO | Runs | HS | Avge | 100 | 50 |
|---|---|---|---|---|---|---|---|---|---|---|
| D.G. Bradman | A v E | 1930 | 5 | 7 | 0 | **974** | 334 | 139.14 | 4 | – |
| W.R. Hammond | E v A | 1928-29 | 5 | 9 | 1 | **905** | 251 | 113.12 | 4 | – |
| R.N. Harvey | A v SA | 1952-53 | 5 | 9 | 0 | **834** | 205 | 92.66 | 4 | 3 |
| I.V.A. Richards | WI v E | 1976 | 4 | 7 | 0 | **829** | 291 | 118.42 | 3 | 2 |
| C.L. Walcott | WI v A | 1954-55 | 5 | 10 | 0 | **827** | 155 | 82.70 | 5 | 2 |
| G. St A. Sobers | WI v P | 1957-58 | 5 | 8 | 2 | **824** | 365* | 137.33 | 3 | 3 |
| D.G. Bradman | A v E | 1936-37 | 5 | 9 | 0 | **810** | 270 | 90.00 | 3 | 1 |
| D.G. Bradman | A v SA | 1931-32 | 5 | 5 | 1 | **806** | 299* | 201.50 | 4 | – |
| E. de C. Weekes | WI v I | 1948-49 | 5 | 7 | 0 | **779** | 194 | 111.28 | 4 | 2 |
| S.M. Gavaskar | I v WI | 1970-71 | 4 | 8 | 3 | **774** | 220 | 154.80 | 4 | 3 |
| D.G. Bradman | A v E | 1934 | 5 | 8 | 0 | **758** | 304 | 94.75 | 2 | 1 |
| D.C.S. Compton | E v SA | 1947 | 5 | 8 | 0 | **753** | 208 | 94.12 | 4 | 2 |
| H. Sutcliffe | E v A | 1924-25 | 5 | 9 | 0 | **734** | 176 | 81.55 | 4 | 2 |
| G.A. Faulkner | SA v A | 1910-11 | 5 | 10 | 0 | **732** | 204 | 73.20 | 2 | 5 |
| G. St A. Sobers | WI v E | 1966 | 5 | 8 | 1 | **722** | 174 | 103.14 | 3 | 2 |
| E. de C. Weekes | WI v I | 1952-53 | 5 | 8 | 1 | **716** | 207 | 102.28 | 3 | 2 |
| D.G. Bradman | A v I | 1947-48 | 5 | 6 | 2 | **715** | 201 | 178.75 | 4 | 1 |
| G.St A. Sobers | WI v E | 1959-60 | 5 | 8 | 1 | **709** | 226 | 101.28 | 3 | 1 |
| G.A. Headley | WI v E | 1929-30 | 4 | 8 | 0 | **703** | 223 | 87.87 | 4 | – |
| G.S. Chappell | A v WI | 1975-76 | 6 | 11 | 5 | **702** | 182* | 117.00 | 3 | 3 |
| K.D. Walters | A v WI | 1968-69 | 4 | 6 | 0 | **699** | 242 | 116.50 | 4 | 2 |
| C.L. Walcott | WI v E | 1953-54 | 5 | 10 | 2 | **698** | 220 | 87.25 | 3 | 3 |
| A.R. Morris | A v E | 1948 | 5 | 9 | 1 | **696** | 196 | 87.00 | 3 | 3 |
| E.H. Hendren | E v WI | 1929-30 | 4 | 8 | 2 | **693** | 205* | 115.50 | 2 | 5 |
| D.G. Bradman | A v E | 1946-47 | 5 | 8 | 1 | **680** | 234 | 97.14 | 2 | 3 |
| L. Hutton | E v WI | 1953-54 | 5 | 8 | 1 | **677** | 205 | 96.71 | 2 | 3 |
| G.M. Turner | NZ v WI | 1971-72 | 5 | 8 | 1 | **672** | 259 | 96.00 | 2 | 2 |
| W.M. Lawry | A v WI | 1968-69 | 5 | 8 | 0 | **667** | 205 | 83.37 | 3 | 2 |
| D.L. Amiss | E v WI | 1973-74 | 5 | 9 | 1 | **663** | 262* | 82.87 | 3 | – |
| J.B. Hobbs | E v A | 1911-12 | 5 | 9 | 1 | **662** | 187 | 82.75 | 3 | 1 |
| V.T. Trumper | A v SA | 1910-11 | 5 | 9 | 2 | **661** | 214* | 94.42 | 2 | 2 |

## HIGHEST AGGREGATES IN A RUBBER – *continued*

| | | | M | I | NO | Runs | HS | Avge | 100 | 50 |
|---|---|---|---|---|---|---|---|---|---|---|
| R.N. Harvey | A v SA | 1949-50 | 5 | 8 | 3 | **660** | 178 | 132.00 | 4 | 1 |
| G. Boycott | E v A | 1970-71 | 5 | 10 | 3 | **657** | 142* | 93.85 | 2 | 5 |
| E. Paynter | E v SA | 1938-39 | 5 | 8 | 0 | **653** | 243 | 81.62 | 3 | 2 |
| R.N. Harvey | A v WI | 1954-55 | 5 | 7 | 1 | **650** | 204 | 108.33 | 3 | 1 |
| J.H. Edrich | E v A | 1970-71 | 6 | 11 | 2 | **648** | 130 | 72.00 | 2 | 4 |
| D.N. Sardesai | I v WI | 1970-71 | 5 | 8 | 0 | **642** | 212 | 80.25 | 3 | 1 |
| C.H. Lloyd | WI v I | 1974-75 | 5 | 9 | 1 | **636** | 242* | 79.20 | 2 | 1 |
| Hanif Mohammad | P v WI | 1957-58 | 5 | 9 | 0 | **628** | 337 | 69.77 | 1 | 3 |
| K.R. Stackpole | A v E | 1970-71 | 6 | 12 | 0 | **627** | 207 | 52.25 | 2 | 2 |
| C.C. Hunte | WI v P | 1957-58 | 5 | 9 | 1 | **622** | 260 | 77.75 | 3 | – |
| A.D. Nourse | SA v E | 1947 | 5 | 9 | 0 | **621** | 149 | 69.00 | 2 | 5 |
| L.G. Rowe | WI v E | 1973-74 | 5 | 7 | 0 | **616** | 302 | 88.00 | 3 | – |
| B. Sutcliffe | NZ v I | 1955-56 | 5 | 9 | 2 | **611** | 230* | 87.28 | 2 | 1 |
| W.R. Hammond | E v SA | 1938-39 | 5 | 8 | 1 | **609** | 181 | 87.00 | 3 | 2 |
| G.S. Chappell | A v E | 1974-75 | 6 | 11 | 0 | **608** | 144 | 55.27 | 2 | 5 |
| D.T. Lindsay | SA v A | 1966-67 | 5 | 7 | 0 | **606** | 182 | 86.57 | 2 | 3 |
| E.J. Barlow | SA v A | 1963-64 | 5 | 10 | 2 | **603** | 201 | 75.37 | 3 | 1 |

## CARRYING BAT THROUGH A COMPLETED INNINGS

| | Score | Total | Opponents | Venue | Rubber |
|---|---|---|---|---|---|
| **ENGLAND** | | | | | |
| R. Abel | 132* | 307 | Australia | Sydney | 1891-92 |
| P.F. Warner‡ | 132* | 237 | South Africa | Johannesburg[1] | 1898-99 |
| L. Hutton | 202* | 344 | West Indies | Oval | 1950 |
| L. Hutton | 156* | 272 | Australia | Adelaide | 1950-51 |
| **AUSTRALIA** | | | | | |
| J.E. Barrett‡ | 67* | 176 | England | Lord's | 1890 |
| W.W. Armstrong | 159* | 309 | South Africa | Johannesburg[1] | 1902-03 |
| W. Bardsley | 193* | 383 | England | Lord's | 1926 |
| W.M. Woodfull | 30* | 66† | England | Brisbane[1] | 1928-29 |
| W.M. Woodfull | 73* | 193† | England | Adelaide | 1932-33 |
| W.A. Brown | 206* | 422 | England | Lord's | 1938 |
| W.M. Lawry | 49* | 107 | India | Delhi | 1969-70 |
| W.M. Lawry | 60* | 116† | England | Sydney | 1970-71 |
| I.R. Redpath | 159* | 346 | New Zealand | Auckland | 1973-74 |
| **SOUTH AFRICA** | | | | | |
| A.B. Tancred | 26* | 47 | England | Cape Town | 1888-89 |
| J.W. Zulch | 43* | 103 | England | Cape Town | 1909-10 |
| T.L. Goddard | 56* | 99 | Australia | Cape Town | 1957-58 |
| D.J. McGlew | 127* | 292 | New Zealand | Durban[2] | 1961-62 |
| **WEST INDIES** | | | | | |
| F.M.M. Worrell | 191* | 372 | England | Nottingham | 1957 |
| C.C. Hunte | 60* | 131 | Australia | Port-of-Spain | 1964-65 |
| **NEW ZEALAND** | | | | | |
| G.M. Turner | 43* | 131 | England | Lord's | 1969 |
| G.M. Turner | 233* | 386 | West Indies | Kingston | 1971-72 |
| **INDIA** | | | | | |
| Nil | | | | | |
| **PAKISTAN** | | | | | |
| Nazar Mohammad | 124* | 331 | India | Lucknow | 1952-53 |

‡ *On debut in Test cricket.*
† *Completed innings in which one or more batsmen were retired or absent.*
*G.M. Turner is the youngest player to carry his bat through a Test match innings; he was 22 years and 63 days old when he first achieved this feat.*
*D.L. Amiss (262*) batted throughout England's innings of 432-9 against West Indies at Kingston in 1973-74. His unbroken tenth-wicket partnership with R.G.D. Willis (3*) added 40 runs in 53 minutes.*

# HIGHEST INDIVIDUAL INNINGS

| | | | | |
|---|---|---|---|---|
| 365* | G.St A. Sobers | West Indies v Pakistan | Kingston | 1957-58 |
| 364 | L. Hutton | England v Australia | Oval | 1938 |
| 337 | Hanif Mohammad | Pakistan v West Indies | Bridgetown | 1957-58 |
| 336* | W.R. Hammond | England v New Zealand | Auckland | 1932-33 |
| 334 | D.G. Bradman | Australia v England | Leeds | 1930 |
| 325 | A. Sandham | England v West Indies | Kingston | 1929-30 |
| 311 | R.B. Simpson | Australia v England | Manchester | 1964 |
| 310* | J.H. Edrich | England v New Zealand | Leeds | 1965 |
| 307 | R.M. Cowper | Australia v England | Melbourne | 1965-66 |
| 304 | D.G. Bradman | Australia v England | Leeds | 1934 |
| 302 | L.G. Rowe | West Indies v England | Bridgetown | 1973-74 |
| 299* | D.G. Bradman | Australia v South Africa | Adelaide | 1931-32 |
| 291 | I.V.A. Richards | West Indies v England | Oval | 1976 |
| 287 | R.E. Foster | England v Australia | Sydney | 1903-04 |
| 285* | P.B.H. May | England v West Indies | Birmingham | 1957 |
| 278 | D.C.S. Compton | England v Pakistan | Nottingham | 1954 |
| 274 | R.G. Pollock | South Africa v Australia | Durban[2] | 1969-70 |
| 274 | Zaheer Abbas | Pakistan v England | Birmingham | 1971 |
| 270* | G.A. Headley | West Indies v England | Kingston | 1934-35 |
| 270 | D.G. Bradman | Australia v England | Melbourne | 1936-37 |
| 266 | W.H. Ponsford | Australia v England | Oval | 1934 |
| 262* | D.L. Amiss | England v West Indies | Kingston | 1973-74 |
| 261 | F.M.M. Worrell | West Indies v England | Nottingham | 1950 |
| 260 | C.C. Hunte | West Indies v Pakistan | Kingston | 1957-58 |
| 259 | G.M. Turner | New Zealand v West Indies | Georgetown | 1971-72 |
| 258 | T.W. Graveney | England v West Indies | Nottingham | 1957 |
| 258 | S.M. Nurse | West Indies v New Zealand | Christchurch | 1968-69 |
| 256 | R.B. Kanhai | West Indies v India | Calcutta | 1958-59 |
| 256 | K.F. Barrington | England v Australia | Manchester | 1964 |
| 255* | D.J. McGlew | South Africa v New Zealand | Wellington | 1952-53 |
| 254 | D.G. Bradman | Australia v England | Lord's | 1930 |
| 251 | W.R. Hammond | England v Australia | Sydney | 1928-29 |
| 250 | K.D. Walters | Australia v New Zealand | Christchurch | 1976-77 |
| 247* | G.S. Chappell | Australia v New Zealand | Wellington | 1973-74 |
| 246* | G. Boycott | England v India | Leeds | 1967 |
| 244 | D.G. Bradman | Australia v England | Oval | 1934 |
| 243 | E. Paynter | England v South Africa | Durban[2] | 1938-39 |
| 242* | C.H. Lloyd | West Indies v India | Bombay[3] | 1974-75 |
| 242 | K.D. Walters | Australia v West Indies | Sydney | 1968-69 |
| 240 | W.R. Hammond | England v Australia | Lord's | 1938 |
| 240 | Zaheer Abbas | Pakistan v England | Oval | 1974 |
| 239 | G.T. Dowling | New Zealand v India | Christchurch | 1967-68 |
| 237 | F.M.M. Worrell | West Indies v India | Kingston | 1952-53 |
| 236 | E.A.B. Rowan | South Africa v England | Leeds | 1951 |
| 234 | D.G. Bradman | Australia v England | Sydney | 1946-47 |
| 234 | S.G. Barnes | Australia v England | Sydney | 1946-47 |
| 232 | D.G. Bradman | Australia v England | Oval | 1930 |
| 232 | S.J. McCabe | Australia v England | Nottingham | 1938 |
| 232 | I.V.A. Richards | West Indies v England | Nottingham | 1976 |
| 231* | W.R. Hammond | England v Australia | Sydney | 1936-37 |
| 231 | A.D. Nourse | South Africa v Australia | Johannesburg[1] | 1935-36 |
| 231 | V.M.H. Mankad | India v New Zealand | Madras[2] | 1955-56 |
| 230* | B. Sutcliffe | New Zealand v India | Delhi | 1955-56 |
| 227 | W.R. Hammond | England v New Zealand | Christchurch | 1932-33 |
| 226 | D.G. Bradman | Australia v South Africa | Brisbane[2] | 1931-32 |
| 226 | G.St A. Sobers | West Indies v England | Bridgetown | 1959-60 |
| 225 | R.B. Simpson | Australia v England | Adelaide | 1965-66 |
| 223* | G.M. Turner | New Zealand v West Indies | Kingston | 1971-72 |
| 223 | G.A. Headley | West Indies v England | Kingston | 1929-30 |
| 223 | D.G. Bradman | Australia v West Indies | Brisbane[1] | 1930-31 |
| 223 | P.R. Umrigar | India v New Zealand | Hyderabad | 1955-56 |

| 223 | V.M.H. Mankad | India v New Zealand | Bombay$^2$ | 1955-56 |
|---|---|---|---|---|
| 220 | C.L. Walcott | West Indies v England | Bridgetown | 1953-54 |
| 220 | S.M. Gavaskar | India v West Indies | Port-of-Spain | 1970-71 |
| 219 | W.J. Edrich | England v South Africa | Durban$^2$ | 1938-39 |
| 219 | D. St E. Atkinson | West Indies v Australia | Bridgetown | 1954-55 |
| 217 | W.R. Hammond | England v India | Oval | 1936 |
| 217 | R.B. Kanhai | West Indies v Pakistan | Lahore$^1$ | 1958-59 |
| 216* | E. Paynter | England v Australia | Nottingham | 1938 |
| 216 | K.W.R. Fletcher | England v New Zealand | Auckland | 1974-75 |
| 214* | V.T. Trumper | Australia v South Africa | Adelaide | 1910-11 |
| 214* | D. Lloyd | England v India | Birmingham | 1974 |
| 214 | L.G. Rowe | West Indies v New Zealand | Kingston | 1971-72 |
| 212 | D.G. Bradman | Australia v England | Adelaide | 1936-37 |
| 212 | D.N. Sardesai | India v West Indies | Kingston | 1970-71 |
| 211 | W.L. Murdoch | Australia v England | Oval | 1884 |
| 211 | J.B. Hobbs | England v South Africa | Lord's | 1924 |
| 210 | W.M. Lawry | Australia v West Indies | Bridgetown | 1964-65 |
| 209* | B.F. Butcher | West Indies v England | Nottingham | 1966 |
| 209 | C.A. Roach | West Indies v England | Georgetown | 1929-30 |
| 209 | Imtiaz Ahmed | Pakistan v New Zealand | Lahore$^1$ | 1955-56 |
| 209 | R.G. Pollock | South Africa v Australia | Cape Town | 1966-67 |
| 208 | D.C.S. Compton | England v South Africa | Lord's | 1947 |
| 208 | A.D. Nourse | South Africa v England | Nottingham | 1951 |
| 207 | E. de C. Weekes | West Indies v India | Port-of-Spain | 1952-53 |
| 207 | K.R. Stackpole | Australia v England | Brisbane$^2$ | 1970-71 |
| 206* | W.A. Brown | Australia v England | Lord's | 1938 |
| 206 | M.P. Donnelly | New Zealand v England | Lord's | 1949 |
| 206 | L. Hutton | England v New Zealand | Oval | 1949 |
| 206 | A.R. Morris | Australia v England | Adelaide | 1950-51 |
| 206 | E. de C. Weekes | West Indies v England | Port-of-Spain | 1953-54 |
| 206 | Javed Miandad | Pakistan v New Zealand | Karachi | 1976-77 |
| 205* | E.H. Hendren | England v West Indies | Port-of-Spain | 1929-30 |
| 205* | J. Hardstaff, jr | England v India | Lord's | 1946 |
| 205 | R.N. Harvey | Australia v South Africa | Melbourne | 1952-53 |
| 205 | L. Hutton | England v West Indies | Kingston | 1953-54 |
| 205 | E.R. Dexter | England v Pakistan | Karachi | 1961-62 |
| 205 | W.M. Lawry | Australia v West Indies | Melbourne | 1968-69 |
| 204 | G.A. Faulkner | South Africa v. Australia | Melbourne | 1910-11 |
| 204 | R.N. Harvey | Australia v West Indies | Kingston | 1954-55 |
| 203* | Nawab of Pataudi, jr | India v England | Delhi | 1963-64 |
| 203* | Hanif Mohammad | Pakistan v New Zealand | Lahore$^2$ | 1964-65 |
| 203 | H.L. Collins | Australia v South Africa | Johannesburg$^1$ | 1921-22 |
| 203 | D.L. Amiss | England v West Indies | Oval | 1976 |
| 202* | L. Hutton | England v West Indies | Oval | 1950 |
| 201* | J. Ryder | Australia v England | Adelaide | 1924-25 |
| 201 | S.E. Gregory | Australia v England | Sydney | 1894-95 |
| 201 | D.G. Bradman | Australia v India | Adelaide | 1947-48 |
| 201 | E.J. Barlow | South Africa v Australia | Adelaide | 1963-64 |
| 201 | R.B. Simpson | Australia v West Indies | Bridgetown | 1964-65 |
| 201 | S.M. Nurse | West Indies v Australia | Bridgetown | 1964-65 |
| 201 | Mushtaq Mohammad | Pakistan v New Zealand | Dunedin | 1972-73 |
| 200* | D.N. Sardesai | India v New Zealand | Bombay$^2$ | 1964-65 |
| 200 | W.R. Hammond | England v Australia | Melbourne | 1928-29 |

## BATSMEN SCORING MOST HUNDREDS

| | | | | | Opponents | | | | |
|---|---|---|---|---|---|---|---|---|---|
| | | 100 | HS | E | A | SA | WI | NZ | I | P |
| D.G. Bradman | Australia | 29 | 334 | 19 | – | 4 | 2 | – | 4 | – |
| G.St A. Sobers | West Indies | 26 | 365* | 10 | 4 | – | – | 1 | 8 | 3 |
| M.C. Cowdrey | England | 22 | 182 | – | 5 | 3 | 6 | 2 | 3 | 3 |
| W.R. Hammond | England | 22 | 336* | – | 9 | 6 | 1 | 4 | 2 | – |
| R.N. Harvey | Australia | 21 | 205 | 6 | – | 8 | 3 | – | 4 | – |

## BATSMEN SCORING MOST HUNDREDS – *continued*

| | | 100 | HS | E | A | SA | WI | NZ | I | P |
|---|---|---|---|---|---|---|---|---|---|---|
| | | | | | | *Opponents* | | | | |
| K.F. Barrington | England | 20 | 256 | – | 5 | 2 | 3 | 3 | 3 | 4 |
| L. Hutton | England | 19 | 364 | – | 5 | 4 | 5 | 3 | 2 | – |
| D.C.S. Compton | England | 17 | 278 | – | 5 | 7 | 2 | 2 | – | 1 |
| H. Sutcliffe | England | 16 | 194 | – | 8 | 6 | – | 2 | – | – |
| G. Boycott | England | 15 | 246* | – | 5 | 1 | 4 | 1 | 1 | 3 |
| J.B. Hobbs | England | 15 | 211 | – | 12 | 2 | 1 | – | – | – |
| R.B. Kanhai | West Indies | 15 | 256 | 5 | 5 | – | – | – | 4 | 1 |
| C.L. Walcott | West Indies | 15 | 220 | 4 | 5 | – | – | 1 | 4 | 1 |
| E. de C. Weekes | West Indies | 15 | 207 | 3 | 1 | – | – | 3 | 7 | 1 |
| G.S. Chappell | Australia | 14 | 247* | 6 | – | – | 4 | 2 | – | 2 |
| I.M. Chappell | Australia | 14 | 196 | 4 | – | – | 5 | 2 | 2 | 1 |
| K.D. Walters | Australia | 14 | 250 | 4 | – | – | 6 | 2 | 1 | 1 |
| S.M. Gavaskar | India | 13 | 220 | 2 | 3 | – | 6 | 2 | – | – |
| W.M. Lawry | Australia | 13 | 210 | 7 | – | 1 | 4 | – | 1 | – |
| P.B.H. May | England | 13 | 285* | – | 3 | 3 | 3 | 3 | 1 | – |
| J.H. Edrich | England | 12 | 310* | – | 7 | – | 1 | 3 | 1 | – |
| Hanif Mohammad | Pakistan | 12 | 337 | 3 | 2 | – | 2 | 3 | 2 | – |
| A.R. Morris | Australia | 12 | 206 | 8 | – | 2 | 1 | – | 1 | – |
| P.R. Umrigar | India | 12 | 223 | 3 | – | – | 3 | 1 | – | 5 |
| D.L. Amiss | England | 11 | 262* | – | – | – | 4 | 2 | 2 | 3 |
| T.W. Graveney | England | 11 | 258 | – | 1 | – | 5 | – | 2 | 3 |
| C.H. Lloyd | West Indies | 11 | 242* | 3 | 4 | – | – | – | 3 | 1 |
| A.L. Hassett | Australia | 10 | 198* | 4 | – | 3 | 2 | – | 1 | – |
| G.A. Headley | West Indies | 10 | 270* | 8 | 2 | – | – | – | – | – |
| A.I. Kallicharran | West Indies | 10 | 158 | 2 | 3 | – | – | 2 | 2 | 1 |
| Mushtaq Mohammad | Pakistan | 10 | 201 | 3 | 1 | – | 2 | 3 | 1 | – |
| R.B. Simpson | Australia | 10 | 311 | 2 | – | 1 | 1 | – | 4 | 2 |

## MOST HUNDREDS IN A RUBBER

*FIVE*
| | | | |
|---|---|---|---|
| C.L. Walcott | | West Indies v Australia | 1954-55 |

*FOUR*
| | | | |
|---|---|---|---|
| D.G. Bradman | (3) | Australia v England | 1930 |
| | | Australia v South Africa | 1931-32 |
| | | Australia v India | 1947-48 |
| D.C.S. Compton | (1) | England v South Africa | 1947 |
| S.M. Gavaskar | (1) | India v West Indies | 1970-71 |
| W.R. Hammond | (1) | England v Australia | 1928-29 |
| R.N. Harvey | (2) | Australia v South Africa | 1949-50 |
| | | Australia v South Africa | 1952-53 |
| G.A. Headley | (1) | West Indies v England | 1929-30 |
| H. Sutcliffe | (2) | England v Australia | 1924-25 |
| | | England v South Africa | 1929 |
| K.D. Walters | (1) | Australia v West Indies | 1968-69 |
| E. de C. Weekes | (1) | West Indies v India | 1948-49 |

## MOST DOUBLE CENTURIES IN A RUBBER

*THREE*
| | | | |
|---|---|---|---|
| D.G. Bradman | | Australia v England | 1930 |

*TWO*
| | | | |
|---|---|---|---|
| D.G. Bradman | (3) | Australia v South Africa | 1931-32 |
| | | Australia v England | 1934 |
| | | Australia v England | 1936-37 |
| W.R. Hammond | (2) | England v Australia | 1928-29 |
| | | England v New Zealand | 1932-33 |
| V.M.H. Mankad | (1) | India v New Zealand | 1955-56 |
| I.V.A. Richards | (1) | West Indies v England | 1976 |
| G.M. Turner | (1) | New Zealand v West Indies | 1971-72 |

# HUNDREDS IN MOST CONSECUTIVE INNINGS

| | | | Opponents | Venue | Rubber |
|---|---|---|---|---|---|
| *FIVE* | | | | | |
| E. de C. Weekes | West Indies | 141 | England | Kingston | 1947-48 |
| | | 128 | India | Delhi | 1948-49 |
| | | 194 | India | Bombay[2] | 1948-49 |
| | | 162) 101) | India | Calcutta | 1948-49 |
| *FOUR* | | | | | |
| J.H.W. Fingleton | Australia | 112 | South Africa | Cape Town | 1935-36 |
| | | 108 | South Africa | Johannesburg[1] | 1935-36 |
| | | 118 | South Africa | Durban[2] | 1935-36 |
| | | 100 | England | Brisbane[2] | 1936-37 |
| A. Melville | South Africa | 103 | England | Durban[2] | 1938-39 |
| | | 189 ) 104*) | England | Nottingham | 1947 |
| | | 117 | England | Lord's | 1947 |
| *THREE* | | | | | |
| W. Bardsley | Australia | 136) 130) | England | Oval | 1909 |
| | | 132 | South Africa | Sydney | 1910-11 |
| G. Boycott | England | 119* | Australia | Adelaide | 1970-71 |
| | | 121* | Pakistan | Lord's | 1971 |
| | | 112 | Pakistan | Leeds | 1971 |
| D.G. Bradman | Australia | 132 ) 127*) | India | Melbourne | 1947-48 |
| | | 201 | India | Adelaide | 1947-48 |
| D.C.S. Compton | England | 163 | South Africa | Nottingham | 1947 |
| | | 208 | South Africa | Lord's | 1947 |
| | | 115 | South Africa | Manchester | 1947 |
| S.M. Gavaskar | India | 117* | West Indies | Bridgetown | 1970-71 |
| | | 124) 220) | West Indies | Port-of-Spain | 1970-71 |
| C.G. Greenidge | West Indies | 134) 101) | England | Manchester | 1976 |
| | | 115 | England | Leeds | 1976 |
| V.S. Hazare | India | 122 | West Indies | Bombay[2] | 1948-49 |
| | | 164* | England | Delhi | 1951-52 |
| | | 155 | England | Bombay[2] | 1951-52 |
| G.A. Headley | West Indies | 270* | England | Kingston | 1934-35 |
| | | 106) 107) | England | Lord's | 1939 |
| C.G. Macartney | Australia | 133* | England | Lord's | 1926 |
| | | 151 | England | Leeds | 1926 |
| | | 109 | England | Manchester | 1926 |
| A.R. Morris | Australia | 155 | England | Melbourne | 1946-47 |
| | | 122 ) 124*) | England | Adelaide | 1946-47 |
| G. St A. Sobers | West Indies | 365* | Pakistan | Kingston | 1957-58 |
| | | 125 ) 109*) | Pakistan | Georgetown | 1957-58 |
| H. Sutcliffe | England | 115 | Australia | Sydney | 1924-25 |
| | | 176) 127) | Australia | Melbourne | 1924-25 |
| P.R. Umrigar | India | 117 | Pakistan | Madras[2] | 1960-61 |
| | | 112 | Pakistan | Delhi | 1960-61 |
| | | 147* | England | Kanpur | 1961-62 |
| E. de C. Weekes | West Indies | 123 | New Zealand | Dunedin | 1955-56 |
| | | 103 | New Zealand | Christchurch | 1955-56 |
| | | 156 | New Zealand | Wellington | 1955-56 |

# HUNDRED IN EACH INNINGS OF A MATCH

| ENGLAND | | | Opponents | Venue | Rubber |
|---|---|---|---|---|---|
| C.A.G. Russell | 140 | 111 | South Africa | Durban[2] | 1922-23 |
| H. Sutcliffe | 176 | 127 | Australia | Melbourne | 1924-25 |
| W.R. Hammond | 119* | 177 | Australia | Adelaide | 1928-29 |
| H. Sutcliffe | 104 | 109* | South Africa | Oval | 1929 |
| E. Paynter | 117 | 100 | South Africa | Johannesburg[1] | 1938-39 |
| D.C.S. Compton | 147 | 103* | Australia | Adelaide | 1946-47 |

| AUSTRALIA | | | | | |
|---|---|---|---|---|---|
| W. Bardsley | 136 | 130 | England | Oval | 1909 |
| A.R. Morris | 122 | 124* | England | Adelaide | 1946-47 |
| D.G. Bradman | 132 | 127* | India | Melbourne | 1947-48 |
| J. Moroney | 118 | 101* | South Africa | Johannesburg[2] | 1949-50 |
| R.B. Simpson | 153 | 115 | Pakistan | Karachi | 1964-65 |
| K.D. Walters | 242 | 103 | West Indies | Sydney | 1968-69 |
| I.M. Chappell | 145 | 121 | New Zealand | Wellington | 1973-74 |
| G.S. Chappell | 247* | 133 | New Zealand | Wellington | 1973-74 |
| G.S. Chappell | 123 | 109* | West Indies | Brisbane[2] | 1975-76 |

| SOUTH AFRICA | | | | | |
|---|---|---|---|---|---|
| A. Melville | 189 | 104* | England | Nottingham | 1947 |
| B. Mitchell | 120 | 189* | England | Oval | 1947 |

| WEST INDIES | | | | | |
|---|---|---|---|---|---|
| G.A. Headley | 114 | 112 | England | Georgetown | 1929-30 |
| G.A. Headley | 106 | 107 | England | Lord's | 1939 |
| E. de C. Weekes | 162 | 101 | India | Calcutta | 1948-49 |
| C.L. Walcott | 126 | 110 | Australia | Port-of-Spain | 1954-55 |
| C.L. Walcott | 155 | 110 | Australia | Kingston | 1954-55 |
| G.St A. Sobers | 125 | 109* | Pakistan | Georgetown | 1957-58 |
| R.B. Kanhai | 117 | 115 | Australia | Adelaide | 1960-61 |
| L.G. Rowe | 214 | 100* | New Zealand | Kingston | 1971-72 |
| C.G. Greenidge | 134 | 101 | England | Manchester | 1976 |

| NEW ZEALAND | | | | | |
|---|---|---|---|---|---|
| G.M. Turner | 101 | 110* | Australia | Christchurch | 1973-74 |
| G.P. Howarth | 122 | 102 | England | Auckland | 1977-78 |

| INDIA | | | | | |
|---|---|---|---|---|---|
| V.S. Hazare | 116 | 145 | Australia | Adelaide | 1947-48 |
| S.M. Gavaskar | 124 | 220 | West Indies | Port-of-Spain | 1970-71 |

| PAKISTAN | | | | | |
|---|---|---|---|---|---|
| Hanif Mohammad | 111 | 104 | England | Dacca | 1961-62 |

*L.G. Rowe achieved this feat in his first Test match.*
*G. Boycott scored 99 and 112 for England v West Indies at Port-of-Spain in 1973-74.*

# HUNDRED ON DEBUT

## IN BOTH INNINGS

| L.G. Rowe | 214 100* | West Indies v New Zealand | Kingston | 1971-72 |
|---|---|---|---|---|

## IN FIRST INNINGS

| C. Bannerman | 165* | Australia v England | Melbourne | 1876-77 |
|---|---|---|---|---|
| W.G. Grace | 152 | England v Australia | Oval | 1880 |
| H. Graham | 107 | Australia v England | Lord's | 1893 |
| R.E. Foster | 287 | England v Australia | Sydney | 1903-04 |

|  |  | *Opponents* | *Venue* | *Rubber* |
|---|---|---|---|---|
| G. Gunn | 119 | England v Australia | Sydney | 1907-08 |
| W.H. Ponsford | 110 | Australia v England | Sydney | 1924-25 |
| A. Jackson | 164 | Australia v England | Adelaide | 1928-29 |
| J.E. Mills | 117 | New Zealand v England | Wellington | 1929-30 |
| Nawab of Pataudi, sr | 102 | England v Australia | Sydney | 1932-33 |
| B.H. Valentine | 136 | England v India | Bombay[1] | 1933-34 |
| S.C. Griffith | 140 | England v West Indies | Port-of-Spain | 1947-48 |
| A.G. Ganteaume | 112 | West Indies v England | Port-of-Spain | 1947-48 |
| P.B.H. May | 138 | England v South Africa | Leeds | 1951 |
| D.H. Shodhan | 110 | India v Pakistan | Calcutta | 1952-53 |
| B.H. Pairaudeau | 115 | West Indies v India | Port-of-Spain | 1952-53 |
| A.G. Kripal Singh | 100* | India v New Zealand | Hyderabad | 1955-56 |
| C.C. Hunte | 142 | West Indies v Pakistan | Bridgetown | 1957-58 |
| C.A. Milton | 104* | England v New Zealand | Leeds | 1958 |
| Hanumant Singh | 105 | India v England | Delhi | 1963-64 |
| Khalid Ibadulla | 166 | Pakistan v Australia | Karachi | 1964-65 |
| B.R. Taylor | 105 | New Zealand v India | Calcutta | 1964-65 |
| K.D. Walters | 155 | Australia v England | Brisbane[2] | 1965-66 |
| J.H. Hampshire | 107 | England v West Indies | Lord's | 1969 |
| G.S. Chappell | 108 | Australia v England | Perth | 1970-71 |
| A.I. Kallicharran | 100* | West Indies v New Zealand | Georgetown | 1971-72 |
| R.E. Redmond | 107 | New Zealand v Pakistan | Auckland | 1972-73 |
| G.J. Cosier | 109 | Australia v West Indies | Melbourne | 1975-76 |
| S. Amarnath | 124 | India v New Zealand | Auckland | 1975-76 |
| Javed Miandad | 163 | Pakistan v New Zealand | Lahore[2] | 1976-77 |

*IN SECOND INNINGS*

|  |  |  |  |  |
|---|---|---|---|---|
| K.S. Ranjitsinhji | 154* | England v Australia | Manchester | 1896 |
| P.F. Warner | 132* | England v South Africa | Johannesburg[1] | 1898-99 |
| R.A. Duff | 104 | Australia v England | Melbourne | 1901-02 |
| R.J. Hartigan | 116 | Australia v England | Adelaide | 1907-08 |
| H.L. Collins | 104 | Australia v England | Sydney | 1920-21 |
| G.A. Headley | 176 | West Indies v England | Bridgetown | 1929-30 |
| L. Amarnath | 118 | India v England | Bombay[1] | 1933-34 |
| P.A. Gibb | 106 | England v South Africa | Johannesburg[1] | 1938-39 |
| J.W. Burke | 101* | Australia v England | Adelaide | 1950-51 |
| O.G. Smith | 104 | West Indies v Australia | Kingston | 1954-55 |
| A.A. Baig | 112 | India v England | Manchester | 1959 |
| G.R. Viswanath | 137 | India v Australia | Kanpur | 1969-70 |
| F.C. Hayes | 106* | England v West Indies | Oval | 1973 |
| C.G. Greenidge | 107 | West Indies v India | Bangalore | 1974-75 |
| L. Baichan | 105* | West Indies v Pakistan | Lahore[2] | 1974-75 |
| A.B. Williams | 100 | West Indies v Australia | Georgetown | 1977-78 |

*A.I. Kallicharran also scored a hundred in his second Test innings — 101 v New Zealand at Port-of-Spain, 1971-72.*

*The following scored 99 in their debut match:*

| A.G. Chipperfield | *(1st innings)* | *Australia v England* | *Nottingham* | *1934* |
|---|---|---|---|---|
| R.J. Christiani | *(2nd innings)* | *West Indies v England* | *Bridgetown* | *1947-48* |

## MOST RUNS IN FIRST TEST MATCH

| 314 | L.G. Rowe | (214, 100*) | West Indies v New Zealand | Kingston | 1971-72 |
|---|---|---|---|---|---|
| 306 | R.E. Foster | (287, 19) | England v Australia | Sydney | 1903-04 |

# HUNDRED BEFORE LUNCH

| *FIRST DAY* | Lunch score | | | |
|---|---|---|---|---|
| V.T. Trumper | 103* | Australia v England | Manchester | 1902 |
| C.G. Macartney | 112* | Australia v England | Leeds | 1926 |
| D.G. Bradman | 105* | Australia v England | Leeds | 1930 |
| Majid Khan | 108* | Pakistan v New Zealand | Karachi | 1976-77 |

| *OTHER DAYS* | Overnight score | Lunch score | | | |
|---|---|---|---|---|---|
| K.S. Ranjitsinhji | 41* | 154* | E v A | Manchester | 1896 |
| C. Hill | 22* | 138* | A v SA | Johannesburg[1] | 1902-03 |
| W. Bardsley | 33* | 150* | A v SA | Lord's | 1912 |
| C.P. Mead | 19* | 128* | E v A | Oval | 1921 |
| J.B. Hobbs | 12* | 114* | E v SA | Lord's | 1924 |
| H.G. Owen-Smith | 27* | 129 | SA v E | Leeds | 1929 |
| W.R. Hammond | 41* | 152* | E v NZ | Auckland | 1932-33 |
| L.E.G. Ames | 25* | 148* | E v SA | Oval | 1935 |
| S.J. McCabe | 59* | 159* | A v SA | Johannesburg[1] | 1935-36 |

## YOUNGEST PLAYERS TO SCORE A HUNDRED

| Years | Days | | | | | |
|---|---|---|---|---|---|---|
| 17 | 78 | Mushtaq Mohammad | 101 | Pakistan v India | Delhi | 1960-61 |
| 19 | 119 | Javed Miandad | 163 | Pakistan v New Zealand | Lahore | 1976-77 |
| 19 | 121 | H.G. Vivian | 100 | New Zealand v South Africa | Wellington | 1931-32 |
| 19 | 121 | R.N. Harvey | 153 | Australia v India | Melbourne | 1947-48 |
| 19 | 152 | A. Jackson | 164 | Australia v England | Adelaide | 1928-29 |
| 19 | 318 | R.G. Pollock | 122 | South Africa v Australia | Sydney | 1963-64 |
| 19 | 357 | K.D. Walters | 155 | Australia v England | Brisbane[2] | 1965-66 |
| 20 | 19 | D.C.S. Compton | 102 | England v Australia | Nottingham | 1938 |
| 20 | 58 | Hanif Mohammad | 142 | Pakistan v India | Bahawalpur | 1954-55 |
| 20 | 129 | D.G. Bradman | 112 | Australia v England | Melbourne | 1928-29 |
| 20 | 131 | A.A. Baig | 112 | India v England | Manchester | 1959 |
| 20 | 148 | H.G. Owen-Smith | 129 | South Africa v England | Leeds | 1929 |
| 20 | 154 | Saeed Ahmed | 150 | Pakistan v West Indies | Georgetown | 1957-58 |
| 20 | 230 | G.A. Headley | 176 | West Indies v England | Bridgetown | 1929-30 |
| 20 | 240 | J.W. Burke | 101* | Australia v England | Adelaide | 1950-51 |
| 20 | 253 | V.L. Manjrekar | 133 | India v England | Leeds | 1952 |
| 20 | 281 | G.R. Viswanath | 137 | India v Australia | Kanpur | 1969-70 |
| 20 | 317 | C. Hill | 188 | Australia v England | Melbourne | 1897-98 |
| 20 | 324 | J.W. Hearne | 114 | England v Australia | Melbourne | 1911-12 |
| 20 | 330 | O.G. Smith | 104 | West Indies v Australia | Kingston | 1954-55 |

*G.A. Headley scored four hundreds in Test matches before his twenty-first birthday.*

## YOUNGEST PLAYERS TO SCORE A DOUBLE CENTURY

| Years | Days | | | | | |
|---|---|---|---|---|---|---|
| 19 | 141 | Javed Miandad | 206 | Pakistan v New Zealand | Karachi | 1976-77 |
| 20 | 315 | G.A. Headley | 223 | West Indies v England | Kingston | 1929-30 |

# MAIDEN FIRST-CLASS HUNDRED IN A TEST MATCH

| | | | | |
|---|---|---|---|---|
| C. Bannerman†‡ | 165* | Australia v England | Melbourne | 1876-77 |
| W.L. Murdoch | 153* | Australia v England | Oval | 1880 |
| P.S. McDonnell | 147 | Australia v England | Sydney | 1881-82 |
| H.J.H. Scott | 102 | Australia v England | Oval | 1884 |
| H. Wood‡ | 134* | England v South Africa | Cape Town | 1891-92 |
| H. Graham† | 107 | Australia v England | Lord's | 1893 |
| A.J.L. Hill | 124 | England v South Africa | Cape Town | 1895-96 |
| J.H. Sinclair | 106 | South Africa v England | Cape Town | 1898-99 |
| P.W. Sherwell | 115 | South Africa v England | Lord's | 1907 |
| R.J. Hartigan† | 116 | Australia v England | Adelaide | 1907-08 |
| H.G. Owen-Smith | 129 | South Africa v England | Leeds | 1929 |
| C.A. Roach | 122 | West Indies v England | Bridgetown | 1929-30 |
| S.C. Griffith† | 140 | England v West Indies | Port-of-Spain | 1947-48 |
| V.L. Manjrekar | 133 | India v England | Leeds | 1952 |
| C.C. Depeiza‡ | 122 | West Indies v Australia | Bridgetown | 1954-55 |
| P.L. Winslow | 108 | South Africa v England | Manchester | 1955 |
| S.N. McGregor | 111 | New Zealand v Pakistan | Lahore[1] | 1955-56 |
| F.C.M. Alexander‡ | 108 | West Indies v Australia | Sydney | 1960-61 |
| Nasim-ul-Ghani | 101 | Pakistan v England | Lord's | 1962 |
| B.R. Taylor† | 105 | New Zealand v India | Calcutta | 1964-65 |
| B.D. Julien | 121 | West Indies v England | Lord's | 1973 |
| W.K. Lees | 152 | New Zealand v Pakistan | Karachi | 1976-77 |

† On Test debut.     ‡ Only hundred in first-class cricket.

# HUNDREDS IN TEST CRICKET

*(‡ Denotes hundred on first appearance against that country.)*

| ENGLAND (444) | | | Opponents | Venue | Rubber |
|---|---|---|---|---|---|
| Abel, R. | (2) | 120 | South Africa | Cape Town | 1888–89 |
| | | 132* | Australia | Sydney | 1891–92 |
| Allen, G. O. B. | (1) | 122‡ | New Zealand | Lord's | 1931 |
| Ames, L.E.G. | (8) | 105 | West Indies | Port-of-Spain | 1929–30 |
| | | 149 | West Indies | Kingston | 1929–30 |
| | | 137‡ | New Zealand | Lord's | 1931 |
| | | 103 | New Zealand | Christchurch | 1932–33 |
| | | 120 | Australia | Lord's | 1934 |
| | | 126 | West Indies | Kingston | 1934–35 |
| | | 148* | South Africa | Oval | 1935 |
| | | 115 | South Africa | Cape Town | 1938–39 |
| Amiss, D. L. | (11) | 112 | Pakistan | Lahore[2] | 1972–73 |
| | | 158 | Pakistan | Hyderabad | 1972–73 |
| | | 138*‡ | New Zealand | Nottingham | 1973 |
| | | 174 | West Indies | Port-of-Spain | 1973–74 |
| | | 262* | West Indies | Kingston | 1973–74 |
| | | 118 | West Indies | Georgetown | 1973–74 |
| | | 188 | India | Lord's | 1974 |
| | | 183 | Pakistan | Oval | 1974 |
| | | 164* | New Zealand | Christchurch | 1974–75 |
| | | 203 | West Indies | Oval | 1976 |
| | | 179 | India | Delhi | 1976–77 |
| Bailey, T. E. | (1) | 134* | New Zealand | Christchurch | 1950–51 |
| Bakewell, A. H. | (1) | 107‡ | West Indies | Oval | 1933 |
| Barber, R. W. | (1) | 185 | Australia | Sydney | 1965–66 |
| Barnes, W. | (1) | 134 | Australia | Adelaide | 1884–85 |
| Barnett, C. J. | (2) | 129 | Australia | Adelaide | 1936–37 |
| | | 126 | Australia | Nottingham | 1938 |
| Barrington, K. F. | (20) | 128‡ | West Indies | Bridgetown | 1959–60 |
| | | 121 | West Indies | Port-of-Spain | 1959–60 |
| | | 139‡ | Pakistan | Lahore[2] | 1961–62 |
| | | 151* | India | Bombay[2] | 1961–62 |
| | | 172 | India | Kanpur | 1961–62 |
| | | 113* | India | Delhi | 1961–62 |
| | | 132* | Australia | Adelaide | 1962–63 |
| | | 101 | Australia | Sydney | 1962–63 |
| | | 126‡ | New Zealand | Auckland | 1962–63 |
| | | 256 | Australia | Manchester | 1964 |
| | | 148* | South Africa | Durban[2] | 1964–65 |
| | | 121 | South Africa | Johannesburg[3] | 1964–65 |
| | | 137 | New Zealand | Birmingham | 1965 |
| | | 163 | New Zealand | Leeds | 1965 |
| | | 102 | Australia | Adelaide | 1965–66 |
| | | 115 | Australia | Melbourne | 1965–66 |
| | | 148 | Pakistan | Lord's | 1967 |
| | | 109* | Pakistan | Nottingham | 1967 |
| | | 142 | Pakistan | Oval | 1967 |
| | | 143 | West Indies | Port-of-Spain | 1967-68 |
| Botham, I. T. | (1) | 103 | New Zealand | Christchurch | 1977–78 |
| Bowley, E. H. | (1) | 109 | New Zealand | Auckland | 1929–30 |
| Boycott, G. | (15) | 113 | Australia | Oval | 1964 |
| | | 117 | South Africa | Port Elizabeth | 1964–65 |
| | | 246*‡ | India | Leeds | 1967 |
| | | 116 | West Indies | Georgetown | 1967–68 |
| | | 128 | West Indies | Manchester | 1969 |
| | | 106 | West Indies | Lord's | 1969 |
| | | 142* | Australia | Sydney | 1970–71 |
| | | 119* | Australia | Adelaide | 1970–71 |

*ENGLAND – continued*

| | | | Opponents | Venue | Rubber |
|---|---|---|---|---|---|
| | | 121* | Pakistan | Lord's | 1971 |
| | | 112 | Pakistan | Leeds | 1971 |
| | | 115 | New Zealand | Leeds | 1973 |
| | | 112 | West Indies | Port-of-Spain | 1973–74 |
| | | 107 | Australia | Nottingham | 1977 |
| | | 191 | Australia | Leeds | 1977 |
| | | | *(His 100th first-class hundred)* | | |
| | | 100* | Pakistan | Hyderabad | 1977–78 |
| Braund, L. C. | (3) | 103* | Australia | Adelaide | 1901–02 |
| | | 102 | Australia | Sydney | 1903–04 |
| | | 104‡ | South Africa | Lord's | 1907 |
| Briggs, J. | (1) | 121 | Australia | Melbourne | 1884–85 |
| Brown, J. T. | (1) | 140 | Australia | Melbourne | 1894–95 |
| Chapman, A. P. F. | (1) | 121 | Australia | Lord's | 1930 |
| Compton, D.C.S. | (17) | 102‡ | Australia | Nottingham | 1938 |
| | | 120‡ | West Indies | Lord's | 1939 |
| | | 147 ) 103*) | Australia | Adelaide | 1946–47 |
| | | 163‡ | South Africa | Nottingham | 1947 |
| | | 208 | South Africa | Lord's | 1947 |
| | | 115 | South Africa | Manchester | 1947 |
| | | 113 | South Africa | Oval | 1947 |
| | | 184 | Australia | Nottingham | 1948 |
| | | 145* | Australia | Manchester | 1948 |
| | | 114 | South Africa | Johannesburg[2] | 1948–49 |
| | | 114 | New Zealand | Leeds | 1949 |
| | | 116 | New Zealand | Lord's | 1949 |
| | | 112 | South Africa | Nottingham | 1951 |
| | | 133 | West Indies | Port-of-Spain | 1953–54 |
| | | 278 | Pakistan | Nottingham | 1954 |
| | | 158 | South Africa | Manchester | 1955 |
| Cowdrey, M. C. | (22) | 102 | Australia | Melbourne | 1954–55 |
| | | 101 | South Africa | Cape Town | 1956–57 |
| | | 154‡ | West Indies | Birmingham | 1957 |
| | | 152 | West Indies | Lord's | 1957 |
| | | 100* | Australia | Sydney | 1958–59 |
| | | 160 | India | Leeds | 1959 |
| | | 114 | West Indies | Kingston | 1959–60 |
| | | 119 | West Indies | Port-of-Spain | 1959–60 |
| | | 155 | South Africa | Oval | 1960 |
| | | 159‡ | Pakistan | Birmingham | 1962 |
| | | 182 | Pakistan | Oval | 1962 |
| | | 113 | Australia | Melbourne | 1962–63 |
| | | 128* | New Zealand | Wellington | 1962–63 |
| | | 107 | India | Calcutta | 1963–64 |
| | | 151 | India | Delhi | 1963–64 |
| | | 119 | New Zealand | Lord's | 1965 |
| | | 105 | South Africa | Nottingham | 1965 |
| | | 104 | Australia | Melbourne | 1965–66 |
| | | 101 | West Indies | Kingston | 1967–68 |
| | | 148 | West Indies | Port-of-Spain | 1967–68 |
| | | 104 | Australia | Birmingham | 1968 |
| | | | *(In his 100th Test match)* | | |
| | | 100 | Pakistan | Lahore[2] | 1968–69 |
| Denness, M. H. | (4) | 118 | India | Lord's | 1974 |
| | | 100 | India | Birmingham | 1974 |
| | | 188 | Australia | Melbourne | 1974–75 |
| | | 181 | New Zealand | Auckland | 1974–75 |
| Denton, D. | (1) | 104 | South Africa | Johannesburg[1] | 1909–10 |

| *ENGLAND – continued* | | | *Opponents* | *Venue* | *Rubber* |
|---|---|---|---|---|---|
| Dexter, E. R. | (9) | 141 | New Zealand | Christchurch | 1958–59 |
| | | 136*‡ | West Indies | Bridgetown | 1959–60 |
| | | 110 | West Indies | Georgetown | 1959–60 |
| | | 180 | Australia | Birmingham | 1961 |
| | | 126* | India | Kanpur | 1961–62 |
| | | 205 | Pakistan | Karachi | 1961–62 |
| | | 172 | Pakistan | Oval | 1962 |
| | | 174 | Australia | Manchester | 1964 |
| | | 172 | South Africa | Johannesburg[3] | 1964–65 |
| D'Oliveira, B. L. | (5) | 109‡ | India | Leeds | 1967 |
| | | 158 | Australia | Oval | 1968 |
| | | 114* | Pakistan | Dacca | 1968–69 |
| | | 117 | Australia | Melbourne | 1970–71 |
| | | 100 | New Zealand | Christchurch | 1970–71 |
| Douglas, J. W. H. T. | (1) | 119‡ | South Africa | Durban | 1913–14 |
| Duleepsinhji, K. S. | (3) | 117 | New Zealand | Auckland | 1929–30 |
| | | 173‡ | Australia | Lord's | 1930 |
| | | 109 | New Zealand | Oval | 1931 |
| Edrich, J. H. | (12) | 120‡ | Australia | Lord's | 1964 |
| | | 310*‡ | New Zealand | Leeds | 1965 |
| | | 109 | Australia | Melbourne | 1965–66 |
| | | 103 | Australia | Sydney | 1965–66 |
| | | 146 | West Indies | Bridgetown | 1967–68 |
| | | 164 | Australia | Oval | 1968 |
| | | 115 | New Zealand | Lord's | 1969 |
| | | 115 | New Zealand | Nottingham | 1969 |
| | | 115* | Australia | Perth | 1970–71 |
| | | 130 | Australia | Adelaide | 1970–71 |
| | | 100* | India | Manchester | 1974 |
| | | 175 | Australia | Lord's | 1975 |
| Edrich, W. J. | (6) | 219 | South Africa | Durban[2] | 1938–39 |
| | | 119 | Australia | Sydney | 1946–47 |
| | | 189 | South Africa | Lord's | 1947 |
| | | 191 | South Africa | Manchester | 1947 |
| | | 111 | Australia | Leeds | 1948 |
| | | 100 | New Zealand | Oval | 1949 |
| Evans, T. G. | (2) | 104 | West Indies | Manchester | 1950 |
| | | 104 | India | Lord's | 1952 |
| Fane, F. L. | (1) | 143 | South Africa | Johannesburg[1] | 1905–06 |
| Fletcher, K. W. R. | (7) | 113 | India | Bombay[2] | 1972–73 |
| | | 178 | New Zealand | Lord's | 1973 |
| | | 129* | West Indies | Bridgetown | 1973–74 |
| | | 123* | India | Manchester | 1974 |
| | | 122 | Pakistan | Oval | 1974 |
| | | 146 | Australia | Melbourne | 1974–75 |
| | | 216 | New Zealand | Auckland | 1974–75 |
| Foster, R. E. | (1) | 287‡ | Australia | Sydney | 1903–04 |
| Fry, C. B. | (2) | 144 | Australia | Oval | 1905 |
| | | 129 | South Africa | Oval | 1907 |
| Gibb, P. A. | (2) | 106‡ | South Africa | Johannesburg[1] | 1938–39 |
| | | 120 | South Africa | Durban[2] | 1938–39 |
| Grace, W. G. | (2) | 152‡ | Australia | Oval | 1880 |
| | | 170 | Australia | Oval | 1886 |
| Graveney, T. W. | (11) | 175‡ | India | Bombay[2] | 1951–52 |
| | | 111 | Australia | Sydney | 1954–55 |
| | | 258 | West Indies | Nottingham | 1957 |
| | | 164 | West Indies | Oval | 1957 |
| | | 153 | Pakistan | Lord's | 1962 |
| | | 114 | Pakistan | Nottingham | 1962 |
| | | 109 | West Indies | Nottingham | 1966 |

*ENGLAND – continued*

| | | | Opponents | Venue | Rubber |
|---|---|---|---|---|---|
| | | 165 | West Indies | Oval | 1966 |
| | | 151 | India | Lord's | 1967 |
| | | 118 | West Indies | Port-of-Spain | 1967–68 |
| | | 105 | Pakistan | Karachi | 1968–69 |
| Greig, A. W. | (8) | 148 | India | Bombay² | 1972–73 |
| | | 139‡ | New Zealand | Nottingham | 1973 |
| | | 148 | West Indies | Bridgetown | 1973–74 |
| | | 121 | West Indies | Georgetown | 1973–74 |
| | | 106 | India | Lord's | 1974 |
| | | 110 | Australia | Brisbane² | 1974–75 |
| | | 116 | West Indies | Leeds | 1976 |
| | | 103 | India | Calcutta | 1976–77 |
| Griffith, S. C. | (1) | 140‡ | West Indies | Port-of-Spain | 1947–48 |
| Gunn, G. | (2) | 119‡ | Australia | Sydney | 1907–08 |
| | | 122* | Australia | Sydney | 1907–08 |
| Gunn, W. | (1) | 102* | Australia | Manchester | 1893 |
| Hammond, W. R. | (22) | 251 | Australia | Sydney | 1928–29 |
| | | 200 | Australia | Melbourne | 1928–29 |
| | | 119*) 177 ) | Australia | Adelaide | 1928–29 |
| | | 138* | South Africa | Birmingham | 1929 |
| | | 101* | South Africa | Oval | 1929 |
| | | 113 | Australia | Leeds | 1930 |
| | | 136* | South Africa | Durban² | 1930–31 |
| | | 100* | New Zealand | Oval | 1931 |
| | | 112 | Australia | Sydney | 1932–33 |
| | | 101 | Australia | Sydney | 1932–33 |
| | | 227 | New Zealand | Christchurch | 1932–33 |
| | | 336* | New Zealand | Auckland | 1932–33 |
| | | 167 | India | Manchester | 1936 |
| | | 217 | India | Oval | 1936 |
| | | 231* | Australia | Sydney | 1936–37 |
| | | 140 | New Zealand | Lord's | 1937 |
| | | 240 | Australia | Lord's | 1938 |
| | | 181 | South Africa | Cape Town | 1938–39 |
| | | 120 | South Africa | Durban² | 1938–39 |
| | | 140 | South Africa | Durban² | 1938–39 |
| | | 138 | West Indies | Oval | 1939 |
| Hampshire, J. H. | (1) | 107‡ | West Indies | Lord's | 1969 |
| Hardstaff, J., jr. | (4) | 114‡ | New Zealand | Lord's | 1937 |
| | | 103 | New Zealand | Oval | 1937 |
| | | 169* | Australia | Oval | 1938 |
| | | 205* | India | Lord's | 1946 |
| Hayes, F. C. | (1) | 106*‡ | West Indies | Oval | 1973 |
| Hayward, T. W. | (3) | 122 | South Africa | Johannesburg¹ | 1895–96 |
| | | 130 | Australia | Manchester | 1899 |
| | | 137 | Australia | Oval | 1899 |
| Hearne, J. W. | (1) | 114 | Australia | Melbourne | 1911–12 |
| Hendren, E. H. | (7) | 132 | South Africa | Leeds | 1924 |
| | | 142 | South Africa | Oval | 1924 |
| | | 127* | Australia | Lord's | 1926 |
| | | 169 | Australia | Brisbane¹ | 1928–29 |
| | | 205* | West Indies | Port-of-Spain | 1929–30 |
| | | 123 | West Indies | Georgetown | 1929–30 |
| | | 132 | Australia | Manchester | 1934 |
| Hill, A. J. L. | (1) | 124 | South Africa | Cape Town | 1895–96 |
| Hobbs, J. B. | (15) | 187 | South Africa | Cape Town | 1909–10 |
| | | 126* | Australia | Melbourne | 1911-12 |
| | | 187 | Australia | Adelaide | 1911-12 |
| | | 178 | Australia | Melbourne | 1911–12 |

| *ENGLAND – continued* | | | *Opponents* | *Venue* | *Rubber* |
|---|---|---|---|---|---|
| | | 107 | Australia | Lord's | 1912 |
| | | 122 | Australia | Melbourne | 1920–21 |
| | | 123 | Australia | Adelaide | 1920–21 |
| | | 211 | South Africa | Lord's | 1924 |
| | | 115 | Australia | Sydney | 1924–25 |
| | | 154 | Australia | Melbourne | 1924–25 |
| | | 119 | Australia | Adelaide | 1924–25 |
| | | 119 | Australia | Lord's | 1926 |
| | | 100 | Australia | Oval | 1926 |
| | | 159 | West Indies | Oval | 1928 |
| | | 142 | Australia | Melbourne | 1928–29 |
| Hutchings, K. L. | (1) | 126 | Australia | Melbourne | 1907–08 |
| Hutton, L. | (19) | 100 | New Zealand | Manchester | 1938 |
| | | 100‡ | Australia | Nottingham | 1938 |
| | | 364 | Australia | Oval | 1938 |
| | | 196‡ | West Indies | Lord's | 1939 |
| | | 165* | West Indies | Oval | 1939 |
| | | 122* | Australia | Sydney | 1946–47 |
| | | 100 | South Africa | Leeds | 1947 |
| | | 158 | South Africa | Johannesburg² | 1948–49 |
| | | 123 | South Africa | Johannesburg² | 1948–49 |
| | | 101 | New Zealand | Leeds | 1949 |
| | | 206 | New Zealand | Oval | 1949 |
| | | 202* | West Indies | Oval | 1950 |
| | | 156* | Australia | Adelaide | 1950–51 |
| | | 100 | South Africa | Leeds | 1951 |
| | | 150 | India | Lord's | 1952 |
| | | 104 | India | Manchester | 1952 |
| | | 145 | Australia | Lord's | 1953 |
| | | 169 | West Indies | Georgetown | 1953–54 |
| | | 205 | West Indies | Kingston | 1953–54 |
| Illingworth, R. | (2) | 113 | West Indies | Lord's | 1969 |
| | | 107 | India | Manchester | 1971 |
| Insole, D. J. | (1) | 110* | South Africa | Durban² | 1956–57 |
| Jackson, Hon. F. S. | (5) | 103 | Australia | Oval | 1893 |
| | | 118 | Australia | Oval | 1899 |
| | | 128 | Australia | Manchester | 1902 |
| | | 144* | Australia | Leeds | 1905 |
| | | 113 | Australia | Manchester | 1905 |
| Jardine, D. R. | (1) | 127 | West Indies | Manchester | 1933 |
| Jessop, G. L. | (1) | 104 | Australia | Oval | 1902 |
| Knight, B. R. | (2) | 125‡ | New Zealand | Auckland | 1962–63 |
| | | 127 | India | Kanpur | 1963–64 |
| Knott, A. P. E. | (5) | 101 | New Zealand | Auckland | 1970–71 |
| | | 116 | Pakistan | Birmingham | 1971 |
| | | 106* | Australia | Adelaide | 1974–75 |
| | | 116 | West Indies | Leeds | 1976 |
| | | 135 | Australia | Nottingham | 1977 |
| Legge, G. B. | (1) | 196 | New Zealand | Auckland | 1929–30 |
| Lewis, A. R. | (1) | 125 | India | Kanpur | 1972–73 |
| Leyland, M. | (9) | 137‡ | Australia | Melbourne | 1928–29 |
| | | 102 | South Africa | Lord's | 1929 |
| | | 109 | Australia | Lord's | 1934 |
| | | 153 | Australia | Manchester | 1934 |
| | | 110 | Australia | Oval | 1934 |
| | | 161 | South Africa | Oval | 1935 |
| | | 126 | Australia | Brisbane² | 1936–37 |
| | | 111* | Australia | Melbourne | 1936–37 |
| | | 187 | Australia | Oval | 1938 |

| *ENGLAND – continued* | | | *Opponents* | *Venue* | *Rubber* |
|---|---|---|---|---|---|
| Lloyd, D. | (1) | 214* | India | Birmingham | 1974 |
| Luckhurst, B. W. | (4) | 131 | Australia | Perth | 1970–71 |
| | | 109 | Australia | Melbourne | 1970–71 |
| | | 108*‡ | Pakistan | Birmingham | 1971 |
| | | 101 | India | Manchester | 1971 |
| MacLaren, A. C. | (5) | 120 | Australia | Melbourne | 1894–95 |
| | | 109 | Australia | Sydney | 1897–98 |
| | | 124 | Australia | Adelaide | 1897–98 |
| | | 116 | Australia | Sydney | 1901–02 |
| | | 140 | Australia | Nottingham | 1905 |
| Makepeace, W. H. R. | (1) | 117 | Australia | Melbourne | 1920–21 |
| Mann, F. G. | (1) | 136* | South Africa | Port Elizabeth | 1948–49 |
| May, P. B. H. | (13) | 138‡ | South Africa | Leeds | 1951 |
| | | 135 | West Indies | Port-of-Spain | 1953–54 |
| | | 104 | Australia | Sydney | 1954–55 |
| | | 112 | South Africa | Lord's | 1955 |
| | | 117 | South Africa | Manchester | 1955 |
| | | 101 | Australia | Leeds | 1956 |
| | | 285* | West Indies | Birmingham | 1957 |
| | | 104 | West Indies | Nottingham | 1957 |
| | | 113* | New Zealand | Leeds | 1958 |
| | | 101 | New Zealand | Manchester | 1958 |
| | | 113 | Australia | Melbourne | 1958–59 |
| | | 124* | New Zealand | Auckland | 1958–59 |
| | | 106 | India | Nottingham | 1959 |
| Mead, C. P. | (4) | 102 | South Africa | Johannesburg[1] | 1913–14 |
| | | 117 | South Africa | Port Elizabeth | 1913–14 |
| | | 182* | Australia | Oval | 1921 |
| | | 181 | South Africa | Durban[2] | 1922–23 |
| Milburn, C. | (2) | 126* | West Indies | Lord's | 1966 |
| | | 139 | Pakistan | Karachi | 1968–69 |
| Milton, C. A. | (1) | 104*‡ | New Zealand | Leeds | 1958 |
| Murray, J. T. | (1) | 112‡ | West Indies | Oval | 1966 |
| Parfitt, P. H. | (7) | 111 | Pakistan | Karachi | 1961–62 |
| | | 101* | Pakistan | Birmingham | 1962 |
| | | 119 | Pakistan | Leeds | 1962 |
| | | 101* | Pakistan | Nottingham | 1962 |
| | | 131*‡ | New Zealand | Auckland | 1962–63 |
| | | 121 | India | Kanpur | 1963–64 |
| | | 122* | South Africa | Johannesburg[3] | 1964–65 |
| Parks, J. M. | (2) | 101*‡ | West Indies | Port-of-Spain | 1959–60 |
| | | 108* | South Africa | Durban[2] | 1964–65 |
| Pataudi, Nawab of, sr | (1) | 102‡ | Australia | Sydney | 1932–33 |
| Paynter, E. | (4) | 216* | Australia | Nottingham | 1938 |
| | | 117‡ )  100‡ ) | South Africa | Johannesburg[1] | 1938–39 |
| | | 243 | South Africa | Durban[2] | 1938–39 |
| Place, W. | (1) | 107 | West Indies | Kingston | 1947–48 |
| Pullar, G. | (4) | 131 | India | Manchester | 1959 |
| | | 175 | South Africa | Oval | 1960 |
| | | 119 | India | Kanpur | 1961–62 |
| | | 165 | Pakistan | Dacca | 1961–62 |
| Radley, C. T. | (1) | 158 | New Zealand | Auckland | 1977-78 |
| Randall, D. W. | (1) | 174‡ | Australia | Melbourne | 1976–77 |
| Ranjitsinhji, K. S. | (2) | 154*‡ | Australia | Manchester | 1896 |
| | | 175 | Australia | Sydney | 1897–98 |
| Read, W. W. | (1) | 117 | Australia | Oval | 1884 |
| Rhodes, W. | (2) | 179 | Australia | Melbourne | 1911–12 |
| | | 152 | South Africa | Johannesburg[1] | 1913–14 |

*ENGLAND – continued*

| | | | Opponents | Venue | Rubber |
|---|---|---|---|---|---|
| Richardson, P. E. | (5) | 104 | Australia | Manchester | 1956 |
| | | 117‡ | South Africa | Johannesburg³ | 1956–57 |
| | | 126 | West Indies | Nottingham | 1957 |
| | | 107 | West Indies | Oval | 1957 |
| | | 100‡ | New Zealand | Birmingham | 1958 |
| Robertson, J. D. B. | (2) | 133 | West Indies | Port-of-Spain | 1947–48 |
| | | 121‡ | New Zealand | Lord's | 1949 |
| Robins, R. W. V. | (1) | 108 | South Africa | Manchester | 1935 |
| Russell, C. A. G. | (5) | 135* | Australia | Adelaide | 1920–21 |
| | | 101 | Australia | Manchester | 1921 |
| | | 102* | Australia | Oval | 1921 |
| | | 140 )<br>111 ) | South Africa | Durban² | 1922–23 |
| Sandham, A. | (2) | 152‡ | West Indies | Bridgetown | 1929–30 |
| | | 325 | West Indies | Kingston | 1929–30 |
| Sharp, J. | (1) | 105 | Australia | Oval | 1909 |
| Sharpe, P. J. | (1) | 111 | New Zealand | Nottingham | 1969 |
| Sheppard, Rev. D. S. | (3) | 119 | India | Oval | 1952 |
| | | 113 | Australia | Manchester | 1956 |
| | | 113 | Australia | Melbourne | 1962–63 |
| Shrewsbury, A. | (3) | 105* | Australia | Melbourne | 1884–85 |
| | | 164 | Australia | Lord's | 1886 |
| | | 106 | Australia | Lord's | 1893 |
| Simpson, R. T. | (4) | 103‡ | New Zealand | Manchester | 1949 |
| | | 156* | Australia | Melbourne | 1950–51 |
| | | 137 | South Africa | Nottingham | 1951 |
| | | 101 | Pakistan | Nottingham | 1954 |
| Smith, M. J. K. | (3) | 100‡ | India | Manchester | 1959 |
| | | 108 | West Indies | Port-of-Spain | 1959–60 |
| | | 121 | South Africa | Cape Town | 1964–65 |
| Spooner, R. H. | (1) | 119‡ | South Africa | Lord's | 1912 |
| Steel, A. G. | (2) | 135* | Australia | Sydney | 1882–83 |
| | | 148 | Australia | Lord's | 1884 |
| Steele, D. S. | (1) | 106‡ | West Indies | Nottingham | 1976 |
| Stoddart, A. E. | (2) | 134 | Australia | Adelaide | 1891–92 |
| | | 173 | Australia | Melbourne | 1894–95 |
| Subba Row, R. | (3) | 100‡ | West Indies | Georgetown | 1959–60 |
| | | 112‡ | Australia | Birmingham | 1961 |
| | | 137 | Australia | Oval | 1961 |
| Sutcliffe, H. | (16) | 122 | South Africa | Lord's | 1924 |
| | | 115‡ | Australia | Sydney | 1924–25 |
| | | 176 )<br>127 ) | Australia | Melbourne | 1924–25 |
| | | 143 | Australia | Melbourne | 1934–25 |
| | | 161 | Australia | Oval | 1926 |
| | | 102 | South Africa | Johannesburg¹ | 1927–28 |
| | | 135 | Australia | Melbourne | 1928–29 |
| | | 114 | South Africa | Birmingham | 1929 |
| | | 100 | South Africa | Lord's | 1929 |
| | | 104 )<br>109* ) | South Africa | Oval | 1929 |
| | | 161 | Australia | Oval | 1930 |
| | | 117‡ | New Zealand | Oval | 1931 |
| | | 109* | New Zealand | Manchester | 1931 |
| | | 194 | Australia | Sydney | 1932–33 |
| Tate, M. W. | (1) | 100* | South Africa | Lord's | 1929 |
| Tyldesley, E. | (3) | 122‡ | South Africa | Johannesburg¹ | 1927–28 |
| | | 100 | South Africa | Durban² | 1927–28 |
| | | 122 | West Indies | Lord's | 1928 |

| *ENGLAND – continued* | | | *Opponents* | *Venue* | *Rubber* |
|---|---|---|---|---|---|
| Tyldesley, J. T. | (4) | 112 | South Africa | Cape Town | 1898–99 |
| | | 138 | Australia | Birmingham | 1902 |
| | | 100 | Australia | Leeds | 1905 |
| | | 112* | Australia | Oval | 1905 |
| Ulyett, G. | (1) | 149 | Australia | Melbourne | 1881–82 |
| Valentine, B. H. | (2) | 136‡ | India | Bombay[1] | 1933–34 |
| | | 112 | South Africa | Cape Town | 1938–39 |
| Walters, C. F. | (1) | 102 | India | Madras[1] | 1933–34 |
| Ward, Albert | (1) | 117 | Australia | Sydney | 1894–95 |
| Warner, P. F. | (1) | 132*‡ | South Africa | Johannesburg[1] | 1898–99 |
| Washbrook, C. | (6) | 112 | Australia | Melbourne | 1946–47 |
| | | 143 | Australia | Leeds | 1948 |
| | | 195 | South Africa | Johannesburg[2] | 1948–49 |
| | | 103* | New Zealand | Leeds | 1949 |
| | | 114‡ | West Indies | Lord's | 1950 |
| | | 102 | West Indies | Nottingham | 1950 |
| Watkins, A. J. | (2) | 111 | South Africa | Johannesburg[2] | 1948–49 |
| | | 137*‡ | India | Delhi | 1951–52 |
| Watson, W. | (2) | 109‡ | Australia | Lord's | 1953 |
| | | 116‡ | West Indies | Kingston | 1953–54 |
| Wood, H. | (1) | 134* | South Africa | Cape Town | 1891–92 |
| Woolley, F. E. | (5) | 133* | Australia | Sydney | 1911-12 |
| | | 115* | South Africa | Johannesburg[1] | 1922–23 |
| | | 134* | South Africa | Lord's | 1924 |
| | | 123 | Australia | Sydney | 1924–25 |
| | | 154 | South Africa | Manchester | 1929 |
| Woolmer, R. A. | (3) | 149 | Australia | Oval | 1975 |
| | | 120 | Australia | Lord's | 1977 |
| | | 137 | Australia | Manchester | 1977 |
| Worthington, T. S. | (1) | 128 | India | Oval | 1936 |
| Wyatt, R. E. S. | (2) | 113 | South Africa | Manchester | 1929 |
| | | 149 | South Africa | Nottingham | 1935 |
| | | | | | |
| *AUSTRALIA* (339) | | | | | |
| Archer, R.G. | (1) | 128 | West Indies | Kingston | 1954-55 |
| Armstrong, W.W. | (6) | 159* | South Africa | Johannesburg[1] | 1902-03 |
| | | 133* | England | Melbourne | 1907-08 |
| | | 132 | South Africa | Melbourne | 1910-11 |
| | | 158 | England | Sydney | 1920-21 |
| | | 121 | England | Adelaide | 1920-21 |
| | | 123* | England | Melbourne | 1920-21 |
| Badcock, C.L. | (1) | 118 | England | Melbourne | 1936-37 |
| Bannerman, C. | (1) | 165*‡ | England | Melbourne | 1876-77 |
| | | *(The first hundred in Test cricket)* | | | |
| Bardsley, W. | (6) | 136) 130) | England | Oval | 1909 |
| | | 132‡ | South Africa | Sydney | 1910-11 |
| | | 121 | South Africa | Manchester | 1912 |
| | | 164 | South Africa | Lord's | 1912 |
| | | 193* | England | Lord's | 1926 |
| Barnes, S.G. | (3) | 234 | England | Sydney | 1946-47 |
| | | 112 | India | Adelaide | 1947-48 |
| | | 141 | England | Lord's | 1948 |
| Benaud, J. | (1) | 142 | Pakistan | Melbourne | 1972-73 |
| Benaud, R. | (3) | 121 | West Indies | Kingston | 1954-55 |
| | | 122 | South Africa | Johannesburg[3] | 1957-58 |
| | | 100 | South Africa | Johannesburg[3] | 1957-58 |
| Bonnor, G.J. | (1) | 128 | England | Sydney | 1884-85 |

| AUSTRALIA – *continued* | | | *Opponents* | *Venue* | *Rubber* |
|---|---|---|---|---|---|
| Booth, B.C. | (5) | 112 | England | Brisbane[2] | 1962-63 |
| | | 103 | England | Melbourne | 1962-63 |
| | | 169‡ | South Africa | Brisbane[2] | 1963-64 |
| | | 102* | South Africa | Sydney | 1963-64 |
| | | 117 | West Indies | Port-of-Spain | 1964-65 |
| Bradman, D.G. | (29) | 112 | England | Melbourne | 1928-29 |
| | | 123 | England | Melbourne | 1928-29 |
| | | 131 | England | Nottingham | 1930 |
| | | 254 | England | Lord's | 1930 |
| | | 334 | England | Leeds | 1930 |
| | | 232 | England | Oval | 1930 |
| | | 223 | West Indies | Brisbane[1] | 1930-31 |
| | | 152 | West Indies | Melbourne | 1930-31 |
| | | 226‡ | South Africa | Brisbane[2] | 1931-32 |
| | | 112 | South Africa | Sydney | 1931-32 |
| | | 167 | South Africa | Melbourne | 1931-32 |
| | | 299* | South Africa | Adelaide | 1931-32 |
| | | 103* | England | Melbourne | 1932-33 |
| | | 304 | England | Leeds | 1934 |
| | | 244 | England | Oval | 1934 |
| | | 270 | England | Melbourne | 1936-37 |
| | | 212 | England | Adelaide | 1936-37 |
| | | 169 | England | Melbourne | 1936-37 |
| | | 144* | England | Nottingham | 1938 |
| | | 102* | England | Lord's | 1938 |
| | | 103 | England | Leeds | 1938 |
| | | 187 | England | Brisbane[2] | 1946-47 |
| | | 234 | England | Sydney | 1946-47 |
| | | 185‡ | India | Brisbane[2] | 1947-48 |
| | | 132 )<br>127*) | India | Melbourne | 1947-48 |
| | | 201 | India | Adelaide | 1947-48 |
| | | 138 | England | Nottingham | 1948 |
| | | 173* | England | Leeds | 1948 |
| Brown, W.A. | (4) | 105 | England | Lord's | 1934 |
| | | 121 | South Africa | Cape Town | 1935-36 |
| | | 133 | England | Nottingham | 1938 |
| | | 206* | England | Lord's | 1938 |
| Burge, P.J.P. | (4) | 181 | England | Oval | 1961 |
| | | 103 | England | Sydney | 1962-63 |
| | | 160 | England | Leeds | 1964 |
| | | 120 | England | Melbourne | 1965-66 |
| Burke, J.W. | (3) | 101*‡ | England | Adelaide | 1950-51 |
| | | 161 | India | Bombay[2] | 1956-57 |
| | | 189 | South Africa | Cape Town | 1957-58 |
| Chappell, G.S. | (14) | 108‡ | England | Perth | 1970-71 |
| | | 131 | England | Lord's | 1972 |
| | | 113 | England | Oval | 1972 |
| | | 116* | Pakistan | Melbourne | 1972-73 |
| | | 106 | West Indies | Bridgetown | 1972-73 |
| | | 247*)<br>133 ) | New Zealand | Wellington | 1973-74 |
| | | 144 | England | Sydney | 1974-75 |
| | | 102 | England | Melbourne | 1974-75 |
| | | 123 )<br>109*) | West Indies | Brisbane[2] | 1975-76 |
| | | 182* | West Indies | Sydney | 1975-76 |
| | | 121 | Pakistan | Melbourne | 1976-77 |
| | | 112 | England | Manchester | 1977 |

| *AUSTRALIA – continued* | | | *Opponents* | *Venue* | *Rubber* |
|---|---|---|---|---|---|
| Chappell, I.M. | (14) | 151 | India | Melbourne | 1967-68 |
| | | 117‡ | West Indies | Brisbane² | 1968-69 |
| | | 165 | West Indies | Melbourne | 1968-69 |
| | | 138 | India | Delhi | 1969-70 |
| | | 111 | England | Melbourne | 1970-71 |
| | | 104 | England | Adelaide | 1970-71 |
| | | 118 | England | Oval | 1972 |
| | | 196 | Pakistan | Adelaide | 1972-73 |
| | | 106* | West Indies | Bridgetown | 1972-73 |
| | | 109 | West Indies | Georgetown | 1972-73 |
| | | 145)<br>121) | New Zealand | Wellington | 1973-74 |
| | | 192 | England | Oval | 1975 |
| | | 156 | West Indies | Perth | 1975-76 |
| Chipperfield, A.G. | (1) | 109‡ | South Africa | Durban² | 1935-36 |
| Collins, H.L. | (4) | 104‡ | England | Sydney | 1920-21 |
| | | 162 | England | Adelaide | 1920-21 |
| | | 203 | South Africa | Johannesburg¹ | 1921-22 |
| | | 114 | England | Sydney | 1924-25 |
| Cosier, G.J. | (2) | 109‡ | West Indies | Melbourne | 1975-76 |
| | | 168 | Pakistan | Melbourne | 1976-77 |
| Cowper, R.M. | (5) | 143 | West Indies | Port-of-Spain | 1964-65 |
| | | 102 | West Indies | Bridgetown | 1964-65 |
| | | 307 | England | Melbourne | 1965-66 |
| | | 108 | India | Adelaide | 1967-68 |
| | | 165 | India | Sydney | 1967-68 |
| Darling, J. | (3) | 101 | England | Sydney | 1897-98 |
| | | 178 | England | Adelaide | 1897-98 |
| | | 160 | England | Sydney | 1897-98 |
| Davis, I.C. | (1) | 105‡ | Pakistan | Adelaide | 1976-77 |
| Duff, R.A. | (2) | 104‡ | England | Melbourne | 1901-02 |
| | | 146 | England | Oval | 1905 |
| Edwards, R. | (2) | 170* | England | Nottingham | 1972 |
| | | 115 | England | Perth | 1974-75 |
| Favell, L.E. | (1) | 101 | India | Madras² | 1959-60 |
| Fingleton, J.H.W. | (5) | 112 | South Africa | Cape Town | 1935-36 |
| | | 108 | South Africa | Johannesburg¹ | 1935-36 |
| | | 118 | South Africa | Durban² | 1935-36 |
| | | 100 | England | Brisbane² | 1936-37 |
| | | 136 | England | Melbourne | 1936-37 |
| Giffen, G. | (1) | 161 | England | Sydney | 1894-95 |
| Gilmour, G.J. | (1) | 101 | New Zealand | Christchurch | 1976-77 |
| Graham, H. | (2) | 107‡ | England | Lord's | 1893 |
| | | 105 | England | Sydney | 1894-95 |
| Gregory, J.M. | (2) | 100 | England | Melbourne | 1920-21 |
| | | 119 | South Africa | Johannesburg¹ | 1921-22 |
| | | *(Including the fastest Test hundred in 70 minutes)* | | | |
| Gregory, S.E. | (4) | 201 | England | Sydney | 1894-95 |
| | | 103 | England | Lord's | 1896 |
| | | 117 | England | Oval | 1899 |
| | | 112 | England | Adelaide | 1903-04 |
| Hartigan, R.J. | (1) | 116‡ | England | Adelaide | 1907-08 |
| Harvey, R.N. | (21) | 153 | India | Melbourne | 1947-48 |
| | | 112‡ | England | Leeds | 1948 |
| | | 178 | South Africa | Cape Town | 1949-50 |
| | | 151* | South Africa | Durban² | 1949-50 |
| | | 100 | South Africa | Johannesburg² | 1949-50 |
| | | 116 | South Africa | Port Elizabeth | 1949-50 |
| | | 109 | South Africa | Brisbane² | 1952-53 |

*AUSTRALIA – continued*

| | | | Opponents | Venue | Rubber |
|---|---|---|---|---|---|
| | | 190 | South Africa | Sydney | 1952-53 |
| | | 116 | South Africa | Adelaide | 1952-53 |
| | | 205 | South Africa | Melbourne | 1952-53 |
| | | 122 | England | Manchester | 1953 |
| | | 162 | England | Brisbane² | 1954-55 |
| | | 133 | West Indies | Kingston | 1954-55 |
| | | 133 | West Indies | Port-of-Spain | 1954-55 |
| | | 204 | West Indies | Kingston | 1954-55 |
| | | 140 | India | Bombay² | 1956-57 |
| | | 167 | England | Melbourne | 1958-59 |
| | | 114 | India | Delhi | 1959-60 |
| | | 102 | India | Bombay² | 1959-60 |
| | | 114 | England | Birmingham | 1961 |
| | | 154 | England | Adelaide | 1962-63 |
| Hassett, A.L. | (10) | 128 | England | Brisbane² | 1946-47 |
| | | 198* | India | Adelaide | 1947-48 |
| | | 137 | England | Nottingham | 1948 |
| | | 112‡ | South Africa | Johannesburg² | 1949-50 |
| | | 167 | South Africa | Port Elizabeth | 1949-50 |
| | | 132 | West Indies | Sydney | 1951-52 |
| | | 102 | West Indies | Melbourne | 1951-52 |
| | | 163 | South Africa | Adelaide | 1952-53 |
| | | 115 | England | Nottingham | 1953 |
| | | 104 | England | Lord's | 1953 |
| Hendry, H.S.T.L. | (1) | 112 | England | Sydney | 1928-29 |
| Hill, C. | (7) | 188 | England | Melbourne | 1897-98 |
| | | 135 | England | Lord's | 1899 |
| | | 119 | England | Sheffield | 1902 |
| | | 142‡ | South Africa | Johannesburg¹ | 1902-03 |
| | | 160 | England | Adelaide | 1907-08 |
| | | 191 | South Africa | Sydney | 1910-11 |
| | | 100 | South Africa | Melbourne | 1910-11 |
| Horan, T.P. | (1) | 124 | England | Melbourne | 1881-82 |
| Iredale, F.A. | (2) | 140 | England | Adelaide | 1894-95 |
| | | 108 | England | Manchester | 1896 |
| Jackson, A. | (1) | 164‡ | England | Adelaide | 1928-29 |
| Kelleway, C. | (3) | 114 | South Africa | Manchester | 1912 |
| | | 102 | South Africa | Lord's | 1912 |
| | | 147 | England | Adelaide | 1920-21 |
| Kippax, A.F. | (2) | 100 | England | Melbourne | 1928-29 |
| | | 146‡ | West Indies | Adelaide | 1930-31 |
| Lawry, W.M. | (13) | 130 | England | Lord's | 1961 |
| | | 102 | England | Manchester | 1961 |
| | | 157 | South Africa | Melbourne | 1963-64 |
| | | 106 | England | Manchester | 1964 |
| | | 210 | West Indies | Bridgetown | 1964-65 |
| | | 166 | England | Brisbane² | 1965-66 |
| | | 119 | England | Adelaide | 1965-66 |
| | | 108 | England | Melbourne | 1965-66 |
| | | 100 | India | Melbourne | 1967-68 |
| | | 135 | England | Oval | 1968 |
| | | 105 | West Indies | Brisbane² | 1968-69 |
| | | 205 | West Indies | Melbourne | 1968-69 |
| | | 151 | West Indies | Sydney | 1968-69 |
| Lindwall, R.R. | (2) | 100 | England | Melbourne | 1946-47 |
| | | 118 | West Indies | Bridgetown | 1954-55 |
| Loxton, S.J.E. | (1) | 101‡ | South Africa | Johannesburg² | 1949-50 |
| Lyons, J.J. | (1) | 134 | England | Sydney | 1891-92 |
| Macartney, C.G. | (7) | 137 | South Africa | Sydney | 1910-11 |

| *AUSTRALIA – continued* | | | *Opponents* | *Venue* | *Rubber* |
|---|---|---|---|---|---|
| | | 170 | England | Sydney | 1920-21 |
| | | 115 | England | Leeds | 1921 |
| | | 116 | South Africa | Durban[1] | 1921-22 |
| | | 133* | England | Lord's | 1926 |
| | | 151 | England | Leeds | 1926 |
| | | 109 | England | Manchester | 1926 |
| McCabe, S.J. | (6) | 187* | England | Sydney | 1932-33 |
| | | 137 | England | Manchester | 1934 |
| | | 149 | South Africa | Durban[2] | 1935-36 |
| | | 189* | South Africa | Johannesburg[1] | 1935-36 |
| | | 112 | England | Melbourne | 1936-37 |
| | | 232 | England | Nottingham | 1938 |
| McCool, C.L. | (1) | 104* | England | Melbourne | 1946-47 |
| McCosker, R.B. | (4) | 127 | England | Oval | 1975 |
| | | 109* | West Indies | Melbourne | 1975-76 |
| | | 105 | Pakistan | Melbourne | 1976-77 |
| | | 107 | England | Nottingham | 1977 |
| McDonald, C.C. | (5) | 154 | South Africa | Adelaide | 1952-53 |
| | | 110 | West Indies | Port-of-Spain | 1954-55 |
| | | 127 | West Indies | Kingston | 1954-55 |
| | | 170 | England | Adelaide | 1958-59 |
| | | 133 | England | Melbourne | 1958-59 |
| McDonnell, P.S. | (3) | 147 | England | Sydney | 1881-82 |
| | | 103 | England | Oval | 1884 |
| | | 124 | England | Adelaide | 1884-85 |
| McLeod, C.E. | (1) | 112 | England | Melbourne | 1897-98 |
| Mann, A.L. | (1) | 105 | India | Perth | 1977-78 |
| Marsh, R.W. | (3) | 118‡ | Pakistan | Adelaide | 1972-73 |
| | | 132 | New Zealand | Adelaide | 1973-74 |
| | | 110* | England | Melbourne | 1976-77 |
| Miller, K.R. | (7) | 141* | England | Adelaide | 1946-47 |
| | | 145* | England | Sydney | 1950-51 |
| | | 129 | West Indies | Sydney | 1951-52 |
| | | 109 | England | Lord's | 1953 |
| | | 147 | West Indies | Kingston | 1954-55 |
| | | 137 | West Indies | Bridgetown | 1954-55 |
| | | 109 | West Indies | Kingston | 1954-55 |
| Moroney, J. | (2) | 118 )<br>101*) | South Africa | Johannesburg[2] | 1949-50 |
| Morris, A.R. | (12) | 155 | England | Melbourne | 1946-47 |
| | | 122 )<br>124*) | England | Adelaide | 1946-47 |
| | | 100* | India | Melbourne | 1947-48 |
| | | 105 | England | Lord's | 1948 |
| | | 182 | England | Leeds | 1948 |
| | | 196 | England | Oval | 1948 |
| | | 111 | South Africa | Johannesburg[2] | 1949-50 |
| | | 157 | South Africa | Port Elizabeth | 1949-50 |
| | | 206 | England | Adelaide | 1950-51 |
| | | 153 | England | Brisbane[2] | 1954-55 |
| | | 111 | West Indies | Port-of-Spain | 1954-55 |
| Murdoch, W.L. | (2) | 153* | England | Oval | 1880 |
| | | 211 | England | Oval | 1884 |
| Noble, M.A. | (1) | 133 | England | Sydney | 1903-04 |
| O'Neill, N.C. | (6) | 134 | Pakistan | Lahore[2] | 1959-60 |
| | | 163 | India | Bombay[2] | 1959-60 |
| | | 113 | India | Calcutta | 1959-60 |
| | | 181‡ | West Indies | Brisbane[2] | 1960-61 |
| | | 117 | England | Oval | 1961 |

| *AUSTRALIA* – *continued* | | | *Opponents* | *Venue* | *Rubber* |
|---|---|---|---|---|---|
| | | 100 | England | Adelaide | 1962-63 |
| Pellew, C.E. | (2) | 116 | England | Melbourne | 1920-21 |
| | | 104 | England | Adelaide | 1920-21 |
| Ponsford, W.H. | (7) | 110‡ | England | Sydney | 1924-25 |
| | | 128 | England | Melbourne | 1924-25 |
| | | 110 | England | Oval | 1930 |
| | | 183 | West Indies | Sydney | 1930-31 |
| | | 109 | West Indies | Brisbane[1] | 1930-31 |
| | | 181 | England | Leeds | 1934 |
| | | 266 | England | Oval | 1934 |
| Ransford, V.S. | (1) | 143* | England | Lord's | 1909 |
| Redpath, I.R. | (8) | 132 | West Indies | Sydney | 1968-69 |
| | | 171 | England | Perth | 1970-71 |
| | | 135 | Pakistan | Melbourne | 197273 |
| | | 159* | New Zealand | Auckland | 1973-74 |
| | | 105 | England | Sydney | 1974-75 |
| | | 102 | West Indies | Melbourne | 1975-76 |
| | | 103 | West Indies | Adelaide | 1975-76 |
| | | 101 | West Indies | Melbourne | 1975-76 |
| Richardson, A.J. | (1) | 100 | England | Leeds | 1926 |
| Richardson, V.Y. | (1) | 138 | England | Melbourne | 1924-25 |
| Rigg, K.E. | (1) | 127‡ | South Africa | Sydney | 1931-32 |
| Ryder, J. | (3) | 142 | South Africa | Cape Town | 1921-22 |
| | | 201* | England | Adelaide | 1924-25 |
| | | 112 | England | Melbourne | 1928-29 |
| Scott, H.J.H. | (1) | 102 | England | Oval | 1884 |
| Sergeant, C.S. | (1) | 124 | West Indies | Georgetown | 1977-78 |
| Sheahan, A.P. | (2) | 114 | India | Kanpur | 1969-70 |
| | | 127 | Pakistan | Melbourne | 1972-73 |
| Simpson, R.B. | (10) | 311 | England | Manchester | 1964 |
| | | 153‡) 115‡) | Pakistan | Karachi | 1964-65 |
| | | 201 | West Indies | Bridgetown | 1964-65 |
| | | 225 | England | Adelaide | 1965-66 |
| | | 153 | South Africa | Cape Town | 1966-67 |
| | | 103 | India | Adelaide | 1967-68 |
| | | 109 | India | Melbourne | 1967-68 |
| | | 176 | India | Perth | 1977-78 |
| | | 100 | India | Adelaide | 1977-78 |
| Stackpole, K.R. | (7) | 134 | South Africa | Cape Town | 1966-67 |
| | | 103‡ | India | Bombay[2] | 1969-70 |
| | | 207 | England | Brisbane[2] | 1970-71 |
| | | 136 | England | Adelaide | 1970-71 |
| | | 114 | England | Nottingham | 1972 |
| | | 142 | West Indies | Kingston | 1972-73 |
| | | 122‡ | New Zealand | Melbourne | 1973-74 |
| Taylor, J.M. | (1) | 108 | England | Sydney | 1924-25 |
| Toohey, P.M. | (1) | 122 | West Indies | Kingston | 1977-78 |
| Trott, G.H.S. | (1) | 143 | England | Lord's | 1896 |
| Trumper, V.T. | (8) | 135* | England | Lord's | 1899 |
| | | 104 | England | Manchester | 1902 |
| | | 185* | England | Sydney | 1903-04 |
| | | 113 | England | Adelaide | 1903-04 |
| | | 166 | England | Sydney | 1907-08 |
| | | 159 | South Africa | Melbourne | 1910-11 |
| | | 214* | South Africa | Adelaide | 1910-11 |
| | | 113 | England | Sydney | 1911-12 |
| Turner, A. | (1) | 136 | West Indies | Adelaide | 1975-76 |
| Walters, K.D. | (14) | 155‡ | England | Brisbane[2] | 1965-66 |

| *AUSTRALIA – continued* | | | *Opponents* | *Venue* | *Rubber* |
|---|---|---|---|---|---|
| | | 115 | England | Melbourne | 1965-66 |
| | | 118 | West Indies | Sydney | 1968-69 |
| | | 110 | West Indies | Adelaide | 1968-69 |
| | | 242) | West Indies | Sydney | 1968-69 |
| | | 103) | | | |
| | | 102 | India | Madras[1] | 1969-70 |
| | | 112 | England | Brisbane[2] | 1970-71 |
| | | 102* | West Indies | Bridgetown | 1972-73 |
| | | 112 | West Indies | Port-of-Spain | 197273 |
| | | 104* | New Zealand | Auckland | 1973-74 |
| | | 103 | England | Perth | 1974-75 |
| Walters, K.D. *(cont.)* | | 107 | Pakistan | Adelaide | 1976-77 |
| | | 250 | New Zealand | Christchurch | 1976-77 |
| Wood, G.M. | (1) | 126 | West Indies | Georgetown | 1977-78 |
| Woodfull, W.M. | (7) | 141 | England | Leeds | 1926 |
| | | 117 | England | Manchester | 1926 |
| | | 111 | England | Sydney | 1928-29 |
| | | 107 | England | Melbourne | 1928-29 |
| | | 102 | England | Melbourne | 1928-29 |
| | | 155 | England | Lord's | 1930 |
| | | 161 | South Africa | Melbourne | 1931-32 |
| Yallop, G.N. | (1) | 121‡ | India | Adelaide | 1977-78 |

| *SOUTH AFRICA* (105) | | | | | |
|---|---|---|---|---|---|
| Balaskas, X.C. | (1) | 122* | New Zealand | Wellington | 193132 |
| Barlow, E.J. | (6) | 114‡ | Australia | Brisbane[2] | 1963-64 |
| | | 109 | Australia | Melbourne | 1963-64 |
| | | 201 | Australia | Adelaide | 1963-64 |
| | | 138 | England | Cape Town | 1964-65 |
| | | 127 | Australia | Cape Town | 1969-70 |
| | | 110 | Australia | Johannesburg[3] | 1969-70 |
| Bland, K.C. | (3) | 126 | Australia | Sydney | 1963-64 |
| | | 144* | England | Johannesburg[3] | 1964-65 |
| | | 127 | England | Oval | 1965 |
| Catterall, R.H. | (3) | 120 | England | Birmingham | 1924 |
| | | 120 | England | Lord's | 1924 |
| | | 119 | England | Durban[2] | 1927-28 |
| Christy, J.A.J. | (1) | 103‡ | New Zealand | Christchurch | 1931-32 |
| Dalton, E.L. | (2) | 117 | England | Oval | 1935 |
| | | 102 | England | Johannesburg[1] | 1938-39 |
| Endean, W.R. | (3) | 162* | Australia | Melbourne | 1952-53 |
| | | 116 | New Zealand | Auckland | 1952-53 |
| | | 116* | England | Leeds | 1955 |
| Faulkner, G.A. | (4) | 123 | England | Johannesburg[1] | 1909-10 |
| | | 204 | Australia | Melbourne | 1910-11 |
| | | 115 | Australia | Adelaide | 1910-11 |
| | | 122* | Australia | Manchester | 1912 |
| Frank, C.N. | (1) | 152 | Australia | Johannesburg[1] | 1921-22 |
| Goddard, T.L. | (1) | 112 | England | Johannesburg[3] | 1964-65 |
| Hathorn, C.M.H. | (1) | 102 | England | Johannesburg[1] | 1905-06 |
| Irvine, B.L. | (1) | 102 | Australia | Port Elizabeth | 1969-70 |
| Lindsay, D.T. | (3) | 182 | Australia | Johannesburg[3] | 1966-67 |
| | | 137 | Australia | Durban[2] | 1966-67 |
| | | 131 | Australia | Johannesburg[3] | 1966-67 |
| McGlew, D.J. | (7) | 255*‡ | New Zealand | Wellington | 1952-53 |
| | | 104* | England | Manchester | 1955 |
| | | 133 | England | Leeds | 1955 |
| | | 108 | Australia | Johannesburg[3] | 1957-58 |
| | | 105 | Australia | Durban[2] | 1957-58 |

| | | | Opponents | Venue | Rubber |
|---|---|---|---|---|---|
| | | 127* | New Zealand | Durban² | 1961-62 |
| | | 120 | New Zealand | Johannesburg³ | 1961-62 |
| McLean, R.A. | (5) | 101 | New Zealand | Durban² | 1953-54 |
| | | 142 | England | Lord's | 1955 |
| | | 100 | England | Durban² | 1956-57 |
| | | 109 | England | Manchester | 1960 |
| | | 113 | New Zealand | Cape Town | 1961-62 |
| Melville, A. | (4) | 103 | England | Durban² | 1938-39 |
| | | 189 ) | England | Nottingham | 1947 |
| | | 104*) | | | |
| | | 117 | England | Lord's | 1947 |
| Mitchell, B. | (8) | 123 | England | Cape Town | 1930-31 |
| | | 113‡ | New Zealand | Christchurch | 1931-32 |
| | | 164* | England | Lord's | 1935 |
| | | 128 | England | Oval | 1935 |
| | | 109 | England | Durban² | 1938-39 |
| | | 120 ) | England | Oval | 1947 |
| | | 189*) | | | |
| | | 120 | England | Cape Town | 1948-49 |
| Murray, A.R.A. | (1) | 109‡ | New Zealand | Wellington | 1952-53 |
| Nourse, A.D. | (9) | 231 | Australia | Johannesburg¹ | 1935-36 |
| | | 120 | England | Cape Town | 1938-39 |
| | | 103 | England | Durban² | 1938-39 |
| | | 149 | England | Nottingham | 1947 |
| | | 115 | England | Manchester | 1947 |
| | | 112 | England | Cape Town | 1948-49 |
| | | 129* | England | Johannesburg² | 1948-49 |
| | | 114 | Australia | Cape Town | 1949-50 |
| | | 208 | England | Nottingham | 1951 |
| Nourse, A.W. | (1) | 111 | Australia | Johannesburg¹ | 1921-22 |
| Owen-Smith, H.G. | (1) | 129 | England | Leeds | 1929 |
| Pithey, A.J. | (1) | 154 | England | Cape Town | 1964-65 |
| Pollock, R.G. | (7) | 122 | Australia | Sydney | 1963-64 |
| | | 175 | Australia | Adelaide | 1963-64 |
| | | 137 | England | Port Elizabeth | 1964-65 |
| | | 125 | England | Nottingham | 1965 |
| | | 209 | Australia | Cape Town | 1966-67 |
| | | 105 | Australia | Port Elizabeth | 1966-67 |
| | | 274 | Australia | Durban² | 1969-70 |
| Richards, B.A. | (2) | 140 | Australia | Durban² | 1969-70 |
| | | 126 | Australia | Port Elizabeth | 1969-70 |
| Rowan, E.A.B. | (3) | 156* | England | Johannesburg² | 1948-49 |
| | | 143 | Australia | Durban² | 1949-50 |
| | | 236 | England | Leeds | 1951 |
| Sherwell, P.W. | (1) | 115 | England | Lord's | 1907 |
| Siedle, I.J. | (1) | 141 | England | Cape Town | 1930-31 |
| Sinclair, J.H. | (3) | 106 | England | Cape Town | 1898-99 |
| | | 101 | Australia | Johannesburg¹ | 1902-03 |
| | | 104 | Australia | Cape Town | 1902-03 |
| Snooke, S.J. | (1) | 103 | Australia | Adelaide | 1910-11 |
| Taylor, H.W. | (7) | 109 | England | Durban¹ | 1913-14 |
| | | 176 | England | Johannesburg¹ | 1922-23 |
| | | 101 | England | Johannesburg¹ | 1922-23 |
| | | 102 | England | Durban² | 1922-23 |
| | | 101 | England | Johannesburg¹ | 1927-28 |
| | | 121 | England | Oval | 1929 |
| | | 117 | England | Cape Town | 1930-31 |
| Van der Bijl, P.G.V. | (1) | 125 | England | Durban² | 1938-39 |
| Viljoen, K.G. | (2) | 111 | Australia | Melbourne | 1931-32 |

*SOUTH AFRICA – continued*

| | | | Opponents | Venue | Rubber |
|---|---|---|---|---|---|
| | | 124 | England | Manchester | 1935 |
| Wade, W.W. | (1) | 125 | England | Port Elizabeth | 1948-49 |
| Waite, J.H.B. | (4) | 113 | England | Manchester | 1955 |
| | | 115 | Australia | Johannesburg³ | 1957-58 |
| | | 134 | Australia | Durban² | 1957-58 |
| | | 101 | New Zealand | Johannesburg³ | 1961-62 |
| White, G.C. | (2) | 147 | England | Johannesburg¹ | 1905-06 |
| | | 118 | England | Durban¹ | 1909-10 |
| Winslow, P.L. | (1) | 108 | England | Manchester | 1955 |
| Zulch, J.W. | (2) | 105 | Australia | Adelaide | 1910-11 |
| | | 150 | Australia | Sydney | 1910-11 |

*WEST INDIES* (202)

| | | | | | |
|---|---|---|---|---|---|
| Alexander, F.C.M. | (1) | 108 | Australia | Sydney | 1960-61 |
| Atkinson, D.St E. | (1) | 219 | Australia | Bridgetown | 1954-55 |
| Baichan, L. | (1) | 105*‡ | Pakistan | Lahore² | 1974-75 |
| Barrow, I. | (1) | 105 | England | Manchester | 1933 |
| Butcher, B.F. | (7) | 103 | India | Calcutta | 1958-59 |
| | | 142 | India | Madras² | 1958-59 |
| | | 133 | England | Lord's | 1963 |
| | | 117 | Australia | Port-of-Spain | 1964-65 |
| | | 209* | England | Nottingham | 1966 |
| | | 101 | Australia | Sydney | 1968-69 |
| | | 118 | Australia | Adelaide | 1968-69 |
| Carew, G.M. | (1) | 107 | England | Port-of-Spain | 1947-48 |
| Carew, M.C. | (1) | 109‡ | New Zealand | Auckland | 1968-69 |
| Christiani, R.J. | (1) | 107‡ | India | Delhi | 1948-49 |
| Davis, C.A. | (4) | 103 | England | Lord's | 1969 |
| | | 125* | India | Georgetown | 1970-71 |
| | | 105 | India | Port-of-Spain | 1970-71 |
| | | 183 | New Zealand | Bridgetown | 1971-72 |
| Depeiza, C.C. | (1) | 122 | Australia | Bridgetown | 1954-55 |
| Foster, M.L.C. | (1) | 125‡ | Australia | Kingston | 1972-73 |
| Fredericks, R.C. | (8) | 163 | New Zealand | Kingston | 1971-72 |
| | | 150 | England | Birmingham | 1973 |
| | | 100 | India | Calcutta | 1974-75 |
| | | 104 | India | Bombay³ | 1974-75 |
| | | 169 | Australia | Perth | 1975-76 |
| | | 138 | England | Lord's | 1976 |
| | | 109 | England | Leeds | 1976 |
| | | 120 | Pakistan | Port-of-Spain | 1976-77 |
| Ganteaume, A.G. | (1) | 112‡ | England | Port-of-Spain | 1947-48 |
| Gomes, H.A. | (2) | 101‡ | Australia | Georgetown | 1977-78 |
| | | 115 | Australia | Kingston | 1977-78 |
| Gomez, G.E. | (1) | 101‡ | India | Delhi | 1948-49 |
| Greenidge, C.G. | (5) | 107‡ | India | Bangalore | 1974-75 |
| | | 134 )<br>101 ) | England | Manchester | 1976 |
| | | 115 | England | Leeds | 1976 |
| | | 100 | Pakistan | Kingston | 1976-77 |
| Headley, G.A. | (10) | 176‡ | England | Bridgetown | 1929-30 |
| | | 114 )<br>112 ) | England | Georgetown | 1929-30 |
| | | 223 | England | Kingston | 1929-30 |
| | | 102* | Australia | Brisbane¹ | 1930-31 |
| | | 105 | Australia | Sydney | 1930-31 |
| | | 169* | England | Manchester | 1933 |
| | | 270* | England | Kingston | 1934-35 |

*WEST INDIES – continued*

| | | | Opponents | Venue | Rubber |
|---|---|---|---|---|---|
| | | 106 ) | England | Lord's | 1939 |
| | | 107 ) | | | |
| Holford, D.A.J. | (1) | 105* | England | Lord's | 1966 |
| Holt, J.K. | (2) | 166 | England | Bridgetown | 1953-54 |
| | | 123 | India | Delhi | 1958-59 |
| Hunte, C.C. | (8) | 142‡ | Pakistan | Bridgetown | 1957-58 |
| | | 260 | Pakistan | Kingston | 1957-58 |
| | | 114 | Pakistan | Georgetown | 1957-58 |
| | | 110 | Australia | Melbourne | 1960-61 |
| | | 182 | England | Manchester | 1963 |
| | | 108* | England | Oval | 1963 |
| | | 135 | England | Manchester | 1966 |
| | | 101 | India | Bombay² | 1966-67 |
| Julien, B.D. | (2) | 121 | England | Lord's | 1973 |
| | | 101 | Pakistan | Karachi | 1974-75 |
| Kallicharran, A.I. | (10) | 100*‡ | New Zealand | Georgetown | 1971-72 |
| | | 101 | New Zealand | Port-of-Spain | 1971-72 |
| | | 158 | England | Port-of-Spain | 1973-74 |
| | | 119 | England | Bridgetown | 1973-74 |
| | | 124‡ | India | Bangalore | 1974-75 |
| | | 115 | Pakistan | Karachi | 1974-75 |
| | | 101 | Australia | Brisbane² | 1975-76 |
| | | 103* | India | Port-of-Spain | 1975-76 |
| | | 127 | Australia | Port-of-Spain | 1977-78 |
| | | 126 | Australia | Kingston | 1977-78 |
| Kanhai, R.B. | (15) | 256 | India | Calcutta | 1958-59 |
| | | 217 | Pakistan | Lahore¹ | 1958-59 |
| | | 110 | England | Port-of-Spain | 1959-60 |
| | | 117 ) | Australia | Adelaide | 1960-61 |
| | | 115 ) | | | |
| | | 138 | India | Kingston | 1961-62 |
| | | 139 | India | Port-of-Spain | 1961-62 |
| | | 129 | Australia | Bridgetown | 1964-65 |
| | | 121 | Australia | Port-of-Spain | 1964-65 |
| | | 104 | England | Oval | 1966 |
| | | 153 | England | Port-of-Spain | 1967-68 |
| | | 150 | England | Georgetown | 1967-68 |
| | | 158* | India | Kingston | 1970-71 |
| | | 105 | Australia | Bridgetown | 1972-73 |
| | | 157 | England | Lord's | 1973 |
| Lloyd, C.H. | (11) | 118‡ | England | Port-of-Spain | 1967-68 |
| | | 113* | England | Bridgetown | 1967-68 |
| | | 129‡ | Australia | Brisbane² | 1968-69 |
| | | 178 | Australia | Georgetown | 1972-73 |
| | | 132 | England | Oval | 1973 |
| | | 163 | India | Bangalore | 1974-75 |
| | | 242* | India | Bombay³ | 1974-75 |
| | | 149 | Australia | Perth | 1975-76 |
| | | 102 | Australia | Melbourne | 1975-76 |
| | | 102 | India | Bridgetown | 1975-76 |
| | | 157 | Pakistan | Bridgetown | 1976-77 |
| McMorris, E.D.A.St J. | (1) | 125‡ | India | Kingston | 1961-62 |
| Martin, F.R. | (1) | 123* | Australia | Sydney | 1930-31 |
| Nurse, S.M. | (6) | 201 | Australia | Bridgetown | 1964-65 |
| | | 137 | England | Leeds | 1966 |
| | | 136 | England | Port-of-Spain | 1967-68 |
| | | 137 | Australia | Sydney | 1968-69 |
| | | 168‡ | New Zealand | Auckland | 1968-69 |
| | | 258 | New Zealand | Christchurch | 1968-69 |

*WEST INDIES – continued*

| | | | Opponents | Venue | Rubber |
|---|---|---|---|---|---|
| Pairaudeau, B.H. | (1) | 115‡ | India | Port-of-Spain | 1952-53 |
| Rae, A.F. | (4) | 104 | India | Bombay² | 1948-49 |
| | | 109 | India | Madras¹ | 1948-49 |
| | | 106 | England | Lord's | 1950 |
| | | 109 | England | Oval | 1950 |
| Richards, I.V.A. | (8) | 192* | India | Delhi | 1974-75 |
| | | 101 | Australia | Adelaide | 1975-76 |
| | | 142 | India | Bridgetown | 1975-76 |
| | | 130 | India | Port-of-Spain | 1975-76 |
| | | 177 | India | Port-of-Spain | 1975-76 |
| | | 232‡ | England | Nottingham | 1976 |
| | | 135 | England | Manchester | 1976 |
| | | 291 | England | Oval | 1976 |
| Roach, C.A. | (2) | 122 | England | Bridgetown | 1929-30 |
| | | 209 | England | Georgetown | 1929-30 |
| Rowe, L.G. | (6) | 214‡ | New Zealand | Kingston | 1971-72 |
| | | 100*‡ | | | |
| | | 120 | England | Kingston | 1973-74 |
| | | 302 | England | Bridgetown | 1973-74 |
| | | 123 | England | Port-of-Spain | 1973-74 |
| | | 107 | Australia | Brisbane² | 1975-76 |
| Shillingford, I.T. | (1) | 120 | Pakistan | Georgetown | 1976-77 |
| Smith, O.G. | (4) | 104‡ | Australia | Kingston | 1954-55 |
| | | 161‡ | England | Birmingham | 1957 |
| | | 168 | England | Nottingham | 1957 |
| | | 100 | India | Delhi | 1958-59 |
| Sobers, G.St A. | (26) | 365* | Pakistan | Kingston | 1957-58 |
| | | 125 ⎫ | Pakistan | Georgetown | 1957-58 |
| | | 109*⎭ | | | |
| | | 142*‡ | India | Bombay² | 1958-59 |
| | | 198 | India | Kanpur | 1958-59 |
| | | 106* | India | Calcutta | 1958-59 |
| | | 226 | England | Bridgetown | 1959-60 |
| | | 147 | England | Kingston | 1959-60 |
| | | 145 | England | Georgetown | 1959-60 |
| | | 132 | Australia | Brisbane² | 1960-61 |
| | | 168 | Australia | Sydney | 1960-61 |
| | | 153 | India | Kingston | 1961-62 |
| | | 104 | India | Kingston | 1961-62 |
| | | 102 | England | Leeds | 1963 |
| | | 161 | England | Manchester | 1966 |
| | | 163* | England | Lord's | 1966 |
| | | 174 | England | Leeds | 1966 |
| | | 113* | England | Kingston | 1967-68 |
| | | 152 | England | Georgetown | 1967-68 |
| | | 110 | Australia | Adelaide | 1968-69 |
| | | 113 | Australia | Sydney | 1968-69 |
| | | 108* | India | Georgetown | 1970-71 |
| | | 178 | India | Bridgetown | 1970-71 |
| | | 132 | India | Port-of-Spain | 1970-71 |
| | | 142 | New Zealand | Bridgetown | 1971-72 |
| | | 150* | England | Lord's | 1973 |
| Solomon, J.S. | (1) | 100* | India | Delhi | 1958-59 |
| Stollmeyer, J.B. | (4) | 160 | India | Madras² | 1948-49 |
| | | 104 | Australia | Sydney | 1951-52 |
| | | 152 | New Zealand | Auckland | 1951-52 |
| | | 104* | India | Port-of-Spain | 1952-53 |
| Walcott, C.L. | (15) | 152‡ | India | Delhi | 1948-49 |
| | | 108 | India | Calcutta | 1948-49 |

| | | | *Opponents* | *Venue* | *Rubber* |
|---|---|---|---|---|---|
| *WEST INDIES – continued* | | | | | |
| | | 168* | England | Lord's | 1950 |
| | | 115 | New Zealand | Auckland | 1951-52 |
| | | 125 | India | Georgetown | 1952-53 |
| | | 118 | India | Kingston | 1952-53 |
| | | 220 | England | Bridgetown | 1953-54 |
| | | 124 | England | Port-of-Spain | 1953-54 |
| | | 116 | England | Kingston | 1953-54 |
| | | 108 | Australia | Kingston | 1954-55 |
| | | 126) 110) | Australia | Port-of-Spain | 1954-55 |
| | | 155) 110) | Australia | Kingston | 1954-55 |
| | | 145 | Pakistan | Georgetown | 1957-58 |
| Weekes, E. de C. | (15) | 141 | England | Kingston | 1947-48 |
| | | 128‡ | India | Delhi | 1948-49 |
| | | 194 | India | Bombay² | 1948-49 |
| | | 162) 101) | India | Calcutta | 1948-49 |
| | | 129 | England | Nottingham | 1950 |
| | | 207 | India | Port-of-Spain | 1952-53 |
| | | 161 | India | Port-of-Spain | 1952-53 |
| | | 109 | India | Kingston | 1952-53 |
| | | 206 | England | Port-of-Spain | 1953-54 |
| | | 139 | Australia | Port-of-Spain | 1954-55 |
| | | 123 | New Zealand | Dunedin | 1955-56 |
| | | 103 | New Zealand | Christchurch | 1955-56 |
| | | 156 | New Zealand | Wellington | 1955-56 |
| | | 197‡ | Pakistan | Bridgetown | 1957-58 |
| Weekes, K.H. | (1) | 137 | England | Oval | 1939 |
| Williams, A.B. | (1) | 100‡ | Australia | Georgetown | 1977-78 |
| Worrell, F.M.M. | (9) | 131* | England | Georgetown | 1947-48 |
| | | 261 | England | Nottingham | 1950 |
| | | 138 | England | Oval | 1950 |
| | | 108 | Australia | Melbourne | 1951-52 |
| | | 100 | New Zealand | Auckland | 1951-52 |
| | | 237 | India | Kingston | 1952-53 |
| | | 167 | England | Port-of-Spain | 1953-54 |
| | | 191* | England | Nottingham | 1957 |
| | | 197* | England | Bridgetown | 1959-60 |
| *NEW ZEALAND* (65) | | | | | |
| Barton, P.T. | (1) | 109 | South Africa | Port Elizabeth | 1961-62 |
| Burgess, M.G. | (5) | 119* | Pakistan | Dacca | 1969-70 |
| | | 104 | England | Auckland | 1970-71 |
| | | 101 | West Indies | Kingston | 1971-72 |
| | | 105 | England | Lord's | 1973 |
| | | 111 | Pakistan | Lahore² | 1976-77 |
| Congdon, B.E. | (7) | 104 | England | Christchurch | 1965-66 |
| | | 166* | West Indies | Port-of-Spain | 1971-72 |
| | | 126 | West Indies | Bridgetown | 1971-72 |
| | | 176 | England | Nottingham | 1973 |
| | | 175 | England | Lord's | 1973 |
| | | 132 | Australia | Wellington | 1973-74 |
| | | 107* | Australia | Christchurch | 1976-77 |
| Dempster, C.S. | (2) | 136 | England | Wellington | 1929-30 |
| | | 120 | England | Lord's | 1931 |
| Donnelly, M.P. | (1) | 206 | England | Lord's | 1949 |
| Dowling, G.T. | (3) | 129 | India | Bombay² | 1964-65 |

*NEW ZEALAND – continued*

| | | | Opponents | Venue | Rubber |
|---|---|---|---|---|---|
| | | 143 | India | Dunedin | 1967-68 |
| | | 239 | India | Christchurch | 1967-68 |
| Guy, J.W. | (1) | 102‡ | India | Hyderabad | 1955-56 |
| Hadlee, W.A. | (1) | 116 | England | Christchurch | 1946-47 |
| Harris, P.G.Z. | (1) | 101 | South Africa | Cape Town | 1961-62 |
| Hastings, B.F. | (4) | 117* | West Indies | Christchurch | 1968-69 |
| | | 105 | West Indies | Bridgetown | 1971-72 |
| | | 110 | Pakistan | Auckland | 1972-73 |
| | | 101 | Australia | Wellington | 1973-74 |
| Howarth, G.P. | (2) | 122) | | | |
| | | 102) | England | Auckland | 1977-78 |
| Jarvis, T.W. | (1) | 182 | West Indies | Georgetown | 1971-72 |
| Lees, W.K. | (1) | 152 | Pakistan | Karachi | 1976-77 |
| McGregor, S.N. | (1) | 111 | Pakistan | Lahore[1] | 1955-56 |
| Mills, J.E. | (1) | 117‡ | England | Wellington | 1929-30 |
| Morrison, J.F.M. | (1) | 117 | Australia | Sydney | 1973-74 |
| Page, M.L. | (1) | 104 | England | Lord's | 1931 |
| Parker, J.M. | (3) | 108 | Australia | Sydney | 1973-74 |
| | | 121 | England | Auckland | 1974-75 |
| | | 104 | India | Bombay[3] | 1976-77 |
| Pollard, V. | (2) | 116 | England | Nottingham | 1973 |
| | | 105* | England | Lord's | 1973 |
| Rabone, G.O. | (1) | 107 | South Africa | Durban[2] | 1953-54 |
| Redmond, R.E. | (1) | 107‡ | Pakistan | Auckland | 1972-73 |
| Reid, J.R. | (6) | 135 | South Africa | Cape Town | 1953-54 |
| | | 119* | India | Delhi | 1955-56 |
| | | 120 | India | Calcutta | 1955-56 |
| | | 142 | South Africa | Johannesburg[3] | 1961-62 |
| | | 100 | England | Christchurch | 1962-63 |
| | | 128 | Pakistan | Karachi | 1964-65 |
| Sinclair, B.W. | (3) | 138 | South Africa | Auckland | 1963-64 |
| | | 130 | Pakistan | Lahore[2] | 1964-65 |
| | | 114 | England | Auckland | 1965-66 |
| Sutcliffe, B. | (5) | 101 | England | Manchester | 1949 |
| | | 116 | England | Christchurch | 1950-51 |
| | | 137*‡ | India | Hyderabad | 1955-56 |
| | | 230* | India | Delhi | 1955-56 |
| | | 151* | India | Calcutta | 1964-65 |
| Taylor, B.R. | (2) | 105‡ | India | Calcutta | 1964-65 |
| | | 124‡ | West Indies | Auckland | 1968-69 |
| Turner, G.M. | (7) | 110‡ | Pakistan | Dacca | 1969-70 |
| | | 223* | West Indies | Kingston | 1971-72 |
| | | 259 | West Indies | Georgetown | 1971-72 |
| | | 101 ) | | | |
| | | 110*) | Australia | Christchurch | 1973-74 |
| | | 117 | India | Christchurch | 1975-76 |
| | | 113 | India | Kanpur | 1976-77 |
| Vivian, H.G. | (1) | 100‡ | South Africa | Wellington | 1931-32 |

*INDIA* (102)

| | | | | | |
|---|---|---|---|---|---|
| Adhikari, H.R. | (1) | 114*‡ | West Indies | Delhi | 1948-49 |
| Amarnath, L. | (1) | 118‡ | England | Bombay[1] | 1933-34 |
| Amarnath, M. | (1) | 100 | Australia | Perth | 1977-78 |
| Amarnath, S. | (1) | 124‡ | New Zealand | Auckland | 1975-76 |
| Apte, M.L. | (1) | 163* | West Indies | Port-of-Spain | 1952-53 |
| Baig, A.A. | (1) | 112‡ | England | Manchester | 1959 |
| Borde, C.G. | (5) | 109 | West Indies | Delhi | 1958-59 |
| | | 177* | Pakistan | Madras[2] | 1960-61 |
| | | 109 | New Zealand | Bombay[2] | 1964-65 |

| INDIA – *continued* | | | Opponents | Venue | Rubber |
|---|---|---|---|---|---|
| | | 121 | West Indies | Bombay² | 1966-67 |
| | | 125 | West Indies | Madras¹ | 1966-67 |
| Contractor, N.J. | (1) | 108 | Australia | Bombay² | 1959-60 |
| Durani, S.A. | (1) | 104 | West Indies | Port-of-Spain | 1961-62 |
| Engineer, F.M. | (2) | 109 | West Indies | Madras¹ | 1966-67 |
| | | 121 | England | Bombay² | 1972-73 |
| Gavaskar, S.M. | (13) | 116 | West Indies | Georgetown | 1970-71 |
| | | 117* | West Indies | Bridgetown | 1970-71 |
| | | 124)<br>220) | West Indies | Port-of-Spain | 1970-71 |
| | | 101 | England | Manchester | 1974 |
| | | 116‡ | New Zealand | Auckland | 1975-76 |
| | | 156 | West Indies | Port-of-Spain | 1975-76 |
| | | 102 | West Indies | Port-of-Spain | 1975-76 |
| | | 119 | New Zealand | Bombay³ | 1976-77 |
| | | 108 | England | Bombay³ | 1976-77 |
| | | 113 | Australia | Brisbane² | 1977-78 |
| | | 127 | Australia | Perth | 1977-78 |
| | | 118 | Australia | Melbourne | 1977-78 |
| Hanumant Singh | (1) | 105‡ | England | Delhi | 1963-64 |
| Hazare, V.S. | (7) | 116)<br>145) | Australia | Adelaide | 1947-48 |
| | | 134* | West Indies | Bombay² | 1948-49 |
| | | 122 | West Indies | Bombay² | 1948-49 |
| | | 164* | England | Delhi | 1951-52 |
| | | 155 | England | Bombay² | 1951-52 |
| | | 146* | Pakistan | Bombay² | 1952-53 |
| Jaisimha, M.L. | (3) | 127 | England | Delhi | 1961-62 |
| | | 129 | England | Calcutta | 1963-64 |
| | | 101 | Australia | Brisbane² | 1967-68 |
| Kripal Singh, A.G. | (1) | 100*‡ | New Zealand | Hyderabad | 1955-56 |
| Kunderan, B.K. | (2) | 192 | England | Madras² | 1963-64 |
| | | 100 | England | Delhi | 1963-64 |
| Manjrekar, V.L. | (7) | 133 | England | Leeds | 1952 |
| | | 118 | West Indies | Kingston | 1952-53 |
| | | 118‡ | New Zealand | Hyderabad | 1955-56 |
| | | 177 | New Zealand | Delhi | 1955-56 |
| | | 189* | England | Delhi | 1961-62 |
| | | 108 | England | Madras² | 1963-64 |
| | | 102* | New Zealand | Madras² | 1964-65 |
| Mankad, V.M.H. | (5) | 116 | Australia | Melbourne | 1947-48 |
| | | 111 | Australia | Melbourne | 1947-48 |
| | | 184 | England | Lord's | 1952 |
| | | 223 | New Zealand | Bombay² | 1955-56 |
| | | 231 | New Zealand | Madras² | 1955-56 |
| Merchant, V.M. | (3) | 114 | England | Manchester | 1936 |
| | | 128 | England | Oval | 1946 |
| | | 154 | England | Delhi | 1951-52 |
| Modi, R.S. | (1) | 112 | West Indies | Bombay² | 1948-49 |
| Mushtaq Ali | (2) | 112 | England | Manchester | 1936 |
| | | 106‡ | West Indies | Calcutta | 1948-49 |
| Nadkarni, R.G. | (1) | 122* | England | Kanpur | 1963-64 |
| Pataudi, Nawab of, jr | (6) | 103 | England | Madras² | 1961-62 |
| | | 203* | England | Delhi | 1963-64 |
| | | 128*‡ | Australia | Madras² | 1964-65 |
| | | 153 | New Zealand | Calcutta | 1964-65 |
| | | 113 | New Zealand | Delhi | 1964-65 |
| | | 148 | England | Leeds | 1967 |
| Patel, B.P. | (1) | 115* | West Indies | Port-of-Spain | 1975-76 |

| *INDIA – continued* | | | *Opponents* | *Venue* | *Rubber* |
|---|---|---|---|---|---|
| Phadkar, D.G. | (2) | 123 | Australia | Adelaide | 1947-48 |
| | | 115 | England | Calcutta | 1951-52 |
| Ramchand, G.S. | (2) | 106* | New Zealand | Calcutta | 1955-56 |
| | | 109 | Australia | Bombay² | 1956-57 |
| Roy, P. | (5) | 140 | England | Bombay² | 1951-52 |
| | | 111 | England | Madras¹ | 1951-52 |
| | | 150 | West Indies | Kingston | 1952-53 |
| | | 100 | New Zealand | Calcutta | 1955-56 |
| | | 173 | New Zealand | Madras² | 1955-56 |
| Sardesai, D.N. | (5) | 200* | New Zealand | Bombay² | 1964-65 |
| | | 106 | New Zealand | Delhi | 1964-65 |
| | | 212 | West Indies | Kingston | 1970-71 |
| | | 112 | West Indies | Port-of-Spain | 1970-71 |
| | | 150 | West Indies | Bridgetown | 1970-71 |
| Shodhan, D.H. | (1) | 110‡ | Pakistan | Calcutta | 1952-53 |
| Solkar, E.D. | (1) | 102 | West Indies | Bombay³ | 1974-75 |
| Umrigar, P.R. | (12) | 130* | England | Madras¹ | 1951-52 |
| | | 102 | Pakistan | Bombay² | 1952-53 |
| | | 130 | West Indies | Port-of-Spain | 1952-53 |
| | | 117 | West Indies | Kingston | 1952-53 |
| | | 108 | Pakistan | Peshawar | 1954-55 |
| | | 223‡ | New Zealand | Hyderabad | 1955-56 |
| | | 118 | England | Manchester | 1959 |
| | | 115 | Pakistan | Kanpur | 1960-61 |
| | | 117 | Pakistan | Madras² | 1960-61 |
| | | 112 | Pakistan | Delhi | 1960-61 |
| | | 147* | England | Kanpur | 1961-62 |
| | | 172* | West Indies | Port-of-Spain | 1961-62 |
| Viswanath, G.R. | (5) | 137‡ | Australia | Kanpur | 1969-70 |
| | | 113 | England | Bombay² | 1972-73 |
| | | 139 | West Indies | Calcutta | 1974-75 |
| | | 112 | West Indies | Port-of-Spain | 1975-76 |
| | | 103* | New Zealand | Kanpur | 1976-77 |
| Wadekar, A.L. | (1) | 143 | New Zealand | Wellington | 1967-68 |
| *PAKISTAN* (71) | | | | | |
| Alimuddin | (2) | 103* | India | Karachi | 1954-55 |
| | | 109 | England | Karachi | 1961-62 |
| Asif Iqbal | (8) | 146 | England | Oval | 1967 |
| | | 104* | England | Birmingham | 1971 |
| | | 175 | New Zealand | Dunedin | 1972-73 |
| | | 102 | England | Lahore² | 1972-73 |
| | | 166 | New Zealand | Lahore² | 1976-77 |
| | | 152* | Australia | Adelaide | 1976-77 |
| | | 120 | Australia | Sydney | 1976-77 |
| | | 135 | West Indies | Kingston | 1976-77 |
| Hanif Mohammad | (12) | 142 | India | Bahawalpur | 1954-55 |
| | | 103 | New Zealand | Dacca | 1955-56 |
| | | 337‡ | West Indies | Bridgetown | 1957-58 |
| | | 103 | West Indies | Karachi | 1958-59 |
| | | 101* | Australia | Karachi | 1959-60 |
| | | 160 | India | Bombay² | 1960-61 |
| | | 111 ) 104 ) | England | Dacca | 1961-62 |
| | | 104 | Australia | Melbourne | 1964-65 |
| | | 100* | New Zealand | Christchurch | 1964-65 |
| | | 203* | New Zealand | Lahore² | 1964-65 |
| | | 187* | England | Lord's | 1967 |

| PAKISTAN – *continued* | | | *Opponents* | *Venue* | *Rubber* |
|---|---|---|---|---|---|
| Haroon Rashid | (2) | 122‡ | England | Lahore² | 1977-78 |
| | | 108 | England | Hyderabad | 1977-78 |
| Imtiaz Ahmed | (3) | 209 | New Zealand | Lahore¹ | 1955-56 |
| | | 122 | West Indies | Kingston | 1957-58 |
| | | 135 | India | Madras² | 1960-61 |
| Intikhab Alam | (1) | 138 | England | Hyderabad | 1972-73 |
| Javed Burki | (3) | 138‡ | England | Lahore² | 1961-62 |
| | | 140 | England | Dacca | 1961-62 |
| | | 101 | England | Lord's | 1962 |
| Javed Miandad | (2) | 163‡ | New Zealand | Lahore² | 1976-77 |
| | | 206 | New Zealand | Karachi | 1976-77 |
| Khalid Ibadulla | (1) | 166‡ | Australia | Karachi | 1964-65 |
| Majid Khan | (5) | 158 | Australia | Melbourne | 1972-73 |
| | | 110 | New Zealand | Auckland | 1972-73 |
| | | 100 | West Indies | Karachi | 1974-75 |
| | | 112 | New Zealand | Karachi | 1976-77 |
| | | 167 | West Indies | Georgetown | 1976-77 |
| Mohammad Ilyas | (1) | 126 | New Zealand | Karachi | 1964-65 |
| Mudassar Nazar | (1) | 114‡ | England | Lahore² | 1977-78 |
| Mushtaq Mohammad | (10) | 101 | India | Delhi | 1960-61 |
| | | 100* | England | Nottingham | 1962 |
| | | 100 | England | Birmingham | 1971 |
| | | 121 | Australia | Sydney | 1972-73 |
| | | 201 | New Zealand | Dunedin | 1972-73 |
| | | 157 | England | Hyderabad | 1972-73 |
| | | 123 | West Indies | Lahore² | 1974-75 |
| | | 101 | New Zealand | Hyderabad | 1976-77 |
| | | 107 | New Zealand | Karachi | 1976-77 |
| | | 121 | West Indies | Port-of-Spain | 1976-77 |
| Nasim-ul-Ghani | (1) | 101 | England | Lord's | 1962 |
| Nazar Mohammad | (1) | 124* | India | Lucknow | 1952-53 |
| Sadiq Mohammad | (5) | 137 | Australia | Melbourne | 1972-73 |
| | | 166 | New Zealand | Wellington | 1972-73 |
| | | 119 | England | Lahore² | 1972-73 |
| | | 103* | New Zealand | Hyderabad | 1976-77 |
| | | 105 | Australia | Melbourne | 1976-77 |
| Saeed Ahmed | (5) | 150 | West Indies | Georgetown | 1957-58 |
| | | 166 | Australia | Lahore² | 1959-60 |
| | | 121‡ | India | Bombay² | 1960-61 |
| | | 103 | India | Madras² | 1960-61 |
| | | 172 | New Zealand | Karachi | 1964-65 |
| Waqar Hassan | (1) | 189 | New Zealand | Lahore¹ | 1955-56 |
| Wasim Raja | (2) | 107* | West Indies | Karachi | 1974-75 |
| | | 117* | West Indies | Bridgetown | 1976-77 |
| Wazir Mohammad | (2) | 106 | West Indies | Kingston | 1957-58 |
| | | 189 | West Indies | Port-of-Spain | 1957-58 |
| Zaheer Abbas | (3) | 274‡ | England | Birmingham | 1971 |
| | | 240 | England | Oval | 1974 |
| | | 101 | Australia | Adelaide | 1976-77 |

## MOST FIFTIES

| | | | | | Opponents | | | | |
|---|---|---|---|---|---|---|---|---|---|
| | | *50* | *E* | *A* | *SA* | *WI* | *NZ* | *I* | *P* |
| M.C. Cowdrey | England | 60 | – | 16 | 10 | 16 | 10 | 5 | 3 |
| G.St A. Sobers | West Indies | 56 | 23 | 10 | – | – | 1 | 15 | 7 |
| K.F. Barrington | England | 55 | – | 18 | 8 | 7 | 4 | 12 | 6 |
| L. Hutton | England | 52 | – | 19 | 11 | 11 | 7 | 4 | – |

## MOST CONSECUTIVE FIFTIES

*SEVEN*

| E. de C. Weekes | West Indies | 141 | 128 | 194 | 162 | 101 | 90 | 56 | 1947-48/1948-49 |
|---|---|---|---|---|---|---|---|---|---|

*SIX*

| J. Ryder | Australia | 78* | 58 | 56 | 142 | 201* | 88 | 1921-22/1924-25 |
|---|---|---|---|---|---|---|---|---|
| E.H. Hendren | England | 77 | 205* | 56 | 123 | 61 | 55 | 1929-30 |
| G.A. Headley | West Indies | 93 | 53 | 270* | 106 | 107 | 51 | 1934-35/1939 |
| A. Melville | South Africa | 67 | 78 | 103 | 189 | 104* | 117 | 1938-39/1947 |
| G.St A. Sobers | West Indies | 52 | 52 | 80 | 365* | 125 | 109* | 1957-58 |
| E.R. Dexter | England | 85 | 172 | 70 | 99 | 93 | 52 | 1962/1962-63 |
| K.F. Barrington | England | 63 | 132* | 101 | 94 | 126 | 76 | 1962-63 |
| K.D. Walters | Australia | 76 | 118 | 110 | 50 | 242 | 103 | 1968-69 |
| G.S. Chappell | Australia | 68 | 54* | 52 | 70 | 121 | 67 | 1975-76/1976-77 |

## OVER 250 RUNS IN A DAY

| 309 | D.G. Bradman (334) | Australia v England | Leeds | 1930 |
|---|---|---|---|---|
| 295 | W.R. Hammond (336*) | England v New Zealand | Auckland | 1932-33 |
| 273 | D.C.S. Compton (278) | England v Pakistan | Nottingham | 1954 |
| 271 | D.G. Bradman (304) | Australia v England | Leeds | 1934 |

## OVER 60% OF A COMPLETED INNINGS TOTAL

| 67.3% | C. Bannerman | 165*/245 | Australia v England | Melbourne | 1876-77 |
|---|---|---|---|---|---|
| 63.5% | C.G. Greenidge | 134/211 | West Indies v England | Manchester | 1976 |
| 62.8% | J.R. Reid | 100/159 | New Zealand v England | Christchurch | 1962-63 |
| 61.8% | S.M. Nurse | 258/417 | West Indies v New Zealand | Christchurch | 1968-69 |
| 61.8% | M. Amarnath | 60/97† | India v West Indies | Kingston | 1975-76 |
| 60.6% | V.T. Trumper | 74/122 | Australia v England | Melbourne | 1903-04 |
| 60.1% | J.T. Tyldesley | 62/103 | England v Australia | Melbourne | 1903-04 |

† *Five men were absent hurt.*
*D.L. Amiss (262*) scored 60.6% of England's total of 432 for 9 against West Indies at Kingston in 1973-74.*

## OVER 600 RUNS ADDED DURING ONE BATSMAN'S INNINGS

| 770 | L. Hutton | 364 | England v Australia | Oval | 1938 |
|---|---|---|---|---|---|
| 720 | A. Sandham | 325 | England v West Indies | Kingston | 1929-30 |
| 703 | G. St A. Sobers | 365* | West Indies v Pakistan | Kingston | 1957-58 |
| 646 | R.B. Simpson | 311 | Australia v England | Manchester | 1964 |
| 628 | Hanif Mohammad | 337 | Pakistan v West Indies | Bridgetown | 1957-58 |

# FASTEST TEST FIFTIES

| | | | | |
|---|---|---|---|---|
| 28 | J.T. Brown | England v Australia | Melbourne | 1894-95 |
| 29 | S.A. Durani | India v England | Kanpur | 1963-64 |
| 30 | E.A.V. Williams | West Indies v England | Bridgetown | 1947-48 |
| 30 | B.R. Taylor | New Zealand v West Indies | Auckland | 1968-69 |
| 33 | C.A. Roach | West Indies v England | Oval | 1933 |
| 34 | C.R. Browne | West Indies v England | Georgetown | 1929-30 |

# FASTEST TEST HUNDREDS

*Minutes*

| | | | | |
|---|---|---|---|---|
| 70 | J.M. Gregory | Australia v South Africa | Johannesburg[1] | 1921-22 |
| 75 | G.L. Jessop | England v Australia | Oval | 1902 |
| 78 | R. Benaud | Australia v West Indies | Kingston | 1954-55 |
| 80 | J.H. Sinclair | South Africa v Australia | Cape Town | 1902-03 |
| 86 | B.R. Taylor | New Zealand v West Indies | Auckland | 1968-69 |

# FASTEST TEST DOUBLE CENTURIES

*Minutes*

| | | | | |
|---|---|---|---|---|
| 214 | D.G. Bradman | Australia v England | Leeds | 1930 |
| 223 | S.J. McCabe | Australia v England | Nottingham | 1938 |
| 226 | V.T. Trumper | Australia v South Africa | Adelaide | 1910-11 |
| 234 | D.G. Bradman | Australia v England | Lord's | 1930 |
| 240 | W.R. Hammond | England v New Zealand | Auckland | 1932-33 |
| 241 | S.E. Gregory | Australia v England | Sydney | 1894-95 |
| 245 | D.C.S. Compton | England v Pakistan | Nottingham | 1954 |

# FASTEST TEST TRIPLE CENTURIES

*Minutes*

| | | | | |
|---|---|---|---|---|
| 287 | W.R. Hammond | England v New Zealand | Auckland | 1932-33 |
| 336 | D.G. Bradman | Australia v England | Leeds | 1930 |

# MOST RUNS IN A DAY BY A BATSMAN

| | | | | |
|---|---|---|---|---|
| 309 | D.G. Bradman | Australia v England | Leeds | 1930 |
| 295 | W.R. Hammond | England v New Zealand | Auckland | 1932-33 |
| 273 | D.C.S. Compton | England v Pakistan | Nottingham | 1954 |
| 271 | D.G. Bradman | Australia v England | Leeds | 1934 |

# MOST RUNS OFF ONE OVER

**EIGHT-BALL**

| | | | | |
|---|---|---|---|---|
| 25 (66061600) | B. Sutcliffe and R.W. Blair (off H.J. Tayfield) | NZ v SA | Johannesburg[2] | 1953-54 |

**SIX-BALL**

| | | | | |
|---|---|---|---|---|
| 22 (116626) | M.W. Tate and W. Voce (off A.E. Hall) | E v SA | Johannesburg[2] | 1930-31 |
| 22 (064066) | R.C. Motz (off D.A. Allen) | NZ v E | Dunedin | 1965-66 |

# MOST SIXES IN AN INNINGS

| | | | |
|---|---|---|---|
| TEN | W.R. Hammond (336*) | E v NZ    Auckland | 1932-33 |

# MOST SIXES OFF CONSECUTIVE BALLS

| | | | |
|---|---|---|---|
| THREE | W.R. Hammond (off J. Newman) | E v NZ    Auckland | 1932-33 |

# MOST RUNS FROM STROKES WORTH FOUR OR MORE IN AN INNINGS

| | 6s | 5s | 4s | | | | | |
|---|---|---|---|---|---|---|---|---|
| 238 | 5 | – | 52 | J.H. Edrich | 310* | E v NZ | Leeds | 1965 |
| 192 | 10 | – | 33 | W.R. Hammond | 336* | E v NZ | Auckland | 1932-33 |
| 184 | – | – | 46 | D.G. Bradman | 334 | A v E | Leeds | 1930 |
| 184 | 2 | – | 43 | D.G. Bradman | 304 | A v E | Leeds | 1934 |
| 177 | – | 1 | 43 | R.G. Pollock | 274 | SA v A | Durban² | 1969-70 |
| 166 | 1 | – | 40 | D.L. Amiss | 262* | E v WI | Kingston | 1973-74 |
| 157 | – | 1 | 38 | G.St A. Sobers | 365* | WI v P | Kingston | 1957-58 |
| 152 | – | – | 38 | R.E. Foster | 287 | E v A | Sydney | 1903-04 |
| 152 | 2 | – | 35 | F.M.M. Worrell | 261 | WI v E | Nottingham | 1950 |
| 152 | – | – | 38 | Zaheer Abbas | 274 | P v E | Birmingham | 1971 |

# SLOWEST INDIVIDUAL INNINGS

| Runs | Minutes | | | | |
|---|---|---|---|---|---|
| 3 | 100 | J.T. Murray (injured) | E v A | Sydney | 1962-63 |
| 5 | 102 | Nawab of Pataudi, jr | I v E | Bombay² | 1972-73 |
| 8 | 120 | T.E. Bailey | E v SA | Leeds | 1955 |
| 9 | 120 | W. Newham | E v A | Sydney | 1887-88 |
| 9 | 125 | T.W. Jarvis | NZ v I | Madras¹ | 1964-65 |
| 10* | 133 | T.G. Evans | E v A | Adelaide | 1946-47 |
| 18 | 194 | W.R. Playle | NZ v E | Leeds | 1958 |
| 20 | 195 | Hanif Mohammad | P v E | Lord's | 1954 |
| 21 | 210 | P.G.Z. Harris | NZ v P | Karachi | 1955-56 |
| 28* | 250 | J.W. Burke | A v E | Brisbane² | 1958-59 |
| 31 | 264 | K.D. Mackay | A v E | Lord's | 1956 |
| 40 | 289 | H.L. Collins | A v E | Manchester | 1921 |
| 45 | 318 | Shujauddin | P v A | Lahore² | 1959-60 |
| 58 | 367 | Ijaz Butt | P v A | Karachi | 1959-60 |
| 68 | 458 | T.E. Bailey | E v A | Brisbane² | 1958-59 |
| 99 | 500 | M.L. Jaisimha | I v P | Kanpur | 1960-61 |
| 105 | 575 | D.J. McGlew | SA v A | Durban² | 1957-58 |
| 114 | 591 | Mudassar Nazar | P v E | Lahore² | 1977-78 |
| 197* | 682 | F.M.M. Worrell | WI v E | Bridgetown | 1959-60 |
| 259 | 705 | G.M. Turner | NZ v WI | Georgetown | 1971-72 |
| 337 | 970 | Hanif Mohammad | P v WI | Bridgetown | 1957-58 |

# SLOWEST HUNDREDS

| Minutes | | | | |
|---|---|---|---|---|
| 557 | Mudassar Nazar (114) | P v E | Lahore² | 1977-78 |
| 545 | D.J. McGlew (105) | SA v A | Durban² | 1957-58 |

## DISMISSED FOR A 'PAIR' MOST TIMES

| FOUR | B.S. Chandrasekhar | India |
|------|--------------------|-------|
| THREE | B.S. Bedi | India |
| | R.W. Blair | New Zealand |
| | R. Peel | England |
| | D.L. Underwood | England |

## HIGHEST PARTNERSHIPS FOR EACH WICKET

| | | | | | |
|------|-----|-----------------------------------------------|--------|------------|---------|
| 1st | 413 | V.M.H. Mankad (231), P. Roy (173) | I v NZ | Madras² | 1955-56 |
| 2nd | 451 | W.H. Ponsford (266), D.G. Bradman (244) | A v E | Oval | 1934 |
| 3rd | 370 | W.J. Edrich (189), D.C.S. Compton (208) | E v SA | Lord's | 1947 |
| 4th | 411 | P.B.H. May (285*), M.C. Cowdrey (154) | E v WI | Birmingham | 1957 |
| 5th | 405 | S.G. Barnes (234), D.G. Bradman (234) | A v E | Sydney | 1946-47 |
| 6th | 346 | J.H.W. Fingleton (136), D.G. Bradman (270) | A v E | Melbourne | 1936-37 |
| 7th | 347 | D. St E. Atkinson (219), C.C. Depeiza (122) | WI v A | Bridgetown | 1954-55 |
| 8th | 246 | L.E.G. Ames (137), G.O.B. Allen (122) | E v NZ | Lord's | 1931 |
| 9th | 190 | Asif Iqbal (146), Intikhab Alam (51) | P v E | Oval | 1967 |
| 10th | 151 | B.F. Hastings (110), R.O. Collinge (68*) | NZ v P | Auckland | 1972-73 |

# HUNDRED PARTNERSHIPS

## ENGLAND – (513) – 1st Wicket

| Partnership | Venue | Rubber | A | SA | WI | NZ | I | P |
|---|---|---|---|---|---|---|---|---|
| L. Hutton (158), C. Washbrook (195) | Johannesburg[2] | 1948–49 | – | 359 | – | – | – | – |
| J.B. Hobbs (178), W. Rhodes (179) | Melbourne | 1911–12 | 323 | – | – | – | – | – |
| M.C. Cowdrey (155), G. Pullar (175) | Oval | 1960 | – | 290 | – | – | – | – |
| J.B. Hobbs (154), H. Sutcliffe (176) | Melbourne | 1924–25 | 283 | – | – | – | – | – |
| J.B. Hobbs (211), H. Sutcliffe (122) | Lord's | 1924 | – | 268 | – | – | – | – |
| G. Boycott (84), R.W. Barber (185) | Sydney | 1965–66 | 234 | – | – | – | – | – |
| J.B. Hobbs (187), W. Rhodes (77) | Cape Town | 1909–10 | – | 221 | – | – | – | – |
| C.J. Barnett (126), L. Hutton (100) | Nottingham | 1938 | 219 | – | – | – | – | – |
| C. Washbrook (102), R.T. Simpson (94) | Nottingham | 1950 | – | – | 212 | – | – | – |
| G. Boycott (93), D.L. Amiss (174) | Port-of-Spain | 1973–74 | – | – | 209 | – | – | – |
| G. Pullar (165), R.W. Barber (86) | Dacca | 1961–62 | – | – | – | – | – | 198 |
| T.W. Hayward (137), F.S. Jackson (118) | Oval | 1899 | 185 | – | – | – | – | – |
| G. Boycott (100*), J.M. Brearley (74) | Hyderabad | 1977–78 | – | – | – | – | – | 185 |
| J.B. Hobbs (119), H. Sutcliffe (82) | Lord's | 1926 | 182 | – | – | – | – | – |
| M.C. Cowdrey (97), G. Pullar (66) | Kingston | 1959–60 | – | – | 177 | – | – | – |
| P.E. Richardson (104), M.C. Cowdrey (80) | Manchester | 1956 | 174 | – | – | – | – | – |
| G. Gunn (85), A. Sandham (325) | Kingston | 1929–30 | – | – | 173 | – | – | – |
| J.B. Hobbs (100), H. Sutcliffe (161) | Oval | 1926 | 172 | – | – | – | – | – |
| J.H. Edrich (146), G. Boycott (90) | Bridgetown | 1967–68 | – | – | 172 | – | – | – |
| G. Boycott (70), B.W. Luckhurst (131) | Perth | 1970–71 | 171 | – | – | – | – | – |
| W.G. Grace (170), W.H. Scotton (34) | Oval | 1886 | 170 | – | – | – | – | – |
| L. Hutton (81), C. Washbrook (143) | Leeds | 1948 | 168 | – | – | – | – | – |
| G. Boycott (76*), J.H. Edrich (74*) | Melbourne | 1970–71 | 161* | – | – | – | – | – |
| R.E.S. Wyatt (54), W.R. Hammond (136*) | Durban[2] | 1930–31 | – | 160 | – | – | – | – |
| J.B. Hobbs (89), W. Rhodes (66) | Johannesburg[1] | 1909–10 | – | 159 | – | – | – | – |
| P.E. Richardson (71), G. Pullar (83) | Bombay[2] | 1961–62 | – | – | – | – | 159 | – |
| C.A.G. Russell (102*), G. Brown (84) | Oval | 1921 | 158 | – | – | – | – | – |
| J.B. Hobbs (115), H. Sutcliffe (59) | Sydney | 1924–25 | 157 | – | – | – | – | – |
| D.L. Amiss (79), D. Lloyd (214*) | Birmingham | 1974 | – | – | – | – | 157 | – |
| J.B. Hobbs (88), H. Sutcliffe (94) | Leeds | 1926 | 156 | – | – | – | – | – |
| J.B. Hobbs (159), H. Sutcliffe (63) | Oval | 1928 | – | – | 155 | NZ | – | – |
| T.W. Hayward (69), A.C. MacLaren (116) | Sydney | 1901–02 | 154 | – | – | – | – | – |
| J.M. Brearley (81), G. Boycott (80*) | Nottingham | 1977 | 154 | – | – | – | – | – |
| A. Sandham (58), C.A.G. Russell (96) | Johannesburg[1] | 1922–23 | – | 153 | – | – | – | – |
| W.G. Grace (68), A.E. Stoddart (83) | Oval | 1893 | 151 | – | – | – | – | – |
| P.E. Richardson (73), M.C. Cowdrey (81) | Nottingham | 1956 | 151 | – | – | – | – | – |
| T.W. Hayward (90), A.C. MacLaren (67) | Adelaide | 1901–02 | 149 | – | – | – | – | – |
| T.W. Hayward (67), P.F. Warner (79) | Adelaide | 1903–04 | 148 | – | – | – | – | – |
| J.B. Hobbs (187), W. Rhodes (59) | Adelaide | 1911–12 | 147 | – | – | – | – | – |
| L. Hutton (206), R.T. Simpson (68) | Oval | 1949 | – | – | – | 147 | – | – |
| W.G.A. Parkhouse (78), G. Pullar (75) | Leeds | 1959 | – | – | – | – | 146 | – |
| D.L. Amiss (50), J.M. Brearley (91) | Bombay[3] | 1976–77 | – | – | – | – | 146 | – |
| T.W. Hayward (47), A.C. MacLaren (140) | Nottingham | 1905 | 145 | – | – | – | – | – |
| J.B. Hobbs (74), H. Sutcliffe (64) | Adelaide | 1928–29 | 143 | – | – | – | – | – |
| L. Hutton (66), J.D.B. Robertson (121) | Lord's | 1949 | – | – | – | 143 | – | – |
| L. Hutton (86), D.S. Sheppard (119) | Oval | 1952 | – | – | – | – | 143 | – |
| W. Rhodes (152), A.E. Relf (63) | Johannesburg[1] | 1913–14 | – | 141 | – | – | – | – |
| L. Hutton (100), C. Washbrook (75) | Leeds | 1947 | – | 141 | – | – | – | – |
| P. Holmes (88), H. Sutcliffe (99) | Cape Town | 1927–28 | – | 140 | – | – | – | – |
| L. Hutton (40), C. Washbrook (112) | Melbourne | 1946–47 | 138 | – | – | – | – | – |
| L. Hutton (94), C. Washbrook (65) | Adelaide | 1946–47 | 137 | – | – | – | – | – |
| J.B. Hobbs (76), H. Sutcliffe (64) | Birmingham | 1924 | – | 136 | – | – | – | – |
| J.B. Hobbs (97), W. Rhodes (35) | Durban[1] | 1913–14 | – | 133 | – | – | – | – |
| L. Hutton (56), W. Watson (116) | Kingston | 1953–54 | – | – | 130 | – | – | – |
| L. Hutton (56), J.D.B. Robertson (64) | Kingston | 1947–48 | – | – | 129 | – | – | – |
| L. Hutton (57), C. Washbrook (65) | Leeds | 1948 | 129 | – | – | – | – | – |
| D. Smith (57), A. Mitchell (72) | Leeds | 1935 | – | 128 | – | – | – | – |
| J.B. Hobbs (66), H. Sutcliffe (143) | Melbourne | 1924–25 | 126 | – | – | – | – | – |
| P.E. Richardson (74), W. Watson (66) | Manchester | 1958 | – | – | – | 126 | – | – |
| J.B. Hobbs (74), H. Sutcliffe (58*) | Nottingham | 1930 | 125 | – | – | – | – | – |
| J.B. Bolus (57), J.G. Binks (55) | Bombay[2] | 1963–64 | – | – | – | – | 125 | – |

| ENGLAND – 1st Wicket – *continued* | Venue | Rubber | A | SA | WI | NZ | I | P |
|---|---|---|---|---|---|---|---|---|
| G. Boycott (47), J.H. Edrich (115) | Lord's | 1969 | – | – | – | 125 | – | – |
| G. Boycott (121*), B.W. Luckhurst (46) | Lord's | 1971 | – | – | – | – | – | 124 |
| C.F. Walters (50*), H. Sutcliffe (69*) | Manchester | 1934 | 123* | – | – | – | – | – |
| J.H. Edrich (62), R.M. Prideaux (64) | Leeds | 1968 | 123 | – | – | – | – | – |
| G. Ulyett (67), R.G. Barlow (62) | Sydney | 1881–82 | 122 | – | – | – | – | – |
| T.W. Hayward (58), P.F. Warner (68) | Melbourne | 1903–04 | 122 | – | – | – | – | – |
| L. Hutton (98*), J.T. Ikin (38) | Manchester | 1951 | – | 121 | – | – | – | – |
| G. Boycott (73), R.W. Barber (74) | Durban² | 1964–65 | – | 120 | – | – | – | – |
| J.B. Hobbs (53), H. Sutcliffe (54) | Manchester | 1928 | – | – | 119 | – | – | – |
| H. Sutcliffe (61), R.E.S. Wyatt (149) | Nottingham | 1935 | – | 118 | – | – | – | – |
| B.W. Luckhurst (53*), R.A. Hutton (58*) | Lord's | 1971 | – | – | – | – | – | 117* |
| Rev.D.S. Sheppard (57), M.C. Cowdrey (182) | Oval | 1962 | – | – | – | – | – | 117 |
| G. Boycott (77), B.W. Luckhurst (38) | Sydney | 1970–71 | 116 | – | – | – | – | – |
| D.L. Amiss (188), D. Lloyd (46) | Lord's | 1974 | – | – | – | – | 116 | – |
| P.E. Richardson (68), T.E. Bailey (80) | Durban² | 1956–57 | – | 115 | – | – | – | – |
| D.L. Amiss (90), D. Lloyd (44) | Melbourne | 1974–75 | 115 | – | – | – | – | – |
| H. Sutcliffe (86), D.R. Jardine (46) | Brisbane² | 1932–33 | 114 | – | – | – | – | – |
| Rev.D.S. Sheppard (53), G. Pullar (56) | Brisbane² | 1962–63 | 114 | – | – | – | – | – |
| J.B. Hobbs (107), W. Rhodes (59) | Lord's | 1912 | 112 | – | – | – | – | – |
| H. Sutcliffe (194), R.E.S. Wyatt (38) | Sydney | 1932–33 | 112 | – | – | – | – | – |
| J.H. Edrich (58), G. Boycott (128) | Manchester | 1969 | – | – | 112 | – | – | – |
| G. Boycott (92), D.L. Amiss (53) | Lord's | 1973 | – | – | – | 112 | – | – |
| A.C. MacLaren (65), E. Wainwright (49) | Sydney | 1897–98 | 111 | – | – | – | – | – |
| A.H. Bakewell (85), C.F. Walters (59) | Madras¹ | 1933–34 | – | – | – | – | 111 | – |
| B. Wood (52), J.H. Edrich (175) | Lord's | 1975 | 111 | – | – | – | – | – |
| J.B. Hobbs (57), H. Sutcliffe (115) | Sydney | 1924–25 | 110 | – | – | – | – | – |
| J.B. Hobbs (31), H. Sutcliffe (74) | Manchester | 1930 | 108 | – | – | – | – | – |
| J.B. Hobbs (66), W. Rhodes (49) | Oval | 1912 | 107 | – | – | – | – | – |
| G. Boycott (58), J.H. Edrich (130) | Adelaide | 1970–71 | 107 | – | – | – | – | – |
| L. Hutton (150), R.T. Simpson (53) | Lord's | 1952 | – | – | – | – | 106 | – |
| J.B. Hobbs (62*), C.B. Fry (35*) | Birmingham | 1909 | 105* | – | – | – | – | – |
| G. Boycott (56*), D.L. Amiss (56) | Birmingham | 1973 | – | – | 105*† | – | – | – |
| J.B. Hobbs (49), H. Sutcliffe (135) | Melbourne | 1928–29 | 105 | – | – | – | – | – |
| M.H. Denness (50), D.L. Amiss (112) | Lahore² | 1972–73 | – | – | – | – | – | 105 |
| H. Sutcliffe (38), C.F. Walters (64) | Oval | 1934 | 104 | – | – | – | – | – |
| L. Hutton (73), C. Washbrook (44) | Manchester | 1949 | – | – | – | 103 | – | – |
| G. Boycott (119*), J.H. Edrich (40) | Adelaide | 1970–71 | 103 | – | – | – | – | – |
| J.B. Bolus (58), J.H. Edrich (41) | Delhi | 1963–64 | – | – | – | – | 101 | – |
| J.B. Hobbs (92), W. Rhodes (35) | Johannesburg¹ | 1913–14 | – | 100 | – | – | – | – |
| L. Hutton (100), C.J. Barnett (62) | Manchester | 1937 | – | – | – | 100 | – | – |
| L. Hutton (76), C. Washbrook (39) | Adelaide | 1946–47 | 100 | – | – | – | – | – |
| **Totals: (102)** | | | **50** | **18** | **11** | **7** | **10** | **6** |

†*119 runs were added for this wicket in two partnerships, G. Boycott retiring hurt and being replaced by B.W. Luckhurst when 105 runs had been scored.*

| ENGLAND – 2nd Wicket | Venue | Rubber | A | SA | WI | NZ | I | P |
|---|---|---|---|---|---|---|---|---|
| L. Hutton (364), M. Leyland (187) | Oval | 1938 | 382 | – | – | – | – | – |
| J.H. Edrich (310*), K.F. Barrington (163) | Leeds | 1965 | – | – | – | 369 | – | – |
| P.A. Gibb (120), W.J. Edrich (219) | Durban² | 1938–39 | – | 280 | – | – | – | – |
| P.E. Richardson (126), T.W. Graveney (258) | Nottingham | 1957 | – | – | 266 | – | – | – |
| J.H. Edrich (155), P.J. Sharpe (111) | Nottingham | 1969 | – | – | – | 249 | – | – |
| M.C. Cowdrey (182), E.R. Dexter (172) | Oval | 1962 | – | – | – | – | – | 248 |
| H. Sutcliffe (102), E. Tyldesley (122) | Johannesburg¹ | 1927–28 | – | 230 | – | – | – | – |
| H. Sutcliffe (114), W.R. Hammond (138*) | Birmingham | 1929 | – | 221 | – | – | – | – |
| D.L. Amiss (188), J.H. Edrich (96) | Lord's | 1974 | – | – | – | – | 221 | – |
| L. Hutton (206), W.J. Edrich (100) | Oval | 1949 | – | – | – | 218 | – | – |
| D. Lloyd (214*), M.H. Denness (100) | Birmingham | 1974 | – | – | – | – | 211 | – |
| M.C. Cowdrey (119), E.R. Dexter (76) | Port-of-Spain | 1959–60 | – | – | 191 | – | – | – |
| H. Sutcliffe (194), W.R. Hammond (112) | Sydney | 1932–33 | 188 | – | – | – | – | – |
| H. Sutcliffe (109*), W.R. Hammond (101*) | Oval | 1929 | – | 187* | – | – | – | – |
| P.A. Gibb (93), E. Paynter (117) | Johannesburg¹ | 1938–39 | – | 184 | – | – | – | – |
| T.W. Graveney (111), P.B.H. May (79) | Sydney | 1954–55 | 182 | – | – | – | – | – |
| H. Sutcliffe (117), K.S. Duleepsinhji (109) | Oval | 1931 | – | – | – | 178 | – | – |

## HUNDRED PARTNERSHIPS – *continued*

### ENGLAND – 2nd Wicket – *continued*

| | Venue | Rubber | A | SA | WI | NZ | I | P |
|---|---|---|---|---|---|---|---|---|
| G. Boycott (116), M.C. Cowdrey (59) | Georgetown | 1967–68 | – | – | 172 | – | – | – |
| J.H. Edrich (130), K.W.R. Fletcher (80) | Adelaide | 1970–71 | 169 | – | – | – | – | – |
| P.A. Gibb (106), E. Paynter (100) | Johannesburg¹ | 1938–39 | – | 168 | – | – | – | – |
| L. Hutton (145), T.W. Graveney (78) | Lord's | 1953 | 168 | – | – | – | – | – |
| D.L. Amiss (158), K.W.R. Fletcher (78) | Hyderabad | 1972–73 | – | – | – | – | – | 168 |
| M.C. Cowdrey (159), E.R. Dexter (72) | Birmingham | 1962 | – | – | – | – | – | 166 |
| G. Pullar (89), K.F. Barrington (113*) | Delhi | 1961–62 | – | – | – | – | 164 | – |
| Rev. D.S. Sheppard (83), E.R. Dexter (85) | Nottingham | 1962 | – | – | – | – | – | 161 |
| L. Hutton (150), P.B.H. May (74) | Lord's | 1952 | – | – | – | – | 158 | – |
| C. Milburn (139), T.W. Graveney (105) | Karachi | 1968–69 | – | – | – | – | – | 156 |
| A. Shrewsbury (81), W. Gunn (77) | Lord's | 1893 | 152 | – | – | – | – | – |
| L. Hutton (122*), W.J. Edrich (60) | Sydney | 1946–47 | 150 | – | – | – | – | – |
| A. Sandham (325), R.E.S. Wyatt (58) | Kingston | 1929–30 | – | – | 148 | – | – | – |
| C. Washbrook (62), W.J. Edrich (89) | Melbourne | 1946–47 | 147 | – | – | – | – | – |
| G. Pullar (165), K.F. Barrington (84) | Dacca | 1961–62 | – | – | – | – | – | 147 |
| P.E. Richardson (107), T.W. Graveney (164) | Oval | 1957 | – | – | 146 | – | – | – |
| L. Hutton (63), R.T. Simpson (137) | Nottingham | 1951 | – | 144 | – | – | – | – |
| A.C. MacLaren (124), K.S. Ranjitsinhji (77) | Adelaide | 1897–98 | 142 | – | – | – | – | – |
| J.B. Hobbs (211), F.E. Woolley (134*) | Lord's | 1924 | – | 142 | – | – | – | – |
| G. Pullar (119), K.F. Barrington (172) | Kanpur | 1961–62 | – | – | – | – | 139 | – |
| G. Boycott (246*), K.F. Barrington (93) | Leeds | 1967 | – | – | – | – | 139 | – |
| G. Ulyett (87), J. Selby (55) | Melbourne | 1881–82 | 137 | – | – | – | – | – |
| A.C. MacLaren (109), T.W. Hayward (72) | Sydney | 1897–98 | 136 | – | – | – | – | – |
| R.W. Barber (97), E.R. Dexter (172) | Johannesburg³ | 1964–65 | – | 136 | – | – | – | – |
| J.B. Hobbs (72), G. Gunn (122*) | Sydney | 1907–08 | 134 | – | – | – | – | – |
| A.E. Fagg (39), W.R. Hammond (167) | Manchester | 1936 | – | – | – | 134 | – | – |
| L. Hutton (87), J.F. Crapp (54) | Cape Town | 1948–49 | – | 134 | – | – | – | – |
| H. Sutcliffe (58), W.R. Hammond (200) | Melbourne | 1928–29 | 133 | – | – | – | – | – |
| T.W. Graveney (60), P.B.H. May (112) | Lord's | 1955 | – | 132 | – | – | – | – |
| G. Boycott (49), C. Milburn (83) | Lord's | 1968 | 132 | – | – | – | – | – |
| J.M. Brearley (49), R.A. Woolmer (120) | Lord's | 1977 | 132 | – | – | – | – | – |
| T.W. Hayward (137), K.S. Ranjitsinhji (54) | Oval | 1899 | 131 | – | – | – | – | – |
| L. Hutton (73), N. Oldfield (80) | Oval | 1939 | – | – | 131 | – | – | – |
| L. Hutton (79), R.T. Simpson (156*) | Melbourne | 1950–51 | 131 | – | – | – | – | – |
| G. Pullar (131), M.C. Cowdrey (67) | Manchester | 1959 | – | – | – | – | 131 | – |
| H. Sutcliffe (51), E. Tyldesley (100) | Durban² | 1927–28 | – | 130 | – | – | – | – |
| D.L. Amiss (99), K.W.R. Fletcher (54) | Karachi | 1972–73 | – | – | – | – | – | 130 |
| J.B. Hobbs (159), E. Tyldesley (73) | Oval | 1928 | – | 129 | – | – | – | – |
| L. Hutton (100), P.B.H. May (138) | Leeds | 1951 | – | 129 | – | – | – | – |
| J.H. Edrich (96), M.C. Cowdrey (101) | Kingston | 1967–68 | – | – | 129 | – | – | – |
| D.L. Amiss (183), D.L. Underwood (43) | Oval | 1974 | – | – | – | – | – | 129 |
| L. Hutton (100), J. Hardstaff, jr (58) | Manchester | 1937 | – | – | – | 128 | – | – |
| W. Rhodes (61), J.W. Hearne (114) | Melbourne | 1911–12 | 127 | – | – | – | – | – |
| H. Sutcliffe (109*), K.S. Duleepsinhji (63) | Manchester | 1931 | – | – | – | 126 | – | – |
| J.H. Edrich (96), D.S. Steele (66) | Oval | 1975 | 125 | – | – | – | – | – |
| W. Rhodes (36), R.H. Spooner (119) | Lord's | 1912 | – | 124 | – | – | – | – |
| C. Washbrook (85*), W.J. Edrich (53) | Manchester | 1948 | 124 | – | – | – | – | – |
| Rev. D.S. Sheppard (113), E.R. Dexter (52) | Melbourne | 1962–63 | 124 | – | – | – | – | – |
| B.W. Luckhurst (101), J.H. Edrich (59) | Manchester | 1971 | – | – | – | – | 123 | – |
| H. Sutcliffe (56), W.R. Hammond (101) | Sydney | 1932–33 | 122 | – | – | – | – | – |
| W.G. Grace (152), A.P. Lucas (55) | Oval | 1880 | 120 | – | – | – | – | – |
| C. Washbrook (97), J.F. Crapp (51) | Johannesburg² | 1948–49 | – | 120 | – | – | – | – |
| D.L. Amiss (174), M.H. Denness (44) | Port-of-Spain | 1973–74 | – | – | 119 | – | – | – |
| C. Washbrook (103*), W.J. Edrich (70) | Leeds | 1949 | – | – | – | 118 | – | – |
| D.S. Sheppard (119), J.T. Ikin (53) | Oval | 1952 | – | – | – | – | 118 | – |
| W.E. Russell (56), M.C. Cowdrey (59) | Auckland | 1965–66 | – | – | – | 118 | – | – |
| G. Boycott (80*), M.C. Cowdrey (71) | Port-of-Spain | 1967–68 | – | – | 118 | – | – | – |
| B.W. Luckhurst (96), P.H. Parfitt (46) | Nottingham | 1972 | 117 | – | – | – | – | – |
| A. Shrewsbury (72), W. Barnes (58) | Melbourne | 1884–85 | 116 | – | – | – | – | – |
| P.A. Gibb (38), E. Paynter (243) | Durban² | 1938–39 | – | 115 | – | – | – | – |
| G. Boycott (60), T.W. Graveney (96) | Lord's | 1966 | – | – | 115 | – | – | – |
| W. Rhodes (73), W.H.R. Makepeace (54) | Melbourne | 1920–21 | 113 | – | – | – | – | – |
| J.B. Hobbs (126*), G. Gunn (43) | Melbourne | 1911–12 | 112 | – | – | – | – | – |
| J.H. Edrich (62), D.S. Steele (73) | Leeds | 1975 | 112 | – | – | – | – | – |

### ENGLAND – 2nd Wicket – *continued*

| | Venue | Rubber | A | SA | WI | NZ | I | P |
|---|---|---|---|---|---|---|---|---|
| E.H. Bowley (109), K.S. Duleepsinhji (117) | Auckland | 1929–30 | – | – | – | 111 | – | – |
| G. Boycott (58), E.R. Dexter (174) | Manchester | 1964 | 111 | – | – | – | – | – |
| R. Subba Row (49), E.R. Dexter (76) | Manchester | 1961 | 110 | – | – | – | – | – |
| R. Subba Row (112), E.R. Dexter (180) | Birmingham | 1961 | 109 | – | – | – | – | – |
| H. Gimblett (67*), M.J.L. Turnbull (37*) | Lord's | 1936 | – | – | – | – | 108* | – |
| J.H. Edrich (88), M.C. Cowdrey (104) | Birmingham | 1968 | 108 | – | – | – | – | – |
| L. Hutton (77), P.B.H. May (62) | Bridgetown | 1953–54 | – | – | 107 | – | – | – |
| A.C. MacLaren (92), J.T. Tyldesley (79) | Sydney | 1901–02 | 106 | – | – | – | – | – |
| H. Sutcliffe (143), J.W. Hearne (44) | Melbourne | 1924–25 | 106 | – | – | – | – | – |
| J.A. Jameson (82), J.H. Edrich (41) | Oval | 1971 | – | – | – | – | 106 | – |
| W.G. Grace (66), R. Abel (94) | Lord's | 1896 | 105 | – | – | – | – | – |
| J.B. Hobbs (123), W.H.R. Makepeace (30) | Adelaide | 1920–21 | 105 | – | – | – | – | – |
| Albert Ward (32), A.E. Stoddart (68) | Melbourne | 1894–95 | 104 | – | – | – | – | – |
| J.H. Edrich (175), D.S. Steele (45) | Lord's | 1975 | 104 | – | – | – | – | – |
| G. Pullar (65), K.F. Barrington (128) | Bridgetown | 1959–60 | – | – | 103 | – | – | – |
| W. Rhodes (179), G. Gunn (75) | Melbourne | 1911–12 | 102 | – | – | – | – | – |
| P. Holmes (56), E. Tyldesley (62*) | Durban[2] | 1927–28 | – | 102 | – | – | – | – |
| J.B. Hobbs (59), J.W. Hearne (57) | Sydney | 1920–21 | 100 | – | – | – | – | – |
| C. Washbrook (143), W.J. Edrich (111) | Leeds | 1948 | 100 | – | – | – | – | – |
| L. Hutton (82), P.B.H. May (39) | Oval | 1953 | 100 | – | – | – | – | – |
| D.L. Amiss (203), D.S. Steele (44) | Oval | 1976 | – | – | 100 | – | – | – |
| **Totals: (102)** | | | **42** | **17** | **14** | **9** | **12** | **8** |

### ENGLAND – 3rd Wicket

| | Venue | Rubber | A | SA | WI | NZ | I | P |
|---|---|---|---|---|---|---|---|---|
| W.J. Edrich (189), D.C.S. Compton (208) | Lord's | 1947 | – | 370 | – | – | – | – |
| L. Hutton (165*), W.R. Hammond (138) | Oval | 1939 | – | – | 264 | – | – | – |
| W.R. Hammond (177), D.R. Jardine (98) | Adelaide | 1928–29 | 262 | – | – | – | – | – |
| E.R. Dexter (174), K.F. Barrington (256) | Manchester | 1964 | 246 | – | – | – | – | – |
| R.E.S. Wyatt (113), F.E. Woolley (154) | Manchester | 1929 | – | 245 | – | – | – | – |
| J. Hardstaff, jr (114), W.R. Hammond (140) | Lord's | 1937 | – | – | – | 245 | – | – |
| E. Paynter (243), W.R. Hammond (120) | Durban[2] | 1938–39 | – | 242 | – | – | – | – |
| W.J. Edrich (191), D.C.S. Compton (115) | Manchester | 1947 | – | 228 | – | – | – | – |
| Albert Ward (93), J.T. Brown (140) | Melbourne | 1894–95 | 210 | – | – | – | – | – |
| T.W. Graveney (258), P.B.H. May (104) | Nottingham | 1957 | – | – | 207 | – | – | – |
| K.F. Barrington (148), T.W. Graveney (81) | Lord's | 1967 | – | – | – | – | – | 201 |
| C.A. Milton (104*), P.B.H. May (113*) | Leeds | 1958 | – | – | – | 194* | – | – |
| K.F. Barrington (139), M.J.K. Smith (99) | Lahore[2] | 1961–62 | – | – | – | – | – | 192 |
| E.R. Dexter (172), K.F. Barrington (121) | Johannesburg[3] | 1964–65 | – | 191 | – | – | – | – |
| J.H. Edrich (85), K.F. Barrington (115) | Melbourne | 1965–66 | 178 | – | – | – | – | – |
| W.H. Scotton (82), W. Barnes (134) | Adelaide | 1884–85 | 175 | – | – | – | – | – |
| E.R. Dexter (93), M.C. Cowdrey (113) | Melbourne | 1962–63 | 175 | – | – | – | – | – |
| R. Subba Row (94), M.J.K. Smith (98) | Oval | 1959 | – | – | – | – | 169 | – |
| A. Sandham (152), E.H. Hendren (80) | Bridgetown | 1929–30 | – | – | 168 | – | – | – |
| P.B.H. May (135), D.C.S. Compton (133) | Port-of-Spain | 1953–54 | – | – | 166 | – | – | – |
| D.W. Randall (174), D.L. Amiss (64) | Melbourne | 1976–77 | 166 | – | – | – | – | – |
| W.J. Edrich (111), A.V. Bedser (79) | Leeds | 1948 | 155 | – | – | – | – | – |
| W. Rhodes (152), C.P. Mead (102) | Johannesburg[1] | 1913–14 | – | 152 | – | – | – | – |
| D.L. Amiss (164*), M.H. Denness (59*) | Christchurch | 1974–75 | – | – | – | 151* | – | – |
| J.F. Crapp (56), D.C.S. Compton (114) | Johannesburg[2] | 1948–49 | – | 150 | – | – | – | – |
| L. Hutton (169), D.C.S. Compton (64) | Georgetown | 1953–54 | – | – | 150 | – | – | – |
| W.R. Hammond (336*), E. Paynter (36) | Auckland | 1932–33 | – | – | – | 149 | – | – |
| J.H. Edrich (70), M.H. Denness (188) | Melbourne | 1974–75 | 149 | – | – | – | – | – |
| E.R. Dexter (110), R. Subba Row (100) | Georgetown | 1959–60 | – | – | 148 | – | – | – |
| E.R. Dexter (205), M.J.K. Smith (56) | Karachi | 1961–62 | – | – | – | – | – | 143 |
| J.B. Hobbs (122), E.H. Hendren (67) | Melbourne | 1920–21 | 142 | – | – | – | – | – |
| R.A. Woolmer (137), D.W. Randall (79) | Manchester | 1977 | 142 | – | – | – | – | – |
| K.F. Barrington (142), T.W. Graveney (77) | Oval | 1967 | – | – | – | – | – | 141 |
| F.E. Woolley (87), E.H. Hendren (127*) | Lord's | 1926 | 140 | – | – | – | – | – |
| C.A.G. Russell (140), C.P. Mead (66) | Durban[2] | 1922–23 | – | 139 | – | – | – | – |
| C.T. Radley (158), G.R.J. Roope (68) | Auckland | 1977–78 | – | – | – | 139 | – | – |
| A. Shrewsbury (106), F.S. Jackson (91) | Lord's | 1893 | 137 | – | – | – | – | – |
| L. Hutton (364), W.R. Hammond (59) | Oval | 1938 | 135 | – | – | – | – | – |
| M.C. Cowdrey (72), K.F. Barrington (143) | Port-of-Spain | 1967–68 | – | – | 134 | – | – | – |

## ENGLAND – 3rd Wicket – *continued*

| | Venue | Rubber | A | SA | WI | NZ | I | P |
|---|---|---|---|---|---|---|---|---|
| M.C. Cowdrey (148), K.F. Barrington (48) | Port-of-Spain | 1967–68 | – | – | 133 | – | – | – |
| W.R. Hammond (231*), M. Leyland (42) | Sydney | 1936–37 | 129 | – | – | – | – | – |
| R.T. Simpson (81), D.C.S. Compton (79) | Christchurch | 1950–51 | – | – | – | 129 | – | – |
| G. Boycott (128), T.W. Graveney (73) | Manchester | 1969 | – | – | 128 | – | – | – |
| E. Tyldesley (78), W.R. Hammond (90) | Durban² | 1927–28 | – | 127 | – | – | – | – |
| W.R. Hammond (167), T.S. Worthington (87) | Manchester | 1936 | – | – | – | – | 127 | – |
| G. Boycott (76), E.R. Dexter (80*) | Lord's | 1965 | – | – | – | 126 | – | – |
| R.E.S. Wyatt (61*), W.R. Hammond (75*) | Sydney | 1932–33 | 125* | – | – | – | – | – |
| W.J. Edrich (88), P.B.H. May (44) | Brisbane² | 1954–55 | 124 | – | – | – | – | – |
| P.B.H. May (117), D.C.S. Compton (71) | Manchester | 1955 | – | 124 | – | – | – | – |
| H. Sutcliffe (194), Nawab of Pataudi, sr (102) | Sydney | 1932–33 | 123 | – | – | – | – | – |
| F.E. Woolley (134*), E.H. Hendren (50*) | Lord's | 1924 | – | 121* | – | – | – | – |
| T.W. Hayward (122), C.B. Fry (64) | Johannesburg¹ | 1895–96 | – | 119 | – | – | – | – |
| W.R. Hammond (75), E.H. Hendren (64) | Johannesburg¹ | 1930–31 | – | 119 | – | – | – | – |
| G. Boycott (115), K.W.R. Fletcher (81) | Leeds | 1973 | – | – | – | 119 | – | – |
| J.H. Edrich (109), K.F. Barrington (63) | Melbourne | 1965–66 | 118 | – | – | – | – | – |
| J.H. Edrich (64), M.H. Denness (181) | Auckland | 1974–75 | – | – | – | 117 | – | – |
| W. Place (107), J. Hardstaff, jr (64) | Kingston | 1947–48 | – | – | 113 | – | – | – |
| L. Hutton (74), D.C.S. Compton (184) | Nottingham | 1948 | 111 | – | – | – | – | – |
| G. Pullar (63), P.B.H. May (95) | Manchester | 1961 | 111 | – | – | – | – | – |
| P.A. Gibb (58), W.R. Hammond (181) | Cape Town | 1938–39 | – | 109 | – | – | – | – |
| L. Hutton (202*), D.C.S. Compton (44) | Oval | 1950 | – | – | 109 | – | – | – |
| A.P.E. Knott (73), J.H. Edrich (79) | Brisbane² | 1970–71 | 109 | – | – | – | – | – |
| P.E. Richardson (81), P.B.H. May (73) | Nottingham | 1956 | 108 | – | – | – | – | – |
| M.C. Cowdrey (159), T.W. Graveney (97) | Birmingham | 1962 | – | – | – | – | – | 107 |
| G. Boycott (246*), T.W. Graveney (59) | Leeds | 1967 | – | – | – | 107 | – | – |
| J.T. Tyldesley (55), J. Sharp (61) | Leeds | 1909 | 106 | – | – | – | – | – |
| W.J. Edrich (57), D.C.S. Compton (65) | Nottingham | 1947 | – | 106 | – | – | – | – |
| W.G.A. Parkhouse (69), J.G. Dewes (67) | Nottingham | 1950 | – | – | 106 | – | – | – |
| W. Rhodes (66), C.B. Fry (62) | Oval | 1909 | 104 | – | – | – | – | – |
| J. Hardstaff, jr (64), C.J. Barnett (83*) | Lord's | 1937 | – | – | – | 104 | – | – |
| Rev.D.S. Sheppard (113), M.C. Cowdrey (58*) | Melbourne | 1962–63 | 104 | – | – | – | – | – |
| W.J. Edrich (54), D.C.S. Compton (66) | Leeds | 1948 | 103 | – | – | – | – | – |
| A.C. MacLaren (47*), Hon.F.S. Jackson (55*) | Lord's | 1902 | 102* | – | – | – | – | – |
| Albert Ward (117), J.T. Brown (53) | Sydney | 1894–95 | 102 | – | – | – | – | – |
| W.J. Edrich (119), D.C.S. Compton (54) | Sydney | 1946–47 | 102 | – | – | – | – | – |
| L. Hutton (101), D.C.S. Compton (114) | Leeds | 1949 | – | – | – | 102 | – | – |
| L. Hutton (145), D.C.S. Compton (57) | Lord's | 1953 | 102 | – | – | – | – | – |
| J.H. Edrich (76*), D.B. Close (36*) | Nottingham | 1976 | – | – | 101* | – | – | – |
| P.B.H. May (97), D.J. Insole (47) | Leeds | 1955 | – | 101 | – | – | – | – |
| M.C. Cowdrey (101), K.F. Barrington (63) | Kingston | 1967–68 | – | – | 101 | – | – | – |
| G. Boycott (112), K.W.R. Fletcher (45) | Port-of-Spain | 1973–74 | – | – | 101 | – | – | – |
| T.W. Hayward (59), C.B. Fry (144) | Oval | 1905 | 100 | – | – | – | – | – |
| D.L. Amiss (118), K.W.R. Fletcher (41) | Georgetown | 1973–74 | – | – | 100 | – | – | – |
| **Totals: (83)** | | | **32** | **16** | **16** | **11** | **3** | **5** |

*Although the 3rd wicket added 145 against Australia (2nd Test – Melbourne) in 1903—04, this consisted of two partnerships: J.T. Tyldesley added 89\* with R.E. Foster (retired ill) and a further 56 with L.C. Braund.*

## ENGLAND – 4th Wicket

| | Venue | Rubber | A | SA | WI | NZ | I | P |
|---|---|---|---|---|---|---|---|---|
| P.B.H. May (285*), M.C. Cowdrey (154) | Birmingham | 1957 | – | – | 411 | – | – | – |
| W.R. Hammond (217), T.S. Worthington (128) | Oval | 1936 | – | – | – | 266 | – | – |
| M.H. Denness (188), K.W.R. Fletcher (216) | Auckland | 1974–75 | – | – | – | 266 | – | – |
| G. Boycott (246*), B.L. D'Oliveira (109) | Leeds | 1967 | – | – | – | – | 252 | – |
| A. Sandham (325), L.E.G. Ames (149) | Kingston | 1929–30 | – | – | 249 | – | – | – |
| L. Hutton (196), D.C.S. Compton (120) | Lord's | 1939 | – | – | 248 | – | – | – |
| E.H. Hendren (205*), L.E.G. Ames (105) | Port-of-Spain | 1929–30 | – | – | 237 | – | – | – |
| W.R. Hammond (240), E. Paynter (99) | Lord's | 1938 | 222 | – | – | – | – | – |
| K.F. Barrington (172), E.R. Dexter (126*) | Kanpur | 1961–62 | – | – | – | – | 206 | – |
| W.R. Hammond (181), L.E.G. Ames (115) | Cape Town | 1938–39 | – | 197 | – | – | – | – |
| M.C. Cowdrey (160), K.F. Barrington (80) | Leeds | 1959 | – | – | – | – | 193 | – |
| M.H. Denness (188), K.W.R. Fletcher (146) | Melbourne | 1974–75 | 192 | – | – | – | – | – |
| B.R. Knight (127), P.H. Parfitt (121) | Kanpur | 1963–64 | – | – | – | – | 191 | – |
| E.R. Dexter (205), P.H. Parfitt (111) | Karachi | 1961–62 | – | – | – | – | – | 188 |

## ENGLAND – 4th Wicket – *continued*

| | Venue | Rubber | A | SA | WI | NZ | I | P |
|---|---|---|---|---|---|---|---|---|
| K.F. Barrington (143), T.W. Graveney (118) | Port-of-Spain | 1967–68 | – | – | 188 | – | – | – |
| P.B.H. May (101), C. Washbrook (98) | Leeds | 1956 | 187 | – | – | – | – | – |
| T.W. Graveney (114), P.H. Parfitt (101*) | Nottingham | 1962 | – | – | – | – | – | 184 |
| P.B.H. May (92), M.C. Cowdrey (100*) | Sydney | 1958–59 | 182 | – | – | – | – | – |
| T.W. Graveney (109), M.C. Cowdrey (96) | Nottingham | 1966 | – | – | 169 | – | – | – |
| K.F. Barrington (126), M.C. Cowdrey (86) | Auckland | 1962–63 | – | – | – | 166 | – | – |
| W.R. Hammond (140), E. Paynter (75) | Durban[2] | 1938–39 | – | 164 | – | – | – | – |
| E.R. Dexter (180), K.F. Barrington (48*) | Birmingham | 1961 | 161 | – | – | – | – | – |
| K.F. Barrington (151*), E.R. Dexter (85) | Bombay[2] | 1961–62 | – | – | – | – | 161 | – |
| R.A. Woolmer (137), A.W. Greig (76) | Manchester | 1977 | 160 | – | – | – | – | – |
| A.J. Watkins (137*), D.B. Carr (76) | Delhi | 1961–62 | – | – | – | – | 158 | – |
| G. Boycott (117), K.F. Barrington (72) | Port Elizabeth | 1964–65 | – | 157 | – | – | – | – |
| P.B.H. May (83*), D.C.S. Compton (94) | Oval | 1956 | 156 | – | – | – | – | – |
| D.C.S. Compton (278), T.W. Graveney (84) | Nottingham | 1954 | – | – | – | – | – | 154 |
| C.B. Fry (144), Hon.F.S. Jackson (76) | Oval | 1905 | 151 | – | – | – | – | – |
| W.R. Hammond (65), M. Leyland (161) | Oval | 1935 | – | 151 | – | – | – | – |
| W.R. Hammond (251), E.H. Hendren (74) | Sydney | 1928–29 | 145 | – | – | – | – | – |
| A.R. Lewis (125), K.W.R. Fletcher (58) | Kanpur | 1972–73 | – | – | – | – | 144 | – |
| K.F. Barrington (121), E.R. Dexter (77) | Port-of-Spain | 1959–60 | – | – | 142 | – | – | – |
| D.C.S. Compton (112). W. Watson (57) | Nottingham | 1951 | – | 141 | – | – | – | – |
| B.W. Luckhurst (109), B.L. D'Oliveira (117) | Melbourne | 1970–71 | 140 | – | – | – | – | – |
| R.E.S. Wyatt (149), M. Leyland (69) | Nottingham | 1935 | – | 139 | – | – | – | – |
| K.F. Barrington (137), M.C. Cowdrey (85) | Birmingham | 1965 | – | – | – | 136 | – | – |
| K.F. Barrington (73), M.C. Cowdrey (78*) | Oval | 1965 | – | 135 | – | – | – | – |
| G. Boycott (112), B.L. D'Oliveira (74) | Leeds | 1971 | – | – | – | – | – | 135 |
| G. Boycott (142*), B.L. D'Oliveira (56) | Sydney | 1970–71 | 133 | – | – | – | – | – |
| W.R. Hammond (100*), L.E.G. Ames (41) | Oval | 1931 | – | – | – | 130 | – | – |
| W.R. Hammond (87*), R.E.S. Wyatt (44) | Leeds | 1935 | – | 129 | – | – | – | – |
| D.L. Amiss (203), P. Willey (33) | Oval | 1976 | – | – | 128 | – | – | – |
| G. Boycott (106), P.J. Sharpe (86) | Lord's | 1969 | – | – | 126 | – | – | – |
| D.C.S. Compton (65), J. Hardstaff, jr (103) | Oval | 1937 | – | – | – | 125 | – | – |
| P.B.H. May (106), K.F. Barrington (56) | Nottingham | 1959 | – | – | – | – | 125 | – |
| J.H. Edrich (164), T.W. Graveney (63) | Oval | 1968 | 125 | – | – | – | – | – |
| T.W. Hayward (122), A.J.L. Hill (65) | Johannesburg[1] | 1895–96 | – | 122 | – | – | – | – |
| D.C.S. Compton (79), W. Watson (79) | Nottingham | 1951 | – | 122 | – | – | – | – |
| T.W. Graveney (151), B.L. D'Oliveira (33) | Lord's | 1967 | – | – | – | – | 122 | – |
| G.R.J. Roope (77), R.A. Woolmer (149) | Oval | 1975 | 122 | – | – | – | – | – |
| P.E. Richardson (117), M.C. Cowdrey (59) | Johannesburg[3] | 1956–57 | – | 121 | – | – | – | – |
| P.B.H. May (84), M.C. Cowdrey (81) | Birmingham | 1958 | – | – | – | 121 | – | – |
| D.S. Steele (106), R.A. Woolmer (82) | Nottingham | 1976 | – | – | 121 | – | – | – |
| W.R. Hammond (63), D.R. Jardine (83) | Manchester | 1928 | – | – | 120 | – | – | – |
| J.B. Bolus (88), K.F. Barrington (80) | Madras[2] | 1963–64 | – | – | – | – | 119 | – |
| G. Gunn (119), L.C. Braund (30) | Sydney | 1907–08 | 117 | – | – | – | – | – |
| E.H. Hendren (127*), A.P.F. Chapman (50*) | Lord's | 1926 | 116* | – | – | – | – | – |
| P.B.H. May (104), M.C. Cowdrey (54) | Sydney | 1954–55 | 116 | – | – | – | – | – |
| G. Gunn (74), J. Hardstaff, sr (63) | Sydney | 1907–08 | 113 | – | – | – | – | – |
| L.C. Braund (47), J. Hardstaff, sr (72) | Adelaide | 1907–08 | 113 | – | – | – | – | – |
| D.C.S. Compton (51*), A.J. Watkins (64*) | Cape Town | 1948–49 | – | 111* | – | – | – | – |
| C.B. Fry (60), A.C. MacLaren (49) | Oval | 1899 | 110 | – | – | – | – | – |
| J.H. Edrich (100*), M.H. Denness (45*) | Manchester | 1974 | – | – | – | – | 109* | – |
| M.J.K. Smith (100), K.F. Barrington (87) | Manchester | 1959 | – | – | – | – | 109 | – |
| J.H. Edrich (310*), P.H. Parfitt (32) | Leeds | 1965 | – | – | – | 109 | – | – |
| J.H. Edrich (146), T.W. Graveney (55) | Bridgetown | 1967–68 | – | – | 109 | – | – | – |
| J.M. Brearley (59), A.W. Greig (54) | Madras[1] | 1976–77 | – | – | – | – | 109† | – |
| L.C. Braund (126), K.L. Hutchings (49) | Melbourne | 1907–08 | 108 | – | – | – | – | – |
| P.B.H. May (117), M.C. Cowdrey (50) | Manchester | 1955 | – | 108 | – | – | – | – |
| J.H. Edrich (109), M.C. Cowdrey (104) | Melbourne | 1965–66 | 105 | – | – | – | – | – |
| K.S. Duleepsinhji (173), E.H. Hendren (48) | Lord's | 1930 | 104 | – | – | – | – | – |
| W.R. Hammond (231*), L.E.G. Ames (29) | Sydney | 1936–37 | 104 | – | – | – | – | – |
| P.E. Richardson (100), M.C. Cowdrey (70) | Birmingham | 1958 | – | – | – | 104 | – | – |
| A. Shrewsbury (66), Albert Ward (55) | Oval | 1893 | 103 | – | – | – | – | – |
| W.R. Hammond (63), M.J.L. Turnbull (61) | Johannesburg[1] | 1930–31 | – | 101 | – | – | – | – |

### ENGLAND – 4th Wicket – *continued*

| | Venue | Rubber | A | SA | WI | NZ | I | P |
|---|---|---|---|---|---|---|---|---|
| F.L. Fane (37), F.E. Woolley (64) | Cape Town | 1909–10 | – | 100 | – | – | – | – |
| K.F. Barrington (93), P.H. Parfitt (122*) | Johannesburg³ | 1964–65 | – | 100 | – | – | – | – |
| **Totals: (78)** | | | **24** | **16** | **12** | **8** | **14** | **4** |

† *111 runs were added for this wicket in two partnerships, R.W. Tolchard retiring hurt and being replaced by A.W. Greig after 2 runs had been scored. Although the 4th wicket added 101 against New Zealand (Christchurch) in 1977-78, this consisted of two partnerships: G.R.J. Roope added 77\* with G. Miller (retired hurt) and a further 24 with C.T. Radley.*

### ENGLAND – 5th Wicket

| | Venue | Rubber | A | SA | WI | NZ | I | P |
|---|---|---|---|---|---|---|---|---|
| K.W.R. Fletcher (113), A.W. Greig (148) | Bombay² | 1972–73 | – | – | – | – | 254 | – |
| W.R. Hammond (227), L.E.G. Ames (103) | Christchurch | 1932–33 | – | – | – | 242 | – | – |
| D.C.S. Compton (163), N.W.D. Yardley (99) | Nottingham | 1947 | – | 237 | – | – | – | – |
| D.L. Amiss (138*), A.W. Greig (139) | Nottingham | 1973 | – | – | – | 210 | – | – |
| E. Paynter (216*), D.C.S. Compton (102) | Nottingham | 1938 | 206 | – | – | – | – | – |
| M.H. Denness (118), A.W. Greig (106) | Lord's | 1974 | – | – | – | – | 202 | – |
| R.E. Foster (287), L.C. Braund (102) | Sydney | 1903–04 | 192 | – | – | – | – | – |
| D.C.S. Compton (278), T.E. Bailey (36*) | Nottingham | 1954 | – | – | – | – | – | 192 |
| E.H. Hendren (132), M. Leyland (153) | Manchester | 1934 | 191 | – | – | – | – | – |
| G.B. Legge (196), M.S. Nichols (75) | Auckland | 1929–30 | – | – | – | 184 | – | – |
| J. Hardstaff, jr (205*), P.A. Gibb (60) | Lord's | 1946 | – | – | – | – | 182 | – |
| M. Leyland (161), L.E.G. Ames (148*) | Oval | 1935 | – | 179 | – | – | – | – |
| R. Subba Row (137), K.F. Barrington (83) | Oval | 1961 | 172 | – | – | – | – | – |
| W. Watson (109), T.E. Bailey (71) | Lord's | 1953 | 163 | – | – | – | – | – |
| A.C. MacLaren (164), R. Peel (73) | Melbourne | 1894-95 | 162 | – | – | – | – | – |
| A. Shrewsbury (164), W. Barnes (58) | Lord's | 1886 | 161 | – | – | – | – | – |
| M. Leyland (83), R.E.S. Wyatt (78) | Adelaide | 1932-33 | 156 | – | – | – | – | – |
| C.P. Mead (181), P.G.H. Fender (60) | Durban² | 1922-23 | – | 154 | – | – | – | – |
| T.W. Graveney (175), A.J. Watkins (80) | Bombay² | 1951-52 | – | – | – | – | 148 | – |
| K.W.R. Fletcher (146), A.W. Greig (89) | Melbourne | 1974-75 | 148 | – | – | – | – | – |
| D.R. Jardine (61), B.H. Valentine (136) | Bombay¹ | 1933-34 | – | – | – | – | 145 | – |
| D.C.S. Compton (158), T.E. Bailey (44) | Manchester | 1955 | – | 144 | – | – | – | – |
| K.F. Barrington (256), J.M. Parks (60) | Manchester | 1964 | 143 | – | – | – | – | – |
| R.W. Tolchard (67), A.W. Greig (103) | Calcutta | 1976–77 | – | – | – | – | 142 | – |
| D.C.S. Compton (84), T.E. Bailey (72) | Sydney | 1954–55 | 134 | – | – | – | – | – |
| C. Milburn (126*), T.W. Graveney (30*) | Lord's | 1966 | – | – | 130* | – | – | – |
| M.C. Cowdrey (93*), K.F. Barrington (54*) | Oval | 1964 | 126* | – | – | – | – | – |
| W.R. Hammond (200), D.R. Jardine (62) | Melbourne | 1928–29 | 126 | – | – | – | – | – |
| Hon. F.S. Jackson (113), R.H. Spooner (52) | Manchester | 1905 | 125 | – | – | – | – | – |
| M.J.K. Smith (87), P.H. Parfitt (46*) | Christchurch | 1965–66 | – | – | – | 125 | – | – |
| J.H. Edrich (164), B.L. D'Oliveira (158) | Oval | 1968 | 121 | – | – | – | – | – |
| D.C.S. Compton (147), J. Hardstaff, jr (67) | Adelaide | 1946–47 | 118 | – | – | – | – | – |
| P.B.H. May (113), M.C. Cowdrey (44) | Melbourne | 1958–59 | 118 | – | – | – | – | – |
| P.H. Parfitt (67), M.C. Cowdrey (151) | Delhi | 1963–64 | – | – | – | – | 115 | – |
| P.F. Warner (39), F.E. Woolley (73) | Lord's | 1912 | – | 113 | – | – | – | – |
| M.J.K. Smith (54), P.H. Parfitt (54) | Christchurch | 1965–66 | – | – | – | 113 | – | – |
| R. Abel (70), W. Barnes (62) | Oval | 1888 | 112 | – | – | – | – | – |
| J.W. Hearne (45), F.E. Woolley (57) | Leeds | 1912 | – | 111 | – | – | – | – |
| D.C.S. Compton (133), T.W. Graveney (92) | Port-of-Spain | 1953–54 | – | – | 110 | – | – | – |
| A.J. Watkins (68), C.J. Poole (55) | Calcutta | 1951–52 | – | – | – | – | 107 | – |
| W.H.R. Makepeace (117), J.W.H.T. Douglas (50) | Melbourne | 1920–21 | 106 | – | – | – | – | – |
| R. Abel (120), H. Wood (59) | Cape Town | 1888–89 | – | 105 | – | – | – | – |
| R.T. Simpson (103), T.E. Bailey (72*) | Manchester | 1949 | – | – | – | 105 | – | – |
| M.C. Cowdrey (119), M.J.K. Smith (44) | Lord's | 1965 | – | – | – | 105 | – | – |
| C.P. Mead (117), F.E. Woolley (54) | Port Elizabeth | 1913–14 | – | 104 | – | – | – | – |
| B.L. D'Oliveira (81*), D.B. Close (36) | Lord's | 1967 | – | – | – | – | – | 104 |
| E. Tyldesley (78*), P.G.H. Fender (44*) | Manchester | 1921 | 102* | – | – | – | – | – |
| K.F. Barrington (132*), T.W. Graveney (36*) | Adelaide | 1962–63 | 101* | – | – | – | – | – |
| A.R. Lewis (70*), A.W. Greig (40*) | Delhi | 1972–73 | – | – | – | – | 101* | – |
| A. Sandham (46), E.H. Hendren (142) | Oval | 1924 | – | 101 | – | – | – | – |
| E.R. Dexter (57), P.J. Sharpe (85*) | Birmingham | 1963 | – | – | 101 | – | – | – |

## ENGLAND – 5th Wicket – *continued*

| | Venue | Rubber | A | SA | WI | NZ | I | P |
|---|---|---|---|---|---|---|---|---|
| D.B. Close (46), P.J. Sharpe (63) | Oval | 1963 | – | – | – | – | 101 | – |
| A.R. Lewis (88), A.W. Greig (48) | Karachi | 1972–73 | – | – | – | – | – | 100† |
| **Totals: (53)** | | | **21** | **9** | **4** | **7** | **9** | **3** |

† *103 runs were added for this wicket in two partnerships, P.I. Pocock retiring hurt after 3 runs had been scored. Although the 5th wicket added 115 v Australia in 1884-85 (5th Test — Melbourne), this consisted of two partnerships: A. Shrewsbury added 73\* with W. Bates (retired ill) and a further 42 with W. Flowers. Similarly, in the Oval Test v Pakistan in 1974, 139 runs were added in two partnerships for the 5th wicket, K.W.R. Fletcher adding 61\* with D.L. Amiss (retired hurt) and a further 78 with A.W. Greig.*

## ENGLAND – 6th Wicket

| | Venue | Rubber | A | SA | WI | NZ | I | P |
|---|---|---|---|---|---|---|---|---|
| P.H. Parfitt (131*), B.R. Knight (125) | Auckland | 1962–63 | – | – | – | 240 | – | – |
| L. Hutton (364), J. Hardstaff, jr (169*) | Oval | 1938 | 215 | – | – | – | – | – |
| G. Boycott (107), A.P.E. Knott (135) | Nottingham | 1977 | 215 | – | – | – | – | – |
| K.F. Barrington (148*), J.M. Parks (108*) | Durban² | 1964–65 | – | 206* | – | – | – | – |
| D.C.S. Compton (116), T.E. Bailey (93) | Lord's | 1949 | – | – | – | 189 | – | – |
| W.R. Hammond (240), L.E.G. Ames (83) | Lord's | 1938 | 186 | – | – | – | – | – |
| H. Sutcliffe (161), R.E.S. Wyatt (64) | Oval | 1930 | 170 | – | – | – | – | – |
| A.W. Greig (148), A.P.E. Knott (87) | Bridgetown | 1973–74 | – | – | 163 | – | – | – |
| T.E. Bailey (82*), T.G. Evans (104) | Manchester | 1950 | – | – | 161 | – | – | – |
| I.T. Botham (103), R.W. Taylor (45) | Christchurch | 1977–78 | – | – | – | 160 | – | – |
| T.W. Graveney (73), T.G. Evans (104) | Lord's | 1952 | – | – | – | 159 | – | – |
| J.T. Tyldesley (112*), R.H. Spooner (79) | Oval | 1905 | 158 | – | – | – | – | – |
| L.E.G. Ames (126), J. Iddon (54) | Kingston | 1934–35 | – | – | 157 | – | – | – |
| C.P. Mead (181), F.T. Mann (84) | Durban² | 1922–23 | – | 156 | – | – | – | – |
| P.H. Parfitt (101*), D.A. Allen (79*) | Birmingham | 1962 | – | – | – | – | – | 153* |
| A.W. Greig (116), A.P.E. Knott (116) | Leeds | 1976 | – | – | 152 | – | – | – |
| R.A. Woolmer (149), A.P.E. Knott (64) | Oval | 1975 | 151 | – | – | – | – | – |
| L.C. Braund (104), G.L. Jessop (93) | Lord's | 1907 | – | 145 | – | – | – | – |
| M. Leyland (153), L.E.G. Ames (72) | Manchester | 1934 | 142 | – | – | – | – | – |
| K.W.R. Fletcher (129*), A.P.E. Knott (67) | Bridgetown | 1973–74 | – | – | 142 | – | – | – |
| Hon. F.S. Jackson (128), L.C. Braun (65) | Manchester | 1902 | 141 | – | – | – | – | – |
| E.H. Hendren (95), M. Leyland (137) | Melbourne | 1928–29 | 140 | – | – | – | – | – |
| M.C. Cowdrey (79), J.M. Parks (89) | Melbourne | 1965–66 | 138 | – | – | – | – | – |
| W.W. Read (52), F.S. Jackson (103) | Oval | 1893 | 131 | – | – | – | – | – |
| M. Leyland (102), M.W. Tate (100*) | Lord's | 1929 | – | 129 | – | – | – | – |
| M. Leyland (109), L.E.G. Ames (120) | Lord's | 1934 | 129 | – | – | – | – | – |
| J.H. Hampshire (107), A.P.E. Knott (53) | Lord's | 1969 | – | – | 128 | – | – | – |
| M.C. Cowdrey (82), A.P.E. Knott (73*) | Georgetown | 1967–68 | – | – | 127 | – | – | – |
| A.P.F. Chapman (121), G.O.B. Allen (57) | Lord's | 1930 | 125 | – | – | – | – | – |
| G.H. Hirst (62), K.S. Ranjitsinhji (175) | Sydney | 1897–98 | 124 | – | – | – | – | – |
| C.A.G. Russell (135*), J.W.H.T. Douglas (60) | Adelaide | 1920–21 | 124 | – | – | – | – | – |
| F.E. Woolley (115*), F.T. Mann (59) | Johannesburg¹ | 1922–23 | – | 124 | – | – | – | – |
| G. Boycott (191), A.P.E. Knott (57) | Leeds | 1977 | 123 | – | – | – | – | – |
| C.P. Mead (182), Hon. L.H. Tennyson (51) | Oval | 1921 | 121 | – | – | – | – | – |
| M.J.K. Smith (99), P.M. Walker (52) | Lord's | 1960 | – | 120 | – | – | – | – |
| A.W. Greig (121), A.P.E. Knott (61) | Georgetown | 1973–74 | – | – | 119 | – | – | – |
| M.J.K. Smith (121), J.M. Parks (59) | Cape Town | 1964–65 | – | 117 | – | – | – | – |
| W.W. Read (66), E.F.S. Tylecote (66) | Sydney | 1882–83 | 116 | – | – | – | – | – |
| Hon. F.S. Jackson (82*), W. Rhodes (39*) | Nottingham | 1905 | 113* | – | – | – | – | – |
| J.T. Ikin (48), N.W.D. Yardley (61) | Melbourne | 1946–47 | 113 | – | – | – | – | – |
| M.C. Cowdrey (148), A.P.E. Knott (69*) | Port–of–Spain | 1967–68 | – | – | 113 | – | – | – |
| A.W. Greig (64), A.P.E. Knott (63*) | Hyderabad | 1972–73 | – | – | – | – | – | 112 |
| Hon. F.S. Jackson (49), G.L. Jessop (104) | Oval | 1902 | 109 | – | – | – | – | – |
| W.G. Quaife (68), L.C. Braund (103*) | Adelaide | 1901–02 | 108 | – | – | – | – | – |
| L. Hutton (205), T.G. Evans (28) | Kingston | 1953–54 | – | – | 108 | – | – | – |
| F.E. Woolley (83), M. Leyland (45) | Leeds | 1929 | – | 106 | – | – | – | – |
| M.J. Horton (58), T.G. Evans (73) | Nottingham | 1959 | – | – | – | – | 106 | – |
| B.L. D'Oliveira (72), R. Illingworth (45) | Leeds | 1971 | – | – | – | – | – | 106 |
| M. Leyland (53), R.W.V. Robins (108) | Manchester | 1935 | – | 105 | – | – | – | – |
| J.W.H.T. Douglas (60), P.G.H. Fender (59) | Melbourne | 1920–21 | 104 | – | – | – | – | – |
| K.W.R. Fletcher (123*), A.W. Greig (53) | Manchester | 1974 | – | – | – | – | 104 | – |

### ENGLAND – 6th Wicket – *continued*

| Player | Venue | Rubber | A | SA | WI | NZ | I | P |
|---|---|---|---|---|---|---|---|---|
| E.R. Dexter (66*), R.W. Barber (39*) | Lahore[2] | 1961–62 | – | – | – | – | – | 101* |
| D.L. Amiss (179), A.P.E. Knott (75) | Delhi | 1976–77 | – | – | – | – | 101 | – |
| F.G. Mann (136*), R.O. Jenkins (29) | Port Elizabeth | 1948–49 | – | 100 | – | – | – | – |
| **Totals: (54)** | | | **23** | **10** | **10** | **3** | **4** | **4** |

*Although the 6th wicket added 121 v. Australia (Oval) 1934, this consisted of two partnerships: M. Leyland added 85\* with L.E.G. Ames (retired hurt) and a further 36 with G.O.B. Allen.*

### ENGLAND – 7th Wicket

| Player | Venue | Rubber | A | SA | WI | NZ | I | P |
|---|---|---|---|---|---|---|---|---|
| M.J.K. Smith (96), J.M. Parks (101*) | Port-of-Spain | 1959–60 | – | – | 197 | – | – | – |
| M.C. Cowdrey (152), T.G. Evans (82) | Lord's | 1957 | – | – | 174 | – | – | – |
| A.P.E. Knott (116), P. Lever (47) | Birmingham | 1971 | – | – | – | – | – | 159 |
| A.P.E. Knott (104), P. Lever (64) | Auckland | 1970–71 | – | – | – | 149 | – | – |
| F.E. Woolley (133*), J. Vine (36) | Sydney | 1911–12 | 143 | – | – | – | – | – |
| J. Sharp (105), K.L. Hutchings (59) | Oval | 1909 | 142 | – | – | – | – | – |
| D.R. Jardine (128), R.W.V. Robins (55) | Manchester | 1933 | – | – | 140 | – | – | – |
| W.W. Whysall (76), R. Kilner (74) | Melbourne | 1924–25 | 133 | – | – | – | – | – |
| K.W.R. Fletcher (122), C.M. Old (65) | Oval | 1974 | – | – | – | – | – | 130 |
| A.F.A. Lilley (84), L.C. Braund (58) | Sydney | 1901–02 | 124 | – | – | – | – | – |
| E.R. Dexter (136*), R. Swetman (45) | Bridgetown | 1959–60 | – | – | 123 | – | – | – |
| J.B. Hobbs (119), E.H. Hendren (92) | Adelaide | 1924–25 | 117 | – | – | – | – | – |
| J.W.H.T. Douglas (119), M.C. Bird (61) | Durban[1] | 1913–14 | – | 115 | – | – | – | – |
| T.W. Hayward (130), A.F.A. Lilley (58) | Manchester | 1899 | 113 | – | – | – | – | – |
| M. Leyland (111*), R.W.V. Robins (61) | Melbourne | 1936–37 | 111 | – | – | – | – | – |
| F.R. Brown (74), W. Voce (66) | Christchurch | 1932–33 | – | – | – | 108 | – | – |
| J. Hardstaff, jr (169*), A. Wood (53) | Oval | 1938 | 106 | – | – | – | – | – |
| L. Hutton (205), J.H. Wardle (66) | Kingston | 1953–54 | – | – | 105 | – | – | – |
| A.P.E. Knott (90), R.A. Hutton (81) | Oval | 1971 | – | – | – | – | 103 | – |
| W. Flowers (56), J.M. Read (56) | Sydney | 1884–85 | 102 | – | – | – | – | – |
| R. Illingworth (50), R. Swetman (65) | Oval | 1959 | – | – | – | – | 102 | – |
| E.H. Hendren (79), G. Geary (53) | Nottingham | 1934 | 101 | – | – | – | – | – |
| **Totals: (22)** | | | **10** | **1** | **5** | **2** | **2** | **2** |

### ENGLAND – 8th Wicket

| Player | Venue | Rubber | A | SA | WI | NZ | I | P |
|---|---|---|---|---|---|---|---|---|
| L.E.G. Ames (137), G.O.B. Allen (122) | Lord's | 1931 | – | – | – | 246 | – | – |
| T.W. Graveney (165), J.T. Murray (112) | Oval | 1966 | – | – | 217 | – | – | – |
| R. Illingworth (107), P. Lever (88*) | Manchester | 1971 | – | – | – | – | 168 | – |
| C.W. Wright (71), H.R. Bromley-Davenport (84) | Johannesburg[1] | 1895–96 | – | 154 | – | – | – | – |
| R.W.V. Robins (76), H. Verity (66*) | Manchester | 1936 | – | – | – | – | 138 | – |
| E.H. Hendren (169), H. Larwood (70) | Brisbane[1] | 1928–29 | 124 | – | – | – | – | – |
| D.C.S. Compton (145*), A.V. Bedser (37) | Manchester | 1948 | 121 | – | – | – | – | – |
| D.A. Allen (88), D.J. Brown (44) | Christchurch | 1965–66 | – | – | – | 107 | – | – |
| R. Illingworth (57), J.A. Snow (48) | Leeds | 1972 | 104 | – | – | – | – | – |
| **Totals: (9)** | | | **3** | **1** | **1** | **2** | **2** | **–** |

### ENGLAND – 9th Wicket

| Player | Venue | Rubber | A | SA | WI | NZ | I | P |
|---|---|---|---|---|---|---|---|---|
| M.C. Cowdrey (128*), A.C. Smith (69*) | Wellington | 1962–63 | – | – | – | – | 163* | – |
| W.H. Scotton (90), W.W. Read (117) | Oval | 1884 | 151 | – | – | – | – | – |
| F.E. Woolley (123), A.P. Freeman (50*) | Sydney | 1924–25 | 128 | – | – | – | – | – |
| T.F. Bailey (134*), D.V.P. Wright (45) | Christchurch | 1950–51 | – | – | – | 117 | – | – |
| R.E. Foster (287), A.E. Relf (31) | Sydney | 1903–04 | 115 | – | – | – | – | – |
| G.A.R. Lock (89), P.I. Pocock (13) | Georgetown | 1967–68 | – | – | 109 | – | – | – |
| G. Geary (35*), G.G. Macaulay (76) | Leeds | 1926 | 108 | – | – | – | – | – |
| **Totals: (7)** | | | **4** | **–** | **1** | **1** | **1** | **–** |

### ENGLAND – 10th Wicket

| Player | Venue | Rubber | A | SA | WI | NZ | I | P |
|---|---|---|---|---|---|---|---|---|
| R.E. Foster (287), W. Rhodes (40*) | Sydney | 1903–04 | 130 | – | – | – | – | – |
| K. Higgs (63), J.A. Snow (59*) | Oval | 1966 | – | – | 128 | – | – | – |
| **Totals: (2)** | | | **1** | **–** | **1** | **–** | **–** | **–** |

### AUSTRALIA – (360) – 1st Wicket

| | Venue | Rubber | E | SA | WI | NZ | I | P |
|---|---|---|---|---|---|---|---|---|
| W.M. Lawry (210), R.B. Simpson (201) | Bridgetown | 1964–65 | – | – | 382 | – | – | – |
| R.B. Simpson (225), W.M. Lawry (119) | Adelaide | 1965–66 | 244 | – | – | – | – | – |
| J.H.W. Fingleton (112), W.A. Brown (121) | Cape Town | 1935–36 | – | 233 | – | – | – | – |
| W.M. Lawry (157), I.R. Redpath (97) | Melbourne | 1963–64 | – | 219 | – | – | – | – |
| A.R. Morris (111), J. Moroney (118) | Johannesburg² | 1949–50 | – | 214 | – | – | – | – |
| W.M. Lawry (106), R.B. Simpson (311) | Manchester | 1964 | 201 | – | – | – | – | – |
| A.R. Morris (111), C.C. McDonald (110) | Port-of-Spain | 1954–55 | – | – | 191 | – | – | – |
| R.B. Simpson (109), W.M. Lawry (100) | Melbourne | 1967–68 | – | – | – | – | 191 | – |
| C.C. McDonald (99), J.W. Burke (189) | Cape Town | 1957–58 | – | 190 | – | – | – | – |
| W. Bardsley (130), S.E. Gregory (74) | Oval | 1909 | 180 | – | – | – | – | – |
| W.H. Ponsford (92*), A. Jackson (70*) | Adelaide | 1930–31 | – | – | 172* | – | – | – |
| C.C.McDonald (170), J.W. Burke (66) | Adelaide | 1958–59 | 171 | – | – | – | – | – |
| W.M. Woodfull (155), W.H. Ponsford (81) | Lord's | 1930 | 162 | – | – | – | – | – |
| J.H.W. Fingleton (118), W.A. Brown (84) | Durban² | 1935–36 | – | 162 | – | – | – | – |
| K.R. Stackpole (142), I.R. Redpath (60) | Kingston | 1972–73 | – | – | 161 | – | – | – |
| W.M. Woodfull (54), W.H. Ponsford (110) | Oval | 1930 | 159 | – | – | – | – | – |
| I.R. Redpath (65), A.Turner (136) | Adelaide | 1975–76 | – | – | 148 | – | – | – |
| C.C. McDonald (91), R.B. Simpson (75) | Melbourne | 1960–61 | – | – | 146 | – | – | – |
| C.C. McDonald (78), J.W. Burke (65) | Lord's | 1956 | 137 | – | – | – | – | – |
| W.M. Lawry (98), R.B. Simpson (71) | Brisbane² | 1962–63 | 136 | – | – | – | – | – |
| K.P. Stackpole (76*), I.R. Redpath (57*) | Georgetown | 1972–73 | – | – | 135* | – | – | – |
| V.T. Trumper (104), R.A. Duff (54) | Manchester | 1902 | 135 | – | – | – | – | – |
| I.C. Davis (56), A. Turner (82) | Melbourne | 1976–77 | – | – | – | – | – | 134 |
| W.M. Woodfull (67), V.Y. Richardson (83) | Brisbane² | 1932–33 | 133 | – | – | – | – | – |
| V.T. Trumper (113), R.A. Duff (79) | Adelaide | 1903–04 | 129 | – | – | – | – | – |
| V.T. Trumper (63), M.A. Noble (64) | Melbourne | 1907–08 | 126 | – | – | – | – | – |
| S.G. Barnes (71), A.R. Morris (57) | Sydney | 1946–47 | 126 | – | – | – | – | – |
| H.L. Collins (104), W. Bardsley (57) | Sydney | 1920–21 | 123 | – | – | – | – | – |
| S.G. Barnes (141), A.R. Morris (57) | Lord's | 1948 | 122 | – | – | – | – | – |
| C.C. McDonald (41), A.R. Morris (99) | Melbourne | 1952–53 | – | 122 | – | – | – | – |
| R.B. Simpson (67), W.M. Lawry (78) | Melbourne | 1965–66 | 120 | – | – | – | – | – |
| R.B. Simpson (65), W.M. Lawry (98) | Johannesburg³ | 1966–67 | – | 118 | – | – | – | – |
| H.L. Collins (59), W. Bardsley (56) | Melbourne | 1920–21 | 117 | – | – | – | – | – |
| S.G. Barnes (61), A.R. Morris (196) | Oval | 1948 | 117 | – | – | – | – | – |
| C.E. McLeod (77), J.Worrall (75) | Oval | 1899 | 116 | – | – | – | – | – |
| H.L. Collins (64), W. Bardsley (51) | Melbourne | 1920–21 | 116 | – | – | – | – | – |
| A.R. Morris (124*), M.R. Harvey (31) | Adelaide | 1946–47 | 116 | – | – | – | – | – |
| W.M. Lawry (45), I.R. Redpath (79) | Brisbane² | 1967–68 | – | – | – | – | 116 | – |
| W.M. Lawry (47*), R.B. Simpson (71) | Calcutta | 1964–65 | – | – | – | – | 115 | – |
| W.M. Lawry (102), R.B. Simpson (51) | Manchester | 1961 | 113 | – | – | – | – | – |
| W.M. Lawry (52), R.M. Cowper (165) | Sydney | 1967–68 | – | – | – | – | 111 | – |
| I.R. Redpath (83),R.B. McCosker (76) | Melbourne | 1974–75 | 111 | – | – | – | – | – |
| A.C. Bannerman (37), W.L. Murdoch (85) | Melbourne | 1881–82 | 110 | – | – | – | – | – |
| C.C. McDonald (46), L.E. Favell (72) | Bridgetown | 1954–55 | – | – | 108 | – | – | – |
| W.M. Woodfull (54), W.H. Ponsford (83) | Manchester | 1930 | 106 | – | – | – | – | – |
| J.H.W. Fingleton (62), W.A. Brown (51) | Johannesburg¹ | 1935–36 | – | 105 | – | – | – | – |
| W. Bardsley (63*), T.J.E. Andrews (49) | Lord's | 1921 | 103 | – | – | – | – | – |
| A.R. Morris (65), C.C. McDonald (50) | Kingston | 1954–55 | – | – | 102 | – | – | – |
| V.T. Trumper (70), R.A. Duff (34) | Cape Town | 1902–03 | – | 100 | – | – | – | – |
| **Totals: (49)** | | | **26** | **9** | **9** | **–** | **4** | **1** |

### AUSTRALIA – 2nd Wicket

| | Venue | Rubber | E | SA | WI | NZ | I | P |
|---|---|---|---|---|---|---|---|---|
| W.H. Ponsford (266), D.G. Bradman (244) | Oval | 1934 | 451 | – | – | – | – | – |
| A.R. Morris (182), D.G. Bradman (173*) | Leeds | 1948 | 301 | – | – | – | – | – |
| W.M. Lawry (205), I.M. Chappell (165) | Melbourne | 1968–69 | – | – | 298 | – | – | – |
| R.B. McCosker (127), I.M. Chappell (192) | Oval | 1975 | 277 | – | – | – | – | – |
| C.C. McDonald (154), A.L. Hassett (163) | Adelaide | 1952–53 | – | 275 | – | – | – | – |
| W.M. Woodfull (161), D.G. Bradman (167) | Melbourne | 1931–32 | – | 274 | – | – | – | – |
| S.G. Barnes (112), D.G. Bradman (201) | Adelaide | 1947–48 | – | – | – | – | 236 | – |
| W.M. Woodfull (141), C.G. Macartney (151) | Leeds | 1926 | 235 | – | – | – | – | – |
| A.P. Sheahan (127), J. Benaud (142) | Melbourne | 1972–73 | – | – | – | – | – | 233 |
| W.M. Woodfull (155), D.G. Bradman (254) | Lord's | 1930 | 231 | – | – | – | – | – |

**AUSTRALIA – 2nd Wicket – *continued***

| | Venue | Rubber | E | SA | WI | NZ | I | P |
|---|---|---|---|---|---|---|---|---|
| W.H. Ponsford (109), D.G. Bradman (223) | Brisbane[1] | 1930–31 | – | – | 229 | – | – | – |
| W. Bardsley (132), C. Hill (191) | Sydney | 1910–11 | – | 224 | – | – | – | – |
| I.R. Redpath (105), G.S. Chappell (144) | Sydney | 1974–75 | 220 | – | – | – | – | – |
| W.M. Lawry (105), I.M. Chappell (117) | Brisbane[2] | 1968–69 | – | – | 217 | – | – | – |
| W.M. Woodfull (111), H.S.T.L. Hendry (112) | Sydney | 1928–29 | 215 | – | – | – | – | – |
| J.W. Burke (161), R.N. Harvey (140) | Bombay[2] | 1956–57 | – | – | – | – | 204 | – |
| K.R. Stackpole (136), I.M. Chappell (104) | Adelaide | 1970–71 | 202 | – | – | – | – | – |
| W.A. Brown (72), S.J. McCabe (137) | Manchester | 1934 | 196 | – | – | – | – | – |
| W.M. Woodfull (117), C.G. Macartney (109) | Manchester | 1926 | 192 | – | – | – | – | – |
| W.M. Woodfull (50), D.G. Bradman (334) | Leeds | 1930 | 192 | – | – | – | – | – |
| H.L. Collins (114), W.H. Ponsford (110) | Sydney | 1924–25 | 190 | – | – | – | – | – |
| I.R. Redpath (72), I.M. Chappell (111) | Melbourne | 1970–71 | 180† | – | – | – | – | – |
| G.M. Wood (90), P.M. Toohey (97) | Kingston | 1977–78 | – | – | 180 | – | – | – |
| J.H.W. Fingleton (40), S.J. McCabe (189*) | Johannesburg[1] | 1935–36 | – | 177 | – | – | – | – |
| W.M. Woodfull (82), D.G. Bradman (299*) | Adelaide | 1931–32 | – | 176 | – | – | – | – |
| I.C. Davis (88), R.B. McCosker (105) | Melbourne | 1976–77 | – | – | – | – | – | 176 |
| A.C. Bannerman (91), J.J. Lyons (134) | Sydney | 1891–92 | 174 | – | – | – | – | – |
| S.G. Barnes (141), D.G. Bradman (89) | Lord's | 1948 | 174 | – | – | – | – | – |
| W.A. Brown (133), D.G. Bradman (144*) | Nottingham | 1938 | 170 | – | – | – | – | – |
| J. Moroney (101*), R.N. Harvey (100) | Johannesburg[2] | 1949–50 | – | 170 | – | – | – | – |
| A.R. Morris (89), K.R. Miller (109) | Lord's | 1953 | 165 | – | – | – | – | – |
| W.M. Woodfull (76), D.G. Bradman (226) | Brisbane[2] | 1931–32 | – | 163 | – | – | – | – |
| W.A. Brown (66), S.J. McCabe (149) | Durban[2] | 1935–36 | – | 161 | – | – | – | – |
| R.B. Simpson (91), R.N. Harvey (64) | Sydney | 1962–63 | 160 | – | – | – | – | – |
| A.R. Morris (77), R.N. Harvey (116) | Adelaide | 1952–53 | – | 157 | – | – | – | – |
| W.M. Woodfull (83), D.G. Bradman (152) | Melbourne | 1930–31 | – | – | 156 | – | – | – |
| K.R. Stackpole (207), I.M. Chappell (59) | Brisbane[2] | 1970–71 | 151 | – | – | – | – | – |
| J. Darling (178), C. Hill (81) | Adelaide | 1897–98 | 148 | – | – | – | – | – |
| C. Kelleway (61), C.G. Macartney (99) | Lord's | 1912 | 146 | – | – | – | – | – |
| P.S. McDonnell (103), W.L. Murdoch (211) | Oval | 1884 | 143 | – | – | – | – | – |
| V.T. Trumper (113), C. Hill (88) | Adelaide | 1903–04 | 143 | – | – | – | – | – |
| I.R. Redpath (93), I.M. Chappell (121) | Wellington | 1973–74 | – | – | – | 141 | – | – |
| W.M. Lawry (89), N.C. O'Neill (88) | Sydney | 1963–64 | – | 140 | – | – | – | – |
| W.M. Lawry (210), R.M. Cowper (102) | Bridgetown | 1964–65 | – | – | 140 | – | – | – |
| R.B. Simpson (72), R.M. Cowper (69) | Port-of-Spain | 1964–65 | – | – | 138 | – | – | – |
| W.M. Woodfull (58), K.E. Rigg (127) | Sydney | 1931–32 | – | 137 | – | – | – | – |
| V.T. Trumper (65), C. Hill (98) | Adelaide | 1901–02 | 136 | – | – | – | – | – |
| F.A. Iredale (108), G. Giffen (80) | Manchester | 1896 | 131 | – | – | – | – | – |
| W.M. Lawry (135), I.R. Redpath (67) | Oval | 1968 | 129 | – | – | – | – | – |
| K.R. Stackpole (122), I.M. Chappell (54) | Melbourne | 1973–74 | – | – | – | 128 | – | – |
| I.R. Redpath (103), G.N. Yallop (47) | Adelaide | 1975–76 | – | – | 128 | – | – | – |
| C.C. McDonald (47), R.N. Harvey (167) | Melbourne | 1958–59 | 126 | – | – | – | – | – |
| A.L. Hassett (104), R.N. Harvey (59) | Lord's | 1953 | 125 | – | – | – | – | – |
| I.C. Davis (105), R.B. McCosker (65) | Adelaide | 1976–77 | – | – | – | – | – | 125 |
| C.E. McLeod (112), C. Hill (58) | Melbourne | 1897–98 | 124 | – | – | – | – | – |
| C.G. Macartney (137), H.V. Hordern (50) | Sydney | 1910–11 | – | 124 | – | – | – | – |
| J.H.W. Fingleton (73), D.G. Bradman (82) | Sydney | 1936–37 | 124 | – | – | – | – | – |
| R. Edwards (170*), I.M. Chappell (50) | Nottingham | 1972 | 124 | – | – | – | – | – |
| H.L. Collins (24), C.G. Macartney (133*) | Lord's | 1926 | 123 | – | – | – | – | – |
| I.R. Redpath (135), I.M. Chappell (66) | Melbourne | 1972–73 | – | – | – | – | – | 123 |
| A.R. Morris (67), A.L. Hassett (115) | Nottingham | 1953 | 122 | – | – | – | – | – |
| C. Kelleway (70), C. Hill (65) | Sydney | 1911–12 | 121 | – | – | – | – | – |
| K.A. Archer (48), A.L. Hassett (70) | Sydney | 1950–51 | 121 | – | – | – | – | – |
| R.B. Simpson (115), I.R. Redpath (40*) | Karachi | 1964–65 | – | – | – | – | – | 119 |
| R.B. McCosker (79), I.M. Chappell (86) | Lord's | 1975 | 119 | – | – | – | – | – |
| R.B. Simpson (153), I.R. Redpath (54) | Cape Town | 1966–67 | – | 117 | – | – | – | – |
| K.R. Stackpole (79), I.M. Chappell (37) | Oval | 1972 | 116 | – | – | – | – | – |
| W.M. Woodfull (67), D.G. Bradman (71) | Sydney | 1932–33 | 115 | – | – | – | – | – |
| H.L. Collins (203), J. Ryder (56) | Johannesburg[1] | 1921–22 | – | 113 | – | – | – | – |
| H.L. Collins (104), C.G. Macartney (69) | Sydney | 1920–21 | 111 | – | – | – | – | – |
| R.M. Cowper (57), I.M. Chappell (71) | Birmingham | 1968 | 111 | – | – | – | – | – |
| W.A. Brown (67), S.G. Barnes (54) | Wellington | 1945–46 | – | – | – | 109 | – | – |
| R. Edwards (74), I.M. Chappell (56) | Port-of-Spain | 1972–73 | – | – | 109 | – | – | – |
| I.R. Redpath (66), G.S. Chappell (56) | Port-of-Spain | 1972–73 | – | – | 107 | – | – | – |

## HUNDRED PARTNERSHIPS – *continued*

### AUSTRALIA – 2nd Wicket – *continued*

| | Venue | Rubber | E | SA | WI | NZ | I | P |
|---|---|---|---|---|---|---|---|---|
| M.A. Noble (50), C. Hill (54) | Nottingham | 1905 | 106‡ | – | – | – | – | – |
| R.B. McCosker (95*), I.M. Chappell (62) | Leeds | 1975 | 106 | – | – | – | – | – |
| A. Turner (136), G.N. Yallop (43) | Adelaide | 1975–76 | – | – | 105 | – | – | – |
| J. Moroney (87), K.R. Miller (58) | Cape Town | 1949–50 | – | 104 | – | – | – | – |
| I.R. Redpath (83), I.M. Chappell (50) | Melbourne | 1974–75 | 104 | – | – | – | – | – |
| W. Bardsley (85), C. Hill (39) | Melbourne | 1910–11 | – | 101 | – | – | – | – |
| A.P. Sheahan (44), I.M. Chappell (196) | Adelaide | 1972–73 | – | – | – | – | – | 100 |
| **Totals: (81)** | | | **43** | **16** | **11** | **3** | **2** | **6** |

† *202 runs were added for this wicket; W.M. Lawry retired hurt and was succeeded by I.R. Redpath after 22 runs had been scored.*

‡ *128 runs were added for this wicket; V.T. Trumper retired hurt and was succeeded by M.A. Noble after 22 runs had been scored.*

*Although the 2nd wicket added 134 v India at Melbourne in 1947-48, this consisted of two partnerships: W.A. Brown added 92\* with D.G. Bradman (retired hurt) and a further 42 with K.R. Miller. Similarly, 105 were added v England at Adelaide in 1958-59. N.C. O'Neill scoring 97\* with C.C. McDonald (retired hurt) and a further 8 with R.N. Harvey.*

### AUSTRALIA – 3rd Wicket

| | Venue | Rubber | E | SA | WI | NZ | I | P |
|---|---|---|---|---|---|---|---|---|
| C.C. McDonald (127), R.N. Harvey (204) | Kingston | 1954–55 | – | – | 295 | – | – | – |
| D.G. Bradman (187), A.L. Hassett (128) | Brisbane² | 1946–47 | 276 | – | – | – | – | – |
| I.M. Chappell (145), G.S. Chappell (247*) | Wellington | 1973–74 | – | – | – | 264 | – | – |
| D.G. Bradman (169), S.J. McCabe (112) | Melbourne | 1936–37 | 249 | – | – | – | – | – |
| C. Kelleway (102), W. Bardsley (164) | Lord's | 1912 | – | 242 | – | – | – | – |
| D.G. Bradman (334), A.F. Kippax (77) | Leeds | 1930 | 229 | – | – | – | – | – |
| R.M. Cowper (143), B.C. Booth (117) | Port-of-Spain | 1964–65 | – | – | 225† | – | – | – |
| R.N. Harvey (133), K.R. Miller (147) | Kingston | 1954–55 | – | – | 224 | – | – | – |
| W.M. Lawry (108), R.M. Cowper (307) | Melbourne | 1965–66 | 212 | – | – | – | – | – |
| H.L. Collins (203), J.M. Gregory (119) | Johannesburg¹ | 1921–22 | – | 209 | – | – | – | – |
| K.R. Stackpole (207), K.D. Walters (112) | Brisbane² | 1970–71 | 209 | – | – | – | – | – |
| W.L. Murdoch (211), H.J.H. Scott (102) | Oval | 1884 | 207 | – | – | – | – | – |
| R.N. Harvey (102), N.C. O'Neill (163) | Bombay² | 1959–60 | – | – | – | – | 207 | – |
| C. Kelleway (114), W. Bardsley (121) | Manchester | 1912 | – | 202 | – | – | – | – |
| A.R. Morris (153), R.N. Harvey (162) | Brisbane² | 1954–55 | 202 | – | – | – | – | – |
| I.M. Chappell (118), G.S. Chappell (113) | Oval | 1972 | 201 | – | – | – | – | – |
| J. Darling (160), J. Worrall (62) | Sydney | 1897–98 | 193 | – | – | – | – | – |
| D.G. Bradman (223), A.F. Kippax (84) | Brisbane¹ | 1930–31 | – | – | 193 | – | – | – |
| I.M. Chappell (106*), K.D. Walters (102*) | Bridgetown | 1972–73 | – | – | 192* | – | – | – |
| D.G. Bradman (254), A.F. Kippax (83) | Lord's | 1930 | 192 | – | – | – | – | – |
| A.R. Morris (122), A.L. Hassett (78) | Adelaide | 1946–47 | 189 | – | – | – | – | – |
| A.R. Morris (157), R.N. Harvey (116) | Port Elizabeth | 1949–50 | – | 187 | – | – | – | – |
| R.B. Simpson (103), R.M. Cowper (108) | Adelaide | 1967–68 | – | – | – | – | 172 | – |
| D.G. Bradman (132), A.L. Hassett (80) | Melbourne | 1947–48 | – | – | – | – | 169 | – |
| W.W. Armstrong (59), C. Hill (142) | Johannesburg¹ | 1902–03 | – | 164 | – | – | – | – |
| I.M. Chappell (74*), G.S. Chappell (109*) | Brisbane² | 1975–76 | – | – | 159* | – | – | – |
| J.W. Burke (81), R. Benaud (100) | Johannesburg³ | 1957–58 | – | 158 | – | – | – | – |
| H. Carter (72), C. Hill (98) | Adelaide | 1911–12 | 157 | – | – | – | – | – |
| R.N. Harvey (109), A.L. Hassett (55) | Brisbane² | 1952–53 | – | 155 | – | – | – | – |
| D.G. Bradman (77), S.J. McCabe (70) | Oval | 1934 | 150 | – | – | – | – | – |
| R.N. Harvey (114), N.C. O'Neill (82) | Birmingham | 1961 | 146 | – | – | – | – | – |
| R. Edwards (170*), G.S. Chappell (72) | Nottingham | 1972 | 146 | – | – | – | – | – |
| C.G. Macartney (137), W. Bardsley (94) | Sydney | 1910–11 | – | 145 | – | – | – | – |
| C. Hill (191), D.R.A. Gehrs (67) | Sydney | 1910–11 | – | 144 | – | – | – | – |
| W.M. Lawry (81), K.D. Walters (81) | Manchester | 1968 | 144 | – | – | – | – | – |
| A.L. Mann (105), A.D. Ogilvie (47) | Perth | 1977–78 | – | – | – | – | 139 | – |
| J.W. Burke (161), P.J.P. Burge (83) | Bombay² | 1956–57 | – | – | – | – | 137 | – |
| R.B. Simpson (71), B.C. Booth (77) | Adelaide | 1962–63 | 133 | – | – | – | – | – |
| P.M. Toohey (122), G.N. Yallop (57) | Kingston | 1977–78 | – | – | 133 | – | – | – |
| J. Ryder (52*), J.M. Gregory (76*) | Melbourne | 1920–21 | 130* | – | – | – | – | – |
| I.M. Chappell (72), G.S. Chappell (106) | Bridgetown | 1972–73 | – | – | 129 | – | – | – |
| W.M. Lawry (58*), N.C. O'Neill (74*) | Bridgetown | 1964–65 | – | – | 126*† | – | – | – |

### AUSTRALIA – 3rd Wicket – *continued*

| | Venue | Rubber | E | SA | WI | NZ | I | P |
|---|---|---|---|---|---|---|---|---|
| W.M. Lawry (205), K.D. Walters (76) | Melbourne | 1968–69 | – | – | 123 | – | – | – |
| I.M. Chappell (109), G.S. Chappell (51) | Georgetown | 1972–73 | – | – | 121 | – | – | – |
| G.N. Yallop (121), P.M. Toohey (60) | Adelaide | 1977–78 | – | – | – | – | 120 | – |
| R.N. Harvey (167), N.C. O'Neill (37) | Melbourne | 1958–59 | 118 | – | – | – | – | – |
| A.P. Sheahan (81), R.M. Cowper (92) | Adelaide | 1967–68 | – | – | – | – | 118 | – |
| R.B. Simpson (153), P.J.P. Burge (54) | Karachi | 1964–65 | – | – | – | – | – | 116 |
| R.A. Duff (146), M.A. Noble (25) | Oval | 1905 | 115 | – | – | – | – | – |
| R.B. McCosker (84), G.S. Chappell (58) | Auckland | 1976–77 | – | – | – | 115 | – | – |
| V.T. Trumper (166), S.E. Gregory (56) | Sydney | 1907–08 | 114 | – | – | – | – | – |
| C.C. McDonald (67), R.N. Harvey (190) | Sydney | 1952–53 | – | 113 | – | – | – | – |
| K.E. Rigg (127), D.G. Bradman (112) | Sydney | 1931–32 | – | 111 | – | – | – | – |
| A.R. Morris (206), R.N. Harvey (43) | Adelaide | 1950–51 | 110 | – | – | – | – | – |
| D.G. Bradman (212), S.J. McCabe (55) | Adelaide | 1936–37 | 109 | – | – | – | – | – |
| A.R. Morris (196), A.L. Hassett (37) | Oval | 1948 | 109 | – | – | – | – | – |
| C.G. Macartney (61), T.J.E. Andrews (94) | Oval | 1921 | 108 | – | – | – | – | – |
| R.N. Harvey (85), N.C. O'Neill (70) | Sydney | 1960–61 | – | – | 108 | – | – | – |
| D.G. Bradman (201), A.L. Hassett (198*) | Adelaide | 1947–48 | – | – | – | – | 105 | – |
| R.B. Simpson (78), P.J.P. Burge (81) | Adelaide | 1963–64 | – | 104 | – | – | – | – |
| G.J. Cosier (67), C.S. Serjeant (85) | Melbourne | 1977–78 | – | – | – | – | 104 | – |
| R.N. Harvey (205), A.L. Hassett (40) | Melbourne | 1952–53 | – | 103 | – | – | – | – |
| W. Bardsley (82), W.W. Armstrong (48) | Melbourne | 1910–11 | – | 102 | – | – | – | – |
| C.G. Macartney (115), C.E. Pellew (52) | Leeds | 1921 | 101 | – | – | – | – | – |
| D.G. Bradman (185), A.L. Hassett (48) | Brisbane[2] | 1947–48 | – | – | – | – | 101 | – |
| I.M. Chappell (99), K.D. Walters (56) | Calcutta | 1969–70 | – | – | – | – | 101 | – |
| I.R. Redpath (39), G.S. Chappell (61) | Melbourne | 1974–75 | 101 | – | – | – | – | – |
| R.N. Harvey (74), W.J. Watson (30) | Bridgetown | 1954–55 | – | – | 100 | – | – | – |
| I.M. Chappell (90), G.S. Chappell (58) | Brisbane[2] | 1974–75 | 100 | – | – | – | – | – |
| **Totals: (69):** | | | **28** | **14** | **13** | **2** | **11** | **1** |

† *228 runs were added for this wicket, N.C. O'Neill retired hurt and was succeeded by B.C. Booth after 3 runs had been scored.*

‡ *147 runs were added for this wicket, W.M. Lawry retired hurt and was succeeded by B.C. Booth after 126 runs had been scored.*

### AUSTRALIA – 4th Wicket

| | Venue | Rubber | E | SA | WI | NZ | I | P |
|---|---|---|---|---|---|---|---|---|
| W.H. Ponsford (181), D.G. Bradman (304) | Leeds | 1934 | 388 | – | – | – | – | – |
| W.M. Lawry (151), K.D. Walters (242) | Sydney | 1968–69 | – | – | 336 | – | – | – |
| G.M. Wood (126), C.S. Serjeant (124) | Georgetown | 1977–78 | – | – | 251 | – | – | – |
| D.G. Bradman (232), A. Jackson (73) | Oval | 1930 | 243 | – | – | – | – | – |
| A.L. Hassett (132), K.R. Miller (129) | Sydney | 1951–52 | – | – | 235 | – | – | – |
| G.H.S. Trott (143), S.E. Gregory (103) | Lord's | 1896 | 221 | – | – | – | – | – |
| I.R. Redpath (132), K.D. Walters (103) | Sydney | 1968–69 | – | – | 210 | – | – | – |
| A.C. Bannerman (70), P.S. McDonnell (147) | Sydney | 1881–82 | 199 | – | – | – | – | – |
| C.G. Macartney (170), J.M. Gregory (93) | Sydney | 1920–21 | 198 | – | – | – | – | – |
| C. Kelleway (147), W.W. Armstrong (121) | Adelaide | 1920–21 | 194 | – | – | – | – | – |
| R.N. Harvey (154), N.C. O'Neill (100) | Adelaide | 1962–63 | 194 | – | – | – | – | – |
| A.F. Kippax (146), S.J. McCabe (90) | Adelaide | 1930-31 | – | – | 182 | – | – | – |
| R.N. Harvey (122), G.B. Hole (66) | Manchester | 1953 | 173 | – | – | – | – | – |
| R.M. Cowper (307), K.D. Walters (60) | Melbourne | 1965–66 | 172 | – | – | – | – | – |
| I.M. Chappell (196), R. Edwards (89) | Adelaide | 1972–73 | – | – | – | – | 172 | – |
| G. Giffen (161), F.A. Iredale (81) | Sydney | 1894–95 | 171 | – | – | – | – | – |
| R.N. Harvey (190), K.R. Miller (55) | Sydney | 1952–53 | – | 168 | – | – | – | – |
| M.A. Noble (65), S.E. Gregory (112) | Adelaide | 1903–04 | 162 | – | – | – | – | – |
| W.H. Ponsford (128), J.M. Taylor (72) | Melbourne | 1924–25 | 161 | – | – | – | – | – |
| A.F. Kippax (100), J. Ryder (112) | Melbourne | 1928–29 | 161 | – | – | – | – | – |
| R.N. Harvey (153), S.J.E. Loxton (80) | Melbourne | 1947–48 | – | – | – | – | 159 | – |
| W.W. Armstrong (132), C. Hill (100) | Melbourne | 1910–11 | – | 154 | – | – | – | – |
| N.C. O'Neill (113), P.J.P. Burge (60) | Calcutta | 1959–60 | – | – | – | – | 150 | – |
| R.N. Harvey (205), I.D. Craig (53) | Melbourne | 1952–53 | – | 148 | – | – | – | – |
| A.L. Hassett (198*), K.R. Miller (67) | Adelaide | 1947–48 | – | – | – | – | 142 | – |
| A.F. Kippax (51), J. Ryder (87) | Adelaide | 1928–29 | 137 | – | – | – | – | – |
| R.N. Harvey (114), K.D. Mackay (78) | Delhi | 1959–60 | – | – | – | – | 132 | – |
| R.N. Harvey (162), G.B. Hole (57) | Brisbane[2] | 1954–55 | 131 | – | – | – | – | – |

| AUSTRALIA – 4th Wicket – *continued* | Venue | Rubber | E | SA | WI | NZ | I | P |
|---|---|---|---|---|---|---|---|---|
| C. Hill (135), M.A. Noble (54) | Lord's | 1899 | 130 | – | – | – | – | – |
| J.W. Burke (189), K.D. Mackay (63) | Cape Town | 1957–58 | – | 130 | – | – | – | – |
| W.M. Woodfull (141), A.J. Richardson (100) | Leeds | 1926 | 129 | – | – | – | – | – |
| A. Jackson (164), J.Ryder (63) | Adelaide | 1928–29 | 126 | – | – | – | – | – |
| R.M. Cowper (81), B.C. Booth (74) | Bombay² | 1964–65 | – | – | – | – | 125 | – |
| W.A. Brown (206*), A.L. Hassett (56) | Lord's | 1938 | 124 | – | – | – | – | – |
| R.N. Harvey (83), K.R. Miller (47) | Melbourne | 1951–52 | – | – | 124 | – | – | – |
| I.R. Redpath (101), G.S. Chappell (68) | Melbourne | 1975–76 | – | – | 124 | – | – | – |
| N.C. O'Neill (117), P.J.P. Burge (181) | Oval | 1961 | 123 | – | – | – | – | – |
| K.R. Miller (58), R.N. Harvey (112) | Leeds | 1948 | 121 | – | – | – | – | – |
| D.G. Bradman (185), K.R. Miller (58) | Brisbane² | 1947–48 | – | – | – | – | 120 | – |
| N.C. O'Neill (82), B.C. Booth (169) | Brisbane² | 1963–64 | – | 120 | – | – | – | – |
| W. Bardsley (54), V.T. Trumper (214*) | Adelaide | 1910–11 | – | 118 | – | – | – | – |
| K.D. Walters (48), I.R. Redpath (77) | Bombay² | 1969–70 | – | – | – | – | 118 | – |
| A.R. Morris (157), A.L. Hassett (167) | Port Elizabeth | 1949–50 | – | 114 | – | – | – | – |
| G.S. Chappell (71), R. Edwards (53) | Brisbane² | 1974–75 | 114 | – | – | – | – | – |
| W.A. Brown (73), S.J. McCabe (88) | Nottingham | 1934 | 112 | – | – | – | – | – |
| A.F. Kippax (67), S.J. McCabe (71) | Melbourne | 1931–32 | 111 | – | – | – | – | – |
| G.S. Chappell (41), K.D. Walters (70) | Port-of-Spain | 1972–73 | – | – | 111 | – | – | – |
| R.B. McCosker (109*), G.S. Chappell (54*) | Melbourne | 1975–76 | – | – | 110* | – | – | – |
| N.C. O'Neill (77), L.E. Favell (54) | Sydney | 1958–59 | 110 | – | – | – | – | – |
| C.G. Macartney (115), J.M. Taylor (50) | Leeds | 1921 | 109 | – | – | – | – | – |
| K.R. Miller (84), A.L. Hassett (53) | Johannesburg² | 1949–50 | – | 109 | – | – | – | – |
| A.L. Hassett (115), K.R. Miller (55) | Nottingham | 1953 | 109 | – | – | – | – | – |
| N.C. O'Neill (73), P.J.P. Burge (103) | Sydney | 1962–63 | 109 | – | – | – | – | – |
| G.S. Chappell (73*), R. Edwards (52*) | Lord's | 1975 | 107* | – | – | – | – | – |
| C. Hill (119), S.E. Gregory (29) | Sheffield | 1902 | 107 | – | – | – | – | – |
| M.A. Noble (133), W.W. Armstrong (48) | Sydney | 1903–04 | 106 | – | – | – | – | – |
| C.G. Macartney (116), J. Ryder (58) | Durban¹ | 1921–22 | – | 106 | – | – | – | – |
| A.L. Hassett (128), K.R. Miller (79) | Brisbane² | 1946–47 | 106 | – | – | – | – | – |
| W.M. Lawry (94), B.C. Booth (74) | Oval | 1964 | 106 | – | – | – | – | – |
| I.R. Redpath (58), I.C. Davis (50) | Christchurch | 1973–74 | – | – | – | 106 | – | – |
| G.N. Yallop (121), R.B. Simpson (100) | Adelaide | 1977–78 | – | – | – | – | 104 | – |
| C.S. Serjeant (81), K.D. Walters (53) | Lord's | 1977 | 103 | – | – | – | – | – |
| G.S. Chappell (70), K.D. Walters (51) | Adelaide | 1976–77 | – | – | – | – | – | 101 |
| G.N. Yallop (75), C.S. Serjeant (49) | Port-of-Spain | 1977–78 | – | – | 101 | – | – | – |
| G.S. Chappell (42), K.D. Walters (94) | Adelaide | 1973–74 | – | – | – | 100 | – | – |
| **Totals: (65)** | | | **33** | **10** | **10** | **2** | **8** | **2** |

| AUSTRALIA – 5th Wicket | Venue | Rubber | E | SA | WI | NZ | I | P |
|---|---|---|---|---|---|---|---|---|
| S.G. Barnes (234), D.G. Bradman (234) | Sydney | 1946–47 | 405 | – | – | – | – | – |
| A.R. Morris (100*), D.G. Bradman (127*) | Melbourne | 1947–48 | – | – | – | – | 223* | – |
| K.R. Miller (109), R.G. Archer (128) | Kingston | 1954–55 | – | – | 220 | – | – | – |
| R.B. Simpson (311), B.C. Booth (98) | Manchester | 1964 | 219 | – | – | – | – | – |
| P.J.P. Burge (120), K.D. Walters (115) | Melbourne | 1965–66 | 198 | – | – | – | – | – |
| W.M. Lawry (166), K.D. Walters (155) | Brisbane² | 1965–66 | 187 | – | – | – | – | – |
| P.J.P. Burge (181), B.C. Booth (71) | Oval | 1961 | 185 | – | – | – | – | – |
| D.G. Bradman (123), A.G. Fairfax (65) | Melbourne | 1928–29 | 183 | – | – | – | – | – |
| W.H. Ponsford (183), W.M. Woodfull (58) | Sydney | 1930–31 | – | – | 183 | – | – | – |
| G.S. Chappell (121), G.J. Cosier (168) | Melbourne | 1976–77 | – | – | – | – | – | 171 |
| R. Edwards (115), K.D. Walters (103) | Perth | 1974–75 | 170 | – | – | – | – | – |
| C.L. Badcock (118), R.G. Gregory (80) | Melbourne | 1936–37 | 161 | – | – | – | – | – |
| A.P. Sheahan (88), I.M. Chappell (73) | Manchester | 1968 | 152 | – | – | – | – | – |
| K.R. Miller (141*), I.W. Johnson (52) | Adelaide | 1946–47 | 150 | – | – | – | – | – |
| G.S. Chappell (116*), R.W. Marsh (74) | Melbourne | 1972–73 | – | – | – | – | – | 146 |
| W.W. Armstrong (132), V.T. Trumper (87) | Melbourne | 1910–11 | – | 143 | – | – | – | – |
| S.E. Gregory (70), J. Darling (74) | Melbourne | 1894–95 | 142 | – | – | – | – | – |
| R.N. Harvey (178), S.J.E. Loxton (35) | Cape Town | 1949–50 | – | 140 | – | – | – | – |
| G. Giffen (161), S.E. Gregory (201) | Sydney | 1894–95 | 139 | – | – | – | – | – |
| D.G. Bradman (212), R.G. Gregory (50) | Adelaide | 1936–37 | 135 | – | – | – | – | – |
| R.N. Harvey (151*), S.J.E. Loxton (54) | Durban² | 1949–50 | – | 135 | – | – | – | – |
| I.R. Redpath (70), A.P. Sheahan (114) | Kanpur | 1969–70 | – | – | – | – | 131 | – |
| S.J. McCabe (187*), V.Y. Richardson (49) | Sydney | 1932–33 | 129 | – | – | – | – | – |

## AUSTRALIA – 5th Wicket – *continued*

| Partnership | Venue | Rubber | E | SA | WI | NZ | I | P |
|---|---|---|---|---|---|---|---|---|
| F.A. Iredale (89), G.H.S. Trott (79) | Melbourne | 1897–98 | 124 | – | – | – | – | – |
| G.S. Chappell (123), R.W. Marsh (48) | Brisbane² | 1975–76 | – | – | 122 | – | – | – |
| D.G. Bradman (138), A.L. Hassett (137) | Nottingham | 1948 | 120 | – | – | – | – | – |
| W. Bardsley (136), V.T. Trumper (73) | Oval | 1909 | 118 | – | – | – | – | – |
| D.G. Bradman (299*), K.E. Rigg (35) | Adelaide | 1931-32 | – | 114 | – | – | – | – |
| G.S. Chappell (52), G.J. Cosier (109) | Melbourne | 1975–76 | – | – | 114 | – | – | – |
| K.D. Walters (71*), R. Marsh (55) | Adelaide | 1974–75 | 112 | – | – | – | – | – |
| K.D. Walters (118), A.P. Sheahan (47) | Sydney | 1968–69 | – | – | 110 | – | – | – |
| V.T. Trumper (166), C. Hill (44) | Sydney | 1907–08 | 108 | – | – | – | – | – |
| T.P. Horan (124), G. Giffen (30) | Melbourne | 1881–82 | 107 | – | – | – | – | – |
| G.H.S. Trott (92), H. Graham (42) | Oval | 1893 | 106 | – | – | – | – | – |
| W.W. Armstrong (77), C.G. Macartney (54) | Melbourne | 1907–08 | 106 | – | – | – | – | – |
| G.S. Chappell (131), R. Edwards (28) | Lord's | 1972 | 106 | – | – | – | – | – |
| R.N. Harvey (112), S.J.E. Loxton (93) | Leeds | 1948 | 105 | – | – | – | – | – |
| N.C. O'Neill (181), K.D. Mackay (35) | Brisbane² | 1960–61 | – | – | 103 | – | – | – |
| B.C. Booth (169), R. Benaud (43) | Brisbane² | 1963–64 | – | 102 | – | – | – | – |
| K.D. Walters (102), I.R. Redpath (33) | Madras¹ | 1969–70 | – | – | – | – | 102 | – |
| J. Ryder (79), O.E. Nothling (44) | Sydney | 1928–29 | 101 | – | – | – | – | – |
| R.B. Simpson (176), S.J. Rixon (50) | Perth | 1977–78 | – | – | – | – | 101 | – |
| J. Darling (71), S.E. Gregory (117) | Oval | 1899 | 100 | – | – | – | – | – |
| P.M. Toohey (83), R.B. Simpson (39) | Perth | 1977–78 | – | – | – | – | 100 | – |
| **Totals: (44)** | | | **26** | **5** | **6** | **–** | **5** | **2** |

## AUSTRALIA – 6th Wicket

| Partnership | Venue | Rubber | E | SA | WI | NZ | I | P |
|---|---|---|---|---|---|---|---|---|
| J.H.W. Fingleton (136), D.G. Bradman (270) | Melbourne | 1936–37 | 346 | – | – | – | – | – |
| I.R. Redpath (171), G.S. Chappell (108) | Perth | 1970–71 | 219 | – | – | – | – | – |
| K.R. Miller (137), R.G. Archer (98) | Bridgetown | 1954–55 | – | – | 206 | – | – | – |
| C. Kelleway (78), W.W. Armstrong (158) | Sydney | 1920–21 | 187 | – | – | – | – | – |
| T.R. Veivers (67), B.N. Jarman (78) | Bombay² | 1964 65 | – | – | – | – | 151 | – |
| J.M. Gregory (77), W.W. Armstrong (123*) | Melbourne | 1920–21 | 145 | – | – | – | – | – |
| S.E. Gregory (57), H. Graham (107) | Lord's | 1893 | 142 | – | – | – | – | – |
| R.M. Cowper (83), T.R. Veivers (88) | Melbourne | 1964–65 | – | – | – | – | – | 139 |
| I.M. Chappell (151), B.N. Jarman (65) | Melbourne | 1967–68 | – | – | – | 134 | – | – |
| C.L. McCool (95), I.W. Johnson (47) | Brisbane² | 1946–47 | 131 | – | – | – | – | – |
| C. Kelleway (147), C.E. Pellew (104) | Adelaide | 1920–21 | 126 | – | – | – | – | – |
| V.Y. Richardson (138), C. Kelleway (32) | Melbourne | 1924–25 | 123 | – | – | – | – | – |
| K.D. Walters (155), T.R. Veivers (56*) | Brisbane² | 1965–66 | 119 | – | – | – | – | – |
| I.M. Chappell (138), H.B. Taber (46) | Delhi | 1969–70 | – | – | – | – | 118 | – |
| G.S. Chappell (182*), R.W. Marsh (38) | Sydney | 1975–76 | – | – | 117 | – | – | – |
| V.T. Trumper (113), R.B. Minnett (90) | Sydney | 1911–12 | 109 | – | – | – | – | – |
| C. Kelleway (59), V.S. Ransford (75) | Melbourne | 1910–11 | – | 107 | – | – | – | – |
| R.N. Harvey (151*), C.L. McCool (39*) | Durban² | 1949-50 | – | 106* | – | – | – | – |
| W.H. Ponsford (80), A.F. Kippax (42) | Sydney | 1924–25 | 105 | – | – | – | – | – |
| B.C. Booth (75), R. Benaud (43) | Sydney | 1963- 64 | – | 100 | – | – | – | – |
| **Totals: (20)** | | | **11** | **3** | **2** | **–** | **3** | **1** |

## AUSTRALIA – 7th Wicket

| Partnership | Venue | Rubber | E | SA | WI | NZ | I | P |
|---|---|---|---|---|---|---|---|---|
| K.D. Walters (250), G.J. Gilmour (101) | Christchurch | 1976–77 | – | – | – | 217 | – | – |
| R.W. Marsh (132), K.J. O'Keeffe (85) | Adelaide | 1973–74 | – | – | – | 168 | – | – |
| C. Hill (188), H. Trumble (46) | Melbourne | 1897–98 | 165 | – | – | – | – | – |
| R. Benaud (90), G.D. McKenzie (76) | Sydney | 1963–64 | – | 160 | – | – | – | – |
| K.S. Miller (145*), I.W. Johnson (77) | Sydney | 1950–51 | 150 | – | – | – | – | – |
| J. Ryder (201*), T.J.E. Andrews (72) | Adelaide | 1924–25 | 134 | – | – | – | – | – |
| A.K. Davidson (80), R. Benaud (52) | Brisbane² | 1960–61 | – | – | 134 | – | – | – |
| K.R. Stackpole (134), G.D. Watson (50) | Cape Town | 1966–67 | – | 128 | – | – | – | – |
| R.W. Marsh (118), K.J. O'Keeffe (40) | Adelaide | 1972–73 | – | – | – | – | – | 120 |
| K.D. Mackay (31), R. Benaud (97) | Lord's | 1956 | 117 | – | – | – | – | – |
| K.D. Mackay (57), A.K. Davidson (71) | Sydney | 1958–59 | 115 | – | – | – | – | – |
| R. Benaud (64), A.T.W. Grout (74) | Melbourne | 1958–59 | 115 | – | – | – | – | – |
| H.L. Collins (61), J.M. Gregory (73) | Oval | 1926 | 107 | – | – | – | – | – |
| B.C. Booth (112), K.D. Mackay (86*) | Brisbane² | 1962–63 | 103 | – | – | – | – | – |
| **Totals: (14)** | | | **8** | **2** | **1** | **2** | **–** | **1** |

## AUSTRALIA – 8th Wicket

| | Venue | Rubber | E | SA | WI | NZ | I | P |
|---|---|---|---|---|---|---|---|---|
| R.J. Hartigan (113), C. Hill (160) | Adelaide | 1907–08 | 243 | – | – | – | – | – |
| C.E. Pellew (116), J.M. Gregory (100) | Melbourne | 1920 -21 | 173 | – | – | – | – | – |
| G.J. Bonnor (128), S.P. Jones (40) | Sydney | 1884–85 | 154 | – | – | – | – | – |
| D. Tallon (92), R.R. Lindwall (100) | Melbourne | 1946- 47 | 154 | – | – | – | – | – |
| R. Benaud (128), I.W. Johnson (27*) | Kingston | 1954–55 | – | – | 137 | – | – | – |
| G.J. Cosier (168), K.J. O'Keeffe (28*) | Melbourne | 1976–77 | – | – | – | – | – | 117 |
| C. Kelleway (73), W.A.S. Oldfield (65*) | Sydney | 1924–25 | 116 | – | – | – | – | – |
| H. Graham (105), A.E. Trott (85*) | Sydney | 1894–95 | 112 | – | – | – | – | – |
| W.W. Armstrong (133*), H. Carter (66) | Melbourne | 1907–08 | 112 | – | – | – | – | – |
| A.L. Hassett (137), R.R. Lindwall (42) | Nottingham | 1948 | 107 | – | – | – | – | – |
| P.J.P. Burge (160), N.J.N. Hawke (37) | Leeds | 1964 | 105 | – | – | – | – | – |
| | | **Totals: (11)** | **9** | **–** | **1** | **–** | **–** | **1** |

## AUSTRALIA – 9th Wicket

| | Venue | Rubber | E | SA | WI | NZ | I | P |
|---|---|---|---|---|---|---|---|---|
| S.E. Gregory (201), J.M. Blackham (74) | Sydney | 1894–95 | 154 | – | – | – | – | – |
| J. Ryder (201*), W.A.S. Oldfield (47) | Adelaide | 1924–25 | 108 | – | – | – | – | – |
| R.W. Marsh (91), J.W. Gleeson (30) | Manchester | 1972 | 104 | – | – | – | – | – |
| A.E.V. Hartkopf (80), W.A.S. Oldfield (39*) | Melbourne | 1924–25 | 100 | – | – | – | – | – |
| M.H.N. Walker (78*), M.F. Malone (46) | Oval | 1977 | 100 | – | – | – | – | – |
| | | **Totals: (5)** | **5** | **–** | **–** | **–** | **–** | **–** |

## AUSTRALIA – 10th Wicket

| | Venue | Rubber | E | SA | WI | NZ | I | P |
|---|---|---|---|---|---|---|---|---|
| J.M. Taylor (108), A.A. Mailey (46*) | Sydney | 1924–25 | 127 | – | – | – | – | – |
| R.A. Duff (104), W.W. Armstrong (45*) | Melbourne | 1901–02 | 120 | – | – | – | – | – |
| | | **Totals: (2)** | **2** | **–** | **–** | **–** | **–** | **–** |

## SOUTH AFRICA – (134) – 1st Wicket

| | Venue | Rubber | E | A | NZ |
|---|---|---|---|---|---|
| B. Mitchell (123), I.J. Siedle (141) | Cape Town | 1930 -31 | 260 | – | – |
| B. Mitchell (113), J.A.J. Christy (103) | Christchurch | 1931–32 | – | – | 196 |
| B. Mitchell (89), P.G.V. van der Bijl (97) | Durban[2] | 1938- 39 | 191 | – | – |
| D.J. McGlew (133), T.L. Goddard (74) | Leeds | 1955 | 176 | – | – |
| D.J. McGlew (108), T.L. Goddard (90) | Johannesburg[3] | 1957–58 | – | 176 | – |
| B. Mitchell (61*), R.H. Catterall (98) | Birmingham | 1929 | 171 | – | – |
| B.A. Richards (81), E.J. Barlow (73) | Port Elizabeth | 1969–70 | – | 157 | – |
| H.W. Taylor (70), J.W. Zulch (82) | Johannesburg[1] | 1913–14 | 153 | – | – |
| D.J. McGlew (104*), T.L. Goddard (62) | Manchester | 1955 | 147 | – | – |
| D.J. McGlew (120), E.J. Barlow (67) | Johannesburg[3] | 1961–62 | – | – | 134 |
| T.L. Goddard (60), E.J. Barlow (96) | Johannesburg[3] | 1964–65 | 134 | – | – |
| A. Melville (78), P.G.V. van der Bijl (125) | Durban[2] | 1938–39 | 131 | – | – |
| H.W. Taylor (87), J.W. Zulch (60) | Port Elizabeth | 1913–14 | 129 | – | – |
| B. Mitchell (73), I.J. Siedle (57) | Durban[2] | 1930–31 | 127 | – | – |
| B. Mitchell (88), R.H. Catterall (67) | Birmingham | 1929 | 119 | – | – |
| T.L. Goddard (40), E.J. Barlow (92) | Wellington | 1963–64 | – | – | 117 |
| T.L. Goddard (63), E.J. Barlow (49) | Dunedin | 1963–64 | – | – | 117 |
| B. Mitchell (128), I.J. Siedle (35) | Oval | 1935 | 116 | – | – |
| H.W. Taylor (71), J.M.M. Commaille (47) | Cape Town | 1927–28 | 115 | – | – |
| T.L. Goddard (73), E.J. Barlow (61) | Auckland | 1963–64 | – | – | 115 |
| T.L. Goddard (61), E.J. Barlow (69) | Port Elizabeth | 1964–65 | 114 | – | – |
| D.J. McGlew (84), J.H.B. Waite (43) | Durban[2] | 1953 54 | – | – | 113 |
| T.L. Goddard (74), E.J. Barlow (46) | Port Elizabeth | 1966–67 | – | 112 | – |
| H.W. Taylor (91), R.H. Catterall (52) | Durban[2] | 1922–23 | 110 | – | – |
| A. Melville (67), P.G.V. van der Bijl (31) | Johannesburg[1] | 1938–39 | 108 | – | – |
| B. Mitchell (53), J.A.J. Christy (53) | Wellington | 1931–32 | – | – | 104 |
| D.J. McGlew (61), R.J. Westcott (43) | Johannesburg[2] | 1953–54 | – | – | 104 |
| B. Mitchell (56), E.A.B. Rowan (37) | Port Elizabeth | 1948–49 | 101 | – | – |
| | | **Totals: (28)** | **17** | **3** | **8** |

## SOUTH AFRICA – 2nd Wicket

| | Venue | Rubber | E | A | NZ |
|---|---|---|---|---|---|
| E.A.B. Rowan (236), C.B. van Ryneveld (83) | Leeds | 1951 | 198 | – | – |
| L.J. Tancred (97), C.B. Llewellyn (90) | Johannesburg[1] | 1902–03 | – | 173 | – |
| E.J. Barlow (138), A.J. Pithey (154) | Cape Town | 1964–65 | 172 | – | – |

## SOUTH AFRICA – 2nd Wicket – *continued*

| | Venue | Rubber | E | A | NZ |
|---|---|---|---|---|---|
| R.H. Catterall (76), H.W. Taylor (68) | Cape Town | 1922–23 | 155 | – | – |
| P.G.V. van der Bijl (87), E.A.B. Rowan (89*) | Cape Town | 1938–39 | 147 | – | – |
| A. Melville (104*), K.G. Viljoen (51*) | Nottingham | 1947 | 145* | – | – |
| P.W. Sherwell (115), C.M.H. Hathorn (30) | Lord's | 1907 | 139 | – | – |
| J.W. Zulch (105), G.A. Faulkner (56) | Adelaide | 1910–11 | – | 135 | – |
| B.A. Richards (126), A. Bacher (73) | Port Elizabeth | 1969–70 | – | 126 | – |
| T.L. Goddard (93), A.J. Pithey (49) | Sydney | 1963- 64 | – | 124 | – |
| B. Mitchell (109), E.A.B. Rowan (67) | Durban² | 1938–39 | 119 | – | – |
| T.L. Goddard (112), A.J. Pithey (39) | Johannesburg³ | 1964–65 | 115 | – | – |
| E.A.B. Rowan (86*), K.G. Viljoen (53) | Johannesburg² | 1948–49 | 113 | – | – |
| T.L. Goddard (67), J.H.B. Waite (61) | Johannesburg³ | 1956–57 | 112 | – | – |
| J.H.B. Waite (62), W.R. Endean (162*) | Melbourne | 1952–53 | – | 111 | – |
| L.J. Tancred (73), G.C. White (147) | Johannesburg¹ | 1905–06 | 110 | – | – |
| J.W. Zulch (42), G.A. Faulkner (204) | Melbourne | 1910–11 | – | 107 | – |
| B. Mitchell (164*), E.A.B. Rowan (44) | Lord's | 1935 | 104 | – | – |
| B. Mitchell (46), J.A.J. Christy (63) | Melbourne | 1931- 32 | – | 102 | – |
| | **Totals: (19)** | | **12** | **7** | |

## SOUTH AFRICA – 3rd Wicket

| | Venue | Rubber | E | A | NZ |
|---|---|---|---|---|---|
| E.J. Barlow (201), R.G. Pollock (175) | Adelaide | 1963–64 | – | 341 | – |
| A. Melville (189), A.D. Nourse (149) | Nottingham | 1947 | 319 | – | – |
| D.J. McGlew (105), J.H.B. Waite (134) | Durban² | 1957–58 | – | 231 | – |
| B. Mitchell (120), A.D. Nourse (112) | Cape Town | 1948–49 | 190 | – | – |
| B. Mitchell (189*), A.D. Nourse (97) | Oval | 1947 | 184 | – | – |
| E.A.B. Rowan (143), A.D. Nourse (66) | Durban² | 1949–50 | – | 167 | – |
| E.A.B. Rowan (156*), A.D. Nourse (56*) | Johannesburg² | 1948–49 | 162* | – | – |
| J.W. Zulch (150), G.A. Faulkner (92) | Sydney | 1910–11 | – | 143 | – |
| E.J. Barlow (110), R.G. Pollock (87) | Johannesburg³ | 1969–70 | – | 139 | – |
| H.W. Taylor (101), A.W. Nourse (63) | Johannesburg¹ | 1922–23 | 134 | – | – |
| A. Bacher (60*), R.G. Pollock (67*) | Durban² | 1966–67 | – | 127* | – |
| B. Mitchell (72), R.H. Catterall (54) | Johannesburg¹ | 1930–31 | 122 | – | – |
| B. Mitchell (95), H.W. Taylor (84) | Adelaide | 1931–32 | – | 121 | – |
| G.C. White (147), A.W. Nourse (55) | Johannesburg¹ | 1905–06 | 120 | – | – |
| B. Mitchell (75), H.W. Taylor (78) | Adelaide | 1931–32 | – | 120 | – |
| A. Melville (117), A.D. Nourse (61) | Lord's | 1947 | 118 | – | – |
| B. Mitchell (73), A.D. Nourse (73) | Johannesburg¹ | 1938–39 | 116 | – | – |
| E.A.B. Rowan (85), B. Mitchell (63) | Johannesburg¹ | 1938–39 | 116 | – | – |
| D.J. McGlew (120), R.A. McLean (78) | Johannesburg³ | 1961–62 | – | – | 112 |
| G.A. Faulkner (204), A.W. Nourse (33) | Melbourne | 1910–11 | – | 110 | – |
| C.N. Frank (152), H.W. Taylor (80) | Johannesburg¹ | 1921–22 | – | 105 | – |
| D.J. McGlew (127), R.A. McLean (63) | Durban² | 1961–62 | – | – | 103 |
| B.A. Richards (140), R.G. Pollock (274) | Durban² | 1969–70 | – | 103 | – |
| B. Mitchell (99), A.D. Nourse (73) | Port Elizabeth | 1948–49 | 101 | – | – |
| G.A. Faulkner (78), A.W. Nourse (53) | Johannesburg¹ | 1909–10 | 100 | – | – |
| H.W. Taylor (91), A.W. Nourse (52) | Durban² | 1922–23 | 100 | – | – |
| | **Totals: (26)** | | **13** | **11** | **2** |

## SOUTH AFRICA – 4th Wicket

| | Venue | Rubber | E | A | NZ |
|---|---|---|---|---|---|
| H.W. Taylor (121), H.G. Deane (93) | Oval | 1929 | 214 | – | – |
| C.N. Frank (152), A.W. Nourse (111) | Johannesburg¹ | 1921–22 | – | 206 | – |
| B. Mitchell (99), W.W. Wade (125) | Port Elizabeth | 1948–49 | 150 | – | – |
| H.W. Taylor (117), R.H. Catterall (56) | Cape Town | 1930–31 | 148 | – | – |
| G.C. White (118), A.W. Nourse (69) | Durban¹ | 1909–10 | 143 | – | – |
| K.J. Funston (39), R.A. McLean (101) | Durban² | 1953–54 | – | – | 135 |
| B. Mitchell (45), A.D. Nourse (231) | Johannesburg¹ | 1935–36 | – | 129 | – |
| A.J. Pithey (76), J.H.B. Waite (77) | Melbourne | 1963–64 | – | 128 | – |
| A.D. Nourse (115), K.G. Viljoen (32) | Manchester | 1947 | 121 | – | – |
| S.J. Snooke (47), G.A. Faulkner (99) | Cape Town | 1909–10 | 120 | – | – |
| E.A.B. Rowan (49), A.D. Nourse (91) | Durban² | 1935–36 | – | 118 | – |
| A.J. Pithey (154), K.C. Bland (78) | Cape Town | 1964–65 | 117 | – | – |
| T.L. Goddard (99), J.H.B. Waite (77) | Oval | 1960 | 115 | – | – |
| G.C. White (72), G.A. Faulkner (76) | Johannesburg¹ | 1909–10 | 114 | – | – |

### SOUTH AFRICA – 4th Wicket – *continued*

| | Venue | Rubber | E | A | NZ |
|---|---|---|---|---|---|
| M.J. Susskind (64), R.H. Catterall (120) | Lord's | 1924 | 112 | – | – |
| H.W. Taylor (176), W.V.S. Ling (38) | Johannesburg[1] | 1922–23 | 111 | – | – |
| J.H.B. Waite (44), K.J. Funston (92) | Adelaide | 1952–53 | – | 108 | – |
| J.F.W. Nicolson (78), R.H. Catterall (76) | Durban[2] | 1927–28 | 107 | – | – |
| W.R. Endean (87), J.C. Watkins (45) | Port Elizabeth | 1953–54 | – | – | 107 |
| A.D. Nourse (129*), W.W. Wade (54) | Johannesburg[2] | 1948–49 | 106 | – | – |
| J.H.B. Waite (115), W.R. Endean (50) | Johannesburg[3] | 1957–58 | – | 104 | – |
| D.J. McGlew (63), R.A. McLean (113) | Cape Town | 1961–62 | – | – | 101 |
| | | Totals: (22) | 13 | 6 | 3 |

### SOUTH AFRICA – 5th Wicket

| | Venue | Rubber | E | A | NZ |
|---|---|---|---|---|---|
| A.J. Pithey (95), J.H.B. Waite (64) | Johannesburg[3] | 1964–65 | 157 | – | – |
| R.H. Catterall (119), H.B. Cameron (53) | Durban[2] | 1927–28 | 135 | – | – |
| W.R. Endean (116), J.E. Cheetham (54) | Auckland | 1952–53 | – | – | 130 |
| J.H.B. Waite (59), W.R. Endean (77) | Johannesburg[3] | 1957–58 | – | 129 | – |
| A.D. Nourse (208), G.M. Fullerton (54) | Nottingham | 1951 | 121 | – | – |
| H.R. Lance (53), D.T. Lindsay (81) | Cape Town | 1966–67 | – | 119 | – |
| R.H. Catterall (120), J.M. Blanckenberg (56) | Birmingham | 1924 | 114 | – | – |
| G.A. Faulkner (115), C.B. Llewellyn (80) | Adelaide | 1910–11 | – | 109 | – |
| E.A.B. Rowan (236), R.A. McLean (67) | Leeds | 1951 | 108 | – | – |
| H.J. Keith (40*), R.A. McLean (76*) | Melbourne | 1952–53 | – | 106* | – |
| K.G. Viljoen (74), A. Melville (103) | Durban[2] | 1938–39 | 104 | – | – |
| | | Totals: (11) | 6 | 4 | 1 |

### SOUTH AFRICA -- 6th Wicket

| | Venue | Rubber | E | A | NZ |
|---|---|---|---|---|---|
| R.G. Pollock (274), H.R. Lance (61) | Durban[2] | 1969–70 | – | 200 | – |
| J.H.B. Waite (113), P.L. Winslow (108) | Manchester | 1955 | 171 | – | – |
| K.C. Bland (144*), G.D. Varnals (23) | Johannesburg[3] | 1964–65 | 124 | – | – |
| K.C. Bland (126), D.T. Lindsay (65) | Sydney | 1963–64 | – | 118 | – |
| R.G. Pollock (137), P.L. van der Merwe (66) | Port Elizabeth | 1964–65 | 113 | – | – |
| R.G. Pollock (209), P.L. van der Merwe (50) | Cape Town | 1966–67 | – | 112 | – |
| H.R. Lance (44), D.T. Lindsay (69) | Johannesburg[3] | 1966–67 | – | 110 | – |
| R.A. McLean (142), H.J. Keith (57) | Lord's | 1955 | 109 | – | – |
| A.D. Nourse (231), F. Nicholson (29) | Johannesburg[1] | 1935–36 | – | 106 | – |
| R.A. McLean (109), S. O'Linn (27) | Manchester | 1960 | 102 | – | – |
| | | Totals: (10) | 5 | 5 | – |

### SOUTH AFRICA – 7th Wicket

| | Venue | Rubber | E | A | NZ |
|---|---|---|---|---|---|
| D.J. McGlew (255*), A.R.A. Murray (109) | Wellington | 1952–53 | – | – | 246 |
| D.T. Lindsay (182), P.L. van der Merwe (76) | Johannesburg[3] | 1966–67 | – | 221 | – |
| H.G. Deane (73), E.P. Nupen (69) | Durban[2] | 1927–28 | 123 | – | – |
| G.C. White (81), A.W. Nourse (93*) | Johannesburg[1] | 1905–06 | 121 | – | – |
| J.E. Cheetham (66), P.N.F. Mansell (52) | Melbourne | 1952–53 | – | 111 | – |
| S. O'Linn (98), J.H.B. Waite (60) | Nottingham | 1960 | 109 | – | – |
| K.G. Viljoen (50), E.L. Dalton (102) | Johannesburg[1] | 1938–39 | 108 | – | – |
| A.D. Nourse (103), R.E. Grieveson (75) | Durban[2] | 1938–39 | 107 | – | – |
| X.C. Balaskas (122*), C.L. Vincent (33) | Wellington | 1931–32 | – | – | 105 |
| D.T. Lindsay (137), P.L. van der Merwe (42) | Durban[2] | 1966–67 | – | 103 | – |
| B. Mitchell (164*), A.B.C. Langton (44) | Lord's | 1935 | 101 | – | – |
| | | Totals: (11) | 6 | 3 | 2 |

### SOUTH AFRICA – 8th Wicket

| | Venue | Rubber | E | A | NZ |
|---|---|---|---|---|---|
| A.W. Nourse (72), E.A. Halliwell (57) | Johannesburg[1] | 1902–03 | – | 124 | – |
| B. Mitchell (189*), L. Tuckett (40*) | Oval | 1947 | 109* | – | – |
| K.G. Viljoen (111), Q. McMillan (29) | Melbourne | 1931–32 | – | 104 | – |
| H.J. Tayfield (75), N.B.F. Mann (46) | Cape Town | 1949–50 | – | 102 | – |
| G.A. Faulkner (62), R.O. Schwarz (61) | Sydney | 1910–11 | – | 100 | – |
| | | Totals: (5) | 1 | 4 | – |

### SOUTH AFRICA – 9th Wicket

| | Venue | Rubber | E | A | NZ |
|---|---|---|---|---|---|
| E.L. Dalton (117), A.B.C. Langton (73*) | Oval | 1935 | 137 | – | – |

**SOUTH AFRICA – 10th Wicket**

| | Venue | Rubber | E | A | NZ |
|---|---|---|---|---|---|
| H.G. Owen-Smith (129), A.J. Bell (26*) | Leeds | 1929 | 103 | – | – |

**WEST INDIES – (211) – 1st Wicket**

| | Venue | Rubber | E | A | NZ | I | P |
|---|---|---|---|---|---|---|---|
| J.B. Stollmeyer (160), A.F. Rae (109) | Madras[1] | 1948–49 | – | – | – | 239 | – |
| R.C. Fredericks (94), L.G. Rowe (120) | Kingston | 1973–74 | 206 | – | – | – | – |
| J.B. Stollmeyer (152), A.F. Rae (99) | Auckland | 1951–52 | – | – | 197 | – | – |
| R.C. Fredericks (109), C.G. Greenidge (115) | Leeds | 1976 | 192 | – | – | – | – |
| R.C. Fredericks (86*), C.G. Greenidge (85*) | Oval | 1976 | 182* | – | – | – | – |
| R.C. Fredericks (83), C.G. Greenidge (82) | Kingston | 1976–77 | – | – | – | – | 182 |
| G.M. Carew (107), A.G. Ganteaume (112) | Port-of-Spain | 1947–48 | 173 | – | – | – | – |
| C.C. Hunte (92), J.K. Holt (123) | Delhi | 1958–59 | – | – | – | 159 | – |
| R.C. Fredericks (52*), C.G. Greenidge (96) | Georgetown | 1976–77 | – | – | – | – | 154 |
| C.C. Hunte (81), B.A. Davis (68) | Bridgetown | 1964–65 | – | 145 | – | – | – |
| C.A. Roach (209), E.A.C. Hunte (53) | Georgetown | 1929–30 | 144 | – | – | – | – |
| J.B. Stollmeyer (76*), A.F. Rae (63*) | Port-of-Spain | 1952–53 | – | – | – | 142* | – |
| C.G. Greenidge (93), A.I. Kallicharran (124) | Bangalore | 1974–75 | – | – | – | 139† | – |
| J.B. Stollmeyer (66), A.F. Rae (104) | Bombay[2] | 1948–49 | – | – | – | 134 | – |
| C.G. Greenidge (80*), D.L. Haynes (55) | Bridgetown | 1977–78 | – | 131 | – | – | – |
| R.C. Fredericks (32), L.G. Rowe (302) | Bridgetown | 1973–74 | 126 | – | – | – | – |
| C.C. Hunte (114), R.B. Kanhai (62) | Georgetown | 1957–58 | – | – | – | – | 125 |
| C.C. Hunte (142), R.B. Kanhai (27) | Bridgetown | 1957–58 | – | – | – | – | 122 |
| G.S. Camacho (87), M.C. Carew (36) | Port-of-Spain | 1967–68 | 119 | – | – | – | – |
| C.C. Hunte (89), B.A. Davis (54) | Port-of-Spain | 1964–65 | – | 116 | – | – | – |
| R.C. Fredericks (50), C.G. Greenidge (101) | Manchester | 1976 | 116 | – | – | – | – |
| R.C. Fredericks (67), L.G. Rowe (123) | Port-of-Spain | 1973–74 | 110 | – | – | – | – |
| R.C. Fredericks (63), G.S. Camacho (67) | Lord's | 1969 | 106 | – | – | – | – |
| R.C. Fredericks (82), L.G. Rowe (47) | Kingston | 1975–76 | – | – | – | 105 | – |
| J.B. Stollmeyer (52*), A.F. Rae (46*) | Nottingham | 1950 | 103* | – | – | – | – |
| S.M. Nurse (73), G.S. Camacho (25) | Kingston | 1967–68 | 102 | – | – | – | – |
| R.C. Fredericks (39), M.C. Carew (64) | Sydney | 1968–69 | – | 100 | – | – | – |
| | | **Totals: (27)** | **12** | **4** | **1** | **6** | **4** |

† *177 runs were added for this wicket, R.C. Fredericks retired hurt and was succeeded by A.I. Kallicharran after 38 had been scored.*

**WEST INDIES – 2nd Wicket**

| | Venue | Rubber | E | A | NZ | I | P |
|---|---|---|---|---|---|---|---|
| C.C. Hunte (260), G.St A. Sobers (365*) | Kingston | 1957–58 | – | – | – | – | 446 |
| G. St A. Sobers (125), C.L. Walcott (145) | Georgetown | 1957–58 | – | – | – | – | 269 |
| R.C. Fredericks (163), L.G. Rowe (214) | Kingston | 1971–72 | – | – | 269 | – | – |
| E.D.A. St J. McMorris (125), R.B. Kanhai (158) | Kingston | 1961–62 | – | – | – | 255 | – |
| L.G. Rowe (302), A.I. Kallicharran (119) | Bridgetown | 1973–74 | 249 | – | – | – | – |
| M.C. Carew (91), S.M. Nurse (258) | Christchurch | 1968–69 | – | – | 231 | – | – |
| R.K. Nunes (92), G.A. Headley (223) | Kingston | 1929–30 | 227 | – | – | – | – |
| J.K. Holt (166), F.M.M. Worrell (76*) | Bridgetown | 1953–54 | 222 | – | – | – | – |
| I. Barrow (105), G.A. Headley (169) | Manchester | 1933 | 200 | – | – | – | – |
| C.A. Roach (209), G.A. Headley (114) | Georgetown | 1929–30 | 192 | – | – | – | – |
| A.F. Rae (109), F.M.M. Worrell (138) | Oval | 1950 | 172 | – | – | – | – |
| M.C. Carew (109), S.M. Nurse (95) | Auckland | 1968–69 | – | – | 172 | – | – |
| D.M. Lewis (88), R.B. Kanhai (85) | Bridgetown | 1970–71 | – | – | – | 166 | – |
| M.C. Carew (83), R.B. Kanhai (94) | Brisbane[2] | 1968–69 | – | 165 | – | – | – |
| C.C. Hunte (79), R.B. Kanhai (115) | Adelaide | 1960–61 | – | 163 | – | – | – |
| C.A. Roach (77), G.A. Headley (176) | Bridgetown | 1929–30 | 156 | – | – | – | – |
| R.C. Fredericks (71), I.V.A. Richards (291) | Oval | 1976 | 154 | – | – | – | – |
| F.R. Martin (123), G.A. Headley (105) | Sydney | 1930–31 | – | 152 | – | – | – |
| C.C. Hunte (182), R.B. Kanhai (90) | Manchester | 1963 | 151 | – | – | – | – |
| C.C. Hunte (114), G.St.A. Sobers (109*) | Georgetown | 1957–58 | – | – | – | – | 135 |
| J.B. Stollmeyer (60), J.K. Holt (94) | Kingston | 1953–54 | 134 | – | – | – | – |
| M.C. Carew (90), R.B. Kanhai (80) | Adelaide | 1968–69 | – | 132 | – | – | – |
| R.C. Fredericks (52), I.V.A. Richards (91) | Bridgetown | 1976–77 | – | – | – | – | 130 |
| E.D.A. St J. McMorris (50), R.B. Kanhai (139) | Port-of-Spain | 1961–62 | – | – | – | 119 | – |
| J.B. Stollmeyer (59), G.A. Headley (106) | Lord's | 1939 | 118 | – | – | – | – |
| J.B. Stollmeyer (59), G.A. Headley (65) | Oval | 1939 | 113 | – | – | – | – |
| C.C. Hunte (108*), R.B. Kanhai (77) | Oval | 1963 | 113 | – | – | – | – |

### WEST INDIES – 2nd Wicket – *continued*

| | Venue | Rubber | E | A | NZ | I | P |
|---|---|---|---|---|---|---|---|
| R.C. Fredericks (138), A.I. Kallicharran (34) | Lord's | 1976 | 113 | – | – | – | – |
| R.C. Fredericks (104), A.I. Kalicharran (98) | Bombay³ | 1974–75 | – | – | – | 113 | – |
| C.G. Greenidge (101), I.V.A. Richards (135) | Manchester | 1976 | 108 | – | – | – | – |
| R.C. Fredericks (43), R.B. Kanhai (69) | Sydney | 1968–69 | – | 103 | – | – | – |
| M.C. Carew (45), C.A. Davis (125*) | Georgetown | 1970–71 | – | – | – | 103 | – |
| J.K. Holt (60), O.G. Smith (104) | Kingston | 1954–55 | – | 102 | – | – | – |
| R.C. Fredericks (76), A.I. Kallicharran (91) | Port-of-Spain | 1972–73 | – | 102 | – | – | – |
| **Totals: (34)** | | | **15** | **7** | **3** | **5** | **4** |

### WEST INDIES – 3rd Wicket

| | Venue | Rubber | E | A | NZ | I | P |
|---|---|---|---|---|---|---|---|
| E. de C. Weekes (206), F.M.M. Worrell (167) | Port-of-Spain | 1953–54 | 338 | – | – | – | – |
| I.V.A. Richards (232), A.I. Kallicharran (97) | Nottingham | 1976 | 303 | – | – | – | – |
| S.M. Nurse (136), R.B. Kanhai (153) | Port-of-Spain | 1967–68 | 273 | – | – | – | – |
| C.L. Walcott (126), E. de C. Weekes (139) | Port-of-Spain | 1954–55 | – | 242 | – | – | – |
| I.V.A. Richards (142), A.I. Kallicharran (93) | Bridgetown | 1975–76 | – | – | – | 220 | – |
| G.A. Headley (270*), J.E.D. Sealy (91) | Kingston | 1934–35 | 202 | – | – | – | – |
| R.B. Kanhai (129), S.M. Nurse (201) | Bridgetown | 1964–65 | – | 200 | – | – | – |
| F.M.M. Worrell (237), E. de C. Weekes (109) | Kingston | 1952–53 | – | – | – | 197 | – |
| I.V.A. Richards (291), L.G. Rowe (70) | Oval | 1976 | 191 | – | – | – | – |
| S.M. Nurse (168), B.F. Butcher (78*) | Auckland | 1968–69 | – | – | 174 | – | – |
| R.B. Kanhai (217), G. St A. Sobers (72) | Lahore¹ | 1958–59 | – | – | – | – | 162 |
| A.F. Rae (62), F.M.M. Worrell (261) | Nottingham | 1950 | 143 | – | – | – | – |
| G.A. Headley (176), F.I. de Caires (70) | Bridgetown | 1929–30 | 142 | – | – | – | – |
| R.B. Kanhai (157), C.H. Lloyd (63) | Lord's | 1973 | 138 | – | – | – | – |
| R.B. Kanhai (89), B.F. Butcher (49) | Georgetown | 1964–65 | – | 135 | – | – | – |
| E.D.A. St J. McMorris (73), G. St A. Sobers (147) | Kingston | 1959–60 | 133*† | – | – | – | – |
| I.V.A. Richards (135), C.H. Lloyd (43) | Manchester | 1976 | 132 | – | – | – | – |
| J.B. Stollmeyer (104*), E. de C. Weekes (55*) | Port-of-Spain | 1952–53 | – | – | – | 127* | – |
| C.L. Walcott (110), E. de C. Weekes (87*) | Port-of-Spain | 1954–55 | – | 127 | – | – | – |
| I.V.A. Richards (101), A.I. Kallicharran (67) | Adelaide | 1975–76 | – | 127 | – | – | – |
| R.C. Fredericks (169), A.I. Kallicharran (57) | Perth | 1975–76 | – | 124 | – | – | – |
| S.M. Nurse (70), R.B. Kanhai (84) | Melbourne | 1960–61 | – | 123 | – | – | – |
| I.V.A. Richards (98), A.I. Kallicharran (44) | Melbourne | 1975–76 | – | 117 | – | – | – |
| C.C. Hunte (81), B.F. Butcher (71) | Kingston | 1964–65 | – | 116 | – | – | – |
| L.G. Rowe (76), A.I. Kallicharran (50) | Kingston | 1972–73 | – | 116 | – | – | – |
| J.B. Stollmeyer (152), E. de C. Weekes (51) | Auckland | 1951–52 | – | – | 115 | – | – |
| R.B. Kanhai (55), G. St A. Sobers (145) | Georgetown | 1959–60 | 115 | – | – | – | – |
| R.B. Kanhai (158*), C.H. Lloyd (57) | Kingston | 1970–71 | – | – | – | 115 | – |
| A.I. Kallicharran (93), C.H. Lloyd (49) | Kingston | 1973–74 | 112 | – | – | – | – |
| G.A. Headley (105), G.C. Grant (62) | Sydney | 1930–31 | – | 110 | – | – | – |
| J.B. Stollmeyer (85), E. de C. Weekes (56) | Bombay² | 1948–49 | – | – | – | 110 | – |
| G. St A. Sobers (147), S.M. Nurse (70) | Kingston | 1959–60 | 110† | – | – | – | – |
| R.B. Kanhai (63), B.F. Butcher (209*) | Nottingham | 1966 | 110 | – | – | – | – |
| F.M.M. Worrell (191*), R.B. Kanhai (42) | Nottingham | 1957 | 109 | – | – | – | – |
| R.B. Kanhai (256), O.G. Smith (34) | Calcutta | 1958–59 | – | – | – | 108 | – |
| G.S. Camacho (71), B.F. Butcher (91) | Leeds | 1969 | 108 | – | – | – | – |
| A.F. Rae (106), E. de.C. Weekes (63) | Lord's | 1950 | 105 | – | – | – | – |
| J.B. Stollmeyer (78), G.E. Gomez (86) | Bridgetown | 1947–48 | 104 | – | – | – | – |
| A.I. Kallicharran (98), C.H. Lloyd (242*) | Bombay³ | 1974–75 | – | – | – | 104 | – |
| L.G. Rowe (123), C.H. Lloyd (52) | Port-of-Spain | 1973–74 | 102 | – | – | – | – |
| A.I. Kallicharran (101), C.A. Davis (40) | Port-of-Spain | 1971–72 | – | – | 101 | – | – |
| **Totals: (41)** | | | **19** | **11** | **3** | **7** | **1** |

† 243 runs were added for this wicket, E.D.A. St J. McMorris retired hurt and was succeeded by S.M. Nurse after 133 had been scored.

### WEST INDIES – 4th Wicket

| | Venue | Rubber | E | A | NZ | I | P |
|---|---|---|---|---|---|---|---|
| G. St A. Sobers (226), F.M.M. Worrell (197*) | Bridgetown | 1959–60 | 399 | – | – | – | – |
| F.M.M. Worrell (261), E. de C. Weekes (129) | Nottingham | 1950 | 283 | – | – | – | – |
| C.L. Walcott (152), G.E. Gomez (101) | Delhi | 1948–49 | – | – | – | 267 | – |
| R.B. Kanhai (150), G. St A. Sobers (152) | Georgetown | 1967–68 | 250 | – | – | – | – |

## WEST INDIES – 4th Wicket – *continued*

| | Venue | Rubber | E | A | NZ | I | P |
|---|---|---|---|---|---|---|---|
| R.B. Kanhai (256), B.F. Butcher (103) | Calcutta | 1958–59 | – | – | – | 217 | – |
| F.M.M. Worrell (237), C.L. Walcott (118) | Kingston | 1952–53 | – | – | – | 213 | – |
| C.H. Lloyd (132), A.I. Kallicharran (80) | Oval | 1973 | 208 | – | – | – | – |
| C.G. Greenidge (107), C.H. Lloyd (163) | Bangalore | 1974–75 | – | – | – | 207 | – |
| L.G. Rowe (107), A.I. Kallicharran (101) | Brisbane[2] | 1975–76 | – | 198 | – | – | – |
| G. St A. Sobers (365*), C.L. Walcott (88*) | Kingston | 1957–58 | – | – | – | – | 188* |
| C.H. Lloyd (178), R.B. Kanhai (57) | Georgetown | 1972–73 | – | 187 | – | – | – |
| C.L. Walcott (110), G. St A. Sobers (64) | Kingston | 1954–55 | – | 179 | – | – | – |
| G. St A. Sobers (132), F.M.M. Worrell (65) | Brisbane[2] | 1960–61 | – | 174 | – | – | – |
| I.V.A. Richards (291), C.H. Lloyd (84) | Oval | 1976 | 174 | – | – | – | – |
| R.B. Kanhai (158*), G. St A. Sobers (93) | Kingston | 1970–71 | – | – | – | 173 | – |
| C.A. Davis (125*), G. St A. Sobers (108*) | Georgetown | 1970–71 | – | – | – | 170* | – |
| A.I. Kallicharran (127), C.H. Lloyd (86) | Port-of-Spain | 1977–78 | – | 170 | – | – | – |
| C.A. Davis (79), G. St A. Sobers (178*) | Bridgetown | 1970–71 | – | – | – | 167 | – |
| C.L. Walcott (220), B.H. Pairaudeau (71) | Bridgetown | 1953–54 | 165 | – | – | – | – |
| L. Baichan (105*), C.H. Lloyd (83) | Lahore[2] | 1974–75 | – | – | – | – | 164 |
| E. de C. Weekes (123), O.G. Smith (64) | Dunedin | 1955–56 | – | – | 162 | – | – |
| B.F. Butcher (117), G. St A. Sobers (69) | Port-of-Spain | 1964–65 | – | 160 | – | – | – |
| S.M. Nurse (201), C.C. Hunte (75) | Bridgetown | 1964–65 | – | 146 | – | – | – |
| R.B. Kanhai (92), G. St A. Sobers (102) | Leeds | 1963 | 143 | – | – | – | – |
| A.I. Kallicharran (115), C.H. Lloyd (73) | Karachi | 1974–75 | – | – | – | – | 139 |
| E. de C. Weekes (86), C.L. Walcott (125) | Georgetown | 1952–53 | – | – | – | 130 | – |
| F.M.M. Worrell (71), C.L. Walcott (65) | Christchurch | 1951–52 | – | – | 129 | – | – |
| B.F. Butcher (71), O.G. Smith (100) | Delhi | 1958–59 | – | – | – | 127 | – |
| C.L. Walcott(73), F.M.M. Worrell (56) | Georgetown | 1954–55 | – | 125 | – | – | – |
| F.I. de Caires (80), J.E.D. Sealy (58) | Bridgetown | 1929–30 | 124 | – | – | – | – |
| I.V.A. Richards (177), C.H. Lloyd (68) | Port-of-Spain | 1975–76 | – | – | – | 124 | – |
| C.C. Hunte (182), G. St A. Sobers (64) | Manchester | 1963 | 120 | – | – | – | – |
| G. St A. Sobers (142*), O.G. Smith (58) | Bombay[2] | 1958–59 | – | – | – | 119 | – |
| R.B. Kanhai (85), C.H. Lloyd (118) | Port-of-Spain | 1967–68 | 116 | – | – | – | – |
| C.C. Hunte (101), C.H. Lloyd (82) | Bombay[2] | 1966–67 | – | – | – | 110 | – |
| C.L. Walcott (155), F.M.M. Worrell (61) | Kingston | 1954–55 | – | 109 | – | – | – |
| R.B. Kanhai (117), F.M.M. Worrell (71) | Adelaide | 1960–61 | – | 107 | – | – | – |
| B.F. Butcher (209*), S.M. Nurse (53) | Nottingham | 1966 | 107 | – | – | – | – |
| E. de C. Weekes (207), C.L. Walcott (47) | Port-of-Spain | 1952–53 | – | – | – | 101 | – |
| C.W. Smith (55), F.M.M. Worrell (82) | Sydney | 1960–61 | – | 101 | – | – | – |
| B.F. Butcher (60), C.H. Lloyd (113*) | Bridgetown | 1967–68 | 101 | – | – | – | – |
| **Totals: (41)** | | | **12** | **11** | **2** | **13** | **3** |

## WEST INDIES – 5th Wicket

| | Venue | Rubber | E | A | NZ | I | P |
|---|---|---|---|---|---|---|---|
| S.M. Nurse (137), G. St A. Sobers (174) | Leeds | 1966 | 265 | – | – | – | – |
| E. de C. Weekes (207), B.H. Pairaudeau (115) | Port-of-Spain | 1952–53 | – | – | – | 219 | – |
| R.B. Kanhai (84), M.L.C. Foster (125) | Kingston | 1972–73 | – | 210 | – | – | – |
| F.M.M. Worrell (100), C.L. Walcott (115) | Auckland | 1951–52 | – | – | 189 | – | – |
| E. de C. Weekes (197), O.G. Smith (78) | Bridgetown | 1957–58 | – | – | – | – | 185 |
| C.A. Davis (105), G. St A. Sobers (132) | Port-of-Spain | 1970–71 | – | – | – | 177 | – |
| B.F. Butcher (209*), G. St A. Sobers (94) | Nottingham | 1966 | 173 | – | – | – | – |
| E. de C. Weekes (194), R.J. Christiani (74) | Bombay[2] | 1948–49 | – | – | – | 170 | – |
| C.H. Lloyd (149), D.L. Murray (63) | Perth | 1975–76 | – | 164 | – | – | – |
| V.H. Stollmeyer (96), K.H. Weekes (137) | Oval | 1939 | 163 | – | – | – | – |
| G. St A. Sobers (142*), B.F. Butcher (64*) | Bombay[2] | 1958–59 | – | – | – | 134* | – |
| S.M. Nurse (74), G. St A. Sobers (67) | Melbourne | 1968–69 | – | 134 | – | – | – |
| G. St A. Sobers (168), S.M. Nurse (43) | Sydney | 1960–61 | – | 128 | – | – | – |
| R.B. Kanhai (104), G. St A. Sobers (81) | Oval | 1966 | 122 | – | – | – | – |
| I.V.A. Richards (130), D.L. Murray (46) | Port-of-Spain | 1975–76 | – | – | – | 122 | – |
| G. St A. Sobers (145), F.M.M. Worrell (38) | Georgetown | 1959–60 | 121 | – | – | – | – |
| E. de C. Weekes (156), D. St E. Atkinson (60) | Wellington | 1955–56 | – | – | 120 | – | – |
| I.V.A. Richards (192*), C.H. Lloyd (71) | Delhi | 1974–75 | – | – | – | 120 | – |
| E. de C. Weekes (141), K.R. Rickards (67) | Kingston | 1947–48 | 116 | – | – | – | – |
| G. St A. Sobers (198), B.F. Butcher (60) | Kanpur | 1958–59 | – | – | – | 114 | – |
| C.G. Greenidge (134), C.L. King (32) | Manchester | 1976 | 111 | – | – | – | – |
| R.B. Kanhai (90), S.M. Nurse (56) | Calcutta | 1966–67 | – | – | – | 105 | – |
| C.H. Lloyd (78*), G. St A. Sobers (53*) | Bombay[2] | 1966–67 | – | – | – | 102* | – |

**WEST INDIES – 5th Wicket –** *continued*

| | Venue | Rubber | E | A | NZ | I | P |
|---|---|---|---|---|---|---|---|
| C.L. Walcott (51*), D. St E. Atkinson (53*) | Port-of-Spain | 1953–54 | 101* | – | – | – | – |
| F.C.M. Alexander (57), G. St A. Sobers (80) | Port-of-Spain | 1957–58 | – | – | – | – | 101 |
| G. St A. Sobers (66), E. de C. Weekes (90) | Lord's | 1957 | 100 | – | – | – | – |
| | | Totals: (26) | 9 | 4 | 2 | 9 | 2 |

**WEST INDIES – 6th Wicket**

| | Venue | Rubber | E | A | NZ | I | P |
|---|---|---|---|---|---|---|---|
| G. St A. Sobers (163*), D.A.J. Holford (105*) | Lord's | 1966 | 274* | – | – | – | – |
| C.A. Davis (183), G. St A. Sobers (142) | Bridgetown | 1971–72 | – | – | 254 | – | – |
| C.H. Lloyd (242*), D.L. Murray (91) | Bombay[3] | 1974–75 | – | – | – | 250 | – |
| C.L. Walcott (168*), G.E. Gomez (70) | Lord's | 1950 | 211 | – | – | – | – |
| F.M.M. Worrell (161), O.G. Smith (81) | Birmingham | 1957 | 190 | – | – | – | – |
| R.B. Kanhai (105), D.L. Murray (90) | Bridgetown | 1972–73 | – | 165 | – | – | – |
| G. St A. Sobers (198), J.S. Solomon (86) | Kanpur | 1958–59 | – | – | – | 163 | – |
| G. St A. Sobers (106*), J.S. Solomon (69*) | Calcutta | 1958–59 | – | – | – | 160* | – |
| C.H. Lloyd (157), D.L. Murray (52) | Bridgetown | 1976–77 | – | – | – | – | 151 |
| C.L. Walcott (108), O.G. Smith (44) | Kingston | 1954–55 | – | 138 | – | – | – |
| G. St A. Sobers (161), D.A.J. Holford (32) | Manchester | 1966 | 127 | – | – | – | – |
| I.T. Shillingford (120), D.L. Murray (42) | Georgetown | 1976–77 | – | – | – | – | 123 |
| G. St A. Sobers (113), S.M. Nurse (137) | Sydney | 1968–69 | – | 118 | – | – | – |
| G.C. Grant (53*), E.L. Bartlett (84) | Adelaide | 1930–31 | – | 114 | – | – | – |
| R.C. Fredericks (150), D.L. Murray (25) | Birmingham | 1973 | 114 | – | – | – | – |
| F.M.M. Worrell (53), F.C.M. Alexander (87*) | Adelaide | 1960–61 | – | 113 | – | – | – |
| G. St A. Sobers (57), B.D. Julien (66) | Kingston | 1973–74 | 112 | – | – | – | – |
| G. St A. Sobers (153), F.M.M. Worrell (58) | Kingston | 1961–62 | – | – | – | 110 | – |
| B.F. Butcher (133), F.M.M. Worrell (33) | Lord's | 1963 | 110 | – | – | – | – |
| G. St A. Sobers (113*), D.A.J. Holford (35) | Kingston | 1967–68 | 110 | – | – | – | – |
| G.E. Gomez (74), J.D.C. Goddard (58*) | Oval | 1950 | 109 | – | – | – | – |
| G. St A. Sobers (178*), M.L.C. Foster (36*) | Bridgetown | 1970–71 | – | – | – | 107* | – |
| E. de C. Weekes (156), A.P. Binns (27) | Wellington | 1955–56 | – | – | 106 | – | – |
| I.V.A. Richards (177), B.D. Julien (47) | Port-of-Spain | 1975–76 | – | – | – | 106 | – |
| O.G. Smith (168), D. St E. Atkinson (46) | Nottingham | 1957 | 105 | – | – | – | – |
| J.D.C. Goddard (44), E. de C. Weekes (128) | Delhi | 1948–49 | – | – | – | 101 | – |
| B.F. Butcher (142), J.S. Solomon (43) | Madras[2] | 1958–59 | – | – | – | 101 | – |
| R.B. Kanhai (217), J.S. Solomon (56) | Lahore[1] | 1958–59 | – | – | – | – | 100 |
| | | Totals: (28) | 10 | 5 | 2 | 8 | 3 |

**WEST INDIES – 7th Wicket**

| | Venue | Rubber | E | A | NZ | I | P |
|---|---|---|---|---|---|---|---|
| D. St E. Atkinson (219), C.C. Depeiza (122) | Bridgetown | 1954–55 | – | 347 | – | – | – |
| G. St A. Sobers (150*), B.D. Julien (121) | Lord's | 1973 | 155*† | – | – | – | – |
| O.G. Smith (168), J.D.C. Goddard (61) | Nottingham | 1957 | 154 | – | – | – | – |
| G.A. Headley (270*), R.S. Grant (77) | Kingston | 1934–35 | 147 | – | – | – | – |
| D. St E. Atkinson (85), J.D.C. Goddard (83*) | Christchurch | 1955–56 | – | – | 143 | – | – |
| G. St A. Sobers (153), I. Mendonça (78) | Kingston | 1961–62 | – | – | – | 127 | – |
| C.H. Lloyd (129), M.C. Carew (71*) | Brisbane[2] | 1968–69 | – | 120 | – | – | – |
| E. de C. Weekes (128), R.J. Christiani (107) | Delhi | 1948–49 | – | – | – | 118 | – |
| D.L. Murray (71), M.A. Holding (55) | Kingston | 1975–76 | – | – | – | 107 | – |
| J.S. Solomon (45), F.C.M. Alexander (70) | Kanpur | 1958–59 | – | – | – | 100 | – |
| A.I. Kallicharran (158), B.D. Julien (86*) | Port-of-Spain | 1973–74 | 100 | – | – | – | – |
| | | Totals: (11) | 4 | 2 | 1 | 4 | – |

† *231 runs were added for this wicket, G. St A. Sobers retired ill and was succeeded by K.D. Boyce after 155 had been scored.*

**WEST INDIES – 8th Wicket**

| | Venue | Rubber | E | A | NZ | I | P |
|---|---|---|---|---|---|---|---|
| I.V.A. Richards (192*), K.D. Boyce (68) | Delhi | 1974–75 | – | – | – | 124 | – |

**WEST INDIES – 9th Wicket**

| | Venue | Rubber | E | A | NZ | I | P |
|---|---|---|---|---|---|---|---|
| D.A.J. Holford (80), J.L. Hendriks (37*) | Adelaide | 1968–69 | – | 122 | – | – | – |
| R.J. Christiani (107), D.St.E. Atkinson (45) | Delhi | 1948–49 | – | – | – | 106 | – |
| | | Totals: (2) | – | 1 | – | 1 | – |

**WEST INDIES – 10th Wicket**
**No instance – Highest Partnership**

| | Venue | Rubber | E | A | NZ | I | P |
|---|---|---|---|---|---|---|---|
| F.M.M. Worrell (73*), W.W. Hall (50*) | Port-of-Spain | 1961–62 | – | – | – | 98* | – |

**NEW ZEALAND – (71) – 1st Wicket**

| | Venue | Rubber | E | A | SA | WI | I | P |
|---|---|---|---|---|---|---|---|---|
| G.M. Turner (259), T.W. Jarvis (182) | Georgetown | 1971–72 | – | – | – | 387 | – | – |
| C.S. Dempster (136), J.E. Mills (117) | Wellington | 1929–30 | 276 | – | – | – | – | – |
| R.E. Redmond (107), G.M. Turner (58) | Auckland | 1972–73 | – | – | – | – | – | 159 |
| G.T. Dowling (83), T.W. Jarvis (55) | Lahore[2] | 1964-65 | – | – | – | – | – | 136 |
| B. Sutcliffe (58), W.A. Hadlee (116) | Christchurch | 1946–47 | 133 | – | – | – | – | – |
| G.O. Rabone (56), M.E. Chapple (76) | Cape Town | 1953–54 | – | – | 126 | – | – | – |
| B.A.G. Murray (74), G.T. Dowling (239) | Christchurch | 1967–68 | – | – | – | – | 126 | – |
| B. Sutcliffe (88), V.J. Scott (60) | Oval | 1949 | 121 | – | – | – | – | – |
| G.T. Dowling (76), G.M. Turner (38) | Christchurch | 1968–69 | – | – | – | 115 | – | – |
| B. Sutcliffe (82), V.J. Scott (43) | Leeds | 1949 | 112 | – | – | – | – | – |
| G.T. Dowling (71), G.M. Turner (40) | Auckland | 1968–69 | – | – | – | 112 | – | – |
| G.M. Turner (72), J.M. Parker (34) | Auckland | 1973-74 | – | 107 | – | – | – | – |
| G.T. Dowling (42), B.A.G. Murray (80) | Hyderabad | 1969–70 | – | – | – | – | 106 | – |
| S.N. McGregor (49), J.G. Leggat (50*) | Delhi | 1955–56 | – | – | – | – | 101 | – |
| | **Totals: (14)** | | **4** | **1** | **1** | **3** | **3** | **2** |

**NEW ZEALAND – 2nd Wicket**

| | Venue | Rubber | E | A | SA | WI | I | P |
|---|---|---|---|---|---|---|---|---|
| G.T. Dowling (143), B.E. Congdon (58) | Dunedin | 1967–68 | – | – | – | – | 155 | – |
| G.M. Turner (95), B.E. Congdon (82) | Port-of-Spain | 1971–72 | – | – | – | 139 | – | – |
| B. Sutcliffe (116), J.R. Reid (50) | Christchurch | 1950–51 | 131 | – | – | – | – | – |
| B. Sutcliffe (230*), J.W. Guy (52) | Delhi | 1955–56 | – | – | – | – | 130 | – |
| J.F.M. Morrison (58), J.M. Parker (121) | Auckland | 1974–75 | 116 | – | – | – | – | – |
| G.M. Turner (117), B.E. Congdon (58) | Christchurch | 1975–76 | – | – | – | – | 114 | – |
| G.M. Turner (79), J.F.M. Morrison (66) | Wellington | 1973–74 | – | 108 | – | – | – | – |
| G.M. Turner (65), J.M. Parker (104) | Bombay[3] | 1976–77 | – | – | – | – | 106 | – |
| | **Totals: (8)** | | **2** | **1** | **–** | **1** | **4** | **–** |

**NEW ZEALAND – 3rd Wicket**

| | Venue | Rubber | E | A | SA | WI | I | P |
|---|---|---|---|---|---|---|---|---|
| B. Sutcliffe (230*), J.R. Reid (119*) | Delhi | 1955–56 | – | – | – | – | 222* | – |
| B.E. Congdon (175), B.F. Hastings (86) | Lord's | 1973 | 190 | – | – | – | – | – |
| J.W. Guy (91), J.R. Reid (120) | Calcutta | 1955–56 | – | – | – | – | 184 | – |
| B.W. Sinclair (130), J.R. Reid (88) | Lahore[2] | 1964–65 | – | – | – | – | – | 178 |
| B.E. Congdon (66), B.F. Hastings (83) | Nottingham | 1969 | 150 | – | – | – | – | – |
| G.T. Dowling (129), R.W. Morgan (71) | Bombay[2] | 1964–65 | – | – | – | – | 134 | – |
| B.E. Congdon (54), J.M. Parker (70) | Auckland | 1975–76 | – | – | – | – | 122 | – |
| C.S. Dempster (120), M.L. Page (104) | Lord's | 1931 | 118 | – | – | – | – | – |
| B. Sutcliffe (137*), J.R. Reid (45*) | Hyderabad | 1955–56 | – | – | – | – | 108* | – |
| G.M. Turner (113), M.G. Burgess (54) | Kanpur | 1976–77 | – | – | – | – | 106 | – |
| G.T. Dowling (27), J.R. Reid (82) | Calcutta | 1964–65 | – | – | – | – | 101 | – |
| B.A.G. Murray (90), B.F. Hastings (80*) | Lahore[2] | 1969–70 | – | – | – | – | – | 101 |
| | **Totals: (12)** | | **3** | **–** | **–** | **–** | **7** | **2** |

**NEW ZEALAND – 4th Wicket**

| | Venue | Rubber | E | A | SA | WI | I | P |
|---|---|---|---|---|---|---|---|---|
| B.E. Congdon (132), B.F. Hastings (101) | Wellington | 1973–74 | – | 229 | – | – | – | – |
| B.E. Congdon (126), B.F. Hastings (105) | Bridgetown | 1971–72 | – | – | – | 175 | – | – |
| B.W. Sinclair (138), S.N. McGregor (62) | Auckland | 1963–64 | – | – | 171 | – | – | – |
| M.L. Page (104), R.C. Blunt (96) | Lord's | 1931 | 142 | – | – | – | – | – |
| B.F. Hastings (72), M.G. Burgess (79) | Wellington | 1972–73 | – | – | – | – | – | 128 |
| G.T. Dowling (78), J.R. Reid (69) | Port Elizabeth | 1961–62 | – | – | 125 | – | – | – |
| J.F.M. Morrison (117), B.F. Hastings (83) | Sydney | 1973–74 | – | 124 | – | – | – | – |
| G.M. Turner (110*), B.F. Hastings (46) | Christchurch | 1973–74 | – | 115 | – | – | – | – |
| G.M. Turner (98), J.M. Parker (41) | Christchurch | 1974–75 | 115 | – | – | – | – | – |
| B.E. Congdon (42), J.R. Reid (97) | Wellington | 1964–65 | – | – | – | – | – | 109 |
| G.T. Dowling (239), M.G. Burgess (26) | Christchurch | 1967–68 | – | – | – | – | 103 | – |
| | **Totals: (11)** | | **2** | **3** | **2** | **1** | **1** | **2** |

**NEW ZEALAND – 5th Wicket**

| | Venue | Rubber | E | A | SA | WI | I | P |
|---|---|---|---|---|---|---|---|---|
| M.G. Burgess (111), R.W. Anderson (92) | Lahore[2] | 1976–77 | – | – | – | – | – | 183 |
| B.E. Congdon (176), V. Pollard (116) | Nottingham | 1973 | 177 | – | – | – | – | – |

### NEW ZEALAND – 5th Wicket – *continued*

| Partnership | Venue | Rubber | E | A | SA | WI | I | P |
|---|---|---|---|---|---|---|---|---|
| J.R. Reid (135), J.E.F. Beck (99) | Cape Town | 1953–54 | – | – | 174 | – | – | – |
| S.N. McGregor (111), N.S. Harford (93) | Lahore[1] | 1955–56 | – | – | – | – | – | 150 |
| P.G.Z. Harris (101), M.E. Chapple (69) | Cape Town | 1961–62 | – | – | 148 | – | – | – |
| M.G. Burgess (104), M.J.F. Shrimpton (46) | Auckland | 1970–71 | 141 | – | – | – | – | – |
| M.P. Donnelly (64), F.B. Smith (96) | Leeds | 1949 | 120 | – | – | – | – | – |
| G.T. Dowling (239), K. Thomson (69) | Christchurch | 1967–68 | – | – | – | – | 119 | – |
| M.P. Donnelly (75), J.R. Reid (50) | Manchester | 1949 | 116 | – | – | – | – | – |
| B.F. Hastings (117*), V. Pollard (44) | Christchurch | 1968–69 | – | – | – | 110 | – | – |
| M.G. Burgess (87), V. Pollard (62) | Leeds | 1973 | 106 | – | – | – | – | – |
| J.R. Reid (84), J.E.F. Beck (38) | Auckland | 1955–56 | – | – | – | 104 | – | – |
| T.W. Jarvis (77), B. Sutcliffe (54) | Delhi | 1964–65 | – | – | – | – | 104 | – |
| **Totals: (13)** | | | **5** | **–** | **2** | **2** | **2** | **2** |

### NEW ZEALAND – 6th Wicket

| Partnership | Venue | Rubber | E | A | SA | WI | I | P |
|---|---|---|---|---|---|---|---|---|
| G.M. Turner (223*), K.J. Wadsworth (78) | Kingston | 1971–72 | – | – | – | 220 | – | – |
| M.G. Burgess (105), V. Pollard (105*) | Lord's | 1973 | 117 | – | – | – | – | – |
| J.M. Parker (121), K.J. Wadsworth (58) | Auckland | 1974–75 | 112 | – | – | – | – | – |
| M.G. Burgess (38), R.J. Hadlee (81) | Auckland | 1976–77 | – | 105 | – | – | – | – |
| H.G. Vivian (100), F.T. Badcock (53) | Wellington | 1931–32 | – | – | 100 | – | – | – |
| **Totals: (5)** | | | **2** | **1** | **1** | **1** | **–** | **–** |

### NEW ZEALAND – 7th Wicket

| Partnership | Venue | Rubber | E | A | SA | WI | I | P |
|---|---|---|---|---|---|---|---|---|
| W.K. Lees (152), R.J. Hadlee (87) | Karachi | 1976–77 | – | – | – | – | – | 186 |
| B. Sutcliffe (151*), B.R. Taylor (105) | Calcutta | 1964–65 | – | – | – | – | 163 | – |
| B. Sutcliffe (53), V. Pollard (81*) | Birmingham | 1965 | 104 | – | – | – | – | – |
| T.C. Lowry (80), H.M. McGirr (51) | Auckland | 1929–30 | 100 | – | – | – | – | – |
| **Totals: (4)** | | | **2** | **–** | **–** | **–** | **1** | **1** |

### NEW ZEALAND – 8th Wicket

| Partnership | Venue | Rubber | E | A | SA | WI | I | P |
|---|---|---|---|---|---|---|---|---|
| B.E. Congdon (166*), R.S. Cunis (51) | Port-of-Spain | 1971–72 | – | – | – | 136 | – | – |
| D.A.R. Moloney (64), A.W. Roberts (66*) | Lord's | 1937 | 104 | – | – | – | – | – |
| B.W. Yuile (47*), D.R. Hadlee (56) | Karachi | 1969–70 | – | – | – | – | – | 100 |
| **Totals: (3)** | | | **1** | **–** | **–** | **1** | **–** | **1** |

### NEW ZEALAND – 9th Wicket
**No instances – Highest Partnership**

| Partnership | Venue | Rubber | E | A | SA | WI | I | P |
|---|---|---|---|---|---|---|---|---|
| M.G. Burgess (119*), R.S. Cunis (23) | Dacca | 1969–70 | – | – | – | – | – | 96 |

### NEW ZEALAND – 10th Wicket

| Partnership | Venue | Rubber | E | A | SA | WI | I | P |
|---|---|---|---|---|---|---|---|---|
| B.F. Hastings (110), R.O. Collinge (68*) | Auckland | 1972–73 | – | – | – | – | – | 151 |

### INDIA – (121) – 1st Wicket

| Partnership | Venue | Rubber | E | A | WI | NZ | P |
|---|---|---|---|---|---|---|---|
| V.M.H. Mankad (231), P. Roy (173) | Madras[2] | 1955–56 | – | – | – | 413 | – |
| V.M. Merchant (114), Mushtaq Ali (112) | Manchester | 1936 | 203 | – | – | – | – |
| S.M. Gavaskar (66), A.D. Gaekwad (81*) | Kingston | 1975–76 | – | – | 136 | – | – |
| F.M. Engineer (66), S.M. Gavaskar (67) | Bombay[2] | 1972–73 | 135 | – | – | – | – |
| S.M. Gavaskar (49), F.M. Engineer (86) | Lord's | 1974 | 131 | – | – | – | – |
| D.N. Sardesai (28), F.M. Engineer (109) | Madras[1] | 1966–67 | – | – | 129 | – | – |
| V.M. Merchant (78), Mushtaq Ali (46) | Manchester | 1946 | 124 | – | – | – | – |
| V.M.H. Mankad (116), C.T. Sarwate (36) | Melbourne | 1947-48 | – | 124 | – | – | – |
| A.V. Mankad (53*), S.M. Gavaskar (64*) | Georgetown | 1970–71 | – | – | 123* | – | – |
| P. Roy (99), N.J. Contractor (34) | Delhi | 1959–60 | – | 121 | – | – | – |
| M.L. Jaisimha (127), N.J. Contractor (39) | Delhi | 1961–62 | 121 | – | – | – | – |
| S.M. Gavaskar (119), A.D. Gaekwad (42) | Bombay[3] | 1976–77 | – | – | – | 120 | – |
| F.M. Engineer (77), A.V. Mankad (64) | Kanpur | 1969–70 | – | 111 | – | – | – |
| V.M.H. Mankad (72), P. Roy (35) | Lord's | 1952 | 106 | – | – | – | – |
| P. Roy (31*), V.M.H. Mankad (71*) | Calcutta | 1951–52 | 103* | – | – | – | – |
| **Totals: (15)** | | | **7** | **3** | **3** | **2** | **–** |

## INDIA – 2nd Wicket

| Batsmen | Venue | Rubber | E | A | WI | NZ | P |
|---|---|---|---|---|---|---|---|
| P. Roy (150), V.L. Manjrekar (118) | Kingston | 1952–53 | – | – | 237 | – | – |
| S.M. Gavaskar (116), S. Amarnath (124) | Auckland | 1975–76 | – | – | – | 204 | – |
| S.M. Gavaskar (127), M. Amarnath (100) | Perth | 1977–78 | – | 193 | – | – | – |
| F.M. Engineer (121), A.L. Wadekar (87) | Bombay² | 1972–73 | 192 | – | – | – | – |
| F.M. Engineer (87), A.L. Wadekar (91) | Leeds | 1967 | 168 | – | – | – | – |
| S.M. Gavaskar (86), E.D. Solkar (102) | Bombay³ | 1974–75 | – | – | 168 | – | – |
| C.P.S. Chauhan (88), M. Amarnath (90) | Perth | 1977–78 | – | 149 | – | – | – |
| S.M. Gavaskar (220), A.L. Wadekar (54) | Port-of-Spain | 1970–71 | – | – | 148 | – | – |
| V.L. Mehra (62), S.A. Durani (104) | Port-of-Spain | 1961–62 | – | – | 144 | – | – |
| B.K. Kunderan (192), D.N. Sardesai (65) | Madras²· | 1963–64 | 143 | – | – | – | – |
| N.J. Contractor (92), P.R. Umrigar (76) | Delhi | 1958–59 | – | – | 137 | – | – |
| M.L. Jaisimha (51), V.L. Manjrekar (84) | Bombay² | 1961–62 | 131 | – | – | – | – |
| V.M.H. Mankad (111), H.R. Adhikari (38) | Melbourne | 1947–48 | – | 124 | – | – | – |
| D.N. Sardesai (106), Hanumant Singh (82) | Delhi | 1964–65 | – | – | – | 123 | – |
| K.C. Ibrahim (85), R.S. Modi (63) | Delhi | 1948–49 | – | – | 121 | – | – |
| S.M. Gavaskar (66), M. Amarnath (70) | Kanpur | 1976–77 | – | – | – | 114 | – |
| N.J. Contractor (56), A.A. Baig (112) | Manchester | 1959 | 109 | – | – | – | – |
| M.L. Jaisimha (70), V.L. Manjrekar (96) | Kanpur | 1961–62 | 109 | – | – | – | – |
| B.K. Kunderan (55), R.G. Nadkarni (122*) | Kanpur | 1963–64 | 109 | – | – | – | – |
| S.M. Gavaskar (102), M. Amarnath (85) | Port-of-Spain | 1975–76 | – | – | 108 | – | – |
| N.J. Contractor (92), R.F. Surti (64) | Delhi | 1960–61 | – | – | – | – | 107 |
| **Totals: (21)** | | | **7** | **3** | **7** | **3** | **1** |

## INDIA – 3rd Wicket

| Batsmen | Venue | Rubber | E | A | WI | NZ | P |
|---|---|---|---|---|---|---|---|
| P.R. Umrigar (223), V.L. Manjrekar (118) | Hyderabad | 1955–56 | – | – | – | 238 | – |
| V.M. Merchant (154), V.S. Hazare (164*) | Delhi | 1951–52 | 211 | – | – | – | – |
| V.M.H. Mankad (184), V.S. Hazare (49) | Lord's | 1952 | 211 | – | – | – | – |
| P. Roy (140), V.S. Hazare (155) | Bombay² | 1951–52 | 187 | – | – | – | – |
| L. Amarnath (118), C.K. Nayudu (67) | Bombay¹ | 1933–34 | 186 | – | – | – | – |
| A.D. Gaekwad (77*), G.R. Viswanath (103) | Kanpur | 1976–77 | – | – | – | 163* | – |
| M. Amarnath (85), G.R. Viswanath (112) | Port-of-Spain | 1975–76 | – | – | 159 | – | – |
| R.S. Modi (112), V.S. Hazare (134*) | Bombay² | 1948–49 | – | – | 156 | – | – |
| R.G. Nadkarni (122*), D.N. Sardesai (87) | Kanpur | 1963–64 | 144 | – | – | – | – |
| P. Roy (100), V.L. Manjrekar (90) | Calcutta | 1955–56 | – | – | – | 143 | – |
| N.J. Contractor (108), A.A. Baig (50) | Bombay² | 1959–60 | – | 133 | – | – | – |
| M. Amarnath (86), G.R. Viswanath (73) | Adelaide | 1977–78 | – | 131 | – | – | – |
| P. Roy (67*), V.L. Manjrekar (74*) | Dacca | 1954–55 | – | – | – | – | 130* |
| R.S. Modi (80), V.S. Hazare (59) | Calcutta | 1948–49 | – | – | 129 | – | – |
| B.K. Kunderan (100), Nawab of Pataudi, jr (203*) | Delhi | 1963–64 | 125 | – | – | – | – |
| P. Roy (78), V.L. Manjrekar (59) | Bahawalpur | 1954–55 | – | – | – | – | 123 |
| S.M. Gavaskar (124), D.N. Sardesai (75) | Port-of-Spain | 1970–71 | – | – | 122 | – | – |
| A.L. Wadekar (99), R.F. Surti (43) | Melbourne | 1967–68 | – | 116 | – | – | – |
| M.L. Apte (64), V.S. Hazare (63) | Bridgetown | 1952–53 | – | – | 112 | – | – |
| M.L. Jaisimha (66), V.L. Manjrekar (59) | Bombay² | 1964–65 | – | 112 | – | – | – |
| S.M. Gavaskar (116), G.R. Viswanath (50) | Georgetown | 1970–71 | – | – | 112 | – | – |
| R.S. Modi (87), V.S. Hazare (58*) | Calcutta | 1948–49 | – | – | 108 | – | – |
| M. Amarnath (72), G.R. Viswanath (59) | Melbourne | 1977–78 | – | 105 | – | – | – |
| N.J. Contractor (86), Nawab of Pataudi, jr (103) | Madras² | 1961–62 | 104 | – | – | – | – |
| A.L. Wadekar (71), R.F. Surti (44) | Dunedin | 1967–68 | – | – | – | 103 | – |
| A.L. Wadekar (55), G.R. Viswanath (59) | Madras¹ | 1969–70 | – | 102 | – | – | – |
| **Totals: (26)** | | | **7** | **6** | **7** | **4** | **2** |

## INDIA – 4th Wicket

| Batsmen | Venue | Rubber | E | A | WI | NZ | P |
|---|---|---|---|---|---|---|---|
| V.S. Hazare (89), V.L. Manjrekar (133) | Leeds | 1952 | 222 | – | – | – | – |
| V.S. Hazare (146*), P.R. Umrigar (102) | Bombay² | 1952–53 | – | – | – | – | 183 |
| P.R. Umrigar (223), A.G. Kripal Singh (100*) | Hyderabad | 1955–56 | – | – | – | 171 | – |
| V.M.H. Mankad (223), A.G. Kripal Singh (63) | Bombay² | 1955–56 | – | – | – | 167 | – |
| D.N. Sardesai (200*), C.G. Borde (109) | Bombay² | 1964–65 | – | – | – | 154 | – |
| P. Roy (85), P.R. Umrigar (117) | Kingston | 1952–53 | – | – | 150 | – | – |
| A.V. Mankad (74), Nawab of Pataudi, jr (95) | Bombay² | 1969–70 | – | 146 | – | – | – |
| V.S. Hazare (134*), L. Amarnath (58*) | Bombay² | 1948–49 | – | – | 144* | – | – |
| R.S. Modi (86), V.S. Hazare (122) | Bombay² | 1948–49 | – | – | 139 | – | – |

## HUNDRED PARTNERSHIPS – *continued*

| INDIA – 4th Wicket – *continued* | Venue | Rubber | E | A | WI | NZ | P |
|---|---|---|---|---|---|---|---|
| S.M. Gavaskar (108), B.P. Patel (83) | Bombay³ | 1976–77 | 139 | – | – | – | – |
| C.G. Borde (87), Nawab of Pataudi,jr (113) | Delhi | 1964–65 | – | – | – | 138 | – |
| G.R. Viswanath (89), D.B. Vengsarkar (44) | Adelaide | 1977–78 | – | 136 | – | – | – |
| M.L. Apte (163*), P.R. Umrigar (67) | Port-of-Spain | 1952–53 | – | – | 135 | – | – |
| R.F. Surti (52), Nawab of Pataudi, jr (74) | Brisbane² | 1967–68 | – | 128 | – | – | – |
| G.R. Viswanath (79), D.B. Vengsarkar (48) | Sydney | 1977–78 | – | 125 | – | – | – |
| C.G. Borde (69), R.F. Surti (70) | Adelaide | 1967–68 | – | 121 | – | – | – |
| A.L. Wadekar (91*), G.R. Viswanath (44*) | Delhi | 1969–70 | – | 120* | – | – | – |
| C.G. Borde (96), H.R. Adhikari (40) | Delhi | 1958–59 | – | – | 108 | – | – |
| P.R. Umrigar (112), C.G. Borde (45) | Delhi | 1960–61 | – ` | – | – | – | 107† |
| R.F. Surti (67), Nawab of Pataudi, jr (52) | Christchurch | 1967–68 | – | – | – | 103 | – |
| F.M. Engineer (75), P. Sharma (49) | Delhi | 1974–75 | – | – | 101 | – | – |
| **Totals: (21)** | | | **2** | **6** | **6** | **5** | **2** |

†*123 runs were added for this wicket, N.J. Contractor retiring hurt and being succeeded by C.G. Borde after 16 had been scored.*

| INDIA – 5th Wicket | Venue | Rubber | E | A | WI | NZ | P |
|---|---|---|---|---|---|---|---|
| S.M. Gavaskar (156), B.P. Patel (115*) | Port-of-Spain | 1975–76 | – | – | 204 | – | – |
| Nawab of Pataudi, jr (203*), C.G. Borde (67*) | Delhi | 1963–64 | 190* | – | – | – | – |
| P.R. Umrigar (117), C.G. Borde (177*) | Madras² | 1960–61 | – | – | – | – | 177 |
| S.A. Durani (73), G.R. Viswanath (113) | Bombay² | 1972–73 | 150 | – | – | – | – |
| C.G. Borde (69), S.A. Durani (71) | Bombay² | 1961–62 | 142 | – | – | – | – |
| Hanumant Singh (73), Nawab of Pataudi, jr (148) | Leeds | 1967 | 134 | – | – | – | – |
| V.L. Manjrekar (189*), C.G. Borde (45) | Delhi | 1961–62 | 132 | – | – | – | – |
| P.R. Umrigar (69), D.G. Phadkar (65) | Port-of-Spain | 1952–53 | – | – | 131 | – | – |
| V.L. Manjrekar (177), G.S. Ramchand (72) | Delhi | 1955–56 | – | – | – | 127 | – |
| R.F. Surti (99), C.G. Borde (65*) | Auckland | 1967–68 | – | – | – | 126 | – |
| G.R. Viswanath (95), A.D. Gaekwad (51) | Bombay³ | 1974–75 | – | – | 121 | – | – |
| D.N. Sardesai (112), E.D. Solkar (55) | Port-of-Spain | 1970–71 | – | – | 114 | – | – |
| C.G. Borde (62), Nawab of Pataudi, jr (153) | Calcutta | 1964–65 | – | – | – | 110 | – |
| A.A. Baig (58), R.B. Kenny (55*) | Bombay² | 1959–60 | – | 109 | – | – | – |
| **Totals: (14)** | | | **5** | **1** | **4** | **3** | **1** |

| INDIA – 6th Wicket | Venue | Rubber | E | A | WI | NZ | P |
|---|---|---|---|---|---|---|---|
| D.N. Sardesai (200*), Hanumant Singh (75*) | Bombay² | 1964–65 | – | – | – | 193* | – |
| V.S. Hazare (116), D.G. Phadkar (123) | Adelaide | 1947–48 | – | 188 | – | – | – |
| Nawab of Pataudi, jr (128*), C.G. Borde (49) | Madras² | 1964–65 | – | 142 | – | – | – |
| D.N. Sardesai (212), E.D. Solkar (61) | Kingston | 1970–71 | – | – | 137 | – | – |
| C.G. Borde (109), H.R. Adhikari (63) | Delhi | 1958–59 | – | – | 134 | – | – |
| V.L. Manjrekar (177), R.G. Nadkarni (68*) | Delhi | 1955–56 | – | – | – | 123 | – |
| M.L. Jaisimha (101), C.G. Borde (63) | Brisbane² | 1967–68 | – | 119 | – | – | – |
| P.R. Umrigar (130), D.K. Gaekwad (43) | Port-of-Spain | 1952–53 | – | – | 118 | – | – |
| G.R. Viswanath (137), E.D. Solkar (35) | Kanpur | 1969–70 | – | 110 | – | – | – |
| V.S. Hazare (56), D.G. Phadkar (64) | Leeds | 1952 | 105 | – | – | – | – |
| D.G. Phadkar (61), P.R. Umrigar (130*) | Madras¹ | 1951–52 | 104 | – | – | – | – |
| E.D. Solkar (75), F.M. Engineer (63) | Delhi | 1972–73 | 103 | – | – | – | – |
| C.G. Borde (121), S.A. Durani (55) | Bombay² | 1966–67 | – | – | 102 | – | – |
| **Totals: (13)** | | | **3** | **4** | **4** | **2** | **–** |

| INDIA – 7th Wicket | Venue | Rubber | E | A | WI | NZ | P |
|---|---|---|---|---|---|---|---|
| D.N. Sardesai (150), E.D. Solkar (65) | Bridgetown | 1970–71 | – | – | 186 | – | – |
| M.L. Apte (163*), V.M.H. Mankad (96) | Port-of-Spain | 1952–53 | – | – | 153 | – | – |
| C.G. Borde (84), S.A. Durani (90) | Bombay² | 1963–64 | 153 | – | – | – | – |
| V.S. Hazare (145), H.R. Adhikari (51) | Adelaide | 1947–48 | – | 132 | – | – | – |
| B.P. Patel (81), S.M.H. Kirmani (49) | Wellington | 1975–76 | – | – | – | 116 | – |
| **Totals: (5)** | | | **1** | **1** | **2** | **1** | **–** |

| INDIA – 8th Wicket | Venue | Rubber | E | A | WI | NZ | P |
|---|---|---|---|---|---|---|---|
| R.G. Nadkarni (75), F.M. Engineer (90) | Madras² | 1964–65 | – | – | – | 143 | – |
| R.G. Nadkarni (63), F.M. Engineer (65) | Madras² | 1961–62 | 101 | – | – | – | – |
| **Totals: (2)** | | | **1** | **–** | **–** | **1** | **–** |

**INDIA – 9th Wicket**

| | Venue | Rubber | E | A | WI | NZ | P |
|---|---|---|---|---|---|---|---|
| P.G. Joshi (52*), R.B. Desai (85) | Bombay² | 1960–61 | – | – | – | – | 149 |
| D.N. Sardesai (212), E.A.S. Prasanna (25) | Kingston | 1970–71 | – | – | 122 | – | – |
| S.M.H. Kirmani (88), B.S. Bedi (36) | Bombay³ | 1976–77 | – | – | – | 105 | – |
| | **Totals: (3)** | | **–** | **–** | **1** | **1** | **1** |

**INDIA – 10th Wicket**

| | Venue | Rubber | E | A | WI | NZ | P |
|---|---|---|---|---|---|---|---|
| H.R. Adhikari (81*), Ghulam Ahmed (50) | Delhi | 1952–53 | – | – | – | – | 109 |

**PAKISTAN – (73) – 1st Wicket**

| | Venue | Rubber | E | A | WI | NZ | I |
|---|---|---|---|---|---|---|---|
| Khalid Ibadulla (166), Abdul Kadir (95) | Karachi | 1964–65 | – | 249 | – | – | – |
| Hanif Mohammad (62), Imtiaz Ahmed (135) | Madras² | 1960–61 | – | – | – | – | 162 |
| Majid Khan (167), Zaheer Abbas (80) | Georgetown | 1976–77 | – | – | 159† | – | – |
| Hanif Mohammad (337), Imtiaz Ahmed (91) | Bridgetown | 1957–58 | – | – | 152 | – | – |
| Sadiq Mohammad (34), Majid Khan (112) | Karachi | 1976–77 | – | – | – | 147 | – |
| Sadiq Mohammad (103*), Majid Khan (98) | Hyderabad | 1976–77 | – | – | – | 136*‡ | – |
| Hanif Mohammad (142), Alimuddin (64) | Bahawalpur | 1954–55 | – | – | – | – | 127 |
| Majid Khan (54), Sadiq Mohammad (81) | Port-of-Spain | 1976–77 | – | – | 123 | – | – |
| Hanif Mohammad (104), Alimuddin (50) | Dacca | 1961–62 | 122 | – | – | – | – |
| Mohammad Ilyas (126), Naushad Ali (39) | Karachi | 1964–65 | – | – | – | 121 | – |
| Majid Khan (76), Sadiq Mohammad (105) | Melbourne | 1976–77 | – | 113 | – | – | – |
| | **Totals: (11)** | | **1** | **2** | **3** | **3** | **2** |

† *219 runs were added for this wicket, Sadiq Mohammad retired hurt and was succeeded by Zaheer Abbas after 60 had been scored.*

‡ *164 runs were added for this wicket, Sadiq Mohammad retired hurt and was succeeded by Zaheer Abbas after 136 had been scored. Although the 1st Wicket added 128 v Australia at Melbourne in 1972-73, this consisted of two partnerships: Sadiq Mohammad added 31\* with Saeed Ahmed (retired hurt) and a further 97 with Zaheer Abbas.*

**PAKISTAN – 2nd Wicket**

| | Venue | Rubber | E | A | WI | NZ | I |
|---|---|---|---|---|---|---|---|
| Zaheer Abbas (274), Mushtaq Mohd (100) | Birmingham | 1971 | 291 | – | – | – | – |
| Hanif Mohammad (160), Saeed Ahmed (121) | Bombay² | 1960–61 | – | – | – | – | 246 |
| Sadiq Mohammad (137), Majid Khan (158) | Melbourne | 1972–73 | – | 195 | – | – | – |
| Hanif Mohammad (103), Saeed Ahmed (78) | Karachi | 1958–59 | – | – | 178 | – | – |
| Hanif Mohammad (96), Waqar Hassan (65) | Bombay² | 1952–53 | – | – | – | – | 165 |
| Imtiaz Ahmed (98), Mushtaq Mohammad (72) | Oval | 1962 | 137 | – | – | – | – |
| Hanif Mohammad (81), Saeed Ahmed (64) | Port-of-Spain | 1957–58 | – | – | 130 | – | – |
| Sadiq Mohammad (105), Zaheer Abbas (90) | Melbourne | 1976–77 | – | 128 | – | – | – |
| Imtiaz Ahmed (122), Saeed Ahmed (52) | Kingston | 1957–58 | – | – | 118 | – | – |
| Mohammad Ilyas (56), Saeed Ahmed (68) | Rawalpindi | 1964–65 | – | – | – | 114 | – |
| Hanif Mohammad (111), Saeed Ahmed (69) | Dacca | 1961–62 | 113 | – | – | – | – |
| Hanif Mohammad (337), Alimuddin (37) | Bridgetown | 1957–58 | – | – | 112 | – | – |
| Majid Khan (98), Zaheer Abbas (240) | Oval | 1974 | 100 | – | – | – | – |
| | **Totals: (13)** | | **4** | **2** | **4** | **1** | **2** |

**PAKISTAN – 3rd Wicket**

| | Venue | Rubber | E | A | WI | NZ | I |
|---|---|---|---|---|---|---|---|
| Mudassar Nazar (114), Haroon Rashid (122) | Lahore² | 1977–78 | 180 | – | – | – | – |
| Zaheer Abbas (240), Mushtaq Mohammad (76) | Oval | 1974 | 172 | – | – | – | – |
| Sadiq Mohammad (166), Majid Khan (79) | Wellington | 1972–73 | – | – | – | 171 | – |
| Saeed Ahmed (97), Wazir Mohammad (189) | Port-of-Spain | 1957–58 | – | – | 169 | – | – |
| Saeed Ahmed (166), Shujauddin (45) | Lahore² | 1959–60 | – | 169 | – | – | – |
| Hanif Mohammad (111), Javed Burki (140) | Dacca | 1961–62 | 156 | – | – | – | – |
| Hanif Mohammad (337), Saeed Ahmed (65) | Bridgetown | 1957–58 | – | – | 154 | – | – |
| Saeed Ahmed (74), Javed Burki (138) | Lahore² | 1961–62 | 138 | – | – | – | – |
| Saeed Ahmed (150), Hanif Mohammad (79) | Georgetown | 1957–58 | – | – | 136 | – | – |
| Zaheer Abbas (72), Mushtaq Mohammad (57) | Leeds | 1971 | 129 | – | – | – | – |
| Majid Khan (99), Mushtaq Mohammad (99) | Karachi | 1972–73 | 121 | – | – | – | – |
| Saeed Ahmed (172), Javed Burki (29) | Karachi | 1964–65 | – | – | – | 114 | – |
| Majid Khan (110), Mushtaq Mohammad (61) | Auckland | 1972–73 | – | – | – | 104 | – |
| Imtiaz Ahmed (122), W. Mathias (77) | Kingston | 1957–58 | – | – | 101 | – | – |
| | **Totals: (14)** | | **6** | **1** | **4** | **3** | **–** |

### PAKISTAN – 4th Wicket

| | Venue | Rubber | E | A | WI | NZ | I |
|---|---|---|---|---|---|---|---|
| Mushtaq Mohammad (201), Asif Iqbal (175) | Dunedin | 1972–73 | – | – | – | 350 | – |
| Javed Miandad (206), Mushtaq Mohd (107) | Karachi | 1976–77 | – | – | – | 252 | – |
| Mustaq Mohammad (101), Asif Iqbal (73) | Hyderabad | 1976–77 | – | – | – | 164 | – |
| Wazir Mohd (189), Hanif Mohd (54) | Port-of-Spain | | – | – | – | 154 | – |
| Javed Burki (138), Mushtaq Mohammad (76) | Lahore² | 1961–62 | 153 | – | – | – | – |
| Maqsood Ahmed (99), A.H. Kardar (44) | Lahore¹ | 1954–55 | – | – | – | – | 136 |
| Hanif Mohd (337), Wazir Mohd (35) | Bridgetown | 1957–58 | – | – | 121 | – | – |
| Mushtaq Mohammad (76), Wasim Raja (53) | Lord's | 1974 | 115 | – | – | – | – |
| Haroon Rashid (108), Javed Miandad (88*) | Hyderabad | 1977–78 | 112 | – | – | – | – |
| Majid Khan (92), Mushtaq Mohammad (121) | Port-of-Spain | 1976–77 | – | – | 108 | – | – |
| Mushtaq Mohammad (100*), Saeed Ahmed (64) | Nottingham | 1962 | 107 | – | – | – | – |
| Majid Khan (75), Zaheer Abbas (48) | Leeds | 1974 | 100 | – | – | – | – |
| Mudassar Nazar (114), Javed Miandad (71) | Lahore² | 1977–78 | 100 | – | – | – | – |
| | | Totals: (13) | 6 | – | 3 | 3 | 1 |

### PAKISTAN – 5th Wicket

| | Venue | Rubber | E | A | WI | NZ | I |
|---|---|---|---|---|---|---|---|
| Javed Miandad (163), Asif Iqbal (166) | Lahore² | 1976–77 | – | – | – | 281 | – |
| Javed Burki (101), Nasim-ul-Ghani (101) | Lord's | 1962 | 197 | – | – | – | – |
| Alimuddin (103*), A.H. Kardar (93) | Karachi | 1954–55 | – | – | – | – | 155 |
| Mushtaq Mohammad (157), Asif Iqbal (68) | Hyderabad | 1972–73 | 153 | – | – | – | – |
| Mushtaq Mohammad (121), Asif Iqbal (65) | Sydney | 1972–73 | – | 139 | – | – | – |
| Javed Miandad (85), Mushtaq Mohammad (67*) | Karachi | 1976–77 | – | – | – | 138 | – |
| Javed Burki (61), Mushtaq Mohd (101) | Delhi | 1960–61 | – | – | – | – | 136 |
| | | Totals: (7) | 2 | 1 | – | 2 | 2 |

### PAKISTAN – 6th Wicket

| | Venue | Rubber | E | A | WI | NZ | I |
|---|---|---|---|---|---|---|---|
| Hanif Mohammad (203*), Majid Khan (80) | Lahore² | 1964–65 | – | – | – | 217 | – |
| Wazir Mohammad (106), A.H. Kardar (57) | Kingston | 1957–58 | – | – | 166 | – | – |
| Mushtaq Mohammad (157), Intikhab Alam (138) | Hyderabad | 1972–73 | 145 | – | – | – | – |
| Mushtaq Mohammad (123), Aftab Baloch (60*) | Lahore² | 1974–75 | – | – | 116 | – | – |
| Mushtaq Mohammad (56), Wasim Raja (70) | Port-of-Spain | 1976–77 | – | – | 116 | – | – |
| Asif Iqbal (120), Javed Miandad (64) | Sydney | 1976–77 | – | 115 | – | – | – |
| Asif Iqbal (135), Wasim Raja (64) | Kingston | 1976–77 | – | – | 115 | – | – |
| Wazir Mohammad (67), A.H. Kardar (69) | Karachi | 1956–57 | – | 104 | – | – | – |
| | | Totals: (8) | 1 | 2 | 4 | 1 | – |

### PAKISTAN – 7th Wicket

| | Venue | Rubber | E | A | WI | NZ | I |
|---|---|---|---|---|---|---|---|
| Waqar Hassan (189), Imtiaz Ahmed (209) | Lahore¹ | 1955–56 | – | – | – | 308 | – |
| Wasim Raja (107*), Wasim Bari (58) | Karachi | 1974–75 | – | – | 128 | – | – |
| Intikhab Alam (64), Wasim Bari (72) | Adelaide | 1972–73 | – | 104 | – | – | – |
| | | Totals: (3) | – | 1 | 1 | 1 | – |

### PAKISTAN – 8th Wicket

| | Venue | Rubber | E | A | WI | NZ | I |
|---|---|---|---|---|---|---|---|
| Hanif Mohammad (187*), Asif Iqbal (76) | Lord's | 1967 | 130 | – | – | – | – |

### PAKISTAN – 9th Wicket

| | Venue | Rubber | E | A | WI | NZ | I |
|---|---|---|---|---|---|---|---|
| Asif Iqbal (146), Intikhab Alam (51) | Oval | 1967 | 190 | – | – | – | – |

### PAKISTAN – 10th Wicket

| | Venue | Rubber | E | A | WI | NZ | I |
|---|---|---|---|---|---|---|---|
| Wasim Raja (71), Wasim Bari (60*) | Bridgetown | 1976–77 | – | – | 133 | – | – |
| Zulfiqar Ahmed (63*), Amir Elahi (47) | Madras¹ | 1952–53 | – | – | – | – | 104 |
| | | Totals: (2) | – | – | 1 | – | 1 |

# PLAYERS' RECORDS – BOWLING

## 100 WICKETS IN TESTS

### ENGLAND

| | Tests | Wkts | Avge | A | SA | WI | NZ | I | P |
|---|---|---|---|---|---|---|---|---|---|
| | | | | | | Opponents | | | |
| F.S. Trueman | 67 | **307** | 21.57 | 79 | 27 | 86 | 40 | 53 | 22 |
| D.L. Underwood | 74 | **265** | 24.90 | 92 | — | 37 | 48 | 52 | 36 |
| J.B. Statham | 70 | **252** | 24.84 | 69 | 69 | 42 | 20 | 25 | 27 |
| A.V. Bedser | 51 | **236** | 24.89 | 104 | 54 | 11 | 13 | 44 | 10 |
| J.A. Snow | 49 | **202** | 26.66 | 83 | 4 | 72 | 20 | 16 | 7 |
| J.C. Laker | 46 | **193** | 21.24 | 79 | 32 | 51 | 21 | 8 | 2 |
| S.F. Barnes | 27 | **189** | 16.43 | 106 | 83 | — | — | — | — |
| G.A.R. Lock | 49 | **174** | 25.58 | 31 | 15 | 39 | 47 | 26 | 16 |
| M.W. Tate | 39 | **155** | 26.16 | 83 | 53 | 13 | 6 | — | — |
| F.J. Titmus | 53 | **153** | 32.22 | 47 | 27 | 15 | 28 | 27 | 9 |
| H. Verity | 40 | **144** | 24.37 | 59 | 31 | 9 | 7 | 38 | — |
| A.W. Greig | 58 | **141** | 32.20 | 44 | — | 36 | 20 | 27 | 14 |
| T.E. Bailey | 61 | **132** | 29.21 | 42 | 28 | 29 | 32 | — | 1 |
| W. Rhodes | 58 | **127** | 26.96 | 109 | 8 | 10 | — | — | — |
| R.G.D. Willis | 35 | **126** | 25.32 | 58 | — | 18 | 16 | 25 | 9 |
| D.A. Allen | 39 | **122** | 30.97 | 28 | 21 | 15 | 13 | 21 | 24 |
| R. Illingworth | 61 | **122** | 31.20 | 34 | 6 | 19 | 22 | 31 | 10 |
| J. Briggs | 33 | **118** | 17.74 | 97 | 21 | — | — | — | — |
| G.G. Arnold | 34 | **115** | 28.29 | 30 | — | 17 | 20 | 27 | 21 |
| G.A. Lohmann | 18 | **112** | 10.75 | 77 | 35 | — | — | — | — |
| C.M. Old | 36 | **111** | 29.39 | 25 | — | 15 | 20 | 43 | 8 |
| D.V.P. Wright | 34 | **108** | 39.11 | 48 | 37 | 11 | 8 | 4 | — |
| R. Peel | 20 | **102** | 16.81 | 102 | — | — | — | — | — |
| J.H. Wardle | 28 | **102** | 20.39 | 24 | 46 | 7 | 5 | — | 20 |
| C. Blythe | 19 | **100** | 18.63 | 41 | 59 | — | — | — | — |

### AUSTRALIA

| | Tests | Wkts | Avge | E | SA | WI | NZ | I | P |
|---|---|---|---|---|---|---|---|---|---|
| | | | | | | Opponents | | | |
| R. Benaud | 63 | **248** | 27.03 | 83 | 52 | 42 | — | 52 | 19 |
| G.D. McKenzie | 60 | **246** | 29.78 | 96 | 41 | 47 | — | 47 | 15 |
| R.R. Lindwall | 61 | **228** | 23.03 | 114 | 31 | 41 | 2 | 36 | 4 |
| C.V. Grimmett | 37 | **216** | 24.21 | 106 | 77 | 33 | — | — | — |
| A.K. Davidson | 44 | **186** | 20.53 | 84 | 25 | 33 | — | 30 | 14 |
| D.K. Lillee | 32 | **171** | 23.49 | 96 | — | 27 | 15 | — | 33 |
| K.R. Miller | 55 | **170** | 22.97 | 87 | 30 | 40 | 2 | 9 | 2 |
| W.A. Johnston | 40 | **160** | 23.91 | 75 | 44 | 25 | — | 16 | — |
| J.R. Thomson | 32 | **145** | 25.51 | 72 | — | 49 | — | 22 | 2 |
| W.J. O'Reilly | 27 | **144** | 22.59 | 102 | 34 | — | 8 | — | — |
| H. Trumble | 32 | **141** | 21.78 | 141 | — | — | — | — | — |
| M.H.N. Walker | 34 | **138** | 27.47 | 56 | — | 37 | 28 | — | 17 |
| A.A. Mallett | 35 | **125** | 27.95 | 47 | 6 | 12 | 19 | 28 | 13 |
| M.A. Noble | 42 | **121** | 25.00 | 115 | 6 | — | — | — | — |
| I.W. Johnson | 45 | **109** | 29.19 | 42 | 22 | 22 | — | 19 | 4 |
| G. Giffen | 31 | **103** | 27.09 | 103 | — | — | — | — | — |
| A.N. Connolly | 29 | **102** | 29.22 | 25 | 26 | 20 | — | 31 | — |
| C.T.B. Turner | 17 | **101** | 16.53 | 101 | — | — | — | — | — |

### SOUTH AFRICA

| | Tests | Wkts | Avge | E | A | NZ |
|---|---|---|---|---|---|---|
| | | | | | Opponents | |
| H.J. Tayfield | 37 | **170** | 25.91 | 75 | 64 | 31 |
| T.L. Goddard | 41 | **123** | 26.22 | 63 | 53 | 7 |
| P.M. Pollock | 28 | **116** | 24.18 | 32 | 52 | 32 |
| N.A.T. Adcock | 26 | **104** | 21.10 | 57 | 14 | 33 |

### WEST INDIES

| | Tests | Wkts | Avge | E | A | NZ | I | P |
|---|---|---|---|---|---|---|---|---|
| | | | | | | Opponents | | |
| L.R. Gibbs | 79 | **309** | 29.09 | 100 | 103 | 11 | 63 | 32 |
| G.St A. Sobers | 93 | **235** | 34.03 | 102 | 51 | 19 | 59 | 4 |
| W.W. Hall | 48 | **192** | 26.38 | 65 | 45 | 1 | 65 | 16 |
| S. Ramadhin | 43 | **158** | 28.98 | 80 | 22 | 32 | 15 | 9 |
| A.L. Valentine | 36 | **139** | 30.32 | 40 | 43 | 23 | 30 | 3 |
| A.M.E. Roberts | 27 | **134** | 24.61 | 31 | 34 | — | 38 | 31 |
| V.A. Holder | 34 | **101** | 30.48 | 33 | 28 | 12 | 23 | 5 |

### NEW ZEALAND

| | Tests | Wkts | Avge | E | A | SA | WI | I | P |
|---|---|---|---|---|---|---|---|---|---|
| | | | | | | Opponents | | | |
| R.O. Collinge | 34 | **114** | 29.02 | 46 | 17 | — | — | 23 | 28 |
| B.R. Taylor | 30 | **111** | 26.60 | 28 | — | — | 32 | 29 | 22 |
| R.C. Motz | 32 | **100** | 31.48 | 28 | — | 21 | 17 | 22 | 12 |

### INDIA

| | Tests | Wkts | Avge | E | A | WI | NZ | P |
|---|---|---|---|---|---|---|---|---|
| | | | | | | Opponents | | |
| B.S. Bedi | 58 | **246** | 26.89 | 78 | 56 | 55 | 57 | — |
| B.S. Chandrasekhar | 50 | **222** | 28.24 | 95 | 38 | 53 | 36 | — |
| E.A.S. Prasanna | 47 | **187** | 29.36 | 41 | 57 | 34 | 55 | — |
| V.M.H. Mankad | 44 | **162** | 32.32 | 54 | 23 | 36 | 12 | 37 |
| S.P. Gupte | 36 | **149** | 29.55 | 24 | 8 | 49 | 34 | 34 |
| S. Venkataraghavan | 37 | **113** | 33.59 | 17 | 14 | 38 | 44 | — |

### PAKISTAN

| | Tests | Wkts | Avge | E | A | WI | NZ | I |
|---|---|---|---|---|---|---|---|---|
| | | | | | | Opponents | | |
| Fazal Mahmood | 34 | **139** | 24.70 | 25 | 24 | 41 | 5 | 44 |
| Intikhab Alam | 47 | **125** | 35.93 | 49 | 9 | 8 | 54 | 5 |

## BEST BOWLING AVERAGES
### (Qualification: 25 wickets)

| | | Tests | Balls | Runs | Wkts | Avge | 5wI | 10wM |
|---|---|---|---|---|---|---|---|---|
| G.A. Lohmann | (E) | 18 | 3821 | 1205 | 112 | **10.75** | 9 | 5 |
| J.J. Ferris | (A/E) | 9 | 2302 | 775 | 61 | **12.70** | 6 | 1 |
| M.J. Procter | (SA) | 7 | 1514 | 616 | 41 | **15.02** | 1 | – |
| W. Barnes | (E) | 21 | 2289 | 793 | 51 | **15.54** | 3 | – |
| W. Bates | (E) | 15 | 2364 | 821 | 50 | **16.42** | 4 | 1 |
| S.F. Barnes | (E) | 27 | 7873 | 3106 | 189 | **16.43** | 24 | 7 |
| C.T.B. Turner | (A) | 17 | 5195 | 1670 | 101 | **16.53** | 11 | 2 |
| R. Peel | (E) | 20 | 5216 | 1715 | 102 | **16.81** | 6 | 2 |
| J. Briggs | (E) | 33 | 5332 | 2094 | 118 | **17.74** | 9 | 4 |
| R. Appleyard | (E) | 9 | 1596 | 554 | 31 | **17.87** | 1 | – |
| W.S. Lees | (E) | 5 | 1256 | 467 | 26 | **17.96** | 2 | – |
| H. Ironmonger | (A) | 14 | 4695 | 1330 | 74 | **17.97** | 4 | 2 |
| G.B. Lawrence | (SA) | 5 | 1334 | 512 | 28 | **18.28** | 2 | – |
| F.R. Spofforth | (A) | 18 | 4185 | 1731 | 94 | **18.41** | 7 | 4 |
| F.H. Tyson | (E) | 17 | 3452 | 1411 | 76 | **18.56** | 4 | 1 |
| C. Blythe | (E) | 19 | 4438 | 1863 | 100 | **18.63** | 9 | 4 |
| G.F. Bissett | (SA) | 4 | 989 | 469 | 25 | **18.76** | 2 | – |
| I.T. Botham | (E) | 5 | 1246 | 513 | 27 | **19.00** | 4 | – |
| A.S. Kennedy | (E) | 5 | 1683 | 599 | 31 | **19.32** | 2 | – |

## MOST FREQUENT WICKET-TAKERS

*(Qualification: 25 wickets)*

| | | Balls/wkt. | Tests | Balls | Runs | Wkts | Avge |
|---|---|---|---|---|---|---|---|
| G.A. Lohmann | (E) | **34.11** | 18 | 3821 | 1205 | 112 | 10.75 |
| M.J. Procter | (SA) | **36.92** | 7 | 1514 | 616 | 41 | 15.02 |
| J.J. Ferris | (A/E) | **37.73** | 9 | 2302 | 775 | 61 | 12.70 |
| B.J.T. Bosanquet | (E) | **38.80** | 7 | 970 | 604 | 25 | 24.16 |
| C.E.H. Croft | (WI) | **39.00** | 7 | 1638 | 846 | 42 | 20.14 |
| G.F. Bissett | (SA) | **39.56** | 4 | 989 | 469 | 25 | 18.76 |
| S.F. Barnes | (E) | **41.65** | 27 | 7873 | 3106 | 189 | 16.43 |

## MOST ECONOMICAL CAREER FIGURES

*(Qualification: 2000 balls)*

| | | Runs/100 balls | Tests | Balls | Runs | Wkts | Avge |
|---|---|---|---|---|---|---|---|
| W. Attewell | (E) | **21.96** | 10 | 2850 | 626 | 27 | 23.18 |
| C. Gladwin | (E) | **26.82** | 8 | 2129 | 571 | 15 | 38.06 |
| T.L. Goddard | (SA) | **27.48** | 41 | 11736 | 3226 | 123 | 26.22 |
| R.G. Nadkarni | (I) | **27.92** | 41 | 9165 | 2559 | 88 | 29.07 |
| H. Ironmonger | (A) | **28.32** | 14 | 4695 | 1330 | 74 | 17.97 |
| J.C. Watkins | (SA) | **29.09** | 15 | 2805 | 816 | 29 | 28.13 |
| K.D. Mackay | (A) | **29.71** | 37 | 5792 | 1721 | 50 | 34.42 |
| A.R.A. Murray | (SA) | **29.90** | 10 | 2374 | 710 | 18 | 39.44 |

## 25 WICKETS IN A RUBBER

| | | | | Opponents | | | | | |
|---|---|---|---|---|---|---|---|---|---|
| *ENGLAND* | | *Venue* | *Tests* | A | SA | WI | NZ | I | P |
| S.F. Barnes | 1913-14 | SA | 4 | — | 49 | — | — | — | — |
| J.C. Laker | 1956 | E | 5 | 46 | — | — | — | — | — |
| A.V. Bedser | 1953 | E | 5 | 39 | — | — | — | — | — |
| M.W. Tate | 1924-25 | A | 5 | 38 | — | — | — | — | — |
| G.A. Lohmann | 1895-96 | SA | 3 | — | 35 | — | — | — | — |
| S.F. Barnes | 1911-12 | A | 5 | 34 | — | — | — | — | — |
| S.F. Barnes | 1912 | E | 3 | — | 34 | — | — | — | — |
| G.A.R. Lock | 1958 | E | 5 | — | — | — | 34 | — | — |
| F.S. Trueman | 1963 | E | 5 | — | — | 34 | — | — | — |
| H. Larwood | 1932-33 | A | 5 | 33 | — | — | — | — | — |
| T. Richardson | 1894-95 | A | 5 | 32 | — | — | — | — | — |
| F.R. Foster | 1911-12 | A | 5 | 32 | — | — | — | — | — |
| W. Rhodes | 1903-04 | A | 5 | 31 | — | — | — | — | — |
| A.S. Kennedy | 1922-23 | SA | 5 | — | 31 | — | — | — | — |
| J.A. Snow | 1970-71 | A | 6 | 31 | — | — | — | — | — |
| J.N. Crawford | 1907-08 | A | 5 | 30 | — | — | — | — | — |
| A.V. Bedser | 1950-51 | A | 5 | 30 | — | — | — | — | — |
| A.V. Bedser | 1951 | E | 5 | — | 30 | — | — | — | — |
| F.S. Trueman | 1952 | E | 4 | — | — | — | — | 29 | — |
| D.L. Underwood | 1976-77 | I | 5 | — | — | — | — | 29 | — |
| F.H. Tyson | 1954-55 | A | 5 | 28 | — | — | — | — | — |
| R. Peel | 1894-95 | A | 5 | 27 | — | — | — | — | — |
| M.W. Tate | 1924 | E | 5 | — | 27 | — | — | — | — |
| J.B. Statham | 1960 | E | 5 | — | 27 | — | — | — | — |
| F.J. Titmus | 1963-64 | I | 5 | — | — | — | — | 27 | — |
| J.A. Snow | 1967-68 | WI | 4 | — | — | 27 | — | — | — |
| R.G.D. Willis | 1977 | E | 5 | 27 | — | — | — | — | — |
| W.S. Lees | 1905-06 | SA | 5 | — | 26 | — | — | — | — |
| C. Blythe | 1907 | E | 3 | — | 26 | — | — | — | — |
| W. Voce | 1936-37 | A | 5 | 26 | — | — | — | — | — |
| J.H. Wardle | 1956-57 | SA | 4 | — | 26 | — | — | — | — |

| ENGLAND – *continued* | | Venue | Tests | Opponents A | SA | WI | NZ | I | P |
|---|---|---|---|---|---|---|---|---|---|
| J.K. Lever | 1976-77 | I | 5 | — | — | — | — | 26 | — |
| A. Fielder | 1907-08 | A | 4 | 25 | — | — | — | — | — |
| J.C. White | 1928-29 | A | 5 | 25 | — | — | — | — | — |
| F.S. Trueman | 1960 | SA | 5 | — | 25 | — | — | — | — |

| AUSTRALIA | | Venue | Tests | Opponents E | SA | WI | NZ | I | P |
|---|---|---|---|---|---|---|---|---|---|
| C.V. Grimmett | 1935-36 | SA | 5 | — | 44 | — | — | — | — |
| W.J. Whitty | 1910-11 | A | 5 | — | 37 | — | — | — | — |
| A.A. Mailey | 1920-21 | A | 5 | 36 | — | — | — | — | — |
| G. Giffen | 1894-95 | A | 5 | 34 | — | — | — | — | — |
| C.V. Grimmett | 1930-31 | A | 5 | — | — | 33 | — | — | — |
| C.V. Grimmett | 1931-32 | A | 5 | — | 33 | — | — | — | — |
| A.K. Davidson | 1960-61 | A | 4 | — | — | 33 | — | — | — |
| J.R. Thomson | 1974-75 | A | 5 | 33 | — | — | — | — | — |
| M.A. Noble | 1901-02 | A | 5 | 32 | — | — | — | — | — |
| H.V. Hordern | 1911-12 | A | 5 | 32 | — | — | — | — | — |
| J.V. Saunders | 1907-08 | A | 5 | 31 | — | — | — | — | — |
| H. Ironmonger | 1931-32 | A | 4 | — | 31 | — | — | — | — |
| R. Benaud | 1958-59 | A | 5 | 31 | — | — | — | — | — |
| D.K. Lillee | 1972 | E | 5 | 31 | — | — | — | — | — |
| R. Benaud | 1957-58 | SA | 5 | — | 30 | — | — | — | — |
| G.D. McKenzie | 1968-69 | A | 5 | — | — | 30 | — | — | — |
| C.V. Grimmett | 1930 | E | 5 | 29 | — | — | — | — | — |
| A.K. Davidson | 1959-60 | I | 5 | — | — | — | — | 29 | — |
| R. Benaud | 1959-60 | I | 5 | — | — | — | — | 29 | — |
| G.D. McKenzie | 1964 | E | 5 | 29 | — | — | — | — | — |
| J.R. Thomson | 1975-76 | A | 6 | — | — | 29 | — | — | — |
| H. Trumble | 1901-02 | A | 5 | 28 | — | — | — | — | — |
| W.J. O'Reilly | 1934 | E | 5 | 28 | — | — | — | — | — |
| A.A. Mallett | 1969-70 | I | 5 | — | — | — | — | 28 | — |
| W.M. Clark | 1977-78 | A | 5 | — | — | — | — | 28 | — |
| E.A. McDonald | 1921 | E | 5 | 27 | — | — | — | — | — |
| W.J. O'Reilly | 1932-33 | A | 5 | 27 | — | — | — | — | — |
| W.J. O'Reilly | 1935-36 | SA | 5 | — | 27 | — | — | — | — |
| R.R. Lindwall | 1948 | E | 5 | 27 | — | — | — | — | — |
| W.A. Johnston | 1948 | E | 5 | 27 | — | — | — | — | — |
| D.K. Lillee | 1975-76 | A | 5 | — | — | 27 | — | — | — |
| E. Jones | 1899 | E | 5 | 26 | — | — | — | — | — |
| H. Trumble | 1902 | E | 3 | 26 | — | — | — | — | — |
| R.R. Lindwall | 1953 | E | 5 | 26 | — | — | — | — | — |
| J.W. Gleeson | 1968-69 | A | 5 | — | — | 26 | — | — | — |
| M.H.N. Walker | 1972-73 | WI | 5 | — | — | 26 | — | — | — |
| C.V. Grimmett | 1934 | E | 5 | 25 | — | — | — | — | — |
| W.J. O'Reilly | 1936-37 | A | 5 | 25 | — | — | — | — | — |
| A.K. Davidson | 1957-58 | SA | 5 | — | 25 | — | — | — | — |
| D.K. Lillee | 1974-75 | A | 6 | 25 | — | — | — | — | — |

| SOUTH AFRICA | | Venue | Tests | Opponents E | A | NZ | | | |
|---|---|---|---|---|---|---|---|---|---|
| H.J. Tayfield | 1956-57 | SA | 5 | 37 | — | — | | | |
| A.E.E. Vogler | 1909-10 | SA | 5 | 36 | — | — | | | |
| H.J. Tayfield | 1952-53 | A | 5 | — | 30 | — | | | |
| G.A. Faulkner | 1909-10 | SA | 5 | 29 | — | — | | | |
| G.B. Lawrence | 1961-62 | SA | 5 | — | — | 28 | | | |
| A.E. Hall | 1922-23 | SA | 4 | 27 | — | — | | | |
| H.J. Tayfield | 1955 | E | 5 | 26 | — | — | | | |
| N.A.T. Adcock | 1960 | E | 5 | 26 | — | — | | | |
| T.L. Goddard | 1966-67 | SA | 5 | — | 26 | — | | | |

# 25 WICKETS IN A RUBBER – *continued*

| *SOUTH AFRICA – continued* | | Venue | Tests | Opponents E | A | NZ |
|---|---|---|---|---|---|---|
| M.J. Procter | 1969-70 | SA | 4 | — | 26 | — |
| C.B. Llewellyn | 1902-03 | SA | 3 | — | 25 | — |
| R.O. Schwarz | 1910-11 | A | 5 | — | 25 | — |
| J.M. Blanckenberg | 1922-23 | SA | 5 | 25 | — | — |
| G.F. Bissett | 1927-28 | SA | 4 | 25 | — | — |
| T.L. Goddard | 1955 | E | 5 | 25 | — | — |
| P.M. Pollock | 1963-64 | A | 5 | — | 25 | — |
| J.T. Partridge | 1963-64 | A | 5 | — | 25 | — |

| *WEST INDIES* | | Venue | Tests | Opponents E | A | NZ | I | P |
|---|---|---|---|---|---|---|---|---|
| A.L. Valentine | 1950 | E | 4 | 33 | — | — | — | — |
| C.E.H. Croft | 1976-77 | WI | 5 | — | — | — | — | 33 |
| C.C. Griffith | 1963 | E | 5 | 32 | — | — | — | — |
| A.M.E. Roberts | 1974-75 | I | 5 | — | — | — | 32 | — |
| W.W. Hall | 1958-59 | I | 5 | — | — | — | 30 | — |
| A.L. Valentine | 1952-53 | WI | 5 | — | — | — | 28 | — |
| M.A. Holding | 1976 | E | 4 | 28 | — | — | — | — |
| A.M.E. Roberts | 1976 | E | 5 | 28 | — | — | — | — |
| W.W. Hall | 1961-62 | WI | 5 | — | — | — | 27 | — |
| S. Ramadhin | 1950 | E | 4 | 26 | — | — | — | — |
| R. Gilchrist | 1958-59 | I | 4 | — | — | — | 26 | — |
| L.R. Gibbs | 1963 | E | 5 | 26 | — | — | — | — |
| L.R. Gibbs | 1972-73 | WI | 5 | — | 26 | — | — | — |
| J. Garner | 1976-77 | WI | 5 | — | — | — | — | 25 |

| *NEW ZEALAND* | | Venue | Tests | Opponents E | A | SA | WI | I | P |
|---|---|---|---|---|---|---|---|---|---|
| B.R. Taylor | 1971-72 | WI | 4 | — | — | — | 27 | — | — |

| *INDIA* | | Venue | Tests | Opponents E | A | WI | NZ | P |
|---|---|---|---|---|---|---|---|---|
| B.S. Chandrasekhar | 1972-73 | I | 5 | 35 | — | — | — | — |
| V.M.H. Mankad | 1951-52 | I | 5 | 34 | — | — | — | — |
| S.P. Gupte | 1955-56 | I | 5 | — | — | — | 34 | — |
| B.S. Bedi | 1977-78 | A | 5 | — | 31 | — | — | — |
| B.S. Chandrasekhar | 1977-78 | A | 5 | — | 28 | — | — | — |
| S.P. Gupte | 1952-53 | WI | 5 | — | — | 27 | — | — |
| E.A.S. Prasanna | 1969-70 | I | 5 | — | 26 | — | — | — |
| V.M.H. Mankad | 1952-53 | I | 5 | — | — | — | — | 25 |
| E.A.S. Prasanna | 1967-68 | A | 4 | — | 25 | — | — | — |
| B.S. Bedi | 1972-73 | I | 5 | 25 | — | — | — | — |
| B.S. Bedi | 1976-77 | I | 5 | 25 | — | — | — | — |

| *PAKISTAN* | | Venue | Tests | Opponents E | A | WI | NZ | I |
|---|---|---|---|---|---|---|---|---|
| Imran Khan | 1976-77 | WI | 5 | — | — | 25 | — | — |

# TEN WICKETS IN A MATCH

*(† On debut)*

| ENGLAND (79) | | | Opponents A | SA | WI | NZ | I | P |
|---|---|---|---|---|---|---|---|---|
| J.C. Laker | 1956 | Manchester | 19-90 | — | — | — | — | — |
| S.F. Barnes | 1913-14 | Johannesburg[1] | — | 17-159 | — | — | — | — |
| J. Briggs | 1888-89 | Cape Town | — | 15-28 | — | — | — | — |
| G.A. Lohmann | 1895-96 | Port Elizabeth | — | 15-45 | — | — | — | — |
| C. Blythe | 1907 | Leeds | — | 15-99 | — | — | — | — |
| H. Verity | 1934 | Lord's | 15-104 | — | — | — | — | — |
| W. Rhodes | 1903-04 | Melbourne | 15-124 | — | — | — | — | — |
| A.V. Bedser | 1953 | Nottingham | 14-99 | — | — | — | — | — |
| W. Bates | 1882-83 | Melbourne | 14-102 | — | — | — | — | — |
| S.F. Barnes | 1913-14 | Durban[1] | — | 14-144 | — | — | — | — |
| S.F. Barnes | 1912 | Oval | — | 13-57 | — | — | — | — |
| D.L. Underwood | 1974 | Lord's | — | — | — | — | — | 13-71 |
| J.J. Ferris | 1891-92 | Cape Town | — | 13-91 | — | — | — | — |
| A.W. Greig | 1973-74 | Port-of-Spain | — | — | 13-156 | — | — | — |
| S.F. Barnes | 1901-02 | Melbourne | 13-163 | — | — | — | — | — |
| T. Richardson | 1896 | Manchester | 13-244 | — | — | — | — | — |
| J.C. White | 1928-29 | Adelaide | 13-256 | — | — | — | — | — |
| G.A. Lohmann | 1895-96 | Johannesburg[1] | — | 12-71 | — | — | — | — |
| J.H. Wardle | 1956-57 | Cape Town | — | 12-89 | — | — | — | — |
| D.L. Underwood | 1970-71 | Christchurch | — | — | — | 12-97 | — | — |
| R. Tattersall | 1951 | Lord's | — | 12-101 | — | — | — | — |
| D.L. Underwood | 1969 | Oval | — | — | — | 12-101 | — | — |
| F. Martin† | 1890 | Oval | 12-102 | — | — | — | — | — |
| G.A. Lohmann | 1886 | Oval | 12-104 | — | — | — | — | — |
| A.V. Bedser | 1951 | Manchester | — | 12-112 | — | — | — | — |
| F.S. Trueman | 1963 | Birmingham | — | — | 12-119 | — | — | — |
| G. Geary | 1927-28 | Johannesburg[1] | — | 12-130 | — | — | — | — |
| J. Briggs | 1891-92 | Adelaide | 12-136 | — | — | — | — | — |
| A.P. Freeman | 1929 | Manchester | — | 12-171 | — | — | — | — |
| G.A.R. Lock | 1957 | Oval | — | — | 11-48 | — | — | — |
| G.A.R. Lock | 1958 | Leeds | — | — | — | 11-65 | — | — |
| R. Peel | 1888 | Manchester | 11-68 | — | — | — | — | — |
| D.L. Underwood | 1969 | Lord's | — | — | — | 11-70 | — | — |
| J. Briggs | 1886 | Lord's | 11-74 | — | — | — | — | — |
| W.H. Lockwood | 1902 | Manchester | 11-76 | — | — | — | — | — |
| G.A.R. Lock | 1958-59 | Christchurch | — | — | — | 11-84 | — | — |
| F.S. Trueman | 1961 | Leeds | 11-88 | — | — | — | — | — |
| A.E.R. Gilligan | 1924 | Birmingham | — | 11-90 | — | — | — | — |
| A.V. Bedser | 1946 | Manchester | — | — | — | — | 11-93 | — |
| C.S. Marriott† | 1933 | Oval | — | — | 11-96 | — | — | — |
| J.B. Statham | 1960 | Lord's | — | 11-97 | — | — | — | — |
| T.E. Bailey | 1957 | Lord's | — | — | 11-98 | — | — | — |
| C. Blythe | 1909 | Birmingham | 11-102 | — | — | — | — | — |
| S.F. Barnes | 1912 | Lord's | — | 11-110 | — | — | — | — |
| J.C. Laker | 1956 | Leeds | 11-113 | — | — | — | — | — |
| C. Blythe | 1905-06 | Cape Town | — | 11-118 | — | — | — | — |
| A.V. Bedser† | 1946 | Lord's | — | — | — | — | 11-145 | — |
| W. Voce | 1929-30 | Port-of-Spain | — | — | 11-149 | — | — | — |
| F.S. Trueman | 1963 | Lord's | — | — | 11-152 | — | — | — |
| H. Verity | 1933-34 | Madras[1] | — | — | — | — | 11-153 | — |
| T. Richardson | 1896 | Lord's | 11-173 | — | — | — | — | — |
| D.L. Underwood | 1974-75 | Adelaide | 11-215 | — | — | — | — | — |
| M.W. Tate | 1924-25 | Sydney | 11-228 | — | — | — | — | — |
| F.E. Woolley | 1912 | Oval | 10-49 | — | — | — | — | — |
| W. Voce | 1936-37 | Brisbane[2] | 10-57 | — | — | — | — | — |
| R. Peel | 1887-88 | Sydney | 10-58 | — | — | — | — | — |
| J.T. Hearne | 1896 | Oval | 10-60 | — | — | — | — | — |
| J.K. Lever† | 1976-77 | Delhi | — | — | — | — | 10-70 | — |

### ENGLAND – continued

| | | | A | SA | WI | NZ | I | P |
|---|---|---|---|---|---|---|---|---|
| | | | \<td colspan=6\>*Opponents*\</td\> | | | | | |
| G.O.B. Allen | 1936 | Lord's | — | — | — | — | 10-78 | — |
| D.L. Underwood | 1972 | Leeds | 10-82 | — | — | — | — | — |
| G.A. Lohmann | 1886-87 | Sydney | 10-87 | — | — | — | — | — |
| A.P. Freeman | 1928 | Manchester | — | — | 10-93 | — | — | — |
| C. Blythe | 1909-10 | Cape Town | — | 10-104 | — | — | — | — |
| A.V. Bedser | 1950-51 | Melbourne | 10-105 | — | — | — | — | — |
| S.F. Barnes | 1913-14 | Durban[1] | — | 10-105 | — | — | — | — |
| S.F. Barnes | 1912 | Leeds | — | 10-115 | — | — | — | — |
| J.C. Laker | 1951 | Oval | — | 10-119 | — | — | — | — |
| H. Larwood | 1932-33 | Sydney | 10-124 | — | — | — | — | — |
| F.H. Tyson | 1954-55 | Sydney | 10-130 | — | — | — | — | — |
| G.A. Lohmann | 1891-92 | Sydney | 10-142 | — | — | — | — | — |
| J.A. Snow | 1967-68 | Georgetown | — | — | 10-142 | — | — | — |
| J. Briggs | 1893 | Oval | 10-148 | — | — | — | — | — |
| A.W. Greig | 1974-75 | Auckland | — | — | — | 10-149 | — | — |
| T. Richardson† | 1893 | Manchester | 10-156 | — | — | — | — | — |
| D.V.P. Wright | 1947 | Lord's | — | 10-175 | — | — | — | — |
| K. Farnes† | 1934 | Nottingham | 10-179 | — | — | — | — | — |
| G.T.S. Stevens | 1929-30 | Bridgetown | — | — | 10-195 | — | — | — |
| T. Richardson | 1897-98 | Sydney | 10-204 | — | — | — | — | — |
| A.P. Freeman | 1929 | Leeds | — | 10-207 | — | — | — | — |

### AUSTRALIA (48)

| | | | E | SA | WI | NZ | I | P |
|---|---|---|---|---|---|---|---|---|
| | | | \<td colspan=6\>*Opponents*\</td\> | | | | | |
| R.A.L. Massie† | 1972 | Lord's | 16-137 | — | — | — | — | — |
| F.R. Spofforth | 1882 | Oval | 14-90 | — | — | — | — | — |
| C.V. Grimmett | 1931-32 | Adelaide | — | 14-199 | — | — | — | — |
| M.A. Noble | 1901-02 | Melbourne | 13-77 | — | — | — | — | — |
| F.R. Spofforth | 1878-79 | Melbourne | 13-110 | — | — | — | — | — |
| C.V. Grimmett | 1935-36 | Durban[2] | — | 13-173 | — | — | — | — |
| A.A. Mailey | 1920-21 | Melbourne | 13-236 | — | — | — | — | — |
| C.T.B. Turner | 1887-88 | Sydney | 12-87 | — | — | — | — | — |
| H. Trumble | 1896 | Oval | 12-89 | — | — | — | — | — |
| A.K. Davidson | 1959-60 | Kanpur | — | — | — | — | 12-124 | — |
| H. Trumble | 1902 | Oval | 12-173 | — | — | — | — | — |
| H.V. Hordern | 1911-12 | Sydney | 12-175 | — | — | — | — | — |
| H. Ironmonger | 1931-32 | Melbourne | — | 11-24 | — | — | — | — |
| E.R.H. Toshack | 1947-48 | Brisbane[2] | — | — | — | 11-31 | — | — |
| H. Ironmonger | 1930-31 | Melbourne | — | — | 11-79 | — | — | — |
| C.V. Grimmett† | 1924-25 | Sydney | 11-82 | — | — | — | — | — |
| C.G. Macartney | 1909 | Leeds | 11-85 | — | — | — | — | — |
| M.A. Noble | 1902 | Sheffield | 11-103 | — | — | — | — | — |
| R. Benaud | 1956-57 | Calcutta | — | — | — | — | 11-105 | — |
| F.R. Spofforth | 1882-83 | Sydney | 11-117 | — | — | — | — | — |
| D.K. Lillee | 1976-77 | Auckland | — | — | — | 11-123 | — | — |
| W.J. O'Reilly | 1934 | Nottingham | 11-129 | — | — | — | — | — |
| G.E. Palmer | 1881-82 | Sydney | 11-165 | — | — | — | — | — |
| D.K. Lillee | 1976-77 | Melbourne | 11-165 | — | — | — | — | — |
| C.V. Grimmett | 1930-31 | Adelaide | — | — | 11-183 | — | — | — |
| A.K. Davidson | 1960-61 | Brisbane[2] | — | — | 11-222 | — | — | — |
| C.T.B. Turner | 1888 | Lord's | 10-63 | — | — | — | — | — |
| C.V. Grimmett | 1935-36 | Cape Town | — | 10-88 | — | — | — | — |
| G.D. McKenzie | 1964-65 | Madras[2] | — | — | — | — | 10-91 | — |
| C.V. Grimmett | 1935-36 | Johannesburg[1] | — | 10-110 | — | — | — | — |
| N.J.N. Hawke | 1964-65 | Georgetown | — | — | 10-115 | — | — | — |
| W.J. O'Reilly | 1938 | Leeds | 10-122 | — | — | — | — | — |
| G.E. Palmer | 1882-83 | Melbourne | 10-126 | — | — | — | — | — |
| H. Trumble | 1902 | Manchester | 10-128 | — | — | — | — | — |
| W.J. O'Reilly | 1932-33 | Melbourne | 10-129 | — | — | — | — | — |
| D.K. Lillee | 1976-77 | Melbourne | — | — | — | — | — | 10-135 |

### AUSTRALIA – *continued*

| | | | E | SA | WI | NZ | I | P |
|---|---|---|---|---|---|---|---|---|
| F.R. Spofforth | 1884-85 | Sydney | 10-144 | — | — | — | — | — |
| A.A. Mallett | 1969-70 | Madras[1] | — | — | — | — | 10-144 | — |
| K.R. Miller | 1956 | Lord's | 10-152 | — | — | — | — | — |
| G.D. McKenzie | 1967-68 | Melbourne | — | — | — | — | 10-151 | — |
| G.D. McKenzie | 1968-69 | Melbourne | — | — | 10-159 | — | — | — |
| G. Giffen | 1891-92 | Sydney | 10-160 | — | — | — | — | — |
| H.V. Hordern | 1911-12 | Sydney | 10-161 | — | — | — | — | — |
| E. Jones | 1899 | Lord's | 10-164 | — | — | — | — | — |
| D.K. Lillee | 1972 | Oval | 10-181 | — | — | — | — | — |
| C.V. Grimmett | 1930 | Nottingham | 10-201 | — | — | — | — | — |
| L.O'B. Fleetwood-Smith | 1936 | Adelaide | 10-239 | — | — | — | — | — |
| A.A. Mailey | 1920-21 | Adelaide | 10-302 | — | — | — | — | — |

### SOUTH AFRICA (9)

| | | | E | A | NZ |
|---|---|---|---|---|---|
| H.J. Tayfield | 1952-53 | Melbourne | — | 13-165 | — |
| H.J. Tayfield | 1956-57 | Johannesburg[3] | 13-192 | — | — |
| S.J. Snooke | 1905-06 | Johannesburg[1] | 12-127 | — | — |
| A.E.E. Vogler | 1909-10 | Johannesburg[1] | 12-181 | — | — |
| A.E. Hall† | 1922-23 | Cape Town | 11-112 | — | — |
| E.P. Nupen | 1930-31 | Johannesburg[1] | 11-150 | — | — |
| S.F. Burke† | 1961-62 | Cape Town | — | — | 11-196 |
| P.M. Pollock | 1965 | Nottingham | 10-87 | — | — |
| C.B. Llewellyn | 1902-03 | Johannesburg[1] | — | 10-116 | — |

### WEST INDIES (13)

| | | | E | A | NZ | I | P |
|---|---|---|---|---|---|---|---|
| M.A. Holding | 1976 | Oval | 14-149 | — | — | — | — |
| A.M.E. Roberts | 1974-75 | Madras[1] | — | — | — | 12-121 | — |
| W.W. Hall | 1958-59 | Kanpur | — | — | — | 11-126 | — |
| K.D. Boyce | 1973 | Oval | 11-147 | — | — | — | — |
| S. Ramadhin | 1950 | Lord's | 11-152 | — | — | — | — |
| L.R. Gibbs | 1963 | Manchester | 11-157 | — | — | — | — |
| A.L. Valentine† | 1950 | Manchester | 11-204 | — | — | — | — |
| W. Ferguson | 1947-48 | Port-of-Spain | 11-229 | — | — | — | — |
| H.H.H. Johnson† | 1947-48 | Kingston | 10-96 | — | — | — | — |
| L.R. Gibbs | 1966 | Manchester | 10-106 | — | — | — | — |
| G.E. Gomez | 1951-52 | Sydney | — | 10-113 | — | — | — |
| A.M.E. Roberts | 1976 | Lord's | 10-123 | — | — | — | — |
| A.L. Valentine | 1950 | Oval | 10-160 | — | — | — | — |

### NEW ZEALAND (3)

| | | | E | A | SA | WI | I | P |
|---|---|---|---|---|---|---|---|---|
| R.J. Hadlee | 1975-76 | Wellington | — | — | — | — | 11-58 | — |
| R.J. Hadlee | 1977-78 | Wellington | 10-100 | — | — | — | — | — |
| J. Cowie | 1937 | Manchester | 10-140 | — | — | — | — | — |

### INDIA (13)

| | | | E | A | WI | NZ | P |
|---|---|---|---|---|---|---|---|
| J.M. Patel | 1959-60 | Kanpur | — | 14-124 | — | — | — |
| V.M.H. Mankad | 1952-53 | Delhi | — | — | — | — | 13-131 |
| B.S. Chandrasekhar | 1977-78 | Melbourne | — | 12-104 | — | — | — |
| V.M.H. Mankad | 1951-52 | Madras[1] | 12-108 | — | — | — | — |
| S. Venkataraghavan | 1964-65 | Delhi | — | — | — | 12-152 | — |
| R.G. Nadkarni | 1964-65 | Madras[2] | — | 11-122 | — | — | — |
| E.A.S. Prasanna | 1975-76 | Auckland | — | — | — | 11-140 | — |
| B.S. Chandrasekhar | 1966-67 | Bombay[2] | — | — | 11-235 | — | — |
| Ghulam Ahmed | 1956-57 | Calcutta | — | 10-130 | — | — | — |
| E.A.S. Prasanna | 1969-70 | Madras[1] | — | 10-174 | — | — | — |

# TEN WICKETS IN A MATCH – *continued*

| INDIA – *continued* | | | Opponents | | | | |
|---|---|---|---|---|---|---|---|
| | | | E | A | WI | NZ | P |
| S.A. Durani | 1961-62 | Madras[2] | 10-177 | — | — | — | — |
| B.S. Bedi | 1977-78 | Perth | — | 10-194 | — | — | — |
| S.P. Gupte | 1958-59 | Kanpur | — | — | 10-223 | — | — |

| PAKISTAN (8) | | | Opponents | | | | |
|---|---|---|---|---|---|---|---|
| | | | E | A | WI | NZ | I |
| Fazal Mahmood | 1956-57 | Karachi | — | 13-114 | — | — | — |
| Fazal Mahmood | 1952-53 | Lucknow | — | — | — | — | 12-94 |
| Fazal Mahmood | 1954 | Oval | 12-99 | — | — | — | — |
| Fazal Mahmood | 1958-59 | Dacca | — | — | 12-100 | — | — |
| Imran Khan | 1976-77 | Sydney | — | 12-165 | — | — | — |
| Zulfiqar Ahmed | 1955-56 | Karachi | — | — | — | 11-79 | — |
| Intikhab Alam | 1972-73 | Dunedin | — | — | — | 11-130 | — |
| Intikhab Alam | 1969-70 | Dacca | — | — | — | 10-182 | — |

# EIGHT WICKETS IN AN INNINGS
### († *On debut*)

| ENGLAND (20) | | | Opponents | | | | | |
|---|---|---|---|---|---|---|---|---|
| | | | A | SA | WI | NZ | I | P |
| J.C. Laker | 1956 | Manchester | 10-53 | — | — | — | — | — |
| G.A. Lohmann | 1895-96 | Johannesburg[1] | — | 9-28 | — | — | — | — |
| J.C. Laker | 1956 | Manchester | 9-37 | — | — | — | — | — |
| S.F. Barnes | 1913-14 | Johannesburg[1] | — | 9-103 | — | — | — | — |
| G.A. Lohmann | 1895-96 | Port Elizabeth | — | 8-7 | — | — | — | — |
| J. Briggs | 1888-89 | Cape Town | — | 8-11 | — | — | — | — |
| S.F. Barnes | 1912 | Oval | — | 8-29 | — | — | — | — |
| F.S. Trueman | 1952 | Manchester | — | — | — | — | 8-31 | — |
| G.A. Lohmann | 1886-87 | Sydney | 8-35 | — | — | — | — | — |
| H. Verity | 1934 | Lord's | 8-43 | — | — | — | — | — |
| D.L. Underwood | 1974 | Lord's | — | — | — | — | — | 8-51 |
| S.F. Barnes | 1913-14 | Johannesburg[1] | — | 8-56 | — | — | — | — |
| G.A. Lohmann | 1891-92 | Sydney | 8-58 | — | — | — | — | — |
| C. Blythe | 1907 | Leeds | — | 8-59 | — | — | — | — |
| W. Rhodes | 1903-04 | Melbourne | 8-68 | — | — | — | — | — |
| L.C. Braund | 1903-04 | Melbourne | 8-81 | — | — | — | — | — |
| A.W. Greig | 1973-74 | Port-of-Spain | — | — | 8-86 | — | — | — |
| T. Richardson | 1897-98 | Sydney | 8-94 | — | — | — | — | — |
| B.J.T. Bosanquet | 1905 | Nottingham | 8-107 | — | — | — | — | — |
| J.C. White | 1928-29 | Adelaide | 8-126 | — | — | — | — | — |

| AUSTRALIA (9) | | | Opponents | | | | | |
|---|---|---|---|---|---|---|---|---|
| | | | E | SA | WI | NZ | I | P |
| A.A. Mailey | 1920-21 | Melbourne | 9-121 | — | — | — | — | — |
| F. Laver | 1909 | Manchester | 8-31 | — | — | — | — | — |
| A.E. Trott† | 1894-95 | Adelaide | 8-43 | — | — | — | — | — |
| R.A.L. Massie† | 1972 | Lord's | 8-53 | — | — | — | — | — |
| A.A. Mallett | 1972-73 | Adelaide | — | — | — | — | — | 8-59 |
| H. Trumble | 1902 | Oval | 8-65 | — | — | — | — | — |
| G.D. McKenzie | 1968-69 | Melbourne | — | — | 8-71 | — | — | — |
| R.A.L. Massie† | 1972 | Lord's | 8-84 | — | — | — | — | — |
| M.H.N. Walker | 1974-75 | Melbourne | 8-143 | — | — | — | — | — |

| SOUTH AFRICA (4) | | | Opponents | | |
|---|---|---|---|---|---|
| | | | E | A | NZ |
| H.J. Tayfield | 1956-57 | Johannesburg[3] | 9-113 | — | — |
| G.B. Lawrence | 1961-62 | Johannesburg[3] | — | — | 8-53 |
| H.J. Tayfield | 1956-57 | Durban[2] | 8-69 | — | — |
| S.J. Snooke | 1905-06 | Johannesburg[1] | 8-70 | — | — |

# EIGHT WICKETS IN AN INNINGS – *continued*

|  |  |  | Opponents | | | | |
|---|---|---|---|---|---|---|---|
| **WEST INDIES (5)** |  |  | E | A | NZ | I | P |
| J.M. Noreiga | 1970-71 | Port-of-Spain | — | — | — | 9-95 | — |
| C.E.H. Croft | 1976-77 | Port-of-Spain | — | — | — | — | 8-29 |
| L.R. Gibbs | 1961-62 | Bridgetown | — | — | — | 8-38 | — |
| M.A. Holding | 1976 | Oval | 8-92 | — | — | — | — |
| A.L. Valentine† | 1950 | Manchester | 8-104 | — | — | — | — |

|  |  |  | Opponents | | | | |
|---|---|---|---|---|---|---|---|
| **INDIA (7)** |  |  | E | A | WI | NZ | P |
| J.M. Patel | 1959-60 | Kanpur | — | 9-69 | — | — | — |
| S.P. Gupte | 1958-59 | Kanpur | — | — | 9-102 | — | — |
| V.M.H. Mankad | 1952-53 | Delhi | — | — | — | — | 8-52 |
| V.M.H. Mankad | 1951-52 | Madras[1] | 8-55 | — | — | — | — |
| S. Venkataraghavan | 1964-65 | Delhi | — | — | — | 8-72 | — |
| E.A.S. Prasanna | 1975-76 | Auckland | — | — | — | 8-76 | — |
| B.S. Chandrasekhar | 1972-73 | Delhi | 8-79 | — | — | — | — |

*NEW ZEALAND & PAKISTAN*

*The best innings analysis for New Zealand is 7 for 23 by R.J. Hadlee against India at Wellington in 1975-76.*
*The best innings analysis for Pakistan is 7 for 42 by Fazal Mahmood against India at Lucknow in 1952-53.*

## OUTSTANDING INNINGS ANALYSES

| O | M | R | W |  |  |  |  |
|---|---|---|---|---|---|---|---|
| 51.2 | 23 | 53 | 10 | J.C. Laker | E v A | Manchester | 1956 |
| 14.2 | 6 | 28 | 9 | G.A. Lohmann | E v SA | Johannesburg[1] | 1895-96 |
| 16.4 | 4 | 37 | 9 | J.C. Laker | E v A | Manchester | 1956 |
| 9.4 | 5 | 7 | 8 | G.A. Lohmann | E v SA | Port Elizabeth | 1895-96 |
| 14.2 | 5 | 11 | 8 | J. Briggs | E v SA | Cape Town | 1888-89 |
| 19.1 | 11 | 17 | 7 | J. Briggs | E v SA | Cape Town | 1888-89 |
| 7.4 | 2 | 17 | 7 | M.A. Noble | A v E | Melbourne | 1901-02 |
| 11 | 3 | 17 | 7 | W. Rhodes | E v A | Birmingham | 1902 |
| 6.3 | 4 | 7 | 6 | A.E.R. Gilligan | E v SA | Birmingham | 1924 |
| 11.4 | 6 | 11 | 6 | S. Haigh | E v SA | Cape Town | 1898-99 |
| 11.6 | 7 | 12 | 6 | D.L. Underwood | E v NZ | Christchurch | 1970-71 |
| 14 | 7 | 13 | 6 | H.J. Tayfield | SA v NZ | Johannesburg[2] | 1953-54 |
| 18 | 11 | 15 | 6 | C.T.B. Turner | A v E | Sydney | 1886-87 |
| 16 | 8 | 15 | 6 | M.H.N. Walker | A v P | Sydney | 1972-73 |
| 2.3 | 1 | 2 | 5 | E.R.H. Toshack | A v I | Brisbane[2] | 1947-48 |
| 7.2 | 5 | 6 | 5 | H. Ironmonger | A v SA | Melbourne | 1931-32 |
| 12 | 8 | 5 | 4 | Pervez Sajjad | P v NZ | Rawalpindi | 1964-65 |
| 9 | 7 | 5 | 4 | K. Higgs | E v NZ | Christchurch | 1965-66 |
| 6.3 | 2 | 7 | 4 | J.C. White | E v A | Brisbane[1] | 1928-29 |
| 5 | 2 | 7 | 4 | J.H. Wardle | E v A | Manchester | 1953 |
| 6 | 3 | 7 | 4 | R. Appleyard | E v NZ | Auckland | 1954-55 |
| 3.4 | 3 | 0 | 3 | R. Benaud | A v I | Delhi | 1959-60 |

## HAT-TRICKS

| | | | |
|---|---|---|---|
| F.R. Spofforth | Australia v England | Melbourne | 1878-79 |
| W. Bates | England v Australia | Melbourne | 1882-83 |
| J. Briggs | England v Australia | Sydney | 1891-92 |
| G.A. Lohmann | England v South Africa | Port Elizabeth | 1895-96 |
| J.T. Hearne | England v Australia | Leeds | 1899 |
| H. Trumble | Australia v England | Melbourne | 1901-02 |
| H. Trumble | Australia v England | Melbourne | 1903-04 |
| T.J. Matthews (2) | Australia v South Africa | Manchester | 1912 |
| M.J.C. Allom† | England v New Zealand | Christchurch | 1929-30 |
| T.W.J. Goddard | England v South Africa | Johannesburg[1] | 1938-39 |

## HAT-TRICKS – *continued*

| | | | |
|---|---|---|---|
| P.J. Loader | England v West Indies | Leeds | 1957 |
| L.F. Kline | Australia v South Africa | Cape Town | 1957-58 |
| W.W. Hall | West Indies v Pakistan | Lahore[1] | 1958-59 |
| G.M. Griffin | South Africa v England | Lord's | 1960 |
| L.R. Gibbs | West Indies v Australia | Adelaide | 1960-61 |
| P.J. Petherick† | New Zealand v Pakistan | Lahore | 1976-77 |

*† On debut*

*T.J. Matthews did the hat-trick in each innings on the second afternoon of the match.*

## FOUR WICKETS IN FIVE BALLS

| | | | |
|---|---|---|---|
| M.J.C. Allom | England v New Zealand | Christchurch | 1929-30 |
| | *(On debut)* | | |

## THREE WICKETS IN FOUR BALLS

| | | | |
|---|---|---|---|
| F.R. Spofforth (2) | Australia v England | Oval | 1882 |
| | Australia v England | Sydney | 1884-85 |
| J. Briggs | England v South Africa | Cape Town | 1888-89 |
| W.P. Howell | Australia v South Africa | Cape Town | 1902-03 |
| E.P. Nupen | South Africa v England | Johannesburg[1] | 1930-31 |
| W.J. O'Reilly | Australia v England | Manchester | 1934 |
| W. Voce | England v Australia | Sydney | 1936-37 |
| R.R. Lindwall | Australia v England | Adelaide | 1946-47 |
| K. Cranston | England v South Africa | Leeds | 1947 |
| | *(He took four wickets in a six-ball over)* | | |
| R. Appleyard | England v New Zealand | Auckland | 1954-55 |
| R. Benaud | Australia v West Indies | Georgetown | 1954-55 |
| Fazal Mahmood | Pakistan v Australia | Karachi | 1956-57 |
| J.W. Martin | Australia v West Indies | Melbourne | 1960-61 |
| L.R. Gibbs | West Indies v Australia | Sydney | 1960-61 |
| K.D. Mackay | Australia v England | Birmingham | 1961 |
| W.W. Hall | West Indies v India | Port-of-Spain | 1961-62 |
| D. Shackleton | England v West Indies | Lord's | 1963 |
| G.D. McKenzie | Australia v West Indies | Port-of-Spain | 1964-65 |
| F.J. Titmus | England v New Zealand | Leeds | 1965 |
| | *(He took four wickets in a six-ball over)* | | |
| G.St A. Sobers | England v West Indies | Leeds | 1966 |
| P. Lever | England v Pakistan | Leeds | 1971 |
| D.K. Lillee (2) | Australia v England | Manchester | 1972 |
| | Australia v England | Oval | 1972 |

## A WICKET WITH FIRST BALL IN TEST CRICKET

| | | | |
|---|---|---|---|
| A. Coningham | Australia v England | Melbourne | 1894-95 |
| E.G. Arnold | England v Australia | Sydney | 1903-04 |
| G.G. Macaulay | England v South Africa | Cape Town | 1922-23 |
| M.W. Tate | England v South Africa | Birmingham | 1924 |
| H.D. Smith | New Zealand v England | Christchurch | 1932-33 |
| T.F. Johnson | West Indies v England | Oval | 1939 |
| R. Howorth | England v South Africa | Oval | 1947 |
| Intikhab Alam | Pakistan v Australia | Karachi | 1959-60 |

## MOST WICKETS BY ONE BOWLER IN A DAY

| | | | | |
|---|---|---|---|---|
| 15 | J. Briggs | 15-28 England v South Africa | Cape Town | 1888-89 |
| 14 | H. Verity | 14-80 England v Australia | Lord's | 1934 |

## OVER 200 RUNS CONCEDED IN AN INNINGS

| O | M | R | W | | | | |
|---|---|---|---|---|---|---|---|
| 87 | 11 | 298 | 1 | L.O'B. Fleetwood-Smith | A v E | Oval | 1938 |
| 80.2 | 13 | 266 | 5 | O.C. Scott | WI v E | Kingston | 1929-30 |
| 54 | 5 | 259 | 0 | Khan Mohammad | P v WI | Kingston | 1957-58 |
| 85.2 | 20 | 247 | 2 | Fazal Mahmood | P v WI | Kingston | 1957-58 |
| 82 | 17 | 228 | 5 | V.M.H. Mankad | I v WI | Kingston | 1952-53 |
| 64.2 | 8 | 226 | 6 | B.S. Bedi | I v E | Lord's | 1974 |
| 71 | 8 | 204 | 6 | I.A.R. Peebles | E v A | Oval | 1930 |
| 75 | 16 | 202 | 3 | V.M.H. Mankad | I v WI | Bombay[2] | 1948-49 |
| 84 | 19 | 202 | 6 | Haseeb Ahsan | P v I | Madras[2] | 1960-61 |

## OVER 300 RUNS CONCEDED IN A MATCH

| O | M | R | W | | | | |
|---|---|---|---|---|---|---|---|
| 105.2 | 13 | 374 | 9 | O.C. Scott | WI v E | Kingston | 1929-30 |
| 63 | 3 | 308 | 7 | A.A. Mailey | A v E | Sydney | 1924-25 |
| 61.3 | 6 | 302 | 10 | A.A. Mailey | A v E | Adelaide | 1920-21 |

## BOWLERS UNCHANGED IN A COMPLETED INNINGS

| ENGLAND | Opponents | | |
|---|---|---|---|
| F. Morley (2-34), R.G. Barlow (7-40) | Australia | Sydney | 1882-83 |
| G.A. Lohmann (7-36), J. Briggs (3-28) | Australia | Oval | 1886 |
| G.A. Lohmann (5-17), R. Peel (5-18) | Australia | Sydney | 1887-88 |
| J. Briggs (8-11), A.J. Fothergill (1-30) | South Africa | Cape Town | 1888-89 |
| J.J. Ferris (7-37), F. Martin (2-39) | South Africa | Cape Town | 1891-92 |
| J. Briggs (6-49), G.A. Lohmann (3-46) | Australia | Adelaide | 1891-92 |
| T. Richardson (6-39), G.A. Lohmann (3-13) | Australia | Lord's | 1896 |
| S. Haigh (6-11), A.E. Trott (4-19) | South Africa | Cape Town | 1898-99 |
| S.F. Barnes (6-42), C. Blythe (4-64) | Australia | Melbourne | 1901-02 |
| G.H. Hirst (4-28), C. Blythe (6-44) | Australia | Birmingham | 1909 |
| F.R. Foster (5-16), S.F. Barnes (5-25) | South Africa | Lord's | 1912 |
| A.E.R. Gilligan (6-7), M.W. Tate (4-12) | South Africa | Birmingham | 1924 |
| G.O.B. Allen (5-36), W. Voce (4-16) | Australia | Brisbane[2] | 1936-37 |

| AUSTRALIA | Opponents | | |
|---|---|---|---|
| G.E. Palmer (7-68), E. Evans (3-64) | England | Sydney | 1881-82 |
| F.R. Spofforth (5-30), G.E. Palmer (4-32) | England | Sydney | 1884-85 |
| C.T.B. Turner (6-15), J.J. Ferris (4-27) | England | Sydney | 1886-87 |
| C.T.B. Turner (5-36), J.J. Farris (5-26) | England | Lord's | 1888 |
| G. Giffen (5-26), C.T.B. Turner (4-33) | England | Sydney | 1894-95 |
| H. Trumble (3-38), M.A. Noble (7-17) | England | Melbourne | 1901-02 |
| M.A. Noble (5-54), J.V. Saunders (5-43) | England | Sydney | 1901-02 |

| PAKISTAN | Opponents | | |
|---|---|---|---|
| Fazal Mahmood (6-34), Khan Mohammad (4-43) | Australia | Karachi | 1956-57 |

## MOST BALLS BY ONE BOWLER IN A MATCH

| 774 | S. Ramadhin | West Indies v England | Birmingham | 1957 |
|---|---|---|---|---|

## MOST BALLS BY ONE BOWLER IN AN INNINGS

| 588 | S. Ramadhin | West Indies v England | Birmingham | 1957 |
|---|---|---|---|---|

# ONLY FOUR BOWLERS IN AN INNINGS OF OVER 300 RUNS

| | *Opponents* | | |
|---|---|---|---|
| England | Australia (349) | Oval | 1893 |
| Australia | England (403-8d) | Oval | 1921 |
| South Africa | England (421-8) | Oval | 1924 |
| Australia | England (342-8d) | Brisbane[1] | 1928-29 |
| New Zealand | England (372) | Leeds | 1949 |
| New Zealand | England (482) | Oval | 1949 |
| England | Australia (426) | Sydney | 1950-51 |
| England | Australia (318) | Manchester | 1953 |
| Pakistan | West Indies (325 & 312) | Port-of-Spain | 1957-58 |
| India | England (361) | Oval | 1959 |
| New Zealand | South Africa (371) | Auckland | 1963-64 |
| England | South Africa (307-3d) | Johannesburg[3] | 1964-65 |
| Australia | England (315) | Lord's | 1975 |
| Australia | New Zealand (357) | Christchurch | 1976-77 |
| West Indies | Pakistan (301-9) | Port-of-Spain | 1976-77 |

## ELEVEN BOWLERS IN AN INNINGS

| | | | |
|---|---|---|---|
| England | Australia (551) | Oval | 1884 |

# ALL-ROUND FEATS

## 1000 RUNS AND 100 WICKETS

| ENGLAND | Tests | Runs | Wkts | Test in which Double was achieved |
|---|---|---|---|---|
| T.E. Bailey | 61 | 2290 | 132 | 47th |
| A.W. Greig | 58 | 3599 | 141 | 37th |
| R. Illingworth | 61 | 1836 | 122 | 47th |
| W. Rhodes | 58 | 2325 | 127 | 44th |
| M.W. Tate | 39 | 1198 | 155 | 33rd |
| F.J. Titmus | 53 | 1449 | 153 | 40th |
| *AUSTRALIA* | | | | |
| R. Benaud | 63 | 2201 | 248 | 32nd |
| A.K. Davidson | 44 | 1328 | 186 | 34th |
| G. Giffen | 31 | 1238 | 103 | 30th |
| I.W. Johnson | 45 | 1000 | 109 | 45th |
| R.R. Lindwall | 61 | 1502 | 228 | 38th |
| K.R. Miller | 55 | 2958 | 170 | 33rd |
| M.A. Noble | 42 | 1997 | 121 | 27th |
| *SOUTH AFRICA* | | | | |
| T.L. Goddard | 41 | 2516 | 123 | 36th |
| *WEST INDIES* | | | | |
| G. St A. Sobers | 93 | 8032 | 235 | 48th |
| *INDIA* | | | | |
| V.M.H. Mankad | 44 | 2109 | 162 | 23rd |
| *PAKISTAN* | | | | |
| Intikhab Alam | 47 | 1493 | 125 | 41st |

## 250 RUNS AND 25 WICKETS IN A RUBBER

| | Runs | Wkts | | |
|---|---|---|---|---|
| G. Giffen | 475 | 34 | Australia v England | 1894-95 |
| G.A. Faulkner | 545 | 29 | South Africa v England | 1909-10 |
| R. Benaud | 329 | 30 | Australia v South Africa | 1957-58 |
| T.L. Goddard | 294 | 26 | South Africa v Australia | 1966-67 |

## MATCH DOUBLE – 100 RUNS AND 10 WICKETS

| A.K. Davidson | Australia v West Indies | Brisbane[2] | 1960-61 |
|---|---|---|---|

*(He scored 44 and 80, and took 5-135 and 6-87 in tied match)*

# WICKET-KEEPING RECORDS

## WICKET-KEEPERS WHO HAVE MADE 100 DISMISSALS

|  |  | Tests | Ct | St | Total |
|---|---|---|---|---|---|
| A.P.E. Knott | England | 89 | 233 | 19 | 252 |
| T.G. Evans | England | 91 | 173 | 46 | 219 |
| R.W. Marsh | Australia | 52 | 190 | 8 | 198 |
| A.T.W. Grout | Australia | 51 | 163 | 24 | 187 |
| D.L. Murray | West Indies | 51 | 150 | 8 | 158 |
| J.H.B. Waite | South Africa | 50 | 124 | 17 | 141 |
| W.A.S. Oldfield | Australia | 54 | 78 | 52 | 130 |
| J.M. Parks | England | 46 | 103† | 11 | 114 |
| Wasim Bari | Pakistan | 39 | 91 | 15 | 106 |

† *Including 2 catches in 3 Tests when not keeping wicket.*

## MOST DISMISSALS IN A TEST RUBBER

| | | | |
|---|---|---|---|
| 26 (26 ct) | R.W. Marsh | Australia v West Indies (6 Tests) | 1975-76 |
| 26 (23 ct 3 st) | J.H.B. Waite | South Africa v New Zealand | 1961-62 |
| 24 (21ct 3 st) | A.P.E. Knott | England v Australia (6 Tests) | 1970-71 |
| 24 (24 ct) | D.T. Lindsay | South Africa v Australia | 1966-67 |
| 24 (22 ct 2 st) | D.L. Murray | West Indies v England | 1963 |

## MOST DISMISSALS IN A TEST MATCH

| | | | | |
|---|---|---|---|---|
| 9 (8 ct 1 st) | G.R.A. Langley | Australia v England | Lord's | 1956 |

## MOST DISMISSALS IN A TEST INNINGS

| | | | | |
|---|---|---|---|---|
| 6 (6 ct) | A.T.W. Grout | Australia v South Africa | Johannesburg[2] | 1957-58 |
| 6 (6 ct) | D.T. Lindsay | South Africa v Australia | Johannesburg[3] | 1966-67 |
| 6 (6 ct) | J.T. Murray | England v India | Lord's | 1967 |
| 6 (5 ct 1 st) | S.M.H. Kirmani | India v New Zealand | Christchurch | 1975-76 |

# FIELDING RECORDS

## FIELDERS WHO HAVE MADE 100 CATCHES

|  |  | *Tests* | *Catches* |
|---|---|---|---|
| M.C. Cowdrey | England | 114 | 120 |
| R.B. Simpson | Australia | 62 | 110 |
| W.R. Hammond | England | 85 | 110 |
| G. St A. Sobers | West Indies | 93 | 109 |
| I.M. Chappell | Australia | 72 | 103 |

## MOST CATCHES IN A TEST RUBBER

| 15 | J.M. Gregory | Australia v England | | 1920-21 |
|---|---|---|---|---|

## MOST CATCHES IN A TEST MATCH

| 7 | G.S. Chappell | Australia v England | Perth | 1974-75 |
|---|---|---|---|---|
| 7 | Yajurvindra Singh | India v England | Bangalore | 1976-77 |

## MOST CATCHES IN A TEST INNINGS

| 5 | V.Y. Richardson | Australia v South Africa | Durban[2] | 1935-36 |
|---|---|---|---|---|
| 5 | Yajurvindra Singh | India v England | Bangalore | 1976-77 |

# PLAYERS' RECORDS – THE CAPTAINS

## RESULTS SUMMARY

| ENGLAND (60) | Tests as Captain | A | SA | WI | NZ | I | P | W | L | D | Toss Won |
|---|---|---|---|---|---|---|---|---|---|---|---|
| James Lillywhite | 2 | 2 | – | – | – | – | – | 1 | 1 | – | – |
| Lord Harris | 4 | 4 | – | – | – | – | – | 2 | 1 | 1 | 2 |
| A. Shaw | 4 | 4 | – | – | – | – | – | – | 2 | 2 | 4 |
| A.N. Hornby | 2 | 2 | – | – | – | – | – | – | 1 | 1 | 1 |
| Hon Ivo Bligh | 4 | 4 | – | – | – | – | – | 2 | 2 | – | 3 |
| A. Shrewsbury | 7 | 7 | – | – | – | – | – | 5 | 2 | – | 3 |
| A.G. Steel | 4 | 4 | – | – | – | – | – | 3 | 1 | – | 2 |
| W.W. Read | 2 | 1 | 1 | – | – | – | – | 2 | – | – | – |
| W.G. Grace | 13 | 13 | – | – | – | – | – | 8 | 3 | 2 | 4 |
| C.A. Smith | 1 | – | 1 | – | – | – | – | 1 | – | – | – |
| M.P. Bowden | 1 | – | 1 | – | – | – | – | 1 | – | – | 1 |
| A.E. Stoddart | 8 | 8 | – | – | – | – | – | 3 | 4 | 1 | 2 |
| T.C. O'Brien | 1 | – | 1 | – | – | – | – | 1 | – | – | – |
| Lord Hawke | 4 | – | 4 | – | – | – | – | 4 | – | – | 4 |
| A.C. MacLaren | 22 | 22 | – | – | – | – | – | 4 | 11 | 7 | 11 |
| P.F. Warner | 10 | 5 | 5 | – | – | – | – | 4 | 6 | – | 5 |
| Hon F.S. Jackson | 5 | 5 | – | – | – | – | – | 2 | – | 3 | 5 |
| R.E. Foster | 3 | – | 3 | – | – | – | – | 1 | – | 2 | 3 |
| F.L. Fane | 5 | 3 | 2 | – | – | – | – | 2 | 3 | – | 3 |
| A.O. Jones | 2 | 2 | – | – | – | – | – | – | 2 | – | 1 |
| H.D.G. Leveson-Gower | 3 | – | 3 | – | – | – | – | 1 | 2 | – | – |
| J.W.H.T. Douglas | 18 | 12 | 6 | – | – | – | – | 8 | 8 | 2 | 7 |
| C.B. Fry | 6 | 3 | 3 | – | – | – | – | 4 | – | 2 | 4 |
| Hon L.H. Tennyson | 3 | 3 | – | – | – | – | – | – | 1 | 2 | 2 |
| F.T. Mann | 5 | – | 5 | – | – | – | – | 2 | 1 | 2 | 3 |
| A.E.R. Gilligan | 9 | 5 | 4 | – | – | – | – | 4 | 4 | 1 | 2 |
| A.W. Carr | 6 | 4 | 2 | – | – | – | – | 1 | – | 5 | 3 |
| A.P.F. Chapman | 17 | 9 | 5 | 3 | – | – | – | 9 | 2 | 6 | 9 |
| R.T. Stanyforth | 4 | – | 4 | – | – | – | – | 2 | 1 | 1 | – |
| G.T.S. Stevens | 1 | – | 1 | – | – | – | – | – | 1 | – | – |
| J.C. White | 4 | 1 | 3 | – | – | – | – | 1 | 1 | 2 | 3 |
| A.H.H. Gilligan | 4 | – | – | – | 4 | – | – | 1 | – | 3 | 1 |
| Hon F.S.G. Calthorpe | 4 | – | – | 4 | – | – | – | 1 | 1 | 2 | 2 |
| R.E.S. Wyatt | 16 | 5 | 5 | 5 | 1 | – | – | 3 | 5 | 8 | 12 |
| D.R. Jardine | 15 | 5 | – | 2 | 4 | 4 | – | 9 | 1 | 5 | 7 |
| C.F. Walters | 1 | 1 | – | – | – | – | – | – | 1 | – | – |
| G.O.B. Allen | 11 | 5 | – | 3 | – | 3 | – | 4 | 5 | 2 | 6 |
| R.W.V. Robins | 3 | – | – | – | 3 | – | – | 1 | – | 2 | 2 |
| W.R. Hammond | 20 | 8 | 5 | 3 | 1 | 3 | – | 4 | 3 | 13 | 11 |
| N.W.D. Yardley | 14 | 6 | 5 | 3 | – | – | – | 4 | 7 | 3 | 9 |
| K. Cranston | 1 | – | – | 1 | – | – | – | – | – | 1 | – |
| F.G. Mann | 7 | – | 5 | – | 2 | – | – | 2 | – | 5 | 5 |
| F.R. Brown | 15 | 5 | 5 | 1 | 4 | – | – | 5 | 6 | 4 | 3 |
| N.D. Howard | 4 | – | – | – | – | 4 | – | 1 | – | 3 | 2 |
| D.B. Carr | 1 | – | – | – | – | 1 | – | – | 1 | – | 1 |
| L. Hutton | 23 | 10 | – | 5 | 2 | 4 | 2 | 11 | 4 | 8 | 7 |
| D.S. Sheppard | 2 | – | – | – | – | – | 2 | 1 | – | 1 | 1 |
| P.B.H. May | 41 | 13 | 10 | 8 | 7 | 3 | – | 20 | 10 | 11 | 26 |
| M.C. Cowdrey | 27 | 6 | 5 | 10 | – | 2 | 4 | 8 | 4 | 15 | 17 |
| E.R. Dexter | 30 | 10 | – | 5 | 3 | 5 | 7 | 9 | 7 | 14 | 13 |
| M.J.K. Smith | 25 | 5 | 8 | 1 | 6 | 5 | – | 5 | 3 | 17 | 10 |
| D.B. Close | 7 | – | – | 1 | – | 3 | 3 | 6 | – | 1 | 4 |
| T.W. Graveney | 1 | 1 | – | – | – | – | – | – | – | 1 | – |
| R. Illingworth | 31 | 11 | – | 6 | 8 | 3 | 3 | 12 | 5 | 14 | 15‡ |
| A.R. Lewis | 8 | – | – | – | – | 5 | 3 | 1 | 2 | 5 | 3 |

| *ENGLAND – continued* | Tests as Captain | A | SA | Opponents WI | NZ | I | P | Results W | L | D | Toss Won |
|---|---|---|---|---|---|---|---|---|---|---|---|
| M.H. Denness | 19 | 6 | – | 5 | 2 | 3 | 3 | 6 | 5 | 8 | 9 |
| J.H. Edrich | 1 | 1 | – | – | – | – | – | – | 1 | – | – |
| A.W. Greig | 14 | 4 | – | 5 | – | 5 | – | 3 | 5 | 6 | 6 |
| J.M. Brearley | 7 | 5 | – | – | – | – | 2 | 3 | – | 4 | 2 |
| G. Boycott | 4 | – | – | – | 3 | – | 1 | 1 | 1 | 2 | 3 |
| | 536 | 230 | 102 | 71 | 50 | 53 | 30 | 199 | 137 | 200 | 264 |

*‡ Excluding toss won in abandoned Melbourne Test of 1970-71.*

| *AUSTRALIA* (35) | Tests as Captain | E | SA | Opponents WI | NZ | I | P | Results W | L | D | Tie | Toss Won |
|---|---|---|---|---|---|---|---|---|---|---|---|---|
| D.W. Gregory | 3 | 3 | – | – | – | – | – | 2 | 1 | – | – | 2 |
| W.L. Murdoch | 16 | 16 | – | – | – | – | – | 5 | 7 | 4 | – | 7 |
| T.P. Horan | 2 | 2 | – | – | – | – | – | – | 2 | – | – | 1 |
| H.H. Massie | 1 | 1 | – | – | – | – | – | 1 | – | – | – | 1 |
| J.M. Blackham | 8 | 8 | – | – | – | – | – | 3 | 3 | 2 | – | 4 |
| H.J.H. Scott | 3 | 3 | – | – | – | – | – | – | 3 | – | – | 1 |
| P.S. McDonnell | 6 | 6 | – | – | – | – | – | 1 | 5 | – | – | 4 |
| G. Giffen | 4 | 4 | – | – | – | – | – | 2 | 2 | – | – | 3 |
| G.H.S. Trott | 8 | 8 | – | – | – | – | – | 5 | 3 | – | – | 5 |
| J. Darling | 21 | 18 | 3 | – | – | – | – | 7 | 4 | 10 | – | 7 |
| H. Trumble | 2 | 2 | – | – | – | – | – | 2 | – | – | – | 1 |
| M.A. Noble | 15 | 15 | – | – | – | – | – | 8 | 5 | 2 | – | 11 |
| C. Hill | 10 | 5 | 5 | – | – | – | – | 5 | 5 | – | – | 5 |
| S.E. Gregory | 6 | 3 | 3 | – | – | – | – | 2 | 1 | 3 | – | 1 |
| W.W. Armstrong | 10 | 10 | – | – | – | – | – | 8 | – | 2 | – | 4 |
| H.L. Collins | 11 | 8 | 3 | – | – | – | – | 5 | 2 | 4 | – | 7 |
| W. Bardsley | 2 | 2 | – | – | – | – | – | – | – | 2 | – | 1 |
| J. Ryder | 5 | 5 | – | – | – | – | – | 1 | 4 | – | – | 2 |
| W.M. Woodfull | 25 | 15 | 5 | 5 | – | – | – | 14 | 7 | 4 | – | 12 |
| V.Y. Richardson | 5 | – | 5 | – | – | – | – | 4 | – | 1 | – | 1 |
| D.G. Bradman | 24 | 19 | – | – | – | 5 | – | 15 | 3 | 6 | – | 10 |
| W.A. Brown | 1 | – | – | – | 1 | – | – | 1 | – | – | – | – |
| A.L. Hassett | 24 | 10 | 10 | 4 | – | – | – | 14 | 4 | 6 | – | 18 |
| A.R. Morris | 2 | 1 | – | 1 | – | – | – | – | 2 | – | – | 2 |
| I.W. Johnson | 17 | 9 | – | 5 | – | 2 | 1 | 7 | 5 | 5 | – | 6 |
| R.R. Lindwall | 1 | – | – | – | – | 1 | – | – | – | 1 | – | – |
| I.D. Craig | 5 | – | 5 | – | – | – | – | 3 | – | 2 | – | 3 |
| R. Benaud | 28 | 14 | 1 | 5 | – | 5 | 3 | 12 | 4 | 11 | 1 | 11 |
| R.N. Harvey | 1 | 1 | – | – | – | – | – | 1 | – | – | – | – |
| R.B. Simpson | 39 | 8 | 9 | 10 | – | 10 | 2 | 12 | 12 | 15 | – | 19 |
| B.C. Booth | 2 | 2 | – | – | – | – | – | – | 1 | 1 | – | 1 |
| W.M. Lawry | 25 | 9 | 4 | 5 | – | 7 | – | 9 | 8 | 8 | – | 8 |
| B.N. Jarman | 1 | 1 | – | – | – | – | – | – | – | 1 | – | 1 |
| I.M. Chappell | 30 | 16 | – | 5 | 6 | – | 3 | 15 | 5 | 10 | – | 17 |
| G.S. Chappell | 17 | 6 | – | 6 | 2 | – | 3 | 8 | 5 | 4 | – | 11 |
| | 380 | 230 | 53 | 46 | 9 | 30 | 12 | 172 | 103 | 104 | 1 | 187 |

| SOUTH AFRICA (24) | Tests as Captain | Opponents | | | Results | | | Toss Won |
|---|---|---|---|---|---|---|---|---|
| | | E | A | NZ | W | L | D | |
| O.R. Dunell | 1 | 1 | – | – | – | 1 | – | 1 |
| W.H. Milton | 2 | 2 | – | – | – | 2 | – | 1 |
| E.A. Halliwell | 3 | 2 | 1 | – | – | 3 | – | 1 |
| A.R. Richards | 1 | 1 | – | – | – | 1 | – | – |
| M. Bissett | 2 | 2 | – | – | – | 2 | – | – |
| H.M. Taberer | 1 | – | 1 | – | – | – | 1 | 1 |
| J.H. Anderson | 1 | – | 1 | – | – | 1 | – | – |
| P.W. Sherwell | 13 | 8 | 5 | – | 5 | 6 | 2 | 5 |
| S.J. Snooke | 5 | 5 | – | – | 3 | 2 | – | 3 |
| F. Mitchell | 3 | 1 | *2 | – | – | 3 | – | 2 |
| L.J. Tancred | 3 | 2 | 1 | – | – | 2 | 1 | 2 |
| H.W. Taylor | 18 | 15 | 3 | – | 1 | 10 | 7 | 11 |
| H.G. Deane | 12 | 12 | – | – | 2 | 4 | 6 | 9 |
| E.P. Nupen | 1 | 1 | – | – | 1 | – | – | – |
| H.B. Cameron | 9 | 2 | 5 | 2 | 2 | 5 | 2 | 3 |
| H.F. Wade | 10 | 5 | 5 | – | 1 | 4 | 5 | 5 |
| A. Melville | 10 | 10 | – | – | – | 4 | 6 | 4 |
| A.D. Nourse | 15 | 10 | 5 | – | 1 | 9 | 5 | 7 |
| J.E. Cheetham | 15 | 3 | 5 | 7 | 7 | 5 | 3 | 6 |
| D.J. McGlew | 14 | 8 | 1 | 5 | 4 | 6 | 4 | 4 |
| C.B. van Ryneveld | 8 | 4 | 4 | – | 2 | 4 | 2 | 3 |
| T.L. Goddard | 13 | 5 | 5 | 3 | 1 | 2 | 10 | 4 |
| P.L. van der Merwe | 8 | 3 | 5 | – | 4 | 1 | 3 | 4 |
| A. Bacher | 4 | – | 4 | – | 4 | – | – | 4 |
| | 172 | 102 | 53 | 17 | 38 | 77 | 57 | 80 |

| WEST INDIES (17) | Tests as Captain | Opponents | | | | | Results | | | | Toss Won |
|---|---|---|---|---|---|---|---|---|---|---|---|
| | | E | A | NZ | I | P | W | L | D | Tie | |
| R.K. Nunes | 4 | 4 | – | – | – | – | – | 3 | 1 | – | 2 |
| E.L.G. Hoad | 1 | 1 | – | – | – | – | – | – | 1 | – | 1 |
| N. Betancourt | 1 | 1 | – | – | – | – | – | 1 | – | – | – |
| M.P. Fernandes | 1 | 1 | – | – | – | – | 1 | – | – | – | 1 |
| G.C. Grant | 12 | 7 | 5 | – | – | – | 3 | 7 | 2 | – | 5 |
| R.S. Grant | 3 | 3 | – | – | – | – | – | 1 | 2 | – | 2 |
| G.A. Headley | 1 | 1 | – | – | – | – | – | – | 1 | – | 1 |
| G.E. Gomez | 1 | 1 | – | – | – | – | – | – | 1 | – | – |
| J.D.C. Goddard | 22 | 11 | 4 | 2 | 5 | – | 8 | 7 | 7 | – | 12 |
| J.B. Stollmeyer | 13 | 5 | 3 | – | 5 | – | 3 | 4 | 6 | – | 7 |
| D. St E. Atkinson | 7 | – | 3 | 4 | – | – | 3 | 3 | 1 | – | 3 |
| F.C.M. Alexander | 18 | 5 | – | – | 5 | 8 | 7 | 4 | 7 | – | 9 |
| F.M.M. Worrell | 15 | 5 | 5 | – | 5 | – | 9 | 3 | 2 | 1 | 9 |
| G. St A. Sobers | 39 | 13 | 10 | 8 | 8 | – | 9 | 10 | 20 | – | 27 |
| R.B. Kanhai | 13 | 8 | 5 | – | – | – | 3 | 3 | 7 | – | 6 |
| C.H. Lloyd | 29 | 5 | 8 | – | 9 | 7 | 13 | 9 | 7 | – | 14 |
| A.I. Kallicharran | 3 | – | 3 | – | – | – | 1 | 1 | 1 | – | 1 |
| | 183 | 71 | 46 | 14 | 37 | 15 | 60 | 56 | 66 | 1 | 100 |

| NEW ZEALAND (15) | Tests as Captain | Opponents | | | | | | Results | | | Toss Won |
|---|---|---|---|---|---|---|---|---|---|---|---|
| | | E | A | SA | WI | I | P | W | L | D | |
| T.C. Lowry | 7 | 7 | – | – | – | – | – | – | 2 | 5 | 5 |
| M.L. Page | 7 | 5 | – | 2 | – | – | – | – | 3 | 4 | 4 |
| W.A. Hadlee | 8 | 7 | 1 | – | – | – | – | – | 2 | 6 | 5 |
| B. Sutcliffe | 4 | – | – | 2 | 2 | – | – | – | 3 | 1 | 4 |
| W.M. Wallace | 2 | – | – | 2 | – | – | – | – | 1 | 1 | – |
| G.O. Rabone | 5 | 2 | – | 3 | – | – | – | – | 4 | 1 | 2 |
| H.B. Cave | 9 | – | – | – | 1 | 5 | 3 | – | 5 | 4 | 5 |
| J.R. Reid | 34 | 13 | – | 8 | 3 | 4 | 6 | 3 | 18 | 13 | 17 |
| M.E. Chapple | 1 | 1 | – | – | – | – | – | – | – | 1 | – |
| B.W. Sinclair | 3 | 2 | – | – | – | 1 | – | – | 1 | 2 | 3 |
| G.T. Dowling | 19 | 5 | – | – | 5 | 6 | 3 | 4 | 7 | 8 | 10 |
| B.E. Congdon | 17 | 5 | 6 | – | 3 | – | 3 | 1 | 7 | 9 | 4 |
| G.M. Turner | 10 | – | 2 | – | – | 6 | 2 | 1 | 6 | 3 | 2 |
| J.M. Parker | 1 | – | – | – | – | – | 1 | – | – | 1 | – |
| M.G. Burgess | 3 | 3 | – | – | – | – | – | 1 | 1 | 1 | 1 |
| | 130 | 50 | 9 | 17 | 14 | 22 | 18 | 10 | 60 | 60 | 62 |

| INDIA (19) | Tests as Captain | Opponents | | | | | Results | | | Toss Won |
|---|---|---|---|---|---|---|---|---|---|---|
| | | E | A | WI | NZ | P | W | L | D | |
| C.K. Nayudu | 4 | 4 | – | – | – | – | – | 3 | 1 | 1 |
| Maharajkumar of Vizianagram | 3 | 3 | – | – | – | – | – | 2 | 1 | 1 |
| Nawab of Pataudi, sr | 3 | 3 | – | – | – | – | – | 1 | 2 | 3 |
| L. Amarnath | 15 | – | 5 | 5 | – | 5 | 2 | 6 | 7 | 4 |
| V.S. Hazare | 14 | 9 | – | 5 | – | – | 1 | 5 | 8 | 8 |
| V.M.H. Mankad | 6 | – | – | 1 | – | 5 | – | 1 | 5 | 1 |
| Ghulam Ahmed | 3 | – | – | 2 | 1 | – | – | 2 | 1 | 1 |
| P.R. Umrigar | 8 | – | 3 | 1 | 4 | – | 2 | 2 | 4 | 6 |
| H.R. Adhikari | 1 | – | – | 1 | – | – | – | – | 1 | 1 |
| D.K. Gaekwad | 4 | 4 | – | – | – | – | – | 4 | – | 2 |
| P. Roy | 1 | 1 | – | – | – | – | – | 1 | – | 1 |
| G.S. Ramchand | 5 | – | 5 | – | – | – | 1 | 2 | 2 | 4 |
| N.J. Contractor | 12 | 5 | – | 2 | – | 5 | 2 | 2 | 8 | 7 |
| Nawab of Pataudi, jr | 40 | 8 | 11 | 10 | 11 | – | 9 | 19 | 12 | 20 |
| C.G. Borde | 1 | – | 1 | – | – | – | – | 1 | – | – |
| A.L. Wadekar | 16 | 11 | – | 5 | – | – | 4 | 4 | 8 | 7 |
| S. Venkataraghavan | 1 | – | – | 1 | – | – | – | 1 | – | 1 |
| S.M. Gavaskar | 1 | – | – | – | 1 | – | 1 | – | – | – |
| B.S. Bedi | 19 | 5 | 5 | 4 | 5 | – | 6 | 9 | 4 | 12 |
| | 157 | 53 | 30 | 37 | 22 | 15 | 28 | 65 | 64 | 80 |

# RESULTS SUMMARY – *continued*

| PAKISTAN (10) | Tests as Captain | Opponents | | | | | Results | | | Toss Won |
|---|---|---|---|---|---|---|---|---|---|---|
| | | E | A | WI | NZ | I | W | L | D | |
| A.H. Kardar | 23 | 4 | 1 | 5 | 3 | 10 | 6 | 6 | 11 | 10 |
| Fazal Mahmood | 10 | – | 2 | 3 | – | 5 | 2 | 2 | 6 | 6 |
| Imtiaz Ahmed | 4 | 3 | 1 | – | – | – | – | 2 | 2 | 4 |
| Javed Burki | 5 | 5 | – | – | – | – | – | 4 | 1 | 3 |
| Hanif Mohammad | 11 | 3 | 2 | – | 6 | – | 2 | 2 | 7 | 6 |
| Saeed Ahmed | 3 | 3 | – | – | – | – | – | – | 3 | 1 |
| Intikhab Alam | 17 | 6 | 3 | 2 | 6 | – | 1 | 5 | 11 | 12 |
| Majid Khan | 3 | 3 | – | – | – | – | – | – | 3 | 1 |
| Mushtaq Mohammad | 11 | – | 3 | 5 | 3 | – | 4 | 3 | 4 | 6 |
| Wasim Bari | 3 | 3 | – | – | – | – | – | – | 3 | 2 |
| | 90 | 30 | 12 | 15 | 18 | 15 | 15 | 24 | 51 | 51 |

## MOST CONSECUTIVE MATCHES AS CAPTAIN

| | | | |
|---|---|---|---|
| England | 35 | P.B.H. May | 1955/1959 |
| Australia | 30 | I.M. Chappell | 1970-71/1975 |
| South Africa | 18 | H.W. Taylor | 1913-14/1924 |
| West Indies | 39 | G.St A. Sobers | 1964-65/1971-72 |
| New Zealand | 34 | J.R. Reid | 1955-56/1965 |
| India | 21 | Nawab of Pataudi, jr | 1961-62/1967 |
| Pakistan | 23 | A.H. Kardar | 1952-53/1957-58 |

## WINNING ALL FIVE TOSSES IN A RUBBER

| Captains | | Venue | |
|---|---|---|---|
| Hon F.S. Jackson | England v Australia | England | 1905 |
| M.A. Noble | Australia v England | England | 1909 |
| H.G. Deane | South Africa v England | South Africa | 1927-28 |
| J.D.C. Goddard | West Indies v India | India | 1948-49 |
| A.L. Hassett | Australia v England | England | 1953 |
| P.B.H. May (3) ) | England v West Indies | West Indies | 1959-60 |
| M.C. Cowdrey (2) ) | | | |
| M.C. Cowdrey | England v South Africa | England | 1960 |
| Nawab of Pataudi, jr | India v. England | India | 1963-64 |
| G. St A. Sobers | West Indies v England | England | 1966 |
| G. St A. Sobers | West Indies v New Zealand | West Indies | 1971-72 |

*I.M. Chappell won the toss in five of the six Tests against England in Australia in 1974-75.*
*G.S. Chappell won the toss in five of the six Tests against West Indies in Australia in 1975-76.*

## MOST TEST MATCH APPEARANCES

| For | Total | | Opponents | | | | | |
|---|---|---|---|---|---|---|---|---|
| | | | E | A | SA | WI | NZ | I | P |
| ENGLAND | 114 | M.C. Cowdrey | – | 43 | 14 | 21 | 18 | 8 | 10 |
| AUSTRALIA | 79 | R.N. Harvey | 37 | – | 14 | 14 | – | 10 | 4 |
| SOUTH AFRICA | 50 | J.H.B. Waite | 21 | 14 | – | – | 15 | – | – |
| WEST INDIES | 93 | G. St A. Sobers | 36 | 19 | – | – | 12 | 18 | 8 |
| NEW ZEALAND | 58 | J.R. Reid | 19 | – | 15 | 6 | – | 9 | 9 |
| | 58 | B.E. Congdon | 19 | 8 | – | 8 | – | 13 | 10 |
| INDIA | 59 | P.R. Umrigar | 17 | 6 | – | 16 | 5 | – | 15 |
| PAKISTAN | 55 | Hanif Mohammad | 18 | 6 | – | 6 | 10 | 15 | – |

# YOUNGEST TEST PLAYERS

| Years | Days | | | | |
|---|---|---|---|---|---|
| 15 | 124 | Mushtaq Mohammad | P v WI | Lahore[1] | 1958-59 |
| 16 | 191 | Aftab Baloch | P v NZ | Dacca | 1969-70 |
| 16 | 248 | Nasim-ul-Ghani | P v WI | Bridgetown | 1957-58 |
| 16 | 352 | Khalid Hassan | P v E | Nottingham | 1954 |
| 17 | 122 | J.E.D. Sealy | WI v E | Bridgetown | 1929-30 |
| 17 | 239 | I.D. Craig | A v SA | Melbourne | 1952-53 |
| 17 | 245 | G.St A. Sobers | WI v E | Kingston | 1953-54 |
| 17 | 265 | V.L. Mehra | I v NZ | Bombay[2] | 1955-56 |
| 17 | 300 | Hanif Mohammad | P v I | Delhi | 1952-53 |
| 17 | 341 | Intikhab Alam | P v A | Karachi | 1959-60 |
| 18 | 26 | Majid Khan | P v A | Karachi | 1964-65 |
| 18 | 31 | M.R. Bynoe | WI v P | Lahore[1] | 1958-59 |
| 18 | 41 | Salahuddin | P v NZ | Rawalpindi | 1964-65 |
| 18 | 44 | Khalid Wazir | P v E | Lord's | 1954 |
| 18 | 105 | J.B. Stollmeyer | WI v E | Lord's | 1939 |
| 18 | 149 | D.B. Close | E v NZ | Manchester | 1949 |
| 18 | 173 | A.T. Roberts | WI v NZ | Auckland | 1955-56 |
| 18 | 186 | Haseeb Ahsan | P v WI | Bridgetown | 1957-58 |
| 18 | 190 | Imran Khan | P v E | Birmingham | 1971 |
| 18 | 197 | D.L. Freeman | NZ v E | Christchurch | 1932-33 |
| 18 | 214 | M. Amarnath | I v A | Madras[1] | 1969-70 |
| 18 | 232 | T.W. Garrett | A v E | Melbourne | 1876-77 |
| 18 | 249 | B.S. Chandrasekhar | I v E | Bombay[2] | 1963-64 |
| 18 | 260 | Mohammad Ilyas | P v A | Melbourne | 1964-65 |
| 18 | 267 | H.G. Vivian | NZ v E | Manchester | 1931 |

## OLDEST PLAYERS ON TEST DEBUT

| Years | Days | | | | |
|---|---|---|---|---|---|
| 49 | 119 | J. Southerton | E v A | Melbourne | 1876-77 |
| 47 | 284 | Miran Bux | P v I | Lahore[1] | 1954-55 |
| 46 | 253 | D.D.J. Blackie | A v E | Sydney | 1928-29 |
| 45 | 237 | H. Ironmonger | A v E | Brisbane[2] | 1928-29 |
| 41 | 337 | E.R. Wilson | E v A | Sydney | 1920-21 |
| 41 | 27 | R.J. Jamshedji | I v E | Bombay[1] | 1933-34 |
| 40 | 345 | C.A. Wiles | WI v E | Manchester | 1933 |
| 40 | 110 | H.W. Lee | E v SA | Johannesburg[1] | 1930-31 |
| 40 | 56 | G.W.A. Chubb | SA v E | Nottingham | 1951 |
| 40 | 37 | C. Ramaswami | I v E | Manchester | 1936 |

## OLDEST TEST PLAYERS

*(Age on final day of their last Test match)*

| Years | Days | | | | |
|---|---|---|---|---|---|
| 52 | 165 | W. Rhodes | E v WI | Kingston | 1929-30 |
| 50 | 320 | W.G. Grace | E v A | Nottingham | 1899 |
| 50 | 303 | G. Gunn | E v WI | Kingston | 1929-30 |
| 49 | 327 | H. Ironmonger | A v E | Sydney | 1932-33 |
| 49 | 139 | J. Southerton | E v A | Melbourne | 1876-77 |
| 47 | 302 | Miran Bux | P v I | Peshawar | 1954-55 |
| 47 | 249 | J.B. Hobbs | E v A | Oval | 1930 |
| 47 | 87 | F.E. Woolley | E v A | Oval | 1934 |
| 46 | 309 | D.D.J. Blackie | A v E | Adelaide | 1928-29 |
| 46 | 206 | A.W. Nourse | SA v E | Oval | 1924 |
| 46 | 202 | H. Strudwick | E v A | Oval | 1926 |
| 46 | 41 | E.H. Hendren | E v WI | Kingston | 1934-35 |
| 45 | 245 | G.O.B. Allen | E v WI | Kingston | 1947-48 |
| 45 | 215 | P. Holmes | E v I | Lord's | 1932 |
| 45 | 140 | D.B. Close | E v WI | Manchester | 1976 |
| 44 | 341 | E.G. Wynyard | E v SA | Johannesburg[1] | 1905-06 |
| 44 | 238 | R.Abel | E v A | Manchester | 1902 |
| 44 | 236 | G.A. Headley | WI v E | Kingston | 1953-54 |
| 44 | 105 | Amir Elahi | P v I | Calcutta | 1952-53 |

# INDIVIDUAL CAREER RECORDS

These career records for all players appearing in official Test matches are complete to 31 May, 1978.
Symbols: * not out;  † left-handed batsman;  ‡ left-handed bowler.

## ENGLAND (478 players)

| | | | BATTING AND FIELDING | | | | | | | | | BOWLING | | | | | |
|---|---|---|---|---|---|---|---|---|---|---|---|---|---|---|---|---|---|
| | Tests | I | NO | Runs | HS | Avge | 100 | 50 | Ct | St | Balls | Runs | Wkts | Avge | BB | 5wI | 10wM |
| Abel, R. | 13 | 22 | 2 | 744 | 132* | 37.20 | 2 | 2 | 13 | — | — | — | — | — | — | — | — |
| Absolom, C.A. | 1 | 2 | 0 | 58 | 52 | 29.00 | — | 1 | — | — | — | — | — | — | — | — | — |
| Allen, D.A. | 39 | 51 | 15 | 918 | 88 | 25.50 | — | 5 | 10 | — | 11297 | 3779 | 122 | 30.97 | 5-30 | 4 | — |
| Allen, G.O.B. | 25 | 33 | 2 | 750 | 122 | 24.19 | 1 | 3 | 20 | — | 4390 | 2379 | 81 | 29.37 | 7-80 | 5 | 1 |
| Allom, M.J.C. | 5 | 3 | 2 | 14 | 8* | 14.00 | — | — | — | — | 817 | 265 | 14 | 18.92 | 5-38 | 1 | — |
| Ames, L.E.G. | 47 | 72 | 12 | 2434 | 149 | 40.56 | 8 | 7 | 74 | 23 | — | — | — | — | — | — | — |
| Amiss, D.L. | 50 | 88 | 10 | 3612 | 262* | 46.30 | 11 | 11 | 24 | — | — | — | — | — | — | — | — |
| Andrew, K.V. | 2 | 4 | 1 | 29 | 15 | 9.66 | — | — | 1 | — | — | — | — | — | — | — | — |
| Appleyard, R. | 9 | 9 | 6 | 51 | 19* | 17.00 | — | — | 4 | — | 1596 | 554 | 31 | 17.87 | 5-51 | 1 | — |
| Archer, A.G. | 1 | 2 | 1 | 31 | 24* | 31.00 | — | — | — | — | — | — | — | — | — | — | — |
| Armitage, T. | 2 | 3 | 0 | 33 | 21 | 11.00 | — | — | — | — | 12 | 15 | 0 | — | — | — | — |
| Arnold, E.G. | 10 | 15 | 3 | 160 | 40 | 13.33 | — | 1 | — | — | 1683 | 788 | 31 | 25.41 | 5-37 | 1 | — |
| Arnold, G.G. | 34 | 46 | 11 | 421 | 59 | 12.02 | — | 1 | 8 | — | 7650 | 3254 | 115 | 28.29 | 6-45 | 6 | — |
| Arnold, J. | 1 | 2 | 0 | 34 | 34 | 17.00 | — | — | 9 | — | — | — | — | — | — | — | — |
| Astill, W.E. | 9 | 15 | 0 | 190 | 40 | 12.66 | — | — | 7 | — | 2182 | 856 | 25 | 34.24 | 4-58 | — | — |
| Attewell, W. | 10 | 15 | 6 | 150 | 43* | 16.66 | — | — | 9 | — | 2850 | 626 | 27 | 23.18 | 4-42 | — | — |
| Bailey, T.E. | 61 | 91 | 14 | 2290 | 134* | 29.74 | 1 | 10 | 32 | — | 9712 | 3856 | 132 | 29.21 | 7-34 | 5 | 1 |
| Bakewell, A.H. | 6 | 9 | 0 | 409 | 107 | 45.44 | 1 | 3 | 3 | — | 18 | 8 | 0 | — | — | — | — |
| Balderstone, J.C. | 2 | 4† | 0 | 39 | 35 | 9.75 | — | — | 1 | — | 96‡ | 80 | 1 | 80.00 | 1-80 | — | — |
| Barber, R.W. | 28 | 45† | 3 | 1495 | 185 | 35.59 | 1 | 9 | 21 | — | 3426 | 1806 | 42 | 43.00 | 4-132 | — | — |
| Barber, W. | 2 | 4 | 0 | 83 | 44 | 20.75 | — | — | 1 | — | 2 | 0 | 1 | 0.00 | 1-0 | — | — |
| Barlow, G.D. | 3 | 5† | 1 | 17 | 7* | 4.25 | — | — | 1 | — | — | — | — | — | — | — | — |
| Barlow, R.G. | 17 | 30 | 4 | 591 | 62 | 22.73 | — | 2 | 14 | — | 2456‡ | 767 | 34 | 22.55 | 7-40 | 3 | — |
| Barnes, S.F. | 27 | 39 | 9 | 242 | 38* | 8.06 | — | — | 12 | — | 7873 | 3106 | 189 | 16.43 | 9-103 | 24 | 7 |
| Barnes, W. | 21 | 33 | 2 | 725 | 134 | 23.38 | 1 | 5 | 19 | — | 2289 | 793 | 51 | 15.54 | 6-28 | 3 | — |
| Barnett, C.J. | 20 | 35 | 4 | 1098 | 129 | 35.41 | 2 | 5 | 14 | — | 256 | 93 | 0 | — | — | — | — |
| Barratt, F. | 5 | 4 | 1 | 28 | 17 | 9.33 | — | — | 2 | — | 750 | 235 | 5 | 47.00 | 1-8 | — | — |
| Barrington, K.F. | 82 | 131 | 15 | 6806 | 256 | 58.67 | 20 | 35 | 58 | — | 2715 | 1300 | 29 | 44.82 | 3-4 | — | — |
| Barton, V.A. | 1 | 1 | 0 | 23 | 23 | 23.00 | — | — | 9 | — | — | — | — | — | — | — | — |
| Bates, W. | 15 | 26 | 2 | 656 | 64 | 27.33 | — | 5 | 9 | — | 2364‡ | 821 | 50 | 16.42 | 7-28 | 4 | — |
| Bean, G. | 3 | 5 | 0 | 92 | 50 | 18.40 | — | 1 | 4 | — | — | — | — | — | — | — | — |
| Bedser, A.V. | 51 | 71 | 15 | 714 | 79 | 12.75 | — | 1 | 26 | — | 15918 | 5876 | 236 | 24.89 | 7-34 | 15 | 5 |
| Berry, R. | 2 | 4† | 2 | 6 | 4* | 3.00 | — | — | 2 | — | 653‡ | 228 | 9 | 25.33 | 5-63 | 1 | — |
| Binks, J.G. | 2 | 4 | 0 | 91 | 55 | 22.75 | — | 1 | 8 | — | — | — | — | — | — | — | — |
| Bird, M.C. | 10 | 16 | 1 | 280 | 61 | 18.66 | — | 2 | 5 | — | 264 | 120 | 8 | 15.00 | 3-11 | — | — |
| Birkenshaw, J. | 5 | 7† | 0 | 148 | 64 | 21.14 | — | 1 | 3 | — | 1017 | 469 | 13 | 36.07 | 5-57 | 1 | — |
| Bligh, Hon. Ivo | 4 | 7 | 1 | 62 | 19 | 10.33 | — | — | 7 | — | — | — | — | — | — | — | — |

ENGLAND – continued

| | | | | BATTING AND FIELDING | | | | | | | BOWLING | | | | | | |
|---|---|---|---|---|---|---|---|---|---|---|---|---|---|---|---|---|---|
| | Tests | I | NO | Runs | HS | Avge | 100 | 50 | Ct | St | Balls | Runs | Wkts | Avge | BB | 5wI | 10wM |
| Blythe, C. | 19 | 31 | 12 | 183 | 27 | 9.63 | — | — | 6 | — | 4438† | 1863 | 100 | 18.63 | 8-59 | 9 | 4 |
| Board, J.H. | 6 | 12 | 2 | 108 | 29 | 10.80 | — | — | 8 | 3 | — | 16 | 0 | — | — | — | — |
| Bolus, J.B. | 7 | 12 | 2 | 496 | 88 | 41.33 | — | 4 | 2 | — | 18‡ | 16 | 0 | — | — | — | — |
| Booth, M.W. | 2 | 2 | 0 | 46 | 32 | 23.00 | — | — | 2 | — | 312 | 130 | 7 | 18.57 | 4-49 | — | — |
| Bosanquet, B.J.T. | 7 | 14 | 3 | 147 | 27 | 13.36 | — | — | 9 | — | 970 | 604 | 25 | 24.16 | 8-107 | 2 | — |
| Botham, I.T. | 5 | 7 | 1 | 237 | 103 | 39.50 | 1 | 1 | 6 | — | 1246 | 513 | 27 | 19.00 | 5-21 | 4 | — |
| Bowden, M.P. | 2 | 2 | 0 | 25 | 25 | 12.50 | — | — | 1 | — | — | — | — | — | — | — | — |
| Bowes, W.E. | 15 | 11 | 5 | 28 | 10* | 4.66 | — | — | 2 | — | 3655 | 1519 | 68 | 22.33 | 6-33 | 6 | — |
| Bowley, E.H. | 5 | 7 | 0 | 252 | 109 | 36.00 | 1 | — | 2 | — | 252 | 116 | 0 | — | — | — | — |
| Boycott, G. | 72 | 125 | 17 | 5516 | 246* | 51.07 | 15 | 32 | 22 | — | 816 | 350 | 7 | 50.00 | 3-47 | 1 | — |
| Bradley, W.M. | 2 | 2 | 1 | 23 | 23* | 23.00 | — | — | — | — | 625 | 233 | 6 | 38.83 | 5-67 | 1 | — |
| Braund, L.C. | 23 | 41 | 3 | 987 | 104 | 25.97 | 3 | 2 | 39 | — | 3737 | 1810 | 47 | 38.51 | 8-81 | 3 | — |
| Brearley, J.M. | 15 | 26 | 0 | 701 | 91 | 26.96 | — | 4 | 21 | — | — | — | — | — | — | — | — |
| Brearley, W. | 4 | 5 | 2 | 21 | 11* | 7.00 | — | — | — | — | 705 | 359 | 17 | 21.11 | 5-110 | 1 | — |
| Brennan, D.V. | 2 | 2 | 0 | 16 | 16 | 8.00 | — | — | — | 1 | — | — | — | — | — | — | — |
| Briggs, J. | 33 | 50 | 5 | 815 | 121 | 18.11 | 1 | 2 | 12 | — | 5332‡ | 2094 | 118 | 17.74 | 8-11 | 9 | 4 |
| Brockwell, W. | 7 | 12 | 1 | 202 | 49 | 16.83 | — | — | 6 | — | 582 | 309 | 5 | 61.80 | 3-33 | — | — |
| Bromley-Davenport, H.R. | 4 | 6 | 0 | 128 | 84 | 21.33 | — | 1 | 1 | — | 155‡ | 98 | 4 | 24.50 | 2-46 | — | — |
| Brookes, D. | 1 | 2 | 0 | 17 | 10 | 8.50 | — | — | 1 | — | — | — | — | — | — | — | — |
| Brown, A. | 2 | 1 | 1 | 3 | 3* | — | — | — | — | — | 323 | 150 | 3 | 50.00 | 3-27 | — | — |
| Brown, D.J. | 26 | 34 | 5 | 342 | 44* | 11.79 | — | — | 7 | — | 5098 | 2237 | 79 | 28.31 | 5-42 | 2 | — |
| Brown, F.R. | 22 | 30 | 1 | 734 | 79 | 25.31 | — | 5 | 22 | — | 3260 | 1398 | 45 | 31.06 | 5-49 | 1 | — |
| Brown, G. | 7 | 12† | 2 | 299 | 84 | 29.90 | — | 2 | 9 | 3 | 35 | 22 | 0 | — | — | — | — |
| Brown, J.T. | 8 | 16 | 3 | 470 | 140 | 36.15 | 1 | 1 | 7 | — | — | — | — | — | — | — | — |
| Buckenham, C.P. | 4 | 7 | 0 | 43 | 17 | 6.14 | — | — | 2 | — | 1182 | 593 | 21 | 28.23 | 5-115 | 1 | — |
| Butler, H.J. | 2 | 2 | 1 | 15 | 15* | 15.00 | — | — | 1 | — | 552 | 215 | 12 | 17.91 | 4-34 | — | — |
| Butt, H.R. | 3 | 4 | 1 | 22 | 13 | 7.33 | — | — | 1 | 1 | — | — | — | — | — | — | — |
| Calthorpe, Hon. F.S.G. | 4 | 7 | 0 | 129 | 49 | 18.42 | — | — | 3 | — | 204 | 91 | 1 | 91.00 | 1-38 | — | — |
| Carr, A.W. | 11 | 13 | 1 | 237 | 63 | 19.75 | — | 1 | 3 | — | — | — | — | — | — | — | — |
| Carr, D.B. | 2 | 4 | 0 | 135 | 76 | 33.75 | — | 1 | — | — | 210‡ | 140 | 2 | 70.00 | 2-84 | — | — |
| Carr, D.W. | 1 | 1 | 0 | 0 | 0 | 0.00 | — | — | — | — | 414 | 282 | 7 | 40.28 | 5-146 | 1 | — |
| Cartwright, T.W. | 5 | 7 | 2 | 26 | 9 | 5.20 | — | — | 2 | — | 1611 | 544 | 15 | 36.26 | 6-94 | 1 | — |
| Chapman, A.P.F. | 26 | 36† | 4 | 925 | 121 | 28.90 | 1 | 5 | 32 | — | 40‡ | 20 | 0 | — | — | — | — |
| Charlwood, H.R.J. | 2 | 4 | 0 | 63 | 36 | 15.75 | — | — | 2 | — | — | — | — | — | — | — | — |
| Chatterton, W. | 1 | 1 | 0 | 48 | 48 | 48.00 | — | — | — | — | — | — | — | — | — | — | — |
| Christopherson, S. | 1 | 1 | 0 | 17 | 17 | 17.00 | — | — | — | — | 136 | 69 | 1 | 69.00 | 1-52 | — | — |
| Clark, E.W. | 8 | 9† | 5 | 36 | 10 | 9.00 | — | — | 1 | — | 1931‡ | 899 | 32 | 28.09 | 5-98 | 1 | — |
| Clay, J.C. | 1 | — | — | — | — | — | — | — | — | — | 192 | 75 | 0 | — | — | — | — |
| Close, D.B. | 22 | 37† | 2 | 887 | 70 | 25.34 | — | 4 | 24 | — | 1212 | 532 | 18 | 29.55 | 4-35 | — | — |

ENGLAND – continued

| | | | | BATTING AND FIELDING | | | | | | | | | BOWLING | | | | |
| --- | --- | --- | --- | --- | --- | --- | --- | --- | --- | --- | --- | --- | --- | --- | --- | --- | --- |
| | Tests | I | NO | Runs | HS | Avge | 100 | 50 | Ct | St | Balls | Runs | Wkts | Avge | BB | 5wI | 10wM |
| Coldwell, L.J. | 7 | 7 | 5 | 9 | 6* | 4.50 | — | — | 1 | — | 1668 | 610 | 22 | 27.72 | 6-85 | 1 | — |
| Compton, D.C.S. | 78 | 131 | 15 | 5807 | 278 | 50.06 | 17 | 28 | 49 | — | 2716‡ | 1410 | 25 | 56.40 | 5-70 | 1 | — |
| Cook, C. | 1 | 2 | 0 | 4 | 4 | 2.00 | — | — | 1 | — | 180‡ | 127 | 0 | — | — | — | — |
| Cope, G.A. | 3 | 3 | 0 | 40 | 22 | 13.33 | — | — | 1 | — | 864 | 277 | 8 | 34.62 | 3-102 | — | — |
| Copson, W.H. | 3 | 1 | 0 | 6 | 6 | 6.00 | — | — | 1 | — | 762 | 297 | 15 | 19.80 | 5-85 | 1 | — |
| Cornford, W.L. | 4 | 4 | 0 | 36 | 18 | 9.00 | — | — | 5 | 3 | — | — | — | — | — | — | — |
| Cottam, R.M.H. | 4 | 5 | 1 | 27 | 13 | 6.75 | — | — | 2 | — | 903 | 327 | 14 | 23.35 | 4-50 | — | — |
| Coventry, Hon. C.J. | 2 | 2 | 1 | 13 | 12 | 13.00 | — | — | — | — | — | — | — | — | — | — | — |
| Cowdrey, M.C. | 114 | 188 | 15 | 7624 | 182 | 44.06 | 22 | 38 | 120 | — | 119 | 104 | 0 | — | — | — | — |
| Coxon, A. | 1 | 2† | 0 | 19 | 19 | 9.50 | — | — | 1 | — | 378 | 172 | 3 | 57.33 | 2-90 | — | — |
| Cranston, J. | 1 | 2† | 0 | 31 | 16 | 15.50 | — | — | 1 | — | — | — | — | — | — | — | — |
| Cranston, K. | 8 | 14 | 0 | 209 | 45 | 14.92 | — | — | 3 | — | 1010 | 461 | 18 | 25.61 | 4-12 | — | — |
| Crapp, J.F. | 7 | 13† | 2 | 319 | 56 | 29.00 | — | 3 | 7 | — | — | — | — | — | — | — | — |
| Crawford, J.N. | 12 | 23 | 2 | 469 | 74 | 22.33 | — | 2 | 13 | — | 2203 | 1150 | 39 | 29.48 | 5-48 | 3 | — |
| Cuttell, W.R. | 2 | 4 | 0 | 65 | 21 | 16.25 | — | — | 2 | — | 285 | 73 | 6 | 12.16 | 3-17 | — | — |
| Dawson, E.W. | 5 | 9 | 0 | 175 | 55 | 19.44 | — | 1 | — | — | — | — | — | — | — | — | — |
| Dean, H. | 3 | 4† | 2 | 10 | 8 | 5.00 | — | — | 2 | — | 447‡ | 153 | 11 | 13.90 | 4-19 | — | — |
| Denness, M.H. | 28 | 45 | 3 | 1667 | 188 | 39.69 | 4 | 7 | 28 | — | — | — | — | — | — | — | — |
| Denton, D. | 11 | 22 | 1 | 424 | 104 | 20.19 | 1 | 1 | 8 | — | — | — | — | — | — | — | — |
| Dewes, J.G. | 5 | 10† | 0 | 121 | 67 | 12.10 | — | 1 | — | — | — | — | — | — | — | — | — |
| Dexter, E.R. | 62 | 102 | 8 | 4502 | 205 | 47.89 | 9 | 27 | 29 | — | 5317 | 2306 | 66 | 34.93 | 4-10 | — | — |
| Dipper, A.E. | 1 | 2 | 0 | 51 | 40 | 25.50 | — | — | — | — | — | — | — | — | — | — | — |
| Doggart, G.H.G. | 2 | 4 | 0 | 76 | 29 | 19.00 | — | — | 3 | — | — | — | — | — | — | — | — |
| D'Oliveira, B.L. | 44 | 70 | 8 | 2484 | 158 | 40.06 | 5 | 15 | 29 | — | 5706 | 1859 | 47 | 39.55 | 3-46 | — | — |
| Dollery, H.E. | 4 | 7 | 0 | 72 | 37 | 10.28 | — | — | 1 | — | — | — | — | — | — | — | — |
| Dolphin, A. | 1 | 2 | 0 | 1 | 1 | 0.50 | — | — | 1 | — | — | — | — | — | — | — | — |
| Douglas, J.W.H.T. | 23 | 35 | 2 | 962 | 119 | 29.15 | 1 | 6 | 9 | — | 2812 | 1486 | 45 | 33.02 | 5-46 | 1 | — |
| Druce, N.F. | 5 | 9 | 2 | 252 | 64 | 28.00 | — | 1 | 5 | — | — | — | — | — | — | — | — |
| Ducat, A.N. | 1 | 2 | 0 | 5 | 3 | 2.50 | — | — | 1 | — | — | — | — | — | — | — | — |
| Duckworth, G. | 24 | 28 | 12 | 234 | 39* | 14.62 | — | — | 45 | 15 | — | — | — | — | — | — | — |
| Duleepsinhji, K.S. | 12 | 19 | 2 | 995 | 173 | 58.52 | 3 | 5 | 10 | — | 6 | 7 | 0 | — | — | — | — |
| Durston, F.J. | 1 | 2 | 1 | 8 | 6* | 8.00 | — | — | — | — | 202 | 136 | 5 | 27.20 | 4-102 | — | — |
| Edmonds, P.H. | 7 | 10 | 1 | 115 | 50 | 12.77 | — | 1 | 14 | — | 1975‡ | 661 | 25 | 26.44 | 7-66 | 2 | — |
| Edrich, J.H. | 77 | 127† | 9 | 5138 | 310* | 43.54 | 12 | 24 | 43 | — | 30 | 23 | 0 | — | — | — | — |
| Edrich, W.J. | 39 | 63 | 2 | 2440 | 219 | 40.00 | 6 | 13 | 39 | — | 3226 | 1693 | 41 | 41.29 | 4-68 | — | — |
| Elliott, H. | 4 | 5 | 1 | 61 | 37* | 15.25 | — | — | 8 | 3 | — | — | — | — | — | — | — |
| Emmett, G.M. | 1 | 2 | 0 | 10 | 10 | 5.00 | — | — | — | — | — | — | — | — | — | — | — |
| Emmett, T. | 7 | 13† | 1 | 160 | 48 | 13.33 | — | — | 9 | — | 728‡ | 284 | 9 | 31.55 | 7-68 | 1 | — |

# INDIVIDUAL CAREER RECORDS – continued

ENGLAND – continued

| | Tests | I | NO | Runs | HS | Avge | 100 | 50 | Ct | St | Balls | Runs | Wkts | Avge | BB | 5wI | 10wM |
|---|---|---|---|---|---|---|---|---|---|---|---|---|---|---|---|---|---|
| | | | | | | BATTING AND FIELDING | | | | | | | | BOWLING | | | |
| Evans, A.J. | 1 | 2 | 0 | 18 | 14 | 9.00 | – | – | – | – | – | – | – | – | – | – | – |
| Evans, T.G. | 91 | 133 | 14 | 2439 | 104 | 20.49 | 2 | 8 | 173 | 46 | – | – | – | – | – | – | – |
| Fagg, A.E. | 5 | 8 | 0 | 150 | 39 | 18.75 | – | – | 5 | – | – | – | – | – | – | – | – |
| Fane, F.L. | 14 | 27 | 1 | 682 | 143 | 26.23 | 1 | 3 | 6 | – | – | – | – | – | – | – | – |
| Farnes, K. | 15 | 17 | 5 | 58 | 20 | 4.83 | – | – | 1 | – | 3932 | 1719 | 60 | 28.65 | 6-96 | 3 | 1 |
| Farrimond, W. | 4 | 7 | 0 | 116 | 35 | 16.57 | – | – | 5 | 2 | – | – | – | – | – | – | – |
| Fender, P.G.H. | 13 | 21 | 1 | 380 | 60 | 19.00 | – | 2 | 14 | – | 2178 | 1185 | 29 | 40.86 | 5-90 | 2 | – |
| Ferris, J.J. | 1 | 1† | 0 | 16 | 16 | 16.00 | – | – | – | – | 272‡ | 91 | 13 | 7.00 | 7-37 | 2 | 1 |
| Fielder, A. | 6 | 12 | 5 | 78 | 20 | 11.14 | – | – | 4 | – | 1491 | 711 | 26 | 27.34 | 6-82 | 1 | – |
| Fishlock, L.B. | 4 | 5† | 2 | 47 | 19* | 11.75 | – | – | 1 | – | – | – | – | – | – | – | – |
| Flavell, J.A. | 4 | 6† | 2 | 31 | 14 | 7.75 | – | – | – | – | 792 | 367 | 7 | 52.42 | 2-65 | – | – |
| Fletcher, K.W.R. | 52 | 85 | 11 | 2975 | 216 | 40.20 | 7 | 16 | 46 | – | 249 | 173 | 1 | 173.00 | 1-48 | – | – |
| Flowers, W. | 8 | 14 | 0 | 254 | 56 | 18.14 | – | 1 | 3 | – | 858 | 296 | 14 | 21.14 | 5-46 | 1 | – |
| Ford, F.G.J. | 5 | 9† | 0 | 168 | 48 | 18.66 | – | – | 5 | – | 210‡ | 129 | 1 | 129.00 | 1-47 | – | – |
| Foster, F.R. | 11 | 15 | 1 | 330 | 71 | 23.57 | – | 3 | 11 | – | 2447‡ | 926 | 45 | 20.57 | 6-91 | 4 | – |
| Foster, R.E. | 8 | 14 | 1 | 602 | 287 | 46.30 | 1 | 1 | 13 | – | – | – | – | – | – | – | – |
| Fothergill, A.J. | 2 | 2† | 0 | 33 | 32 | 16.50 | – | – | 4 | – | 321‡ | 90 | 8 | 11.25 | 4-19 | – | – |
| Freeman, A.P. | 12 | 16 | 5 | 154 | 50* | 14.00 | – | 1 | 4 | – | 3732 | 1707 | 66 | 25.86 | 7-71 | 5 | 3 |
| Fry, C.B. | 26 | 41 | 3 | 1223 | 144 | 32.18 | 2 | 7 | 17 | – | 10 | 3 | 0 | – | – | – | – |
| Gatting, M.W. | 2 | 3 | 0 | 11 | 6 | 3.66 | – | – | 3 | – | 8 | 1 | 0 | – | – | – | – |
| Gay, L.H. | 1 | 2 | 0 | 37 | 33 | 18.50 | – | – | 3 | 1 | – | – | – | – | – | – | – |
| Geary, G. | 14 | 20 | 4 | 249 | 66 | 15.56 | – | 2 | 13 | – | 3810 | 1353 | 46 | 29.41 | 7-70 | 4 | 1 |
| Gibb, P.A. | 8 | 13 | 0 | 581 | 120 | 44.69 | 2 | 3 | 3 | 1 | – | – | – | – | – | – | – |
| Gifford, N. | 15 | 20† | 9 | 179 | 25* | 16.27 | – | – | 8 | – | 3084‡ | 1026 | 33 | 31.09 | 5-55 | 1 | – |
| Gilligan, A.E.R. | 11 | 16 | 3 | 209 | 39* | 16.07 | – | – | 3 | – | 2404 | 1046 | 36 | 29.05 | 6-7 | 2 | 1 |
| Gilligan, A.H.H. | 4 | 4 | 0 | 71 | 32 | 17.75 | – | – | 1 | – | – | – | – | – | – | – | – |
| Gimblett, H. | 3 | 5 | 1 | 129 | 67* | 32.25 | – | 1 | 1 | – | – | – | – | – | – | – | – |
| Gladwin, C. | 8 | 11 | 5 | 170 | 51* | 28.33 | – | 1 | 2 | – | 2129 | 571 | 15 | 38.06 | 3-21 | – | – |
| Goddard, T.W.J. | 8 | 5 | 3 | 13 | 8 | 6.50 | – | – | 3 | – | 1563 | 588 | 22 | 26.72 | 6-29 | 1 | – |
| Gooch, G.A. | 2 | 4 | 0 | 37 | 31 | 9.25 | – | – | 2 | – | – | – | – | – | – | – | – |
| Gover, A.R. | 4 | 1 | 1 | 2 | 2* | – | – | – | 1 | – | 816 | 359 | 8 | 44.87 | 3-85 | – | – |
| Grace, E.M. | 1 | 2 | 0 | 36 | 36 | 18.00 | – | – | 1 | – | – | – | – | – | – | – | – |
| Grace, G.F. | 1 | 2 | 0 | 0 | 0 | 0.00 | – | – | 2 | – | – | – | – | – | – | – | – |
| Grace, W.G. | 22 | 36 | 2 | 1098 | 170 | 32.29 | 2 | 5 | 39 | – | 663 | 236 | 9 | 26.22 | 2-12 | 1 | – |
| Graveney, T.W. | 79 | 123 | 13 | 4882 | 258 | 44.38 | 11 | 20 | 80 | – | 260 | 167 | 1 | 167.00 | 1-34 | – | – |
| Greenhough, T. | 4 | 4 | 1 | 4 | 2 | 1.33 | – | – | 1 | – | 1129 | 357 | 16 | 22.31 | 5-35 | 1 | – |
| Greenwood, A. | 2 | 4 | 0 | 77 | 49 | 19.25 | – | – | 2 | – | – | – | – | – | – | – | – |
| Greig, A.W. | 58 | 93 | 4 | 3599 | 148 | 40.43 | 8 | 20 | 87 | – | 9802 | 4541 | 141 | 32.20 | 8-86 | 6 | 2 |

ENGLAND – continued

| | Tests | I | NO | Runs | HS | Avge | 100 | 50 | Ct | St | Balls | Runs | Wkts | Avge | BB | 5wI | 10wM |
|---|---|---|---|---|---|---|---|---|---|---|---|---|---|---|---|---|---|
| | | | | | | *BATTING AND FIELDING* | | | | | | | | *BOWLING* | | | |
| Grieve, B.A.F. | 2 | 3 | 2 | 40 | 14* | 40.00 | – | – | – | – | – | – | – | – | – | – | – |
| Griffith, S.C. | 3 | 5 | 0 | 157 | 140 | 31.40 | 1 | – | 5 | – | – | – | – | – | – | – | – |
| Gunn, G. | 15 | 29 | 1 | 1120 | 122* | 40.00 | 2 | 7 | 15 | – | 12 | 8 | 0 | – | – | – | – |
| Gunn, J. | 6 | 10† | 2 | 85 | 24 | 10.62 | – | – | 3 | – | 903‡ | 387 | 18 | 21.50 | 5-76 | 1 | – |
| Gunn, W. | 11 | 20 | 2 | 392 | 102* | 21.77 | 1 | 1 | 5 | – | – | – | – | – | – | – | – |
| Haig, N.E. | 5 | 9 | 0 | 126 | 47 | 14.00 | – | – | 4 | – | 1026 | 448 | 13 | 34.46 | 3-73 | – | – |
| Haigh, S. | 11 | 18 | 3 | 113 | 25 | 7.53 | – | – | 8 | – | 1294 | 622 | 24 | 25.91 | 6-11 | 1 | – |
| Hallows, C. | 2 | 2† | 1 | 42 | 26 | 42.00 | – | – | – | – | – | – | – | – | – | – | – |
| Hammond, W.R. | 85 | 140 | 16 | 7249 | 336* | 58.45 | 22 | 24 | 110 | – | 7967 | 3138 | 83 | 37.80 | 5-36 | 2 | – |
| Hampshire, J.H. | 8 | 16 | 1 | 403 | 107 | 26.86 | 1 | 2 | 9 | – | – | – | – | – | – | – | – |
| Hardinge, H.T.W. | 1 | 2 | 0 | 30 | 25 | 15.00 | – | – | 1 | – | – | – | – | – | – | – | – |
| Hardstaff, J., sr | 5 | 10 | 0 | 311 | 72 | 31.10 | – | 3 | 9 | – | – | – | – | – | – | – | – |
| Hardstaff, J., jr | 23 | 38 | 3 | 1636 | 205* | 46.74 | 4 | 10 | 9 | – | – | – | – | – | – | – | – |
| Harris, Lord | 4 | 6 | 1 | 145 | 52 | 29.00 | – | 1 | 2 | – | 32 | 29 | 0 | – | – | – | – |
| Hartley, J.C. | 2 | 4 | 0 | 15 | 9 | 3.75 | – | – | 2 | – | 192 | 115 | 1 | 115.00 | 1-62 | – | – |
| Hawke, Lord | 5 | 8 | 1 | 55 | 30 | 7.85 | – | – | 3 | – | – | – | – | – | – | – | – |
| Hayes, E.G. | 5 | 9 | 1 | 86 | 35 | 10.75 | – | – | 2 | – | 90 | 52 | 1 | 52.00 | 1-28 | – | – |
| Hayes, F.C. | 9 | 17 | 1 | 244 | 106* | 15.25 | 1 | – | 7 | – | – | – | – | – | – | – | – |
| Hayward, T.W. | 35 | 60 | 2 | 1999 | 137 | 34.46 | 3 | 12 | 19 | – | 869 | 514 | 14 | 36.71 | 4-22 | – | – |
| Hearne, A. | 1 | 1 | 0 | 9 | 9 | 9.00 | – | – | 1 | – | – | – | – | – | – | – | – |
| Hearne, F. | 2 | 2 | 0 | 47 | 27 | 23.50 | – | – | 1 | – | – | – | – | – | – | – | – |
| Hearne, G.G. | 1 | 1† | 0 | 0 | 0 | 0.00 | – | – | 1 | – | – | – | – | – | – | – | – |
| Hearne, J.T. | 12 | 18 | 4 | 126 | 40 | 9.00 | – | – | 4 | – | 2976 | 1082 | 49 | 22.08 | 6-41 | 4 | 1 |
| Hearne, J.W. | 24 | 36 | 5 | 806 | 114 | 26.00 | 1 | 2 | 13 | – | 2926 | 1462 | 30 | 48.73 | 5-49 | 1 | – |
| Hendren, E.H. | 51 | 83 | 9 | 3525 | 205* | 47.63 | 7 | 21 | 33 | – | 47 | 31 | 1 | 31.00 | 1-27 | – | – |
| Hendrick, M. | 14 | 19 | 5 | 45 | 15 | 4.50 | – | – | 16 | – | 2758 | 1162 | 44 | 26.40 | 4-28 | – | – |
| Heseltine, C. | 2 | 2 | 0 | 18 | 18 | 9.00 | – | – | 3 | – | 157 | 84 | 5 | 16.80 | 5-38 | 1 | – |
| Higgs, K. | 15 | 19† | 3 | 185 | 63 | 11.56 | – | 1 | 4 | – | 4112 | 1473 | 71 | 20.74 | 6-91 | 2 | – |
| Hill, A. | 2 | 4 | 0 | 101 | 49 | 50.50 | – | 1 | 1 | – | 340 | 130 | 7 | 18.57 | 4-27 | – | – |
| Hill, A.J.L. | 3 | 6 | 1 | 251 | 124 | 62.75 | 1 | 1 | 1 | – | 40 | 8 | 4 | 2.00 | 4-8 | – | – |
| Hilton, M.J. | 4 | 6 | 1 | 37 | 15 | 7.40 | – | – | 1 | – | 1244‡ | 477 | 14 | 34.07 | 5-61 | 1 | – |
| Hirst, G.H. | 24 | 38 | 3 | 790 | 85 | 22.57 | – | 5 | 18 | – | 3967‡ | 1770 | 59 | 30.00 | 5-48 | 3 | – |
| Hitch, J.W. | 7 | 10 | 3 | 103 | 51* | 14.71 | – | 1 | 4 | – | 462 | 325 | 7 | 46.42 | 2-31 | – | – |
| Hobbs, J.B. | 61 | 102 | 7 | 5410 | 211 | 56.94 | 15 | 28 | 17 | – | 376 | 165 | 1 | 165.00 | 1-19 | – | – |
| Hobbs, R.N.S. | 7 | 8 | 3 | 34 | 15* | 6.80 | – | – | 8 | – | 1291 | 481 | 12 | 40.08 | 3-25 | – | – |
| Hollies, W.E. | 13 | 15 | 8 | 37 | 18* | 5.28 | – | – | 2 | – | 3554 | 1332 | 44 | 30.27 | 7-50 | 5 | – |
| Holmes, E.R.T. | 5 | 9 | 2 | 114 | 85* | 16.28 | – | 1 | 4 | – | 108 | 76 | 2 | 38.00 | 1-10 | – | – |
| Holmes, P. | 7 | 14 | 1 | 357 | 88 | 27.46 | – | 4 | 3 | – | – | – | – | – | – | – | – |
| Hone, L. | 1 | 2 | 0 | 13 | 7 | 6.50 | – | – | 2 | – | – | – | – | – | – | – | – |

# INDIVIDUAL CAREER RECORDS – continued

ENGLAND – continued

| | | | | BATTING AND FIELDING | | | | | | | BOWLING | | | | | | |
|---|---|---|---|---|---|---|---|---|---|---|---|---|---|---|---|---|---|
| | Tests | I | NO | Runs | HS | Avge | 100 | 50 | Ct | St | Balls | Runs | Wkts | Avge | BB | 5wI | 10wM |
| Hopwood, J.L. | 2 | 3 | 1 | 12 | 8 | 6.00 | – | – | – | – | 462‡ | 155 | 0 | – | – | – | – |
| Hornby, A.N. | 3 | 6 | 0 | 21 | 9 | 3.50 | – | – | – | – | 28 | 0 | 1 | – | 1-0 | – | – |
| Horton, M.J. | 2 | 2 | 0 | 60 | 58 | 30.00 | – | 1 | 2 | – | 238 | 59 | 2 | 29.50 | 2-24 | – | – |
| Howard, N.D. | 4 | 6 | 1 | 86 | 23 | 17.20 | – | – | 4 | – | – | – | – | – | – | – | – |
| Howell, H. | 5 | 8 | 6 | 15 | 5 | 7.50 | – | – | – | – | 918 | 559 | 7 | 79.85 | 4-115 | – | – |
| Howorth, R. | 5 | 10† | 2 | 145 | 45* | 18.12 | – | – | 2 | – | 1536‡ | 635 | 19 | 33.42 | 6-124 | 1 | – |
| Humphries, J. | 3 | 6 | 1 | 44 | 16 | 8.80 | – | – | 7 | 3 | – | – | – | – | – | – | – |
| Hunter, J. | 5 | 7 | 2 | 93 | 39* | 18.60 | – | – | 8 | 3 | – | – | – | – | – | – | – |
| Hutchings, K.L. | 7 | 12 | 2 | 341 | 126 | 28.41 | 1 | 1 | 9 | – | 90 | 81 | 1 | 81.00 | 1-5 | – | – |
| Hutton, L. | 79 | 138 | 15 | 6971 | 364 | 56.67 | 19 | 33 | 57 | – | 260 | 232 | 3 | 77.33 | 1-2 | – | – |
| Hutton, R.A. | 5 | 8 | 2 | 219 | 81 | 36.50 | – | 2 | 9 | – | 738 | 257 | 9 | 28.55 | 3-72 | – | – |
| Iddon, J. | 5 | 7 | 1 | 170 | 73 | 28.33 | – | 2 | – | – | 66‡ | 27 | 0 | – | – | – | – |
| Ikin, J.T. | 18 | 31† | 2 | 606 | 60 | 20.89 | – | 3 | 31 | – | 572‡ | 354 | 3 | 118.00 | 1-38 | – | – |
| Illingworth, R. | 61 | 90 | 11 | 1836 | 113 | 23.24 | 2 | 5 | 45 | – | 11934 | 3807 | 122 | 31.20 | 6-29 | 3 | – |
| Insole, D.J. | 9 | 17 | 2 | 408 | 110* | 27.20 | 1 | 1 | 8 | – | – | – | – | – | – | – | – |
| Jackson, Hon. F.S. | 20 | 33 | 4 | 1415 | 144* | 48.79 | 5 | 6 | 10 | – | 1587 | 799 | 24 | 33.29 | 5-52 | 1 | – |
| Jackson, H.L. | 2 | 2 | 1 | 15 | 8 | 15.00 | – | – | 1 | – | 498 | 155 | 7 | 22.14 | 2-26 | – | – |
| Jameson, J.A. | 4 | 8 | 0 | 214 | 82 | 26.75 | – | 1 | – | – | 42 | 17 | 1 | 17.00 | 1-17 | – | – |
| Jardine, D.R. | 22 | 33 | 6 | 1296 | 127 | 48.00 | 1 | 10 | 26 | – | 6 | 10 | 0 | – | – | – | – |
| Jenkins, R.O. | 9 | 12 | 1 | 198 | 39 | 18.00 | – | – | 4 | – | 2118 | 1098 | 32 | 34.31 | 5-116 | 1 | – |
| Jessop, G.L. | 18 | 26 | 0 | 569 | 104 | 21.88 | 1 | 3 | 11 | – | 672 | 354 | 10 | 35.40 | 4-68 | – | – |
| Jones, A.O. | 12 | 21 | 0 | 291 | 34 | 13.85 | – | – | 15 | – | 228 | 133 | 3 | 44.33 | 3-73 | – | – |
| Jones, I.J. | 15 | 17 | 9 | 38 | 16 | 4.75 | – | – | 4 | – | 3546‡ | 1769 | 44 | 40.20 | 6-118 | 1 | – |
| Jupp, H. | 2 | 4 | 0 | 68 | 63 | 17.00 | – | 1 | 2 | – | – | – | – | – | – | – | – |
| Jupp, V.W.C. | 8 | 13 | 1 | 208 | 38 | 17.33 | – | 1 | 5 | – | 1301 | 616 | 28 | 22.00 | 4-37 | – | – |
| Keeton, W.W. | 2 | 4 | 0 | 57 | 25 | 14.25 | – | – | – | – | – | – | – | – | – | – | – |
| Kennedy, A.S. | 5 | 8 | 2 | 93 | 41* | 15.50 | – | – | 5 | – | 1683 | 599 | 31 | 19.32 | 5-88 | 2 | – |
| Kenyon, D. | 8 | 15 | 0 | 192 | 87 | 12.80 | – | 1 | 5 | – | – | – | – | – | – | – | – |
| Killick, E.T. | 2 | 4 | 0 | 81 | 31 | 20.25 | – | – | 2 | – | – | – | – | – | – | – | – |
| Kilner, R. | 9 | 8† | 1 | 233 | 74 | 33.28 | – | 2 | 6 | – | 2368‡ | 734 | 24 | 30.58 | 4-51 | – | – |
| King, J.H. | 1 | 2† | 0 | 64 | 60 | 32.00 | – | 1 | – | – | 162‡ | 99 | 1 | 99.00 | 1-99 | – | – |
| Kinneir, S.P. | 1 | 2† | 0 | 52 | 30 | 26.00 | – | – | – | – | – | – | – | – | – | – | – |
| Knight, A.E. | 3 | 6 | 1 | 81 | 70* | 16.20 | – | 1 | 1 | – | – | – | – | – | – | – | – |
| Knight, B.R. | 29 | 38 | 7 | 812 | 127 | 26.19 | 2 | 1 | 14 | – | 5377 | 2223 | 70 | 31.75 | 4-38 | – | – |
| Knight, D.J. | 2 | 4 | 0 | 54 | 38 | 13.50 | – | – | 1 | – | – | – | – | – | – | – | – |
| Knott, A.P.E. | 89 | 138 | 14 | 4175 | 135 | 33.66 | 5 | 28 | 233 | 19 | – | – | – | – | – | – | – |
| Knox, N.A. | 2 | 4 | 1 | 24 | 8* | 8.00 | – | – | – | – | 126 | 105 | 3 | 35.00 | 2-39 | – | – |

# INDIVIDUAL CAREER RECORDS – *continued*

## ENGLAND – *continued*

| | | | BATTING AND FIELDING | | | | | | | | BOWLING | | | | | | |
|---|---|---|---|---|---|---|---|---|---|---|---|---|---|---|---|---|---|
| | Tests | I | NO | Runs | HS | Avge | 100 | 50 | Ct | St | Balls | Runs | Wkts | Avge | BB | 5wI | 10wM |
| Laker, J.C. | 46 | 63 | 15 | 676 | 63 | 14.08 | – | 2 | 12 | – | 12027 | 4101 | 193 | 21.24 | 10-53 | 9 | 3 |
| Langridge, James | 8 | 9† | 0 | 242 | 70 | 26.88 | – | 1 | 6 | – | 1074‡ | 413 | 19 | 21.73 | 7-56 | 2 | – |
| Larter, J.D.F. | 10 | 7 | 2 | 16 | 10 | 3.20 | – | – | 5 | – | 2172 | 941 | 37 | 25.43 | 5-57 | 2 | – |
| Larwood, H. | 21 | 28 | 3 | 485 | 98 | 19.40 | – | 2 | 15 | – | 4969 | 2212 | 78 | 28.35 | 6-32 | 4 | 1 |
| Leadbeater, E. | 2 | 2 | 0 | 40 | 38 | 20.00 | – | – | 3 | – | 289 | 218 | 2 | 109.00 | 1-38 | – | – |
| Lee, H.W. | 1 | 2 | 0 | 19 | 18 | 9.50 | – | – | – | – | | | | | | | |
| Lees, W.S. | 5 | 9 | 3 | 66 | 25* | 11.00 | – | – | 2 | – | 1256 | 467 | 26 | 17.96 | 6-78 | 2 | – |
| Legge, G.B. | 5 | 7 | 1 | 299 | 196 | 49.83 | 1 | – | 1 | – | 30 | 34 | 0 | – | – | | |
| Leslie, C.F.H. | 4 | 7 | 0 | 106 | 54 | 15.14 | – | 1 | 1 | – | 96 | 44 | 4 | 11.00 | 3-31 | – | – |
| Lever, J.K. | 13 | 19 | 3 | 199 | 53 | 12.43 | – | 1 | 8 | – | 2562‡ | 1058 | 44 | 24.04 | 7-46 | 2 | 1 |
| Lever, P. | 17 | 18 | 2 | 350 | 88* | 21.87 | – | 2 | 11 | – | 3571 | 1509 | 41 | 36.80 | 6-38 | 2 | – |
| Leveson-Gower, H.D.G. | 3 | 6 | 2 | 95 | 31 | 23.75 | – | – | 1 | – | | | | | | | |
| Levett, W.H.V. | 1 | 2 | 1 | 7 | 5 | 7.00 | – | – | 3 | – | | | | | | | |
| Lewis, A.R. | 9 | 16 | 2 | 457 | 125 | 32.64 | 1 | 3 | 3 | – | | | | | | | |
| Leyland, M. | 41 | 65† | 5 | 2764 | 187 | 46.06 | 9 | 10 | 13 | – | 1103‡ | 585 | 6 | 97.50 | 3-91 | – | – |
| Lilley, A.F.A. | 35 | 52 | 8 | 903 | 84 | 20.52 | – | 4 | 70 | 22 | 25 | 23 | 1 | 23.00 | 1-23 | – | – |
| Lillywhite, James | 2 | 3† | 1 | 16 | 10 | 8.00 | – | – | 1 | – | 340‡ | 126 | 8 | 15.75 | 4-70 | – | – |
| Lloyd, D. | 9 | 15† | 2 | 552 | 214* | 42.46 | 1 | 2 | 11 | – | 24‡ | 17 | 0 | – | – | | |
| Loader, P.J. | 13 | 19 | 6 | 76 | 17 | 5.84 | – | – | 2 | – | 2662 | 878 | 39 | 22.51 | 6-36 | 1 | – |
| Lock, G.A.R. | 49 | 63 | 9 | 742 | 89 | 13.74 | – | 3 | 59 | – | 13147‡ | 4451 | 174 | 25.58 | 7-35 | 9 | 3 |
| Lockwood, W.H. | 12 | 16 | 3 | 231 | 52* | 17.76 | – | 1 | 4 | – | 1970 | 884 | 43 | 20.55 | 7-71 | 5 | 1 |
| Lohmann, G.A. | 18 | 26 | 2 | 213 | 62* | 8.87 | – | 1 | 28 | – | 3821 | 1205 | 112 | 10.75 | 9-28 | 9 | 5 |
| Lowson, F.A. | 7 | 13 | 0 | 245 | 68 | 18.84 | – | 2 | 5 | – | | | | | | | |
| Lucas, A.P | 5 | 9 | 1 | 157 | 55 | 19.62 | – | 1 | 1 | – | 120 | 54 | 0 | – | – | | |
| Luckhurst, B.W. | 21 | 41 | 5 | 1298 | 131 | 36.05 | 4 | 5 | 14 | – | 57‡ | 32 | 1 | 32.00 | 1-9 | – | – |
| Lyttelton, Hon. A. | 4 | 7 | 1 | 94 | 31 | 15.66 | – | – | 2 | – | 48 | 19 | 4 | 4.75 | 4-19 | – | – |
| Macaulay, G.G. | 8 | 10 | 4 | 112 | 76 | 18.66 | – | 1 | 5 | – | 1701 | 662 | 24 | 27.58 | 5-64 | 1 | – |
| MacBryan, J.C.W. | 1 | – | – | – | – | – | – | – | – | – | | | | | | | |
| McConnon, J.E. | 2 | 3 | 1 | 18 | 11 | 9.00 | – | – | 4 | – | 216 | 74 | 4 | 18.50 | 3-19 | – | – |
| McGahey, C.P. | 2 | 4 | 0 | 38 | 18 | 9.50 | – | – | 1 | – | | | | | | | |
| MacGregor, G. | 8 | 11 | 3 | 96 | 31 | 12.00 | – | – | 14 | 3 | | | | | | | |
| McIntyre, A.J.W. | 3 | 6 | 0 | 19 | 7 | 3.16 | – | – | 8 | – | | | | | | | |
| Mackinnon, F.A. | 1 | 2 | 0 | 5 | 5 | 2.50 | – | – | – | – | | | | | | | |
| MacLaren, A.C. | 35 | 61 | 4 | 1931 | 140 | 33.87 | 5 | 8 | 29 | – | | | | | | | |
| McMaster, J.E.P. | 1 | 1 | 0 | 0 | 0 | 0.00 | – | – | – | – | | | | | | | |
| Makepeace, W.H.R. | 4 | 8 | 0 | 279 | 117 | 34.87 | 1 | 2 | – | – | | | | | | | |
| Mann, F.G. | 7 | 12 | 2 | 376 | 136* | 37.60 | 1 | 1 | 3 | – | | | | | | | |
| Mann, F.T. | 5 | 9 | 1 | 281 | 84 | 35.12 | – | 2 | 4 | – | | | | | | | |
| Marriott, C.S. | 1 | 1 | 0 | 0 | 0 | 0.00 | – | – | 1 | – | 247 | 96 | 11 | 8.72 | 6-59 | 2 | 1 |

# INDIVIDUAL CAREER RECORDS – continued

ENGLAND – continued

| | Tests | I | NO | Runs | HS | Avge | 100 | 50 | Ct | St | Balls | Runs | Wkts | Avge | BB | 5wI | 10wM |
|---|---|---|---|---|---|---|---|---|---|---|---|---|---|---|---|---|---|
| | | | | BATTING AND FIELDING | | | | | | | BOWLING | | | | | | |
| Martin, F. | 2 | 2† | 0 | 14 | 13 | 7.00 | – | – | 2 | – | 410‡ | 141 | 14 | 10.07 | 6-50 | 2 | 1 |
| Martin, J.W. | 1 | 2 | 0 | 26 | 26 | 13.00 | – | – | – | – | 270 | 129 | 1 | 129.00 | 1-111 | – | – |
| Mason, J.R. | 5 | 10 | 0 | 129 | 32 | 12.90 | – | – | 3 | – | 324 | 149 | 2 | 74.50 | 1-8 | – | – |
| Matthews, A.D.G. | 1 | 1 | 1 | 2 | 2* | – | – | – | 1 | – | 180 | 65 | 2 | 32.50 | 1-13 | – | – |
| May, P.B.H. | 66 | 106 | 9 | 4537 | 285* | 46.77 | 13 | 22 | 42 | – | – | – | – | – | – | – | – |
| Mead, C.P. | 17 | 26† | 2 | 1185 | 182* | 49.37 | 4 | 3 | 4 | – | – | – | – | – | – | – | – |
| Mead, W. | 1 | 2 | 0 | 7 | 7 | 3.50 | – | – | 1 | – | 265 | 91 | 1 | 91.00 | 1-91 | – | – |
| Midwinter, W.E. | 4 | 7 | 0 | 95 | 36 | 13.57 | – | – | 5 | – | 776 | 272 | 10 | 27.20 | 4-81 | – | – |
| Milburn, C. | 9 | 16 | 2 | 654 | 139 | 46.71 | 2 | 2 | 7 | – | – | – | – | – | – | – | – |
| Miller, A.M. | 1 | 2 | 2 | 24 | 20* | – | – | – | – | – | – | – | – | – | – | – | – |
| Miller, G. | 9 | 12 | 1 | 328 | 98* | 29.81 | – | 2 | 5 | – | 1130 | 514 | 11 | 46.72 | 3-99 | – | – |
| Milligan, F.W. | 2 | 4 | 0 | 58 | 38 | 14.50 | – | – | 1 | – | 45 | 29 | 0 | – | – | – | – |
| Millman, G. | 6 | 7 | 2 | 60 | 32* | 12.00 | – | – | 13 | 2 | – | – | – | – | – | – | – |
| Milton, C.A. | 6 | 9 | 1 | 204 | 104* | 25.50 | 1 | – | 5 | – | 24 | 12 | 0 | – | – | – | – |
| Mitchell, A. | 6 | 10 | 0 | 298 | 72 | 29.80 | – | 2 | 9 | – | 6 | 4 | 0 | – | – | – | – |
| Mitchell, F. | 2 | 4 | 0 | 88 | 41 | 22.00 | – | – | 2 | – | – | – | – | – | – | – | – |
| Mitchell, T.B. | 5 | 6 | 2 | 20 | 9 | 5.00 | – | – | 1 | – | 894 | 498 | 8 | 62.25 | 2-49 | – | – |
| Mitchell-Innes, N.S. | 1 | 1 | 0 | 5 | 5 | 5.00 | – | – | – | – | – | – | – | – | – | – | – |
| Mold, A. | 3 | 3 | 1 | 0 | 0* | 0.00 | – | – | 1 | – | 491 | 234 | 7 | 33.42 | 3-44 | – | – |
| Moon, L.J. | 4 | 8 | 0 | 182 | 36 | 22.75 | – | – | 4 | – | – | – | – | – | – | – | – |
| Morley, F. | 4 | 6† | 2 | 6 | 2* | 1.50 | – | – | 4 | – | 972‡ | 296 | 16 | 18.50 | 5-56 | 1 | – |
| Mortimore, J.B. | 9 | 12 | 2 | 243 | 73* | 24.30 | – | 1 | 3 | – | 2162 | 733 | 13 | 56.38 | 3-36 | – | – |
| Moss, A.E. | 9 | 7 | 1 | 61 | 26 | 10.16 | – | – | 1 | – | 1657 | 626 | 21 | 29.80 | 4-35 | – | – |
| Murdoch, W.L. | 1 | 1 | 0 | 12 | 12 | 12.00 | – | – | 1 | 1 | – | – | – | – | – | – | – |
| Murray, J.T. | 21 | 28 | 5 | 506 | 112 | 22.00 | 1 | 2 | 52 | 3 | – | – | – | – | – | – | – |
| Newham, W. | 1 | 2 | 0 | 26 | 17 | 13.00 | – | – | – | – | – | – | – | – | – | – | – |
| Nichols, M.S. | 14 | 19† | 7 | 355 | 78* | 29.58 | – | 2 | 11 | – | 2565 | 1152 | 41 | 28.09 | 6-35 | 2 | – |
| Oakman, A.S.M. | 2 | 2 | 0 | 14 | 10 | 7.00 | – | – | 7 | – | 48 | 21 | 0 | – | – | – | – |
| O'Brien, T.C. | 5 | 8 | 0 | 59 | 20 | 7.37 | – | – | 4 | – | – | – | – | – | – | – | – |
| O'Connor, J. | 4 | 7 | 0 | 153 | 51 | 21.85 | – | 1 | 2 | – | 162 | 72 | 1 | 72.00 | 1-31 | – | – |
| Old, C.M. | 36 | 54† | 6 | 701 | 65 | 14.60 | – | 2 | 21 | – | 6704 | 3263 | 111 | 29.39 | 6-54 | 3 | – |
| Oldfield, N. | 1 | 2 | 0 | 99 | 80 | 49.50 | – | 1 | – | – | – | – | – | – | – | – | – |
| Padgett, D.E.V. | 2 | 4 | 0 | 51 | 31 | 12.75 | – | – | – | – | 12 | 8 | 0 | – | – | – | – |
| Paine, G.A.E. | 4 | 7 | 1 | 97 | 49 | 16.16 | – | – | 5 | – | 1044‡ | 467 | 17 | 27.47 | 5-168 | 1 | – |
| Palairet, L.C.H. | 2 | 4 | 0 | 49 | 20 | 12.25 | – | – | 2 | – | – | – | – | – | – | – | – |
| Palmer, C.H. | 1 | 2 | 0 | 22 | 22 | 11.00 | – | – | – | – | 30 | 15 | 0 | – | – | – | – |
| Palmer, K.E. | 1 | 1 | 0 | 10 | 10 | 10.00 | – | – | – | – | 378 | 189 | 1 | 189.00 | 1-113 | – | – |

# Individual Career Records – *continued*

| | | | | BATTING AND FIELDING | | | | | | | BOWLING | | | | | | |
|---|---|---|---|---|---|---|---|---|---|---|---|---|---|---|---|---|---|
| | Tests | I | NO | Runs | HS | Avge | 100 | 50 | Ct | St | Balls | Runs | Wkts | Avge | BB | 5wI | 10wM |
| Parfitt, P.H. | 37 | 52† | 6 | 1882 | 131* | 40.91 | 7 | 6 | 42 | – | 1326 | 574 | 12 | 47.83 | 2-5 | – | – |
| Parker, C.W.L. | 1 | 1 | 1 | 3 | 3* | – | – | – | – | – | 168‡ | 32 | 2 | 16.00 | 2-32 | – | – |
| Parkhouse, W.G.A. | 7 | 13 | 0 | 373 | 78 | 28.69 | – | 2 | 3 | – | | | | | | | |
| Parkin, C.H. | 10 | 16 | 3 | 160 | 36 | 12.30 | – | – | 3 | – | 2095 | 1128 | 32 | 35.25 | 5-38 | 2 | – |
| Parks, J.H. | 1 | 2 | 0 | 29 | 22 | 14.50 | – | – | – | – | 126 | 36 | 3 | 12.00 | 2-26 | – | – |
| Parks, J.M. | 46 | 68 | 7 | 1962 | 108* | 32.16 | 2 | 9 | 103 | 11 | 54 | 51 | 1 | 51.00 | 1-43 | – | – |
| Pataudi, Nawab of, sr | 3 | 5 | 0 | 144 | 102 | 28.80 | 1 | – | – | – | | | | | | | |
| Paynter, E. | 20 | 31† | 5 | 1540 | 243 | 59.23 | 4 | 7 | 7 | – | | | | | | | |
| Peate, E. | 9 | 14† | 8 | 70 | 13 | 11.66 | – | – | 2 | – | 2096‡ | 682 | 31 | 22.00 | 6-85 | 2 | – |
| Peebles, I.A.R. | 13 | 17 | 8 | 98 | 26 | 10.88 | – | – | 5 | – | 2882 | 1391 | 45 | 30.91 | 6-63 | 3 | – |
| Peel, R. | 20 | 33† | 4 | 427 | 83 | 14.72 | – | 3 | 17 | – | 5216‡ | 1715 | 102 | 16.81 | 7-31 | 6 | 2 |
| Penn, F. | 1 | 2 | 1 | 50 | 27* | 50.00 | – | – | 1 | – | 12 | 2 | 0 | – | – | – | – |
| Perks, R.T.D. | 2 | 2† | 2 | 3 | 2* | – | – | – | 8 | – | 829 | 355 | 11 | 32.27 | 5-100 | 2 | – |
| Philipson, H. | 5 | 8 | 1 | 63 | 30 | 9.00 | – | – | – | 3 | | | | | | | |
| Pilling, R. | 8 | 13 | 1 | 91 | 23 | 7.58 | – | – | 10 | 4 | | | | | | | |
| Place, W. | 3 | 6 | 1 | 144 | 107 | 28.80 | 1 | – | – | – | | | | | | | |
| Pocock, P.I. | 17 | 27 | 2 | 165 | 33 | 6.60 | – | – | 13 | – | 4482 | 2023 | 47 | 43.04 | 6-79 | 3 | – |
| Pollard, R. | 4 | 3 | 2 | 13 | 10* | 13.00 | – | – | 3 | – | 1102 | 378 | 15 | 25.20 | 5-24 | 1 | – |
| Poole, C.J. | 3 | 5† | 1 | 161 | 69* | 40.25 | – | 2 | 1 | – | 30‡ | 9 | 0 | – | – | – | – |
| Pope, G.H. | 1 | 1 | 1 | 8 | 8* | – | – | – | – | – | 218 | 85 | 1 | 85.00 | 1-49 | – | – |
| Pougher, A.D. | 1 | 1 | 0 | 17 | 17 | 17.00 | – | – | 2 | – | 105 | 26 | 3 | 8.66 | 3-26 | – | – |
| Price, J.S.E. | 15 | 15† | 6 | 66 | 32 | 7.33 | – | – | 7 | – | 2724 | 1401 | 40 | 35.02 | 5-73 | 1 | – |
| Price, W.F.F. | 1 | 2 | 0 | 6 | 6 | 3.00 | – | – | 2 | – | | | | | | | |
| Prideaux, R.M. | 3 | 6 | 0 | 102 | 64 | 20.40 | – | 1 | 2 | – | 12 | 0 | 0 | – | – | – | – |
| Pullar, G. | 28 | 49† | 4 | 1974 | 175 | 43.86 | 4 | 12 | 2 | – | 66 | 37 | 1 | 37.00 | 1-1 | – | – |
| Quaife, W.G. | 7 | 13 | 1 | 228 | 68 | 19.00 | – | 1 | 4 | – | 15 | 6 | 0 | – | – | – | – |
| Radley, C.T. | 2 | 2 | 0 | 173 | 158 | 86.50 | 1 | – | – | – | | | | | | | |
| Randall, D.W. | 16 | 26 | 2 | 631 | 174 | 26.29 | 1 | 3 | 9 | – | 16 | 3 | 0 | – | | | |
| Ranjitsinhji, K.S. | 15 | 26 | 4 | 989 | 175 | 44.95 | 2 | 6 | 13 | – | 97 | 39 | 1 | 39.00 | 1-23 | – | – |
| Read, H.D. | 1 | – | – | – | – | – | – | – | – | – | 270 | 200 | 6 | 33.33 | 4-136 | – | – |
| Read, J.M. | 17 | 29 | 2 | 463 | 57 | 17.14 | – | 2 | 8 | – | 60 | 63 | 0 | – | – | – | – |
| Read, W.W. | 18 | 27 | 1 | 720 | 117 | 27.69 | 1 | 5 | 16 | – | 1764 | 624 | 25 | 24.96 | 5-85 | 1 | – |
| Relf, A.E. | 13 | 21 | 3 | 416 | 63 | 23.11 | – | 1 | 14 | – | 449 | 244 | 9 | 27.11 | 4-50 | – | – |
| Rhodes, H.J. | 2 | 1 | 1 | 0 | 0* | – | – | – | – | – | | | | | | | |
| Rhodes, W. | 58 | 98 | 21 | 2325 | 179 | 30.19 | 2 | 11 | 60 | – | 8231‡ | 3425 | 127 | 26.96 | 8-68 | 6 | 1 |
| Richardson, D.W. | 1 | 1† | 0 | 33 | 33 | 33.00 | – | – | 1 | – | | | | | | | |
| Richardson, P.E. | 34 | 56† | 1 | 2061 | 126 | 37.47 | 5 | 9 | 6 | – | 120 | 48 | 3 | 16.00 | 2-10 | – | – |
| Richardson, T. | 14 | 24 | 8 | 177 | 25* | 11.06 | – | – | 5 | – | 4497 | 2220 | 88 | 25.22 | 8-94 | 11 | 4 |

# INDIVIDUAL CAREER RECORDS – continued

ENGLAND – continued

| | | | | BATTING AND FIELDING | | | | | | | BOWLING | | | | | | |
| | Tests | I | NO | Runs | HS | Avge | 100 | 50 | Ct | St | Balls | Runs | Wkts | Avge | BB | 5wI | 10wM |
|---|---|---|---|---|---|---|---|---|---|---|---|---|---|---|---|---|---|
| Richmond, T.L. | 1 | 2 | 0 | 6 | 4 | 3.00 | – | – | – | – | 114 | 86 | 2 | 43.00 | 2-69 | – | – |
| Ridgway, F. | 5 | 6 | 0 | 49 | 24 | 8.16 | – | – | 3 | – | 793 | 379 | 7 | 54.14 | 4-83 | – | – |
| Robertson, J.D.B. | 11 | 21 | 2 | 881 | 133 | 46.36 | 2 | 6 | 6 | – | 138 | 58 | 2 | 29.00 | 2-17 | 1 | – |
| Robins, R.W.V. | 19 | 27 | 4 | 612 | 108 | 26.60 | 1 | 4 | 12 | – | 3318 | 1758 | 64 | 27.46 | 6-32 | – | – |
| Roope, G.R.J. | 17 | 27 | 3 | 724 | 77 | 30.16 | – | 6 | 29 | – | 172 | 76 | 0 | – | – | – | – |
| Root, C.F. | 3 | – | – | – | – | – | – | – | 1 | – | 642 | 194 | 8 | 24.25 | 4-84 | – | – |
| Rose, B.C. | 5 | 8† | 1 | 100 | 27 | 14.28 | – | – | 2 | – | – | – | – | – | – | – | – |
| Royle, V.P.F.A. | 1 | 2 | 0 | 21 | 18 | 10.50 | – | – | 2 | – | 16 | 6 | 0 | – | – | – | – |
| Rumsey, F.E. | 5 | 5 | 3 | 30 | 21* | 15.00 | – | – | 2 | – | 1145‡ | 461 | 17 | 27.11 | 4-25 | – | – |
| Russell, C.A.G. | 10 | 18 | 2 | 910 | 140 | 56.87 | 5 | 2 | 8 | – | – | – | – | – | – | – | – |
| Russell, W.E. | 10 | 18 | 1 | 362 | 70 | 21.29 | – | 2 | 4 | – | 144 | 44 | 0 | – | – | – | – |
| Sandham, A. | 14 | 23 | 0 | 879 | 325 | 38.21 | 2 | 3 | 4 | – | – | – | – | – | – | – | – |
| Schultz, S.S. | 1 | 2 | 1 | 20 | 20 | 20.00 | – | – | – | – | 35 | 26 | 1 | 26.00 | 1-16 | – | – |
| Scotton, W.H. | 15 | 25† | 2 | 510 | 90 | 22.17 | – | 3 | 4 | – | 20‡ | 20 | 0 | – | – | – | – |
| Selby, J. | 6 | 12 | 1 | 256 | 70 | 23.27 | – | 2 | 1 | – | – | – | – | – | – | – | – |
| Selvey, M.W.W. | 3 | 5 | 3 | 15 | 5* | 7.50 | – | – | 1 | – | 492 | 343 | 6 | 57.16 | 4-41 | – | – |
| Shackleton, D. | 7 | 13 | 7 | 113 | 42 | 18.83 | – | – | 1 | – | 2078 | 768 | 18 | 42.66 | 4-72 | – | – |
| Sharp, J. | 3 | 6 | 2 | 188 | 105 | 47.00 | 1 | 1 | 1 | – | 183 | 111 | 3 | 37.00 | 3-67 | – | – |
| Sharpe, J.W. | 3 | 6 | 4 | 44 | 26 | 22.00 | – | – | 2 | – | 975 | 305 | 11 | 27.72 | 6-84 | 1 | – |
| Sharpe, P.J. | 12 | 21 | 4 | 786 | 111 | 46.23 | 1 | 4 | 17 | – | – | – | – | – | – | – | – |
| Shaw, A. | 7 | 12 | 1 | 111 | 40 | 10.09 | – | – | 4 | – | 1099 | 285 | 12 | 23.75 | 5-38 | 1 | – |
| Sheppard, Rev. D.S. | 22 | 33 | 2 | 1172 | 119 | 37.80 | 3 | 6 | 12 | – | – | – | – | – | – | – | – |
| Sherwin, M. | 3 | 6 | 4 | 30 | 21* | 15.00 | – | – | 5 | 2 | – | – | – | – | – | – | – |
| Shrewsbury, A. | 23 | 40 | 4 | 1277 | 164 | 35.47 | 3 | 4 | 29 | – | 12 | 2 | 0 | – | – | – | – |
| Shuter, J. | 1 | 1 | 0 | 28 | 28 | 28.00 | – | – | 1 | – | – | – | – | – | – | – | – |
| Shuttleworth, K. | 5 | 6 | 0 | 46 | 21 | 7.66 | – | – | 1 | – | 1071 | 427 | 12 | 35.58 | 5-47 | 1 | – |
| Simpson, R.T. | 27 | 45 | 3 | 1401 | 156* | 33.35 | 4 | 6 | 5 | – | 45 | 22 | 2 | 11.00 | 2-4 | – | – |
| Simpson-Hayward, G.H.T. | 5 | 8 | 1 | 105 | 29* | 15.00 | – | – | 1 | – | 898 | 420 | 23 | 18.26 | 6-46 | 2 | – |
| Sims, J.M. | 4 | 4 | 0 | 16 | 12 | 4.00 | – | – | 6 | – | 887 | 480 | 11 | 43.63 | 5-73 | 1 | – |
| Sinfield, R.A. | 1 | 1† | 0 | 6 | 6 | 6.00 | – | – | – | – | 378 | 123 | 2 | 61.50 | 1-51 | – | – |
| Smailes, T.F. | 1 | 1 | 0 | 25 | 25 | 25.00 | – | – | 1 | – | 120 | 62 | 3 | 20.66 | 3-44 | – | – |
| Smith, A.C. | 6 | 7 | 3 | 118 | 69* | 29.50 | – | 1 | 20 | – | – | – | – | – | – | – | – |
| Smith, C.A. | 1 | 1 | 0 | 3 | 3 | 3.00 | – | – | 1 | – | 154 | 61 | 7 | 8.71 | 5-19 | 1 | – |
| Smith, C.I.J. | 5 | 10 | 0 | 102 | 27 | 10.20 | – | – | 1 | – | 930 | 393 | 15 | 26.20 | 5-16 | 1 | – |
| Smith, D. | 2 | 4† | 0 | 128 | 57 | 32.00 | – | 1 | 1 | – | – | – | – | – | – | – | – |
| Smith, D.R. | 5 | 5 | 1 | 38 | 34 | 9.50 | – | – | 2 | – | 972 | 359 | 6 | 59.83 | 2-60 | – | – |
| Smith, D.V. | 3 | 4† | 1 | 25 | 16* | 8.33 | – | – | – | – | 270‡ | 97 | 1 | 97.00 | 1-12 | – | – |
| Smith, E.J. | 11 | 14 | 1 | 113 | 22 | 8.69 | – | – | 17 | 3 | – | – | – | – | – | – | – |
| Smith, H. | 1 | 1 | 0 | 7 | 7 | 7.00 | – | – | 1 | – | – | – | – | – | – | – | – |

# INDIVIDUAL CAREER RECORDS – continued

ENGLAND – continued

| | | | | BATTING AND FIELDING | | | | | | | BOWLING | | | | | | |
|---|---|---|---|---|---|---|---|---|---|---|---|---|---|---|---|---|---|
| | Tests | I | NO | Runs | HS | Avge | 100 | 50 | Ct | St | Balls | Runs | Wkts | Avge | BB | 5wI | 10wM |
| Smith, M.J.K. | 50 | 78 | 6 | 2278 | 121 | 31.63 | 3 | 11 | 53 | — | 214 | 128 | 1 | 128.00 | 1-10 | — | — |
| Smith, T.P.B. | 4 | 5 | 0 | 33 | 24 | 6.60 | — | — | 1 | — | 538 | 319 | 3 | 106.33 | 2-172 | — | — |
| Smithson, G.A. | 2 | 3† | 0 | 70 | 35 | 23.33 | — | — | — | — | — | — | — | — | — | — | — |
| Snow, J.A. | 49 | 71 | 14 | 772 | 73 | 13.54 | — | 2 | 16 | — | 12021 | 5387 | 202 | 26.66 | 7-40 | 8 | 1 |
| Southerton, J. | 2 | 3 | 1 | 7 | 6 | 3.50 | — | — | 2 | — | 263 | 107 | 7 | 15.28 | 4-46 | — | — |
| Spooner, R.H. | 10 | 15 | 0 | 481 | 119 | 32.06 | 1 | 4 | 4 | 2 | — | — | — | — | — | — | — |
| Spooner, R.T. | 7 | 14† | 1 | 354 | 92 | 27.23 | — | 3 | 10 | 2 | — | — | — | — | — | — | — |
| Stanyforth, R.T. | 4 | 6† | 1 | 13 | 6* | 2.60 | — | — | 7 | 2 | — | — | — | — | — | — | — |
| Staples, S.J. | 3 | 5 | 0 | 65 | 39 | 13.00 | — | — | — | — | 1149 | 435 | 15 | 29.00 | 3-50 | — | — |
| Statham, J.B. | 70 | 87† | 28 | 675 | 38 | 11.44 | — | — | 28 | — | 16056 | 6261 | 252 | 24.84 | 7-39 | 9 | 1 |
| Steel, A.G. | 13 | 20 | 3 | 600 | 148 | 35.29 | 2 | — | 5 | — | 1364 | 605 | 29 | 20.86 | 3-27 | — | — |
| Steele, D.S. | 8 | 16 | 0 | 673 | 106 | 42.06 | 1 | 5 | 7 | — | 88‡ | 39 | 2 | 19.50 | 1-1 | — | — |
| Stevens, G.T.S. | 10 | 17 | 1 | 263 | 69 | 15.47 | — | 1 | 9 | — | 1186 | 648 | 20 | 32.40 | 5-90 | 2 | 1 |
| Stewart, M.J. | 8 | 12 | 1 | 385 | 87 | 35.00 | — | 2 | 6 | — | — | — | — | — | — | — | — |
| Stoddart, A.E. | 16 | 30 | 2 | 996 | 173 | 35.57 | 2 | 3 | 6 | — | 162 | 94 | 2 | 47.00 | 1-10 | — | — |
| Storer, W. | 6 | 11 | 0 | 215 | 51 | 19.54 | — | 1 | 11 | 1 | 168 | 108 | 2 | 54.00 | 1-24 | — | — |
| Street, G.B. | 1 | 2 | 1 | 11 | 7* | 11.00 | — | — | — | 1 | — | — | — | — | — | — | — |
| Strudwick, H. | 28 | 42 | 13 | 230 | 24 | 7.93 | — | — | 60 | 12 | — | — | — | — | — | — | — |
| Studd, C.T. | 5 | 9 | 1 | 160 | 48 | 20.00 | — | — | 5 | — | 384 | 98 | 3 | 32.66 | 2-35 | — | — |
| Studd, G.B. | 4 | 7 | 0 | 31 | 9 | 4.42 | — | — | 8 | — | — | — | — | — | — | — | — |
| Subba Row, R. | 13 | 22† | 1 | 984 | 137 | 46.85 | 3 | 4 | 5 | — | 6 | 2 | 0 | — | — | — | — |
| Sugg, F.H. | 2 | 2 | 0 | 55 | 31 | 27.50 | — | — | — | — | — | — | — | — | — | — | — |
| Sutcliffe, H. | 54 | 84 | 9 | 4555 | 194 | 60.73 | 16 | 23 | 23 | — | — | — | — | — | — | — | — |
| Swetman, R. | 11 | 17 | 2 | 254 | 65 | 16.93 | — | 1 | 24 | 2 | — | — | — | — | — | — | — |
| Tate, F.W. | 1 | 2 | 1 | 9 | 5* | 9.00 | — | — | 2 | — | 96 | 51 | 2 | 25.50 | 2-7 | — | — |
| Tate, M.W. | 39 | 52 | 5 | 1198 | 100* | 25.48 | 1 | 5 | 11 | — | 12523 | 4055 | 155 | 26.16 | 6-42 | 7 | 1 |
| Tattersall, R. | 16 | 17† | 7 | 50 | 10* | 5.00 | — | — | 8 | — | 4228 | 1513 | 58 | 26.08 | 7-52 | 4 | 1 |
| Taylor, K. | 3 | 5 | 0 | 57 | 24 | 11.40 | — | — | 1 | — | 12 | 6 | 0 | — | — | — | — |
| Taylor, R.W. | 7 | 9 | 1 | 159 | 45 | 19.87 | — | — | 16 | 2 | — | — | — | — | — | — | — |
| Tennyson, Hon. L.H. | 9 | 12 | 1 | 345 | 74* | 31.36 | — | 4 | 6 | — | 6 | 1 | 0 | — | — | — | — |
| Thompson, G.J. | 6 | 10 | 1 | 273 | 63 | 30.33 | — | 2 | 5 | — | 1367 | 638 | 23 | 27.73 | 4-50 | — | — |
| Thomson, N.I. | 5 | 4 | 1 | 69 | 39 | 23.00 | — | — | 3 | — | 1488 | 568 | 9 | 63.11 | 2-55 | — | — |
| Titmus, F.J. | 53 | 76 | 11 | 1449 | 84* | 22.29 | — | 10 | 35 | — | 15118 | 4931 | 153 | 32.22 | 7-79 | 7 | — |
| Tolchard, R.W. | 4 | 7 | 2 | 129 | 67 | 25.80 | — | 1 | 5 | — | — | — | — | — | — | — | — |
| Townsend, C.L. | 2 | 3† | 0 | 51 | 38 | 17.00 | — | — | 1 | — | 140 | 75 | 3 | 25.00 | 3-50 | — | — |
| Townsend, D.C.H. | 3 | 6 | 0 | 77 | 36 | 12.83 | — | — | 1 | — | 6 | 9 | 0 | — | — | — | — |
| Townsend, L.F. | 4 | 6 | 0 | 97 | 40 | 16.16 | — | — | 2 | — | 399 | 205 | 6 | 34.16 | 2-22 | — | — |
| Tremlett, M.F. | 3 | 5 | 2 | 20 | 18* | 6.66 | — | — | — | — | 492 | 226 | 4 | 56.50 | 2-98 | — | — |
| Trott, A.E. | 2 | 4 | 0 | 23 | 16 | 5.75 | — | — | — | — | 474 | 198 | 17 | 11.64 | 5-49 | 1 | — |

# INDIVIDUAL CAREER RECORDS – continued

ENGLAND – continued

| | | | | BATTING AND FIELDING | | | | | | | | | BOWLING | | | | |
|---|---|---|---|---|---|---|---|---|---|---|---|---|---|---|---|---|---|
| | Tests | I | NO | Runs | HS | Avge | 100 | 50 | Ct | St | Balls | Runs | Wkts | Avge | BB | 5wI | 10wM |
| Trueman, F.S. | 67 | 85 | 14 | 981 | 39* | 13.81 | – | – | 64 | – | 15178 | 6625 | 307 | 21.57 | 8-31 | 17 | 3 |
| Tufnell, N.C. | 1 | 1 | 0 | 14 | 14 | 14.00 | – | – | 1 | 1 | – | – | – | – | – | – | – |
| Turnbull, M.J.L. | 9 | 13 | 2 | 224 | 61 | 20.36 | – | 1 | 1 | – | – | – | – | – | – | – | – |
| Tyldesley, E. | 14 | 20 | 2 | 990 | 122 | 55.00 | 3 | 6 | 2 | – | 3 | 2 | 0 | – | – | – | – |
| Tyldesley, J.T. | 31 | 55 | 1 | 1661 | 138 | 30.75 | 4 | 9 | 16 | – | – | – | – | – | – | – | – |
| Tyldesley, R.K. | 7 | 7 | 1 | 47 | 29 | 7.83 | – | – | 1 | – | 1615 | 619 | 19 | 32.57 | 3-50 | – | – |
| Tylecote, E.F.S. | 6 | 9 | 1 | 152 | 66 | 19.00 | – | 1 | 5 | 5 | – | – | – | – | – | – | – |
| Tyler, E.J. | 1 | 1† | 0 | 0 | 0 | 0.00 | – | – | – | – | 145‡ | 65 | 4 | 16.25 | 3-49 | – | – |
| Tyson, F.H. | 17 | 24 | 3 | 230 | 37* | 10.95 | – | – | 4 | – | 3452 | 1411 | 76 | 18.56 | 7-27 | 4 | 1 |
| Ulyett, G. | 25 | 39 | 0 | 949 | 149 | 24.33 | 1 | 7 | 18 | – | 2627 | 1020 | 50 | 20.40 | 7-36 | 1 | – |
| Underwood, D.L. | 74 | 100 | 31 | 824 | 45* | 11.94 | – | – | 39 | – | 18979‡ | 6600 | 265 | 24.90 | 8-51 | 16 | 6 |
| Valentine, B.H. | 7 | 9 | 2 | 454 | 136 | 64.85 | 2 | 1 | 2 | – | – | – | – | – | – | – | – |
| Verity, H. | 40 | 44 | 12 | 669 | 66* | 20.90 | – | 3 | 30 | – | 11173‡ | 3510 | 144 | 24.37 | 8-43 | 5 | 2 |
| Vernon, G.F. | 1 | 2 | 1 | 14 | 11* | 14.00 | – | – | – | – | – | – | – | – | – | – | – |
| Vine, J. | 2 | 3 | 2 | 46 | 36 | 46.00 | – | – | – | – | – | – | – | – | – | – | – |
| Voce, W. | 27 | 38 | 15 | 308 | 66 | 13.39 | – | 1 | 15 | – | 6360‡ | 2733 | 98 | 27.88 | 7-70 | 3 | 2 |
| Waddington, A. | 2 | 4 | 0 | 16 | 7 | 4.00 | – | – | 1 | – | 276‡ | 119 | 1 | 119.00 | 1-35 | – | – |
| Wainwright, E. | 5 | 9 | 0 | 132 | 49 | 14.66 | – | – | 2 | – | 127 | 73 | 0 | – | – | – | – |
| Walker, P.M. | 3 | 4 | 0 | 128 | 52 | 32.00 | – | 1 | 5 | – | 78‡ | 34 | 0 | – | – | – | – |
| Walters, C.F. | 11 | 18 | 3 | 784 | 102 | 52.26 | 1 | 7 | 6 | – | – | – | – | – | – | – | – |
| Ward, Alan | 5 | 6 | 1 | 40 | 21 | 8.00 | – | – | 3 | – | 761 | 453 | 14 | 32.35 | 4-61 | – | – |
| Ward, Albert | 7 | 13 | 0 | 487 | 117 | 37.46 | 1 | 3 | 1 | – | – | – | – | – | – | – | – |
| Wardle, J.H. | 28 | 41† | 8 | 653 | 66 | 19.78 | – | 2 | 12 | – | 6597‡ | 2080 | 102 | 20.39 | 7-36 | 5 | 1 |
| Warner, P.F. | 15 | 28 | 2 | 622 | 132* | 23.92 | 1 | 3 | 3 | – | – | – | – | – | – | – | – |
| Warr, J.J. | 2 | 4 | 0 | 4 | 4 | 1.00 | – | – | 1 | – | 584 | 281 | 1 | 281.00 | 1-76 | – | – |
| Warren, A.R. | 1 | 1 | 0 | 7 | 7 | 7.00 | – | – | 1 | – | 236 | 113 | 6 | 18.83 | 5-57 | 1 | – |
| Washbrook, C. | 37 | 66 | 6 | 2569 | 195 | 42.81 | 6 | 12 | 12 | – | 36 | 33 | 1 | 33.00 | 1-25 | – | – |
| Watkins, A.J. | 15 | 24† | 4 | 810 | 137* | 40.50 | 2 | 4 | 17 | – | 1364‡ | 554 | 11 | 50.36 | 3-20 | – | – |
| Watson, W. | 23 | 37† | 3 | 879 | 116 | 25.85 | 2 | 3 | 8 | – | – | – | – | – | – | – | – |
| Webbe, A.J. | 1 | 2 | 0 | 4 | 4 | 2.00 | – | – | 2 | – | – | – | – | – | – | – | – |
| Wellard, A.W. | 2 | 4 | 0 | 47 | 38 | 11.75 | – | – | 2 | – | 456 | 237 | 7 | 33.85 | 4-81 | – | – |
| Wharton, A. | 1 | 2† | 0 | 20 | 13 | 10.00 | – | – | – | – | – | – | – | – | – | – | – |
| White, D.W. | 2 | 2† | 0 | 0 | 0 | 0.00 | – | – | – | – | 220 | 119 | 4 | 29.75 | 3-65 | – | – |
| White, J.C. | 15 | 22 | 9 | 239 | 29 | 18.38 | – | – | 6 | – | 4801‡ | 1581 | 49 | 32.26 | 8-126 | 3 | 1 |
| Whysall, W.W. | 4 | 7 | 0 | 209 | 76 | 29.85 | – | 2 | 7 | – | 16 | 9 | 0 | – | – | – | – |
| Wilkinson, L.L. | 3 | 2 | 1 | 3 | 2 | 3.00 | – | – | – | – | 573 | 271 | 7 | 38.71 | 2-12 | – | – |
| Willey, P. | 2 | 4 | 0 | 115 | 45 | 28.75 | – | – | – | – | 24 | 15 | 0 | – | – | – | – |

# INDIVIDUAL CAREER RECORDS – continued

ENGLAND – continued

| | Tests | I | NO | Runs | HS | Avge | 100 | 50 | Ct | St | Balls | Runs | Wkts | Avge | BB | 5wI | 10wM |
|---|---|---|---|---|---|---|---|---|---|---|---|---|---|---|---|---|---|
| | | | | *BATTING AND FIELDING* | | | | | | | | | *BOWLING* | | | | |
| Willis, R.G.D. | 35 | 52 | 28 | 299 | 24* | 12.45 | — | — | 18 | — | 6759 | 3191 | 126 | 25.32 | 7-78 | 8 | – |
| Wilson, C.E.M. | 2 | 4 | -1 | 42 | 18 | 14.00 | – | – | 1 | – | 1472‡ | 466 | 11 | 42.36 | 2-17 | – | – |
| Wilson, D. | 6 | 7† | 1 | 75 | 42 | 12.50 | – | – | 1 | 1 | 123 | 36 | 3 | 12.00 | 2-28 | – | – |
| Wilson, E.R. | 1 | 2 | 0 | 10 | 5 | 5.00 | – | – | – | 1 | | | | | | | |
| Wood, A. | 4 | 5 | 1 | 80 | 53 | 20.00 | – | 1 | 10 | 1 | 80 | 48 | 0 | – | – | | |
| Wood, B. | 11 | 20 | 0 | 440 | 90 | 22.00 | – | 2 | 6 | – | – | | | | | | |
| Wood, G.E.C. | 3 | 2 | 0 | 7 | 6 | 3.50 | – | – | 5 | 1 | | | | | | | |
| Wood, H. | 4 | 4 | 1 | 204 | 134* | 68.00 | 1 | 1 | 2 | 1 | – | | | | | | |
| Wood, R. | 1 | 2† | 0 | 6 | 6 | 3.00 | – | – | – | – | | | | | | | |
| Woods, S.M.J. | 3 | 4 | 0 | 122 | 53 | 30.50 | – | 1 | 4 | – | 195 | 129 | 5 | 25.80 | 3-28 | – | – |
| Woolley, F.E. | 64 | 98† | 7 | 3283 | 154 | 36.07 | 5 | 23 | 64 | – | 6495‡ | 2815 | 83 | 33.91 | 7-76 | 4 | 1 |
| Woolmer, R.A. | 15 | 26 | 1 | 920 | 149 | 36.80 | 3 | 2 | 8 | – | 546 | 299 | 4 | 74.75 | 1-8 | – | – |
| Worthington, T.S. | 9 | 11 | 0 | 321 | 128 | 29.18 | 1 | 1 | 8 | – | 633 | 316 | 8 | 39.50 | 2-19 | – | – |
| Wright, C.W. | 3 | 4 | 0 | 125 | 71 | 31.25 | – | 1 | – | – | | | | | | | |
| Wright, D.V.P. | 34 | 39 | 13 | 289 | 45 | 11.11 | – | – | 10 | – | 8135 | 4224 | 108 | 39.11 | 7-105 | 6 | 1 |
| Wyatt, R.E.S. | 40 | 64 | 6 | 1839 | 149 | 31.70 | 2 | 12 | 16 | – | 1395 | 642 | 18 | 35.66 | 3-4 | – | – |
| Wynyard, E.G. | 3 | 6 | 0 | 72 | 30 | 12.00 | – | – | – | – | 24 | 17 | 0 | – | – | – | – |
| Yardley, N.W.D. | 20 | 34 | 2 | 812 | 99 | 25.37 | – | 4 | 14 | – | 1662 | 707 | 21 | 33.66 | 3-67 | – | – |
| Young, H.I. | 2 | 2 | 0 | 43 | 43 | 21.50 | – | – | 1 | – | 556‡ | 262 | 12 | 21.83 | 4-30 | – | – |
| Young, J.A. | 8 | 10 | 5 | 28 | 10* | 5.60 | – | – | 5 | – | 2368‡ | 757 | 17 | 44.52 | 3-65 | – | – |
| Young, R.A. | 2 | 4 | 0 | 27 | 13 | 6.75 | – | – | 6 | – | | | | | | | |
| Substitutes | – | – | – | – | – | – | – | – | 59 | 1 | – | | | | | | |
| AUSTRALIA (296 players) | | | | | | | | | | | | | | | | | |
| A'Beckett, E.L. | 4 | 7 | 0 | 143 | 41 | 20.42 | – | – | 4 | – | 1062 | 317 | 3 | 105.66 | 1-41 | – | – |
| Alexander, G. | 2 | 4 | 0 | 52 | 33 | 13.00 | – | – | 2 | – | 168 | 93 | 2 | 46.50 | 2-69 | – | – |
| Alexander, H.H. | 1 | 2 | 1 | 17 | 17* | 17.00 | – | – | – | – | 276 | 154 | 1 | 154.00 | 1-129 | – | – |
| Allan, F.E. | 1 | 1† | 0 | 5 | 5 | 5.00 | – | – | – | – | 180‡ | 80 | 4 | 20.00 | 2-30 | – | – |
| Allan, P.J. | 1 | – | – | – | – | – | – | – | – | – | 192 | 83 | 2 | 41.50 | 2-58 | – | – |
| Allen, R.C. | 1 | 2 | 0 | 44 | 30 | 22.00 | – | – | 2 | – | – | | | | | | |
| Andrews, T.J.E. | 16 | 23 | 1 | 592 | 94 | 26.90 | – | 4 | 12 | – | 156 | 116 | 1 | 116.00 | 1-23 | – | – |
| Archer, K.A. | 5 | 9 | 0 | 234 | 48 | 26.00 | – | – | – | – | | | | | | | |
| Archer, R.G. | 19 | 30 | 1 | 713 | 128 | 24.58 | 1 | 2 | 20 | – | 3576 | 1318 | 48 | 27.45 | 5-53 | 1 | – |
| Armstrong, W.W. | 50 | 84 | 10 | 2863 | 159* | 38.68 | 6 | 8 | 44 | – | 8022 | 2923 | 87 | 33.59 | 6-35 | 3 | – |

AUSTRALIA – *continued*

| | Tests | I | NO | Runs | HS | Avge | 100 | 50 | Ct | St | Balls | Runs | Wkts | Avge | BB | 5wI | 10wM |
|---|---|---|---|---|---|---|---|---|---|---|---|---|---|---|---|---|---|
| | | | | | | *BATTING AND FIELDING* | | | | | | | | *BOWLING* | | | |
| Badcock, C.L. | 7 | 12 | 1 | 160 | 118 | 14.54 | 1 | – | 3 | – | 292 | 163 | 4 | 40.75 | 3-111 | – | – |
| Bannerman, A.C. | 28 | 50 | 2 | 1108 | 94 | 23.08 | – | 8 | 21 | – | – | – | – | – | – | – | – |
| Bannerman, C. | 3 | 6 | – | 239 | 165* | 59.75 | 1 | – | – | – | – | – | – | – | – | – | – |
| Bardsley, W. | 41 | 66† | 5 | 2469 | 193* | 40.47 | 6 | 14 | 12 | – | – | – | – | – | – | – | – |
| Barnes, S.G. | 13 | 19 | 2 | 1072 | 234 | 63.05 | 3 | 5 | 14 | – | 594 | 218 | 4 | 54.50 | 2-25 | – | – |
| Barnett, B.A. | 4 | 8† | 1 | 195 | 57 | 27.85 | – | 1 | 3 | 2 | – | – | – | – | – | – | – |
| Barrett, J.E. | 2 | 4† | 0 | 80 | 67* | 26.66 | – | 1 | 1 | – | – | – | – | – | – | – | – |
| Benaud, J. | 3 | 5 | 0 | 223 | 142 | 44.60 | 1 | – | 1 | – | 24 | 12 | 2 | 6.00 | 2-12 | – | – |
| Benaud, R. | 63 | 97 | 7 | 2201 | 122 | 24.45 | 3 | 9 | 65 | – | 19108 | 6704 | 248 | 27.03 | 7-72 | 16 | 1 |
| Blackham, J.M. | 35 | 62 | 11 | 800 | 74 | 15.68 | – | 4 | 36 | 24 | – | – | – | – | – | – | – |
| Blackie, D.D.J. | 3 | 6† | 3 | 24 | 11* | 8.00 | – | – | 2 | – | 1260 | 444 | 14 | 31.71 | 6-94 | 1 | – |
| Bonnor, G.J. | 17 | 30 | 0 | 512 | 128 | 17.06 | 1 | 2 | 16 | – | 164 | 84 | 2 | 42.00 | 1-5 | – | – |
| Booth, B.C. | 29 | 48 | 6 | 1773 | 169 | 42.21 | 5 | 10 | 17 | – | 436 | 146 | 3 | 48.66 | 2-33 | – | – |
| Boyle, H.F. | 12 | 16 | 4 | 153 | 36* | 12.75 | – | – | 10 | – | 1744 | 641 | 32 | 20.03 | 6-42 | 1 | – |
| Bradman, D.G. | 52 | 80 | 10 | 6996 | 334 | 99.94 | 29 | 13 | 32 | – | 160 | 72 | 2 | 36.00 | 1-8 | – | – |
| Bright, R.J. | 3 | 5 | 1 | 42 | 16 | 10.50 | – | – | 2 | – | 433‡ | 147 | 5 | 29.40 | 3-69 | – | – |
| Bromley, E.H. | 2 | 4† | 0 | 38 | 26 | 9.50 | – | – | 2 | – | 60 | 19 | 0 | – | – | – | – |
| Brown, W.A. | 22 | 35 | 1 | 1592 | 206* | 46.82 | 4 | 9 | 14 | – | – | – | – | – | – | – | – |
| Bruce, W. | 14 | 26† | 2 | 702 | 80 | 29.25 | – | 5 | 12 | – | 954‡ | 440 | 12 | 36.66 | 3-88 | – | – |
| Burge, P.J.P. | 42 | 68 | 8 | 2290 | 181 | 38.16 | 4 | 12 | 23 | – | – | – | – | – | – | – | – |
| Burke, J.W. | 24 | 44 | 7 | 1280 | 189 | 34.59 | 3 | 5 | 18 | – | 814 | 230 | 8 | 28.75 | 4-37 | – | – |
| Burn, K.E. | 2 | 4 | 0 | 41 | 19 | 10.25 | – | – | 1 | – | – | – | – | – | – | – | – |
| Burton, F.J. | 2 | 4 | 2 | 4 | 2* | 2.00 | – | – | 1 | 1 | – | – | – | – | – | – | – |
| Callaway, S.T. | 3 | 6 | 1 | 87 | 41 | 17.40 | – | – | 1 | – | 471 | 142 | 6 | 23.66 | 5-37 | 1 | – |
| Callen, I.W. | 1 | 2† | 2 | 26 | 22* | – | – | – | 1 | – | 440 | 191 | 6 | 31.83 | 3-83 | – | – |
| Carkeek, W. | 6 | 5† | 2 | 16 | 6* | 5.33 | – | – | 6 | 21 | – | – | – | – | – | – | – |
| Carter, H. | 28 | 47 | 9 | 873 | 72 | 22.97 | – | 4 | 44 | 21 | – | – | – | – | – | – | – |
| Chappell, G.S. | 51 | 90 | 13 | 4097 | 247* | 53.20 | 14 | 20 | 73 | – | 3752 | 1399 | 32 | 43.71 | 5-61 | 1 | – |
| Chappell, I.M. | 72 | 130 | 9 | 5187 | 196 | 42.86 | 14 | 25 | 103 | – | 2873 | 1316 | 20 | 65.80 | 2-21 | – | – |
| Charlton, P.C. | 2 | 4 | 0 | 29 | 11 | 7.25 | – | – | – | – | 45 | 24 | 3 | 8.00 | 3-18 | – | – |
| Chipperfield, A.G. | 14 | 20 | 3 | 552 | 109 | 32.47 | 1 | 2 | 15 | – | 924 | 437 | 5 | 87.40 | 3-91 | – | – |
| Clark, W.M. | 9 | 17 | 2 | 89 | 33 | 5.93 | – | – | 5 | – | 2489 | 1162 | 43 | 27.02 | 4-46 | – | – |
| Colley, D.J. | 3 | 4 | 0 | 84 | 54 | 21.00 | – | 1 | 1 | – | 729 | 312 | 6 | 52.00 | 3-83 | – | – |
| Collins, H.L. | 19 | 31 | 1 | 1352 | 203 | 45.06 | 4 | 6 | 13 | – | 654‡ | 252 | 4 | 63.00 | 2-47 | – | – |
| Coningham, A. | 1 | 2† | 0 | 13 | 10 | 6.50 | – | – | – | – | 186‡ | 76 | 2 | 38.00 | 2-17 | – | – |
| Connolly, A.N. | 29 | 45 | 20 | 260 | 37 | 10.40 | – | – | 17 | – | 7818 | 2981 | 102 | 29.22 | 6-47 | 4 | – |
| Cooper, B.B. | 1 | 2 | 0 | 18 | 15 | 9.00 | – | – | 2 | – | – | – | – | – | – | – | – |
| Cooper, W.H. | 2 | 3 | 1 | 13 | 7 | 6.50 | – | – | 1 | – | 466 | 226 | 9 | 25.11 | 6-120 | 1 | – |
| Corling, G.E. | 5 | 4 | 1 | 5 | 3 | 1.66 | – | – | – | – | 1159 | 447 | 12 | 37.25 | 4-60 | – | – |

AUSTRALIA – continued

| | | | BATTING AND FIELDING | | | | | | | | BOWLING | | | | | |
| | Tests | I | NO | Runs | HS | Avge | 100 | 50 | Ct | St | Balls | Runs | Wkts | Avge | BB | 5wI | 10wM |
|---|---|---|---|---|---|---|---|---|---|---|---|---|---|---|---|---|---|
| Cosier, G.J. | 16 | 28 | 1 | 845 | 168 | 31.29 | 2 | 3 | 12 | – | 803 | 306 | 5 | 61.20 | 2-26 | – | – |
| Cottam, J.T. | 1 | 2 | 0 | 4 | 3 | 2.00 | – | – | 1 | – | | | | | | | |
| Cotter, A. | 21 | 37 | 2 | 457 | 45 | 13.05 | – | – | 8 | – | 4633 | 2549 | 89 | 28.64 | 7-148 | 7 | – |
| Coulthard, G. | 1 | 1 | 1 | 6 | 6* | – | – | – | – | – | | | | | | | |
| Cowper, R.M. | 27 | 46† | 2 | 2061 | 307 | 46.84 | 5 | 10 | 21 | – | 3005 | 1139 | 36 | 31.63 | 4-48 | – | – |
| Craig, I.D. | 11 | 18 | 0 | 358 | 53 | 19.88 | – | 2 | 2 | – | | | | | | | |
| Crawford, W.P.A. | 4 | 5 | 2 | 53 | 34 | 17.66 | – | – | 1 | – | 437 | 107 | 7 | 15.28 | 3-28 | – | – |
| Darling, J. | 34 | 60† | 2 | 1657 | 178 | 28.56 | 3 | 8 | 27 | – | | | | | | | |
| Darling, L.S. | 12 | 18† | 1 | 474 | 85 | 27.88 | – | 3 | 8 | – | 162 | 65 | 0 | – | – | – | – |
| Darling, W.M. | 4 | 8 | 0 | 164 | 65 | 20.50 | – | 2 | 1 | – | | | | | | | |
| Davidson, A.K. | 44 | 61† | 7 | 1328 | 80 | 24.59 | – | 5 | 42 | – | 11587‡ | 3819 | 186 | 20.53 | 7-93 | 14 | 2 |
| Davis, I.C. | 15 | 27 | 1 | 692 | 105 | 26.61 | 1 | 4 | 9 | – | | | | | | | |
| De Courcy, J.H. | 3 | 6 | 1 | 81 | 41 | 16.20 | – | – | 3 | – | | | | | | | |
| Dell, A.R. | 2 | 2 | 2 | 6 | 3* | – | – | – | – | – | 559‡ | 160 | 6 | 26.66 | 3.65 | – | – |
| Donnan, H. | 5 | 10 | 1 | 75 | 15 | 8.33 | – | – | 1 | – | 54 | 22 | 0 | – | – | – | – |
| Dooland, B. | 3 | 5 | 1 | 76 | 29 | 19.00 | – | – | 3 | – | 880 | 419 | 9 | 46.55 | 4-69 | – | – |
| Duff, R.A. | 22 | 40 | 3 | 1317 | 146 | 35.59 | 2 | 6 | 14 | – | 180 | 85 | 4 | 21.25 | 2-43 | – | – |
| Duncan, J.R.F. | 1 | 1 | 0 | 3 | 3 | 3.00 | – | – | – | – | 112 | 30 | 0 | – | – | – | – |
| Dymock, G. | 4 | 5† | 1 | 13 | 13 | 3.25 | – | – | – | – | 1352‡ | 452 | 14 | 32.28 | 5-58 | 1 | – |
| Dyson, J. | 3 | 6 | 0 | 101 | 53 | 16.83 | – | 1 | – | – | | | | | | | |
| Eady, C.J. | 2 | 4 | 1 | 20 | 10* | 6.66 | – | – | 2 | – | 223 | 112 | 7 | 16.00 | 3-30 | – | – |
| Eastwood, K.H. | 1 | 2† | 0 | 5 | 5 | 2.50 | – | – | – | – | 40‡ | 21 | 1 | 21.00 | 1-21 | – | – |
| Ebeling, H.I. | 1 | 2 | 0 | 43 | 41 | 21.50 | – | – | 1 | – | 186 | 89 | 3 | 29.66 | 3-74 | – | – |
| Edwards, J.D. | 3 | 6 | 1 | 48 | 26 | 9.60 | – | – | 1 | – | | | | | | | |
| Edwards, R. | 20 | 32 | 3 | 1171 | 170* | 40.37 | 2 | 9 | 7 | – | 12 | 20 | 0 | – | – | – | – |
| Edwards, W.J. | 3 | 6† | 0 | 68 | 30 | 11.33 | – | – | – | – | | | | | | | |
| Emery, S.H. | 4 | 2 | 0 | 6 | 5 | 3.00 | – | – | 2 | – | 462 | 249 | 5 | 49.80 | 2-46 | – | – |
| Evans, E. | 6 | 10 | 2 | 82 | 33 | 10.25 | – | – | 5 | – | 1247 | 332 | 7 | 47.42 | 3-64 | – | – |
| Fairfax, A.G. | 10 | 12 | 4 | 410 | 65 | 51.25 | – | 4 | 15 | – | 1520 | 645 | 21 | 30.71 | 4-31 | – | – |
| Favell, L.E. | 19 | 31 | 3 | 757 | 101 | 27.03 | 1 | 5 | 9 | – | | | | | | | |
| Ferris, J.J. | 8 | 16† | 4 | 98 | 20* | 8.16 | – | 3 | 4 | – | 2030‡ | 684 | 48 | 14.25 | 5.26 | 4 | – |
| Fingleton, J.H.W. | 18 | 29 | 1 | 1189 | 136 | 42.46 | 5 | 3 | 13 | – | | | | | | | |
| Fleetwood-Smith, L.O'B. | 10 | 11 | 5 | 54 | 16* | 9.00 | – | – | – | – | 3093‡ | 1570 | 42 | 37.38 | 6-110 | 2 | 1 |
| Francis, B.C. | 3 | 5 | 0 | 52 | 27 | 10.40 | – | – | 1 | – | | | | | | | |
| Freeman, E.W. | 11 | 18 | 0 | 345 | 76 | 19.16 | – | 2 | 5 | – | 2183 | 1128 | 34 | 33.17 | 4-52 | – | – |
| Freer, F.W. | 1 | 1 | 1 | 28 | 28* | – | – | – | – | – | 160 | 74 | 3 | 24.66 | 2-49 | – | – |

AUSTRALIA – continued

| | | | | BATTING AND FIELDING | | | | | | | BOWLING | | | | | | |
|---|---|---|---|---|---|---|---|---|---|---|---|---|---|---|---|---|---|
| | Tests | I | NO | Runs | HS | Avge | 100 | 50 | Ct | St | Balls | Runs | Wkts | Avge | BB | 5wI | 10wM |
| Gannon, J.B. | 3 | 5† | 4 | 3 | 3* | 3.00 | – | – | 3 | – | 726‡ | 361 | 11 | 32.81 | 4-77 | – | – |
| Garrett, T.W. | 19 | 33 | 6 | 339 | 51* | 12.55 | – | 1 | 7 | – | 2708 | 970 | 36 | 26.94 | 6-78 | 2 | – |
| Gaunt, R.A. | 3 | 4† | 2 | 6 | 3 | 3.00 | – | – | 1 | – | 716 | 310 | 7 | 44.28 | 3-53 | – | – |
| Gehrs, D.R.A. | 6 | 11 | 0 | 221 | 67 | 20.09 | – | 2 | 6 | – | 4 | 4 | 0 | – | – | – | – |
| Giffen, G. | 31 | 53 | 0 | 1238 | 161 | 23.35 | 1 | 6 | 24 | – | 6325 | 2791 | 103 | 27.09 | 7-117 | 7 | 1 |
| Giffen, W.F. | 3 | 6 | 0 | 11 | 3 | 1.83 | – | – | 1 | – | – | – | – | – | – | – | – |
| Gilmour, G.J. | 15 | 22† | 1 | 483 | 101 | 23.00 | 1 | 3 | 8 | – | 2661‡ | 1406 | 54 | 26.03 | 6-85 | 3 | – |
| Gleeson, J.W. | 29 | 46 | 8 | 395 | 45 | 10.39 | – | – | 17 | – | 8857 | 3367 | 93 | 36.20 | 5-61 | 3 | – |
| Graham, H. | 6 | 10 | 0 | 301 | 107 | 30.10 | 2 | – | 3 | – | – | – | – | – | – | – | – |
| Gregory, D.W. | 3 | 5 | 2 | 60 | 43 | 20.00 | – | – | 1 | – | 20 | 9 | 0 | – | – | – | – |
| Gregory, E.J. | 1 | 2 | 0 | 11 | 11 | 5.50 | – | – | – | – | – | – | – | – | – | – | – |
| Gregory, J.M. | 24 | 34† | 3 | 1146 | 119 | 36.96 | 2 | 7 | 37 | – | 5582 | 2648 | 85 | 31.15 | 7-69 | 4 | – |
| Gregory, R.G. | 2 | 3 | 0 | 153 | 80 | 51.00 | – | 2 | 1 | – | 24 | 14 | 0 | – | – | – | – |
| Gregory, S.E. | 58 | 100 | 7 | 2282 | 201 | 24.53 | 4 | 8 | 25 | – | 30 | 33 | 0 | – | – | – | – |
| Grimmett, C.V. | 37 | 50 | 10 | 557 | 50 | 13.92 | – | 1 | 17 | – | 14513 | 5231 | 216 | 24.21 | 7-40 | 21 | 7 |
| Groube, T.U. | 1 | 2 | 0 | 11 | 11 | 5.50 | – | – | – | – | – | – | – | – | – | – | – |
| Grout, A.T.W. | 51 | 67 | 8 | 890 | 74 | 15.08 | – | 3 | 163 | 24 | – | – | – | – | – | – | – |
| Guest, C.E.J. | 1 | 1 | 0 | 11 | 11 | 11.00 | – | – | – | – | 144 | 59 | 0 | – | – | – | – |
| Hamence, R.A. | 3 | 4 | 1 | 81 | 30* | 27.00 | – | – | 1 | – | – | – | – | – | – | – | – |
| Hammond, J.R. | 5 | 5 | 2 | 28 | 19 | 9.33 | – | – | 2 | – | 1031 | 488 | 15 | 32.53 | 4-38 | – | – |
| Harry, J. | 1 | 2 | 0 | 8 | 6 | 4.00 | – | – | 1 | – | – | – | – | – | – | – | – |
| Hartigan, R.J. | 2 | 4 | 0 | 170 | 116 | 42.50 | 1 | – | 1 | – | 12 | 7 | 0 | – | – | – | – |
| Hartkopf, A.E.V. | 1 | 2 | 0 | 80 | 80 | 40.00 | – | 1 | – | – | 240 | 134 | 1 | 134.00 | 1-120 | – | – |
| Harvey, M.R. | 1 | 2 | 0 | 43 | 31 | 21.50 | – | – | – | – | – | – | – | – | – | – | – |
| Harvey, R.N. | 79 | 137† | 10 | 6149 | 205 | 48.41 | 21 | 24 | 64 | – | 414 | 120 | 3 | 40.00 | 1-8 | – | – |
| Hassett, A.L. | 43 | 69 | 3 | 3073 | 198* | 46.56 | 10 | 11 | 30 | – | 111 | 78 | 0 | – | – | – | – |
| Hawke, N.J.N. | 27 | 37 | 15 | 365 | 45* | 16.59 | – | – | 9 | – | 6974 | 2677 | 91 | 29.41 | 7-105 | 6 | 1 |
| Hazlitt, G.R. | 9 | 12 | 4 | 89 | 34* | 11.12 | – | – | 4 | – | 1563 | 623 | 23 | 27.08 | 7-25 | 1 | – |
| Hendry, H.S.T.L. | 11 | 18 | 2 | 335 | 112 | 20.93 | 1 | 1 | 10 | – | 1706 | 640 | 16 | 40.00 | 3-36 | – | – |
| Hibbert, P.A. | 1 | 2† | 0 | 15 | 13 | 7.50 | – | – | – | – | – | – | – | – | – | – | – |
| Higgs, J.D. | 4 | 7 | 4 | 10 | 4* | 3.33 | – | – | 1 | – | 836 | 384 | 15 | 25.60 | 4-91 | – | – |
| Hill, C. | 49 | 89† | 2 | 3412 | 191 | 39.21 | 7 | 19 | 33 | – | 606 | 273 | 8 | 34.12 | 3-35 | – | – |
| Hill, J.C. | 3 | 6 | 3 | 21 | 8* | 7.00 | – | – | 2 | – | 232 | 156 | 2 | 78.00 | 2-68 | – | – |
| Hoare, D.E. | 1 | 2 | 0 | 35 | 35 | 17.50 | – | – | 2 | – | 136‡ | 84 | 6 | 14.00 | 2-7 | – | – |
| Hodges, J.H. | 2 | 4† | 1 | 10 | 8 | 3.33 | – | – | 2 | – | 398 | 126 | 3 | 42.00 | 1-9 | – | – |
| Hole, G.B. | 18 | 33 | 2 | 789 | 66 | 25.45 | – | 6 | 21 | – | – | – | – | – | – | – | – |
| Hookes, D.W. | 6 | 11† | 0 | 356 | 85 | 32.36 | – | 3 | 2 | – | – | – | – | – | – | – | – |
| Hopkins, A.J.Y. | 20 | 33 | 2 | 509 | 43 | 16.42 | – | 1 | 11 | – | 1327 | 696 | 26 | 26.76 | 4-81 | 1 | – |
| Horan, T.P. | 15 | 27 | 2 | 471 | 124 | 18.84 | 1 | 1 | 6 | – | 373 | 143 | 11 | 13.00 | 6-40 | 1 | – |

AUSTRALIA – *continued*

| | | | | BATTING AND FIELDING | | | | | | | BOWLING | | | | | | |
|---|---|---|---|---|---|---|---|---|---|---|---|---|---|---|---|---|---|
| | Tests | I | NO | Runs | HS | Avge | 100 | 50 | Ct | St | Balls | Runs | Wkts | Avge | BB | 5wI | 10wM |
| Hordern, H.V. | 7 | 13 | 2 | 254 | 50 | 23.09 | – | 1 | 6 | – | 2148 | 1075 | 46 | 23.36 | 7-90 | 5 | 2 |
| Hornibrook, P.M. | 6 | 7† | 1 | 60 | 26 | 10.00 | – | – | 7 | – | 1579‡ | 664 | 17 | 39.05 | 7-92 | 1 | – |
| Howell, W.P. | 18 | 27† | 6 | 158 | 35 | 7.52 | – | – | 12 | – | 3892 | 1407 | 49 | 28.71 | 5-81 | 1 | – |
| Hughes, K.J. | 3 | 5 | 0 | 65 | 28 | 13.00 | – | – | 2 | – | – | – | – | – | – | – | – |
| Hunt, W.A. | 1 | 1† | 0 | 0 | 0 | 0.00 | – | – | 1 | – | 96‡ | 39 | 0 | – | – | – | – |
| Hurst, A.G. | 2 | 3 | 1 | 42 | 26 | 21.00 | – | – | 1 | – | 408 | 154 | 3 | 51.33 | 2-50 | – | – |
| Hurwood, A. | 2 | 2 | 0 | 5 | 5 | 2.50 | – | – | 2 | – | 517 | 170 | 11 | 15.45 | 4-22 | – | – |
| Inverarity, R.J. | 6 | 11 | 1 | 174 | 56 | 17.40 | – | 1 | 4 | – | 372‡ | 93 | 4 | 23.25 | 3-26 | – | – |
| Iredale, F.A. | 14 | 23 | 1 | 807 | 140 | 36.68 | 2 | 4 | 16 | – | 12 | 3 | 0 | – | – | – | – |
| Ironmonger, H. | 14 | 21† | 5 | 42 | 12 | 2.62 | – | – | 3 | – | 4695‡ | 1330 | 74 | 17.97 | 7-23 | 4 | 2 |
| Iverson, J.B. | 5 | 7 | 3 | 3 | 1* | 0.75 | – | – | 2 | – | 1108 | 320 | 21 | 15.23 | 6-27 | 1 | – |
| Jackson, A. | 8 | 11 | 1 | 474 | 164 | 47.40 | 1 | 2 | 7 | – | – | – | – | – | – | – | – |
| Jarman, B.N. | 19 | 30 | 3 | 400 | 78 | 14.81 | – | 2 | 50 | 4 | – | – | – | – | – | – | – |
| Jarvis, A.H. | 11 | 21 | 3 | 303 | 82 | 16.83 | – | 1 | 9 | 9 | – | – | – | – | – | – | – |
| Jenner, T.J. | 9 | 14 | 5 | 208 | 74 | 23.11 | – | 1 | 5 | – | 1881 | 749 | 24 | 31.20 | 5-90 | 1 | – |
| Jennings, C.B. | 6 | 8 | 2 | 107 | 32 | 17.83 | – | – | 5 | – | – | – | – | – | – | – | – |
| Johnson, I.W. | 45 | 66 | 12 | 1000 | 77 | 18.51 | – | 6 | 30 | – | 8780 | 3182 | 109 | 29.19 | 7-44 | 3 | – |
| Johnson, L.J. | 1 | 1 | 1 | 25 | 25* | – | – | – | 2 | – | 282 | 74 | 6 | 12.33 | 3-8 | – | – |
| Johnston, W.A. | 40 | 49† | 25 | 273 | 29 | 11.37 | – | – | 16 | – | 11048‡ | 3826 | 160 | 23.91 | 6-44 | 7 | – |
| Jones, E. | 19 | 26 | 1 | 126 | 20 | 5.04 | – | – | 21 | – | 3748 | 1857 | 64 | 29.01 | 7-88 | 3 | 1 |
| Jones, S.P. | 12 | 24 | 4 | 432 | 87 | 21.60 | – | 1 | 12 | – | 262 | 112 | 6 | 18.66 | 4-47 | – | – |
| Joslin, L.R. | 1 | 2† | 0 | 9 | 7 | 4.50 | – | – | – | – | – | – | – | – | – | – | – |
| Kelleway, C. | 26 | 42 | 4 | 1422 | 147 | 37.42 | 3 | 6 | 24 | – | 4363 | 1683 | 52 | 32.36 | 5-33 | 1 | – |
| Kelly, J.J. | 36 | 56 | 17 | 664 | 46* | 17.02 | – | – | 43 | 20 | – | – | – | – | – | – | – |
| Kelly, T.J.D. | 2 | 3 | 0 | 64 | 35 | 21.33 | – | – | 1 | – | – | – | – | – | – | – | – |
| Kendall, T. | 2 | 4† | 1 | 39 | 17* | 13.00 | – | – | 2 | – | 563‡ | 215 | 14 | 15.35 | 7-55 | 1 | – |
| Kippax, A.F. | 22 | 34 | 1 | 1192 | 146 | 36.12 | 2 | 8 | 13 | – | 72 | 19 | 0 | – | – | – | – |
| Kline, L.F. | 13 | 16† | 9 | 58 | 15* | 8.28 | – | – | 9 | – | 2373‡ | 776 | 34 | 22.82 | 7-75 | 1 | – |
| Langley, G.R.A. | 26 | 37 | 12 | 374 | 53 | 14.96 | – | 1 | 83 | 15 | – | – | – | – | – | – | – |
| Laughlin, T.J. | 2 | 3† | 0 | 80 | 35 | 26.66 | – | – | 1 | – | 316 | 202 | 6 | 33.66 | 5-101 | 1 | – |
| Laver, F. | 15 | 23 | 6 | 196 | 45 | 11.52 | – | – | 8 | – | 2361 | 964 | 37 | 26.05 | 8-31 | 2 | – |
| Lawry, W.M. | 67 | 123† | 12 | 5234 | 210 | 47.15 | 13 | 27 | 30 | – | 14‡ | 6 | 0 | – | – | – | – |
| Lee, P.K. | 2 | 3 | 0 | 57 | 42 | 19.00 | – | – | 1 | – | 436 | 212 | 5 | 42.40 | 4-111 | – | – |
| Lillee, D.K. | 32 | 40 | 14 | 448 | 73* | 17.23 | – | 1 | 9 | – | 8783 | 4017 | 171 | 23.49 | 6-26 | 12 | 4 |
| Lindwall, R.R. | 61 | 84 | 13 | 1502 | 118 | 21.15 | 2 | 5 | 26 | – | 13650 | 5251 | 228 | 23.03 | 7-38 | 12 | – |
| Love, H.S.B. | 1 | 2 | 0 | 8 | 5 | 4.00 | – | – | 3 | – | – | – | – | – | – | – | – |
| Loxton, S.J.E. | 12 | 15 | 0 | 554 | 101 | 36.93 | 1 | 3 | 7 | – | 906 | 349 | 8 | 43.62 | 3-55 | – | – |
| Lyons, J.J. | 14 | 27 | 0 | 731 | 134 | 27.07 | 1 | 3 | 3 | – | 316 | 149 | 6 | 24.83 | 5-30 | 1 | – |

AUSTRALIA – continued

| | Tests | I | NO | Runs | HS | Avge | 100 | 50 | Ct | St | Balls | Runs | Wkts | Avge | BB | 5wI | 10wM |
|---|---|---|---|---|---|---|---|---|---|---|---|---|---|---|---|---|---|
| | | | | BATTING AND FIELDING | | | | | | | | | | BOWLING | | | |
| McAlister, P.A. | 8 | 16 | 1 | 252 | 41 | 16.80 | – | – | 10 | – | – | – | – | – | – | – | – |
| Macartney, C.G. | 35 | 55 | 4 | 2131 | 170 | 41.78 | 7 | 9 | 17 | – | 3555‡ | 1240 | 45 | 27.55 | 7-58 | 2 | 1 |
| McCabe, S.J. | 39 | 62 | 5 | 2748 | 232 | 48.21 | 6 | 13 | 41 | – | 3746 | 1543 | 36 | 42.86 | 4-13 | 3 | – |
| McCool, C.L. | 14 | 17 | 4 | 459 | 104* | 35.30 | 1 | 1 | 14 | – | 2504 | 958 | 36 | 26.61 | 5-41 | 3 | – |
| McCormick, E.L. | 12 | 14† | 5 | 54 | 17* | 6.00 | – | – | 8 | – | 2107 | 1079 | 36 | 29.97 | 4-101 | – | – |
| McCosker, R.B. | 22 | 40 | 5 | 1498 | 127 | 42.80 | 4 | 9 | 18 | – | | | | | | | |
| McDonald, C.C. | 47 | 83 | 5 | 3107 | 170 | 39.32 | 5 | 17 | 14 | – | 8 | 3 | 0 | – | – | – | – |
| McDonald, E.A. | 11 | 12 | 5 | 116 | 36 | 16.57 | – | – | 3 | – | 2885 | 1431 | 43 | 33.27 | 5-32 | 2 | – |
| McDonnell, P.S. | 19 | 34 | 1 | 950 | 147 | 28.78 | 3 | 2 | 6 | – | 52 | 53 | 0 | – | – | – | – |
| McIlwraith, J. | 1 | 2 | 0 | 9 | 7 | 4.50 | – | – | 1 | – | | | | | | | |
| Mackay, K.D. | 37 | 52† | 7 | 1507 | 89 | 33.48 | – | 13 | 16 | – | 5792 | 1721 | 50 | 34.42 | 6-42 | 2 | – |
| McKenzie, G.D. | 60 | 89 | 12 | 945 | 76 | 12.27 | – | 2 | 34 | – | 17681 | 7328 | 246 | 29.78 | 8-71 | 16 | 3 |
| McKibbin, T.R. | 5 | 8† | 2 | 88 | 28 | 14.66 | – | – | 4 | – | 1032 | 496 | 17 | 29.17 | 3-35 | 1 | – |
| McLaren, J.W. | 1 | 2 | 2 | 0 | 0* | – | – | – | – | – | 144 | 70 | 1 | 70.00 | 1-23 | – | – |
| McLeod, C.E. | 17 | 29 | 5 | 573 | 112 | 23.87 | 1 | 4 | 9 | – | 3374 | 1325 | 33 | 40.15 | 5-65 | 2 | – |
| McLeod, R.W. | 6 | 11† | 0 | 146 | 31 | 13.27 | – | – | 3 | – | 1089 | 384 | 12 | 32.00 | 5-55 | 1 | – |
| McShane, P.G. | 3 | 6† | 1 | 26 | 12* | 5.20 | – | – | 2 | 1 | 108‡ | 48 | 1 | 48.00 | 1-39 | – | – |
| Maddocks, L.V. | 7 | 12 | 2 | 177 | 69 | 17.70 | – | 1 | 18 | – | | | | | | | |
| Mailey, A.A. | 21 | 29 | 9 | 222 | 46* | 11.10 | – | – | 14 | – | 6119 | 3358 | 99 | 33.91 | 9-121 | 6 | 2 |
| Mallett, A.A. | 35 | 47 | 13 | 393 | 43* | 11.55 | – | – | 29 | – | 9136 | 3494 | 125 | 27.95 | 8-59 | 6 | 1 |
| Malone, M.F. | 1 | 1 | – | 46 | 46 | 46.00 | – | – | – | – | 342 | 77 | 6 | 12.83 | 5-63 | 1 | – |
| Mann, A.L. | 4 | 8† | 0 | 189 | 105 | 23.62 | 1 | – | 2 | – | 552 | 316 | 4 | 79.00 | 3-12 | – | – |
| Marr, A.P. | 1 | 2 | 0 | 5 | 5 | 2.50 | – | – | 2 | – | 48 | 14 | 0 | – | – | – | – |
| Marsh, R.W. | 52 | 82† | 9 | 2396 | 132 | 32.82 | 3 | 12 | 190 | 8 | | | | | | | |
| Martin, J.W. | 8 | 13† | 1 | 214 | 55 | 17.83 | – | 1 | 5 | – | 1846‡ | 832 | 17 | 48.94 | 3-56 | – | – |
| Massie, H.H. | 9 | 16 | 0 | 249 | 55 | 15.56 | – | 1 | 5 | – | | | | | | | |
| Massie, R.A.L. | 6 | 8† | 1 | 78 | 42 | 11.14 | – | – | 7 | – | 1739 | 647 | 31 | 20.87 | 8-53 | 2 | 1 |
| Matthews, T.J. | 8 | 10 | 1 | 153 | 53 | 17.00 | – | 1 | 7 | – | 1081 | 419 | 16 | 26.18 | 4-29 | – | – |
| Mayne, E.R. | 4 | 4 | 1 | 64 | 25* | 21.33 | – | – | 2 | – | 6 | 1 | 0 | – | – | – | – |
| Mayne, L.C. | 6 | 11† | 3 | 76 | 13 | 9.50 | – | – | 3 | – | 1251 | 628 | 19 | 33.05 | 4-43 | – | – |
| Meckiff, I. | 18 | 20 | 7 | 154 | 45* | 11.84 | – | – | 9 | – | 3738‡ | 1423 | 45 | 31.62 | 6-38 | 2 | – |
| Meuleman, K.D. | 1 | 1 | 0 | 0 | 0 | 0.00 | – | – | – | – | | | | | | | |
| Midwinter, W.E. | 8 | 14 | 1 | 174 | 37 | 13.38 | – | – | 5 | – | 949 | 333 | 14 | 23.78 | 5-78 | 1 | 1 |
| Miller, K.R. | 55 | 87 | 7 | 2958 | 147 | 36.97 | 7 | 13 | 38 | – | 10461 | 3906 | 170 | 22.97 | 7-60 | 7 | 1 |
| Minnett, R.B. | 9 | 15 | 0 | 391 | 90 | 26.06 | – | 3 | 6 | – | 589 | 290 | 11 | 26.36 | 4-34 | – | – |
| Misson, F.M. | 5 | 5 | 3 | 38 | 25* | 19.00 | – | – | 6 | – | 1197 | 616 | 16 | 38.50 | 4-58 | – | – |
| Moroney, J. | 7 | 12 | 1 | 383 | 118 | 34.81 | 2 | 1 | – | – | | | | | | | |
| Morris, A.R. | 46 | 79† | 3 | 3533 | 206 | 46.48 | 12 | 12 | 15 | – | 111‡ | 50 | 2 | 25.00 | 1-5 | – | – |
| Morris, S. | 1 | 2 | 1 | 14 | 10* | 14.00 | – | – | 1 | – | 136 | 73 | 2 | 36.50 | 2-73 | – | – |
| Moses, H. | 6 | 10† | 0 | 198 | 33 | 19.80 | – | – | 1 | – | | | | | | | |

AUSTRALIA – continued

| | | | | BATTING AND FIELDING | | | | | | | BOWLING | | | | | | |
| | Tests | I | NO | Runs | HS | Avge | 100 | 50 | Ct | St | Balls | Runs | Wkts | Avge | BB | 5wI | 10wM |
|---|---|---|---|---|---|---|---|---|---|---|---|---|---|---|---|---|---|
| Moule, W.H. | 1 | 2 | 0 | 40 | 34 | 20.00 | – | – | 1 | 1 | 51 | 23 | 3 | 7.66 | 3-23 | – | – |
| Murdoch, W.L. | 18 | 33 | 5 | 896 | 211 | 32.00 | 2 | 1 | 13 | 1 | – | – | – | – | – | – | – |
| Musgrove, H. | 1 | 2 | 0 | 13 | 9 | 6.50 | – | – | – | – | – | – | – | – | – | – | – |
| Nagel, L.E. | 1 | 2 | 1 | 21 | 21* | 21.00 | – | – | – | – | 262 | 110 | 2 | 55.00 | 2-110 | – | – |
| Nash, L.J. | 2 | 2 | 0 | 30 | 17 | 15.00 | – | – | 6 | – | 311 | 126 | 10 | 12.60 | 4-18 | – | – |
| Nitschke, H.C. | 2 | 2† | 0 | 53 | 47 | 26.50 | – | – | 3 | – | – | – | – | – | – | – | – |
| Noble, M.A. | 42 | 73 | 7 | 1997 | 133 | 30.25 | 1 | 16 | 26 | – | 7109 | 3025 | 121 | 25.00 | 7-17 | 9 | 2 |
| Noblet, G. | 3 | 4 | 1 | 22 | 13* | 7.33 | – | – | 1 | – | 774 | 183 | 7 | 26.14 | 3-21 | – | – |
| Nothling, O.E. | 1 | 2 | 0 | 52 | 44 | 26.00 | – | – | – | – | 276 | 72 | 0 | – | – | – | – |
| O'Brien, L.P.J. | 5 | 8† | 0 | 211 | 61 | 26.37 | – | 2 | 3 | – | – | – | – | – | – | – | – |
| O'Connor, J.D.A. | 4 | 8† | 1 | 86 | 20 | 12.28 | – | – | 3 | – | 692 | 340 | 13 | 26.15 | 5-40 | 1 | – |
| Ogilvie, A.D. | 5 | 10 | 0 | 178 | 47 | 17.80 | – | – | 5 | – | – | – | – | – | – | – | – |
| O'Keeffe, K.J. | 24 | 34 | 9 | 644 | 85 | 25.76 | – | 1 | 15 | – | 5384 | 2018 | 53 | 38.07 | 5-101 | 1 | – |
| Oldfield, W.A.S. | 54 | 80 | 17 | 1427 | 65* | 22.65 | – | 4 | 78 | 52 | – | – | – | – | – | – | – |
| O'Neill, N.C. | 42 | 69 | 8 | 2779 | 181 | 45.55 | 6 | 15 | 21 | – | 1392 | 667 | 17 | 39.23 | 4-41 | – | – |
| O'Reilly, W.J. | 27 | 39† | 7 | 410 | 56* | 12.81 | – | 1 | 7 | – | 10024 | 3254 | 144 | 22.59 | 7-54 | 11 | 3 |
| Oxenham, R.K. | 7 | 10 | 0 | 151 | 48 | 15.10 | – | – | 4 | – | 1802 | 522 | 14 | 37.28 | 4-39 | – | – |
| Palmer, G.E. | 17 | 25 | 4 | 296 | 48 | 14.09 | – | – | 13 | – | 4517 | 1678 | 78 | 21.51 | 7-65 | 6 | 2 |
| Park, R.L. | 1 | 1 | 0 | 0 | 0 | 0.00 | – | – | – | – | 6 | 9 | 0 | – | – | – | – |
| Pascoe, L.S. | 3 | 5 | 2 | 23 | 20 | 7.66 | – | – | – | – | 826 | 363 | 13 | 27.92 | 4-80 | – | – |
| Pellew, C.E. | 10 | 14 | 1 | 484 | 116 | 37.23 | 2 | 1 | 4 | – | 78 | 34 | 0 | – | – | – | – |
| Philpott, P.I. | 8 | 10 | 1 | 93 | 22 | 10.33 | – | 1 | 5 | – | 2262 | 1000 | 26 | 38.46 | 5-90 | 1 | – |
| Ponsford, W.H. | 29 | 48 | 4 | 2122 | 266 | 48.22 | 7 | 6 | 21 | – | – | – | – | – | – | – | – |
| Pope, R.J. | 1 | 2 | 0 | 3 | 3 | 1.50 | – | – | – | – | – | – | – | – | – | – | – |
| Ransford, V.S. | 20 | 38† | 6 | 1211 | 143* | 37.84 | 1 | 7 | 10 | – | 43 | 28 | 1 | 28.00 | 1-9 | – | – |
| Redpath, I.R. | 66 | 120 | 11 | 4737 | 171 | 43.45 | 8 | 31 | 83 | – | 64 | 41 | 0 | – | – | – | – |
| Reedman, J.C. | 1 | 2 | 0 | 21 | 17 | 10.50 | – | – | 1 | – | 57 | 24 | 1 | 24.00 | 1-24 | – | – |
| Renneberg, D.A. | 8 | 13 | 7 | 22 | 9 | 3.66 | – | – | 2 | – | 1598 | 830 | 23 | 36.08 | 5-39 | 2 | – |
| Richardson, A.J. | 9 | 13 | 0 | 403 | 100 | 31.00 | 1 | 2 | 1 | – | 1812 | 521 | 12 | 43.41 | 2-20 | – | – |
| Richardson, V.Y. | 19 | 30 | 0 | 706 | 138 | 23.53 | 1 | 1 | 24 | – | – | – | – | – | – | – | – |
| Rigg, K.E. | 8 | 12 | 0 | 401 | 127 | 33.41 | 1 | 1 | 5 | – | – | – | – | – | – | – | – |
| Ring, D.T. | 13 | 21 | 2 | 426 | 67 | 22.42 | – | 4 | 5 | – | 3024 | 1305 | 35 | 37.28 | 6-72 | 2 | – |
| Rixon, S.J. | 10 | 19 | 3 | 341 | 54 | 21.31 | – | 2 | 31 | 4 | – | – | – | – | – | – | – |
| Robertson, W.R. | 1 | 2 | 0 | 2 | 2 | 1.00 | – | – | – | – | 44 | 24 | 0 | – | – | – | – |
| Robinson, R.D. | 3 | 6 | 0 | 100 | 34 | 16.66 | – | – | 4 | – | – | – | – | – | – | – | – |
| Robinson, R.H. | 1 | 2 | 0 | 5 | 3 | 2.50 | – | – | 1 | – | – | – | – | – | – | – | – |

# INDIVIDUAL CAREER RECORDS – continued

## AUSTRALIA – continued

| | | | | BATTING AND FIELDING | | | | | | | | | | BOWLING | | | |
|---|---|---|---|---|---|---|---|---|---|---|---|---|---|---|---|---|---|
| | Tests | I | NO | Runs | HS | Avge | 100 | 50 | Ct | St | Balls | Runs | Wkts | Avge | BB | 5wI | 10wM |
| Rorke, G.F. | 4 | 4† | 2 | 9 | 7 | 4.50 | – | – | 1 | – | 703 | 203 | 10 | 20.30 | 3-23 | – | – |
| Rutherford, J.W. | 1 | 1 | 0 | 30 | 30 | 30.00 | – | – | – | – | 36 | 15 | 1 | 15.00 | 1-11 | – | – |
| Ryder, J. | 20 | 32 | 5 | 1394 | 201* | 51.62 | 3 | 9 | 17 | – | 1897 | 743 | 17 | 43.70 | 2-20 | – | – |
| Saggers, R.A. | 6 | 5 | 2 | 30 | 14 | 10.00 | – | – | 16 | 8 | – | – | – | – | – | – | – |
| Saunders, J.V. | 14 | 23† | 6 | 39 | 11* | 2.29 | – | – | 5 | – | 3565‡ | 1796 | 79 | 22.73 | 7-34 | 6 | – |
| Scott, H.J.H. | 8 | 14 | 1 | 359 | 102 | 27.61 | 1 | 1 | 8 | – | 28 | 26 | 0 | – | – | – | – |
| Sellers, R.H.D. | 1 | 1 | 1 | 0 | 0 | 0.00 | – | – | 1 | – | 30 | 17 | 0 | – | – | – | – |
| Sergeant, C.S. | 12 | 23 | 1 | 522 | 124 | 23.72 | 1 | 2 | 13 | – | – | – | – | – | – | – | – |
| Sheahan, A.P. | 31 | 53 | 6 | 1594 | 127 | 33.91 | 2 | 7 | 17 | – | – | – | – | – | – | – | – |
| Shepherd, B.K. | 9 | 14† | 2 | 502 | 96 | 41.83 | – | 5 | 2 | – | 26 | 9 | 0 | – | – | – | – |
| Sievers, M.W. | 3 | 6 | 1 | 67 | 25* | 13.40 | – | – | 4 | – | 602 | 161 | 9 | 17.88 | 5-21 | 1 | – |
| Simpson, R.B. | 62 | 111 | 7 | 4869 | 311 | 46.81 | 10 | 27 | 110 | – | 6881 | 3001 | 71 | 42.26 | 5-57 | 2 | – |
| Sincock, D.J. | 3 | 4 | 1 | 80 | 29 | 26.66 | – | – | 2 | – | 724‡ | 410 | 8 | 51.25 | 3-67 | – | – |
| Slater, K.N. | 1 | 1 | 0 | 1 | 1* | – | – | – | – | – | 256 | 101 | 2 | 50.50 | 2-40 | – | – |
| Slight, J. | 1 | 2 | 0 | 11 | 11 | 5.50 | – | – | – | – | – | – | – | – | – | – | – |
| Smith, D.B.M. | 2 | 3 | 1 | 30 | 24* | 15.00 | – | – | – | – | – | – | – | – | – | – | – |
| Spofforth, F.R. | 18 | 29 | 6 | 217 | 50 | 9.43 | – | 1 | 11 | – | 4185 | 1731 | 94 | 18.41 | 7-44 | 7 | 4 |
| Stackpole, K.R. | 43 | 80 | 5 | 2807 | 207 | 37.42 | 7 | 14 | 47 | – | 2321 | 1001 | 15 | 66.73 | 2-33 | – | – |
| Stevens, G.B. | 4 | 7 | 0 | 112 | 28 | 16.00 | – | – | 2 | – | – | – | – | – | – | – | – |
| Taber, H.B. | 16 | 27 | 5 | 353 | 48 | 16.04 | – | – | 56 | 4 | – | – | – | – | – | – | – |
| Tallon, D. | 21 | 26 | 3 | 394 | 92 | 17.13 | – | 2 | 50 | 8 | – | – | – | – | – | – | – |
| Taylor, J.M. | 20 | 28 | 0 | 997 | 108 | 35.60 | 1 | 8 | 11 | – | 114 | 45 | 1 | 45.00 | 1-25 | – | – |
| Thomas, G. | 8 | 12 | 1 | 325 | 61 | 29.54 | – | 3 | 3 | – | – | – | – | – | – | – | – |
| Thompson, N. | 2 | 4 | 0 | 67 | 41 | 16.75 | – | – | 3 | – | 112 | 31 | 1 | 31.00 | 1-14 | – | – |
| Thoms, G.R. | 1 | 2 | 0 | 44 | 28 | 22.00 | – | – | – | – | – | – | – | – | – | – | – |
| Thomson, A.L. | 4 | 5 | 4 | 22 | 12* | 22.00 | – | – | – | – | 1519 | 654 | 12 | 54.50 | 3-79 | – | – |
| Thomson, J.R. | 32 | 43 | 7 | 424 | 49 | 11.77 | – | – | 13 | – | 7158 | 3699 | 145 | 25.51 | 6-46 | 6 | 3 |
| Thurlow, H.M. | 1 | 1 | 0 | 0 | 0 | 0.00 | – | – | – | – | 234 | 86 | 0 | – | – | – | – |
| Toohey, P.M. | 8 | 15 | 0 | 705 | 122 | 47.00 | 1 | 6 | 2 | – | – | – | – | – | – | – | – |
| Toshack, E.R.H. | 12 | 11 | 6 | 73 | 20* | 14.60 | – | – | 4 | – | 3140‡ | 989 | 47 | 21.04 | 6-29 | 4 | 1 |
| Travers, J.P.F. | 1 | 2† | 0 | 10 | 9 | 5.00 | – | – | 1 | – | 48‡ | 14 | 1 | 14.00 | 1-14 | – | – |
| Tribe, G.E. | 3 | 3† | 1 | 35 | 25* | 17.50 | – | – | – | – | 760‡ | 330 | 2 | 165.00 | 2-48 | – | – |
| Trott, A.E. | 3 | 5 | 3 | 205 | 85* | 102.50 | – | 2 | 4 | – | 474 | 192 | 9 | 21.33 | 8-43 | 1 | – |
| Trott, G.H.S. | 24 | 42 | 0 | 921 | 143 | 21.92 | 1 | 4 | 21 | – | 1890 | 1019 | 29 | 35.13 | 4-71 | – | – |
| Trumble, H. | 32 | 57 | 14 | 851 | 70 | 19.79 | – | 4 | 45 | – | 8099 | 3072 | 141 | 21.78 | 8-65 | 9 | 3 |
| Trumble, J.W. | 7 | 13 | 1 | 243 | 59 | 20.25 | – | 1 | 3 | – | 600 | 222 | 10 | 22.20 | 3-29 | – | – |
| Trumper, V.T. | 48 | 89 | 8 | 3163 | 214* | 39.04 | 8 | 13 | 31 | – | 546 | 317 | 8 | 37.62 | 3-60 | – | – |
| Turner, A. | 14 | 27† | 1 | 768 | 136 | 29.53 | 1 | 3 | 15 | – | – | – | – | – | – | – | – |
| Turner, C.T.B. | 17 | 32 | 4 | 323 | 29 | 11.53 | – | – | 8 | – | 5195 | 1670 | 101 | 16.53 | 7-43 | 11 | 2 |

# INDIVIDUAL CAREER RECORDS – *continued*

## AUSTRALIA – *continued*

| | Tests | I | NO | Runs | HS | Avge | 100 | 50 | Ct | St | Balls | Runs | Wkts | Avge | BB | 5wI | 10wM |
|---|---|---|---|---|---|---|---|---|---|---|---|---|---|---|---|---|---|
| | | | | *BATTING AND FIELDING* | | | | | | | *BOWLING* | | | | | | |
| Veivers, T.R. | 21 | 30† | 4 | 813 | 88 | 31.26 | – | 7 | 7 | – | 4191 | 1375 | 33 | 41.66 | 4-68 | – | – |
| Waite, M.G. | 2 | 3 | 0 | 11 | 8 | 3.66 | – | – | 1 | – | 552 | 190 | 1 | 190.00 | 1-150 | – | – |
| Walker, M.H.N. | 34 | 43 | 13 | 586 | 78* | 19.53 | – | 1 | 12 | – | 10094 | 3792 | 138 | 27.47 | 8-143 | 6 | – |
| Wall, T.W. | 18 | 24 | 5 | 121 | 20 | 6.36 | – | – | 11 | – | 4812 | 2010 | 56 | 35.89 | 5-14 | 3 | – |
| Walters, F.H. | 1 | 2 | 0 | 12 | 7 | 6.00 | – | – | 2 | – | | | | | | | |
| Walters, K.D. | 68 | 116 | 12 | 4960 | 250 | 47.69 | 14 | 30 | 38 | – | 3211 | 1378 | 49 | 28.12 | 5-66 | 1 | – |
| Ward, F.A. | 4 | 8 | 2 | 36 | 18 | 6.00 | – | – | 1 | – | 1268 | 574 | 11 | 52.18 | 6-102 | 1 | – |
| Watkins, J.R. | 1 | 2 | 1 | 39 | 36 | 39.00 | – | – | 1 | – | 48 | 21 | 0 | – | – | – | – |
| Watson, G.D. | 5 | 9 | 0 | 97 | 50 | 10.77 | – | 1 | 1 | – | 552 | 254 | 6 | 42.33 | 2-67 | – | – |
| Watson, W.J. | 4 | 7 | 1 | 106 | 30 | 17.66 | – | – | 2 | – | 6 | 5 | 0 | – | – | – | – |
| Whitty, W.J. | 14 | 19† | 7 | 161 | 39* | 13.41 | – | – | 4 | – | 3357‡ | 1373 | 65 | 21.12 | 6-17 | 3 | – |
| Wilson, J.W. | | | | | | – | | | | – | 216‡ | 64 | 1 | 64.00 | 1-25 | – | – |
| Wood, G.M. | 6 | 12† | 0 | 521 | 126 | 43.41 | 1 | 4 | 7 | – | – | | | | | | |
| Woodcock, A.J. | 1 | 1 | 0 | 27 | 27 | 27.00 | – | – | 1 | – | – | | | | | | |
| Woodfull, W.M. | 35 | 54 | 4 | 2300 | 161 | 46.00 | 7 | 13 | 7 | – | – | | | | | | |
| Woods, S.M.J. | 3 | 6 | 0 | 32 | 18 | 5.33 | – | – | 1 | – | 217 | 121 | 5 | 24.20 | 2-35 | – | – |
| Worrall, J. | 11 | 22 | 3 | 478 | 76 | 25.15 | – | 5 | 13 | – | 255 | 127 | 1 | 127.00 | 1-97 | – | – |
| Yallop, G.N. | 8 | 15† | 2 | 641 | 121 | 49.30 | 1 | 4 | 5 | – | 18‡ | 8 | 0 | – | – | – | – |
| Yardley, B. | 6 | 11 | 2 | 254 | 74 | 28.22 | – | 1 | 5 | – | 1447 | 573 | 19 | 30.15 | 4-35 | – | – |

## SOUTH AFRICA (235 players)

| | Tests | I | NO | Runs | HS | Avge | 100 | 50 | Ct | St | Balls | Runs | Wkts | Avge | BB | 5wI | 10wM |
|---|---|---|---|---|---|---|---|---|---|---|---|---|---|---|---|---|---|
| | | | | *BATTING AND FIELDING* | | | | | | | *BOWLING* | | | | | | |
| Adcock, N.A.T. | 26 | 39 | 12 | 146 | 24 | 5.40 | – | – | 4 | – | 6391 | 2195 | 104 | 21.10 | 6-43 | 5 | – |
| Anderson, J.H. | 1 | 2 | 0 | 43 | 32 | 21.50 | – | – | 1 | – | – | | | | | | |
| Ashley, W.H. | 1 | 2 | 0 | 1 | 1 | 0.50 | – | – | – | – | 173 | 95 | 7 | 13.57 | 7-95 | 1 | – |
| Bacher, A. | 12 | 22 | 1 | 679 | 73 | 32.33 | – | 6 | 10 | – | – | | | | | | |
| Balaskas, X.C. | 9 | 13 | 1 | 174 | 122* | 14.50 | 1 | – | 5 | – | 1572 | 806 | 22 | 36.63 | 5-49 | 1 | – |
| Barlow, E.J. | 30 | 57 | 2 | 2516 | 201 | 45.74 | 6 | 15 | 35 | – | 3021 | 1362 | 40 | 34.05 | 5-85 | 1 | – |
| Baumgartner, H.V. | 1 | 2 | 0 | 19 | 16 | 9.50 | – | – | 1 | – | 166 | 99 | 2 | 49.50 | 2-99 | – | – |
| Beaumont, R. | 5 | 9 | 0 | 70 | 31 | 7.77 | – | – | 2 | – | 6 | 0 | 0 | – | – | – | – |
| Begbie, D.W. | 5 | 7 | 0 | 138 | 48 | 19.71 | – | – | 2 | – | 160 | 130 | 1 | 130.00 | 1-38 | – | – |
| Bell, A.J. | 16 | 23 | 12 | 69 | 26* | 6.27 | – | – | 6 | – | 3342 | 1567 | 48 | 32.64 | 6-99 | 4 | – |
| Bisset, M. | 3 | 6 | 2 | 103 | 35 | 25.75 | – | – | 2 | 1 | – | | | | | | |
| Bissett, G.F. | 4 | 4 | 2 | 38 | 23 | 19.00 | – | – | 2 | – | 989 | 469 | 25 | 18.76 | 7-29 | 2 | – |

# INDIVIDUAL CAREER RECORDS – *continued*

## SOUTH AFRICA – *continued*

| | Tests | I | NO | Runs | HS | Avge | 100 | 50 | Ct | St | Balls | Runs | Wkts | Avge | BB | 5wI | 10wM |
|---|---|---|---|---|---|---|---|---|---|---|---|---|---|---|---|---|---|
| | | | | *BATTING AND FIELDING* | | | | | | | | | | *BOWLING* | | | |
| Blanckenberg, J.M. | 18 | 30 | 7 | 455 | 59 | 19.78 | – | 2 | 9 | – | 3888 | 1817 | 60 | 30.28 | 6-76 | 4 | – |
| Bland, K.C. | 21 | 39 | 5 | 1669 | 144* | 49.08 | 3 | 9 | 10 | – | 394 | 125 | 2 | 62.50 | 2-16 | – | – |
| Bock, E.G. | 1 | 2 | 2 | 11 | 9* | – | – | – | – | – | 138 | 91 | 0 | – | – | – | – |
| Bond, G.E. | 1 | 1 | 0 | 0 | 0 | 0.00 | – | – | – | – | 16 | 16 | 0 | – | – | – | – |
| Botten, J.T. | 3 | 6 | 0 | 65 | 33 | 10.83 | – | – | 1 | – | 828 | 337 | 8 | 42.12 | 2-56 | – | – |
| Brann, W.H. | 3 | 5 | 0 | 71 | 50 | 14.20 | – | 1 | 2 | – | – | – | – | – | – | – | – |
| Briscoe, A.W. | 2 | 3 | 0 | 33 | 16 | 11.00 | – | – | 1 | – | – | – | – | – | – | – | – |
| Bromfield, H.D. | 9 | 12 | 7 | 59 | 21 | 11.80 | – | – | 13 | – | 1810 | 599 | 17 | 35.23 | 5-88 | 1 | – |
| Brown, L.S. | 2 | 3 | 0 | 17 | 8 | 5.66 | – | – | 1 | – | 318 | 189 | 3 | 63.00 | 1-30 | – | – |
| Burger, C.G.de V. | 2 | 4 | 1 | 62 | 37* | 20.66 | – | – | – | – | – | – | – | – | – | – | – |
| Burke, S.F. | 2 | 4 | 1 | 42 | 20 | 14.00 | – | – | – | – | 660 | 257 | 11 | 23.36 | 6-128 | 2 | 1 |
| Buys, I.D. | 1 | 2 | 1 | 4 | 4* | 4.00 | – | – | – | – | 144 | 52 | 0 | – | – | – | – |
| Cameron, H.B. | 26 | 45 | 4 | 1239 | 90 | 30.21 | – | 10 | 39 | 12 | – | – | – | – | – | – | – |
| Campbell, T. | 5 | 9 | 3 | 90 | 48 | 15.00 | – | – | 7 | 1 | – | – | – | – | – | – | – |
| Carlstein, P.R. | 8 | 14 | 1 | 190 | 42 | 14.61 | – | – | 3 | – | – | – | – | – | – | – | – |
| Carter, C.P. | 10 | 15 | 5 | 181 | 45 | 18.10 | – | – | 2 | – | 1475 | 694 | 28 | 24.78 | 6-50 | 2 | – |
| Catterall, R.H. | 24 | 43 | 2 | 1555 | 120 | 37.92 | 3 | 11 | 12 | – | 342 | 162 | 7 | 23.14 | 3-15 | – | – |
| Chapman, H.W. | 2 | 4 | 1 | 39 | 17 | 13.00 | – | – | 1 | – | 126 | 104 | 1 | 104.00 | 1-51 | – | – |
| Cheetham, J.E. | 24 | 43 | 6 | 883 | 89 | 23.86 | – | 5 | 13 | – | 6 | 2 | 0 | – | – | – | – |
| Chevalier, G.A. | 1 | 2 | 1 | 0 | 0* | 0.00 | – | – | 1 | – | 253‡ | 100 | 5 | 20.00 | 3-68 | – | – |
| Christy, J.A.J. | 10 | 18 | 0 | 618 | 103 | 34.33 | 1 | 5 | 3 | – | 138 | 92 | 2 | 46.00 | 1-15 | – | – |
| Chubb, G.W.A. | 5 | 9 | 3 | 63 | 15* | 10.50 | – | – | – | – | 1425 | 577 | 21 | 27.47 | 6-51 | 2 | – |
| Cochran, J.A.K. | 1 | 1 | 0 | 4 | 4 | 4.00 | – | – | 1 | – | 138 | 47 | 0 | – | – | – | – |
| Coen, S.K. | 2 | 4 | 2 | 101 | 41* | 50.50 | – | – | 1 | – | 12 | 7 | 0 | – | – | – | – |
| Commaille, J.M.M. | 12 | 22 | 1 | 355 | 47 | 16.90 | – | – | 1 | – | 366 | 103 | 2 | 51.50 | 1-40 | – | – |
| Conyngham, D.P. | 1 | 2 | 2 | 6 | 3* | – | – | – | 1 | – | – | – | – | – | – | – | – |
| Cook, F.J. | 1 | 2 | 0 | 7 | 7 | 3.50 | – | – | – | – | – | – | – | – | – | – | – |
| Cooper, A.H.C. | 1 | 2 | 0 | 6 | 6 | 3.00 | – | – | 1 | – | – | – | – | – | – | – | – |
| Cox, J.L. | 3 | 6 | 1 | 17 | 12* | 3.40 | – | – | 1 | – | 576 | 245 | 4 | 61.25 | 2-74 | – | – |
| Cripps, G. | 1 | 2 | 0 | 21 | 18 | 10.50 | – | – | – | – | 15 | 23 | 0 | – | – | – | – |
| Crisp, R.J. | 9 | 13 | 1 | 123 | 35 | 10.25 | – | – | 3 | – | 1428 | 747 | 20 | 37.35 | 5-99 | 1 | – |
| Curnow, S.H. | 7 | 14 | 0 | 168 | 47 | 12.00 | – | – | 5 | – | – | – | – | – | – | – | – |
| Dalton, E.L. | 15 | 24 | 2 | 698 | 117 | 31.72 | 2 | 3 | 5 | – | 864 | 490 | 12 | 40.83 | 4-59 | – | – |
| Davies, E.Q. | 5 | 8 | 3 | 9 | 3 | 1.80 | – | – | – | – | 768 | 481 | 7 | 68.71 | 4-75 | – | – |
| Dawson, O.C. | 9 | 15 | 1 | 293 | 55 | 20.92 | – | 1 | 10 | – | 1294 | 578 | 10 | 57.80 | 2-57 | – | – |
| Deane, H.G. | 17 | 27 | 2 | 628 | 93 | 25.12 | – | 3 | 8 | – | – | – | – | – | – | – | – |
| Dixon, C.D. | 1 | 2 | 0 | 0 | 0 | 0.00 | – | – | 1 | – | 240 | 118 | 3 | 39.33 | 2-62 | – | – |
| Dower, R.R. | 1 | 2 | 0 | 9 | 9 | 4.50 | – | – | 2 | – | – | – | – | – | – | – | – |

# INDIVIDUAL CAREER RECORDS – continued

## SOUTH AFRICA – continued

| | | | BATTING AND FIELDING | | | | | | | | BOWLING | | | | | |
| | Tests | I | NO | Runs | HS | Avge | 100 | 50 | Ct | St | Balls | Runs | Wkts | Avge | BB | 5wI | 10wM |
|---|---|---|---|---|---|---|---|---|---|---|---|---|---|---|---|---|---|
| Draper, R.G. | 2 | 3 | 0 | 25 | 15 | 8.33 | – | – | – | – | – | | | | | – | – |
| Duckworth, C.A.R. | 2 | 4 | 0 | 28 | 13 | 7.00 | – | – | 3 | – | | | | | | – | – |
| Dumbrill, R. | 5 | 10 | 0 | 153 | 36 | 15.30 | – | – | 3 | – | 816 | 336 | 9 | 37.33 | 4-30 | – | – |
| Duminy, J.P. | 3 | 6 | 0 | 30 | 12 | 5.00 | – | – | 2 | – | 60 | 39 | 1 | 39.00 | 1-17 | – | – |
| Dunell, O.R. | 2 | 4 | 1 | 42 | 26* | 14.00 | – | – | 1 | – | | | | | | – | – |
| Du Preez, J.H. | 2 | 2 | 0 | 0 | 0 | 0.00 | – | – | 2 | – | 144 | 51 | 3 | 17.00 | 2-22 | – | – |
| Du Toit, J.F. | 1 | 2 | 2 | 2 | 2* | – | – | – | 1 | – | 85 | 47 | 1 | 47.00 | 1-47 | – | – |
| Dyer, D.V. | 3 | 6 | 0 | 96 | 62 | 16.00 | – | 1 | – | – | – | | | | | – | – |
| Elgie, M.K. | 3 | 6 | 0 | 75 | 56 | 12.50 | – | 1 | 4 | – | 66‡ | 46 | 0 | – | – | – | – |
| Endean, W.R. | 28 | 52 | 4 | 1630 | 162* | 33.95 | 3 | 8 | 41 | – | – | | | | | – | – |
| Farrer, W.S. | 6 | 10 | 2 | 221 | 40 | 27.62 | – | – | 2 | – | – | | | | | – | – |
| Faulkner, G.A. | 25 | 47 | 4 | 1754 | 204 | 40.79 | 4 | 8 | 20 | – | 4227 | 2180 | 82 | 26.58 | 7-84 | 4 | – |
| Fellows-Smith, J.P. | 4 | 8 | 2 | 166 | 35 | 27.66 | – | – | 2 | – | 114 | 61 | 0 | – | – | – | – |
| Fichardt, C.G. | 2 | 4 | 0 | 15 | 10 | 3.75 | – | – | 2 | – | | | | | | – | – |
| Finlason, C.E. | 1 | 2 | 0 | 6 | 6 | 3.00 | – | – | – | – | 12 | 7 | 0 | – | – | – | – |
| Floquet, C.E. | 1 | 2 | 1 | 12 | 11* | 12.00 | – | – | – | – | 48 | 24 | 0 | – | – | – | – |
| Francis, H.H. | 2 | 4 | 0 | 39 | 29 | 9.75 | – | – | 1 | – | – | | | | | – | – |
| Francois, C.M. | 5 | 9 | 1 | 252 | 72 | 31.50 | – | 1 | 5 | – | 684 | 225 | 6 | 37.50 | 3-23 | – | – |
| Frank, C.N. | 3 | 6 | 0 | 236 | 152 | 39.33 | 1 | – | – | – | 58 | 52 | 1 | 52.00 | 1-52 | – | – |
| Frank, W.H.B. | 1 | 2 | 0 | 7 | 5 | 3.50 | – | – | – | – | | | | | | – | – |
| Fuller, E.R.H. | 7 | 9 | 1 | 64 | 17 | 8.00 | – | – | 3 | – | 1898 | 668 | 22 | 30.36 | 5-66 | 1 | – |
| Fullerton, G.M. | 7 | 13 | 0 | 325 | 88 | 25.00 | – | 3 | 10 | 2 | – | | | | | – | – |
| Funston, K.J. | 18 | 33 | 1 | 824 | 92 | 25.75 | – | 5 | 7 | – | – | | | | | – | – |
| Gamsy, D. | 2 | 3 | 1 | 39 | 30* | 19.50 | – | – | 5 | 3 | – | | | | | – | – |
| Gleeson, R.A. | 1 | 2 | 1 | 4 | 3 | 4.00 | – | – | 2 | – | – | | | | | – | – |
| Glover, G.K. | 1 | 2 | 1 | 21 | 18* | 21.00 | – | – | – | – | 65 | 28 | 1 | 28.00 | 1-28 | – | – |
| Goddard, T.L. | 41 | 78† | 5 | 2516 | 112 | 34.46 | 1 | 18 | 48 | – | 11736‡ | 3226 | 123 | 26.22 | 6-53 | 5 | – |
| Gordon, N. | 5 | 6 | 4 | 8 | 7* | 2.00 | – | – | 1 | – | 1966 | 807 | 20 | 40.35 | 5-103 | 2 | – |
| Graham, R, | 2 | 4 | 0 | 8 | 4 | 1.50 | – | – | 2 | – | 240 | 127 | 3 | 42.33 | 2-22 | – | – |
| Grieveson, R.E. | 2 | 2 | 0 | 114 | 75 | 57.00 | – | 1 | 7 | 3 | – | | | | | – | – |
| Griffin, G.M. | 2 | 4 | 0 | 25 | 14 | 6.25 | – | – | – | – | 432 | 192 | 8 | 24.00 | 4-87 | – | – |
| Hall, A.E. | 7 | 8 | 2 | 11 | 5 | 1.83 | – | – | 4 | – | 2361 | 886 | 40 | 22.15 | 7-63 | 3 | 1 |
| Hall, G.G. | 1 | 1 | 0 | 0 | 0 | 0.00 | – | – | – | – | 186 | 94 | 1 | 94.00 | 1-94 | – | – |
| Halliwell, E.A. | 8 | 15 | 0 | 188 | 57 | 12.53 | – | 1 | 9 | 2 | – | | | | | – | – |
| Halse, C.G. | 3 | 3 | 3 | 30 | 19* | – | – | – | 1 | – | 587 | 260 | 6 | 43.33 | 3-50 | – | – |
| Hands, P.A.M. | 7 | 12 | 0 | 300 | 83 | 25.00 | – | 2 | 3 | – | 37 | 18 | 0 | – | – | – | – |
| Hands, R.H.M. | 1 | 2 | 0 | 7 | 7 | 3.50 | – | – | – | – | – | | | | | – | – |

SOUTH AFRICA – continued

| | Tests | I | NO | Runs | HS | Avge | 100 | 50 | Ct | St | Balls | Runs | Wkts | Avge | BB | 5wI | 10wM |
|---|---|---|---|---|---|---|---|---|---|---|---|---|---|---|---|---|---|
| | | | | | | BATTING AND FIELDING | | | | | | | | BOWLING | | | |
| Hanley, M.A. | 1 | 1 | 0 | 0 | 0 | 0.00 | – | – | 1 | – | 232 | 88 | 1 | 88.00 | 1-57 | – | – |
| Harris, T.A. | 3 | 5 | 1 | 100 | 60 | 25.00 | – | 1 | 1 | – | – | – | – | | | – | – |
| Hartigan, G.P.D. | 5 | 10 | 0 | 114 | 51 | 11.40 | – | 1 | – | – | 252 | 141 | 1 | 141.00 | 1-72 | – | – |
| Harvey, R.L. | 2 | 4 | 0 | 51 | 28 | 12.75 | – | – | – | – | | | | | | | |
| Hathorn, C.M.H. | 12 | 20 | 1 | 325 | 102 | 17.10 | 1 | – | 5 | – | – | | | | | – | – |
| Hearne, F. | 4 | 8 | 0 | 121 | 30 | 15.12 | – | – | 2 | – | 62 | 40 | 2 | 20.00 | 2-40 | – | – |
| Hearne, G.A.L. | 3 | 5 | 0 | 59 | 28 | 11.80 | – | – | 3 | – | | | | | | | |
| Heine, P.S. | 14 | 24 | 3 | 209 | 31 | 9.95 | – | – | 8 | – | 3890 | 1455 | 58 | 25.08 | 6-58 | 4 | – |
| Hime, C.F.W. | 1 | 2 | 0 | 8 | 8 | 4.00 | – | – | – | – | 55 | 31 | 1 | 31.00 | 1-20 | – | – |
| Hutchinson, P. | 2 | 4 | 0 | 14 | 11 | 3.50 | – | – | 3 | – | – | | | | | | |
| Innes, A.R. | 2 | 4 | 0 | 14 | 13 | 3.50 | – | – | 2 | – | 128 | 89 | 5 | 17.80 | 5-43 | 1 | – |
| Ironside, D.E.J. | 3 | 4 | 2 | 37 | 13 | 18.50 | – | – | 1 | – | 985 | 275 | 15 | 18.33 | 5-51 | 1 | – |
| Irvine, B.L. | 4 | 7† | 0 | 353 | 102 | 50.42 | 1 | 2 | 2 | – | – | | | | | | |
| Johnson, C.L. | 1 | 2 | 0 | 10 | 7 | 5.00 | – | – | 1 | – | 140 | 57 | 0 | – | – | – | – |
| Jones, P.S.T. | 1 | 2 | 0 | 0 | 0 | 0.00 | – | – | – | – | – | | | | | | |
| Keith, H.J. | 8 | 16† | 1 | 318 | 73 | 21.20 | – | 2 | 9 | – | 108‡ | 63 | 0 | – | – | – | – |
| Kempis, G.A. | 1 | 2 | 1 | 0 | 0* | 0.00 | – | – | – | – | 168 | 76 | 4 | 19.00 | 3-53 | – | – |
| Kotze, J.J. | 3 | 5 | 0 | 2 | 2 | 0.40 | – | – | 3 | – | 413 | 243 | 6 | 40.50 | 3-64 | – | – |
| Kuys, F. | 1 | 2 | 0 | 26 | 26 | 13.00 | – | – | – | – | 60 | 31 | 2 | 15.50 | 2-31 | – | – |
| Lance, H.R. | 13 | 22 | 1 | 591 | 70 | 28.14 | – | 5 | 7 | – | 948 | 479 | 12 | 39.91 | 3-30 | – | – |
| Langton, A.B.C. | 15 | 23 | 4 | 298 | 73* | 15.68 | – | 2 | 8 | – | 4199 | 1827 | 40 | 45.67 | 5-58 | 1 | – |
| Lawrence, G.B. | 5 | 8 | 0 | 141 | 43 | 17.62 | – | – | 2 | – | 1334 | 512 | 28 | 18.28 | 8-53 | 2 | – |
| Le Roux, F.L. | 1 | 2 | 0 | 1 | 1 | 0.50 | – | – | – | – | 54 | 24 | 0 | – | – | | |
| Lewis, P.T. | 1 | 2 | 0 | 0 | 0 | 0.00 | – | – | – | – | – | | | | | | |
| Lindsay, D.T. | 19 | 31 | 1 | 1130 | 182 | 37.66 | 3 | 5 | 57 | 2 | – | | | | | | |
| Lindsay, J.D. | 3 | 5 | 2 | 21 | 9* | 7.00 | – | – | 4 | 1 | – | | | | | | |
| Lindsay, N.V. | 1 | 2 | 0 | 35 | 29 | 17.50 | – | – | 1 | – | | | | | | | |
| Ling, W.V.S. | 6 | 10 | 0 | 168 | 38 | 16.80 | – | – | 1 | – | 18 | 20 | 0 | – | – | – | – |
| Llewellyn, C.B. | 15 | 28 | 1 | 544 | 90 | 20.14 | – | 4 | 7 | – | 2292 | 1421 | 48 | 29.60 | 6-92 | 4 | 1 |
| Lundie, E.B. | 1 | 2 | 1 | 1 | 1 | 1.00 | – | – | – | – | 286 | 107 | 4 | 26.75 | 4-101 | – | – |
| Macaulay, M.J. | 1 | 2 | 0 | 33 | 21 | 16.50 | – | – | – | – | 276‡ | 73 | 2 | 36.50 | 1-10 | – | – |
| McCarthy, C.N. | 15 | 24 | 15 | 28 | 5 | 3.11 | – | – | 6 | – | 3499 | 1510 | 36 | 41.94 | 6-43 | 2 | – |
| McGlew, D.J. | 34 | 64 | 6 | 2440 | 255* | 42.06 | 7 | 10 | 18 | – | 32 | 23 | 0 | – | – | – | – |
| McKinnon, A.H. | 8 | 13 | 7 | 107 | 27 | 17.83 | – | – | 1 | – | 2546‡ | 925 | 26 | 35.57 | 4-128 | – | – |
| McLean, R.A. | 40 | 73 | 3 | 2120 | 142 | 30.28 | 5 | 10 | 23 | – | 4 | 1 | 0 | – | – | – | – |

SOUTH AFRICA – continued

| | | | | BATTING AND FIELDING | | | | | | | | BOWLING | | | | | |
|---|---|---|---|---|---|---|---|---|---|---|---|---|---|---|---|---|---|
| | Tests | I | NO | Runs | HS | Avge | 100 | 50 | Ct | St | Balls | Runs | Wkts | Avge | BB | 5wI | 10wM |
| McMillan, Q. | 13 | 21 | 4 | 306 | 50* | 18.00 | – | 1 | 8 | – | 2021 | 1243 | 36 | 34.52 | 5-66 | 2 | – |
| Mann, N.B.F. | 19 | 31 | 1 | 400 | 52 | 13.33 | – | 1 | 3 | – | 5796‡ | 1920 | 58 | 33.10 | 6-59 | 1 | – |
| Mansell, P.N.F. | 13 | 22 | 2 | 355 | 90 | 17.75 | – | 2 | 15 | – | 1506 | 736 | 11 | 66.90 | 3-58 | – | – |
| Markham, L.A. | 1 | 1 | 0 | 20 | 20 | 20.00 | – | – | – | – | 104 | 72 | 1 | 72.00 | 1-34 | – | – |
| Marx, W.F.E. | 3 | 6 | 0 | 125 | 36 | 20.83 | – | – | 3 | – | 228 | 144 | 4 | 36.00 | 3-85 | – | – |
| Meintjes, D.J. | 2 | 3 | 0 | 43 | 21 | 14.33 | – | – | – | – | 246 | 115 | 6 | 19.16 | 3-38 | – | – |
| Melle, M.G. | 7 | 12 | 4 | 68 | 17 | 8.50 | – | – | 4 | – | 1667 | 851 | 26 | 32.73 | 6-71 | 2 | – |
| Melville, A. | 11 | 19 | 2 | 894 | 189 | 52.58 | 4 | 3 | 8 | – | – | – | – | – | – | – | – |
| Middleton, J. | 6 | 12 | 5 | 52 | 22 | 7.42 | – | – | 1 | – | 1064 | 442 | 24 | 18.41 | 5-51 | 2 | – |
| Mills, C. | 1 | 2 | 0 | 25 | 21 | 12.50 | – | – | 2 | – | 140 | 83 | 2 | 41.50 | 2-83 | – | – |
| Milton, W.H. | 3 | 6 | 0 | 68 | 21 | 11.33 | – | – | 1 | – | 79 | 48 | 2 | 24.00 | 1-5 | – | – |
| Mitchell, B. | 42 | 80 | 9 | 3471 | 189* | 48.88 | 8 | 21 | 56 | – | 2519 | 1380 | 27 | 51.11 | 5-87 | 1 | – |
| Mitchell, F. | 3 | 6 | 0 | 28 | 12 | 4.66 | – | – | – | – | – | – | – | – | – | – | – |
| Morkel, D.P.B. | 16 | 28 | 1 | 663 | 88 | 24.55 | – | 4 | 13 | – | 1704 | 821 | 18 | 45.61 | 4-93 | – | – |
| Murray, A.R.A. | 10 | 14 | 1 | 289 | 109 | 22.23 | 1 | 1 | 3 | – | 2374 | 710 | 18 | 39.44 | 4-169 | – | – |
| Nel, J.D. | 6 | 11 | 0 | 150 | 38 | 13.63 | – | – | 1 | – | – | – | – | – | – | – | – |
| Newberry, C.J. | 4 | 8 | 0 | 62 | 16 | 7.75 | – | – | 3 | – | 558 | 268 | 11 | 24.36 | 4-72 | – | – |
| Newson, E.S. | 3 | 5 | 1 | 30 | 16 | 7.50 | – | – | 3 | – | 874 | 265 | 4 | 66.25 | 2-58 | – | – |
| Nicholson, F. | 4 | 8 | 1 | 76 | 29 | 10.85 | – | – | 3 | – | – | – | – | – | – | – | – |
| Nicolson, J.F.W. | 3 | 5 | 0 | 179 | 78 | 35.80 | – | 1 | – | – | 24 | 17 | 0 | – | – | – | – |
| Norton, N.O. | 1 | 2 | 0 | 9 | 7 | 4.50 | – | – | – | – | 90 | 47 | 4 | 11.75 | 4-47 | – | – |
| Nourse, A.D. | 34 | 62 | 7 | 2960 | 231 | 53.81 | 9 | 14 | 12 | – | 20 | 9 | 0 | – | – | – | – |
| Nourse, A.W. | 45 | 83† | 8 | 2234 | 111 | 29.78 | 1 | 15 | 43 | – | 3234 | 1553 | 41 | 37.87 | 4-25 | – | – |
| Nupen, E.P. | 17 | 31 | 7 | 348 | 69 | 14.50 | – | 2 | 9 | – | 4159 | 1788 | 50 | 35.76 | 6-46 | 5 | 1 |
| Ochse, A.E. | 2 | 4 | 0 | 16 | 8 | 4.00 | – | – | – | – | – | – | – | – | – | – | – |
| Ochse, A.L. | 3 | 4 | 1 | 11 | 4* | 3.66 | – | – | 1 | – | 649 | 362 | 10 | 36.20 | 4-79 | – | – |
| O'Linn, S. | 7 | 12† | 1 | 297 | 98 | 27.00 | – | 2 | 4 | – | – | – | – | – | – | – | – |
| Owen-Smith, H.G. | 5 | 8 | 2 | 252 | 129 | 42.00 | 1 | 1 | 4 | – | 156 | 113 | 0 | – | – | – | – |
| Palm, A.W. | 1 | 2 | 0 | 15 | 13 | 7.50 | – | – | 1 | – | – | – | – | – | – | – | – |
| Parker, G.M. | 2 | 4 | 2 | 3 | 2* | 1.50 | – | – | – | – | 366 | 273 | 8 | 34.12 | 6-152 | 1 | – |
| Parkin, D.C. | 1 | 2 | 0 | 6 | 6 | 3.00 | – | – | 1 | – | 130 | 82 | 3 | 27.33 | 3-82 | – | – |
| Partridge, J.T. | 11 | 12 | 5 | 73 | 13* | 10.42 | – | – | 6 | – | 3684 | 1373 | 44 | 31.20 | 7-91 | 3 | – |
| Pearse, C.O.C. | 3 | 6 | 0 | 55 | 31 | 9.16 | – | – | 1 | – | 144 | 106 | 3 | 35.33 | 3-56 | – | – |
| Pegler, S.J. | 16 | 28 | 5 | 356 | 35* | 15.47 | – | 1 | 5 | – | 2989 | 1572 | 47 | 33.44 | 7-65 | 2 | – |
| Pithey, A.J. | 17 | 27 | 1 | 819 | 154 | 31.50 | 1 | 4 | 3 | – | 12 | 5 | 0 | – | – | – | – |
| Pithey, D.B. | 8 | 12 | 1 | 138 | 55 | 12.54 | – | 1 | 6 | – | 1424 | 577 | 12 | 48.08 | 6-58 | 1 | – |
| Plimsoll, J.B. | 1 | 2 | 1 | 16 | 8* | 16.00 | – | – | – | – | 237‡ | 143 | 3 | 47.66 | 3-128 | – | – |

SOUTH AFRICA – *continued*

| | Tests | I | NO | Runs | HS | Avge | 100 | 50 | Ct | St | Balls | Runs | Wkts | Avge | BB | 5wI | 10wM |
|---|---|---|---|---|---|---|---|---|---|---|---|---|---|---|---|---|---|
| | | | | BATTING AND FIELDING | | | | | | | | | | BOWLING | | | |
| Pollock, P.M. | 28 | 41 | 13 | 607 | 75* | 21.67 | – | 2 | 9 | – | 6522 | 2806 | 116 | 24.18 | 6-38 | 9 | 1 |
| Pollock, R.G. | 23 | 41† | 4 | 2256 | 274 | 60.97 | 7 | 11 | 17 | – | 414 | 204 | 4 | 51.00 | 2-50 | – | – |
| Poore, R.M. | 3 | 6 | 0 | 76 | 20 | 12.66 | – | – | 3 | – | 9 | 4 | 4 | 4.00 | 1-4 | – | – |
| Pothecary, J.E. | 3 | 4 | 0 | 26 | 12 | 6.50 | – | – | 2 | – | 828 | 354 | 9 | 39.33 | 4-58 | – | – |
| Powell, A.W. | 1 | 2 | 0 | 16 | 11 | 8.00 | – | – | 2 | – | 20 | 10 | 1 | 10.00 | 1-10 | – | – |
| Prince, C.F.H. | 1 | 2 | 0 | 6 | 5 | 3.00 | – | – | – | – | – | – | – | – | – | – | – |
| Procter, M.J. | 7 | 10 | 1 | 226 | 48 | 25.11 | – | – | 4 | – | 1514 | 616 | 41 | 15.02 | 6-73 | 1 | – |
| Promnitz, H.L.E. | 2 | 4 | 0 | 14 | 5 | 3.50 | – | – | 2 | – | 528 | 161 | 8 | 20.12 | 5-58 | 1 | – |
| Quinn, N.A. | 12 | 18 | 3 | 90 | 28 | 6.00 | – | – | 1 | – | 2922‡ | 1145 | 35 | 32.71 | 6-92 | 1 | – |
| Reid, N. | 1 | 2 | 0 | 17 | 11 | 8.50 | – | – | – | – | 126 | 63 | 2 | 31.50 | 2-63 | – | – |
| Richards, A.R. | 1 | 2 | 0 | 6 | 6 | 3.00 | – | – | – | – | – | – | – | – | – | – | – |
| Richards, B.A. | 4 | 7 | 0 | 508 | 140 | 72.57 | 2 | 2 | 3 | – | 72 | 26 | 1 | 26.00 | 1-12 | – | – |
| Richards, W.H.M. | 1 | 2 | 0 | 4 | 4 | 2.00 | – | – | – | – | – | – | – | – | – | – | – |
| Robertson, J.B. | 3 | 6 | 1 | 51 | 17 | 10.20 | – | – | 2 | – | 738 | 321 | 6 | 53.50 | 3-143 | – | – |
| Routledge, T.W. | 4 | 8 | 0 | 72 | 24 | 9.00 | – | – | 2 | – | – | – | – | – | – | – | – |
| Rowan, A.M.B. | 15 | 23 | 6 | 290 | 41 | 17.05 | – | – | 7 | – | 5193 | 2084 | 54 | 38.59 | 5-68 | 4 | – |
| Rowan, E.A.B. | 26 | 50 | 5 | 1965 | 236 | 43.66 | 3 | 12 | 14 | – | 19 | 7 | 0 | – | – | – | – |
| Rowe, G.A. | 5 | 9 | 3 | 26 | 13* | 4.33 | – | – | 4 | – | 998 | 456 | 15 | 30.40 | 5-115 | 1 | – |
| Samuelson, S.V. | 1 | 2 | 0 | 22 | 15 | 11.00 | – | – | 1 | – | 108 | 64 | 0 | – | – | – | – |
| Schwarz, R.O. | 20 | 35 | 8 | 374 | 61 | 13.85 | – | 1 | 18 | – | 2639 | 1417 | 55 | 25.76 | 6-47 | 2 | – |
| Seccull, A.W. | 1 | 2 | 1 | 23 | 17* | 23.00 | – | – | 1 | – | 60 | 37 | 2 | 18.50 | 2-37 | – | – |
| Seymour, M.A. | 7 | 10 | 3 | 84 | 36 | 12.00 | – | – | 2 | – | 1458 | 588 | 9 | 65.33 | 3-80 | – | – |
| Shalders, W.A. | 12 | 23 | 1 | 355 | 42 | 16.13 | – | – | 3 | – | 48 | 6 | 1 | 6.00 | 1-6 | – | – |
| Shepstone, G.H. | 2 | 4 | 0 | 38 | 21 | 9.50 | – | – | 2 | – | 115 | 47 | 0 | – | – | – | – |
| Sherwell, P.W. | 13 | 22 | 4 | 427 | 115 | 23.72 | 1 | 1 | 20 | 16 | – | – | – | – | – | – | – |
| Siedle, I.J. | 18 | 34 | 0 | 977 | 141 | 28.73 | 1 | 5 | 7 | – | 19 | 7 | 1 | 7.00 | 1-7 | – | – |
| Sinclair, J.H. | 25 | 47 | 1 | 1069 | 106 | 23.23 | 3 | 3 | 9 | – | 3598 | 1996 | 63 | 31.68 | 6-26 | 1 | – |
| Smith, C.J.E. | 3 | 6 | 1 | 106 | 45 | 21.20 | – | – | 2 | – | – | – | – | – | – | – | – |
| Smith, F.W. | 3 | 6 | 1 | 45 | 12 | 9.00 | – | – | 2 | – | – | – | – | – | – | – | – |
| Smith, V.I. | 9 | 16 | 6 | 39 | 11* | 3.90 | – | – | 3 | – | 1655 | 769 | 12 | 64.08 | 4-143 | – | – |
| Snooke, S.D. | 1 | 1 | 0 | 0 | 0 | 0.00 | – | – | 2 | – | – | – | – | – | – | – | – |
| Snooke, S.J. | 26 | 46 | 1 | 1008 | 103 | 22.40 | 1 | 5 | 24 | – | 1620 | 702 | 35 | 20.05 | 8-70 | 1 | 1 |
| Solomon, W.R.T. | 1 | 2 | 0 | 4 | 2 | 2.00 | – | – | 1 | – | – | – | – | – | – | – | – |
| Stewart, R.B. | 1 | 2 | 0 | 13 | 9 | 6.50 | – | – | 2 | – | – | – | – | – | – | – | – |
| Stricker, L.A. | 13 | 24 | 0 | 342 | 48 | 14.25 | – | – | 3 | – | 174 | 105 | 1 | 105.00 | 1-36 | – | – |
| Susskind, M.J. | 5 | 8 | 0 | 268 | 65 | 33.50 | – | 4 | 1 | – | – | – | – | – | – | – | – |
| Taberer, H.M. | 1 | 1 | 0 | 2 | 2 | 2.00 | – | – | – | – | 60 | 48 | 1 | 48.00 | 1-25 | – | – |
| Tancred, A.B. | 2 | 4 | 1 | 87 | 29 | 29.00 | – | – | 2 | – | – | – | – | – | – | – | – |

# INDIVIDUAL CAREER RECORDS – continued

| | Tests | I | NO | Runs | HS | Avge | 100 | 50 | Ct | St | Balls | Runs | Wkts | Avge | BB | 5wI | 10wM |
|---|---|---|---|---|---|---|---|---|---|---|---|---|---|---|---|---|---|
| | | | | | *BATTING AND FIELDING* | | | | | | | | *BOWLING* | | | | |
| Tancred, L.J. | 14 | 26 | 1 | 530 | 97 | 21.20 | – | 2 | 3 | – | – | – | – | – | – | – | – |
| Tancred, V.M. | 1 | 2 | 0 | 25 | 18 | 12.50 | – | – | 1 | – | – | – | – | – | – | – | – |
| Tapscott, G.L. | 1 | 2 | 0 | 5 | 4 | 2.50 | – | – | 1 | – | – | – | – | – | – | – | – |
| Tapscott, L.E. | 2 | 3 | 1 | 58 | 50* | 29.00 | – | 1 | – | – | 12 | 2 | 0 | – | – | – | – |
| Tayfield, H.J. | 37 | 60 | 9 | 862 | 75 | 16.90 | – | 2 | 26 | – | 13568 | 4405 | 170 | 25.91 | 9-113 | 14 | 2 |
| Taylor, A.I. | 1 | 2 | 0 | 18 | 12 | 9.00 | – | – | – | – | – | – | – | – | – | – | – |
| Taylor, D. | 2 | 4 | 0 | 85 | 36 | 21.25 | – | – | – | – | – | – | – | – | – | – | – |
| Taylor, H.W. | 42 | 76 | 4 | 2936 | 176 | 40.77 | 7 | 17 | 19 | – | 342 | 156 | 5 | 31.20 | 3-15 | – | – |
| Theunissen, N.H. | 1 | 2 | 1 | 2 | 2* | 2.00 | – | – | 1 | – | 80 | 51 | 0 | – | – | – | – |
| Thornton, P.G. | 1 | 1 | 1 | 1 | 1* | – | – | – | – | – | 24 | 20 | 1 | 20.00 | 1-20 | – | – |
| Tomlinson, D.S. | 1 | 1 | 0 | 9 | 9 | 9.00 | – | – | 1 | – | 60 | 38 | 0 | – | – | – | – |
| Traicos, A.J. | 3 | 4 | 2 | 8 | 5* | 4.00 | – | – | 4 | – | 470 | 207 | 4 | 51.75 | 2-70 | – | – |
| Trimborn, P.H.J. | 4 | 4 | 2 | 13 | 11* | 6.50 | – | – | 7 | – | 747 | 257 | 11 | 23.36 | 3-12 | – | – |
| Tuckett, L. | 9 | 14 | 3 | 131 | 40* | 11.90 | – | – | 9 | – | 2104 | 980 | 19 | 51.57 | 5-68 | 2 | – |
| Tuckett, L.R. | 1 | 2 | 1 | 0 | 0* | 0.00 | – | – | 2 | – | 120 | 69 | 0 | – | – | – | – |
| | | | | | | | | | | | | | | | | | |
| Van der Bijl, P.G.V. | 5 | 9 | 0 | 460 | 125 | 51.11 | 1 | 2 | 1 | – | – | – | – | – | – | – | – |
| Van der Merwe, E.A. | 2 | 4 | 1 | 27 | 19 | 9.00 | – | – | 3 | – | – | – | – | – | – | – | – |
| Van der Merwe, P.L. | 15 | 23 | 2 | 533 | 76 | 25.38 | – | 3 | 11 | – | 79‡ | 22 | 1 | 22.00 | 1-6 | – | – |
| Van Ryneveld, C.B. | 19 | 33 | 6 | 724 | 83 | 26.81 | – | 3 | 14 | – | 1554 | 671 | 17 | 39.47 | 4-67 | – | – |
| Varnals, G.D. | 3 | 6 | 0 | 97 | 23 | 16.16 | – | – | – | – | 12 | 2 | 0 | – | – | – | – |
| Viljoen, K.G. | 27 | 50 | 2 | 1365 | 124 | 28.43 | 2 | 9 | 5 | – | 48 | 23 | 0 | – | – | – | – |
| Vincent, C.L. | 25 | 38 | 12 | 526 | 60 | 20.23 | – | 2 | 27 | – | 5863 | 2631 | 84 | 31.32 | 6-51 | 3 | – |
| Vincent, C.H. | 3 | 6 | 0 | 26 | 9 | 4.33 | – | – | 1 | – | 369 | 193 | 4 | 48.25 | 3-88 | – | – |
| Vogler, A.E.E. | 15 | 26 | 6 | 340 | 65 | 17.00 | – | 2 | 20 | – | 2764 | 1455 | 64 | 22.73 | 7-94 | 5 | 1 |
| | | | | | | | | | | | | | | | | | |
| Wade, H.F. | 10 | 18 | 2 | 327 | 40* | 20.43 | – | – | 4 | – | – | – | – | – | – | – | – |
| Wade, W.W. | 11 | 19 | 1 | 511 | 125 | 28.38 | 1 | 3 | 15 | 2 | – | – | – | – | – | – | – |
| Waite, J.H.B. | 50 | 86 | 7 | 2405 | 134 | 30.44 | 4 | 16 | 124 | 17 | – | – | – | – | – | – | – |
| Walter, K.A. | 2 | 3 | 1 | 11 | 10 | 3.66 | – | – | 3 | – | 495 | 197 | 6 | 32.83 | 4-63 | – | – |
| Ward, T.A. | 23 | 42 | 9 | 459 | 64 | 13.90 | – | 2 | 19 | 13 | – | – | – | – | – | – | – |
| Watkins, J.C. | 15 | 27 | 1 | 612 | 92 | 23.53 | – | 3 | 12 | – | 2805 | 816 | 29 | 28.13 | 4-22 | – | – |
| Wesley, C. | 3 | 5† | 0 | 49 | 35 | 9.80 | – | – | 1 | – | – | – | – | – | – | – | – |
| Westcott, R.J. | 5 | 9 | 0 | 166 | 62 | 18.44 | – | 1 | 1 | – | 32 | 22 | 0 | – | – | – | – |
| White, G.C. | 17 | 31 | 2 | 872 | 147 | 30.06 | 2 | 4 | 10 | – | 498 | 301 | 9 | 33.44 | 4-47 | – | – |
| Willoughby, J.T. | 2 | 4 | 0 | 8 | 5 | 2.00 | – | – | – | – | 275 | 159 | 6 | 26.50 | 2-37 | – | – |
| Wimble, C.S. | 1 | 2 | 0 | 0 | 0 | 0.00 | – | – | 1 | – | – | – | – | – | – | – | – |
| Winslow, P.L. | 5 | 9 | 0 | 186 | 108 | 20.66 | 1 | 1 | 1 | – | – | – | – | – | – | – | – |
| Wynne, O.E. | 6 | 12 | 0 | 219 | 50 | 18.25 | – | 1 | 3 | – | – | – | – | – | – | – | – |
| | | | | | | | | | | | | | | | | | |
| Zulch, J.W. | 16 | 32 | 2 | 985 | 150 | 32.83 | 2 | 4 | 4 | – | 24 | 28 | 0 | – | – | – | – |

# INDIVIDUAL CAREER RECORDS – continued

WEST INDIES (171 players)

| | Tests | I | NO | Runs | HS | Avge | 100 | 50 | Ct | St | Balls | Runs | Wkts | Avge | BB | 5wI | 10wM |
|---|---|---|---|---|---|---|---|---|---|---|---|---|---|---|---|---|---|
| | | | | | | BATTING AND FIELDING | | | | | | | | BOWLING | | | |
| Achong, E.E. | 6 | 11 | 1 | 81 | 22 | 8.10 | – | – | 6 | – | 918‡ | 378 | 8 | 47.25 | 2-64 | – | – |
| Alexander, F.C.M. | 25 | 38 | 6 | 961 | 108 | 30.03 | 1 | 7 | 85 | 5 | – | – | – | – | – | – | – |
| Ali, Imtiaz | 1 | 1 | 1 | 1* | – | – | – | – | – | – | 204 | 89 | 2 | 44.50 | 2-37 | – | – |
| Ali, Inshan | 12 | 18† | 2 | 172 | 25 | 10.75 | – | – | 7 | – | 3718‡ | 1621 | 34 | 47.67 | 5-59 | 1 | – |
| Allan, D.W. | 5 | 7 | 1 | 75 | 40* | 12.50 | – | – | 15 | 3 | – | – | – | – | – | – | – |
| Asgarali, N.R. | 2 | 4 | 0 | 62 | 29 | 15.50 | – | – | – | – | – | – | – | – | – | – | – |
| Atkinson, D.St E. | 22 | 35 | 6 | 922 | 219 | 31.79 | 1 | 5 | 11 | – | 5201 | 1647 | 47 | 35.04 | 7-53 | 3 | – |
| Atkinson, E.St E. | 8 | 9 | 1 | 126 | 37 | 15.75 | – | – | 2 | – | 1634 | 589 | 25 | 23.56 | 5-42 | 1 | – |
| Austin, R.A. | 2 | 2 | 0 | 22 | 20 | 11.00 | – | – | 2 | – | 6 | 5 | 0 | – | – | – | – |
| Bacchus, S.F.A. | 2 | 4 | 0 | 42 | 21 | 10.50 | – | – | 3 | – | – | – | – | – | – | – | – |
| Baichan, L. | 3 | 6† | 2 | 184 | 105* | 46.00 | 1 | – | 2 | – | – | – | – | – | – | – | – |
| Barrett, A.G. | 6 | 7 | 1 | 40 | 19 | 6.66 | – | – | 17 | – | 1612 | 603 | 13 | 46.38 | 3-43 | – | – |
| Barrow, I. | 11 | 19 | 2 | 276 | 105 | 16.23 | 1 | 1 | 17 | 5 | – | – | – | – | – | – | – |
| Bartlett, E.L. | 5 | 8 | 1 | 131 | 84 | 18.71 | – | 1 | 2 | – | – | – | – | – | – | – | – |
| Betancourt, N. | 1 | 2 | 0 | 52 | 39 | 26.00 | – | – | – | – | – | – | – | – | – | – | – |
| Binns, A.P. | 5 | 8 | 1 | 64 | 27 | 9.14 | – | – | 14 | 3 | – | – | – | – | – | – | – |
| Birkett, L.S. | 4 | 8 | 0 | 136 | 64 | 17.00 | – | 1 | 4 | – | 126 | 71 | 1 | 71.00 | 1-16 | – | – |
| Boyce, K.D. | 21 | 30 | 3 | 657 | 95* | 24.33 | – | 4 | 5 | – | 3501 | 1801 | 60 | 30.01 | 6-77 | 2 | 1 |
| Browne, C.R. | 4 | 8 | 1 | 176 | 70* | 25.14 | – | 1 | 1 | – | 840 | 288 | 6 | 48.00 | 2-72 | – | – |
| Butcher, B.F. | 44 | 78 | 6 | 3104 | 209* | 43.11 | 7 | 16 | 15 | – | 256 | 90 | 5 | 18.00 | 5-34 | 1 | – |
| Butler, L.S. | 1 | 1 | 0 | 16 | 16 | 16.00 | – | – | 4 | – | 240 | 151 | 2 | 75.50 | 2-151 | – | – |
| Bynoe, M.R. | 4 | 6 | 0 | 111 | 48 | 18.50 | – | – | 4 | – | 30‡ | 5 | 1 | 5.00 | 1-5 | – | – |
| Camacho, G.S. | 11 | 22 | 0 | 640 | 87 | 29.09 | – | 4 | 4 | – | 18 | 12 | 0 | – | – | – | – |
| Cameron, F.J. | 5 | 7 | 1 | 151 | 75* | 25.16 | – | 1 | – | – | 786 | 278 | 3 | 92.66 | 2-74 | – | – |
| Cameron, J.H. | 2 | 3 | 0 | 6 | 5 | 2.00 | – | – | – | – | 232 | 88 | 3 | 29.33 | 3-66 | – | – |
| Carew, G.M. | 4 | 7 | 1 | 170 | 107 | 28.33 | 1 | – | 1 | – | 18‡ | 2 | 0 | – | – | – | – |
| Carew, M.C. | 19 | 36† | 3 | 1127 | 109 | 34.15 | 1 | 5 | 13 | – | 1174 | 437 | 8 | 54.62 | 1-11 | – | – |
| Challenor, G. | 3 | 6 | 0 | 101 | 46 | 16.83 | – | – | – | – | – | – | – | – | – | – | – |
| Christiani, C.M. | 4 | 7 | 2 | 98 | 32* | 19.60 | – | – | 6 | 1 | – | – | – | – | – | – | – |
| Christiani, R.J. | 22 | 37 | 3 | 896 | 107 | 26.35 | 1 | 4 | 19 | 2 | 234 | 108 | 3 | 36.00 | 3-52 | – | – |
| Clarke, C.B. | 3 | 4 | 1 | 3 | 2 | 1.00 | – | – | – | – | 456 | 261 | 6 | 43.50 | 3-59 | – | – |
| Clarke, S. | 1 | 2 | 1 | 11 | 6 | 11.00 | – | – | 1 | – | 294 | 141 | 6 | 23.50 | 3-58 | – | – |
| Constantine, L.N. | 18 | 33 | 0 | 635 | 90 | 19.24 | – | 4 | 28 | – | 3583 | 1746 | 58 | 30.10 | 5-75 | 2 | – |
| Croft, C.E.H. | 7 | 10 | 8 | 60 | 23* | 30.00 | – | – | 7 | – | 1638 | 846 | 42 | 20.14 | 8-29 | 1 | – |
| Da Costa, O.C. | 5 | 9 | 1 | 153 | 39 | 19.12 | – | – | 5 | – | 372 | 175 | 3 | 58.33 | 1-14 | – | – |
| Daniel, W.W. | 5 | 5 | 2 | 29 | 11 | 9.66 | – | – | 2 | – | 788 | 381 | 15 | 25.40 | 4-53 | – | – |

# INDIVIDUAL CAREER RECORDS – continued

WEST INDIES – continued

| | Tests | I | NO | Runs | HS | Avge | 100 | 50 | Ct | St | Balls | Runs | Wkts | Avge | BB | 5wI | 10wM |
|---|---|---|---|---|---|---|---|---|---|---|---|---|---|---|---|---|---|
| | | | | **BATTING AND FIELDING** | | | | | | | **BOWLING** | | | | | | |
| Davis, B.A. | 4 | 8 | 0 | 245 | 68 | 30.62 | - | 3 | 1 | - | - | - | - | - | - | - | - |
| Davis, C.A. | 15 | 29 | 5 | 1301 | 183 | 54.20 | 4 | 4 | 4 | - | 894 | 330 | 2 | 165.00 | 1-27 | - | - |
| De Caires, F.I. | 3 | 6 | 0 | 232 | 80 | 38.66 | - | 2 | 4 | - | 12 | 9 | 0 | - | - | - | - |
| Depeiza, C.C. | 5 | 8 | 2 | 187 | 122 | 31.16 | 1 | - | 7 | 4 | 30 | 15 | 0 | - | - | - | - |
| Dewdney, D.T. | 9 | 12 | 5 | 17 | 5* | 2.42 | - | - | 7 | - | 1641 | 807 | 21 | 38.42 | 5-21 | 1 | - |
| Dowe, U.G. | 4 | 3 | 2 | 8 | 5* | 8.00 | - | - | 3 | - | 1014 | 534 | 12 | 44.50 | 4-69 | - | - |
| Edwards, R.M. | 5 | 8 | 1 | 65 | 22 | 9.28 | - | - | - | - | 1311 | 626 | 18 | 34.77 | 5-84 | 1 | - |
| Ferguson, W. | 8 | 10 | 3 | 200 | 75 | 28.57 | - | 2 | 11 | - | 2568 | 1165 | 34 | 34.26 | 6-92 | 3 | 1 |
| Fernandes, M.P. | 2 | 4 | 0 | 49 | 22 | 12.25 | - | - | - | - | - | - | - | - | - | - | - |
| Findlay, T.M. | 10 | 16 | 3 | 212 | 44* | 16.30 | - | 1 | 19 | 2 | - | - | - | - | - | - | - |
| Foster, M.L.C. | 14 | 24 | 5 | 580 | 125 | 30.52 | 1 | 1 | 3 | - | 1776 | 600 | 9 | 66.66 | 2-41 | - | - |
| Francis, G.N. | 10 | 18 | 4 | 81 | 19* | 5.78 | - | - | 7 | - | 1619 | 763 | 23 | 33.17 | 4-40 | - | - |
| Frederick, M. | 1 | 2 | 0 | 30 | 30 | 15.00 | - | - | - | - | - | - | - | - | - | - | - |
| Fredericks, R.C. | 59 | 109† | 7 | 4334 | 169 | 42.49 | 8 | 26 | 62 | - | 1187‡ | 548 | 7 | 78.28 | 1-12 | - | - |
| Fuller, R.L. | 1 | 1 | 0 | 1 | 1 | 1.00 | - | - | - | - | 48 | 12 | 0 | - | - | - | - |
| Furlonge, H.A. | 3 | 5 | 0 | 99 | 64 | 19.80 | - | 1 | - | - | - | - | - | - | - | - | - |
| Ganteaume, A.G. | 1 | 1 | 0 | 112 | 112 | 112.00 | 1 | - | - | - | - | - | - | - | - | - | - |
| Garner, J. | 7 | 10 | 1 | 97 | 43 | 10.77 | - | - | 6 | - | 1690 | 883 | 38 | 23.23 | 4-48 | - | - |
| Gaskin, B.B.M. | 2 | 3 | 0 | 17 | 10 | 5.66 | - | - | 1 | - | 474 | 158 | 2 | 79.00 | 1-15 | - | - |
| Gibbs, G.L. | 1 | 2† | 0 | 12 | 12 | 6.00 | - | - | 1 | - | 24‡ | 7 | 0 | - | - | - | - |
| Gibbs, L.R. | 79 | 109 | 39 | 488 | 25 | 6.97 | - | - | 52 | - | 27115 | 8989 | 309 | 29.09 | 8-38 | 18 | 2 |
| Gilchrist, R. | 13 | 14 | 3 | 60 | 12 | 5.45 | - | - | 4 | - | 3227 | 1521 | 57 | 26.68 | 6-55 | 1 | - |
| Gladstone, G. | 1 | 1 | 1 | 12 | 12* | - | - | - | - | - | 300‡ | 189 | 1 | 189.00 | 1-139 | - | - |
| Goddard, J.D.C. | 27 | 39† | 11 | 859 | 83* | 30.67 | - | 4 | 22 | - | 2931 | 1050 | 33 | 31.81 | 5-31 | 1 | - |
| Gomes, H.A. | 5 | 9† | 0 | 276 | 115 | 30.66 | 2 | - | 1 | - | 96 | 34 | 0 | - | - | - | - |
| Gomez, G.E. | 29 | 46 | 5 | 1243 | 101 | 30.31 | 1 | 8 | 18 | - | 5236 | 1590 | 58 | 27.41 | 7-54 | 1 | - |
| Grant, G.C. | 12 | 21 | 5 | 413 | 71* | 25.81 | - | 3 | 10 | - | 24 | 18 | 0 | - | - | - | - |
| Grant, R.S. | 7 | 11 | 1 | 220 | 77 | 22.00 | - | 1 | 13 | - | 986 | 353 | 11 | 32.09 | 3-68 | - | - |
| Greenidge, A.T. | 2 | 4 | 0 | 142 | 69 | 35.50 | - | 2 | 2 | - | - | - | - | - | - | - | - |
| Greenidge, C.G. | 19 | 36 | 2 | 1641 | 134 | 48.26 | 5 | 9 | 22 | - | 8 | 0 | 0 | - | - | - | - |
| Greenidge, G.A. | 5 | 9 | 2 | 209 | 50 | 29.85 | - | 1 | 3 | - | 156 | 75 | 0 | - | - | - | - |
| Grell, M.G. | 1 | 2 | 0 | 34 | 21 | 17.00 | - | - | 1 | - | 30 | 17 | 0 | - | - | - | - |
| Griffith, C.C. | 28 | 42 | 10 | 530 | 54 | 16.56 | - | 1 | 16 | - | 5631 | 2683 | 94 | 28.54 | 6-36 | 5 | - |
| Griffith, H.C. | 13 | 23 | 5 | 91 | 18 | 5.05 | - | - | 4 | - | 2663 | 1243 | 44 | 28.25 | 6-103 | 2 | - |
| Guillen, S.C. | 5 | 6 | 2 | 104 | 54 | 26.00 | - | 1 | 9 | 2 | - | - | - | - | - | - | - |

# INDIVIDUAL CAREER RECORDS – continued

## WEST INDIES – continued

| | | BATTING AND FIELDING | | | | | | | | BOWLING | | | | | | |
|---|---|---|---|---|---|---|---|---|---|---|---|---|---|---|---|---|---|
| | Tests | I | NO | Runs | HS | Avge | 100 | 50 | Ct | St | Balls | Runs | Wkts | Avge | BB | 5wI | 10wM |
| Hall, W.W. | 48 | 66 | 14 | 818 | 50* | 15.73 | – | – | 11 | – | 10421 | 5066 | 192 | 26.38 | 7-69 | 9 | 1 |
| Haynes, D.L. | 2 | 3 | 0 | 182 | 66 | 60.66 | – | 3 | 1 | – | – | – | – | – | – | – | – |
| Headley, G.A. | 22 | 40 | 4 | 2190 | 270* | 60.83 | 10 | 5 | 14 | – | 398 | 230 | 0 | – | – | – | – |
| Headley, R.G.A. | 2 | 4† | 0 | 62 | 42 | 15.50 | – | – | 2 | – | – | – | – | – | – | – | – |
| Hendriks, J.L. | 20 | 32 | 8 | 447 | 64 | 18.62 | – | 2 | 42 | 5 | – | – | – | – | – | – | – |
| Hoad, E.L.G. | 4 | 8 | 0 | 98 | 36 | 12.25 | – | – | 1 | – | – | – | – | – | – | – | – |
| Holder, V.A. | 34 | 51 | 9 | 603 | 42 | 14.35 | – | 1 | 15 | – | 7877 | 3079 | 101 | 30.48 | 6-28 | 3 | – |
| Holding, M.A. | 13 | 20 | 1 | 213 | 55 | 11.21 | – | 1 | 3 | – | 2910 | 1348 | 57 | 23.64 | 8-92 | 4 | 1 |
| Holford, D.A.J. | 24 | 39 | 5 | 768 | 105* | 22.58 | 1 | 3 | 18 | – | 4816 | 2009 | 51 | 39.39 | 5-23 | 1 | – |
| Holt, J.K. | 17 | 31 | 2 | 1066 | 166 | 36.75 | 2 | 5 | 8 | – | 30 | 20 | 1 | 20.00 | 1-20 | – | – |
| Howard, A.B. | 1 | –† | – | – | – | – | – | – | – | – | 372 | 140 | 2 | 70.00 | 2-140 | – | – |
| Hunte, C.C. | 44 | 78 | 6 | 3245 | 260 | 45.06 | 8 | 13 | 16 | – | 270 | 110 | 2 | 55.00 | 1-17 | – | – |
| Hunte, E.A.C. | 3 | 6 | 1 | 166 | 58. | 33.20 | – | 2 | 5 | – | – | – | – | – | – | – | – |
| Hylton, L.G. | 6 | 8 | 2 | 70 | 19 | 11.66 | – | – | 1 | – | 965 | 418 | 16 | 26.12 | 4-27 | – | – |
| Johnson, H.H.H. | 3 | 4 | 0 | 38 | 22 | 9.50 | – | – | – | – | 789 | 238 | 13 | 18.30 | 5-41 | 2 | 1 |
| Johnson, T.F. | 1 | 1 | 1 | 9 | 9* | – | – | – | 1 | – | 240‡ | 129 | 3 | 43.00 | 2-53 | – | – |
| Jones, C.M. | 4 | 7† | 0 | 63 | 19 | 9.00 | – | – | 3 | – | 102‡ | 11 | 0 | – | – | – | – |
| Jones, P.E. | 9 | 11 | 2 | 47 | 10* | 5.22 | – | – | 4 | – | 1842 | 751 | 25 | 30.04 | 5-85 | 1 | – |
| Julien, B.D. | 24 | 34 | 6 | 866 | 121 | 30.92 | 2 | 3 | 14 | – | 4542‡ | 1868 | 50 | 37.36 | 5-57 | 1 | – |
| Jumadeen, R.R. | 10 | 12 | 9 | 26 | 11* | 8.66 | – | – | 4 | – | 2638‡ | 933 | 26 | 35.88 | 4-72 | – | – |
| Kallicharran, A.I. | 45 | 76† | 7 | 3331 | 158 | 48.27 | 10 | 17 | 35 | – | 151 | 73 | 1 | 73.00 | 1-7 | – | – |
| Kanhai, R.B. | 79 | 137 | 6 | 6227 | 256 | 47.53 | 15 | 28 | 50 | – | 183 | 85 | 0 | – | – | – | – |
| Kentish, E.S.M. | 2 | 2 | 1 | 1 | 1* | 1.00 | – | – | 1 | – | 540 | 178 | 8 | 22.25 | 5-49 | 1 | – |
| King, C.L. | 4 | 7 | 1 | 211 | 63 | 35.16 | – | 2 | 3 | – | 276 | 113 | 2 | 56.50 | 1-30 | – | – |
| King, F.M. | 14 | 17 | 3 | 116 | 21 | 8.28 | – | – | 5 | – | 2871 | 1159 | 29 | 39.96 | 5-74 | 1 | – |
| King, L.A. | 2 | 4 | 0 | 41 | 20 | 10.25 | – | – | 2 | – | 476 | 154 | 9 | 17.11 | 5-46 | 1 | – |
| Lashley, P.D. | 4 | 7† | 0 | 159 | 49 | 22.71 | – | – | 4 | – | 18 | 1 | 1 | 1.00 | 1-1 | – | – |
| Legall, R.A. | 4 | 5 | 0 | 50 | 23 | 10.00 | – | – | 8 | 1 | – | – | – | – | – | – | – |
| Lewis, D.M. | 3 | 5 | 2 | 259 | 88 | 86.33 | – | 3 | 8 | – | – | – | – | – | – | – | – |
| Lloyd, C.H. | 65 | 113† | 8 | 4594 | 242* | 43.75 | 11 | 22 | 43 | – | 1710 | 621 | 10 | 62.10 | 2-13 | – | – |
| McMorris, E.D.A.St J. | 13 | 21 | 0 | 564 | 125 | 26.85 | 1 | 3 | 5 | – | – | – | – | – | – | – | – |
| McWatt, C.A. | 6 | 9† | 2 | 202 | 54 | 28.85 | – | 2 | 9 | 1 | 24 | 16 | 1 | 16.00 | 1-16 | – | – |
| Madray, I.S. | 2 | 3 | 0 | 3 | 2 | 1.00 | – | – | 2 | – | 210 | 108 | 0 | – | – | – | – |
| Marshall, N.E. | 1 | 2 | 0 | 8 | 8 | 4.00 | – | – | – | – | 279 | 62 | 2 | 31.00 | 1-22 | – | – |
| Marshall, R.E. | 4 | 7 | 0 | 143 | 30 | 20.42 | – | – | 1 | – | 52 | 15 | 0 | – | – | – | – |
| Martin, F.R. | 9 | 18† | 1 | 486 | 123* | 28.58 | 1 | 2 | 2 | – | 1346‡ | 619 | 8 | 77.37 | 3-91 | – | – |

WEST INDIES – continued

| | | | | BATTING AND FIELDING | | | | | | | BOWLING | | | | | | |
| --- | --- | --- | --- | --- | --- | --- | --- | --- | --- | --- | --- | --- | --- | --- | --- | --- | --- |
| | Tests | I | NO | Runs | HS | Avge | 100 | 50 | Ct | St | Balls | Runs | Wkts | Avge | BB | 5wI | 10wM |
| Martindale, E.A. | 10 | 14 | 3 | 58 | 22 | 5.27 | – | – | 5 | – | 1605 | 804 | 37 | 21.72 | 5-22 | 3 | – |
| Mendonca, I. | 2 | 2 | 0 | 81 | 78 | 40.50 | – | 1 | 8 | 2 | | | | | | – | – |
| Merry, C.A. | 2 | 4 | 0 | 34 | 13 | 8.50 | – | – | 1 | – | | | | | | – | – |
| Miller, R. | 1 | 1 | 0 | 23 | 23 | 23.00 | – | – | – | – | 96 | 28 | 0 | – | – | – | – |
| Mudie, G.H. | 1 | 1† | 0 | 5 | 5 | 5.00 | – | – | – | – | 174‡ | 40 | 3 | 13.33 | 2-23 | – | – |
| Murray, D.A. | 3 | 6 | 0 | 67 | 21 | 11.16 | – | – | 6 | 3 | | | | | | – | – |
| Murray, D.L. | 51 | 80 | 8 | 1705 | 91 | 23.68 | – | 10 | 150 | 8 | | | | | | – | – |
| Neblett, J.M. | 1 | 2† | 1 | 16 | 11* | 16.00 | – | – | – | – | 216‡ | 75 | 1 | 75.00 | 1-44 | – | – |
| Noreiga, J.M. | 4 | 5 | 2 | 11 | 9 | 3.66 | – | – | 2 | – | 1322 | 493 | 17 | 29.00 | 9-95 | 2 | – |
| Nunes, R.K. | 4 | 8† | 1 | 245 | 92 | 30.62 | – | 2 | 2 | – | | | | | | – | – |
| Nurse, S.M. | 29 | 54 | 1 | 2523 | 258 | 47.60 | 6 | 10 | 21 | – | 42 | 7 | 0 | – | – | – | – |
| Padmore, A.L. | 2 | 2 | 1 | 8 | 8* | 8.00 | – | – | – | – | 474 | 135 | 1 | 135.00 | 1-36 | – | – |
| Pairaudeau, B.H. | 13 | 21 | 0 | 454 | 115 | 21.61 | 1 | 3 | 6 | – | 6 | 3 | 0 | – | – | – | – |
| Parry, D.R. | 5 | 9 | 2 | 193 | 65 | 27.57 | – | 2 | 3 | – | 748 | 360 | 12 | 30.00 | 5-15 | 1 | – |
| Passailaigue, C.C. | 1 | 2 | 1 | 46 | 44 | 46.00 | – | – | 3 | – | 12 | 15 | 0 | – | – | – | – |
| Phillip, N. | 3 | 6 | 1 | 120 | 46 | 24.00 | – | – | 2 | – | 660 | 391 | 9 | 43.44 | 4-75 | – | – |
| Pierre, L.R. | 1 | – | – | – | – | – | – | – | – | – | 42 | 28 | 0 | – | – | – | – |
| Rae, A.F. | 15 | 24† | 2 | 1016 | 109 | 46.18 | 4 | 4 | 10 | – | | | | | | – | – |
| Ramadhin, S. | 43 | 58 | 14 | 361 | 44 | 8.20 | – | – | 9 | – | 3939 | 4579 | 158 | 28.98 | 7-49 | 10 | 1 |
| Richards, I.V.A. | 28 | 47 | 2 | 2500 | 291 | 55.55 | 8 | 8 | 26 | – | 644 | 235 | 4 | 58.75 | 2-34 | – | – |
| Rickards, K.R. | 2 | 3 | 0 | 104 | 67 | 34.66 | – | 1 | – | – | | | | | | – | – |
| Roach, C.A. | 16 | 32 | 1 | 952 | 209 | 30.70 | 2 | 6 | 5 | – | 222 | 103 | 2 | 51.50 | 1-18 | – | – |
| Roberts, A.M.E. | 27 | 36 | 5 | 229 | 35 | 7.38 | – | – | 5 | – | 6858 | 3298 | 134 | 24.81 | 7-54 | 9 | 2 |
| Roberts, A.T. | 1 | 1 | 0 | 28 | 28 | 14.00 | – | – | – | – | | | | | | – | – |
| Rodriguez, W.V. | 5 | 7 | 0 | 96 | 50 | 13.71 | – | 1 | 3 | – | 573 | 374 | 7 | 53.42 | 3-51 | – | – |
| Rowe, L.G. | 24 | 38 | 2 | 1706 | 302 | 47.38 | 6 | 5 | 13 | – | 56 | 40 | 0 | – | – | – | – |
| St Hill, E.L. | 2 | 4 | 0 | 18 | 12 | 4.50 | – | – | 1 | – | 558 | 221 | 3 | 73.66 | 2-110 | – | – |
| St Hill, W.H. | 3 | 6 | 0 | 117 | 38 | 19.50 | – | 1 | 1 | – | 12 | 9 | 0 | – | – | – | – |
| Scarlett, R.G. | 3 | 4 | 1 | 54 | 29* | 18.00 | – | – | 2 | – | 804 | 209 | 2 | 104.50 | 1-46 | – | – |
| Scott, A.P.H. | 1 | 1 | 0 | 5 | 5 | 5.00 | – | – | – | – | 264 | 140 | 0 | – | – | – | – |
| Scott, O.C. | 8 | 13 | 3 | 171 | 35 | 17.10 | – | – | 1 | – | 1405 | 925 | 22 | 42.04 | 5-266 | 1 | – |
| Sealy, B.J. | 1 | 2 | 0 | 41 | 29 | 20.50 | – | – | – | – | 30 | 10 | 1 | 10.00 | 1-10 | – | – |
| Sealy, J.E.D. | 11 | 19 | 2 | 478 | 92 | 28.11 | – | 3 | 6 | 1 | 156 | 94 | 3 | 31.33 | 2-7 | – | – |
| Shepherd, J.N. | 5 | 8† | 0 | 77 | 32 | 9.62 | – | – | 4 | – | 1445 | 479 | 19 | 25.21 | 5-104 | 1 | – |
| Shillingford, G.C. | 7 | 8† | 1 | 57 | 25 | 8.14 | – | – | 2 | – | 1181 | 537 | 15 | 35.80 | 3-63 | 1 | – |
| Shillingford, I.T. | 4 | 7 | 0 | 218 | 120 | 31.14 | 1 | – | 1 | – | | | | | | – | – |

## WEST INDIES – continued

| | Tests | I | NO | Runs | HS | Avge | 100 | 50 | Ct | St | Balls | Runs | Wkts | Avge | BB | 5wI | 10wM |
|---|---|---|---|---|---|---|---|---|---|---|---|---|---|---|---|---|---|
| | | | | BATTING AND FIELDING | | | | | | | BOWLING | | | | | | |
| Shivnarine, S. | 3 | 6 | 0 | 217 | 63 | 36.16 | – | 3 | 1 | – | 264‡ | 139 | 1 | 139.00 | 1-13 | – | – |
| Singh, C.K. | 2 | 3 | 0 | 11 | 11 | 3.66 | – | – | 2 | – | 506‡ | 166 | 5 | 33.20 | 2-28 | – | – |
| Small, J.A. | 3 | 6 | 0 | 79 | 52 | 13.16 | – | 1 | 3 | – | 366 | 184 | 3 | 61.33 | 2-67 | – | – |
| Smith, C.W. | 5 | 10 | 1 | 222 | 55 | 24.66 | – | 1 | 4 | 1 | – | – | – | – | – | – | – |
| Smith, O.G. | 26 | 42 | 0 | 1331 | 168 | 31.69 | 4 | 6 | 9 | – | 4431 | 1625 | 48 | 33.85 | 5-90 | 1 | – |
| Sobers, G. St A. | 93 | 160† | 21 | 8032 | 365* | 57.78 | 26 | 30 | 109 | – | 21599‡ | 7999 | 235 | 34.03 | 6-73 | 6 | – |
| Solomon, J.S. | 27 | 46 | 7 | 1326 | 100* | 34.00 | 1 | 9 | 13 | – | 702 | 268 | 4 | 67.00 | 1-20 | – | – |
| Stayers, S.C. | 4 | 4 | 1 | 58 | 35* | 19.33 | – | – | – | – | 636 | 364 | 9 | 40.44 | 3-65 | – | – |
| Stollmeyer, J.B. | 32 | 56 | 5 | 2159 | 160 | 42.33 | 4 | 12 | 20 | – | 978 | 507 | 13 | 39.00 | 3-32 | – | – |
| Stollmeyer, V.H. | 1 | 1 | 0 | 96 | 96 | 96.00 | – | 1 | – | – | – | – | – | – | – | – | – |
| Taylor, J.O. | 3 | 5 | 3 | 4 | 4* | 2.00 | – | – | – | – | 672 | 273 | 10 | 27.30 | 5-109 | 1 | – |
| Trim, J. | 4 | 5 | 1 | 21 | 12 | 5.25 | – | – | 2 | – | 794 | 291 | 18 | 16.16 | 5-34 | 1 | – |
| Valentine, A.L. | 36 | 51 | 21 | 141 | 14 | 4.70 | – | – | 13 | – | 12953‡ | 4215 | 139 | 30.32 | 8-104 | 8 | 2 |
| Valentine, V.A. | 2 | 4 | 1 | 35 | 19* | 11.66 | – | – | – | – | 288 | 104 | 1 | 104.00 | 1-55 | – | – |
| Walcott, C.L. | 44 | 74 | 7 | 3798 | 220 | 56.68 | 15 | 14 | 53 | 11 | 1194 | 408 | 11 | 37.09 | 3-50 | – | – |
| Walcott, L.A. | 1 | 2 | 1 | 40 | 24 | 40.00 | – | – | 1 | – | 48 | 32 | 1 | 32.00 | 1-17 | – | – |
| Watson, C.D. | 7 | 6 | 1 | 12 | 5 | 2.40 | – | – | – | – | 1458 | 724 | 19 | 38.10 | 4-62 | – | – |
| Weekes, E. de C. | 48 | 81 | 5 | 4455 | 207 | 58.61 | 15 | 19 | 49 | – | 122 | 77 | 1 | 77.00 | 1-8 | – | – |
| Weekes, K.H. | 2 | 3† | 0 | 173 | 137 | 57.66 | 1 | – | 1 | – | – | – | – | – | – | – | – |
| White, A.W. | 2 | 4 | 1 | 71 | 57* | 23.66 | – | 1 | 1 | – | 491 | 152 | 3 | 50.66 | 2-34 | – | – |
| Wight, C.V. | 2 | 4 | 0 | 67 | 23 | 22.33 | – | 1 | – | – | 30 | 6 | 0 | – | – | – | – |
| Wight, G.L. | 1 | 1 | 0 | 21 | 21 | 21.00 | – | – | – | – | – | – | – | – | – | – | – |
| Wiles, C.A. | 1 | 2 | 0 | 2 | 3 | 1.00 | – | – | – | – | – | – | – | – | – | – | – |
| Willett, E.T. | 5 | 8† | 3 | 74 | 26 | 14.80 | – | – | 4 | – | 1326‡ | 482 | 11 | 43.81 | 3-33 | – | – |
| Williams, A.B. | 3 | 6 | 0 | 257 | 100 | 42.83 | 1 | 1 | 2 | – | – | – | – | – | – | – | – |
| Williams, E.A.V. | 4 | 6 | 0 | 113 | 72 | 18.83 | – | 1 | – | – | 796 | 241 | 9 | 26.77 | 3-51 | – | – |
| Wishart, K.L. | 1 | 2† | 0 | 52 | 52 | 26.00 | – | – | – | – | – | – | – | – | – | – | – |
| Worrell, F.M.M. | 51 | 87 | 9 | 3860 | 261 | 49.48 | 9 | 22 | 43 | – | 7141‡ | 2672 | 69 | 38.72 | 7-70 | 2 | – |

## NEW ZEALAND (141 players)

| | Tests | I | NO | Runs | HS | Avge | 100 | 50 | Ct | St | Balls | Runs | Wkts | Avge | BB | 5wI | 10wM |
|---|---|---|---|---|---|---|---|---|---|---|---|---|---|---|---|---|---|
| | | | | BATTING AND FIELDING | | | | | | | BOWLING | | | | | | |
| Alabaster, J.C. | 21 | 34 | 6 | 272 | 34 | 9.71 | – | – | 7 | – | 3992 | 1863 | 49 | 38.02 | 4-46 | – | – |
| Allcott, C.F.W. | 6 | 7† | 2 | 113 | 33 | 22.60 | – | – | 3 | – | 1206‡ | 541 | 6 | 90.16 | 2-102 | – | – |
| Anderson, R.W. | 6 | 12 | 0 | 381 | 92 | 31.75 | – | 3 | 1 | – | – | – | – | – | – | – | – |
| Anderson, W.M. | 1 | 2† | 0 | 5 | 4 | 2.50 | – | – | 1 | – | – | – | – | – | – | – | – |
| Andrews, B. | 2 | 3 | 2 | 22 | 17 | 22.00 | – | – | 1 | – | 256 | 154 | 2 | 77.00 | 2-40 | – | – |

NEW ZEALAND – continued

| | | | | BATTING AND FIELDING | | | | | | | | BOWLING | | | | | |
| --- | --- | --- | --- | --- | --- | --- | --- | --- | --- | --- | --- | --- | --- | --- | --- | --- | --- |
| | Tests | I | NO | Runs | HS | Avge | 100 | 50 | Ct | St | Balls | Runs | Wkts | Avge | BB | 5wI | 10wM |
| Badcock, F.T. | 7 | 9 | 2 | 137 | 64 | 19.57 | – | 2 | 1 | – | 1608 | 610 | 16 | 38.12 | 4-80 | – | – |
| Barber, R.T. | 1 | 2 | 0 | 17 | 12 | 8.50 | – | – | – | – | – | | | | | | |
| Bartlett, G.A. | 10 | 18 | 1 | 263 | 40 | 15.47 | – | – | 8 | – | 1768 | 792 | 24 | 33.00 | 6-38 | 1 | – |
| Barton, P.T. | 7 | 14 | 0 | 285 | 109 | 20.35 | 1 | 1 | 4 | – | – | | | | | | |
| Beard, D.D. | 4 | 7 | 2 | 101 | 31 | 20.20 | – | – | 2 | – | 812 | 302 | 9 | 33.55 | 3-22 | – | – |
| Beck, J.E.F. | 8 | 15† | 2 | 394 | 99 | 26.26 | – | 3 | 1 | – | – | | | | | | |
| Bell, W. | 2 | 3 | 3 | 21 | 21* | – | – | – | 1 | – | 491 | 235 | 2 | 117.50 | 1-54 | – | – |
| Bilby, G.P. | 2 | 4 | 0 | 55 | 28 | 13.75 | – | – | 3 | – | – | | | | | | |
| Blair, R.W. | 19 | 34 | 6 | 189 | 64* | 6.75 | – | 1 | 5 | – | 3525 | 1515 | 43 | 35.23 | 4-85 | – | – |
| Blunt, R.C. | 9 | 13 | 1 | 330 | 96 | 27.50 | – | 1 | 5 | – | 936 | 472 | 12 | 39.33 | 3-17 | – | – |
| Bolton, B.A. | 2 | 3 | 0 | 59 | 33 | 19.66 | – | – | 1 | – | – | | | | | | |
| Boock, S.L. | 3 | 5 | 1 | 7 | 4 | 1.75 | – | – | 2 | – | 475‡ | 129 | 7 | 18.42 | 5-67 | 1 | – |
| Bradburn, W.P. | 2 | 4 | 0 | 62 | 32 | 15.50 | – | – | 2 | – | – | | | | | | |
| Burgess, M.G. | 41 | 75 | 5 | 2291 | 119* | 32.72 | 5 | 12 | 32 | – | 498 | 212 | 6 | 35.33 | 3-23 | – | – |
| Burke, C. | 1 | 2 | 0 | 4 | 3 | 2.00 | – | – | – | – | 66 | 30 | 2 | 15.00 | 2-30 | – | – |
| Burtt, T.B. | 10 | 15 | 3 | 252 | 42 | 21.00 | – | – | 2 | – | 2593‡ | 1170 | 33 | 35.45 | 6-162 | 3 | – |
| Butterfield, L.A. | 1 | 2 | 0 | 0 | 0 | 0.00 | – | – | – | – | 78 | 24 | 0 | – | – | – | – |
| Cairns, B.L. | 9 | 16 | 4 | 238 | 52* | 19.83 | – | 1 | 3 | – | 1890 | 738 | 16 | 46.12 | 5-55 | 1 | – |
| Cameron, F.J. | 19 | 30 | 20 | 116 | 27* | 11.60 | – | – | 2 | – | 4570 | 1849 | 61 | 30.31 | 5-34 | 3 | – |
| Cave, H.B. | 19 | 31 | 5 | 229 | 22* | 8.80 | – | – | 8 | – | 4074 | 1467 | 34 | 43.14 | 4-21 | – | – |
| Chapple, M.E. | 14 | 27 | 1 | 497 | 76 | 19.11 | – | 3 | 10 | – | 248‡ | 84 | 1 | 84.00 | 1-24 | – | – |
| Chatfield, E.J. | 4 | 7 | 3 | 31 | 13* | 7.75 | – | – | 1 | – | 1054 | 485 | 8 | 60.62 | 4-100 | – | – |
| Cleverley, D.C. | 2 | 4 | 3 | 19 | 10* | 19.00 | – | – | – | – | 222 | 130 | 0 | – | – | – | – |
| Collinge, R.O. | 34 | 48 | 13 | 514 | 68* | 14.68 | – | 2 | 10 | – | 7473‡ | 3309 | 114 | 29.02 | 6-63 | 3 | – |
| Colquhoun, I.A. | 2 | 4 | 2 | 1 | 1* | 0.50 | – | – | 4 | – | – | | | | | | |
| Coney, J.V. | 4 | 7 | 0 | 123 | 45 | 17.57 | – | – | 6 | – | 16 | 13 | 0 | – | – | – | – |
| Congdon, B.E. | 58 | 108 | 7 | 3374 | 176 | 33.40 | 7 | 19 | 42 | – | 5218 | 2028 | 59 | 34.37 | 5-65 | 1 | – |
| Cowie, J | 9 | 13 | 4 | 90 | 45 | 10.00 | – | – | 3 | – | 2028 | 969 | 45 | 21.53 | 6-40 | 4 | 1 |
| Cresswell, G.F. | 3 | 5† | 3 | 14 | 12* | 7.00 | – | – | 1 | – | 650 | 292 | 13 | 22.46 | 6-168 | 1 | – |
| Cromb, I.B. | 5 | 8 | 2 | 123 | 51* | 20.50 | – | 1 | 1 | – | 960 | 442 | 8 | 55.25 | 3-113 | – | – |
| Cunis, R.S. | 20 | 31 | 8 | 295 | 51 | 12.82 | – | 1 | 1 | – | 4250 | 1887 | 51 | 37.00 | 6-76 | 1 | – |
| D'Arcy, J.W. | 5 | 10 | 0 | 136 | 33 | 13.60 | – | 1 | 1 | – | – | | | | | | |
| Dempster, C.S. | 10 | 15 | 4 | 723 | 136 | 65.72 | 2 | 5 | 2 | – | 5 | 10 | 0 | – | – | – | – |
| Dempster, E.W. | 5 | 8† | 2 | 106 | 47 | 17.66 | – | – | 1 | – | 544‡ | 219 | 2 | 109.50 | 1-24 | – | – |
| Dick, A.E. | 17 | 30 | 4 | 370 | 50* | 14.23 | – | 1 | 47 | 4 | – | | | | | | |
| Dickinson, G.R. | 3 | 5 | 0 | 31 | 11 | 6.20 | – | – | 3 | – | 451 | 245 | 8 | 30.62 | 3-66 | – | – |
| Donnelly, M.P. | 7 | 12† | 1 | 582 | 206 | 52.90 | 1 | 4 | 7 | – | 30‡ | 20 | 0 | – | – | – | – |
| Dowling, G.T. | 39 | 77 | 3 | 2306 | 239 | 31.16 | 3 | 11 | 23 | – | 36 | 19 | 1 | 19.00 | 1-19 | – | – |
| Dunning, J.A. | 4 | 6 | 1 | 38 | 19 | 7.60 | – | – | 2 | – | 830 | 493 | 5 | 98.60 | 2-35 | – | – |

## INDIVIDUAL CAREER RECORDS – continued

NEW ZEALAND – continued

| | BATTING AND FIELDING | | | | | | | | | | BOWLING | | | | | | |
|---|---|---|---|---|---|---|---|---|---|---|---|---|---|---|---|---|---|
| | Tests | I | NO | Runs | HS | Avge | 100 | 50 | Ct | St | Balls | Runs | Wkts | Avge | BB | 5wI | 10wM |
| Edwards, G.N. | 3 | 6 | 0 | 209 | 55 | 34.83 | – | 3 | 3 | – | – | | | | | – | – |
| Emery, R.W.G. | 2 | 4 | 0 | 46 | 28 | 11.50 | – | – | – | – | 46 | 52 | 2 | 26.00 | 2-52 | – | – |
| Fisher, F.E. | 1 | 2 | 0 | 23 | 14 | 11.50 | – | – | – | – | 204‡ | 78 | 1 | 78.00 | 1-78 | – | – |
| Foley, H. | 1 | 2† | 0 | 4 | 2 | 2.00 | – | – | – | – | – | | | | | – | – |
| Freeman, D.L. | 2 | 2 | 0 | 2 | 1 | 1.00 | – | – | – | – | 240 | 169 | 1 | 169.00 | 1-91 | – | – |
| Gallichan, N. | 1 | 2 | 0 | 32 | 30 | 16.00 | – | – | – | – | 264‡ | 113 | 3 | 37.66 | 3-99 | – | – |
| Gedye, S.G. | 4 | 8 | 0 | 193 | 55 | 24.12 | – | 2 | – | – | – | | | | | – | – |
| Guillen, S.C. | 3 | 6 | 0 | 98 | 41 | 16.33 | – | – | 4 | 1 | – | | | | | – | – |
| Guy, J.W. | 12 | 23† | 2 | 440 | 102 | 20.95 | 1 | 3 | 2 | – | – | | | | | – | – |
| Hadlee, D.R. | 26 | 42 | 5 | 530 | 56 | 14.32 | – | 1 | 8 | – | 4883 | 2389 | 71 | 33.64 | 4-30 | – | – |
| Hadlee, R.J. | 20 | 36† | 4 | 697 | 87 | 21.78 | 1 | 2 | 10 | – | 4707 | 2541 | 76 | 33.43 | 7-23 | 3 | 2 |
| Hadlee, W.A. | 11 | 19 | 1 | 543 | 116 | 30.16 | 1 | 2 | 6 | – | – | | | | | – | – |
| Harford, N.S. | 8 | 15 | 0 | 229 | 93 | 15.26 | – | 2 | – | – | – | | | | | – | – |
| Harford, R.I. | 3 | 5† | 2 | 7 | 6 | 2.33 | – | – | 11 | – | – | | | | | – | – |
| Harris, P.G.Z. | 9 | 18 | 1 | 378 | 101 | 22.23 | 1 | 1 | 6 | – | 42 | 14 | 0 | – | – | – | – |
| Harris, R.M. | 2 | 3 | 0 | 31 | 13 | 10.33 | – | – | – | – | – | | | | | – | – |
| Hastings, B.F. | 31 | 56 | 6 | 1510 | 117* | 30.20 | 4 | 7 | 23 | – | 22 | 9 | 0 | – | – | – | – |
| Hayes, J.A. | 15 | 22 | 7 | 73 | 19 | 4.86 | – | – | 3 | – | 2681 | 1217 | 30 | 40.56 | 4-36 | – | – |
| Henderson, M. | 1 | 1 | 1 | 8 | 6 | 8.00 | – | – | 1 | – | 90‡ | 64 | 2 | 32.00 | 2-38 | – | – |
| Hough, K.W. | 2 | 3 | 2 | 62 | 31* | 62.00 | – | – | 1 | – | 462 | 175 | 6 | 29.16 | 3-79 | – | – |
| Howarth, G.P. | 11 | 21 | 1 | 568 | 122 | 28.40 | 2 | 2 | 4 | – | 240 | 109 | 2 | 54.50 | 1-13 | – | – |
| Howarth, H.J. | 30 | 42† | 18 | 291 | 61 | 12.12 | – | 1 | 33 | – | 8833‡ | 3178 | 86 | 36.95 | 5-34 | 2 | – |
| James, K.C. | 11 | 13 | 2 | 52 | 14 | 4.72 | – | – | 11 | 5 | – | | | | | – | – |
| Jarvis, T.W. | 13 | 22 | 1 | 625 | 182 | 29.76 | 1 | 2 | 3 | – | 12 | 3 | 0 | – | – | – | – |
| Kerr, J.L. | 7 | 12 | 1 | 212 | 59 | 19.27 | – | 1 | 4 | – | – | | | | | – | – |
| Lees, W.K. | 9 | 18 | 1 | 452 | 152 | 26.58 | 1 | – | 15 | 7 | 5 | 4 | 0 | – | – | – | – |
| Leggat, I.B. | 1 | 1 | 0 | 0 | 0 | 0.00 | – | – | 2 | – | 24 | 6 | 0 | – | – | – | – |
| Leggat, J.G. | 9 | 18 | 2 | 351 | 61 | 21.93 | – | 2 | 1 | – | – | | | | | – | – |
| Lissette, A.F. | 2 | 4 | 2 | 2 | 1* | 1.00 | – | – | 1 | – | 288‡ | 124 | 3 | 41.33 | 2-73 | – | – |
| Lowry, T.C. | 7 | 8 | 0 | 223 | 80 | 27.87 | – | 2 | 8 | – | 12 | 5 | 0 | – | – | – | – |
| MacGibbon, A.R. | 26 | 46 | 5 | 814 | 66 | 19.85 | – | 3 | 13 | – | 5659 | 2160 | 70 | 30.85 | 5-64 | 1 | – |
| McGirr, H.M. | 2 | 1 | 0 | 51 | 51 | 51.00 | – | 1 | – | – | 180 | 115 | 1 | 115.00 | 1-65 | – | – |
| McGregor, S.N. | 25 | 47 | 2 | 892 | 111 | 19.82 | 1 | 3 | 9 | – | – | | | | | – | – |

# INDIVIDUAL CAREER RECORDS – continued

NEW ZEALAND – continued

| | | | | BATTING AND FIELDING | | | | | | | BOWLING | | | | | | |
| --- | --- | --- | --- | --- | --- | --- | --- | --- | --- | --- | --- | --- | --- | --- | --- | --- | --- |
| | Tests | I | NO | Runs | HS | Avge | 100 | 50 | Ct | St | Balls | Runs | Wkts | Avge | BB | 5wI | 10wM |
| McLeod, E.G. | 1 | 2† | 1 | 18 | 16 | 18.00 | – | – | – | – | 12 | 5 | 0 | – | – | – | – |
| McMahon, T.G. | 5 | 7 | 4 | 7 | 4* | 2.33 | – | – | 7 | 1 | – | – | – | – | – | – | – |
| McRae, D.A.N. | 1 | 2† | 0 | 8 | 8 | 4.00 | – | – | – | – | 84‡ | 44 | 0 | – | – | – | – |
| Matheson, A.M. | 2 | 2† | 0 | 7 | 7 | 7.00 | – | – | – | – | 282 | 136 | 2 | 68.00 | 2-7 | – | – |
| Meale, T. | 2 | 4† | 0 | 21 | 10 | 5.25 | – | – | 2 | – | – | – | – | – | – | – | – |
| Merritt, W.E. | 6 | 8 | 1 | 73 | 19 | 10.42 | – | – | 2 | – | 936 | 617 | 12 | 51.41 | 4-104 | – | – |
| Meuli, E.M. | 1 | 2 | 0 | 38 | 23 | 19.00 | – | – | – | – | – | – | – | – | – | – | – |
| Milburn, B.D. | 3 | 3 | 2 | 8 | 4* | 8.00 | – | – | 6 | 2 | – | – | – | – | – | – | – |
| Miller, L.S.M. | 13 | 25† | 0 | 346 | 47 | 13.84 | – | – | 1 | – | – | – | – | – | – | – | – |
| Mills, J.E. | 7 | 10† | 1 | 241 | 117 | 26.77 | 1 | – | 1 | – | 2 | 1 | 0 | – | – | – | – |
| Moir, A.M. | 17 | 30 | 8 | 327 | 41* | 14.86 | – | – | 2 | – | 2644 | 1418 | 28 | 50.64 | 6-155 | 2 | – |
| Moloney, D.A.R. | 3 | 6 | 0 | 156 | 64 | 26.00 | – | 1 | 3 | – | 12 | 9 | 0 | – | – | – | – |
| Mooney, F.L.H. | 14 | 22 | 2 | 343 | 46 | 17.15 | – | – | 22 | 8 | 8 | 0 | 0 | – | – | – | – |
| Morgan, R.W. | 20 | 34 | 1 | 734 | 97 | 22.24 | – | 5 | 12 | – | 1114 | 609 | 5 | 121.80 | 1-16 | – | – |
| Morrison, B.D. | 1 | 2† | 0 | 10 | 10 | 5.00 | – | – | 1 | – | 186 | 129 | 2 | 64.50 | 2-129 | – | – |
| Morrison, J.F.M. | 14 | 24 | 0 | 610 | 117 | 25.41 | 1 | 3 | 9 | – | 24‡ | 9 | 0 | – | – | – | – |
| Motz, R.C. | 32 | 56 | 3 | 612 | 60 | 11.54 | – | 3 | 9 | – | 7034 | 3148 | 100 | 31.48 | 6-63 | 5 | – |
| Murray, B.A.G. | 13 | 26 | 1 | 598 | 90 | 23.92 | – | 5 | 21 | – | 6 | 0 | 1 | 0.00 | 1-0 | – | – |
| Newman, J. | 3 | 4 | 0 | 33 | 19 | 8.25 | – | – | – | – | 425‡ | 254 | 2 | 127.00 | 2-76 | – | – |
| O'Sullivan, D.R. | 11 | 21 | 4 | 158 | 23* | 9.29 | – | – | 2 | – | 2744‡ | 1219 | 18 | 67.72 | 5-148 | 1 | – |
| Overton, G.W.F. | 3 | 6† | 1 | 8 | 3* | 1.60 | – | – | 1 | – | 730 | 258 | 9 | 28.66 | 3-65 | – | – |
| Page, M.L. | 14 | 20 | 0 | 492 | 104 | 24.60 | 1 | 2 | 6 | – | 379 | 231 | 5 | 46.20 | 2-21 | – | – |
| Parker, J.M. | 26 | 45 | 2 | 1223 | 121 | 28.44 | 3 | 3 | 23 | – | 40 | 24 | 1 | 24.00 | 1-24 | – | – |
| Parker, N.M. | 3 | 6 | 0 | 89 | 40 | 14.83 | – | – | 2 | – | – | – | – | – | – | – | – |
| Petherick, P.J. | 6 | 11 | 4 | 34 | 13 | 4.85 | – | – | 4 | – | 1305 | 687 | 16 | 42.93 | 3-90 | – | – |
| Petrie, E.C. | 14 | 25 | 5 | 258 | 55 | 12.90 | – | 1 | 25 | – | – | – | – | – | – | – | – |
| Playle, W.R. | 8 | 15 | 0 | 151 | 65 | 10.06 | – | 1 | 4 | – | – | – | – | – | – | – | – |
| Pollard, V. | 32 | 59 | 7 | 1266 | 116 | 24.34 | 2 | 7 | 19 | – | 4421 | 1853 | 40 | 46.32 | 3-3 | – | – |
| Poore, M.B. | 14 | 24 | 1 | 355 | 45 | 15.43 | – | – | 1 | – | 788 | 367 | 9 | 40.77 | 2-28 | – | – |
| Puna, N. | 3 | 5 | 3 | 31 | 18* | 15.50 | – | – | 1 | – | 480 | 240 | 4 | 60.00 | 2-40 | – | – |
| Rabone, G.O. | 12 | 20 | 2 | 562 | 107 | 31.22 | 1 | 2 | 5 | – | 1385 | 635 | 16 | 39.68 | 6-68 | 1 | – |
| Redmond, R.E. | 1 | 2† | 0 | 163 | 107 | 81.50 | 1 | 1 | 1 | – | – | – | – | – | – | – | – |
| Reid, J.R. | 58 | 108 | 5 | 3428 | 142 | 33.28 | 6 | 22 | 43 | 1 | 7725 | 2835 | 85 | 33.35 | 6-60 | 1 | – |
| Roberts, A.D.G. | 7 | 12 | 1 | 254 | 84* | 23.09 | – | 1 | 4 | – | 440 | 182 | 4 | 45.50 | 1-12 | – | – |
| Roberts, A.W. | 5 | 10 | 1 | 248 | 66* | 27.55 | – | 3 | 4 | – | 459 | 209 | 7 | 29.85 | 4-101 | – | – |
| Rowe, C.G. | 1 | 2 | 0 | 0 | 0 | 0.00 | – | – | 1 | – | – | – | – | – | – | – | – |

# INDIVIDUAL CAREER RECORDS – *continued*

NEW ZEALAND – *continued*

| | Tests | I | NO | Runs | HS | Avge | 100 | 50 | Ct | St | Balls | Runs | Wkts | Avge | BB | 5wI | 10wM |
|---|---|---|---|---|---|---|---|---|---|---|---|---|---|---|---|---|---|
| | | | | *BATTING AND FIELDING* | | | | | | | | | | *BOWLING* | | | |
| Scott, R.H. | 1 | 1 | 0 | 18 | 18 | 18.00 | – | – | – | – | 138 | 74 | 1 | 74.00 | 1-74 | – | – |
| Scott, V.J. | 10 | 17 | 1 | 458 | 84 | 28.62 | – | 3 | 7 | – | 18 | 14 | 0 | – | – | – | – |
| Shrimpton, M.J.F. | 10 | 19 | 0 | 265 | 46 | 13.94 | – | – | 2 | – | 257 | 158 | 5 | 31.60 | 3-35 | – | – |
| Sinclair, B.W. | 21 | 40 | 1 | 1148 | 138 | 29.43 | 3 | 3 | 8 | – | 60 | 32 | 2 | 16.00 | 2-32 | – | – |
| Sinclair, I.M. | 2 | 4† | 1 | 25 | 18* | 8.33 | – | – | 1 | – | 233 | 120 | 1 | 120.00 | 1-79 | – | – |
| Smith, F.B. | 4 | 6 | 1 | 237 | 96 | 47.40 | – | 2 | 1 | – | – | – | – | – | – | – | – |
| Smith, H.D. | 1 | 1 | 0 | 4 | 4 | 4.00 | – | – | – | – | 120 | 113 | 1 | 113.00 | 1-113 | – | – |
| Snedden, C.A. | 1 | – | – | – | – | – | – | – | – | – | 96 | 46 | 0 | – | – | – | – |
| Sparling, J.T. | 11 | 20 | 2 | 229 | 50 | 12.72 | – | 1 | 3 | – | 708 | 327 | 5 | 65.40 | 1-9 | – | – |
| Sutcliffe, B. | 42 | 76† | 8 | 2727 | 230* | 40.10 | 5 | 15 | 20 | – | 538‡ | 344 | 4 | 86.00 | 2-38 | – | – |
| Taylor, B.R. | 30 | 50† | 6 | 898 | 124 | 20.40 | 2 | 2 | 10 | – | 6334 | 2953 | 111 | 26.60 | 7-74 | 4 | – |
| Taylor, D.D. | 3 | 5 | 0 | 159 | 77 | 31.80 | – | 1 | 2 | – | 21 | 9 | 1 | 9.00 | 1-9 | – | – |
| Thomson, K. | 2 | 4 | 1 | 94 | 69 | 31.33 | – | 1 | – | – | – | – | – | – | – | – | – |
| Tindill, E.W.T. | 5 | 9† | 1 | 73 | 37* | 9.12 | – | – | 6 | 1 | 180‡ | 116 | 1 | 116.00 | 1-69 | – | – |
| Troup, G.B. | 1 | 1 | 0 | 0 | 0 | 0.00 | – | – | 1 | – | – | – | – | – | – | – | – |
| Truscott, P.B. | 1 | 2 | 0 | 29 | 26 | 14.50 | – | – | 1 | – | 12 | 5 | 0 | – | – | – | – |
| Turner, G.M. | 39 | 70 | 6 | 2920 | 259 | 45.62 | 7 | 14 | 40 | – | – | – | – | – | – | – | – |
| Vivian, G.E. | 5 | 6† | 0 | 110 | 43 | 18.33 | – | – | 3 | – | 198 | 107 | 1 | 107.00 | 1-14 | – | – |
| Vivian, H.G. | 7 | 10 | 0 | 421 | 100 | 42.10 | 1 | 5 | 4 | – | 1311‡ | 633 | 17 | 37.23 | 4-58 | – | – |
| Wadsworth, K.J. | 33 | 51 | 4 | 1010 | 80 | 21.48 | – | 5 | 92 | 4 | – | – | – | – | – | – | – |
| Wallace, W.M. | 13 | 21 | 0 | 439 | 66 | 20.90 | – | 5 | 5 | 1 | 6 | 5 | 0 | – | – | – | – |
| Ward, J.T. | 8 | 12 | 6 | 75 | 35* | 12.50 | – | – | 16 | 1 | – | – | – | – | – | – | – |
| Watt, L. | 1 | 2 | 0 | 2 | 2 | 1.00 | – | – | – | – | – | – | – | – | – | – | – |
| Webb, M.G. | 3 | 2 | 0 | 12 | 12 | 6.00 | – | – | – | – | 732 | 471 | 4 | 117.75 | 2-114 | – | – |
| Weir, G.L. | 11 | 16 | 2 | 416 | 74* | 29.71 | – | 3 | 3 | – | 342 | 209 | 7 | 29.85 | 3-38 | – | – |
| Whitelaw, P.E. | 2 | 4 | 2 | 64 | 30 | 32.00 | – | – | 1 | – | – | – | – | – | – | – | – |
| Wright, J.G. | 3 | 6† | 0 | 107 | 55 | 17.83 | – | 1 | 1 | – | – | – | – | – | – | – | – |
| Yuile, B.W. | 17 | 33 | 6 | 481 | 64 | 17.81 | – | 1 | 12 | – | 2897‡ | 1213 | 34 | 35.67 | 4-43 | – | – |

INDIA (140 Players)

| | Tests | I | NO | Runs | HS | Avge | 100 | 50 | Ct | St | Balls | Runs | Wkts | Avge | BB | 5wI | 10wM |
|---|---|---|---|---|---|---|---|---|---|---|---|---|---|---|---|---|---|
| | | | | BATTING AND FIELDING | | | | | | | BOWLING | | | | | | |
| Abdul Hafeez – see Kardar, A.H. | | | | | | | | | | | | | | | | | |
| Abid Ali, S. | 29 | 53 | 3 | 1018 | 81 | 20.36 | – | 6 | 32 | – | 4164 | 1980 | 47 | 42.12 | 6-55 | 1 | – |
| Adhikari, H.R. | 21 | 36 | 8 | 872 | 114* | 31.14 | 1 | 4 | 8 | – | 170 | 82 | 3 | 27.33 | 3-68 | – | – |
| Amarnath, L. | 24 | 40 | 4 | 878 | 118 | 24.38 | 1 | 4 | 13 | – | 4241 | 1481 | 45 | 32.91 | 5-96 | 2 | – |
| Amarnath, M. | 18 | 33 | 1 | 1183 | 100 | 36.96 | 1 | 8 | 20 | – | 1803 | 726 | 17 | 42.70 | 4-63 | – | – |
| Amarnath, S. | 7 | 13† | 0 | 403 | 124 | 31.00 | 1 | 2 | 4 | – | – | – | – | – | – | – | – |
| Amar Singh, L. | 7 | 14 | 1 | 292 | 51 | 22.46 | – | 1 | 3 | – | 2182 | 858 | 28 | 30.64 | 7-86 | 2 | – |
| Amir Elahi | 1 | 2 | 0 | 17 | 13 | 8.50 | – | – | – | – | – | – | – | – | – | – | – |
| Apte, A.L. | 1 | 2 | 0 | 15 | 8 | 7.50 | – | – | – | – | – | – | – | – | – | – | – |
| Apte, M.L. | 7 | 13 | 2 | 542 | 163* | 49.27 | 1 | 3 | 2 | – | 6 | 3 | 0 | – | – | – | – |
| Baig, A.A. | 10 | 18 | 0 | 428 | 112 | 23.77 | 1 | 2 | 6 | – | 18 | 15 | 0 | – | – | – | – |
| Banerjee, S. | 1 | 1 | 0 | 0 | 0 | 0.00 | – | – | 3 | – | 306 | 181 | 5 | 36.20 | 4-120 | – | – |
| Banerjee, S.N. | 1 | 2 | 1 | 13 | 8 | 6.50 | – | – | – | – | 273 | 127 | 5 | 25.40 | 4-54 | – | – |
| Baqa Jilani, M. | 1 | 2 | 1 | 16 | 12 | 16.00 | – | – | – | – | 90 | 55 | 0 | – | – | – | – |
| Bedi, B.S. | 58 | 91 | 26 | 621 | 50* | 9.55 | – | 1 | 24 | – | 19135‡ | 6615 | 246 | 26.89 | 7-98 | 14 | 1 |
| Bhandari, P. | 3 | 4 | 0 | 77 | 39 | 19.25 | – | – | 1 | – | 78 | 39 | 0 | – | – | – | – |
| Borde, C.G. | 55 | 97 | 11 | 3061 | 177* | 35.59 | 5 | 18 | 37 | – | 5695 | 2417 | 52 | 46.48 | 5-88 | 1 | – |
| Chandrasekhar, B.S. | 50 | 72 | 35 | 162 | 22 | 4.37 | – | – | 23 | – | 14253 | 6270 | 222 | 28.24 | 8-79 | 15 | 2 |
| Chauhan, C.P.S. | 9 | 17 | 0 | 368 | 88 | 21.64 | – | 1 | 12 | – | 516 | 205 | 1 | 205.00 | 1-130 | – | – |
| Chowdhury, N.R. | 2 | 2 | 1 | 3 | 3* | 3.00 | – | – | – | – | – | – | – | – | – | – | – |
| Colah, S.H.M. | 2 | 4 | 0 | 69 | 31 | 17.25 | – | – | 2 | – | – | – | – | – | – | – | – |
| Contractor, N.J. | 31 | 52† | 1 | 1611 | 108 | 31.58 | 1 | 11 | 18 | – | 186 | 80 | 1 | 80.00 | 1-9 | – | – |
| Dani, H.T. | 1 | 1 | – | – | – | – | – | – | 1 | – | 60 | 19 | 1 | 19.00 | 1-9 | – | – |
| Desai, R.B. | 28 | 44 | 13 | 418 | 85 | 13.48 | – | 1 | 9 | – | 5597 | 2761 | 74 | 37.31 | 6-56 | 2 | – |
| Dilawar Hussain | 3 | 6 | 0 | 254 | 59 | 42.33 | – | 3 | 6 | 1 | – | – | – | – | – | – | – |
| Divecha, R.V. | 5 | 5 | 0 | 60 | 26 | 12.00 | – | – | 5 | – | 1044 | 361 | 11 | 32.81 | 3-102 | – | – |
| Durani, S.A. | 29 | 50† | 2 | 1202 | 104 | 25.04 | 1 | 7 | 14 | – | 6446‡ | 2657 | 75 | 35.42 | 6-73 | 3 | 1 |
| Engineer, F.M. | 46 | 87 | 3 | 2611 | 121 | 31.08 | 2 | 16 | 66 | 16 | – | – | – | – | – | – | – |
| Gadkari, C.V. | 6 | 10 | 4 | 129 | 50* | 21.50 | – | 1 | 6 | – | 102 | 45 | 0 | – | – | – | – |
| Gaekwad, A.D. | 14 | 26 | 2 | 742 | 81* | 30.91 | – | 4 | 5 | – | 76 | 53 | 0 | – | – | – | – |
| Gaekwad, D.K. | 11 | 20 | 1 | 350 | 52 | 18.42 | – | 1 | 5 | – | 12 | 12 | 0 | – | – | – | – |
| Gaekwad, H.G. | 1 | 2† | 0 | 22 | 14 | 11.00 | – | – | 1 | – | 222‡ | 47 | 0 | – | – | – | – |
| Gandotra, A. | 2 | 4† | 0 | 54 | 18 | 13.50 | – | – | 1 | – | 6‡ | 5 | 0 | – | – | – | – |

INDIA – continued

| | Tests | I | NO | Runs | HS | Avge | 100 | 50 | Ct | St | Balls | Runs | Wkts | Avge | BB | 5wI | 10wM |
|---|---|---|---|---|---|---|---|---|---|---|---|---|---|---|---|---|---|
| Gavaskar, S.M. | 37 | 71 | 5 | 3226 | 220 | 48.87 | 13 | 14 | 35 | — | 172 | 72 | 0 | — | — | — | — |
| Ghavri, K.D. | 11 | 19† | 3 | 333 | 64 | 20.81 | — | 1 | 8 | — | 1550‡ | 833 | 30 | 27.76 | 5-33 | 1 | — |
| Ghorpade, J.M. | 8 | 15 | 0 | 229 | 41 | 15.26 | — | 1 | 4 | — | 150 | 131 | 0 | — | — | — | — |
| Ghulam Ahmed | 22 | 31 | 9 | 192 | 50 | 8.72 | — | — | 11 | — | 5650 | 2052 | 68 | 30.17 | 7-49 | 4 | 1 |
| Gopalan, M.J. | 1 | 2 | 1 | 18 | 11* | 18.00 | — | — | 3 | — | 114 | 39 | 1 | 39.00 | 1-39 | — | — |
| Gopinath, C.D. | 8 | 12 | 1 | 242 | 50* | 22.00 | — | 1 | 2 | — | 48 | 11 | 1 | 11.00 | 1-11 | — | — |
| Guard, G.M. | 2 | 2† | 0 | 11 | 7 | 5.50 | — | — | 2 | — | 396‡ | 182 | 3 | 60.66 | 2-69 | — | — |
| Guha, S. | 4 | 7 | 2 | 17 | 6 | 3.40 | — | — | 2 | — | 674 | 311 | 3 | 103.66 | 2-55 | — | — |
| Gul Mahomed | 8 | 15† | 0 | 166 | 34 | 11.06 | — | — | 3 | — | 77‡ | 24 | 2 | 12.00 | 2-21 | — | — |
| Gupte, B.P. | 3 | 3 | 2 | 28 | 17* | 28.00 | — | — | — | — | 678 | 349 | 3 | 116.33 | 1-54 | — | — |
| Gupte, S.P. | 36 | 42 | 13 | 183 | 21 | 6.31 | — | — | 14 | — | 11284 | 4403 | 149 | 29.55 | 9-102 | 12 | 1 |
| Hanumant Singh | 14 | 24 | 2 | 686 | 105 | 31.18 | 1 | 5 | 11 | — | 66 | 51 | 0 | — | — | — | — |
| Hardikar, M.S. | 2 | 4 | 1 | 56 | 32* | 18.66 | — | — | 3 | — | 108 | 55 | 1 | 55.00 | 1-9 | — | — |
| Hazare, V.S. | 30 | 52 | 6 | 2192 | 164* | 47.65 | 7 | 9 | 11 | — | 2840 | 1220 | 20 | 61.00 | 4-29 | — | — |
| Hindlekar, D.D. | 4 | 7 | 2 | 71 | 26 | 14.20 | — | — | 3 | — | — | — | | | | | |
| Ibrahim, K.C. | 4 | 8 | 0 | 169 | 85 | 21.12 | — | 1 | — | — | — | | | | | | |
| Indrajitsinhji, K.S. | 4 | 7 | 1 | 51 | 23 | 8.50 | — | — | 6 | 3 | — | | | | | | |
| Irani, J.K. | 2 | 3 | 2 | 3 | 2* | 3.00 | — | — | 2 | 1 | — | | | | | | |
| Jahangir Khan, M. | 4 | 7 | 0 | 39 | 13 | 5.57 | — | — | 4 | — | 606 | 255 | 4 | 63.75 | 4-60 | — | — |
| Jai, L.P. | 1 | 2 | 0 | 19 | 19 | 9.50 | — | — | — | — | — | | | | | | |
| Jaisimha, M.L. | 39 | 71 | 4 | 2056 | 129 | 30.68 | 3 | 12 | 17 | — | 2097 | 829 | 9 | 92.11 | 2-54 | — | — |
| Jamshedji, R.J. | 1 | 2 | 1 | 5 | 4* | 5.00 | — | — | 2 | — | 210‡ | 137 | 3 | 45.66 | 3-137 | — | — |
| Jayantilal, K. | 1 | 1 | 0 | 5 | 5 | 5.00 | — | — | — | — | — | | | | | | |
| Joshi, P.G. | 12 | 20 | 1 | 207 | 52* | 10.89 | — | 1 | 18 | 9 | — | | | | | | |
| Kanitkar, H.S. | 2 | 4 | 0 | 111 | 65 | 27.75 | — | 1 | — | — | — | | | | | | |
| Kardar, A.H. | 3 | 5† | 0 | 80 | 43 | 16.00 | — | — | 1 | — | — | | | | | | |
| Kenny, R.B. | 5 | 10 | 1 | 245 | 62 | 27.22 | — | 3 | 1 | — | — | | | | | | |
| Kirmani, S.M.H. | 20 | 32 | 4 | 795 | 88 | 28.39 | — | 5 | 35 | 15 | — | | | | | | |
| Kishenchand, G. | 5 | 10 | 0 | 89 | 44 | 8.90 | — | — | 4 | — | — | | | | | | |
| Kripal Singh, A.G. | 14 | 20 | 5 | 422 | 100* | 28.13 | 1 | 2 | 4 | — | 1518 | 584 | 10 | 58.40 | 3-43 | — | — |
| Krishnamurthy, P. | 5 | 6 | 0 | 33 | 20 | 5.50 | — | — | 7 | 1 | — | | | | | | |
| Kulkarni, U.N. | 4 | 8† | 5 | 13 | 7 | 4.33 | — | — | — | — | 448‡ | 238 | 5 | 47.60 | 2-37 | — | — |
| Kumar, V.V. | 2 | 2 | 0 | 6 | 6 | 3.00 | — | — | 2 | — | 605 | 202 | 7 | 28.85 | 5-64 | 1 | — |
| Kunderan, B.K. | 18 | 34 | 4 | 981 | 192 | 32.70 | 2 | 3 | 23 | 7 | 24 | 13 | 0 | — | — | — | — |
| Lall Singh | 1 | 2 | 0 | 44 | 29 | 22.00 | — | — | 1 | — | — | | | | | | |

INDIA – continued

| | | | | BATTING AND FIELDING | | | | | | | | | | BOWLING | | | |
|---|---|---|---|---|---|---|---|---|---|---|---|---|---|---|---|---|---|
| | Tests | I | NO | Runs | HS | Avge | 100 | 50 | Ct | St | Balls | Runs | Wkts | Avge | BB | 5wI | 10wM |
| Madan Lal, S. | 16 | 30 | 6 | 428 | 55* | 17.83 | – | 1 | 8 | – | 2457 | 977 | 29 | 33.68 | 5-72 | 2 | – |
| Maka, E.S. | 2 | 1 | – | 2 | 2* | – | – | – | 2 | 1 | – | – | – | – | – | – | – |
| Manjrekar, V.L. | 55 | 92 | 10 | 3208 | 189* | 39.12 | 7 | 15 | 19 | 2 | 204 | 44 | 1 | 44.00 | 1-16 | – | – |
| Mankad, A.V. | 22 | 42 | 3 | 991 | 97 | 25.41 | – | 6 | 12 | – | 41 | 43 | 0 | – | – | – | – |
| Mankad, V.M.H. | 44 | 72 | 5 | 2109 | 231 | 31.47 | 5 | 6 | 33 | – | 14685‡ | 5236 | 162 | 32.32 | 8-52 | 8 | 2 |
| Mantri, M.K. | 4 | 8 | 1 | 67 | 39 | 9.57 | – | – | 8 | 1 | – | – | – | – | – | – | – |
| Meherhomji, K.R. | 1 | 1 | 1 | 0 | 0* | – | – | – | 1 | – | – | – | – | – | – | – | – |
| Mehra, V.L. | 8 | 14 | 1 | 329 | 62 | 25.30 | – | 2 | 1 | – | 36 | 6 | 0 | – | – | – | – |
| Merchant, V.M. | 10 | 18 | 0 | 859 | 154 | 47.72 | 3 | 3 | 7 | – | 54 | 40 | 0 | – | – | – | – |
| Milkha Singh, A.G. | 4 | 6† | 0 | 92 | 35 | 15.33 | – | – | 2 | – | 6 | 2 | 0 | – | – | – | – |
| Modi, R.S. | 10 | 17 | 1 | 736 | 112 | 46.00 | 1 | 6 | 3 | – | 30 | 14 | 0 | – | – | – | – |
| Muddiah, V.M. | 2 | 3 | 1 | 11 | 11 | 5.50 | – | – | 3 | – | 318 | 134 | 3 | 44.66 | 2-40 | – | – |
| Mushtaq Ali | 11 | 20 | 1 | 612 | 112 | 32.21 | 2 | 3 | 7 | – | 378‡ | 202 | 3 | 67.33 | 1-45 | – | – |
| Nadkarni, R.G. | 41 | 67† | 12 | 1414 | 122* | 25.70 | 1 | 7 | 22 | – | 9165‡ | 2559 | 88 | 29.07 | 6-43 | 4 | 1 |
| Naik, S.S. | 3 | 6 | 0 | 141 | 77 | 23.50 | – | 1 | – | – | – | – | – | – | – | – | – |
| Naoomal Jeoomal | 3 | 5 | 1 | 108 | 43 | 27.00 | – | – | 1 | – | 108 | 68 | 2 | 34.00 | 1-4 | – | – |
| Navle, J.G. | 2 | 4 | 0 | 42 | 13 | 10.50 | – | – | 1 | – | – | – | – | – | – | – | – |
| Nayudu, C.K. | 7 | 14 | 0 | 350 | 81 | 25.00 | – | 2 | 4 | – | 858 | 386 | 9 | 42.88 | 3-40 | – | – |
| Nayudu, C.S. | 11 | 19 | 3 | 147 | 36 | 9.18 | – | – | 3 | – | 522 | 359 | 2 | 179.50 | 1-19 | – | – |
| Nazir Ali, S. | 2 | 4 | 0 | 30 | 13 | 7.50 | – | – | – | – | 138 | 83 | 4 | 20.75 | 4-83 | – | – |
| Nissar, Mahomed | 6 | 11 | 3 | 55 | 14 | 6.87 | – | – | 2 | – | 1211 | 707 | 25 | 28.28 | 5-90 | 3 | – |
| Nyalchand, S. | 1 | 2† | 1 | 7 | 6* | 7.00 | – | – | – | – | 384‡ | 97 | 3 | 32.33 | 3-97 | – | – |
| Pai, A.M. | 1 | 2† | 0 | 10 | 9 | 5.00 | – | – | – | – | 114 | 31 | 2 | 15.50 | 2-29 | – | – |
| Palia, P.E. | 2 | 4† | 1 | 29 | 16 | 9.66 | – | – | – | – | 42‡ | 13 | 0 | – | – | – | – |
| Parkar, R.D. | 2 | 4 | 0 | 80 | 35 | 20.00 | – | – | – | – | – | – | – | – | – | – | – |
| Patankar, C.T. | 1 | 2 | 0 | 14 | 13 | 14.00 | – | – | 3 | – | – | – | – | – | – | – | – |
| Pataudi, Nawab of, sr | 3 | 5 | 0 | 55 | 22 | 11.00 | – | – | – | – | – | – | – | – | – | – | – |
| Pataudi, Nawab of, jr | 46 | 83 | 3 | 2793 | 203* | 34.91 | 6 | 16 | 27 | – | 132 | 88 | 1 | 88.00 | 1-10 | – | – |
| Patel, B.P. | 21 | 38 | 5 | 972 | 115* | 29.45 | 1 | 5 | 17 | – | – | – | – | – | – | – | – |
| Patel, J.M. | 7 | 10 | 1 | 25 | 12 | 2.77 | – | – | 2 | – | 1725 | 637 | 29 | 21.96 | 9-69 | 2 | 1 |
| Patiala, Yuvaraj of | 1 | 2 | 1 | 84 | 60 | 42.00 | – | 1 | 1 | – | – | – | – | – | – | – | – |
| Patil, S.R. | 1 | 2 | 1 | 14 | 14* | – | – | – | 2 | – | 138 | 51 | 2 | 25.50 | 1-15 | – | – |
| Phadkar, D.G. | 31 | 45 | 7 | 1229 | 123 | 32.34 | 2 | 8 | 21 | – | 5994 | 2285 | 62 | 36.85 | 7-159 | 3 | 2 |
| Prasanna, E.A.S. | 47 | 81 | 18 | 720 | 37 | 11.42 | – | – | 18 | – | 13867 | 5491 | 187 | 29.36 | 8-76 | 10 | 2 |
| Punjabi, P.H. | 5 | 10 | 0 | 164 | 33 | 16.40 | – | – | 5 | – | – | – | – | – | – | – | – |
| Rai Singh, K. | 1 | 2 | 0 | 26 | 24 | 13.00 | – | – | – | – | – | – | – | – | – | – | – |
| Rajindernath, V. | 1 | 1 | – | – | – | – | – | – | – | 4 | – | – | – | – | – | – | – |

# INDIVIDUAL CAREER RECORDS – continued

| INDIA – continued | Tests | I | NO | Runs | HS | Avge | 100 | 50 | Ct | St | Balls | Runs | Wkts | Avge | BB | 5wI | 10wM |
|---|---|---|---|---|---|---|---|---|---|---|---|---|---|---|---|---|---|
| | | | | | | *BATTING AND FIELDING* | | | | | | | | *BOWLING* | | | |
| Rajinder Pal | 1 | 2 | 1 | 6 | 3* | 6.00 | – | – | – | – | 78 | 22 | 0 | – | – | – | – |
| Ramaswami, C. | 2 | 4† | 1 | 170 | 60 | 56.66 | – | 1 | – | – | – | – | – | – | – | – | – |
| Ramchand, G.S. | 33 | 53 | 5 | 1180 | 109 | 24.58 | 2 | 5 | 20 | – | 4976 | 1899 | 41 | 46.31 | 6-49 | 1 | – |
| Ramji, L. | 1 | 2 | 0 | 1 | 1 | 0.50 | – | – | 1 | – | 138 | 64 | 0 | – | – | – | – |
| Rangachari, C.R. | 4 | 6 | 3 | 8 | 8* | 2.66 | – | – | – | – | 846 | 493 | 9 | 54.77 | 5-107 | 1 | – |
| Rangnekar, K.M. | 3 | 6† | 0 | 33 | 18 | 5.50 | – | – | 1 | – | – | – | – | – | – | – | – |
| Ranjane, V.B. | 7 | 9 | 3 | 40 | 16 | 6.66 | – | – | 1 | – | 1265 | 649 | 19 | 34.15 | 4-72 | – | – |
| Rege, M.R. | 1 | 2 | 0 | 15 | 15 | 7.50 | – | – | 1 | – | – | – | – | – | – | – | – |
| Roy, A. | 4 | 7† | 0 | 91 | 48 | 13.00 | – | – | 1 | – | – | – | – | – | – | – | – |
| Roy, P. | 43 | 79 | 4 | 2442 | 173 | 32.56 | 5 | 9 | 16 | – | 104 | 66 | 1 | 66.00 | 1-6 | – | – |
| Sardesai, D.N. | 30 | 55 | 4 | 2001 | 212 | 39.23 | 5 | 9 | 4 | – | 59 | 45 | 0 | – | – | – | – |
| Sarwate, C.T. | 9 | 17 | 1 | 208 | 37 | 13.00 | – | – | – | – | 658 | 374 | 3 | 124.66 | 1-16 | – | – |
| Saxena, R. | 1 | 2 | 0 | 25 | 16 | 12.50 | – | – | – | – | 12 | 11 | 0 | – | – | – | – |
| Sen, P. | 14 | 18 | 4 | 165 | 25 | 11.78 | – | – | 20 | 11 | – | – | – | – | – | – | – |
| Sengupta, A.K. | 1 | 2 | 0 | 9 | 8 | 4.50 | – | – | 1 | – | – | – | – | – | – | – | – |
| Sharma, P. | 5 | 10 | 0 | 187 | 54 | 18.70 | – | 1 | 1 | – | 24 | 8 | 0 | – | – | – | – |
| Shinde, S.G. | 7 | 11 | 5 | 85 | 14 | 14.16 | – | – | 1 | – | 1515 | 717 | 12 | 59.75 | 6-91 | 1 | – |
| Shodhan, D.H. | 3 | 4† | 1 | 181 | 110 | 60.33 | 1 | – | 1 | – | 60‡ | 26 | 0 | – | – | – | – |
| Sohoni, S.W. | 4 | 7 | 2 | 83 | 29* | 16.60 | – | – | 2 | – | 532 | 202 | 2 | 101.00 | 1-16 | – | – |
| Solkar, E.D. | 27 | 48† | 6 | 1068 | 102 | 25.42 | 1 | 6 | 53 | – | 2265‡ | 1070 | 18 | 59.44 | 3-28 | – | – |
| Sood, M.M. | 1 | 2 | 0 | 3 | 3 | 1.50 | – | – | – | – | – | – | – | – | – | – | – |
| Subramanya, V. | 9 | 15 | 1 | 263 | 75 | 18.78 | – | 2 | 9 | – | 444 | 201 | 3 | 67.00 | 2-32 | – | – |
| Sunderam, G.R. | 2 | 1 | 1 | 3 | 3* | – | – | – | – | – | 396 | 166 | 3 | 55.33 | 2-46 | – | – |
| Surendranath, R. | 11 | 20 | 7 | 136 | 27 | 10.46 | – | – | 4 | – | 2602 | 1053 | 26 | 40.50 | 5-75 | 2 | – |
| Surti, R.F. | 26 | 48† | 4 | 1263 | 99 | 28.70 | – | 9 | 26 | – | 3870‡ | 1962 | 42 | 46.71 | 5-74 | 1 | – |
| Swamy, N.V. | 1 | – | – | – | – | – | – | – | – | – | 108 | 45 | 0 | – | – | – | – |
| Tamhane, N.S. | 21 | 27 | 5 | 225 | 54* | 10.22 | – | 1 | 35 | 16 | 114‡ | 72 | 0 | – | – | – | – |
| Tarapore, K.K. | 1 | 1 | 0 | 2 | 2 | 2.00 | – | – | – | – | – | – | – | – | – | – | – |
| Umrigar, P.R. | 59 | 94 | 8 | 3631 | 223 | 42.22 | 12 | 14 | 33 | – | 4725 | 1473 | 35 | 42.08 | 6-74 | 2 | – |
| Vengsarkar, D.B. | 11 | 20 | 1 | 472 | 78 | 24.84 | – | 1 | 11 | – | 5 | 7 | 0 | – | – | – | – |
| Venkataraghavan, S. | 37 | 55 | 8 | 660 | 64 | 14.04 | – | 2 | 32 | – | 10301 | 3796 | 113 | 33.59 | 8-72 | 3 | 1 |
| Viswanath, G.R. | 43 | 82 | 7 | 3154 | 139 | 42.05 | 5 | 21 | 33 | – | 24 | 18 | 0 | – | – | – | – |
| Vizianagram, Maharajkumar of | 3 | 6 | 2 | 33 | 19* | 8.25 | – | – | 1 | – | – | – | – | – | – | – | – |
| Wadekar, A.L. | 37 | 71† | 3 | 2113 | 143 | 31.07 | 1 | 14 | 46 | – | 61‡ | 55 | 0 | – | – | – | – |
| Wazir Ali, S. | 7 | 14 | 0 | 237 | 42 | 16.92 | – | – | 1 | – | 30 | 25 | 0 | – | – | – | – |
| Yajurvindra Singh | 2 | 4 | 0 | 50 | 21 | 12.50 | – | – | 8 | – | 6 | 2 | 0 | – | – | – | – |

PAKISTAN (79 Players)

| | | | BATTING AND FIELDING | | | | | | | | BOWLING | | | | | | |
|---|---|---|---|---|---|---|---|---|---|---|---|---|---|---|---|---|---|
| | Tests | I | NO | Runs | HS | Avge | 100 | 50 | Ct | St | Balls | Runs | Wkts | Avge | BB | 5wI | 10wM |
| Abdul Kadir | 4 | 8 | 0 | 272 | 95 | 34.00 | – | 2 | 1 | 1 | 1056 | 305 | 12 | 25.41 | 6-44 | 1 | – |
| Abdul Qadir | 3 | 3 | 0 | 36 | 21 | 12.00 | – | – | 2 | – | 240 | 106 | 1 | 106.00 | 1-40 | – | – |
| Afaq Hussain | 2 | 4 | 4 | 66 | 35* | – | – | – | 2 | – | 44 | 17 | 0 | – | – | – | – |
| Aftab Baloch | 2 | 3 | 1 | 97 | 60* | 48.50 | – | 1 | – | – | 6 | 4 | 0 | – | – | – | – |
| Aftab Gul | 6 | 8 | 0 | 182 | 33 | 22.75 | – | – | 3 | – | – | | | | | | |
| Agha Saadat Ali | 1 | 1 | 1 | 8 | 8* | – | – | – | 3 | – | | | | | | | |
| Agha Zahid | 1 | 2 | 0 | 15 | 14 | 7.50 | – | – | – | – | | | | | | | |
| Alimuddin | 25 | 45 | 2 | 1091 | 109 | 25.37 | 2 | 7 | 8 | – | 84 | 75 | 1 | 75.00 | 1-17 | – | – |
| Amir Elahi | 5 | 7 | 1 | 65 | 47 | 10.83 | – | – | – | – | 400 | 248 | 7 | 35.42 | 4-134 | – | – |
| Anwar Hussain | 4 | 6 | 0 | 42 | 17 | 7.00 | – | – | – | – | 36 | 29 | 1 | 29.00 | 1-25 | – | – |
| Arif Butt | 3 | 5 | 0 | 59 | 20 | 11.80 | – | – | – | – | 666 | 288 | 14 | 20.57 | 6-89 | 1 | – |
| Asif Iqbal | 45 | 77 | 4 | 2748 | 175 | 37.64 | 8 | 10 | 29 | – | 3574 | 1401 | 50 | 28.02 | 5-48 | 2 | – |
| Asif Masood | 16 | 19 | 10 | 93 | 30* | 10.33 | – | – | 5 | – | 3038 | 1568 | 38 | 41.26 | 5-111 | 1 | – |
| D'Souza, A. | 6 | 10 | 8 | 76 | 23* | 38.00 | – | – | 3 | – | 1587 | 745 | 17 | 43.82 | 5-112 | 1 | – |
| Farooq Hamid | 1 | 2 | 0 | 3 | 3 | 1.50 | – | – | – | – | 184 | 107 | 1 | 107.00 | 1-82 | – | – |
| Farrukh Zaman | 1 | –† | – | – | – | – | – | – | – | – | 80‡ | 15 | 0 | – | – | – | – |
| Fazal Mahmood | 34 | 50 | 6 | 620 | 60 | 14.09 | – | 1 | 11 | – | 9834 | 3434 | 139 | 24.70 | 7-42 | 13 | 4 |
| Ghazali, M.E.Z. | 2 | 4 | 0 | 32 | 18 | 8.00 | – | – | – | – | 48 | 18 | 0 | – | – | – | – |
| Ghulam Abbas | 1 | 2† | 0 | 12 | 12 | 6.00 | – | – | – | – | | | | | | | |
| Gul Mahomed | 1 | 2† | 1 | 39 | 27* | 39.00 | – | – | – | – | | | | | | | |
| Hanif Mohammad | 55 | 97 | 8 | 3915 | 337 | 43.98 | 12 | 15 | 40 | – | 206 | 95 | 1 | 95.00 | 1-1 | – | – |
| Haroon Rashid | 9 | 16 | 1 | 694 | 122 | 46.26 | 2 | 3 | 6 | – | 8 | 3 | 0 | – | – | – | – |
| Haseeb Ahsan | 12 | 16 | 7 | 61 | 14 | 6.77 | – | – | 1 | – | 2835 | 1330 | 27 | 49.25 | 6-202 | 2 | – |
| Ibadulla, K. – see Khalid Ibadulla | | | | | | | | | | | | | | | | | |
| Ijaz Butt | 8 | 16 | 2 | 279 | 58 | 19.92 | – | 1 | 5 | – | – | | | | | | |
| Imran Khan | 15 | 26 | 2 | 503 | 59 | 20.95 | – | 1 | 8 | – | 4129 | 2045 | 62 | 32.98 | 6-63 | 4 | 1 |
| Imtiaz Ahmed | 41 | 72 | 1 | 2079 | 209 | 29.28 | 3 | 11 | 77 | 16 | 6 | 0 | 0 | – | – | – | – |
| Intikhab Alam | 47 | 77 | 10 | 1493 | 138 | 22.28 | 1 | 8 | 20 | – | 10475 | 4492 | 125 | 35.93 | 7-52 | 5 | 2 |
| Iqbal Qasim | 8 | 11† | 4 | 29 | 8* | 4.14 | – | – | 7 | – | 2380‡ | 766 | 23 | 33.30 | 4-84 | – | – |
| Israr Ali | 4 | 8† | 1 | 33 | 10 | 4.71 | – | – | 1 | – | 318‡ | 165 | 6 | 27.50 | 2-29 | – | – |
| Javed Akhtar | 1 | 2 | 1 | 4 | 2* | 4.00 | – | – | – | – | 96 | 52 | 0 | – | – | – | – |
| Javed Burki | 25 | 48 | 4 | 1341 | 140 | 30.47 | 3 | 4 | 7 | – | 42 | 23 | 0 | – | – | – | – |
| Javed Miandad | 10 | 17 | 4 | 917 | 206 | 70.53 | 2 | 6 | 8 | – | 1144 | 496 | 14 | 35.42 | 3-74 | – | – |

# INDIVIDUAL CAREER RECORDS – continued

## PAKISTAN – continued

| | Tests | I | NO | Runs | HS | Avge | 100 | 50 | Ct | St | Balls | Runs | Wkts | Avge | BB | 5wI | 10wM |
|---|---|---|---|---|---|---|---|---|---|---|---|---|---|---|---|---|---|
| | | | | | BATTING AND FIELDING | | | | | | | | BOWLING | | | | |
| Kardar, A.H. | 23 | 37† | 3 | 847 | 93 | 24.91 | – | 5 | 15 | – | 2712‡ | 954 | 21 | 45.42 | 3-34 | – | – |
| Khalid Hassan | 1 | 2 | 1 | 17 | 10 | 17.00 | – | – | – | – | 126 | 116 | 2 | 58.00 | 2-116 | – | – |
| Khalid Ibadulla | 4 | 8 | 0 | 253 | 166 | 31.62 | 1 | – | 3 | – | 336 | 99 | 1 | 99.00 | 1-42 | – | – |
| Khalid Wazir | 2 | 3 | 1 | 14 | 9* | 7.00 | – | – | – | – | – | – | – | – | – | – | – |
| Khan Mohammad | 13 | 17 | 7 | 100 | 26* | 10.00 | – | – | 4 | – | 3157 | 1292 | 54 | 23.92 | 6-21 | 4 | – |
| Liaquat Ali | 3 | 3 | 1 | 12 | 12 | 6.00 | – | – | 1 | – | 448‡ | 165 | 2 | 82.50 | 1-43 | – | – |
| Mahmood Hussain | 27 | 39 | 6 | 336 | 35 | 10.18 | – | – | 5 | – | 5910 | 2628 | 68 | 38.64 | 6-67 | 2 | – |
| Majid Khan | 37 | 64 | 2 | 2651 | 167 | 42.75 | 5 | 13 | 47 | – | 2668 | 1066 | 24 | 44.41 | 4-45 | – | – |
| Maqsood Ahmed | 16 | 27 | 1 | 507 | 99 | 19.50 | – | 2 | 13 | – | 462 | 191 | 3 | 63.66 | 2-12 | – | – |
| Mathias, W. | 21 | 36 | 3 | 783 | 77 | 23.72 | – | 3 | 22 | – | 24 | 20 | 0 | – | – | – | – |
| Miran Bux | 2 | 3 | 1 | 1 | 1* | 1.00 | – | – | – | – | 348 | 115 | 2 | 57.50 | 2-82 | – | – |
| Mohammad Aslam | 1 | 2 | 0 | 34 | 18 | 17.00 | – | – | – | – | – | – | – | – | – | – | – |
| Mohammad Farooq | 7 | 9 | 4 | 85 | 47 | 17.00 | – | – | 1 | – | 1422 | 682 | 21 | 32.47 | 4-70 | – | – |
| Mohammad Ilyas | 10 | 19 | 0 | 441 | 126 | 23.21 | 1 | 2 | 6 | – | 84 | 63 | 0 | – | – | – | – |
| Mohammad Munaf | 4 | 7 | 2 | 63 | 19 | 12.60 | – | – | 1 | – | 769 | 341 | 11 | 31.00 | 4-42 | – | – |
| Mohammad Nazir | 4 | 5 | 2 | 84 | 29* | 84.00 | – | – | 1 | – | 1066 | 353 | 10 | 35.30 | 7-99 | 1 | – |
| Mohsin Khan | 1 | 1 | 0 | 44 | 44 | 44.00 | – | – | – | – | 8 | 3 | 0 | – | – | – | – |
| Mudassar Nazar | 4 | 7 | 0 | 344 | 114 | 49.14 | 1 | 2 | 2 | – | 8 | 1 | 0 | – | – | – | – |
| Mufasir-ul-Haq | 1 | 1 | 1 | 8 | 8* | – | – | – | 1 | – | 222‡ | 84 | 3 | 28.00 | 2-50 | – | – |
| Munir Malik | 3 | 4 | 1 | 7 | 4 | 2.33 | – | – | 1 | – | 684 | 358 | 9 | 39.77 | 5-128 | 1 | 1 |
| Mushtaq Mohammad | 49 | 88 | 7 | 3283 | 201 | 40.53 | 10 | 17 | 33 | – | 4063 | 1770 | 62 | 28.54 | 5-28 | 1 | 2 |
| Nasim-ul-Ghani | 29 | 50† | 5 | 747 | 101 | 16.60 | 1 | 2 | 11 | – | 4406‡ | 1959 | 52 | 37.67 | 6-67 | 2 | – |
| Naushad Ali | 6 | 11 | 0 | 156 | 39 | 14.18 | – | – | 9 | – | – | 4 | 0 | – | – | – | – |
| Nazar Mohammad | 5 | 8 | 1 | 277 | 124* | 39.57 | 1 | 1 | 7 | – | 12 | 4 | 0 | – | – | – | – |
| Niaz Ahmed | 2 | 3 | 3 | 17 | 16* | – | – | – | 1 | – | 294 | 94 | 3 | 31.33 | 2-72 | – | – |
| Pervez Sajjad | 19 | 20 | 11 | 123 | 24 | 13.66 | – | – | 9 | – | 4145‡ | 1410 | 59 | 23.89 | 7-74 | 3 | – |
| Rehman, S.F. | 1 | 2 | 0 | 10 | 8 | 5.00 | – | – | 1 | – | 204 | 99 | 1 | 99.00 | 1-43 | – | – |
| Sadiq Mohammad | 31 | 57† | 2 | 2120 | 166 | 38.54 | 5 | 8 | 23 | – | 170 | 78 | 0 | – | – | – | – |
| Saeed Ahmed | 41 | 78 | 4 | 2991 | 172 | 40.41 | 5 | 16 | 13 | – | 1980 | 802 | 22 | 36.45 | 4-64 | – | – |
| Salahuddin | 5 | 8 | 2 | 117 | 34* | 19.50 | – | 1 | 3 | – | 546 | 187 | 7 | 26.71 | 2-36 | – | – |
| Salim Altaf | 20 | 31 | 12 | 276 | 53* | 14.52 | – | 1 | 3 | – | 3827 | 1640 | 45 | 36.44 | 4-11 | – | – |
| Sarfraz Nawaz | 24 | 34 | 5 | 401 | 53 | 13.82 | – | 2 | 15 | – | 6038 | 2574 | 77 | 33.42 | 6-89 | 1 | – |
| Shafiq Ahmed | 4 | 7 | 1 | 82 | 27* | 13.66 | – | – | – | – | 8 | 1 | 0 | – | – | – | – |
| Shafqat Rana | 5 | 7 | 0 | 221 | 95 | 31.57 | – | 2 | 5 | – | 36 | 9 | 1 | 9.00 | 1-2 | – | – |

## INDIVIDUAL CAREER RECORDS – continued

PAKISTAN – continued

| | | | | BATTING AND FIELDING | | | | | | | | | BOWLING | | | | |
|---|---|---|---|---|---|---|---|---|---|---|---|---|---|---|---|---|---|
| | Tests | I | NO | Runs | HS | Avge | 100 | 50 | Ct | St | Balls | Runs | Wkts | Avge | BB | 5wI | 10wM |
| Shahid Israr | 1 | 1 | 1 | 7 | 7* | – | – | – | 2 | – | | | | | | – | – |
| Shahid Mahmood | 1 | 2† | 0 | 25 | 16 | 12.50 | – | – | 2 | – | 36‡ | 23 | 0 | – | – | – | – |
| Sharpe, D.A. | 3 | 6 | 0 | 134 | 56 | 22.33 | – | 1 | 2 | – | | | | | | – | – |
| Shujauddin | 19 | 32 | 6 | 395 | 47 | 15.19 | – | – | 8 | – | 2313‡ | 801 | 20 | 40.05 | 3-18 | – | – |
| Sikander Bakht | 4 | 4 | 3 | 11 | 7* | 11.00 | – | – | 1 | – | 824 | 368 | 11 | 33.45 | 3-55 | – | – |
| Talat Ali | 5 | 9 | 1 | 201 | 57 | 25.12 | – | 1 | 3 | – | 20 | 7 | 0 | – | – | – | – |
| Waqar Hassan | 21 | 35 | 1 | 1071 | 189 | 31.50 | 1 | 6 | 10 | – | 6 | 10 | 0 | – | – | – | – |
| Wasim Bari | 39 | 59 | 15 | 736 | 72 | 16.72 | – | 4 | 91 | 15 | 8 | 2 | 0 | – | – | – | – |
| Wasim Raja | 17 | 30† | 5 | 1041 | 117* | 41.64 | 2 | 6 | 4 | – | 1184 | 517 | 16 | 32.31 | 3-22 | – | – |
| Wazir Mohammad | 20 | 33 | 4 | 801 | 189 | 27.62 | 2 | 3 | 5 | – | 24 | 15 | 0 | – | – | – | – |
| Younis Ahmed | 2 | 4† | 0 | 89 | 62 | 22.25 | – | 1 | – | – | – | | | | | | |
| Zaheer Abbas | 26 | 47 | 1 | 1583 | 274 | 34.41 | 3 | 6 | 18 | – | 20 | 2 | 0 | – | – | – | – |
| Zulfiqar Ahmed | 9 | 10 | 4 | 200 | 63* | 33.33 | – | 1 | 5 | – | 1285 | 366 | 20 | 18.30 | 6-42 | 2 | 1 |

## COMPLETE TEST RECORD FOR PLAYERS REPRESENTING TWO COUNTRIES

| | | | | | BATTING AND FIELDING | | | | | | | | | BOWLING | | | | |
|---|---|---|---|---|---|---|---|---|---|---|---|---|---|---|---|---|---|---|
| | Teams | Tests | I | NO | Runs | HS | Avge | 100s | 50s | Ct | St | Balls | Runs | Wkts | Avge | BB | 5wI | 10wM |
| Amir Elahi | I/P | 6 | 9 | 1 | 82 | 47 | 10.25 | – | – | 2 | – | 400 | 248 | 7 | 35.42 | 4-134 | – | – |
| J.J. Ferris | A/E | 9 | 17† | 4 | 114 | 20* | 8.76 | – | 1 | 4 | – | 2302‡ | 775 | 61 | 12.70 | 7-37 | 6 | 1 |
| S.C. Guillen | WI/NZ | 8 | 12 | 2 | 202 | 54 | 20.20 | – | 1 | 13 | 3 | – | | | | | – | – |
| Gul Mahomed | I/P | 9 | 17† | 1 | 205 | 34 | 12.81 | – | – | 3 | – | 77† | 24 | 2 | 12.00 | 2-21 | – | – |
| F. Hearne | E/SA | 6 | 10 | 0 | 168 | 30 | 16.80 | – | – | 3 | – | 62 | 40 | 2 | 20.00 | 2-40 | – | – |
| A.H. Kardar | I/P | 26 | 42† | 3 | 927 | 93 | 23.76 | – | 5 | 16 | – | 2712† | 954 | 21 | 45.42 | 3-34 | – | – |
| W.E. Midwinter | E/A | 12 | 21 | 1 | 269 | 37 | 13.45 | – | – | 10 | – | 1725 | 605 | 24 | 25.20 | 5-78 | 1 | – |
| F. Mitchell | E/SA | 5 | 10 | 0 | 116 | 41 | 11.60 | – | – | 2 | – | – | | | | | – | – |
| W.L. Murdoch | A/E | 19 | 34 | 5 | 908 | 211 | 31.31 | 2 | 1 | 12 | 2 | – | | | | | – | – |
| Pataudi, Nawab of, sr | E/I | 6 | 10 | 0 | 199 | 102 | 19.90 | 1 | – | 4 | – | – | | | | | – | – |
| A.E. Trott | A/E | 5 | 9 | 3 | 228 | 85* | 38.00 | – | 2 | 4 | – | 948 | 390 | 26 | 15.00 | 8-43 | 2 | – |
| S.M.J. Woods | A/E | 6 | 10 | 0 | 154 | 53 | 15.40 | – | 1 | 5 | – | 412 | 250 | 10 | 25.00 | 3-28 | – | – |

# INDEX OF TEST CRICKETERS

Every cricketer who appeared in official Test matches before June 1978 is listed alphabetically within his country's section of the index. Players who appeared for two countries are listed within both sections. The numbers in brackets show the total number of Test match appearances by the player for that country. The numbers that follow are the reference numbers of the matches in which he played; only the prefix of each match number is listed (e.g. *Test No. 596/102* is shown as '596').

## ENGLAND (478 players)

Abel, R. (13): 28, 29, 30, 31, 32, 35, 36, 37, 50, 51, 52, 72, 73.
Absolom, C.A. (1): 3.
Allen, D.A. (39): 487, 488, 489, 490, 491, 495, 496, 507, 509, 510, 511, 512, 513, 514, 515, 516, 517, 518, 519, 530, 531, 532, 534, 539, 543, 544, 561, 571, 572, 573, 575, 597, 598, 599, 600, 602, 603, 604, 605.
Allen, G.O.B. (25): 195, 209, 210, 211, 220, 221, 222, 223, 224, 225, 226, 227, 235, 237, 252, 253, 254, 255, 256, 257, 258, 259, 296, 297, 298.
Allom, M.J.C. (5): 186, 187, 188, 189, 206.
Ames, L.E.G. (47): 185, 190, 191, 192, 193, 209, 210, 211, 219, 220, 221, 222, 223, 224, 225, 226, 227, 228, 229, 233, 234, 235, 236, 237, 238, 239, 240, 241, 242, 243, 244, 246, 255, 256, 257, 258, 259, 260, 261, 262, 263, 264, 267, 268, 269, 270, 271.
Amiss, D.L. (50): 609, 619, 620, 623, 637, 687, 688, 689, 690, 703, 704, 705, 719, 720, 721, 722, 723, 724, 725, 726, 727, 731, 732, 733, 734, 735, 739, 740, 741, 742, 743, 744, 750, 752, 753, 754, 755, 758, 759, 760, 761, 781, 788, 789, 790, 791, 792, 803, 804, 805.
Andrew, K.V. (2): 391, 543.
Appleyard, R. (9): 388, 392, 393, 394, 395, 401, 402, 408, 425.
Archer, A.G. (1): 59.
Armitage, T. (2): 1, 2.
Arnold, E.G. (10): 78, 80, 81, 82, 83, 84, 86, 87, 93, 94.
Arnold, G.G. (34): 622, 623, 658, 698, 701, 702, 703, 705, 706, 707, 719, 720, 721, 722, 723, 724, 725, 726, 727, 733, 734, 735, 740, 741, 742, 743, 744, 751, 753, 754, 755, 758, 759, 760.
Arnold, J. (1): 209.
Astill, W.E. (9): 168, 169, 170, 171, 172, 190, 191, 192, 193.
Attewell, W. (10): 17, 18, 19, 20, 21, 27, 33, 35, 36, 37.

Bailey, T.E. (61): 314, 315, 316, 317, 323, 326, 327, 328, 329, 331, 332, 333, 334, 337, 372, 373, 374, 375, 376, 382, 383, 384, 385, 386, 387, 388, 389, 391, 392, 393, 394, 395, 401, 402, 408, 409, 410, 411, 412, 425, 426, 427, 428, 434, 435, 436, 437, 438, 439, 440, 441, 443, 454, 455, 456, 458, 464, 465, 466, 467, 468.
Bakewell, A.H. (6): 209, 210, 229, 232, 245, 246,.
Balderstone, J.C. (2): 780, 781.
Barber, R.W. (28): 492, 512, 513, 514, 515, 516, 517, 518, 519, 565, 571, 572, 573, 574, 591, 592, 593, 594, 595, 596, 597, 598, 599, 600, 601, 608, 609, 637.
Barber, W. (2): 244, 245.
Barlow, G.D. (3): 788, 789, 804.
Barlow, R.G. (17): 5, 6, 7, 8, 9, 10, 11, 12, 13, 14, 15, 16, 22, 23, 24, 25, 26.
Barnes, S.F. (27): 65, 66, 67, 72, 96, 97, 98, 99, 100, 103, 104, 105, 116, 117, 118, 119, 120, 122, 123, 124, 126, 128, 129, 130, 131, 132, 133.
Barnes, W. (21): 4, 9, 10, 11, 12, 13, 14, 16, 17, 18, 19, 20, 21, 23, 24, 25, 28, 29, 30, 33, 34.
Barnett, C.J. (20): 229, 230, 231, 232, 254, 255, 256, 257, 258, 259, 260, 261, 262, 263, 264, 265, 286, 287, 288, 299.

Barratt, F. (5): 184, 186, 187, 188, 189.
Barrington, K.F. (82): 408, 409, 474, 475, 476, 477, 478, 487, 488, 489, 490, 491, 493, 494, 495, 496, 507, 508, 509, 510, 511, 512, 513, 514, 515, 516, 517, 518, 530, 531, 532, 534, 535, 536, 537, 538, 539, 540, 541, 542, 543, 544, 545, 546, 547, 553, 561, 562, 563, 564, 565, 571, 572, 573, 574, 575, 591, 593, 594, 595, 596, 597, 598, 599, 600, 601, 605, 606, 618, 619, 620, 621, 622, 623, 628, 629, 630, 631, 632, 638, 639, 640.
Barton, V.A. (1): 38.
Bates, W. (15): 5, 6, 7, 8, 10, 11, 12, 13, 17, 18, 19, 20, 21, 25, 26.
Bean, G. (3): 35, 36, 37.
Bedser, A.V. (51): 276, 277, 278, 279, 280, 281, 282, 283, 284, 285, 286, 299, 300, 301, 302, 303, 309, 310, 311, 312, 313, 314, 317, 324, 325, 326, 327, 328, 329, 330, 331, 332, 333, 334, 335, 336, 337, 338, 351, 352, 353, 354, 372, 373, 374, 375, 376, 388, 389, 391, 410.
Berry, R. (2): 323, 324.
Binks, J.G. (2): 554, 555.
Bird, M.C. (10): 106, 107, 108, 109, 110, 130, 131, 132, 133, 134.
Birkenshaw, J. (5): 706, 707, 721, 734, 735.
Bligh, Hon. Ivo (4): 10, 11, 12, 13.
Blythe, C. (19): 65, 66, 67, 68, 69, 85, 88, 89, 90, 91, 92, 93, 94, 95, 96, 101, 104, 109, 110.
Board, J.H. (6): 58, 59, 88, 89, 91, 92.
Bolus, J.B. (7): 546, 547, 553, 554, 555, 556, 557.
Booth, M.W. (2): 130, 134.
Bosanquet, B.J.T. (7): 78, 80, 81, 82, 83, 84, 85.
Botham, I.T. (5): 806, 807, 817, 818, 819.
Bowden, M.P. (2): 31, 32.
Bowes, W.E. (15): 219, 221, 226, 234, 236, 237, 242, 244, 245, 246, 265, 266, 272, 273, 276.
Bowley, E.H. (5): 183, 184, 187, 188, 189.
Boycott, G. (72): 561, 563, 564, 565, 571, 572, 573, 574, 575, 591, 592, 594, 595, 597, 598, 599, 600, 601, 602, 603, 606, 607, 608, 609, 618, 620, 622, 628, 629, 630, 631, 632, 637, 638, 639, 653, 654, 655, 656, 657, 658, 674, 675, 676, 677, 678, 688, 689, 690, 698, 699, 722, 723, 724, 725, 726, 727, 731, 732, 733, 734, 735, 739, 806, 807, 808, 814, 815, 816, 817, 818, 819.
Bradley, W.M. (2): 63, 64.
Braund, L.C. (23): 65, 66, 67, 68, 69, 70, 71, 72, 73, 74, 78, 79, 80, 81, 82, 93, 94, 95, 96, 97, 98, 99, 100.
Brearley, J.M. (15): 777, 778, 788, 789, 790, 791, 792, 803, 804, 805, 806, 807, 808, 814, 815.
Brearley, W. (4): 86, 87, 103, 122.
Brennan, D.V. (2): 337, 338.
Briggs, J. (33): 17, 18, 19, 20, 21, 22, 23, 24, 25, 26, 27, 28, 29, 30, 31, 32, 35, 36, 37, 40, 41, 42, 43, 44, 45, 46, 51, 53, 54, 55, 56, 57, 62.
Brockwell, W. (7): 41, 42, 43, 44, 45, 46, 63.
Bromley-Davenport, H.R. (4): 47, 48, 49, 58.
Brookes, D. (1): 295.
Brown, A. (2): 512, 513.
Brown, D.J. (26): 594, 596, 597, 599, 600, 601, 602, 604, 605, 619, 620, 628, 629, 630, 631, 638, 639, 640, 641, 647, 648, 649, 653, 654, 655, 656.

# AUSTRALIA (296 players)

717, 718, 728, 729, 730, 736, 737, 738, 750, 751, 752, 753, 754, 755, 760, 761, 762, 763, 764, 765, 766, 767, 768, 769.
Charlton, P.C. (2): 33, 34.
Chipperfield, A.G. (14): 233, 234, 235, 236, 237, 247, 248, 249, 250, 251, 255, 256, 258, 264.
Clark, W.M. (9): 809, 810, 811, 812, 813, 820, 821, 822, 823.
Colley, D.J. (3): 698, 699, 700.
Collins, H.L. (19): 135, 136, 137, 138, 139, 140, 143, 144, 145, 146, 147, 158, 159, 160, 161, 162, 163, 164, 167.
Coningham, A. (1): 43.
Connolly, A.N. (29): 548, 549, 550, 567, 568, 598, 624, 625, 626, 637, 638, 639, 640, 641, 642, 643, 644, 645, 646, 665, 666, 667, 668, 669, 670, 671, 672, 673, 676.
Cooper, B.B. (1): 1.
Cooper, W.H. (2): 5, 17.
Corling, G.E. (5): 561, 562, 563, 564, 565.
Cosier, G.J. (16): 766, 767, 768, 793, 794, 795, 796, 797, 803, 809, 811, 812, 813, 820, 821, 822.
Cottam, J.T. (1): 26.
Cotter, A. (21): 81, 82, 83, 86, 87, 96, 97, 101, 102, 103, 104, 105, 111, 112, 113, 114, 115, 116, 117, 118, 119.
Coulthard, G. (1): 6.
Cowper, R.M. (27): 563, 567, 568, 569, 570, 583, 584, 585, 586, 587, 597, 598, 599, 601, 613, 614, 615, 616, 617, 624, 625, 626, 627, 637, 638, 639, 640.
Craig, I.D. (11): 364, 428, 429, 430, 431, 433, 444, 445, 446, 447, 448.
Crawford, W.P.A. (4): 426, 431, 432, 433.

Darling, J. (34): 42, 43, 44, 45, 46, 50, 51, 52, 53, 54, 55, 56, 57, 60, 61, 62, 63, 64, 65, 66, 67, 70, 71, 72, 73, 74, 75, 76, 77, 83, 84, 85, 86, 87.
Darling, L.S. (12): 223, 224, 233, 234, 235, 236, 247, 248, 249, 250, 251, 257.
Darling, W.M. (4): 813, 821, 822, 823.
Davidson, A.K. (44): 372, 373, 374, 375, 376, 392, 394, 395, 425, 429, 430, 432, 444, 445, 446, 447, 448, 464, 465, 466, 467, 468, 479, 480, 481, 482, 483, 484, 485, 486, 502, 503, 504, 506, 507, 508, 509, 510, 511, 535, 536, 537, 538, 539.
Davis, I.C. (15): 728, 729, 730, 736, 737, 738, 793, 794, 795, 796, 797, 803, 805, 806, 807.
De Courcy, J.H. (3): 374, 375, 376.
Dell, A.R. (2): 679, 728.
Donnan, H. (5): 35, 37, 50, 51, 52.
Dooland, B. (3): 281, 282, 292.
Duff, R.A. (22): 66, 67, 68, 69, 70, 71, 72, 73, 74, 75, 76, 77, 78, 79, 80, 81, 82, 83, 84, 85, 86, 87.
Duncan, J.R.F. (1): 677.
Dymock, G. (4): 730, 736, 737, 755.
Dyson, J. (3): 810, 811, 812.

Eady, C.J. (2): 50, 69.
Eastwood, K.H. (1): 679.
Ebeling, H.I. (1): 237.
Edwards, J.D. (3): 28, 29, 30.
Edwards, R. (20): 699, 700, 701, 702, 708, 810, 714, 715, 716, 717, 718, 750, 751, 752, 753, 755, 760, 761, 762, 763.
Edwards, W.J. (3): 750, 751, 752.
Emery, S.H. (4): 121, 123, 126, 127.
Evans, E. (6): 5, 6, 13, 19, 23, 24.

Fairfax, A.G. (10): 180, 194, 195, 197, 198, 199, 200, 201, 202, 203.
Favell, L.E. (19): 391, 392, 393, 395, 406, 407, 466, 467, 479, 480, 481, 482, 484, 485, 486, 502, 503, 504, 505.
Ferris, J.J. (8): 25, 26, 27, 28, 29, 30, 33, 34. *(Also Test No. 38 for England.)*

Fingleton, J.H.W. (18): 216, 220, 221, 222, 247, 248, 249, 250, 251, 255, 256, 257, 258, 259, 263, 264, 265, 266.
Fleetwood-Smith, L.O'B. (10): 247, 248, 249, 257, 258, 259, 263, 264, 265, 266.
Francis, B.C. (3): 698, 699, 700.
Freeman, E.W. (11): 626, 627, 639, 640, 643, 644, 645, 646, 668, 671, 672.
Freer, F.W. (1): 280.

Gannon, J.B. (3): 810, 811, 812.
Garrett, T.W. (19): 1, 2, 3, 6, 7, 8, 9, 10, 11, 12, 19, 20, 21, 22, 23, 24, 25, 26, 27.
Gaunt, R.A. (3): 446, 511, 551.
Gehrs, D.R.A. (6): 82, 86, 111, 112, 113, 114.
Giffen, G. (31): 5, 7, 8, 9, 10, 11, 12, 13, 14, 15, 16, 17, 20, 21, 22, 23, 24, 35, 36, 37, 39, 40, 41, 42, 43, 44, 45, 46, 50, 51, 52.
Giffen, W.F. (3): 26, 36, 37.
Gilmour, G.J. (15): 728, 729, 738, 762, 764, 765, 767, 768, 769, 793, 794, 795, 796, 797, 803.
Gleeson, J.W. (29): 624, 625, 626, 627, 637, 638, 639, 640, 641, 642, 643, 644, 645, 646, 665, 666, 667, 670, 671, 672, 673, 674, 675, 676, 677, 678, 698, 699, 700.
Graham, H. (6): 39, 40, 41, 45, 46, 50.
Gregory, D.W. (3): 1, 2, 3.
Gregory, E.J. (1): 1.
Gregory, J.M. (24): 135, 136, 137, 138, 139, 140, 141, 142, 143, 144, 145, 146, 147, 158, 159, 160, 161, 162, 163, 164, 165, 166, 167, 176.
Gregory, R.G. (2): 258, 259.
Gregory, S.E. (58): 33, 34, 37, 39, 40, 41, 42, 43, 44, 45, 46, 50, 51, 52, 53, 54, 55, 56, 57, 60, 61, 62, 63, 64, 65, 66, 67, 68, 69, 70, 71, 72, 73, 74, 75, 76, 77, 78, 79, 80, 81, 83, 84, 85, 99, 100, 101, 102, 103, 104, 105, 120, 121, 123, 125, 126, 127, 129.
Grimmett, C.V. (37): 162, 165, 166, 167, 176, 177, 178, 179, 180, 194, 195, 196, 197, 198, 199, 200, 201, 202, 203, 212, 213, 214, 215, 216, 220, 221, 222, 233, 234, 235, 236, 237, 247, 248, 249, 250, 251.
Groube, T.U. (1): 4.
Grout, A.T.W. (51): 444, 445, 446, 447, 448, 464, 465, 466, 467, 468, 479, 480, 481, 482, 484, 485, 486, 502, 503, 504, 505, 506, 507, 508, 509, 510, 511, 538, 539, 548, 549, 550, 551, 552, 561, 562, 563, 564, 565, 566, 569, 583, 584, 585, 586, 587, 597, 598, 599, 600, 601.
Guest, C.E.J. (1): 537.

Hamence, R.A. (3): 283, 291, 292.
Hammond, J.R. (5): 714, 715, 716, 717, 718.
Harry, J. (1): 44.
Hartigan, R.J. (2): 98, 100.
Hartkopf, A.E.V. (1): 159.
Harvey, M.R. (1): 282.
Harvey, R.N. (79): 293, 294, 302, 303, 318, 319, 320, 321, 322, 327, 328, 329, 330, 331, 344, 345, 346, 347, 348, 360, 361, 362, 363, 364, 372, 373, 374, 375, 376, 391, 392, 393, 394, 395, 403, 404, 405, 406, 407, 425, 426, 427, 428, 429, 430, 431, 432, 433, 445, 446, 447, 448, 464, 465, 466, 467, 468, 479, 480, 481, 482, 483, 484, 485, 486, 502, 503, 504, 506, 507, 508, 509, 510, 511, 535, 536, 537, 538, 539.
Hassett, A.L. (43): 263, 264, 265, 266, 275, 279, 280, 281, 282, 283, 290, 291, 292, 293, 299, 300, 301, 302, 303, 318, 319, 320, 321, 322, 327, 328, 329, 330, 331, 344, 345, 347, 348, 360, 361, 362, 363, 364, 372, 373, 374, 375, 376.
Hawke, N.J.N. (27): 539, 549, 550, 551, 552, 561, 562, 563, 564, 565, 566, 569, 570, 583, 584, 585, 586, 587, 597, 599, 600, 601, 613, 615, 627, 637, 638.
Hazlitt, G.R. (9): 96, 97, 120, 121, 123, 125, 126, 127, 129.

Mallett, A.A. (35): 641, 642, 665, 666, 667, 668, 669, 670, 676, 678, 701, 702, 708, 709, 728, 729, 730, 736, 737, 738, 751, 752, 753, 754, 755, 760, 761, 762, 763, 764, 765, 766, 767, 768, 769.

Malone, M.F. (1): 808.

Mann, A.L. (4): 809, 810, 811, 812.

Marr, A.P. (1): 18.

Marsh, R.W. (52): 674, 675, 676, 677, 678, 679, 698, 699, 700, 701, 702, 708, 709, 710, 714, 715, 716, 717, 718, 728, 729, 730, 736, 737, 738, 750, 751, 752, 753, 754, 755, 760, 761, 762, 763, 764, 765, 766, 767, 768, 769, 793, 794, 795, 796, 797, 803, 804, 805, 806, 807, 808.

Martin, J.W. (8): 503, 504, 506, 549, 566, 567, 569, 617.

Massie, H.H. (9): 5, 6, 7, 8, 9, 10, 11, 12, 19.

Massie, R.A.L. (6): 699, 700, 701, 702, 708, 710.

Matthews, T.J. (8): 118, 119, 121, 123, 125, 126, 127, 129.

Mayne, E.R. (4): 125, 126, 146, 147.

Mayne, L.C. (6): 583, 584, 585, 669, 672, 673.

Meckiff, I. (18): 444, 445, 447, 448, 464, 465, 466, 468, 479, 480, 482, 483, 484, 485, 486, 502, 504, 548.

Meuleman, K.D. (1): 275.

Midwinter, W.E. (8): 1, 2, 13, 14, 15, 16, 25, 26. *(Also 5, 6, 7, 8 for England.)*

Miller, K.R. (55): 275, 279, 280, 281, 282, 283, 290, 291, 292, 293, 294, 299, 300, 301, 302, 303, 318, 319, 320, 321, 322, 327, 328, 329, 330, 331, 344, 345, 346, 347, 348, 360, 361, 362, 363, 372, 373, 374, 375, 376, 391, 393, 394, 395, 403, 404, 405, 406, 407, 425, 426, 427, 428, 429, 430.

Minnett, R.B. (9): 116, 117, 118, 119, 120, 121, 125, 127, 129.

Misson, F.M. (5): 503, 505, 506, 507, 508.

Moroney, J. (7): 318, 319, 320, 321, 322, 327, 347.

Morris, A.R. (46): 279, 280, 281, 282, 283, 290, 291, 292, 293, 299, 300, 301, 302, 303, 318, 319, 320, 321, 322, 327, 328, 329, 330, 331, 344, 345, 346, 347, 360, 361, 362, 363, 364, 372, 373, 374, 375, 376, 391, 392, 393, 394, 403, 404, 405, 407.

Morris, S. (1): 18.

Moses, H. (6): 25, 26, 27, 35, 36, 45.

Moule, W.H. (1): 4.

Murdoch, W.L. (18): 2, 3, 4, 5, 6, 7, 8, 9, 10, 11, 12, 13, 14, 15, 16, 17, 33, 34. *(Also Test No. 38 for England.)*

Musgrove, H. (1): 18.

Nagel, L.E. (1): 220.

Nash, L.J. (2): 216, 259.

Nitschke, H.C. (2): 212, 213.

Noble, M.A. (42): 54, 55, 56, 57, 60, 61, 62, 63, 64, 65, 66, 67, 68, 69, 70, 71, 72, 73, 74, 75, 76, 77, 78, 79, 80, 81, 82, 83, 84, 85, 86, 87, 96, 97, 98, 99, 100, 101, 102, 103, 104, 105.

Noblet, G. (3): 322, 346, 364.

Nothling, O.E. (1): 177.

O'Brien, L.P.J. (5): 221, 224, 255, 251, 256.

O'Connor, J.D.A. (4): 98, 99, 100, 101.

Ogilvie, A.D. (5): 809, 810, 811, 822, 824.

O'Keeffe, K.J. (24): 677, 679, 708, 709, 714, 715, 716, 717, 718, 728, 729, 730, 736, 737, 738, 793, 794, 795, 796, 797, 803, 804, 805, 806.

Oldfield, W.A.S. (54): 135, 136, 137, 144, 146, 158, 159, 160, 161, 162, 163, 164, 165, 166, 167, 176, 177, 178, 179, 180, 194, 195, 196, 197, 198, 199, 200, 201, 202, 203, 212, 213, 214, 215, 216, 220, 221, 222, 224, 233, 234, 235, 236, 237, 247, 248, 249, 250, 251, 255, 256, 257, 258, 259.

O'Neill, N.C. (42): 464, 465, 466, 467, 468, 479, 480, 481, 482, 483, 484, 485, 486, 502, 503, 504, 505, 506, 507, 508, 509, 510, 511, 535, 536, 537, 538, 539, 548, 550, 551, 552, 561, 562, 564, 565, 566, 567, 583, 584, 585, 586.

O'Reilly, W.J. (27): 215, 216, 220, 221, 222, 223, 224, 233, 234, 235, 236, 237, 247, 248, 249, 250, 251, 255, 256, 257, 258, 259, 263, 264, 265, 266, 275.

Oxenham, R.K. (7): 178, 179, 180, 201, 202, 203, 212.

Palmer, G.E. (17): 4, 5, 6, 7, 8, 10, 11, 12, 13, 14, 15, 16, 17, 20, 22, 23, 24.

Park, R.L. (1): 136.

Pascoe, L.S. (3): 804, 806, 807.

Pellew, C.E. (10): 135, 136, 137, 138, 140, 141, 142, 143, 144, 147.

Philpott, P.I. (8): 583, 584, 585, 586, 587, 597, 598, 599.

Ponsford, W.H. (29): 158, 159, 160, 161, 162, 166, 167, 176, 177, 194, 195, 197, 198, 199, 200, 201, 202, 203, 212, 213, 214, 215, 220, 222, 223, 233, 235, 236, 237.

Pope, R.J. (1): 18.

Ransford, V.S. (20): 96, 97, 98, 99, 100, 101, 102, 103, 104, 105, 111, 112, 113, 114, 115, 116, 117, 118, 119, 120.

Redpath, I.R. (66): 549, 561, 562, 563, 564, 565, 566, 568, 569, 597, 613, 614, 615, 616, 617, 624, 625, 626, 637, 638, 639, 640, 641, 642, 643, 644, 645, 646, 665, 666, 667, 668, 669, 670, 671, 672, 673, 674, 675, 676, 677, 678, 679, 708, 709, 710, 714, 715, 716, 717, 718, 736, 737, 738, 750, 751, 752, 753, 754, 755, 764, 765, 766, 767, 768, 769.

Reedman, J.C. (1): 42.

Renneberg, D.A. (8): 613, 614, 615, 616, 617, 624, 625, 626.

Richardson, A.J. (9): 158, 159, 160, 161, 163, 164, 165, 166, 167.

Richardson, V.Y. (19): 158, 159, 160, 177, 178, 194, 195, 196, 197, 220, 221, 222, 223, 224, 247, 248, 249, 250, 251.

Rigg, K.E. (8): 203, 213, 214, 215, 216, 257, 258, 259.

Ring, D.T. (13): 294, 303, 344, 345, 346, 347, 348, 360, 361, 362, 363, 364, 373.

Rixon, S.J. (10): 809, 810, 811, 812, 813, 820, 821, 822, 823, 824.

Robertson, W.R. (1): 18.

Robinson, R.D. (3): 804, 806, 807.

Robinson, R.H. (1): 255.

Rorke, G.F. (4): 467, 468, 482, 483.

Rutherford, J.W. (1): 432.

Ryder, J. (20): 135, 136, 137, 138, 139, 145, 146, 147, 160, 161, 162, 163, 164, 165, 166, 176, 177, 178, 179, 180.

Saggers, R.A. (6): 302, 318, 319, 320, 321, 322.

Saunders, J.V. (14): 68, 71, 72, 73, 74, 76, 77, 78, 79, 96, 97, 98, 99, 100.

Scott, H.J.H. (8): 14, 15, 16, 17, 19, 22, 23, 24.

Sellers, R.H.D. (1): 568.

Sergeant, C.S. (12): 804, 805, 808, 809, 810, 811, 812, 820, 821, 822, 823, 824.

Sheahan, A.P. (31): 624, 625, 626, 627, 637, 638, 639, 640, 641, 642, 643, 644, 645, 646, 665, 666, 667, 668, 669, 670, 671, 672, 673, 674, 675, 701, 702, 708, 709, 728, 729.

Shepherd, B.K. (9): 537, 538, 549, 550, 551, 552, 570, 586, 587.

Sievers, M.W. (3): 255, 256, 257.

Simpson, R.B. (62): 444, 445, 446, 447, 448, 465, 502, 503, 504, 505, 506, 507, 508, 509, 510, 511, 535, 536, 637, 538, 539, 548, 549, 550, 551, 552, 561, 562, 563, 564, 565, 566, 567, 568, 569, 570, 583, 584, 585, 586, 587, 598, 600, 601, 613, 614, 615, 616, 617, 624, 625, 627, 809, 810, 811, 812, 813, 820, 821, 822, 823, 824.

Sincock, D.J. (3): 570, 587, 599.

Slater, K.N. (1): 466.

Slight, J. (1): 4.

Smith, D.B.M. (2): 123, 129.

Spofforth, F.R. (18): 2, 3, 8, 9, 10, 11, 12, 13, 14, 15, 16, 19, 20, 21, 22, 23, 24, 25.

Stackpole, K.R. (43): 600, 601, 613, 614, 615, 616, 617, 642, 643, 644, 645, 646, 665, 666, 667, 668, 669, 670, 671, 672, 673, 674, 675, 676, 677, 678, 679, 698, 699, 700, 701, 702, 710, 714, 715, 716, 717, 728, 729, 730, 736, 737, 738.
Stevens, G.B. (4): 480, 481, 483, 484.

Taber, H.B. (16): 613, 614, 615, 616, 617, 639, 646, 665, 666, 667, 668, 669, 670, 671, 672, 673.
Tallon, D. (21): 275, 279, 280, 281, 282, 283, 290, 291, 292, 293, 294, 299, 300, 301, 303, 327, 328, 329, 330, 331, 372.
Taylor, J.M. (20): 135, 136, 137, 138, 139, 140, 141, 142, 143, 144, 145, 146, 158, 159, 160, 161, 162, 163, 164, 165.
Thomas, G. (8): 583, 584, 585, 586, 587, 599, 600, 601.
Thompson, N. (2): 1, 2.
Thoms, G.R. (1): 348.
Thomson, A.L. (4): 674, 675, 677, 678.
Thomson, J.R. (32): 709, 750, 751, 752, 753, 754, 760, 761, 762, 763, 764, 765, 766, 767, 768, 769, 793, 804, 805, 806, 807, 808, 809, 810, 811, 812, 813, 820, 821, 822, 823, 824.
Thurlow, H.M. (1): 215.
Toohey, P.M. (8): 809, 810, 811, 812, 813, 820, 823, 824.
Toshack, E.R.H. (12): 275, 279, 280, 281, 282, 283, 290, 293, 299, 300, 301, 302.
Travers, J.P.F. (1): 69.
Tribe, G.E. (3): 279, 280, 283.
Trott, A.E. (3): 44, 45, 46. *(Also 58, 59 for England.)*
Trott, G.H.S. (24): 28, 29, 30, 33, 34, 35, 36, 37, 39, 40, 41, 42, 43, 44, 45, 46, 50, 51, 52, 53, 54, 55, 56, 57.
Trumble, H. (32): 33, 34, 39, 40, 41, 43, 50, 51, 52, 53, 54, 55, 56, 57, 60, 61, 62, 63, 64, 65, 66, 67, 68, 69, 72, 73, 74, 75, 79, 80, 81 82.
Trumble, J.W. (7): 18, 19, 20, 21, 22, 23, 24.
Trumper, V.T. (48): 60, 61, 62, 63, 64, 65, 66, 67, 68, 69, 70, 71, 72, 73, 74, 75, 76, 77, 78, 79, 80, 81, 82, 83, 84, 85, 86, 87, 96, 97, 98, 99, 100, 101, 102, 103, 104, 105, 111, 112, 113, 114, 115, 116, 117, 118, 119, 120.
Turner, A. (14): 760, 761, 763, 764, 765, 766, 767, 768, 769, 793, 794, 795, 796, 797.

Turner, C.T.B. (17): 25, 26, 27, 28, 29, 30, 33, 34, 35, 36, 37, 39, 40, 41, 42, 43, 45.

Veivers, T.R. (21): 548, 549, 552, 561, 562, 563, 564, 565, 566, 567, 568, 569, 570, 597, 598, 600, 601, 613, 614, 615, 616.

Waite, M.G. (2): 265, 266.
Walker, M.H.N. (34): 709, 710, 714, 715, 716, 717, 718, 729, 736, 737, 738, 750, 751, 752, 753, 754, 755, 760, 761, 762, 763, 765, 766, 767, 794, 795, 796, 797, 803, 804, 805, 806, 807, 808.
Wall, T.W. (18): 180, 194, 195, 196, 197, 198, 199, 212, 213, 214, 220, 221, 222, 223, 233, 234, 235, 236.
Walters, F.H. (1): 21.
Walters, K.D. (68): 597, 598, 599, 600, 601, 626, 627, 637, 638, 639, 640, 641, 643, 644, 645, 646, 665, 666, 667, 668, 669, 670, 671, 672, 673, 674, 675, 676, 677, 678, 679, 698, 699, 700, 701, 710, 714, 715, 716, 717, 718, 728, 729, 730, 736, 737, 738, 750, 751, 752, 753, 754, 755, 760, 761, 762, 763, 793, 794, 795, 796, 797, 803, 804, 805, 806, 807, 808.
Ward, F.A. (4): 255, 256, 257, 263.
Watkins, J.R. (1): 710.
Watson, G.D. (5): 614, 616, 617, 698, 702.
Watson, W.J. (4): 395, 404, 405, 406.
Whitty, W.J. (14): 101, 111, 112, 113, 114, 115, 116, 117, 121, 123, 125, 126, 127, 129.
Wilson, J.W. (1): 432.
Wood, G.M. (6): 813, 820, 821, 822, 823, 824.
Woodcock, A.J. (1): 730.
Woodfull, W.M. (35): 163, 164, 165, 166, 167, 176, 177, 178, 179, 180, 194, 195, 196, 197, 198, 199, 200, 201, 202, 203, 212, 213, 214, 215, 216, 220, 221, 222, 223, 224, 233, 234, 235, 236, 237.
Woods, S.M.J. (3): 28, 29, 30. *(Also 47, 48, 49 for England.)*
Worrall, J. (11): 18, 27, 28, 29, 30, 44, 57, 61, 62, 63, 64.

Yallop, G.N. (8): 767, 768, 769, 813, 820, 821, 823, 824.
Yardley, B. (6): 813, 820, 821, 822, 823, 824.

# SOUTH AFRICA (235 players)

Adcock, N.A.T. (26): 377, 378, 379, 380, 381, 408, 409, 410, 411, 434, 435, 436, 437, 438, 444, 445, 446, 447, 448, 492, 493, 494, 495, 496, 523, 524.
Anderson, J.H. (1): 76.
Ashley, W.H. (1): 32.

Bacher, A. (12): 594, 595, 596, 613, 614, 615, 616, 617, 670, 671, 672, 673.
Balaskas, X.C. (9): 204, 205, 217, 218, 243, 249, 250, 251, 268.
Barlow, E.J. (30): 520, 521, 522, 523, 524, 548, 549, 550, 551, 552, 558, 559, 560, 571, 572, 573, 574, 575, 594, 595, 596, 613, 614, 615, 616, 617, 670, 671, 672, 673.
Baumgartner, H.V. (1): 130.
Beaumont, R. (5): 121, 127, 128, 131, 132.
Begbie, D.W. (5): 309, 310, 311, 321, 322.
Bell, A.J. (16): 182, 183, 184, 205, 206, 208, 212, 213, 214, 215, 216, 217, 218, 243, 244, 245.
Bisset, M. (3): 58, 59, 110.
Bissett, G.F. (4): 169, 170, 171, 172.
Blanckenberg, J.M. (18): 130, 131, 132, 133, 134, 145, 146, 147, 148, 149, 150, 151, 152, 153, 154, 155, 156, 157.
Bland, K.C. (21): 520, 521, 522, 523, 524, 549, 550, 551, 552, 558, 559, 560, 571, 572, 573, 574, 575, 594, 595, 596, 613.

Bock, E.G. (1): 248.
Bond, G.E. (1): 267.
Botten, J.T. (3): 594, 595, 596.
Brann, W.H. (3): 148, 149, 150.
Briscoe, A.W. (2): 248, 268.
Bromfield, H.D. (9): 520, 521, 522, 523, 524, 573, 574, 575, 594.
Brown, L.S. (2): 213, 218.
Burger, C.G. de V. (2): 447, 448.
Burke, S.F. (2): 522, 573.
Buys, I.D. (1): 148.

Cameron, H.B. (26): 168, 169, 170, 171, 172, 181, 182, 184, 185, 204, 205, 206, 207, 208, 212, 213, 214, 215, 216, 217, 218, 242, 243, 244, 245, 246.
Campbell, T. (5): 106, 107, 108, 109, 122.
Carlstein, P.R. (8): 448, 492, 493, 494, 495, 496, 548, 551.
Carter, C.P. (10): 122, 124, 133, 134, 145, 146, 147, 155, 156, 157.
Catterall, R.H. (24): 148, 149, 150, 151, 152, 153, 154, 155, 156, 157, 168, 169, 170, 171, 172, 181, 182, 183, 184, 185, 204, 205, 206, 207.
Chapman, H.W. (2): 133, 145.
Cheetham, J.E. (24): 313, 318, 319, 320, 334, 335, 336, 337, 338, 360, 361, 362, 363, 364, 370, 371, 377, 378, 379, 380, 381, 408, 409, 412.
Chevalier, G.A. (1): 670.

# WEST INDIES (171 players)

# NEW ZEALAND (141 players)

Smith, F.B. (4): 284, 314, 315, 349.
Smith, H.D. (1): 225.
Snedden, C.A. (1): 284.
Sparling, J.T. (11): 456, 457, 458, 472, 473, 520, 522, 524, 540, 558, 559.
Sutcliffe, B. (42): 284, 314, 315, 316, 317, 332, 333, 349, 350, 370, 371, 377, 378, 379, 380, 381, 401, 402, 413, 414, 415, 416, 417, 418, 419, 420, 421, 422, 455, 456, 457, 458, 472, 473, 579, 580, 581, 582, 588, 589, 590, 591.

Taylor, B.R. (30): 580, 581, 582, 588, 589, 590, 592, 593, 604, 633, 635, 636, 650, 651, 652, 656, 658, 659, 661, 663, 694, 695, 696, 697, 711, 712, 713, 722, 723, 724.
Taylor, D.D. (3): 284, 423, 424.
Thomson, K. (2): 634, 635.
Tindill, E.W.T. (5): 260, 261, 262, 275, 284.
Troupe, G.B. (1): 786.
Truscott, P.B. (1): 578.
Turner, G.M. (39): 650, 651, 652, 656, 658, 659, 660, 661, 664, 685, 686, 693, 694, 695, 696, 697, 711, 712, 713, 722, 723, 724, 728, 730, 736, 737, 738, 758, 759, 770, 771, 772, 782, 783, 785, 786, 787, 796, 797.

Vivian, G.E. (5): 580, 694, 695, 696, 697.
Vivian, H.G. (7): 210, 211, 218, 225, 260, 261, 262.

Wadsworth, K.J. (33): 656, 657, 658, 659, 660, 661, 662, 663, 664, 685, 686, 693, 694, 695, 696, 697, 711, 712, 713, 722, 723, 724, 728, 729, 730, 736, 737, 738, 758, 759, 770, 771, 772.
Wallace, W.M. (13): 260, 261, 262, 275, 284, 314, 315, 316, 317, 332, 333, 370, 371.
Ward, J.T. (8): 558, 578, 579, 580, 581, 582, 593, 636.
Watt, L. (1): 401.
Webb, M.G. (3): 686, 693, 736.
Weir, G.L. (11): 187, 188, 189, 209, 210, 211, 217, 218, 225, 226, 262.
Whitelaw, P.E. (2): 225, 226.
Wright, J.G. (3): 817, 818, 819.

Yuile, B.W. (17): 540, 541, 576, 577, 578, 579, 580, 581, 588, 593, 633, 650, 651, 652, 660, 662, 663.

# INDIA (140 players)

Abdul Hafeez, see Kardar, A.H.
Abid Ali, S. (29): 624, 625, 626, 627, 633, 634, 635, 636, 659, 660, 661, 665, 680, 681, 682, 683, 684, 690, 691, 692, 703, 704, 706, 707, 739, 740, 741, 745, 746.
Adhikari, H.R. (21): 290, 291, 292, 293, 294, 304, 305, 306, 307, 308, 339, 340, 342, 352, 353, 354, 355, 357, 431, 432, 463.
Amarnath, L. (24): 230, 231, 232, 276, 277, 278, 290, 291, 292, 293, 294, 304, 305, 306, 307, 308, 340, 341, 343, 355, 356, 357, 358, 359.
Amarnath, M. (18): 669, 770, 771, 772, 773, 774, 775, 776, 785, 786, 787, 788, 790, 809, 810, 811, 812, 813.
Amarnath, S. (7): 770, 771, 772, 773, 774, 791, 792.
Amar Singh, L. (7): 219, 230, 231, 232, 252, 253, 254.
Amir Elahi (1): 291. *(Also 355, 356, 357, 358, 359 for Pakistan.)*
Apte, A.L. (1): 476.
Apte, M.L. (7): 357, 358, 365, 366, 367, 368, 369.

Baig, A.A. (10): 477, 478, 482, 483, 484, 497, 498, 499, 610, 611.
Banerjee, S. (1): 306.
Banerjee, S.N. (1): 308.
Baqa Jilani, M. (1): 254.
Bedi, B.S. (58): 611, 612, 618, 619, 620, 626, 627, 633, 634, 635, 636, 659, 660, 661, 665, 666, 667, 668, 669, 680, 681, 682, 683, 684, 690, 691, 692, 703, 704, 705, 706, 707, 739, 740, 741, 746, 747, 748, 749, 771, 772, 773, 774, 775, 776, 785, 786, 787, 788, 789, 790, 791, 792, 809, 810, 811, 812, 813.
Bhandari, P. (3): 400, 418, 433.
Borde, C.G. (55): 459, 460, 462, 463, 474, 476, 477, 478, 482, 483, 484, 485, 486, 497, 498, 499, 500, 501, 513, 514, 515, 516, 517, 525, 526, 527, 528, 529, 553, 554, 555, 556, 557, 566, 567, 568, 579, 580, 581, 582, 610, 611, 612, 618, 619, 620, 624, 625, 626, 627, 633, 634, 635, 636, 665.

Chandrasekhar, B.S. (50): 554, 555, 556, 557, 567, 568, 581, 582, 610, 611, 612, 618, 619, 620, 624, 625, 690, 691, 692, 703, 704, 705, 706, 707, 739, 740, 745, 747, 748, 749, 770, 771, 772, 773, 774, 775, 776, 785, 786, 787, 788, 789, 790, 791, 792, 809, 810, 811, 812, 813.

Chauhan, C.P.S. (9): 659, 660, 669, 705, 706, 810, 811, 812, 813.
Chowdhury, N.R. (2): 307, 339.
Colah, S.H.M. (2): 219, 230.
Contractor, N.J. (31): 417, 418, 419, 420, 433, 459, 460, 461, 462, 463, 474, 475, 477, 478, 482, 483, 484, 485, 486, 497, 498, 499, 500, 501, 513, 514, 515, 516, 517, 525, 526.

Dani, H.T. (1): 357.
Desai, R.B. (28): 463, 474, 475, 476, 477, 478, 482, 485, 486, 497, 498, 499, 500, 501, 513, 515, 516, 517, 525, 526, 527, 555, 556, 580, 581, 582, 625, 633.
Dilawar Hussain (3): 231, 232, 254.
Divecha, R.V. (5): 341, 343, 353, 354, 358.
Durani, S.A. (29): 484, 513, 514, 515, 516, 517, 525, 526, 527, 528, 529, 553, 554, 555, 556, 557, 566, 567, 568, 579, 580, 581, 610, 680, 681, 682, 704, 705, 707.

Engineer, F.M. (46): 514, 515, 516, 517, 525, 526, 527, 579, 580, 581, 582, 612, 618, 619, 620, 624, 625, 626, 627, 633, 634, 635, 636, 659, 660, 665, 666, 667, 668, 669, 690, 691, 692, 703, 704, 705, 706, 707, 739, 740, 741, 745, 746, 747, 748, 749.

Gadkari, C.V. (6): 365, 368, 369, 397, 398, 399.
Gaekwad, A.D. (14): 747, 748, 749, 773, 775, 776, 785, 786, 787, 788, 789, 791, 792, 813.
Gaekwad, D.K. (11): 351, 356, 359, 365, 366, 463, 474, 476, 477, 478, 500.
Gaekwad, H.G. (1): 356.
Gandotra, A. (2): 661, 666.
Gavaskar, S.M. (37): 681, 682, 683, 684, 690, 691, 692, 703, 704, 705, 706, 707, 739, 740, 741, 745, 749, 770, 771, 772, 773, 774, 775, 776, 785, 786, 787, 788, 789, 790, 791, 792, 809, 810, 811, 812, 813.
Ghavri, K.D. (11): 747, 748, 749, 786, 787, 788, 791, 792, 811, 812, 813.
Ghorpade, J.M. (8): 367, 369, 419, 432, 461, 475, 476, 478.
Ghulam Ahmed (22): 306, 307, 308, 342, 343, 351, 352, 353, 354, 355, 356, 357, 359, 396, 397, 398, 399, 416, 431, 433, 460, 461.
Gopalan, M.J. (1): 231.
Gopinath, C.D. (8): 340, 341, 343, 351, 358, 397, 398, 486.

Guard, G.M. (2): 459, 484.
Guha, S. (4): 618, 666, 667, 668.
Gul Mahomed (8): 276, 290, 291, 292, 293, 294, 355, 356. *(Also Test No. 430 for Pakistan.)*
Gupte, B.P. (3): 500, 557, 580.
Gupte, S.P. (36): 341, 357, 358, 365, 366, 367, 368, 369, 396, 397, 398, 399, 400, 416, 417, 418, 419, 420, 431, 432, 433, 459, 460, 461, 462, 463, 474, 475, 476, 477, 478, 497, 498, 499, 514, 515.

Hanumant Singh (14): 556, 557, 566, 567, 568, 579, 580, 581, 582, 611, 612, 618, 620, 659.
Hardikar, M.S. (2): 459, 460.
Hazare, V.S. (30): 276, 277, 278, 290, 291, 292, 293, 294, 304, 305, 306, 307, 308, 339, 340, 341, 342, 343, 351, 352, 353, 354, 355, 357, 358, 365, 366, 367, 368, 369.
Hindlekar, D.D. (4): 252, 276, 277, 278.

Ibrahim, K.C. (4): 304, 305, 306, 308.
Indrajitsinhji, K.S. (4): 566, 567, 568, 661.
Irani, J.K. (2): 290, 291.

Jahangir Khan, M. (4): 219, 252, 253, 254.
Jai, L.P. (1): 230.
Jaisimha, M.L. (39): 475, 486, 498, 499, 500, 501, 513, 514, 515, 516, 517, 526, 527, 528, 529, 553, 554, 555, 556, 557, 566, 567, 568, 579, 580, 581, 582, 610, 611, 626, 627, 633, 634, 635, 636, 661, 680, 683, 684.
Jamshedji, R.J. (1): 230.
Jayantilal, K. (1): 680.
Joshi, P.G. (12): 339, 342, 356, 365, 366, 368, 462, 474, 475, 477, 482, 497.

Kanitkar, H.S. (2): 745, 746.
Kardar, A.H. (3): 276, 277, 278. *(Also 23 appearances — 355–359, 387–390, 396–400, 413–415, 430, 449–453 — for Pakistan.)*
Kenny, R.B. (5): 461, 483, 484, 485, 486.
Kirmani, S.M.H. (20): 770, 771, 772, 773, 774, 775, 776, 785, 786, 787, 788, 789, 790, 791, 792, 809, 810, 811, 812, 813.
Kishenchand, G. (5): 290, 291, 293, 294, 356.
Kripal Singh, A.G. (14): 416, 417, 418, 420, 431, 433, 462, 475, 513, 514, 515, 553, 556, 566.
Krishnamurthy, P. (5): 680, 681, 682, 683, 684.
Kulkarni, U.N. (4): 624, 626, 627, 634.
Kumar, V.V. (2): 501, 513.
Kunderan, B.K. (18): 484, 485, 486, 500, 501, 513, 528, 529, 553, 554, 555, 556, 557, 580, 610, 611, 619, 620.

Lall Singh (1): 219.

Madan Lal, S. (16): 739, 740, 747, 748, 770, 771, 772, 773, 774, 775, 776, 785, 789, 790, 809, 810.
Maka, E.S. (2): 358, 367.
Manjrekar, V.L. (55): 341, 342, 351, 352, 353, 354, 355, 356, 359, 366, 367, 368, 369, 396, 397, 398, 399, 400, 416, 417, 418, 419, 420, 431, 432, 433, 459, 460, 461, 463, 474, 475, 497, 498, 499, 500, 501, 513, 514, 515, 516, 517, 525, 526, 527, 528, 529, 553, 554, 555, 557, 566, 567, 568, 579.
Mankad, A.V. (22): 659, 660, 665, 666, 667, 668, 669, 681, 682, 683, 690, 691, 692, 741, 748, 785, 786, 787, 790, 809, 811, 812.
Mankad, V.M.H. (44): 276, 277, 278, 290, 291, 292, 293, 294, 304, 305, 306, 307, 308, 339, 340, 341, 342, 343, 352, 353, 354, 355, 357, 358, 359, 365, 366, 367, 368, 369, 396, 397, 398, 399, 400, 416, 417, 419, 420, 431, 432, 433, 462, 463.
Mansur Ali Khan, see Pataudi.
Mantri, M.K. (4): 340, 351, 352, 396.
Meherhomji, K.R. (1): 253.

Mehra, V.L. (8): 417, 418, 516, 525, 528, 529, 553, 554.
Merchant, V.M. (10): 230, 231, 232, 252, 253, 254, 276, 277, 278, 339.
Milkha Singh, A.G. (4): 485, 500, 501, 513.
Modi, R.S. (10): 276, 277, 278, 304, 305, 306, 307, 308, 339, 357.
Muddiah, V.M. (2): 482, 498.
Mushtaq Ali (11): 231, 232, 252, 253, 254, 277, 278, 306, 307, 308, 343.

Nadkarni, R.G. (41): 418, 459, 474, 476, 477, 478, 482, 483, 484, 485, 486, 497, 498, 499, 501, 517, 525, 526, 527, 528, 529, 553, 554, 555, 556, 557, 566, 567, 568, 579, 580, 581, 582, 610, 624, 626, 627, 633, 634, 635, 636.
Naik, S.S. (3): 741, 746, 747.
Naoomal Jeoomal (3): 219, 231, 232.
Navle, J.G. (2): 219, 230.
Nayudu, C.K. (7): 219, 230, 231, 232, 252, 253, 254.
Nayudu, C.S. (11): 231, 232, 252, 253, 276, 278, 290, 291, 292, 294, 342.
Nazir Ali, S. (2): 219, 232.
Nissar, Mahomed (6): 219, 230, 231, 252, 253, 254.
Nyalchand, S. (1): 356.

Pai, A.M. (1): 659.
Palia, P.E. (2): 219, 252.
Parkar, R.D. (2): 703, 704.
Patankar, C.T. (1): 419.
Pataudi, Nawab of, sr (3): 276, 277, 278. *(Also 220, 221, 233 for England.)*
Pataudi, Nawab of, jr (now Mansur Ali Khan) (46): 515, 516, 517, 527, 528, 529, 553, 554, 555, 556, 557, 566, 567, 568, 579, 580, 581, 582, 610, 611, 612, 618, 619, 620, 625, 626, 627, 633, 634, 635, 636, 659, 660, 661, 665, 666, 667, 668, 669, 705, 706, 707, 745, 747, 748, 749.
Patel, B.P. (21): 739, 740, 745, 746, 749, 770, 771, 772, 774, 775, 776, 785, 786, 787, 788, 789, 790, 791, 792, 809, 810.
Patel, J.M. (7): 400, 420, 431, 432, 483, 485, 486.
Patiala, Yuvraj of (1): 232.
Patil, S.R. (1): 417.
Phadkar, D.G. (31): 291, 292, 293, 294, 304, 305, 307, 308, 339, 341, 342, 343, 351, 352, 353, 354, 358, 359, 365, 366, 367, 368, 396, 399, 400, 416, 417, 419, 420, 432, 461.
Prasanna, E.A.S. (47): 517, 526, 612, 618, 619, 620, 624, 625, 626, 627, 633, 634, 635, 636, 659, 660, 661, 665, 666, 667, 668, 669, 680, 681, 684, 704, 705, 706, 740, 741, 745, 746, 747, 748, 749, 770, 771, 772, 773, 789, 790, 791, 792, 809, 811, 812, 813.
Punjabi, P.H. (5): 396, 397, 398, 399, 400.

Rai Singh, K. (1): 292.
Rajindernath, V. (1): 357.
Rajinder Pal (1): 554.
Ramaswami, C. (2): 253, 254.
Ramchand, G.S. (33): 351, 352, 353, 354, 355, 358, 359, 365, 366, 367, 368, 369, 396, 397, 398, 399, 400, 416, 417, 418, 419, 420, 431, 432, 433, 459, 460, 462, 482, 483, 484, 485, 486.
Ramji, L. (1): 230.
Rangachari, C.R. (4): 293, 294, 304, 305.
Rangnekar, K.M. (3): 290, 292, 293.
Ranjane, V.B. (7): 460, 513, 514, 516, 529, 553, 566.
Rege, M.R. (1): 307.
Roy, A. (4): 660, 661, 667, 668.
Roy, P. (43): 339, 340, 341, 342, 343, 351, 352, 353, 354, 355, 356, 359, 366, 367, 368, 369, 396, 397, 398, 399, 400, 416, 419, 420, 431, 432, 433, 459, 460, 461, 462, 463, 474, 475, 476, 477, 478, 482, 483, 484, 485, 486, 497.

## PAKISTAN (79 players)